FILM REVIEW ANNUAL

1990

**With Cumulative Title Index
1981-1990**

FILM REVIEW ANNUAL

1990

With Cumulative Title Index
1981-1990

Film Review Publications
JEROME S. OZER, PUBLISHER

Editor: Jerome S. Ozer
Associate editor: Richard Zlotowitz

Reviews from THE CHRISTIAN SCIENCE MONITOR reprinted by permission from *The Christian Science Monitor.* © 1989 The Christian Science Publishing Society. All rights reserved.

Reviews from CINEASTE reprinted by permission from *Cineaste — A Magazine on the Art and Politics of the Cinema.*

Reviews from FILM QUARTERLY reprinted by permission. © 1989, 1990 by The Regents of the University of California.

Reviews from FILMS IN REVIEW reprinted by permission granted by Films in Review.

Reviews from the LOS ANGELES TIMES copyright, 1989, Los Angeles Times. Reprinted by permission.

Reviews from MONTHLY FILM BULLETIN reprinted by kind permission of the British Film Institute, London.

Reviews from THE NEW LEADER reprinted with permission from *The New Leader,* 1989. Copyright © The American Labor Conference on International Affairs, Inc.

Reviews from the NEW STATESMAN & SOCIETY reprinted by kind permission of, the *New Statesman,* London.

Reviews from NEW YORK copyright © 1989 by the New York Magazine Company, Inc. Reprinted with the permission of NEW YORK Magazine.

Reviews from the NEW YORK POST reprinted by permission of the New York Post. © 1989, New York Post Corporation.

Reviews from NEWSDAY reprinted by permission. © Newsday, Inc.

Reviews from NEWSWEEK copyright © 1989 by Newsweek, Inc. All rights reserved. Reprinted by permission.

Reviews from SIGHT AND SOUND reprinted by kind permission of the British Film Institute, London.

Reviews from TIME reprinted by permission from TIME, The Weekly Newsmagazine; Copyright Time Inc., 1989.

Reviews from THE VILLAGE VOICE reprinted by permission of The Village Voice. Copyright © News Group Publications, Inc., 1989.

ISBN 0-89198-142-X
ISSN 0737-9080

Manufactured in the United States of America

Jerome S. Ozer, Publisher
340 Tenafly Road
Englewood, NJ 07631

TABLE OF CONTENTS

PREFACE
FILM REVIEWS

ADDENDUM   1488

PREFACE

The FILM REVIEW ANNUAL provides, in a convenient format, a single reference volume covering important reviews—*in their entirety*—of full-length films released in major markets in the United States during the course of the year.

The format of the FILM REVIEW ANNUAL has been kept as clear and simple as possible. Films are reviewed in alphabetical order by title. Following each film title, we provide production information, cast and crew listings, the running time, and the MPAA rating. The reviews for each film are arranged alphabetically by publication. Each review is identified by the name of the publication, the date of the review, the page number, and the name of the reviewer. After the last review of a film, there is an *Also reviewed* section which lists other publications in which the film was reviewed. Because of restrictions in obtaining permission, we were unable to include reviews from certain publications. However, we felt that users of the FILM REVIEW ANNUAL should have help in gaining access to those reviews. Therefore, we included the *Also reviewed* section.

At the end of the FILM REVIEW ANNUAL, we provided full listings of the major film awards, including the nominees as well as the winners.

There are ten Indexes in the FILM REVIEW ANNUAL: Film Critics, Publications, Cast, Producers, Directors, Screenwriters, Cinematographers, Editors, Music, and Production Crew.

We have not attempted to force a single editorial style upon the reviews for the sake of achieving consistency. The reader will readily recognize that some reviews were written under deadline pressure and that others were prepared in a more leisurely and reflective style. Some reviews were written to help the moviegoer determine whether or not to see the film. Other reviews assumed the reader had already seen the film and was interested in getting another point of view. We believe this diversity of purposes and styles is one of the major strengths of the FILM REVIEW ANNUAL.

Because of our respect for the integrity of the writers' styles, we made changes from the original only where absolutely necessary. These changes were confined to typographical errors in the original review and errors in the spelling of names. When the reviewer made a reference to another film, we inserted the name of that film. Otherwise the reviews remain as written. British spelling used in English publications has been kept.

We have tried to make the FILM REVIEW ANNUAL pleasurable to read as well as useful for scholars and students of film, communications, social and cultural history, sociology, and also for film enthusiasts. We, the editors, would appreciate your suggestions about how we might make subsequent editions of the FILM REVIEW ANNUAL even more useful.

FILM REVIEWS

ABYSS, THE

A Twentieth Century Fox Film Corporation release. *Producer:* Gale Anne Hurd. *Director:* James Cameron. *Screenplay:* James Cameron. *Director of Photography:* Mikael Salomon. *Editor:* Joel Goodman. *Music:* Alan Silvestri. *Music Editor:* Kenneth Karman. *Sound:* Lee Orloff and (music) Dennis S. Sands. *Sound Editor:* Dody Dorn. *Production Designer:* Leslie Dilley. *Art Director:* Peter Childs. *Set Designer:* Andrew Precht, Thomas Wilkins and Gershon Ginsburg. *Set Decorator:* Anne Kuljian. *Set Dresser:* Jim Ferrell. *Special Effects:* Joe Unsinn. *Special Visual Effects:* Laura Buff. *Costumes:* Deborah Everton. *Make-up:* Kathryn Miles Kelly. *Stunt Coordinator:* Dick Warlock. *Running time:* 136 minutes. *MPAA Rating:* PG-13.

CAST: Ed Harris (Bud Brigman); Mary Elizabeth Mastrantonio (Lindsey Brigman); Michael Biehn (Lt. Coffey); Leo Burmester (Catfish De Vries); Todd Graff (Alan "Hippy" Carnes); John Bedford Lloyd (Jammer Willis); J.C. Quinn ("Sonny" Dawson); Kimberly Scott (Lisa "One Night" Standing); Capt. Kidd Brewer Jr. (Lew Finler); George Robert Klek (Wilhite); Christopher Murphy (Schoenick); Adam Nelson (Ensign Monk); Richard Warlock (Dwight Perry); Jimmy Ray Weeks (Leland McBride); J. Kenneth Campbell (DeMarco); Ken Jenkins (Gerard Kirkhill); Chris Elliot (Bendix); Peter Ratray (Captain); Michael Beach (Barnes); Brad Sullivan (Executive); Frank Lloyd (Navigator); Joe Farago (Anchorman); William Wisher (Bill Tyler); Phillip Darlington (Crew Member); Joseph Nemec III (Crew Member); Super Sea Rover (Big Geek); Mini Rover Mk II (Little Geek).

CHRISTIAN SCIENCE MONITOR, 8/18/89, p. 10, David Sterritt

If a look at the ocean cools you off in the summertime, you might be curious about "The Abyss," which was filmed about 40 percent underwater. But don't expect a relaxing, warm-weather plunge from this picture. It was written and directed by James Cameron, whose other movies are "The Terminator" and "Aliens," and, as you might expect from his record, it isn't stingy with action scenes and violence.

Or publicity, for that matter. "The Abyss" is the most loudly hyped movie since "Batman" flapped into our lives a few weeks ago. Advance word from the studio, Twentieth Century-Fox, told us it would be an adventure with a difference—not just thrills and spills, but complex human relationships, and even a bit of mysticism to get us all thinking. Was the public-relations buzz true? Or would this underwater thriller turn out to be (if you'll pardon the expression) all wet?

I'm sorry to report that "The Abyss" is a little on the soggy side. It's big and fast-moving, and it has plenty of energy. But the plot is silly, and for a picture that claims to be out of the ordinary, a lot of its scenes look awfully familiar.

The story begins when a military submarine has an accident, littering the ocean with nuclear warheads. Who's going to clean up this radioactive mess? The workers on an underwater oil rig—who aren't crazy about the job, but have no choice, especially when a Navy crew arrives to supervise the operation.

The big subplot involves the oil rig's boss and his engineer wife, who's in the middle of divorcing him. To top things off, one of the Navy men is well on the way to insanity. This becomes quite interesting when he gets his hands on a nuclear bomb and decides to become a one-man army.

Where does the mysticism come in? Well, every now and then a character sees something that looks like an underwater UFO, and at one point an alien—a kind of snake made out of water—slithers in for a visit.

At the climax, our hero finds himself all alone 25,000 feet under the sea, and there he runs into a whole alien headquarters, where folks are happy to lend him a helping hand. Or fin, or pod, or whatever you want to call it.

The trouble is: This isn't very original. The first 90 minutes are full of ideas that were new in pictures like "Alien" several years ago: The settings are messy and lived-in, and many of the characters are rough-and-ready workers who don't look anything like movie heroes. But this isn't exactly startling nowadays.

In the last 45 minutes, the picture tries to be more exotic than ever, but strangely enough it gets even more hackneyed. Most of the aliens look like Steven Spielberg puppets, and the climax is lifted right out of "2001: A Space Odyssey," which has never been pilfered so eagerly in the 21 years since its première.

"The Abyss" is expensively made and action-packed, and if that's all you're looking for this summer, it'll entertain you well enough.

A nod of appreciation also goes to Ed Harris and Mary Elizabeth Mastrantonio, whose solid performances keep the movie on a reasonably even keel—dramatically speaking—even when other performers (including Michael Biehn, who overacts like crazy as the villain) threaten to sink it.

If you want an adventure that's really surprising, though, you'd better head for another theater. "The Abyss" isn't abysmal, but it's a replay of hits we've already seen—a recycled "close encounters of the wet kind" with far too few ideas of its own.

LOS ANGELES TIMES, 8/9/89, Calendar/p. 1, Sheila Benson

"The Abyss" is the most hardware-cluttered movie imaginable, full of dials and valves and pressure locks and daunting technical gear, yet it leaves you feeling sappily euphoric. This must be like rapture of the deep: Machines crash against other machines underwater with a slo-mo bounce and a bell-like clanggggg; the ocean begins to collect as many floating spare parts as space and we look at it all benignly, "Thasssss nice." All stress washes away in this intense, mindless blueness; it's like 2 hours and 20 minutes in an immersion tank full of Scope.

With all its numskullness, "The Abyss" is at heart a sweet movie, full of people dying and then living for love, and nothing new to add on the subject of other-worldlings than "Close Encounters of the Third Kind" offered 12 years ago: "Give 'em a chance. You don't hurt them; they don't hurt you. Who knows, we might learn something from them."

But the climax of "Close Encounters" was breathtaking and the climax of "The Abyss" is downright embarrassing; in the light of day, its payoff effect looks like a glazed ceramic what's-it your 11-year-old made in crafts class. It's criminal, because the undersea effects are glowingly beautiful and one gimmick used by the "non-terrestrial intelligence" (jargon theirs) is jaw-dropping. Perhaps, to keep us in its spell, this final effect should have surfaced at night.

It's not at all hard to believe that writer-director James Cameron has carried this film in his head since he was 17; it's a 17-year-old's vision, complete with men who say "Steady, big fella" to each other without a trace of irony. In the meantime, however, Cameron and his producer and former co-writer, Gale Anne Hurd, have learned to make movies like "The Terminator" and "Aliens" that move with a headlong, punishing pace. So here we are, taking turns between free-floating and being propelled forward with a whoosh. And all in the service of a truly footling script.

In brief, Cameron strands a nuclear submarine, armed with a bomb-to-end-all-bombs, on a shelf in the Caribbean. Two teams are involved in a rescue against the clock to get the dee-vice: the (mostly) hairy, brawny, wisecracking crew of Deepcore, a "submersible hyperbaric drilling platform" lodged at sea bottom—the gang we may think of as *us*. And there are the militaristic crew-cut Navy SEAL (Sea, Air and Land) commandos, who are definitely *them*. Threatening them all is a malady called High-Pressure Nervous Syndrome, a sort of underwater PMS, which causes irrationality and galloping Oliver Northism. There's also a hurricane battering the Navy forces topside. And that bomb.

Now you add the personalities. Returning to Deepcore during this crisis is Lindsey Brigman (Mary Elizabeth Mastrantonio), who seems to revel in her widespread reputation as "a cast-iron bitch." She has designed every inch of the steel monster and goes through it turning wheels and tapping valves like someone tidying up her kitchen after others have been messing in it.

Foreman of Deepcore is Bud Brigman (Ed Harris), her estranged husband, seemingly thrilled about the split. Head of the loyal SEAL opposition is Lt. Coffey (Michael Biehn), whose eyes begin rolling like marbles within minutes of arriving at Deepcore's niche on the ocean floor. Before long, he is carving hash marks on his forearm with his assault knife. Not hard to tell where the dreaded nervous syndrome has struck this time.

Most prominent of the crew members are Catfish (Leo Burmester), Harris' huge, ginger-bearded decompression expert, company for his scarier swims; the paranoid Hippy (Todd Graff), who has a pet white rat, and a roughneck, no-nonsense underwater tractor pilot, One Night (Kimberly Scott). If your heart sinks at names like this, it has every reason to. Not a single surprise of dialogue or character awaits you.

As these men and women take to the depths in crab-like pods with pincer claws, or in extended-time diving helmets, or immersed in a liquid that lets Ed Harris "breathe fluid instead of air," we await the appearance of The Other. Imagine the surprise of discovering that it's a neon flittering Tinker Bell that leaves mortals all the better for encounters with its presence.

There are more: rounded glowing transparent creatures in sea shapes. Most mysterious of all these visions is something like a mercury-glass pseudopod, a probe with a worm-like shape that can assume any shape and moves with the liquidity of water. *This* is the movie's payload, and in this blue, watery womb-like state it's tempting to float free and just enjoy it and the picture's frail message about the power of love. If only Cameron knew what to do with his otherworldlings; an explanation of their world, even a use for them except as a nifty, power-assisted forklift. So his picture simply dribbles away.

In the matter of hardware (and excepting its final effect) "The Abyss" is flawless in each technical department; unfortunately, they can't all be credited here. Cinematographer Mikael Salomon's camera seems to race down steel corridors, only milliseconds in front of walls of water, and it seems to have been his formidable job to light up this Stygian universe. The business of non-gurgling voices at every depth would seem to be a horrendous task, conquered by sound mixer Lee Orloff. The veteran Leslie Dilley's production designs are both realistic and properly otherworldly.

But apart from its technical geewhizzery, "The Abyss" has more than its share of eyebrow-raisers. As Harris looks unconvinced about taking liquid fluorocarbon into his lungs in place of air, a wiser source says soothingly, "We all breathe liquid for nine months, Bud. Your body will remember." That may be news to *many* of us ex-babies.

Forget "Quest for Fire," where the half-naked cast huddled under pelts that must have smelled like wet Airedales. "The Abyss's" permanently drenched crew wins the Most Pathetic vote in a dog-paddle, including the estimable Mastrantonio, who must willingly drown herself in another plot-line mind-boggler. She and the ice-blue-eyed Harris do manage to bring fire to all this damp tinder, but it can't have been easy.

It's perfectly possible to have a mindlessly pleasant time in the intense Tidy-Bowl blueness of "The Abyss." You just relax and let go. You may just wonder when you come out if you haven't pruned a little.

MONTHLY FILM BULLETIN, 11/89, p. 328, Julian Petley

When the nuclear submarine "U.S.S. Montana" suffers a power failure and crashes on to the edge of the Cayman Trough after encountering a bright, fast-moving object, a team of civilian divers working on Deepcore, a prototype underwater drilling rig, is reluctantly pressed into a rescue operation by the U.S. Navy. The nine-man team led by rig foreman Bud Brigman (whose estranged wife Lindsey, the project's chief engineer, also insists on coming along) is joined by four men from the navy's SEALS led by Lieutenant Coffey. No survivors are found from the submarine, but a strange blue light is glimpsed around the hull and one of the team, Jammer, convulses and goes into a coma. Coffey insists on arming one of the submarine's nuclear missiles and taking it back to Deepcore. Meanwhile, Hurricane Frederick is raging on the surface and Russian surveillance vessels are homing in on the scene of the disaster. A collapsing crane drags the Deepcore rig close to the edge of the trough; Lindsey encounters a mysterious blue presence outside the rig and photographs it, though the developed pictures reveal nothing. Coffey, who is convinced that the whole thing is a Russian plot, accuses her of hysteria. An object like a silvery sea serpent, which has the ability to mimic the crew's faces and seems to be trying to make room for the missile, appears in Deepcore. It is destroyed by Catfish, one of the crew, while Jammer suddenly recovers consciousness. Coffey escapes from Deepcore in a small submersible, Cab Three, armed with the missile with which he intends to destroy what he takes to be the Russians. He is pursued by Bud and Lindsey in Cab One, and in the course of a battle Coffey is killed while the missile plunges to the bottom of the trough. Stranded, Bud swims with Lindsey back to the rig, and then descends into the trough to defuse the missile. Without enough oxygen to regain Deepcore, he is calmly awaiting death when he is visited by a strange luminous being who takes him to a vast, radiant structure on the bottom of the trough. He takes off his equipment and is able to breathe. On the surface the storm abates. The structure rises from the ocean floor, taking Deepcore with it and coming up under the U.S. Navy vessels, which find themselves stranded on what appears to be a vast spaceship. Bud emerges from within, and is reunited with the Deepcore crew.

Rumoured to have cost in the region of sixty million dollars, *The Abyss* is the most elaborate of the current slew of undersea adventure films, which also includes *DeepStar Six, Leviathan* and the Roger Corman-produced *Lords of the Deep*. To the inevitable toll of costly logistical problems during production (the sets were built in two multi-million gallon tanks, both of which sprang leaks, at the never completed Cherokee nuclear power station in South Carolina, in which it proved extremely difficult to simulate the endless night of the deep sea while still allowing enough light for filming), was added James Cameron's estrangement from his wife, the film's producer Gale Anne Hurd, who also produced *Aliens* and *The Terminator* and cowrote the latter. None of these problems are too evident in the final product, which for the most part is as exciting an undersea drama as one could imagine. A horribly convincing sense of claustrophobia and imminent danger is maintained throughout, and the scene in which Bud and Lindsey take their leave of one another in the rapidly filling Cab One, followed by Bud's desperate bid to reach Deepcore with the unconscious Lindsey in tow, is quite agonising.

More visceral thrills are provided by the tremendous battle between Cabs One and Three (a reminder of Cameron's way with hardware in *The Terminator*), while the film's eeriest scene is that in which the divers enter the wrecked submarine and find a floating world of corpses and everyday objects. However, *The Abyss* is by no means just a special-effects bonanza. Ed Harris and Mary Elizabeth Mastrantonio are most convincing as the estranged couple who nevertheless work together (some autobiographical element here?), and the scene in which Bud tries desperately to bring Lindsey back to life has an emotional charge that transcends the will-she-won't-she-recover level. Likewise the other members of the two teams are nicely individualised—in particular Todd Graff as a nervous, and occasionally somewhat paranoid, member of Bud's team (shades of *Dark Star*), while Michael Biehn inverts his positive characterisations in Cameron's last two films to present a chilling picture of the obsessive and finally demented military mind.

What is finally rather unsatisfying about *The Abyss*, however, is its "Close Encounters Beneath the Sea" aspect, which doesn't sit very happily with the rest of the film. One wonders why the film-makers bothered with the friendly-alien sub-text (which also features in *Lords of the Deep*, incidentally), and why, having once introduced the idea, they then fail to develop it adequately. The aliens prove to be ideologically 'green', i.e. anti-nuclear, and evidently in one version of the script threatened the world's cities with tidal waves unless nations stopped their drift towards nuclear destruction. As the story now stands, however, the Good Aliens threaten to mutate from awesome superbeings into sentimental harbingers of the New Age: the 'heavenly choirs' scoring simply isn't wholehearted enough in the John Williams manner to drown one's doubts, while the alien who rescues Bud comes across as a curious amalgam of monster dragonfly and neon-lit Tinker Bell. The brio and conviction that mark the earlier passages seem somewhat exhausted by this stage—as is one's capacity to take in any more of anything, especially benevolent aliens on the seabed. As Nietzsche put it, even if not apropos this film, "If you gaze for long into an abyss, the abyss gazes also into you".

NEW YORK, 8/21/89, p. 126, David Denby

The characters in The Abyss, James Cameron's briny-depths adventure spectacle, do much of their work in the damp. They fall down under avalanches of ocean water; they ride submersibles into a bottomless crevasse; they take water into their stomachs and lungs, "drowning" and then coming back to life, rising out of the ocean in what is intended to be a spiritual rebirth. They cough up water, *shpritzing* it all over the room. I came out of the movie appalled by the idea of even taking a bath. *The Abyss* has its own look and tempo—it's a physically impressive work by a talented filmmaker. It's also one of the most doggedly humorless adventure films in years, and the narrative, which Cameron also devised, is a water-soaked mess.

Somewhere in the Caribbean, a submerged nuclear submarine, armed to the teeth with missiles, encounters a speeding freak—a Russian supertoy, a force, a something—which sends the sub barreling into a Big Hole (familiarly known as "the abyss"). The cavity in the ocean floor is called the Cayman Trough, and as the sub smashes into its rocky walls, it cracks open and sinks. Immediately, the crew of an experimental underwater oil rig, working nearby, is told to go see if anybody's left alive. Living in a huge container thousands of feet down, the oil riggers have grown a little odd, but they're still a swell bunch of guys. Bud Brigman (Ed Harris) is their leader—until the designer of the rig shows up, stepping out of a helicopter on a ship above in high heels. She's Lindsey Brigman (Mary Elizabeth Mastrantonio), the "cast-iron bitch" who is Bud's wife. When she shows up on the rig, it's immediately clear that Lindsey thinks her husband is a stupe and a wimp; he loves her and suffers.

James Cameron and Gale Anne Hurd (she produces) are themselves a former husband-and-wife team; together they have introduced something new to American action movies, the bristling female superhero, tougher and smarter than any man. Mary Elizabeth Mastrantonio's role here is equivalent to Sigourney Weaver's monster-busting turn in *Aliens*. I suppose the new heroines are a sign of progress, but they're also an instant cliché: These women kick butt. Lindsey's war with her husband is stale stuff—we can tell, after one look at Ed Harris's plaintive face, that he's going to try to prove himself in this crisis to win her back.

And there's much else in the plotting that's stale. A team of SEALS, led by Lieutenant Coffey (Michael Biehn), also come down to the rig; their mission is to disarm the sub and, if necessary, detonate one of the nuclear warheads, destroying the sub so it can't fall into the hands of the Russians. Biehn, a sincere but crude actor who was rather touching in Cameron's B-movie masterpiece, *The Terminator*, can't do anything amusing with the paranoid Coffey, who is slowly going crazy from the increased air pressure below the surface; Coffey is supposed to be a Cold War military hardball who sees everything in outdated anti-Soviet terms, and from the beginning he's set up as a bug-eyed psycho.

The oil riggers, led by Lindsey, who doesn't want her rig blown up, wind up fighting the military, all of them racing around the many compartments of the rig or chasing one another in small underwater craft that look like beautiful floating bump-'em cars with lights. There's a wild card thrown into all this fine hugger-mugger: The thing that spooked the sub turns out to be some kind of creature, a waving emanation of light. Translucent, it glows pink and pretty, like the neon decoration in a downtown disco; the being is an emissary from a gigantic mother ship, a higher form of intelligence that has taken up residence below the sea. Suddenly, we're thrown into a white-light, transcendental, Spielbergian mode: Lindsey confronts the being and, like the dazzled Richard Dreyfuss in *Close Encounters of the Third Kind*, has a conversion experience. She is cleansed of all bad thoughts about the Russians and anyone else. Redeemed, she is. And Lindsey has to persuade the others to love too. Which is all very well, but what does it have to do with the rest of *The Abyss*? Still, there are exciting passages; the movie is a wonderful big deepwater production. Cameron, as we know from *The Terminator* and *Aliens*, has an advanced Erector Set mentality; he likes to set up some grand piece of industrial technology and then burn it, wreck it, turning it into blackened, twisting junk. Enclosed in their steel structure, the characters are sitting ducks; at one point, an elaborate crane on the oil company's ship way above collapses in a hurricane and comes hurtling down through the thousands of feet of water, heading straight for them. The way the broken, heavy mess falls through water—smoothly and implacably, like a car going off a cliff in slow motion—is one of the scariest sights in recent movies.

There's also a mysteriously terrifying sequence in which Harris, chasing a nuclear warhead that has fallen to the bottom of the trough, sinks and sinks through blackness into what looks like eternity itself. Harris and the others appear to suffer great discomfort from all that liquid coming out of their ears, but they establish a new screen reality, too—they live and talk and even act underwater. I would have been happier, however, had certain corny touches been left in the world above—Harris slapping the water-logged Mastrantonio back to life ("Fight, you bitch!"), and she, in turn, melting from cast iron to jelly when he sinks to the bottom ("Oh, Bud, you're not alone..."). The beatific conclusion of the movie, which tries to rival the end of *Close Encounters*, is not only ridiculous, it's cheesy. In *The Terminator*, the supernatural stuff was organic to the whole fable, but here the ersatz Spielbergism is merely grafted onto a hardworking action film. It's as if Madame Blavatsky had shown up at a meeting of the United Auto Workers. And I suppose no one in the audience is supposed to notice or care that while Lindsey and her crew are undergoing sublime religious experiences, the ruined sub, with its 150 corpses, has been completely forgotten.

NEW YORK POST, 8/9/89, p. 23, David Edelstein

The costly deep-sea sci-fi romance "The Abyss" is private film making on an undreamed-of scale; the movie is a teensy, egocentric fantasy pumped up to cosmic dimensions—aliens, threats of nuclear annihilation, symbolic death and rebirth. There's even a quote from Nietzsche: "When you look long into an abyss, the abyss also looks into you." This "Abyss" doesn't look back, however; you look into it and your head swims.

Directed and written by James Cameron ("The Terminator," "Aliens"), the film is also meant as the story of a saved marriage—of two competitive, antagonistic people forced by monstrous circumstances to work together and make big sacrifices for each other (not to mention all of mankind).

Bud Brigman (Ed Harris) is the foreman of an underwater oil-drilling rig; during a routine operation, his team of grunts is dispatched by the Navy to investigate the nearby crash of a nuclear submarine 2,000 feet beneath the surface. Along for the expedition is the project engineer, Brigmen's soon-to-be ex-wife, Lindsey (Mary Elizabeth Mastrantonio), known to all as a brusque, officious bitch.

But underwater, Lindsey is mysteriously feminized. Near the shattered sub, she sees floating beings—luminous jellyfish or skate, transparent, with pink filaments. With New Age fervor, Lindsey tells the incredulous crew that these aren't Soviet probes but good, inquiring extraterrestrials.

In the language of '50s Cold War sci-fi, she's either a commie dupe about to receive a nasty shock (as in "The Thing") or the first human mature enough to drop her backward suspicions and welcome a new era of interstellar camaraderie (as in "The Day the Earth Stood Still").

Clues to the creatures' true intentions are their beatific expressions and the angelic choir that underscores their appearances. Another is that Cameron harbors doubts about the military-industrial complex, which was the true villain in "Aliens." It's represented here by Lt. Coffey (Michael Biehn, the hero of Cameron's last two films), a jittery Cold Warrior who wigs out and tries to drop a nuclear warhead on these smiley, glowing squiggles.

Perhaps the secret of Cameron's appeal is that he combines a macho, military-hardware style with a reverence for things feminine; he might act like a steel-jawed bridge-builder, but in his heart he's just a baby mewling for mama's bosom. That heart compensates for some leaden film making, while his testosterone-heavy technique gives heft to his amazingly infantile fantasies.

The upshot is weirdly schizoid. The underwater rig is full of poker-faced roughnecks and constricted iron corridors, all shot with a rattling Steadicam. But outside it's lyrical and blue, pierced by jeweled rays of light. When a luminous pink alien probe darts around the mammoth gray vessel, it's as if Tinker Bell had decided to drop in on the U-boat soldiers of "Das Boot."

Except for huge pieces of machinery crunching and exploding (Cameron's signature shots), all the imagery is borrowed (mostly from Spielberg in "Close Encounters of the Third Kind," "E.T." and even "Jaws"). Yet the scale of the effects is always impressive, and there's a great sequence in which the crew waits in fear for a crane knocked into the water thousands of feet above them to land on their bow—its cables go by like the ropes on a descending dumb waiter.

On its primitive level, "The Abyss" can hook you—the nervous camerawork and high-pressure editing let you share in the characters' panic and claustrophobia, if that's your idea of a good time. Even so, you can't avoid the dialogue, which never clunks louder than when it toils for cleverness. (The only actor who transcends the script is the gifted Todd Graff as the resident conspiracy buff; sallow, with hammy proletarian inflections, he's like a young Harvey Pekar).

The most harrowing sequence is one of those what-would-you-do-if-you-had-one-oxygen-tank-for-two-people dilemmas; in a flooded submersible "cab," Lindsey, weeping with terror, lets herself drown so that her husband can swim back to the rig—and perhaps revive her. (Mastrantonio, a likable actress, deserves a Purple Heart for her contortions.)

Bud also gets to lay his life on the line, chasing the warhead in a diving suit to the unprecedented depth of 25,000 feet, at which point the pressure makes him delirious, euphoric. And the deeper he sinks, the dumber "The Abyss" gets.

What happens, I'm convinced, is that Cameron identifies so strongly with his hero that his brain begins to swell from lack of exygen; he gets euphoric, drunk on the nobility of his self-sacrifice. You could predict the film's finale, but not its overflowing silliness: The couple and their marriage are reborn from the dark waters, baptized; the rig becomes the Love Boat on a Sea of Dreams.

It's not hard to see what's going on here. Cameron, whose marriage was in trouble when he wrote the script, indulged in a stellar bout of wish-fulfillment—he modeled the relationship on his own with producer Gale Anne Hurd (whom Mastrantonio slightly resembles) and dreamed of extraterrestrial marriage counselors.

That the couple split for good during "The Abyss" is more an issue for the gossip columns than this review, but it does suggest that Cameron's howlingly funny vision of eternal love might be one reason he couldn't hold his marriage together (or keep from alienating his cast and crew during the reportedly torturous shoot).

It is, after all, the most egomaniacal people who are most obsessed with self-sacrifice. When the abyss looked into him, it must have caught the next plane out.

NEWSDAY, 8/9/89, Part II/p. 3, Mike McGrady

The same producer-director creative team that brought you "The Terminator" and "Aliens" has done it again—well, almost. Writer-director James Cameron, that master of lean screenplays and muscular cinematography, has made another four-star thriller—for about three-fifths of the way. Actors Ed Harris and Mary Elizabeth Mastrantonio have breathed life and fire into a pair of pulp-fiction characters—before finally going under beneath one of the sap-happiest movie endings in memory.

As a fully armed nuclear submarine struggles for survival 2,000 feet below the surface, "The Abyss" opens as an adventure-lover's dream. Through much of the flick, whenever danger flashes up from the darkest depths, you'll find yourself perched on seat's edge holding onto that last breath. The unfortunate decision to wind up "The Abyss" with some sunny Spielbergian amalgam of fantasy and magic, however, undoes much of the good that has come before.

Ed Harris (only Hackman and De Niro wear hard hats with equal grace) is the foreman overseeing a raggedy team of divers stationed on a futuristic underwater oil rig loosely anchored to the floor of the Caribbean. When the sub carrying 192 nuclear warheads sinks nearby, the oil workers are drafted to join a team of crewcut Navy divers on what at first seems to be a search-and-rescue mission but is actually one with a search-and-destroy goal.

A late arrival to the scene, Mary Elizabeth Mastrantonio is Harris' soon-to-be-ex-wife, a tough executive who begins to soften when she makes contact with her first underwater aliens: "There is something down there. Something that's not us. Something not human but intelligent."

Writer-director James Cameron is, of course, a past master of hardware—and as long as the drama is confined to the brilliantly photographed and choreographed underwater movements and battles, all goes swimmingly. It's only when the humans take off their diving apparatus and relate without benefit of machinery that some problems develop.

The presence of underwater alien life provides the crew with what one member describes as "a sphincter factor of about 9.5." And as long as the aliens are not fully defined iridescent presences and as long as the oil-rig crew is trying to contain a psychopathic Navy diver (Michael Biehn), the film itself has approximately the same sphincter factor.

Moreover, the central performers generate enough electricity individually and together to almost compensate for mawkish moments. (Mastrantonio radios to a husband stranded three miles below the surface: "There are some things I need to say. It's not easy being a castiron bitch. ...Bud, I know how alone you feel, alone in the cold darkness. ...Bud, you're not alone, I'll always be with you.")

Although there are reasons to see the movie, the ending—think of it as a close encounter of the weird kind—is totally contrary to Cameron's normally gritty and darkside style. It's so ludicrously magical that it makes the final scenes of "Cocoon" look like hard-bitten realism. And the aliens themselves, when fully defined, bear an unfortunate relationship to the lovable E.T.

It was Nietzsche who observed, "When you look long into an abyss, the abyss also looks into you." I'm not at all sure what "The Abyss" will see when it looks back, but this is one abyss into which I wouldn't advise looking too long, too hard or too deep.

NEWSWEEK, 8/14/89, p. 56, David Ansen

The Abyss stands apart from the other action movies this summer: it's the only one that doesn't dilute its tension with irony. James Cameron, director of the smashing B movie "The Terminator" and the spectacularly intense "Aliens," is a genre fundamentalist, a True Believer in back-to-basics suspense. In his new deep-sea thriller, there are variations on scenes you've seen a hundred times (and often in disreputable B movies), yet Cameron renders them with such white-knuckle conviction they regain their primal force. Take, for example, the Resuscitation Scene, that old standby in which our hero desperately labors to bring a corpse back to life with mouth-to-mouth, electric shocks, whatever it takes. In the hands of Cameron and his two ferociously effective stars, Ed Harris and Mary Elizabeth Mastrantonio, this cliché is redeemed with heart-stopping flair. There's nothing significantly novel about the staging, it's simply done better than you've ever seen it. Much of "The Abyss" is like that: B movie parts reorchestrated with such perfectionist's zeal that the whole genre seems resuscitated.

Cameron composes from borrowed parts, but the worlds he creates are distinctly his own. Though most of "The Abyss" takes place underwater, it's recognizably Cameronland, a gritty, blue-collar industrial landscape dominated by clanky, squat machinery and decorated with valves and rusty pipes: it's like being inside a metallic womb, some cosmic Detroit of the soul.

Cameron takes a little time to set up his high-jeopardy plot: under mysterious circumstances, a nuclear sub is grounded on the underwater cliffs of an abyss. Above ground, a hurricane rages. Below the Atlantic, a team of underwater oil drillers—led by Harris—is conscripted by the Navy to disarm the nuclear sub before catastrophe strikes. A second team of SEAL divers—at odds with the civilian crew—gets into the act, led by the increasingly psychotic Michael Biehn. Meanwhile, Harris has to work beside his estranged wife (Mastrantonio), the oil drillers' much despised project engineer, who's as determined and macho as he is. There are enough plot threads going to sustain several movies, but Cameron adds another, extraterrestrial dimension, and it's here that he runs into trouble. There's Something Unearthly down in the depths, and we wait with bated breath to see what mystical rabbit Cameron pulls out of his hat.

The rabbit, I'm sorry to say, is pretty mangy. Without giving anything away, it must be said that the payoff to "The Abyss" is pretty damn silly—a portentous *deus ex machina* that leaves too many questions unanswered and evokes too many other films. Cameron has based his movie on a story he dreamt up in high school, and that may be the problem: it feels like a high-school idea. But whatever you think of the concept, the technical brillance of Cameron's accomplishment can't be denied. "The Abyss" holds the viewer in a vise grip for 2¼ hours. It's thrilling, dumb and irresistible.

TIME, 8/14/89, p. 79, Richard Schickel

Water is not the director's friend. Actors immersed in it do not have many opportunities for sharp repartee. It provides no cover for the villain to sneak up on the hero. It turns action sequences into exercises in slow motion. It is costly to work in and obscures expensive and imaginative special-effects work.

All of this having been made obvious by dozens of subaqueous movies, one has to wonder why James Cameron, whose *Aliens* and *The Terminator* were among the smartest and most frugally made recent entertainments, plunged into the $50 million-plus *Abyss*. Or, if he was sending his cast on a dive into a bottomless ocean trough, why he didn't at least arrange to have a monster paddle up to meet them.

The situation seems promising. A nuclear submarine has a mysterious accident at the edge of an ocean canyon, and the only hope for rescue is the crew of a futuristic underwater oil-drilling rig working nearby. The rig's designer (Mary Elizabeth Mastrantonio), who is the estranged wife of its master (Ed Harris), drops down to help and bicker. So does a Navy diving team whose leader (Michael Biehn) suffers a psychotic break caused by the great depths. He becomes particularly obstreperous after he recovers a warhead from the wreck.

A good thing, too, because he is the only menace around—not nearly enough to sustain this endless tale. As it turns out, there is nothing else in the deep except some benign escapees from Steven Spielberg country. Harris and Mastrantonio do have a strong death and resurrection sequence, but long before that, one is pining for a rubber shark or a plastic octopus—anything, in fact, out of a good old low-tech thriller.

VILLAGE VOICE, 8/15/89, p. 61, Amy Taubin

The *Abyss* is a very likable $43 million movie (low-end estimate). As an experience, it's a bit like two hours in a bumper car with a special someone—you get shook up and adrenalized, but the risks are pretty minimal. An action-adventure love story in a setting that's both fresh and suitable to 70mm (40 per cent of the film was actually shot under water), this high-tech wet dream tries its best to follow the guidelines for a mega-hit. And since it's the first studio epic since *Aliens* (also directed and written by James Cameron) with a woman character who's more than a sidekick or a send-up, I wish it the very best.

Set in the imminent future, *The Abyss* features underwater technology so advanced it might as well be sc-fi. The basic interiors—an underwater oil drilling facility nicknamed Deepcore and its smaller satellite submersibles—correspond to outer-space crafts except in one important particular. Rather than (supposedly) gliding through space, thus providing a stable frame for the image, the submersibles rock 'n' roll in the water. Their movement adds an extra dimension to Cameron's habitually hyperactive camerawork. Kinetic impact and visual excitement compensate for the low level of suspense and lack of dramatic conflict.

In part, *The Abyss* is about a marriage (although that's probably not the reason Cameron favors something old, something new, a lot of borrowing, and the Big Blue). Virgil "Bud" Brigman (Ed Harris) is the foreman of Deepcore; his wife, Lindsey (Mary Elizabeth Mastrantonio), is its chief engineer. When an American nuclear submarine runs aground on an underwater reef at the edge of the Cayman Trough, a two-and-a-half-mile abyss in the Atlantic, the navy enlists Deepcore in a search-and-rescue mission. The ambitious Lindsey is all too willing, but Bud fears for the safety of his crew. "Virgil, you weiner," she scoffs, "you never could stand up to a fight." "God, I hate that bitch," he mutters. "I probably never should have married her." Shortly after, Bud throws his wedding ring down the chemical toilet, instantly repents, and has to stick his hand in the yucky blue—um, abyss—to get it out. Cameron wants us to believe this marriage, like the nuclear sub, is on the rocks and ready to explode, but it's obvious from the first that these two are extremely well-matched. They just have a combative style.

With Bud and Lindsey basically on the same side, Cameron has to rely on some shopworn devices to get things going. The very paranoid Lieutenant Coffey (Michael Biehn), head of the navy SEAL team involved in the operation, suspects that the Soviets have sabotaged the sub and wants to nuke them out of the water. Since Cuba is less than 100 miles away, this could become another Bay of Pigs. Then Hurricane Fred knocks out communication with the surface and leaves Deepcore itself disabled, with only enough fuel and air for 12 hours.

After this plausible, if overblown, opening, Lindsey goes down to investigate the sub and has a close encounter with something "better than a UFO, a nonterrestrial intelligence." As you may have observed in the TV trailers, the NTIs look like big, transparent, pink-and-blue flying fish. Tucked between their fins are tiny E.T.-like heads, and they trail their attenuated E.T.-like fingers in the H_2O. When Lindsey sees them, her eyes light up with childlike wonder. (Mastrantonio is extremely good at this.) Cameron spends about three minutes fooling around with the notion that NTIs mirror the inner state of whoever's around (i.e., they have both creative and destructive potential), then drops it. With the "queen bee" gushing about how the NTI was the most beautiful thing she'd ever seen, there's no doubt we're drifting toward Speilbergia.

To put it gently, the script is a run-of-the-mill patchwork. It wants to have it all ways—to be both a children's and an adult movie, a nonthreatening, life-affirming, special-effects fantasy, and a hi-tech *noir*. Cameron conceives the abyss as a metaphoric as well as geological space. But the film is nonstop action; its notion of subjectivity, of the dark recesses of the psyche, is purely aerobic. Lindsey and Bud overcome their differences (ostensibly a class issue—she's management, he's labor) because they both exhibit enormous courage under extraordinary physical circumstances. They risk drowning and are thereby reborn. Lindsey's second coming has overtones of Tinker Bell's in *Peter Pan*. Bud is less fortunate in that he has to go through a deep sea version of the *2001* Stargate sequence (Kubrick's Waterloo). Given 20 years of development in computer animation, what's amazing is that infinity still looks like an infrared aerial shot of the Santa Monica Freeway.

Like *Batman, The Abyss* is nothing if not a set. Cameron didn't shoot in the open sea. He converted two tanks in an abandoned nuclear reactor into underwater sound stages, flooded them with seven and a half million and two million gallons of water respectively, and lit them with state-of-the-art HMI lights converted for underwater photography. But where the *Batman* set, after its initial presentation, recedes into mere background, Cameron's set dynamically defines the action. On a visual and technical level, as a tour de force of one seemingly impossible and never-before-realized shot after another, about 20 per cent of *The Abyss* is brilliantly inventive filmmaking. Cameron sends the camera careening down corridors that are too narrow for a Steadicam and have to be lit with fiber-optic tubes, because there's no place to hide regular movie lights. Even more remarkable than the image is the quality of the sound—not postdubbed but recorded live underwater, so that the actors' voices are the direct expression of their moment-by-moment physical situation. Mastrantonio and Harris give not only energetic but at times emotionally compelling performances. The argument between them is whether Lindsey, like Millamant in Congreve's *The Way of the World*, will consent "to dwindle into a wife." And it's revealing that although the word *wife* gets batted around (it even comes up on the screen in giant letters at the climax), the word *husband* is never mentioned.

An expert action director, Cameron is much too good at covering his tracks—directing the audience's attention to what's supposed to be happening as opposed to how it actually gets on the screen. If this is a film about redemption through endurance, then a shot of Cameron—hanging from a rope, half submerged in the water with an oxygen tube up his nose, decompressing after five hours of underwater shooting—would reveal more about this brand of megalomania than anything in the actual film. (My advice—read the location stories before you buy your ticket.)

In the end, the operative myth in *The Abyss* is about distinguishing oneself as a director (as opposed to strengthening a marriage or saving the world). For all its gritty stylistics, the film has almost no psychological or social resonance; it's relevant only to other blockbusters. (Because Cameron treats women and men as equals, and locates villainy squarely in the military, he comes out to the left of most mainstream product.) A technical and financial groundbreaker, *The Abyss* is no deeper than its surface.

Also reviewed in:
NEW YORK TIMES, 8/9/89, p. C13, Caryn James
NEW YORKER, 9/4/89, p. 89, Terrence Rafferty
VARIETY, 8/9-15/89, p. 20
WASHINGTON POST, 8/9/89, p. Cl, Rita Kempley
WASHINGTON POST, 8/11/89, Weekend/p. 37, Desson Howe

ADVENTURES OF BARON MUNCHAUSEN, THE

A Columbia Pictures release of a Prominent Features/Laura Film production. *Executive Producer:* Jake Eberts. *Producer:* Thomas Schuhly. *Director:* Terry Gilliam. *Screenplay:* Charles McKeown and Terry Gilliam. *Director of Photography:* Giuseppe Rotunno. *Editor:* Peter Hollywood. *Music:* Michael Kamen. *Music Editor:* Chris Brooks. *Sound:* Frank Jahn and (music) Stephen McLaughlin. *Sound Editor:* Peter Pennell. *Production Designer:* Dante Ferretti. *Art Director:* Massimo Razzi. *Set Decorator:* Francesca Lo Schiavo. *Special Effects:* Richard Conway, Adriano Pischiutta, and Antonio Parra. *Costumes:* Gabriella Pescucci. *Make-up:* Maggie Weston. *Stunt Coordinator:* Tony Smart and Riccardo Mioni. *Running time:* 126 minutes. *MPAA Rating:* PG.

CAST: John Neville (Baron Munchausen); Eric Idle (Desmond/Berthold); Sarah Polley (Sally Salt); Oliver Reed (Vulcan); Charles McKeown (Rupert/Adolphus); Winston Dennis (Bill/Albrecht); Jack Purvis (Jeremy/Gustavus); Valentina Cortese (Queen Ariadne/Violet); Jonathan Pryce (Horatio Jackson); Bill Paterson (Henry Salt); Peter Jeffrey (The Sultan); Uma Thurman (Venus/Rose); Alison Steadman (Daisy); Ray Cooper (Functionary); Don Henderson (Commander); Sting (Heroic Officer); Andrew MacLachlan (Colonel); Jose Lifante (Dr. Death); Mohamed Badrsalem (Executioner); Ray D. Tutto [Robin Williams] (King of the Moon); Kiran Shah (Executioner's Assistant); Franco Adducci (Treasurer); Ettore Martini (First General); Antonio Pistillo (Second General); Michael Polley and Tony Smart (Gunners).

CHRISTIAN SCIENCE MONITOR, 3/14/89, p. 11, David Sterritt

Terry Gilliam is best known as the only American member of Monty Python, the British comedy group. He's also the one member who never appeared in person, instead providing the wacky animations that kept popping into their TV show. As a filmmaker, Mr. Gilliam has cultivated a live-action style that's still proudly cartoonlike. And as director for pictures like "Time Bandits" and "Brazil," he concocted a nonstop flow of visions, fantasies, and dreams that flooded the screen with vigor and invention.

In some ways, "The Adventures of Baron Munchausen" is Mr. Gilliam's most flamboyant creation yet. To call it larger than life is an understatement—it's downright gigantic in every department, from its exuberant performances to its pulsating colors and unstinting energy. Even with all this going for it, though, the movie doesn't quite succeed. In the end, it's more tiring than triumphant.

The tale begins in the 18th century—it's "the age of reason," a caption informs us—during a war that's anything but reasonable. In a European city that's besieged by Turkish troops, a theater company is presenting its latest diversion, an account of Baron Munchausen's mythical adventures. Suddenly, who shows up but the real baron, telling the players they've got things all wrong. He's willing to set their story straight, a favor they're not eager to receive. Since he's an unstoppable yarn-spinner, we're soon caught up in his account of one impossible feat after another.

The movie announces its epic intentions from the beginning. Gilliam's camera soars, swoops, dives, and runs rings around its subjects, bestowing a heroic importance on everything it encounters—much of which is pretty heroic to begin with, since the story's basic setting is full of ferocious combat, insidious politics, and (somehow surviving side-by-side with all this) the zany theatrics that interest Baron Munchausen more than anything else in sight.

For sheer spectacle, "The Adventures of Baron Munchausen" is unbeatable by any other film in recent memory. The plot is full of whimsy and magic, whether our hero is riding a cannonball through the skies, reminiscing in the belly of a fish, or matching wits with the King of the Moon, whose (intellectual) head is conveniently detachable from his (lusty) body. What's missing, though, is a sense of lightness, of ease, of *humor* as opposed to labored ingenuity and monumental cuteness. The movie sweats and strains to earn our affection. There's not a relaxed moment in it, and after a while you feel as if Gilliam and Co. had grabbed you by the lapels (like the inescapable Munchausen himself) and won't let go until you *laugh* and *have a good time* whether you feel like it or not.

While the film's trouble stems partly from its visual style, there are also problems with the screenplay. Written by Charles McKeown and Gilliam, it just isn't *funny* most of the time. The casting also contributes to the difficulty. John Neville looks and sounds right in the title role, but his performance smacks more of makeup and costuming than real, human charm. Gilliam regular Jonathan Pryce is priceless, as usual, but his small role as a political bad guy doesn't let him develop the comic mannerisms he has wielded so well in the past.

Python member Eric Idle suffers from a similar problem, although he provides some of the picture's few moments of laid-back laughter. In the spirit of the proceedings talented performers like Oliver Reed and Bill Paterson seem to be working too hard to enjoy themselves. Ditto for Robin Williams, who puts his usual hyperactivity into an (uncredited) turn as the moon-king. Other names in the cast, including Sting and Valentina Cortese, make little impression, although young Sarah Polley is likable as the baron's little-girl sidekick.

I don't mean to come down on "The Adventures of Baron Munchausen" too strongly. Many moviegoers may be captivated by its sweeping ambition, its visual lavishness, and its determination to be the most extravagant film comedy since "It's a Mad, Mad, Mad, Mad World" ended an era of overblown Hollywood farce. I sorely missed the sense of childlike wonder that charged through Gilliam's earlier "Time Bandits," though, and the sardonic social commentary that enriched "Brazil," his most underrated movie.

FILMS IN REVIEW, 6-7/89, p. 365, Roy Frumkes & Denise Labelle

The Spielberg/Lucas fantasy factory, which has been unable to break new ground in the '80s, might take a glance at two recent films: a little experiment called *Paper House* and an enormous adventure story by Terry Gilliam which have demonstrated that there is still plenty of creative room left in the genre.

Paper House is a first feature, a child's nightmare played out on the often irrational landscape of the Id. It cost less than anything Spielberg or Lucas have done for theatrical release. *Munchausen* (the tail end of a trilogy including *Time Bandits* and *Brazil*) cost more than anything from the Spielberg/Lucas arsenal, with the possible exception of *Howard The Duck*.

Working from the right (intuitive) side of his brain, Gilliam forces us to judge his phantasmagorical film using personal taste alone, which isn't such a terrible thing, except perhaps to the critical community, who need rigid criteria, and to the distributors, who need hard and fast genres in order to sell their product. Not this time. Children may be able to absorb it uninterrupted by a bewildered left lobe.

In that respect it will remind the viewer of the work of Dario Argento, whose films bear some resemblance to Hitchcock, only without the benefit of anything vaguely resembling logical thought processes.

The Adventures Of Baron Munchausen follows the kaleidoscopic exploits of the towering, sturdy old codger, who seems to have been struck from a C. Aubrey Smith mold, then garnished with prop hair, latex wrinkles, and a nose appliance. Pursued by the aggressive spectre of death, and accompanied by an unduly cynical little girl, the Baron tracks down his motley bank of supergifted former cohorts, and together they rout the Turkish forces of wartorn 18th century Europe.

One can approach *Munchausen* by comparing it to Gilliam's past works. Like them, it is full of energy, yet boring. This is due primarily to major characters being unlikeable, which causes each scene to stand or fall on its own merits. The protagonists bring no forward motion to the story. Also Munchausen's framing story, set inside a theater, is leaden despite a flurry of action.

Other Gilliam signatures abound. There's always a horse that jumps over someone's head, giants who either wear ships on their heads or swing ships around, other giants coming out of the water. . . .

More broadly, his films are like raging, chaotic cancers of the Art Department, overdecorated with props, mixing time periods with what appears to be an intent to confuse rather than to inform.

Being in *Brazil* was akin to being in quicksand—what world were we really in? *Munchausen*, happily, is mostly true to a particular style. The period is baroque, with billowing yellow-browns, golds, and muddied reds, giving a feeling of being lush rather than color rich.

There is, however, one sequence that *does* stand on its own. It features a friend of Gilliam's who did his guest stint as a favor but insisted on going creditless. So while I respectfully will not print the RW name, I must mention that not only does his performance make the moon sequence pulsate with euphoric energy, but I liked him better here than in any of his past film roles, including the one for which he was Academy Award nominated in 1987.

Munchausen, like *Last Temptation*, may be remembered as much for what went on outside the theater as for what appears on screen. Gilliam is a classic example of the renegade filmmaker at war with the powers that be. Unfortunately, despite all his generally accurate campaigning against the evil bureaucrats, he is also giving business people fodder for their arguments against leaving artistic control in the hands of the directors.

Gilliam's concept wasn't economically capable of being filmed on the $23.5 million budget, nor even on the final budget, possibly more than double the original estimate. Much was edited during production and copious amounts were deleted during post production. Despite the debacle of *Heaven's Gate, Munchausen* demonstrates that we live in a cyclical world where nothing really changes. The same mad fiascos are still unfolding.

It may be premature to be looking forward to the laser disc on *Baron Munchausen*, but after hearing that Gilliam cut 38 minutes out to make the present version more commercial, and that he prefers the longer cut to the one we're seeing....

LOS ANGELES TIMES, 3/10/89, Calendar/p. 1, Sheila Benson

We wouldn't really want to be children again. Mumps. Chicken pox. First day of school. Big dogs. But to find the world an adventure, an astonishment. *Believable* again. Who wouldn't want that?

That is Terry Gilliam's gift: He spins his yarn about an elegant old duffer who has waltzed round and round through the air with the goddess Venus, who has been to the moon and has the moon dust in his shoes to prove it and we are his, our eyes as round as the fullest moon.

Children won't know that "The Adventures of Baron Munchausen" is the most sophisticated vision imaginable. That a treasure-chest of references—from movies, old and new, animated and otherwise; from the history of art and from music and mythology—is being spilled out for them. That their imaginations as well as their funny bones are being tickled and that, actually, they are being taught to prefer the beautiful to the gaudy, the perfect to the shoddy. (You hate to think what the Care Bears will look like after "Munchausen.") Children will simply accept the movie's magic matter-of-factly, the way they do a book by Maurice Sendak or a movie as effortlessly fine as "The Black Stallion." They don't yet know how great a present it is, and that's probably best.

The rest of us have no such stake in keeping our cool, and from its very first minutes, "Munchausen's" witty splendor is reason enough to lose ours. In an unnamed European city under siege from the Turks in the late 18th Century, a very tatty theater company is attempting to tell the miraculous adventures of a semi-fraud, Karl Friedrich Hieronymus, the Baron von Munchausen.

The Theater Royal itself, backstage and onstage, is enough to hook us: There is an enormous sea monster with sea-blue-green scales who might have swum straight out of Sendak and seductive mermaids (the most seductive Uma Thurman from "Dangerous Liaisons" and Valentina Cortese, in the first of their double roles). Suddenly, just as we are entering a Turkish harem, the performance is interrupted by a tottering old gentleman (John Neville) who says he is the baron himself.

To prove it, he will save the city from the siege *and* set a few facts about himself straight. But to do this, he needs his four friends: Berthold (Eric Idle), the fastest man alive; Albrecht (Winston Dennis) the strongest; Adolphus (Charles McKeown) the most farsighted and Gustavus (Jack Purvis) the most leather-lunged.

Only the spirited Sally Salt, 10-year-old daughter of the troupe's impresario, believes him, but she's enough for Gilliam: The adventures are off and rolling. Salt is played by Sarah Polley, a marvelously feisty, blessedly un-cute Canadian actress who seems to have been raised oblivious to any child-acting cliches. A perfect foil for the richly classic shadings of Neville's Baron, Polley is irresistible. (Kids will recognize her at once as Ramona Quimby, from the splendid PBS series based on Beverely Cleary's "Ramona" books.)

And so we glide back into the harem again, which this time is "real," staffed by Fellini-esque harem ladies so pinkly voluminous they appear to be made out of folds of salt-water taffy. It's the domain of a cheerfully lethal Sultan (Peter Jeffrey), and the consequences of a bet he makes with Munchausen are the bombardment of the city.

That is how things began, Munchausen explains to a skeptical audience. If he can leave the besieged city and seek out his four invaluable friends, he will raise the siege. And so, in a hot-air balloon made from the silken knickers of the town's ladies, and with Sally, who has secretly stowed away on board, Munchausen soars off, to hover between faith and disbelief, reality and illusion, old age and virile manhood.

"He won't get far on hot air and fantasy," sneers his nemesis, the Right Ordinary Horatio Jackson (Jonathan Pryce, terrifying behind his Three Blind Mice glasses), chief bureaucrat of the city. Ah, but how wrong he is. Those are exactly the qualities the world needs a shot of—and that movies soar upon.

(That, and money, and how *ever* much this extravaganza cost, it is, as they say, all up there on the screen a thousandfold. Frankly, it is beside the point of this film, anyway, not its big news).

The baron is a terribly reassuring hero. Not all of us have adjusted to the Age of Reason, no matter how long it's been upon us. For those discombobulated by astronauts and space stations, who can barely manage daylight savings time and who are put off by an invention with more moving parts than a fly swatter, the baron is our man.

And Gilliam is our man too. Ironically, he has harnessed the most advanced side of movie technology to make poetry, not hard-edged hardware. To give us a shimmering, tide-rippled moonscape, littered with giant heads like some silent De Chirico vista; to offer a theater that Piranesi might have etched, an angel of darkness that Goya would recognize.

But its best moments go straight into our filmic unconscious, as unerringly as "The Thief of Baghdad" or "Pinocchio" or Moliere, to create new pockets of wonder. There are the King and Queen of the Moon, whose heads and bodies can be—and frequently are—separated: reason and carnality, nicely differentiated. If the king, "Ray D. Tutto"/*Rei di Tutto*/King of Everything, sounds madly familiar, it is an unbilled Robin Williams, creating his own amazing universe.

There is the baron's dalliance with no less than Venus herself (Uma Thurman, naturally), who has stepped daintily out of her Botticelli clam shell. The sight of them, waltzing upward into the sky, attended by angels whose wings flutter like hummingbirds, is enough to make steam shoot from the ears of her hairy husband, Vulcan (Oliver Reed, also naturally).

And more and more and more. But it is "Munchausen's" theme, that in the face of logic and reason, there is still a place for the imagination, that is its greatest gift. "We cannot fly to the moon. We must face facts. We must live in the modern world," gloats archvillain Pryce.

For all those whom the modern world unsettles slightly, there is Munchausen. And small, sturdy Sally. And, thank the Lord, Terry Gilliam, captaining his magnificent artisans: production designer Dante Ferretti, cinematographer Giuseppe Rotunno, costume designer Gabriella Pescucci, special effects man Richard Conway, editor Peter Hollywood and composer Michael Kamen. And whoever it was who persuaded that horse to *sit*.

MONTHLY FILM BULLETIN, 3/89, p. 71, Mark Finch

The late eighteenth century. In a war-torn city, Henry Salt's debilitated theatre troupe enact the tales of famed adventurer Baron Munchausen. They are suddenly interrupted by an eccentric who claims to be the real Baron, and who proves his authenticity by giving an account of his culpability in the current war—the result of a bad bet with the Turkish Sultan. Won over, the townspeople assist Munchausen in trying to locate his band of four followers: Berthold (the fastest man alive), Adolphus (blessed with super-vision), Gustavus (capable of causing a hurricane), and Albrecht (the world's strongest man). In a makeshift hot-air balloon, Munchausen and Sally—Henry Salt's stowaway daughter—set sail for the moon. He promises to return to the town with his army of four in time to stop the Turks' final attack. On the moon, Munchausen and Sally are imprisoned by the King of the Lunar City, whose body and head are at constant odds. In jail, he finds grey-haired Berthold, and all three are rescued by the Queen; the trio fall back to earth and into the bowels of Mount Etna, where Vulcan entertains them at tea—served by Albrecht, who now just wants to be gentle. Inconveniently, Munchausen becomes enamoured of Vulcan's wife, Venus; Albrecht and the three visitors are tossed by Vulcan into a whirlpool. Emerging on the other side of the world, they are immediately consumed by a giant sea monster, within the belly of which they are reunited with Adolphus and Gustavus, who seem to have lost their respective skills. The five men are persuaded by Sally, however, to return and defend the town from the Turks. Recovering their super-powers at the last moment, they win the battle but the Baron is shot by the town's crazed captain, the Right Ordinary Horatio Jackson...Back at the theatre, Munchausen concludes his story to the townspeople, who open the city gates to find that the Turks have mysteriously fled.

The making of *The Adventures of Baron Munchausen*, a cautionary tale of the 'Brazilian' ways of movie financing and Europroduction, is probably a taller tale than anything recounted by the Baron. It is sad, though, to find that it is also more fantastic than anything in the finished film. Where *Brazil* represented a consummate, idiosyncratic yoking of political paranoia and comic precocity, these ingredients have separated unappetisingly in *Munchausen*. The film opens with the siege of a walled town, under bombardment by the Turks, but there's no sense of madness or even of genuine confusion. Jonathan Pryce, as the Right Ordinary Horatio Jackson, crazed commander of the town, delivers some relishable *non sequiturs*; but Gilliam strikes some banal and embarrassing anti-war postures (inside Mount Etna, Vulcan and his miners will make weapons "for anyone who'll buy"; at the end of each adventure, Sally has a vision of the Angel of Death).

The flipside of this heavy-handed observation is the gory humour, which peaks early on with the Sultan's Organ of Human Torture: "You won't want to miss this aria", he enthuses, as keys trigger tuneful shrieks from prisoners. "It reminds me of my schooldays in England." A panorama of Pythonesque decapitations chimes wittily enough with the original text's fondness for splitting or slicing bodies—commonly horses, dogs and diverse wild beasts. But this disconnection between politics and jokes has a deadly effect on the film's pace, and looks like a misguided attempt to keep the young audience in mind (*Time Bandits* and Rob Reiner's *The Princess Bride* were able to keep their integrity while operating within similar terms). *Munchausen's* inability to get into gear rather defeats what would seem to be the point of the picture: whereas the source is adroit at slipping between fantasy and reality, Gilliam's fiction can't even handle a flashback.

Throughout the novel, the Baron insists on his veracity, often by comparison with other narrators' more extravagant inventions. Munchausen's surreal stories are also bookended by serial testimonials (signed Gulliver, Sinbad and Aladdin). The original Munchausen dramatises and parodies the process of storytelling (and then...and then...), but instead of subverting notions of truthfulness, this *Munchausen* has enough difficulty relating a story. In a particularly unsatisfactory finale, the Baron's adventure is discounted as a mad monologue. Although it is implied that events may really have happened, this misses the original's giddy pleasure in aggressive exaggeration. In this context, there's something unnerving about so much effort being expended to make *Munchausen* 1988 look like *Munchausen* 1943, or the novel's original line drawings. On the credit side are some spirited cameos by the non-English performers, including Robin Williams in a pseudonymous role as the Lunar King and Valentina Cortese as his long-suffering but spirited Queen.

NEW LEADER, 3/6/89, p. 21, John Morrone

As an antidote [to *New York Stories*] let me offer, briefly, a story about another city in Terry Gilliam's big, noisy, tumultuous fantasy, *The Adventures of Baron Munchausen*. The time, we are told, is "the late 18th century...the Age of Reason...Wednesday," and cannonbursts from Turkish artillery are shattering Vienna. The city, run by callow bureaucrats (the slimiest one is played by Jonathan Pryce), is on the point of surrender when the aged Baron Munchausen (John Neville) arrives. He has come to reacquaint the citizens with his exploits involving various villains on earth, in space and under the sea, in order to arouse their courage and revive their taste for heroism.

A Vienna about to fall, the Baron sings, is "no place for cucumber trees, no place for three-legged cyclops, no place for me." To subdue the Turks he then travels far and wide to reunite his former cohorts, who have given up their own peculiar talents (superstrength, superspeed, super*breath*, among others) and become salves to other potentates. The Baron renews their faith in themselves, they return with him to Vienna, and inspire the people to triumph.

Baron Munchausen is all pyrotechnics, Eastern splendor, and bathroom humor—poised, one might say, somewhere between Orientalia and genitalia. And the oddest people keep appearing: Sting, as an Austrian soldier about to be executed, Valentina Cortese as a slave girl, Robin Williams (unbilled) as the frantic, oversexed King of the Moon.

The film is in many ways Gilliam's thematic follow-up to *Brazil*, but this fable of how imagination conquers bureaucratic inertia is happier, brighter, even more unpredictable. Although the character of Baron Munchausen has been seen before in films (as the hero in both a Czech animated feature of the early '60s and one of Germany's biggest Nazi-era entertainments), Gilliam creates him anew. His adventures are a tonic—wildly fantastic yet spirit-affirming—the work of a storyteller who prefers not fact but phosphorescence.

NEW YORK, 3/20/89, p. 73, David Denby

Terry Gilliam's gigantic comic fantasy *The Adventure of Baron Munchausen* offers one brilliantly outlandish image after another—and yet I couldn't wait for the movie to be over. Since I was also made restless by an earlier Gilliam film, the 1981 *Time Bandits*, I think it's fair to surmise that what's boring in *Munchausen* may be endemic to the way Gilliam structures movies. *Munchausen* doesn't have a story, just passages from nowhere to nowhere; it doesn't have characters, just flamboyant eccentrics or mythical creatures. Gilliam's emotional distance from his audience is frightening. The whole gibbering, riotous movie could be taking place at the end of a tunnel.

I say this while recognizing that the American-born Monty Python veteran, director of *Brazil*, has very great gifts. *Munchausen* is a late-eighteenth-century period reconstruction in which we appear to travel through a skewed version of the art of the era—a trip to the moon, for instance, surreally drifts through old, elegantly geometric astronomical drawings. And in the beginning of the movie, his camera outside a city under siege, Gilliam achieves the enchanted-minarets style of the classic *Thief of Baghdad*. Gilliam's is a truly fantastical mind; he never does anything straight. In *Munchausen*, the nattering, nagging, cluttered style of Python excess reaches its apotheosis in an explosion of eyeball-assaulting comic detail. Every corner of the frame jumps.

As the Turks storm a seaside city, the golden haze of dust kicked up by the war is tinged with red flames shooting from the mouths of ornately fanged cannons. In a half-wrecked theater, actors are putting on a show dramatizing the preposterous adventures of Baron Munchausen, a grandiloquent officer in Frederick the Great's cavalry—at which point the old hollow-voiced Munchausen himself (John Neville) breaks in, waving his sword, and denounces the slanders perpetrated against his name. We then see Munchausen's own version of his exploits, his attempts to reassemble his four comrades in arms (who have appeared, teasingly, as actors in the play) and lift the siege against the city.

The movie plays the kind of neo-Borges representation-and-reality tricks that leave me cold (outside of Borges stories themselves). Munchausen's epic adventures end with him back onstage, narrating, but then it turns out the stories have been true all along, etc. Wheels within wheels, and who cares? The shifts from "story" to "reality" carry little emotional or dramatic meaning—they're just games. Rather than find some way of engaging us, Gilliam and Charles McKeown, who wrote the movie together, use the shifts to demonstrate the primacy of imagination over the supposedly arid and tyrannical properties of reason. With the ayatollah's followers aflame all over the earth, "reason" would hardly seem to be man's worst enemy, but Gilliam rides his high horse. The movie is an elaborate undergraduate attack on the Enlightenment's pretensions to rationality. Munchausen himself, traveling on cannonballs, riding aloft in a balloon made of women's underwear, is pure dream. His nemesis is the maniacally logical governor of the beleaguered city, played by the rascally Jonathan Pryce, who performs wonders of comic malignancy with bushy eyebrows and tiny dark glasses.

In the course of his adventures, Munchausen first visits the sultan's palace, a lemony seraglio filled with fatties, freaks, and dwarfs. Gilliam out-Fellinis Fellini here, adding a touch of Mel Brooks in the sultan's torture machine, which produces musical sounds from the cries of the sufferers. Later, on the moon, Munchausen encounters the ecstatic, chattering head of Robin Williams; he is the king of the moon, pure intellect separated from his body and whirling through space on a silver platter. In middle earth, the bellowing Oliver Reed, covered with hair and bent over, a round, roaring beast, is the sulfurous Vulcan, enslaved by a naked Venus (Uma Thurman) rising from her Botticellian half-shell. Thurman, her long locks covering her dainties, is truly radiant.

There's much more. But extravagantly imagined as the material is, it's also phenomenally boring. Part of the problem is that Munchausen is a force of will, not a protagonist—and the stiff-backed, bristling Neville is completely impersonal. Yet I doubt that a better actor would have transformed the material. The movie may itself be proof of the powers of imagination, but it's also a depressing example of how futile "pure" imagination, floating free from narrative or emotions, can be. Fantasy filmmaking, I have begun to think, is the last refuge of the emotionally disconnected.

NEW YORK POST, 3/10/89, p. 25, David Edelstein

Give a visionary director like Terry Gilliam ("Time Bandits," "Brazil") a decent-sized topic (say, "The Case for Fantasy") and a spot of cash (say, $50 million) and he's apt to run brilliantly, picturesquely riot.

In his exhausting, wizardly epic, "The Adventures of Baron Munchausen," Gilliam can't stop at one or two visual conceits; he piles layer on layer of soot, carnage, period clutter and phantasmagorical bric-a-brac. It's almost too much to take in all at once; you might find yourself wishing for an extra eye. Or an Excedrin.

The picture is already infamous for its cost overruns, but every penny is on screen and working—hard. Gilliam doesn't set out to make a mere fantasy; he sets out to make the fantasy to end all fantasies, the conquering fantasy—the Fantasy Über Alles.

His hero, Baron Karl Friedrich Hieronymus von Munchausen (John Neville) is an 18th century adventurer who trots the globe with a quartet of superhuman servants, among them the fastest man in the world (Eric Idle) and the strongest man in the world (Winston Dennis).

At least, that's according to rascally fabulist himself. For the film is a story-within-a-story. As Turkish cannons fire on a German city, the ancient eccentric Neville disrupts a performance of a play about the exploits of Baron Munchausen. Throwing the actors and audience into an uproar, he claims that he's the real Baron and that only he can end the war that threatens to wipe out the entire population.

Is there a place for this fanciful dreamer in an enlightened, rational world? That's the rather boring question posed by the city's chief executive officer, a dessicated. Teutonic bureaucrat (Jonathan Pryce) who proclaims the superiority of logic and science over fairytales and fantasy.

"There's no room now for three-legged cyclopses, cucumber trees, oceans of wine..." moans the old baron. "No place for me." Wearily surrendering to a great black bird with a rotted-skull head—the gruesome incarnation of death that haunts him—Munchausen is summoned back to life by a little girl, Sally (Sarah Polley), who still believes in the imagination, and who exhorts him to reassemble his team of aging miracle-workers and save the city.

And so the pair charges forward, the baron growing younger with each success and withered with each setback. He and Sally escape the walled city in a hot-air balloon fashioned from ladies' knickers; sail to the moon and tussle with its king (an unbilled Robin Williams); fall into the volcanic abode of the god Vulcan (Oliver Reed) and his wife Venus (Uma Thurman); and hurtle all the way through the earth to the South Seas, where they're swallowed and then disgorged by a sea-monster. Get the picture?

No, you couldn't possibly get the picture; the picture is too wondrous and sprawling. Gilliam, who designed the animation for "Monty Python's Flying Circus," loves the rickety artifice of old theaters and their magnificent gewgaws.

He is most buoyant, in fact, in the unveiling of splendid new sets, and in spectacular entrances and exits. The emergence of Thurman's Venus is a lollapolooza: Little angels, their wings fluttering, rise up from the sea bearing a giant pink shell, which opens to reveal the naked goddess draped in her long auburn hair.

Thurman's Venus does not compare unfavorably to Botticelli's: Her expression suggests she is magnificently (and justifiably) pleased with herself, as if to say, "It might have cost $50 million, but this alone is worth all of *Ishtar.*"

Nothing in "Munchausen" is similarly ethereal. Elsewhere, the effects have a lumbering quality—you're always conscious of gravity. And Pythonesque cruelty abounds. In Gilliam's universe, heads are unceremoniously lopped off, and when one of them lands on the startled lap of a female bystander, it winks. Gilliam doesn't chase rainbows; he laboriously erects and then defaces them.

Columbia reportedly made the director tighten his belt before shooting began, but we can certainly make do with this K-Mart "Munchausen." The narrative surges deliriously, evoking the teeming panoramas of Bosch and Fellini, and when Eric Idle does his Road Runner thing the action has a cartoon charge.

The heave-ho is part of why the film, for all its glories, isn't a fantasy classic. There's something self-congratulatory about its miracles. And pretentiousness doesn't do much for a kiddie movie: You don't cheer the baron, you cheer Fantasy: You don't applaud heroic silliness, you applaud the Triumph of the Will. (It's no surprise that the most famous treatment of the Munchausen story was a 1943 rallying cry for the Third Reich).

Gilliam's satire of a murderous, totalitarian bureaucracy is meant to be contemporary, but it feels dated. (Doesn't Gilliam know that encouraging people to lose themselves in fantasy is also, in our escapist age, a potent tool of repression?) In its lack of complexity, "Munchausen" could be one more pipe dream of the director's broken "Brazil" hero—a doomed romantic obsessed with flight and transcendence.

It's hard to compete with so many miracles, and the fine cast, with one exception, is mostly upstaged. As the King of the Moon, Williams appears as a giant, white, disembodied head ("I am Rei di Tutto; you may call me Ray"), and proceeds to wage a titanic battle with his rapaciously horny body, which he regards as a distraction from the cerebral task of being at one with every molecule in the universe. The wildly funny sequence exposes the folly of trying to repress one's physical impulses, which have a way of rebounding with a vengeance.

Williams—himself a costly but inexhaustible special effect—holds his own against Gilliam's designs: He's the only performer whose rhythms briefly dominate the film. In context, that's a blessing—a true illustration of the triumph of the will.

NEWSDAY, 3/10/89, Part III/p. 5, Mike McGrady

Frail, old Baron Munchausen (John Neville), surrounded by the wounded and dying, exposed to a rain of Turkish cannonballs, lies in a besieged fortress awaiting death. After a full life of adventure and prevarication (not for nothing was he known as "Lugenbaron," or "the lying baron") he wants only to perish in peace.

"But *why*?" asks the tiny waif who has become his constant companion.

"Because I'm tired of the world," he explains. "Because it's all logic, all reason now... There's no room for three-legged cyclops in the south, no place for cranberry trees...no place for me."

Those lines had to be penned by writer-director Terry Gilliam, a man who has spent recent years battling bankers and busting budgets in his quest for the cinematic equivalent of a three-legged cyclops or, at the very least, a cranberry tree.

With "The Adventures of Baron Munchausen," Gilliam concludes a trilogy that began with "Time Bandits" and "Brazil." So dissimilar are these three movies that the concept of trilogy requires a word of explanation. What unites the films is not character or storyline; it is theme, a celebration of imagination over logic.

In "Time Bandits" a boy is able to dream his way into history's great romantic adventures. The hero of "Brazil" unravels bureaucratic red tape through his daydreams. "The Adventures of Baron Munchausen," the wildest film in the packet, is a free-flowing argument for magic in an era of reason. While the theme is adult, the results are a child's delight—an explosively imaginative fantasy catering to the youngster who survives within all of us.

Baron Munchausen, trapped in a fortress under Turkish siege, escapes by constructing a huge hot-air balloon out of whatever material happens to be at hand, primarily the underwear worn by actresses attached to a traveling troupe: "Kindly be so good as to remove your knickers." Later, floating high above the ramparts, he explains his basic military strategy to a young stowaway: "Fantasy is the only way to escape the Turks."

The first stop—why not?—is the moon where the king (Robin Williams) and queen (Valentina Cortese) have detachable heads—they also have most of the film's best moments. From there, it's but a short hop to the center of the Earth and the kingdom of Vulcan (Oliver Reed) where the baron finds time for a flirtation with Venus (Uma Thurman). Then on into the belly of a sea monster where he rejoins former comrades at arms before venturing back to a fortress still under siege and a final battle with the Turks.

Director Gilliam has mentioned an early infatuation with that magical movie, "Thief of Baghdad." Throw in a bit of "Alice in Wonderland" and a soupçon of "The Wizard of Oz"— then carefully excise logic, reason and coherence and you'll have something roughly approximating "The Adventures of Baron Munchausen." While a lunatic Robin Williams and a devilish Oliver Reed steal every scene within reach, it is Gilliams's bravura cinematic techniques that make all the hullabaloo bearable.

My reasonable, logical side is dazzled by his work but has some difficulty applauding his thesis. In fact, fullest appreciation of the film would seem to entail one of two prerequisites. Either one should be a youngster not yet ensnared in logic's nets. Or one must be able to see the film through that most special of viewing devices, rose-colored glasses.

NEWSWEEK, 3/13/89, p. 69, Jack Kroll

The movies are the only place where a childlike sense of wonder can wind up costing an unchildlike $45 million. That's the amount of money that reportedly has been spent on making *The Adventures of Baron Munchausen*, which was originally budgeted at about half of that. Director Terry Gilliam (of Monty Python fame) is the guy with the childlike sense of wonder. It turned out he needed all that money to play with in a runaway operation that nearly cost him his job. "Munchausen" is one of those movies in which art and business collide and affect each other. Just because a film costs so much to make doesn't mean that it will be a bomb—or that it deserves to be. A lot depends on how a studio—Columbia in this case—distributes and promotes it. And of course, how good is it? "Munchausen" is flawed but fascinating, a Pythonesque fantasy with awesome special effects. And win or lose, Terry Gilliam is a talent to reckon with.

In the original, 18th-century stories, Baron Munchausen was an epic liar, part of a cultural tradition that stretches from Ananias in the Bible to Ted Baxter from "The Mary Tyler Moore Show." For Gilliam the baron represents fantasy, the imagination, against the chilly dictates of reason and logic. Gilliam's version is an 18th-century magical mystery tour in which Baron Munchausen (John Neville) suddenly appears in an unnamed town that's being bombarded by the Turks and boasts that he will save the city.

The baron takes off in a balloon made out of a mountainous pile of ladies' bloomers, accompanied by 10-year-old Sally (Sarah Polley), who is the Alice of this wonderland. They land on the moon, ruled by a king whose head detaches itself from his body, so the head can concentrate on higher things while the body engages in carnal congress with the queen (Valentina Cortese). "I haven't time for flatulence and orgasms," explains the king's disembodied head. As that brashly surrealist line might indicate, the moon king is played with perfect lunacy by Robin Williams, unidentified in the credits.

From the moon the expedition plummets to the lair of the fire-god Vulcan (roaring Oliver Reed) who crushes coals into diamonds for his bride, Venus (exquisite Uma Thurman). One of the film's most magical scenes is the dance of Venus and Munchausen, who whirl in midair through her floorless ballroom laced with waterfalls. Touching all elements—space, earth, water—Munchausen & Co. plop into the belly of a giant sea monster, where he meets up with his old servants: Adolphus (Charles McKeown, who cowrote the screenplay with Gilliam) is the world's greatest marksman. Gustavus (Jack Purvis) is a dwarf whose mighty lungs can blow away armies. Albrecht (Winston Dennis) is the world's strongest man, who carries off everything in the Turkish sultan's treasury. Berthold (Eric Idle) is the fastest man on earth, who can cross Europe in minutes. This 18th-century SWAT team defeats the Turks and discomfits the city's boss, the puritanical, Robespierre-like Horatio Jackson (Jonathan Pryce), who hates fantasy and fun.

Much of "Munchausen" is truly astonishing, as was Gilliam's Orwellian fantasy "Brazil." But like "Brazil," "Munchausen" sometimes mistakes astonishment for delight. "Munchausen" lacks what one of Gilliam's models, the English classic "The Thief of Bagdad," had—an enchanting balance of technical wizardry, narrative and character. Gilliam crams the screen with so many marvels that it's hard for his characters and the audience to breathe. Yet few movies contain the authentic prodigies in "Munchausen"; Terry Gilliam is one of the rare directors who can create an entire world. "Munchausen" is like a huge, flawed emerald, a real gem that has cracked under pressure.

TIME, 3/13/89, p. 82, Richard Corliss

The grandest film folly since *Heaven's Gate*! The $40 million pratfall! The project that put Columbia Pictures in the commode! Even Baron Karl Friedrich Hieronymus von Münchausen, the 18th century adventurer and fabulist on whose alleged exploits this film is based, might pause before telling such tales of artistic profligacy. But Terry Gilliam has the wounds to prove it.

Gilliam, who learned from his days with Monty Python to be truculent and never truckle, had earlier fought Universal Pictures when it was reluctant to release his film *Brazil*—a masterpiece at a mere $15 million. This time he would run up a higher tab—say, $17 million to $20 million over budget—and into bigger trouble. David Puttnam, *Munchausen's* Hollywood sponsor, soon departed as boss of Columbia. Film Finances Inc., which stepped in to supervise the picture, threatened to fire Gilliam if he didn't scale back on the spiraling costs. A producer sued Columbia, claiming that five years ago it agreed to a *Munchausen* project based on a 1942 German movie he owns.

Is Gilliam's picture worth all the fuss? Sure, because he has tapped the cinema's capacity for lying with a straight face. If you can create a vision onscreen, then it's true. At the start, Baron Munchausen (John Neville) strides onstage to recount his hoodwinking of a sulky Sultan (Peter Jeffrey), his dalliance with the Queen of the Moon (Valentina Cortese), his flirtation with the goddess Venus (Uma Thurman), his captivity inside a giant fish, and his long-odds battle with the Turkish army. Except for young Sally (Sarah Polley), his listeners don't know if he's telling the truth. But his viewers know; Gilliam has used the magic of film to show them the wonders Munchausen has limned. Lovers dance in midair in an underworld waterfall ballroom. The baron sails to the moon in a ship wafted by a hot-air balloon. One of his servants (Eric Idle) outruns a speeding bullet. A terrifying angel of death hovers over the baron, like a fiendish C.P.A. over Gilliam's pricey dreams.

A few episodes test the viewer's patience, and there is considerably more wit in the film's sumptuous design than in its dialogue. But anyone with an educated eye and a child's love of hyperbole can take delight in Gilliam's images and incidents. Starlight spangles a lunar beach as the baron's ship drifts ashore for his interview with an Italianate creature (Robin Williams, unbilled and hilarious) who identifies himself as "the King of Everything—*Rei di Tutto*. But you may call me Ray." The king's body is detachable from his head, which provokes schizophrenia of celestial proportions. "I got tides to regulate!" the head shouts to his errant anatomy. "I got no time for flatulence and orgasms!"

Everything about *Munchausen* deserves exclamation points, and not just to clear the air of the odor of corporate flop sweat. So here it is! A lavish fairy tale for bright children of all ages! Proof that eccentric films can survive in today's off-the-rack Hollywood! The most inventive fantasy since, well, *Brazil*! You may not believe it, ladies and gentlemen, but it's all true.

VILLAGE VOICE, 3/14/89, p. 57, J. Hoberman

The least you can say for *The Adventures of Baron Munchausen*, whose budget *Variety* puts at $50 million, is that the money is there on the screen. Droll and clamorous, Terry Gilliam's latest epic—a self-described example of "18th century science fiction," opening Friday—suggests the overamplified confluence of Federico Fellini and Ronald Searle, a gibbering, capering merry-go-round, full of wacky wigs, funny accents, and throwaway grottiness.

A few performances may be detected amid the impressive special effects: John Neville plays the dynamically doddering baron to prating perfection, Oliver Reed makes a roistering Vulcan, and Uma Thurman confirms her status as the Enlightenment's reigning sex goddess with a turn as Venus. Still, as with Gilliam's 1985 cause célèbre *Brazil*, the sets are the real star. Dante Ferretti has concocted Turkish harems with pajama-striped walls, lunar cities based on false Renaissance perspective, and a perpetual battlefield populated by ruined statues, dragon-mouthed cannons, and actual elephants. There's a Disneyland attention to architectural detail. The miniature work is impeccable, and even a primitive playlet is performed in the context of a backstage as vast as Carlsbad Caverns.

Munchausen has an entertaining 45 minutes before the floating, long-winded, uncredited head of Robin Williams rolls in to impose his own mechanical comic rhythms, reinforce Gilliam's thesis about the duality of mind and body, and send the movie plummeting back to earth. Although *Munchausen* quotes *Pinocchio* and Gilliam has cited *The Thief of Bagdad* as his model, the film seems far too programmatic to exert the same fairytale fascination. Less quirky than *Time Bandits*, *Munchausen* is ultimately as didactic as *Brazil*, nostalgically presenting its hero (director?) as the implacable foe of progress, reason, and science—the last fabulist—who meets his antithesis in authority figure Jonathan Pryce (the rational man, meant to suggest Robespierre).

Abstractly splendiferous as *Munchausen* is, the most impressive thing about its director is his ability to mooch off the age of Spielberg in indulging his own penchant for costly, curdled fantasy.

Like Spielberg, Gilliam is always strenuously on the side of imagination, even if his position seems overly theoretical; he lacks Spielberg's grounding in suburbia and Hitchcock. Narrative and character not being Gilliam's strong suits, his mode is less rollercoaster than fireworks display—which may account for Hollywood's love/hate relationship with this prodigal prodigal. Legend has it that after attending a screening of *Brazil* Spielberg excitedly told Gilliam: "That's amazing! You've just shown me my nightmares." Presumably he wasn't referring to the movie's commercial prospects.

Also reviewed in:
NATION, 3/27/89, p. 427, Stuart Klawans
NEW REPUBLIC, 3/20/89, p.32, Stanley Kauffmann
NEW YORK TIMES, 3/10/89, p. C8, Vincent Canby
NEW YORKER, 4/3/89, p. 103, Pauline Kael
VARIETY, 1/18-24/89, p. 8
WASHINGTON POST, 3/24/89, p. C1, Hal Hinson
WASHINGTON POST, 3/24/89, Weekend/p. 39, Desson Howe

ADVENTURES OF MILO AND OTIS, THE

A Columbia Pictures release of a Fujisankei Communications film. *Executive Producer:* Haruo Shikanai and Hisashi Hieda. *Producer:* Masaru Kakutani and Satoru Ogata. *Director:* Masanori Hata. *Screenplay:* Mark Saltzman. *Based on the Story by:* Masanori Hata. *Director of Photography:* Hideo Fujii and Shinji Tomita. *Editor:* Chizuko Osada. *Music:* Michael Boddicker. *Music Editor:* Nancy Fogarty and Bill Bernstein. *Sound:* Minoru Nobuoka and Tetsuya Ohashi. *Production Designer:* Misaki Miyauchi. *Art Director:* Takeharu Sakaguchi. *Special Effects:* Yoshio Kojima. *Narrator:* Dudley Moore. *Running time:* 76 minutes. *MPAA Rating:* G.

LOS ANGELES TIMES, 8/25/89, Calendar/p. 8, Michael Wilmington

There's something delightfully pure and fresh about the children's film "The Adventures of Milo and Otis."

This epic fairy tale about male bonding between an orange kitten and a pug-nosed puppy, refashioned from Masanori Hata's Japanese movie "The Adventures of Chatran." is full of clean sunlight and waving grass. Populated entirely with animals from Hata's private island menagerie—bears, foxes and snakes as well as the usual barnyard assortment—it generates the blissfully dry sense of wonder the best children's books or movies often do.

Hata creates a little world, as magically detailed as Oz, Wonderland or Pooh Corner. And he draws us into it, serenely, effortlessly—guiding us along a rushing river where the frightened kitten, Milo, is swept along in a runaway crate; following the puppy, Otis, as he chases along the banks; pausing quizzically over the antics of a fox, the stately stare of an owl and the relentless pursuit by a bear; lingering on the snowy forest that eventually imprisons Milo, Otis and their respective families. Then gazing out to the sea, as Otis stands stranded on a tide-lashed rock, ultimately rescued by a disgruntled but duty bound sea turtle.

The basic story deals with the friendship of all animals, exemplified by Otis's yearlong expedition to rescue his childhood companion. It's an idealistic theme. Obviously, it translates to universal community among all species. Yet there's nothing sticky about the movie's visual execution. In its original Japanese form, "Milo and Otis" may well be a classic. And even in its shortened American version—with roguish narration by Dudley Moore, a bouncy score and a rickytick country-Western theme song that's a real mistake—it's engrossing, genuinely heartwarming stuff.

It's certainly unique. Hata hasn't used the conventional method of training the animals to perform according to a pre-existing scenario, tricking or teasing them. The animal actors, including as many as 30 roughly identical kittens or puppies pressed into service as Milo or Otis, were filmed in their natural environment responding to situations Hata and his crew helped create. This makes the movie the animal equivalent of an "improvised" drama like John Cassavetes' "Shadows" or Henry Jaglom's "Always."

The movie is full of what François Truffaut called "privileged moments": little jolts of charm or reality. One scene, where Milo and Otis watch a chick emerging from his egg and then nuzzle him as he stretches out, strikes me as a more impressive achievement—at least a more heartening one—than anything in "Batman."

Hata worked on the film for more than four years, turning to one of the great masters of the Japanese cinema, Kon Ichikawa, to help him edit the unwieldly mass; Ichikawa's title here is "associate director." The director of "Fires on the Plain" and "The Makioka Sisters" is no stranger to animal or children's films, and he helps give the movie a seamless shape and flow.

"The Adventures of Milo and Otis" (MPAA-rated G) is an unabashed children's film, made with a wit and intelligence that adults can enjoy too. It reminds us that sometimes it takes the purest sophistication to see with an innocent eye. Just as Milo and Otis, drifting kitten and determined pup, learn that they're not alone in the world—so, perhaps, will the children and parents who will see, and love, this movie.

NEWSDAY, 8/25/89, Part III/p. 3, Terry Kelleher

The trouble with most animal movies is the people in them. They tend to be dumb.

Zoologist and author Masanori Hata (pen name Mutsugoro) decided to eliminate this problem when he realized his long-held dream of making a feature film at his private menagerie in Hokkaido, Japan. There are no humans in Hata's movie—just a cat and a dog and all sorts of animal supporting players.

Hata proved to be a true "actor's director." Allowing his cast to perform naturally and spontaneously within the loose framework of the story, Hata shot some 400,000 feet of film over four years. Somebody forgot to tell him he was a madman who'd never be offered so much as a lunch meeting in Hollywood.

The result of Hata's efforts was released in Japan three years ago, and moviegoers over there flocked to this simple tale of a cat and a dog whose friendship endures adversity. Now Columbia Pictures has brought the movie to America under the title "The Adventures of Milo and Otis," with narration by Dudley Moore.

Don't worry, parents. The English-language version isn't another "What's up, Tiger Lily?" Moore doesn't say anything outrageously inappropriate or tell a story totally different from the one Hata intended. His tone is occasionally impish but consistently gentle, and he has fun providing various animals with distinctive voices (e.g., a weary, stuffy, veddy British sea turtle). There's nothing too jarring in Mark Saltzman's screenplay, except for the expressions "Make my doggy day" and "You're dead meat."

And those amazing animals do the darndest things under the direction of Hata and his associate, documentary film maker Kon Ichikawa. Milo the cat fishes for trout with his tail. Otis the dog, stranded at sea, hitches a ride on the turtle's back. Some of the best shots aren't the trickiest. Young children, and many of their elders, are guaranteed to "awwwwww" at the close-up of a drenched and shivering Milo emerging from the drink.

The camera doesn't always avert its gaze from the less tidy aspects of animal life. Milo lunched on a muskrat, not a mixed green salad. His mate gives birth in a scene that's a bit more graphic than you might expect. But "The Adventures of Milo and Otis" should leave kids with a warm and fuzzy feeling, like an hour and a quarter at the petting zoo. Maybe they'll be entranced enough to forget the opening song, "Walk Outside," which even Mister Rogers would reject as too sappy.

A final note: The tree-star award for "The Adventures of Milo and Otis" comes with a CG (Child Guidance) rating. Adults are urged to behold it only through a kid's eyes.

NEW YORK POST, 8/25/89, p. 25, V.A. Musetto

Milo is a cute little kitten. Otis, a pug-nosed puppy, is his best pal. They live on a farm with lots of other adorable animals. Like Gloria the chicken, who asks Milo and Otis to keep her eggs warm for her.

One bright and sunny day the frisky Milo (is there any other kind of kitten?) finds himself in a wooden box being swept down a river. Otis takes off in hot pursuit, determined to save his pal and bring him back to the farm. He does, but not before encounters with a waterfall, a swamp, a bear, a sea turtle, snakes and a snowy winter. And not before Milo finds true love with a beautiful white cat named Joyce and Otis has his heart stolen by Sandra, a dog with a French accent.

"The Adventures of Milo and Otis" is an all-animal, live-action movie made in Japan, where it is reported to be one of that country's highest grossing pictures ever. The version that opens here today is in English, with Dudley Moore providing the narration and all the voices.

Only a curmudgeon would dare say anything nasty about a movie like this. But I must advise you that the three-star rating is meant for kids under 10. People older than that are on their own.

TIME, 9/18/89, p. 93, Richard Corliss

[*The Adventures of Milo and Otis* was reviewed jointly with *Honey, I Shrunk the Kids*; see Corliss' review of that film.]

VILLAGE VOICE, 9/5/89, p. 80, Renee Tajima

If the horrors wrought by human beings are too much to take [the reference is to *Weapons of the Spirit*], join the toddlers at a Saturday matinee of *The Adventures of Milo and Otis*—a charming tale of a kitten and puppy gamboling about Japan's Hokkaido idyll.

Adventures is like a live-action bedtime story, inhabited by talking animals and narrated with great gusto (in its cut American version) by Dudley Moore. Feline Milo and canine Otis have their start on a rustic farm, where they do heartwarming things like guard a chicken egg and tumble about the livestock. The story quickly turns to a road picture when mischievous Milo is accidentally swept away downriver on a wood crate, with buddy Otis in hot pursuit. Along the way, separately and together, the two encounter a world of adventurous escapades, even love.

A sweet, harmless tale directed by well-known author Masanori Hata (the associate director is the renowned Kon Ichikawa), *Adventures* will probably appeal to smaller children here. There are the usual spatterings of animal stereotypes—evil predators include black vultures and a big, black bear, and Milo falls for a platinum blond number named Joyce—that are unfortunate leftovers of the traditional children's oeuvre. But parents will be hooked by Mark Saltzman's clever script and Moore's talented mimicry. As Milo's feline mom ("Milo! I told you not to walk on the chickens!") or a prissy Joyce replying to Milo's marriage proposal ("Oh, I don't know, a farm isn't exactly my lifestyle"), Moore proves himself a virtual Rich Little of the animal voices—a purr-fect 10.

Also reviewed in:
NEW YORK TIMES, 8/25/89, p. C10, Stephen Holden
VARIETY, 5/21/86, p. 25

ALL DOGS GO TO HEAVEN

A United Artists Pictures release in association with Goldcrest Films of a Sullivan Bluth Studios Ireland Ltd. production. *Executive Producer:* George A. Walker and Morris F. Sullivan. *Producer:* Don Bluth, Gary Goldman, and John Pomeroy. *Director:* Don Bluth. *Screenplay:* David N. Weiss. *Story:* Don Bluth, Ken Cromar, Gary Goldman, Larry Leker, Linda Miller, Monica Parker, John Pomeroy, Guy Schulman, David Steinberg, and David N. Weiss. *Editor:* John K. Carr. *Animation Film Editor:* Lisa Dorney. *Music:* Ralph Burns. *Music Editor:* Michael Connell. *Sound:* Gerry Humphreys, Dean Humphreys, and (music) Keith Grant. *Sound Editor:* John K. Carr. *Production Designer:* Don Bluth and Larry Leker. *Directing Animator:* John Pomeroy, Linda Miller, Ralph Zondag, Dick Zondag, Lorna Pomeroy-Cook, Jeff Etter, and Ken Duncan. *Special Effects Directing Animator:* Stephen B. Moore. *Running Time:* 84 minutes. *MPAA Rating:* G.

VOICES: Dom De Luise (Itchy); Burt Reynolds (Charlie); Daryl Gilley (Dog Caster); Candy Devine (Vera); Charles Nelson Reilly (Killer); Vic Tayback (Carface); Melba Moore (Whippet Angel); Judith Barsi (Anne-Marie); Rob Fuller (Harold); Earleen Carey (Kate); Anna Manahan (Stella Dallas); Nigel Pegram (Sir Reginald); Loni Anderson (Flo); Ken Page (King Gator); Godfrey Quigley (Terrier); Jay Stevens (Mastiff); Cyndi Cozzo (Puppy); Thomas Durkin (Gambler Dog); Kelly Briley (Puppy); Dana Rifkin (Fat Pup).

LOS ANGELES TIMES, 11/17/89, Calendar/p. 6, Peter Rainer

I've always loved the *idea* of feature-length animated movies more than I've loved the movies themselves. Although there are many notable exceptions, animation seems to work best in the short form; few feature-length animated movies have the sustained snap and invention of, say, the best Disney and Warners shorts.

This is to some degree a matter of economics. The cost of producing an animated feature is so prohibitive, and the labor so painstaking, that most film makers opt for the commercially safe "family entertainment" mode. Irreverence is generally the first casualty of the long form.

"All Dogs Go to Heaven," the latest animated feature from Don Bluth ("The Land Before Time," "An American Tail"), is in the comfy fun-for-the-entire-family category. Except, as is so often the case with such movies, it's not really a whole lot of fun for anyone. The animation is of variable quality; the story is a garbled pastiche of "Oliver Twist" and "Little Miss Marker;" the songs, including four by Charles ("Annie") Strouse, are eminently unhummable. Adults probably won't find the story transporting enough to stifle yawns; children won't pop their eyes at the animation.

Even on a product tie-in level, the film falls short. Charlie, the junkyard dog at the film's center, is rather mangy and uncuddly. Do the Wendy's executives who arranged the marketing tie-ins with this movie really believe that rubber figurines of a flea-specked mutt will sell burgers? The most memorable thing about Charlie is that he is voiced by Burt Reynolds. Charlie/Burt actually gets to sing a few songs, making this the first time Reynolds has crooned on-screen—sort of—since "The Best Little Whorehouse in Texas" and before that, "At Long Last Love." Some milestones are millstones.

Charlie and his dachshund chum Itchy (Dom De Luise) break out of prison at the start of the film and make their way back to the Louisiana nightclub Charlie co-owns with the bulldog Carface (Vic Tayback).

When Charlie is rubbed out by Carface, he zooms off to heaven, where he pirouettes with a cloud-borne whippet angel (Melba Moore) before sneaking back to Earth for some pay back. There, he snatches from Carface's clutches an orphan girl, Anne-Marie (Judith Barsi), who has the ability to talk to animals—which comes in handy when betting on rat races and kangaroo boxing matches.

With Anne-Marie in tow, Charlie and Itchy put their new-found booty into their own nightclub, Charlie's Place. But then innocence rears its ugly head. Anne-Marie wants Charlie to find her parents; And she disapproves of gambling.

Considering how integral Anne-Marie has been to Charlie's betting success, her sudden disapproval has the hollowest ring since Claude Rains was shocked—shocked—to discover *gambling* going on at Rick's place in "Casablanca." Don Bluth and his screenwriter, David Weiss, may be able to sleep better at night because of this little tyke's willed naivete, but her virtuousness is a drag on the action. The only time the movie jolts to life is when Carface and his underlings are scampering and slavering.

A tip-off to the film's vacuity is its vision of heaven, which appears to have been color-coordinated in shades of Pepto Bismol. Shouldn't a movie keyed to the wonderment of childhood look more wonderful? When animation falls short, as it does here, we feel the lack more severely than we would in a live-action film, since the expressive possibilities of animation seem limitless. Virtually anything can be made to happen.

A great animated film delineates the entrancements and poetic leaps of imagination that are central to a child's fantasy life—and an adult's fantasy life too. That's why, when we're in the presence of great animation, we feel as if our childhoods have overwhelmed us. Suddenly, everything is possible. In "All Dogs Go to Heaven," the possible is the mundane.

MONTHLY FILM BULLETIN, 4/90, p. 93, Julian Stringer

New Orleans, 1939. After escaping from the local dog pound, Charlie and his best friend Itchy return to the gambling casino run by the vicious pitbull Carface, Charlie's old business partner. Unwilling to share the riches of his growing success, Carface orders his henchman Killer to dispose of his former friend. Charlie is struck by a runaway automobile and drowned in the bay, but immediately finds himself at the Gates of Heaven, met by a sweet Whippet Angel. She explains that all dogs go to Heaven because of their innate virtue—though she has difficulty in finding any record of Charlie's good deeds. Seeking revenge on Carface, Charlie decides to return to earth; he steals the heavenly watch inscribed with his name, thus prolonging his life. Reunited with Itchy, the two dogs stumble across the secret of Carface's operation. He has been using the talents of Anne-Marie, a young orphan girl who can talk to animals, to predict racing winners. Anne-Marie escapes with Charlie and Itchy, on the understanding that they will find her new parents. At the races, with money stolen from a young couple, Kate and Harold, the trio place a bet on an inept 1000-1 long shot whom Anne-Marie knows will be allowed to win on its birthday, and with their subsequent winnings the friends set up their own bar, named Charlie's Place. In the meantime, Anne-Marie has won the affections of Kate and Harold, and is eventually asked to live with them. After a violent confrontation with Carface and Killer, Charlie finds his business burnt to the ground; a bruised and beaten Itchy accuses him of going soft over his fondness for Anne-Marie. On hearing that she has again been grabbed by Carface, Charlie rushes to the rescue and is trapped by Carface. The latter eventually meets his end at the hands of King Gator, an underworld character infatuated with Charlie's singing voice. Charlie saves Anne-Marie's life but loses his heavenly watch in the process; although he dies once more, this sacrificial deed allows Charlie back into Heaven. At Kate and Harold's home, his ghost visits Anne-Marie, imploring her to look after the tired and lame Itchy. In Heaven, Charlie spies Carface stealing another watch and heading back to earth, bent on revenge.

Walt Disney's model for the animated feature (Don Bluth, although no longer at that company, is, with *The Secret of Nimh* and *An American Tail*, one of its major revivalists) usually pays harmonious attention to the separate workings of story and spectacle. It is as important for characters to act naturalistically as it is for songs and set-pieces to be staged with some sense of timing and visual panache. Early on in *All Dogs Go to Heaven*, the hero, Charlie (voiced with resistable assurance by Burt Reynolds), performs his vaudevillian "You Can't Keep a Good Dog Down" in the less than salubrious surroundings of a gambling den. A happy client screams that the place needs more such theatre, and it's a cry that the film repeatedly tries, but fails, to live up to. Lavish scenes (not just the above, but also the ones set in Heaven and, particularly, the grossly offensive visit to King Gator) are jarringly inserted into an already clumsy narrative, so the drama and pacing found in many Disney films is lacking, a weakness only accentuated by the general structural confusion. Here is a buddy film that starts by gently parodying gangster movies, races into a chase and rescue plot, and ends up in Lord only knows what mode of celestial satire. *All Dogs Go to Heaven* moves in and out of its reference points like a speedy fiddler's elbow.

The resulting unevenness is especially felt in the extreme ambiguity surrounding Charlie. As a hero/anti-hero he is consistently doubled, shadowed and compared to the utterly rogueish Carface, both being small-minded capitalists who exploit the other characters. Although this moral ambivalence is explicitly stated (Charlie revealing himself to be Anne-Marie's kidnapper, not just her liberator), it is never satisfactorily resolved. Anne-Marie is the innocent yet sensual girl whom Charlie wants to possess—and not simply as a means of making money. Like any number of children's fictions, *All Dogs Go to Heaven* can be read as a rape parable, the intention of which is to control and use a virgin orphan child. One scene closes with a show of affection (Anne-Marie kissing Charlie), sealed by an iris shot which harks back to an earlier period of popular American film, the silent cinema, whose sexual dynamic was often exactly this need to have narrative power over an innocent female.

Almost inevitably, Anne-Marie gets lodged with new parents (an anodyne yet grisly couple who lack even the mild temper tantrums of *Lady and the Tramp*'s Mr. and Mrs.). This is perfectly in keeping with the loss and absence concerns of family animation, though one cannot find any interesting or dynamic tension here between the pulls of an absent, 'natural' family and the alternative appeals of an 'unnatural', surrogate one (productively explored, for all its faults, in Disney's *Song of the South*). This rather gets in the way of the film's first half, where the moments that work do so precisely because there's no need for the story to worry about setting up representations of family. The early pastiche of gangster movies is not without its appeal, and there are occasional scenes of some vividness and colour, such as the play of light and dark in the opening break-out underground, the moment when Charlie and Itchy's buddy relationship is first established.

The film's weak final quarter—despite a brief but memorable incantation of the New Orleans back streets, when all the neighbourhood dogs hear of Anne-Marie's abduction and rush to help track her down—tries to turn Charlie into a jumped-up Lassie. However, *All Dogs Go to Heaven* can't muster the pull or emotional effect of even the most cloying films in that series. In the end, the fact that a sad yet sub-standard death and farewell scene can be quickly juxtaposed with a jokey epilogue in Heaven suggests a fundamental lack of faith in the story and characters, an indifference at odds with the moral sentiments so pointedly expressed elsewhere.

NEW YORK POST, 11/17/89, p. 31 Jami Bernard

Don Bluth's animated features have included "The Land Before Time" and "An American Tail," both of which dealt with the animal equivalents of children being abandoned in scary, uncharted worlds. This theme has particular resonance for children and for adults who haven't forgotten, which—along with Bluth's detailed and sometimes foreboding animation—may account for those movies' success.

His latest, "All Dogs Go to Heaven," is the first complete production from Bluth's Sullivan-Bluth Studios in Ireland, and it has a few kinks to work out. The abandonment theme is present in the form of an orphaned girl who speaks to animals, but obscured by the story's main character, a rover of a dog who returns from the great beyond, "Heaven Can Wait"-style, to right a few wrongs. The movie is dark and confusing.

Charlie B. Barkin (Burt Reynolds) is a German shepherd who has not done all the good deeds that dogs are supposed to do (which is why, ostensibly, they all go to heaven). When his former gambling partner, Carface Malone (Vic Tayback), has Charlie bumped off before his time, Charlie finesses his way out of heaven (guarded over by whippet Melba Moore) and returns to Earth to get even.

Charlie and his canine pal Itchy (Dom De Luise) appropriate the thing that has made Carface rich—a little girl whose ability to talk to animals helps her determine the winner of races (rat races and horse races). This girl, Anne-Marie (Judith Barsi), wants Charlie to help her find a nice set of parents.

The nastiness of the canine underworld of 1939 New Orleans does not juxtapose well with the suffocatingly, cloyingly cute orphan's quest for a home. Another problem is that Reynolds' voice is somehow inappropriate for an animated character—his low-key, breezy delivery, interacting with De Luise's more frenzied Itchy, tends to get lost in the crazy quilt of cartoonland.

Reynolds' wife, Loni Anderson, also has a minor voice role, leading one to expect more from her stay-at-home girl-doggie character than we get. Charles Nelson Reilly, however, is memorable as bad dog Carface's sidekick.

There is an interesting aspect to the background paintings—the sky is unfamiliar looking, sort of roiling and moody, very dramatic. The animators were clearly influenced by their Irish environment.

"All Dogs" is a musical, although the only thing I can remember about the music is that Reynolds sings some of it, and shouldn't. It's good that he's attempting to stretch, what with his old-time burglar in the recent "Breaking In," but when it comes to singing, he shouldn't stretch, he shouldn't reach. Not until he can reach the notes.

Despite all the effort that has obviously gone into this, the movie never really seems to come together, plotwise or otherwise. It is one of those "Flintstones" type cartoons, where humans could easily be substituted and the story wouldn't suffer (nor would it improve). The animation seems almost beside the point, and that won't help much in the movie's box office competition with Disney's "The Little Mermaid," which opened earlier this week.

NEWSDAY, 11/17/89, Part III/p. 5 Bill Kaufman

Children who see "All Dogs Go to Heaven" will get their fill of cartoon characters; happily, not the stilted Saturday morning garden variety of high-tech zappers, but a colorful cast of animal figures, each thoughtfully imbued with endearingly human traits.

Ask anyone who fondly remembers some of the classic animated films of decades back, most notably Walt Disney's Golden Age creations of the 1930s and '40s: A key element was the wonderful way life was sketched into the drawing-board characters. In this new film, the fanciful flight of the animator's art is set in a rather offbeat milieu—New Orleans, circa 1939. The hero, Charlie B. Barkin, a pugnacious German shepherd, a rogue with a heart of kibble and the instincts of a bookie, embarks on a quest for such thoroughly human virtues as love and kinship. Burt Reynolds supplies the familiar voice for the dog, who dwells in a hulk of a scrapped car in a sort of junkyard Oz.

The only human character drawn into the movie is Anne-Marie, a wide-eyed, doleful little orphan who has the ability to speak with animals. Each of the other pooches in the film displays human behavior traits. Count among them greediness, foolishness, loyalty and a touch of evil. Then there's Itchy, a hyperactive dachshund with Dom De Luise's voice, and a nasty pit bull sporting Vic Tayback's Brooklynese. Charles Nelson Reilly's unmistakable voice comes from a near-blind mongrel, who bumps into obstacles.

The Mardi-Gras-flavored New Orleans setting combined with sophisticated animation offers an effective, constantly changing panorama of colors and art styles that shift swiftly from vivid to subdued, keeping pace with the dramatic context of the moment. Just about the only disappointments are the movie's maudlin, uninspired songs. Only one of the tunes, "You Can't Keep a Good Dog Down," written by Charles Strouse ("Annie") and sung by Reynolds and De Luise, has some pizzazz. Then again, youngsters tend to care more for believable characters and stimulating action than a quality musical score, things they'll find in abundance in this movie.

TIME, 11/20/89, p. 91, Richard Corliss

These days, nearly every popular movie wants to be a cartoon. For proof, check out 1989's five top hits: *Batman; Indiana Jones and the Last Crusade; Lethal Weapon 2; Honey, I Shrunk the Kids, Ghostbusters II.* They all aspire to the freedom of form and story that any animated film takes for granted. Problem is, real life gets in the way. Location shooting is at the whim of weather; special effects can look chintzy onscreen. And actors! They cost the moon, and their bodies aren't elastic enough to perform the comic contortions that Daffy Duck can give you with the wave of an animator's pen. So here's a tip for the '90s, Hollywood: junk the live-action movie. Just make cartoons.

Disney and Don Bluth can lead the way. Walt Disney, after all, created the genre, turning barnyard animals into superstars and a Sunday-supplement curiosity into the movie's most enduring subspecies. Bluth, a Disney renegade, showed his old masters that the cartoon possessed a social vitality for the '80s. Bluth's *The Secret of NIMH* was a parable on animal experimentation; *An American Tail* found much to say, endearingly, about melting-pot prejudice; *The Land Before Time* found love and death among the dinosaurs. Now Disney and Bluth have launched a welcome new Thanksgiving tradition, each producing a feature cartoon for the rescue of baby-sitters and the beguilement of the child in every moviegoer.

In *All Dogs Go to Heaven*, Bluth takes a vacation from portent and dips into anecdote. Listen for familiar echoes *(Little Miss Marker. Heaven Can Wait*, even Disney's 1988 cartoon *Oliver & Company)* in the story of Charlie, a German shepherd who is reprieved from death and befriends a little girl kidnaped by his scurvy old gang. Visually, the picture is swathed in Bluth's trademark golden browns and moody blues. Aurally, it's a reunion of the Burt Pack: Burt Reynolds is the voice of Charlie, Loni Anderson is the moll Flo, the exuberantly flustered Dom De Luise is Charlie's pal Itchy. *All Dogs* dawdles a bit, but it offers the requisite charm and a poignant moral: some things, like friendship and honor, are worth dying for.

The end of *The Little Mermaid* wrestles with no such ambiguities. It comes with flourishes, a rainbow and a perfect kiss—full heartstring accompaniment. But from the first frame, Disney's suave storytellers cue you to wonderment in their adaptation of the Hans Christian Andersen fairy tale. Ariel is a mermaid princess with a teenager's yen to travel beyond her world and become part of the forbidden one above. To her father, King Triton of the Mer-people, humans are "spineless, savage, harpooning fish eaters." To Ariel they are skyrockets and sea chanteys and buried treasure—the thrilling unknown. Then she spies hunky, lonely Prince Eric, and it's impossible love at first sight. For Eric, when he is saved by the mermaid and nursed by her caressing song, it's love at first sound. A cross-species *Romeo and Juliet:* boy meets gill.

Around these mismatched romancers, writer-directors John Musker and Ron Clements have assembled enough entertaining creatures to stock a theme park. Sebastian the crab (voiced by Samuel E. Wright) is a Caribbean Jiminy Cricket, fussing avuncularly over Ariel but bound to break into calypso croon. Louis the French chef (René Auberjonois) brings sadistic élan to his dicing, flaying and serving of *les poissons*. Ursula (Pat Carroll) the sea witch is a fat, shimmying squid with malefic revenge in mind—the sort of Disney horror queen who has given kids nightmares for a half-century. All these characters are given witty, hummable pop songs by Howard Ashman and Alan Menken (the *Little Shop of Horrors* team), a reminder that the Hollywood cartoon has become the last, best refuge of the Broadway musical.

The film's vocal, musical and painterly talents mesh ecstatically in the big water-ballet production number *Under the Sea.* As Sebastian limns the aquatic virtues, a Noah's aquarium of sea creatures animates a joyous Busby Berkeley palette. If ever a cartoon earned a standing ovation in mid-film, this would be it. But the whole movie is canny magic. For 82 minutes, *The Little Mermaid* reclaims the movie house as a dream palace and the big screen as a window into enchantment. Live-action filmmakers, see this and try to top it. Go on and try.

VILLAGE VOICE, 11/21/89, p. 96, Elliott Stein

When Don Bluth, frustrated at the routine work that had become the norm at Disney, left its animation department in 1979 after nearly 10 years there, animation freaks were all rooting for him. Three uneven films later, we're slightly impatient, but still rooting.

All Dogs, made at Bluth's studios in Ireland, is far from a total success. It does contain some exquisitely designed scenes, notably the haunting and superbly detailed long shots of the New Orleans skyline, under a bulging moon, full to bursting. The script's the rub. Its two cannie principals—Itchy (voice of Dom De Luise), a cowardly dachshund, and Charlie (voice of Burt Reynolds), a German shepherd bowwow-about-town and con pooch—escape from prison, resume their roguish lives, and alas, adopt a dreary, twee human moppet orphan, Anne-Marie (voice of Judith Barsi). The dark, convoluted, episodic story has Charlie murdered by a shifty pit bull; he goes to heaven, returns to earth, and...

I do expect I've just about had it with celebrity voiceovers in animation. This path has become a blind alley, invariably producing dialogue overload. Other than a handful of specialists, did anyone know or care who did the voices for *Snow White, Dumbo*, or *Bambi*? I'm genuinely fond of Burt Reynolds; when I hear his voice, it makes me want to look at him, not a German shepherd. And if Bluth really wants to divaricate from Disney, why doesn't he consider endowing *his* animals with genitals?

Also reviewed in:
NEW YORK TIMES, 11/17/89, p. C12, Janet Maslin
VARIETY, 11/15/89, p. 21
WASHINGTON POST, 11/17/89, p. D7, Rita Kempley
WASHINGTON POST, 11/17/89, Weekend/p. 51, Desson Howe

ALL'S FAIR

A Moviestore Entertainment release. *Executive Producer:* David G. Stern. *Producer:* Jon Gordon. *Director:* Rocky Lang. *Screenplay:* Randee Russel, John Finegan, Tom Rondinella, and William Pace. *Story:* John Finegan and Watt Tyler. *Director of Photography:* Peter Lyons Collister. *Editor:* Maryann Brandon. *Music:* Bill Myers. *Running Time:* 89 minutes. *MPAA Rating:* PG-13.

CAST: George Segal (Colonel); Sally Kellerman (Florence); Robert Carradine (Mark); Jennifer Edwards (Ann); Jane Kaczmarek (Linda); Lou Ferrigno (Klaus); John Kapelos (Eddie).

LOS ANGELES TIMES, 2/7/89, Calendar/p. 6, Kevin Thomas

"All's Fair..." is such a dismal comedy that not even Sally Kellerman's style and panache can salvage it. Kellerman plays the elegant estranged wife of an obnoxious, military-minded candy manufacturer (George Segal) who insists that his corporate staffers, armed with paint guns, join him in war games every weekend as a test of their mettle.

When Kellerman learns that a young executive (Jennifer Edwards) is blocked from a vice presidency because she's a woman and therefore effectively barred from participating in the games, Kellerman rallies to her cause. Edwards rounds up some women friends, and Kellerman hires a mercenary (Lou Ferrigno) to get them in shape to declare war on Segal and his guys, including Robert Carradine as Edwards' competition for the vice president slot.

A quartet of writers and director Rocky Lang create only tedium with their protracted battle of the sexes. In such dire circumstances, only Kellerman is able to make an impression. "All's Fair..." (rated PG-13 for language), which has terrible sound and lighting, is really wretched business.

NEW YORK POST, 4/1/89, p. 20, Jami Bernard

What do actors with recognizable names do when they need a little extra cash to put in a pool deck? They probably take roles in stupid movies like "All's Fair," which opened yesterday and will probably close before you finish reading this.

George Segal, Sally Kellerman, and Robert Carradine star in this adolescent comedy about the war between the sexes, set on the battlefield of an office where women can't advance and where the men keep in shape by playing war games on the weekends. When the women (wives of the staff, mostly) team up to play a war game of their own, the men get nervous and cover their vitals.

Segal plays—or overplays—the militaristic head of the company. Carradine is the employee most likely to succeed him, although a female co-worker is more qualified. Kellerman embarrasses herself as Segal's emasculating, materialistic wife, spouting tired double entendres about her husband's lack of muscle in bed.

Jane Kaczmarek is the only likable member of the cast, an intelligent-looking actress playing a disgruntled housewife who turns into a fighting machine with the help of ninja-for-hire, Lou Ferrigno. The Incredible Hulk weighs in with his usual annoying speech impediment. "See these fingers?" he asks, holding up two. "They are wegistered weapons in three countries."

The war between the sexes, as waged in this movie, is the one that fizzled out about 15 years ago when people were still wondering whether being a sensitive man meant he had to wear a frilly apron, and whether being a strong woman meant she had to wear army fatigues. (Actually, the women look pretty good in their army fatigues, while the frilly apron does nothing for Ferrigno.)

There are some occasional watchable moments, which is all one can hope for from a movie this lame. Ferrigno gingerly picking up a crying baby to comfort her is worth rousing yourself from your torpor for a moment. Then the moment passes.

NEWSDAY, 4/8/89, Part II/p. 17, Bill Kaufman

It seems that the inspiration for "All's Fair" came from the so-called survival game, a popular pastime in some circles, in which the participants dress up in combat gear and play war by shooting each other with pellets that splatter paint.

A wispy premise indeed that is padded to witless extremes when the bombastic military-buff president of the Hunky Chunk candy bar company known as The Colonel, played heavy-handedly by George Segal, decides to wage marital and corporate warfare against his wife, Florence (Sally Kellerman). He mutters to her, "I notice you look lousy in pink. You look like cotton candy upchuck."

Kellerman is totally miscast as the woman, who is in the process of suing her hunsband for divorce as well as trying to take control of the floundering firm's stock.

The film sputters along lamely as Florence herds together a group of disgruntled women for a mock war with The Colonel and his all-male troops to decide who gets the company. Everyone scurries around preparing for the Big Battle.

The movie spares no one: Lou Ferrigno ("The Hulk") looks woefully miscast as Rambo-like buffoon who is hired to train the women for battle.

To top off this slug of a motion picture, there is a streak of tacky dialogue, including a thoroughly tasteless scene at a bar, where Kellerman and two other women end up giving scatology a bad name.

Also reviewed in
VARIETY, 2/8-14/89, p. 24

ALWAYS

A Universal Pictures release. *Producer:* Steven Spielberg, Frank Marshall, and Kathleen Kennedy. *Director:* Steven Spielberg. *Screenplay:* Jerry Belson. *Based on "A Guy Named Joe" Directed by:* Victor Fleming; *Screenplay by:* Dalton Trumbo; *Adaptation by:* Frederick Hazlitt Brennan; *Story by:* Chandler Sprague and David Boehm. *Director of Photography:* Mikael Salomon. *Editor:* Michael Kahn. *Music:* John Williams. *Music Editor:* Kenneth Wannberg. *Choreographer:* Bob Banas. *Sound:* Willie Burton. *Sound Editor:* Richard Hymns. *Production Designer:* James Bissell. *Art Director:* Christopher Burian-Mohr. *Set Designer:* Carl Stensel. *Set Decorator:* Jackie Carr. *Special Effects:* Michael Wood. *Costumes:* Ellen Mirojnick. *Make-up:* James L. McCoy and Don Cash. *Stunt Coordinator:* Steve Lambert. *Running time:* 125 minutes. *MPAA Rating:* PG.

CAST: Richard Dreyfuss (Pete Sandich); Holly Hunter (Dorinda Durston); Brad Johnson (Ted Baker); John Goodman (Al Yackey); Audrey Hepburn (Hap); Roberts Blossom (Dave); Keith David (Powerhouse); Ed Van Nuys (Nails); Marg Helgenberger (Rachel); Dale Dye (Fire Boss); Brian Haley (Alex); James Lashly (Charlie);

Michael Steve Jones (Grey); Jim Robillard (Air Traffic Controller); Jim Sparkman (Dispatcher); Doug McGrath (Bus Driver); Shereil L. Bowens, Acencion Fuentes, Todd Jacobson, and DeMarious T. Morganfield (Children on Bus); Mike O'Neal, Larry Landless, Steve Shatynski, and James Pruitt (Ground Pounders); Joseph McCrossin (Mechanic #1); J.D. Souther (The Singer); David Jackson, David Kitay, and Gene Strimling (Band); Roy Harrison and Ted Grossman (Fishermen); Gerry Rothschild (Carl the Barkeep); Loren Smothers (Bartender); Taleena Ottwell (Bar Girl).

CHRISTIAN SCIENCE MONITOR, 1/23/90, p. 11, David Sterritt

Steven Spielberg is a powerful force in Hollywood, and—such is the extent of his popularity—in world cinema generally. During the '80s alone he's given us such top moneymakers as "E.T.: The Extra-Terrestrial" and the Indiana Jones pictures, not to mention "Steven Spielberg presents" movies like "Gremlins" and "Back to the Future," Parts 1 and 2.

What those movies have in common is that they're fantasies, appealing to mostly young audiences. Indeed, skeptical critics have criticized Spielberg for being a storytelling wizard with a permanently 12-year-old mind. In recent years, though, he's been trying desperately to grow up—if not in every film with his name over the tittle, at least in the pictures he's directed personally. "The Color Purple" had mature characters and touched on difficult challenges faced by American blacks. "Empire of the Sun" had a young boy as its main character, but dealt with such hard issues as war and the growing threat of mass destruction in the world.

Spielberg's new movie, "Always," marks another step in his cinematic growing up. It's a fantasy, but it's also a genuine love story. Every single character is an adult. And except for the action scenes (just a few) there's not a special effect in sight. You'd think Spielberg had finally left childhood and adolescence behind. The only trouble is, "Always" is a bore—the most tedious and washed-out picture this energetic filmmaker has ever done.

"Always" is based on "A Guy Named Joe," a hit movie from 1943, with Richard Dreyfuss and Holly Hunter replacing Spencer Tracy and Irene Dunne in the leading roles. The star is Mr. Dreyfuss as Pete, a man who dies, returns to Earth as a ghost, and finds himself still crazy about the woman he loved when he was alive. Spielberg has updated the story and made Pete a flyer who earns his living by extinguishing forest fires from an airplane. As a ghost, his assignment is to be guardian angel for a younger pilot, who happens to be in love with—you guessed it—Pete's old girlfriend. Which means Pete now needs the strength and wisdom to let go of what he once loved most.

That's a good theme for a movie, and Spielberg plays it straight. The ghost character might have been covered with ectoplasm and gussied up with weird camera tricks, for instance, but Spielberg makes him completely down-to-earth: He looks like Richard Dreyfuss, plain and simple. Pete's heavenly mentor, likewise, is played by veteran star Audrey Hepburn in a way that's as quiet as it is majestic.

Spielberg isn't yet the grownup filmmaker he wants to be, though. In his hands, the story seems superficial rather that resonant or thoughtful. A friend of mine puts it very well. Spielberg tries to plumb the depths of a big subject: loss, and the need to let go of things we cherish. But seen with his sensibility, Pete's doomed love seems as tragic as a kid's dog running away. You feel bad for a while, and soon you feel better.

"Always" is a nice try for Spielberg, and the cast gives it a game try. Dreyfuss plays Pete as winningly as he can; Holly Hunter has a fair amount of spunk; and John Goodman is likable, as always. (By contrast, newcomer Brad Johnson is completely out of his depth as the young pilot.) The movie's generally dull effect makes it clear, however, that Spielberg still has some maturing to do before he's ready to scan the depths of human—not to mention cosmic—psychology.

LOS ANGELES TIMES, 12/22/89, Calendar/p. 1, Sheila Benson

A better title for "Always", directed by Steven Speilberg, might be "Forever," which is roughly its running time.

Strange, the material that directors seize upon to update. "A Guy Named Joe" was dreadful the first time around, a soppy 1943 movie in which flying ace Spencer Tracy was killed and allowed by crusty old angel Lionel Barrymore to come back to help new pilot Van Johnson become the hot-shot that Tracy himself had been. At the same time, Tracy helped his love, ferry pilot Irene Dunne, get over her grief at his death and made his own regretful farewell.

This bathos might work in wartime, except that Dalton Trumbo's dialogue, paraphrased only slightly, about the wave of free children who would take to the free air that Tracy was helping keep free in the name of freedom, was questionable even then. And the film's vision of the uses of heaven prompted critic James Agee to call it "stonily impious."

Working from a screenplay by Jerry Belson, from material begun by the late Diane Thomas, Spielberg has kept the story almost intact and, in an homage to those Victor Fleming/Howard Hawks kind of films, has created a world in which nothing feels right. Here in the late 1980s, guys call their gals "funny face" and get called "you big lug" in return; fliers have "moxie" until that moment when "their number is up."

Richard Dreyfuss is now our flying ace, and since there isn't a popular war to throw him into, he drops water bombs on forest fires. Well, red, sandy extinguishing stuff. And Holly Hunter, the Irene Dunne in his life, wears khaki jumpsuits and can bomb the sizzle out of those fires as spiffily as he can.

Pilot John Goodman, playing Dreyfuss' best buddy—charmingly—tries to put his finger on it when he says their flying base is like a World War II movie, full of bombing raids and B-26s, with only Glenn Miller left out. Not exactly. This is a slavish copy of bogus reality: It's imitation ersatz.

Nevertheless, Dreyfuss and Hunter are one fun couple, matching cute for cute, spunk for spunk. He's even thought up a great present for her birthday: a white dress, in the spirit of the white dress Karen Allen wore on the run through most of "Raiders of the Lost Ark." The kind of clinging white dress that makes audiences perk up, and Hunter gurgle "Gurl clothes!"

So, Dreyfuss is cool. He is supportive. He will make sacrifices for his gurl, D'rinda. All he cannot say is the "I" word, as in "I ———— you," although you and I and that yellow Caterpillar tractor over there know gosh darn well he does.

All of us who fell under Holly Hunter's spell in "Broadcast News" and stuck to her through "Miss Firecracker" are in for a rough time of it. That wonderful directness and energy, that crackly voice and careening timing—bolting to the end of a phrase and catching herself just before she drops off the end of it—have been pushed into mannerism. She has a terribly affecting moment as, in that white dress, she dances to "their song," and Dreyfuss, dead and invisible, dances with her. But cuteness turning overripe is not a pleasant sight.

Opposite her is the pro himself. Richard Dreyfuss has made his career breathing reality into schlock, giving heart and warmth and sometimes a cutting edge to not-great material and making it seem better and finer and truer than it is. And he's really in peak form here, even if he's a little bookish for a "fly-boy." Of all of them, Dreyfuss is the one who hits us with a sense of loss; even with Hunter twinkling away at his side, it's his face and voice and eyes that draw us. But he can do no better than his dialogue or his situation—or his direction, and all of that is, as they say, tooth-rotting.

As the next fly-boy in line for Dorinda, newcomer Brad Johnson fits the description "big lug" eerily well. He is forgetability in motion. That leaves Lionel Barrymore's role as the angelic overseer. Director Spielberg has had a nice idea of turning this over to Audrey Hepburn, who is warmly offhanded in white nubbly sweaters and pants. Then he marooned her on what looks like the set for a Glade commercial—all Astroturf and fake daisies—had her trim Dreyfuss' hair as her first, unfathomable angelic act, and called her "Hap." It's tough to smile through plaque like this.

Finally, there are vast fiery action sequences, unclearly edited, involving the safety of brave firefighters we've barely met and can't be persuaded to care about. So we've got an unrealized heaven and a banal and noisy Earth. That leaves only hell, and that may feel realized enough by those who pay money to see this gargantuan nonsense.

MONTHLY FILM BULLETIN, 4/90, p. 94, Richard Combs

Pete Sandich is a daredevil pilot with a fire-fighting unit in the forests of the American North-West, his risk-taking being a constant provocation to his girlfriend, air controller (and would-be pilot herself) Dorinda Durston. After the airfield holds a birthday party for Dorinda, joined by Ted Baker, owner of Wings 'n' Prayer courier service and much smitten by Dorinda, she has an intimation that Ted's number is up, and begs him to take a safe instructor's job in Colorado, in return for which she will give up her flying ambitions. He accepts, but is then called out on an emergency operation, and after dousing a fire on his friend Al Yackey's plane in mid-air, himself catches fire and is blown up. Subsequently bemused to find himself wandering through the burntout forest, he meets Hap, a guardian angel who tells him that he is indeed dead and that now his mission is to lend spiritual support to another up-and-coming flyer—Ted Baker. At Flat Rock, Colorado, where Al has taken the job as chief instructor, the awkward Ted gets off to a bad start and is banished by Al. The latter then finds Dorinda, languishing at an air base in San Diego since Pete's death, and insists that she return with him to Flat Rock. Ted and his invisible mentor Pete also return, after the latter is convinced that Ted should find the girl he is pining for—although he doesn't realise who this is. He becomes jealously possessive when Ted and Dorinda do meet again, and through his spectral presence begins interfering in their budding relationship. Hap warns him that, his life being over, anything he does for himself is a waste of spirit and he must release Dorinda. With Pete's telepathic encouragement, Ted becomes a fully fledged pilot, but when he, volunteers to rescue a group of 'firejumpers' (ground firefighters) trapped by a blaze, Dorinda realises that he will be running the same risks as Pete. She takes off in his plane herself, and flying through intense heat (with Pete behind her, 'sending' instructions) creates a path for the firejumpers. He then helps her escape (on the point of joining him in death) from a crashlanding in a lake, and as she and Ted are reunited, Pete is finally able to withdraw from their lives.

Of the setting of *Always*, a saga of sky jockeys dousing forest fires in the north-western U.S., Spielberg has said: "I wanted the story to be somewhat timeless. A lot of the old World War II bomber pilots have kept their old aeroplanes, or at least restored, bought and used parts and turned them into fire-fighting equipment...It's a contemporary movie. It feels like it's set in the 40s, but in fact is set today". Which suggests what a special time frame 'always' is, both in *Always* and other Spielberg films: it comprises a transcendental or other-worldly future (here an after-life ruled, pixieishly, by none other than Audrey Hepburn) and a present that is simply old movies remembered. The present, in other words, doesn't really exist, except as another version of the past, and a past with (compared to the nebulous hereafter) peculiarly specific co-ordinates: World War II movies, aeroplane games, boyish dreams of heroism.

One more peculiarity is that the wartime ambience so often seems to be British rather than American. *Always* is a remake of Victor Fleming's 1944 *A Guy Named Joe*, in which Spencer Tracy as the dear departed had to learn to surrender his hold on Irene Dunne and leave her to Van Johnson. In relocating this from wartime New Guinea to the contemporary U.S.A., Spielberg has also kept other co-ordinates in mind: as Richard Dreyfuss' pal John Goodman declares, enthusing over their front-line airfield in the forests, the permanently grease-stained ground crew and the pilots lounging between missions, "It's England!", circa 1940 (or 1941, *the* Spielberg date), lacking only Glenn Miller. What this act of cultural projection signifies is a little hard to say. It could suggest that, although Michael Powell has become symbiotically linked with Martin Scorsese among American directors, the ur-Spielberg movie might be *A Matter of Life and Death*. It could have to do with his admiration for David Lean and something similar in the emotional themes if not temper of their films: if *Empire of the Sun* rebuilt *The Bridge on the River Kwai*, *Always*, about the necessity of renouncing love and embracing (existential? heavenly?) loneliness, is Spielberg's *Brief Encounter* or *Summer Madness*.

The connection does explain why Spielberg should have found his most rewarding vehicle in J. G. Ballard's story of an English schoolboy, obsessed with aeroplanes, who must reunite a world that begins in memory, a colonial dream of 'home', and ends, after Nagasaki, in another kind of after-life. (Spielberg had originally intended Lean to direct *Empire of the Sun*.) *Always* is the lighter, jokier, popcorn-Spielberg version of that scenario, the Spielberg who is meant when critics talk of the *Wunderkind* who refuses to grow up, because his protagonists are either children or adults playing movie games. *Empire* was tough enough, and fascinating enough in its equation of the family its young hero was trying to put back together with the reconstructive alchemy (words and light) of author and director, to render the complaint redundant. And perhaps *Always* demonstrates that, even when turned back into a game, the scenario has its charms and uses.

Although it is cast as a romance—with Dreyfuss in the Spencer Tracy role, as the pilot whose number comes up, and is sent back as spiritual guide to a young protégé only to find that he has to guide him into the arms of his former lover—this really plays as another kind of family drama. If *Empire* is about putting it back together, *Always* is about the necessity of 'letting go', with Dreyfuss' Pete Sandich constantly referring to his earthly rival in love as "my boy". The final shot has him receding into the night sky, faintly glowing like one of the visitors in *Close Encounters*, perhaps a proper 'heavenly father' now that he has helped Ted Baker not only as a trainee pilot but a learner in love. In being released to Pete's ex-lover, Ted (the possible merging of their names is toyed with) is also entering an implicit Oedipal scenario akin to the one blithely raised by the Spielberg-produced *Back to the Future*, and jokily by Harrison-Connery in the last Indiana Jones film.

But then, the romance between Pete and Dorinda celebrated in the early scenes has itself been a rather chaste one—screwball-comedy badinage (even cartoon talk), *1941*-type shenanigans (a dance set-piece; tough, dungareed Dorinda melting—"Girl clothes!"—when she opens Pete's birthday present). If there is an excluded present in Spielberg's films, between a movie-made past and an ethereal future, then obviously part of what is excluded is sexual love and mature romance. Such renunciation or postponement may be a refusal to grow up, but it's also a key to something central, creatively playful, about what the cinema keeps 'in suspense', and which Spielberg plugs into with his fantasias about hypothetical worlds, movie-identity conundrums and familyless children. No wonder that he is prepared to take cues from that master of renunciation whose never-to-be lovers laugh at a movie trailer for *"Flames of Passion*—all next week".

NEW STATESMAN & SOCIETY, 3/30/90, p. 46, Suzanne Moore

It may not be possible to be too thin or too rich, but is it possible, I wonder, to be too popular? Take Steven Spielberg. He is the most popular filmmaker ever: he has directed half of the ten most successful films of all time. So it's strange that he has never won an Oscar and is not revered in the way that Scorcese or even Woody Allen is. Spielberg's films are still generally thought to be manipulative entertainment rather than anything else. How could something this popular ever be regarded as art, let alone great art?

The cynical dismissal of his work is littered with the well-worn put downs that are always summoned in the presence of truly popular culture: it is banal, sentimental, predictable and shallow, say the critics. But, even the critics have to admit grudgingly that somewhere along the line Spielberg manages to key into something this makes his movies a success from La Paz to Leeds. And though *Always* his latest film, has opened to mixed reaction in the States, I think he's done it again.

Always, a love story, has been widely represented as Spielberg's first grown-up film. In fact, he has already made a love story. What else was *ET* but the tale of a little boy's romance with an alien? *Always* is perhaps more conventional in that it does feature a man and a woman. On the cards for some ten years, it is essentially an adaptation of the 1943 Spencer Tracy film *A Guy Named Joe*, though at moments it has flashes of Powell's *A Matter of Life and Death*. Like the Indiana Jones films it is full of knowing nostalgia for an age of purity and faith and a hankering for a kind of security that is no longer possible either in modern life or in modern movies.

The love story of Dorinda (Holly Hunter) and Pete (Richard Dreyfuss) is set amongst firefighting pilots. He is, of course, a courageous flier while she is a dispatcher who waits patiently on the ground while he does his derring-do. All this gives Spielberg the chance to inject some spectacular flying scenes using old war planes without the intrusion of anything so morally suspect as real war. Instead, Dreyfuss is a positively green hero risking his neck for the sake of a few trees and his best friend Al—the ubiquitous John Goodman of *Roseanne* fame, whom, you might like to know, has just been voted the sexiest man in America.

Dorinda, though tough on the outside (she wears boiler suits) is actually soft on the inside— she's worried sick about her man. Their relationship, outlined in a long opening sequence, is somewhat overstretched. It even includes a musical number in which Pete gives Dorinda "girl-clothes" in the form of a horrid dress that only some retard like Diana Spencer would consider wearing. Needless to say, Dorinda is immediately transformed from spunky tomboy to drippy female and waltzes around the canteen with a set of fighter pilots.

The whole thing gets a lot better when, in one too many feats of bravery, Pete pops off and finds himself in a field of daisies with none other than Audrey Hepburn. She plays Hap—a kind of New Age angel in white slacks and sweater who sends him back to earth to be a young man's guiding spirit. The young man just happens to be Ted Baker, a young pilot who is himself in the process of falling in love with Dorinda. Here the gears begin to shift and Pete has to come to terms with giving up his "girl" to Ted.

True love, the movie suggests, means letting go. And Hap mouths a lot of New Age/hippy platitudes in a thoroughly convincing way: "To gain your freedom you have to give it" and "The love that we hold back is the only thing that follows us here" and, best of all, "Time's funny stuff,

Pete." The "here" she refers to might be heaven (if your idea of heaven is a meadow) or it might just mean death. This is the heaven of an agnostic. But Spielberg manages to play out his personal themes—around love, belief and sacrifice—in a way that mixes naivety with profundity.

This is Spielberg's forte because, whether you feel his philosophising is cosmic or comic, you cannot deny the way he taps into concerns that everybody has. Normally, we only refer to them in an off-hand kind of way, like the embarrassing area of spirituality. It is evident in all those action adventure movies that he can make with his eyes closed, but comes to the fore in his more personal work such as *ET, Close Encounters* and *Empire of the Sun*. In this context you can see why he was drawn to the transcendental humanism of Alice Walker's *The Colour Purple*.

There is a consistent refusal to accept death as the end (even *ET* comes alive again) and a continuing emphasis on communication and connections that cannot be explained rationally—the telepathic messages of Close Encounters feature again in *Always*—that is both enormously attractive and resonant for audiences everywhere. Such popular mysticism is routinely dismissed by the left whether in the guise of intellectual anti-humanism or morbidly literal readings of materialism.

In the real world, however, we read our horoscopes, consult psychics and bore our friends with everyday instances of synchronicity. This world remains completely outside the realms of politics, mainly because it is continually belittled by it.

Spielberg does just the opposite. He elevates these concerns and integrates them into the most traditional of genres, whether it's the love story or the adventure movie. Some have read his preoccupation with loss and separation as a result of the childhood trauma of his parents' divorce. Yet this doesn't explain his universal appeal to all age groups. Officially, Steven Spielberg is now more successful than Disney. And for someone who provides "mere entertainment", he has an instinctive grasp of one of modernity's deepest secrets: that underneath we just want to believe. We really do.

NEW YORK, 1/8/90, p. 58, David Denby

At the very beginning of Steven Spielberg's *Always*, two old geezers sitting in a rowboat, half asleep, dangle their fishing poles negligently in the water. In the distance, across a mountain lake, a large seaplane touches down and heads straight for them. The plane rushes across the water, drawing nearer and nearer; the men, now thoroughly alarmed, bestir themselves—and at the last moment, just as it's on the verge of wiping the two guys out, the plane takes off, roaring over their heads.

Always can best be enjoyed as a series of shimmering, borderline-outrageous images. Spielberg, master of clashing, multiple levels of action, charges up the frame in a way that no other director can match, and *Always*, at its peaks, is filled with the nostalgic romance of daredevil flying— beautiful propeller planes surging through the smoke and flames of a raging forest fire or swooping low, wings tilted rakishly, over a landing field. We're not meant to take the feats of derring-do— the preposterous rescues and show-off stunts—as literal truth. What's being celebrated is the pictorial excitement of flying, not the reality of flying. *Always* has the heady exuberance of an aerial-adventure film from the thirties, but with color and blazingly successful special effects added. The movie never goes dead visually, even when the material is junk. And most of it—gently whimsical stuff about a dead flier watching his girl fall in love with another guy—*is* junk. Mysticism for soft-heads.

Perhaps I'm overly fond of rationalism—or have the horse sense of a mule—but whatever the reason, movies about dead people coming back to life or showing up as ghosts or unseen observers have always left me cold (*Topper*'s charm wears thin after about half an hour). Like the recent *Field of Dreams*, Spielberg's movie is about the guilt a man feels over withholding love from someone and his relief at being able, at last, to unload his shame. Rebirth—or, at least, ghostly visitation—is apparently now available to us all as a second chance to correct mistakes and sort things out. Which is certainly a sweet dream. Perhaps I'll get the opportunity to make peace with my long-gone stepgrandfather, Freddy, whose smelly cigars I once hid in the back of a toy closet in 1952. *Freddy, I'm coming!* At least Spielberg, unlike Phil Alden Robinson, the ethereally silly writer-director of *Dreams*, uses his gimmick for comedy But I still find the material tiresome— kitsch passing for spirituality.

Always is a remake of Victor Fleming's *A Guy Named Joe*, which starred Spencer Tracy, Irene

Dunne, and Ward Bond—one of those cheerful stairway-to-Heaven jobs so fashionable in the forties. In spirit, however, the first half of *Always* bears a greater resemblance to 1939 Howard Hawks classic *Only Angels Have Wings*, in which Cary Grant, Thomas Mitchell, and Jean Arthur made a gallant and smashingly glamorous entertainment out of some nonsense about fliers and girls hanging out at a little airstrip in South America. Here the airstrip is in the American Northwest, and instead of running the mail across the Andes, our heroes are dousing forest fires in the timber region, flying low, dangerously low, so they can aim a heavy spritz of red flame-retardant chemicals at just the right spot.

Richard Dreyfuss is Pete, the ace who takes insane risks every time he goes up; Holly Hunter is his stouthearted girl, an ace herself, who mostly stays on the ground and suffers; and roly-poly John Goodman is his lovable sidekick, who insults Pete and loves him and always has grease on his face, the big puddy-tat. After Dreyfuss's Pete cheats death again, these three, and all the other guys at the base, unwind at a bar, dancing, drinking, scoring off one another. It's a perfect dream of comrades at play, especially when Goodman screws up his face and begins to dance, rolling about like a huge rubber duckie in a waterfall, dancing even more orgiastically than he did in *Sea of Love*.

Yet, entertaining as it is, the scene at the base is still a little odd. Spielberg, as I've said before, doesn't so much tell his stories as hype them to us. Everything is worked up, larger than life, and suddenly the movie almost turns into a musical. Holly Hunter's Dorinda, the only woman around, takes off her drab flying suit and appears in the "girl clothes" Pete has bought for her. All in white, she's a honey with sparkling eyes and small, perfectly shaped breasts outlined by the clinging dress. Gosh, she's purty. Awed, the men stand silently, as reverent as church mice. They take turns dancing with her, one after the other.

It's the most purely sexless moment in Spielberg's long, long career as a boy, and it made me realize to what extent sex in his movies is a matter of dreams and idealization. Dorinda, now feminized, persuades Pete that night to quit his fire-fighting gig. But sure enough, he is called out for one last time, and in the course of an incredible act of bravery, he dies. So ends the entertaining part of the movie.

Audrey Hepburn would probably be everybody's choice to play an angel, but Hepburn, holding forth to the dead Pete in wheat fields or sanctified clearings in a forest, is no more interesting than any other actor required to twinkle. She sends Pete back to the world as an unseen inspiration for a handsome young flier, Ted Baker (Brad Johnson), a hero in the making who has great ability but no judgment. People can't see or hear Pete, but when he's around, they are gently disturbed by a mental breeze, a ruffling of the unconscious. Spielberg has put as many charming wrinkles into this conceit as possible. Ted, it turns out, is a bit of a doofus and misinterprets the messages his unconscious is receiving from Pete. He heads off after Dorinda, leaving Pete in a sorry state of posthumous jealousy. The girl to whom he never said "I love you" is in danger of falling in love with someone else. *Always* turns out to be a rather sickly movie about dead people learning to give up their selfishness—their claim on the living. It's a character flaw that not all of us may have to face.

People ask, When is Spielberg going to grow up? The answer is, Probably never. Because he can't. His interests, the kind of imagery he likes, the kind of emotions he is drawn to producing onscreen, limit him to certain kinds of boyish, semi-satirical, but essentially awestruck pop fantasies. *Empire of the Sun* is the closest he has come to "mature" filmmaking, and in that movie he used all his resources to illuminate the point of view of a boy. In *Always* there's a disproportion between Spielberg's skill and what the movie is about. But at least he *does* have skill. *Always* is exciting to look at right down to the last shot.

NEW YORK POST, 12/22/89, p. 31, David Edelstein

"Always" is the story of a fire-fighting pilot (Richard Dreyfuss) who dies in an explosion and comes back as a ghost to watch over the woman (Holly Hunter) he loves but could never quite tell he loved. Directed by Steven Spielberg, it's an adolescent boy's romantic daydream instead of a little kid's romantic daydream (like "E.T." or "Close Encounters"); Spielberg wants us to know he's growing up.

The film is a remake of a 1943 Dalton Trumbo/Victor Fleming war weepie called "A Guy Named Joe" with Spencer Tracy and Irene Dunne. A variation on "Cyrano de Bergerac," it blends romance, heartbreak, supernatural comedy and inspirational action-adventure. It idealizes women as loyal, supportive, endlessly worrying creatures who try to keep their men from sticking their necks out too far.

You can see what tempted Spielberg. The mogul—who wants to dazzle mainstream audiences as well as the older segment of Hollywood that resents him—has a chance to charge the action sequences with the emotion lacking in his Indiana Jones sagas. He can also try his hand at love scenes, with the supernatural gimmick to protect him from falling on his face. He can also renew his undying faith in the opposite sex.

But Spielberg, whose best works are seamless expressions of his passion, seems so divided that he can't get anything going. "Always" is a heartfelt effort, but when he tries to get misty and poetic about women and relationships, the faking shows. He's always losing the emotional pulse of the story, getting distracted by set-pieces. Nothing plays way it's supposed to.

Dreyfuss, who has been Spielberg's stand-in for two of the director's best movies ("Jaws" and "Close Encounters"), plays Pete, a hot-dog pilot who stays out dropping water on a fire until his plane runs low on gas and he has to glide back into the runway, shearing off treetops while the little woman in the tower curses him and prays he'll make it home in one piece.

Dreyfuss looks fit and in good spirits, but the role uses none of his gifts. It amplifies his showoffy instincts and his smugness, and he doesn't have the kind of physical daring—the easy, heroice presence—the role calls for.

It's hard to convey the weirdness of the movie's attitude toward women, which often seems straight out of the '40s. In an early scene, Pete thinks it's his girl's birthday and buys the little tomboy a frilly white prom dress—whereupon all the firefighters in the camp ooh and ahh and take turns dancing with her while Pete strolls around the lodge, beaming at having the gal who's the envy of every guy on the base.

But as if to remind themselves this is the end of the '80s and women are equals, Spielberg and company have Hunter's Dorinda doing stupid, reckless things—charging into airplanes and flying into forest-fires. She doesn't like the boys to get all the laurels; she'll call attention to her own needs if it kills her.

Dorinda wants Pete to give up his daredevil ways—she has a premonition his time is up. But before the issue is fully settled, he jumps into a plane and gets himself killed.

When Pete dies, he wanders the smoldering forest and meets up with Audrey Hepburn, looking even more drawn and bright-eyed than she used to. She tells Pete he has to return to earth and be a source of inspiration to a clumsy young pilot named Ted Baker (Brad Johnson), just as a ghost was once an inspiration to him. Alas, the young man Pete's supposed to be inspiring has the hots for the woman he still loves—the woman he can't give up, despite his incorporeal status.

The idea that inspiration is an actual spirit whispering in one's ear has charm, but the script (by Jerry Belson) is so gummy and the movie's style so labored that it belies the premise: Whoever was supposed to be whispering in Belson and Spielberg's ear must have caught the first plane to the pearly gates.

At bottom, "Always" is a reverie about what would happen to the person you love if you were to die—how you'd want to come back and watch them grieve, how it would tear you up if they got interested in someone else, how you could rise to the occasion by giving your blessing and ascending to heaven.

This is a deeply narcissistic daydream, and there are some eerie and moving scenes in Dorinda's bedroom as she dances with herself while the ghost of Pete purrs he'll never leave her, she'll always be his. ("Always" might have made a good horror movie.) But the script is more interested in the sentimental idea that there are things we can't say to those we love until it's too late.

Hunter looks elfin and sparkly, and it's fun to watch her drawling mouth as it twists around a word. You can see the acting, though—she often overpowers the camera. Newcomer Brad Johnson, who has the widest neck in movies, is a Ken doll with no histrionic resources; this is the sort of bland work that makes you appreciate the wit that Christopher Reeve—a hunk who never seemed at home in his body—brought to the "Superman" series.

The only real diversion is Goodman, who's shaping up to be a real movie star. What's startling about him is his delicacy—as a dancer, he surprisingly twinkle-toed, like Astaire with 100 extra pounds. Sucking the cream out of a Twinkie, he's a paradigm of elegance.

NEWSDAY, 12/22/89, Part III/p. 3, Terry Kelleher

Next time Steven Spielberg feels the urge to remake a picture directed by Victor Fleming, he ought to show a little more ambition and have a go at "Gone With the Wind."

But, please, not Richard Dreyfuss as Rhett Butler.

In "Always," the Spielberg version of Fleming's 1943 hit "A Guy Named Joe," Dreyfuss has the Spencer Tracy role of the risk-taking pilot who dies in a crash and goes on to earn his wings as a guardian angel.

This is Dreyfuss' third job for Spielberg (after "Jaws" and "Close Encounters of the Third Kind"), and no one's saying he's not a fine actor in the right vehicle. However, that vehicle is not the A26 he flies in "Always." Tracy got off his share of wisecracks in "A Guy Named Joe," but here Dreyfuss oversells the jokes as if he's nervous about how they'll go over. What's more, he "laughs like a donkey," as the aviator's girlfriend (Holly Hunter) points out. She finds the trait endearing, viewers may not. Though the makeup department has outfitted Dreyfuss with a little extra hair to enhance his daredevil image, he's unconvincing dead or alive.

Not that Dreyfuss is all that's wrong with "Always." He can't be blamed for the script, unless he served as guardian angel to screenwriter Jerry Belson. In "A Guy Named Joe," the pilots were bombing Nazis for the Army Air Corps; in "Always," they're dousing fires for the U.S. Forest Service. The aircraft's similar, but the situation's a comedown. John Goodman, playing the big funny sidekick again, observes: "You know what this place reminds me of? The war in Europe." Someone should tell him he's been watching too many old movies.

Bad dialogue abounds in the early going. Radioing ground controller Hunter from his red-hot cockpit, Dreyfuss says: "I love it in the kitchen, baby." She calls him "you big lug." He calls her "funny face." She threatens to leave him and "find my own piece of the sky" if he doesn't quit defying death. "Fighting fires is what I do," he responds heatedly.

Some will argue that "Always" is supposed to sound old-fashioned and slightly hokey in homage to Hollywood's heartwarming past. Then why not forget the update and retain the World War II setting? But, some will counter, there's no point in bothering to remake "A Guy Named Joe" if you're not going to fiddle with it. No point in bothering? Now we're getting somewhere.

Fact is, this story was rather flabby and mawkish the first time around. For "Always," sweet Audrey Hepburn replaces crusty Lionel Barrymore as the deceased pilot's heavenly counselor, and a hunky newcomer named Brad Johnson takes over for Van Johnson as the eager flyboy our hero is assigned to guide and inspire. What hasn't changed is that the flyboy falls for the hero's girlfriend, and who says guardian angels are above jealousy? "If I'm really dead, how come I hurt so bad?" Dreyfuss asks. Tracy would've had trouble with that line.

Dreyfuss and Hunter aren't an especially appealing couple when their characters are both living, but they have a couple of touching moments when his ghost tries to woo her with loving words too long unspoken. The aerial action, while not quite edge-of-your-seat stuff, is good for a thrill here and there.

Unfortunately, the movie never gains the emotional altitude Spielberg intended, even when Hunter jumps into the cockpit herself in defiance of death *and* logic. "Always" leaves us wondering: Is the director losing his touch at the controls, or was he hamstrung by his attachment to an outdated flight plan?

NEWSWEEK, 1/1/90, p. 60, David Ansen

In *Always*, Steven Spielberg labors mightily to recapture the swooning romanticism of the '40s movies he loved as a kid. He's got the right moves but he's picked the wrong movie to remake. "A Guy Named Joe" (1944) starred Spencer Tracy as a brave, reckless pilot who's killed in action. Returning to earth as a ghost, he passes on the flyboy spirit to a younger pilot (Van Johnson), who falls for the girl (Irene Dunne) Tracy loved. Can Tracy selflessly help her get over her grief and find a new life? Victor Fleming's movie was no gem, but in a nation of war widows it must have packed an inspirational punch.

"Always" updates the same story among flying firefighters in Montana, but without its wartime resonance the fable looks even daffier. As romantic fantasies go, this one is oddly masochistic: do we really want to watch a ghostly Richard Dreyfuss watch Holly Hunter fall in love with a big, square-jawed hunk (Brad Johnson), while guardian angel Audrey Hepburn bucks up Dreyfuss's spirits with heavenly homilies?

At the start, it seems as if Spielberg will pull off some movie-movie magic. As lovers, Dreyfuss and Hunter have charm, chemistry and conviction. Spielberg choreographs their romance with a luscious lyricism that's as stylized as a musical. But once Dreyfuss becomes Otherworldly—which is when most supernatural films get fun—"Always" runs into trouble. Jerry Belson's script isn't funny or edgy enough to prevent restlessness. There's only one possible outcome, and it's not particularly gratifying. How can we root for Hunter to connect with the good-hearted klutz Johnson when his character is so bloodlessly unreal? It's like rooting for Christian over Cyrano in pursuit of Roxane. And while the spitfire Hunter is acting with all her heart (it wouldn't hurt if she held a little in reserve), the inexperienced Johnson seems to switch personalities from scene to scene.

Spielberg doesn't differentiate between the good ideas in the script and the bad ones: everything is given an emphatic, production-number treatment, whether it's fliers cleaning their dirty hands at a dance, a runaway-vehicle gag or a daredevil flying sequence. His ultraslick, seductive technique can be a pleasure to watch in itself, but it can't disguise the fact that "Always" is a decidedly uneternal fantasy.

VILLAGE VOICE, 12/26/89, p. 102, Georgia Brown

Steven Spielberg opens *Always* with a devilish bit of prologue that never really gets explained. (Call it his version of Spike Lee's alarm clock, his "Wake up!" to the species.) Two fishermen in a small boat on a lake, dozing, listening to birdsong, are blissfully unaware of a giant PLANE bearing down on them. When one of them wakes up to this bad dream, he tries to start the outboard. It doesn't catch. Men and boat were about to be pulverized when I covered my eyes.

What's this here for, this signature exercise in visual shock? It's the old *Jaws* setup: Man, taking his leisure in nature, is suddenly threatened by a monster from out of the big blue. (The mechanical shark, which turned into a Japanese sub in *1941*, harked back to the sinister truck in Spielberg's *Duel*. Since *Close Encounters*, machines come from the sky.) Spielberg's movies play on dangers in taking the world for granted; they're all about death, but a hopeful death.

Pete Sandich (Richard Dreyfuss)—whom we now see flying his tanker bomber through a curtain of flames—is the star pilot for a squadron of forest-fire fighters in the American West. This is an occupation that suffers greatly (at least in a movie) from not being one of the traditional major branches of risk-taking, and writer Jerry Belson includes a number of opportunities for the pilots to lament that they are not flying midnight missions over the channel.

Down below, as usual, waits the maiden. When Pete has to "come in dead-stick" because both his engines have conked out, Dorinda Durston (Holly Hunter) talks to him from the tower in a sequence that looks for a moment out of the opening of Powell and Pressburger's *Stairway to Heaven*. (It is and it isn't. The film is more directly based on the Spencer Tracy World War II picture, *A Guy Named Joe*.) But Dorinda chafes with conflicts of her own. She wants to *be* one of the fliers, and she wants *her* flier, Pete, grounded because she can't bear the anxiety. She resists the domestic and needs it. (Trying valiantly here to get it right about women, Spielberg even takes a noble detour from convention at the end in order to give his heroine a shot at saving herself from being adjunct.)

The premise of *Always*—which the reader will no doubt learn elsewhere, even if I could avoid mentioning it—has Pete dying in a flaming crash, waking in a singed forest (like Bambi, he glimpses a stag), where he meets an angel called Hap (Audrey Hepburn). Hap sends Pete back to become invisible copilot to a fledgling flier, Ted Baker (Brad Johnson), who's also in love with Dorinda. One question is whether the short, dead Pete can relinquish Dorinda to tall, live (and handsome) Ted. In life, Pete has failed to speak his feelings. Like George Lucas's Han Solo, when his woman says "I love you," he says "I know."

If this sounds like extremely maudlin material, you're right. And depending on your weakness for this kind of corn, you'll love it or hate it. I actually loved it—well, parts of it. (And this is no Spielberg fan talking.)

Dorinda wears distressed leather jackets, says things like "None of your beeswax," and rides a boy's bike. When Pete gives her "girl's clothes!" for her birthday, though, she's delighted: "It's not the dress, it's the way you see me!" This scene in a dance club—where Dorinda's and Pete's relationship is established—struck me as terribly strained and overwrought. Dorinda, who resembles the Karen Allen tomboy in *Raiders of the Lost Ark*, is almost weirdly intense. Hunter's childlikeness occasionally borders on hysteria, and her manic mannerisms seems to invite Dreyfuss, who's also prone to such excesses, to follow suit. It's as if they're being egged on to find some '80s correlative for '50s-style melodramatic acting. John Goodman, who plays Al, their pal, may dance like an indestructible Humpty Dumpty, but he can't put this mess together. Spielberg, who has a gift for the-way-we-live-now details, really can be off.

The good news is that there are breathtaking scenes here, too. Love scenes: The guardian angel tries to be human again, to keep his woman for himself, yet he's required to give his protégé (son) the means to win her. Death in movies is used to induce audience feeling, and the afterlife conceit, always good for generating pathos, here places two lovers in the same frame who can never talk and who have to part. In a wistful dance number, Pete and Dorinda dance to their song, "Smoke Gets in Your Eyes," without touching. Giving up one's true love (from *Back Street* to *The Last Temptation of Christ*) is always about parents and children, and parting signifies both liberty *and* death. For Spielberg, this is the Saddest Story.

Always may be flawed, but the director is back where he's comfortable, with the great beyond, the outside unknown—the arena of *E.T., Close Encounters*, even *Poltergeist*—and with a homegrown American mysticism grounded in the anguish of human relationships and the ardor of human ambitions. In this *E.T.* for adults (well, some of us), Spielberg begins looking more and more like Frank Capra. Stretching for iconography, he looks both silly and brave.

Also reviewed in:
NEW YORK TIMES, 12/22/89, p. C12, Janet Maslin
NEW YORKER, 1/8/90, p. 92, Pauline Kael
VARIETY, 12/20/89, p. 22
WASHINGTON POST, 12/22/89, p. D1, Rita Kempley

ANIMAL BEHAVIOR

A Millimeter Films release. *Executive Producer:* Randolph Clendenen. *Producer:* Kjehl Rasmussen. *Director:* H. Anne Riley (Jenny Bowen) and Kjehl Rasmussen. *Screenplay:* Susan Rice. *Director of Photography:* David Spellvin. *Editor:* Joseph Weintraub. *Music:* Cliff Edelman. *Sound:* John Pritchett. *Production Designer:* Jeannine Oppewall. *Art Director:* David Brisbin. *Set Decorator:* Lisa Fischer. *Running time:* 85 minutes. *MPAA Rating*: PG.

CAST: Karen Allen (Alex Bristow); Armand Assante (Mark Mathias); Holly Hunter (Coral Grable); Josh Mostel (Mel Gorsky); Richard Libertini (Dr. Parrish); Alexa Kenin (Sheila Sandusky); Michael (Michael); Jon Mathews (Tyler Forbes); Nan Martin (Mrs. Norton); Crystal Buda (Cleo Grable).

LOS ANGELES TIMES, 10/27/89, Calendar/p. 4, Kevin Thomas

There's warm sensibility and an engaging cast in "Animal Behavior," but it's too slight to recommend it. Dusted off after three years on the shelf since its completion, it's the kind of film you want to like—and wish there was more to it to like.

The ads are misleading, overemphasizing Holly Hunter's importance in the film. It's not Hunter but a chimpanzee who is standing in the way of Karen Allen and Armand Assante falling in love. Allen is Alex Bristow, a psychologist at a New Mexico university who is so intensely absorbed in an interspecies study with her adorable chimp, Michael, that she tries to persuade herself that she has no time for love, even though she is as attracted to Assante's Mark Mathias, the new music professor, as he is to her.

Even though "Animal Behavior" was directed by two people, Jenny Bowen and Kjehl Rasmussen, the film's producer who replaced her, its problem seems mainly in Susan Rice's undeveloped script. Allen and Assante seem to keep playing the same scene over and over, with Alex pushing away Mark in the name of work. "Animal Behavior" is too talky by a mile yet it seems superficial. Throughout, there is the feeling that the film makers never quite decided how seriously to take Alex's research project or her attachment to Michael. We're never quite sure whether the chimp is, on some level, Mark's rival or whether Alex is simply a workaholic.

Allen and Assante are so terrific together you regret that "Animal Behavior," goes for whimsy and sentimentality rather than the screwball humor and sophistication of "Bringing Up Baby." Holly Hunter, who made this film before "Broadcast News," has only a small role as Assante's good ol' gal neighbor, who has a mute little daughter taught to sign by the chimp. Actually, Josh Mostel has more to do as Mark's breezy sidekick, an art professor, and Richard Libertini scores as Alex's arrogant, jealous superior, a nasty academic with whom she had a fling when she was his student.

Unfortunately, "Animal Behavior" (rated PG) is filled with repetitive and inane humor, culminating in a silly and contrived ending. It's not enough that Allen and Assante are such a pleasure.

NEW YORK POST, 10/27/89, p. 23, Jami Bernard

Any movie that makes Holly Hunter and Karen Allen look ridiculous should be deep-sixed.

"Animal Behavior" attempts to draw a connection between the lack of communication among humans and the attempts to teach a chimpanzee sign language. Allen plays Alex Bristow, a lab scientist so wrapped up in her research with Michael the chimp that she fails to relate to master cellist Mark Mathias (Armand Assante).

Mark has come to the university to teach music but is probably so confused by his incredibly awful haircut—I know I am—that he starts monkeying around in Alex's lab, hoping for love or musical inspiration or some sign-language indication that this excruciating movie will soon be over.

Mark is renting a room from landlady Coral Grable. As the director of this movie is using a pseudonym in the credits, it seems unfair that Holly Hunter can't do the same, but anyway, there's no mistaking that pert, wonderful actress, even when she has been goosed into overplaying Coral as a young unwed mother of an adorable, mute child.

Exercise videos often interrupt the proceedings for a quick pulse check. Let's try one now. No, not to see if you are awake, but whether you know where a movie could be heading that features a chimp who speaks in sign language and an adorable child who doesn't speak at all.

Now, back to the review. Someone, I don't know who, encouraged Allen to portray shyness as a sort of *petit mal* exercise in stuttering, gesticulating and looking at her feet. She is actually awkward at being awkward. And this is the actress who did such a sensitive job of the shy daughter in the 1987 movie version of "A Glass Menagerie."

And someone, I don't know who, must have blackmailed Hunter into depicting "young and working class" by being excessively mannered and loud.

And someone, I don't know who, cut handsome Armand Assante's hair while harboring a personal vendetta.

Michael the chimp, appearing here as himself, does just fine, although you'd think a movie with a chimp and a child could arouse a little emotion from an audience. What else are they there for?

And the relaxed Josh Mostel as a flaky art professor wanders around happily and aimlessly like a line-prompter who would be more than happy to cue the others in if they would just let him.

But they don't. So everyone flounders like a chimp out of diapers until a ridiculous haystack-maze chase scene and an awkward child-chimp scene. The movie makes a monkey of everyone.

NEWSDAY, 10/27/89, Part III/p. 3, Mike McGrady

The new movie, "Animal Behavior," completed more than four years ago, is just now arriving at the movie screens. Why all the shelf time? Well, I've been informed that the producers spent all that time in court battling first-time director H. Anne Riley for the right to cut her work. If one may judge by the results, cutting was not enough. For a film like this, nothing less than stabbing will do.

"Animal Behavior" centers on a college professor (Karen Allen) doing research in inter-species communication. She has taught her chimpanzee, Ameslan, the sign language used by the deaf, and now has even greater ambitions for him: "I want him to conceptualize, to put together combinations."

After allowing herself a one-afternoon stand with the new music professor (Armand Assante), Allen mistakenly concludes her lover is married, an erroneous assumption that is not straightened out until movie's end and provides the film with what little tension it possesses. The misunderstanding is entirely due to a personal failing shared by both principals, an embarrassing inability to communicate with humans.

Matters are complicated, but not in the least enlivened, by the presence of Assante's next-door neighbor (Holly Hunter) and her little girl, who is unable to speak. (If you're already thinking in terms of miraculous breakthroughs, you're way too sophisticated for this film. Even if you aren't thinking in those terms, the same probably applies). Hunter, a cashier at a video-arcade, is a non-stop talker with nothing to say. You may wonder how the star of "Broadcast News" could emote so raggedly and ineffectually—well, "Animal Behavior" was made so long ago that it must be considered nothing more than a learning experience for her.

The monkey (Michael, playing himself) absolutely steals the movie, an act of petit larceny if there ever was one. I particularly liked the scene where, using sign language, he calls Assante "a bug." Whether he was describing the actor's appearance or performance is unclear but in either event, the observation shows an ability to conceptualize and put together combinations that places the animal light years ahead of the scriptwriter.

NEWSWEEK, 11/13/89, p. 92, Jack Kroll

Animal Behavior is of interest not as a movie but as a piece of Hollywood sociology. A big ad in the Sunday New York Times features Holly Hunter standing over Armand Assante and Karen Allen, with text clearly suggesting the three costar in this "very funny movie about getting serious." Wrong, Blurb Breath. This very unfunny movie about nothing in particular bears a copyright date of 1989, but the movie was made almost five years ago, before Hunter's Oscar-nominated performance in "Broadcast News" and even before her splendid work in "Raising Arizona." In "Animal Behavior" Hunter only has a minor role. It's Allen and Assante who star in director H. Anne Riley's movie about a psychologist (Allen) and a music teacher (Assante) at Lamont University in the Southwest. Nor is there any such person as director H. Anne Riley, which is merely a space-filler for Jenny Bowen, who demanded that her name be removed from the film.

So, no costar Holly, no director H. Anne. (What's the H for, Hiatus?) Is there anything real about "Animal Behavior?" Yes, badness. You can't blame Bowen for wanting her name tag cut from this pile of unlaundered campers' shorts. She directs her stars in the ghastliest kind of undergrad "comedy" acting—they stumble and stammer and don't finish their sentences. While Assante is conducting the "Lamont Philharmonic," an ear-grating bunch of screechers, Allen is researching inter-species communication with a chimp named Michael. Michael is wonderful. He finishes his sentences. You can learn dental hygiene by watching him use his toothbrush. And when he puts his picture on a pile of human photographs, signaling that he is claiming the status of homo sapiens, he's earned it, at least in this movie. He can direct the next flick for the studio, Millimeter Films. H. Michael Riley directs his first feature, "Human Behavior."

VILLAGE VOICE, 10/31/89, p. 84, Manohla Dargis

You know there's something wrong with a movie when there's no director's bio included in the press kit; it looks particularly bad when the director's credit turns out to be a pseudonym. *Animal Behavior* is credited to H. Anne Riley, but the real director is Jenny Bowen. Shot in 1984–85, it's taken half a decade to get *Animal* released; its distributor, Millimeter (an arm of Miramax), shouldn't have bothered. Another five years in the editing room couldn't save this mess. According to producer Kjehl Rasmussen, Bowen asked that her name be removed from the film when it ran into delays and she—by then directing *The Wizard of Loneliness*—wasn't available for postproduction. Karen Allen and Holly Hunter, both of whom perform at a shrill, unappealing pitch, are completely wasted, as are romantic lead Armand Assante and a supporting cast that includes a chimpanzee and Zero Mostel's son, Josh.

Also reviewed in:
NEW YORK TIMES, 10/27/89, p. C18, Vincent Canby
VARIETY, 11/1/89, p. 35

APARTMENT ZERO

A Skouras Pictures release. *Executive Producer:* Stephen J. Cole. *Producer:* Martin Donovan and David Koepp. *Director:* Martin Donovan. *Screenplay:* Martin Donovan and David Koepp. *Story:* Martin Donovan. *Director of Photography:* Miguel Rodriguez. *Editor:* Conrad M. Gonzalez. *Music:* Elia Cmiral. *Music Editor:* Allan K. Rosen. *Sound:* Jorge Stavropoulos and (music) Gary Denton. *Sound Editor:* Martin Maryska. *Production Designer:* Miguel Angel Lumaldo. *Costumes:* Angelica Fuentes. *Make-up:* Mirta Blanco. *Running time:* 124 minutes. *MPAA Rating:* Not Rated.

CAST: Colin Firth (Adrian LeDuc); Hart Bochner (Jack Carney); Dora Bryan (Margaret McKinney); Liz Smith (Mary Louise McKinney); Fabrizio Bentivoglio (Carlos Sanchez-Verne); James Telfer ("Vanessa"); Mirella D'Angelo (Laura Werpachowsky); Juan Vitali (Alberto Werpachowsky); Francesca d'Aloja (Claudia); Miguel Ligero (Mr. Palma); Elvia Andreoli (Adrian's Mother); Marikena Monti (Tango Singer); Cipe Lincovsky (Mrs. Treniev); Luis Romero (Projectionist); Oca Spirito and Micky Chapman (Women in Cinema); Claudia Rosenblat and Sandra Calderon (Nurses); Max Berliner, Mane Auauz and Maria José Catino (Prospective Tenants); Debora Bianco (Girl in Café); Federico D'Elia (Boy in Cafe); Veronica Gambini (Girl with Carlos in Building); Rosario Varela (Girl with Carlos at Tango); Raul Florido (Jack's Argentine Contact); Claudio Ciacci (Young Man in Cinema); Gabriel Posniak (Dead Man); Guillermo Willart and Javier Balina (Paramedics); Darwin Sanchez (Police Inspector); Daniel Queirolo (Young Cop); Miguel Angel Porro (Taxi Driver); Daniel Astesano (Immigration Officer); Alfredo Quesada (Speaker at Group Meeting); Stephen Cole (Strange-looking Man in Airport); Nicolas Pereyra (Doctor at Institution); Gabriel Corrado (Victim in Hotel Room); Jorge Caseres (Young Man with Vanessa).

LOS ANGELES TIMES, 10/20/89, Calendar/p. 13, Kevin Thomas

The one thing you can say for "Apartment Zero" is that they've got that numeral in the title right. This overwrought and underdeveloped psychological thriller with heavy-handed political implications adds up to exactly nothing.

It's the kind of genre piece in which logic must be airtight, yet fledgling film maker Martin Donovan would have us believe that you can fall down a stairwell and emerge with only a cut over your eye, and that a shrewd serial killer would leave incriminating photos in a dresser drawer.

Nothing, however, makes much sense right from the start. We soon learn that Hart Bochner's handsome, insinuating Jack Carney has every reason to seek privacy and security, yet he rents a room from Colin Firth's Adrian LeDuc, who clearly spells trouble for him. A fussy, overattentive and intensely repressed film buff with an incestuous passion for his crazy hospitalized mother, LeDuc registers an instant attraction to Jack, who responds with a laid-back, tantalizing seductiveness. Since there is no credibility in Jack accepting Adrian as a landlord—let alone toying with such an up-tight, obvious weirdo—there is really no credibility in all that follows.

Donovan seems to have overdosed on Losey's "The Servant," Polanski's "The Tenant" and the Roeg-Cammell "Performance"—just for starters. He strives to establish Jack and Adrian as one of those calamitous but inevitable teams, reminiscent of Chicago child-killers Leopold and Loeb, in which we're supposed to perceive larger meanings. The setting of "Apartment Zero" is present-day Buenos Aires, with Adrian as a native Argentine who insists on speaking English after having been raised in Great Britain and Jack as an American ostensibly there on some sort of corporate training program. Donovan and co-writer David Koepp attempt, in their increasingly morbid horror-picture context, to comment on the evil of the notorious death squads of Argentina's former military regime and to suggest further that killing becomes addictive.

Unfortunately, the long-winded "Apartment Zero" is awkward to the point of ludicrousness. Firth has the determination and skill to make Adrian consistently pathetic and believable, but Bochner is allowed to lapse into striking attitudes and poses. British actresses Dora Bryan and Liz Smith play the nosiest of Adrian and Jack's neighbors as caricatures. With its tango-tinged score and moody lighting, "Apartment Zero" (Times-rated Mature) looks and sounds far better than it is.

MONTHLY FILM BULLETIN, 9/89, p. 265, John Pym

Buenos Aires, 1988. A serial killer is on the loose. With attendance at his small art cinema plummeting and the tenants of the neglected family apartment building in which he lives growing restive, Adrian LeDuc is forced to take in a lodger, Jack Carney, a personable American who claims to be on an exchange with the Intercomp computer company. Radiating sympathy and sexual promise, Jack soon has the fastidious, anti-social Adrian and all the tenants—Laura, a lonely married woman; the McKinney sisters, elderly English spinsters; Carlos, a thwarted ladies man; and "Vanessa", a self-pitying transvestite—innocently eating out of his hand. It transpires, however, that Intercomp knows nothing of Jack and that hidden in his bedroom are snapshots of himself with a gang of tough men in military fatigues. A human-rights group hires the cinema and at a screening of some clandestine footage Adrian learns that Jack, with whom he is now half in love, was in fact a hired killer for the former military dictatorship. Jack attempts to flee the country; and in order to obtain a valid passport kills a man he has picked up at the airport. Meanwhile, Adrian breaks down at the death in a clinic of the mother on whom he is fixated. Suspecting their landlord of the murder of their beloved Jack, the tenants set upon Adrian and in the ensuing mêlée he is accidentally tipped down the central stairwell. Jack returns and tenderly sews up Adrian's head wound. Claudia, the manager of Adrian's cinema, finally unmasks Jack as the murderer. He kills her and without difficulty persuades Adrian to help him dispose of the corpse. Adrian proposes they decamp to California. Back at the apartment, however, he has a change of heart: a fight develops and a shot goes off. Later, Adrian raises a glass to his friend's propped-up remains. Clad in leather, the emotionless Adrian now runs a porn cinema. . .

The title suggests something sinister and symbolic, and the apartment building where most of the action occurs contains a cross-section of sexual tastes. In Apartment Zero, however, where Adrian launders his lodger's shirts and brings out the best china every morning for a formal English breakfast, there is no sex, unless one counts a son's unrequited love for his absent, demented and dying mother. What this long, portentous film finally serves up is a frantic mixture: a salute to all those movies which have taken an obsession with cinema as their theme (Adrian, however, is the most plodding of film buffs); an undernourished thriller about a serial killer (Jack is certainly a psychopath, but is he this particular bogeyman?); a cautionary tale about tyranny and its aftermath, in which the hired killers always, it seems, escape judicial retribution.

Among the devices used to bind the mixture together are the elliptical fade and the lingering facial shot. The first works well enough, up to a point. The chameleon Jack empathises with all the lost souls in the building; but just how each of his therapeutic sessions ends, we never know. The second device is more crudely handled. When Jack is prevailed on to rescue the McKinney sisters' cat, an angry black face glowers from a niche in immense close-up; Jack, standing on a ladder, stares unblinkingly back in extreme close-up. The performances of the principals, Colin Firth, the grating, priggish, honorary Englishman, and Hart Bochner, the self-consciously charming American with his concerned eyes and gleaming, faithless grin, in a sense spin clear of the director's intentions. Their closed drama of sexual repression and manipulation, played out with considerable intensity, seems to develop independently of the rest of the action. Beside this, the film's expressionist flourishes—the camera looking up from the floor at a circle of plotting faces; a shot from inside the LeDuc mausoleum, as if from the point of view of mother's coffin—appear incongruously out of place.

NEW YORK POST, 10/18/89, p. 31, Jami Bernard

"Apartment Zero" can be viewed as a cautionary tale—the kind of movie you usually get when a former film school student goes mad with power. It is full of pseudo-arty self-reference: Adrian LeDuc (Colin Firth) runs a Buenos Aires cinema club, keeps photos of his favorite sexually ambiguous screen idols around his apartment and plays a game with his new roommate, Jack Carney (Hart Bochner), in which one names the stars and the other names the movie in which they appeared.

That, plus borrowed cinematic clichés, neither add to nor subtract from this tediously enigmatic thriller. All those visual flourishes are irrelevant.

Adrian, a control freak who denies his Argentine roots by adopting a British accent, takes in a handsome American boarder to help pay his ailing mother's medical costs. He is immediately consumed with Jack, but then so are the neighbors in this weirdo apartment complex.

And why not? Jack is charming, rakish, all things to all people. To the old lady downstairs, he is the reincarnation of her long-dead fiance. To the woman next door, he is the caring daddy she never had. To the skittish transvestite, he is an old friend.

A string of murders is being committed in the neighborhood, supposedly by a former death squad mercenary, and believe me, it could be any of the wackos.

What the death squad has to do with James Dean is beyond me, except that it gives the movie a chance to flirt with homoerotic overtones as the two roomies gaze soulfully at one another.

Director Martin Donovan makes that same mistake so many directors make—writing the script himself. "You calling me a freak?" twitters Adrian. "I'm calling you special," soothes his all-purpose roommate.

The best that can be said about "Apartment Zero" is that it is perverse; the worst is that it is ridiculous. Donovan has seen "Psycho" one too many times, and, in any case, has appropriated images and themes from Hollywood movies but with an alien, star-struck sensibility. Much as we all love James Dean and Montgomery Clift, you cannot just idly summon up their spirits and expect them to perform miracles on movies more comatose than they.

NEWSDAY, 10/18/89, Part II/p. 5, Terry Kelleher

Adrian LeDuc, one of the two principal characters in "Apartment Zero," says everybody's entitled to "one or two hundred idiosyncrasies." Adrian is over the limit.

He runs a movie revival house in Buenos Aires, and you might say he takes his work home with him. His apartment is filled to capacity with framed photos of film stars.

He's paranoid and reclusive, shrinking from even routine contact with his nosy neighbors.

He has an unhealthy fixation on his institutionalized mother, whom he visits regularly for anguished, one-sided conversations.

He's "an Argentine born and bred," but speaks only English with a lordly British accent.

Strapped for cash, Adrian (Colin Firth) places an "apartment to share" ad in the newspaper. In walks smilin' Jack Carney (Hart Bochner) and Apartment Zero becomes the strangest pad in town.

Martin Donovan, himself born in Argentina, has made a movie that is part psychological drama, part political thriller, part black comedy, part lighter comedy—and totally self-conscious. "Apartment Zero" is not boring, but it is very trying.

While we're attempting to determine whether Jack is a mercenary assassin or merely a hunk who drives men and women equally wild, the director's visual style continually calls attention to itself.

Donovan likes to get up close. After two hours with his characters, you may not really know them, but you'll never forget their faces. It's one tight closeup after another, until the viewer feels a powerful urge to move back several rows for a little breathing room. When Jack goes on a crying jag, we get such a close look at his dripping nose that we're almost in danger of catching something.

Among Donovan's other camera tricks, the showiest are the extreme low-angle shots and the Ping-Pong panning between Adrian and Jack as the roommates shoot glances at each other over the breakfast table.

As for the script by Donovan and David Koepp, it doesn't bear close-up inspection. Why does Jack carry around photos linking him with a rightist death squad—to remind himself of who he is? And why on earth does he hide them in Adrian's desk? Indeed, why would Donovan keep showing us newspaper headlines and TV reports about political murder if Jack *weren't* eventually to be revealed as a political murderer?

Logic is beside the point anytime those dizzy British biddies, the McKinney sisters (Dora Bryan and Liz Smith), dish the apartment-house dirt. And it flies completely out the window toward the end, when the film takes a sharp turn toward the surreal and the grotesque.

To be sure, it's not insignificant that Jack, this beautiful angel of death, is all things to all residents—gallant protector to the drag queen (James Telfer); sexy father-substitute to the lonely beauty down the hall (Mirella D'Angelo); rouser of homoerotic feelings in two very different men, Adrian and the more macho Carlos (Fabrizio Bentivoglio). Somewhere in "Apartment Zero" there's a statement concerning the pornographic lure of violence and the perverse thrill of fascism.

But any substance in this movie is obscured by the directorial flourishes. The characters are mere furnishings, like all those pictures on the cineast's walls.

VILLAGE VOICE, 10/24/89, p. 73, Elliott Stein

Aficionados of the bizarre will have a field day with *Apartment Zero*, a mannered and overwrought odd couple saga set in a mysterious Buenos Aires, where Pidgin English seems to be the lingua franca. Creepy and schizzy, teasingly erotic, it's wildly uneven, brilliant in patches, irritating and ponderous in others, yet by and large one of the most singular new films in recent months.

The eponymous apartment belongs to Adrian (Colin Firth), an Anglophile Argentinian movie nut who runs a dying revival house. He shows "real movies on a real screen," but videos are putting him out of business. His flat is chockablock with portraits of Monty Clift and Charles Laughton. He knows the casts and credits of every film ever made. He's unbearable. A tightass closet case, snotty, bitter, and asocial, he, out of snobbishness, even pretends not to speak Spanish. His lifestyle is suddenly enriched and contaminated the day he rents a room to Jack (Hart Bochner), a glamorous and amicable American hunk who works for a computer company. Adrian gets into preparing elaborate breakfasts for them and lets Jack know he can spit in the coffee if he wants to; he also takes immoderate pleasure in doing his boarder's smelly laundry. And he can't wait to rush off and bring the news to Mother at her nursing home. "You'll like him. He has a certain James Dean *je ne sais quoi.*" The demented old lady nods unfathomably.

This blithe ménage is soon clouded. After an outbreak of killings, the work of mercenaries once in the employ of the former military government and now in league with rightist death squads, it becomes apparent that the clean-cut jock from Connecticut is not exactly what he seems. The film's gruesome, somewhat incoherent finale ventures into very dark comedy.

What is clear is that director Martin Donovan, who was raised in Argentina and worked as an assistant to Visconti on *Ludwig* and *Conversation Piece*, has a fine eye for atmosphere. Marvelous footage shot all around the Argentine capital—sinuous Gaudiesque buildings, sexy public statuary, cemeteries, ominously observed boulevards—all serve to place this disturbing narrative in an appropriate frame: a haunted, ambiguous, and sensual metropolis. It's a story about masks in a city where role-playing has become the norm for many, and about the fascination of fascism. There are echoes of *Performance*, *The Servant*, and *Kiss of the Spider Woman*.

Firth is excellent, and Bochner extraordinary as the demonic bisexual charmer who doesn't care whom he fucks. In a memorably grotesque seduction scene, he makes out with Carlos (Fabrizio Bentivoglio), a nebbishy neighbor snubbed by Adrian because the poor guy had never heard of Geraldine Page.

At over two hours, *Apartment Zero* rambles more than a bit, but I can't be too harsh on a movie that sends its cinephilic protagonist for a stroll up Calle Herman Weinberg, the first street in motion picture history named after an ex-*Voice* film columnist.

Also reviewed in:
NEW YORK TIMES, 10/18/89, p. C18, Vincent Canby
VARIETY, 10/5/88, p. 18
WASHINGTON POST, 11/3/89, Weekend/p. 37, Desson Howe
WASHINGTON POST, 11/4/89, p. G7, Rita Kempley

ARIEL

A Villealfa Filmproductions film. *Producer:* Aki Kaurismaki. *Director:* Aki Kaurismaki. *Screenplay (Finnish with English subtitles):* Aki Kaurismaki. *Director of Photography:* Timo Salminen. *Sound:* Jouko Lumme. *Production Designer:* Jaakko Talaskivi. *Set Designer:* Risto Karhula. *Costumes:* Tuula Hilkamo. *Running Time:* 74 minutes. *MPAA Rating:* Not Rated.

CAST: Turo Pajala (Taisto Kasurinen); Susanna Haavisto (Irmeli); Matti Pellonpaa (Mikkonen); Eetu Hilkamo (Riku); Erkki Pajala (Miner); Matti Jaaranen (Mugger); Hannu Viholainen (Accomplice); Jorma Markkula (Tallyman); Tarja Keinanen (Woman in the Harbor); Eino Kuusela (Man on the Beach); Kauko Laalo (Night Hostel Warden); Jyrki Olsonen (Man in the Night Hostel); Eskko Nikkari (Car Dealer); Marja Packalen (Judge); Mikko Remes (Prison Doctor); Veikko Uusimaki (Mayor); Esko Salminen (Crook); Hannu Kivisalo (Doorman); Pekka Wilen (Skipper).

MONTHLY FILM BULLETIN, 10/89, p. 295, Tim Pulleine

When the mine in Lapland where he works closes down, Taisto Kasurinen is, like the rest of the workforce, made redundant. A senior colleague makes him a present of his prized white Cadillac, prior to committing suicide. Drawing his redundancy pay, Taisto heads south in the car, but at a roadside snack bar is robbed by two muggers. He subsequently obtains casual work at the docks and a bed in a flophouse; Irmeli, a divorcée and traffic warden who is about to book him, impulsively throws up her job instead and invites him home. They sleep together, and next morning Taisto meets her young son, Riku. Unable to find further work, Taisto feels compelled to sell his car to an unscrupulous second-hand dealer. The same evening, he spots one of the muggers in a shopping precinct and gives chase; but after a fight, Taisto (who has not reported being mugged) is arrested, charged with assault, and sentenced to prison. He shares a cell with Mikkonen, who has been convicted of manslaughter, and they form a friendship of sorts. Taisto asks Irmeli, now working at a meatpacking plant, to marry him, and she later smuggles a file to him hidden inside a book. He and Mikkonen escape, Taisto forcibly reclaims the Cadillac from the dealer, and he and Irmeli are married at a registry office. Shortly afterwards, the police arrive at Irmeli's flat and Taisto has to flee. In order to arrange fake passports for passage to Mexico,he and Mikkonen are forced to participate in a bank robbery. They are double-crossed, and Mikkonen is mortally knifed. But Taisto shoots dead their two contacts and makes off with the money. Taisto and Irmeli bury Mikkonen then make for the harbour with Riku. They are taken aboard the cargo ship "Ariel", which is bound for South America.

Very much a hybrid, *Ariel* combines elements of road movie and deterministic social melodrama with some stray intimations of antirealism in the style of early Godard. Up to a point, it succeeds in both imbuing these with a local flavour and yoking them together through a deliberately artificial plot, a chapter of accidents with a fantasised happy ending. Road movie conventions are utilised to pointed effect, notably in the chance meeting between Taisto and Irmeli and the latter's impulsive surrender to him. Earlier, the incongruity of the huge American convertible in the Nordic landscape, with the driver uncharismatically swathed in scarves because he can't figure out how to operate the roof, makes its own comment, offset by the alternation between American rock and Scandinavian schmalz which issues from radios and juke-boxes. Music is used evocatively elsewhere, with a blues lament accompanying the montage of Taisto looking for work; and the social commentary aspect is reinforced by a kind of 1930s-style determinism: for instance, in the foreshadowing of Taisto's incarceration in the prison-like images of the opening mine sequence.

But though the film has both vigour and a commendable economy, its contrivance begins to look increasingly out of place. Despite some quasi-surreal details (Mikkonen becomes instantly insensate after taking a tranquilliser), the film does little to justify the stylisation of the jailbreak, or such glaring implausibilities as Taisto and Irmeli getting married in the midst of the police hue and cry. In fact, this problem of tone manifests itself earlier, particularly in the black comedy of the initial suicide. In consequence, the climactic burst of violence looks more like a duplication of B-movie shorthand than any suggestive fantasia upon it, and the upbeat conclusion (for all that it is fetchingly underscored by the strains of "Over the Rainbow" in Finnish) leaves a rather indeterminate impression.

NEWSDAY, 9/25/89, Part II/p. 11, Terry Kelleher

The feature attraction on tonight's 6:15 [New York Film Festival] program is "Ariel," a dark, resolutely deadpan comedy from Finnish director Aki Kaurismaki. It's the story of a miner from Lapland who chucks it all (which isn't much) and heads for adventure in the big city of Helsinki. He gets mugged, abused, arrested, imprisoned and married before leaving the country in something of a hurry. It's all played so straight that the laughs can come as a shock. "Ariel" is an oddly appealing movie that will whet your appetite for more of Kaurismaki's work, which includes such intriguing titles as "Hamlet Goes Business" and "Leningrad Cowboys Go America."

Also reviewed in:
NEW YORK TIMES, 9/24/89, p. 71, Caryn James
VARIETY, 3/22/89, p. 23

ASHIK KERIB

An International Film Exchange release of a Gruziya Film Studios film. *Director:* Sergei Paradjanov *Screenplay (Russian with English subtitles):* Georgy Badridze. *Based on themes from "Ashik Kerib" by:* Mikhail Lermontov. *Director of Photography:* Albert Yavuryan. *Music:* Djavashir Kuliev. *Sound:* G. Kuntsev. *Production Designer:* Shota Gogolashvili and Nikolai Zandukeli. *Costumes:* E.Magalashvili. *Running time:* 78 minutes. *MPAA Rating:* Not Rated.

CAST: Yuri Goyan (Ashik Kerib); Veronika Metonidze; Levan Natroshvili; Sofiko Chiaureli; R. Chkhlkvadze; K. Stepanov; C. Dvalishvili; D. Dovlatyan; N. Dugladze.

LOS ANGELES TIMES, 7/14/89, Calendar/p. 11, Michael Wilmington

The allegories in "Ashik Kerib" are on a child's level. They are not philosophical. If you are a poet, armor will interfere with your song; if you see the blind, give them a caress.

—Sergei Paradjanov

Watching Paradjanov's tender little masterpiece, "Ashik Kerib" is almost like gazing at a delicate Persian miniature that suddenly flames into life and begins to shake and dance. The film is a feast of color, a banquet of music, an orgy of poetry and sensuality, yet it's also over-poweringly strange. It really transports us into another world—not the world of the past, the medieval Caucasus, where it supposedly takes place, or the 19th-Century Russia of its writer, Mikhail Lermontov—but a realm that seems somehow outside time, of pure poetry, childhood delight.

There's an ecstatic abandon about this movie, a curious mixture of extreme sophistication and conscious naiveté. It's a rapturously strange, eccentric fairy tale about a poor minstrel's seven-year odyssey to save his loved one from forced marriage by her Turkish merchant father. This simple story becomes a visual feast, filled with fruits, silks, castles, camels, birds, magical landscapes, mysterious hills and plans—as Paradjanov and co-director David Abachidze give us the tale in painterly images, constant music and two layers of narration, dialogue and mime. ("Ashik" was shot in the Muslim dialect Azerbaijani and the Georgian translation is dubbed on top of it, making for a cross-babble that might ordinarily annoy you. Here, it seems magically appropriate.)

Lermontov's tale of love triumphant becomes, for Paradjanov, something else: the odyssey of a young artist and lover through a hostile and treacherous world. The film's minstrel, Ashik (Yuri Goyan), naively tries to woo and buy his love with a bowl full of flowers, but though her heart is won, her father explodes in anger and ridicule, demanding something more tangible: money.

Ashik's journey to get it for him is an odyssey of absurdity and woe. When the lover leaves to earn his fortune, his unscrupulous rival steals his clothes and declares him dead; the kind old musician who teaches him dies in his arms, pomegranate juice bleeding over his lips. His most attentive audience is blind; the nabobs and warlords who hire him are lunatics and voluptuaries who will kill him if they dislike his song. In this world, death and ruin are everywhere, but miracles abound: two-headed tigers whirl, winged horses take flight. Love is a frail flower blooming on a crazy battlefield.

Paradjanov shapes this luminous film poem, which he dedicates to his late colleague, Andrei Tarkovsky, as if for a children's stage show. The actors face front and caper. The scenes, done in the rigid tableau style of his earlier "The Color of Pomegranates," look like creches filled with toys. Most film directors, even the fantasists, try to persuade us of the reality of their stories. Paradjanov's style, which has the straightforward look of a documentary or of Renoir's 1928 version of "The Little Match Girl," instead keeps insisting on unreality.

There's a dark substratum here. This film about an artist in conflict with society was directed by a Soviet film maker who, after shooting to world prominence in 1965 with the lyrical masterpiece "Shadows of Forgotten Ancestors," was convicted on charges that included homosexuality and spent 11 years in prison. You can sense this current vaguely beneath the bright, toylike surfaces of "Ashik Kerib" (Times-rated: Family), but it's remarkably free of bitterness. It's like a spectacular but delicate flower that blooms in darkness and confinement, banishing the squalor with its childlike joy.

MONTHLY FILM BULLETIN, 9/89, p. 265, Tony Rayns

Azerbaijan, sometime in the past. The handsome young minstrel Ashik Kerib is betrothed to Magul, daughter of the rich Turkish merchant Mekhar. But Mekhar rudely rejects the impoverished suitor, preferring to marry his only daughter to the wealthy Kurshid-Bek. Ashik and Magul pledge eternal loyalty to each other before the minstrel leaves to seek his fortune. An overly friendly horseman (actually Kurshid-Bek in disguise) pretends to help Ashik cross a river, but steals his clothes and returns to his home village, claiming that he has seen Ashik drown. Ashik's mother goes blind with grief. Reclothed by a kindly stranger, Ashik is led to a village by two women who have found his *saz* (Turkish balalaika) on the river bank. There he teams up with an elderly, dying minstrel and they take to the camel trails together. The old man dies on the road (as minstrels are fated to do), and Ashik buries him. Sleeping rough, Ashik is summoned by Aziz and Vale, the patrons of minstrel songs, to play first at the wedding of the blind, and then at the wedding of the deaf and dumb. Continuing his journey west, Ashik enters the domain of Nadir

Pasha, who petulantly imprisons him when he declares himself too exhausted to sing. But Ashik is released by adoring women from the Pasha's harem, only to be enslaved (as prophesied by his patron saints) by the villainous Sultan Aziz, who encases him in chain mail and orders him beheaded when he protests that he can no longer sing. Two boy angels trick the Sultan, and a life-size doll is beheaded in Ashik's place. Ashik is next set upon by xenophobic horsemen, who beat him and leave him for dead. Recovering, he approaches a church to do penance for his sins, but finds it invaded by wild animals and evil spirits. He preserves his soul by thinking of his mother. St. George on a white horse comes to Ashik in a field and warns him that Magul is about to be pressed into marriage with Kurshid-Bek. They fly back to Ashik's village on the horse; the saint counsels the minstrel to wipe dust from the horse's hoof and await a miracle. Ashik enters Kurshid-Bek's house, where his claim to have flown the distance of a hundred-day journey in a single day is met with anger and derision. But the dust from the horse's hoof restores the sight of his mother—a miracle that wins Ashik the hand of Magul. Ashik kisses and releases a white dove in honour of his new father-in-law. The dove alights on a movie camera.

Ashik Kerib, rooted in Azerbaijan, completes what must be thought of as a Caucasus trilogy, alongside The Colour of Pomegranates (Armenia/Georgia) and The Legend of the Suram Fortress (Georgia). And if current, sad reports that Paradjanov is terminally ill can be trusted, then it may well also turn out to be the final chapter in his extended, oblique autobiography. Here, more than in the earlier films, the protagonist is transparently a surrogate for the author, and the picaresque plot a cypher for the triumphs, travails and doubts that beset the artist. The nominal derivation from a Lermontov story is the merest pretext for a film that is profoundly personal. As in Suram Fortress, the direction is co-credited to the actor Dodo Abashidze, but no-one doubts that Paradjanov is the sole "true" author.

In the sense that it deals with an artistic career blighted by uncomprehending audiences and cruel paymasters, not to mention all manner of physical temptations and spiritual anxieties, Ashik Kerib aligns itself with 8½ and its neurotic variant Stardust Memories. But Paradjanov—who has suffered real-life setbacks beyond the worst dreams of Fellini and Woody Allen—has junked whatever self-pity he may be prone to, along with all the other "psychological" trappings that go with conventional storytelling. Paradjanov characteristically refuses to internalise the issues to produce anguished soul-searching, but instead joyfully externalises them—to produce dance, pantomime and mystery-play. His film has less in common with Western studies of The Artist than with a movie like Tian Zhuangzhuang's Horse Thief, which equally values poetry above banal narrative pedantry and prefers images to drama and colour to dialogue. This connection is cemented, incidentally, by Tian's decision to follow Horse Thief with his own extraordinary film about the plight of persecuted artists, Gushu Yiren (The Street Players, 1987).

In form, this is another of Paradjanov's pageant-films, loosely in the vein of Pomegranates and Suram Fortress, but this time taking its tone and design from ancient Persian and other Middle-Eastern art. The director helpfully clarified his use of visual sources in his 1985 short Arabesques on Themes of Pirosmani; he has little interest in duplicating the compositions of paintings per se, but loves abstracting colours, shapes and figures from paintings and co-opting them into his own idiosyncratic fantasies. Here, there is much less use of tableau compositions than in the earlier films and a proportionally greater use of actual paintings as inserts to propel or comment on the narrative line. A montage of camel paintings, for instance, signifies the extent and duration of Ashik's journey; and a montage of paintings of same-sex couples (twins?) provides a thoroughly ambiguous coda to the scene of Ashik's seduction at the hands of the women of Nadir Pasha's harem.

Equally, there is more camera movement than before, although nothing to compare with the florid excesses of Shadows of Our Forgotten Ancestors, made by Paradjanov in what must now seem like an earlier life. Most often the camera pans to take in the full scale of a location or a camel train or the movements of a large group of extras. Sometimes camera movement is synonymous with digression, as when the narrative stops while the camera drifts admiringly over the ornate woodwork inside a belltower. On the whole, though, as in the two preceding features, there is a clear preference for containing a sense of movement within a more or less static frame. Ashik Kerib offers two startling new extensions of this principle: the drastic rack-focus shots (as extreme as anything in Leone's films) that render the mother's descent into and recovery from blindness; and the shots that represent the magic flight back home on St. George's horse, which pose two boy angels blowing conch horns against a huge spinning globe.

As these examples may suggest, Ashik Kerib is significantly lighter and more playful in tone than its predecessors. As a pageant, it could easily have been costumed and made-up by Lindsay Kemp and choreographed by Michael Clark. To call it "camp", though, would be to confuse the character of the spectacle with the underlying thrust of the narrative. Paradjanov loves festooning his macho protagonist in silk robes and lipstick as much as he loves his dazzling array of antique props, from pewter jugs to Persian carpets, but the element of indulgence that seems basic to the camp sensibility is crucially absent. Like *Pomegranates* and *Suram Fortress*, the film chronicles a spiritual journey in profane, worldly terms, and it is the earthy vulgarity of the detail that gives the spirituality its edge. To reach for yet another point of reference, Paradjanov here matches his beloved Pasolini (specifically, the Pasolini of *Arabian Nights*) in achieving a paradoxical pleasure in and detachment from his storyline. He has nothing to prove, but everything to show and endless stories to tell.

The tension between free will and predestination that ran through *Pomegranates* and *Suram Fortress* here finds its clearest focus. Ashik's artistry is a postulate, not something that needs to be demonstrated, and so the film feels free to effect a radical separation of image and soundtrack. Ashik's songs are *heard* throughout, but he is rarely seen playing, and when he is, it is never in sync with the soundtrack. The soundtrack thus functions as a commentary on the images, an anthology of love songs and religious songs that counterpoints the visual anthology of scenes from the life of the artist. Ashik himself chooses whether to perform (as in the remarkably imagined scenes of the blind wedding and the deaf and dumb wedding) or to withhold his songs (as in the courts of the Pasha and the Sultan), but the soundtrack songs continue regardless, like the artist's inner life. Carefully placed details like the precisely timed arrival of the stranger with clothes to cover Ashik's nakedness and the interventions of the patron saints of minstrel songs indicate that Ashik's journey is predestined; hence the total elimination of "drama" and "suspense" from the narrative. At the same time, though, Ashik lives through all the vagaries of a rich and colourful life, and his exploits yield continuously provocative events and images, whether coarse or exquisite, vulgar or sublime. Paradjanov does not *deny* drama; rather, he takes it out of the narrative and relocates it in the play between image and sound. This, of course, is a modernist strategy, and that is what gives the film's poetry its polemic thrust and makes it so compulsive.

Ashik Kerib moves through every colour in the spectrum towards the purest and most dazzling white. It ends on the image of a white dove perching on a black movie camera, together with a dedication to Tarkovsky. One vein of imagery in the film seems intended as a direct homage to the late director, who was Paradjanov's chief ally in the struggle to uphold the Dovzhenko tradition in Soviet cinema: the fruit on the bough in Magul's garden, which changes colour from red to black to white according to twists of fate. But even this little gesture towards expressionism is integrated into what can only be called the Paradjanov aesthetic. It relates, for instance, to the scene of the old minstrel's death on the road, where Ashik squeezes a pomegranate and lets the blood-red juice trickle over the corpse's mouth. As ever, Paradjanov achieves his effects in the simplest and most direct way, trusting handpicked faces, bodies, objects, textures and colours to yield enough spectacle to fire the dullest imagination. His film has no whiff of the "industrial" about it. It offers the light and magic of a true artisan.

VILLAGE VOICE, 6/20/89, p. 87, J. Hoberman

Local color is too tepid a term to describe the work of Sergei Paradjanov, the Soviet filmmaker who resumed his career four years ago after spending most of the '70s in prison and disgrace. More than a professional backwoods bard, the 65-year-old Paradjanov is the reigning master of Carpathian-Armenian-Azerbaijani ethnofunk; his movies are the visual equivalent of the Bulgarian State Radio and Television Female Vocal Choir.

Half Edgar G. Ulmer (the '30s impresario of bargain-basement Yiddish, Ukrainian, and all-black talkies), half Jack Smith (the '60s maestro of *Flaming Creatures* and admirer of Maria Montez's *Arabian Nights*), Paradjanov specializes in impenetrably gestic, impossibly exotic folk pageants—typically composed of a few well-deployed elements. There's no mistaking Paradjanov's world: His is the realm of the snow-white dove and the blood-red pomegranate, the planet where a torrent of rose petals flutters down upon antique, intricately patterned carpets, while a troupe of dromedaries saunters across the weathered stones of some ancient courtyard. Paradjanov doesn't edit so much as compile individual tableaux, punctuated with Persian miniatures and little groupings of museum-quality artifacts.

Paradjanov's *Ashik Kerib*, which had its local premiere at the last New York Film Festival and settles in Thursday for a 10-day run at Anthology Film Archives, is the tale of a medieval Turkish troubador's trans-Caucasian wanderings. (It's liberally embroidered from the story by Mikhail Lermontov, the 19th century Russian poet who spent much of his brief life exiled to the Caucasus.) Ridiculed by the wealthy merchant whose daughter he is courting, the eponymous hero sets off in search of bride money—traveling from court to court, enduring all manner of betrayal and oppression before benefiting from the miraculous intercession of St. George. (In a scene with an unmistakable directorial touch, the elderly saint has onions braided in his long white beard.)

The material seems like *echt*-Paradjanov, and maybe that's the problem. Formula supersedes feeling—*Ashik Kerib* might have been directed by a clumsy acolyte. If Paradjanov's sense of humor is more evident here than previously, the movie's jocular tone brings the proceedings to the brink of self-parody. While some devices are adapted from traditional puppet-plays (a red silk scarf pulled out of a dummy's severed neck, an outsize tiger that rotates its head), others are straight out of Fractured Flickers: The exaggerated, eye-rolling performances and slight undercranking give the action a herky-jerky silent-movie flavor. (Paradjanov plays on the anachronism at one point by arming a bevy of courtesans with plastic machine guns.) Worse, the film is hampered by the inexpressive, if not befuddled, male ingenue in the title role. (Where is Sabu when you need him?)

Ashik Kerib has its moments: The guests at "the wedding of the blind, deaf, and dumb" wear blindfolds decorated with jewel-encrusted eyes, and everyone gropes about as the bard launches into his trademark keening song. It is in keeping with the metaphor that this would be the first Paradjanov film to receive the blessing of *The New York Time*'s tireless ideological *meshiach*, Walter Goodman. After mocking Paradjanov's comeback opus, *The Legend of Suram Fortress*, when it played the Film Forum in early '87, the shameless Goodman has evidently concluded that Paradjanov *was* a legitimate subject of Soviet persecution and has recognized that *Ashik Kerib* none-too-subtly lends itself to such an interpretation. (To underscore the point, the movie is dedicated to Tarkovsky, another belated *Times* enthusiasm.)

Perhaps Goodman's indulgence will encourage his more adventurous readers to trek down to Anthology, but the sad truth is that *Ashik Kerib* is mediocre Paradjanov at best. His movie is a lot less stringent and a lot more strident than *Suram Fortress*, not to mention Paradjanov's beleaguered 1969 masterpiece, *Sayat Nova*. Only the flow has the director's eccentric rhythms—time frequently appears to go backward (or maybe Ashik is simply a precog). The mise-en-scène feels like dress-up. The narrative takes center stage (for Paradjanov, *Ashik Kerib* is virtually an action film). The shrill, tinny sound mix approaches the threshold of pain.

"I think the absolute best filmmaking would be for the deaf and dumb," Paradjanov is quoted as saying in the current *Film Comment*. Would that *Ashik Kerib* were! Shot in Azerbaijani with a dubbed Georgian voiceover and a surfeit of overamplified lute music, the movie might benefit immeasurably from being shown silent at the slower speed of 16 frames per second. Even then it would probably look facile: If Anthology really wanted to break your heart, they'd show it with something victimized by our local gulag, a reel of Jack Smith's unfinished *Normal Love*.

Also reviewed in:
NEW YORK TIMES, 6/15/89, p. 17, Walther Goodman
VARIETY, 9/14/88, p. 26

AVANTI POPOLO

A Film Ventures International release. *Producer:* Rafi Bukaee. *Director:* Rafi Bukaee. *Screenplay (Arabic and Hebrew with English subtitles):* Rafi Bukaee. *Director of Photography:* Yoav Kosh. *Editor:* Zohar Sela. *Music:* Uri Ofir. *Sound:* Itamar Ben-Yaakov, Dani Matalon, Ronny Berger, and Shmuel Ettinger. *Art Director:* Ariel Glazer. *Make-up:* Irith Elazar. *Running time:* 84 minutes. *MPAA Rating:* Not Rated.

CAST: Salim Daw (Haled); Suhel Hadad (Gassan).

LOS ANGELES TIMES, 11/4/88, Calendar/p. 13, Kevin Thomas

"Avanti Popolo," the third offering in the Israeli series at the Monica 4-Plex, is the kind of picture that, dealing as it does with the Six-Day War, might be expected to stir audiences on home ground in spite of itself. But it's too heavy-handed and obvious in its expression of its anti-war sentiments, noble as they are, to travel well.

Haled (Salim Daw) and Gassan (Suhel Hadad) star as two Egyptian soldiers trying to make their way back to Cairo from the Sinai Desert in the wake of the cease-fire. Their grimly realistic plight gives way to a more surreal and comic mood as they encounter various people, culminating with a lost Israeli patrol that takes them in when Haled, a struggling actor, recites a scene in broken English from his greatest role, Shylock. But as surely as brotherhood between the two Egyptians and the Israelis flowers, it contains the seeds of tragedy.

Writer-director Rafi Bukaee makes "Avanti Pololo" hard going all the way. Daw and Hadad are not especially engaging in their woebegone Everyman portrayals; at best they evoke unwelcome memories of Warren Beatty and Dustin Hoffman being similarly stranded in "Ishtar." The film's curious title refers to the Italian revolutionary song that the Egyptians and the Israelis sing together without understanding its words, an act meant to symbolize the way in which men are sent off to battle without comprehending why.

NEW YORK POST, 4/19/89, p. 25, V.A. Musetto

"Avanti Popolo" starts out slowly, unsurely. The 1967 Middle East war has just ended and two Egyptian soldiers, separated from their unit, stumble across the desert, hoping to reach friendly territory. You're not sure just what Rafi Bukaee, the 31-year-old Israeli who wrote, directed and produced the film, is up to.

The Egyptians come upon a white U.N. jeep, abandoned in the desert, with a peace-keeping soldier sitting in the back seat. He's dead. The Egyptians search the vehicle for badly needed water. All they find is an umbrella and a bottle of liquor.

"Even when they're dead they look better than we do," one of the unkempt wanderers observes, glancing nervously at the dead soldier. It is about this point, as the Egyptians settle down to get plastered on the whiskey, that you realize that "Avanti Popolo" is a comedy—an unlikely one, as it turns out. For here you have an Israeli director making a comedy in which enemy soldiers in a deadly war turn out to be the most, if not the only, sympathetic characters.

This did not go unnoticed in Jerusalem. Politicians reacted angrily when the movie, which enjoyed box-office success in Israel, was nominated as the country's official entry for an Oscar as Best Foreign Language film of 1987. "Avanti Popolo," the detractors said, is unflattering toward Israeli troops, who are depicted as petty, argumentative and not especially bright.

Replied Bukaee: The film "isn't about Israeli soldiers at all"—its true concern is the stupidity of war.

As such, "Avanti Popolo" (the title is taken from an Italian revolutionary song and is translated as "Forward, the people") is a sly, if uneven, success. The script lacks depth, and the direction often is indecisive and meandering. Still there are moments of ingenious farce and black humor.

Consider: a run-in with a loudmouthed British TV reporter bellowing for "blood, burned-out tanks"; the two heroes gliding through the sand in the U.N. jeep, the umbrella opened, the dead Swede still upright in the rear seat, his head bobbing up and down; one of the Egyptians, an actor whose career has been interrupted by the war, using Shylock's monologue from "The Merchant of Venice" to get water from Israeli troops with whom they have struck up a friendship of sorts.

These scenes ripple amiably and largely compensate for the more serious moments, which seem thrown in and not fully thought out. But the finely tuned comic performances of Salim Daw as the desert Shylock and Suhel Hadad as his war buddy are the sympathetic heart of a film that comes tantalizingly close to victory.

VILLAGE VOICE, 4/25/89, p. 68, Amy Taubin

Plumbing the metaphor of war as theater, Israeli filmmaker Rafi Bukaee follows two hapless and buffoonish Eygptian soldiers who are stranded in the glorious set of the Sinai Desert at the end of the 1967 Six Day War. The heroes of *Avanti Popolo* aren't waiting for Godot; they're walking, walking, walking, desperately trying to reach the border, but because the sand and sky look the same from all directions, they might as well be standing still center-stage. *Avanti Popolo*'s interest lies chiefly in the fact that it's an Israeli film portraying Egyptian soldiers as innocent victims and the Israelis as callous and cunning, although no less dupes of the state. The entire narrative is dependent on the Egyptians finding a bottle of whiskey in an abandoned jeep. Since it's the first liquid they've seen in two days, they drink half of it for breakfast. This allows them to behave in a charmingly reckless manner when captured by an Israeli patrol. I found it impossible to believe that two totally dehydrated persons who had never tasted alcohol before wouldn't have expired minutes after imbibing. Problems of credibility aside, *Avanti Popolo* is nearly devoid of politics, and Bukaee, who wrote as well as directed, lacks the graveyard poetics and everything else that distinguishes Samuel Beckett from his puerile imitators.

Also reviewed in:
NEW YORK TIMES, 4/19/88, p. C19, Caryn James
VARIETY, 7/23/86, p. 16

BABAR: THE MOVIE

A New Line release of a Canada-France co-production with the participation of Telefilm Canada, Ontario Film Development Corporation, and Centre National de la Cinématographie. *Producer:* Patrick Loubert, Michael Hirsh and Clive A. Smith. *Director:* Alan Bunce. *Screenplay:* Peter Sauder, J.D. Smith, John De Klein, Raymond Jaffelice, and Alan Bunce. *Story:* Peter Sauder, Patrick Loubert, and Michael Hirsh. *Based on characters created by:* Jean de Brunhoff and Laurent de Brunhoff. *Director of Animation:* John Laurence Collins. *Editor:* Evan Landis. *Running time:* 80 minutes. *MPAA Rating:* G.

VOICES: Gordon Pinsent (King Babar); Gavin Magrath (Boy Babar); Elizabeth Hanna (Queen Celeste); Sarah Polley (Young Celeste); Lisa Yamanaka (Isabelle); Marsha Moreau (Flora); Bobby Becken (Pom); John Stocker (Zephir); Charles Kerr (Rataxes); Amos Crawley (Alexander).

LOS ANGELES TIMES, 7/28/89, Calendar/p. 8, Sheila Benson

Funny to see the influences of "Indiana Jones" and "'Crocodile' Dundee" casting their shadows on the film version of a character as presumably sturdy and indelible as Babar the Elephant, but they're there, sure as grosses are grosses.

To be sure, the ample young king of "Babar: The Movie" doesn't crack a bullwhip and he still wears a crown, not a Stetson, but the perils that lurk for him, Celeste and the mischievous monkey Zephir have a distinctly Indiana-ish flavor. And the Crocodile, who turns out to be such an ally to these brave little elephants, has a broad Australian accent.

Very young children, who will be this movie's best audience, may not get the joke, particularly the Dundee one. But it's interesting to see that, with all the approaches that could have been taken in adapting the classic Jean and Laurent de Brunhoff books for today's action-saturated children, the choice was to make this first feature an elephant action-adventure; granted that it's a warm, family elephant action-adventure.

Those who worry that a beloved set of characters has been properly treated needn't worry...too much. Toronto's Nelvana animation house—which has done the "Ewoks" and "Droids" for television with Lucasfilm, as well as "The Care Bears" series and the "Babar" segments on Nickelodeon—has seen to it that Babar still looks like his dear self, pin-dots for eyes, natty green suit, gold crown and all. We recognize too his lifelong love, Celeste, seen here both as a slip of a thing and as a suitably matronly mama of four. Only the sage old Cornelius seems to have shed a few of his wiggly lines, which represented his extreme age. Would it were that simple.

Presumably down the line we can get to the details that kids also love about Babar: the little, just-orphaned elephant who was found, outfitted, loved and tutored by the Old Lady who lived in such a sophisticated (and thoroughly French) city. And how he grew into such authority and wisdom that when he became homesick and journeyed back to Elephantland, proving himself in the process, the elephant elders crowned him their new king.

"Babar: The Movie" plunges right in, assuming that the children have a few of those introductions under their belts. After a witty, full-scale Elephantland Victory Parade, including a drum major doing baton tricks and the royal family on a float, with the royal children throwing peanuts, King Babar tells his four wiggly children the tale of their country's victory against the rhinos as a bedtime story.

As we shift back to the past, Babar and Celeste have little-children voices, a bit more trying than the splendid voice Gordon Pinsent gives the mature Babar. The rhinos are still led by the malevolent Rataxes, although there's been a subtle shift in his characterization since the books.

You'd be hard-pressed, looking at Rataxes, to believe that this took place in or around Africa, in spite of the all-African-animal cast. Rataxes' soldiers wear conquistadors' armor and all the architectural details around him are Mayan, not African. It may be better, in this day and age, than making your villain into a rhino Idi Amin, but it's something of a geographic leap.

Babar's ingenuity in defeating Rataxes at Elephantland's very gates is, if memory serves, right from the book and thunderingly, ground-shakingly splendid. The film is also full of songs, mostly unmemorable, with the exception of a sprightly number in praise of red tape. It's done in razzmatazz style by two fussy courtiers, Cornelius and Pompadour, sung by their actors, Chris Wiggins and Stephen Ouimette, respectively, and written by Phil Balsam. If more of "Babar" hit this tone, it would be an enchantment. As it is, "Babar: The Movie" is pleasant, occasionally delightful and certainly a safe niche for the young'uns.

NEW YORK POST, 8/25/89, p. 23, Jami Bernard

They're calling it "Babar: The Movie," but I'm suspicious. Seems more like "Babar: The Merchandising Campaign."

In addition to "The Movie," there's Babar: The Series, composed of 26 episodes for HBO, and Babar: The Licensing Kingdom, in which pajamas, bedding, calendars, lunch kits, bendable toys and more are capitalizing on the spare, linear, charming drawings made long ago by Jean de Brunhoff to illustrate the children's stories told by his wife, Cecile.

So now we have Babar: The Lunch Box. But long ago in a wonderful series of children's books we had Babar: The Boy King—of the elephants, that is. Babar was a pointy-eyed little tusker of great kindness and jungle savvy who saved his kingdom from evil rhinos and grew to be an adult king with a queen and little Babars of his own.

This movie version has Babar: The King reminiscing to his young'uns about his royal boyhood and the battle royale with the rhinos, about how he saved the future Queen Celeste and Celeste's mother, and how he outwitted and then befriended a snapping crocodile and a wiseacre monkey.

Babar's mission to save the elephants from being pressed into slavery by the rhinos is impeded by the plodding deliberations of his trusted advisers, but Babar does a "Prince and the Pauper" switch with a lookalike and sets out to save the day.

The story's just fine, but its execution—in unimaginative and clunky animation—is cloyingly cutesy. There is a catchy song about bureaucracy of elephantine proportions, but otherwise the adults who accompany their wee ones to the movie will have to bring along a book and a penlight to keep themselves occupied.

The elephants in this movie have no distinct personalities. Even Babar is only distinguished by having a bigger speaking role and being able to devise plans, something his fellow elephants have not been able to achieve as they lumber up the evolutionary ladder. These pachyderms—who wear clothes, by the way—are really humans in disguise. If you close your eyes (and you'll want to), you won't be able to distinguish this from any human-based adventure story.

The monkey Zephir at least does a little shtick, but otherwise this is adventure as strained through cheesecloth.

"You do something for me and I do something for you—that's the law of the jungle" is an odd maxim to promote for kids, since it is most certainly not the law of the jungle—quite the opposite.

The film, short on its own ideas (part of the lure of the children's books was their simplicity) borrows a bit from "Indiana Jones" and "The Wizard of Oz" to bulk up the adventure.

"Babar: The Movie" is inoffensive, if that's all you're looking for in a children's movie. Even Babar: The Bedding might prove more exciting for children whose own fervid imaginations are not impeded by marketing schemes.

NEWSDAY, 8/25/89, Part III/p. 5, Terry Kelleher

When you see "The Movie" in the title of a movie, you know you're dealing with a multi-media marketing phenomenon.

"Babar: The Movie" is primarily for kids (and parents) who are already sold on Babar books, Babar merchandise and the "Babar" television series. Like "Babar" on HBO, "Babar: The Movie" comes from Nelvana, the Canadian animation house that did "The Care Bears Movie," "The Care Bears Movie II" and the syndicated "Care Bears" TV show.

King Babar is an anthropomorphic elephant, but he's known to resemble a Care Bear in his gentle wisdom and solid family values. A benevolent-looking leader in his crown and three-piece suit, he tells his children a bedtime story about his heroic days as boy monarch of Elephantland, when he defeated the evil Lord Rataxes and his rampaging rhinoceros army.

The tale gets off to an unpromising start, wisdomwise. When his friend Celeste reports that the rhinos are threatening her village, Babar's senior advisers counsel cautious diplomacy ("A war isn't something we want to rush into," say the fuddy-duddies), but the young king is clearly inclined to use force as a first resort.

Frustrated by his country's lack of military preparedness, Babar joins Celeste on an undercover mission behind enemy lines, leaving her brother Arthur to pose as king. "All us little elephants look the same," Arthur says in accepting the assignment.

Unfortunately, he's exactly right. All the pachyderms in "Babar: The Movie" have dots for eyes, stumps for hands and generally expressionless features, just as they do in the Babar books. The Nelvana animators try to compensate by giving the elephants extremely useful trunks. They write with them, they hammer with them, they swing by them. Babar even employs his to suck a bird out of the air.

Trunk versatility notwithstanding, the elephants are awfully *gray*—in both complexion and personality. "Babar: The Movie" grows more colorful when Babar and Celeste encounter a rambunctious band of monkeys, led by a wiseacre named Zephir. Realizing this picture needs a touch of show biz, Zephir introduces himself by doing his impression of an elephant. He may not qualify as the Rich Little of the jungle, but his verve is much needed here. A hungry, mischievous crocodile soon appears and adds to the fun.

The rhino-elephant conflict is played out in terms that recall "The Ten Commandments" (rhino/Egyptians enslave elephant/Israelites) and "The Alamo" (gallant, outnumbered elephants, hold the fort against the rhino hordes). Serious violence is averted at the last minute, but it's trickery, not gentle wisdom, that saves the day.

With grays, browns and pastels so much in evidence, the 80-minute cartoon seldom delights the eye. The few songs are forgettable and the voices, except for Charles Kerr's gravelly Rataxes, do little to enhance the characterizations.

Though it should be met with approval by the many devoted followers of the elephant king, "Babar: The Movie" seems unlikely to attract millions of new converts to Babarism.

Also reviewed in:
NEW YORK TIMES, 8/25/89, p. C14, Stephen Holden
VARIETY, 7/26–8/1/89, p. 16
WASHINGTON POST, 7/28/89, p. B7, Rita Kempley

BACK TO ARARAT

A First Run Features release. *Producer:* PeA Holmquist. *Director:* PeA Holmquist, Jim Downing and Suzanne Khardalian. *Screenplay (French, Armenian and English with English subtitles):* PeA Holmquist and Goran Gunner. *Director of Photography:* PeA Holmquist. *Editor:* PeA Holmquist and Toby Trotter. *Music:* Komitas. *Running time:* 100 minutes. *MPAA Rating:* Not Rated.

LOS ANGELES TIMES, 5/25/89, Calendar/p. 2, Michael Wilmington

"Back to Ararat" is a Swedish documentary about one of the most horrible and piteous events of this century: the forced deportation and slaughter of vast numbers of Armenian people by the government of Turkey in April, 1915, during World War I. This appalling event reverberates like the echo of some hideous cataclysm over the entire film.

Eyewitnesses recount gruesome forced marches, families riven apart, mass executions. They tell of thousands of people herded into caves to be burned alive by Turkish soldiers, of the handful of survivors crawling their way out of the carnage, forced to sustain themselves for days on the burnt human flesh all around them.

As a counterpoint to these recollections, we visit the descendants of those victims and Armenia as it is today: the small wedge—one-sixth of the old land mass—of Soviet Armenia and the rest of the old Turkish-ruled country, near Ararat and the sea. It's a halcyon-seeming but very empty-looking place, where barely a handful of Armenians now exist. Yet it's the touchstone for many of the displaced people we meet.

Directors PeA Holmquist and collaborators Jim Downing and Suzanne Khardalian interview them everywhere: in Decines, France (near Lyon), New York City, Boston, Fresno or Bourdj Hamoud in Beirut. A pattern emerges. The older Armenians, some of them actual refugees from the terror, try to accept, forget or somehow transcend the past. Many of the younger Armenians, furious, talk of revenge or reclaiming the turf, even cultivate a pseudo-military tough-guy facade.

Representatives of Turkey appear, too. Here, as with some of the scenes of the Armenian "Young Turks," the movie is at its most disturbing. Few histories cast any doubt on the Turkish army's wholesale massacre of the Armenian citizenry. Yet these representatives vehemently lecture young Turkish-Americans in workshops, or blandly address the camera, exuding an air of wounded reason, their eyes shifting or glazing over.

They all agree: there was no massacre. A huge mistake. The explanation for the disappearance or scattering of over a million people? It was a war, full of mass confusion, bloodshed, people running here and there, getting killed. Who could keep track? It was nobody's fault. It was awful. And the worst victims of all, one spokesman blandly assures us, were the Turks themselves, maligned for something they never did.

"Back to Ararat" is well shot by Holmquist and his crew, and beautifully scored to the mournful tunes of Armenian composer Komitas, who never composed again after the massacre. It's difficult to watch it without a sense of outrage: not directed against the Turkish people, but against the brutal tyrants who ruled over them in 1915 and hatched the inhuman stratagem of emptying an entire land. And it's hard not to feel anguish, not just for the million or more Armenians, but for every helpless group of people in the history of this world, whether Armenians, European Jews, Ukrainians, American Indians, Africans or Cambodians, crushed in the juggernaut of politics, enslaved or slaughtered by callous, cruel and vain leaders who believe themselves above the law and humanity.

"Back to Ararat" (Times-rated: Mature, for adult themes and content) should probably be seen by every person of Armenian and Turkish descent in this city. (In a strange way, one hopes it might reconcile them, at least in a mutual recognition of this terrible history.) And it should be seen as well by those of us who may forget the sheer murderous enormity of what our leaders sometimes do in the name of history's necessity and their nation's rightful destiny.

NEW YORK POST, 5/19/89, p. 32, V.A. Musetto

"Back to Ararat" is a competently made, sometimes-moving documentary about the "forgotten genocide"—the death of 1.5 million Armenians and the forced evacuation of hundreds of thousands more by Turkish authorities in 1915. Unfortunately, it breaks the most important rule of documentary-film making: appeal to everyone, not just to those with a vested interest in your subject.

The English-language film by a team of Swedish film makers headed by PeA Holmquist is best when it lets survivors of the tragedy tell their stories.

The most chilling account comes from a retired silk worker named Garabed Hovakimian. Sitting on a sofa at his home in Lyon, France, his wife by his side, he recalls how at age 8 he was one of 2 million people forced into a three-week "death march." Sobbing, he tells how his 17-year-old brother and 60 other children were herded into a house and shot to death while his mother hid him under her skirt.

When she was dying from lack of water, the child had to stop her from using a well into which bodies had been thrown.

In a tiny village in what was once old Armenia and today is part of Turkey, a wrinkled 92-year-old grandmother, a member of the town's only Armenian family, warns Holmquist: "Why do you ask about this? It all happened 70 years ago. Return to your own lives. Be wise, the police can arrest you." Then, fingering a worn Armenian Bible, she tells about the day in 1915 that villagers were forced into cellars and killed with knives and axes. Her family was spared, she says, because her father made oil lamps for the authorities.

Meanwhile, an Armenian terrorist matter-of-factly describes how he shot and killed a Turkish envoy in Yugoslavia: "I walked calmly up to the car. I cocked my pistol. Then I shot him." The assassin was sentenced to 20 years in prison but set free early for reasons never explained. "I don't feel I've paid a great price," he says now. "It was my duty."

"Back to Ararat" might have succeeded had it devoted itself to scenes like the above. Instead, Holmquist lulls us with talk about Armenians one day returning to their former homeland in the shadow of Mount Ararat (the Soviet republic of Armenia contains one-sixth of their ancient land). The director seems more interested in the impassioned rhetoric of people like Raffy, a young New York newlywed whose entire life seems to revolve around a return to Ararat, than he does in the chilling tales of those who survived a living hell.

The result is a sympathetic but overlong and not very compelling film that should make believers in the cause even more fervent while leaving others unmoved.

NEWSDAY, 5/22/89, Part II/p. 11, Lynn Darling

It has been nearly three quarters of a century since the Armenian people saw their homeland destroyed by the Turks in a genocide that left 1.5 million dead and their survivors scattered throughout the world. As Swedish film maker PeA Holmquist emphasizes in "Back to Ararat," the longing for nationhood and the memory of the horror have continued, like the aching of a phantom limb, in the memories of both the old and the young.

Old men living now in France and Syria break down in tears before the camera as they describe the horror they survived and the members of their family who were not so fortunate. A young man in New York talks angrily of regaining a homeland he has never seen and of the importance of keeping a flickering culture alive in the hearts of the next generation. A gunman talks calmly of patriotism from the wheelchair in which he has been confined since he tried to assassinate the Turkish ambassador to Yugoslavia on behalf of the cause. A 92-year-old woman in a fly-specked shawl wants to know why the film makers are asking so many questions. It's meaningless, she says. It all happened 70 years ago.

Holmquist punctuates these interviews with meditative shots of old Armenia, now a part of Turkey, a barren and brooding land that looks as if it is in mourning for its lost people. The camera returns again and again to Mount Ararat, the sacred symbol of the Armenian people, in mute illustration of the sorrow of exile.

But "Back to Ararat" devotes very little attention to the background, history and context of the terrible events that led to the massacre. Nor does it explore in any depth the culture, sensibility and temperament of that now vanished country, as it once was or as it exists in places like Soviet Armenia or in the various exile communities. The Armenians are a people swallowed up by history: Unfortunately this film does little to bring them back compellingly into the present.

VILLAGE VOICE, 5/23/89, p. 64, Amy Taubin

Most documentaries are only interesting to those with a direct connection to their subject matter. *Back to Ararat* and *A Night in Havana: Dizzy Gillespie in Cuba* [see Taubin's review] are no exceptions to the rule.

When I watched the TV coverage of the earthquake in Soviet Armenia, I dimly realized that the disaster was but the capper to a century-long raw deal for the Armenians. *Back to Ararat*, directed by Swedish filmmaker PeA Holmquist, relies on the testimony of survivors of the events of 1915 to fill in the details of the "first genocide of the 20th century." One and a half million Armenians perished when they were forced from their homes and marched across the desert to Syria. Those who survived starvation were thrown into caves and burned to death or drowned or shot. The Turkish authorities maintain their own claim to the Armenian homeland by denying the charge of genocide, admitting only that people on both sides were killed during a period of unrest.

Although Holmquist was approached to make a film about the Armenian diaspora on the basis of *Gaza Ghetto*, his pro-Palestinian documentary, he draws no parallels. As a result, the film is compassionate and informative but limited in scope—oddly ahistorical and apolitical. The Turkish government won't like it; the Armenians will. But for everyone else, *Back to Ararat* is neatly noncontroversial. It makes no connections.

Also reviewed in:
NEW YORK TIMES, 5/19/89, p. C18, Richard Bernstein
VARIETY, 3/8-14/89, p. 25

BACK TO THE FUTURE PART II

A Universal Pictures release. *Executive Producer:* Steven Spielberg, Frank Marshall, and Kathleen Kennedy. *Producer:* Bob Gale and Neil Canton. *Director.* Robert Zemeckis. *Screenplay:* Bob Gale. *Story:* Robert Zemeckis and Bob Gale. *Director of Photography:* Dean Cundey. *Editor:* Arthur Schmidt and Harry Keramidas. *Music:* Alan Silvestri. *Music Editor:* Kenneth Karman. *Sound:* William B. Kaplan and (music) Dennis S. Sands. *Sound Editor:* Charles L. Campbell and Louis L. Edemann. *Production Designer:* Rick Carter. *Art Director:* Marjorie Stone McShirley. *Set Designer:* Martha Johnston, Stephen Homsy, Paul Sonski, Beverli Eagan, Steven Wolff, Nancy Nickelberry, Larry Hubbs, and Joseph G. Pacelli. *Set Decorator:* Linda De Scenna. *Set Dresser:* Lee Orlikoff, Tony Piller, John Rankin, and Larry Boyd. *Special Effects:* Michael Lantieri. *Visual Effects:* Ken Ralston. *Costumes:* Joanna Johnston. *Make-up:* Ken Chase. *Stunt Coordinator:* Walter Scott. *Running time:* 105 minutes. *MPAA Rating:* PG.

CAST: Michael J. Fox (Marty McFly/Marty McFly Jr./Marlene McFly); Christopher Lloyd (Doctor Emmett Brown); Lea Thompson (Lorraine); Thomas F. Wilson (Biff Tannen/Griff); Harry Waters Jr. (Marvin Berry); Charles Fleischer (Terry); Joe Flaherty (Western Union Man); Flea (Needles); Elizabeth Shue (Jennifer); James Tolkan (Strickland); Jeffrey Weissman (George McFly); Casey Siemaszko (3-D); Billy Zane (Match); J.J. Cohen (Skinhead); E. Casanova Evans (Michael Jackson); Jay Koch (Ronald Reagan); Charles Gherardi (Ayatollah Khomeini); Ricky Dean Logan (Data); Darlene Vogel (Spike); Jason Scott Lee (Whitey); Elijah Wood and John Thornton (Video Game Boys); Theo Schwartz and Lindsey Barry (Hoverboard Girls); Judy Ovitz (Antique Store Saleswoman); Stephanie E. Williams (Officer Foley); Marty Levy (Cab Driver); James Ishida (Fujitsu); Nikki Birdsong (Loretta); Al White (Dad); Junior Fann (Mom); Shaun Hunter (Harold); Buck Flower (Bum); Neil Ross (Museum Narrator); Tamara Carrera and Tracy D'Aldia (Jacuzzi Girls); Jennifer Brown, Irina Cashen, Angela Greenblatt, Cameron Moore, and Justin Mosley Spink (Baseball Kids); Lisa Freeman (Babs); John Erwin (Radio Sportscaster); David Harold Brown, Tommy Thomas, Lloyd L. Tolbert, and Granville "Danny" Young (Starlighters); Wesley Mann (CPR Kid); Freddie (Einstein); Kevin Holloway (Marty Photo Double); Charles F. Fitzsimmons (Biff Photo Double).

CHRISTIAN SCIENCE MONITOR, 12/4/89, p. 10, David Sterritt

"Back to the Future" came out in 1985, and when the box-office receipts were added up it turned out that Universal Pictures had earned more than $100 million with its science-fiction comedy—a fact as fantastic as anything in the movie.

With that kind of money at stake, it was inevitable that a sequel would come racing down the space-time continuum. And sure enough, "Back to the Future Part II" has arrived. Once again the filmmakers are director Robert Zemeckis (who also made "Who Framed Roger Rabbit") and screenwriter Bob Gale, his frequent collaborator. Another key player this time is the Vistaglide camera, a computerized device that helps a performer do two roles in the same scene, which happens quite a lot in this picture. It facilitates some impressive special effects, as it did in "Roger Rabbit," but it's also reaping the blame for a lackluster photographic style that makes the movie less than eye-boggling. (Dean Cundey did the cinematography, with help from Jack Priestley.)

Unless *you've* been back in the future for the past few years, you already know the main characters of the yarn. Marty McFly is a nice young man who dreams of being a rock star but lives an ordinary life. Not so ordinary is his friend, Emmett Brown, the maddest mad scientist in the world. He's invented a time machine—made from a DeLorean automobile—and in the first movie, he and Marty had some deliciously goofy adventures together, especially when they visited 1955 and played matchmaker for Marty's own mother and father.

The new picture starts exactly where the first one left off, with Marty and Doc Brown zooming to the year 2015 to save Marty's future children from a catastrophe. They take care of the crisis easily, but during his trip to the future Marty gets an idea: If he picked up a 2015 sports almanac and brought it back to 1985, he could win all kinds of wagers on sporting events, just by looking up the final scores.

Doc talks him out of this mercenary idea, but it's overheard by the movie's nastiest character, Biff, who takes a time-trip of his own to put such an almanac in the hands of his own, earlier self. The young Biff gets rich and famous by winning every bet he makes, becomes even more insufferable than he was in the first movie, and causes some awful changes in the world around him. Marty and Doc have a big job to do: altering the future and the past, so the present will turn out all right.

If this sounds confusing—it is, a little. Fans of the original "Back to the Future" may enjoy figuring it all out, and it's amusing to see scenes from the first movie reappear in the sequel, but with new meanings.

I also liked the portrait of what 2015 might be like; among other predictable things, "Jaws 19" is playing at the local movie theater. The ever-likable Michael J. Fox is good as Marty (and briefly hilarious as Marty's future daughter), and Doc Brown is still the best movie part Christopher Lloyd has ever played.

Unlike the first "Back to the Future," though, the sequel doesn't stay fresh and surprising all the way through. After a few good scenes, the plot gets too tricky, and the filmmakers keep walloping us with one chase scene after another. On top of this, we have to wait for another sequel (which has already been partly filmed) to see how the story comes out. It's going to be a western, and I'm sure it'll pack some surprises. But for the moment, I'm tired of the future, and I suspect other moviegoers will be, too.

FILMS IN REVIEW, 3/90, p. 165, Edmond Grant

"To be continued. . ." read the closing titles of the Saturday morning serials of the 30s and 40s. An acceptable ending, considering that these serials were a staple of a movie-goer's diet when entry to a picture palace only cost a dime. Now it's the 90s, when movies can cost up to $7.50 for a single entry, theater screens are smaller than ever before, and every major release winds up as a $1.00 video rental a few months later. No wonder the repellent "cliff-hanger" ending of *Back To The Future II* has been greeted with boos, hisses and general disgust in movie theaters all over America.

The picture that precedes this colossal let down of an finale isn't as predictable as one might expect. In fact, it's almost necessary that each viewer keep in mind the time chart constructed by Doc Brown (Christopher Lloyd) in one scene in order to follow what's going on. It's also absolutely necessary that every person watching the sequel have the original *Back* memorized by heart, as it is impossible to follow the sequence of events, or decipher the many in-jokes (like the repetition of dialogue) without having a steady, cable viewer familiarity with the original.

With this in mind, it was only natural that this picture begin with the last sequence of the original, wherein Doc Brown frantically informs Marty and his gal pal that he's discovered trouble in the future with their off-spring. Here the new narrative takes over, and we find out in short order that, in the year 2015, Marty's wimpy son will be arrested for his involvement in a robbery. Marty and the Doc swiftly correct this situation, and then the real insanity begins. The Doc, Marty, and Jennifer (Marty's girl-friend, who is quickly disposed of) return to 1985—every event in the overstuffed plotline takes place on the day following Marty's original trip into the past—and find that their wholesome little town has turned into a dangerous slum owned by Biff (Thomas Wilson), the perpetual nemesis of the McFly family. It seems that (here comes the pivotal plot twist), the old Biff "borrowed" the time machine in 2015, without Marty and the Doc's knowledge, and returned to 1955 to give his younger self a comprehensive sports almanac. And thus was all of history changed, as the young Biff grew rich and influential as the result of the sucker bets he made with the help of the almanac. To correct these changes, Marty and the Doc travel back to 1955, in order to destroy the almanac and, coincidentally, relive nearly all the major moments they experienced in the first film.

This last plot point is technically fascinating, as Fox is seen interacting with footage from the first *Back*, passing right by himself and his teenage "mom," peering out of the wings to view his performance at the prom, etc. It is also indicative of a major problem—namely, the fact that co-scripters Robert Zemeckis (who also directed) and Bob Gale get so carried away with their inventive time-travel play that the needlessly complicate the storyline to the point where one ends up longing for the simpleminded charm that characterized the original picture (which still stands as the most *innocent* and wholesome version ever of the Oedipus myth). And, despite our time-traveling duo's placid acceptance of every enigma they encounter, it's almost impossible not to spend some of the film's running time wondering about the many loose ends and ludicrous new twists on time travel thought up by Zemeckis and Gale to get their characters out of tight logical corners. The most disturbing of these loose ends being the fact that Marty's girlfriend Jennifer is left sleeping on a porch in the alternate 1985 and is abruptly forgotten. Later Marty makes a quick reference to her and is assured by the Doc that if they change the past, their hometown will "transform itself around her," and she'll be right back in her regular existence. This whole development is obviously a result of the scripters' need to get rid of the character (only Marty and Doc Brown can really share the adventures) and their desire to reassure the audience that she won't (as logic demands) disappear with the "bad" alternate present when it is eradicated.

To make up for the profusion of logical gaffes created by the topheavy storyline, Zemeckis directs the film at a very fast clip, in hopes that the established charm of the performers will smooth out any difficulties. Fox is as golly-gee wholesome as he's always been (although it is quite depressing to see him follow up the impressive and disturbing *Casualties Of War* with this piece of Spielberg-financed fluff); along for the ride, Christopher Lloyd isn't as funny here as he was in any selected episode of TV's *Taxi*; and the irresistibly cute Lea Thompson and the thoroughly forgettable Wilson share the most alter-egos/ugly prosthetic makeup jobs.

And then there's the film's final slap in the face, the inconclusive ending, which, we're assured in a trailer (making this the first movie to present an actual complete coming attraction for the next sequel before the closing credits), will be resolved when Marty rescues the Doc from the Old-West perils of the year 1885. This rank money grubbing ploy ("pay $7.50 next summer to find out if our heroes survive") isn't the only way in which *Back II* gives a preview of things to come: in the 2015 sequence, it is mentioned that Marty experienced a traumatic car wreck which ruined his chances of becoming a rock star; most likely a plot portent for the fourth installment of the series.

Perhaps it won't be necessary for Zemeckis and company to actually make a fourth film; perhaps they, and all other sequel producing moviemakers, can simply have their actors "interact" with footage from past installments. Just think what Sly (*Rocky IV*) Stallone will do when he finds out about this.

LOS ANGELES TIMES, 11/22/89, Calendar/p. 1, Sheila Benson

If "Back to the Future" made you bored and querulous, then the tumbling inventiveness in its sequel may come as a pleasant surprise. Of course, if you were among the 92% of the world who loved the ride in Dr. Emmett Brown's diabolical DeLorean back in 1985, then "Back to the Future Part II" is your oyster. Well, your hamburger with onions.

If it proves anything, it's that director Robert Zemeckis ("Who Framed Roger Rabbit") is getting cooler and even more adept at controlled mayhem. Actually, "Future II's best moments are like a Tex Avery cartoon with live actors, crammed to the edges of the frame with nutsy touches.

This is not to say that it isn't one of the year's noisiest films, nor one of the most dizzying. It not only zooms up to the year 2015, but back again to that fateful high school dance of Marty McFly's parents in 1955, then up for a while to 1985. And not 1985 as the characters knew it, but a sort of *faux* 1985, the Ghost of 1985-yet-to-come-in-the-worst-of-all-possible-worlds.

Now, *you* may whiz up and back and sideways with the ease of Isaac Asimov, but not this time traveler, So it is invigorating to report that screenwriter Bob Gale has had pity on the spaced-out. When he begins his backs and forths in the Chrono-Synclastic Infundibulum or whatever, he has the eminent Doc Brown (Christopher Lloyd) diagram it all out on a blackboard for us. Thus, even the dimmest among us can appreciate exactly why McFly and Doc must risk time-warp whiplash to keep their universe, and perhaps even ours, on an even keel.

It all begins with danger in the year 2015 to Marty McFly's son, Marty Jr. (conveniently played by McFly "himself," Michael J. Fox, surely one of the world's oldest high school students and one of the more bearable). Scanning the future, Doc Brown knows there is big trouble if Marty Jr. goes along with the scuzzy plans of a guy named Griff, so McFly and Brown nip up to 2015 in the gull-winged DeLorean to see if they can change history, or future history. With them is McFly's girlfriend, Jennifer, played by the talented and, in this instance, vastly wasted Elizabeth Shue. Also wasted are the talents of "Breaking In's" Casey Siemaszko, almost unfindable here as a third thug.

"Future"-ites will already be onto the fact that Griff is the son of Biff Tannen (Thomas F. Wilson, both times), who made the life of the McFly family father, George, such a living hell. Frankly, the braying of Crispin Glover's George McFly in the first film made some of *our* lives living hell too, so it came as good news that Glover appears in the sequel only in brief silent scenes taken from footage in the first film. The grandfather George McFly is played in the year 2015 by Jeffrey Weissman.

When film makers' visions of the future spin off nearly familiar technology, the results are more fun than brainstorming wild inventions that take forever to understand. We might not want to live in Zemeckis and Gale's 21st Century but we can grasp its systems quickly enough to feel comfortable and even smug. In the town square, hologram movie trailers do more than put you in the picture; the ads for "Jaws 19" ("directed by Max Spielberg") are enough to give you cardiac arrest. Then there's the town's retro restaurant, "Cafe '80s," a sort of free-fall Cafe 50's, updated and feverishly realized by Zemeckis.

Here, nostalgia buffs can ride Lifecycles and have their orders taken by video waiters Ronald Reagan, Michael Jackson or the Ayatollah Khomeini. Outside, skateboards float magically a few feet off the ground, and Doc Brown's car is now completely airborne. As Marty browses in the window of an antiques store, there is even an ancient computer, right next to a Sport Almanac listing the winners in every sporting event from 1950 to 2000.

That almanac becomes the story's prize, when first Marty, then doddering grandfather Biff in the year 2015, realize its potential as a solid-gold betting guide—if one were to go back to the 1950s and lay bets according to the book's documented winners.

As the movie ricochets all over the calendar, Gale and Zemeckis are profligate with throwaway sight gags, almost as many as there are blatant product plugs, and a vast improvement over the sometimes skimpy invention of "Future I." There are also lavish visual quotes from that first film, so if you have—*somehow*—missed it, "Future II" will fill you in on everything but its Calvin Klein joke. That had to do with an unconscious Marty being identified by the citizenry of 1955 by the label in his underwear: Calvin Klein. (Plug.)

Technically, the film brings multiple role-playing to new deftness: among Fox's endearing McFlys there is cute Marlene McFly in 2015, a role for which Fox gets a close shave and an auburn wig. In addition to doubling and sometimes tripling his actors in the same, seamless scene, Zemeckis also folds in footage from the first movie, making the continuity person perhaps the most heroic figure on the project. The sheer personal pull of Lloyd and Fox cannot be underestimated. Lloyd keeps his even when he's delivering speeches with the velocity of a railroad train. Amazing.

The film ends with a quote from its own sequel, Doc and Marty in 1885, a shockingly tacky coda to such charm. If "Future II" had the wit and daring of some of its best moments, or of that masterly satire "This Is Spinal Tap," it would end it all now, and let these quotes be from a nonexistent sequel—one that looks as though it may snap the trio's winning streak. No such luck; we are all expected Back in the summer of 1990.

MONTHLY FILM BULLETIN, 1/90, p. 7, Tim Pulleine

Hill Valley, California, 1985. Marty McFly and inventor Doc Brown have recently returned from their journey back to 1955 (see M.F.B., December 1985) when the agitated Doc informs Marty and his girlfriend Jennifer that he has made an alarming discovery about their future. The three travel in his DeLorean time machine to 2015, where it transpires that the couple's son, Marty Jnr., will shortly be involved in a robbery led by Griff Tannen (grandson of Biff Tannen, one-time bully of Marty's father George). Masquerading as his own son, Marty contrives to forestall the robbery and have Griff arrested. Jennifer, however, is found unconscious by police and taken 'home', where she is dismayed to find that the middle-aged Marty is a run-down failure. Doc and Marty rescue her, but not before the aged Biff has over-heard talk between Doc and Marty and consequently made off (it later emerges) in the time machine, taking with him a sports almanac. This he presents to his youthful self in 1955, enabling him to place bets on guaranteed winners and become vastly wealthy. When Marty and the others return to 1985, they find Hill Valley completely altered, a sink of iniquity presided over by Biff, who is now married to Marty's mother Lorraine, having (as Marty finds out at the near cost of his own life) had George murdered in 1973. Doc tells Marty that they can forestall this 'alternative reality' by going back to 1955 and destroying the almanac (taking care in the process not to create a 'paradox' by directly confronting their own other selves, who at this point were making their previous trip in the past). During the high-school dance at which Marty's parents fell in love, Marty regains the almanac; Biff steals it back, and only after a frantic skateboard chase does Marty recover and destroy the book. Subsequently, bad atmospherics abruptly cause Doc and his time machine to 'disappear'. Then a Western Union messenger arrives with a letter for Marty, which has been awaiting him for seventy years. It is from Doc, who has transported himself to the West of 1885. (A caption announces "To be continued", with glimpses of the forthcoming *Back to the Future Part III*.)

"There's something familiar about all this", muses a bystander during a futuristic variation on the skateboarding set-piece of its predecessor. It's a sentiment that proves only too apt during the rerun of material that was invested with real momentum and originality in the first film, but here seems not only second-hand in conception but curiously half-hearted in scripting and realisation. The thirty-years on sequences manage only a toy-shop notion of future living, annotated by nothing more inventive than advertisements for 'antique computers' and remarks about traffic jams on the 'skyways'. The narrative—especially as regards Biff's purloining of the time machine—remains a muddle, and while Michael J. Fox now looks a little past it for seventeen, the middle- and old-age versions of himself and the other principals constitute an even less convincing charade.

The return to discover a drastically worsened version of 1985 is the most arresting aspect of the plot—its echoes of the nightmare vision of *It's a Wonderful Life* underlining just how influential that film has been to film-makers within the Spielberg ambit. But the latter passages, with Marty and Doc returning to 1955 to head off the 'alternative' history they have just witnessed, fail to develop the time-warp farce of the protagonists having to avoid contact with their own 'other' selves, and does not even make much of the moment-to-moment business of retrieving the fatal almanac. The 'open' ending, which leaves in the air the question of whether Marty's mid-life situation will be as discouraging as has been intimated, feels more like a cheat, compounded by the tagging on of what amounts to a trailer for the forthcoming (if now none too eagerly awaited) third instalment.

NEW STATESMAN & SOCIETY, 12/1/89, p. 42, Suzanne Moore

Mae West, in her infinite wisdom once said: "Too much of a good thing can be wonderful." I'm inclined to agree. Though, when it comes to the ever-increasing number of blockbuster sequels that are being blasted at us these days, I'm not so sure. Too much of a good thing may be highly lucrative but it is fast becoming less and less wonderful with each part two, three and four. The biggies this month are *Back to the Future 2* and *Ghostbusters 2* released in time for the Christmas holidays.

If the purpose of a sequel is to develop some of the original film's distinguishing features, neither of these films can be described as such. Rather they are re-makes of the first movie, which strikes me as a highly cynical exercise.

This cynicism runs through both the lacklustre *Ghostbuster 2* and *Back to the Future 2*. No amount of jokey self-referentiality can disguise it and no amount of clever-clever postmodern critique can justify it. The thinking behind *Back to the Future 2* seems to have been to give us more of everything: more action, more special effects, more gadgets, more volume. This is one of the *loudest* movies I've sat through in a long time. Director Robert Zemeckis and producer Steven Spielberg seem to have taken as their maxim "nothing succeeds like excess.".

Yet, in criticising the sequel a strange thing happens. One elevates the "original" to the dizzy heights of authenticity. The real thing unto which everything else is referred. *Back to the Future 2* in a way anticipates this and recreates the first film within itself. This exercise in movie-brat slickness inevitably fails to duplicate the charm of the original because, once you introduce such a degree of self-consciousness into any film, notions like innocence fly out of the window. The exception is Spielberg's own *Indiana Jones* where Spielberg has perfected this trick. Here everyone is trying very hard to do the same thing which results in a blustering and busy movie, but not much else.

The original had Michael J. Fox (Marty) going back to 1955 in Doctor Brown's time machine with a mission to get his parents to fall in love with each other. This resulted in some nicely perverse Oedipal cock-ups when his mother makes a pass at him—"You mean my mother's got the hots for me"—and some inventive sendups of eighties mores. Marty keeps getting called Calvin Klein as that was the name stitched into his underpants.

In the sequel this inventiveness is there, not I'm afraid in the plot or the dialogue, but in the sets. This time Marty goes both forward in time to the year 2015 and backwards to 1955, back to the original film. Can you feel yourself being manipulated here? As in *Batman* the sets are the star rather than the Pepsi-guzzling Fox or even the wonderful Christopher Lloyd as crazed Doctor Brown. Hill Valley, California 2015 looks like a version of the future designed exactly in 1955 but with the advantage of modern special effects: hover boards instead of skate boards, self-lacing training shoes, and so on. Eventually all this time travel creates a paradox, hiccups in the space-time continuum. It certainly creates difficulty for the dialogue so that the characters spend their time explaining or rather shouting the plot to one another.

It's all pretty much what you would expect. Marty's girlfriend is knocked unconscious in the first five minutes and spends the rest of the movie that way—so much for roles for women in the future. Blatantly shameless product placement also appears capable of time travel.

What really jars, however, is the mania of the whole thing. Everything is too excessive, too manic, too much. In that way it's a very contemporary movie. It is stuffed full of *things*, material things, as though this could make up for what it lacks—coherence, vision and meaning. Its pleasures are decidedly of the Diet Coke kind. The ending, simply a trailer for *Back to the Future 3*, exemplifies its cocksure, almost contemptuous, attitude to its audience. All its excesses lead nowhere except back to itself, they aren't allowed to spill off screen. Part 3 should be called "Back to the Box Office". It would at least be honest.

NEW YORK, 12/11/89, p. 116, David Denby

As I was out buying a quart of milk the other day, the leadership of Czechoslovakia's Communist Party fell from power. The revolution sweeping Central Europe has come deliriously hard and fast, so fast that staying interested in new movies like *Back to Future Part II* and *Harlem Nights* has been a little tough. Whole governments collapse between chase scenes. The possibility of a future in which America is irrelevant teases us, haunting our lockjawed president, a man frightened not only of events but of words. De Tocqueville correctly predicted 150 years ago that Russia and America would someday hold sway. But a united Europe may dominate the next century, which will change the way Americans think of themselves. It may even change the movies.

At the moment, America is supplying movies to the entire world. Many Europeans resent the popularity of our films in their own markets. When people flock to American movies, less money flows back to local film industries. As a result, some countries have established quotas—restricting American movies to, say, 50 percent of the theaters. These quotas may be reinforced or expanded when the European Community becomes a single market in 1992. At the same time, many Europeans, surrounded and overwhelmed by American pop, fear the corruption of their own cultures.

I have contradictory, unresolvable feelings about this. On the one hand, American mass culture is a liberator. German students threw themselves a party on top of the Berlin Wall a few weeks ago—and what were they singing? Ray Parker Jr.'s theme from *Ghostbusters*. Bopping on the wall, they zapped the communist phantoms. Pow, you're dead! Pop is an important element in the seduction of the East by the West, the seduction of Communism by capitalism. It's easy pleasure, quick satisfaction; it's one of the things that Communists are not very good at. For years, the longing of Eastern-bloc youth for American and British rock has amounted to a de facto aesthetic rejection of drably bureaucratic regimes. Governments trying to persuade people to give up good times in return for a future Utopia have lost their credibility. Western mass culture helped do them in.

At the same time, many educated Europeans fight American movies. In 1978, I showed George Lucas's *American Graffiti* to some very serious students at the Polish state film school in Lodz, and they roared with laughter from beginning to end. But afterward, they told me that the movie was trash, completely without value. Europeans can sound awfully priggish when putting down American movies (the students weren't amused when I accused them of hypocrisy). Of course, this was a state school and someone from the Party may have been listening. The students—all of whom would move into the government-sanctioned film apparatus if they behaved—may have been priggish out of necessity. I trust their first, spontaneous reactions.

Pop can be good for the soul. As for quotas, I'm instinctively against them, since they amount to a form of censorship. People should be able to watch what they want. On the other hand, I'm also repelled by the idea of American junk playing every small town in France and Germany—and soon, presumably, every town in Hungary and Poland too. The habit of easy, violent pleasures could discourage more thoughtful kinds of local filmmaking. Some people say it already has. As a counterforce, the new European pride—the reemergent sense of Europe as the rightful center of Western civilization—may well lead to increased demands for cultural protectionism; the resistance to American pop may stiffen, which might not be such a bad idea. Americans could resist their own mass culture a little more.

Intimacy is certainly not a quality anyone could find in Robert Zemeckis's *Back to the Future, Part II*. In the original, Michael J. Fox's struggle to bring his parents together so they could mate and produce *him* had a wrenching force. And with that wild man Crispin Glover giving a painfully expressive performance as the wimpy father, the comedy veered recklessly into pathos and back. But the sequel is just noise and frenzied activity. Fox and Christopher Lloyd, as the mad doctor, fly forward and then backward in time, running into other versions of themselves from the first movie's trip back in time. We get plot complexity without any point—a desperate attempt to double and redouble the central gimmick so it will explode like the grand finale of a fireworks display. The wild-eyed Lloyd, shouting gibberish, is desperately unfunny, and Fox is little more than a shuttlecock with mussed feathers. I don't care how much money it makes; the movie is a brutal setback for Zemeckis's career.As for Eddie Murphy's *Harlem Nights*, this promisingly swank fantasy of black club owners and white gangsters in thirties Harlem falls into racial and sexual taunting of frightening crudity. Eddie Murphy the mass-entertainment genius seems to be turning into Eddie Murphy the pop demagogue.

NEW YORK POST, 11/22/89, p. 33, David Edelstein

"Back to the Future Part II" is a lunatic riff on the dumb ideas of part one, and it's an epic goof, a mighty blow-out. The movie takes place after, before and during the first film—in the margins of the first film, sometimes darting in and out of it—and you can go bonkers keeping track of all the parallel universes and nightmare permutations.

Sound confusing? Let me attempt an explanation. At the end of "Back to the Future," Marty McFly (Michael J. Fox), Doc Brown (Christopher Lloyd) and Marty's girlfriend Jennifer (now Elizabeth Shue) took off in a flying DeLorean time-machine for the year 2015, on a mission to save the couple's kids from disaster.

That mission is accomplished with relative ease (only one madcap chase and one hysterical detour), but it's amazing how much trouble you can get into with a time machine.

We know from the first film (and from common sense) that if you change something in the past you start a chain reaction that potentially alters the present.

When Marty realizes an almanac listing results of all sports contests between 1950 and 2000 could make him the richest man alive, he buys a copy, discards it after a lecture from Doc, then learns to his horror that their conversation had a witness: the elderly Biff Tannen (Thomas F. Wilson), who was bested by Marty in 1955 and has now resolved to pass the almanac on to himself as a teen-ager—back in 1955!

So Marty and Doc go back to the present (1985) and boom! It isn't the present but an alternate present, a parallel time where all hell has erupted—thanks to Biff. The only way to set things right is to go back to past, to the very dance where Marty's mom fell in love with Marty's dad and where Marty rocked the crowd with "Johnny B. Goode."

The basic ingredients of "Back to the Future" get whirred around and scrambled and gleefully topped. Jokes are turned inside-out, famous gags viewed from different angles. The core idea is dizzyingly sustained: Director Robert Zemeckis and writer Bob Gale have created a time-travel farce, in which people hurry out of dimensions instead of doors and have to dodge not angry spouses but themselves at another age.

The floor is littered with metaphorical eggshells: In the past, one misstep and the present is forever altered; in the future, the trauma comes from learning too much about your own depressing destiny. And in the past and future, you can't let yourself see yourself or a kind of temporal shock sets in, potentially rupturing the space/time continuum.

Frantic and bewildering as it sounds, this is wonderful pop movie making. Zemeckis and Gale use the original—which was pleasant but a little tidy—as the foundation for something much wilder; its inspiration isn't just "Back to the Future" but the breathless opening cartoon of Zemeckis' "Who Framed Roger Rabbit," in which the distance between cliffhangers was terrifyingly short.

Marty spends a lot of time fleeing from Biff in various incarnations, and the chases and spills don't have the visual grace of Spielberg at his best. But Zemeckis and Gale's story has so much wit and momentum that it almost doesn't matter.

The film makers and designer Rick Carter have envisioned 2015 as a nightmare extension of '80s pop culture, in which you can't seem to get away from assaultive celebrity replicants. A Max-Headroom style Michael Jackson takes your order at a coffee shop; "Jaws 19" occupies the movie house; and capitalism has rescued the center of town from ruin—it's now a park and shopping mall.

Cars fly through the air, clothes conform to all body-sizes at the touch of a button, and food is sold dried and then magically rehydrated. But Americans seem just as stupid as ever, and there's a bleakness to it all: Marty and his family have taken nothing but wrong turns; a world that was once full of possibilities is now sadly fixed.

"Back to the Future Part II" doesn't have anything as weird and unsettling as the Oedipal confusions of the first film, but it does have a strange "Hamlet"-style sequence, a vision of Marty's mother soiled physically as well as spiritually—Biff's concubine, affixed with mammoth breasts and slinking drunkenly around a garish suite high atop a gambling casino.

It's hard to talk about the acting in a film like this—the performers just have to hit their marks. But Fox is a more accomplished farceur than he was the first time out. He's springy and still game, and he gets his effects with marvelous economy, never letting the anger and grief slow him down. And Lloyd remains a wide-eyed marvel, an actor who always holds something spooky in reserve. (He seems to have an authentic streak of madness).

My only serious complaint is the trailer for Part III tacked onto the end of the film—it makes this feel like a TV series. That's a pity, because Zemeckis and Gale have transcended the sitcom mentality that dragged down much of the original. They've deliriously upped the stakes—and triumphed.

NEWSDAY, 11/22/89, Part II/p. 7, Mike McGrady

Time travel is not without its perils. As wild-haired "Doc" Brown (Christopher Lloyd) warns young Marty McFly (Michael J. Fox), there is a danger: It might just "destroy the entire world—granted, that's a worst-case scenario."

In "Back to the Future Part II," our two intrepid time commuters have dashed off to the year 2015 to prevent Marty's future son from committing a criminal act. While they're busy righting future wrongs, Biff, the town bully (once again, Thomas F. Wilson) borrows their time machine, goes back to the year 1953 and gives himself, young Biff, a 2015 sports almanac that enables him to make millions wagering on upcoming sports events while, simultaneously, altering the course of history and creating an "alternate reality."

Returning to year 1985, Marty discovers just how much havoc Biff's mischief has caused. Young Biff's sudden gambling prowess has made him the wealthiest man on Earth, and once-bucolic Hill Valley is now dominated by a towering skyscraper casino, "Biff's Pleasure Palace." Home windows are barred, gates are locked, the school principal trades shotgun blasts with roaming truants, rotting car-hulks line the streets and bands of motorcyclists are drawn by the "Bikers Welcome" signs. In the new, revised Hill Valley, Doc Brown is in an insane asylum, McFly's father has been murdered and his mother, complete with breast implants, is married to Biff. Observes Marty, "it's like we're in hell or something."

Not exactly. It's more like we're back in Pottersville in "It's a Wonderful Life." Pottersville, you'll remember, is what would have happened to Bedford Falls if good old George Bailey had never lived—a perfect illustration of that movie's message, the difference that one decent man makes to a community and to every person in that community.

While the revised vision of Hill Valley seems a direct ripoff of that vastly superior film, it dramatically illustrates the weaknesses of "Back to the Future Part II." There seems little import or impact to McFly's nightmarish world—none of the meaning, none of the terror, that made "It's a Wonderful Life" so memorable.

While director Robert Zemeckis' technical wizardry (in addition to the initial "Back to the Future," he did "Roger Rabbit") will always draw praise, the special effects come at the expense of human effects. However, what draws the strongest audience response is neither his sometimes dazzling vision of the future nor his romanticized image of the past, but his lighthearted commentary on our present. Future executives, for example, are Japanese and future criminals are sentenced within hours of the crime because, "The justice system works well...now that we've abolished all lawyers."

The humor tends to be mild, and while the funnybone is being gently tickled, the eye is constantly diverted. Unfortunately, and I find this true of every Zemeckis movie, neither the mind nor the heart is ever fully engaged.

Considering that the original "Back to the Future" made $350 million and was the top-grossing film of 1985, a trip ahead to the past was inevitable. The irony is this: A Zemeckis film gets its strength from novelty, and sequels are, by definition, the enemy of novelty. The closing words of the current film—"To Be Concluded..."—indicate there will be only one additional sequel (already filmed, at the same time as this one) and I sincerely hope that is not just an idle promise.

NEWSWEEK, 12/4/89, p. 78, David Ansen

Picking up right where the original ended, *Back to the Future Part II* starts in midfrenzy as

"Doc" Emmett Brown (Christopher Lloyd), Marty McFly (Michael J. Fox) and his future bride Jennifer (Elizabeth Shue) bid farewell to 1985, leap into the DeLorean time machine and go whisking off to the year 2015 to save Marty's future children from disgrace and disaster. No sooner is that problem solved than a bigger catastrophe ensues: while they're fixing the future, Marty's old rival Biff (Thomas F. Wilson), having stolen the DeLorean and an almanac of sporting results up to the year 2000, is tampering with the past. When they return to 1985 it's actually an alternate 1985. Good old Hill Valley has been transformed into an infernal combat zone where Marty's mother (Lea Thompson) is now married to the ultra-rich crime czar Biff, who has murdered Marty's father and made a killing betting on sports. And the only way to get the original, benign 1985 back is to travel further back to 1955 and try to stop Biff from altering the future he's already altered.

From its frenetic opening to its abrupt conclusion, "Future II" barely stops to catch its breath. Director Robert Zemeckis and writer Bob Gale assume you've seen the original and are ready to swallow whatever zany time-travel notion they offer. They're not wrong. As unapologetically broad and silly as this sequel is, it's also a good deal of fun, and its relentless velocity is part of the joke. Between the first and second installments, Zemeckis has had the experience of "Who Framed Roger Rabbit" under his belt, and it seems to have encouraged him to make this sequel even more of a live-action cartoon than the first. Deliberately garish (but did the makeup jobs have to be so phony?), generously inventive and sophisticatedly childish, the movie manages to sustain its breathless mixture of gung-ho adventure and pointed social satire almost to the end, when it simply collapses in a heap. For the finale, the filmmakers tackily append a trailer for next summer's Part III. It's a shame that this high-spirited romp has to sign off with a shameless blast of hucksterism.

The actors all seem to be on Zemeckis's "let's party" wavelength. Fox gets the chance to play his own son Marty at 47, two versions of his younger self, and even (hilariously) his own daughter Marlene, with bangs and a coy tilt to her head. Lloyd has to do all the script's bogus-scientific explication, but he's such an inspired lunatic he manages to turn this burden to his comic advantage. The sequel's pleasures are all on the surface (it has none of the clever Oedipal undertones the original offered) and the viewer who somehow missed part one will be baffled by certain references (like why Marty is sometimes called "Calvin Klein" in 1955). But even those rare viewers left in the dark should find Zemeckis's roller-coaster kineticism infectious. "Back to the Future Part II" leaves you exhausted but happy.

TIME, 12/4/89, p. 101, Richard Schickel

Time travel is the thinking person's UFO, an improbability that nevertheless resonates with mysterious and sometimes marvelous possibilities. But it has become a rather tired topic. It is almost as hard nowadays to create fictional vehicles capable of reawakening childhood reveries about zapping through the years as it is to invent a scientific instrument actually able to journey up and down the old continuum.

All the more remarkable then that the director-writer team of Bob Zemeckis and Bob Gale has created, in the space of just four years, two terrific movies on this subject. Like its predecessor, *Back to the Future Part II* does not merely warp time; it twists it, shakes it and stands it on its ear. But as before, the film's technical brilliance is the least of its appeals. Satirically acute, intricately structured and deftly paced, it is at heart stout, good and untainted by easy sentiment.

Future II opens with a deceptively simple errand to run. Doc Brown (Christopher Lloyd) wheels up to Marty McFly (Michael J. Fox) in that lovable time machine (a goofily customized DeLorean) with bad news: Marty's son—not yet even a gleam in his father's eye—is in trouble in the year 2015, and there is just enough time to save him from a life of crime. The dauntless duo, accompanied, of course, by Marty's girlfriend Jennifer (Elizabeth Shue), must head off to give future history a quick fix.

The world they find is not entirely disagreeable: shoelaces tie themselves; the criminal-justice system works efficiently because lawyers have been eliminated; the Chicago Cubs have finally won the World Series. Young McFly's salvation, though it requires a certain strenuousness, is quite simply accomplished. On the other hand, the personal future that Marty and Jennifer discover is not what they dreamed it would be. Something has gone quite nastily wrong.

That brutal jerk Biff Tannen (Thomas F. Wilson)—he who almost destroyed Marty's parents' lives in 1955, and from whom Marty rescued them in the earlier film—has survived into the 21st century too. What's worse, on their voyage into the future Marty and Doc unwittingly provide him with the means to construct a dark alternate history beginning in 1955. Over its course, Biff has managed to turn pleasant little Hill Valley, Calif., into a hellish variant of Las Vegas, with himself as its czar. He has even contrived to make Marty's mother a widow and marry her, turning her into an alcoholic and Marty into an abused stepson.

Doc and Marty have no choice. They must return again to the scene of their first intervention in history, that high school dance that climaxed *Future I*. All along this story line, Marty has been encountering variations on himself, his progenitors and heirs. But when he is reinserted into this moment in time and starts to meet himself and the situations of the previous movie, *Back to the Future II* ceases to be a sequel. It becomes instead a kind of fugue, brilliantly varying and expanding on previously stated themes. And it accomplishes this while retaining its powerful narrative drive and its infectious geniality.

Coming right after Zemeckis' *Who Framed Roger Rabbit*, which was equally rich in invention and astonishment, the movie establishes him as today's most exciting young director. And makes next summer, when the concluding episode in this saga will be released, a season to anticipate.

VILLAGE VOICE, 12/5/89, p. 117, J. Hoberman

With *Back to the Future Part II*—the intricate, clever, fast-paced bridge between the 1985 original and the *Back to the Future Part III* already in the can—Robert Zemeckis's teen comedy bids to become a full-fledged pop mythology. Far more than *Star Wars* and *Indiana Jones* (and maybe even *The Godfather*), this baroque tale of teenage Oedipus Marty McFly (Michael J. Fox) and his increasingly convoluted coming of age allegorizes the story of American postwar rise and decline.

Unlike that of *Ghostbusters*, which in a burst of avaricious nostalgia simply cloned itself, *BTTF*'s belated sequelization is grandiose as well as pragmatic, at once jerry-built and overweening. Architecturally speaking, the expansion of the original movie is somewhere between the absurd splendor of the discarded Michael Graves design for the enlarged Whitney Museum, which simply assimilated the modernist original into an eccentric postmod superstructure, and Neil Sedaka's homemade basement mix for "Breaking Up Is Hard To Do"—albeit the techniques are state-of-the-art, post-*Roger Rabbit*.

After reprising the punchline of the first *BTTF*—mad scientist Doc Brown (Christopher Lloyd) returning to the "new, improved" 1985 from 30 years hence—*BTTF Part II* barely pauses for credits before pulling Marty away from his newly acquiescent girlfriend Jennifer (Elizabeth Shue) and blasting off into the midair freeway frenzy of 2015. Lawyers have been abolished but sequels thrive. Marty receives his first taste of future shock from a holographic advertisement for *Jaws 19*. Not surprisingly, the future (an even more cramped theme park than *BTTF*'s "1955") is defined entirely in terms of consumer products—auto-Velcro Nikes, computerized down jackets, hovercrafts—and references to the original film.

In the first of several revisionist views of the Reagan New Morning that the first *BTTF* both celebrated and parodied, Marty visits Café '80s—the 2015 equivalent of the hyperreal '50s diners that first appeared half a dozen years ago and are currently wearing out their welcome. Given the pop stridence of '80s culture, it's a little disappointing to find Michael Jackson's "Beat It" video dominating a TV wall barely worthy of a third-rate Tokyo department store. This, however, is in keeping with the film's mediacentric, dystopian view: Windows have been replaced by the Scenery Channel, teenagers watch six TV shows at once and wear telephone necklaces. (At the screening I attended, however, it was the instant dehydrated pizza that got spontaneous applause.)

As a director, Zemeckis has an infectious passion for detail (a poster advertising "Surf Vietnam" is another 2015 pleasure) and an unfortunate addiction to the Spielberg rollercoaster. *BTTF Part II* has far more than its share of frantic chases; the strident hues and propulsive camerawork could leave you with a candy-colored headache. It's enough that the movie maintains a constant level of hysteria by simply plunging from one alternate universe to another.

As notions of time travel, like attempts at historical reconstruction, tend to render the past as shorthand, the first *BTTF* was necessarily thin and artificial. This naive ahistoricism notwithstanding, the film's particular piece of the zeitgeist was to propose, as the still attainable summit of American civilization, the sanitized '50s that haunted so much of '70s and '80s pop culture. (The future is then.) Like our last president, *BTTF* provided an ersatz national past, while optimistically suggesting that we still might be free to tinker with it. Although lasting the better part of a decade, this conjuring trick is, of course, a lot less stable than the San Andreas Fault. Appropriately then, the heart of *BTTF Part II* is a nightmare version of the original's now periodicized "1985." This amounts to the dark side of the Reagan boom—although here, as in *BTTF*, social forces are conceptualized as something like viral infections imported from the future.

Although the contradictions in the original *BTTF* were implicit in the very name of Marty's hometown, Hill Valley, the presence of a black family in Marty's house (as well as the unconscious racism of the premise) sets the scene for the more radical transformation of his suburban neighborhood into an inner-city wasteland of wrecked cars and chalk body outlines. Hill Valley is a cross between Watts and Reno, Main Street dominated by the skyscraper casino-cum-museum that marks the transformation of working-class villain Biff Tannen (Thomas F. Wilson) into the resident Donald Trump. Biff's triumph, which is explicitly a perversion of Marty's own *echt*-'80s drive towards wealth and power, further fuels the *BTTF* saga's Oedipal subtext. Acting out the desire that our teenage hero only barely repressed in the first installment, Biff has murdered Marty's father and married his mother (Lea Thompson), her sexuality hilariously reified with a prosthtetic chest.

Again, Marty is compelled to return to the Golden Age. When *BTTF Part II* plunged back to "1955," I experienced a sense of despair. Silly me. The '50s will never die; as Marty exclaims, "This is heaven!" Since "1955" is already being visited by the Doc and Marty of that other "1985," screenwriter Bob Gale has patched together the sort of metaphysical rules governing parallel worlds and imaginary futures that it took the Superman cosmos at least two decades and seven varieties of kryptonite to establish. Meanwhile, Zemeckis adroitly superimposes new activities upon the original action, thus creating what amounts to a conceptual version of *Dead Men Don't Wear Plaid*—recycling the "Enchantment Under the Sea" dance from a completely different angle, and shamelessly redeploying the first movie's climax.

"There is something very familiar about this," one character remarks. Already the sort of movie in which everything happened twice, the original *BTTF* soon became a media hall of mirrors—amplifying the hit sitcom *Family Ties* as well as its Washington equivalent. (When Ron Reagan hosted *Saturday Night Live*, a week after his father managed two allusions to *Back to the Future* in his state-of-the-union address, he played at being Michael J. Fox.) The new movie is totally ingrown. Virtually every gag in the original is reflexively replayed. Rather than the bigger-and-better rehabilitation of *Batman* or the simple rerun of *Ghostbusters II*, *BTTF's* sequel feeds upon itself in a parody of sequelization. While not exactly a substitute for depth, this frantic, self-referential surface creates a more interesting flatness.

Although often cheerfully unconscious, Gale and Zemeckis seem intuitive enough to explore the myth of American orgins that precedes the '50s, and thus consign Marty to the funhouse forever. *BTTF Part II* ends with a coda of coming attractions from *BTTF Part III* that suggest the ultimate Disneyfication of the official (and obsolete) America of the western. Despite the tantalizing image of the time-traveling DeLorean speeding through Monument Valley, I suspect that, being as he still hasn't had his date at the lake, Marty will have to venture back one last time to that idyllic November day in 1955, the hidden wellspring of the 20th century—or at least the yuppified 1985 he has yet to enjoy. Which is another way of saying that he hasn't yet consummated his date with Jennifer.

Also reviewed in:
NEW REPUBLIC, 12/25/89, p. 26, Stanley Kauffmann
NEW YORK TIMES, 11/22/89, p. C9, Janet Maslin
NEW YORKER, 12/11/89, p. 139, Pauline Kael
VARIETY, 11/22/89, p. 19
WASHINGTON POST, 11/22/89, p. D1, Rita Kempley

BATMAN

A Warner Bros. release. *Executive Producer:* Ben Melniker and Michael Uslan. *Producer:* Jon Peters and Peter Guber. *Director:* Tim Burton. *Screenplay:* Sam Hamm and Warren Skaaren. *Story:* Sam Hamm. *Based upon Batman Characters Created by:* Bob Kane. *Director of Photography:* Roger Pratt. *Editor:* Ray Lovejoy. *Music:* Danny Elfman. *Music Editor:* Bob Badami and Robin Clarke. *Sound:* Tony Dawe and (music) Eric

Tomlinson. *Sound Editor:* Don Sharpe. *Production Designer:* Anton Furst. *Art Director:* Les Tomkins. *Set Decorator:* Peter Young. *Special Effects:* John Evans. *Special Visual Effects:* Derek Meddings. *Costumes:* Bob Ringwood. *Batsuit Designer:* Vin Burnham and Paul Barrett-Brown. *Make-up:* Paul Engelen. *Joker Make-up:* Nick Dudman. *Stunt Coordinator:* Eddie Stacey. *Running time:* 124 minutes. *MPAA Rating:* PG-13.

CAST: Jack Nicholson (The Joker/Jack Napier); Michael Keaton (Batman/Bruce Wayne); Kim Basinger (Vicki Vale); Robert Wuhl (Alexander Knox); Pat Hingle (Police Commissioner Gordon); Billy Dee Williams (District Attorney Harvey Dent); Michael Gough (Alfred); Jerry Hall (Alicia); Jack Palance (Carl Grissom); Tracey Walter (Bob the Goon); Lee Wallace (Mayor); William Hootkins (Eckhardt); John Sterland (Accountant); Edwin Craig (Rotelli); Vincent Wong (1st Crime Lord); Joel Cutrara (2nd Crime Lord); John Dair (Ricorso); Christopher Fairbank (Nic); George Roth (Eddie); Kate Harper (Anchorwoman); Bruce McGuire (Anchorman); Richard Durden (TV Director); Kit Hollerbach (Becky); Lachelle Carl (TV Technician); Keith Edwards and Leon Herbert (Reporters); Steve Plytas (Doctor); Anthony Wellington (Patrolman at Party); Amir Korangy (Wine Steward); Hugo E. Blick (Young Jack Napier); Charles Roskilly (Young Bruce Wayne); Philip O'Brien (Maftre d')' Michael Belfour (Scientist); Liza Ross (Mom); Garrick Hagon (Dad); Adrian Meyers (Jimmy); David Baxt (Dr. Wayne); Sharon Holm (Mrs. Wayne); Clyde Gatell (Other Mugger); Jon Soresi (Medic); Sam Douglas (Lawyer); Elliott Stein (Man in Crowd); Dennis Lill (Bob the Cartoonist); Paul Birchard (Another Reporter); Paul Michael (Cop).

CHRISTIAN SCIENCE MONITOR, 6/29/89, p. 10, David Sterritt

Indiana Jones or no Indiana Jones, movie insiders say "Batman" has a strong chance of becoming the summer's biggest hit. Which raises a big question about the masked crusader: Why now? Is there a cultural reason why this particular comic-book myth should be capturing the public's fancy at this particular time? Or is the current "Batman" craze simply the result of well-orchestrated hype by Warner Bros. and other commericaly interested parties?

The film itself provides a mixed answer. On one hand, it's basically a standard action picture, with the usual blend of heroic feats, dastardly villains, and coy romance, all assembled into a smoothly running and impeccably timed entertainment machine.

Yet there's more to "Batman" than this. The atmosphere of the movie is surprisingly gloomy. Many of the settings and backgrounds are downright grim, and there's an undertone of urban malaise that grows oddly unsettling after a while. This reaches its high point in the villain's most evil deed: He adulterates consumer products with deadly poisons, becoming the first Hollywood bad guy to capitalize on one of the most awful phenomena to make real-life headlines during the 1980s. He also attempts a mass poison-gas attack that has distuibingly genocidal implications.

All these elements make "Batman" very different from the popular 1960s television show, which imitated the light-heartedness of its comic-book source as eagerly as this version repudiates its lighter roots. If audiences do make it their summertime favorite, that may testify to a general darkening of the American mood.

This doesn't mean the new "Batman" is great cinema or flawless entertainment. It would be a lot better if it didn't lean exclusively on bone-crunching action for its climactic thrills, and the story continues long after its ideas have started to sag.

For a movie anchored in contemporary myth, moreover, it takes surprisingly little interest in the origins of Batman's methods: We learn that his crime-hating nature stems from the murder of his parents, but we never find out why bats—not ostriches or frogs, for example—became his obsessional motif. Parents should also be warned that its *angst*-ridden violence makes it a highly questionable choice for younger children.

For older spectators, though, the picture has a haunting tone that sets it aside from most of its action-packed cousins, and, while Michael Keaton doesn't make the Batman of one's dreams, Jack Nicholson provides the most memorable villain to seize the screen in ages.

The story pulls together sundry elements from the "Batman" comic books that have enticed young readers for decades. Bruce Wayne is a millionaire playboy by day, a mysterious crime-fighter by night. Ilis disguise is a bat-mask, his lair a bat-filled cave, his getaway car is the aptly named Batmobile.

Battling criminals one evening, he tosses a particularly manic foe into a vat of chemicals, giving the once-ordinary man a deformed new face and a twisted new identity: the Joker, an insane but ingenious evildoer whose mission is to terrorize Gotham City just for the dreadful fun of it—and to steal Batman's girlfriend, infuriating our hero all the more.

Joining in the fray are Commissioner Gordon of the police, photographer Vicki Vale of the local newspaper, and a butler named Alfred from Bruce Wayne's mansion, all of whom I remember from the comic books I grew up with in the 1950s.

The movie's producers made their most important decision when they recruited Tim Burton to direct it. In his previous films, "Pee-wee's Big Adventure" and "Beetlejuice," he showed a rare talent for dreaming up loony but striking images that zoom across the screen with madcap energy. What better director for a comic-book epic than a *cinéaste* whose style has been proudly cartoonish from the beginning?

"Batman" is more somber than his earlier pictures, but he packs it with the odd compositions and explosive colors that are already his trademark. Support comes from cinematographer Roger Pratt and production designer Anton Furst, whose Gotham City settings are as detailed and intricate as anything in "Blade Runner," the dour fantasy that "Batman" visually echoes at moments. (It echoes or borrows from other films, too, including the Orson Welles classic "Touch of Evil.")

Mr. Keaton plays our hero in the straight-faced manner he developed in "Clean and Sober," his first noncomedy picture; if he's not an exciting Batman, he's at least a credible one. Top honors go to Mr. Nicholson as the Joker, though—a villain of delirious creepiness, played with a bizarre intensity that passes the lunacy Nicholson assumed in "The Shining" and "The Witches of Eastwick." True, the screenplay gives him all the memorable lines, but few actors could have grabbed them with the fervor of Nicholson at his best and strangest.

The supporting cast, including such talents as Billy Dee Williams and Jack Palance, is merely adequate most of the time, and the music—especially the songs that rock star Prince serves up—is a sop to '80s tastes that mixes poorly with the film's other components.

Less fashionable, but far more eerie, are the snippets from such tunes as "Theme From A Summer Place" and "Beautiful Dreamer" that show up surrealistically on the sound track, suggesting what a wild ride we might have if David Lynch ever sets his hand to a "Batman" sequel.

The movie's rating is PG-13, reflecting its violence as well as some foul language and talk about sex.

FILMS IN REVIEW, 10/89, p. 480, Ken Hanke

Batman is—if not a work of genius—a work of brilliance. But, after all, how can a film by Tim Burton that stars Jack Nicholson and Michael Keaton, and boasts a Danny Elfman musical score fail? It can't and it doesn't, but I do confess that I'm surprised by its popularity with mainstream audiences. On the surface, it may play a little like a stylish version of Paul Verhoeven's stomach churning fantasy, *RoboCop*, if that film had been made by people who were troubled by the crypto-Nazi implications of this kind of "get-a-rope" vigilante mentality. That to one side for the moment, Burton's film is a relatively slow paced, elegant, and often thoughtful work that would seem to have no place in a summer otherwise devoted to *Indiana Jones And The Last Crusade* and *Star Trek V: The Final Frontier* (I want promises *in writing* from all concerned on the use of those words, "Last" and "Final"). Yet the film is well on its way to becoming *the* all time box office champ. A weird triumph of art through hype? (Now, wouldn't that be an ironic treat?) Or does the film simply work on the mass level thanks to a handful of one liners, Nicholson in a purple suit, and a couple of unnecessary—and pretty ghastly—songs by Prince? Time and repeat business will undoubtedly tell.

Popularity apart, *Batman* triumphs in the main by creating a separate world in which to take place. Beautifully designed by Anton Furst and utilized for maximum effect by Burton, the world of *Batman* has been rather oddly likened to that of Fritz Lang's silent *Metropolis*. That may well be accurate in terms of the stunning Gotham Cathedral at the film's climax (though the sequence itself has overtones of Hitchcock's *Vertigo*), however, the film, more aptly, might be likened to Roland West's silent *The Bat* and his own talkie remake of that film, *The Bat Whispers*. (One shot of the bat plane in the new film is in fact straight out of *The Bat*.) And Burton's film takes not only its visual cue from those lesser known masterpieces of eccentricity, but its attitude as well. This is as it should be, since Batman creator Bob Kane was inspired to create his character by the West films, especially the silent. (In Burton's film, a character at the newspaper office produces a drawing of the Batman that is very like the silent Bat's nightmarish outfit—and the drawing is boldly signed, "Bob Kane!") The character of Batman here is very nearly as psychotic as that of Chester Morris' Detective Anderson in *The Bat Whispers*, though Keaton's playing, the devotion of Alfred the butler (a wonderful performance by the ever underrated Michael Gough), and the romance element all help to soften and humanize his mental imbalance.

The script's most audacious move was the decision to personalize the conflict between Keaton's

Batman and Nicholson's Joker in a very complex psychological manner, so that each character is, in turn, responsible for the existence of the other. Indeed, without the joker there would be no Batman and without Batman there would be no Joker. Each mirrors the other's psychosis. This, of course, is the stuff from which great melodrama is made—from the schizophrenic dual incarnations of Detective Anderson and the Bat in *The Bat* to Count Dracula and Professor Van Helsing in *Dracula*—but it is all too rarely remembered today. The only problem with the approach is that the villainous side is likely to come off as far more interesting than the heroic one. That problem *does* surface here—in part due to Nicholson's bravura theatrics, which threaten to overbalance the film—but Keaton's Batman is sufficiently unhinged and quirky to head it off. In his first appearance as Batman, the character is pure comic book fascism, easily as terrifying as any of the criminals he tackles—and much more mystifying. In his first appearance as his real self, Bruce Wayne, he is strangely distracted and distanced. The two fully merge in a scene where Wayne as himself stands up to the Joker, suddenly raising a fireplace poker to strike his opponent, but first swinging wildly, smashing a vase on the mantle for dramatic effect. Voice raised and eyes blazing, the "real" Bruce Wayne and his secret self are fleetingly one, and that one is obviously and alarmingly insane. Yes, Nicholson is more fun than Keaton, but Keaton balances this by being more disturbing than Nicholson.

The depth of the characterization is the thing that keeps *Batman* from falling into the realm of a film like *RoboCop*, where the virtuous are oh-so-virtuous and the bad are oh-so-bad. Burton, his cast, and writers are clearly uncomfortable with the usual line of thought in such films that any excess on the part of the "hero" is justified simply because he *is the hero*. (So troubled are they, in fact, that the film contains one shot of Batman standing in front of a giant neon sign that reads, "Axis," leaving little doubt as to the implications of his actions.) Peter Weller's character in *RoboCop*, for example, maims, kills, and, in one memorably tacky piece of law-and-order chauvinism, even castrates his prey to the chilling admiration of both filmmaker and audience. Not so Batman. The voice of conscience is never far away, whether it comes from Alfred (who is even handed a piece of Jesse Jackson rhetoric—"If not now, when?"—for a line of dialogue), romantic interest Vickie Vale, the Joker, or Batman himself. It's not for nothing that Batman is slated to go into semi-retirement at the film's end, where *RoboCop* marches back onto the streets, presumably to pump some more lead into those forces of evil before the "wishy-washy" court system gets its hands on them. Batman does not, which makes its commercial success all the more mysterious. What place have these complex shadings of grey in a world that seems to have an increasingly black-and-white viewpoint? Apparently, there is greater room for such than the sociopolitical times would have us believe.

On its own terms, *Batman* is both a triumph and a breakthrough for director Burton and Composer Elfman (who also scored Burton's previous films, *Pee-wee's Big Adventure* and *Beetlejuice*, and whose work is inseparable from Burton's). In the earlier films, Burton proved himself a stylistic whiz kid, but, as with so many stylists, his work seemed devoid of much beyond that surface style. It was engaging, even briliant, but ultimately empty. With *Batman* he abandons none of that stylishness. The film is his most beautiful and accomplished to date, and his delayed unveiling of the Joker's face (though ruined by the use of that face in trailers and advertising) is a tour de force equal to James Whale's *Frankenstein*. This time, however, the style is finally allied with a sense of purpose and point. Using much of Nicholson's manic "Wait till they get a load of me" campiness as the false-whiskers (Nicholson essentially performs the function of Pee-wee Herman in *Big Adventure* and Michael Keaton in *Beetlejuice*) to bamboozle an audience into watching a dark edged, disconcerting film that finally subverts the conventions of its own genre, Burton proves himself a master filmmaker. Previously, Burton hadn't made a film that was as good as his direction. Much the same is true of Elfman, who'd never scored a film equal to his music. Finally, they have. Burton's style and Elfman's musical wit are still very much with us, but for a change they don't overshadow the slightness of the overall work at hand.

If we must have big budget summer releases (and it seems we must), let more of them be like this. I hate to think how many years it will be before I run into something more than mindless juvenilia and Spielbergian confections during the hot months, but I suspect it will be a while.

LOS ANGELES TIMES, 6/23/89, Calendar/p. 1, Sheila Benson

As its trailer has already hinted, "Batman" is very much a movie and a hero for the '80s. Is it interesting? Fitfully. Is it fun? Not much, Gotham City fans, not much.

It's a murky, brooding piece, set in a twisted city almost choked with evil and inertia, and Bruce

Wayne, half of its hero's dual identities, is very nearly in the same fix. Driven to right a naughty world the best that one man can, he's withdrawn, cerebral, severely absent-minded. As director Tim Burton sees him, he's practically the Hamlet of millionaire philanthropist socialites.

When he puts on his Batmuscles and his Bathat, his Batjock, His Batgauntlets and his world heavyweight's Batbelt, almost nothing is left of him but glitteringly blue-gray eyes and a voluptuously full mouth. If a costume alone could stop crime, this one would, since it almost stops Michael Keaton.

In the opposite corner, wearing purple satin, clown white, green hair and a permanent rictus, is the picture's big noise, the Joker, the dirtiest trickster since G. Gordon Liddy. Never still for a millisecond, Jack Nicholson's Joker preens and prances, drum major for a squad of sociopaths, detonating his noxious jokes like cherry bombs. ("You're insane!" Joker: "I thought I was a Pisces.")

Director Burton has sensibly turned his back on the camp of the '60s "Batman" TV series, and has drawn his menacing atmosphere from the Gotham City of "Batman's" creator, Bob Kane. Burton read his audience right in that respect. And with the production designs of Anton Furst ("The Company of Wolves," "Full Metal Jacket") and Danny Elfman's darkly enveloping score, he has a shiveringly dense and poetic city against which to set his characters.

Unfortunately, the screenplay, credited to both Sam Hamm and Warren Skaaren from Hamm's story and Kane's characters, doesn't give those characters a fighting chance. It flops about, unsure of which of its scarred protagonists it finds the most seductive, and it's disastrously low on the sort of wit that can make a gargantuan movie lovable.

The movie's first half hour is a thicket of exposition, yet it never answers a few basic Batquestions in every mind. The Joker we learn almost everything about: his plans to take over first the girlfriend (Jerry Hall), then the chair of crime lord Carl Grissom (Jack Palance). Batman, his savvy butler Alfred (the estimable Michael Gough) and the Batgadgets remain annoyingly uninvestigated. So does the moment when Kim Basinger's Vicki Vale notices it's Bruce Wayne fiddling away in that Batcave.

So Bruce Wayne was traumatized by witnessing the murder of his parents when he was 9, and that has led him into this double life of midnight vigilantism. Why bats? Wherefore bat caves? The fact that he's mortal makes him especially fascinating, yet the movie (and that Batrig) never lets us worry for a second that anything can happen to him.

The volatile Keaton, an extremely interesting casting choice if he had a chance to let some of his dangerousness out, remains tamped-down and muted. His Bruce Wayne is as magnetic as one can make a character carved out of soap, but it's hardly Keaton's fault. As "ace photographer Vicki Vale," Basinger again does her magic of making a stock character warm, interesting and irreplaceable through some mysterious chemistry all her own. Meanwhile, Nicholson (quoted this week as saying, "I wanted to see how far I could go and I've never hit my head on top") has corkscrewed through the roof and is reaching into the ozone.

The Joker begins as Gotham City gangster Jack Napier before a confrontation with Batman tips him into a vat of toxic waste, turning him into a party-hearty misanthrope. His notion is to paralyze Gothamites with Smylex gas and lethal toiletries. His target? Apparently anything that moves, including his own henchmen, and a few things that don't, like a museum's worth of the art treasures of the Western world, which go under in an orgy of slashing and splashing. He does spare one: a shrieking nightmare vision by contemporary *Angst*-master Francis Bacon that the Joker kinda likes.

The vandalism is supposed to suggest the lengths to which this sadist will go. There may even be a lost Ted Turner-colorizing joke somewhere in the melee. But not even the fact that the paintings look like K-Mart repros can keep this sequence from being a true stomach churner. Not in today's world of indiscriminate art whackos.

Nicholson's Joker will be the pivotal point for many. It's his energy, spurting like an artery, that keeps the picture alive; it's certainly not the special effects, the editing, which has no discernible rhythm, or the flaccid screenplay. Nicholson keeps things moving higher and higher, even with his reading of the line, "It's time to retire," throwing in a voice that's pure John Huston.

But it's also a performance of such draining intensity and so few really quotable lines, most of which have been packed into the trailer, that it has us on the ropes begging for mercy long before the Joker waltzes into his climax. To a diehard Nicholson fan, it's unthinkable that a day would come when you wished Jack Nicholson would get off the screen, just so this headache would let up for a minute. But "Batman" has managed it. Talk about a toxic waste. . . .

(The Joker, with his gruesome death dealing, is also the cautionary figure for parents of young children. Take that PG-13 very seriously; this is where bad dreams are born.)

The Joker's screaming machinations become so exhausting that to get away from them, we begin looking past him, straight into some puzzling inconsistencies. The gag of the TV anchorpersons, getting progressively scuzzy because they're afraid of sampling the Joker's line of killer-toiletries, is a funny one. Then why don't we see dapper Dans like Dist. Atty. Harvey Dent (Billy Dee Williams, thrown away in a sub-cameo) also getting frayed in the personal daintiness department? Does he have his own line of after shave?

When, in a riotous parade through Gotham's scrunched-up streets, the Joker kills about a quarter of the revelers with poison gas, why don't the other hundreds swarm over him and beat that silly grin off his face? And in the bell tower "Vertigo" finale, after the three principals have inched their way perilously to the top, where in the name of holy Bat guano did those Joker henchmen come from?

Sidestepped most disastrously is the meaning of the conflict between Batman and the Joker. Batman is hardly Superman, unscarred psychically, and his duel with a man who could have been another facet of his own personality should have resonated. Instead, the Joker has been demoted into a broadscale sociopath, without a tempter's power or a mythic villain's complexity. And that's the movie's real undoing.

MONTHLY FILM BULLETIN, 9/89, p. 268, Kim Newman

Gotham City. Crime czar Carl Grissom learns that his girlfriend Alicia has been seeing his associate Jack Napier, and sets Jack up to be killed during a raid on the Axis chemical works. Jack escapes Grissom's gunmen, but Batman, a masked, black-cloaked vigilante who has been terrorising petty crooks, arrives on the scene and Jack, wounded by a ricochet, falls into a vat of chemicals. Investigative reporters Vicki Vale and Alexander Knox are covering the Batman story, and happen to meet reclusive millionaire Bruce Wayne, with whom Vicki has a one-night stand. Jack emerges from the chemicals as a white-faced, green-haired, eternally grinning freak, The Joker, and murders Grissom before taking over Gotham City's underworld. Vicki is hurt because Bruce has been avoiding her, and happens to see the millionaire leaving a floral tribute in a back alley. The Joker sees Vicki's picture and decides to pay court to her, inviting her in Bruce's name to the Flugelheim Museum where he is defacing works of art. When Bruce's butler Alfred informs him that Vicki has left a message referring to their non-existent date, Batman appears at the museum and rescues her. The Joker contaminates a run of cosmetics products and terrorises the city. Knox discovers that Bruce Wayne's parents were murdered in front of him when he was a child in the alley where he laid the flowers, and Bruce realises that the hoodlum who set him on course to become the Batman was the young Jack Napier. The Joker issues a challenge to Batman to face him in a duel, and stages a parade during which he passes out millions of dollars and plans to dose the crowds with lethal gas from giant balloons. Batman turns up in a Batwing aircraft and cuts the balloons free, then crashes on the steps of the Gotham City cathedral. The Joker takes Vicki, who has guessed that Bruce is Batman, to the top of the cathedral, where he is finally tackled by Batman. The Joker falls to his death and Batman presents the city with a signalling device which Commissioner Gordon can use to summon him if he is ever needed again.

Tim Burton signals his new approach to the world of *Batman* with his first vision of Gotham City, a tainted Metropolis of neon and steam, resembling a 40s vision of a hellish future and populated by criminals and their unwary victims. A family from out of town—bumbling parents and wide-eyed son—fall prey to a pair of psychotic muggers and a black batshape detaches itself from the shadows to descend on the villains, wreaking a rough justice and telling the criminals to spread the word about the Batman. Like Alan Moore in *The Killing Joke*, Burton and screenwriters Sam Hamm and Warren Skaaren see Batman and The Joker as dramatic antitheses, and the film deals with their intertwined origins and fates to an even greater extent than any of the comic-strip stories that have played variations on their oft-told tales. Here, not only is The Joker created partially due to Batman's intervention in the Axis Chemicals raid (as in the comic story "The Man Behind the Red Hood"), but the young Jack Napier is the mugger who attacked the Wayne family—echoing the innocents of the first sequence—and triggered off the neuroses that led young Bruce to become the fearsome Batman (in the comics, the killer was another character entirely, Joe Chill).

The major switch in this version is that the monstrousness of Batman is emphasised to an even greater degree than in the darkest of the comic stories (Frank Miller Jnr.'s *The Dark Knight*

Returns). The first reports of his activities suggest that he is a vampire who drains the blood of his victims, and the redesigned costume—all black rather than shades of blue and gray—is rather more reminiscent of Dracula or the Phantom of the Opera than of Batman's red-white-and-blue-hued superheroic competitors, Superman and Captain America. For most of the film, the authorities of Gotham City are as keen to track down the vigilante as The Joker, and the Laurel and Hardy-style one-upmanship that characterises the relationship of hero and villain is nicely crystallised in the moment, at once funny and genuinely chilling, in which The Joker, annoyed by the headline "WINGED FREAK TERRORISES CITY", chortles "Terrorises? Wait until they get a load of me". There is some confusion towards the end, in the moment of mutual revelation when Batman and The Joker admit that each has made a monster of the other, when The Joker seems suddenly and with no narrative explanation to be aware of Batman's secret identity ("I was just a kid when I knocked off your parents"). But this pays off in the powerful confrontation between the two characters in the belltower ("I have a bat in my belfry") of godless Gotham City's apparently abandoned cathedral.

During the production of the film, a great deal of hostility was generated in the fan press by the selection of a director and star known best for their comedic work, on the assumption that a Burton-Keaton *Batman* would echo the camp approach of the influential but much despised television series with Adam West. In the event, the film has found a great deal of humour in the subject but also diluted the laughter with a Gothic horror tone in keeping with Denny O'Neil's ghost-haunted approach to the character in the 70s—to such an extent, however, that it would never get past the "A" comics code. Jack Nicholson's Joker differs from the previous representations of the character by remaining Jack (Napier or Nicholson) under the make-up rather than, as in the original, being a nonentity (unlike the Riddler, the Penguin and the Catwoman, The Joker has, until now, had no "real" name). Through Nicholson, Burton works cruel humour very much in the vein of *Beetlejuice* or his underappreciated short *Vincent*, as a joy-buzzer is used to reduce a gangland figure to a smoking skeleton while The Joker snaps off a series of one-liners, or a museumful of classical pieces is desecrated ("I am the world's first fully functional homicidal artist").

In the climax, when the villain's schemes are foiled, he gratuitously shoots dead his best friend and asks his goons to kill everyone in sight: "Because I want a minute to myself". Beside this star turn, the figure of the hero becomes necessarily shadowy—as if areas were deliberately being left in the dark for future instalments—but Keaton holds his own remarkably well as the detached, emotionally bruised Bruce Wayne and as the Schwarzenegger-armoured dark knight. When Vicki Vale asks which of the guests at a party in Wayne Manor is Bruce Wayne, "the most useless man in the world", Wayne honestly and disturbingly replies, "I don't know", a meeting-cute device that establishes how fragile the multi-millionaire's identities are. Later, Keaton manages to bridge his usual bumbling image—unable to tell Vicki the truth during a tense confrontation, he mumbles "I'm Batman" over and over behind her back as she answers the door—and the obsessional quality necessary for the Caped Crusader.

Batman is very sparingly used in the film, always located in *noir*-ish shadows and vast rooftop sets, which means that the film isn't as overbalanced in his favour as such recent superheroic endeavours as *Superman* or *Raiders of the Lost Ark*. The little compromises necessary in any film with a budget in the $50 million region don't do any serious harm. Prince's songs, which interrupt an outstandingly old-fashioned score by Danny Elfman, could have been as disastrous as Queen's contribution to *Flash Gordon*, but only get gratuitously in the way during two scenes in which The Joker insists on a musical accompaniment to his crime sprees. And the casting of Kim Basinger—a last-minute replacement for Sean Young—never quite comes off because, although she is established as an independent photojournalist and war correspondent in the mould of Margot Kidder's Lois Lane, the film mainly has her get into danger and be rescued.

Other well-remembered aspects of the Batman story—faithful Alfred the butler, irascible Commissioner Gordon, the sleek black batmobile and batplane, the cavernous batcave, the crusading status of DA Harvey Dent (who, when scarred by a vindictive convict, becomes Batman's number two foe, Two-Face)—are unobtrusively but effectively worked in. The giant balloons and Flugelheim Museum even capture the wiseass New York humour of Bob Kane's original strips, in which Gotham City was full of giant but fully functional typewriters or umbrellas, but such mainly unwelcome and "silly" additions as Batwoman, Batgirl (two of them),

Bat-mite (an extra-dimensional imp), Ace the Bat-Hound and, worst of all, Robin the Boy Wonder, have thankfully been left back in the batcave.

NEW STATESMAN & SOCIETY, 8/4/89, p. 32, Suzanne Moore

Let's be honest about this, it doesn't really matter one way or the other what I think about *Batman*. Which is just as well because I'm at the stage where I can't *think* about *Batman* any more. It's enough to sit mesmerised by the statistics, the publicity, the buzz. Look I know that this isn't what you expect from a film review but I admit it—the hype has actually got to me. My critical faculties had been zapped, shot to pieces, immobilised before I even saw the bloody film.

It's not that I've been whipped into a frenzy by Batmania. Quite the opposite, in fact. I'm suffering from a total excess of information. Lost in a whirlwind of press releases and interviews, sneak previews and predictions, of Batman badges and backpacks and boxer shorts, of test screenings and market research, I have to keep reminding myself that somewhere there is a movie. And that I have actually seen it. Or at least I think I have. Perhaps it was just a premonition of the sequel—"Batman 2". Perhaps I'm thinking of the Batdance video. I don't know.

You see that's the worst thing about Batfatigue. You get confused. All that you can hold on to is the merchandise. You don't even have to want all this useless stuff. You know it's real when your kids start whingeing for it. And if that fails, you can cite all those vast and meaningless figures. All those millions of dollars it cost to make—35 to be precise—and all those millions of dollars it's going to make. How it took $40.49 million in the first opening weekend alone in the states and $160 million in the first month—outgrossing every other film in movie history. These are the facts.

But if you're suffering from Batfatigue the whole thing takes on the nightmarish air of an extreme conspiracy theory. Warner Brothers owns the film, owns the record company that has just released Prince's best-selling soundtrack; it owns DC comics and it owns the Batman licence. In the UK alone Warner Brothers has licensed 30 different companies to sell 150 products. The movie itself may or may not be phenomenal but the process surely is—further proof of the concentration of ownership at the top end of the media industries.

This hellish scenario seems so all powerful, so all encompassing that one is numbed into the fatal strategy of going with the flow rather than trying to swim against the tide. And anyway what's the point of feigning interest in popular culture if you lose heart once culture gets *this* popular? Yet even in the sweaty delirium of Batfatigue, and the dull fascination with which we watch this glob of media conglomerates selling us its secrets, discussing its PR exercises in loving detail, presenting itself as seamlessly and inevitably powerful, it's good to see that even capitalism isn't as smoothly efficient as it might be.

Warner Brothers has issued a set of particularly paranoid press releases urging "all concerned citizens to help battle (video) piracy". With the Batman video not scheduled till 1990, illegally duplicated prints are changing hands for large sums. I don't know who would actually want to see a poor quality video that's been shot directly from a cinema screen with a handheld camera—which apparently happens. But I'm kind of glad they do.

They have also, in Britain at least, screwed up the chance to cash in on marketing tie-ins by not giving its UK subsidiary enough advance warning of its release date. In other words, *Batman* may be everywhere but at least not on your cereal packets: even vertical integration begins to disintegrate under pressure.

The logic and logistics of making consumption so conspicuous eventually takes its toll; consumer exhaustion replaces consumer exhilaration and we all look around for the next big deal. Judging by most of the interviews given by director Tim Burton and Michael Keaton (who plays Batman in the film), they have been similarly affected. Burton is depressed and drained by the experience. It is, after all, only his third film. To recover he suggests: "A month in a little hospital somewhere hooked up to an IV unit. And then a short documentary on Abba." Michael Keaton, meanwhile, has responded to the hype with a series of spectacularly bland "I'm just a regular guy" style interviews that manage to make even Kim Basinger sound interesting by comparison.

Burton is understandably sick of being compared incorrectly to Spielberg. The only similarity is that they were given the chance to direct big budget movies at a relatively young age. Spielberg, like Burton, was 29 when he made *Jaws*, the movie that established his reputation. Other than that they are miles apart. While Spielberg's fantasies are of a universal and mythical lost innocence, Burton's are altogether more wayward and warped, deriving specifically from the cultural detritus of the ultimate consumer society. Both *Pee-wee's Big Adventure* and *Beetlejuice* depend for their humour on upturning established notions of good taste. Pee-wee Herman, suspended for ever between childhood and adulthood, is perversely unsettling in his adoration of trash. While *Betelgeuse*, the farting bio-exorcist, is monstrous simply because he is truly tasteless—unacceptable to homely preppies and pretentious yuppies alike.

In *Batman* it is Jack Nicholson as The Joker who fulfils this role. Lewd and lascivious, in garish outfits, The Joker becomes the ultimate eco-villain polluting the cosmetics of Gotham City from his chemical plant. Nicholson steals the show as The Joker. He has all the best lines (which are few and far between) but there is no way that the scriptwriters' strike in Hollywood can be used to excuse the lack of good plot or good writing. Though film is primarily a visual medium, I'm sure that I'm not alone in tiring of the increasing number of blockbusters that rely totally on dramatic imagery.

Perhaps Burton was simply overwhelmed by the fact that there were already so many Batman storylines that he forgot to work out one for himself. The decision to go back to the source—the darker character of the comic books—rather than trying to rework the camp television series, was a brave one. And, at times, there are hints that this lone obsessive vigilante may be psychotic and and that part of this psychosis is the symbiotic relationship that Batman has with his alter-ego The Joker. But, on the whole, these ambiguities get lost, not least because Bruce Wayne (Batman) is required to have a relationship with photographer Vicki Vale (Basinger). This attempt to normalise Wayne runs counter to the isolated, emotionally damaged and morally ambiguous figure of the later comic books—*The Killing Joke* and Frank Millar's *Dark Knight*. There is no point trying to make him into a Superman-type hero because it is his flawed humanity that makes the character interesting in the first place.

These sinister aspects emerge most sucessfully in a brilliant noirish set which designer Anton Furst describes as based on "the worst aspects of New York City...A city where there has been no planning or zoning controls." This is a cleverly retro vision of the future, a deliberately postmodern ragbag of styles, a threatening and shadowy contrast to *Superman*'s sunny, wide open spaces—and one that externalises the scarred psyche of the dark knight, the ever-youthful vigilante better than Keaton's subdued performance.

But all of this pales into insignificance besides the everpresent Bat insignia. As the media saturates itself with Bat stories already creating the hype for the sequel, the film remains somehow the least important part of the whole business. The empty heart in the corporate body. The soul is elsewhere in the transcendental business deals, in Burton's clichéd struggle for artistic control, in our desire to buy into a second-hand version of a second-hand fantasy. Like I said, if I haven't described exactly what I think about the film it's because I can't think about it anymore. I have had enough. The point is that I went to see it or I think I did. And now it really doesn't matter one way or the other. ...

NEW YORK, 7/17/89, p. 45, David Denby

A married couple and their little boy, walking down a cruddy street in the big city, are attacked by muggers, and the father is knocked out. But the family, it turns out, is not alone. High above, perched on some ridge in the concrete canyons, a man watches the thugs divide up the loot. Silently, darkly, he floats to the street, his black cape outstretched, looking less like a bat than like a ballet dancer slowing the pull of gravity. The great thing about comic-book movies is that a director can go all the way into the fantastic. Reality is there only to be stylized. But who knows what the figure of Batman means? Drifting down in the murk, he's wonderfully beautiful, a portent of something. But of what?

Tim Burton's *Batman* is the grandest of the pop visions and also, as you may have heard, the darkest and most pessimistic. It's not a joyride or a redemptive fantasy or a feast of action. And even though Batman triumphs, you couldn't say that the movie ends happily. Batman (Michael Keaton) and his vile nemesis the Joker (Jack Nicholson) are two halves of the same obsession, linked by personal history and by temperament, both disfigured (though in very different ways), both at home in the corrupted city. As characters, however, they aren't equals, and that's a big problem. *Batman* is out of balance—witty and flamboyant, but also depressed.

The movie begins and ends in darkness. Here is a grand mock-up of the old comicbook metropolis, with gigantic gray towers bunched together, a sunless island city ready to sink, like Altantis, into nowhere. In Anton Furst's production design, the dulled-out skyscrapers go straight up forever but have odd protuberances affixed to their sides, as if the builders ran out of imagination but couldn't stop violating their own creations.

In this filthy, demoralized, abandoned city, gangsters run the show and pols are either weak or on the take. Burton, the exuberant young director of *Beetlejuice*, goes all the way with his aestheticized vision of corruption. The movie is art of a specialized and limited variety; it's probably pointless to say, as Vincent Canby did, that the movie offers the décor and forbidding moods of Fritz Lang's silent films (*Metropolis*, etc.) without Fritz Lang's substance. Burton, whose first feature was *Pee-wee's Big Adventure*, is a pop director through and through. He thinks in gaudily colored absolutes. In *Batman*, the scenes go vividly, abruptly; each gesture is outlined, burlesqued. *Batman* is a very grandiose cinematic comic book. The trouble with Burton is that he isn't very good at WHAP! BANG! violence: He botches the two encounters between Batman and a Ninja swordsman, and some other things are either poorly staged or just too dark to see clearly.

But Tim Burton is a bolder, crazier talent than many a more competent director. Just as Milton's fiery iconoclasm led him to make the rebellious angel Satan the most stirring character in *Paradise Lost*, Burton's macabre temperament leads him to glorify the Joker. As this happy anarch, Jack Nicholson is scarifyingly brilliant. Preening and twirling, the master of revels, he embodies a truly frightening nihilistic idea—that a completely witty man, who sees everything as absurd and lives only for his own amusement, would have to be a killer.

When Batman throws him into a vat of acid and his flesh is burned away, leaving a grin permanently fixed on his face, he is freed to be himself. Clowns strike us as sinister because they're stuck with only one expression; we fear the man may become the mask. Nicholson and Burton renew and enlarge this old nightmare. The Joker becomes his face and turns death into a carnival. He's all show business, playing with his disfigurement, sometimes actually wearing whiteface and harlequin suits of purple silks with soft, floppy hats. His killings and outrages become scenes from an ongoing show he's staging for his own entertainment, tests of his imagination. Nicholson's whole personality becomes jocular and vicious, so that freakish smile actually looks natural on his face. In the most bizarre joke devised by screenwriters Sam Hamm and Warren Skaaren, he reproduces himself by marketing poisoned cosmetics that give anyone who uses them the same terrifying rictus.

Some of this mock ghoulishness is exhilarating fun. But at the risk of sounding like a nanny eager to protect American moviegoers from uneasy thoughts, I want to say that parts of *Batman* are genuinely unsavory. A few of the movie's nastier larks rival the more scabrously offensive scenes in *A Clockwork Orange*. When the Joker waltzes into a museum and defaces one famous painting after another, I can see the outrageous wit in his caper, but when he defaces his girlfriend (Jerry Hall), the wit turns a little too malicious and personal for laughter.

The unsavoriness, I know, is an overflow of Burton's daredevil talent. And, paradoxically, it may also have been produced by his decision to do the material seriously. With that morbid do-gooder Batman in his cape and hood as his hero, Burton was trapped—it became inevitable that the Joker would dominate the movie. Michael Keaton, who had the wild role in *Beetlejuice*— another Joker, though not a killer—tries to give a completely serious and internalized performance, as if he were playing a real character with a complex psychological makeup. But the writing doesn't support his ambition.

As the millionaire Bruce Wayne, handsome in his beautiful suits, Keaton shows us a man all tied up inside; Wayne, of course, saw his parents killed when he was a child, and he's become a control freak, incapable of feeling. Keaton, playing a man who goes out in bat drag at night—a pretty strange dude at the midnight madball—pares his voice down to a sincere monotone. He doesn't make much of a connection with plush Kim Basinger, who looks great as Vicki Vale, the photographer who falls in love with Wayne. And when he puts on his cape, he's transformed only physically and remains as earnest as ever. The cape functions more like a cloak—only Keaton's eyes and soft lips, enigmatically pursed, appear below the hood. All of which makes him awfully recessive in his own movie.

Some of *Batman* is funny, but the movie isn't high-spirited like *Beetlejuice*. It's more like Wagnerian pop, grand and gloomy, with gargoyle witticisms providing the relief. And it's not about much of anything but its own ambitions. One man, orphaned, becomes obsessed with stopping crime. The other man looks like a nightmare, and so he becomes a nightmare. Each becomes his obsession. The pop abstractions don't allow for any dramatic development. Burton ends up repeating himself, over and over, setting off one firecracker after another, until the picture finally blows itself into the dark void.

NEW YORK POST, 6/23/89, p. 23, David Edelstein

Bob Kane, creator of "Batman" for DC comics, made his title character an obsessive, even twisted vigilante—a man who watches his parents murdered and vows to purge the city of scum. Through pure will, Bruce Wayne turns himself into a superhero. He's a nutcase, but Wayne's choice of costume exerts a mythic power: as the shadowy, nocturnal Batman, he swoops down on villains like an avenging angel—a dark knight.

That tension between lunacy and superheroism is the core of director Tim Burton's freakily magnificent new movie. This isn't the campy, pop-art "Batman" of TV; it's the dreamy, brooding "Batman" of Freud, Gaudi, Fritz Lang and a new breed of graphic novels such as "The Dark Knight" and "The Killing Joke."

More than anything, it's the "Batman" of Burton, the 30-year-old director ("Pee-wee's Big Adventure," "Beetlejuice") whose passion for wacko individualists makes him the best person alive to bring out the operatic grandeur of a guy in a bat suit duking it out with a homicidal clown.

People buoyed by the hype—who go in hoping for the giddy high of a comic-book film like "Superman"—might feel baffled by this "Batman." It's constricted, dissonant, often droopy; it revels in ambiguity, which is dangerous in the blockbuster business. It doesn't leave you feeling that anything on earth is possible, which is what the craving for superheroes is all about.

But "Batman" feeds other, more subterranean cravings, and every frame is haunting, visionary. That vision is sad and strange, as much about a world that calls forth superheroes as the superheroes themselves. It's about the impulses that turn men—in their dreams—into gargoyles. And it's sublime: beautiful and funny and horrifying at once.

Burton and his brilliant designer, Anton Furst, have crammed Gotham City with elongrated skyscrapers and needlelke spires—it's all of Manhattan stretched out vertically and bunched together on a San Francisco hill.

Sunlight doesn't fall on its streets: the city is eternally gray and overcast, as if developers were allowed to run wild and blot out the sky. Filled with gargoyles, Gothic arches and Deco slashes of light, it's a place where humans lose touch with their higher instincts.

The cold, futurist City Hall suggests how far the ordinary citizen is from the workings of justice. Most of the cops are on the take; Commissioner Gordon (Pat Hingle) is inept; and the city is ruled by mobster Carl Grissom (Jack Palance) and his right-hand man, Jack Napier (Jack Nicholson). This is the moral void on which the damaged Wayne seeks to impose his sense of order.

The part is underwritten, but Michael Keaton gives a scarily suggestive performance, and a great one: if you know someone orphaned at an early age, you'll recognize its accuracy. Keaton's Wayne keeps things in. He can't begin to articulate his motives or his feelings—they scurry for cover in the batcave he carries inside him. He's always out of place.

He moves through the action like a sleepwalker, bug-eyed, and Burton lets us contemplate the vertical crevice in the middle of his forehead, which looks as if it might sink in on itself—like those houses built over hollowed-out coal mines. He really needs therapy. Why does he have video cameras all over his manor? Will he someday spy on his wife? His kids?

When he's Wayne, Keaton's movements are lurching, as if monitoring himself, but as Batman he's balletic. Confronting his prey, he's a statuesque Dracula; leading photojournalist Vicki Vale (Kim Basinger) up the steps of his batcave, he's the Phantom of the Opera. (Indeed, Batman and the Joker trade off the Phantom role—that's one of the ways Burton connects them visually.)

When Adam West was Batman, there was no tension between the costume and the man. But Keaton is a guy in a suit of armor. Its sharp angles clash with his soft chin and peevish lips, and his voice is a spooky put-on: low, hoarse, the voice of someone who can never smile. There's wit in pitting him against a villain who can never not smile, and whose flaming green hair and purple suits mock the knight's somber black.

The script by Sam Hamm and Warren Skaaren makes Batman and the Joker doubles—two freaks, neither of whom is at home in the world. Both have been violated, sent spiraling off into a hell of isolation. And both have chosen to come back and remake society in the image they think just. The Joker, in fact, calls himself a "homicidal artist"—a man who's fully alive only when he maims and kills.

Wattled, sneaky-eyed, Nicholson is a dandified psychotic even before he's the Joker, but his plunge into a vat of toxic chemicals liberates him, gives him absolute freedom. He can do or say anything now; he's dead.

As an actor he's liberated, too—he gives a performance of Olympian silliness. Watch him bulge his eyes, wiggle his new features, find the jaunty moves and laugh to match the white skin and red lips and green hair, the cheeks stretched out as if he's swallowed an anvil.

Nicholson and Burton conjure up a childlike terror of clowns, which most kids have before they're taught to laugh instead of cry. This Joker really slays people with his gags—he fries a man black with his joy buzzer, then speaks of "the healing power of laughter." And Burton's camera is in Nicholson's thrall, holding on the actor as he giggles and snorts, and waves his arms like a mechanical funhouse dummy. This Joker, who goes from deadpan to hysteria—zero to 90—in two seconds flat, makes his own rules.

It's a pity that the Joker's plans are so nebulous and that, structurally speaking, the script is such a mess. The story has no momentum, and Burton blows some opportunities. He robs us of a key emotional moment when Basinger's Vicki discovers that Wayne is Batman—off screen! And while Basinger's ravaged-cover-girl face is dazzling, the character exists only to be wooed and slung around.

Burton isn't a fluid director. He works frame by frame, like a comic artist, and he can't bring off the epic action scenes: an attack on City Hall by the Joker's men (disguised as mimes) seems truncated; and Batman's batplane attack on the Joker's lethal parade float is a botch. (The song by Prince doesn't help—it's too '80s.)

The fight scenes are high-impact—the blows make your head rock—but Batman's triumphs aren't always rousing, the way they'd be in, say, "Lethal Weapon." There's something disturbing, in principle, about his interventionist policies, about a man so obsessed with tracking down villains that he can't wake up to life. (Clearly, if Wayne did succeed in ridding Gotham City of all criminals, he'd be at a loss—he'd probably have to become one himself.)

On the other hand, the climax atop the Gotham City cathedral is gorgeous, breathtaking. High above the city in the moonlight, the Joker waltzes to Muzak with a sagging Vicki, while Batman fights off one warrior after another, and then turns on the clown with cathartic fury.

The Joker's exit is the most poetic imaginable—the man whose soul has been weighted down by gargoyles gets just what he deserves. And he doesn't seem to mind: the artist in him knows it's time to go. Our last sight and sound of him is Burton's grand punch line for this dizzying, traumatic, and imperfect masterpiece.

NEWSDAY, 6/23/89, Part III/p. 3, Mike McGrady

Gotham City. The night streets are teeming with scavenging hookers and belligerent panhandlers, with brazen muggers and corrupt politicians, with the hunters and the hunted. But on the rooftops, well above the streets, a man wearing the costume of a bat has just decided to spare the life of a petty criminal.

"I want you to do me a favor," he explains. "I want you to tell all your friends about me."

"What—what are you?" the hoodlum asks.

"I'm...Batman."

So begins one of the most interesting comic-book movies ever made, a movie that vividly illustrates where most of the others have gone wrong. As a rule, moviemakers assigned to comic books either go in for outlandish overstatement, exaggerating what is already an exaggeration, or aim for camp, making fun of the work even as they're filming it.

What makes "Batman" radically different, arresting in its freshness, is that young director Tim Burton has done the unheard-of; he has taken his source material seriously and has made a movie that is dark, somber, impressive and involving on more than a single level.

Burton, who demonstrated such cinematic elan with "Beetlejuice," now demonstrates unique respect for his subject. Going back almost 50 years, he has drawn on the earliest portraits of "The Bat-Man," as he was then known, "a mysterious and adventurous figure, fighting for righteousness and apprehending the wrongdoer, in a lone battle against the evil forces of society."

This was the Caped Crusader before Robin or the Penguin or any of the other ornithological additions. Batman, as he came to be known, was *not* as fast as a speeding locomotive, was wholly unable to leap tall buildings in a single bound, was not in the least indestructible. He was just a human being, just another brooding millionaire-philanthropist seeking to avenge the murder of his parents by combating crime. His real edge came from strength, ingenuity, resolve and, to be sure, enough money to buy a Batmobile, a Batplane, a Batarang and a host of other dandy little crime-fighting devices.

By honoring these antecedents, Burton has put together a film that is unusually somber for a comic-book movie; much of the action takes place in shadows and night, a perfectly apt backdrop for a film with a psychological focus.

Production designer Anton Furst ("Full Metal Jacket"), largely responsible for the tone of the film, has translated Gotham City into a mood poem, a teeming Dickensian cross between the Manhattan of today and the Los Angeles of "Blade Runner." In this hellish setting, a photojournalist (Kim Basinger), aided by a newspaperman (Robert Wuhl), tracks down the strange bat-like figure who has been fighting crime from the rooftops. Quickly, Basinger becomes romantically involved with Batman (Michael Keaton) while being pursued by Batman's nemesis, the fiendishly evil Joker (Jack Nicholson).

One of the great strengths of the film is the utter conviction the actors bring to their roles. Keaton is likable, distracted, complicated enough to handle a double life. As he understates it to Basinger, "My life is...very complex." Nicholson's Joker, a work of pure genius, is a murderous cutup, a vicious criminal jealous of Batman's public acclaim: "Can somebody tell me, what kind of world we live in where a man dressed up as a bat gets all of my press?"

The Batman-Joker connection is the twine that keeps the parcel together. Each is responsible for creating the other—the Joker murdered young Bruce Wayne's parents, forcing him into a life of crime-fighting, and Batman caused the Joker's disfigurement by dumping him into a vat of chemical sludge. They represent two sides of a single coin, a Jekyll-Hyde union of the manic and the depressed.

So unique is the film's approach that I can think of only one comparable experience; it recalls that time, many years ago, when most of us picked up our first "Batman" comic book, started thumbing through it and got hooked—swept along by the powerful visual dynamics and enthralled by the stark drama of good fighting evil on an essentially human battlefield.

NEWSWEEK, 1/23/89, p. 68, Jack Kroll

Holy Hollywood, at last "Batman's" a major movie! Drop those campy old comic-book expletives, this "Batman" is strictly new wave. It's got a hot young director, Tim Burton (1988's surprise box-office bonanza, "Beetlejuice"), a hot young actor, Michael Keaton ("Beetlejuice," "Night Shift"), as Batman, an always-hot superstar, Jack Nicholson, as the Joker, and Kim Basinger, who's...well, *hot*, as love interest Vicki Vale. But the new high-tech, high-concept, highbudget ($30 million) Batpic has already thrown Batfans into a Batfit even before it finishes shooting. In a front-page story The Wall Street Journal reported that Batties fired off letters to Warner Brothers protesting that Keaton, known mainly for comedy roles in movies like "Mr. Mom" and "Johnny Dangerously" and who drew critical praise for his role as a cocaine addict in "Clean and Sober," is simply not cut from the right heroic capecloth to play their hero.

But that's the whole point of the new "Batman." On the set recently at the vast Pinewood Studios outside London, Burton stoutly defended his postmodern Batman from the forces of reaction: "Our Batman is not somebody from another planet, he's not this mythic thing. It's very easy to go for a square-jawed hulk, but I find it much more interesting to go our way. If some guy is 6-foot-5 with gigantic muscles and incredibly handsome, why does he need to put on a batsuit? Why doesn't he just put on a ski mask and kick the crap out of people?" Burton sees Bruce Wayne, Gotham City's leading young socialite who becomes the caped crusader, as a real human being with interesting psychological problems. "He has no agenda, like Superman's "Truth, justice and the American way." If this Batman knew so specifically why he was doing it, he wouldn't be doing it. That's the audience hook. Everybody has a bit of the split personality, everybody wants to do *something*, everybody does something they don't know why they do."

When he was first approached by Burton to play Batman, Keaton didn't see himself as a comic-book hero. "I read the script out of politeness, and Batman wasn't this guy with arms akimbo, legs apart, chest out, standing on a parapet." There's barely enough of the slim, 5-foot-10 Keaton to be akimbo anyway. But his Batman operates out of the head rather than the body. "In the script Bruce Wayne was this complex, weird guy. What interested me in the project was, what kind of man would do this, would put on the bat uniform?" For Keaton, Bruce-Batman is something of a schizophrenic. "I get up in the morning, look in the mirror and try to see what damage this character has done to my head." It's clear that Keaton, Burton and Nicholson are working hard to subvert the traditional, or neoconservaBat, concept of the basic story.

The original "Batman" comic strip, the brainchild of cartoonist Bob Kane (a consultant on the movie), first appeared in 1939 in Detective Comics. The movie will be released this June, in time to celebrate the hero's 50th anniversary. There were a couple of movie serials in the '40s, and the popular TV series of the '60s, with square-jawed Adam West, who also starred in a quickie movie in 1966 with Cesar Romero as the Joker. And of course there was Robin, Wayne's teenage sidekick, a partnership that was characterized by prominent—but part-pooping—psychiatrist Frederic Wertham as "a wish dream of two homosexuals living together." In his stead, fellowship is provided by Kim Basinger playing photojournalist Vicki Vale.

The script, credited to the rhyming team of Warren Skaaren ("Beverly Hills Cop II") and Sam Hamm ("Never Cry Wolf"), is a tricky but deft attempt to fuse fantasy and reality, pastiche and put-on. At one point Bruce tells Vicki: "I wear a cape. You take pictures. It is not a perfect world." Into this world comes the Joker, whose face has been fixed in a satanic smile by a fall into a vat of industrial acid. "I'm the world's first fully functioning homicidal artist," he proclaims, and makes his point in true pop-artist fashion by disposing of his victims through such means as handshakes with a 40,000-volt Joy Buzzer, filling parade balloons with the deadly gas Smylex and blazing away with the world's longest gun.

The anchorman for this delicate operation is clearly the unflappable Nicholson. "What I like about the Joker," he says, "is that he has no taste in his humor." As for the strip itself, "I remember as a kid I liked 'Batman' because it was the only comic book that took place at night." At an early meeting with Burton "to see if we could get along," the first thing he told the director was "Just make sure you don't lose that old black-purple-night ominous feeling." They *are* getting along: "This is the most carefree production I've ever done," says Nicholson. "I've even stopped watching dailies [unedited footage of the previous day's scenes]. At least half of what you see in dailies is junk, and you're always petrified that they're gonna pick the junk. But Tim and I like the same things, so I don't have to worry about it."

Shooting a climactic scene on the huge Pinewood set of Gotham City's main street (the biggest set since "Cleopatra," says the studio), Nicholson appears in the Joker's killer-clown haberdashery of purple tail coat, purple and green check pants, purple gloves, green shirt, green waistcoat, purple tie, an orchid in his lapel that shoots acid, his face a chalk-white mask inset with grinning blood-red lips and topped with luminescent green hair. The Joker is harassing Vicki while she frantically tries to extricate Batman from his Batwing aircraft, which has been shot down on the steps of Gotham City's neo-Gothic cathedral. As flames and smoke swirl in the biting winter wind, Kim Basinger's long blond locks dance about her hip-angel face. Off to one side, Tim Burton watches the scene on a TV monitor. "Cut," he calls, and asks for more debris to be brought in.

"I'd do anything for Tim," says Basinger between takes. "He's a freak and I'm a freak—we're two freaks in the wind." The increasingly stunning, increasingly stylish actress keeps getting good reviews in not-so-good movies, the latest being "My Stepmother Is an Alien." "Being in this movie is like being inside a surrealist painting," she says with her Georgia lilt. "Gotham City is a place where forbidden things happen and good things come out of forbidden things. And that's the ultimate fantasy. I love being the female, sometimes the strength and sometimes the weakness." Will this be her breakthrough movie? "Oh, I don't think so, not for me. But if this is magical, it'll be an event instead of a movie. I don't think it's anything that anyone expects."

The key is Tim Burton. Just turned 30, looking 20, this spectrally thin, black-clad Californian with long bedraggled hair may be the first breakaway talent since the Spielberg-Lucas-Coppola-Scorsese movie brats came along. He studied animation at the California Institute of the Arts, went to work at the Disney studio as an animator and a designer, made a couple of short films that did well at festivals. That got him the chance to direct Pee-wee Herman in "Pee-wee's Big Adventure," which made $45 million. That led to "Beetlejuice," which earned twice that. Now he's handling one of those blockbusters that make ("Roger Rabbit") or break ("Dune"). "I'm a firm believer in doing movies at a lower cost," he says. "A movie like 'Batman' has to be one of the biggest of the year. Well, if the studio isn't worried about it I'm not gonna worry about it, but they seem incredibly worried about it so I'm incredibly worried about it." This isn't a wisecrack; it sounds rather like the voice of a new breed: sophisticated innocence. "Actually I feel good about 'Batman'," says Burton. "I feel as if it's gonna be this big movie and still have some feel to it. Some style."

TIME, 6/19/89, p. 60, Richard Corliss

The familiar blue sky behind the Warner Bros. shield grows dark. The clouds gain some menacing heft. A cumulus of urban steam shrouds the camera as it goes cruising for trouble in Gotham City. Nighttime is the right time for...Batman.

Not "*Baat-maaaan!*" Not the bleating trumpets and Pop art facetiousness of the '60s TV series, which turned Bob Kane's superhero into a camp crusader. Director Tim Burton's approach is dead serious. He renounces the bright palette, the easy thrills, to aim for a psychodrama with the force of myth. He creates a Gotham City that looms like a rube's nightmare of Manhattan. He strips the Bruce Wayne legend legend down to its chassis, dumping Robin and the goony rogues' gallery. This is a face-off between two men in weird masks: one in a leathery black item out of a dominatrix's pleasure chest, the other with a grin frozen into a rictus. One man obsessed with good, the other enthralled by evil: Batman (Michael Keaton) and the Joker (Jack Nicholson).

Ambitious goals, most of which are not realized. The film stints on narrative surprise. It prowls—slowly, so slowly—in search of grandeur, but it often finds murk. It permits a few inside jokes (a cartoon of a bat in a suit, drawn by Kane), but mines its main humor from the Joker's ribald misanthropy ("This town needs an enema"). *Batman*'s style is both daunting and lurching; it has trouble deciding which of its antagonists should set the tone. It can be as manic as the Joker, straining to hear the applause of outrage; it can be as implosive as Batman-Bruce, who seems crushed by the burden of his schizoid eminence. This tension nearly exhausts the viewer and the film.

Inconsistencies abound. The Joker falls into a vat of toxic slime that eats the skin off his body but doesn't damage his signature deck of cards; when he gaily vandalizes some classic paintings, the film spells the museum's name two different ways; and when he starts tossing $20 million in cash onto the street, the good people of Gotham don't go into a looting frenzy and attack his perch. More important, the picture's first hour poses one big question: How will ace photographer Vicki Vale (Kim Basinger) react when she learns that Bruce is Batman? We never find out; the revelation occurs offscreen.

Anyone can take pleasure in the matching of Keaton and Nicholson, their dueling eyebrows poised like crossed swords. And Keaton does locate the troubled human inside Batman's armature. He is amusingly awkward wrestling with the threat that Vicki's inquisitive love represents. He knows the world is not quite worth saving, and yet, "It's just something I have to do," he says, "because nobody else can." Same with Nicholson. Who else could play the Joker? He has a patent on satanic majesty. His performance is high, soaring, gamy. He is as good, and as evil, as the film allows him to be. Which, finally, is not enough.

Here's why. At the end, Batman and the Joker realize they must destroy each other because, in a way, they have created each other. It would be nice to say that the Joker is Batman's lost, twisted twin; then his clumsy antics could be seen as an expression of existential anguish. He could feel as much pain as he dishes out. He could be Hamlet dressed as a clown. But the Joker's malignancy is neither seductive nor poignant. His power never tempts Vicki or compromises Bruce. His soul must have been stripped away with his skin, and what's left is the spirit of anarchic violence, giggling at its own enormity.

What's left in *Batman* is the skeleton of a nifty film. Its heart got lost on Tim Burton's storyboard.

VILLAGE VOICE, 7/4/89, p. 69, J. Hoberman

It's not exactly a yuppie fad, but for months now the crowds on 14th Street have been sporting the jagged, curvilinear Batman logo on their jackets, backpacks, and T-shirts like a magic talisman or a negative campaign pin. Are they organizing for chaos or warding it off? So see *Batman* and be confused: The logic by which the city's proles and school kids have been transformed into unpaid human advertisements for Warner Bros.'s $35- (or is it $50-?) million gamble is reproduced in the movie itself.

The class structure in Tim Burton's long-awaited epic is nearly as brutal as the one in its distant progenitor, Fritz Lang's *Metropolis*. Indeed, the sensational opening tracking shot is like something shot on Berlin's vast UFA soundstage in 1927: beggars rummaging through garbage on a mock Fifth Avenue as affluent crowds stream from an ersatz Radio City to battle for taxis. *Batman's* Gotham City is New York seen through a glass darkly—an anguished realm of unbridled authority and eternal night, a citadel of overdesigned power pads and blast-furnace skyscrapers where everything seems built in the iron shadow of the El. City Hall is a lysergic version of the Tombs, and even the heart of Midtown has been put through the trash compactor—the skyline is a frenzied jumble, the avenues seems narrow as alleyways.

Batman is nothing if not a look. The atmosphere is as foggy as Victorian Eastcheap and no less pestilent. The production design is as elaborate and detailed as that of *Blade Runner* or *Dune*—albeit without the former's grandiose lyricism or the latter's psychosexual obsessions. The mode is that of the Archaic Future, the No Future, the Dreadful Now. As the villainous Joker (Jack Nicholson) sneers, watching the Koch-clone mayor mouth some televised anticrime piety, "Decent people shouldn't live here."

Fueled by Danny Elfman's pseudo-Wagnerian score, populated by corroded power brokers in double-breasted, three-piece pin-striped suits, *Batman's* early scenes seem lit by lightning. A brutal mugging brings down the vengeance of the sinister hero (Michael Keaton). A shoot-out at the local Con Ed-cum-Chemical Death plant is a festival of disfiguration, with criminals dangling over vats of acid and seeking refuge with back alley plastic surgeons. The first 20 minutes move like a Phil Karlson episode of *The Untouchables*; still, after a while, the beginning seems like a miracle. Burton has no shortage of comic ideas, and he can choreograph a 20-car crack-up, complete with cascading cabbages. But *Batman* is undone by its package. The movie sputters, stalls, and turns inert because it's the prisoner of its set—and Jack Nicholson's relentless desire to devour it.

Dancing, singing, mugging, and shrugging, Nicholson establishes an energy level that nothing else in this brooding cosmos approaches—least of all his costar and nemesis. Just about everything in *Batman* is overwrought except Keaton, whose self-effacement borders on the masochistic. His Bruce Wayne is disarmingly bumbling, his Batman a bondage-cowled stiff. In the role of a modified Lois Lane named Vicki Vale, Kim Basinger is essentially decorative. (Her masklike face is as sculpted as the set—this is one environment where those lushly chiseled features seem perfectly at home.) But Basinger's voluptuous, white-clad heroine is bizarrely innocent, and, as Keaton too is posing as *faux naïf*, the movie nods off whenever the two play a scene. No wonder Nicholson absorbs maximum screen time. Although his excess initially helps, it's a Pyrrhic victory that only serves to gut the film.

The least one can say is that *Batman* has the grandeur of its own ruins. Despite the scene where Nicholson prances about in a purple satin beret, improving the paintings in the Flugelheim Museum (the epitome of production designer Anton Furst's Deco-Aztec-Bathyscaphe look), Burton's movie is a far cry from the tinny delirium of the post-Pop Art TV show. *Batman* is violent and filled with physical pain (even more disturbing for being delivered cartoon-style). There's a megalomaniacal Brothers Grimm quality to the molded black leather, deep blue highlights, and universal plate armor that, in the end, only constrains the movie more tightly than Nicholson's prosthetic cheeks or Keaton's rubber bodysuit.

Batman aspires to be a primeval rhapsody: flame and steel, night and fog, surging music and Götterdämmerung textures. But the movie doesn't have the courage of its own perversity. (It ultimately lacks Lang's lunatic conviction.) The idea that, having already had Vicki in his Bruce Wayne mode, our schizoid hero might want her again, this time as Batman, is flirted with and hastily dropped—as is the notion that Batman and the Joker are in some way symbiotic. The reconstruction of Batman's childhood trauma is drearily self-obvious. The Joker's parade of triumph seems feeble, constricted—a geriatric notion of evil. The climactic confrontation between the alter egos is so one-sided as to be embarrassing.

Devoid of subtext (not to mention the "Boy Wonder," Robin), the film is reduced to sub-Nietzschean nonsense, with two supercartoons running around an infernal Disneyland, modeling their heavy-metal Gothic accessories. In lieu of a narrative motor, the movie depends on the staggered introduction of ancillary merchandise—the arsenal of harpoon Batguns, the swooping, boomerang-shaped Batwing, the fortress-on-wheels Batmobile that suggest Albert Speer's design for a Porsche. "Where does he get those wonderful toys?" Nicholson whines. Not on 14th Street. Yuppies, take heed.

By the time you read this, *Batman* will likely have broken the opening-weekend record set by

Ghostbusters II (which broke that set by *Indiana Jones and the Last Crusade*). It would be pleasing to see *Batman*'s record fall to yet another saga of Gotham City. As Spike Lee has gotten almost as much press as the Caped Crusader, I'll have my say next issue. In the meantime, this weekend: *Do The Right Thing*.

Also reviewed in:

NATION, 7/17/89, p. 100, Stuart Klawans
NEW REPUBLIC, 7/13/89. p. 24, Stanley Kauffmann
NEW YORK TIMES, 6/23/89, p. C12, Vincent Canby
NEW YORKER, 7/10/89, p. 83, Pauline Kael
VARIETY, 6/14-20/89, p. 7
WASHINGTON POST, 6/23/89, p. D1, Hal Hinson
WASHINGTON POST, 6/23/89, Weekend/p. 37, Desson Howe

BEAR, THE

A Price Entertainment release. *Producer:* Claude Berri. *Director:* Jean-Jacques Annaud. *Screenplay:* Gerard Brach. *Based on "The Grizzly King" by:* James Oliver Curwood. *Director of Photography:* Philippe Rousselot. *Editor:* Noelle Boisson. *Music:* Philippe Sarde. *Sound:* Laurent Quaglio. *Sound Editor:* Eric Mauer, Fabienne Alvarez, Roberto Garzelli. *Production Designer:* Toni Ludi. *Art Director:* Heidi Ludi, Antony Greengrow, and Georg Dietz. *Special Effects:* Willy Neuner, Uli Nefzer, and Johann Fickel. *Costumes:* Corinne Jorry and Françoise Disle. *Make-up:* Hans-Jurgen Schmelzle. *Running Time:* 93 minutes. *MPAA Rating:* PG.

CAST: Bart (Kaar); Douce (Youk); Jack Wallace (Bill); Tcheky Karyo (Tom); Andre Lacombe (The Dog Handler).

CHRISTIAN SCIENCE MONITOR, 11/8/89, p. 11, David Sterritt

Bears have a special place in the animal world, as we humans see it. True, there's never been a great bear character like, say, Lassie the dog or Dumbo the elephant. But bears are always popular in circuses, and the way we think about them is unusual: We know they're big, strong, and even scary, yet they're also sort of cuddly. The teddy bear, after all, must be the most popular snuggling companion of all time.

Add up the different qualities we associate with bears, and it's not surprising that Jean-Jacques Annaud's new movie, "The Bear," has been one of the year's biggest hits in Europe—and has now arrived on American screens, beginning with a debut at the annual Festival of Festivals here. It's a likable movie, and at times an adorable one. I think it would be better, though, if it paid more attention to the world of nature—which is its subject, after all—and less attention to the world of moviemaking tricks.

The story is simple, so I won't give much of it away. The heroes are two Kodiak bears, a cub and an adult, living in the British Columbia wilds. These aren't cartoon creatures but real, live, majestic animals. And at the moment, both of them are unusually vulnerable: The cub is an orphan, and the grownup has been wounded by hunters. They meet up with each other, and it looks as if they might have a nice future together—except that hunters are still after the big one; so they must flee for their lives across the wilderness. They have various adventures along the way, and the big bear even has a quick love affair, with a little on-screen sex.

The stars of "The Bear" are compulsively watchable. Just the way they move their bodies is endlessly fascinating. Ditto for the magnificent Canadian scenery.

The trouble with "The Bear" is that it's such self-conscious filmmaking. The joy of watching a wilderness movie is feeling a sense of the wilderness itself; that's why nature movies are usually best when the filmmakers just film it, calling little attention to themselves. But director Annaud, whose films include "Quest for Fire" and "The Name of the Rose," is always manipulating things, usually through editing, to make the plot more powerful—even though this often means less natural.

This raises a fascinating issue that film theorists have written about for decades: the tension between film's ability to capture the real world (or a reasonable facsimile) and the filmmaker's ability to manipulate filmed material so it suits a particular (usually narrative) purpose.

In the early days of cinema, filmmakers such as D.W. Griffith and Sergei Eisenstein were overwhelmed by the power of montage—the editing of shots into carefully arranged sequences—to bestow new meanings on the material they photographed. For decades, beginning in the 1920s, most filmmakers considered montage to be the essence of cinema. This didn't change until the 1942s, when such directors as Orson Welles and William Wyler started using new methods (camera movements, deep focus, and "takes" lasting a long time) to crowd more information into each individual shot, thus avoiding the need for constant shot-to-shot cutting. This gave a new kind of realism to cinema, since it allowed images to flow in a lifelike way.

French critic André Bazin wrote eloquently on the advantages of this approach. A magic trick may be very impressive if it's filmed in one uninterrupted shot, he noted, but if there's single cut—however insignificant—the audience will assume things were manipulated while the camera was turned off, and lose faith in the magician's skill. Bazin found a special need for avoiding montage in nature films. He praised a movie in which the camera grinds patiently away while a hunter waits for his prey to come in view, forcing the audience to share his suspense; if editing were used, "real time" would be condensed into "movie time" and the realistic effect would be lost.

Montage certainly has important uses and Mr. Annaud is clearly a competent filmmaker. But he has failed to learn Bazin's lessons. To arrive at the story he's after—a highly anthropomorphic story, which is also part of the problem—he continually chops his footage into bits and pieces that diminish the sense of conviction we might have felt regarding the bears, their training, and even the Canadian background of their story.

Most moviegoers will love "The Bear" anyway, since it's like a traditional Disney kind of film made with grown-up audiences in mind. I think it would be more effective, though, if it showed us the profound charm of the real world captured spontaneously on film.

FILM QUARTERLY, Spring 1990, p. 30, Derek Bouse

Jean-Jacques Annaud has been both praised and criticized in recent years for his attempts to film massive, unwieldy, and what some have even considered "unfilmable" stories by resorting to conventionalized narrative frameworks. In *Quest for Fire* (1981) and *The Name of the Rose* (1986) he eschewed "epic" pretensions for the drama of one or two characters in pursuit of a single (and deceptively simple) goal. In each case the thing sought, the secret which promised to bring light—literal as well as symbolic—to an age of relative darkness, was, at bottom, knowledge itself.

It might be tempting to try to fit Annaud's most recent film, *The Bear*, into just this sort of basic *auteurist* framework. In it, an innocent young cub is introduced to the mysterious ways of life by a wise, older bear, while a hunter who stalks them learns the life-affirming value of allowing them to survive. Thus, the North American frontier civilization, virtually built on the trapping and slaughter of animals (not to mention genocide), gives way to a new age of enlightened, peaceful co-existence. As in the earlier films then, we see one of history's small pivot-points of change and progress, a quiet chapter in the story of humanity's advancement.

Yet, forcing interpretations of this film to conform to the context of Annaud's others, especially given the diverse range of subject matter he has taken on since *Black and White in Color* (1977), imposes severe limitations on our appreciation of *The Bear* for what it is. For despite claims, at the time of its American release, of its uniqueness and innovation, *The Bear* is very likely the most *conventional* film Annaud has ever made—his first real genre piece. Critics, however, have long tended to deny wildlife film the status of a full-fledged film genre, though it is an old and established form with a history and tradition as rich and diverse as any. The popularity of wildlife films on television has made them just the sort of thing "serious" critics have preferred to overlook or dismiss. The success of *The Bear* should indicate that the wildlife genre is creatively viable, and, more importantly, in need of a critical re-evaluation.

Annaud has shown, as other film makers have often discovered, that working within any well-defined genre need not be a constraint on creativity, but instead can provide a familiar "ground" against which one's own work stands out all the more clearly in relief. The idea, of course, is that this figure/ground distinction works because audiences have a *tacit* familiarity with the genre's conventions, and so are likely to respond to subtle variations on familiar themes far more readily than to something truly unique and original, for which they may have no "language." Thus, much of what may seem new or original about *The Bear* stems precisely from the fact that it is, after all, old and familiar.

Though the novel on which *The Bear* is based, James Oliver Curwood's *The Grizzly King* (1916), is virtually unknown today, Curwood's stories were once widely read, and a number of them were made into films both during his lifetime and after. Curwood died in 1927, but it was in the very next year that Felix Salten published his novel *Bambi*. Disney's film version of this story is, arguably, the single work that exerted the most influence on the development of the wildlife genre for decades—despite the fact that *Bambi* was an animated film.[1] Salten followed it up a few years later with *Perri*, the "biography" of a squirrel, which Disney filmed in 1956, this time as a live action feature using real, though *untrained* animals (an essential difference from Annaud's film). The film version of *Perri* was oxymoronically advertised as a "True Life *Fantasy*," but it represented the culmination of nearly every narrative device and storytelling convention the Disney team had perfected in eight years of making their series of "True Life *Adventures*." Though these earlier films had been widely (and wrongly) considered "documentaries," *Perri* emerged nonetheless as the quintessential Disney wildlife film, and showed how far the genre had evolved by the mid-1950s in the direction of pure storytelling. Moreover, by focusing on the lives of animal protagonists, Disney effectively projected the nuclear family structure into nature. Partly as an outcome of increasing "ecological" consciousness during the 1960s (resulting in, for example, passage of the Endangered Species Act), Disney's highly anthropomorphic model of wildlife filmmaking fell into decline after *Charlie the Lonesome Cougar* (1968). Television programs professing a more "scientific" interest in wildlife soon became the norm. Yet as recently as 1988, wildlife filmmaker Marty Stouffer has suggested that Disney's model, the one "devoted to the life story of one particular animal" remains the "classic format for wildlife films."[2] It is this context in which Annaud's *The Bear* can be best appreciated.

Though the absence of voice-over narration in *The Bear* is the most obvious departure from tradition, some have been led to deny emphatically that the film has anything in common with the classic Disney model.[3] Yet even the much talked-about dream sequence, held up as the true token of Annaud's unique and innovative determination to portray the animals' point of view, has its precedent in Disney's *Perri*. Though *Perri*'s visually surrealistic dream occurs during winter hibernation, the one experience by Annaud's cub is the result of eating wild mushrooms. (They appear to be the highly toxic *Amanita muscaria*, incidentally, and nobody should be tempted into eating them for hallucinogenic purposes!) Yet, even here Disney is not easily one-upped; one need only recall the episode in *Dumbo* (1941) in which the under-aged protagonist becomes accidentally intoxicated, and hallucinates a frightening onslaught of pink elephants. One could argue that animation is another genre entirely, and that cartoons are full of animal characters whose points of view are routinely depicted; yet at the Disney studios the separation between the two types of production was never clear. Ben Sharpsteen, who directed *Dumbo*, also directed the "documentary" film *Water Birds* (1951). James Algar, a sequence director on *Bambi*, went on to direct Disney's first two feature-length "True Life Adventures," *The Living Desert* (1953) and *The Vanishing Prairie* (1954), both of which won Academy Awards for "Best Documentary Feature."

What all of this intermingling of novels, animation, and so-called "documentary" film resulted in was the development of a set of clearly codified narrative conventions which survive even today, and which unite film-makers as diverse as Stouffer and Annaud. Thus, *The Bear*, like Stouffer's *The Man Who Loved Bears* (1977), a number of Disney's films, and several others from around the world, wastes no time in making an orphan of its young protagoinst. The matter of the mother's death might seem only an unfortunate accident until it is seen in the context of the entire genre, where it is typical. In some cases the use of the orphan device takes the form of a temporary separation, as in Disney's *Yellowstone Cubs* (1963) and *Flash, the Teenage Otter* (1964); in *The Bear* the death of the mother during the first reel completely eliminates the possibility of a happy reunion in the end, and so focuses attention on the drama of survival more than on frolicsome comedy.

Though seemingly unwarranted, this tragic occurrence is also necessary to set up the "incredible journey" motif which often forms the dynamic of these pictures' narratives. In *Flash*, this takes the form of a variation on the heroic quest tale: a foundling is set adrift on the waters, embarks on a perilous voyage in search of his origins, along the way undergoes ritual trials which initiate him into adulthood, and returns to otter society in triumph, where he is rewarded with a companion of the opposite sex. The same is true for *Charlie, the Lonesome Cougar*, and to some degree for *Perri*, though these two, like the cub in Annaud's film, are true orphans. In each case, an idyllic paradise is first established, then threatened or lost through the action of predators or natural cataclysms, and finally, after a series of trials, joyously regained. More specifically, the nuclear family is reaffirmed in the end, if not completely reconstituted, and ready to begin the cycle anew.

At this structural level, another break with convention that Annaud appears to make in *The Bear* involves his treatment of the surrogate family theme, though, ultimately, this too is guided by convention. Soon after the cub is orphaned, it meets a bullet-wounded adult male grizzly, and the two embark on their incredible journey together. Though we know from animal behavior research since Curwood's time that adult male bears have no paternal instincts or duties beyond copulation, that they often attack and kill cubs out of instinctive defense of their territory against competitors, and that a wounded adult male is the most dangerous kind, wildlife films nonetheless have a way of putting aside such niggling details in pursuit of a good story. What makes an "incredible journey" truly incredible is, after all, the very unlikelihood of the companions and, further, the mysterious bond that unites them. In Disney's film of Sheila Burnford's novel *The Incredible Journey* (1963) the companions were two dogs and a cat; in *A Tale of Two Critters* (1977), they are a bear cub and a raccoon, and so forth. in the classic model of wildlife film, narrative drives always override instinctual drives when the two come into conflict.

Indeed, these stories can often be seen as parables of suppressed instincts, extolling the values of community and brotherhood among the animals (an extension of the nuclear family structure) especially in times of crisis. Disney's films constantly constructed whole scenes in order to make the point visually: in *Perri*, a cataclysmic fire forces a skunk and a procupine to share a floating log that whisks them to safety together, while elsewhere a squirrel clings to the back of a bobcat as it fords the current. The lesson is that "hostilities" (technically not present in an actual predator/prey relationship) can be overcome, or suspended, when animals rationally face the necessity of banding together against a common peril. In the case of *The Bear*, that peril is embodied by armed human beings, making the unlikely partnership between the bears seem all the more necessary.

Still, a question remains regarding the mother's death: why kill off one adult guardian and companion only to replace it with another? Many wildlife films actually do center on the relationship of a mother and her young through the seasons, but the particular narrative pattern that characterizes *The Bear* (journey, trial, struggle, etc.) is more in the line of a *male* outdoor adventure, and make no mistake, despite a brief "love scene" between the male grizzly and a passing female, this is an all-male film. Also, as indicated earlier, much of the drama in these stories comes from seeing the family unit sundered, then mended or reconstituted through struggle, sacrifice, and *love*.

Yet there are other, more literary conventions at work in Curwood's story (which, reportedly, was drawn from personal experience). The fact is, for there to be a climactic confrontation with humans (an essential ingredient in the incredible journey narrative), the particular humans portrayed here need an adversary who is sufficiently deadly and menacing for them to prove themselves against. In such a scenario, there would be little enough glory in shooting a female in the first place, let alone one who is only defending her offspring. Yet the story demands that the mother be discarded nonetheless so that: (a) her cub is tutored in survival skills by an acknowledged "master" grizzly, one who shows supreme cunning and strength in "battle," and (b) so that the conflict with the human hunters can be played out as a traditional, primal struggle between warrior males.

At this point, Kaar, the huge grizzly (played by Bart, a seasoned film veteran), takes on some of the mythic, totemic proportions of Faulkner's "Old Ben," in his classic story also called *The Bear*. Indeed, Curwood's original title, *The Grizzly King*, clearly refers to the fearsome larger bear, while Annaud's retitled version centers on Youk, the cub. One reason for this is that Annaud has taken a story from a different genre and adapted it to meet the demands of wildlife film conventions. Though Curwood's bear-hunter character allows his prey to live in the end, the story up to that point falls into the same basic category as Faulkner's, as well as Walter Van Tilburg Clark's *Track of the Cat*. In these, the totem animal becomes an open symbol onto which characters project personal obsessions of mythical and metaphysical dimensions, but in the guise of a profound and abiding respect. Then they kill it. When an animal in western literature becomes "the god of the wilderness," it will usually be worshipped in a most destructive fashion. As Freud argued in *Totem and Taboo*, this death does not serve to demystify the victim, but only to elevate him to a higher level of symbolic (totemic) abstraction—and further misunderstanding. The deep respect the protagonists claim to have for their victims, and the dignity they pretend to accord them, achieve their apotheosis in ritual slaughter. Though Curwood's resolution (the hunter's humanitarian epiphany in the story's denouement) reverses this, as well as the traditional theme of the heroic conquest of nature, the novel remains essentially a drama of man against beast. Annaud's film, in focusing on the cub's coming-of-age experience, tells the story even less as a tale of masculine combat, and more as one of "education" in the wilds—for both the cub and the hunter. The parallel underscores Curwood's live-and-let-live theme, while the close-up drama of an animal's survival in nature remains in the tradition of Salten and, yes, Disney.

There have been other film-makers all along doing interesting things with the wildlife genre; Sweden's Arne Sucksdorff and Canda's Bill Mason come to mind, though, like the others, they have been largely unrecognized. There are also a number of structural variations in addition to the "classic" model of which *The Bear* is an example. It is, after all, but a small step from Annaud's film to Carroll Ballard's *Never Cry Wolf*, and from there into the cinematic mainstream. It is too early to tell if Annaud leaves the wildlife genre behind having brought it a new measure of respect; certainly he has left his indelibled mark on it, but whether this is enough to raise the general level of reception of these films from a vague apprehension to an enlightened appreciation remains to be seen. Ultimately, while *The Bear* is inescapably a genre film, Annaud is anything but a genre director, and no doubt his next work will be characteristically exploratory and provocative.

NOTES

[1] In his book *The Disney Films* (New York: Crown, 1973), Leonard Maltin unproblematically asserts that the theme and format of *Bambi* actually "*became the basis* for many of the True Life features" (p. 53—emphasis mine). Though having Maltin's word here is not the same as having Disney's, the mere possibility that *Bambi* was the "basis" for films both Disney and the Academy described as "documentary" may be a case of *True Life* imitating art. Reviewers were quick to pick up on at least the surface similarities to *Bambi*, et al. *Variety* (Oct 7, 1953), for example, described one of the ground squirrels in *the Living Desert* as "exhibiting all of the charm of a Disney cartoon character" (p. 6). *Time* (Nov. 16, 1953) described the film's strong points as "vitiated by cuteness. . .reducing the picture sometimes to the level of recent Donald Duck cartoons" (p. 108), while *Newsweek* (Nov. 23, 1954) also saw "a good deal of the cuteness to be expected from the Disney office" (p. 100). Bosley Crowther in the *New York Times* summed up the situation, saying simply that the Disney team was "inclined to do with nature pictures pretty much what they have always done with cartoons" (quoted in Maltin, 1973, p. 114).

[2] The entire quotation reads: "I think I will always be more inclined to film programs devoted to the life story of one particular animal. This is the classic format for wildlife films, and though I've never beeen reluctant to break the rules, it really is the most satisfying approach for a cinematographer." From his book, *Wild America* (New York: Times Books, 1988), p. 219.

[3] See, for example, Desmond Ryan, "Animal Magnetism," in *The Philadelphia Inquirer*, Oct. 29, 1989; also, Sean O'Gara, "The Bear" (review) in *The Animals' Agenda*, Dec. 1989, pp. 50–51.

LOS ANGELES TIMES, 10/25/89, Calendar/p. 1, Michael Wilmington

In a world squandering its natural resources and slaughtering its wildlife, we sometimes sentimentalize over the carnage. As we strip the land, we mourn its passing. As we kill off one species after another, we cluck, often impotently, over their destruction.

Remarkably, Jean-Jacques Annaud's new film, "The Bear," avoids most of these sentimental traps. Based on a 1916 children's book by the American naturalist James Oliver Curwood, it's the story of two bears—a fierce grizzly and a lovable cub—pursued implacably by two human hunters in the Canadian Rockies.

And though the outline of the movie's story—the cub Youk losing its mother in a landslide triggered by her addiction to honey, its introduction to the wounded grizzly Kaar and their shifting relationship with the relentless hunters—may suggest a male-bonding version of "Bambi," the material never gets weepy or cloying. Annaud and his collaborators charge it with a sweep and exhilaration startling for a family-oriented movie. You'd have to go back to the island section of Carroll Ballard's 1979 "The Black Stallion" to find something comparable.

Part of that exhilaration comes from the landscapes. Inspired by the paintings of Albert Bierstadt and Caspar Friedrich, Annaud shot much of "The Bear" in the Bavarian Alps, in a spectacular environment of 10,000-foot-high peaks, snowy slopes and pine forests. The cinematographer, the great color stylist Philippe Rousselot ("Diva," "The Emerald Forest"), bathes them in frosty, clear light, an almost glacial purity and depth.

Some of the exhilaration comes from the astonishing empathy the movie develops with and between the bears—partly, of course, through sheer trickery (the many dubbed yaps and yelps of adorable Youk), but also through staggering work by trainers Doug and Lynn Seus and Clint Youngreen. When you watch Youk waving goodby to some human friends, craning to get a better look and then slumping disconsolately to the ground, you never think of how he is being manipulated. The action and the shot have an almost magical rightness.

And much of the charge comes simply from the movie's philosophy, the reverence for life in the Curwood quote—"The greatest thrill is not to kill but to let live"—used as the epigraph. The film makers involve you with the animals, make you see the world through their eyes, romping with them, running fearfully or attacking in anger, mourning death or curling up gratefully together in the chilly darkness—even, in some surreal sequences, dreaming their dreams.

Equally, we get the viewpoint of the two hunters (Jack Wallace and Tcheky Karyo). These men aren't disembodied villains. Their pursuit of Kaar comes not through viciousness but vendetta and pride; they want to avenge the horses and dogs he has clawed or killed. He is also, for them both, a symbol of prowess and mystical strength, like the prey in Faulkner's "The Bear."

Kaar (played by the Montana-based Kodiak, Bart) becomes like the master warrior of a Kurosawa film. When he rubs his back magisterially against a swaying tree, it's a gesture of gaudy machismo not unlike Toshiro Mifune's shoulder twitch in "Yojimbo." By contrast, the gray, tender little Youk (played by the French cub, Douce) is an orphaned mite lost in a beautiful, threatening world, like the child protagonists of many European art films. He is the quintessential innocent, watching wide-eyed the sports and swaggering of Kaar.

Annaud has a taste for epic subjects. He is a flamboyant visual stylist who is drawn to vast or elemental stories: the World War I anti-war, anti-racist fable of "Black and White in Color"; the dawn-of-man picaresque of "Quest for Fire"; the medieval eschatological murder mystery of "The Name of the Rose." But Annaud doesn't treat these subjects solemnly. He makes grandiose images—and sometimes bizarrely baroque ones, like the shot of the moon from a bullet's-eye view in "The Bear." But there is also a humorous edge in his visuals, a childlike wonder, a witty relish in the absurd mechanisms of man viewed against the awesome unity of nature.

In "The Bear," he gets the "Once upon a time. . ." inflection of a good Spielberg or Disney picture, but it's steeped in hints of real horror or darkness. "Quest," "Rose" and "The Bear" were all written by Roman Polanski's regular scenarist, Gerard Brach—an agoraphobic who has not left his Parisian apartment in two decades—and the sense of entrapment, sexy absurdity or hip paranoia in his Polanski films isn't entirely absent here. (There's even some bear-faced voyeurism.) In a way, the Annaud-Brach movies are like those glass balls that contain immaculate little worlds. Despite the illusion of a limitless universe, they're confined, stylized, imprisoned.

These hints of bleakness don't dampen the joyous surge of the movie's climax. They heighten it. There has been a glut of animal movies in the last few years. But, of them all, "The Bear" (MPAA-rated PG, despite some violence and bear bawdiness)—sympathetically imagined, meticulously organized and grandly executed—is easily the period's epic. These movie makers want you to feel the thrill of life, of all life. At their best, they do.

MONTHLY FILM BULLETIN, 10/89, p. 295, John Pym

British Columbia, 1885. After the death of its mother, a brown bear cub sets off to make its way in the world. A hunter, Tom, wounds a large male bear in the shoulder; his companion, Bill, returns to civilisation to collect a pack of dogs. The cub tags after the male bear, which limps off into the wilderness, and is eventually permitted to lick its wound. Later, while the male mates with a female bear, the cub eats mushroom and is perplexed by a psychedelic dream. Bill returns with the dogs and their handler Joseph, and the hunt is resumed. Despite the male bear's attempt to lead the dogs away, the cub is captured and taken to the hunters' camp as a pet. Next morning, having bitten through its tether, the cub is found asleep on a bearskin. The hunters set an ambush for the male bear in a ravine. The tables are turned, however, when the creature corners Tom, who has put aside his rifle to quench his thirst. But the bear declines to kill its terrified prey. A little later, when Bill has the male bear in his sights, Tom philosophically pushes the rifle aside. The cub is returned to nature and the hunters go home. Having saved the cub from a puma, the male bear leads its charge to a cave for a long, untroubled winter sleep.

For Jean-Jacques Annaud's previous saga of elemental life, *Quest for Fire* (1981), Anthony

Burgess devised a "language" for the prehistoric hunter-gatherers who roamed the African plains. Here, a different sort of care has been taken with the soundtrack. The noises of the bears, from the first frenzied grunt of the mother as she digs for honey, to the heavy swish of a paw towards the head of cowering Tom, are rendered with striking vividness. The sounds of nature are as immediate as its sights; and it is not going too far to assert that the great male Kodiak bear—1,500 lbs, no natural enemies except man, slavering grey lower lip—is as mesmerically compelling in its own way as that other invincible cinematic loner, Spielberg's mechanical white shark.

Annaud, however, has an advantage: his bears are real, and although not wild, but painstakingly trained from birth, register thus on screen. (The preparation of the principals, two adult Kodiaks, a Kodiak cub and a male grizzly, the "female" mate, has been painstakingly recorded in Columbia TriStar's 79-page pressbook.) Animatronic models from the Henson workshop were sometimes necessary, chiefly for the violent scenes, though for the most part, in keeping with the moral that unnecessary killing is abhorrent, these occur decorously off-screen or in long shot. The seams are expertly hidden, and after a while most spectators, one imagines, will stop wondering if this or that bear is live. What they may question, though, is whether two fanciful dream sequences, realised with Czech animation, really reflect the workings of a bear cub's mind.

The Tyrol and the national parks of northern Italy stand in for the fastness of British Columbia; the effect, however, in almost every panoramic long shot, is of a virgin landscape in which bears, and all other wild creatures, are as scarce as human beings. The overwhelming feeling is one of loneliness. Tom, his more experienced companion having gone for the dogs, is terrified by the solitude of the night and takes pot shots at ominous shapes; the cub longs for companionship and, when captured, prefers to curl up on a comforting bearskin than to escape into the wilderess. *The Bear* carries a simple, timely message, knocked squarely and unapologetically home. It is handsomely photographed by Philippe Rousselot, battlehardened to tough location shoots through service on John Boorman's more mystical eco-saga *The Emerald Forest*. The human players, though essentially supernumerary, are suitably self-effacing; and, most importantly, the bears are allowed their natural dignity.

NEW STATESMAN & SOCIETY, 9/29/89, p. 41, Suzanne Moore

There are as many brands of nature these days as there are soap powder. You can have your nature Martin Amis style—raw, angry, terrifying, vengeful, full of shattered ozone layers and disasters waiting to happen. Or there is the sensible greeny model where nature is seen as exhausted, worn out, the poor old thing in need of a good rest to restore her innate balance and get her back on her feet. Or there is the sweet and cuddly version of nature, full of wide- eyed baby seals and caring voice-overs.

The Bear, this week's "epic film", fits the last category minus, thank God, the voice-over. Instead of a hyperventilating David Attenborough-style commentary we have real bear grunts, a marginal improvement and one that much impressed the French. *The Bear*, apparently a smash hit in France, outgrossed *Roger Rabbit* and is doing very well in every country it has reached.

It is, as you might have guessed, about bears, and the story line as summarised by the director is astonishingly simple: "A big solitary bear; an orphan bear cub; two hunters in the forest; the animals' point of view." And, for once, all the production notes that come with the film are a good read because, like so many of these kind of films, what happened during the shooting is often a damned sight more interesting than the film itself.

In the first instance, there was the problem of finding the bears—sorry, "animal actors"—and then getting them to perform for the camera. This apparently required dedicated trainers—sorry, "animal advisers"—prepared to commit themselves to such an enterprise. So what you end up with are bears that have been brought up in captivity having to be trained to *act* like wild bears in the wilderness.

Why anyone would spend years of his or her life wanting to do this is quite beyond me, but I guess I've never been a natural kind of woman. Jean-Jacques Annaud, the director, not only managed to put the whole thing together but, in the process, got mauled by one of his "stars". Klaus Kinski's squabbles with Herzog rather pale into insignificance when compared to Annaud's scarred backside.

The Bear is also unusual in that it has hardly any dialogue apart from dubbed animal noises. Annaud's previous film *Quest for Fire* shares this quality. Set in the palaeolithic era, it was done entirely in an ancient primitive language concocted by that ancient old primitive Anthony Burgess. Instead—and to his credit—Annaud makes the bears communicate with each other and with us through various looks and noises and manages to involve us in the story. The real nature in the film—fighting and killing scenes—is ironically done through animatronics à la Jim Henson of *The Muppets* fame.

Set in turn-of-the-century British Columbia (actually Austria and Switzerland) the scenery is fantastic and the range of emotions that Annaud elicits from his stars is often greater than that of their human counterparts. But the film lapsed too often into sentimental anthropomorphism to really work. The poor little orphaned cub is like a real-life cuddly toy and Annaud has sequences where it—sorry she—dreams about dear little frogs and things like that. Do bears dream in colour? It all became too much when the cub ate some hallucinogenic mushrooms and rolled around having a trip in the dewy grass. Bears are higher mammals, yes. They have certain emotions, yes. They re-enact scenes from Woodstock in their spare time? No.

Although Annaud does go beyond the Disneyesque, and the film comes stamped with approval from all sorts of wildlife authorities, *The Bear* falls prey to the myth that to touch an audience you have to show animals as more or less human. In order to care about bears we somehow have to believe that they are the same as us. Isn't it possible to care about an endangered species on the grounds that it is endangered rather than because it shares qualities we value? At one point the bear chooses not to kill an unarmed hunter, as though it has some sense of fair play.

It seems once again that we can't or won't accept the concept of difference. However much bears or monkeys remind us of ourselves, they are not human beings. That does not, however, give us the right to destroy them. As Julie Christie says in *The Animals Film*, how we treat animals tells us a lot about our relationship to each other.

By ascribing human qualities to *ursus arctos horribilis* (the grizzly bear), the film eventually tells us much more about our prejudices than it does about bears. This is especially apparent during the mating scene where ridiculous clichés are trotted out. The female bear seduced the male by supremely coquettish behaviour, and off they go into the bushes together where we hear orgasmic moaning, or at least the bear equivalent of it. And just in case you thought this film sounds a little too wholesome, you not only see a sex scene but a gay sex scene, as the bear plying the female is apparently "an incredibly effeminate male", according to the production notes.

What the hell is effeminate behaviour in a bear? At the end of the film a notice comes up which informs us that none of the animals has been mistreated and that some of the scenes have been simulated. You could say the same about some of the emotions.

NEW YORK, 10/30/89, p. 70, David Denby

I would like to be able to recommend *The Bear* as a movie that parents and children could see together, but I'm afraid there's a scene in the middle that would have to be...*explained*.

Directed by Jean-Jacques Annaud (*Quest for Fire, The Name of the Rose*), *The Bear* is about a young cub, in the British Columbia of the 1880s, who loses his mother in a rock slide, wanders alone for a while, and then takes up with a gigantic, roaring male (let's call him Big Bear). The huge old fighter and the tiny cub hunt together, help each other out of scrapes, lick each other's wounds, and evade two hunters who track them for days. Shot in the Bavarian Alps (doubling for Canada), *The Bear* is a satisfyingly emotional animal story, old-fashioned in construction yet modern in the way that it emphasizes the malevolence of men without softening the malevolence of nature. The movie steps over into the anthropomorphic rather more often than it should, but I'm far from being a purist in such matters. Give me an adorable cub swatting bees from his nose, and an old warrior fighting for honor, and I am perfectly happy.

The scene that would require explanation involves a female bear that Big Bear and the cub run into. Big Bear roars and pushes down a few trees and then takes the lady off aways, where they commence smooching rhythmically, leaving the cub to watch with his little head resting sadly on folded paws. Oh, dear. If you're a coward (like me) about confronting such things with the children, you have a problem. Perhaps it would be best to go out for Raisinets.

NEW YORK POST, 10/25/89, p. 31, David Edelstein

The opening of Jean-Jacques Annaud's "The Bear" inspires the kind of awe reserved exclusively for things non-human. A mother bear breaks open a beehive, scoops up the honey with her long, thin tongue and shares it with her cub, who laps greedily at the sweetness. For a few seconds, mother and child tongue each other happily.

Annaud makes these actions momentous. The texture of the bears' fur leaps out at you, and the sound—even the silence—seems amplified: The air is filled with buzzing; the bears swat at bees with heavy paws, in a motion that could be human but feels slurred, hallucinatory.

Despite this strangeness, the point of "The Bear" is that these animals are just like us and should not, therefore, be hunted for sport. (One could argue that even were they nothing at all like us they should not be hunted for sport.)

A huge hit in Europe and likely to be one here, "The Bear" turns into the agreeable story of a cute little cub whose mom gets squashed in a landslide. After some scary nights alone, the cuddly thing finally falls in with a huge kodiak, a mighty loner, and together they try to get away from the guys who shot Bambi's mom.

Based on the 1916 novel "The Grizzly King" by James Oliver Curwood, the movie's formula is recognizable: A little kid attaches himself to a grizzled, macho loner, who responds in spite of himself. Here the loner is a bit more grizzled than usual, but Bart (the bear's real name) is the Wallace Beery of quadrupeds; he's especially warmed when the li'l cub licks the blood off some ugly bullet wounds.

Curwood wrote the book to atone for years of bear hunting. He tells the story through the eyes of a grizzly called Thor, interrupting the narrative only for some flatfooted campfire discussions among the hunters. (One of them, a naturalist, comes to realize that nature is sacred.)

Annaud, who made the primeval epic "Quest for Fire," isn't interested in the hunters. He's into pre-verbal experiences. Last time, he showed us how ugga-wugga cavemen could at heart be as banal as we are; this time, he shows us how bears feel as we feel and love as we love and suffer as we suffer.

It's not a point worth disputing, but if bears do feel as we feel, etc., the way we organize our perceptions is vastly different. Part of the pleasure of watching wild animals is that they're not like us, that getting on their wavelengths is a challenge. Even then we never do completely—there are always mysteries.

There's no mystery about "The Bear," however: Translating the life of a bear into terms we can effortlessly understand diminishes it. What remains is a heartwarming cartoon with some texture and a powerful anti-hunting message, pretty much a Disney movie if you don't count the scene with two big bears noisily fornicating.

Annaud's style isn't expressive, but he and his excellent cinematographer, Philippe Rousselot, have a lot to work with. The bears, which can walk on hind legs and gesture with their arms, seem at once familiar and strange, huggable and terrifying.

There are marvelous images of them up on their haunches, noses in the air, listening and smelling for man and dogs. And when the kodiak angrily confronts a hunter, his neck seems to stretch to twice its length, his jaws stretching too as he roars and roars into the petrified human's face. You can almost smell the bear's breath.

"The Bear" also has its embarrassments, especially the scene where the little bear eats some odd-looking mushrooms and has what I'm convinced is the first bad acid trip ever taken by a movie bear.

Annaud thinks that by making films with non-verbal types he has done something radical, almost holy. But spoken language has never been paramount in cinema, and his storytelling is actually pretty simple-minded. Kids will love "The Bear," and grownups will find it more than, er, bearable. But it's an animal adventure without a sense of wonder. It's tame.

NEWSDAY, 10/25/89, Part 11/p. 5, Mike McGrady

French director Jean-Jacques Annaud is evidently a man of few words. In fact, the starting point for "The Bear" was a terse four-sentence note that he handed to producer Claude Berri in June, 1982. Annaud had just directed one dialogueless movie, the caveman epic "Quest For Fire," and his note outlined the plot for another film with little possibility of conversation: "An orphan bear cub. A big solitary bear. Two hunters in the forest. The animals' point of view."

Seven years—and $25 million—later, Annaud completed work on "The Bear," the most ambitious animal flick ever made, and his unique film set opening-day records across Europe, then went on to gross more than $100 million before arriving on these shores.

The story behind the making of "The Bear" is as fascinating as anything that appears on screen. Readying the 1,800-pound Bart for his starring role took four years (he was featured in such other movies as "The Great Outdoors" and "Clan of the Cave Bear"). Much of that training went in to teaching him to behave in bear-like fashion.

"The Bear" begins on a tragic note with a scene that will awaken "Bambi" memories. A mother bear and her cub, covered with bees, are breaking into a mountainside hive when the mother's efforts prompt a rock fall that does her in. The cub (Douce) attaches itself to a large male grizzly and the two are then tracked by hunters and Dobermans through the spectacular visual backdrops provided by the Bavarian Alps.

At times "The Bear" seems something of a cross between a Walt Disney fairy tale and a National Geographic nature study. Although I would imagine it might qualify as a four-star thriller for the impressionable, some of the grizzly scenes will be more than a little grisly for the very young. However, adults along for the ride should find the going painless.

The outline of the story may reveal its simple nature but it doesn't indicate the dramatic moments that have to be seen to be believed. And although the bears have been made more human than the humans (it's extremely unlikely a large male bear would ever "adopt" a cub), that doesn't dilute the effect of the film's most gripping scenes, especially the dramatic windup as the cub is being hunted and mauled by a mountain lion.

The humans on hand have little to do other than hunt. In fact, the three actors have a grand total of 657 words, almost all of them utilitarian. The director who makes do without dialogue must compensate with visual excitement and Annaud has done precisely that; the images that make up "The Bear" are absolutely amazing.

NEWSWEEK, 11/13/89, p. 92, David Ansen

What can you say about a movie that has about 10 minutes of dialogue and a star who weighs 2,000 pounds? If the movie is Jean-Jacques Annaud's *The Bear*, whose leading actors are a seriously adorable bear cub named Douce and a gigantic kodiak named Bart, you could say that this is a movie as difficult to classify as it is easy to enjoy. No wildlife documentary, this audacious movie is a fiction scripted, rehearsed and acted by a cast that includes three humans, four bears and a supporting team which includes a puma, a herd of deer, 10 Dobermans, an Airedale and assorted trout, frogs and bees. Annaud, who attempted in "Quest For Fire" (1981) to re-create the world of prehistoric man, here attempts to show us life from a bear's point of view. He even goes so far as to visualize their dreams. These reveries may be dubiously anthropomorphic—then again, who can say for sure? What is undeniable is that Annaud has pulled off a unique and enchanting film. Certainly no one has ever gotten such performances from this species before (or was crazy enough to try) and no small part of the film's fascination is wondering how on earth the filmmakers achieved these results.

Based on a 1916 novel, "The Grizzly King" by James Oliver Curwood and set in British Columbia in 1885 (though shot in the magnificent landscapes of northern Italy and the Austrian Tyrol), "The Bear's" story is simple, violent and sweet. Like many fables, it starts with an orphan. After the death of his mother, our cub hero ventures out into the world alone. Soon it has found a surrogate father, a huge wounded kodiak that has survived an ambush by trappers. The hunters (Jack Wallace and Tcheky Karyo), by no means evil men, are determined to finish the job, and send for dogs to aid in the chase. This hunt gives Gerard Brach's screenplay its form, but there's much more to the tale than a chase: this being an '80s movie, animal sex and even drugs enter the picture, when the cub nibbles on a psychedelic mushroom and trips out on the rather tacky animated vision of a flapping butterfly. In what may be the most astonishing scene, a puma, sleek and hungry, pursues Douce to a riverbank and out onto a log straddling the river, from which Douce plunges into the river to try to escape. It's a scene of peril that harkens back at least as far as D.W. Griffith, but you've never seen it enacted by a fourlegged cast.

Annaud's film is designed to evoke our reverence for an endangered species—it's a plea against killing wildlife—but it doesn't soft-pedal the carnivorous strength of the bear itself, which is capable of toppling a pine tree or feasting on a horse. Philippe Rousselot's superb cinematography captures nature's beauty as well as suggestions of its ferocity.

"The Bear" should not be ghettoized as a children's film, though kids will love it. Disarming as Douce is, there's more than cuteness here. And while Annaud (who was clawed in the buttocks by Bart during the shooting) deserves most of the credit for his perseverance and talent, it would be criminal to fail to mention the animal trainers, Doug Seus and Mark Wiener among others. They must be the Stanislavskys of their field. Just to teach Bart to walk with a limp took two years of effort. It seems safe to say that this is one hit—"The Bear" has already grossed $100 million in Europe—that will not have a sequel.

TIME, 10/30/89, p. 97, Richard Schickel

An orphan bear cub.
A big solitary bear.
Two hunters in the forest.
The animals' point of view.

That may be the shortest treatment in the history of the movies. It is surely one of the most truthful because, seven years and $25 million later, the four modest sentences that set this film in motion still accurately summarize *The Bear*. And, ironically, they send exactly the wrong signals to the sophisticated filmgoers who should be its most appreciative audience.

The outline could as well describe a nature documentary or even a children's picture—anyway, something bland, earnest or otherwise simpleminded. This is not to imply that *The Bear*, which is an adaptation by French filmmakers of a 1916 novel by the American outdoorsman James Oliver Curwood, lacks educational value. Or that children will not be charmed by the misadventures of its bouncy, cuddly hero. But the highest pleasures of this wondrous movie lie not in its apparently artless narrative but in the artful ways it transcends it.

The trick is quite simple to describe, ridiculously hard to execute. As director Annaud says, he and screenwriter Brach only placed their animals in very basic survival situations "in which a bear or a man would respond in the same ways." That is to say, by resorting to their common store of instincts: to fight or flee, to seek food, shelter, sex. The difficulties of capturing all this on film, using actors that are willful, dangerous and, of course, nonverbal, requires awesome patience and artifice, both on location and in postproduction. At the level of technique, *The Bear* is to other films about nature what *Star Wars* was to science-fiction movies: a redefinition of the state of the art.

But like George Lucas' film, *The Bear* works not because of the connections it makes with primal emotions. We form an instant attachment to a near helpless creature whose mother is killed by falling rocks. Nor can we entirely avoid anthropomorphizing the cub's attempts to survive on his own or to attach himself to a full-grown male as a protector-mentor. He is such a vulnerable little guy, infinitely curious and dangerously, comically distractible—whether by a passing butterfly or the moon's reflection in a pond.

Indeed, as humans, with a powerful sense of our own species' capacity for evil, we are more alarmed by the intrusion of hunters into the animals' territory than these creatures, guided by untutored instinct rather than bitter experience, can possibly be. We fear for the older bear's life as he does not; we imagine the degradations of captivity as the cub cannot. But these emotions are not imposed by the movie. There is almost no dialogue, no voice-over narration to cue audience response, and composer Philippe Sarde's lovely score is similarly discreet. This very pure picture entrusts all its meaning to images, and then trusts the audience to read them correctly.

VILLAGE VOICE, 10/31/89, p. 78, Georgia Brown

Bears need families too. Jean-Jacques (*Quest for Fire*) Annaud's $100 million-grossing *The Bear* takes the familiar Bambi tale into the mountains of British Columbia. (Whoops. Another ersatz location; the landscapes were shot in the Austrian Alps.) It's a film that's generated a number of production stories about the use of the creatures themselves—trained kodiak bears—as actors in a fictional story. Fans of PBS tooth-and-claw nature shows (like the wife in *The Documentator*) might be curious, but they'll miss that degree of authenticity. It's hard to watch *The Bear* without being continually aware of trick editing and camerawork. (Cinematography is by Philippe Rousselot, editing by Noelle Boisson. Jim Henson's studio also gets a credit.)

Annaud wastes no time getting into his story. Little Bear's mother dislodges a tree when going for a honey bee nest, and a rock ledge collapses on her head. (Not to worry; there's a disclaimer at the film's beginning: "No animal was mistreated during this film. Some scenes were simulated." The last is an understatement; in the sense of being staged and manipulated, all the movie's scenes are simulated.) Little Bear nuzzles up to her, but Mom doesn't budge. Meanwhile (ominous music), two white hunters arrive in the area, tracking a two-ton grizzly. The movie's 1885 time frame explains why their equipment is primitive and inefficient. They only wound the big one. Little Bear finds a father (syrupy score) and affectionately licks the big one's wounds. What follows are further confrontations with the hunters in which the daddy succeeds in instilling some respect and the little guy gets to mess up a camp site.

Although the cub, who dreams and free-associates, is played by a female, *The Bear* tells a familiar male coming-of-age story: The boy is forced to turn from Mom and discover Dad. (The hunters have a complementary father-son relation.) Annaud told a *Film Comment* interviewer that he wanted a John Wayne type for the big guy, and that he used an effeminate male—"a transvestite"—for the mother. Of course, you could tell the kids that the first bear is the daddy and the big one is Mom.

Which brings me to the question of audience. Who are those Europeans who flocked to *The Bear*, who will probably keep it and Luc Besson's *The Big Blue* playing Paris into the next century? I think sophisticated kids might find this one a bit cute. Under-sevens woulds probably get restless.

Also reviewed in:
NEW YORK TIMES, 10/25/89, p. C15, Janet Maslin
NEW YORKER, 11/13/89, p. 121, Pauline Kael
VARIETY, 10/26/88, p. 14
WASHINGTON POST, 10/28/89, p. C9, Rita Kempley

BERT RIGBY, YOU'RE A FOOL

A Warner Bros. release of a Lorimar Film Entertainment presentation of a Clear production. *Producer:* George Shapiro. *Director:* Carl Reiner. *Screenplay:* Carl Reiner. *Director of Photography:* Jan De Bont. *Editor:* Bud Molin. *Music:* Ralph Burns. *Music Editor:* Dan Garde. *Choreographer:* Larry Hyman. *Sound:* Joe Kenworthy and (music) Dennis S. Sands. *Sound Editor:* James J. Klinger. *Production Designer:* Terence Marsh. *Art Director:* Dianne Wager. *Set Decorator:* John Franco Jr. *Costumes:* Ruth Myers. *Make-up:* Wes Dawn and Greg LaCava. *Stunt Coordinator:* Victor Paul and Nick Gillard. *Running time:* 95 minutes. *MPAA Rating:* R.

CAST: Robert Lindsay (Bert Rigby); Anne Bancroft (Meredith Perlestein); Corbin Bernsen (Jim Shirley); Robbie Coltrane (Sid Trample); Cathryn Bradshaw (Laurel Pennington); Jackie Gayle (I. I. Perlestein); Bruno Kirby (Kyle DeForest); Liz Smith (Mrs, Rigby); Lila Kaye (Mrs. Pennington); Fanny Carby (Aunt Aggie); Carmen Du Sautoy (Tess Trample); Mike Grady (Mick O'Grady); George Wallace (Bartender); Frank Lugo (Latin Bar Patron); Santos Morales (Jesús); Mark Crowdy (Clyde); Liberty Mounten (Elvis Impersonator); George Malpas (Minister); Diana Weston (Young Mrs. Rigby); Sydney Laura Stevenson (Kelly Astaire Rigby); Robert Hines (Crown Royal Commercial Boy); Dominique Barnes (Crown Royal Commercial Girl); Slaughterhouse Five (Landed Gentry); Ian Hawks (Young Bert); Ken Eastwell (Bingo Master); Tubby Andrews, Bill Rogers, Roger Bingham, and Paul Butterworth (Bert's Mates); Michael Rice (Pianist); Alison Jane Frazer (Stewardess); Gela Nash (Mona); Ted Hayden (Martin); Israel Juarbe (Bellhop); Julie Ow (Cashier); Ben Ryan Ganger (Jim Shirley Jr.); Ernest (Ernie) W. Brown (Security Guard); Johnny Dark (Customer at Improv); Judy Nagy (Waitress at Improv); Anthony Mazzola (Bus Boy at Improv); Zoey Wilson (Miss Fogelson); Brad Rijn (Thief); Jordan Bennett (Director/Improv Customer); Harry Murphy and Murray MacLeod (Beer Distributors); Barbara Stamm and Monique August (Dinner Guests); Arsenio "Sonny" Trinidad (Oriental Gardener); Tomas Trujillo (Gang Leader; James Clark (Train Engineer); Andrea Lund (Artist's Model); Ron Barker (English Butler); Brenda Kristina Lee (Mail Carrier); Katie Graves and Mic Thompson (Joggers); Jude Van Wormer (Beverly Hills Dancing Lady).

FILMS IN REVIEW, 4/89, p. 234, Michael Buckley

Carl Reiner, so the story goes, was so impressed with Robert Lindsay's Tony Award winning performance in the Broadway musical/London import, *Me And My Girl* , that he vowed to make Lindsay a movie star. *Bert Rigby, You're a Fool* is Reiner's attempt and it fails. An end credit reads: "This film is lovingly dedicated to Gene Kelly." Fortunately, the star is not dead; unfortunately, by then, the movie (a long 90 minutes) has long since expired.

Reiner, who wrote and directed, has taken a rags-to-riches *Merton Of The Movies*-type plot and infused it with Lindsay's singing, dancing and comedy (including an embarrassingly bad capsule version of *Singin' In The Rain*) talents. However, as happens with some stage stars, Lindsay's appeal does not transfer to the screen.

This might have made a funny sketch for Sid Caesar on *Your Show Of Shows*, back when Reiner was one of its writers and performers; but, stretched to feature length, the material suffers. Reiner and another *Your Show* alumnus, Mel Brooks (both of whom seem to have senses of humor that permanently stalled during puberty) went on to perform together and make films separately. Herein, Reiner works with Mrs. Brooks, Anne Bancroft, but she is playing Madeline Kahn—right down to the lisp: "Oh, Mr. *Wigby*..."

The jokes probably seem funny on paper: "Let's do a fantasy dance number—but the girl is pregnant. See?" (Obviously, no one here saw *Funny Girl*.) A chauffeur is pointing out places in Beverly Hills to Rigby and says, "That's the street where Fred Astaire walked." Asks an excited Rigby: "In what film?" "Not in a movie. When he was alive, he loved to walk." (These are the jokes, folks!)

A non-bowed Lindsay has a scene where he promises himself: "Bert, you're not leaving Hollywood till you've kicked the s---out of it." Let's hope that Lindsay scores with his second movie (*Loser Takes All*, costarring Molly Ringwald) since neither he nor anyone else gets much of a kick out of this one.

LOS ANGELES TIMES, 2/24/89, Calendar/p. 8, Kevin Thomas

Watching "Bert Rigby, You're a Fool" you can understand how its English star, Robert Lindsay, was such a sensation on stage in the revival of the 50-year-old British musical, "Me and My Girl"—and how Carl Reiner could get sufficiently carried away when seeing him perform to write and direct this misfired movie especially for him.

Lindsay is an affable, old-fashioned song-and-dance man but lacks charisma on screen. (Mary Martin and Ethel Merman had the same problem.) Not that he gets much help from Reiner, who encourages him to strive to please so endlessly that he becomes tiresome and bland. Lindsay's repeated homages to Fred Astaire and Gene Kelly end up underlining the inimitableness of the originals. (His Chaplin and Keaton are far crisper.) "Bert Rigby, You're a Fool" overdoses on nostalgia.

You know that you're in vintage musical comedy fantasy land when Rigby, a naive North of England coal miner dreaming of music hall stardom, emerges at the end of the day from the colliery performing "The Continental" and his fellow miners don't think he's out of his mind. Chance and a labor strike take him to Hollywood to do a Keaton routine for a jogging shoe commercial (easily the best thing in the film), but he's soon met with a struggle for survival rather than the promised fame and fortune.

At this point the innocuous slides into the tedious, especially when Bert encounters Anne Bancroft, the least likely woman ever to have been a dancer in "Royal Wedding" and "Silk Stockings." Bancroft seems to be giving us her impression of Marilyn Monroe, had Monroe lived to a sexually predatory middle age, married a crass studio mogul (the late Jackie Gayle) and somehow acquired Kay Francis' well-known problem in pronouncing *r*. The total effect is simply appalling. More on target are Corbin Bernsen with his relaxed portrayal of an amiably caddish big star to whom Bert teaches a North of England accent and Robbie Coltrane as Bert's shamelessly ruthless English manager. Cathryn Bradshaw is Rigby's pert childhood sweetheart, wondering when he'll ever return home.

Most everyone professes a longing for the return of the musical, but "Bert Rigby, You're a Fool" (rated R for crude language, much of it needless) and the more vital "Tap," both of which should have been set no later than the '50s, reveal how badly the form needs to be brought up to date.

MONTHLY FILM BULLETIN, 12/89, p. 358, John Pym

Bert Rigby, down and out in Hollywood, tells his story to a barfly... With his fellow coalminers of Langmoor in the North of England about to strike, Bert grasps an opportunity to fulfil his dream of reopening the town's defunct cinema by making his fortune as a song-and-dance man. To the dismay of his sweetheart Laurel, he joins Sid Trample's Original Travelling Amateur Show, as the tame amateur who beats all comers with his fluffed rendering of "Isn't It Romantic". Spotted by American director Kyle DeForest, Bert is whisked to California with his "agent" Sid to play Buster Keaton in a running-shoe advertisement. A promised contract evaporates, however, and Sid disappears leaving Bert with their bills. Bert becomes handyman to lascivious Meredith Perlestein and subsequently "Northern" dialogue coach to Jim Shirley, the star of I.I. Perlestein's latest picture. Out for the day with Jim's small son, Bert inadvertently foils a stick-up at an art gallery. Later, however, he ruins his chances of a career in the movies by refusing to sleep with Mrs. Perlestein (Laurel is pregnant) and accidentally setting fire to Mr. Perlestein's newly acquired

Van Gogh...In the bar, Bert goes into a song-and-dance routine in praise of Old Peculiar, his favourite beer. Two ad-men promptly sign him up. Nine months later, with Laurel and their baby in the audience, Bert hosts the glittering reopening of the Langmoor Ritz.

Devised as a vehicle for Robert Lindsay, the modest star of the musical *Me and My Girl*, an immensely successful transfer from the West End to Broadway, *Bert Rigby, You're a Fool* mixes sentimentality with vulgarity with reckless abandon. One strength of writer-director Carl Reiner, demonstrated with effect in "The 2,000-Year-Old Man" recordings, in which he played the straight man to Mel Brooks' Methuselah, was an ability to pass off the preposterous as the commonplace. Here, however, it is hard to accept that a bomb-shelter separating two back gardens would be the cosy trysting spot of Bert and Laurel; or that director Kyle DeForest would really be putting a couple, dressed as Tudor noblefolk, through a contraceptive advertisement (he seeks solace from this fiasco in a night out at Sid's show...). The preposterous in this instance simply registers as carelessness.

Lindsay himself is an agreeable, open actor, an accomplished dancer with a pleasant voice and a gift for restrained mimicry. One of his chief assets, it seems, is an ability to sing *and* dance simultaneously without the post-synching showing. The film is "lovingly dedicated" to Gene Kelly; and Lindsay does possess a modest measure of the great star's charm, but the vehicle in which he finds himself is a hotch-potch lacking the essential fluidity which carries an audience over the time-honoured improbabilities. Robbie Coltrane, as Sid Trample, and Anne Bancroft, as Mrs. Perlestein, vigorously impose themselves on character roles as old as Chaplin's boots, and in the process effectively smother the star. Only Cathryn Bradshaw, as the pretty, forbearing Laurel seems really in tune with what should have been the innocent tone of the proceedings. For the rest, this slapped-together homage attempts to get by on that brand of archness which has already worn more than a little thin in Carl Reiner's old partner, the indefatigable Mel Brooks.

NEW YORK, 3/20/89, p. 75, David Denby

Carl Reiner's *Bert Rigby, You're a Fool* is a sweet, sad pass at the musical Reiner can only dream about making, but Robert Lindsay is charming.

NEW YORK POST, 2/24/89, p. 23, Jami Bernard

British actor Robert Lindsay has the kind of talent that would have made him a firecracker back in the days of the Hollywood musical: he's lithe, charming, can sing and dance and twirl a cane and bobble a straw hat atop his head. The only other place that has much use for that kind of thing is the occasional Broadway musical, such as "Me and My Girl."

Carl Reiner, whose face is carved into the Mount Rushmore of comedy, took in "Me and My Girl" one night, was duly impressed and decided that Robert Lindsay was the kind of rare bird for whom a movie ought to be written.

He was probably right. But the resulting "Bert Rigby, You're a Fool," written and directed by Reiner, is not that movie. It is a sad, directionless, listless thing, whose reverential production numbers come off as rather pedestrian.

It does not appear to be Lindsay's fault. He gives the role of Bert Rigby, the fool of the title, all the gusto of a make-or-break audition. But that's just not enough to save the picture.

Bert Rigby is a happy-go-lucky coal miner (now, *there's* a concept) in a depressed town in northern England. He enlivens the workday with renditions of "The Continental," hopping about the mineshaft in his orange uniform, his pith helmet at a rakish angle. He's perfectly happy dating the curly-headed, sweet-faced girl next door (Cathryn Bradshaw), and his life's ambition is to amass enough money to reopen the town's one movie theater, which has been reduced to a Bingo hall.

A coal miners' strike coincides with Bert winning a traveling amateur show, where his *hommage* to the old movie musicals is mistaken for comedy because he performs it during a nosebleed. The sleazy stage manager (Robbie Coltrane) hires Bert as a permanent "amateur" whose job it is to win each night and thus save the manager from paying out the prize money.

Producers, directors and other influential people are constantly scouting Rigby—in fact, he makes it as far as Hollywood, but his career mostly consists of odd menial jobs. Meanwhile, the girl he left behind is pregnant and lonely.

All this is presented in flashback as Bert, down to his last shilling, spills his guts to a fellow barfly.

Along the way, Robert Lindsay gets to break into song a lot, including a rendition of "Singin' in the Rain" with a bottle of seltzer as part of a near-hysterical (and I don't mean that in the sense of "funny") show-tune medley. The musical numbers are uninspired and have a cluttered look.

Also along the way, Bert meets some "zany" characters, including bizarre older women who try to seduce him. One of these is played by an offensively mugging Anne Bancroft.

The worst sin (aside from the cumbersome title) is that "Bert Rigby" is just not funny. Many scenes drift aimlessly until some after-thought narration brings them mercifully to a sheepish close. Neither is it dramatically gratifying: Bert's transition from pizza-boy to movie dialect coach (for Corbin Bernsen as a spoiled actor) is circuitous and uninvolving.

Sure, everyone misses those grand old musicals. But this production, as devoted as it is to musicals past, is joyless and does not have enough irony to carry off a tacky dream-dance sequence between Bert and his very pregnant girlfriend.

Astaire danced for the love of the dance, and often for the love of a girl. Bert Rigby's driving force is for money, pure and simple, and very '80s. If musicals are escapist fare, this one doesn't take you very far.

NEWSDAY, 2/24/89, Part III/p. 5, Lynn Darling

Watching the talented Robert Lindsay singing "The Continental" while dancing through an English coal mine raises interesting expectations—"Bert Rigby, You're a Fool" looks as if it might be making use of the sort of musical dislocation that worked so effectively in Dennis Potter's "Pennies From Heaven" and "The Singing Detective."

But no such luck. Instead director Carl Reiner serves up a harmless homage to the musical entertainments of yesteryear, where plot and character are merely excuses for a lot of musical numbers, or at least for fragments of a lot of musical numbers. The result is a hybrid movie, committed neither to the story it's telling nor to the music it's honoring.

"Bert Rigby" is an innocent's odyssey through the sharpsters and comic weirdness of the world of show business, as seen through a lens of gauzy nostalgia and deliberate naivete. The title character (Robert Lindsay) is a happy-go-lucky coal miner stuck, quite comfortably, it appears, in the fantasies that fired his mother's generation; he worships Gene Kelly and Fred Astaire and the other stars of a vanished era.

When he wins an amateur talent contest and is invited by the manager to take his act on the road, he gets big ideas: He's going to make enough money to buy the broken-down, old movie theater in his dying hometwon and return it to the glorious palace of dreams it had been in his childhood.

His plans go awry, of course. Before long he's stranded in Hollywood, prey to the machinations of his agent (Robbie Coltrane), a handsome movie star (Corbin Bernsen) and the predatory wife (Anne Bancroft) of a millionaire movie mogul, while back home his sweetheart (Cathryn Bradshaw) waits for him none too patiently. Reiner, who also wrote the script, left his wit in the same closet where he found the originals of these all-too-stock characters.

The movie is "lovingly dedicated to Gene Kelly," and Rigby's adventures are punctuated throughout by lots of opportunities to showcase Lindsay doing his imitations of both Kelly and Astaire. He does them very well, though he's never in danger of upstaging the memory of his mentors. Curiously, the musical numbers aren't given much room to shine; they're presented in bits and pieces before a camera that pays only distracted attention to the action taking place before it.

TIME, 2/27/89, 83, Richard Schickel

Show business having turned into a vast antechamber for the Betty Ford Center, one has to have a certain sympathy for Bert Rigby (Robert Lindsay), whose career is founded on nothing more complicated or newsworthy than a nosebleed.

In Carl Reiner's funny fable about an English coal miner's search for fame and fortune, Bert suffers this affliction as he sings and dances *Isn't It Romantic?* in an amateur-night competition. Since the attempt to cope with it and finish his number is both hilarious and heartwarming, Bert wins the contest. Next he is hired by the show's corrupt promoter to tour as a perpetual competitor, getting paid only if he beats the authentic contestants. This he can do only by faking the bloody nose night after night.

Being an honest chap, with a genuine passion for the great show-biz tunes and turns, Bert finally rebels against this demeaning chicanery. The reward for his pains: a trip to Hollywood and a chance to discover that its streets are paved with poseurs, among whom lurks a comically glorious Anne Bancroft, playing a randy Beverly Hills princess.

Will Bert somehow succeed in his quest for stardom? Yes. In a nice manageable sort of way. As his autobiographical *Enter Laughing* shows, Reiner has always believed that show biz is a circle more charmed than vicious, that its most characteristic derangement is a sort of addled innocence. In Lindsay, star of the London-Broadway hit *Me and My Girl*, Reiner has found a perfect, gently insinuating instrument. Together they have created a sweet anachronistic counterpoint to the depressing hubbub of today's celebrity world.

VILLAGE VOICE, 3/7/89, p. 64, Bruce Handy

The musical *Me and My Girl* made Robert Lindsay a star on Broadway—but not enough of a star to carry the film *Bert Rigby, You're a Fool*, which, unfortunately, is predicated upon the English song-and-dance man's ability to do song and dance. Writer/director Carl Reiner is so enamored of Lindsay's charms that he seems to have designed the movie as a testament. Inevitably, it comes to feel like one continuous, long-winded exhortation: "You're gonna love this guy!" it assures us over and over again with its adoring, lapdoggish direction, with its endless scenes of Lindsay winning over hardhearted audiences on screen. Most of us, however, will require more convincing.

The script has Lindsay as the eponymous hero, a dim, sweet-natured coal miner from a depressed town in Northern England. Bert Rigby lives for old movies and can't seem to pass a lightpole without breaking into a number from *Singin' in the Rain*. Hey—this is a guy who's got a song in his heart, a dance in his feet, and a straw boater on his head that's just gotta be cocked. Through a series of uninteresting and, needless to say, implausible plot turns, he finds himself in Hollywood. (Along the way, Anne Bancroft turns up in her familiar, humiliating role as the vain, horny old JAP—this time with a breathy, little-girl voice that makes her sound like a nightmare hybrid of Mia Farrow and Great Neck.)

I never saw *Me and My Girl*, so I can't say I know what Lindsay has to offer beyond what he offers here, where he's made to recreate a number of Fred Astaire and Gene Kelly routines, mock up an imitation Buster Keaton sequence, and romp through some hoary music-hall choreography. An athletic dancer and a seemingly able clown (at least when Reiner's clumsily placed cameras allow you to get a decent look at him), Lindsay moves with swing and grace all well as vigor, but *Bert Rigby*'s borrowed steps and styles look as if they've been forced on him; they don't quite fit— indeed, why should they? And as you get accustomed to him, Lindsay starts to look cramped, constricted, as if he's wearing his shoes and underwear a size or two or three too snug. Despite his best intentions, Reiner in effect sabotages Lindsay's showcase.

Also reviewed in:
NEW YORK TIMES, 2/24/89, p. C17, Janet Maslin
VARIETY, 3/1–7/89, p. 20
WASHINGTON POST, 4/22/89, p. C3, Rita Kempley

BEST OF THE BEST, THE

A Taurus Entertainment release. *Executive Producer:* Michael Holzman and Frank Giustra. *Producer:* Phillip Rhee and Peter E. Strauss. *Director:* Bob Radler. *Screenplay:* Paul Levine. *Story:* Phillip Rhee and Paul Levine. *Director of Photography:* Doug Ryan. *Editor:* William Hoy. *Music:* Paul Gilman. *Production Designer:* Kim Rees. *Running time:* 95 minutes. *MPAA Rating:* PG-13.

CAST: Eric Roberts (Alex); James Earl Jones (Coach Couzo); Sally Kirkland (Wade); Phillip Rhee (Tommy); Christopher Penn (Travis); John Dye (Virgil); David Agresta (Sonny); Tom Everett (Don); Louise Fletcher (Mrs. Grady); John P. Ryan (Jennings).

LOS ANGELES TIMES, 11/10/89, Calendar/p. 15, Kevin Thomas

"Best of the Best" is a by-the-numbers martial-arts movie graced by several celebrated actors marking time between more rewarding assignments and crowned by an appallingly brutal Tae Kwan Do competition. There's nothing here except for karate fanatics.

The title refers to five young men recruited for the U.S. Karate Team by its coach (James Earl Jones) to take on the world champion South Korean team. The U.S. athletes are played by Eric Roberts, Phillip Rhee (who wrote the film's story with screenwriter Paul Levine), Christopher Penn, John Dye and David Agresta, and none of their characters are interesting or individual enough to warrant description.

After predictable friction, they shape up under the fire-breathing Jones and trainer Sally Kirkland, an expert on Eastern philosophies who is to sharpen their concentration. Kirkland has her work cut out for her as we see flashes of just how rugged the training of the South Koreans is. (Why are the Americans eating junk food? Why are they frequenting a roadhouse, except as a pretext for them to show their stuff in a barroom brawl?)

The film's familiar names, which include Louise Fletcher as Roberts' concerned mother, all acquit themselves as well as doggedly trite material and Bob Radler's uninspired direction permit. Cast as a karate champ making a comeback three years after suffering a shoulder injury, Roberts works up an impassioned determination that helps breathe some life into the film. Kirkland has never looked so attractive on the screen, but even this canniest, most distinctive of actresses cannot help but draw unintended laughter when she's required to exclaim to Roberts, after his shoulder is severely damaged a second time and he's floundering about in bloody, unspeakable agony, "Put your mind somewhere else! There is no pain!"

Considering its brutality, "Best of the Best's" PG-13 rating seems lenient.

NEW YORK POST, 11/11/89, p. 17, V. A. Musetto

Take the worst plot devices of "Rocky" and "The Karate Kid." Throw in some talented actors—Eric Roberts, James Earl Jones and Sally Kirkland—and give them nothing to do but look befuddled. Result: a simplistic, predictable and boring movie called "Best of the Best."

Jones is the bellowing, win-at-any-cost coach of the official U.S. karate team, which is training for a big match against a bunch of sinister looking South Koreans. "You will eat, sleep and s--- competition," Jones warns his guys.

And what a bunch they are. If ever a set of characters had just come from central casting, it's this huffing-and-puffing crew: the widower with a 5-year-old son and a gimpy arm (Roberts), the belligerent wise guy (a too-fat Christopher Penn), the quiet brain named Virgil (John Dye), the Detroit street kid named Sonny (David Agresta) and, of course, the troubled young man (Phillip Rhee) who has a grudge to settle with the Korean fighter who killed his brother in a match.

And then there's Kirkland, who turns up as an assistant trainer who "studied Eastern philosophy all my life" and quotes Vince Lombardi in pep talks. As far as I can see, the character's sole purpose is to allow the camera to linger over Kirkland's long and lean legs, which she displays in short, tight skirts more suited to streetwalking than sports training.

First-time director Bob Radler and writer Paul Levine leave no cliche unturned. The boys spend their "last night out" before training starts at a honky-tonk bar full of rednecks and wanton women. Don't you just know that there's going to be a big brawl. And don't you just know the karate kids are going to wipe the floor with the locals then walk away as if nothing had happened.

Roberts' son is hospitalized in a coma after he's hit by a car. Don't you just know that Daddy is going to rush to his side and almost miss going to Korea. And don't you just know that the boy is going to miraculously pull through and—even more miraculously—show up just a few days later in Seoul to cheer on the U.S. team. (Judging by the badly done intercutting, his presence was an afterthought on the part of the movie makers.)

The training scenes—lots of grimacing faces and sweating bodies—are nothing you haven't seen before. Worse, the shots of the Koreans going through *their* paces remind you of the racist stereotypes that '40s Hollywood employed to portray the Japanese in World War II movies.

Only in its bloody finale—the big match—does "Best of the Best" attempt to break away from the tried and true. But instead of being uplifting, as intended, the sequence comes off as mawkish, laughable—and just plain dumb.

NEWSDAY, 11/11/89, Part II/p. 17, Bill Kaufman

Seems just about the only martial arts expert missing from "Best of the Best," a predictable karate film, is Chuck Norris.

However unlike most kung-fu epics and martial arts pictures, in this film the theme is not good guys against bad guys, but good guys against their own character flaws. Here, five handchosen athletes—each representing a different ethnic cliché—arrive at a training camp for three months of preparation for world class competition in Korea, and coach Frank Couzo (James Earl Jones) starts the standard army-movie discipline process. He tells them there will be no women, no alcohol and no drugs for the duration. Then comes the standard locker room lecture on team spirit. Last night on the town, of course, features a bar brawl and some tacky pick-up banter.

The five karate contenders display increasingly dismal personal problems. There's Alex Grady (Eric Roberts), a long-haired widower with a young son; and Travis (Christopher Penn), a loud-mouthed bully. As the hard-driving coach, Jones comes across like a weak caricature. But the movie's most ludicrous part went to Sally Kirkland, who manages only to look like a primping fashion model in mini-skirts. In a laughable piece of scripting, Kirkland plays a consultant hired to use meditation and eastern philosphy techniques to sharpen the team's concentration.

About the only thing "Best of the Best" has going for it is an abundance of elaborately choreographed karate sequences accompanied by appropriate bodycrunching sound effects.

Also reviewed in:
NEW YORK TIMES, 11/11/89, p. 16, Stephen Holden
VARIETY, 11/8/89, p. 34

BIG PICTURE, THE

A Columbia Pictures release of an Aspen Film Society production. *Executive Producer:* William E. McEuen and Richard Gilbert Abramson. *Producer:* Michael Varhol. *Director:* Christopher Guest. *Screenplay:* Michael Varhol, Christopher Guest, and Michael McKean. *Director of Photography:* Jeff Jur. *Editor:* Martin Nicholson. *Music:* David Nichtern. *Music Editor:* Sally Boldt. *Sound:* Jon Huck and (music) Dennis S. Sands. *Sound Editor:* Dody Dorn and Blake Leyh. *Production Designer:* Joseph T. Garrity. *Art Director:* Patrick Tagliaferro. *Set Decorator:* Jerie Kelter. *Set Dresser:* Richard A. Frisch, G. Roger Abell, and Michael George Miller. *Special Effects:* Gary P. D'Amico. *Costumes:* Karen Patch. *Make-up:* Lizbeth Williamson. *Stunt Coordinator:* Richard Lundin. *Running time:* 100 minutes. *MPAA Rating:* PG-13

CAST: Kevin Bacon (Nick Chapman); Martin Short (Nick's Agent); Emily Longstreth (Susan Rawlings); J.T. Walsh (Allen Habel); Jennifer Jason Leigh (Lydia Johnson); Michael McKean (Emmet Sumner); Kim Miyori (Jenny Sumner); Teri Hatcher (Gretchen); Dan Schneider (Jonathan Tristan-Bennet); Jason Gould (Carl Manknik); Tracy Brooks Swope (Lori Pressman); Don Franklin (Todd Marvin); Gary Kroeger (Mark); Alice Hirson (Mrs. Chapman); Grant Owens (Mr. Chapman); Fran Drescher (Polo Habel); Suzy Cote (Mindy Habel); Eddie Albert Sr. (M.C.); June Lockhart (Janet Kingsley); Stephen Collins (Attorney); Roddy McDowall (Judge); Robert Bauer (Wounded Soldier); Vladimir Skomarovsky (Man in Nick's Movie); C.W. Hemingway (Joey); Holly Fields (Daughter); Yvonne Peattie (Mrs. Feldzar); Stan Ivar (Charlie); David Hayward (George); Caitlin Clarke (Sharon); Nancy Valen (Young Sharon); Wesley Pfenning (Woman in Cabin); John Cleese (Bartender); Richard Blake (Abe Lincoln); Walter Olkewicz (Babe Ruth); T. Scott Coffey (Waiter); Bruce Kirby (Businessman); Richard Belzer (Video Show Host); Tom Maier (Building Manager); Scott Williamson (Restaurant Manager); Victor Steinbach (Andres Vargiak); Arlene Lorre (Cleopatra); George Rogan (Security Guard/Nazi); Perla Walter (Housekeeper); Pamela Morris (Cheryl); Lulie Newcomb (Receptionist); Patty Howeth (Woman with Fridge); Brad Zutaut (Surfer); Matthew Eichler (Piano Player); Nadine Lenore Patterson (Twin).

LOS ANGELES TIMES, 9/15/89, Calendar/p. 8, Michael Wilmington

"The Big Picture" is an attempted satire on the banalities and venalities of Hollywood that turns into a kind of celebrity roast. Somehow, the jokesters and their target get promiscuously intertwined.

This is supposedly a movie about idealistic film makers trapped in the Hollywood system. Yet it looks like a standard '80s sell-out comedy, full of lame dialogue, guest stars and shticky gags, with a young hero seduced away from his steadfast girlfriend by the daffy, goofy, corrupt Establishment—and then finding himself, and integrity, in time for the rock song under the closing credits.

This attack on compromise—in which Nick Chapman (Kevin Bacon), a student-film prize winner, is wooed and dumped by the dream factory—looks like all the other rib-digging sex-and-success comedies: the end result of the same marketing-research, cookie-cutter methods it's trying to spoof. It's as if a film maker wanted to make a satire about a young genius trying to make another "Persona" inside the Hollywood system, and being forced to turn it into "Beach Blanket Bingo"—and then somebody decided to play it safe by sticking in sex and beaches and shooting it in the style of "National Lampoon's Vacation."

Writer-director Christopher Guest blows his wad early. He and his hip cinematographer, Jeff Jur ("Dirty Dancing"), stage a student film awards banquet with four amusing parodies of typical student films. This scene, emceed by Eddie Albert, is clever but no gem. And, if it weren't for later appearances by Martin Short (unbilled) as an effete agent and J.T. Walsh and Don Franklin as a bland exec and his crafty secretary, it would be the best the movie has to offer.

"The Big Picture" has the same flaws as most student films. It's underwritten and overdirected. the laborious, one-note gags include old movie parodies of Bogart, "Psycho" and "The Lost Weekend," opulent parties with starlets who ditch you when you're down, funny fat snobs, rock videos and swishy agents. Guest, who has wonderful delayed comic timing when he acts, delays the timing too much here: The whole picture seems sapped.

Scriptwriters Guest and Michael McKean ("This Is Spinal Tap") and Michael Varhol ("Pee-wee's Big Adventure") have amusing credits; McKean also doubles as a lovable buddy cinematographer. But their dialogue here has the monomaniacally spare quality of the average '80s studio screenplay, as if the speeches were being held under seven to 10 words apiece to keep readers from eye-strain. The few observant bits of Hollywood jargon ("Call my secretary and I'll call you back") rattle around like manufactured bon mots in a sea of tinseled blather.

What can you say about a Hollywood satire whose idea of mordant humor is to make fun of Chuck Barris and "The Gong Show"? One of the gags in the film is that Nick reshapes his rigorous Bergmanesque drama into a jiggle movie called "Beach Nuts." But "The Big Picture" doesn't look much different from "Beach Nuts"—which might have been a movie about a lifeguard with integrity who defies the daffy, goofy, corrupt parks administration.

Guest's heart is in the right place. But "The Big Picture" (MPAA-rated PG-13) is closer to a jiggle movie than to a truly trenchant Hollywood satire like Preston Sturges' "Sullivan's Travels" or Ben Hecht's "Woman of Sin." And, as for the brilliant personal drama that Chapman wants to shoot: It looks pretty terrible, too—as if Nick were trying to remake "The Passion of Anna" on a set built for a Frosty the Snowman commercial. If you're going to mock commercialism and stand up for art, you'd better make sure you know the difference between them.

NEW YORK, 9/25/89, p. 130, David Denby

There are three great performances in Christopher Guest's spoof of contemporary Hollywood, *The Big Picture.* As a blandly dominating studio boss with awful ideas for movies, J.T. Walsh has pleasant terrible eyes, and Fran Drescher, in a bit part, is extremely funny as Walsh's nasal, up-from-Brooklyn wife, Polo, with her exposed midriff and her happy admission to a stranger, "You know how much this house cost? 4.6 mil." And the brilliant Martin Short outdoes himself as an insinuatingly effete, coked-up agent, all hands and mouth, devouring, hysterical, ghoulish, with a fabulous false candor, each manipulative remark prefaced by "I wouldn't want to bullshit you, but. . . ."

Despite other nifty bits of malice, satirist Guest, directing for the first time, has only minimal dramatic abilities—enough for skits but not enough, really, to make a full-length movie. The story that holds the movie together is a bummer. Nick Chapman (Kevin Bacon) is a student filmmaker who suddenly becomes hot. On the basis of one little film, everyone in Hollywood starts talking about him, everyone wants him, and just as suddenly he's dropped and forgotten. Such things happen every year, but Nick Chapman has no substance; he's just a nice, sheepish kid, without any apparent talent, who becomes a jerk when everyone fusses over him. Guest, Michael Varhol, and Michael McKean, who worked together on the screenplay, clearly wanted to show how innocence can be corrupted, but their trashing of their own hero destroys any emotional interest in the story. A young artist who fights for something worth believing in would be someone to care about. But who cares about a patsy?

NEW YORK POST, 9/15/89, p. 23, David Edelstein

Christopher Guest, the writer and director of the satirical Hollywood comedy "The Big

Picture," has a gift for getting into the heads of the people he skewers: He doesn't stop at their mannerisms or wardrobe, he works his way down to their most primal insecurities.

Taking on the sycophants and studio heads and poseurs who populate Tinseltown, Guest (a marvelous actor) understands the pressures to adopt a strong style whether you have one instinctively or not. And so even his broadest caricatures are laced with a kind of sympathy. Which makes them funnier.

"The Big Picture" is Guest's first shot at directing (he co-wrote "This Is Spinal Tap") and it's a more than respectable debut—it may, in fact be too respectable. The movie is crammed with brilliant caricatures and riffs, but as a performer he's missed, and to enjoy the film you have to overlook the draggy morality-play structure.

Guest tells the story of the rise and corruption and fall and redemption of a hot-shot film-school graduate, Nick Chapman (Kevin Bacon). The winner of a prize for a broad, expressionistic short about a first date, Nick is approached by studio head Allen Habel (J.T. Walsh), who offers him a juicy development deal.

Immediately Nick is set upon by agents, ambitious starlets and sundry hangers-on, all of whom know exactly which part of him to stroke. In no time, he has moved out on his sweet, simple girlfriend (Emily Longstreth), blown off his cinematographer buddy (cowriter Michael McKean) and leased himself a fancy car.

"The Big Picture" is about selling out big: Nick abandons his vision because the studio says audiences like movies with teen-agers instead of adults (a somewhat dated idea now, as we witness the rebirth of sincere movies for grown-ups). Once he's immersed in the lifestyle, the women and the competitive atmosphere, Nick's only concern is for status.

The problem is that Nick himself is a cipher, and the movie he wants to make sounds so frozen and pretentious that I kept hoping he's meet up with some Roger Corman type who'd set him straight. Integrity doesn't mean much when it's this bland and generalized; the movie's frame is so insipid that Guest appears to have knuckled under to the very forces he's satirizing.

The glory of "The Big Picture" is its parade of outrageous caricatures, all of them grounded in observation. Jennifer Jason Leigh is sublimely kooky as a performance artist and Fran Drescher, as Mrs. Habel, restores the Jewish American princess to gaudy respectability: There's no artifice here, she's *genuinely* tacky.

After his non-performance as Bob Woodward in "Wired," J.T. Walsh comes back with a beaut. His Habel is a man with no taste and no intelligence making profound decisions about works of art—every ponderous, idiot whim becomes carved in stone (or celluloid). Ensconced in his ridiculous office (with its Southwestern motif), he's equipped with a sleek yes-man named Todd (Don Franklin); Guest and Franklin wisely make Todd a *brilliant* yes-man, an artist.

But "The Big Picture" belongs to Martin Short, who gives an (unbilled) performance of dizzying brilliance—the most riotous turn since Michael Keaton's in "Beetlejuice." He plays an agent, Neil, and appears to have been born without bones. Curly-haired and cross-eyed, he wears a sickly, self-infatuated smile and lets the fawning words gush out of him.

He'll say anything he thinks you want to hear, yet the genius of the performance is that Neil seems convinced he's the most honest, b.s.-free person on earth. This is more than great acting: Short has shown us a new life form, a Hollywood mutation.

NEWSDAY, 9/15/89, Part III/p. 5, Mike McGrady

The boyish movie director Nick Chapman (Kevin Bacon) is outlining the plot of his first film to the big-time producer (J.T. Walsh): "It's a love story. It's a triangle, really. It's how people change...The whole thing takes place in a country home in the middle of winter."

As he sketches out the story, his words simultaneously come to life on a large movie screen in the background. We see three 40-ish individuals sharing a remote home in the middle of a snowstorm. Two rugged men are seen battling winter and each other for the love of the woman who is with them.

At this point, the producer interrupts and the picture in the background changes radically. Why not make it two women and a man? And why not have the two women involved in a lesbian love relationship? Then the producer questions the whole business with the snowstorm: "The winter is depressing. What if it took place in the summer? At the beach?" Moreover, since so many moviegoers are in their late teens, why must the characters be in their 40s? "This is a bad age, Nick." And although the young director has hitherto envisioned his film in stark black and white without a trace of background music, the producer sees flamboyant color and, "Oh, fifteen or twenty pop hits."

Before Nick realizes what has hit him, he's making something called "Beach Nuts." It's a film featuring three fun-loving college guys and three stewardesses who, if you can follow this, are actually ghosts. This is reality—Hollywood style. And at that, it's better than the suggestion offered Nick by another producer, one who wants to make the ultimate buddy movie, a buddy movie bringing together two of the most beloved figures in American history, a president and a ballplayer. His working title: "Abe and the Babe."

Writer-director Christopher Guest (he co-wrote "This Is Spinal Tap" and was a regular contributor to "Saturday Night Live") obviously understands the process whereby Hollywood regularly transforms silk purses into sows' ears. His inside-movieland portraits—student film makers, agents, cinematographers, party animals, vamp trainees—are sharp, though uneven.

Quite a few familiar faces—Eddie Albert, John Cleese, Stephen Collins, Roddy McDowall, June Lockhart, Elliott Gould, Richard Belzer—pop in to make unbilled guest appearances and to take part in the general merriment. But it is an unbilled Martin Short who absolutely steals the movie with his hilarious portrait of a Hollywood agent, a portrait that has reportedly prompted half the agents in Hollywood to consult with their libel lawyers. Wonderfully malevolent and malicious, Short's characterization is strong enough to warrant a more elaborate reprise at some later date.

But when the spoofery slows down, so does the film. And this happens whenever the focus shifts to the love affair going on between Nick and his live-in lover (Emily Longstreth), a relationship complicated by the sudden appearance of a Hollywood starlet (Teri Hatcher), a character in search of a casting couch. By this time, Nick has learned to take meetings, leased a Porsche and taken to saying "Ciao."

Despite the film's unevenness—one long segment detailing his making of a rock video is particularly tiresome—"The Big Picture" is a pleasantly lighthearted effort to strip the phony tinsel off Hollywood and get to the real tinsel underneath.

VILLAGE VOICE, 9/19/89, p. 68, Georgia Brown

Before alighting on planet Earth, first-time director Christopher Guest contemplates the starry sky. His film's main theme is perspective—relative size, immutable values—which is one reason it's called *The Big Picture*. (This play on scale—big and little people, cars, houses, souls, stars—accounts, I suppose, for the glimpse at one point of a midget leaving a theater and, later, a passing dwarf.) Another reason for the title is that the tacky corner of the planet the camera pans down to is Hollywood. This gentle, deceptively "small," low-budget comedy is a morality tale about an eager young director seduced away from friendship and principles by glamour and fakery.

Guest (formerly of *The National Lampoon Lemmings* and *Saturday Night Live*, cowriter of Rob Reiner's *This Is Spinal Tap*) teams here with longtime cohorts, Michael Varhol (cowriter of *Pee-wee's Big Adventure* and *Pee-wee's Playhouse*, which also play on size) and Michael McKean (*Laverne and Shirley* and fellow writer of *This Is Spinal Tap*). What they put together is irreverent in ways that one would expect; the film's an amusing spoof on studio heads, agents, other minions, and sychophants. What's unexpected is the movie's reverence—its tenderness and sincerity.

Nick Chapman (Kevin Bacon) drives his tiny car up to the gates of the National Film Institute, gives one of the guards his name, and hallucinates a scene from a World War II espionage thriller—the kind in which an undercover hero enters a Nazi stronghold. Nick's a graduating film student, and *The Big Picture* is dotted with parodic versions of old movies. (The idea may be promising, but the execution tends to be lame.) Inside the NFI compound, Eddie Albert hosts the 10th annual awards ceremony, quoting Frank Capra ("Don't compromise, for only the valiant can create...only the daring will make films"), and introducing clips from four distinctly unpromising student efforts.

One contender, *The Trial of Janet Kingsley*, is by Carl Manknik, "born into the business," says the MC (Carl's the son of his agent). The in-joke is that Carl is played by Jason Gould, son of Elliott Gould and Barbra Streisand, with Elliott appearing as prosecuting attorney (together with Roddy McDowall and June Lockhart) in Carl's courtroom drama. Carl later turns up as a prissy agent. (Guest himself married into the business as husband of Jamie Lee Curtis.) Then there's the whimsical *Afterbirth of a Notion* by Nick's flaky friend Lydia (Jennifer Jason Leigh, daughter of Vic Morrow), and *Crossed Sabres of Truth* by the huge and pretentious Jonathan Tristan-Bennet (Dan Schneider).

Nick's *First Date*—in which an unsuspecting teen calls on a girl and finds himself in a house of ghouls—takes first prize and his acceptance speech gives special thanks to his best friend and cameraman, Emmet Sumner (McKean)—who can't be present because he's doing Lamaze classes—and to girlfriend Susan Rawlings (Emily Longstreth) for bearing with him. Little do his friends know what they'll have to beat when industry ghouls sink their fangs into the fledgling director.

This is as good a place as any to mention Martin Short's outrageous unbilled appearance—it's more than a cameo—as the foppish agent who takes Nick on. Neil ("Nobody calls me a douchebag") is pale, cross-eyed, a wicked crocheter, and intensely fey. In contrast, the deadpan J.T. Walsh (fresh from *Wired*'s Bob Woodward) plays Allen Habel, a studio chief who options Nick's new script. Habel has the trick of making slowness look vaguely like profundity. He collects commemorative thimbles, works in an office that looks like a Zona showroom, and manipulates Nick's screenplay according to personal fetish and trade wisdom. (Later, Habel gets canned, and his severe-looking female replacement sits on what looks like a high-tech throne; she's not Dawn Steel, however. The script, Guest assures all who inquire, was written four years ago.)

When Nick mentions that his characters are in their early forties, Habel objects: "That's a bad age." Movie audiences, he points out, are predominantly between 14 and 24. "If kids want to see people in their forties, they don't go to movies, they go home and look at their parents." Nick's "mature" love story set in a cabin in the snow turns into something at a beach house ("Snow is depressing," says Habel) with stewardesses. Rapidly seduced by power, glamour, and an actress named Gretchen, Nick begins making principal script changes himself.

If *The Big Picture* were simply a satire, it would rate at the level of an extended *Saturday Night Live* skit—very funny at times; sophomoric and belabored at others. But the movie has a much rarer, more impressive side—probably most easily located in Longstreth's gentle, dowdy Susan; McKean's shaggy, genial Emmet; and Leigh's schizy Lydia. (Bacon's very good here too, although he may just be too far into the actor's mode to pull off the anti-acting the others do.) The intensity of these secondary characters' reality—simple, genuine, truthful presence—provides the moral antidote to Hollywood's parasites, impostors, and buffoons, all of whom are warped and plastic. A measure of the movie's comic vision is that the bad guys are not so much wicked as ridiculous.

The archkook Lydia, contemplating a documentary on people who abandon shopping carts, matches Short's fop in eccentricity; the two are comic counterparts, one from the world of the authentic, the other from the world of the artificial. It's fitting, then, that Lydia's apartment is in a former mannequin factory; the leftover zombies look like a poor girl's George Segal. "Do you live here alone?" Nick asks. "As far as I know," she says. Guest has a gift for lingering on the seemingly innocuous—small details of decor, mannerism, wardrobe—until a simple quirk turns oddly touching.

As an architect, Nick's girlfriend Susan is clearly interested in quality of life over lifestyle. At moments toward the end, her plainness becomes a small miracle. What Guest achieves with Susan, Lydia, and Emmet is rare. With the sainted Capra as its touchstone, *The Big Picture* may often look amateurish and klutzy, but it contemplates a world where good people work creatively in community and actual friendship.

Also reviewed in:
NATION, 10/9/89, p. 398, Stuart Klawans
NEW YORK TIMES, 9/15/89, p. C6, Vincent Canby
NEW YORKER, 9/18/89, p. 103, Terrence Rafferty

BILL AND TED'S EXCELLENT ADVENTURE

An Orion Pictures release of a Nelson Entertainment presentation of an Interscope Communications production. *Executive Producer:* Ted Field and Robert Cort. *Producer:* Scott Kroopf, Michael S. Murphey, and Joel Soisson. *Director:* Stephen Herek. *Screenplay:* Chris Matheson and Ed Solomon. *Director of Photography:* Timothy Suhrstedt. *Editor:* Larry Bock and Patrick Rand. *Music:* David Newman. *Music Editor:* Scott Grusin. *Choreographer:* Brad Jeffries. *Sound:* Ed White and (music) Tim Boyle. *Production Designer:* Roy Forge Smith. *Art Director:* Gordon White. *Set Decorator:* Jennifer Williams. *Set Dresser:* Theresa Pedemonte. *Visual Effects:* Barry Nolan. *Costumes:* Jill Ohanneson. *Make-up:* Daniel Marc. *Neanderthal Make-up:* Kevin Yagher. *Stunt Coordinator:* Dan Bradley. *Running time:* 90 minutes. *MPAA Rating:* PG.

CAST: Keanu Reeves (Ted "Theodore" Logan); Alex Winter (Bill S. Preston); George Carlin (Rufus); Terry Camilleri (Napoleon); Dan Shor (Billy the Kid); Tony Steedman (Socrates); Rod Loomis (Freud); Al Leong (Genghis Khan); Jane Wiedlin (Joan of Arc); Robert V. Barron (Abraham Lincoln); Clifford David (Beethoven); Hal Landon Jr. (Captain Logan); Bernie Casey (Mr. Ryan); Amy Stock-Poynton (Missy/Mom); J. Patrick McNamara (Mr. Preston); Frazier Bain (Deacon); Diane Franklin (Princess Joanna); Kimberley LaBelle (Princess Elizabeth); Will Robbins (Ox); Steve Shepherd (Randolf); Anne Machette (Buffy); Traci Dawn Davis (Jody); Duncan McLeod (Bartender); John Clure (Tattooed Cowboy); Jim Cody Williams (Bearded Cowboy); Dusty O'Dee (Old West Ugly Dude); Heather Pittman (Kerry); Ruth Pittman (Daphne); Dick Alexander (Bowling Alley Manager); James Bowbitch (John the Serf); John Karlsen (Evil Duke); Jeanne Hermine Herek (Mother at Waterslides); Jonathan Bond (Waterslide Attendant); Jeff S. Goodrich (Music Store Salesman); Lisa Rubin (Girl at Mall); Marjean Holden (Student Speaker); Claudia Templeton (Aerobic Saleswoman); Carol Gossler (Aerobic Instructor); J. Donovan Nelson (Mall Photographer); Marcia Darroch (Store Clerk); Steve Rotblatt (Police Psychiatrist); Ed Solomon (Stupid Waiter); Chris Matheson (Ugly Waiter); Mark Ogden (Neanderthal #1); Tom Dugan (Neanderthal #2); Ron R. Althoff (Security Guard).

LOS ANGELES TIMES, 2/17/89, Calendar/p. 8, Chris Willman

"Bill and Ted's Excellent Adventure" is cultural arbiter Allan Bloom's worst nightmare come to horrifying cinematic life. It's a rock 'n' roll time-travel comedy in which two high-school dimwits with no discernible blips on the brain-wave chart act as the 20th Century's emissaries to some of the great figures of history. And it's no meeting of the minds.

Bill and Ted, played with blank, imbecilic enthusiasm by Keanu Reeves ("River's Edge") and Alex Winter, are interchangeable in their personality quirks and their willful ignorance. Both of them are sad clones of a movie character: Jeff Spiccoli, sketched so spookily by Sean Penn in "Fast Times at Ridgemont High." Bill and Ted differ from Spiccoli, their "stoner" predecessor, only in that there are no drug references here to account for their allegedly jocular lack of ambition or interest in education or self-improvement.

The day before they're to be expelled, the two are thrust by a futuristic visitor (George Carlin) into a time vortex, allowing them to kidnap eight of the more important figures of Western Civilization for an all-important history-class oral report.

Bill and Ted convince Lincoln, Beethoven, Joan of Arc, Freud, Socrates, et al. to stop being so stuffy and high-minded and just loosen up, dudes, 1989 California-style.

Thus: Napoleon trades in Waterloo for a day at the water slides. Joan of Arc gives up the spiritual life for hard-core aerobics. Beethoven starts doing squealing hardrock solos on a synthesizer and learns to love Bon Jovi. Socrates tries to pick up girls at the mall. And swingin' Abe Lincoln sagely advises an assembly of history students: "Be excellent to each other, and... *party on, dudes!*"

Are we in hell yet, dudes?

Make no mistake, "Bill and Ted's Excellent Adventure" (MPAA-rated PG) is *not* a satire of mindlessness; it's unabashed glorification of dumbness for dumbness' sake. Bill and Ted are heroic in their ability to reduce some of history's great minds to their level— a notion that will be of comfort mainly to the dudes' fellow sufferers in after-school detention and others in the under-17 target audience. As for Mr. Bloom's minions (as well as most grown-ups considerably to his left), in lieu of excellent laughs, one can strain to hear the sound of a theater's worth of American minds snapping shut.

MONTHLY FILM BULLETIN, 4/90, p. 96, Mark Kermode

On the penultimate day of term, Californian high-school friends Bill and Ted are informed that they will fail their history course unless they make an outstanding presentation the next day on the subject of "How would a famous historical person view the modern world?" Ted's policeman father warns him that he will be sent to the Oats Military Academy in Alaska, thus terminating his and Bill's endeavour to launch their rock band Wyld Stallyns. That evening, the pair are visited by Rufus, a bespectacled benefactor from 700 years in the future who travels the "circuits of history" in a cosmic telephone box. Given another such vehicle to travel through history and obtain information for their presentation, Bill and Ted visit eighteenth-century France and abduct Napoleon (whom they deposit in the care of a younger schoolfriend at home), before travelling to New Mexico and Ancient Athens, enlisting the help of Billy the Kid and Socrates en route, and then fifteenth-century Britain where they are captured while attempting to rescue beautiful princesses Joanna and Elizabeth from arranged marriages. Saved by the latter from sentence of death, Bill and Ted pilot the telephone box randomly through time, rounding up Sigmund Freud,

Beethoven, Joan of Arc, Genghis Khan and Abraham Lincoln. Returning to their own time, two hours before their presentation deadline, Bill and Ted take the group to a shopping mall, where they are left to their own devices while their hosts search for the missing Napoleon. Havoc ensues in the mall (Genghis Khan destroys a sports shop, Joan of Arc hijacks an aerobics class, and Beethoven commandeers a music store), resulting in the arrest of the entire group. Locating Napoleon at a waterslide park named Waterloo, the pair detour to the city jail to liberate the others, and arrive at school in time to present a spectacular stage show featuring the amassed historical celebrities, and thus pass their course. They are visited once again by Rufus, who presents them with expensive modern guitars and informs them that in the future the music of Wyld Stallyns will "unite life-forms" and "align the spheres", becoming the very basis of society. His mission, it is revealed, was to guarantee that Bill and Ted would continue to play together, and thus ensure the tranquillity of the future.

Despite its s-f trappings, *Bill & Ted's Excellent Adventure* is first and foremost a verbal comedy, predicated on the rarefied form of 'valley speak' (a now somewhat passé Californian slang) used by the eponymous heroes who describe everything in terms of extremes: situations are either "excellent" and "triumphant", or "bogus" and "non-triumphant". Their quick-fire dialogue is thus the centre of interest throughout, which is just as well since the surrounding plot is both inconsistent and largely derivative of *Back to the Future* (from the opening scene in which our heroes blow up a guitar amp with a particularly enthusiastic power-chord to a peculiar Oedipal sub-plot involving Bill's nubile young stepmother, who seduces his father in Bill's bedroom and with whom the teenager cannot cope as a mother figure).

Director Stephen Herek (who worked as an editor for Roger Corman and subsequently directed *Critters*) employs efficient computer graphics to depict the 'circuits of time' travelling sequences. But such accomplishments are peculiarly tangential: the time-travelling element serves only as a device for landing the boys in a number of situations wherein their language is laughably incongruous, first-time scriptwriters Chris Matheson and Ed Soloman (perhaps wisely) making no attempt whatsoever to render the plot believable or to paste over its gaping inconsistencies and impossibilities: Props miraculously appear from nowhere throughout the various adventures, most notably in the climactic 'presentation' scene in which choreographed lighting, sound and smoke machines accompany a splendid stage show which utilises Roman columns, weaponry, psychiatrists' couches and an entire bank of synthesizers, all of which are conjured from thin air.

But Keanu Reeves and Alex Winter provide a warmly entertaining central double-act, portraying the two friends as both incredibly dopey and attractively sharp, locked into a world view which none of their peers can understand, or indeed tolerate. In an early scene, Bill is upbraided by a magnificently deadpan Bernie Casey for describing Napoleon as "as a short, dead dude", to which his companion adds that Joan of Arc was probably "Noah's wife". The pair's ignorance of history is subsequently exploited to the hilt; discovering the Socratic maxim that "True wisdom is knowing you know nothing", they gleefully exclaim, "That's us!". And there are occasional subtleties, such as the noisy arrival of the time machine going unnoticed by an apparently deaf Beethoven. Herek also amusingly handles the future-world scenes wherein the linguistic joke is neatly reversed. While Bill and Ted's language is out of place everywhere else, the future-worlders solemnly intone the greetings "Be excellent to each other" and "Party on dude" with due reverence, creating an environment in which the errant pair's every utterance is considered not only fitting but profound.

NEW YORK POST, 2/17/89, p. 27, Jami Bernard

Like, hey dude, here's a movie for teens who are *rilly* out of touch with the King's English, or any English, for that matter. It's all about two *totally excellent* dudes who go back and forward in a time-travel telephone booth picking up famous dudes from history to help them in their high school oral exam, and getting to say the word "dude" a lot. But, like, how about some *rilly rad* subtitles for those of us who are not privileged California dudes and do not speak with our bodies vibrating all over the map like a Gumby?

"Bill and Ted's Excellent Adventure" is a teen movie whose comedy relies mostly on the repetition of certain key phrases—"dude," party on, dudes," and "be excellent to each other, dudes" are a few that come to mind.

In fact, those last two phrases—well, maybe all three—are the kind that make Bill (Alex Winter) and Ted (Keanu Reeves) unlikely prophets of the future. A dude from that future time (played straight by George Carlin) arrives in a phone booth to help the kids out on their history project;

it seems that the safety of the free world depends on these guys passing their course and forming a rock band in their garage. It's like "The Terminator" for teens.

Even if the future of the civilized world did not rest on this, it's lucky the kids are getting some help; they think that Caesar is "the salad dressing dude" and that Napoleon is "the short, dead dude."

As completely stupid and silly as this movie is, it has its moments. When they find Socrates (or Sew-craytz, as they call him), he is philosophizing in ancient Greece. "The only true wisdom lies in knowing you know nothing," he says. "That's us, dude!" whispers Bill excitedly.

Once our Val-boy heroes round up their historical role models, most of whom go by a single name—Lincoln, Napoleon, Freud (for extra credit), Beethoven, Socrates, Billy the Kid, Joan of Arc, and Genghis Khan—they plop them down in a mall. Genghis takes apart a sporting goods store, Beethoven entertains the shoppers on a synthesizer, Freud tries to pick up babes. You get the picture, dude. As a remedial history lesson for idiots—which is how the movie culminates when Bill and Ted give their oral exam—"B&T" is not such a bad idea.

Alex Winter as Bill is The Smart One, if there can be such a thing.

The floppy-haired Keanu Reeves (who was so good in the somber "River's Edge") is completely loose-limbed, arms akimbo, as he plows through his "Adventure" as if no harm could come to him in this world or the next, or in Hollywood either. Clarence Clemons, from Springsteen's E Street Band, plays one of three Most Important People in the World of the future.

What we learn from this nutty movie is that if Genghis Khan were alive today, he'd be eating Twinkies "for the sugar rush," and Joan of Arc would be leading her troops in aerobics. As a "Saturday Night Live" skit, this would have been a winner. As a full-length movie, its funny moments are undermined by a creeping feeling that no dudes is good dudes.

NEWSDAY, 2/17/89, Part III/p. 5, Lynn Darling

At least "Bill and Ted's Excellent Adventure" has a compassionately anesthetic effect: By the time Abraham Lincoln exhorts an auditorium full of teenagers to "party down," any sense of outrage has been dulled by the inanities that have already passed before one's eyes.

Who cares if two hours have been wasted watching a film that flits over history like a dragonfly over pond scum? By the end, critical judgment has been replaced by an almost toxic sense of apathy.

Bill (Alex Winter) and Ted (Keanu Reeves) are the best of friends living the life of the virtually brain dead in San Demas, Calif. They want to become famous as rock-and-roll singers without bothering to learn how to play music—they've adopted the same attitude toward graduating from high school.

When their history teacher threatens them with failure and flunking out, the two chums receive help from an unexpected quarter. It turns out that together, their music will usher in the dawn of a new era; the leaders of San Dimas in the year 2688 have decided to make sure they don't blow it.

Rufus (George Carlin), an emissary from the future, instructs them in the use of a time-traveling telephone booth that will take them to different eras in history.

That way, they can learn enough history to keep Ted out of military school and prevent a separation that would eventually mean the end of civilization as we know it.

By the time it's all over, we've seen Joan of Arc leading an aerobics class, Sigmund Freud trying to pick up girls in a shopping mall and Napoleon Bonaparte in love with a water slide.

There's nothing clever or satirical or ingratiating in any of this. The movie merely wants to reduce the past to the world view of two adolescent airheads.

Of course this may be an all-too-accurate portrait of the sense of history imbibed by contemporary teenagers, but that's a possibility too ghastly to contemplate.

VILLAGE VOICE, 2/28/89, p. 61, Bruce Handy

It might sound ungrateful to complain that a movie featuring Napoleon Bonaparte on a Southern California water slide suffers from anemia. On a happier note, *Bill and Ted's Excellent Adventure* has managed to bring off the cinema's very first water slide point-of-view shot, so one can't be too critical. Plus, the film features a stepmother who's only three years older than the teenaged heroes. Ted: "Remember when we were freshmen and she was a senior?" Bill: "Shut up, dude."

SoCal burnouts with a hereditary debt to Sean Penn's character in *Fast Times at Ridgemont High*, Bill and Ted are in danger of failing their history class—"flunking most heinously," in Bill's words. (The school follows the kind of scattershot yet traditional curriculum of which Edward Bennett and Allan Bloom would approve: "Who was Napoleon?" demands the teacher. "Who was Joan of Arc?" "Noah's wife," Ted answers with undue confidence.) Fortunately for Bill and Ted, uncharismatic film presence George Carlin soon visits from the future and gives the boys a time machine—it looks like a telephone booth—so that they can visit the past, collect some major historical figures, and bring them back to San Demas High for an oral report. Which, give or take a couple of minor complications—such as addressing Socrates as "Soh-craits"—is pretty much all that happens. Compared to the more interesting teen fantasy movies, like *Back to the Future* or Joe Dante's failed, bizarre *Explorers, Bill* and *Ted* feels schematic, ground-out. It's *Back to the Future* without the Oedipal juice.

The actors, Keanu Reeves as Ted and Alex Winter as Bill, hit the exact same notes again and again, cocking their heads, hanging their mouths open to register glee, shock, dismay, whatever. Yes, they're supposed to be stupid. No, they don't have to be so predictable. Reeves at least has long bangs to play with, but he's a disappointment here after his convincingly shaded performance in *River's Edge*. Winter you may remember as the Penn-ish looking actor (more Christopher, actually, then Sean) in *Lost Boys*; he suffers for the comparison. Stephen Herek is the journeyman director.

Still, there are some boneheaded laughs to be had. At one point, Bill and Ted berate Ted's younger brother, who was supposed to be babysitting the piggish Napoleon, but has instead abandoned the emperor in a bowling alley. "Do you realize you've stranded one of history's great personages?" they scream.

"He was a dick," the kid explains—with considerable historical accuracy.

Also reviewed in:
NEW YORK TIMES, 2/17/89, p. C12, Vincent Canby
VARIETY, 2/22–28/89, p. 18
WASHINGTON POST, 2/17/89, p. C7, Hal Hinson.

BLACK RAIN (*Japan*)

An Imamura Productions and Hayashibara Group film in association with Tohokuhinsha Film Company. *Producer:* Hisa Iino. *Director:* Shohei Imamura. *Screenplay (Japanese with English subtitles):* Toshiro Ishido and Shohei Imamura. *Based on the novel by:* Masuji Ibuse. *Director of Photography:* Takashi Kawamata. *Editor:* Hajime Okayasu. *Music:* Toru Takemitsu. *Art Director:* Hisao Inagaki. *Running time:* 123 minutes. *MPAA Rating:* Not Rated.

CAST: Yoshiko Tanaka (Yasuko Takamaru); Kazuo Kitamura (Shigematsu Shizuma); Etsuko Ichihara (Shigeko Shizuma); Shoichi Ozawa (Shokichi); Tomie Ume (Tane); Norihei Miki (Kotaro); Hisako Hara (Grandmother); Shoji Kobayashi (Katayama); Keisuke Ishida (Yuichi); Masa Yamada (Yuichi's Mother).

CHRISTIAN SCIENCE MONITOR, 2/15/90, p. 10, David Sterritt

A few months ago, Hollywood released a movie called "Black Rain" about a New York policeman chasing a Japanese criminal. Now another film with the same title has arrived on American screens, but this one comes from Japan and deals with a very different subject.

The phrase "black rain" refers to the radioactive fallout that poured from the skies, with devastating results, after an atomic bomb was dropped on Hiroshima and on Nagasaki at the close of World War II.

Many artists, from Japan and elsewhere, have dealt with that tragedy either as a metaphor (as in the Hollywood "Black Rain") or as a historical event.

The new treatment comes from Shohei Imamura, a respected Japanese filmmaker. His movie was among the most controversial and actively discussed entries in last year's Cannes Film Festival, and prompted more talk during the New York filmfest. Now moviegoers on a wider scale have the opportunity to make up their minds about it, although it's so quiet and subdued that it probably won't be shown in theaters everywhere, and you may have to hunt a bit to find it.

The main character is a young woman named Yasuko, who's caught with her aunt and uncle in the aftermath of the Hiroshima bombing. They are all survivors, coming through the blast in pretty good shape, unlike so many others who are killed or mutilated.

But their story is just beginning. After the war has ended, radiation sickness begins to take its toll—an effect never expected by people who thought the disaster was behind them. Yasuko is in her early 20s and wants to marry. But the black rain has brought to Japan a new set of social behaviors and conventions. No one wants to marry a survivor of it, even when her uncle gets a certificate stating she's in perfect health. Overcoming objections from her family, she strikes up a relationship with a soldier who has been traumatized by his own wartime experiences. But when her health does begin to fail, even this match fades away.

"Black Rain" tells an unhappy story, but one that shouldn't be ignored. The movie takes its plot and characters from a celebrated novel by Japanese author Masuji Ibuse, who used actual diaries and interviews as the foundation of his book.

Just as important, the film is never sensationalized. It's less wry and ironic than the book, but it's still exceptionally understated, except for brief scenes when we revisit the nuclear bombing itself—and even these moments are bearable, partly because the movie is photographed not in color but in delicate shades of black and white.

Mr. Imamura's films usually deal with strange and violent subjects, reflecting a pressimistic view of human affairs. The very titles of his movies (from "Vengeance Is Mine" to "The Pornographers" and "Pigs and Battleships") signal his gloominess, which found one of its most complex expressions in "The Ballad of Narayama," perhaps his most widely praised film.

"Black Rain" maintains Imamura's usual grim outlook, but it has an unexpected subtlety that both strengthens and weakens its impact. On one hand, the film-maker deserves credit for shedding light on an important historical subject, and doing this through remarkably quiet performances and photography. Yet the movie is so airless and static that it's hard to get deeply involved with its unhappy characters.

I know thoughtful and insightful *cinéastes* who consider it a masterpiece. But they can't sweep away the shortcomings of the film itself.

LOS ANGELES TIMES, 3/29/90, Calendar/p. 7, Kevin Thomas

Shohei Imamura's "Black Rain"—not to be confused with the recent Ridley Scott set-in-Japan action-thriller—takes its title from a phenomenon that occurred in the aftermath of the atomic bombing of Hiroshima and Nagasaki. Moisture in the air, permeated by radioactive ash, condensed into rain and fell in dark, lethal drops.

The heart of the matter is the psychological torment of those who must live with the uncertain, unpredictable nature of having been exposed to such radioactive fallout. They worry for themselves and for each other; they are terror-struck by merely feeling under the weather. Imamura makes palpable the agony of living with the unknown.

"Black Rain," which was shot appropriately in black-and-white and has a discreet Toru Takemitsu score, is of course implicitly an anti-nuclear protest and a very strong one at that. But it also a protest of discrimination against the atomic bomb survivors, who number today approximately 370,000, and it furthermore belongs to a large group of Japanese films concerned with exposing the terrible price exacted of ordinary citizens by World War II.

Based on a 1969 novel drawn from diaries and interviews with actual Hiroshima survivors, "Black Rain" opens in the immediate aftermath of the bombing of Hiroshima and tells the story of a family of survivors, a middle-aged couple, Shigematsu and Shigeko Shizuma (Kazuo Kitamura, Etsuko Ichihara) and their niece Yasuko (Yoshiko Tanaka). Only the aunt and uncle actually were in Hiroshima at the time of the bombing, although Yasuko was exposed to the black rain.

Of all the major films of Imamura, one of the most distinctive and powerful filmmakers in the world, "Black Rain" is the most conventional, perhaps because of the enormity of the catastrophe with which he is trying to come to terms. It is in fact a tribute to his ability to compel us that his film recovers and develops a timeless sense of urgency from what seems a major miscalculation at its start. For instead of relying upon archival footage, Imamura re-creates the immediate after-effects of the bombing upon the citizens of Hiroshima, with scores of people wandering about with their flesh literally melting like wax. Their hideous wounds, however, are patently fake yet so horrible as for us to resist suspending disbelief—we're relieved and glad to be able to realize that it's all just make-up. As a result, it takes a considerable amount of time to get caught up in the story—to accept its reality in all its relentlessness.

Eventually, however, Imamura's abiding preoccupation, which is obsessive behavior, comes into play. The Shizumas commence resuming a semblance of normal existence at the country estate of the uncle, a wealthy landowner and the dominant figure in a small, idyllic-looking rural community. All three seem perfectly healthy, and they look forward happily to Yasuko's imminent arranged marriage. But when the engagement is broken off—Yasuko's prospective in-laws fear she really is not healthy—a heartbreaking pattern is set in motion, for Yasuko discovers she is permanently stigmatized by her exposure to the black rain. Meanwhile, the Shizumas and their neighbors are learning that the atom bomb has in effect set off within all exposed to it a time bomb in the form of radiation sickness.

Imamura is most effective at getting his actors to suggest what it is like to confront and live with an enduring, slowly-consuming sense of horror. By the time "Black Rain" (Times-rated Mature) is over its impact is akin to that of Lynne Littman's glavanic nuclear holocaust drama "Testament."

NEW YORK, 2/5/90, p. 58, David Denby

Shohel Imamura's *Black Rain* (not to be confused with last year's rubbishy Ridley Scott movie) is dignified and shocking. It's 1950, five years after the bombing of Hiroshima. Three survivors, Yasuko (Yoshiko Tanaka) and her aunt and uncle, live with the bomb as if it were yesterday. For years, they have been pursued by a sense of unworthiness. The inky black rain that fell on them after the blast—moisture permeated by radioactive ash—has left a stain on their self-possession. Yasuko has received a clean bill of health from a sympathetic doctor, but one suitor after another, hearing of her past, drops off, and at some level, she acquiesces in their betrayal. When actual tumors develop, they seem to Yasuko a mere confirmation of her uncleanliness. Only a shell-shocked survivor of conventional warfare, a sculptor, accepts her and cares for her.

Watching the movie, I was split between contradictory responses. From moment to moment, I was grateful for *Black Rain*'s somber matter-of-factness, its stoic refusal of melodrama or self-pity. Yasuko's uncle, who tries to hold things together and keep going, is a truly heroic figure. And yet, by the end, I longed for something more than the uncle's self-contained courage. I wanted to feel the rage that the director and so many in Japan must have felt. Imamura works in black-and-white, with restraint and taste. In the flashbacks to the blast itself and its immediate aftermath, horribly burned, half-dead people stumble blindly in the ruins; horses; people, and buildings are literally shocked into collapsing. Yet his treatment of the events, though frightening, is still inadequate.

The subject may be vulnerable to every kind of exploitation and sensationalism, but I wish some modern Dante of the cinema would take it on. I'm told that in Japan, the dominant method of dealing with Hiroshima and Nagasaki is denial. Judging by the way outbreaks of radiation poisoning have been ignored or forgotten in the United States, one could say that denial is universal, and that fear of radiation goes so deep that a frozen silence is the only attitude possible. Yet an artist of genius, wielding a strong enough ax, could break up that frozen sea within us and let the emotions flow.

NEW YORK POST, 2/2/90, p. 27, David Edelstein

The black rain that falls from the sky in "Black Rain" has nothing to do with yakuza or Michael Douglas charging down wet, neon-lit streets in an Armani trenchcoat.

The title of Shohei Imamura's funereal Japanese drama (which had its premiere at the New York Film Festival) refers to fall-out from the bomb that roasted Hiroshima: radioactive ash that condensed into tar-like drops which stuck to the skin and slowly, over time, poisoned those whom it caressed.

The director is known for his cruel, sardonic epics like "The Ballad of Narayama" and

"Vengeance is Mine." But "Black Rain" (based on a popular Japanese book about Hiroshima and its aftermath) is a rigorous and compassionate piece of film making—its coldness ails, freezes the bones, imbues its own form of radiation sickness.

The movie begins on Aug. 6, 1945, when a tiny package descends from the sky on a parachute. The explosion makes no sound—it's just a flash, followed, several seconds later, by a gale that shatters glass and sends people flying out windows.

The brief scenes that follow are difficult to watch—shots of scorched humans trudging dumbly through the city, past tangles of charred, husk-like corpses. A woman cradles her blackened infant. A young boy whose face is burned off and fingers melted to look like string cheese must convince his older brother that he is who he says he is. The recognition, when it comes, does not make the heart soar.

But this is only an overture: "Black Rain" is primarily about the aftermath of the bomb and its impact on the lives and the culture of those who survived the initial blast.

Outside the city, the black rain falls on a boat containing the beautiful Yasuko (Yoshiko Tanaka), dribbling silently down her young, clear face. Yasuko lives in a small village with her uncle (Kazuo Kitamura) and aunt (Etsuko Ichihara), both of whom were with her in Hiroshima and exhibit, five years later, signs of the cancer that will kill them.

The uncle has two passions: stocking a dead stream with carp and convincing a doctor to give his niece a certificate of health, so that suitors will no longer retreat from his so-far unblemished niece.

But suitor after suitor suspects that she will ultimately perish from the black rain, and the more frustrated (and sick) the uncle and aunt become, the more cheerful their assertions that Yasuko will soon be married.

At times, "Black Rain"—which is shot in high-contrast black and white—is a grim meditation on the Japanese impulse to repress. Doctors refuse to attribute the disease to the bomb, and Yasuko's uncle maintains adamantly that his niece is in perfect health. Only the girl herself admits the end can begin anytime.

The haunting, ominous, dirge-like music (by Toru Takemitsu) hints at the leukemia these people carry inside them. (Of the 340,000 living in Hiroshima, 120,000 were killed instantly; another 90,000 had died by 1950.) But if "Black Rain" is to be believed, what happened and continued to happen to these people was too horrible to address openly.

This muted, minor key is a strange one for the usually splashy Imamura, and the film is not as moving as you'd hope. Imamura intends a gentle critique of post-war Japanese culture, of its denial, cynicism and superstition. He points hopefully to an anti-nuclear movement and a realistic assessment of the damage that has been done (and must never be done again).

But after the initial conflagration, "Black Rain" seems cold, remote and unfocussed. It's only when people begin to drop that the movie comes to life—when this community, bound by the bomb, begins to waste away and the funeral processions come one after another. Then the melancholy irony gets to you—you respect Imamura for his refusal to pander.

The whole cast is superb, but Yoshiko Tanaka manages to be radiant even while succumbing to radiation sickness, assuring her uncle that she's fine, she's getting better, in a voice so calm and life-affirming that you know she's not long for this world.

NEWSDAY, 9/27/89, Part II/p. 5, Terry Kelleher

Shohei Imamura's "Black Rain," definitely not to be confused with Ridley Scott's action flick of the same title, is a moving, disturbing but extremely slow-paced study of Hiroshima's effect on one family. Though the black-and-white film opens with a quietly horrifying depiction of the atomic attack, most of the story takes place five years later in as rural village. By Imamura's estimate, 70 percent of "Black Rain" consists of people sitting on the floor talking. However worthwhile, it's a long sit.

NEWSDAY, 2/1/90, Part II/p. 7, Terry Kelleher

A motion picture about show death hardly can help being painfully slow. You have to live with that.

So it is with Shohei Imamura's "Black Rain," opening commercially today after winning praise last fall at the New York Film Festival. The viewer's patience is required and, to a great extent, rewarded.

Based on the novel by Masuji Ibuse, "Black Rain" chillingly depicts the immediate horror of the atomic attack on Hiroshima, but its focus is on three survivors at a five-year remove from the bombing.

Shiegematsu (Kazuo Kitamura) and his wife, Shigeko (Etsuko Ichihara), have provided a loving home for their pretty niece, Yasuko (Yoshiko Tanaka). The young woman is overdue to wed, but prospective suitors are put off by fears that Hiroshima fallout (the "black rain" that fell after the bomb) left her with latent radiation sickness. Acutely conscious of the traditional obligation to arrange a marriage for Yasuko, Shigematsu enlists the aid of a matchmaker, decries "nasty rumors" about his niece's condition and even obtains a doctor's certificate attesting to her good health. The clean bill only arouses further suspicion. In fact, Yasuko, Shigematsu and Shigeko are all fooling themselves—or pretending to be fooled, for want of a more useful way to behave under the circumstances. Each is dying of radiation sickness. It's simply a matter of sooner or later.

Imamura ("The Ballad of Narayama") maintains a quiet, elegiac tone throughout this black-and-white film. Breast-beating and recrimination would be unthinkable for most of these characters. None ask for pity, and very few even question the political and military decisions that shook down the nuclear thunder from the sky. Their calm is admirable but also somewhat exasperating—particularly given the fact that 70 percent of "Black Rain," by the director's reckoning, consists of people sitting on the floor talking. The only source of emotional turbulence is Yuichi (Keisuke Ishida), a shell-shocked veteran who experiences combat flashbacks whenever a motor vehicle rumbles past his shack. Imamura draws a compassionate kind of comedy from Yuichi's addled state, until he and Yasuko begin to establish a tender relationship. In a theatrical scene that strikes one of the film's few false notes, Yuichi acts out a war-time trauma and touches Yasuko's heart.

Ever so slowly, we come to know these Hiroshima survivors as a family that shares a bequest of death.

The beauty of "Black Rain" lies in the immense dignity with which the legatees carry on what remains of their lives. But this is not to say we don't wish someone would get up from the floor and cry out against cruel fate and nuclear folly. Exquisite restraint can be as difficult to observe as it is to practice.

VILLAGE VOICE, 10/10/89, p. 90, Georgia Brown

I'm reeling from an overnight reading of *Black Rain*, Masuji Ibuse's semidocumentary novel about Hiroshima survivors. Delicate, subversively witty, and elegiac, it's a bit like Jane Austen meets the atomic bomb. You might catch the flavor from the novel's original title, *The Niece's Marriage*, and its opening sentence: "For several years past, Shigematsu Shizuma, of the village of Kobatake, had been aware of his niece Yasuko as a weight on his mind." I came belatedly to the book, first published here in 1969, by way of Shohei Imamura's reverberating *Black Rain* (no, not the one with Michael Douglas on his motorbike), which played recently in the New York Film Festival.

Imamura and co-writer Toshiro Ishido wisely concentrate on the novel's present—the postwar '50s—adding subplots and characters of their own. The novel is much more hermetic. But the blunt and daring Imamura doesn't shy from re-creating some of the bomb's horrors, which the novel, incorporating actual survivor diaries, relates at greater length. (The movie's bomb sequences are its weakest, but they serve as a shorthand reminder.) Black-and-white imparts an implicit reticence, though, as well as historical verity. You'll find it hard to believe you're watching a 1989 film. In the same vein, Imamura has commissioned a wonderfully lush, old-fashioned string score by Toru Takemitsu.

Three Hiroshima survivors—a couple, Shigematsu (Kazuo Kitamura) and Shigeko (Etsuko Ichihara), and their niece Yasuko (Yoshiko Tanaka)—pick their way across the inferno without suspecting that they're exposing themselves to radiation. Though Yasuko was outside the city when the bomb hit, some black rain has fallen on her. (This was the strange precipitation formed when radioactive dust and debris were sucked up into the mushroom cloud and then condensed. Drops were the size of marbles. Medically, the rain itself turns out not to have been lethal.) All three are potential victims of radiation sickness—a syndrome that, at the time they were exposed, wasn't even named.

A few years later, living in a rural village, Yasuko becomes the subject of malicious gossip. Each time a suitor declares himself, he soon drops her because of rumors that she's been exposed. (Who wants deformed children?) Her aunt and uncle, suffering symptoms themselves, are anxious to discharge their obligation to her dead mother, and to see her married before either of them dies. At first, Shigematsu is convinced that Yasuko is pure; later he discovers she's been hiding sores and trying to treat them herself. The community trots the survivors out for memorial festivals, but views the victims as pariahs. As Shigematsu records in his diary, "Yasuko, my wife, and I are a community based on the bomb."

Black Rain may have the look of Ozu, but thematically it's absolutely consistent with Imamura's long preoccupation with the cursed and outcast—particularly with those who huddle on the fringes of postwar economic miracles. Madness, which accompanied some cases of radiation sickness, gets considerably more prominence in the movie than it does in the novel, probably because madness for Imamura has tended to signify access to higher reality. A perpetually dying man (with many funerals), Shigematsu has privileged access to death.

Accused by the moderator of the festival press conference of finally having made peace with Ozu, Imamura said wryly, "I haven't changed in my dislike for Ozu," and then went on to admit to visiting Ozu's grave with cameraman Takashi Kawamata. In *Black Rain*'s planning stages, he'd used *The Niece's Marriage* as a working title, keeping him conscious of its Ozu-type narrative. And having attained the age of 63, he said, he may have moved somewhat toward a contemplative style. "Seventy per cent of the film is made up of people sitting on *tatami*, and no doubt filming people on *tatami* brought me closer to Ozu."

VILLAGE VOICE, 2/6/90, p. 68, Renee Tajima

For a subject as gripping as the bombing of Hiroshima, it is perplexing that *Black Rain*, Shohei Imamura's chronicle of one family's slow, simmering death from atomic radiation, falls short. Promising elements for a powerful film are in place: an intimate family drama posed against insidious social malady; imagery fired by moments of dreamlike illusion, then memories of unspeakable horror.

The problem may lie somewhere in the immutability of the movie's heroine and emotional center. Yasuko (Yoshiko Tanaka), a young *hibakusha* (A-bomb survivor), was spared the deadly blast, but was washed instead by the "black rain" of radioactive fallout. She and her adoring guardians, Uncle Shigematsu (Kazuo Kitamura) and Aunt Shigeko (Etsuko Ichihara), manage to flee through the vile remains of the city. Arriving in a rural village, the three set about to regain an elusive normality, symbolized by Shigematsu and Shigeko's determination to find a husband for Yasuko, whom the black rain has branded for life like a scarlet letter.

The film is mercifully shot in black and white, but the stylized flashbacks of the bomb's aftermath—combined with a ponderous musical score—seem surreal, like a Cold War-era B movie. A mother holds a stiff, charred baby to her nipple; a young boy reaches for his brother, skin dripping from his fingers like a marsh creature. Scenes of the holocaust reappear throughout the film, like a running motif, penetrating the illusion of rural tranquility.

The village is the kind of microcosm of common folk and eccentrics that evokes postwar Italian Neorealism. There are the family's fellow war survivors, all physically or emotionally crippled: Shokichi (Shoichi Ozawa), the kind doctor who falsifies Yasuko's health certificate to mollify prospective suitors; or the otherwise scarred Yuichi (Keisuke Ishida), the village's seriocomic mad artist figure, given to attacking oncoming buses he imagines to be enemy tanks. They are symbolic of a dying society, stricken yet humane, and they make *Black Rain* an essentially bleak social comment. The real survivors are the unseen suitors, their bigoted parents, the gossiping neighbor and her bargirl daughter—a tenacious new Japan with all its ignorance and prejudice intact.

In Imamura's tradition of long-suffering heroines, the asexual, romantic Yasuko recognizes the true values of life. Rather than marry her first willing suitor—the robust and modern Aono— Yasuko chooses to remain ensconced in the womb of her doomed, loving family. In fact, through most of the film she is relentlessly enduring. She doesn't come alive dramatically until the end, when, in a breathtaking scene, she deliriously imagines a flying carp, sending her into reverie among a flurry of feathers.

Perhaps it is a statement on the limits of cinematic/cultural interpretation that Yasuko's character seems to lack dimension—we are accustomed to a more vital breed of heroine. Imamura elevates these ordinary people to the level of myth, but perhaps we would be moved more by the anguish of humans, not symbols.

Also reviewed in:

NATION, 3/5/90, p. 322, Stuart Klawans
NEW REPUBLIC, 2/12/90, p. 27, Stanley Kauffmann
NEW YORK TIMES, 2/1/90, p. C17, Vincent Canby
VARIETY, 5/24–30/89, p. 26
WASHINGTON POST, 4/27/90, p. D1, Hal Hinson
WASHINGTON POST, 4/27/90, Weekend/p. 39, Desson Howe

BLACK RAIN (*United States*)

A Paramount Pictures release. *Executive Producer:* Craig Bolotin and Julie Kirkham. *Producer:* Stanley R. Jaffe and Sherry Lansing. *Director:* Ridley Scott. *Screenplay:* Craig Bolotin and Warren Lewis. *Director of Photography:* Jan De Bont. *Editor:* Tom Rolfe. *Music:* Hans Zimmer. *Music Editor:* James Flamberg. *Sound:* Keith Wester, James Sabat, and (music) Jay Rifkin. *Sound Editor:* Milton C. Burrow and William L. Manger. *Production Designer:* Norris Spencer. *Art Director:* John Jay Moore and Herman F. Zimmerman. *Set Designer:* Alan S. Kaye, Robert Maddy, and James R. Bayliss. *Set Decorator:* John Alan Hicks, Leslie Bloom, and Richard C. Goddard. *Special Effects:* Stan Parks. *Costumes:* Ellen Mirojnick. *Make-up:* Richard Dean, Christina Smith, and Monty Westmore. *Stunt Coordinator:* Bobby Bass. *Running time:* 125 minutes. *MPAA Rating:* R.

CAST: Michael Douglas (Nick); Andy Garcia (Charlie); Ken Takakura (Masahiro); Kate Capshaw (Joyce); Yusaku Matsuda (Sato); Shigeru Koyama (Ohashi); John Spencer (Oliver); Guts Ishimatsu (Katayama); Yuya Uchida (Nashida); Tomisaburo Wakayama (Sugai); Miyuki Ono (Miyuki); Luis Guzman (Frankie); John A. Costelloe (The Kid); Stephen Root (Berg); Richard Riehle (Crown); Bruce Katzman (Yudell): Edmund Ikeda (Japanese Businessman); Tomo Nagasue (Japanese Translator); Clem Caserta (Abolofia); Tim Kelleher (Bobby); George Kyle (Farentino); Vondie Curtis-Hall, Joe Perce, and Louis Cantarini (Detectives); Doug Yasuda (Japanese/American Translator); Toshio Sato (Japanese Embassy Official); Jun Kunimura (Yoshimoto); Roy Ogata and Shiro Oishi (Sato's Men); Professor Toru Tanaka, Rikiya Yasuoka, and Joji Shimaki (Sugai's Men); Goro Sasa, Taro Ibuki, and Daisuke Awaji (Ohashi's Men); Keone Young (Karaoke Singer); Jim Ishida (Escort Officer); Shotaro Hayashi and Toshihiro Obata (Mediators); Michiko Tsushima (Noodle Woman); Linda Gillen (Peggy); John Gotay (Danny); Matthew Porac (Patrick); Ken Kensei (Masahiro's Son); Josip Elic (Bartender); Mitchell Bahr (Friend).

FILMS IN REVIEW, 1–2/90, p. 40, Edmond Grant

Only rarely can a big-budget American film be referred to as a triumph of form over content. *Black Rain* is just that rarity—an exciting tough cop thriller that rises above its own plot clichés by the sheer force of its dazzling imagery.

The roller coaster ride begins with a well done (but of course superfluous) motorcycle racing scene that establishes the devil-may-care attitude of police detective Nick Conklin (Michael Douglas). Under investigation on suspicion of corruption. Conklin gets assigned the demeaning task of escorting an especially violent Japanese killer back to his home country. Of course, the killer gets away from Conklin, and so Nick and his amiable Italian-American sidekick, with the able assistance of a subdued local cop (Ken Takakura), set out to find him and bring down the criminal empire he's part of.

There's not much that's original about *Black Rain*'s plotline; in fact, the big confrontation scene near the film's end bears more than a passing resemblance to the stirring conclusion of *The Yakuza* (1975), another cross cultural cop drama.

With director Ridley Scott at the helm, though, the banality of incident and dialogue is more than absorbed by a sumptuous profusion of atmosphere; with Scott, it's not only the storyline—be it innovative (*Alien, Blade Runner*) or lame (*Legend*)—that's important, but also the way the story is told.

Scott and cinematographer Jan De Bont (*The Fourth Man*) shot the film's exteriors on location in the streets of New York and Osaka. Out of these real locales Scott fashions a landscape that has the ambience of both the classic film noirs and contemporary high tech music videos. Scott perfected this unique visual approach in his cult masterwork *Blade Runner*, and the similarities between this film and that are fascinating—where *Blade Runner* took place in a future where neon signs written in Japanese, colored lights, and sky high commercial billboards were everywhere, *Black Rain* shows a contemporary Osaka that looks practically identical. Scott also effectively counterposes images of the "old-fashioned" Japan, such as factory workers bicycling to work or the isolated rural area where the finale takes place, with elements of its current lifestyle, like a crowded pachinko parlor that serves as one site for a chase scene, or the golf range where Conklin goes to meet the aged crime overlord.

Scott's particular genius at creating atmosphere isn't simply limited to selecting the right milieu for his characters to inhabit (or in this case, intrude upon). His stylization is pervasive at every level: from the "busy" soundtrack to the expertly slick camerawork and the remarkably intricate lighting, his work here calls to mind the noir visions of that other legendary stylist, Orson Welles. The cast members are another integral part of Scott's scheme. Michael Douglas is no pretty boy hero this time around; as Nick, he's a scarred and embittered veteran of the streets who is played off nicely against the easygoing charm of Garcia as the sidekick and popular Japanese actor Takakura as the reserved Japanese detective. The generally uninteresting Kate Capshaw is wisely used only sporadically as Nick's informant, a possible love interest who never gets a chance to ignite, due to the nonstop action that comes as a result of the actions of the truly nasty looking villain (played by another popular Japanese actor, Yusaku Matsuda).

Some major problems do enter on the level of scripting, such as the totally illogical manner in which two non-Japanese speaking police officers are sent to Japan to accompany a native criminal. Or the way the film gradually reduces its scope to become a buddy film toward the end. Or the rather heady two-hour running time. These are small qualitications, though, when you consider that *Black Rain* key moments have an undeniable visual power and a clear aesthetic vision that's light years away from anything currently appearing on American screens.

LOS ANGELES TIMES, 9/22/89, Calendar/p. 1, Michael Wilmington

In "Black Rain," director Ridley Scott and his team pump in so much pyrotechnic razzle-dazzle that the movie becomes a triumph of matter over mind. It's a blast of pure sensation, shallow but scintillating, like a great rock melody, superbly produced, where the music pumps you up even as the lyrics drag you down.

"Rain" focuses on a macho cop from Manhattan who runs head-first into two sides of modern Japan: the rigid formalities on top, the crazy danger of the underworld below. It's more movie culture-clash, with Michael Douglas' rude and surly Nick Conklin, the ultimate fish out of water, trying to blast his way through an Asian sea of red tape to recover an extradited murderer, while the city around him becomes the movie's dominant character.

This material has rich potential. It suggests current American paranoia about Japan's emerging economic supremacy, as well as the skewed modern visions of the new high-tech Orient in Juzo Itami films like "The Funeral" or "A Taxing Woman." But the story is standard '80s shtick: boy meets killer, boy loses killer, boy gets killer. The screenwriters, Craig Bolotin and Warren Lewis, show little inspiration. They seem to have transplanted bodily Don Siegel's 1968 "Coogan's Bluff"—in which Clint Eastwood was a brusque Arizona lawman chasing a crazy extradited criminal all over New York—and juiced it up with a lot of *yakuza* movie bits and a doomed cop buddy named Charlie (Andy Garcia). Charlie figures in the script's nadir of invention, a dopey scene where he plays torero with his jacket to a gang of maniacal motorcycle punks.

The *yakuza* references are deliberate. Ken Takakura, the Eastwood of that genre, is cast here as the representative of old-style Japanese decency and honor: a cop assigned to help Conklin. He seems to be the only sane man in the entire movie, the foil for Conklin's belching rage and his what-the-hell approach to law enforcement. Takakura plays him with dignity and restraint— even when he and Andy Garcia do their big male-bonding number, a duet to Ray Charles' "What'd I Say" in an Osaka nightclub.

But Scott and his visual team—including cinematographer Jan De Bont and production designer Norris Spencer—give this unimaginative plot a dazzling, dangerous, overwhelming surface. The images seem to explode right in your face: a coruscating cabaret street that looks like pop Dante, towering angular skyscrapers poking like huge computer blocks into a misty black-night sky aflame with neon, a factory shooting off iridescent sparks, a weird modernistic golf range jutting over the edge of the city, huge plumes of Scott's trademark mist spilling out into the black, rain-slickened streets.

Scott may have composed more knock-out frames per movie than any other modern director, and "Black Rain" knocks your eyes out all over again. It's hellaciously gorgeous. Much of this movie was actually shot in Osaka, but somehow Scott seems to have found part of the world he helped imagine in "Blade Runner": a huge, multimedia hybrid of a city that promiscuously smears together West and East.

In "Blade Runner," Scott, Laurence Paull and Jordan Cronenweth seemed to have invented a new visual style: a kind of *film noir* refracted through the voluptuously mechanical imagery of movies like "2001: A Space Odyssey." It became *film noir* cubed: a world in which night, rain, rot and melancholy shadows mingled with blazing neon and super-electronic gadgetry, where those dark "Citizen Kane" camera angles had gone kaleidoscopic and hot. Here, Scott re-creates the same kind of imagery, minus the rot. You don't watch this movie, you get drenched in it.

Douglas, who's played great, smooth, shifty slicksters in his last two movies—the stock-manipulator Gordon Gekko in "Wall Street" and the adulterous lawyer of "Fatal Attraction"—seems to be liberated here. He gets to snarl at everyone, wear leather and get gutty, honest, and low-down. It's a big, sexy, swaggeringly self-confident movie-star performance, and it plays nicely against the crisp, knife-like work of Garcia, Takakura, Yusaku Matsuda (the young killer) and the others.

But Nick isn't really a character. He's another archetype, a stubblefaced superman who's usually right and whose battering-ram tactics are better suited to running down psychos than the slow-but-steady style of the local police. It's hard to take seriously the idea, which the movie suggests, that he's learned anything from this culture—other than to be fond of Ken Takakura—because the cops we see are tradition-bound fuddy-duddies and the *yakuzas* are weirdos or rich, conniving scum, and the only girl Nick flirts with is Kate Capshaw as a bar hostess from Chicago.

"Black Rain" is not an anti-Japanese film. (The title, which Shohei Imamura also used for his most recent film, refers to the rain that poured on Hiroshima.) But it suffers from the same problem as 90% of the big movie thrillers these days. It divides its characters between the superhuman, the inhuman and the irrelevant—with an occasional Kate Capshaw. The movie's penultimate scene, its idea of a grand ethical resolution, works viscerally because of the force of the editing and the grandiose bravura of the last big action scene. But it's feeble on reflection: more market-researched morality from the Jaffe-Lansing producing team.

Still, action movies are one genre where clichés can be transcended and execution can triumph over content. That's what happens here. "Black Rain" (MPAA-rated R for sex, violence and language) has a sheen and pace that puts it in the high class of glossy new urban thrillers like "RoboCop," "Die Hard" and "True Believer": mad, overheated, overviolent movies that keep driving up over the top and taking you with them. Ridley Scott makes you see the world in new ways. When he and his colleagues are cooking visually, they're in a class by themselves. Even with an albatross of an action script around their necks, they can make the world hot, fantastic, wild, make the ragged skies split open, make hell come raining down.

MONTHLY FILM BULLETIN, 1/90, p. 8, Richard Combs

New York detective Nick Conklin, separated from his wife and struggling financially to maintain his family, is called to testify at a police Internal Affairs enquiry, and angrily defends other officers who he feels have to be 'on the take' to make ends meet. Later, in a diner with his colleague Charlie Vincent, he sees mafiosi meeting with Japanese yakuza, and then the object of their transaction, a package, being stolen by a younger Japanese, Sato. He is caught after a chase with Conklin and Charlie, and they are detailed to escort him back to Osaka. At the airport, they are tricked into turning him over to other gangsters posing as police, and they are grudgingly allowed to remain as observers in the subsequent hunt, with the English-speaking cop Masahiro Matsumoto as their liaison. After a murder (of one of the bogus cops) at the Club Miyako, Conklin realises they are involved in a gang war, and he and Charlie join in a raid (over Matsumoto's objections) on Sato's newly discovered headquarters. Conklin realises, after taking some dollars found at the scene, that they are counterfeit; Matsumoto, after being up-braided by Masahiro "Mas" Matsumoto (Ken Takakura), an impressively grave, softspoken gentleman who talks about disgrace and the value of team play. (He's the character Sean Connery played in *The Untouchables*.) In turn, Nick—who operates under the assumption that "New York is one big his superior for the irregular behaviour of the Americans, assumes he is stealing and reports him. Charlie is killed by Sato, and Matsumoto and Conklin, though still arguing over their respective ethics—Matsumoto's 'honour' versus Conklin's street-wise pragmatism (he admits that he too has been on the take)—begin to collaborate. They trail a girl from the Miyako, who leads them to a meeting between Sato and crime overlord Sugai. Once a lieutenant of Sugai's, Sato has violated underworld codes by turning on him and stealing (in New York) one of two counterfeiting plates which can produce perfect replicas of U.S. currency. The watching cops are involved in a shoot-out with Sato and his men, but the gangster escapes and Conklin is officially ordered off the case. Matsumoto refuses to go against his superiors to help him any further, but through an American girl, Joyce Kingsley, working at the Miyako, Conklin manages to meet Sugai. He promises to take care of Sato if Sugai will smuggle him into a forthcoming meeting of four 'oyabans' (gang chiefs), where the breach with Sato will supposedly be healed. At the scene, Conklin is unexpectedly joined by Matsumoto, who realises that Sato has set up his own double-cross. As war breaks out between the two factions, Conklin pursues and catches Sato. Bidding Matsumoto farewell, Conklin leaves him a present of the two counterfeiting plates—which the Japanese cop half-suspected he would make off with himself.

Is Ridley Scott the new Fritz Lang? Do, say, *Blade Runner, Someone to Watch Over Me* and now *Black Rain*, taken together, constitute a reworking and updating of *Metropolis* (if anything can 'update' what was always an amalgam of old mythologies and new dreads)? Like the nightmarishly steam-driven vision of the 'future' in *Metropolis, Blade Runner* looked backwards (to a rain-sodden approximation of 40s mean streets) for its view of the future as essentially used up, technologically over-developed and in every other way impoverished. If it seems more than impertinent to compare Lang's architectural grandeur with Scott's relentless visual filigree—a sort of designer shabby notion of the way we might be—it's interesting how in both design dominates drama. Or how grandiloquent décor becomes the films' major dramatic statement, 'state of the art' film technology turning into a kind of expressionism for inspiring fear and loathing, within which other motifs, political fables, Freudian fears, can be alluded to but don't have to be developed.

Within this orchestrated cinema, it's not surprising that *Metropolis* lent itself rather well to Giorgio Moroder's 'rock video' reconstruction, a style achieved by Scott's films at the other end of the time warp, as it were. Between the motifs that ricochet round the two directors' décors, dramatic conceits never really anchored in a drama, a certain continuity is also observable. In *Blade Runner*, there is the robot woman and the robot slaves, the latter looking for the 'father' who can make them whole (the unity of head, heart and hands promised by the patriarch of *Metropolis*); class divisions in the future are not removed but technologically, architecturally underpinned (*Someone to Watch Over Me*, also with its double heroine, an unreal, ultra-chic, fabricated one and a down-to-earth one). And the decadence of the ruling classes becomes so extreme that it also becomes unfathomably exotic: the Yoshiwara, fabled pleasure palace of *Metropolis*, now has a twin in Osaka's glittering Club Miyako in *Black Rain*.

The title of the latter is another compression of past and present-future horrors, a reference to post-Hiroshima climatic conditions beginning to have more general relevance. That it *is* the title is something of an oddity, since this is not an s-f jeremiad but a *policier*, and one with a now thoroughly worn-out plot about the hero so hardened by his own street wisdom that he has to be sent abroad to learn something new (as well as to get his man). The 'black rain', of course, is also a metaphoric contagion, the mutual pollution of cultures which exchange poisons as readily as wisdom. Hence the similarly smoky, sulphurous vistas of New York and Osaka; these pretty parallels are more the film's subject than its trite plot, just as the detailed debris of urban life exerted more fascination in *Someone to Watch Over Me* than the ostensible drama.

The senior Japanese gangster, Sugai, who was there when the bomb fell, explains the phenomenon of black rain to Michael Douglas' 'barbarian' cop, and relishes flooding the U.S. with counterfeit currency as a kind of revenge. He also claims that the new breed of local gangster, the tearaway Sato who has tried to co-opt his operation, is another spawn of American influence, flouting the old ways (Sato goes through with the yakuza finger-chopping ritual of repentance, but he doesn't mean it) just as Nick Conklin has upset the Japanese cops by not going by their book. But the cultural plays-offs, and any cross-cultural bonding between Conklin and Sato, are not worked through in a psychological or dramatic sense. Anything that can't be expressed in the design slides away, and one learns as much from the film's poster (Conklin, gun in hand, posed blade runner-like over a double exposure of the city, with Sato's face emerging from 'within') as from the film itself. The problem of the 'fathers' who created Lang's future, a problem the film could only resolve perfunctorily or cynically, is replaced by a problem of brothers here (the brotherhood of nations?), for which only readymade genre situations—the death of Conklin's buddy Charlie presages a new understanding with his Japanese colleague—are supplied.

NEW STATESMAN & SOCIETY, 2/3/90, p. 44, Suzanne Moore

[*Black Rain* was reviewed jointly with *Yaaba*; see Moore's review of that film.]

NEW YORK, 10/2/89, p. 66, David Denby

Black Rain, directed by the hollowly talented Ridley Scott, is an expensive, state-of-the-art junk thriller. Here we are at the cutting edge: Japan as the future of technology, America as the home of anarchic individualism—all the thrilling clichés. Scott sends steam rising from city streets; he produces a mass of gleaming black surfaces spangled with neon. If only he would design boutiques or disco floors. But instead he makes movies: Along with his brother, Tony Scott, and Adrian Lyne, he's one of the British advertising-world hotshots who are destroying what's left of American film aesthetics. For all its sparkle, *Black Rain* is just another genre film about one cop who won't play by the rules and another who does.

Michael Douglas, sneering and grinning balefully at an evil world, is Nick Conklin, raffish New York homicide detective. Nick won't shape up; he's profane, reckless, hostile to his superiors, and a little corrupt, too, though of course he's a great policeman. Douglas takes him well over the edge; he makes Nick a man who thinks he must live crazily or else choke on the taste of his own mortality. At the same time, Nick *needs* to be violent to be a good cop—at least that's what we're meant to believe. Nick is yet another of the rebel cops who have dominated American movies for almost twenty years.

Why this hero, over and over? As anyone can see, the rebel cop isn't much of a rebel, since his job, in the end, is to uphold authority. But that's probably why he keeps showing up. He embodies authoritarian and antisocial attitudes at the same time; he's useful to moviemakers and gratifying to audiences. He gives us the charge of aggression, but aggression placed at the service of Right. And his loathing of his safe-playing superiors is a convenient outlet for frustration over crime—as if petty-minded bureaucrats were the only thing stopping the police from restoring order to our cities. In the real world, however, everyone goes crazy when a policeman doesn't obey the rules. Which suggests that Dirty Harry and his many imitators should most likely be laid to rest as movie heroes. Dirty Harry anticipated Reagan, but now, after the failure of Reaganism to do anything but increase urban crime, the rebel cop throwing off bureaucracy and cleaning up the city is an illusion that has pooped out.

Grabbing a little lunch in New York, Nick and his charming young partner, Charlie (Andy Garcia), find themselves in the middle of a Japanese gang war—the black-clad, freaky Sato (Yusaku Matsuda) enters the restaurant and with many weird flourishes murders a Japanese man and a mafioso sitting at the same table. Nick and Charlie capture Sato and escort him back to Japan. But at the Osaka airport, they are tricked into handing him over to some of his own men posing as cops. The Osaka police try to send the Americans home, but our boys want a piece of the action, cursing and blundering in front of the sternly decorous Japanese, who, it turns out, understand their obscene insults all too well. Screenwriters Craig Bolotin and Warren Lewis set up the Americans as bulls in the Japanese china shop. If you think American bureaucrats are stopping Michael Douglas from doing his job, wait till you see the *Japanese* police! Let Michael Douglas be Michael Douglas!

The Americans-bumbling-in-Japan theme is initially played for all the crude paranoia and bravado that can be squeezed out of it. The Americans are taunted and fooled, surrounded by murderous motorcycle thugs in a deserted, neonized tenderloin district (*deserted*—in Japan?). A guttural crime lord tells Nick that the Americans A-bombed the Japanese, then corrupted them during the Occupation, and now must be paid back. Is war between Japan and America about to break out? Nick huffily lectures a glittering American doll (Kate Capshaw) who works as a hostess at an Osaka club, talking to her as if she were a "compromised" woman sleeping with Germans in an anti-Fascist movie of 1939. Capshaw's role is the stuff of camp.

After titillating us with xenophobia and cultural contempt, the filmmakers turn on the across-the-Pacific homilies. Inspector Masahiro (Ken Takakura) of the Osaka police department is recognizably human, though he's a stiff. Takakura, a huge star in Japan, has a handsomely stoic face and an aura of resigned melancholy. In his country, Inspector Masahiro explains, the police work cautiously and as a group; Nick's individualistic methods won't do. "Sometimes you just have to go for it," Douglas responds, eyes glowing, and at the action climax, when the inspector comes out with guns ablaze, the dignified Takakura growls, "You-have-to-go-for-it." American brazenness wins out. On the other hand, the Japanese cop's unyielding sense of honor restores the American's idealism. Reconciled to each other, the clichés shake hands over the sunset.

Ridley Scott's Japan is like the best avant-garde commerical for electronic equipment we've ever seen. He makes Osaka a multitiered toy city—the interconnected levels of plazas and malls, held together by circuits of light, could be the transistorized interior of a computer. There's huge, garish club, a steel plant with fires blazing. It's all very vivid but just décor, an advertising vision of sinister techno-Japan with no connection to the warring-gang-lords plot. Scott, thank God, does have some fun with the Japanese actors, particularly with Yusaku Matsuda as the vicious Sato. Matsuda, tall, with hair standing straight up in a brush, acts in a broader, funkier, less realistic tradition than we're used to. He's full of bug-eyed scorn for the men he murders. He commits violence with so much irrelevant style that he seems to be sending up the solemnly stupid movie all around him.

NEW YORK POST, 9/22/89, p. 27, Jami Bernard

The buddy cop movie is predicated on pairing two opposites who, through shared adversity and a dawning respect for each other's methods, come to care about each other and laugh at each other's jokes. ''Black Rain'' has a good enough premise—a tough New York loner of a cop who teams up with a company-man counterpart in Japan to track down a rogue extradited killer. But soon enough, movie genres collide like angry clouds, and ''Black Rain'' becomes a gorgeous-looking but disappointing washout.

The drizzle begins about two-thirds of the way through. Nick Conklin and his amiable partner, Charlie Vincent, have taken their vicious punk quarry, Sato, all the way to Japan to turn him over to authorities. By mistake, they turn him over to the wrong authorities, leaving Nick and Charlie in the care of local cop Masahiro, more a babysitter for the Americans, as the wheels of Japanese criminal policework grind slowly. When Sato does Nick a deadly injustice, Nick and Masahiro team up to exact a Rambo-like revenge on the *yakuza* (gangster).

Like an international pact gone sour, the opportunities for the movie to explore and reconcile an interesting, Machiavellian culture clash are abandoned, and ''Black Rain'' instead takes on a strident pro-Americanism that does a disservice to both cultures. The Japanese cops are reduced to caricatured yes-men, the *yakuza* to sneering goons, the women to giggly geishas, all of them hopelessly culture-bound in Neanderthal tradition.

Michael Douglas plays Nick, a world-weary, rebel motorcycle cop who kicks up spare cash for his alimony and child support payments by recklessly racing the leather-jacket set on bikes under the FDR. He's under investigation for being on the take, which is why it is initially so important for him to recoup his escaped convict. Otherwise, it would look like he took a payoff.

This is Douglas' first film since his Oscar'ed financial shark in ''Wall Street.'' In that movie, he was edgily smooth, crudely sophisticated, a bundle of power lust. As Nick Conklin, he is dissipated, angry, crude, desperate, a borderline nut case. He has a thinly veiled lust for cruelty; when beating the stuffing out of his nemesis he has an open-mouthed, drooly eagerness. It's an interesting, unlikable character who is done in by the Rambo factor—the script-sanctioned revenge frenzy that is meant to be cheered. (Not helping is an overblown plot thing involving counterfeit money and Mafia wars. When it rains, it pours.)

That the elegantly reserved Osaka detective (Ken Takakura, a renowned actor in Japan) would secretly be envious of Nick's drive and tactics is unlikely, as Nick embodies all that the Japanese probably don't like about obnoxious Americans.

The detective's friendship with the other American, Charlie (the delightful Andy Garcia), is much more believable. Charlie gets Masahiro to shed enough inhibitions to get up in front of a *karaoke* mike and self-consciously sing a rock tune. Takakura looks politely embarrassed; even a language barrier cannot deceive him that he and his countrymen are being played for fools.

There is no dramatic tension between the *gaigin* (strangers) and the Japanese police force, depicted as a bunch of plodding, humorless bureaucrats hopelessly mired in pokey tradition. Unless, of course, you count the ongoing and predictable jokes about translating the niceties of American vulgarities, most of which revolve around the male organ.

Following Nick's loner tradition, he keeps an emotional distance throughout the movie from the only two people he knows in Osaka: the detective, and a hard-bitten American hostess Joyce Kingsley (Kate Capshaw, whose perm mysteriously straightens out for one scene).

Nevertheless, American moxie will out; Nick manages to coerce Masahiro into helping him exact his revenge, and then the movie begins to rain clichés.

Even the shiny alien landscape groans beneath the weight of the ponderous *yakuza* straight out of Osaka Central Casting, with their various stalkings, grimaces, threats and sneers. There is an odd preponderance of slasher-type gore, probably aimed at attracting the Japanese market down the road.

Director Ridley Scott uses his "Blade Runner" and "Alien" sensibilities to make a lush-looking (and somewhat overproduced) movie, hard and beautiful (like the unnecessarily blunt Capshaw; I suppose her vitriol could very well uncurl any perm).

Osaka apparently has never been used as a film backdrop because of the difficulties of congestion and crowd control; the film makers manage gloriously—really gloriously—but the look of the movie can't save "Black Rain" from springing those leaks.

The title refers to the sooty fallout after the U.S. dropped The Bomb—the implication being that America is to blame for the breakdown of Japanese culture, and that only American toughness can restore it to something better, something more...American. If only Nick had learned to blend his entrepreneurship with his Japanese colleague's sense of teamwork, maybe the sun would have come out on "Black Rain."

NEWSDAY, 9/22/89, Part III/p. 3, Mike McGrady

I'm sitting here trying to imagine Beethoven slaving over the newest Pepsi jingle. I'm conjuring up visions of Van Gogh churning out a daily comic strip. Absurd? Of course, but not all that much sillier than assigning a director like Ridley Scott to oversee a piece of pulp fiction like "'Black Rain."

Not that you'll realize immediately that "Black Rain" is pulp fiction. The extravagantly gifted Scott, responsible for the look of "Blade Runner" and "Someone to Watch Over Me," always comes up with enough knock-your-socks-off visuals to keep you distracted long after the screenplay has settled into the predictable.

The film begins promisingly enough, with the NYPD's Internal Affairs Division investigating a crooked New York cop (Michael Douglas) who has been effectively busting drug dealers, then skimming a percentage of their loot for his personal needs, which include child support and alimony. When Douglas and his partner (Andy Garcia) observe a gangland killing by a Japanese hitman (Yusaku Matsuda), they make the collar and wind up being assigned to escort the killer back to Japan.

Not until their jet lands in Japan—Scotts nightmarish vision of an Osaka painted in smoke and neon immediately brings to mind the gloomily futuristic terrain of "Blade Runner"—does the plot begin to take its familiar turns. Scriptwriters Warren Lewis and Craig Bolotin give us such action staples as a prisoner escape, a brutal cop-stabbing, battles with the Japanese police bureaucracy, bloody shoot-outs, and so forth.

As the plot of "Black Rain" becomes more heavily cliched, the tremendous skill that has gone into the making of the movie begins to seem like artistic overkill. By the end of the film, as we're dipping into our final bloodbath, the highly stylized camera work is no longer enough to cover up the flaws.

Although I have no quibbles with the performance of Douglas, who won an Oscar for "Wall Street" his last time out, his character hardly seems worth all the effort. For starters, he's an openly crooked cop. The fact that he's so macho he makes pin money by challenging New York City hoodlums to motorcycle races is not exactly an endearing trait. Once he's in Japan, going head to head with the rigid Japanese police bureaucracy, he seems increasingly bullheaded and always less than likable.

But then, most of the American characters live up to the ugly American stereotype. Garcia, who scored in "The Untouchables" and "Eight Million Ways to Die," fares slightly better as the uncrooked cop, but he is saddled with too many unlikely moments. Kate Capshaw as the American geisha girl with the heart of gold is nothing more than an old cliché in a new setting.

The veteran Japanese actors, headed by Matsuda as the hitman and Ken Takakura as the Osaka detective assigned to the Americans, are excellent, and their restraint would have been most welcome in other areas of the film.

Without all the high-tech hoopla, the film's dramatic failings might not have seemed so glaring. But the overly amplified sound track, the booming foreground music and the exploding closeups only seem to underscore the script's crudenesses and simplicity. As the story itself gives way to violence—beautifully filmed violence, but still and all, violence—all of the cinematographic excitement first seems misplaced, later wearisome and finally faintly ludicrous.

NEWSWEEK, 10/2/89, p. 70, David Ansen

Remember the quaint "The Teahouse of the August Moon" and "Sayonara," with delicate-as-a-bird Miyoshi Umeki? That was the kind of movie we made about Japan in the 1950s, after we'd nuked them into submission and could afford, from our victor's vantage point, the luxury of benign cultural condescension. Now we make *Black Rain*, a churlish and violent Rambo-era revenge fantasy that suggests, through its furiously overcompensating macho posturing, that we are no longer so sure who's No. 1. This is not, let's make it clear, an admission this movie makes. But how else to explain, other than a mood of besieged national insecurity, the peculiarly surly and swaggering tone this Ridley Scott movie adopts? Now that the Japanese are beating us at our own industrial games, Hollywood feels free to indulge in a little Asia-bashing again.

So who do we send to teach the Japanese a lesson in unfettered individualism? Michael Douglas as tough-as-nails New York cop Nick Conklin, and his slightly more affable partner Charlie Vincent (Andy Garcia). Nick and Charlie are supposed to deliver a dangerous young *yakuza* mobster (Yusaku Matsuda) they've arrested in New York to the Osaka police, but they bungle the job and turn him over to the mob instead. This really ticks Nick off, and he vows to get his man his own way, not by playing by the Japanese rules of teamwork but in true Rambo fashion. He even says, swear to God, "Sometimes you gotta go for it." He also says things like "Sometimes you gotta choose a side." Somebody should have told the writers, Craig Bolotin and Warren Lewis, that sometimes you gotta write an original line of dialogue.

We are obviously meant to cheer Nick Conklin as a hero for all seasons, but why? Rude, sadistic, charmless and a corrupt cop to boot, his outstanding attribute is the chip on his shoulder. From the minute he lands in Osaka he starts slurring his hosts (they're "Nips" to him, and every epithet is preceded by "little"), making fun of the way they talk and their suspiciously unmanly self-control. When Andy Garcia's character, who at least flashes a smile now and then, gets viciously dispatched early on, your heart sinks: Douglas has to carry the rest of the movie himself. You almost feel sorry for the puffy, miscast actor, glowering strenuously as he tries to convince us he's the next Chuck Norris. For a while, it seems the movie must be setting Conklin up to learn a lesson in humility from the Japanese. On the contrary, it's they who have to learn from us. The lesson: sometimes you have to, yes, go for it.

"Black Rain" is the sort of movie where, if you see a motorcycle race at the start, you know you'll get one in the climax. The script is routine formula swill, at best. It's worse when it tries for "significance," dragging in Hiroshima as "motivation" for the yakuza chieftain, who, we're told, is producing perfect counterfeit U.S. money as an act of revenge for the bomb. (The title is a reference to nuclear fallout!)

But the movie certainly doesn't *look* routine: it's got Ridley Scott at the helm. As you would expect from the man who made "Blade Runner," "Alien" and more than 2,000 commercials, "Black Rain" is swimming in smoky "style." Having borrowed from urban Japan for "Blade Runner," he descends on Osaka and turns it into an oppressive, neon-streaked, soul-shrinking industrial landscape. But there's no fun in Scott's flashy, neoexpressionist filigree this time: it's too cold and alienating a style for the dumb Rambo fantasy he's trying to sell. There's not a moment of honest emotion in the whole movie. Only Ken Takakura, quietly effective as Nick's reluctant Japanese partner, manages to suggest a man with some life behind the eyes. Poor Kate Capshaw is saddled with a thankless role as a bar girl and polished off by an unkind, lopsided haircut.

It's sad to see Scott sinking to this level, but he's not the first talented Brit to fall into the clutches of Stanley Jaffe and Sherry Lansing, the producing team who brought you Adrian Lyne's rancidly successful "Fatal Attraction." "Black Rain" bears their inimitable touch, cleverly designed to tap into the national neurosis of the day. With their talent for pandering to our worst instincts with slickly packaged product, they ought to be running presidential campaigns, not making movies.

TIME, 10/2/89, p. 90, Richard Corliss

This fall the moviegoer has a choice of two *Black Rains* set in Japan, but they're not hard to tell apart. One is Shohei Imamura's stark meditation on Hiroshima 1945. The other is a cop movie backed by some heavy Hollywood artillery: the producers of *Fatal Attraction*. Michael Douglas and Andy Garcia are two New York City detectives on the trail of a cool, vicious Japanese gangster (Yusaku Matsuda). Their contact in the Osaka constabulary is a by-the-book gent (Ken

Takakura) afronted by Douglas' bullying. You've seen this picture before; last year it was called *Red Heat*. "Theft is theft—there is no gray area," Takakura observes, and Douglas ripostes, "New York is one big gray area."

There are no gray areas in Ridley Scott movies; the director of *Blade Runner* tosses color and atmosphere into every shot. The man has never photographed a dry sidewalk in his life; the tiles have got to glisten like Bakelite in heat. Neon glyphs snake around each lurid shop sign. An ominous bike boy threads his Suzuki around columns in a Japanese mall-cathedral.

Is this the pinnacle of Scott's luscious style or a parody of it? Maybe it's the spectacle of a director running for cover. Scott's last hit was *Alien*, a decade ago; these days his brother Tony directs the block busters (*Top Gun, Beverly Hills Cop II*). So *Black Rain* catches a gifted imagist between inspirations, biding his time without quite wasting ours.

VILLAGE VOICE, 10/3/89, p. 71, Georgia Brown

There are two *Black Rain*s in town, both named for the ash that fell on Hiroshima and Nagasaki after the bomb. Shohei Imamura's at the New York Film Festival actually is about the bomb's aftermath (more on this next week). The other, directed by Ridley Scott, is a bloody, baroque thriller about two New York City cops who track a killer in Japan. This one includes a bit of dialogue blaming the bomb for present-day Japanese corruption and violence, but you know that someone just loved the title's tough, sorrowful ring.

"Someone" wasn't necessarily Scott, who, in *The Duellists*, *Alien*, and *Blade Runner*, reveled in offbeat metaphysical/psychological content. (*Blade Runner*, many things to many people, for me was a poignant study of the struggle to gain memory of humanness.) *Black Rain* is more Michael Douglas's project; he bought the script from writers Craig Bolotin and Warren Lewis, brought in *Fatal Attraction* producers Sherry Lansing and Stanley Jaffe, and signed Scott for flamboyance. Scott's visual and aural hyperactivity almost distracts us from the still, chill void at the center.

If you were hoping for something like *The Untouchables*, Brian De Palma's over-the-top exercise in style, maybe the producers had something similar in mind when they cast that movie's discovery, Andy Garcia, as the hero's sidekick. Garcia's Charlie is neat, amiable, by-the-books—a "kid" foil to Douglas's weathered, scuzzy, glowering detective, Nick Conklin. The beleaguered Nick's got alimony payments and private school bills due, and is facing a department inquiry into whether he skimmed cash during a drug bust.

Charlie and Nick are eating in a luncheonette that caters to the mob when a tall, sneering Japanese ostentatiously slits a diner's throat. They bring him in but are told that diplomatic channels insist they take the killer back to Japan. Before deplaning in Osaka, Nick has mistakenly handed the guy over to the wrong people. The local cops take away their guns, yet Nick stubbornly refuses to leave Japan until he gets his man—even though he and Charlie are sitting ducks in a strange land, and in the middle of a Yakuza (Japanese mafia) war.

The human being can take a certain amount of improbability in a movie. She goes along happily with givens and a few contrivances. At a point, though, the mind balks. And when improbabilities pile up, it craves something to take the place of credible narrative.

Such human frailty may look like ample justification for Scott's pyrotechnics. Around hooks (a meat locker), blades (knives, fans, swords, a windmill), stakes, and staves, Scott—who hadn't been to Japan before scouting locations—constructs a world of naked spokes and jagged edges, a kind of barbed field. Impalement seems to be a Scott fetish, or phobia. (Consider the titles, *The Duellists* and *Blade Runner*; in *Alien* the thrust comes from inside out.)

Scott's Japan resembles *Blade Runner*'s Hong Kong/L.A.: a tangled, seamy mishmash of forward-looking past and contemporary future. He's edited out both the yesteryear quaint and the contemporary bland, and instead found some striking deco architecture and furnished it accordingly (great lamps!). A climactic scene takes place around Frank Lloyd Wright's Ennis-Brown house (actually located in the Hollywood Hills). Other locations are an eerie tiered driving range, a belching steel plant, and a sleek nightclub, where Kate Capshaw, still working the Orient (*Indiana Jones and the Temple of Doom*), turns up as hostess. In dark, artfully cluttered frames, Scott sculpts with lighting and with gleaming reflections on wet or shiny surfaces. Color schemes shift dramatically from one sequence to the next. Rain comes in black and blue. You could say the movie is about bruise.

Ostensibly *Black Rain* is about the taming of Nick—how Japanese tradition and code of conduct begin to civilize the cocky, can-do American. One agent of change is Osaka policeman gray area''—teaches Mas the efficacy of bluntness and disobedience. None of this makes much sense when Scott's Japan looks thoroughly anarchic, corrupt, and menacing—like one big black area.

NEW STATESMAN & SOCIETY, 2/3/90, p. 44, Suzanne Moore

[*Black Rain* was reviewed jointly with *Yaaba*; see Moore's review of that film.]

Also reviewed in :
NEW REPUBLIC, 10/16/89, p. 31, Stanley Kauffmann
NEW YORK TIMES, 9/22/89, p. C12, Vincent Canby
VARIETY, 9/20–26/89, p. 28
WASHINGTON POST, 9/22/89, p. B1, Rita Kempley

BLACK SUN 731

A Grand Essex Enterprises release of a Sil-Metropole film. *Executive Producer:* Chu Hung. *Producer:* Fu Chi. *Director:* T.F. Mous. *Screenplay (Japanese with English subtitles):* Mou Wen Yuan, Teng Dun Jing, Liu Mei Fei. *Running time:* 90 minutes. *MPAA Rating:* No Rating.

CAST: Wang Kang (General Ishii).

NEW YORK POST, 3/24/89, p. 27, V.A. Musetto

First, I highly recommend ''Black Sun 731.'' Second, I must warn you that the film is so graphic in its depiction of horrors that a Japanese army unit perpetrated on prisoners during World War II that I was unable to watch parts of the film.

''Black Sun 731'' is the work of T.F. Mous, a Hong Kong-based Chinese filmmaker. It tells of Japan's top-secret 731 Corps, set up, some say, on the orders of the late Emperor Hirohito, who, it has been reported, enjoyed experimenting with germs so much that a fully-equipped lab was set up in the Imperial Palace.

According to evidence only recently unearthed, Unit 731 was based in central Manchuria from 1931 to the end of the war. It operated under the direction of a Lt. Gen. Ishii, a surgeon who was questioned by U.S. Occupation authorities but never prosecuted. He died several years ago.

Critics of the U.S. action contend that even as German officers were being prosecuted for experimenting on humans, Washington struck a deal with the Japanese: No action against their scientists and officers in return for receiving results of their tests.

Under Ishii, evidence indicates, 2,000 to 3,000 Chinese, Korean and Soviet POWs died. (Reports that some victims were Americans has been denied by Washington.) Some of the human guinea pigs—the Japanese called them ''marutas,'' or ''logs of wood''—fell victim to deliberate infection with organisms responsible for tetanus, typhus and other diseases. Other POWs were killed so that researchers could study their bodies as the diseases progressed.

''Black Sun 731'' is a valiant and vivid attempt to recreate these events. The detail includes relatively benign scenes: a crying infant being grabbed from the arms of its sobbing mother and thrown into the snow to die; escaping prisoners being electrocuted as they climb a barbed-wire fence.

But there are also sequences that forced me to cover my eyes. One involves an experiment on a young woman to determine how best to treat frostbite. Another concerns horrific surgery performed on a mute boy—I can't tell you more because I was unable to look at the screen.

Much to Mous' credit, the violence never seems gratuitous. Rather, it comes across as a means to an end—creating awareness of an ugly and mostly unpublicized part of history. As such, ''Black Sun 731'' chillingly succeeds. The actors, especially Wang Kang as the commandant, are convincing, as is the direction and color photography.

If the film has a fault, it is the failure to develop the character of Gen. Ishii. Other than several brief glimpses of him relaxing with a young geisha (whom he treats rather sadistically), we learn little about what makes this brutal man tick.

"Black Sun 731" opens today at the out-of-the-way Essex Theater in downtown New York City, after a screening at this year's Berlin Film Festival. Here's hoping it gets the wider distribution it deserves.

VILLAGE VOICE, 4/4/89, p. 63, Elliott Stein

It's not easy to come to terms with the "docudrama" *Black Sun 731*, a Hong Kong production shot in mainland China, now on view at the Essex, a new venue for Chinese films on the Lower East Side. This is the first screen dramatization of a recently unearthed major horror story—germ warface experiments carried out by the Japanese beginning in camps around Harbin, Manchuria, in the '30s and continuing until the 1945 Soviet invasion.

Thousands of live "subjects" were apparently tortured and killed. The local Chinese used as human guinea pigs were called *marutas*—Japanese for "logs of wood"—and, once dehumanized, were inoculated with plague, boiled, flayed, or frozen in the name of "science." Although Manchuria was ruled by a puppet government, the area of the camps was under the direct control of the Japanese, even considered Japanese territory. The film's researchers claim that these torture labs were created by a secret order from Emperor Hirohito. Operations were headed by a surgeon and bacteriologist, Lt. General Shiro Ishii. It is further claimed that, after the war, Ishii and his aides cut a deal with the occupying U.S. military authorities: They supplied the Americans with full documentation on their experiments, and, in return, were not indicted as war criminals. (A tagline to *Black Sun 731*'s final credits suggests that virulent strains of hemorrhagic fever that appeared during the Korean War may have been introduced by the U.S. military using organisms acquired from the Japanese).

The facts recounted in the film are also the subject of a recent book, *Unit 731, The Japanese Army's Secret of Secrets*, by Peter Williams and David Wallace, published early this year in England by Hodder & Stoughton. Reports on the experiments were first discovered by a Japanese researcher in 1984; the first detailed account in this country was delivered to a scientific congress held in San Diego last August, covered at some length by the *Los Angeles Times*.

Veteran director T.F. Mous has made 25 films. He was born in Shantung, studied in Taiwan, now lives in Hong Kong, and shoots films there and in mainland China. He maintains that he has "toned down" the violence for *Black Sun 731*, because anything approaching the true story would be unbearable for audiences. Unfortunately, in spite of some memorable imagery and a few scenes that do have the ring of truth, a good deal of his movie is an unrelieved litany of horrors depicted in nauseating splatter opus style. Even though it is somewhat lacking in skill, I believe it will be of interest to those who can stomach it.

Also reviewed:
VARIETY, 4/5-11/89, p. 18

BLAZE

A Touchstone Pictures release in association with Silver Screen Partners IV of an A & M Films production. *Executive Producer:* David Lester and Don Miller. *Producer:* Gil Friesen and Dale Pollock. *Director:* Ron Shelton. *Screenplay:* Ron Shelton. *Based on the book "Blaze Starr: My Life as Told to Huey Perry":* Blaze Starr and Huey Perry. *Director of Photography:* Haskell Wexler. *Editor:* Robert Leighton. *Music:* Bennie Wallace. *Music Editor:* Scott Stambler. *Sound:* Kirk Francis and (music) Bruce Botnick. *Sound Editor:* Gordon Ecker and Bruce Stambler. *Production Designer:* Armin Ganz. *Art Director:* Edward Richardson. *Set Designer:* Harold Fuhrman. *Set Decorator:* Michael J. Taylor and Rosemary Brandenburg. *Special Effects:* Dan Lester. *Costumes:* Ruth Myers. *Make up:* Monty Westmore and Christina Smith. *Running time:* 120 minutes. *MPAA Rating:* R.

CAST: Paul Newman (Earl Long); Lolita Davidovich (Blaze Starr); Jerry Hardin (Thibodeaux); Gailard Sartain (LaGrange); Jeffrey DeMunn (Tuck); Garland Bunting (Doc Ferriday); Richard Jenkins (Picayune); Brandon Smith (Arvin Deeter); Jay Chevalier (Wiley Braden); Robert Wuhl (Red Snyder); Michael Brockman (Bobby); Eloy Casados (Antoine); James Harper (Willie Rainach); Teresa Gilmore Capps (Tamara Knight); Diane Brill (Delilah Dough); Blaze Starr (Lily); Gilbert Lewis (Reverend Marquez); Gary Sturgis (Marquez' Son); Louanne

Stephens (Lora Fleming); Emily Warfield (Debbie Fleming); Ben Cook (Younger Brother); John Fertitta (Hospital Director); Harlan Jordan (Dr. Cheeseborough); Rod Masterson (Town Talk Reporter #1); Bill Dunleavy (Town Talk Reporter #2); King Cotton (Jimmie Davis); Mike Baer (Secretary of Legislature); Bob Cherry, Sid Lacey, and Harold G. Herthum (Earl's Cronies); Frederick F. Lewis (Heckling Reporter); Al Robinson (Magnolia Local); Dick Person (General Store Owner); Brooks Read (Reporter in Store); Bill Mesman (Representative Davis); John A. Barber (Representative Hebert); Patrik Baldauff (Representative Kennon); Carey Rauhman Holliday (Representative Alexander); Robert Earle (Representative Elfin); Thomas Radcliffe Atkins (Representative Johnson); Thomas C. Smith-Alden (Asylum Spokesman); Donald J. Lee Jr. (Donut Shop Man); Pat Snow (Johnnie Mae); George Wyatt (Drunken Officer #1); Deano Thornton (Drunken Officer #2); David R. Conly (Drunken Sailor); Janet Shea (Crony Wife #1); Glynn Rubin (Crony Wife #2); Bran Leland (Dufee).

LOS ANGELES TIMES, 12/13/89, Calendar/p. 1, Sheila Benson

In "Blaze", the raucous and selectively true story of the love affair of Earl K. Long, the 63-year-old governor of Louisiana, and red-haired, 28-year-old burlesque queen Blaze Starr, Paul Newman throws himself into bringing every eccentric, disrespectful quirk of Ol' Earl's to life and he succeeds fiercely well.

A handful even for his day, Earl Long was a real pistol, the younger brother of the state's greatest demagogue, Huey Long, and a genuine if unlikely advocate of black voting rights in 1959. To watch Newman's frowsy-haired Long sweep confidently into a rowdy Bourbon Street strip joint is to reflect on what a tepid, joyless bunch politicians have shriveled into, post-television surveillance. Growly voiced and lickerish-eyed, Newman is audacious.

The one who has pulled back is writer-director Ron Shelton, How the maker of "Bull Durham" could have come this close and then have tip-toed away from a portrait as wild and as flamboyant as his subject's is a question to ponder.

Ol' Earl carried "progressive" ideas about the rights of the poor and blacks into action. He was considered outright crazy, there were questions of tax evasion, alcoholism, womanizing. And when he began his public affair with Starr, no stranger to publicity herself, his wife conspired with his political enemies to have him locked away in a Louisiana mental institution—three times. From this beleaguered position, because he couldn't succeed himself as governor more than three times, he went on to run for Congress in 1960.

The movie truncates the political skirmishing that *was* Earl Long, leaving us with more questions than answers. Those who know nothing about him, going in, won't even be sure that his stand against white supremacists in the Louisiana state legislature was real. It was.

And probably because the family wouldn't allow it, there's no mention of Long's wife of almost 30 years. With no wife, we're at a loss to understand what kept these two from marrying after Long's public, ring-brandishing proposal. They so clearly loved each other.

Shelton certainly got the casting right, though. With her tumbling red hair and her pansy-shaped face, Lolita Davidovich is luscious and endearing all at once. There's a nice easy style to her that seems a natural part of this fantasy woman. Lust aside, you can see how Long, this political animal, might also like talking to this bright, down-homey girl—whether a panther took her clothes off onstage or not.

Blaze's transformation from Fannie Belle Fleming of Twelve Pole Creek, W. Va., to a savvy Baltimore stripper probably isn't long enough for some. It's positively streamlined from the book she wrote with Huey Perry, which provided the backbone of Shelton's screenplay.

We don't see enough of her act to know the sort of headliner Starr was, the kick she got from dreaming up her trademark gimmicks—like the panther, or a couch that seemed to burst into flame at the end of her routine. And Shelton doesn't linger on the pleasure she took from her dancing. You only need to remember Valerie Perine's strip in "Lenny," courtesy of Bob Fosse, to know how powerful this material can be. Having whetted our interest, Shelton downplays that whole side of Blaze.

We do see her beginnings, as a scared, aspiring country singer in a servicemen's bar during the Korean War, whistled onto a stage and asked if she won't shed her clothes and undo her formidable white cotton bra "for America." Bob Wuhl has a grand moment as the creepo emcee who lures her into it.

By the next scene, she's trying to teach herself clockwise and counterclockwise with the tassels and before we know it, she's a star, er, Starr. She's learned patter, she's learned back-combing and she knows exactly where to glue the sequins. And she's learned to offer men a powder puff from the stage, to dust the derriere she also offers.

As for Long, his spellbinding side goes almost undemonstrated. The press notes, not the movie, give us the great Long quote: "The three best friends the poor people have ever had are Jesus Christ, Sears & Roebuck and Earl K. Long." It's electrifying to hear the old reprobate's own voice under the closing credits and it gives a good idea how close Newman has come to capturing him. But speechifying like this comes on a roll, and "Blaze" never really gets its roll going.

As it stands, "Blaze" is hugely enjoyable, with fluid, sensual camera work by Haskell Wexler and Ruth Myer's cheerfully outrageous costumes that savor every inch of Davidovich. There's real feeling about Long's henchmen, Gailard Sartain in particular, as the aide who hates what Blaze is doing to the boss' chances, but grudgingly comes to admire her spirit.

But "Blaze" is also puzzling. It peaks too soon, and having teased us with these legendary characters, it goes almost prim when it comes to seeing them in action. Short-sheeting, from the maker of "Bull Durham"? Who would have thought?

MONTHLY FILM BULLETIN, 2/90, p. 37, Pam Cook

1950. Teenager Fannie Belle Fleming leaves her poverty-stricken family in Twelve Pole Creek, West Virginia, hoping to become a singer. While working as a waitress she is approached by club manager John "Red" Snyder, who promises to further her singing career. Belle is shocked to discover she is expected to take off her clothes, but Snyder overcomes her initial resistance, renaming her "Blaze Starr". When he makes a pass, however, Blaze leaves, going on to make her name as an exotic dancer. Some years later, she is noticed in a New Orleans night-club by Earl Kemp Long, the sixty-five-year-old governor of Louisiana, whose weakness for women does not please his Democrat cronies. Blaze rebuffs the governor's crude sexual advances several times, but agrees to accompany him on a campaign visit to a local parish, where he reaffirms his controversial stand on Negro rights. Long takes Blaze to his broken-down farm, The Pea Patch, where they make passionate love. The governor's fellow Democrats warn him that his affair with Blaze, coupled with tax evasion charges and his support for Negro voting rights, will destroy his chances of re-election, and Long agrees to stay clear of the State Legislature when the voting rights bill is debated. At the last minute, however, he turns up and delivers a diatribe against racism which causes uproar in the chamber. Subsequently, Long is abducted and committed to a mental hospital, but obtains his own release by firing the state medical hierarchy and appointing one of his cronies, Doc Ferriday, as hospital head. His reputation is now seriously damaged and to save him further scandal, Blaze decides to leave him. He loses the election and, convinced that Blaze will not come back, storms the night-club with a shotgun. They are reconciled, but Earl is deeply depressed in retirement and Blaze persuades his cronies to allow him to run for congress in John F. Kennedy's campaign. On polling day, Long suffers a heart attack but refuses to go to hospital until the polls close. He dies in Blaze's arms before he can learn of his victory.

After the success of the amiably droll *Bull Durham*, Ron Shelton here turns to more spicy subject matter in the political scandal surrounding the affair in the 50s and 60s of the 'mad' governor of Louisiana, Earl K. Long, brother of Huey, and a young 'exotic' dancer. Blaze Starr's autobiography provides the basis for the screenplay, and she makes a guest appearance as Lily, one of the dancers in the New Orleans night-club where the sixty-five-year-old Long first falls for the voluptuous twenty-nine-year-old who becomes the companion of his final years. The combination of sex and political intrigue would probably be enough to make *Blaze* a winner, but Shelton's characteristically quirky perspective and surreal ear for dialogue propels the film into a higher league.

Despite its title and ostensible focus on the love story, the real interest lies in the character of Earl K. Long, portrayed with outstanding comic verve by Paul Newman as a wily, tough, loud-mouthed megalomaniac whose progressive views and unconventional sexual habits were a continual embarrassment to his fellow Democrats. Nevertheless, in spite of tax evasion charges, a notorious fondness for low-life activities and support for Negro voting rights, he was an immensely popular 'man of the people', serving three terms as governor. As with *Bull Durham*, Shelton has chosen an ageing hero at the crossroads, unwilling to relinquish the power he has spent a lifetime acquiring, and unable to accept defeat. A completely political animal, Long is able to turn every banana skin to his advantage, until he finally skids on the Negro rights issue.

Although there has obviously been some glossing over this scandalous episode in American history, leaving notable gaps in the plot, Newman and Shelton pull no punches when it comes to Long himself, a contradictory mixture of corruption and idealism whose total lack of guile bulldozes through the hypocrisy of white Southern society and the deviousness of his fellow politicians. His storming of the State Legislature to deliver a ranting indictment of racism, and subsequent abduction and confinement to a psychiatric institution, is the stuff of high melodrama, while his turning the tables on his enemies by sacking the medical hierarchy and appointing his cronies from his hospital room is all the more outrageous for being true. That Long was unhinged is not denied by the film, which celebrates his eccentric individualism and relishes the fact that the conservative political system failed to control him. The ultimate vindication of his integrity lies in his vision of the future, the 60s civil rights movement he would not live to see.

Blaze Starr's own poverty-to-burlesque-queen story appears conventional in comparison, though Blaze herself, played by statuesque newcomer Lolita Davidovich as an independent, strong-minded woman, more than holds her own against Long, and delivers lines rich in off-beat Southern vernacular with impressive aplomb. Although their relationship is mostly played for laughs (their hilarious first sexual encounter offers Newman a comic challenge to which he rises with gusto), it is clearly a love match, and the romance is sufficiently unorthodox to sustain its place centre stage. But though Blaze was important enough in Long's private life for him to refuse to give her up in the face of pressure from his cronies, her role in the political sphere is less clear. The obvious allusions to the similarity between politics and show business apart, and her unconditional support of him throughout their affair notwithstanding, Blaze is little more than another of Long's follies. Her own dreams of finding a lucrative career and a good man go sadly awry, though she achieves some financial reward and notoriety as Long's mistress. In a poignant scene after his defeat in his re-election campaign, Long rampages into the club where Blaze dances dementedly brandishing a shotgun and railing against her for leaving him. As they come face to face, he breaks down and she tenderly leads him away, a beaten, frail old man. An improbable couple, both trapped in their dependency.

But Blaze has no inkling of being trapped, and her devotion appears absolute. Indeed, the brash innocence of both central characters shines forth, given added luminosity by Haskell Wexler's vibrant cinematography and wittily enhanced by carefully chosen musical numbers. The real Long himself is given the last word: over the end titles his fading voice is heard in a radio interview castigating the media (who plagued him all his life) for misrepresentation. Sounding very far away, in time and place, he declaims the film's closing line: "I got one language, and that's the truth".

NEW YORK, 1/15/90, p. 55, David Denby

In *Blaze*, Paul Newman, playing Earl K. Long—the combustible Louisiana governor of the fifties—walks stiffly, in sudden spurts, with his shoulders turned out and his arms hanging loose. Newman is a man of perfect grace suggesting the eager awkwardness of a stiff-jointed old rooster; at the same time, he talks in a low, raspy growl. The performance is extremely funny—though not always audible—and deeply eccentric. At times, it has a wonderfully happy spirit. Long, the younger brother of the demagogue Huey, was a lifetime Democratic politican, and Newman makes him preternaturally alert. Bursting into a room, he sizes up the crowd, darting in a quick, Groucho-like shuffle toward some likely voters; after shaking hands and offering an instant's eye contact, he darts away.

His brain moves fast, and he's a great buffoon, as eager to astonish as Norman Mailer holding a drink in his hand. This clowning old pol is not quite cynical. He gives a touch of his personality to whomever he looks at, and his straight-in-the-eye glance is what counts in the end. Earl is a man who delivers. And he has to be shrewder and faster than anyone else because he's that vulnerable creature, a true democrat, as well as a Democrat, and he believes (in 1959) that the time of the black man in the South has come. In *Blaze*, writer-director Ron Shelton lionizes Long as a racial progressive done in by a combination of white racism and sexual hypocrisy. In his last years, the governor, a man over 60, falls for a fleshy young stripper named Blaze Starr. The center of the movie is their relationship and the effects it had on Earl's career.

A great subject, but apart from Newman, *Blaze* isn't very good. Shelton, whose sex scenes were so earthy and direct in *Bull Durham*, plays the action here for embarrassing waggish comedy. A flaky joker even in bed, Earl hops into action with his boots on. Blaze, played by the newcomer Lolita Davidovich, receives him calmly, impassively, like a mother gentling an excitable child. Their encounters are the opposite of sensual, but then Davidovich, though abundant, is not a sensual performer. Her large face is doughy; she doesn't have much smartness or spark. When she tries to be exuberant, one can hear a high-school drama class. Nothing much gets going between her and Newman, who tries to carry the scenes by himself.

Blaze, whose self-serving memoir forms the basis of the movie, turns out to be smarter than anyone expects, a tough cookie who rejuvenates Earl after he's been defeated for a fourth term (partly because of bad publicity generated by her liaison with him). She gets him to run (successfully) for Congress. But the scenes of her turning him around aren't very convincing; and the political satire throughout is affectionate yet thin. Not only is Newman the sole source of energy in the movie, Earl K. Long appears to be the sole intelligence in the state of Louisiana. Some of the actors are good, especially Jerry Hardin and Gailard Sartain as Earl's cronies, but they all have to play flunkies, racists, and low hacks. Shelton skids over Earl's tax problems, and brushes aside as a mere naughty trick the governor's attempt to bypass the state constitution and stay in power a fourth term. Oh, what a delicious scoundrel! Newman is great, but Shelton uses him for some ripely sentimental mythmaking.

NEW YORK POST, 12/13/89, p. 29, David Edelstein

Earl Long Jr., brother of Huey, was immortalized in A.J. Liebling's "The Earl of Louisiana" as one of the most effective (and surprising) civil-rights advocates in the pre-1960 South. An outrageous showman and rabble-rouser, always competing with his late brother's legend, he was a great character even before his scandalous liaison in 1960 with a stripper named Blaze Starr (and his incarceration in a mental hospital) boosted him to tabloid immortality.

The affair occupies only 60 pages of Starr's autobiography, but it's the soul of Ron Shelton's lovely and muted new film—a disappointment, given Shelton's crackerjack work in "Bull Durham," but with more flaky dialogue and sweet-tempered laughs than any 10 ordinary big-studio productions. It's a wry celebration of the loonier side of democracy.

Young Blaze, whom we meet as she leaves her West Virginia shack for a career as a singer, is played by Lolita Davidovich, a young Canadian actress with a relaxed and sunny presence. She has creamy skin and clear eyes and wide-apart cheekbones, and you can see how happy it makes her to drive men crazy with her body. Yet there's no malice in her stripping—it's clean work.

It's also a little underwhelming. Shelton doesn't give her any super-colossal eye-poppers, and Haskell Wexler's filtered cinematography seems subdued for a subject this juicy. When Earl appears in his limo outside the Bourbon Street club, he's seen in shadow, at a distance—too far away to make as much of an impression as we'd like him to.

Earl is played by Paul Newman with a thatch of white hair, a sharper nose and a mumbly delivery—he chews his words 10 times before he swallows them. The real Earl was short and stout and old beyond his 63 years; Newman—he can't help it—is fit and handsome. Lord knows, he tries to be play Earl as a codger. But impersonation has never been Newman's gift and it takes a while for him to find his footing.

He gets much better as he goes along, though, and "Blaze" gets less mumbly, too—maybe beacuse we're pulled in by Shelton's glee at capturing Earl's amazing (true) story on screen. He lingers happily over scenes of Earl and his cronies talking shop and plotting strategy, drawn by the easiness of these old-time Louisiana politicians' rapport and their unflappability in the face of Earl's antics.

Shelton is one of the least puritanical film makers in America—he understands how democratic politics and big appetites go together naturally. This extends to sex, into which Earl hurls himself like a kid coming back to the ocean after a year's painful absence. The fun is splashy and guiltless and oral.

Blaze stood by her man when her tried to pass a bill that would abolish literacy tests at the polls so that uneducated blacks could vote, too. Shelton recreates the day that Long marched into the legislature and harangued the assembly about the rights of blacks—the day that really ended his career as governor. (His slogan in his subsequent run for congress was "I Ain't Crazy.")

There's something sentimental about the way the relationship is recreated—you can tell as you watch that it's based on the memoirs of someone still living. (There's little mention of Long's wife, and for all the movie tells you, Blaze was a virgin when she met the governor.)

But Earl himself would have responded to the tall-tale spirit of Shelton's inventions and interpolations. When, early in their relationship, Blaze won't sleep with the governor, he has her fill out a voter-registration form to keep the evening from being a total loss. If Earl didn't do that in real life, he'd have slapped himself on the side of the head and wished he had.

NEWSDAY, 12/13/89, Part II/p. 7, Mike McGrady

Gov. Earl Long, brother of Huey and scion of the Louisiana Longs, was a hard-drinking, hell-raising, crowd-pleasing political oddball who once described himself, accurately, as "half-crazy and half-intelligent." The intelligent half of Earl Long made him a formidable political presence, a populist who soaked the oil companies to pay for progressive welfare programs and a voting-rights advocate who bucked segregationist trends and managed to win a congressional nomination even after a stopover in an insane asylum.

Long's crazier half, the half that dominates the new movie "Blaze," prompted him to shoot off shotguns in public bars, to grab microphones and disrupt meetings of the state Ligislature and to get involved with a stripper named Blaze Starr.

As a basic movie situation, this union of a 65-year-old, highly public figure and a 28-year-old striptease *artiste* seems all but unimprovable. And while "Blaze" *is* entertaining, this colorful look at a colorful affair never gets much beyond situation, never quite covers the distance from colorful to meaningful.

To be sure, the novelty of a governor openly carrying on with a stripper is enough to hold one's interest for a considerable spell. And the presence of old pro Paul Newman, clowning it up in and out of the governor's baggy trousers, is certainly worth a look-see.

Writer-director Ron ("Bull Durham") Shelton has a gift for creating flamboyant characters. He also has a weakness for giving those characters little to do, and neither Earl Long nor Blaze Starr change one iota during the course of the film, giving the whole enterprise a somewhat static quality.

Still, it can be fun. Charged with buying congressman, Long snorts, "Never bought a congressman in my life. I rent 'em. It's cheaper." Explaining his decision to ignore scandal and to run again for public office: "I don't want to be a ex-governor; I ain't *ex*-governor material." Caught up in one peccadillo or another, he could be eloquently critical of himself: "Man in public life, he's got to be discreet in his indiscretions." Well, Earl Long may have been guilty of many things—cronyism, graft, truth-stretching—but no one ever charged him with discretion.

Since this is Earl Long as viewed through the eyes of his stripper-mistress, one should not be overly surprised that some of the facts are awry. Moreover, since the source material is the book "Blaze Starr: My Life as Told to Huey Perry," one may not be persuaded when the stripper herself is pictured as sweet, innocent, charming, bright and all but virginal. However, a little-known Canadian actress with the unlikely name of Lolita Davidovich does bring considerable natural warmth to the role.

Blaze's view of the governor, and Newman does all in his power to reinforce that view, is of a good-natured buffoon, a man who is to ordinary politics what hillbilly music is to opera. Admittedly, there are occasional nuggets of information not available to such other Long scholars as A.J. Liebling: Before first bedding down his young stripper, Earl took the time to don his heaviest boots.

On the other hand, hardly a truth passes unembellished. The fact that the governor was married (albeit unhappily) is not deemed worth a reference. And where "Blaze" pictures the governor perishing quietly in his lover's arms in a hotel suite on the very day of winning his last election, the truth is somewhat more prosaic—he perished some nine days later in a hospital room after drinking a cup of coffee. Such flaws, of course, can be attributed to the fact that we're not dealing with history here, but with her story.

NEWSWEEK, 12/18/89, p. 69, David Ansen

Writer-director Ron Shelton is a funky romanticist. His lovers in "Bull Durham" had a down-to-earth grit and larger-than-life panache. Larger still are the lovers in "Blaze," a chronicle of the flamboyant affair between Blaze Starr (Lolita Davidovich), the renowned redheaded stripper, and the late governor of Louisiana, Earl K. Long (Paul Newman). When they met in New Orleans in 1959, she was in her 20s and he was 63. She was a voluptuous country girl from West Virginia and he, brother of Huey Long, was a reckless and shrewd power broker with a bad heart, progressive ideas about black voting rights, and a colorfully corrupt approach to lubricating the wheels of government. Some folks thought "Ole Earl" was crazy—he was incarcerated in a mental hospital while still in office—and it wouldn't be hard to read venal motives into Blaze Starr's alliance with this powerful man. But Shelton, taking generous poetic license with Starr's autobiography, is a celebrant. He loves their swagger, their disregard for propriety, their last-of-the-breed romantic exhibitionism.

There's a lot to savor in Shelton's stylish movie, particularly in its sprightly and funny first hour. Newcomer Davidovich, looking like a hillbilly Rubens goddess, is a beguiling mix of innocent and tramp. Newman, obviously relishing old Earl's garrulous oratorical bombast, has a field day playing this bawdy old rooster with startled eyes. Yet for those who loved "Bull Durham," "Blaze" ultimately proves disappointing. Shelton, surprisingly, so idealizes this love story he takes too much of the sleaze out. A tale this outrageous would seem to demand a more freewheeling style, but Shelton never really lets his hair down. His movie peaks too early: it feels over when Long loses the gubernatorial election; the last half hour seems redundant. But if "Blaze" isn't quite the movie it could have been, it's much too good a tale to pass up. And it may make you ponder with nostalgia what we've given up in our age of rigorous ethical scrutiny and TV journalism: a political wild card like Long wouldn't survive and hour on "Phil Donahue."

TIME, 12/18/89, p. 93, Richard Corliss

It was an affair made in tabloid heaven: stripteaser Blaze Starr ("Miss Spontaneous Combustion, and I do mean *bust*-ion!") and Earl K. Long, fine Governor of the great state of Louisiana. Long was too full of his princely power to be discreet about his indiscretions. Blaze could have told him—and in this lengthy, clever, depressing film she does—that "your political instincts are clouded by the aroma of my perfume." By 1959, when Long's campaign slogan was the forthright "I ain't crazy," his liaison with the stripper was as controversial as his tax evasion and support for Negro voting rights. He lost. It was a little American tragedy, played as farce.

Ron Shelton *(Bull Durham)* directs *Blaze* with plenty of pungent wit, but from a high, disinterested view. He never gets steam into the affair. Paul Newman approaches Earl from the outside too, as a growly-bear clown who doesn't realize he's King Lear. Lolita Davidovich, making the most of her first big break, plays Blaze as a sensible, loving career gal with an overripe body. But the picture is nòt mainly about sex or even love; it is about an aging man's loss of sexual, political and personal power.

The film ends with a great shot. Blaze walks out of the state house where Earl's corpse lies, and the camera ascends to take in Long's old domain. Randy Newman's poignant song *Louisiana 1927*—a cracker's lament about a devastating flood—reaches its apogee of symphonic paranoia with the line "They're tryin' to wash us away." Just then, the camera discovers the Mississippi roaring past, washing away Earl and his wily, wild, pre-TV tradition of Southern politics. What has happened down there is that the wind has changed, and for its last three minutes *Blaze* finds potent film poetry to express that change. The rest of the movie lacks Earl's heroic craziness. And the stars could use a dose of Blaze's spontaneous combustion.

VILLAGE VOICE, 12/19/89, p. 91, J. Hoberman

Ron Shelton's *Blaze*, a glorified account of the madcap affair between Louisiana governor Earl Long and stripper Blaze Starr, means to be as voluptuously innocent as its heroine and as lovably eccentric as its hero. The movie is never less than obvious, but, frisking out of the gate, it's limber and zippy, almost debonair. Paul Newman plays the wacko gov with such flinty concentration one excepts to see flames shoot from his ears.

Far nuttier film fodder than the dank Profumo scandal (which followed it by three years), the Long-Starr coupling has a goofy Barnum & Bailey appeal. The 63-year-old, three-time governor—a garrulous good ol' boy with a talent for invective—hit the bottle and hooked up with Blaze during the course of a several-month, pre-election spree that ultimately landed him in a Texas mental hospital. It's midlife crisis as political screwball, and one can only imagine what David Lynch and Dennis Hopper might have made out of this star-spangled breakdown. Shelton, however, is more stolid and folksy.

As the big-hearted stripper, sweet-faced, ample Lolita Davidovich is stuck animating the world's corniest conception. She's a neophyte, though, so she takes the role seriously—her poise presaged in the early, Starr-is-born scene where a teenage Blaze, the yummiest-looking pastry in a D.C. diner, is tricked into doing a striptease at a sailor bar for a bunch of boys en route to Korea. As meta-eploitation, the sequence is at least good-naturedly simpering. Suddenly, it's 1959 in

New Orleans, with Blaze, now a tousle-haired strip-goddess, ogled by the governor as though she'd dropped down from Mars.

Not nearly as rubelike as his entrance suggests, Newman gives his most dapper character performance to date. Haggard yet trim, he seems to be signaling inner life by pushing his jaw out and gnawing his face from within. (This craggy preoccupation suggests a close study of the mad televangelist in the Werner Herzog doc, *God's Angry Man*.) As *Bull Durham* demonstrated, Shelton can write a juicy role: When Long fails to muster an erection, he rises quizzically from Blaze's embrace and starts lecturing his rebellious member: "You're on the state payroll, now wake up!" It's the movie's best joke on the nature of the body politic.

Earl Long was undoubtedly in major-league character; Shelton's mistake is to make him heroic. The movie sweetens Long's story (if not his language) and even hints that the old crock was a proto-'60s free spirit. Hardly a belated bon vivant slugging gin from a Coke bottle, Newman's Long is a visionary who keeps insisting that "the future's coming." The gov is crazy like a fox. Even when transfixed by Blaze's formidable "pair of rascals," he has the presence of mind to register her to vote. The very next morning, he makes a bid for *our* approval by tricking a state hospital into integrating its staff. (*Blaze* exaggerates Long's commitment to civil rights. While this liberal populist was never a race-baiter, he did—when pressured by white supremacist opponents—declare himself for segregation "one million per cent .")

Of course, Earl's situation was complicated by the fact that he had a nephew in the U.S. Senate and a wife—both written out of the tale. But then Shelton is more interested in simplifying (rather than sending up) American electoral politics. Just because Blaze realizes that she and Earl are both in show biz is no reason to provide a number of key characters with presidential totems: A sleazebag seducer has a portrait of Ike in his boudoir; Blaze watches JFK on the tube, while her salt-of-the-earth mother keeps a photo of FDR on the wall of her Appalachian shack. The connections are so thin they might be random.

Shelton is drawn to sexy, oddball Americana, with generic regional flavor and feel-good potential. But if *Blaze* starts like nouveau-Preston Sturges—an irreverent foible-fest stocked with weird-talking baritones—it ultimately turns cloyingly mythic. Scratch an American satirist and find a Frank Capra wannabe. Forget the Cajun hot sauce; this film is strictly molasses. Half an hour too long and a heartwarmer besides, *Blaze* turns an epic bender into a fairy-tale romance. The movie is so gently rollicking that it ends up rollicking itself to sleep.

Also reviewed in:
NEW YORK TIMES, 12/13/89, p. C24, Janet Maslin
NEW YORKER, 12/11/89, p. 136 Pauline Kael
VARIETY, 12/13/89, p. 28
WASHINGTON POST, 12/13/89, p. B1, Rita Kempley
WASHINGTON POST, 12/15/89, Weekend/p.65, Desson Howe

BLOODHOUNDS OF BROADWAY

A Columbia Pictures release of an American Playhouse Theatrical Film production. *Executive Producer:* Lindsay Law. *Producer:* Howard Brookner. *Director:* Howard Brookner. *Screenplay:* Howard Brookner and Colman deKay. *Director of Photography:* Elliot Davis. *Editor:* Camilla Toniolo. *Music:* Jonathan Sheffer. *Music Editor:* Alex Steyermark. *Choreographer:* Diane Martel. *Sound:* Allan Byer. *Sound Editor:* Wendy Hedin. *Production Designer:* Linda Comaway-Parsloe. *Art Director:* Jefferson Sage. *Set Decorator:* Ruth Ammon. *Set Dresser:* David Williams. *Special Effects:* David Scott Gagnon and Arthur Lorenz. *Costumes:* Beatrix Aruna Pasztor. *Make-up:* Nina Port. *Stunt Coordinator:* Jery Hewitt and Danny Aiello III. *Running time:* 93 minutes. *MPAA Rating:* PG.

CAST: Josef Sommer (Waldo Winchester); Madonna (Hortense Hathaway); Tony Azito (Waiter); Jennifer Grey (Lovey Lou); Tony Longo (Crunch Sweeney); Rutger Hauer (The Brain); Matt Dillon (Regret); Stephen McHattie (Red Henry); Anita Morris (Miss Missouri Martin); Ethan Phillips (Basil Valentine); Alan Ruck (John Wangle); Dinah Manoff (Maud Milligan); David Youse (Busboy); Randy Quaid (Feet Samuels); Julie Hagerty (Harriet MacKyle); Louis Zorich (Mindy); Esai Morales (Handsome Jack); Fisher Stevens (Hotfoot Harry);

Richard Edson (Johnny Crackow); Howard Brookner (Daffy Jack); John Rothman (Marvin Clay); Mark Nelson (Sam the Skate); Madeleine Potter (Widow Mary); Stellar Bennett (Thelma); Nicole Burdette (Woman on Corner); Colman deKay (Nosmo); Gerry Bamman (Inspector McNamara); Jane Brucker (Charlotte); Googy Gress (McGinty); Robert Donley (Doc Bodeeker); Grant Forsberg (Cab Driver); Shelly Abend (Long George); Veryle Rupp (Whitey); Helmar Augustus Cooper (Brother Divine); George Ede (Judge Witherspoon); William Burroughs (Butler); Michael Wincott (Soupy Mike); Herschel Sparber (Big Shelley); Black Eyed Susan (Minnie the Shrimp); Steve Buscemi (Whining Willie); Patrick Garner (Rodent Ralph); Tobin Wheeler (Fleming Meeks); Jean Brookner (Woman); Tamara Tunie (Cynthia Harris); Cathryn De Prume (Showgirl); Katherine Monick (Bobby Baker); Sara Driver (Yvette); William Murray Weiss (Joey the Toothpick); Leonard Termo (Goodtime Nate Fishkin); Graham Brown (Doc Frischer); Ed Zang (Hymie Weisberger); Vince Giordano and The Nighthawks ("300 Club" Musicians).

LOS ANGELES TIMES, 11/3/89, Calendar/p. 17, Sheila Benson

Heigh ho, if style were all, "Bleedhounds of Broadway" would be a romp. Instead, this star-crammed exercise in Roaring '20s fashion and atmosphere is a handsomely mounted, joyless dead end.

It does have one glimmering moment, when Madonna, one of its clutch of stars, punches right through the screen, singing "I Surrender, Dear," but it's not enough to stay awake for.

Meanwhile, Rutger Hauer, Matt Dillon, Jennifer Gray, Randy Quaid, Josef Sommer, Esai Morales, Julie Hagerty and the less-well-known but lovely Madeleine Potter are enmeshed in this complicated adaptation of four Damon Runyon short stories, strung together with a remarkable lack of urgency.

All the patented Runyon Broadway types are here, so many monikers that the mind soon gives up on them. A Walter Winchell-like newspaperman, Waldo Winchester (Josef Sommer), presides over the various problems.

Will friendly, goofus Feet Samuels (Quaid) persuade a dish like Hortense Hathaway (Madonna) to take him seriously? Will inveterate bettor Regret (Dillon) ever make an honest woman of songstress Lovey Lou (Grey)? Will socialite Harriet MacKyle (Hagerty) forswear her pet parrot for the attentions of gangster Basil Valentine (Ethan Phillips), who is less of a gunsel than she thinks he is? And will the Brain (Hauer), the dapper gangland leader knifed in the first scene and trucked around throughout this freezing 1928 New Year's Eve, finally find some guy or doll to take him in?

The movie itself has been trucked hither and yon. It was begun when Madonna was a brunette, in December of 1987. Reportedly in an effort to clarify its story line, Columbia, its present releasing studio, has re-cut it, adding a narration that was absent in the version by its producer-director-co-adapter, Howard Brookner, a documentary film maker ("Burroughs," "Robert Wilson and the CIVIL warS") whose first feature this was. Brookner, 35, died in April from AIDS.

It may not be possible to discern what Brookner's style was, with so many other hands involved. Certainly he had a beautiful eye for faces and characters: "Stranger Than Paradise's" flattened-nosed Richard Edson is shown off to great advantage, as is Steve Buscemi ("Parting Glances"), Michael Wincott, who plays the nicely ironic bartender, Soupy Mike, and Potter, in a pivotal role as the flower girl, Mary. (You may remember her debut in "The Bostonians." She is better here.) And it's clear that the look of the film was crucial to Brookner, from the witty costuming to the brilliant production design to the careful hair styles, accurate if not always flattering. (The exception is Madonna's Louise Brooks helmet of hair.)

Unfortunately, none of this is proof against this rat's nest of stories, which unravel with nothing like the audacity needed to sustain anyone's interest, beyond a passing one in this Art Deco ceiling fixture or that pearl-studded flapper dress.

NEW YORK POST, 12/8/89, p. 31, Jami Bernard

Here's a movie that got Madonna to work for scale as a jazz-baby nightclub singer but fails to have a single scene in which she sings solo. If problems were bugle beads, "Bloodhounds of Broadway" could outfit an entire chorus line.

This ill-fated amalgam of four Damon Runyon stories would need a bloodhound of its own to sniff out where things went wrong. After all, there is a dynamite, "in-crowd" cast, with everyone from the aforementioned Madonna to William Burroughs as a butler. There is a slew of colorful, prototypically Runyonesque characters, with names like The Brain, Sam the Skate and Handsome

Jack. There's the late-'20s world of New York gambling, drinking, romancing and welching on bets. And the movie is set in the frivolous gaiety of New Year's Eve, 1928, a party night aswirl with assignations, practical jokes, dangerous liaisons.

Yet the movie is dead, flat, confusing, disappointing, ill-cut, lifeless, and draining. *And* Madonna doesn't sing, a crime much worse than the The Brain being stabbed, Lovey Lou's romantic heartache, Feet Samuels' deadly pact with medical science, Regret's unerring nose for the wrong horse, and, oh, I could go on.

The film itself has had a history almost as convoluted as one of the tales it tells. It was produced, directed and co-written with much effort by Howard Brookner, who found out he had AIDS before filming was underway and who died last April without having final cut or, needless to say, seeing his film open. Even without knowing under what sad and difficult circumstances it was made, "Bloodhounds of Broadway" lacks the vibrancy and fascination that characterizes Runyon's prose.

Instead, holding sway are such faux-pearls as the suddenly marriage-minded Madonna saying, without a shred of irony: "I want to hear the patter of little feet." Or Jennifer Grey, similarly cast as a chanteuse fatale (but with no singing scenes), scolding her lover with a flat-footed delivery of: "If your excuses were snowflakes, we'd be digging out 'til winter."

You know you're in for trouble when the opening credits show outtakes of the film with captions like "Madonna…as Hortense Hathaway." Since this sort of thing is usually done at the end of a film, it's a sure sign that confusion is to follow. Who is who? Which one is Hotfoot Harry and why can't we see the scene where Widow Mary gets what's coming to her, or hear the song that Miss Missouri Martin (Anita Morris) dedicates to The Brain?

The plot, in short: It's New Year's Eve, the end of the delirious gangster era, and the hoods are living it up at Mindy's restaurant, and later at a society party. Romances are blooming and fading, craps are being shot, feuds are simmering, erupting and cooling, and getting underfoot are a pair of bloodhounds that are trying to sniff out a murderer.

Matt Dillon, looking just right for the part, is small-time gambler and womanizer Regret, named after the only horse he ever picked correctly. He's playing head games with Lovey Lou (a teary Grey), who spies him going off with Maud Milligan (Dinah Manoff). Randy Quaid is appropriately hapless as the lovestruck Feet Samuels, named for the big feet he has pre-sold to a scalpel-sharpening doc in return for cash with which to woo Hortense Hathaway (Madonna in a husky voice, Louise Brooks hairdo, and no solo).

There's more, although not enough screen time to do any of them justice. The Brain (Rutger Hauer) is finding out after being stabbed that you can buy some women's affections but you can't make them dress a wound; Julie Hagerty plays high-strung society lady Harriet MacKyle, who vows revenge when Handsome Jack (Esai Morales) shoots her macaw; and, probably the best and certainly the liveliest, Morris as nightclub owner Missouri Martin does, in fact, get to sing, although the camera frequently cuts away from her as it desperately tries to keep up with the bloodhounds, the bleedings, the intrigues and the amours.

Josef Sommer is Waldo Winchester, the Walter Winchell-style columnist, narrating in a hard-boiled '40s manner. And yes, that is Burroughs in a butler's uniform.

The period look is rich but surprisingly somber, often brownish, interrupted by frequent key-lighting of faces, as if a rectangle of illumination could compensate for the overall lack of electricity.

There is one scene where Madonna appears in a chorus line, cranks her neck Egyptian-style, swings on a stage swing and seems about to burst into song—but that footage must have gone the way of the bugle-bead dress.

NEWSDAY, 12/8/89, Part III/p. 5, Terry Kelleher

As far as New York movies are concerned, nostalgia truly ain't what it used to be.

First, Eddie Murphy's "Harlem Nights" made it appear that Harlem nightlife in 1938 wasn't nearly as funny or exciting as we'd like to think. Now here's "The Bloodhounds of Broadway," a comedy set on New Year's Eve, 1928. If this is all the roaring they did in the '20s, the Depression couldn't have been too drastic a change.

"The Bloodhounds of Broadway," which interweaves four Damon Runyon stories, must have seemed like a good idea at the time. But "Guys and Dolls" it's definitely not, though it introduces us to more of Runyon's guys and dolls than we can possibly keep straight in 80 minutes or so.

The late Howard Brookner's film, made under the aegis of public television's American Playhouse, is sometimes too arch, sometimes too sober and never much fun.

Julie Hagerty is the archest of 'em all as Harriet MacKyle, a dizzy rich dame fascinated by the raffish lower strata of society. My, how she envies gossip columnist Waldo Winchester (Josef Sommer), who gets to consort with such "marvelous types" night after night. So she rings out the old year with a lavish party and invites just about everybody in Gotham with a colorful nickname.

Before the MacKyle bash begins, we meet most of Waldo's winners at Mindy's, the extremely popular (though dimly lit) Broadway restaurant. The crew includes: Regret (Matt Dillon), a chronically unlucky horseplayer; Lovey Lou (Jennifer Grey), the showgirl who loves him; "Feet" Samuel (Randy Quaid), a likeable but impecunious lug with the largest shoe size in town; Hortense Hathaway (Madonna), the showgirl he loves; "Mizzou" Martin (Anita Morris), owner of a hotsy speakeasy called the 300 Club; the stylish gambling boss known as The Brain (Rutger Hauer); Handsome Jack (Esai Morales), the bootlegger whose sobriquet says it all; Basil Valentine (Ethan Phillips), Jack's schnooky sidekick... The guest list runs on and on till it reaches Hotfoot Harry (Fisher Stevens), a devilish gagster who sneaks around warming the soles of the unwary.

Harry would serve the cause better by lighting a fire under the audience. Though there are two gunshots, a knifing and a couple of brief outbreaks of fisticuffs, "The Bloodhounds of Broadway" seems almost devoid of purposeful activity. Madonna and Morris each get to start a sexy musical number, but they're barely warmed up before we cut away to something distinctly less interesting.

Few of the characters are given enough screen time to establish an identity, and few of the cast members seem to grasp the humor in the dialogue. As a result, some of the actors talk past the jokes while others tell them in italics. Exceptions are Quaid, who brings a certain sweetness to Feet, and Dillon, whose New York manner of speaking is naturally Runyonesque.

Grey is hardly the angel puss her part calls for, but the most-miscast award must go to Hauer, who might have looked more comfortable if his underworld character had been nicknamed "Dutch."

Beatrix Aruna Pastor's costume design may be the movie's biggest asset, and Madonna's hairstyle and makeup are the cat's meow. Perhaps she can put together a video from the outtakes.

VILLAGE VOICE, 12/19/89, p. 94, Georgia Brown

A Damon Runyon-inspired farce, *Bloodhounds of Broadway* seems conceived as a loose bundle of miniperformances by a clutch of notable actors. Produced by public television, it was the first feature by the talented Howard Brookner (*Burroughs, Robert Wilson and the Civil Wars*), who died last spring of AIDS just before his 35th birthday. *Bloodhounds*, infused with a gentle nostalgia, has a lovely bluish cast to it. It looks as if it were shot with a Camel smoke filter.

Columnist Waldo Winchester (Josef Sommer)—"My beat is Broadway"—narrates a peripatetic, hard-to-follow tale of the Great White Way. A "strangely shaped gentleman," Feet Samuels (Randy Quaid), has sold his feet to science for a few dollars, but, just as his forfeit is due, gets lucky at craps and discovers he has a chance to win Hortense (Madonna), a fresh-mouthed showgirl sporting a Louise Brooks helmet. A top gangster known as The Brain (Rutger Hauer) is knifed by mobsters from Brooklyn, but can't get any of his fair-weather mistresses to take him in. A loser at the horses called Regret (Matt Dillon), after the only horse he ever won on, tries to regain his miffed and pouting sweetheart (Jennifer Grey). An anorexic society matron (Julie Hagerty) has a yen for babyfaced gunmen. The door to her mansion is tended by an ancient butler (William Burroughs), whose line, "Your coat, Sir," receives the Runyonesque comeback, "What about it?"

Since Brookner's lovesong to Runyon (co-written with Colman deKay) fails to generate even a halfway gripping story, involvement is moot. For the most part, the characters simply sit around speakeasies and jazz joints and set out to look ravishing. That they do. Special mention should go to chief hairdresser Bruce Geller and to whoever came up with the spectacular pearls and rhinestones, the boas, cloches, and fringes, for this homage to a world on the cusp of 1929.

Also reviewed in:
NEW YORK TIMES, 12/8/89, p. C12, Vincent Canby
VARIETY, 6/7/89, p. 30

BORN ON THE FOURTH OF JULY

A Universal Pictures release of A. Kitman Ho & Ixtlan production. *Producer:* Oliver Stone and A. Kitman Ho. *Director:* Oliver Stone. *Screenplay:* Oliver Stone and Ron Kovic. *Based on the book by:* Ron Kovic. *Director of Photography:* Robert Richardson. *Editor:* David Brenner. *Music:* John Williams. *Music Editor:* Kenneth Wannberg. *Sound:* Tod A. Maitland and (music) Armin Steiner. *Sound Editor:* Wylie Stateman and Michael Minkler. *Production Designer:* Bruno Rubeo. *Art Director:* Victor Kempster and Richard L. Johnson. *Set Decorator:* Derek R. Hill. *Set Dresser:* George Toomer Jr., Craig H. Pittman, J. Grey Smith, Don Clark, and John Timothy Williams. *Special Effects:* William Oliver Purcell. *Costumes:* Judy Ruskin. *Make-up:* Sharon Ilson. *Special Effects Make-up:* Gordon Smith. *Stunt Coordinator:* Gil Arceo. *Running time:* 145 minutes. *MPAA Rating:* R.

CAST: Tom Cruise (Ron Kovic); Bryan Larkin (Young Ron); Raymond J. Barry (Mr. Kovic); Caroline Kava (Mrs. Kovic); Josh Evans (Tommy Kovic); Seth Allen (Young Tommy); Jamie Talisman (Jimmy Kovic); Sean Stone (Young Jimmy); Anne Bobby (Susanne Kovic); Jenna von Oy (Young Susanne); Samantha Larkin (Patty Kovic); Erika Geminder (Young Patty); Amanda Davis (Baby Patty); Kevin Harvey Morse (Jackie Kovic); Kyra Sedgwick (Donna); Jessica Prunell (Young Donna); Frank Whaley (Timmy); Jason Klein (Young Timmy); Jerry Levine (Steve Boyer); Lane R. Davis (Young Steve); Richard Panebianco (Joey Walsh); John Pinto (Young Joey); Rob Camilletti (Tommy Finnelli); J.R. Nutt (Young Tommy); Stephen Balwin (Billy Vorsovich); Philip Amelio (Young Billy); Michael McTighe (Danny Fantozzi); Cody Beard (Young Danny); Ryan Beadle (Ballplayer); Harold Woloschin (Umpire); Richard Grusin (Coach); Tom Berenger (Recruiting Sergeant); Richard Haus (2nd Recruiting Sergeant); Mel Allen (Mel Allen); Ed Lauter (Legion Commander); Liz Moore (Fat Lady at Parade); Sean McGraw (Young Donna's Father); Oliver Stone (News Reporter); Dale Dye (Infantry Colonel); Norma Moore (Massapequa Mom); Stacey Moseley (Young Donna's Friend); Bob Tillotson (Truck Driver); John Getz (Marine Major); David Warshofsky (Lieutenant); Jason Gedrick (Martinez); Michael Compotaro (Wilson); Paul Abbott, Bill Allen, William Baldwin, Claude Brooks, Michael Smith Guess, James Le Gros, William R. Mapother, Christopher W. Mills, Byron Minns, and Ben Wright (Platoon); Markus Flanagan (Doctor); R.D. Call (Chaplain); John Falch, Dan Furnad, Fred Geise, Greg Hackbarth, and Don Wilson (Corpsmen). Corkey Ford (Marvin); Rocky Carroll (Willie); SaMi Chester, Chris Pedersen, Chris Walker (Aides); Willie Minor (Eddie); David Herman, Bruce MacVittie, Damien Leake, David Neidorf, Paul Sanchez, Richard Lubin, Norm Wilson, Peter Benson, Sergio Scognamiglio (Patients); Billie Neal (Nurse Washington); Richard Poe (Frankie); Bob Gunton (Doctor #1); Vivica Fox (Hooker); Mark Moses (Optimistic Doctor); Abbie Hoffman (Strike Organizer); Jake Weber (Donna's Boyfriend); Reg E. Cathey (Speaker); Edie Brickell (Folksinger); Keri Roebuck (Loudspeaker); Geoff Garza (Young Radical); Joseph Reidy (Student Organizer); Holly Marie Combs (Jenny); Mike Starr, Beau Starr, and Rick Masters (Men); John Del Regno, Gale Mayron, and Lisa Barnes (Friends); Melinde Ramos Renna (Bar Maid); Willem Dafoe (Charlie); Tom Sizemore, Andrew Lauer and Michael Wincott (Vets); Ivan Kane, Ed Jupp Jr., and Michael Sulsona (Villa Vets); Cordelia Gonzalez (Maria Elena); Karen Newman (Whore); Begonia Plaza (Charlie's Whore); Edith Diaz (Madame); Anthony Pena (Bartender); Eduardo Ricardo (Cab Driver); Tony Frank (Mr. Wilson); Jayne Haynes (Mrs. Wilson); Lili Taylor (Jamie Wilson); Elbert Lewis (Cab Driver); Peter Crombie (Undercover Vet); Kevin McGuire, Ken Osborne, and Alan Toy (Paraplegics); Chuck Pfeiffer (Secret Service Agent); Frank Girardeau and William Wallace (Agents); Chip Moody (T.V. Anchor); Eagle Eye Cherry, Brian Tarantina, Frank Cavestani, and Jimmy L. Parker (Vets); William Knight (Chief Cop); David Carriere (Miami Hippie); John Galt (Fat Republican); Jack McGee (Democratic Delegate); Keri Roebuck, Kristel Otney, and Pamela S. Neill (Women); Jodi Long and Michelle Hurst (Reporters); John McGinley and Wayne Knight (Officials).

FILMS IN REVIEW, 3/90, p. 177, C.M. Fiorillo

Oliver Stone cuts deep into this nation's psyche. His latest film, *Born on the Fourth of July*, is a powerful assault on our minds and emotions. Based on the autobiography of Vietnam veteran Ron Kovic, and adapted for the screen by Kovic and Stone, the film is both a strong anti-war statement and a tribute to the courageous disabled veterans it portrays.

Tom Cruise—in an Oscar caliber performance—takes us on the journey of Kovic's life, from gung ho Marine to disillusioned paraplegic. [Kovic's spine was shattered by a V.C. bullet during his second tour in 'nam. He is paralyzed from the chest down.]

The most brutal episodes depict Kovic's stay in a Bronx V.A. hospital severely bereft of adequate staff and equipment. Rats roam freely, as American servicemen lie helpless in their own excrement. There, Kovic's frustration and rage become ours.

After a brief and bitter sojourn at home where he rails against the very things he once believed in—God, Mother, and Country—a distraught Kovic escapes to a Mexican community created by other wheelchair-bound vets. At Villa Dulce they do nothing all day except play poker, drink mescal, and carouse with whores to their hearts' content. It is here that Kovic spends his first night with a woman. Watching him confront his impotence is heartwrenching. A fellow paraplegic named Charlie is the catalyst for Kovic's return to America. (It is a small but urgent role, skillfully handled by the captivating Willem Dafoe.) Charlie generates the pangs that give birth to vehement war protester Ron Kovic.

Used to playing feisty, strong young men, Cruise is astonishing in a role that limits his physicality. Because of this restraint, Kovic's struggle and passion must come from inside. Cruise's intense, fiery eyes and impassioned words bring us deeply into Kovic's being. He hammers home the daily indignities of life in a wheelchair, and the sense of loss and frustration. That he also brings to life Kovic's will to survive is a sign of Cruise's depth and range as an actor. Surely he is the best of his generation.

Cruise is backed by a solid cast of supporting players. These include Raymond J. Barry and Caroline Kava as Kovic's parents; Kyra Sedgwick as Donna, his childhood sweetheart; Frank Whaley as Timmy, his close friend and fellow war survivor; and Josh Evans as Tommy, his tormented younger brother. The late Abbie Hoffman appears as a strike organizer; Tom Berenger appears as a Marine sergeant. Serving as director of photography is Stone regular Robert Richardson. Music is by John Williams.

Academy Award-winning director Oliver Stone's genius is his ability to horrify, to throw emotional knockout punches. His films take your breath away and leave you weak. His direction is intense; his style, aggressive. Strong, passionate men are his signature. With *Born on the Fourth of July*, he has again proven himself an extraordinarily gifted director. His latest film is a harrowing journey, yet one we are obliged to take. Stone peels back our skin and reveals the truth, however painful it may be. His film sears our conscience. Though him and his gifted star Cruise, we see ourselves, finally. Stone relates Kovic's near-tragic story vividly through several memorable scenes. Each scene is a beautiful facet of the gem that is *Born on the Fourth of July*. (That these moments are loosely stiched together and never form a fluid picture is but a minor distraction.) Stone surrounds us with sights and sounds to horrify us, yet compel us to keep watching, keep listening. Even the most minute detail is rendered with precision. The film works because Oliver Stone created it, because he makes us *believe*, makes us *feel*.

As Ron Kovic's story comes full circle (he is about to address the 1976 Democratic National Convention), this heartwrenching film comes to an end. Our glimpse into one man's anguished and painful journey is over. But there is no sense of relief. That is the vision of a great director and the mark of a great film.

LOS ANGELES TIMES, 12/20/89, Calendar/p. 1, Sheila Benson

In "Born on the Fourth of July's" best scene, young, wheelchair-bound Ron Kovic and another traumatically wounded Vietnam War vet sit in the dark of Kovic's back yard, drinking a liberating number of beers and remembering high school classmates who've been killed—already, in the early years of the war.

For the first time with someone who speaks the same language, the two men joke irreverently about the fate—and the stupidity—that got one buddy blown up by a land mine and another pair of twins killed.

In this casually profane byplay, Kovic comes alive, almost for the first time. Before this, Tom Cruise, who plays him with previously untapped eloquence, has had virtually no chance to dig in and show us the real man. In director Oliver Stone's extended prologue, we've seen Kovic as a youngster, playing war in the Massapequa, N.Y., woods; as a driven high school athlete; as a star-crossed high-school lover and as one of the few good men the Marine Corps was looking for. He's been turned into an idealized figure in Stone's furious moral lesson on the macho American mentality that led us to Vietnam.

No one can doubt Stone's sincerity, any more than they can his talent for bravura emotionalism. But when his film needs to lower its voice and make crucial points clear, like the issues behind Kovic's political transformation, Stone turns up the volume and blasts over any such pantywaist distinctions. It turns "Fourth of July" into passionate pyrotechnics; you gasp as they go off, but they touch your emotions, not your mind.

Stone is a punishing director, never more so when he deals with Vietnam, clearly one of the central experiences of his life. In his deeply moving, tightly focused "Platoon," he was able to re-create that war so personally that its sounds, its dangers, its terrifying randomness came alive to every audience.

With "Born on the Fourth of July," he is dealing with a wider time frame, the mid-'50s through the Vietnam War and the birth of the anti-war movement. His trickier challenge is to convey one veteran's political journey from right-wing patriot to anti-war activist and his private journey from inchoate rage to a modicum of peace. However, possibly because Stone empathizes so enormously with co-writer Kovic, who came back from Vietnam at the age of 21 paralyzed from the chest down, the director has lost the specificity that made "Platoon" so electrifying. In its place he uses bombast, overkill, bullying. His scenes, and their ironic juxtapositioning, explode like land mines.

The explosions do their job. One would have to be granite not to be moved by these painful sequences. Kovic's Vietnam action is a maelstrom of confusion and accident, where civilian women and babies are maimed and destroyed and where he mortally wounds a fellow Marine. The actuality of this field hospital is a scene from hell, not "MASH." And there is the purgatory of Kovic's Bronx VA hospital, an overtaxed, filthy, rat-ridden facility. Quieter moments have their own tension: the happy-face surface of his return home and the repression underneath. But because we never know the characters except as symbols, and because Stone pulls out all the stops almost all the time, he undermines the story he wishes to tell so fervently to tell.

He has chosen his central figure well, however. Cruise is not deep and you never catch a watchful intelligence lurking in his eyes. Playing Kovic may require other priorities: fierce physicality, empathy and the ability to work full throttle for virtually every scene. Cruise delivers all that and a quality of defenselessness that is terribly touching.

But just how do you build a "Yankee Doodle boy," a love-it-or-leave-it patriot? From "Fourth of July" we learn that it was his devout, repressed-hysteric mother (Caroline Kava) who fed young Ron every jingoistic message. The script makes her prescient as well; watching Kennedy's inaugural address, she tells little Ronnie that in her dream, *he* was making a speech too, and everyone was listening. Then, as though we weren't listening, Stone plays her dream-prediction again at the film's end, just as he *is* about to speak, thus making an otherwise tactful closing scene overstated and obvious.

Perhaps this is just what Kovic's mother said. Perhaps she also told him, as she does here, that it was God's will that he should go and fight the communists. But the direction of Kava has turned her into a looming Mom From Hell. She was subtle and fine as Mickey Rourke's murdered wife in "Year of the Dragon."

And still to come is the nightmare of a scene in which the drunk, tortured Kovic confronts his mother with the blood on his conscience and his howling fury at his impotence. Aghast, she shrieks, "Don't you *dare* say *penis* in his house!," causing him to scream nothing but that word for what seems like eons. This is quintessential Oliver Stone; it's also patently unplayable. (Language like this and the film's extremely realistic battle and hospital scenes give it its R rating.)

In the film's 2 hours and 25 minutes, there seems to be warfare on the screen every 15 minutes: in Vietnam, then at home in intrafamily dissension between Kovic and an anti-war younger brother, then between Kovic and his mother. There's a surreal sort of war in Mexico when Kovic, desperately trying to regain his manhood, takes refuge in a small village whose neighboring brothel caters to disabled men. Here, he butts heads and wheelchairs with fellow vet Willem Dafoe. In this vast cast, only Dafoe, Kava, Frank Whaley from the back-yard scene and Josh Evans as Kovic's younger activist brother have a chance to stand out.

Then there are the political wars: campus protests after Kent State, melees at the Republican convention at Miami Beach, where a thoroughly radicalized Kovic now leads a group of vets in protesting Nixon's acceptance speech in Miami Beach in 1972. The screen is a virtual battleground and you leave the theater battered in the onslaught.

You may not leave it feeling you *know* Ron Kovic, however. You have met him, suffered with him, shuddered at his pain, hoped that he would find a modicum of peace. But know him? Unfortunately for us, such crucial introductions are not Oliver Stone's strong suit.

MONTHLY FILM BULLETIN, 4/90, p. 97, Richard Combs

Massapequa, Long Island. In the late 50s and early 60s, growing up in a large working-class Catholic family, Ron Kovic unquestioningly accepts his mother's belief in a healthy body in a healthy mind, the community's patriotism and Communist phobia, and the national success ethic. Heartbroken when he fails his school in a wrestling match, Ron eagerly accepts the challenge when a Marine recruiting sergeant comes to lecture the students on the élite requirements of the corps and its vital role in Vietnam. On the eve of his departure, having failed through a misunderstanding to take his childhood sweetheart Donna to the high-school prom, Ron runs through the rain to join her in a last dance. In 1967, near the Cua Viet River in Vietnam, Ron's unit attacks a village that turns out to contain only old people and children, until an NVA ambush leads to a confused retreat and Ron's accidental killing of another, recently arrived Marine, Wilson. After trying unsuccessfully to report this, Ron is himself wounded in an attack, and with his spine severed winds up crippled from the chest down. After a spell in a filthy veterans' hospital in the Bronx, he returns to Massapequa in a wheelchair. He is the guest of honour in a 4th of July parade disrupted by anti-war demonstrators, and argues with his younger brother who is against the war. He visits Donna, now a student in Syracuse, and one of the organisers of the campus anti-war movement; caught up in a demonstration, Ron is himself hassled by police. Returning home, he feels himself to be an embarrassing freak, unable to talk about his condition (particularly his impotence), and in 1970 leaves for Mexico. There other Vietnam paraplegics (particularly the bellicose Charlie) encourage him to think that a life of debauchery is still possible, until some of the same problems re-emerge. He returns to the U.S. and visits Wilson's poor Georgia family, where he finds some release by confessing what happened. He joins the Veterans Against the War movement, and angrily disrupts the 1972 Republican Party Convention in Miami. In 1976, having written a book about his experiences, and feeling that he has at last come home, Ron addresses the nation from his wheelchair at the Democratic Party Convention in New York.

Although its hero's Catholic boyhood is very much to the point, as part of the baggage of fear and repression, self-abnegation and self-betterment, that drives him into the arms of the Marine recruiting sergeant, *Born on the Fourth of July* is Oliver Stone's most secular parable yet of fall and redemption. There's a significant explanation for this in the title itself. *Salvador* elided the country of that name with the Salvation its hero obscurely sought by involving himself in its politics; *Platoon* described a one-man (or one-soul) military band containing good and evil, innocence and experience, moving into the hinterland of its own imagination, which for dramatic convenience could be called Vietnam. But *Born on the Fourth of July* reverses this solipsistic process: the date commemorates Ron Kovic's birthday and simultaneously buries it in the national one. The film's primary project becomes not to save its hero, not to redeem him from the baseness that is a given from Charlie Sheen's first voice-over in *Platoon* about why he volunteered for Vietnam, but to discover him, to unearth him from all the hoopla of parades and twirling batons and the ideology that goes with it.

Ron Kovic goes to Vietnam not at the behest of private demons but national ones, or domestic and cultural ones—hysterical mother, kill-crazy wrestling coach, fear of Commie infiltration—which he internalises and reduces to one manically repeated phrase about his country, "Love it or leave it". Such a processed man would make a suitable case for study but he can hardly make a very sympathetic hero for a director who believes that the real struggle is that between God and the Devil in the solitary soul. Stone may blame the processing and false values for sending young men off to die or be crippled in Vietnam, but he cannot convincingly organise his scenario around these themes, and the first part of his film has a curiously detached quality. On the one hand it is slightly defensive about its hero so easily swallowing the 'better dead than Red' ethic (the only one of his schoolfriends to poohpooh the Red scare does so out of blatant self-interest, a character who later 'matures' into a fast-food entrepreneur), and on the other it mechanically invokes all kind of social conditioning but doesn't really explore it. In the opening sequence, Ron and his boyhood friends playing war games in the woods might be boys being boys, victims of gun lore, of Cold War propaganda or of other myths about what it takes to be a man. But all that the sequence delivers, with its headlong camera movement and vertiginous angles, are heavy intimations of the danger into which this play acting will soon lead them.

The dizzying, headlong movement is characteristic of the film as a whole, and rather uncharacteristic of Stone up to now, except in such isolated sequences as the 'feeding frenzy' scenes in the trading room of *Wall Street*. What it seems to express here is not any dynamic within scenes but one that Stone needs to create around his hero. Eventually the restless movement will be a kind of compensation for Kovic's physical immobility, but initially, with the camera plunging through crowds and parades, elaborate 50s and 60s set-pieces, there's a sense of it desperately searching out its hero. If there's a frenzy here it's that of a director who must set up this social context to explain what happened to Kovic, when he cannot really identify with heroes who are made this way. And the frenzy to turn Kovic into a Stone hero can be attributed to the obvious ways in which he is Stone's *alter ego*: as a Vietnam veteran himself, Stone first attempted to film Kovic's story over ten years ago, and then revived the project after *Platoon* instead of doing a sequel based on his own post-war experiences.

All the 50s and 60s scene-setting echoes much adolescent and family drama of the period but doesnt 'take' in its own right; it comes with no added psychological acuity or interest. In the scope format, these scenes also appear to be framing movie memories of the period, though again recreating their mood without any insight. Stone is no Movie Brat, and if his films don't connect in an immediate visceral way, they don't connect at a more reflective level. Where the viscera are engaged, of course, is in Vietnam. There is an immediate lift in the film's confidence, as well as a raising of the spiritual stakes, as soon as it shifts from "Moon River" and Kovic running through the rain to the high-school prom (in a surely accidental memory of *Breakfast at Tiffany's*) to this new terrain. Stone's evocation of Vietnam is no period recreation like the Massapequa scenes but an immersion in a physical environment at once so intense yet terrifyingly fluid and unreal that to pass through it is necessarily a rebirthing experience. (The coastal firefights here have a liquescent, shimmering, dimly burning air very different from the green hell of *Platoon*, yet equally stunning as combat footage.) Kovic's rebirth will involve the death of his innocence, doubly signalled: first by his own shooting of another, newly landed Marine, in the confusion of battle, and then by the wound that will leave him crippled from the chest down for the rest of his life.

Kovic's suffering through this, and subsequently through his 'rehabilitation' in a Veterans Administration hospital, certainly primes him for redemption. But in *Salvador* and *Platoon*, the heroes were already fallen men when they arrived on their foreign venture; it was by surviving this alien hell, transcending it and themselves in the process, that they achieved redemption. Kovic has to be returned home to find his portion of grace, and this returns Stone to the scenario he had problems with at the beginning: he has to find a social rationale for his hero's change of heart rather than having it spring from inner necessity, by fiat of a director who always works from the vitals outwards. The rationale will be Kovic's growing involvement in the anti-war movement, where one feels Stone going through the motions of a political conversion just as he did earlier through the processing (even the scenes of demonstration and confrontation lack grip and conviction, despite the authenticating presence of such as Abbie Hoffman on the Syracuse campus).

What exercises more grip is the scene of Kovic's visit to the Wilson home, where he confesses his (double?) murder—a scene not in Kovic's own account—and the detour to Mexico, which briefly holds out the promise of another self-confirming foreign venture (a friendlier Vietnam). But it turns out more like the false promise of Peckinpah's *Bring Me the Head of Alfredo Garcia*, and Kovic must needs return home a second time. His assertion, though, on the podium of the 1976 Democratic Convention, that he feels like he is finally home, has the ring of false confidence. It is not the hero's peace of mind which is in doubt so much as that of a director who has been forced to resolve familiar conflicts on this unfamiliar terrain.

NEW STATESMAN & SOCIETY, 3/9/90, p. 44, Suzanne Moore

Who knows where Vietnam is any more? Who can remember how the war started and exactly when it ended? Who really needs to know, when fiction is somehow so much more *definite* than the blur of history? When Hollywood has demarcated a territory called "Vietnam" so well that we no longer need a map or a fact to help us along. For Hollywood's Vietnam has been a new frontier where history and geography melt into air. An imaginary place which, as Gilbert Adair points out in his astute book on the subject, eventually tells us more about Hollywood than it ever could about Vietnam.

This brave new war zone lies somewhere between Kilgore's immortal line of dialogue in *Apocalyse Now:* "I love the smell of napalm in the morning," and Stallone's plea at the end of *Rambo:* "All I want, and all any guy who ever fought in Vietnam wants, is for our country to love us as much as we love it." The Vietnam of the movies is strung out somewhere between *Taxi Driver's* Travis Bickle preparing to fight his own personal war ("It's a jungle out there") and Jon Voight's disabled veteran in *coming Home* who gives Jane Fonda not only her first orgasm but instantaneously frizzy hair.

Vietnam is forever grunts and gooks and geeks, John Wayne's green beret and Coppola's choppers, the fabricated Russian roulette of *The Deer Hunter* and the all-engulfing jungle of *Platoon*. Somewhere in the midst of all this is that distant war, a collective trauma that still troubles the sleep of the American conscience, that makes it sit bolt upright in bed at night as the long-repressed memory floods back.

Born on the Fourth of July, Oliver Stone's powerful new film based on Ron Kovic's autobiography, is important not because of all those Oscar nominations but because it publicly accepts the emotional cost of Vietnam without trying to justify it. It's a loud, showy, rambling and at times incoherent movie that pushes through the confusion not to make some universal statement about war being a "bad thing", but rather to say quite simply that what America did in Vietnam was wrong. Through Kovic's story of an impossibly athletic and idealistic clean-cut American boy who gets his spine shattered whilst serving in Vietnam, Stone overturns many of the conventions of the Nam movie.

Stone, as he has reminded us in interview after interview, has a handle on the truth because he was *there*, and Kovic who co-wrote the script was obviously there. The late Abbie Hoffman, who advised on the anti-war demonstrations in the film, was also there in a sense. This leaves Tom Cruise to convince us that he too was there, which he does in a brilliant performance. This obsession with authenticity has been worked into the script of many Nam movies, with characters often declaring that only those who have been through the Vietnam experience can know what it was like. John Rambo on returning to Vietnam says he has "come home", which is doubly ironic when you consider that Stallone spent the war coaching tennis in a girls' school.

Cruise transforms himself during the course of the film from goody-goody patriot to hairy peace activist and Stone, whilst terrific at portraying a man raging at his disability, is less good at showing us the more complex process of politicisation that Kovic goes through. Where Stone excels is in the portrayal of combat and its aftermath. The familiar inland swamp iconography which he managed to create so viscerally in *Platoon* is exchanged for the blinding glare of the coast. Jerky camera movements convey the impossibility of seeing amongst the sand dunes. The Vietnamese are here at least glimpsed as ordinary soldiers and Kovic's accidental killing of another American is a reminder of the staggeringly high number of US soldiers killed in so-called "friendly fire". The Americans are no more at home here than they are in the jungle and its is these hostile, hallucinatory landscapes that wore them down despite their more advanced weaponry.

Returning home, Kovic (paralysed from his mid-chest down) doesn't receive a hero's welcome but is shunted into an unbelievably squalid veteran's hospital. These episodes are as harrowing as any war scenes. He cannot walk, he is impotent, he has been betrayed by that which he loved most—his country. The whore-houses of Mexico are no more of a consolation than the oblivion of drugs and alcohol. The character who cannot accept what has happened to him seems a million miles from the benign Kovic who recently appeared on *Wogan*.

Stone's achievement is in underlining the fact that patriotism and anti-war activism were not mutually exclusive activities as the hawks so often painted them. However, as in so many portrayals of the war, women come off badly. Here they are literally whores, virginal sweethearts and repressed mothers. Kovic's impotence and the resulting exploration of what it means to be a man run parallel with the American realisation that phallic fire power didn't for once guarantee absolute victory.

This is why so many of these films endeavour to explain the war to America with scant regard for the Vietnamese. They take place in some ahistorical time, crucial for successful mythmaking. They play on our ignorance and historical confusion. How many people now, ffor instance, realise that Robert Altman's *MASH* was about Korea and not Vietnam at all? Or that the first Rambo movie, *First Blood*, was set entirely in the States? It is through this device that, as Adair argues, the war is kept going.

This mythical quality of so many Nam movies is further enriched by presenting Vietnam as an internal war, a psychic and psychedelic war, a civic war. "The enemy was in us," says one character in Platoon. "There is a war going on right here," says a black nurse in the Bronx hospital in *Born on the Fourth of July*. The real victims of the war, we are led to believe, were not the Vietnamese but the Americans.

Stone's latest film may be guilty of some of this; yet it triumphs finally because it grabs at all those fantasies, media constructions and obscene images and forces them to confront the passing of time and the changing of the world—in other words, history. It pulls the whole bloody mess that was Vietnam back into the American dream. It plucks it out of the timeless genre of the war film and puts it back in the past. Which means that despite strenuous efforts by Rambo and the others to keep fighting, to keep the war alive, to say the war isn't over yet, Stone is brave enough to utter the unutterable. That not only did the war end a long, long time ago but that America lost.

NEW YORK, 12/18/89, p. 103, David Denby

Ron Kovic, the decorated Vietnam vet who was wounded in combat—paralysed, at the age of 21, from the chest down—is not the kind of man to spare others his suffering. Condemned to his wheelchair, miserable over acts he had committed in the war, he lost faith not only in the conflict but in mother, country, and God—everything. From *Born on the Fourth of July* the pulverizing epic movie Oliver Stone has made out of Kovic's account of his life, we can see that Kovic (Tom Cruise) was as hard on himself as on everyone else. The movie takes him down to the depths of degradation, and then part of the way back. All through it, he wails and howls, like a figure in a Greek tragedy crying out to the gods.

He shares some other things with those heroes—courage and a driving need to face disaster openly. His conviction that what matters to him should matter to other people as well can seem, at times, like righteous showing-off. It can also seem like inspiration. *Born on the Fourth of July* is a relentless but often powerful and heartbreaking piece of work, dominated by Tom Cruise's impassioned performance. His Ron Kovic is not a natural winner like other Cruise characters but a clenched, patriotic, working-class boy—a "Yankee-Doodle dandy" who has to fight for every bit of intellectual and moral clarity he gets.

Cruise has dropped his confident smile, his American-eagle look. In the past, he has seemed callow, a failing he disguised with cockiness. But Ron Kovic, who believed everything his parents and his country told him, was himself callow, and when Cruise shrieks in dismay he sounds right. His work may lack the precision, the sense of proportion, the feeling for climax that a great actor would bring to suffering, but he does, undeniably, have power. Raging against helplessness, he gives a brave and vulnerable performance that many people, I think will find harrowing—not just young men but women and Cruise's natural audience, teenage girls, who may be shocked and moved as Cruise picks fights in bars and throws himself drunkenly on girls and screams at his religious and priggish mother about his limp penis.

Oliver Stone has become as unrelenting as Kovic. From his earlier films (*Salvador, Platoon, Wall Street, Talk Radio*), we understood that he was enraged by the softness of American mythmaking—the lies, the evasions, the Reaganite media scam that turned greed into public virtue and the disaster of Vietnam into an illusion of noble endeavor undermined by weakhearted liberals. But *Platoon* was almost consoling in comparison with *Born on the Fourth of July*.

Stone and Kovic have consciously created an anti-myth. Born on July 4, 1946, Kovic is raised in a large family in Massapequa, Long Island. At first, Stone makes everything exemplary, almost dreamy in its sunshiny Americanness: a slow-motion homer in a baseball game; a pretty girl kissing Kovic. But he also plants intimations that Kovic can fail: Kovic trains for and then fights hard in a championship wrestling match, which (in a startling reversal of movie convention) he loses. Uneasiness creeps in.

From the beginning, Kovic is primed with patriotism, war, and God. His mother (Caroline Kava) enters the family dining room in the early sixties saying things like "Those Communists have to be stopped." Stone makes every line, every moment, part of Kovic's conditioning, as if the boy had no secret life, no *self*. Trying to show us the perfect American hero-dummy (Mom's victim), Stone holds the movie in too tight a grip. The war scenes, set along a sparkling river rather than in the usual lush jungle, are a frenzied horror of confusion and panic. Recovering from his wounds in a Bronx V.A. hospital, Kovic encounters a new horror, the decrepitude of urban America. Rats roam the squalid wards. The nurses and aides—urban blacks, alien to Kovic—are alternately cheerful and callously indifferent; one aide, caring only for the civil-rights struggle, lectures the half-dead Kovic on the futility of the war. Stone, a liberal, demonstrates almost Purple Heart courage himself in putting this painful stuff on the screen.

Obsessed with making sexual contact with a girl, Kovic turns against his mother. It's Mom, socializing America's youth with patriotic drivel while trying to subdue their sexual drives, who gets the most shocking abuse in the movie. Escaping from home, Kovic heads for a vacation village in Mexico that caters to crippled men, and he finds solace with a beautiful whore. For a while, the savagery breaks free into a bitter joyousness. Willem Dafoe, in magnificent voice, shows up as a Vietnam vet who's in even worse shape than Kovic. In a hilarious scene, the two men in their wheelchairs fight in the middle of the Mexican desert. They could be figures out of Samuel Beckett—Zed and Zero, lunging at an empty universe. Kovic, hitting bottom, pulls himself together and heads home.

Through most of the movie, Stone directs as if he were in as much pain as his impotent hero—as if he didn't have an obligation as an artist to shape his anger and then turn it loose when it counts most. Mistakenly, he tries to blow us away in every scene. Watching the movie is like being held in the grip of a brilliant monomaniac. In scene after scene, Stone jams the camera right up against people's faces, as if he were grabbing them by the lapels; or he gets cinematographer Robert Richardson to jerk the camera from one place to another in a rough, heart-stopping blur.

What Stone wants, of course, is not only to re-create Kovic's experiences from the inside but to bring us closer to mess and suffering—the blood and puke and disorder—so we can't escape into consoling "aesthetic" responses. Sometimes, I admit, the power of the movie is over-whelming. After Kovic's unit has accidentally wiped out a Vietnamese family in a chaotic battle, Kovic accidentally kills an American Marine as well. A pious Catholic boy, he wants to confess the act to his commanding officer, but the officer won't listen to him (and therefore won't absolve him), and the close-ups of the two men sweating in the officer's tent are anguishing. Later, back home, an anti-war protester along with other vets, Kovic enters the 1972 Republican National Convention in Miami, and from his point of view, as he looks up, the outraged faces, swollen under their straw boaters, look obscene in their contempt for him.

But there's a problem in staying so close to Kovic's anger: His personal torments rather than any reasoned political arguments, appear to be what turned him against the war. The movie seems out of balance. A young man's loss of potency is equated with the country's loss of honor.

Stone, better than anyone before him, has caught the combined nightmarish and exhilarating quality of the 1966–1972 period, a time when many young people, mesmerized by the government's lies about the war, wanted to waste themselves, wanted to become filthy and obscene as a way of bearing witness, in their own bodies, to the truth. Truth is all-important to Oliver Stone. At a noisy Fourth of July parade, the *pop-pop-pop* of firecrackers makes the World War II veterans flinch. Yet there's a damaging literal-mindedness in Stone's work. He's often overexplicit. He doesn't really trust us to get his point, and although he has the instincts and the courage to tackle major themes, he doesn't really trust his art either. Someday, he may discover that art can be a way to truth rather than an escape from it.

NEW YORK POST, 12/20/89, p. 23, David Edelstein

Few images of the anti-war protests of the '60s and '70s provoked more shock and rage than Ron Kovic—a soldier who'd been paralyzed from the mid-chest down in Vietnam—when he and other Vietnam Veterans Against the War crashed the Republican National Convention in 1972, on the night Richard Nixon accepted his renomination for president.

For those who believed in the war's immorality, Kovic's rant about massacred Vietnamese civilian and young American men sentenced to death and dismemberment by a deceitful government became the ultimate weapon in their passionate struggle; for those whose retort was, "My country right or wrong," Kovic symbolized the ultimate betrayal.

Oliver Stone ("Platoon") has rekindled these tumultuous emotions in "Born on the Fourth of July," his powerful, bombastic and furiously uneven new film, based on Kovic's autobiography. Taking his cue from that title (Kovic was actually born on July 4, 1946) Stone has recast Kovic's life as the story of Every Patriotic American Boy who is misled by the country he loves, morally compromised, maimed and then resurrected by the anti-war movement.

A vet himself, Stone is furious that under Reagan the loss of the war was blamed on liberals. He wants to show Vietnam as a murderous fraud—a big, bloody screw-up—and to take back the '90s for the Left.

As a propagandist, he works you over with brutal efficiency; there are moments when "Born" feels like those cliche-ridden biographies used to introduce a candidate to a convention. To the elegiac, Coplandesque music of John Williams, we meet the young Ron playing war games with his buddies, hitting the home run that wins the little-league championship, making eyes at the redheaded girl he knows he'll someday marry.

The teenage Ron (Tom Cruise) wants to fight Communism and earn a place in history like his dad and grandfather. Stone gives him a cornball prom scene in which he comes in out of the rain and seizes the girl (Kyra Sedgwick) he loves while "Moon River" swoons on the soundtrack. But policymakers deny Kovic his storybook coming-home; kissing his princess, he has no idea that the next time he sees her he'll have left his manhood in the jungles of Southeast Asia.

The battle scenes that follow are technically brilliant, as Stone employs a hand-held camera to express the jitter and disorientation of combat. Everything is subjective: when a gun jumps, so do we, and when we're hit all ambient noise drops away, leaving only the sickening squish of a bullet severing our spine; we fall into the dry grass, staring up at the bleached-out sky. In the operating room the camera veers crazily over the carnage, pausing briefly over geysers of blood or bodies blown in half.

There's little doubt that Stone believes in the morality of his techniques—he's a righteous ghoul. He wants every back-seat patriot to see what men and women look like when they've been eviscerated by bullets; he wants you to smell the urine and excrement that clogs up their catheters in rat-infested veterans' hospitals.

It might be easier to justify all this if Stone's touch were lighter outside of combat scenes. But there's no calm between storms: he hurtles from storm to storm. (A relative of Stone's once said, "Oliver is the only person ever sent to Vietnam to cool out.") His work is pure sensationalism. Armed with his invasive camera, Stone is less an artist than a dictator.

"Born on the 4th of July" is a long, long dive—from the VA hospital to anti-war rallies in which police move in with tear-gas and billy-clubs to a Mexican resort full of macho paraplegics. His heart broken by a prostitute, Kovic knows he has hit bottom when he finds himself exchanging drunken blows and obscenities with a paraplegic (Willem Dafoe) even more burned-out than he is. It's about half an hour after we know we've hit bottom.

How is Cruise? He rises to the occasion once or twice. When he confesses to the accidental shooting of an American, he's movingly tongue-tied; later, when he cries drunkenly to his mother "Thou shalt not kill women and children," he hits a note of genuine anguish. (Too bad the scene is botched by his cries of "Penis! Penis!" while his prudish mom plugs her ears. It's like a "Saturday Night Live" sketch.)

But Cruise isn't a smart or imaginative enough actor to make Kovic's rabid patriotism more than a hollow pose. The way he blurts "Love it or leave it" telegraphs his future conversion—he's signalling too clearly that he doesn't believe what he's saying.

There are times when Cruise is doing DeNiro, but that might be because Stone is doing Scorcese. The director constructs Kovic's story as a Catholic odyssey of crime, punishment, confession and resurrection. Kovic sins by enlisting and then accidentally killing babies, women and—in the middle of a confusing battle—a soldier on his own side. He is punished by maiming and castration and is then sent to hell (Mexico).

The key to salvation is confession, first to the backwoods Georgia family of the man he killed, then to the nation. At the Republican Convention he is spit on and reviled by the Pharisees (young Nixonites), betrayed by a Judas (a buddy who turns out to be a cop) and metaphorically crucified.

But lo: hoisted from the cross by comrades, Kovic leads a military-style campaign to take back the hall. (He's Christ and Rambo). Resurrection comes at the Democratic convention of 1976, where Kovic make his grand appearance to cheering crowds—the light making clear that he's apotheosized.

What's wrong with his scheme? Apart from the heavy-handed mythmaking, there's something creepily self-serving about it. The way the tale is pitched, the anti-war movement offers Kovic his only shot at recovering his potency, and Stone behaves with the same frenzied opportunism.

The movie doesn't question Kovic's infantile John Wayne fantasies—it just says this John Wayne had the bad luck to get duped into fighting a land war in Southeast Asia. It's calculated to appeal to our most primitive emotions. The war at home is a consolation prize for not kicking Vietcong butt.

NEWSDAY, 12/20/89. Part II/p. 2, Mike McGrady

Director Oliver Stone, who caught the full ugliness of the Vietnam War with "Platoon," now captures the devastating effect of that war at home with "Born on the Fourth of July."

The gut-wrenching biography of Ron Kovic chronicles a young man's transition from a clean-cut, athletic, all-America boy born on the Fourth—a real-life Yankee Doodle Dandy—into an embittered and scruffy war-hero-turned-protester sentenced to life in a wheelchair.

Those who have thought of Tom Cruise as just another pretty face are in for a major revelation. Not only is his portrayal of Kovic his finest role (and he was superb in both "Rain Man" and "The Color of Money"), it is a shattering piece of work, one of the strongest performances of the year.

Stone, at his angriest here, catches more than the painful transition of one young man; he also gets some of the agony of a nation that shared in the young man's valor, in his confusion, in his bitterness and his disillusion.

Kovic, born in Massapequa in 1946, grew up normally enough, playing suburban soldier games ("You're dead and you know it!"). His birthdays are marked by parades with fireworks, prancing drum majorettes, orating politicos and, almost unnoticed in the near sexual excitement, a few ancient veterans with empty sleeves, black glasses, canes or wheelchairs.

Kovic comes of age listening to the promises of a vigorous new president: "We shall pay any price, bear any burden. . ." Listening to a brutal gym instructor: "You gotta sacrifice. . . you gotta pay the price." Listening to a marine recruiting officer: "We want the best! And we will accept nothing less than the best!" Listening to a puritanical mother: "Those Communists have to be stopped." Listening, listening, listening—then deciding: "If we don't sign up soon, we're going to miss it."

But Kovic doesn't miss it, doesn't miss a thing. As a marine sergeant signing up for two tours in Vietnam, he witnesses the killing of innocent women and children. At one point, he accidentally kills one of his own men. And then he is severely wounded; the first bullet tears up his foot and the next one severs his spinal cord, permanently erasing all sensation from the chest down.

The American dream becomes a nightmare. Suffering from horrendous injuries, Kovic receives grotesquely uncaring medical treatment. Forever bound to his wheelchair, the young soldier comes back to a country that doesn't know what to do with him. To some he has become a nagging reminder of a less than glorious excursion; to others, a living symbol of a hateful policy.

Kovic can find solace only in the company of other damaged vets and, for a while, retreats with them to a Mexican town offering a steady supply of pot, booze and prostitutes who have learned to accommodate themselves to the men's limitations.

Watching all of this is an extraordinarily moving experience, one that can hardly be done through dry eyes. Stone and cinematographer Robert Richardson, shooting much of the film from wheelchair level, have imparted the full feel of the wounded man's limits; the use of hand-held cameras and sudden, jolting close-ups adds immediacy to both wars, the one over there and the one at home.

Although I found myself terribly involved, I do have a few quibbles. Stone's strength has never been subtlety, and this is a full frontal assault that never lets up. For more than two hours there is no loosening of the tension, no alteration of the pace. It might have been more effective if there had been pauses, moments of release, if perhaps some time had been spent clarifying the specifics behind Kovic's radicalization. Despite these caveats, no movie this year has shaken me, moved me, disturbed me as much as "Born on the Fourth of July."

NEWSWEEK, 12/25/89, p. 74, David Ansen

Oliver Stone's *Born on the Fourth of July* is a primal scream of a movie. Fueled by rage, pain, self-pity and political outrage, this long, relentless movies tries for a knockout in almost every scene. It's impossible not to be shaken by the onslaught and equally hard not to feel you're being manhandled by a cinematic bully. The movie is a tirade against the authoritarian macho mentality that led us into Vietnam, but Stone fights back with his own brand of emotional authoritarianism.

Stone has been trying to get Ron Kovic's book made into a movie for over a decade. Tom Cruise plays Kovic, the gung-ho, working-class kid from Massapequa, N.Y., who went off to Vietnam with a head full of John Wayne fantasies and returned in a wheelchair, paralyzed from the chest down. Back home, Kovic's rage turned against the war he had once embraced: joining with other disillusioned veterans, he became one of the war's most effective protesters, reaching a moment of media glory at the 1972 Republican convention in Miami when he shouted down Nixon.

Kovic, who collaborated with Stone on the screenplay, is one in a long line of last-angry-men Stone protagonists. But Stone identifies so closely with Kovic's victimization that he threatens to turn him into a generic Everyman. The problem is clearest in the opening encapsulation of Kovic's flag-waving, baseball-playing childhood. It's trying so hard to be archetypal it ends up feeling unreal. You can't connect to the characters because they've been deprived of personality: they're simply white-bread symbols of deluded American patriotism.

Of course Stone is setting us up for a shock. From a phony romantic prom-night scene we're hurtled into the inferno of Vietnam: Kovic's patrol mistakenly massacres women and children, and in the confusion of battle, he kills one of his own men—the nightmare event that will haunt his life. These war scenes—and the queasy moment when Kovic is wounded in battle, his spinal cord shattered—come at us like hallucinatory MTV Highlights from Hell. You're dizzy and disoriented by the violence, but because you haven't been grounded in the story, the effect of these atrocities (unlike the similar scenes in Stone's "Platoon") is strangely abstract.

It isn't until the horrific sequence at the Bronx veterans hospital, where Kovic encounters the shockingly bad treatment that wounded vets often faced, that the movie begins to settle in. Stone spares us nothing: the rats, the junkies, the excrement. It's the film's most effective passage, harrowing and filled with fury.

Quotidian events don't interest the expressionistic Stone. When, finally, a relatively calm scene occurs—Kovic sitting in his Massapequa backyard reminiscing about the war with his childhood friend and fellow vet Timmy (Frank Whaley)—you're grateful for the relief. But the breathing space doesn't last long: next we're off on an alternately brilliant and overwrought sexual interlude in Mexico, where Kovic, wracked by the loss of his manhood, finds respite in booze and the arms of Mexican whores.

What gets lost in all the visceral pyrotechnics is any clear understanding of Kovic's political conversion. Stone is conversant only in the politics of emotionalism. Anyone too young to have lived through the '60s will come away from this movie with only the vaguest sense of the issues.

Few of the actors in the huge cast—except Whaley, Willem Dafoe, and Caroline Kava, as Kovic's hysterical, repressed mother—get to make an impression. It's up to Cruise to carry the film, and he traces Kovic's transition from naive jock to agonized survivor with fierce conviction. There's a blunt power in Cruise we haven't seen before, and great physicality. It's not his fault that the movie's Kovic seems blander, less complex than the real Kovic, with his lusty mixture of braggadocio and outrage. Stone uses his star's All-American persona for ironic generalizations. He wants primal effects, not particular truths.

There's no denying that Oliver Stone has a vision; his conviction, his anger and his talent are for real. It's impossible to be indifferent to "Born on the Fourth of July," and hard to shake its brutal images from your mind. But Stone's esthetics of hysteria can take you only so far: it's the cinematic equivalent of heavy metal, awesome fragments buried in a whole lot of bombast. This movie offers you two choices: you can be overwhelmed by it, or do battle with it. Either way it leaves you drained.

VILLAGE VOICE, 12/26/89, p. 99, J. Hoberman

Born on the Fourth of July is the most visceral of weepies—a vast oozing wound of a movie. Oliver Stone's second Vietnam film, based on a harrowing memoir by the severely disabled Vietveteran Ron Kovic, is awash with bodily fluids. Powerful and unflinching, crude but compelling, this is a movie to remind you that blood and guts (not to mention sweat and tears) are the sort of abstractions that leave a puddle on the floor.

Nearly two-and-a-half hours long, *Born* opens like an episode of *The Wonder Years*, with Tom Cruise's incantatory voiceover: "It was a lo-o-o-ng time ago." The sun is refracted in the trees, the kids are playing war ("You're dead and you know it!"). This reference to the last scene in *Platoon* provides the first proof that Stone has no fear of the obvious. Indeed, he wants to get your tear ducts pumping even before the credits end. Stone piles "innocent" patriotic displays upon Little League heroics, ladles family togetherness over JFK's inaugural address. The air swirls with spring buds, it's the last American paradise. This is the "American Pie" of movies—a distended dirge, as coarse as it is clever, that bids to lodge itself in your brain. Permanently.

The eldest son of a large Catholic family from Massapequa, Long Island, Ron (Cruise) grows up during the postwar boom in thrall to a mother whose rampant Momism (an odd remnant of '50s pop psychology) combines anti-Communist rhetoric and sexual repression in equal measure. Young Ron is totally gung ho, wrestling for God and country (and crying when he loses), mouthing better-dead-than-red platitudes to his more cynical friends, enlisting in the marines as soon as he graduates high school. Vietnam is the fall, and Stone builds upon his prior mythology by having the robotic recruiter played by Tom Berenger, the evil angel from *Platoon*.

If the archetypal movie 'Nam is green jungle, the terrain here is parched and brown, as if drained of its vibrance by constant reproduction. Combat is signaled as unrepresentable. A confused firefight is made more so by the alternation of stolid pans and brain-slamming returns—as though the camera were mounted on a typewriter carriage—while the sound comes and goes of its own accord. Indeed, Stone's visualization of the scene in which Ron suffers his wound is far less graphic than Kovic's unforgettable written account of paralysis and panic (grown marines calling on Jesus and screaming for their mothers).

Not until Ron winds up in the field hospital—a butcher shop piled with leaking, twitching bodies—does *Born on the Fourth of July* wrap its hands around your throat. The next circle of hell (and one of the most horrific sequences in any American movie) is a Bronx VA hospital, a miserable hovel with urine on the floor, rats in the bedpans, and junkies in the closet. Disaffected black orderlies give enemas and hose down the wounded, while the still-avid Ron watches a telecast of the '68 Chicago police riot ("Love it or leave it, you fucking bastards") and wonders what he, a Vietnam veteran, is doing in this world of excremental slime.

It's to Stone's credit that *Born on the Fourth of July* never forgets that the ultimate purpose of war is to inflict injury—to puncture, maim, and destroy human body tissue. Nor does it allow the viewer to repress the nature of the metaphoric injury that the Vietnam war wreaked on American manhood. To see *Born on the Fourth of July* is to understand, once again, Rambo's profound, quasi-therapeutic importance as an American icon. Indeed, as *Platoon*'s relatively naturalistic battlefield challenged *Rambo*'s fantasy arena, *Born* unmasks *Rambo*'s compensatory appeal. While Stallone's perfect Nautilus-built pecs assuaged America's mutilated masculinity, Kovic's book, Stone's movie, and Cruise's gritty performance are all intimately concerned with the failure of the body.

This collapse extends to the dissolution of Ron's patriotic character armor. In the film's most disturbingly choreographed scene, he spins drunkenly around a Massapequa barroom (as it spins around him). More than an act of will, Cruise's performance has the quality of a convulsive rebirth. Moist and drooling, shooting pool and picking fights, desperately hitting on a half-amused, half-petrified hippie chick, he's rapping and wheeling under the strobe until he falls out of his chair—then goes home to complete his degradation, waking up the neighborhood, blubbering about killing women and children, and screaming the word *penis* until his mother breaks down in tears. It's a scene as painful as the dry heaves: "Who's gonna love me? Who's ever gonna love me, Dad?" the drunken paraplegic wants to know.

Although nothing else in the movie has the horror and pathos of these middle sequences, they are sufficient to propel the events to an uncertain conclusion—Ron's moral regeneration as an antiwar activist—and even overwhelm the film's obvious flaws. *Born on the Fourth of July* can be as operatically strident as *The Deer Hunter*, it's only rival as a there-and-back-again epic. Stone has a simple belief in catharsis and a maddening propensity to nudge the audience. The film is thick with unnecessary voiceovers and superfluous flashbacks. Does Kovic enlist out of high school? Let's have the prom feature the Shirelles' "Soldier Boy." Is Mom in an advanced stage of denial? Let's have her change channels from a demonstration to a rerun of *Laugh-In*. Is there a scene in a hippie coffeehouse? How about a Baez-oid chanteuse singing "A Hard Rain's A-Gonna Fall" (a golden oldie even then). Is there a student demo? Get the actual Abbie Hoffman to address the crowd, and never mind that he looks closer to 60 than the '60s.

Naïve as can be, *Born on the Fourth of July* lacks the evil humor of the year's other major Viet-film, *Casualties of War*. While the detached De Palma is coolly working something out, the overinvolved Stone is struggling to work something through. (If he were any more earnest, he'd be the Elie Wiesel of Vietnam.) Thus, it's difficult to gauge the irony of Kovic's turning-point rehabilitation in another Third World brothel. As neither *Born* nor *Platoon* addresses Vietnam as a realm for sexual acting out, one wonders if Stone recognizes this Mexican interlude as the symbolic return to the 'Nam that it is. (It is here too that Ron encounters a "good," if fallen, angel in the *Platoon*ic form of Willem Dafoe.)

Ultimately, Stone's solipsism is more generous than De Palma's narcissism—he wants to relive Vietnam for all of us, for the national good. For all the muscle-flexing camera pyrotechnics, Stone is always ready to go slow and tragic. More than any other American filmmaker, he's in touch with his grief over Vietnam—but what is that grief exactly? Stone's heartbroken evocation of American innocence betrayed is indistinguishable from his celebration of American superficiality. What happened to that suburban Eden where every A&P seemed an arena of possibility? Why did Vietnam bring the fast-food degradation of the national life?

Despite (or maybe because of) a decade spent stripmining our resources, it's increasingly apparent that the Vietnamese conflagration marked the acme of American empire. *Born on the Fourth of July* is like the jolt that failed. Stone's sincerity is weirdly self-congratulatory. He denies his nostalgia even as he indulges it.

Also reviewed in:
NATION, 1/1/90, p. 28, Stuart Klawans
NEW REPUBLIC, 1/29/90, p. 26, Stanley Kauffmann
NEW YORK TIMES, 12/20/89, p. C15, Vincent Canby
NEW YORKER, 1/22/90, p. 122, Pauline Kael
VARIETY, 12/20/89, p. 21
WASHINGTON POST, 1/5/90, p. B1, Hal Hinson
WASHINGTON POST, 1/5/90, Weekend/p. 22, Desson Howe

BRAVE LITTLE TOASTER, THE

A Hyperion Entertainment release. *Producer:* Donald Kushner and Thomas L. Wilhite. *Director:* Jerry Rees. *Screenplay:* Jerry Rees and Joe Ranft. *Based on a novella by:* Thomas M. Disch. *Music:* David Newman. *Running time:* 90 minutes. *MPAA Rating:* Not Rated.

VOICES: Jon Livitz; Tim Stack; Timothy Day; Thurl Ravenscroft.

NEW YORK, 6/12/89, p. 78, David Denby

The Brave Little Toaster, which is playing the Film Forum until June 13, is the best American full-length animated feature since the glory days of Disney. There is *no* reason this touching little masterpiece shouldn't have major distribution.

NEW YORK POST, 5/31/89, p. 27, David Edelstein

"The Brave Little Toaster" is one of the loveliest full-length cartoons ever made, a buoyant and sometimes melancholy ode to the gizmos that once meant more to us than—as grown-ups—we can unblushingly explain.

It's not a dazzler the way "Fantasia" or "Pinocchio" or even the techno-wonder "Who Framed Roger Rabbit" are. It's old-fashioned, low-tech.

But the point of the movie, which is based on a novella by Thomas M. Disch, is that simple, outdated objects can absorb and reflect so much more of our souls than their newfangled upgrades can. In the picture's spell, we return to a state when the world was, er, pre-user-friendly.

This is a universe where our most beloved possessions have distinct personalities—and needs. The strongest link among the toaster, blanket, radio, lamp and vacuum cleaner in a country cabin is the love they share for the little boy ("the Master") who arrives every summer to play with them.

As they sit one day waiting for the car to pull up and the little boy to rush in (an occasion we relive in their fantasies), they see a "For Sale" sign pounded into the ground outside the cabin. Oh, woe.

They've been squabbling among themselves—the radio has been waving its antenna around and dueling with the lamp and the blanket has been drooping like a...wet blanket.

But the prospect of losing their master snaps them out of their anomie, and they decide to travel to the city and rejoin him—not an easy task for a bunch of inanimate objects.

How do they travel scores of miles, braving forests and gorges and quicksand and destructive humans? Best to let you marvel at their (and the animators') inventiveness—at how they employ their cords and bulbs and antennae and rollers to cover the distance and even save one another's lives.

The look of the characters is rarely more complicated than in your average Hanna Barbera cartoon—they have broad lines and big, round eyes with black-marble pupils. But they're mobile emotionally; there's nothing cartoonish about their hearts.

By the end we know them well—their quirks, their moods, their pet peeves. The stalwart toaster—who acts as the peacemaker—gestures with his black handles, so that in bringing forth a piece of perfect toast he seems to throw up his arms in ecstasy.

The needy blanket, always wanting to cuddle, enfolds itself in hastily fashioned arms and mews adorably. The lamp is nice and dim and sounds like a Muppet. The curmudgeonly vacuum cleaner, Kirby, has a bass voice that's instantly familiar as the one that sang the songs in "How the Grinch Stole Christmas."

Maybe best of all is the wiseguy radio (brilliantly played by John Lovitz), who provides a constant spew of '30s and '40s aural memorabilia—game shows, speeches, slogans, famous sports broadcasts. He calls the brave little toaster "Slots."

The director, Jerry Rees, is a real film maker. It's odd to speak of camera angles since, technically speaking, there aren't any (everything is drawn). But Rees has storyboarded the film as if the toaster and its comrades were actors instead of cartoons, and lo, they become so.

David Newman's music exalts their quest. Newman gives their entrance into a redwood forest a Coplandesque grandeur, and he sets the stage lovingly for Van Dyke Parks' seductive pop songs, which are laced with mini-parodies. In the end, when the toaster, blanket and the rest approach the junkyard—with its fierce compactor—the music takes us into another realm: modern, resigned, accepting of chaos and death.

The emotions really are tragic. In the junkyard, cars about to be mashed tell anyone who'll listen they were once the top of the line. On the brink of extinction they still don't understand what happened—why people stopped cherishing them.

"The Brave Little Toaster" suggests why some people keep cellars and attics full of stuff they can't use but can't bear to throw away: They don't want to imagine a beloved object's wail of grief as it's compacted.

This isn't meant to make the movie sound highfalutin'—only to suggest that it's more than an idle fancy, this idea that objects can exist and accept our love and love us back.

The film doesn't traffic in the fake piety of most full-length cartoons, which really want to sell you breakfast cereals and lunch boxes. The love it speaks of is the sort that infuses the world with meaning—a child's love.

It doesn't seem irrelevant to recall that, in "1984," the first sign that Winston Smith can't fit into the Party of Big Brother is his mysterious affection for a rain-watery paperweight. And Orwell, too, believed that knowing how to invest meaning in something old and useless and beautiful is the key to our humanity.

"The Brave Little Toaster" suggests that modern society is, in that regard, diminished. In one scene, the toaster and its friends meet the heartless, high-tech appliances of the master's city apartment and grow convinced they've outlived their usefulness. And so begins their anguished trek to the junkyard—and to the magnificent, rejuvenating climax.

This low-budget animated marvel was in danger of similar neglect: it couldn't find a distributor in 1987 and went right to the Disney Channel and video. Its two-week exhibition at the Film Forum—itself an old-fashioned specialty moviehouse—is joyously appropriate.

NEWSDAY, 5/31/89, Part II/p. 5, Bill Kaufman

Refreshingly, the spunky heroes of this animated movie for youngsters don't reflect most Saturday morning children's TV—instead of spacy and violent creatures that have bizarre powers, here we merely have a few old household appliances with big hearts.

An adventure tale with hardly a message to impart except that maybe perseverance is a good thing, "The Brave Little Toaster" uses five 1950s-era appliances as its stars. Each has a personality of its own and, as required by the laws of animated films, they talk, sing and romp.

Toaster, Radio, Lampy, Kirby the Vacuum Cleaner and Blankey, an electric blanket, have been quietly languishing in a rural cottage for years, fighting off a sort of AC/DC ennui, while awaiting the return of an often-absent family. There's appliance trauma aplenty when the cottage is put up for sale and their existence is put in jeopardy. So, despite the cool cynicism of a bitter old air-conditioner, the quintet of aging but serviceable appliances unplug themselves and sashay off to the big city to find the household's teenage resident. Perhaps he can save them. Their mode of transportation, quite logically, is the vacuum, who takes them in tow like a swooshing steam locomotive.

Looking like refugees from a Newmark & Lewis warehouse, the band and its adventures are what make the movie fun. There are some charming touches, such as when the vintage radio talks and, for the benefit of any adult moviegoers, the klunky box drops a few 1950s references, including a Little Richard send-up.

The animation is straightforward, lacking the graphic eloquence of a major Disney flick or some other megabudget production. The same goes for its musical score. But as anyone who shepherds a youngster through a movie matinee knows, kids usually enjoy the basics while being oblivious to most artistic fine points.

"The Brave Little Toaster" is a well-wrought movie filled with enough joyful basics to give any youngster a happy 90-minute journey to Appliance Fantasyland.

VILLAGE VOICE, 6/6/89, p. 66, J. Hoberman

If anthropomorphism is the secret pleasure of the animated cartoon, then *The Brave Little Toaster* deserves some sort of historical footnote for making our discarded household hardware as cute 'n' cuddly as R2D2. A *ballet mécanique* wobbling around a quintet of household appliances that leave the summer cabin where they have been abandoned to seek their "master" in the city. *The Brave Little Toaster* is the anti-*Frankenstein*—it's as gratifying an example of techno-subservience as films have ever offered.

Opening today at Film Forum 1, long a bastion of animation *maudit*, Jerry Rees's movie takes an offbeat premise and gives it a familiar spin. Led by the perky, optimistic toaster, the scrapped conveniences—an irrepressibly raucous radio (he tunes in FDR for inspiration, uses "Tutti-Frutti" as cleanup music), a surly (but golden-hearted) vacuum cleaner, a childish electric blanket, and a vagued-out reading lamp—traverse a wilderness of mountains and precipices to find the now teenaged human who used to own them. The machines seem to have little problem in the garden (such as it is). The movie's best bits have them interacting with "nature"—visualized as chorus lines of goofy frogs and fish.

The *BLT* is reasonably well animated—the design suggests the clean once-upon-a-time modernity of Disney's *Alice in Wonderland*. What's missing are the nuts and bolts. The structure is ramshackle, the pace creaky, the score shrill and undistinguished. Not even disaster is much fun: The blanket blows away in a storm and returns wetter than ever; the lamp gets his bulb smashed and can only riposte, "I really thought I turned in my warranty that time." The intrepid travellers are found by a fat junkman and have to be rescued from the dump. Long before he gets there, the movie pulls its own plug.

Also reviewed in:
NEW YORK TIMES, 5/31/89, p. C14, Stephen Holden
VARIETY, 7/15/87, p. 15
WASHINGTON POST, 3/20/90, p. F3, Richard Harrington

BREAKING IN

A Samuel Goldwyn Company release. *Executive Producer:* Andrew Meyer and Sarah Ryan Black. *Producer:* Harry Gittes. *Director:* Bill Forsyth. *Screenplay:* John Sayles. *Director of Photography:* Michael Coulter. *Editor:* Michael Ellis. *Music:* Michael Gibbs. *Music Editor:* Denise McCormick. *Sound:* Les Lupin. *Sound Editor:* Wayne Griffin. *Production Designer:* Adrienne Atkinson and John Willett. *Set Decorator:* Woody Crocker. *Set Dresser:* William Martin. *Special Effects:* Larry L. Fuentes. *Costumes:* Louise Frogley. *Make-up:* Manlio Rocchetti and Jean Black. *Running time:* 91 minutes. *MPAA Rating:* R.

CAST: Burt Reynolds (Ernie); Casey Siemaszko (Mike); Sheila Kelley (Carrie); Lorraine Toussaint (Delphine); Albert Salmi (Johnny Scat); Harry Carey (Shoes); Maury Chaykin (Tucci); Stephen Tobolowsky (District Attorney); Richard Key Jones (Lou); Tom Laswell (Bud); Walter Shane (Boss); Frank A; Damiani (Waiter); David Frishberg (Nightclub Singer); John Baldwin (Sam the Apostle); Eddie Driscoll (Paul the Apostle); Melanie Moseley (Young Woman Apostle); Galen B. Schrick (Choir Master); Duggan L. Wendeborn (Faith House Member); K. Gordan Scott (Counterman); Clifford Nelson (Old Man #1); Roy McGillivray (Old Man #2); Kim Singer (Anchorwoman); Charles E. Compion (Real Estate Agent); Earl Taylor (Mr. Withrow); Julianne R. Johnson (Cashier); Rod Long (Garbage Truck Driver); Daryl Olson (Security Guard #1); George Catalano (Security Guard #2); Aaron Cooley (Teenage Boy on Skates); John R. Knotts (Detective #1); Russ Fast (Detective #2); Eddie Gove (Scavenger); Alan Fudge (Detective #3); Joseph Burke (Ted); Gene Dynarski (Brock); Ted Bryant (Newscaster); Garcia Phelps (Gerry Hacker); Douglas Mace (Prison Guard #1); Stephan Adam Szymel (Prison Guard #2); Jack Esformes (Mike's Prison Buddy); Charles Bernard (Judge).

LOS ANGELES TIMES, 10/12/89, Calendar/p. 1, Sheila Benson

The pairing of director Bill Forsyth and John Sayles, this time as a screenwriter, to create the delightful "Breaking In" seems so felicitous you wonder that it didn't happen sooner. These are both men who know when to leave well-enough alone and when the smallest grace note will set a scene tingling.

The same might be said for Burt Reynolds and Casey Siemaszko, whose pairing as the steady old hand and the decidedly sharky new one sets the precise tone for this smart, affectionate comedy about chemistry and larceny.

Dapper Ernie (Reynolds), a man for whom the action-back golf shirt was invented, is careful about his appearance, his habits and the impression he leaves behind. With his very slight limp and his handsome silver hair and mustache, he might be a Portland high school principal, although his business card says "Ernest Mullins, Sculptor." What's it supposed to say: "Ernest Mullins, Safecracker"?

Ringleted Mike (Siemaszko), the goofoff at Bob's Tire and Body Shop, is half bouncing ball, half Labrador puppy. You'd swear his tongue was hanging out as he panted; the only thing Mike is likely to leave behind is a banana peel, with predictable results. Ernie calls him a wacko and Ernie is rarely ever wrong.

They are both set to become partners in the serious business of safecracking. With the care that he would use to case a job, Ernie sizes up the goofy Mike and thinks just *maybe* there's the making of a working relationship there, since he has recently lost his longtime partner, Red. For his part, once he really believes that Ernie's true calling is as a master of "grease" (i.e., nitroglycerin), Mike is giddy with the prospect. You half expect him to get cards printed too, but you shudder to think what they'd say.

"Breaking In" is decidedly minor-key, done on the notes between the solid, expected chords. Like everything Forsyth has put his hand to, but especially "Local Hero" and "Comfort and Joy," the humor as well as the character development is cumulative. Forsyth is in no hurry to crank up the voltage; he's assured enough to let the observations pile up until the audience does his work for him, chortling when they can foresee a reaction because they understand the characters so well.

And Sayles has given him gorgeous characters. Ernie's two poker cronies, for example: Shoes (Harry Carey, who has at last abandoned the *Jr.* at the end of his name) and Johnny Scat (Albert Salmi), who set their considerable experience to coming up with the right moniker for Mike. The Artichoke Kid would be a natural, given Mike's home town of Castroville, but there *was* an Artichoke Kid, so of course that would be disrespectful. The Tire and Body Shop does it: Mike is hereafter the Firestone Kid, and he's as pleased as a general who's gotten his fourth star to be so called. (The payoff on this little gag is delayed and delovely.)

There are also the ladies whom Ernie brings into their relatively sedate lives. You and I and your smart 10-year-old know these are ladies of the evening. Mike thinks that big-eyed Carrie (Sheila Kelley) has a thing for him. What he makes of Delphine (Lorraine Toussaint), Ernie's statuesque regular, the good Lord alone can fathom.

But even after Mike learns the truth, that Carrie is neither an actress nor a musician—the impression he got when she explained gravely that her acting is "Not at performance level yet— I'm still developing my instrument"—he finds her irresistible. That's pretty much our reaction too, since Kelley (seen so far as the artistic one of the three beautiful young sisters in "Some Girls") seems not to be troubled that the warmhearted hooker is the oldest role playable, and chooses to make it divinely hers. As Carrie, Kelley is earnest, impulsive, dizzyingly eager to please and deliriously funny. And she may certainly be in demand for poetry readings, if her delivery of Carrie's ode "What Would I Do?" is any indication. (It and other language and mores are the reason for the film's R rating.)

Forsyth must have finished the film with calluses from reining Reynolds in instead of pushing him down the path of broad reactions and least resistance that far too many directors have encouraged in recent years. And both actor and director should be elated at the result. It is a superb job, the equal to Ernie's deftness with the "grease," not an ounce wasted, not an excess motion, with the most satisfying *pop* to cap things off. To hear Reynolds' comic timing when it's being calibrated to a minisecond is an absolute joy, and there are more than one of those moments lurking here.

Siemaszko, whose forte is unpredictability and a certain irrepressible energy (and whose name is pronounced Sheh-mash-ko), gives absolutely full measure as Reynold's sparring partner. Besides, there's always the danger that Mike will be a little more of the wacko than even Ernie expects. It gives this luxuriously civilized movie its edge.

NEW YORK, 10/23/89, p. 128, David Denby

In *Breaking In*, Burt Reynolds gives an expert, soft-shoe performance as an aging safecracker who begins to work with a stupid, sly, inexperienced kid (Casey Siemaszko). Director Bill Forsyth (*Local Hero*) can do humbling comedy without slapstick; he takes the vulgarity out of it, just as he takes the violence out of crime. But Forsyth's glancing touch is perhaps too glancing for what is essentially genre material. *Breaking In* is charming and has its share of underplayed little moments, but the story never quite settles in. (Denying that one is making a genre film doesn't make it less true.) Affably cool, Forsyth undercuts dramatic involvement as much as he does the standard chichés.

NEW YORK POST, 10/13/89, p. 27, David Edelstein

It takes a while to zone in on Bill Forsyth's trim comedy "Breaking In." The story of a stoic, old-time burglar (Burt Reynolds) who takes on a happy-go-lucky apprentice (Casey Siemaszko), it has a flatness that at first you might confuse with ineptitude. (Like, is anyone home?) But its dry wit creeps up on you until just about everything on screen makes you giggle.

The role is quite a change for Reynolds, whose hair (or whatever he sports) has been streaked with gray and neck affixed with modest wattles. As the 61-year-old Ernie, a veteran Oregon safecracker, he looks like a dour, small-time businessman: neat hair, glasses, a briefcase.

In the opening, he watches a well-heeled man drive away from a house and then moves, in measured steps, to the door. Above, the home is being simultaneously invaded by Mike (Siemaszko), who climbs a ladder—which he lets fall with a clatter—and scrambles into an upstairs window.

The two meet up in the living room, where Mike is heading to watch TV with a snack from the fridge—he doesn't steal anything, it turns out, he just likes to mess up people's houses so they'll freak out when they get home. Ernie, charmed in spite of himself by the kid's prankishness and reckless disregard for consequences, gives him a share of the loot.

Everything about "Breaking In" is small and finely calibrated, yet it has a bubbly air, as if the Scottish director had synthesized the most attractive traits of his two protagonists. He tells the tale in gorgeous, deadpan non-sequiturs, which somehow add up to a thoughtful, rather sad vision of this world on the fringes of society.

You know in the larger sense where the picture is going, but you're constantly surprised by its sneakiness—by how Forsyth sets you up to go one way and then serenely goes the opposite. There's a tiny, insanely funny bit with a vicious-looking watchdog that, during a break-in, trots along to the safe with the burglars, as if happy for the company. Every time you see the dog, you grin at its amiability—until the punchline of the sequence, when you laugh at how blithely you've been hoodwinked.

Forsyth's jokes never blow when you expect them to. You see them, register them, and then they detonate—they're on a time-delay. A thief who's about to be snagged walks along whistling to himself, picking up litter, while behind him what looks like half the Portland police force converges and follows along, closing the distance ever so slowly, as if everyone's out on a Sunday stroll. (Buster Keaton would have loved this shot.)

John Sayles' script, written 10 years ago, is a reminder of how good he can be when he keeps his writing small and nuanced. It's just an exercise, but a graceful one; without moralizing. Sayles suggests that Ernie—who refuses to let himself think about the people he steals from—is emotionally arrested.

This must have been a challenge for Reynolds—to give a performance free of mugging and coyness. He rises to it. Understated and immaculate, his Ernie is the work of a real craftsman instead of a fatuous clown. Siemaszko gives every scene a lift—he's so buoyant, he looks as if he might drift away. As a hooker for whom he falls, Sheila Kelley brings down the house with a poem about her lover's private parts, and Lorraine Toussaint is perfect as her wry mentor.

Forsyth has said he chose Portland because it reminded him of Glasgow, and he treats these Americans as transplanted Scots. To be frank, I miss the vitality you'd find in a major American comedy—or even a minor American slob comedy. But in movies as in baseball, much can be achieved by going the opposite way.

NEWSDAY, 10/9/89, Part II/p. 5, Mike McGrady

In the world of movies there are many kinds of funny. Funny can be a custard pie to the kisser or an open manhole lurking just beyond a banana peel. However, my favorite kind of funny is less obvious, gentler; it's humor that rests on whimsy and irony, humor that springs from small eccentricities and unexpected happenings.

No one does gentle humor better than Scotland's Bill Forsyth. His finest film, "Local Hero," brought us into a small Scottish coastal village just as an American oil company was planning to build a huge oil refinery there. His "Comfort and Joy" chronicled the fierce competition between ice cream companies. And "Breaking In," the saga of an old safecracker who takes on a young petty thief as his apprentice, mines that same gentle comic vein.

I suspect that if "Breaking In" is to be noted, it may well be because it is the best movie Burt

Reynolds has been associated with in many years. While this may not be saying much, not after such an all-lemon lineup as "Switching Channels" and "Rent-a-Cop" and "Heat," it is well to be reminded that Reynolds has a great deal of natural charm and intelligence—qualities generally more visible during his talk-show appearances than in the macho posturings common to most of his films.

Here, Reynolds plays a 61-year-old safecracker who lives modestly, plays the horses, confines his romances to women of the night and sculpts in his spare time. He is soft-spoken, restrained, quietly humorous and subscribes to his favorite hooker's philosophy: "You gotta be careful when you start getting involved with people."

Despite his suspicion of outsiders, he finds himself becoming involved with a young petty thief (Casey Siemaszko) whom he meets while cracking a safe in a quiet suburban home. Well, any movie that begins with two thieves breaking into the same suburban home on the same quiet night is clearly not asking to be taken too seriously. The boy, however, is there to raid the icebox, watch television and short the sheets, and he is impressed by Reynolds' loftier achievements: "I never met anyone did crime for a living."

Casey (I refuse to struggle with Siemaszko more than once in a review) may look less like an actor than anyone in movies today, but he has appeared in many flicks (most recently "Young Guns") and is perfectly credible as the youngster who learns the safecracking arts. He learns how to case a joint, how to gentle Dobermans, how to manufacture "grease" (nitroglycerin), how to handle various vintages of safes and (imperfectly) how to lay low after a major score.

The story, written some 10 years ago by writer-director John Sayles ("Matewan," "Eight Men Out"), could not conceivably have received more considerate treatment than this. What makes a Forsyth movie work is never plot; it's the richness of the characters, none of whom seems artificial in the least. The humor, that very gentle humor, comes directly from the characters, never from the story.

I didn't hear anyone howling or see a single soul rolling in an aisle. The phrase laff-riot doesn't apply.

I guess I'd call it a smile-a-minute experience. And while I may not have personally laughed out loud, I thought about doing so on at least a half-dozen occasions.

VILLAGE VOICE, 10/17/89, p. 87, J. Hoberman

Breaking In, which closed the New York Film Fest with a whimper and opens theatrically Friday, deserves better than short shrift, but not much. Directed by Bill Forsyth from John Sayles's script, it's slight stuff—a cross-generational buddy film about a pair of inland California burglars. The title suggests an initiation, and from the opening meet-cute wherein a grungy whacko from Castroville (Casey Siemaszko) stumbles upon the suave safecracking Ernie (Burt Reynolds) while both are sneaking around the same suburban house, that's what it is—in more ways than one. This is Burt Reynolds's *Atlantic City*; playing a man a decade or so his senior presents him an unaccustomed opportunity to parlay his stiff walk and debonair bulk into a performance.

Sayles's script is amply stocked with actor-friendly foibles, and Forsyth gives the proceedings a self-consciously "American" look (one nice bit: Reynolds's rented shoebox under the spreading airport flight path). Although too cute by half, and relentlessly overscored with generic Dixieland, *Breaking In* hobbles briskly along before succumbing to the cozy lethargy that Forsyth's *Housekeeping* so adroitly played against. Reynolds's innate affability raises the sunshine quotient, but, considering *Breaking In* is basically a tale of betrayal and corruption, there's an underlying bitterness Forsyth seems determined not to acknowledge.

Also reviewed in:
NEW REPUBLIC, 10/23/89, p. 24, Stanley Kauffmann
NEW YORK TIMES, 10/9/89, p. C18, Vincent Canby
NEW YORKER, 10/16/89, p. 109, Pauline Kael
VARIETY, 5/24–30/89, p. 30
WASHINGTON POST, 10/13/89, p. C1, Hal Hinson

'BURBS, THE

A Universal Pictures release of an Imagine Entertainment presentation of a Rollins-Morra-Brezner production. *Producer:* Michael Finnell and Larry Brezner. *Director:* Joe Dante. *Screenplay:* Dana Olsen. *Director of Photography:* Robert Stevens. *Editor:* Marshall Harvey. *Music:* Jerry Goldsmith. *Music Editor:* Kenneth Hall. *Sound:* Ken King and (music) Bruce Botnick. *Sound Editor:* George Simpson. *Production Designer:* James Spencer. *Art Director:* Charles L. Hughes. *Set Designer:* Judy Cammer, Erin Cummins, Michael Johnson, and James E. Tocci. *Set Decorator:* John Anderson. *Special Effects:* Ken Pepiot. *Costumes:* Rosanna Norton. *Make-up:* Michael Germain and Daniel C. Striepeke. *Stunt Coordinator:* Jeff Smolek. *Running time:* 102 minutes. *MPAA Rating:* PG.

CAST: Tom Hanks (Ray Peterson); Bruce Dern (Mark Rumsfield); Carrie Fisher (Carol Peterson); Rick Ducommun (Art Weingartner); Corey Feldman (Ricky Butler); Wendy Schaal (Bonnie Rumsfield); Henry Gibson (Dr. Werner Klopek); Brother Theodore (Uncle Reuben Klopek); Courtney Gains (Hans Klopek); Gale Gordon (Walter); Dick Miller and Robert Picardo (Garbagemen); Cory Danziger (Dave Peterson); Franklyn Ajaye and Rance Howard (Detectives); Heather Haase (Ricky's Girlfriend), Nick Katt (Steve Kuntz); Bill Stevenson and Gary Hays (Ricky's Friends); Kevin Gage and Dana Olsen (Cops); Brenda Benner (Walter's Daughter); Patrika Darbo (Art's Wife).

LOS ANGELES TIMES, 2/17/89, Calendar/p. 6, Kevin Thomas

It's a safe bet that Universal slated "The 'burbs" for its citywide opening today, hoping that Tom Hanks would get nominated for "Big." Certainly, this grimly unfunny comedy needs all the help that it can get. It's so bad it doesn't deserve the boost a Hanks nomination may give it.

Whatever persuaded Hanks, especially now that he has hit his stride as a star actor and comedian of the first rank, to do this picture? For that matter, why was this turkey ever given the green light in the first place? (Didn't anyone remember Columbia's wretched and all-too-similar 1981 Belushi-Aykroyd "neighbors"?) What was it that the savvy director Joe Dante saw in co-producer Dana Olsen's script?

It's inconceivable that "The 'burbs" looked good on paper. Yet its makers are far from amateurs: This is the first film financed by Brian Gazer and Ron Howard's Imagine Entertainment and the initial production in the company's multipicture distribution deal with Universal.

So much for speculation. What we're confronted with is the endlessly labored spectacle of three grown men (Hanks, Bruce Dern and Rick Ducommun) behaving like little boys when a weirdo family—a Bela Lugosi-like doctor (Henry Gibson), his surly, monosyllabic brother (Brother Theodore) and a dim, goofy-looking kid (Courtney Gains)—moves in the ramshackle Victorian in their cul-de-sac in Hinkley Hills. (True, the newcomers do seem to have installed a particularly ferocious furnace in the cellar.)

At any rate, the three men get completely carried away when an elderly man (Gale Gordon) who lives at the end of their cul-de-sac disappears. (Why don't they—or at least Hanks' marginally sensible wife, Carrie Fisher, or their bright teen-age neighbor Corey Feldman—call the cops or check with Gordon's daughter as to his whereabouts?)

Not only is there nothing amusing, or frightening about the men's foolishness but there's no discernible point to it, except perhaps to suggest that the dullness of suburbia can rot your brain. A momentary plea for tolerance gives way to the apparent proposition that it's all right to torment your "different" neighbors because they may be a bad lot up to no good after all. It's hardly a wholesome message to send to the impressionable young audience for whom the film seems primarily intended. "The 'burbs" (rated PG) is the pits.

MONTHLY FILM BULLETIN, 8/89, p. 233, Kim Newman

Hinckley Hills, U.S.A. Against the wishes of his wife Carol, Ray Peterson has decided to spend his vacation lazing around his suburban home. His neighbours—ex-soldier Mark Rumsfield and general layabout Art Weingartner—encourage him in his fantasies about the Klopeks, a seldom-seen family of newcomers whose bizarre habits include digging in the garden after midnight during thunder storms. When Walter, an old man who also lives on the block, disappears, leaving behind his treasured toupée, the men suspect that the Klopeks have done away with him. Ray's dog digs up a human femur from under the Klopeks' fence. Carol and Bonnie, Mark's wife, think their husbands are being ridiculous and force them to pay a call on the Klopeks to see what the neighbours are really like. The party meet Reuben Klopek and his nephew Hans, who are sinister and grotesque, but also the mild-mannered and charming Dr. Werner Klopek, who allays their fears. However, Ray finds Walter's toupée in the house, and is suspicious of the peculiarly large incinerator in the basement. The next day, while the Klopeks are away, Ray, Art and Mark break into the house and search for Walter's remains, digging fruitless holes in the backyard and basement. Walter, who has actually been in hospital, returns home just as Ray breaks through the gas main. The Klopek house explodes, and Ray turns on Art and Mark, accusing them of being the crazies. Wounded in the explosion, Ray is taken away in an ambulance, and attacked by Werner, who believes his neighbour has found his collection of human skulls in the furnace and confesses to the murders of the couple who lived in the house before. Ricky Butler, a teenager, finds an assortment of human remains in the boot of the Klopek car, and the Klopeks are dragged away by the police. Ray, shaken by Werner's attack, departs with Carol and his son for a holiday.

Throughout his career, Joe Dante has been presenting us with average, normal American communities and asking, "What's wrong with this picture?" In *Piranha, The Howling* and *Gremlins*, the tensions between anarchy (toothy monsters) and repression (reactionary values) are made manifest, while *Explorers* shows the struggle to escape from a cycle of intolerance that oppresses both misfit kids and movie aliens. Even comparatively throwaway credits like his contributions to *Twilight Zone the Movie* and *Amazon Women on the Moon*, or his instalments for the *Twilight Zone* ("The Shadow Man") and *Amazing Stories* ("Boo!") anthology series, deal with the confrontation of ordinary, everyday cruelty with the bizarre and dangerous. *The 'burbs*—like many other aspects of the movie, the title is a pointed and witty film reference—is a literal return to Earth after the commercial disappointment of *Explorers* and the impersonal blandness of *InnerSpace*. The film opens with a dazzling Industrial Light & Magic zoom from the revolving globe of the Universal logo down to Mayfield Place, one residential close in the anonymous suburbs within whose confines the rest of the action takes place. "I can't think of many pictures since *Lifeboat* that all take place in the same area", claims Dante. "There was a lot of temptation to broaden it and go outside the neighbourhood, but it seemed to violate the spirit of the piece".

Dante brings along his trademarked cameo players, Dick Miller and Robert Picardo, as briefly glimpsed garbagemen, but otherwise avoids the pandering-to-the-buffs casting for which he is known. The only iconic pieces of casting are of off-beat performance artist Brother Theodore as one of the sinister Klopeks, and Gale Gordon—Lucille Ball's perennially exasperated boss, as is confirmed by a framed photograph of the two—as prissy old Walter. Dante's other trademark, the filmic in-reference, is brilliantly employed as Ray and his friends fantasise about the horrific possibilities of the Klopek house: the night digging evokes memories of Elizabeth Taylor's suspect neighbours in *Night Watch*, and when the trio's suspicions turn to Devil worship, Ray is able to dig up a suggestive textbook from his basement written by Julian Karswell (the villain of Tourneur's *Night of the Demon*).

Dante is able to make points with his in-jokes, and even satirise movies through subtleties like music cues and camera movements. There are references to the key works of "family" horror in Ray's nightmare, inspired by earlier clips on television from *The Devil Rides Out, The Exorcist* and *The Texas Chain Saw Massacre, Part 2* (ironically, we get to see one of the more offensive scenes from the film that has been refused a certificate outright by the BBFC), in which a chain saw invades Ray's house and he finds himself sacrificed on a giant barbecue by Uncle Reuben. A great deal of humour is gained from the juxtaposition of the Klopeks' Old Dark House with the surrounding dwellings, and from the James Whale-style expressionism Dante uses whenever the suburbanites come into contact with the sinister family. The funniest scene in the film is a parody of *Once Upon a Time in the West* with Jerry Goldsmith spoofing Ennio Morricone on the soundtrack as the camera homes in on the squinting eyes of all the residents of Mayfield Place, including Walter's distressed poodle.

For the most part, *The 'burbs* follows *Explorers* in its unusual (and unpopular) narrative strategy—presenting a situation filled with threat and mystery that then turns out to be entirely innocent, thus forcing the audience to reassess its attitude to the "normal" point of view. The key speech, marvellously delivered by Tom Hanks at the climax of another apparently effortless but actually marvellous performance, has Ray turning on Rumsfield and Weingartner as the Klopek house burns: "Don't you see, *we're* the ones who are acting suspiciously!" Shot on the same lot as the archetypal retro sit-com *Still the Beaver* (the sequel to the 50s classic, *Leave It to Beaver*), the film deliberately evokes that artificial world in which nobody seems to go out to work because only one major set exists ("That was my nod to the Nelsons and Ward Cleaver", says scenarist Dana Olsen, referring to *Ozzie and Harriet* and *Leave It to Beaver*, "they were always home"). Sadly, for all its spirited playing, pointed dialogue and sure-handed direction, the film fumbles at the last moment and can't quite make the break with traditional menace-dominated storylines. After Ray's impassioned speech, Werner's half-hearted revelation of genuine evil is disappointing because it neither contradicts nor exceeds the neighbours' paranoia, merely confirms it. Still, for the most part, this is one of the most extraordinary major studio films of the late 80s.

NEW YORK, 3/6/89, p. 57, David Denby

I'm told that there used to be an editor at a leading magazine in this city who would wander about the office, pick up a manuscript offered for publication, read a few paragraphs, and then exclaim, "Who are these people? Why are we interested in them?" These queries, simple enough in form, often stopped the article dead or sent it back for revision. I wish the same common sense had been applied to Dana Olsen's script for The 'Burbs.

The 'Burbs is set on a typical suburban street and stars Tom Hanks as a typical wage earner, husband, and father. Spending a week's vacation at home, Hanks, lounging about in his bathrobe, becomes obsessed with the new next-door neighbors, a shadowy bunch who never leave their house and whose basement emits strange rumblings and flashes. In this obsession Hanks's householder is egged on by a wild-eyed Vietnam vet (Bruce Dern) and his Barbie-doll wife (Wendy Schaal), an infantile husband deserted by his wife (Rick Ducommun), an old man whose toupee falls off (Gale Gordon), and a teenager who utters a dozen variations on the aria "Woww! Cool, duuu-ude!" (Corey Feldman). If ever a more dreary group has been collected in a single movie, I'm not aware of it. Even Tom Hanks is bad, and director Joe Dante's talent disappears. The physical comedy is graceless and obvious, the jokes leaden, the scares pathetic. The movie lies on the screen like a sitcom waiting to be canceled.

NEW YORK POST, 2/17/89, p. 25, David Edelstein

There is no accounting for "The 'Burbs," a comedy so lifeless that even the most dogged of coroners must finally throw up his hands and say, "What can I tell you? It's just dead. It could never have lived."

Acted with grim, poker-faced irony, this Gothic "Twilight Zone" sitcom feels like a disastrous "Saturday Night Live" sketch in which the cast waits helplessly for the arrival of a commercial but the commercial, like Godot, never comes. They must go on. They do go on.

There's a good, if not novel, satiric idea here: the notion of suburbia as a battlefield, in which residents' manicured lawns and bucolic lifestyles can't conceal the subterranean struggle of monstrous egos.

Neighbors peer out windows and speculate on each other's activities; animals—agents of unconscious aggression—jump fences to poop on rivals' lawns; and the children—hip, postmodern—invite their dates to sit on their porches and hear them comment, like a new breed of sportscaster, on the nocturnal comings-and-goings of the lunatics next door and across the street.

But "The 'Burbs" isn't content to explore this scene. It introduces figures from a more cartoonish kind of Gothic comedy—a spooky family of recluses called the Klopeks (Brother Theodore, Henry Gibson and Courtney Gains), from whose basement come flashing lights and who, after dark, may be seen wearing cowls and digging in their back yard.

Thanks to listless pacing and a witless script, whether the Klopeks are murderers or not becomes a matter of crashing indifference. The film's only funny gag—in which Tom Hanks and Rick Ducommun hold up what may be the femur bone of a vanished neighbor and the camera zooms in and out hysterically—is already stale from TV commercials.

Reported reshoots and cuts might explain the picture's two endings, but nothing can explain why Hanks would accept this non-role. There is no expression like that of an actor who knows he is dying, yet knows that a fight in this context will only prolong the agony—that the best thing one can do is bite one's lip, see it through and go into hiding.

After "The Howling," "Gremlins," and his wonderful episode of the "The Twilight Zone—The Movie," director Joe Dante looked to be the premier pop-surrealist of his generation—a brash, satiric visionary with a liberating style. But his work here is desultory, burnt-out.

There's a cute Sergio Leone parody and a jokey Jerry Goldsmith score, but so little invention that I passed the time recalling a more sophisticated variation on this theme—an episode of "The Flintstones" in which Fred and Barney think their neighbor (Alfred Hatchrock, I believe) has murdered his wife. To think we have regressed so far.

NEWSDAY, 2/17/89, Part III/p. 3, Lynn Darling

Question: JUST how bad could a movie starring Tom Hanks be? The man played a 12-year-old, after all, and just got an Oscar nomination for it; now he's in a movie that pokes fun at suburbia, an easy target if ever there was one.

Answer: Real, real bad.

Not that this tedious failure is Hanks' fault in particular—director Joe Dante can take most of the credit for that. "The 'burbs" is the sort of fat-headed comedy that has to frantically signal every time a joke is about to arrive because otherwise there's no way of knowing when it hits. Characters tend to scream a lot while the camera simultaneously goes into its own form of hysterics; you know you're in real trouble when one of the movie's lesser figures periodically has to inform us that he loves the street he lives on while merry mayhem erupts all around him.

The mayhem involves a mysterious family that has moved into a seedy looking house right next door to one Ray Peterson (Hanks), a mild-mannered suburbanite who plans to enjoy a much-needed vacation at his home on a tree-lined cul de sac. Strange doings distract him, however: The new neighbors appear only at night to dig giant holes in their back yard, and mysterious sounds and lights emanate from their basement.

Petersen is not the only resident obsessed by the mystery: so are his slovenly, gluttonous friend Art (Rick Ducommun) and Rumsfield (Bruce Dern) who is, it almost goes without saying in a movie up to its ears in stock characters, a slightly deranged ex-Special Services type.

"The 'burbs" looks and sounds vaguely contemporary: The cars, the clothes, the teenagers in sunglasses, all point to a version of contemporary suburban living. But the shtick is all broken-down Ozzie and Harriet: The husbands act like overgrown adolescents who are kept in line by their much more sensible wives, none of the women (or men for that matter) seems to have any sort of job, and there's no sense of any of the action being anchored to even a skewed reality.

Such relentless '50s-style stereotyping, while boring, might even have worked in its fashion if it were filtered through the perspective of one character who was equally baffled by the anachronistic goings-on. But the likely candidate, Hanks' character, simply alternates between befuddlement and a hysteria on a par with the prevailing norm.

Before long, the three neighbors have broken nearly every law in the books, blacked out the neighborhood and suffered substantial bodily harm in their efforts to find out what is going on behind the peeling walls and shuttered windows next door. About the only aspect of this movie less interesting than wondering what the new neighbors will reveal themselves to be is to stick around for the revelation.

NEWSWEEK, 3/6/89, p. 58, David Ansen

Director Joe Dante's "Gremlins" served up a wicked vision of the curdled American Dream. He goes back to the well in *The 'Burbs* and comes up dry. Attempting a slapstick satire of suburban paranoia and xenophobia, Dante lavishes his considerable skills on a one-note, repetitive Dana Olsen screenplay which, at best, contains enough invention for a 20-minute skit. Tom Hanks, Bruce Dern and Rick Ducommun play three overgrown American boys whose macho terrors are unleashed by the arrival of a weird Slavic family on their quiet suburban street. Convinced that these mysterious, nocturnal strangers are performing murderous deeds in their cellar, our heroes turn into lawbreaking suburban commandos in defense of their sacred neighborhood. Hanks, as the skeptic among the gung-ho guys, gives yet another deft and seemingly effortless comic performance. Would that the script allowed him more to do. Brother Theodore has some curtly funny moments as the sourest of the Slavs.

But in the end, "The 'Burbs" lacks even the courage of its satirical conviction. After spelling out a message about addled middle-class macho, the moviemakers tack on a frenetic second ending that undercuts all that has come before. The victims are revealed to be villains; the booboisie antiheroes suddenly become defenders of the faith. After the endless windup, the feeble and cynical double delivery just leaves you depressed. About Hollywood, not suburbia.

TIME, 2/27/89, p. 82, Richard Corliss

Here it is, folks: the movie that hates its own audience. In mall-town America, a modest queue forms at the local Googolplex to see a new comedy starring Tom Hanks, exemplary nice guy. This time, the overgrown kid from *Big* is playing Ray Peterson, an amiable businessman whose idea of an O.K. vacation is to hang around his pleasant home in numbingly normal Hinckley Hills and be lazy. Let his wife (Carrie Fisher) and son go to their lakeside cottage; he'll just veg out, watch TV and keep an eye on those. . . well, darned *odd* neighbors who recently moved next door. These people talk funny; they don't socialize; they probably smell bad. So Ray and his friends will just, oh, break into the new family's house, dig up the backyard, wreck the basement and leave the place in cinders. They'll destroy the neighborhood in order to save it.

What's got into moviemakers lately, that they are so enthusiastically trashing their most genteel patrons? Bob Balaban's recent comedy *Parents*, a kind of robin's-egg *Blue Velvet*, limned a '50s family, as placid and telegenic as the Andersons on *Father Knows Best*, that devours human flesh. New Middle America gets a return visit from Joe Dante, guerrilla terrorist in Spielbergian suburbia. His *Gremlins* was a comic nightmare in which midget monsters invade a wonderful-life town and act up like the Hell's Angels in a malt shop. In *The 'Burbs*, the gremlins are the townspeople themselves, driven to posse paranoia by their suspicions about people whose only sin may be eccentricity. It's sort of a lynch-mob movie for laughs—laughs that are meant to catch in the back of your throat, like movie-house popcorn that turns out to be all kernels. One of the new neighbors is described as "about a nine on the tension scale." And so is this smart, crafty, off-putting movie.

Well, satire was never meant to ingratiate, and *The 'Burbs* is unsparing in its cauterizing of provincialism. One neighbor (played by Bruce Dern with wonderfully psychotic poise and a barbed-wire halo of gray hair) responds to every real or imagined threat to his property values as if he were commanding a platoon in Nam—with trusty telescope, walkie-talkie and a K ration of animal crackers. Another friend (Rick Ducommun) is your basic bully-wimp who goads Ray into all manner of illicit snooping. And Ray is the mild soul caught in the middle; with no special convictions, he mutates from a slightly curious homeowner to a horribly singed home wrecker. Hanks throws himself into this antiaudience movie with such suave energy that he seems determined to torpedo his hard-won rep as Hollywood's most comfortable new star.

Dante, a gifted parodist, adds spice to the gruel with glancing references to vintage cartoons, Sergio Leone movies and *The Texas Chainsaw Massacre*. His sight gags can be as nimble as a house number that, when budged, somersaults from a nine to a six, revealing the new neighbors' address as 666, the sign of the Antichrist. But like many a Hollywood Voltaire, Dante wants his *Candide* candied. This is satire that hedges its bets. By the end, Ray and his friends must be heroes as well as oafs; the new neighbors must be villains as well as victims. All of them are "neighbors from hell," but the old residents are revealed to have done the right thing, if for the wrong reasons. And so Dante, like the viewer, is left straddling a white picket fence, perched between admiration and an urge to move out of this neighborhood pretty darned quick.

VILLAGE VOICE, 2/28/89, p. 62, Elliott Stein

The 'Burbs begins with a spectacularly beautiful shot—created by George Lucas's Industrial Light & Magic—of the planet Earth spinning. The camera homes in slowly down to this country and plunks us somewhere in the Midwest on a residential suburban street. (The locale will be familiar to many—*'Burbs* was shot on Colonial Street on Universal's back lot, site of countless TV shows.) After this sequence, the ride is all downhill for the rest of a movie originally scheduled for release at Easter, but which seems to have been rushed into completion to profit from Tom Hanks's expected Best Actor Oscar nomination for *Big*.

The simplistic story concerns three neighbors, young married Ray (Hanks), xenophobic super-patriot war veteran Mark (Bruce Dern), and bumbling nerd Art (Rick Ducommun). They are obsessed by the new guys on the block, the Klopeks, a three-man family who live in a rambling, unkempt Charles Addamsy house and do not socialize. Ray, Mark, and Art suspect the newcomers of chopping people up and burying them in the yard.

This shaggy neighbor tale treats us to a spate of routine slapstick pratfalls, predictable mayhem, and a lame double whammy climax. Joe Dante's agitated direction does little to flesh out the vacuous screenplay by coproducer Dana Olsen. Hanks's boyish charm and limpid green eyes are well in evidence, but he has not been required to do much more than blink cute while doors are slammed in his face. Also wasted is the talent of performance artist Brother Theodore, who turns up as the Klopek uncle—this master of paranoiac satire (who bears an odd resemblance to Gertrude Stein) should have been permitted a hand in the script. *'Burbs* could have used a bit of genuine vitriol. The clangorous, nudgingly insistent and inconsequential musical score is by Jerry Goldsmith (*Freud, In Harm's Way, The Sand Pebbles*), who used to be a good film composer. *The 'Burbs* is the first production from Ron Howard and Brian Grazer's Imagine Entertainment's multipicture deal with Universal. It is not an auspicious starter.

Also reviewed in:

NEW YORK TIMES, 2/17/89, p. C12, Vincent Canby
VARIETY, 2/22–28/89, p. 18

CAMILLE CLAUDEL

An Orion Classics release of a Films Christian Fechner/Lilith Films/Gaumont/A2 TV France/Films A2/DD Productions film. *Producer:* Bernard Artigues. *Director:* Bruno Nuytten. *Screenplay (French with English subtitles):* Bruno Nuytten and Marilyn Goldin. *Based on the book by:* Reine-Marie Paris. *Director of Photography:* Pierre Lhomme. *Editor:* Joëlle Hache and Jeanne Kef. *Music:* Gabriel Yared. *Sound:* François Groult and (music) William Flageollet. *Sound Editor:* Claire Pinheir L'Heveder. *Set Designer:* Bernard Vezat. *Set Decorator:* Daniele Lagrande, Emmanuel de Chauvigny, and Charles Marty. *Costumes:* Dominique Borg. *Make-up:* Thi Loan N'Guyen and Dominique Germain. *Running time:* 149 minutes. *MPAA Rating:* R.

CAST: Isabelle Adjani (Camille Claudel); Gérard Depardieu (Auguste Rodin); Laurent Grevill (Paul Claudel); Alain Cuny (Camille's Father); Philippe Clevenot (Blot); Katrine Boorman (Jessie); Danielle Lebrun (Rose Beuret); Maxime Leroux (Claude Debussy); Jean-Pierre Sentier (Limet); Roger Planchon (Morhardt); Aurelle Doazan (Louise); Madeleine Marie (Victoire); Madeleine Robinson (Camille's Mother); Flaminio Corcos (Schwob); Roch Leibovici (P'tit Louis); Gerard Darier (Marcel); Benoit Vergne (Auguste Beuret); Philippe Paimblanc (Giganti); Denise Chalem (Judith Claudel); Hester Wilcox (Adèle); Ariane Kah (Kneeling Woman); Patrick Palermo (Photographer); Anne-Marie Pisani (Singer); François Berleand (Doctor Michaux); Martin Berleand (Robert); Claudine Delvaux (Concierge); Lison Bonfils (Landlady); Eric Lorvoire (Ferdinand de Massary); Dany Simon (Madame Morhardt); Michel Beroff (Conductor); François Revillard (Usher).

FILMS IN REVIEW, 3/90, p. 176, Eva H. Kissin

This essentially true story of the beautiful, driven young sculptor, Camille Claudel, who studied with the greatest artist of her time, August Rodin, is based on a biography published in 1984, which was written by her grand niece, Reine-Marie Paris. The biography, in turn, was based on letters written by Camille to her famous and adored brother, Paul, the writer and diplomat.

The material itself is fascinating. By now, the nineteenth century is just far enough removed to titillate us with its differences. In addition, the "woman problem" as it was known in that era (from Jane Eyre to Emma Bovary to Anna Karenina) is intrinsic to understanding contemporary feminism. It was certainly almost impossible for women to become serious artists. The usual paths of study and exhibitions were barred. Women might paint delicate flowers on china while baby napped—but full fledged artistic careers were almost unheard of. The few who made it like Mary Cassatt, were extremely disciplined spinsters who had the time and money to sustain their efforts. Women artists were generally considered contrary to nature, bizarre.

The obviously talented twenty-year-old, Camille Claudel, managed to become apprenticed to Rodin, who was busy at work on The Gates of Hell, a prophetic title. Her next, perhaps inevitable step, was to become the mistress of the artist, twenty-three-years her senior. A passionate love affair followed which inspired Rodin's most productive period. Claudel gloried in her role in the beginning, but found little time to do her own work. When Rodin refused to reject his common-law wife for the young artist, the passionate girl, now a woman forced to have an abortion, became hostile, competitive, bitter, and eventually mad. She was permanently committed to an institution for the insane by her proper but caring brother who could not bear the stain of her derangement on his own career. It is a terrible tale of wasted talent and misery. All that remains of it in the Rodin archives is an empty envelope with her name on it.

What about the film itself—a huge success in France—the winner of five Cesars (the French Oscar) for best film and best actress? It is far from completely satisfying.

Indeed, the material *is* significant. And the production *is* lavish. Its emphasis on era—the half-built Eiffel Tower, the wasp-waisted female silhouette right out of La Grand Jatte, the ardent young artist in her straw hat, the gas lit interiors—all seduce us visually. We might well be walking through a gallery of nineteenth century French painting.

In addition, the concern with the artist's studio has its own particular cach with the living plasters, marbles and bronzes—and the old world talk of life in the stone. We can't help but enjoy watching the chisel free the sculpture from its imprisoning material.

What is wrong then? The film is overly long and drastically overdone. The emotions are melodramatic verging on the soap opera. Wildly passionate music pours in to underline significant moments. The editing is also inadequate both in numerous dead spots and the seam-showing transitions which frequently lack smoothness. A sculpture of lovers on a studio turn of lovers in a carriage. Furthermore, the lines are often awkward and puerile. "I worked hard for you; now I'll work for myself" hardly exemplifies the feelings of a spurned woman and artist.

The entire film is stereotyped from Isabelle Adjani's overacted mad scenes as Camille to a gothic horror moment when the distraught artist haunts Rodin's house as a streak of lightening illuminates it.

Gérard Depardieu is, as always, convincing. He's appropriately strong and tender, and properly projects what our grandparents referred to as artistic temperament. He *never* overplays, even if the vehicle does. Adjani, a genuine force behind the production and obviously aware of its significance, overdoes her role after the first quarter of the film and seems almost ruled by it.

This quintessentially melodramatic film trivializes its aim to delineate the role of the nineteenth-century woman in the arts. The entire message, almost vulgarly underlined, might well be summed up as an admonition to separate the bedroom and the studio lest *you* fall in love with the boss.

LOS ANGELES TIMES, 12/21/89, Calendar/p. 11, Kevin Thomas

The two most important lines in Bruno Nuytten's soaring, heart-breaking "Camille Claudel" are "She has the talent of a man," which is quickly followed by "She is a witch." The remarks are made by friends of the great French sculptor Auguste Rodin (Gérard Depardieu) just after he has feverishly chipped away the cast of a bust of himself sculpted from memory by Camille Claudel (Isabelle Adjani), who at this very moment has progressed from his apprentice, model, muse and lover to the dangerous position of rival. Those two observations, both uttered by men, of course, help seal the fate of Claudel.

Rodin (1840-1917), creator of "The Thinker," remains one of the most famous sculptors of all time, and virtually every student of literature is familiar with the French poet, playwright and diplomat Paul Claudel (1868-1955). Even so, it is quite possible never to have heard of the tragic woman who linked the two men until this film or the recent Reine-Marie Paris book, which Nuytten and Marilyn Goldin adapted to the screen. This terrible and unjust obscurity is the very point of the film.

"Camille Claudel," which is France's official Academy Award entry, is a romantic tragedy in the grand manner, accompanied by a stormy score and unfolding amid settings that are period perfect, right down to cutlery and stemware. It's a rich, darkly gorgeous film, with tempestuous lovers played with bravura and bristling intelligence by Adjani and Depardieu in what are surely two of their best performances. Yet "Camille Claudel" is more than a Bohemian "Wuthering Heights," because it is told from a contemporary perspective of controlled feminist rage. One of the most distinguished cinematographers of the international cinema, Nuytten makes a dazzling directorial debut with this film, which never loses its briskness and energy throughout its 149-minute running time.

When 21-year-old Camille and Rodin cross paths in February 1885, he instantly recognizes her talent and backs her decision to leave her academic studies, convinced that she can learn by doing. "Work with the clay, inspiration doesn't exist," Rodin declares, but soon he is telling the beautiful Camille that she is his only inspiration, and art scholars today have declared her impact upon him as decisive, rescuing him from an academicism that eventually did overtake him.

From the start, Camille displays a determination so single-minded that she gets up in the middle of the night to steal clay from a deposit in the woods. For all her fierce independence of spirit, Camille is eventually swept off her feet by the man called "the greatest seducer since Victor Hugo." Depardieu's expansive, virile Rodin and Adjani's exquisite Camille are the apotheosis of romantic lovers, working intensively in a derelict 18th-Century mansion in front of an immense dump.

Eventually, Camille realizes that the master sculptor himself has feet of clay, unwilling finally to forsake his longtime mistress (Danielle Lebrun) when she demands he choose between them. She has good reason to do so but has too much pride and self-respect to want to ensnare him. Striking out on her own, she works feverishly, but her life has begun its ever-accelerating downward spiral even as she approaches the brink of renown.

Camille's story is one of gradual betrayal and abandonment by the three most crucial men in her life Rodin, who after their initial break finds he can't stand the possibility that Camille might just be his artistic equal (or, heaven forbid, better); her father (the splendid Alain Cuny), who had always encouraged her until her sculpture, so expressive of her sensuality and anguish, fails to gain public acceptance, and finally by her beloved brother Paul (Laurent Grevill), so long her defender.

Only her devoted dealer Eugene Blot (Philippe Clevenot) stands by her, but there is no way he can make people buy Camille's sculpture for all the good reviews they receive.

There is no doubt that in the face of so many setbacks the always emotionally turbulent Camille commences to lurch out of control, becoming obsessed that Rodin is actively trying to destroy her while engaging in increasingly eccentric behavior that can only harm her career. Camille does fall prey to a persecution complex, but her father, Rodin and finally Paul reveal themselves as being bourgeois to the core in their overriding concern with what people will think of the now-erratic Camille, whose mother was always her greatest enemy, to make matters much worse. The manner and finality with which Paul deals with his sister is shocking, yet not really when you consider what men have tried to do with troublesome women from the beginning of time.

That the film unfolds with such illuminating and persuasive psychological insight, much of it necessarily conjectural considering the scarcity of documentation concerning Camille, doubtless has much to do with the fact that Reine-Marie Paris, who served as the film's technical adviser, is the grandniece of Camille and the granddaughter of Paul. If conflict is the handmaiden of creativity, then Camille and Paul Claudel were exposed to it in abundance, caught between an intellectual father of high expectations and a mother (Madeleine Robinson) of harsh, narrowly puritanical views.

Indeed, "Camille Claudel" (rated R for adult situations), beyond either star-crossed romance or feminist tract, captures what seems to the essence—or at least the myth—of the French character as a unique distillation of pride, severity, elegance and passion.

MONTHLY FILM BULLETIN, 4/89, p. 108, Tom Milne

Paris, 1885. Camille Claudel, a twenty-two-year-old sculptress, shares dreams of glory with her brother Paul, an aspiring poet: her mother disapproves, taxing her with leading Paul astray, but her father secretly supports her. Uncertain of her talent, in awe of the forty-four-year-old Rodin as an acknowledged genius, Camille seeks to become his pupil. Non-committal but impressed by her work, Rodin eventually takes her on as an apprentice. Rapidly disillusioned by the feeling that he is using her to stoke his flagging inspiration, Camille nevertheless falls in love with him. The pair are ecstatically happy, despite stirrings of scandal and the hostility of Rodin's long-time companion, Rose. But when Camille becomes pregnant and begs Rodin to marry her, he (unaware of the pregnancy) pleads that he cannot simply sack Rose like a servant, while the furious Rose attacks her with a red-hot poker. Leaving Rodin, to the relief of her father, who feels that Rodin's use of her work lessens her chance of making her reputation, Camille determines on an abortion, horrifying Paul, who has meanwhile found God and become a promising Catholic writer. Camille resumes her own career, not without success. But after a brief reconciliation with Rodin, ending in mutual recrimination (both personal and artistic), Camille takes to drink and drugs. A one-woman exhibition results in favourable reviews but no sales (and the defection of Paul, appalled by the change in her); and obsessed by the conviction that Rodin is trying to destroy her, she is arrested for breaking his windows, strewing garbage on his doorstep, and screaming abuse. Becoming totally paranoid, virtually destitute after rejecting all attempts to help her (including Rodin's), she destroys her work; and in 1913 is committed to a sanatorium, where she remained until her death in 1943.

Easy to see why Isabelle Adjani stubbornly nursed this project into being, since it not only provides her with a meaty role, but resurrects a fascinating, feminist-oriented, almost forgotten byway of artistic history. Easy, too, to see why the film has not only been a fêted success in Paris, but received an unprecedented round dozen nominations for César awards. As a cultural coffee-table artefact, it has everything, from central theme of artistic creativity (agonies and ecstasies of, in best Hollywood tradition) to gutter-press whiff of dirty linen being washed (blots exposed on the copybooks not just of the great Rodin, but of Paul Claudel, one of France's most revered Catholic literary treasures).

Directed with careful if slightly stolid competence, and graced with fine, actorly lead performances from Adjani and Depardieu (though both are outplayed by Alain Cuny, who brings uncanny reverberations to the placid waters of his characterisation as Camille and Paul's father), the film is not as bad as the foregoing implies. It has some excellent scenes, two in particular going some way towards illuminating the mysterious processes of creativity: one in which Rodin, finding Camille allowing her model Giganti a breather from his pose, advises her never to spare the model; and a complementary sequence in which, preoccupied by his vision for "The Gates of Hell",

Rodin absently manipulates a naked female model into what appears to be an anatomically impossible, tightly stylised ball of torment.

One is surprised, on the other hand, to realise that twenty-eight years passed between Camille's first meeting with Rodin and her eventual incarceration in the Maison de Santé at Saint-Evrard (with their relationship spanning fifteen of those years). In the film, what we are offered is one of those conventional renderings of *amour fou*: one day passion and ecstasy; the next, despairing descent into madness. Dramatic compression is of course to be expected; but instead of troubling to evoke the passage of time, the film seems to be much more concerned with name-dropping tactics.

Fair enough in the context to have Madame Claudel cite Rimbaud as a token of unease as to the downward path along which her fallen daughter is leading her young brother. Fair enough, too, at a pinch, the fact that Camille's model Giganti should be reading Victor Hugo ("the most important thing in my life"), thus planting a signpost to the portentous nature of the later announcement, "Victor Hugo Is Dead!" Much less justifiable is the way Marcel Schwob is briefly trotted out as a buddy for Paul, Debussy for Camille. The clumsy nature of this aspect of the film is not unfairly represented by a scene in which Camille visits her doctor to learn of her pregnancy; as she leaves, the camera pans dramatically up; and there is the Eiffel Tower, under construction and still only half-completed. In similar vein, but subscribing to the pathetic fallacy, the nadir of Camille's degradation is staged against the backdrop of the great Paris '*inondation*'.

More crucially, given the fact that it impugns Rodin's creativity, is the film's failure to establish Camille's identity as a sculptress. We are simply not afforded sufficient opportunity to consider her work, to correlate it with Rodin's, and to judge from there. But that, presumably, is something consumers of coffee-table movies are not expected to require.

NEW YORK POST, 12/22/89, p. 33, David Edelstein

Ah, the French, they do love their tales of *amour fou*, their broken-hearted femmes wandering glassy-eyed under streetlamps, robbed of essence by caddish or indecisive lovers. The queen of unrequited ardor was heretofore Adele Hugo (Isabelle Adjani) in Truffaut's scorching "The Story of Adele H." It took Adjani more than a decade to find another heroine who could lead her once more into those dark byways of madness and obsession.

She is the sculptor Camille Claudel, disciple, model and lover of Rodin—who flowered in her company and thereafter settled into musty celebrity. Camille, meanwhile, sank into obscurity and depression when the long affair expired, and was finally committed to an asylum until her death in 1943. She believed (erroneously) that Rodin had put her and kept her there, jealous of her talent.

"Camille Claudel," directed by cinematographer Bruno Nuytten ("Jean de Florette" and "Manon of the Spring"), is prettily unfocussed and interminable, but is flecked, at least, with moments of passion. Adjani is in her element, which is to say elemental.

We meet young Camille wandering through the dark streets at night. When she returns home we discover she has been to the quarry to dig for clay—she has, her mother says, "the madness of the mud." We are told that her work consumes her, and when she goes to work for the notoriously lecherous, disagreeable Rodin (Gérard Depardieu) on the "Gates of Hell" project, she promptly recognizes a fellow zealot.

The two share the madness for the mud. They smell it, they hold it in their hands, they run their hands over it like blind people, nourishment pouring in through their fingertips. The movie is best when it's most tactile, when we're allowed, voyeuristically, to participate in that madness.

There is one breathtaking scene. Rodin, attempting to sculpt a woman's naked back, sends away his nude model, unsatisfied. Camille, who knows what he wants, drapes herself over a platform: we see the sinews and muscles in her back—which, ivory-colored and unblemished, seems halfway to marble already. Entranced, Rodin sculpts.

They had more than sex, they had sculpture.

But repeatedly "Camille Claudel" tells rather than dramatizes: We hear the lines, we note them, but we don't feel their meaning in our bloodstream. (Impressionable young women who dream of having their hearts broken in Paris may be another matter. If you are among them, forgive my insensitivity. ...)

Based on a brief, handsomely illustrated biography by Camille's grandniece (the granddaughter of her brother Paul, a well-known poet and playwright), the actors can't do much with the literary, rarefied script, which hoards known utterances of Camille's or Rodin's and wedges them unceremoniously into scenes. The scholarship is sound, the drama deadly.

It's easy to see why the film makers thought that no one but Depardieu could play the giant Rodin, but I wish anyone but Depardieu had. A titanic actor, he has become almost generically titanic—he lacks specificity, focus. Those large hands! That great body! That hunger for life! So what else is new?

Adjani, with that strange, hooded mouth and those dark blue eyes, is both seductive and frightening. You can see what attracts Rodin and also what drives him away, and Adjani's later scenes are startling: She's puffy and garish, that mouth developing a slatternly curl.

But the script hedges its bets on the nature of her crack-up. A 20th century woman with the misfortune to achieve in the 19th and so be ignored and punished by society? A woman robbed of her essence by a man? A true delusional paranoid? Her face pressed against the glass of the van that takes her away, she is, like so many of her sculptures, struggling to be formed. So is "Camille Claudel."

NEWSDAY, 12/22/89, Part III/p. 3, Terry Kelleher

"Camille Claudel" is like a great museum with too many rooms. Impressive as it is, this film may end up exhausting even its most determined admirers.

Released a year ago in France, where it won the Cesar Award as best picture of 1988, "Camille Claudel" tells the tragic story of the woman who was Auguste Rodin's muse, mistress and victim, Claudel herself was a brilliant artist, but she became known less for her work than for her involvement with the most celebrated sculptor of his day. She inspired him, loved him, rivaled him, hated him, but always she was obsessed with him. According to the screenplay by Marilyn Goldin and director Bruno Nuytten (based on a biography by the subject's grandniece, Reine-Marie Paris), this obsession destroyed Claudel's life—with help from turn-of-the-century sexual prejudice, malicious gossip and her own ferocious individualism.

Nuytten, a distinguished cinematographer making his directorial debut, has mounted a production that is at once somber and ravishing. His camera makes love to the sculpture, just as his main characters make love to a mound of clay until it brings forth a statue. We see that body, soul and work are as one in Camille Claudel, so we can begin to understand her pain when she feels that Rodin has "stolen" all three.

The lead performances are equally fine. Adjani, whose production company developed the project, rightly saw that she is an ideal actress to convey Claudel's boldness, complexity, volatility and desperation. In his skillful portrayal of her lover, Gérard Depardieu hews to a fine line between Rodin the artist and Rodin the operator, between the unconventional man who follows his heart (or his libido) and the cultural politician who covers his tracks.

Leading the able supporting cast are Laurent Grevill as the poet-diplomat Paul Claudel, Camille's adoring but increasingly priggish brother; Alain Cuny as her doting father; Madeleine Robinson as her harshly unsupportive mother; and Philippe Clevenot as the loyal art dealer who champions Claudel's work after her bitter split with Rodin.

The problem with "Camille Claudel" is its weakness for overstatement and histrionics. Rodin accuses Claudel of getting "drunk on pain," and the same could be said of this film before the anguish runs its 2½-hour-plus course. Of course, it would be wrong to gloss over Claudel's raging paranoia—her mother and brother were not wholly without grounds in eventually having her committed to a mental institution—but the suspicion rises in the last 30 minutes or so that Nuytten was duty-bound to fulfill Adjani's quota of mad scenes. "Why? Why?" she cries. "RODIIIIIIN!" she screams. The hysteria level grows so high that we realize it's only a matter of time before Claudel goes berserk in the studio and smashes her *oeuvre* to bits.

In fact, this scene is less shattering than a somewhat quieter one that precedes it: Resolved to keep her from slipping into obscurity and madness, her dealer and friend, Eugene Blot (Philippe Clevenot), arranges an exhibit of Claudel's work. She arrives late and drunk for her own show, just in time to disrupt a speech by brother Paul. "My sister is a mystery in full light," says Paul, not only embarrassed but revolted.

"There's a way to approach a mystery," Blot replies. "Gently."

Probably the gentle approach would not have worked here, but "Camille Claudel" could benefit from a touch more moderation.

VILLAGE VOICE 12/26/89, p. 107, Elliott Stein

At the recent Sarasota French Film Festival, a good deal of *le kvetching* could be heard about French cinema's declining visibility on American screens. Well, *ne kvetchez pas*, guys. No less than three Gallic imports are premiering locally this week in a diverse mix of genres that seems to offer a decent overview of what's happening in Mitterlandia: Jacques Rivette's *The Gang of Four*, an extremely personal, low-budget work from one of the surviving pillars of the New Wave; new director Jeanne Labrune's *Sand and Blood*, featuring Patrick Catalifo, a charismatic young actor already being promoted as "a sex symbol for the '90s"; and Bruno Nuytten's *Camille Claudel*, a very high-budget, mainstream blockbuster, winner of five French Césars and a showpiece for the combined histrionics of two of France's biggest stars, Isabelle Adjani and Gérard Depardieu. [See Stein's reviews of *The Gang of Four* and *Sand and Blood*.]

The talented sculptor Camille Claudel only began to come into her own in 1984: The Rodin Museum in Paris organized the first major retrospective of her work, and two biographies were available, one (unauthorized by the Claudel family) from 1982 by the feminist writer Anne Delbée, the other by the granddaughter of poet and playwright Paul Claudel, Reine-Marie Paris. Until then, Camille had been known, if at all, as Paul's sister, and as Auguste Rodin's lover for several years. She was an accomplished artist in her own right, but her creative achievements had been largely forgotten.

Camille had been Rodin's first female apprentice, then his model, muse, and collaborator (she sculpted parts of some of his most famous works). When he refused to marry her, she broke with him, began drinking, complained that Rodin was persecuting her, and was eventually forcibly placed by her embarrassed family in an asylum, where she spent the final 30 years of her life.

On the heels of her rediscovery, there were several proposals for a filmed biography. Claude Chabrol planned a movie starring Isabelle Huppert as Camille, based on the Delbée bio; the Claudel family blocked the project by withholding the right to reproduce any of her sculptures they owned. Nuytten's film is based on the Reine-Marie Paris, or "family," version, which apparently tones down the Claudels' culpability in her internment.

Nuytten has been one of France's leading cinematographers (*Jean de Florette*, *Going Places*) for over 15 years. *Camille Claudel* is his directorial debut, and as expected, it has turned out to be a cameraman's field day (the director of photography is Pierre Lhomme), with swoops and fancy backtracking and circular waltzes around statuary. The lighting at times seems inspired by de la Tour or Poussin. Some scenes are even flecked by whitish tonalities suggesting plaster casts. Luscious slow dissolves evoke classics of the silent cinema; huge closeups of unhappy faces loom. Some of these applications are effective; others coat Camille's tragic life story in ponderous artsy-fartsiness.

The opening reels work; they are dominated by Depardieu, who wisely underplays Rodin, yet powerfully inhabits the role. Throughout the film, eroticism is treated with some singularity. (There are a few conventional love scenes of no particular interest.) The sexually charged moments have naught to do with penetration and everything to do with tactility: Rodin, arriving to examine Camille's sculptures, turns out the light and gropes around in the room to feel them first; Paul (Laurent Grevill), jealous of Rodin and possibly harboring incestuous feelings for Camille, slowly runs his hand over the back of a statue of his sister; Camille, standing in a ditch, lasciviously scoops up wet clay with her bare hands and dumps it into an old suitcase ("She's got the madness for mud," a friend remarks); Camille, after the break with Rodin, returns home, then abuses, almost violates, a large head of clay.

The American release version of *Camille Claudel* has been cut by about 20 minutes (Nuytten made the trims himself, he told me, "to the great relief of the distributor"), but at a tad less than three hours, it still seems longish and less than the sum of a few imaginative parts. One is constantly aware of a work attempting to impress. Drama is smothered by packaging. Nuytten has constructed his movie with a myriad of short, pointillistic scenes; none lasts long enough to gain dramatic momentum. Gabriel Yared's overweeningly aggressive score is instant migraine. This glossy and largely academic movie strives to make big statements about artistic creation but can't even manage to come up with any satisfactory small ones.

The movie is Adjani's baby. She initiated the project; her company, Lilith Films, coproduced. The last section is thoroughly dominated by her Camille, in isolation, Rodin gone from her life. Her transition from vibrant young artist to bleary middle-aged alcoholic is abrupt and unconvincing—the fault may lie in the cuts. Nothing can mitigate the film's primary failure: A conspicuously self-adoring star, in a one-dimensional performance, has vitiated the urgency of a fascinating true-life story.

Also reviewed in:
NATION, 1/1/90, p. 31, Stuart Klawans
NEW YORK TIMES, 12/22/89, p. C20, Vincent Canby
VARIETY, 1/4–10/89, p. 14
WASHINGTON POST, 12/21/89, p. D1, Hal Hinson

CANNIBAL TOURS

A Direct Cinema release. *Producer:* Dennis O'Rourke. *Director:* Dennis O'Rourke. *Screenplay (Numerous languages with English Subtitles). Director of Photography:* Dennis O'Rourke. *Editor:* Tim Litchfield. *Sound:* Tim Litchfield and Chris Owen. *Running time:* 70 minutes. *MPAA Rating:* Not Rated.

NEW YORK POST, 8/23/89, p. 28, Jami Bernard

When the first Europeans arrived for a look-see at Papua, New Guinea, the tribesfolk called out in alarm: "Our dead ancestors have returned!" Today, when the tourist boats drop anchor, the villagers still say, "The dead have come back," only, as one confides in his native tougue to Australian film maker Dennis O'Rourke's camera, "We don't really believe it, but we say it."

"Cannibal Tours" is a unique and discomfiting documentary about the tourist trade in the South Pacific, shown from both perspectives—the tourists who delight in the adventure of seeing far-off lands but whose only urge once there is to mill about and take pictures, and the New Guineans who are confused, bemused and resentful at the invasion. Through it all, that tourist staple, the camera, emerges as the supreme icon.

O'Rourke gently, and with humor, juxtaposes the two cultures. The film opens with an horizon of luxuriant blue water, over which plays the incongruous chamber-music sound of Mozart. That gives way to static-filled interceptions of pop music from the closest outposts; civilization has come so far.

As the tourist boat cruises up the Sepik River, crocodiles and parrots observe and Nikon lenses watch back; natives swat at flies on their legs with rags while a beautiful Italian tourist bares her creamy, pampered skin in a bikini. (Among the many things that evidently the tourists have but the islanders don't is bug repellent.)

Sensitive through O'Rourke is, it doesn't take a master documentarian to make tourists of any nationality look like jerks. Fleshyfaced, abrasive, self-righteous, these armchair adventurers congratulate themselves on bargaining down the prices of already cheap local handicrafts. They are nervous and giggly over items that are new to them, smugly superior about a culture they've traveled so far to see but have little active interest in.

"They're happy and well-fed," rationalizes one tourist. "Nature provides them with the necessities of life."

The New Guineans might disagree. One embittered woman, angrily gnawing on a root, complains that the tourists never buy her wares, that they just stand around and look and then walk away without sharing their obvious wealth.

"I want them to pay me without any fuss," says another, speaking of that tourist habit, encouraged in guidebooks, of haggling.

A village elder, who with the aid of subtitles sounds much like any man in the street back home, admits that he charges tourists $2 to take photos in a religious shrine because it's the village's only income, and it's the only way to part the visitors from their money. He mentions more than once that he's baffled by the endless barrage of photo-taking. "We sit here confused while they take pictures," he says, adding that he has no idea what the tourists have really come for.

The tourists are equally perplexed. A florid German who is so well-traveled he can proclaim that "Iran used to be interesting" watches as a descendant of cannibals points out a marker where heads were once cut off. "And you like to keep these stones?" the German asks. Then he hands his camera to O'Rourke, behind his own camera, and instructs the film maker on how to snap a picture.

Although O'Rourke, too, is an intruder in his way, at least he has a purpose, which is neither to civilize the heathen nor chide the wealthy, but to show a corner of the earth where worlds collide.

VILLAGE VOICE, 8/29/89, p. 71, J. Hoberman

The most powerful ethnographic films inevitably turn in on themselves to reflect on the notion of what it means to document someone's life. Although Dennis O'Rourke's *Cannibal Tours*—one of the hits of the last Margaret Mead Film Festival, opening today for a week's run at Film Forum 1—is often funny enough to suggest a sitcom pilot (the postmod *Gilligan's Island*), the underlying tone is more like rueful pathos. This social satire can't help enjoying the objectification it decries.

O'Rourke, an Australian, makes pugnacious, enjoyable documentaries that share a common theme with his national art cinema. From his early account of Papua New Guinea's first election through such ethno cult films as *Yap...How Did You Know We'd Like TV?* to the controversial *Half Life*, a blistering account of American nuclear testing in the Marshall Islands, each of his movies has detailed the impact of Western technology on the lives of "primitive" peoples. *Cannibal Tours*, which documents a pleasure cruise up New Guinea's Sepik River, is the soft version of this cultural imperialism. Here, the Western technology in question is the vacation.

The filmmaker has called *Cannibal Tours* a tale of two journeys. The first is a more elaborate version of Disneyland's jungle cruise, "the packaged version of *Heart of Darkness*." On this trip, the American and European tourists are the stars of the predetermined movie, using video cameras or sound Super 8 to supply their own mock-travelogue narrations. The second journey, O'Rourke writes, is the more subterranean and unconscious "attempt to discover the place of 'the Other.'" Perhaps that was true for Captain Cook. Now the Other seems more like a photo op prop and souvenir connection.

Whatever the psychic attraction of the primitive, the basic transaction between native and tourist is commercial. Watching his extremely entertaining film, one soon notices that tribal discourse has been heavily contaminated by the English words *money* and *camera*. As O'Rourke suggests in his ironic use of Mozart to score parts of the film, these tourists are a new elite—the aristocrats of leisure, vanguard of an international bourgeois revolution. As such, they constitute objects of ridicule and envy for the natives, who, in order to facilitate commodity exchange, have learned to see themselves through foreign eyes.

Alienation is complete. "At that stone, we would dance and cut off heads," a New Guinea tribesman tells an avid German in safari garb. "Now I need a photograph," the tourist cries, demonstrating the tacit complicity between wealthy stranger and improverished native to produce the Exotic. Indeed, when the native begins to dance as the tourists click off snapshots, it's unclear whose ritual is more practiced—or more stimulating to whom.

Also reviewed in:
NATION, 9/4-11/89, p. 253, Stuart Klawans
NEW YORK TIMES, 8/23/89, p. C14, Caryn James
VARIETY, 1/6/88, p. 60

CARNIVAL OF SOULS

A Panorama Entertainment release. *Producer:* Herk Harvey. *Director:* Herk Harvey. *Screenplay:* John Clifford. *Director of Photography:* Maurice Prather. *Editor:* Dan Palmquist and Bill DeJarnette. *Music:* Gene Moore. *Sound:* Ed Down. *Running time:* 92 minutes. *MPAA Rating:* Not Rated.

CAST: Candace Hilligoss (Mary Henry); Sidney Berger (John); Herk Harvey (Ghoul).

NEW YORK POST, 7/19/89, p. 27, David Edelstein

"Carnival of Souls," a horror film from 1962, bobs to the surface of the modern cinema like a waterlogged car full of perfectly preserved bodies; time hasn't corroded it, but has given its contents an eerie luster. Made for a mere $30,000, the movie anchors itself in the subconscious; even when it's laughable, it gives you the creepy-crawlies.

Directed by Harold "Herk" Harvey, this cult classic never had an official New York opening. Tonight, that will change. With Harvey in attendance, it kicks off the Film Forum 2's Summer Festival of Fantasy and Science Fiction.

The shocks in "Carnival of Souls" aren't of the gut-bucket variety; the movie is all doomy atmosphere, its catatonia pitched on the edge of hysteria. In the opening, a car with three women plunges off a bridge into a river. Hours later, Mary Henry (Candace Hilligoss) sloshes out of the water, unable to remember the accident or its aftermath. The camera lingers suggestively on the river's dark, glassy surface.

That glassiness marks the movie's surface too, and it's suspicious; you sense that the sterile black-and-white images are concealing something, that underneath the zombie-like performances and pristine surface (with its '50s hairdos and sexless clothing) there's a hellish undertow.

Mary, whose blond, high-cheek-boned prettiness is equally pristine, takes a job as a church organist in a mingy small town in Utah, where the pastor advises her to "play with her soul." (The movie is full of heavily ironic dialogue like that.)

He gets more than he bargained for. Mary's music is suffused with a feverish lyricism, as if the spirits of the dead are speaking through her. And she's haunted in other ways. A tall, wheyfaced ghoul (played by the director) appears in her rooming-house window; attempting to flee him, she seems to leave the world altogether—for several minutes, no one can see or hear her.

"Carnival of Souls" takes place in a bell jar, a vacuum—there's no ambient noise, only the organ's quivering peals and subterranean moans. It's as remote and otherworldly as a silent movie, and so is its heroine.

Isolated from the human race—without friends, lovers or convictions—Mary isn't certain if she's dead or alive; she drifts through the film in a twilight zone. Drawn to an abandoned amusement park on a mile-long pier by the Great Salt Lake, she watches white-faced ghouls dance wildy under the pavilion.

Coldly pretty, her wide eyes topped with huge false lashes, Hilligoss is crucial to the movie's power. Her Method-actress readings give these soap-opera lines a whisper of hysteria, sexual panic; neither a bad nor an expressive actress, she's as spookily unmoored as Mary.

In fact, Harvey's lack of skill with actors only adds to the surrealism. Watching the landlady twitter monotonically (on the verge of forgetting her lines) or Mary's lecherous neighbor (Sidney Berger) drape himself in her doorway with Jon Lovitz-like salaciousness, you can't tell if this is bad or brilliantly stylized acting.

And eventually that doesn't matter—you accept Harvey's vision. The camera is always in the right place because the director is making his own rules. Even when the tone slips and the movie spills into camp, the mood isn't dispelled—you laugh gratefully, clutching at your rationality; as you do watching "Night of the Living Dead." (George Romero, director of "Night," credited Harvey as an inspiration. So did Rod Serling.)

After the commercial failure of "Carnival of Souls," Harvey didn't make another feature. We'll never know if this was a freak—a series of happy accidents—or the work of a genuine visionary.

VILLAGE VOICE, 7/25/89, p. 65, J. Hoberman

Another sort of low-budget tale of a back-country gal in a weird town [the reference is to *Four Adventures of Reinette and Mirabelle*], Herk Harvey's subterranean classic *Carnival of Souls* gets its alleged and belated New York theatrical premiere today as the opening attraction of Film Forum 2's annual fantasy/horror/sci-fi summerfest.

Made in 1962 by a group of industrial filmmakers in Lawrence, Kansas—with appropriately stark location work in Salt Lake City, Utah—this crudely poetic, genuinely creepy item impressed *Variety* ("a creditable can of film, considering it was put together for less than $100,000") but went nowhere as a theatrical release and became a perennial on *Creature Features*. *Carnival of Souls* is a movie that, like *Plan 9 From Outer Space* and *The Wizard of Oz*, found its cult on television—as befits its morbid treatment of Middle America. Harvey makes excellent use of the outsized Reuter Organ Factory in Lawrence and the abandoned Saltair Resort outside Salt Lake City; the film's sustained atmosphere is its strong suit.

As cost-conscious supernatural fantasy, *Carnival of Souls* looks back to Val Lewton's moody Bs and forward to *Night of the Living Dead*'s rampaging regionalism, while suggesting a heavy infusion of *The Twilight Zone* (just past its peak when the movie was made). Even before the credits, a desultory drag race sends a car full of young lovelies on a turgid plunge off a lonely bridge into the river. As the local authorities despair of even finding the bodies, one of the victims miraculously staggers out onto the sandbar—cue for Rod Serling and the first commercial break.

Much of the film's distinctive flavor comes from the heroine's nonlovability. A haughty, querulous creature (played by Candace Hilligoss, a Method actress imported from New York), she turns out to be a professional church organist whose disdain for religion is matched by her indifference to family, friendship, and men. A Rohmer *moraliste* might point out that, as the Hilligoss character was only barely alive, she doesn't even realize that she's died. Scarcely pausing to change into dry clothes, she leaves Kansas for a new job in Utah. There, when not lapsing into temporary invisibility (typically at high noon, in the middle of a crowded department store), Hilligoss spends her time fending off the advances of her droolingly lascivious neighbor (Sidney Berger, now chairman of the drama department at the University of Houston) and fleeing from a spook (director Harvey) who looks like Uncle Fester of *The Addams Family*.

Carnival of Souls may sound ridiculous, but it exudes psychic disassociation. The protagonist's flickering existence is matched by the narrative's unresolved dream-within-a-dream structure. The most powerful scenes are not Harvey's shock appearances in white pancake and lipstick so much as Hilligoss's attempts to articulate her alienation to a series of hostile or noncomprehending characters.

There are at least three ways to read this movie: Hilligoss as literal lost soul, Hilligoss as figurative lost soul, Hilligoss as flaming schizo. Not mutually exclusive, the three come together in the scene where, as Berger starts to paw her, she sees the death angel in a mirror, screams, "That man's after me!," then spends the rest of the night barricading her room—fending off a Blue Hour that promises to be permanent.

Also reviewed in:
NEW YORK TIMES, 7/19/89, p. C14, Stephen Holden
NEW YORKER, 9/4/89, p. 88, Terrence Rafferty
VARIETY, 10/3/62, p. 7

CASUALTIES OF WAR

A Columbia Pictures release. *Producer:* Art Linson. *Director:* Brian De Palma. *Screenplay:* David Rabe. *Based on the article and book by:* Daniel Lang. *Director of Photography:* Stephen H. Burum. *Editor:* Bill Pankow. *Music:* Ennio Morricone. *Music Editor:* Suzana Peric. *Sound:* Gary Wilkins. *Sound Editor:* Maurice Schell. *Production Designer:* Wolf Kroeger. *Art Director:* Bernard Hydes. *Set Decorator:* Hugh Scaife. *Special Effects:* Kit West. *Costumes:* Richard Bruno. *Make-up:* Paul Engelen. *Stunt Coordinator:* Jeff Jensen. *Running time:* 120 minutes. *MPAA Rating:* R.

CAST: Michael J. Fox (Eriksson); Sean Penn (Meserve); Don Harvey (Clark); John C. Reilly (Hatcher); John Leguizamo (Diaz); Thuy Thu Le (Oahn); Erik King (Brown); Jack Gwaltney (Rowan); Ving Rhames (Lt. Reilly); Dan Martin (Hawthorne); Dale Dye (Capt. Hill); Steve Larson (Agent #1); John Linton (Agent #2); Vyto Ruginis (Prosecutor); Al Shannon (Wilkins); Wendell Pierce (MacIntire); Sam Robards (Chaplain Kirk); Maris Valainis (Streiberg); Darren Burrows (Cherry); Sherman Howard (Court Martial President); J.J. (M.P.); Holt McCallany (Lt. Kramer); Kady Tran (Yen); Scott Gregory (Soldier Charlie 1); Ennalls Berl (Soldier Charlie 2); Vinh Tran (V.C. Interpreter); Somsak (ARVN Interpreter); Hataya Sarmount (Girl Villager); Ba Thuan T Le (Oahn's Mother); Nootch (Child Villager); Kwan (Child Villager); J. Chalerm (Villager Old Man Farmer); Sigma (Villager Woman); Po Powpi (Villager Old Man); Shaun Shea (Soldier); Kristopher Dunn (Soldier); Donal Gibson (Soldier); Shane Kerwin (Soldier); Niran (V.C. in Tunnel).

CHRISTIAN SCIENCE MONITOR, 8/23/89, p. 11, David Sterritt

Movies have explored the Vietnam war from a number of angles. To name a few: "Apocalypse Now" and "Full Metal Jacket" showed the literal insanity of war, while "Coming Home" studied the problems of veterans and "Platoon" looked at the brutal conflicts within an army unit.

"Casualties of War," the new movie by Brian De Palma, uses Vietnam as a background for its story, but it's less interested in the war itself than in certain fundamental questions of morality and responsibility. These could be examined in other settings, but take on tremendous power when magnified by the horror of wartime, which De Palma portrays in all its terrifying ferocity.

Based on an actual Vietnam incident that was reported in 1969 by a New Yorker magazine article, the story centers on a five-man patrol unit. Early in the film, its newest member (played by Michael J. Fox) gets trapped in a Viet Cong tunnel, and barely escapes death when his sergeant (Sean Penn) pulls him free. Shortly later, the squad's amiable radio man is killed, just weeks before he's due to leave for home.

This has a morbid effect on the sergeant, who begins to lose whatever humanity the war had still left in him. At the start of another long march through the countryside, he masterminds a criminal act—kidnaping, raping, and eventually killing a Vietnamese woman. Only the newcomer to the squad refuses to join this awful crime, and, when it's over, he has to face his conscience. Should he keep quiet about it, as everyone wants him to? Or should he turn in his former mates, including the one who saved his life, and make sure they're punished?

This is the moral question at the heart of "Casualties of War," and it's hardly new or startling. To make it as pungent as possible, Mr. De Palma rubs our faces in the awfulness of the circumstances, especially in the long sequence involving the Vietnamese captive. De Palma is the right person for this job, since he's famous for horror yarns like "Sisters" and "The Fury" and suspense pictures like "Scarface" and "The Untouchables," among others. He's also famous for pouring on violence and gore in his movies, a practice that raises moral questions quite beyond those in the story of this film.

In his own defense, De Palma has long insisted that he's a serious visual stylist who doesn't particularly like violence or even suspense, but turns to harrowing subjects because they offer the best opportunities for cinematic inventiveness.

In making "Casualties of War," De Palma and screenwriter David Rabe seem to have been genuinely concerned not only with "visual style," but also with the moral issues their characters face. The war itself is so vast and upsetting, however, that the filmmakers must be faulted for using it not as a social microcosm or philosophical crucible, but simply as a backdrop for melodramic events.

The film's most effective scenes are invariably the most horrifying ones—the abduction of the helpless woman, the rape and captivity she goes through, and her bloody murder. De Palma clearly sympathizes with this woman and hates the evil that she suffers. Yet he depicts that evil very graphically, and he allows the victim to show no real personality of her own. That's a serious limitation of the movie, and it's likely to rouse particular ire among women who've accused De Palma of an antifemale streak in past movies like "Dressed To Kill" and "Body Double."

Considered in terms of visual style, "Casualties of War" is steeped in the best tradition of classical Hollywood filmmaking. De Palma wields the camera efficiently and sometimes eloquently, and he knows how to inject a sequence with extra urgency by wholly cinematic means, as when at carefully chosen moments he wrenches his camera through the air instead of simply cutting from shot to shot. His tactics seem calculated and cold at times, as when he resorts to mathematically precise montage during the climactic murder scene. Yet the pathos of many key episodes is undeniable and testifies to De Palma's growing maturity.

Sean Penn gives a surprisingly strong and nuanced performance as the bad sergeant, and Michael J. Fox is likable as the hero, but his acting doesn't have much force and weakens parts of the story—including the end, which is droopy and sentimental. Other noteworthy performances are Erik King as the radio man, Sam Robards as an Army chaplain, and especially Thuy Thu Le as the Vietnamese woman.

"Casualties of War" is a flawed movie, and at times a terribly violent one. But it's also a powerful experience. And in a summer dominated by Ghostbusters and Batmen, it's good to have a film that gives us something to think about—even something as troubling as the horrors of Vietnam.

CINEASTE, Vol. XVII, No. 3, 1990, p. 40, Cindy Fuchs

Casualties of War is a movie of at least two minds. On the one hand, there is director Brian De Palma's typical concern—some would say obsession—with the male spectator who must take responsibility for what he sees. Here the hesitant voyeur is Private Eriksson (Michael J. Fox), a freckle-faced midwesterner who must confront his complicity in a wartime atrocity. On the other hand, the film presents screenwriter David Rabe's interest in a culturally conditioned intersection of sex and war, as embodied in Sergeant Meserve (Sean Penn), an unhinged boy-man loose in Vietnam, the closest approximation of amoral hell in the current American mindscape.

The issues raised by *Casualties* are not nearly so categorical as this breakdown would suggest, despite its insistence on closure and just punishment. Indeed, the film's unconscionable finale hoists Eriksson to ethical heaven (unabashedly proclaimed by a choir on the soundtrack as he looks skyward and the camera cranes out), while damning Meserve (he is banished to an off-screen jail sentence). Nevertheless, persistent political, ideological, and, yes, moral complications rupture this resolution. The film's designation of characters as good and evil hardly eases the tension created by the film's governing metaphor: Vietnam as rape.

This figure is not new to American films about the war. In *Platoon*, for example, an out-of-frame gang rape impels the young Chris Taylor to take a moral stand against his fellow troops; and in *Full Metal Jacket*, the act of rape is barely displaced by a pointedly phallic shooting of a female Vietcong sniper. In *Casualties*, the symbolic stake is raised considerably. The rape and its moral fallout become the war in microcosm, with the woman's body the territory to be saved or destroyed by American action.

The material seems tailor-made for De Palma (well-known for his slick reprises of Hitchcock and cinematic assaults on women's bodies) and Rabe, a Vietnam vet whose play *Streamers* effectively examines wars conflation of sex and death. Based on Daniel Lang's 1969 *New Yorker* article about a 1966 incident, the film traces the extended moral twitching of Eriksson, who accompanies and watches four fellow Air Cavalry patrol members as they kidnap, rape, and murder a Vietnamese girl. "If I do nothing," the private worries after the fact, "she just vanishes."

She doesn't vanish, but she is effaced by the movie's elaborate efforts to right the wrong. The film is structured as an extended flashback, triggered when Eriksson sees a Vietnamese woman on a San Francisco trolley car. By making little guy Eriksson our moral(istic) center, however, the film opts out of the mess of Vietnam. He seems less a participant making choices than an anguished tag along, watching with the movie's audience or, perhaps more to the point, the war's own concurrent television audience.

Eriksson is from the start an outsider, a helpless schmuck in over his head, almost literally. The first scene in country signals the loss of principled ground: in the darkening jungle, the earth literally collapses beneath Eriksson as he falls into a Vietcong tunnel. From beneath, we see his legs swinging wildly from the tunnel ceiling as a black-pajamaed soldier with a knife between his teeth crawls toward him. The tension builds like an episode of *The Perils of Pauline*, the camera shifting from the wide-eyed Eriksson, to the enemy below, to the approaching Meserve, who arrives at the last moment to rescue Eriksson from certain death. The sergeant empties his rifle into the sinister "VC gook" who erupts from the earth. "Some mad fuckin' minute!," Meserve exults, himself wide-eyed and breathless with his absolute power.

Ineffectual and ingenuous, Eriksson at this point might easily be Craig Wasson in *Body Double* or John Travolta in *Blow Out*, for the quandary here is vintage De Palma: Eriksson's reluctant voyeurism leads directly to his personal crisis. At first he simply doesn't see anything: he misses a fellow soldier's shooting by a sniper when it takes place behind him; then he misses the escaping sniper because his gaze is locked on the victim as Meserve works to stop the bleeding.

Appropriately, it is the horribly seductive Meserve who forces Eriksson to watch the war, while instigating the film's carefully delineated moral climax. When the frustrated Sarge reveals his plan to "requisition" a girl for "a little portable R and R," Eriksson can't believe it. When the kidnapping does take place (the invading GIs' point of view indicated by a hand-held camera, horror movie style), Eriksson turns away and faces the camera while the action continues in the background. Fox's familiarity underlines the absurdity and terror of this scene; he's Alex Keaton lost in the boonies.

But not looking doesn't absolve him or us. Eriksson's culpability begins with a lack of options drilled into him by the military, a lack which in turn emerges from a culture condoning sexual violence, and, in particular, male aggression. Meserve is the end result of this system, punchy with his own courageous audacity. Once the five-day patrol is underway, complete with the "VC whore" taken for "interrogation" (Vietnam's bankruptcy of language has been well-charted by Michael Herr, Gustav Hasford, and others), the sergeant seems as schizophrenic as the villagers he accuses of being "confused themselves if they're Cong or not Cong."

This messiness makes Meserve all the more threatening and interesting, before he is relegated to De Palma's Rogue's Gallery: Meserve operates according to a grim logic of survival that insists he maintain authority. At one moment tenderly feeding aspirin to the girl. Oahn (Thuy Thu Le), Meserve brutalizes her in an instant when he is challenged by Eriksson ("Ya gotta give me a minute on this thing we're doin' here," the private whines). Combining *Platoon*'s ungainly 'two fathers' theme in one person. Meserve is both Elias and Barnes, savior and menace. His confusion and complexity suggest as well the collapse of us/them thinking that undermined any sense of American mission in Vietnam. The 'dinks' all looked alike. Americans were killed by 'friendly fire.' Official Rules of Engagement existed only on military paper.

Meserve's henchmen—the psychotic, knife-wielding Clark (Don Harvey) and the jug-eared, complacently pernicious Hatcher (John C. Reilly)—lack his venomous ingenuity, but appreciate his grandeur: Meserve is "like Ghengis Khan...This is what armies do, man!" rejoices Hatcher. Unfortunately, this *is* what armies do, and Eriksson's complaint that "This ain't the army" seems hopelessly naive. The enemy, as the men have learned since Basic Training, is inhuman, a 'gook' or a 'dink,' a body to be fucked, this time literally. When Clark spouts U.S. good guy bromides— "We're gonna win her heart and mind, if she's got one"—or whispers pop cultural schtick in Oahn's ear—"Hello, I love you, won't you tell me your name?"—the extent of these American boys' immature self-absorption is stunningly clear.

Meserve, especially—with his flashes of lunatic tyranny and apparently infinitely perverse nature—is simply more than the literal-minded Eriksson can comprehend. But he's much more than that. Meserve's vile masculine hostility was honed to a fever pitch long before he arrived in Vietnam. Cagey, swaggering, and almost goofily smug, Meserve is the perfect product of the military's exchange of sex and death: a killing and fucking machine. His most effective strategy when trying to enlist Eriksson in the rape is both adolescent and macho-paranoid: he attacks the kid's manhood. "Ain't you got a pair?," he taunts. Not being a 'man' is tantamount to being the enemy. Meserve sticks his rifle in his own mouth to imply that "Maybe Eriksson's *homo*-sexual!," surely the worst fate imaginable in this man's army. It's only when Meserve threatens to "hump" him after the girl that Eriksson pulls out his rifle. But the contest is already over. Meserve grabs his genitals and asserts his power, more effective than any conventional weapon: "This is for fighting," he smirks, and saunters off to do battle with the enemy Oahn.

Turning to look at Eriksson and us, Meserve accuses us all: "You gonna watch?!" We do, of course, the camera positioned on the hill where the private sits out in an artfully staged downpour, having been assigned, of course, the 'watch.' As the rapists relax after the assault, one of them asks. "When's the last time you had a real woman, Sarge?" "She was real," he answers laconically. "I think she was real." But this reality is lost to Eriksson and to the film, which would rather forget that Meserve is no aberration, but the raging result of a successful system of indoctrination. There is no lapse in logic for him: the rape is a mission.

Left alone with Oahn. Eriksson is devastated by her battered face and whimpering Vietnamese. "I don't understand," he says. "I don't know what you're saying." So alien as to be animalistic, the woman is reduced to a spectacle of abuse. Her subsequent death (she is shot down by the patrol members) is similarly fetishized as an emblem of conspicuous, inexplicable American cruelty: her crumpled, bloody body is accented in the film frame by a red flower.

After the fateful patrol, Eriksson articulates the film's crucial question: "If you were me," he asks a friend, "What would you have done?" The answer here is much too simplistic (Eriksson reports the event and the offenders are court martialed), but the question is a good one, given the rampantly willful ignorance (still) engendered by Vietnam and its aftermath (recall Reagan's wistful 1980 declaration of our "noble cause").

If Eriksson can feel forgiven years later when the woman in San Francisco tells him he's had a "bad dream," the overwhelming ugliness that precedes this epiphany belies its validity. If De Palma's precise imagery is recognizably resonant (as the kidnapped girl stumbles along the path behind the men, a snake slithers across the path behind her), the profoundly unruly question of responsibility lingers.

That our boy Eriksson does the right thing when he reports the incident is less compelling, finally, than the questions raised by Meserve's very scary potency. For Meserve embodies the paradox of the American military system: he plans and carries out a reprehensible atrocity, yet he is also a good grunt, a ruthless, energetic killer who takes care of his own. Penn's performance is both shrewd and outrageous in its combination of boyish unself-consciousness and gear-stripping malevolence. Although this virile monster would seem to exemplify the cultural apparatus that grinds out American Manhood, *Casualties* beats a hasty retreat from such a troublesome insight: by film's end, the system proves morally sound and the significantly named Meserve is renamed a forgettable nightmare.

The fact that Thuy Thu Le plays both the Vietnamese victim and the woman Eriksson meets after the war appears to tie up all the film's unruly threads. Such an elision, however, only exacerbates the extremely disturbing relation between sex and war that *Casaualties of War* seeks to organize into a coherently moral tale. If the Other and the Woman can look so alike as to be identical, what does this say about the subjective observer's ability to see?

FILMS IN REVIEW, 12/89, p. 615, Edmond Grant

Coming at what is hopefully the end of Hollywood's cycle of Vietnam movies, *Casualties Of War* proved to be both profoundly disturbing and decidedly unpopular at the same time. It was clear the two factors were definitely related.

After *Platoon*'s across the board acceptance by the critics and the public, open season began for films about the "Nam experience." Now even as the cycle is dying out, with such "readjustment pictures" as *Welcome Home* and *In Country*, Vietnam has even reached the home screen, so now American viewers can relive the war, albeit in a highly sanitized, routinely plotted condition, on two weekly network series.

These two programs point up the problematic aspects of America's fixation with Vietnam: the simultaneous urge to purge our national guilt about the fruitless, genocidal conflict, and, at the same time, the desire to revel in what is likely to be America's last real shooting war—to witness healthy young men (and, in the case of TV's *China Beach*, women) bopping around to the latest Motown and psychedelic pop tunes while they dodge enemy mortar fire and read sentimental letters from home. *Casualties Of War* did not fit into this aspect of America's Vietnam fixation, and was downright adamant about not doing so, thus winding up being shunned by the public and tossed aside by the critics.

Based on a real incident, the film tells the story of an all-American sort, played by the appropriately wholesome Michael J. Fox, who is forced to confront the brutal and inhuman behavior that can become commonplace during wartime. He confronts it in the form of his fellow soldiers who, having been denied a weekend pass, decide to create their own entertainment. They kidnap a local Vietnamese girl and take her along on a reconaissance mission, raping her repeatedly and ultimately killing her. Fox's character is thus faced with a classic dilemma—to inform and salve his own conscience, or go along with the scheme and remain secure within the ranks.

A simple storyline, to be sure, but one that is intended to serve as a metaphor for the war as whole. And unlike the lengthy, symbolic "sniper" sequence that serves as the conclusion of Kubrick's *Full Metal Jacket*, *Casualties'* plot is all the more disturbing because the incident it recounts really took place.

Director Brian De Palma and noted writer David Rabe bring the events surrounding the kidnapping and subsequent murder into sharp focus, detailing the inhuman conditions which bring about such an act, but also revealing the cold premeditation with which the act was committed. Rabe's screenplay as rendered by De Palma is spare and no-nonsense grim, casting an unflinching eye toward the proceedings. Because of this, several critics labelled the film as sexist and exploitative, thereby missing the film's point entirely. For *Casualties* is an account of sexist and exploitative behavior, a movie that does not mirror its less savory characters' attitudes, but merely chooses to depict them as clearly as possible. And, for those who have followed the career of the talented but inconsistent De Palma, it definitely represents a departure from his *truly* exploitative Hitchcockian thrillers of a few years back.

De Palma and director of photography Stephen H. Burum work hard to transform the jungles of Southeast Asia into Fox's own personal hell. Standing as his chief antagonist is his sergeant, played to the hilt by Sean Penn. Penn does an impeccable job of lending a human face to the man who instigates the incident: he swaggers about with an excess of masculine bravado, grinning manically like Robert DeNiro, and recklessly incarnating the sort of schoolyard/barroom bully we've all the misfortune of encountering.

Given Penn's strengths as a performer, it should come as no surprise that he overshadows the very white-bread Mr. Fox. However, Fox's boy-next-door quality is exactly what is needed for the character of the film's hero. *Casualties* is indeed a very dark view of America's fighting men in Vietnam, and Eriksson (Fox's character and the real-life individual who blew the whistle on his fellow soldiers) is the answer. Eriksson's inherent goodness and his disbelief at the cruelty displayed by his cohorts may seem naïve at points, but these qualities are nonetheless essential, if only to serve as a sort of balance, to show that not all American soldiers in Vietnam were morally bankrupt characters like the one played by Penn. Thus, Fox's reticent and somewhat dull-edged screen persona is used to good effect by De Palma to show that virtue may have been in recess in the intolerable jungles of Vietnam, but it still had its place.

In the final analysis, *Casualties'* grim outlook (which is not dispelled by an odd framing device showing an older Fox seeing a Vietnamese girl on a San Francisco bus years later) was undoubtedly what caused the public to avoid it in droves. It is a fine, disturbing drama, though, that points to a deep, unsettling truth about the nature of Vietnam—namely, that the enemy within posed the greatest danger.

Missing from the film is a necessary footnote—that none of the soldiers ever served their prison terms and that Ericksson is still in hiding, living under an assumed name somewhere in the middle west.

LOS ANGELES TIMES, 8/18/89, Calendar/p. 1, Michael Wilmington

In the late '60s, TV coverage of the Vietnam War gave it the repetitiveness of a bad dream. That's probably what Brian De Palma is after in "Casualties of War:" a nightmare, reeking with blood, tears and cold sweat.

Taken from a real-life incident, De Palma's movie turns into a battle epic with a screw loose. It conveys a sense of moral quagmire, of sinking into squishily dangerous terrain, honeycombed with tunnels and traps, all hell exploding around it. That's the imagery of the movie's first battle scene, a taut prologue for a superb film.

De Palma may have found here the perfect arena for his darkly voluptuous expertise. Working with a David Rabe script that uses Daniel Lang's New Yorker reportage, he gets a bad-dream Vietnam. This isn't reality but hyper-reality: war as experienced in the oscillations between fatigue and terror, or recalled by someone fighting back the horror of his recollections. There's moral charge to the action, but it's also swooningly exciting, coldly scary. Every friend may be an enemy, every innocent a traitor.

Lang's book revolved around a brutally shocking 1966 incident in which the leader of a five-man reconnaissance squad, Sgt. Tony Meserve, informed his men that, before setting out on their mission, they would kidnap a Vietnamese farm girl, rape her en masse and then murder and dump her to cover their tracks. Astonishingly, all the men went along with this plan, except for one upright Minnesota farm boy, Sven Eriksson—like the others, a fictitious name—who refused to participate and later tried to bring his squad mates to justice.

The horror of the premise soaks right into the movie's bones. In its scheme, everyone is a casualty of war: not only the poor, brutalized girl but the men themselves, turned by this hell into monsters or cowardly bystanders. The movie contrasts two temperaments: Eriksson's thoughtful reserve, Meserve's posturing bravado. And two styles of heroism: Meserve's undeniable bravery in battle, and the moral courage Eriksson needs to report the crime. The story becomes a battle between men who pervert the system to their own uses and others who, out of passionate conviction, try to buck it.

Michael J. Fox and Sean Penn, who play Eriksson and Meserve, respectively, have such dissimilar styles that, at times, they seem to be inhabiting different movies. Fox, in his best dramatic performance to date, has the laid-back, tamped-in, deferential quality of a skilled TV performer. Penn, on the other hand, bursts the boundaries of his role with his gargoyle intensity, his drilling gaze, his jaws perpetually chewing a plug of tobacco. Grabbing his crotch or waving his rifle, he's like a young kid's parody of a warrior: a macho paradigm.

The whole Vietnam episode is part of a reverie—Eriksson's—triggered when he sees a woman who looks just like the victim Oahn (played by the same actress, Thuy Thu Le). Meserve's excesses seem part of that nightmare; so do the excesses of the rest of the cast. As the near-psychotic Clark, Don Harvey has a werewolf glower and an ominous mad-dog grim. John Reilly's Hatcher is a gangling, slack-jawed goof, Erik King's Brownie a florid clown and Ving Rhames' Lt. Reilly a coldblooded rationalist.

"Casualties of War" is De Palma's 19th movie and easily his best. His detractors saw his Hitchcock-pastiche thrillers as manipulative and sadistic, but here he's not dealing with stylish slashers or bloody set-pieces. He doesn't have to reach for a shock. He's dredging up a deeper horror: the hell that lies beneath every man's skin, waiting to erupt.

There may be a conflict here between De Palma and Rabe's temperaments—Rabe is said to dislike the movie—and, in a way, it's understandable. Rabe probably tried to make the nightmare real; De Palma turned it back into a nightmare.

But that hallucinatory framework is what makes the movie uniquely his. The old virtuosity is there—the murderously complicated long-take tracking shots, the macabre jokes at the edge of the frame, the deep-focus compositions. But they're buried in the story, they don't draw attention to themselves. And the themes and ideas are typical for De Palma too: the interplay of voyeurism and guilt, the heroine who can't escape, the linkage of violence and repressed or twisted sex, the obsession with a system's secret rot, with a nightmare taking over your life.

"Casualties of War" questions the whole current movie idea of heroism in war: the blood-spattered boy's fantasies and one-against-a-hundred lollapaloozas of the '80s. Oddly enough, Meserve is more heroic and sympathetic in the movie than he was in Lang's book; he saves Eriksson's life and staunchly ministers to a dying black buddy (both fictitious episodes). We don't have the satisfaction of regarding Meserve as a coward, a hypocrite, a phony; he's a good soldier who's come to believe he has the right to rape and kill innocents.

"Casualties of War" (MPAA-rated R for sex and violence) is no indictment of the American soldier—indeed, Vietnam combat veterans may be among those most moved by it—but it is an indictment of the idea that individual brutality can be cloaked by a system. For Eriksson, the horror of the episode was its anonymity; he refused to let the girl suffer and die for nothing. That's the bravest and finest part of the film, what all the people involved—De Palma, Rabe, Penn, Fox, composer Ennio Morricone, cinematographer Stephen Burum, all of the cast and crew—should be proudest of celebrating.

The heroism of the real-life Eriksson lay not in revenge, but in his devotion to the victim. For all those who suffered or died anonymously in the juggernaut of the Vietnam War, or any war—or the victims in their mass graves, the demonstrators shot down in a city square, the millions of bystanders caught and killed in the crossfire—the movie makes its lonely plea. The leitmotif Morricone uses for Oahn, the mournful pan flute that underscores her plight, comes back like an anguished cry, pushed up past breath, past hope, the last call of the suffering in a world in which death and horror are not only the province of night.

MONTHLY FILM BULLETIN, 2/90, p. 38, John Pym

In 1974, a young man, Eriksson, dozing on a San Francisco subway, is transfixed by a girl whose face takes him back to Vietnam...During a night-time jungle engagement, Sergeant Meserve saves the life of the inexperienced Eriksson who has fallen through the roof of a Vietcong tunnel. Next day, however, Meserve's unit, which includes the simple Hatcher and the ruthless Clark, is ambushed in a village and the good-natured Sergeant Brown mortally wounded. Back at Basecamp Wolf, Meserve and his men are infuriated when the nearby village—where they intend to find compliant girls—is placed off limits. The following morning, the unit, including Brown's replacement, the quiet Private Diaz, embarks on a long-distance reconnaissance. Eriksson is shocked when Meserve, determined not to be denied a woman, orders the kidnapping of a village girl, Oahn. In a tumbledown jungle hut, finding no support from the initimidated Diaz, Eriksson levels a gun at Meserve, but the latter outfaces him. Meserve leads the gang rape on Oahn, while Eriksson stands watch in the rain. Next day, Clark stops Eriksson from freeing Oahn and returns them both to an escarpment where the unit is about to attack an arms cache. Eriksson and Hatcher refuse Meserve's order to kill the girl. Diaz is about to stab her, however, when Eriksson fires in the air and alerts the enemy. In the ensuing firefight, which is joined by a U.S. patrol boat and a fleet of helicopters, Clark butchers the girl, who nevertheless staggers to her feet and is blasted off an elevated railway track by all the frenzied Americans except Eriksson. Back at camp, Captain Hill declines to institute a court martial until Eriksson, who survives Clark's attempt to kill him, confesses the crime to an army chaplain. Diaz, Hatcher, Clark and Meserve all receive prison terms (though Hatcher's conviction is reversed on appeal)...Eriksson follows the girl from the train to return a scarf she has left behind.

Based on a true story by Daniel Lang first serialised in *The New Yorker*, Brian De Palma's blood-drenched movie begins in a bright, claustrophobic, faintly unreal tunnel and ends in the liberating sunshine of a green California slope on the long-awaited day of President Nixon's resignation. When Oahn was kidnapped, her mother begged the soldiers to take the girl's scarf, as a symbolic reminder of home; at the end, Eriksson returns another scarf to a poised young woman who somehow understands his turmoil and, it seems, releases him from it. (The closing titles omit a credit for the woman on the train, and one guesses that the Vietnamese non-professional Thuy Thu Le, who plays Oahn, acted as a body double.)

De Palma tells the story straight and old-fashioned: everyone is a casualty of war, and the two rabbit's feet which cheerful Sergeant Brown, three weeks away from the end of his tour of duty, wears round his neck will not, of course, save him; one survives in Vietnam by chance, despite Meserve's admonition, invalidated by Brown's death, that his men bring only good-luck charms on their long-distance mission. Meserve and his men are not exactly guilty; but Eriksson, a Lutheran family man, is definitely an all-American hero; the Vietnamese are as voiceless as Oahn.

It is, too, an unambiguously signposted picture for a director who, before *The Untouchables* (1987), was known for his embellishments and trailed cinematic references: Meserve is denied sexual relief on the night before the mission, and consequently takes his revenge on the army, the war, on everything, by kidnapping a girl who can be raped at leisure. Motives are kept simple: one soldier is slow, another psychotic, another a coward, the officers are pragmatic, the padre is honest. The story boils down to whether Eriksson (the still babyfaced Michael J. Fox) has the moral courage to withstand Meserve (Sean Penn, with a permanently twisted lip), the man who saved his life; and then whether he has the physical courage—a grenade rolls into a latrine as he pauses to light a cigarette—to see his fellow soldiers brought to justice.

De Palma's is not, by current standards, a particularly apocalyptic war. The jungle engagement, for instance, has none of the terrifying confusion of the similar scene in *Platoon*. There is little sense of anger on the part of the film-makers at the atrocity which is their subject: De Palma has, perhaps, spilt too many buckets of blood in the cause of Grand Guignol; and now, when it comes to showing how a real person is brutally destroyed, his credit has in a sense been used up. Clark is a psychotic, he is—one can tell from his face—destined to kill someone; and the Vietnamese girl, whose anguish registers chiefly through her moans, is not the first victim of a frenzied cinematic knifeman who proves more difficult to despatch than her murderer expected.

NEW YORK, 8/28/89, p. 53, David Denby

Terrified most of the time, men in war may come to feel something like love for the platoon leader who takes them through the worst. War stories are full of such bursts of admiration. A brutal sergeant who gets his squad back to the base in one piece may even seem like a great man. He's not an officer, not distant, fussy, or calculating, not worried about strategy or his career. Profane and intimate, a bruising, foulmouthed familiar, he knows all about fear. As far as the men are concerned, the tougher he is, the better; his brutality is the mark of his insight into the nature of the war.

All of which goes to explain one of the central motivating factors in Brian De Palma's powerful Vietnam movie, *Casualties of War*. At least three of the men on a patrol in the Central Highlands early in the war adore (and fear) their young sergeant, Tony Meserve (Sean Penn), and when Meserve, a great soldier, decides that the squad should kidnap a Vietnamese peasant girl for a bit of "fun," the three men, battle-weary, demoralized, filled with loathing for the Vietnamese, go along with him. Two of them enjoy themselves, taking license from Meserve's pleasure in the crime. For them, the kidnap and rape is a wild adventure—a midnight joyride. The third man is uneasy, guilt-ridden, yet too weak to resist the others.

There's a fifth man on the patrol. Sven Eriksson (Michael J. Fox) won't take part in the rape and tries to protect the girl. It's not that Eriksson doesn't admire Meserve, too—earlier, Meserve saved his life. But Eriksson has something else alive in him—instinctive decency, a painfully stubborn sense of justice. Fox's performance in this difficult, even booby-trapped role is a major achievement. Certainly the slightest hint of sanctimoniousness in its star would have pushed the movie into a soft, sticky bed of self-righteousness. But Fox, far from being priggish, offers decency as an unhappy burden, a fate neither asked for nor enjoyed. His Eriksson is appalled not only by what his friends do but by his own excruciating role as the only man who could have stopped them—and later as the only man in the Army who wants to bring them to justice. Who wants to be a goody-good with bodies falling everywhere?

When Eriksson fails to prevent the girl's destruction, an agonizing sweat of self-recrimination breaks out all over his body and douses his spirit—permanently. His misery speaks volumes about the quandary of liberalism during the war, when goodness became a kind of consuming nausea. In wartime, no one is going to love Eriksson the way they do Meserve.

The men's devotion to Meserve is not the only reason for the crime. Playwright David Rabe, who wrote the screenplay, adapting Daniel Lang's 1969 *New Yorker* account of an actual incident, has dissociated himself from the finished movie, but despite Rabe's unhappiness, what comes through of the men's motivation has considerable psychological density. Rabe and De Palma have created the incident as a foul but inevitable product of the degraded atmosphere of the war. It is the American disaster in Vietnam in miniature. *Casualties of War* is steady, fully felt, fully dramatized, a nobly serious and responsible movie. The only trouble with it—the reason that it's not quite a great film—is that morally, it's too simple, Shrewed and humane as it is, *Casualties of War* lacks, finally, the boldest powers of discovery, an exploration of the tangled web of good and evil.

For Eriksson, the war is never anything but an experience of cruel absurdity and helplessness. At the beginning, on night patrol, as enemy mortar fire comes closer and closer, he falls through the collapsed roof of a Vietcong tunnel and just hangs there, half in, half out, his lower body vulnerable to a VC soldier crawling through the tunnel with a knife. Meserve pulls him out and kills the VC, but De Palma has already got us seeing the war as a nightmare of total vulnerability.

Eriksson is a "cherry"; he's been in Vietnam only three weeks. But the other men aren't charmed by his innocence; as they see it, inexperience attracts death. In a peasant village, Eriksson is shocked by the men's rudeness, a scruple that strikes the others as ludicrous. A few minutes later, as the squad relaxes by the side of a rice paddy, one of them, the beloved radio man Brownie (Erik King), takes a bullet in the neck. In the background—it is one of De Palma's masterstrokes—the villagers who set up the Americans for the ambush can just barely be seen scurrying away. The men feel exposed, defenseless; they aren't about to understand how those villagers might have been bullied by the VC. From their point of view, betrayal lurks behind every yellow skin. Casual and deadly, the scene is a classic.

Screaming with fear and excitement, Meserve loves to kill Vietnamese. The exhilaration that he feels in killing is part of his hold over the men. And the excitement of Sean Penn's acting—at least for a while—is that he makes Meserve a mean, calculating, sadistic little punk who has moments of greatness. He's the most physical of actors, working with his jaw and bullet head and his sneering, sculpted lips; his being small yet overmuscled, a would-be neighborhood bully, is just right for this role. It's the most Brandoish of his performances: He brings out the swaggering beauty, the thrusting insolence inside the punk's aggressiveness.

The death of Brownie, Meserve's soul mate, threatens his sense of invulnerability, and he struggles mightily to get it back. Rabe and De Palma demonstrate an impressive acquaintance with all the sickening, stunted rationalizations of criminality. In obscene tirades, the Americans vilify the Vietnamese as scum; the men even convince themselves that they are exercising the historical privilege of conquerors. Their self-justification is stupid yet understandable because they have every reason to be frightened. Under pressure, a common macho delusion—the men's belief that by crushing women they will enlarge themselves—blots out everything.

The girl, Oahn (Thuy Thu Le), is young and beautiful and terrified; and she has a nagging cough that strikes Eriksson each time like a knife thrust. Eriksson's bond with her is painful to watch, because there is little he can do but comfort her and argue with Meserve. At the same time, he's never tempted to touch her himself, and this makes the movie less interesting than it might have been. Eriksson is simply *good*. And Meserve, on his side, is never tempted to mercy. Penn's performance turns into the gleeful display of an actor making himself high on evil. By the end, partly because Penn's work becomes inhuman, we see Meserve as merely degraded and stupid—a vicious bum. Any hope of an enriching moral ambiguity fades.

Still, the movie is a remarkable development in De Palma's career. Earlier, in such hair-raising films as *Carrie* and *Dressed to Kill*, De Palma brought a dizzying sensuality to pulp horror stories. He was showing how much fun he could have by letting go, relaxing the moral sense. But *Casualties of War* can only be seen as a stern self-reckoning. De Palma has cut up his share of women, but this time, the girl is viewed with complete sympathy; this time, horror is really horrible—sordid, even disgusting. Yet De Palma's ease, his mastery of filmmaking, his command of the emotional charge of violent spectacle, makes the movie an intensely pleasurable experience, however painful the material. Just after Oahn's death, in the midst of a battle, with Americans and Vietnamese dying all around, Michael J. Fox comes to after blanking out for a while and takes in the mess. Though we share his dismay, we may also think—for the scene is stunning—"God, how beautiful!"

NEW YORK POST, 8/18/89, p. 23, David Edelstein

To most people, the phrase "war is hell" suggests a buddy getting shot down in the trenches or a landscape littered with dead and mangled bodies. No one can dispute the horror of such images; but a work of art owes us more than literal horrors.

"Casualties of War," the fact-based account of an atrocity committed by American soldiers in Vietnam, depicts a horror so much more profound than loss of human life that silence is the only fit response. The film is inconsolably moving. The casualties of its title aren't simply human: They're the qualities that emblemize what's human, chief among them, pity.

The incident itself was reported by New Yorker writer Daniel Lang in 1969. His article (later a book) detailed in terse and unhysterical prose how a squadron of five men kidnapped, raped and eventually murdered a young Vietnamese woman. The one soldier who refused to participate turned the others in; on screen, it is through his unblinking eyes that we in the audience bear witness.

The film, directed by Brian De Palma from a script by David Rabe, begins with this man, Eriksson (Michael J. Fox), on a San Francisco streetcar in 1974. Bleary and furrowed with grief, he sees a Vietnamese woman sitting across from him (she is Thuy Thu Le, who also plays the victim, Oahn), and his nightmare recollection comes again.

We are now in the dark forest, prowling alongside Eriksson and his squadron, and De Palma's camera moves with gorgeous fluidity and expressiveness; it conveys both the suppleness and fear—the heightened receptivity—of these absurdly youthful warriors, these children slung with bazookas and bullets and automatic rifles.

The images have a mythic terror. When Eriksson sinks halfway into a Vietcong tunnel, a VC crawls toward his legs while up above the ground the helpless soldier sees trees explode in flames and topple closer and closer, as if elbowed aside by an invisible dragon. Eriksson's savior is his sarge, Meserve (Sean Penn), the man who later suggests they requisition "a little portable R&R"—a girl.

De Palma has often led with his style, but here he respects Lang's austerity, and his storytelling has a purity and compression that's mesmerizing. It's still a lush, enveloping style, but the boldness of his imagery suggests black-and-white expressionism: In every shot, De Palma sets up palpable tensions between the men and each other and the men and their environs. This is a landscape of the soul.

He and Rabe lay the groundwork for the coming atrocity, the assaults that, in the soldiers' mind, give them license to do anything they please. They're aliens in this deceptively pastoral, agrarian society, this land of rice paddies and water buffaloes; every encounter has an unplumbable subtext, a hidden tunnel that may suddenly open up and swallow them.

They're always waiting for the next bullet, which could come at any time, from any direction. It leaves you "humpbacked and crooked," declares a boisterous, entertaining soldier, Brownie (Erik King), before he learns that he isn't armor-plated. De Palma makes these Yankees increasingly vulnerable in the frame; every second they survive makes them eligible in their heads for "payback." Entitlement reigns.

Muscle-bound and rock-jawed, Penn's Meserve is like a boy playing Rambo and swelling to fill the mold. He isn't a good soldier, he's a great one: alert, precise in his movements and fearless. But there's a little something extra: When he kills he gives himself completely to the madness of the moment—he leans back from his gun and rocks out.

In carrying off Oahn, asleep beside her sister and mother in a hooch, his instincts are those of a caveman; to flourish in this war he has deadened himself to whatever we mean by civilization. (What characters said about Brando's Kurtz in "Apocalypse Now," Penn's Meserve embodies.) True, Penn gets hammy—his emphatic dumb-prole accent undermines him—but few other actors could be this scarily remote. He's on his own wavelength.

After the wailing girl is kidnapped, "Casualties of War" becomes grueling, a theater of cruelty. Eriksson tries to reason with his sergeant, but is a voice in the wilderness. Clark (Don Harvey) with his Neanderthal jawline and psycho eyes, can't wait to mess her up; Hatcher (John C. Reilly) goes dumbly along for the ride; Diaz (John Leguizamo), who has a conscience, fears the chaos of the jungle without the affection of his squadron—he succumbs to peer pressure.

Oliver Stone got at this frightening sense of entitlement in the atrocity scene in "Platoon," but gummed up his film with specious allegory. What's remarkable is that De Palma and Rabe never lose their focus: They're as clear-eyed as Goya in "Disasters of War," but without the bitter irony that kept Goya from losing his mind.

Irony is absent from "Casualties of War"—its tone is rigorous and heartsick, as is Fox's wrenching performance. He is, as always, baby-faced, but there were plenty of kids in Vietnam. More important, there's no TV glibness in Fox's acting—like Eriksson, he's raw, a clear pool. When he blurts "It isn't right," it seems involuntary, a reflex of a decency that hasn't been allowed to die.

De Palma has been accused of eroticizing violence, especially toward women, but no film has ever made rape so repulsive—the violation of a human soul. He doesn't permit his camera to ogle Oahn: We glimpse only segments of her body, and during the act itself he washes the frame in blue and putrid yellow and cocks his camera on the hooch a sickening 30 degrees, as if he can't bear to look straight on but knows he musn't flinch.

The cries the bruised, sick young woman makes the following morning are the purest sounds of anguish I've ever heard, and De Palma pushes it beyond what you think would be the limit. The climax, set on a railroad bridge—and on the widest screen imaginable—dissolves into pure insanity; cruelty and terror merge into a single, bottomless wail. Agony so prolonged should be unwatchable, but you don't want to look away. Too much is at stake.

There is a falling off in power after the central events of the film, and I could sense that the audience welcomed the chance to pull back—to laugh at some of the clunky ways that Rabe and De Palma try to wind things up.

A speech Eriksson makes—close to what the actual Eriksson told Lang—articulates the movie's theme of entitlement in ways we don't want it articulated. It's a brilliant insight, but the set-up is hokey, and this is the only point in the film where Fox looks foolish. That said, it's important that De Palma and Rabe do wrap up "Casualties of War"—that they send us out with something more substantial than our devastation.

I have described the film as inconsolably moving, but there is one consolation: that goodness persists with even more stubbornness than evil. In "Full Metal Jacket," Stanley Kubrick portrayed the dehumanization of men by war, and he seemed to accept and participate in that dehumanization.

De Palma never accepts it, and in the sorrow of the movie is its hopefulness. When, after the rape, Meserve emerges from the hooch and stares at Eriksson, Fox's eyes and mouth fill the frame—the camera couldn't be much closer. Around his face, a blue rain falls in thick, gelatinous drops: it's as if the celluloid itself were weeping.

NEWSDAY, 8/18/89, Part III/p. 3, Mike MCGrady

In any confrontation with true horror, our first instinct is to put distance between ourselves and the event. So it was that Daniel Lang's original New Yorker article, "Casualties of War," appeared in print three years after the incident it described. And so it was that 20 more years passed before director Brian De Palma got around to making his movie based on that same episode.

"Casualties of War," the based-on-truth story of a squad of soldiers who kidnap and rape a Vietnamese woman, gives strong dramatic substance to the thought expressed in "Arrogance of Power" by J. William Fulbright: "...in the course of dehumanizing an enemy—and this is the ultimate fallout from any war—a man dehumanizes himself."

Sean Penn's Sgt. Meserve is cold-eyed and combat-weary, thoroughly dehumanized; his misquote of the 23rd Psalm ("Yeah, though I walk through the valley of evil, I shall fear no death...") seems right, as does his entire performance. After matter-of-factly rescuing a green arrival from a Viet Cong tunnel, Meserve sees his closest buddy killed by a sniper and he finally snaps—not outwardly, where others might notice it, but inwardly, where the audience can only feel it.

The lurking presence of death has dehumanized others in his command. Clark (Don Harvey) is a knife-flashing psycopath; Hatcher (John C. Reilly) is both slow-witted and insensitive; Diaz (John Leguizamo) is too cowardly to stand up against the others. And Eriksson (Michael J. Fox) is still so wet behind the ears that he'll accept a possibly booby-trapped gift from a villager because "I didn't want to do something rude."

Something *rude*? In this dirty little "sorry-'bout-that" war, rudeness is never an issue. And what Meserve is now contemplating goes a few clicks beyond rudeness; shortly before dawn, he detours his squad into a remote hamlet and kidnaps a screaming young woman from her home: "We're gonna requisition ourselves a girl, a little portable R & R."

As they carry the woman off into the jungle, some of his men are enthusiastic: "This is *unbelievable*!" Others see themselves as either pioneers of modern warfare ("Why didn't someone think of this before?'') or part of a long-standing tradition (''Just like Genghis Khan!''). Eriksson's objection (''Jesus, we're supposed to be here to *help* these people'') are brushed aside by Meserve with, ''We've incarcerated a VC suspect, is that what you're talkin' about?''

The girl is to be terrorized, brutalized, raped and perhaps murdered. Afterward, in the monsoon rains, Meserve joins Eriksson for a smoke.

''I hate the army,'' the sergeant says, explaining all.

''This ain't the army,'' Eriksson says. ''This ain't the army, Sarge.''

While De Palma may seem to dwell overlong on the gruesome details, he sees the episode as an apt metaphor for our entire involvement in Vietnam. Unfortunately, and I hold this against the film, he seeks to strengthen that metaphor through numerous small but significant departures from Lang's report and the real-life situation.

I can accept the film's dramatic frame as a necessary contrivance, but I'm unsure why De Palma or playwright David Rabe (''Streamers'') tampered with so many of the reported facts—the actual makeup of the squad, what was said and when, the preliminary events, the resultant prison sentences and so forth.

While Penn has enough savvy to moderate the villainy, to make his own dehumanization an understandable byproduct of war, Michael J. Fox has been saddled with more than his share of nobler-than-thou sentiments. While not in 'Nam long enough to be dehumanized by the war, he is never quite humanized by the script. Given these limitations, the intensity and feeling the young actor brings to his performance are remarkable.

Until recently, De Palma (''Dressed to Kill,'' ''Body Double,'' ''The Untouchables'') has made a career out of murder most stylish. All too often De Palma's successes have been triumphs of style over substance. Now, by toning down the visuals and keeping the cinematographic showing-off to a minimum, he enters a new area of movie-making. In the past, De Palma has specialized in stylish horror, mock horror, Hitchcockian horror; here, for the first time, he confronts real horror, and the results are devastating.

NEWSWEEK, 8/21/89, p. 58, David Ansen

It's getting harder and harder to pigeonhole Brian De Palma. Though he began his career as a counterculture satirist (''Greetings,'' ''Hi, Mom!'') he has long been type-cast as a hip, sadistic Hitchcock heir, thanks to such suspense exercises as ''Carrie,'' ''Obsession'' and ''Dressed to Kill.'' But this fails to take into account the epic ambitions of ''Scarface'' (perhaps his most unjustly maligned movie), his detour into gangster comedy, ''Wise Guys,'' or his greatest commercial success, ''The Untouchables.''

Audiences expecting baroque plot twists and cynical sensationalism may be quite astonished by his Vietnam drama, *Casualties of War*. It's as harrowing as anything he's made, but in an entirely different way—straightforward, emotionally direct, even bordering on the earnest. Middle age seems to have wrought a change in De Palma's sensibility: the moralist who was perhaps always lurking under the irreverent, thrill-happy surface has come to the fore.

Written by the playwright David Rabe, based on a wartime incident reported by Daniel Lang in The New Yorker in 1969, this is De Palma's first real-life horror story. Five young soldiers are sent into the jungle on a reconnaissance mission. At the instigation of their commanding sergeant (Sean Penn), they kidnap a Vietnamese girl (Thuy Thu Le), then rape and murder her. Only one man in the squad, Private Eriksson (Michael J. Fox), protests and refuses to participate. Haunted by the girl's grisly fate, he reports the incident to his superiors; to his astonishment, they try to dissuade him from pressing charges. But Eriksson, risking his own life, persists in his quest for justice.

De Palma keeps his focus tight. Though ''Casualties of War'' feels like a big movie, it's the most dramatically contained of the Vietnam films. De Palma and Rabe aren't reaching, like Oliver Stone or Francis Coppola or Michael Cimino, for metaphysical dimensions or grand summations. Surprisingly for De Palma, the movie shies away from political metaphors. It's the story of the price of keeping one's moral sanity in a war in which indecency, paranoia and murder have become the norm. The thinnest line separates bravery from depravity, the courageous from the craven. In a speech a bit too explicit for its dramatic context, Eriksson spells out the movie's moral: that living under the constant threat of death makes our actions more, not less, important—that we cannot act as if nothing mattered, but as if everything does.

What is unmistakably De Palma is the breathtaking craft he brings to bear on this unbearable tale. The most premeditated stylist in Hollywood (De Palma first story-boarded every shot of the movie on his home computer), he uses his style to serve the story, but at the same time he never lets you forget you're watching a movie. From vast crane shots to gigantic close-ups to vertiginously tilted angles, he uses screen space to suggest the moral disorientation of his characters. The complex choreography of the murder of the Vietnamese girl—in midbattle, on a trestle, with choppers looming in the skies overhead—is bravura film-making but without the show-offy taint of the set pieces in "The Untouchables." And he knows when to keep it simple, as in the surprising scene when Eriksson reports the atrocity to his lieutenant (Ving Rhames), a black man who uses his own experience of racial discrimination to argue Eriksson *out* of making waves.

Feminists who have attacked De Palma for the alleged glee he takes in victimizing women may have to rethink their position. Perhaps they will see "Casualties of War" as his apologia: this is as savage a critique of male sexual aggression as you could want, and the rape itself is presented without a whiff of exploitation. Penn is truly scary as the hopped up, supermacho sergeant, a man whose undeniable bravery has been twisted into obscene shapes. At moments his strutting "business" seems actorish, but there's no denying his demonic charisma. Penn has the flashy role, but Fox has the tougher one: it's not easy playing "goodness," and he pulls it off beautifully, without strain. You believe in Eriksson's innate decency and understand the courage it takes to remain a boy scout in hell.

When a movie is this well made, the occasional lapses stick out. It seems too cheap to have Don Harvey play the brutal Clark as such a glowering B-movie psycho. And the final scene, a brief "redemptive" coda set in San Francisco, is awful—it ends the movie on a phony rhetorical note. "Casualties of War" is De Palma's best work in years—it's powerful, meticulous filmmaking—yet it may be a movie easier to admire than love. Ultimately the drama seems too cut and dried; Eriksson wrestles with his conscience, but the audience never has to. "Casualties" has the visceral impact of a good movie; it lacks the resonance of a great one.

SIGHT & SOUND, Winter 1989/90, p. 62, Terrence Rafferty

For American moviemakers, as, perhaps, for most Americans, the war in Vietnam has signified an almost unimaginable chaos: a moral swamp, a jungle of ambiguity, an acid-rock inferno, a purple haze in which nothing can be seen clearly. To watch the war on the nightly news in the late 60s was to experience it as a nightmare or a bad trip—there was never enough context to allow us to interpret the horrors before our eyes—and that, for the most part, is the Vietnam the movies have given back to us: the war that took place inside our stunned minds, the one that wasn't so much about Vietnam as about *us*.

Looking at *Apocalypse Now* or *The Deer Hunter* or *Full Metal Jacket*, you'd think that the real obscenity wasn't that a small country was invaded by America, but that America's consciousness was invaded by what it most feared: doubt, self-consciousness, the everyday awareness of mortality. Even Oliver Stone's *Platoon*, less solipsistic than the others, fell back on the egregious notion that the primary conflict was within the souls of Americans.

Brian De Palma's *Casualties of War* transcends the chaos. De Palma isn't interested in expressing his shock at the treacherousness of the world: he's known about that for quite some time. *Casualties of War* is the strongest, the simplest and the most painful of all the Vietam movies because it isn't about how terrible it is not to understand what's going on around us—it's about the agony of seeing terrible things too clearly. The screenplay, by the play-wright David Rabe (*The Basic Training of Pavlo Hummel, Streamers*), is based on an incident reported by Daniel Lang in the *New Yorker* in 1969: the rape and murder of a young Vietnamese woman by the members of a US Army patrol.

What makes the story extraordinary is that we see it through the eyes of the one member of the five-man patrol who refused to participate (and later brought charges against his comrades), an ordinary Midwesterner named Eriksson (Michael J. Fox), who can't believe the evil that's taking place in front of him. The leader of the squad, Meserve (Sean Penn), a tough soldier nearing the end of his tour of duty, is the organiser of the kidnapping: the movie shows us the factors that have driven him to this—the sudden death of a close friend, the denial of a pass and the constant, corrosive unease of living in a treacherous landscape, never knowing where the enemy might be coming from. De Palma, as we might expect, does full justice to the dangerous unpredictability of this environment, but he isn't dazed by it. His vision has a bracing clarity: he never allows us to suspend our moral judgment, to believe, even for a moment, that disorientation excuses everything.

De Palma doesn't treat Vietnam as if it were a remote, totally alien place, the great exception to all we've learned. It's a landscape he knows well, the ferocious and intricately threatening world for which his thrillers have provided such potent metaphors—a traumatised world, in which unspeakable crimes are played out before helpless witnesses, then replayed endlessly in their dreams. Doubt, self-consciousness and mortality invaded him a long, long time ago. Acknowledging them isn't an issue for De Palma anymore: living with them is.

In a sense, he has been making films about Vietnam his whole life, using a painstaking exploration of the thriller technique as a way of dealing with his fear and outrage. (His thriller and horror movies have always made audiences more uncomfortable than even the most graphic slasher pictures, perhaps because we sense something more urgent and serious in his images than a simple desire to shock.) In *Casualties of War*, he seems to have arrived, finally, at the terrifying source of his sensibility; and his unmistakable style feels not so much simplified as purified. The suspense here is heartfelt and unendurable. It's tragic suspense.

The longest and most brilliant section of the film is its middle hour—from the brutal abduction of the young woman, Oahn (Thuy Thu Le), to her murder—and there are few passages in movies in which terror is so agonisingly sustained. Oahn has no English, but her tears and her struggles and her screams speak directly to us, the sounds of her suffering isolated from the undifferentiated din of the war. Her pain is a constant presence that can't be ignored, or taken for something else, or forgotten when it's over. It registers, with a piercing clarity, in us as it does in Eriksson. Michael J. Fox's unremarkable, sympathetic face is the ideal screen for her horror to be projected on, and his performance is quietly astonishing: the soldier's anguish is plain and eloquent.

The crime is not more awful because this decent American is seeing it, but it *feels* more awful because Eriksson's awareness provided a moral (and physical) tension that we couldn't experience so powerfully if we were simply watching a unanimous bunch of madmen. Eriksson is us, saying (as we do in any great suspense sequence), "This can't be allowed to happen." And for a few, heart-stopping moments he takes us to the verge of believing that it won't: although he feels trapped by his role as a grunt taking orders (and it's clear that the deranged Meserve wouldn't hesitate to kill him if he stepped too far out of line), he tries, after a good deal of delay and indecision, to take Oahn away from her tormentors. But there's no escape.

Finally, Oahn is killed by the squad in the midst of a hectic skirmish with the enemy, and Eriksson, fighting for his own life, can't save her. De Palma's staging of this climatic sequence, which takes place on a set of railway tracks on the side of a hill, is both a formally stunning bit of action filmmaking and the embodiment of the movie's rigorous morality. All hell is breaking loose, everything's happening at once, yet, in the middle of the chaos, our attention remains— passionately, almost obsessively—on Oahn, who's always somewhere in the frame and always in focus. The fate of this Vietnamese woman is all that matters; she's running towards us along the straight, clear lines of the tracks as she dies.

TIME, 8/21/89, p. 54, Richard Schickel

Why are we in Viet Nam? Again. At this late date. In the case of *Casualties of War*, there can be only one answer: for further diagnostic tests on the national conscience. For the story it tells, based on an incident first reported in *The New Yorker* by Daniel Lang two decades ago, is too brutally horrific to contemplate unless some moral edification can be derived from it, some guide to the larger enigmas of human conduct.

The story, recounted in a grinding, realistic style that is unlike Brian De Palma's usual manner of playing fast and loose with death, is simple to describe. A small unit under the command of a Sergeant Meserve (Sean Penn, in an uncompromising performance) sets off on a long-range reconnaissance mission. On Meserve's orders, it stops at a peasant village, where it abducts a young girl and sadistically binds and gags her for the many awful hours of their trek. The girl, who is heartbreakingly played by a delicate newcomer named Thuy Thu Le, will serve as "portable R, and R," In other words, Meserve intends that he and his men will gang-rape her. This they eventually do, with only one among them, Eriksson (Michael J. Fox), refusing to participate and trying to rescue the girl. She is murdered in a fire fight, and ultimately Eriksson, despite threats to his own life and the indifference of his commanding officers, succeeds in bringing charges against his sometime buddies. They receive, at last, stern punishment from a court-martial.

Its surface realism notwithstanding, this movie must be read symbolically, especially since it is presented as a dream that overtakes Eriksson years later, when he encounters a young Oriental woman on a train who reminds him of the long-ago victim. In the dream, Meserve—arrogant, competent, headlong (in short, a born American leader)—is an archetype of the worst in the national character. Eriksson—frail-looking but articulate and morally alert—is the beleaguered best. The remainder of the unit is, of course, the hulking, muddled majority, all too willing to be conned by anyone who seems to be sure of his goals, however, perverse. Their victim represents all of the innocents who, by accident, find themselves in the path of Yankee imperialism.

The script, by playwright David Rabe (*Streamers, Hurlyburly*), introduces some complexities into this schematic story. Eriksson owes his life to Meserve's military skills. The sergeant, who is not presented as a psychopath, and the other men are in a furor because a buddy has been killed in an ambush at a supposedly pacified village. Eriksson has an interesting speech in which he argues that the standard rationale for bad wartime behavior ("We might at any second be blown away") is exactly wrong. It is precisely because soldiers live inches from death that they should be "extra careful about what we do." The ending, in which Eriksson is awakened from his nightmare and, in effect, offered absolution by his trainmate, seems to propose that decent Americans may, at last, enjoy sleep untroubled by the naggings of historical conscience. It is, at least in popular-cultural terms, novel.

But still the movie does not work. Its true story is too singular to serve as the basis for moral generalizations. The ideas advanced by the film are, in any case, not significantly different from the ones put forward by opponents of the war while it was going on. But it is its distant and curiously monotonous tone that finally betrays *Casualties of War*. It numbs the conscience instead of awakening it.

VILLAGE VOICE, 8/22/89, p. 77, J. Hoberman

The unnatural verdancy of Brian De Palma's *Casualties of War* has intimations of tropical madness. The landscape is revoltingly fecund, a gaudy green hell. The air is thick, the colors iridescent, the fireworks spectacular. A battle scene is lit like a page from *Sgt. Rock*—orange highlights and blue flares illuminating the green-on-green foliage. This Vietnam flick is less *Tour of Duty* than tour de force; the music that accompanies a soldier drowning in his own blood is as sickeningly sweet as overripe papaya.

No less than Coppola or Kubrick, De Palma treats Vietnam as his arena—although he has a far more developed sense of the tawdry than those proudly solipsistic maestros. After a brief framing scene, *Casualties* goes totally "Look, ma!"—plunging headlong into bravura, sweat-sopped, nocturnal chaos. Retreating grunts run through the jungle, screaming in terror as mystery explosions close in on them. Their confusion is hallucinatory—not to mention wildly entertaining. "Some mad fucking minute, huh, Cherry?" cocky Sergeant Meserve (Sean Penn) asks trembling Private Eriksson (Michael Fox), the raw recruit whose life he's just saved. "You survive the 'Nam, you get to live forever, man."

By now we know that, in movies at least, nobody *really* survives the 'Nam. Still, *Casualties of War*, adapted by David Rabe from Daniel Lang's lengthy article (first published in *The New Yorker* in late 1969), has an aggressive quality that sets it apart from such aggrieved grunt ensemble pieces as *Platoon* and *Hamburger Hill*. Despite some perfunctory softening around the edges, De Palma and Rabe approximate the furious tone with which Lang reported on the genesis and aftermath of an American war atrocity. Indeed, they make its evil humor a universal condition.

There are no happy campers in this outfit. Everyone is keyed up, spaced out, twisted around—contorted with hatred for the "slugs" and "roaches" they're supposed to fight (and defend). "This place is bullshit, man. I hate this fucking place. ...If the gooks had half a brain, they'd be fighting to get out of this stinkhole instead of keeping it." When Meserve and Eriksson's unit is restricted to base, with the local whorehouse placed off-limits, the sergeant announces that as part of the next day's recon mission, they'll simply requisition a woman. De Palma underscores his fatal declaration with a burst of thunder and lightning. This is a movie with a lot of weather—scenes dissolve into rain; the infinite blue is often peering over someone's shoulder.

Casualties of War reeks of frustration and megalomania and, beyond its grim story of a Vietnamese civilian's abduction-rape-murder at the hands of an American patrol, it's disturbingly sensual: GIs smoke Thai stick in some superstoned Eternal Now (the eternal Asia of peasant and water buffalo materializing in the background). No previous Vietnam film, not even *Apocalypse Now*, has quite this sense of humid, paralyzed stupor: "Am I talking?" one zonked soldier asks as the camera peers down at him in one of De Palma's trademark overheads. "I can't tell if I'm talking or not, man."

Reality is continually up for grabs. Penn has a transcendent moment, telling a dying buddy to "look in my fucking eyes" so he can hypnotize him into thinking he's fine. It's a stunning bit of business. Would that the actor were always so mesmerizing. For the most part Penn plays the out-of-control Meserve as meta-De Niro, barking out phrases in stage Brooklynese. (In the intricately choreographed murder scene, he works his face like a wad of bubble gum.) Indeed, Penn so relentlessly overmasticates the part that the diminutive Fox, in the thankless role of the squad's lone nonparticipant in the gang rape (and subsequent whistleblower), trots off with the film by merely acting determined and looking anxious on cue.

If *The Untouchables* established that De Palma could make money, *Casualties of War* represents his follow-up push for artistic respectability. There's no mistaking this for a routine combat film. The movie is laden with tilted angles and mannerist close-ups. The camera hunkering down in some manicured rice paddy gives you the same suave nudge as the Ennio Morricone score. Perhaps it's not surprising that Penn's performance should be fragmented when the movie itself is so lush and uneven a series of set pieces. While some scenes are so grotesquely distended they suggest a record caught in a groove, others are brilliantly staccato. De Palma crosscuts reaction shots endlessly, then does more with a single glimpse of the obligatory rescue chopper than most Viet films do with an entire fleet carpet-bombing the countryside.

In any case, De Palma is rarely predictable: The abduction sequence sets the camera prowling through a dog-ridden village, then he makes even more expressive use of offscreen space. ("You gonna suck this, you fucking hoo-ah?" the unseen Meserve growls at his unknown prey.) Flagged months before the movie's release in De Palma's *New York Times Magazine* profile, the murder-attack sequence cries out for shot-by-shot analysis. Modulating sound, animating corpses, shifting viewer interest from foreground to background, it's made for the Steenbeck, a blatant bid for the sort of textbook explication lavished on *Psycho*'s shower or *Potemkin*'s Odessa Steps. Still, in making his first war film, De Palma gives new meaning to the term "army brat"; *Casualties of War* never delivers on the promise of its most scuzzy, exalted moments.

De Palma thrives on shock effect and surface tension, and while this bold, virtuoso flatness has tremendous verve, it serves to drain the emotional content out of whatever he touches. He's not exactly Mr. Soul. (*Blow Out*'s Möbius strip ending seems a remarkably self-aware illustration of this quandary.) Five minutes into the movie, Eriksson falls halfway into a hole, his legs dangling through the roof of an underground tunnel, while a ferret-faced VC slithers toward him. When at the last second Meserve yanks him out (the VC lunging in vain), the effect is so chintzy that it's funny: war as a scene out of *Halloween XXXII*. This isn't the first movie De Palma's made in which a nubile young woman is terrorized by a mad slasher, but it's certainly the most ambitious. What's puzzling is how the movie eviscerates itself.

While Rabe's dialogue has a percussive, slangy lyricism, his script is oddly heartless, begging a number of crucial (even can't-miss) scenes. Why, for example, is so much made of Eriksson's wife and child, only to have them dropped from the film's final reckoning? Even more unsatisfying is the perfunctory final confrontation between Eriksson and Meserve, a moment which should crystallize the former's moral dilemma, but drifts by with disarming "Strangers in the Night" casualness. The feeble ending wherein Eriksson is absolved from our national "bad dream" lacks the guts of *Carrie*, or even *Dressed To Kill*. If it weren't for bad taste, De Palma might not have taste at all—which is why you have to wonder where this film will go at the box office.

It's not just that Oliver Stone has already preempted the moral high road. *Casualties of War* flies in the face of half a dozen years of Viet vet recuperation. The least you can say about De Palma is that he hasn't pinned his rehab on theirs.

Also reviewed in:
NATION, 9/4–11/89, p. 252, Stuart Klawans
NEW REPUBLIC, 10/2/89, p. 26, Stanley Kauffmann
NEW YORK TIMES, 8/18/89, p. C10, Vincent Canby
NEW YORKER, 8/21/89, p. 76, Pauline Kael
VARIETY, 8/16–22/89, p. 20
WASHINGTON POST, 8/18/89, p. D1, Hal Hinson
WASHINGTON POST, 8/18/89, Weekend/p. 37, Desson Howe

CHANCES ARE

A Tri-Star Pictures release. *Executive Producer:* Andrew Bergman and Neil A. Machlis. *Producer:* Mike Lobell. *Director:* Emile Ardolino. *Screenplay:* Perry Howze and Randy Howze. *Director of Photography:* William A. Fraker. *Editor:* Harry Keramidas. *Music:* Maurice Jarre. *Music Editor:* Dan Carlin Sr. *Choreographer:* Miranda Garrison. *Sound:* Bill Nelson and C. Darin Knight. *Sound Editor:* Charles L. Campbell and Richard C. Franklin Jr. *Production Designer:* Dennis Washington. *Set Designer:* Perry Gray and Richard McKenzie. *Set Decorator:* Robert R. Benton. *Set Dresser:* Gary Kudroff, Mike Higelmire, and Greg Lynch. *Special Effects:* Stan Parks. *Costumes:* Albert Wolsky. *Make-up:* Cheri Minns. *Stunt Coordinator:* John Moio. *Running time:* 108 minutes. *MPAA Rating:* PG.

CAST: Cybill Shepherd (Corinne Jeffries); Robert Downey Jr. (Alex Finch); Ryan O'Neal (Philip Train); Mary Stuart Masterson (Miranda Jeffries) Christopher McDonald (Louie Jeffries); Josef Sommer (Judge Fenwick); Joe Grifasi (Omar); Henderson Forsythe (Ben Bradlee); Susan Ruttan (Woman in the Bookstore); Lester Lanin (Conductor); Richard DeAngelis (Hot Dog Vendor); Franchelle Dorn (Receptionist); Jacquelyn Drake (Bradlee's Secretary); Don Richards (Bonino's Defense Attorney); June Thorne (Clerk of the Court); Nat Benchley and Cliff McMullen (Marshalls); Carey Hauser and Laura Lee Stetzel (Paramedics); Max Trumpower (First Minister); Dennis Mancini (Second Minister); Katie Schwarz, Margi Holland, and Andrew Reilly (Limbodrome Staff); Fran Ryan (Mavis Talmadge); James Noble (Dr. Bailey); Marc McClure (Richard); Mimi Kennedy (Sally); Kathleen Freeman (Mrs. Handy); Dennis Patrick (Archibald Blair); Martin Garner (Mr. Zellerbach); Gianni Russo (Anthony Bonino); Channing Chase (Aide at Smithsonian).

FILMS IN REVIEW, 6–7/89, p. 367, C.M. Fiorillo

Chances Are is a romantic comedy injected with a heady dose of saccharin. As written by sisters Perry and Randy Howze (*Maid To Order*), reincarnation and unrequited love are sugar coated for mass consumption. Directed by Emile Ardolino (*Dirty Dancing*), the film stars Cybill Shepherd, Robert Downey, Jr., Mary Stuart Masterson and Ryan O'Neal. Their considerable talents are considerably lackluster in this outing, although Downey and Masterson manage to emit some sparkle.

In a time worn premise, museum curator Corinne Jeffries' (Shepherd) long dead husband Louie (Christopher McDonald returns to her in the guise of Alex Finch (Downey). Louie's reincarnation wreaks havoc on the lives of Miranda Jeffries (Masterson) who had first dibs on Alex's bod before he metamorphosized into dad, and long suffering Philip Train (O'Neal) who has wanted second dibs on Corinne's bod since Louie's death 20 years ago.

Louie's reappearance is the catalyst for the re-emergence of Corinne's passions. Which man will win Corinne's latent affections?

In *Chances Are*, Shepherd, whose last foray onto the big screen was 1980's. *The Return*, doesn't stray far from her well known TV persona Maddie Hayes of *Moonlighting*. Here she plays another working woman with passion frozen—a cooly detached ice queen. Downey (*The Verdict*) is the firecracker aimed at warming this woman's heart. When the occasion arises for quick comic flare, Downey's sense of immediacy is on target. But big chunks of the Howze duo's screenplay are mere pablum for this gifted actor, as they are for his co-star Masterson. Both shine when given the opportunity. Masterson (*Some Kind Of Wonderful*) has a tougher time of it with a less defined role. Both young stars outclass veteran actor O'Neal (*Tough Guys Don't Dance*) who seems cruelly wasted as milquetoast Philip.

It's too bad there isn't more development of the McDonald-as-Louie character. Christopher McDonald (*Outrageous Fortune*) engages the screen in a pleasant manner until Louie's untimely demise. Nothing of Louie's personality is truly captured by Downey's performance. There's nothing to link the two actors as Louie, just supposition. (Audience gullibility only goes so far—studio culpability, much further.)

Emile Ardolino's direction is adequate. This is what *Dirty Dancing* would have been like without the dance sequences.

Unfortunately, the Howze sisters' screenplay and characters ring false and familiar (the Cohen's, they're not). Dead-end plot lines, such as Downey's finagling his way into the offices of *The Washington Post,* and unfulfilled characters, such as Louie Jeffries, mar this film. *Chances Are* is lighthearted fluff, and irritatingly ordinary.

NEW YORK POST, 3/10/89, p. 29, David Edelstein

Robert Downey Jr., the talented young actor from "The Pick-up Artist," "Less Than Zero" and other forgettable flicks, will probably become a big star with the woozy romantic fantasy "Chances Are."

This is Downey's first coy, self-consciously "dreamboat" performance, and as these things go it's a beaut. He's all moist, moo-cow ingenuousness, and those round eyes and fat lips make him laughably handsome, like a cartoon prince.

The picture needs his charm, but it needs a lot of other things it doesn't get. Downey plays the reincarnation of Cybill Shepherd's husband, a hotshot lawyer who's hit by a car in the soft-focus prologue.

Although her husband's buddy, Ryan O'Neal—a moist Romeo of another era, now stuck playing second banana—is hopelessly smitten with her, she's still (20 years later) faithful to her darling departed: She has taped his photo to her sun-visor and butter dish, and she continues to prepare him his favorite meals.

The character is a loon, but the way Shepherd plays her she's more like a Village idiot—serenely dazed. It's the dopiest performance of the year. She meets Downey, a Yale classmate of her daughter (Mary Stuart Masterson), when he spends the night in her tony Georgetown town house after getting blown off for a job by The Washington Post.

Because the young man didn't get an injection in heaven to make him forget his past life, memories inevitably bleed through to his present consciousness. Like, he knows instinctively at dinner where Shepherd keeps those corn-on-the-cob holders. Just blurts it out. And soon he's repelling the advances of Masterson—who doesn't realize that this adorable young body houses the soul of the dad she never met—and making a big play for his half-wit ex-wife.

Obsession with past-life experiences could be the subject of a great comedy, but "Chances Are" is directed by Emile Ardolino with the same swooning, saccharine hand that wrecked the last 15 minutes of "Dirty Dancing" Cottony and inane, it's watchable the way Muzak, when you're in a dentist's chair, is preferable to the sound of a drill.

("Chances Are," by the way, will be the last independent Tri-Star production; the studio has this week been absorbed by Columbia.)

NEWSDAY, 3/10/89, Part III/p. 3, Mike McGrady

When someone says, "They don't make movies like that anymore," chances are they're talking about a movie like "Chances Are."

And what kind of movie is that?

The kind of movie where an accident victim arrives in a cloudcarpeted heaven and pleads with functionaries for a chance to return to his lovely wife back on Earth. The kind of movie where, years later, a boy (Robert Downey Jr.) falls in love with a girl (Mary Stuart Masterson) and suddenly realizes that in his last life he was married to the girl's mother and, therefore (gulp!), he's in love with his own daughter. The kind of movie where his lovely widow (Cybill Shepherd) from a former life has remained chaste while keeping company with her former husband's best friend (Ryan O'Neal) for 23 years. The kind of movie, in short, they don't make anymore.

What keeps "Chances Are" from seeming either dated or overly sentimental is a light touch that brightens every corner of the film. In last year's "Mystic Pizza," screenwriting sisters Randy and Perry Howze revealed a wit that served as antidote to sentiment; here they add an economy the earlier movie could have used. We knew that director Emile Ardolino ("Dirty Dancing") could move audiences; what we didn't know was that he could also move them in such funny directions.

But why is it so hard for Hollywood to make a film like this, the kind of light comedy that once would star a Cary Grant or a Carole Lombard? In this, the era of Dan Aykroyd and Chevy Chase, Hollywood increasingly seems to be adopting TV's hit-you-over-the-head style—to its own detriment.

"Chances Are" is a throwback in its pleasantly understated style as much as in subect matter. When the basic situation defies rationality—for example, returning to Earth in a new body—the secret is to play it straight, with no extra comic embroidery.

Typical of the film's gentle approach to humor is the moment the 23-year-old collegian tries to explain to his girlfriend's confused mother that he is, in actuality, her deceased husband. The laughline is thrown in almost as an after-thought and that's precisely what makes it work "My memory came back of my last life, with you...I am Louie. I got recycled. You look great, by the way."

Ryan O'Neal's choice of projects in recent years (his most recent outing was in Norman Mailer's "Tough Guys Don't Dance") hasn't inspired much confidence. Here he finds himself once again in a good picture and he happens to be one reason it is so good. Modest, understated and lifelike, he also seems a throwback to a gentler comic era. And Cybill Shepherd, who has been unable to find film work during her past, half-dozen years of television success, is at her very best.

However, much of the film's credibility rests on the shoulders of Robert Downey Jr. After all, he's the one who must make us accept the whole reincarnation business, a feat he accomplishes with ease. In Hollywood's only other decent movie this year, "True Believer," Downey shines, and even when trapped in a turkey like "Less Than Zero," he was able to produce a shatteringly effective performance. The combination of talent and range make him the most promising young actor in films today. And this is a fine opportunity to see him at work.

"Chances Are" you're going to enjoy it all very much.

NEWSWEEK, 3/20/89, p. 83, David Ansen

This is "Heaven Can Wait" plus incest. In every one of Hollywood's reincarnation fantasy movies from "Here Comes Mr. Jordan" to "Made in Heaven" there are certain irresistible scenes. Here we have the moment when young Yale grad Robert Downey Jr., who has fallen for a pretty co-ed (Mary Stuart Masterson), enters the Georgetown home of her mother (Cybill Shepherd) and realizes he's the reincarnation of Mama's dead husband. Which means (a) that he's his girlfriends's father and has to rebuff her advances; and (b) that he's madly in love with Shepherd and has to persuade her to fall in love with a man young enough to be her son. Further complicating matters is the journalist (Ryan O'Neal) who has stood by all these years helplessly in love with Shepherd, still grieving over her husband's premature death. The preposterousness of the premise (concocted by writers Perry Howze and Randy Howze) is the appeal of "Chances Are." The problem is the execution. Where "Heaven Can Wait" seduced you into belief with its expert comic timing and romantic urgency, director Emile ("Dirty Dancing") Ardolino's fantasy grows increasingly labored as it piles improbability upon psychological impossibility. You'll have no trouble believing the reincarnation plot, but why would O'Neal give up his life in helpless worship of an eternal widow, and why wouldn't she ever notice he was in love with her? Even the most farfetched romantic fantasy must be made with conviction, but the symmetrical resolution of the plot's tangled web seems the work of computer programmers, not writers. Nor does the lightweight casting of Shepherd and O'Neal produce any emotional *frisson*. The engaging Downey gets to have the most fun, as a guy caught in a New Age romantic dilemma even Shirley MacLaine would find hard to explain. "Chances Are" will make you laugh, but you won't feel good about it in the morning.

VILLAGE VOICE, 3/14/89, p. 68, Renee Tajima

A comedy with the same perceptiveness is *Jacknife* [see Tajima's review], *Chances Are* is a modern twist on the *Heaven Can Wait* and *Topper* stories. Louie (Christopher McDonald) and Philip (Ryan O'Neal) are two rising young professionals during Washington's Camelot years. They share an undying friendship, despite the amiable Philip's love for Louie's wife, Corinne (Cybill Shepherd), until Louie is indelicately "turned to cream sauce on Wisconsin Avenue" by oncoming traffic. Louie stops in heaven to sign up for rebirth, but an angel forgets to give him an amnesia innoculation. All hell breaks loose when he returns to Washington years later in the body of Alex Finch (Robert Downey Jr.) the beau-to-be of his posthumously born daughter, Miranda (Mary Stuart Masterson).

Thus the trio becomes a quintet, or at least four and a half. Corinne never got over Louie's death and still cooks for him despite her therapist's advice to form a meaningful relationship "with a man who has a body." She and Miranda are like a little family with surrogate father Philip, but without the sex: Philip, still flush with love after 23 years, says he doesn't want to rush Corinne. Although *Chances Are* begins with a whimper—some necessary but awkward story line to set up the complications that follow—it turns to hilarious farce when Finch, a newly minted Yalie, wanders into their lives.

Both *Chances Are* and *Jacknife* revolve around two men competing for the affections of one woman. The triangle is a vehicle for delving the emotional matrices of our relationships to one another, all woven and frayed by love, tragedy, the unhealed past. The women in these configurations are neither icons of sex nor objects of male power, but fully drawn characters living in what was once an actress's neverworld, the approach of middle age. In *Chances Are*, Shepherd is a more vulnerable version of *Moonlighting*'s Maddie Hayes, sometimes looking decidedly unglamorous—in one frazzled moment squirting hairspray under her armpits. She really *hasn't* done it in 23 years, and the prospect of finally getting some sends her into comic disarray. In these films, Baker and Shepherd seem like regular women. They glow at the prospect of romance or dressing up for a dance, but otherwise look tired around the eyes from the accumulated years of loneliness and everyday living. Their portrayals are a respite from the land of t&a that dominated the screen 10 years ago.

Also reviewed in:
NEW YORK TIMES, 3/10/89, p. C13, Janet Maslin
VARIETY, 3/8-14/89, p. 20

CHECKING OUT

A HandMade Films release. *Executive Producer:* George Harrison and Denis O'Brien. *Producer:* Ben Myron. *Director:* David Leland. *Screenplay:* Joe Eszterhas. *Director of Photography:* Ian Wilson. *Editor:* Lee Percy. *Music:* Carter Burwell. *Art Director:* Richard Hoover. *Set Decorator:* Nancy Haigh. *Set Dresser:* Victoria Spader and Claire Gaul. *Special Effects:* Robbie Knott. *Sound:* Mark Ulano and (music) Shawn Murphy. *Sound Editor:* Susan Dudeck and Richard King. *Production Designer:* Barbara Ling. *Costumes:* Adelle Lutz. *Make-up:* Valli O'Reilly. *Running time:* 93 minutes. *MPAA Rating:* R.

CAST: Jeff Daniels (Ray Macklin); Melanie Mayron (Jenny); Michael Tucker (Harry); Kathleen York (Diana); Ann Magnuson (Connie); Allan Havey (Pat); Jo Harvey Allen (Barbara); Felton Perry (Dr. Duffin). Ian Wolfe (Mr. D'Amato); Billy Beck (Father Carmody); Adelle Lutz (Dr. Helmsley); John Durbin (Spencer Gittinger); Trudi Dochtermann (Val); Allan Rich (Dr. Haskell); Danton Stone (Dr. Wolfe); Stephen Tobolowsky (Pharmacist); Matthew Hurley (Joey Macklin); Courtney Sonne (Mo Macklin); Joe Gosha (Andrews); Mark Lowenthal (Phillips); Randy Pelish (Spencer's Driver); Dean Abston (Security Guard); Ruth Manning (Dr. Duffin's Receptionist); William Kerr (Policeman); Dan Leegant (Drunk); Douglas Koth (Workman); David Byrne (Bartender); Joe Unger (Joe); Kristen Trucksess (Stewardess); Martin Doyne (Surgeon); Robert Goyett (Doctor); Benjamin Wendel (Young Ray); Kevin Mockrin (Young Pat), Jimi Wisner (Pat Hagen Jr.); Denis Wisner (Denis Hagen); Lydia Nielson (Mrs. Feldman); John Cherrod (Coffin Truck Driver).

LOS ANGELES TIMES, 4/21/89, Calendar/p. 13, Michael Wilmington

Jeff Daniels is such a resolutely healthy-looking actor that the idea of a comedy in which he becomes convinced he is going to die seems to have a built-in humorous kick. But "Checking Out," with Daniels as an airline executive on a death trip, isn't funny at all.

It's a strange movie, an attempt to do a gentle fairy-tale satire on the corruption of American values, and it has a cleverly stylized candy-floss look. Every once in a while, there is something surprising or nice: the Las Vegas heaven scene or the end-credit song by the Traveling Wilburys. (George Harrison is the movie's co-executive producer.) Ninety-three-year-old Ian Wolfe—whom I'll always remember fondly for the wedding scene in "They Live By Night"—does a wonderful bit as a mortuary owner who keeps telling frantic Daniels how great business is.

Otherwise, this movie tends to crumble like a day-old coffee shop doughnut.

In the film, Ray Macklin (Daniels) becomes terrified of impending death when his boss, Pat (Allan Havey), expires from a heart attack at an outdoor tiki barbecue. Macklin goes haywire; he besieges his doctor, demands checkups, refuses to believe the results, and then runs out and buys home heart monitors, pulse-taking wrist clips and hydraulic therapeutic shower extensions. He interprets everything that happens as a dark omen and, at one point, he dives out of his bedroom window in his boxer shorts and, in daylight, stands on his car roof and screams incoherently to the entire neighborhood.

There isn't a clue as to why Macklin has become such a fruitcake. Insanity didn't sneak up on him; it possessed him all of a sudden, like Freddy Kreuger. Instead, there is a symbolic reason for the crackup. This overly complacent guy has become gorged on a the yuppie life style of frantic acquisition and inner terror until he's choking.

The major running gag of the film is a bad ethnic joke—"Why don't Italians like barbecues?"—which the boss was blaring out crassly as he suffered the attack. He died before getting to the punch line. This joke obsesses Macklin. It's like the movie's lost chord, but its absence is symbolic. The script is full of lost gags and missing punch lines, and, ironically, it's been directed in the dry, understated, style of a British comedy or a Robert Altman film, as if the literary material were something special.

"Checking Out's" director, David Leland, is capable of something special. He co-wrote "Mona Lisa" with Neil Jordan and wrote and directed "Wish You Were Here." In those films, Leland showed an affinity for outsiders and a bracing mixture of wit, satire and romanticism. But here he is working with a script by Joe Eszterhas of "F.I.S.T.," "Flashdance" and "Betrayed," the man who turns class drama into MTV, sexual politics into gothic soap opera and iconoclastic ideas into slam-bang movie trailers.

Eszterhas is onto something potentially rich—he always is—but as usual, he has cranked out, or collaborated on, a script without a single character you can believe, full of attitudes and archetypes and banging, clanging plot twists. Particularly undeveloped here is Macklin's wife, Jenny (Melanie Mayron), a suburban porcelain scold who starts kvetching and demanding sex while Macklin struggles with the hydraulic pump. Later on, Macklin gets raped by his secretary in his car. Is hypochondria supposed to be a wild turn-on?

The satiric vision of America that bubbles under "Checking Out" (MPAA rated R for sex, nudity and language) surfaces in only one extended scene: a nightmare of a horrible Las Vegas-TV heaven with sterile bungalows and people with Diane Arbus faces, where, instead of God, the boss is Howard Hughes. This is such a great idea it almost redeems the movie. But it's gone before we can savor it: one more missing punch line, one more lost joke.

MONTHLY FILM BULLETIN, 10/89, p. 296, Philip Strick

Ray Macklin, advertising executive for the Californian airline Bon-Aire, leads a comfortable suburban existence with his wife Jenny and their two children. Then the sudden death of his wisecracking colleague Pat Hagen, who has a coronary in mid-joke at a barbecue party, shatters Ray's peace of mind. As well as puzzling over the punchline to Pat's joke, he begins to suspect symptoms of his own imminent collapse. His doctor tells him that he's healthy, and his boss, Harry Lardner, trusts him to restore Bon-Aire's flagging reputation, but Ray becomes increasingly depressed following Pat's funeral. While visiting a specialist, Dr. Duffin, Ray meets the hypochondriac Spencer Gittinger, whose obsession with physical ailments is so extreme that Ray decides to shake off his fears. He throws himself into his work and is appointed vice-president by the delighted Lardner. But within days comes the news that Dr. Duffin has dropped dead and that Ray's heart tests reveal a minor imperfection. Rushing to a medical supply store, he buys a mass of equipment to help monitor his health; he has to reveal the diagnosis to Jenny, who scornfully dismisses the ailment (shared by millions, including her) and, fed up with his neurotic behaviour, throws him out. After a lonely night on the town, during which he is beaten up by a barfly he has tried to warn about the dangers of drink, Ray is assigned by Lardner to fly to the site of a crash-landed Bon-Aire plane to reassure the press and public. No sooner has he boarded the flight than Ray panics, yells that there's a bomb on the plane and, fleeing with the other passengers, collapses on the runway with a ruptured appendix. On the operating table he suffers a cardiac arrest and finds Pat Hagen standing by with a limousine to welcome him. They drive to a holiday camp in the desert, where Ray is assigned a beach hut which he has to share with a silent stranger. At the crowded poolside, everybody sings but swimming is not permitted. Plunging in defiantly, Ray finds himself back in the hospital with the punchline to Pat's final joke. He grabs a wheelchair and rushes joyfully home to Jenny and the kids.

If, on the strength of *Mona Lisa, Personal Services* and *Wish You Were Here*, David Leland might tentatively be identified as a champion of the unconventional, *Checking Out* is suitably in character. Distraught at realising the brevity of existence in general and of his own with possibly immediate effect, an ordinary family man turns wildly menopausal and "checks out" from his suddenly meaningless daily routine. If he took his cue from the cinema, he would have a wide range of options at this point: he could save the tiger, get lost in America, visit the Mosquito Coast, or even get ahead in advertising. Instead, although his drop-out phase begins promisingly enough with him standing on a car roof in his underwear, his panic measures are quickly confined to medical research in the expectation that, contrary to normal experience, he just might find a cure for mortality. This in turn could have produced some satirical reflections on the American way of self-preservation. But again, despite some echoes of *The Loved One* (which after all these years still stands unchallenged as the terminal word on termination), this new quest twists aside and proceeds to facelift itself into the domain of surgical comedy. Fun and frolics on the operating table ("Look at the junk in here", sighs the specialist, scooping disgustedly at some intestines) are followed smartly by a time-sharing vacation in the hereafter, a convenient reawakening, and a screwball reconciliation with domestic bliss in all its corrosive vitality.

Leland's defiant existentialists have all taken much the same cyclical route in pursuit of survival at minimum risk to their personal inclinations. The satisfaction they have gained from ending up where they started, which already seemed a hollow enough victory in the case of the pram-wheeling rebel in *Wish You Were Here*, looks merely self-defeating in *Checking Out*, where all that rebellion gains is the answer to a ridiculous puzzle. Leland's interest in eccentricity leads to each of his characters being played as misfit. But the fragmentary delirium of such encounters as the professional hypochondriac Gittinger and his limousine furnished with do-it-yourself medical manuals, the gleeful undertaker D'Amato who suggests that his business card be kept on top of the freezer, or the Macklin daughter who dances in the garden to a mysterious litany of nursery rhymes, leave any semblance of legitimate argument in tatters. Although *Checking Out* is packed with diversions including, with help from the Travelling Wilburys, a tribute to the late Roy Orbison (and, inevitably, to *Blue Velvet*), it belies and belittles the hollow-eyed anguish of its naive protagonist (played by Jeff Daniels with an air of harassed integrity) as he industriously researches his prospects. Like Karel Reisz's Morgan he's a suitable case for treatment—but a day-trip to "Heaven", despite its visual amusements, makes an unconvincing remedy.

NEW YORK POST, 4/21/89, p. 29, Jami Bernard

Quick—why don't Italians have barbecues?

You'll have to sit through all 93 creeping minutes to get the answer to this teaser that runs through the course of "Checking Out." And when you finally hear the punchline, you'll find it's hardly worth the wait—just as when hypochondriac Ray Macklin finally gets a glimpse of heaven and it's not the paradise he had hoped.

Not that watching "Checking Out" is complete hell. Jeff Daniels is not bad as an airline executive who begins to check his pulse obsessively after his loudmouth boyhood friend, Pat (stand-up comedian Allan Havey), keels over with a fatal heart attack during a tacky barbecue and in the midst of a tacky Italian joke. There are some funny bits: Ray, tormented by not knowing the punchline to the joke, walks distractedly through his office skimming a book of stupid ethnic jokes. Or when Ray appears at his lustful wife's bedside strapped head to toe in pulse and heart monitoring devices.

The several doctors in the film come off like real doctors, which seems funny in and of itself, and there is some humor derived from Ray running for a plane with a portable oxygen tank swinging from his shoulder.

But the movie, like its subject, lacks fever. (Which is not to say it is not feverish; Daniels is made to howl insanely to show just how much his hypochondria is getting to him.) There is a surprisingly slow pace to this comedy, considering that it is directed by David Leland, who wrote the scripts for "Mona Lisa" and "Personal Services" and directed the excellent "Wish You Were Here." This is a man who has shown a great deal of sensitivity to the interplay of human drama and comedy, yet the timing and pacing is all off. Daniels gazes in mirrors or at his late pal's belongings like a wounded beagle for long periods.

There is also a discomfiting edge for a movie this bland. A scene in a shrink's waiting room spends a lot of time scrutinizing a Howard Hughes-type disgusto looney as he meticulously attacks junk food and makes obnoxious sounds. Leland used the same cameraman (Ian Wilson) for "Wish You Were Here," where various oddballs are shot with bemused affection. Leland doesn't seem to like the characters in "Checking Out"; why should we?

There is also a rather tasteless scene involving quickie sex in the company parking garage; after some efforts to make the wife a sympathetic character, it seems odd that Ray's messy infidelity would go uncommented upon.

As Ray delves further into his psychosis, his life falls apart. In fact, he begins to resemble his dead pal, who was an ebullient jerk—now Ray, who has been heretofore sober and responsible, is pushing condoms across the desk at his secretary and giggling. Maybe it was jerkiness that killed his friend, not a heart attack after all; and if that is the case, then Ray really is next.

Meanwhile, Ray's wife (Melanie Mayron of "thirtysomething") is frustrated by lack of attention, and one of the kids is going to sleep at night with a pulse-meter strapped to his fingers. Ray's trip to the shrink results in his jacket being ripped by a car door, a scene that takes an inordinate amount of time. Euphemisms like "he's passed on" and "we've lost him" pervade the movie without much comic effect.

Why Jeff Daniels has to run around the last quarter of the film in a hospital gown with his butt hanging out is also as elusive as the punchline to that barbecue joke. It's almost as if the subject of hypochondria just couldn't cough up enough laughs on its own.

Despite some presentable acting, life signs are weak for "Checking Out."

NEWSDAY 4/21/89, Part III/p. 5, Mike McGrady

"Why don't Italians have barbecues?" Just as he begins to tell his final bad joke, the young executive suffers a massive coronary. He has already told us what is Irish and stays out all night. "Paddy O'Furniture." He's told the one about the womanizer in the confessional. He's been sexist and racist, bawdy and blasphemous, but then just as he asks that final question, he crumples, perishing on the spot.

Naturally, the young man's death deeply affects his lifelong buddy (Jeff Daniels) who suffers from his own illness, a case of massive hypochondria. Daniels spends the rest of "Checking Out" experiencing nightmares, chest pains and anxiety attacks. He visits a heart specialist, a psychiatrist, a medical-supply store, a tough waterfront bar and his secretary's apartment late at night. He searches for health tips, marital happiness and the answer to one haunting question, "Why don't Italians have barbecues?"

While neither death nor hypochondria has ever been declared off-limits to Hollywood (dozens of movies ranging from "The End" to "Send Me No Flowers" feature a grinning reaper), the gap between death and laughter is never easily bridged, certainly not by a film that tends to be as ragged, overstated, and generally unfunny as "Checking Out."

Since I suspect that this will represent today's majority report from the critical fraternity, allow me to add a small footnote or two. While I cannot in good conscience urge anyone to actually go out and see "Checking Out," honesty compels me to confess that there were flashes of lunatic humor that made me laugh despite a general feeling of distaste.

Prior to writing "Checking Out," Joe Eszterhas ("Flashdance," "Jagged Edge") had never been noted for success in the field of broad comedy. The same can be said of Eszterhas after writing "Checking Out." But director David Leland, who wrote "Mona Lisa" and directed "Wish You Were Here," has hitherto revealed a flair for the offbeat, the unexpected, the nutty. And "Checking Out" has enough of this inspired craziness to at least ease the general pain.

Such as: The appearance of a billionaire hypochondriac living in a stretch limo filled with junk food, garbage cans and health books bearing such titles as "The Joy of Colonic Irrigation." An ancient and solemn undertaker raving about business: "Oh, they're dropping like flies out there...I can't stop making money." A surgeon watching his patient die on the operating table: "I don't know his name—but he sure screwed up *my* day." A startling vision of an afterlife ruled not by God but by...Howard Hughes.

However, remembering the film's brighter moments falls under the category of being grateful for small favors. "Checking Out" is not just uneven, it's one-sided—with the preponderance of the film being shrill and witless. No, no need to check out "Checking Out," and certainly not to learn why Italians don't have barbecues. While I'm reluctant to give away punch lines, exceptions sometimes seem in order, especially when they reflect the film's overall level of attainment. It's because spaghetti falls through the grill.

VILLAGE VOICE, 5/2/89, p. 70, Renee Tajima

In *Checking Out*, the narrative is driven by a search for the punchline to the joke, "Why don't Italians have barbecues?" The movie—a comedy—is about as funny as the answer. Don't bother finding out either. Set in 49ers country, in what looks like the suburban homesteads of Silicon Valley, it's the story of Ray (Jeff Daniels), husband to a dowdy wife, Jenny (Melanie Mayron), and father to two forgettable kids. When jokester pal Pat Hagen (Allan Havey) dies suddenly of massive coronary occlusion, Ray is sent plummeting into hypochondriac hell.

What Woody Allen did to endow hypochondria with an edgy comic mania, *Checking Out* manages to undo. It's full of clever stuff: campy suburban motifs and a few promising, morbid takes on themes like death and airline safety. But the film is not intrinsically funny, and Ray's hypochondria never manages to connect to the normal fears we all face—the touch that makes Woody Allen's renditions work.

Also reviewed in:
NEW YORK TIMES, 4/21/89, p. C12, Caryn James
VARIETY, 4/26–5/2/89, p. 26

CHEETAH

A Walt Disney Pictures release in association with Silver Screen Partners III. *Executive Producer:* Roy Edward Disney. *Producer:* Robert Halmi. *Director:* Jeff Blyth. *Screenplay:* Erik Tarloff, John Cotter, and Griff du Rhone. *Based on the book "The Cheetahs" by:* Alan Caillou. *Director of Photography:* Tom Burstyn. *Editor:* Eric Albertson. *Music:* Bruce Rowland. *Music Editor:* Roy Prendergast and Richard Luckey. *Sound:* Bill Daly and (music) Robin Gray. *Sound Editor:* Ron Kalish and Jesse Soraci. *Production Designer:* Jane Cavedon. *Art Director:* Caroline Woodall. *Set Dresser:* Colin Athanasius and Bruce Trzebinski. *Costumes:* Elizabeth Ryrie. *Make-up:* Norma Hill. *Running time:* 83 minutes. *MPAA Rating:* G.

CAST: Keith Coogan (Ted); Lucy Deakins (Susan); Collin Mothupi (Morogo); Timothy Landfield (Earl Johnson); Breon Gorman (Jean Johnson); Ka Vundla (Kipoin); Lydia Kigada (Lani); Kuldeep Bhakoo (Patel); Paul Onsongo (Abdullah); Anthony Baird (Nigel): Rory McGuinness (Larry); Rod Jacobsen (David); David Adido (Mwangi); Konga Mbandu (Police Captain); Martin Okello (Friendly Policeman); Allaudin Qureshi (Patel's Cousin); William Tsuma (Cabbie); Waigwa Wachira (Racetrack Policeman); James Ward (Announcer); Jan MacCoy (Stewardess); Evalyne Kamau (Nyambura); Jane Gelardi (Announcer's Girlfriend); Thomas Akare, Denis Doughty, Siddik Ebrahim, Lee Harvin (Bettors); Aloysius Lazarus, Njorogue M. Ngoima, Frank C. Turner (Greyhound Owners): Richard Clarke (Voice of Announcer); Michael Rogers (Voice of Racetrack Policeman).

NEW YORK POST, 8/18/89, p. 27, Jami Bernard

Nature specials have the mesmerizing quality that Paul Hogan had when he got vicious animals to roll over for him in "Crocodile Dundee." You start watching with a snarl, then roll over and find yourself glued to images of wildebeests cavorting, cute insects, and all those darling forest creatures.

You can't go wrong with shots of gazelles a-leapin', but "Cheetah," packaged with a bland, sappy script and predictable moves, is as safe and unthreatening as a cheetah cub raised in captivity.

Which is what "Cheetah" is about. Two typical teens from L.A. visit Kenya for half a year, where their parents are working on a research project. To amuse themselves, they hook up with a local kid, a mini-Masai warrior who is quite charming and practically indistinguishable from his white counterparts except for the spear and the accent. Although there is a hint at the "Crocodile Dundee" formula—the kids teaching each other how to survive in alien territory—that aspect never really gets off the ground.

While doing such fun Kenyan things as piling stones on sleeping hippos and outrunning stampeding elephants, the teens find a motherless cheetah cub and raise her.

The cheetah, named Duma, is a luscious animal—sinewy and sleek. Maybe she's not as whimsical as one of those movie canines, but always the most interesting thing on the screen. The plot hinges around the kids' attempts to reintegrate the big cat into the wilds, and of their pursuit of unscrupulous poachers who kidnap Duma and give her the undignified fate of racing against greyhounds.

The kids' adventure with their native friend is par for the course in a Disney film; if only the adventure were just a little harrowing. Surely today's young audience can stand something a little stronger than a gosh-darn-it outing in a Kenya no more threatening than the average car wash.

And the brother and sister are unbearably white-bread teens, played by Keith Coogan and Lucy Deakins. Their pal Morogo, played by Collin Mothupi, is more interesting, and even more sarcastic. Coogan is expert at playing the smart-mouth ("Adventures in Babysitting," "Hiding Out"), but he's rendered toothless here.

Even the smiling natives seem suspiciously Americanized. When the two sets of concerned parents sit down in the living room to discuss their wayward kids, it could pass for any sitcom on TV.

"Cheetah" takes a perfectly acceptable teen adventure and blandifies it until it's embarrassing. If I were a parent, I suppose I'd be grateful there was *something* I could take the kids to, but, golly gee! Are we protecting their sensibilities or removing them?

NEWSDAY, 8/18/89, Part III/p. 3, Terry Kelleher

A teenage brother and sister from California get to spend six months in Kenya while their father works at a research center outside Nairobi. But Mom says no exploring, stick close to the house. Some adventure, huh?

"When I close my eyes, I think I'm still in Pasadena," complains Susan (Lucy Deakins). Ted (Keith Coogan) says he feels that way when his eyes are open.

Whether they know it or not, Susan and Ted are giving us a mini-review of "Cheetah," the new Disney movie that tells their story. For even when the kids start having adventures, they seem to be having them in Adventureland.

The script is loaded with cliches and coincidences. The acting and characterization are of the quality and depth expected in TV commercials. If Tom Burstyn's location photography didn't provide attractive evidence to the contrary, we might think the cast and crew never got closer to Kenya than a Southern California theme park. It may not be coincidental that director Jeff Blyth, here making his feature debut, has done short films for exhibition at such sites as Tokyo Disneyland and Epcot Center.

Shaking off the Pasadena blues, Ted and Susan put some excitement in their life by adopting a cheetah cub and befriending a Masai youngster named Morogo (Collin Mothupi). Duma the cheetah—a fast grower, fortunately—is handsome and shows some spirit.

Where's the conflict? Coming right up. There's this Indian shopkeeper (Kuldeep Bhakoo) who's *so* obsequious he must be up to no good. The Indian fellow, a black Kenyan and a British ex-colonialist type form a tri-ethnic poaching team that snatches Duma for the nefarious purpose of running the cat in a rigged race against greyhounds. The poachers are cruel to the captive animal—the surest sign of Disney villainy.

Ted, Susan and Morogo set off in pursuit of the bad guys, and before their mission is accomplished we learn a couple of cultural lessons: American and Kenyan kids are pretty much alike, except the Kenyans eat termites and drink cow's blood; American and Kenyan parents are pretty much alike in that they're best kept in the dark.

Even if Susan and Ted and the audience never quite dispel a Pasadena state of mind, "Cheetah" is good outdoor exercise. But must Disney's wild kindom be so tame?

TIME, 9/18/89, p. 93, Richard Corliss

[*Cheetah* was reviewed jointly with *Honey, I Shrunk the Kids*; see Corliss' review of that film.]

Also reviewed in:
NEW YORK TIMES, 8/18/89, p. C14, Lawrence Van Gelder
VARIETY, 8/23–29/89, p. 28
WASHINGTON POST, 8/19/89, p. C9, Richard Harrington

CHOCOLAT

An Orion Classics release of a Cinémanuel/Marin Karmitz-MK 2 Productions/Cerito Films/Wim Wenders Produktion/La S.E.P.T./Caroline Productions/Le F.O.D.I.C./TFI Films Production co-production. *Executive Producer:* Alain Belmondo and Gérard Crosnier. *Director:* Claire Denis. *Screenplay (French with English subtitles):* Claire Denis and Jean-Pol Fargeau. *Director of Photography:* Robert Alazraki. *Editor:* Claudine Merlin. *Music:* Abdullah Ibrahim. *Sound:* Jean-Louis Ughetto and Dominique Hennequin. *Sound Editor:* Jean-Christophe Winding. *Art Director:* Thierry Flamand. *Set Decorator:* François Ejenguele Bollo, Franck Proix, Scott Kirby, Christian Delhome, Siddi Djaouro. *Costumes:* Christian Gasc. *Make-up:* Jean-Pierre Eychenne. *Running time:* 105 minutes. *MPAA Rating:* PG-13.

CAST: Isaach De Bankolé (Protée); Giúlia Boschi (Aimée Dalens); François Cluzet (Marc Dalens); Cécile Ducasse (France Dalens, as a child);Jean-Claude Adelin (Luc Segalen); Kenneth Cranham (Jonathan Boothby); Jacques Denis (Delpich, the Coffee Planter); Edwige Nto Ngon A Zock (Thérèse, Delpich's Companion); Laurent Arnal (André Machinard); Emmanuelle Chaulet (Mireille Machinard); Jean Bediebe (Prosper); Didier Flamand (Captain Vedrine); Jean-Quintin Chatelain (Courbassol, the co-pilot); Donatus Ngala (Enoch, the cook); Clémentine Essono (Marie-Jeanne); Essindi Mindja (Blaise); Philemon Blake Ondoua (Wadjiri); Mireille Perrier (France Dalens, as adult); Emmet Judson Williamson (Mungo Park).

CINEASTE, Vol. XVII, No. 2, 1989, p. 52, Peter Bates

Claire Denis's first film, *Chocolat*, begins quietly, almost casually. A young French woman returns to northern Cameroon to visit the home of her youth. She accepts a ride with William Park, an American black. When he finds out her name is France, he replies ironically, "Vive la

France." Then the flashback begins: Cameroon of 1958, shortly before independence, at the remote estate of provincial governor Marc Dalens.

The countryside of *Chocolat* is parched badland where few animals thrive, except vulture and pack mules. Like *Coup de Torchon*, Tavernier's film of French West Africa, only human tensions flourish in the oppressive climate. Claire Denis's oblique style cleverly contains the sexual and racial stress coursing underneath the surface. She dilutes the tension by relating her story through multiple points of view. Within the flashback, there are frequent shifts from child to parent, visitor to host, victim to master. When passions do flare up, they erupt in short bursts and are soon buried by another shift in perspective.

Chocolat's flashback shows France as a young girl, watched over by Protée, the family's house servant. She travels to market with him, orders him when to come and go, even symbolically feeds him. Since she is virtually ignored by her mother, Denis builds sympathy for Protée by assigning him the role of surrogate parent. He teachers her his language, how to eat ants on bread, takes her hyena hunting, and once, when the local missionary's animals are killed, ritualistically smears chicken blood on her.

Soon the point of view shifts to Aimée, France's mother, the jaded wife of Marc, a liberal governor more involved in appeasing herdsmen than pleasing her. He does not even hear her request more books from Paris. When he goes on trips, she becomes unhappy and feels doomed. In a striking scene, she is tending the local European plot when France asks her if they too will be buried there. She turns in horror.

While Marc is away, Aimée develops a sexual attraction for Protée, which she simultaneously suppresses and encourages. She stops him from putting away her clothes, then shortly afterward asks him to help dress her. When a neighbor tells her she has a "handsome boy," she feigns disinterest, then a day later (with her husband at home), she tries to seduce Protée.

From his point of view, any mingling with whites can only lead to disaster. Yet Protée is also attracted to the taboo of miscegenation. After she orders him out of her bedroom, he sobs while showering outside. He becomes morose and spends less time amusing France. But as much as Denis wants to show his anguish, and through him the anguish of all blacks, she can only provide brief glimpses into his persona. Once, when he talks to another black on the property, their animated discussion—inexplicably—has no subtitles.

Protée knows he must, like the mythical Proteus, change his essence to suit his environment. So he suffers in silence, only once reacting ironically. When Aimée asks him to stand guard all night against an imagined hyena attack, he smiles to himself. That is all he is allowed. Like many others around him, he may be disaffected, but does not harbor the spirit of revolt.

Claire Denis has said she didn't want her film to be a tract against colonialism; she believes that "has already been done." Rather, she wanted to show the human toll this primitive, oppressive system wreaked on everyone, black and white. Even the world *chocolat* is French slang for frustrated. Not only do Aimée and Protée want what they cannot have, but other characters are thwarted too. When a disabled plane lands nearby for repairs, a panoply of racial bias emerges. The rabid Delpiche keeps a black mistress on sustenance level. He cannot get a ride into town, or even a decent cup of coffee. Honeymooner Mr. Machinard will not let a black doctor treat his wife. She screams in pain. Ex-seminarian Luc works and eats with blacks, believing they are superior beings. Few take him seriously.

Denis's massive intentions, however, sometimes fall short. Although intriguing, none of her characters are fully developed. They are brief, occasionally even ludicrous snippets, making their point in two or three scenes and then passing out of the frame. Occasionally they function as foils augmenting the central tension; other times, their actions impede and confuse the story line.

It is clear that Luc exists as a contrast to the others, a gadfly to their smug conceptions. It is not apparent, however, why Marc asks him to stay on with them after the plane is repaired. Perhaps he is amused by his confrontational style, so different from his own. After Luc publicly mocks the Machinards for expelling the black doctor, Marc tells him, "One day we'll get kicked out of here," they laugh, and the scene dissolves. It is not clear whether they are laughing at the same thing. Just who will do the kicking? The colonial government in power? Or the blacks, whose discontent seethes in the shadows? Shortly afterward, a conflict arises between Protée and Luc. When he tries to goad the servant to "stand up to his bosses," Protée kicks Luc out of his domain, demonstrating that blacks do not need liberal whites to tell them what to do. Yet nothing comes of it—no epiphany, no flight to the wilderness. Protée simply plunges into the next crisis.

Denis skillfully shows how political domination throws priorities askew and forces people to act haphazardly. Some, like Aimée, perform illogical, self-destructive acts. Others, like Marc, muddle through and miss the point entirely. Yet despite occasional potent scenes, *Chocolat* lacks a cumulative dramatic strength, partly because its characters lack some important human traits.

Marc catches a whiff of anti-colonial agitation, but it quickly passes. When they drive to pick up the black doctor, they find him attending an evening meeting at the school. "What are they doing there this late?" he asks. "Just talking," replies Protée. "Talking about what?" could have been the governor's next question, but he says nothing, even seems to think nothing.

Chocolat sometimes dilutes its social points with a moody minimalism that avoids showing characters reacting plausibly to events. Their roles may be clear-cut, but interactions between them seldom are. Revolution is in the air in *Chocolat*, but it is not a strong wind. Some of the whites, like Delpich, can sense it and relate tales of white settlers being massacred. When the blacks refuse to drive him into town during Ramadan, he rails "What, do *they* run things around here?" Aimée grimaces at such crude sarcasm, unable to see how close Delpich is to the mark. By 1960, blacks *will* be running things and her world will collapse.

Denis's most powerful statement occurs when Aimée banishes Protée to the garage for sexually attracting her. He puts his hand on a hot pipe and tempts France to copy him. They both burn their hands, but after she runs off, he stoically walks into the night. Denis, like France, also grew up in Cameroon during its colonial era and must have been scarred by it. Her often eloquent account tells how easily human values twist when caught in unnatural conditions. But how well does she understand the legacy of colonialism? The answer can be found in the coda.

While the adult France travels with the voluble Park, he tells her he came to Africa with delusions of black solidarity. Then a native cabbie ripped him off and he realized "they don't give a shit about guys like me. If I died today, I'd disappear forever." France is apparently attracted to his knee-jerk cynicism, his cavalier jabs at indifference, so she asks him to go for a drink. Like Protée before him, he declines her advances, then warns her, "You better get out of here soon, they'll eat you up."

Is Denise trying to say that nothing has changed? That the black population of Cameroon, after twenty-eight years of independence, mistrusts whites as much as ever? That the heritage of colonialism is an uneasy separatism? Not only are these implications politically shaky, they also occur too late in the film to explore.

In the end, *Chocolat*'s atmosphere is bleak, constricted, and alienated. The film does not show France returning to her childhood estate, because that would have involved making a further statement, perhaps revealing a typical phenomenon of converting colonial manors into schools. It is also curious that France catches a ride with an American black rather than a local, whose outlook would have cast her tale into more immediate relief. Such choices distance this film from the land and its people and dilute some of its power. Like Chekhov, however, Denis provides a jarring glimpse into a dying regime and, against a landscape cloudy with ennui, poses some reasonable and unsetting questions.

LOS ANGELES TIMES, 4/20/89, Calendar/p. 1, Sheila Benson

In her first film, "Chocolat," co-writer/director Claire Denis, who has worked closely with Jim Jarmusch and Wim Wenders, treasures the elliptical and the allusive. She makes her portrait of 1950s white French colonials in black Cameroon out of fragments, snapshots ragged at the edge, snippets of observation.

"Chocolat" is a film of some subtley. It has good, even memorable moments to it, and it's beautiful looking. It is very, very *very* French, which may or may not be your cup of *chocolat*. It is also a suffocatingly precious film, enough to try the patience of an oyster, and one that primly refuses to detonate the mounting numbers of erotic situations it sets up.

That is precisely Denis' way; to do otherwise would clearly be a vulgarity in her eyes. Yet it may have an opposite effect. By denying her black central character, Protée, any outlet for the sexual rage and humiliation building up in him, instead of the statement Denis imagines she is making, she actually takes away his humanity. He becomes ennobled, pure and beautiful as a living statue and as objectified.

The film is one long flashback, a truncated, brooding return to the places of her childhood by a reflective adult, France Dalens (Mireille Perrier). Her reveries as she speeds across this shimmering landscape move her back roughly 25 years, to when her youngish father, Marc Dalens (François Cluzet) was the colonial district officer for the area. (Cluzet is familiar to Americans as Dexter Gordon's stalwart French fan in "'Round Midnight.")

His position provides Dalens and his beautiful, tensed-up wife, Aimée (Giúlia Boschi), with a big, pleasant house, soldiers under Dalens' command and a house staff, including the enormously capable African "boy" Protée (Isaach de Bankolé), frequently in charge of the house during Dalens' excursions.

Protée and the 7-year-old France (Cécile Ducasse), an observant child, mostly silent under her little straw helmet, spend most of their time together in mutual invisibility. They are friends, although as Denis, who co-wrote the screenplay with Jean-Pol Fargeau, sees France, the child is already an imperious little white colonial too. Frankly, it doesn't leave us many people to give a tinker's damn about. Marc Dalens, who loves the country and possibly even its people and is prescient enough to know that the French will not be astride it forever, is the best of the bunch but he's not the world's most charismatic leader.

It might help if the film makers let us in on the Dalenses' relationship. Mostly, lonely, bored *maman* smokes, drinks endless cups of espresso and alternately yearns for and is imperious toward Protée. (Boschi was Christopher Lambert's bride in "The Sicilian," and the jury is still out on whether her attitudes constitute acting but she certainly is decorative.)

About a third of the way into the film, the emergency landing of a small plane brings its passengers to the Dalens household, while mechanical parts are sent for and a runway is built. They are, in varying degress, a loathsome bunch, arrogant and condescending, with an ingrained, unearned sense of superiority. The foulmouthed, bullying coffee planter, Delpich (Jacques Denis), seems the worst of the lot. Then, in the film's best scene, as Delpich lounges under a canvas with a few of the men after their noontime meal, he unexpectedly sings a refrain from a childhood song. Coming from such a despicable soul, his voice is unexpectedly sweet and poignant; it's a surprising, humanizing moment.

Actually, the most dangerous guest is Luc Segalen (Jean-Claude Adelin), a muscular ex-seminarian currently walking across the continent, who prides himself on truth-telling and a "simple" way of life more native than that of the natives. More precisely, he's a sexual predator who has already cut a considerable swath among the French ladies at one after another remote outpost. Anyone with a good memory for the '70s will recognize Segalen; he's a variation on the earnest young Americans who become more Indian than the Navajos; more peaceable than Gandhi. Today they are commodities traders and movie producers.

"Chocolat" is a compendium of telling moments, so self-consciously pointed that they form a connect-the-dots map of colonialism. What makes it a bore is that audiences are encouraged to think that by picking up these vast, looming clues, they are on to something deep.

Jarmusch works in fragments, too, but they finally lead to something, and his films have a buoyancy that comes from his bushwhacking humor. Denis is cautious, joyless, as though she regarded levity from her film's few possible comic moments or characters (Segalen is one) as inappropriate to the toniness of her message. So the film's natural light moments are stifled.

"Chocolat" broods, it teases with consummate adroitness, then it skitters away from confrontation. (The film is MPAA rated PG-13 for brief nudity.) It has no driving rhythm to it, only nicely captured moments in isolation. In a slightly different context, Denis has called her film "suffused with a sense of frustration." Audiences may agree with her completely.

MONTHLY FILM BULLETIN, 4/89, p. 109, Jill Forbes

France, whose father was a *commissaire* in the French colonial administration, visits the remote region of the Cameroons where she spent much of her childhood. She hitches a lift from the airport to catch a plane into the bush from Mungo Park, a black American who has settled in the country. Her mind flashes back to scenes of her youth: she remembers her friendship with the black servant Protée; the Englishman, Boothby, arriving for dinner when her father was away and her mother hastily unpacking her evening dress from a trunk; the upheaval caused when a plane crashed nearby and the house was invaded by the crew and passengers, including a white coffee planter and his black mistress, a young couple on their first trip to Africa who refuse to accept treatment from the local doctor, and Luc, an ex-priest who has gone native. Luc detects an attraction between France's mother Aimée and Protée, and taunts the latter. When Aimée makes a half-hearted attempt to seduce Protée, he turns her down and is banished, at Aimée's request, from the house to the garage, where France visits him secretly. The plane is finally repaired and the guests depart. France's reverie ends and she arrives at the airport. Mungo Park, assuming she is an ordinary tourist, asks if she is disappointed that he is not a real "native".

In this highly accomplished first feature, Claire Denis, who previously worked as assistant to

Wim Wenders, Jim Jarmusch and Jacques Rivette, has produced a subtle portrait of a colonial society which displays extremely varied attitudes towards Africa, and in which a greater role than usual is given to the Africans. The relationship between the young girl, France, and Protée, the black servant, is a prelapsarian view of inter-racial friendship: idealised, unattainable and doomed by outside forces. France's parents are the benevolent, paternalistic administrators, upright and fearless in applying the rule of law to all and on excellent terms—their own—with their black servants. The plane crew are the intrepid explorers, reluctant to remove bomber jackets and goggles even in the heat, speaking in a jargon of camaraderie that is also paternalistic. Each of the passengers represents a different perspective on Africa (the young couple are terrified by the dark continent, while the other two men have attempted to assimilate, with disastrous results).

Luc, the defrocked priest, sleeps outside and showers with the blacks, until Protée sternly tells him not to; Thérèse, whose lover is white, is not allowed to eat with the whites and is forced to maintain appearances by creeping into his bed at night after everyone else has gone to sleep. The framing sequences involving the adult France and the American Mungo Park are nicely ironic: the black man feels like an outsider, while the white girl is thoroughly at home. Many films and novels about the colonial era refer to the fear of miscegenation. In *White Mischief* and *Coup de torchon*, the white woman is portrayed as nymphomaniac, transgressing racial barriers purely for sexual gratification. Here, the seduction scene between France's mother Aimée and Protée is sensitively handled. Aimée's tentativeness derives from her dependence on Protée for material comfort and protection, while he has sufficient dignity to turn her down, at which point she becomes petulant (Claire Denis secures superb performances from her actors, especially Isaach de Bankolé as Protée).

Chocolat is undoubtedly over-generous, fictionalised and nostalgic, but it is also well paced, well observed and shot through with a dry sense of humour. The episode in which Boothby comes to dinner, forcing his hostess into evening dress, occasions a hilarious exchange with Enoch, the English-speaking cook who has been unable to produce the French dishes Aimée orders but is saved, *in extremis*, from dismissal in order to produce "pouding" for the British visitor. Yet this sequence has a serious point too: the whites in an Africa not yet overrun by package tours relied on a tribal solidarity which no longer exists. Altogether, the world of *Chocolat*, policed by men on horseback and overflown by propeller planes, is far gentler than the one we live in.

NEW STATESMAN & SOCIETY, 4/28/89, p. 52, Suzanne Moore

Chocolat, a quietly self-assured film by Clare Denis is also an investigation into other cultures and about being an outsider. [The reference is to *The Serpent and the Rainbow*.] Set in the Cameroons of the fifties, its flashback structure takes a young Frenchwoman back to her colonial childhood. Through her eyes we see racism, not in some monolithic form but in all its complicated nuances, through the relationships between the little girl, her family, the black servants and some white visitors. Understated, and at times ambiguous, *Chocolat* never gives us the answers or questions on a plate. It simply observes the strangeness and pain of a colonial past and the impossibility of being truly at home in a culture that is not your own. There is a sadness and emptiness about the film which avoids right-on political statements and instead concentrates on the minute gestures and expressions that constitute racism. This sparseness is in marked contrast to the lavishness and nostalgia for Africa and India that we have lately seen so much of in the cinema, and shows that, as they say in the beer adverts, less is sometimes more.

NEW YORK, 3/27/89, p. 70, David Denby

The strengths of *Chocolat*—and finally its limitations, too—lie in its avoidance of the obvious. In this beautifully made memory piece, the first-time director Claire Denis demonstrates an art of understatement and suggestion. A young woman, France Dalens, traveling through the former French colony Cameroon, falls into a reverie, dreaming of her girlhood there in the fifties, when the French still ruled and she lived in the middle of a golden plain near the mountains. As a girl, France has all the time in the world to listen to her own heartbeat: In her fine-looking house live her lovely, tense, bored mother, Aimée (Giúlia Boschi), and her father, Marc (François Cluzet), a district superintendent who is often away on territorial business and who leaves the women in the care of the house "boy," Protée (Isaach de Bankolé). Protée, France's friend and fellow outsider, a forbearing, nobly handsome native servant, swallows his sexual pride and rage, suffering the indignities of his status in silence. The movie is told largely (but not exclusively) from the point of view of the girl, who observes the repressed attraction between mother and servant and the general brutality of the French visitors—ratty colonial types who exhibit the perverse and peremptory habits acquired in their long rule.

Awkward and tentative with actors, Denis has built a dramatic method based on what people don't say—or do—to one another. Many scenes lead toward an explosion but then stop just before they detonate. We are in a beautiful but sinister country, baking and still, where repression may well be necessary if people are not to murder one another. The movie, with considerable precision, establishes the thin line between security and fear, contentment and unease. But I don't think *Chocolat* quite delivers the revelations we need—I was left expecting more than was there—and I wonder as well if Denis does not idealize Protée too much. Still, *Chocolat* is an extremely auspicious directorial debut and an exquisite-looking piece of work.

NEW YORK POST, 3/10/89, p. 27, David Edelstein

Many films seek to portray the quality and tempo of life among white Europeans in the waning years of French West Africa, but few have the sensual texture of Claire Denis' first feature, "Chocolat," or convey so vividly the small and yet shattering cruelties experienced by blacks under colonialism.

A hushed, entrancing work, the film is set on an outpost in Cameroon, where a French sheriff, Marc Dalens (François Cluzet), his wife, Aimée (Giúlia Boschi) and young daughter, France (Cécile Ducasse), live in relative concord with their black servants and the local population on parched, insect-ridden land.

The film is a reminiscence, kindled in the adult France by her return to Cameroon after two decades. Most of her memories revolve around her family's "boy," a handsome, efficient black man named Protée (Isaach de Bankolé), who has a reserved but affectionate bond with the girl.

France slips out of her room at night to sit with the servants, and Protée enjoys giving her glimpses of his true culture. Standing formally behind her while she eats, Protée sees her contemplate the ants on the dining room table and calmly demonstrates the consumption of live moths. "You make me sick," she announces. "Dirty nigger," says Protée, laughing.

Lithe and muscular, the Ivory Coast actor de Bankolé is like a panther, and the movie presents him as an erotic object—his muscles, coated with sweat, gleam white. France is drawn to him, and so is her mother, who stares at him with silent lust, perhaps contrasting him with the fops who drift through the remote region, and with her kind but unexciting husband.

Sexual tension gives the film a dramatic spine. Protée is equally enthralled, but clearly furious at being desired as a man and treated as an inferior. Soaping himself in the "boys" outdoor shower, he watches her pass with her daughter and then cries out when she goes, striking the wall repeatedly with his shoulder.

Denis loves shots of water flowing over black skin—they reinforce the visual thesis, that the blacks are part of this land. And she has one character read from a book about a white woman in Africa who eventually finds her own pallor strange: "Who can blame the blacks for thinking the whites unnatural?"

The first half hour, which includes the prologue, is only fitfully interesting; Denis isn't skilled at giving us our bearings. But here and there an image leaps out, especially when Protée carries France on his shoulders while hunting a hyena: swinging his rifle and chanting, he becomes another person.

Slowly, without realizing it, we're pulled into the frame. Denis, who has worked as an assistant for Wim Wenders and Jim Jarmusch, has a style all her own. Visually, "Chocolat" is mesmerizing. Photographed by Robert Alazraki, the compositions—with the cream-colored dwellings and distant, jagged mountains—have extraordinary depth.

The film's small revelations create an overwhelming sense of melancholia; both blacks and whites are profoundly isolated. Revolutionary feeling simmers among the natives, and while the servants say nothing of their secret political meetings, their faces suggest misery and anger. They're waiting.

The turning point in "Chocolat" comes when a small plane busts a propeller and has to make an emergency landing; its colorful passengers, most of whom treat the blacks as slaves, rupture the delicate equilibrium.

Dennis doesn't have much control over her supporting cast—there are some awful, broad performances, and the script goes in for untranslatable French puns. (The title itself is a lost pun: *chocolat* means both dark-skinned and "to be cheated.")

But there is one fascinating character, the sort of complicated racist that movies never show: Luc Segalen (Jean-Claude Adelin), an ex-seminarian and wanderer who likes to eat with blacks and shower in their quarters but who also taunts them with his social superiority. (He taunts whites, too, by suggesting they're not natural, like blacks.)

Luc becomes unhinged by the attraction between Aimée and Protée. The fight he provokes sets in motion a chain of events that leads to the final, devastating act of cruelty—Protée's betrayal of France, which haunts her even as an adult.

The sexual aspect of "Chocolat" is its most intriguing, since the film concludes with France being gently rebuffed by an American black man (Emmet Judson Williamson), who advises her to leave Cameroon or be burned.

Denis herself was the daughter of a French civil servant in Africa. She insists in interviews that "Chocolat" isn't autobiographical, but she's clearly working out her fascination with the black males who surrounded her as an adolescent. Protée's sexual power infuses the film; he's even there in spirit in the joyous (and narratively inexplicable) final shot.

"Chocolat" has many small flaws, but in conveying Dennis' mix of attraction, guilt and unease, it's an indelible first film.

NEWSDAY, 3/10/89, Part III/p. 7, Lynn Darling

There's scene early in Claire Denis' "Chocolat" that embodies the finely etched attention to character and relationships that distinguishes her first feature film.

It's a dusty afternoon, one that emphasizes the slowness of time and the enervating heat of French colonial Africa at empire's end. A little white girl on a donkey watches the black children at play in the schoolyard; her own loneliness plays on her face until she catches sight of the young black man who is the chief servant, "the boy" as her parents call him. Illiterate himself, he is dictating a letter to his fiancee. Arrogantly, peremptorily, she calls him to her side. The young man walks over, to the derision of the blacks who watch him. He is caught in the middle, between the white rulers who employ him and depend so heavily on him, and the blacks whose country and culture will remain a mystery to those who nominally control it.

Hardly a word is spoken, but Denis captures all the tensions implicit in the isolated, fading world she explores. With an unblinking observant eye, "Chocolat" delineates the shifting tidal quality of the emotions that govern her characters' relationship: Marc Dalens (François Cluzet), a French colonial administrator; Aimee, his beautiful young wife (Giúlia Boschi) and Protée (Isaach de Bankolé), the young man who runs their household, protects them and explains the world to their young daughter, France (played as a child by Cécile Ducasse and as an adult by Mireille Perrier).

"Chocolat" focuses most closely on Protée and Aimée. When her husband goes off on an extended trip, it's Protée upon whom Aimée depends to guide and organize her life, from mediating with the cook to zipping up her dress for dinner. He is both a servant, and in unspoken, hesitant ways, a trusted intimate. At the same time, he is denied even the most elemental privileges of personal dignity—he must wash himself outside, hiding himself from whoever might be strolling by. When an arrogant young white outsider (Jean-Claude Adelin) amuses himself by deliberately crossing the carefully established borders between the two worlds in which Protée functions, the tense, precarious balance begins to unravel.

Denis has a sure hand in establishing the complications and nuances of these relationships, and de Bankolé and Boschi do a lovely job of etching their attitudes and emotions toward one another. But Denis is less steady when she opens her drama up by importing a host of unexpected guests whose plane has inconveniently crashed; most of them hang around to little avail through much of the movie. She also has a rather mannered affection for long, elegiac sweeps of the camera and the lingering, perfectly composed frame.

The bigger problem, however, lies in the story's structure. "Chocolat" is told mainly in flashback. It begins with the grown-up France returning to the country of her youth, a trip that plunges her into memories of her childhood. At the end, the movie returns to the present, where it finds itself with little to say and nowhere to go. By then, however, Denis has established a mood and a tone that imbue the world she has rendered with impressive clarity.

NEWSWEEK, 3/27/89, p. 68, Jack Kroll

In French slang, *Chocolat* means both to be dark-skinned and to "get caught." Director Claire Denis's subtle, shimmering movie about the waning years of French colonialism in Africa during the '50s deals with both senses of the word. Everyone in the film is caught—the blacks are trapped in a decayed political system, the whites cling to the paternalism of a "superior" race. But "Chocolat" is not about the politics of imperialism, it's about the texture of human lives under a system where injustice has become mere routine. Denis grew up in colonial Africa, and her film (her first) pivots about a child named France (Cécile Ducasse), the daughter of a district officer in French Cameroon (François Cluzet) and his wife (Giúlia Boschi).

The central relationship in the film is between France and Protée (Isaach de Bankolé), the Dalenses' black house "boy." Protée is France's friend and mentor—he teaches her the native language, he shows her how to eat ant sandwiches, he spends more time with her than her beautiful, jaded mother and her always-traveling father. For little France it's a kind of paradise, but when a plane is forced down nearby, disgorging a motley band of characters, that paradise begins to unravel, exposing the buried tensions of race, culture and sex. Moving like a dream that explodes into reality, "Chocolat" is blessed with superb acting, especially by its star, the African-born Bankolé. His quiet eloquence and suppressed passion express the human cost of an unjust political system.

VILLAGE VOICE, 3/14/89, p. 68, Elliott Stein

From northern France [the reference is to *Under the Sun of Satan*], we hippety-hop to north Cameroon with another French release, *Chocolat*. This semi-autobiographical first feature was directed by Claire Denis, who grew up in Africa and then, once grown, worked as an assistant to Wim Wenders on *Wings of Desire* and Jim Jarmusch on *Down by Law*. *Chocolat*'s point of view is that of a young Frenchwoman (her name is France) who returns to Cameroon and, in a long flashback that composes the bulk of the film, reminisces about her childhood. The plot is largely concerned with the unconsummated mutual sexual attraction that torments France's mother (the district officer's wife) and a young black houseboy.

This engaging and largely successful movie is filled with stately pictorial compositions. The characters include a few of the usual overdrawn empire outpost boors and bores, but on the whole, it's a tale of decent and fairly ordinary, likable people trapped in a racist colonial society. The interracial adultery motif is not of consuming interest; far more intriguing are the scenes of near-sexual complicity between the hulky houseboy, Protée (Isaach de Bankolé), and the young blond France (Cécile Ducasse). She feeds him soup; when her parents are not around, he stains her hands with chicken blood and prepares live ant sandwiches that she devours unhesitatingly. De Bankolé's Protée is a nicely understated marvel of humiliated dignity and muted love. In his big scene, he weeps in solitude while taking a shower. Beefcake and pathos—it's irresistible. If this man is not destined for stardom, I'll eat an ant club sandwich.

Also reviewed in:

NEW REPUBLIC, 4/17/89, p. 28, Stanley Kauffmann
NEW YORK TIMES, 3/10/89, p. C17, Vincent Canby
VARIETY, 5/18/88, p. 38
WASHINGTON POST, 4/14/89, p. C1, Hal Hinson
WASHINGTON POST, 4/14/89, Weekend/p. 33, Desson Howe

CHOCOLATE WAR, THE

A Management Company Entertainment Group release. *Producer:* Jonathan D. Krane. *Director:* Keith Gordon. *Screenplay:* Keith Gordon. *Based on the book by:* Robert Cormier. *Director of Photography:* Tom Richmond. *Editor:* Jeff Wishengrad. *Sound:* Mary Jo Devenney. *Art Director:* David Ensley. *Set Decorator:* Melissa Matthies. *Costumes:* Elizabeth Kaye. *Running time:* 103 minutes. *MPAA Rating:* R.

CAST: John Glover (Brother Leon); Ilan Mitchell-Smith (Jerry); Wally Ward (Archie); Doug Hutchison (Obie); Corey Gunnestad (Goober); Bud Cort (Brother Jacques); Adam Baldwin (Carter); Brent Fraser (Emille).

LOS ANGELES TIMES, 11/23/88, Calendar/p. 13, Sheila Benson

"The Chocolate War" is a first-rate adaptation of Robert Cormier's dark, cautionary tale about personal freedom, as an idealistic freshman at a Catholic high school for boys unexpectedly defies the system and learns firsthand about the power of manipulation and intimidation.

Years from now, its haunting allegory may be best remembered as the directing debut of Keith Gordon. Although he has co-written and co-produced before ("Static"), Gordon's primarily known as an exceptional young actor ("Christine" "Dressed to Kill"). As "The Chocolate War" proves, he's also a terrifyingly assured director.

The look of the film, its Shaker-like visual severity and the taut control that Gordon exercises is almost astringent. However, his work with his actors is anything but clinical; Gordon, who also adapted the story, has a lovely feeling for nuance and for ensemble.

Brother Leon (John Glover, splendidly malevolent), is not yet head of St. Trinity's, one of the hubs of this Northwestern city, but he's palpably close and hotly ambitious for the job. To cement his position as the acting chief administrator, he has come up with an unprecedented quota for the annual chocolate sale: The boys will have to sell twice as many chocolates at double the price of last year.

Almost equal in power to Brother Leon are the Vigils, the secret school club. As the film opens, a pair of the club's officers, Archie (Wally Ward) and his assistant Obie (Doug Hutchison) sit alone above the football field, picking boys for Vigil "assignments," excruciating secret tests of loyalty or stamina. It's an almost surreal scene that reminds you of one of those "angels come to earth" sequences; however the manipulative Archie and the covertly ambitious Obie are anything but angels.

Jerry Renault (Ilan Mitchell-Smith), a smallish freshman whose tenacity at the football tryout catches Archie's eye, receives one of these assignments. When every boy at St. Trinity's routinely accepts his quota of chocolates, Jerry's orders are to refuse; then, after the Vigil-created ban is over, to agree to take his 50 boxes.

Even in the face of Brother Leon's most sardonic "persuasion"—a masterly display of bullying in which the priest's cobra-quick changes of logic and mood terrorize the entire class—Jerry holds fast. He's seen as a nut, then a menace, then as a symbol. Then something in Jerry snaps, almost audibly. Even after his Vigil time-frame is over, Jerry still refuses to sell the chocolates.

Systems work only as long as we let them. Jerry stands firm, a tangible threat to every side. In no time, the Vigils are fighting among themselves and with Brother Leon over absolute control of the school. And in the center is Jerry, thoughtful, resolute and wretched. (Mitchell-Smith gives a beautifully detailed performance.) He has virtually no support at home. His mother has died of cancer just as the school term begins, and his pharmacist-father sees Jerry through a miasma of mourning.

Significantly, the film doesn't spell out Jerry's reasons, but we can speculate that it's in reaction to his father's resignation and passivity.

Gordon mixes fantasy (not all of it completely successful), flash-forward and an eclectic range of music, from Yaz to Joan Armatrading to Peter Gabriel, to tell his story. It's not the sort that sends audiences out inspired by the best in their fellow man. Goodness has a very hard time of it, even up through the film's punishing ending. It's not accidental that in granting the film rights to two of his songs, Peter Gabriel cites his support of human rights and of Amnesty International. Human rights are clearly at the heart of the darkness here.

However, even with its chilling message, "The Chocolate War" (MPAA-rated R) is a fascinating film done with style, with care and with excellence in every department, from the actors (Hutchison's owlish Obie; Brent Fraser's sleek, preternaturally experienced wise guy, Emile Janza, and a delightful moment by Bud Cort as Brother Jacques) to Tom Richmond's beautiful camera work and David Ensley's art direction, which is both witty and understated.

NEW YORK POST, 1/27/89, p. 30, Jami Bernard

If it walks like a duck and quacks like a duck, it's a duck.

On the surface, "The Chocolate War" is a silly teen movie, the kind the studios dump on a stultified public during summer break. It has all the elements of a silly teen movie: high school hazings and a wimp-turned-hero who defies the sadistic secret society and gets to beat up the sniveling bully in the end, to the cheers of the entire school.

Beneath that surface, actor Keith Gordon has written and directed in such a way as to distract the viewer from the teen movie angle. On closer inspection, the ending is actually a dark moment of humiliation and self-knowledge for the wimp-turned-hero, an acknowledgment of his fundamental wimpiness and of The System's triumph over the will.

But one can detect a suspicious waddling. "The Chocolate War" does not quite make it as a clever piece of dark comedy. It's a duck after all.

If you want to watch a movie about the cruelty of schoolboys with interesting heroes and villains, go back to the old Masterpiece Theater version of "Tom Brown's Schooldays."

Archie (Wally Ward) is the oily school bully who, as taskmaster for The Vigils secret society at St. Trinity High School, is out scouting the new recruits for the football team. Sitting on the empty bleachers, he ticks off names to his social secretary, then invents an appropriate punishment for each one.

One kid is going to have to unscrew all the desks in Brother Eugene's homeroom, so that when the students sit down everything will go boom. Another kid is going to do some other ridiculous thing. And Jerry (Ilan Mitchell-Smith), our wimp-hero, still in his wimp phase, is going to refuse to sell his quota during the annual chocolate drive, run with undue enthusiasm by the dangerously loony Brother Leon (John Glover, played with lip-smacking, sadistic glee).

Jerry does as he's asked by The Vigils, but when his 10-day punishment is up, he still refuses to sell the chocolates. He just won't be goaded into doing the bidding of Brother Leon or of The Vigils either.

The students, weary of selling, come to look on Jerry as a saint on a hunger strike. Here at last is a kid who will stand up to authority. Naturally, Archie is beside himself—this is making The Vigils look bad, and besides, Brother Leon has forcefully enlisted Archie's support. If the chocolate sale breaks all records, Leon gets a promotion.

Unfortunately, both Jerry and Archie are bland characters, Jerry because of his impassiveness (and his "arty" nightmares about his dead mother), Archie because of his superficiality. The only interesting person is Glover as he goes chatteringly over the top, brandishing his blackboard pointer like a riding crop and tormenting his students.

There is a scene in which Leon chides the class for letting a particular torture go on too long. The same lesson can be applied to director Gordon, who seems to have left the camera rolling while he tiptoed on out.

Even a potentially funny scene is ruined by poor cutting, a scene in which a teacher catches on to why his students are acting crazy every time he pronounces a certain word.

With this ham-handed direction, including scenes in which Archie tries to break down his subjects in The Vigils' conference room, at least we are spared endless shots of the chocolates themselves. In a regular old teen comedy, we'd see stacks of unsold boxes teetering all over the place and kids secretly stuffing their faces. Here the students accept their allotment of boxes as if they were taking communion.

Everyone talks in a kind of dreamy, psychotic way, but the script is pretty tame. "Like all great plans, this has the beauty of simplicity," salivates Archie after figuring out how to get Jerry's goat. "We can make your life very bad, very sad," is a typical threat.

Actor Gordon, who played Rodney Dangerfield's son in the unpretentiously silly "Back to School," has shown his predilection for more serious filmmaking by co-producing and co-writing the dark (but static) comedy "Static." It is possible he means stinging indictment of a world that encourages survival of the mediocre.

Unfortunately, "Chocolate" quacks like a duck.

NEWSDAY, 1/27/89, Part III/p. 7, Lynn Darling

Maybe it's all of those repressed adolescent hormones, maybe it's the atmosphere of barely controlled anarchy, but private boys' schools can usually be counted on to provide a suitably feverish arena for imaginative film makers. When the concept works—as it did in Lindsay Anderson's "If"—the result can be an admirably twisted microcosm of society at large.

When it doesn't—and in "The Chocolate War" it most definitely does not—the result is an embarrassing confusion of the obvious, the banal and the painfully dreary.

"People are two things, greedy and cruel," Archie (Wally Ward), the sadistic, young villain of "The Chocolate War" declaims to one of his henchmen. The movie puts this thesis rather pointlessly to the test. Archie is one of the leaders of the Vigils, a secret society devoted to tormenting the younger members of the school by forcing them to carry out mean and pointless pranks. The task Archie devises for young Jerry Renault (Ilan Mitchell-Smith), a football player who is still in mourning for his dead mother, seems harmless enough—he must refuse to participate in the annual school sale of chocolate candies for 10 days.

But the chocolate standoff puts Renault at odds with one Brother Leon (John Glover), the maniacal chocolate sale leader who is gunning for a chance to become the school's headmaster. Before long Renault has become the increasingly persecuted scapegoat in an interminable battle between conformity and conscience that never rises above the stupefying.

Director Keith Gordon (who starred in "Christine" and "Back to School" and also wrote the script for this movie) has stocked his film with a numbing selection of uninteresting characters whose motivations remain for the most part obscure. To vary the action a little, he interpolates a handful of surreal scenes—Renault hallucinates his mother's coffin resting in front of the goal posts, for instance—that add nothing but a little self-consciously fancy footwork to the action. "The Chocolate War" eventually winds down to its mystifying conclusion—an ironic twist that invalidates whatever point there might have been to the whole thing in the first place. By then, the movie has come to resemble a familiar sort of exorcism—it's a way of expelling all the half-articulated rage and undigested ideas that come with the territory in adolescence. It's just too bad that they appear in the same form on the screen as well.

VILLAGE VOICE, 1/31/89, p. 67, Bruce Handy

Teenagers, as a social class, suffer from a profound lack of irony. Indeed, this failing may be the age group's single worst trait—and it certainly sinks *The Chocolate War*, a hymn to adolescent pains as morose and unrelentingly self-serious as you and I were at 15.

Talk about your imitative fallacies.

The film, written and directed by the actor Keith Gordon (he was the car owner in *Christine* and Angie Dickinson's son in *Dressed To Kill*), takes place in a Catholic boys' school in the state of Washington. A freshman, Jerry (Ilan Mitchell-Smith), bucks both the administration and an outlaw secret society when he refuses to take part in a fundraising drive. (The boys sell chocolates, hence the film's title.) Not only does Jerry draw the enmity of the school's headmaster, he also gets beaten up, finds turds in his locker, and is otherwise ostracized by his peers. The point, of course, is that both the powers that be and the ostensible rebels have a stake in the status quo; individualism is a threat to everyone.

Certainly no one in his or her right mind would want to tromp around drizzly Washington selling chcolates door-to-door. The problem is, that's not an interesting enough motivation to hang a movie on, and Jerry is given none better. Well, okay, that's not entirely true: As the film opens, his mother has just died—an easy bit of characterization that director Gordon literally runs to the ground with a series of dream sequences in which Jerry watches as his mom is interred in the high school football field. (No doubt the grass will grow just a wee bit greener on the 40-yard line.) What Mom's absence really means to Jerry (besides TV dinners every night) and what his grieving entails (besides not selling chocolates) are issues the film chooses not to explore—for Gordon's purposes, it's enough that she's dead, just as it was enough for Nicholas Ray that James Dean's dad wore an apron in *Rebel Without a Cause*.

Jerry's main antagonist is a premature fop named Archie (Wally Ward). Evil and manipulative, he's a prep Henry Kissinger, a master of high school realpolitik. He's also a nihilist. We know this because he announces early on that "Life is shit"—a sentiment that in various guises is repeated at regular intervals throughout the film, with such solemnity, and followed by such resonant silence on the soundtrack, that you soon fear Gordon means for us to take this pearl of schoolboy wisdom as a profundity. These are the moments when *The Chocolate War* threatens to implode, when the movie, its slight conceits frieghted with a ponderous mise-en-scène, out-*September*s *September*. You may have the claustrophobic feeling you're on the inside looking out of one colossal snit.

It's too bad Gordon is so enamored of his own ideas, because he evinces some considerable, if unencumbered, raw talent as a filmmaker. This is a handsome, sturdily crafted movie, made on the cheap ("$700,000," a publicist hissed as the lights dimmed). The actors are mostly capable, although it might have been nice if some of them had looked like kids instead of waiters at Odeon. Ward as Archie and John Glover (the smarmy, golden-boy producer in *Scrooged*) as the headmaster, Brother Leon, are the standouts. But with their drawn, horsey faces, their high foreheads brushed by epicene bangs, the two make physically similiar baddies, and in case we've missed the mild political point, Jerry has a dream envisioning Archie cloaked in Brother Leon's robes. If only real dreams were as numbingly obvious: The analysands among us would save a fortune on therapy.

Also reviewed in:
NEW YORK TIMES, 1/27/89, p. C8, Janet Maslin
VARIETY, 11/9/88, p. 16
WASHINGTON POST, 1/20/89, Weekend/p. 33, Desson Howe

CHORUS OF DISAPPROVAL, A

A Southgate Entertainment release. *Producer:* Michael Winner. *Director:* Michael Winner. *Screenplay:* Alan Ayckbourn and Michael Winner. *Based on the play by:* Alan Ayckbourn. *Director of Photography:* Alan Jones. *Editor:* Arnold Crust. *Music:* John du Prez. *Art Director:* Peter Young. *Running time:* 92 minutes. *MPAA Rating:* PG.

CAST: Anthony Hopkins (Dafydd Ap Llewellyn); Jeremy Irons (Guy Jones); Prunella Scales (Hannah Ap Llewellyn); Jenny Seagrove (Fay Hubbard); Gareth Hunt (Ian Hubbard); Lionel Jeffries (Jarvis Huntley-Pike); Sylvia Sims'(Rebecca Huntley-Pike); Alexandra Pigg (Bridget Baines).

LOS ANGELES TIMES, 9/1/89, Calendar/p. 14, Michael Wilmington

Scarborough, the English coastal resort city that is the setting of "A Chorus of Disapproval"—and also the home of its writer, Alan Ayckbourn—looks a lovely, eccentric place. Cold cliffs sweep to a paved esplanade, and the town is full of hilly streets that wind up between gingerbread houses, dingy pubs and Victorian hotels. In such a town, Alec Guinness, in a fey '50s comedy, might have wandered bemusedly, lamb to the slaughter for the flamboyant zanies inside.

Instead of Guinness, this hacked-up adaptation of Ayckbourn's wry play has Jeremy Irons, playing the befogged Guy Jones, haplessly seeking companionship in a Scarborough community production of "The Beggar's Opera."

Guy is right: The theater is the place to meet people, the place where wallflowers become *femmes fatales*, wimps become superstuds. Though he has the aggressiveness of a lily pad and the sexual smolder of a pressed tweed suit, he soon tumbles into one adulterous amour with the director's neglected wife, Hannah (Prunella Scales, of "Fawlty Towers"), and another with voracious Fay (Jenny Seagrove), a woman who pumps undreamed-of lascivious metaphor into the word *veal*.

Like many amateur groups, this one is riddled with good intentions, high hamminess and sexual intrigue. The director, Dafydd Ap Llewellyn (Anthony Hopkins), is a temperamental tyrant: a sentimental Welsh lawyer who throws tantrums with geyser regularity and seems less concerned with hearing the actors than playing to them, springboards for his weird, dreamy malice.

But instead of a Robert Hamer or an Alexander Mackendrick—a director in tune with classic British movie comedy—to handle all this, "Chorus" has producer-director Michael Winner. Like Jack the Ripper, Winner has a crucial flaw: He likes to cut.

From "I'll Never Forget What's 'is Name" to "Death Wish I, II and III," Winner has never been a man to shoot one set-up when seven will do. And Ayckbourn's humor depends on keeping his characters within a habitable universe, letting the action grow organically around them.

There's not a bad actor in the cast but barely a complete performance. Seagrove has a nice, brittle lewdness, but Winner's camera seems so transfixed by her derrière, he reverses strategy and holds her shots too long. Irons is such a limp Guy that he seems capable of dribbling into the crannies—and in one Royal Hotel Tea Room row, when he's handed some telltale underwear, Winner has him brandish it to the kibitzing old ladies.

As Dafydd, the play's great part, Hopkins gives his most contorted performance since the Hunchback of Notre Dame, whose posture he almost duplicates. Scrunched-up, stiff-shouldered, roaring, whispering, rasping, Dafydd is a piece of spiced ham, burnt to a crisp. His melancholy eyes pop at you out of the charred lines.

It's a shame that Winner the producer—who's assembled a splendid cast, fine script and locations—is so ill-served by Winner the director, who treats the play's wit like salami thrown into the slicer of his movieola. He's as shameless as Guy fingering his drawers. The material suggests the deft whimsy of "The Man in the White Suit" or "Tight Little Island." But the execution is just that: a slaughter. Winner keeps chopping off the heads of his scenes, battle-axing his actions. Behind every Ayckbourn on-target *mal mot* you can practically hear a directorial growl: "Arf a mo', mate. *I like to cut!*"

MONTHLY FILM BULLETIN, 11/89, p. 329, John Pym

Seeking new friends, Guy Jones, a widower, relocated to Scarborough by the electronics firm GRV, nervously auditions for an amateur production of *The Beggar's Opera*. Cast as Crook-Fingered Jack (one line, Act 2), he is immediately pitched into another overheated drama. Dafydd

Ap Llewellyn, a solicitor, the production's put-upon director, is anxious to learn on behalf of an unidentified client whether Guy's firm plans to expand; meanwhile, Dafydd's neglected wife Hannah sets out to seduce the susceptibly weak-willed newcomer. To add to his confusion, Guy is also rapidly embroiled with vampish Fay, spouse of wife-swapping Ian Hubbard, who also has a business interest in GRV's future. A sub-plot of the off-stage drama has Bridget, the calculating stage manager, vying with spitfire Linda (Lucy Locket), for the affections of lank Crispin (Macheath). Guy is promoted to the role of Matt of the Mint; and then to Filch, Ian having resigned the part anticipating that this business "backhander" will somehow be reciprocated by the naive Guy. Later, a third member of the company, Jarvis Huntley-Pike, a powerful local businessman, attempts to win Guy's confidence over the GRV expansion, backing his offer with a cash bribe. Crispin quits the show and Guy takes his part—not realising that his elevation was set up by Jarvis. Guy unwittingly double-crosses Ian over the GRV information; whereupon Ian, Dafydd's client, takes his revenge by telling the director he has been cuckolded by his leading man. With his life in ruins—dumped by Hannah, whom he intended to leave anyway; dressed down by Dafydd, who nevertheless wishes him well as Macheath—Guy faces opening night. He carries the evening, but afterwards is shunned by the cast. Outside the theatre, he throws away Jarvis' money.

Hanging over Alan Ayckbourn's play *A Chorus of Disapproval* is a curiously intangible disquiet, attributable chiefly, perhaps, to the shadow of Guy's dead wife. Guy makes a fearful muddle of his life, business and private, but at the curtain one is left wondering whether he deserves pity or contempt: has bereavement made him incapable, or is he merely a weak man who thought he could play both ends against the middle—in his private life at least—with impunity. In this, the first of Ayckbourn's thirty-seven plays to have been translated to the cinema, Jeremy Irons lacks the lugubriousness of Bob Peck, who played Guy in the original London production at the National Theatre in 1985; he does, on the other hand, perfectly convey the amateur actor's unbecoming vanity and, linked to it, a certain sort of sexual fecklessness, a chronic inability to say no. This makes Guy peculiarly dislikeable in a way, and gives the film a bitter after-taste which the original production lacked.

The cast fall upon their roles with relish, making more of a meal of the foibles of their amateur counterparts than the National cast. Anthony Hopkins' tendency to rant is exactly suited to Dafydd Ap Llewellyn's mordantly overblown frustration; and his first scene in the chilly rehearsal room, showing off as he mercilessly extracts "All Through the Night" from the timid Guy, is an immensely enjoyable *tour de force*. All the other players, from wispy Pete Lee-Wilson, through foursquare Alexandra Pigg, to the regal and indestructible Sylvia Syms who, as Jarvis' wife, has the task of explaining the facts of life to Guy, likewise give an admirable account of themselves. On the night, the company, as one would expect, turns in a remarkably assured production of Gay's comic opera.

The backstage side of the film, one imagines, pretty much took care of itself. Less satisfactory is the elucidation of the business shenanigans: the stormy passage of the production, for all its predictability, has the awful ring of truth; the wheeling and dealing round the electronics firm's plans for expansion is never, regrettably, much more than a device, and a mind-twisting one at that. Michael Winner has elected to play up the plot's farcical moments (a wife-swapping interlude, for instance, to which Guy brings an aged relative) with raw gusto and some unambiguous camera angles. And this, too, sits somewhat uneasily beside the fluid, unforced and universal comedy of amateurs gamely struggling to do a professionals' job.

NEW YORK POST, 8/18/89, p. 25, Jami Bernard

Gentle, nervous, recently widowed Guy Jones is new in town. He joins the local theater troupe as a way of integrating himself into the community and staving off loneliness. But he gets more than he bargained for—and, delightfully, so do we—when he walks into rehearsals of "The Beggar's Opera" in "A Chorus of Disapproval," a congenially off-center ensemble comedy adapted by director Michael Winner and playwright Alan Ayckbourn from the latter's award-winning play.

Jeremy Irons erases all traces of his wonderfully creepy gynecologist twins of "Dead Ringers" to play the earnest, awkward Guy Jones, transferred by his company to a faded English seaside resort town. Bumbling, apologetic, naive, he shows up to audition a stiff "All Through the Night" for Anthony Hopkins, the director of the chaotic, interbred little group of local amateurs.

"It's a song that sings itself!" booms Hopkins' character, Dafydd Ap Llewellyn, interrupting Guy's audition with theatrical relish.

Guy wins a walk-on part and the eager confidence and attentions of his fellow thespians, hearty oddballs including man-hungry women, schemers, love rivals. Helplessly, Guy is buffeted by their various needs. He is suddenly and bafflingly involved in real estate speculation. He is pursued by two aggressive women, one the wife of a '60s-styled "swinger," the other the frustrated wife of the director. As he gradually replaces errant cast members in more important roles, he becomes both the savior of the play and the source of town gossip.

Director Winner, who started out with a succession of British comedies but who is more closely identified with Charles Bronson's "Death Wish" series, imbues the film with a boisterous theatricality befitting the story's origin as a play. The characters bounce around with gusto and are disarmingly amusing. During a typically stiff rehearsal for this mess of a "Beggar's Opera," Dafydd assures the cast: "I will be stuffing it full of gestures at a later time...you won't be able to see the stage for arm movements."

Thanks to Ayckbourn's deft and daft script, every moment is an odd one, although, oddly enough, not always an apt one. A conversation about who will be missed when dead and by whom is poignantly revealing; a misunderstood wife-swap dinner party is not.

Hopkins has the showiest role as the obstreperous director, who fumes and spits and reduces his players to tears. "You can breathe offstage, on your own time," he snaps at an actress who cannot concentrate on her lines because they are being prompted by her love rival (saucily played with Mack-truck bitchiness by Alexandra Pigg of "A Letter to Brezhnev").

Hopkins also manages to plumb the depths of his curmudgeon with a single wounded look.

Irons is not an altogether convincing wimp; he overuses his reedy body to achieve the kind of haplessness that more often characterized those nerd-into-hero teen comedies.

Prunella Scales is excellent as the director's lumpy, sad-eyed wife, finding new excitement in secretly doing Guy's laundry and matching his socks at midnight. Others in the supporting cast are also strong.

Despite a somewhat overzealous stab at zaniness from Winner—he focuses his camera squarely on faces as if taunting kittens to play with the yarn again—"A Chorus of Disapproval" retains an underlying affection for its quirky characters.

NEWSDAY, 8/18/89, Part III/p. 3, Mike McGrady

The peculiarly solemn young man (Jeremy Irons) travels by rail across the fields of northern England, stopping finally in Scarborough, a quaint seaside village of cobbled roadways and Georgian homes. A recent widower, he climbs steep hills and even steeper stairs to his genteel but very ordinary new flat. He visit his new office in an electronics firm and, desperately anxious to make contact with others, wears his loneliness as plainly as if it were a shabby winter coat. That afternoon, while thumbing through the local paper, he runs across a small ad placed by an amateur theater group and the words leap out to greet him: "Meet People—Have Fun."

All this occurs before the completion of the opening credits of "A Chorus of Disapproval," an enormously entertaining British import that features a literate and amusing script by Alan Ayckbourn, sterling performances by Anthony Hopkins and Jeremy Irons and direction by Michael Winner that is as deft and lighthearted as the prize winning play it's based on.

Oh, how Winner must have *loved* making this film! A Cambridge graduate and art collector, Winner began his career directing small English comedies that attracted small English audiences, little-known movies such as "The Jokers" and "I'll Never Forget What'sisname." He then had the great fortune—or misfortune, depending on your viewpoint—of teaming up with Charles Bronson to film "The Mechanic," "The Stone Killer" and the first three "Death Wish" movies. In short order, Winner became known as a guts-and-glory guy, an action specialist. "A Chorus of Disapproval," says Winner, is "the first film I've made in years where all the cast are alive at the end."

Alive *and* well. In fact, even Anthony Hopkins' fans are going to be pleasantly surprised by his portrait of a crotchety, droopy-eyed, sarcastic, dictatorial and ultimately lovable director of a very amateur troupe of actors. Hopkins' recent stage triumphs—he played both Lear and Macbeth at Britain's National Theater—seem to have freed him up, allowing him to pull out all the stops and deliver one of those juicy, broadly stated performances that recall Charles Laughton at his best.

By contrast, Jeremy Irons is diffident and shy as the young man who turns to amateur theatrics as a way of rejoining the human race. Once he's back among the living, he also finds himself back among them loving—involved with two women who happen to be married to others. With romance and adventure come infusions of charm and warmth and joy, qualities one has not always found in Irons' past roles. Buffs will be delighted to note the presence of such old favorites as Lionel Jeffries and Sylvia Sims along with such new favorites as Patsy Kensit, costar of the current "Lethal Weapon II."

Alan Ayckbourn, sometimes described as England's Neil Simon, has written 37 plays, many of them broad sex comedies and including such hits as "Bedroom Farce" and "Absurd Person Singular." The 1985 production of "A Chorus of Disapproval" at Britain's National Theater won that year's best-play and best-comedy honors. Strangely enough, this is the first film ever made of an Ayckbourn play. There will be others.

VILLAGE VOICE, 8/22/89, p. 92, Julie Phillips

Theoretically, *A Chorus of Disapproval* is one of those mild, eccentric little English comedies. Based on an Alan Ayckbourn play, it's about a shy man (Jeremy Irons) who joins an amateur theater group rehearsing *The Beggar's Opera*, and gets caught up in the small-town actors' years of accumulated grudges and affections. Grateful for a new face, the other players take him into their confidence and their sleeping arrangements; as they warm to him, and to the valuable information they think he has about his employer's building plans, they reward him with better and better parts. Finally they make him their leading man, and then, when he disappoints, their archvillain as well.

But director Michael Winner, a maker of vigilante thrillers including the *Death Wish* series, has a lot to unlearn before he goes back to doing comedies. He drives the pace too hard, overrunning the play's slow, erratic rhythms; films people from funny angles, for no reason; and cuts anxiously from one harmless face to another, as if his small-town people were really alien spies, and their exchanged looks held something darker and more chilling than gossip and spite. Very much an ensemble piece, *Chorus* translates strangely into the language of loner movies: Jeremy Irons doesn't bear much resemblance to Charles Bronson.

As the despotic Welshman who directs the drama group, Anthony Hopkins does manage to nourish the belief that the true basis of the English character is not cuteness but psychosis. He overacts in one direction, raving in a thick (and inconsistent) accent, while Irons shuffles off in another, wringing his hands and grimacing in an unconvincing agony of shyness. Jenny Seagrove (*Local Hero*), as a scheming young wife, is a parody of platinum blondness, and Patsy Kensit (*Lethal Weapon 2*) is sniffly as a spurned girlfriend. A light in this fog of overacting, Prunella Scales (*Fawlty Towers*), is gracious and funny as the tyrant's neglected wife.

The material itself seems a little outdated, or something. Do swinger couples still exist? Are they still funny? Were catfights—women scratching and biting and pulling hair over men—ever really funny? And sex itself, and affairs and cheating and all, seem to have used up their potential for cute, innocuous embarrassment. But when Winner finally slows down, toward the end, he allows a pleasure in the ordinary oddness of these people that is genuine and unforced. It helps, somehow, to see them onstage in their all-purpose Elizabethan costumes. It deflects some of the meanness of their scheming, and reminds us that in their own English way, these people are probably having a good time.

Also reviewed in:
NEW REPUBLIC, 9/11/89, p. 26, Stanley Kauffmann
NEW YORK TIMES, 8/18/89, p. C15, Vincent Canby
VARIETY, 5/31–6/7/89, p. 34
WASHINGTON POST, 9/23/89, p. C10, Hal Hinson

CITY OF SADNESS, A

An ERA International and 3-H Films Limited production. *Executive Producer:* H.T. Jan and Michael Yang. *Producer:* Chiu Fu-Sheng. *Director:* Hou Hsiao-hsien. *Screenplay (Chinese with English subtitles):* Wu Nien-jen and Chu Tien-wen. *Director of Photography:* Chen Hwa-In. *Editor:* Liau Ching-Sown. *Music:* Chang Hong-Yi. *Running time:* 158 minutes. *MPAA Rating:* Not Rated.

CAST: Tony Leung (Lin Wen-ching); Hsin Shu-fen (Hinomi); Chen Sown-yung (Lin Wen-heung); Kao Jai (Lin Wen-leung); Li Tien-Lu (Lin Ah-lu); Wu Yi-fang (Hiuoe); Nakamura Ikuyo (Shisuko); Kenny Cheung (Ah-ga); Chen Shu-fang (Mio); Lin Yang (Ko-san); H.T. Jan (Lin-san).

NEWSDAY, 10/6/89, Part III/p. 5, Terry Kelleher

After a press screening of "A City of Sadness" earlier this week, someone asked whether two male characters in the Taiwanese saga are supposed to have sexual feelings for each other.

Laughter spread on the stage at Alice Tully Hall as a translator relayed the query to director Hou Hsiao-hsien, actor Chen Sown-yung and screen writers Wu Nien-jen and Chu Tien-wen. Finally, the replay came: This interpretation was definitely a "misunderstanding".

In all fairness to the questioner, it should have been added that "A City of Sadness" is easy to misunderstand. And there's nothing else easy about it.

"A City of Sadness," winner of the Golden Lion Award as best picture in competition at last month's Venice Film Festival, will have two new York Film Festival showings: today at 6:15 p.m. and Sunday at 8 p.m. This one may well be worth seeing twice, especially for those who can't keep the story straight the first time.

Set in 1945–49, "A City of Sadness" focuses on one family as representative of Taiwan's post-World War II identity crisis. At the start of the film, the island is reverting to Chinese rule after 50 years under Japanese control. At the end, the Communists have taken over the Chinese mainland and Chiang Kai-shek's forces have turned Taiwan into "Nationalist China," crushing dissenters who want the island to pursue its own destiny.

Over two hours and 38 minutes, the movie conveys the idea that Taiwan is a colonial pawn, "eaten by everyone, ridden by everyone, sympathized with by no one." Loyalties are ambiguous; patriotism is a matter of whose flag is flying at the moment. With the variety of languages and dialects spoken on the island, communication is obviously a problem. The most sympathetic character is a deaf-mute who expresses himself by writing notes.

The larger themes come through, but the particulars of plot and relationships get lost somewhere in the subtitles (Chinese and English) and protracted silences. Hou tends to hold one distanced shot for what seems like forever, often filming whole scenes through doorways. Important action repeatedly takes place out of camera range. Near the end, knife fights break out for no clear reason. It's hard to tell who's slashing whom, much less why.

The director explained that he relied on long takes because the nonprofessional actors in his cast needed extra time to work up the required emotions. He said it's difficult to find the proper physical environment for a period drama in Taiwan, and therefore his choice of camera angles was limited. For whatever reason, "A City of Sadness" induced restlessness, confusion and mild eyestrain in this viewer. A second look might be more rewarding.

Also reviewed in :
NEW YORK TIMES, 10/6/89, p. C13, Caryn James
VARIETY, 9/20-26/89, p. 30

COLD FEET

An Avenue Pictures release, *Producer:* Cassian Elwes. *Director:* Robert Dornhelm. *Screenplay:* Tom McGuane and Jim Harrison. *Director of Photography:* Brian Duggan. *Editor:* David Rawlins and Debra McDermott. *Music:* Tom Bähler. *Production Designer:* Bernt Capra. *Art Director:* Cory Kaplan. *Running time:* 94 minutes. *MPAA Rating:* R.

CAST: Keith Carradine (Monte); Sally Kirkland (Maureen); Tom Waits (Kenny); Bill Pullman (Buck); Rip Torn (Sheriff); Kathleen York (Laura); Tom McGuane (Cowboy in Bar); Jeff Bridges (Bartender).

FILMS IN REVIEW, 12/89, p. 619, Edmond Grant

One can honestly wonder whether *Cold Feet,* a sporadically funny but directionless oddball comedy, would have ever gotten filmed were it not for the fact that noted novelist Thomas McGuane co-authored the screenplay.

The film follows the exploits of three outlaws who hide a cache of jewels in the stomach of a horse (this can be chalked up to the fact that none of the three is any too bright). When one of the three, a bored-looking cowpoke played by Keith Carradine, absconds with the horse and its highly valued innards, the other two give chase. One of them—a middle-aged, "loose woman" clad in skintight fashions (Sally Kirkland)—is out to recapture Carradine's heart; the other—a delightfully whacked-out hit man (Tom Waits) wants his hide.

McGuane and co-scripter Jim Harrison clearly intended *Cold Feet* as an all-out screwball comedy, a kind of New West version of the tacky-lifestyle comedies made popular (and to better effect) by Jonathan Demme and Susan Seidelman. If the film worked solely on that level, it might have had a fighting chance. But, in addition to the moments of broad comedy appearing around every turn, there is also a rather dull subtext running throughout, something to the effect that there *is* a better life that these three could be aspiring to, if only they'd forget their greedy obsessions. That lifestyle is embodied by Carrandine's brother and sister-in-law, who are trying to start up their own ranch. These characters are so pure and innocent that they seem to blunt the film's otherwise wild and off-handed spirit.

This spirit is best incarnated by Waits, who seems to have taken a leaf from his *Ironweed* co-star, Jack Nicholson, and decided to play the role of Kenny the hit man to the hilt, adding more gusto and dynamism to his moments on screen than any other cast member. Except, that is, for Sally Kirkland, who with her broad turn as the day-glo clad, hot-to-trot heroine, seems to react with similar abandon (this abandon was also displayed in Ms. Kirkland's promotional interviews for the film, wherein she would set about personally seducing her television interviewers, or as in one late night example, dancing/gyrating with another interviewee).

On the other hand, the talented Keith Carradine is left with next to nothing to do except react to his co-stars delightful excesses. Though cast in a central role, Carradine seems, like co-stars Rip Torn and Jeff Bridges (in an unbilled cameo), to have simply wandered onto the film's set.

The film ultimately suffers from a case of the title condition; it's a broad farce that's afraid to give in to its only positive element, the raging, over-the -top work done by Waits and Kirkland.

LOS ANGELES TIMES, 5/19/89, Calender/ p. 12, Sheila Benson

"Cold Feet," which moves in abrupt spurts and jagged gyrations, features three enormously deft and funny actors, Sally Kirkland, Tom Waits and Keith Carradine, as partners in a bizarre emerald smuggling scheme. Their deft larcenies are played out with all Montana as a dwarfing background.

Cowboy and habitual liar Monte (Carradine) arrives at his brother Buck's spread in Montana with Infidel, a handsome stallion. The horse's services may let Buck (Bill Pullman) and his wife Laura (Kathleen York) make a go of the family ranch at last. However, Infidel is actually the property of Monte's partners, the marriage-minded Maureen (Kirkland) and the suntanned, frowzy Kenny (Waits), a talented contract killer. With Monte, they have arranged to transport a container of emeralds into the country along Infidel's rib-cage, courtesy of a now-dead veterinarian.

"Cold Feet" is schizoid; smart yet untiringly vulgar; exquisitely played yet out of control most of the time. It's no secret that its director, Robert Dornhelm ("She Dances Alone," "Echo Park") is unhappy with the released version, which certainly has none of the insights or gentle observations of his earlier features.

The screenplay is the work of two of Montana's proudest literary lights, novelist/screenwriter and occasional director Tom McGuane ("92 in the Shade," "Rancho Deluxe") and poet/novelist Jim Harrison ("Legends of the Fall" and the current "Dalva"). It's full of McGuane earmarks: characters like Waits' malevolent Kenny, muttering to himself in verbal footnotes. Kenny is reluctant to grow old as just another murderer. He sees himself as *executive* material, and in the climate of today he may be exactly right. Such zingers, enriched by the special Waits body English, may not exactly advaqnce the action, but they do make for a rich dallying place while all else flows by.

But action isn't the point, it's character that counts or should count in "Cold Feet." The soulful Maureen, for example, she of the spray-painted Spandex wardrobe and the voracious appetites, whose dream of finding a completely dishonest cowboy and snuggling down for all time has been mistakenly realized in Monte.

There was a hint in "Anna" of Kirkland's potential for humor; it's unfurled here in her quick-change range, from sunny to stormy in two sentences. It takes a powerful inner gyroscope to make this work, but Kirkland never falters, even with the editing working tirelessly against her. (Two editors are credited.) By contrast, Carradine's Monte is almost a goofball straight man to this bent pair. It's up to him and Pullman—and these lush cobalt blue skies—to make the pull of Montana tangible, and this they do emphatically.

There was the chance that "Cold Feet" could have been another "Bagdad Cafe," bringing a distinctly European eye to the peculiarities of the American West. (Director Dornhelm is Romanian born, Austrian educated.) But just as the charm of these characters gets a chance to work, some flagrant crassness shrivels the moment. It remains a bungled beguilement, one of the screen's wistful might-have-beens.

MONTHLY FILM BULLETIN, 5/90, p. 12, Philip Strick

On their ranch in Montana, Buck and Laura get a call from Buck's brother Monte in Mexico to say he's coming to stay. Laura suspects this is connected with one of Monte's crooked deals, and indeed Monte is as usual up to his neck in trouble. He has acquired a magnificent stallion, Infidel, a bag of emeralds, and two demented partners—Kenny, an unstable gunman, and Maureen, an unscrupulous siren whose one aim in life is to marry Monte. The plan is to smuggle the emeralds into the U.S. inside Infidel, at which point Monte's private intention is to lose Kenny and Maureen and go into hiding. Monte and Kenny duly negotiate the horse across the Mexican border while Maureen flies ahead, appropriates a trailer, and waits for them on the other side. When she and Kenny find Monte has given them the slip, the chase is on; their first destination is Colorado where Monte's daughter Rosemary is in summer camp. Meanwhile, riding Infidel, Monte reaches Buck and Laura's ranch, settles in, and tries to work out how to extract the emeralds without irreparable damage. Convinced that he is up to something, and irritated at his reluctance to share their work load, Buck and Laura console themselves with the prospect of profits to be made from Infidel's services as a stud. Monte summons Rosemary to join him and she is in transit by the time Maureen and Kenny reach the camp. They find out her destination and arrive shortly before her bus, attraction considerable attention in their attempts to trace Monte. Their antics are brought to the notice of the Sheriff, whose precautionary visit to the ranch alerts Monte that trouble is on the way. He has hidden Infidel by the time his former partners arrive in the middle of the night, Maureen passionately protecting him from excessive damage by Kenny. She forces Monte to announce their impending wedding, for which the Sheriff, suspicious of them all, decides to officiate as non-denominational minister. Monte enlists Buck's help to hide Infidel in a herd of other horses bound for the local slaughterhouse, but Kenny forces Buck to take him to find the animal. The remains of the horses are being boiled down in huge vats; Buck pushes Kenny into one of them and makes his escape. He finds that Infidel has been saved by the slaughterhouse owner, who sells him back to Buck. The marriage ceremony completed, Monte and Maureen are promptly arrested by the Sheriff, confident that he will also capture Kenny within days. Unleashing Infidel among their herd at the ranch, Buck and Laura settle down with Rosemary to a bright future, unaware that Kenny has survived the vat with unfinished business in mind.

The "Nouveau Western", intermittently invented by sporting columnists and co-writers Tom McGuane and Jim Harrison across a thirty-year friendship, occupies a territory which, fortunately, has not yet defined its limits. Somewhere between the landscapes of Tex Avery and John Ford, it may in due course by throttled by barbed wire or choked with an excess of mobile homes, but for the moment there seems enough space to accommodate a modest army of persistent cowboys drifting between motels. With his scripts for *The Missouri Breaks* and *Tom Horn*, McGuane contributed to the image of the West as a land without a future, occupied by loners distracted by the compulsion only to look backwards, as if trapped by imperturbable geography into unchangingly primitive rituals of survival. But what is "nouveau" about the McGuane-Harrison approach is that it shoves irreverently past this impasse; today's Western, way beyond innocence, carries the payload of Larry McMurtry and W.R. Burnett, recalls Monte Hellman and Sam Shepard, and combines road-movie rivalries with the uncomfortable reliability of W. S. Hart. In the colours of Hoch and Ballard, a shot may evoke Mann or Boetticher, but another might as easily be from Rudolph or Jarmusch. And so *Cold Feet* offers a lyrical opening of horses fording a stream, only to switch, some moments later, to a disorienting chaos like something out of Wes Craven, as stolen jewels are bloodily concealed inside a recumbent stallion.

Such collisions of genre are more likely to appeal to fans of Jim Thompson than of John Wayne, but *Cold Feet* refuses to decelerate for the sake of the undecided. The remarkable chemistry between Tom Waits, Sally Kirkland and Keith Carradine, one-liners crackling between them, creates an infectious hysteria that invades every scene, transforming even the extras. By the time Monte's vengeful partners reach the summer camp to kidnap his daughter, it's no surprise to find the place packed with kids in combat gear, apparently ready for civil war and having to be fought off at gunpoint. Dead Rock, Montana (McGuane's favourite fictional desert town, often used as a setting to his stories), borders on *Last Picture Show* territory with the slightly bemused (and uncredited) appearance of Jeff Bridges behind the bar, and is engagingly populated by a handful of whiskered drunks (McGuane among them) alongside a lavishly over-equipped store of Stetsons, boots and buckskin jackets. Presiding over this ragged community, Rip Torn gleefully parodies the role of sheriff as if having awaited the opportunity for years. The scene in which he hastily turns preacher in an empty house, barely hiding the "For Sale" board and securing his trousers in time to greet his unsuspecting visitor ("I work for God, son, and He don't like me foolin' around"), is glorious and unashamed farce.

Constructed as a series of incidents not necessarily vital to the central pursuit, *Cold Feet* improvises random volleys of asides and comments. "1962 was the year of the Surgeon General's Report", says somebody in passing. "Damn bad year for smokers". As the stolen trailer careers the highways, with Kenny trying to stay on the road while Maureen watches television, rearranges the furniture, sunbathes noisily on the roof, and changes into one skintight outfit after another, they both review their lives in rueful argument. Kenny considers himself executive material, disinclined to remain a common murderer for the rest of his days, while Maureen's dream has always been to find herself a completely dishonest cowboy, and now she has but Monte won't marry her. "If I got myself a vibrator and learned how to shoot", she pouts at her volatile companion, "I wouldn't need you at all". And when, restless for physical stimulation, she decides they must stop at the next town, Kenny claims it's a uranium mining camp. "Your ass'll glow in the dark", he warns her. Nearing their prey, she primly reminds the hit man, who boasts of once making 23 hits in a row, "We don't want an orgy of violence", adding a thoughtful "Don't hurt him!" as Kenny's glinting razor approaches the sleeping Monte's throat.

In all of this, ruthlessly mugged by Waits and Kirkland but played tolerably straight by Carradine, the film's title remains oddly unsubstantiated. Nothing to do with Lefty Frizzell's classic cowpoke number, it's explained by McGuane as a reference to lack of commitment ("We are the "cold feet" generation", he says), which might just about be relevant to Monte, who can't bring himself to get married, or work, or extract the emeralds from their messy hiding place, but seems sparsely illustrated in general. McGuane's writings are indeed inhabited by vague and passive characters drifting amiably from one crisis to the next, but the spine of this story is in fact provided by the good ol' couple Buck and Laura who, toiling away at their fields and fences, periodically appear in poses of conventional domesticity to comment on the mysterious conduct of everyone else. The film ends with them romping in sunlit hay as Buck comments: "There's nothin' like a woman's laughter to tell you you're doin' the right thing". No cold feet for *them*.

Robert Dornhelm responds to the pantomime as if plucking his *Echo Park* trio straight off the mountain where we last saw them to resume their search for fulfilment. His indulgent approach to hyperbole and slapstick, not far distant from that of fellow European Percy Adlon, suggests that McGuane and Harrison's new West has previously unremarked origins in the writings of Karl May. Certainly Dornhelm shares the vivid affection of Brian Duggan's camera for the Montana vistas enviable surrounding McGuane's own home, but the sense of *Echo Park* continuity was undoubtedly the main attraction: the muscleman, the dreamer and the vacillating entrepreneur, no longer aspiring to Hollywood but, in a sense, already beyond it, are given their heads in a frenetic replay. Now a more macabre unit, they have acquired an ardent fatalism ("Oo, I kinda like this!" squeaks Maureen as the handcuffs shackle her to Monte) and wind up appropriately behind bars. But Buck and Laura, cannily enclosed by Dornhelm in barbed wire for their final shot, are available if required for further quests, and the triangle is completed with the wicked insert of Kenny's resurrection during the end credits. If McGuane's heroes suffer a kind of in-built fatigue, one senses that Dornhelm's will show, on the contrary, a cheery resilience.

NEW YORK POST, 5/19/89, p. 31, David Edelstein

The shrill, pushy mess of a comedy that calls itself "Cold Feet" isn't for everyone, but I had a happy time cackling like an idiot at it. Sometimes you have to go with your idiot. It's a movie with no particular story but some great macho-nihilist dialogue and a what-the-hell attitude toward plot and character. I'd like to buy the studio head a bourbon for having the guts to release it.

What plot there is, is a tired ol'thing about a horse named Infidel with some emeralds sewn up in its gut and smuggled across the Mexican border into the United States. The smugglers (Keith Carradine, Sally Kirkland, Tom Waits) are going to cut open its belly on the other side, but ne'er-do-well Carradine likes the horse and doesn't much like the floozy (Kirkland) who wants to marry him and her vicious hit-man sidekick (Waits).

So he gallops away to the Montana ranch of his honest, hard-working brother (Bill Pullman) and sister-in-law (Kathleen York), and the steamed-up Waits and Kirkland follow—in a Winnebago. When they get to Montana, Waits buys some ugly lizard-skin boots for $400 to get the owner to draw him a map to the ranch and then contemptuously slings them into the garbage. "I don't want this to turn into an orgy of violence," says Kirkland.

Novelists Tom McGuane and Jim Harrison co-wrote "Cold Feet" by mail in the days(1974) before modems and fax machines, and I'll bet each tried to break the other up with his smartass lines. At the same time McGuane was writing "Panama," about a screenwriter who stumbles around Key West in a drug haze trying to win back his girlfriend by doing things like nailing his hand to her front door. The people who wrote "Cold Feet" know about nothin' left to lose.

They do best with blowhard Waits, a runty little jerk with a load of macho airs to compensate for his height and looks. Waits, with his strained and bellowing voice, is doing a neat Warren Oates impersonation, and that's appropriate: The movie has been made by people who never got over the death of Warren Oates.

He does situps out a moving car window; he antagonizes customs officials; he walks into a ranchers' bar and loudly (and pointlessly) orders "a round of Shirley Temples for those homosexuals over there." "Those homosexuals"—very big cowboys—are not amused.

Sally Kirkland's exhibitionism can be hard to take, but this is certainly a good exhibition for her. She lolls around in her Day-Glo minidresses, an absurd sight against the big skies and pale prairies of Montana. Drunk and slobbering over Waits as he drives, she purrs, "Oooh, my skin is alive," and it is, it is. (If you don't laugh when Waits tells her to "Go sit on a wheel well and feel the bumpy road," you probably won't laugh at much else.)

The movie was reportedly cut by its studio to the fury of most of those involved; there's no composer listed; the big climax is lame; you feel like a slob for enjoying yourself. (Actually, you feel like a hip slob for enjoying yourself.)

But the actors are all amiable weirdos. Pullman makes the ingenuous rancher brother a fidgety dufus. He looks a little like Robin Williams here—crinkly eyes, upturned chin—and he's very sweet when he asks his wife, "You think maybe we can get started on that herd of our own?"

If that isn't enough incentive to see this sucker, there's Rip Torn as an ugly cuss of a sheriff who disguises himself as a preacher to catch the smugglers and Montana resident Jeff Bridges in a peculiar cameo as a bartender. (McGuane shows up too as a cowboy.)

John Waters once wrote that Tom Waits sings like a man who doesn't change his underwear daily. "Cold Feet" is a movie for people who don't change their underwear daily. Excuse me while I do my laundry.

NEWSDAY, 5/19/89, Part III/ p. 3, Mike McGrady

Has anyone else noticed Hollywood's new passion for eccentricity? I'm not talking about the warm, lovable nuttiness of a "Harvey" or the small idiosyncrasies of a "Columbo." No, what I've noticed lately is eccentricity on the grand scale, eccentricity for eccentricity's sake...eccentric eccentricity.

The arrival of "Cold Feet," a comic western scripted by novelists Tom McGuane and Jim Harrison, is yet another example of what is fast becoming a major Hollywood growth industry. In fact, there are now enough examples of on-screen eccentricity that we could submit formal applications for genre status. Included in that genre would have to be Beth Henley ("Miss Firecracker"), John Patrick Shanley ("Five Corners" and "Moonstruck") and newcomer Daniel Waters ("Heathers").

The modern eccentrics see reality as but a starting point, a backdrop against which highly improbable characters do highly unlikely things. When eccentricity works at its best (as with Shanley's "Moonstruck") there is enough laughter to gloss right over all those tenuous connections with real life. And even when eccentricity fails, with results ranging from overly theatrical to ludicrous, there is still as sense of surprise, a pleasure that comes from the determined avoidance of cliches.

The main sources of eccentricity in "Cold Feet" are its characters, none of whom will seem familiar to students of either the cinema or life.

The oddball heroine, played by Sally Kirkland, is a nymphomaniacal outlaw who sunbathes atop a speeding motor home while dreaming of marrying her worthless cowpoke: "All I want is to settle down and eat well." Her main ongoing task is to calm down her traveling companion, a psychotic hit man who is getting restless: "I know you, Kenny, you want to spread your wings and kill some one."

The hitman (Tom Waits) doesn't much like her soothing ways. ("*Stop calming me down!*" he screams.) Between murders, Kenny sends inaccurate postcards to his mother ("Dear Mommy, I've been promoted to chief executive branch manager..."), all the while taking pride in his record of 23 consecutive hits whithout a miss: "That's the problem with the world today. There's no more professionalism...No one wants to take reponsibility for the bottom line."

Then there's Keith Carradine, a shiftless ranch hand who sends out for prostitutes; his 9-year-old, fatigues-wearing daughter who is being educated in a "survival school", and, well, you get the idea. An all-oddball lineup directed by Robert Dornhelm, who established his own eccentricity credentials with an earlier feature, "Echo Park," the saga of a stripper, a body builder and a pizza delivery boy.

The story? It's a shaggy-horse story that McGuane and Harrison wrote through the mail, sending a script back and forth until it was sufficiently weird. McGuane has a nice ear for what he calls "quickie poetry," and the writing quality lured some genuine talents. Rip Torn and an unbilled Jeff Bridges show up, one suspects, simply to be in on the gag.

McGuane describes the results as a "nouveau western," but it is no more a western than "Blazing Saddles" was a western. The truth is, it's an eccentric and has all the earmarks of the genre. The expected number of unexpected moments, the usual number of surprises, the normal lineup of wackos, and the prerequisite pointlessness. Yes, definitely a prime example of The Eccentric School of Moviemaking.

VILLAGE VOICE, 5/23/89, p. 64, Amy Taubin

Remember *Straight to Hell* (Alex Cox)? Remember *Siesta* (Mary Lambert)? Well, *Cold Feet* is more pretentiously incoherent than both of them put together. Which might mean that next year Robert Dornhelm, whose prior claim to fame was the Academy Award-nominated documentary *The Children of Theatre Street,* could have as big a success as *Pet Sematary.* or, then again, maybe not.

Co-written by Tom McGuane and Jim Harrison, and filmed down-home style mostly on McGuane's Paradise Valley ranch, *Cold Feet* is a treacly attempt at a postmodern western. A trio of opportunists smuggles a bag of emeralds across the border by having it sewn inside the belly of a prize racehorse (I swear). Tom Waits is psycho—we know because he foams at the mouth when, to cover their tracks, he shoots the vet. Keith Carradine is his usual noncommittal self, and Sally Kirkland's just after Carradine. Carradine splits with the horse (probably because he's nauseated by Kirkland's taste in clothes). Waits and Kirkland follow him, having what the press materials describe as picaresque adventures en route. I'd be more specific if I could just remember one of them.

You know the producers are worried when they slug in a voiceover narration by a minor character to keep the audience apprised about what's supposed to be happening and the significance of it all. Carradine's experience in many Alan Rudolph films stands him in good stead here. He brings a certain panache to the incomprehensible. The other two are less fortunate. The harder Kirkland works, the less presence she has. She seems to be going for some sort of composite of Dolly Parton and Jerry Hall, but the only way I could identify her shot to shot was by the omnipresent fake desert flower in her platinum locks.

While the movie itself raised not a chuckle, the press packet is a hoot and a half. If you have the misfortune to be in a theater where *Cold Feet* is playing, just remember that "a native of Rumania, director Dornhelm was a bit nervous about creating in a world of horses, cowboys, and lizard skin boots."

Also reviewed in:

NEW YORK TIMES: 5/19/89, p. C10, Caryn James
VARIETY, 5/24-30/89, p. 30
WASHINGTON POST, 5/22/89, p. B2, Hal Hinson

COMIC BOOK CONFIDENTIAL

A Cinecom Pictures release of a Sphinx Productions film. *Executive Producer:* Don Haig. *Producer;* Ron Mann. *Director:* Ron Mann. *Screenplay:* Ron Mann. *Director of Photography:* Robert Fresco and Joan Churchill. *Editor:* Robert Kennedy and Ron Mann. *Art Director:* Gerlinde Scharinger. *Music:* Keith Elliot, Gerard Leckey, Nicholas Stirling, and Dr. John (Mac Rebennack). *Sound:* David Joliet, Tod A. Maitland, Brenda Ray, Nick Broomfield, Greg von Buchau, Alan Barker, Steve Bull, and Byron Patchett. *Sound Editor:* Bruce McDonald, Gordon McClellan, and Peter Wintonick. *Running time: 90 minutes. MPAA Rating:* Nor Rated.

CINEASTE, Vol. XVII, No. 2, 1989, p. 44, David Segal

Comic Book Confidential is the third in a series of cultural history documentaries produced and directed by Toronto based filmmaker Ron Mann. *Imagine the Sound* (1981) was about the jazz avant-garde of the Sixties, and featured Paul Bley, Bill Dixon, Archie Shepp, and Cecil Taylor. *Poetry in Motion* (1982) covered contemporary poetry, with an emphasis on the Beats and post-Beats, including Allen Ginsberg, Charles Bukowski, Robert Creeley, Ntozake Shange, Jim Carroll, William Burroughs, Amiri Baraka, and Anne Waldman, among others.

The use of archival footage gives *Comic Book Confidential* a wider scope than Mann's previous films. While focussing on the development of the medium over the past fifty-five years, the film touches on the key events of American history that ran parallel with that development.

For example, America's entry into World War II led to the enlistment of the superheroes in the propaganda effort, as well as the creation of others (Jack Kirby's Captain America) specifically for that purpose. In the Fifties, comic books were blamed as the cause of juvenile delinquency, as rock and roll would later be. This led to Congressional investigation which echoed other witch hunts of the era. The main target was William Gaines's line of EC comics *(Tales from the Crypt, Two-Fisted Tales),* which were accused of being excessively violent. The industry was forced to censor itself, and Gaines had to fold all of his books, with the exception of the influential *Mad* magazine.

The repressed returned with a vengeance in the Sixties, not only in the work of underground artists such as Robert Crumb, who felt obliged to commit to paper every perversion their febrile minds could come up with, but also in other media (Stephen King and George Romero have often acknowledged the influence of EC comics on their work). The retrenchment of the life-style-oriented Seventies is represented by the ultimate consumer, Zippy the Pinhead, whose creator, Bill Griffith, confesses to the serious satirical intent behind Zippy's seemingly innocuous non sequiturs.

For the Eighties, we have some of the artists associated with the postpunk graphics magazine *RAW*, including Art Spiegelman (*Maus*), Charles Burns (*Big Baby*), and the hard core politico Sue Coe. Mann features another group of artists who specialize in portraying the quotidian, such as Jaime Hernandez (*Love and Rockets*), Harvey Pekar (*American Splendor*), and the incomparable Lynda Barry.

Mann covers this expanse of history well, although sometimes rather cursorily. Adapting a strategy from *Poetry in Motion*, Mann has the artists read their own work. In addition to these readings and interviews, he keeps the film moving with a lively use of Filmograph animation and a well-chosen musical accompaniment.

This is not to say that the film doesn't have its problems. Some momentum is lost when the historical line of the narrative reaches the present. At this point the film just seems to present one artist after another, with a somewhat arbitrary choice of artists. While Mann commendably has Shary Flenniken talk about the role women have played in the industry, I would have liked to have seen a black artist—say, Denys Cowan—describe typical experiences of cartoonists. Along similar lines, aficionados will be annoyed at the inevitable exclusion of some of their favorites. Nevertheless, Mann deserves credit for providing a fascinating survey of this often despised art form.

LOS ANGELES TIMES, 6/23/89, Calendar/ p. 12, Charles Solomon

For most of its 56-year history, the comic book has been treated as an unloved stepchild by critics of the graphic arts and literature.

Ron Mann's "Comic Book Confidential," is the first documentary feature on the subject. Anyone who is interested in the comics should plan to see it, but anyone who knows much about them will probably be disappointed by its lack of depth.

"Confidential" includes interviews with artists representing the superhero genre (Will Eisner, Jack Kirby), the underground "comix" of the late '60s and early '70s (R. Crumb and Gilbert Shelton) and contemporary graphic novels (Frank Miller and Art Spiegelman). But these artists really don't get a chance to say anthing about their work; instead, Mann has them read pages of their comics as the camera pans slowly over the panels, a device that quickly cloys.

Although he has assembled an impressive array of comic book talent, Mann neglects some of the most important names in the medium: Bob Kane, who wrote and drew the first Batman comic; Joel Seigel and Jerry Shuster, the co-creators of Superman. No mention is made of Carl Barks, who devised the adventures of Uncle Scrooge, Donald Duck et al., or of the late Bob Montana, the originator of the Archie series. But the film does include Lynda Barry (Ernie Pook), Sherry Flenniken (Trots and Bonnie) and Bill Griffith (Zippy, the Pinhead), who draw comic strips, not comic books.

One of the key events in the history of the comics was the national clean-up campaign led by Frederic Wertham, which culminated in hearings by a Senate subcommittee on juvenile delinquency in 1954. Some "Reefer Madness"-style scare footage of adolescent boys reading comic books, then stabbing tree limbs with their pocket knives looks hilariously *outré* in 1989. But Mann ignores the questions of sex, sexism, violence and racism in comic books, which are being raised again today.

"Confidential" offers some truly memorable images: Crumb and Shelton at work in San Francisco during the heyday of Haight-Ashbury; Spiegelman describing how Maus reflects his relationship with his father; Eisner shyly confessing that he always regarded The Spirit as a significant work, but could never admit it to anyone.

These moments seem few and far between in a very slow 90-minute film. Mann devotes far too much time to cheesy animation of cut-out figures and montages of comic book covers set to inane songs. At a time when a record number of films based on the comics are in production, he fails to explore the ties between comic books and film making (animated and live action).

As it's the only documentary on the subject, "Comic Book Confidential" (Times-rated: Mature for language and drug references) is perforce the best documentary on the subject. But people who want to know more about comic books will find that almost any issue of The Comics Journal contains more information—and doesn't bore them with those silly montages.

MONTHLY FILM BULLETIN, 12/89, p. 360, Kim Newman

Having tackled jazz in *Imagine the Sound* and performance poetry in *Poetry in Motion,* Ron Mann claims to be completing here "a trilogy of feature-length documentaries about North American cultural history, all focusing on new waves of artistic expression". The demands of the subject matter, at once visually kinetic and frame-frozen, are more subtly difficult than his previous topics, which were essentially performance-based. Without succumbing to the lure of full animation, Mann attempts to recreate the impact of comic-book stories, with the original creators reading the speech balloons while the frames are shuffled creatively on and off the screen. One or two of these mini-movies really click—Harvey Pekar's hyper-realistic tale of a compulsive jazz record collector, Charles Burns' surreal horror story about the Big Baby and the sinister neighbours—but others, like Lynda Barry's funny piece about sex education, are little more than illustrated readings.

The film avoids the art-documentary talking heads syndrome by putting the comic images on the screen and pulling in appropriate snippets of popular music, progressing from swing and doo-wop to illustrate the patriotic spirit of WW II comics, epitomised by Jack Kirby's Captain America, through to rock 'n' roll for the 50s (when McCarthy- style commissions attacked the wave of horror comics spearheaded by William M. Gaines' classic *Tales from the Crypt*), and "I Had too Much to Dream Last Night" weirdness for the Haight-Ashbury 'underground comix' scene of the late 60s. The approach is roughly chronological, deftly interweaving straight historical 'what I was trying to do' anecdotes with a sub-theme about the various attempts by government or moral authorities to censor, repress or marginalise comics. The implication of Gaines' works, which include an anti-racist space opera that aroused censorial ire, is taken up by committed political comic creators like Spain Rodriguez (*Trashman*) and Sue Coe (*How to Commit Suicide in South Africa*), who admit a subversive, propagandist intent.

Gaines recalls his father's role in inventing the comic book in the early 30s by spinning off from the 'talking animal' strips of the Sunday supplements; superheroes arrive on the scene in the late 30s, and are discussed by Jack Kirby (but not, strangely enough, by Bob Kane or any other survivors from the early days of Superman and Batman). Will Eisner steps in to talk about his *film noir*-influenced Spirit, and Gaines returns to recount the struggles the horror titles of the 50s went through before their suppression, which came about with the introduction of a comics code by which the publishers themselves regulated their product and drove Gaines out of the business. Harvey Kurtzman, who worked with Gaines, talks about *MAD* magazine and then pops up later as "the godfather of underground comix"; Stan Lee and Frank Miller claim to have revitalised mainstream comics with their 'realistic' revisions of the superhero, introducing Spider Man, a hero with everyday problems, and the Dark Knight, a vigilante rereading of the Batman character; Robert Crumb (*Fritz the Cat, Mr. Natural*), Victor Moscoso, Gilbert Shelton (*The Fabulous Furry Freak Brothers*) and Dan O'Neill recall a lengthy attempt to sue him for defiling Mickey Mouse in *Air Pirates*. And current practitioners like Art Spiegelman (*Maus*), Shary Flenniken (*Toots and Bonnie*), Jaime Hernandez (*Love and Rockets*), Françoise Mouly (*Raw*) and Bill Griffith (*Zippy the Pinhead*) talk about their work.

Mann rarely steps in to pass comment, but much of his material throws up inescapable associations. 50s newsreel footage from an anti-comics documentary is at once amusing and chilling, with a concerned narrator suggesting that *Tales from the Crypt* leads children into juvenile delinquency and violence, while mass comic-burning ceremonies resonate eerily with Art Spiegelman's later descriptions of his work on *Maus*, a comic dealing with the rise of Nazism. Less stressed is the irony of Robert Crumb rebelling against designing greetings cards by dropping out, going to San Francisco, drawing underground comics and creating, in the "Keep on Truckin" logo, one of the key merchandising images of the twentieth century. Although the breadth of scope means that the film cannot go deeply into any one type of comic, *Comic Book Confidential* is a consistently watchable, intellectually lively introduction to its subject.

NEW YORK POST, 6/14/89, p. 31, Jami Bernard

The word "documentary" has all the appeal of a trip to the mortuary, but occasionally one comes along that is as entertaining as a movie with, you know, plot and stuff. "Comic Book Confidential," an overview of the American comics scene, has all the wacky vibrancy of its subject and manages to satisfy the discriminating aficionado while enlightening those who think comics means Archie.

Directed by Ron Mann, who has previously explored such cultural fringes as jazz and performance poetry, "Comic Book Confidential" uses the driving theme of censorship to examine the lives and work of 22 of the industry's big guns. No, not everyone is included, but it is a fair cross-section of people from William M. Gaines, the publisher of the satirical Mad Magazine (the bane of many a parent), to the Winesburg, Ohio-esque musings of Harvey Pekar, who writes a comic book based on his own mundane life.

There are superheroes, pinheads and persecuted mice, and the men and women—some of them incredibly geeky looking, others mild and unpretentious, and a new crop who are cooler than thou—who drew them out of thin air.

Best of all, Mann manages—with lively cut-out animation, a snappy score and the Rorschach-like device of having the cartoonists read their work aloud—to show what a complicated and subtle art form comics can be.

Throughout the documentary are snippets of '50s ultra-scare TV, the kind in which an authority figure rails mightily against the dangers of comics. To illustrate, he shows a group of children reading these spawn of the devil. Within moments, the children begin gouging tree bark with pocketknives and pounding rocks together. Comic books, you see, turn children into monsters.

These monsters grew up to become, in many cases, the very people who are giving comics the exciting, sophisticated edge they have today. For every superhero, there is a "Love and Rockets," and for every Archie, there is Lynda Barry with a cynical take on modern relationships. The one-gag funny has given way to highly stylized graphic novels.

The world of comics has often been dogged by controversy and threats of censorship. Some of that controversy is not covered in "Comic Book Confidential"—things such as creators rights and just who is responsible for what over at collaborative Marvel—but the film does make the point that comics has been a lightning rod for controversy and the perfect medium for combating it.

From the comics-world pantheon appear some of the *real* superheroes of the art: Jack Kirby, who gave much of his soul to Marvel, raises a frail voice to dramatize Captain America for the camera; Will Eisner claims he was inept as a painter and inept as a writer, but when he brought those talents together to create The Spirit, "I came out with an eptitude."

Gaines, his snowy beard flowing, recalls with a mixture of bitterness and irony how he began publishing Mad to escape the insanity of the 1950s Comics Code, the kind of organization that in another era would have whited out portions of the Sistine Chapel. Gaines' famous, gory "Tales From the Crypt" died a horrible death at the hands of the code, which arbitrarily outlawed the words "horror," "terror" and "weird."

From the grave of "Crypt" rose the phoenix of Mad magazine, whose parodies of pop culture galvanized a generation bored with bland. "Mad created the same crazy fear that the Marx Brothers created in their day," say Harvey Kurtzman, Mad's creator and first editor. "It was outrageous and audacious."

R. Crumb, who teamed up with other "lost souls" in Haight-Ashbury to help create the pulsating underground comix sense of the late '60s, tells how he gave up making greeting cards once and for all: "I could not do another card." But, as his famous cartoon goes, he kept on truckin'.

Dan O'Neill discusses his protracted lawsuit with Disney while in the background a couple of underclad females play pool, certainly a fantasy shared by the predominantly male-adolescent comic fans. O'Neill lost the suit over his portrayal of a horny Mickey Mouse, but the publicity helped spotlight the comics cause. "If you're going down in flames, hit something big," he says.

Over the years, comics have both reflected and advanced the culture. "In my secret studio, I fantasized I was working on a primitive art form," admits Eisner shyly. "Comic Book Confidential" shows just how prescient he was.

NEWSDAY, 6/14/89, Part II/p. 5, Lynn Darling

There's always been something innately subversive about the comics. From the beginning, 50 years ago, they have held up a cracked mirror to the times and reflected a telling, if often thoroughly warped, image of contemporary values.

Their disruptive potential didn't escape notice for long: The documentary "Comic Book Confidential" begins with TV footage from the 1950s in which one would-be guardian of the public morals rants on about why there ought to be law against the comics, charging them with perverting the morals of the country's youth.

In fact, a congressional investigation in the 1950s and increasingly hysterical fulminations from the usual bluenoses did result in self-imposed censorship on the part of the industry: Comic books like "Tales From the Crypt" were replaced by ones celebrating "Cowboy Love." But not for long: Ever since the 1960s, when unabashedly twisted artists like R. Crumb felt free to explode every taboo they could put their pens to, the comic book has become an increasingy pointed and expressive medium for the darker visions abroad in the land.

Using interviews, jazzy collages of the comics themselves and sequences in which the artists give voice to their characters' dialogue, director Ron Mann presents a fast-paced overview of the history of comics and the people attracted to the art form. "Someone has to stand outside and tell you what's going on—it's a dirty job, but someone has to do it," observes Bill Griffith, creator of the kitschy anti-hero Zippy. And as this easygoing documentary makes clear, it's a job that attracts an engagingly eccentric cast of farsighted volunteers.

"I always felt I was involved in a literary form," says Will Eisner, creator of "The Spirit." Others see their contributions in less exalted terms. "We were getting grosser and grosser, no doubt about it," Bill Gaines says about the "Crypt" books, in which a typical storyline might be, "Guy murders his wife and eats her."

Gaines went on to publish Mad magazine, thereby doing his bit to introduce several generations to the pleasures of crude satire and to set the stage for the surrealistic wildness of the underground comics that followed.

Mann does a fine job of rescuing these and other efforts from the dustbin of the trivial, pointing out their social significance without becoming ponderous or losing sight of the breezy nature of the subject matter.

But the director gives fairly short shrift to more recent developments in the world of comics. Mann pays attention to the efforts of social satirists like Lynda Barry, and to the haunting creations of Art Spiegelman, whose magazine RAW ("the graphic magazine that lost its faith in nihilism") and novel "Maus" have pushed the frontier in dazzling directions. But the amount of time he devotes to them is frustratingly short. These are minds and points of view worth exploring in depth, but we're confined to a perspective almost as two-dimensional as the frames in which this art form flourishes.

VILLAGE VOICE, 6/20/89, p. 90, Georgia Brown

Any temptation to put down *Star Trek* [see Brown's review] as comic book-level entertainment ought to be resisted. See Ron Mann's *Comic Book Confidential* if you need reminding that comics can be a lot wittier, ranker, and just generally more sophisticated. At least you'll admit that Mann's interviewees—22 artists from Will Eisner to our own Lynda Barry—are. Aficionados, though, may find Mann's survey short on substance and graphic stimulation.

Mann frames and interweaves his pedestrian, if evocative, cultural history with clips from heavy-handed cautionary tracts from the '50s warning about the corruptions of comic consumption. There's one deliciously dotty scene in which four boys steal away to the woods to indulge in the latest issues. As they read, the blood begins to rise. (A sinister narrator warns how a kid can become "a mass of jangled nerves before he's through.") While one boy stabs at a tree trunk with his jackknife, another budding mass murderer picks up a good-sized rock and looks around for a head to bash in. *Comic Book Confidential*'s point, which few would dispute, is that comics have always been under "worried" attack (read Joe Queenan's lame exposé in *The New York Times Magazine* a few weeks ago), and that exceptional spirits keep on drawing them.

As a stab at style, the movie's transitions are announced with such comic headlines as "In the Beginning," "Meanwhile," "The Plot Thickens." In the very Beginning, apparently, was William M. Gaines's father, who in 1933—according to chip-off-the-enterprising-block—folded a newspaper sheet into quarters and sold the books for a dime. (Gaines Jr. founded EC [Entertaining Comic] and, later, *Mad*.) In 1938, *Superman* appeared, followed by the likes of *Captain Marvel, Wonder Woman, Batman*. Will Eisner created *The Spirit* in the early '40s, and one of the movie's fairly rare visual treats—despite its visual subject—is seeing some of Eisner's exquisite frames blown up.

On to the '50s. As "the guys in the barracks" settled into civilian life, they needed something to read. Gaines and Al Feldstein at EC obliged with "grosser and grosser" material: "What we were doing was writing up to our readers." (A Feldstein sample: "Guy murders own wife and eats her—to get rid of the evidence.") In 1954 the Kefauver hearings on juvenile delinquency resulted in formation of the puritanical Comic Code (clips of censors brushing whiteout over offending drawing). Gaines recalls that "all the good words," like *horror, terror,* and *weird*, became taboo. After the code, comics appeared with such titles as *Nature Boy, Cowboy Love,* and *Psychoanalysis*. Thus *Mad* was born.

Although superheroes were subsequently rejuvenated, notably by Stan Lee, the '60s gave rise to a thriving comic underground. R. Crumb recalls how he gave up designing greeting cards in Cleveland and journeyed to Haight-Ashbury. (Victor Moscoso: "The psychedelic poster was to the comics what the Kingston Trio was to Bob Dylan.")

From here on, Mann zeros in on the cool comics, the exceptional graphic books like Art Spiegelman and Françoise Mouly's *Raw*, and pretty much ignores the stuff kids are buying in the corner candy store. He begins showing intact segments of strips, mini-narratives usually read by their creators, such as Bill Griffith, Harvey Pekar, Jaime Hernandez, Charles Burns. Shary Flenniken does a *Trots and Bonnie* episode, "The Execution of Elrod" (capital punishment by toaster in a wading pool). One of the film's few laughs comes when Lynda Barry reads "Tina's Special Day," about the time when hopeful Tina finally "found a red flower in her underpants."

Also reviewed in:
NEW REPUBLIC, 7/17 & 24/89, p. 24, Stanley Kauffmann
NEW YORK TIMES, 6/14/89, p. C19, Caryn James
WASHINGTON POST, 8/18/89, p. D7, Rita Kempley
WASHINGTON POST, 8/18/89, Weekend/p. 37, Desson Howe

COMING OUT

A Counterproductions, Inc. film. *Director:* Susan Bell and Ted Reed. *Director of Cinematography:* Ted Reed, John Baynard, and Lowry Stewart. *Editor:* Ted Reed. *Running time:* 63 minutes. *MPAA Rating:* Not Rated.

VILLAGE VOICE, 3/21/89, p. 64, Renee Tajima

Ted Reed and Susan Bell use cinema vérité—the quintessential '60s-era cultural weapon for exposing the Establishment—in *Coming Out*, their humorous tribute to Reagan youth in '80s society. The movie follows the elaborate preparations for a debutante cotillion, a highborn tradition that's been appropriated by the nouveau classes. *Coming Out* expresses vérité's contradiction within the image but lacks the potent irony of such masters of the style as Leacock and the Maysles.

Also reviewed in:
NEW YORK TIMES, 3/19/89, p. 60, Vincent Canby

COMMUNION

A New Line Cinema release of a Pheasantry Films production in association with Allied Vision Ltd. and The Picture Property Company. *Executive Producer:* Paul Redshaw. *Producer:* Philippe Mora, Whitley Strieber, and Dan Allingham. *Director:* Philippe Mora. *Screenplay (based on his book):* Whitley Strieber. *Director of Photography:* Louis Irving. *Editor:* Lee Smith. *Music:* Eric Clapton and Allan Zavod. *Sound:* Ed White. *Production Designer:* Linda Pearl. *Art Director:* Dena Roth. *Set Dresser:* Danielle Simpson. *Special Visual Effects:* Michael McCracken. *Costumes:* Malissa Daniel. *Make-up:* Michelle Buhler. *Running time:* 107 minutes. *MPAA Rating:* R.

CAST: Christopher Walken (Whitley); Lindsay Crouse (Anne); Joel Carlson (Andrew); Frances Sternhagen (Dr. Janet Duffy); Andreas Katsulas (Alex); Territ Hanauer (Sara); Basil Hoffman (Dr. Freidman); John Dennis Johnston (Fireman); Dee Dee Rescher (Mrs. Greenberg); Aileen Fitzpatrick (Mother #1); R.J. Miller (Father #1); Holly Fields (Praying Mantis Girl); Paula Shaw (Woman from Apartment); Juliet Sorcey (2nd Grade Girl); Kate Stern (Woman on Bus); Johnny Dark (Lab Tech); Irene Forrest (Sally); Vince McKewin (Bob); Sally Kemp (Laurie); Maggie Egan (Nancy); Paul Clemens (Patrick); Andrew Magarian (Man in Hallway); Madeleine Mora (Baby Girl).

LOS ANGELES TIMES, 11/10/89, Calendar/p. 10, Kevin Thomas

"Communion," a serious, often persuasive attempt to dramatize writer Whitley Strieber's purported contact with aliens, affords Christopher Walken his showiest role to date.

As the life-loving, happily married Strieber, Walken is a prankish, playful charmer whose wife Anne (Lindsay Crouse) laughs a great deal but is in fact a solid, sensible type. They're smart enough to know they have it all, including an adored small son Andrew (Joel Carlson) and a chic Manhattan apartment.

They also have a large, equally chic cabin in the mountains. On a weekend in October, 1985, Strieber, his son and another couple (Andreas Katsulas, Terri Hanauer) are awakened by a blinding light. In short order Strieber seems to be hallucinating and sinking into paranoia. A calm, dedicated parapsychologist (Frances Sternhagen) tries to help, but he tends to resist her.

Under the assured, easy direction of Philippe Mora, working from Strieber's adaptation of his own best seller, Walken dazzles, giving us an intelligent, talented man caught in a nightmare and fearing for his sanity. Crouse matches him as a strong woman determined to put up a ferocious fight to help her husband and save their marriage. Mora and his stars take "Communion" far above standard sci-fi schlock, yet the film stumbles in its presentation of the aliens.

Even those open to the possibility that Strieber did have a series of close encounters of the third kind with a bunch of jolly blue gnomes and some spindly, doe-like creatures with Keane eyes may have a problem with the literalness with which these aliens are presented. They seem right out of the pages of the National Enquirer. Clearly, Mora means to be faithful to Strieber, but a more ethereal approach to the non-humans might have been more effective.

Even so, "Communion," a most handsome production, does take us on an incredible journey that comes full circle in satisfying fashion. And Walken and Crouse are terrific.

NEW YORK POST, 11/10/89, p. 29, Jami Bernard

The story of a frenzied novelist who has a series of close encounters of the third kind,

"Communion" is one big brassy paeon to writer's block. It's stylish, creepy, mystifying and, while not really very good, it's a delightful read, like a trashy novel.

And speaking of novels, the movie is based on the bestseller of the same name, the supposedly true experiences of writer Whitley Strieber, who made the talk show circuit with his tale of curious aliens who repeatedly abducted him from his country home, probed him in a sort of intellectual sense but in other senses as well (shrink alert!), trained bright lights on him, and never quite explained what they were after.

Neither does the movie. In being faithful to Strieber's experiences, the lack of resolution is the movie's weakest link. Theories are bandied about, ranging from, "It is narcissistic to think we are alone in the universe," to the possibility that Strieber saw what the Star Trek crew failed to see in "The Final Frontier"—namely, God itself.

Strieber enlisted his friend, director Philippe Mora, to produce and direct—which explains all the wolf imagery (Mora directed the two "Howling" sequels).

Christopher Walken plays Whitley Strieber, which is an interesting choice right away, since Walken, despite his cat's-feet grace, cannot walk a straight line acting wise. His novelist is an odd combination of self-indulgent eccentricity (he wears a hat to write and videotapes himself at the computer keyboard) and banal yuppiedom (he cooks duck for the family dinner, is dressed by Perry Ellis, and is constantly stymied by an elaborate security alarm system).

Why the aliens would choose Whitley is a mystery. But then, judging by the members of an alien-rape-victim support group that Whitley joins, the visitors from outer space are only interested in upscale white people.

With the stiff, angry Lindsay Crouse (she's been hanging around her husband, David Mamet, too long) as Whitley's wife, Anne, and Joel Carlson as their young son, Andrew, the movie creates a happy modern New York family. They laugh together, brunch together, spend weekends at their country cottage.

Their normalcy is quickly unbalanced by the arrival of the aliens—short, squat, blue ones and tall, slender, big-eyed ones. Andrew seems to see them in his dreams, and a couple of spooked houseguests sense their presence, but it is Whitley who gets the rectal probe.

Later, his memory prodded by children's Halloween masks and by the pygmy statues in the exotically lavish home of his shrink (Frances Sternhagen, concerned and underused), Whitley recalls the alien bacchanal.

Is Whitley going crazy? Is his marriage on the rocks? Does he have the courage to face the "little blue doctors," as his son calls the aliens? And will he ever learn the correct code for his burglar alarm system?

One of the women in the screening room where I saw this told me she is a real-life member of that support group that Whitley joined. I don't know if her little friends were around, but I backed away from her—all I need is a rectal probe by spacemen while I'm working.

Strieber is either a master of self-promotion or self-deception. The press notes inform us that he and his terrorized family still reside in the country cabin where the aliens hung out. His ghostly, behind-the-scenes presence may be part and parcel of the movie, but you'll go crazy trying to figure out if it's true or if it's hokum.

My advice is to watch and enjoy it as you would any science-fiction movie. It doesn't have the big pay-off of a "Close Encounters" or an "E.T.," but it nicely captures the horrors of the ordinary—that stuffed bear in the closet, the hint of a shadow behind a door.

And it makes a nice bedtime ghost story for yuppies as they turn off their pasta makers, froth the milk for one last cappuccino, and procrastinate on finishing their screenplays.

NEWSDAY, 11/10/89, Part III/p. 7, Terry Kelleher

Was he dreaming or did extraterrestrials actually pay repeated calls on author Whitley Strieber?

Whether visitations or mere hallucinations, there were definitely strange goings-on in his head and household. And the reason for this outbreak of weirdness is clear from the movie version of Strieber's bestseller "Communion": an overabundance of scary art in his life.

Poor Strieber (Christopher Walken) wakes up in the middle of the night, convinced that aliens are stealing into his bedroom and sticking needles in his noggin. Is it any wonder when his Manhattan apartment is filled with odd *objects* to haunt his slumbers?

After his wife (Lindsay Crouse) persuades Strieber to seek professional counseling, the psychiatrist (Frances Sternhagen) suggests he submit to hypnosis—not in her office but in her sculpture-crammed duplex. With the shrink's outerspace collection to put him in the mood,

Strieber feels his eyelids growing heavy, heavy, and soon relives his terrifying abduction by aliens bent on playing biology lab with his body.

Late in the movie, when Strieber and spouse have the leisure for a reflective discussion of their otherworldly encounters, director Philippe Mora poses them before large abstract paintings at the Whitney Museum. Next thing you know, they're on the roof of their apartment building, scanning the night sky for spaceships. The obvious explanation: They're having scary-art flashbacks.

Linda Pearl's production design notwithstanding, "Communion" is less a work of art than a document of personal history. Strieber arranged financing for the film, wrote the script himself and handpicked his friend Mora to make sure his experiences would be accurately represented on screen. (Perhaps the director's chief qualification is that he's one of 19 visitors to have witnessed, or imagined, something unearthly in Strieber's upstate cabin.)

With "The Beast Within" and "Howling II and III" among his credits, Mora might be expected to turn "Communion" into a horror show. Early on, however, the movie gives signs of being a comparatively restrained psychological thriller. The most effective scene comes at a Halloween party, where Strieber nearly jumps out of his skin at the sight of a child's mask. "I was frightened," he explains, with a simplicity that's frightening.

But once the hypnosis begins and we start seeing a lot of the aliens, we're inclined to wish they'd go back where they came from. The majority are short, pudgy and blue. Strieber's 7-year-old son (Joel Carson), who seems to share his visions, calls them "the little blue doctors," though they look more like little blue monks. A few have elongated white faces and almond-shaped black eyes, like the creature on the cover of the "Communion" paperback. At one point they subject the earthling to a "rectal probe" with a device resembling a lounge singer's microphone. But later they make nice and invite him to a dance party, sort of an "American Bandstand" for nerdy nonhumans. I give it a 70; it's more pleasant than an invasive medical procedure.

Strange dudes are a specialty of Walken's, but his Strieber is too off-center from the outset. Even before he starts consorting with aliens, you suspect his roots are on another planet. He's also surprisingly inarticulate for a successful novelist, even one suffering from writer's block (until the little blue docs inject him with literary inspiration).

Strieber has made a lot of money from "Communion" and a follow-up book, "Transformation." If he invests his movie profits in art, this nightmare may never end.

VILLAGE VOICE, 11/14/89, p. 119, Gary Giddins

It may have been possible for a clever filmmaker to concoct a comedy or even a suspense thriller out of his bestseller *Communion*, but with Strieber himself writing and producing and an old friend, Philippe Mora, the hack director behind *Howling II* and *III*, directing, there was no chance. Strieber has sold five million or so books detailing his honest-to-God kidnapping by tiny little black, rubbery-faced aliens in jogging suits, who stripped him naked, sat him in a vat filled with ominous alien mist, and performed a rectal probe. Permit me my cynicism. I know if I were an alien, I'd have done my research the Nixon way—simply break into a proctologist's office in dead of night and steal his records. Of course, the aliens may have valued the hands-on experience more than the information, and it is odd that Strieber is absolutely convinced that they very specifically wanted his ass, as it were.

What distinguishes, if that's not too highfalutin a word, Strieber from other loonies is that he's a novelist and goes around insisting, "Hey, I didn't believe it either!" Such sincerity! Such courage in accepting the inevitable truth! According to the movie, his response to the invasion was to scream at his wife and see a shrink. Frances Sternhagen, the divine Frances Sternhagen, whose current performance in *Driving Miss Daisy* should have all aliens lining up at her door, plays Dr. Janet Duffy, who analyzes her patients in an office roughly the size of a football field, complete with a roaring fireplace and a small population of pygmy-sized statues. Her method is hypnotism, which she accomplishes faster than you can say *drowsy*; if that doesn't work she suggests group. She just happens to have a group that consists exclusively of people who were abducted and intimately probed by the same aliens. What a coincidence!

The movie isn't merely stupid; it's lifeless. Christopher Walken, with his hair standing at attention, plays Strieber as the kind of writer who wears funny hats and headphones and videotapes himself in the throes of creation. Before the aliens came, he and his wife (played, no, emoted by Lindsay Crouse) were one happy couple. They giggle as incessantly as Richard Dreyfuss on a bad day. But the aliens make Strieber testy; he even accidentally fires a gun at his wife. Unfortunately, there's no place for this story to go. The aliens aren't particularly personable or highly motivated. The more earnest Walken becomes (his alien-like eyes grow increasingly limpid), the more ridiculous his search for an explanation. The shrink didn't to him any good, so he does the next best thing—cuts a deal with a publisher. The movie ends with Strieber back in the throes of creation, bounding into the bedroom to read his wife passages from his new book, just like the old days. The idea of writing as purgative analysis was popular among the beats 30 years ago. Of course, the difference is that Kerouac had something on his mind. Strieber doesn't have a mind—the aliens got it when they did that rectal probe.

Also reviewed in:
NEW YORK TIMES, 11/10/89, p. C8, Janet Maslin
VARIETY, 5/10-16/89, p. 24
WASHINGTON POST, 11/11/89, p. C5, Hal Hinson

COMRADES

A Gavin Film release of a Skreba Productions film in association with The National Film Finance Corporation, Film Four International, and Curzon Film Distributors. *Producer:* Simon Relph. *Director:* Bill Douglas. *Screenplay:* Bill Douglas. *Director of Photography:* Gale Tattersall. *Editor:* Mick Audsley. *Music:* Hans Werner Henze and David Graham. *Sound:* Clive Winter. *Sound Editor:* Alan Bell, Richard Dunford, and Jupiter Sen. *Production Designer:* Michael Pickwoad. *Art Director:* Henry Harris. *Costumes:* Doreen Watkinson. *Make-up:* Elaine Carew. *Stunt Coordinator:* Peter Armstrong. *Running time:* 180 minutes. *MPAA Rating:* Not rated.

CAST: Robin Soans (George Loveless); William Gaminara (James Loveless); Philip Davis (Young Stanfield); Stephen Bateman (Old Tom Stanfield); Keith Allen (James Hammett); Patrick Field (John Hammett); Jeremy Flynn (Brine); Robert Stephens (Frampton); Michael Hordern (Mr. Pitt); Freddie Jones (Vicar); Barbara Windsor (Mrs. Wetham); Murray Melvin (Clerk); Imelda Staunton (Betsy Loveless); Amber Wilkinson (Hetty Loveless); Katy Behean (Sarah Loveless); Sandra Voe (Diana Stanfield); Valerie Whittington (Elvi Stanfield); Harriet Doyle (Charity Stanfield); Heather Page (Bridget Hammett); Patricia Healey (Mrs. Brine); Shane Down (Joseph Brine); Joanna David (Mrs. Frampton); Trevor Ainsley and Malcolm Terris (Gentlemen Farmers); Dave Atkins (Mr. Frampton's Foreman); Collette Barker (Frampton's Servant Girl); Michael Clark (Sailor); Alex McCrindle (Jailor); Jack Chissick (Policeman); Sarah Reed (Blonde Girl); Nicola Hayward (Dark Girl); Mark Brown (Legg); Sophie Randall and Emma Tuck (Legg's Children); John Holman and Jan Holman (Gypsy Band); Bevan James (Escapologist); John Lee (Juggler); Vanessa Redgrave (Mrs. Carlyle); James Fox (Norfolk); Arthur Dignam (Fop); John Hargreaves (Convict); Simon Parsonage (Charlie); Charles Yunipingu (Lone Aboriginal); Simon Landis (Flower); Anna Volska (Woman in White); Brian McDermott (Auctioneer); Shane Briant (Official); Tim Eliot (Registrar); David Netheim (Fop's Officer); Ralph Cotterill (Bertie the Guard); David McWilliams (Digger); Lynette Curran (Prostitute); Alex Norton (Lanternist/Sergeant Bell/ Diorama Showman/Laughing Cavalier/Mr. Wetham/Wollaston/Ranger/Tramp/Sea Captain/McCallum/ Silhouettist/Mad Photographer/Usher/Witch).

MONTHLY FILM BULLETIN, 9/87, p. 259, David Wilson

Dorset, the early 1830s. After witnessing the repression of an outbreak of machine-breaking by farm labourers discontented with their poor wages, an itinerant lanternist arrives in the village of Tolpuddle. Here the farm workers and their families can barely make ends meet on the wages paid them by local landowner Frampton. When their wages are further reduced after the harvest festival, one of the labourers—Methodist lay preacher George Loveless—travels to Dorchester where, after a chance encounter with Frampton, he sees a sympathetic magistrate, Pitt. With his brother James and several others, George has set up a local Friendly Society lodge, whose members are admitted under an oath of secrecy. One of them is a lackey of Frampton's. George asks the local vicar to intercede on the men's behalf, and at a meeting at Frampton's house they are promised a better deal. In fact, their wages are further reduced. The men refuse to work, and six of them—George and James Loveless, Brine, Old Tom Stanfield and his son, and James Hammett, who is mistaken for his carpenter brother John—are arrested and charged with administering unlawful oaths. Despite Pitt's intervention, they are tried and sentenced to seven years' transportation to Australia. A London-Dorchester Committee, of which Pitt is a leading member, is set up to lobby for the men's release and raise funds for their families. But the six men are hurriedly shipped to Australia. Here, George is ordered to walk the three hundred miles to his work. In the outback, he meets and befriends a runaway boy convict, Charlie, who robs him. Brine is sent to work in a stone-breaking chain-gang, whose members eventually wreak a deadly revenge on their sadistic overseer. Old Stanfield works as a servant to the Governor of New South Wales, with whom Charlie also finds brief employment. After he is dismissed by the Governor, Charlie sends young Stanfield on the wrong track as he journeys to visit his father. James Loveless meanwhile works on a sheep ranch for a rich widow, Mrs. Carlyle, who unsuccessfully tries to persuade him to stay after revealing that she has withheld from him a letter from George with the news that the men have been pardoned. The Loveless brothers, the Stanfields and Brine are finally reunited. But James Hammett has been sold at auction to a fop, who uses him and other men to shunt his private railway carriage. Charlie, who has been abducted by the fop, is in the carriage with him when James engineers a crash. Injured, the fop later arranges for James to be transported to the penal settlement on Norfolk Island. In London, the London-Dorchester Commitee celebrates the return of five of the Tolpuddle Martyrs (James Hammett is released a year later) with a presentation on stage, orchestrated by the lanternist and chaired by Pitt. George Loveless delivers a speech calling on the working classes to unite.

Comrades is at its primary level a narrative account of the Tolpuddle Martyrs, the six Dorset farm labourers who, in 1834, after they had formed what was in effect a trade union branch, were sentenced to be transported to Australia under a catch-all law which penalised the administering of "unlawful oaths". The Tolpuddle men, as the appellation "Martyrs" reveals, have attained iconic status in British labour history, and the film celebrates their act and relates the circumstances of their exemplary punishment with due respect. But for all its historical accuracy, which extends to the use of authentic locations, *Comrades* is less a historical film than a film *about* history. It tells its story conventionally, in linear progression (if not always with clarity); but simultaneously it invites those who watch it to consider what they see and how they perceive it. It is, essentially, a film about seeing: about light and illumination, projection and perception. "What you offer, sir, is illusion", George Loveless says to a Diorama showman he meets in Dorchester. "It's the real world I'd like to see. In our short lives...we see so little". In one of the film's several playful ironies, the Diorama show is entitled "Journey through the Antipodes". And of course the central and (in a literal sense also) brilliant irony of *Comrades* is that we see it through the greatest of all illusions, the cinema.

We are alerted to this from the beginning. The film is presented as "A Lanternist's Account of the Tolpuddle Martyrs", and in various guises the lanternist appears at intervals, played in all his manifestations by the same actor. The lanternist's story begins with a full moon, which in a series of dissolves is seen to wane, immediately suggesting the aperture of a camera. There follows a visual essay in light and shadow: a coach with side lanterns; a house with lighted windows; a maid with a candle opening the door to the lanternist; two men glimpsed through a window in a silhouette of yellow light; the lanternist walking away under a yellow moon; shadows, made by artifice, cast on a wall. In effect, a history in miniature of the creation of images through light (and perhaps including an incidental tribute to Kubrick's candle-lit effects in *Barry Lyndon*). But since the cinema as we know it has sound as well as light, the lanternist, denied his show of silent images, remonstrates with a show of sound—watched by a wide-eyed child.

This sequence, in narrative terms apparently marginal, is the key to Bill Douglas' extraordinary film. At first sight, *Comrades* seems an astonishing departure for a filmmaker previously known for the intimist autobiographical trilogy which began with *My Childhood*. Another illusion. One of the distinctive qualities of Douglas' trilogy was that, within their small canvas, the films allowed time—indeed insisted on it—to linger on a detail: the spectator was invited to gaze at the contours of an object or a human face in close-up, or to contemplate a landscape in long shot. This is rare in any cinema, not least (if not particularly) in British cinema. But Douglas shares with filmmakers like Dovzhenko and Ozu, Tarkovsky and Angelopoulos, the will to ask his audience to look—to see—as well as to watch. The Dorset sequences of *Comrades* reveal to the full this painterly aspect of his cinema. The camera (both lit and operated by Gale Tattersall) holds on a series of *tableaux vivants*. Within a narrative scarcely lacking in drama, there is time to contemplate a quiet domestic scene, like the breaking of bread at a family meal; or to look at—in the way we look at a pastoral painting—a yoke of horses on the brow of a field, the implements of farm labour, the chairs which a carpenter has crafted.

It may be that there are rather too many of these compositionally precise images (were those dark clouds scudding across the sky caught on the wing?), so that at times during its first half the film appears over-studied. Their effect, nevertheless, is to subvert narrative expectations, to point up the illusion of a straightforward linear account of the events at Tolpuddle. George Loveless demonstrates the point tellingly when he meets squire Frampton in a Dorchester print shop. He places a (borrowed) silver coin over the head of the infant Christ in an engraving: Frampton sees the point but does not "see" it, and after the trial he is glimpsed nervously fingering the same coin as he reflects that "It is almost as if *he* had won". A single image conveys a point both of politics and of perception.

This counterpoint of illumination and illusion is sustained by a recurring artifice. Throughout the film there are references to various optical devices of the pre-cinema era. Apart from the magic lantern and the Diorama, there is a Thaumatrope, a mezzotint photographer with his steam heliotype, a silhouette artist. The transportation to Australia is represented by a moving illustrated map animated by sound effects; and the lanternist's final theatrical presentation of the men's story includes a fleeting reference to *Ars magna lucis et umbrae*, Kircher's seventeenth-century treatise on the principles of magic-lantern projection. Set against these apparatuses, revealing their illusory purpose, are the film's images of the real world, as in the extraordinary scene at the harvest festival when the villagers are entranced by the physical grace of a sailor dancing the hornpipe; or the moment when James Loveless inadvertently destroys the photographer's heliotypes by letting in the light.

The image and its artifice are challenged by the reality of experience, of what is really seen if we look closely enough. The members of the Tolpuddle men's trade union are blindfolded during their initiation ceremony until the light is revealed to them ("Give the strangers sight"): the implication is that they are enlightened by their commitment to unite, not to accept what the Tolpuddle vicar has called "the natural order of things". In a sustained counterpoint of sound and light, Douglas moves from the gloom of the Anglican church, where this acceptance of the *status quo* is ordained, to the white-walled Methodist chapel where light streams through the windows and the prayer is for change ("Help us to stretch ourselves").

The Australian sequences, which depend more on direct narrative, slightly undermine this play of artifice and its revelation. The colourful locations seem here to announce themselves as spectacle (spectacular though they are), and there are some rather too easy ironies obtained from the portraits of colonial administrators. But if *Comrades* is not without its miscalculations, the final sequence triumphantly vindicates its confident ambition. As the Tolpuddle men are feted with theatrical pomp and circumstance, George Loveless moves to the centre of the stage to call on the working classes to unite in action. As he speaks, direct to camera, the theatre lights slowly dim until he is picked out by a single spotlight. We cannot fail to see him, and to see what he means.

NEW STATESMAN, 8/28/87, p. 16, Judith Williamson

So often films about politics seem lacking in a passion for the medium they're made in; or, conversely, a passion for cinema becomes divorced from any sense of how it might function politically. Here at last are two films [The reference is to *Good Morning Babylon*; see Williamson's review in *Film Review Annual, 1988.*] which—different as they are in both style and content—deal with the politics *of* cinema: with both its materiality and its purpose in the real world that film is at once in and about.

For film consists of light, thrown on to the screen; and just as this literal illumination must inevitably have a direction, so must the politics of its content. We are used to the apparently sourceless light of bourgeois cinema, offering us a vision of the world as if it were the only one possible; yet these films each in their way remind us that that light can be thrown differently, and can illuminate people and events that have been hidden in the shadows of conventional history.

Bill Douglas' *Comrades*, subtitled "A Lanternist's Account of the Tolpuddle Martyrs and What Became of Them", has the clear purpose of commemoration: and at a time when trade union politics are unfashionable not only on the right but on much of the left, the Tolpuddle labourers' fight to unionise in the face of wage cuts is as relevant as ever. Their story has to be told and remembered; *Comrades* not only tells it, but engages with the problems of preserving and passing on working-class stories in a culture which works to suppress them.

For there *are* problems with telling "history from below" and one which besets *Comrades* very seriously is that of style: the tale of hardship, struggle, arrest and deportation is told in the conventional realist form that we have become accustomed to in historical dramas. Maybe working people really didn't wear bright colours; nevertheless the grim greys and greens that characterise the lives of the worthy poor in movies seem so familiar that some of their impact in presenting the experience of rainy, muddy, rural poverty is blunted. Part of this style is the way the goodies all look ruggedly honest, the baddies vicious and leering; but even worse, the good men are all good and masculine, the good women all good and womanly, while the baddies contain a disproportionate number of campy, effeminate figures, from the squire's ring-laden agent to the creepy Australian landlord with his pet boy. Not only is this whole mode of representation crude, its sense of sexual politics (the very worst character has sex with his *dog*) verges on the tabloid.

Yet *Comrades* differs from conventional dramas in two ways. First, it is a narrative without a single hero and instead of being drawn into the structures of imaginary identification invited by most mainstream films, we follow the characters as onlookers. Second, this position is one we are reminded of throughout the film. A harvesting sequence begins with close-ups of the heavily exhausting, repetitive labour; shot by shot, the camera pulls out and the light falls, until from a distance we see in a golden evening glow what looks like a peaceful harvest scene, familiar from countless paintings and postcards. At this moment the film cuts to a reverse shot of the squire's family driving by in a carriage, so that this image becomes *what they see*; picturesqueness is shown to be a middle-class view of labour.

The rich also have the power to preserve their image; the Australian governor has his arrogance crisply outlined for posterity by a silhouette cutter. The poor must struggle to pass on their messages; throwing poems on scrumpled paper through prison bars. And the filmmaker must take sides: *Comrades* casts the lanternist (a succession of different characters played by the same actor) as witness, right from the opening scene where he watches the brutal suppression of a rebellion.

We next see him by night at the door of the manor; and as the squire's maid walks the length of the house, its wealthy inhabitants loom large in the giant looping shadows thrown by her candle, reminding us at once of the fluidity of light and its capacity for changing the shapes of our perceptions. Film is illusion, Douglas insists, yet it must be used; and *Comrades* ends with the solidarity committee hosting a lantern show of the Tolpuddle story where the chairman says to the presenter, "Go then, and make a union of lanternists."

NEW YORK POST, 1/13/89, p. 27, V.A. Musetto

Watching the three-hour British epic "Comrades," you're left with no doubt where director Bill Douglas stands in the worker-vs-boss struggle. The 19th-century Dorchester laborers are a pleasant, good-natured lot, struggling to keep body and soul together against overwhelming odds. When things get too tough, they gather together for a song.

The local Simon Legree is a fork-tongued tyrant who promises an extra shilling a week but instead *cuts* wages by a shilling. His friend the Anglican minister is a glutton who admonishes the workers to "accept our lot in life and work for our rewards" and not dare question "His decision." When it comes time to testify on the men's behalf, the clergyman fingers a crucifix—and lies.

"Comrades" is based on England's real-life "Tolpuddle martyrs," who in the 1830s banded together in a "union of friendship" to battle their oppressors and as a result found themselves shipped off to an Australian penal colony for seven years.

Douglas is in no hurry to tell his story. He deliberately and convincingly builds up his case for the downtrodden—a peasant wife gives birth in a field, a family burns books for warmth. By the time six of the rebels are led off in chains—the camera slowly panning their faces, then pulling back to a medium shot, then to a long one—we're ready to stand up and join them in their rallying cry, "We will, we will, we will be free."

But "Comrades" is too leisurely for its own good once the story shifts to New South Wales. There *are* some superb moments, particularly the gruesome death meted out by ax-wielding prisoners against a sadistic chain-gang guard. And Vanessa Redgrave provides a pleasant respite in a too-brief cameo as a lonely widow. But in following each prisoner separately, the film has difficulty maintaining its momentum.

Still, the ambitious "Comrades" has more going for it than against it—sensitive acting, beautiful color photography, and a story painfully pertinent to the age of Bush and Reagan.

SIGHT & SOUND, Winter 1986–87, p. 66 Jill Forbes

"Comrades, to whom our thoughts return/Brothers . . ." Bill Douglas has much in common with the author of those lines: populism tempered with virtuosity, the religion of his art and the courage of the apostate. Douglas is no more the hero of the right-thinking Left than Auden was a cadre of the Communist movement. Whatever the resonance of the title, *Comrades* is not a film about labour history, or even a film that is morally uplifting; it is a story about making sense of experience—highly political for that very reason although not, perhaps, in a way that designer socialism would recognise.

It is so long since Britain had a rural population of any size that the folk memories have long since departed. *Comrades* attempts to resurrect them, possibly with a degree of anachronism although that is unimportant, by situating its narrative just at the moment when the men of toil were ceasing to be the besmocked yokels of pastoral tradition and were coming to have a sense of their own worth. What more crucial to this than the value of work? The central scene in the Tolpuddle episode, therefore, is the weekly distribution of wages. Here we see the conflict between the literate, the illiterate and the becoming literate enacted with brilliant economy. As the paltry coins slide across the counter under the baleful gaze of the overseer (Murray Melvin), the labourers are required to sign the ledger in receipt. Half mark a cross and half their full name; half can count and half rely on the amount being signalled by their more numerate brethren; half submit with docility to the roll call imposed and half dispute with the overseer the alphabetical order in which he summons them to receive their due. Knowledge is power, so it is said, and unity is strength...

What was it that instructed these men and gave them a sense of justice, against the one inflicted by the "natural order of things"? Hunger, certainly, but also religion. Another scene, this time brilliant in its exploitation of stereophonic sound, dramatises the impact of non-conformism with its emphasis on individual responsibility and self-help, when one of the Martyrs literally runs out of the parish church in which the parson is intoning the ritual message that whatever is, is right, and "goes over" to Methodism to find an amateur orator improvising in the chapel a sermon of hope and comfort. As he runs, the sound of one voice and one hymn is imperceptibly but unmistakably modulated into another until the new haven is reached.

These things are splendidly observed, as is the detail of the rural landscape—the hedges, ditches, barns and cottages, dress and furniture and even the animals. We are reminded in the Hardyesque touches, such as silhouettes against a darkening landscape of figures watching the beacons light up across the hills, that Hardy himself was another determined nostalgic. We see the rich man in his hall and the poor man at the gate; the craftsman trapped by insufficient remuneration of a craft that today would earn him thousands of pounds and held there by the church's prohibition of Sunday labour.

But the most fascinating thing about the Tolpuddle Martyrs is that they were an anachronism in their own times. Not for nothing were they martyrs, their lives reduced for the purposes of moral fable to exemplary tableaux in the tradition of the narratives preceding the novel. The implied narrator of this film is the *colporteur*, the man with the magic lantern show, moving from village to village peddling his ballads and his tales in pictures, while the implied viewer is a throwback to a past when simple stories aroused strong emotions, you knew whose side you were on and it was God's.

Another theme of Douglas' film is thus the development of popular, industrial entertainment, for just when the novel was discovering psychology and throwing off its simplistic moral mode, forms of industrial reproduction began to perpetuate its erstwhile regimes and genres—the images d'Epinal, the dioramas of the Battle of Waterloo or the Execution of Louis XVI, or indeed any scene of popular excitement. Of course, this is not the first time a film has attempted to look back into its own sources, but Douglas approaches the subject with a lightness of touch and an immensely appealing aestheticism. To take just one example, Michael Clarke, disguised as an itinerant performer, executes the Sailor's Hornpipe on a platform in the middle of a field, with such grace and agility that one could wish for a brief moment that the whole film had been enacted as ballet; for we, the modern sophisticated audience, are as spellbound as the open-mouthed rustics.

The various travelling performers and entertainers, lanternists, owners of dioramas, circus masters, operators of patent steam heliotypes and, when the scene shifts to Australia, it is implied the colonial administrators themselves, are all, I believe, mobilised to suggest that somehow Tolpuddle was a last-ditch struggle destined almost to be won before it began because it caricatured the world that was swept away with the industrial revolution. It should not, after all, be forgotten that this episode was almost contemporaneous with the first Reform Bill and that the influence of the London-Dorchester Committee, or the industrial lobby, was such that the Martyrs were brought back from transportation and feted precisely on the London stage.

Comrades is a big film on a broad canvas, authentically located in Dorset and Australia, which will come as quite a shock to some admirers of Douglas' intimist autobiographical pieces. There is the same brilliant exploitation of faces and physical types; invidious as it may be to single out any individual, Robin Soans' George Loveless will surely go down in cinema history as a great performance. There are also the same moments of slapstick which surprise and delight by their unexpectedness. Another clever touch is to use the well-known faces—the Robert Stephenses, James Foxes, Vanessa Redgraves—for the bit parts, the nobs that ordinary folk look up to. By contrast, the narrative exposition does not shine by its clarity, and I seriously wonder how many of those who had not already boned up on the history will have come away from the film with even a minimal grasp of the names of the principals, let alone what happened to them. Ellipsis is a fine and private thing, but surely not in the popular cinema?

I also query the length of the Australian sequences. They are not uncharacteristic of Douglas, to be sure: admirers of the trilogy will remember those Egyptian scenes forever; and it is also true that the colonial system was the ultimate cause of the fall in agricultural wages. But the connection is never made explicit here—nor could it be in this kind of film—and while there must be a fascinating movie to be made on the British in the Australian outback, *Comrades* surely is not it. Perhaps, indeed, Auden should have the last word: "Comrades/Remember that in each direction/Love outside our own election/Holds us in unseen connection/O trust that ever."

VILLAGE VOICE, 1/17/89, p. 69, Manohla Dargis

Shot while Thatcher strong-armed the 1984–85 British coal miners' strike, Bill Douglas's *Comrades* is a three-hour historical epic that carries the unsung refrain, "I Ain't Gonna Work on Maggie's Farm No More." The film is based on events surrounding England's Tolpuddle martyrs—six agricultural laborers exiled for the crime of administering "unlawful oaths"—and it's difficult not to see contemporary parallels. What these Dorchester plebes were up to in the 1830s was trade unionizing working-class solidarity that was subsequently quashed by seven years "transportation" to an Australian penal colony.

Douglas's previous works, an autobiographical trilogy set in the small, Scottish mining village where he was raised, are concentrated, grim chronicles of a child's damaged life. *Comrades*, with its Bressonian mise-en-scène, is no less stylized, but it's less austere—due in part to sublime color photography. The peasants (looking a bit too postcard robust and orthodontial-perfect), while not Rousseauistic, have a sentimental gloss nonetheless. Whether rejecting high Anglicanism for poor-but-righteous Methodism, or stooped like Millet's gleaners, these folk are posed for enobling sacrifice.

The director makes few concessions to his audience. Intricacies of British history are left unexplained, and, except for Robin Soan's crumple-faced George Loveless, actors aren't used as sympathetic entries into the narrative. The film's leisurely pace (which may drive some crazy) works well while in England, but—despite scenic exotica, greater character development, and notable villains (Ralph Cotterill as an outback guard does a splendid whip dance)—it drags Down Under.

Comrades begins and ends through the lens of a magic lantern. Threaded throughout are other precinematic entertainments—dioramas, hand shadows, engravings, silhouettes, steam heliotypes—all presented by a Douglas stand-in, a lanternist in a variety of guises (the versatile Alex Norton), metaphoric attempts to explore film's social function. Such cinematic reflexivity, however, can easily develop into a weird and annoying tic. The final scene in *Comrades* sounds like Marx's Communist Manifesto and looks like Scorsese's *The King of Comedy*.

The moral of the Dorchester laborers' story (like that of the coal miners) does not necessarily depend upon who won, but on the importance of solidarity itself. *Comrades* makes its American premiere at the Public Theater on the eve of the Bush inauguration and well into Thatcher's third term—timing that's either prescient or perversely ironic.

Also reviewed in:

NEW YORK TIMES, 1/13/89, p. C6, Vincent Canby

VARIETY, 12/10/86, p. 18

COOKIE

A Warner Bros. release of a Lorimar Film Entertainment Company film. *Executive Producer:* Susan Seidelman, Nora Ephron, and Alice Arlen. *Producer:* Laurence Mark. *Director:* Susan Seidelman. *Screenplay:* Nora Ephron and Alice Arlen. *Director of Photography:* Oliver Stapleton. *Editor:* Andrew Mondshein. *Music:* Thomas Newman. *Music Editor:* Kenneth Karman. *Sound:* Tom Maitland. *Sound Editor:* Maurice Schell. *Production Designer:* Michael Haller. *Art Director:* Bill Groom. *Set Decorator:* Les Bloom. *Set Dresser:* Dick Tice, Jim Archer, Bruce Swanson, and Bob Klatt. *Special Effects:* Connie Bink. *Costumes:* Albert Wolsky. *Make-up:* Richard Dean. *Stunt Coordinator:* Jery Hewitt. *Running time:* 93 minutes. *MPAA Rating:* R.

CAST: Peter Falk (Dino); Dianne Wiest (Lenore); Emily Lloyd (Cookie); Michael V. Gazzo (Carmine); Brenda Vaccaro (Bunny); Adrian Pasdar (Vito); Lionel Stander (Enzo Della Testa); Jerry Lewis (Arnold Ross); Bob Gunton (Segretto); Ben Rayson (Henry Solomon); Ricki Lake (Pia); Joe Mantello (Dominick); Thomas Quinn (Vinnie); David Wohl (Alvin Diamond); Joy Behar (Dottie); Frank Gio (Frankie); Mario Todisco (Sloppy Louie); Tony LaFortezza (Angelo); F.X. Vitolo (Motorcycle Cop); Ira Flitter (State Trooper); Joseph Pentangelo (Fed #1); David K. Reilly (Fed #2); William Jay Marshall (Frank Pearl); George Bartenieff (Andy O'Brien); Ed Setrakian (Mike Fusco); Paul Slimak (Priest); Sydney Sheriff (Vendor); Mark Boone Jr. (Transit Cop); Arto Lindsay (Court Clerk); Ralph Monaco (Judge); Evan Bell (Court Guard); Kim Chan (Hong Kong Tailor); Marshall Anker (Parole Board Member); Aida Linares (Carmen); Delphi Harrington (Rosa Tarantino); Margaret Knopf (Recipe Woman); Crystal Field (Angela); J.D. DeKranis and J.P. (Cookie's Friends); Alfred De La Fuente (Maitre 'D); Lynn White (TV Reporter); Teresa Bellettieri (Vito's Girlfriend); Isabell Monk (Matron); Richard Caselnova (Driver); Tony Devon (Bodyguard); Steve DeLuca (Bomb Squad Man); Ben Spell (Justice of the Peace); Jerry Blavat (D.J. at Chateau Mer); Bob Martana (Ritz Truck Driver); Marv Albert (Voice of the New York Knicks).

FILMS IN REVIEW, 12/89, p. 620, Edmond Grant

A bright and funny Mafia fairy tale, *Cookie* can best be described as utterly delectable. This is due to its fast pacing, some cute character quirks, but most of all, to the absolutely charming group of performers who make up its cast.

At the forefront is Peter Falk, who stars as Dino Capisco, a mob bigwig who exits prison after more than a decade only to find that he's been shafted by his "partner" (Michael V. Gazzo). In addition, his mistress (Dianne Wiest) decides it's high time he got to know his teenage daughter Cookie (Emily Lloyd) better. So, after witnessing Cookie's unorthodox but effective driving technique, he hires her as his personal chauffeur. When mob war erupts as a result of Dino's attempts to regain his former power, Cookie proves to be particularly useful in helping her old man get even, and wins some respect for herself in the process.

Cookie blends the old and the new with splendid results—Director Susan Seidelman peppers the film with familiar faces, reminding one of the Damon Runyon comedies of yesteryear (like *Pocketful Of Miracles*, the film which offered Falk his first comic role), while the nonconformist character of Cookie and the focus the film places on the women in Dino's life makes it as contemporary as Seidelman's biggest hit, *Desperately Seeking Susan*.

The measure of Falk's excellence as a performer is that he not only shines as a comic actor, but also makes a terrific straight man for the other oddball characters surrounding him. Dianne Wiest has some amusing moments as the perpetually sobbing mistress with superbly tacky taste (and what a relief to see her without her usual "cropped" hairdo), but Brenda Vaccaro supplies the real laughs as Dino's shrewish wife, who runs a dog-grooming service to make some "real money." Dino's fellow gangsters are played by two fellows with inimitable gravel-voices, Michael V. Gazzo and Lionel Stander; and a somber Jerry Lewis takes the part of an old chum who's gone legit in Altantic City. Even the smaller supporting players are immaculately chosen, from Cookie's best girlfriend (Ricki Lake) to Gazzo's menacing henchmen.

And then there's Emily Lloyd. To say that Ms. Lloyd has shown versatility in her three roles on screen thus far would have to be an understatement. At only 19, Lloyd has already essayed the parts of a rebellious British girl (*Wish You Were Here*), a Kentucky teen (*In Country*), and here, an outspoken Brooklyn street kid. Her New Yorkese is flawless, her diction (or lack of it) directly on target. Though her character is supposed to be rather obnoxious for the film's first half, at no time does she come off as less than endearing, and succeeds in holding her own in her moments with Falk, himself an inveterate scene-stealer.

The script by Nora Ephron and Alice Arlen isn't surprisingly original in any respect (in fact, the movie's paperback novelization has a better, more conclusive ending than the film's own). But (dare it be repeated again) the characters are charismatic enough that any excessively silly plot logic can be excused. On the directorial side, Susan Seidelman plays down the knicknackery that dominated her last three films, and chooses instead to keep the plot moving while letting the actors deliver fully blown characterizations. The choice of actual New York/New Jersey locations adds to the film's coolly contemporary quality.

LOS ANGELES TIMES, 8/23/89, Calendar/p. 1, Sheila Benson

The funniest observation that "Cookie" makes about its New York Mafioso subjects is the mobsters's routine greeting at home each night. After a hard day's labor racketeering, drug dealing and money laundering, as the men hit the door, their wives call out brightly, "So, honey, d'ya have a nice day?"

It's a touch that makes you smile, the sort of perfect detailing with which another director, Elaine May, studs her scripts and her films. Here, director Susan Seidelman keeps her frame busy and lively, and her eye for the right actor in every small role is still precise. But May's lethal observations always come with a core of humanity, quite missing from "Cookie's" frail farce.

Nora Ephron and Alice Arlen's script, for all its individual moments, can't seem to decide whether it's the story of Mafia father Dino Capisco (Peter Falk), who learns to appreciate his headstrong daughter Cookie (Emily Lloyd), or whether it's the story of gum-chewing, chain-smoking 18-year-old Cookie, who outsmarts the mob and the D.A. and becomes a sort of ruling Mafia princess herself.

If it's a father-daughter story, that humanistic element dissolves with the movie's conclusion. Actually, whichever story it's supposed to be, the audience gets short-sheeted. Our sympathies lie with Peter Falk and his dogged inamorata, Lenore (Dianne Wiest), Cookie's mother. They are supposed to rest with Cookie, who may be smart and has hidden talents as a getaway driver, but Cookie's a pill and a bore—another in that Seidelman catalogue of heroines like Madonna in "Desperately Seeking Susan" or Susan Berman in "Smithereens," where brashness is supposed to be charm enough. *Enough.*

Cookie is understandably teed off when the father she hasn't seen since she was 5 years old bursts back on the scene and, worse yet, begins giving her orders. Complicated arrangements in the Mafia hierarchy—and his parole—make it impossible for Dino to marry Lenore, but his lust for her is pure and unabated.

The Wiest-Falk scenes, even within the framework of rowdy farce, have a nice adult appreciation to them, and a few lines that make them sing: Lenore flutteringly complains that she's faded during Dino's 13 years away. Putting his hand on her face, he says to her—and means it— "You used to have a baby face. Now you're beautiful." *That's* the way to charm the birds out of the trees. Be nice if the rest of the movie were as persuasive.

It's a plot-heavy story of elaborate double-dealing as Dino schemes to get even with his cheating ex-partner, Carmine Tarentino ("Godfather II" icon Michael V. Gazzo), while avoiding a tail that the politically ambitious D.A. Segretto (Bob Gunton) has on him. Segretto is waiting for Dino's first misstep, which will land him back in the slammer.

Decorating the plot is Dino's legal wife Bunny (Brenda Vaccaro), who seems to groom and sell stolen dogs at Bunny's Bark Place; Vito (Adrian Pasdar, an interesting presence), the young gangster Cookie sets her sights on, and ex-mobster Arnold Rose (Jerry Lewis), now an Atlantic City developer but, like Dino, also cheated by the powerful Tarentino. And lurking with not half enough to do but to show his leonine presence is Lionel Stander as the Capo of Capos, Enzo Della Testa.

The film comes alive with Wiest's Lenore, the lustiest, most full-blooded characterization in the place—although the idea veers dangerously close to Mia Farrow's Mafia-madonna in "Broadway Danny Rose." Smoothing her dress over her hips as she awaits her reunion with Dino, using breath spray, hair spray and room spray until the whole apartment is probably toxic through the year 2000, Wiest rules the movie. Although her method of getting her way with Dino has always been by sofa-moving sobs, there's tensile steel just under Lenore's surface. Luckily, with the handsome Falk in the opposite corner, Wiest gets back as good as she gives; the two are a very palpable couple. (The film is rated R for its occasional raunchy language and behavior.)

In the way that Hollywood is notorious for, England's Emily Lloyd is doing a transplanted equivalent of her first success, as Lynda the hellion-in-training in "Wish You Were Here," Lloyd seems to have a good ear; she has no real problems with her Brooklyn-Italian speech, nor with her bubble gum. But "Wish You Were Here's" plucky, emotionally ripped-off 15-year-old single mother had heart, among other notable qualities. Like most of Seidelman's women, Cookie has brass, and that must serve.

Lynda was desperately vulnerable, which made her all the more appealing. Cookie is ticked-off, noisy, shrewd, self-absorbed, inventive and iron-willed. Vulnerable she's not. And played against Wiest's warm-hearted if small-brained expansiveness, it makes Cookie seem even more of a brat, which may not have been the desired effect.

So where does the conclusion of "Cookie" leave its plucky heroine? Eighteen years old. Mudduhless. Fadduhless. Educationless. Ambitionless. With that teeny-tiny chain-smoking habit. And the pluses? She snags the hood of her choice. And she's sitting on more money than anyone but movie makers (or hoods) probably ever see in the course of one lifetime.

Is this cynical, tinny view of "success" really the best that three lively film makers could conjure up for a character they *like*? Hard to imagine what they'd wish for someone on their hit list.

MONTHLY FILM BULLETIN, 12/89, p. 330, Pam Cook

Brooklyn. The funeral takes place of ex-labour racketeer Dominick "Dino" Capisco, apparently murdered by rival mobsters. A few months earlier...Carmella "Cookie" Voltecki, Dino's illegitimate daughter by his mistress Lenore, is taken by his henchmen to visit her father, whom she has not seen for thirteen years, in Lewisburg prison. Dino, worried that her irresponsible behaviour will affect his chances of parole, insists that she get a job in the garment factory of his former partner, Carmine Tarantino. In spite of attempts by District Attorney Richard Segretto, who hopes to become governor by busting the crime syndicates, to block it, Dino obtains his parole on condition that he live with his wife Bunny. He visits successful builder Arnold Ross in Atlantic City for his share of their racketeering profits, only to learn that Arnold bought him and Carmine out seven years ago. Angry at Carmine's betrayal, Dino sets out to even the score and retrieve his money. At Carmine's Christmas party, Cookie aggressively rejects the advances of his son Dominick, and she and Dino have to leave in a hurry; impressed by the way Cookie loses the police car tailing them, Dino hires her as his driver. Dino makes contact with former Mafia associates and, under close surveillance by Segretto, moves in on Carmine's operations. Carmine retaliates with attempts on Dino's life, and he is forced to go into hiding. Though warned off by Dino's young henchman Vito, to whom she is attracted, Cookie determines to help her father, suggesting to Segretto that he give Dino a new identity and immunity in exchange for what she knows. Segretto agrees, but Dino resists, until Cookie suggests that they fake his death prior to his disappearance. Arnold and Dino doublecross Carmine by hijacking the $2,000,000 he was pretending to invest in a phoney deal intended to trap Dino, while the federal agents, using a body from the morgue, plan Dino's "death" in a car explosion. Carmine, who is holding Cookie hostage after the hijack, demands his money back from Dino, and arranges to meet him later that night under Brooklyn Bridge. When he gets into Dino's limousine, the car is blown up by one of Dino's associates, prior to the bomb squad's planned explosion. Dino, Arnold and Cookie share out Carmine's money and Segretto (believing his men to be responsible for Carmine's death), agrees to Dino starting a secret new life with Lenore. Cookie and Vito get together, and at Dino's "funeral" Cookie is acknowledged by "capo" Enzo Della Testa as the heir to Dino's operations...

It's difficult to see how a project with these credentials could go awry, but even a script by Nora Ephron and Alice Arlen, high calibre performers like Peter Falk, Emily Lloyd, Dianne Wiest and Brenda Vaccaro, and a knowingly ironic music soundtrack do not prevent this potentially interesting story from falling flat. All the Seidelman trademarks are there—screwball capers, feminist fantasy, female friendship, play with style and fashion—but laboured direction and ponderous plot development combine to reduce them to tired formulae.

Mafia movies, with their patriarchal family sagas, generational conflicts and macho ethics, offer fertile ground for post-feminist satire. This one, which charts the rise of quick-witted teenager Cookie Voltecki to the upper echelons of syndicate power, swings valiantly, if rather heavy-handedly, at a number of targets: the air-freshened romantic dreams of Cookie's mother and her aspirations to conventional family life; the Mafia milieu in which sons inherit from fathers, relegating women to swapping recipes or running small-time businesses like Bunny's pet-grooming service (a cover for selling stolen dogs); and the respectable suburban veneer covering murderous mob activities. Some fun is had from playing feminine (domestic) and masculine (business) values off against one another, but for the most part the performances, though carried off with panache, are so exaggerated that they obscure many of the more subtle jibes.

But the main problem is with the central father/daughter relationship, which sadly fails to spark. A gum-chewing Emily Lloyd is not strong enough to tip the balance from the redoubtable Peter Falk and the host of ageing mafiosi who dominate the screen, and the relegation of Cookie's peers (Ricki Lake as her friend Pia and Adrian Pasdar as Dino's henchman Vito) to passive bit parts does not help. (Jerry Lewis is equally disappointing in a woodenly executed cameo.) All in all, *Cookie* has the feel of a worn-out vehicle grinding to a halt. Perhaps it's time to change to a new model.

NEW YORK POST, 8/23/89, p. 25, David Edelstein

The comedy "Cookie" glides by like a pink cloud—quirky-looking but vaporous. It's a felicitous waste of time. The picture opens promisingly with two teens (Emily Lloyd and Ricki Lake) buying a pink camera from an East Village street vendor, jumping a subway turnstile and snapping a triumphant photo of two cops banging on the doors as their train pulls away.

The director, Susan Seidelman, did a variation of this scam in her first movie, "Smithereens," but that was when her work had some grit—before she became a stylist. From all the creamy pans and gimmicky dissolves and Candyland colors in "Cookie," you'd swear *she* was using a pink camera, too.

At least the hefty Lake (the star of "Hairspray") makes a vivacious camera subject. Too bad she never reappears. The heroine is actually Lloyd (of "Wish You Were Here"), who plays the ornery, illegitimate daughter of an imprisoned mobster, Dino (Peter Falk).

When Cookie's arrested for jumping that turnstile, Dino has her bailed out and brought to the jail to see him. "No one even knows you're my father," she tells him, witheringly, "including me."

That's a good line, but the script, by Nora Ephron and Alice Arlen, doesn't have many more. When Dino gets out of prison, he by-passes his crass wife (Brenda Vaccaro) for Cookie's mom (Dianne Wiest), his mistress. The two smooch while Cookie, shut up in her bedroom, watches "The Brady Bunch"—as if longing for a normal home life.

Meanwhile, Dino tries to recover the money he's owed by his old partner, Carmine (Michael V. Gazzo), and a casino owner, Ross (Jerry Lewis in his spooky deadpan mode). Carmine thinks Dino should be happy just being free and alive; when Dino isn't, Carmine decides to have him killed.

"Cookie" turns into a conventional caper comedy with twists and double-crosses and car chases. It's about how Cookie becomes her father's chauffeur, outwits the mob, brings her parents together (legally) and lands a groovy guy. She's a Disney heroine with clothes from Trash and Vaudeville.

The movie is smoothly made, and once or twice the action is cleverly staged, but we don't feel any of Dino's pain over being double-crossed by his old compadres or discover just when it is that Cookie stops hating him and starts to want to fight his battles. (Lloyd and Falk have zero chemistry; they look as if they want to have as little to do with each other as possible.)

At heart, this is a little-girl fantasy about recapturing the love of a distant daddy; Cookie gets to be wilier and gutsier than any other man's son. Lloyd looks terrific (especially in a jacket, tie, fedora and miniskirt) and sports a flawless American accent, yet she isn't as open—as emotionally naked—as in "Wish You Were Here." She doesn't pull us in. It's as if Seidelman never figured out how to get into her head—or never much though about it.

It's not that Seidelman doesn't care about the emotional aspects of the movie; it's that she wants at all costs to keep it bounching along prettily, because that's what she thinks people responded to in "Desperately Seeking Susan" and missed in "Making Mr. Right." But her style doesn't help "Cookie" slide down more easily; it blands it out, lobotomizes it.

Physically, there are similarities between "Cookie" and Jonathan Demme's "Married to the Mob": Both proceed from the jokey assumption that gangsters and kitsch go together. (It's a sign of conspicuous consumption.) But in Demme's film it was the pain and revulsion that the heroine (Michele Pfeiffer) felt for the gangster's way of life that gave the ridiculous decor a kick; here it's just a source of cheap laughs.

Ben Rayson has an amusing, Zero Mostel-ish theatricality as Dino's lawyer, but no one else (aside from Lake) registers: not Falk, who's in a stupor, as if waiting to be roused by a Cassavetes-style improvisation that never comes; not Wiest, who's all icky, dumb-blonde niceness after her great performance in "Parenthood"; not Bob Gunton as a Giuliani-like prosecutor; and not Vaccaro, who's made to look hideous.

Technically, this is Seidelman's most proficient film; it's also (by miles) her most mannered, full of deadpan, "quirky" reaction shots—her trademark.

The '60s thriller "Chamber of Horrors" had a neat device to let the squeamish know when to avert their eyes: Before something awful happened, the "horror horn" blasted and the screen turned blood-red. "Cookie" should have a "quirky horn," which would sound before an offbeat reaction shot or visual curlicue. The screen would turn—what else?—pink. And we could hide.

NEWSDAY, 8/23/89, Part II/p. 2, Mike McGrady

Oh, she's one smart cookie, this Cookie of "Cookie." Her studded black leather jacket supports more gold braid than a Latin American junta, more graffiti than your average city block. Her never-motionless mouth is busy pulverizing either bubblegum or the English language. She's bright, sassy, funny, gaudy and beautifully sketched by English actress Emily Lloyd as the centerpiece of a funny new movie by director Susan Seidelman.

Seidelman has always been fascinated by characters like Cookie, all those feisty, nervy, amoral, warm-hearted women unwilling to accept the dull hand fate has dealt them. The women in "Desperately Seeking Susan" and "Smithereens" were refugees from New Jersey anxious to recarve their destinies and just be themselves—once they figured out who that might be. And their quests were always conducted in the company of colorful oddballs who tended to do unpredictable and, at times, violent things.

The Nora Ephron-Alice Arlen script (they wrote "Silkwood" together; Ephron's "When Harry Met Sally..." is this year's sharpest screenplay) is—and this, too, is typical of a Seidelman flick—generally preposterous, alway fascinating and usually fun.

Teenager Cookie, nabbed for "turnstile jumping," is surprised to find a high-priced criminal lawyer defending her in court. As it turns out, her father, Dino (Peter Falk), a big-time labor racketeer, is up for parole and doesn't want anything to distract from his unblemished prison record. Cookie is thereupon forced to hear him set down the law: "You're gettin' a job, nine-to-five, in bed early, after a little TV."

One need take only one glance at Cookie to realize this regimen doesn't fit into her blueprint for life. However, she goes so far as to start work at a Garment District sweatshop, where she learns to sew Calvin Klein labels over the original "Made in Hong Kong" tags. After complaining to her father ("I'm practically the only one there who's not an alien"), Cookie becomes her father's chauffeur, which, as it turns out, is approximately the same thing as a getaway driver.

As the story unfolds, we see the two strong clashing personalities, father and daughter, slowly coming to appreciate one another. The buffer between the two is the woman who is Cookie's mother and Dino's mistress; count this as another marvelous performance from Dianne Wiest. Despite a tendency to lubricate her complaints with tears, Wiest is wonderfully funny as an all-frills female who also knows a thing or two about strength: "I was a single mother long before they were talking about it on 'Oprah Winfrey.'"

Still another bit comes from Brenda Vaccaro as Dino's wife, who makes a living regrooming stolen pets, running a kind of chop shop for expensive animals. Jerry Lewis plays it straight as a real estate developer and, of course, Peter Falk is no stranger to gangster roles; by this time he can handle it beautifully, taking what might have been a cartoon character and softening it before remolding it into human form.

Despite all this talent, the movie is effectively stolen by Lloyd, who won both raves and awards for her last performance in "Wish You Were Here." Living for a time with a Brooklyn family enabled Lloyd to master the nuances of a New York accent. Not so easily explained is her ability to take this very complicated character—this combination of innocent and gun moll, this brassplated gold figurine—and bring her to life. It's no small accomplishment.

NEWSWEEK, 9/4/89, p. 68, David Ansen

Emily Lloyd, the delightful English star of "Wish You Were Here," makes her American debut as the title character of Susan Seidelman's raggedly executed Mafia comedy. As the gum-chewing, foulmouthed, illegitimate daughter of a charming Mafia don (Peter Falk) just sprung from Sing Sing, Lloyd cuts a fetchingly rude figure, but the script by Nora Ephron and Alice Arlen gives her little to do but strike poses of sullen exasperation. Lloyd becomes Falk's driver in this complicated story of mob revenge, double cross and father daughter reconciliation. The fine cast—Dianne Wiest as Falk's foxy mistress and true love, Brenda Vaccaro as his shrill wife, Michael Gazzo and Lionel Stander as fellow mafiosi—helps make "Cookie" watchable, but their best efforts are undermined by Seidelman's maladroit timing. Instead of shaping her scenes, the director seems more interested in accessorizing them.

TIME, 8/28/89, p. 64, Richard Corliss

We gather to praise the forgettable comedy. Some movies can be faulted for nothing but low ambition. They aim not for the Academy Award. They disdain the zillion-dollar gross. Not for them a double-domed debate on the op-ed page. But some sweltering August evening, they afford easy wit, engaging performances and, for moviegoers, the satisfaction of 90 minutes well wasted.

Such a one is the film under consideration—a Mafia comedy. Already the mind contracts with diminished expectations! Non-Italian actors gesturing rambunctiously, speaking with cotton candy in their mouths, plotting elaborate revenge with dim-bulbed resources. Cast Peter Falk as Dino Capisco, a dapper don just sprung from Sing Sing. Give him a score to settle with his weaselly partner Carmine Tarantino (Michael V. Gazzo) and a slick, Rudolph Giuliani-style D.A. (Bob Gunton) with an eye to nailing Dino's hide on the front page. Saddle him with a dog-stealing wife (Brenda Vaccaro) and a devoted but ditsy mistress (Dianne Wiest). And do make sure his life finally depends on the skeptical love and untested intelligence of his daughter Carmela Maria Angelina Theresa Voltecki, a.k.a. Cookie (Emily Lloyd).

Lloyd, the English teenager who won prizes for her role in *Wish You Were Here*, imports a fetching presence and an acute mimicry to her Brooklyn punkster. The rest of the cast has fun playing in a farce summer-stocked with plot twists and cunning character studies. A perfect forgettable comedy—now what was its name? Ah, yes. Tasty, brittle, sweet, of no nutritional value...*Cookie*.

VILLAGE VOICE, 8/29/89, p. 63, Georgia Brown

Susan Seidelman's *Cookie* intends to be cute. It has a promising narrative idea—how can a mafioso's daughter earn the attention of her macho mobster father who thinks only males count—but this plotline is more nominal than real. It's the sort of plot you need to have spelled out for you, and then you think, oh, yes, that's what that movie is about! Except that it really isn't. Seidelman is more focused on maintaining a hyper, hysterical pace than on character or action. The script is written by the *Silkwood* team of Nora Ephron and Alice Arlen but contains little evidence of their talents. *Cookie* is loud, frenetic, and jangly.

As for mafioso girl children, Cookie can't hold a candle to Anjelica Huston's sublime Maerose Prizzi, or to Michelle Pfeiffer's beleaguered daughter-in-law in *Married to the Mob*. Lanky British actress Emily Lloyd (*Wish You Were Here*) does a credible Brooklynese and snaps gum fine, but she's not required to do much more than pout and spout off. She's all attitude problem, although she's shown to have good reason for having one.

Her father, Dino Capisco (Peter Falk), is serving time, and since he's not formally her dad, he rarely acknowledges her existence. Only when she gets into minor trouble (jumping a turnstile) and his parole is jeopardized, does he pay attention. Her mom, Lenore (Dianne Wiest), is Dino's mistress, a dewy-eyed, traditionaly subservient sweetheart. The tease is that even in this stock role, Wiest manages to seem a more promising comic focus than her sullen daughter. Dino's loudmouth wife (Brenda Vaccaro) steals dogs to groom them and dress them for weddings. Lionel Stander and Jerry Lewis are fun to see as Mafia bigshots.

Posters for the movie show Cookie lounging beside the dapper Dino in a pose that vaguely recalls Madonna and Rosanna Arquette's ads for Seidelman's *Desperately Seeking Susan*. Like that film, *Cookie* relies heavily on decor, costume, and location. In an opening scene Cookie shops the sidewalks of the Lower East Side with her friend (*Hairspray's* Ricki Lake), wearing the obligatory piled-on junk and a motorcycle jacket that in the fall's $700 Donna Karan version is known as the St. Marks. Seidelman obviously gets a kick out of locations—finding the genteel, tacky heart of Bay Ridge or shooting the parking lot at Bamonte's restaurant under the BQE.

When Dino gets paroled and has to fight his way back to credibility in the mob, Cookie puts herself in his way until he begins to acknowledge her usefulness. What she does seems slight, however, and the transformation isn't what it might be. Falk's ease is everything, and his presence continually dwarfs Lloyd's. In effect, we're back to *The Godfather*. Seidelman manages to subvert her feminist thesis; poor Cookie is a nebbish.

Also reviewed in:
NEW YORK TIMES, 8/23/89, p. C13, Vincent Canby
NEW YORKER, 9/4/89, p. 90. Terrence Rafferty
VARIETY, 8/23-29/89, p. 29
WASHINGTON POST, 8/24/89, p. C1, Hal Hinson
WASHINGTON POST, 8/25/89, Weekend/p. 33, Desson Howe

COURIER, THE

A Vestron Pictures release of a Euston Films and Palace Production presentation of a City Vision film. *Executive Producer:* Neil Jordan, Nik Powell, and John Hambley. *Producer:* Hilary McLoughlin. *Director:* Frank Deasy and Joe Lee. *Screenplay:* Frank Deasy. *Director of Photography:* Gabriel Beristain. *Editor:* Annette D'Alton. *Music:* Declan MacManus [Elvis Costello]. *Sound:* Pat Hayes. *Sound Editor:* Nigel Galt. *Production Designer:* David Wilson. *Special Effects:* Gerry Johnston. *Costumes:* Consolata Boyle. *Make-up:* Rosie Blackmore. *Stunt Coordinator:* Dominick Hewitt. *Running time:* 85 minutes. *MPAA Rating:* R.

CAST: Padraig O'Loingsigh (Mark); Cait O'Riordan (Colette); Gabriel Byrne (Val); Ian Bannen (McGuigan); Patrick Bergin (Christy); Andrew Connelly (Danny); Michelle Houlden (Sharon); Mary Ryan (Carol); Dave Duffy (Dunne); Joe Savino (Video Editor); Caroline Rothwell (Receptionist); Mary Elizabeth Burke Kennedy (Doctor); Stuart Dunne (Tony); Martin Dunne (Alfie); Mick Egan (Barman); Mark Flanagan (Sharon's Baby); Anne Enright (Pregnant Girl); Liz Bono (Girl in Bank); Lucy Vigne-Welsh (Assistant in Jewelers); Owen Hyland (Schoolboy); Kevin Doyle (Boy at Val's Shop); Albert Fahy (Val's Assistant); Alec Doran (Man in Pub); Aidan Murphy (Boy Picked Up by Val); Aisling Cronin (Girl in Alfie's); Tony Coleman (Special Branch #1)); Seay Ledwidge (Special Branch #2)).

MONTHLY FILM BULLETIN, 2/88, p. 41, Philip Strick

On a delivery assignment, young Dublin motorcycle messenger Mark visits the office of Colette, whose brother Danny was once his close friend; she responds to Mark's new interest in her. Danny, now a helpless addict, is being unscrupulously exploited by crime boss Val, whose drug-dealing activities have made him a prime target for Police Detective McGuigan. When Danny is offered a chance to help the police set a trap for Val, he is disfigured by the dealer to ensure his loyalty. After a minor accident during a delivery, Mark realises that the courier company is controlled by Val and he has unknowingly been carrying drugs and cash between the dealer and his customers. Danny dies from a dose of poisoned heroin supplied by Val, and Mark is determined to avenge him for Colette's sake; he uses his opportunities as courier to plant evidence that will implicate the dealer for McGuigan. Val learns about Mark's plans just in time to thwart a police raid, and sends his henchman, Christy, on a revenge hunt to Mark's home. There Christy kills Sharon, manager of the courier office, who has come to warn Mark, and this crime leads the police first to Christy and in turn to Val's hideout. They arrive just as he is about to kill Mark, who has been threatening him with a shotgun, and Val is picked off by a police marksman. Fed up with Dublin, Mark sells his home and sets out with Colette in search of a new life.

This is an enterprise it would be satisfying to be able to welcome. The two co-directors (Deasy controlled script and actors, Lee controlled the camera) have graduated to a first feature through community video projects for their own company City Vision, and a short fiction film, *Sometime City*, shown at the London Film Festival in 1986. Guidance and financial support for *The Courier* came from the Irish Film Board (currently in limbo), the ever-valuable Euston Films, and Palace Productions whose management team, already rich in *wunderkinder,* has recruited Neil Jordan for substantial extra muscle. Given the declared purpose of making "a commercial thriller but at the same time a film about life in modern-day Ireland", the potential for an explosion of freshness and originality would seem considerable, Sadly, no such event has materialised: *The Courier* is remarkable only for its frequency of cliché in text, situation and staging, and for its portrait of a shapeless environment which, aside from the occasional Dublin landmarks, could be anywhere.

The conventional urban glimpses of shopping precincts, offices and decaying houses are populated by itinerants of no clear purpose or nationality, among whom a cops-and-robbers yarn more suitable to an episode of *The Sweeney* is perilously attenuated.

If there are echoes of *Angel* (as well as of that other Palace discovery, *Diva*) in the story of an Irish youth taking arms against a sea of betrayals, his bike and helmet emblematic of speedy purpose and courage in a labyrinth of greed and conspiracy, these are quickly muffled by the amiable but dull performance at the centre of *The Courier*. No particular anguish emerges from the steel-eyed impassivity of the biker, whether uttering aphorisms at the cemetery or posing for his girl with the shotgun he has conveniently unearthed from a pile of rags. "You think you're Clint Eastwood", she sneers as he blocks her path, and he doesn't argue—but the allusion is not much help: where Dirty Harry had a certain charisma and his opponents were nonentities, this messenger-boy warrior is outclassed by both lawbreakers and lawbringers. Gabriel Byrne, effortlessly villainous in all sorts of obvious ways (the white suit, the vulpine smile, the penchant for rent-boys), is matched in overbearing professional skill by Ian Bannen who, like the manipulative McAnally in *Angel,* arrives peevishly late on all occasions with a threat, a promise, and a whiff of brimstone.

Carefully composed by Gabriel Beristain (cameraman for *Caravaggio*), the film's images perpetually capture glossy moments resembling jeans and drinks commercials, all moody lighting and breathless pauses, requiring the exaggerated positions of the cast frequently to be held beyond the point of comfort, theirs and ours. There is a sequence of anticipated ambush, as hunter and victims creep around a house of creaking doors and restless curtains, which is clearly a rehearsal for some other drama—it makes little sense in the present narrative, except as an exercise in suspense. And there is a street scene in the French *policier* style, for which an army of gunmen stroll into a picturesque pattern of confrontation with the crook they've been waiting for.

Hints of the unusual (or could we, after all, be in *Odd Man Out* territory?) are momentarily conveyed by a small accordionist whose amazing voice rings out over the discovery of a death, but the apparition is rendered meaningless by the cheap joke that curtails it. Having finally dashed our hopes of any startling occurrence (even the baddie falls from a height), the innocents make their getaway along the shore (where else?) as the city dwindles behind them. "You were somebody else out there", comments the girl, which might explain a loose end or two. Unfortunately, whoever he may have been, his intricate manoeuvring with packets of drugs and money have done little to rescue him from anonymity. Commercial thrillers may be made from the likes of this, but life in modern-day Ireland—or anywhere else, for that matter—is surely a lot more interesting.

NEW YORK POST, 6/2/89, p. 25, Jami Bernard

One intention of the Irish-made "The Courier" seems to be to dissuade us of the notion that Dublin is all leprechauns and ruddy-faced peasants. It is the kind of drug-underworld picture that crawls out from under enough rocks on these shores, about life and addiction in the teeming, filthy city.

Perhaps because Ireland is fairly new to this, "The Courier" lacks the necessary street smarts to grab its audience. In fact, aside from the obvious, I hadn't the foggiest idea what was going on, or going down, or going bad.

There is a drug network headed by Val, a jewel heist, a murder disguised as a suicide, revenge, homo-erotic overtones in the steam bath and a strong suggestion that bad childhoods are to blame for the snorting o' the white.

Whew. Let's see. Mark (Padraig O'Loingsigh) is the motorcycle courier of the title. With his helmet on, he looks like a spaceman as he makes his rounds, always picking up and dropping off little brown envelopes of the same size and heft. A New York preschooler could tell him he's working for a drug syndicate, but Mark only catches on after a spill off his bike leaves a lot of Irish green flapping around the streets.

Gabriel Byrne plays Val, whose day job consists of putting price stickers on toy bunnies, but whose real calling is directing drug traffic.

On one of his runs, Mark meets up with the sister of his old friend Danny. Concurrently, Danny dies of a snort of strychnine. Mark is mad, the sister is confused, the police chief (Ian Bannen) is well-meaning but clumsy, and various henchmen and secretaries come and go with no clear purpose.

Frank Deasy co-directed from his own screenplay—often a sign of trouble. When he was writing a line like "Just cool it now" to defuse a high-tension hostage situation, someone should have taken him aside and said, "Frank, baby, stick to directing."

But no one did Frank this favor, so we have Mark and the girl prefacing their first romantic kiss with this reminiscence from their childhood:

He: You had acne!

She: You used to have blackheads!

Smooch!

For a fairly violent drug movie, "The Courier" has a slow, folksy exposition and takes its concerns about the drug problem seriously. Occasionally there are appalling lapses into bad taste—a scene in an almost-topless bar, for instance, or one in which a displeased Val mashes a jagged light bulb into someone's eye.

NEWSDAY, 6/2/89, Part III/p. 5, Mike McGrady

When the Irish Film Board backed the production of "The Courier," it obviously wasn't considering image. The Ireland familiar to most film-goers is a beautiful land of green fields, ancient castles, amiable leprechauns and friendly brawls in noisy pubs. Well, that Ireland never makes so much as a cameo appearance in "The Courier."

This grim little darkside movie stars an Ireland most Americans have never imagined: an industrialized nation of slums, factories, traffic jams and dreary rowhouses. An Ireland of cocaine dealing, armed robbery, male prostitution, great violence, murder.

Mark (Padraig O'Loingsigh), a young courier, inadvertently discovers he's the middle man in a cocaine operation—delivering drugs in one direction and huge amounts of cash in the other. Most of the cash is heading toward an unsavory businessman named Val (Gabriel Byrne.) When Val murders Danny, an informer (Andrew Connelly), he makes a bad career decision. You see, Danny was Mark's friend, also the brother of his sweetheart. And, in the process of exacting revenge, the leather-garbed Mark reveals that he has seen far too many "Rambo" and "Dirty Harry" movies.

One of the few commercial "thrillers" ever made in Ireland, "The Courier" illustrates the many ways a film can go bad. The writing ignores normal human motivation to concentrate relentlessly on gratuitous violence. The direction, from newcomers Frank Deasy and Joe Lee, achieves no flow at all between actors. And the acting (with the sole exception of Dublin-born veteran Gabriel Byrne) comes from stage-trained performers who show no ease at all before the cameras.

Also reviewed in:
NEW YORK TIMES, 6/2/89, p. C15, Caryn James
VARIETY, 2/24/88, P. 12

COUSINS

A Paramount Pictures release. *Executive Producer:* George Goodman. *Producer:* William Allyn. *Director:* Joel Schumacher. *Screenplay:* Stephen Metcalfe. *Based on the Film "Cousin, Cousine" by:* Jean-Charles Tacchella. *Director of Photography:* Ralf Bode. *Editor:* Robert Brown. *Music:* Angelo Badalamenti. *Music Editor:* Jim Weidman. *Sound:* Larry Sutton, Rob Young, and (music) Joel Moss. *Sound Editor:* George Watters II.

Groves, and Gordon A. Clapp. *Special Effects:* William H. Orr. *Costumes:* Michael Kaplan. *Make-up:* Fern Buchner. *Running time:* 111 minutes. *MPAA Rating:* PG-13.
Production Designer: Mark Freeborn. *Set Decorator:* Linda Vipond. *Set Dresser:* Patrick Kearns, Jane
CAST: Ted Danson (Larry); Isabella Rossellini (Maria); Sean Young (Tish); William Petersen (Tom); Lloyd Bridges (Vince); Norma Aleandro (Edie); Keith Coogan (Mitch); Gina DeAngelis (Aunt Sofia); George Coe (Phil); Katie Murray (Chloe Hardy); Alex Bruhanski (Herbie); Stephen E. Miller (Stan); Gerry Bean (Kevin Costello); Gordon Currie (Dean Kozinski); Saffron Henderson (Terri Costello); Michele Goodger (Claudia); Andrea Mann (Rosanna); Mark Frank (Arnie Slevins); Leroy Schultz (Cousin Harry); Gloria Harris (Terri's Mother); John Civitarese (Terri's Father); Kate Danson (Wedding Killer Listener); David Hurwitz and John Hurwitz (Twins); Babs Chula (Mrs. Davidow); Bernadette Leonard (Bernadette); Denalda Williams (Olga);

Margot Pinvidic (Natalie); Tom McBeath (Mr. Dionne); Dolores Drake (Mrs. Dionne); Michael Naxos (Mr. Bergman); Lorraine Butler (Mrs. Greenblatt); Ann Leong (Chinese Fish Salesperson); Harold MacDonald (Priest at Funeral); Lorena Gale (Cosmetic Demonstrator); Monica Marko (Cosmetic Customer); Wes Tritter (Waiter); David W. Rose (Maître d'); Sharon Wahl (Weddingland Hostess); George Goodman (Jewish Father of Bride); Tom Heaton (Farmer on Tractor); Sheila Paterson (Cottage owner); Gary Pembroke Allen (Oil Painting Teacher); Antony Holland (Wedding Priest); Cathy Bayer (Cathy); John Paterson (Magician); Michele Moyier (Magician's Assistant).

FILMS IN REVIEW, 5/89, P. 300, Charles Epstein

What better way to show appreciation for two of France's more adored films than to appropriate and try bettering them? First came the charming *Three Men And A Baby,* easily surpassing its French predecessor. But that wasn't hard; the original wasn't a particularly distinguished film. *Cousins,* however, is based on one of the more delightful and enduring of French romps; *Cousin Cousine.* While *Cousins* pulls up well short of the original (lacking its pathos and light touch), it does acquit itself surprisingly well.

As in the original, the story is threaded through a tapestry of weddings (and one funeral) where a host of relationships are played out in capsule form: families are joined, romances bud, affairs develop, fights erupt. It is at the film's first of many weddings, between middle-aged Mitch and Edie, that the central relationships emerge. Tom, the womanizing husband of Edie's daughter Maria, prevails on the wife of Mitch's nephew Larry to take a "test drive" in his Subaru (he's a car salesman). As the band leaves at the end of the affair, Larry and Maria strike up a casual conversation as they wait for their spouses to return. When they do return it's obvious that Tom has shown Tish more than just what's beneath the car's hood. Initially, Larry and Maria are discreet about their respective spouse's infidelity; Maria is inured to her husband's philandering and Larry, a forgiving husband in liberal marriage, pretends to be unfazed. It is only when Maria, who's not really sure her husband is having an affair, asks Larry whether her suspicions are justified, that they both acknowiedge what they knew all along and, gradually, acknowledge their attraction for each other.

What might have started partially as a stunt to get back at their unfaithful spouses (a series of platonic rendezvous) escalates into the real thing. Larry and Maria, and Tish and Tom all tacitly realize they married the wrong partner. The narcissistic, career-driven Tish is a complement to the narcissistic/career-driven Tom. And the zany, warm Larry ("a failure at everything but life") meshes with the warm, sensitive Maria. However, sobriety ultimately intervenes, the two couples decide to patch things up and return to the status quo, But destiny is a stubborn thing; it can be deferred, but not denied. Their attraction resurfaces at a wedding between—naturally—their respective parents and after a brief verbal skirmish between Larry and the pugnacious Tom, the soundtrack swells and well, you can figure the rest out for yourself.

Although the script reflects no small degree of demographic calculation (the principles span three loveable generations, giving a little something for everyone), it is in the main spirited and winning. Ted Danson, an engaging presence, imbues Larry with a quirky charm and develops an easy, although sometimes shaky chemistry with Isabella Rossellini, who is just fine as the demure Maria (although she is encumbered with some clunky lines). William Petersen, however, is unconvincing as the perpetually contentious womanizer and the beautiful Sean Young is, well, let's just say she's never been more beautiful. Miss Young is most believable when she "affects" boredom, which, unfortunately, is most of the time. In lesser, albeit pungent roles, the protean Norma Aleandro is colorful as Maria's spunky mother, Lloyd Bridges is predictably workmanlike as Larry's ribald dad and young Gordon Currie contributes an unaffected turn as Larry's camera-toting, somewhat clichéd teenage son. After the breathless opening shots, Director Joel Schumacher settles in and escorts us through a breezy, if occasionally heavy-handed, light romantic comedy.

LOS ANGELES TIMES, 2/10/89, Calendar/p. 1, Sheila Benson

To add to the long list of translations from the French, we now have our American "Cousins," which began as 1975's vastly successful "Cousin, Cousine." As directed by Joel Schumacher, what moments of genuine emotion "Cousins" has can be traced directly to Isabella Rossellini; the rest is bustling, prettified, thoroughly bogus but intermittently entertaining.

It traces a tender friendship that begins between a couple (Isabella Rossellini and Ted Danson) with nothing initially in common other than the fact that their respective spouses (car salesman

William Petersen and cosmetics demonstrator Sean Young) have begun a very public affair. It ignites during the raucous second marriage celebration of Rossellini's mother (Norma Aleandro) to Danson's uncle, and at frequent intervals thereafter.

Danson, who drives a motorcycle with a sidecar in preference to a car, is supposed to be charmingly irresponsible about the material world. At present, he has a job as a dance instructor; in the past he's been an investment banker and a trumpeter in a jazz band. Rossellini, who works as a legal secretary, seems bemused but not particularly disturbed by this thoroughly out-of-step original.

Their partners' deceptions hurt them both: Danson takes refuge in an attitude that everyone has a right to freedom of choice; in Rossellini's case, the wound is clearly not a new one. She has chosen to overlook Petersen's countless affairs in the past because of their little daughter. It's only when an almost inadvertent (and charmingly written) affection grows between her and Danson that she wakes up to the real emptiness of her life.

"Cousins" has a palpable glow when Rossellini is on the screen, radiating a charm and a pure inviolable honesty that will make you think of only one other actress: her mother, Ingrid Bergman. It's an aura that spills over to include co-star Danson in its warmth. In their presence you *will* a lot to work that might, frankly, founder in other hands.

What makes "Cousins" feel splintered is that while so much of it is delicately written, there is also a jarring crassness at times, surefire cuteness, "boffo lines" or characters, like fake-wood siding tacked on to a beautifully constructed house.

Since these embarrassments come on the heels of deftly funny lines (like Rossellini's and Danson's deadpan zingers when Petersen brings Young back to the wedding site hours late), it's a peculiar mix. It's hard to know from simply scanning the credits *where* the problem lies. Usually it's with platoons of writers, but in this case, only one screenwriter is credited, playwright Stephen Metcalfe, whose first produced screenplay this is.

Yet Metcalfe has solved the original film's toughest story problem: how to keep from feeling real pity for the Sean Young character, who was a ditz and a neurotic, but clearly undeserving of the pain inflicted on her. In "Cousin, Cousine," it was easy to dislike her paramour, the compulsively straying husband, and to feel that he was getting what he deserved, but at some point, the flaunted infidelity of the "wronged" couple (our Danson-Rossellini pair) felt too insensitive, even for the romantically tolerant French.

This screenplay gets around our queasy feelings of cruelty by strengthening Young's character (nicely played) and by the very gently dawning affection between the odd couple out. Rossellini's character, with 12 years of marriage behind her, is clearly struggling with moral reservations about dashing into a love affair, and Danson, who has never crossed this line of infidelity before, is in love with her when he finally does. This delicacy of writing and performance is the film's real plus.

But "Cousins" has its exasperating side too: ersatz ethnicity (to these film makers there are no differences between Italians and Argentines, and a cartoon sense of what a real Italian wedding feels like); the broad obnoxiousness of Danson's teen-age son (Keith Coogan) and marriages and remarriages that have been made entirely too symmetrical. When Lloyd Bridges as Danson's father enters the picture with his blunt aphorisms, it's far too pat to team him up with Aleandro. (The French didn't push that in "Cousin, Cousine": Mama sampled what this new widower had to offer, found it wanting and settled for her freedom. Why must tidiness be such a besetting American trait?)

"Cousins" (rated PG-13 for the decorousness of its love scenes) is *such* a patent fairy tale that it's impossible to guess in what city or even which part of the country it's supposed to take place. From the scenery you'd say Colorado/France/Switzerland, although it was shot in British Columbia. It's no wonder the "Italian" part of its ethnicity comes with all the authenticity of Chef Boy-Ar-Dee boxed dinner. By the movie's last, satiric slapstick quarter, in which all production stops are pulled at a nuptial extravaganza palace called Wedding Land, its style has undergone another wrenching change. It remains only for that swarmy, home-movie tableau at the close to signal "Cousins'" final bankruptcy.

MONTHLY FILM BULLETIN, 8/89, p. 235, Tim Pulleine

Businessman Phil Kozinski is married to the widowed Edie Costello at a lavish ceremony. Among the guests are Phil's nephew Larry, a semi-bohemian who after sundry jobs has become a ballroom dancing teacher, with his second wife Tish, a beautician, Mitch, his teenage son by his former marriage, and Edie's daughter Maria, with her husband of eleven years, car salesman

Tom Hardy, and their young daughter Chloe. During the reception, Tom is attracted to Tish; under the pretext of looking at his car, they steal away to make love. Meanwhile, Maria and Larry have met, both half-suspecting the infidelity. Next day, Tom seeks out Tish at her workplace, and half-heartedly tries to convince her that the affair must not develop; at the same time, Maria is visiting Larry to share her growing suspicions; the upshot of the latter meeting is a strong bond of mutual attraction. A platonic friendship develops, though Tom and Tish each assume it is more than that. During a family party, Phil suffers a fatal heart attack; mourners at his funeral include his brother Vince (Larry's father), who moves in to Larry's Chinatown apartment. Vince subsequently finds himself drawn to Edie, though she reacts guardedly. Larry and Maria eventually become lovers, but her concern for Tom and particularly for Chloe (alleged by her teacher to be showing signs of disturbance) causes her to break off the relationship. However, Tish severs ties not only with Larry but also with Tom, with whom she has had one further, unsatisfactory, assignation. Some time later, Vince proposes to Edie, who to his surprise accepts. At their wedding, Larry confronts Maria, and asks her to choose between Tom and himself; she impulsively opts for a new life with Larry.

The Gallic influence of *Cousin, Cousine,* from which *Cousins* derives, may well be apparent in the new film's energetically textured mix of humour and sentiment. However, in both observational tone and visual manner (including an unforced used of focal distortion), the film appears more in line with American comedies of two decades ago like *Goodbye Columbus* (which may themselves have served partly as models of *Cousin, Cousine*). *Moonstruck* is probably the recent movie which *Cousins* most resembles in generic terms, but where the former updated "old" Hollywood protocols, the latter cleaves to "new" Hollywood in the sense that the figure of Larry, with his declared preference for happiness over success, could be considered a protagonist fit for the late 60s, although he has some resemblance to a tuba-playing Capra hero of the 30s.

Cousins, anyway, looks completely at home in an American milieu, and combines satire, near-farce, and incipient fantasy with great dexterity, due to the seamless interaction of script and direction. The narrative is structured round the rituals of family relationships: the action begins with the elaborately choreographed set-piece of the reception following Phil and Edie's wedding; subsequently it takes in the gathering at which the video of this event is shown, and at which Phil succumbs to a heart attack, making the transition directly from this to his funeral; and after taking in another wedding en route, the finale comes with the marriage of Edie and Vince. There is an emphasis on the participants' parents and on their children (the film's first shot is a close-up of the recalcitrant Chloe), extended into the recurring byplay between Vince and his grandson as well as into the former's courtship of his widowed sister-in-law, which provides a stylistic scaffolding around the edifice of the central situation, at the same time amplifying its emotional context.

A carefully selective presentation has led to a heightening in other ways. Conventional scene-setting and exposition has been reduced and is complemented by the symbolic resonance of apparently incidental detail, whether it be Maria running "against the tide" through the throng of commuters ot meet Larry at the railway station, or the unexpected equilibrium conferred on Maria and the camera in the dancing school sequence, where Larry's dauntingly stout lady pupil proves to be wondrously light on her feet. Then, too, the satirical asides, as in the jargon-laden utterances of Chloe's teacher, throw into relief the reality of the feelings underlying them.

Strangely, the relationship between Larry and Tish is fairly presented from both points of view, while the longer-standing bond between Maria and Tom is left mainly unexplored. But this potential weakness is overcome by the skill with which the presentation of the go-getting salesman combines satire with intimations of genuine vulnerability. Similarly, the suddenness of Maria's final capitulation to Larry is turned to positive advantage by the sleight-of-hand transition from that scene to a coda in which the couple are seen realising their "impossible" fantasy of life together. The playing is unfailingly accomplished, enlivened by the way in which Isabella Rossellini and Sean Young appear to have been cast in each other's expected role.

NEW YORK, 2/27/89, p. 143, David Denby

Why are critics fussing over whether *Cousins*—an American remake of *Cousin, Cousine*—is faithful to the spirit of the original? It's the nonissue of the decade. *Cousin, Cousine* was not a masterpiece but a slick commercial comedy about adultery that was slightly better acted and written than the other mid-seventies French comedies about adultery. The American version is not as good, but its alterations of the original do not amount to sacrilege. The movie is bland, pleasant, pretty to look at (it was shot in and around that great American city Vancouver), and it features two good actors—William Petersen, playing a shallow, self-disappointed philanderer who feels himself outclassed by his wife, and Isabella Rossellini, as the lady in question, a grave, matronly madonna who becomes progressively lighter on her feet and more sensual as she falls in love. Rossellini has a touchingly tentative smile, as if she would be punished for feeling good. Unfortunately, the object of her affections is the bucking, sashaying Ted Danson, who, apart from his peculiar body gyrations, gives a boring, neo-Alan Alda performance as a Mr. Nice Guy.

NEW YORK POST, 2/10/89, p. 19 David Edelstein

The 1975 French comedy "Cousin, Cousine"—which has been remade in English as "Cousins"— asks the question, "When is cheating on your wife or husband morally OK?" The answer is multi-part. It's OK, says the film, if he or she has cheated on you first; if he or she is a vacuous brute or ninny; and if you do it openly, proudly, without bourgeois guilt.

Indeed, in the last 10 minutes the "good" man and woman (cousins by marriage) retreat to bedroom during their extended family's Christmas dinner (*sacre bleu!*), fornicate passionately while young-'uns peer through the keyhole, and emerge to bid their respective children and spouses adieu. Stuff that in your stocking, the finale says.

"Cousin, Cousine" was a huge hit, and was hailed as a breath of fresh air by mainstream critics. But that was the '70s; I have no doubt that today many of those same writers would wrinkle their noses and furrow their brows at the picture's strenuously cheerful disregard for the sanctity of marriage and family.

An American remake in 1989 has a ticklish problem: How, in the age of pro-family horror movies like "Fatal Attraction," do you serve up a giddy romantic comedy about marital infidelity without incurring the wrath of our nation's moral guardians?

The solution is that you fudge it. In place of the original's blithely righteous ending, you substitute half an hour of talk, hand-wringing, and self-denial; instead of celebrating the abandonment of family, you show how *this* infidelity leads to a new, improved family. Ees not very French, but ees very commercial.

"Cousins" is actually a skillful piece of work, and part of me admires the way director Joel Schumacher and writer Stephen Metcalfe pirouette so deftly around the problem. The movie works hard to seem playful and ingratiating, and Isabella Rossellini is meltingly beautiful—at last, she gives a genuine star performance. But the price of all the compromises is that the picture has no core: half an hour later, you'll probably forget you've seen it.

As before, there are two couples; one partner in each is quirky and sensitive, the other shallow. The nice ones are Larry (Ted Danson), a dance instructor who plays a soulful trumpet and rides a motorcycle, and Maria (Rossellini), a warmly maternal legal secretary.

Their spouses are thoroughbred yuppie: the hot-tempered philanderer Tom (William Petersen) sells Subarus and BMWs but doesn't like to mention the former in public; Tish (Sean Young) works as a manager in a tony department store, and pays a psychic to teach her how to approve of herself.

Tom and Tish gaze lustfully at each other during the long wedding sequence that opens the film—the marriage of Maria's mother (Norma Aleandro) to Danson's uncle (George Coe). Long after their mates have snuck off into the bushes, Larry and Maria wait grimly in the empty banquet hall, making embarrassed small talk as their children yawn and complain.

Having abandoned their families, Tom and Tish must be punished, and soon a rich, platonic friendship blossoms between Larry and Maria. We feel a surge of satisfaction when the two begin to spend time together, much to the horror of their suddenly possessive spouses. It's even better that they don't make love for the longest while—more of an insult to the boobish Tom and Tish that these lovebirds can get off on each other's *minds.*

You'd be able to guess this was based on a European movie even if you hadn't seen the original. The look of "Cousins" is Continental, soft-focus, with lots of relaxed, airy group shots and almost no assaultive closeups. In the party scenes, Schumacher cuts from frolicsome children to frolicsome grown-ups—and the children are better behaved. What *joie de vivre!* I felt out of place without a glass of wine in my hand.

It's quite a menagerie. The characters drink too much, belch loudly, and pull down their trousers, but not everyone's having fun: off to one side, Maria's pious Italian grandmother (Gina DeAngelis) glowers disapprovingly. Larry's son (Keith Coogan) is a video-maven borrowed from

"Down and Out in Beverly Hills", his lurid video of the proceedings (intercut with starving Ethiopians and surgical footage) is a high point. And the picture gets a lift from the arrival of Lloyd Bridges—a sly, sprightly actor in his old age—as Larry's irreverent dad.

With his long, rectangular face, Neanderthal brow and sitcom glibness, Danson would seem a natural not for Larry but for Tom. He's too clenched for the nonconformist hero—there's no spark of a personality under his granite facade. A better choice, oddly enough, would have been Petersen, a terrific actor (especially in "Manhunter") who gives Tom an exciting edginess. It's not a great character, but Petersen gets hold of the insecurity beneath the blowhard persona, and strikes some funny—and recognizable—notes.

The same can't be said for his partner, the appealingly plastic Sean Young, whose huffy delivery gets stale pretty fast, and who seems bonier and more angular with every film. Someone buy this woman a milk shake.

It's Rossellini who holds the picture together. She looks ravishingly fit, and she gives Maria a dazed, effervescent quality—a shiny-eyed delight in new things. Yet she isn't addled or ditzy; it's a lucid daze, the daze you're in when you fall in love for real. Even when the tone changes in the last half hour—when "Cousins" sobers up in preparation for its conscientious finale—she doesn't let the movie droop. This is an intoxicating performance.

NEWSDAY, 2/10/89, Part III/p. 3, Mike McGrady

Back in 1975, When the frothy French comedy "Cousin, Cousine" was setting foreign-film, box-office records, it was cited as evidence of changing mores. A lighthearted spoof of bourgeois morality, the film suggested that what really went together like a horse and carriage was infidelity and marriage; its notion of a happy ending was a mate-swap that endured.

When it was first announced that Hollywood was remaking "Cousin, Cousine," one had to wonder how on earth Hollywood would handle themes this touchy, this volatile, this... well...essentially un-American. The answer, as evidenced in the new film "Cousins," is simplicity itself. Hollywood does what it is famous for doing: It chickens out.

Blame must rest on the shoulders of director Joel Schumacher ("St. Elmo's Fire," "The Lost Boys"). Not only is he guilty of startlingly mediocre moviemaking (the film is all dimness and long shots that keep the principal characters and their problems at arm's length), but he is also guilty of effecting a 180-degree attitude reversal.

Perhaps this should have been foreseen. Schumacher has been quoted as dismissing the original film as "a product of the sexual revolution" and now, in this post-sexual-revolution calm, "people are rediscovering the importance of commitment in their relationships and the joys of romance, marriage and the family."

The main result: An appealingly irreverent French film has been transformed into an appallingly reverent American movie. Whimsy has become lead, charm has become guilt, froth has become suds and comedy is now soap opera.

While much of the fabled charm of the original escaped me, at least there was some charm. Stephen Metcalfe's knuckleheaded script has replaced that charm with belches, with boorishness, with crude infidelities that lack either the comic or the human touch.

The actors play their parts with a minimum of energy. Of course, few American performers could match the French cast—headed by Victor Lanoux and the beautiful Marie-Christine Barrault—in charm or wit. Although Isabella Rossellini is lovely and Ted Danson is likable, neither comes close to the original. Oddly, this Americanized "Cousins" doesn't approach the original on even a technical level. A scene-by-scene comparison, reveals the most common change to be a kind of defanging.

Both films, for example, use weddings as principal settings—what more suitable event for satirizing middle-class values? However, consider what happens to the November-October romance between Lloyd Bridges and Norma Aleandro. In the original, the two oldsters go off on a romantic fling and after several weeks of geriatric lovemaking return home separately, apparently deciding enough is enough. In the new, unimproved version, they head directly for the altar. As does everyone else in sight. Only in America.

Each change is designed to enhance the same middle-class values the original film satirized. While this doubtless provides American audiences with the comfort of the conventional, something has definitely been lost in the translation. No, not something. Everything.

NEWSWEEK, 2/20/89, p. 65, David Ansen

Any American remake of a French comedy, as bitter experience has taught us, is guilty until proven innocent. Surprise. *Cousins*, a glossy, clever refurbishing of Jean-Charles Tacchella's popular 1976 "Cousin, Cousine," is a real charmer. Unabashedly romantic but laced with wit, it's the sort of feel-good Hollywood fantasy in which all the settings look idyllic, all the people are attractive, and even though the adulterous lovers, Ted Danson and Isabella Rossellini, make their livings as a dance instructor and a legal secretary, they seem to lead a leisure-filled existence without a money care in the world.

Danson and Rossellini play distant cousins, both married to incompatible spouses, who meet at a big family wedding—her Italian mother (Norma Aleandro) is marrying his wealthy uncle (George Coe). While their spouses—the ditsily attractive Sean Young and the philandering car salesman William Petersen—drive off from the party for a quickie, Danson and Rossellini begin a pristinely platonic affair that has the whole family clucking.

Structured around weddings and funerals and huge family gatherings, "Cousins" has the crowded, cluttered, warm feel of an extended family. Adding considerably to the mirth are Lloyd Bridges, delightful as Danson's widowed father, who moves in on Aleandro when her new husband suddenly dies, and Keith Coogan as Danson's teenage son, who video-tapes the wedding and splices in shots of starving Africans as social protest.

Director Joel ("The Lost Boys") Schumacher and screenwriter Stephen Metcalfe follow the original with nearly scene-by-scene fidelity. (A few details, like the groom mooning at his wedding, strike a sociologically false note in their new context.) What's fascinating, however, is what's been changed, to suit a different decade and a different culture. The central jest of Tacchella's comedy was the serene indifference of the lovers—played by Victor Lanoux and Marie Christine Barrault—to the outrage of their families. Lanoux felt no jealousy over his wife's infidelity; he announced that he had too much respect for people's freedom to be bothered by such bourgeois feelings.

In the American version, Danson says the same things, then explodes with jealous rage and admits he's full of bull. A true American love story in the '80s—especially an adulterous one—must be star-crossed and guilt-ridden, exactly what the French version wasn't. Once the platonic gives way to the carnal, Rossellini feels the guilty pull of husband and daughter. If this is more conventional, it is also more emotionally honest and saves the film from the smugness that crept into the edges of "Cousin, Cousine," whose success could only have come at the height of the Me Decade.

"Cousins" shows everyone off in top form: Danson and Rossellini have never been more likable, Young is deliciously gauche and Petersen gives his loutish, overgrown baby a surprising touch of pathos. It's an expert, richly produced entertainment offering up such a gauzily romantic vision that only the most confirmed cynic would want to resist it.

VILLAGE VOICE, 2/21/89, p. 77, Manohla Dargis

Isabella Rossellini has her mother's luminous face, and her guileless presence is the very soul of *Cousins*. Without her, the remake of the insipid 1975 French hit *Cousin, Cousine* would fade instantly—and deservedly—from memory.

Cousins mimics its Gallic predecessor with few notable changes. At a large wedding, Maria (Rossellini) meets her new cousin by marriage, Larry (Ted Danson), and soon this most unlikely pair, allied by their respective spouses' infidelities, is deep in Hallmark-card dew.

Any difference between *Cousins* '75 and '89 is due less to the transatlantic shift than to the social and psychic distance between the mid-'70s and late '80s. The no-frills look of the original is replaced by art-directed tableaux of bourgeois comfiness. Directed by Joel Schumacher (*The Lost Boys, St. Elmo's Fire*) and shot in British Columbia, *Cousins* looks like a California wine commercial; every scene seems shot through shimmering mists of gauze. Topicality, obligatory for recycled material, means strategically placed '80s icons. Knowing references—heavy metal, condoms, *The Brady Bunch*, and interior design that's "postmodern Jetsons"—reveal Hollywood hip rather than the provincial charm of coastal anytown.

Danson walks through the film with his familiar TV affability. His Larry is an implausible hipster who plays blues horn, rides a panhead Harley, and lives in Chinatown. (The decorative use of people of color to give white folks cultural capital marches on.) Rossellini's Maria is an

'80s Nora trapped in a Laura Ashley doll house. He's Sensitive Man: a caring dad, a gentle lover; she can't cry. He's dropped out '80s style, having left securities and real estate to teach ballroom dancing; she's a legal secretary. Stephen Matcalfe's uncharitable script leaves Rossellini little to do but register a sampler of reactions, but, with her grace and unaffected presence, it's still her film. You want this sad madonna to be happy. In 1989, however, a woman finding herself means trading in a boor for a Republican in drag.

Also reviewed in:
NEW YORK TIMES, 2/10/89, p. C12, Janet Maslin
NEW YORKER, 3/6/89, p. 97, Pauline Kael
VARIETY, 2/8-14/89, p. 18
WASHINGTON POST, 2/10/89, p. D1, Rita Kempley

CRIMES AND MISDEMEANORS

An Orion Pictures release. *Executive Producer:* Jack Rollins and Charles H. Joffe. *Producer:* Robert Greenhut. *Director:* Woody Allen. *Screenplay:* Woody Allen. *Director of Photography:* Sven Nykvist. *Editor:* Susan E. Morse. *Music:* Joe Malin. *Sound:* James Sabat. *Sound Editor:* Robert Hein. *Production Designer:* Santo Loquasto. *Art Director:* Speed Hopkins. *Set Decorator:* Susan Bode. *Set Dresser:* Dave Weinman. *Costumes:* Jeffrey Kurland. *Make-up:* Fern Buchner and Frances Kolar. *Running time:* 104 minutes. *MPAA Rating:* PG-13.

CAST: Bill Bernstein (Testimonial Speaker); Martin Landau (Judah Rosenthal); Claire Bloom (Miriam Rosenthal); Stephanie Roth (Sharon Rosenthal); Gregg Edelman (Chris); George Manos (Photographer); Anjelica Huston (Dolores Paley); Woody Allen (Cliff Stern); Jenny Nichols (Jenny); Joanna Gleason (Wendy Stern); Alan Alda (Lester); Sam Waterston (Ben); Zina Jasper (Carol); Dolores Sutton (Judah's Secretary); Joel S. Fogel, Donna Castellano, Thomas P. Crow (T.V. Producers); Mia Farrow (Halley Reed); Martin Bergmann (Professor Louis Levy); Caroline Aaron (Barbara); Kenny Vance (Murray); Jerry Orbach (Jack Rosenthal); Jerry Zaks (Man on Campus); Barry Finkel and Steve Maidment (T.V. Writers); Nadia Sanford (Alva); Chester Malinowski (Hit Man); Stanley Reichman (Chris' Father); Rebecca Schull (Chris' Mother); David S. Howard (Sol Rosenthal); Garrett Simowitz (Young Judah); Frances Conroy (House Owner); Anna Berger (Aunt May); Sol Frieder, Justin Zaremby, Marvin Terban, Hy Anzell, and Sylvia Kauders (Seder Guests); Victor Argo (Detective); Lenore Loveman, Nora Ephron, Sunny Keyser, Merv Bloch, Nancy Arden, Thomas Bolster, Myla Pitt, and Robin Bartlett (Wedding Guests); Grace Zimmerman (Bride); Randy Aaron Fink (Groom); Rabbi Joel Zion (Rabbi).

CHRISTIAN SCIENCE MONITOR, 10/27/89, p. 10, David Sterritt

When a new Woody Allen movie comes out, the first thing people want to know is: Will this one make us laugh?

It's a natural question because, while Mr. Allen made his reputation as a comedy filmmaker, he also has a philosophical streak running through him. You might call this his Ingmar Bergman streak, since he's heavily influenced by Bergman, and it often tends toward the gloomy side. His work runs from farces like "Sleeper" and "Take the Money and Run" to somber dramas like "September" and "Another Woman."

At his very best—in "Hannah and her Sisters," for instance—Allen manages to combine both sides of his personality into a single excellent movie. That's what he aims for in "Crimes and Misdemeanors," his new picture. The attempt doesn't quite work; there are lots of lumpy and unsatisfying moments. But it's such an odd and ambitious film that it's always absorbing to watch, and you never know what's going to happen next. One moment, it's a romantic comedy in the "Annie Hall" mode. The next, it's threatening to become Woody Allen's version of "Fatal Attraction."

The movie has two main storylines. One features Allen himself as a wistful comic character: a second-rate filmmaker who falls in love with an attractive producer, only to face competition from his brother-in-law, a slick TV director. Mia Farrow and Alan Alda play the love interest and the rival, respectively.

The more involving story is about a physician (Martin Landau) who's going through a major crisis in his life. Although he's been happily married for years, he's fallen into an affair with another woman (Anjelica Huston) who's threatening to tell his wife. The doctor is an educated, successful man, but in his desperation to find a way out of this predicament, he turns to his brother—a thug who suggests murdering the woman before she can blow the whistle and undermine the seeming stability of his household.

This may sound melodramatic, and at times, that's exactly what the movie is. It also does a weak job of integrating this plotline with the comic one about the lovelorn filmmaker.

What makes the picture fascinating are its philosophical undercurrents. "Crimes and Misdemeanors" is no mere entertainment; it's an exploration of moral and even spiritual issues. The ability to see clearly is a key metaphor in the story of the doctor, an ophthalmologist who treats other people's eyes while wondering (prodded by his conscience) if the eyes of God might be on his criminal behavior. Another key character is a deeply religious rabbi who keeps his faith and optimism even though he's going blind. Allen carries the metaphor of "vision" into the very fabric of the movie, until even a camera movement to the headlights of a car reinforces our awareness that enlightenment—as a literal circumstance, a symbolic process, and a spiritual necessity—is the quality he's seeking to explore.

What conclusions does Allen reach as his tale comes to a close? I'm sorry to report that they're surprisingly pessimistic, even cynical in their views of guilt, innocence, and justice. (There's that Ingmar Bergman streak again.) And yet, in a last scene with faint echoes of "Hannah and Her Sisters," the filmmaker does leave some hope for the future—if not the future of these characters, at least that of their children and later generations. In the end, "Crimes and Misdemeanors" isn't exactly a comedy or a tragedy, and it certainly isn't a wholehearted success. But it has a lot of interesting things on its mind, and its ability to mingle all sorts of ideas and attitudes—an important ability in our increasingly crowded and complex age—is as stimulating as it is provocative.

FILMS IN REVIEW, 12/89, p. 613, Kenneth M. Chanko

When Spike Lee's first feature, *She's Gotta Have It*, opened three years ago, critics dubbed him the black Woody Allen for being not just a triple-threat filmmaker (writer, director and actor), but for his *Annie Hall*-esque look at contemporary love in New York. So, it's only fair to turn the tables and call *Crimes and Misdemeanors* Woody Allen's *Do The Right Thing*.

Crimes and Misdemeanors is Woody's most serious comedy to date. In fact, it's more serious minded than any of his three dramas (*Another Woman, September* and *Interiors*). It's the story of how two sets of brothers—along with their wives, in-laws and other relatives—choose to live their lives. Woody's world, of course, is far removed from Spike's; yet, for the first time, Allen has his central character confront an act of violence and its moral implications. The murder-for-hire in Crimes and Misdemeanors takes on the same importance that the racially motivated murder and resulting riot does in *Do The Right Thing*, even though the particular problems that plague Woody's characters are radically different from the deep rooted feelings that bedevil Spike's characters.

Here are the plot basics: Judah Rosenthal (Martin Landau) is a middle-aged, wealthy and respected Jewish ophthalmologist who's been married for 25 years. Yet he's been having an affair with an emotionally volatile woman, Dolores (Anjelica Huston), for the past two years. He now wants to break things off, but she's threatening to not only have it out with his wife but to expose some financial irregularities if he unceremoniously dumps her. At the end of his rope, Judah—who was brought up religiously by his orthodox father but has long since strayed from anything resembling a religious life—turns to his less successful but street tough younger brother, Jack (Jerry Orbach), who has mob connections. Though the two are estranged, Jack offers his services, saying he knows some people who would "handle" the situation with his mistress if Judah wishes to go that route.

Meanwhile, there's another set of brothers: Ben (Sam Waterston), a rabbi and patient of Judah's who is going blind; and his brother, Lester (Alan Alda), an insufferably egotistical but powerful TV producer. Ben and Lester also have a sister, Wendy (Joanna Gleason), who's married to Cliff (Allen), a struggling documentary filmmaker whose topics of choice include terminal diseases and natural disasters. Reluctantly, Cliff, though he can't stand him, agrees to do a documentary on Lester at his loveless wife's urgings. On the set, Cliff becomes attracted to an associate producer, Halley (Mia Farrow), who shows interest in a documentary Cliff's putting together on an elderly professor of philosophy, Louis Levy (Martin Bergmann), whose concerns include God, ethics and love. Yet, much to Cliff's chagrin, Lester is also vying for Halley's attentions.

How things work out among the principal characters won't be revealed here. However, things don't go so well for the most sympathetically drawn characters, while the ones who will rub most audiences the wrong way get a far better deal. How things work out for Judah, who's responsible for a heinous crime, might surprise you. And Prof. Levy's fate is a telling—if perhaps overly cynical—comment on all that's transpired.

Crimes and Misdemeanors is probably Woody Allen's most mature film to date, and not just in the context of his past work. This is his "biggest" movie as well, for it not only deals with human frailties as they relate to romantic love, but it delves into the very heart of the human condition. Before, Allen's cracked amusing existential jokes about the difficulties of making one's way through life in an uncaring—or godless—world; here, however, he doesn't just pontificate on man's plight, or bury it as mere subtext. This time that formidable subject is addressed—honestly, pointedly, brilliantly—through the choices made and actions taken by his characters.

Conclusions beyond this-is-the-way-of-the-world are as difficult to draw here as they were in *Do The Right Thing*. Very few movies, though, are as magnificently convincing—not to mention as enormously entertaining—in their depiction of the-way-things-are within a particular milieu as *Crimes and Misdemeanors* and *Do The Right Thing*.

Allen's film also functions on another level: that of the artist and his role—and responsibilities—in society. At one point in the film, as his character, Cliff, and Halley watch a murder scheme being hatched in a melodramatic black-and-white movie, Cliff says, "That only happens in the movies." Meanwhile, Judah and his brother have gotten the ball rolling on their plot to do away with Dolores. And, in a luminously conceived closing sequence, Allen—through Cliff—addresses the issue head on. Cliff, after hearing Judah's "murder story" (the first and only meeting between these two characters), says that he'd have the murderer turn himself in. Judah tells him, "Yes, but this is real life...You've seen too many movies...If you want a happy ending, go see a Hollywood movie." The scene works in context, revealing Cliff to be a hopeless—even naive—romantic, and it also can be read as self-criticism on the part of Allen-as-artist. Up until *Crimes and Misdemeanors*, has Allen been tiptoeing around the "big" issues? Has *he* been a tad naive by not confronting murderous human acts and attempting to draw meaning from their consequences?

It's also no coincidence that Woody Allen's most successfully ambitious work yet happens to be leavened by significant doses of drollery. It's becoming ever more obvious that Allen is at his best—freer, more confident, more incisive—when, in addition to writing and directing, he puts himself in front of the camera. (Although, with *Hannah And Her Sisters* and now *Crimes and Misdemeanors*, his presence creates a somewhat fractured tone, with almost all the humor emanating exclusively from the scenes in which Allen's character is present.)

Who needs deathly serious drama from Woody Allen w' en he's able to produce something of the caliber of *Crime and Misdemeanors* and still make us laugh?

LOS ANGELES TIMES, 10/13/89, Calendar/p. 12, Michael Wilmington

In a contemporary movie world where, too often, technological bravura is wedded to moral vacuity, let's give thanks again for Woody Allen. He may not have all the answers, but he can make sweet, sad and hilarious music out of the questions.

In the brainy, poignant "Crimes and Misdemeanors," Allen splits his private world into two equal halves—the funny and the fatal, the dreamy and the real. On a simple level, he's joining the two kinds of movies he's made since 1978's "Interiors" into a kind of seriocomic fugue or jazzy sonata.

On another level, he's juxtaposing two kinds of moral dilemmas: some simple (sexual and professional peccadilloes), some more cataclysmic.

One half of "Crimes and Misdemeanors" follows a rich ophthalmologist, Judah Rosenthal (Martin Landau), who is besieged by the mistress (Anjelica Huston) he's trying to discard as he decides to silence her with murder. The other half has a nebbishy new Woody persona, threadbare documentary film maker Cliff Stern, enamored of Halley, a co-worker (Mia Farrow), who's also being romanced by his hated, and successful, brother-in-law, Lester (Alan Alda).

Success is Cliff's *bete noire* and the film's as well. It's a movie about how success poisons you, corrupts your values—and, in Cliff's case, how envy of success poisons you too. The two stories only intersect briefly, mostly at parties that bring together the two clans, the Rosenthals and Cliff's in-laws. But in a way, both men are the same character, split: lecherous dreamers obsessed with moral questions, the past and heritage. Cliff films Jewish philosophers. Judah returns in reverie to the dinner-table moralizing of his father, a rabbi who chooses faith over truth. The movie, more skeptical, chooses truth—but remains nostalgic for faith's simple joys.

Self-destructive Cliff keeps his idealism, his sensibility. Clinging to romantic dreams at old Hollywood movies at the Bleecker Street Cinema with his young niece (Jenny Nichols), he sabotages himself by juxtaposing Lester, in a TV documentary, with shots of Mussolini and Francis the Talking Mule. There's a pathos in Allen's acting here that he doesn't always achieve, a sadness beneath Cliff's tart quips. He's an aging clown, his innocence ravaged and fissured. And the parallel plot—Judah's murder—is the shadow behind Cliff's story.

It's also a great antidote to a pop infidelity hit like "Fatal Attraction," which turned its audience into a howling lynch mob. Landau, Huston and Jerry Orbach give the story a dark, pathetic edge, especially Landau, whose quietly satanic features are held in a strange, soft, falsely compassionate mask. When Cliff's face crinkles with disgust at his sister's S&M story and says that it's the worst thing he ever heard, we know he's wrong. There is much worse.

Allen has often been criticized for draining all the humor out of movies like "September" and "Another Woman," inflating them into frosty, WASPy Bergman pastiches, with none of the robust, self-kidding wit of his Jewish comedies. But in "Crimes and Misdemeanors," there's a crucial difference. Both worlds are Jewish, filled with the same things: infidelity, betrayal, hypocrisy and the perils of success.

And where "Hannah and Her Sisters" ended happily at Thanksgiving, punishing vice, rewarding the virtuous, "Crimes and Misdemeanors" (MPAA-rated PG-13) pushes us toward chaos and the dark, with its major moral spokespeople either blind or dead.

In a random or cruel world, where we are defined by every choice we make, these are the compensations: friends, family, love, art. And, surprisingly, this becomes a powerfully affirmative coda. Like a match flickering bravely in the midst of howling darkness, it casts a pure little flame. Does it break? Does it bend? Either way, we can laugh.

NEW YORK, 10/23/89, p. 124, David Denby

In *Crimes and Misdemeanors*, Woody Allen's most ambitious and complexly organized film yet, the principal character, Judah Rosenthal (Martin Landau), a rich, distinguished doctor, is faced with the kind of dilemma that he thinks occurs only in movies. The woman who has secretly been his mistress for the past two years has gone crazy. A harried loner whose cigarette ash drops to the floor in mid-conversation, Dolores (Anjelica Huston) can wait no longer for Judah to leave his wife. Enraged, she threatens to talk to the wife, expose Judah's financial misdeeds, even commit suicide. Dolores dogs his every step, and Judah, too weak to even confess the affair to his wife, begins to listen to his gangster brother (Jerry Orbach), who proposes that Dolores be gotten rid of.

Judah and the pathetic Dolores have what could only be called a destiny. So does an unlucky New York woman in the movie, a lonely divorcée who advertises in the personals columns only to wind up with a date who ties her to her bed and defecates on her. (To be dumped on is nothing if not your destiny.) In *Crimes and Misdemeanors*, the characters may be faced with terrible choices or they may fall into ludicrous and humiliating misadventures, but either way, they aren't merely neurotic, like the tremulously self-conscious wraiths in Allen's three earlier *serioso* efforts, *Interiors, September*, and *Another Woman*. (*Crimes and Misdemeanors* is *serioso* with laughs.) A glum drizzle of lassitude and inanition fell on those movies. But *Crimes and Misdemeanors* is vigorous and lively. The movie suffers from patches of poor writing, from occasional obviousness (the minor characters who "stand" for one thing or another), but it's still extremely entertaining—swift, resourceful, exciting, with surprising twists and turns.

Woody Allen, to our relief, has decided to embrace the movies—a *story*, dramatic tension, complications—rather than "art," with the result that he's more of a moviemaker and perhaps more of an artist than before. The movie-ness is explicit: There are repeated scenes of Allen's character, an embittered documentary filmmaker, going to old Hollywood features. One of the pictures he sees is the forties thriller *This Gun for Hire*, and it's satisfying to think of *Crimes and*

Misdemeanors, which is filled with passionate obsessions and lightning flashes in the night, as Allen's *film noir*. Sometimes a director has to go through a lot of "non-narrative" experiments before he realizes the moral power of stories all over again. This time, when Allen introduces a philosophical debate, the ideas don't rattle off the walls of an angst-lined echo chamber, they're woven into the plot—in fact, they *are* the plot. *Crimes and Misdemeanors* asks such things as, Is there any real punishment for crime? Is God, or anyone else, paying attention and keeping score? If someone is murdered or humiliated, does anyone care? To Judah's amazement, life turns into a movie—but will it end like one? The resolution to these questions is the movie's main line of suspense.

Another Woman was pretty bad, but at least Allen was developing a remarkably fluid way with structure. He folded scenes within scenes; he used flashbacks to introduce fresh characters who then turned up later, and so on. *Crimes and Misdemeanors* is even more supple. Allen now moves from one character to another with no apparent strain; he's become the master of casually linked exposition. The milieu of *Crimes and Misdemeanors* is upper-middle-class Jewish life in New York and Connecticut, and a whole web of relationships is established, a system of manners and ethics exposed.

The silver-haired doctor with his lurid, scandal-sheet love affair might have seemed banal if he were the whole movie. But there's also a highly developed subplot, which begins, we think, as comic relief but develops its own rather painful fascination. Lester (Alan Alda) a big-shot TV producer—the glib creator of many Emmy-winning sitcoms—tries to do his sister a favor by getting her filmmaker husband, Cliff (Woody Allen), a job. Public television, it seems, wants a documentary on Lester the genius, and Cliff needs work. After Cliff accepts, both he and Lester start pursuing Halley (Mia Farrow), the lovely (and available) producer of the documentary. Desperate for success, Cliff wants to use the film to do in Lester while making off with Halley. But Cliff is such an envious little creep—can he pull it off? Is he gauging Halley's attitude correctly? Allen gather all these characters at the beginning of the movie, disperses them in twos and threes, and then gathers them again for a wedding celebration at the end.

What holds the two disparate stories together is not the occasionally overlapping characters but Woody Allen's fascination with the drama of winners and losers—the strong and the weak—in a world without safety nets. *Interiors* trembled with the unwanted triumph of two talented and beautiful sisters (Diane Keaton and Kristin Griffith) over an untalented and plain one (Mary Beth Hurt). In *September*, a self-confident battle tank of a mother (Elaine Stritch) crushed her anxiety-plagued daughter (Mia Farrow). Allen seemed to admire the vulgar strength of his obstacle-smashing characters while offering his sympathy to the insulted and the injured. But now I'm not so sure. His attitude has become harsher.

Judah Rosenthal is the kind of success—a lion of the Jewish medical-philanthropy circuit—who can hide his sins behind an ivied façade of respectability. When Martin Landau was young, his lean angularity and deep-set eyes made him seem odd-looking, almost sinister, but now, heavier, with thick, patriarchal brows, he's craggily handsome, a middle-aged monument. Landau gives a strong, detailed performance; his doctor, normally masterful (in a ponderous sort of way), retreats into stuffy outrage when his mistress makes more demands on him than he can handle. Landau brings out the selfishness in Judah's most self-righteous moments. And when Judah passes from simple deceit into criminality, Landau suffers, but without much pain. Judah's suffering becomes a form of luxury, a way of assuring himself he has moral reflexes.

From an occasional look at Judah's anxiously proper wife (Claire Bloom), we can see that volatile Dolores gave Judah an emotional charge lacking in his long, prosperous marriage. But after two years, Dolores has become a weepy, blackmailing woman. The normally glamorous Anjelica Huston, pacing and smoking furiously, races ahead, biting off her words; she looks pale, almost frumpy, and, for the first time, awkwardly large. It's a flaw in the movie that Allen doesn't give Dolores the kind of big scene that would make us understand her better. Except for a few flashbacks, where she appears loving and relaxed, she's seen distantly, through Judah's eyes, as a squalling, misery-inducing crank. Since Judah is a coward protecting himself, neither of them is in the right.

It's not that Allen has become pitiless, but he's making a stern effort to see things for what they are. Is the movie ever funny? Yes, but in an intentionally curdling way—the jokes are there to expose the weakness of the joker. Allen's own character, Cliff, is a witty man yet also one of the bitterest studies in failure ever put on the screen. High-minded Cliff, who makes documentaries about toxic waste, puts himself and everyone else down. Rolling his eyes in disgust, Allen gives

Cliff sarcasm without courage, intelligence without self-knowledge. Cliff falls in love with Halley but can't see that his pitch to her is based almost entirely on making fun of another man's success. And every time he ridicules Lester, he's drawing on Lester's energy while offering nothing of his own. Again, a simple rooting interest has been replaced by a more complex judgment. Cliff deserves a comeuppance. And Lester? As Alan Alda plays him—exuberantly, noisily, head bobbing—he's an egotistical jerk. But you also see why he's such an all-American success: He pleases people; he brings them to life; he's generous as well as self-important.

In Allen's new view, the strong, by definition, are great at shucking things off and moving on; they have talent, and they see the way to their own advantage in every situation. They beat down the weak—who get stuck in the glue of their own tastes, their own sense of honor—or merely discard them. Fatalism has replaced pathos.

And who is to stop the stone-crushers? A kind of pained ethical debate runs through *Crimes and Misdemeanors*, a debate between two visions of life. In one view, upheld by a stoic rabbi who is going blind (Sam Waterston, who makes goodness almost comically saccharine), and also by Judah's Orthodox father, seen holding forth at a seder long, long ago, the world is morally coherent. Evil is punished in one way or another, either by God or through the suffering of the guilty. In the competing view, expounded by a German Holocaust survivor Cliff has been filming, as well as by Judah's freethinking Socialist aunt, who also holds forth at that memorable long-ago seder, the universe is coldly indifferent and morally neutral; and belief in right and wrong, however admirable, is just a personal myth that people use to make sense of their lives. Dostoevski chewed over such ideas a full 120 years ago, but originality may not be the point. Woody Allen brings the old arguments dramatically to life. I don't want to give away which view prevails, but I'll interpret the title for you: More pessimistic than ever, Allen gives us a pleasant social world in which crime goes unpunished while misdemeanors are greeted with a scorn close to annihilation.

NEW YORK POST, 10/13/89, p. 23, David Edelstein

These days, Woody Allen doesn't so much make a movie as worry it. Insistently (almost perversely) high-minded, he goes to the mat with the sort of questions that, in comedy, he made a habit of shrugging off. Allen the comic asked, "Is there an afterlife and if so, can they change a 20?" Allen the tragedian leaves out the punchline.

His new film "Crimes and Misdemeanors," is concerned with nothing less than universal justice, and for once Allen has made a pointy-headed problem drama that keeps you in your seat.

Unlike his excruciating parlor play, "September" (source: "Uncle Vanya") and his pristine paean to life, "Another Woman" (source: "Wild Strawberries") "Crimes and Misdemeanors" has a compelling plotline, terrific acting and a structure closer to "Hannah and Her Sisters." That doesn't mean it's a barrel of laughs, but it works.

Allen supplies two protagonists. The most vivid is a wealthy ophthalmologist, Judah Rosenthal (Martin Landau) who has been having an affair for two years with Caroline, an airline stewardess (Anjelica Huston) he met on a business trip. The woman, however, is high-strung and vindictive and threatens to expose both the affair and the good doctor's business maneuvers.

Backed against the wall, this pillar of society summons his brother (Jerry Orbach), a shady underworld type,, for advice, half-knowing he'll suggest a contract killing. As the scheme nears completion, however, Judah recalls with escalating horror the words of his pious Jewish father: That God is all-seeing and crimes will be punished.

This would be enough for one movie, but Allen has learned that his films do better when he's in them and can relieve some of the gloom with his one-liners. (You get the feeling, though, that in his ideal movie he wouldn't have a place.)

In "Crimes and Misdemeanors," the dispirited clown plays Cliff Stern, an unsuccessful, high-principled documentary director working on a movie about an NYU professor called Levy (modeled, I'd guess, on Primo Levi)—a man who survived a concentration camp and now speaks of love as the only sustaining force in a cold universe.

Stuck in a loveless (and sexless) marriage, the impoverished Cliff is further humiliated when he accepts a job working on a public-TV documentary about his brother-in-law Lester (Alan Alda), an oily and pretentious producer who's like a cross between Norman Lear and Warren Beatty.

On the set, Cliff falls for a demure, matronly producer named Halley (Mia Farrow); to his horror, he sees that the salacious Lester has fallen for her, too, spurred by her reluctance to be wooed by him.

With all the movie's pontifications, Allen could not define what's at stake more clearly. In a

Hollywood film, Cliff's documentary would be made and the professor acclaimed, the murderer would confess and Woody would get the girl he so poignantly deserves. But—as Allen's characters take pains to point out—life is not a Hollywood film.

"Crimes and Misdemeanors," in fact, is defeatist even in its look. I doubt Sven Nykvist, Ingmar Bergman's longtime collaborator, has ever shot a film so drably. The joy Cliff worships in musical comedy would never be possible in a world so gray and muddy. Joy = Escapism. Despair = Here.

So what does it boil down to? Either God sees everything and punishes wrongdoers or we create our own meaning (and define ourselves) through action. Allen believes the second answer and it bugs him: Why should be and not God be compelled to create meaning? And who's to say he'll be rewarded if he does create it? (Women are so messy, people so untrustworthy.)

This world view is neither appealing nor illuminating, but Allen does work it through with skill and feeling. Love is the answer, says Professor Levy, but he can't stave off despair. Eyes are the windows of the soul, we're told, but the infinitely loving rabbi (Sam Waterston in a goofy and lovable performance) goes blind while scoundrels return one's gaze.

Too bad Allen is so tin-eared these days: he writes as if he learned English from Constance Garnett, William Archer and other turn-of-the-century translators of the Russians and Norwegians.

Fortunately, the roles he creates are juicy and his actors resourceful. With his thick, black brows, the saturnine Landau brings Old Testament stature to Judah and works excitingly with the sallow, flinty Orbach. Anjelica Huston is shockingly vivid; fleshy and ravaged by self-loathing, she's determind to act out her rage at being abandoned. And the oily Lester liberates Alda, who gives his most deft performance in years. This feminist-liberal-do-gooder should never be allowed to play a nice guy again.

NEWSDAY, 10/13/89, Part III/p. 3, Mike McGrady

To appreciate the originality of Woody Allen—no, let's make that the genius of Woody Allen—one has only to imagine how Hollywood would have handled the very serious themes and ideas explored in "Crimes and Misdemeanors."

For starters, can you imagine a murder movie that never bothers to show the killing itself? Next, imagine a murderer who is neither insane nor lowlife but is, instead, enormously successful, a paragon of virtue, a pillar of the community. Then, consider what happens to the murderer. Nothing. In fact, as a result of the killing, the killer apparently goes on to enjoy a richer, fuller, happier existence.

Even the subplots violate all the basic canons of moviedom. One subplot centers on an idealistic, intellectual film maker (Woody Allen) who is assigned to do a film bio of his brother-in-law, a smug, egomaniacal, fatuous, womanizing TV producer (Alan Alda). And who gets the girl? Guess again. The pure-of-heart Allen winds up losing the woman he loves (Mia Farrow) to the charlatan he despises.

Unhappy endings? Help yourself, there are plenty to go around. A mistreated mistress is cruelly murdered. A lonely woman places a personal ad and, for her trouble, is subjected to grotesque sexual abuse. A saintly rabbi (Sam Waterston) is going blind. An elderly professor (Martin Bergmann) seems to have the answer to all of mankind's ailments but winds up leaping out a window. In fact, the only ones who seem to triumph in "Crimes and Misdemeanors" are the sleazy and the corrupt, the criminals and killers.

To envision the film's everyday occurrences, you have to conjure up a world in which no noble instinct goes unpunished and no evil act goes unrewarded. To some, of course, this will seem distressingly close to real life. Others will observe that it is refreshingly far removed from the usual tidy packages of myth and Technicolor manufactured in that great movie-making town slightly to the west of reality.

The new Woody Allen film, his best work since "Hannah and Her Sisters," violates your every expectation. The tale of a leading citizen, an opthamologist-philanthropist being driven to the murder of his mistress, would be gripping of its own account. But Allen, precisely like Dostoevsky with "Crime and Punishment," uses the killing as a mere starting point and goes on to explore psychological areas ignored by most other moviemakers.

For example, religion—after all, the murderer is an upright citizen raised in a religious household. It may well have been his father's simply stated religious beliefs ("The eyes of God see all. ...there is absolutely nothing that escapes His sight") that led to his choice of ophthalmology as a profession, as well as to the guilt that tortures him before and after the act.

Stressing the serious nature of "Crimes and Misdemeanors" may do the film a disservice. It also happens to be very funny. The lines gleam with wit and irony. While Allen once again shows the ability to balance and counterbalance many complicated characters doing many complicated things, what separates this from his most recent Bergmanesque efforts is the return of humor; even the horror of the central situation fails to dim the hilarity.

There are several performances of brilliance. Martin Landau, Oscar-nominated for his fine work in last year's "Tucker," is again superb, showing many facets of a most complex man. Alan Alda—and I never dreamed I'd write these words—is perfect, just perfect, as the pontificating TV producer. And Woody Allen—well, Woody is Woody, and he has done it once again—provoked, excited, amused, entertained, and made one of the year's best movies.

NEWSWEEK, 10/16/89, p. 67, Jack Kroll

In each of Woody Allen's movies, he changes the ratio of comic elements to dramatic or tragic ones. Between the extremes of, say, "Bananas" (comedy 100, tragedy 0) and "Interiors" (the exact opposite) his films are collages of light and dark, laughter and lament. In *Crimes and Misdemeanors* it's 50–50, and the result is a tension that makes this one of his most affecting movies and perhaps his most disquieting portrait of the urban psyche-scape.

The title's two nouns almost suggest two interlocking films. The comic one centers on Cliff Stern (Allen), who makes documentary films that are seen by nobody. The tragic one deals with Judah Rosenthal (Martin Landau), a successful ophthalmologist who panics when his unstable mistress (Anjelica Huston) threatens to destroy his life if he doesn't divorce his wife (Claire Bloom). Stern's marriage is a casualty of his unsuccessful career. As he says: "The last time I was inside a woman was when I visited the Statue of Liberty."

There are no gags in Dr. Rosenthal's story. As his mistress gets increasingly hysterical, he turns to his brother Jack (Jerry Orbach), a businessman with underworld connections. Jack's advice is brutally simple: for a price he can arrange for the mistress to be liquidated. Rosenthal is horrified by the idea, but more horrified when he realizes he's considering it. Meanwhile Stern reluctantly undertakes to make a documentary about his brother-in-law Lester (Alan Alda), a big-shot TV producer. Stern despises the pretentious, crass, lecherous Lester. And when Lester scores with Halley (Mia Farrow), whom Stern has fallen for, Stern goes bananas.

Allen has directed his screenplay with a precise eye for its ironic turns and subversive twists. His mix of the absurd and the appalling exactly registers the schizoid soul of New York. The "Crimes" represent the domestication of evil: "good" people make murderous decisions as if conscience had simply been exhausted. The "Misdemeanors" are farcical foul-ups, phonies beating out schlemiels. Allen whipsaws you between dismay and laughter. If the result lacks the warmth of "Hannah and Her Sisters," it rings truer than anything he's ever done.

As in all his best films, Allen's cast works together like a good repertory company. Huston provides a scary study of neurotic desperation. Alda, going against type (or is he?), is repellently funny as a successful supercreep. In his best screen role Landau gives his finest performance as a man who loses his humanity in the private hell of self-interest. And Allen does an engaging variation on his classic loser. Frozen out by his wife, rejected by his girlfriend, humiliated by his brother-in-law, Stern's truest relationship is with his adorable young niece (Jenny Nichols). Referring to his own plight, Stern tells her: "You'll find as you go through life that great depth and smoldering sensuality don't always win."

TIME, 10/16/89, p. 82, Richard Schickel

Judah Rosenthal (Martin Landau) is possessed by a primal memory: a rabbi instructing the boy Judah that the eye of God is all seeing; no crime ever escapes it. Now successful and middle aged, Judah self-deprecatingly suggests to the audience at a testimonial dinner on his behalf that perhaps he became an ophthalmologist because he is haunted by that recollection.

Seeing is also a subject that Cliff Stern (Woody Allen) takes seriously. A documentary filmmaker, he is driven not by God but by the demands of an unyielding conscience to make his camera—his eye—bear witness to the inequities of his careless time.

Cliff's only connection to Judah—until the concluding sequence of this thematically unified but somewhat bifurcated movie—is through Ben, another rabbi (Sam Waterston), who is one of Cliff's brothers-in-law. The rabbi is Judah's patient, and his eye trouble is quite literal; by the end of the movie he has gone blind. But this blindness is also symbolic. By visiting this affliction on the only character in his movie who has remained close to God, Allen is suggesting that if the Deity himself is not dead, then he must be suffering from severely impaired vision.

All the crimes and misdemeanors Allen records in this film go not merely unpunished; they are generously rewarded. Upstairs, on the melodramatic story line, a hypocritical Judah gets away with murder, arranging for the assassination of his mistress (Anjelica Huston), who threatens to make their affair—and his equally shabby financial affairs—public, thereby destroying his family, wealth reputation.

Downstairs, on the funny line, is Cliff's other brother-in-law Lester, a sleek TV producer (played by Alan Alda in a gloriously fashioned comic performance). He offers Cliff a sinecure: filming a documentary that will make Lester look like a philosopher-king among the pompous nitwits who produce prime-time TV. Cliff agrees, but because he tries to turn Lester's story into a truthful exposé, the project collapses. Along the way he loses the woman he loves (Mia Farrow), as well as a serious film to which he had been profoundly committed.

This is the funny stuff? Yes, because Allen puts a deliberately farcical spin on Cliff's frenzies. It is good showmanship, a way of relieving the itchy ironies of Judah's discomfiting story. It also rings with irony. If neither Judah's guilty musings on his own crimes—and he does exhibit a strong desire to be caught and punished—nor decent Cliff's frantic quest for some kind of fulfillment can awaken heaven's sleeping eye, then what in this world can? If *Manhattan*, coming at the end of the '70s, was Woody Allen's comment on that decade's besetting sin, self-absorption, then this is his concluding unscientific postscript on the besetting sin of the '80s, greed. At times the joints in the movie's carpentry are strained, at times the mood swings jarring. But they stir us from our comfortable stupor and vivify a true, moral, always acute and often hilarious meditation on the psychological economy of the Reagan years.

VILLAGE VOICE, 10/17/89, p. 87, J. Hoberman

Woody Allen has shown a remarkable capacity to reinvent himself, and with *Crimes and Misdemeanors*, opening Friday, he's done it again. This is Allen's first successfully "serious" film. It's the breakthrough he's been laboring toward in the decade since *Interiors*, and it's actually most exciting when its maker is groping in the dark.

Although hardly unfunny, *Crimes and Misdemeanors* is deeper and more mysterious than any previous Allen excursion into domestic drama. Like *Interiors* or *September, Crimes* can be read as his attempt to place his irrepressible (y)id under the genteel superego of high (Episcopalian) art, but here the tension is palpable. Fraught with ritual, *Crimes* opens at a testimonial dinner and ends with a wedding. In between, the movie manages to engage *Fatal Attraction*, satirize Woody's own romantic love stories, and integrate Betty Hutton. The tale of two families linked by their common connection to a blind rabbi, *Crimes and Misdemeanors* is Allen's most structurally complex movie since *Annie Hall*, and a far more interestingly Jewish one than the overrated *Hannah and Her Sisters*.

The film's resident patriarch, Judah Rosenthal (Martin Landau), is a fabulously successful ophthalmologist—the rabbi (Sam Waterston) is his patient—with a well-developed public persona. As his name suggests, Judah is a lion of integrity, adored by his wife (Claire Bloom), revered by his peers. Landau's characterization personifies the Jewish mystique of doctor as priest. He also carries the burden of an Allen protagonist's self-pity and -absorption with corroded, solitary grandeur, as he attempts to disentangle himself from the frenzied clutches of pill-popping Dolores (Anjelica Huston), an airline stewardess with whom he's carried on a clandestine affair that's lasted two years.

In contrast to the majestically tormented Landau, Allen's second icon is himself—as the nebbish Cliff, a maker of documentaries on toxic waste, married to the rabbi's sister, Wendy (Joanna Gleason). Terminally irritated with her loser husband, Wendy, a sour English professor, has stopped sleeping with him—beginning, he claims, "on Hitler's birthday." One of Allen's greatest gifts is the ability to reduce all Jewish history to a family affair; consequently Cliff gets the movie's best one-liner, the mordant Julius and Ethel Rosenberg joke with which he characterizes his other brother-in-law, Lester, the king of primetime comedy.

Superbly embodied by Alan Alda with a tan rich enough to match his alpaca topcoat, Lester is as much found object as artistic creation—he's wholesome sleaze, the most cheerily impervious of the demonic sellouts, nightmare alter egos, that haunt Woody's world. Lester is rich, famous, and surrounded by babes; the college he dropped out of now offers a course on "existential motifs" in his situation comedies. As a favor to Wendy, Lester hires Cliff to direct the profile being made on him for public TV. Few miseries are more communicable than Cliff's, watching

Lester hold forth in some *echt*-Manhattan location on his love for New York, or earnestly explicate his theory of comedy. Cliff is more characteristically interested in documenting Dr. Louis Levy, a venerable New School type (named, 'I'd like to think, after a Chinatown men's store) who offers psychoanalytic wisdom with a heavy Middle European accent and provides the movie its grimmest punchline.

That *Crimes and Misdemeanors* manages its huge cast of characters with adroit visual shorthand—the cultural artifacts that furnish Judah's posh Connecticut estate have their equivalents in Cliff's cluttered, funky apartment—suggests the movie would amply repay a second viewing. The sibling relationships in particular are a film in themselves: Wendy, whom the talented Gleason gives the angst-ridden zing of active unhappiness, shamelessly blossoms whenever she's with brother Lester; Judah and his brother Jack (Jerry Orbach) make a sensational pair, two hustlers with extravagant, mournful profiles, pondering their father's dictum that "the eyes of God see all."

Moving from the *haimish* environs of early Philip Roth to the icier climes of Bellowland, *Crimes and Misdemeanors* doesn't lack for literary motifs. (Rather too much is made of the notion that the eyes are the windows of the soul.) Most impressive is the novelistic harshness of certain scenes. The story Cliff's sister Barbara (Caroline Aaron) tells of a date met through the personals is a joke gone off the radar screen and then horribly back. The outrageous final solution to the Dolores question, a sequence unlike any other in the Allen oeuvre, is hauntingly played against a Schubert quartet. The scene in which Judah revisits his childhood home and remembers a family seder is, if initially clunky, an audacious attempt to map the religious worldview of American Jews. Even if Allen's notion of Judaism sometimes seems an uneasy amalgam of ethical culture, ethnic couture, and Catholic theology, the film has the tribal conviction and moral complexity of a Jewish *Do the Right Thing*.

What's particularly fascinating is that, while none of Allen's set pieces are completely successful, they are all far darker and more resonant than the pop Bergmanesques with which he used to adorn life's little tragedies. This toughness extends to the Allen persona itself. A typical Woodman, Cliff romances dream shiksa Halley (Mia Farrow) with jokes, junk food, and prewar movies. *Crimes and Misdemeanors*, however, never buys these illusions; the documentarian's powers of denial far exceed his amorous yearnings. Still, shabby and unredeemed, Cliff gives the movie its soul. No previous Allen film has been more skillful (or less pretentious) in integrating movie clips and show tunes. The parallel scenes from *Happy Go Lucky* or *This Gun for Hire* that punctuate the narrative underscore Cliff's power as a filmmaker when, in a documentary that rivals the avant-garde bar mitzvah movie in *The Apprenticeship of Duddy Kravitz*, he match-cuts from Lester to Mussolini.

This small misdemeanor is Cliff's greatest triumph. In the last scene, he and Judah meet—for a story conference of sorts. "I was plotting the perfect murder," Cliff remarks, and suddenly Judah's face appears in closeup, an Old Testament mask of tragedy. As Cliff recounts his scenario, the memory of justice drains from the world. Like Lester, Judah embodies the reality principle, the winner's violence. Indeed, he is killer reason, obliterating fantasy, irrationality, passion. "If you want a happy ending," he tells Cliff with rich duplicity, "you should see a Hollywood movie."

That line notwithstanding, *Crimes* ends on a quasi-affirmative note; had the laughs been more sustained, Allen might have opted for the bleak conclusion that the material seems to demand. At one point, the insufferable Lester defines comedy as "tragedy plus time." It's an asinine formula but, like much of what Allen gives this surrogate to say, not altogether untrue. If Woody had taken more time, *Crimes and Misdemeanors* might have been a comic masterpiece; the wit beneath the surface is certainly savage enough. As it is, this is a smart, absorbing, inventive movie, with startling intimations of greatness. Woody Allen hasn't simply caught up to his ambition, in some ways he's run past it.

Also reviewed in:

NATION, 11/13/89, p. 575, Stuart Klawans
NEW REPUBLIC, 11/13/89, p. 22, Stanley Kauffmann
NEW YORK TIMES, 10/13/89, p. C19, Vincent Canby
NEW YORKER, 10/30/89, p. 76, Pauline Kael
VARIETY, 10/11-17/89, p. 32
WASHINGTON POST, 10/13/89, p. C1, Rita Kempley

CRIMINAL LAW

A Hemdale Film release. *Producer:* Robert MacLean and Hilary Heath. *Director:* Martin Campbell. *Screenplay:* Mark Kasdan. *Director of Photography:* Phil Meheux. *Editor:* Christopher Wimble. *Production Designer:* Curtis Schnell. *Running time:* 112 minutes. *MPAA Rating:* Not Rated.

CAST: Gary Oldman (Ben Chase); Kevin Bacon (Martin Thiel); Karen Young (Ellen Faulkner); Joe Don Baker (Detective Mesel); Tess Harper (Detective Stillwell); Ron Lea (Gary Hull); Karen Woolridge (Claudia Curwen); Elizabeth Sheppard (Martin's mother).

LOS ANGELES TIMES, 4/28/89, Calendar/p. 19, Kevin Thomas

"Criminal Law" is a doggedly routine thriller that doesn't deserve the vital presence of Gary Oldman, not to mention that of Kevin Bacon and Tess Harper. Ever since Oldman first attracted attention in "Sid and Nancy," the young British actor has been a brash, distinctive force on the screen. As a hotshot Boston attorney successfully defending Bacon's rich aristocrat for murder, Oldman is once again electrifying, but he and the capable, rather than inspired, British TV director, Martin Campbell, are short-circuited at every turn by Martin Kasdan's trite plotting and often pretentious dialogue.

In a bravura display of courtroom maneuvers, Oldman successfully defends Bacon on a charge of an exceptionally brutal murder of a young woman. Too flush with lucrative success to examine his conscience about the possibility that Bacon might well have been guilty, Oldman agrees to meet his client at a park during a rainstorm, only to stumble over the still-burning corpse of a second young woman. Certain details convince Oldman that Bacon is in fact her murderer, perhaps even a budding serial rapist-killer, whom he vows to nail.

Why isn't Oldman, who reports his discovery of the smoldering body to the police, ever for an instant under suspicion himself, especially considering that the investigating detective (Joe Don Baker) loathes him and that Baker's partner (Harper) has become disillusioned with him? The innocent man turning detective to save his own skin was a favorite Hitchcock device, and it could have given Oldman's quest much-needed dimension and urgency.

Unfortunately, "Criminal Law" proceeds from one weakness to another. Bacon's perpetual smirk, coupled with the icy demeanor of his dominating mother (Elizabeth Sheppard), telegraphs the plot needlessly from Day One. And why should the roommate (Karen Young) of the woman murdered in the park so speedily begin an affair with Oldman, whom she has angrily blamed for her friend's death? At one point writer Kasdan actually resorts, Hardy Boys/Nancy Drew-style, to the discovery of a secret tunnel to further a plot with even more holes than have already been related.

Kasdan points up the chasm between law and justice—hardly news—overlaid with Freudian notions of behavior and Nietzschean considerations of the nature of evil. (Not once but twice Oldman has conversations with his tiresomely sage old professor.) Yet we know absolutely no more about Oldman's background at the end of the film than at the beginning; Oldman's excellent American accent sounds as if it might be meant to be smoothed-over Boston blue-collar Irish.

The film also could have benefited from Oldman and Bacon spending more time together, from them having developed a kind of friendship. As it is, Bacon has a decidedly supporting role, one that requires him only to sound the same note of clever craziness over and over. Baker is straitjacketed in a standard tough, angry cop role, but Harper's detective is actually the film's best-written part, that of a smart, sensible professional. She's the kind of cop you want when you're in trouble, and Harper plays her beautifully.

"Criminal Law" (rated R for sex and graphic depictions of the result of extreme violence against women) is the latest in the unending parade of films in which Canadian cities stand in for American ones and here Montreal and Quebec City are ineffective stand-ins for Boston. Seeming neither truly American or truly Canadian in flavor "Criminal Law" is in trouble right from the start.

NEW YORK POST, 4/28/89, p. 29, Jami Bernard

A flamboyant, self-assured lawyer and his psycho-killer client play a dangerous game of yuppie cat-and-mouse in the courtroom thriller "Criminal Law," a dishearteningly anti-abortion movie that bites off more than it can chew. But then anything that kicks off with a quote from Nietzsche deserves what it gets.

"Whoever fights monsters should see to it that in the process he does not become a monster. And when you look long into the abyss, the abyss also looks into you," is the quote, something defense attorney Ben Chase (Gary Oldman) and bright-eyed killer Martin Thiel (Kevin Bacon) probably both read in their Philosophy 101 courses at their respective Ivy League schools.

The movie begins (post-Nietzsche) with a grisly crime scene in a nighttime deluge. (Don't put those rain machines away yet, crew—more storm-tossed murders to come.) We jump to the trial where Ben successfully defends a smirkily impassive Martin, mostly by reducing the one eyewitness to tears. The case is closed.

But of course it is not closed, or there would be no movie. For one thing, it doesn't take a fortuneteller to see right away that Thiel is a psycho-killer. (Later, he will demonstrate that one quality that really gives him away—the psycho-killer's insistence on stalking prey with baby-steps instead of pouncing and slashing when given the chance.)

Psycho-killers must stay busy too; no sooner is Martin acquitted than he is hard at work raping, burning and killing women joggers in the park. (It is unfortunate that this movie happens to open on a week when all of New York—except the psycho-killer segment—is in shock over what happened in Central Park.)

Martin has taken a shine to Ben; to reward the lawyer, Martin sort of dedicates the next couple of murders to him, both as a sign of affection and as a test of his loyalty. After all, Martin will be needing a good lawyer again real soon.

Ben greets these offerings as he might a dead mouse that his loyal cat has dragged in. He does what many a conflicted movie lawyer or cop or priest or stock trader has done with inside information—he bends the rules of his profession and feels real bad about it. He starts by exploring the caverns under Martin's gynecologist-mother's Addams-family-type mansion.

Nietzsche fans are probably getting all excited here about the lovely monster/abyss possibilities in the mere casting of Oldman as the lawyer who has second thoughts about justice. Oldman played Sid Vicious in "Sid and Nancy" and playwright Joe Orton in "Prick Up Your Ears," both doomed and self-destructive characters. In this movie, he goes at his role with concentrated zest (and an American accent), but his transformation to Martin's doppelganger is never really complete, or even possible. That's because Chase is a man who has everything except moral fiber; stalking the beast is more a response to the serial killer's cheek than to Ben's own indignation. He could almost as easily have gone on safari, like other yuppies for whom winning is no big deal any more.

Oldman gives it the old college try, though, his hair pumped up into a pompadour, anger and disdain roiling beneath a controlled veneer.

Bacon seems playfully intrigued by his role. In place of remorse or other introspective emotions, his Martin has a feverish, bright-eyed curiosity, a quality you wouldn't normally associate with rabid anti-abortionists, which is what Martin essentially turns out to be. It is the movie's grisly anti-abortion subtext that is its most horrifying and infuriating element. Lots of movies make women the victims of gruesome, senseless sex murders, but "Criminal Law" tries to justify it. That's as sick as anything any psycho-killer ever dreamed up.

NEWSDAY, 4/28/89, Part III/p. 5, Mike McGrady

Until now, British actor Gary Oldman's career has been an extended freak show, a one-man gallery of sick, twisted, demented souls. After exploding onto the screen as punk rocker Sid Vicious in "Sid and Nancy," Oldman went on to portray a sadistic playwright ("Prick Up Your Ears"), a sinister stranger wooing a woman who may be his mother ("Track 29") and a key part of a romantic triangle that includes a dog ("We Think the World of You").

Now for something completely new. Something normal. In his new film, "Criminal Law," Oldman hazards a rather ordinary sort, an up-and-coming American attorney who defends an insane rapist-murderer and then suffers anguish because of his courtroom prowess.

Piece of cake, right? One might guess that anyone so adept at portraying weirdos and wackos would have little difficulty handling mere normalcy. Not so. As Oldman strives for restraint, Krafft-Ebing is replaced by ebbing craft. Supposedly normal, he remains tortured, emotive, hysterical.

While writer Mark Kasdan (director Lawrence's brother) is intent on drawing psychological parallels between the defense attorney and his murderous client, Oldman's shrill performance forces these parallels together. He doesn't so much speak lines as sob them. But perhaps there's no proper way to deliver a line like this: "They had that animal locked up, and I let him out to kill again!"

American actor Kevin Bacon fares somewhat better as the madman. Although he has been provided with lines every bit as difficult ("I love the rain. After the purifying fire, the cleansing rain..."), he manages to give them credibility. Just as Oldman has to escape his past roles, so Bacon must abandon his solid, all-American image to play a demented killer. How much easier to reverse roles and play to type, but that must have seemed too unchallenging.

And this is but one of many questionable choices. When your central character is a madman who sees himself as a heavenly avenger, an emissary of death dispatched to punish practicing pro-choicers, you have a clear decision to make about direction. You can concentrate on thoughts and motives, or you can simply record actions; you can go inward and explore the psyche, or you can go outward and show results.

The more interesting, more difficult direction would have been internal. The other path, Hollywood's preferred choice, calls for the rain machines, the thunderclaps, the explosions, the guns, the mad killer stalking lonely women in deserted office buildings. Bring out the slowly turning door handles, the creaking hinges, the amplified footsteps. Whenever faced with such a choice, "Criminal Law" opts for the road most traveled, the road that leads to mechanically contrived suspense.

Director Martin Campbell, a veteran of British telly best known for directing the BBC series "Edge of Darkness," does much better with environment than with people. He is at his very best snooping around old mansions, uncovering secret tunnels, finding clues in remote glass-walled gazebos. Unfortunately, the inhabitants of these spooky environments never do quite come to life. You keep hoping "Criminal Law" will become a true psychological thriller, but wind up settling for superficial melodrama.

VILLAGE VOICE, 5/2/89, p. 67, Georgia Brown

Corruptions of class American-style is a peripheral subject of *Criminal Law*, written by an American, Mark Kasdan (brother of director Lawrence), and directed by the British Martin Campbell (director of the gripping BBC series *Edge of Darkness*). A movie has to be either nervy or obtuse to open, as this one does, with that Nietzsche chestnut about the abyss looking back at you. *Criminal Law*, unhappily, is more the second.

Watching Gary Oldman play a hotshot Harvard alum (at least that's the T-shirt he wears for squash) and rising Boston criminal lawyer—American accent and all—is a lot like watching James Woods in *True Believer*: These actors, much better than their material, work hard and look good anyway. When Oldman's pompadoured Ben Chase addresses the jury in *Criminal Law*'s opening scene, he seems more authentic for a practicing attorney than Woods's histrionic counterpart. Ben, on his way up rather than down, is defending the heir to a New England family fortune, Martin Thiel (Kevin Bacon), who's accused of a gory murder on a rainy night. Hardly does Ben get his client off than it turns out Martin is suspected of being a serial killer whose trademark is to mutilate a woman's body and stuff a Pamper in her mouth.

Criminal Law looks good for a while, in the beginning establishing a colorful sense of daily life among young legals. But soon the movie gets caught up in a very farfetched plot. What seemed destined to be a snappy courtroom drama turns into a most improbable thriller, in which the psycho killer is a right-to-lifer avenging the aborted fetus. Tess Harper plays a dedicated policewoman investigating sex crimes, and Joe Don Baker has a too-small role as chief dectective.

As he pursues his quarry, Ben has to face the fact that he is a violent man himself (you should see him on the squash court), but the killer-in-the-mirror psychology that Kasdan works up seems more a screenwriter's idea than true to his characters. The movie does succeed in making the idle rich look like a doomed species.

Also reviewed in:
NEW YORK TIMES, 4/28/89, p. C16, Vincent Canby
VARIETY, 9/28/88, p. 17
WASHINGTON POST, 4/28/89, p. D4, Hal Hinson

CRUSOE

An Island Pictures release. *Producer:* Andrew Braunsberg. *Director:* Caleb Deschanel. *Screenplay:* Walon Green. *Director of Photography:* Tom Pinter. *Editor:* Humphrey Dixon. *Music:* Michael Kamen. *Music Editor:* Bob Hathaway. *Sound:* Ray Beckett, Paul Le Mare, and (music) Stephen McLaughlin. *Sound Editor:* John Foster. *Production Designer:* Velco Despotovic. *Art Director:* Nemanja Petrovic. *Set Decorator:* Vladislav Tomanovic and Ivan Ujevic. *Special Effects:* John Evans. *Costumes:* Nada Perovic. *Make-up:* Radmila Invatovic and Saveta Kovac. *Stunt Coordinator:* Eddie Stacey. *Running time:* 95 minutes. *MPAA Rating:* PG-13

CAST: Aidan Quinn (Crusoe); Elvis Payne (Runaway Slave); Richard Sharp (Colcol); Colin Bruce (Clerk); William Hootkins (Auctioneer); Shane Rimmer (Mr. Mather); Jimmy Nail (Tarik); Patrick Monkton (Cook); Chris Pitt (Kitchen Lad); James Kennedy (Captain Harding); Tim Spall (Reverend Milne); Scampy (Scamp the Dog); Adé Sapara (The Warrior); Hepburn Graham (Lucky); Raymond Johnson (1st Victim); Ricco Ross (2nd Victim); Warren Clarke (Captain Lee); Michael Higgins (Dr. Martin); Keith Alan (Mr. Mipps); Oliver Platt (Mr. Newby).

LOS ANGELES TIMES, 4/7/89, Calendar/p. 13, Kevin Thomas

With the handsome, well-meaning "Crusoe" director Caleb Deschenal and writer Walon Green attempt to rework the Daniel Defoe tale into a parable on the evil folly of racism. Unfortunately, the undertaking is far too obvious and contrived to generate much impact.

Deschanel and Green have moved up the story nearly a century, setting it in Virginia in 1808. In his greed, the slave trader Crusoe (Aidan Quinn) has launched a risky late season voyage to Africa to capture more natives. Anyone with the slightest acquaintance with the Defoe classic can tell you that this Crusoe will end up shipwrecked on a remote island—yet it takes the film 25 minutes to get us there. Worse, it takes a full hour into what is only a 95-minute movie for anything significant to happen, by which time it scarcely matters.

Meanwhile, we're stuck in this gorgeous tropical paradise with the least sympathetic of men. It's no fault of the personable, capable Quinn, but rather the simple and damning fact that his Crusoe has been shown to be a thoroughly callous dealer in human beings. Why should we care whether he prevails in his solitary struggle for survival? Only a confirmed white supremacist could get worked up over his lonely predicament. (Throughout this long stretch Crusoe never seems to reflect on how he has brought about his own fate.)

The film makers need to get to the heart of the matter more quickly, especially when what's in the offing is so predictable anyway. It's hardly difficult to guess that eventually Crusoe will meet his match (and then some) in a black man (Adé Sapara, a young British actor of imposing presence) who will finally raise his consciousness. Regrettably, the considerable craftsmanship that has gone in the filming of "Crusoe" (rated PG-13 for violence) only convinces you that it wasn't worth making in the first place.

MONTHLY FILM BULLETIN, 8/89, P. 230, Sylvia Paskin

Tidewater, Virginia, 1808. Crusoe, a wealthy slave owner, persuades a merchant to loan him a ship to go on a slave-buying expedition. During a storm at sea, a fire breaks out on board and the ship is wrecked. Crusoe is washed up on the shore of a desert island amidst the drowned bodies of the crew and debris from the ship, although the ship's dog is saved. Crusoe begins to learn to survive on the island, swimming back to the ship to retrieve a number of useful items, including a gun. He builds a stockade, plants seeds, raises geese and hens. He tries to build and launch a boat but this fails. When the dog falls sick and dies, he is grief-stricken. Cannibals come to the island with some prisoners for sacrifice, but Crusoe manages to save one of them and brings him to his cave. The cannibals appear to leave, but in the morning the man is missing and Crusoe finds his body in the forest, bedecked with flowers like the other sacrificial victims. Just as another cannibal warrior appears, Crusoe's leg is caught in a trap and he is left swinging helplessly in the air. The warrior lets him down then ties him up and disappears. After Crusoe escapes, the two men meet and fight and Crusoe falls into quicksand. The warrior saves him by bending a tree in his direction, and an uneasy alliance develops between the two. They build a boat together. Eventually a ship arrives: the warrior is captured and Crusoe welcomed by the white crew. he learns that they intend to take the warrior back to "civilisation" and exhibit him. That night,

Crusoe releases his companion from his cage and he escapes on the boat they built together. Crusoe returns to his cabin and begins to shave. The ship sails at dawn, leaving the island once more peaceful and deserted.

Daniel Defoe's classic novel of 1719 has been called "the first epic of bourgeois man", tracing as it does one man's voyage of self-discovery through guilt, puritanical diligence, religious moral fervour and a considerable aptitude for accounting. It has inspired several film versions, silent as well as sound, including such curiosities as *Ein Robinson* (1940) by Arnold Franck (spiritual father to Leni Riefenstahl), an extraordinary brew of anti-British propaganda, anti-Communist rhetoric and grandiose "mountain-film" imagery infused with mystical and, of course, nationalistic overtones. Buñuel's *The Adventures of Robinson Crusoe* (1954) accentuated the maddened anguish of a man without human company: it is only his trust in the love and companionship of Friday that restores him to sanity. Jack Gold's *Man Friday* (1976) told the story from Friday's point of view, suggesting that the white man's prejudice, puritanical paranoia and bitter repressiveness made any real understanding between the races impossible.

Caleb Deschanel's *Crusoe* is not of the visionary and limpid order of Buñuel's film, but it has a similar economy, gentleness and optimism. Deschanel, whose *Black Stallion* was another tale of shipwreck, survival and self-discovery, has apparently drawn as much on the memoirs of Alexander Selkirk, the Scottish seaman who inspired Defoe's character, and who was abandoned on the island of Juan Fernandez, off the coast of Chile, and only rescued four years later. This *Crusoe* tells of the character's getting of wisdom, and in focusing on the detail of Crusoe's struggle for survival, and the concomitant spiritual changes he undergoes, it has appropriately combined as screenwriters Walon Green (from *The Wild Bunch*) and the poet Christopher Logue. "What attracted me to the story", Deschanel has said, "was the idea of concentrating on a single character and the changes he goes through. Although there is plenty of action in the film—the shipwreck, slave auctions, warriors, sacrifices, the real drama comes from watching the central character and how he deals with the situation he finds himself in...".

Aidan Quinn's Crusoe begins the film as an elegant and rangy slave owner, hunting runaways on horseback with his dogs. He deals, with proud self-assurance, in human flesh, discussing the price of a "fine buck". He can barely bother to converse with his few fellow passengers on the ship, and is in turn despised by the crew (one of whom urinates into his shaving water before the cabin boy brings it to him). Once he is marooned on the island, there is genuine pathos in his initial attempts to cling to civilised rituals and manners. He tries for many days to shave before giving up. He dresses for dinner and tries at first to wear a dead comrade's shoes before deciding to go barefoot. Aspects of his colonial self come to the fore in his meeting with the runaway slave ("I'll call you Lucky. You are a lucky man because I have no one to sell you to"), whom he teaches to wash before he eats and to pray; he encourages him to use a napkin by holding a gun to his head.

This encounter, however, is short-lived. Crusoe's meeting with the warrior brings him into contact with someone as highly self-possessed as he, full of a supple grace and dignity. When Crusoe tries to teach him the word "meat", the warrior responds in his own tongue; when Crusoe sings "One man went to mow", the warrior chants his own song. The warrior offers Crusoe sustenance at the point of a spear, and it is this mutuality and reciprocity that in the end makes it possible for them to work together on the boat as equals. By the end of the film, Crusoe has travelled much further than the sumptuous desert island on which he was marooned; he is sufficiently changed to set the warrior free rather than allow him to be taken as cultural bounty to England ("You can give lectures about him", says the amiable ship's naturalist). Deschanel gives us a picture of solitude in which the simplest actions, the tiniest gestures, fascinate, and he makes of the island a strange, silent and beautiful world. The transition in Crusoe's character is marked with dignity, and the maturing of trust between the warrior and the erstwhile slave owner is touching, credible and humorous.

NEW YORK POST, 3/31/89, p. 29, David Edelstein

Aidan Quinn, who plays the lone survivor of a shipwreck in "Crusoe," is a classic movie dreamboat. But there's something dorky about him, too. His arms would fit a scarecrow, and his nasal inflections make him sound a bit like Charles Grodin. As adventure heroes go, he's lightweight, but he has a silly streak—a hint of self-mockery—and he's wonderful in this small, tidy version of Daniel Defoe's work.

Directed by Caleb Deschanel, the great cinematographer of "The Black Stallion," "Crusoe" is everything you'd want in a big-book adaptation—and less. This Robinson Crusoe is a slave trader, and in the opening sequence he hunts down an escaped black man in the Virginia swamps. Inspecting the human goods at the auction block, he stares into the captured slave's face with a tiny smirk; he could almost be Sylvester Stallone.

Naturally, being shipwrecked en route to Africa (to buy more slaves) will turn out to be the best thing that ever happened to the man—his rebirth as a human being.

The movie says that blacks and whites are, underneath the skin, equal and that slavery is morally wrong. Obviously, I couldn't agree more, but all this brotherhood-of-man stuff reduces the Crusoe story quite a bit: it turns a complex tale of survival into a Sunday school lesson.

Yet "Crusoe" is so amiable and so deftly made that it never seems preachy. In the first part of the movie, Deschanel and screenwriter Walon Green get fairly specific about the economics of slavery, and the images are constricted, airless. Crusoe seems like a prisoner of a capitalist system that encourages him to be less than human. But when he washes up on the island, the images begin to breathe.

"Crusoe" could actually catch on—it plays like a yuppie fantasy of escape. Nasty Wall Street trader gets shipwrecked, grows a beard, befriends a mangy cur, acquires some muscle tone. There's even exotic cuisine. The director gives us a National Geographic-style close-up of snail and then cuts to Crusoe eating something squishy. Then there's a beautiful shot of a chameleon, followed by Crusoe eating something...bony. Then there's a shot of a centipede and...no, I can't go on.

Even with the furious storms, menacing surf and craggy shorelines, there's no wildness in Deschanel's technique. Everything is smooth and pretty and simple. But the film has a great deal of picture-postcard charm. And when Crusoe saves a black man from being executed by cannibals and then tries to turn him into a valet—ordering him to use a napkin at gunpoint, for instance—cultural imperialism does indeed get a satisfying comeuppance.

NEWSDAY, 3/31/89, Part III/p. 5, Lynn Darling

Even though it's set in 1808, "Crusoe" is a decidedly contemporary version of Daniel Defoe's novel. The story, cut and spliced from the original as well as from other sources, takes its themes from a far more contemporary attitude toward man and his place in the world.

In the version presented by director Caleb Deschanel and screenwriter Walon Green, Crusoe (Aidan Quinn) is a kind of proto-yuppie—a greedy, ambitious colonial American slave trader who thinks of nothing but the profit margins on his human assets. Greed drives him to make an ill-advised late-season crossing in search of more human cargo; his gamble is rewarded by a storm that washes him up on the shores of a lushly verdant island.

"Crusoe" is about a man's capacity for change when released from the context of the conventions, values and ambitions that drive him. The result is a movie that is true neither to the world view of the era in which it is set nor the contemporary one to which it owes the most allegiance. In the end, "Crusoe" simply doesn't have a lot to say.

The director, a cinematographer by training, tells his hero's story primarily in long, slowly developed scenes in which dialogue plays a necessarily minor part. Slowly, very slowly, we watch Crusoe form a more committed relationship with his dog Scamp, grow his hair long and cut it short again. Eventually he meets up with a fellow human being, a hapless native who has been ear-marked for human sacrifice by a visiting tribe. Crusoe rescues the man, whom he names Lucky, but his act of kindness doesn't indicate much of a change in attitude—he tries to make Lucky his slave. When Lucky ends up dead, Crusoe gets a second chance with another, unnamed visitor (Adé Sapara) to the island. This time around he learns a few humbling lessons about relating to his fellow man.

There is no man Friday in this version of the Crusoe tale, and the decision to eliminate him spares the movie Defoe's patronizing, anachronistic assumptions of white man's superiority and benevolence. But instead of substituting a relationship with its own resonance and complexity, the movie opts for corny, slow-witted exchanges in which slave-trader and "savage" learn to appreciate each other's humanity. Since Crusoe and his new friend never learn each other's language, this appreciation is necessarily extremely primitive.

Aidan Quinn is a good-looking young actor who has done fine by the very contemporary roles he's played in productions such as the television drama "An Early Frost" and the film

"Desperately Seeking Susan." But in this movie he seems more preoccupied with the cut of his hair than with the predicament his character's in. Quinn does manage to convey the loneliness Crusoe feels, but he's done in by the demands of being an essentially one-man band and by the camera's obvious preference for pretty scenarios.

Writers from Rousseau to William Golding have been tantalized by the question of what man's nature and identity would be like freed from the constraining influence of civilization. Unfortunately, according to "Crusoe," the best we can hope for is the evolution of a jerk into a man qualified to lead human-potential seminars. Even Scamp showed the potential for more complexity than that.

VILLAGE VOICE, 4/4/89, p. 56, Georgia Brown

Caleb Deschanel tackles the subject of white pretension to supremacy by way of Daniel Defoe's *Robinson Crusoe*, one of those indestructible texts that generously lend themselves to rewrites and cultural updates. In 1952, Luis Buñuel filmed a revisionist *Robinson Crusoe* that lifted Defoe's 17th century bourgeois hero out of his acquisitive capitalist mind-set and gave him capacity for moral growth. Turning Crusoe into a Virginia slave trader, circa 1800, as Deschanel and writer Walon Green have done, is not in itself a dumb idea.

The sinking of Crusoe's ship is considerably less spectacular than the shipwreck Deschanel photographed for *The Black Stallion*. No horse on board this time; there is a dog, Scamp, played plaintively by a well-trained mongrel who's subject of a good many coy reaction shots. Crusoe's treatment of Scamp is meant to bear on his expectations for the black man he adopts soon after Scamp expires.

Defoe's hero spent 28 years on his island, but Aidan Quinn, whose performance lacks any gravity, looks more like a college kid separated from his buddies for a week at spring break. Deschanel—occupied with sunsets and nature-world blowups of some creepies and crawlies—has no good way of indicating the passage of time or the difficulty of labor. Crusoe is shown building, the camera looks away and, presto, a tree turns into boards. Compare this to the "two and forty days" it took Defoe's Crusoe to make one board for use as a shelf.

With access to razor, tools, utensils, clothes, and wine, situated on a pristine cove, always fair weather, no wonder Crusoe's in good spirits. He talks gaily to himself and his creatures. "See you at supper," he reminds his penned geese. "Goin' to the general store," he tells Scamp, referring to the ship sticking up just off the beach.

When a few boatloads of painted natives arrive for some sacrifical business, the spying Crusoe inadvertently saves one from having his throat ceremonially slit and names him Lucky. "You're lucky I have no one to sell you to," he cackles, informing Lucky that *his* name is Master. At the dinner table, Master instructs Lucky (holding a gun to his head) in the use of a napkin. The lesson goes for naught, however, when Lucky is stolen and Crusoe finds him headless, as his tribespeople intended.

It turns out that a warrior considerably more cunning and less compliant than Lucky was left on the island, too. Crusoe and the new man (Adé Sapara) play cat and mouse (Crusoe the mouse), until it is Master who is more or less tamed. Each time Crusoe smacks him, the man smacks back, harder. When Crusoe touts an English word for something, the man sticks with his own word. It's witty reversal on the Eurocentric white man's version; too bad the execution is pitifully inadequate.

Everything poetic about Defoe's *Crusoe* is missing—effects of solitude or bitter frustration, fascination with nature, materials, and technology that went into the painstaking reinvention of bourgeois civilization. *Poetic* to this style of filmmaking means picturesque slow-motion shots of the warrior running on the beach. For a supposedly enlightened look at racial prejudice, this looks suspiciously like *The Return of the Black Stallion*.

Also reviewed in:

NEW YORK TIMES, 3/31/89, p. C13, Vincent Canby
NEW YORKER, 4/17/89, p. 114, Pauline Kael
VARIETY, 5/25/88, p. 29
WASHINGTON POST, 4/21/89, p. C7, Rita Kempley

CYBORG

A Cannon Entertainment release. *Producer:* Menahem Golan and Yoram Globus. *Director:* Albert Pyun. *Screenplay:* Kitty Chalmers. *Director of Photography:* Philip Alan Waters. *Editor:* Rozanne Zingale and Scott Stevenson. *Music:* Kevin Bassinson. *Music Editor:* Joachim H. Hansch. *Sound:* Alan Selk and Gary Dowling. *Sound Editor:* Tony Garber. *Production Designer:* Douglas Leonard. *Set Decorator:* Yvonne Hegney. *Set Dresser:* Dawn Serody. *Special Effects:* Joe Digaetano and R.J. Hohman. *Costumes:* Heidi Kaczenski. *Make-up:* Teri Blythe. *Stunt Coordinator:* Tom Elliott. *Running time:* 85 minutes. *MPAA Rating:* R.

CAST: Jean-Claude Van Damme (Gibson Rickenbacker); Deborah Richter (Nady Simmons); Vincent Klyn (Fender Tremolo); Alex Daniels (Marshall Strat); Dayle Haddon (Pearl Prophet); Blaise Loong (Furman Vox); Rolf Muller (Brick Bardo); Haley Peterson (Haley); Terrie Batson (Mary); Jackson "Rock" Pinckney (Tytus); Janice Graser (Vorg); Robert Pentz (Base); Sharon K. Tew (Prather); Chuck Allen (Vondo); Stefanos Miltsakakis (Xylo); Kristina Sebastian (Young Haley); Thomas Barley (Willy); Dale Frye (Sather); Jophery Brown (Saloon Owner); Jim Creech (Roland Pick).

LOS ANGELES TIMES, 4/7/89, Calendar/ p. 12, Chris Willman

"I like scars—really," says a girlish, love-starved refugee in "Cyborg," trying to woo the bloodied beefcake hero with a little idle flattery about his battle blemishes. This movie too, jam-packed with clockwork bits of the old ultraviolence, is mostly for people who like scars—really.

It imagines nasty future in which the survivors of an overwhelming plague slice and dice each other at length, often for no reason other than that they're bad, they're bad, they're really, really bad. If you experience a little *deja vu* over this future, it's because we've seen it dozens of times before, most notably in the "Mad Max" trilogy. There's no vehicular manslaughter in this one, though; everyone just walks, all the better to engage in sudden sword and knife fights along the way.

The lead villain, a predictably leather-clad young hunk named Fender Tremolo, is the sort of unsavory fellow who will, as they used to say, kill a man just to watch him die. (Women and children too. Barbed-wire torture and crucifixion are a couple of his favorite time-killers.) As played by Vincent Klyn, this indestructible behemoth bellows homicidal instructions to his followers with the sweet voice and good will of a professional wrestler—or like the very similar sadist-in-chief of "The Road Warrior"

On the other side, there will of course be a sullen, silent type who turned mercenary after losing his wife and children to the savage pirates. He will of course be prodded back into righteous activism by the nagging of a new woman in his life. He is not Mel Gibson, but rather Gibson Rickenbacker, a.k.a. muscly Jean-Claude Van Damme—you know, "the first hero of the 21st Century."

The musicians among us may have sussed by now that virtually all the characters are named after guitars or amplifiers. That little in-joke is the beginning and end of the wit to be found in "Cyborg," which has as humorless and stupefyingly awful a screenplay as you'll see playing on a screen this year. Script credit goes to a mysterious Kitty Chalmers—which, if it isn't a pseudonym, probably should be.

But how much script can there be in a movie that almost never lets five minutes pass without unleashing another bone-snapping, blood-spilling epic fight scene? And although director Albert Pyun ("Sword and the Sorcerer") brings out nothing but the worst in the mercifully brief recitations of dialogue, he does know how to stage and pile up effectively brutal action sequences till you feel as though you've been through four world wars in under 85 minutes. It's desensitizing violence in all its glory: You may cheer during the rousing slugfests, then hate yourself afterward.

Credit for the dumb fun must also go to cinematographer Philip Alan Waters and editors Rozanne Zingale and Scott Stevenson, who keep the carnage-filled proceedings as pretty as they are fast—and to sound effects editor Bill Van Daalen, who may have been the busiest man in post-production, given hundreds of loud jaw-socks and jugular-slashes to juggle.

"Cyborg" (MPAA-rated R for every manner of unpleasantness) doesn't offer much hope for man's civilized nature in the wake of disaster, but viewers may find one glimmer of light in its future: the seeming absence of firearms. These gangs *were* able to stockpile sharp kitchenware, but apparently the semiautomatic weapon ban had some effect in the 1990s after all.

NEW YORK POST, 4/8/89, p. 19, Jami Bernard

The time is the future, a time that, if you follow the post-apocalyptic genre of moviemaking, features much inclement weather, deterioration of verbal skills, fenced-off areas where people are dying of undisclosed diseases and a surprising number of Nautilus-fresh bodies.

"First there was the Palazzo Civilization," intones a narrator over a matte painting of a crestfallen New York as "Cyborg" begins. "Then we came down with The Plague." Things can only go downhill from there, and they do.

It's April (in the real world, that is) and we're in The Wasteland (according to a road sign). A cyborg is on the run to Atlanta, the only place, apparently, that is not burning. Atlanta is where the few remaining doctors are trying to find a cure for The Plague, and the cyborg is carrying vital information in her computer-for-brains.

Frankly, The Plague is the least of the future world's troubles. There is a bigger immediate threat from Fender Tremolo (Vincent Klyn), a one-man whirlwind of destruction. Fender wants to own the cure for The Plague so he can be master of the universe. He wears a metal-mesh shirt somewhat like what Cher wears in those ads for Jack La Lanne; when he really means business he takes off his high-tech sunglasses and reveals blazing blue contact lenses.

The cyborg—half human, half computer, but very beautiful (the actress Dayle Haddon was the cat-eyed model for the Scoundrel perfume ads)—hopes to enlist handsome Gibson Rickenbacker, a "slinger," or soldier for hire, to help her get to Atlanta. But he's got other fish to fry, and before you can kick someone upside the head with a knife-studded boot, the cyborg has been kidnapped by Fender and his gang of nogoodniks.

Well, enough with the plot. Let's discuss those names the characters are saddled with—Gibson Rickenbacker, Fender Tremolo, Furman Vox, Xylo. The press notes report that the names are derived from guitar equipment, although the name "Gibson" brings something else to mind, a drink that could make this movie more palatable.

Whoops! Now Fender is removing his glasses. Something must be up. Bring on the bone-crunching!

And much bone-crunching there is. In addition to specialized homoerotic tortures—one guy gets a battering ram down his throat—there are snapping limbs, slashed faces, car doors slammed against heads, thwack! thwack! The harsher the punishment (the hero even gets nailed to a mile-high cross) the livelier the next fight scene, and the manlier the grunting on the soundtrack. Men display their weapons like male birds display their plumage.

The hero Gibson is played by a handsome, genial Schwarzenegger wannabe, Jean-Claude Van Damme. Cannon, which was also responsible for Van Damme's previous "Bloodsport," is trying to build the guy up to stardom, and he certainly has the looks for it. He has the cheekbones of Arnold S., the determined mouth of Arnold S., even a "Terminator" brush-cut. Better yet, he's a former bodybuilder (dubbed "Muscles from Brussels") who wants an acting career but is hampered by a pungent accent. Maybe he's dating a Kennedy, too; the press notes don't say.

Gibson is one of those beefcake heroes whose chest is larger than the heroine's and who kills with perfunctory gusto. "I didn't make this world," he says simply, but then, he says everything simply.

He is paired with a succession of women who are not quite right for him. One dies early. Another, a feisty road companion, is too young and petulant ("There's a cure for The Plague you don't give a s...!" she rails at Gibson).

Not for me to ruin the ending—we're talking not only about the end of a film here, but of the human race—but the final *mano-a-mano* fight between good and evil involves a level of bellowing not heard since Mothra was brough out of mothballs to save Japan.

Director Albert Pyun ("The Sword and the Sorcerer," "Radioactive Dream") and his music-video cinematographer, Philip Waters, have strung together many music-vid-type fight scenes, snap snap snap, and thrown in lots of religious imagery (in case we don't catch on during the crucifixion scene). If they were half as interested in plot or script as in creating a colorfully forbidding look, "Cyborg" would not be as tedious as it is. Can the future really be this bleak?

NEWSDAY, 4/8/89, Part II/p. 17, Bill Kaufman

Though the only thing "Cyborg" has going for it is its nice, succinct title, more expansively the movie might better be called "The A-Team Meets the Bionic Woman With Guest Star Who Looks Like Arnold Schwarzenegger."

With its backdrop of junkyard trash, burned-out cities and a worldwide death plague, this movie is a study in things grotesque; a stylized piece of black fantasy that exudes a ghoulish mood throughout. The leftovers in this world devoid of civilization are roving gangs, Flesh Pirates, who ruthlessly slice-and-dice anyone in their way, and a team of more charitable mercenary warriors known as Slingers.

In a futuristic limbo where might makes right, the hero is Gibson Rickenbacker, a fighter hired to escort a young woman and her family to a safer city. Rickenbacker is played with an intensity bordering on suppressed rage by Belgian body-builder Jean-Claude Van Damme. His shimmering pectorals and accent unavoidably bring Arnold Schwarzenegger to mind. (According to the movie's production notes, Van Damme describes himself as "Muscles From Brussels.")

At one point, Rickenbacker looks momentarily happy when he saves an attractive woman named Pearl Prophet (Dayle Haddon) who is being terrorized by the Flesh Pirates. But the relationship stays platonic after she rips off her face and reveals a pulsating mechanism. "I'm a Cyborg," she tells him.

This schizoid mix of sword-and-sorcery and science-fiction loses control of its identity somewhere during the first 15 minutes, ending up a melange of mindless action and violence. Its weapons include everything from electric daggers to crossbows that blast lasers. Unfortunately, there is no aspirin-coated popcorn.

Also reviewed in:
NEW YORK TIMES, 4/8/89, p. 16, Stephen Holden
VARIETY, 4/5-11/89, p. 20
WASHINGTON POST, 4/11/89, p. D3, Richard Harrington

DAD

A Universal Pictures release of an Amblin Entertainment presentation. *Executive Producer:* Steven Spielberg, Frank Marshall, and Kathleen Kennedy. *Producer:* Joseph Stern and Gary David Goldberg. *Director:* Gary David Goldberg. *Screenplay:* Gary David Goldberg. *Based on the novel by:* William Wharton. *Director of Photography:* Jan Kiesser. *Editor:* Eric Sears. *Music:* James Horner. *Music Editor:* Jim Henrikson. *Sound:* Ron Judkins. *Sound Editor:* Stephen H. Flick. *Production Designer:* Jack DeGovia. *Art Director:* John R. Jensen. *Set Decorator:* Thomas L. Roysden. *Set Dresser:* Ramiro Arrendondo. *Special Effects:* Gary Zink. *Costumes:* Molly Maginnis. *Make-up:* Ken Diaz and (Jack Lemmon) Dick Smith. *Running time:* 117 minutes. *MPAA Rating:* PG.

CAST: Jack Lemmon (Jake Tremont); Ted Danson (John Tremont); Olympia Dukakis (Bette Tremont); Kathy Baker (Annie); Kevin Spacey (Mario); Ethan Hawke (Billy); Zakes Mokae (Dr. Chad); J.T. Walsh (Dr. Santana); Peter Michael Goetz (Dr. Ethridge); John Apicella (Dr. Delibro); Richard McGonagle (Victor Walton); Bill Morey (Hal McCarthy); Mary Fogarty (Gloria McCarthy); Art Frankel (DMV instructor) Ray Girardin (Butcher); Vickilyn Reynolds (CCU Nurse); Jimmy Higa (Chris); Edith Fields, Takayo Fischer and Andi Chapman (Jake's Nurses); Emily Kuroda (Vicki); Gregory Itzin (Ralph Kramer); Richard Fiske (Bingo Caller); Tony Kienitz (Bank Executive); Terry Wills (Dry Cleaner); Patti Arpaia (Receptionist); Donna Porter (Surprised Neighbor); Erin Strom and Lisa Rae (Nurses); Chris Lemmon (Young Jake); Gina Raymond (Young Bette); Justin Petersen (Young John); Sprague Grayden (Young Annie); Lucas Hall (Hank); Katie Kissell (Lizbeth).

FILMS IN REVIEW, 1-2/90, p. 42, Edmond Grant

Dad is not ideal family viewing. That's not a putdown; it's a warning to those with aged and infirm relatives that, at its most effective, the film is a terribly sad account of the ravages of old age that will certainly play on the heartstrings of anyone who has (or has had) such relatives, and will deeply disturb the older members of the audience.

The film is a tearjerker-in-three-acts which features a number of definite changes in mood and intensity. The first section details how the heart attack suffered by his strong willed mother (Olympia Dukakis) brings a businessman (Ted Danson) back home to take care of his slow-moving near-helpless father (Jack Lemmon). Danson gradually re-educates Lemmon in the fine art of surviving without Mom (who eventually recovers). And then the real tragedy occurs—Lemmon is informed that he has cancer and then slips into a coma induced by shock. Danson is so incensed at what he sees as the hospital's cavalier attitude towards his father that he decides to personally care for him at home.

These first two sections are manipulative—we are made to like Dad, then his life is put in jeopardy—but Lemmon's passive, sympathetic performance and the emotionally charged circumstances draw the audience into the harrowing situation faced by Danson. The sequences which show Lemmon's physical and psychological breakdown tap a powerful fear common to us all, the fear that this sort of condition could befall someone we love, or that we, too, may someday wind up like Lemmon's character.

Amidst all the emotional intensity, though, there is one weak link—namely, the affable Ted Danson. Danson is a pleasant comic performer who has become a saleable big screen commodity since the success of *Three Men And A Baby*, but he is severely lacking the sort of intensity that is called for here. The situations are indeed so emotional that they can't help but affect the viewer, but throughout, one can't help but wonder how much better the film might have been if a powerhouse dramatic performer had been cast in the role played by Danson.

The film's third section provides a definite turn, as Lemmon's character has a sudden recovery, and all the heavily realistic doom and gloom is swept away only to be replaced by an artificial sense of apple-pie homegrown optimism that rings of the film's executive producer, Steven Spielberg. One fascinating plot element is introduced, a fantasy that Lemmon has carried around with him for years. This fantasy lends some depth to the final sequences of the film, but the sharp switch in tone that occurs once the Lemmon character "wakes up" from his comatose, nearly senile state betrays the direction the film had been taking, making it less a film that audiences can *relate* to, and more a film they can *escape* into.

Director-screenwriter Gary David Goldberg, best known for his work on TV's *Family Ties*, lets the film slip into Spielberg territory early on (even one charming scene where Danson and Lemmon play catch for the first time in many years is shot in soft-focus and underscored by smarmy music), but toward the end, Goldberg lends a thick sugar coating to the proceeding, tying up all the loose ends in the neat manner of the standard TV movie.

The cast are all (save weak link Danson) fine in their respective family roles, with Olympia Dukakis aptly unpleasant as Lemmon's stubborn wife, the very talented (and underused here) Kathy Baker and Kevin Spacey as Danson's sister and brother-in-law and young Ethan Hawke as Danson's teenage son.

Dad is a movie that gradually sells out the bitter truths it takes such pains to establish, but it does nonetheless accomplish something significant by drawing attention to the difficulties and anguish that crop up in our relatives' "golden years."

LOS ANGELES TIMES, 10/27/89, Calendar/p. 1, Sheila Benson

"Dad" wants desperately to deal frankly with old age. Not just the wise old Polident-commercial variety, with golden oldsters arm in arm, but the part that every one of us fears: intrusive medical procedures, pitiless physicians, loss of our abilities and our very functions, the encroachment of real or imagined terrors.

The fact that all these terrors are mirrored in Jack Lemmon's performance as 75-year-old retiree Jake Tremont, and in the interaction between him and Ted Danson, who plays his son, is all to the credit of the film's director/adaptor, Gary David Goldberg, of television's "Family Ties."

Lemmon's work is extraordinary; notably unsentimental for an actor who has, at times, become awash with sentiment and something of a marvel physically. It's nice too that Goldberg has been true to the essence of the character of Jake's wife, Bette (Olympia Dukakis), who is, through and through, a really nasty piece of work. In the original novel, her son dispassionately describes his mother's 50-year-long run as a wife as "a simple matter of miscasting."

But also at Goldberg's door is the fact that the film has no clear through-line; that it branches off onto limbs that should have been pruned back, and that eventually it succumbs to a prettified sentimentality that its performers have gone to some lengths to avoid.

Goldberg has picked a diabolically difficult book to adapt: William Wharton's 1981 novel of the same name, with more than a hint of personal experience about it. The book too is cluttered and diffuse, but it still has nice, uncompromisingly rough edges to it that this film adaptation has planed away. It was an honest, painful record; it has been nudged into family-style uplift.

Everything is now within our experience, or within the experience of a devoted television viewer. Rather than an expatriate American painter with children and a French wife, Danson's John

Tremont is now a Wall Street go-getter, attached umbilically to his computer and detached from his family. It includes his ex-wife and his teen-age son, Billy (Ethan Hawke, of "Dead Poet's Society"). Useless to wonder, of course, why he *couldn't* have been a painter, or why we had to suffer again through the cliché of the overachieving American executive who cannot feel but will learn to.

It's Dukakis' heart attack that brings Danson to California, but it's his father's deteriorating condition that shocks him into staying a while. After more than 40 years with a domineering, overprotective wife, any will that the elderly man had has been eroded. He cannot even pick out his pajamas or butter his toast.

While his mother recovers in the hospital, as a pure act of conscience, Danson taps through to the man he once knew—bringing him back to a degree that Danson's sister (the splendid Kathy Baker) and brother-in-law (Kevin Spacey) find almost miraculous. The line here between sitcom timing and truth is a fine one, and for the most part, truth wins out. These scenes may be kitsch, but it's kitsch that works. It's sweet to see the habits and bywords that once linked these men surfacing again.

Then medical mishandling by a stubborn,heedless doctor reduces Lemmon to childlike senility, wiping out the loving advancements his son has made and taking the story into new areas, a violent roller coaster ride full of them.

Disaster. Shamanlike doctors. Recovery. Violent swings of behavior. Fathers and sons. Doctors and sons. Sons and fathers. Wives and husbands. Mothers and sons. Mothers and neighbors. Much of a muchness.

No movie can retain its intent with this much cluttering up the plumb line of its story. "Dad" certainly can't. And that's without even doing much with the subplot about Lemmon's "successful schizophrenia," his 40-year retreat from his wife's nagging to a powerful and completely imaginary other life as a farmer in rural New Jersey.

It's a pity, because there are individual moments here of surpassing tenderness and compassion. It's unlikely that anyone who sees it will forget Lemmon's physical regression, in which he literally seems to shrink to an 80-pound wraith, or the moment in which Danson climbs onto his father's bed for the sort of farewell that most sons (of daughters) wish they could make.

These truths don't seem to satisfy the film makers, though. (This is a movie made under the Amblin banner, after all.) With all that Olympia Dukakis has done to keep this unpleasant wife true to herself, she is undercut by a smarmy ending, which insists that she would begin to act utterly contrary to the habits of 70 years. The film is determined to wear a smile button at its close, and damn the consequences to the material. So damned it remains.

Impossible to discuss "Dad" without mentioning the truly magical job of Lemmon's makeup, designed by Dick Smith. It's matched, of course, by the actor's physical contributions, but even in a decade of extraordinary realistic makeup (Edward James Olmos in "Stand and Deliver," Shirley MacLaine through the decades in "Terms of Endearment" among them), this stands out. Dukakis' makeup designer has no individual credit, but should; the overall credited makeup artist is Ken Diaz. Bravo, gentlemen.

MONTHLY FILM BULLETIN, 4/90, p. 101, Tom Milne

John Tremont, a Wall Street broker, flies to Los Angeles on learning that his mother Bette is in hospital following a heart attack. He finds his seventy-eight-year-old father Jake confused and helpless. Realising that Jake is terrified of the possibility of cancer, John helps him face up to the reality of his wife's illness. Further realising the extent to which Bette dominated Jake, doing everything for him, John rearranges his schedule so as to stay longer than the weekend originally planned, relieving his sister Annie and her husband Mario of some of the burden. Fondly remembering his own childhood as he looks after Jake, John reawakens his father's zest for living by making a game of showing him how to do his own cooking and cleaning, by coaxing him out to the Bingo sessions he used to enjoy, and by encouraging him to take up driving again. When Bette finally gets home, and John's son Billy has turned up from Mexico, the entire family is amazed at Jake's rejuvenation. But Jake starts passing blood; cancer is diagnosed; and when Jake suffers panic-stricken convulsions, John realises that Dr. Santana, against his strict instructions, has told Jake about the cancer. Furious, John storms out of the hospital with Jake in his arms, but is soon forced to bring him back, now in a coma but under the more sympathetic care of Dr. Chad, who waives regulations to let John sleep in his father's room (while Billy, impatiently told by his father to rejoin his friends in Mexico, keeps an anxious vigil of his own). Abruptly waking from the coma, Jake is seemingly his old self, with the cancer gone. The episode effects a reconciliation between John and Billy: long separated from his wife and inclined to view Billy as a worthless college dropout, John comes to a new understanding of his son's true values. Jake himself starts living out a repressed fantasy life, buying gaudy new clothes, cultivating the neighbour's children, and becoming a joyously gregarious extrovert. Only Bette is less than delighted by the change, seeing it as a rejection of their married life. The cancer returns; Jack calmly accepts his fate; and his death brings Bette into the family circle to share their new understanding of the meaning of love.

By the time *Dad* reaches the most crucial of a seemingly endless succession of cruxes, with everybody uttering choked cries of "I love you!" and falling ecstatically into everybody else's arms, one might be forgiven for feeling like an explorer stumbling across a lost colony of live-action Care Bears. Sincerity is writ large over the film, most obnoxiously in the tailor's-dummy presence of Ted Danson (all but sporting a mark-down price tag announcing "Caring Son"), most acceptably in the sheer professionalism of Jack Lemmon.

But not even Lemmon's skill, carefully and persuasively deployed in the opening scenes to sketch a sympathetic portrait of an old man teetering confusedly on the brink of senility, can cope with a script which subjects the character to a rollercoaster of metamorphoses—highlighted by cartoon-style explosions of joy and despair—with the aid of an obligingly appearing and disappearing cancer. By the time Dad has romped into second childhood (or as the film puts it, achieved successfuly schizophrenia and liberated his repressed inner self), one feels more than slight sympathy with his supposedly termagant wife in her expressions of appalled disbelief as he dons funny clothes and drags her round bearing gifts and bonhomie for the surprised neighbours.

Punctuated by nostalgia-tinted glimpses of a tranquil rustic past (why do all idealised Hollywood families have roots down on the farm?), the film is so hell-bent on promoting its message about love of family as life's magic formula that it neglects to secure even one toe in reality. Danson's John Tremont, for instance, is presented as a company executive with a busy boardroom schedule, yet he is apparently able to take off all the time he needs (several months, at least) to reap the rewards of caring: a not inconceivable situation, but one which demands at least some reference to the complications entailed. His son Billy is similarly pulled out of the hat, a one-dimensional caricature of the disaffected youth cliché, purely in order to demonstrate that caring (and being *seen* to be caring, apparently) can bring new understanding to heal the generation gap. The whole thing, in other words, is emotional exploitation at its most objectionable.

NEW STATESMAN & SOCIETY, 3/2/90, p. 41, Suzanne Moore

There is a question in the film *Parenthood*, that prolonged advert for procreation, where Steve Martin asks his own father:"Who's to say who is a shitty father?" Well, I hate to break it to you Steve, but I don't mind saying that lots of men are shitty fathers. Germaine Greer didn't call her latest book *Daddy, I Hardly Knew You* for nothing.

Yet, however shitty they may be, there is nothing more vomit-inducing than the current superdad competitions. The designer dad can now be found selling us everything from cars to clothes, as cute as the babies he is cuddling. Is this progress? Years ago I wrote an article bemoaning the lack of images of fatherhood that were available for the modern man and now I am surrounded by them.

Perhaps I should be pleased. Perhaps, if reality didn't ever poke its ugly head into this gloriously glossy world, I would be. Yet survey after survey shows that although men would like to, or even think that they *are* spending more time with their kids, they are not.

As Angela Phillips pointed out recently in the *Guardian*, it's not simply a case of men paying lipservice to the idea of shared parenting. As many British fathers tend to work longer hours than most of their European counterparts, so many men don't even get home in time to say "goodnight" to their kids. Needless to say someone has to tuck them in and sacrifice career opportunities. There are no prizes for guessing who.

What I see happening more and more is that the few women I know who stay with the fathers of their children have long ago stopped battling for anything like co-parenting. It just adds to the exhaustion. It's easier in fact to regard their children's father as just another kid to look after. With divorce on the increase the family actually means women and children with men drifting in and out of these basic units.

That half of the men who get divorced lose contact with their kids within two years makes you wonder how strong the paternal instinct really is. With Hollywood itself in the throes of some mid-life crisis, brought on by the changing demographics of cinema audiences, the paradise of paternity is back on the agenda. Apart from any ideological implications it also provides work for the older generation of actors. Sean Connery has a great career ahead of him playing eccentric fathers—he was Harrison Ford's father in *Indiana Jones* and Dustin Hoffman's in *Family Business*. Now Jack Lemmon has got in on the act playing Ted Danson's (of *Cheers* fame) father in a film called appropriately enough *Dad*.

Dad, like the recently released *Family Business* and *Parenthood* and the forthcoming *See You In The Morning*, wants to prove not only that daddies can do it, but that eventually they can do it better than any mummy. To achieve this implausible position the fathers in these films compete in the over-compensation stakes. When Danson's dad is ill he not only cares for his but moves into the same hospital room as him. In *See You In The Morning* Jeff Bridges sorts out the problems of both his old family and his recently acquired new family. And Steve Martin in Fatherhood (sorry *Parenthood*) solves his son's emotional difficulties with that new found cure, baseball.

Baseball may symbolise some bygone time when men were men, America was great and paternity was a matter of fact rather than opinion, but men's ballgames hardly transcend every major societal shift. Mike Gatting take note. This doesn't stop Jack Lemmon croaking on in his hospital bed about baseball, as the sunlight floods the room—a sure sign in this saccharine world that death is imminent.

But Lemmon doesn't snuff it until we see just how caring his son is and how good Lemmon is at acting senile, William Wharton's novel, on which the film is based, is a far more ambiguous exploration of father/son relationships than is allowed for here. In the film version, on hearing that his mother is ill, Danson drops his Wall Street career to come home and look after his ageing parents. Of course he looks after his dad better than his mother ever did, encouraging his dad's independence and sense of fun. When Lemmon also gets ill, Danson stays put; his brilliant career can apparently wait.

Just like last week's *Sea of Love*, which sets a woman up as a serial killer when this is a predominantly male occupation, so too in *Dad*, caring for elderly relatives is being done by a man. In reality, as we know, most women don't just drop everything to look after dependants. Rather, they work and continue to look after the rest of their family as well as taking on this extra responsibility. This being Hollywood however, Danson doesn't just excel in the sensitivity stakes but also manages to achieve the dreaded goal of every baby boomer—he "finds himself".

In re-establishing his relationship with his father he realises that he has neglected his own son because: "It's tough for guys my age to reach out". With dialogue like this, thank god, guys his age have kept themselves to themselves for all these years! His college drop-out son is actually the only character with any sense of irony about the whole ludicrous enterprise. "Quality time? Take it easy dad, let's not get carried away".

All these "family" films get uncontrollably carried away with this idea of quality time. Every father/child interaction is painted in glowing colours as though a few minutes with junior is enough to make up for all those nights spent working late. These fantasies, propelled by male guilt and female dissatisfaction, obscure the everyday hassle of childcare that so many of these designer dads are not around to see. This is quantity time. It's the blood and guts business of parenting and it's not particularly cinematic.

While some men may want to kid themselves that quality is more important *than* quantity, those of us who put in more than six hours a week—the average amount of time that men take responsibility for their kids—know differently.

NEW YORK POST, 10/27/89, p. 23, Jami Bernard

A sort of "Terms of Endearment" for the menfolk, "Dad" is a cry-fest that will probably put Jack Lemmon up for an Oscar as a frail, old man on the cusp of death.

The movie's instincts lie somewhat along the faultline of a more sophisticated TV movie of the week, replete with a bizarre psychological twist that mars this often hilarious tear-jerker.

Despite its slick deficiencies, you simply cannot ignore the movie's emotional power or the scarily fine performances by Lemmon as an ailing oldster and Olympia Dukakis as his sarcastically domineering wife.

Shot in mostly warm, nostalgic yellows designed to tug at the heart (Steven Spielberg is an executive producer), "Dad" begins with a typical morning in the life of Jake and Bette Tremont

(Lemmon and Dukakis). Their days are ordered around order itself; each morning brings more of the same, from breakfast to grocery shopping in which ball-buster Bette (no surprise that her name is spelled like the late Miss Davis') commands the butcher to give her the choicer cut at the lower price.

The routine changes when a heart attack sidelines Bette to the hospital. Their successful and somewhat remote son John (Ted Danson), a high-powered Type A businessman with a good heart, comes to care for dad (shades of "Nothing in Common") and gradually coaxes him into a more independent life, teaching him simple household chores and taking him to a Bingo game.

Soon, Jake is buying outrageous outfits on Venice Beach, befriending neighborhood children and holding a weekly Foreign Food Night.

Jake's metamorphosis at this point has more to do with a near-miss of his own, healthwise, and some psychological ramifications that are so curious they undermine the tragicomedy at hand. They also give Dukakis a chance to steal the show.

Bette, rooted in routine and control, tries to go along gamely with her husband's new zest for life. Her barely masked horror is priceless when Jake volunteers their services as neighborhood babysitters or when he babbles about a fantasy past he believes is real.

Danson's character is the one through whose eyes the action is seen. Despite his strong jaw and rugged good looks, the actor exudes a gentleness, a niceness really and a physical sturdiness that handily offsets the frailties and difficult natures of his screen parents. Danson's easygoing humor also grounds the movie when it threatens to take off into illness-of-the-week-land.

By the sniffles in the screening audience, the movie touched a raw nerve, but Lemmon's outstanding performance must be prefaced with a nod to Dick Smith, whose natural-looking, wrinkly makeup aged the actor 20 years. Lemmon also lost 30 pounds for the role and shaved his head, save for a wisp of white hair. He looks like hell, and it's a shock.

To that, Lemmon adds a slow and debilitating body language. I couldn't bear to watch the scene in which the son feeds him, the camera clenched on Lemmon's face like a death mask.

The Oscar people may be moved as well, as they go for physically arduous roles (Sigourney Weaver in "Gorillas in the Mist," Dustin Hoffman in "Rain Man"). Lemmon has an equal in Dukakis, in a dead-on performance that gives Bette just the right, light touch of irony and self-awareness.

NEWSDAY, 10/27/89, Part III/p. 3, Mike McGrady

Seventy-eight-year-old Jake Tremont (Jack Lemmon) is slow to awaken. His eyes blink open but remain just slightly out of focus as he seems to be seeing his bedroom for the first time. His wife (Olympia Dukakis) is laying out his clothing for the day ("It's a little chilly, I'll put out a sweater") as he moves with evident difficulty to the bathroom where his toilet articles have been laid out for him in order of use; the first item is a toothbrush carrying a ribon of freshly squeezed toothpaste.

At the breakfast table, Jake blinks at the decaffinated coffee as though it might carry some not easily deciphered message while his wife maintains a running commentary: "I already put sugar in. One's enough. Here your napkin. You want that buttered? Here you go." Then it's off to the supermarket where he hobbles along after his wife's shopping cart, blinking mutely as she negotiates the price of pork chops and cashes in coupons.

"Dad" opens with an incredibly chilling portrait of age. And I don't suppose I'm going to sell many tickets by revealing the film then goes on to touch upon such subjects as heart attack, senility, schizophrenia, cancer, coma and death. You must be thinking: With a movie like "Dad," who needs real life?

The truth is that "Dad " is not only profoundly moving, it's also strangely elating. And one reason for its being such a genuine heart-warmer is the performance by Lemmon in the title role. As Lemmon ages as an actor, he has gone beyond an uncanny knack for capturing modern types to the vastly more difficult feat of breathing life into individuals. "Dad" represents his very best work.

When Jake's wife suffers a heart attack, he must attempt to get by with a little help from his businessman-son (Ted Danson) who moves in to help out. Getting by is no cinch. The old man seems lost in another world, unable to even locate his pajamas without his wife's help. Once the pajamas are located, he fumbles at the buttons and finally surrenders.

With his son offering basic survival lessons, Jake learns how to dress himself, how to wash clothes, how to prepare food and slowly, very slowly, returns to the land of the living. By the time his recuperating wife can return home from the hospital, he has even gotten his driver's license back. So deeply involved have we become by this time that every advance—and every setback—is taken personally.

I don't recall any film that draws responses from a deeper emotional well. As three generations of Tremont family males—all pursuing quite separate existences—become bound together by this aging and ailing parent, the accumulation of truths has a shattering impact.

Although the film is billed as a comedy, it is never quite that. Most of the laughs are prompted by Dukakis' portrayal of a tough old bird ("They told me I have the willpower of a woman half my age!" she says from her hospital bed.), but the emotions tend to follow deeper currents. Danson, who has not always been lucky in his choice of past film roles, here gets lucky and does well.

Based on the William Wharton novel, "Dad" also draws on writer-director-producer Gary David Goldberg's own experiences in caring for a dying father. The creator of television's "Family Ties,"Goldberg's first feature film is terribly ambitious, gaining its strength from truths revealed about such basic family concerns as life and death and love—mostly love, as it turns out. Everyone involved is excellent except for Jack Lemmon—and he's a miracle.

VILLAGE VOICE, 10/31/89, p. 84, Manohla Dargis

Jack Lemmon is a convicing septuagenarian. With his droopy pants, bowed legs and superb makeup, Lemmon is Jake, the paterfamilias of *Dad*, the first feature film by director Gary David Goldberg (who helped make neoconservativism cuddly for the '80s with his hit TV series *Family Ties*). This dewy drama aspires to be a *Terms of Endearment* for the *Golden Girls* set, but without the bite of Jack Nicholson or even Bea Arthur.

For a short while, even as it stockpiles clichés, *Dad* isn't half bad. A restrained Olympia Dukakis is Mom to Lemmon's Dad; crusty but kind, domineering but well-meaning, Mom bustles about in mauve pantsuits, monitoring the details of Dad's life as bloodlessly as a CPA. She squeezes paste on his toothbrush, lays out his clothes, sugars his coffee. Jake shuffles about in a fog; the weight of his ordered life has sucked him dry.

While pricing processed cheese in the dairy section, Mom has a heart attack. John (Ted Danson), their A-type executive son, flies in to babysit Dad While Mom is hospitalized. Mortified by Jake's enfeebled state John gives his father a hasty, impatient lesson in male liberation. In a series of dissolves Dad is soon revitalized, but when Jake is stricken ill, Lemmon shifts into cuteness and *Dad* becomes unbearable. Bathed in the suffocating golden glow familiar from executive coproducer Spielberg's homilies, *Dad* lacks guts; it trivializes old age while it flees the messiness of death.

Also reviewed in:
NEW YORK TIMES, 10/27/89, p. C15, Vincent Canby
NEW YORKER, 11/13/89, p. 119, Pauline Kael
VARIETY, 10/25–31/89, p. 29
WASHINGTON POST, 10/27/89, p. B1, Hal Hinson

DANCE OF HOPE

A First Run Features release of a Copihue production. *Producer:* Deborah Shaffer and LaVonne Poteet. *Director:* Deborah Shaffer. *Director of Photography:* Jaime Reyes. *Editor:* Marcelo Navarro. *Music:* Sting and Wendy Blackstone. *Sound:* Mario Diaz and Patricio Valenzuela. *Running time:* 75 minutes. *MPAA Rating:* Not Rated.

NEW YORK POST, 12/1/89, p. 29, V.A. Musetto

"Dance of Hope" is a no frills but compelling indictment of the dictatorship that has gripped Chile since Augusto Pinochet seized power from Salvador Allende in a 1973 coup. The movie is directed by Deborah Shaffer, whose previous documentaries include the Oscar-winning "Witness to War: Dr. Charlie Clements," and it opens today at the Public Theater.

"Dance" is dedicated to the tens of thousands of Chileans—those arrested, killed and exiled under Pinochot's regime—"whose lives have been sacrificed in the struggle for democracy and justice." With Chile preparing for Dec. 14 elections, the first since Pinochet took power, it is particularly timely.

"Dance" makes its point with a minimum of commentary, allowing juxtaposed images and interviews to do the job.

Soldiers in riot gear use tear-gas and armored vehicles to break up peaceful rallies. Asked about what has just happened, one soldier will say only: "Everything is normal. Thank you." A stern-faced Pinochet—decked out in an ornate uniform—receives the blessing of a Roman Catholic cardinal.

Women tell why they have turned to prostitution to survive. A man collects paper from the street to sell for four cents a pound in order to feed his family. A woman says her family subsists on "teapot soup"—a piece of bread and a cup of tea.

But the film makes its point best when it interviews eight women whose sons and husbands have disappeared in government crackdowns. One woman tells how her husband was arrested during the 1973 coup because he refused to shut down the radio station that he managed. He was sentenced to 60 days in jail. But, as his wife was to learn in what she calls "a scene out of a nightmare," he instead was executed by a firing squad. The government never returned his body.

Says another woman, whose son disappeared after his arrest in 1976: "Our family continues to search for him to this day."

But probably the most devastating comments come from the wife of another of the missing: "They [the government] know where the bodies are buried. For 15 years they have tortured us, not physically, but psychologically... We've searched for them in the desert, and we will continue to search. As long as we're alive we will not lose hope of finding them. Maybe not today or tomorrow, but we will find them."

VILLAGE VOICE, 12/12/89, p. 109, Juile Phillips

Dance of Hope, a documentary of current events in Chile by Deborah Shaffer (*Fire From the Mountain*), also [the reference is to *Mapantsula*] illuminates the possibilities of the answer "No." The film was shot last year at the time of the October 5 plebiscite, in which Chileans were given the choice of continuing the Pinochet regime, or not. Over the course of Shaffer's interviews with women on both sides of Chilean politics, it becomes clear that the majority who said "No" to Pinochet were rejecting not only the tortures and disappearances, but the more commonplace miseries of the current situation: unemployment, prostitution, hunger.

Again, the familiarity of the demonstrations, tear gas, soldiers, water cannon does not take away from their disturbing quality. Shaffer has a nice sense of irony, and shots of a vague, Reaganesque Pinochet wandering through a sea of government-sponsored pageantry are intercut with the real thing: women dancing the *cueca sola*, a campesino courtship dance performed alone to protest the disappearances. (Sting's two cents on the subject, "They Dance Alone," makes a mercifully brief appearance on the soundtrack.) A better sense of history might have been in order—the film as it is could as easily be about any repressive Latin American country. Still, with elections in Chile scheduled for December 14, *Dance of Hope* dóes give a useful account of the situation now.

Also reviewed in:
NEW YORK TIMES, 12/1/89, p. C12, Vincent Canby
VARIETY, 12/20/89, p. 24

DANCING FOR MR. B: SIX BALANCHINE BALLERINAS

A Seahorse Films production in association with WNET/New York. *Producer:* Anne Belle. *Director:* Anne Belle and Deborah Dickson. *Director of Photography:* Don Lenzer. *Editor:* Deborah Dickson. *Sound:* Peter Miller. *Running time:* 86 minutes. *MPAA Rating:* Not Rated.

WITH: Maria Tallchief, Mary Ellen Moylan, Melissa Hayden, Allegra Kent, Merrill Ashley, and Darci Kistler.

NEW YORK POST, 10/7/89, p. 19, Jami Bernard

With reverence and affection and their own dear egocentricities *en pointe*, six well-known ballerinas recall being taught and mesmerized by George Balanchine, the late mastermind of the New York City Ballet, in "Dancing for Mr. B" at the New York Film Festival tonight.

One dancer decided early on that she wanted to work for this man because she read in Vogue that he chose the perfume for each of his girls. Maria Tallchief, who was married to Balanchine briefly, fondly recalls how he used to refer to her "lousy barre." They discuss the elongated "Balanchine look" and his dislike for fussy costumes, his devotion to his ballerinas, his exquisite choreography and the grand effect he had on their lives.

The portrait that emerges is not only of the great Balanchine, but of his ballerinas' emotional lives as well. Other-wordly Allegra Kent remembers wanting to excel at something, anything, that would separate her from her overbearing mother. Merrill Ashley's rivalry with newcomer Suzanne Farrell is painfully evident despite her attempt to conceal it.

"He was always giving me myself," says the young Darci Kistler, who is shown floating through "La Sonnambula" as if she were a feather.

"Dancing for Mr. B" is a wonderful, low-key testimonial; the man's effect on the dance world emerges second only to the powerful effect he had on his ballerinas, whose need for him even after his death practically bleeds through the celluloid.

Also reviewed in:
NEW YORK TIMES, 10/7/89, p. 14, Caryn James
VARIETY, 10/18-24/89, p. 32

DEAD-BANG

A Lorimar Film Entertainment release. *Executive Producer:* Robert L. Rosen. *Producer:* Steve Roth. *Director:* John Frankenheimer. *Screenplay:* Robert Foster. *Director of Photography:* Gerry Fisher. *Editor:* Robert F. Shugrue. *Music:* Gary Chang. *Music Editor:* Don Sanders. *Sound:* Claude Hazanavicius and Charles Wilborn. *Sound Editor:* Anthony Palk and Mike Le Mare. *Production Designer:* Ken Adam. *Art Director:* Richard Hudolin and Alan Manzer. *Set Decorator:* Art Parker. *Set Dresser:* Tedd Kuchera and Janice Blackie. *Special Effects:* Cliff P. Wenger. *Costumes:* Jodie Tillen. *Make-up:* Jamie Brown. *Stunt Coordinator:* Mic Rodgers and Brent Woolsey. *Running time:* 109 minutes. *MPAA Rating:* R.

CAST: Don Johnson (Jerry Beck; Penelope Ann Miller (Linda); William Forsythe (Arthur Kressler); Bob Balaban (Elliot Webly); Frank Military (Bobby Burns); Tate Donovan (John Burns); Antoni Stutz (Ray); Mickey Jones (Sleepy); Ron Campbell (Crossfield); William Taylor (Elton Tremmel); Hy Anzell (Captain Waxman); Michael Jeter (Dr. Krantz); Tim Reid (Chief Dixon); James B. Douglas (Agent Gilroy); Brad Sullivan (Chief Hillard); Phyllis Guerrini (Louisa); Darwyn Swalve (Biker #1); David H. Van Dalsem (Biker #2); Ron Jeremy Hyatt (Biker #3); Sam Scarber (Detective Bilson); Mic Rodgers (Sergeant Kimble); Tiger Haynes (Edwin Gates); Garwin Sanford (Officer #1); Lon Katzman (Officer #2); Daniel Quinn (James "Hard Rock" Ellis); Jarion Monroe (L.A.P.D. Officer); Ricardo Ascencio (Ponchito); William Taylor (Officer Franklin); Trudy Forbes (Female Officer); Michael Hibbins (Reverend Gebhardt); Evans Evans (Mrs. Gebhardt); Stephen E. Miller (Bogan, Oklahoma Officer); Dawn Mortensen (Daughter); Frank C. Turner (Cottonwood Officer); Lennard Camarillo (Juancho); Jerome Beck (Detective John); Louis Clark (Man in Car); Billy Boyle (Priest); Justin Stillwell (Mark Beck); Christine Cable (Karen Beck); Maureen Thomas (Teacher); Ron Carothers (Dixon's Men #1); Ernie Jackson (Dixon's Men #2); Juliana Carter (Dixon's Wife).

LOS ANGELES TIMES, 3/27/89, Calendar/p. 12, Michael Wilmington

In John Frankenheimer's "Dead-Bang," Don Johnson, playing a scruffy Los Angeles cop hot on the trail of a fascist underground group, has a squeezed-up, desperate look. He keeps grabbing onto things—bottles, people, his own clothes—like a bleary golden boy after an all-night binge.

Johnson and Frankenheimer cannily play up the character's near-alcoholism, his hair-trigger temper, vulnerability to insult and his shame-faced littleboy shuffle when he gets in a jam.

Johnson's Jerry Beck gives the movie some internal tension, which it really needs. Supposedly "Dead-Bang" is based on fact—Beck is a real-life L.A. cop—but it's been hammered into the usual one-man vendetta saga. The movie's Beck, his glasses falling apart, his taxes overdue, his sanity in question, has become, superficially, Columbo crossed with James Dean. Johnson makes him a sweating never-say-die bulldog racing through the metallic jags and cold corners of the plot: a sleek, formula "message" thriller with no exits.

Arrayed against him are bureaucrats, smirking fascists, an obnoxious ex-wife, uncooperative local police and hidebound FBI agents (William Forsythe, playing a reactionary robot after his radical robot in "Patty Hearst"). There's also the apparent killer himself (Frank Military) popping up regularly with three maniac buddies and an endless supply of attack rifles.

The story is a weird unjelled mixture of fact and fancy, fiction and formula. The best scenes have a real smack of truth: the frenzied street chase that begins with the kidnapping of a testy parole officer (Bob Balaban) and ends with an exhausted Beck up-chucking on his tackled suspect. The worst of them rattle around in an exploding gutter of gratuitous, bloody kitsch.

In the '60s, Frankenheimer was a master of the topical political thriller; then, his style seemed a curious blend of Orson Welles tracks and angles, film-noir urban cynicism and the electronic shorthand of TV journalism. When he's working at top pressure, he still knows how to tighten the vise. Some of "Dead-Bang" is gratifyingly fast, sharp and mean, full of acrobatic camera movements, offbeat, crammed frames and salty, sarcastic confrontations. But where his '60s movies, like "Manchurian Candidate," were verbally adroit and audacious, "Dead-Bang" clots its social observations with hack repetition and the usual paranoid lone-wolf '80s affectations. (Beck bullies almost everyone, including his psychiatrist.)

Like his contemporaries Arthur Penn in "Target" or Sidney Lumet in "The Morning After," Frankenheimer is wasting his time with material like this. What can he do besides showcase Johnson, get in a few little grace notes on alcoholic torment and keep the ball, and the camera, moving? "Dead-Bang" (rated R) not only falls short compared to Frankenheimer's best '60s work, but from his best '80s work, too—like the Elmore Leonard-scripted "52 Pickup," with its startling sadism and perversity, its cruel humor and its great psycho-villain by John Glover. By comparison, "Dead-Bang," ends not with a bang, but a simper.

MONTHLY FILM BULLETIN, 6/89, p. 178. Richard Combs

Los Angeles homicide detective Jerry Beck, in the middle of a divorce, returns to his cheap apartment beneath the Burbank airport flight paths to find a court injunction forbidding him from seeing his children. That night, a convenience store owner and a patrolman are cold-bloodedly gunned down, and Beck comes up with a likely suspect in the recently paroled Bobby Burns. Insisting that Burns' parole officer, Elliot Webly, meet him the next day, Christmas Day, Beck attends a police party and spends the night with a woman, Linda, who leaves hurriedly the next morning. With Webly, Beck busts into the Hell's Angels hang-out where he expects to catch Burns, but finds only his younger brother John. Beck is further frustrated by a phone call to his wife, and angered to realise that Linda was the dead patrolman's ex-wife, who now asks Beck to kill his killer. A murderous raid by Burns and his henchmen on a bar in Cottonwood, Arizona, leads Beck and the local sheriff's men to a ranch from which the killers escape, leaving behind a storehouse of white supremacist literature. FBI agent Arthur Kressler arrives on the scene, and though pooh-poohing the significance of the racist organisation, joins Beck in following its trail to Oklahoma and the Aryan Nation Church run by Reverend Gebhardt. The two law officers argue over tactics, and the uptight Kressler protests at Beck's belligerent attitude; when Beck is then nearly kidnapped by Burns, and involved in a messy shoot-out from which the killer escapes, his superior officer insists he has behavioural problems and should see a psychiatrist. Beck offends the latter, Dr. Krantz, by finding his attempt at bonhomie comical, and threatens him when Krantz intimates that he won't be passed as fit for duty. He follows the supremacists' trail to Boulder, where he is joined again by Kressler and , with a team of black cops led by Chief Dixon, they plan an assault on the group's nearby training camp. They surprise Gebhardt and his fascist "congregation", but can find no trace of Burns and his sidekicks until Beck stumbles on an underground hideaway and arms cache. In a running battle through the network of tunnels, Burns' henchmen are killed, but the dying Burns tells Beck that he didn't commit the initial murders of the storeowner and the patrolman. Beck and Kressler are then surprised by the crazed

John Burns, who claims he committed the murders to prove to his brother that he had the requisite "fire and ice" to serve his organisation. He is shot by Beck, who—now apparently more philosophical about his problems—bids Chief Dixon farewell after watching Kressler claim most of the credit at a press conference.

Its dim, Mickey Spillane-ish title notwithstanding, *Dead-Bang* is John Frankenheimer's boldest, most enjoyable, and at least partially successful attempt both to recreate the halcyon days of his early 60s reputation, and to adapt them to changing times. For one thing, it's about a conspiracy to take over America—the kind of plot that always seems to call out the baroque, overheated best in Frankenheimer—and for another it detours that plot through all sorts of incidental paranoia, scenes that should bear on the main business but seem more like playlets of the psychopathology of everyday life, proof that Frankenheimer was always better at scenes than plots, however tightly wound their paranoia. He has been wont to complain (most recently in *American Film*, March 1988) that he was early typecast as an action director when what he really wanted to do was "intimate things and character things". But the restless, combustible style of those first films, full of the pushy compositions and unfamiliar rhythms of TV drama, was not really a cinema of action *or* intimacy—the declamatory, TV style of dialogue was more theatrical, abstracting, caricaturing, and the busy plots always turned in on themselves, seizing up around their obsession with technology, with the myriad of internal "monitors" Frankenheimer liked to include, and again becoming caricature, action going in circles.

Hence the usefulness of conspiracy plots (*The Manchurian Candidate, Seconds, Seven Days in May*) within a mood that seemed to swing between crazed melodrama and satire of same. Two things put paid to that period when Frankenheimer seemed the golden boy of the American cinema: the TV dynamics of his films calcified of their own accord and, after the uncertain 60s, genre cinema reestablished itself with a vengeance in the 70s, a context in which Frankenheimer has been mostly at sea. In *Dead-Bang*, he finds his way back mostly to dry land, ably setting up the familiar situation of the effective but undisciplined cop, who is not only out of favour with his department but down on his luck personally (his wife is divorcing him, he can't see his kids, the bills are piling up as unheeded as the dishes), but who finds that he has stumbled on to something Big in a nationwide, well-organised, raring-for-Armageddon white-supremacist conspiracy. But having established this, it's a measure of Frankenheimer's return to form that to some extent he can let it go. Don Johnson's cop (the epitome-of-style actor playing a painfully short-of-style character) trails across country after one obvious psychopath while encountering other eccentrics, like the fiercely clean-cut and boy-scoutish FBI agent played by William Forsythe (late of the Symbionese Liberation Army), who suggest, à la *The Manchurian Candidate*, a certain bewildering criss-cross of conspiracies, that Big Brother has a number of identically evil, but ideologically opposite, siblings.

It's back, in other words, to scenes that relate tangentially, theatrically, to the main plot, the piecemeal effect emphasised by the fact that the script for *Dead-Bang* was put together from the reminiscences of real, and still-practising, Los Angeles detective Jerome Beck. Sometimes the effect is just dissatisfyingly discontinuous, as with the dead cop's wife (Penelope Ann Miller) who beds Beck, asks him to kill her husband's killer, then disappears—and she is the only significant female character in the film, apart from Frankenheimer's wife, Evans Evans, in one scene silently serving apple turnovers as wife to the pastor of the Aryan Nation Church. At other times, the effect plays humorously against the grain, as when Beck pulls Bob Balaban's disgruntled parole officer away from his family on Christmas Day and turns him into an unwilling partner, but their expected odd-couple pairing also goes no further than the one scene. Or in the off-centre comedy of Beck's interview with a psychiatrist, at his superiors' orders, which he flunks when he can't stop thinking of the doctor as looking like Woody Allen, until he is finally forced to extort a passing grade from him. But plot, and vigilante-cop conventions, finally catch up with *Dead-Bang,* and now that conspiracies have become so everyday, Frankenmheimer can't make anything too fancifully baroque out of this one. Nor does the final revelation that Beck has been chasing the wrong psychopath—that it's his kid brother who is the real supremacist fanatic—have the absurdity, the comic-horror pathology of family life, of *The Manchurian Candidate*.

NEW YORK POST, 3/25/89, p. 17, David Edelstein

The high point of "Dead-Bang" is when Don Johnson, as a homicide cop, chases a white-supremicist slimeball through the streets of L.A., tackles him, kicks him in the groin and then throws up all over him.

No joke—it's a heck of a scene. See, Big Don partied rather hard the night before and wasn't up for the pounding run and fisticuffs, and the chase itself would make anyone queasy: The men leap over fences, weave through traffic and engage in all manner of manly manhandling shortly before our hero dribbles all over his fallen quarry.

This isn't the only arresting sequence. Directed by John Frankenheimer, who once upon a time made "The Manchurian Candidate," "Seconds" and other nifty thrillers, "Dead-Bang" studs a couple of savory action scenes like truffles through its chopped-liver storyline. Not to carry the metaphor too far, but a lot of this picture is mush.

Despite its ejaculatory title, "Dead-Bang" is not a porn flick for morgue attendants, although they would certainly enjoy its cadaverous emotional tone and body-spattering shootouts. It begins like a lot of sadistic cop movies: A neo-Nazi punk shoots up an elderly black man in a convenience store and then blows the bejesus out of a cop at close range.

Big Don gets called in because it's almost Christmas and he doesn't have a family. In fact, he lives in the style of most divorced, sloppy, hard-drinking movie cops—they must all have the same interior decorator. As a gang of Aryan goons shoots up the countryside on its way to a convention, our hero tracks them to Arizona, Oklahoma and then Colorado. Funny how it all looks like Canada, where most of the picture was actually shot).

In between the action stuff, Big Don squints through his granny glasses at assorted maps and documents, talks dirty to his fellow officers and gets on people's nerves.

The filmmaker's idea is to surround him with a lot of prissy white guys—Bob Balaban as a parole officer, William Forsythe as a religious, by-the-book FBI agent and Michael Jeter as a Jewish psychiatrist—and show how hard it is for a tough guy like Don to get the dirty job done.

He meets his soulmate only after he gets to Colorado—a rocksolid, black police captain named Dixon (Tim Reid). "Would there be anyone afraid to go through a door with me?" he asks the assembled SWAT team, and the men, including Dixon, eye him fishily.

I don't know what that question means exactly—it sounds like male prison shower-talk—but no one stays behind. And, appropriately enough, the movie's explosive climax takes place deep inside a mine shaft.

Unshaven, raspy and in fighting shape, Big Don has a lot of vanity close-ups, but he's still quite likable. There's a long shot in which he tries to talk to his ex-wife about why she won't let him see his kids: He pleads, wheedles, gets hung-up on, smashes his phone, hurls his papers across the room and kicks over a chair—all in one take.

Oh, he might not have much range as an actor, but there are plenty of less ingratiating leading men around. Don't worry, Don—there are millions of Americans who'd go through a door with you anytime.

NEWSDAY, 3/25/89, Part II/P. 15, Drew Fetherston

A guy walks into a convenience store on Christmas Eve, loots the till, shoots the black clerk. A few minutes later, he shoots a cop who accosts him.

Case lands on the desk of homicide cop Don Johnson. (Yeah, he has a name but it doesn't matter. He's playing Don Johnson.) No sweat. He doodles with his computer for a few minutes, comes up with a suspect. One suspect. Gets to work. Breaks some rules. Breaks some heads.

Square FBI guy hates him. So do the small-town cops he meets as he pursues the killer. So do his bureaucrat bosses.

Big shootout. Bad guys conveniently leave behind a marked map and a stack of hate literature. Light bulb goes off in our hero's head.

He hooks up with six black cops to attack the Neo-Nazis' mountain stronghold. FBI guy comes along. Approximately 500,000 shots are fired, most from Uzis in the hands of the wrong people. Casualties nonetheless tip in favor of the good guys.

Right triumphs. The FBI takes all the credit.

Standard stuff, and if that's all there was to "Dead-Bang," the film would be easier to respect. Straightforward action doesn't necessarily mean it's not a nice film; some such even rise to respectable heights.

But "Dead-Bang" is careless with its plot and characters, and thereby contemptuous of its audience. The cop gets a firm suspect in five minutes at the computer, and law enforcement mobilizes to track him down? Come on, folks, that doesn't happen in good movies, much less real life.

The hero has a one-night stand with someone he meets less than 24 hours after the cop is murdered—and it turns out to be the dead cop's estranged wife? Who would believe that?

Well, maybe you could make me believe it if you took the time to give the wife (played by Penelope Ann Miller) a motive. Not in "Dead-Bang"; she comes in, comes on, takes off her clothes and leaves the next morning. End of subplot.

"Dead-Bang" leaves the field littered with such discarded characters. Bob Balaban shows up as a parole officer dragged along on a questionable raid by the hero. He looks like a good candidate for a quirky buddy relationship, but gets written out of the action in short order.

In the midst of this character assassination, one scene shines: The hero is sent to a department shrink, who is to decide if he can stay on the case. The interview and its aftermath are funny and cleverly handled. One wishes there were at least a few more like it to enliven "Dead-Bang."

VILLAGE VOICE, 4/4/89, p. 59, Georgia Brown

Since *Dead-Bang* didn't press-screen, I saw it at the seedy Eighth Street Theater, as did a number of single (unaccompanied) men. As a star vehicle for Don Johnson, directed by John Frankenheimer, the film isn't intended for the ladies. Still, I developed a muted fondness for it, despite having to change seats when the theater's roof began to leak precisely onto my head.

A cop's wife troubles are becoming a staple subplot to policiers. Whereas *Dead-Bang* isn't in the same league with *Die Hard, Someone To Watch Over Me,* or *Tightrope,* its harried cop hero evoked a lot of empathy in my audience, maybe from other men with tough jobs who are at a loss when it comes to emotional matters. Down-and-out homicide detective Jerry Beck (Johnson) is first seen carrying groceries into his cheerless apartment, while reading a restraining order that seems designed to keep him from even peering wistfully through the chainlink fence into his daughters' schoolyard. What Jerry has done to merit a court order isn't clarified, but he does have a temper. When he phones to wish his daughters Merry Christmas and his wife hangs up on him, he smashes the phone—an act that got big laughs.

Frankenheimer cuts from Jerry's domestic problems to his job-related ones: A psycho brutally shoots an ancient, quaking grocery store owner and a young cop. The camera conceals the killer's features but shows he's wearing jeans and a V-neck T-shirt, just as Jerry is—establishing the obligatory link between hunter and hunted. (The identification, like Jerry's marital troubles, isn't pursued.) The search for the killer takes tenacious Jerry out of the L.A. smog into the cold, clear air of Colorado, where a white supremacy group ("Aryans Awake" is its credo) has built its fancy headquarters, a cross between hunt club and fortress. *Dead-Bang* loses steam the more it focuses on this neo-Nazi conspiracy—even though fascism connects in an elemental way to the movie's only real theme: male impotence, male rage.

Jerry Beck fumes at his unseen wife, takes on some huge ex-con bikers (arresting one, he vomits all over the guy, who then looks up and says, "Why don't you just shit on me while you're at it?"), and deliberately infuriates a series of petty, prissy professionals. There are three of these: a fusspot parole officer (Bob Balaban); a self-righteous Christian FBI agent (William Forsythe), who thinks Jerry says "fuck" much too often; and a tiny, uptight department shrink (Michael Jeter), whose resemblance to Woody Allen sends Jerry into a giggling fit. "No one responds well to ridicule, Mr. Beck," says bitter Dr. Krantz, "not even psychiatrists."

Back in the days when John Frankenheimer was considered an artist, I wasn't a believer, but with his pictures now opening furtively, as studio embarrassments, it's plain at least that his work has more sstyle and definition than most studio fare. *Dead-Bang*, for all its lamebrain incoherence, has strong, graceful moments.

Also reviewed in:
NEW YORK TIMES, 3/25/89, p. 12, Vincent Canby
VARIETY, 3/29–4/4/89, p. 14
WASHINGTON POST, 3/25/89, p. D7, Hal Hinson

DEAD CALM

A Warner Bros. release of a Kennedy Miller production. *Producer:* Terry Hayes, Doug Mitchell, and George Miller. *Director:* Phillip Noyce. *Screenplay:* Terry Hayes. *Based on the novel by:* Charles Williams. *Director of Photography:* Dean Semler. *Editor:* Richard Francis-Bruce. *Music:* Graeme Revell. *Sound:* Ben Osmo. *Production Designer:* Graham (Grace) Walker. *Costumes:* Norma Moriceau. *Running time:* 96 minutes. *MPAA Rating:* R.

CAST: Nicole Kidman (Rae Ingram); Sam Neill (John Ingram); Billy Zane (Hughie Warriner); Rod Mullinar (Russell Bellows); Joshua Tilden (Danny); George Shevtsov (Doctor); Micahel Long (Specialist Doctor).

LOS ANGELES TIMES, 4/7/89, Calendar/ p. 1, Sheila Benson

Cracking-good thrillers are harder to find these days, possibly because the audiences for them seem to have gotten more demanding. They insist that smart people not do dumb things—like walk downstairs alone in the dark toward the source of that nasty sound, that fright come from sources other than slathering, 30-foot monsters with toxic slime dripping from their teeth, and that if women are in danger they should do something clever about getting themselves out of it, beyond screaming or ripping a nail dialing 911.

Into this void sails "Dead Calm," a spare, smart, seductive piece of real movie making with (almost) every loophole covered, a superlative cast and enough tension to keep us all hyperventilating for hours.

It should be tense; it's from the Australian-based film production group Kennedy Miller—which, among its other virtues, gave us the "Mad Max" films—and it has been directed by "Newsfront's" crackerjack Phillip Noyce.

A prologue dramatizes why this extended South Pacific voyage of the Ingrams, John (Sam Neill) and Rae (Nicole Kidman), is so important. Some months earlier they lost a young son to an automobile accident that almost killed Rae as well. So it's a voyage of healing and forgetting on the Saracen, their handsome, well-equipped yacht, with John, a career Royal Australian Navy officer, securely in charge and tenderly aware of his wife's emotionally fragile state.

On their 32nd day out, their tranquility is shattered as they sight another sailing ship on the horizon, then a dinghy being furiously rowed toward them from that boat. In it is Hughie Warriner (Billy Zane) a terrified young American survivor of a grotesque bout of food poisoning that has killed everyone aboard his ship, the Orpheus, out of Santa Barbara.

John notices an ad among Hughie's things: "Free South Seas Cruise. Four young women wanted—must be attractive." In spite of Hughie's panicky, desperate condition and his warning that the Orpheus is shipping water and beginning to sink, John takes his own small boat over to investigate.

However, because this is a different sort of thriller, he locks the exhausted Hughie's cabin door prudently behind him, and also leaves the terrific family dog there with his singularly beautiful wife. ("Dead Calm" is also different enough and smart enough that when this young, burly stranger appears, Rae changes from her swimming clothes to something less provocative. Nice sensibilities prevail.)

But no thriller fan worthy of the name will be surprised that, within minutes, John has made an horrific discovery; Hughie is not where he should be, and every jot of Rae's ingenuity and stamina will be called upon to stay on top of an increasingly desperate situation.

"Dead Calm" becomes a film maker's brilliant chess game: two boats, three characters—actually four, since the dog is so memorable—a dinghy and a prescribed amount of ocean. How to build the maximum tension with these simple elements and with only these locations possible?

It begins with Terry Hayes' taut screenplay, adapted from Charles Williams' 1963 novel. (As "The Deep" it was made once before, beginning in 1968, by Orson Welles, although it has never been shown and possibly never completed.) Hayes, a Kennedy Miller principal and also co-producer here with Doug Mitchell and George Miller, has pared away a few of the novel's characters who might slow the film's juggernaut momentum, although he has found an ingenuous way of our "meeting" some of the missing members anyway.

Director Noyce seems to have been energized by his story's physical limitations. He uses these elements like a symphony conductor calling on sections of his orchestra: now physical emotion, now the sea itself, now a rainstorm, now technological gadgetry, now brute force, now brute cunning.

And his cast is brilliant. Kidman is known to any who saw the Australian miniseries "Vietnam." For the rest of us, she is a magnificent discovery. Five-feet-10 and dark-red-haired, she looks a bit like Samantha Egger, but mostly like her arresting self. "Dead Calm" (rated R for violence, sexual and otherwise) is almost non-stop action, much of it brutal, but Kidman seems to approach it from a reservoir of intelligence and with an arc of her character's growth clearly in her mind. And, of course, there's this script, which presumes that having spent so much time on a boat, she has learned something useful about her surroundings. How delightful.

Neill is probably one of the screen's most underrated actors, witness the general overlooking of his exceptional work in "A Cry in the Dark." He is a man who is called in to star opposite the heaviest hitters (it's hardly accidental that he has acted twice with Meryl Streep), when unquestionable authority and a soupçon of sexuality is needed. "Dead Calm" was probably far and away his nastiest assignment physically, yet his presence, sexuality and all, is absolutely vital to the balance of the story.

Zane is the second newcomer, a thick-lashed, black-haired monster with a pretty face, whose derangement we learn about only gradually. It's a strong, careful, merciless performance and an interesting debut.

Ever since "Carrie" we've had after-endings, which by now are commonplace instead of heart-stopping. This ultra-violent one *never* would be missed, and although the prologue is there to refer to a crucial life-or-death decision that Rae faces later, I'm not sure it was absolutely needed either.

Graham (Grace) Walker's marvelous production designs, the superb editing of Richard Francis-Bruce, Dean Semler's camera work, Norma Moriceau's canny costuming and the strangely eerie part-vocal score of Graeme Revell all contribute to "Dead Calm's" beautifully controlled tone. For those who like their terror smart but merciless, help is here at last.

MONTHLY FILM BULLETIN, 11/89, p. 332, Verina Glaessner

John Ingram returns home from a tour of duty with the Royal Australian Navy to find that his young son has been killed in a road accident, which has also left his wife Rae in a coma. When she recovers, the couple attempt to come to terms with the tragedy by taking off on board their yacht the "Saracen" (though Rae continues to be plagued by feelings of guilt). Their boat is becalmed, and on the horizon they notice another vessel, the "Orpheus", which fails to respond to the radio; a distressed American, Hughie Warriner, approaches them in a lifeboat and tells them of a failed attempt to cross the Pacific and how the rest of the crew died of a virulent outbreak of botulism. The suspicious John rows out to the "Orpheus", and sets about putting the sinking vessel to rights, in the process discovering the dismembered bodies of several women and a videotape which replays the hellish events which preceded the killings. Meanwhile, on the "Saracen", Hughie knocks Rae unconscious, and when she recovers John has been left far behind on the sinking "Orpheus" and the crazed Hughie refuses to turn back. Rae contrives to send a message by radio to John (who has been unable to repair the leak), promising to return for him. When Hughie makes sexual advances to her, she seizes the opportunity to spike his drink with a sedative; before it takes effect, she locks herself in the cabin with a harpoon gun which she fires at random when Hughie tries to break down the door. She emerges from the cabin when she sees blood under the door, but it is the dog that has been killed and she is attacked again. She wounds Hughie and finally ties him up when the sedative takes effect. She set sail for the "Orpheus", where John is trapped in the hold of the rapidly sinking vessel. When Hughie revives she is forced to shoot him again and set him adrift in a lifeboat. John meanwhile escapes from the "Orpheus", and clings to a makeshift raft while using a flare gun to set the boat on fire as a beacon. He is rescued by Rae, but the couple are once again threatened by Hughie, who has managed to clamber aboard in secret. He is finally despatched by John with the flare gun.

Dead Calm is derived from the same Charles Williams novel which served as the basis for *The Deep*, one of Orson Welles' last, still unseen productions, filmed in 1968 with Laurence Harvey and Jeanne Moreau off the coast of Yugoslavia. Phillip Noyce has claimed that, rather than any suppositions about what Welles might have made of the project, he took his inspiration from Hitchcock, and in particular *Notorious*. One might see a trace of Wellesian surrealism, none the less, in some haunting shots of the death ship—a veritable terrain of the unconscious, full of Orphic horrors—although there is little of this elsewhere in the film, which delivers a routine woman-in-jeopardy chiller. Noyce was attracted by the novel's "minimalism", and he has pared this down even further until he is left with a three-hander confined to two sets. But the film is sunk precisely by its inability to handle its minimal props in any evocative way: there is nothing to disguise the fact that Billy Zane spends an awful lot of time kicking down doors, and stalwart Sam Neill an almost equal amount of time being gradually submerged.

The relentlessly glossy appearance lent the film by Noyce's (presumed) use of "state of the art" technology remains entirely inappropriate. The time has also long passed when the spectacle of a woman essaying macho violence on screen could carry any progressive intimations. A possible psychological reading is suggested in the film's opening scenes, which imply that the attack is rooted in Rae's guilt, or in John's inability to respond to her needs. But this remains unexplored in Noyce's mechanical and entirely unreflective direction. He retains a knack for projecting a sense of malevolence about everyday objects and situations (the sequence with Rae and her son in the car is filled with more menace than anything else in the film), but steadily casts himself adrift, figuratively as well as literally, from the sources of his directorial strength.

NEW YORK, 4/24/89, p. 98, David Denby

Back at film school in the sixties, there was a student from paris—a structuralist with many theories—who once stopped conversation cold in the cafeteria by insisting that movies set on sailboats must always, by their very nature, turn into triangle dramas (the reason had something to do with water imagery). He was thinking of René Clément's *Purple Noon*, Polanski's *Knife in the Water*, and I don't remember what else. I scoffed at the time, but now here's the new thriller *Dead Calm*, an Australian movie set on a sailboat, and the main trouble with the picture, apart from its general squalor, is that it isn't *enough* of a triangle drama.

A sea captain (Sam Neill) and his beautiful young red-haired wife, Rae (Nicole Kidman), vacationing on their boat on the Great Barrier Reef, pick up an overwrought young man (Billy Zane) who is rowing away from his own boat. Hughie, as the young man is called, turns out to be a psychotic murderer. When the husband goes to check out Hughie's craft, he gets trapped in the slowly sinking vessel and spends most of the movie trying not to go down with the psycho's ship; Rae is left behind to fight off Hughie, using arms, legs, tranquilizers, rope, harpoon gun, shotgun, and flares.

Shot in both stormy and placid seas, and in all sorts of light, *Dead Calm* looks great and easily holds your attention. Yet I have to admit that the movie genre in which beautiful women are menaced by nuts is not one of my favorites. It's true that the women have grown bigger, stronger, and more resourceful since the days when blind, stick-armed Audrey Hepburn fought off Alan Arkin in *Wait Until Dark*. But the nuts have grown more resourceful, too; they now tend to rise, over and over, from the dead. The hammer-headed stupidity of *Dead Calm* makes one indifferent to how well made it is. Rae Kidman, who has the stature and beauty of Sigourney Weaver, is an exciting physical presence, and it would be nice to see her do something in a movie besides get pulled around by the hair and thrown to the deck. Despite an ambiguous and rather arousing sex scene between Rae and Hughie, the director, Phillip Noyce, doesn't work out the three-way tensions implicit in the material—through most of *Dead Calm*, the husband isn't even *there*. Does the movie's ineptitude at triangular construction disprove my friend's theory? Try the Sorbonne for an answer.

NEW YORK POST, 4/7/89, p. 27, David Edelstein

In a thriller, there are few things as spooky as utter tranquility—no music, the gentlest rocking of a boat, miles of water. In "Dead Calm," John and Rae Ingram (Sam Neill and Nicole Kidman) go to sea in their yacht to forget the loss of an infant boy, who hurtled through the windshield when his mother lost control of her car in a storm.

As they drift—guilty, forlorn, alone with each other and their thoughts—the audience waits anxiously for...something.

Something comes.

"Dead Calm," directed by the Australian Phillip Noyce and produced by the team behind "The Road Warrior," has a golden hue, and the waters of the Great Barrier Reef glow aqua. The suspense is voluptuous. Noyce's style is built on opposites: on claustrophobic dread and space without end; on taut, slashing cuts and overripe images; on paradisical settings and deep-dark, floating rot.

The movie is so beautifully made—so lush and colorful and alive with primal terrors—that it's a shock to discover that at heart it's just a dumb horror movie. But a knockout dumb horror movie, a corker.

This formula worked for "Fatal Attraction," too: Tease us with psychological complexity and then bring on the loony. And "Dead Calm" provokes the same sort of fury in its audience, the same collective "Kill the psycho!" howl. There's art in manipulation this brilliant, but also a cunning that has nothing to do with art. You leave feeling giggly, wiped out, unsure if you've been entertained or violated (or both).

The stranger who disrupts the couple's nervous idyll is a slim, muscular young man (Billy Zane) who rows frantically towards the yacht on a dinghy. On the horizon sits his boat, an old-fashioned schooner with the ominous name of "Orpheus." The man, Hughie Warriner, staggers onto the yacht and heads straight into the cabin, where he blurts out the story of a crew and passengers succumbing one by one to botulism. Only he survived.

Ingram, a veteran sailor, rows over to the flooded, slowly-sinking Orpheus to investigate. What he discovers—and what happens when he tries to return to his yacht—would be wrong to reveal. But it's possible to say that for the next tumultuous hour it's man vs. the elements and wife vs. nutcase.

Of all the movie's images, none is more provocative—and vulnerable—than Kidman. Noyce shoots her corkscrew-curled red hair against the electric blue of the sea, which matches her eyes. The 22-year-old actress wears bathing suits and body-hugging shorts and at one point nothing at all, and she's a troubling figure—an object of drooling lust and also an avenger, a feminist heroine, the protector of the family.

On one level, young Hughie—a delusional paranoid, stupid, coarse, brutal—could have sprung fully-formed from the brain of a jealous, angry husband. Noyce and the screenwriter Terry Johnson don't carry the story to this depth, but their hallucinatory opening—in which John makes his way to the hospital to identify the body of his child—suggests an enraged male's nightmare.

Perhaps the power of "Dead Calm" comes as much from its buried symbolism as its juicy, cat-and-mouse thrills. In one scene, the wife is pawed by a sweaty freak while miles away the husband works desperately and in vain to pump out the water from an opening in the schooner. Run that one up your mast.

Based on a book by Charles Williams, the story was filmed by Orson Welles in 1968 as "The Deep." (It featured Laurence Harvey and Jeanne Moreau.) The picture, unreleased, remains shut up in Welles' vaults somewhere, but it's obvious what attracted him in the subject matter.

Noyce and Johnson keep the action focused, a succession of tiny cliffhangers: getting the radio to work, maneuvering to get close to a gun. And two-thirds of the acting shines. In the late scenes, Kidman sets her big jaw while her eyes blaze like Sigourney Weaver's in "Gorillas in the Mist." Neill, superb last year in "A Cry in the Dark," gives a star performance: personable, understated, unassumingly masculine.

Zane, alas, isn't in their league. He looks startlingly like a young Marlon Brando—they have the same big, obscenely self-satisfied lips. But his line readings are Psycho Killer 101—he never cracks the surface of the part.

As usual with these kind of thrillers, there's one ending too many. Villains don't die once anymore—they have to keep springing back to life so that they can be shot or stabbed or exploded yet again. Somewhere Rasputin watches amazed, envying his descendants' longevity.

NEWSDAY, 4/7/89, Part III/p. 3, Mike McGrady

What makers a horror film work is neither the murder nor the mayhem, not those corpses rising from misty graves or those ax-wielders stalking babysitters. What makes horror effective is what occurs outside the circle of horror itself—the humanity of the people, the believability of the backdrop, the calm stretches that separate the storms.

"Dead Calm," a new Australian horror film starring Sam Neill, would qualify as a beautifully made movie in any genre. It is well-paced, suspenseful, brilliantly acted and directed with great flair.

"Dead Calm" begins on a gruesome note, one of many such notes, with an automobile accident, a head-on collision that kills a toddler and critically injures the mother. The father (Neill), a naval officer, identifies the baby's body and then sets about helping his wife (Nicole Kidman) survive her nightmares and get over the tragedy; they decide on a long cruise through remote seas.

After three weeks of calm waters, they sight a black schooner lying dead in the water. A young stranger, the only survivor, explains that his shipmates were felled by food poisoning: "There were six of us. The others died ten days ago. One by one. It all happened in a day."

There is no sense of haste, no rush to violence, just a gradually increasing sense of uneasiness. One small, logical step after another, set in bright sunlight on misleadingly calm seas, leading inevitably toward a collision with insanity. The husband, suspicious, decides to row over and inspect the sinking black schooner while the new passenger sleeps. The young man awakens, notes the absence, commandeers the ship, shanghais the wife and sets off for points unknown.

While the film's basic situation, a beautiful woman trapped in close quarters with a psychotic killer, is hardly novel, the treatment seems fresh. The sense of peril and sexuality in a nautical setting may bring to mind Roman Polanski's first film, "Knife in the Water," but here the terror is more physical and less psychological, more concrete and less subtle, as both the stranded husband and kidnaped wife reach deep within themselves to work out their salvations.

My only quibble with "Dead Calm" are those few occasions when it resorts to the basic horror-film formulas. I'm thinking specifically of the familiar Lazarus ploy, the prerequisite that calls for all villains to rise repeatedly from the dead. A cliche this familiar, this expected, undermines the very suspense it is intended to create.

But the way most of the rest of the film is carried out is a credit to director Noyce, represented here some weeks back by the lushly romantic "Echoes of Paradise." As the danger to both husband and wife mount, he all but dispenses with dialogue, allowing fantastic detail work, particularly nautical detail, to carry the story forward. The telling of the tale then rests largely in the excellent hands of cinematographer Dean Semler ("The Road Warrior").

Sam Neill seen here most recently in "A Cry in the Dark," is again attractive and effective. He is paired with talented 22-year-old Nicole Kidman, who bears an uncanny physical resemblance to Sigourney Weaver. An unknown Chicago actor, Billy Zane, 23, offers enough novel quirks and tics to individualize the psychopath. Final credit: A mongrel named Benji, portraying a yacht-bound pet, must be reckoned an early candidate for 1989's animal-of-the-year honors.

NEWSWEEK, 4/17/89, p. 72, David Ansen

Phillip Noyce, the Australian director, made his name 10 years ago with "Newsfront," a beguiling film about Aussie newsmen in the '50s. *Dead Calm*, a seabound suspense thriller, will no doubt make Noyce a hot Hollywood property. Based on a Charles Williams novel that was the source for Orson Welles's unreleased film "The Deep" (filmed in the late '60s with Jeanne Moreau), "Dead Calm" begins dazzlingly, as its husband-and-wife heroes (Sam Neill and Nicole Kidman), recovering from the tragic death of their child, set out on a recuperative yacht trip. Their moment of peace is shattered when they take aboard a freaked-out young American (Billy Zane) fleeing his sinking schooner. The American, it soon becomes clear, is a paranoid psychopath who commandeers Neill's wife and yacht while Neill is off investigating the leaking schooner.

Noyce orchestrates the suspense with impressive visual flair, using the constricted setting to great advantage. But an hour into the tale impatience sets in when it becomes clear that neither he nor screenwriter Terry Hayes has anything more in mind than pressing our fear buttons. Ultimately, this is just a waterlogged damsel-in-distress movie. The death of the child is meaningless; the promise of psychological subtleties comes to nothing. Except for Zane's creepy villain, a callow and vain psycho, there is little characterization. "Dead Calm" even resorts to the most hackneyed post-"Carrie" device of all: the last-minute horror-movie jolt. Since everybody expects it, the only way to redeem this cliché would be if nothing at all happened. Noyce's stylishness keeps this vehicle afloat, but his portentousness raises expectations he can't deliver. "Dead Calm" will buy him a ticket into the mainstream; let's hope he uses it next time to make a movie that's about something.

VILLAGE VOICE, 4/18/89, p. 63, Georgia Brown

A sailboat may seem like cramped quarters, but John and Rae Ingram seem to have spare room to burn on their luxury yacht *Saracen*—plenty of space to accommodate Hughie, the spooked survivor of the sinking schooner *Orpheus*. *Dead Calm*, directed by Australian Phillip Noyce (*Newsfront*) from a mystery novel by cult favorite Charles Williams, starts promisingly and with style, as if it will be some sort of *Knife in the Water* Oedipal psychodrama (especially since the Ingrams are taking a "healing cruise," having just lost their young son in an auto accident), but it turns too readily into a perfunctory, if tense, thriller.

Sam Neill again is required to be the steady, loving husband that he was in *A Cry in the Dark*, and Nicole Kidman is Rae, his beautiful, improbably resilient wife. But Hughie (Billy Zane, who looks like a demented Ron Darling) is a psycho from the starting gun, and there are too many violations of credibility that keep giving him a new lease on life. *Dead Calm* has notions of making the woman into the film's hero—a female Orpheus turning back to rescue her mate from a ghastly underworld. (Speaking of claustrophobia, you should see the fix husband John gets himself into.) But the movie's plot sloshes around in cheap thriller effects too long to warrant a serious reading. *Dead Calm* is the same old woman-in-jeopardy narrative—let's count the ways she can be surprised. If Rae were actually suffering the trauma of a car accident during which her child was killed, she'd be a basket case by the time Hughie finished terrorizing her. I won't say what happens to her nosy little dog.

In 1968, Orson Welles started filming his own screenplay of *Dead Calm*, called *The Deep*, using Jeanne Moreau, Laurence Harvey, Oja Kodar (then Olga Palinkas), and himself. Apparently, the unreleased print rests in the vaults of Welles's estate. Let's wait for that one.

Also reviewed in:
NEW YORK TIMES, 4/7/89, p. C19, Caryn James
VARIETY, 4/5–11/89, p. 18
WASHINGTON POST, 4/7/89, p. C1, Rita Kempley
WASHINGTON POST, 4/7/89, Weekend/p. 37, Desson Howe

DEAD POETS SOCIETY

A Touchstone Pictures release in association with Silver Screen Partners IV. *Producer:* Steven Haft, Paul Junger Witt, and Tony Thomas. *Director:* Peter Weir. *Screenplay:* Tom Schulman. *Director of Photography:* John Seale. *Editor:* William Anderson. *Music:* Maurice Jarre. *Music Editor:* Dan Carlin Sr. *Sound:* Charles Wilborn. *Sound Editor:* Alan Splet. *Production Designer:* Wendy Stites. *Art Director:* Sandy Veneziano. *Set Designer:* Carleton E. Reynolds. *Set Decorator:* John Anderson. *Special Effects:* Allen Hall. *Costumes:* Eddie Marks. *Make-up:* Susan A. Cabral. *Running time:* 124 minutes. *MPAA Rating:* PG.

CAST: Robin Williams (John Keating); Robert Sean Leonard (Neil Perry); Ethan Hawke (Todd Anderson); Josh Charles (Knox Overstreet); Gale Hansen (Charlie Dalton); Dylan Kussman (Richard Cameron); Allelon Ruggiero (Steven Meeks); James Waterston (Gerard Pitts); Norman Lloyd (Mr. Nolan); Kurtwood Smith (Mr. Perry); Carla Belver (Mrs. Perry); Leon Pownall (McAllister); George Martin (Dr. Hager); Joe Aufiery (Chemistry Teacher); Matt Carey (Hopkins); Kevin Cooney (Joe Danburry); Jane Moore (Mrs. Danburry); Lara Flynn Boyle (Ginny Danburry); Colin Irving (Chet Danburry); Alexandra Powers (Chris Noel); Melora Walters (Gloria); Welker White (Tina); Steve Mathios (Steve); Alan Pottinger (Bubba); Pamela Burrell (Directing Teacher); Allison Hedges (Actor/Fairy); Christine D'Ercole (Titania); John Cunningham (Mr. Anderson); Debra Mooney (Mrs. Anderson); John Martin Bradley (Bagpiper); Charles Lord (Mr. Dalton); Kurt Leitner (Lester); Richard Stites (Stick); James J. Christy (Spaz); Catherine Soles (Stage Manager); Hoover Sutton (Welton Professor); James Donnell Quinn (Procession Alumnus); Simon Mein (Welton Vicar); Ashton W. Richards (Phys. Ed. Teacher); Robert Gleason (Father of Spaz); Bill Rowe (Dormitory Porter); Robert J. Zigler III (Beans); Keith Snyder (Russell); Nicholas K. Gilhool (Shroom); Jonas Stiklorius (Jonas); Craig Johnson (Dewey); Chris Hull (Ace); Jason Woody (Woodsie); Sam Stegeman (Sam); Andrew Hill (Senior Student).

CINEASTE, Vol. XVII, No. 3, 1990, p. 43, Burns Raushenbush

A band of students in black capes cavort across a dark and misty landscape as they steal away to an Indian cave to revive the 'Dead Poets Society.'

The image—like the language—suggests nightly revels, paganism, witchcraft. It belongs to a powerful and distinct movement in literature and the arts, the romantic movement, notable for its rebellion against all constraints imposed on the individual by church, state, and tradition. Romanticism lifted taboos on expression of feelings; it glorified the primitive and broke ground for humanist studies like psychology and anthropology. One dictionary definition of 'Romantic' is: "Marked by the imaginative or emotional appeal of the heroic, adventurous, remote, mysterious, or idealized."

Readers familiar with the films of Peter Weir will recognize that this definition fits his work like a glove. *The Third Wave* explored the magical culture of Australian aborigines with their reliance on a psychic "dream time." *Picnic at Hanging Rock* portrayed upper class school-girls disappearing into some vast, inexplicable maw of nature. Both of these brilliant, haunting films gave voice to one of the key beliefs of romanticism: that there is something out there, some force in nature or the human soul, far more powerful than anything in 'civilization' as we know it. Now, after a couple of stylish thrillers, Peter Weir has returned to his true subject, or domain, and fixed his unsparing gaze on the United States.

The setting is Welton Academy, a prestigious boarding school in the East. It's the sort of school to which the wealthiest members of society send their children. The year is 1959. On Opening Day students carry banners embroidered with the words "Honor," "Excellence," "Discipline," "Tradition." There is a new English teacher, John Keating, a Welton alumnus who is now in his early 30s. He has a different approach to teaching than the other instructors.

During his first class he has the students fellow him out into the corridor, where they look at old photos of Welton classes from years past. Keating (Robin Williams) asks his boys to listen to what their predecessors are saying. "*Carpe diem*," he intones. "Seize the day!" At the next class he insists that they tear out a pseudo-scientific introduction to the poetry text. He has them "huddle up" around him as he explains, with quiet passion, why poetry is essential. He makes witty comments, jokes and mimics, allaying their fears of daunting material like Shakespeare. He stands up on his desk—to demonstrate the importance of having a different perspective—and has each of them do the same. In short, he wows them and wins them over.

One of the most captivated students, Neil Perry (Robert Sean Leonard), digs up an old yearbook from Keating's class. Among the memberships listed there is the Dead Poets Society. Led by Neil, a group of Keating's students hail him during recess and question him about it. His answer inspires them and they decide to revive the Society. Maps are brought, the meeting place located, and the students, black-clad, slip away into the night.

The secret meetings quickly become the high point of the term. The students shed inhibitions, gain confidence. They smoke, play music, make declarations, chant and dance—all within a framework of poetry read aloud. A talented sax player named Charlie (Gale Hansen) renames himself Nuanda and brings a couple of girls to the cave. Chubby, self-conscious Overstreet (Josh Charles) spurs himself on with the mantra of *carpe diem* and calls up a beautiful girl, whom he pursues with love poems. Neil reaches the buoyant realization that what he wants to be is an actor, not the lawyer his strict father expects him to be. Like Keating in class, Neil tries to draw out his morose roommate. Todd (Ethan Hawke), who is at Welton only because his brother was there. While Neil fakes a letter from his father granting permission to be in a local play. Nuanda is emboldened to mention the Dead Poets Society in an article in the school paper calling for girls on campus.

These two developments quickly bring reactions. The administration under Headmaster Nolan (Norman Lloyd) comes crashing down on Charlie/Nuanda. He is beaten with a paddle and eventually expelled. Neil's ruse is discovered by his father, who snatches him away from a triumphant opening night in the lead role and tells him he's being transferred to military school. He also tells him he can forget all about this acting "stuff." Unable to influence—or to obey— his father, Neil commits suicide. Welton is in an uproar. Nolan convenes an assembly at which he promises a "thorough inquiry, at the request of Neil's parents" into his death. The inquiry turns out to be a set of trumped-up charges against Keating, who is held responsible for Neil's death. Five students belonging to the Dead Poets Society are called into the headmaster's study, with their parents present, and told to sign a paper accusing Keating. The teacher is ousted, and leaves, but not before a number of his students show their loyalty to him, in a memorable and moving way, by standing on their desks during the English class that Nolan is trying to take over.

This basic sketch of the plot may help to explain the rather literal or superficial interpretation of the film by many critics. According to this general view, it is an eccentric movie about an exotic school where a gifted teacher comes a cropper with an authoritarian headmaster peculiar to the 1950s. Sort of an historical flick, if you will, safely distant from the world of 1989. But the movie is hardly the quaint, innocuous entertainment it has been made out to be. It is a compelling restatement of a dangerous romantic credo: that the spirit of poetry is sharply at odds with the conservative values of a business society, that imagination does not respect authority and tradition any more than they respect it. The links between romanticism and revolution—from Rousseau and Buchner all the way to the Surrealists and beyond—are very strong.

It is important to recognize, however, the Keating, as portrayed in the film, is no political activist. He is an idealist who doesn't realize the extent to which his teaching goes against the grain. This becomes clear in a talk with the headmaster, who says he has heard rumors of "unorthodox teaching methods." Keating naively replies that he has only trying to teach the students the dangers of conformity. He is taken aback by Nolan's rejoinder that conformity is all to the good. Another incident underscores Keating's ambivalence. Following Nuanda's paddling, he joins the students to urge caution. When asked by Nuanda "Whose side are you on?," he is evasive. He is truly a divided soul who does not fully understand the rottenness of the institution he serves. Even as he takes his leave, teary-eyed at the show of support by half the English class, his political allegiance is in doubt. Of course, none of this has prevented the administration from making him a scapegoat.

The search for scapegoats marks a society that is unable to confront and remedy its own failings, to change and grow. Americans are taught that Nazi Germany and Stalinist Russia exemplify such rigid societies. Through this microcosmic parable, though, Peter Weir indicates that the U.S. is also that kind of society. The problem is that he says it so quietly, so obliquely, that many viewers will miss the point. A comparison with Lindsay Anderson's *If...*—also set in an elite boarding school (in England)—is instructive. There is never any doubt in *If...* that the school is an extension of, and recruiting ground for, the military-industrial establishment. In *Dead Poets Society*, this role is understated. The rural aspect of the campus, with its images of meadows and geese, suggests isolation. Another difference is that in *If...* specific injustices fuel the revolutionary momentum. *Dead Poets Society* bypasses such incidents early-on, preferring instead to paint a backdrop of fearful drudgery against which Keating's enthusiasm stands out. The focus on Keating's magnetism means that the evil character of the school is played down—until the end. Too much of the burden of villainy falls onto Neil Perry's boorish father (Kurtwood Smith).

Hovering about the film is an eerie sense that Welton is a place where rich parents send kids to get rid of them and have their spirits broken into the bargain. The idea that this may be the real 'tradition' of Welton is too subtly conveyed. Some viewers may simply come away relieved that they never went to prep school. Few will grasp the irony that Welton is *exactly* the kind of school politicians have in mind when they talk about "excellence in education"—the kind of school whose graduates become excutives of major corporations, leading members of government, and even occupants of the White House. Peter Weir and his writer, Tom Schulman, could have made these connections clearer without jeopardizing the film's swift flow.

Another possible weakness is the ending. It can persuasively be argued that the ending is a fantasy, that in reality the kids would've had no chance to show their loyalty to the fired teacher, or, given the chance, would have been too intimidated to do so. Yet I believe the ending succeeds in intensifying the emotional power of the film. It engages the audience, saying, "Do not forget this man."

Today, the voices of rebel poets—alive *and* dead—have been drowned out by a much more commercial, devalued din. Demagogues and frauds are widely heard, and admired, but the American public rarely hears from any John Keatings, much less any real, live radicals. The mainstream of opinion is sluggish and full of crud, jingoism crowding out justice. Adrift in the stink, the American people accept a politics that is two parts hucksterism, one part hype. Banana Republicanism rules.

In this context, *Dead Poets Society* is a film that raises high the banner of romanticism in a numbed-out, Who Cares? age. It has mystery and beauty and sensibility. It illuminates mechanisms of denial and repression that go to the heart of our society.

FILMS IN REVIEW, 12/89, p. 617, Frank Scheck

The casting of Robin Williams, white hot after his success in *Good Morning, Vietnam*, as an English professor exhorting his students about the glories of poetry was an inspired move by the ever savvy executives of Touchstone Pictures. Williams' past movie roles have proven to be uneasy vehicles for his talents; his manic energy has only rarely been taken advantage of. Except for an occasional classroom sequence such as the one where he performs Macbeth as interpreted by John Wayne, the same is true here. But his restraint fits the character, an unconventional and irrepressible English teacher struggling against the confines of an autocratic school bureaucracy.

The casting probably saved the movie, both in commercial and artistic terms. The film is a tired rehash of every inspiring teacher plot for the past fifty years, and it plays like an anachronism. Williams portrays John Keating, a former student, and new teacher, at the Welton Academy, a boarding school in the hills of Vermont. The year is 1959, a time of innocence and tradition, and Keating is a breath of fresh air in the musty classroom. On his first day, he orders the students to actually rip out pages from their textbooks, and soon he is schooling them in the importance of individuality.

Eventually, the boys are led to the rebellious act of re-forming Keating's Dead Poets Society, a secret club that meets late at night off campus in a secluded cave to read poetry aloud. The dramatic centerpiece of the film involves a sensitive young man rebelling against his dictatorial father by taking time out from his studies to act in a school production of Shakespeare.

John Seale's photography is gorgeous, giving the film an autumnal glow that is bound to increase enrollment at New England schools. Peter Weir's canny direction easily skirts the script's blend of comedy and drama, and he has managed the great feat of reining Williams in while at the same time exploiting his appeal. The success of that difficult balancing act has made *Dead Poets Society* one of the year's biggest—and most unlikely—successes.

LOS ANGELES TIMES, 6/2/89, Calendar/p. 1, Michael Wilmington

"Dead Poets Society" is set in 1959, in an East Coast prep school, which the Australian director Peter Weir turns into an evil ice palace. The grounds are green and immaculate, the forests are deep and dark, the school a network of echoing hallways, grandiose chapels and tiny, fusty classrooms. It's a place of crystalline but dangerous beauty, against which Weir's star, Robin Williams, blazes like a poetry-spewing comet.

The film, one of the best American movies of a so-far undistinguished year, keeps trying to expand its barriers, to become an allegory of the dark side of adolescence and family, a romantic fable about the destruction of beauty in a conformist world. Even if it doesn't succeed, its feverish grappling becomes impressive. A movie's reach should exceed its grasp, or what's a heaven for?

"Poets'" hero, played with a fine lyric-comic frenzy by Williams, is John Keating, a brilliant teacher who wants his students to gorge themselves on dreams and the music of Whitman, Shakespeare and Keats. A one-time star student of this stuffy academy, Keating takes over a class, leaps on desk tops and gets his boys to tear out the deadening cant of their English anthology, emit barbaric Whitmanesque yawps.

Poetry is the real hero of the movie: Robin Williams plays its spirit. An eccentric grandstander, Keating throws his milieu into relief: the craggily beautiful Welton Academy, another of those citadels of class, sex and privilege catering to a society obsessed with money and surfaces. "Carpe Diem!" ("Seize the Day!") is his motto. And "Oh, Captain! My Captain!" is what he encourages his class to call him—after Whitman's lament for the fallen Abraham Lincoln.

Williams doesn't dominate the movie physically. Indeed, his character is off-screen for most of the important action—which revolves around the septet from his class, who revive his old club, the Dead Poets Society. These seven are like a Hollywood bomber's crew of prep school rebels. There's the frustrated actor (Robert Sean Leonard's Neil), the tongue-tied writer (Ethan Hawke's Todd), the bespectacled brain (Allelon Ruggiero's Meeks), the gawky goon (James Waterston's Pitts), the love-struck romantic (Josh Charles' Knox), the wise-cracking trouble-maker (Gale Hanson's Dalton) and the pragmatic apple-polisher (Dylan Kussman's Cameron). Kussman seems to be playing a symbolic personification of the ex-Communist informers of the early '50s; he draws him as a nasty, self-serving little creep.

In the movie, Perry is the group's leader, but he's also the one most repressed and bullied by his father, an up-by-his-bootstraps doctor, who's planned out his son's life in advance, supported by the school's reptilian headmaster. (These villains are hatefully well played by Kurtwood Smith and Mercury theater veteran Norman Lloyd.) That's the major collision: soul and form, desire and duty, art and commerce, poetry and money.

Screenwriter Tom Schulman tries to do so many unusual things here—celebrate language, poetry and dissidents; allegorize the plight of the blacklist victims; crystallize very inspirational teacher in the person of Keating—that it might seem churlish to complain about what the script lacks. But right from the beginning, it has a melodramatic, selfconsciously theatrical mode. You might ask why the authorities are so bewildered by the Dead Poets Society when Keating's membership in an earlier version is memorialized under his old yearbook photo, or why Keating doesn't attend any of their meetings. And, the catastrophe at the end is also hard to accept; it hints at something more primal—perhaps an attack on sexual identity—buried under the surface events.

Peter Weir has suggested that "Dead Poets Society" resembles his previous anti-war epic, "Gallipoli," also a tale of beautiful, idealistic young men careening toward a disaster engendered by stubborn, shortsighted elders. And it's clear that he connects with his subject here, more than in his previous two American films: the overrated "Witness" and the underrated "Mosquito Coast." Weir, the cinematic heir of directors such as Stanley Kubrick or John Huston, has a similar taste for doom-drenched adventures and super-aestheticized movie traps. He and cinematographer John Seale give the movie a gorgeous look and smashing rhythms. The climax, the jaws of the trap closing, is done with hammer-blow force and intensity: a rage against injustice that's almost palpable. And the classroom scenes have a mad, joyous obullience.

Right now, Robin Williams may be the most exciting performer in American movies, perhaps less for what he does than for what the audience, by now, knows he can do. "Good Morning, Vietnam" soared when it used his genius for the maniacal, cross-media, multi-referential spritz. In "Dead Poets Society," he spritzes only occasionally. But the threat is always there—and that sense of an explosion thrumming beneath the surface, gives a charge to Williams' Keating that a more gifted dramatic actor might not have managed. (Apparently more of these semi-improvisations were shot, but excised as extraneous or disruptive. This may have been a mistake: usually, the more Williams' disruptions there are in a movie—or an Oscar show—the better.)

Ultimately, whatever its flaws, "Dead Poets Society" (MPAA rated PG, despite salty language) commands respect and affection. It becomes—in ways that most movies don't even attempt—a cry of passion and rage against the brutality of a conformist society, against the deadening of our capacity for beauty. And, it's also a moving elegy for every inspired teacher who suddenly opened up a world before their wondering students—let them catch the pulse of poetry, the flesh and soul of art.

MONTHLY FILM BULLETIN, 9/89, p. 272, Richard Combs

Fall, 1959. Among the new pupils gathering at Welton Academy, a traditional boys' preparatory school in Vermont, are shy Todd Anderson, whose famous brother was valedictorian at the school, and Neil Perry, whose controlling father intends that nothing should distract him from his programme of study to become a doctor. The headmaster, Mr. Nolan, introduces the assembled pupils and parents to the new English teacher, John Keating, himself once a pupil at Welton. In their first class with Keating, Neil and Todd (who are room-mates) and their fellow students are startled when he declares his exuberant philosophy of life and poetry, telling them to seize the day and to make their lives extraordinary, and later demanding that they rip out the introduction from the set, pedantic text on poetry. From an old school year book, the boys learn of the Dead Poets Society, a secret group which Keating ran dedicated to an ecstatic approach to life and literature. Seven of his pupils decide to reconstitute the group; apart from Neil and Todd, they include the class clown and would-be "beat" Charlie Dalton, the more cautiously respectful Cameron, and the "odd couple" of studious Meeks and gangling Pitts. The seventh member of the group, Knox Overstreet, is already distracted by the passion he has conceived for a local girl, Chris Noel. In class, Keating forces Todd to reveal some of the poetry he has locked inside him, while Neil forges a letter of consent from his father to Nolan when he is offered the part of Puck in a production of A Midsummer Night's Dream. Encouraged by the others, Knox calls Chris and is invited to a party, where he gets in a fight with her jock boyfriend Chet Danburry. Charlie, meanwhile, brings two girls, Gloria and Tina, to the cave in the woods where the society meets, and later gets himself and the society in trouble with a prank at school to demand that girls be admitted to Welton. Neil is forbidden by his father to indulge his passion for acting, but performs, and is a hit, nevertheless, in A Midsummer Night's Dream (which Knox attends with Chris). Taken home by his father, and told that he will be removed from Welton and sent to a military academy, Neil commits suicide that night. To defuse the scandal, Nolan, the other staff and the parents settle on Keating as a scapegoat, and the members of the Dead Poets Society are forced to sign an affadavit attesting to his corrupting influence. Keating is forced to resign, but before he goes his pupils defy Nolan to make a final show of their love and solidarity.

Is there any relationship between Dead Poets Society and the last time Peter Weir essayed a film on the joys and sorrows of schooldays, Picnic at Hanging Rock, nearly fifteen years ago? There is one—although this film takes place in firmly ordered groves of academe in Vermont (filmed in Delaware), and Picnic was perched closer to actual wilderness—of setting. In the latter, three schoolgirls were lost when they gave in to the haunted aura of Hanging Rock, evidently compounded of their own sexual fears and longings, here a group of schoolboys periodically desert their cultivated campus and in a candlelit cave read poetry to each other, play the saxophone, and talk of "sucking the marrow out of life", reviving the dead society of the dead poets inaugurated by their subversive teacher, John Keating. Their hideaway was modelled on a real historic site in Delaware, known as the Wolf Cave—a fit complement to Hanging Rock, and also sexually complementary if one thinks of the possible symbolism of the places to which these schoolboys and schoolgirls are drawn.

There is, then, an air not just of social taboo-breaking but of ghostliness about these "secret" activities, an awe and a dread which suggests that the mysteries of life in which both sets of characters are trying to initiate themselves are practically supernatural. This, in a way, is appropriate enough to the state of mind in which the adolescent protagonists might approach them—as is the mood of fearful excitement, of tremulousness, which it produces in the films. There, unfortunately, Weir—ever a tactful conductor of journeys to the wilder shores, as in *The Mosquito Coast*—stops. The veils which his characters are fearful to look behind, he also leaves undisturbed, and the tremulousness more or less defines the films. The same diffidence comes out slightly differently: *Picnic at Hanging Rock* seems to be all atmosphere, as if the film had surrendered to the girls' swooning incomprehension before those mysteries; *Dead Poets Society* so earnestly sets up its moral conflicts that it finally has no convincing atmosphere at all, although this may be because it has surrendered to a rather naive, one-dimensional, schoolboyish notion of moral conflict.

Characteristic enough is the way the date, 1959, serves as a convenient, cut-and-dried emblem—the stuffy, conformist 50s about to meet the libertarian 60s—without the period ever becoming part of the film's ambience. The human exemplars of that conflict are equally, irritatingly cut-and-dried: Welton's headmaster, Mr. Nolan, who can always be counted on to huff and bluster at any affront to authority or the "four pillars" of academic discipline, and John Keating, poet by name and mischievously puckish in Robin Williams' playing of him, who sounds Walt Whitman's "barbaric YAWP" without ever seeming dangerous, overweening or even particularly unruly. How he came to be, or survives as, a teacher in academies like Welton is a mystery, subverting them it seems without compromise, conflict or contradiction, as easily as he encourages his students to rebellion without disturbing anything. When one of his acolytes does stage an amusing prank, and gets a beating for his trouble, Keating advises that "there's a time for daring and a time for caution", and the film leaves it at that. Keating remains as purely liberating a force as the school is patently a repressive one, and out of this manufactured scheme the film can only produce the manufactured tragedy of Neil Perry and his frustrated acting ambitions to bring things to a head. It proves a point that has been obvious, and obviously specious, every painstaking, tactful step of the way.

NEW YORK, 6/12/89, p. 77, David Denby

Self-importance in a movie can be a greater blight than the cynicism of ordinary movie trash. Peter Weir's *Dead Poets Society* takes the cake for high-mindedness. Set in a straitlaced Wasp boys' school in 1959, *Poets* is about a group of caution-bound students who fall under the spell of a flamboyant English teacher (Robin Wiliams). The poetry-loving Mr. Keating, whose rebel god is Thoreau, rouses the boys not only to the beauty and power of words but to their own powers as individuals, and they lose their fears. But after this awakening, the world closes in on them, and the movie ends ambiguously, in both tragedy and triumph.

Weir, the first-time screenwriter Tom Schulman, and the fellows at Disney must have wanted to get away from the coarse-grained tone of most summer-season teen movies; they must have wanted to do something sincere and delicate and even vulnerable. It is infinitely to be regretted, therefore, that while taking so many risks they also covered every bet in sight. For all its unfashionable, hard-to-sell ardor for literature, *Dead Poets Society* has been calculated to hit teens right where they live: The villains of the film are absurdly repressive fathers and schoolmasters, the victims teenagers who innocently want to express themselves.

Peter Weir, the director of such soft-headed mystical movies as *Picnic at Hanging Rock* and *The Last Wave* (as well as the excellent *Witness*), has produced a work of pedagogical lyricism. Clean-limbed preppies romp in the crisp New England air and ride their bicycles through flocks of birds. The movie is set 30 years ago, but it's really set in a mythical land and time—Great Prepschoolvania. No trace of Elvis pollutes the autumn air, no Fabian, no Doris Day or Jerry Lewis, no students sneaking out to the movies or even smuggling a radio into the dormitory. The high-toned cultural limbo of the period setting is itself a kind of cop-out. If the movie had been set in 1989, when even the children of the highly educated don't read much, a teacher hoping to excite seventeen-year-olds with Byron and Keats would need all the Devil's own cleverness to succeed. What a triumph if he did wake anyone up! By placing the movie in the past, the filmmakers make a love of literature seem quaint, as if it had nothing to do with today.

A stuffy, autocratic place, Welton Academy exudes both self-satisfaction and hysterical vigilance. Terrorized on all sides, the boys, who address their fathers as "sir," seem nice and rather bland, especially Neil Perry (Robert Sean Leonard), who is so dominated by his old man (Kurtwood Smith) that he can barely speak in his presence. The other students are pleasant but unmemorable types—a wise guy, a boy who chases a blonde, a what's-in-it-for-me pragmatist, a nerdy electronics whiz, and so on.

Enter God, bearing a volume of Walt Whitman. The teaching sequences, a mixture of cornball romantic platitudes and genuine fun, are by far the liveliest things in the movie. A baritonal charmer with leprechaun eyes, Williams appears in his Mr. Wonderful, or high-humanist, mode. His Keating seduces the kids with comedy, keeping them off balance, shocking them with his unorthodox methods. He imitates different styles of playing Shakespeare (British priss, Brando, etc.); he tells the boys to stand on his desk for a different view of the world; he even gets each of them to walk across the quadrangle in his own style—anything to break down their conformity and self-consciousness. By teaching them poetry, he is saving their souls. Poetry, he tells them, is sex and power, a matter of life and death. "Words and ideas can change the world," he insists (George Bush obviously went to a different prep school).

Keating isn't meant to be a fraud, but we may not see things the same way as the filmmakers. The details of the portrait are worth arguing about because Keating's success is presented as nothing less than the birth of sensibility: The boys respond to him, and all the angels begin singing at once. (Beethoven's Ninth rings out on the soundtrack while they play soccer.) I can accept such bits of impassioned classroom doggerel as Keating's "The powerful play goes on, and you might contribute a verse," and even, pushing charity to its limits, his description of his own student days: "We didn't just read poetry; we let it drip from our tongues like honey." This is the kind of bluster that actors love, and Williams is probably right to give it a ripened glow. We can believe that a teacher who combines wit and enthusiasm might really shake up students.

It's something of a bad joke, therefore, that this emancipator turns out to have such square, anthology taste in poetry and that he never seems to get past the famous first lines. (Wouldn't a hip teacher 30 years ago have read e. e. cummings and Dylan Thomas to his kids?) And the filmmakers' glorification of teaching as theater finally collapses into glorifying teaching as therapy breakthroughs. When Keating bullies a self-conscious boy into making up a poem, laying on hands and literally pulling it out of him, Weir's camera spins around in ecstasy. *Thus spake the boy!* Soon the students are traipsing off to a forbidden cave in the woods, reciting poems and ghost stories, culminating in a group-choral rendition of Vachel Lindsay's ineffably absurd "study of the Negro race," the boom-boom classic "The Congo." Weir, who has often lamented the disappearance of the primitive in our lives, must think the boys in the cave are renewing the sacred springs of art.

Weir has talent. You certainly won't see a film with a more active camera style, or one without violence that nevertheless moves along with so much energy and tension. The boys' abashed reverence for their teacher is touching, and so is their sudden, awkward enthusiasm for poetry. But Weir is working with a sapheaded, essentially dishonest script and doing so without irony. When the boys become nonconformists, no one else at the school jeers at them or even notices; only the authority figures jump on them. The teachers and administrators tear their hair over the boys' going off to recite poetry—my God, what a scandal! What the students do is almost hilariously innocent, so the enraged authorities seem as mad as hatters. (But no one says as much.) Indeed, if anything so miraculous should happen today, the students and their teacher would be hauled onto *60 Minutes* as harbingers of a national renewal.

And what Neil does—acting in *A Midsummer Night's Dream*—would fill most fathers with delight. But in this movie, Neil's father, mysteriously enraged, bans his son from the stage, and the ban causes the choked-up, inarticulate boy to fall completely to pieces. What's going *on* here? The amount of emotion generated by these impacted father-son scenes would make sense if Neil were announcing to his father that he was gay, but the filmmakers stay miles from any such idea. This call for freedom seems rather conformist and repressed itself. *Dead Poets Society*, a Daddy-done-him-wrong story, is an exploitation of teenage self-pity under the guise of being a celebration of creativity. Boom, boom, BOOM.

NEW YORK POST, 6/2/89, p. 25, David Edelstein

"Dead Poets Society" must be the most severe, high-toned movie ever made about passionate non-conformity—about breaking senseless rules and following your heart. It's "Animal House" for the "Masterpiece Theatre" set.

Set in a rigid boys' prep school in the '50s, the picture offers Robin Williams as an English teacher who liberates his students' minds with the cry "Carpe diem!" ("Seize the day!") But Tom Schuman, who based the script on his own experiences, doesn't write like a man whose mind has been liberated. He writes like a man who has a head full of old movies. He wants to seize the Oscar.

You know what you're in for as soon as Williams—as John Keating, the new teacher at stuffy Welton—strolls out of his classroom, whistling and then impishly waves his pasty-faced students into the hall, calling their gaze toward pictures of the school's athletes in their prime. Now, he says, even the fastest is "food for worms."

Keating shows the boys how poetry isn't just something in an old book. It's alive and irreverent and the key to immortality; it will keep them from leading lives of quiet desperation and dying without ever having lived.

And while we're puzzling out why Williams—who squinches up his eyes and lets a moist, beatific smile spread like melted butter over his face—would play a role so wet and righteous and constricted, we watch the boys drink in his words.

Inspired, a group of them treks, cowled, to a dank cave, where they stretch out and read poetry to one another, formally opening their meetings with the preface to "Walden," in which Thoreau speaks of "sucking the marrow out of life." And gradually they begin to ignore the unreasonable demands of their repressive parents.

Wide-eyed, affirmative Neil (Robert Sean Leonard), who dreams of acting, defies his stern father (Kurtwood Smith) and wins the role of Puck in "A Midsummer Night's Dream." Knox (Josh Charles) chases a beautiful, unattainable girl (Alexandra Powers) and serenades her with honeyed verse. Todd (Ethan Hawke) gives voice to his anger against his family for neglecting him.

You'd think parents and teachers would be thrilled about their kids reading poetry, acting in plays and penning heartfelt stanzas, but in this sort of film such activities are viewed by authority figures as akin to a communist plot—deeply threatening to the status quo.

The way the script is contrived, the boys' passion provokes such rage in these grim disciplinarians that life becomes hell. We're talking beatings, expulsion. We're talking kids pushed to the brink and over. For reading the wrong kind of poetry! (Williams teaches the Romantics and the headmaster prefers the Realists. Except someone should tell Schulman that there was never any Realist school in poetry.)

There's a neat, counterculture joke at the movie's heart: that poets and philosophers taught in dry, academic settings are often subversive. It's true: A student who takes either Whitman or Thoreau to heart could easily get chucked out of school.

But these are counterculture sentiments minus the rudeness and messiness of real drama; they're affixed with a Good Housekeeping Seal of Approval. Some scary rebels, these sensitive, choir-boy poets!

For all the picture's non-conformist tootings, the tender young fellows and their monstrous dads conform to an ancient Hollywood code, the one that says, "No shades of gray." This movie carries the loudest "anti-dad" message since the axe-wielding patriarch of "The Stepfather."

It also carries good, progressive messages. Lord knows, we should all seize the day. And more of us should make gestures of defiance when a person with integrity becomes a scapegoat. But you can agree with the film's politics and still think it's all too easy.

"Dead Poets Society" will mean a lot to some people, though, especially if they're 12 years old. It's "A Separate Peace," "Catcher in the Rye," "One Flew Over the Cuckoo's Nest" and "Stand By Me" rolled into one.

It has two (count 'em) martyrs. And although it's downer, it ends with the kind of stand-up-and-cheer act of rebellion that makes TV critics blow their gaskets. ("You'll laugh and cry and feel good about being alive! Not since last week has a masterwork moved me to such heights of wonderment!")

Director Peter Weir ("The Last Wave," "Witness") does tasteful, tony work, and he gets credible performances. There's evidence he believes in this material. He doesn't sugar it with music, and he and his photographer, John Seale, give the images an overlay of myth: Dancing out of the cave, one of them twanging a mouth-harp, the boys seem mysteriously transformed, aboriginal.

Williams, who appears only intermittently, is transformed as well. Into Jell-O. By turning a great, anarchic comedian into a salesman for the life force, "Dead Poets Society" robs him of his power—it neuters him. It's understandable that Williams wants to be loved on screen, but if he plays any more saintly cut-ups, he'll be ready for Cheerios commercials.

NEWSDAY, 6/2/89, Part III/p. 3, Mike McGrady

At Welton Academy, a stone-walled fortress set in rolling New England farmlands, all the old verities are observed. In this graceful monument to the established order, the boys wear ties and jackets, conjugate Latin verbs and follow well-marked paths toward the Ivy League and, beyond that, toward medicine and the law and the boardroom. It is a sedate, orderly world built on four clearly labeled pillars: "Tradition," "Honor," "Discipline," "Excellence."

To this bastion of tradition comes a new English teacher (Robin Williams) preaching the poetry of Whitman and the philosophy of Thoreau, a free spirit who takes his text from Rabelais as he urges his young charges to "suck the marrow from the bone" and echoes Horace with his: *Carpe Diem*, lads. Seize the day. Make your lives extraordinary!"

What tends to make "Dead Poets Society" extraordinary in these frenzied times is that it is a film about young people dealing with the clash of ideas, not the crash of autos, a film that looks beyond the next junior prom to question whether we are living lives or simply marking time. Not only is it a film of ideas, it's also—*mirabile dictu!*—a film that takes and uses poetry seriously, only fitting since this is an argument for the poetic life over the prosaic existence.

Although writer Tom Schulman's original screenplay for "Dead Poets Society" is constructed around a familiar literary theme, how to find freedom in a world of stupifying conformity, films are not always hospitable to such serious notions. Peter Weir is one director who has never shied away from ideas, with generally splendid results ("Witness," "The Year of Living Dangerously," "Gallipoli") and, at least once, some not entirely splendid results ("The Mosquito Coast").

Although one cannot help but join in the laughter prompted by another brilliant performance from Robin Williams, "Dead Poets Society" is not a comedy. Its concerns are deadly serious. And as each young man seeks to apply his teacher's message to his life—"*Carpe Diem*! Seize the day!"—the drama races from high comedy to heartbreak to tragedy.

Perhaps my only complaint, and it's a minor one, is that Schulman tends to load the argument. The parents are domineering to a hateful degree ("Don't you *ever* dispute me in public!") and the academicians are smug to the point of simplism ("Prepare them for college, and the rest will take care of itself.").

But the students themselves are never predictable, never ordinary. Though most attempt to seize the day, it is for different reasons and in different ways. The simple act of reclaiming a life from the grip of a parent or a teacher or a tradition requires enormous courage, and not everyone has that. Although all have been deeply stirred by the passions of this singularly passionate teacher, there is no uniformity to the responses. While all the performances ring true, young Robert Sean Leonard, as one who would rather be an actor than a doctor, is a standout.

Williams, so it seems, will always be cast in the role of the individual challenging orthodoxy. But his performances don't repeat themselves, and here he is at his most restrained and believable and likable, perfectly able to fit into the very world he is challenging.

Although the teacher's own narrow Prufrockian life, a life of intellect and books and afternoon teas, seems to contradict his message, that irony is the truest notion in the film. Most of us have heard the occasional different drummer, but we go on marching in lockstep to Sousa all the way to our graves. Perhaps you're such a free spirit, you feel the film won't apply to you. Maybe you're even considering letting it slip by unseen. I would offer but two words of advice: *Carpe Diem!*

NEWSWEEK, 6/12/89, p. 67, David Ansen

It is tempting to call *Dead Poets Society* the best movie of the year 1959. This is neither a put-down nor a reflection of the film's style, which in terms of acting and cinematography could only be of the '80s. But no small part of the appeal of Peter Weir's lovely, stirring look at a boys' prep school in the late '50s is the nostalgia it evokes for a simpler time, when the burning adolescent issue was conformity vs. nonconformity, when it took your last ounce of courage to talk back to an authority figure and when the concept of self-realization, soon to become a pop-psych cliché, was still a subversive notion. For the sensitive, repressed, privileged boys of Welton Academy, rebellion takes the form of clandestine meetings in the lcoal cave, where cigarettes are puffed amid ardent midnight readings of verse.

The catalyst for these white boys' soul searchings is their eccentric, beloved English teacher Mr. Keating (Robin Williams), the antithesis of the strict, starchy academics who want them to take their appointed places in the world of commerce. Stirring their souls with romantic poetry and exhortations to seize the day, he's both teacher and therapist, and a harbinger of the '60s

Dionysian spirit soon to descend on campuses. Keating himself is not the real subject of "Dead Poets Society"—he's a colorful classroom virtuoso with only the sketchiest of private lives in Tom Schulman's fine screenplay. It's the kids whose lives are transformed by Keating's influence—for both good and ill—who hold our rapt attention. The key figure is Neil (Robert Sean Leonard), a model student and dutiful son whose secret desire to act runs fatally up against his father's unyielding ambitions for him. There's also Todd (Ethan Hawke), Neil's painfully shy, self-doubting roomate, whom Keating helps to emerge from his shell.

Director Weir gets wonderfully unaffected performances from all the boys. As he showed in "Gallipoli," he has his own poetic instinct for the spectacle of martyred innocence. This movie has some of the same elegiac sadness as that wartime epic, and the same propensity to divide the world between strict, inhuman adults and pure, vulnerable youths. It's a simple-minded but undeniably powerful vision.

The risk of casting Williams is obvious: audiences will be expecting "Good Morning, Schoolchildren." Here and there the stand-up comic breaks through—reciting Shakespeare in a John Wayne drawl, invoking "Uncle Walt" Whitman. But Williams plays by Weir's rules, scaling himself back enough to be a credible figure in tweed, letting enough anarchic spirit shine so that we feel the magic that ignites his impressionable charges. How will this revised "Goodbye, Mr. Chips" play in the very unrepressed moviehouses of 1989? To some it may seem as distant as science fiction. But to anyone with a memory for the adolescent agonies of yore, it's bound to strike some primary emotional chords.

TIME, 6/5/89, p. 78, Richard Schickel

Good old Welton: blue blazers, compulsory chapel, imitation Gothic architecture. A headmaster (Norman Lloyd) with a mellifluous voice and a pinched spirit. A student body harboring a minority of disaffected spirits awaiting rebellious mobilization. And over in the English department, a passionate eccentric, John Keating—played by Robin Williams—who is just the man to stir the lads up.

In the '50s, when *Dead Poets Society* takes place, prep schools of this type were basically boot camps for male Establishment offspring. They were also essential literary institutions. In those days hardly a month seemed to pass without the publication of some novel recounting a hormonal fire storm in one of these supposedly serene, and unquestionably enviable, settings. As traditional private schools changed, the fictional form they spawned fell into disuse, and, frankly, that engenders no deep sense of loss. All that quivering sensitivity! All that earnest soul-searching! All that whining about absent and misunderstanding parents, present and misunderstanding trigonometry teachers!

These attitudes are revisited in *Dead Poets Society*, which assiduously apes the manner of this antique genre, and they may put off viewers who will recollect having heard this song before. But the film is also at pains not to exploit or endorse the lowest impulses of its core audience, which is, of course, composed of adolescents. It contains no har-har pranks. No one wrecks a car, gets drunk or does anything more with a girl than hold hands.

Mostly the fine ensemble of young actors who are members of the film's eponymous secret society (notably Robert Sean Leonard and Ethan Hawke) grope with energetic sobriety toward an idea that Keating keeps putting to them every way he can. It is this: the business of education is not to gather facts but to find a ruling passion, something around which you can organize your life. This is a point that seems to elude most kids nowadays, probably because it is one that their popular culture rarely troubles to make to them.

Certainly it never does so as fairly as this picture does. Encouraged by his mentor, Leonard's character defies parental and school authority to reach out for his dream (he wants to be an actor, not the doctor his father insists he must become) and finds that it is beyond his emotional grasp. Though director Weir, who is good at unspoken menace (*Picnic at Hanging Rock* and *The Last Wave*), has created a subtly dark and claustrophobic atmosphere, the final tragedy is nonetheless somewhat implausible.

There are times when Keating's colorful nonconformity verges on the tiresome (he whistles Beethoven and declaims Whitman a little too self-consciously). But basically Williams, who has comparatively little screen time, has come to act, not to cut comic riffs, and he does so with forceful, ultimately compelling, simplicity. Like everyone else involved in this movie, he is taking a chance on an odd, imperfect but valuable enterprise. He and the movie deserve attention, respect and finally gratitude. Especially at the start of sequel summer.

VILLAGE VOICE, 6/13/89, p. 59, Georgia Brown

Dead Poets Society is so old-fashioned it's almost daring. In a year that has delivered the ultra-hip *Heathers*, here is a high school movie—more like last year's *Stand and Deliver*, only with a dark outcome—actually about curriculum. Directed by Peter Weir (*The Last Wave, The Year of Living Dangerously, Witness*) from Tom Schulman's screenplay and starring a bravely suppressed (or ruthlessly edited) Robin Williams, this determinedly retro, formulaic tearjerker—an elegy to lost promise—has a naïve charm. It stirred in me nostalgia for the days when to become an English major was to gain the world. Remember when reading actually changed lives?

Williams plays John Keating [sic], the new English instructor at Welton Academy, a fictitious boys' prep school in Vermont. Its campus (actually St. Andrews in Delaware) is mock-Gothic, and its rituals Episcopal and Scot—e.g., bagpipes on the dock at sundown. (Maybe because Weir is Australian, the whole affair never quite looks American.) Set in the late '50s—but feeling like 1910—this is a quasi-military world where visiting fathers call their sons Son, young men defer to Dad as Sir, and teachers address students as Gentlemen. Uniforms are charcoal-gray flannels, gray sweaters and, for outside, hooded duffle coats (which in Weir's conspicuous moonstruck silhouettes make the boys look like Druids). For casual time they wear chinos; everyone has a plaid flannel bathrobe to wear for brushing his teeth.

As if belaboring a point about '50s conformity, the four main boys are cast looking so alike—tall, with straight brown hair in similar cuts—it takes a while to sort them out. The movie opens on a new term; after a ceremony in chapel, parents begin their leave-taking. Neil (Robert Sean Leonard) gets chastised by his martinet father (*Robocop*'s villainous Kurtwood Smith): "Don't you ever dispute me in public again!" All Neil has said is that he will be letting people down if he has to quit the extracurricular journal as his father has ordered.

Todd (Ethan Hawke), Neil's roommate and the new boy at school, is the painfully shy, insecure younger brother of a recently graduated, overachieving valedictorian. Another buddy, Knox (Josh Charles), pursues a crush on a girl at a neighboring coed high school, and Charlie (Gale Hansen) shows he's temperamentally more defiant than the others. If these characterizations sound limp, they are.

Enter Robin Goodfellow. The beamish Keating is himself a Welton graduate—a recently returned Rhodes scholar with a sweetheart he writes to in England. At Welton, he performs the English teacher's function at the time: prying open shut minds. (Such was the function performed by many college humanities instructors until the early '70s, when students began to enter the universities sullen and impenetrable. No longer able to inspire, English departments gave themselves over to semiotics.)

A shrewd and gentle Puck, Keating arrives with a bag of vision-altering tricks. He has his class ripping out a foolish anthology introduction, taking turns standing on his desk ("I stand on my desk to remind myself we must constantly see things in a different way"), trying out silly walks, shouting lines from poems as they kick rubber balls. "We are food for worms, lads." He informs them that they're going to die. (It was Matthew Arnold who observed, "No young man thinks that he will ever die.") He teaches carpe diem poems beneath a portrait of Whitman and tells students, after Thoreau, to "suck out all the marrow of life." He warns them against the sin of being ordinary.

Some kids begin to idolize Keating. "O Captain, My Captain," they call him after one of his jokes. ("Oh, Charlie, my Charlie, another film is done..." was D.H. Lawrence's misfiring joke on Whitman, meaning he would have just as well idolized Chaplin as Lincoln. Why not, indeed.) When they discover Keating's picture in an old yearbook and read underneath that he was a member of something called "The Dead Poets Society," Neil, Charlie, Knox, and a few others decide to revive the society—stealing off at night to read poetry in a nearby cave. Todd is allowed to come too, though he's too timid to read. Meetings are opened with a reading of Thoreau's declaration of purpose: "I went into the woods to live deliberately...and not, when I came to die, discover that I had not lived." Not trusting the texts, the movie finds it necessary to convert these poetry readings into light entertainment, when it would have been much more affecting if kept straight.

Apparently, according to interviews, some scenes were shot with classes taught by Williams in hyper gear, but next to nothing of this mad spirit business is left in. Well, there's his John Wayne doing *Macbeth*. (Using the manic scenes would have meant a truly schizophrenic picture.) But Williams in his quiet mode has a beatific beam and genuine force. It's the students' movie more than it is his—although without Williams's charisma the film probably wouldn't have much life.

The individual dramas of Neil and Todd trying to break out of their repressions, of Knox's infatuation and Charlie's rebellions, tend to be sketchy or clichéd.

When Neil defies his father and takes the role of Puck in a local production of *A Midsummer Night's Dream* ("I'm going to act!"), tragedy results, and Keating, naturally, becomes the scapegoat. *Dead Poets* is dead accurate about the '50s rites of witch-hunting. The school's headmaster wields his paddle ("Assume the position!") to get students to name names, or bullies them, with the help of their parents, into signing prepared confessions. An "inquiry" turns quickly into an inquisition. Keating's message to "think for yourself" is anathema to Welton's petty officials and officious pedants.

Dead Poets is simplified and earnest, and in this imitates many dramatic pieces of its period. But in trying to revive some near-dead, lost values, it's a sweet, brave effort. Hail, subdued Robin.

Also reviewed in:
NEW REPUBLIC, 6/26/89, p. 26 Stanley Kauffmann
NEW YORK TIMES, 6/2/89, p. C8, Vincent Canby
NEW YORKER, 6/26/89, p. 70, Pauline Kael
VARIETY, 5/31–6/7/89, p. 26
WASHINGTON POST, 6/9/89, p. C1, Rita Kempley
WASHINGTON POST, 6/9/89, Weekend/p. 43, Desson Howe

DEALERS

A Skouras Pictures release of a Euston Films production. *Executive Producer:* Andrew Brown, and John Hambley. *Producer:* William P. Cartlidge. *Director:* Colin Bucksey. *Screenplay:* Andrew MacLear. *Director of Photography:* Peter Sinclair. *Editor:* Jon Costelloe. *Music:* Richard Hartley. *Sound:* David John. *Sound Editor:* Richard Dunford. *Production Designer:* Peter J. Hampton. *Art Director:* Ken Wheatley. *Set Decorator:* Stephanie McMillan. *Costumes:* Dizzy Downs. *Make-up:* Beryl Lerman. *Running time:* 95 minutes. *MPAA Rating:* R.

CAST: Paul McGann (Daniel Pascoe); Rebecca DeMornay (Anna Schuman); Derrick O'Connor (Robby Barrell); John Castle (Frank Mallory); Paul Guilfoyle (Lee Peters); Rosalind Bennett (Bonnie); Adrian Dunbar (Lennox Mayhew); Nicholas Hewetson (Jamie Dunbar); Sara Sugarman (Elana); Dikran Tulaine (Wolfgang); Douglas Hodge (Patrick Skill); Annabel Brooks (Lucy); Simon Slater (Tony Eisner); Rohan McCullough (Carla Mallory); Richenda Carey (Mallory's Secretary); Paul Atkinson (Whitney Paine Guard); Paul Stacey (Private Eye); Willie Ross (Anna's Doorman); Choy Ling Man (Riki); Beverley Hills (Tape-room Girl); Andrew Baker (Barman); Irene Marot (Taxi Passenger); Barry Ewart (Commissionaire); Kit Hollerbach (Newscaster); Georgia Byng (Bar Girl); Amanda Dickinson (Whitney Paine Clerk); Marissa Dunlop (Little Girl).

LOS ANGELES TIMES, 11/3/89, Calendar/p. 19, Michael Wilmington

"Dealers" looks like the sort of movie that might have resulted if some would-be high-rollers caught a screening of Oliver Stone's "Wall Street" and decided that its setting—the sleek world of high finance—had potential but its concept had to be turned around.

After all, what's wrong with a little inittiative, a lot of money? Instead of a downer of a movie about amoral, greed-crazed hustlers who live glittering high lives, get exposed and go to jail, why not send the audience out happy by making the hustlers into heroes and by making the movie into a slightly disguised celebration of mindless hedonism, conspicuous consumption and reckless money manipulation?

If the sleazier characters in "Wall Street" ever dreamed, this is the sort of dumb fantasy they might conjure up. They would have aggressive, sexy young brokers life Briton Daniel Pascoe (Paul McGann) who live on a country lake and commute to the city by seaplane. And they would cook up heroines like American Anna Schuman (Rebecca DeMornay), as blond, svelte sex bomb with a mind like a steel trap, whose favorite salutation is "Let's make money!" and who cruises the computer aisles with a walk that might be described as a power jiggle.

They would give us lonely, salty father figures like Robby Barrell (Derrick O'Connor)—a boozed-out, coked-out paterfamilias, fired from the bank and content to putter around Pascoe's house, cook up gourmet meals and plan stock strategies. The villain, of course, would be the conservative, play-it-safe boss (John Castle) who doesn't understand that to win big, you've got to risk big.

There would be a fairy godfather of a character in power (Paul Guilfoyle), preferably a look-alike for Lee Iacocca, and instead of a big fight or a last-minute rescue, the ending would turn on a rise in the American GNP. The other dealers would be a daffy, crazy, lovable bunch—a real team: comical Germans and big, loud Welshwomen (Sara Sugarman).

"Dealers" is soggy with the sentimentalism of people who kid themselves that they're not sentimental. Halfway through, Pascoe—whose name suggests a softer version of "Wall Street's" monster, Gordon Gekko—sneaks into Anna's hotel and fills up her room with more balloons than you've seen since "A Thousand Clowns." Would a movie that wasn't wearing its greed on its sleeve, like this one, try so hard to persuade us there's a heart in its pocket?

The director, Colin Bucksey, ("Blue Money"), has too much style for his own good. It's like a chrome trim laid over all a malfunctioning engine full of empty characters and vacuous ethics. Bucksey apes the super-salesman panache of the prime British TV ad directors, the metallic surfaces and gleaming, lucid setups. But we might guess we're in for trouble when, shortly after a major character commits suicide, the movie blares out, unsatirically, a rock song by Pray for Rain called "Corporate World."

"Dealers" has one superb performance: O'Connor's, poking some believability and bitterness into this fancy trash. But the film's bottom line suggests that it's all right to play havoc with the market, spy on and blackmail your bosses into bed, accumulate illegal insider information and parasitic paper fortunes—and possibly wreck jobs just like Wall Street's Gekko—as long as you're a cute guy with a nice smile, a seaplane and a lot of balloons. There's a lot of hardware in "Dealers" (MPAA rated R for sex and language)—much of it supplied by Reuters' financial services—but, emotionally, artistically and morally, it's bankrupt.

MONTHLY FILM BULLETIN, 8/89, p. 237, Philip Strick

Responsible for a $100-million trading loss, a leading dealer at the City bank of Whitney Paine commits suicide in the boardroom. Dealing supervisor Robby Barrell is confident that the brightest member of his team, young and dynamic Daniel Pascoe, can take over the dollar account to recover the loss, but the directors of the bank, Lee Peters and Frank Mallory, unexpectedly appoint an outsider, Anna Schuman, to the job. Anna is a tough but attractive American, to whom Daniel is drawn despite his initial antagonism towards her as an unwelcome rival. He leads a flashy and luxurious life style which has finally driven his regular girlfriend Bonnie to leave him, and he begins to concentrate on Anna, quickly disovering that the real reason behind her appointment is that she is Frank's mistress. Inviting her to his mansion in the Kent countryside, which they reach in his private seaplane from a mooring by Tower Bridge, he confronts her with his discovery; she promptly walks out and flies the plane back to London on her own. Their relationship now on a new level, Anna and Daniel are required to work in partnership by the bank, her cautious trading style balanced by his risk-taking flair. Finding Robby, now unemployed, on the brink of poverty, Daniel makes him a permanent house guest until he can find his feet again; his old colleague still has useful tips to offer on trading strategy. Meanwhile, despite Frank's jealousy, Anna and Daniel at last become lovers. With Robby's guidance, Daniel plans a secret coup that will completely recover the dollar loss, but which involves a huge temporary risk to the bank. Anna accidentally finds out what he has done, and finds that Frank has discovered it too but said nothing, hoping it will mean the end of Daniel. She goes to Lee with the information, but he is willing to trust her instinct that Daniel's gamble will pay off. Robby dies suddenly, broken by alcohol and drugs, and Daniel finds himself at the centre of crisis with only Anna to defend his refusal to sell until the right moment in what appears to be a disastrous market. Suddenly the tide turns, potential ruin is converted to substantial profit, and Daniel triumphantly quits his job while Frank is fired and Anna is left to run the business. That evening, when Daniel arrives at Tower Bridge to collect his plane, he finds Anna waiting for him in the cockpit and they fly off into the sunset.

Although the Stock Market has more or less reassembled itself after the October Crash, the average investor, now a more nervous and cynical creature than in the hot summer of the raging bull, is unlikely to be amused by *Dealers*. Confirming all worst fears about fast-lane yuppie life styles, the film shows the naked face of capitalism in high-gloss hues of treachery, lechery and greed, while revealing that the professional manipulation of money involves hardly more skill than quick reaction to an electronic bingo game. A tunnel-vision single-mindedness is perhaps essential to any specialist while he's doing his job, but the girls and sports cars of his spare time are no concern of his customers. The trouble with *Dealers*, however, is that it has a lot of spare time to fill, and in plumbing the shallows of its chosen milieu it merely confirms a dispiriting lack of depth. Away from the boisterous excitement of their phones and monitors, the film's traders become several shades more uninteresting except in the curiously ill-formed nature of their emotions. The best that maturity can offer in the dealing game, on this evidence, is disgrace, a drug habit, and a lonely death beside somebody else's private lake.

Antonioni made much the same point (lake included) nearly thirty years ago with *L'Eclisse*, when financial collapse and a failed romance seemed part of an inescapable global malaise. If *Dealers* had similarly externalised its crises, or even included some memorable malevolence in the manner of *Wall Street*, it might have acquired a few small hints of significance. instead, Colin Bucksey's experience in directing episodes of *Miami Vice* allows him to disguise the vapid nature of his material with energetic volleys of images, above and beyond the call of narrative, spiralling down on his performers from dizzy heights, setting them off against unexpected colours and busy backgrounds, or chopping whole sequences into piecemeal information (like the seduction scene which contrives to take place in a welter of balloons before the participants actually arrive). Often hasty to the point of ugliness, *Dealers* also comes up with a generous ration of visual surprises to compensate for its largely inanimate cast (although Derrick O'Connor is pleasingly vehement as a veteran trader who has endured most of the world's injustices), and gets full value for money from the dealing arena designed as a furnace of flashing figures and fake marble. With its beautiful glimpses of the City's architectural contrasts, the film might encourage the tourist industry, but as a guide to survival in these inflationary times it is best ignored.

NEW YORK POST, 11/3/89, p. 27, V.A. Musetto

Daniel Pascoe is a brash, young money trader at Whitney Paine, a conservative London bank. He lives in a castle on an estate in Kent and commutes to work each day by private seaplane (20 minutes each way). He gets results for his bosses, but he takes big risks in the process.

So when one of the bank's top traders blows his brains out in the opening minutes of "Dealers," leaving behind an embarrassing $100 million default, the "reckless" Daniel (Paul McGann) is passed over as replacement. Instead, the spot goes to Anna Schuman (Rebecca DeMornay), a touched-up blonde with awesome legs and a wiggle that would have made Marilyn Monroe jealous. Of course, the fact that Anna is sleeping with one of the bank's married honchos doesn't hurt her upward mobility.

You don't need a degree from Harvard Business to figure out what's going to happen when Daniel feasts his eyes on Anna. His girlfriend has just dumped him in favor of "something more stable." And Anna isn't exactly the monogamous type, although she makes Daniel work harder for her than he does for most of his big-bucks deals.

Less predictable is Daniel's friendship with Robby Barrell (Derrick O'Connor), a Scotch-guzzling, cocaine-snorting, cigar-puffing banker who unceremoniously gets the bounce from Whitney Paine. (Robby receives the bad news from the security guard who has just changed the lock on his office door, then proceeds to use a computer to smash his way back in.)

Daniel lets the broke Robby stay at his mansion, giving him the run of the place and trying to get the older guy to straighten up. Daniel may be a super-yuppie, but he's got a heart.

"Dealers" has one big problem: credibility. I know that Daniel makes lots of dough—but enough for a fairy-tale lifestyle that outstrips even his bosses'? And the rah-rah finale, which sends Daniel dashing through London in search of an advance look at the GNP figures that will make or break him? Too much!

If you can put aside such matters, however, there's no reason why you shouldn't enjoy this one. The director, Colin Bucksey, spent much of his career in TV (three episodes of "Miami Vice," for instance). And it shows. "Dealers" is slick, escapist entertainment. It keeps your attention with fast-paced acting, direction and camera work that captures the energy of the frantic world of Big Money.

The bottom line: "Dealers" isn't a bad way to invest 95 minutes.

NEWSDAY, 11/3/89, Part III/p. 5, Mike McGrady

Dawn. London's Whitney Paine Bank is all but deserted. Wall clocks steadily tick away the minutes in London, Hong Kong, New York, Tokyo—those distant cities where international currencies are bought and sold. The long rows of video display terminals are darkened now but a radio somewhere is reporting that the dollar "continues to decline."

Apparently this is bad news for the lone dealer—striped suit, striped shirt, dotted tie—who is moving a cigarette toward his lips with a trembling hand. He has just lost a $100-million gamble with his company's money and that still trembling hand now reaches into an attache case to extract a snub-nosed revolver.

So begins "Dealers," a careening roller-coaster ride of a movie that leaves "Wall Street" in its dust and an audience trying to grab its breath. It's all as sexy and as exciting and as dangerous as a 200-point day on the stock market.

At Whitney Paine there is a new opening at the top that must be filled. Also a $100-million loss that must be made up. Daniel, the logical successor to the post, is brash and young and reckless: "This is a respected financial institution, Daniel, not a bloody casino." His competition for the top job is the lovely American, Anna, who has a track record for reliability and, oh, yes, another factor in her favor: She just happens to be the boss' lover.

Daniel (Paul McGann) drives the perfect car, commutes from downtown London to his Kent home by seaplane, enjoys the company of a striking array of women, subscribes to Fast Lane magazine and carries a small Reuters terminal to keep himself constantly abreast of financial fluctuations. Anna (Rebecca DeMornay) is slower and steadier, the perfect counterweight. As the two battle each other for power, they begin to merge romantically.

Oh, to be sure, these elements reveal "Dealers" to be the slick fiction it is. But so fast is the pace, so smooth the track, so exciting the ride, that there's simply no time to pause and raise questions of credibility. Besides, this is a flick, not a film—a movie intended to be enjoyed, not scrutinized.

Ensuring our enjoyment is a group of performances that manage to ring truer than will any brief plot outline. McGann brings just the proper flair and intensity to the young trader gutsy enough to risk hundreds of millions on his hunches and tough enough to stick with his bets through the roughest of times.

While the entire cast is fine—at times, England seems to be an island of gray skies and superb character actors—a particularly fine performance comes from Derrick O'Connor as McGann's free-wheeling, coke-sniffing, high-rolling boss, who winds up every morning's pep talk with a rousing, "All right, let's make money."

Andrew MacLear's script is understated, economical, funny, sexy. His story simply streaks along, always well accompanied by Richard Hartley's uptempo background music, then explodes like a stock market suddenly gone out of control

Director Colin Bucksey, a former cameraman, is a veteran BBC hand who won a variety of television awards before coming here to direct segments of "Miami Vice" and "Crime Story." His one previous feature film was 1986's "The McGuffin." Although there's no denying Bucksey's slickness or visual style, he never loses sight of his story, and he manages the mix of man's three favorite pursuits—money, power, sex—with great flair and pacing.

VILLAGE VOICE, 11/7/89, p. 74, Georgia Brown

According to Freud, the money market has to be the capital of excrement. *Dealers*, a small English film directed by Colin Bucksey, is titled after the hyperactive players who mess around with great big piles of dough.

One dealer begins with a messy act: He shoots himself while sitting at the board table of the respected bank known as Whitney Paine. (Screenwriter Andrew MacLear may have meant this as a reference to the mental institution, though nothing else in the script shows this degree of wit.) As a replacement for the suicide, who leaves the bank with a $100 million default, the boss (John Castle) overlooks next-in-line Daniel Pascoe (Paul McGann), a hotshot risk-taker, to hire his more prudent (at least businesswise) American mistress, Anna Schuman (Rebecca DeMornay), away from the rival Merrill.

As Daniel and Anna sit at their respective computers, their eyes flash complex messages. Daniel's girlfriend has just left him because she's fed up with the pace of his life. "None of this is real!" she has tried to tell him. In a display of unreality, Daniel commutes to his castle in Kent in his own plane, which he lands and parks on the Thames near the office. (He seems to have air rights and river rights to himself.) Not having learned to dress for success in her home country, Anna has made a hit in the land of tradition with tight short skirts and bottom-wagging.

When Whitney Paine makes a scapegoat ("dis-fucking-missed!") of Daniel's friend Robby

Barrell (Derrick O'Connor), whose trademark is fancy silk vests, Daniel invites Robby to join him in the castle. He wants to wean the older man, and the movie's most sympathetic character, from booze and cocaine. This subplot is meant to make Daniel look capable of human feeling.

Dealers's attitude toward dealing shifts casually from the former girlfriend's critique to uncritical support of its hero. In the beginning one of the bosses chews out Daniel: "This is a respected financial institution, not a bloody casino." But when Daniel goes on to gamble the bank's funds without his bosses' knowledge, the movie plays this as if it's any old suspense finish and assumes we're rooting reflexively for the hero to pull it off.

The lesson Daniel learns is not the usual Hollywood moral for characters of his type—humility, sacrifice, and good works. Daniel discovers he can get what he wants when he wants it. It's hard to tell if *Dealers* is cynical or just wistful.

Also reviewed in:
NEW REPUBLIC, 12/25/89, p. 27, Stanley Kauffmann
NEW YORK TIMES, 11/3/89, p. C4, Vincent Canby
VARIETY, 5/17–23/89, p. 38
WASHINGTON POST, 11/3/89, p. C7, Rita Kempley

DEEPSTAR SIX

A Tri-Star Pictures release. *Executive Producer:* Mario Kassar and Andrew Vajna. *Producer:* Sean S. Cunningham and Patrick Markey. *Director:* Sean S. Cunningham. *Screenplay:* Lewis Abernathy and Geof Miller. *Story:* Lewis Abernathy. *Director of Photography:* Mac Ahlberg. *Editor:* David Handman. *Music:* Harry Manfredini. *Sound:* Hans Roland and (music) Ron Capone. *Sound Editor:* Fred J. Brown and Gene Corso. *Production Designer:* John Reinhart. *Art Director:* Larry Fulton and Don Diers. *Set Designer:* Scott Herbertson. *Set Decorator:* Christina Volz. *Set Dresser:* Denise Dugally and Tito Blasini. *Visual Effects:* James Isaac. *Creature Effects:* Mark Shostrom. *Creature Supervisor:* Greg Nicotero. *Costumes:* Amy Endries. *Make-up:* Robert Arrollo. *Stunt Coordinator:* Kane Hodder. *Running time:* 99 minutes. *MPAA Rating:* R.

CAST: Taurean Blacque (Laidlaw); Nancy Everhard (Joyce Collins); Greg Evigan (McBride); Miguel Ferrer (Snyder); Nia Peeples (Scarpelli); Matt McCoy (Richardson); Cindy Pickett (Diane Norris); Marius Weyers (Van Gelder); Elya Baskin (Burciaga); Thom Bray (Hodges); Ron Carroll (Osborne).

LOS ANGELES TIMES, 1/13/89, Calendar/p. 6, Kevin Thomas

"DeepStar Six" tries to be the underwater "Alien" but ends up a dull, routine action-adventure in which the suspense is mechanical at best. Although there are a couple of gory moments, those expecting the jolts director Sean Cunningham brought to the original "Friday the 13th" are sure to be disappointed.

Fledgling writers Lewis Abernathy and Geof Miller trap 11 people in a secret undersea naval laboratory base, Deepstar Six, and have them menaced by an unseen monster—"something very big and very fast." Their predicament is not as exciting as it should be.

First of all, they are a fairly colorless lot, and instead of allowing them some individuality the writers weigh them down heavily with a tremendous amount of technical jargon; so much that the film seems more complicated than it really is. Little is made of the fact that the mission is a trade-off involving potentially conflicting goals: the crew is to be allowed to pursue an undersea exploration project in return for installing a missile base.

We're not allowed a good look at the monster until one hour and 16 minutes into the one hour and 39-minute movie. After such a long tease, the creature had better seem pretty scary, but it looks merely like a reptilian variation of King Kong, improbable rather than fearsome. Worst of all, "Deepstar Six" is virtually humorless, which means that the grimmer it gets for its people the more unintended laughter it evokes.

The cast, headed by Nancy Everhard and Greg Evigan, is uniformly competent and conscientious. Only Miguel Ferrer, as a stir-crazy communications expert, has the chance to express some personality. "Deepstar Six" itself (rated R for some grisliness and some four-letter words) seems likely to be deep-sixed quickly.

MONTHLY FILM BULLETIN, 8/89, p. 238, Julian Petley

In the near future, the U.S. Navy has established a secret undersea laboratory, DeepStar Six; the operation is led by Dr. John Van Gelder, who is interested primarily in undersea colonisation, but the navy's support is conditional on his installing a deepsea missile base. During construction, the crew discover a huge cavern under the ocean floor and, needing a solid base for the missile launch site, Van Gelder orders it to be destroyed. Subsequently, the command centre is violently attacked and severely damaged, and two excavation and reconnaisance vehicles are destroyed with the loss of Captain Laidlaw and crewmen Burciaga, Hodges and Osborne. Scarpelli, a marine biologist, realises that they may have disturbed a creature of the deep and suggests that it might have turned aggressive after being suddenly exposed to light. As the monster continues to attack the base, the missiles are fired in error, thereby setting off the countdown to an irreversible auto-destruct mechanism. The reactor is becoming supercritical and the air supply is running out. The creature manages to enter the rapidly flooding base via an air lock, and kills Scarpelli and Richardson. Snyder becomes increasingly crazed and is beaten up by McBride. While hunting the monster, Snyder accidentally kills Van Gelder and has to be forcibly sedated; attempting to escape to the surface, he is killed by the rapid pressure change. As the three remaining crew members, McBride, Joyce Collins (who are romantically involved) and Diane Norris, try to repair the escape craft, the monster takes over more and more of the flooding base. Eventually it is electrocuted by Norris, who dies in the process. McBride and Collins escape to the surface just before the base explodes. The monster also abruptly surfaces and McBride destroys it with fire, barely escaping incineration himself.

With the imminent release of *The Abyss, Leviathan* and *Lords of the Deep*, undersea adventure looks like being the next flavour of the month in horror films. *DeepStar Six* is a relatively modest, low-budget curtain raiser and, as the title suggests, is really an aquatic variation on the familiar monster-at-large-in-spaceship theme. The crucial ingredient in all such stories is a gripping sense of claustrophobia, and in this respect *DeepStar Six* works rather well. The film was shot in a large, specially designed tank capable of holding 110,000 gallons of water and thirteen modular sets. As the story progresses and the crew are gradually wiped out, the survivors find themselves driven from one refuge to another, until only one small room is safe from the monster's attacks. meanwhile, of course, the air is running out, the water is running in, and the whole base is about to self-destruct. The early attacks, before the monster enters the base itself, are signalled by fast-moving subjective shots from the monster's point of view, and the creature itself is revealed only gradually. This generates an effective degree of suspense, and the final revelation of what resembles a vast, ferocious, armour-plated crayfish does not disappoint.

On the debit side, the external shots are murky and blurry—the long shots of the base make it look rather like a floodlit football pitch in a night-time cloudburst—and script and characters uninteresting. There are some nice *Dark Star*-style laconic exchanges between two crew members of an excavation vehicle, but these are the monster's first victims and after their demise the script returns to the level of weak banter punctuated by scientific-sounding jargon and Snyder's none-too-convincing ravings. Equally hard to take are Norris' final electrocution (given the amount of electrical cable lashing about in the water all of the crew should have died after the monster's first attack), and McBride emerging unscathed from the final seaborne inferno.

NEW YORK POST, 1/13/89, p. 28, Jami Bernard

You'd think they learned from "Aliens" that you can't just start a colony in a far-flung corner of the cosmos without first conducting a check for slime-monsters.

But it's not as if the makers of "DeepStar Six" did not learn anything from "Aliens." They learned quite a bit, certainly enough to pilfer a number of main story elements, even the fashion statement made by Sigourney Weaver's tank-top T-shirts. In fact, only the locale is different. Instead of outer space, this experimental colony is six miles beneath the surface of the ocean.

What's important in a movie, however, is not location, location, location, but characters, characters, characters. And although "DeepStar Six" is derivative and occasionally ridiculous, it has a congenial cast and makes for easy watching, a sort of humanistic science-fiction fantasy for those who don't usually like them.

After six months under water, the crew is getting a little testy. Standing between them and "going topside" is the discovery of a cavern beneath their colony site. Anxious to get on with it, they blow up the cavern, inadvertently freeing a long-dormant sea creature who becomes even crankier than the crew and takes it out on the movie's cast and sets.

As the 10 or 11 Little Indians predictably dwindle to three or four, the race is on to decompress and get the hell out of that leaky vessel.

Of course, six months in cramped quarters can lead to lots of things, including romance. The main lovebirds are McBride (Greg Evigan) and Joyce Collins (Nancy Everhard), both smart and attractive crew members who have a little secret that is quite apparent from the first scene, if you're paying attention.

McBride is not the marrying type, at least not unless it's the right woman or until the traumas of the deep remind him of his mortality. In fact, the monster's claustrophobic pinch is probably nothing compared to that suffocating feeling McBride gets in the face of commitment. "She don't need no submarine pilot from New Jersey who can't keep a week's pay in his pocket," he rationalizes.

There is a judicious use of special effects, at least in the first half, to establish the underwater routine. Later, there is much thrashing about with the monster and a graphic case of the bends.

Like Cecil the Seasick Sea Serpent, whose bottom was always concealed in a barrel, we never see the beast in full figure; he'd never make it as a partner for Fred Astaire, who insisted on being framed from head to toe.

Okay, it's not the scariest movie around, but there is a charming ordinariness to it. Not one of these crew members is as efficient as a cyborg, neither is anyone completely insane (with the possible exception of Miguel Ferrer, who suffers from anxiety attacks). You can really imagine these are regular people who signed on with the Navy because it sounded like fun.

So far, all has been affable, but gradually the stupidities threaten to overtake the picture like a rubbery sea monster trying to break into an airlock and the refreshing lack of techno-jargon becomes a hindrance when things reach the panic level.

"It'll go super-critical in a few hours!" warns one crew member.

"What'll happen at super-critical?" asks another.

"We explode!"

At any rate, this movie is not so much about creatures of the deep as about human and technological breakdown. With its carefully established underwater world and inter-crew relationships, it might have made the basis for a "Star Trek"-like TV series, where its silliness would be part of its charm. It's not super-critical that you see it, but for all its stupid moments, "DeepStar Six" is bland good fun.

NEWSDAY, 1/13/89, Part III/p. 5, Bill Kaufman

Wouldn't you know it? Computer expert Tony Snyder (Miguel Ferrer) one of the 11 crew members cooped up inside the submerged exploration station for the past six months, is getting the whimwhams—the antsy scientist pleads with the doctor to send him topside as soon as possible.

In addition to the guy with a case of nerves, the stock ensemble of very familiar characters in "DeepStar Six" is all here in awfully close quarters: We have a couple of beautiful female researchers (one of them pregnant), a stern captain of the submerged base and a cocky young diver who is the office jokester.

On a mission to construct a secret underwater missile site, the sink tank team aboard DeepStar Six is being hassled to get the job done quickly. Using a bulldozer-like vehicle on the seabed, two of the scientists set off a blast that causes a vast cave-in of the ocean floor. Before anyone can say "Uh-Oh!," a really ugly creature of prehistoric origins arises from the gap in the sea floor and attacks, causing not a little havoc aboard DeepStar Six.

From this point on, the movie is mostly a suspenseful hunt-and-chase, sink-or-swim drama where everyone gets doused repeatedly as various compartments of the craft spring leaks and the crew attempts to track down and fight the monster.

Greg Evigan, known from his television days in "B.J. and the Bear" is just fine as McBride, a scientist lucky enough to have his love interest along for the tour of duty. She's played by Nancy Everhard, who manages to look fresh and suntanned even after half a year in the submerged laboratory. Early on, before all the bulkheads began spraying everyone, there's even a brief romantic interlude in a hot shower.

Taurean Blacque, another small-tube expatriate (Det. Neal Washington in "Hill St. Blues") comes off as a believable captain, an authoritative leader well-suited to the task of keeping his crew relatively intact and rallying the unit against the offending creature. As for the monster, it has moments where it steals the picture—a sort of Godzilla-Jaws-Leviathan You-Name-It, that benefits from well-conceived special effects.

VILLAGE VOICE, 1/24/89, p. 64, Amy Taubin

Directed by Sean (*Friday the 13th*) Cunningham, *DeepStar Six* is so formulaic that no amount of gore could relieve the boredom. This *Alien* ripoff has the crew of a Navy deep-sea missile base getting in a wrangle with a prehistoric monster, which, when it finally looms into view halfway through the interminable 90 minutes, looks more Maurice Sendak Wild Thing than Loch Nessie. Many of the scenes were shot in a very crowded underwater tank, and I hope the actors—good swimmers all—were well paid, because they did not seem to be having fun. There *are* two novelties in the film—both ideological bludgeons. First, the protagonist is not one character but a nuclear family—man, woman, and developing embryo. The adults share equally in the crucial actions and almost never leave each other's sides. (The embryo obviously has no choice in the matter.) *DeepStar Six* may be the only horror film that stops dead for two minutes just before the climax, while the pregnant bride-to-be prays for the salvation of her family. Second-guessing the audience's predictable reaction—that a plot like this can only be taken on faith—the script proclaims that what we're about too see is nothing less than an act of God.

Also reviewed in:
NEW YORK TIMES, 1/13/89, p. C13, Janet Maslin
VARIETY, 1/18/89, p. 20
WASHINGTON POST, 1/14/89, p. C2, Richard Harrington

DETAILS OF A DUEL

A Focine production in cooperation with Producciones Fotograma and Icaic. *Executive Producer:* Abelardo Quintero. *Director:* Sergio Cabrera. *Screenplay (Spanish with English subtitles):* Humberto Dorado. *Director of Photography:* José Medeiros. *Editor:* Justo Vega. *Music:* Juan Márquez. *Sound:* Heriberto Garcia. *Art Director:* Enrique Linero. *Running time:* 97 minutes. *MPAA Rating:* Not Rated.

CAST: Frank Ramirez (Teacher); Humberto Dorado (Butcher); Florina Lemaitre (Miriam); and Vicky Hernandez; Kepa Amuchastegui; Angelo Javier Lozano; Edgardo Roman; Manuel Pachon; Luis Chiappe; Antonio Aparicio; Fausto Cabrera; Elio Mesa; Yolanda Garcia; Humberto Arango; Alberto Sanchez; Dario Valdivieso; Julian Roman; Alicia De Rojas; Carlos Parruca; Miguel Ignacio Vanegas; Teresa Ibañez; Cecilia Ricardo.

VILLAGE VOICE, 3/21/89, p. 64, Katherine Dieckmann

Less fanciful and more picaresque than Ruy Guerra's García Márquez adaptations, Sergio Cabrera's gentle *Chronicles of a Death Foretold*-like tale takes place in one day, as a village anticipates a duel between the local schoolteacher and butcher. They are to kill each other for reasons never adequately explained (though Cabrera's cross-cutting hints that the egghead has diddled the prole's wife). The movie is really about dismantling Latin machismo, Sartrian being-towards-death, and the self-serving needs of church and state. Pleasant but insubstantial, *Details* also offers a political allegory lite: The opposition must stick together.

Also reviewed in:
NEW YORK TIMES, 3/18/89, p. 16, Janet Maslin
VARIETY, 10/19/88, p. 262

DIRECTED BY ANDREI TARKOVSKY

A Swedish Film Institute presentation. *Producer:* Lisbet Gabrielsson. *Director:* Michal Leszczylowski. *Screenplay (Swedish with English subtitles):* Michal Leszczylowski. *Director of Photography:* Arne Carlsson. *Editor:* Michal Leszczylowski and Lasse Summanen. *Sound:* Lars Ulander. *Reading Voice:* Erland Josephson. *Voiceover Narrator:* Brian Cox. *Running time:* 101 minutes. *MPAA Rating:* Not Rated.

LOS ANGELES TIMES, 6/19/89, Calendar/p. 7, Kevin Thomas

Andrei Tarkovsky once said that each man contains a universe within himself, and no director illuminated that universe with more imagination or rigor. Tarkovsky, who died of cancer at 54 in Paris on the last day of 1986, made only seven features in his 24-year career, but each of them is astonishing in the often surreal power of their vision.

Tarkovsky had an abiding preoccupation with the memory as the great shaping force of the individual psyche. He also said that the purpose of our lives was to develop ourselves spiritually, and he believed that the function of art was to serve that purpose.

Consequently, much could rightly be expected of a documentary called "Directed by Andrei Tarkovsky," but that title is misleading. It is simply a record of Tarkovsky shooting his last film, "The Sacrifice," made by his editor, Michael Leszczylowski. It is overlaid by quotations from "Sculpting in Time," Tarkovsky's book on his theories of film, and interspersed with scenes from "The Sacrifice" and interviews with Tarkovsky culled from earlier documentaries. As a memento of a great film maker cut down in his prime, the film is deeply affecting; for anyone who loved and admired Tarkovsky's work it is thrilling simply to see him at work, collaborating with two of Ingmar Bergman's most esteemed colleagues, actor Erland Josephson and cinematographer Sven Nykvist.

Leszczylowski assumes that we have a great deal of familiarity with Tarkovsky and his films. There's not a word on the director's life and career, his tremendous difficulties in working in his native Soviet Union and his eventual, deeply painful emigration to the West. No one on the set of "The Sacrifice," which takes place in Swedish Gotland around a large house by the sea, is identified, and the only person Leszczylowski interviews for his film is Tarkovsky's elegant, gracious widow Larissa, who insists proudly that her husband was the only Soviet director who always got exactly what he wanted (but does not say at what high cost, even of the banning of his work).

It essential to have seen "The Sacrifice," a profound meditation on the imperiled future of humanity, for there's nary a clue as to what it's about or what's going on. (It screens Wednesday and Thursday at the New Beverly Cinema, along with "L'Argent," by director Robert Bresson, the man at the top of Tarkovsky's list of film makers.) Instead of the quotes from "Sculpting in Time," which sound self-evident and platitudinous when heard on a sound track, Leszczylowski might better have had his narrator, the well-spoken Brian Cox, tell us something about "The Sacrifice" and its maker.

Leszczylowski unintentionally reminds us that a motion picture set is a great leveler: If you didn't already know, you would never guess that this particular cast and crew, as professional and conscientious as countless others, is in fact working at the highest level of artistic aspiration. Tarkovsky once said that directors could be divided into those who imitated the world around them and those that created their own. There's no question as to which category Tarkovsky belonged, but Leszczylowski hasn't really taken us into the world of the man he called Maestro.

MONTHLY FILM BULLETIN, 4/89, p. 121, Philip Strick

During the making of Andrei Tarkovsky's last film *The Sacrifice* in 1985, some fifty hours of behind-the-scenes footage was shot on video by the Swedish assistant cameraman Arne Carlsson. Part of this was used for the Swedish Film Institute production *The Making of "The Sacrifice"*, a forty-minute promotional film released in 1986. From the raw material, all of which he viewed, Tarkovsky also proposed to assemble with the help of his film editor Michal Leszczylowski a two-hour study of his working methods, incorporating a commentary and specially filmed interview sequences. But after completing *The Sacrifice* in 1986 in time for the Cannes Festival, Tarkovsky was too weak to collaborate on the project, which Leszczylowski finally had to construct without him, using extracts from *The Sacrifice*, from Tarkovsky's book *Sculpting in Time*, and from previous interviews.

The first shot of Tarkovsky is of an intense profile suddenly hidden by an imperious hand. Relenting, the shield is lowered, and the director turns towards us, eyes anxious then closed for a nod of reluctant acceptance. In fact concentrating on a rehearsal, acting and steering it simultaneously and apparently unaware of being observed, Tarkovsky is perceptively introduced through this performance. Although very much a public figure during his European exile, his interviews were habitually guarded, as if, by lapses into spontaneity, he might expose himself to accusations of being mundane, or worse, deliberately obscure. It is remarkably difficult to find a record of Tarkovsky talking with precision about *any* of his films, although by using the convenient pauses for thought afforded by conversing through interpreters, he was able to theorise at length about film in general. Here, the only work referred to is *The Sacrifice*, and what it says and why he made it remains a perpetual conundrum.

What is no longer mysterious, thanks to Leszczylowski's tribute, is how Tarkovsky functioned once, with script complete, he was in a position to embark on a production. Nosing into discussions already complicated by the presence of translators, technicians, actors and other bystanders, Carlsson's camera reveals a sternly meditative figure constantly gliding around the furniture like one of his own tracking shots, smoothing, polishing and rearranging as he goes. He insisted he was poet rather than cinematographer, but the austere, glowing interiors of *The Sacrifice*, slowly assembling themselves as we watch until, with triumphant footage from the finished film, we see them exactly in context, demonstrate the precision of his draughtsman's gaze. At the same time, it is fascinating to watch the choreographic consequences of his staging, as chairs and tables ferried by scuttling conspirators float into position and out again while the camera and the actors prowl among them in uninterrupted collusion. Preparing for the sequence of the postman's arrival with the ancient map in its huge frame, director and cast work out a clumsy bit of business that will turn the thing towards the camera, and the movement, as performed, looks perfectly rational. More elusively, Tarkovsky shows Allan Edwall how to stand thoughtfully at a window, and with a signalling finger the actor makes the gesture completely his own. In one of the brightest clues to his philosophy, the director even admits, while instructing Erland Josephson to drop to his knees, that he doesn't know why the character is behaving like this. But as the scene falls into place, there's no question that it's the right move.

At times of major crisis, Tarkovsky's reaction appears as more sorrow than anger, his words emerging through translation as if phrased for diplomacy. The Swedes can't produce a cherry tree in blossom which, according to the script, is to shed white petals on Josephson's bicycle, and Tarkovsky with incredulous fury gives them ten minutes to clear the offending foliage from his sight. But Josephson, with good reason, is more worried about a flock of sheep that has to rush across his path, and so, in another sense, should we be. White petals or sheep, a vast miscellany of enigmatic items form the substance of Tarkovsky's drama. The famous production crisis during *The Sacrifice* was the burning of the house which, first time round, happened in front of a jammed camera; a drama of despair as enthralling as anything in the final work, this footage is a vivid reminder that the compulsiveness of many Tarkovsky images lies in their sheer stubborn impracticality, the suspense of waiting for them to lead somewhere. Only Tarkovsky could insist that the six-minute burning be in one take, that the house be reconstructed in order to be destroyed again, and only the experience of watching the result (in which, as a matter of fact, the house is *not* on screen for at least two of those minutes) allows us to understand that there was no other way.

What we do learn about *The Sacrifice* is that there's another forty minutes of it somewhere, of which we see some tantalising moments (the white horse, the startling assembly of witnesses at Josephson's bedside) before they were pruned by Tarkovsky and Leszczylowski. Tarkovsky's wife Larissa tells us about the two original stories on which the film was based, the family memories that it contains, the "real" dreams to which it refers. The soundtrack quotations from Tarkovsky's writing, elaborate, tortuous, sometimes verging on the incomprehensible, are occasionally so obtrusive that they point up the simple truth that words were never his happiest form of communication. As a postscript, Leszczylowski show us Tarkovsky in his hospital bed, studying on a movieola a sequence in which, ironically, another spokesman on another screen admits that the end is at hand. Briefly it seems to contradict Tarkovsky's earlier answer to an Italian interviewer in a rare, unpremeditated glimpse, that he is, almost certainly, immortal. But the concluding shot of boy and tree from *The Sacrifice* is mesmerising affirmation that, in terms of pure film, he knew exactly where he was heading.

NEW STATESMAN & SOCIETY, 7/21/89, p. 38, Suzanne Moore

The films of Russian director Andrei Tarkovsky epitomise all that is right or wrong (depending on your point of view) with "art" cinema. It's certainly true that apart from being very long, slow and subtitled, it's not everyone's idea of a good night out to spend two and a half hours watching obscure characters endlessly discussing the meaning of life, love and the universe, however beautifully bleak the settings are. Yet for fans of Tarkovsky's films, *Solaris, Mirror, Nostalgia,*

Stalker, The Sacrifice, it is precisely the depth and purity of his work that marks him out as one of the cinema's great directors. His total disdain for commercial cinema—the celluloid strip as commodity, as he refers to it—and his absolute insistence on cinema as one of the highest art forms, produced films that were not afraid to deal with deeply unfashionable spiritual questions.

Tarkovsky's questioning of the nature of faith, of prayer, of sacrifice in the modern world, alongside his elevation of personal experience eventually lead to his exile from the Soviet Union. By the mid-sixties the liberal attitude to cultural affairs was hardening. Cuts were demanded by the authorities on *Andrei Roubleuv*, his film about the life of a medieval icon painter. Tarkovsky's work was increasingly denounced as "elitist" and his continued emphasis on the profundity rather than the reactionary nature of Christian faith was taken as a subtle critique of communism and indeed of the Soviet state.

These issues are alluded to but not explored in *Directed by Andrei Tarkovskij*, a Swedish documentary by Michal Leszczylowski. From the opening shot of Tarkovsky himself, face screwed up in intense concentration, you know that this is going to be very much in the portrait-of-the-artist-as-god genre. And you would be right. Filmed during the making of *The Sacrifice*, it is given extra significance as Tarkovsky died of cancer shortly after editing the film from his hospital bed.

Despite the over-reverent attitude and moving interviews with his widow, Larissa, the film almost inadvertently allows an occasional critical edge to poke through. These surface not in the interviews with Tarkovsky or his wife, or in the scenes where he is describing his theories of cinema to adoring students, but when we see him on set actually working. While the respectful voice-over describes Tarkovsky's meticulous attention to detail, to every aspect of the film from set-design to make-up, we see before us a tyrant, interfering everywhere, refusing to let anyone else make a decision. This may be a little harsh because without a doubt his charm, brilliance and sheer determination to find the exact image inspired enormous admiration in those working with him.

Nonetheless, the documentary unwittingly highlights the problems of *auteur*-theory, of looking at films as the product of a single mind. While Tarkovsky is an *auteur* if ever there was one—every film uncompromisingly his own—the process of making a film involves hundreds of other individual talents as this documentary graphically illustrates.

He is at his most impressive when expounding his ideas on what film should do, on "sculpting in time". Seeing himself as a poet rather than a cinematographer, his films are mosaics of memory and time. The past is always a resource and cinema, he says, is the only medium that can take an impression of time. At his best his films excel in doing what film should do—they show things visually rather than saying them narratively. For Tarkovsky is not interested in the intellectual response of an audience but in its spiritual illumination—in a pure moment of what he calls "aesthetic acceptance of the beautiful on an emotional level". This is the truth he strives for through creating his own world, directly perceiving it, not by commenting on or imitating reality.

His absolute faith expressed time and time again in his book is in the ability of the right image to communicate directly. He dislikes metaphors and searches for images that are "innocent of symbolism": that in the beloved style of the Japanese haiku expresses a "specific, unique, actual, fact"—a precise observation of life. Fittingly, he doesn't like Freud or Eisenstein both of whom, in different ways, elevate the ambiguity of images and facts, their potential for multiple meanings. Eisenstein's use of the third meaning—that derives from the interplay of two images—is for Tarkovsky incompatible with the nature of cinema: he believes the image exists within time, within the frame, for the spectator to make of it what she or he will. Editing, he insists, is to bring out the essential nature of the filmed material rather than to tell the audience how to read the imagery. Indeed, he is famous for the rhymes and rhythms of his films, his single takes, scenes lasting five or six minutes and shot in real time such as the house burning down in *The Sacrifice*.

What is fascinating about Tarkovsky, regardless of whether or not you like his films, is the way that both thematically and stylistically his work runs counter to nearly everything that could be called "contemporary".

His almost Zen-like characters are strong because they are weak, their passivity and humility is valued above all. We need to return to the time before we lost the ability to pray, to believe, to offer ourselves to the "greater good". Some find this visionary, fluid quality in his films full as they are of water, fire and wind. Others have described his work as cold, sanctimonious, egotistical, over-intellectual and lacking in warmth or humanity.

Above all, as Mark Le Fanu points out in his excellent book *The Cinema of Andrei Tarkovsky*, Tarkovsky stands in opposition to most modern atheistic directors such as Bergman and Bresson whom he admires. Tarkovsky believes in the power of "the word" and in the reality of "the self"—two concepts that have been undermined with equally religious zeal by many modern western theorists. Tarkovsky clearly believes that there is a correlation between truth and language and that inner experience proves the existence of the individual, of the soul. Thus, it is possible both to believe and to tell the "truth", to have faith even in the modern world.

As we well know Tarkovsky's sadness at the secularisation of society both in the east and the west is a view strongly held by many people. Whether you find the films of this " poet of memory" radical or irritatingly anachronistic, his visions of the time we have lost or are yet to have remain real and heartfelt and unique. They are quite unlike anything else: disturbingly beautiful and evocative and always too strangely lucid to be dismissed as mere nostalgia.

Also reviewed in:
NEW YORK TIMES, 5/26/89, p. C10, Caryn James
VARIETY, 5/25/88, p. 19

DISORGANIZED CRIME

A Touchstone Pictures release in association with Silver Screen Partners IV. *Executive Producer:* Rob Cohen and John Badham. *Producer:* Lynn Bigelow. *Director:* Jim Kouf. *Screenplay:* Jim Kouf. *Director of Photography:* Ron Garcia. *Editor:* Frank Morriss and Dallas Puett. *Music:* David Newman. *Music Editor:* Tom Villano and Segue Music. *Sound:* Douglas Axtell. *Sound Editor:* Michael Hilkene. *Production Designer:* Waldemar Kalinowski. *Art Director:* David Lubin. *Set Designer:* Florence Fellman. *Set Dresser:* Jon David Charpentier. *Special Effects:* Burt Dalton. *Costumes:* Stephanie Maslansky. *Make-up:* Joann Wabisca. *Stunt Coordinator:* Dan Bradley. *Running time:* 98 minutes. *MPAA Rating:* R.

CAST: Hoyt Axton (Sheriff Henault); Corbin Bernsen (Frank Salazar); Rubén Blades (Carlos Barrios); Fred Gwynne(Max Green); Ed O'Neill (George Denver); Lou Diamond Phillips (Ray Forgy); Daniel Roebuck (Bill Lonigan); William Russ (Nick Bartkowski); Marie Butler Kouf (Wanda Brem); Gregory Wurster (Deputy Greg); Patrick Collins (Deputy Monroe); Mitch Carter (Deputy Larry); Dean Norris (Deputy Joe); Thomas Schellenberg (Deputy Jim); Robert Feldmann (Dispatcher); David Hart (Proprietor); Jeff Duus (Stock Truck Driver); Noah Keen (Farmer); Marie Stelin (Farmer's Wife); Dena Dietrich (Judge D. Greenwalt); Monica Rapalli (Young Girl/Gina); John Oblinger (Store Owner); Tony Lecce (Shooter #1); Mark Lewis (Shooter #2); Al Gile (Bank President); Todd Irwin (Mechanic); Gina Lecce (Girl on Bike); Kitty Lecce (Blonde Bomshell); Cliff Buhler (Farmer in Bank).

LOS ANGELES TIMES, 4/14/89, Calendar/p. 8, Kevin Thomas

Jim Kouf's "Disorganized Crime" is a pleasant comedy caper enlivened by enjoyable actors and a couple of belly laughs, but it's stretched too thin for its own good. As a result, it's acceptably routine rather than truly successful.

Rubén Blades, Fred Gwynne, Lou Diamond Phillips and William Russ play a quartet of ill-assorted crooks who haven't met before and have been summoned by a mutual friend (Corbin Bernsen) to a remote, ramshackle farmhouse outside a small Montana town, where Bernsen intends to rob the local bank. Before Bernsen can make his own rendezvous he's nabbed by a pair of New Jersey cops (Ed O'Neill, Dan Roebuck), but only temporarily.

Kouf, who also wrote "Stakeout," parallels the quartet's querulous efforts to go ahead with the heist with the cops chasing Bernsen across the wilds of Montana. Since it's clear that the film is headed for a climactic "Rififi"-"Asphalt Jungle" robbery, Kouf puts off getting there for far too long. (How many cuts to Bernsen racing through the woods do we really need?) "Disorganized Crime" suffers from a slack, wearying middle, a common flaw in genre films made by fledgling directors.

If the plot meanders and is resolved evasively, the cast is nonetheless terrific. Looming, lantern-jawed Gwynne is a special pleasure as the senior member of the gang, a career criminal who has no intention of spending the rest of his life behind bars. Russ is the gang's safecracker with a short fuse, liked by no one but obviously indispensable. Phillips, the hot-wire and Blades provide the group with some ballast. "Disorganized Crime" offers the usually suave Bernsen a nice change of pace as a hapless scruffy type who is subjected to one indignity after another in his scramble to escape; he emerges as adept at slapstick as he is with more sophisticated comedy.

"Disorganized Crime," however, is stolen by the cops rather than the criminals. O'Neill and burly Roebuck are actors with solid experience in theater and TV whose perfectly average looks serve them well playing obnoxious, smug, city boys whose mishaps in the hinterlands prove a hilarious comeuppance. Observing them with a certain amount of glee is local sheriff Hoyt Axton.

Also on the plus side is all that gorgeous Montana scenery (captured by cinematographer Ron Garcia) and a lively score by David Newman. Refreshingly, "Disorganized Crime" (rated a rather stiff R for language) isn't cynical, doesn't glamorize larceny and doesn't make anyone a numskull, but it sure does drag.

NEW YORK POST, 4/14/89, p. 37, David Edelstein

At the start of "Disorganized Crime," robber Corbin Bernsen strolls into a Montana bank and surveys an impressive-looking safe. But it's nowhere near as impressive as his tan. He looks as if he has been dipped in caramel. Then the movie tells you he's from Newark. The only people with tans like this in Newark are arsonists who stand too close.

It's downhill from there. "Disorganized Crime" is a broad, aimless caper picture without enough laughs to sustain a coming attraction. Bernsen summons a team of crack bank robbers (Rubén Blades, Fred Gwynne, Lou Diamond Phillips, William Russ) to Montana, but before he can tell them what they're there for he gets nailed by a pair of doltish Newark cops.

Virtually dropped from the picture, Bernsen gets the best deal. The other actors are stranded on the screen, each with his quota of temper tantrums and four-letter words. Blades, so ingratiating in "The Milagro Beanfield War," pushes the hardest and fares the worst. Russ, as the group paranoid, gives the picture some wild-eyed jitters, but most of his gags are pushing up daisies.

Gwynne adds the one touch of poetry. He moves superbly for a giant—age and weight have given him immense gravity, and expressions pass slowly over his long face, as if top and bottom were in different hemispheres. His voice has deepened, too, so that his deadpan has majesty. Always an inventive clown—in everything from sitcoms to Shakespeare to "The Cotton Club"— Gwynne appears to have his best years ahead of him.

For one thing, "Disorganized Crime" is behind him. Caper pictures have a certain inherent suspense—they build, after all, to a heist but writer-director Jim Kouf lays out too many parallel plot strands, so momentum is continually defused.

The movie does have one amazing piece of plunder: composer David Newman's central motif, which sounds suspiciously like the opening bars of Ennio Morricone's "Untouchables" score. At least someone on "Disorganized Crime" had light fingers.

NEWSDAY, 4/14/89, Part III/p. 3, Mike McGrady

From the moment they step off the train in the small Montana town at the foot of the Rockies, the four new arrivals are noticeably out of place. Neckties. Hangovers. Unruddy complexions. Moreover, each of the visitors seems to be carrying a duffel bag that makes loud, clanking sounds when moved. Why have these unsavory types carried mysterious tools into this pristine land of blue skies, green forests, unsophisticated sheriffs and small-town banks holding large sums of money?

You guessed it. The arrivals though strangers to one another, are all veteran thieves invited to Montana by a master criminal (Corbin Bernsen), a widely wanted man who has just been tracked to his hideaway by two of New Jersey's funniest (Ed O'Neill, Daniel Roebuck). In fact, even as his gang is arriving, Bernsen is being arrested, thus leaving the four felons to their own devices, most of them comic.

"Disorganized Crime" is essentially a one-joke movie and the title spells out that joke rather completely. It also might have been called "The Hole in the Head Gang" or "The Gang That Couldn't Rob Banks Straight" or "The Four Stooges Meet the Keystone Kops" or...well, you get the general idea. It's a comic caper, a bumbling contest, a not-altogether unfamiliar tale of law-enforcement snafus, wild chases through the wilderness and rather elaborate efforts to rob a local bank.

Don't be misled by those ads pointing out that "Disorganized Crime" is "from the creators of 'Stakeout.' " While that's true, the creators have swapped hats. Jim Kouf, who wrote

"Stakeout," is both writer *and* director here, while the original director, John Badham, serves as executive producer this time out.

These alterations may explain the change in emphasis. The first film, benefitting from solid work by Richard Dreyfuss and Forest Whitaker, was amusing without ever losing its grip on the real world. Entertaining, yes, but also involving, with the laughter never getting in the way of the suspense.

The criminal caper in "Disorganized Crime" soon takes a back seat to the comedy. All the performances are broad, and much of the humor is physical. Bernsen, temporary escapee from the "L.A. Law" television series, starring in his second film opening in as many weeks (the other was "Major League"), again shows a nice touch. Since his enmeshment with the law keeps him from participating in the robbery he has masterminded, he does what is essentially a solo comic turn—and he pulls it off.

Fred Gwynne's presence is a steadying factor; William Russ as the least reliable gang member, delivers a fair Peter Falk imitation; Ed O'Neill draws laughs as the dumbest of cops. But the most pleasant surprise in the film is the work of Rubén Blades as one of the gang. In each appearance, most recently in "The Milagro Beanfield War," Blades has added nice touches to characters who would otherwise be forgettable.

While "Disorganized Crime" tries to have it both ways—as both comedy and suspense—the real emphasis is on the garnering of bellylaughs. Never have so many grown men, both cops and criminals, fallen down so often and gotten so wet and lost their trousers so frequently. If this thought makes you smile, then "Disorganized Crime" will make you laugh.

Also reviewed in:
NEW YORK TIMES, 4/14/89, p. C17, Caryn James
VARIETY, 4/19-25/89, p. 24
WASHINGTON POST, 4/14/89, p. C7, Rita Kempley

DO THE RIGHT THING

A Universal Pictures release of a 40 Acres and a Mule Filmworks production. *Producer:* Spike Lee. *Director:* Spike Lee. *Screenplay:* Spike Lee. *Director of Photography:* Ernest Dickerson. *Editor:* Barry Alexander Brown. *Music:* Bill Lee. *Music Editor:* Alex Steyermark. *Sound:* Skip Lievsay. *Sound Editor:* Philip Stockton. *Production Designer:* Wynn Thomas. *Set Decorator:* Steve Rosse. *Set Dresser:* Keith Wall. *Special Effects:* Steve Kirshoff. *Costumes:* Ruth Carter. *Make-up:* Matiki Anoff. *Stunt Coordinator:* Eddie Smith. *Running time:* 120 minutes. *MPAA Rating:* R.

CAST: Danny Aiello (Sal); Ossie Davis (Da Mayor); Ruby Dee (Mother Sister); Richard Edson (Vito); Giancarlo Esposito (Buggin Out); Spike Lee (Mookie); Bill Nunn (Radio Raheem); John Turturro (Pino); Paul Benjamin (ML); Frankie Faison (Coconut Sid); Robin Harris (Sweet Dick Willie); Joie Lee (Jade); Miguel Sandoval (Officer Ponte); Rick Aiello (Officer Long); John Savage (Clifton); Samuel L. Jackson (Mister Senor Love Daddy); Rosie Perez (Tina); Roger Guenveur Smith (Smiley); Steve White (Ahmad); Martin Lawrence (Cee); Leonard Thomas (Punchy); Christa Rivers (Ella); Frank Vincent (Charlie); Luis Ramos (Stevie); Richard Habersham (Eddie); Gwen McGee (Louise); Steve Park (Sonny); Ginny Yang (Kim); Sherwin Park (Korean Child); Shawn Elliot (Puerto Rican Ice Man); Diva Osorio (Carmen); Travell Lee Toulson (Hector); Joel Nagle (Sargeant); David E. Weinberg (Plain Clothes Detective).

FILM QUARTERLY, Winter 1989-90, p. 35, Thomas Doherty

Young, gifted, and bankable, Spike Lee is the first black film-maker America has looked at seriously. Forebears there were, but despite the ongoing work of recovery and reclamation—of Oscar Micheaux, of the All-American Newsreels, of all the anonymous workers in a segregated industry—they remain obscure, names known to archivists alone. The spaces opened up by the civil rights movement of the 1960s and the "blaxploitation" cycle of the early 1970s were limited and the few anomalies who squeezed in—Melvin Van Pebbles (*Sweet Sweetback's Baadasssss Song*, 1971) and Gordon Parks *père* (*Shaft*, 1971) and *fils* (*Superfly*, 1972)—soon found their Hollywood dreams deferred. Of the 25 films recently deemed sacrosanct by the Film Preservation Board, only one—Gordon Parks's *The Learning Tree* (1969)—is by a black American, a nod to affirmative action not a mark of aesthetic qualification.

So Lee is different, unprecedented in the history of American film and culture. He makes movies that play in multipled malls, that inspire think pieces in *The New Republic* and *National Review*, that spark serious discussions on *Oprah* and *Nightline*. Most significantly, though, his quick elevation to the ranks of marquee auteur is unquestionably a promotion on merit. The visible skill and manifest originality of his progressively ambitious work silences the whispers of tokenism and special treatment that demean so much black achievement in the post-movement era. On the cover of *American Film*, Lee is suited up in a Dodger uniform, the Jackie Robinson of another American pastime, a pioneer with all the privilege and pressure that comes with crossing frontiers.

In a summer of comicbook superheroes and sequels by-the-numbers, *Do the Right Thing* was the only mainstream release that came within boom-box range of a concept. What's more, it blasted out the one issue that almost never disturbs the American screen, the nature of race relations in American screen, the nature of race relations in America *today*—not a retreat back in time to Jim Crow Mississippi or a displacement in space to the smug antiapartheid politics of, say, *Lethal Weapon II* (the summer blockbuster that, with typical pop-cult schizophrenia, demonizes South African *herrenvolk* at the same time it situates its black lead on a toilet with his trousers at his ankles). Even if *Do the Right Thing* were not accomplished, activist, and acid-tongued, it would stand out as a rebuke to what usually passes for socially conscious cinema as well as to cineastes whose idea of an urgent black and white issue is colorization.

An acute businessman and a passionate advocate, Lee has won a twin victory over what he calls "the cutthroat film industry." Though the name of his production company ("Forty Acres and a Mule") bespeaks the modest aspirations of a sharecropper, he may well end up owning the mansion on the hill. Involving himself in financing, marketing, and promotion, he plays a skillful hand against a stacked deck. He also knows the importance of keeping product in the pipeline. After Columbia botched the distribution of *School Daze*, he quickly cut a deal with Universal for the next project. "It's important I follow up *School Daze* right away," he wrote in the movie journal published with *Do the Right Thing*. "This is crucial, no recent black film-maker has been able to go from film to film like the white boys do."

If Lee's managerial attitude is money-wise, his artistic stance is blood loyal. Refusing to filter black life through a racial prism, to record a dialogue in which whites name the topic and define the terms, he sets his sights at street level and frames his own conversations. As Toni Morrison wrote in *Beloved*, "definitions belong to the definers not the defined." Committed to projecting black experience through its own lens, Lee brings to American cinema a strategy that has animated black literature since the Harlem Renaissance.

It is militant aesthetics that cuts both ways. With whites literally out of the picture, blacks bear a greater burden of blame for their choices, failures, and lives. In his journal, Lee writes that "Black people cannot be held responsible for racism. We are not in that position. We are, and have been, the victims." However, his films consistently refuse to grant any dispensation for victim status. As early as his project for NYU, *Joe's Bed-Stuy Barbershop: We Cut Heads* (1983), the admonition is to look inside, to the souls of black folk, not outside to the support of white folk. Hence the double edge to the numbers racketeer in the film, a black mobster who preaches the gospel of economic self-sufficiency and personal uplift. In seizing control of the local rackets from the Mafia, he has done the right thing—and though a parasite on the community, he is at least *of* the community. Not incidentally, *Joe's Bed-Stuy Barbershop* introduced the Lee wit along with the wisdom. "He just needs direction," says a social worker about one of her young charges. Pointing east, her companion cries, "Rikers Island is that way!"

Lee's first feature film, made on the storied shoestring budget (an hilarious trailer had the director hawking athletic socks on the streets of New York to secure financing), was the feminist *She's Gotta Have It* (1986). A double-barrelled defiance of stereotypes (racial and sexual), it featured a free-spirited siren named Lola Darling getting not only her share of the antecedent but the better of three would-be black knight. Fluid, frank, and really funny, it was also well timed: had it been closer to the epidemic of minority AIDS, it would have missed its moment.

From sex and color Lee moved to class and color in his second film, the underrated *School Daze* (1988), a reworking of the director's own undergraduate years at Morehouse College. Again, the focus was *intra*-racial, the issue the meaning of black brother- (and sister-) hood. It builds to a harrowing climax, an act of willful self-degradation wherein the hotshot sorority sister and a male pledge engage in sex at the behest of the fraternity kingpin. Prostitution is the logical culmination and appropriate metaphor for what the pair has been doing throughout the film: sacrificing personal integrity for social ambition, black identity for white assimilation.

Though hardly a black version of *Animal House*, the film is more noteworthy for its hijinks than highmindedness. Lee's call to student protest paled against his portrait of student life—the dance craze "da butt," the brief vogue for Washington DC's indigenous go-go music, the ritual chants and choral dance steps of the black fraternity system, and, strikingly, the causal expose of the social shadings to pigmentation among the talented tenth. Reversing the color hierarchy of Oscar Micheaux, Lee set the "high yeller" Wannabees against the deep dark "Jigaboos," hypocrisy against authenticity, in a hair-curling musical interlude called "Straight and Nappy."

The alarm bell polemical line ("WAKE UP!") notwithstanding, *School Daze* rang truest as a series of finely drawn character studies. Lee's penchant for extended speechifying never quite managed to smother his generosity of spirit or his insights into private motives. On camera, each voice gets a fair hearing, each character a fair shake. Thus, the antiapartheid organizer Dap Dunlap may be politically correct, but he's also a major pain in the neck; the sharecropper's son Grady is understandably reluctant to jeopardize his chance at a college education to fulfill Dap's agenda; and even the odious frat leader Big Brother Al-might-ty scores a direct hit when he sneers at Dap's naive Garveyism: "Back to Mother Africa, that's bullshit. We're all Black *Americans*. You don't know a goddamn thing 'bout Africa. I'm from *Chi-town*."

Above all, Lee himself is riveting. The hormonal urgency of his performances as Mars Blackmon in *She's Gotta Have It* ("please baby, please baby, please baby, baby, baby, please!") gave way to a wrenching desperation in his portrayal of Half-Pint, the fraternity pledge only too willing to withstand whatever ritual humiliation the BMOCs can conjure. Like Woody Allen, the director's attempts to submerge his acting persona into an ensemble are never quite succcessful: he's always more magnetic than the rest of the crew. He's also more bottled up, tightly wound, pissed off. Unlike Robert Townsend—for a short time, the synchronicity of the timing of *She's Gotta Have It* and *Hollywood Shuffle* paired these two directors who have nothing in common but youth, talent, and color—Lee has an edge, a bitterness, one that probably owes as much to height as color.

As with the blaxploitation cycle, part of the appeal of Lee's films is pure ethnography: his people and stories are simply not accorded a celluoid rendering anywhere else. Hollywood has absolutely no idea what these folks are about. Coppola and Scorsese know the Italians, Allen and Brooks the Jews, Spielberg and Hughes the whitebread 'burbs, but no brandname director has inside-dopster access to the vernacular, manners, and values of black America, still less the black underclass. Lee—a product of the black middle class to be sure—is as close as mainstream American cinema is likely to get.

In *Do the Right Thing* the director crossed the color line. On the hottest day of the summer, black subculture rubs against white culture and ignites a conflagration that burns them both. Set on the streets of Brooklyn's Bedford-Stuyvesant, the main locus of activity is Sal's Famous Pizzeria, a hangout that serves up hot slices and heated dialogue, cheese being extra. Sal (Danny Aiello), the proprietor, is a crusty small businessman who employs his two rather dimwitted sons, the bigot Pino (John Turturro) and the befuddled Vito (Richard Edson), and a shiftless deliveryman, Mookie (Lee). Outside the pizzeria—on stoops, sidewalks, in sweltering apartments—a parade of characters mingle in a sun-drenched mosaic of tracking shots and angular compositions: the expository d.j. with the nonstop patter, Mister Señor Love Daddy (Sam Jackson), three Corner men doing the dozens and acting as Greek chorus (Paul Benjamin, Robin Harris, and Frankie Faison), the self-styled "Da Mayor" (Ossie Davis), the watchful matriarch Mother Sister (Ruby Dee), the glaring agitator Buggin' Out (Giancarlo Esposito), the boom box-toting Radio Raheem (Bill Nunn), a Mom and Pop pair of Korean grocers (Steve Park and Ginny Yang), and the brain-addled Smiley (Roger Guenveur Smith) waving the famous photo of Martin Luther King and Malcolm X, shaking hands and forcing smiles.

The title sequence is a showcase for the editing skills of Barry Alexander Brown and the feverish choreography of Rosie Perez (who doubles as Mookie's long-suffering girlfriend Tina). In three different outfits, she's quick-cut punching out an athletic hip-hop to Public Enemy's "Fight the Power." Dreamy pull back, long takes, and off-kilter close-ups (Lee calls them "Chinese angles" after the awed, skewed gaze of the kung fu films) define the directorial style; the color scheme is steamy yellow and dull red, a cinematographic slow burn conjuring the equatorial oppression of summer in the city. Location shoot notwithstanding, this feels like a soundstage nighborhood, clean, drug-free, secure. Like Sam Goldwyn in *Dead End*, Lee removes the unsightly refuse from his ghetto street. Still, neither authorial control nor commercial success has dulled Lee's street reflexes. The vertiginous tight close-up of Buggin Out after a hapless Celtics fan (John Savage) scuffs his Air-Jos is a sidewalk vignette accessible only to the kind of director who still personally scouts his locations on bicycle. Her remains as fluent in street patois as film grammar.

Like most socially conscious cinema, the film is at its worst when it tries hardest to articulate its Meaning. A race-conscious exchange between Mookie and Pino plays like an instructive afternoon special on PBS. In sports, movies, and music, the Italian's subconscious is as colonized by black American performers (Magic Johnson, Eddie Murphy, and Prince) as his conscious is poisoned by racism. The rhetorical premediation with which Mookie sets up Pino is plausible; the ability of this racist working-class Italian to quote verbatim the words of Louis Farrakhan is not. Tellingly, the film's falsest moments come at the limits of Lee's own iconoclasm. Jesse Jackson (whose New York primary ads Lee directed) and "Minister Farrakhan" (whose personal bodyguards provided security for the location shoot) are sacred figures, beyond satire. Lee exults in stinging the brothers over style—announcing the torrid weather forecast, Mister Señor Love Daddy issues a "jerry curl alert," and Buggin Out gets what may be the single best shot in a screenplay loaded with them when one of the Corner Men tells him to "boycott that goddamn barber that fucked up your hair"—but over some things he is not willing to break ranks. In the interest of racial solidarity, Lee sometimes puts his brain on hold: a scrawled injunction in graffiti—"Tawana Told the Truth"—is displayed conspicuously and unironically when Mookie warns his sister Jade (Joie Lee) to stay away from what he does not see as the innocent paternal attentions of Sal.

Still, it is a measure of the triumph of the intuitive over the ideological that the humanism of the old pros, not the militancy of the young toughs, attracts the deepest affections of both Lee and the audience. Backed by a Showboat-era musical motif, Ossie Davis's "Da Mayor" presides with dignity over his sidewalk community—and commands every sequence he occupies. Likewise, Danny Aiello's warmth in two key "character-building" scenes—a moving conversation with his son explaining his pride in feeding pizza to the community's kids and the smitten welcome he gives to the beautiful Jade—lends Sal a full dimension of personality deined Buggin Out, Radio Raheem, or Mookie. On this point, St. Clair Bourne's documentary record of the location shoot, Making Do the Right Thing (1989), offers an intriguing glimpse into the way an actor can overwhelm an auteur. In a discussion about Sal's character, Lee declares flatly that he thinks Sal is racist. Aiello disagrees—and on the screen if not in the screenplay his portrayal wins the argument.

But always simmering on, not below, the surface of the heart-warming moments provided by Da Mayor, Mother Sister, and Sal, is the white heat of racism. The interethnic, interracial animosity explodes in a montage of face-front slurs—blacks slam Italians, Italians slam blacks, Latins slam Koreans, whites slam Latins, Koreans slam Jews—that serve as warm-ups for the ultimate bonfire. The immediate kindling is Buggin Out's presumptuous call for Sal to add a "brother" to the portraits on his American-Italian Wall of Fame, but the spark that sets off the community is Radio Raheem's stadium-wattage sound system.

As an Ur-symbol of interracial animosity and class style wars, the boom box is a perfect radiator for black anger and white noise (and vice versa). Next to semi-automatic weaponry, the ghetto blaster is the easiest way for the underclass to exact vengeance and aggression on an unwary bourgeois. In New York, Boston, Chicago—any metropolis with public transportation—a black youth strolling onto a subway car with his personal, multidecibel sound track sends up red-alert signals and draws out palpable racial vibes. An urban commonplace, it has become something of a mass-media leitmotif. In The Survivors (1983), Robin Williams comically counsels Walter Matthau to aim for a black teenager's boom box because without music "they lose the will to fight"; in Star Trek IV (1986), Spock silences an obnoxious punk rocker with a Vulcan pinch; and, in the most vivid exposure of the racial undertones of the musical overmix, a commercial for the NY yellow pages features a boom box blaring rap music as a mild accountant type methodically opens his briefcase, assembles a sledgehammer, and pounds the offending black box into scrap. Lee—who knows his public transportation as well as his Public Enemy—is the only director capable of shouldering the boom box from the other side of the speakers.

Powered by 20 "D" batteries, Radio Raheem makes his entry to the beat-machine blare of rap music, specifically the tough agit-rap of Public Enemy. Like every other musical subgenre from the Delta blues to downtown disco, rap has been neatly contained and regrooved by the entertainment conglomerates it originally arose in opposition to. Not all rap groups, however, have been domesticated by ad jingles or heavy rotation on MTV. Public Enemy—currently in disarray over the anti-Semitic tirades of its "Minister of Information"—is not politically engaged in the approved I-ain't-gonna-play-Sun-City mold; these guys are authentically bad in the Webster Dictionary sense. To pressure cooker backbeats they spew out incendiary lyrics less shocking for their obscenity than for their casual blasphemy of the most sacred icons of American culture ("Elivs was a hero to most/but he never meant shit to me/you see/ straight out racist/the sucker was/simple and plain/motherfucker! ain't John Wayne").

Egged on by Buggin Out, Radio Raheem turns up the volume on Sal and Sal explodes in apoplectic rage, pounding the radio to scrap with a baseball bat. Radio Raheem lunges for Sal's throat and all hell breaks loose. The established rhythm of slow tracking shots and extended takes explodes in a cacophony of violent noise and quick-cut action. The riot pours out into the street, the cops arrive and strangle Radio Raheem to death in what Lee describes as "the infamous Michael Stewart chokehold." Here the casting of Nunn—a man of imposing build, whose enraged character has just been forcibly removed from a middle-aged man's throat, who is struggling with manic frenzy—may have worked against the demonization of the cops. Also, the killing scene itself is poorly rendered cinematically: the choke-hold seems too brief and unlikely to inflict death. Regardless, the crowd sees the death as a summary execution. With calm deliberation, Mookie— heretofore a shiftless worker and an absent father, whose girlfriend has to order a pizza to get him to come by and visit his son—tosses a garbage can through Sal's window and sets off the fire this time. The community becomes a wailing, destructive mob and Sal watches helplessly as the flames engulf his life's work.

After the epochal firebombing of the pizzeria, a brief coda is careful to exculpate Mookie and the citizenry from guilt and thus prevent Sal from becoming a martyr to misdirected black rage— we are assured that the insurance will recoup his loss. The same equivocation motivates the closing credit crawl that pairs dueling statements from Martin Luther King and Malcolm X on What Is To Be Done. King's sentiment is idealistic and Gandhian, Malcolm's is pragmatic and Jeffersonian—and totally noncontroversial, simply according to the governed that right to withdraw consent from oppressive authority and take up arms. Like Smiley peddling his grainy photo, like Radio Raheem's own imitation of Robert Mitchum's love-hate preaching from *Night of the Hunter*, Lee's two-roads-diverge strategy unifies two main lines of the civil rights movement and puts side by side two men who had little use for one another. It also sidesteps the meaning of the imperative title. As vague on causation as solution, the director seems really certain only about one mitigating factor—the weather.

Lee has sneered at a mass (not just white) audience upset because *Do the Right Thing* didn't conclude with Mookie and Sal joining arms to sing "We Are the World." But the wider cultural matrix around the movie—the ancillary marketing (book, T-shirts, CDS), public relations (Lee has become a designated media spokesman for black America), and, one assumes, Academy Award recognition—offers more hope for reconciliation and progress than the fiery climax. (By the way, the album jacket for the sound track actually *does* feature Sal and Mookie arm and arm.) On a recent NBC special on Race in America, Lee declaimed against the "pie in the sky" ethos of America that promises reward for hard work and initiative. "Your own example disproves your point," Boston University president John Silber snapped at him. Just as Tracy Chapman can no longer sing "Mountain o' Things" with a straight face, this authentic success story and uneasy Positive Role Model is going to find it increasingly difficult to inveigh against racist limitations. The soothing, smothering embrace of American culture may yet blunt the sharpness of Spike Lee and modulate the volume on his dissonant rap.

FILMS IN REVIEW, 10/89, p. 484, Edmond Grant

One of the most unusual and thought provoking comedies in recent years, *Do the Right Thing* has a concluding segment that works on such an overpowering emotional level that it all but eclipses everything that has gone before it. However, to give the film its due, let us put aside for a moment the issues raised by its very disturbing and somewhat heavy handed finale, and concentrate instead on director-producer-star Spike Lee's unique approach, which successfully elicits laughter while depicting some terribly tense situations.

The setting for the film is an idealized version of the multiracial community of New York's Bedford-Stuyvesant, a melting pot microcosm that's just at the point of boiling over. Mookie (Lee), our hero of sorts, is a laid back young Black man who delivers pizza for Sal, a middle-aged Italian-American (played with a great amount of depth by Danny Aiello) who proudly boasts that the Black community of Bed-Stuy have grown up eating his pizza. Also figuring heavily in the ensuing drama are Sal's two sons, Pino and Vito (John Turturro and Richard Edson), who take varying positions regarding their customers: Radio Raheem (Bill Nunn), an imposing figure whose blasting boom-box precipitates most of the trouble; Buggin Out (Giancarlo Esposito), a comic figure who later turns out to be deadly serious; and the only two level-minded characters, Da Mayor, a chivalrous old drunkard who utters the eponymous piece of advice (played to perfection by Ossie Davis); and Mookie's sister Jade (played by Spike's real life sister, Joie Lee).

Lee chronicles the interaction between these characters on the hottest day of the summer, the day that Raheem and Buggin Out decide it is imperative that pictures of noted Black celebrities be added to Sal's "Wall of Fame" in the pizzeria, a collection of framed portraits of Italian-American notables. This absurd demand, when combined with Sal's obstinate refusal, leads up to the much talked about finale wherein Sal's pizzeria is torched and decimated by the neighborhood Blacks in response to the killing of Raheem by a White police officer.

Given all this, it seems almost impossible to believe that *Do The Right Thing* could be a comedy. And yet it is, for most of its length, thanks to Lee's fine ear for ethnic nonsense dialogue, whether it be African-American or Italian-American in origin, Mookie, Buggin Out, and a Greek chorus of elderly Black men on a street corner communicate in their own distinctive way, as do Sal and his sons; it's the near-surreal, but always authentic, quality of these exchanges that provides the first sign of Lee's unstated but strongly felt message which indicates that, despite their cloaked loathing for each other, these characters are all extremely alike.

The second factor contributing to the film's vibrant tone is the refreshingly kinetic camerawork devised by Lee and cinematograper Ernest Dickerson. Visually, Lee's films have much in common with the best of Godard and Scorsese; the camera work and editing move and breathe along with the characters, while always clearly drawing attention to the director's sense of enthusiasm and eagerness for visual experimentation. One particular sequence here encapsulates Lee's experimental urges and his perceptive comic approach: the instant where we leave temporarily the narrative after a heated exchange between Mookie and Pino, and are suddenly confronted with Pino, Mookie, and then a host of other ethnic "types" from the film, each addressing the camera in single shots spewing out a laundry list of choice racial epithets. Therefore, illustrating Lee's point, that everyone in the neighborhood has some kind of axe to grind, and someone they're willing to blame their troubles on. At first, the hate-filled epithets make the average viewer cringe, but as it becomes clear that Lee's is going to allow everyone his say, the scene increases in hilarity. The characters' words, which could be seen as threatening and inflammatory, instead come across as facile and ridiculous.

This is Lee at his best, making a point while he entertains. Certain moments in the film conspicuously avoid this level of subtlety, such as the instant where Mookie and his sister go off-camera and it lingers on a wall where the graffiti "Tawana told the Truth" is prominently displayed. At a moment like this, or the later one where the characters participating in the riot at Sal's call out the names of real life Black victims of police brutality, the film stops being informative and analytical, and instead becomes uncomfortably didactic, a shrewd piece of pop propaganda, reminiscent of Godard's more strident Marxist films.

Lee's finely honed characterizations seem to wither in the heat of the moment—witness the awkwardly scripted final exchange between Sal and Mookie after the fiery debacle in which Mookie dismisses the destruction with the immediate mention of the insurance payments Sal will be receiving, and Sal responds with equal militance by tossing some balled up hundred dollar bills at Mookie's chest. This scene purports to show that "life goes on" between the races, but neglects to let the humanity of either character seep through the dialogue, as it had previously.

In essence, the riot scene shows most of the characters at their worst and Spike the director at his weakest. For the leap from the initial absurdity of the "Wall of Fame" situation to the final explosive riot doesn't come across clearly. One senses in the earlier stages of the film that something is bound to erupt, but the gravity with which Lee surrounds the incident seems to undercut the film's earlier direction, wherein *all* of the characters are seen as foolishly disposed towards being narrow minded. Suddenly and irrevocably with the death of Raheem, we are thrown into a situation where one side is seen as "right" and the other as "wrong."

And setting aside the N.Y.C. Police force, who certainly are not depicted in any three dimensional manner, it's important to make note of the other group discriminated against in this film, which protests the difficulty of racial harmony in current society: the Koreans, represented by the couple who own the local deli. This man and woman are grudgingly accepted by the rioting

Blacks as being similarly disadvantaged in not being white and privileged, which is ironic in light of the fact that Lee has up to this point used them as the butt of jokes—primarily jokes about their inability to understand their English customers. In this light, the final concession that they, too, are human beings does not wash away the earlier stereotyping.

And yet, despite all the aforementioned difficulties, it still must be stressed that the troublesome part of the film (except if you're Korean or a N.Y.C. police officer) only comprises about a quarter of its length. *Do The Right Thing* is a complex work, one that's ripe with conflicts, humor, and some inevitable contradictions. At points a joy to watch, at others a demanding viewing experience, it consistently challenges its audience to discuss the issues it's focusing on.

LOS ANGELES TIMES, 6/30/89, Calendar/p. 1, Sheila Benson

Under the opening credits of "Do the Right Thing," Tina (Rosie Perez), a young, great-looking honey blond in satin boxing trunks and a halter top, punches out a message of sexual aggressiveness steamy enough and serious enough to melt the grommets in your Air Jordans.

Working to the song "Fight the Power," she pouts, jabs, double-punches and, for a little emphasis, puts her boxing gloves behind her head and tosses off a series of hip thrusts vicious enough to pop contact lenses in the back row.

She's sexy and she's funny about it. She is also writer-director-producer Spike Lee's way of putting us on warning: People are mad here. Watch out.

The deliberate stylization of her number, shot against rear projections of Brooklyn streets and brownstones, and its electrifying intensity says something else: This is a director working with absolute assurance and power. This stylization carries over to the body of the film; Lee has cleared out his scene of anything extraneous (including, as many have already noted, drugs), the better to concentrate on the larger issue at hand, which is racism. That would seem to be his choice to make.

Spike Lee has never lacked confidence. "She's Got to Have It" and "School Daze" radiated a cheeky bravado that sometimes did and sometimes didn't quite cover weak performances or shaky artistic choices. But the leap he has made here—as a writer; working with his actors, and directing a molten flow of action—is phenomenal. "Do the Right Thing" announces the coming-of-age of an important film maker with something urgent and uncomfortable to say.

Lee's intent is no less than a behind-the-scenes guide to a racial conflagration; an epic portrait on a block-square scale, one small neighborhood in Brooklyn's Bedford-Stuyvesant area. If Lee's vehicle is humor—quick, light, knowing, even loving—it's a humor he uses cathartically.

On the hottest day of a hot summer and against this faintly surreal backdrop, which seems to intensify the furnace-like glow of the day, Lee has created at least four ages of this Bed-Stuy community. There are the Elders, Ossie Davis' proud, alcoholic "Mayor" and Ruby Dee's Mother Sister, unrelated but mother and father figures to much of the neighborhood. (Lee's use of this magnificent pair of director-actors can also be seen as an homage to a great earlier generation of black film making.)

Next are the three Corner Men, perennial onlookers somewhere in their 50s, one of whom (rumbling comedian Robin Harris) rejoices in the name "Sweet Dick Willie." Jobless but never opinionless, these three wrangling sideline quarterbacks, who pass around some of the movie's most pungent lines, form a sort of hilarious chorus.

Then there are the young men, the hysterically confrontational Buggin Out (Giancarlo Esposito), and the silent giant Radio Raheem (Bill Nunn) with his maddening boom box. There is a second chorus of youngsters, four watchful teen-agers whom Lee's script calls The Posse, and a passel of kids, from Tina's baby to an 8-year-old boy, crucial to the action.

And there are three daily commuters. When Sal (Danny Aiello, working with masterly shading and complexity) built Sal's Famous Pizzeria some 25 years ago, this was an Italian neighborhood. Now it's mainly black, with some Latino families such as Tina's; Sal's Famous is a landmark, and Sal and his sons Pino (John Turturro) and Vito (Richard Edson) drive in to work every day from all-Italian Brownsville.

Folding in and out of the action is Mookie, pizza-deliverer to the neighborhood, father of Tina's baby son, watchful, likable but not admirable. He's too cantankerous and too flaky for that, living week to week, running out on his obligations to Tina and their son, rooming for free with his sister Jade (Lee's actual sister, Joie). However, Mookie is played by Lee himself, and by the force of Lee's personality he becomes someone we care about. It makes his part in the film's last quarter hour both painful and deeply disturbing.

Yet it touches on the film's prickly core. With the possible exception of Sal's purely racist son Pino and an overzealous New York cop with a fatally bad attitude, the film has no clear-cut villains. It has flawed, complex human beings, almost none of whom do the right thing all the time. Lee is not advocating violence, nor does his masterly cameraman, Ernest Dickerson, revel in it cinematographically (not the way "Mississippi Burning" did). Mother Sister's dreadful scream in the glow of her neighborhood in flames is a sound from the heart of the film makers.

What Lee *is* showing is a series of abrasive incidents, trivial by themselves that, combined with soaring heat and in a climate of oppressiveness, finally ignite. In fact, Lee suggests that the actual point from which the fury builds is petty, if not ridiculous: Buggin Out's demands that Sal put a few black faces up there with Sinatra, Pacino, DeNiro and DiMaggio in the pizzeria's fly-specked, Italian-American wall of fame. And Lee makes it clear that Buggin Out's proposed boycott gets no support anywhere in the community until, by accident, he hooks up with the one person nursing a grudge against Sal.

Lee's point is that, like the Howard Beach tragedy in New York or the case of Vincent Chin in Detroit, what follows comes from a mixture of fear, sociology, economics and feelings buried so deep that those who carry them would deny they exist.

And in that context, the two quotations Lee has chosen to close his film—lines from Martin Luther King on the immorality of violence, others from Malcolm X describing violence in self-defense as intelligence—hang there, reflecting choices to ponder.

As he has in three past films, Spike Lee is commanding people to wake up—not only the black community but all of us—before we are over the brink. Since its Cannes unveiling, "Do the Right Thing" (MPAA-rated R for language) has stirred up impassioned debate everywhere; it would seem the greatest compliment that could be paid a stunning entertainment.

MONTHLY FILM BULLETIN, 7/89, p. 202, Tom Milne

It's a hot day and getting hotter when Sal arrives to open up his pizza parlour, an Italo-American enclave in New York's predominantly black/Puerto Rican neighbourhood of Bedford-Stuyvesant, more or less reluctantly assisted by his sons Pino and Vito, and his black delivery boy Mookie. Established there for twenty years, Sal feels like a benevolent local patriarch, and refuses to listen when Pino urges him to sell up and return to their own kind. Pino takes out his frustration on Vito; the easygoing Vito turns to Mookie for advice on how to stand up for himself; and Mookie, lodging on sufferance at his sister Jade's place, ponders the problem of money for an apartment for himself, his Puerto Rican girlfriend Tina, and their baby. Sticking by his ethnic pride, Sal refuses to make any changes when Buggin' Out, the neighbourhood's loud-mouth exponent of Black Awareness, demands that the pictures of famous Italo-Americans on the walls be replaced by famous blacks. Trying to drum up support for a boycott of Sal's place, Buggin' Out is laughed at. But tempers, suffering in the heat, are frayed by a number of incidents: in particular, Radio Raheem, who walks around playing the same Black Power number at full blast on his radio cassette, is resentful at being told to turn it down when he comes in for a pizza; and Mookie, rightly or wrongly suspecting that Sal is making a play for his sister, exchanges heated words with his boss. Late that night, tempers finally explode when Radio Raheem again walks in playing his music; Sal smashes the radio; and a fight ensues which escalates—after cops intervene, and one contrives to strangle Radio Raheem in subduing him—into a riot. This ends, as Koreans who have just opened a delicatessen across the road nervously watch, with the pizza parlour being burned to the ground by a rampaging mob.

Shrugging off the mainstream miscalculations of *School Daze*, Spike Lee here returns to a variation, more pointillist than Brechtian, on the method of *She's Gotta Have It*. The above synopsis is at best incomplete, at worst misleading, since it extracts a plot where the film simply strings incidents like beads on a thread of combustible racial tension. At its centre is the pizza parlour's delivery boy Mookie (played by Lee himself, and obviously to some extent representative of his own position), a black who has established a *modus vivendi* with the white world. Secure enough to return barb for barb when dealing with Pino's embryonic racism (one very funny scene has him reduce Pino to desperate casuistry in justifying his fan worship of Prince and Eddie Murphy: "They're not *black*, they're *more* than black"), he is nevertheless kept constantly and uncomfortably aware, by the climate of the street as much as anything else, that he is clinging precariously to coat tails.

Sharing centre stage, the other half of the racial equation, is Sal the Italo-American, a paterfamilias who has created his world and finds it well. A man of goodwill, he benignly masks his handout of a dollar to the local drunk as a fee for nominally sweeping out each day; he angrily berates his son for shooing away the tongue-tied retard who hangs around the place, importunately hawking a dog-eared collection of postcard photographs (of black personalities); and he basks in a warm glow of contented achievement as he contemplates this neighbourhood that he has made his own, this family that he has fed and nurtured through the sweat of his brow. Is his attitude genuinely benevolent or simply patronising, the contentment of the master able to point to a community of happy, wellfed, profit-bearing slaves? Is he, as Mookie thinks, working up to a seduction of his sister, or simply delighted at the chance reunion with someone he watched grow up as a child? It's impossible to tell, but Lee's point is that, in *this* context, it's easy to assume the worst. Mookie's sensibilities, one suspects, wouldn't have been half so ruffled had he suspected his sister of taking up with a *black* widower.

The message is nothing new: people doing what seems, rather than is, the right thing. As Spike Lee puts it, "If Radio Raheem had turned down his radio, nothing would have happened. If Sal had put up a black person's picture on his Wall of Fame, there wouldn't have been any static". Beyond that, however, in evoking the street life of the Bed-Stuy neighbourhood, Lee vividly illustrates the heavy residue of static in the air, just waiting for the right amount of friction to generate a lethal charge of electricity. He shot the film on location in Bedford-Stuyvesant (taking over a short block on Stuyvesant Avenue), with a lick or two of paint and crafty set decoration turning reality into a wonderfully formalised stage setting, within which the characters' movements are choreographed with the formality of a dance. As the fool's parade goes by—Radio Raheem blasting all other sources of music into submission with ceaseless replays of his favourite number (Public Enemy's "Fight the Power"); black teenagers needling a white yuppie houseowner who asserts his right to *choose* where to live; a passing white motorist stopping to holler blue murder because black kids cooling off under the street hydrant splash his car—a chorus of three middle-aged black men, clearly out of work and not uncontent to be so, pass idle comment. For all the world like gentlemen of leisure lolling on a Riviera café terrace (actually it's just a table and beach umbrella, set against a red brick wall on a disused segment of pavement), they are not entirely partisan in their attack. Only a year off the boat, one grumbles about the new Korean delicatessen, and already they've got their own business. Must be because we're black, the second concurs. All excuses, the third snaps, "you'll just go on sittin' ".

The one element never quite comfortably integrated involves Ruby Dee as a sternly disapproving matriarch watching over the street from her porch, and Ossie Davis as the disreputable local drunk, forever harking back to the heroic struggles of the old days and trying to win favour in her eyes (he finally does so by saving a child from being run over). Evidently intended to evoke the persistence of outmoded but ingrained Uncle Tom attitudes, they in fact come over as sharing an irrelevant romantic sub-plot. Otherwise, the film is funny, graceful, and paradoxically charming even in its more abrasive moments, like the one where Mookie runs into Radio Raheem and stops to admire his new rings, in effect massive knuckle-dusters, spelling out "Love" and "Hate". "The story of life is this", says Raheem, echoing Mitchum's Preacher Powell as he demonstrates how the fingers intertwine, "One is always fightin' the other".

NEW LEADER, 9/18/89, p. 21, John Morrone

In *Do the Right Thing* Spike Lee returns to the setting of his 1983 short feature, *Joe's Bed-Stuy Barbershop: We Cut Heads*, and offers a stylized look at 24 hours in the life of an impoverished inner-city neighborhood. His slice of Brooklyn's Bedford-Stuyevsant—once an Italian community, now predominantly black and Hispanic—is a raucous, fibrillating urban machine whose many moving parts are its underclass inhabitants constantly caroming off each other. The center of this turbulence is the local pizzeria, run by the conspicuously white Sal and his two sons from the not-too-distant Italian enclave of Bensonhurst.

Music—rhythm-and-blues, rap, reggae, soul—wakes the people of this neighborhood every hot summer morning and, punctuated by the endless patter of DJ Mister Señor Love Daddy, keeps them company as they make their way through a day of fights, chill-outs, domestic fracases, idle street gossip, and spells of dozing. Their voices raised in contrapuntal chatter, what comes most naturally to these folks is mouthing off at each other, to the beat of music, music, music.

Do the Right Thing is, in fact, a kind of pulsing fugue; with some qualification it could be called a musical featuring extended dialogue and one riot. Even that riot, the cause of much of the controversy surrounding the film, does not disrupt the production's formal orderliness. While the fictional lives Lee has created are distinct, crisp and complementary, the street (the corner of

Lexington and Stuyvesant Avenue, to be exact) is the real main character and unifying element of the plot. It is not too difficult to imagine *Do the Right Thing* adapted for the stage, the members of Lee's ensemble acting out their frustrations within a big unit set bristling with tenement tensions. *Street Scene*, though distant, is a direct antecedent. More recent ones are the performance works by Ntozake Shange and Vinnette Carroll that fuse the call-and-response cadences of traditional gospel conventions with the rhythms of contemporary black poetry. The cast of Lee's drama actually plays it as if the script were blank verse set to an inner rap beat that regularly bursts through to the surface.

Most movies by independent film-makers have an offbeat quality and Lee retains much of the flip, seemingly improvisational tone of maverick works (including his own *She's Gotta Have It*). Yet this latest offering is deeply indebted to traditional storytelling. Its frame of time and place has a classical unity, and its jigsaw-puzzle precision is almost Hitchcockian.

Small details pile up and weave the film's dense texture. The occasionally deserved but mostly undeserved insults received by Mookie, the pizza delivery boy (portrayed by Lee himself), are refractions of the film's prismatic point of view. Half supported by his flashy, no-nonsense sister Jade (played by real-life sister Joie Lee), he is called a bum by his Hispanic girlfriend Tina (Rose Perez), who has borne his son, nudged and needled by Sal (Danny Aiello) the *pizzero*, who would like to get a little work out of him, and repeatedly made a scapegoat by Sal's older son Pino (John Turturro), who resents his obligations to his father, the restaurant and Bed-Stuy with a virulent racist rage.

If Mookie is not particularly attached to Sal or his pizza, the neighborhood is. ("They grew up on my food," says Sal, tired but still proud after 25 years on the same block, behind the same storefront). Nevertheless, on this most sweltering Saturday an argument over a trivial matter erupts in Sal's Famous Pizzeria that will lead to the day's violent climax. A complaint by Buggin' Out (Giancarlo Esposito), a vain big-month, about paying more for extra cheese quickly escalates into a gripe over the absence of "brothers" on Sal's "Wall of Fame." Frank Sinatra and Sophia Loren are displayed, he protests, but no Michael Jackson, no Jesse Jackson.

At first, Buggin' Out's call to boycott Sal's is ignored by the people in the street. It gains supporting muscle when he joins up with Smiley (Roger Guenveur Smith), the area half-wit who hawks photos to passersby of Malcolm X and Martin Luther King, and Radio Raheem (Bill Nunn), the belligerent carrier of a boombox equal in size to the chip on his shoulder. The chip has been made even heavier by Sal's refusal to serve him unless he keeps the deafening noise turned off.

Here is where Lee really pours on the heat, making everything that subsequently happens foreshadow the slugout between Sal and Raheem. That vicious fight, when it finally occurs, becomes a free-for-all involving Sal, his sons and an angry mob, which brings the mostly white and openly hostile police to the scene. Whether inadvertently or not, they strangle Raheem while restraining him.

The large crowd of onlookers and the participants in the brawl are stunned. Mookie, until now the cooling voice of mediation, very calmly and deliberately seizes a garbage can and (after politely removing the plastic bag inside) heaves it through Sal's large plate-glass window. At this extended floating moment, with the camera focused expectantly on Sal, one feels further violence can be avoided if he says something conciliatory, echoing the neighborhood's outrage over Raheem's death. But Sal's world has been turned upside down; he has been beaten up and suddenly repulsed by the people who for half his life had coexisted with him in peace. He says nothing. Then—a riot and the pizzeria is wrecked. Gratified by the carnage, Smiley pins the pictures of Malcolm X and Dr. King to the coveted wall.

In casting himself as Mookie, Lee has taken an enormous risk. His performance is so vivid that it is hard not to assume he agrees with his character that the destruction of Sal's store is the symbolically apt response (the "right thing") to whites' abuse of blacks. But could Lee in good conscience have put himself in the role of anyone other than the film's most controversial figure? It seems to be his way of emphasizing his responsibility for a movie that starkly represents a large spectrum of racial, ethnic and religious hatred.

Indeed, many whites have perceived *Do the Right Thing* as an endorsement of the kind of "justified" violence advocated by Malcolm X. At the same time, a number of blacks have protested the absence of any positive images of black inner-city dwellers. Both of these responses, albeit unsurprising, I think ultimately miss the film's balance and detachment, have failed to catch its intimation of hope beneath all the cruel bigotry.

Ironically, the movie does have a serious flaw that has been overlooked in the heated debate it has stirred. Lee's portrayal of the two Korean greengrocers who have a store across the street from Sal's is as unfortunate as the attitudes he wants to expose. Prejudice against Koreans is frequently as comfortably tolerated as the yuppie novel caricatures of feckless Gulf State millionaires hobnobbing on Rodeo Drive. Sadly, Lee presents this Asian ehtnic group as a cultural imponderable, the "other" whose special trouble with English, astonishing commercial enterprise, unflagging tenacity, etc. arouse suspicion and resentment.

In one of *Do the Right Thing*'s funniest scenes, characters representing most of the city's main ethnic and racial groups face the camera and, one at a time, attack each other by spitting out the vilest slurs imaginable. It is an orgiastic moment of absurd let-it-all-hang-out hostility intended to defuse the audience's own anger, artfully provoked during the film's first half. At that Lee succeeds. We laugh nervously, but laugh nevertheless at ridiculous expressions like "spearchucker," "slanty-eyes," "garlic breath," "mañana-man," and so on. The Korean comes last, spewing anti-Semitic insults. But there are no Jews in the movie; the attack has no reference point. This underscores how shallowly drawn the Korean grocer and his wife are, and that Lee did not construct a personality for them because he naturally assumed their real-life counterparts lacked one.

So Spike Lee is prone to racism, too. One could argue that this lapse in the script appropriately reflects one of the film's main themes: When pushed we're all of us just a little prejudiced. To his credit, Lee keeps stressing the point that such harmful attitudes come in unexpected varieties. Mookie, for example, is not pleased that Tina's mother, who considers him a bum, rants at him in Spanish as she babysits her grandchild. "Speak English!" he shouts, "I want my son to learn English. It's bad enough his name is Hector." White viewers are reminded that an affair between a black and a Hispanic is also interracial.

Later, Mookie is none too thrilled by the attention Sal pays Jade, the comeliest girl on the block, when she saunters in for a slice. Is Sal being courtly or seductive? There is no question about it for Mookie, whose face shows a rage usually associated in the popular mind with the reaction of white men who notice "their" women being eyed by blacks. At such moments Lee enters regions films rarely approach.

In a manner that reminds one of John Sayles, another iconoclast who tells unfashionable truths about controversial issues, Lee scorns the achingly earnest style of features like *Mississippi Burning* and television's "social problem" packages. Those efforts, usually labeled "docudramas," have unfortunately set the standard for the cinematic treatment of troubling subjects. Consequently, commercial filmmakers feel compelled to ignore almost everything that does not somehow uplift, entertain or blandly inform. Recall how television's recent *Roe vs. Wade* fretted so anxiously over equal-time representation that you might have thought it was a dramatization of FCC guidelines. This kind of "neutrality," of course, is no more than a strategy for covering one's behind.

Spike Lee, unafraid of losing sponsors, does not play this game. *Do the Right Thing* offers no apologies for its savage polyphony of voices. Even I was at first taken aback by the film's aggressive rap theme song, "Fight the Power," performed by Public Enemy and danced by Rosie Perez under the credits. No getting around it—it's nasty. But like the film it graphically lays bare the reality of a choice that has long faced poor urban blacks: Fight the powers that be peacefully or with violence. A pair of quotations from Martin Luther King and Malcolm X pointedly appears just before the closing credits.

If anything about *Do the Right Thing* strikes me as utterly perfect, it is the title. For were you to ask 20 different people swept up into the kind of extreme social situation enacted here what should be done, 10 would choose one path and 10 would choose the other. Spike Lee's rich, intense film has the effect of shrewdly holding up a blank slate to the face of racism. He leaves it up to you to write a message of peace. Or to smash the tablet to bits.

NEW YORK, 6/26/89, p. 53, David Denby

In *Do the Right Thing*, filmmaker Spike Lee does the right thing, the wrong thing, and finally everything. This immensely skillful, humane, and richly detailed movie about racism in New York suffers from trying to satisfy everyone—black, white, middle-class, and "street." It's a comedy that ends in tragedy; a spectacle of black victimization by whites and white victimization by blacks; a demonstration of the pointlessness of violence that is also a *celebration* of violence. Confusing? *Do the Right Thing* is going to create an uproar—in part because Lee, a middle-class black hoping to capture the anger of the underclass, is thoroughly mixed up about what he's saying.

Much of the movie, which is set on a single block in Brooklyn's Bedford-Stuyvesant section, is genial and fond-hearted. But Lee, who both writes and directs, lays the groundwork, in many small, sandpapery confrontations between black and white characters, for disaster. The explosion at the end of the movie, an outburst intimate in scale but truly frightening, should divide the audience, leaving some moviegoers angry and vengeful, others sorrowful and chastened. Divided himself, Lee may even be foolish enough to dream, alternately, of increasing black militance and of calming it. But if Spike Lee is a commercial opportunist, he's also playing with dynamite in an urban playground. The response to the movie could get away from him.

After making the lovely erotic comedy *She's Gotta Have It* in 1986, Lee could have pleased a great many moviegoers by cultivating his charming satirical talent in a series of small, fashionable pictures. But instead, two years later he tried something messy and ambitious—*School Daze*, a sort of race-consciousness musical in which groups of dark- and light-skinned blacks at a southern black college danced and sang out their arguments over assimilation. *School Daze* was disorganized and muddled; I found it hard to sit through, yet I admired Lee's courage and also his determination to find some flexible and open-ended form for what he was trying to say. He rejects the stiff earnestness of most politically "engaged" filmmaking. He wants to become—if such a thing is possible—a lyricist of racial tension.

In *Do the Right Thing*, Lee doesn't mount musical numbers, but, allowing for a didactic or sentimental line here or there, the first three quarters of the movie has the jumping vitality and buoyant, light touch of a good musical. The single-block setting recalls the tenement plays and studio-bound movies of the thirties and forties, though this movie was shot on an actual Bed-Stuy street with brownstones and rubble, and features language never heard in those entertainments. Through a long hot day, the neighborhood regulars come out of the background, make a few jokes, blow off steam, then recede. Cinematographer Ernest Dickerson, whose black-and-white work made *She's Gotta Have It* so elegant to look at, shoots this time in bold, bright colors, producing the look of a glaring, reddened summer light. And Spike Lee weaves his anecdotes together in a casual "simultaneous" structure, so that at any one moment we seem to be taking the pulse of the entire neighborhood. All the same, the movie builds inexorably to its climax.

The center of *Do the Right Thing* is a corner store, Sal's Famous Pizzeria, run by Italians who drive in from Bensonhurst in their old Eldorado. Sal (Danny Aiello) is a tough patriarch proud of the business he has built up over the decades and unafraid of the black hostility gathering in the neighborhood. A big, solid man, he feels a rough affection for black people, and not just because they are customers. "These kids *grew up* on my food," he boasts. The imposing, heavy-browed Aiello has blustered his way through some of his movie roles, but this time he gives a full-scaled, emotionally expansive performance; he makes Sal a hot-tempered but generous man who's been through a lot and doesn't panic easily. Sal dominates his two grown sons. The older, Pino (John Turturro), is an Italian tribal racist, venomous, soulless, irrational, a man humiliated by working among "niggers"; his brother, Vito (Richard Edson), has black friends and is ready to accommodate.

Sal and his two sons run a thriving business in a black neighborhood where many people are just barely getting by. Among the loafers and unemployed, there are three middle-aged clowns—the Corner Men—sitting at their post, chairs against a wall, beached, immobile, excoriating one another and themselves with the scandal of their defeat. The great powerhouse Ossie Davis also is on hand to play a philosophical old drunk, "da mayor" (i.e., the neighborhood conciliator), a ponderously sentimental role that only Davis could have saved from embarrassment.

Lee doesn't caricature the whites, and in his treatment of the older black characters he shows an appreciation for rumpled and messed-up people—people who have lost something or failed but still have good words to say. The younger men on the block, however, are stupider—fools, really. Radio Raheem (Bill Nunn), a bruiser with a woodblock face, carries his boom box everywhere, refusing as a matter of pride to turn the thing down; his whole life is his blaster. Buggin Out (Giancarlo Esposito), a yammering, high-pitched advocate of "black consciousness," is obsessed with the pictures of Italians—Frank Sinatra, Al Pacino—on the wall at Sal's. Why can't there be pictures of *blacks?* His voice burns the air like hot electric wires.

These young black men are meant to be infantile, and so is Mookie, played by Lee himself, who delivers Sal's pizzas to the neighborhood, racing around in his Brooklyn Dodgers jersey and shorts. Mookie, who gets along with everybody, cross-polinates the block, visiting, reviving up, carrying information. He's also a minor-league trickster and liar, playing games with his Hispanic grilfriend, Tina (Rosie Perez), who raises his little son and who scorches him with foulmouthed scorn whenever he drops in for a quickie.

Mookie cools her down by running an ice cube all over her body (the camera shares his enjoyment). He's a good-natured man looking for a little pleasure around the edges of his irritation. All the characters live with dissatisfaction; life may not be great for them, but it has its moments. The worst thing is that people get on one another's nerves, though Lee's version of a poor neighborhood is considerably sanitized, without rampaging teenagers, muggers, or crack addicts. The block has its chronicler and troubadour, an FM disc jockey, Mister Señor Love Daddy, who broadcasts from a brownstone facing the street (and who serves the same unifying function as Wolfman Jack in *American Graffiti*), and it has a kind of village idiot, too, a retarded man selling pictures of Martin Luther King Jr. and Malcolm X shaking hands and smiling. Spike Lee wants to put on the screen a black neighborhood that is stable, benign, even organic, like a medieval town. But in 1989, this is a form of false nostalgia (in real life, the film crew cleared out crack dealers so it could shoot the movie).

The heat turns petty grievances into choking rage. In a startling and funny sequence, one character after another (white, black, Korean) lets loose an aria of racial slurs, right into the camera. The slurs are almost quaint, but when Buggin Out, with his pictorial obsession, and Radio Raheem, with his boom box, descend on Sal's, all hell breaks loose. Trivial matters—noisy music, some pictures on a wall—lead to a violent fight. The triviality is Lee's point. By temperament, he is a comic and satirist, and most of these characters are seen as slightly ridiculous. The tragedy in the movie—and the source of its power—is that such silly-ass, affectionately observed people are dying to lay hands on one another. Once the façade of civility collapses, we watch, aghast, as they bite, kick, punch, and strangle.

When some white policemen arrive and kill a black boy, the crowd, enraged, riots, taking revenge on the nearest white property. Rather than attacking the police, the rioters attack a symbolic target, and that part of the movie is hard to justify. Defenders will say this is what happens in the ghetto after a police atrocity, but Lee appears to be endorsing the outcome: His own character, Mookie, starts the riot (unbelievably, I thought) by hurling a garbage can through a window, and as the violence gathers steam it's presented as a form of deliverance; nor does anyone in the community express repentance the next day. Though there's been plenty of police brutality in New York, Spike Lee the writer and director invented this particular crime; he also created the dramatic structure that primes black people to cheer the explosion as an act of revenge. It's his fiction; it's not life.

At the end of the film, Lee runs balancing quotations, the first, from Martin Luther King Jr., attacking violence, and the second, from Malcolm X, praising violence in self-defense as a form of intelligence. But the crowd doesn't commit violence in self-defense, it trashes a neighborhood institution that it has always liked—an absurd, self-defeating act (no one points this out). Only the willfully deluded will take the riot as an attack on the white power structure.

If an artist has made his choices and settled on a coherent point of view, he shouldn't be held responsible, I believe, if parts of his audience misunderstand him. He should be free to be "dangerous." But Lee hasn't worked coherently. The end of this movie is a shambles, and if some audiences go wild, he's partly responsible. Lee wants to rouse people, to "wake them up." But to do what? Those matching quotations are little more than a confession of artistic and moral impotence: My guess is that Spike Lee thinks that violence solves nothing, but he'd like to be counted in the black community as an angry man, a man ready, despite his success, to smash things. The end of the movie is an open embrace of futility.

NEW YORK POST, 6/30/89, p. 23, David Edelstein

That Spike Lee, he sure likes to stir things up. Lee knows how tense things are between the races in New York City and why they're tense; he understands what it's like to feel powerless in one's own society—slighted, oppressed, rendered almost speechless with impotent rage.

The plot of "Do The Right Thing" takes off on that feeling of impotence, but the picture is about power in other, less obvious ways: It's the act of a film maker testing his own power, of a talented provocateur who knows the tenderest spot to wale on.

He has set the film on a block in Bedford-Stuyvesant on the hottest day of the year. We know it's the hottest because people say so, repeatedly, and there's a whiff of apocalypse in the air. The cinematographer, Ernest Dickerson, gives the brownstones a reddish, clay-oven cast; the moving camera views the world at a tilt, in a kind of musky delirium.

The action revolves around Sal's Pizzeria, a white-owned business in a virtually all-black neighborhood. Sal (Danny Aiello) could have left Bed-Stuy when the neighborhood turned black, but this romantic believes in tradition, and he sees himself as sort of a Great White Father—a man who's helping Bed-Stuy's children grow into healthy adults.

In between selling slices (for a whopping $1.50) the Italian argues with his two sons, the belligerent bigot Pino (John Turturro) and the amiable Vito (Richard Edson). Their helper (and delivery person) is Mookie (Spike Lee), a black from the neighborhood who plays by the rules but gets ragged on constantly by Pino and Sal.

Mookie is the hub of "Do The Right Thing," and Lee uses his deadpan brilliantly. His beautiful, heavy-lidded eyes stay open a second too long; he suggests how Mookie holds himself in check as the insults hit home. His sister (Joie Lee) is a do-gooder, prevailing on him to achieve something; he also has a son by his Hispanic girlfriend, Tina (Rosie Perez).

The movie catalogs insults big and small—they're a constant. At first Lee directs them for comedy. An old-timer known as "Da Mayor" (Ossie Davis) handles slights gracefully: He bows and scrapes in the old-fashioned, Uncle Tom way, sweeping Sal's sidewalk for a couple of bills and relishing his morning beer.

But they add up, those insults, so that in the sweltering heat even something relatively minor can trigger a confrontation—a white yuppie (John Savage) spilling Tropicana on the shoe of Buggin Out (Giancarlo Esposito), the absence of black faces from the photos on the wall of Sal's.

There's tension in the smallest transactions: Korean grocers treat the joshing blacks with brusque impatience; white cops cruise the street and glare menacingly at three old guys shooting the breeze under a parasol. A piece of graffiti on a wall screams "Tawana Told the Truth."

Through all this, the film provides an enormous amount of pleasure—its universe envelops you. The community is sustained by the 24-hour DJ Mister Señor Love Daddy (Sam Jackson), whose advice often ends with, "And that's the truth, Ruth." Another prophet is Radio Raheem (Bill Nunn), an inarticulate behemoth whose boom box blasts the Public Enemy anthem "Fight The Power."

Radio Raheem is looking for trouble, but there's something touching about his straightforward worship of the music's militant energy and his determination to impose it on everyone else—you understand what he's trying to express, even if you're disturbed by it.

There's also a chillingly suggestive character called Smiley (Roger Guenveur Smith), a mentally handicapped stutterer who wanders around the neighborhood showing people a weathered photo of Malcolm X and Martin Luther King. Like Radio Raheem, he's the prisoner of an anger he can't quite put into words.

Lee does some things better than anyone else. In a sex scene, he and Dickerson make Tina's dark flesh tactile under a melting ice cube and Mookie's roving hands. And Lee has a knack for bravura rants. The camera rides in on Mookie as he lashes out obscenely at Italians, then on Pino as he lashes out at blacks, on a Puerto Rican at Koreans, on a white cop at Puerto Ricans, on a Korean at Jews.

The sequence conjures up a city in which people of all races carry tirades inside them, and Lee builds masterfully to the inevitable eruption. But here the film turns didactic and disingenuous—this is the scary part of "Do The Right Thing," in which Lee doesn't simply depict rioting, he endorses and then prescribes it.

That Lee romanticizes the Bed-Stuy neighborhood isn't much of a problem when the picture is all threat, implication, portent. We accept this vision as we would that of a folk opera. But when the film shifts gears, this looking-on-the-bright-side seems like cheating, a way of shifting the responsibility onto virulent white oppressors. The outcome is skewed: the white police, in their vicious enthusiasm, kill a man, but the blacks—inflamed by his murder—only vent their wrath on property, as if whites have a monopoly on homicidal impulses.

In interviews, Lee expresses anger at white reporters who ask why he left the crack and the crime out of his movie, responding that the question is racist, that it wouldn't be asked of a white film maker. But any director, black or white, who doesn't mention drugs or crime in what's meant to be a panoramic portrait of a place like Bed-Stuy isn't telling the whole truth, Ruth.

The tragedy of a society that treats blacks as abominably as this one does is that it can drive them to commit acts of violence—acts that are met, in turn, by even more murderous repression. That's the lesson Martin Luther King tried to teach, but Lee throws the weight of his film behind Malcolm X, who preached violence as a form of self-defense.

When Mookie, the decent, centrist character, launches the climactic riot, Lee treats his gesture not as a horrifying act of rage, something that diminishes his humanity, but as the reasoned, deliberate, moral act of someone pushed too far. Obviously, that's his right, and the sentiment is easy to understand in light of the killings of Michael Stewart, Eleanor Bumpurs and other victims of white lethal force.

But the murder, whatever its real-life inspiration, doesn't rise organically out of this material. It's as if Lee conceived of it and the riot first and then built the film as a pedestal. (It's really a testament to his artistry that the two halves don't meet.) And the violence that Lee is so proud of isn't directed against the right people—it's directed at Sal's Pizzeria.

Sal, the film says, deserves to have his business destroyed. He deserves it for not having photos of blacks on his wall, for looking at Mookie's sister the wrong way, for not permitting someone to play a boom box at deafening volume. He deserves it for not recognizing the merits of black culure (in case we've forgotten, Mister Señor Love Daddy reels off a long list of estimable black artists). And, for that matter, he deserves it for not moving out of a black neighborhood when he should have.

Spike Lee is an important film maker, and the movie is vital to see—but as a black artist's subjective vision and not as a prescription. It's good that "Do The Right Thing" makes us nervous, that it shows us another side to a tragedy that is tearing our cities apart.

What scares me is not the chip on his shoulder the size of a planet. It's that he sees no difference between Eleanor Bumpurs and Tawana Brawley. It's that—if I read him right—he thinks collective violence is warranted in response to both the killing of a young man in police custody and to a pizzeria owner's failure to pay tribute to black culture.

For the last month people have been saying that "Do The Right Thing" will incite a race riot, and Lee has been giving heated interviews. According to Stanley Crouch in the Village Voice, when Lee's film lost the prize at Cannes, the director said he'd been robbed because "they are always looking for a golden white boy." Is he angry, I wonder, that the pavilion in Cannes still stands?

NEWSDAY, 6/30/89, Part III/p. 3, Mike McGrady

Seldom have I been so uneasy, so thoroughly unentertained watching a movie as when watching "Do the Right Thing." But then, Spike Lee's sizzling study of racial hostilities is not meant to be another harmless little diversion. Intended to get strong reactions, it hits that target on the mark.

The film's title comes from Da Mayor (Ossie Davis), an aging Uncle Tom figure who sweeps out the corner pizza parlor for beer money, then spends the hottest day of summer offering slurred advice to youngsters living on the same block in the Bedford-Stuyvesant section of Brooklyn. One of those young men is Mookie (Spike Lee), pizza deliverer, who listens closely to Da Mayor's profound counsel: "Always do the right thing."

At those words, Mookie smiles agreeably—yes, he can do the right things, whatever that is. However, director-writer-producer-actor Spike Lee's idea of the right thing is not going to thrill all moviegoers. Despite Lee's avowals to the contrary, "Do the Right Thing" is a clear call to blacks to solve their problems with whites through direct action; violence is seen as a sane reaction to economic oppression. In fact, the film's final quote is given over to Malcolm X: "I don't even call it violence when it's self-defense; I call it intelligence."

Pulsating with energy and life, fairly exploding with its varied hatreds, "Do the Right Thing" centers on the way people respond to the last white business on the block. Sal (Danny Aiello), who has worked the counter of Sal's Famous Pizzeria for 15 years, thinks of his customers in sentimental terms: "These kids grew up on my food. *My* food!"

But Sal's customers do not return the sentiment. Da Mayor fraternizes with the enemy but saves his real ire for the new Korean grocer who has stopped carrying Miller High Life: "You askin' a lot, you askin' a man to change his beer." Mother Sister (Ruby Dee), an old-fashioned matriarch, is made of sterner stuff but also, like Da Mayor, mired in the past. Uninvolved.

Younger blacks, no longer capable of such forebearance, include the menacing Radio Raheem (Bill Nunn), who uses his barely portable squawk box as a weapon, booming rap music into the pizzeria. And the militant Buggin Out (Giancarlo Esposito), upset by the lack of black faces on the parlor's Italian "Wall of Fame," urges a pizza boycott. A restless peace is maintained only through the efforts of Mookie, who finds time to negotiate small truces between pizza deliveries and stolen visits with his Hispanic girlfriend (Rosie Perez) and their child.

There is no questioning the accuracy of Spike Lee's eye or ear; he has unerringly caught both individuals and types, and he has introduced them with all the perception and some of the humor that marked his earlier "She's Gotta Have It." While Lee's movie-making techniques have improved markedly, any discussion of "Do The Right Thing" will not long concern itself with esthetics. This is a political movie and what caused all the shock waves at Cannes, reportedly costing Lee a top prize, is his clear and uncompromising message.

The message is there in the music that opens and closes the movie, a song by the rap group Public Enemy to a driving beat, an exhortation to "Fight the power...fight the power...fight the powers that be." It's found most clearly in the person of Mookie, the bright young peacemaker who finally rebels ("Slave days is over; my name ain't Kunte Kinte") and leads a ferocious mob in rioting and torching the pizza parlor.

The portraits of whites (this is Danny Aiello's best work by far) are almost all unpleasant. A fat, white Cadillac-driver is loud and bellicose. White police officers, hostile and smug in their patrol cars, are capable of murdering a black without a second thought. The ugliness of prejudice is personified by one of Sal's sons (John Turturro): "I'm sick of niggers. Every time I come to work, it's 'Planet of the Apes.'"

If it accomplished nothing else, "Do the Right Thing" would be applauded for vividly reminding us how far the races are from any kind of harmony. A glimpse of graffiti spray-painted against the side of a building—"TAWANA TOLD THE TRUTH"—draws a laugh, but it's a nervous laugh, a laugh cut short by recognition of the vastness separating black and white perceptions. Spike Lee's movie draws laughs, too, but they are also cut short and for the same reason.

NEWSWEEK, 7/3/89, p. 65, David Ansen

Somewhere near the midpoint in Spike Lee's "Do the Right Thing"—as the summer heat in Bedford-Stuyvesant reaches the boiling point—there occurs an astonishing outpouring of racial invective, five short soliloquies of ethnic slurs directed straight at the camera. A black man insults Italians. An Italian defames blacks. A Puerto Rican castigates Koreans. A white cop rips into Puerto Ricans. A Korean slanders Jews. At which point Lee cuts to the neighborhood radio deejay, Mister Señor Love Daddy, screaming into his mike "Time out! ...Cool that shit out!"

Nigger, dago, kike, spic. There they are, America's dirtiest words, hurled across the screen in Lee's nervy, complex, unsettling movie. The sequence makes you catch your breath, but you also laugh as you laughed when Lenny Bruce or Richard Pryor touched a raw nerve of publicly unspoken experience. And Lee's rude comic impulse is the same as theirs: unless we air these noxious fumes, and acknowledge just how dire the racial situation has become, this great unmelted pot might well explode.

When white filmmakers deal with race (from Stanley Kramer's "The Defiant Ones" to Alan Parker's "Mississippi Burning"), no matter how fine their intentions, they tend to speak in inflated, self-righteous tones, and they always come down to Hollywood's favorite dialectic, bad guys versus good guys. They allow the audience to sit comfortably on the side of the angels. In "Do the Right Thing," Lee blows away the pieties and the easy answers. He prefers abrasion and ambiguity to comfort and tidiness. As a black filmmaker, he's too close to the subject—and too much the artist—to oversimplify the issues. The beauty of "Do the Right Thing" is that all the characters, from the broadest cartoons to the most developed, are given their humanity and their due.

At the end of the story there is violence, police brutality, a riot. Sal's pizzeria, a white-run business that has existed peacefully in the black community for 25 years, suddenly becomes the target of pent-up rage. The owner, Sal (Danny Aiello, who's never been better), is no ogre—he's a sympathetic figure, a peacemaker who's arguably an unconscious racist. His son Pino (John Turturro), on the other hand, is blatantly antiblack, the closest to a villain the movie gets. Lee isn't saying the violence is inevitable, or even just. But we see how it comes to pass, a combination of heat, irritation, insensitivity, stubbornness and centuries of systematic oppression.

Lee trusts his audience: he doesn't need to stack the deck. You can feel he's working out his own ambivalence on screen. His rich portrait of the Bed-Stuy community is both affectionate and critical. Take the character of Buggin' Out (Giancarlo Esposito). He's the most militant black in the movie, but Lee shows his rage as misplaced and foolish. His attempt to boycott Sal's because there are no pictures of blacks on the walls—only Italian-Americans—is greeted by most with derision. When Mother Sister (Ruby Dee), the block's wise old watchdog, sees Sal's go up in flames we're startled by her exhilaration at the violence. But moments later she's wailing in despair at the destruction. It's one of the movie's points that we are all nursing wildly contradictory impulses: our heads and hearts aren't always in sync. This is no cop-out, it's unusually honest reporting.

"Do the Right Thing" is a kind of compacted epic played out in jazzy, dissonant scenes that dance in and out of realism. Lee's deliberately discordant style didn't jell in "School Daze," an ambitious but turgid look at the divisions in a black college. Here the clashing styles add up and pay off. You leave this movie stunned, challenged and drained. To accuse Lee of irresponsibility—of inciting violence—is to be blind to the movie he has made. The two quotes that end the film—Martin Luther King's eloquent antiviolent testament and Malcolm X's acknowledgment that violence in self-defense may be necessary—are the logical culmination of Lee's method. There can be no simple, tidy closure. Not now. Not yet. Lee's conscience-pricking movie is bracing and necessary: it's the funkiest and most informed view of racism an American filmmaker has given us.

NEWSWEEK, 7/3/89, p. 64, Jack Kroll

Spike Lee's *Do the Right Thing* is the most controversial movie in many years. To put it bluntly: in this long hot summer, how will young urban audiences—black and white—react to the film's climactic explosion of interracial violence? This incendiary subject, coupled with the brilliance of Lee's filmmaking talent, makes this question inescapable. People are going to argue about this film for a long time. That's fine, as long as things stay on the arguing level. But this movie is dynamite under every seat. Sadly, the fuse has been lit by a filmmaker tripped up by muddled motives.

With three movies in four years, the 32-year-old producer-writer-director-actor has become the most important black filmmaker working today. With astonishing guts he's muscled his way into the mainstream with films uncompromisingly about black lives, black problems. The 1986 "She's Gotta Have It" dealt with a young black woman who insists on a sex life as free as any man's; the 1988 "School Daze" concerned conflicts of identity (and skin color) at a black college. Both movies were propelled by an essentially comic sensibility, and so is most of "Do the Right Thing."

The film deals with the events of one day on one block in Brooklyn's Bedford-Stuyvesant section. Lee provides a mother lode of characters: three funky philosophers, the Corner Men; two senior citizens; a boozy sage called Da Mayor (Ossie Davis); and Mother Sister (Ruby Dee), watching eternally from her window. There's a hip-hopping swarm of people including the hyped-up Buggin' Out (Giancarlo Esposito), the stuttering Smiley (Roger Smith) and Radio Raheem (Bill Nunn), whose ghetto blaster is the power pack of his pride. Dozens of others include Mookie (Spike Lee), who delivers pizza for the film's whites, Sal (Danny Aiello) and his sons Pino (John Turturro) and Vito (Richard Edson), who run the landmark Sal's Famous Pizzeria.

Acted with epic charm by a marvelous ensemble cast, these profanely eloquent street people criss-cross through the hottest day of the year. The solar glow that Lee and his master cinematographer Ernest Dickerson pour over everything isn't just the heat, it's the aura of an idealized ghetto reminiscent of old studio-shot films like "Street Scene" and "Dead End." Lee's dream Bed-Stuy omits too many things to justify his claim of reality: most startlingly, there's not a single reference to drugs. When journalists at the Cannes Film Festival asked Lee about this, he snapped: "When you see 'Working Girl' or 'Rain Man' you don't ask where the drugs are'"— a silly response for such a smart guy.

In the companion book to "Do the Right Thing," Lee's own journal records his agonized grappling with the drug question. "Not to acknowledge that drugs exist might be a serious omission in this film," he writes. "The drug epidemic is worse than the plague... My goal is to show how the different social pressures that lead to this are all connected." Lee's movie crew had to close down some crack houses before filming could begin. The drug dealers, comments Lee, just "moved around the corner." And right out of the film. A good guess is that Lee simply couldn't handle the dense, hardly comic reality of the drug problem, or all those "different social pressures," at this stage of his career.

The explosion at Sal's pizzeria occurs because Sal refuses the demand by Buggin' Out, Radio Raheem and Smiley to place black heroes on his "wall of fame," which features only Italian-Americans like Sinatra, Stallone and DiMaggio. The riot that escalates from this triviality results in a brutal death that's meant to recall the deaths of blacks like Michael Stewart and Eleanor Bumpurs at the hands of the New York police. But Lee's substitution of pizza politics for the hard realities of urban racial conflict is an evasion of the issues.

The real problem with "Do the Right Thing" is that it's not radical enough. Lee appears caught between his desire to be both the ironic humanist and the "black nationalist with a movie camera," as he has called himself. This ambivalence is compounded by the two quotes he puts on screen at the end: one from Martin Luther King denouncing violence and one from Malcolm X validating violence as intelligent self-defense. But it's too late for these Post-it Notes; their implied equality has already been overwhelmed by Lee's images of violence. In his attempt to be both ingratiating and militant, Lee has done the wrong thing.

SIGHT & SOUND, Autumn 1989, p. 281, Geoffrey Nowell-Smith

The place: Bedford Stuyvesant, a poor black district of Brooklyn. The time: the hottest day of the New York summer. The action: a little edge of racial tension that stupidly and yet somehow inevitably becomes a riot. Spike Lee's new film, *Do the Right Thing*, observes all the classical unities but refuses quite to be a tragedy. Sure enough there's a death, but the person who dies is not the hero. More importantly, that is not inevitable, and the point of the film is to question the process which made it seem so.

The action centres around Sal's Famous Pizza joint. Sal is an Italian immigrant, who has built up his business in Bed-Stuy over twenty-five years, likes the place, likes the people and has no intention of quitting. Sal is not a racist, but he is a sort of cultural nationalist and he decorates his joint exclusively with pictures of Italian and Italian-American heroes, from Rocky Marciano to Sophia Loren. It is Sal's "Wall of Fame" combined with the class and racial attitudes of his eldest son, Pino, which provide the provocation for the eventual riot.

The film's hero (sort of) is Mookie, played by Spike Lee himself. Mookie has a three-year-old son, whom he does not support. He is charming, feckless, unwilling to settle down with the boy's mother, and he has never had a proper job: he is now working as Sal's delivery boy for $250 a week. Mookie is peaceable and gets on with everybody except the graceless Pino. It is therefore somewhat shocking—to the audience, but also to the other characters—when he picks up the garbage can and throws it at Sal's window to set off the looting which is the climax of the film.

On the black side, the stirrer is Buggin' Out, a would-be activist who first fails and then eventually succeeds in making an issue of the Wall of Fame. Buggin' Out wants black pictures on the wall, since all the customers are black, and he has a point but of a quite utopian kind. Sal's Famous Pizzas is Sal's private property. Sal is only in Bed-Stuy because he wants to run a business to pass on to his children. More than his whiteness, or his Italianness, that Wall of Fame represents Sal's rights as a property owner. In a sense, the whole American system is invested in that wall, and Buggin' Out is in no position to take on the system, nor is he smart enough to understand why.

Most of the other characters understand all too well the limitations on their power to act, and Buggin' Out's call for a boycott of Sal's gets no community support ("Boycott, man, you should boycott the barber who fucked up your hair style," says one member of the chorus of bystanders). Eventually, round about midnight on a hot evening when Sal has opted out of friendliness to stay open later than usual, an incongruous team of three turns up to challenge him about the pictures on his wall. These are Buggin' Out, a loner called Radio Raheem whose self-esteem is entirely tied up in his ghetto-blaster, and the half-witted Smiley, who spends his day handing out pictures of a meeting between Malcolm X and Martin Luther King. Sal objects to the noise of the ghetto-blaster and, when Raheem won't turn it down, smashes it with a baseball bat. Raheem attacks Sal. The cops come and in the fighting a white cop throttles Raheem with his nightstick. Stunned silence follows. Then Mookie picks up that garbage can, Sal's is looted and burnt. Smiley puts his picture of Malcolm X and Martin Luther King up on the charred Wall of Fame.

The violence, though unwanted, is curiously cathartic. It has the effect of bringing the community to its senses, making people more aware of their responsibilities towards each other. Enemies are reconciled. Mookie looks set to get back together with Tina and their son. The film then closes with two long quotations about violence, one from Martin Luther King arguing that it is always degrading, and one from Malcolm X declaring that it may sometimes be necessary. There is something both sententious and sentimental about this ending (as there is about the ending of Lee's earlier *School Daze*), as if the audience needed to be cheered up and enlightened at the same time. The ending also gives the impression that the film is about violence, when actually it is about impotence, frustration and the sense of being nowhere and getting nowhere. Although the film is constructed to lead up to a violent ending, that ending is contrived—for the sake of the catharsis, not because violence is either endemic in the situation or a key political issue.

The two quotations represent opposed points of view which are, in a sense, equally irrelevant.

The problem for Lee, I would argue, is that he seems intent on making a drama out of a situation which is inherently undramatic. The Bedford Stuyvesant of the film is a listless, dissociated community, unstructured and purposeless. A few people work, more are on welfare. Everyone is aware of being black, which is a shared condition making them different from cops (white or Hispanic) and shopkeepers (Italian or Korean). There is a lot of talk about being black and bandying about of terms of endearment such as blackass. But there is no black consciousness or political struggle. Raheem has his music, Smiley has his icons, Buggin' Out has his pose, but for everyone in the film life is mostly a matter of carrying on. There is a great deal of cultural energy, which has to do with blackness. But there is nothing black people can do except banter about things in general and blackness in particular.

So long as the film sticks to the level of recording the entropic energy and the diffuse impotence of community life in Bedford Stuyvesant it is both funny and—I would say—truthful. When it tries to become a drama and to use that drama to underscore its own truthfulness, it falls into a trap and manages to undermine its point rather than underline it. Bed-Stuy and places like it need a new politics that relates to the new situation and is neither that of King nor that of Malcolm, just as the students of *School Daze* need a politics that is neither separatist not integrationist.

Lee does not know what this politics will be like, but he is aware of the problem and honest enough to put both the problem and his ignorance of the solution on the agenda. What he cannot do is articulate his consciousness of the political problem into a narrative form. For all its apparent roughness, *Do the Right Thing* is aesthetically very sophisticated, particularly in the first half. But at the end it collapses both aesthetically and politically because on both fronts it is seeking a closure which denies everything that is specific and novel about what has come before. If Lee finds an aesthetic solution in his next film, it will probably be a sign that he and the characters of his film are nearer a political solution as well.

TIME, 7/3/89, p. 62 Richard Corliss

On the hottest day of the year, good people can do bad things. Especially in Bedford-Stuyvesant, Brooklyn's black ghetto where the crime rate sizzles and hopes evaporate in the summer glare. Spike Lee's *Do the Right Thing* is the story of a day in the death of the American Dream.

The day starts calmly enough, as if the people on Lee's Stuyvesant Avenue are the cheerful graduating class of *Sesame Street*. Da Mayor (Ossie Davis) spreads inebriated wisdom, Uncle Remus-style. Sal (Danny Aiello), the Italian American who runs the corner pizzeria, brags that the locals "grew up on my food." His delivery boy, Mookie (Lee), doles out advice while dodging duties to his girlfriend and their child. Radio Raheem (Bill Nunn) keeps the block pulsing to the rap song, *Fight the Power*, that bleats from his boom box. By day's end, though, the neighborhood has erupted. Sal and Raheem start fighting about the loud music; the cops arrive and, in the struggle, kill Raheem; Mookie throws a trash can through his employer's window; the place goes up in a puff of black rage.

The rage of race is exactly what has stirred a righteous debate over Lee's movie. After it lost the top prize at last month's Cannes Film Festival (to a comedy by another young American, Steven Soderbergh's *sex, lies and videotape*), jury member Sally Field told Lee she fought to get him a prize. The film's detractors called it facile and irresponsible; Lee responded by accusing his critics of racism.

With this week's U.S. release of *Do the Right Thing*, the furor goes Stateside. Not since the Black Panthers cowed Manhattan's glitterati 20 years ago has there been such a virulent outbreak of radical chic—or so many political-disease detectives ready to stanch the epidemic. A single issue of the *Village Voice* ran eight articles on the movie, with opinions running from raves to cries of "fascist" and "racist." A political columnist for *New York* magazine charged that Lee's film could undermine the New York City mayoral campaign of a black candidate. Everywhere, the film has polarized white liberals for whom Bed-Stuy is as exotic and unknowable as Burkina Faso. Some see Lee as the movies' great black hope; others tut till they're tuckered. A few fear that *Do the Right Thing* could trigger the kind of riot it dramatizes and perhaps condones.

The 32-year-old auteur (*She's Gotta Have It, School Daze*) must be enjoying his prominence as the angry young man of the don't-worry, be-happy '80s. Of all the blacks who have strutted through the studio door that Eddie Murphy kicked down, Lee is the one who won't settle for being a Murphy manqué. Sure, he markets himself cannily, as a performer in Air Jordan commercials, and with books and *The Making of...* spinoffs of his own movies. But Lee will not be ingratiating; he wants to be accepted on his own rude terms. Same goes for *Do the Right Thing*.

To accept the film, though, one must first understand its point of view, and that is maddeningly difficult. All we know for certain is that *Do the Right Thing* is not naturalistic. Golden sunset hues swathe the street at 10 in the morning. The color scheme is chicly coordinated, as if Jerome Robbins' Sharks and Jets were about to dance onscreen; the picture could be called *Bed-Stuy Story*, full of Officer Krupkes and kindly store owners. At first, the dilemmas are predictably pastel too: populist clichés brought to life by an attractive cast. Even the racial epithets have a jaunty tinge, as in a series of antibrotherhood jokes made by blacks, Italians, Hispanics, white cops and Korean grocers—the film's best sequence. On this street there are no crack dealers, hookers or muggers, just a 24-hour deejay named Mister Señor Love Daddy (Sam Jackson), who punctuates every mellow bellow with "And that's the truth, Ruth!"

But what is the truth of *Do the Right Thing*? Whose side is Lee on? Is the Movie a revolutionary scream or a fatalistic shrug? Lee leaves plenty of hints—contradictory epigrams from Martin Luther King Jr. and Malcolm X, a dedication to families of blacks slain by police, graffiti proclaiming TAWANA [Brawley] TOLD THE TRUTH—but no coherent clues. Lee cagily provides a litmus test for racial attitudes in 1989, but he does so by destroying the integrity of his characters, black and white. They vault from sympathetic to venomous in the wink of a whim. One minute, Sal delivers a moony monologue about how much he loves his black neighbors; the next, he is wielding a baseball bat, bound to crack skulls. One minute, Mookie urges caution; the next, he trashes the one store the brothers can call home.

In Hollywood the black man's burden is to be all things to all people: stoic Sidney Poitier and sassy Eddie Murphy, angelic sitcom kid and fuming rapmaster. Lee's movie bravely tries both approaches. It gives you sweet, then rancid, but without explaining why it turned. He holds the film like a can of beer in a paper bag—the cool sip of salvation on a blistering day—until it is revealed as a Molotov cocktail.

The morning after igniting the riot, Mookie slinks back to demand that Sal pay him his week's wages. Behind the camera, Lee wants the same thing: to create a riot of opinion, then blame viewers for not getting the message he hasn't bothered to articulate. Though the strategy may lure moviegoers this long hot summer, it is ultimately false and pernicious. Faced with it, even Mister Señor Love Daddy might say, "Take a hike, Spike!"

VILLAGE VOICE, 7/11/89, p. 59, J. Hoberman

There's been a lot of ink spilled already on *Do the Right Thing*, and there's sure to be a lot more—the new Spike Lee Film may be the only summer movie that encourages any discussion beyond the "oh, wow." You can't avoid having a point of view; this film won't just wash over you. Indeed, some commentators seem to think that the operative fluid won't be ink, but blood and tears.

The effect of motion pictures on human behavior is a question that's been debated for nearly a century, but *Do the Right Thing* is being treated in some quarters as a blueprint for catastrophe. Let's start by observing that the experience of this movie is complicated and perhaps chastening, but also skillfully organized and not exactly unpleasurable. *Do the Right Thing* is bright and brazen, and it moves with a distinctive jangling glide. Set on a single block in the heart of Brooklyn on the hottest Saturday of the summer, it offers the funniest, most stylized, most visceral New York street scene this side of Scorseseland.

Lee is a deft quick-sketch artist. His Bed-Stuy block—a dank pizza stand, a Korean grocery, a storefront radio station, a half dozen decrepit brownstones—is as humid as a terrarium and as teeming with life. Taunted by a moving chorus of heedless high school kids, the tormented, borderline Radio Raheem (Bill Nunn) stalks the neighborhood with his humongous boombox. Meanwhile, a retarded stammerer (Roger Guenveur Smith) peddles a double portrait of Malcolm X and Martin Luther King. The irascible Mother Sister (Ruby Dee) stares contemptuously out her window at the beer-sozzled busybody known as Da Mayor (Ossie Davis), as a trio of street corner philosophers shoot the breeze beneath their portable beach umbrella, badmouthing Mike Tyson, the Korean greengrocer, and the proud and foolish Buggin' Out (Giancarlo Esposito), an irate hiphopster looking for a fight. Someone opens the hydrant. The cops turn it off. People get on each other's nerves. Da Mayor saves a kid running for the Mister Softee truck. The sun starts going down; you're waiting for the catastrophe.

Do the Right Thing has a surplus of data; it's filled with low angles and crowded, panoramic frames, the characters peering over each other's shoulders like good and bad angels in a medieval morality play. Everyone interacts with everybody else; the diminutive hero Mookie (played by Lee) threading his way among them, delivering pizzas, dispensing advice, dropping in on his girlfriend. The other unifying presence is Mister Señor Love Daddy, the DJ who broadcasts 24 hours a day. If Mookie is a black everyman, Mister Señor Love Daddy is the celestial spirit of the neighborhood, at one moment offering a celebratory litany of black artists, at another calling time out to end a cathartic montage of ethnic slurs.

Lee, himself, isn't quite so mellow; his portraits are affectionate but not exactly flattering. Few black filmmakers have ever been this bold and it's telling that, in a movie as filled with intricate checks and balances as this, he would make the most obnoxious, least articulate character the ultimate victim. Everyone has his or her own agenda. Mookie is introduced counting his money, then nuzzling awake his sister Jade (the filmmaker's sister, Joie Lee) as Sal (Danny Aiello) pilots his battered white Cadillac toward his "famous" pizzeria, warning his squabbling sons, "I'm gonna kill somebody today,"

Do the Right Thing is Lee's first film with white characters and, if not as vivid as the blacks, they're not exactly faceless stereotypes. The bored cops cruising in and out of the neighborhood are hardly identical to the guy who gets drenched, or the gentrifier who inadvertently scuffs Buggin' Out's sneakers; the passive, easygoing Vito (Richard Edson), who drops out of the narrative, is distinguished from the stupid, angry Pino (John Turturro), who *wants* to move out: "I'm sick of niggers. It's like working on Planet of the Apes." And, given a weary dignity by Aiello, the patriarch Sal is a complex creation.

Crude but hard-working, the pizza-man is the movie's sole embodiment of the American Dream. "I never had no trouble with these people," he tells unhappy Pino. "They grew up on my food, and I'm very pround of that." It's Sal's fantasy that his sons will someday inherit this empire of nourishment—in a moment of generosity he even declares that there will always be a place for the hired hand Mookie. Sal's success is comprehensible, his paternalism has a human face. "Who does he think he is," Radio Raheem wants to know when Sal compels him to turn down his boombox, "Don Corleone and shit?"

Lee, who hates comparison as much as the next filmmaker, has more than once expressed his distaste for being dubbed "the black Woody Allen." Still, one would be hard-pressed to come up with another auteur who has as much of himself invested in his work. Like Allen, Lee is a control freak who typically has his own person inscribed at the center of his films. But, unlike Allen, Lee has no firmly established persona. What exactly is the relation between Mookie and Lee?

Do the Right Thing's fictional pressure cooker suggests Lee's own. In this steaming Saturday world, Mookie (brilliantly named after the most lovable of Mets, so that his name will haunt us all summer long) is responsibility writ small. He works, he maintains some interest in the mother of his child. He counsels his friends. So when the crunch comes, what right thing will Mookie do?

A daring mix of naturalism and allegory, agitprop and psychodrama, *Do the Right Thing* begins, literally, where *School Daze* leaves off—with a Brechtian call to "wake up"—and, as confrontational as it is, the movie sustains more moment-to-moment interest than most of the year's releases combined. The choppy, fragmented narrative seems much smoother on second viewing, once you get the spiral structure. The flow is teasingly eruptive: Like Julien Temple, Lee designs his production numbers with an eye toward MTV. The movie opens with a surge of rock-video energy and a burst of prurient militance as Rosie Perez in boxer shorts pugnaciously gyrates to Public Enemy's "Fight the Power." This anthem has an irony that only becomes apparent when the film is over.

Someone is sure to call *Do the Right Thing* a rap movie. Certainly, it's a language-intoxicated film, filled with mainly feckless, fast-talking men and invariably judgmental, fast-talking women. "What I ever done to you?" Da Mayor asks haughty Mother Sister. "You a drunk fool," she spits back like a gatling gun. "Beside that?" he demands. Jade is usually on Mookie's case, while Tina (Perez), his awesomely strident lady friend, is in a class by herself: "If you listened to me, I wouldn't have to repeat myself like a fucking radio." *Do the Right Thing* is clamorous with sign language, but this is the only negative reference to the medium that, supporting Marshall McLuhan's notion of the tribal drum, provides Lee's somewhat idealized village with its social cohesion.

Lee has already taken a fair amount of criticism for sanitizing his street scene. But the real issue is not the absence of drugs or street crime; the real issue is racial solidarity. No black character, on this street may exploit another for economic gain. Thus, no black character can operate any sort of business or hold any real authority. No black character, save Mookie (and the ethereal Mister Señor Love Daddy), is shown to be gainfully employed. Where *School Daze* offered a critique of black racism and class conflict, *Do the Right Thing* presents no essential divisions within the black community. Discontent is signaled by the endless series of personal turf wars, the movie touching lightly on the pain in having your sense of self bound up in a pair of sneakers or a radio, the relative merits of this major league pitcher or that pop music superstar.

Like Scorsese, Lee fills his films with his own fetish objects and family members. The latter subtext comes complete with an undercurrent of sexual paranoia. When Jade (who is, after all, the woman with whom Mookie lives) visits Sal's and gets fawningly special treatment, Mookie flips out. "All Sal wants to do is play hide the salami," he tells his disbelieving sister. That the scene is played in front of a "Tawana Told the Truth" graffito gives it an added ambiguity. Is Jade an unwitting candidate for abduction and gang rape? Does Mookie believe Tawana told the truth? Does Lee? Or is the sign only a sign of the times, a bit of street scene verisimilitude?

Walls are important in this movie, mainly for what they say. A Hispanic mural is visible in many scenes. And the site of the *Kulturkampf*, after all, is the sweaty wall of Sal's Famous, covered with (and restricted to) framed publicity photos of the Italian celebs who, whatever else they do, will never ever drop in for a slice.

Another director might be satisfied putting stuff on the screen that's never been there before, but Lee is driven by his own demons, not to mention constituencies ranging from the Fruit of Islam, who protected his set, to the Universal executives who bankrolled the film (after Paramount, the studio of Eddie Murphy, put the project in turnaround). Thus, *Do the Right Thing* is not a career move in any conventional sense of the term. As Da Mayor tells Mookie in a fit of melancholy, "Always do the right thing." Yeah, sure. But just what is that anyway?

There are a number of powerful black personalities in American show business, but Lee is unique, having gone further on his own terms than any other black filmmaker in American history. Neither Ossie Davis nor Sidney Poitier, Melvin Van Peebles nor Michael Schultz, has been able to move from success to success, generating his own projects and controlling his own persona, to become a spokesman, a symbol, and a force to be reckoned with. For that alone, Lee is destined to be patronized and slighted, lionized and attacked, spoiled and abused, put in his place and denied his place. (Why was it not immediately recognized, for example that his was the missing voice in *New York Stories*—and not only for the obvious demographic reasons?).

Lee's films are markedly free of film-school references (*Do the Right Thing*'s homage to *The Night of the Hunter* is a rare exception), but to a certain degree his project seems to involve rewriting the movies of the '70s. If his first feature, *Joe's Bed-Stuy Barbershop: We cut Heads*, was an archetypal regional/independent, his breakthrough, *She's Gotta Have It*, can be seen as a cannily revisionist *Sweet Sweetback's Baadasssss Song* for the '80s. *School Daze*, his would-be blockbuster, combines, overhauls, rewires, and subverts a number of mondo youth films, including *Animal House, Grease,* and *Saturday Night Fever*. Not as grandiose as its predecessor, *Do the Right Thing* appears to address Michael Schultz's 1976 *Car Wash,* coincidentally the last movie directed by an American black to be shown in competition at Cannes (where, less problematic than Lee's, Schultz's film won an award for its score).

Anticipating *Do the Right Thing* in its workday structure and radio mysticism, as well as its high-grade ensemble acting, *Car Wash* is suffused with frustration and powerlessness. What Lee does, among other things, is to bring the story back home, moving the L.A. car wash owned by a middle-aged white ethnic to a black neighborhood and transforming it into a pizzeria (even as the car wash's mainly black labor force is reduced to Mookie). That the whites in *Do the Right Thing* are virtually all Italian-American not only suggests Howard Beach but an assault on the media counterrevolution begun by *The Godfather* and effected with *Rocky*, by which, with the blessing of white America, Italians supplanted blacks as the national minority of choice.

Do the Right Thing is truly tribal; it lacks the horror of the industrial world. Indeed, *Car Wash*'s space-age shoeshine parlor makes Lee's movie seem cozily old-fashioned. (A kindred social realism might have dictated the replacement of Sal's Famous with a bombed-out Burger King—half junk food factory, half armed camp.) But while *Car Wash* reeks of mid-'70s post-Orgy burnout—it's one of the saddest movies ever made about the cost of earning a living in America (there's never been a more chilling disco refrain than the title song's exhortation to "work and work and work and work'')—*Do the Right Thing* seems more a metaphor for the '60s. It requires human sacrifice and a taste of the apocalypse for the climactic integration of Sal's Wall of Fame.

Do the Right Thing might have ended there, with flames devouring the image of Al Pacino (making room for a picture of Eddie Murphy?). But, didactic as he is, Lee reserves the right to tie up some loose ends and balance a few equations with a coda that stops the film dead. Even the well-choreographed riot is clumsily adjusted to "do the right thing" by evoking Selma, Alabama, as well as Michael Stewart, while allowing the industrious Koreans—previously hassled by Da Mayor, Coconut Sid, and Radio Raheem—to be accepted into Lee's particular rainbow coalition.

"I built this place with my bare fucking hands," Sal tells Mookie on the grim morning after. "Do you know what that means?" Mookie may not, but Lee certainly does—something effaced in the closing minutes. This final scene, which should have the impact of the father-son battle the narrative never delivers, disintegrates into feeble self-justification. Mookie accepts his pitiful reparations (something less than 40 acres and a mule) and, less than convincingly, promises to go back to Tina and his son (oddly adding, "if it's all right with you"). Mister Señor Love Daddy informs us that the mayor has convened a blue ribbon panel to protect private property, and suggests that his listeners register to vote; Lee delivers an antiviolence quote from Martin Luther King and an apparently contradictory, pro-self-defense quote from Malcolm X.

If Lee's convoluted ending hedges his bets, that shouldn't obscure the enormous risk that the film takes. In addressing racism and racial violence, while refusing to take an unambiguous stance for (white) civil order, Lee risks being blamed as the messenger of bad news—if not an outright demagogue. Already Joe Klein, *New York*'s expert on race relations, has speculated at length as to whether *Do the Right Thing* will cost David Dinkins the primary: Not only do "a great many white New Yorkers" hold Dinkins answerable for the gang-rape of a white jogger, Klein reports, but "unfortunately, Dinkins will also have to pay the price for Spike Lee's reckless new movie...which opens on June 30 (in not too many theaters near you, one hopes)."

So will Ed Koch have to play the price for the urban bad vibes in the reckless *Ghostbusters II*? *New York*'s target audience notwithstanding, Klein predicts that while white liberals debate *Do the Right Thing*'s message, "black teenagers won't find it so hard...*white people are your enemy.*" In spite of this hysterical accusation of cinematic wilding, it seems obvious that (1) most black teenagers don't have to see *Do the Right Thing* to have feelings about white people; (2) there is no monolithic, unthinking response to this film, anyway; and (3) the vast majority of Lee's fans would probably rather star in his next movie than torch the bijou where its shown.

But even if black teenagers are angry enough to burn it down, Spike Lee didn't invent that destructive rage or American racism. Did George Bush need *Do the Right Thing* to get himself elected by running against Willie Horton? Americans spent the past eight years under a Teflon smile button whose pleasure it was to deny that racism had *ever* existed in America—let alone that it might actually be a live social problem. New Yorkers have lived for the last 12 years with a mayor who has recklessly played one ethnic group off against another and then congratulated himself for his evenhandedness. And whatever one thinks about them, these experiences (as even Klein must know) are qualitatively different, depending on your race.

The ending of *Do the Right Thing* is certainly upsetting (and upsettingly incoherent), but its pathos and self-defeat are real. In the absence of an organized movement, honest political leadership, and a realistic sense of American life, the alternative for those this system denies will be to fight whatever comes to hand, even if they are only the powers that *seem* to be.

Also reviewed in:

NATION, 7/17/89, p. 98, Stuart Klawans
NEW REPUBLIC, 7/3/09, p. 24, Stanley Kauffmann
NEW YORK TIMES, 6/30/89, p. C16, Vincent Canby
NEW YORKER, 7/24/89, p. 78, Terrence Rafferty
VARIETY, 5/24-30/89, p. 26
WASHINGTON POST, 6/30/89, p. B1, Hal Hinson
WASHINGTON POST, 6/30/89, Weekend/p. 29, Desson Howe

DOCUMENTATOR, THE

A Hunnia Film Studio production in cooperation with the Hungarian Ministry of Education. *Director:* István Dárday and Györgyi Szalai. *Screenplay (Hungarian with English subtitles):* István Dárday and Györgyi Szalai. *Director of Photography:* Péter Tímár and Sándor Csukás. *Editor:* Klára Majoros and Hajnal Veil. *Music:* József Czencz, János Molnár, and Péter Kaszás. *Sound:* Gábor Erdélyi and István Fehér. *Set Designer:* László Gárdonyi. *Costumes:* Tamás Nagy. *Running time:* 215 minutes. *MPAA Rating:* Not Rated.

CAST: Mihály Dés (Raffael); Lilla Pászti (Chip); János Agoston (Rambo).

NEWSDAY, 10/2/89, Part II/p. 5, Terry Kelleher

"The Documentator" is about a gal, two guys and an extensive videotape collection. The last element is all that makes the movie interesting, and most of what makes it boring.

Raffael (Mihály Dés) owns a prosperous video store that appears to specialize in porn. His icy blond girlfriend, Chip (Lilla Pászti), waits on the customers when she's not getting it on with Raffael's sullen delivery man (János Agoston), who's called "Rambo." Meanwhile, Raffael holes up in his private office and watches tape, tape and more tape as he compiles a "video encyclopedia" of modern history. Quite a hobby, eh? And we get to watch right along with him.

Like any encyclopedia, Raffael's could be educational if consulted on a specific subject. But film makers István Dárday and Györgyi Szalai expect viewers to plow from A to Z at one sitting. Just when you fear you'll go blind from the sight of blown-up, fuzzed-out video footage filling the movie screen, Dárday and Szalai switch to an even more torturous screen-within-a-screen technique. By positioning their camera in front of a television set, they allow the audience to share fully in Raffael's experience as Eastern Europe's foremost couch potato/archivist. So you have to squint for seven or eight minutes at a time. Small price to pay.

Brace for a flurry of action at the 2¼-hour mark. Raffael catches Chip and Rambo having sex, locks them in, sets up his video camera to record their every move, gets drunk and eats fried eggs. Chip and Rambo free themselves, though we never see how. That part must have been edited out to save time.

Be sure to note that at three hours and counting, the cops raid the establishment and discover Raffael has hidden U.S. currency inside a book about Karl Marx. At a press conference for the 30-or-so hardy souls who persevered to the conclusion of last week's advance screening, Szalai explained through a translator that Raffael comes to an inevitably tragic end after attempting to exploit the opportunities presented by Hungary's nascent capitalism. On the other hand, as Raffael's video encyclopedia makes abundantly clear, communism is no bargain, either.

VILLAGE VOICE, 10/3/89, p. 61, J. Hoberman

The New York Film Festival is always good for a Sunday think piece, and this year there's no shortage of movies to think about. Some even address the contemporary world—the ramifications of communications technology, the not-unrelated end of Russian hegemony in Eastern Europe, the corresponding loss of American economic preeminence.

A three-and-a-half-hour evocation of the Hungarian home-video business, *The Documentator* (showing Sunday afternoon and Monday evening) is set in 1987—two years after the local leadership realized that the VCR revolution posed a threat to "socialist morality,' even though, unlike in Poland, Magyar home video was less a matter of guerrilla newreels than black-market porn. (Now socialist morality has all but vanished; last month, the Hungarian Workers Party cynically created a corporate entity with an English-language name, "Next 2000," to protect its portfolio of resorts, garages, and computer systems.) If events have overtaken this film, *The Documentator* is still the first postcommunist movie I've seen, albeit no less Marxist for that.

This epic assemblage, made by István Dárday and Györgyi Szalai from all manner of archival footage, depicts Budapest as a sleazy Eurotown where the Diners Club logo has replaced the hammer and sickle, and a single day's take at the protagonists video store is 10 times the monthly salary of the average Hungarian worker. A vast, visually exciting political cartoon, *The Documentator* has an abundance of sight-gags, very little dialogue, and all manner of juxtaposition. In some respects, it's a throwback to '60s hubris; Dárday and Szalai, who call their movie a "film novel," are groping for a new form. The credit sequence offers a compressed history of 20th century warfare from grainy battlefields to brash color-and-disco video games. A subsequent montage introduces all the film's elements: sex, violence, advertising, surveillance.

Russian tanks may be irrelevant, but the legacy of Soviet filmmakers remains: The movie engages Sergei Eisenstein's sensational "montage of attractions," Dziga Vertov's encyclopedic kino-eye, Esther Shub's historical compilation films. The intellectual categories are Marxist too. (From time to time, the proles appear—getting drunk in a dive named "Hell," dressing up on TV in 18th century costumes—complaining about low pay, high prices, and constant work.) *The Documentator* continually flips the dialectic of glitz and squalor, fiction and documentary, personal drama and history.

Virtually everything in this mad, ambitious movie is mediated by the TV monitor, punctuated by the squeals of car tires and orgasm. Vérité-style monologues alternate with mindless sensationalism, sometimes in the same frame. The use of archival footage takes the last few Márta Mészáros films several steps further: In one set piece, newsreels of Budapest '56 occupy one large monitor and three smaller ones, the soundtrack segueing from a '30 paean to the Five Year Plan to a radio report of Stalin's death. *The Documentator* is a film taxonomy, quoting everything from Italian horror flicks to Wim Wenders's *State of Things*; a so-called "intermission" offers five minutes of Hungarian commercials for toilets, bikinis, tax helpers, designer work clothes, state objet d'art insurance, "superbike" motorcycles, and *The Documentator II*.

The minimal plot concerns a sordid romantic triangle consisting of the middle-aged Raffael, the dour, bearded intellectual of East European tradition (here, the owner of a white Oldsmobile and mighty mogul of the bootleg video market), his smashing concubine Chip—a blond bombshell with cheekbones up to her hairline—and the leather-clad second-in-command they call Rambo (although his mode of attire more closely suggests RoboCop). Healthy young animals, Chip and Rambo live in their own romantic movie, which Raffael ultimately turns into a closed-circuit spectacle.

The eponymous documentator is not only hooked on surveillance devices, he's a history-junkie, obsessed with the idea of creating a video lexicon of the 20th century. Thus the self-absorption of everyday life, parodied in the narrative and magnified by commercials, is set against the televised drama of Great Events. Even as his feckless employees cavort in the nude, Raffael spends his free time cross-referencing his image archive. (Undermining his lack of commitment, the filmmakers ponder images of Prague '68 with Raffael wondering how to categorize them: *war, coup d'état, demonstration, reform, revolution, counterrevolution,* or *fight for freedom*?) A visionary who narcissistically tapes his own Nietzschean credo while maintaining that cheap video will democratize expression, Raffael embodies the dilemma of the Hungarian movie industry as it maneuvers between a 40-year tradition of state-subsidized "research" and the new imperative to create crowd-pleasing blockbusters.

The filmmakers have this problem themselves: They identify their techniques with advertising even as they make visible much of what we have become immune to. The juxtaposition of rural poverty with a televised speech by Party Secretary Károly Grosz (his platitudes interpersed with random quacking from the barnyard) aside, *The Documentator's* most politically daring moment is the pithy critique one economist offers of the current crisis. Citing the traumas of modern Hungarian history, the tradition of national self-deception, and the unexpected violence of 1956, he raises the possibility that public ignorance of the country's real economic situation could lead to a similar explosion. (Indeed, *The Documentator* has a quintessential Hungarian ending—the police arrive and everything comes to naught.)

This is a film of high energy and deep pessimism. The failure of socialism creates a vacuum that can only be filled by the shit of capitalism.

Also reviewed in:
NEW YORK TIMES, 10/1/89, p. 61, Vincent Canby
VARIETY, 2/22/89, p. 257

DREAM A LITTLE DREAM

A Vestron Pictures release of a Lightning Pictures production. *Executive Producer:* Lawrence Kasanoff and Ellen Steloff. *Producer:* D.E. Eisenberg and Marc Rocco. *Director:* Marc Rocco. *Screenplay:* Daniel Jay Franklin, Marc Rocco, and D.E. Eisenberg. *Story:* Daniel Jay Franklin. *Director of Photography:* King Baggot.

Editor: Russell Livingstone. *Music:* Derek Alpert. *Music Editor:* Mary Bram. *Sound:* Blake Wilcox. *Sound Editor:* Barney Cabral. *Production Designer:* Matthew C. Jacobs. *Art Director:* Melody Levy. *Set Dresser:* Kim Barofsky. *Costumes:* Kristine Brown. *Make-up:* Marie Clark. *Stunt Coordinator:* John Cade. *Running time:* 99 minutes. *MPAA Rating:* PG-13.

CAST: Corey Feldman (Bobby Keller); Corey Haim (Dinger); Jason Robards (Coleman Ettinger); Piper Laurie (Gena Ettinger); Harry Dean Stanton (Ike Baker); Meredith Salenger (Lainie Diamond); William McNamara (Joel); Ria Pavia (Maureen); Lala (Shelley); Laura Lee Norton (Marge); John Ward (Derek); Matt Adler (Dumas); Josh Evans (Low Life #1); Jody Smith (Low Life #2); Kent Faulcon (Low Life #3); Alex Rocco (Gus Keller); Victoria Jackson (Kit Keller); Russell Livingstone (Neighbor Next Door); Mickey Thomas (Mr. Pattison); Fran Taylor (Shelia Baker); Susan Blakely (Cherry Diamond); John Ford Coley (Ron).

LOS ANGELES TIMES, 3/3/89, Calendar/p. 10, Kevin Thomas

In the sweet-natured but hopelessly confused "Dream a Little Dream" Jason Robards' whimsical Coleman Ettinger says he's searching for that point "where dreams and reality intersect." He's hoping to enter a dream state so that he and his wife Gena (Piper Laurie) can possibly live forever. (Coleman and Gena are one of those mature screen couples directed to act like honeymooners.) Gena is as perplexed as we are by her husband's notion, but she agrees to join Coleman in some "transcendental" tai chi exercises on the front lawn of their spacious house in a picture-post card small city.

Just then Bobby (Corey Feldman), a dreamy 16-year-old, happens by, colliding with the bike-riding Lainie (Meredith Salenger), the most gorgeous girl in his high school. Both are knocked momentarily unconscious; when they come to, the spirits of Coleman and Gena have entered their bodies. Or so it seems, for "Dream a Little Dream" compounds its handicap of being at least the *fifth* body exchange comedy recently, by a self-defeating level of obscurity. You can never be certain at any given moment at which level of reality—or in whose dreams, perhaps—the film is unfolding. Coleman doesn't exactly take over Bobby's personality, yet Bobby seems to have acquired a 65-year-old's perspective. Gena seems to have little effect on Lainie until much later, when Lainie starts dreaming about her.

Director Marc Rocco and his writers are trying to show us young people and older people discovering what each has to offer the other, certainly a noble sentiment. They would have been far better off without the overused body swap gimmick, especially since they don't seem to have their hearts in it anyway. Overlong, repetitive and self-indulgent, "Dream a Little Dream" reveals its makers to be so enchanted with their characters that they lose all perspective. Although they do have a quartet of charmers in the central roles—augmented by Harry Dean Stanton as Coleman's sensible best friend—they can't overcome such a heady dose of muddled sentimentality.

"Dream a Little Dream," which has a very busy, noisy score, does allow Feldman and Salenger to shine, making us eager to see them in more rewarding circumstances. Feldman, who has a bright, rebellious intensity, continually makes unpredicatable choices that set him apart from most young actors, and Salenger has a cool, assured presence. Feldman plays off Corey Haim, his likable sidekick in both this film and last year's "License to Drive" especially well. Susan Blakely, as Lainie's shallow mother, heads "Dream a Little Dream's" (PG-13 for language) substantial supporting cast.

NEW YORK POST, 3/3/89, p. 27, Jami Bernard

The latest entry in that new and annoying category, the body-switch movie, opens with the two Coreys—Haim and Feldman—being their cool-dude selves. "Dogfight!" yells Haim, and the two start snarling and barking at each other. In quick MTV-style blackouts, backed by pounding music, the Coreys have a sleep-over, cut holes in their jeans and talk about girls. Male bonding in the late '80s consists of applying hair mousse in front of the same mirror.

The Coreys have appeared in enough movies together ("The Lost Boys" and "License to Drive") to be a well-matched set, and they really have a certain easy charm together that makes them if not the great comic duo of their age, at least easy on the eyes. Haim is puppy-dog anxious to please; Feldman's growly voice belies his coming-of-age insecurity.

But the Coreys do not switch bodies with each other in "Dream a Little Dream"—they're too similar. Instead, Feldman switches bodies with the oldster down the block (Jason Robards), who has been practicing weird Tai Chi with his wife (Piper Laurie), in hopes of just such an event, so that he can prolong their lives together.

Something goes wrong. Instead of "Eugene O'Neill meets MTV,' which could have been a disaster anyway, "Dream" is an awkward, ill-conceived confusion that is jogged along by an incessant rock score and is filmed in choppy, short-attention-span cuts.

Haim is sidelined with a broken leg (apparently what really has happened to him). Piper Laurie fares even less well—like Brundlefly in "The Fly"—only some of her is unconsciously imbedded in the luscious Meredith Salenger, on whom Feldman has a crush. The rest of her is off in the ozone of Robards' bad dreams.

Of course, the whole idea of a body-switch is, you know, to walk a mile in another man's shoes. But the old geezer in the young body mostly learns to mousse his hair like Michael Jackson and do a self-conscious moonwalk, while the irreverent teen does not ever develop Robards' body at all (whaa?) but lounges around in the ozone basking in the thought of never going to school again.

Harry Dean Stanton puts in an enigmatic appearance as a sort of helpmate who rarely comes down off his porch, a Boo Radley for the sleep set.

Most of the action revolves around Feldman's pursuit of Salenger, who twirls appealingly in her modern dance class, but many of the scenes appear to have been filmed, and edited together, at random. A high-drama showdown at the end is especially unconvincing, and an odd, lip-synched duet between Robards and Feldman just goes to show that there *is* a generation gap. "Dream a Little Dream" does nothing to bridge it.

NEWSDAY, 3/3/89, Part III/p. 8, Terry Kelleher

"Something happened. I don't know what. But I got trapped in this body and I can't get out."

As teen star Corey Feldman speaks these words, a terrible sense of deja vu sweeps over the audience. "Like Father, Like Son," "Vice Versa," "18 Again" and "Big" obviously were not enough. The generational-body-swap movie *can* be done again—and done worse.

"Dream a Little Dream" induces sleep from the start, with its interminable credit sequence. An inane conversation between Feldman and Corey Haim is followed by Jason Robards lip-synching Mel Torme's rendition of the title song. Maybe his agent meant to book him on "Puttin'on the Hits."

Robards plays a charming eccentric in his 60s who has strange theories about dreams and eternal life. He's outdoors one night conducting a wacko experiment with his wife (Piper Laurie) when Feldman and the girl of his dreams (Meredith Salenger) collide while cutting through the older folks' back yard. Presto: Robards' mind is in Feldman's body, Robards' body is in the movie only when he's dreaming about talking to Feldman, and Feldman's trying to convince Salenger that she's Laurie and he's Robards. Meanwhile, Haim says, "Chill out, dude," and other best-pal stuff.

Daniel Jay Franklin's flimsy, confused screenplay leaves numerous gaps that director Marc Rocco fills with rock videos. Just when it seems that "Dream a Little Dream" will consist of nothing but Feldman and Salenger dancing, walking and brooding to today's hits the movie turns into "Rebel Without a Script." Feldman's romantic rival (William McNamara) gets drunk, grabs a gun and goes after a punk who, for the viewer's convenience has the label "PUNK" sewn on his jacket. Passing on the wisdom of Robards' years, Feldman intercedes with a rambling speech on the futility of violence.

The adults in "Dream a Little Dream" should've stayed in bed. Robards and Laurie act like blissed-out refugees from "Cocoon." Harry Dean Stanton is to Robards what Haim is to Feldman—faithful and superfluous. As Feldman's parents, Alex Rocco (father of the director) and Victoria Jackson are one-note dolts. Salenger's mother (Susan Blakely) is bitch enough to drug her child as a means of control.

Feldman's no prize as the young hero. We never see Robards in him, and we never see what Salenger sees in him. But his performance is only part of the problem. What dooms "Dream a Little Dream" is its failure to develop the gimmick in any way that's funny, dramatic or even coherent.

VILLAGE VOICE, 3/7/89, p. 60, Amy Taubin

Enervatingly inept, *Dream a Little Dream* tries to goose up a belated addition to the grownup-in-a-boy's-body genre—the age differential here is 50 years—with MTV fast-and-fragmented cutting, but the beat is strictly oompah, oompah, ad infinitum. Clearly desperate, the producers introduce a song roughly every two minutes, but the film's puerile sentiments manage to dull even the sounds of Otic Redding and Van Morrison. Vestron Pictures is obviously aiming this release at the home market, but I wouldn't rent it if it were the last tape in the store. My sympathies to the excellent actors who had the misfortune to be involved. I bet someone described the project to them as *very* special.

Also reviewed in:
NEW YORK TIMES, 3/3/89, p. C16, Walter Goodman
VARIETY, 3/1-7/89, p. 16
WASHINGTON POST, 3/6/89, p. C3, Richard Harrington

DREAM TEAM, THE

A Universal Pictures release of an Imagine Entertainment film. *Executive producer:* Joseph M. Caracciolo. *Producer:* Christopher W. Knight. *Director:* Howard Zieff. *Screenplay:* Jon Connolly and David Loucka. *Director of Photography:* Adam Holender. *Editor:* C. Timothy O'Meara. *Music:* David McHugh. *Music Editor:* Kathleen Bennett and Segue Music. *Sound:* Bruce Carwardine, Glen Gauthier, Gary Parker, and (music) Greg Townley. *Sound Editor:* Fred J. Brown. *Production Designer:* Todd Hallowell. *Art Director:* Christopher Nowak and Greg Keen. *Set Decorator:* John Alan Hicks. *Set Dresser:* Bruce Swanson. *Special Effects:* Neil N. Trifunovich. *Costumes:* Ruth Morley. *Make-up:* Patricia Green. *Stunt Coordinator:* Danny Aiello III and Anton Tyukodi. *Running time:* 113 minutes. *MPAA Rating:* PG-13.

CAST: Michael Keaton (Billy Caulfield); Christopher Lloyd (Henry Sikorsky); Peter Boyle (Jack McDermott); Stephen Furst (Albert Ianuzzi); Dennis Boutsikaris (Dr. Weitzman); Lorraine Bracco (Riley); Milo O'Shea (Dr. Newald); Philip Bosco (O'Malley); James Remar(Gianelli); Jack Gilpin (Dr. Talmer); MacIntyre Dixon (Dr. Verboven); Michael Lembeck (Ed); Bill Goffi (Singer/Accordionist); Jack Duffy (Bernie); Brad Sullivan (Sgt. Vincente); Larry Pine (Canning); Harold Surratt (Pastor Lester); The Frierson Family Singers (Gospel Group); Kenneth Raybourne and Alphonsus E. Platt (Gospel Musicians); Robert Weil (Caesar); Janet Feindel (Senior Nurse); Tico Wells (Station Attendant); Barry Flatman (Arrogant Yuppie); Ted Simonett and Bruce Hunter (Yuppies); John Stocker (Murray); Lizbeth Mackay (Henry's Wife); Olivia Horton (Henry's Daughter); Richard Fitzpatrick (Dr. Bauer); Jack Jessop (Dr. Meekum); Ron James (Dwight); Dennis Parlato and Freda Foh Shen (T.V. Newscasters); Donna Hanover and Greg Beresford (Field Reporters); Wayne Tippit (Captain Lewitt); Eric Fink (Priest); A. Frank Ruffo (Relative); Michael Copeman (Con Ed Man); Victor Ertmanis (Man in Mets Jersey); Cynthia Belliveau (Nurse); Stewart Bick (Paramedic); James O'Regan (Litterbug); Dick Callahan (Bartender); Shelley Goldstein (Waitress); Jihmi Kennedy (Tow Man); Marty Waldman (Salesman); Michelyn Emelle (Duty Nurse Harriet); Michael Beatty (Intern); Jane Luk (Admissions Nurse); Marilyn Peppiatt and Myra Fried (Floor Nurses); J.R. Zimmerman (Hospital Guard); Maxine Miller (Newald's Secretary); Pat Idlette (Woman at Police Station); Max Haines and Henry Gomez (Guards); Ellen Maguire (Canning's Secretary); Al Therrien and Don Saunders (Security Guards); John Liddle (Cop); Dwayne MacLean (Old Gent); Kay Hawtrey and Patricia Carol Brown (Nurses); Chick Roberts (Old Guard); Nicholas Pasco (Man Out Window).

LOS ANGELES TIMES, 4/7/89, Calendar/p. 10, Michael Wilmington

Howard Zieff's new comedy "The Dream Team" is so clearly derived from the movie "One Flew Over the Cuckoo's Nest" that you might begin to wonder when Jack Nicholson will show up. This mechanically funny, amiably slick farce seems to expand, perhaps unconsciously, on the "Cuckoo" scene where Nicholson's McMurphy took his fellow inmates on an unauthorized field trip—jazzed up with another "fish out of water" comic thriller plot.

These "loonies " don't mean to be unauthorized. They're stranded in Manhattan when their psychiatrist (Dennis Boutsikaris), driving them to a Yankee game, is beaten into a coma after witnessing a murder. The only witness is the one member of the quartet who can't communicate (Stephen Furst, as Iannuzzi, babbling out catch-phrases from TV commercials and Phil Rizzuto's Yankee broadcasts). The foursome is left on the streets with everyone pitted against them.

You'd like to see Nicholson pop up here, perhaps in a restaurant scene, ordering some toast, but his part—the rebellious, wisecracking hothead—has already been taken by Michael Keaton. Is it just an illusion, or is Keaton consciously pushing Nicholson mannerisms in this performance? They've always had a certain kindred attitude: black, sarcastic, sexually opportunistic, defiantly flaky and quick. But here, the screenwriters have Keaton's Billy Caulfield doing Jersey drawls and throwing a tantrum every 10 minutes or so.

The other three also resemble "Cuckoo's Nest" characters. Christopher Lloyd's anal-compulsive play-doctor suggests William Redfield's Harding; Stephen Furst's Iannuzzi recalls Danny DeVito's Martini, and Peter Boyle's religious fanatic McDermott, going full circle, suggests Lloyd's old, "Cuckoo" part, howling Taber. Boutsikaris' Dr. Weitzman—who's always kiding everybody and advising them to cheer up—bears an eerie resemblance to Steven Spielberg.

All this may suggest that "Dream Team" is a weak, derivative, somehow disreputable movie, which is somewhat true. If you compare it to its obvious source, it has a coy, flip attitude toward illness, skating over the surface of tragedy, dementia and pain without breaking the ice. The union of four oddballs—rebel-writer, obsessive noodge, religious fanatic and couch potato—is almost too schematic, as if the writers were somehow trying to define '80s dissidence. But even though you can predict virtually everything that happens from the first five minutes on, the director and actors manage to hook you in.

Keaton, Lloyd and Boyle are carnivorously funny: three scene-stealers whose specialty has always been offbeat intensity, quirky, flamboyant energy. And though Furst ("Animal House's" Flounder) is playing the weakest role, he has a great comic waddle, running along helplessly behind them like a chafed turtle.

Zieff's outstanding comedy merit is the way he seems to let his casts open out and take over. Here, the fugitives get to do insane upstaging exhibitions—at the beginning, they rarely even seem to be looking at each other—followed by sentiment, guns and car chases, romps with Lorraine Bracco and cutesy camaraderie. All three of them respond. Boyle, as an ad executive with a messiah complex, an F.D.R. grin and a compulsion to undress in public, hasn't been this funny in years. (If it were better written and more convulsively developed, the scene where Boyle gives his testimony and strips in a black storefront church might have been a little classic on the scale of Red Skelton's "Guzzler's Gin.")

"The Dream Team" (MPAA rated PG-13, for violence and language) isn't unusual, but it's funnier than, say, "Twins" or "Fletch Lives." It can't really hit any classic highs, perhaps because it regards rebellion as cute and paranoia as a running gag. The jokes, to stick, need grittier, sawtooth edges. Life may be a madhouse, but if we were all patients in asylums where the doctors looked and acted like Steven Spielberg, none of us might want to call home.

MONTHLY FILM BULLETIN, 6/89, p. 179, John Pym

On an outing from Cedarbrook, their New Jersey hospital, four psychotic patients—volatile Billy, silent Albert, punctilious Henry, and Jack who believes he is Jesus—find themselves alone in Manhattan when their keeper, Dr. Weitzman, mysteriously disappears. As Albert knows, but cannot say, Weitzman was witness to a professional killing and, having been beaten unconscious, has been whisked away by ambulance. After a night of misadventures, with Billy discovering that his girl Riley has found another man and Jack stripping off at a black revival service, the four madmen uneasily band together and unsuccessfully seek the help of the police. (It was, it transpires, two policemen—O'Malley and Gianelli—who had clubbed Weitzman after they had killed a colleague who was about to expose them for corruption.) Albert having intimated as best he can that Weitzman's disappearance has something to do with ambulances, the quartet set about checking all the city infirmaries. At Mercy Hospital, Albert again gives a warning, and the men narrowly succeed in frightening off O'Malley and Gianelli who are about to complete their job on Weitzman. Billy, the most rational of the lunatics, begins to fathom what has happened, but receives no help when he telephones Dr. Newald, the by now panic-stricken Cedarbrook administrator. The police find their murdered colleague and suspicion falls on the madmen, who despite their best efforts are soon collared. Billy implores the visiting Riley to hasten to Mercy to save Weitzman. Having now discovered a capacity for independent action, the madmen bury their mutual animosity and effect an escape by switching roles with the doctors who have come to return them to hospital. With Riley's help, Weitzman is saved and O'Malley and Gianelli overcome. Later, the four men again set out from Cedarbrook in a second attempt to see a baseball game in New York City.

There are two moments when this sharp and punchily acted picture slip-slidingly reminds one that Howard Zieff, before putting his name to *Private Benjamin* and a string of other well-arranged mainstream entertainments, made his début with the original and gloriously strung-out comedy *Slither*. The first is when the four patients nervously en route to New York pick up on the driver's lead and give a throwaway rendition of "Hit the Road Jack": the script may have called for it, but this scatty, privileged and above all unstressed moment occurred before the camera. The second is when Weitzman, having taken Albert down a sinister alley to relieve a call of nature, chances on the murder: the scene is straight out of *Point Blank*, and for a tingling second it seems one might just possibly be watching a wholly different film, one liable to go shooting off in unpredictable directions. In the event, *The Dream Team* ends exactly how and where one would expect, but that initial, revivifying uncertainty is never wholly absent.

Zieff has a way with actors—Goldie Hawn has never been better than as the Jewish princess turned Private Benjamin—and here he is royally served by his four principals. Christopher Lloyd may have played one too many madmen; Peter Boyle, a deadpan zany, may perhaps have wondered about the wisdom, at his time in life, of removing all his clothes in front of the camera; and Michael Keaton, an actor fuelled by high-octane fizz, has not yet wholly recovered from the effects of the manic Beetlejuice. Here, however, admirably partnered by the dumpling Stephen Furst, the straight guy for all the crackerjack energy, they manage notably fresh ensemble performances. Lost in New York, they are like children separated from their teacher, rather than the sort of roaming psychopaths familiar from a hundred lesser pictures. Only when they find themselves in a tight corner do they threaten to behave like "real" lunatics. They are not exactly sainted 60s madmen; but they accept their condition—Cedarbrook being little more than a benevolent country club—and, the film suggests, they have lessons to teach us.

It is here that *The Dream Team*—note the candied title—veer into the realm of insidious sentimentality. Its most cloying moment, for example, has Henry return home, shortly before he is arrested, for a reunion which ends with father giving his adoring little girl a clipboard, the cherished emblem of Henry's delusion that he is an all-controlling doctor. There is, too, something a shade schematic about the villainy of the real world—not the dyed-in-the-wool evil of the two cops but the ease, for example, with which Jack, once a whizz advertising copywriter, is turned in by the former colleague to whom he has appealed for help. These madmen are not up against a world crazier than themselves, but one marked chiefly by its predictability. This said, however, in the end, the film's bite, and its imprinting star performances particularly, carry the day.

NEW YORK POST, 4/7/89, p. 29, David Edelstein

"The Dream Team" sets you up for a wild and crazy ride. It's the story of four psychotics left to fend for themselves in Manhattan after their guardian gets bonked on the head—not exactly a G.B. Shaw premise, but no more lamebrained than a lot of slapstick setups.

The possibilities for clowning are obvious, and the clowns, in this case, are tops: Michael Keaton (fresh from his triumphs in "Beetlejuice" and "Clean and Sober"), Christopher Lloyd and Peter Boyle. They can be gonzo performers, recklessly inventive, but in "The Dream Team" they wear their caricatures like strait-jackets. The movie is depressingly sane.

Keaton plays a man with an "attitude problem"—he can't stand authority, he's a compulsive liar and he's prone to violence. But in this New Jersey psychiatric hospital, he's the closest thing to a Regular Guy.

Lloyd, with his prissy lips and pinstriped suit (with two pens in his breast pocket) is the ultimate anal-retentive, a delusional neat freak. Stephen Furst repeats lines from TV programs and nothing else. Boyle believes he is the Son of God and frequently strips to his birthday suit because "We are all naked in the eyes of the Lord."

Their do-good therapist, Dr. Weitzman (Dennis Boutsikaris), thinks it's time for these yo-yos to take a field trip to Yankee Stadium. In some respects, he gets what he deserves, since anyone can tell you that you don't go from Jersey to Yankee Stadium via the Holland Tunnel. Somewhere around Times Square Furst has to empty his bladder, and Weitzman witnesses a homicide at the hands of two bad cops (James Remar and Philip Bosco). For his trouble he gets his skull bashed in, and the loonies drift into the night.

It's hard to account for the subsequent tedium of "The Dream Team," since the actors are inventive and some of the lines have wit. Its studio has dubbed it "a comic odyssey," but it has no momentum; the picture goes around in circles like an electric wheelchair with an expired passenger—director Howard Zieff? After 10 minutes I had to restrain myself from going out for Gummi Bears; after half an hour I wanted a shot of Thorazine.

Even if the movie had been properly paced, it would still be a stiff. The borders around each character are too thick, and the formula weighs the actors down: instead of getting crazier, they're forced to band together to save their therapist. It turns out they're not really psychotics—they're just lovably dotty. And they have big hearts. The icky piano score by David McHugh keeps "The

Dream Team'' dear, responsible—the music functions like the "sleep" button on your bedside clock radio.

His huge body naked , a serene smile wiggling across his face, Boyle supplies the picture's only shot of dementia. When, in the group's van, he sings along with the instrumental fills in "Hit the Road, Jack,'' he finds the perfect balance between the ecstatic highs of bebop and the lunatic freedom of a padded cell.

Keaton is terrific, too, but he's at half-speed. Wiry and alert, his face has a pickled, incredulous look, like an octopus sucking a lemon, and he gives the movie jolts of danger: When he hurls a chair against a window and mashes an insolent yuppie's head down on a restaurant table, he doesn't soften the rage or make it comic. He's mad.

But Keaton also has the snorting impatience of a racehorse held unconscionably long in a paddock—he can't wait to tear loose and Go For It. Keaton has flown so high in his last few pictures that he can't seem to settle anymore for the sitcom silliness of movies like "The Dream Team.'' He must have related to his character—locked up, patronized restrained.

NEWSDAY, 4/7/89, Part III/p. 3, Lynn Darling

"The Dream Team'' is based on an innately funny premise—four acknowledged crazy people on their own in New York, a city that's no slouch in bringing out the insanity lurking in most of its inhabitants.

But instead of these elements combining into the smoothly accelerating screwball comedy it obviously means to be, "The Dream Team'' coughs and sputters along in the breakdown lane, unable to keep up any momentum.

It's too bad, because the combination of actors playing the crazoids is so promising: Michael Keaton as a writer with an overdeveloped fantasy life and a right hook ready to deck anyone who challenges him, Christopher Lloyd as a compulsive postal clerk who thinks he's on the other side of the doctor-patient relationship, Peter Boyle as an advertising executive with a Christ complex, and Stephen Furst as a gentle catatonic who speaks in koans derived from a life of constant TV watching.

The four patients form a fractious therapy group at a psychiatric hospital, where they are considered lifelong inmates. They're just coming off medication when their therapist (Dennis Boutsikaris) takes them to watch a game at Yankee Stadium. The doctor is beaten unconscious after witnessing a murder along the way, and they're suddenly on their own—it's up to them to rescue the doctor and, for that matter, themselves.

The best moments in "The Dream Team'' come in the confrontations between the wackos and the world of the supposedly sane.

There's a funny scene in a fancy apartment where Peter Boyle comments in perfect yuppie-speak on the esthetic qualities of a trendy sculptor, only to segue without warning into his biblical mode. And Keaton has a zippy encounter with a bunch of sexist jerks who are harassing his girlfriend (Lorraine Bracco) in a trendy restaurant. The scenes work because we're given the pleasure of anticipation—we know going into them that these guys are crazy, something the people they're interacting with aren't hip to.

But too much of the movie is taken up in shtick among the loonies themselves; their fixations and delusions don't play off each other particularly well. Christopher Lloyd probably has the toughest time in that regard, since his character is devoted mostly to being a pain-in-the-neck neatness freak.

As the ringleader, Michael Keaton has a role that ought to make full use of his manic, out-on-the-edge persona, and occasionally director Howard Zieff lets him loose—there's a nice scene where he's facing down a cop who is at least as psychotic as he is. But most of the time, the slow-moving script and lame direction do a better job of strait-jacketing him than any more tangible restraints.

VILLAGE VOICE, 4/11/89, p. 64, Georgia Brown

On one point *The Dream Team*, directed by Howard Zieff and written by Jon Connolly and David Loucka, meets *Voyage to Cythera* [see Brown's review of this film]: Each recounts a journey in which the literal goal (Cythera, Yankee Stadium) is never glimpsed. One fine day, a four-patient therapy group and its ambitious leader set out from their home base in bucolic New Jersey for a Yankee game. Heading uptown on Sixth Avenue, they are waylaid when they stop their van at a deserted gas station because one member has to go to the "bathroom.'' The leader,

Dr. Weitzman (Dennis Boutsikaris), takes Albert into an alleyway and, as will happen in the Big Apple, stumbles onto a murder—which happens to be committed by two crooked cops—then is knocked unconscious and taken away in an ambulance.

Thus, four mental patients, with $10 hot dog and soda money each, are left to their own devices on the sidewalks of New York. After some escapades in which each fends separately, the four just happen to run into one another, discover that Dr. Weitzman is in danger, and—since their credibility is not the highest—realize it is up to them to save his life.

This comedy starts very lamely back at the institution, with setups giving each member of the team many chances to demonstrate his particular psychosis. Henry (Christopher Lloyd) is the obsessive-compulsive who thinks he's the doctor and scolds the others for messiness, profanity, and so forth. Verbally and physically aggressive, Billy (Michael Keaton) is his violent antagonist. The traumatized Albert (Stephen Furst) speaks only as if giving a play-by-play; for example, he might say "close play at second" when someone has just avoided being caught. Jack (Peter Boyle) is a former senior vice-president "with a corner office" in an advertising agency, who developed, somewhere in the heat of battle, a Christ complex. He recalls his mission as having been the attempt to "put Jesus Christ back into advertising where he belongs." Back in the world of the sane, women wait, patiently or not, for their men to return.

The Dream Team loosens up a bit from its initial dreariness to deliver a few good laughs. Stiff-upper-lip Lloyd tries to clean up the streets of the city and reform the slovenly habits of its citizens. (He has something of our mayor's old maid fussiness.) As a Peter Boyle fan, I liked him best but found myself wishing his delusion were more imaginative. By the end, one is supposed to have grown fond of the four "madmen." Michael Keaton's antagonistic humor continues to be so aggressive, however, that the movie—which on the surface seems genial enough—wound up making me tense. I couldn't wait to flee their company.

Also reviewed in:
NEW REPUBLIC, 5/8/89, p. 28, Stanley Kauffmann
NEW YORK TIMES, 4/7/89, p. C6, Vincent Canby
NEW YORKER, 4/17/89, p. 113, Pauline Kael
VARIETY, 4/5–11/89, p. 18
WASHINGTON POST, 4/7/89, p. C1, Rita Kempley

DRESSMAKER, THE

A Euro-American Films release of a Freeway/Shedlo film for Film Four International and British Screen. *Executive Producer:* John McGrath. *Producer:* Ronald Shedlo. *Director:* Jim O'Brien. *Screenplay:* John McGrath. *Based on the novel by:* Beryl Bainbridge. *Director of Photography:* Michael Coulter. *Editor:* William Diver. *Music:* George Fenton. *Choreographer:* Isobel Hurll. *Sound:* Sandy MacRae. *Sound Editor:* Peter Joly. *Production Designer:* Caroline Amies. *Art Director:* Chris Townsend. *Costumes:* Judy Moorcroft. *Make-up:* Kezia De Winne. *Stunt Corrdinator:* Jim Dowdall. *Running time:* 92 minutes. *MPAA Rating:* Not Rated.

CAST: Joan Plowright (Nellie); Billie Whitelaw (Margo); Jane Horrocks (Rita); Tim Ransom (Wesley); Peter Postlethwaite (Jack); Pippa Hinchley (Valerie Manders); Rosemary Martin (Mrs. Manders); Tony Haygarth (Mr. Manders); Michael James-Reed (Chuck); Sam Douglas (Corporal Zawadski); Bert Parnaby (Mr. Barnes); Lorraine Ashbourne and Mandy Walsh (Factory Girls); Margi Clarke (Shop Woman); Andrew Moorcroft (Butcher's Boy); Marie Jelliman (Mrs. O'Toole); Rita Howard (Producer); Pamela Austin and Gerry White (Singers); Dorothy Dearnley (Pianist); Anthony Benson (Terrence); Al Mossy (Mr. Betts); Val Elliott (Secretary); Mandy Humphrey, Jayne Male, Bradley Lavelle, and Andrew Woodman (Party Guests); Freda Kelly and Terry Channing (Couple in Doorway).

CHRISTIAN SCIENCE MONITOR, 4/12/89, p. 11, David Sterritt

Sometimes a movie is made by its acting—by first-rate performers just getting up in front of the camera and letting their talent run free. "The Dressmaker" is one of these.

Its story is nothing special, and its settings are anything but glamorous. There's real pleasure in watching its performances, though, which are as lifelike and vivid as anything a film has given us lately.

"The Dressmaker" takes place in 1944. The setting is Liverpool, England, and the main characters are three women of two generations. Rita is a 17-year-old, facing problems of life and love that aren't unusual for teen-agers, especially in the movies. She lives with two middle-aged aunts, who raised her and are now trying to guide her into adult life.

The problem is, these two ladies can't agree on many things—including tough questions like "What should a nice girl do on a date?" and "Should Rita keep seeing the dim-witted American soldier who's been paying so much attention to her?"

Rita herself is confused about these things, and when she turns to her aunts for guidance, she gets nothing but mixed signals. One says you can't be too careful about being proper. But the other says you shouldn't pay attention to grownups: They say the things they're *supposed* to say, and youngsters are supposed to disobey now and then. Meanwhile the everhopeful GI is on the sidelines waiting for Rita to respond a little to his passion.

These characters are no more attractive than Liverpool itself during the World War II period—it appears to be a drab and chilly place, with few comforts and no luxuries to offer.

What makes Rita and the others so fascinating to spend time with is the way they're acted, by performers who bring their joys and sorrows to life without ever condescending to them or making their behavior seem ridiculous.

The old pros of the movie are Joan Plowright and Billie Whitelaw, two fine British actresses with a talent for making the ordinary seem extraordinary. It's no surprise to see them give superb performances, but the movie's extra treat is a newcomer named Jane Horrocks, who gives Rita an amazingly complex personality beneath her oh-so-plain exterior. She's an actress of unusual talent, and I'm sure we'll see more of her before long.

Even with its excellent acting, "The Dressmaker" seems kind of stodgy at first, with its main characters always chattering about a party or a date that seem more important to them than to us. But the movie isn't as timid as it may appear.

It includes some nudity, and a last-minute story twist that's downright melodramatic—leading to a final scene that's the best thing in the whole picture.

Directed by Jim O'Brien, a capable British filmmaker, "The Dressmaker" is a small but impressive movie that hits you hardest when you least expect it.

FILMS IN REVIEW, 3/89, p. 169, Pat Anderson

A marvelous Joan Plowright is Nellie, the movie's title character. She is an unmarried, self-righteous woman whose life is lived and governed by the mores of the Victorian era; completely unattuned to contemporary morality; contemptuous of men in general but especially of the American soldiers stationed in Liverpool in 1944. Nellie's tight-lipped disapproval comes out in many ways and is aimed at *everything* that is different or done differently from the days of her childhood. Her younger sister Margo (a fine performance by Billie Whitelaw), by contrast, a war widow, is a munitions worker who is high-spirited, full of life and ready for anything the Twentieth Century has to offer.

Together, these disparate women have raised their niece Rita (promising newcomer, Jane Horrocks) since her father Jack (Peter Postlethwaite), the local butcher, turned her over to his sisters on his wife's death. Jack is a good enough man in his own way, but clearly has little understanding of his family females. Certainly he can't cope with his own daughter, and knows so little of his elder sister that he is upset when she scrupulously spurns his offer of a little black market meat.

Rita, at 17, is predictably a bundle of nerves. The opposite pull of the two aunts leaves her confused, guilt ridden and prey to constant nightmares. When she meets Wesley (Tim Ransom) a simple young man from Mississippi, she is really torn. Margo gleefully encourages Rita to date her Yank, while Nellie, of course, is ignorant of his existence. Rita, though, has imbibed enough of Nellie's strictures to equivocate in her attitude to her erstwhile lover; she shrinks when he touches her—the idea of sex both fascinates and repels her—and she knows enough to realize she is trying his patience. But not enough to see that he is not in love with her at all. Wesley wants only the obvious from Rita: when he doesn't get it, his eyes light on Margo. The interplay between the three women and the only man who has entered their world in years, furnishes the catalyst for a natural, but shocking climax.

The picture is from a prize winning Beryl Bainbridge novel, nicely adapted by John McGrath. And director Jim O'Brien has really captured wartime Liverpool. One can almost smell the drabness of the city, with its shortages and endless queues. And the differences between the local men and the U.S. troops are not glossed over: jealousy of the Americans' freedom with money, nylons and various PX goodies to win the Liverpool women, results in frequent fights. No punches are pulled in showing the tribal antagonisms in this still male dominated society, giving the film the veracity it deserves.

LOS ANGELES TIMES, 12/16/88, Calendar/p. 8, Michael Wilmington

Wartime, home-front movies, even great ones like "Hope and Glory," often go a little dewy with sentiment, self-sacrifice and solidarity. But in "The Dressmaker," we get a more disturbing view, drained of exhilaration or uplift.

The film—adapted from a Beryl Bainbridge novel, beautifully acted, full of grimness and irony—is set in Liverpool in 1944. In the city outside, the cigarettes and meat are rationed, the British and American soldiers feud and brawl, the streets are full of soot and rain. Inside, something worse is brewing. "The Dressmaker" imprisons the audience in one of those terrible claustrophobic households we get in plays by Harold Pinter or Tennessee Williams: veined with dark secrets, buried hatreds and fears, where propriety battles sexuality and both lose.

It's a bleak view. But what gives "The Dressmaker" its own exhilaration is the acting: especially the mesmerizingly powerful lead performances by Joan Plowright and Billie Whitelaw. These two great stage actresses make a strikingly opposite pair. Plowright's face has a mother-hen sternness and glistening eyes. Whitelaw's is harsh and angular; her eyes like molten, angry flakes of blue.

The seemingly antipathetic sisters they play are engaged in a sort of moral war over their niece, Rita (Jane Horrocks), a sad girl tentatively approaching womanhood, in love with the first man who has noticed her: a carefree, illiterate soldier from Mississippi. Rita's heart may be broken because she refuses this shallow, opportunistic farm boy the only thing he really wants from her—sex.

Neither aunt is quite what she seems. Good-time Margo (Whitelaw) is a florid extrovert who breaks up her factory line with horrible renditions of old pop songs. Nellie (Plowright), at first, seems the paradigm of the long-suffering, kindly maiden aunt.

Yet, we gradually see that Nellie has evolved into a family tyrant, stern guardian of the Victorian values of her youth, while Margo is steadily growing sillier, louder, a chain-smoking devotee of radio serials and shameless flirtations. Their brother, Rita's father Jack (Peter Postlethwaite), who lives elsewhere, is a sallow butcher who spouts racist prejudices and all but swoons at the sight of human blood.

The two women seem so morally and physically opposed that it comes as a shock when we discover that they still sleep in the same bed. That moment is the key to the special horror of the film, crystallizing the family's entrapment, the dark side that begins to steadily reveal itself.

"The Dressmaker" is about the intrusion of sexuality into a household built on a tacit, but finally murderous rejection of all sex. Much of the family's careful routine is based on lies, hypocrisy, role-playing. Margo inwardly blames Nellie for the death of her World War I soldier-husband and the loss of potential suitors. Nellie views sexuality with fascinated distaste, while, ironically, she earns her living making dresses for local girls to catch their beaux. Rita, caught between them, is simultaneously pulled toward devious sensuality by Margo, and self-flagellating chastity by Nellie.

Playwright John McGrath, who adapted the novel, has created a shrewdly anti-sentimental family portrait. It's all the more effective, because, for the first half of "The Dressmaker," you may suspect it *will* be sentimental: that it's about long-suffering Nellie's old-fashioned devotion, the good heart that beats under Margo's bursting decolletage, and about poor sweet Rita, who will emerge sadder but wiser, yet still cherishing her handsome Yank memories.

No such luck. The film has another side, the kind of horrific cul-de-sac you might find in the sordid family dramas of Balzac, Zola or Celine.

"The Dressmaker's" director, Jim O'Brien, comes from British TV; he was the co-director of the miniseries made from Paul Scott's "Jewel in the Crown" quartet. O'Brien doesn't have a strong, visual style. Nor does he really develop the right ensemble rhythm with this cast. The individual performances—including a brief nasty bit by Margie Clarke of "Letter to Brezhnev"—while excellent, don't always seem to blend or connect with each other. The movie lacks spontaneity.

Interestingly enough, this doesn't necessarily hurt the story, which is about alienation and role-playing. What O'Brien has done is choose a trenchant, evocative tale, and then put his talents completely at the service of superb actors.

They respond brilliantly. Few actors' moments in any other 1988 movie are as charged or memorable as the sight of Horrocks' Rita burying her mother's little pearl necklace in the sand, or Plowright's dressmaker Nellie scurrying around on her punctilious errands, or the look on Whitelaw's face as she waits in the night air to seduce another, improbable lover.

Whitelaw makes Margo—her face pathetically painted and powdered, voluptuously silly, full of desire and shame—a woman so frustrated and cramped that she's become besotted with her own dime-novel romances. It's as if Margo's most squalid little sins were mad flights of passion, as if the household were a cliff of repression from which she had to hurl herself, while keeping chains of propriety wrapped around her ankles. In "The Dressmaker" (Times-rated: Mature) that's exactly what they are.

MONTHLY FILM BULLETIN, 1/89, p. 14, Pam Cook

Liverpool, September 1944: Since her mother died when she was very young, seventeen-year-old Rita has lived with her unmarried aunts Nellie and Margo, while her father Jack lives alone above his butcher's shop. A neighbour, Valerie Manders, invites Rita to a party, and the fun-loving Margo decides to go along. The party is attended by rowdy GIs, and while Margo becomes merry, Rita gets to know Wesley, a gauche young American soldier. She starts to go out with him secretly, and though shocked by his clumsy sexual advances, becomes infatuated. Margo finds out about Wesley and Rita when Valerie's mother lets it slip. Knowing that the puritanical Nellie and the Yank-hating Jack will object, she keeps the secret, feeling that Rita needs experience. Frustrated by Rita's lack of passion, Wesley cools off, and the desperate Rita sends him letters via Chuck, Valerie's GI fiancé. One night, she returns home from a date with Wesley to find that Margo has told Nellie and Jack, who insist on inviting the young man to tea. Margo flirts with him and he responds, to Rita's dismay. A few days later, Wesley visits the house when he knows Margo is alone and asks her to tell Rita he wants to end the relationship. Disturbed by his suggestive behaviour, Margo packs him off. Rita finds out from Valerie that Wesley is poorly educated so that Chuck has to read her letters to him, and that he is no longer interested in her. At home, Margo tells Rita about Wesley's visit. Rita is angry, and goes to Valerie's engagement party with Nellie in sullen mood, while Margo stays at home with a headache. Returning home early, Nellie hears noises upstairs and investigates, taking her dressmaker's scissors. She surprises Margo and Wesley in bed; as he stumbles past her, Nellie stabs him and he falls down the stairs to his death. Nellie and Margo dispose of the body with Jack's help, and the household returns to normal.

Beryl Bainbridge's 1973 novel, set in wartime Liverpool, is a savage vignette of Northern working-class life disturbed by the intrusion of American hedonism on traditional puritan values. Born in Liverpool herself, Bainbridge approaches her subject with a mixture of affection and malice, injecting a bizarrely surreal note into her characters' attempts to keep the lid on their lives in the face of the promise of abundance held out by the American Dream.

John McGrath's faithful adaptation and Jim O'Brien's low-key direction tend towards realism, stressing (as do so many British films about Britishness) confined spaces and constrained lives, allowing carefully observed details to convey the sense of normality coming apart at the seams: Nellie, the dressmaker, ritualistically dusting her dead mother's furniture to keep change at bay; her frustrated sister Margo's moments of manic hysteria; and Rita, their repressed seventeen-year-old ward, on the verge of sexual awakening, coveting a pearl necklace which belonged to her mother.

The film is carried by the faultless performances of Joan Plowright as Nellie and Billie Whitelaw as Margo, each of whom in different ways tries to protect Rita when she becomes involved with a young GI. They are both ambivalent figures: Nellie on the one hand capable and strong, on the other obsessively concerned with respectability, disapproving of Margo's open sexuality, yet displaying a hidden violent streak as she beheads and skins one of brother Jack's rabbits. Nellie's frustrations are turned inwards, while Margo, who blames her sister for spoiling her chances of marriage, is openly, aggressively bitter. Afraid that Rita's chances will be similarly ruined, she encourages the relationship with Wesley, until her desires take over and she goes to bed with him herself, provoking the climactic murder.

Rita is caught in the middle, pathetically vulnerable and emotionally undernourished, she dreams of escaping the narrow red-brick terraces for the freedom of suburban America, seeing Wesley as her way out. But she is too crippled by her background either to see through Wesley or cope with the desires he arouses in her. Rita has none of the tough independence displayed by Northern heroines from Jo in *A Taste of Honey* to Teresa and Elaine in *A Letter to Brezhnev*; she is profoundly damaged, a sullen victim of puritanism's iron grip. What saves this from being a thoroughly depressing account of working-class life is, on the one hand, the *joie de vivre* of the neighbouring Manders family, with their parties and unashamed enjoyment of American favours, and on the other, the almost terrible strength of the two sisters, especially Nellie. After murdering Wesley, she quickly organises Margo into clearing up the mess while she stitches a shroud for the body and gets Jack to dispose of it. By the time Rita returns home, everything is back in place and the familiar bed-time rituals of turning down the gas lamps and removing the corsets carried on

It is perhaps inevitable that this straightforwardly realist adaptation sacrifices some of the original novel's psychological complexity. Bainbridge's description of Nellie's almost uncontrollably violent inner anger, when the shop assistant refuses to give her Margo's cigarettes, translates into a scene of comic self-righteous bluster, and the links between Nellie's bottled-up feelings and her murderous impulses are a little too tenuous. Similarly, Margo's often febrile state of mental disarray is less easy to depict through this exterior, observational style. Most marked is the absence of Rita's nightmares, described graphically and disturbingly in the novel (at the end of the film, as the household returns to normal and Rita lies in bed between her aunts, her nightmare wakes her up and the camera slowly zooms out...). But in spite of losing some of Bainbridge's unpleasantness, this version of *The Dressmaker* quietly and insidiously strikes a chill in the heart.

NEW YORK, 3/6/89, p. 56, David Denby

Belatedly, I want to add to the swelling chorus of praise for the fine English film *The Dressmaker*. In Liverpool, in 1944, a rather timid, pale seventeen-year-old girl, Rita (Jane Horrocks), lives with two aunts—the formidable, disapproving Nellie (Joan Plowright), a spinster who heads the household and works at home as a dressmaker, and the kindly Margot (Billie Whitelaw), a munitions worker who was widowed in World War I but still looks for men and a good time in life. Based on a novel by Beryl Bainbridge (John McGrath did the dramatically effective adaptation), *The Dressmaker* uses the materials of a gothic fairy tale—good and bad witches controlling a motherless young girl—but in a realistic way that builds in power to a shocking yet entirely convincing conclusion.

The dowdy house they live in is a shadowy horror, a mausoleum ruled by the spinster's love of her very strict dead mother, which she has somehow fetishized and transformed into an iron law of propriety. Greedily, Nellie clings to the pictures, the furniture, the manners and prohibitions that once marked the family's standing in the world. At the same time, Margot, desperate but squelched by her sister, tries to keep up some spirit. The mutual recriminations between these two, encompassing a possible crime committed decades earlier, reach a climax when their niece falls in love with an American soldier stationed in England. Thin and quiet, Rita has a face that hasn't come alive yet. Her boyfriend, Wesley (Tim Ransom), a rangy and broad-shouldered Southerner, illiterate, practically inarticulate, awakens in her a ravaging desire to be loved. But Rita is frightened by sex, and the boy's sexual hunger, reverberating uneasily in the repressive household, leads to catastrophe.

The direction, by Jim O'Brien, is extraordinarily precise in mood and color—plain, even matter-of-fact, but never obvious—and the movie is superbly acted. Billie Whitelaw may remind you of an aunt unlucky in love (everyone has one) who drinks too much, sings too much, flirts with all the available men; she is heartbreaking. Plowright's villainess could have been a standard movie turn—the kind of showy thing that Gladys Cooper did in old Hollywood pictures. But Plowright makes Nellie's rage against sexuality, her clinging to propriety and discipline, a true passion, not some huffy shrinking from life. Indeed, Nellie is not afraid of anything. Throughout, we get hints of how terrifying a person she can be, but you don't quite understand her until the astonishing and ironic ending.

NEW YORK POST, 1/6/89, p. 25, David Edelstein

As Margo, a lusty widow, Billie Whitelaw begins "The Dressmaker" by hurling water onto the fire in her bedroom furnace. The steam hisses, the cat leaps up with a shriek, and Margo throws back her head and roars, toothsome in her hairnet. The image is rude, unnerving—even more so because, in the background, Margo's prudish sister Nellie (Joan Plowright) glowers at her like a bull.

The two—residents of Liverpool during the final, black days of the second World War—are diametric opposites. Nellie, the dressmaker, is a prig who thinks that England, overrun with American GIs and "painted" young girls, is going to the devil.

But the war has liberated Margo, who was thrashed as a child by a mother a lot like her sister; now she loves nothing more than making a spectacle of herself. At the factory where she works, she warbles "Please don't take my sunshine away" over sacks of machine-gun bullets.

"The Dressmaker," based on a novel by Beryl Bainbridge, is a queer, intense sort of comedy—small-scale but overflowing. In its droll way, it's a profile of an entire country wracked with tension. And yet all of this is compressed into the relationship of these two middle-aged sisters (who loathe each other but sleep in the same bed) and the gawky 17-year-old niece, Rita (Jane Horrocks), whom they've stepped in to raise. (Their widower brother, a butcher who recoils from blood, is an ineffectual father.)

The film tells what happens when Rita tumbles for an American soldier, Wesley (Tim Ransom), who worms his way into the girl's lonely life for the sake of a little nooky. Margo counsels her niece to give in to the Yank's demands for sex and even longs for a bit herself; Nellie, on the other hand, gives you the feeling she'd kill to keep such depravity out of her house. Rita, sandwiched between repression and exhibitionism, is going mad.

Snuffling and drizzling tears, her reddish hair hanging limply, Horrocks makes a lovely film debut. With her huge eyes and slightly bulbous nose, her face has a clownish cast; depending on what the rest of her features are doing, she can look ravishingly pretty or painfully homely.

Horrocks has a ducky, stuffed-up Liverpudlian voice, and her impish attempts at slang are touching. When she meets the American at a "sing-along" (really a make-out party), they climb onto the toilet and stare through a skylight at the grayish Mersey. Wesley says it's nothing compared to the rivers back home; then he clasps her hand.

Later, at the movies, Rita sees Technicolor horses and rivers, a vision of the life she could lead in America. And while she watches, Wesley moves his hand up her leg. When he reaches her underpants, her forehead furrows and she bops him. It's funny, but not to her. Sleeping between her aunts, Rita wakes up whimpering "Don't go"—terrified of losing him but unable to surrender.

As Wesley, the New York actor Ransom has a big, gummy grin and a lock of hair over his forehead. His hands in pockets, he shuffles idly, hiding his intentions behind a gee-whiz-ma'am politeness. The conception of the character is a little flat, but that's the point: Wesley is a cipher. He's amoral, casually exploitive, and "The Dressmaker" is useful as a portrait of how our GIs must have seemed to the countries they helped to liberate, throwing their money around and seducing the women.

The director, Jim O'Brien, has worked only in television (albeit on a large scale—he co-directed "The Jewel in the Crown"); cinematically, "The Dressmaker" feels a bit hemmed in. But it's full of sneaky throwaways and darting images, and its drabness has witty gradations. The wallpaper and costumes abound with yellow flowers and leafy bits of lace, yet this is ironic: nothing's growing in this country except anger and psychosis.

The sly, terse script is by John McGrath, who founded the rousing Scottish agit-prop troupe called 7/84 (so named because 7 percent of the population owns 84 percent of the wealth). McGrath loves bawdy subversive musicals. For him, the Nellies of British society are the true enemies of the people.

But "The Dressmaker" is more complicated than that—it's swamped with ambiguity. With spasms of passion, Margo acts out her anger over all those years of beatings; with spasms of violence, Nellie stamps out the objects of her sister's passion. They have a strange equilibrium.

Whitelaw's magnificent performance floods you with contradictory emotions; she's so reckless that on one level she seems to cry out for the smack that will keep her in her place. Margo is a haunting example of how repression warps even those who have the courage to rebel.

Plowright's Nellie—who makes clucking noises as she walks past Americans and over-made-up young women—isn't the ogre you'd expect. Given the sleaziness of the Yanks, you might even feel a surge of affection when she executes her idea of justice. At least this dressmaker can stitch up the mess so that no one will see it.

But the point here is that a stitch in time doesn't save nine: In the long run, repression kills. The last shot of Rita in bed is a stupendous, macabre joke: You're left with a portrait of English youth utterly possessed by irresolvable conflict. "The Dressmaker" is an eerily funny portrait of a spooked generation.

NEWSDAY, 1/6/89, Part III/p. 3, Mike McGrady

To everything—even the release of movies—there is a season. The recently observed holiday was clearly the time of blockbusters and top-tenners. The summer—ah, that's traditionally the time for the heat-beaters, for comedy and froth. But January is dead winter in the movie-releasing world, the time for films of high aspiration and low budget, for foreign films with serious themes and laughable prospects, for... "The Dressmaker."

"The Dressmaker" goes beyond small to cozy, beyond personal to intimate, at times beyond serious to deadly. This story of three related women sharing cramped quarters in Liverpool in 1944 has a closeness to it approaching claustrophobia. That's the bad news. The good news is that in this highly contained setting we come to know the central characters intimately.

Nellie (Joan Plowright), the dressmaker and oldest sister, is a self-appointed keeper of the old order, spokeswoman for the established way of doing things. Nellie keeps one room in the home locked as a shrine to her mother and to the past, a somber room filled with Victorian artifacts and graceful *objets d'art* that have trouble surviving in the new world.

Nellie's sister Margo, extremely well played by Billie Whitelaw, is transitional, not traditional—high-spirited and fun-loving, refusing to be bound by ties to a past yet unprepared to cope in a different kind of world.

Caught between Nellie and Margo, tugged in both directions, is their 17-year-old niece Rita (Jane Horrocks), who has had the misfortune to fall in love with an American GI (Tim Ransom), who represents something different to each of the three women.

To the niece, he is young, handsome, a possible passport to a less restrictive future. Margo, whose free spirit has brought only pain and loss in the past, sees the young man as a symbol of what might have been, as possibly her one last chance. To Nellie, he's an intruder, simply, the enemy, the crude slayer of the old order.

The drama, which may be too strong a word, centers on the girl's fear of the young man's advances and the clash of all three women as they try to adjust to him and to a new era. A coming-of-age movie with a "Hope and Glory" backdrop, "The Dressmaker" addresses more than the problems of the youngster—it illuminates the problems faced by all three women coming to terms with a world that is harder, more harsh and dangerous.

Young Jane Horrocks, making her movie debut as Rita, is just a trifle too dour for my liking, just too much the born victim. Joan Plowright is solid in the title role but Billie Whitelaw shines as the more adventurous aunt. Director Jim O'Brien, making his movie debut, is well known for putting together television's "The Jewel in the Crown" and in his favor it must be observed that he's no compromiser.

"The Dressmaker," based on a 1973 Beryl Bainbridge novel, was a long time coming to the screen. The producers delayed filming because at that time Steven Spielberg busily was reinventing film through the addition of megabucks, megaexplosives and megaeffects. "The Dressmaker" is the very opposite of the "hardware movies"—it's thoughtful, personal, intimate and...seasonal. Yes, if it's "The Dressmaker," it must be January.

NEWSWEEK, 1/9/89, p. 54, David Ansen

[*The Dressmaker* was reviewed jointly with *Pelle the Conqueror*; see Ansen's review in *Film Review Annual, 1989.*]

VILLAGE VOICE, 1/10/89, p. 53, Elliott Stein

The sexual awakening of an adolescent girl is at the heart of both Jim O'Brien's *The Dressmaker* and Catherine Breillat's *36 Fillette* [see Stein's review]—yet the peripheries of these two coming-of-age stories could not be more dissimilar. *The Dressmaker*, based on a novel by Beryl Bainbridge, is set in 1944 Liverpool, its territory akin to that of *Hope and Glory* and *Distant Voices, Still Lives*, but this latest retrospection on family life in Britain during World War II eschews John Boorman's joyful nostalgia and the complex narrative structures of Terence Davies.

In a working-class family of women, 17-year-old Rita (Jane Horrocks) has been raised since her mother's death by two aunts: Nellie (Joan Plowright), a puritanical dressmaker who has never married, and Margo (Billie Whitelaw), a chain-smoking, high-spirited widow who livens up the arms factory where she works with her squawky songs. Latent domestic tensions erupt into a war of temperaments when Rita falls madly in love with a hillbilly GI (Tim Ransom), who couldn't care less for romance—he just wants to get his rocks off. Rita's not ready for sex without romance and a proper courtship—when he wants to ball, all she can think of to say it, "You've got nice white socks." All the while, the confused girl is caught in a vise between Nellie's respressive, nearly crazed sense of respectability and Margo's brazen encouragement to enjoy those pleasures that the widowed aunt has been without for so long.

Intermittent comic moments lighten things up, mostly supplied by Rita's father (Peter Postlethwaite), an idiotic racist who works as a butcher, yet faints at the least sight of human blood. He lives in deadly fear that his daughter will "marry a white-looking GI and give birth to a pickaninny." Bleakness does gradually gain the day, and this claustrophobic tale ends with a shattering bit of unexpected Grand Guignol.

This is O'Brien's first theatrical film—he was codirector of the TV miniseries, *The Jewel in the Crown*. He doesn't go for directorial flourishes, but almost humbly, and quite prudently, makes room for the performances—they're what count in this movie. Horrocks is extremely moving as the smitten and downcast Rita. Plowright is fearsome, a benign mother hen on the outside, a monster of repression within. Whitelaw, a legendary figure on the London stage for her appearances in Beckett's plays, now gains commensurate stature on screen. Though *The Dressmaker* is mostly concerned with teenage yearnings, it is Whitelaw's extraordinary depiction of thwarted middle-age sexuality that dominates this small but rewarding film.

Also reviewed in:
NEW YORK TIMES, 1/6/89, p. C8, Vincent Canby
VARIETY, 5/11/88, p. 32
WASHINGTON POST, 2/10/89, p. D1, Hal Hinson
WASHINGTON POST, 2/10/89, Weekend/ p. 37, Desson Howe

DRIVING MISS DAISY

A Warner Bros. release of a Zanuck Company production. *Executive Producer:* David Brown. *Producer:* Richard D. Zanuck and Lili Fini Zanuck. *Director:* Bruce Beresford. *Screenplay (based on his play):* Alfred Uhry. *Director of Photography:* Peter James. *Editor:* Mark Warner. *Music:* Hans Zimmer. *Music Editor:* Laura Perlman. *Sound:* Hank Garfield and (music) Jay Rifkin. *Sound Editor:* Gloria S. Borders. *Production Designer:* Bruno Rubeo. *Art Director:* Victor Kempster. *Set Decorator:* Crispian Sallis. *Set Dresser:* Wren Boney. *Special Effects:* Bob Shelley. *Costumes:* Elizabeth McBride. *Make-up:* Manlio Rocchetti. *Stunt Coordinator:* Danny Mabry. *Running time:* 99 minutes. *MPAA Rating:* PG.

CAST: Morgan Freeman (Hoke Colburn); Jessica Tandy (Daisy Werthan); Dan Aykroyd (Boolie Werthan); Patti Lupone (Florine Werthan); Esther Rolle (Idella); Joann Havrilla (Miss McClatchey); William Hall Jr. (Oscar); Alvin M. Sugarman (Dr. Weil); Clarice F. Geigerman (Nonie); Muriel Moore (Miriam); Sylvia Kaler (Beulah); Carolyn Gold (Neighbor Lady); Crystal R. Fox (Katie Bell); Bob Hannah (Red Mitchell); Ray McKinnon (Trooper #1); Ashley Josey (Trooper #2); Jack Rousso (Slick); Fred Faser (Insurance Agent); Indra A. Thomas (Soloist).

CHRISTIAN SCIENCE MONITOR, 1/23/90, p. 10, David Sterritt

How refreshing to have a pair of new movies that focus on black characters and situations related to their lives.

But how frustrating to face an all-too-familiar question once again: Will the filmmakers of Hollywood ever give us a movie about black Americans that doesn't fill the screen with white Americans as often as possible?

Two new pictures, "Driving Miss Daisy" and "Glory", help correct Hollywood's longtime racial imbalance by placing African-American characters in central roles. Both pictures also have a constructive attitude that's as welcome as it is unmistakable.

But neither has enough courage to put all its emphasis on black experiences. "Driving Miss Daisy" is about a dignified and intelligent black man facing the difficulties of life in the South—yet he is flanked by *two* white characters, and their family life keeps popping into the story while his stays completely invisible. "Glory" features a whole regiment of African-Americans earning glory in the Civil War—yet the movie's central character is the white colonel who leads them, and the story gives almost as much attention to his problems as to the sufferings of all the black men combined.

I don't mean to criticize these films too strongly. Both are attempts to deal honestly and sensitively with characters and issues that rarely get *any* attention on the wide screen.

Still, it's disappointing that Hollywood won't go the last mile and make a film that gives black people all the attention for a change. Independent filmmakers do this once in a while, as when John Sayles gave us "The Brother From Another Planet" a few years ago. But the movie world has done some backsliding since then. Even the militant black filmmaker Spike Lee injected a white star (Danny Aiello) into his explosive "Do the Right Thing" when he decided it was time for his work to reach a mainstream American audience.

Looking beyond this issue, "Driving Miss Daisy" and "Glory" both have assets worth noting—especially the presence of Morgan Freeman, who dominates much of "Daisy" and lends an extra touch of sensitivity to "Glory," although he plays only a supporting role in that picture.

Mr. Freeman's role in "Driving Miss Daisy" is quiet, and therefore particularly challenging. He plays Hoke Colburn, a working man whose need for a job leads him to accept a near-impossible task: becoming the chauffeur of Daisy Werthan, and aging and eccentric woman who's so stubborn that several scenes go by before she'll even admit she needs a chauffeur. The movie follows their relationship over many years, revealing subtle but important changes in Daisy—who grows closer to Hoke than she's probably aware of—and in Southern society, working its way through the Martin Luther King era.

What we don't see, regrettably, are changes in Hoke himself: He's great guy at the beginning of the picture, and he's exactly the same great guy at the end. Nor do we see how the changing South affects his life beyond working for Miss Daisy, since the movie never shows him at home, or with his family, or in any situation outside Daisy's natural habitat.

This is a major shortcoming of the film, which is pleasant and even touching in other ways. Jessica Tandy gives a versatile performance as the title character, who has her own challenges (as a Jew and as a woman) to tackle in everyday life. Dan Aykroyd surely deserves an Academy Award nomination for his unexpectedly nuanced portrayal of her long-suffering son. And filmmaker Bruce Beresford gives a solid lift to his uneven career with his careful and colorful directing of Alfred Uhry's screenplay, based on Mr. Uhry's prize-winning stage play.

"Glory" focuses on the 54th Massachusetts Volunteer Infantry, the first regiment of black soldiers in American history. They were as valiant as they were unprecedented, and Abraham Lincoln cited their fighting as a turning point in the Civil War. Their virtually unknown story is well worth heeding—to correct the historical record, and to emphasize the overlooked fact that African-Americans contributed to their own hard-won freedom from the evils of slavery.

"Glory" shows how the idea of a black regiment was developed by some Boston abolitionists, who felt freedom should extend to military service. It chronicles the long, hard training of the soldiers, in scenes that recall pictures like "Full Metal Jacket" and Clint Eastwood's raucous "Heartbreak Ridge." It also shows a long, frustrating time when the soldiers are ready to fight but no one takes them seriously enough to send them into battle. Finally they get their chance, and we witness their courage and self-sacrificing spirit.

While these events are fascinating and important, "Glory" is less inspiring and enlightening than it ought to be. A key problem is the main character—partly because he's white, and thus a distraction from the film's real heroes, and partly because he's poorly acted. Matthew Broderick is a skillful and likable actor, and at first I thought he was trying a bold approach to his role, deliberately playing the young colonel as a wishy-washy twerp. But it soon becomes evident that the shortcomings are less in the concept than in the performance, which becomes more ordinary and lame as it proceeds.

Other performances are much better: It's a rare treat to see superb talents like Freeman and Denzel Washington on screen together. Yet the script, by Kevin Jarre, rarely lives up to their abilities. The screenplay is also slippery on the issue of war in general. It's hard to tell whether the filmmakers are just saluting the 54th Infantry soldiers and their moment in history, or celebrating warfare itself—which isn't such a good idea.

"Glory" was directed by Edward Zwick and photographed by Freddie Francis, who comes up with some powerful images of war and struggle. They obviously care about the story and the little-known historical details it reveals. Yet their movie seems almost too earnest at times, like an educational or classroom film. Although one learns from it, one rarely feels exhilarated by it.

FILMS IN REVIEW, 4/90, p. 231, James M. Welsh

Driving Miss Daisy, starring Morgan Freeman, Jessica Tandy, and Dan Aykroyd (in his best movie role to date), directed by Bruce Beresford, and adapted by Alfred Uhry from his own Pulitzer Prize-winning play, is a small miracle of a picture, beautifully done and sure to have both an emotional and nostalgic advantage in the Academy Award competition. Even if the film were not as splendid as it is, there would be the temptation to reward Jessica Tandy with recognition for a career that spans 64 years. She has won three Tony Awards for her stage work. She made her motion picture debut in 1932 with *The Indiscretion Of Eve*. She has won the Obie and the Emmy Award for Best Actress. Now here is an excellent chance to give her an Oscar. She is, after all, one of the first ladies of the theatre.

Her performance shows Miss Daisy aging over three decades. The film starts in 1948, when this Southern Jewish matron backs her new Chrysler into her neighbor's garden. Concluding that she is no longer competent to drive, her son Boolie (Dan Aykroyd), who runs the family mill in Atlanta and is obviously well off, hires Hoke Colburn (Morgan Freeman) to be her chauffeur. At first her feelings are hurt, but eventually she comes to accept Hoke's services. She is at first haughty and proud, but over the years she comes to like and respect Hoke. She has worked as a teacher and she teaches him to read. After her temple is bombed by racists, she begins to show interest in civil rights and Martin Luther King's message to the New South (though she does not translate her convictions into actions as fully as she might have done). Finally, as her mind begins to fail at the end, she comes to realize that her black chauffeur is probably her best friend.

The film, of course, opens up the play, fleshing out some of the characters who were not central to the play (for example, Patti Lupone as Boolie's wife Florine, a social climber, and Esther Rolle as Idella, Miss Daisy's long suffering housekeeper, as well as a number of Miss Daisy's women friends). But at the heart of his film is Morgan Freeman, who created the role of Hoke on stage. The playwright credits Freeman with creating "things that I couldn't write and can barely explain," bringing to the role "a combination of irony, dignity and humility that's quite indefinable."

Not only is the acting peerless, but the art direction is also extraordinary. The action stretches from 1948 to 1973, and the shifts in time are entirely suggested by subtle shifts in visual details—a 1953 Chevrolet glimpsed down the street, for example, a billboard advertising a 1955 Plymouth, the changing technology at Boolie's factory, the vintage of heard Christmas music. An Academy Award for art direction also seems possible, and best adapted screenplay, and direction. The play is intelligently expanded to fill cinema space. The performances are simply wondrous.

LOS ANGELES TIMES, 12/13/89, Calendar/p. 6, Peter Rainer

Morgan Freeman's performances this year in "Lean on Me," "Johnny Handsome," and, now, "Driving Miss Daisy," have been among the best reasons to go to the movies. (He's also in "Glory," the Civil War drama opening tomorrow.) Freeman has an infuriating habit of being extraordinary even in mediocre movies; his presence, alas, makes them must-sees.

"Driving Miss Daisy," directed by Bruce Beresford and adapted by Alfred Uhry from his Pulitzer Prize-winning 1987 play, isn't mediocre. It's musty and schematic, though, with a measured pace that's meant to incur our respect. This is "quality" theater transferred relatively intact to the screen.

The central relationship is between Daisy Werthan (Jessica Tandy), a cranky Atlanta widow and Hoke (Freeman), the chauffeur hired by Daisy's son Boolie (Dan Aykroyd) to keep her from plowing her brand-new '48 Packard into the neighbor's flower beds. The film takes us through 25 years of winsome acrimony between these two. Their mellowing relationship is meant to mirror the growth of civil rights in the South. Daisy is Jewish, and so the movie is structured as a tale of two outcasts bonded by their stubborn pride.

It is to everybody's credit that the stubbornness never gets mushed into sentimentality, at least not overtly. Freeman and Tandy have their own performer's pride, and that transfers to their characters. Tandy, in particular, is almost astringent in her denial of easy emotion. When something heartfelt occurs in this movie, you accept it without too much squirming. The disciplined yet intuitive way in which these actors connect is a model of ensemble performance.

One of the film's pleasant oddities is that Hoke and Daisy seem to look younger as they grow older. Bickering brings out their human contours; it gets their spirit up. Hoke plays a canny game with Daisy; he does her bidding without lapsing into servility.

It would have been easy for Freeman to distance himself from this character by cuing us with modern attitudes. Instead, he accepts Hoke's subservience as a characteristic of the man's innate graciousness . Daisy is, in fact, subservient to him, but he never throws her helplessness back at her. The shadow play between Hoke and Daisy is immensely subtle, even though the film is structured as a series of mini-revelations about the nature of interracial brotherhood. The actors know those lessons don't come easily.

The predictability of "Driving Miss Daisy" (rated PG) derives from the play's tone of civic uplift. The tensions between Hoke and Daisy exist only to be resolved. Their 25-year communion is more than a personal triumph; it is intended as a moral triumph as well. This may be too much baggage for such a frail vehicle, and the occasional bulletins from the front—like the bombing of the local synagogue or a speech by Martin Luther King—don't seem to be taking place in Hoke and Daisy's shuttered universe.

Since Uhry bothered to "open up" the play, he should have opened up the cast of characters a bit more, too. The sequences in which Hoke talks with his friends, or with Daisy's maid, Idella (Esther Rolle), are revelatory. We can see how he drops his guard with them, how he moves freer, talks more animatedly. There's more of an edge to his sequences with Idella, in fact, than with Daisy, and that's largely because in those moments Uhry isn't pushing his customary principled restraint.

Rolle's role is small, but it's a major performance. The same indignities that Hoke has braced himself against all his life have all but destroyed her. But Idella isn't anybody's mammy, and her sass gives the movie a much-needed jolt of rage.

It's the sort of rage that would be out of place in Hoke's life, or in Freeman's performance. I hope nobody chooses to jump on Freeman's work here as a species of Uncle Tom-ism. By staying within the modest restraints of the role, Freeman does justice to Hoke's circumstances. The performance is not an apologia, it's a tribute. Freeman recognizes the heroism of a man who creates a life for himself based on kindness in an unkind world.

MONTHLY FILM BULLETIN, 3/90, p. 66, Tom Milne

Atlanta, Georgia, 1948. Daisy Werthan, a wealthy seventy-two-year-old Jewish widow, crashes her car while taking it out of the garage. Despite her protests, her son Boolie—a budding tycoon whose wife Florine is held in contempt by Daisy because of her efforts to ingratiate herself with Episcopalian society—hires a chauffeur for her: Hoke Colburn, a black in his sixties. Furious at the threat to her independence, Daisy refuses to let Hoke do anything, and berates him for distracting her back cook Idella from her work. Patient and amused, Hoke follows in the car when, on the sixth day, Daisy sets off on foot to buy much-needed groceries; to avoid neighbourly gossip, Daisy gets into the car; and from then on, despite a hiccup when Daisy mistakenly assumes Hoke has stolen a tin of salmon from her larder, their relationship blossoms into something akin to friendship. Respectful distances are nevertheless maintained: though insisting that she is not prejudiced, Daisy automatically assumes blacks to be idle and dishonest. In 1954, driving in Alabama on a trip to Mobile for her brother Walter's ninetieth birthday party, Daisy is outraged when Hoke defies her order to drive on (they are late) by stopping to relieve himself in a wood; but she is silenced when he explains that he cannot use the "whites only" toilets at gas stations. In 1958, the realities of prejudice are brought closer to home when Daisy, caught in in a traffic jam while out driving with Hoke, learns that the cause is the bombing of the Temple, Atlanta's oldest synagogue. In 1965, annoyed when Boolie announces that he is unable to accompany her to a banquet honouring Martin Luther King at the Dinkler Plaza Hotel, Daisy taxes him with having no regard for the great black leader; but when Boolie retorts that Hoke would like to go and that she should take him instead, she relays the suggestion so negatively that Hoke naturally refuses, and she goes alone. In the early 70s, Hoke is distressed to find Daisy lapsing into senile dementia, and she is committed to a home. In 1973, his visits less frequent now that he is too old to drive, Hoke is taken to the home by Boolie. It is one of Daisy's good days, and she packs Boolie off to charm the nurses: it is her beloved Hoke she wants to see . . .

Bruce Beresford's third venture into the American South is closer in spirit to the showy theatrics of *Crimes of the Heart* than to the emotional honesty of *Tender Mercies*, making one wonder all over again whether Robert Duvall may not have been the auteur responsible for the lyrically charged understatement of the latter film. *Driving Miss Daisy*, adapted from Alfred Uhry's long-running off-Broadway success, is not exactly stagy (Uhry himself has managed the screen transfer very neatly), but its does retain a theatrical taste (however discreet) for declamatory effects.

Essentially an extended version of the old meeting-cute gambit, the film indulges itself a little coyly over the scenes in which Miss Daisy plays hard to get for the benefit of the black chauffeur clearly destined to become her best friend, meanwhile usefully establishing both that she is racially prejudiced, and that she is a candidate for racial prejudice who despises those trying to escape by passing themselves off as other than they are. It then tentatively develops the relationship into areas where Hoke and Daisy are each prodded into revealing more of themselves to the other than they intended. A scene in a cemetery, for instance, in which Hoke, sent to lay flowers on a gravestone, is forced to admit that he doesn't know how to read (having started him on his way, Miss Daisy rather charmingly later presents him, at Christmas but not as a Christmas present—"If I had a nose like Florine", she tartly comments, "I wouldn't go around saying Merry Christmas to anybody"—with a treasured memento from her own childhood: a Victorian calligraphy copybook in which to practise his new-found art). Or the sequence in which Hoke, picking Miss Daisy up again after driving her to the synagogue in her new car, is unable to comprehend her fury; she is forced to explain that, by parking right outside, he has made her seem guilty of the unpardonable sin of vulgarity by flaunting her wealth (if *he* had her wealth, Hoke mutters, he surely would flaunt it).

Played with charm, humour and authority by Jessica Tandy and Morgan Freeman (with Dan Aykroyd excellent in the thankless role of amiable liberal buffer), the relationship is often tender, often funny, and even rather moving in the final scene in the old people's home where, with convention at last overtaken by senility, Hoke's gesture in tenderly helping Daisy to eat, and her blissful enjoyment of his attentions, ring out like a declaration of love. But the film, ranging over twenty-five years (with the characters either not changing at all, in Freeman's case, or suddenly sporting rubber wrinkles, like Tandy when senility strikes) also has sociological pretensions. The progress of the central relationship is punctuated, rather in the manner of cliff-hanging curtain lines, by a number of key moments intended to indicate changing times and attitudes: the bombing of the Temple, the Martin Luther King banquet, and (earlier) the trip to segregation-torn Alabama, involving two hard-faced highway patrolmen who come upon Daisy and Hoke peacefully picnicking by their car, and who, getting nowhere with their hassling, drive off again complaining, "An old nigger and an old Jewish woman takin' off down the road, and that is one sorry sight".

The raw realities of White Lynching and Black Power of course remain discreetly and dimly in the background, along with any threat of miscegenation: obviously intentionally, and perhaps quite rightly, given that Miss Daisy is sheltered from reality by her age and wealth. But the interpolations, arbitrarily touting broader significance for what should have been content to remain the story of a relationship, are really no more than flim-flam, conning the audience into thinking they have witnessed a heart-warming tale of victory over prejudice. Actually, like all those Hollywood movies in which the Southern belle loved her dear old mammy, *Driving Miss Daisy* merely demonstrates that Miss Daisy loved her dear old chauffeur who was respectful enough to know his place.

NEW YORK, 12/18/89, p. 104, David Denby

In the mild but pleasing *Driving Miss Daisy*, Bruce Beresford's adaptation of Alfred Uhry's play, the great Jessica Tandy plays a wealthy old Georgia widow of German-Jewish descent, and Morgan Freeman her black chauffeur of many years. The movie, passing in time from the fifties through the civil-rights period, lovingly measures the precise shadings of irritation, affection, and dependence that flow back and forth between the two characters as they shift, ever so slowly, from mistress and servant to friends.

NEW YORK, 4/16/90, p. 68, David Denby

Now that the triumph of *Driving Miss Daisy* is complete, it's time for me to drop a few poisoned sprinkles onto the party cake. Not an enjoyable task: The movie has abundant charm. Further, the success of so intelligent and graceful a work could be viewed as exactly the kind of rebuke that our slaphappy movie culture so badly needs. But something has been nagging at me: Why is *Miss Daisy*—a small, quiet movie—so great a box-office hit? Some may consider its observations about aging and friendship as timeless. But universality of theme is not, I believe, the cause of the movie's success. On the contrary, the film is a hit because it's about something very specific—a twenty-five-year relationship between an elderly southern Jewish woman and her black chauffeur—that the audience appears eager to accept and be soothed by. I mean the white audience.

Let's try not to reduce this to a purely political argument. A movie, especially a good movie, may appeal to people for a great many reasons. *Miss Daisy* offers a variety of small insights, and an emotionally satisfying and poignant image of the passing of time. Alfred Uhry's adaptation of his own play shrewdly camouflages what's coy and self-congratulatory in the whole conception. The acting is beyond praise, the direction by Bruce Beresford exquisitely modulated—Beresford brings to the material a feeling for silence and contrast and the power of many half-crescendos. He has become a master of film syntax. Leaving aside its racial theme, so harmonious and calming a movie may well represent a generalized longing for peace, for the solid bourgeois life—the big house, the regular habits, the solid, heavy old cars—that the film celebrates and that now seems gone forever. *Miss Daisy* offers relief from not only the noise and disorder of life but from the noise and disorder of contemporary movies. The aging film audience has received its first real bouquet.

But even a good movie may cater to some weakness or half-understood longing in its audience. I realize that this statement puts me in the self-appointed position of accuser, and I accept the complaint of overpresumption. But I can't get away from the idea that *Miss Daisy* is part of the Bush era's hypocrisy—the public fantasy that everything is just swell in this country, when in fact we have catastrophic problems. In the United States, in particular, an immense dismay has settled over race relations. On the two sides of this relationship, blacks are often testy or withdrawn, whites stonyhearted or silently guilty. A nauseating abyss of fear, hatred, and distaste, manifesting itself as a general indifference, makes closeness increasingly difficult. Even to bring up the subject of friendship is to invite ridicule. (Who *wants* it?) But *Miss Daisy* is about friendship. Against the background of our current reality, the movie's long stillness, its paring away of the world to a small space in which two elderly people can work out their problems of respect and affection—well, the movie seems more than peaceful. It seems a pure dream.

But it's a dream whose innocence and charm cannot conceal the essential point that the white character has all the power. It's true that in the course of the movie, power will in some ways shift. The wealthy mistress and her servant will become friends, and in the end, Hoke, the chauffeur, old but still younger than Miss Daisy, will turn into her principal life support. Hoke attains *personal* power, in the sense of dignity and authority. But not social power. Although he stands up for himself as a man, he never really challenges Miss Daisy. He's a supremely mature and companionable fellow, self-sufficient, shrewd yet accommodating. We don't, however, know much about him or his life. Miss Daisy has a past and a lineage; he is defined by, and transfigured in, his role as servant and friend to his mistress.

Since the movie is set in the South, and in the past, it could hardly be otherwise. I'm not quarreling with the accuracy of *Miss Daisy*, only pointing out that a movie (which, by the way, always feels like the present tense, whenever it is set) becomes a hit because it fulfills a certain need. This movie provides an image of a black man, and a relationship with a black man, that a white audience can feel comfortable with. For many whites, it may be the *only* kind of relationship with blacks that they can feel at ease with. From the top looking down, it's easy to see the dignity of black people. But isn't it about 30 years too late for mere perceptions of dignity?

Our avoidance of responsibility in this country is total. At the moment, America is a society in which, on the one hand, expressions of prejudice by whites (Jackie Mason, Andy Rooney) are forbidden in public, yet, on the other, the white majority is unwilling to help take the steps necessary to alleviate the conditions that give rise to prejudice. An enforced public gentility coincides with an atmosphere of brute indifference in which a significant section of the black population slips into complete degradation. "Everyone" has long known that blacks and whites are equal. Yet at the moment, the country is mooning over a movie in which a black servant is content with his lot, and his white mistress learns to trust the goodness of his soul. In a more vigorous and purposeful time, the movie would have been considered sweet but embarrassing. Now we are so defeated and sick at heart, it seems like a necessary balm.

NEW YORK POST, 12/13/89, p. 32, David Edelstein

"Driving Miss Daisy," based on the Pulitzer-Prize winning play by Alfred Uhry, charts a predictable and sentimental course. When a proud, aging Jewish widow, Daisy Werthan (Jessica Tandy) backs her car over a hedge, her prosperous son, Boolie (Dan Aykroyd), decides it's time to hire a chauffeur.

Over his mother's noisy objections, Boolie brings in Hoke (Morgan Freeman), an old, friendly black man who gets along with everyone. But Daisy, who routinely badgers the help, refuses to be driven. She's proud of her working-class roots and liberal values, and won't be squired around Atlanta like "the Queen of Romania."

Eventually, Hoke's affable entreaties to let him drive her wear her down, and she agrees, somewhat imperiously, to be chauffeured to the Piggly-Wiggly. Thereafter, we observe them at random years. At the graveside of her husband she learns Hoke can't read; the next Christmas she gives him a gift to improve his penmanship; a year or so later they drive to Alabama for a birthday party and experience more aggressive forms of prejudice—against both blacks and Jews.

The two grow old and close, and as they do, Uhry skirts the obvious pitfalls. He keeps their banter light and funny, with Hoke good-naturedly debunking Miss Daisy's more prickly assertions. Uhry doesn't spell anything out when he can quietly suggest it, and both Hoke and Daisy manage to be more complicated than they initially appear.

It helps that they're played by two of the sharpest actors on the planet. At first, Freeman's courtly, deliberate Hoke seems to border on Uncle Tom-ism: peppering his speech with yassers and yaz'ms, he lets his voice fly up into the higher registers, and mmms in agreement after everything his white employers say.

But soon you realize that Freeman has transferred some of his own caginess to Hoke, who answers maltreatment and condescension with a reasonableness that defuses it. Ironic without a trace of impertinence, he gets exactly what he wants—a raise from Boolie, kindness from Miss Daisy. The performance tears you up: you wince at the ways in which he has to be accommodating; you marvel at his refusal to be victimized.

It feels terrific after movies like "Dad" and "Steel Magnolias" to be in the hands of two actors who aren't going to tug on your heartstrings as if they were dog-leashes. Tandy's Daisy isn't a fussbudget with a heart of gold. A former schoolteacher, she's disgusted by hypocrisy yet blind to her own—trumpeting both her lack of prejudice and her belief that all black people steal.

Her Daisy is permanently vexed, perceiving slights and insults in ways that suggest intense self-hatred. Conscious of her increasing isolation, Daisy is too stiffened by pride to reach out; in one of the sadder ironies, only senility can fully liberate her feelings.

But the film is about more than the isolation of age. When Daisy leaves Hoke in the car so she can attend a lecture by Martin Luther King, the minister's harsh words hit home: In the fight for freedom, he says, the enemy is "not the vitriolic words and violent acts of the bad people, but the silence and apathy of the children of light."

At bottom, "Driving Miss Daisy" is about the failure of white liberalism to do more than congratulate itself for its sensitivity, proclaiming the equality of blacks in principle while dismissing them in person. The movie ends in the '70s, after the civil rights movement has changed the way both races regard themselves. Both Daisy and Hoke are the last of a line.

In places the cinematography may be a little too golden-hued and muzzy, but otherwise Bruce Beresford's direction is a model of taste and self-respect. There's too little Esther Rolle and maybe too much Dan Aykroyd (reviving his Jimmy Carter accent). But if by lending his presence Aykroyd helped to get the movie made, he can be forgiven almost anything.

NEWSDAY, 12/13/89, Part II/p. 12, Terry Kelleher

Alfred Uhry's play "Driving Miss Daisy" has been running Off-Broadway for almost three years. Successful productions of the comedy-drama have been mounted in cities coast-to-coast and in Europe.

If you've yet to see this enormously popular, Pulitzer Prize-winning play, you'll be charmed and touched by the movie version. If the stage work is fairly fresh in your mind, you're bound to be somewhat less affected by the film. But you'll be pleased, perhaps relieved, at the artfulness of the adaptation.

Australian director Bruce Beresford's touch hasn't always been golden since "Breaker Morant" established his reputation. ("King David" and "Her Alibi" come to mind.) But with "Tender Mercies," "Crimes of the Heart" and now "Driving Miss Daisy," Beresford has made himself more than comfortable in the American South. Like "Tender Mercies," this is an intimate, low-key study of honestly drawn, life-sized characters. There's none of the sense of movie stars playing it fey that intruded on "Crimes of the Heart."

On stage, "Driving Miss Daisy" had a cast of just three: Daisy Werthan, a flinty Jewish widow living in Atlanta; Daisy's businessman son Boolie, who insists on hiring her a chauffeur when her motoring skills become dangerously suspect; and a black gentleman named Hoke Colburn, who spends the next quarter-century as Daisy's driver and (though she's terribly slow to admit it) friend.

On screen, these parts are taken by Jessica Tandy, Dan Aykroyd and Morgan Freeman, respectively. Freeman, of course, earned an Obie Award for originating the role of Hoke, and he inhabits it here with consummate grace, dignity and understanding. Tandy is superb as Miss Daisy, capturing her self-deception and vulnerability, as well as her sharp tongue and strong spine.

The casting of Aykroyd was something of a gamble, though he had ample opportunity to hone his Georgia accent when mimicking Jimmy Carter in the halcyon days of "Saturday Night Live." On the whole, the comedy star is restrained and believable as Boolie, a solid citizen who appreciates the humor in a situation but is seldom inclined to add to it. Unfortunately, as his character advances in years, Aykroyd is burdened by a makeup job that makes him look more and more like a senior member of the Conehead Chamber of Commerce.

In fashioning the film script, Uhry has added a couple of secondary parts: Idella (Esther Rolle), the black maid who knows Miss Daisy's quirks like the back of her hand, and Florine (Patti LuPone), Boolie's acutely status-conscious wife. He also has opened up the play in ways that serve the story well.

When Hoke drives Miss Daisy to Mobile for a relative's birthday party, they are subjected to petty harassment by a couple of Alabama troopers who obviously group blacks and Jews in the same "undesirable" category. Later, Miss Daisy makes a noble "New South" gesture by attending a testimonial dinner for the renowned Martin Luther King Jr., but can't bring herself to invite the humble black man she's seen every day since 1948. The camera shows us Miss Daisy in the hotel ballroom, listening to King politely reproach "white people of good will," while Hoke sits in the car, waiting for a summons to drive the lady home from this gala celebration of racial tolerance. It's a telling moment, and very much a movie moment.

"Driving Miss Daisy" has made the trip from stage to screen with its virtues intact. It still has the quiet courage to present human beings in all their blindness and foolishness, and persuade us to care for them anyway.

NEWSWEEK, 12/18/89, p. 68, David Ansen

Is it possible that Jessica Tandy, at the age of 80, is still reaching her peak as an actress? Can it be that Morgan Freeman, who was so terrifyingly brilliant as the pimp in "Street Smart," is equally convincing as a soft-spoken, quietly dignified old Southern chauffeur? Watching these two superb performers light up "Driving Miss Daisy" is an experience no student of great acting—and no moviegoer in search of a satisfying tug at the heart—will want to miss. Freeman originated the role of Hoke in Alfred Uhry's Pulitzer Prize-winning play. Tandy is new to the role of Miss Daisy Werthan, the stubborn, bossy, Jewish Atlanta widow who—at the insistence of her son Boolie (Dan Aykroyd)—begrudgingly takes on Hoke as her chauffeur after she's crashed her new 1948 Packard into a hedge. Over the course of the next 25 years, as she ages from 72 to 97, Hoke and Miss Daisy progress from a strained master/servant relationship into an enduring—but never informal—friendship. Tandy may not be the most Jewish of Daisys, but in every other way she is definitive. It's an incandescent performance: sharp, droll and deeply moving.

Uhry should be a happy man: Bruce Beresford's movie of his delicate, slight play is a model of stage-to-screen adaptation. Uhry has added new characters and settings to his three-character play—we get to meet Boolie's socially ambitious wife Florine (Patti LuPone) and Idella (the terrific Esther Rolle), Miss Daisy's longtime housekeeper—without sacrificing any of the intimacy. The added flesh is becoming: the movie actually strikes richer emotional chords.

Beresford, the Australian director, has had plenty of experience in stage-to-screen adaptations ("Breaker Morant," "Crimes of the Heart") but his touch has never before been this sure. He resists the many easy temptations a more insecure director would jump at—never going for the mawkish, never overplaying the themes of anti-Semitism and black-white racial relations that Uhry discreetly but resonantly leaves in the background. He knows that what remains unsaid between Hoke and Miss Daisy is as important as what is stated, and that much of the play's pathos is in the always proper distance across which they must communicate their true feelings. This lovely, quietly powerful movie would be worth seeing for the final image alone: the childlike, beatific expression on Tandy's face will haunt you forever.

TIME, 12/18/89, p. 91 Richard Schickel

It is the season when movies are ablaze with self-importance, urging us to contemplate, through various fictive metaphors, the great issues of our time. And, by the way, to spare some kindly thoughts for the high-mindedness of their makers and their worthiness for Oscar nominations. Such a metaphor is available in *Driving Miss Daisy*. If you look hard, you can find in this account of the 25-year relationship between Daisy Werthan (Jessica Tandy), a genteel Southern, Jewish matriarch, and her black chauffeur, Hoke Colburn (Morgan Freeman), a microcosmic study of changing racial attitudes in a crucial time and place (Atlanta, circa 1948–73). What you will not find in this marvelously understated movie is overtly inspirational comments on that subject, broad sentimentality or the slightest pomposity about its own mission. In other words, Alfred Uhry's adaptation of his Pulitzer-prizewinning play aspires more to complex observation of human behavior than to simple moralism about it. Precisely because it has its priorities straight, it succeeds superbly on both levels.

Director Bruce Beresford's tone is cool and shadowy—like Miss Daisy's fine old house. Hoke is introduced into it by her son Boolie (Dan Aykroyd, displaying full credentials as an actor), when at 72 Miss Daisy careers her car into a neighbor's yard. She has objections, suspicions. She harbors—yes—more racial prejudice than she has ever been forced to admit.

But Hoke is a wise and patient man. And Miss Daisy is a woman worthy of those qualities. She may be comically set in her small ways, but she casts a shrewd eye on her immediate world. As she ages, that world shrinks, so that Hoke looms ever larger within it. As a result, she is forced to think harder about the growing civil rights struggle than she might otherwise have. An encounter with menacing red-neck cops on a country road, the bombing of her synagogue, a distant but moving exposure to the force of Martin Luther King Jr.'s oratory all have their effect on her. But mostly it is the simple presence of a good man that grants her age's greatest benison, expanding rather than shrinking her humanity.

One cannot speak too highly of the subtlety that two great actors, Freeman and Tandy, bring to their roles. Or of the faith that Beresford places in their ability to convey large emotions through an exchange of glances in a rearview mirror. Or of his trust in a script that speaks most eloquently through silences and indirection. All, finally, have placed their faith in the audience's ability to read their delicately stated work with the responsiveness it deserves. It would be a shame to fail them.

VILLAGE VOICE, 12/19/89, p. 98, Gary Giddins

Chutzpah is perhaps the only word to describe Alfred Uhry's decision to offer the '80s a play in the Faithful Old Retainer mode. *Driving Miss Daisy*, which continues to enjoy a long run Off-Broadway, generates one new variation on the theme: The lady to whom all those yessums and no'ms are addressed is Jewish. Somehow, the play works, and not just because it offers dreamy roles for an elderly white woman and a middle-aged black man, two habitually underemployed classes of actors. The specificity of the characterizations mitigates the clichés, and so does the sketchlike humor of fleeting scenes that cover 25 years and make both the imperious Miss Daisy and the quietly dignified driver, Hoke, increasingly appealing.

If audiences tend to get all weepy about how much better the world was when you could get good colored help, that isn't the play's fault. The central encounter takes place in the early '60s, when Miss Daisy goes to a dinner honoring Martin Luther King. She can't bring herself to invite Hoke, though she'd like him to accompany her, and he won't invite himself. He ignores her while she makes her way to the dinner, a long and lonely walk to the wings. They will never stop playing mistress and servant.

One indication of why the movie doesn't quite work is the undermining of that scene, sacrificing the pathos of Daisy's recalcitrance in a badly staged tiff that is followed immediately by a shot of her listening to King, his voice booming on the soundtrack. This may be the only time in history when King's voice is an intrusion. In expanding a three-character play (Daisy's son brings them together) for the movies, Uhry vitiates the tension between his principals. And director Bruce Beresford has no feeling at all for sketch humor. He shows the passage of time by shooting foliage, which is acceptable, but the transitions are generally awkward. The first encounter between Hoke and Daisy's son, Boolie, cries out for interplay; yet instead of a two-shot, Beresford alternates an endless series of close-ups. One of the movie's conceits comes off rather well—the contrast between a staid synagogue service early on and a tempestuous Baptist memorial service (with Indra A. Thomas gloriously leading the choir) toward the end. The business of the stolen salmon, a send-up of Captain Queeg and the strawberries, is also given a nicely exaggerated comic twist. The introduction of two cops, who remark on "the old nigger and the old Jew woman," however, is a pointless gesture to the galleries.

Dan Aykroyd is an amiable Boolie, though it takes him a couple of scenes to figure out his accent, and if the seat of his pants isn't padded he's done a De Niro in adapting his girth to a role. He's built like Esther Rolle, who has a couple of laugh lines as the maid Idella. Patti Lupone is wasted in the thankless role of Boolie's wife, who was more vivid when you had to imagine her entirely as filtered through Daisy's contempt. It's still a two-character show, and the key performers generally hold their own against a director who doesn't always know how to photograph them.

Morgan Freeman's Hoke is a Tom in the sense of Stowe, which is entirely different from the sense of, say, Stokely Carmichael: He's dignified, accomplished, faithful, knows just how far he can press, and is determined to hold his own in a patient war of wills. It should be his film, but Beresford's perspective leans toward Daisy, who, as played by Jessica Tandy, is a touch harder than seems appropriate. Her final scenes are effective (especially, "Hoke, you're my best friend"), but as she reaches her middle nineties, her makeup disconcertingly suggests Dustin Hoffman's aged Little Big Man. Peter James's quasidaguerrotype photography and the detailed set direction (the house is a museum of *chotchkes, Gentleman's Agreement* is on at the local theater) are convincing enough. Strangely, Robert Lowell's damning observation inspired by the Saint-Gaudens's relief of the 54th is more descriptive of *Driving Miss Daisy* than of *Glory*: "a savage servility," he wrote, "slides by on grease."

Also reviewed in:
NEW REPUBLIC, 1/22/90, p. 26, Stanley Kauffmann
NEW YORK TIMES, 12/13/89, p. C13, Vincent Canby
NEW YORKER, 12/25/89, p. 73, Pauline Kael
VARIETY, 12/13/89, p. 28
WASHINGTON POST, 1/12/90, p. D1, Rita Kempley
WASHINGTON POST, 1/12/90, Weekend/p. 39, Desson Howe

DRUGSTORE COWBOY

An Avenue Pictures release. *Executive Producer:* Cary Brokaw. *Producer:* Nick Wechsler and Karen Murphy. *Director:* Gus Van Sant Jr. *Screenplay:* Gus Van Sant Jr. and Daniel Yost. *Based on the novel by:* James Fogle. *Director of Photography:* Robert Yeoman. *Editor:* Curtiss Clayton. *Music:* Elliot Goldenthal. *Music Editor:* Bill Bernstein. *Sound:* Ron Judkins, Mark "Frito" Long, and (music) Joel Iwataki. *Sound Editor:* Dane A. Davis. *Production Designer:* David Brisbin; *Art Director:* Eve Cauley. *Costumes:* Beatrix Aruna Pasztor. *Make-up:* Lizbeth Williamson. *Stunt Coordinator:* David Boushey. *Running time:* 100 minutes. *MPAA Rating:* R.

CAST: Matt Dillon (Bob); Kelly Lynch (Dianne); James Le Gros (Rick); Heather Graham (Nadine); Beah Richards (Drug Counselor); Grace Zabriskie (Bob's Mother); Max Perlich (David); William S. Burroughs (Tom the Priest); Eric Hull (Druggist); James Remar (Gentry); John Kelly (Cop); George Catalano (Trousinski); Janet Baumhover (Neighbor Lady); Ted D'Arms (Neighbor Man); Neal Thomas (Halamer); Stephen Rutledge (Motel Manager); Robert Lee Pitchlynn (Hotel Clerk); Roger Hancock (Machinist); Mike Parker (Crying Boy); Ray Monge (Accomplice).

FILM QUARTERLY, Spring 1990, p. 27. Steve Vineberg

The astonishingly lyrical and quick-witted *Drugstore Cowboy* is set in Portland, Oregon, in 1971, and every movie it reminded me of comes from the sixties and early seventies—*Bonnie and Clyde,* Godard's *Band of Outsiders, Mean Streets, M*A*S*H,* and the long-forgotten Ivan Passer film *Born to Win.* In *Born to Win,* George Segal played the first legitimate junkie hipster in the movies, a man who had to shoot up because being straight was too boring, and in *Drugstore*

Cowboy Bob (Matt Dillon), chief of a quartet of low-grade desperadoes who rob drugstores and filch pills and Dilaudid from hospitals, explains that staying high releases the pressures of the everyday—like tying your shoes. Bob and his band—his wife Dianne (Kelly Lynch), soft-spoken, rabbitty Rick (James Le Gros) and his novice girl friend Nadine (Heather Graham)—are rebels against respectability. They're not much different from thousands of enclaves of young people of the same era, who sat around getting stoned and laughing at anti-dope ads on TV—the lame propaganda of the straight world—except they use pharmaceuticals instead of grass and hallucinogens, and that's *all* they do; scoring and staying ripped form the wobbly arc of their lives. And director Gus Van Sant, whose style is rambunctious and playfully experimental and ragtaggle-poetic, keeps up with them by creating a leapfrogging rhythm out of odd, slanted angles and quick cuts, and a skewed vision of the world out of his unpredictable, often magical focus on unexpected objects (or ordinary objects seen in extraordinary ways). When Bob boils water for tea in a little tin pot in his room, Van Sant's camera practically dives into the bubbles (like Godard zeroing in on the cup of coffee in *Two or Three Things I Know About Her*); when Bob switches on a light, Van Sant gets in close enough that we can read the wattage on the bulb. And there are free-form sequences where the implements of Bob's lifestyle—capsules, spoons, matches—as well as tiny trees and at one point a blue gun float by like the uprooted bits of Dorothy's farm during the cyclone in *The Wizard of Oz*. They're the disconnected shreds of Bob's consciousness; Van Sant allows us to see the world as he figures a junkie must see it.

A painter with a film degree from the Rhode Island School of Design, Van Sant has a gift for this kind of lopsided allusiveness and home-grown collage surrealism. He also has a gift for conveying outsiders' perspectives. His previous movie, *Mala Noche*, based on a short story by Walt Curtis, was shot (also in Portland) in black and white and 16 millimeter, and though it has a perfectly linear narrative, everything in it seems to be communicated indirectly, by feeling. The hero, Walt (played by the wonderfully expressive Oregonian actor Tim Streeter), is a young man, working in a convenience store, who falls in love with a Mexican teenager, Johnny (Doug Cooeyote), an illegal alien, and subjects himself to a protracted—and futile—series of games and humiliations to earn his affection. In place of his love object, who first refuses his advances and then disappears, Walt sleeps with Johnny's friend, Pepper (Ray Monge), who later gets shot by cops during a drug deal. The movie is about the follies of passion; plaintive and deeply impassioned itself, it takes the point of view that these can't be explained and don't need to be defended. Walt allows himself to be left on the outside of Johnny's and Pepper's camaraderie—to be the gringo they can take their frustrations with white society out on. He's smart enough to know that when Pepper has sex with him, his aggressiveness is meant to victimize Walt, and he's sane enough to resent it—but he's also strung out on his own homosexual romanticism, and he keeps exposing himself. When he wrestles with Pepper and gets on top of him, Streeter's Walt looks ravaged, melted down by his desire for the boy, and there's desperation behind the good-buddy grin he flashes at Johnny on the street when he invites him to come by the store for a visit. Lacerated Walt is the most nakedly emotional gay character in a movie since the runaway Lilica in *Pixote*, and *Mala Noche*, with its manic-depressive tone and its mysterious ashcan lyricism (Pepper's shooting is like a classic *film noir* scene that's been split apart—it's shot like a pointillist photograph), seems to ride on his brain waves.

Working on a budget of $7 million in *Drugstore Cowboy*—many times what it cost him to bring in *Mala Noche* (which was his second independent feature)—Van Sant manages to sacrifice remarkably little of the looseness, the adventurousness, the improvisatory feel of the earlier picture; he still has a knack for taking us into corners we've never come across before. And his actors seem to trust him completely, as Tim Streeter must have in *Mala Noche*. Matt Dillon gives his best performance as Bob, whose peculiar gift as a put-on artist is that, on some level, he's always telling the truth—he's straight and bent at the same time. He and Dianne unsettle Nadine with a rap about the superstitions that govern their lives, several of which they claim she's stepped right into; it's hilarious—a blitzed Nichols and May routine—but when the motel that Bob's gang is holed up in turns out to be housing a cops' convention, Bob blames the hex he says Nadine's inadvertently put on them, and he's dead serious. Dillon's grown smarter and surer and a lot more skillful as an actor, but I think it's his on-camera instinct—the quality that made him a star when he was a teenager—that makes him the perfect actor for Van Sant; I doubt the director could have connected with a more technical actor in quite this way, or gotten him to skate on his mood shifts as Dillon does here. This is Altman-caliber acting, where the performer manages to pick up the *feeling* of a film—which is semisubmerged in the script but evident in the camera movement, the photography (by Robert Yeoman, in this case) and the editing (Curtiss Clayton)—the way a vocalist can catch on to the subtleties of a jazz combo.

Tall, aristocratic Kelly Lynch, who was a sour, leggy blank in *Cocktail* and *Roadhouse*, riffs superbly with Dillon, especially in a wonderful serio-comic gag where she tries to get him into bed but he's more turned on by making another score. Lynch's Dianne has a tough, swinging presence, but she's lost underneath it; when Bob, fed up with the turn his luck has taken, decides to enroll in a methadone program, she feels betrayed—she wants him to explain how he can consider taking such an alternative when he knows she *can't*. Lynch has worked out her performance fully in physical terms—when she leaves him for the last time, the way she bops down the corridor of his apartment building, slightly disconnected from her surroundings, is touching, pathetic.

Bob isn't always likeable; when Nadine OD's on Dilaudid (shooting up more than she can handle is a gesture of rebellion against the oddly parental authority Bob and Dianne exert on her and Rick), his response is callous and self-absorbed. And one of his pranks almost gets a cop killed. Van Sant isn't interested in dividing up his characters so we'll know which ones we're supposed to like; the officer on Bob's case, Gentry (James Remar), is capable of both brutality (provoked by the injury to his partner, he beats Bob up) and generosity (when Bob resurfaces in Portland, in the methadone program, Gentry warns him that he might be in danger). What Van Sant looks for in his characters are surprises, the unanticipated twists that people are always capable of—the ones that throw us and then lead us to uncover unsuspected areas of those we thought we knew: Bob's capacity for lonely contemplation, Dianne's blurry vulnerability, Nadine's bravado, Rick's tenderness.

The entire cast is excellent—Le Gros and Graham, James Remar (cast against type), Grace Zabriskie as Bob's mother, Max Perlich as a druggy teen (a Michael J. Pollard type) who's a lot creepier than he seems at first, William S. Burroughs, with his weird, distended drawl and his hawk face, in an uncategorizable cameo as a junkie priest. Burroughs isn't really an actor, but he has a mesmerizing presence, and he stirs our associations with him as the literary junkie gospel—you can't help wondering if he wrote his own lines. Van Sant mixes his tones with a painter's confidence, setting up the big transition, two-thirds of the way through, from anarchic comedy (in the *Bonnie and Clyde*-ish robbery scenes and the scenes involving the gang relaxing) to bluesy low gear (once Bob makes up his mind—with no feeling of triumph or joy or even simple satisfaction—to give up dope). The scene that prepares us for where the movie's going is Bob and Dianne's visit to his mother, a diminutive, apple-cheeked woman in a bouffant and high heels, who, screaming that Bob's a dope fiend and Dianne's a nymphomaniac, refuses to open the door until she's hidden her valuables. It's wild sketch with a core of melancholy that kicks in a moment or two before Van Sant passes on to something else—and in that moment you get a glimpse of what's underneath the movie's wayward knock-about humor. In a way, the end of this scene, seeping into our consciousness, is like the opening shot of the Mexican kids traveling in boxcars in *Mala Noche*—Van Sant never returns to it, but its mood haunts the film. Alienation's a great deal funnier in *Drugstore Cowboy* than it is in *Mala Noche*, but both movies come from the same impulse: to find a style appropriate to characterizing the lifestyles of people who are closed out—of close themselves out—from the mainstream. The downshift in *Drugstore Cowboy* is Van Sant's way of keeping faith with that impulse.

LOS ANGELES TIMES, 10/11/89, Calendar/p. 1, Sheila Benson

"Drugstore Cowboy," an electrifying movie without one misstep or one conventional moment, makes us voyeurs in the world of 1970s "dope fiends," as junkie Matt Dillon likes to call them.

Because it's a pretty limited world, airless and crushingly dumb, in which the impulse is simply to move from high to high, the wonder is that a movie this alert, this razor-funny and this compulsively watchable can be made about it without betraying its blitzed-out characters. Somehow, in only his second feature, director and co-writer Gus Van Sant has managed it.

From his actors, especially Matt Dillon, Van Sant has gotten hauntingly beautiful performances. There is street poetry and genuine revelation in Dillon's first-person narration as Bob, the acknowledged leader of this dopey little band, expert at boosting any kind of pharmaceutical from any unwary drugstore in Portland, Ore.

This flaky foursome includes Bob's wife, Dianne (Kelly Lynch, in a performance that eradicates all memory of movies like "Cocktail" or "Roadhouse"); Rick (James Le Gros), the dim-bulb muscle of the group, and Rick's teen-age girlfriend Nadine (Heather Graham), the newcomer, whose specialty is faking seizures in the drugstores that divert attention from Bob's practiced lunge behind the pharmacist's counter, clearing out bins as he moves.

Bizarrely, although they gloat over its street value, the gang rarely sells its loot; it goes straight into keeping them all muzzily high—all the time. As a vision from inside a junkie's mind, is there anything about the movie to make this drug-bound existence even remotely appealing? Hardly. It seems like the most vacant, frightful life imaginable, full of intricate, obsessive schemes that fade with the first rays of light, as the dosage wears off.

There's a drug-crossed love story here too, as Bob and Dianne can't seem to get their highs in sync. The same fix that arouses her makes lovemaking the last thing on his mind. "Bob's like a rabbit," Dianne muses, as he hits a hospital for bigger drug stakes. "In and out in no time with no fuss." Then in a measured afterthought she adds, "That goes for more than hospitals." It might be funny, except for the poignancy of Lynch's and Dillon's performances, giving their situation a hell-on-Earth irony.

But when it wants to be, "Drugstore Cowboy" is laconically comic, humor that comes from a mix of precise language and the slow-mo reaction time of people moving under drugs. Try watching Bob, one of the world's masters of arcane superstition, laying out a few ground rules about the taking off of hexes, when his mouth, his eyes and his brain aren't exactly lined up in order.

Other humor is decidedly macabre, particularly when the gang's highway motel becomes host to a sheriff's convention—at the same time the dopers must dispose of a gradually stiffening, overdosed corpse. "Why couldn't it have been a *Tupperware* convention," Bob rages, fighting down waves of paranoiac hysteria.

Brackishly awful though the scene is, it's the turning point for Bob, who doesn't make promises to God lightly. You know, the just-get-me-out-of-this-and-I'll-go-straight pledge? His dead-earnestness about his pact may be another thing that separates Bob from the rest of us.

It's a move he knows will doom his marriage, because Dianne has no desire to let go of her highs. Nevertheless, Bob goes into a methadone program and the straight world of factory work and sleazy rooming houses. We hold our breaths that he can make it. Writer and guru William S. Burroughs enters here as a defrocked priest and serious addict who had led more than one altar boy, Bob included, into the world of drugs.

As the two cross paths again, Burroughs' presence, his sly-fox delivery as he smacks his lips over 160 milligrams of Dilaudid, have a dry, unassailable authenticity. It's like having W.C. Fields run a practiced eye over your liquor cabinet, separating the vintage stuff from the hooch.

The picture keeps its own authenticity all the way down the line, from the dreadfully reminiscent '70s clothes by Beatrix Aruna Pasztor to the period-perfect hair insisted upon by Gina Monaci, to production designer David Brisbin's eye for tacky Portland motel rooms, rooming houses and suburban cracker-boxes. Cameraman Robert Yeoman has a postmodernist's eye and a combat photographer's heart, and Curtiss Clayton's editing is swift and to the point. Among a faultless cast, Max Perlich's weasely young David is disturbingly memorable.

In the way that "Straight Time's" screenplay, based on experiences by convicted thief Eddie Bunker, was utterly believable, "Drugstore Cowboy's" script gets its insider's tone from a writer who knows the territory. (It is MPAA-rated R for just that.)

In San Quentin and Soledad for pharmaceutical robberies in the 1970s, James Fogle wrote a novel that came to the attention of Oregon magazine writer Dan Yost. Corresponding with Fogle, Yost was struck by his storytelling abilities and offered to help edit it; after his release, Fogle submitted his novel to 30 publishers. It was rejected, and Fogle next became involved in another series of drugstore thefts that earned him a 22-year term in the Walla Walla, Wash., prison.

A copy of the novel stayed with Yost, however, and when Van Sant—whose electrifying black-and-white first feature, "Mala Noche," won the Los Angeles Film Critics' prize as the best independent feature of 1987—was looking for a subject for his second film, he read it. The screenplay credit is to Van Sant and Yost.

Fogle is now 52, and when he finishes his current sentence he goes to a Wisconsin state prison for additonal time on a drugstore robbery there. Statistics like this do not in any way heighten the allure of the drug life.

MONTHLY FILM BULLETIN, 12/89, p. 362, Michael O'Pray

Portland, Oregon, 1971. Street-wise but superstitious Bob Hughes leads a gang, comprising his wife Dianne and another couple, the impressionable Rick and the young Nadine, who support their drug habit by stealing from local drugstores and hospitals. David, a young junkie acquaintance, sees them return from one raid and tries to negotiate a drug deal, despite being treated with contempt by Bob. After their house is wrecked during a search led by narcotics officer Gentry (who has sworn to bust Bob), Bob and Dianne visit his mother to get some clothes, and Bob steals from her purse. Gentry keeps them under surveillance, and Bob lays an elaborate plan which results in one of Gentry's men being injured by a shotgun-toting neighbour. Gentry and his men beat up Bob, who decides to move the gang across country. One night, Bob and Rick pick up a particularly strong drug during a raid, and thinking that his luck has changed, Bob organises a hospital raid which goes wrong. He escapes only to find the others standing over the dead Nadine, who has overdosed on the drug. They have to move her body from their motel when it becomes the venue for a police conference, and after burying her in the countryside Bob decides to return to Portland and give up drugs. In a rehabilitation clinic, he meets Tom, a priest from his childhood, and with counselling is able to overcome his addiction. He is visited first by Gentry, who warns him that the injured police officer is intent on revenge, and then by Dianne, who is now with Rick, and who leaves a bag of drugs with him after rejecting his appeal to join her. Bob gives the drugs to Tom. A masked David and an accomplice hold Bob at gunpoint for the drugs, and in frustration beat him up and then shoot him. As he is taken away by ambulance, Bob refuses to tell Gentry who shot him.

   The opening shot of *Drugstore Cowboy*, the drawn, handsome features of Matt Dillon as the drug addict *in extremis* and romantic martyr (faint echoes of Martin Sheen sweating it out on a bed in Saigon in that other romantic parable, *Apocalypse Now*), sets the tone of the film. According to director Gus Van Sant, it represents the world as perceived by the junkie, and to this end is freewheeling and quirky in style, imaginatively shot and avoiding any facile sensationalism. In many ways, it is primarily about the mundanities and mechanics of the gang's appropriation and consumption of drugs, and the emotional minimalism of those who are driven in the end not by personal love or loyalty. Instead of a full-blown plot, it is made up of a loosely connected series of episodes in which the robberies themselves are played rather cutely. As one would expect from a portrayal of drug addicts, characterisation is shallow to the extent that Nadine's death (her name being an anagram of the older Dianne) leaves us unmoved, and Bob's reaction to it is unconvincing.

   Set in 1971, the film has no need to take on AIDs, and in many ways there is a nostalgia at work for a bygone innocent era. The hard-drugs junkie is one of the most potent and literally fatally attractive romantic images of the last two centuries. At a time when drugs is high on the agenda of the American authorities, *Drugstore Cowboy* is a rather strange affair in that it avoids many of the clichés of the usual representations of drugtaking, while trying to trace more realistically the psychic and psychological profile of the young drug-user. There are no harrowing scenes of cold turkey (*á la* Popeye Doyle in *French Connection II*) when Bob kicks the habit, and (this must be accounted a sort of realism. But overall the film is compromised by a romanticisation of the drug world.

   It does bring to mind two memorable cinematic images of the junkie—the late Ondine jacking up in the infamous final reel of Warhol's *Chelsea Girls*, and William S. Burroughs doing the same with much more matter-of-factness in Antony Balch's early 60s classic *Towers Open Fire*. Van Sant's use of the close-up and edgy editing has an avant-garde feel which unfortunately becomes rather self-consciously stylish at times, and the film takes its aesthetic lead from Balch/Burroughs in more ways than one. For example, the drug-induced images of floating objects (hats, animals and abstract textures) superimposed over close-ups of Dillon are direct homages to Balch's film and underline the incipient surrealism.

   But what is powerful about both those films is the fact that they are documents and use real junkies. Van Sant's second feature is based on an unpublished novel by James Fogle, currently serving a twenty-two-year sentence in Washington State Penitentiary for drug-related crimes, and it is unhysterical in its presentation of drug-taking. But it also fatally casts real-life addict and cult author Burroughs in a cameo role as the junkie priest who originally introduced Bob to drugs. And it's the militancy and intellectual stance of Warhol's and Balch's junkie figures which Van Sant's film is never able to incorporate. In a crucial scene towards the end, Burroughs expresses his familiar paranoid theory when he tells Bob of the hate he has for a society which does not allow those who cannot tolerate its cruelties and inanities to take refuge in drugs. This rationale together with the emaciated figure of Burroughs disrupts and stands outside what is in the end a rather thoughtless and unenlightening film about drug addiction.

NEW YORK, 10/9/89, p. 82, David Denby

Drugstore Cowboy is a good American independent feature in which Matt Dillon and Kelly Lynch play a bedraggled and stoned young outlaw couple—a bumbling Bonnie and Clyde for the pill-head age. Too out of it and giddy-limp for work or sex, they spend their days plotting the ripoffs, the getaways, the desperate journeys that make up a druggie's weirdly purposeful existence. Their planning sessions turn into a vicious parody of a normal couple's anxious hedging against disaster: What they are arranging is not a trip to the beach with the kids but a heist at a local drugstore, where, as often as not, Matt will thrust his hand into a behind-the-counter drawer of pills and come up with stool softener rather than morphine or Dilaudid.

Drugstore Cowboy is both sordid and funny—much of it plays at the edge of absurdist comedy. Set in Portland, Oregon, in the seventies (before crack changed the drug scene) and based on an unpublished novel by James Fogle, a lifelong addict and thief currently serving a 22-year term in Walla Walla, *Drugstore Cowboy* doesn't offer the usual warnings and clichés (except for the no-longer-shocking shots of needles going into veins). The writer-director Gus Van Sant Jr., working on Fogle's material with screenwriter Daniel Yost, tries to capture the addict's life from the inside; *Drugstore Cowboy* takes the point of view of Bob Hughes (the Dillion character), a young doper-thief with a cracked sense of himself as an existential adventurer.

Having been a successful (i.e., surviving) junkie for years, Bob has developed the mentality of a gambler, depending on his instincts and the mystique of "hot streaks" to keep him from the ultimate bummer of an empty drug stash. The movie allows Bob his self-romanticization but as often as not pulls the rug out from under him; most of his plans lead to messy disaster. Playing this strange mixture of rationalism and criminality, Dillon is a good deal more alert now than he was when he broke into movies a decade ago as a moodily beautiful but affectless teenager. The dreamy narcissism is gone; he projects enough intelligence to keep us interested in Bob's ups and downs; he even show some promising comic talents.

Here and there Van Sant tries for hallucinatory imagery—little black animals and the like flying through the air upside down. But lyrical bliss is not his thing. He's best at the funny-sinister everyday life of young dopers, the frozen stupidity and sneaky smarts, the rhythm of frenzied activity and bombed-out catatonia. Van Sant indulges in a bit of romanticization of his own. He sees the characters as gallant losers—stupid, perhaps, but not entirely without courage. And at the end, he brings in the patron saint of drugs himself, novelist William S. Burroughs, who plays an old junkie priest. Pressing his lips together dryly, Burroughs utters his usual semi-psychotic witticisms, putting down those idiots who dare think that a drug addict can't exist happily. *He's* happy, so he thinks drugs are a great life. I guess he has the right.

NEW YORK POST, 10/6/89, p. 27, Jami Bernard

Society at large is largely ignorant of or flagrantly insensitive ("just say no") to the ins and outs of the drug culture, which makes "Drugstore Cowboy" such a welcome relief. It is as accurate a portrayal as any of the peculiarly insulated life and concerns of the addict.

Sure, not everyone's high translates visually to Dorothy's tornado, with objects floating by in a vortex of confusion. And not every addict's habit is supported by knocking over—what else?—drugstores, as the characters do in "Drugstore Cowboy."

But the young director Gus Van Sant has a sympathy for that through-the-looking-glass world of the junkie, in which superstition passes for reason, lying for communication, and shared desperation for relationships.

Matt Dillon plays Bob Hughes, the leader of a quartet of young addicts in early '70s Portland, Ore. Bob & Co. live from drugstore heist to drugstore heist, a modern-day Bonnie & Clyde gang whose booty is a drawer full of capsules. A particularly good haul is one which includes a specialty item—say, Dilaudid. Money would buy dope too, but these kids cut out the middleman and go straight for the fix.

The high of the actual heist is then replaced by the blissful daze of a junk high. Bob literally can't wait till he gets home to shoot up; like a kid digging into the Halloween take before the trick or treating is done, Bob does his share in the backseat of the getaway car.

Except for "the drug thing," as Bush might call it, Bob's life could pass for middle-class. He and his high school sweetheart wife Dianne (former model Kelly Lynch) sit around their suburban house making desultory small-talk about their day, their plans (most of which never come to fruition) and, you know, *stuff*.

They share their abode of the moment with another couple, Bob's friend Rick (James Le Gros), a dim bulb who is learning the ropes from Bob, and Rick's new girlfriend, Nadine (Heather Graham). A former drugstore clerk who cast her lot with the robbers, Nadine is young, naive, and fatally anxious to please.

Despite the occasional dust-up with the police, these are kids with the Peter Pan syndrome—they don't want to grow up, they just want to fly. Their habits define their lives. The movie accepts the lure of getting high without glorifying it, and allows Bob the strength to change his destiny without moralizing.

Matt Dillon gives a fine, true performance, as true as he was in his very first role in the underrated (or just under-shown) "Over the Edge." Bob is just smart and devious enough to be a leader of junkies, with his alternating lethargy and mania, bound by ridiculously earnest superstitions (no hats on the bed, no dogs in the house).

Kelly Lynch is good as Bob's seemingly urbane but really unpolished wife, whose chief complaints are with Bob's lack of sex drive and with having to steer the getaway car all the time.

Noted author and drug-culture icon William S. Burroughs has a small role as a junkie ex-priest. He's no actor—he glances frequently and edgily at the camera—but his mere presence lends the movie credulity. Burroughs sifts through a stash with finicky fingers and circumlocuted asides ("I'm on the [methadone] program but sometimes I get a little ahead of my schedule"). He may be in danger of becoming the William Hickey of the drug set, but boy, does he have style.

NEWSDAY, 10/6/89, Part III/p. 3, Terry Kelleher

Warning: this film is not a propaganda broadside in America's latest all-out war against drugs.

It contains no sermons, no cold-turkey scenes, none of the usual anti-drug paraphernalia. It does not openly aspire to Social Responsibility.

"Drugstore Cowboy" is about a group of young people in the 1970s whose lives revolve around the acquisition and consumption of drugs. It aims to show in gritty detail what their existence is like—from *their* point of view, not that of the straight world.

The difficulty with "Drugstore Cowboy" is that the characters stubbornly refuse to do the expected thing. Their behavior can seem illogical, unmotivated, implausible—and therefore unacceptable. It fails to jibe with what we know about drug addiction. Or what we *think* we known.

Matt Dillon gives an impressive performance as Bob, the leader of a gang of four that robs narcotics from pharmacies in the Pacific Northwest and gets high on the haul. The character is loosely modeled on James Fogle, an inmate in Walla Walla, Wash., who wrote the unpublished novel on which Daniel Yost and director Gus Van Sant based their screenplay.

The Bob we see, the Bob of the past, is a dedicated junkie and thief. The Bob we hear in voice-over is a somewhat detached narrator looking back on his folly with irony, relief, a certain amount of regret and no apologies.

The rest of Bob's gang includes his wife, Dianne (Kelly Lynch), who seems too smart to be in her situation; Rick (James Le Gros), who seems too dumb to handle any situation, and Nadine, Rick's girlfriend, who knows enough to challenge Bob's arbitrary, superstitious dictates but not nearly enough to call her own shots and survive.

They pull jobs, they shoot up, they bicker, they snicker at an anti-drug message on television, they stay one step ahead of a pursuing Portland narc (James Remar). There's an edge to the life, the occasional thrill of outlawry, but Van Sant also shows its pettiness and tedium. Although Bob and Dianne, when the mood is upon them, envision their exploits as the stuff of legend, the lot of the daring junkie-bandit often seems scarcely more glamorous than that of the common wage slave.

Maybe this realization is a factor in Bob's abrupt decision to enroll in a methadone program and take a factory job. Maybe, as Bob claims, he made a silent promise to "lead a virtuous life" if the gods allowed his escape from a particularly tight spot. regardless, his conversion is less dramatic than pragmatic.

"I like drugs," Bob explains to a counselor (Beah Richards). "I like the lifestyle. But it didn't pay off."

Credible as Dillon's characterization has been to this point, the suddenness of Bob's turnaround and the cool firmness of his new resolve are not easy to accept. Say some human beings are stronger than others and let it go at that. You may even be right.

William Burroughs, "literary outlaw" and ex-addict, lends authority to the small role of Father

Tom, a confirmed junkie and lapsed cleric who grouses to Bob that conservatives will use anti-drug hysteria to limit freedom for all. And *he* may even be right.

That's the way of the world depicted in "Drugstore Cowboy": Old hopheads can be wise. Intelligent young women can be tragically foolish. Sniveling small-time dealers can be more dangerous than they look. If you can't depend on anybody, neither can you write anybody off.

NEWSWEEK, 10/23/89, p. 84, David Ansen

"Most people, they don't know how they're going to feel from one minute to the next, but a dope fiend has a pretty good idea: all they gotta do is look at the labels on the little bottles." If you're looking for insight into the junkie personality, that quote—spoken by the "shameless full-time dope fiend" Bob (Matt Dillon) in *Drugstore Cowboy*—is about as revealing as they come. For the characters in Gus Van Sant's extraordinary movie, the pursuit of the perpetual high is a full-time occupation, requiring complex planning, dedication and guile. Like any compulsive behavior—workaholism, for one—the goal is control, the enemy the terror of emotional (dare one call it existential?) uncertainty. That's the abyss: not knowing how you're going to feel from one minute to the next.

"Drugstore Cowboy," which is set in Portland, Ore., in 1971, is a brave movie to be made amid the anti-drug hysteria of 1989. Not that it's pro-drug. Not that it glamorizes the junkie lifestyle. Far from it. But Van Sant doesn't stand outside, wagging a judgmental finger at his characters. The trouble with most well-meaning anti-drug dramas is their refusal to acknowledge one obvious fact: the very real, albeit dangerous, *pleasure* of drugs. After all, if they weren't, momentarily, better than "reality," who'd bother to use them? Van Sant's compelling, unnerving and often darkly funny movie is an inside job. Based on an unpublished novel by prison inmate James Fogle (the first-rate screenplay is by Van Sant and Daniel Yost), "Drugstore Cowboy" may be the most honest moive about drug addicts ever made—it gets the details right, and lets the audience draw its own conclusions.

It's a movie about a makeshift family. They're losers all, but temporarily they're on a roll. Bob is the leader. He's no mental giant, but he's a little bit sharper and savvier than the others—he organizes their robberies of drugstores and hospital pharmacies. His childhood sweetheart and wife, Dianne (Kelly Lynch), is his devoted partner in dope and crime, and their "kids" are the dimwitted Rick (James Le Gros) and his young, junkie-in-training girlfriend Nadine (Heather Graham), their running partners.

They are a scuzzy bunch, but all too human in their banality, bravado and wild superstition. (Bob is always worrying about hexes and throws a fit if someone leaves a hat on the bed.) Van Sant finds both the humor and the horror in their day-to-day, fix-to-fix existence. And what perfect-pitch performances he gets from the entire cast: Dillon, who has done more posturing than acting of late, is startlingly good here—the postures he strikes are always Bob's, not his own. And Lynch, known for her glamour-girl roles, faultlessly vanishes inside this jaundiced, half-sophisticated girl/woman. Their unsentimental love story (largely asexual, for Bob is always fixated on his next job when she's interested in sex) owes nothing to generic formulas, yet it's strangely touching. When Bob finally decides to kick drugs after Nadine ODs on Dilaudid, Dianne feels betrayed. Between love and junk, she doesn't have a choice.

The novelist William Burroughs makes a striking appearance as an old junkie priest, spouting patented Burroughs rants about police-state conspiracies. It's a riveting "guest appearance," but his sepulchral presence jolts you out of the story. This may be the movie's only minor miscalculation. The emergence of the 36-year-old Van Sant, who lives in Portland, is the most heartening news from the American "independent" cinema since Steven ("sex, lies and videotape") Soderbergh. Van Sant's first feature was the gritty "Mala Noche." Made on a shoestring, it chronicled a skid-row store clerk's unrequited homosexual passion for an illegal Chicano immigrant. Van Sant has an unforced lyrical touch and a feel for low life that's free of both condescension and macho romanticizing. Every minute of "Drugstore Cowboy" is vital and alive, even when its junkie protagonists seem barely to be breathing.

VILLAGE VOICE, 10/10/89, p. 85, J. Hoberman

Now that Woodstock's 20th anniversary has come and gone, the '60s revival seems destined to sputter. Altamont, Manson, and Kent State don't lend themselves to quite the same mega-maudlin treatment. Still, anyone interested in a taste of late countercultural lifestyle should investigate Gus

Van Sant Jr.'s remarkable (and remarkably timely) *Drugstore Cowboy*, opening here Friday and set, toward the rat's-ass end of the Vietnam era, in 1971 Portland.

A tough, funny film made with considerable verve and no small amount of guts, *Drugstore Cowboy* opens on prone Matt Dillon in sweaty close-up and his voiceover confession that he "was once a shameless, full-time dope fiend." *Shameless* is the operative word: Given the hypocritical rhetoric the drug scourge inevitably inspires, Van Sant's lack of easy moralizing would in itself make *Drugstore Cowboy* an unusual film. (One has to return to the original period—to Ivan Passer's *Born To Win* of Floyd Mutrux's *Dusty and Sweets McGee*—to find a comparable attitude.) But what pushes *Drugstore Cowboy* beyond social tract is the jagged aplomb of Van Sant's style.

Drugstore Cowboy exhibits the same low-budget panache and sardonic edginess that characterized Van Sant's estimable 1987 *Mala Noche*. Like that $25,000 cheapster, a moody drizzle of images in which the manager of a skid row convenience store falls hopelessly in love with a Mexican street kid, *Drugstore Cowboy* takes a wryly nonjudgmental view of so-called deviant behavior. Where *Mala Noche*'s hero is both romantically impulsive and hardheadedly calculating, *Drugstore Cowboy*'s Bob Hughes (Dillon) is a similarly contradictory case. Bob lives by his wits, inside his head, and his drug-addled mind games are as dependent on primitive superstition as they are fueled by native cunning. His most exalted moment is a cleverly orchestrated prank on the cops, and Van Sant celebrates it by superimposing the dope fiend's demonic grin over a whirling storm of greenish confetti as if he were as cosmic a joker as the man in the moon.

Matt Dilon is not exactly a sell point, but the narcissistic self-absorption of his previous performances is here a positive element. Dillon's star mannerisms help account for the hold this arrogant doper has over his "crew"—his wife Dianne (played with steely composure by former model Kelly Lynch), his dim-witted protégé Rick (James Le Gros), and Rick's jailbait pickup Nadine (Heather Graham). The four specialize in burglarizing pharmacies and hospitals for drugs, not money; they're existential outlaws, and, in a sense, *Drugstore Cowboy* is a "real-life" imitation of *Bonnie and Clyde*. Indeed, Dianne, who pockets a copy of *Love Story* during one pharmacy heist, has the same problems as Bonnie in attracting her Clyde's attention. In one violent evocation of the superego, their lone attempt at lovemaking is interrupted by cops splintering down the door.

Albeit not quite sleazy enough—one misses the rancid panorama afforded by the early '70s dope scene—*Drugstore Cowboy* captures both the excitement and the idiocy of junkie life. When Bob goes to see his mother, she reflexively locks the door and hides her purse; when Bob, an erstwhile golf enthusiast, sentimentally picks up a club to demonstrate his backswing, he topples a lamp. Throughout, the sordid comedy of Bob's dope-driven stratagems is played against the physical splendor of the great Northwest. Taking to the road, Bob and Dianne send their drugs ahead by Greyhound, cut a hole in the car floor for quick stash disposal, then wind up sharing a rural motel with the delegates to a sheriffs' convention.

The fetishistic close-ups of Bob cooking, shooting, and booting his dope are complemented by the megalomania of his humorously tacky heroin "hallucinations"; the movie's truest ending would be its hero on methadone clumsily learning how to operate a drill press. Van Sant, a 36-year-old ex-adman who understands a bit about audience expectations, has something more spectacular in mind. Still, mordant as it is, *Drugstore Cowboy* has an elegiac quality. Bob, at 26, is already given to a generational rap, referring to the younger, more violent dopers as "TV babies." And, here, as in *Mala Noche*, Portland's skid row exudes a forlorn nostalgia—for the days of Robert Frank as well as the Wild West. There's an unabashed beatnik quality to Van Sant's worldview, as well as to his jagged camera style. (He'd be well-suited to adapt Charles Bukowski.) Toward the end of the movie, William S. Burroughs appears as a cadaverous, defrocked junkie priest: "Narcotics have been systematically scapegoated and demonized," he intones in his clipped foghorn, half-W.C. Fields, half-P.A. system.

What's stunning about this slice of low-life is its frank acknowledgment that people do drugs because they want to, that drugs provide some pleasure their ordinary lives lack, and that—however destructive—this addiction is not simply a character failure, but a child's pitiful yearning for some fun utopia of thrills and sunshine. Interviewed by a social worker, Bob explains that

people use drugs "to relieve the pressures of their everyday life—like having to tie their shoes."
It's a hilarious moment, but then, there are no shoelaces in Heaven.

Also reviewed in:
NEW YORK TIMES, 10/6/89, p. C17, Stephen Holden
VARIETY, 8/30–9/5/89, p. 30
WASHINGTON POST, 10/27/89, p. B1, Hal Hinson
WASHINGTON POST, 10/27/89, Weekend/p. 43, Desson Howe

DRY WHITE SEASON, A

A Metro-Goldwyn-Mayer release. *Executive Producer:* Tim Hampton. *Producer:* Paula Weinstein. *Director:*
Euzhan Palcy. *Screenplay:* Colin Welland and Euzhan Palcy. *Based on the novel by:* André Brink. *Director
of Photography:* Kelvin Pike and Pierre-William Glenn. *Editor:* Sam O'Steen and Glenn Cunningham. *Music:*
Dave Grusin. *Music Editor:* Else Blangsted. *Sound:* Roy Charman. *Sound Editor:* Bill Phillips. *Production
Designer:* John Fenner. *Art Director:* Alan Tomkins. *Set Decorator:* Peter James. *Special Effects:* David Harris.
Costumes: Germinal Rangel. *Make-up:* Tommie Manderson. *Stunt Coordinator:* Marc Boyle. *Running time:*
106 minutes. *MPAA Rating:* R.

CAST: Donald Sutherland (Ben); Janet Suzman (Susan); Zakes Mokae (Stanley); Jurgen Prochnow (Captain
Stolz); Susan Sarandon (Melanie); Marlon Brando (McKenzie); Winston Ntshona (Gordon); Thoko Ntshinga
(Emily); Leonard Maguire (Bruwer); Gerard Thoolen (Col. Viljoen); Susannah Harker (Suzette); Andrew
Whaley (Chris); Rowen Elmes (Johan); Stella Dickin (Susan's Mother); David De Keyser (Susan's Father); John
Kani (Julius); Sophie Mgcina (Margaret); Bekhithemba Mpofu (Jonathan); Tinashe Makoni (Robert); Precious
Phiri (Wellington); Richard Wilson (Cloete); Derek Hanekom (Viviers); Michael Gambon (Magistrate); Ronald
Pickup (Louw); Paul Brooke (Dr. Herzog); Ernest Ndlovu (Archibald Mabaso); Stephen Hanly (Sgt. Van Zyl);
Andre Proctor (Jaimie); Kevin Johnson (Gert); Grant Davidson (Lt. Venter); Ndu Gumede (Douma); Sello
Maake (Johnson Seroke); Charles Pillai (Dr. Hassiem); Rosemary Martin (Mrs. Beachley); Willie Zweni
(Aubrey Kunene); Mercia Davids (Sadie); Mannie De Villiers (Police Commandant); Anna Manimanzi (Soweto
Girl).

FILMS IN REVIEW, 1–2/90, p. 46, Pat Anderson

Like many South Africans, Ben du Toit (Donald Sutherland) is abysmally ignorant of the
oppression of blacks in his nation. A prep school master, he has a good home and loving family
and is a sort of big white father to his black gardener Gordon Ngubene (Winston Ntshona).

Ben's education in the consequences of apartheid starts when Gordon's son Jonathan
(Bekhithemba Mpofu) is beaten up during a Soweto student demonstration, and Ben naively
assumes that the boy must have provoked the authorities. But then Jonathan's arrest rapidly
follows. Gordon badgers and alienates officials while trying to find his son; until the stark
announcement of Jonathan's death in jail.

Gordon goes to Ben asking him to help find out how Jonathan died. But now, following
Gordon's agitations, the whole Ngubene family is being watched. Gordon himself is arrested and
soon his wife Emily (Thoko Ntshinga) is informed that her husband has committed suicide in
prison. A bitter Emily seeking support from Ben, infuriates his wife Susan (Janet Suzman) and
his family. Susan is even more outraged when her troubled husband agrees that Gordon's death
is suspicious and innocently begins making enquiries. He just isn't prepared for the run-around
from his government acquaintances; the revelation of the brutal treatment of the blacks; and
especially not for the personal hostility he encounters from his friends and colleagues.

Gradually Ben's world is turned upside down. Estranged from friends and family (except his
young son Johan (Rowen Elmes) who was Jonathan's friend), he finds his only acceptance in
people like the lawyer McKenzie (Marlon Brando, looking, and even sounding a bit, like Orson
Welles), larger than life defender of lost causes; crusading reporter Melanie (Susan Sarandon), and
the blacks he comes to know as real people for the first time in his life. Fighting for what he now

realizes is simple justice, Ben gets deeper and deeper into the political mire of apartheid politics until there is no escape.

A Dry White Season, based on an André Brinks novel, was conceived as a film by Euzhan Palcy. She herself directed and, with Colin Welland, co-wrote the screenplay, giving the black story as much weight as the white—both pro and anti government. All the blacks in the cast as well as the whites—except for the principal, big name, American stars—are South African, thus lending an authenticity that other pictures about apartheid have lacked, as well as giving international recognition to these fine actors.

This is a movie that combines an exceptionally entertaining suspense story with an issue that is constantly with us.

LOS ANGELES TIMES, 9/22/89, Calendar/p. 1, Kevin Thomas

"A Dry White Season" moves so swiftly, catching you up into its hellish chain of events, that you're left reeling. That's exactly the effect it should have, for no other contemporary mainstream film takes us so deeply, so unflinchingly, into the tragically divided heart of South Africa.

It combines the artistry of "A World Apart" with the scope of "Cry Freedom" and also manages to generate the kind of suspense that brings back fond memories of that definitive political thriller, Costa-Gavras' "Z". It is in all ways a superior achievement, the very model of what a protest film ought to be, involving and entertaining, angry rather than preachy.

In bringing Andre Brink's novel to the screen, producer Paula Weinstein and writer-director Euzhan Palcy pull absolutely no punches; they lay bare the limitless evil of apartheid for the whole world to see.

The film, which was shot largely in Zimbabwe, opens with the Soweto uprising of 1976. A bright adolescent, Jonathan (Bekhithemba Mpofu) insists on joining a student demonstration against second-rate education for blacks, despite the fears of his father Gordon (Winston Ntshona). Jonathan's brave decision triggers seemingly endless and ever-widening tragic consequences, and eventually involves his father's employer, Afrikaner schoolteacher and former rugby star Ben du Toit (Donald Sutherland), who lives in a Johannesburg suburb that could pass for one of the nicest areas of Brentwood.

Right off, Palcy defines the vast difference between the white and black worlds by relentlessly cutting back and forth between the slaughter of black children in Soweto and a white children's happy rugby match, in which Du Toit's son Johan (Rowen Elmes) participates.

Like "Cry Freedom," "A Dry White Season' centers on a white South African's gradual loss of naiveté and growing commitment to the struggle against apartheid. But it does so with more economy, more dispatch, and illuminates the Afrikaner psyche as no other fiction film has.

Unsparingly, but without lingering morbidity, Palcy shows us the atrocities with which whites afflict blacks on the flimsiest of pretexts. Then she allows us to understand how and why this occurs so endlessly. The Afrikaner society Palcy depicts with such conviction sustains itself on a lethal mixture of fear and indifference.

We see that Jurgen Prochnow's steely Special Branch captain is not merely a sadist but is also consumed with fear, just as Du Toit's wife (Janet Suzman) is. These two really believe that South Africa is *their* country and that they are at war with the black majority, who they are certain would surely destroy them given the chance. It's this terrible fear that permits the most unspeakable torture and oppression.

At the same time, the whites live in considerable comfort, pursuing a stable, settled way of life with a strong sense of community that(insulates them from the horrible realities the blacks must endure from cradle to grave. "A Dry White Season's" key accomplishment is to make believable that a decent, intelligent and loving family man like Du Toit could have reached middle age and still be able to deceive himself as to the true condition of the blacks and the brutal treatment routinely accorded them.

Palcy is able to convey all this and more because she and her co-writer, Colin Welland, have written from Brink's 1979 novel a remarkably succinct yet comprehensive and multilayered script, one of the year's best. To be sure, there are sharp exchanges over apartheid throughout the film, but the effect escapes preachiness because the film has such a fullness of life.

Escalating slaughter culminates in an inquest, which brings Marlon Brando into the picture at just the right moment. He is there not merely to defend good against evil but to give us some respite. Magnificently bulky, he plays a brilliant, eccentric barrister of as much wit and humor as courage. In his first film in eight years, Brando fills the screen with his presence, providing a showy, pivotal distraction, allowing the film to shift gears from fiery exposé to suspense thriller.

From this superbly constructed plot, we are able to see that one loving father and son—Ben and Johan—are gradually taking the places of another loving father and son, Gordon and Jonathan. This is what commitment to change really means: risking being subjected to all the dangers, injustice and suffering of those who have been so systematically victimized. It is in this melding of two worlds, so long deliberately separated, that "A Dry, White Season" becomes so stunning an accomplishment.

There's not a false note in the performances Palcy has elicited from a large and varied cast, which includes Susan Sarandon as a tough-minded journalist; Zakes Mokae as a canny, sarcastic black taxi driver who serves as Du Toit's conscience; Thoko Ntshinga as Gordon's distraught but determined wife, and Susannah Harker as Du Toit's grown daughter who wishes that everything could get back to "normal."

"A Dry White Season" represents the high point of Donald Sutherland's career. Never before has he had a part that demanded such range. Of his many splendid moments is one in which he lets us know he is being betrayed by someone he loves. Refreshingly, the romance between Sutherland and Sarandon that would be obligatory in a lesser film is resisted here.

Five years ago, the Martinique-born Palcy made a terrific feature debut with "Sugar Cane Alley," an intimate West Indian film of much charm and grit about a grandmother determined that her bright grandson will escape the grueling existence of a sugar-cane worker. "A Dry White Season" (rated R for violence) is only her second feature, but working on an epic scale—and in English—she displays the assurance of a David Lean.

MONTHLY FILM BULLETIN, 1/90, p. 12, Pam Cook

South Africa, 1976. When Gordon Ngubene's son Jonathan disappears following the massacre by police of peacefully demonstrating schoolchildren in Soweto, he asks Ben du Toit, the Afrikaner schoolteacher for whom he works as a gardener, for help. Ben discovers that Jonathan is supposed to have been killed during the riots. Against Ben's advice, Gordon begins his own investigation with the help of lawyer Julius and family friend Stanley Makhaya. Special Branch raid Gordon's house and arrest him, taking statements he has collected from witnesses to Jonathan's imprisonment and torture. Ben visits Colonel Viljoen and the sinister Captain Stolz but gets little satisfaction. He is shocked when he hears from Stanley that Gordon is dead, having apparently committed suicide in his cell, and insists on going to Soweto with Stanley to see the body. Deeply distressed when Gordon's scars point to vicious torture, Ben is moved to approach civil rights lawyer Ian McKenzie to represent Gordon's wife Emily at the inquest. The jaded McKenzie reluctantly agrees, but in spite of overwhelming evidence that Gordon was tortured to death by Stolz, the security forces are cleared. Ben is rescued from the angry scenes outside the court by Melanie Bruwer, a journalist on the liberal *Rand Daily Mail*, who questions his naive idealism but offers to help. Ben joins forces with Emily, Julius and Stanley to collect affidavits from witnesses to Gordon's torture, building a hiding place in his tool box. He manages to obtain a truthful autopsy report, but because of his activities he is fired and his son Johan expelled. At Christmas, a visit from a drunken Stanley bearing news of Emily's death while being forcibly evicted causes uproar in Ben's family, and his disenchanted wife Susan leaves him, while Johan insists on staying with his father. Ben's daughter Suzette discovers the tool-box hiding place and informs the police, who blow up Ben's garage. However, Johan has secreted the papers elsewhere. Having gone to Zambia to collect a witness' statement, Melanie is detained on her return and deported to England, but manages to get the affidavit to Stanley. With the police closing in, Ben entrusts his account of events and the statements to Johan to deliver to the *Rand Daily Mail*, while he acts as a decoy, passing false papers to Suzette, who then gives them to Stolz. Incensed, Stolz runs Ben down and kills him. Some time later, Stanley shoots Stolz dead, and Ben's story is printed.

Martinique-born director Euzhan Palcy's five-year struggle to complete *A Dry White Season* is a sign both of the ambition of the project and the difficulties of translating André Brink's momentous story of a white South African's traumatic politicisation into a manageable screenplay. Brink's novel (and Colin Welland's initial script) concentrated on the perspective of Ben du Toit, the mild-mannered Afrikaner schoolteacher whose life is torn apart when he becomes involved in a black family's battle against the corruption and brute force of the South African legal system. Ben's encounter with the realities against which he has been comfortably cushioned has devastating effects: his own family is destroyed, he loses his job and finally his life, but not before his ideals and aspirations have been painfully stripped away.

Brink's book is a powerful indictment of a country whose original tenets of freedom have withered away, leaving a stunted, distorted society (the "dry white season", taken from a poem by Mongane Wally Serote, is a central metaphor for the traumatic drought conditions which destroy lives and livelihoods, and Brink's South Africa is a dusty place in which little flourishes). But an inevitable consequence of mediating the horrors of apartheid through white consciousness (symptomatic also of *Cry Freedom* and *A World Apart*) is that the black experience becomes secondary: the "white eye", to use Stuart Hall's term, however sympathetic, cannot help but colonise. The same is true, in Brink's novel, of Ben's "male eye". His alienation from his wife Susan and affair with journalist Melanie Bruwer are presented entirely from the point of view of a man in moral, sexual and political crisis: the conservative Susan neurotically trying to hang on to the vestiges of their moribund marriage and the progressive Melanie representing Ben's last chance of real passion.

Palcy's revamped script attempts to redress the balance by shifting the emphasis from one white man's psychological disintegration to the real physical brutality inflicted on blacks by apartheid. Instead of allowing Ben's mental pain to stand in for black suffering, she depicts the latter graphically, showing both the sadistic methods of police torture and its horrific results. These shocking scenes are among the strongest in the film, as are those of black resistance. The opening sequence portraying the massacre of Soweto's schoolchildren is deeply disturbing, filmed with an edgy energy which goes for maximum emotional impact. In spite of this shift, however, Palcy retains sympathy with the white characters, and exacts a finely nuanced performance from Donald Sutherland as Ben. Paradoxically, in heavily curtailing the roles of Susan (Ben's wife and an unsympathetic character in Brink's book) and journalist Melanie Bruwer, Palcy has dispensed with much of the novel's sexism, though without entirely escaping the implication that women are marginal to the political fight.

The major relationships of solidarity in the film are between men, often between father and son: Gordon Ngubene and his son Jonathan, Gordon and Ben, Ben and his son Johan, or Ben and Stanley, the cynic who becomes an ally. A telling image occurs near the end, as Ben, betrayed by his daughter Suzette, lies in the street crushed to death by Captain Stolz's car, while Johan and Stanley embrace jubilantly after delivering Ben's story into the right hands. Future resistance is clearly passed on through male alliances (Stanley later kills Stolz, as if to seal his brotherhood with Ben).

Palcy's ending is relatively hopeful, suggesting the possibility of change through black/white partnership, breaking out of the vicious circle of Brink's paranoid conclusion (the novel appeared in 1979 and was immediately banned in South Africa). The pessimism expressed by the world-weary civil rights lawyer Ian McKenzie, "Justice and the law are not on speaking terms in South Africa", is undercut to a certain extent by the newspaper publication of Ben's story, and by the "rough justice" meted out to Stolz by Stanley. But though there is no doubting the passionate commitment sustaining Palcy's *A Dry White Season*, something has been lost: the relentless, tragic lyricism which lends Brink's novel and epic scope the film never quite achieves.

NEW YORK, 10/2/89, p. 75, David Denby

In *A Dry White Season*, Marlon Brando looks enormous—as big as King Farouk after swallowing Orson Welles—but when he performs, he's still light on his feet. Sporting a slightly fussy Anglo accent and perfect manners, Brando plays a British-born South African lawyer who appears at an inquest conducted by a sham court. The dead man in question, a black, has been murdered by the police; the witnesses have been tortured. As the judge toadies to the government side, Brando sinks deeper and deeper into ironic politesse. His delicate "Your Worship," addressed to the corrupt judge, is high comedy.

But Brando is one of the few watchable things in the movie. Donald Sutherland, the star, struggles manfully with a dummy role—an Afrikaner who slowly awakens to the injustice of apartheid. Sutherland plays virtually the same role that Kevin Kline played in *Cry Freedom*, only his character is far less intelligent and resourceful. He is at the center of the movie not because he's an interesting man but because he discovers his conscience; and since he sees nothing, anticipates nothing, understands nothing, and puts his family in jeopardy without even warning them, we can hardly stay involved in the drama of his enlightenment. He seem less a man with a newfound soul than a dunce manipulated by the unconscious hostility of the filmmakers into sacrificing himself to the black cause.

Written by Colin Welland and Euzhan Palcy (from a novel by André Brink) and directed by Palcy, the Martinique-born woman who made *Sugar Cane Alley* (1984), *A Dry White Season* is unbearably stiff. The slaughter of black children and the scenes of intimidation and torture are shot academically, without rage or poetry. The African actors, with the exception of Zakes Mokae, are implacably noble and dignified. No one says anything not absolutely required by the situation; the movie, impersonal, guarded, and correct, is a procession of attitudes—like a school play written by the faculty.

NEW YORK POST, 9/20/89, p. 23, David Edelstein

In dramatizing a government's brutal, unscrupulous behavior, an artist may feel that he or she has the right to be brutal and unscrupulous, too. If police shoot down innocent children, why not show close-ups of those children as they die? If the police torture a man to death, why not linger on his bloody agony? The brutality, the artist reasons, is more than justified. This is about truth.

Well, it is and it isn't. "A Dry White Season," the new anti-apartheid melodrama, is a miserably bad piece of film making that is also extremely powerful. How could it not be? It's set in South Africa under a violent, repressive regime that tortures and kills members of its black majority—people who ask for little more than the most basic human freedoms.

It's about the killing of little boys, the fathers who try to find out what happened to them and the mothers who have the audacity to grieve for both. And it's the kind of propaganda that makes you sick and angry—not because it's true, but because the film makers have resorted to fascist techniques to make their anti-fascist case. The movie feels cheap and ugly and obvious.

"A Dry White Season" opens with an image of a young black boy playing soccer with a young white boy. Look at this vision, it says: We're all equal in the radiant innocence of childhood. Now look what the grownups are doing: bad things.

The white boy, Chris (Andrew Whaley) is the son of Ben du Toit (Donald Sutherland), a happy contented South African schoolteacher. The black boy, Jonathan (Bekhithemba Mpofu), belongs to du Toit's gardener, Gordon (Winston Ntshona), and he burns with a fierce political commitment. (This does not, however, keep him from making nice-nice with oblivious white boys.)

Jonathan attends a peaceful demonstration on which the police open fire, shooting men, women and children in the backs as they flee. He tries to help a small child and is roughly thrown into a van; that is the last we see of him.

Gordon, determined to learn how his son died, is finally arrested and tortured to death: The police call it suicide, but we have seen his mashed, pulpy face and heard his screams. Stunned by the loss of his gardener, du Toit—who has never been involved in politics—decides to seek justice.

The director, Euzhan Palcy, is a young black woman from Mozambique with one other feature to her credit, the overpraised "Sugar Cane Alley." Her work is even clumsier here, and the obviousness would be laughable if the subject weren't so tragic. Palcy was determined not to make another "Cry Freedom"—a movie primarily about the ennoblement and self-sacrifice of a white South African.

Still, that's essentially what she has made. "A Dry White Season" sticks to the formula: An apolitical (white) person has his eyes opened to injustice and is compelled to speak out, with the result that he is ostracized from his community and his family. He's the man who tells the truth and so becomes an enemy of his own kind, much like the hero of "Romero" and the heroine of "Heart of Dixie."

Sutherland, with his reddish hair and drooping face, gives an amiable and shambling performance, but this man has no inner life. He's as purely good as the white South Africans are purely evil. Yet the film makers go to such lengths to show how uninformed du Toit is that they unconsciously make him a simpleton—he's a blur, a dead spot on the screen.

In the beginning, his encounters with the police are very formal and polite, and Palcy captures the tension in any such encounter with people who have disproportionate amounts of power. But the casting is dull-witted: the principal villain is played by Jurgen Prochnow, the blue-eyed Aryan from "Das Boot," and it's a generic Nazi-swine performance.

The only offbeat touch is the presence of Marlon Brando, who returns to the screen (for about 15 minutes) after a nine-year absence. Brando plays a civil-rights lawyer named McKenzie, and the first shot of him, his back to the camera, is startling.

It's a huge back now, stretching all the way across the screen, and when we see his face it's wide, with shivering wattles. His McKenzie has the nasal Englishness of his Fletcher Christian, and his timing is even woozier and more eccentric.

As usual, Brando perversely shrugs off his pedestal, launching into a rambling account of his allergies and the lozenges he must take for them. ("They're totally ineffective but they're rather tasty. Would you like one?") As we watch him we think, "How many gallons of ice cream did this?" (Brando never does anything halfway, including gaining weight.)

Yet it's a terrific performance—Brando seems like the only human being on screen. His McKenzie is a man who has been forced to cloak his outrage in morbid amusement, the knowledge that he's but a poor player in a ghastly farce. "Every time I win a case," he say sadly, "they simply change the law."

Stirringly, he summons up that outrage once more in court, bearing down on the shaken Prochnow with a startling recitation of the dead man's injuries: "His jaw—broken; his nose—broken; his cheekbone—crushed." The courtroom scene is the apex of "A Dry White Season," a charade so ludicrous that it becomes high black comedy.

It's too bad Brando has no scenes with Zakes Mokae, who plays Stanley, a black cab driver who's du Toit's chief co-conspirator. Mokae, best known here for his performances in Athol Fugard plays, has a twisted mouth and snaggle teeth that give his face a wry, subversive cast.

His performance is lean and tough, but the script makes him go through the usual contortions: first telling the white man that it's not his fight and that he doesn't know anything about blacks; then welcoming the white man into the fold as a brother. At least Mokae gets better material than Susan Sarandon, who has a tiny part as a left-wing journalist and who's obviously only here because of her (exemplary) activism.

Palcy proves she knows how to push our buttons. The blacks sing hymns before the police start shooting. Someone we care about gets run down by a car, the driver backing up over the body and driving over it again. And the picture ends with a vigilante killing that satisfies our bloodlust. Apart from the courtroom scene, then, "A Dry White Season" is morally no more complex than "Lethal Weapon II." It's a holier-than-thou exploitation movie.

NEWSDAY, 9/20/89, Part II/p. 2, Terry Kelleher

Last week the government of South Africa made no overt attempt to stop some 20,000 demonstrators from marching to police headquarters at John Vorster Square in Johannesburg and calling for an end to brutality and repression.

A hopeful sign? Perhaps. But "'hope' is a white man's word," as a black man remarks in "A Dry White Season."

Like Richard Attenborough's "Cry Freedom," which got a tepid reception two years ago, "A Dry White Season" deals with a white South African's awakening to the terrible reality of apartheid. The difference is that Euzhen Palcy's film avoids getting carried away with its great white hope.

Although his naivete is maddening and not fully credible, the fictional Afrikaner teacher in "A Dry White Season" is far more sympathetic than the real-life liberal journalist of English descent in "Cry Freedom." We feel his crisis of conscience more keenly, yet we understand that the price he pays is only a small installment on his country's staggering moral debt.

At the start of "A Dry White Season," set in 1976, Ben du Toit (Donald Sutherland) is an apolitical, complacent, benignly paternalistic figure. Noblesse oblige moves him to pay tuition for Jonathan, the son of his black gardener, Gordon (Winston Ntshona). When Jonathan is beaten by police, Ben reflexively decides that "they must have had a reason." When the boy is missing and feared dead after a police slaughter of protesting schoolchildren, Ben is concerned enough to inquire of the authorities, but compliant enough to accept their diversionary assurances. Sutherland, fine throughout, is especially effective in this scene, as Ben politely confines his troublemaking to the minimum required to maintain manly dignity.

Soon Gordon is arrested, hauled to John Vorster Square and tortured to death under the direction of a sadistic police captain (Jurgen Prochnow). Ben now insists that Gordon's friend Stanley (Zakes Mokae), a cabbie, drive him to the black township of Soweto to view the body. What he sees shocks him into actions that alienate his professional colleagues, cost him the support of his wife (Janet Suzman) and daughter (Susannah Harker), and eventually imperil his life.

A 32-year-old film maker from Martinique with just one prior feature ("Sugar Cane Alley") to her credit, Palcy revamped a screenplay by Colin Welland and succeeded in turning the original Andre Brink novel into a movie that works more than acceptably as a thriller. But the relationships form the heart of the story. Foremost among these is the uneasy alliance between Ben and Stanley, who requires more than a goodwill gesture or two before he'll respect, much less trust, a member of the white ruling class. Both men call themselves "Africans," but the teacher has only begun to learn the definition of the term.

It's debatable how much the picture profits from the comparatively brief appearances of Marlon Brando and Susan Sarandon. Playing an aging, weighed-down lawyer retained by Ben to pursue the inquest into Gordon's death, Brando captures the character's disillusionment and abiding contempt for official mendacity, but his slurry diction undercuts his half-hearted English accent and his line readings bespeak a notorious aversion to memorization. Sarandon hasn't much to do in the role of a journalist.

Ben's wife warns him that South Africa is at war, that he must choose sides with his own people or "have no people." Palcy elects to end "A Dry White Season" by showing a true act of war, which some will see as a denial of hope, others as an affirmation of justice.

TIME, 9/25/89, p. 78, Richard Schickel

Here it is, then, our annual antiapartheid movie. In moral thrust, *A Dry White Season* is exactly like its immediate predecessors, *Cry Freedom* and *A World Apart*. Once again a white liberal comes to radical consciousness after intimate confrontations with the murderous brutality of South African racism and suffers dreadfully as a result.

Artistically, *A Dry White Season* may aspire to less than the previous movies, since it lacks both the epic ambition of Richard Attenborough's *Freedom* and the psychological delicacy of Chris Menges' *World*. Emotionally, however, it has a force unmatched by the other movies on this subject. For the new film does not stir you to thought (if you still need to think over apartheid, you are probably brain damaged) or sympathy (if you still lack compassion for South Africa's blacks, you probably need a heart implant). It stirs you to outrage.

One reason for the picture's impact is its straight-ahead melodramatic structure. At its simplest level the movie functions as a well-constructed mystery story. A black man, a gardener named Gordon Ngubene (Winston Ntshona), comes to his employer, Ben du Toit (Donald Sutherland), asking him to help find his son. The boy was taken into police custody during the Soweto protests of 1976 and has disappeared. Du Toit, a calm and rational man, believes this is surely just a bureaucratic muddle that can be easily ameliorated by a solid citizen's firm but polite intervention.

But we are not talking bureaucracy here. We are talking about a strangely imperturbable menace. Searching for his son, Ngubene is also arrested; father and boy are tortured and then murdered in prison. And because Du Toit continues to seek justice on their behalf, he is himself victimized by state terror that is the more frightening because of the bland face with which it covers its institutionalized psychopathy. Du Toit is subjected to steadily escalating harassment. Eventually he loses his job and his wife (Janet Suzman in a good, dour performance), and he must deal with the fact that his daughter is willing to betray him to the police.

He is not entirely isolated in his struggle. His young son stands by him. So do a scrappy journalist (Susan Sarandon in an underdeveloped role) and a weary, canny lawyer, played by Marlon Brando. In his first movie role in eight years, Brando is shockingly bloated in appearance, but his full authority as an actor is mobilized by a part in which he obviously believes (he was paid union scale).

But it may be that the best thing about *A Dry White Season* is that it does not practice unconscious apartheid. Our attention may be focused on the political education of Ben du Toit, but the Ngubene family is well particularized and their torments set forth unblinkingly, not to say horrifically. And Ben is provided with a guide to the realities of life on the other side of the color line: the tough, suspicious, ultimately compassionate taxi driver named Stanley (Zakes Mokae). He is a man who turns up in surprising places in unpredictable moods. He provides the bestartlements that shake Du Toit, who is appropriately all stunned introspection.

If Du Toit is the white audience's surrogate, Stanley must be director Euzhan Palcy's surrogate. Imparting energy and waywardness to her film, he helps give it the pulse of popular fiction without in any way diminishing its moral seriousness.

VILLAGE VOICE, 9/26/89, p. 70, Amy Taubin

Progressive films can blunder into theatricality as readily as conservative ones. Though shot on location in Zimbabwe, *A Dry White Season*, directed by Euzhan Palcy (*Sugar Cane Alley*) and adapted from the novel by Andre Brink, is not only devoid of a sense of place, it's populated by excellent actors performing as if they were on stage and obliged to project for the second balcony.

The film, set during the Soweto uprising of 1976, is the story of two families, one white and one black, destroyed by apartheid. Ben du Toit (Donald Sutherland), an Afrikaner schoolteacher who's never thought twice about the righteousness of the regime, has his eyes opened when his gardener, Gordon (Winston Ntshona), is tortured to death for attempting to find the body of his son, who has been disappeared after a demonstration. Enlisting a celebrated, but disillusioned, radical attorney (Marlon Brando) to represent Gordon at the inquest and to take on the head of the secret police (Jurgen Prochnow), he learns that justice cannot be won legally in a fascist state. With Stanley (Zakes Mokae), a wily and militant taxi driver, he begins to take more radical steps to expose the murderous rulers of South Africa.

Palcy can't resolve the contradictions involved in attempting to make a political film—and particularly a film about a black struggle—that will draw mass audiences and not just preach to the converted. The justification for focusing the story on a white man is obviously that it's whites who need their consciousness raised about South Africa, and it's Hollywood axiom that white audiences won't go to films with black heroes (Eddie Murphy excepting). Palcy tries to aviod the problem of *Mississippi Burning* or, worse, *Mandela* by making the Sutherland character more a mediator than an active hero. But in eschewing scenes that would make the audience identify with du Toit, she leaves the film without a center. There's also a failed attempt to graft on elements of a thriller, and any number of embarrassingly clichéd scenes (like black children and white children romping together in the grass), which, I suppose, are meant to personalize the political. By buying into Hollywood conventions, Palcy guarantees that *A Dry White Season* will draw fewer people than an "arthouse" success like *A World Apart*.

Also reviewed in:

NATION, 10/30/89, p. 507, Stuart Klawans
NEW REPUBLIC, 10/9/89, p. 24, Stanley Kauffmann
NEW YORK TIMES, 9/20/89, p. C19, Janet Maslin
NEW YORKER, 10/2/89, p. 101, Pauline Kael
VARIETY, 9/13-19/89, p. 31
WASHINGTON POST, 9/22/89, p. B1, Rita Kempley
WASHINGTON POST, 9/22/89, Weekend/p. 37, Jeanne Coopar

DYBBUK, THE

A restoration of The National Center for Jewish Film. *Director:* Michal Waszynski. *Screenplay (Yiddish with English subtitles):* Alter Kacyzne and Marek Arnshteyn [Andrzej Marek]. *Based on the play by:* S. Ansky. *Director of Photography:* A. Wywerka. *Editor:* George Roland. *Music:* Henoch Kon. *Choreographer:* Judith Berg. *Production Designer:* Alexander Marten. *Running time:* 123 minutes. *MPAA Rating:* Not Rated.

CAST: Leon Liebgold (Khonnon); Lili Liliana (Leah); Abraham Morewski (Tsaddik); Isaac Samberg (Messenger); Moshe Lipman (Sender); Dina Halpern (Frade, Leah's Aunt); Gershon Sirota (Cantor); Max Bozyk (Nuta); Gerszon Lamberger (Nisan); Samuel Landau (Zalman); S. Bronecki (Nachman); M. Messinger (Menashe); Z. Katz (Mendel); A. Kurc (Michoel); D. Lederman (Meyer).

NEW YORK POST, 9/15/89, p. 25, Jami Bernard

A dybbuk is a Yiddish expression for a ghost, or, as the opening of the majestical, newly restored 1937 Polish film "The Dybbuk" explains, "When a man dies before his time, his soul returns to earth."

The dybbuk in this case is the spirit of Khonnon, a young yeshiva student who dies while trying to procure Satan's assistance in getting the woman he loves, who is betrothed against her will to a richer man. The dybbuk takes hold of his beloved's body on her wedding night and it takes heaven and earth to exorcise him

Based on a popular play by S. Ansky, "The Dybbuk" is a rich tapestry of Polish-Jewish customs and mores of the time. Ritual, superstition, religion, folkore, song and dance fill the frames of this solemn, star-crossed love story, a sort of Yiddish "Wuthering Heights" played out in the *shtetls* (villages) of pre-World War II Poland instead of on the moors.

Years of painstaking restoration by the National Center for Jewish Film—this movie is its 15th such restoration—have yielded a fine, clear print, with new English subtitles and a haunting score.

At the center of the tragedy is the avarice of the old man Sender, who has forgotten his youthful pledge to his best friend that their children would one day wed. When it is time to marry off his daughter, Leah, he pledges her to the wealthiest contender, instead of to Khonnon, who, unbeknownst to Sender, is the son of his long-dead friend.

There is a heavy overlay of mysticism in "The Dybbuk." The lovers Leah and Khonnon pause by a grave in the center of town, where are buried a bride and groom who were killed under their wedding canopy; it's a harbinger of the grief to come.

And speaking of harbingers, a mysterious and mysteriously wise character (simply called "Messenger") keeps fading in and out over the years, advising, commenting, helping to usher in fate.

There is an eerie scene in which Leah visits her mother's grave to invite her to the wedding; as long as she's in the graveyard, Leah extends the same invitation to the spirit of Khonnon, whose Satanic invocations have backfired and killed him.

Other haunting images include Leah's sleepy, swaying dance with a death-masked figure and with the throngs of the poor who crowd around her rich father's house during the wedding. There is also mondo creepiness in a scene in which the religious leader holds a trial and calls up the dead to attend from behind a billowing curtain.

The movie is not without humorous counterpoint, such as when the wealthy bridegroom cowers before his impending marriage as if he were being led to the gallows. Director Michal Waszynski orchestrates all these elements at a stately pace, as if he has all the time in the world—when in fact, right after filming, the war marched in and took the lives of many of the cast and crew.

Certainly some of the acting is dated and theatrical, a product of its time, but Lili Liliana as the reluctant bride has an introspective serenity, her face framed by two prim braids, and manages her scenes of spirit possession so forcefully you'd think it was a dybbuk talking when she opens her mouth.

"The Dybbuk" is a jewel of nearly forgotten (and nearly lost!) film history; catch it during its two-week run at the Festival.

VILLAGE VOICE, 9/19/89, p. 63, J. Hoberman

S. Ansky's *The Dybbuk* is the most celebrated play in the Yiddish theatrical canon and hardly unknown in New York. Still, it's not every day that a lovingly restored and newly subtitled version of a 52-year-old Polish film opens in a midtown movie house, and you might well wonder why this *Dybbuk* is different from all others.

Stately and brooding, Michal Waszynski's adaptation is the most heavily atmospheric and obviously "artistic" of the 40 or so Yiddish talkies produced in the U.S., the Soviet Union, and Poland between 1930 and World War II. From the opening image of a candle-lit synagogue, through the series of nightmarish dances that accompany the unconsummated wedding, to the climactic exorcism, *The Dybbuk* is steeped in religious ritual—as well as folkways, superstitions, and more than a bit of variety theater. The pageantry is sometimes threadbare, the expressionism crude, but this slow and deliberate film has a cumulative power that transcends its limitations.

The Dybbuk evokes a specifically Jewish sense of the uncanny with a particular sort of cultural distance. The power of the past is continually made tangible. The living mingle with the dead—who manifest themselves as spirits, as hobgoblins, and as monuments. The climax offers the fantastic spectacle of a lawsuit in which the plaintiff has been dead for 20 years. Not only does the heroine visit the cemetery to invite her dead mother to her wedding, their village itself is almost a cemetery—the "holy grave" in the town marketplace memorializes a bride and groom who were murdered during a pogrom 200 years before.

Even more than most films, *The Dybbuk* is a collective expression. The play was originally titled *Between Two Worlds* and developed out of the complex interplay of at least three or four. Ansky, the self-educated son of a Vitebsk innkeeper, was an agrarian socialist who spent years as a farm laborer, suffered exile for his political activities, and, late in life, became a pioneer Jewish folklorist. Between 1911 and 1914, he led an expedition for the Jewish Historic-Ethnographic Society that combed the west Ukrainian provinces of Podolia and Volhynia for Jewish tales and artifacts. Among the fruits of this research was *The Dybbuk*.

In a sense, Ansky was *The Dybbuk*'s vehicle. Drawing on Hasidic legends and shtetl folklore, he wrote the play in Russian and offered it to the Moscow Art Theater. Stanislavsky demurred but suggested adding the crucial character of the Messenger (a dour equivalent of the prophet Elijah). His was not the only revision. As the original Russian draft was lost, poet Chaim Bialik's Hebrew translation formed the basis for Ansky's Yiddish version. The play was never produced during the author's lifetime; performed by the Vilna Troupe, its premiere took place in Warsaw on December 9, 1920, 30 days after Ansky's death (and less than two months after the armistice between reconstituted Poland and the new Soviet Union).

Although the Vilna Troupe originally intended only a short run to honor Ansky's memory, *The Dybbuk* proved so astonishingly popular that it became the mainstay of their repertoire, running for 300 performances. (Reportedly trolley conductors approaching the theater would call out "Ansky!" or "*Dybbuk* stop!") This production—a romantic folk pageant, at once lyrical and grotesque, mysterious and nostalgic—established a new mode for the still raw Yiddish theater and brought a new degree of self-consciousness. "With *The Dybbuk*, a new era in Yiddish theater begins," an original member of the troupe recalled. "One began to play for gentiles."

With *The Dybbuk*, the Yiddish stage entered world theater (rather than the reverse). The Vilna Troupe toured Western Europe. In 1922, the Hebrew-language Habima staged an even more expressionistic version in Moscow; the same year, the play was performed in America by Maurice Schwartz. By the mid-'20s, *The Dybbuk* was synonymous with Yiddish art theater—David Vardi directed an English version in New York, Max Reinhardt staged a German one in Berlin, Andrzej Marek presented a Polish production in Warsaw, and the play was subsequently translated into French, Czech, Bulgarian, Ukrainian, Swedish, Serbian, and Japanese.

Although *The Dybbuk* lends itself to a number of metaphoric readings, it is, on the surface, a love story. Betrothed by their fathers at birth, Khonnon and Leah grow up unaware of each other's existence. When Khonnon, a poor and other-worldly student, appears in the town of Brenits, Leah is drawn to him, as he is to her. Her avaricious father, however, prefers a wealthier suitor. The desperate Khonnon uses cabalistic magic to influence the situation and, as a result, dies; his spirit then enters Leah at the moment she is to be wed. A Hasidic wonder-rabbi, the venerable Tsaddik of Miropol, discovers the source of this possession and attempts to redress the wrong done Khonnon and his father—but it is only the threat of excommunication that exorcises the dybbuk (wandering soul). Leah's spirit then joins Khonnon's in death.

For all the emphasis on Jewish mysticism, this drama is less religious than tribal. The Tsaddik embodies the authority of the Jewish folk community; the play emphasizes the fear of the darkness that lies beyond its bounds, the isolation of living apart from its laws. In *shtetl* folklore it is most often young women who are possessed by spirits, and, no less than his contemporary Sigmund Freud, Ansky gives this hysteria a sexual content. *The Dybbuk* hardly shies away from linking love and death: "I feel as if I were being dragged to the gallows," whimpers Leah's hapless groom as he joins her under the wedding canopy. In the film, an unusually grim *badkhn* (wedding jester) cues the most powerful scene—a grotesque danse macabre in which a deathmasked figure, shrouded in a prayer shawl, embraces the entranced bride, who, hallucinating Khonnon, snuggles in the specter's embrace.

The Dybbuk was the most ambitious Yiddish movie of its day and as such involved much of literary and theatrical Warsaw—not to mention Poland's heavily Jewish film industry. Although the impetus came from Ludwig Prywes, whose uncle had been the angel for the original production, the producers were likely encouraged by the precedent of Julian Duvivier's 1936 *Le Golem*, a spectacular, widely distributed, and philo-Semitic French-Czech coproduction with a Jewish supernatural theme. In any case, *The Dybbuk* was a rare international success for the often beleaguered Polish cinema. (The restored print makes use of material discovered in Poland, France, the Netherlands, Britain, Australia, Israel, and the U.S.)

The screenplay was written by the playwright-journalist Alter Kacyzne (Ansky's protégé and literary executor) and the playwright-showman Mark Arnshteyn (who, as Andrzej Marek, had previously staged *The Dybbuk* in Polish). The distinguished historian Majer Balaban served as a consultant; the popular composer Henoch Kon wrote an original score, while his wife, Judith Berg, choreographed the half dozen dance sequences (appearing herself as the Angel of Death).

The film was produced at Warsaw's newest, best-equipped sound studio, using leading designers and technicians (several of them refugees from Nazi Germany). It was directed by the industry's flamboyant wunderkind, 33-year-old Michal Waszynski, who claimed to have studied with Stanislavsky and assisted F.W. Murnau.

After making the first Polish talkie in 1929, Waszynski directed some 30 more over the next decade—virtually all of them money-makers. Waszynski worked in almost every genre, demonstrating a speed, range, and impersonality that suggest a Polish equivalent of W.S. Van Dyke. (His oeuvre includes melodramas, musicals, farces, military films, a Polish-Czech coproduction of *The Twelve Chairs*, even an adventure film shot in Morocco.) A Ukrainian Jew, born in Volhynia less than a decade before the Ansky expedition, Waszynski directed *The Dybbuk* in Polish, with Arnshteyn on hand as translator and, as one actor told me, the production's *"mazhgiekh"* (kosher authority).

The result is an astute popularization. While the play opens in medias res with the announcement of Leah's engagement, the movie supplies a lengthy prologue—filmed largely in the picturesque resort town Kazimierz, a hundred miles south of Warsaw—wherein the two Yeshiva students pledge their unborn children in marriage, thus accentuating the fatalism that characterizes virtually all Polish Yiddish films. As familiar as the material was, the filmmakers felt free to present it as a series of set pieces. (If you've seen the dupey, incomplete prints that have circulated for years, you haven't seen the film: The current version restores scores of details and textural bits of business.)

Most of the digressions are musical: Gershon Sirota, the best-known cantor in Poland (if not Europe), is given a leisurely solo. The filmmakers created a major part—and provided a song—for the popular character actor Max Bozyk (an axiom of the Polish Yiddish cinema, whose widow made her film debut as Amy Irving's *bube* in *Crossing Delancey*). As a movie, *The Dybbuk* is less old-fashioned than it is archaic. The mood suggests the relaxed, ritualistic pace of a dusk-to-dawn Bengali theatrical.

Culled from Warsaw's various Yiddish ensembles, the cast spans several theatrical generations. Leon Liebgold and Lili Liliana, a striking young couple from the satirical revue Yiddishe Bande, play the ill-fated lovers. (In another addition, the slender, severe Liliana—who had wide experience in Yiddish cabaret, or *kleynkunst*—has the opportunity to display her surprisingly strong singing voice.) As the Tsaddik, Abraham Morewski recreates the role he originated in the 1920 Vilna production—haunted and trembling, he's an instrument tuned to emissions no one else can hear. In contrast, the rough-hewn Isaac Samberg—a specialist in proletarian roles (as well as an organizer for the Yiddish Actors Union)—plays the implacable Messenger, his frozen glare fixing each of the principals in turn.

Perhaps the greatest contribution is Berg's. Both she and Kon grew up in Hasidic families (as did David Herman, the play's first director) and, working through their own modernity, took Hasidic folk forms as the basis for a new Jewish art. Berg's choreography ranges from traditional wedding dances to elaborations on the symbolic masques featured in both the Vilna and Habima productions. In one, the already half-possessed Leah is swept into a procession of ragged and misshapen mendicants (some recruited from the streets of Warsaw). These Brueghelian passages are the heart of the film; Kon's haunting music is faintly reprised at the end, when the dybbuk is exorcised and Leah briefly comes to herself.

One almost wishes that Berg had directed the entire movie. Waszynski may have worked on Murnau's *Faust* but he doesn't altogether trust the play's evocative mood, discreetly goosing it with bits of movie magic: The Messenger vanishes and reappears at will, Khonnon's transparent spirit rises from the grave. In the direction of actors, however, his instincts are sure. The possessed Leah speaks with her own vice (albeit deepened and hoarse). In general, the performances are extremely nuanced. Liebgold, who had made one previous film, is a robust Khonnon; Leah's hysteria is eerily freefloating, mitigated by Liliana's austerity and picked up in Morewski's brilliant portrayal of the sick and dying wonder-rabbi.

The Dybbuk was also an act of cultural solidarity, produced in a time of escalating anti-Semitism. Under General Edward Smigly-Rydz, hero of the 1919–20 Russian campaign, Poland moved toward an indigenous fascism. Nationalist politicians in the Sejm and the church blamed the Jewish minority for all Poland's ills.

It would not be too much to say that from the mid-'30s on, Jews were a national obsession. A debate on kosher slaughtering preoccupied the Sejm for two years; at the same time, Poland petitioned the League of Nations for a mandate to relocate its Jewish population in Madagascar.

Nationalist gangs attacked Jewish university students, and, after 15 years of relative calm, there were pogroms in provincial towns. According to Dina Halpern (who plays Leah's aunt in the film), *The Dybbuk*'s bearded extras had to run a gauntlet of toughs who waited on the street corners outside the studio, which was located far from the Jewish neighborhoods: "Practically every day during the peak of the filming, the production was held up as we bound their wounds."

Still, *The Dybbuk* opened at a major Warsaw cinema, where it ran for the last three months of 1937. The film had its New York premiere at a Broadway movie house the following January and received more press than any previous Yiddish (or Polish) film to date—even reviewed by *Time* and *Newsweek*. (The American surrealist Parker Tyler was a particular champion, including it in his *Fifty Classics of the Foreign Film*.) But, if most critics were enthusiastic or at least respectful, it is not altogether surprising that a film so boldly Jewish in its imagery would provoke outright hostility. *The Dybbuk* was not yet the middlebrow classic it would become; nor were Polish Jews the subject of sentimental remembrance.

In *The New York Times*, Frank Nugent termed the film "oppressively tedious...hamstrung (excuse the sacrilege) by a frequently infantile groping after the mystic." *The Dybbuk*, he wrote, "strikes of stupidity, silly superstition, outmoded religion. ...[It is] as incredible in its way as a documentary film of life among the pygmies or a trip to the Middle Ages."

In fact, *The Dybbuk* is a time capsule, though not in the way that Nugent imagined. For a play about eternity, it lends itself extremely well to topical inflection. For Andrzej Wajda, whose feeble production was staged this July at SummerFare, *The Dybbuk* is a parable of contemporary Poland, with a wonder-rabbi who suggests Pope John Paul II. (One could easily imagine a version, directed by Tadeusz Kantor, about another Polish exorcism.) Habima's Yevgeny Vakhtangov, a non-Hebrew-speaking Armenian, expanded the second act "Beggar's Dance" to dramatize class struggle and the spirit of revolution, while his actors interpreted the dybbuk as a metaphor for the Hebrew language.

Historically, *The Dybbuk* is the quintessential example of that style variously termed "Hasidic grotesque" or "Hasidic gothic," which, thanks to the popularity of Ansky's play, Leivick's *Golem*, Schwartz's stage version of *Yoske Kalb*, and the writings of Isaac Bashevis Singer, has misleadingly come to seem the mainstream of modern Yiddish literature. But if this 1937 *Dybbuk* suggests Singer, it is in a less overt way.

As in one of Singer's "American" stories, the film's few now-octogenarian principals represent the triumph of arbitrary fate, the interpenetration of two disparate worlds. Most of those who survived World War II did so only because they were on tour when the Nazis invaded Poland. (Bozyk was in Argentina; delays in the filming of Maurice Schwartz's *Tevye* on a Long Island potato farm, 50 years ago this summer, caused Liebgold and Liliana to miss the last boat to Warsaw.) Others, including Berg, escaped into the Soviet zone. Waszynski, who settled in Rome after the war, served as Orson Welles's assistant on *Othello* and art director on *Roman Holiday*. (At some point, he began passing himself off as Polish royalty; his 1965 obituaries list him as "Prince Michael Waszynski.")

No wonder this *Dybbuk* is different from the others. Drama intensifies a given moment, film freezes it. Whatever the movie's original intentions, events have dictated that its themes will be read as harbingers of exile and oblivion. "For me every road is blocked, every gate is shut," the rebellious dybbuk cries. In the end, history alone remains. "I have forgotten who I am," the spirit whispers. "Only in your thoughts can I remember myself."

Also reviewed in:
NEW YORK TIMES, 1/28/83, p. 17, Frank S. Nugent
VARIETY, 8/30–9/5/89, p. 31

EARTH GIRLS ARE EASY

A Vestron Pictures release of a Kestrel Films production. *Producer:* Tony Garnett. *Director:* Julien Temple. *Screenplay:* Julie Brown, Charlie Coffey, and Terrence E. McNally. *Director of Photography:* Oliver Stapleton. *Editor:* Richard Halsey. *Music:* Nile Rodgers. *Music Editor:* Kenneth Karman. *Sound:* Jon Huck. *Sound Editor:* William Stevenson. *Production Designer:* Dennis Gassner. *Art Director:* Dins Danielsen. *Set Decorator:* Nancy Haigh. *Special Visual Effects:* Dream Quest Images. *Costumes:* Linda Bass. *Make-up:*

Richard Arrington. *Alien Make-up:* Jeffrey Judd. *Stunt Coordinator:* Corey Eubanks. *Running time:* 100 minutes. *MPAA Rating:* PG.

CAST: Geena Davis (Valerie); Jeff Goldblum (Mac); Jim Carrey (Wiploc); Damon Wayans (Zeebo); Julie Brown (Candy); Michael McKean (Woody); Charles Rocket (Ted); Larry Linville (Dr. Bob); Rick Overton (Dr. Rick); Diane Stillwell (Robin); June Ellis (Mrs. Merkin); Felix Montano (Ramon); Richard Hurst (Joe the Cop); Leslie Morris (Mike the Cop); Lisa Fuller (Kikki); Stacey Travis (Tammy); Nicole Kramer (Missy); Wayne "Crescendo" Ward (Demone); Tita Omeze (Tanya); T.C. Diamond (Deca Dance Dancer); Victor Garron (Deca Dance Valet); Steve Lundquist (Body Factory Attendant); Angelyne (Gas Girl); Jory Husain (Mini Mart Cashier); Jake Jundeff (Bryan); Susan Krebs (Bryan's Mother); Lucy Lee Flippin (Receptionist); Gail Neely (Head Nurse); Rob Large (Boy in Body Cast); Terrence E. McNally (Soap Opera Doctor); April Giuffria (Soap Opera Nurse); Cristy Dawson (Soap Opera Wife); Carol Infield Sender (Amy); Helen Infield Siff (Mamie); Nedra Volz (Lana); Yetta (Mrs. Gurtzweiller); Crystal Lujan (Butch Girl); Ismael Araujo Jr. (Gardener).

FILMS IN REVIEW, 8–9/89, p. 424, Edmond Grant

In the years to come, it's entirely possible that this film will be included in "Golden Turkey" festivals as a good example of camp/cult filmmaking gone wrong. As it stands, *Earth Girls* is an exercise in excess that has that curious property common to a lot of outrageously bad movies: it becomes eminently watchable at the moments when it loses all semblance of reason, and standards of quality.

It took a while for the film to get released commercially (it was originally produced for the defunct DEG studios), and it's not exactly difficult to figure out why: it's an oddball sci-fi musical comedy that goes overboard right at the beginning with a scene depicting three fuzzy aliens crashlanding into a swimming pool.

The aliens, who definitely get high marks for being the least interesting E.T.s in screen history, land in the pool of Valley Girl Geena Davis (whose recent Best Supporting Acress Oscar, one suspects, was the real reason why *Earth Girls* finally acquired a distributor). Geena is, like, totally into the latest trends, keeps up a really tacky household, and gets tips on how to lure back her out-of-it fiance from her friend, an intensely with-it hairdresser, played by demented rock comedienne Julie Brown. With Julie's help, the trio of aliens (thank God there aren't more) are turned into (supposedly) "rad" surfer-dudes, and Geena is quickly entranced by their leader, played by a man who shows here that he has no pride, Davis's real life mate, Jeff Goldblum.

Two overactive imaginations—those of director Julien Temple and co-star and co-scripter Brown—are responsible for *Earth Girls* being the way it is, warts and all. Temple came to film from the world of rock video, but his sensibility is decidedly cinematic. His work on *Absolute Beginners* and the most vibrant segment of *Aria* betrays a Busby Berkeley/Francis Coppola-like grandiosity that seems out of place in this quirky L.A. comedy. At times, the film seems to be literally bursting with Temple's visual concepts (as in one black-and-white dream sequence which even includes clips from Cocteau's *Beauty and the Beast!*), but his visual experimentation is for naught, when all that really matters—the plotting and lopsided humor—don't score at all.

The very funny Ms. Brown can carry some of that blame. As a humorous singer/songwriter— her supporting performance here includes two all out Temple production numbers which come across as the only focused moments in the entire movie—she is immensely enjoyable. As a scripter, her talents are more questionable—the script (co-written by Brown's two fellow songwriters, Charlie Coffey and Terrence E. McNally) is a coagulation of snappy patter, some very bad musical moments (including one absolutely wretched "dance-off" which guarantees the film will appear miserably dated when seen in the future) and just plain, unfunny silliness.

The cast do try to grin and bear it. Some, like stand up comic Jim Carrey (as one of the fuzzy aliens) grate almost instantly, while others, like star Goldblum, seem to take the whole thing for the brainless lark it really is. Surprisingly, Geena Davis comes through with her pride intact, and looking quite attractive (that's sometimes all that her role calls for—in a scene where she first encounters the aliens she is seen wearing a quite small white bikini for close to ten minutes).

Considering Mr. Temple's roots, and Ms. Brown's current home (she had done a series of specials for MTV), it can be said with no trace of malice that *Earth Girls* has all the soul of an indefinitely extended (and oh, is it padded toward the end) music video.

LOS ANGELES TIMES, 5/12/89, Calendar/p. 6, Michael Wilmington

"Earth Girls Are Easy" takes place in Los Angeles, but it's L.A. through cracked sunglasses with purple stardust frizzies on the lens.

The movie is a jazzy, snazzy rock-musical comedy about a dumped-on Valley Girl who ushers three girl-crazy extraterrestrials around town after they crash-land in her swimming pool. And its virtuoso director, Julien Temple ("Absolute Beginners"), turns Los Angeles into a candy-frosted, slick dream mall, where Melrose Avenue, the San Fernando Valley and Ocean Avenue seem to have swallowed up everything.

The city is creamed over visually with Temple's wit and impudence. He's like a guy who dreamed up Los Angeles out of TV and movies and then went out and found all the places he dreamed: found the nutty drive-ins, goofball specialty shops, the huge plaster doughnuts, the palm trees slashing the smoggy sky. He's even found Angelyne, the puffy-bosomed blonde in lavender sunglasses whose only *raison d'etre* seemed to be her omnipresent L.A. billboards—she pops up here as a sultry bimbo in a BMW.

It's the look of the movie, supposedly filtered through alien eyes, that's special. But the core of "Earth Girls" is too easy: slick fluff that's been ingeniously lacquered over, a mix of Valley Girl shop-and-chop sarcasm and cutie-pie sci-fi effects with the laid-back, benignly trashy mood of an old beach party musical.

The script and four songs were co-written by Julie Brown, MTV's resident put-down specialist, as a vehicle for herself. Instead, Brown's part, Valerie the dippy manicurist, went to Geena Davis, with Brown recast as her girlfriend, boss of the Curl Up and Dye hair salon. The rest of the cast is equally anachronistic: Michael McKean as a burnt-out surfer and pool cleaner; Jeff Goldblum, Jim Carrey and Damon Wayans as the aliens from Jhazzalan, and ex-"Saturday Night Live" bad-mouth Charlie Rocket, as Valerie's faithless boyfriend, looking something like Dan Quayle as a sour-faced yuppie swinger.

Brown's songs are cute; as Temple stages and shoots them, they're the high spots of the movie. But the movie is a weird hybrid. The visual satire is ingenious and even entrancing, like an old '50s Frank Tashlin comedy or a musical number by Stanley Donen and Bob Fosse. But the verbal humor has a mean, sluggy tartness, like the condescending cracks of rich kids at the hicko culture of the local styleless boobs.

Temple has a weakness for this kind of humor; he's a wealthy Cambridge boy who must have liked the punks and rockers for their freedom and contempt for authority. But, sometimes, he seems to lack the real populist flair that a pop-music specialist needs, and this may be why, except for his superb rock videos, he hasn't caught the public fancy yet.

In the end, though, the visuals triumph. "Earth Girl Are Easy" may be a classic case of a director getting more out of his material than it really deserves. Temple has spectacular gifts for making musical movies. He is a witty formalist, a light-hearted virtuoso, and, like all the best movie-musical directors, he's able to create images that breathe in tempo with the songs or cut against them jaggedly, exhilaratingly.

There is one terrific example of that here: " 'Cause I'm a Blonde," a bimbos-on-the-beach satirical number in which Julie Brown redeems herself for all the script's lazy one-liners and its paucity of invention and real style. She gives the number a languorous, wooly-headed self-infatuated buzz, and Temple makes the air around her crackle. "Earth Girls Are Easy" (MPAA rated PG, despite sexual innuendo and partial nudity) may be the weakest piece of material Temple has had to work with, but he transforms it anyway. In his hands, the whole style of this movie becomes an apotheosis of glitz.

MONTHLY FILM BULLETIN, 12/89, p. 363, Steve Jenkins

The San Fernando Valley, California. Manicurist Valerie Dale is frustrated by the lack of romantic attention paid her by her fiancé Dr. Ted Gallagher. At the Curl Up and Dye Beauty Salon, Valerie is given a new, sexy look by her boss Candy Pink, but that night, when Ted comes back accompanied by a nurse, she throws him out and wrecks their home. The next day, a spaceship from the planet Jhazzala, crewed by three aliens, Mac, Wiploc and Zeebo, crashlands in Valerie's pool. Overcoming her initial fear, she takes the aliens in and calls the surfing-obsessed Woody to drain the pool. After learning something of life on Earth from television, the aliens are taken by Valerie to the salon, where Candy transforms them into three good-looking men. They then visit a disco, where Zeebo wins a dance duel, while Mac and Valerie begin to feel attracted to each other. Valerie and the aliens arrive home to be confronted by an angry Ted, who has called the police. They take Ted away, however, when he attacks Wiploc. Mac and Valerie then make love. The next morning, Woody takes Wiploc and Zeebo to Zuma Beach, where they witness a Blonde of the Month contest and then cause havoc on the freeway during a high-speed chase with the police. Summoned by Woody, Mac and Valerie are also arrested but Mac uses his alien powers to get them to the hospital where Wiploc and Zeebo are being treated by Ted. Discovering that the aliens have two heartbeats, Ted sees fame and fortune in the offing, but they bamboozle him into taking them back to Valerie's. Ted wants to marry Valerie but, realising the aliens' true nature, fears she may have been contaminated. Mac brings the couple together, but for Valerie the magic has gone. Declaring her love for Mac, she joins the aliens as they head for outer space.

Julien Temple's first feature since *Absolute Beginners* has in many ways an air of running for cover. Certainly there is no suggestion here of an entire film industry's future being at stake. Instead, the thin central premise of a close encounter between alien and Valley girl becomes a peg on which to hang not very much. The musical numbers hardly advance what Temple has achieved in his pop-promo work (although the context does allow songs like "Brand New Girl" and "Cause I'm a Blonde" to be staged with a pleasing degree of brash vulgarity), and for the rest, it is largely a matter of jokes about sex with extraterrestrials and car chases. However, the fact that the narrative and characters are so underdeveloped, and that one is given no reason to care about the developing relationship between Valerie and Mac, is actually the inevitable result of the film's basic strategy.

This is summed up by Temple in the film's production notes: "The climate, the entertainment industry, and the pioneering attitude of the West Coast combine to create a distinctive look. Being British and therefore a sort of alien in L.A. myself, I thought that I could bring to the audience a feel for what these Jhazzalians must have first experienced when they landed in the Valley". This is a polite way of saying that the view of the Valley and its inhabitants is relentlessly and appropriately one-dimensional, reducing characters and settings to a tacky mix of stupidity and garish tastelessness that is both engaging and convincing. In fact, Temple's Britishness is rather misleading as regards the film's style, particularly in tandem with producer Tony Garnett, who is so firmly linked with the 60s social realism of *Kes, Cathy Come Home, Family Life*, etc. Instead, Jeff Goldblum's Mac borrows lines from *The Nutty Professor* ("Go rest your thumbs—I'll drive", as he takes over at the piano) and it is Lewis and Tashlin, rather than Ken Loach, who provide inspiration here. Visually, Temple overloads and saturates the images with colours and objects which make his aliens' furry suits (red, green and yellow) seem the epitome of restrained good taste.

The lurid hues of Ted's tropical fish tank, for example (with its tenants "Aston" and "Martin"), are matched in both the characters' look (Valerie blow-drying her red and blue fingernails as she arrives at the Curl Up and Dye Salon) and their attitudes. "Waste your brains; wax your board; pray for waves" advises Woody the pool man (a very funny performance by Michael McKean), when asked by Valerie how she should survive with her pool out of action. And Valerie's observations on geography ("This is the Valley. Finland is the capital of Norway"), nutrition ("Spray-on cheese. This is great"), and the nature of Mac's home planet ("Tell me about Zimbabwe") ensure that she is at least as unappealing as the duplicitous Ted. In the end, the satire here is no more profound than the culture under scrutiny, but the film is rendered with an odd kind of throwaway intensity that is highly enjoyable.

NEW YORK, 5/15/89, p. 101, David Denby

Earth Girls Are Easy, an alien-in-my-bed comedy set in the San Fernando Valley and designed in candy colors, is obviously the most enjoyable bad movie of the year (put *that* in your ad). Geena Davis, stretching her long, long torso in a bikini, plays the manicurist Valerie, sweet as sugar but not too bright, who's puzzled by her fiancé's habit of turning his back on her in bed every night. At the same time, three aliens from the planet Jhazzala are buzzing about in a spaceship. These creatures lack Michael Rennie's distinguished bone structure and impeccable diction in *The Day the Earth Stood Still*, and they're not soulful Spielbergian gremlins either. They are just three ordinary guys, though a bit furry and colored orange or blue or yellow; and they're awfully horny from their long trip through the Milky Way.

After they land in Val's swimming pool, she and her boss (the garish Julie Brown) make them over at the beauty parlor where she works, and they almost look human. Jeff Goldblum, their leader, who is stern of demeanor, as if he were seeing to a serious problem in the afterburners, introduces Val to the pleasures of Jhazzalan love, and you can figure out the rest. Director Julien Temple (*Absolute Beginners* and lots of rock videos) proves once again that he can't structure a movie; *Earth Girls* takes forever to get going, and it has that queasy, shifting facetiousness that I associate with MTV—it's just *images*, and nothing in it means anything. But Temple turns cheesiness into a form of likability, and Goldblum and Davis (who are married) snuggle ardently. Imitative and empathetic, the three men mimic bits of Valley speech, and there's a very funny scene at a disco in which a black alien (Damon Wayans) picks up on the moves of a white-suited local stud, and they dance each other to a draw.

NEW YORK POST, 5/12/89, p. 25, David Edelstein

The Valley Girl musical "Earth Girls Are Easy" is like a beach ball with a slow leak—plastic and colorful and bouncy and fun until you notice it's not staying airborne. The movie opens with a blast of infantile silliness. In a passing spaceship, two totally hairy aliens—one bright blue (Damon Wayans), one bright yellow (Jim Carrey)—turn their telescope on Southern California, where they sight the astounding Geena Davis in a skimpy bikini.

Unlike the females of their planet, she's peculiarly hairless. But hey, they've been up there more than a year, and this "bald thing" looks so good to the sex-starved extraterrestrials that they lose control of their ship and splash down in her pool—much to the annoyance of their bright red, hitherto dozing leader (Jeff Goldblum). Welcome to the Valley, spacedudes.

In the beginning, the picture has a nearly-irresistible shallowness—it's full of candy land colors and jokey, surfin'-U.S.A. pop songs. The cartoon credit sequence conjures up tacky '50s and '60s posters for movies about aliens carrying off bikini-clad women, and the spaceship looks like something out of a 5-year-old's bathtub—more "Sesame Street" than "Star Wars."

But there isn't a wealth of plot here. The joke is that broken-hearted Valley Girl Valerie (Davis)—who has just caught her doctor-fiance (Charles Rocket) wearing little more than a stethoscope with one of his nurses—accepts these bitchin' E.T.s without protest, filling their heads with her airhead lingo and their bellies with Low-Cal Pop Tarts. ("These are natural.")

The fuzzballs from space have to wait around for the pool to be drained and their ship to dry; they learn English from watching TV, like most movie aliens, and snack on live goldfish—another trend. Val sneaks them to the salon (Curl Up & Dye) where she works as a manicurist and lets the perky blond hairdresser, Candy (Julie Brown, one of the picture's writers), snip away. Candy introduces each hunky, newly-shorn spaceman with a flourish. Then they all go dancing.

The Valley Girl jokes are, fer sher, a little tired by now, but the lines have zip, and if the movie had been directed halfway decently it might have been a romp—better, at least, than any beach-blanket picture. But it's fractured and sloppy, and it can't seem to work up any momentum.

The English director, Julien Temple, is highly esteemed for his music videos and his feature "Absolute Beginners," but he has as much flair for comedy as Woody Allen has for tragedy. In "Earth Girls," Temple's work has the kind of galumphing energy that impresses the hell out of you on MTV—when your television is one more piece of furniture in a room full of distractions.

Few of Temple's shots last longer than five seconds. More to the point, he mangles the performers' rhythms, and steps on all the jokes. (The hallmark of most great comedies is seamlessness, whereas the MTV aesthetic is to spotlight the seams.)

Temple does fine with the musical numbers. There's one outright music video: Julie Brown's "Cause I'm a Blonde," and it's sensationally funny—a blithe, infectious pop song about the assets of being B-L-O-N-D-E. ("I talk like a baby and I never pay for drinks...")

But outside the realm of MTV, Temple's sense of rhythm deserts him. He botches a sure-fire scene in a nightclub—a dance-off between the supernaturally limber Zeebo (Wayans) and a woman's jealous boyfriend—by chopping it into dozens of teensy-weensy shots. You can barely see the dancers' bodies.

Geena Davis gets by because she pops her eyes and cocks her head and does her darnedest to be pixieish, and she's spectacularly willowy in her bikini. She has chosen to do without the traditional Valley Girl inflections, and while I admire her for fighting the caricature, I kept thinking she'd be funnier if she were dubbed by Moon Zappa.

Goldblum, whose dithery readings can border on genius, gets confined by his role to monosyllables. He's spectacular-looking—like a hero out of the "Arabian Nights"—but you can't help resenting the picture for wasting his gifts. (He's in good company: Michael McKean and Wayans are also left standing around.)

"Earth Girls" has a limp, slapped-together climax that's a bummer even if you like what has preceded it, although it's somewhat redeemed by the finale—a sci-fi variation on the smutty last shot of "North By Northwest." How they got the rocket ship through that donut-hole I'll never know.

NEWSDAY, 5/12/89, Part III/p. 3, Lynn Darling

"Earth Girls Are Easy" has a great title going for it and the wit to present the San Fernando Valley as a place just as alien and weird as any planet one could imagine. When a spaceship containing three furry aliens crash-lands in a swimming pool belonging to a quintessential Valley Girl, they find themselves fitting in easily—everyone's so strange in the Valley that a few more oddities only add to the sense of freaky possibility.

It's a nice idea that's drowned early and often in a series of glitzy production numbers that only the most die-hard fans of MTV can love. I don't doubt that the sight of Geena Davis in a pink lace corset and white stockings singing a love song while she microwaves a football will have its admirers. I'd just like to think that I don't know any of them.

This is the story of Valerie, a sweet but not very bright manicurist (Davis) engaged to a philandering turkey of a doctor (Charles Rocket). Her life is complicated one afternoon by the sudden appearance of three aliens covered in psychedelic fur, and gets more complicated when she falls in love with the leader of the trio (Jeff Goldblum). I don't know what talented actors like Goldblum and Davis are doing in a movie like this, but they must have had their reasons.

The plot is thin, the dialogue is thinner, and the aforementioned production numbers are choreographed to some of the most cacophonous sounding music this side of a Waring blender. In such a desperate climate, one takes what one can get. In this case, there's the energetic Julie Brown as Valerie's friend Candy, Michael McKean as a stoned surfer, and many shots of interestingly designed fingernails, which leads to thoughts about just how exhausted a culture can get before it finally bottoms out. It's not much, but in this case, it's all there is.

TIME, 5/15/89, p. 74, Richard Corliss

It's been a rough day for Valerie the Valley Girl (Geena Davis), manicurist at the Curl Up and Dye hair salon. Her icky beau Dr. Ted (Charles Rocket) hasn't made love—to her, anyway—in *two weeks!* "At the rate we're having sex," she pouts becomingly, "we may as well be married already." She has discovered Ted in a compromising costume with another woman and responded by trashing their condo: microwaving his football, toasting his funny cigarettes in the VCR, dropping his gold watch in the Disposall. And now, she notes, "there's a giant blow-dryer in my pool." Well, a UFO actually, with three horny, color-coordinated aliens (Jeff Goldblum, Jim Carrey, Damon Wayans) itching to spend the night. Valerie had better listen to her cute boss Candy (Julie Brown): "Sit down. Relax. Have a mental margarita."

That is sage advice for viewers of *Earth Girls Are Easy*, the movies' first postmodernist musical comedy. This divine diversion is best approached in a fruit-cocktail state of mind. With its amiable aliens getting their pop culture out of a TV set and its hydraulic surf bunnies singing "I can't spell VW but I got a Porsche,/ 'Cause I'm a blonde," *Earth Girls* sounds like a quick mix of *E.T.* and *Beach Blanket Bingo.* But it's really a revved-up tribute to postwar Hollywood style: the vulgar vitality, the supersaturated colors, the new aristocracy of teen taste. Gaud is in the details here. A glimpse in Valerie's refrigerator reveals a package of lo-cal Pop-Tarts; the movie is a hi-cal Pop-Tart to go. At the Deca Dance disco, a teenybopper flashes past wearing earrings cut from American Express cards. "They're my dad's," she confides in a gag that doesn't waste a millisecond of screen time.

If the film's tempo comes from '80s MTV, the story is straight '40s MGM. Like *On the Town,* *Earth Girls* sets three naive voyagers down in a bustling American fun world (the San Fernando Valley) for 24 hours of dance and romance. This is, after all, a love story about people from two different worlds. Or, as Davis explains to Goldblum, "You're an alien and I'm from the Valley. We many not even be anatomically correct for each other."

Earth Girls is a movie that takes its cues from sources as disparate as *The Wizard of Oz* and Chantal Akerman's avant-garde French musical *The '80s.* But everything blends neatly in the witty, zippy script; everybody has a good time. Davis, a living windup doll, plays Everygal to Goldblum as he exercises his ingratiating leer. Carrey (a randy mime) and Wayans (with his turbo terpsichore) give unearthly pleasure. So does *Earth Girls*, the tastiest thing to come out of a space program since Tang.

VILLAGE VOICE, 5/23/89, p. 69, J. Hoberman

Earth Girl Are Easy is British music video-wiz Julien Temple's dream of a drive-in movie— young love, rock 'n' roll, monsters from outer space. This silly but savvy exercise in meta-pop is a goodnatured genre blur: *The Jetsons Meet Repo Man* or *Beach Blanket Bingo Goes Liquid Sky*. The film isn't nearly as ambitious as Temple's iridescent, gaseous *Absolute Beginners*. That was the hipster's *Grease*; this is as sweet, stylishly colored, and disposable as a pack of Necco Wafers.

In celebrating interspecies romance, *Earth Girls* more or less reverses the trajectory of David Cronenberg's *Fly* remake, which also starred Geena Davis and Jeff Goldblum. Here, the "monstrous" descends from the sky—a trio of space dudes (Goldblum, Jim Carrey, and Damon Wayans) traversing the universe in a tinny-looking spaceship that's half Flash Gordon blimp, half vintage De Soto. Wearing costumes that scarcely update those in the archetypal cheapster *Robot Monster* (Greek helmets and primary-colored apesuits), Temple's aliens roar and leer at each other; they're lascivious stuffed animals, overaroused wookies who, in a paroxysm of horniness, crash-land their spacecraft in Davis's San Fernando Valley backyard.

As the lead earth girl, a manicurist at the Curl Up & Dye beauty salon, Davis sports two-tone nail polish and keeps her characterization aloft on a stream of ditsy chatter. She's a benign, quotidian version of that terrifying Hollywood innocent whose lack of complexes so fascinated Aldous Huxley and Nathanael West half a century ago; her response to discovering her doctor fiancé (Charles Rocket) in would-be flagrante is a plaintive, "You were gonna have sex without *me*?"

Davis is no Kenny Scharf, but her house is a modest museum of Americanarama—the aliens, too, are superb consumers. They eat the fish out of her Day-Glo fishbowl, drink the lava out of her lava lamp. And, like their landsmen in *E.T.*, *Space Man*, and *Explorers*, they can imitate anything—beginning here with Jerry Lewis's impersonation of Dean Martin in *The Nutty Professor*. The Lewis reference is an apt one, for, no less than Lewis or Frank Tashlin, Temple has a gift for gags that are more impressively elaborate than laugh-out-loud funny: Davis using a bowling ball to pulverize Rocket's PC, the aliens wedging their car in the colossal, rotating trademark of a roadside doughnut emporium.

Earth Girls is airy, if flat-footed, fun. The last reel drags a bit, and most of the musical numbers are scarcely more than interpolated music videos. ("Brand New Girl," the big beauty salon dramatization of Davis's "makeover," goes up against *Funny Face*'s "Think Pink" and *School Daze*'s "Straight and Nappy" and loses.) The TV set is always talking to you: Ronald Reagan proclaiming, "You are Americans," followed by James Dean screaming, "You're tearing me apart." After Davis and Goldblum make love, she has a dream combining Ray Harryhausen's *Earth vs. the Flying saucers* with Jean Cocteau's *Beauty and the Beast*. Temple has a total video mentality; his mastery of quote and pastiche gives *Earth Girls* a shallow, persistent subtext that matches "Brand New Girl"'s parodic mono beat. Not for nothing does Davis attempt to pass off her extraterrestrial visitors as "a band from MTV."

The pop-vid ambience is further enhanced by the presence of rock comedian Julie Brown in the Eve Arden role. Brown, credited as one of the film's three writers, plays a seasoned, suntanned cliché. ("Relax, have a mental margarita," she firmly advises Davis at one highstress moment.) Brown is the closest thing the movie has to a guru, leading the aliens on a magical mystery tour to a neighborhood disco. ("You guys are so lucky you crashed in the Valley!") The sub-*2001* atmospherics create ample comic opportunities for Wayans and, particularly, the hilariously rubber-faced Carrey. "I'm going home with him!" one girl spontaneously announces after watching the alien clean out a glass with his monstrous tongue.

It's not hard to see who Temple identifies with in this galaxy. A quick detour to a ratty-looking beach occasions the most idiotic declaration of American superiority imaginable—Brown, uncredited, as a well-worn bathing beauty tweeting a manic mock-'50s anthem about being a blonde ("yeah, yeah, yeah"). Temple already made California's Madonna Inn a star of his *Aria* segment. Now, having landed in the acme of postcivilization, he doesn't need a set. The funniest thing about *Earth Girls* is the gee-whiz mise-en-scéne: the rubber duck on the telephone receiver, the elderly woman exiting Curl Up & Dye on her walker, the fridge covered with novelty magnets. Filled with tacky, totemic monuments, this is the America envisioned by Claes Oldenburg. "There's a giant blow-dryer in my pool," Davis cries when the spaceship splashes down.

Also reviewed in:
NEW YORK TIMES, 5/12/89, p. C13, Caryn James
VARIETY, 9/14/88, p. 27
WASHINGTON POST, 5/12/89, p. D1, Hal Hinson
WASHINGTON POST, 5/12/89, Weekend/p. 39, Desson Howe

EAT A BOWL OF TEA

A Columbia Pictures release of An American Playhouse theatrical film. *Executive Producer:* Lindsay Law and John K. Chan. *Producer:* Tom Sternberg. *Director:* Wayne Wang. *Screenplay (English and Chinese with English subtitles):* Judith Rascoe. *Based on the novel by:* Louis Chu. *Director of Photography:* Amir Mokri. *Editor:* Richard Candib. *Music:* Mark Adler. *Sound:* Curtis Choy and (music) Samuel Lehmer and Michael Ahearn. *Sound Editor:* Teresa Eckton. *Production Designer:* Robert Ziembicki. *Art Director:* Timmy Yip. *Set Decorator:* Lisa Dean. *Costumes:* Marit Allen. *Make-up:* Yam Chan Hoi. *Running time:* 102 minutes. *MPAA Rating:* PG.

CAST: Victor Wong (Wah Gay); Lee Sau Kee (Bok Fat); Yuen Yat Fai (Letter Writer); Lau Siu Ming (Lee Gong); Russell Wong (Ben Loy); Hui Fun (Ben Loy's Mom); Law Lan (Aunt Gim); Ng Yuen Yee (Third Sister); Cora Miao (Mei Oi); Wu Ming Yu (Mei Oi's Mother); Lui Tat (Movie Translator); Eric Tsang Chi Wai (Ah Song); Wong Wai (Chuck Ting); Philip Chan (Henry Wang); Tang Shun Nin (Fat Man); Michael Lee (Old Lum); Z. Greenstreet Kam (Chong Loo); Woo Wang Tat (Sam Woo); Stephen Fong (George); Paul Carr (Fry Cook); Tony Souza (Dr. Bing); Lee Lai Ha (Cowgirl); Franklin Yee (Fortune Cookie Boss); Lane Nishikawa (Ben Loy's Friend in Bar); Lydia Sham (Mrs. Chan); Hui Kin Shun (Mr. Chan); Stephen Horowitz and Nigel Kat (Policemen); Joe Paulino and Peter Scarlett (Other Voices).

CHRISTIAN SCIENCE MONITOR, 9/6/89, p. 11, David Sterritt

Wayne Wang burst on the filmmaking scene a few years ago with "Chan Is Missing," an exciting and innovative comedy-mystery about a vanished Chinatown taxi driver. Even its title announced Mr. Wang's intention to create a new kind of Chinese-American cinema in which the old stock characters-like detective Charlie Chan, the granddaddy of them all—would be totally and pointedly absent. Wang seemed the ideal artist for this enterprise, a gifted young *cinéaste* steeped in film theories, yet eager to entertain as well as enlighten.

It's no fun to report that his later films haven't quite lived up to his early promise. The family drama "Dim Sum" was gentle and charming but unfortunately slight, and the rambunctious "Slamdance" seemed a failed attempt to cook up a mass-market entertainment by giving fashionable formulas a pallid new twist. While his newest release, "Eat a Bowl of Tea," marks of bit of a comeback after the "Slamdance" disaster, it's not strong enough to be called a full-scale success.

The story takes place in New York's teeming Chinatown shortly after World War II, when immigration laws didn't allow Asian-American men to bring their families into their adopted country. When the legal situation abruptly changes in 1949, the hero of the movie takes himself promptly to China and returns with an attractive young bride. This delights the older men of the community, but it isn't enough for them—they want the couple to produce a baby, too, and as quickly as possible. The resulting pressure on the newlyweds is the source of much of the movie's comedy—and drama, especially when the wife's affections start straying from her uptight husband and eventually fix themselves on a local gambler who's one of the neighborhood's sleaziest characters.

"Eat a Bowl of Tea" is partly a look at the manner in which folkways and mores continue to hover over a culture even when people are transplanted into very new surroundings and situations. (In this way it resembles the Japanese drama "Black Rain," about the aftermath of the Hiroshima bombing, a much more somber film due in the United States soon.) It's also a study of loneliness, particularly when it focuses on the young bride, who finds herself transported almost instantly to an unfamiliar land full of unfamiliar—and often rowdily rude—people she must deal with on a daily basis. Unfortunately, the film doesn't delve very deeply into either of these potentially fascinating areas. Instead, it puts far too much of its energy into detailing the amiable crudeness of the male Chinese community, filling the screen with characters whom Wang finds a lot more charming than many moviegoers will. Even the title, which has little to do with anything substantive that happens in the film, seems less an effort to illuminate the story than a rote attempt to let us know that cuteness and a kind of domestic exoticism are the movie's main concerns.

"Eat a Bowl of Tea" has appealing performances by Russell Wong and Cora Miao as the married couple. (Ms. Miao is Wang's wife, and they have a strong professional rapport in each of their films together.) Wang's frequent collaborator Victor Wong has a lot of energy, if not much else, as the young man's pushy father. They keep the movie jogging along even when the screenplay fails to recognize its own best possibilities—quite missing the depths and subtleties of the bride's plight, for example, and allowing her poignant situation to be overtaken by movie-style melodrama.

Since completing "Eat a Bowl of Tea," the busy Wang has made another film called "Life Is Cheap . . . But Toilet Paper Is Expensive," which I won't comment on since it hasn't opened yet—except to note that it moves back toward the unconventional and even experimental urges that set "Chan Is Missing" apart from the common herd. This indicates that Wang hasn't lost his aspiration to accomplish something new and different in cinema. More's the pity that little of this aspiration is visible in "Eat a Bowl of Tea," which falls into patterns as unoriginal as they are unexciting.

LOS ANGELES TIMES, 8/4/89, Calendar/p. 14, Michael Wilmington

Wayne Wang gets shadows and a honey-soft glow into the images of his fine new film "Eat a Bowl of Tea." Pinned down in darkness, the flesh tones gleam like peach-skin pearls. Like his last movie, the vacuous but gaudily shot thriller "Slamdance," "Tea" resembles a sort of *film noir* under glass. But it's a delicate, rummy little *film noir* that doesn't heave murder and cliches at us. The melodramatic plot points are buried within a naturalistic, nostalgic story, set in an era and place—the late '40s in New York's Chinatown—that begins to seem stylized as a Czech puppet film.

Based on Louis Chu's 1961 novel, "Tea" is about a young Chinatown couple pressured so outrageously to produce children that, finally, they can't even make love. This is no smutty joke. The Exclusion Laws, in effect for 60 years until they were repealed in the mid-'40s, had banned women and new immigrants from entering the country. Chinatown, in the late '40s, was a community of aging virtual bachelors.

So, swarming around the movie's young couple—Army vet Wang Ben Loy (Russell Wong) and his immigrant bride Mei Oi (Cora Miao, the wife of director Wang)—are an enclave of grinning old voyeurs who can barely contain their lascivious curiosity. Deprived of marital sex and family, they turn the wedding pair into both heroes and butts. Worst of all is Ben Loy's father, Wang Wah Gay (Victor Wong), who's seen his prestige rise as a result of the marriage and fears it will topple if they can't produce. The joker in this randy deck is a wily, chubby Lothario named Ah Song, played with beaming panache by Hong Kong comedy star Eric Tsang Chi Wai.

The couple, in turn, are drowned in romantic fantasy: the plush, moonstruck images they've flushed out of movies and pop songs. Wang stages the action against creamy '40s pop ballads—a Chinese chanteuse, languorously crooning "Slow Boat to China"—scat songs and standards. And he surrounds his lovers with great lustrous images out of movies. When Ben Loy woos Mei Oi in her village, they're before a huge screen showing Capra's "Lost Horizon." Later on, the couple get hot with Orson and Rita in Welles' "Lady From Shanghai," and, still later, the romanticism has shriveled to pint-size: a scene from Cukor's "Holiday" on a tiny TV, which they all but ignore.

Wang's major subject is the fusion of Chinese and American cultures. In "Eat a Bowl of Tea"—a vernacular phrase that roughly means "Take your medicine"—he's again examining it with irony and affection. One of his funniest insights in the way he replaces cliched images of smiling, remote, somewhat sinister Sino-Americans with earthy and pragmatic urban wise guys, more realistic cousins of the slangy, extroverted hipsters Keye Luke played in the '40s. Indeed, one flaw in the film may be that Mei Oi is *too* Americanized, acclimated too rapidly. This Chinese girl, fresh from the countryside, in the end, cops attitudes that seem more compatible with post-'70s liberation.

The youngsters are good but sometimes facile. The oldsters around them shine. As Wah Gay, Wong gives another eccentric and endearing comic performance. He is a great oddball camera subject: His face looks like a withered fruit split down the middle and pasted back together slightly askew, with a crooked, slithery grin and the eyes popping frenziedly in either direction. His character here isn't like the warmhearted "uncle" he played in Wang's "Dim Sum." This is a warm-hearted, patriarchal nut-case and Wong acts him with the unabashed comic fervor of Charley Grapewin's Grampaw Joad in "The Grapes of Wrath."

Judith Rascoe's screenplay is so briskly compressed, the movie feels almost distilled. Shot in Hong Kong, in sets that are like a dollhouse vision, the characters are seen flailing around in their little rituals of love, cultural adjustment, betrayal, shame and violence, just as trapped in the plot as they are in conventions and culture. But there's nothing stifling or ragged about the imagery in "Eat a Bowl of Tea" (MPAA-rated PG-13, despite sexual content). It's like a photo album with the pages being precisely turned, one after the other. That's the key to the movie: a mixture of love and sarcasm. Like those medicinal herb teas, it's steeped in bitterness and warmth, soaked in tradition and life.

MONTHLY FILM BULLETIN, 12/89, p. 364, John Pym

New York, 1949. With the end of the Exclusion Laws, Wah Gay, a member of the powerful Wang family, despatches his son Ben Loy, a thoroughly American ex-serviceman, to China to marry Mei Oi, daughter of his old friend Lee Gong, the owner of a laundry. The match seems an immediate success. At the feast welcoming home the newlyweds, Chuck Ting, head of the Wang Family Association, makes Ben a restaurant manager. Ben, however, is barely up to the job, and as a result finds he cannot perform his conjugal duties. Matters are not improved by Wah Gay's heavy hints that he expects a grandchild as soon as possible. A second honeymoon, in Washington DC, seems to rectify the marriage, but back in New York, and with the reappearance of one of Ben's former girlfriends, things are in fact no better. Mei Oi reluctantly begins an afternoon affair with the complacent Ah Song and in due course becomes pregnant. Word gets out of Ben's condition and Mei Oi's affair, whereupon Ah Song takes a diplomatic trip to Florida. The two fathers are furious with their offspring. Ben appeals to Chuck Ting and is given a menial job in a New Jersey fortune-cookie factory. On his return, Ah Song pays a call on the now single Mei Oi only to have his ear sliced off by the irate Wah Gay. In the incorrect belief that he has committed murder, Wah Gay flees to Havana. Lee Gong thinks it politic to leave for Chicago. In due course, Ben and Mei Oi are reconciled and leave for a new life on the West Coast. In San Francisco, Wah Gay and Lee Gong dote over their first grandchild.

Eat a Bowl of Tea is prefaced with a historical note about the Exclusion Laws, framed in the 1880s, and the changed social climate after the Second World War, in which Chinese Americans had, as it were, fought for their right to become full U.S. citizens and for the first time were permitted to marry and bring back to the United States Chinese brides. What follows, based on a novel by a prominent Chinese-American New Yorker, Louis Chu (1915–70), is a slight case history—decorated with many glancing observations on post-war life in America's Chinese community—of one of the first of these long-forbidden marriages. Wayne Wang who, one feels, still has a great deal of buried Chinese-American history inside him, evokes the period with a cool and sympathetic eye; and his cameraman, Amir Mokri, recreates the tone of the times—of light just beginning to break through into a closed, well-ordered but claustrophobic immigrant society—with his careful framing and a palette of predominantly rich, dark colours.

The story, however, has been adapted by a practised Hollywood scriptwriter, Judith Rascoe and, unlike the director's two best-known films, *Chan Is Missing* and *Dim Sum*, runs for the most part along inescapably conventional West Coast lines. Even a neatly turned sequence such as Ben Loy's trip to mainland China does not seem uniquely Chinese: one could equally well imagine a young Italian American going to Sicily for the first time to meet the bride picked out for him. The tone of the story and its archetypal characters are also almost wilfully homogenised: the doting fathers; the beautiful, cheerful bride; the put-upon groom, not at first up to his duties as a householder; the oily suitor who comes to Mei Oi when the all-clear is signalled by a goldfish bowl on the fire-escape. One does not expect quirky or offbeat behaviour from any of them. *Eat a Bowl of Tea* remains in many ways an engaging and welcome picture. Good-humoured, sincere, it is nothing more than it modestly aspires to be; and only at the close, with its reassertion of family values, does its inherent sentimentality run out of control.

NEW LEADER, 8/7–21/89, p. 20, John Morrone

Wayne Wang's *Eat a Bowl of Tea*, produced by PBS' American Playhouse, is a welcome exception to the customary public television-inspired torpor. Based on the novel by Louis Chu and shot almost entirely in Hong Kong (although set in 1949 New York), the film's television techniques—constant close-ups, claustrophobic two-shots—capture the insularity and cramped intimacy of Chinatown.

Life in the cold-water flat that U.S.-born Ben Loy (Russell Wong) occupies with his newly arrived Chinese bride, Mei Oi (Cora Miao), is closely monitored by Ben's father, Wah Gay (Victor Wong). The pressures he puts on his son to succeed, to rise to a position of respect in the community, and most of all to provide grandchildren have a crushing effect, as Ben struggles to cope with problems at work, sexual insecurity, and Mei Oi's affair with one of the "uncles" in the local Family Association. After about an hour of domestic strife the film threatens to slow to a halt, but Wang's utter lack of manipulation and one character's shocking act of revenge keep it vibrantly alive.

In Wang's first feature, *Chan Is Missing*, he represented Chinese-Americans as spiritual entities—unpredictable, undefined and enigmatic (not to be confused with "the inscrutable Oriental"). Next came *Dim Sum*, where he portrayed them as family men and women trying to reconcile the dicta of Chinese ancestor worship with contemporary American attitudes about parents and children. In *Eat a Bowl of Tea* Wang's characters are creatures of passion, often reacting to each other in hot, primal outbursts. Their world may be as small as a bowl of tea, but they drink deeply from it. Not since Joan Micklin Silver's *Hester Street* a decade ago has there been so rich and unsentimental an American film about immigrants and their new lives.

NEW YORK, 8/21/89, p. 128, David Denby

In the years prior to World War II, immigration to America from China was heavily restricted, and thus New York's Chinatown became a neighborhood with few women or young children. In Wayne Wang's *Eat a Bowl of Tea*, set in the immediate postwar years, a young, handsome Chinese-American goes to China and brings a shy village beauty back with him as his bride. Then—disaster. The community of old men, including the boy's father, are so furiously eager for a baby that the husband feels as if the men are peeking under the bed covers; he can't perform, and his wife, more avid than she looks, falls into the arms of a cheap gambler. The persistence of village customs in the New World is meant to be the source of amusement here, but the comedy is so enmeshed in waggishness—scenes of old men cackling over jokes about the marriage bed— that the movie could have been made in the mother country.

Eat a Bowl of Tea has lovely period touches and fine performances by Russell Wong and Cora Miao as the young couple (though Victor Wong, as the lunging, shouting father, is lamentable), but it feels like a very familiar and tepid folktale. It lacks the stronger colors of eroticism and the sharpening of mood that could raise it above its safe, harmless status as an *American Playhouse* production destined for public television. The result is the kind of respectable, slightly boring whimsy that always seems to delight the *Times* and lifetime contributors to Channel 13—the ever-so-mild comedy of "cultural contrasts."

NEW YORK POST, 7/21/89, p. 25, Jami Bernard

By the looks of "Eat a Bowl of Tea"—Wayne Wang's charmingly eccentric new movie about a community's overweening interest in a young couple's personal life—New York's Chinatown was one big bachelor party until right after World War II. That's when the immigration ban that kept Chinese women out of the country was lifted; suddenly it was open season on arranged marriages and mail-order brides.

Wang is back in familiar territory. His previous "Chan is Missing" and "Dim Sum" also took place in a stir-fry of Chinese and American cultures. Here he recreates a 1949 ambiance of smoky, narrow, dim interiors where the crumbling pillars of Chinatown society play mah-jongg, gamble, gossip, and meddle in each other's affairs.

Due to the Exclusion Laws, which pretty effectively kept the Asian population in the United States from growing for about 60 years, Chinatown society was top-heavy with old men; their hope for the next gneration and for the survival of the community was to send their grown sons back to China for war brides.

Old Wah Gay (Victor Wong) has decided it's high time for sonny boy Ben Loy (Russell Wong) to stop hanging out at cheap dance halls, where women lean against him singing "Slow Boat to China." Ben Loy is dispatched to the mother he hasn't seen in 20 years, where he is to endure an old-fashioned matchmaking, the kind that can't proceed unless the horoscopes are in sync.

Well, the moon must be in the seventh house, because Ben Loy takes a shine to adorable Mei Oi (Cora Miao, the director's real-life wife), and brings her back to the States to an all-male wedding feast that is a circus. "We've got the big face tonight," crows Wah Gay, grabbing his son drunkenly by the lapels.

The neighborhood immediately takes an active interest in the couple's life and livelihood. Mei Oi's belly—and whether there's anything cooking in it—is the topic du jour at the barber shop. Ben Loy is pressed into a career managing a fractious restaurant, which could lead one day to the plum—being head of the Wang Family Assn., an umbrella group for anyone named Wang, of which Ben Loy is a member.

Feeling the pressure, Ben Loy goes half-mast in the marital bed. "I feel like everyone's watching us," he complains, and he's not wrong. Dad shows up at the restaurant with a little fatherly advice: "*Do you know what to do with this?*" he screams, clutching his crotch.

Mei Oi quickly sheds her Old Country ways and takes a lover, whose only softness is the fleshy part around his insinuating face.

New the cue-ball gossip hound at the barber shop really has something to talk about, and inlaws are losing face like crazy. The illicit lover, a local gambler, becomes the scourge of the Wang Family Assn., and Ben Loy has a close brush with a Jersey fortune-cookie factory, a fate worse than death.

Lush with music and allusions to movies of the era, "Eat A Bowl of Tea" is as personal and internecine a work as Woody Allen's, as delicately funny, too. Like his characters, Wang is interested in "family values," the ways in which networks of people adapt to new circumstances. The movie is playful, affectionate and self-assured enough not to founder when events take a turn for the dramatic.

Victor Wong as the boy's father is especially appealing, with his lopsided slit of a smile. Eric Tsang Chi Wai as the lover is likably unctuous and looks a little Orson Wellesian. Cora Miao is by turns hilarious and touching as the naive bride whose early infatuation with Western gewgaws, like faucets, quickly wanes when she finds that the life she has been prescribed is emotionally bereft.

The meaning of the title becomes clear at the very end, when the ordinary takes on new significance, something like what Wang has done to Chinese-American assimilation in this picture.

NEWSDAY, 7/21/89, Part III/p. 3, Mike McGrady

"Eat A Bowl of Tea," the title of the new Wayne Wang movie, is a literal translation of an all-purpose remedy often prescribed by Chinese herbal physicians. Ailments ranging from the flu to ingrown toenails are routinely treated with a bitter herbal brew and these simple instructions: "Eat a bowl of tea." It's the Asian version of "Take two aspirins and call me in the morning."

Unfortunately, as we know, not all ailments respond to such uncomplicated remedies, and Ben Loy (Russell Wong, the handsome young bridegroom, is the victim of an ailment that resists any simple treatment. The ailment is discovered while he's in bed, embracing the beautiful bride Mei Oi (Cora Miao) recently imported from China.

"Wait a minute," Ben Loy says. "Stop! I don't think I'm going to be able to do this."

"What's wrong?" the bride asks.

"I don't know," he says. "I just feel like everyone is watching us."

This is not far off the mark. The year is 1949, and the scarcity of Chinese women in America makes the birth of any baby an event of considerable importance to the Chinese community. Ben Loy's failure to impregnate his bride causes locals to give him a nickname with an Oriental ring, but a clearly Occidental derivation: "No-Can-Do." The despicable gambler Ah Song (Eric Tsang Chi Wai) takes advantage of Ben Loy's husbandly failures and rapidly impregnates Mei Oi, at the same time transforming "Eat a Bowl of Tea" into a peculiarly mawkish soap opera.

When Ben Loy learns of his wife's indiscretions, his reaction seems peculiarly sophisticated.

"Frankly, I'm a little disappointed in your taste."

"At least he's a man," his bride responds, revealing that she has spent entirely too much time parked in front of their brand new television set.

The primary value of director Wayne Wang's past offorts has been the presentation of a sharp and often funny picture of the Chinese-American community. In both "Chan Is Missing" and "Dim Sum," Wang was able to highlight the conflicts between old ways and new ways, between Chinese traditions and American modernism.

What makes "Eat a Bowl of Tea" noteworthy at all is, once again, its picture of a way of life. At the heart of both the film and the original 1961 Louis Chu novel are the Exclusion Laws—an American policy that for many years limited Asian immigration to this country. Although Chinese laborers were allowed in to build railroads, wives and daughters were not allowed to follow. The result, just before World War II, was a Chinese population that was 96 percent male and 4 percent female.

"Eat a Bowl of Tea" begins after the war with a Chinese-American GI returning to China in search of a bride. The backdrop is consistently fascinating, beginning with the young man's quest, courtship and marriage in China and carrying over to his dealing with the "bachelor society" back home, the aging unmarried men who meet in the family associations and in the gambling rooms, offering commentary and advice while serving as an Asian version of a Greek chorus. What is consistently less than fascinating—trite, maudlin, melodramatic and creaky—is the drama that takes place in the foreground.

VILLAGE VOICE, 8/1/89, p. 67, Renee Tajima

Reading the book always ruins the movie for me, especially if it's a story I love. So I had to watch Wayne Wang's adaptation of *Eat a Bowl of Tea* twice: once to expunge myself of the novel by Louis Chu, then again to try and watch the film with a cleansed slate. *Eat a Bowl of Tea*, The Movie, is long-awaited among Asian Americans. For a community that gets nervous whenever cherished literary properties are sold off to white directors—some still have a bitter taste from John Korty's version of *Farewell to Manzanar*—the adaptation of a landmark novel by a favorite son like Wang is an event.

Chu's story of the Wang family (no relation to the director) depicts a raw, funny, even vulgar Chinatown, New York, circa 1949—a dying society of aging bachelors kept wifeless by laws of exclusion. When the War Brides Act nudges the borders for Chinese women, Wang Wah Gay, the irascible mah-jongg operator, sends his GI son Wang Ben Loy to China to bring back a new wife, Mei Oi, who in turn would bring an heir. These types of marriages spawned the family-filled Chinatown you see today. But for Ben Loy, pressed by the fertile expectations of his father, the future seems, well, soft; and his frustrated wife is moved to find consolation with a local dandy.

Upon its release, the novel was all but ignored. After all, it was published in 1961, the same year as *Flower Drum Song*, a Rodgers and Hammerstein ode to Grant Avenue assimilation that offered up more palatable Chinese Americans in the age of model minorities. A generation of '60s activists rediscovered the book a decade later, embracing it for the same reasons it was first rejected. Here was a story of inner-city poverty and sex, of life on the edge with a dialogue that reads, "Wow your mother...you manymouthed bird, go sell your ass." No sanitized exoticism, but a long-sought testament to what we'd all been searching for: Asian-American soul.

Director Wang, who has already plumbed the world of American Chinatowns in *Chan Is Missing* and *Dim Sum*, gives Chu's story another incarnation, part drama, part romantic comedy. The film is gorgeous to watch. Wang and director of photography Amir Mokri endow it with a stylized beauty that plays on dark Chinatown interiors—a torch song to '40s-era black-and-white cinematography. But this visual elegance transforms the setting in much the same way Spielberg gave *The Color Purple* a hue far different from Alice Walker's vision—muting the story's edge, its passion.

Russell Wong and Cora Miao as the newlyweds are appealing enough, although the script calls on Mei Oi to be irritatingly coy for much of the film, matched by a relatively lifeless Ben Loy. (Wong's visual appeal is not to be underestimated. There are women I know who speak of seeing him on the street with the same air of reverence my eight-year-old nephew reserves for Orel Hershiser.) As Ben Loy lighting his first cigar, the grinning and open-faced Wong could be Jeff Bridges's Tucker: a vision of the buoyant optimism in postwar America. Wah Gay's only son isn't one to take charge of the future. A transitional character between the old bachelor laborers and the new Chinatown bursting at its seams with children, Ben Loy is the kind of guy who you'd ask to be the dummy at bridge—pleasant enough, but the other players call the shots. Wong and Miao play an immigrant version of Redford and Fonda in *Barefoot in the Park*, the attractive young couple starting a new life in Manhattan under the gaze of meddling inlaws, and with all the typical newlywed problems. Except Ben Loy can't get it up or keep it up, at least within the city limits. Not the usual malady for young marrieds.

Ben Loy's impotence is no wonder. Says one of Wah Gays gambling cronies, "For Chinese people, the old ones want children, and the young ones produce them." The entire bachelor community seems to be tracking Mei Oi's ovulation and Ben Loy's performance. His harshest critic is Wah Gay—a role that actor Victor Wong, with his wheezing laugh and twisted smile, seems to have been born to play. In one hilarious scene, exasperated that his son has been nicknamed "No Can Do," Wah Gay corners Ben Loy at work, grabs his own groin, and asks, "Do you know what to do with this?"

Mei Oi does. Lonely and one of Chinatown's first TV widows (Ben Loy would rather watch boxing on his new set), she's been putting out the fishbowl for Uncle Ah Song. Hong Kong comedian Eric Tsang Chi Wai is superbly unctuous as the dapper gambler: You'd think he leaves a trail of grease from the tip of his Panama hat to the spats on his shoes. When Ah Song seduces Mei Oi, the two virtually slithering down a tenement hallway, Tsang is a chubbier version of Jack Nicholson's reptilian drifter in *The Postman Always Rings Twice.* Wang's stylized vision, together with Mark Adler's voluptuous music, produces the same visual choreography. But what's missing is palpable sexual tension. (I don't know if it's due to public-television sensibilities—the movie is made for *American Playhouse*—or because Wang, married to Miao, doesn't belong to the John Derek school of directing one's own wife.) That is my biggest complaint about most of what I've seen in Asian-American film or theater. Where's the beef? Wang's underrated *Slam Dance,* starring Tom Hulce and Virginia Madsen, certainly had its stab at sexuality. Wang's approach reminds me of an old boyfriend. In front of Americans, he could get positively raunchy, but in front of other Asians, he was Mother Teresa.

Whereas the stylized noir and experimentation of *Chan Is Missing* was liberating—I still remember the euphoria upon first seeing it—*Eat a Bowl of Tea* is somehow restrained. What Wang does best is to build the texture of place, populated by ensembles that virtually sing with humor, whether the gaggle of village women checking to see that Ben Loy has all four limbs intact, or the gossiping old men at Wah Gay's club, the Money Come. In all his films there is an economy of frame—a foyer of shoes in *Dim Sum,* the young jook sing gazing at the lo-fan taxi dancers in *Eat a Bowl of Tea*—that summarizes a world of meaning.

Wang has an eye for incongruities, especially of ordinary lives posed between two worlds (East/West, feudal/modern), without resorting to exoticism or novelty. Mei Oi and Ben Loy's union is blessed by both their horoscopes and mutual attraction at an outdoor picture show in the Chinese village. An old man recites the dialogue from *Lost Horizon:* "When I kiss you, my darling, the whole world belongs to me," and the young lovers are posed for the future, set against the blue gaze of Ronald Colman and Jane Wyatt. (Later the two try a dose of Orson Welles and Rita Hayworth in *The Lady From Shanghai* at a New York movie house to prime Ben Loy for his own performance.) Wang not only refers cinematically to the era, but in a stunning way explicitly incorporates the big screen as metaphor for the American Dream. Mei Oi and Ben Loy's story ultimately has a Hollywood ending—which seems a long time coming—replete with attempted murder, mayhem, an illegitimate child, and finally a vision of a Technicolor suburban future far away from Chinatown.

Also reviewed in:
NEW YORK TIMES, 7/21/89, p. C13, Caryn James
VARIETY, 5/24–30/89, p. 27
WASHINGTON POST, 9/1/89, p. B9, Hal Hinson
WASHINGTON POST, 9/1/89, Weekend/p. 31, Desson Howe

ECHOES OF PARADISE

A Quartet Films Inc. release of a Laughing Kookaburra Productions film. *Executive Producer:* Jan Sharp. *Producer:* Jane Scott. *Director:* Phillip Noyce. *Screenplay:* Jan Sharp. *Director of Photography:* Peter James. *Editor:* Frans Vandenburg. *Music:* Bill Motzing. *Production Designer:* Clarissa Patterson. *Running time:* 92 minutes. *MPAA Rating:* R.

CAST: Wendy Hughes (Maria); John Lone (Raka); Steven Jacobs (George); Peta Toppano (Judy); Rod Mullinar (Terry); Gillian Jones (Mitty); Claudia Karuan (Julia).

LOS ANGELES TIMES, 4/14/89, Calendar/p. 6, Michael Wilmington

Hard on the heels of Phillip Noyce's smashing new sea-and-sex chase thriller "Dead Calm" comes a much different movie, one which Noyce shot several years ago: "Echoes of Paradise."

In "Calm," Noyce shows that he knows how to make a smoking melodrama. In "Echoes of Paradise," he's trying something softer, gentler: a psychological love story about an Australian mother and wife (Wendy Hughes) who leaves her would-be politician husband after discovering his incessant infidelities and takes up with a Balinese dancer (John Lone) in a Thai tourist paradise.

Trying to cauterize her own pain and humiliation, Hughes' Maria McAvoy drifts into a languorous, little alternative community: with the homosexual hotel-owner, Terry (Rod Mullinar) and his seductive and ambiguously charming guest, Raka (Lone). As she falls, or slides, into an extramarital affair, Maria has the self-conscious stance of an uncertain actress, edging into a bewildering role. Raka and Terry, theatrical to the core, manipulate their performances more adroitly: Raka with a silken, lazy ease; Terry more flamboyantly, with witty lines and troubled eyes.

Do some directors keep making the same film, in various guises? Both of Noyce's recent films are about triangles, about a husband and wife kept physically apart after a crisis in their marriage, and with a third male character—strange, sexually aggressive, possibly with a pathological edge—coming in to roil the waters and to keep them apart.

"Dead Calm" was like "Knife in the Water" with an electric chainsaw; it was all swift mechanics, with a technical gleam that burned your eyes. "Echoes of Paradise," written and executive-produced by Noyce's wife, Jan Sharp, digs deeper into its characters. It keeps its edges cloaked in mist, the sunlight dropped and filtered in a latticework of Asian shadows, the love scenes unfolding serenely, by candlelight. Both lovers are on vacation, Raka on an extended retirement from the stage, and Noyce and Sharp give us a sense of what happens when ordinary time hits a stop.

It's a subtle film that doesn't make any obvious errors. And it has two splendid, all but faultless, leading performances—by Wendy Hughes and John Lone. They mesh seamlessly, quietly reversing our usual conceptions of male-female movie personas. Despite her soft, wounded expression, Hughes' acting has the keener edge, the more aggressive, searching attack, while Lone, in a role that predated "The Last Emperor," gives his Raka more rounded, voluptuous contours, a honeyed smile, eyes like flaming liqueur.

But, somehow it doesn't go far enough, doesn't open up enough possibilities. Like the wife, this movie is somewhat trapped; it has lovely moments, but it's restrained, hemmed in—and the cinematography, by Peter James, is a disappointment.

Fuzzy and muted and soft, it suggests Maria's repressed home life when she's in Australia, but, in Thailand, it doesn't change. It doesn't release you into the hot exoticism of her new surroundings, or suggest, even subliminally, the danger, glamour or flukey romance that might be sucking her in.

Part of what the film suggests is that interludes are dangerous, that marriage is a serious affair, that the world outside can never be avoided. But "Echoes of Paradise" (MPAA rated R, for sex and language) also tries for the poetics of the unplanned impulse. It's a shame that more of its moments aren't up to Hughes' and Lone's best. You're left at the end with two finely delineated, perfectly etched performances and a mood that stays languorous, pensive, drifting. The paradise vanishes and only the echoes remain.

NEW YORK POST, 3/10/89, p. 27, Jami Bernard

There is no Club Med on the island of Phuket, off the coast of Thailand, but there is the equivalent—a quaint little hotel with thatched-roof bungalows, run by an expatriate Australian who knows what his guests need in order to unwind. When Maria comes to get away from her philandering husband back in Sydney, the hotelier sets her up in a little hut near an exotic Balinese dancer who will give her the full Club Med treatment.

"Echoes of Paradise" is essentially the oft-told (or daydreamed) story of a troubled tourist's soul being soothed by the restorative powers of an island affair, the kind of hype that keeps travel agents in business. But the story is presented here with the kind of beatified dramatic flourish that makes "Echoes" seem to be about something more. Certainly it tries to be.

Maria, played by cat-eyed Australian actress Wendy Hughes, is a doting mother of three and wife to a political hopeful and noted philanderer. The wife being the last to know in these stories, Maria is devastated to learn at a dinner party that her husband and another woman are "having lunch quite often—perhaps 'lunch' is too euphemistic a word."

Outraged and disoriented, Maria does what many a woman has done—she goes off for a week's vacation with a girlfriend.

Thailand works on Maria like a tonic. After years of playing happy homemaker, Maria is surrounded by dreamy flora and fauna and local men with fabulous bodies wanting her to teach them English, or maybe body English.

The Balinese dancer next door who constantly trains but never performs is hypnotically played by John Lone ("The Last Emperor"), who is magnificent at being enigmatic. When the hotel proprietor (Rod Mullinar) explains to Maria that this dancer, Raka, has "extraordinary power, as though he'd touched the source," you can believe it.

The innkeeper has a crush on Raka, which is why he keeps him around, but Raka also earns a nominal existence as proprietor of a lonely tropical bar, the kind of place tourists go wild for, decorated with ceremonial candles and statues and local artifacts. Raka invites Maria there for cocktails.

The cocktails don't move her, but the sensuous massage does. Soon they are lovers, and Maria is canceling her reservations for home. Hubby and the kids are annoyed, but Maria's neck muscles are no longer tense. (The subtext is an unfortunate one: the traditional notion that there's nothing wrong with a woman that a liberating affair can't cure.)

Directed by Phillip Noyce this affair between two temporarily lost souls takes on cosmic proportions—helped by mystic Buddhist ceremonies in bat caves, during which Maria trembles and is perhaps touched by the source.

If "Echoes" doesn't hold up to scrutiny, you can't fault the acting. Even the movie itself knows its imperfections. "You have to decide what's real" and accept "the need to dream," it concludes lamely.

People who come back from their wonderful times at Club Med often can't believe, in retrospect, that they really quacked like ducks and sang the happy hands song, either.

VILLAGE VOICE, 3/21/89, p. 68, Amy Taubin

Even seemingly purposeless pictures have their uses. Naively racist and maudlin, *Echoes of Paradise* nevertheless jogged memories of Alain Resnais and Marguerite Duras's risky, rigorous *Hiroshima, Mon Amour*, now available on home video. Need I say more?

Echoes of Paradise, like *Hiroshima*, describes an intense and impossible love affair between a white woman and an Asian man. Whereas in *Hiroshima*, their difference is a function of history—specifically irreconcilable experiences of World War II—*Echoes* defines the otherness strictly through skin tone and crude *Jungle Book* stereotypes. Set on an island off the coast of Thailand, *Echoes*'s frame of reference excludes Vietnam and a century of war in Indochina.

Maria McEvoy (Wendy Hughes—a slightly Anglicized version of Resnais's Emmanuelle Riva), devoted mother of three young children, discovers within days of her father's death that her husband, an Australian MP, is an avid womanizer. Unnerved and unmoored, she takes off with a friend for a vacation on the exotic island of Phuket, where beach houses rent for $2 a month. There she meets Raka (John Lone), a famous Balinese dancer, who, corrupted by success in Paris, has lost his divine inspiration and is now trying to find himself while freelancing as a bartender. He offers her a "pressure point" massage (a fairly dangerous proposition since he sports a couple of three-inch fingernails), and within 30 seconds they are rolling around behind some discreet black lace curtains.

Hughes clearly deserves better material and a less hack director than Phillip Noyce. Judging from his brilliant performance in *The Last Emperor*, I might have said the same for Lone, had not his characterization here—all flashing teeth, tossing ponytail, and monotonously questioning inflection—suggested that, on some level, he buys into the colonizers' myth of brown people as innocent children. Or maybe he just doesn't know how to play a nice guy.

The print I saw had a distinctly green cast. Just carelessness, or was some astute lab technician placing the proper patina on a thoroughly tarnished endeavor?

Also reviewed in:
NEW YORK TIMES, 3/10/89, p. C10, Janet Maslin

EDDIE AND THE CRUISERS II: EDDIE LIVES!

A Scotti Brothers Picture release in association with Aurora Film Partners of a Les Productions Alliance film. *Executive Producer:* Victor Loewy and Denis Heroux. *Producer:* Stephane Reichel. *Director:* Jean-Claude

Lord. *Screenplay:* Charles Zev Cohen and Rick Doering. *Based on characters created by:* P.F. Kluge. *Director of Photography:* Rene Verzier. *Editor:* Jean-Guy Montpetite. *Music:* Marty Simon and Leon Aronson. *Art Director:* Dominic Ricard. *Set Decorator:* Gilles Aird. *Costumes:* Ginnette Magny. *Make-up:* Jocelyne Bellemare. *Running time:* 100 minutes. *MPAA Rating:* PG-13.

CAST: Michael Pare (Eddie Wilson/Joe West); Marina Orsini (Diane); Bernie Coulson (Rick); Matthew Laurance (Sal); Michael Rhoades (Dave Pagent); Anthony Sherwood (Hilton); Mark Holmes (Quinn); David Matheson (Stewart); Paul Markle (Charlie); Kate Lynch (Lyndsay); Harvey Atkin (Lew Eisen); Vlasta Vrana (Frank); Larry King (T.V. Talk Show Host); Bo Diddley (Legendary Guitarist); Martha Quinn (Music Video Hostess); Merrill Shindler (Musicologist); Sunny Joe White (Radio Disc Jockey); James Rae (Tom); Michael "Tunes" Antunes (Wendall Newton); Ulla Moreland (Art Critic); Bruno Verdoni (Rick's Keyboard Player); Phil Mattera (Rick's Bass Player); Kim Lombard (Rick's Drummer).

LOS ANGELES TIMES, 8/18/89, Calendar/p. 12, Kevin Thomas

"Eddie and the Cruisers" was a 1983 sleeper, an engaging and modest little movie about a new Jersey rock star who apparently drowned in the summer of 1964 when he drove his blue-and-white '57 Chevy convertible off a bridge and into the Raritan River. Almost 20 years later, a TV reporter, played by Ellen Barkin, delves into Eddie's never-explained demise because all of a sudden Eddie's records were bigger than ever. (Shades of Jim Morrison.) Although effective as a contemplation of the past's hold on the present, the film ended unsatisfactorily.

With "Eddie and the Crusiers II: Eddie Lives!," a new set of film makers has been given a chance to round out Eddie's story, and writers Charles Zev Cohen and Rick Doehring got on the right track. Although their script could have used some polish, it is fortunately sturdy enough to withstand some unintended laughs and the pedestrian quality of the contributions of director Jean-Claude Lord, cinematographer Rene Verzier and editor Jean-Guy Montpetite. The result is a pleasant, entertaining picture sparked by Michael Pare, returning as Eddie, by the driving music of Marty Simon and Leon Aronson and by the straightforward songs of John Cafferty, who once again supplies Eddie's singing voice.

Eddie is alive and well and living in Montreal as construction worker Joe West. It's 1982—something the production notes, not the film itself, make clear—and the executives of Eddie's old record company intend to cash in on the renewed interest in Eddie. He may hate this hype, but it stirs him sufficiently to resume performing under his assumed name, taking over a young rock group.

There's a certain sweet squareness to the film and to Eddie himself, who drills into his new colleagues the importance of hard work and practice in creating a great band. Eddie's reasons for dropping out are credible, as is his increasing uncertainty about making a grab for the brass ring a second time around. Since all the pressures and contradictory feelings surrounding Eddie are so very familiar, it's too bad the film spells them all out so literally.

In the first film, we had to take it on faith that Eddie was the stuff of legend, but you can believe it here when the sexy and charismatic Pare goes into action, in a perfect lip-sync with Cafferty's voice, as deep as his own. He has developed considerable muscle since the first film, and is convincing as a man in his late 30s. He also effectively projects the isolation, the shy vulnerability of the spectacularly good-looking individual. (The rest of the cast is OK but fades into the background.)

If nothing else, "Eddie II" (mild for its PG-13 rating) could just give Pare another shot at the kind of big-screen opportunities Ellen Barkin and Tom Berenger (as one of the original Cruisers) have enjoyed since their appearances in "Eddie I."

NEW YORK POST, 8/18/89, p. 25, Jami Bernard

With all the starkness of the latest title of a slasher series, this sequel to 1983's "Eddie and the Cruisers" announces: "Eddie Lives!"

Eddie's no Jason or Freddie, but he is just as tormented.

In Part I, Eddie Wilson, the greatest rock legend-to-be of the '60s, drove his car off a pier and died. With the healing powers of the sequel, it turns out he didn't die (they never recovered the body anyway), he just went to Montreal to be a hardhat.

Now with the discovery of some "lost" Eddie tapes and an unscrupulous record promoter's campaign to revive the Eddie legend—on the par of the "Paul is Dead" thing or today's various

Elvis sightings—Eddie comes out of retirement under the name of Joe West and starts another band. With all the Eddiemania going on, no one recognizes him or his voice—or his songs.

Straining the bounds of credulity, "Eddie and the Cruisers II" does boast a lively, angst-ridden, Springsteen-ish sound track by John Cafferty (an extra star rating just for that) and some mighty creditable lip-synching by Michael Pare as the haunted Eddie. Plenty of performance scenes happily distract from the weirdo plot. Terrible decision, though, to disguise Eddie in Robert Goulet-type hairdo and wedged sideburns.

The love interest is provided by Marina Orsini, notable mostly for the Geena Davis corners of her mouth, as an artist who has exhausted her reds—don't ask—and who adores Eddie/Joe despite his alarming mood swings and suicidal tendencies. As far as rock mythology goes, Eddie Wilson is more in need of a shrink and a shave than a comeback record.

NEWSDAY, 8/18/89, Part III/p. 5, Bill Kaufman

Moviegoers who caught the original "Eddie and the Cruisers" always knew that Eddie Wilson didn't really die, because his body was never found after his car plunged off the Raritan Bridge.

The 1983 limited-release film about a rock and roller obsessed with finding just the right sound for his band turned out to be something of a sleeper that went on to do gangbuster business on pay TV and videocassette. At the same time, John Cafferty and the Beaver Brown Band, the Jersey Shore rock group that played the movie's sound track, sold 3 million albums as a spinoff.

"Eddie and the Cruisers II" picks up 20 years after Eddie Wilson's disappearance, and right from the start, as the camera closes in on a handsome Montreal construction worker, we know who he is. Michael Pare re-creates his role as Eddie Wilson, now an introspective, bitter man hiding behind a pseudonym, sideburns and a mustache because he feels he isn't ready for the world. Or is it the other way around?

When a record firm that once rejected his music puts out unreleased tapes of Eddie Wilson jamming, and his sound throbs from every radio, we see a tear rolling down the hardhat's face. Succumbing to much gentle persuasion by his lover, played with sensitivity by the beautiful Canadian actress Marina Orsini, and more emphatic encouragement from his buddy, guitarist Rick DeSal (Bernie Coulson), Wilson gives in and forms a new band. A hard taskmaster with his musicians, Wilson doesn't reveal his true identity, even to them.

Much of the movie features flashy music scenes of the powerhouse band practicing and in concert. Pare displays a keen intensity as the driven musician—even if at times his inflection sounds like a nasal version of Sylvester Stallone's Rocky. The performers that make up the new "Cruisers" are also convincing; two of them, Mark Holmes and Paul Markle, are members of the rock band Platinum Blonde. This wellmade music movie nicely captures some of the backstage rock milieu, and showcases a handful of new songs that, if the producer's expectations come true, may once again make it to the charts.

VILLAGE VOICE, 8/22/89, p. 93, Julie Phillips

Eddie and the Cruisers II: Eddie Lives! is based on faith in the purity and manliness of rock 'n' roll. It's also based on the assumption that former rock stars, even ones believed dead, don't lose their hair, get fat, or become temperamental: They become wiser and more Zen, and make Pat Morita-like pronouncements about what you can do if you really *believe*. Eddie—who drove his car off a bridge in the original, ending his band's dreams of the big time—has survived, grown a mustache, and gone into hiding as a construction worker in Montreal. Elusive in the first movie—which was more about his buddies than about him—he is the center of the second. As he assembles a band and begins his incognito comeback, he is revealed to be (what else?) a sensitive, tormented blue-collar hero.

The sequel lacks some of the charm of the first one, which was about nostalgia: Eddie was a minor Elvis, a symbol of the half-remembered rock 'n' roll energy of growing up in Asbury Park. *Eddie II* is more of a straightforward music success story, in which the good musicians win out over the evil art capitalists. Michael Pare returns as Eddie; he looks nice close up, although he's not as interesting as Tom Berenger, the narrator Wordman in the original. Marina Orsini is the all-purpose girlfriend, who hangs around the band all day though she doesn't even get to sing backup. Filmed mostly in Canada (do Canadians have rock 'n' roll?), it loses that Jersey edge, but the Springsteen-type music, by John Cafferty and the Beaver Brown Band, is good and solid, and for the kind of movie that it is, you can't really ask for much more than that and good lip-synching.

Also reviewed in:
NEW YORK TIMES, 8/18/89, p. C16, Caryn James
VARIETY, 8/16-22/89, p. 22
WASHINGTON POST, 8/18/89, p. D1, Rita Kempley

EDGE OF SANITY

A Millimeter Films release of an Allied Vision film. *Executive Producer:* Peter A. McRae. *Producer:* Edward Simons and Harry Alan Towers. *Director:* Gerard Kikoine. *Screenplay:* J.P. Felix and Ron Raley. *Director of Photography:* Tony Spratling. *Editor:* Malcolm Cooke. *Music:* Frederic Talgorn. *Sound:* Paul Sharkey. *Production Designer:* Jean Charles Dedieu. *Art Director:* Fred Carter and Tivadar Bertalan. *Costumes:* Valerie Lanee. *Make-up:* Gordon Kaye. *Running time:* 86 minutes. *MPAA Rating:* R.

CAST: Anthony Perkins (Dr. Jekyll/Mr. Hyde); Glynis Barber (Elisabeth Jekyll); Sarah Maur-Thorp (Susannah); David Lodge (Underwood); Ben Cole (Johnny); Ray Jewers (Newcomen); Jill Melford (Flora); Lisa Davis (Maria); Noel Coleman (Egglestone).

LOS ANGELES TIMES, 4/14/89, Calendar/p. 4, Kevin Thomas

"Edge of Sanity" is an elegant, bloody new version of Robert Louis Stevenson's "Dr. Jekyll and Mr. Hyde," reworked by writers J.P. Felix and Ron Raley to turn Hyde into Jack the Ripper.

Anthony Perkins brings just the right degree of tongue-in-cheekery to his dual role; would that director Gerard Kikoine had exercised the same restraint in showing the Ripper's victims and had left more to the imagination. The result is a stylish, imaginative picture too morbid and graphic for mainstream audiences in its sex-and-violence juxtapositions—but one that may have enough bizarre panache to become a cult film.

Perkins' Dr. Henry Jekyll is an eminent, upper-crust London physician who becomes the victim of an accident in his laboratory when the fumes of an anesthetic he is developing unleash in him a second personality, which he calls Jack Hyde. An opening credit sequence reveals that Jekyll is still haunted in nightmares by an especially traumatic, humiliating adolescent discovery of sex. In Hyde he will release all the twisted sexual rage he has long suppressed as a dignified, respected professional and as a devoted husband (to a lovely Glynis Barber).

Shot largely in Budapest by Tony Spratling, a gifted cinematographer, "Edge of Sanity" makes fine use of light and shadow and distorted camera angles to convey Jekyll/Hyde's progressive mental disintegration. The film has much of the stylized, decadent look and mood of the better efforts of Italian horrormeister Dario Argento, and production designer Jean-Charles Dedieu deserves credit for his handsome settings, which range from the Jekylls' charming period boudoir to a lurid red-and-gold bordello that would have delighted the Marquis de Sade (and probably Oscar Wilde as well).

For all its fine sense of time and place, "Edge of Sanity" has a highly contemporary arid tone, finding dark amusement rather than pathos in the predicament of the pompous, very proper Victorian Dr. Jekyll, and Perkins' Jekyll/Hyde is as outrageous as he is tormented. The bravura of his dual portrayal is much like his performance as the sexually obsessed priest in Ken Russell's flamboyant "Crimes of Passion." It can't be denied that "Edge of Sanity" (rated R) has the courage of its kinky material, but all the same: Let the buyer beware.

NEW YORK POST, 4/14/89, p. 38, Jami Bernard

It is possible that Tony Perkins has more of a range than playing morally ambiguous, sexually ambivalent psychos, but when he takes on roles like the ones he played in "Crimes of Passion" and "Edge of Sanity," it's hard to cry for him. Okay, he doesn't wear a dress this time, but that's a minor sticking point.

"Edge of Sanity" is a new take on the Dr. Jekyll and Mr. Hyde story, about a mild-mannered doctor whose evil side takes over now and again and causes him to kill kill kill (and get very cranky with his wife).

This version is a hack-fest, with the interesting twist that the baser side of the good doctor is not only Mr. Hyde, but *Jack* Hyde, or Jack the Ripper. The concept has a bizarre logic of its own, and yet making Perkins' doppelganger into a familiar mass murderer also takes some of the sting out of Robert Louis Stevenson's original concept, in which the darker side of the soul was dark enough. Did the Werewolf have to be a *famous* werewolf to make his transition any more frightening?

This Jekyll is a nerdy milquetoast, saccharined to death by his cloying Grace Kelly-pure wife (Glynis Barber), toiling away in his basement lab of gleaming white tile and blue bottled liquids. The only other item on hand is a spitoon-full of fine white powder, which the good doctor frequently puts up his nose.

Yes, he's experimenting with the anaesthetic qualities of a powdery white drug. (That's the equivalent of reading girlie magazines for the literature.) Let's see, we've got Jekyll, Hyde, Jack the Ripper and now Freud (who was a big cocaine advocate around the turn of the century). Can Sybil be far behind?

If we want to read even more into it—perhaps more than warranted—Jekyll's curved glass bong looks something like the pipe of Sherlock Holmes, and in fact, the local police enlist Jekyll's aid in trying to solve the Ripper murders.

But even with this "Bill & Ted" approach to literary history, director Gerard Kikoine is restless. So whenever Jekyll, in his coke-induced paranoid fog, becomes Jack Hyde, the East End goes modern and the fuschia-clad tarts to whom Hyde is inexorably drawn each night (he gets his jollies by slitting their throats to make up for a childhood sexual trauma) are Madonna clones, with single crucifix earrings.

Jekyll's transition into Hyde (just say no, doc!) is accomplished with some brown eyeliner and by Perkins setting his teeth and lowering his head to the camera like a charging bull. Amidst lots of crucifix imagery and women's mocking laughter, Hyde confesses to one painted lady, "I can't...because I'm *bad*!"

Not having had the kind of guilt-inducing religious traumas that Jekyll did (or Tony Perkins for that matter), I find movies that prey on religious sexual fetishes rather uninvolving. Nevertheless, Hyde is most certainly bad, just as he says. The women he has done the nasty with (or thought about doing the nasty with) are found the next morning "ripped open clean as a codfish from Billingsgate Market," according to Scotland Yard.

If the transition from Jekyll to Hyde were as distinct as the schism the movie presents between "good girls" and "bad girls," we might have something here. But Perkins looks quite mad all the time. No wonder he's not doing light comedy.

NEWSDAY, 4/14/89, Part III/p. 4, Bill Kaufman

More than two dozen movies have been inspired by Robert Louis Stevenson's Victorian masterpiece "Dr. Jekyll and Mr. Hyde," a terrorizing glimpse into the duality of human nature that is considered one of the first psychological thrillers, a genre that is, for the most part, well represented by this latest film version.

Admittedly, "Edge of Sanity" is not a straightforward adaptation of the classic horror tale, but a version that weaves in a couple of new themes—specifically, territory dealing with sexual hang-ups of the sort explored by Freud and Krafft-Ebing, as well as the problem of drug abuse.

Anthony Perkins plays Dr. Jekyll, the ostensibly kindhearted, methodical London physican who divides his time between treating beaten-up streetwalkers in a charity hospital and experimenting with a new anesthetic in his laboratory. Glynis Barber is fine as Elisabeth, his beautiful and devoted wife who ultimately discovers her husband's dark side.

Early on, to account for Jekyll's bent psyche, the film establishes how, as a youth, he was emotionally and phsycially scarred while peeking at a couple making love. Discovered in his voyeurism after accidentally falling from a hayloft, the young Jekyll is beaten bloody by the enraged man while the woman looks on, laughing.

Later, in adulthood, using a drug he has discovered, Jekyll transforms himself into Hyde, a killer who viciously murders a number of prostitutes in a plot deviation that borrows from the infamous Jack-the-Ripper murders of the time. We're shown Jekyll not only habitually sniffing a white powder, but also smoking it in a glass pipe. Not only is he a crackpot, but could he also be a crackhead, circa 1888?

Perkins, his face etched with torment, is excellent in the dual role of the sexually repressed killer. When he transforms into madman Hyde, vacant eyes peering from a contorted face, audiences will undoubtedly remember Norman Bates, the deranged motel owner with whom Perkins has been associated since the "Psycho" sagas began in 1960.

Filmed in Hungary, "Edge of Sanity" nicely conveys the atmosphere of Victorian London's back alleys, opulent brothels and elegant mansions. Director Gerard Kikoine maintains a taut level of suspense throughout, while the competent cast, including Ben Cole as a decadent pimp, adds luster to the horror-thriller.

VILLAGE VOICE, 4/18/89, p. 71, Elliott Stein

The path from *Brightness* [see Stein's review] to *Edge of Sanity* is a descent from the sublime to the pernicious. This incoherent exploitation movie, starring Tony Perkins as Dr. Jekyll and Mr. Hyde, was shot in Budapest by a French director (Gerard Kikoine) of no observable gifts. It should be given a wide berth, except by those with an express interest in the sight of Victorian tarts besmirched with stage blood. The climax is a scene in which the suspicious Mrs. Jekyll (Glynis Barber) is sliced by her husband, and the crime is pinned on Jack the Ripper; however pointless, this is a new twist. Even newer might be a return to Robert L. Stevenson. His much-mangled story has been filmed dozens of times, but the movie versions have always added both pure and promiscuous women to parallel the two sides of Jekyll's nature. Stevenson's superb tale is a strictly all-male affair—it would be interesting to see it that way on screen at least once.

Also reviewed in:
NEW YORK TIMES, 4/14/89, p. C15, Vincent Canby
VARIETY, 4/12–18/89, p. 24

EGG

Producer: René Scholten. *Director:* Danniel Danniel. *Screenplay (Dutch with English subtitles):* Danniel Danniel. *Director of Photography:* Erik van Empel. *Editor:* Menno Boerema. *Music:* Michel Mulders. *Sound:* Mark Glynne. *Production Designer:* Michal Shabtay. *Running time:* 58 minutes. *MPAA Rating:* Not Rated.

CAST: Johan Leysen (Johan); Marijke Veugelers (Eva); Coby Timp (Johan's Mother); Jake Kruyer (Paul); Peter Smits (Peter); Piet Kamerman (Gerard).

NEW YORK POST, 4/5/89, p. 21, Jami Bernard

Film Forum has joined two interesting short films at the hip; what they have in common, aside from being short, is that they feature simplistic, elemental forms. The narrative "Egg" has a lot of ovals; the documentary "Stones and Flies" has a lot of circles and lines (and stones and flies).

"Egg" is a sweetly humorous old-fashioned sort of story about a 35-year-old baker named Johan who lives with his mother in elemental bliss in a small Dutch village. Johan's main pleasures are baking, balancing eggs on their ends and sitting on a park bench with his pals and skipping stones toward the village square. For big excitement, they wave at the bus as it makes its daily stop.

Johan's two like-looking friends egg him on to find himself a woman through the personals. The baker begins a correspondence with a woman from "foreign climes," who one day startles them all by descending from the bus with her bags; she has come to marry the baker. Embarrassment, awkwardness, silences all do nothing to prevent romance from taking its timeless course.

The structure of the little film is as simple and serene as the baker's eggs. There is very little dialogue, and changes in venue are introduced with old-fashioned, oval title cards and peppy theme music, like a silent picture. Director Danniel, an Israeli who has settled in Holland for his video- and film-making career, has an ear for, of all things, *lack* of dialogue, and his fondness for his insular, small-world villagers makes such a light dish as "Egg" a satisfying meal.

If skipping stones is Johan's delight, then picking them up and placing them in new positions is something the artist Richard Long likes to do. "Stones and Flies" follows Long during a trek through the Sahara, as he creates little sculptures along the way to commemorate his passage.

Long doesn't exactly keep banker's hours. The British artist trudges along with a backpack, occasionally dragging a straight line out of the sand with his heel, or making sneaker-tread marks in a big circle, or toeing out an ever-radiating circle like a hypnotist's tool against a majestic desert background. He makes snaky rivers in the dust from a watering can; he piles rocks into mini-Stonehenges. "I have made walking into sculpture," he says. "Something is happening in the middle of nothing."

Your first temptation may be to laugh this off as an aberrant hiker's pretensions, but the finished "sculptures" really do resonate with the environment. After 20 years of making these walking sculptures in highly inaccessible geographies, Long can make the straightest line and the roundest circle. He has an impeccable eye for composition, even when he's standing in the middle of it.

Now he gathers some twigs, leaving little stripes in the sand where they lay. Whoops—that's no sculpture he's making, that's a fire. Even artists must relax after a hard day making geometric patterns in the wilderness.

"A walk is a line of footsteps, a sculpture is a line of stones...they're interchangeable, they're complementary." Before you know it, there'll be a walking, sculpturing exercise-video out. Meanwhile, "Stones and Flies" is visually stimulating, almost in spite of itself.

VILLAGE VOICE, 4/11/89, p. 71, Katherine Dieckmann

Droll and subdued, the Dutch film *Egg* is as ideally balanced as nature's oval, and as its Israeli director's name, Danniel Danniel. This 58-minute fable, set in an uneventful village where the daily arrival of a bus and the pregnancy of the Van der Kirks' dog are cause for excitement, is about unruffled surfaces (monotonous pale tile interiors, the bleached white of bakers' uniforms) and the feelings that hide beneath the shell, threatening to spill out once it's cracked.

Johan (Johan Leysen) is a 35-year-old baker who still lives with his mother. With his slightly glazed appreciation for the extraordinary in the ordinary, Johan is reminiscent of the angels spouting aphorisms about quotidian beauty in *Wings of Desire*. The texture and smell of kneaded bread and the feel of dog fur send him into quiet rapture. His two employees at the bakery—in Danniel's comedy of sameness, the three tend to dress alike even off the job—are a little worried. So they pore over the personals, and Johan picks a likely candidate: Eva (Marijke Veugelers), who lives in a place referred to simply as the "Foreign Climes." As the correspondence develops, Johan reveals odd details about his tiny world, while Eva's given to lyrical confessions like 'I lie in bed and listen to the night. It makes me feel so lonely.'

Taking Johan's descriptions for intimacy, Eva shows up in town one day, stepping off the bus dressed in pink and a straw hat, like some midlife Fragonard. But reality of a certain sort is too much for Johan. The remainder of *Egg* traces his emerging communication with Eva—at first they're still writing letters to each other in their heads, incapable of translating it into dialogue. But slowly they find a way to talk to each other, much to the surprise of the ever-watchful village.

Realizing that silence is the characters' dominant mode, the director plays on silent film conventions, finding humor in camera movements and subtle facial expressions, and using intertitles that appear in egg-shaped ovals. In his press bio, Danniel says, "I hope that I can send people home feeling nice." That sounds schmaltzy, but *Egg* is pleasurable—an astringent feel-good movie.

One of Johan's pet activities in *Egg* is stacking small stones by the river. Conceptualist-minimalist-earth workist Richard Long has made that a vocation. Since the mid-'60s, Long has walked barren landscapes the world over, marking his trail with repeated forms—small-scale spiral jetties, stone circles, and straight lines scuffed in the ground with his feet. In the 38-minute *Stones and Flies: Richard Long in the Sahara*, Philip Haas (who has also made documentaries on David Hockney and Gilbert & George) follows Long into a particularly forbidding part of the Sahara to film the artist picking up rocks, then knocking them down ("to use each place with respect"), drawing in the dirt with his shoes, and always walking, walking, walking.

Haas's spare camerawork and restrained use of music gives *Stones and Flies* a suitably reverent feeling. (It's as austere in its way as *Egg*.) So it's unfortunate that he includes the artist speaking in voiceovers and to the camera about his work, generally belaboring the obvious with comments such as "Sculptures are stopping places along the journey." Using titles for this commentary would have better preserved the ritualistic feeling of the setting and the work; as it is, Long's explications start to sound premeditated, precious, and the act of roaming exotic lands, the heroism of laboring for the concept, starts to seem pretty self-aggrandizing. And arid.

Also reviewed in:
NEW YORK TIMES, 4/5/89, p. C18, Caryn James
VARIETY, 5/18/88, p. 42

84 CHARLIE MOPIC

A New Century/Vista Film Co. release of a Charlie Mopic production. *Producer:* Michael Nolin. *Director:* Patrick Duncan. *Screenplay:* Patrick Duncan. *Director of Photography:* Alan Caso. *Editor:* Stephen Purvis. *Sound:* Michael Moore and Craig Woods. *Special Effects:* Eric Rylander. *Art Director:* Douglas Dick. *Costumes:* Lyn Paolo. *Make-up:* Ron Wild. *Technical Advisor:* Capt. Russ "Gunny" Thurman. *Running time:* 95 minutes. *MPAA Rating:* R.

CAST: Jonathan Emerson (L.T.); Nicholas Cascone (Easy); Jason Tomlins (Pretty Boy); Christopher Burgard (Hammer); Glenn Morshower (Cracker); Richard Brooks (O.D.); Byron Thames (Mopic); Russ Thurman, Joesph Hieu, and Don Schiff.

LOS ANGELES TIMES, 4/7/89, Calendar/p. 1, Michael Wilmington

The people who made "84 Charlie Mopic" don't want you to be superficially amused by their re-creation of the Vietnam War. They don't want to pump you up with any apocalyptic razzle-dazzle or the old Stallone baloney. Instead, they want to hurl that war in your face, let you feel the heat and wind of the forest, the sweat of a long march, the stench of carnage, the blast of bullets or trip-mines tearing flesh. They want to rub your noses in fatigue, fear, casual profanity, graveyard yocks—all the naturalistic detritus and gritty minutiae of men facing death and trying to beat it.

Surprisingly often, they do.

"84 Charlie Mopic" has been somewhat overpraised, but the best of it has a cutting edge, a hard-bitten damn-your-eyes integrity. It's a small, dedicated film with a killingly clear focus. It gives you the feeling of war by fixing on the little stuff: the way one G.I. keeps a pet lizard or another carefully washes his own socks, the modus operandi for defusing mines or fooling the enemy with phony cigarette litter—and all around, the ominous bird-song of the forest.

Writer-director Patrick Duncan tries for an ultrarealist illusion. He turns the film into a fake documentary: a collection of apparently unedited (and uncensored) footage shot by a Mopic, or Army motion-picture cameraman, accompanying a six-man reconnaissance team into the Central Highlands in 1969. This footage is intended for a mundane purpose, a training film to instruct raw recruits in the routines of jungle warfare: checking for mines, surviving in the forest, scouting enemy positions.

But the Mopic (Byron Thames) is an opportunist who keeps going further, digging into the men's personal lives. He goads them into self-revelations, accompanies them everywhere.

At one point he is belly-down in the brush, while Viet Cong walk by several feet away, and a nearby soldier whose had his hand stabbed with a bamboo spear tries to keep from screaming. At another, he has got his camera practically in the face of a man being shot to pieces by a sniper and begging his buddies to kill him. And, at yet another, he lays down his equipment to throw himself into the action and rescue a comrade; it goes on recording the bloody action even after he leaves.

This Mopic is obviously getting footage that the Army is never going to show—in a training film or anyhere else. And he is shooting things that more than likely, the men on this mission—a five-man intelligence unit, bolstered by the Mopic and a young lieutenant (Jonathan Emerson)—wouldn't even have allowed him to record: like the extreme close-up execution of a V.C. prisoner.

In the script, the conceit of the training film keeps breaking down. One moment, the steely-nerved leader, O.D. (Richard Brooks), is brusquely shoving Mopic away. But, shortly afterward, O.D. pays no attention, even though lens and microphone are hovering inches away while he: 1) confesses to the lieutenant that he pulled a gun on him, 2) taunts L.T. about the unlikelihood of a court martial without other officer witnesses and 3) promises to pull the trigger next time. (Talk about being comfortable in front of a camera. . . .)

Duncan's script keeps swinging back and forth between his initial idea of the mock *cinéma vérité* framework, a really brilliant notion, and much of the plot he has cooked up, which is heavy on archetypal war-movie stories. Duncan has an ear for grunt jargon. He is an award-winning writer (for TV's "Vietnam War Story") and a Vietnam infantry veteran—but he has obviously seen a lot of movies as well.

We get the baptism of fire ("Platoon" and its many antecedents), the G.I. community in tight quarters ("The Story of G.I. Joe," "A Walk in the Sun"), the squad picked off one by one on a dangerous mission ("Attack!" "Men in War"). And we also get prototypical characters: the wisecracker and the craven psycho (combined in Nicholas Cascone's Easy); the hipster delinquent (Christopher Burgard's Hammer), the Good ol' Boy, (Glenn Morshower's Cracker), the callowly ambitious officer (Jonathan Emerson's L.T.) and the hard-as-nails, soft-as-tears sergeant (Brooks' O.D.). Other than making the leader a black man, the movie isn't exactly unpredictable. There's a golden boy (Jason Tomlins' Pretty Boy) whose luck is obviously running out; you can tell by the way his voice cracks. And there are soldiers who buy it seconds after being told it's their last mission, and one more argument about shooting prisoners.

Duncan probably errs in one sense: believing he can make a Vietnam War movie without an overarching moral or mythic viewpoint, making himself into a camera, making a fiction that has the impersonality of truth caught on the fly. More than likely, he really wants to make a left-wing war film that won't offend Vietnam veterans by preaching or making silly mistakes. There *is* an attitude here, and you can see it readily in L.T.'s speech about the war being a great business opportunity and Cracker's about the Army being an equal-opportunity employer.

But what's different, and what gives "84 Charlie Mopic" its undeniable force and feeling, is the framework: the sheer intensity generated by the limited-camera setups, the long takes and the purposely abrupt pans within a scene, the absence of background music, and the ingenious sound recording (by Michael Moore and Craig Woods)—which gives us the eerie bright chirpiness of a forest laden with death. And, more than anything, the quiet, deliberately offhand rhythms of the acting. Duncan and his fine young cast sustain the mood of lassitude and paranoia beautifully. They put a deceptively still, nervy edge into this film that almost hypnotizes you. This, we gradually begin to feel, is what war must be like: a long wait in deadly sunlight, a walk with banality and terror, nerves and boredom followed by chaos and the dark.

NEW YORK, 4/3/89, p. 70, David Denby

The audience for *84 Charlie Mopic* will understand the terrors of jungle warfare in a way that few audiences for Vietnam movies ever have before. Another exciting independent production, the movie establishes a unique fictional situation: An Army cameraman joins a patrol in the Central Highlands in 1969, and we see only what the cameraman, gathering material for training films, takes in while hoisting his camera through the jungle. This tense, original movie, written and directed by Patrick Duncan, a Vietnam vet, draws strength from its limited point of view. We are stuck inside the skull of a single observer, trapped and isolated in a frightening way that we couldn't be in a normal movie that uses the resources of multiple angles and editing to get the best possible view. When a bullet comes flying out of the jungle and one of the soldiers drops, writhing in the mud, the camera swings his way wildly; the absence of warning is terrifying.

I don't mind that *84 Charlie Mopic* is essentially a conceit; in fact, I would have preferred that the gimmick be extended even further. I longed for a scene, for instance, in which the cameraman gets himself out in front of the riflemen and faces the VC in the bush unprotected. The only trouble with the film is that dropping conventional cinematic technique as it does, it's still too theatrical. Too much of the dialogue, for all its profanity, has a pre-processed sound, and Duncan has constructed a rather conventional clash between a new platoon leader—a callow second lieutenant (Jonathan Emerson) who sees the war as an opportunity for career advancement—and the tough, resourceful black sergeant (Richard Brooks) whom the men trust to keep them alive. What's best in *84 Charlie Mopic* is the most intimate perceptions—the men's lonely self-protecting rituals and fetishes, the incantations murmured at dawn and again, gratefully, as night falls.

NEW YORK POST, 3/22/89, p. 29, Jami Bernard

We need another Vietnam picture like we need a shrapnel wound, but fortunately, "84 Charlie Mopic" provides a substantially different kind of experience. It succeeds in creating a gripping drama without the kind of faceless, stock-footage bloodlettings we have come to expect from most of the genre.

A camera detail is assigned to follow a small Army reconnaisance team into the jungle, to record the mission and make a training film for the green recruits back home. The trick here is that the entire movie is presented from a hand-held, point-of-view camera, like a cinema verite documentary made under duress. The word "mopic" stands for motion picture, and what we see on the screen is ostensibly the raw footage of that training film in progress.

When the cameraman stumbles, so does the camera; the audience has to reckon with the camera as a presence in the movie and to identify with the cameraman behind it.

The goal of the training film is "to record procedures peculiar to this situation." The members of the company greet this intrusion with mixed emotions on one hand; lugging a heavy piece of whirring equipment through the underbrush can be a liability. On the other hand, being part of a movie is a welcome diversion from the boring, agonizing down-time between skirmishes.

Some members of the company are initially shy. Others prove that the urge to mouth "Hi, mom" when a camera is pointed at you is universal. One soldier named Easy, the one who's "short" (meaning he has the least time left to serve), makes wisecracks. OD, the unit's hard-boiled commander, seethes into the lens; it wasn't his idea to take this show on the road.

Eventually, the men oblige with awkward little interviews. They demonstrate how to wire and defuse booby traps, how to load a rifle, how to bury garbage so you can't be tracked, the importance of dry socks. ("During a monsoon, dry socks are better than sex.")

And as they talk, they reveal much about themselves and about the wartime bond that results years later in movies like this (writer/director Patrick "I Was There" Duncan is this year's Oliver Stone).

A cabinetmaker's son tells of how a customer asked that a beautiful piece of black walnut be painted over, which his father did, painting it "whiter than milk," to show how he views his orders in "the Nam." You do the job, and you do it well. Who said anything about right or wrong?

Another tells of how he was able to place a call back home to his wife, and how after she got over the surprise of hearing from him, they had nothing to say. "There was dead silence, not word one."

"84 Charlie Mopic" packs an emotional wallop, and it does so without two staples of the Vietnam movie. One is the pounding '60s soundtrack; the only music these men hear in the jungle is a minute or so of tinny Donovan, tuned in on the shortwave radio. The rest of the time, they are alert only to the snapping of twigs and other potentially hostile sounds. After a while, so is the audience.

There is also an absence of Victor Charlie. The enemy is glimpsed only occasionally, at a distance, through the brush. We may not see the enemy, but evidence of him abounds—tripwires, sharp stakes along the side of the trail. The view we get of this Army unit is very insular.

These choices are the work of director Duncan, whose personal vision rules as completely as the largely unseen cameraman who is getting all this down for his training film. Duncan's take on the war is unique enough to personalize the film.

Duncan also largely steers clear of the morality play that was central to "Platoon." The tug at the heart of "Mopic" is not between good and evil, but between being a soldier and staying alive.

The carnage scenes are left to the last third of the picture, but the scene that really drives home the horror of war is when the commander of the unit gently and lovingly wraps the stillwarm corpse of one of his men into a body-bag. That scene tells more about what it was like to lose a buddy than all the revenge flicks put together.

The script, although containing the obligatory "lock and load" macho stuff, is also nicely idiosyncratic. The "short" guy jokes that he's so short, he could parachute off a dime. Later, reflective, but with the same protective sarcasm, he explains, "When you get short, you get paranoid, *beaucoup*."

Of the seven roles, two stand out. Richard Brooks, as the sturdy, compassionate commander, also happens to be black. I wouldn't mention that except it was refreshing to find a black lead where race is not a big plot device.

Also, edgy and ingratiating is Nicholas Cascone as Easy, the "short" guy whose jokes barely conceal his anxiety.

"84 Charlie Mopic" derives its power from personal drama.

NEWSDAY, 3/22/89, Part II/p. 7, Drew Fetherston

Judged by its own standards and stated aim, "84 Charlie Mopic" is a thorough success.

"My goal is to show the audience what happened to the young men in the Vietnam conflict," writer/director Patrick Duncan has written. "Not on a soul-searching level, but what physically happened to them."

This mission, and more, is accomplished. Though only a veteran could judge the claim of authenticity, the audience certainly gets a harrowing plunge into the bush with a six-man American reconnaissance unit. It is, for film, an unusually unsentimental view of war, presented in daring fashion: Everything is seen through the hand-held camera of an all-but-unseen character, an Army combat cameraman assigned to document the patrol for a training film.

It's not a new technique, but "84 Charlie Mopic" carries it to its logical extreme: The characters speak to the person behind the camera, recognize that they are being filmed, alter their behavior at times to make it fit to be seen by others. There's no music track. The method has perils, and "84 Charlie Mopic"—the title is the miliary designation of the film-within-the-film, Mopic being shorthand for motion picture—does not escape unscathed.

It probably is impossible to counterfeit documentary reality, even with a good cast of unknown actors. Professional actors, trained to wring everything possible from each word and gesture, here supply verisimilitude, but fall short of absolute, unaffected authenticity. By striving for documentary realism, Duncan alerts every viewer to watch for slipups. To make sense, the characters must introduce themselves and reveal their histories, but this costs some realism. Dramatic effect also demands compromises; the soldiers sometimes are crazy about keeping silent; at other times they make noise without evident concern. Some of the night scenes would have been impossible to capture on film.

Still, the device is used to good effect, and overall it is well maintained. The personalities of the soldiers emerge from what they do and say to each other, from the minutiae of daily life on a patrol in enemy territory. They never emerge fully—that would have required major departures from the technique—but gradually they become known and familiar.

The dynamics of the group are particularly convincing; the complex bonds that link the men (who are themselves satisfyingly complex) are nicely rendered.

The film neither shrinks from violence nor dwells upon it. Some of the action takes place at the periphery of the camera's vision, or, indeed, behind the camera. Some events are missed simply because the cameraman has fallen down. But when killing and suffering take place within the camera's vision, it does not blink.

Everything is confused, as it should be. The cameraman is excess baggage; nobody on the patrol explains much to him. Their only concern is that he not get them discovered and killed. So they discuss their plans in terms known only to the initiate; the cameraman follows through the undergrowth, bent-over but still filming. The pacing is realistically ragged; bouts of wild action interperse slow scenes of silent movement.

"84 Charlie Mopic" succeeds beyond its self-drawn perimeter of literal realism. It is a good, professional effort that takes risks and casualties but gets its job done. It is a gut experience that, despite Duncan's disclaimer, still opens some souls to the audience's view.

NEWSWEEK, 4/3/89, p. 67, David Ansen

There have been more shattering, more ambitious and more stylish films about the Vietnam War, but Patrick Duncan's low-budget job captures better than any of them the nuts-and-bolts reality of jungle warfare. As we follow a six-man reconnaissance team into the Central Highlands, we gain a graphic familiarity with not only the men but with the objects and strategies vital to their survival: the radio that is their only lifeline to the outside world; the body bags; the gum wrappers and cigarette butts that can betray your location. Every piece of equipment has its use, and its danger.

Duncan has chosen an unconventional strategy to convey his claustrophobically intimate view of warfare: the entire film is seen through the eyes of an Army cameraman, sent along to document the mission for the benefit of future troops. (Mopic is short for motion picture.) We see only what his camera records. This proves both fascinating and frustrating, for the viewer can't escape into the protection—and visual relief—of an omniscient narrator. "84 Charlie Mopic" deliberately refrains from any political or philosophical overview and thus stands as an implicit rebuke to the

Manichaean symbolism of "Platoon." Duncan, a vet himself, writes pungent, profane dialogue, and he gets some remarkable performances from his largely unknown cast—particularly Richard Brooks as the black commanding sergeant. True to tradition, the least sympathetic is the highest ranked, the career officer who sees war as an opportunity for advancement. After his harrowing mission he may change his mind. In Duncan's tense, grueling view of war, there is great courage but no glory.

TIME, 4/17/89, p. 83, Richard Schickel

We have been soldiering with this lost patrol since we were kids: the gruff but caring sergeant, preternaturally wise in the ways of the enemy and the equally hostile terrain; the street wisecracking kid; the slow-drawling bumpkin; a man called Hammer and another called Pretty Boy. And, of course, a lieutenant who is both green and ambitious and therefore more dangerous to friend than foe. Such characters have been AWOL from most movies about Viet Nam, and *84 Charlie Mopic* would have curiosity value if it only brought them back and restored them to their chief role: demonstrating the masculine need for bonding.

What gives this film a somewhat higher value is the addition of one new character. "84 Charlie Mopic" is an Army term for a documentary cameraman, and all of this film was shot on super-16 mm, as if through his lens. But Mopic provides more than the title; he is responsible for the film's unique point of view. There is no editing in the formal sense. In the field the cameraman must pan from face to face to cover a scene and use his zoom for close-ups. Tracking shots are handheld, often on the run. Sequences end when the cameraman decides to shut off—or when he runs out of film. We see Mopic only fleetingly, when, for laughs or in a final desperate moment, his comrades turn his camera on him.

This mostly unseen star is played by Byron Thames, but special citations must go to Richard Brooks, Nicholas Cascone and Glenn Morshower, as his most sharply delineated subjects. It is, however, first-time director Duncan's raw technique that jolts, transforms and grants powerful immediacy to basically banal material. In these bland days, more famous directors, operating on bigger budgets, are not managing to do as well.

VILLAGE VOICE, 3/28/89, p. 60, Georgia Brown

My father, an ex-tank battalion commander, refuses to see war movies on the principle that they never get "it" right. Once someone persuasive dragged him to *Patton*—Patton was one of the generals he served under—but couldn't make him stay awake.

If I read Viet vet Patrick Duncan right, he thinks war movies are crap as far as representing war goes. On the program notes for *84 Charlie Mopic*, writer/director Duncan is quoted as saying, "I don't want to work out any good versus evil mythic symbolism in my film." (Could he be talking about the celebrated *Platoon*?) "I wanted to make the most intimate war film that could possibly be made." One translation of this might be: No one would see it and enlist. Has there been a war movie yet that wasn't good for recruitment? *84 Charlie Mopic* could be the first. It scared the daylight out of me.

Mopic's conceit is that it is an on-site training film in the making. In Vietnam's central highlands, a reconnaissance team going into the bush to locate enemy buildups takes along a cameraman to document its operation. This mock-documentary is the visual equivalent of a notebook novel—daily life minutiae make it tick. The job of the eponymous cameraman (the film's title is taken from his ID badge) is to record details, to get "it" down.

The opening title is written in sand, so to speak, drawn with a bayonet in the dirt at an army base, as Mopic starts his film by having members of the six-man recon team introduce themselves. The unit's new leader, a lieutenant fresh out of training callled L.T. (Jonathan Emerson), has a speech prepared, stumbles over his lines, and goes blank. A voluble wiseguy called Easy (Nicholas Cascone)—the unit's requisite New Yorker—horses around, and for a time his compulsive mugging and chatter make him into a narrator of sorts. "Don't look at me," Mopic instructs one subject, "look at the camera." Joke: The guy's eyes shyly shift to what is obviously the body of the camera, not the lens. The unit's seasoned mainstay, a tall, severe black sergeant known as O.D. (Richard Brooks), hardly keen on the movie business, stiff-arms the camera, "Get that thing outta my face." Conflict between O.D., the skilled warrior, and L.T., the unit's only college boy and a jungle ingenue, has already kindled. (Defending his use of stock characters and this rather worn plot, Duncan told a screening audience, "Clichés happen to be true.")

Mopic trains his lens on lowly details. There's the diligent application of foot powder, for example. Pretty Boy (Jason Tomlins) shows how he takes care of his socks. Rations come in bright foil packs. When Mopic sees someone taking a pill before his meal, he asks what it is. Tetracycline for the clap. Easy, showing off, flashes his stash at the camera; the no-nonsense O.D. spots this and scatters the contents on the ground. "I'll come back in six months and harvest it," complains Easy. Talk tends to be crude and generally witless. (Riddle: "What's the difference between fish and meat?" Answer: "You beat your fish and it'll die." This happens to be one of the jollier lines.) But it doesn't take long for lessons to turn somber, for Mopic to record the proper, reverent way of dressing one of the men in a body bag—inserting dog tags in the mouth before sealing shut the lips with duct tape.

Shot in just 16 days near Magic Mountain outside L.A., *Mopic* is visually, certainly scenically, myopic. The subjective camera keeps its focus inside the unit—no vistas, long shots, or overheads, just the characterless nearby vegetation. And since this doesn't, in the way of conventional war movies, show the enemy creeping up (or tip you off with tension music), there's no real letup to anxiety. Sound, too, stays naturalistic. (If Duncan couldn't afford the obligatory array of '60s tunes, he makes a case for not using them.) Once, the radio picks up a Donovan song on Armed Forces Radio; it also, chillinghly, makes contact with a fellow unit while it's in the process of being wiped out.

At night O.D. rigs an alarm system as primitive as one out of a Cub Scout manual—strings with tin cans precariously balanced. Moving through underbrush, soldiers have to be alert for nearly invisible trip wires attached to deadly explosives. If they're really quiet, they hear VC before VC hear them. (First blood: A soldier hits the deck into a trap where a sharpened stalk punctures his arm.) What becomes almost immediately apparent is that luck—known variously as "karma, voodoo, or God"—is the only flimsy armor these poor souls have been issued, and they know it. One soldier, preoccupied with reading omens as a means of staving off panic, becomes convinced he has now inherited the luck of his buddy who's just been ambushed; you can see it begin to dawn on him that, if true, this make him dead.

Duncan's narrative strategy intentionally violates conventional rhythm, in which violent episodes are balanced with lulls, soft spots, for character development. Character here barely has time to develop, although O.D.'s heroism comes through clear. This booby trap school of filmmaking tries to throw off viewer timing by making the usual safe places lethal.

Indicating how inapplicable the old rules are may be one way of simulating both the narrow and the wider Viet debacle, but it's futile for the movie to make too many claims—claims that just as easily distract viewers by rendering them attentive to all the glaring impossibilities: When's the film going to run out? Where's the sound equipment? How come these guys can talk loud when the enemy's out there? Mopic—a fiction, after all—can't escape being "another war movie," but in its feisty, frugal way it may be the scariest look yet at the horror of soldiering in Vietnam. I'd call it the movie most likely to make you thank God if you weren't there and praise those who were.

Also reviewed in:
NEW REPUBLIC, 4/24/89, p. 24, Stanley Kauffmann
NEW YORK TIMES, 3/22/89, p. C 24, Richard Bernstein
VARIETY, 1/25–31/89, p. 15
WASHINGTON POST, 5/2/89, p. C7, Hal Hinson

EMMA'S SHADOW

An Angelika Films release of a Metronome Film production with the Danish Film Institute. *Producer:* Tivi Magnusson. *Director:* Soeren Kragh-Jacobsen. *Screenplay (Danish with English subtitles):* Soeren Kragh-Jacobsen and Joern O. Jensen. *Director of Photography:* Dan Laustsen. *Editor:* Leif Axel Kjeldsen. *Music:* Thomas Lindahl. *Sound:* Morten Degnbol. *Art Director:* Lars Nielsen. *Costumes:* Jette Termann. *Make-up:* Birte Christiansen. *Running time:* 98 minutes. *MPAA Rating:* Not Rated.

CAST: Line Kruse (Emma); Borje Ahlstedt (Malthe Eliasson); Henrik Larsen (Emma's Father); Inge Sofie

Skovbo (Emma's Mother); Ulla Henningsen (Malthe's Lady Friend); Bent Nalepa Steinert (Gustav); Ken Vedsegaard (Albert); Otto Brandenburg (Eatery Owner); Jesper Christiansen (Chauffeur); Eric Wedersoe (Chief of Detectives).

NEW YORK POST, 9/29/89, p. 23, Jami Bernard

Inspired by an overheard conversation about the Lindbergh baby kidnapping, Emma, an 11-year-old poor little rich girl in 1930s Copenhagen, stages her own abduction to rouse her parents from their emotional torpor in "Emma's Shadow," a sweet, touching Danish film debuting today at downtown's new Angelika Film Center.

Emma (Line Kruse) is a lonely rebel, finding solace within her parents' stark void of a home by fantasizing about her aunt Mogga, a Russian noblewoman who—as the glamorous family history goes—narrowly escaped the Bolsheviks.

Emma's "kidnapping" gets off to a lonely start when Malthe, a simple Swedish sewer worker and ex-con, knocks her down as he's running from neighborhood hecklers. Malthe takes Emma in, treats her scraped knee and seems to accept Emma's story—that she is Mogga, on the run from the Bolsh...Bol...well, whatever they're called.

The two form an unlikely friendship that is closer than any they've had before. After all, Malthe is ridiculed and preyed on by his co-workers and his drunken landlady, and Emma's only companion previously was a kitten, which her mother tossed out.

Emma and Malthe look out for each other in their own ways—Emma intercedes when people make fun of Malthe, Malthe is the first adult to take a genuine interest in the little girl.

"Emma's Shadow" is slow and lyrical, with a quiet, graceful rhythm that you'd never find in a Hollywood picture in which there is even a hint of kidnapping. The mother's emotional aloofness is demonstrated by her langorous afternoon massages; the father's by his reaction to a routine question by police investigators. "What sort of child is she? Is she happy?" they ask, and the father, truly baffled but not stupidly so, recoils.

Borje Ahlstedt plays a heartbreakingly touching Malthe, a slow-witted, good-hearted drunk whose life is a series of heavy, inevitable persecutions.

And Line Kruse is spectacular as the lonely, bratty child, her wide forehead creased in confusion or smooth with triumph, her nose and chin jutting out with determination, uplifted with affection, downtilted with shame. The ending provokes an unexpected gasp of something horribly familiar.

The Danes are having a good couple of seasons here, what with "Babette's Feast" and "Pelle the Conqueror." With the addition of "Emma's Shadow," there seems to be an emphasis on spirit and humanity flowering amid an emotional tundra. It's a welcome thaw.

NEWSDAY, 9/29/89, Part III/ p. 5, Mike McGrady

Sometimes a movie grows on you slowly. During the opening scenes of "Emma's Shadow," I was charmed but a bit fidgety; it seemed a cute idea, little more. The setting is Denmark in the early 1930s, and the entire world is caught up in the fever surrounding the kidnaping of the Lindbergh baby. The starting point: Poor-little-rich-girl Emma is startled to overhear her mother express concern over the kidnaped baby—"It must be terrible to lose your most precious possession."

Most precious possession? If Emma is, indeed, her parents most precious possession, they've maintained that secret well. In fact, both parents are too busy to take much note of Emma. The father is forever on the phone dealing deals, while his beautifully coiffed wife pampers herself with visiting masseuses and all the modern gadgets of a new age.

Emma, ignored and spoiled, is the kind of brat who airily discards soiled clothes wherever she happens to find herself. Cruel to the servants, disdainful of all "the proles," she is heard snapping at the scullery maid: "Any fool can do the kind of woman's work you do."

Seemingly on a whim, the uncharming Emma stages her own kidnaping, constructing a ransom note from newspaper headlines, then stealing off to the wrong side of the tracks. Engaging, but my mind still felt free to wander—possibly because Emma seemed spoiled beyond redemption.

But from the very instant Emma's unlikely rescuer appears, the film begins to take hold. Malthe (Borje Ahlstedt)—unshaven, unwashed, inarticulate—is a crude sewer worker, a bear of a man who offers the child a plate of hot food and a bed for the night. Emma borrows the life story of favorite aunt and explains to Malthe that she is a Russian of royal birth fleeing the Bolsheviks: "They killed my nanny. Actually, they shot my whole family."

And at this point, as this grizzled, lice-ridden hulk and the cunning little rich girl connect and begin to help one another, the film grabs full attention. Emma, noting that Malthe is bullied by everyone, including girlfriend and co-workers, prods him into standing up and fighting back. If Malthe learns courage from his guest, Emma learns about generosity and selflessness from him. This impoverished sewer rat manifests more genuine affection for her in a few days than her parents have managed in a lifetime.

Malthe brings the rich girl into his life, and she reciprocates by introducing him to her world— with terribly touching results all around. Her ransom money gets Malthe a new suit of clothes and a suite at the Grand Hotel, where he and two local urchins are exposed to such extravagances as a telephone, a radio, a hot shower and a lavish feast. Malthe, high on Dom Perignon, observes, "That night we bumped into each other, that was my lucky night."

Not entirely. Hot-on-the-trail police are understandably convinced that Malthe is a kidnaper. A more profound excitement comes from the ever-deepening relationship between the two central figures. Nor are they alone in their involvement. By the time it reaches its superb windup, the film has made an almost mystical connection with the viewer. And the involvement doesn't end with the film's conclusion. "Emma's Shadow" won't let you go; it comes back to haunt you long after the final fade to black.

VILLAGE VOICE, 8/22/89, p. 86, Georgia Brown

The title *Emma's Shadow,* which sounds like the name of a racehorse, obviously loses something in the translation from the Danish. I'm not sure what it means, but Soeren Kragh-Jacobsen's gentle fairy tale is set in the shadowy interiors of Copenhagen in the '30s. Emma (Line Kruse) is a striking, blond 11-year-old, a poor little rich girl whose aloof socialite parents have no time for their only child. In desperation, she uses her wits and joins an underworld richer than what her parents can offer.

A motorized plastic massage tool is shown inching over Mama's pale skin; the spunky Emma is out muddying her lace gloves and stockings while buying a black kitten from a foundry worker. When Mama discovers the kitten, she turns it over to a kitchen maid, who in turn offers it to two errand boys—whom Emma then denounces as "proles with lice." Making enemies of the servants, who see her as a spoiled brat, Emma has no allies.

Eavesdropping on one of her parents' soirees, she overhears the adults lamenting the kidnapping of the Lindbergh baby. Her usually pouty, glazed-over mother seems all sympathy for the poor Lindberghs losing "their most prized possession." Thinking to evoke the same concern, Emma stages her own kidnapping. She runs away from her chauffeur and wanders about until meeting up with Malthe (Borje Ahlstedt), a Swedish ex-con and sewer worker with a strong stench, as well as lice and fleas.

Emma's Shadow is photographed in rich tones used to suggest the period (cinematography by Dan Laustsen). Most of the sets are interiors. Emma's home is pristine and stark, but once she finds Malthe, she seems to inhabit a nighttime world, filled with shadows, cushions, and rags (harboring the lice). lit softly by his kerosene lamp. This mild and tasteful fantasy has sexual undertones, but studiously avoids the kinkiness it keeps suggesting.

Malthe has liquid, hound dog eyes (Ahlstedt looks like Mickey Rourke with a few years and a few pounds), and he's a gentle, simpleminded creature, passive while being tormented by fellow workers and by his landlady, Ruth, who wants him to herself. Ruth and Emma become rivals for Malthe, but he clearly prefers the youug one to the one his age. Not that Emma's less demanding. She orders him around too; a master-servant relation seems to both their likings.

That *Emma's Shadow* avoids the obvious tragic ending it seems headed for—where Malthe would be killed by the police defending Emma—is to its credit. Instead, the denouement is touching and would probably be appreciated by children. I kept waiting for the lice to itch, but they seem not to affect blonds.

Also reviewed in:

NEW YORK TIMES, 9/29/89, p. C20, Stephen Holden

VARIETY, 2/10/88, p. 10

ENEMIES, A LOVE STORY

A Twentieth Century Fox release of a Morgan Creek production. *Executive Producer:* James G. Robinson and Joe Roth. *Producer:* Paul Mazursky. *Director:* Paul Mazursky. *Screenplay:* Roger L. Simon and Paul Mazursky. *Based on the novel by:* Isaac Bashevis Singer. *Director of Photography:* Fred Murphy. *Editor:* Stuart Pappé. *Music:* Maurice Jarre. *Music Editor:* Dan Carlin Sr. *Sound:* Don Cohen and (music) Bobby Fernandez. *Sound Editor:* John Stacy and David A. Whittaker. *Production Designer:* Pato Guzman. *Art Director:* Steven J. Jordan *Set Dresser:* Gilles Aird. *Special Effects:* Jacques Godbout. *Costumes:* Albert Wolsky. *Make-up:* David Craig Forrest. *Running time:* 118 minutes. *MPAA Rating:* R.

CAST: Ron Silver (Herman); Anjelica Huston (Tamara); Lena Olin (Masha); Margaret Sophie Stein (Yadwiga); Alan King (Rabbi Lembeck); Judith Malina (Masha's Mother); Rita Karin (Mrs. Schreier); Phil Leeds (Pesheles); Elya Baskin (Yasha Kotick); Paul Mazursky (Leon Tortshiner); I.J. Dollinger (Reb Nissen Yaroslaver); Zypora Spaisman (Sheva Haddas); Arthur Grosser (Doctor); Burney Lieberman (Yom Kippur Cantor); Nathaniel Katzman (Wedding Cantor); Gayle Garfinkle (Mrs. Lembeck); Shelley Goldstein (Mrs. Regal); Henry Bronchtein (Benny); Howard Rushpan (Onlooker); Doris Gramovot (Yadwiga's Neighbor); Vera Miller (Masha's Neighbor); Shimon Aviel (Windbag); Jacob Greenbaum (Rabbi at Catskills); Rhona Shekter (Rabbi's Wife); Bobby Pierson (Rhumba Instructor); Edward Sebic (Fitness Instructor); Shirley Merovitz (Catskill Woman); Robin Bronfman (Catskill Woman); Tyrone Benskin (Cabbie); Rummy Bishop (Waiter at Dairy Restaurant); Brian Dooley (Man on Ladder); Kevin Fenlon (Desk clerk); Manal Hassib (Hooker); Libby Owen (Cashier); Sam Sperber (Violinist); Tommy Canary (Cotton Candy Man); Terry Clark (Beach Acrobat); Wally Roberts (Barker); Mark Robinson (Snowcone Vendor); Joe Viviani (Newsstand Vendor); Michael Dunetz (Customer); Mick Muldoon (Doorman).

FILMS IN REVIEW, 3/90, p. 170, Edmond Grant

Numerous movies have been made in which one man has to choose between several different ideal women. But *Enemies, A Love Story*, based on the novel by Isaac Bashevis Singer, is more, much more than that simple plot description.

What it is is a slice of life. An uncommon life, to be sure, but one that contains elements which are the stuff of fantasy, such as the choice of women, and others which come straight out of a nightmare. Like the literal nightmare which opens the film and the attendant paranoid visions that haunt the protagonist, Herman Broder (Ron Silver). Herman survived the Holocaust without imprisonment, and now (the "now" here being 1949) lives in Coney Island with the loving but terrifyingly subservient Yadwiga (Margaret Sophie Stein). Yadwiga, it turns out, saved Herman's life in Europe when she hid him in a hayloft; then his servant, she is now his wife. What she doesn't know is that he's got a mistress, Masha (Lena Olin), an unhappily married concentration camp survivor who loves Herman with wild abandon and does know about "that peasant." And, as if Herman's attentions weren't already divided, he soon finds out that his wife (Anjelica Huston), whom he believed had died in the camps, is alive and living on the Lower East Side. Masha subsequently announces that she is pregnant, so, since his other (current) marriage is not in the Jewish faith, he marries Masha in a religious ceremony, thereby giving him, for all intents and purposes, three spouses at once.

Director-screenwriter Paul Mazursky and his co-scripter Roger L. Simon handle all of the silly ramifications of Herman's situation with deft skill. There is no air of farce in these proceedings, no moments where all three women are "juggled" at the same location by the male lead, or where all three encounter each other in a public setting.

Mazursky has always been a filmmaker who knows when to go for the laugh, and when to just let the story unfold and the characters' contradictions emerge. In any ordinary movie about a man involved with more than one woman, the man is always a Casanova who has no real feeling for the women he uses, and who usually winds up an emotional wreck (*Alfie* is the best example of this scenario). As conceived by Singer, and executed by Mazursky and Simon, Herman is a tortured individual who tries to love to keep on living; he does actually feel for all three women, he just can't decide what to do.

Further, all three women embody one particular element for Herman, elements which, if taken together, would indeed compose the "ideal woman" for most men. Tamara is his past, a woman whom he has shared experiences with and can talk to at length about his problems. Though a victim herself, she is also a listener, who really does want the best for him. Yadwiga is the old-fashioned sort of wife whose entire existence is chained to that of her man and her duties around the house. Of the three, she is the most blissfully innocent of the pain that life inflicts; she also must be a little slow not to catch on to Herman's other major affair. And finally Masha is the sensual woman, always ready to physically love Herman. Though Tamara suffered the most in the death camps, it is Masha who is one of the walking wounded, an individual who suffers manic depressive swings from happiness to complete despair.

And thus the perfection of this creation. Mazursky is able to convey all of Singer's complex themes with a minimum of high tragedy and an excess of vivid characterization. In this regard, the actors all distinguish themselves. Silver, who has gone from sitcom characters to roles of great complexity and keeps getting better and better, plays Herman not as a heel or an outright victim, but as a confused man who has some very nice fringe benefits but never will be able to enjoy his existence. Alan King scores nicely in his brief turn as the class-conscious rabbi who employs Herman as his ghost writer, but most attention is rightly focused on the actresses who play Herman's three loves. Stein has the unglamorous role, but she does invest her character with sensitivity and compassion. Both Anjelica Huston and Lena Olin do remarkable work as two women who have survived hell, and are not certain what part, if any, Herman should play in their future. Huston's characterization subtly shifts as the film goes on, as Tamara becomes a friend and companion to Yadwiga as well as Herman (although at the end the ex-servant still addresses her as "Mistress Tamara"). Olin's character here is much like the one she played in *The Unnatural Lightness Of Being*. Both are highly emotionally and primally erotic.

The cast operate in a wonderfully vivid recreation of New York, circa 1949–50 (shot, like most contemporary American films, in Canada), which Mazursky carefully uses to situate the film firmly in the past, while avoiding the temptation to indulge in nostalgia for that period.

As a body of work, and of course with certain bigger budgeted exceptions (*Down And Out In Beverly Hills*), Mazursky's films have always stressed the personal, indulging in sentiment without becoming saccharine. In certain ways, his concerns and methods are that of an independent filmmaker—witness here the way he underscores Silver's answering a late night phone call with shaky handheld camerawork that is straight out of the work of John Cassavetes. At his best, as he is here, he is able to draw very real characters, who aren't entirely likeable, but are, more importantly, identifiable and realistic.

LOS ANGELES TIMES. 12/12/89, Calendar/p. 1, Sheila Benson

You might hope that the pairing of Isaac Bashevis Singer, a writer who couples eroticism with wisdom, and Paul Mazursky, whose best films have been both juicy and insightful, would be a good one. But who could have predicted this?

"Enemies, A Love Story" is stunning, a richly satisfying, perfectly realized film. Although there are still a few more movies to see before the season's end, this one may be the year's finest and most complex; clearly it's the best of Mazursky's career. But it's something more, the brilliant dovetailing of a writer's intentions and a film maker's mature craft.

There's the same wholeness of understanding here that permeated the best of John Huston's films, "The African Queen" or "Fat City" or "The Dead"; adaptations that felt so full and so right that when you re-read the books, the characters and the actors merged. Now Mazursky, who co-adapted this screenplay with Roger L. Simon, has found in Singer his perfect author and the pleasure is all ours.

The time is 1949, the place is New York; more specifically the corners of New York that have become havens for Jewish refugees from Hitler's deviltry. In Coney Island we find Herman Broder (Ron Silver), who eluded the Nazis by hiding in the hayloft of a Polish farm but whose nightmares about his ordeal are far from behind him. With him is his blond Polish wife Yadwiga (Margaret Sophie Stein), his family's former servant, who saved his life and whom he has since married, as much from gratitude as anything else.

In the Bronx lives Herman's passionate mistress Masha (Lena Olin, she of the bowler hat in "Unbearable Lightness of Being"), who with her mother (Judith Malina) has survived the camps. And soon on the scene is the first of the shocks to Herman's somewhat jangled system: Tamara (Anjelica Huston), his first wife, whom eyewitnesses had reported shot by the Nazis and dumped into a pit with hundreds of other bodies. Although their two children were lost in the camps, Tamara has returned to life, acerbic as ever, and has emigrated to Manhattan's Lower East Side.

One note is common to these survivors: a sense of being dead among the living. Even though Herman avoided the camps, the same miasma grips him too; pain at the loss of his children possibly complicated by guilt at *not* having been captured. Only Yadwiga is exempt; stubborn and optimistic, she is the film's positive spirit.

A man in whose body sensuality and intelligence are in constant civil war, Herman tries to keep up with the demands of all three women with *relative* openness. He tells Tamara and Masha, the two most able to cope with the news, of the other's existence. The pathologically jealous Masha believes none of it; Tamara sophisticated and unflappable, isn't surprised to learn he has a mistress, "What can you talk about with Yadwiga?" she says, sensibly.

The danger, of course, in telling even a snippet of "Enemies'" plot is that mentioning Herman's serial wives and sweethearts may make it sound like an ethnic "Worth Winning," one of the nastier ideas of the decade. "Enemies" is actually dark farce told in carefully detailed character studies, which rely entirely on the actors' perfect pitch to keep them airborne.

Well, casting and subtle performance were always Mazursky's long suits, yet even for him this cast is exceptional. At first glance, the biting, ironic brilliance of Anjelica Huston's Tamara seems to be the film's strongest asset, a performance which makes her Academy Award-winning Maerose in "Prizzi's Honor" seem anemic by comparison. It still seems to be the film's most informative creation: watching her we learn everything about caste, aristocracy and a life-long sense of loss.

However, there is also Lena Olin's mercurial Masha, playful, haunted, at peace only in one scene. Masha is an even more adept liar than Herman and certainly his equal in sensuality. In her hilarious comic sequence, we see the dimensions to Maragaret Sophie Stein's gentle, long-suffering Yadwiga, whose strengths emerge slowly until she blossoms into someone far more forceful than a put-upon house wren.

But then you realize Ron Silver's complex shadings have made Herman the flint against which all three women strike fire. His life may be untenable, but if for a moment Herman becomes foolish in his moral confusion or if he becomes a scurrying wimp, the movie is lost. He never does; there's a deep, pained intelligence behind Silver's eyes; if finally, Herman Broder becomes as indecisive as Hamlet, he's no less interesting a man.

Swirling around them all is a second ring of characters, most notably the great comic-poignance of Judith Malina as Masha's mother, Phil Leeds as the crucial Mr. Pesheles, Mazursky as the hateful Leon Tortshiner and the slightly debatable theatricality of Alan King as Rabbi Lembeck.

Finally there is the sense of the city itself, conjured up by Mazursky's usual team of craftsmen, particularly his veteran production designer Pato Guzman, whose crowded apartments or melancholy beachfronts become the story's fifth character and his masterly costume designer Albert Wolsky, whose details for these 1949 clothes—crocheted snoods or cross-stitched peasant blouses—deliberately mirror a slightly earlier period that these refugees might still cling to.

Cinematographer Fred Baker uses a palette subtle as a hand-tinted postcard, and Maurice Jarre's addition of klezmer rhythms to his score gives it just the authentic buzz that's needed.

But it is Mazursky who has filled his teeming frame with these indelible faces, who sketches the activities at a Catskill resort with such affectionate satire and who so clearly understands the knife edge between laughter and tears on which Singer constantly balances. And it is Mazursky whose underlining at the close of "Enemies, A Love Story" (rated R for its steamy love scenes) gives it its soaring sense of continuity and healing.

MONTHLY FILM BULLETIN, 4/90, p. 103, Louise Sweet

New York, 1949. Concentration camp survivor Herman Broder lives in Coney Island with his second wife, Yadwiga, who used to be the family servant to Herman and his first wife Tamara, and their two children David and Sarah. Yadwiga saved Herman's life by sheltering him from the Nazis, while Tamara and the children apparently perished. Herman is simultaneously involved in a passionate affair with another camp survivor, Masha, separated from her husband and living with her mother in the Bronx. When the latter sees an advertisement in the paper trying to locate Herman, it turns out that it was placed by cousins of Tamara, who survived the war with a bullet lodged in her hip. Reunited, he tells her that he was married in a civil ceremony to the non-Jewish Yadwiga, and confesses that he has a mistress. Tormented when alone by nightmares of the war, and scrambling indecisively between Yadwiga (who serves his every need and wants to convert to Judaism) and Masha (who thinks she is pregnant), Herman finds that he is most at peace with Tamara. In order to obtain a divorce, Masha agrees to sleep again with her husband; the latter tells Herman, who breaks off with Masha and devotes himself to studying the Talmud and helping Yadwiga to convert. Yadwiga becomes pregnant, but despite Tamara's insistence that Herman remain with her, he cannot decide. Masha loses what the doctor diagnoses as a phantom six-month pregnancy; Herman marries Masha in a Jewish ceremony to the approval of his go-getter boss, Rabbi Lembeck, for whom Herman writes speeches and who has his own eye on Masha. Trying to comfort Masha when her mother, herself a survivor of the camps, dies, Herman agrees to commit suicide with her. But when he learns that Masha really did sleep with her former husband to obtain the divorce, he leaves in anger and subsequently disappears. Alone in her desolate apartment, Masha swallows the tablets. From different places, Herman sends money to Yadwiga, whose baby girl, named Masha, is cared for by her and Tamara.

Among his many gifts, Isaac Bashevis Singer can evoke the ambivalence, the half-life and the many shadings, the in-between states, of the human condition with a glancing, impish and accurate touch. Paul Mazursky has tackled *Enemies, A Love Story*, a film about characters—many of them survivors of the camps—indeed living in a kind of half-light, with obvious affection but also in a bolder, more head-on style. Conflicts are underscored as emphatically as the signs—Manhattan, the Bronx, Brooklyn—which mark Herman's indecisive rushing from subway to subway, each borough housing another compartment of his life. Around these, the scene-setting is equally signposted: at the beginning, the Nazis in their mint uniforms and conspicuous swastikas storming the barn where Yadwiga, the peasant girl, is sheltering Herman; then street life in Coney Island, 1949, rendered in bright artificial colours rather than shades of beige and grey.

In Singer's less primary-coloured world, credible ghosts and dybbuks also live amongst the furniture, in the cafés and delicatessens where men drink tea in glasses and read Yiddish papers (not *The New York Times*), symptoms of the furtiveness and displacement of the refugee, of people marginal to the material world. Despite the episodic style and the predictable filming of recollection and nightmare, in what is at once too fast-moving and overly long a film, some of the nuances of the material do emerge through the performances. Anjelica Huston, in particular, has a familiarity, a toughness and directness which allows her relationship with Herman to reveal something which stems not just from a shared past but which is on-going and to some extent genuinely unpredictable. With Tamara, not just a stereotypic survivor of the concentration camps, there is the capacity to transcend the half-life. She is allowed to feel love for but not dependence on the man she recognises as lost. With Masha (Lena Olin), who needs Herman to absolve her memories, the theme is passionate groping and lies; with Yadwiga (Margaret Sophie Stein), who remains a servant and dependant, it is tender boredom.

But the larger themes are all too evident: survivor guilt, making do yet the inability to make a unity of anything (self, belief, community). The film skims along, as if noting the signs of life in shorthand—a brief episode in the synagogue on Yom Kippur, shots of the neighbourhood market, signs in Hebrew, men in frock coats—failing to capture the layers, the patina of émigrés' lives. Given its bold style, the film is at its best when situations are at their most extreme: when the supposedly dead Tamara suddenly appears on Yadwiga's doorstep, and the peasant girl is not certain that she is not a ghost. But Mazursky's pacing and timing inevitably imposes a certain sit-com quality, and in the end the ensemble playing of *Bob and Carol and Ted and Alice* does not transfer well to the world of Herman and Tamara and Yadwiga and Masha.

NEW YORK, 12/18/89, p. 103, David Denby

In Paul Mazursky's superb *Enemies, A Love Story,* survivors of the Nazi Holocaust, washed up on the shores of New York in the late forties, look at the teeming, improbably prosperous society around them with a mixture of fearfulness and hope. The war is over and they can breathe—but they are afraid to breathe too deeply. Then they fill their lungs to bursting. Their actions are an inconsistent cross between habitual caution and wild abandon. Sex is the one thing they trust: It blots out the past and reaches to the future. Mazursky, adapting (with Roger L. Simon) Isaac Bashevis Singer's entertaining 1973 novel, has caught the healing spirit of Singer's lustfulness. I've never seen a movie that more convincingly presented sex as the life force at work.

Having been saved from the Nazis by his Polish servant, Mazursky's hero, Herman Broder (Ron Silver), lives with the adoring, subservient woman (Margaret Sophie Stein), now his wife, in lordly boredom in Coney Island. Clambering onto the IND, Herman, a down-at-the-heels literary man, leaves home and rushes to the Bronx to visit his passionate, crazy mistress (Lena Olin, in a magnificent performance). Then his haughty first wife (Anjelica Huston), whom he has long thought dead, shows up on the Lower East Side. He spends his life on the subway and in bed, the ultimate passive-aggressive male, loving and disappointing all three of them.

The period re-creation that Mazursky's team has put together is glowingly perfect down to the peculiar faded tones of the wallpaper in the dowdy apartments, the moldy, cabbagey, yet ebullient atmosphere of old-country Jewish households in the new World. Mazursky could have played the man-with-three-women situation for low farce. Instead, he plays it for the deepest feeling—gallantry and desperation at the edge of the grave. *Enemies* is a beautiful, full-bodies success.

NEW YORK POST, 12/13/89, p. 29, David Edelstein

One of the best things about Paul Mazursky's magnificent new film "Enemies: A Love Story" is that what it's "about" is so vast and imponderable that you can't quite believe how it bobs along so lightly, half sex-farce and half tragedy—a deceptively potent mix.

The movie, closely based on the novel by Isaac Bashevis Singer, centers on a Polish Jew named Herman Broder (Ron Silver), who has moved to Coney Island in the late '40s with his Gentile wife Yadwiga (Margaret Sophie Stein).

A servant of Broder's before the Nazi invasion, Yadwiga hid Herman in a hayloft for four years, taking him food and carrying out his excrement; as a result, Herman escaped the fate of his murdered wife and children. Out of gratitude he married Yadwiga, a simple girl who worships him and continues to behave as a servant—which suits the Jewish prince just fine.

Now Herman is a ghostwriter for a wealthy rabbi (Alan King) and spends many of his nights with a gorgeous and explosive mistress, Masha (Lena Olin), a concentration camp survivor who lives with her mother (Judith Malina) in the East Bronx. Over dinner, the three argue about the meaninglessness of life, after which Herman and Masha retire to the bedroom and make sweaty, ferocious love.

The plot, already complicated, becomes even more dizzying with the arrival from the dead of Herman's first wife, Tamara (Anjelica Huston), who crawled away from a heap of bodies with two bullets in her and spent years in a Soviet work camp.

Hope has been bled out of Tamara, who, even before the war, had grown accustomed to Herman's infidelities. She clearly loves him—if for no other reason as a reminder of when she was "alive"—yet reconciles herself to being his friend and confidante.

Unwilling to abandon the woman who saved his life, unable to give up the beauty whose nihilism and tumultuousness enthralls him, and strangely comfortable with the visitor from his former world, Herman writhes in indecision, scurrying from Brooklyn to the Lower East Side to The Bronx, refusing to be pinned down.

"Enemies" won't be pinned down, either. Mazursky has done something amazing—he has made a comedy about despair, about a man's inability to make a meaningful decision in a world he's convinced has no meaning. What complicates matters is that he's a jerk: he'd have some of these tendencies even if he hadn't lived through the holocaust.

Mazursky doesn't try to make Herman more attractive, and he keeps him inarticulate, dazed. For something more explicit you have to consult Singer, who writes of Herman's life as a game of stealth based on the precariousness of existence and impossibility of certainty. Herman insists on fidelity yet offers nothing in return; he forms deep attachments and then flees them, gasping for air.

Ron Silver doesn't make Herman's agony seem universal, the way a more titanic actor—a movie star—might have. But the performance is flawless and then some. Silver's Herman is fatally self-centered, doomed because he can't outgrow his rich-boy sense of entitlement. Even when he's torn up his mouth betrays a trace of smugness; like many Jewish princes, he revels in the depth of his own suffering.

Mazursky is at the peak of his artistry: Nothing, including the marvelous period detail and deep-focus, sepia-toned cinematography, feels labored. There are shots of Herman and Yadwiga on the boardwalk in Coney Island—Herman with his shirt hanging out over baggy pants—that seem so authentic you'll want to rush down and visit the neighborhood.

Apart from some awkward extras, Mazursky gets rich, incisive performances. Stein, a Polish actress living in New York, makes the obedient-dog Yadwiga an anxious mixture, regarding Herman less as a husband than a son. (After all, she gave him life.)

Olin has the same breathtaking sensuality she had in "The Unbearable Lightness of Being" but with something furious behind it—she's a moth in love with the flame that will incinerate her. She speaks in an uninflected, husky voice, almost a man's voice—rough and exhausted, yet capable still of animal moans and screeches. She shares with Herman the urge to act out her despair; what she doesn't share is his narcissism, which will keep him alive.

At first Huston's Tamara hobbles out of the shadows, wearing a look of hope that's swiftly extinguished by Herman's unease. Guarded and wisecracking thereafter, she can't help but let the sadness and anger bleed through her skin, mixing it with humor when it does. Huston's Tamara is the movie's emotional anchor—a great performance.

"Enemies" could be a farce, but the characters' pain is too real. Masha's moodiness is so spooky it wipes the smile off your face, and if Tamara is like a witty '40s second banana, she's one who has had her children murdered. These people have been to hell and are making up new rules in this new world—this amusement park called America with a God they no longer believe in and bonds they no longer trust.

From his window, Herman gazes at the ferris wheel of Coney Island and the words "Wonder Wheel" on its side. It's a funny, eerie sight gag—the kind of symbol that absorbs the movie's themes like a giant sponge and sits there, glowing. The tone can change from second to second—from ironic to compassionate to giddy to melancholy. This stupendous film is itself a wonder wheel.

NEWSDAY, 12/13/89, Part II/p. 2, Mike McGrady

Every so often a film comes along that has the feel of literature; in most such cases, the moviemakers have so admired an original novel that they have not compromised it during the transfer to film. Director Paul Mazursky's "Enemies, A Love Story" is just such a film, a film that seems more book than movie—loosely constructed and at times enigmatic, but rich in characterization, texture, mood, tone and meaning.

Ron Silver, Tony winner for "Speed-the-Plow" on Broadway and a delight in such offbeat movies as "Garbo Talks," has finally been given a film to challenge his talents. His Herman Broder is a Jewish writer who escaped the Nazis by hiding out in a hayloft and now, living in Coney Island in the year 1949, finds himself besieged by nightmares that carry him back to Poland and the war.

Broder also finds himself involved with three women. More than involved, actually. He has married Yadwiga (touchingly portayed by Polish actress Margaret Sophie Stein), the simple gentile peasant who shielded him from the Nazis during the war and who now waits on him hand and foot, going so far as to draw his bath and soap him down while he concentrates his energies on a perusal of the morning paper.

Broder's beautiful but mercurial mistress Masha (another fine performance by Lena Olin, remembered from "The Unforgettable Lightness of Being") is a survivor of Nazi death camps. When the temperamental Masha announces her pregnancy, she also insists on a temple wedding, despite Broder's civil marriage to Yadwiga.

"The Torah is such a great book," Broder moans. "How come it doesn't explain what a man should do with two wives?"

Whoops, make that *three* wives. Things become complicated, to say the least, when Broder's first Polish wife (Anjelica Huston), long presumed dead at the hands of the Nazis, suddenly reappears and makes contact with him. And complicated anew when two of the three wives announce simultaneous pregnancies. As pressure mounts, the Talmudically trained intellectual retreats to his familiar nightmare; once again, he is hiding in a hayloft while German soldiers accompanied by snarling dogs search the barn for Jews.

Broder is a strangely passive person who tells partial truths to each of his wives, but never reveals more than can be shown safely. His mistress is quite correct in observing, "The truth is you're still hiding in that hayloft."

All four central characters have endured the Holocaust, and all four carry scars. Broder's two young children were killed in the death camps, and it is no wonder that he lives his life as if no relationship can be permanent. He is, in fact, perpetually distracted, unable to make decisions. Mazursky, director of "Down and Out in Beverly Hills," has done a marvelous job of extracting all available humor from a situation that is, at heart, deadly serious. And, along with production designer Pato Guzman, he has beautifully recreated the geography and the feel of postwar New York.

If this were a book, it would not be a spellbinder, not a page-turner. It would be a character study, an evocative novel that gets its message across in the most subtle of ways. It would be, in sum, a book very much like the original Isaac Bashevis Singer novel, also titled "Enemies, A Love Story."

NEWSWEEK, 12/18/89, p. 69, David Ansen

Paul Mazursky's stunning movie of Isaac Bashevis Singer's "Enemies, a Love Story" achieves a complexity of feeling, a richness of tone that Hollywood movies rarely even try for. It's the most ambitious project Mazursky ("Blume in Love," "Down and Out in Beverly Hills") has tackled, and the darkest, but Mazursky doesn't get stiff with self-importance at the prospect of adapting a Nobel Prize-winning author. Singer's wonderful story has the structure of farce and the undertones of tragedy, and Mazursky mingles these quicksilver moods with the spontaneity and warmth that infuse all his best work.

But there's a new, graver tone under the jest. The characters in "Enemies," which is set in 1949 in Coney Island, the Bronx and Manhattan, have all been irrevocably touched by the Holocaust. For Herman Broder (Ron Silver), tragedy has improbably landed him in a situation resembling a bedroom farce: he ends up with three wives. Thinking that his first wife was killed by the Nazis along with their two children, he's married the Polish servant girl, Yadwiga (Margaret Sophie Stein), who saved his life. Meanwhile, he's carrying on a passionate affair with the married Masha (Lena Olin), a beautiful, dangerously volatile survivor of the camps. As if his life were not deceitful enough, his strong, sardonic first wife Tamara (Anjelica Huston), limping but very much alive, now reappears.

Mazursky and his co-writer Roger L. Simon are not telling the tale of some rakish Don Juan here. The tragicomic "Enemies" is a kind of ghost story about people who've lost their lives but somehow go on living. The tormented Broder, an intellectual who makes a living ghostwriting for a flashy, successful rabbi (Alan King), is not an admirable hero. A pathological liar, he's a man afraid to give his address, afraid to make a decision, afraid that at any moment the barking German dogs that hound his dreams will pursue him down the streets of New York. All these characters are haunted by death, but they find a lifeline in their erotic relationships. "Enemies" gives off a palpable sensuous glow.

At the paralyzed center of this romantic storm, Silver gives a subtle, fiercely contained performance that never asks for sympathy but somehow earns it. Huston, wry, stirring and powerful, hasn't been this fine since "Prizzi's Honor." Stein is both touching and funny as the servile Yadwiga. And Olin—so good in "The Unbearable Lightness of Being"—is astonishing here: her heartbreaking, mercurial presence invites comparison to Garbo. In scene after scene, the wise and invigorating "Enemies" catches you by surprise. It's not like any other movie.

SIGHT & SOUND, Spring 1990, p. 136, Jonathan Rosenbaum

"Although I did not have the privilege of going through the Hitler holocaust," Isaac Bashevis Singer ironically begins his Author's Note, "I have lived for years in New York with refugees from this ordeal. I therefore hasten to say that this novel is by no means the story of the typical refugee, his life, and struggle. Like most of my fictional works, this book presents an exceptional case with unique heroes and a unique combination of events. The characters are not only Nazi victims but victims of their own personalities and fates. If they fit into the general picture, it is because the exception is rooted in the rule. As a matter of fact, in literature the exception *is* the rule."

Forewarned is forearmed: Singer's tragi-comic 1972 novel is a holocaust story, but a far from typical one. Set in New York in 1949–50, it focuses on a Jewish survivor named Herman Broder who finds himself living what amounts to three separate, if sometimes distractingly overlapping lives as a direct consequence of the holocaust's traumatic upheavals. In Coney Island, he is married to Yadwiga, his former maid in Poland, a non-Jew who kept him alive during the war by hiding him in a hayloft, and who now happily waits on him hand and foot. Herman tells her he is a travelling book salesman who has to spend much of his time in remote American cities. But in fact he ghosts speeches for a wealthy Manhattan rabbi, and is carrying on a torrid affair with Masha, another holocaust survivor, married but separated, who lives with her mother in the Bronx.

It's a fairly manageable arrangement—at least until Herman discovers that his first wife, Tamara, whom he had heard was killed along with their two children by the Nazis, is alive and well in Manhattan. Herman makes no attempt to conceal his second marriage from Tamara, and before long she learns about Masha too, but wisened and battle-weary from her life in the camps, Tamara makes no marital claims on her husband, serving instead as his friend, adviser and occasional lover. Masha, however, who knows about Herman's marriage to Yadwiga, is beset with jealousy, and wants to marry him as well, largely for the sake of her mother. Eventually, Herman finds himself with three separate wives in three separate New York boroughs.

The comic side of this situation makes it prime material for a film-maker like Paul Mazursky, but the no less tragic undertones would seem to make it an unlikely subject for a writer-director whose usual stomping ground is the contemporary, upwardly mobile middle-class. From *Bob & Carol & Ted & Alice* to *Down and Out in Beverly Hills*, Mazursky has been the staunch defender and celebrator of American bourgeois values, for all his fascination with various kinds of "deviance". Despite periodic efforts to dramatize the dissatisfactions of his usually well-heeled characters that suggest a desire to break out of boulevard comedy, Mazursky generally follows Hollywood formula by coming down squarely on the side of conventional values after extended weekend flirtations with transgression.

All of which leaves one quite unprepared for the absence of glibness in Mazursky's first real adaptation, *Enemies, a Love Story*—an exception in his career that does not quite become the rule (by altering one's judgment of his earlier films), but which does an exceptional job of trying. While he and co-writer Roger L. Simon have needlessly broadened some of the farcical and/or caricatural elements of Singer's novel—the hamminess of Alan King's first scene as the rabbi; the contrived comic complications to Herman and Masha's holiday in the Catskills—they have in general stuck to the tone of the original. And thanks to a superb cast—Ron Silver (Herman), Anjelica Huston (Tamara), Margaret Sophie Stein (Yadwiga), Lena Olin (Masha)—much of the complexity and nearly all the poignancy of Singer's conception is well served.

What is mainly missing is Singer's richer sense of the characters—Tamara's former activities as a Communist and Zionist, Herman's paranoid revenge fantasies, and the tangled underpinnings of Masha's suicidal impulses—although the story's slightly amended conclusion could arguably be defended as an improvement. What remains is Singer's beguilingly deceptive structure, which begins by positing Herman as the hero of the tale—cynically defeated in his emotional indecisiveness, though hardly unsympathetic—and then gradually allows his three wives to overtake him, mitigating and eventually subverting most of the story's male-chauvinist fantasy capers as the trio steadily grow in strength and prominence. Although practically all the story is told from Herman's viewpoint, he literally vanishes from the plot by the final scene, and it is a crucial part of both Singer and Mazursky's uncommon achievement that he isn't missed at all, either by the characters or the audience.

TIME, 1/8/90, p. 76, Richard Corliss

[*Enemies, a Love Story* was reviewed jointly with *Triumph of the Spirit;* see Corliss' review of that film.]

VILLAGE VOICE, 12/19/89, p. 94, Georgia Brown

A squad of burly Nazis with dogs and bayonets swarms into a barn to flush out one terrifed Jew: This is the nightmare of being discovered—found out—that opens *Enemies, A Love Story*. Down below the hayloft where Herman Broder (Ron Silver) is hiding, Yadwiga (Margaret Sophie Stein), the Polish peasant who's been secretly keeping him, tries to stop the goons and gets slapped around for her effort. Herman's nightmare ends with a shot of Yadwiga's wide-open, screaming, and copiously bleeding mouth—an interpolation of director Paul Mazursky, since there's no Yadwiga in the similar opening to Isaac Bashevis singer's 1972 Yiddish novel on which the movie is based. Mazursky's point, I take it, is that Herman is afraid—petrifed—not only of the Nazis, but of the open, bloody jaws of women.

Something is quite the matter with Herman Broder. He spends his days furtively, compulsively shuttling between his homespun shiksa wife in Coney Island—the same blond Yadwiga whom he's gratefully married and brought to the States—and sultry Masha (Lena Olin) of the Bronx, tormented survivor of Auschwitz. Not long into our story, Tamara (Anjelica Huston), Herman's statuesque, difficult wife from before the war, turns up and settles in on the Lower East Side. (He'd thought she had been killed along with their two children.) When Masha gets pregnant and insists on marrying him too, Herman becomes a man with three wives in three boroughs.

Not so different from the lives of many other philanderers, gentiles included. (Audience identification, begin here.) The Holocaust contributes to Herman's situation, but does not explain It. In Singer's novel (though not Mazursky's movie), Herman was practicing some of the same disappearing tricks before the war when he'd more or less abandoned his wife and children. It's as if trauma serves to focus character. In this case it puts a point on one man's flight to and from women (my enemy, my life). The plot's central question: When will Herman be flushed out of his hiding?

Enemies also addresses the *Crimes and Misdemeanors* issue: Since Hitler proved that God isn't just, we may as well forget about punishment and let out all the stops. Or, as Singer puts it in his novel, "...anything was possible among modern people stripped of all faith. What did civilization consist of if not murder and fornication?'' Herman's taste runs to fornication. Lust has always ranked high in Singer's scale of values and Mazursky, who shares the bias, does the best he can here to keep the faith. (It's my impression that lust on the screen—licking of torsos seems to be in fashion right now—becomes more and more an obligatory squirm-through. Yet each new wrinkle or kink gets applauded as a steamy breakthrough.)

Herman and Masha excite themselves with end-of-the-world sex fantasies, one of which runs something like this: He: "If there were no men left, would you do it with a woman?'' She: "Of course. And you, would you do it with a man?'' He: "Never....But an *animal*...''

A man's fixation on a disturbed, sexy woman—*Jules and Jim* to *Betty Blue*—is one of those mythic psychological patterns that particularly in our country often gets tipped on its axis—*Maltese Falcon* to *Chinatown,* and recently in an ugly way with *Fatal Attraction.* Men kill women in many ways, and Herman is one of the meek murderers, wearing soft gloves instead of jackboots, whose suffering offers him license to strike again.

Singer provides an arresting exchange between Tamara and Herman, after Tamara, trying to sort out Herman's mess, advises sending the housebound, non-English-speaking Yadwiga back to Poland where at least she'll be comfortable:

"Tamara, she saved my life.''

"Is that why you want to destroy her?''

Fascinating business, but *Enemies* the movie never sprouts wings. If you know the book, you're left feeling the loss in adaptation. Those who don't know the novel will recognize the material's pull, know they should be pulled, but I doubt they'll *be* pulled. Mazursky was obviously attracted to Singer's often droll treatment of heavy subjects, and he adds some funny touches (I liked when Herman, flustered in a rabbi's apartment, tries to make a quick exit and stalks into the bathroom), but it's clear that Mazursky's just noodling. The script, co-written with Roger L. Simon, and the visual elaborations are all too mild and inconsistent. (That bloody mouth at the beginning isn't supported with a coherent view of Herman's terror.) Silver's Herman—dark eyes boring out of deep sockets—is a cipher to the end.

Praise might go to period recreations of New York's postwar emigrant communities—the streets, the *shmattes,* and some New World parlors—yet one doesn't leave the movie feeling illuminated about men and women, crimes and punishment, or the character of recently traumatized Jews, but rather with a vague sense of, What a pickle this schmuck got himself into.

Singer's point, by the way, about Jewish angst—long habits of stealth, smuggling, flight—is nicely compressed into this passage: "The Bible, the Talmud, and the Commentaries instruct the Jew in one strategy: flee from evil, hide from danger, avoid showdowns, give the angry powers of the universe as wide a berth as possible.'' And this: "In Herman's private philosophy survival itself was based on guile.'' Singer's point—one that *Crimes and Misdemeanors* wanted, I think, to make—is that old, atavistic (undeserved) guilt begets real crimes.

Also reviewed in:
NEW REPUBLIC, 1/1/90, p. 26, Stanley Kauffmann
NEW YORK TIMES, 12/13/89, p. C22, Janet Maslin
NEW YORKER, 12/25/89, p. 73, Pauline Kael
VARIETY, 12/13/89, p. 31
WASHINGTON POST, 1/19/90, p. B1, Hal Hinson
WASHINGTON POST, 1/19/90, Weekend/p.33, Desson Howe

ERIK THE VIKING

An Orion Pictures release of a Prominent Features production. *Executive Producer:* Terry Glinwood. *Producer:* John Goldstone. *Director:* Terry Jones. *Screenplay:* Terry Jones. *Director of Photography:* Ian Wilson. *Editor:* George Akers. *Music:* Neil Innes. *Sound:* Bob Doyle and (music) Austin Ince. *Sound Editor:* Alan Bell. *Production Designer:* John Beard. *Art Director:* Gavin Bocquet and Roger Cain. *Set Decorator:* Joan Woollard. *Special Effects:* Peter Hutchinson. *Costumes:* Pam Tait. *Make-up:* Jenny Shircore. *Stunt Coordinator:* Martin Grace. *Running time:* 104 minutes. *MPAA Rating:* PG-13.

CAST: Tim Robbins (Erik); Mickey Rooney (Erik's Grandfather); Eartha Kitt (Freya); Terry Jones (King Arnulf); Imogen Stubbs (Aud); John Cleese (Halfdan the Black); Tsutomu Sekine (Slavemaster); Antony Sher (Loki); Gary Cady (Keitel Blacksmith); Tim McInnerny (Sven the Berserk); Charles McKeown (Sven's Dad); John Sinclair (Ivar the Boneless); Richard Ridings (Thorfinn Skullsplitter); Samantha Bond (Helga); Freddie Jones (Harald the Missionary); Danny Schiller (Snorri the Miserable); Jim Broadbent (Ernest the Viking, a Rapist); Jim Carter (Jennifer the Viking, another Rapist); Matyelok Gibbs (Erik's Mum); Tilly Vosburgh (Unn-the-Thrown-at); Jay Simpson (Leif the Lucky); John Scott Martin (Ingemund the Old); Sian Thomas (Thorhild the Sarcastic); Sarah Crowden (Grimhild Housewife); Bernard Padden (Mordfiddle the Cook); Bernard Latham (Ulf the Unmemorable); Julia McCarthy (Thorfinn's Mum); Allan Surtees (Thorfinn's Dad); Sandra Voe (Ivar's Mum); Angela Connolly (Thorkatla the Indiscreet); Sally Jones (Leif's Pregnant Girlfriend); Andrew MacLachlan (Ornulf/Chamberlain/Dog Soldier); Tim Killick (Bjarni/Halfdan's Guard/Musician); Graham McTavish (Thangbrand/Citizen/Dog Soldier); Cyril Shaps (Gisli the Chiseller); Peter Geeves (Eilif the Mongol Horde/Musician); Paddy Joyce, Colin Harper, Harry Jones, Barry McCarthy, and Gary Roost (Prisoners); Neil Innes (Hy-Brasilian); Simon Evans (Odin); Matthew Baker (Thor); Dave Duffy (Horribly Slain Warrior); Frank Bednash (Even More Horribly Slain Warrior).

LOS ANGELES TIMES, 11/1/89, Calendar/p.3, Chris Willman

There's no joy in Montyville tonight. First came the recent death of Monty Python troupe member Graham Chapman; now there's the release of the sadly moribund "Erik the Viking," which makes idle use of the talents of Pythonites Terry Jones and John Cleese as well as such frequent collaborators as composer Neil Innes. Post-mortem to follow.

Jones wrote, directed and took a small role in which he has given himself some of the movie's unfunniest lines. "Erik" was purportedly his dream project, but it's more like a paying audience's nightmare—a stillborn comedy in which minutes sometimes mysteriously go by between even attempted gags, and in which virtually no comic scene works up to any kind of viable punch line or payoff.

Berobed and baffled, Tim Robbins founders in the underdeveloped title role. His character— vaguely heroic, a little clumsy—is set up in a pre-credit sequence (the movie's funniest) as a first-time plunderer who tries and fails to rape a young woman and then falls in love with her before skewering her by mistake. Erik's properly barbaric Viking dad, played in a cameo by Mickey Rooney, approves of his son's accidental method of dealing with contentious women: "That's my boy!"

It's downhill from there as Erik consults with earth-mama Eartha Kitt (in another of the movie's many cameos) for cosmic advice, learning that a trip to Valhalla, land of the dead, might land him the Grail-like horn that would awaken the gods, conclude the Ice Age and maybe even end all human savagery. Pacifistic motives aside, Erik also would like to visit the afterlife to bring back the girlfriend he so quickly impaled in Scene 1. But she is irretrievable, and so is the film's sense of wit.

This is the cinema of cruelty, waxing outrage at the mindless violence of the millennia and bemusement at the banalities of history—all proper black-comic Python fodder, to be sure. It's also the kind of territory well-mined in movies by former partner Terry Gilliam, whose brilliant "Adventures of Baron Munchausen" bears many resemblances to this—all the way down to nearly identical scenes in the two movies in which giant sea monsters are made to sneeze away ships with actor Charles McKeown aboard! (You'd think McKeown surely must have warned Gilliam or Jones.)

But similarities aside, there's no confusing the 1989 work of the two Terrys: "Erik" is as consistently unamusing as "Munchausen" was magical. Jones isn't a visonary like Gilliam, and his fantasy sequences, in which the Vikings sail over the edge of the world, fall flat as the Earth from which they departed. So do about nine out of 10 jokes.

As a primitive judge who has his prisoners begging for execution rather than torture, Cleese plays his sadistic part with mild-mannered restraint and, though he's hardly trying, may be the best thing about the picture; he's also only in it for about two minutes.

As the quest finally nears Valhalla, one character intones, gravely, "We're going where only the dead have gone before"—a sentiment likely to be echoed in many theaters where "Erik the Viking" (MPAA-rated PG-13 for violence and language) unspools to an eerie hush. *Requiescat in pace.*

MONTHLY FILM BULLETIN, 10/89, p. 299, Geoff Brown

It is the Age of Ragnarok: Fenrir the Wolf has swallowed the Sun, and the Great Winter blankets the world, causing turmoil and violence. After falling in love with the beautiful Helga, whom he accidentally kills, Erik, a Viking warrior, begins to question the daily round of rape and pillaging. The seeress Freya advises him that he can only end the Age of Ragnarok by waking the Gods, who reside over the Edge of the World in Asgaard. Erik sets sail with an unruly band of followers; one of them, the blacksmith Keitel, is working to sabotage the mission on behalf of the evil Loki and Halfdan the Black, the local warlord. Halfdan's men go in pursuit, but are shaken off. After a clash with the Dragon of the North Sea, Erik's expedition reaches Hy-Brasil, resting place of the Horn Resounding—the magic instrument that will carry them over the Edge of the World. King Arnulf and his Hy-Brasilians live in fear of violence; according to an old curse, if any blood is spilt, their continent will sink beneath the waves. Halfdan's forces reappear; when Erik defeats them without bloodshed Arnulf awards him the Horn. Then a Viking is killed in one of Loki's sabotage attempts; Erik's crew and the beautiful Princess Aud escape safely from the sinking continent, but the water engulfs Arnulf and his loyal subjects. Through the horn's magic notes, the expedition reaches the Halls of Asgaard. The Gods are woken, and Erik finds Helga in Valhalla. After hearing Erik's pleas to let her return to the land of the living, Odin, the supreme God, condemns the intruders to the Pit of Hell. But Princess Aud's quick-wittedness rescues them, and the voyagers soon crash through the sky back home, landing in a duck pond. The sun rises; the violent Age of Ragnarok has ended. "Now it's up to us", Erik says.

"What's it all about, grandpa?" Erik asks, pondering the mysteries of the violent Viking life. Viewers might be wondering the same thing as the film plods on through brooding fantasy, showy displays of special effects, some perilous over-acting, and unfunny chunks of Pythonesque humour. Terry Jones first developed Erik the Viking's character in a 1983 collection of stories, aimed at children. But the film that has resulted six years later is an adult's plaything—all puffed up with pukka Norse mythology and warning notes about mankind's fatal itch for violence.

Technically, Erik's fantastic voyage is a decent enough piece of work, and Tim Robbins—picked for his engaging performance as the bumptious pitcher in *Bull Durham*—plays the doubtful warrior with a fetching, bemused air. But his restraint goes for little when all around, from Antony Sher to John Cleese, are thwacking their slender material to death: Terry Jones himself, as the foppish King Arnulf who delights in singing but cannot hold a tune, is one of the worst offenders. If Jones had abandoned his Python past and jettisoned the unrewarding comic rigmarole, his film might possibly have come to heel as a straight, if *recherché*, fantasy adventure, pitting good against evil. As it is, we are left floundering in a thunderous, unfunny jumble.

NEW YORK POST, 10/28/89, p. 15, Jami Bernard

Pity the poor Viking who doesn't like to rape and pillage. What's left for him, making ice sculptures?

Erik is one such Viking, and he decides to pay a visit to the gods, who are slumbering through a bleak portion of world history.

"Erik the Viking" was written and directed by Terry Jones ("Personal Services") and numbers among its cast Jones and John Cleese, former members of the Monty Python troupe. But don't get your hopes up too high. The movie is a blithe but lackluster adventure yarn that fails to raise the hackles even when its characters are battling the dread Dragon of the North and tumbling over the Edge of the World.

Not every movie is for every taste. "Erik" will attract Python fans, but they are bound to be disappointed. There is about enough droll British humor and swashbuckling adventure for a crowd of 12-year-olds cutting class.

Which is not so surprising, as the project derives from a series of children's stories written by Jones. The result is an adventure too tame for adults, a comedy too adult for children.

Robbins, the boyish galoof from "Bull Durham," plays Erik, a reluctant Viking who is unfit to die a hero's death and thus enter the halls of Valhalla because, although he will grudgingly kill and pillage he can't bring himself to rape. "You haven't done this before, have you?" asks a potential victim disgustedly.

Erik is no longer fulfilled by lusty brawling, throwing axes at young ladies and holding punchouts in the icy fjords. With the help of an aged seer (Eartha Kitt in one of several "celebrity" bit parts), he decides to wake the gods with the Horn Resounding and urge them to end the Age of Ragnarok, where Fenrir the Wolf has swallowed the sun and made everything frosty cold.

The other Vikings, eager for any activity in which they can grunt and inflict pain and look even more sweaty and bedraggled, pack their bags immediately. In a typical example of the kind of

Humor of the Inappropriate that this movie goes for, the Norsemen delay their important journey by arguing over seating arrangements on the Viking ship.

Once all the Svens and Olafs are settled, they paddle away to the peaceful isle of Hy-Brasil, where toga-clad merry makers sing off-key and loll in the sun. Jones plays the idyll's king, who maintains to the last gulp that his island is not sinking.

In pursuit of the vikings is an evil gang, led by the very funny Cleese as a sort of finicky despot, like the Grand Inquisitor of "Candide," handing out vile sentences of torture to his subjects. "Flay him alive, then behead him," Cleese suggests delicately, as if choosing a Beaujolais.

Mickey Rooney, white hair flowing, plays Erik's grandfather, congratulating Erik on having slain a woman with, "That's my boy!"

Shot on the island of Malta, mostly in a huge open-air water tank that is an artifact from the movie "Raise the Titanic," "Erik" features fine production values that tend to overwhelm the dead-pan actors. With all that money and talent, it's too bad "Erik" is never more than amusing. Round up the 12-year-olds.

NEWSDAY, 10/28/89, Part II/p. 15, Terry Kelleher

It's rather unmanly of a Norse warrior to sneak into town unannounced.

But Erik the Viking is an odd sort of Viking, and "Erik the Viking" is an odd sort of movie. Released with an absolute minimum of fanfare by Orion Pictures, "Erik the Viking" was written and directed by Monty Python's Terry Jones, and it contains considerable Pythonic absurdity of widely varying quality. Every once in a while, however, the raucous comedy subsides and everything gets still and serious and mythic. And there are other times when the would-be wit and wisdom are crowded off the screen by action and special effects.

Our tale begins with the Vikings giving a village a good pillaging and Erik (Tim Robbins) poised to rape a saucy female (Samantha Bond). He hesitates, saying he prefers sex with "mutual feeling." A conversation follows, and the woman accuses Erik of advancing a "circular argument." Aha, we think, so that's the kind of movie it's going to be: a genre spoof playing on anachronistic language, attitudes and situations.

There's plenty of that, all right. Also a fair share of gross humor involving vomiting, foaming at the mouth and such. One bit of casting—Mickey Rooney as Erik's grandfather—is designed to be a cheap laugh in itself.

Of course, Eartha Kitt isn't the first person you'd think of to play an Eighth Century Scandinavian soothsayer, but she's not here to amuse. Erik confides that killing and looting have lost their appeal, and she introduces the fantasy-adventure element by sending him to find the Rainbow Bridge, blow the Resounding Horn and wake the gods. (Please don't ask for particulars.) The hero recruits a motley crew of Vikings for a voyage that takes them past of fearsome dragon to an idyllic island with "terribly nice" inhabitants (and Jones as their mincing king). Then it's on to Valhalla, the Pit of Hell and other fantastic places where the jokes tend to get lost in the hubbub.

"Erik the Viking" has its moments, chiefly provided by John Cleese in the regrettably small role of the villainous Halfdan the Black. Halfdan has an exquisitely polite way of ordering his henchmen to dispose of captives: "Uh, flay them both alive, would you please?"

Unfortunately, one sterling cameo and a few good gags don't seem nearly enough to rescue "Erik the Viking" from early consignment to the video store. Better to let sleeping gods lie.

Also reviewed in:
NEW YORK TIMES, 10/28/89, p. 13, Vincent Canby
VARIETY, 9/6–12/89, p. 22
WASHINGTON POST, 10/28/89, p. C9, Rita Kempley

ERRORS OF YOUTH, THE

A Lenfilm Studio Production. *Producer:* Evgeny Volkov. *Director:* Boris Frumin. *Screenplay (Russian with English subtitles):* Edward Topol and Boris Frumin. *Director of Photography:* Alexei Gambarian. *Editor:* Tamara Denisova. *Music:* Victor Lebedev. *Sound:* Galina Lukina. *Production Designer:* Yuri Pugatch. *Running time:* 87 minutes. *MPAA Rating:* Not Rated.

CAST: Stanislav Zhdanko (Dimitry Gurianov); Marina Neyelova (Polina); Natalia Varley (Zina); Mikhail Vaskov (Burkov); Nikolai Karatchetsov (Gena); Nikolai Penkov (Kostik); Marina Maltseva (Kostik's Wife); Bella Tchirina (Alyena); A. Kotchetkow (Gurianov's Father); N. Mamayeva (Gurianov's Mother); V. Marenkov (Captain Risakov); A. Garitchev (Lieutenant Burtchalkin); A. Gorin (Frolikov); A. Vedenskaya (Lusya).

NEWSDAY, 3/18/89, Part II/p. 17, Mike McGrady

When Soviet director-writer Boris Frumin completed rough work on"The Errors of Youth" in 1978, he was told that the film was too true to life to be released in the Soviet Union. In 1979, the young director emigrated from the Soviet Union and made his way to NYU where today he teaches film making. However, the current softening of Soviet attitudes led to Frumin being invited last year to finish his film and it is now making its debut as part of the New Directors/New Films series.

"The Errors of Youth," with just a few new segments roughly patched in to complete the narration, traces the path of a young man from remote farm to big city, from first love to marriage, from idealism to cynicism. And while Stanislav Zhdanko gives a solid performance as Dimitry, the young man unable to find his niche, the most revealing portrait of all is the picture of Soviet society.

The realism of that picture, reportedly the quality that kept the film on the shelf, is what makes it worth watching. While the young man's personal problems are universal, the specifics are fascinating.

"The Errors of Youth" covers varied Soviet terrains. As Dimitry is being discharged from the army, we come to know the resort world of the Black Sea. We return with him to an impoverished family farm. We meet the small-town bureaucrat who doesn't want to give him permission to leave the area for the construction job. We join the construction team where he manages to impregnate a girlfriend but decides against marriage. Finally, there is his descent into a modern city where nothing can be accomplished without brutality or bribery as an accompaniment.

There are many surprises in "The Errors of Youth" and not the least of these is the presence of so many decidedly capitalistic urges in a socialistic society, a world where everyone is scrambling after the almighty ruble. Although the film does lack cohesion, especially toward the end, the fascination doesn't fade.

VILLAGE VOICE, 3/21/89, p. 64, Katherine Dieckmann

USSR. Begun over a decade ago and completed only recently, Boris Frumin reportedly abandoned his third feature because its "critical realism" was untenable at home. But his real problem is an aimless plot and a surly, womanizing protagonist whose angst seems less tied to the problems of Soviet life than to a nasty disposition. *Errors* begins as a kind of grown-up *Biloxi Blues,* with a comic look at military life, then devolves into disjointed scenes: an awkward homecoming, illicit dealmaking, drunken nights in discos, and girls, girls, girls.

Also reviewed in:
NEW YORK TIMES, 3/18/89, p. 16, Walter Goodman
VARIETY, 3/15-21/89, p. 14

EVE OF IVAN KUPALO, THE

A Dovzhenko Film Studio production. *Director:* Yuri Ilyenko. *Screenplay (Ukrainian with English subtitles):* Yuri Ilyenko. *Director of Photography:* Vadim Ilyenko. *Running time:* 71 minutes. *MPAA Rating:* Not Rated.

CAST: Larisa Kadochnikova (The Woman); Boris Khmelnitsky (The Man); B. Friedman (The Devil).

NEW YORK POST, 1/11/89, p. 22, V.A. Musetto

It's a cryptic mix of Faust, Gogol, the Marx Brothers and a Ukrainian folk tale. It's called "The Eve of Ivan Kupalo" and it's one of the six movies, collectively known as "The Cutting Edge II," that are in residence today through Jan. 24 at Film Forum 1.

"Eve" was written and directed in 1968 by Ukrainian Yuri Ilyenko. It was shown briefly, then hidden away until 1987 by Soviet censors. Based on Gogol's story of the same name, which, in turn, owes much to the legend of Faust, "Eve" tells of a young man who makes a pact with the devil to gain great wealth and thus take the beautiful white-clothed woman he loves away from the wealthy landlord her father has promised her to.

The devil commands that the man be the first to "pluck the fern" that blooms only on the eve of Ivan Kupalo Day and, more drastically, pay for it with the blood of a young boy he must kill. The orders are followed, the fern turns promptly to gold, and the suitor gains the woman's hand. But, alas, his happiness is short-lived: He is set aflame by pangs of conscience and turned into a pile of ashes. In hopes of regaining her husband, the bride carries his ashes to Kiev for what the production notes call "a replaying of the history of the Ukraine."

Actually, I must take the press notes' word for much of the above summary. As befits his tale, Ilyenko eschews standard narrative, preferring a dreamy series of eye-filling, mind-testing visuals. People fly through the air. They stand at 45-degree angles. One scampers around a room with an urn over his head, a bit straight out of the Marx Brothers' "Duck Soup." Two other characters engage in some fast talk that I'd swear was inspired by Abbott and Costello. Blood flows from a loaf of bread. Fires burn in the night. If I couldn't always be sure what was happening, at least I enjoyed trying.

VILLAGE VOICE, 1/17/89, p. 61, J. Hoberman

Now in its second edition, "The Cutting Edge" is an invaluable supplement to "New Directors/New Films" and even the new New York Film Festival, introducing or reprising a half-dozen imports deemed insufficiently commercial to acquire American distribution. Last year's series brought Tian Zhuangzhuang's superb *Horse Thief* and Raul Ruiz's foxy *Life Is a Dream*. This year's selection is, if anything, even more varied and toughminded, as it ranges from several varieties of visionary excess to assorted examples of austere narrativity.

The films are showing in repertory at Film Forum 1 through January 24 but, such is the current revision of Soviet cinema history that the venue is giving pride of place to a 21-year-old movie, Yuri Ilyenko's *The Eve of Ivan Kupalo*. Ilyenko, the cinematographer on Sergei Paradjanov's ethno-delirious *Shadows of Our Forgotten Ancestors* (1964) and the director of several long-shelved films, is a cultural nationalist—the heir to Alexander Dovzhenko and Ivan Kavaleridze, the beleaguered Ukrainian cine-poets of the '20s and '30s. Lyrical and grotesque by turns, the feverish *Ivan Kupalo* suggests that *Shadows of Our Forgotten Ancestors* was not an isolated achievement, but the recovery of a tradition. (It also confirms that, in the Soviet Union as elsewhere, the mid-'60s were a time of considerable cinematic ferment.)

Inspired by the supernatural story that initiated Nicolai Gogol's literary career, *Ivan Kupalo* is at once folky and modernist—a kind of visual jazz in which Ilyenko's ravishing wide-screen compositions and L. Grabovsky's jaunty, Prokofiev-like score combine with all manner of embroidered finery and the gardens painted on whitewashed walls to create a sort of peasant surrealism. There are moments when the film suggests a Technicolor equivalent of Spencer Williams: Heaven and Earth are hopelessly mingled; the world is populated by endearingly earthy devils and angels; a loaf of bread sheds blood.

The narrative is basically a Ukrainian version of the Faust legend. A poor laborer named Peter strikes a bargain with the devil, embodied in the brawling figure of the red-haired Cossack Basavryuk, to win Pidorka, the daughter of a wealthy peasant. The film's title comes from the local—here, madly solarized—*Walpurgisnacht*, in which the befuddled hero is compelled to pluck a magic flower and then seal the bargain by murdering Pidorka's younger brother. Peter represses the memory of his crime and eventually goes mad, but the reason *Ivan Kupalo* was shelved for 20 years lies less in lurid depravity than in Pidorka's climactic trip to Kiev—an addition to Gogol's story that provides an allegorical account of the Ukraine's colonization by Russia. Near the end of the sequence, a childlike Catherine the Great appears, manipulated like a puppet by her prime minister, Potemkin. "Why are my people not dancing?" she asks.

Why indeed? The barbed ending notwithstanding, the mode here is exuberantly primitivist—full of herky-jerky moves and slapstick materializations. The ease with which a peasant hut becomes the autumn birch wood, the fiery wheels that the villagers roll down the hills into the river, the island with its miniature church from which Peter and Pidorka's flowered wedding boat casts off—all have the quality of events imagined by a child. The film is at once earthy and ethereal. Ilyenko's people seem elongated; they stand at odd angles and occasionally defy gravity.

Ivan Kupalo's blue cows and capsule description notwithstanding, this fantasmagorical Mirgorod-a-rama doesn't evoke Marc Chagall so much as it suggests a Ukrainian quality to Chagall's own insouciant antinaturalism. (Similarly, the affinities between Gogol's mock-down-home narrative voice and several of Sholom Aleichem's give one a sense of the latter as both a Ukrainian and a Yiddish writer.) This film isn't for every taste—still, who knows? In the aftermath of Gorbymania, the appreciation of Slavic soul that made the Bulgarian State Radio and Television Female Vocal Choir last year's flavor-of-the-week might not carry over here.

Also reviewed in:
NATION, 2/13/89, p. 208, Stuart Klawans
NEW YORK TIMES, 1/11/89, p. C21, Walter Goodman

EVENING BELL

An August First Film Studio production. *Director:* Wu Ziniu. *Screenplay (Chinese with English subtitles):* Wu Ziniu and Wang Yifei. *Director of Photography:* Hou Yong. *Editor:* Zong Lijiang. *Music:* Ma Jianping. *Sound:* Wang Lewen and Zhang Lei. *Running time:* 89 minutes. *MPAA Rating:* Nor Rated.

CAST: Tao Zeru (Patrol Leader); Sun Min (Japanese Prisoner); Cong Peipei (Japanese Platoon Leader); Liu Ruolei, Ge Yaming, Ye Nanqin and Zhao Qi (Soldiers).

NEWSDAY, 3/28/89, Part II/p. 11, Lynn Darling

There is a ravishing scene near the beginning of ''Evening Bell,'' in which the camera pans slowly over leathery, ancient hills suffused in a dusky light. A squad of Chinese soldiers sits on a barren, windswept knoll, each deep within the well of his own thoughts. Beyond them, a group of women mourn their losses in the war that has recently ended in Japan's surrender. Their keening wails find their echo in the men's thoughts of what life will be like now that the war is over and of the price that has been exacted in the long, bitter years of fighting.

But one last paroxysm of war awaits them, in this lyric drama by Chinese director Wu Ziniu. On patrol, they come across a starving, half-mad Japanese soldier who is unaware that the war has ended. Hatred, anger and reluctant compassion vie in their treatment of him.

The conflict between revenge and humanity becomes more pronounced, more bitter when he leads them to a cave in which a platoon of his starving comrades are hiding.

The Japanese soldiers waver between surrender and last-ditch loyalty to the emperor; the Chinese between their anger and horror at the atrocities committed by their enemies and their fundamental sense of decency.

''Evening Bell'' conveys the harsh choices and the desperation to which both sides have been driven in a series of compelling images, one that lends a grandeur, an almost operatic quality to its harsh, simple examination of the erosions of humanity under the ravages of war. Dialogue is minimal: When the Chinese squad offers the renegade troop some food, the men totter silently out of their cave, propped up on the last shreds of their discipline. They wait motionless until their commander gives the order that releases them to yield ravenously to their hunger Later, in the flickering light of their last night in the cave, the Japanese soldiers crouch together in a long line and bathe each other's naked backs, in a scene of ritualistic beauty.

Occasionally, this is carried to heavy-handed symbolic excess—lots of flaring sunsets descending behind silhouetted, serpentine hills. And Wu Ziniu has no compunctions about reducing the Japanese soldiers to an almost cartoon savagery in order to emphasize the purity of the moral choices his protagonists must make. But seen as a tone poem, ''Evening Bell'' is an often compelling look at the warring demands of vengeance and mercy.

VILLAGE VOICE, 3/28/89, p. 64, J. Hoberman

The heirs to Western maestros Anthony Mann and Sergio Leone have turned out to be the young directors of China's fifth generation. Wu Ziniu's briefly shelved *Evening Bell* is another laconic landscapefest—as ruthlessly symmetrical as it is blandly titled, grimly violent, and wildly pictorial. Working for the army's August 1st studio, Wu treats Japanese wartime atrocities in the taciturn, widescreen mode developed by his film school contemporaries Chen Kaige and Tian Zhuangzhuang. Unfortunately, he isn't in the same league as a director.

Also reviewed in:
NEW YORK TIMES, 3/28/89, p. C20, Richard Bernstein
VARIETY, 2/15–21/89, p. 21

EVERLASTING SECRET FAMILY, THE

An International Film Exchange release of an FGH presentation for International Film Management Ltd. *Executive Producer:* Anthony I. Ginnane. *Producer:* Michael Thornhill. *Director:* Michael Thornhill. *Screenplay (based on his short story collection):* Frank Moorhouse. *Director of Photography:* Julian Penney. *Editor:* Pam Barnetta. *Music:* Tony Bremner. *Choreographer;* Nina Veretnnikova. *Sound:* John Schiefelbein and Grant Stuart. *Sound Editor:* Andrew Plain. *Art Director:* Peta Lawson. *Set Dresser:* Eugene Intas. *Costumes:* Graham Purcell and Anthony Jones. *Make-up:* Noriko Spencer. *Running time:* 93 minutes. *MPAA Rating:* Not Rated.

CAST: Arthur Dignam (The Senator); Mark Lee (The Youth); Heather Mitchell (Senator's Wife); John Meillon (The Judge); Dennis Miller (Eric); Paul Goddard (Son); Beth Child (Pottery Woman); John Clayton (Mayor); Nick Holland (New Chauffeur); Bogdan Koca (Medical Specialist); Michael Kozuki (Mr. Akutangana); Tim Page (New Judge); Anna Volska (Wife's Friend); Michael Winchester (School Teacher); Alan Carey (Doctor at Oval); Marcus Cornelius (Teacher at Oval); Ken Keen (Headmaster); Allan Penney (Gardener); Dominic Barry (Bell Captain); Louis Nowra (Shop Assistant); Drew Norman (Oil Boy); Paul Davies (1st Waiter); Victor Ramon (1st Maître d'); Robert Carne (Japanese-speaking Boy); Alexander Brown (1st boy); Bruce Hughes (2nd Boy); James Maddox (1st Painter); Johnny H (1st Drag Queen); Julia Moody (1st Woman Judge); Vanessa Downing (2nd Woman Judge); Jayme Sargent (1st School Child); Jeffrey Davey (2nd School Child); Melany England (3rd School Child); Vicki Luke (Political Secretary); Helen O'Connor (Judge's Associate); Andrew Dawes (Office Person); Alton Harvey (Cleaner); Richard Linger (2nd Drag Queen); Martin Raphael (Embracing Man); Mark Stuckert (2nd Waiter); Tom Kennedy (Synthesizer Player); Tony Bremner (Piano Singer).

LOS ANGELES TIMES, 2/16/90, Calendar/p. 6, Sheila Benson

What *is* an "Everlasting Secret Family" anyway? Either an old boy's network with a tough dress code and some pretty fancy rituals, or a not-uninteresting metaphor for generations of homosexuality flourishing underground in supermacho Australia.

In either case, it's a deliberately stylized and detached film by director Michael Thornhill, whom the press notes quote as "having made the film for straight audiences to observe how sex and power are always intertwined." Except when novelist/screenwriter Frank Moorhouse's conceits get a bit florid or Victorian—and aside from the fact that the 1987-made film is a period piece now in the age of AIDS—Thornhill has done a sleekly impressive job of it. His cool extends to his film's palette, so that these young gods and their older appreciators dress entirely in black black black or blazing white white white. Diana Vreeland would have loved it.

"Gallipoli's" Mark Lee plays the Youth, a blond dazzler theoretically 16 when he is plucked out of a private boy's academy and into the lap of one of Australia's most aggressive and successful politicians, the Senator (Arthur Dignam). It's done covertly; the Senator's eye sweeps across a playing field crammed with adolescents in blinding white, eye contact is made and the Senator retreats to the shade of his Bentley, chauffeured by the omnipresent and interesting Eric (Dennis Miller).

Eric is the only one in the film to have a name. Senator, Judge, Senator's eventual wife and Senator's eventual son presumably all have blanks on their I.D. bracelets. It only gets a little silly when, in a cozy family chat, Wife (Heather Mitchell) must say to Senator/husband, "Our son is well past puberty. ..." It does break our concentration somewhat.

Eric was also once a Lover. Now he is a Chauffeur. Roles are strictly defined, of exquisite importance. Our Youth comes to appreciate that as he and the Senator pass years together, control passing from one to the other, always under the authority of the Everlasting Secret Family. Secret Family members meet in a grand old mansion, wear white poet's shirts, go through the masked ritual of the white rose and obey the watchwords Ecstasy, Secrecy, Silence.

Actually, the ecstasy is demure, no one is ever silent for a minute, and secrecy goes out the window the first time that Bentley arrives and the Youth is excused from class without so much as a hall pass or a note from his mother.

As our hero reaches 25, he begins to obsess about his vanishing youth, prying the name of a doctor who will keep him young from a Judge with whom he has a sadomasochistic relationship. (Demure, believe it, demure.) The doctor's warning of dreadful side effects from his ministrations seems excessive; we follow our Youth to the tottering age of 35 and even though *he's* seen signs of dropped buns, they're not visible to the inquiring camera. (The sight of them, however, and the film's subject matter are the source of the Times' Mature rating.)

The film is actually quite poignant as it contemplates a not-otherwise-stupid young man who equates the loss of his youth and beauty with death. It's borderline hilarious in the casting and character of the Youth's seductive, blowzy art teacher(unnamed in the press kit), apparently an eternal mother figure maintained by the Family. And it is most memorable in Arthur Dignam's incisive and urbane performance as the Senator, redeeming a lot that is unsubtle with his subtlety and control.

MONTHLY FILM BULLETIN, 12/88, p. 362, Philip Strick

Selecting a new recruit from St. Michael's Private School for Boys, the Senator educates him in homosexual activity. The Youth is at first bored with his duties but soon becomes devoted to the Senator, abandoning his education in order to serve him at all times; it is a role he realises he has taken over from Eric, now the Senator's middle-aged chauffeur. The Senator introduces the Youth to a secret fraternity of similarly trained young men and their employers, men of influence like the High Court Judge who clearly indicates his own admiration for the Youth. When the Senator allows himself to be courted by a girl, recognising that marriage would be a useful step in his career, the Youth is fiercely jealous. Anxious that his looks might be fading, he offers himself to the Judge in return for the address of a rejuvenation specialist, with whose help he successfully resists the signs of ageing. Unfortunately, the Judge is so effectively entertained by the Youth that he dies of a heart attack, and the Senator and Eric have to arrange a cover-up to avoid scandal. Reassuring the Youth that he will always be part of the family, the Senator continues after his marriage to keep him in employment, despite the objections of his wife; in time, the Youth becomes baby-sitter and companion to their Son who, like the Senator, finds his seemingly unchanging charms irresistible. When the Son approaches adulthood, Eric claims entitlement to him and, when the Senator refuses permission, attempts a seduction with the aid of a long-term associate, the Pottery Woman. But the Son rejects their approaches, foils his mother's attempt to have the Youth thrown out of the house, and with his father's support and approval undergoes the initiation ceremony of the secret fraternity. At his next birthday party, he expresses to the Youth his dearest wish: that they become lovers. In granting this request, the Youth celebrates the completion of his plan to have both father and son within his power.

Adapted by writer Frank Moorhouse from his collection of six short stories described as erotic memoirs based on experiences in his youth, *The Everlasting Secret Family* wanders precariously and indecisively between various possible identities. Its first signals indicate that we might expect a revelation of the debauchery and corruption among higher ranks of Australian society, but while a network of homosexual collusion is hinted at (no objections are raised to the Youth's frequent departures from the classroom for dalliance with his mentor), the range or quantity of such liaisons is clearly not under investigation. The quaint rigmarole of the initiation ceremonies and a glimpse or two of some vaguely unsavoury cocktail parties do indicate that the Senator and the Judge are not alone in the peculiarity of their private entertainments, but the film notably avoids illustrating any 'secret family' connections with, or influence on, the conduct of bureaucracy at any level, national or local. The closest the screenplay gets to politics is a wonderfully naive lesson in diplomatic science whereby the Youth, nude on a bed, discovers that armies and governments are not always in alliance.

Devoting itself instead to the tale of an eccentric individual enclosed like a pop star or a hot-house plant in temporarily idolatrous slavery, Moorhouse's scenario tinkers with ideas from *Victim, The Servant* and *Performance,* fails to integrate any of them and, for the sake of something to do other than repeating the 'shock' shots of masculine embrace, embarks audaciously on a new version of *The Picture of Dorian Gray.* Inexplicably anxious to retain the affections of his employer, possibly because nobody else is likely to tolerate him ("Do you think my bum has dropped?" he demands archly at one point), the Youth insists on a course of rejuvenation that will ensure he wears less make-up than the rest of the cast (a wise move, given the array of artificial wrinkles and the hair of caked blue that the Senator acquires with the passing of the years).

The son's submission to this smug parasite, a development marked in true Romantic style by some billowing curtains and an open window, is presented not as a revenge (the Senator could, after all, have averted it at any time but instead encourages the relationship) but as a manoeuvre in some grand plan about which, despite the occasional and unexpected comments addressed to us by the Youth on the soundtrack, we have been left in ignorance. Endeavouring to find plausible images for these elusive events, Michael Thornhill directs with an evident preference for comedy, as with the daft scene in which a Japanese dignitary has to be sexually serviced with some unimaginable ritual involving a live crab. But where Moorhouse found in Makavejev a kindred spirit of callous extravagance in the screen version of *The Coca-Cola Kid,* his wild malevolence in *The Everlasting Secret Family* seems less heartily embraced by its director. The extraordinary concept of the Pottery Woman, for example, the callipygous lady available as both mother and mistress to those who have briefly lost their way in the 'family', is elaborately enfolded by Thornhill in artworks and foliage but fails to avoid complete absurdity.

NEW YORK POST, 11/17/89, p. 30, V.A. Musetto

"The Everlasting Secret Family," which comes our way from Australia, is the story of sleazy politicians and kinky sex. But before you rush out to catch it, be advised: It also is a bit of a bore.

At the center is a distinguished-looking, middle-aged senator who makes his campaign rounds in a Rolls-Royce. He also is a leech who likes young, blond guys.

His latest plaything—referred to only as the Youth—attends an exclusive private school. In one of the movie's more preposterous contrivances, the Youth is free to walk out in mid-class to be chauffeured to a motel. There, with a TV quiz show droning on in the background, he sips a glass of creme de menthe on the rocks and "gives pleasure" (the Senator's term) to the older man. Then it's back to class, where the comings and goings raise nary an eyebrow from the instructor. Hard to believe? You bet!

The first half of "Family" laboriously follows the Youth through this and other trysts (both straight and gay), most of them carried on with the senator's blessing. One involves a menage a trois—the Youth, a Japanese businessman and a giant crab. (Fortunately, we never get to see what the three are up to in the privacy of the bedroom, although we do get to hear the Youth's scream from within that bedroom.) Another concerns an aging and respected judge who drops dead during some S & M shenanigans.

Flash forward 14 years. The Senator is now married and the father of a handsome adolescent boy who has caught the eye of the Youth, who, we're asked to believe, has aged not a day because of a "highly experimental" drug. (Where are you when we need you, Oscar Wilde?) At this point, you might be tempted to call it quits. Don't. The last scene is a real doozy (and that's no compliment).

If voyeurism and "forbidden" sex are your thing, you might not mind sitting through "The Everlasting Secret Family." But if you'd like more, like a reason—any reason—to care about these aloof, self-absorbed people, you're going to be gravely disappointed.

NEWSDAY, 11/17/89, Part III/p. 7, Terry Kelleher

"The Everlasting Secret Family" closes with talk of "endless dark possibilities," which is another way of saying "wild improbabilities,"

But as long as it manages to stay within the outer limits of plausibility, you'll want very much to see what happens next.

The movie opens at a private boys' school in Australia. It appears the whole student body is out taking light exercise. A limousine rolls up; an important looking gentleman emerges and scans the scene. His attention is directed to a blond lad of particularly pleasing aspect. A glance, a nod, and in a moment the visitor is gone.

The big shot turns out to be a politician (Arthur Dignam), and this is how he selects young talent for his staff. Next day, when the limo returns, the attractive student (Mark Lee) is pulled out of art class for his first homosexual tryst with the great man. The school quietly approves the relationship, apparently as a matter of routine. Just another internship.

It's a heady change of status for the teenager (identified in the dramatis personae only as "The

Youth''), who soon starts flaunting his privileges as the senatorial catamite. But the politician (no name, just "The Senator") seems to have seen all this before. Though mildly vexed at The Youth's flashes of temperament, The Senator knows how to feed his insecurity and compel his submission. Meanwhile, he tends scrupulously to his public image as the sort of officeholder any mother would trust to kiss her baby.

Thanks to Dignam's magisterial performance and the assured direction of Michael Thornhill— cool and understated, yet taut and erotic—"The Everlasting Secret Family" draws the viewer in as conflict simmers on several fronts. Extending his political contacts, The Youth begins servicing a masochistic judge (John Meillon). Feeling the need for an actual family to illustrate his family values, The Senator decides to marry a colleague's proper daughter (Heather Mitchell).

As if that weren't enough to make The Youth a bit anxious about his future, he discovers that The Senator's chauffeur (Dennis Miller) is a former lover who was demoted when his looks began to go.

Part of this movie's fascination, of course, lies in the potential for political sex scandal. By now we Americans are well schooled in such things. Blackmail, leaks, headlines—let the games begin. But gradually it becomes evident that "The Everlasting Secret Family" is not operating in the real world of media-age politics. Writer Frank Moorhouse, who based the screenplay on his book of short stories, is constructing a tall metaphor on the patterns of power and manipulation. The short-term consequences of a leader's double life are overshadowed by those endless dark possibilities.

The Youth finds a doctor who can arrest the aging process, and perhaps spare him the chauffeur's fate. The story skips ahead 14 years, at which point The Senator has a tall blond son. The Youth, who now looks like a prep schooler with crow's feet, holds the job of permanent "babysitter." And the viewer learns more—though not nearly enough to make sense—about the rituals of a secret homosexual society that has been pulling *everybody's* strings since time immemorial.

As absurdity and pretension creep into "The Everlasting Secret Family," dramatic tension recedes. What was sinister now seems silly, and you wonder how this film hooked you in the first place. The Youth may provide an answer as he reflects on his sexual entanglements: "I couldn't help enjoying the cheap novelty of it."

VILLAGE VOICE, 11/21/89, p. 96, Elliott Stein

Out of deepest left field comes *The Everlasting Secret Family*, an Australian film depicting a world of corruption and sexual manipulation dominated by gay males. The movie takes place in modern, straight-appearing Australia, which is seen as some sort of never-never land of sempiternal masquerade. The authority figures are all members of a ritualistic homosexual s&m secret society with the rose as its emblem ("The thorns supply the ecstasy"). And, what is more, all this has been going on for generations.

The protagonists/antagonists of this untoward tale are the Youth (Mark Lee), a young and very blond person, snatched from his studies to become an influential politican's willing love slave, and the Senator (Arthur Dignam)—no one has a proper name in this abstruse account of upper-class shenanigans except for the single working-class character, Eric (Dennis Miller), the Senator's former lover, who does most of his pimping and dirty work. After a number of labyrinthine events, we last see the Youth when he is fast approaching middle age; thanks to an experimental drug that prevents aging, this Down Under Dorian Gray, still a cutie-pie, is about to walk into the sunset with the Senator's adolescent son.

Family has been directed by Michael Thornhill in a series of elliptical, tableau-like scenes, occasionally punctuated by scooping, swoony Steadicam shots of obscure significance. The script, by Frank Moorhouse, is based on one of his own short stories. Moorhouse is quoted in the pressbook as saying that as a young man he was "forced into promiscuity by a harsh ideology," and, at that time, for him "homosexuality was a fascinating, strange, romantic cult." There's a cult in the movie all right, and some sex, but no romance. The characters are cold, distant, unloving, soigné, and obnoxious.

Moorhouse does have his kinky classics down pat—a scene involving an Asian gentleman comes right out of one of the great brothel sequences in Buñuel's *Belle de Jour*; another, in which the Judge (John Meillon) grovels and licks the Youth's shoes, is direct recall of the Judge-and-Thief scene in Jean Genet's *The Balcony*. Is this gross pilferage or "homage"? Hard to say. I can't even be sure whether this entire grotesquerie was meant as a brazen commentary on Australian mores or as a send-up of a gay soap opera. It may very well all be tongue-in-cheek—but whose tongue and whose cheek is not readily clear. Of this I've no doubt: Made by gays or not, it *smells* homophobic (unlike Moorhouse's original story, which posits a raunchy but nonmalevolent gay milieu). This art film could accommodate Jesse Helms's most paranoid fantasies.

Also reviewed in:
NEW YORK TIMES, 11/17/89, p. C16, Janet Maslin
VARIETY, 3/9/88, p. 10

EXQUISITE CORPSES

An Upfront Films release. *Executive Producer:* David Mazor and Glenn Dubin. *Producer:* Temistocles Lopez and Ken Schwenker. *Director:* Temistocles Lopez. *Screenplay:* Temistocles Lopez. *Director of Photography:* Stephen McNutt. *Editor:* John Murray. *Music:* Gary Knox. *Sound:* Joseph McGirr. *Art Director:* Carlos De Villamil. *Costumes:* Alfredo Villoria and Frederico Macquhae. *Running time:* 96 minutes. *MPAA Rating:* R.

CAST: Zöe Tamerlaine Lund (Belinda Maloney); Gary Knox (Tim Lee); Frank Roccio (Lou); Ruth Collins (Sue); Daniel Chapman (Joe); Chuck Perley (Pat Maloney); David Ilku (Jim); Lucy Ree (Gueneviere); Robert Lund (Club Owner).

NEW YORK POST, 3/24/89, p. 25, V.A. Musetto

Attitude is the most important tool for survival in Manhattan,'' intones Lou, a lascivious gay casting agent, in ''Exquisite Corpses.'' Attitude, he might have added, is also essential to how you feel about the film. Written, directed and produced on a $135,000 shoestring by Temistocles Lopez, a London Film School grad making his feature debut after several shorts and documentaries, ''Corpses'' is one big in-joke that can be appreciated best (and probably only) by the downtown types it portrays.

Tim (Gary Knox, the film's songwriter, too) is an Okie cowboy just arrived in New York to marry his childhood sweetheart, Sue (Ruth Collins). But, Tim discovers upon his unexpected arrival at Sue's East Village flat, the small-town gal has changed into a big-city peroxide blonde with a live-in lover.

After a string of rip-offs and insults that seasoned New Yorkers accept without second thoughts, Tim hooks up with casting agent Lou (Frank Roccio) and overnight sheds his drawl and cowboy boots to become a downtown sophisticate and singer in a seedy cabaret.

There are some nice touches along the way. Learning just the right pronunciation of Indochine, that chi-chi East Village dining spot, is part of Tim's transformation. His act is, in Lou's well-put words, designed to please ''the postcrash yuppie crowd looking for the cheap downtown thrill.'' Two Weillian production numbers have a certain satisfying sizzle. And Stephen McNutt's cinematography nicely evokes '40s noir.

Enter Belinda, a chanteuse provocatively portrayed by Zöe Tamerlaine Lund, who looks like a cross between Bianca Jagger and a young Lauren Bacall. Belinda and her super-rich husband complicate Tim's life—and the movie. The ensuing murder plot is, at best, imperceptible. The film's charm is gone, to be recaptured only in the Parisian finale.

Should you see ''Exquisite Corpses''? It all depends on attitude. If you can relate to the characters and situations, by all means visit the Bleecker Street Cinema, where the movie opens today. If, on the other hand, your world is removed from that on the screen, stay away.

NEWSDAY, 3/24/89, Part III/p. 3, Drew Fetherston

''Exquisite Corpses'' is not nearly a three-star film in all its aspects.

It has an inane retread plot, dialogue that is ofter lumpy and banal, acting that sometimes falls short of common competence. The last section is too long.

On the other hand, it has such flashes of cinematic brilliance that anyone serious about the form should see it. As an evocation of Downtown, the rind of the city where art and decadence rub against poverty and filth, it is superb.

Additionally, it has an excuse for its cinematic failings: Poverty. It was not done on the proverbial shoestring, it was done on $135,000, which is hardly gossamer. (The average Hollywood movie costs $13 million.) Its creator, Temistocles Lopez, wrote, produced and directed the film in fevered haste (before promised money could disappear) in two separate segments.

The haste shows, though not in the visual quality of the film. "Exquisite Corpses" is the story of Tim Lee (played by Gary Knox, who was hired to do the music and got the starring role when casting came to a crunch), an Oklahoma trombonist who comes to New York to find and marry his back-home sweetheart.

New York, or at least the lower right-hand corner of Manhattan, has already altered said sweetheart, and the town quickly gets to work on the poor rube as well. He loses his cash, clothes, instrument and dignity before he can cross 14th Street,.

He is seduced, seduces in turn, and shortly turns from an object of loathing into an object of veneration. He overreaches himself and, in falling, perceives that he has been the dupe of shadowy, sinister figures.

Lame stuff, but presented with so much flair it would be churlish to complain. Perfect shots form the facets of gemlike scenes, which are stitched in gaudy array on the fabric of the tale. Lopez may not have had much money, but he has a flawless eye for tawdry and garish wonders. Knox's musical score is eclectic and good.

Lopez recognized that cost-cutting might damage a serious work, and shrewdly chose to make this a black comedy-mystery. It is all done with a sweet humor that comes across even through the whiffs of decadence: A desperate thief collapses in tears after holding up the flat-broke hero at the point of a pair of hedge clippers. "This is pathetic, man," he sobs.

The film is confident and able in dealing with location shooting in the city (a necessity in a film that only got to use a club, The World, as a studio for a few days).

"The shower's down on the second floor," a clerk says cheerfully as he leads the lad to a hell-hole hotel room. "The bathroom's on the fourth floor, the phone is in the lobby. So now you know where everthing is. Welcome to New York." Later, after the hero has become a no-pay nuisance, the same clerk sips from a bottle of Pepto-Bismol as he tells him get out.

Because the film is really two separate pieces stitched together, it is hard to apportion credit for the best and blame for the rest. It is disturbing to note that some of the least interesting stretches of "Exquisite Corpses" seem to have been done when money was most plentiful.

The film certainly shows that Lopez, a Venezuelan who has also worked in France and Italy, can create remarkable film, out of extremely modest resources. "Exquisite Corpses" should bring him—and his next, better-financed film—deserved attention.

VILLAGE VOICE, 3/28/89, p. 69, Michael Musto

Written in two days by producer/director Temistocles Lopez and shot on a budget of $135,000, *Exquisite Corpses* wears all the pros and pitfalls of the fast-and-cheap genre like tattoos. As if throwing spaghetti against the wall to see if it'll stick, Lopez tries anything in his portrayal of New York as an alternately corrupt and magical place, striving for a calculated weirdness that's not quite soup yet.

Gary Knox (the film's songwriter, who replaced the leading man two days before shooting began) plays Tim, a Joe Buck-type cowboy who's transformed into a decadent—and bad—cabaret star and possible murderer. Zöe Tamerlaine Lund, all mouth, like a sexier, even more petulant Sandra Bernhard, is the vamp who complicates his life. And in the course of Tim's evolution, he meets dozens of others on the edge, stepping in everything from dog shit to performance art along the way. "Attitude is the most important tool for survival in Manhattan," a gay letch casting agent, played by Frank Roccio, informs him before teaching the correct pronunciation of Indochine. Later, Roccio gets to utter the film's underlying plea: "Does love fucking exist?"

Gratuitous attempts at shock mingle with Mack truck-like stabs at winsomeness ("It's a long way to Avalon," says a supposedly wise woman who sings to her Chihuahua), and the tone is never steady, as the genre edges from dark comedy to Weill musical to murder mystery and back again. When the film goes totally over the top, as in Lund's festively sinister production number, it can dazzle with daffiness. But for the most part, Lopez elevates that sacred attitude more into a religion than an entertainment.

Also reviewed in:

NEW YORK TIMES, 3/24/89, p. C8, Richard Bernstein
VARIETY, 7/20/88, p. 14

FABULOUS BAKER BOYS, THE

A Twentieth Century Fox Film release of a Gladden Entertainment Corp. production. *Executive Producer:* Sydney Pollack. *Producer:* Paula Weinstein and Mark Rosenberg. *Director:* Steve Kloves. *Screenplay:* Steve Kloves. *Director of Photography:* Michael Ballhaus. *Editor:* William Steinkamp. *Music:* Dave Grusin. *Music Editor:* Else Blangsted. *Sound:* Stephan Von Hase. *Sound Editor:* J. Paul Huntsman. *Production Designer:* Jeffrey Townsend. *Art Director:* Clay A. Griffith. *Set Designer:* Don Gibbin Jr. *Set Decorator:* Anne H. Ahrens. *Set Dresser:* Amy Feldman and Ross Harpold. *Special Effects:* Robert E. Worthington. *Costumes:* Lisa Jensen. *Make-up:* Ronnie Specter. *Stunt Coordinator:* Jon Pochron. *Running time:* 114 minutes. *MPAA Rating:* R.

CAST: Jeff Bridges (Jack Baker); Michelle Pfeiffer (Susie Diamond); Beau Bridges (Frank Baker); Ellie Raab (Nina); Xander Berkeley (Lloyd); Dakin Matthews (Charlie); Ken Lerner (Ray); Albert Hall (Henry); Terri Treas (Girl in Bed); Gregory Itzin (Vince Nancy); Bradford English (Earl); David Coburn (Kid at Vet); Todd Jeffries (Theo); Jeffrey J. Nowinski (Hotel Masseur); Nancy Fish (Laughing Bar Patron); Beege Barkette (Waitress); Del Zamora (Man with Cleaver); Howard Matthew Johnson (Bathroom Attendant); Stuart Nisbet (Veterinarian); Robert Henry (Doorman); Drake (Eddie); Martina Finch, Winifred Freedman, Wendy Goldman, Karen Hartman, D.D. Howard, Lisa Raggio, Vickilyn Reynolds, Krisie Spear, and Carole Ita White (Bad Singers); Jennifer Tilly (Monica Moran).

FILMS IN REVIEW, 1–2/90, p. 41, Michael Buckley

A first feature for writer-director Steve Kloves, *The Fabulous Baker Boys* is a most enjoyable picture that contains an award caliber performance by The Fabulous Michelle Pfeiffer.

She steals the film as the sensuous singer who spruces up the faltering twin piano act of the Baker brothers (played by the Bridges brothers, Jeff and Beau) and causes sparks to fly all around. Pfeiffer does her own singing (quite well) and performs a memorable rendition of "Makin' Whoopee," while slithering all over the top of a piano.

Jack Baker (Jeff Bridges) is an excellent musician who has sold himself short by teaming up with his brother. Jack lives alone, but is visited frequently by an Orphan Annie type (well played by Ellie Raab). Frank (Beau) has a wife and family—though they're never seen—and handles the finances and bookings for the act. Though they boast, "We've never held a day job in our lives," the Baker boys are experiencing dire times—until Pfeiffer arrives on the scene. A radical (she compares the standard "Feelings" to "*less* than parsley"), she unsettles Frank and, in a romantic way, does the same for Jack.

The sequence where the brothers audition singers, before Pfeiffer (number 38) shows up, is very funny—although it does go on too long. Jennifer Tilly is particularly good as a would-be singer who gives her all with "Candyman."

Like its musical background, *The Fabulous Baker Boys* doesn't miss a note.

LOS ANGELES TIMES, 10/13/89, Calendar/p. 1, Sheila Benson

You've heard "The Fabulous Baker Boys" everywhere. They play under expense-account dinners at restaurants with little paper umbrellas in the banana daiquiris. Their unyielding patter has intruded on more than one businessman's proposition to the new girl in Accounts Receivable. They played "Feelings" and "People" and "The Girl From Ipanema" 358 times last year, and with any luck, they'll play them again next year.

They've shown us no mercy, why should we cut them any slack? Because "The Fabulous Baker Boys," a clear-eyed look at an unpromising end of show biz, is as salty and sexy and unhousebroken a movie as you could hope to find. Because writer-director Steve Kloves has a keen eye, a mean wit and a romantic's heart. And because the fabulous Bridges boys are just that, and Michelle Pfeiffer is delectable, even for her. It does not seem fair that she can sing, too. Maybe she can't cook. Things have to even out somewhere.

As Frank Baker (Beau Bridges) *will* confide to us, want him to or not, he and Jack (Jeff Bridges) have been across the 88 keys from each other, gosh, how many years now? Thirty-one? Fifteen of them on-stage as professionals.

That's a long time on two piano stools. And the funny-dreadful opening scenes make it clear what a long, slow trip down it's been. Fluorescent luau shirts at Tiki-Bob's. Tuxedos at the Starfire Lounge. Apathetic, half-sloshed audiences everywhere, 30 years older than they are. Frank would keep grinding on, night after night, but when an old client pays them *not* to play one night, it's sign that the act needs resuscitation.

The 37 girls who audition to be their singer are pretty grand. Their gestures all seem to have been coached by the same folks who do the Junior Miss America pageant, and not one of them can carry a tune. (OK, so the audition-routine-sequence owes everything Milos Forman's "Taking Off." Almost every audition scene since then has; it's still fiendishly funny.) At least these damsels succeed in getting Jack's total, mesmerized attention, although it's probably just an untapped strain of masochism.

Enter Susie Diamond (Pfeiffer), whose most recent professional experience has been on call for the Triple-A escort service, and who has to park her gum before she sings. Her number? "More Than You Know," and right away we know; my do we know.

With just the right rough edges on this Diamond (and with some really witty music and visual editing effects), we watch these three pound together an act while keeping their lives almost separated. Frank has an (unseen) wife, family and house in the suburbs. Tough cookie Susie has A Past. And Jack has an aging Labrador and Nina, the adoring pre-teen-ager from the upstairs apartment who may not even need a T-shirt that reads "Dramatic Device."

After a wonderfully rocky start, Susie becomes more and more experienced, until the boys find themselves in the astonishing position of being sought after instead of being barely tolerated. This upward curve to the story is lovely; especially a delicately staged and brilliantly photographed scene on a resort hotel balcony, as the longings of all three are revealed in a scene that's almost a subtle aria. (The cinematographer is Michael Ballhaus, which should explain everything.)

The movie's musical high point is a New Year's Eve scorcher when an emergency calls Frank away and, left to program their own gala, Jack and Susie greet the incoming year with a version of "Makin' Whoopee" that takes no prisoners. The love scene that follows—staged tenderly, so that we just see Jack's mouth on the exquisite trench of Susie's naked back—is one that's been building since these two bedroom veterans set eyes on one another.

Then, the story seems to take an unexpected bounce. While we're braced for the plot line about the show-business team that breaks up because one member is offered bigger things, writer Kloves is more interested in the relationship of the boys themselves, as musicians and as brothers. Susie becomes the force needed to have Jack face how much he really hates his life. And the movie requires first a lover's quarrel, then a brother's, before things are right again.

Even with patches of tired dialogue about her checkered past, Pfeiffer's Susie fills the screen so vividly that a lot of the life leaves it when she does, even briefly. Normally, Jeff Bridges' presence would make up for any imbalance, but he's playing a man whose psyche is so retracted it's barely there. Between that and what passes for declarations of attraction on the modern American scene these days, we are not talking major affect here. For an ending to a picture this delicious, it's like a crepe compared to triple-decker strawberry shortcake. You may just have to learn to love crepes.

The performances, at least, couldn't be improved upon. Les Boys have honed their timing so their exchanges, like the one about Frank's touch-up paint for his bald spot, or the fruit war in their hotel suite, are lethally funny without losing their sense of underlying love. Now singing too, Pfeiffer seems to be in the same niche that Ava Gardner was in after "The Flying Dutchman," as the screen's reigning goddess. No objections here.

MONTHLY FILM BULLETIN, 3/90, p. 67, Tom Milne

Seattle. For fifteen years, Frank Baker, a devoted family man, and his brother Jack, an inveterate womaniser, have enjoyed moderate success on the cabaret circuit as a piano duo. Bored by their act's unvarying routine, drinking heavily and relieving his frustrations in backstreet jazz clubs, Jack (the one with the talent) listlessly agrees when Frank (the business manager, always worrying about financial security and determined to keep the act together despite declining bookings) suggests the added attraction of a chanteuse. Discouraged when thirty-seven auditions turn up no one remotely able to carry a tune, both brothers are amazed when a late arrival—dishevelled, loud-mouthed, gum-chewing Susie Diamond, for the last two years on call for the Triple-A Escort Service—proves to be startlingly good. Hurriedly redressed and groomed, she is a resounding success on her début with the act, and bookings take a distinct turn for the better. Meanwhile Jack, though attracted to Susie—his love being reserved for an ancient Labrador with halitosis and a neglected child in his apartment house—remains suspicious of her supposed commerce with men. Susie is equally attracted, but Frank, growing increasingly fond of her, warns Jack off in fear that she may be hurt if Jack follows his usual practice of loving and leaving. Eventually, after a New Year booking when Frank takes time off to be with his family, while Jack and Susie seize the opportunity to jazz the act up, the pair become lovers. As bored as Jack with the set routines Frank insists on, Susie tells Jack she has been offered a job singing in TV commercials; disappointed when he advises her to take it instead of asking her to stay, she quits. Once more a duo with Frank, Jack contrives to turn their appearance on a cretinous charity telethon into disaster. A quarrel, fist fight and eventual reconciliation ensue. So Frank understands when Jack, at last coming out from under his brother's protective management of his chaotic life, announces that he has accepted a job in a jazz club. Jack then hurries to see Susie, and they tentatively agree to reopen their relationship.

There is a marvellously funny scene quite early on in Steve Kloves' film where Beau and Jeff Bridges, after a frantic rush to make Michelle Pfeiffer look suitably sleek and soignée, expectantly take their places at the two pianos, with Beau suavely launching into his usual corny patter. Nervously cadging a swig from a drink being delivered by a passing waitress ("OK", says the latter obligingly, "but no lipstick"), Pfeiffer makes her entry, has trouble adjusting the microphone, audibly snaps "What fucking switch?" in response to prompting, and dives out of frame in pursuit of the dropped mike. Desperately the brothers try to cover by stammering into song themselves, only to be cut short by the first riveting line of Pfeiffer's rendition of "Ten Cents a Dance", heralding her smiling reappearance in frame.

It's an electrifying moment, making one realise what it must have been like to be in on the early revelation of such luminaries as Billie Holiday or Helen Morgan. Good as she is in her début as a singer, Michelle Pfeiffer may not be *that* good (her delivery is perhaps a little too studied), but she effortlessly carries the film's point about creative interpretation in music. Equally effortlessly (thanks both to Kloves' direction and to Dave Grusin's arrangements), *The Fabulous Baker Boys* sidesteps the embarrassing pretensions almost invariably encountered (even Scorsese's *New York, New York* makes a semi-hash of it) in movies trying to explore the frustrations of a musician torn between the world of commerce and jazz.

Here, with the music circulating amiably through a range of standards ("Candy Man" is a favourite of Jack Baker's, but he draws the line at "Bali Ha'i"), the point is to show someone not so much struggling to find a new note and become another Bessie Smith or Charlie Parker, as merely yearning for the right to interpret a song instead of reducing it to its basic Palm Court formula. When Jack and Susie break out during Frank's New Year absence, the item they choose for the occasion is "Makin' Whoopee". No great shakes as songs go, but as performed blues-style by Jack and Susie, complete with sexily choreographed, red velvet-clad piano-top gyrations, it is reborn bursting with vitality.

At the same time, the music offers a codebook to characters, emotions and motivations. When Susie watches unobserved as Jack sits alone at the piano playing for himself, it is the music, obviously, which defines her attraction to him as one kindred spirit recognising another. Less obviously, it provides a complete biographical scenario adumbrating the relationship between the borthers: Frank, the elder and assuming responsibility as such, clinging to the concept of family and devoting all his energies to the pursuit of security; Jack, wayward but the one with the talent, relying on big brother to keep his head above water as he retreats into a world of uncertain dreams. The one comparative weakness in the film is its use of the Labrador with teeth problems and the lonely little girl as stand-ins for the domestic warmth which Jack has turned his back on in pursuit of a chimera. Not that these scenes aren't both delightful and to the point; but they do tend to lower the film, momentarily, towards conventional Neil Simon territory.

Elsewhere in this astonishingly accomplished first feature, Steve Kloves handles his material with an elliptical subtlety that is a pleasure to watch. Crucial to the film's constantly ravelling and unravelling emotional threads is a long, serpentine sequence set in adjoining hotel rooms (the brothers sharing one, Susie occupying the other) and on their connecting balcony as the trio celebrate their success. To the accompaniment of "Moaning Low", Frank dreamily reminisces about boyhood days, starts to dance with Susie, absently suggests that she might like to partner Jack; she demurs, pleading that Jack might not want to; he does, and as the pair move into each other's arms, Frank quietly disappears. The scene later comes to mind, seemingly in verification, when Susie angrily accuses Frank of a lifetime of pimping for Jack in his one-night-stand love life. Yet the implied feelings and resentments are qualified, here as elsewhere, by subsequent scenes tracing their subterranean evolution.

One, for instance, in which Jack unexpectedly interrupts Frank's usual introductory patter on stage, blurting for all to hear, "I love you, Frank . . . I just wanted to say it". Another in which, the morning after their celebration with Frank, Jack sneaks into Susie's room in her absence, examining possible evidence of call girl activities but (in gestures reminiscent of the bedroom-caressing sequence in *Queen Christina*) betraying quite different preoccupations. A third in which Frank, not jealous or resentful but paternally solicitous, misinterprets Jack's attitude to Susie and warns him off. Far from being arbitrary, the happy ending for Jack and Susie ("Hey, am I gonna see you again?"—"What do you think?"—"Yeah, I think I am gonna see you again") becomes a logical inevitability after the delightfully offhand penultimate scene in which the two brothers, reminiscing inconsequentially over the mementoes charting the way stations in their life together, come to an unspoken understanding of how they have used each other as crutches. Superlatively performed by all three leads (with the sibling intimacy between Jeff and Beau Bridges a distinct bonus), directed with high promise and more, *The Fabulous Baker Boys* is a film difficult to imagine anyone disliking, easy to see being underrated because it chooses to proceed by indirections.

NEW STATESMAN & SOCIETY, 3/16/90, p. 42, Suzanne Moore

Whoever it was who said that it was their ambition to die without ever having been to California has my deepest sympathy. For these days you don't even have to get on a plane to get a dose of sickly Californian imperialism. You just need to go to the movies and you are in a strange land where everyone emotes endlessly, the sun always shines, no one smokes and the language is a peculiar kind of therapy-speak. This world is peopled by *individuals* who believe that the root of all evil is simply that we don't know how to "relate" to each other. The goal of these saccharine-coated characters is to "come to terms" with everything it is impossible to come to terms with, like sex, death or growing up.

So in this sanitised, anti-smoking atmosphere of user-friendly smiles, it is a pleasure to see two films which blow smoke in the face of clean living. The first looks as if it was sponsored by the tobacco industry and the other examines the fag end of a marriage.

The Fabulous Baker Boys stars Jeff Bridges as Jack Baker, a man who has "had a cigarette in his mouth for five years." He and his older brother Frank, played by real-life sibling Beau Bridges, are the fabulous Baker boys: a low-key cocktail lounge act whose dire repertoire includes the dreadful song "Feelings" as well as a lot of schmaltzy patter. Early on in the film, written and directed by Steve Kloves, Jack is established as the epitome of cool: ie, besides chain-smoking, he fucks waitresses and doesn't really talk to anyone except children (the little girl upstairs) and animals (his dog).

His brother holds the whole thing together with the help of spray-on hair and smarmy small talk. He has to for the sake of his wife and kids, but even he realises, "Things have changed. Two pianos aren't enough any more." So they recruit a singer and end up with ex-call girl Susie (Michelle Pfeiffer), whose breathy renditions and horrible outfits go down a storm with audiences. Predictably enough she falls for Mr Cool who, surprise, surprise, actually wants to be a black jazz pianist.

But the centre of the film is not so much this affair but the relationship between the two brothers. This is played out beautifully, as is the portrait of life on the road, so that despite the clichés (strong, silent type meets tart with heart of gold), this is a film that is consistently watchable. But Pfeiffer—touted as the new sex-goddess—wiggles so obviously on the top of a piano that it makes you long for the likes of Bette Davis who could suggest more by smoking a cigarette than any amount of bump'n'grind. The days when screen idols had a cigarette *instead* of having sex rather than *after* having sex are long gone. In the era of New Prohibition no one has either any more, they're too busy air-brushing those unhealthy urges and flossing their feelings to meet the exacting standards of moral hygiene currently required by Holly-wood.

NEW YORK, 10/16/89, p. 73, David Denby

The camera rises out of a bubbling fish tank, and there they are, aglow in purple-pink light, sliding their hands up and down the piano—Frank (Beau Bridges) and Jack Baker (Jeff Bridges), the heroes of *The Fabulous Baker Boys*. For fifteen years, they've been working together as a two-piano team, doing the same moldy patter night after night, playing "Feelings" in mossy Seattle hotel lounges for people who talk through their act. With their pasted-on tuxedos and their swelling, shiny hair, the Bakers have merged into their glossies. *Tronkling,* my fastidious dad used to call their kind of playing.

The Fabulous Baker Boys is a great movie about a subject normally taken for granted—the irritations and compromises that lodge between two brothers who love each other and know each other's character all too well; it's also one of the best movies about the dim, dreary lower ranks of show business, with their acrid dissatisfactions, its road-weariness and endless routine. Yet *Baker Boys* isn't all melancholy. Dead in the water, the boys are roused from their sleep by Susie Diamond (Michelle Pfeiffer), a beautiful singer who joins the act. Pfeiffer gives a taut, thrilling performance; she brings sex and the colors of fierce ambition to the movie. *Baker Boys* is both hard-nosed and lyrical, both bluesy and exhilarating. In fact, it's a bloody miracle. Steve Kloves, the 29-year-old writer-director whose only previous credit is the screenplay for Richard Benjamin's *Racing With the Moon,* has made something lovely and fragile, a portrait of show-business seediness that is mysteriously charged with romantic longing.

They are utterly different, these brothers. Frank is the musician as suburbanite, a satisfied family man just earning a living. For him, music is neither ecstasy nor torment; he has long stopped caring, or noticing, that the act is musically pathetic, though he likes to think he's putting on a good show. (Tronkling away and smiling fatuously at the audience, he imagines he's Mr. Entertainment.) Beau Bridges, heavier and jowlier than he used to be, plays this happy man with a touch of anxiety that keeps the character from falling into priggishness. Frank is hard to dislike.

Frank arranges the bookings and the travel, designs the shows, and keeps a motherly watch over his kid brother, Jack, who's surly and unreliable. Always busy, he has developed a fussbudget's sense of martyrdom; he may complain about carrying all the burdens, but actually he revels in it. Beau Bridges is sweaty and hyperactive (he seems to be always packing something); he shows us Frank's sentimentality and his self-righteousness. What saves Frank from smugness is his exasperated appreciation of his talented brother, and when round-faced Beau Bridges looks at *his* talented kid brother, who gets more handsome and virile as he grows older, the relationship makes perfect psychological sense. Frank's resentment is held in check by adoration.

Jack lives in a downtown loft, and his only friends are his sick old dog (a Lab) and a rather inexpressive, sour-faced little girl from upstairs who lets herself in via the fire escape every time her mother entertains a male guest. Grouchy and silent, a cigarette hanging from his mouth, he seems to be punishing himself with isolation and loneliness. Jack's idea of cool is so far out of date it's almost a joke, and he probably knows that. He doesn't say much; Jeff Bridges gives him a small, distant, uncommitted voice (as if the smoking had eaten up his lungs) and furtive sexual impulses—nothing too eager.

When Jack has to play something like "The Girl From Ipanema" for the 200th time, he looks grim, like a volunteer fireman handling a corpse. Jack won't *entertain*—not himself or anyone else. We gather, from little hints, that the intelligence, the musical talent, the courage were once all in place, but the greatness in him is now thoroughly hidden. It's a shock to see him playing at a black jazz club, a basement dive: Liberated at last from the rippling trash of the piano lounge, and free to improvise, he's completely happy, his face animated, almost distorted, with pleasure. Jeff Bridges gives a classic performance as a self-protecting loser. In his cutoff way, Jack *is* cool, but he's weak, too, trapped by fear and his love for his brother into a life he loathes. He's a man choking on self-disgust.

Steve Kloves is a terse and elegant writer of dialogue. For a long time, the movie's moods are not directly articulated but grow out of silent gestures and glances. What most movies lack is a sense that the characters are truly familiar with one another, but *The Fabulous Baker Boys* has it in spades. Appearing together for the first time, the Bridges brothers make their rapport seem instinctive and subverbal. The Baker boys can be abrasive with each other yet relaxed the next moment because, after all, they're brothers. Frank's fussy primness bounces off the wall of Jack's nasty silence—until Jack suddenly shows, with a word, that he has been listening and has understood his brother's lame little point. The ebb and flow of aggression, never consummated and never resolved, keeps the movie in tension.

Michelle Pfeiffer's Susie is an ex-hooker who quickly sees that the Baker boys are in desperate need of her. She is a tough, practical working girl—and the way Pfeiffer plays her is a wonder. At the microphone, Pfeiffer, who does her own singing, has a small voice, but she sings with style and authority; she's sultry yet decisive, a Julie London without the foggy masochism. And her acting is more precise and stronger than ever, taking its power from her amazing beauty, which, like Katharine Hepburn's beauty at her peak, strikes us as an intense clarifier of whatever emotions she is bringing out—we seem to perceive the meaning of what she's saying through the sharp cut of her features, the devastating curve of her lips. This is Pfeiffer's most sensual work yet.

With this dazzler singing, the twin-piano act suddenly becomes a smash, and Kloves's camera, which has been mostly steady, starts sweeping and dipping; the movie turns glamorous, even exultant. But only when the trio is performing. Off-stage, Kloves holds the tentative and inarticulate moods; the three look at one another warily, frightened of what might happen, but now the reticence develops suspense, for Susie and Jack are perfect for each other, hipsters alike in talent, joined by the painful experience of living as whores and hating every moment of it. Will they or won't they? The old romantic question hovers through scene after scene, but Kloves isn't just teasing us. Susie is making it as a singer for the first time, and she doesn't want to louse it up.

Frank sees what's going on and, fearing for his future with his brother, tries to prevent anything from happening. But when he takes a few days off, and Jack accompanies Susie himself, she climbs onto the piano for a version of "Makin' Whoopee" so powerfully erotic that any hesitation is inconceivable. Pfeiffer furls and unfurls herself and slides down Jeff Bridges's back, and he looks stunned. When the seduction finally comes, it's a marvelously satisfying payoff for all our waiting. Roused, Jack has to decide whether he'll live or sink back into slumber.

Watching *The Fabulous Baker Boys*, we may feel vaguely that we've seen elements of it before and that we know how the story is going to work itself out. Still, the way Kloves gets from one point to the next is entirely fresh: The movie has its own hypnotic rhythm of silence, longing, and fear. It trembles with the hipster's terror of saying how much he cares about something—for once he says it, he'll be responsible for what he loves. Young as he is, Kloves nevertheless lets the affection flow out of him. *The Fabulous Banker Boys* is an astoundingly expressive debut film.

NEW YORK POST, 10/13/89, p. 23, David Edelstein

As Jack, half of a lousy brother-brother piano act in "The Fabulous Baker Boys," Jeff Bridges wears a dyspeptic smirk and spins a cobweb of irony around each line.

Viewing the world through eyes half-shut, Jack leaves business to his overbearing older brother, Frank (Beau Bridges), and then drives Frank crazy showing up late for gigs, rumpled and with a butt stuck in his mouth. He's dodgy, as maybe you'd have to be with a brother so bossy and excitable; at the end of the evening he leaves with waitresses or hatcheck girls, none of whom he sees again. It's the darkest, sexiest, most magnetic performance of Jeff Bridges' life.

The Fabulous Baker Boys play Sheraton and Hilton lounges when they're lucky and Polynesian restaurants when they're not. Throughout their set, which includes such numbers as "Feelings" and "The Girl From Ipanema," Frank maintains a level of unctuous show-biz patter while his little brother ("88 keys to my left") sits stonefaced, quietly appalled. Later, Jack sometimes goes to a black-owned basement jazz club and plays with his heart, hunched over the piano. It's the only time he lets his loneliness show.

The "fabulous" in "The Fabulous Baker Boys" is ironic, but the movie sure isn't. Now smart and satirical and effervescent, now sultry and romantic, now depressed and piercingly honest, it can scarcely contain all its disparate moods and feelings. Yet somehow this marvelous comedy-drama—the directorial debut of writer Steve Kloves—seems all of a piece.

It's actually the story of two brothers locked into a neurotically dependent relationship, but you wouldn't know it from the opening hour. With bookings dwindling, Frank proposes the duo incorporate a singer into their act. As they hold auditions, Kloves serves up a montage of the most appallingly off-key and off-beat warblers you've ever heard, to Jack's amusement and Frank's horror. (A hefty percentage of the movie's laughs are reaction shots, and owe much to William Steinkamp's fleet and crackerjack editing.)

Late and the last to audition, Susie Diamond (Michelle Pfeiffer) is what in movies they used call "a real piece of work"—mugging, gum-cracking, her hand on her hip. Pfeiffer is almost too ethereally beautiful for the part—you wonder why the brothers don't drop dead when she walks in—but she proves in this film that she's a great comedienne, a real movie star.

Her singing voice, moreover, is terrific—improbably husky and soulful, with the timbre you'd expect from Mae West or Lauren Bacall. Her phrasing is even more accomplished. It doesn't matter that it's two tacky pianists in a nowhere hotel lounge: With Pfeiffer framed by pianos, singing "Ten Cents a Dance" as the rain falls blue out the window, it's beautiful.

In her short, thigh-high dresses, Susie greets Jack's offer to walk her home with a hardboiled request not to go soft on her, and he smirks and says, "Forget it." To her shock, he does, and she goes soft on him. Their relationship becomes a kind of parody of cool, and the suspense in the movie comes from how these two gorgeous people get under each other's skins.

When Frank has to leave a resort where they're booked for New Year's (his kid has an accident), Jack and Susie bring their foreplay into the open. Rolling and reclining on the piano in a long red dress with a slit to the top of her thighs, she comes on to Jack as no one's been come on to since Bacall offered Bogart a cigarette. The song is "Making Whoopee," and the scene—with the camera revolving around the piano—is a classic.

Yet the beauty of the drifting "Fabulous Baker Boys" is that Susie is a catalyst—she brings the brothers' relationship to a head. Jack's sexy cool comes to seem like a prison, a defense against his older brother, and both seem emotionally stunted.

As Kloves explores this, the evening grows long and some of the audience restless. You don't expect him to keep pushing and plumbing the way he does, edging the material into darker, more subterranean areas. The movie never loses its poise, though. The tone oscillates between musical comedy and something jazzy and melancholy and free-form—between Frank's world and Jack's.

Beau respects Frank too much to send up his showmanship—he knows it's Frank who runs everything, and that what Frank does takes skill. And even though Frank is bossy and repressive—an enemy of the life force—there's something childlike and likable about him, too. He's just out of control.

"The Fabulous Baker Boys," however, is gorgeously balanced—a romantic musical comedy for adults.

The three actors work together with such exuberance that Kloves doesn't have to spell much out. When a delighted Beau erupts into mock-punches and slaps with his baby brother, it doesn't look carefully choreographed; it's just something they do. And when they pound on each other (in the movie's ugliest moment) there's a little something extra in that, too.

There's a little something extra in everything about "The Fabulous Baker Boys." Kloves has clearly seen a lot of musicals from the '40s and '50s, but no one could mistake what he does for recycling—what comes with the old-fashioned glamor are modern neuroses. When Pfeiffer sings, the rest of the world falls away. Her Susie wakes Jack up from his stupor, reminds him what it's like to love what you do. Kloves reminds us what it's like to nestle in a movie instead of just watch one.

NEWSDAY 10/13/89, Part III/p. 3, Mike McGrady

When Hollywood historians get around to summing up the year 1989, they may very well decide to dub this the Year of the Prodigy. First came 26-year-old writer-director Steven Soderbergh with his memorably different "sex, lies, and videotape." Now comes still another wunderkind, Steve Kloves, who wrote "The Fabulous Baker Boys" when he was a lad of 23 but didn't get around to directing it until reaching the ripe old age of 27.

"The Fabulous Baker Boys" is pure dazzle built around three characters who are so distinct, so electric, so real that at times you get the feeling they're making up the script as they go along.

Jeff and Beau Bridges are Jack and Frank Baker, piano-playing brothers described by director Kloves as "blue-collar entertainers"—not unlike assembly-line workers as they hunch over matching pianos and deliver the same pop standards and the same slightly cloying line of patter to cocktail-lounge lizards and their ladies 250 nights out of every year.

Frank (Beau), the square brother, is a family man, a suburbanite, the responsible sort who handles the bookings, the cash flow, the song selections. Jack (Jeff) is a loner who shares his rented skid-row room with an ailing dog; late at night, after working with his brother, he sneaks off to little jazz clubs, where he comes alive briefly until the booze puts out his lights.

Business for the Fabulous Baker Boys has not been good, and it is Frank who comes up with the idea of adding a female vocalist to the act. Enter Susie Diamond (Michelle Pfeiffer), fresh from the Triple-A Escort Service, a natural blues singer who gets every ounce of oomph from great old songs like "More Than You Know" and "Makin' Whoopee."

Susie is more than a new meal ticket for the brothers Baker, she's also the discordant element that forces them to examine their relationship and ask themselves what they've been doing with their lives. Although it may seem as though nothing much is happening, in fact, everything is; lives are changing direction.

The script—funny, tough, human, sexy—is a humdinger, and it's all but impossible to believe that Kloves wrote it at the age of 23; it's equally hard to believe this is the first film he has ever directed. (His only other credit was the script for "Racing With the Moon.") The young man is at home with the written word; he knows what to leave out as well as what to put in. In fact, so good is his script and so hip is his direction that it may never cross your mind this is the oldest movie plot of them all—the vaudeville team being broken up by the arrival of a new love.

When a script is this economical, it's up to the actors to fill in the spaces, and I can't imagine performers better able to do this than these three. Beau Bridges has the relatively thankless job of being the stiffo. Jeff Bridges' part—he is the drifter, the loner, the boozer, the jazzman—enables the actor to do what he does so well: be tough and sensitive, restless and likable.

However, the real surprise of the movie is Michelle Pfeiffer. Not that I'm surprised by the quality of her performance, not after her recent triumphs in "Married to the Mob," "Tequila Sunrise" and "Dangerous Liaisons." But here she must live up to the name Susie Diamond—she must be as spunky and fresh as a Susie and as hard as any diamond. Not only does she manage both sides of the equation, her way with a torch song will astonish. That way, incidentally, is sexy, very sexy.

But everyone, including world-class cinematographer Michael Ballhaus, will find their reputations enhanced by association with "The Fabulous Baker Boys." And in one case, the case of writer-director Kloves, it's not so much that his reputation will be enhanced. It will be established.

NEWSWEEK, 10/23/89, p. 84, David Ansen

The piano-playing Baker brothers, Frank and Jack (Beau and Jeff Bridges), have been doing their cocktail-lounge act for so long they could play "People" in their sleep. Their 15-year gig, playing old chestnuts in second-rate Seattle hotels and bars to bored, increasingly dwindling crowds, is running out of gas. So they decide to hire a singer to jazz up their act, which is how Susie Diamond (Michelle Pfeiffer) enters their lives. Susie isn't the world's most accomplished vocalist, but this dazzling former escort girl doesn't need to be: with her smoldering sexuality, she could sell tickets to a tax audit. Susie turns business around, as intended, but her effect on the brothers is downright disruptive.

The Fabulous Baker Boys is set in the present, but its spiritual model is the moody romanticism of a '40s flick. Exquisitely lit by cinematographer Michael Ballhaus, it has a languid, offbeat ambience that pulls you right in. Twenty-nine-year-old writer ("Racing With the Moon") Steve Kloves, making his directorial debut, has a refreshing faith in understatement and style to burn. His movie is a character study of two brothers and the woman who forces them to reassess their unexamined lives. Frank (Beau) is the responsible, dogged family man, who takes care of business. But the unmarried Jack (Jeff), who's squandered his deep musical talent, is sullen and embittered, a womanizer with crippling fear of commitment. Will Susie, a tough cookie herself, force him out of his shell?

Perhaps. Kloves doesn't want to play by conventional romantic comedy rules, but he hasn't quite figured out what to replace them with. After the first seductive hour, which dances on the edge of comedy and melancholy, "The Fabulous Baker Boys" grows increasingly frustrating. The audience is enjoying Kloves's hip, knowing update of romantic conventions, but the director seems to think he's making "realism": he misjudges the gravity of his story, and his touch becomes more ponderous. Through no fault of Jeff Bridges, Jack's shut-off, self-pitying behavior begins to wear out its welcome. An '80s audience may be less likely to forgive his boorishness because of his "artist's soul." Kloves, in his youth, probably identifies with the romantic posture of the compromised artist, not realizing what a cliché it's become.

Still, this intriguing, imperfect movie is worth rooting for. Pfeiffer is slinky, brittle perfection as the latest whore-with-heart-of-gold—she's never been so alluring. Beau Bridges gives a wonderfully shaded rendition of a decent man with deeply buried sibling resentments, while Jeff broods with imploded panache. These real brothers work together like a charm. Kloves is loaded with talent, no doubt about it. He's made half a terrific movie; with a little more seasoning, he'll get it all right.

TIME, 10/23/89, p. 85, Richard Schickel

In small-time show biz, fading but persistent optimism is always engaged in a losing struggle with slowly metastasizing despair. Since Jack and Frank Baker (Jeff and Beau Bridges) are approaching middle age and still playing duo cocktail piano in Seattle's lesser lounges, an air of hopelessness has begun to hang heavy. Stardom is no longer an option; survival, even on the bottom rung, is becoming a question.

The Baker boys need to refurbish their tired act. But Susie Diamond (Michelle Pfeiffer) is not at first glance an answered prayer. She totters into their lives on a broken high heel, late for her audition and not exactly thrilled to be there in any case. But wonder of wonders, she can sing. And both onstage and off, she combines worldliness and vulnerability in a way that shakes up audiences as well as her new employers.

Can a partnership based on the habit of failure deal with the potential for success she offers? That question preoccupies first-time director Steve Kloves' realistic-romantic, wry-funny, altogether delightful movie. And it is not easily solved.

Banality is a security blanket for Frank. He has been playing the standards in a routine fashion for years, stitching the songs together with chipper-inane prattle as featureless as his musicianship. He's just a guy supporting his offscreen wife, kids and mortgage in a way he finds more congenial than, say, selling aluminum siding. Banality is a hair shirt for Jack. His life is all squalid improvisation and silent disgust at tinkling out "piano stylings." He knows better, and he might do better, as a jazzman.

By transforming their act, Susie of course changes the brothers' lives. To deal with her, they finally have to confront themselves and a relationship based far more on shared genes than on common ideals. The wary way in which she and Jack circle in on a relationship is one of the truest representations of modern romance that the modern screen has offered. The gradual stripping away of false issues between the brothers (Why is Jack always late for gigs? Why does Frank fuss so much about his bald spot?) as they get down to the true ones (involving, naturally, their childhood and piano lessons) is done with similar subtlety. Kloves' delicacy as a writer is, moreover, matched by his restraint as a director. It would have been easy to patronize or satirize the less than fabulous milieu of *The Fabulous Baker Boys*. Instead he and his fine cinematographer, Michael Ballhaus, have created a gently dislocating *noir*ish mood—not quite menacing but not exactly comfortable either—and let it speak for itself.

It is a setting where actors can live and breathe like real people, and the Bridges boys are better than fabulous in it—Jeff not quite falling over the line into unredeemable cynicism, Beau never succumbing to the pull of moral blandness. Pfeiffer, who does her own singing, is a cat with at least nine dimensions ever aflicker in her eyes.

What emerges here is a Hollywood rarity these days, a true character comedy. Because it is a form the studios no longer trust commercially, Kloves lingered four years on the street of broken deals before getting his script onscreen. His persistence deserves a reward. And as a near perfect example of an endangered species, *The Fabulous Baker Boys* deserves the protection only large, enthusiastic audiences can provide.

VILLAGE VOICE, 10/17/89, p. 100 Gary Giddins

It looked promising on paper—the nearly fabulous Bridges boys in a low-key anecdote set against a scrim of nightclubs so seedy that Bill Murray's lounge singer could get by as the real thing. Yet *The Fabulous Baker Boys* is a mess, though not even the relentless piling on of clichés and arty conceits in the service of movietown's most shameless theme (we are all whores) can completely diminish the pleasures of watching Jeff, increasingly rumpled but a born leading man, and Beau, free of his baby fat and ready to assume the mantle of a masterful character actor. Poor Michelle Pfeiffer, unflatteringly photographed and stuck with the role of the gold-hearted hooker-turned-singer whose honesty shows up everyone else's blahblahblah, emotes so hard and well she seems to be in the wrong picture. Emoting is out of place here.

The Baker Boys are a piano act, Ferrante & Teicher without the hits. Frank (Beau), who spray-paints his bald spot and has an offscreen family in the suburbs, takes care of the business end, makes the announcements, chooses the repertory ("Feelings," "People"). His brother Jack (Jeff) goes through the motions, banging cocktail waitresses between sets, and looking amiably morose. You know he's soulful because (a) he loves his dog and his neighbor's neglected little girl, and (b) he hangs out in jazz clubs and keeps photos of Bird and Diz and Bill Evans on the walls of his pad. Beau gets laughs and Jeff wears his tux the way real nightclub hacks do (as though it were pajamas). The characters are established quickly enough, you're ready for a story.

But there isn't one. From the moment early on when they hold auditions for a singer, you know everything that's going to happen—everything. You know that, contrary to real auditions where most applicants are merely mediocre, these will be Grand Guignol bad, except for Susie (Pfeiffer), who arrives late and has to convince them to give her a chance. Need I go on? You know she'll be a hit, even though she sings "More Than You Know" as though she were coming out of general anesthesia. You know Jack and Susie will get it on, which makes their prolonged mating dance (including a scene in which they sniff each other's toiletries) excruciating. You know Jack and Frank will fight and make up. You know Jack and Susie will fight and make up. You know, but you still don't believe it, that Jack will recover his soul by becoming a jazz pianist. A black club-owner offers him two nights a week, every week, just like that—even though Jack plays exactly like Dave Grusin, who did the score. The irony of Grusin being passed off as a deep musician in a movie about whoring is heavier than any of the intended ironies.

Steve Kloves is a first-time director, so you may forgive the endless and pointless overhead tracking of a dance floor, the yellow ocher mist, the depiction of nightclub owners as leftovers from postwar melodramas. His unforgivable error (other than making Pfeiffer look haggard) was in not replacing Steve Kloves the writer. Even clichés can be acceptable when they aren't administered with a sledge. It seems to me you could possibly get away with a scene in which Jack and Susie call each other whores and Frank a pimp, or a scene in which all three perform "Ten Cents a Dance," but not both. Nor do more mundane traits have to be telegraphed every five minutes—by the time we see Frank in a full wardrobe of sweaters, not to mention a Santa suit, and learn that he collects ashtrays but doesn't smoke, the lily has been painted with a dozen coats of Lucite. By way of compensation, much good music adorns the soundtrack: Susie spends her spare time listening to Ellington. You wonder why it doesn't improve their act.

Also reviewed in:
NEW REPUBLIC, 11/20/89, p. 28, Stanley Kauffmann
NEW YORK TIMES, 10/13/89, p. C14, Janet Maslin
NEW YORKER, 10/16/89, p. 107, Pauline Kael
VARIETY, 10/18-24/89, p. 25
WASHINGTON POST, 10/13/89, p. C1, Rita Kempley
WASHINGTON POST, 10/13/89, Weekend/p. 43, Desson Howe

FAMILY BUSINESS

A Tri-Star Pictures release. *Executive Producer:* Jennifer Ogden and Burtt Harris. *Producer:* Lawrence Gordon. *Director:* Sidney Lumet. *Screenplay (based upon his novel):* Vincent Patrick. *Director of Photography:* Andrzej Bartkowiak. *Editor:* Andrew Mondshein. *Music:* Cy Coleman. *Sound:* Allan Byer. *Sound Editor:* Maurice Schell. *Production Designer:* Philip Rosenberg. *Art Director:* Robert Guerra. *Set Decorator:* Gary Brink. *Costumes:* Ann Roth. *Make-up:* Joseph Cranzano. *Stunt Coordinator:* Jery Hewitt and Danny Aiello III. *Running time:* 114 minutes. *MPAA Rating:* R.

CAST: Sean Connery (Jessie); Dustin Hoffman (Vito); Matthew Broderick (Adam); Rosana De Soto (Elaine); Janet Carroll (Margie); Victoria Jackson (Christine); Bill McCutcheon (Doheny); Deborah Rush (Michele Dempsey); Marilyn Cooper (Rose); Salem Ludwig (Nat); Rex Everhart (Ray Garvey); James Tolkan (Judge); Marilyn Sokol (Marie); Thomas A. Carlin (Neary); Tony DiBenedetto (Phil); Isabell Monk (Judge); Wendell Pierce (Prosecutor); James Carruthers (Clerk, 1st Court); Jack O'Connell (Police Lieutenant); John Capodice (Tommy); Luis Guzman (Torres); Dermot A. McNamara (Casket Mourner); John P. Connel (Wake "Suit" Cop); Raymond H. Bazemore ("Caper" Guard); Willie C. Carpenter ("Caper" Cop); Conrad Fowkes ("Caper" Detective); B.D. Wong (Jimmy Chiu); Hal Lehrman (Assistant D.A.); Nick Discenza (Detective #1); Ed Crowley (Charlie); Arthur Pierce (Convict); Alberto Vazquez (Prisoner #1); Jose Machado (Prisoner #2); June Stein (Diner Waitress); David Warshofsky (Parking Attendant); John E. Byrd (Van Guard); Joe Lisi (Desk Sergeant); Elizabeth A. Reilly (Phil's Girlfriend); Tom Dillon (Tenor); Paul Forrest (Tenor #2); Karen Needle (Denise); Susan Korn (Margo); Aideen O'Kelly (Widow Doheny); George Kodisch (Wake Cop #1); Mary T. Fay (Lady Mourner #1); Patricia Fay (Lady Mourner #2).

FILMS IN REVIEW, 4/90,p. 231, C.M. Fiorillo

Director Sidney Lumet has fired off one of the biggest disappointments of the year with *Family Business*. The concept must sound terrific on paper—Connery! Hoffman! Broderick!—but it's a disaster on celluloid. Dustin Hoffman sprung from the loins of Sean Connery? Too great a leap of faith for this reviewer.

The "family business" of the title is larceny. What this comedy caper tries to do is gather the intergenerational McMullen clan together for a million dollar heist. The idea is Adam's (Broderick), a recent M.I.T. drop-out a few months shy of graduating. Adam, however improbably, has rejected his middle-class father Vito's (Hoffman) values in exchange for those of his thieving grandfather Jessie's (Connery). The young thief-in-the-rough sees something glamorous in his grandfather's way of life that his father never provided. Jessie encourages grandson Adam's fledgling criminal career much to the chagrin of his son. For his part, Vito rails against his father for steering Adam wrong. Neither Adam nor Vito respects their respective dads. To protect his son, Vito agrees to go along with the robbery. It's no surprise when Adam is caught.

What is surprising is the mashed potato plot that follows: Jessie discovers that the heist was a farce and Vito turns himself and Jessie in—thus losing his son altogether. Some incredibly maudlin scenes of Jessie dying in a prison hospital come next, followed by a reconciliation between Adam and Vito that is thoroughly contrived.

Sean Connery is his usual suave self as Jessie. He gets to spout the best lines and enjoy his life. Matthew Broderick is oddly ill-at-ease as Adam, an over-educated, unappreciative brat. Dustin Hoffman gets the worst of both worlds: his father *and* his son dislike him.

In supporting roles, James S. Tolkan has a brief but shining moment as the judge who sentences all three McMullens. And B.D. Wong makes a mysterious, even briefer, appearance as D.N.A. double-crosser Jimmy Chiu.

Sidney Lumet tried to direct this picture with panache and verve. The theft in the laboratory is exciting and suspenseful. But two Irish wakes? And two renditions of "Danny Boy"? Lumet can't save *Family Business* from sinking into the mire.

Vincent Patrick, author of *The Pope Of Greenwich Village*, adapted the screenplay from his own novel. But even he can't overcome the plot problems inherent in the choice of the three lead actors.

Family Business sinks like a dead weight.

LOS ANGELES TIMES, 12/15/89, Calendar/p. 1, Peter Rainer

"Family Business" is a frail little caper movie that's overawed by its cast. With Sean Connery, Dustin Hoffman and Matthew Broderick playing three generations of a family you've got a lot of talent at your disposal.

Forget for the moment the fact that, in this movie about the persistence of family genes, none of the actors remotely resembles each other. Forget, too, that Dustin Hoffman is seven years younger than Connery, who plays his father here. Years of agent-inspired casting have inured audiences to weirder confabs than this.

But there should be a pay-off to the oddness, some compelling dramatic reason for these three to get together. Like a good script, maybe.

Instead, the movie lays out a slew of half-baked ideas and never turns on the burner. The contrived plot is set in motion by Adam (Matthew Broderick), a science whiz who has recently dropped out of a master's program in molecular biology. What he wants to become is a thief like his grandfather, Jessie (Connery), whom he helps bail out of jail when the film opens.

It turns out that Adam's father, Vito (Hoffman), now the owner of a meat packing company, was also a thief. Both Jessie and Vito served time in jail. The difference between them is that Vito has renounced the life while Jessie isn't adverse to a stretch in the slammer. He thinks it builds character.

Sidney Lumet, who directed from a script by Vincent Patrick, based on his own novel, is highly regarded as an "actor's director." That encomium only applies however, when he's dealing with material his actors can chew on. In "Family Business," watching these three extraordinarily talented performers try to breathe some life into the story is a bit like watching a magic show that never takes off.

The actors seem to know it, too, at least Hoffman and Broderick. They don't supply much relish. Connery has a better time of it, largely because he dispenses with the film's dour realism and tries for something folkloric, larger-than-life.

Connery's performance is immensely entertaining while not being believable for a moment. How can it be? The role is a screenwriter's conceit. Jessie's free spiritedness is supposed to link up with Adam's. Adam wants to be a thief because he rejects the middle-class safety of his father's life style. When he cooks up a robbery that could net $1 million, Jessie is delighted, Vito aghast. Still, is it any surprise that they end up pulling off the job as a family?

In his best work, Hoffman has generally sought an edge in the characters he plays, some streak of eccentricity. It may come as a relief to see Hoffman playing a normal, worn-down guy in "Family Business" after all his flibbertigibbet acting tricks in "Rain Man." But the role doesn't inspire him. Maybe he felt he had already covered this terrain in the 1978 "Straight Time," where he played an ex-con who falls back into crime. That is still probably his best performance, and it may have used him up for this kind of material.

Broderick conveys the vast intelligence we keep hearing Adam possesses, but he can't make sense of the role. No one could. Adam is supposed a covet a life of crime because he finds no excitement in the humdrum law-abiding world. But Broderick doesn't look famished for excitement; his alert features, this quickness, belie the character's needs. There is also the suggestion here that Adam is turning criminal as a way to spite his father and provoke some love, but the notion is never developed. Nothing in this film is.

This might be a good time to declare a moratorium on any further over-the-hill oldster roles for Sean Connery. It's not that Connery can't play them to the hilt. It's just that, at 59, he is such a hale and vigorous presence (hey, he's the Sexiest Man Alive cover boy for the current issue of People) that he always seems to leave younger actors winded. His dynamism throws "Family Business" completely and deservedly out of whack.

MONTHLY FILM BULLETIN, 3/90, p. 59, Richard Combs

Vito McMullen, manager of a meat-packing business in New York, son of a Sicilian mother and a Scots father, Jessie, goes for a Passover meal with the Jewish parents of his wife Elaine. There he is surprised to find his young son Adam, who has just dropped out of college prior to completing his Master's degree in molecular biology. During the evening, Adam takes a call from Jessie, who needs bailing out of jail after assaulting a policeman; Vito reluctantly lends Adam the money, anxious as he is to keep his son away from the father whose small-time criminal activities so much affected his childhood, and from which he has now saved himself with a respectable life and business. But Adam, resenting the way his father has pushed him to "succeed", sympathises with the old man's unrepentant amorality and contempt for a life devoid of risk. Adam even proposes a "job" to Jessie: a biologist, Jimmy Chiu, recently pushed out of a company researching the genetic improvement of crops, will pay a million dollars for the "plasmets" he was working on to be stolen so that he can start his own company. Vito is horrified to hear of the plan, but eventually agrees to go along to keep an eye on Adam. The three break into the plant and steal the plasmets, but when Adam returns for vital logbooks he is caught by police. Vito and Jessie begin negotiations with a lawyer (their involvement in the robery has not been revealed), and learn that Adam's sentence will be light if the plasmets are returned. Afraid that Jessie will try to take off with the vials, Vito is relieved when his lady friend hands them over, only to learn later from the lawyer that they contain only water. Jessie realises that they were set up by Jimmy Chiu (who was helping the company cover for the fact that they had raised finance based on developments they had not yet made), and sets about blackmailing Chiu. But pressured by Elaine, Vito turns himself and Jessie in to save Adam; he and his son receive sentences of supervised probation, but as a known felon Jessie is sent to prison. Though talking confidently of his ability to survive, and the money he has made from Chiu, Jessie soon sickens and dies. Adam is unforgiving of Vito, until a rooftop wake for Jessie draws father and son together in a tentative reconciliation.

Family Business is a curiously split-level piece of work. Not split in the way of those cross-section dramas which have been Sidney Lumet's most productive, out of which have spilled diverse urban spirits and diverse moral attitudes towards (or moral possibilities within) the divided heroes of, say, *Serpico* or *Prince of the City*. Here the cross-section runs more across Lumet's career itself—that busy, multi-faceted scrambling of directorial personality, through which runs a tougher, brighter contradiction, between one of the most old-fashioned and most modernist sensibilities in American cinema. *Family Business* is a generation-gap or melting-pot drama (or comedy, or bittersweet romance: it also cheerfully cross-sections genre possibilities) which 50s or 60s Lumet might have made. If one were to take its internecine family conflicts and betrayals more seriously, its sense of the city as conflicting codes of honour, it could have stemmed from *A View from the Bridge*. Or if its ethnic comedy were removed from the caper plot, it could be another *Bye, Bye Braverman*.

All the diverse roots of conflict it puts out into the past count for little, however, because it is also latterday Lumet in the style, if not of *Prince of the City* then *Dog Day Afternoon*, in which all the insanity, venality and corruption of the city is treated in a half-accepting, half-celebratory way, as if it were the closest thing to community. At times the mood is that of Damon Runyon-with-anthropology. The film opens, inevitably, with a long shot traversing the New York skyline, which then, less inevitably, is reversed beneath the closing credits, suggesting that the whole landscape is being summoned and dismissed with a musical flourish. Where the shot initially comes to rest is on a rooftop ledge and a large white splash of some waste matter—the work of a prodigious pigeon perhaps, certainly a sarcastic end note to the usual "big city" opening. When the shot takes off again at the end, starting from this same blot, it is revealed to be human ashes, those of the McMullen family patriarch Jessie, Scottish immigrant in the 1940s, married to a Sicilian, father of Vito, who has merged those two strands with the Jewish and in turn fathered Adam, a bespectacled WASP now creating his brave New World in test tubes.

The city indeed breeds and absorbs its own, and the sentimentality of the rooftop wake for Jessie ("Danny Boy" sung by massed mourners of cops and petty con men; a breach healed between Vito and Adam) is offset in rough and ready Runyon fashion by an earlier, identical wake played against the sentimental grain. The first wake is for a minor character—he only appears in one scene—the proprietor of Doheny's bar, about whom we are, however, told a lot in one conversation (an ex-cop modestly on the make in the days when Jessie ran a numbers racket). If he's not a character in the central family drama, he is curiously, a better indicator of the way the city grows and changes through its mutual accommodations and petty corruptions than are the central three-some. Their exemplary American history of how, as Adam puts it, each generation does a little better than the one before it, is as blithely schematic as their all-round ethnic component. Danny Doheny is connective tissue in the film, as are the mourners he brings out of the woodwork (his tipsy widow, the cops who never do any policing but are present at every ceremony, the hustler who enters the funeral home with a rack of suits "just fallen off a lorry"), the kind of connective tissue out of which even the central characters were made in *Dog Day Afternoon*, allowing social and psychological themes to be broached without pushing any explanations.

With the McMullens, however, *Family Business* is on different ground, the kind of theatrical entertainment which is also part of Lumet's repertoire, where the shifting viewpoints of his other crime films are fixed in some definite explanations of behaviour, and the pleasure lies in how many actorly inflections can be brought to an unshifting scenario. Vito resents Jessie for dragging him through a childhood of crime; Adam resents Vito for pushing him into super-respectability and academic achievement; Jessie remains proudly Nietzschean in his view that the criminal is the only free man. (Along the way, old-style Irish-Italian-Jewish freebooting is upheld against the yuppie equivalent, like property dealing with insider knowledge of which tenants have terminal cancer, or the plasma scam that puts Adam in prison.) There's not much interest or impact in the flurry of family betrayals and trade-offs with which this scenario ends—compared, say, with the double and triple binds in which the hero of *Prince of the City* finds himself—and Lumet's constant, and often incongruous, shifting between comedy and drama is a way of insuring that the McMullens never get to be too big for the drama, or the city. They remain slightly emblematic, even documentary, in social function, mixed with the feeling that these star turns bear as little family resemblance to each other as the passengers on the Orient Express.

NEW STATESMAN & SOCIETY, 2/16/90, p. 41, Suzanne Moore

The name of Sidney Lumet's latest film starring Sean Connery and Dustin Hoffman is *Family Business*. Though the movie itself leaves a lot to be desired, its title seems to sum up the mood of the moment perfectly. For The Family it seems is back in vogue. Right across the media the image of the ruthless individual is caving in to the cosy picture of the family man who cares more about his catalytic converter than his cash card. Those who monitor such trends use words that you can't even say without yawning to suggest the mood of the new decade—caring, cocooning, marriage, stability. And the thing that will hold this mind-numbing vision of the nineties together is the big one. The Family.

Maybe I've been missing something here but how can something come back when it's never been away? To read the reports you would think that the whole of the population had spent the last 20 years in weird communes plotting the devastation of the few surviving nuclear families. But now, free at last, these poor misunderstood people can come out of the closet. The latest Mintel publication, *British Life-styles 1990*, cites families as "the key consumer group of the decade". Family business indeed.

The demographic shift to an older population and the end of the credit boom undoubtedly means new patterns of spending with more emphasis on savings, pensions and insurance schemes. But, to what extent such trends are influenced by the break-up of the welfare state rather than by some popular resurgence of family values, is debatable. Certainly, within the public rhetoric that refuses the notion of society and talks only of "individuals and families", is hidden one of the most despicable privatisation schemes of all—the privatisation of the family.

Yet, while this monolithic notion of the family may be held up as an ideal it seems to me a kind of smokescreen. Leisure activities, for instance, be they films or computer games, are targeted so specifically to individual members of the family (infants, young children, teenagers, wives, husbands) that very little exists these days that can truly be described as entertainment for all the family. So, while many new films celebrate variously the sanctity of the family, they are actually aimed at specific markets that are defined by something other than familial relationships.

NEW YORK, 1/8/90, p. 61, David Denby

I don't suppose Sean Connery, Dustin Hoffman, and Matthew Broderick (again) are remotely possible as the three male generations of a single family, but I so enjoyed watching them in Sidney Lumet's *Family Business* that the implausibility bothered me very little. The story, based on a Vincent Patrick novel, is about the irresistible excitement of criminality and the jealousies and tensions between generations. As the roistering old reprobate, Connery has the broadest lines and delivers them superbly; Hoffman is complexly moving in the pivotal role of a man with larcenous instincts who has forced himself to go straight and will never be happy without danger; and Broderick is steady and strong as his genteelly brought-up son, disgusted with what his father has exacted from him as the price of respectability. See this movie. It's better than reviewers have said. Both Patrick's script and Lumet's direction are pungent and deeply rooted in time and place—in New York Irishness and Jewishness. And the allure of crime—the way it strikes some people as the ultimate source of happiness—has never been made clearer.

NEW YORK POST, 12/15/89, p. 41, David Edelstein

In "Family Business," the painfully serious exploration of ties among three generations, Dustin Hoffman plays the son of Sean Connery and—stop right there: Who was the mother, Dr. Ruth? Was there a mix-up in the maternity ward? The lack of resemblance is explained as follows: Connery was married to a small Sicilian. The mind boggles trying to imagine what she looked like.

I'm sorry for dwelling on such surface issues. But in movies, surfaces are everything, and the earnest, probing "Family Business" is crippled from the get-go.

The film, ironically, is about resemblances that can't be shaken off: It's a meditation on the reactionary tendencies of fathers and sons. A father pushes a way of life on his son, who rebels and goes to the opposite extreme; the son pushes his new way of life on *his* son, who rebels and takes after grandpa.

It's a resonant subject, and the script by Vincent Patrick (from his novel) cleverly makes the grandfather a thief and spiritual gypsy so that the conflicts are as vivid as possible. The director, Sidney Lumet, does thoughtful work, but the film isn't expressive enough to overcome its nutty casting. We want it to mushroom; it stays small and drab.

Connery's Jessie is a career thief and rogue who raised Hoffman's Vito to be a chip off the old block. Apparently he succeeded, but Vito got caught during a robbery, jailed, and emerged with the will to shake off the old man's influence.

For 20 years, Vito has behaved legally and prudently and made a success of himself in the meat business. But as far as his son, Adam (Matthew Broderick), is concerned, Vito is dour and joyless—cut off from life.

Adam is more taken with his grandfather, and as the movie opens, he has just abandoned his masters thesis and come to Jessie with a fool-proof heist: A Chinese chemist will pay a million dollars if they steal some plasma from a corporation that double-crossed him. To keep things simple, Jessie and Adam attempt to persuade Vito to join the family business again: the robbery offers a chance for the three to bond.

Visually, the film is dead on the screen, but it still holds your interest. Patrick lays the issues out carefully, showing how Vito can't resist his own nature and the chance to win his son's respect. When disaster strikes, we experience his pain like a blow to the head. He's caught between saving his son and betraying his father, and the safe, upper-middle-class world he has so painstakingly erected ends up in rubble.

Hoffman, tense and bug-eyed until now, handles the strain by getting even more uptight. The role isn't much of a stretch for him, but he's fine—especially when exploding into fisticuffs. (He has a scary temper.) And even though Connery seems too open and heroic for the well-made-play construction, this party need his rascally good humor and unflagging spirit. Hoffman and Broderick are saddled with the heavy stuff; Connery stands outside the conflict, chuckling.

Still, the actors are in different universes. The crabbed, introspective Hoffman and the easy, larger-than-life Connery are opposites, all right, but when Hoffman alludes to all the bad genes he got from dad that he's been fighting against all these years, we think, "You should be so lucky." (Oddly, Broderick acts in a third style, resembling neither Hoffman nor Connery.)

Lumet is good at making actors comfortable. Rosana DeSoto and Janet Carroll have some pungent moments, Deborah Rush gives good meeting as a brusque attorney and Marilyn Sokol is wonderfully tart as Hoffman's secretary. Lumet is also a gentleman: Given the opportunity to jerk your tears near the end, he takes off his hat and backs out the door apologetically.

An unfailingly moral film maker, he lets his standards slip in only one scene, where Jessie humiliates Broderick's real-estate-broker girlfriend (Victoria Jackson) after she brags at the dinner table about how she snaps up apartments. (She has a friend who works in a hospital and gives her the names of terminal cases.)

With the movie's blessing Jessie announces that what he does isn't legal but is moral, whereas what she does is legal but immoral. (He calls her a parasite.) With all due respect to the sleaziness of certain real-estate brokers, I wonder what Jessie's victims would think of the morality of his actions. Sometimes it's best just to shut up and eat.

NEWSDAY, 12/15/89, Part III/p. 3, Mike McGrady

Some movies are irresistible on paper. Personally, I wouldn't care what any critic said about "Family Business," I'd stand in line to see any flick that stars Sean Connery, Dustin Hoffman and Matthew Broderick as three generations of criminals from the same family.

And as long as they are involved in the same complicated caper, the million-dollar theft of genetic research material from a Long Island laboratory, the film itself *is* irresistible.

Although the three generations all bear the same name, McMullen, they could not be more dissimilar. Broderick is Adam, a bespectacled scientific genius who dropped out of MIT just before earning his master's degree and has now come up with his very own criminal caper. His dad, Vito (Hoffman), runs a meat-packing business and is attempting to go straight after spending a portion of his adult life behind bars. And Sean Connery is Jessie, Hoffman's father and a brawling, thieving, charming rogue who has never relinquished his brogue or his criminal tendencies.

Connery, like most of life's finer things, only improves with age. From his first appearance in "Family Business," he is some piece of work. As the inveterate thief, Connery steals everything that isn't nailed down—and that includes every scene in the movie and, in fact, the movie itself. Needless to say, when an actor steals a movie from Dustin Hoffman, it is not petty theft, it's grand larceny.

Following a victorious bar brawl against, alas, an off-duty cop, the strapping Connery pleads self-defense ("I did what little I could for a man of my age") and later he modestly describes himself as just another "man tryin' his best to enjoy his golden years." However, his truer self is exposed as he offers advice to a grandson contemplating a life of crime. Advice about lifestyle: "Always remember, Adam, it only costs one hundred percent more to go first class." Advice about love: "Nothing wrong with an older woman...for a young man."

Despite their shared name, the three generations seem to have little in common. We are told that mixed marriages, specifically the effect of Italian and Jewish mothers, has significantly altered the biological makeup without apparently diluting the family's genetic disposition toward crime. Jessie needs minimal encouragement to go along on the caper, while Vito is reluctant to risk his currently respectable life; his motivation, finally, is to offer his son what protection he can.

And while Hoffman has an undemanding role, he does have his moments. At one point, when he is in deepest despair, the camera catches him from the back, and we are given a lingering closeup of the back of his scalp. Don't ask me how the actor manages it, but his every emotion comes through clearly.

The steps that go into setting up the heist and the heist itself are pure fun. However, as the caper itself begins to unravel, the picture also undergoes a bit of unraveling. The Vincent Patrick screenplay, based on his novel of the same name, is brisk and funny most of the way. However, with the arrest of one member of the family, it turns mawkish. Oh, there's nothing wrong with a touch of sentiment, but this is not honest sentiment; it's an added ingredient tacked on in the interest of completing a package.

Still and all, how could one *not* see "Family Business"? It's definitely one of those movies that is irresistible—on paper. It's only during the transfer to celluloid that some small problems develop.

VILLAGE VOICE, 12/26/89, 114, Stuart Klawans

Consider what Hollywood has offered us this year in the name of holiday merriment: Kathleen Turner and Michael Douglas snarling at each other, Roseanne Barr lumbering around with a mole on her lip, Sean Penn delivering heartfelt sermons, and now Sean Connery in *Family Business*, languishing in an infirmary with a tube stuck up his nose.

The horror. The horror.

Make no mistake—these movies represent something more than just a run of bad comedies. They are the funeral shroud of America, neatly wound in spools. Though the Rockefellers have sold their splendid center to Japan; though *glasnost* has thrown Henry Kissinger out of work; though the subway needs more bailing than the S&Ls, still America as we knew it might stand, if only it could guarantee production of its last remaining industrial commodity, fantasy. Yet the evidence of ruin is before us: at least two years of labor from script idea to projection print, at a cost of millions and millions of dollars, all on the proposition that people will think of *Family Business* as entertainment.

Please remove your hats. We are gathered today above the corpus of a New York caper film, starring Connery as an old thief, Dustin Hoffman as his son and onetime accomplice, and Matthew Broderick as the grandson, who gets the whole family involved in a million-dollar burglary. If the imaginary lineage troubles you, picture this: Hoffman is supposed to be Scots and Sicilian, while Broderick claims to be half-Jewish. In what I presume to be a gesture of actorly valor, both men have waived their right to prosthetic makeup. This yields the advantage to Connery, who is supposed to be all-Scots and probably has never felt more grateful for it. On the other hand, Connery has to deliver the script's wittiest line—"Up yours, guinea midget"—so the score is more or less even.

Connery, by the way, plays a life-affirming rogue, whereas Hoffman is the moralizing, upwardly mobile son who wants to go straight. Broderick sides with the former; the audience is supposed to do so, too. Yet the only reward of *Family Business* lies in the spectacle of Hoffman acting his ass off just on principle—a demonstration of the work ethic that completely undermines the movie's premise.

So much the better. *Family Business* tries with tedious fervor to persuade you that tough guys and crooks live more fully than do working stiffs, and that they offer their love more freely as well. But every once in a while, one of the characters will raise his hand to another, and you think about how there must be one more link among these men: a history of child-beating. And I used to think it was creepy seeing Natalie Wood on Santa's lap.

Also reviewed in:
NEW YORK TIMES, 12/15/89, p. C28, Vincent Canby
VARIETY, 12/13/89, p. 30
WASHINGTON POST, 12/15/89, p. D1, Rita Kempley

FAR FROM HOME

A Vestron Pictures release of a Lightning Pictures presentation. *Executive Producer:* Lawrence Kasanoff and Ellen Steloff. *Producer:* Donald P. Borchers. *Director:* Meiert Avis. *Screenplay:* Tommy Lee Wallace. *Story:* Ted Gershuny. *Director of Photography:* Paul Elliott. *Editor:* Marc Grossman. *Music:* Jonathan Elias. *Sound:* William Fiege. *Production Designer:* Victoria Paul. *Costumes:* Donna Linson. *Running time:* 90 minutes. *MPAA Rating:* R.

CAST: Matt Frewer (Charlie Cross); Drew Barrymore (Joleen Cross); Richard Masur (Duckett); Susan Tyrrell (Agnes Reed); Jennifer Tilly (Amy); Andras Jones (Jimmy Reed); Karen Austin (Louise); Anthony Rapp (Pinky Sears); Dick Miller (Sheriff).

NEW YORK POST, 6/24/89, p. 21, Jami Bernard

The memory of sweet little Drew Barrymore in "E.T." that jumps most readily to mind is her first confrontation with the extraterrestrial. She opens her mouth into a big fat "O" and lets go an ear-piercing scream.

Little Drew is a young teen now, with the body of a sex queen and come-hither eyes set in a baby-fat face. And she's still screaming.

In "Far From Home" she plays Joleen, an adolescent on the brink of womanhood. Her voiced-over diary entries and her choice of apparel (midriff tops and tight bottoms) betray her growing curiosity about boys. Her secret wish for her 14th birthday is to be kissed by a brooding youth whose appearance on screen is marked by an angry heartbeat on the soundtrack, never a good sign.

Joleen is finishing up a boring summer of touring theme parks with her divorced dad (Matt "Max Headroom" Frewer). He's run out of gas in the middle of the Nevada desert (hmmmm...), and they are sidetracked to a one-horse, one-pump trailer park town full of the meanest characters you'd ever want to find.

The garage owner (Richard Masur) packs some serious heat but is the sanest guy in town. The trailer park manager (Susan Tyrrell) is one mean mother who is later done in, presumably by her son, with a little electrolysis session in the bathtub. Then there are numerous other weird and black-hearted denizens of Banco, Nev., population 132 and falling rapidly.

It is during this dry, dusty lay-over that Joleen decides to test her effect on the local boys. Basically, there are only two of them—Jimmy, the one with the over-amped heartbeat, and Pinky, a sunny smiling one who turns out to be no bargain either.

Wistfully, Joleen confides to her diary that she's eager for a kiss and tests the sound of her heartthrob's name on her tongue: "Jimmy, Jim, James." Light of her life, fire of her loins?

Within the movie's 90 or so minutes, Drew Barrymore is saved from rape, pillage, murder, a wet T-shirt tussle, a signal tower, a car explosion and a tornado. And what does she have to say about all this?

Eeeeyaaiii!

Dad is, as Joleen has suspected all along in her diary entries, pretty darn geeky for a father. "Stay put!" he commands his peripatetic daughter as she bounces around town in her midriff and cowboy boots with spurs, while behind every trailer door is a dead body or a heavy breather.

Barrymore plays what she quite possibly is in real life: an exasperated and headstrong teen who cannot believe the geekiness of others. "I almost got raped by a guy I trusted," she pouts, "and he turns out to be a killer!"

Tyrrell burlesques her role as the ultimate evil mother, leaning down to scream into her daughter's ear, "DINNER TIME!" and hurling frozen fish sticks at her kids.

Those responsible for the look of Banco should be commended. This is genuinely the ugliest, most depressing little town ever, with cheap, demoralizing trailers dumped amidst the shimmer of dry heat. The only sounds are from the bug zapper, and the only light is the bluish one that emanates from tired old TV sets.

In fact, there is some attempt to link the murder and mayhem to television, as if the steady, unseen leak of radioactivity has poisoned the bloodstream. The movie's climax is set atop a signal tower, the only steeple in this Godforsaken land.

But let's not get too worked up about the symbolism. Basically, "Far From Home" is an exploitative bit of cinema that capitalizes on Barrymore's breasts—no, she doesn't bare them, but the camera lingers, hoping. It's a dumb and mean-spirited movie which, like its stranded travelers, has nowhere to go.

Also reviewed in:
VARIETY, 6/28–7/4/89, p. 16

FAREWELL TO THE KING

An Orion Pictures release. *Producer:* Albert S. Ruddy and Andre Morgan. *Director:* John Milius. *Screenplay:* John Milius. *Based on the novel "L'Adieu au Roi" by:* Pierre Schoendoerffer. *Director of Photography:* Dean Semler. *Editor:* John W. Wheeler. *Music:* Basil Poledouris. *Music Editor:* Tom Villano. *Choreographer:* Anne Semler. *Sound:* Donald Connolly and (music) Eric Tomlinson. *Sound Editor:* Tom McCarthy. *Production Designer:* Gil Parrondo. *Art Director:* Bernard Hides. *Set Dresser:* Virginia Bieneman. *Special Effects:* Gene Grigg. *Costumes:* David Rowe. *Make-up:* Jose Perez. *Stunt Coordinator:* Terry Leonard. *Running time:* 114 minutes. *MPAA Rating:* PG-13.

CAST: Nick Nolte (Learoyd); Nigel Havers (Fairbourne); Frank McRae (Tenga); Gerry Lopez (Gwai); Marilyn Tokuda (Yoo); Choy Chang Wing (Lian); Aki Aleong (Colonel Mitamura); Marius Weyers (Conklin); William Wise (Dynamite Dave); Wayne Pygram (Bren Armstrong); Richard Morgan (Stretch Lewis); Elan Oberon (Vivienne); James Fox (Ferguson); Michael Nissman (General Sutherland); John Bennett Perry (General MacArthur).

LOS ANGELES TIMES, 3/3/89, Calendar/p. 8, Michael Wilmington

Like many movie makers preoccupied with heroism, John Milius seems to have both a little boy and a wild tiger clawing each other within his breast. And sometimes they run after each other with such savage persistence that one or both are churned into butter.

"Farewell to the King" should have been a major Milius film, maybe even a great one. It's based on the same themes, the Conradian descent into a heart of darkness during warfare, that animate his script for "Apocalypse Now." And it's full of majestic scenery, flourishes, big sweeping gusts of machismo.

It's shot on location in Borneo and Milius' cinematographer, Dean Semler, gets the feel of the jungle. It's rotten and murky, heavy with disease and bugs, sticky with heat, so tangled up with undergrowth and rot that when the characters break through to a hilltop, you get a stabbing sense of relief.

But there's something almost gelded about "Farewell." It has the musculature it needs, even whispers of the soul, but not the raw, seething guts.

Based on Pierre Schoendoerffer's novel, it's about a rebellious American G.I. in World War II, deserting, descending into the jungle, becoming an emperor of the native headhunters, the Dayaks, and then suffering betrayal by the British after his tribe is recruited for jungle warfare against the Japanese.

The hero, Learoyd (Nick Nolte) is real Milius wish fulfillment, despite the fact that he's an ex-Communist who probably wouldn't have bought a ticket to see "Red Dawn." Learoyd is the man in flight from society and rules—the deserter who opts out of civilization, who believes in primitive loyalties, simple pleasures and natural nobility. And Nolte plays him just as Gary Busey played the wild-man surfer, Leroy, in Milius' best film, "Big Wednesday," with charged, animalistic movements, a mixture of explosiveness and tigerish reserve.

Learoyd has two communities around him: the Dayaks, who have made him king, and the little band of British commandos, including his eventual bond-buddy, the narrator-botanist (Nigel Havers). Facing them is the Japanese Army, resorting to cannibalism to survive, led by Learoyd's chief nemesis, a ghostly equestrian colonel.

But the Japanese warriors are only ghost enemies, the test. The real scourge are the distant bureaucrats who hate the smoke of battle and regard the soldiers as their pawns. Prissy Col. Ferguson, (James Fox), betraying by the book, wrinkling his lip in disgust at what he has to do, is a prototypical Milius villain: the mercenary, the numbers man, the creep king.

There's lots of potential here, but it's muffed. "Farewell" doesn't have the dark power of "Apocalypse," the rowdy adventure of "Conan," the sheer Fordian beauty and reverie of "Big Wednesday." Sometimes it sinks to condescension, as in Milius' attempt to make noble savages of the Dayaks—Learoyd's "Comanches."

Milius has always had a weakness for rhetoric, and, in "Farewell" (MPAA rated PG-13 for language and violence), he's trapped himself somewhere between Akira Kurosawa and David Lean. But what he needs is the liberating spontaneity and perverse humor of his other great model, John Ford. Ford had the strategy down. Sing your ballad of nobility, of tragedy, of history's price, then have somebody tumble. That kind of invigorating kick is exactly what "Farewell" lacks.

MONTHLY FILM BULLETIN, 7/89, p. 197, Tom Milne

February 15, 1945. Fairbourne, a British army captain, is parachuted into the Borneo jungle; his mission, to enlist the support of Dayak headhunters against the Japanese invaders. Taken prisoner by tribesmen along with his black radioman, Sergeant Tenga, Fairbourne is astonished to discover that their ruler is Learoyd, a former American soldier (and Communist) who deserted on Corregidor in 1942 when MacArthur pulled out and succeeded in reaching Borneo by boat. After suffering terrible privations and seeing his companions executed by the Japanese, he fell into the hands of headhunters (who were fascinated by his blue eyes, reminiscent of the sea and therefore of salt, essential to their lives), won respect in a trial by combat, and became "king" by uniting the tribes in peace for the first time. Aware that to harry the Japanese will be to drive them into the unexplored interior, Learoyd—unwilling to jeopardise a way of life in which he has found freedom—is reluctant to cooperate until the Japanese, monitoring Fairbourne's radio signals, pinpoint an air attack on his village. He then agrees, demanding a treaty guaranteeing the Dayaks their freedom after the war. Fairbourne has a Special Forces unit of four NCOs parachuted in to train the Dayaks and—hopefully—subvert Learoyd's authority. But already learning to respect the "king", who saves his life in a skirmish with Japanese troops, Fairbourne flies to Allied HQ in the Dutch East Indies and persuades MacArthur to sign a treaty, honouring Learoyd like any other sovereign. When Fairbourne returns, Learoyd shows him the reason for his reluctance to cooperate—an idyllic community in the jungle, untouched by evil, reached by a pass which Learoyd intends to seal off with dynamite. In the bitter skirmishes that follow (August 1945), Learoyd's village and family are wiped out by Japanese now reduced to cannibalism and other atrocities, just as news is received of the first atom bomb. Shattered, Learoyd withdraws with his surviving people. Wounded and sent back to base hospital, Fairbourne learns that his CO, Colonel Ferguson, intends to blast Learoyd out of the jungle (on the principle that an autonomous king is a threat), and suggests depriving the Dayaks of salt as an alternative. Eventually returning to Borneo, Fairbourne finds that Learoyd—having surrendered himself and the Japanese colonel (who surrendered to him) to Australian troops in exchange for the salt desperately needed by his people—faces court martial as a deserter. Impulsively, Fairbourne contrives his escape.

Although finally it must be set down as something of a mess, this adaptation of Pierre Schoendoerffer's novel is at least an encouraging sign that Milius is as unhappy as any of his admirers—lately driven into indefensible corners—about the way his earlier resonant (and usually delightful) sport with macho myths of power and personality has degenerated into the hard-line hawkish barbarisms of films like *Conan the Barbarian* and *Red Dawn*. "I'm tired of carnage", he is quoted as saying, "I've had my fill of it. You'll not see bloodshed or heads being taken in this picture". True, despite the opportunities offered, and despite the intimations of apocalypse now which Milius offers in describing his scouting of Borneo for locations: "We found every location we needed—misty mountains, winding rivers, ocean and the jungle—a jungle that has a distinctive look. This is the true Conrad jungle, out there *is* the heart of darkness". Thematically speaking, the admixture of the heart of darkness and the man who would be king promises a heady brew, but what emerges, alas, is a cup of weak tea. Milius, to belabour the metaphor, forgot to warm the pot, to make sure the water boiled, to let it stand.

Cast as a nostalgic reminiscence (Fairbourne's voice-over saying, "Borneo...For most of you, Borneo doesn't exist. I was there...my war, my youth"), the film opens on an unfortunate note of risibility, presumably intentional but none the less miscalculated, as Captain Fairbourne and his black radio operator, slung upside-down from Dayak poles like Klaus Kinski in *Cobra Verde*, are carried into the village for their first glimpse of the King of the Headhunters. "He's as white as we are!" Fairbourne gasps in astonishment, the little dig at British arrogance (reinforced when Fairbourne later has to warn his black sergeant against going native: "Remember, you're English"—"No, I'm African, practically a savage") no more to the point than Nick Nolte's grotesque initial appearance, more frizz-wigged punk rocker than Wild Man of Borneo (fortunately, as Nolte's performance takes hold, so his appearance steadies).

We then slip into flashback for an account of Learoyd's adventure which is both too long and too short. Too long, in the sense that the semi-impressionistic exposition of his trials and tribulations (fever, starvation, leeches, isolation, fear, hallucination, capture) could have been incorporated more economically and more expressively into his verbal comment ("I died once...had to give up everything, even the will to live"). Too short, in that Learoyd's comments on his elevation to a position of authority and worship ("The people here want to revere the ancient heroes. For them, the *man* counts") are not given visual correlation by an abrupt single-combat sword duel with a Dayak warrior, neither adequately explained nor adequately resonant.

After Learoyd's claim to royalty is authenticated (for Fairbourne, if not for the audience) through a would-be Brechtian parable about a child disputed between two villages (evidently intended to demonstrate that Learoyd rates humanity first, regality second), the film starts describing slightly aimless circles. The Special Forces NCOs and the black radioman tentatively begin the process of going native (presumably seduced by the much-vaunted but little demonstrated local commodity of freedom); the "secret valley" introduces a silly echo of *Lost Horizon* and Shangri-La; and credibility is stretched by dramatic licence when Fairbourne's flying visit to General MacArthur not only reunites him with his fiancée (conveniently on hand in uniform), but also trots out James Fox as Fairbourne's CO to make it quite clear that MacArthur's grandiloquent gesture in signing the treaty will *not* be honoured. But despite the heavy underlining, resonances are clumsily muffled in the later stages of the film. As with the rather tentatively raised matter of Learoyd's Communism, the parallel adumbrated between public and private betrayal never quite surfaces. Awkward editing and flurried dialogue leave motivations disastrously muddled, so that by the end it is unclear what anybody is up to (most notably, whether Fairbourne is protecting or betraying Learoyd by suggesting the salt blockade as an alternative to military assault).

By this time lost en route, with the question of kingship lying around in a mosaic of fragments, the film zones interestingly in on the heart of darkness. Something of myth and horror is evoked as the moon shines darkly in the sky, the Japanese colonel on his white horse leads his wraith-like guerrillas through the jungle, and stories of cannibalism and unspeakable atrocities begin to circulate. Captured and justifying his campaign ("That's my duty, to fight, stay alive, and fight again"), the colonel ruefully adds, "We sank as much into horror as human nature could". Milius, too late, is just starting to get somewhere.

NEW STATESMAN & SOCIETY, 7/14/89, p. 49, Suzanne Moore

Boys will be boys and, given half the chance, so will most men. Growing up is hard to do. Maybe it is easier to switch from infantile selfishness to senile dementia without so much as a glimmer of maturity in between. It is hard enough to live with this fact, let alone see it culturally endorsed by the kind of dreadful films I've seen this week. While *Farewell to the King* is about a white man who becomes king of a tribe in Borneo and *Skin Deep* about a compulsive womaniser in LA, the kinds of macho posturing on display in both movies is not only utterly charmless but completely contemptible. Forget homosexuality—it is the promotion of masculinity *per se* that needs legislating against.

OK, so I've had a hard week. But perhaps I wouldn't loathe these films so much if they were funny or well made. Even on a bad day, I can take a reactionary message if it is wrapped up in shiny enough packaging. If the medium is slick enough, the message matters less. Who can resist a Hollywood blockbuster or, more importantly, who wants to when the *will to resist* is massaged away by the millions of dollars spent on these films? This week's movies, however, are a timely reminder that no amount of money, exotic locations, or grown women impersonating Barbie Dolls, can confer that elusive quality of *irresistibility* on to turkeys such as these.

Farewell to the King is described by director John Milius as the best film he has ever made. He has long been fascinated by a mythical, macho heroism that saw its best moment in the screenplay he wrote for *Apocalypse Now*. But his passion for a raw or "natural" maleness has led him in search of some pretty dubious heroes. In *Big Wednesday*, Californian surfers were portrayed as lonely existential figures living only for the next wave, while the ridiculous *Red Dawn*, based on the premise of a Soviet invasion of America, led to him being branded a Nazi.

His new film combines his quest for "real men" with his other abiding theme—that of "getting back to nature", to a primitive but somehow purer state of being that is freed from the niceties of civilisation. In *Farewell to the King*, Nick Nolte, sounding like Tom Waits and looking like the lion from the *Wizards of Oz*, plays such a figure. One suspects Milius would have preferred Klaus Kinski who, after all, has made a living from roaming round jungles, acting the wild man in various Herzog enterprises. But we have to make do with Nolte as Learoyd, an American deserter who ends up in Borneo at the end of the second world war, and who unbelievably becomes king of a tribe of native people.

Living the life of Riley—complete with blow-pipes and subservient Malaysian women—his blissful existence is rudely interrupted by "history" in the form of Nigel Havers, a British officer whose mission is to get the tribes to fight the invading Japanese troops. It all results in jungle warfare and a ludicrous bit of male bonding between Havers and Nolte. As Nolte scampers about grunting and communing with nature, Havers tries to convince him that he "can no longer avoid history". Havers, whom it is impossible to imagine having a primitive urge in his life, grows to respect and love Learoyd—though both have suitably dumb women to reassure us that it is not *that* sort of male bonding going on. James Fox, as Havers's commanding officer has the best line: "You've done a hell of a piece of soldiering, but that's not the point". Exactly.

If *Farewell to the King* expresses, in a botched way, the notion that going back to—or regressing into—an illusory primal existence is laudable, it does so precisely at the expense of "history" and in doing so validates a particular kind of masculinity as the real thing. Learoyd becomes king of the jungle because colonial and patriarchal impulses don't feel like "history" or the despised "civilisation" but like some God-given and perfectly natural right.

Of course the whole point about regression is that you have to grow up to be able to regress in the first place. Which cannot honestly be said for the central character of Blake Edward's sex-comedy *Skin Deep*. The bearded and bland John Ritter is the archetypal Edwards hero, an affluent LA writer with writer's block. He is also a compulsive (and repulsive) womaniser who mouths the old lie—that he can't help it because he loves women so much—rather than the truth, which is that he has a mental age of 13 and more money that is good for him. This is the excuse for a series of encounters with interchangeable Californian girls. To call them bimbos is the equivalent of describing Maria Whittaker as an intellectual.

What this little-boy-lost needs is the love of a good and mature woman, though any sensible female would have more fun blowing her brains out than getting involved with this emotional retard. Still, if you subscribe to the "wicked willy" view of male sexuality (and sometimes it's difficult not to) and think that men are led around by the dicks, you might like this garbage. Certainly the middle-aged hack sitting next to me in the cinema could identify with this mid-life crisis. He seemed to think the very idea of a condom was hysterically funny.

The clothes, designed by Nolan Miller of *Dynasty*, are incredibly tacky. As Dolly Parton (a woman with more wit in her little finger than this film in its entirety) said of her own wardrobe: "It costs a lot of money to look this cheap." It also costs a lot of money to make movies this bad.

The saddest thing of all, however, is the complete lack of a model of mature masculinity. The choice men are offered is to continue to play toy soldiers—which Milius indulges to the hilt—or to be naughty boys, "wicked willies", which Edwards milks for its sheer ridiculousness.

Yet, surely we only regress both culturally and individually when we cannot face the present, when we cannot accept the consequences of being adult? What saves us from this fate is not the love of a good woman, or even Nigel Havers, but the recognition that regression doesn't work because it is based on an imaginary place that exists only outside both personal and political history.

That is what finally makes the difference between self-awareness and self-indulgence. In other words it is what separates the men from the boys.

NEW YORK POST, 3/3/89, p. 25, Jami Bernard

Deep in the jungles of Borneo, living it up with a native woman, wearing a golden crown around a leonine mane of hair, is a deserter from the U.S. Army. His name, appropriately enough, is—or was—Sgt. Learoyd, and now he is basically *le roi*, the king. uniting the headhunting tribes under one hedonistic banner.

It's near the end of World War II. The last time we saw this Learoyd, he was busy deserting, washed ashore by mighty waves, his pals executed by Japanese soldiers. Thrashing his way through the dense underbrush—and this was filmed in Borneo, where the underbrush really *is* dense—Learoyd vowed to live the rest of his life a free man, although at that point he was a nervous wreck.

What a difference a day, or three years, make. Learoyd escapes being beheaded because of the fierce dragon tattoo on his chest, bests the tribal bully at his own game, sticks a pig, drinks the sacrificial wine, marries a beautiful native girl, unites the tribes, and eats pomegranates (or the Borneo equivalent) every day. The only drawback is that the tribe must keep itself in salt to avoid fainting from the heat.

Our first sight of *le roi*, as opposed to Learoyd, is almost humorously magnificent. He looks like the Cowardly Lion after getting his medal for bravery. Two British airmen parachute down and are transported most unceremoniously to the "longhouse" where the king awaits. There he is, hair aflame, blue eyes piercing, a white man—and Nick Nolte to boot.

Flamboyant, regal, compassionate, fearless, driven—these are things Nolte is good at being, especially with all that hair and his bear-like presence. (Actually, he seems much slimmed down since playing a similarly flamboyant, regal, driven artist in Martin Scorcese's segment of "Tales of New York," which opened Wednesday.)

Coming upon Nolte in the jungle is like coming upon Marlon Brando upriver in "Apocalypse Now," and that's not too surprising, seeing that writer/director John Milius wrote the screenplay for that other Conradian tale.

Nolte speaks with a guttural sound, as if this peace-loving rajah were unaccustomed to language. "I died once," he says. "I had to give up everything, even the will to live."

Nolte's striking physical appearance and a lush, mythical look and feel are the main attractions of "Farewell to the King." It is also, however, an overwrought and sentimental tale of a battle for turf between your basic noble savages and your basic look-alike enemy—in this case, silent Japanese soldiers who scavenge the local villages like lost army ants looking for a way back to the anthill.

The two Brits who have parachuted down are there to enlist the king's help in rallying the natives to oust the Japanese, something the natives would really like to do but are too ill-equipped or too busy sticking pigs and drinking ceremonial wine.

Somehow, the very fate of the war rests on whether this local god will lend a hand; even Gen. Douglas MacArthur is just a little awed, vowing to send supplies and respect the king's integrity. ("History is written by interesting men," he rationalizes.)

A wan Nigel Havers (his parachuter character contracts malaria midway through the eventual fighting) narrates the story with even more awe of the flame-haired king. Initially stupefied at finding an American being fanned and catered to by headhunters who call themselves "Comanches," Havers is quick to become a disciple, marveling at Nolte's jungle know-how and affectionate relationship with his local Sheena. (The native women, by the way, are modestly wrapped in absolutely matching, color-coordinated sarongs and bandana tops, like a Broadway chorus line.)

You can't escape history, Havers prods him, but we have here a reluctant king—that is, until World War II comes knocking at his door, rat-a-tat-tat.

The natives love the war at first—it's like a cavalry charge out of the Comanche Old West and provides an excellent opportunity to bag a few heads. But soon the island paradise Learoyd has created is going up in smoke, women and children first.

"Farewell to the King" has an air of high adventure, a mix of thrilling adolescent genres—pirates, shipwrecks, Indiana Jones. But it goes a bit mawkish, especially when noble Nolte is whipped and tied to a stake yet again. Too much nobility can sap your attention span. Learoyd could probably reign over a beach-side coconut concession stand if he had to, and with the ending the way it is, maybe he will.

NEWSDAY, 3/3/89, Part III/p. 7, Lynn Darling

You have to say this for "Farewell to the King": It has the courage of its own shamelessness. It's all here, every dream ever dreamt by a 12-year-old boy—captured in the unabashed clash of swords glinting in the firelight, the epic and thoroughly ridiculous tale of war and friendship and men being men, the stirring but meaningless tale of freedom and bravery and destiny. Director John Milius ("Conan the Barbarian," "Red Dawn"), no slouch in the macho-pipe-dream department, has outdone even his previous attempts at bombastic vainglory.

What we have here is an upwardly mobile adventure comic, one that helps itself to generous portions of, among many others, "Lawrence of Arabia," "The Man Who Would Be King" and "South Pacific." It's the tale of a bedraggled American deserter (Nick Nolte) who washes up on the shores of Borneo in the waning days of World War II. Before long he's become the king of the Dayaks, a large band of adoring headhunters ready to follow him anywhere. His name is Learoyd—(yes, that's right, Learoyd, as in Leroy, as in the French for king. Subtlety is not one of Milius' priorities).

"I brought them the joy of song and the fellowship of the Round Table," Learoyd tells Capt. Fairbourne (Nigel Havers) in a typical piece of boneheaded dialogue. In return Learoyd has found freedom, true freedom, manly freedom, the kind of freedom that allows him to walk around in a red sash and a fetching pair of black capri-length pants, and to grow his tawny locks to leonine proportions. And to have many, many children.

In the beginning, young Fairbourne is somewhat perplexed by all of this, suspecting that his host might be just a little bit loonytunes, but gosh darn it, that impression fades quickly enough and the two of them become the best of friends. This is a little troubling because Fairbourne has his own fish to fry: He's out to convince Learoyd to lead his people into battle with the Japanese (who conveniently stay out of sight until Fairbourne and his henchmen can get everyone trained in the finer points of military warfare). Fairbourne knows he's going to have to betray good old Learoyd after it's all over, but not before he gets Gen. MacArthur himself to sign a treaty recognizing the sovereign rights of his new pal.

It's all piffle, of course, presented without irony or intelligence or humor. Instead, the camera dwells lovingly, in slow-motion caress, on the scenes of battle, scenes like the one where Learoyd charges along, a six-gun in each hand, shouting, "Advance the colors, men!" War is heck.

If there was any way of making the character of Learoyd any less ridiculous, Nick Nolte doesn't find it: Every now and then there surfaces the sneaking suspicion that he's actually into the nonsensical drivel he has to spout in both English and in Iban, the language of the headhunters.

You have to feel sorry for just about every other actor in this misbegotten bit of romantic bluster, though Nigel Havers got most of my sympathy. He seemed to be trying to turn in a creditable performance in a film in which just keeping a straight face must have been difficult.

VILLAGE VOICE, 3/14/89, p. 68, Amy Taubin

If the measure of a screen actor rests not only on how he shines in the best situation, but also on how he maintains his dignity in the worst, then Nick Nolte—currently to be found giving a deliciously befuddled comic performance in Martin Scorsese's section of *New York Stories* and a genially athletic one in John Milius's unintentionally parodic *Farewell to the King*—is very good indeed.

The opening of Milius's Kiplingesque saga—giant Pacific white caps tossing a tiny rowboat—reminds us of the promise of his early film *Big Wednesday,* making the ludicrousness of what follows even harder to take. Adapted from the novel by Pierre Schoendoerffer, *Farewell to the King* pulls a kind of *Apocalypse Now/Heart of Darkness* reversal and shows us how great it can be when the right white man meets up with the right noble savages.

Maddened by the brutality of war (specifically World War II's action in the Pacific), Sergeant Learoyd (Nolte) deserts the U.S. army and is found by a tribe of innocent Borneo headhunters who are so charmed by him that they make him their "Rajah." This idyll is cut short by the arrival of Captain Fairbourne (Nigel Havers), a British army botanist, and his sidekick, Sergeant Tenga of His Majesty's African Forces (veteran Milius actor Frank McRae). They bring the news that the Japanese are coming, and that the only way Learoyd can save his people is to arm them and put them through boot camp. Thus, while the first half of the film has an abundance of young girlish flesh (breasts discreetly covered by black halters to satisfy PG-13), the second is filled with fire power and rivers red with blood. *Farewell to the King* has all the elements of an old boy's dream—women, guns, and the glories of empire. But I think even political sympathizers will hear the creaking. There's one gorgeous sequence, however—the opposing forces positioning themselves for battle in the moonlight. Under the circumstances, however, a good eye hardly matters.

Also reviewed in:
NEW YORK TIMES, 3/3/89, p. C23, Vincent Canby
VARIETY, 2/15–21/89, p. 20
WASHINGTON POST, 3/3/89, p. D7, Hal Hinson

FAT MAN AND LITTLE BOY

A Paramount Pictures release of a Lightmotive production. *Executive Producer:* John Calley. *Producer:* Tony Garnett. *Director:* Roland Joffé. *Screenplay:* Bruce Robinson and Roland Joffé. *Director of Photography:*

Vilmos Zsigmond. *Editor:* Françoise Bonnot. *Music:* Ennio Morricone. *Choreographer:* Marilyn Corwin and Kurt Kaynor. *Sound:* William J. Randall. *Sound Editor:* Stephen H. Flick and David A. Whittaker. *Production Designer:* Gregg Fonseca. *Art Director:* Peter Lansdown Smith and Larry Fulton. *Set Decorator:* Dorree Cooper. *Special Effects:* Fred Cramer. *Costumes:* Nick Ede. *Make-up:* Monty Westmore. *Stunt Coordinator:* Warren Stevens. *Running time:* 126 minutes. *MPAA Rating:* PG-13.

CAST: Paul Newman (General Leslie R. Groves); Dwight Schultz (J. Robert Oppenheimer); Bonnie Bedelia (Kitty Oppenheimer); John Cusack (Michael Merriman); Laura Dern (Kathleen Robinson); Ron Frazier (Peer de Silva); John C. McGinley (Richard Schoenfield); Natasha Richardson (Jean Tatlock); Ron Vawter (Jamie Latrobe); Michael Brockman (William "Deke" Parsons); Del Close (Dr. Kenneth Whiteside); John Considine (Robert Tuckson); Alan Corduner (Franz Goethe); Joseph d'Angerio (Seth Neddermeyer); Jon De Bries (Johnny Mount); James Eckhouse (Norbert Harper); Todd Field (Robert Wilson); Mary Pat Gleason (Dora Welsh); Clark Gregg (Douglas Panton); Peter Halasz (George Kistiakowsky); Gerald Hiken (Leo Szilard); Arthur Holden (Oakridge Doctor); Ed Lauter (Whitney Ashbridge); Donald Mackechnie (James Tuck); Madison Mason (Boris Pash); Christopher Pieczynski (Otto Frisch); Don Pugsley (Bronson); Logan Ramsey (Brehon Somervell); Fred Dalton Thompson (Melrose Hayden Barry); Jim True (Donald Hornig); Barry Yourgrau (Edward Teller); Marek Alboszta (Scientist); Steven Baigelman (Doctor Avenell); Frank Benettieri Jr. (Messenger); David Brainard (Samuel Allison); Roger Cubicciotti (Frank Oppenheimer); Franco Cutietta (Enrico Fermi); Robert Peter Gale (Dr. Louis Hempelmann); Wesley and Brent Harrison (Peter Oppenheimer); Tom McFarlane (Scientist); David C. Parnes (Raincoat Man); Allen Poirson (Howard McDonald); David Politzer (Robert Serber); Bill Rubenstein (Times Reporter); Ken Strausbaugh (Observation Officer); Walter Sullivan (Henry Stimson); Brian Wandell (Dennis Talmudge); John Williams (Mack Stoddard).

FILMS IN REVIEW, 3/90, p. 167, Frank Scheck

Roland Joffé takes on serious subjects. His most recent films, *The Killing Fields* and *The Mission,* dealt with Cambodian genocide and 18th century Jesuit missionaries in Brazil. His new film is about nothing less than the creation of the atomic bomb and the ushering in of the nuclear age. The title refers to the two devices that were dropped on Hiroshima and Nagasaki, ending World War II.

It is a subject rich with possibilities and filled with fascinating characters, as was proved with last year's award winning television film *Day One.* But Joffé, who has previously brought much passion to his polemical projects, has delivered a curiously detached work. *Fat Man And Little Boy* is not a bomb, but it does misfire.

The central conflict in the story is between General Leslie Groves (Paul Newman), the hard driving, fanatical military man in charge of the project, and J. Robert Oppenheimer (Dwight Schultz), the chief scientist and "father of the bomb," whose doubts about the project were superseded by his desire to achieve the impossible. In the film, neither characterization is fully developed. Newman plays Groves with a mustache, a gravelly voice, and the rigid bearing of a career military man. He lends the portrayal an intensity and righteousness that is not unsympathetic. But there is such a stiffness about the character that, despite his obvious talents for manipulation, it is hard to see how he could have managed his disparate group of scientists and pulled the project together. Schultz's Oppenheimer is curiously uninteresting, especially when one considers the rich Faustian possibilities of the figure. Both the actor and the character are overwhelmed by Newman's Groves, and the film seems unbalanced as a result.

Bruce Robinson's screenplay never does much with the myriad political and social aspects of the story. The bomb was created by a polyglot team of scientists living together in a makeshift community carved out of the desert in Los Alamos, New Mexico, but little is conveyed about what the atmosphere of that chaotic situation was like. The film is more concerned with Oppenheimer's extramarital affair with a suspected Communist (Natasha Richardson) and the trials of his suffering wife Kitty (Bonnie Bedelia). When Groves and Kitty square off over the potentially disastrous results of Oppenheimer's creation, it's like a wife and mistress having a nasty spat for the husband's affections. There's also a disastrous subplot involving an idealistic young scientist played by John Cusack (some of the scientists were young, but were they that young?) and his affair with a beautiful nurse (Laura Dern). One of the film's dramatic centerpieces occurs when Cusack's character becomes accidentally contaminated and dies a vividly depicted death from radiation poisoning. Both the character and the event are fictional, presumably designed to convey the human horror that was about to occur, but it comes off as melodramatic and manipulative.

The film is visually impressive, with a beautiful recreation of the 1940s designed by Gregg Fonseca and gorgeously sunbaked cinematography by Vilmos Zsigmond that is redolent of both vintage photographs and the glow created by the bomb. Joffé has staged the testing of the bomb effectively, with an eerie close up of Oppenheimer, his features distorted by the effects of the blast, watching the birth of his creation. It is a hideously poetic image that has more power than most of the rest of the film.

LOS ANGELES TIMES, 10/20/89, Calendar/p. 1, Sheila Benson

As the first atomic bomb roars to life in "Fat Man and Little Boy," we see a chilling image, as horrific in its way as the roiling cloud overhead: project director J. Robert Oppenheimer, his mouth an opened O, the flesh of his face rippling like a sheet of rubber from the bomb's air blast, twin yellow fireballs reflected in his black goggles.

This is the "mad scientist," late 20th-Century-style; the cornerstone image of the film and director Roland Joffé's cyanide-capsule comment on the intellectual tempted into playing God.

With co-writer Bruce Robinson, Joffé understandably sees this temptation as one with irrevocable consequences for the planet. But while his film makes that point with the fullest poignance, it also takes until its last quarter to gather its power, and its poetic eye is paired with a flat voice and an oddly tin ear.

It's Gen. Leslie Groves (Paul Newman), a hefty, politically conservative engineer who becomes the unlikely Devil to Oppenheimer's Faust. Not one to be argued with, Groves picks Oppenheimer (Dwight Schultz) to head the Manhattan Project because he suspects the man's genius and chooses to ignore Army counterintelligence warnings about the scientist's left-wing background. Sports, Groves once conceded to an interviewer, were the only things *he* could see that Oppenheimer didn't know everything about.

Newman and Schultz are arrestingly matched and *not* playing the title characters (Little Boy was the code name of the bomb dropped on Hiroshima Aug. 6, 1945, and Fat Man was the Nagasaki bomb, dropped three days later). Schultz's "Oppie," charismatic from his first exchange with Groves, is a believably complicated figure, a commanding, prideful, prickly egghead. It's said that his style and his skill at the romantic gesture also make him irresistible to women, a quality harder to see. Oppie's wife, Kitty (Bonnie Bedelia), and mistress, Jean Tatlock (Natasha Richardson), go through their own form of hell for him, but we're never exactly sure why.

Newman's Groves, unconvincing only at being bulky, is far from Oppenheimer's disdainful appraisal of him as a meatball and a cipher. In an entirely different way, Groves is equally commanding, the sort of man who can say—and believe—that God is on the side of the bomb-builders. And in the film, he is the steam that drives the engine of Oppenheimer's darkest ambitions. It's one of Newman's biggest stretches and most complex achievements.

The film cuts background explanations short, so that after Groves checks with Chicago-based nuclear physicist Leo Szilard (Gerald Hiken)—reduced here to a waggish bit role in the bathtub—to learn whether such a weapon could even be created, the focus quickly shifts to Los Alamos, built almost under our eyes. There, the Oppenheimer-picked team of physicists, biochemists and mathematicians, and their families, are literally isolated, and Groves' strict code of secrecy and the scientists' habits of sharing each discovery communally clash almost daily.

Along with the towering figures of the project—the Tellers, the Fermis, et all., whom we meet offhandedly as "Edward" or "Enrico," and really never get to know as individuals—there is a fictitious pair, young Michael Merriman (John Cusack, supposedly a composite of several scientists) and an outspokenly dove-ish nurse, Kathleen Robinson (Laura Dern). Put there clearly to be the film's young lovers-in-optimism, they are fine actors who give sweetness and reality to characters of the purest papier-maché.

Like the bomb itself, stirring to life over years, the film comes to life slowly. The push and pull of Groves and Oppenheimer remains the fascination of the story, but between them and the frustrations in bomb-building, the rest of the characters have to be content with little scraps of scenes. That's especially hard when you have an actress like Bedelia, whose presence and complexities make you want to see more, not less of her. (Incidentally, showing Kitty Oppenheimer glowingly pregnant, then just as glowingly thin again, without explanation, is a terrible mistake. Birth? Death? Trauma? Diapers? Directors shouldn't do this; audiences worry, even subliminally.)

There is tension throughout the movie, but its last quarter contains the film's real philosophical meat, the moral dilemma of some of the scientists about whether, in the wake of V-E Day, the bomb they have raced to build should ever be detonated, even as a threat. To make this quandary immediate to us—here *before* August, 1945—the writers have created a lab accident that exposes one of the young scientists to a lethal dose of radiation, then intercut his agonies with preparations for the pre-dawn test in the desert. (There was a real accident, but it came after the war ended, and the length of time it took that scientist to die was more extended.)

This barefaced device does exactly what it's meant to: No one seeing this suffering can help but multiply this young man by 200,000—the number of Japanese dead in both blasts. It might possibly be considered a forgivable invention.

But another, almost throwaway statistic, delivered by John McGinley's doctor, that the government has been "injecting the old and mentally ill with plutonium" at Oak Ridge is more electrifying and harder to authenticate. It's not mentioned in the bible on the subject, Richard Rhodes' "The Making of the Atomic Bomb," and in a New York Times interview last week, Rhodes was quoted as being "bothered" by the scene because he "doubted that it happened."

Ironically, that last statistic is actually extraneous. Remove it, and the last 20 minutes of "Fat Man and Little Boy" still qualify as civilization's most authentic nightmare. Whatever his film's contrivances as it builds, with this closing, Joffé has made a permanent contribution to our national insomnia.

MONTHLY FILM BULLETIN, 3/90, p. 77, David Wilson

1942. General Leslie R. Groves reluctantly leaves his senior post in the Pentagon to oversee a top-secret project—the making of the first atomic bomb. The man chosen to lead the scientific team is brilliant physicist Robert Oppenheimer, whose known leftist political connections are considered to be controllable within the high-security confines of the hurriedly built base in Los Alamos, New Mexico. Groves and Oppenheimer are soon forced to swallow their initial misgivings about one another as Goves makes plain his military authority and Oppenheimer sets about instilling an operational discipline into his disparate team of scientists. For several months, the project is beset with technical difficulties, including a serious test accident. Meanwhile Oppenheimer, whose wife Kitty is one of the few women allowed to live on the base, is still privately communicating with an old flame, Jean Tatlock. When Groves tells him to end the relationship—closely monitored because Jean is a Communist—Oppenheimer reluctantly breaks the news to Jean as they spend a last night together in a hotel. Oppenheimer is supervising the testing of a new theory—fission through implosion—when Groves hands him a delayed telegram about Jean's suicide. With the war in Europe about to end, Oppenheimer begins to voice his increasing strategic and moral doubts about the project. Groves insists that the work must continue, not least because both his and Oppenheimer's careers depend on a successful outcome. And when one of his young colleagues, Michael Merriman, presents him with a petition signed by many of the back-up scientists in Chicago—that the bomb should only be demonstrated—Oppenheimer's response is ambivalent. Under continuing pressure from Groves, Oppenheimer uncertainly opts to continue with the project. Merriman is fatally irradiated in an accident, to the horror of his girlfriend Kathleen, a nurse at the base, and army doctor Richard Schoenfield, who makes a final plea to Oppenheimer to call a halt to the project. But now the bomb is at last ready for testing. And for all his misgivings, Oppenheimer agrees to go ahead with the test. The tremendous power of the explosion exceeds all expectations. And in less than a month, the world's first atom bombs are dropped on Hiroshima and Nagasaki.

The first atomic bombs, dropped on the citizens of a country now known (and then thought) to have been ready to sue for peace, changed the politics of the post-war world beyond the wildest fantasies of the scientists who developed them and the generals and politicians who sanctioned their use. Einstein thought that the splitting of the atom "changed everything save our mode of thinking". His predictions about a drift towards "unparalleled catastrophe" have of course—so far—not been realised, although the finger has been pretty close to the button on several occasions in the last forty years. With Cold War sabre-rattling presently quieted, the story of the making of the first bomb, fraught with ethical and scientific tensions as it was, ought to have provided a timely opportunity for rehearsing the moral and military issues which have been widely debated ever since. Particularly at a time when Hiroshima and Nagasaki are finding reborn apologists for the "saving" of lives.

Disappointingly, and surprisingly given the credentials of its creators, *Shadow Makers* (formerly *Fat Man and Little Boy*) turns out to be something of a damp squib. Here, the making of the bomb is dramatically dovetailed into the personal conflict and final accommodation between two of the leading players: the brilliant physicist Robert Oppenheimer, who led the scientific team at Los Alamos, and the sturdy General Groves, who ensured that this motley crew of scientific "longhairs" got on with the job. Time and again, the ethical and strategic issues of the opening of this twentieth-century Pandora's Box are raised as though they were mere dramatic ballast to this central clash of powerful personalities. The film's strategy is evident from the start, as a portentous low-angle shot finds Paul Newman as Groves glowering behind his Pentagon desk ("I built this place, so I'll be glad to eat it", he growls as his cringing aides bring in a monstrous farewell cake modelled after the inhuman architecture of the place). When Oppenheimer is introduced opining that Groves is "a provincial windbag ... a meatball, a cypher", it's clear that we are about to be shown that the general is anything but a pushover for opinionated physicists.

The stage is set for a whole series of bristling encounters, as though for Groves and Oppenheimer the question of the bomb were a mere stalking-horse for a clash of outsize personalities. The closest they get to the moral debate is over a meal in a top-brass cafeteria, and even then the argument is predicated on Groves' sense of a class difference between the two men. The effect is to reduce Oppenheimer's elsewhere well attested crisis of conscience to a minor inconvenience. "I'm in a dark place", he tells his wife, in one of the few direct references to his own moral qualms as he begins to appreciate the awesome power of the monster he has created. Similarly diminished is the gathering opposition among the scientific community itself. A petition is raised, but treated almost casually, the film preferring to focus internal misgivings in the character of a young scientist and occasional extracts from the journal he writes for his father. The question of Oppenheimer's own politics—later to cost him dear—is subsumed within a dramatic interlude involving Oppenheimer's ending of his affair with the Communist Jean Tatlock.

The pivoting of the film on a personal conflict has the effect of reducing the central drama of the bomb's making to another kind of implosion through fission. The centre does not hold, and extraordinarily the dramatic build-up to the first testing in the New Mexico desert lacks the very suspense inherent in its enormous implications. Impossible to say how much this is owed to the changes in the screenplay which Bruce Robinson is evidently unhappy about. But it could have something to do with Roland Joffé's direction, which not for the first time demonstrates a capacity for the big scene at the expense of a coherent and modulated narrative development.

NEW YORK, 11/6/89, p. 102, David Denby

The Manhattan Project (the rush-rush construction of the A-bomb during World War II) could, conceivably, make a good movie. What ambitions, what fears, what rivalries must have boiled over in that New Mexico mountain redoubt! Alas, two high-minded Brits—Roland Joffé, the director of *The Killing Fields* and *The Mission,* and screenwriter Bruce Robinson—have brought the subject only partly to life. *Fat Man and Little Boy* is not a disaster, but it's movieish and obvious, a project thoroughly compromised.

Joffé mounts a handsomely authentic large-scale production, and he gives us an eerily exciting test explosion, a blast so powerful that J. Robert Oppenheimer's lips and cheeks are distorted by the shock waves. He looks, at that moment, like a monster—a Faust who has turned into the Devil he bargained with. But most of the scenes of scientific breakthrough are unconvincing, and the human drama is suffocated in banality. Joffé and Robinson don't get into the comedy of the milieu—the oddity of Americans and refugee Europeans, who must have been culturally ill matched, thrown together in this pressure-cooker atmosphere during the bobby-soxer age. The Europeans among the staff seem not just young but callow; major personalities like Edward Teller and Enrico Fermi are a blur, though the veteran actor Gerald Hiken gives a strong, eccentric performance as Leo Szilard.

Most of all, Joffé needed a magnetic young star as the arrogant and subtle Oppenheimer, who ran the scientific side of the project. Dwight Schultz has the requisite slenderness and high forehead but no apparent sense of humor, and the script betrays him into conventionality. As a hotshot young physicist, the charming John Cusack projects all the intellectual energy of a rookie second-baseman reporting for spring training. A basic mistake: trying to convey the arcane passions of young scientific geniuses while making them regular guys at the same time. But pointy-heads have their own special fascination; keel-billed toucans should not be turned into robins pecking at worms. As for the women, played by some very accomplished actresses (Bonnie Bedelia, Natasha Richardson, Laura Dern), they utter variations on "Oh, darling, don't go back to the lab to build that nasty thing tonight." They are like the wives in old Westerns who try to argue the men out of their foolish gun battles.

The best part of *Fat Man and Little Boy* is the power struggle between Oppenheimer and General Leslie R. Groves (Paul Newman). Appointed by the Army to run the project, Groves at first seems like nothing more than a gruff military hardball, all bluster and will, with a brutally reductive mind. Oppenheimer is sure he can dominate him, but actually it is Groves, a master psychologist with a shrewd understanding of Oppenheimer's vanity, who does the dominating. Newman, speaking in a gravelly voice, makes Groves cogent and fierce—so powerful, in fact, that his Groves overwhelms the arguments made by Oppenheimer and some of the other scientists against using the bomb on the Japanese. The filmmakers lose control of the film—their doubts about the bomb only half come across.

NEW YORK POST, 10/20/89, p. 25, Jami Bernard

A glorious orange sun rises over the desert, silhouetting two huge, sleek black objects that are suspended by their tails like fish. "Fat Man and Little Boy," referring to the code names of the first two atomic bombs that changed the course of modern history and cast a shadow over its future, is an ambitious study of the bomb's invention and the moral and psychological fallout among its creators.

Paul Newman is Gen. Leslie R. Groves, the taskmaster who coordinated the mammoth effort at Los Alamos and a figure generally overlooked in the annals of history. There may be good reason to overlook him, too—his genius evidently was in picking J. Robert Oppenheimer to lead the scientists, and in manipulating him off unstable moral high ground to the safer realm of total dedication to the project at hand, unencumbered by second thoughts.

But this is not a psychological thriller, and Groves' appeal as the main character is limited, despite Newman's commanding performance, all gruffness, raspy-voiced, ambition confined in the straitjacket of being a company man.

Dwight Schultz is J. Robert Oppenheimer, or Oppie, the brilliant but unpopular choice as head of the select army of other brilliant minds, all of them fenced in at the giant, $2 billion think-tank-on-a-deadline. Through a unique and cleverly designed combination of leadership and creative stress, these minds together discovered a way to transform life-sustaining forces into destructive ones. Oppie is the more interesting character, a man whose parting words to his Berkeley students are, "May your life be rich and sweet." He is a man who sacrifices his politics, ideals, lover, and his marriage to a cause completely at odds with his conscience. If the physicist's greatest contribution (if you can call it that) was the technology to destroy the planet, then Groves' greatest contribution was in manipulating Oppenheimer to do his bidding. The bond between the two men is an integral part of the movie.

Director Roland Joffé (who teams again with his "The Killing Fields" screenwriter, Bruce Robinson) manages to convey the excitement, competition, and strain of young scientists sparking each other to greater heights of achievement. A euphoric, window-smashing baseball game is just as exciting as when someone hits upon the theory of implosion while squeezing an orange. The movie's swift pace imparts the immediacy of the deadline, plus the ease with which extraneous matters—like conscience—could be dispensed.

It was during WWII that the U.S. pumped $2 billion into the Manhattan Project, charged with inventing a "device" that would put the war to rest and make the U.S. supreme in military might. The movie oddly stops just short of the actual dropping of the bombs on Hiroshima and Nagasaki. To bomb or not to bomb is central to the characters' moral dilemma; possibly it should have been to the film as well.

Where "Fat Man and Little Boy" fails is precisely where the inventors of the bomb failed: on the level of basic humanity. A subplot romance between nurse Laura Dern and young physicist John Cusack falls flat. With the possible exception of Natasha Richardson as the distraught lover with whom Oppie must sever all ties, the script has only the clunkiest ideas about women, love and how to make human values compete in the marketplace of scary technology. When Cusack is caught in a scientific quagmire, Dern asks, "But can you dance?" Dern deserves better, and so does the movie.

Shot in lovely, dusty browns and ochres, there are some stunning visual moments, such as when Oppie, in gas mask and unlit cigarette, the force of the test explosion blowing his gums back from his teeth, is happily, crazily astounded by his invention, looking like a survivor of the dismal future he has created.

NEWSDAY, 10/20/89, Part III/p. 3, Mike McGrady

Though physicist J. Robert Oppenheimer was chosen to head the team of scientists making history's first atomic bomb, he was never fully trusted by the military minds overseeing his work. For one thing, his mistress was a known Communist. Secondly, he drank carrot juice. Leading one of the officers to conclude, rightly, "Oppenheimer ain't one of us."

Just as the military doesn't trust Oppenheimer (Dwight Schultz) and his highbrow cadre, the scientists assigned to the Los Alamos branch of the Manhattan Project underestimate the general who is running the show. Leslie R. Groves (Paul Newman) is a by-the-book officer, hard-nosed and slow to compromise, and, after their first meeting, Oppenheimer guesses, incorrectly, "This general is a meatball, a cipher; he'll be eating out of my hand in a week."

What happens is quite the reverse. During the more than two years it takes to construct and explode the first atomic bomb, Oppenheimer is, in fact, won over by the general. Not only does he build the weapon, he is instrumental in overriding other sicientists' objections to ever using it. "Fat Man and Little Boy" suggests that Oppenheimer had to subvert his own humanity in creating a bomb that would claim 200,000 lives, and that man may be too primitive to be trusted with his own technological accomplishments.

There's no doubt that the story of the secret development of that first nuclear weapon—Oppenheimer heads the think tank to end all think tanks—is fertile soil for drama, as has been demonstrated in earlier books and television shows. But Hollywood's great love for rewriting once again goes beyond script to include history itself.

Roland Joffé, the director of "The Killing Fields" and "The Mission," has his own agenda, one that requires the altering of history. When the facts don't fit, they are either reshaped or rearranged. Since the central story of the general and the scientist lacks sufficient conflict (in real life, the two men came to share a cool respect for one another), the film's dramatic emphasis shifts to a key subplot.

Physicist Michael Merriman (John Cusack) falls in love with a lovely nurse (Laura Dern) who has clearly listened to too many soap operas: "Tonight I want to make love. And I want a future. For me and you." Hmmm. A line like that, in Hollywood, is almost definitely a preamble to tragedy, and that very day Merriman courageously saves the lives of co-workers by exposing himself to radioactive material. slowly then, with the nurse sobbing in the background, we watch the young man lose his hair, become bloated and slowly die, at the same time providing the movie with its metaphorical object lesson, the price science pays when it plays God.

What's wrong with all this? What's wrong is it never happened. There was no Merriman, no adoring nurse, no fatal act of heroism. A call to Joffé educes the explanation that Merriman is a "composite portrait" based on the deaths of scientists Harry Daghlian and Lewis Slotin. But those fatalities occurred some time later—the end of the war. While this may qualify as truth, Hollywood style, it has no place in a film that asks to be taken as history.

Possibly it was felt that the central conflict wasn't powerful enough and, indeed, that's the film's other major problem. Newman passes his first test as a character actor with flying colors; the general doesn't change one iota during the course of the movie. And unknown stage actor Dwight Schultz plays Oppenheimer as the ambiguous figure he may very well have been. The two central characters, then, are either static or enigmatic, not qualities that tend to inspire great drama.

NEWSWEEK, 10/30/89, p. 75, David Ansen

The task of telling the story of the making of the atomic bomb in one 126-minute movie would daunt any film-maker, but Roland Joffé, the director of "The Killing Fields," "The Mission," and now *Fat Man and Little Boy,* is nothing if not ambitious. The question that must have cost Joffé and his co-writer Bruce Robinson many sleepless nights was how to find a dramatic form to contain so rich and complex a tale, enacted by the most brilliant scientific minds of the time, and resonating with the thorniest moral questions of the age. Their solution was to focus on the two utterly disparate men who brought the Manhattan Project to fruition—Gen. Leslie R. Groves (Paul Newman) and the physicist he picked to mastermind the creation of the bomb at Los Alamos, J. Robert Oppenheimer (Dwight Schultz).

With the finest team of international scientists at their disposal, and a 19-month deadline to produce a weapon they hope will end the war, these unlikely allies usher in the atomic age. Groves is the patriotic bulldog, an unscrupulous but crafty taskmaster with a single-minded purpose: to see that "the gadget" gets made, and once made, used. The brilliant, arrogant Oppenheimer, viewed by many in the government as a security risk for his leftist views, thinks Groves will be easy to handle, but he's consistently outmaneuvered by the gruff, Machiavellian military man. As his doubts about the consequences of his work grow, Groves accelerates the pressure.

"Fat Man and Little Boy" casts a wide net, but it never really traps its subject. The screenplay simply isn't up to the job. Only in the last half hour, as Trinity approaches, does dramatic fission occur. Merriman (John Cusack), a young physicist, is fatally exposed to radiation when an experiment goes awry, and his agony drives home the antinuclear message on a gut level. Ironically, this event is fictionalized, drawn from later incidents.

The missed opportunities add up. While we're treated to a banal love story between Merriman and a nurse (Laura Dern), we have no sense of the other scientists at work and no sense of the heady group dynamics. Joffé keeps the pace jumping, but sacrifices depth: the big moral debate at Oppenheimer's house about the consequences of the bomb is maddeningly attenuated.

Perhaps most crucially, the conflict between Groves and Oppenheimer never ignites. As screen presences, Newman and Schultz are mismatched. By casting a bona fide star as Groves—ideologically, Joffé's foe—the balance unintentionally tilts toward the "can do" general. This is true even though Newman's not at his best—he doesn't seem at ease playing a man with this kind of blunt swagger. The Faustian Oppenheimer, torn between ambition and conscience, is one of the great conflicted figure, but neither Schultz nor the script gets inside the man's edgy, haunted soul. Perhaps this stylish, overreaching movie was doomed from the start to be an honorable failure.

VILLAGE VOICE, 10/31/89, p. 75, J. Hoberman

The least that can be said for *Fat Man and Little Boy* is that director Roland Joffé sets himself an interesting problem: How does one make an entertainment that treats the Manhattan Project, the guilt surrounding the creation of the atom bomb, and the birth of the American national security state? Will it be myth or miniseries or some, as yet unknown, third way?

The past dozen years brought plenty of myths—*Star Wars, Superman, Raiders of the Lost Ark*, and *Ghostbusters* each in its fashion deals with the issue of nuclear Armageddon. Still, Joffé is a man whose utter seriousness has been amply established with *The Killing Fields* and *The Mission* (he's a cross between Stanley Kramer and Werner Herzog, attacking Big Themes in Difficult Locations). Thus, *Fat Man and Little Boy* is structured like a miniseries, albeit a compressed one—a full flowering would have had parts for Harry Truman, Albert Einstein, David Greenglass, and a Japanese kamikaze pilot with a wife and kids in Hiroshima.

As a filmmaker, Joffé has more finesse than fellow water buffalo Sir Richard Attenborough; he surrounds himself with skillful performers and heavy-hitting techies (here composer Ennio Morricone and cinematographer Vilmos Zsigmond). Although largely confined to Los Alamos as it follows the progress of the Manhattan Project from 1942 to the summer of 1945, *Fat Man and Little Boy* sets the viewer a crisp martial pace (you can hear *The March of Time*). The film proceeds in little flurries of events—often doubled-up for emphasis. Thus, a playful scientist smacks a home run through the window just as the project's military honcho, General Leslie R. Groves (Paul Newman), warns top scientist J. Robert Oppenheimer (Dwight Schultz) to drop his "known Communist" mistress (Natasha Richardson). This is the sort of winsome, lose-some movie in which—painful irony!—the first successful test of the "gadget" is preceded, by one split-second, with news of personal tragedy for one of the perpetrators.

Even in less portentous moments, Joffé's characteristic mode is to cut from a solemn Hallmark sentiment to a jangle of visual noise (making strategic use of rain and propellers) to achieve a distinctively monotonous checkerboard pattern. You have to wonder whether the movie will ever include anything more surprising than the tire that an irate general rolls into Groves's office, or the lazy anachronisms ("That's the good news, now the bad news"; "It's not over till it's over") peppering the script. Considering that the combined IQs of the characters at hand would probably balance the national budget, Joffé and co-scenarist Bruce Robinson might have concocted some less threadbare dialogue. Instead, the assembled geniuses are a background crowd of vaudeville-accented eccentrics, like the syndicate of professors in Hawks's 1942 *Ball of Fire*, or even Disney's seven dwarves (Barry Yourgrau plays saturnine Edward Teller as Grumpy). Their main function is to glorify the all-American normals (Laura Dern and John Cusack) who are forever discussing the meaning of life.

"Gee, we're trying to tap into the energy that fuels the universe—it's petrifying when I stop to think about it," Cusack muses at one point. The last time Hollywood tackled this dilemma so . . . nakedly was some 42 years ago with MGM's *The Beginning or the End*—a relatively lavish prestige project that opens with a pseudo-newsreel of atomic scientists burying their records, including (why not?) *The Beginning or the End*, in a time capsule intended for the year 2446. Although this dramatization of the Manhattan Project was intended for Spencer Tracy and Clark Gable, Groves and Oppenheimer ended up being played by the rather less glamorous pair of Brian Donlevy and Hume Cronyn. Nevertheless, as *Times* critic Bosley Crowther opined, "In making this picture, Metro has seemed to confuse the humbleness of its achievement with the magnitude of atomic power."

If *Fat Man and Little Boy* has no small sense of its own importance (according to a production piece in the last *Premiere*, the crew is all but running a pool on the number of prospective Oscars), it is in no way as meretricious as *The Beginning or the End* (which, among other things, claimed that the Japanese had 10 days of warnings before Little Boy fell on Hiroshima and, in any case, were working on an atomic bomb of their own). Still, *Fat Man* does resemble a colorized version of its precursor in similarly focusing on an invented scientist who suffers doubts about the project and dies of radiation poisoning, leaving behind a young wife (here fiancée), thus imploding the story of the century down to a highly charged individual tragedy.

Ultimately, *Fat Man and Little Boy* is a miniaturized Faust story. While Schultz must have been told to blink when nervous, then tilt toward the camera, Newman agonizes through the honcho role with growly assurance. Although the script allows him too much easy authority (lots of ordering people to "get in the car" or "get out of the car"), there's a crotchety Walter Brennan quality to his irate homilies. Groves, in the view of Joffé and Robinson, is totally manipulative—an activated military animal for whom all means are legitimate ways to baby Oppenheimer along. By the end of the movie, the pair has been reduced to the two eponymous bombs, malignly glinting in the sun.

Reportedly, Harrison Ford was originally considered for the role of Oppenheimer—a casting coup that might have made *Fat Man* seem a good deal more subversive. Still, Schultz, whose long face and high-strung lope are iconically perfect, does suggest a revisionist view of Indiana Jones. In the realm of dueling fedoras, a twist of his hat brim brings Japan to its knees. Indeed, Joffé's finale does show an irresponsible flare for the mythic—conflating elements of *The Fly*, *Fantasia*, and *Dr. Strangelove* before pushing the button for the inevitable Industrial Light and Magic Show.

Also reviewed in:
NATION, 11/13/89, p. 577, Stuart Klawans
NEW REPUBLIC, 11/20/89, p. 28, Stanley Kauffmann
NEW YORK TIMES, 10/20/89, p. C15, Vincent Canby
NEW YORKER, 11/13/89, p. 121, Pauline Kael
VARIETY, 10/18–24/89, p. 24
WASHINGTON POST, 10/20/89, p. B1, Hal Hinson
WASHINGTON POST, 10/20/89, Weekend/p. 43, Desson Howe

FEAR, ANXIETY AND DEPRESSION

A Samuel Goldwyn Company and Polygram Movies release of a Propaganda Films production. *Executive Producer:* Michael Kuhn and Nigel Sinclair. *Producer:* Stanley J. Wlodkowski, Steve Golin, and Sigurjorn Sighvatsson. *Director:* Todd Solondz. *Screenplay:* Todd Solondz. *Director of Photography:* Stefan Czapsky. *Editor:* Peter Austin, Emily Paine, and Barry Rubinow. *Sound:* Michael Sabo and Joe Earle. *Production Designer:* Marek Dobrowolski. *Art Director:* Susan Block. *Set Decorator:* Susan P. McCarthy, Roza Fitzgerald, and Taylor Black. *Costumes:* Susan Lyall. *Make-up:* Nancy Tong and Cidele Curo. *Running time:* 94 minutes. *MPAA Rating:* Not Rated.

CAST: Todd Solondz (Ira); Bob Martana (Ira's Boss); Alexandra Gersten (Janice); Max Cantor (Jack); Jill

Wisoff (Sharon); Yvonne Roome (Mother, Play #1); Eric Guttierez (Son, Play #1); Helen Hanft (Roz); J.J. Barry (Sam); Jane Hamper (Junk); Stanley Tucci (Donny); Anne Desalvo (Sylvia); Alison Gordy (Kim); Alan Leach (Doctor); Janice Jenkins (Nurse); Mark Webster (Intern); Daniel Neiden (Actor, Play #2).

LOS ANGELES TIMES, 3/23/90, Calendar/p. 10, Michael Wilmington

Todd Solondz, the young writer-director-star of "Fear, Anxiety and Depression," wants to be the new Woody Allen so badly, he should walk around with a sandwich board emblazoned, "Generic Woody: All the urban neuroses, One tenth the cost." And, unfortunately, less than one tenth the laughs. Of "Interiors."

Solondz, a recent NYU graduate, has a subject ripe for satire: the proto-punk Lower Manhattan scene, not quite-starving artists in a landscape of creeping gentrification. But, with all this Allen mimicry, he's like Rich Little run amok. He sees everything through a double screen: the world as a Woody Allen movie.

Solondz appropriates everything: glasses, shaggy wardrobe, nervous oververbal dialogues, anhedonia and self-pity. He uses that draggy, nasal whine. He flops his arms, stammers. At one point, he even copies Woody's little blissed out mating dance: those stiff-legged, dopey, smirky pirouettes. His own frizzy mop is black, but otherwise, he's copied everything but the freckles. And the soul.

Given this performance, one might expect the major character, Ira Ellis (Solondz), to be a young film school graduate obsessed with Woody Allen. But Solondz shows greater hubris. Instead, Ira is fixated on Samuel Beckett; he's a struggling playwright, a nebbish-in-excelsis who inexplicably gets bad plays produced at the Public Theater.

Ira's neurasthenic roundelay of sexual encounters also swarms with Allen archetypes. His stud-buddy Jack, the poseur pop painter (Max Cantor) is Solondz's Tony Roberts. His clinging, sniveling girlfriend Sharon (Jill Wisoff) suggests Louise Lasser. The coldly promiscuous punk performance artist, Junk (Jane Hamper), whom Ira vainly pursues, is not an obvious Diane Keaton clone—though Jack's failed actress girlfriend Janice (Alexandra Gersten) is in the ballpark. And there's a smarmy yuppie success named Donny (Stanley Tucci), who suggests any number of Allen nemeses from Paul Simon to Alan Alda.

Some of this is clever, but little of it is funny. Solondz has the husk of Woody, but not the heart or the mechanics. The movie is frenetic, pushy, thin, obvious—and Solondz's comic sense tends toward overblown, over-telegraphed slapstick.

But, though "Fear, Anxiety and Depression" (Times-rated mature for theme and language) is a pretty complete failure, its stabs at wit, *Angst* and Manhattan occasionally nudge their targets and cinematographer Stefan Czapsky ("Vampire's Kiss") and Solondz get some zippy-stylish long-take scenes and sidewalk tracking shots. And Tucci, Gersten and Cantor have their moments. Unfortunately for all of them, Woody still owns the franchise.

NEWSDAY, 12/11/89, Part II/p. 7, Drew Fetherston

This is a film made by a funny twerpy guy. He's short and slight, with kind of wild long hair around a receding hairline. Nervous. Horn rim glasses he's always pushing up on his nose. He wrote and directed the film, and in it he plays a really insecure guy who gets so shaky around attractive women that he blabbers and stammers.

Always has a furrowed brow, a pained visage with a mouth that tends to drop open. He plays a writer, a serious guy who's always losing out to phonies and empty suits. Nice New York location shots, bookstores and the 59th Street bridge.

No, not Woody Allen. Todd Solondz.

You haven't heard of him. He's only recently out of film school. To judge from this first feature effort, the saga of a shlumpf struggling for Downtown success, Solondz is neither shy nor without promise.

The story is pretty much standard Woody Allen, transplanted to the lower right section of Manhattan from Uptown. We meet Ira Ellis (Solondz) as he is composing a letter to Samuel Beckett, offering praise and proposing a collaboration. Ira has written a play, and manages to get it produced with some financial help from his parents. The single review, in the Village Voice, is brutally negative. (It charges him with, among other things, homophobia.)

Meanwhile, Ira's shallow and undeserving friends are flourishing in the Downtown art world, readying themselves for imminent jumps uptown. Ira meets a jerk of a high school buddy who, inspired by his first exposure to a Broadway play, went home and in two weeks wrote a play of his own. It's to be produced at the Public, as soon as the jerk decides if he wants to have Bob Duvall star in it.

He takes up with Sharon (Jill Wisoff), whose artistic ambitions are clouded by neuroses that prod her incessantly toward suicide. He longs to take up with Junk (Jane Hamper), a soulless performance artist, but she's understandably uninterested. He courts her rejection avidly, while simultaneously burning with guilt for so jeopardizing loving, unstable Sharon.

All of this failure and guilt makes Ira seem to be perpetually at the point of tears or perhaps full nervous collapse, a state that enhances his resemblance to Woody Allen. This isn't to say that "Fear, Anxiety and Depression" isn't funny in its own right. The film is a series of vignettes, many of them well constructed and witty. The cast is good, though they are often asked to play the comedy too broadly.

Solondz is cannily aware of the erosion of creative Downtown: His circle of chums groans nobly about the conversion of performance spaces into Cal-Mex restaurants, without recognizing that they themselves are success-hungry corrupters.

But Solondz tries too hard for too many laughs, and there are some embarrassing lapses. When Ira tries to adapt to Junk, the result is merely dumb. And while he acknowledges his debt to Woody Allen and other film makers, Solondz seems as yet unaware that homage is a symbolic, not explicit, act.

Also reviewed in:
NEW YORK TIMES, 12/18/89, p. C18, Caryn James
VARIETY, 10/4–10/89, p. 32

FEW DAYS WITH ME, A

A Galaxy International release of a Sara Films/Cinéa/Films A2 production. *Producer:* Alain Sarde and Philippe Carcassonne. *Director:* Claude Sautet. *Screenplay (French with English subtitles):* Claude Sautet, Jacques Fieschi and Jérôme Tonnere. *Based on the novel by:* Jean-François Josselin. *Director of Photography:* Jean-François Robin. *Editor:* Jacqueline Thiedot. *Music:* Philippe Sarde. *Sound:* Pierre Lenoir and Jean-Paul Loublier. *Art Director:* Carlos Conti. *Costumes:* Olga Berlutti. *Running time:* 127 minutes. *MPAA Rating:* PG-13.

CAST: Daniel Auteuil (Martial); Sandrine Bonnaire (Francine); Danielle Darrieux (Mme. Pasquier); Jean-Pierre Marielle (Fonfrin); Dominique Lavanant (Mme. Fonfrin); Vincent Lindon (Fernand); Therese Liotard (Régine); Gérard Ismael (Rocky).

LOS ANGELES TIMES, 6/28/89, Calendar/p. 2, Michael Wilmington

Mad passion—the grand amour that unhinges you, makes you throw away your life—is a frequent movie subject. But it's rarely handled with the intense observation or generous good humor writer-director Claude Sautet brings to "A Few Days With Me."

Focusing on the cross-class liaison of an alienated young man, heir to a French supermarket chain, and the maid of one of his family's managers, this movie has an almost irresistible narrative drive. Sautet, one of the great artisans of the naturalistic French screenplay, is dealing with life and death, love that destroys, but he mixes his moods expertly. He keeps "A Few Days With Me" incongruously light, deft, humorous.

He portrays pathology by giving it an unflinching gaze, by filling the story with amusingly eccentric characters and unexpected twists. It's a seeming romantic tragedy or melodrama told in an engaging comic style. The deceptive, often lackadaisical-seeming rhythm keeps you constantly off balance, until the trap is sprung.

Sautet's lovers are played by Daniel Auteuil, the guilt-ridden nephew of "Jean de Florette" and Sandrine Bonnaire, the almost scarily independent hoyden of "A Nos Amours" and "Vagabonde." It's a brilliant piece of double casting. Auteuil, without his grotesque "Florette" prosthesis and makeup, has the yearning eyes and delicate, wary features of an obsessive swain. When we first meet his Martial, recovering from depression in an asylum, he seems vaguely dislocated, insulated by his family's wealth from life's shocks, oddly unaffected by everything, including his wife's infidelity.

Bonnaire, on the other hand, has exactly the stuff a man like this—dreamy, sarcastic, sensitive, bored—might get obsessed with. As Francine, whom Martial meets in Limoges while checking the books of her genial employer, Fonfrin (Jean-Pierre Marielle), she projects something earthy and unfettered, seductive in a seemingly uncalculated way. (Bonnaire is the actress audiences wish Madonna could be.) A practical femme fatale, Francine matches Martial's mad plunges and rich boy's self-indulgence with a working girl's shrewd self-interest. And, as he journeys through degradation and disgrace to possess her, she watches not bitchily or malignly, but curiously, almost bemusedly.

In the 1974 "Vincent, François, Paul and the Others," Sautet proved himself a poet of friendship. He excels at the portrayal of communities and the three groups he draws here—the glassy artificiality of the Pasquier family, the provincial pretensions of the Limoges bourgeois who run the Pasquier stores and the raw roughhouse swagger and cunning of Francine's friends—make for a marvelous collision. It also inspires a marvelous ensemble. Marielle, as the amiably corrupt Fonfrin and the legendary beauty Danielle Darrieux, as Martial's mother, give perfect performances; the rest of the cast, notably Dominique Lavanant as the neurotic Mme. Fonfrin and Gérard Ismael as the sinister Rocky, are nearly as good.

Sautet indulges all his actors, helps them to their best form. But he doesn't indulge his lovers. He shows exactly what happens when their worlds clash, never losing this innate sympathy or his comic, urbane perspective. That's why the film sustains so well the classic narrative virtues of surprise and inevitability, and why, in the end, Sautet, Auteuil and Bonnaire can give us such a devastating last few shots. And it's why "A Few Days With Me" (MPAA rated PG-13, despite partial nudity) can reveal so convincingly the tigerish passions that smolder beneath a surface that's deceptively calm, charmingly funny, insidiously smooth.

NEW YORK POST, 4/14/89, p. 35, Jami Bernard

Martial Pasquier has just been released from the mental hospital, apparently none the worse for his three years of refusing to speak. He still opens his mouth only when he has something to say; his intelligent, deadpan silences make the chatter around him seem that much more foolish.

Out of the hospital he walks and into the sunshine (stormy clouds come later) of Claude Sautet's "A Few Days With Me," a film that is mostly an amusing sendup of social pretensions and relationships, until it runs aground from angst.

Pop psychologists might surmise that Martial (Daniel Auteuil) got the quiets when his wife's lover moved in with them, but he seems to have adjusted with the same emotionless equanimity with which he treats everything else.

Anyway, it's good to be home—profits are off in the family-owned supermarket chain. Martial is elected to make a tour of the branch stores for a look at the books.

He starts with Limoges. The manager there, Leo G. Carroll lookalike Fonfrin (Jean-Pierre Marielle), nervously presents the books. We know they're doctored, the same way we're certain that the asylum-sprung Martial is sane: Auteuil's subtle, earnest deadpan wrings mirth out of scene after scene. That is, until about two-thirds of the movie, when Martial must inexplicably pay for the spree he's been having by going morose and introspective.

By all reckoning, Limoges should be a 15-minute stopover. It's a city awash in the kind of silliness Martial tends to avoid (a twittering dinner party makes frequent mention of the "porcelain show" that's in town, and one guest says, "I hate terrorists, but they are idealists"). But the city seems to hold a fascination for him. Perhaps it is *zee pretty Frensh maid* in Fonfrin's employ?

Within hours, Martial has rented a huge, empty flat and invited *zee pretty Frensh maid* (Sandrine Bonnaire of "Vagabond") to share it with him. As suddenly as he had once decided to stop talking, Martial now decides that the maid, Francine, is "the first person I've wanted to talk to in years."

Martial has chosen Limoges and Francine from the finger-on-spinning-globe school of decision making. What follows is an unorthodox, hedonistic spree in which much money is spent on patio furniture and much social convention ignored. Martial invites Francine's jealous boyfriend to dinner, then throws a garish costume party during which he serves noxious blue drinks and plays sadistic, possibly liberating jokes on his guests. The party is the natural culmination of Martial's passive-aggressive control mania, of which his silences may be a part.

Now the movie's tone changes, and it's not for the better. "Thank you for spending a few days with me," says Martial in that impenetrable tone he has. He leaves Francine and Limoges behind. But those "few days" have changed him; he goes from enigmatic, ironic, urbane silence to the wistful, moony-eyed, alarming withdrawal of the lovesick. His feelings, once aroused, prove to be beastly and obsessive.

Martial's final, noble, useless act of humanity is an exasperating puzzle. After all, people who refuse to make small talk at parties should be rewarded, not punished.

NEWSDAY, 4/14/89, Part III/p. 5, Mike McGrady

What is it that makes Martial so different, so unacceptable? Well, just consider his elevator meeting with a young business associate. Martial, heir to a chain of discount stores, asks the junior executive about the progress of his current love affair and is assured that it is entirely satisfactory. "But is it intense, fulfilling, *exciting?*" Martial wants to know.

"I think so," his perspiring associate says.

Why perspiring? Well, Paul's love affair happens to be with Martial's own beautiful wife, and this is a romance Martial has encouraged from the outset. Clearly, Martial (Daniel Auteuil) takes a different approach to life than most of us; he has a genius for the unexpected.

Dispatched to Limoges to find out why a family-owned store is losing money, Martial quickly learns the manager has been taking from the till. Instead of firing the man on the spot, he gives him a second chance, befriends him, goes to his house that night for a supper party.

It is there that Martial first observes a surly maid (Sandrine Bonnaire). The very next morning, he leases an old-fashioned apartment on the other side of town and invites the maid to move in with him. The following morning he takes her on a shopping spree, allowing her to furnish his apartment in Patio Modern. After outfitting her in pure flash, he encourages her to quit her job, then allows her to get behind the wheel of a new Mercedes. When she seeks permission to visit her unemployed boyfriend for an overnight, he insists on first taking the two of them out to dinner and later finds a job for the young man.

So begins "A Few Days With You," a film that finds its fascination in the blatant eccentricities of its central figure.

Another eccentricity: He always tells the truth while those around him jargonize. The store manager assures a jilted lover that "there are other fish in the sea" and that, furthermore, "time heals all wounds." A wealthy woman announces, "I like terrorists—they're such idealists!" A hostess claims, "The provinces are so ... provincial." When someone apologizes for all this banality, he assures them he very much enjoys "the steady flow of cliches—very musical, very soothing."

It's only later on, as the plot takes a series of conventional turns, that the film loses some of its magic. That magic is tied in so closely to the personality of the central figure there is no separating the two; Martial is given a quietly moving rendition by Daniel Auteuil, the fine actor who portrayed the ill-favored Ugolin in "Jean de Florette."

But what is the root difference between Martial and others? What makes him such an oddball, such a pariah, man seemingly destined to spend his life in one asylum or another?

The central factor that separates Martial from everyone else is that he scrupulously practices the Golden Rule. In every encounter, with lovers and murderers, with family or strangers, he inevitably treats people the way he would want to be treated. Unfortunately, in real life—at least this is the unsettling conclusion of "A Few Days With Me"—that's just not permitted.

VILLAGE VOICE, 4/18/89, p. 71, Stuart Klawans

Why must a would-be Dostoyevski lurk in the heart of every comedian? At its best, *A Few Days With Me* recalls the giddy pleasures of *The Palm Beach Story*, as Martial (Daniel Auteuil), heir to a chain of retail stores, goes on a binge with Francine (Sandrine Bonnaire), a young woman whose highest aspiration is to work as a barmaid. But then Martial turns into Prince Myshkin.

When first seen, Martial is in a posh loony bin, recovering from a breakdown. Returned to his family—which is synonymous with the business—he quickly accepts the assignment of inspecting some stores in the provinces. His tour stops abruptly in Limoges, though, when he discovers not only an embezzlement scheme but also Francine, working as a servant in the home of the store's manager.

The ensuing idyll with Francine involves a shopping spree, a party, some slumming with

Francine's pals, and similar forays into the philosophy of *je-m'en-foutisme*. Neither the audience nor Francine knows whether Martial is frittering away his time or digging up proof of the embezzlement. As long as Martial's motives remain thus mixed, the film has the lively, if undemanding, charm of Gallic screwball comedy. The performances are uniformly engaging (including Jean-Pierre Marielle's impersonation of the unctuous store manager); the direction is assured and unpretentious; the level of political consciousness is high enough to allow you to relax and enjoy the goings-on.

But then Martial makes up his mind about what he wants in life. Moralism and doom set in. Scenes begin to drag, and even the editing loses its sense of purpose. I don't often complain about films taking unexpected turns; the problem here is that the shift from comedy to tragedy, once signaled, plays itself out so predictably.

Admirers of French cinema will note that Danielle Darrieux picks up a paycheck in the role of Martial's no-nonsense mother.

Also reviewed in:
NEW YORK TIMES, 4/14/89, p. C8, Vincent Canby
VARIETY, 10/5/88, p. 154

FIELD OF DREAMS

A Universal Pictures release of a Gordon Company production. *Executive Producer:* Brian Frankish. *Producer:* Lawrence Gordon and Charles Gordon. *Director:* Phil Alden Robinson. *Screenplay:* Phil Alden Robinson. *Based on the book "Shoeless Joe" by:* W.P. Kinsella. *Director of Photography:* John Lindley. *Editor:* Ian Crafford. *Music:* James Horner. *Music Editor:* Jim Henrikson and Nancy Fogarty. *Sound:* Russell Williams II and (music) Shawn Murphy. *Sound Editor:* Sandy Gendler. *Production Designer:* Dennis Gassner. *Art Director:* Leslie McDonald. *Set Designer:* Dawn Snyder and Kathleen McKernin. *Set Decorator:* Nancy Haigh. *Set Dresser:* Claire Gaul and Leslie Linville. *Special Effercts:* Robbie Knott. *Costumes:* Linda Bass. *Make-up:* Richard Arrington. *Stunt Coordinator:* Randy Peters. *Running time:* 106 minutes. *MPAA Rating:* PG.

CAST: Kevin Costner (Ray Kinsella); Amy Madigan (Annie Kinsella); Gaby Hoffman (Karin Kinsella); Ray Liotta (Shoeless Joe Jackson); Timothy Busfield (Mark); James Earl Jones (Terence Mann); Burt Lancaster (Dr. "Moonlight" Graham); Frank Whaley (Archie Graham); Dwier Brown (John Kinsella); James Andelin (Feed Store Farmer); Mary Anne Kean (Feed Store Lady); Fern Persons (Annie's Mother); Kelly Coffield (Dee, Mark's Wife); Michael Milhoan (Buck Weaver, 3B); Steve Eastin (Eddie Cicotte, P); Charles Hoyes (Swede Risberg, C); Art LaFleur (Chick Gandil, 1B); Lee Garlington (Beulah, the Angry PTA Mother); Mike Nussbaum (Principal); Larry Brandenburg, Mary McDonald Gershon, and Robert Kurcz (PTA Hecklers); Don John Ross (Boston Butcher); Bea Fredman (Boston Yenta); Geoffrey Nauffts (Boston Pump Jockey); Anne Seymour (Chisolm Newspaper Publisher); C. George Baisi (First Man in Bar); Howard Sherf (Second Man in Bar); Joseph Ryan (Third Man in Bar); Joe Glasberg (Costumer); Brian Frankish (Clean-shaven Umpire); Jeffrey Neal Silverman (Clean-shaven Center Fielder).

CHRISTIAN SCIENCE MONITOR, 5/2/89, p. 11, David Sterritt

About halfway through "Field of Dreams," a radical author (played by James Earl Jones) compliments a visionary baseball fan (Kevin Costner) on pursuing his ideals with such a passion—a passion that's "misdirected," he says with some scorn, but still a *passion*.

During its first few scenes, I thought "Field of Dreams" deserved the same remark.

Its energies were certainly misdirected, it seemed to me as I watched: The story kept wandering from one interest to another, focusing on baseball and 1960s radicalism and the 1980s farm crisis, among other subjects, in no particular order.

Yet there *is* a kind of passion in its goofy idealism about the American way of life. You can't help liking a movie, no matter how corny, that's goggle-eyed about subjects you just don't see in the movies very often nowadays—like mom, and baseball, and kindly old doctors who solve everyone's problems with a twinkle in their eyes. The picture almost overwhelms you with sheer niceness.

Unfortunately, this effect doesn't last; eventually the movie goes too far and overdoses on its own saccharine. Also, fantasies must be careful to establish their ground rules clearly and then stick by them, no matter what. But this one has the consistency of a wildly pitched knuckleball.

"Field of Dreams" begins with a fast trip through the '50s and '60s, showing how an ordinary guy named Ray grew up, flirted with progressive '60s politics, got married, and became what he never dreamed he'd be: a middle-class Iowa farmer with a family and a mortgage.

The plot thickens when he has (you guessed it) a dream in a field, hearing mysterious words from a disembodied voice. The words tell Ray to build a baseball diamond on his farm—and then Shoeless Joe Jackson, a member of 1919's scandal-ridden Chicago White Sox, will return to life and start belting home runs right there in the cornfield.

Ray obeys, and Shoeless Joe's ghost does come to visit. But this isn't enough for the powers that have chosen Ray as their assistant. Next he has to befriend a writer who lost his idealism when the '60s ended, and then they have to visit a small town where a lovable country physician once lived.

All these plot-threads are woven into a single strand after a while, but not very convincingly, and only after some arbitrary maneuvers. The ending is happy, sentimental, and far-fetched.

At a time when most movies suffer from an appalling lack of ambition, I don't like chiding any picture for attempting too much. But the main trouble with "Field of Dreams" is that it tries to cram about three films' worth of material into one overstuffed story.

It might have worked better as a series, with Ray having a different adventure in three different movies. The tale keeps taking off in new directions, and the underriding logic is so weak that each new twist seems half-baked and contrived. Least successful of all are the movie's stabs at social awareness, which seem hopelessly superficial even though they mean well.

The terrible Midwest farm crisis is handled so weakly that it's almost an insult to people who have suffered directly from it; and when Ray's wife takes a '60s-style stand against censorship at a school meeting, her arguments are as flabby as they are feisty.

On the plus side, Kevin Costner gives a winning performance as our hero, and Amy Madigan is likable as his wife. James Earl Jones is in good form as the aging author, and it's a pleasure to watch Burt Lancaster do just about anything these days, as his talent continues to mellow and mature.

In the Shoeless Joe role, by contrast, Ray Liotta recaptures little of the phenomenal energy he showed in "Something Wild" not long ago. The movie was written and directed by Phil Alden Robinson, based on a W.P.Kinsella novel. John Lindley did the warmly glowing cinematography, which makes the film a pleasure for the eyes even when its inspiration sags.

FILMS IN REVIEW, 8-9/89, p. 420, Kenneth M. Chanko

Field of Dreams is the film version of a little known 1982 novel called *Shoeless Joe,* a remarkable piece of conjuring that posits baseball as not only the most beautiful and grandest of sports, but as as redeemer of lost souls. If Gabriel Garcia Marquez were ever to write a baseball novel, it might turn out something like W.P. Kinsella's *Shoeless Joe.* A powerfully seductive magical realism permeates this story of a baseball obsessed Iowa farmer who one day, walking through his fields, hears a voice tell him, "If you build it, he will come." He knows immediately and exactly what the message means—if he builds a baseball diamond in his cornfield, Shoeless Joe Jackson, the great Chicago White Sox outfielder who was banned from the sport for his part in throwing the 1919 World Series, will appear. Shoeless Joe, though he died in 1951, does indeed show up—and that's just the beginning of this fantastic, lyrical novel.

A movie adaptation of such a tale has its inherent dangers. Like being laughed off the screen. I mean, we're talking a *big* suspension of disbelief here. Some necessary but mostly subtle changes have been made, things like it taking the farmer, Ray Kinsella (Kevin Costner), a bit longer to figure out what the voice means, and like the players who come to Ray's baseball field being quite solidly human in appearance, rather than the half-formed, ghost-like apparitions that the book describes.

Phil Alden Robinson, who wrote the screenplay and directed, has a sure feel for the material. He's also a smooth and resourceful filmmaker. An opening montage of photographs, with Costner's whimsical voice-over description of his life from his baseball dominated childhood to his unlikely occupation as farmer, succinctly establishes character and tone.

Ray has a loving wife, Annie (Amy Madigan), and a young daughter, Karin (Gaby Hoffman), and he's managing to make ends meet at farming. But Ray's a bit of a lost soul. He's worried that he's settled into a middle-aged existence ("Just like my father") before he's even reached the age of 40. An aspiring major league ballplayer, Ray's father had always wanted his son to play professional baseball, but Ray rebelled and gave up on the sport while still in his early teens. Now he's starting to regret it, as well as how he treated his father, who was just trying to live out his unfulfilled dream through his son (his father never made it to the big leagues). Yet Ray's troubled feelings aren't heavy-handedly served up at the film's beginning; they're naturally revealed during the course of his increasingly bizarre voyage of self-discovery.

After building the field and having his father's all-time favorite player, Shoeless Joe (Ray Liotta), appear, Ray is invigorated, even though his farm is in danger of going under. Ray spends his time chatting and shagging flies with Joe, who soon calls on the 7 other banned White Sox team players so he can practice with them. Following that, an all star team from earlier in the century shows up so an actual game can be played. Ray is in grandstand heaven.

But then he hears another message: "Ease his pain." He's stumped again, but only for a short while. After a wonderful scene at a nearby school where censorship of a legendary 60's writer is being debated, Ray realizes whose pain he's supposed to ease—that of the 60's writer himself, Terence Mann (James Earl Jones), who is now a recluse (in the novel, it was J.D. Salinger). Ray does some research on Mann and finds an old interview in which Mann said he always wanted to see a game at the Polo Grounds. So Ray is convinced that "easing his pain" involves finding Mann and bringing him to a Red Sox game at Fenway Park (the Polo Grounds were torn down in 1964), where something important will happen.

Without revealing any more plot specifics, let's just say that after Ray finds Mann and takes him to the game, his quest turns in the direction of an obscure old timer named Moonlight Graham (Burt Lancaster), who played just a half inning of a big league game in 1905 (it's true—you can look it up in your *Baseball Encyclopedia*). Finally, Ray returns home, where he meets one last figure from the past.

If all these events unfolded in a heavy-with-wonder or portentous way, *Field Of Dreams* would have been in early-inning trouble. But the humor is abundant and frequently self-mocking. There's also a sneaky, instant myth-making nature to much of it, with references to *The Wizard of Oz, Harvey* and especially *Citizen Kane* (Madigan's "It says he had a bat named Rosebud"). Songs heard on radios in the background early in the film include "Crazy" and "What A Day For A Day Dream."

The casting itself makes a key contribution to the make-us-believe factor. After starring in last summer's *Bull Durham,* Costner is immediately convincing as a man who could have been a great ballplayer and is still passionate about the game. The enormous presence and dignity of James Earl Jones is essential not just to the viability of the Mann character, but to the success of the film itself—it's Jones's speeches toward the end that define the movie's vision. The serene spirit of Lancaster is perfect for the poignant Moonlight Graham episode, and Madigan's warm, spontaneous and spunky nature makes Annie surprisingly memorable, considering all the larger-than-life characters around her.

As rich in history as it is, baseball lends itself to symbolism and myth like no other sport. Using baseball to somehow define ourselves and/or our country is an undeniable lure; many of America's best 20th century writers at one time or another wrote about baseball—not football, basketball or hockey. Also, it's no coincidence that in both *The Natural* (based on the Bernard Malamud novel) and *Field of Dreams,* the final, uplifting image is that of a father and son playing catch—the archetypal across-the-generations connection. (I've always believed that the special, timeless quality of baseball has a lot to do with the fact that—unlike any other team sport—it has no use for a clock.)

The Natural (the movie version) was an uncomplicated good-versus-evil tale of mythic proportions. In *Field of Dreams,* baseball—pure, beatific, transcendent—is a vehicle for self-knowledge and for righting old wrongs: Shoeless Joe gets to play baseball with big leaguers again, Ray gets a second chance with his father. Baseball can help make dreams come true, and *Field of Dreams* is a sublime celebration of the power of love and the romance of baseball. Not only could it be the ultimate baseball movie for the loving fan, but it might just make believers out of us all.

LOS ANGELES TIMES, 4/21/89, Calendar/p. 1, Michael Wilmington

"Field of Dreams" is a movie about crazy dreams and impossible reunions, and it presents baseball as a kind of national sacrament, the instrument of near-holy reconciliation between the generations. The film is set in an Iowa cornfield, where an obsessed young farmer has built a baseball diamond because he heard voices promising him, "If you build it, he will come." Who? When? Is the movie a Christ fable, a sports comedy, or both?

Director-writer Phil Alden Robinson certainly has his heart in the right place. He wants to make a film about loving your parents, chasing your wildest hopes, finding and accepting your past. He wants to heal all the wounds of the post-'60s, salve and soothe and bind them up. And he doesn't do any of this in a cheap or sensationalized way. "Field of Dreams" is about as heartfelt a movie as any major studio has given us recently.

But there's something missing, something tentative and uncertain. In order to pull off a magic trick, you often have to distract the audience with smooth patter, clever detail or indirection. And this movie tries to play it so pure and unabashed that we can see right up its sleeves.

In the film, adapted from the W.P. Kinsella novel "Shoeless Joe," Robinson tries to create a symbolic fable about the children of the '60s finding their way back to their more conservative parents via the common ground of baseball. The farmer, Ray Kinsella (Kevin Costner), came to Iowa via New York City and college years in Berkeley; an ex-campus radical who parted with his elderly dad on bad terms. Costner plays Ray with the stolid no-nonsense stance of a casual jock and eyes that always seem to be inviting you into a shared joke.

It's the right contrast, because everything that Ray does seems crazy. After the voice beckons him from the corn, he blows all his family's money on the diamond, setting himself up for a foreclosure, sitting there in the long, empty Iowa afternoons apparently staring at nothing, waiting for the ineffable. His wife Annie (Amy Madigan), with a saint's patience, stands behind him. Finally the mists and the cornstalks part, and a Christlike figure appears: Shoeless Joe Jackson (Ray Liotta), baseball's ultimate outsider-hero, and the central figure in John Sayles' "Eight Men Out" and, a few years ago, "The Natural," where he's the inspiration for Robert Redford's Roy Hobbes.

Like a prophet, speaking in the crepuscular Midwestern light, Shoeless Joe greets his deliverer, and the voice proceeds to send Ray off again after a missing writer: who, in the novel, was J.D. Salinger, the catcher in the rye following the outfielder into the corn. But Robinson abandons the Salinger reference and turns recluse-writer Terence Mann (James Earl Jones) into a bizarre Pulitzer-Prize winning novelist and black ex-activist who abandoned fiction for poetry about whales and devising computer software programs for children. Jones, amazingly, brings off this absurd role, cowing us with his majestic presence, his wonderfully baleful glare and wry delivery. Burt Lancaster, who can be equally majestic, brings off another peculiar role equally well, a mixture of Norman Rockwell, Jean Hersholt and "The Twilight Zone."

The movie invites us into what seems a cracked *idée fixe*, then suggests that the core of the obsession is perfectly true: a mystical gig. The Iowa locations are lit by cinematographer John Lindley ("True Believer," "The Stepfather") as a flat but radiant heartland, and at one point Ray makes a joking connection between "Iowa" and "heaven."

All of this would work better if Robinson built up the reality of the town more, made the citizens a more palpable presence, as Frank Capra did in Hollywood's greatest fable-fantasy, "It's a Wonderful Life." You begin to wonder why the Kinsellas get so few non-celestial visitors, why no one in the area asks Ray if they can use his baseball diamond for a game or two. The family seems weirdly isolated, and when they attend a PTA meeting and Annie wins over a book-banning audience by arguing that censorship smacks of Stalinism, the crowd caves in *en masse*. It's like a version of "Harvey" where we see James Stewart and the rabbit, but not the wondering or dyspeptic people around them.

But should baseball be presented as a sacrament? Some cold, stylized, supernatural rite where the greats of the past move in stately rhythms across a perfect, barren field with hardly any spectators? Where are the hot dogs, the sweat, the beer, the savage imprecations against the umpire's sight and sanity, the wild frenzy when the tying run reaches third? Robinson trying to use baseball as a metaphor for America's common ground ends up diminishing, in a way, what makes it a common ground: the fact that it's a game full of sunlit frenzy and excitement. He gets the legend of excellence but not the thrill of combat.

It's a tossup. "Field of Dreams," (MPAA rated PG), like any wild fantasy, will work if you want it to work, inspire belief if you believe it. The director and actors—especially Kevin Costner, James Earl Jones and Burt Lancaster—are obviously giving it their all. The movie tries to dispel cynicism or doubts, by ignoring the world around it, serving up its magic pure and raw. And, if you want it, it will come.

MONTHLY FILM BULLETIN, 12/89, p. 365, Kim Newman

Partially thanks to his unresolved relationship with his one-time baseball player father, Ray

Kinsella has drifted aimlessly through life. At thirty-six, he and his wife Annie and daughter Karin are living on a less than successful Iowa farm when Ray starts hearing a voice, and becomes convinced that if he ploughs under part of his cornfield and builds a baseball pitch then the ghost of "Shoeless" Joe Jackson will appear. Although the community—especially his real-estate broker brother-in-law Mark—think him mad, Annie supports him as he creates his pitch. Shoeless Joe, and the other disgraced players from the 1919 Chicago White Sox team, do appear and thank Ray for the chance to play again. The voice returns, and Ray is compelled to look up first vanished 60s radical author Terence Mann, and then small-town doctor Archie Graham. Ray finds Mann in Boston and convinces the disillusioned writer to join him in his search for Graham, who turns out to be dead. But Ray is briefly transported back to 1972 and meets Graham, who played one inning in a brief baseball career in 1922 and always regretted never coming to bat against a major-league pitcher. Driving back to Iowa, Ray and Mann pick up a teenage hitch-hiker who claims to be Archie Graham, but Ray finds Mark—who can't see the baseball-playing ghosts—about to foreclose the mortgage on the farm. Archie gets to play with the White Sox, who have recruited other ghosts from the baseball Hall of Fame and, his ambition achieved, is willing to sacrifice his happy afterlife to become again the aged Doc Graham when Karin is about to choke to death. Mark is suddenly able to see the players, and the Kinsellas believe that people will pay to watch the game, enabling them to keep their farm. The players vanish for the night into the cornfield, taking the reformed Mann with them, leaving behind only John Kinsella, Ray's father. Ray and John play catch, and finally come to terms with each other, while a convoy of cars converges on the field.

Field of Dreams is fortunate in arriving in Britain *after* the release of John Sayles' *Eight Men Out,* without which it would be difficult for a non-American audience to appreciate the status of Shoeless Joe and the other ghosts who appear magically out of the corn to play on Ray Kinsella's magical ball-park. Kevin Costner, who trails his association with *Bull Durham,* has also been prepared for this role by a screen identification with the national sport. Like *Eight Men Out* and *Bull Durham,* and even the comparatively lightweight *Major League, Field of Dreams* sees baseball as an almost sacred aspect of America's fantasy life and moral fibre. Linking the pleasures of the sport to his own vanished 60s radicalism, Terence Mann—a character, based on J.D. Salinger, whose novel *The Boat Rocker* is supposed to have first encouraged young Ray to rebel against his father's attempts to turn him into a baseball star—declares "the one constant through all the years has been baseball ... it reminds us of all that once was good, and could be again".

Although this is essentially a charming fantasy, *Field of Dreams* does contrast such strong, good-willed characters as Burt Lancaster's Dr. "Moonlight" Graham (confronted with his lifelong trauma, he wisely declares "Now if I had only been a doctor for five minutes, that would have been a tragedy") and the embittered but still passionate Mann with the Iowa Moral Majority representatives who want to burn Mann's books and the bankers who want to foreclose on the Kinsellas' struggling farm. Like *Twilight Zone* sports fanatic Rod Serling, who wrote several baseball fantasies ("The Mighty Casey"), Phil Alden Robinson is a sentimentalist but knows a good wish-fulfilment movie has to be laced with genuine darkness to have any power. Even in the ball-playing afterlife, there are arguments between players and umpires, and—in reference to a notoriously right-wing and unpleasant baseball great—Shoeless Joe comments, "Ty Cobb wanted to play, but none of us could stand the sonofabitch when we were alive, so we told him to stick it".

Tactfully underplayed, with some very discreet Industrial Light & Magic sparkle to the ghostly scenes, *Field of Dreams* has all the earmarks, like *Harvey, It's a Wonderful Life* and *The Wizard of Oz*—all of which it refers to—of a perennially popular fantasy. It is salted with good lines—confronting a book-burner who claims to have lived through the 60s, Annie snaps, "I think you had two 50s and moved right on into the 70s"—and delicate supporting performances (the dignified and ghostly Ray Liotta and Burt Lancaster make the most of their scenes). The sequences in which the Kinsellas, perfectly played by Costner and Amy Madigan, tackle the problems of life down on the farm in the 80s have a realistic, cranky edge that prevents the sugar from running away with the movie. It even overcomes its bizarre story structure—with the theoretically awkward time-travel interlude and the never-quite-justified plot detour to bring in Terence Mann seeming exactly in place—and emerges as a delightful one-off film, marking Robinson, whose earlier *The Woo Woo Kid* was slight but accomplished, as a talent to watch.

NEW YORK, 4/24/89, p. 96, David Denby

I am one of those people who go all soft and ardent in the spring. Over wildflowers and gurgling brooks? No, over baseball, the delicate, infinitely complex game of baseball, a yearly renewal of life, art, and humanity—of everything in the world that is good. But even baseball transcendentalists like me know that our worship of the game can turn maudlin. Every year, baseball writers gather beatitudes to their breasts in limp, damp clusters. The smell of freshly mowed grass, the crack of the bat, the acrid brown tobacco spittle, the scrawny hot dogs and peeling, splintered bleachers. . . .

I have become impatient with the lyrical and nostalgic tones of higher baseball journalism, even when it's well done. Instead, my soul cries out for cold statistics—for the hard-edged analysis and skepticism and digressive convolutions of writer Bill James and his rivals and followers. Enough static pastoral poetry. Give us baseball as a series of dynamic but interlocking, definable acts.

In the movies, the sentimentalization of baseball comes and goes. Years ago, there was *Bang the Drum Slowly,* with its dumb young catcher (Robert De Niro) who dies of a mysterious disease, thereby evoking the compassion of a sensitive, intellectual pitcher (Michael Moriarty). There was the mythico-whimsical fable *The Natural,* about a valiant, haloed outfielder. Last year's *Bull Durham,* on the other hand, was filled with the authentic melancholy twilight of dog days in the bus leagues. But now, in *Field of Dreams,* the etherealizing of baseball returns—so aggressively, in fact, that baseball gets etherealized out of existence. *Field of Dreams* is about a man who, well, pursues his dream, He uses baseball to sew up all the wounds in his life and everyone else's too.

"My name's Ray Kinsella," says Kevin Costner in the forthright and brisk narration that begins the movie. Ray tells us that his dead father was a minor-league player whose heart was broken by Shoeless Joe Jackson and the Black Sox and that he himself loves baseball but has unaccountably bought a farm in Iowa. The narration ends, and there he is, working his cornfields in the very heart of America, surrounded by blue skies. Suddenly he hears a solemn voice saying to him very distinctly, *"If you build it, he will come."*

Gee.

Ray decides, after mulling the matter over, that the voice is telling him to build a baseball field on his farm so the shade of Shoeless Joe can come back to play on it. Yup, that's what he thinks. Ray is obsessed with Jackson, who played hard in the 1919 World Series despite taking the gangsters' money yet was banned from baseball along with the truly crooked players. Ray is meant to be a normal sort of guy (and boy, does Costner play him straight down the middle—not even Fred MacMurray or Van Johnson or Tom Hanks could be so likably and plausibly a normal sort of guy). He has a lovely little daughter and a spunky, right-as-rain wife (Amy Madigan), both of whom Believe in His Dream. He plows his cornfields and puts up bleachers and a diamond.

And, it comes to pass. Shoeless Joe (Ray Liotta) shows up one night, and soon he and the other Black Sox are regularly playing pepper games on Ray's field. Ray, meanwhile, embarks on another quest. For the Voice has spoken again: *"Ease his pain,"* it says. Whose pain? Well, Ray decides that the voice is talking about a famous novelist of the sixties (James Earl Jones) who hasn't published in years and who once mentioned in an interview that he was all broken up about never having played next to Jackie Robinson on the old Brooklyn Dodgers. So Ray drives to Boston, looks up the crusty old genius, and takes him to a Red Sox game. Whereupon the Big Guy delivers yet another message—this time on the Fenway scoreboard.

The two men then set out for Minnesota in search of the grizzled Burt Lancaster, another would-be ballplayer. Had enough? Suffice it to say that in the end, they all return to Ray's farm in Iowa and fulfill their dreams by playing in If-You-Build-It-He-Will-Come Stadium. The heart of the movie, it turns out, is Ray's damaged relationship with his father. One afternoon Ray refused to play catch with the old man, and he has felt awful about it ever since. Just awful.

The writer-director Phil Alden Robinson (*In the Mood*), adapting a novel by W.P. Kinsella (recognize the name?), has obviously put his heart and soul (though perhaps not his brains) in this strange movie, this plastic mold lined with fleece. *Field of Dreams* is calm and spacious; John Lindley's limpid cinematography flatters the Iowa fields and skies. (We know we're in heaven well before Kevin Costner says as much.) And here and there the narrative gives off the pleasantly hokey warmth of a tall tale recited around the campfire at night. *Field of Dreams* is not without humor: There's a wonderful moment when Shoeless Joe makes his first ghostly appearance at the field and he and Ray shyly shake hands; and Amy Madigan and James Earl Jones are both very funny. But just when I was thinking the whole thing wasn't so silly after all, the atmosphere changed, and as involuntary shivers traveled up and down my spine, Robinson sprang an epiphany on me.

Suddenly the movie becomes a homelier version of *The Robe* or perhaps an episode of *The Twilight Zone* toned up by Kahlil Gibran. As the story waits for God to throw another pitch, characters stand around soliloquizing about the smell of the grass, the roar of the crowd. ...

They also keep saying things like "This is crazy," thereby telling us we are right to find the movie gaga. But that's a trick—flattery intended to cozen us out of our cynicism. Robinson wants us to believe—but in what? In baseball as America, baseball as the past, baseball implacably forging the links of our personal history. If we deny baseball, we deny our fathers. Indeed, we kill our fathers, just as Ray has become convinced he killed his father by not throwing the ball to him.

Whew! A baseball transcendentalist is humbled by so profound a message. What more can I say? Only that the movie made me feel guilty, once again, about the time I refused to play Ping-Ping with my mother. There we were, long ago in that summer of 1950, at Atlantic Beach. The ocean breezes blew softly across the patio, and my mother stood holding her paddle, as beautiful as Paulette Goddard. She looked at me imploringly, but I went back into the house, slamming the screen door behind me, and drank a whole pitcher of Kool-Aid. For years, this memory has remained lodged in my soul like a knife. The other night, a Voice spoke to me out of the VCR. But I'm lucky, I don't have to chop down my bookcases and put up a table and net in my dining room. I can simply call her up and say, "Sorry, Ma!" and she'll come over.

NEW YORK POST, 4/21/89, p. 29, Jami Bernard

One day Ray Kinsella is working in the cornfield of his Iowa farm when he hears The Voice. "If you build it, he will come," says The Voice in an authoritative whisper. A further revelation explains things: If Ray carves a baseball diamond from his cornfield, Shoeless Joe Jackson will come back from the dead to play there.

If you can buy this admittedly crazy opening gambit—Kevin Costner as the puzzled but dogged farmer keeps asking wife Amy Madigan if he's going insane—then "Field of Dreams" is a rewarding fantasy. It's as saccharine as they come, but don't let that stop you from choking up (not on the bat, silly).

Anyway, who has not wished for all one's dead heroes to rise from the grave and play with you in the back yard?

Surprisingly, in view of the recent hemorrhage of baseball movies, "Field of Dreams" is not so much about the boys of summer as it is about following your dreams, and beyond that, about faith and redemption, and tying up loose ends, about recognizing what's important in life.

"Is this heaven?" people keep asking Ray. "This is Iowa," he says, *quod erat demonstrandum*. Happiness is in your own back yard or cornfield or, as the movie says, "Heaven is the place where dreams come true." You just have to plow a few fields first.

So Ray bulldozes the cornfield and creates an eerie stadium bounded by corn as high as a dead man's eye. Soon the wraiths come to play ball, Shoeless Joe first, in the fit and energetic and vaguely challenging form of Ray Liotta, then all the other disbarred members of the shamed Black Sox (see "Eight Men Out" on video to bone up on your history).

Ray and wife, nostalgic products of the '60s, plus their young daughter, sit out on the risers all day watching the famed ballplayers get right back into the swing of things, cursing each other and spitting and doing all those things baseball-lovers go all misty over during the off-season. The Kinsella family is entranced; no wonder their neglected farm is about to go belly-up.

But The Voice isn't done with Ray. It starts piling on the requests: "Ease his pain," "Go the distance," etc. Ray's journeys are so far-fetched you simply have to suspend disbelief and travel cheerfully along with him. Soon he's roped in a Very Famous Recluse Novelist (James Earl Jones) and an Almost-Was Ballplayer (Burt Lancaster). They all wind up casting their lot on the playing field of Iowa and therein finding their heart's desire.

In the novel from which this was adapted, Jones' character was J.D. Salinger, which makes more sense, but Salinger probably would have blown a gasket if he'd been appropriated for Hollywood. Now the novelist is "Terence Mann," voice of the '60s, and Jones does a credible job as the curmudgeonly author whose writer's block just may be knocked out of the stadium by the heavy hitters of the Iowa League. Burt Lancaster is a good choice for the old doctor who missed out on his big chance to play in the majors. His face and voice alone evoke the kind of longing for olden days (and better movies?) that fills everyone's heart in this film.

Amy Madigan as the wife does her hyper best to fill up a role that is mostly relegated to the cheering section; next to the super-restrained Costner, her charisma is like having a bullhorn in your ear.

Writer-director Phil Alden Robinson includes just enough humor to keep "Field of Dreams" from choking on its sentimentality. "Why can't The Voice send Shirley MacLaine, what is she, too busy?" grouses Ray at one point.

Without the usual cut & splice Game Glorious sequences most baseball movies resort to, "Field of Dreams" manages to evoke passion for the game and at the same time extend the metaphor to include the folks in the bleacher seats. Ultimately, this is about a man coming to terms with his dead father.

As Terence Mann once wrote, when he was still writing, every now and then "cosmic tumblers click into place, the universe opens," and all possibilities are laid bare.

And every now and then a movie comes along that, though bizarre, can be very affecting.

NEWSDAY, 4/21/89, Part III/p. 3, Mike McGrady

"Field of Dreams" is another movie about our national pastime. No, I'm not referring to baseball. I'm thinking of our love of fantasy, our belief in magic, our willingness to believe the unbelievable. In fact, I wonder whether anyone is even going to blink twice when this film's Iowa farmer (Kevin Costner), strolling through his shoulder-high corn, hears a mystical wind-borne voice saying, "If you build it, he will come."

His no-nonsense wife (Amy Madigan) does have a moment, but only a moment, of skepticism before asking, "Hey, what if the voice calls while you're gone?"

"Take a message," he replies.

Needless to say, the voice does call again. And again. Through a peculiarly intricate deductive reasoning process, Costner translates the message: If he builds a baseball diamond on his corn field, the late Shoeless Joe Jackson will come to play baseball. (Psychologically, this reflects a never-resolved dispute with his father over the merits of the great Chicago player involved in fixing the 1919 World Series.)

Costner briefly wonders how his father might have responded to the mysterious voice: "He must've had dreams but he never did anything about them . . . I want to build that field. Do you think I'm crazy?"

"Yes," his wife says, "but I also think that if you really feel you should do it, you should do it."

So he does. He plows down his corn and creates a baseball field, perfect right down to chalk lines and night lights. All this expense hastens the arrival of the foreclosure people, but before long, Shoeless Joe also appears, along with the rest of the disgraced White Sox, followed by Mel Ott and other long-dead greats. Unfortunately, they can only be seen by the pure of heart, which includes Costner, his wife, his child, a reclusive writer (James Earl Jones), a doctor (Burt Lancaster) who once played one inning of major leage baseball and almost no one else.

Incidentally, the mystical voice keeps reappearing, emitting pithy aphorisms—"Ease his pain" and "Go the distance"—that only Costner can translate.

Writer-director Phil Alden Robinson, basing his work on W.P. Kinsella's 1982 novel, "Shoeless Joe," has given the film every cinematic benefit. Technically, the movie is superb. A terrific cast headed by a well-grounded actor like Costner proves to be an antidote to much of the magic. And the follow-your-dream message has an undeniable emotional appeal.

No game captures the American imagination quite the way baseball does, and the daily sports pages show just how easily legend combines with the game. That it can become the stuff of mythology was seen in a movie like "The Natural." Less successful flicks (does anyone remember 1952's "Angels in the Outfield"?) have combined baseball and fantasy with less impressive results.

"Field of Dreams" goes beyond fantasy into the realm of pure magic. I very much suspect your tolerance of the movie, which is made with considerable love and care, will depend in no small part upon your tolerance of magic. Mine, as it turns out, is minimal. In fact, I just heard a strange disembodied voice saying "Two-and-a-half stars is too many," but, unlike Costner, I never listen to such voices.

NEWSWEEK, 4/24/89, p. 72, David Ansen

Ray Kinsella (Kevin Costner), a veteran of Berkeley in the '60s and now a farmer in Iowa with a wife and daughter, is standing in his cornfield on a lovely late afternoon when he first hears The Voice. "If you build it, he will come," commands this disembodied rumble, which may or may not be the voice of God. A vision soon reveals what Ray must build: a baseball field in the midst of his cornfield. And "he" turns out to be the legendary Shoeless Joe Jackson, the late great left fielder who was suspended from baseball for his role in throwing the 1919 World Series. Now Ray is a man who, by his own description, has never done a crazy thing in his life, but he knows this Voice must be heeded. Down go the cornstalks, back from the dead comes Shoeless Joe (Ray Liotta) and off on a magical and moving ride goes *Field of Dreams*.

Writer-director Phil Alden Robinson clearly knows the risks involved in adapting W.P. Kinsella's lyrical, wonderfully loopy 1982 novel "Shoeless Joe" to the screen. To locate the singular quality of Kinsella's flight of fancy you might place it on a wide-eyed continuum that includes Norman Rockwell, "The Twilight Zone," Ray Bradbury, Garrison Keillor and Richard Brautigan: it's a distinctly American reverie that, in pursuit of its mythical goals, is unafraid to court sentimentality at every turn. This is the sort of movie you either swallow whole or not at all. But for viewers who leave their hearts open to Kinsella's grave, whimsical conceit, the rewards are plentiful.

"Field of Dreams" has more on its mind than the subject of baseball as American religion. As the Voice leads Ray on an odyssey from Iowa to Boston to Minnesota, and literally back into the past, the tale gathers layers of meaning. Robinson's fable is about coming to terms with one's legacy—as an American, as a child of the '60s, as a son. For Ray and his feisty wife, Annie (Amy Madigan), this means reacquainting themselves with their old capacity to dream. Ultimately, Ray's quest is about coming to terms with his dead father, whom he never forgave for growing old and giving up.

In Boston, following a second command from the Voice, Ray recruits another participant in his crazy project: a famous rabble-rousing novelist of the '60s, Terence Mann (James Earl Jones), who has stopped publishing and withdrawn from the world. (In the novel, the character was J. D. Salinger.) Jones gives a robustly humorous performance as a belligerent recluse dragged kicking and screaming back into belief. He even *almost* pulls off the script's sappiest moment, an overripe ode to the glory of the game.

Robinson's fine cast includes Burt Lancaster as a former ballplayer and small-town doctor and Timothy Busfield as Ray's skeptical brother-in-law, who's trying to buy his failing farm out from under him. But it is Costner's regular-guy reality that anchors the movie and keeps the whimsy under control. His understated relish at these supernatural events ("This is so cool!") and the subtle but deeply felt ways in which he conveys his love for his family provide the movie's emotional ballast. "Field of Dreams," with its delicate mix of counterculture wit and traditional heartland values, is a movie that could have been made only in the U.S.A. It is at once radical and deeply conservative, a lovely pipe dream about a country that exists only in our imaginations. "Is this heaven?" asks a character. "It's Iowa," comes the answer, and no contradiction is intended.

TIME, 4/24/89, p. 78, Richard Corliss

[*Field of Dreams* was reviewed jointly with *Major League;* see Corliss' review of that film.]

VILLAGE VOICE, 4/25/89, p. 59. J. Hoberman

Once surefire movie death, jazz and baseball are ripe subjects for national introspection. *Let's Get Lost* [see Hoberman's review] is like a smoky, diffident dream of the '50s; in the more strenuously mythological *Field of Dreams*, American history—as mediated by the movies of the Reagan era—flashes on the screen as though before a drowning man's eyes.

Recombining last season's *Bull Durham* and *Eight Men Out, Field of Dreams* puts a new spin on the religion of baseball: the spirit of "Black Sox" slugger Shoeless Joe Jackson is conjured up as a martyr of lost national innocence while the summer game itself is a ritual affirmation of an eternal America. "It reminds us all of what was good and could be again," muses Ray Kinsella (Kevin Costner), a New York-born, Berkeley educated Iowa farmer who has hewn a baseball diamond out of his cornfield because a disembodied voice told him to.

W.P. Kinsella's 1982 novel, the source for this harmless fantasy of masculine redemption, is a romantic melange of time travel, sports lore, and laconic magic realism, pitched somewhere between Richard Brautigan's hippie haikus and Ray Bradbury's sardonic nostalgia. As adapted and directed by Phil Alden Robinson, *Field of Dreams* serves up the novel as liberal Spielbergism freshened with *thirtysomething* self-pity. Robinson coarsens the original, sixties the characters, and, no doubt of necessity, removes the novel's best element—the use of J.D. Salinger as Ray's comic foil. ("Salinger leans towards me. 'And I thought I had a good imagination,' he says. 'I could never dream up a plot as bizarre as this.' ") Instead, the reclusive novelist who Ray ropes into his world is Terence Mann (James Earl Jones), a/k/a "the Voice of the '60s."

Although the Voice of the Cornfields, a ballpark announcer in the novel, is here a portentous whisper (played, according to the credits, by an actor called "Himself") and Shoeless Joe (Ray Liotta) speaks in lousy blank verse, the most egregious thing about *Field of Dreams* is its demographic pandering. The Kinsella farmhouse boasts a reproduction of a Warhol Marilyn, the Kinsella van sports a weathered peace symbol, the Kinsella stereo is perpetually playing the Lovin' Spoonful's "Daydream." By the time Mrs. Kinsella (Amy Madigan) outwits a brainless bookbanner at the local PTA, yor're braced for her triumphant whoop: "It's just like the '60s again!"

The usually nuanced Madigan goes hyperkinetic trying to work with this material—she's like a kid on a sugar high. (Costner meanwhile sidles through the proceedings pretending he doesn't quite grasp how sappy they are.) After a while, you expect to welcome Puff the Magic Dragon. Small wonder that Mann reaches for the Flit when Ray appears on his doorstep. "Back to the '60s! This is no place for you here in the future." So far as contemporary mass culture goes, the most interesting thing about those so-called '60s may be Hollywood's continuing inability to successfully repackage them.

What's wild in a movie so nostalgic is the total celebration of '80s values—the family is heaven, make-believe works, it's a new morning in America. *Field of Dreams* might have been scripted by the old ex-baseball announcer himself. (Instead, Burt Lancaster is on hand, reprising the codger role he's been trotting out for the past 15 years.) If *field of Dreams* doesn't put a softball-sized lump in your throat, it's not exactly unproductive either. Watch where you put your feet, Shoeless Joe. There's enough horseshit here to fertilize Ray's farm, the rest of the county, and Iowa, too.

Also reviewed in:
NATION, 5/15/89, p. 678, Stuart Klawans
NEW REPUBLIC, 5/8/89, p. 26, Stanley Kauffmann
NEW YORK TIMES, 4/21/89, p. C8, Caryn James
NEW YORKER, 5/1/89, p. 76, Pauline Kael
VARIETY, 4/19-25/89, p. 24
WASHINGTON POST, 4/21/89, p. C1, Rita Kempley
WASHINGTON POST, 4/21/89, Weekend/p. 33, Desson Howe

FIGHT FOR US

A Pathe Europa release. *Producer:* Salvatore Picciotto. *Director:* Lino Brocka. *Screenplay (Tagalog with English subtitles):* Jose F. Lacabra. *Director of Photography:* Rody Lacap. *Editor:* George Jarlego, Sabine Mamoli, and Bob Wade. *Running time:* 96 minutes. MPAA Rating: R.

CAST: Phillip Salvador (Jimmy Cordero); Dina Bonnevie (Trixie); Bembol Roco (Commander Kontra); Ginnie Sobrino (Sister Marie); Abbo De La Cruz (Django).

NEW YORK POST, 10/13/89, p. 28, Jami Bernard

Philippine director Lino Brocka's evidently risky undertaking, "Fight For Us," is perhaps an important film for the sake of pointing up human-rights violations in his country, but unfortunately it is not a good film. And it can't even claim the halo of having its heart in the right place.

Against the thinly fictionalized backdrop of a revolution that has replaced a dictator with a Corazon Aquino-like democracy, former priest Jimmy Cordero (Phillip Salvador) fights the pull of the resistance movement as he watches innocent friends and loved ones mercilessly beaten, raped, killed and imprisoned by a fanatical group of vigilantes headed by the foaming at the mouth Commander Kontra (Bembol Roco).

Kontra's lawless band—there is a portrait in their hideout of Sylvester Stallone as "Rambo"— enjoys the tacit support of the military as it goes about undermining the country's already fragile stability by shooting villagers in the back and hacking off their ears.

The final straw for Jimmy is when a former girlfriend, who has a 6-year-old son by him, is carted off on trumped-up charges of communism.

While human-rights violations are rampant in many countries and the more the public is aware of it the better, this movie doesn't do itself any favors by putting such black hats on its villains. Kontra is stupid evil incarnate. Who knows what his motivations are? Even he certainly doesn't think any of the people he kills are commies. He just likes to be cruel. And the military is a collection of bitter, dumb thugs.

The good guys, of course, are noble, peace-loving folk. There is no attempt to define the issues or make a connection between the new regime and the new (old?) lawlessness.

Further, the movie's women—Jimmy's pregnant wife and his ex-girlfriend—are given such suffering roles that it's hard in a way to side with the supposed good guys. Whoever wins, women will still be serving up the dinner and bearing the children and having to tolerate their men's lost loves in their houses. Predicating Jimmy's moral decision on the graphic gang rape of his ex-girlfriend—that scene has since been cut for an R rating—is a disgusting and classic use of degrading females to motivate men to action.

Ultimately, "Fight For Us" is an exercise in cheap Rambotics, using its noble human-rights theme as a shield. I doubt if that is what the director intended, because you don't risk a government's enmity simply for cheap thrills—and yet that is what he has achieved. It cheapens the movie and deadens the public's awareness of the real issues.

NEWSDAY, 10/13/89, Part III/p. 4, Terry Kelleher

There are two sides to Philippine director Lino Brocka. He's a prolific maker of lightweight, profitable films in the soap-opera mold. But he also turns out serious, controversial pictures, the kind that earned him the hostility of the repressive Ferdinand Marcos regime.

With "Fight for Us," Brocka wanted to dramatize the argument that anticommunist "vigilantes" and some segments of the military are still trampling on human rights in his country, more than 3½ years into the "people power" presidency of Corazon Aquino. To avoid government scrutiny of the production, Brocka shot "Fight for Us" in only three weeks, moving quickly from location to location. Meanwhile, he was also filming a popular musical, which served as a cover of sorts.

The central character is Jimmy Cordero (Phillip Salvador), an ex-priest and former political prisoner under Marcos who has become a human-rights advocate in the Aquino era. A polite critic of the government whose favorite battleground is the TV talk show, Jimmy is moved to take a more aggressive stance after investigating the atrocities of Ora Pro Nobis, a cult-like vigilante group led by a raving monster (Bembol Roco).

Jimmy's increasingly dangerous activities cause him personal problems that Brocka handles in a style more suitable for one of his escapist films. The arguments between Jimmy and his pregnant wife (Dina Bonnevie) are at times unintentionally amusing. (He: "I'm going on a fact-finding mission." She: "What about our Lamaze exercises?") And it just so happens that one of the villagers threatened by Ora Pro Nobis is Jimmy's old girlfriend (Gina Alajar), mother of the 6-year-old son he never knew he had.

But gradually the soapy interludes are overwhelmed by the scenes of violence and terror, which manage to be gripping even when the director yields to excess (trims were necessary to obtain an "R" rating). The most disturbing moment comes when the Manila police invade a school sheltering refugees driven from the countryside by the vigilantes. Wearing a basket over his head to shield his identity, an informer walks through the crowd pointing out suspected communist rebels, who are immediately torn away from their families and taken into a custody that will be anything but protective. Here Brocka creates an atmosphere of almost palpable dread.

Subtlety is absent from "Fight for Us." Brocka pounds his point home, perhaps because there was no time to save his strength.

VILLAGE VOICE, 10/17/89, p. 99, Coco Fusco

The leftist action pic has, in the '80s, become the genre that can propel Third World directors into international recognition. It confirms what many assume about those other worlds—that their reality is wilder than our fiction. These filmmakers have learned since the '70s that the First World audiences that yawn and change the channel at the sight of a TV news report will eagerly swallow the same story packaged as entertainment.

The recent death of Ferdinand Marcos will undoubtedly compel the media to turn its attention to the current political chaos in the Philippines, a subject that has been dealt with for well over a decade by that country's leading cineaste, Lino Brocka. Brocka has divided his time between bread-and-butter melodramas and more overtly ideological, critically acclaimed (and sometimes nationally banned) features. *Fight for Us*, his latest exposé on right-wing vigilante violence, combines soap opera romance with social consciousness. In his story of an ex-radical priest turned human rights activist who has to choose between revolution and reform, Brocka unmasks Third World "democratization" as rhetorical manipulation. Sadly like too many do-good directors, he sacrifices most of his cinematic flourishes, turning in a lopsided movie with its heart in the right place.

Filipino matinee idol Phillip Salvador plays Jimmy Cordero, a former clergyman released from prison just as Marcos is forced into retirement. Marrying a nice bourgeois human rights activist named Trixie, Jimmy believes at first that the new Aquino government will put an end to state-sponsored or-condoned aggression against progressives and the poor. But Brocka proves him wrong from the start by introducing us to Ora Pro Nobis, a right-wing death squad that looks like a pack of Hell's Angels with too many rifles. Led by the crazed neofascist commander Kontra, they roam around rural areas in search of anyone they can accuse of being a rebel—and then kill. Jimmy is stirred by testimony of an Ora Pro Nobis attack given by a peasant who was once his lover and embarks on a fact-fiding mission. Instead of receiving support from the government for its efforts, his human rights team is stonewalled by military officials who consider the vigilantes to be grassroots representatives of the peoples' will. The struggle quickly escalates as attacks begin on urban-based activists, including Jimmy himself.

More interesting than Jimmy's personal dilemma over whether or not to join the underground rebel forces is Brocka's striking ability to get under the skin of this fledgling neocolonial "democracy." He illustrates how its radical cultural heterogeneity is a psychic effect of American domination. The higher up on the social scale, the more the characters inhabit a hybrid world with a spoken language that incorporates Chinese, Spanish, and English terms. Commander Kontra behaves like a psychotic whose maniacal worldview is determined by *Soldier of Fortune* and *Rambo*. Nonetheless, though Brocka brings the dangers of American militarism Filipino-style to life, he trips up by practically leaving the left out of the picture. His bad guys are ready to label anyone a communist, but Brocka doesn't seem to want to tell us what the real ones are like, or what they are actually up to.

Also reviewed in:
NEW YORK TIMES, 10/13/89, p. C13, Vincent Canby
VARIETY, 6/14-20/89, p. 23

FISTFIGHTER

A Taurus Entertainment release. *Producer:* Carlos Vasallo. *Director:* Frank Zuniga. *Screenplay:* Max Bloom. *Based on a story by:* Carlos Vassalo. *Directior of Photography:* Hans Burman. *Editor:* Drake Silliman. *Music:* Emilio Kauderer. *Boxing Choregrapher:* Jimmy Nickerson. *Running time:* 96 minutes. *MPAA Rating:* R.

CAST: George Rivero (C.J. Thunderbird), Mike Connors (Billy Vance); Edward Albert (Harry "Punchy" Moses); Brenda Bakke (Ellen).

LOS ANGELES TIMES, 5/12/89, Calendar/p. 8, Chris Willman

As played by Jorge Rivero, the quiet but quick-fisted title character of the handsome Mexican-American production "Fist Fighter" has no character, other than an essential decency. Devoid of apparent past or future, hero C.J. Thunderbird has nothing to interrupt a dull existence of menial jobs other than occasionally going to great lengths to avenge the deaths of his friends.

He has a lot of friends who die, so it's not as though he isn't busy. There's the pal whose head was caved in at the hands of a brutal boxer before the film begins, sending Thunderbird down to South America in search of the killer for a score-settling slugfest. In the course of this justice, the hero makes more buddies who will kiss their mortal coils goodbye.

Thunderbird does put aside fisticuffs long enough to romance a comely blonde (Brenda Bakke), the south-of-the-border equivalent of a gun moll to the chief gambling, fight-fixing villain (Mike Connors, of "Mannix"). Inexplicably, though, our man leaves this fine woman behind at the climax to walk off alone into the sunset and, presumably, into another lonely construction job till the next acquaintance gets axed.

It's too bad Thunderbird isn't fleshed out at all because Rivero—largely unknown here, but a star in Latin American countries—is a likable action hero, one too personable to be the mysterious high plains drifter Max Bloom's lazy script seems designed for. Rivero (sometimes known as *George* Rivero in more Anglicized projects, and even some of this film's ads) projects a rarely seen burly wholesomeness, like a matinee idol from a gentler, less cynical era.

He also really knows how to fight, unless the editors have done a spectacular job of fooling us. The rousing scenes of bloody, gloveless boxing have been choreographed by Jimmy Nickerson ("Raging Bull," "Rocky"). And for those with a jones to see men pummeled unconscious, but without a month's pay saved up for the next closed-circuit Tyson match, this may be a reasonable—and certainly lengthier—alternative.

Notable among the supporting cast are Edward Albert, as a downtrodden ex-fighter, and personification-of-evil Connors, who gets to end almost every sentence with "my friend" (as in "Don't threaten me, my friend") and is so over-the-top dastardly he lacks only a waxy mustache to twirl.

"Fistfighter" (rated R) may be weak on character but looks fine and moves efficiently under the direction of Frank Zuniga, who made a number of Disney's wildlife adventure shorts (a la "The Owl That Didn't Give a Hoot"). Perhaps the inclusion of a sidekick dog for the hero is an homage to that work; perhaps the violent death of said canine is Zuniga's wry way of kissing the genre goodbye?

NEW YORK POST, 5/12/89, p. 30, Jami Bernard

Every now and then a movie comes along that is SO BAD you almost feel a certain affection for it. "Fistfighter" is not just bad in that mediocre way of teen schlock or body-switch movies. "Fistfighter" is so unbelievably atrocious that a tear comes to the eye—as a loser, this one's a winner.

Our hero, C.J. Thunderbird—a George Hamiltonish piece of granite with salt and pepper hair and a weathered face—is looking for bad guy Rhino Reinhart in order to avenge the death of a friend.

But enough with the plot! It only gets in the way of inappropriate dialogue, too-dark shots, cardboard characters and unconvincing fight scenes.

Perhaps there are no weapons in this action adventure because of a low budget; in any case, fists are the weapons of choice, surely a throwback to simpler times. C.J. is not going to fire a rocket launcher at Rhino, he's going to PUNCH HIM IN THE NOSE!

C.J. is accompanied by an overly cute dog. Director Frank Zuniga did not know what to do between the numerous fistfights, so he spends a lot of time on "cute" reaction shots from the dog. C.J. also gets a friend so he has someone to whom he can direct what little dialogue there is. This friend, Punchy (Edward Albert), is a former fistfighter (this is a Mexican town where fistfighting and betting on fistfighting are the town's main occupations) who has a voice like the kind you find in one of those badly dubbed kung-fu flicks.

We first meet Rhino Reinhart, a South of the Border Swede, as he is being challenged by another fistfighter who wants to PUNCH HIM IN THE NOSE. To show he means business, this challenger stubs out a cigar on his own forehead. Methinks there's been a *leetle* too much inbreeding in this town.

Now, I may not know much about boxing, but aren't you supposed to keep those fists up to protect your face? And aren't you supposed to hop around a lot so you're not a sitting duck? Rhino, a trained killer, keeps his fists somewhere down around his chest like he's doing a dog-paddle, and stands there like a slug.

Enter Chuck "Mannix" Connors, a wealthy bastard in a white dinner jacket who disrupts the fight just when our hero was really getting ready to PUNCH RHINO IN THE NOSE. Connors' character sends C.J. and Punchy off to jail, where suddenly it's "Fistfighter Meets the Wolfman." Evidently prison entertainment consists of watching a half-man-half-beast tear inmates limb from limb while bellowing ferociously.

By this time we know that we have progressed beyond the realm of a mere B movie. This is truly Grade Z, the stuff cult films are made of. "I can make your life very unpleasant here," says a prison official. Yeah! Bring on the werewolf again!

And there is more ludicrousness to come. As C.J. cradles the head of an ailing man, the stiff's dying words are: "Rhino telegraphs every punch with his chest! Aargh!"

"Fistfighter" was made in utter earnestness, which in this case is in its favor. George Rivero plays C.J. from the Billy Jack school of acting; it's one of those movies where you'd like to round up all those responsible and PUNCH THEM IN THE NOSE.

Also reviewed in:
NEW YORK TIMES, 5/12/89, p. C17, Stephen Holden
VARIETY, 5/17–23/89, p. 30

FLETCH LIVES

A Universal Pictures release. *Executive Producer:* Bruce Bodner and Bob Larson. *Producer:* Alan Greisman and Peter Douglas. *Director:* Michael Ritchie. *Screenplay:* Leon Capetanos. *Based on characters created by:* Gregory McDonald. *Director of Photography:* John McPherson. *Editor:* Richard A. Harris. *Music:* Harold Faltermeyer, *Music Editor:* Bob Badami. *Sound:* James Alexander, Les Lazarowitz, and (music) Brian Reeves. *Sound Editor:* Ronald A. Jacobs. *Art Director:* Cameron Birnie, Jimmie Bly, W. Steven Graham, and Donald Woodruff. *Set Decorator:* Gary Fettis and Susan Bode. *Set Dresser:* Robert Good,, Edward Shavers,. and Brian P. Brophy. *Special Effects:* Clifford P. Wenger. *Costumes:* Anna Hill Johnstone. *Make-up:* Tom Miller and Michael Mills. *Special Make-up:* Ken Chase. *Stunt Coordinator:* Chuck Waters. *Running time:* 95 minutes. *MPAA Rating:* PG.

CAST: Chevy Chase (Fletch); Hal Holbrook (Ham Johnson); Julianne Phillips (Becky Culpepper); R. Lee Ermey (Jimmy Lee Farnsworth); Richard Libertini (Frank); Randall "Tex" Cobb (Ben Dover); Cleavon Little (Calculus); George Wyner (Gillet); Patricia Kalember (Amanda Ray Ross); Geoffrey Lewis (KKK Leader); Richard Belzer (Phil); Phil Hartman (Bly Manager); Titos Vandis (Uncle Kakakis); Don Hood (Tom Barbour); Dennis Burkley (Joe Jack); Noelle Beck (Betty Dilworth); William Traylor (Mr. Underhill); Barney D. Arceneaux (Party Guest); Roy Babich (Klansman); Mary Battilana (Bly Assistant); Don Brockett (Sheriff); Walter Charles (Tony); Robert M. Dawson (Tour Guide); Darren Dublin (Ancient Copy Boy); R. Bruce Elliott (Info Technician); Patrick Farrelly (O'Reilly); Grace Gaynor (Mrs. Underhill); Richmond Harrison (T'Boo Ted); Catherine Hearne (Lyda Perl); Charlie Holliday (Security Guard); Christian Kauffman (Bruce); Matthew Kimbrough (Bly Guard); Johnny Kline (Usher); Clarence Landry (Damon Feather); Marcella Lowery (Selma); Jordan Lund (Deputy Sheriff); Thom McCleister (Klansman #2); Patricia G. McConnell (Deputy's Wife); Dick McGarvin (Announcer); Keith R. Mills (Church Elder); Michael P. Moran (Morgue Attendant); Louis M. Rapaport (Walter Bob Buggem); Constance Shulman (Cindy Mae); Robert Silver (Kakakis' Brother); Ebbe Roe Smith (Jim Bob); R. David Smith (Gordon Joe); John Wylie (Accountant).

FILMS IN REVIEW, 6-7/89, p. 367, Ken Hanke

Chevy Chase is one of the most likable comic leads at work in film today—he just generally happens to end up in thoroughly unlikable movies. On those rare occasions where this isn't the case, there's always the danger of overpraising the results. Fortunately, Michael Ritchie's *Fletch Lives* manages to be both likable and surprisingly worthwhile. Granted, its premise—city-oriented hero inherits ramshackle mansion in out-of-the-way small town (southern or otherwise) where he is greeted with suspicion and ill will by the locals (save a young lady or two) and one or two mysterious types who want his land for some nefarious purpose—is a shockingly regressive one to encounter in a film from the tail end of the 1980s. Moreover, the mystery element in *Fletch Lives* is woefully lacking (name stars with nothing to do and precious little screen time to do it in are *invariably* guilty). And, apart from a beautifully realized, singularly bizarre, and weirdly all white *Song Of The South*-styled fantasy production number, there are few surprises along the way. what *is* worthwhile about *Fletch Lives* is the rich vein of pointed satire with which the film is blessed.

Though one would hardly guess it from recent films like the execrable Eddie Murphy "comedy," *The Golden Child*, director Ritchie is no stranger to satire. Yet here, thanks to Leon Capetanos' screenplay and Chase's performance, he has crafted a film that is considerably less heavy handed than such earlier, more highly regarded, works as *The Candidate* and *Smile*. His touch throughout is light—even non-aggressive—as befits a film where the serious overtones cannot be allowed to take precedence over the purely comedic. The undeniably exaggerated picture of the "New South"—where Ku Klux Klansmen are so inept they can't get their cross to burn, where culture and economy revolves around a TV ministry (complete with an evangelical monkey—"God's simian, the ring-tailed revivalist") and its attendant theme park (Bibleland), and where the forces of law and order come across like refugees from an old Dodge sheriff commercial—is agreeably accomplished without losing its bite in the process. When it becomes apparent that, loathesome and unscrupulous though he may be, used car salesman turned televangelist Farnsworth (an hysterically on-target turn by R. Lee Ermey) isn't the heavy in the piece, the film appears to be back pedaling into calculated inoffensiveness—a strange move for a work that is never going to make Jerry Falwell's required viewing list under any circumstances— only to turn around and offer a real villain motivated by insanity brought on by another sacred cow: obsessive mother love. (Similarly, Farnsworth's character is never wholly softened. The last we hear of him is his plan to rerun the episode of his TV show in which the villain is shot to death by the police "every night during Sweep's Week.")

First and foremost, though, *Fletch Lives* is a Chevy Chase vehicle, and Ritchie (who directed Chase in the first *Fletch* picture) seems to trust his star to carry the show (as opposed to *The Golden Child*, where he swamped Eddie Murphy in special effects sequences), while never allowing him to descend to the level of shtick. (For the record, Chase is only allowed one outright pratfall and a brief bout of his patented clumsiness throughout the film's length.) Instead, Ritchie and Chase create a genuine sense of character within the confines of Chase's established personality, much in the manner of the better Bob Hope comedies of the 1940's. Chase's disguises, makeshift identities (ranging from Elmer Fudd Gantry to Billy Gene King), wisecracks ("All it needs is a little spackling and some napalm to turn it into a really nice mausoleum," he observes upon seeing his crumbling inheritance), and a running gag with an aged pink Cadillac (for which stops must be planned well in advance), all work within the film's old fashioned star comedy approach. Neither too big (the film boasts two of the currently obligatory comic chases without succumbing to overkill), nor too small (production values are never wanting), *Fletch Lives* isn't going to change the world, cure cancer, or even start a new wave of film comedy, but it does afford a pleasant 90-odd minutes of entertainment with something on its mind other than non-stop car crashes and under-whelming technocentric displays of special effects. Today, that's no mean feat.

LOS ANGELES TIMES, 3/17/89, Calendar/p. 8, Chris Willman

"Fletch Lives" is the ultimate comedy of condescension, a movie with a hero whose every other line of dialogue is a snide wisecrack directed at a fool. In this meager sequel, as in its popular predecessor, Chevy Chase demolishes every easy target in sight with a quip of the tongue. Some of the lines are funny, but after a while you just want to smack him.

The original "Fletch" film nearly four years ago had Chase, as investigative reporter Irwin Fletcher, sardonically reducing everyone and everything in Los Angles to its proper level. Having exhausted all possible prey for his comic patronization in this town, what better place to go next and be painfully superior about than the Deep South? Uh-oh.

Welcome to Louisiana, land of obese lawmen. sex-hungry belles, KKK goons, crooked TV evangelists, redneck motorcycle gangs, 'possum hunters, plain folks who like to dress up in Confederate regalia and enough suckers to keep P.T. Barnum in business for five lifetimes. Everyone there has two first names—Jim Bob, Joe Jack, Cindy Mae and almost every other possible combination except John Paul.

These dusty clichés are set up like big plastic ducks in a shooting gallery by screenwriter Leon Capetanos, to be knocked flat by cosmopolitan Chevy, who isn't playing a character (least of all the character first created by novelist Gregory McDonald) so much as reprising his nonplussed, punchline-spouting "Weekend Update" anchor role.

This jester ends up in Louisiana after inheriting a mansion from his recently deceased aunt. It's a given that our hero will offer more rejoinders than remorse about the aunt. It's a little more shocking when, 20 minutes into the movie, its most appealing character (a sexy Southern lawyer played by Patricia Kalember) is killed off as she lies in bed next to Fletch, and all he can do when the police show up is crack jokes: "It was good but not *that* good." Would *you* want to sleep with this guy, knowing that he might be playing Henny Youngman over your naked corpse the next morning?

But sleep with him another woman does, knockout real estate agent Becky Ann Culpepper (Julianne Phillips, she of the angel face and wildly wavering accent), whose land-grubbing TV-preacher father just happens to be a prime suspect in the murder.

It's a brilliant stroke of casting to have R. Lee Ermey—the formidable drill sergeant of "Full Metal Jacket"—take on the role of evangelist Jimmy Lee Farnsworth. And when the picture finally gets to this fake faith-healer's massive church, it looks all set to take off into satirical set-piece heaven. The atrocious baby-blue color scheme of the set design and suits (from costume designer Anna Hill Johnstone and five art directors) is hysterical and—for any students of the TBN or PTL cable networks—dead on-target.

There's more reason to be hopeful still: Director Michael Ritchie is the man who took on such American institutions as politics ("The Candidate"), juvenile sports ("Bad News Bears"), beauty pageants ("Smile") and est seminars ("Semi-Tough") in the '70s. Why not institutionalized religion now?

But this is the Michael Ritchie of the '80s, a coaster more apt to cook up gilded turkeys like "The Golden Child" and last year's career low, "The Couch Trip." *This* Ritchie lets sophomoric scatology predominate over satire at every turn, and even in the two church scenes—including an amusing bit with Fletch impersonating a guest healer—the gags are more crass than corrosive. the whole dumb mess bottoms out (so to speak) when a parishioner pulls down his pants to show the congregation his hemorrhoids.

Comedy this smug is bound to find its TV-weaned audience, but moviegoers might think twice about signing on as the film makers' partners in put-down when they're clearly also its targets. It's also a bad sign of the faith Ritchie and editor Richard A. Harris have in their audiences when every time Chase does something funny with his hands, they cut to a closeup of the hands— as if they're afraid we might miss the gag.

Beware: "Fletch Lives" (MPAA—rated PG, in spite of its raunchy-mindedness) may assume that all Southerners are dim bulbs, but it doesn't think you're so bright yourself.

MONTHLY FILM BULLETIN, 5/89, p. 135, Tom Milne

Still badgered over back alimony, refused a vacation after completing an assignment for his Los Angeles paper, Fletch abruptly quits and heads for Louisiana on learning that he has inherited a plantation property from an aunt. Somewhat dashed when his mansion proves to be derelict, his spirits revive when his aunt's executor, Amanda Ray Ross, turns out to be beautiful, spends the night with him, and tells him of an anonymous offer of $250,000 for the land. In the morning, Fletch wakes to find Amanda Ray dead beside him. Arrested on suspicion of murder, he is rescued from the attentions of a brutish cellmate by a lawyer, Hamilton Johnson, who effects his release. A friend of his late aunt, Johnson confides (with reference to the $250,000 offer) that his own mother was swindled out of her land by Jimmy Lee Farnsworth, an evangelist with grandiose plans to expand his "Bibleland" into religion's answer to Disneyland. Fletch, with help from Calculus—the lackadaisical black caretaker on his property—resists an attempt by hooded Ku Klux Klanners to scare him away; he discovers, by burgling Amanda Ray's files, that his aunt was apparently to marry Farnsworth, but changed her mind and her will shortly before her death. When the $250,000 offer is repeated by Becky Culpepper, a pretty girl who turns out to be Farnsworth's daughter, Fletch masquerades as a faith healer on Farnsworth's TV show, gleaning evidence of his expansion plans while prowling backstage. Becky, horrified to learn his suspicions, insists that her father is no killer. Meanwhile, Fletch's property is razed by arson; he is shot at during a coon hunt (a jaunt arranged, somewhat suspiciously, by Calculus); and in escaping, picks up some noxious substance on his shoes. Analysed, this proves to be toxic waste ordered by Johnson. Confronted, Johnson admits to a revenge plot against Farnsworth for swindling his mother (the toxic waste would ruin Bibleland; the murder and other crimes would be blamed on Farnsworth). Pursuing Fletch and Becky with intent to kill, Johnson is shot by Calculus, an undercover FBI agent. Fletch, with Becky and a $100,000 insurance cheque for the house, returns to Los Angeles and his job. Gillet, his ex-wife's lawyer and (secretly) lover, demands a half share in Fletch's inheritance in lieu of further alimony. Fletch happily sings over the non-existent house for Gillet and his ex-wife to live in.

The trouble with this second adventure for Gregory McDonald's engaging journalist/private eye—no better and no worse than *Fletch* four years ago—is that it shows such scant respect for its plot, its characters and its audience. The opening sequence, for instance, has Fletch disguised as a waitress to eavesdrop in Mafia deliberations: his pantomime dame appearance would fool no one, and it's an insult to all concerned to suppose that Mafia hoods would be taken in, that Fletch couldn't do any better, and that the audience will buy it. Similarly, there's the outline of a perfectly serviceable plot here, but it keeps getting shunted aside to allow Chevy Chase to indulge yet another dressing-up act. Some of these are really quite funny, as when he adopts a sad-sack voice and manner, Jerry Lewis-style, to beard a fearsome gang of Hell's Angels in their den; then, just as he is about to be torn to pieces, making angels of Angels by announcing that he is "young Harley... of Harley-Davidson". Others are embarrassingly crude, like the sequence in which Fletch appears on the evangelist's TV Show as a visiting healer.

Funny or not, these interludes are just that: excuses for a comedian to shine while the *raison d'être* of the scenes (Fletch supposedly on the trail of evidence) is lamely stretched out before coming to a dead end. Chase times his one-liners nicely ("On top of everything else", he grumbles while facing a wall of frustrations, "I think I'm getting my period"). He shows a Groucho Marxian ability to make nonsense spiral absurdly into logic (as when, pretending to be a bug exterminator for the benefit of an inquisitive cop, he persuades the latter to kneel on the floor and squeal like a pig to prevent a bug, supposedly accidentally dropped into his ear, from multiplying: "They breed by masturbation!"). He can make no headway, however, against a script and direction which look for the laugh and let the character go hang. Michael Ritchie's gift for bringing even marginal characters vividly alive is evident throughout, not least in Patricia Kalember's brief appearance as Amanda Ray Ross. When she is murdered, one feels a pang of regret; but Fletch, waking to find her lifeless body beside him, merely remarks, "It was good, but not *that* good". It is hard to take much pleasure in the company of someone *that* anxious to display his wit.

NEW YORK POST, 3/17/89, p. 21, David Edelstein

Whenever I write about a Chevy Chase movie, I spend a lot of time catching up on phone calls, sucking down cans of Tab and schmoozing with office mates. It's not that the pictures are so terrible. "Fletch Lives"—the hopefully titled sequel to the breezy "Fletch"—had me chortling now and then, and it's more inventive than it needs to be. But something about Chase's smarmy, laid-back delivery makes me want to stuff the deadline and go shoot some hoops. His low wattage is infectious.

In "Fletch Lives," the smart-aleck reporter with a yen for goofball disguises inherits a dilapidated Louisiana plantation from an aunt he hasn't seen in years. Yes, this is Fletch Goes to Cracker Country; for the next 90 minutes this urban skeptic makes monkeys out of jowly Southern sheriffs, bumbling Klansmen, Neanderthal bikers and sleazy, Jim Bakker-ish televangelists.

They're easy targets, and the movie is full of white-trash cliches. But it's all blandly tolerable (if you're not from the South, that is). One of Chase's disguises is a bespectacled, snaggle-toothed faith healer named Smoots, and the scene in which he cures the migraine of a man named Jim Bob on national TV has some tension and wit. But there's almost nothing else to think back on. "Fletch Lives" is like one of those new "dry" beers—no aftertaste.

On last week's "West 57th St." Chase talked with disarming candor about how lousy his films have been over the years, and I admire his honesty. Yet this is a guy who, in many of those movies, didn't appear to have the energy to *shave*, let alone to give a spirited performance.

The Fletch character, from that standpoint, makes sense for him—it's been engineered to run on almost no gas. Chase is deadpan and smug while the people he comes up against are blustery or garrulous or foolishly sincere. To Fletch the entire world is a stooge, meant to be one-upped with an ironic aside or cheerful double-entendre; he dispatches each chump and moves on.

There's nothing wrong with that in theory—Groucho did little but put people down, and so did W.C. Fields. But their insults were brilliant, epigrammatic, endlessly quotable; Chase's Fletch vanquishes these dummies with easy one-liners and bored off-screen glances. David Letterman is funnier on a slow night.

To be fair, Chase is alert here, sharper than usual. He still can't make you believe that the more complicated put-downs are rolling naturally off his tongue, the way Bill Murray or Tom Hanks can. But he doesn't look zonked-out, the way he did in, say, "Spies Like Us," and he's a graceful physical comedian.

The problem is that he can't play a human being. When a woman with whom he has spent the night is dead in the morning (injected with poison while the couple sleeps), Chase's Fletch can't muster any horror, let alone grief. His reaction ("It was good, but it wasn't *that* good") is meant to be a hoot, but you might feel distant from him after that: Why should anyone care about a man (or a movie) that can't even kiss off a likable character with a decent joke?

Speaking of decent jokes, Julianne Phillips' performance (and accent) wobbles all over the place, but no one could have made much of this bimbo part. R. Lee Ermey gives a spooly intensity to the televangelist, and Geoffrey Lewis, as a Klan leader who can't get his cross to burn, is wonderfully dopey. (The joke is that he's doing a "contract job"—you can hire the Klan to demonstrate on someone's lawn the way you hire musicians for your wedding or bar-mitzvah.)

Cleavon Little comes up with so outrageous a Stepin Fetchit turn that he *can't* be what he seems; there's no way a black actor would consent to do this drawling, shuffling routine in 1989.

And while we're on the subject of racial sensitivity, "Fletch Lives" has a bright dream sequence in which Fletch imagines himself presiding over a happy Southern plantation and skipping under the magnolias singing Zip-A-Dee-Doo-Dah with cartoon animals. The only problem is that his hordes of smiling workers are white, not black—which sort of kills the Great White Father joke. Toothlessness doesn't do much for satire.

NEWSDAY, 3/17/89, Part III/p. 3, Mike McGrady

Chevy Chase, in his second outing as wiseacre investigative reporter Fletch, master of disguise and smirking, delivers the kind of comically contrived lines that bring to mind early Bob Hope movies and the kind of contorted expressions that bring to mind early Jerry Lewis movies.

In "Fletch Lives," Chevy inherits a rundown mansion in the South ("With a little spackling and some napalm, this place would make a nice mausoleum"), wakes up to find a brand-new lover lying dead beside him ("It was good—but not that good"), is asked by the police to make a statement ("A statement? Ask not what your country can . . ."), is arrested ("So far the only real suspect in Amanda's death was me. And I was pretty sure I didn't do it") and so on.

How does one explain why "Fletch Lives" doesn't? Well, since the original "Fletch" wasn't altogether awful, a sequel was clearly in order. However, judging from the evidence at hand, no one wanted to go to the trouble of constructing a sequel from the ground up. In fact, it sometimes seems as though someone found an old, previously unused, script poking fun at the South—knocking such easy targets as the KKK, rednecks, Bible Belt TV preachers and raccoon hunts—and then inserted Chevy Chase into the proceedings, asking him to manufacture contrivances and contortions periodically.

One final note: Much of "Fletch Lives" was shot in the Newsday city room, which just goes to show how the most well-intentioned promotional efforts can backfire. However, some of those blurry background figures are real-life reporters and editors, thus giving the film its sole contact with reality.

NEWSWEEK, 3/20/89, p. 83, David Ansen

You don't go to the "Fletch" movies—this one, like the first, starring Chevy Chase and directed by Michael Ritchie—for mystery or suspense. The fun is watching compulsive wisecracker and investigative reporter I.M. Fletcher outflank the various boobs, fools and ruffians who stand between him and the solution of the utterly irrelevant crime. Fletch lives or dies by the quality of his quips. Here, most of the time, he lives. Leon Capetanos's reasonably witty script sends Fletch into the kind of Deep South that only exists in the minds of middle-aged liberal Hollywood screenwriters, complete with clumsy Ku Klux Klanners, TV evangelists (R. Lee Ermey), moss-laden mansions, biker gangs and courtly Southern gentlemen who dress up in confederate costumes (Hal Holbrook). Low-keyed but amiable, "Fletch Lives" gives Chase the opportunity to put on funny teeth and pass himself off as a smarmy faith healer, an insect exterminator named Billie Gene King and the nerdy scion of the Harley-Davidson company, all of which he does with his usual never-break-a-sweat savvy. Ritchie has the most fun scoring points off the media ministry (he could have gone further) and seems the least engaged when having to bring his murder mystery to its action-packed conclusion. "Fletch Lives" feels like TV, but at least it's clever, unpretentious TV.

Also reviewed in:
NEW YORK TIMES, 3/17/89, p. C17, Vincent Canby
VARIETY, 3/15-21/89, p. 13
WASHINGTON POST, 3/17/89, p. D7, Rita Kempley
WASHINGTON POST, 3/17/89, Weekend/p. 37, Desson Howe

FLY II, THE

A Twentieth Century Fox Film Corporation release of a Brooksfilms production. *Executive Producer:* Stuart Cornfeld. *Producer:* Steven-Charles Jaffe. *Director:* Chris Walas. *Screenplay:* Mick Garris, Jim Wheat, Ken Wheat, and Frank Darabont. *Story:* Mick Garris. *Based on characters created by:* George Langelaan. *Director of Photography:* Robin Vidgeon. *Editor:* Sean Barton. *Music:* Christopher Young. *Music Editor:* Jay Ignaszewski and Earl Ghaffari. *Sound:* Rob Young and (music) Eric Tomlinson. *Sound Editor:* Douglas Murray. *Production Designer:* Michael S. Bolton. *Art Director:* Sandy Cochrane. *Set Decorator:* Rose Marie McSherry. *Set Dresser:* Mark Davidson and Mark Lane. *Effects Creator/Designer:* Chris Walas. *Special Effects:* John Thomas. *Creature Effects:* Jon Berg. *Costumes:* Christopher Ryan. *Make-up:* Jayne Dancose. *Special Effects Make-up:* Stephan Dupuis. *Stunt Coordinator:* John Wardlow. *Running time:* 104 minutes. *MPAA Rating:* R.

CAST: Eric Stoltz (Martin); Daphne Zuniga (Beth); Lee Richardson (Bartok); John Getz (Stathis); Frank C. Turner (Shepard); Ann Marie Lee (Jainway); Gary Chalk (Scorby); Saffron Henderson (Ronnie); Harley Cross (10-year-old Martin); Matthew Moore (4-year-old Martin); Rob Roy (Wiley); Andrew Rhodes (Hargis); Pat Bermel (Mackenzie); William Taylor (Dr. Trimble); Jerry Wasserman (Simms); Duncan Fraser (Obstetrician); Janet Hodgkinson (Nurse); Sean O'Byrne (Perinatologist); Mike Winlaw (Neonatologist); Allan Lysell (Guard A); Kimelly Anne Warren (Marla); Ken Camroux (Linder); Bruce Harwood (Technician); Lorena Gale (Woman); David Mylrea (Flywalker); Tom Heaton (Manager); Cecilia Warren (Anchorwoman); Andrea Mann (Cute Girl); Sterling Cottingham (Baby Martin).

FILMS IN REVIEW, 5/89, p. 301, Edmond Grant

An utterly uncalled for sequel, *The Fly II* actually displays some genuine emotion in its first half, but quickly disintegrates to the point where its final scenes are a gory recreation of the oft-imitated end section of *The Terminator*.

Eric Stoltz plays the wide eyed progeny of the characters played by Jeff Goldblum and Geena Davis in the last version of *The Fly*. Stoltz isn't aware of his unique genetic heritage, but he does sense that all is not well with the staff of the scientific compound who spend their days studying his every move.

And surely every boy—even one who is soon to degenerate into an oversized insect—must have a girl, and so Stoltz meets up and makes cute with Daphne Zuniga, an understanding worker at the institute. Some nicer moments early on in the film concern Stoltz's accelerated growth process, and his interactions with Zuniga and a dog whose fate is rather unpleasant.

But, eventually, Stoltz begins disintegrating just as Goldblum's character had in the film. As he changes, the film too undergoes a transformation and drops all of its melodrama and pathos to go where the big box office pay off is—special effects and gore.

Stoltz disappears entirely once the transformation is complete, and is replaced by a giant prosthetic fly that mercilessly slaughters all of the evil scientific personnel who manipulated his (Stoltz's) existence.

Fly II concentrates on gore and mayhem in a manner totally antithetical to that of the Goldblum film. Director David Cronenberg did focus on the repellent nature of the physical transformation process, but with an eye towards the desperate anxiety of Goldblum's character, and his tongue-in-cheek attitude towards the process, as evidenced in Goldblum's wonderful moments staring at his own decaying reflection in the mirror. *Fly II* dwells on the transformation with an eye towards audience reaction (confusing, as many horror films do, fear and disgust), as in the scene where, in close-up, Stoltz picks at a swelling sore for an extended amount of time.

Like many other sequels, *Fly II* is a pale imitation of its predecessor containing all of the same elements, but none of the original's stylish attitude toward the grotesque, and grim humor in the face of degeneration and death.

LOS ANGELES TIMES, 2/11/89, Calendar/p. 3, Kevin Thomas

That "The Fly II" isn't called "Son of the Fly" typifies the earnestness with which this lame sequel to the 1986 smash attempts to set a serious tone. But it *is* "Son of the Fly" and just might have been more entertaining had its makers owned up to that.

As it is, the film becomes faintly silly in its dead-seriousness, then slides into tedium and triteness.

Essentially a bare-bones replay of "The Fly," it more closely resembles countless other routine sci-fi horror pictures. So much dogged determination, plus considerable technical flourish, have gone into "The Fly II" that it can't be said to be truly terrible, merely ponderous and uninspired.

If you saw the poignant and oddly poetic 1986 film, you'll recall that Dr. Seth Brundle (Jeff Goldblum) inadvertently mixed his molecules with those of a common housefly during an experiment in the transmission of matter. Now we're told that his girlfriend was pregnant and, as the sequel opens, she's giving birth at an industrial complex whose owner (Lee Richardson) holds the rights to Brundle's cursed device. The woman dies giving birth to a monstrous creature, but out of its entrails comes a perfectly formed baby boy.

This is not to say that the kid is exactly normal. He's incredibly brilliant, and his growth, carefully monitored, is so accelerated that by the time he's 5, he's played by the grown-up Eric Stoltz. And then there are those still-dormant "aberrant chromosomes. . . . ''

It's easy to see what's coming; not helping matters is that there is nothing distinctive in the romance that develops between Stoltz and a young scientist at the lab (Daphne Zuniga). Richardson proves to be a stock megalomaniacal villain. Indeed, so much is so dull that the sheer nastiness of Richardson's bullying, dirty-minded head guard (Gary Chalk) livens things up in welcome—albeit pointless—relief.

"The Fly II" (rated R for much repulsive gore, some sex) is a sleek production, featuring a portentous score and an elaborate sound design but its makers had better be braced for unintended laughter.

MONTHLY FILM BULLETIN, 10/89, p. 300, Philip Strick

Veronica Quaife dies after giving birth to the offspring of Seth Brundle, the computer scientist whose experiments at Bartok Industries with a teleportation device led to his fusion with a fly and subsequent death. Although born within a cocoon which has to be stripped away, the child appears normal; under the direction of ruthless industrialist Anton Bartok, he is closely supervised in a specially constructed nursery. Called Martin, the boy never sleeps but matures at an astonishing speed: within five years he has the physical appearance of a seventeen-year-old-and an uncannily advanced intelligence. Gaining access with his computer skills to all sections of the Bartok building, he befriends a dog which to his horror is subsequently used in a teleportation experiment that leaves it a deformed wreck. On his fifth birthday, Martin is given his own apartment where Bartok guarantees complete privacy; in return, Bartok asks him to continue his father's researches to make teleportation safe for human use. One night, Martin meets a computer filing clerk, Beth Logan, and they become friends. He also discovers that the deformed dog is still being kept alive; he puts it out of its misery and, with renewed effort, works out the computer programme which will teleport living creatures without damage. He conceals the information within the computer under a secret password. Now lovers, Martin and Beth are kept apart on Bartok's orders, enforced by vindictive security chief Scorby. Convinced by this that he is still under surveillance, Martin smashes up his apartment and finds hidden video-cameras and tapes of his father's metamorphosis, revealing symptoms which Martin now shares. Bartok admits that they currently have no idea how to cure him but mastery of the shape-changing process could eventually mean world domination. Breaking out, Martin collects Beth and they visit his father's former colleague, Stathis Borans, hoping he knows of an antidote. Borans suggests the answer must lie within the matter transmitters themselves, and Martin realises—as he and Beth continue to dodge Bartok's search parties—that the insect cells in his body could only be exchanged for human cells during teleportation with another human being. After a night in hiding, Martin's body has enveloped him in a new cocoon and Beth desperately gets this back to the Bartok laboratories for help. Hatching as a monstrous hybrid, Martin terrorises Bartok's men, confronts Bartok in the teleportation chamber, and drags the industrialist into one of the transmission pods as Beth releases the controlling computer programme. Two shapes emerge from the receiving telepod—a reconstituted Martin and a hideously mutated Bartok.

As a sign of the times, the technical miracle at the centre of the new *Fly* species has become precisely what was the basis for horror in George Langelaan's original story in which, as well as turning part-fly the hapless French scientist also acquired parts of the family cat. The cunning financier Bartok, emerging from the Cronenberg shadows to take his rightful place as father to the entire project, has detected that the doubtful blessing of instant matter-transmission, while having its uses, would be fiercely opposed by the international freight interests and would probably ruin the world economy. Way ahead of the rest of us, who only get to know the master plan quite late in the proceedings, he has concentrated instead on the *transformation* of matter which, along with its medical implications (cancer cells, for example, could be conveniently erased during the transmission programme), points us along the fashionable path of genetic engineering towards the ultimate (according to Stapledon) evolutionary objective—the superhuman.

Sadly, the visionary Bartok becomes conventional megalomaniac at this prospect. "Bartok Industries", he chortles, "will control the form and function of all life on earth!" And since he has ruthlessly betrayed and exploited the one genius within his grasp who might deliver the goods, he pays the crippling price of vaulting ambition and undergoes a helplessly monstrous transformation of his own. Thus the sins of the scientist are transferred to the shoulders of today's new villain, the entrepreneur. And where Cronenberg's *Fly*, characteristically, was an allegory about the disgusting physical decay which follows on the heels of maturity, *Fly II* has an appealingly joyous sub-text about the emergence of the wholly complete and sparklingly new adult from the glutinous carapace of adolescence. Presiding over this rebirth, which balances the foetal arrival at the beginning of the film, is the mother/mistress who initially rejected the newcomer in horror but who now embraces him in surrogate reconciliation.

In these terms, *Fly II*, far from being any old sequel, has an unexpected integrity as the account of how knowledge—and the changes that it brings—is transferred, sometimes obscured, and ultimately understood between parent and child. Carefully but not drastically underscored throughout the action, Martin's realisation of and atonement for his father's errors is sealed by the ingenuously obvious computer codeword that protects his future—"DAD"—with a meaning that his "false" father, Bartok, understands too late. As a sign of the times, Chris Walas is special-effects-man turned director, promoted on the strength of his Oscar-winning designs for Cronengerg's *Fly*. His début had every excuse to be an excess of nasty shocks, but while there is indeed a rampaging monster sequence which, complete with exploding head (Walas also worked on *Scanners*), is irrelevant to anything but commercial considerations, *Fly II* is constructed with a refreshing intricacy and visual panache.

The Bartok environment, a warren of glacial observation points, centres around the vast proscenium of the telepod test area (to be pedantic about it, "teleportation" is a hypothetical *mental* skill, but maybe Walas knows that too), where the vital elements of Martin's Oedipal struggle are consistently staged. A polished arena of puzzles and fears, it inspires the director to appreciative flights like the high-angle shot with which he studies the courtship dance of Beth and Martin as k. d. lang's sweetly acerbic "Lock, Stock and Teardrops" is deservedly played in full. Such interludes are worth a galaxy of special effects. Even when horror is the name of the game, there are spectacular meditations with the camera—as when, spiralling down a stairway past one corpse, it has us peering along a conjunction of corridors in expectation of the next. One might complain that the mutated dog looks too much like a regurgitated sock (although the mercy killing is handled with redeeming tact), that the hyperactive and over-acted security guard Scorby is pointlessly malicious, that flies don't need teeth, and so on. But with the support of a central trio of excellent performances (Lee Richardson, in particular, shows a baleful authority worthy of John Houseman), the buzz has to be that Walas has emerged from the gestative phase with an assured stretching of his cinematic wings.

NEW YORK POST, 2/11/89, p. 17, David Edelstein

When we left Seth Brundle (Jeff Goldblum), the scientist-hero of "The Fly," he was splattered all over the walls. For the sequel, "The Fly II," Seth does not, logically enough, come bounding back to resume his experiments ("It's just a flesh wound!").

But never fear—in Hollywood, no successful invention is discarded after only one use. Seth's teleportation pods are still churning out squishy approximations of human flesh, and he now has a son, Martin (Eric Stoltz), to carry on the lepidopterous legacy.

Directed by special-effects whiz Chris Walas (who was responsible for the creature in the last film), "The Fly II" is clunky and lame-brained and generally laughable, but it vaults along fearlessly, and I had a pretty good time hooting and screeching. It's a major comedown, but it isn't a downer.

David Cronenberg's "The Fly" was actually a serious—and powerful—work, and the transformation of Brundle into "Brundlefly" was meant as a metaphor for aging and terminal disease. Of course, the movie was also a monumental goo-fest, and probably no one except us pointyheaded critics paid attention to much beyond the gag-me-with-a-shovel special effects.

The sequel doesn't repeat the old plot; it uses Cronenberg's devices as the premise for a cornball, paranoid melodrama about an evil corporation that's out to alter the form of life on this planet.

Martin—born to a stand-in for Geena Davis in the films cruel, ugly overture—is their unwitting tool, the only person alive with the brains to figure out how the teleportation pods really work. (Seth forgot to leave an instruction manual, and those darned things have a way of turning your favorite house pets into steak tartare.)

Because of Martin's peculiar DNA, his growth is accelerated, and on his fifth birthday he already looks like Eric Stoltz—lucky for us, since Stoltz is such an agreeable actor. He's marvelous in the fine, revisionist "Our Town" on Broadway, and here he seems to have been newly-hatched.

Martin needs no sleep, and working late one night in the corporation he calls home, he meets a pretty technician, Beth (Daphne Zuniga), and asks her up to his top-secret, Sector Four lab. This, you'll recall, is how Goldblum drew Davis into his life in the last picture; obviously, teleportation pods are great way to pick up babes.

But ladies, a word of warning: Do not get emotionally involved with a guy who teleports stuff, even if he seems, like, really nifty. Trust me, he'll go to pieces on you.

These kids do get it on, but the atmosphere is too high-pressure for domestic bliss, especially when the "genetic metamorphosis" begins and Martin's skin develops the texture of a toasted marshmallow. Nevertheless, Beth continues to hug her suppurating lover: In the noble tradition of the first film, she stands by her fly.

Unlike "The Fly," however, there are real bad guys in this one. When Martin begins to turn, the corporation shows its true, Kafkaesque colors, and the grandfatherly president (Lee Richardson) proves there's no corporate substitute for a genuine dad. Throw in some heartless scientists and sneering security guards and you have lots of fodder for fly-acid. Hardcore gore hounds will not be disappointed.

It must be said that even when he's a 10-foot Superfly spewing milky geysers of acid into the faces of humans, Martin is still capable of patting a dog—which puts him well above these big-business types on the evolutionary ladder. It's nice to see a horror movie with its priorities straight.

NEWSDAY, 2/11/89, Part II/p. 15, Terry Kelleher

Talk about extreme right-to-lifers.

Pregnant by Seth (The Fly) Brundle—the biggest, most hideous, most destructive man-insect in sci-fi history—Veronica Quaife chose not to have an abortion. (Of course, she was seriously considering one near the end of "The Fly," until Brundle buzzed into her doctor's office and made like King Kong.)

Veronica's decision, whether based on ethical or commercial concerns, provides the premise for "The Fly II." This sequel to David Cronenberg's 1986 horror hit, which in turn was taken from the 1958 Vincent Price classic, is more than disgusting enough to satisfy the "gross me out" crowd and just imaginative enough to allay the worst fears of those averse to movies with Roman numerals in the title.

The director this time is Chris Walas, who did special effects and makeup (the latter won him an Oscar) for "The Fly." Like Cronenberg, he eases into the distasteful stuff, preferring to spend the first 45 minutes or so on plot, character and even a little sly humor. But when the time comes to get icky and gory, he really lets you have it.

The picture opens with a Geena Davis stand-in-having a devil of a time in the delivery room. Lifting a page from Cronenberg's book, Walas shows Veronica giving birth to a horrifying mutation—but it's only a dream. And a cheat.

Martin Brundle, son of Seth, grows up under observation/confinement at Bartok Industries, his dad's old employer. Boy, does he grow up. By age 5, he's grown to the point where Eric Stoltz can step into the part. At first, Martin is a test subject. The sinister folks in the white coats claim to be studying his "accelerated growth syndrome." When Martin is 5-going-on-30, Mr. Bartok (Lee Richardson) urges him to continue his father's experiments in "teleportation," the matter-transmission trick that went terribly awry in "The Fly." To get a feel for the project, Martin watches a videotaped interview of his dad (Jeff Goldblum in a brief reprise).

For a while, Walas settles into the pattern of the previous film. Martin finds a girlfriend in Beth (Daphne Zuniga), a Bartok computer programer with an interest in Fly-fishing (chuckle here). But soon Martin starts turning seriously ugly. The skin gets blotchy and swollen and oozy. Oh, you know. He learns Mr. Bartok is holding him as part of a diabolical scheme to "control the form and function of all life on earth." Martin and Beth take it on the lam, until his raging aberrant chromosomes render him as unfit companion. As Martin grows larger, stronger and ever more revolting, he finds unpleasant ways of dispatching Bartok employees we've come to dislike.

Any redeeming features in all this? The strenuous pace, for one. Stoltz, for another. He's appealing in the character's awkward-genius stage and, as "Mask" established, he functions well in heavy makeup. Then there's John Getz' acerbic apperarance as Veronica's ex-boyfriend, Stathis, whose memories of Seth Brundle are less than fond. "He dissolved my hand and foot with Fly vomit," Stathis explains to Martin. "I had no love for the man."

The best part of "The Fly II" is the end, and not only because the Fly vomit finally stops flowing. Mick Garris and three other screenwriters have devised a conclusion that sets up another sequel while meting out some audience-pleasing poetic justice. A "Fly III" is probably inevitable. Might as well be a half-decent excuse for it.

VILLAGE VOICE, 2/21/89, p. 77, Manohla Dargis

The repackaged schmaltz of *Cousins* [see Dargis' review] is far scarier than *The Fly II*, which opens like *It's Alive!* but quickly turns into the saga of David the Bubble Boy. This latest version of human-insect metamorphosis picks up with the birth of Brundlefly's genetically recombined offspring, some nine months after *Fleischmeister* David Cronenberg's prequel ended. A ward of Bartok Industries, Brundlebaby is raised in laboratory isolation to become Eric Stoltz. In *Fly II*, adolescence (as with disease for *Fly* père) should have been a trope for terrors of the body. But, despite its predictable bloody finale and some loving effects from first-time director Chris Walas (an F/X whiz), *The Fly II* remains more John Hughes than Kafka.

Also reviewed in:
NEW YORK TIMES, 2/11/89, p. 14, Janet Maslin
VARIETY, 2/15-21/89, p. 20
WASHINGTON POST, 2/13/89, p. B2, Richard Harrington

FOR QUEEN AND COUNTRY

An Atlantic Releasing Corporation release of a Working Title film. *Producer:* Tim Bevan. *Director:* Martin Stellman. *Screenplay:* Martin Stellman and Trix Worrell. *Director of Photography:* Richard Greatrex. *Editor:* Stephen Singleton. *Music:* Michael Kamen, Goeff MacCormack and Simon Goldenberg. *Sound:* Simon Fraser, Mike Turner, and (music) Geoff MacCormack and Simon Goldenberg. *Sound Editor:* Kevin Brazier. *Production Designer:* Andrew McAlpine. *Art Director:* Charmian Adams. *Special Effects:* Arthur Beavis. *Costumes:* Sandy Powell. *Make-up:* Morag Ross. *Stunt Coordinator:* Gareth Milne. *Running time:* 106 minutes. *MPAA Rating:* R.

CAST: Denzel Washington (Reuben); Dorian Healy (Fish); Amanda Redman (Stacey); Sean Chapman (Bob); Bruce Payne (Colin); Geff Francis (Lynford); George Baker (Kilcoyne); Craig Fairbrass (Challoner); Michael Bray (Bryant); Stella Gonet (Debbie); Lisa O'Connor (Hayley); Anselm Peters (Oscar); Colin Thomas (Feargal); James Harkishin (Sadiq); Carlton Dixon (Stylee); Jo Martin (Pearl); Frank Harper (Mickey); Titiana Strauss (1st French Girl); Valerie Chassigneaux (2nd French Girl); Suzette Llewellyn (Girl with Bull Terrier); Debbie Killingback (1st Girl); Judith Conyers (2nd Girl); Ken Stott (Civil Servant); Brian McDermott (Harry); Chris Pitt (Chris); Mike Smart (Peelhead); Paul McKenzie (Sean); Peter McNamara (Pete); Dan Armour (Drunken

Man); Charlie Appleby (Fairground Stallholder); Stewart Harwood(Cab Office Owner); Peter Spraggon (Landlord); James Warrior (LEB Man); Joginder Singh Lal (Sikh Minder); Graham McTavish (Lieutenant).

LOS ANGELES TIMES, 5/19/89, Calendar/p. 13, Kevin Thomas

"For Queen and Country" presents Margaret Thatcher's Britain as utterly bleak and hopeless, its racism symptomatic of a rapidly accelerating disintegration. Alongside it, other such broadsides against contemporary Britain, even "Sammy and Rosie Get Laid," seem positively cheery.

The film is convincing, bad news being so easily persuasive, but it smacks of a rigid determinism on the part of writer-director Martin Stellman. He is so intent on hammering out a totally negative statement that he misses a more powerful and subtle fade-out some moments before his actual finish.

If "For Queen and Country" is unsparing, it is also involving, thanks largely to the charismatic, intelligent presence of Denzel Washington, accent-perfect as a young Londoner who leaves the service because he has not been promoted after eight years.

But he finds opportunities in civilian life for blacks no better—and probably worse—than when he joined up. Like many a troubled youth before him, British or American, black or white, Washington's Reuben saw the service as a chance to straighten up and make something of himself.

Reuben has certainly done that, but nobody cares, and his old friends believe he thinks he's better than they are. (They also think he is naive, and rightly so.) The best job he can land is as a cabbie, and that's thanks to the attractive, hearty new woman (Amanda Redman) in his life, herself a cabbie and a single mother.

Happiness, however, has never been more fleeting. More crucial in Reuben's life is his army buddy Fish (Dorian Healy), a young white man who lost his leg in service and who had saved Reuben's life. Fish is now drowning in drink, too many babies and too many bills, and Reuben feels obligated to shore him up, no matter how.

Contributing strongly to the film's gritty realism are its stark inner-city settings, particularly the immense housing project where Reuben lives, a monolithic concrete structure that looks more like a prison than an apartment building. There is much to admire in "For Queen and Country" (rated R for violence, language), although it's too obvious and contrived for its own good.

MONTHLY FILM BULLETIN, 1/89, p. 15, Nigel Floyd

After serving nine years as a British Army paratrooper, with tours of duty in Northern Ireland, Kenya, Belize and the Falklands, sometime football hooligan and small-time thief Reuben returns to his council flat on a run-down South London estate. A former friend, Colin, offers him a job as a paid heavy; he is also harassed by racist policeman Challoner, until seasoned detective Kilcoyne intervenes. Reuben visits Tony (known as "Fish "), an embittered ex-paratrooper now confined to a wheelchair, and repays £200 which Fish owes to Bob, a mutual army buddy now serving with the police firearms division. After catching teenager Hayley and a younger boy burgling his flat, Reuben confronts the girl's mother, Stacey. In the local pub, Reuben is offered stolen goods by his old friend, Lynford, and is later asked by Fish (who has just won £800 on the horses) to join him for a "dirty weekend" in Paris. Visiting a funfair with Stacey and Hayley, Reuben scores well on the shooting range, which prompts Stacey to tell him that her husband was imprisoned for armed robbery and that she will have nothing to do with a man who uses guns. On the way back, Reuben and Stacey see a gang of black youths drop a concrete slab from an overhead walkway on to a police squad car, killing popular beat copper Harry. Questioned by an angry Kilcoyne, Reuben and Stacey claim to have seen nothing. Encouraged by Stacey, Reuben gets a job as a mini-cab driver, but when he tries to renew his out-of-date passport, he is told that under the terms of the 1981 British Nationality Act, those born in St. Lucia are no longer considered British citizens. He contacts Colin and agrees to act as bodyguard for a drugs transaction, but after Indian dealer Sadiq is arrested by drugs squad officers, Reuben terminates the partnership. On Guy Fawkes' night, Reuben finds Fish drunkenly firing his rifle in his council flat; his wife has left him and taken the children back to Ireland. Reuben's St. Lucia passport arrives, but Stacey refuses to accompany him to Paris on the tickets Fish has given him. On his way back to his flat, Reuben follows youngsters pushing supermarket trolleys into an underground car park, where he finds Lynford supplying armed black youths with home-made petrol bombs. Finally giving in to Kilcoyne's pressure, Reuben tells him what is happening; Lynford makes a run for it, and a police squad car is firebombed. Having failed to persuade Fish to flee with him to St. Lucia, Reuben is confronted by a gun-wielding Lynford. Fish talks him into giving up his gun, but he is then shot by Challoner. As the riot continues, Reuben kills Challoner before being shot dead in turn by a police marksman, his former army pal Bob.

In his script for David Drury's *Defence of the Realm*, Martin Stellman succeeded in blending political topicality with the narrative economy and crisp pacing of genre film-making. The pre-credits sequence of Stellman's début feature as a director—in which off-duty soldiers Reuben and "Fish" are ambushed at a set of traffic lights by masked Irish gunmen—generates similar expectations. Sadly, this promise is soon dispelled, as we are bludgeoned into submission by: the heavy-handed presentation of Reuben's social milieu, the over-emphatic and/or speechifying tone that Stellman and Trix Worrell's dialogue employs to ram home already obvious political points, and Stellman's clumsy handling of the action scenes.

The council tower-block estate to which Reuben returns is the antithesis of "a land fit for heroes". In a very early scene, as Reuben makes his way across a desolate wasteland dividing the tower blocks, a frightened old lady scurries past in the opposite direction, her front door key already in her hand. According to production designer Andrew McAlpine, this was a fortuitous, unplanned moment, yet its simple effectiveness contrasts starkly with what follows. Reuben can go nowhere on the estate without finding a man urinating in the lift, seeing children "chasing the dragon" in a corridor, or being subjected to physical and verbal abuse by racist policemen.

This density of social detail also leads to problems of credibility, since Reuben is on hand to witness every significant development. When he sees Kilcoyne and Challoner's harassment of Lynford in the pub, a valid point is made: forced to verify Lynford's obviously false alibi, Reuben is caught between his delinquent black peers and the white forces of law and order with which his career as a soldier tends to align him. However, by the time Reuben has also caught the young burglars redhanded, been on hand when the concrete slab is dropped on the police squad car, witnessed a drugs raid on a party, and stumbled on Lynford's bombmaking factory, one's suspension of disbelief has been stretched to breaking point.

With the exception of the excellent, but unfortunately atypical, pre-credits sequence, the handling of the action scenes is at best adequate and at worst painfully inept. When the drunken Fish and Reuben beat up three Electricity Board employees, the decision to film the whole sequence in medium shot deprives it of any visceral impact. Similarly, the climactic riot scenes derive their power more from the obvious parallels with their real-life counterparts in Brixton and at the Broadwater Farm estate than from the way they are presented. Finally, the commercially motivated decision to cast American actor Denzel Washington as Reuben brings mixed rewards. Washington's powerful screen presence is used to some advantage in what is essentially a passive, brooding role. But apart from the problem of accepting him as a product of this London council estate, Washington is too clean-cut to convey either a street-wise toughness or an undercurrent of simmering violence.

NEW LEADER, 5/1/89, p. 21, John Morrone

Another British Export [the reference is to *Scandal*], *For Queen and Country*, an urban melodrama set in the housing estates of Southeast London, not only moves its characters toward defeat, it starts them off that way. As Reuben, a congenial and intelligent working-class black,American actor Denzel Washington brings more quiet strength than he can actually use in a role designed to show how the best of blokes are targeted for cultural disenfranchisement by racism and an untrustworthy police.

Returning home from his final tour of duty as a soldier in the Falklands, Reuben sees his neighborhood turned into a battleground of antipolice hatred, fueled by the routine abuse local detectives inflict upon the communtiy. Punks, the chronically unemployed, even ordinary looking adolescents are primed for violence because of the undue pressure exerted by "the old Bill" on nonwhites suspected of a variety of crimes. In these circumstances any expectation of protection under the law is at least naïve, and director Martin Stellman hardly lets pass an opportunity to place Reuben in a threatening situation.

Written by the director and Trix Worrell, the film's strongest suit is its uncommonly well-conceived ensemble of supporting roles—Fish, Reuben's disabled Army mate; Stacey, his white girlfriend; Colin, the sleek blond buddy who has made a fortune in drug deals with Arabs. But the pace is slow to the point of being debilitating. To make matters worse although it requires little effort to sympathize with Reuben and his friends, the script saddles them with so many economic limitations and so much environmental squalor that *For Queen and Country* is turned into an exercise in futile measures. And the political lesson it aims to teach us—that the underdog usually loses—is of course painfully unsubtle.

Reuben is forced to choose, metaphorically, between "queen"—the false view of law and order to be maintained by white Brits—and "country"—the sometimes sordid yet immediate realities of living in a slum where people of every color are one's neighbors and, all too often, one's alibi. Thematically, this is awfully familiar terrain. In its schematic way, *For Queen and Country* is virtually identical to *The Kitchen Toto*, Harry Hook's superior 1987 film set in mid '50s Kenya. There a young Kukuyu boy is torn between allegiance to his white protectors or to his Mau Mau compatriots. That the problems of contemporary London are less remote than those of colonial Kenya does not give Stellman's effort any edge, and it is not simply that Africa is prettier.

NEW STATESMAN & SOCIETY, 1/27/89, p. 40, Suzanne Moore

[*For Queen and Country* was reviewed jointly with *Stormy Monday*; see Moore's review in *Film Review Annual, 1989.*]

NEW YORK POST, 5/19/89, p. 29, David Edelstein

The bleak, inflammatory English drama "For Queen and Country" opens with a question from one of Cromwell's soldiers: "Why risk your life fighting for a country if you have no rights in that country?"

This quotation serves as a blueprint for the movie's first scenes. We meet a black soldier, Reuben (Denzel Washington), and watch him risk his life for England, first in Northern Ireland, where he's shot by the IRA, then in the Falklands, where he parachutes into a bloody battle.

In the next scene, we're shown (right on cue) that he has no rights in the country he has defended. Discharged from the army, Reuben walks to his inner city housing project through an underground tunnel and gets roughly accosted by thuggish policemen hissing racist slurs.

The pressure to turn to crime—for reasons both economic and social—is relentless. His childhood buddies feel betrayed by his patriotism and when they ask him why, after serving his country for nearly 10 years, he's back where he started—he has no answer. Humiliatingly, he can't even get a British passport: He was born in St. Lucia, and all the medals and war wounds in the world can't win him his citizenship.

"For Queen and Country" is like a politically responsible "Rambo," and I only wish it were less contrived and that its hero weren't so passive and uninteresting a figure.

It's a thesis movie, and the thesis is that a poor man in England can't win—he's destroyed if only because he has to protect himself against the fascist state. If he somehow outwits the cops, he's destroyed when he comes to the aid of a weaker buddy. It all goes like clockwork.

The buddy is Fish (Dorian Healy), who saved Reuben's life in Northern Ireland, lost a leg in the Falklands and is now a reckless alcoholic. To get money for Fish, Reuben agrees to participate in a drug deal with a sleazy mate called Colin (Bruce Payne). As a result of that, he can be blackmailed by a policeman into becoming an informer. As a result of that, the friend on whom he informs can come after him and Fish; the police can bust in; and in the melee...

"For Queen and Country" is superb on everyday life in a housing project, but the authentic feeling of these scenes gets undercut by the movie's creaky construction and by exchanges such as the one between Colin and Reuben about the latter's military record:

"What you gotta show for it?" says Colin. " Honor? Pride?"

"Thass' right."

"Well, my pride is sittin' out there in the car park—all 30 grand of it."

Still, it's hard to argue with reasoning like that, just as it's hard to tell a Harlem kid who can make six figures selling crack that he'd be better off working at McDonald's. He would be, but the advice doesn't sound so compelling at the current (or even future) minimum wage in a city as status-oriented as this one.

The problem is that Reuben is more an idealized construction than a character—he's a hero and a saint. What if he were a roughneck and a braggart? Would he be less deserving of his rights? Would he then deserve to be trampled by society? Movies that stack the deck like this, for fear of losing the audience's sympathy, remind you constantly of their artifice.

Fortunately, the gifted American actor Denzel Washington doesn't fall into dignified, Sidney Poitier cadences. There's caginess in his silence, and his voice is a crafty purr. (Washington's working-class English accent is good enough to be frequently unintelligible to Americans)

"For Queen and Country" does make one point powerfully: that police repression can turn even passive people into law-breakers, creating an Us-versus-Them mentality that—in the minds of the underclass—justifies acts of violence.

The *movie* doesn't justify that violence. It merely suggests that it's a human response to being treated like an animal. And that's a powerful warning for a city that, like this one, seems on the verge of unprecedented racial upheaval.

NEWSDAY, 5/19/89, Part III/p. 3, Mike McGrady

I can't shake the feeling that British writer-director Martin Stellman never got his copy of the moviemaking primer "Hollywood Guidelines and Ground Rules." In the first place, he keeps making dark little movies with political motifs and unhappy endings. Worse, he creates perfectly splendid heroes and then insists on killing them off shortly before the final credits.

Even without the doom and gloom, Stellman would seem to have a packaging problem. His movies are unwieldy, poorly tied together, all loose ends and disconnected segments. While all this violates basic moviemaking tenets, it also explains why his films tend to have a different feel to them, an unpredictability that can at times be most refreshing.

Stellman's script for "Defense of the Realm" a couple of seasons ago was so fragmented that the audience was forced into unusual exertions; it was as though we were given pieces to a puzzle, then asked to assemble the picture ourselves.

"For Queen and Country"—this time Stellman both writes and directs—presents no such challenge. It does open much the same way as the earlier film, spotlighting a highly charged political situation that shows England in a less than favorable light. In "Defense," Stellman saw his native land run by coldblooded bureaucrats who order up killings and bombings as calmly as other bureaucrats might order up file folders.

"For Queen and Country" pictures an England that neglects its lower classes and blacks, abandoning them to inner-city high-rises and then ignoring their basic needs, brutalizing them, finally forcing them into a Molotov cocktail insurrection.

Reuben (Denzel Washington), a black paratrooper born in St. Lucia and raised in England, has spent the past nine years fighting in Northern Ireland and the Falklands. He returns to a country that is considerably less than appreciative. The only job offers come from drug dealers; the police manhandle him at every turn; unkindest cut of all, his passport is revoked on a technicality and all that military service is apparently not enough to right matters. Reuben has always operated within the establishment and now, though severely mistreated by that establishment, he finds it difficult to join other blacks and Third Worlders in violent rebellion.

Washington, Oscar-nominated for his role in "Cry Freedom!" continues to impress as he provides clarity and definition along with, in this instance, a surprisingly effective Cockney accent. He is close kin to the old gunfighter who wants only to lay down his sixshooters. But neither the sheriff nor the bandits will permit this, and he is constantly pressed to join the fight.

Despite strong work by Washington and George Baker as a one-legged former army buddy, this is a movie about issues rather than people. Symbolism runs riot; a brief romance is not merely with a woman, it's with a woman with a near pathological hatred of the gun Reuben is being asked to carry. There is a feeling that every role and every scene has been squeezed to fit a prearranged shape. Events happen but they happen on cue; they don't unfold naturally, and this takes some of the edge off "For Queen and Country."

VILLAGE VOICE, 5/23/89, p. 61, George Brown

Product of a very Old Realism, *For Queen and Country* brings apocalypse to a London housing project. Predictable from the titles on, all this film requires of viewers is that they sit still and endure the inevitable. Recent movies I winced and squirmed through with a similar mounting desire to flee the theater were *Salaam Bombay!* and *Chocolat*. *For Queen and Country* happens to be cruder and it lacks the exoticism (sufficiently foreign locale) that gives those two their art-house cachet, but the premise remains the same: Watch the handsome, brooding, dark-faced hero be done in by inexorable social forces, despite his apparent nobility and innocence. In this case, it's a bit like witnessing a ritual dismemberment.

The deck is really stacked against Reuben (Denzel Washington) when he returns home after nine years as a British Army paratrooper. He's been ambushed in Northern Ireland, he's jumped into the fray in the Falklands. None of this training prepares him for life in the projects—although you'd think it might, given that the cityscape is a battle zone. Cynical 10-year-old thieves are better equipped than Reuben. No sooner does he settle in than his flat is trashed and robbed by two little kids; they even take his combat medals. He's attracted to Stacey (Amanda Redman), the mother of one junior burglar, though she is convinced that all men are thugs at heart and keeps pushing him away. Looking up old friends, he discovers one is a big-time drug dealer, one a brutal local gang leader, and his paraplegic buddy from the army, Fish (Dorian Healy), with baby and pregnant wife, is on the verge of eviction.

Director/writer Martin Stellman and co-writer Trix Worrell do supply some infuriating details about present-day life for the English underclasses. When Reuben wants to take a weekend in Paris with Stacey and goes to renew his passport, he's told that, according to Parliament's act of 1981, he is no longer a British citizen—no matter that he came to England from St. Lucia at age four and has fought nine years in the British Army. Nor does there seem any way to get an honest job or to avoid police harassment.

But the film is excruciatingly, didactically one-note: Whenever Reuben steps out, he trips over some harsh truth, large or small. (Washington is required only to change his expression from gloomy to grim.) He drives a cab, and a drunk tries to skip without paying his fare. He goes partying with the boys, and wouldn't you know, he's the one who gets left out of the elevator; the next elevator opens, and there's a guy pissing in it. Poor Reuben. They call him Rube, but Rue would do. There's a taste, I suppose, for this sort of fare, but I haven't decided if it's masochistic or sadistic.

Also reviewed in:
NEW YORK TIMES, 5/19/89, p. C14, Caryn James
VARIETY, 5/25/88, p. 18

FORCED MARCH

A Shapiro Glickenhaus Entertainment release. *Executive Producer:* Richard Karo and George Zelma. *Producer:* Dick Atkins. *Director:* Rick King. *Screenplay:* Dick Atkins and Charles K. Bardosh. *Director of Photography:* Ivan Mark. *Editor:* Evan Lottman. *Production Designer:* Laszlo Rajk. *Running time:* 100 minutes. *MPAA Rating:* Not Rated.

CAST: Chris Sarandon (Benjamin Kline/Miklos Radnoti); Renee Soutendijk (Mira van der Meer/Fanni Radnoti); Josef Sommer (Richard Kline)); John Seitz (Walter Hardy).

NEW YORK POST, 11/3/89, p. 25, Jami Bernard

It's pretty rare to get a picture about the Holocaust that raises little emotion, but we have one in "Forced March," a movie within a movie about a TV actor who takes on a big film role and struggles to come to terms with it.

Ben Kline (Chris Sarandon), the star of the TV action series "Derringer," is trying to go legit by signing on with a low-budget Hungarian production about the Hungarian poet Miklos Radnoti, who died while in a World War II labor camp. The name of the film being shot is "Forced March," which is the name of the framework movie, which just adds to the confusion. We'll call the real movie Big March and the movie within the movie Little March.

While trying to find a way to play his role in Little March, Ben begins to sort out his family's past—his dad, a Hungarian expatriate, refuses to talk about the old days, and Ben never knew his mom, who died during the war. All he has of her is a photograph, which he readily hands to a friend who promises to find information about her.

The incremental personal revelations that supposedly enable Ben to play his big death scene more accurately are too uninvolving or too bizarre to be of much use to the audience. For instance, a blow-up of the mother's photograph reveals a cross around her neck, so Ben is not Jewish after all—but then his religious views have not really been introduced into Big March, or Little March, for that matter.

As delving into his past hasn't helped much, it's time to trot our Method acting. Ben moves out of the Hungarian Holiday Inn, or its equivalent, and starts bedding down on the stark Little March set of the concentration camp.

Ben also has to contend with a particularly sadistic director (John Seitz), who might have been the more interesting character. He calls for take after take of scenes in which Ben has to do something punishing, like hang with his arms tied behind his back.

Director Rick King—now we're talking about the director of Big March—handles his movie within a movie as if it were already shot and in the can. In other words, we rarely see the characters making a movie, we just see long passages of it.

The problem of movies within movies, from "The French Lieutenant's Woman" to the ridiculous "A Man in Love," is that the anxieties of the modern actor usually pale in comparison to those of their more dramatic roles. Whatever went through the mind of the Hungarian poet as he marched to his death makes Ben's spats with his director seem insultingly small-time.

The film makers seem in utter earnest about "Forced March," but the peculiarly passionless result makes this more like forced viewing.

NEWSDAY, 11/3/89, Part III/p. 5, Terry Kelleher

Occasionally you'll be discussing a movie and someone will say an actor's performance got better as the picture went along. Cinema-wise person that you are, you immediately expose the fallacy in this observation, pointing out that feature films are routinely shot out of sequence.

Well, Chris Sarandon's work *does* become more convincing as "Forced March" progresses. That's just one of the reasons this American-Hungarian co-production makes a fascinating conversation piece.

Ben Kline (Sarandon), longtime star of a TV private-eye series, goes all the way from Beverly Hills to Budapest to stretch his acting muscles. He's to play the lead in a film about Miklos Radnoti, a real-life Jewish poet who was sent to a Nazi labor camp and ultimately murdered during World War II. The director, Walter Hardy (John Seitz), is openly skeptical of Ben's talent and commitment, but he knows his financing depends upon a big name at the head of the cast.

Walter rides Ben from the start, and indeed the star appears to be gliding on the surface of his role, more interested in pursuing an off-camera affair with Mira (Renee Soutendijk), the actress portraying his wife. When the story shifts to the labor camp, however, Ben identifies with Radnoti more and more—studying his life, reading his poetry, pondering his motivation. Spurning the comforts of the Budapest Hyatt, he spends his nights on the prison-camp set, holding talks between himself and his character. After a while, Sarandon makes both ends of the conversation sound surprisingly credible.

Director Rick King maintains a critical balance in the film-within-a-film structure, managing to avoid the sin of trivialization as he juxtaposes an actor's personal growth with a poet's struggle for physical and spiritual survival. While Ben discovers the difference between playing a hero and being one, the script by Charles Bardosh and Dick Atkins contrasts the "realism" of film with the reality of history, and notes that the former tends to supplant the latter in the public mind.

In fact, "Forced March" could stand to be more realistic. The writers must strain to contrive a pretext for Ben's father (Josef Sommer), a Hungarian refugee, to rush from the States to Budapest to satisfy the actor's curiosity about his mother's death. The character of the tough director is overdrawn and somewhat overacted. Next to Walter, Otto Preminger would look like a pussycat.

Nevertheless, "Forced March" is to be saluted for originality and ambition, and for allowing Sarandon to show he can stretch with the best of them.

VILLAGE VOICE, 11/7/89, p. 77, Elliott Stein

In Rick King's *Forced March*, Ben Kline (Chris Sarandon), a TV star of Hungarian-Jewish origin, jumps at a chance to cancel his current trivial but successful series in order to leave the fleshpots of Tinseltown and travel to Hungary. He has been offered the lead in a film about the life of a Hungarian-Jewish poet who was killed during a forced march from a concentration camp.

Ben soon becomes obsessed with the character he's portraying; he leaves the hotel where the company is billeted and takes to sleeping in the movie set of the camp barracks. He ruins a key sequence by fighting back against the actors playing Nazis, whereas the script calls for the poet to be shot in cold blood, unresisting. A number of scenes from this World War II movie-within-a-movie are abruptly intercut with shots of the contemporary framing story; these fleeting ambiguities come across as mere ham-handed attempts at style.

After the wrap of the war film (it looks dreadful, but *Forced March* is so muddled, it's hard to know if this is intentional), we get a last glimpse of Ben, pondering deep dish thoughts in his Beverly Hills swimming pool. He seems to have learned something—I wish I had. This is the most pointless and uninvolving movie about the Holocaust I've ever seen.

Also reviewed in:
NEW YORK TIMES, 11/3/89, p. C4, Vincent Canby
VARIETY, 10/4-10/89, p. 38

FOUR ADVENTURES OF REINETTE AND MIRABELLE

A New Yorker Films release of a C.E.R./Les Films Du Losange film. *Producer:* Eric Rohmer. *Director:* Eric Rohmer. *Screenplay (French with English subtitles):* Eric Rohmer. *Director of Photography:* Sophie Maintigneux. *Editor:* Maria-Luisa Garcia. *Music:* Ronan Girre and Jean-Louis Valero. *Sound:* Pierre Camus and Pascal Ribier. *Running time:* 95 minutes. *MPAA Rating:* Not Rated.

CAST: Joëlle Miquel (Reinette); Jessica Forde (Mirabelle); Philippe Laudenbach (The Waiter); Yasmine Haury (The Kleptomaniac); Marie Rivière (The Hustler); Beatrice Romand (The Inspector); Gérard Courant (The Inspector); David Rocksavage (The Tourist); Jacques Auffray (The Cadger); Haydée Caillot (The Charitable Lady); Fabrice Luchini (The Picture Dealer); Marie Bouteloup and Françoise Valier (Visitors).

CHRISTIAN SCIENCE MONITOR, 8/21/89, p. 11, David Sterritt

Movies by French director Eric Rohmer often arrive in the United States during the summer. It always feels right to see these films in the warm-weather season, because Rohmer's stories have a summery kind of atmosphere.

One of the best was actually called "Summer" when it opened on American screens, even though its original French title was "The Green Ray."

Rohmer hasn't always been so mellow. He first earned attention from American moviegoers with "My Night at Maud's," a highly intellectual film with characters who spent most of their time discussing philosophical questions—and that was part of a whole series called "Six Moral Tales," about people faced with ethical problems.

In recent years, though, Rohmer has been lightening up. His most recent series, "Comedies and Proverbs," was full of smart characters, yet it often had a winsome and amusing touch.

The new Rohmer romance, "Four Adventures of Reinette and Mirabelle," may be the lightest movie of his career. Although it's not as memorable as his best films, it has a lot of charm and a steady current of the intelligence that's his most important trademark.

The story is a kind of "city mouse and country mouse" fable. Mirabelle is a student in Paris. She's young and inexperienced, but she thinks she knows the secret of life: that you have to bend your principles to get along. Reinette is from the country. She arrives in the big city to study art, and she's also convinced that she understands how to prosper in the world—by knowing exactly what's right and what's wrong, and never bending an inch.

Their adventures are little ones, on the surface: They meet up with a rude waiter, a beggar, and other city characters, and have to decide how they'll respond to unfamiliar situations.

The movie's interest lies in what's going on *beneath* the surface—as both young women learn there's more to life, and to being a responsible adult, than they ever suspected.

We watch them struggle through their small dilemmas, and we watch their friendship grow deeper and more complex.

Rohmer began his filmmaking career as a member of the French "new wave" in the early 1960s. Although he was the most openly intellectual of these filmmakers, he has always had a special affection for young people, and a special talent for exploring their little problems of love and loneliness.

"Four Adventures of Reinette and Mirabelle" is one of his minor films. But as a summertime entertainment, it's as likable as can be.

LOS ANGELES TIMES, 8/11/89, Calendar/p. 15, Kevin Thomas

The art of Eric Rohmer is that of inviting us to perceive the universe in a conversation between two people. For more than 25 years, the French writer-director has made films in which people mainly sit around and talk, yet as we listen to their everyday conversations we discover all manner of cosmic implication. This occurs not merely because of what is being said but because we have been beguiled by his people.

Nearly 70, Rohmer seems as never before to be commenting on his own role as a moralist with a passion for language—and finding great good humor in his artist's presumption. The human comedy, vast category that it is, has always been his subject, and even though he remains as detached as ever, he seems to be acknowledging that he too must surely have his own foibles. His delightful "Four Adventures of Reinette and Mirabelle" suggests that as there are limitations in language, there may be blind spots in the vision of even the most Olympian of moralists.

Typically, he provokes such heavy-duty thoughts in the simplest and slightest of circumstances. In his film's first "adventure," Mirabelle (Jessica Forde), an ethnology major at the Sorbonne, is bicycling in the countryside when she has a flat tire near the gate of a lovely old farm, long in the family of Reinette (Joëlle Miquel).

These young women are adorable and beautiful in different ways. (Don't bother looking for unattractive or unfashionable people in a Rohmer film.) The demure Reinette, who has long dark hair, is an aspiring painter who likes to place Degas-like ballet dancers in a Dali-esque dream world. (Later on, she will amusingly deny any such influences, in Rohmer's wicked send-up of art criticism). She is most eager to share with the patrician, sophisticated Mirabelle *l'heure bleu*, that "blue hour" just before dawn breaks when the world is completely silent (as long as there's no truck rumbling by on a nearby highway).

In what is essentially a prologue, Rohmer digresses, risking tedium with Reinette's love-of-nature sentiments as the two take their time becoming acquainted. The film gets in gear once Mirabelle offers to share her apartment with Reinette, who will soon be going to Paris to study art. The film's next three "adventures" are vignettes devised to make us aware that virtually everything we do involves a moral choice. Yet there's nothing of the Sunday-school lesson about them; they are as witty and amusing as they are reflective.

In the second adventure, Reinette encounters what everyone who has ever gone to Paris experiences: the ineluctable, stern rudeness of the true Parisian. It occurs when she sits at an outdoor table at a cafe and orders a coffee with nothing smaller than a 200-franc note to pay for it. Philippe Laudenbach is hilarious as her outraged waiter, yet the incident ends in such a way to allow us to realize how consciously Reinette is concerned with the morality of her every action, something that has never occurred to Mirabelle.

The establishing of this fundamental difference between the two young women leads deftly to the next and most complex sequence, in which they are confronted with a beggar, a shoplifter and a woman (the last played exquisitely by Marie Rivière, the star of the key French-Canadian film "Good Riddance") whose begging seems to be a con. This is the heart of the film, in which Rohmer seems to be challenging his own assumptions as well as ours and those of his heroines. This "adventure's" talkiness sets up perfectly the concluding sequence. It's too inspired and funny to be revealed here, but it involves Reinette's declaration of her wariness of words, only to be reminded by Mirabelle of her garrulousness and her tendency to continue explaining things to people long after they've understood them. (You may wince here in self-recognition).

Except for No. 3, each of the four episodes proceeds as the blithest of sketches, as Rohmer has long learned how to direct with grace and even, when appropriate, with dispatch, despite all the talk. Amazingly, Rohmer has said that he let his young stars improvise; for all its spontaneity, his film has not a self-conscious or awkward moment. Rohmer has said his films belong to the "cinema of thought rather than action" and that he tells stories "which deal less with what people do than with what is going on in their minds while they're doing it." There could be no better description of "Four Adventures of Reinette and Mirabelle" (Times-rated Mature for complex themes).

MONTHLY FILM BULLETIN, 2/88, p. 49, Tom Milne

L'HEURE BLEUE/THE BLUE HOUR: Mirabelle, a Parisian student on holiday with her parents, encounters Reinette, a country girl living in a derelict barn who persuades her to stay overnight so that she can witness "The Blue Hour"—a moment of absolute silence at dawn as nocturnal sounds give way to those of day. At dawn, Reinette wakes a sleepy Mirabelle, but the moment is ruined by a noisy tractor. Mirabelle decides to stay another day, this time getting up herself, followed by a reluctant Reinette, and successfully experiencing "The Blue Hour".

Reinette, a self-taught painter anxious to study in Paris, accepts Mirabelle's offer to share her flat. LE GARCON DE CAFE/THE WAITER: Now installed in Mirabelle's flat, Reinette arrives first at a rendezvous in a Montparnasse café. Offering to pay for her 4.50 franc coffee with a 200 franc note, Reinette is subjected to a tirade of abuse by the waiter, who argues that the customer should have the right money, that she has lingered all day over one coffee, and that she is trying to bilk him. When the tirade intensifies as Mirabelle arrives and proves to have no change either, Mirabelle persuades Reinette to slip away without paying. But annoyed because she has seemingly confirmed the waiter's suspicions, Reinette returns the following day, leaving the money—since the waiter is off-duty—with a replacement who is amazed that she bothered. LE MENDIANT, LA CLEPTOMANE, L'ARNAQUEUSE/THE BEGGAR, THE KLEPTOMANIAC, THE HUSTLER: Refusing to follow suit when Reinette gives money to a beggar, Mirabelle explains that she didn't like the look of him; Reinette says she always gives what she can afford. In a supermarket, Mirabelle spots two detectives eyeing an obviously wealthy woman who is shoplifting. She saves the woman from arrest by surreptitiously appropriating the bag of stolen goods at the checkout counter, only to see the baffled woman drive away before she can return the bag. Delighted to think that Mirabelle remembered her birthday (the bag includes champagne and salmon), Reinette is indignant when Mirabelle explains about saving the woman from jail, taxing her with confirming the woman in her wrong-doing. Later, at a railway station, Reinette misses her train while giving money to a tearful woman who says her purse was stolen, leaving her unable to get home. Exasperated when her efforts to acquire change for the telephone result only in the loss of her last coin to a beggar, Reinette intervenes on overhearing the tearful woman spinning the same yarn to another woman. Angrily, Reinette demands her money back, but when the tearful woman spins a persuasive new yarn about being turned out of house and home, settles for the franc she needs for the telephone. LA VENTE DU TABLEAU/SELLING THE PICTURE: Short of money for the rent, Reinette contacts a friend who knows a gallery owner interested in her work. Meanwhile, chattering volubly as usual despite her insistence that words cheat while painting lets the heart talk, Reinette is stung by Mirabelle's amusement into making a twenty-four-hour vow of silence, during which she is summoned to the art gallery. With Reinette intriguing the dealer by her enigmatic silence, then Mirabelle working on his conscience by explaining that she is a deaf-mute, he is pushed into paying in advance the entire 1,000 francs due on an agreed price of 2,000 francs. After they leave triumphantly and two customers show an interest in the painting, the dealer announces its price as 4,000 francs.

A film of great delicacy and charm, but distinctly fragile by comparison with the best of Rohmer, 4 aventures de Reinette & Mirabelle is exactly what it seems: an interlude in the mainstream of his development. Improvised on the basis of anecdotes of personal experience told to Rohmer by Joëlle Miquel, it was largely filmed—apparently for Rohmer's own pleasure— during an enforced interval while he was waiting to shoot the final sequence for La Rayon vert. Very obviously made for peanuts, it occasionally betrays—probably for reasons of economy—a lack of Rohmer's usual formal ambition. Compared to the mysterious enchantment of the moment when the Green Ray finally puts in its appearance at the end of La Rayon Vert, for instance, the analogous phenomenon of the Blue Hour is rendered with a casual offhandedness which is a trifle—if not exactly anti-climatic, at least not exactly magical.

In compensation, as it were, the terms of the production seem to have enabled Rohmer to recapture the spirit of his own youth, so that 4 aventures de Reinette & Mirabelle, with its airy delight in the flora and fauna and quirky fringes of the Latin Quarter, seems almost like a throwback to the Nouvelle Vague revolution. Here, lathering himself into a state of wayward emotional frenzy exactly like the Belmondo of Charlotte et son Jules, is the reductio ad absurdum of all Parisian waiters verbalising a lifetime of frustrations into a moment of devastatingly logical illogicality; here, too, the amused tolerance in observing youth's high-handed way with moral imperatives, the delight in throwaway jokes (note the way Reinette, having broken her own rule in refusing a beggar, gets her comeuppance when she inadvertently approaches the same man in quest of change and he simply annexes her last coin), of the characteristic little mortes saisons in which nothing happens but which are a joy to watch (like the one in which, as if we didn't know, Reinette solemnly demonstrates the method to be used in mending a punctured bicycle tyre).

If it is amazing that Rohmer, well into his sixties, should have made a film that could easily pass for a first feature by a highly promising twenty-year-old, it is equally amazing that he should also have contrived to underpin it with his usual complex, if largely subterranean, moral basis. Essentially, Rohmer is here retelling the story of the town mouse and the country cousin, with

Mirabelle applying the pragmatic view of the sophisticate to life's little problems, while Reinette tries to live by the absolutes that rule her more limited horizons. Kleptomania is a vice, says Reinettte, insisting that the woman in the supermarket deserved to go to jail; no, it's a sickness, the more enlightened Mirabelle insists. That this town/country opposition is not an exact reflection of the nature of experience of the two girls is made clear from the outset, partly by a sequence in which Reinette takes Mirabelle on a guided tour of the countryside (including a visit to an ancient and obviously real-life farmer who poses as self-consciously yet as enchantingly for the camera as any African tribesman in a Frank Buck adventure), during which it becomes evident that Mirabelle is much more at home in the rural wilds than Reinette; and partly by the fact that Reinette's surrealist-styled paintings, featuring one which equates a woman's semi-unveiled posterior with the rising sun, testify to far more sophistication than Mirabelle possesses.

Mirabelle, in other words, *accommodates* herself to the world, rejecting authority, principles or preconceptions where they demonstrably fail to match the demands of humanity or necessity. Their adventures sketch the process whereby Reinette makes slow progress along the same road towards a healthy disabusement. Her gleeful (if tacit) role in conning the picture dealer at the end of the film would, by her own earlier judgment, have testified to a criminal absence of moral self-discipline; but already as much of a free-thinker as Mirabelle in an immoral world where the picture dealer effortlessly out-cons her con, she is soon, one senses, likely to outstrip her mentor. But to analyse the film in such terms is to place a weight upon it that was hardly intended. Made purely for pleasure, perfectly cast and directed with the sureness of touch of Rohmer at his best, it should simply be accepted and gratefully enjoyed.

NEW STATESMAN, 2/5/89, p. 25, Judith Williamson

The images were there as new—innocent and shy and strong. The line is Godard's from *Lear*: but it applies almost perfectly to the latest release from another old-New-Wave director, Rohmer, whose *4 Adventures of Reinette & Mirabelle* recently opened. It is fascinating to compare the work of these two old colleagues, both exponents of a kind of filmmaking that fits badly with the present climate: Godard goes on going on about what he does, Rohmer goes on doing what he does, until you feel that his constant refining of his particular style is itself a kind of resistance. There are other comparisons to be made, not least in the relation of these now middle-aged male directors to young women: Godard's increasing, infuriating voyeurism contrasts strongly with Rohmer's evident, and most unusual, liking and respect for them. He seems able to grasp physicality—a crumpled nightdress, sleep—precisely without sexualising it, in the same way that he produces a heightened sense of light and colour, movement and sound, the rhythms of speech and the nuances of expression. Sometimes, as in *The Blue Hour*—the first story—the grain of the film itself, pushed to the limit in night light, seems part of that magnifying glass Rohmer holds against the daily world to show the texture of life as one experiences it when young—at once expanded and intensified.

If Rohmer's imagery here is as luminous and tactile as ever—sunlight on fabrics, thunder in the sky seem almost tangible in a way that makes his use of film far from transparent—his social eye and moral questioning are also at their funniest—and most forgiving. This "light" and incredibly low-budget film takes in issues like begging, stealing, lying, art dealing—and, as so often, indulgently lets one of its excellent heroines talk for ages and ages about silence. All this has its own gentle bearing on filmkmaking: but Rohmer does, as Godard says, "Show, not tell".

NEW YORK, 8/14/89, p. 80, David Denby

In his *Four Adventures of Reinette and Mirabelle*, Eric Rohmer, chewing on smaller and smaller anecdotes, matches up a worldly, relaxed young Parisienne with a stiff, high-principled country girl who is naïve yet full of theories. The movie has characteristic moments of charm and even revelation, but Joëlle Miquel, who plays the country girl, is so awkward that I found it hard to look at her.

NEW YORK POST, 7/21/89, p. 27, Jami Bernard

Nothing much going on in "Four Adventures of Reinette and Mirabelle," but this Eric Rohmer bagatelle about two Paris roommates making minor ethnical choices is a lazy, amusing pleasure.

Reinette and Mirabelle are an unlikely match as friends. Reinette is a deceptively simple country girl who makes paintings of twisted female nudes with their derrieres prominently on display, working out of the barn loft she calls home. She is fiercely proud of her girlish connection to nature and wants to share it with the self-contained Parisienne whose bicycle gives out on a nearby road.

Mirabelle, the bicyclist, is studying something *tres chic* at school (ethnology), and is intrigued by nature in the way that city folks have when on a bus tour that passes by some cows. (Where do the cows go during the day?'' she asks a local farmer without embarrassment.) She also learns firsthand where salad comes from.

The two meet in the first segment, when Reinette cheerfully repairs Mirabelle's bicycle tire with the childish absorption she brings to everything she does. Mirabelle accepts an invitation for a sleep-over. The girls get up early to catch the "blue hour," nature's quiet time between night and dawn; the experience is such a bonding one that Mirabelle invites Reinette to be her roommate in Paris when she comes to study art.

The next three segments take place in Paris. There is no reciprocation here—Mirabelle does not teach her country cousin the ins and outs of the *metro* or anything like that. These vignettes are studies in ethics (and how dopey people are when they try to formulate a stand on them) as the pals are challenged by a succession of beggars, surly waiters and con artists.

Not only do they spare some change or not spare some change, they also drone on about it.

Our country girl turns out to be obtusely, grandly naive, a rigid, bossy moralizer and a petty chatterbox whose charm would wear thin if not for the fact that clear-eyed Mirabelle seems to take it in stride.

The final section is the funniest. Reinette finally agrees to shut up for a day even though this is the day that a gallery owner may buy a painting from her. Plus, silence scares her, as she already made clear during the "blue hour."

Although similar to Rohmer's "Comedies and Proverbs" series, this movie is not meant to be part of it. Both characters do go on, and it's interesting how intimately you get to know them through this technique. Joelle Miquel is convincing as the self-deluded artist, wearing a stupid, defensive smile whenever challenged. And Jessica Forde as Mirabelle starts out aloof and gradually, as the on-screen friendship progresses, gives the audience more, too.

The early friendship, by the way, is the kind that men imagine women have (or would like us to have): a slightly eroticized, oblivious playfulness in Barbie doll clothes. I don't remember Barbie and Tressie ever chattering this much, though.

NEWSDAY, 7/21/89, Part III/p. 3, Mike McGrady

Eric Rohmer movies, like the taste of caviar, take some getting used to. But there are ways to prepare for the singular experience of watching a Rohmer movie, steps one can take before actually attempting to acquire the taste.

Begin by reading the complete works of Marcel Proust. Start your own stamp collection. Take a course in the art of tying flies, then learn to cast them out onto slow-flowing streams. Carve delicate cameos in ivory, take up three-cushion billiards, visit nursing homes and record the recollections of the elderly.

When you've learned patience and have acquired the ability to appreciate life's more fragile beauties, begin with the film that first brought Rohmer to international attention, "My Night at Maud's." Move on to "Claire's Knee" and "Pauline at the Beach." And in due time, when a new Rohmer movie opens—say, "Four Adventures of Reinette and Mirabelle"—you may discover that not only is Rohmer an acquired taste, he can become an addiction.

In many ways, "Four Adventures" is typical Rohmer. There's no standard storyline, no conflict, no resolution. Instead of story, there is situation: A freewheeling young city woman meets a slightly rigid country woman and the two share an apartment in Paris. They also share involvement in several incidents and a few lengthy discussions.

Where then is the payoff? With Rohmer, the rewards are never the expected ones. The virtue is not in the story itself so much as in the way it is told. Rohmer is a miniaturist, and he works with ordinary people in mundane situations. You come to know the people not through any external events but through their own behavior and conversation. It is, in Rohmer's apt phrase, a cinema of thoughts rather than of actions.

When you have people being themselves, of course, you also have comedy. Each of the film's four segments—anecdotes, really—offers an abundance of ironic humor.

The final incident, "Selling the Picture," begins when the city girl, Mirabelle (Jessica Forde), complains that the country girl, Reinette (Joëlle Miquel), talks too much and, worse, tends to be repetitive. Reinette vows to remain quiet for one full day. Unfortunately, the chosen day turns out to be the day she is scheduled to negotiate the sale of one of her paintings to a prestigious art dealer. How can she possibly do this without uttering a single word?

Rather simply, as it turns out. The art dealer is so completely taken with himself, so self-important, so anxious to dispense esoteric nuggets of nonsense, that he scarcely notices the artist's silence. For long moments he delves deeper and deeper into his own fatuousness while Reinette's silence causes the price of her painting to skyrocket. Perhaps Rohmer is having a bit of sly fun with the entire critical fraternity here, with all of us who bend over backward trying to explain something as inexplicable as the impact of art.

So let me say no more about "Four Adventures..." Anyone who has developed the Rohmer habit will need no encouragement. And those who haven't yet acquired the taste—well, no need to just plunge in cold. Prepare yourself first. Piece together a patchwork quilt, listen to recordings of Shakespearean plays, take up diagramless crossword puzzles, crochet an afghan. Full appreciation of a Rohmer movie, like so many good things, takes a bit of time.

SIGHT & SOUND, Summer 1988, p. 210, Tom Milne

[4 *Adventures of Reinette and Mirabelle* was reviewed jointly with *L'Ami de mon amie*; see Milne's review in *Film Review Annual, 1989.*]

VILLAGE VOICE, 7/25/89, p. 65, J. Hoberman

Although each new Eric Rohmer films feels slighter than the last, one of the lessons you learn from this former schoolteacher is to be grateful for small pleasures. Ever since an American art movie distributor chose to forgo the New York Film Festival and release *Pauline on the Beach* in the depths of August, the annual Rohmer has become as much a part of summer as the latest *Star Trek* or *Karate Kid*—a modest ritual that, even if you partake of it on the Upper West Side, is pleasantly redolent of sandy hair, sun-sizzled skin, and a white-wine buzz.

Rohmer's somewhat delayed *Four Adventures of Reinette and Mirabelle*, opening Friday at the Lincoln Plaza, is a lowbudget effort produced in 1986 during a hiatus on the production of *Summer*. The film is thus a vacation within a vacation, featuring a pair of neophyte ingenues improvising to save their lives. The meetcute is simple: Bicycling deep in the verdant French countryside, city mouse Mirabelle (Jessica Forde) gets a punctured tire. The rustic Reinette (Joëlle Miquel) ambles by in time to fix it. Squarefaced and rawboned, Reinette lives in an abandoned barn . The sleek and snooty Mirabelle studies ethnography in Paris. "You have a cute place," she tells Reinette, who promptly invites her to stay.

The two girls make conversation, taking their meals alfresco and grooving on nature. Meanwhile, the film idles by, inviting you to vegetate along with the action. Rohmer flirts with self-parody, orchestrating an elaborate tilt to honor a century-old pear tree and including a rainstorm, despite an old peasant's grave assurances of fair weather. Indeed, part of the film seems a petulant riff on his other movie-in-progress. In their first adventure, Reinette and Mirabelle awake before dawn to partake of the "Blue Hour," the minute of silence that separates the sounds of the night from those of the day. Less magical than the appearance of the Green Ray that climaxes *Summer*, the moment is absurdly disrupted by a sputtering tractor. Reinette is no less shattered, and, to make her stop crying, Mirabelle offers to remain another day.

By now it's clear that, despite her schoolgirl getup, Reinette is something other than a provincial Ms. Natural. (Ultimately, she will emerge as far more rigid than her new, only apparently brittle, friend.) Although not exactly clever, the movie is full of quotidian mysteries. Like, where did Mirabelle get the change of clothes, too chic to belong to Reinette? And how did Reinette learn to dance so well when she claims to have never been off the farm? The best gag by far, however, is making Reinette an amateur painter of dreamily masochistic, comic-strip nudes, contorted like mandalas around their plump derrieres. "I like it, it's the prettiest part of a woman—so soft, so round. That's why I put it in the center," the artist explains to Mirabelle (who confuses her by pronouncing the paintings "surreal").

Learning that Reinette hopes to study art, Mirabelle invites her to share a Paris apartment. We're all understandably curious to see how this nature girl handles metropolitan life, but Rohmer is somewhat less ambitious. The heart of the movie is a series of vintage New Wave digressions ranging from encounters with urban types (a paranoid, a waiter, an elegant shoplifter, an assortment of panhandlers) to long-winded anecdotes retailed by the principal actresses. Although Rohmer's handheld camera gets jostled in the crowd, Reinette's adjustment is flawless—or nearly so. The country fades as quickly as last night's dream, while the city becomes a kind of ethical proving ground. *Four adventures* is not one of Rohmer's "Comedies and Proverbs," but it has a similarly moralizing tone. As casual as the movie's interactions are, they all raise issues of charity and honesty and situational ethics.

As relentlessly self-explanatory as only a Rohmer heroine can be, Reinette chatters on about her painting so compulsively that she is ultimately challenged by Mirabelle not to speak—thus bringing the movie full circle back to the notion of the Blue Hour. Only now, nature has given way to civilization. In the last adventure, Reinette poses as a deaf-mute, hoping to sell her paintings to a chic gallery. Her miming notwithstanding, the scene becomes a solo for the gallery owner, played by Rohmer's master fatuist, Fabrice Luchini: "These are close to mature male fantasies," he exclaims in wonder, examining one of Reinette's pastel *Metal Hurlant* knockoffs.

Is the gallery owner speaking for the director? Rohmer loves these girls. He deploys them like paper dolls—changing their outfits, stage-managing their meetings, organizing their spats. Given this overdetermination, what's truly extraordinary is how fresh their adventures seem to be. *Reinette and Mirabelle* isn't slight, it has the callowness of youth. Indeed, the underlying fifth adventure is the movie's prolonged balancing act, teetering as it does on a knife edge between contrivance and spontaneity.

Also reviewed in:
NEW REPUBLIC, 8/28/89, p. 26, Stanley Kauffmann
NEW YORK TIMES, 7/21/89, p. C10, Caryn James
VARIETY, 4/1/89, p. 14
WASHINGTON POST, 8/25/89, p. D7, Rita Kempley

FOXTROT

A Viking Film/Filmeffekt presentation of a Frost Film production. *Executive Producer:* Dag Alveberg. *Producer:* Hlynur Oskarsson. *Director:* Jon Tryggvason. *Screenplay (Icelandic with English subtitles):* Svienbjorn I. Baldvinsson. Director of Photography: Karl Oskarsson. *Editor:* Russel Lloyd. *Music:* Erik Gunvaldsen and Stein B. Svendsen. *Sound:* Gunnar Hermannsson. *Production Designer:* Geir Ottarr. *Running time:* 97 minutes. *MPAA Rating:* Not Rated.

CAST: Steinarr Olafsson (Tommy); Valdimar Flygenring (Kiddy); Maria Ellingsen (Lisa).

VILLAGE VOICE, 3/28/89, p. 64, Katherine Dieckmann

Using the road trip as stage set for sibling rivalry and bonding, like some embittered *Rain Man*, Jon Tryggvason's *Foxtrot* tracks two brothers, the elder a hard-assed soccer star, the younger an impressionable wanna-be, as they haul goods across a forbidding Icelandic landscape. When a ripe blond girl hops on board and drives a wedge between the already troubled twosome, the violence ticking at the edges of the story erupts. Tryggvason handles the brutality smoothly, but there's too much of it. And wouldn't an enterprising production lose the moody electronic music and have the Sugarcubes singing "Motorcrash"?

Also reviewed in:
NEW YORK TIMES, 3/28/89, p. C20 Janet Maslin
VARIETY, 5/25/88, p. 23

FRIDAY THE 13th PART VIII— JASON TAKES MANHATTAN

A Paramount Pictures release. *Producer:* Randolph Cheveldave. *Director:* Rob Hedden. *Screenplay:* Rob Hedden. *Director of Photography:* Bryan England. *Editor:* Steve Mirkovich. *Music:* Fred Mollin. *Production Designer:* David Fischer. *Special Effects:* Martin Becker. *Special Effects Make-up:* Jamie Brown. *Costumes:* Carle Hetland. *Stunt Coordinator:* Ken Kirzinger. *Running time:* 100 minutes. *MPAA Rating:* R.

CAST: Jenson Daggett (Rennie Wickham); Scott Reeves (Sean Robertson); Peter Mark Richman (Charles McCulloch); Barbara Bingham (Colleen Van Deusen); V.C. Dupree (Julius Gaw); Kane Hodder (Jason); Sharlene Martin (Tamara Mason); Kelly Hu (Eva Watanabe); Martin Cummins (Wayne Webber); Gordon Currie (Miles Wolfe); Warren Munson (Admiral Robertson); Saffron Henderson (J.J.); Todd Shaffer (Jim); Tiffany Paulsen (Suzy).

LOS ANGELES TIMES, 7/31/89, Calendar/p. 4, Chris Willman

Picture this imaginary (but not unlikely) scenario: It's late 1988 and an early planning meeting is under way for the inevitable "Friday the 13th Part VIII." A production executive outlines the obvious: "So we figure out another hokey way to resurrect Jason from the briny, then he kills a dozen and a half campers at Crystal Lake, then the last surviving bimbette kills him again. We shoot sheap in Canada and recoup the first weekend. Miss Smith, could you please find some soulless TV hack to write and direct, and we'll see you all in the spring. Morton's, anyone?"

Suddenly the clouds part as some brave soul in the back of the room—a mail-room boy with auteur aspirations, perhaps—timidly raises his hand and squeaks out: "Sir, what if we had Jason slaughter teen-agers somewhere besides Crystal Lake this time?" He is, of course, immediately fired for gross insolence but later, a higher-up arrives at the same ingenious epiphany: Perhaps the eighth installment isn't too soon to throw the slightest of wrinkles into a largely plotless series? Talk about high concept, dude: Jason takes a road trip!

Whatever its creative genesis, we now have the would-be departure from formula that is "Friday the 13th Part VIII—Jason Takes Manhattan." Funny ad campaign; a real dunghill of a major motion picture. To begin with the very least of complaints, they went ahead and shot the bleedin' thing in Canada anyway. It takes the plot a full hour just to get Jason and his victims away from camp and sea and onto the title island, and even then, except for a few fleeting scenes set in Times Square, It's all too obviously set-bound. Try singing "Vancouver, B.C." to the tune of "New York, New York": It just doesn't work.

This time, our ripe-for-the-maiming Crystal Lake teens are on a senior cruise to Manhattan; only a few of them make it even that far, as this is mostly a slasher-on-board sea snooze. Once the survivors finally reach dry land, Jason—who by this time has spent so much time underwater that he's a dead ringer for Swamp Thing—lurches after them and does his share to carve up the Big Apple.

Satirical potential is rife, to be sure, in the idea of Jason coming to the biggest of big cities, only to have his mere homicidal monstrousness dwarfed by the real-life horrors of drugs, rape, homelessness, disease, despair and all-around urban decay, all of it unrealized in a script as witless and willfully imbecile as any of the preceding seven.

And there can be no suspense when—as usual—Jason goes after whomever he goes after, usually quickly, until the last couple of survivors. Not that this urgency means there aren't still a few lingering shots of cowering femmes screaming as the invincible stalker takes his time going for the final kill. Whether you're a callow teen coke fiend or a courageous athlete, you die violently anyway, so why bother being virtuous, kids? Given the degree of slow-mo sadism on view, whether this was made by sick minds or for sick minds is a distinction that finally matters little.

Rob Hedden wrote and directed this, his first feature; there's no reason here to look forward to his second. Meanwhile, since it seems like just about anyone who's taken a film school class or two can get a shot at doing one of these, we'd like to take this opportunity to pitch the only possible palatable scenario for another sequel. It's a little treatment we like to call "Friday 13th Part IX: Jason Disembowels Bill and Ted," to be shot on location, of course, in the Great White North. Morton's, anyone?

NEW YORK POST, 7/29/89, p. 17, Jami Bernard

The folks who were upset about the movie poster that showed maniac killer Jason slashing an "I Love New York" logo can breathe easy—Jason doesn't get anywhere near the city.

Despite the title, Jason doesn't "take" Manhattan in "Friday the 13th Part VIII" until two-thirds of the way through, and then he makes a wrong turn and takes Vancouver instead, where a not very convincing looking Manhattan was staged for the film.

Before that, the killer in the hockey mask spends most of his time slicing and dicing aboard a cruise ship loaded with recent high school graduates, knocking them off in descending order with the naughtiest going first.

Seven sequels ago, Jason drowned unceremoniously at summer camp, and he's been fabulously cranky ever since, reappearing at the box office every now and again to kill teens according to the prime directive of slasher movies: Those engaging in drugs and promiscuous sex must die.

The grads are cruising to Manhattan for a night of fun: There's an athlete, a science honors student, a prom queen, a camcorder nerd, the spineless but cute son of the captain, a girl trying to get over her fear of drowning, an up-tight chaperone who already looks like he's embalmed and a few assorted others. No time for character development; let the hacking begin!

The first guy who dies gets his innards ripped out. A naked girl gets a trident in the chest. A would-be rocker is beaten to death with an electric guitar. A molten rock is buried in a guy's stomach as he takes a sauna. A sexpot gets it with a shard of mirror. The first-mate is harpooned, someone's throat is slit, the honors student takes one too many turns around the disco, there's an electrocution and several ax murders. Someone dies in the ship's crow's-nest. Jason punches a guy's head clear off and over a rooftop.

There's more, although flooding out some leftover kids is a gyp and ruined my death count, since I assumed they'd stick around long enough to be picked off one by one.

The count as it stands is 17 dead, plus whoever was in the flood. So let's just say for argument's sake it's 22.

Problem is, they come so fast and furious (appoximately every four minutes, like the IRT at rush hour), the killings seem less scary than perfunctory. Jason himself looks a little bushed, standing there in the mist surveying his next victim with a worldweary sigh. A maniac slasher's work is never done.

By the time the few survivors row ashore to a Vancouver-ized Manhattan (the trash in the alleys largely consists of paper confetti, as if a big prom party just let out), there are very few weapons left in the Jason arsenal to surprise us.

Seeing as how if you walk 10 minuites in any direction in Manhattan you'd be bound to come upon some form of civilization, however primitive, it's odd that the survivors keep running around some kind of wharf district where toxic waste is stored in open vats and the occasional passing cop has a distinct Canadian accent, eh?

"I think it will be more productive if we split up," says the stiff of a chaperone, his suit hardly wrinkled, as one of the group is dragged off to be shot up with drugs and raped, probably a Vancouver high school senior's conception of a typical night in New York. The set designer, by the way, has seemingly never visited our fair city. The subway graffiti is a very lovely pink design, outlined in black, and seems to say something in French. Watch out for the third rail, Jason!

The Rasputin-descended Jason gets kicked around a little—he staggers once or twice—and he finally treats us to a glimpse of what's under the hockey mask. It's...why, it's...SOMETHING FROM THE SPECIAL EFFECTS DEPARTMENT!

Oh, now I've gone and spoiled it for you. But no more so than Jason has spoiled it for all of us. The hockey-mask in the mist used to scare me to pieces, but now Jason's just a big lug with an ax to grind in this, his eighth rampage. The movie isn't even opening on a Friday the 13th; even the marketing department has abandoned Jason (although the production notes are printed in red ink).

We know he'll be back, like the swallows to Capistrano, but Jason, if you're listening , please believe me: VIII is enough.

NEWSDAY, 7/29/89, Part II/p. 15, Terry Kelleher

You may have read that Vincent Tese, our fair state's director of economic development, cried foul over Paramount Pictures' advertising for "Friday the 13th Part VIII—Jason Takes Manhattan." Transit ads and theater lobby displays have shown Jason, the superhuman slayer in the hockey mask, slashing through an I ♥ New York poster.

Don't sweat the trademark abuse, Vince. It's the consumer protection boys who ought to come down on Paramount.

The title's a snare. "Take" Manhattan? Jason doesn't even reach the isle of joy until the movie's more than an hour old.

The commercials are a scam. "Part VIII" is nearly over before it delivers the scenes used in the TV spots. You saw Jason scare the bejabbers out of those New York street punks and you thought this might be a horror variation on "Crocodile Dundee"? In fact, "Part VIII" offers only a smidgen of humor—about half a star's worth if you're scoring.

When the story opens, Jason lies dead as usual at the bottom of Crystal Lake. In a few minutes, he climbs onto a pleasure boat and surprises two teenagers trying to have sex. As "Friday the 13th" fans know, nobody interrupts coitus quite like Jason.

Next, Jason boards a ship bearing the Crystal Lake High School senior class on a graduation cruise to New York. And guess what? Somebody says, "There's a big storm predicted for tonight."

'Tis a dark and stormy night, indeed, and among Jason's victims are: the class bitch, the Joan Jett wanna-be, the "dweeb" with film-making aspirations, the pretty science scholar—in fact, the whole passenger list except the sensitive girl with a deathly fear of water (Jensen Daggett), the stuffed-shirt teacher who's her legal guardian (Peter Mark Richman), her boyfriend (Scott Reeves), her kindly English teacher (Barbara Bingham) and her dog.

The survivors wind up in a rowboat bound for The Apple, which was neatly depicted in the opening credit sequence as the vermin capital of the universe. Jason, apparently, swims to the city. In this blood-drenched movie's most distasteful scene—and that's saying something—Jason kills a mugger who's about to rape little Miss Sensitive. Why so distasteful? Because he'd really rather kill her himself.

Since Jason's basically indestructible (when it appears otherwise, he's only playing possum), the ending leaves open the possibility that he'll be around town long enough for a Grayline tour before he starts scouting locations for "Part IX." How about "New Jersey and Jason: Perfect Together"?

Also reviewed in:
NEW YORK TIMES, 7/29/89, p. 12, Caryn James
VARIETY, 8/2-8/89, p. 20
WASHINGTON POST, 7/29/89, p. C9, Richard Harrington

FUNNY

An Original Cinema release of an Associates and Ferren production. *Producer:* Bran Ferren. *Director:* Bran Ferren. *Director of Photography:* Bran Ferren. *Running time:* 81 minutes. *MPAA Rating:* Not Rated.

LOS ANGELES TIMES, 9/22/89, Calendar/p. 2, Chris Willman

Did you hear the one about the wanna-be director who made his first film simply by setting up his camera and inviting hundreds of wanna-be gagsters to tell the funniest joke they'd ever heard? And how the resulting talking-heads filmic funfest turned out to be, in the words of that great comic pundit Pee-wee Herman, so funny we forgot to laugh?

No? It's no joke.

In directing "Funny—The Movie," Bran Ferren took the lazy and/or underfunded man's approach to debut film making and shot roughly 2,000 actors, students, bartenders show-biz types and other jes' plain folks spilling quips. About 100 made the intermittently amusing, often dull, listlessly long final cut; there doesn't appear to be a Robert Benchley *or* a Henny Youngman in the bunch.

Well, just one Henny Youngman (the real one). He's one of several actual comedians who ply their professional wares for the camera. Most of the crop, though, are amateurs who force some of the same puns usually perpetrated at coffee breaks, the local tavern or lulls in family reunions. We get long stories about Jesus and Moses playing golf that lead to impossibly anticlimactic punch lines; lovingly related racial slurs ("What do you get when you cross a Jewish-American princess with a hooker?"; "Did you hear about the new black-Jewish temple?"), down-and-dirty sex talk (told mostly by women), your basic cruelty-to-animal jokes. Rim shots 'n' all.

Ferren, who sets the tone for the film with a lowbrow spoken intro, has taken the onus of tastelessness off himself and put it onto his subjects by claiming that "Funny" is not about what's funny but what people think is funny. If so, the thesis of his picture—an unwitting one, no doubt—is that intellectual humor is pushing up daisies in America.

That warning stated, most viewers will probably find at least a few guffaws among the groaners.

Your subjective reviewer chuckled out loud two or three times and smiled inwardly another dozen or so, winced frequently at some of the older and oft-heard offenders but never laughed so hard he fell of his dinosaur.

"Funny—The Movie" (Times-rated Mature) will probably work better as "Funny—The Home Video Rental," where partying chortle-seekers can take in its 83 minutes in segments, punctuated by beer runs and recitations from Playboy's Party Jokes.

NEW YORK POST, 6/28/89, p. 24, Jami Bernard

Despite its title, "Funny" isn't very , and that's a real drawback for a movie that purports to be an anthology of jokes.

In fact, "Funny" just goes to prove what we all suspected—that most Americans' idea of humor is sexist, racist, coarse and about as subtle as a car chase. Then again, Americans like car chases, so there you go.

This odd movie is a collection of 120 celebrities and just-folks in blackout vignettes telling the funniest joke or story they've ever heard. Some are seated nervously on a stool under hot lights, as if posing for a high school graduation picture. Others are captured in more natural settings—on the roof of a hotel, in the back yard of a summer house. Eli Wallach and Anne Jackson are sitting at their dining room table; Alan King sits behind a grand polished desk as if he's in the Oval Office.

"Funny" proves that few people can tell a joke well. Most of them shamble about, embarrassed. Or pull their punch lines, or tangle them. Even the most secure often preface a joke with self-defeating apologies. Go ahead, try to think of someone you know who is truly funny and ask yourself this: Is Joe really funny, or is it just that I belong to the same lodge?

And so "Funny" gives us a fair share of self-inflated jerks who think the longer they draw out a story, the better the punch line—along with an assortment of pleasant, unprepossessing folks who release their joke into the ozone, hoping for the best, and then stare uncertainly at the camera as if expecting to be run out of town on a rail.

The movie opens with the "ki-ki" joke, which I've heard before as the "unga-bunga" joke. Belligerently, I believe "unga-bunga" is the funnier way to go, and the movie's best moments are when it takes off on people's differing ideas of how a story should be told, intercutting among several raconteurs until the carcass of the joke is laid bare. Unfortunately, "Funny" tries this only a couple of times; otherwise it makes no comment on its material.

In fact, the camera sits there, waiting after the joke is told, chronicling that uneasy aftermath in which the joke teller, mission accomplished, fidgets and looks ashamed. "This is like talking to an oil painting," complains one jokester after a deafening silence broken only by the camera's whir. On a certain level, these reactions are interesting, but "Funny" doesn't aspire to anything more lofty than a series of punch lines. It is not exactly a Freudian treatise on the nature of humor.

There are rape jokes, JAP jokes, penis jokes, old Jewish man jokes, a few puns. Did you hear about the new Jewish congregation up in Harlem, at Temple Beth You Is My Woman Now? Or the paper-goods customer who asked the saleswoman, "Do you keep stationery?" To which she replied: "For the first few minutes—then I go crazy."

Some jokes have little payoff, like the movie itself. Others sound like they'd be pretty funny in someone else's hands. Among the many shaggy dog stories, the most insufferable is from a journalist who goes on and on about meeting Russian spy Kim Philby. You could go to any bar where journalists hang out and hear a dozen such stories (and be just as bored).

Whether you laugh, and when, probably says more about you than about the joke. "What's the most useless thing on a woman's body? An Irishman," says one woman saucily into the camera. I laughed. My Irish companion didn't (and boy, did I hear about it later).

The upshot of the gorilla-rape joke—the victim finally comes to and moans, "He doesn't write, he doesn't call." There are two jokes about deaf people, one that makes fun of them, and one that is simultaneously translated into sign language—making all the difference. No one wants to be the butt of someone else's bad joke.

The movie was made by Bran Ferren and his special effects company, seemingly as a group effort. The concept of people telling their favorite jokes on camera has been done before, by MPI Home Video; Ferren and company pass up opportunities to make something cohesive of these jokes or to use their directorial or editing powers to make "Funny" more than the sum of its parts.

Among the jokesters: Dick Cavett (wearing short-shorts) Frank Zappa, Bob Balaban, Fred Ebb,

Gene Saks, Melissa Gilbert, Dan Greenburg, Marshall Brickman, Adolph Green, Chris Oyen, Peter Boyle (with his little daughter) and Sidney Lumet.

Comedian Alan King tells not a joke—after all, he gets paid for doing that—but shares an anecdote about Henny Youngman. The anecdote is intercut with Youngman doing his take-my-wife shtick. The anecdote is not particularly funny (you had to be there), and Youngman's jokes are so old he hadn't even met his wife yet when he dreamed them up. Ba-boom.

It leads you to wonder whether jokes were ever very funny.

NEWSDAY, 6/28/89, Part II/p. 2, Mike McGrady

I hate jokes. Let someone start in with, "So this midget walks into his doctor's office . . ." and I start seeking the nearest egress. Someone says, "Pat and Mike were having a beer one day . . ." and I'm gone, history, outta there. The next person who begins, "Stop me if you've heard this one before," is going to be stopped on the spot.

Why this aversion to formula humor? Possibly because joke-telling is one of many talents to elude me. In the past, like everyone else, I've tried to recite the latest "in" joke—stumbling over setups, omitting key ingredients, mangling punchlines. There was even a time—I was young, *very* young—when I tried to tell a joke to Bob Hope; never before and never since have I seen such cold, unyielding eyes.

Bearing this in mind, you may understand my reluctance to watch a movie where 120 people get in front of a movie camera to tell their favorite jokes. On my personal laffmeter, it breaks down this way: 120 jokes, 28 laughs, 15 snickers, three giggles and two guffaws. While it's true that not many movies can guarantee 28 laughs, or even two guffaws, it's also true that not many movies can guarantee the same number of grumbles and groans.

Funnily enough, most of the laughs were not prompted by superb deliveries of hilarious punchlines; most of the laughs came from the sight of so many people telling jokes just as badly as you or I might. Of course, no mere joke could ever hope to compete in the area of humor with the sight of people simply being themselves.

In fact, in many ways "Funny" illustrates how *not* to tell a joke, or precisely what kind of joke not to tell. I can assure you that pretty young women of innocent demeanor should never tell jokes about vibrators, that jokes involving Christ on the cross tend to seem less than hilarious, that the word "Hiiroshima" should never be part of any joke's punchline.

I must confess there were some—three of four, oh, maybe five at the outside—absolutely superb storytellers. What made their stories work were not the gaglines but the narrative construction, the near literary skill that went into the buildup. the jokes themselves covered the gamut—windy personal narratives, shaggy dog stories, morsels of pure filth, jokes to offend every religious and ethnic group along with many nationalities.

Once again you will hear of the girl in the paper goods store being asked if she kept stationery: "For the first couple of minutes and then I go crazy." The elderly Jewish gentleman who goes to St. Patrick's to confess a wild affair with a teenager and the priest asking why he's telling *him* about this: "Because I'm telling *everyone!*" The Pope and the prostitute, Quasimodo and the assistant bell-ringer the miracle horse who doesn't understand the word "posse" . . .

As the jokes kept coming, one after another, endlessly, repetitively, tiresomely, viewers kept rising to their feet and wandering out of the screening room. Which is just what would happen at a party that went on this long and then degenerated into a joke-telling contest.

VILLAGE VOICE, 7/4/89, p. 79, Stuart Klawans

If I lose an hour and a half of my life watching a not-terrific documentary, it's tragic. But if *you* pay to see 85 people stare into a camera and recite their favorite jokes—now, that's *Funny*.

Almost all of the people in question are show-biz types. This does not guarantee that their jokes are either funny or well-told; it just means that they involve a lot of Yiddish accents. You also hear a handful of Jesus jokes (which may be considered a subset of the Jewish ones), plus two insults to the Irish and two to the Poles. Deaf people are the subjects of three stories requiring sign language. There is one joke about a Scot and his kilt. Jokes that are embarrassing to blacks, gays, and women (other than young, moneyed Jewish women, that is) are confined to a brief introductory segment that serves as a ghetto of the politically incorrect. When a working-class man (one of the very few in the film) breaks out of this ghetto, he tells a joke so nasty that you wonder what insights *Funny* might have offered had it employed a little more courage and a much wider ethnographic sample.

As it is, you can draw only one conclusion from the film: Some people laugh at their own jokes, and some don't. The latter are at a disadvantage here, since their punchlines play to a mute camera crew. There's a lot of anticlimactic shrugging. And there's nothing for you to do about it but fidget, since these are not your friends. You don't have to put up with them, you're not abusing substances in their company, and you certainly have no way to stop them if you've heard it before, The latter point, of course, is supposed to be part of the fun. In two sequences, the film cuts among various people telling the same story. But if that's the sort of thing you like, you should drop by Bellevue to visit the folks with repetition compulsions. They're really a scream.

Funny was directed by Bran Ferren, who has heretofore honed his comedic skills designing special effects for Brian De Palma and robotics for the U.S. Naval Surface Weapons Center. This chucklesome experience has no doubt contributed to his lightness of touch.

Also reviewed in:
NEW REPUBLIC, 7/17–24/89, p. 25, Stanley Kauffmann
NEW YORK TIMES, 6/28/89, p. C15, Vincent Canby
VARIETY, 2/22-28/89, p. 229

GANG OF FOUR, THE

A Metropolis Films release of a Pierre Gris Productions film. *Director:* Jacques Rivette. *Screenplay (French with English subtitles):* Jacques Rivette, Pascal Bonitzer, and Christine Laurent. *Director of Photography:* Caroline Champetier. *Editor:* Catherine Quésemand. *Running time:* 150 minutes. *MPAA Rating:* Not Rated.

CAST: Bulle Ogier (Constance); Benoît Régent (Thomas); Laurence Côte (Claude); Fejria Deliba (Anna); Bernadette Giraud (Joyce); Inès de Medeiros-D'Almeida (Lucia); Nathalie Richard (Cécile).

NEW YORK POST, 12/22/89, p. 33, V.A. Musetto

Jacques Rivette was one of the founders of the French New Wave 30 years back, but the 15 or so films he has made since have never received the same popularity (or, in some cases, notoriety) as works by peers such as Godard, Truffaut and Rohmer.

Rivette's latest, "The Gang of Four," playing today through Jan. 11 at the Public in the East Village, may help rectify that oversight. It is fresh, intelligent, accessible and, to keep restless American audiences happy, suspenseful.

"Gang" opens with a shot of Anna, an aspiring actress, in a Paris cafe, then follows her down a cobblestone street, through a door and onto a stage, where she is suddenly in the midst of a rehearsal for a play.

Anna is one of four young female roommates (they share an old house outside Paris) who are members of an all-female acting class presided over by a demanding instructor portrayed by Bulle Ogier, who often pops up in Rivette films.

Meanwhile, outside class, the four roomies find themselves mixed up with a mysterious man who uses a variety of names, may or may not be a cop, and is looking for a key hidden in the house by a fifth woman. Rivette expertly intercuts these suspenseful doings with scenes of the rehearsals. The play involves false identities and allows the director to indulge in one of his favorite themes, the relationship between performance and life.

"Gang" is superbly acted, from the veteran Ogier to the four women (neophytes Laurence Côte, Fejria Deliba, Bernadette Giraud, Inès D'Almeida) to the enigmatic troublemaker (Benoît Régent). Also notable are Caroline Champetier's cinematography and Rivette's concern with small details—an opened book, the ingredients of a breakfast shared by the four women, a wall decorated with a Parisian newspaper reporting the death of Rita Hayworth ("A Star is Dead," shouts the headline).

"The Gang of Four" is 150 minutes long, but (except for some of the rehearsal scenes) it moves along painlessly. In any event, the dramatic payoff is well worth the wait.

VILLAGE VOICE, 12/26/89, p. 108, Eilliott Stein

The Gang of Four is Rivette's most engaging and accessible film in over a decade. It opens observing a young woman in a Paris café. She leaves, a few shots later goes through a door, and, without losing a beat, is emoting in an 18th century play that seems an outgrowth of the modern scene. (It's the Marivaux *Double Infidelities*, a comedy about false identities.) The theme broached here, as in several of the director's earlier films, is the interplay of performance and life. This is a gracefully fluent and deceptively simple work, nearly three hours long but consistently engrossing.

Nearly all the action is set in two locales: a suburban villa, inhabited by four aspiring young actresses, and a studio in Paris where Constance (Bulle Ogier) conducts her drama course. The lady is a true sacred monster, a high priestess of classical French theater. She doesn't seem to have a private life; she lives in her studio. It's the hottest drama course in town; she only accepts women students—the place is a bit like the convent in *The Nun*. The enigmatic narrative involves the pursuit of all the gang of four by a mystery man (cop? crook? spy?) who attempts to seduce them in order to trace the lover of one of their fellow students. This thriller plot intersects with the play rehearsals, creating odd tensions.

Gang is beautifully lit, its camera work discreetly expert. Director of photography: Caroline Champetier. I can't think of a woman cinematographer working in Hollywood today—can anyone?

Not the least of the film's delights is the impressive roster of fresh talent (Bernadette Giraud, Ines D'Almeida, Fejria Deliba, Nathalie Richard), all excellent and most in their first important roles. Veteran Ogier is superb; her performance during the rehearsal scenes is a marvel of timing, controlled interiority, and sheer craft. Isabelle Adjani might well profit from one of her courses.

Also reviewed:
NEW YORK TIMES, 12/22/89, p. C14, Caryn James

GETTING IT RIGHT

A Management Company Entertainment Group release. *Executive Producer:* Rusty Lemorande. *Producer:* Jonathan D. Krane and Randal Kleiser. *Director:* Randal Kleiser. *Screenplay (based on her novel):* Elizabeth Jane Howard. *Director of Photography:* Clive Tickner. *Editor:* Chris Kelly. *Music:* Colin Towns. *Sound:* John Midgley and (music) David Hines. *Sound Editor:* Leslie Hodgson. *Production Designer:* Caroline Amies. *Art Director:* Frank Walsh. *Costumes:* Hazel Pethig. *Make-up:* Sue Black. *Running time:* 102 minutes. *MPAA Rating:* R.

CAST: Jesse Birdsall (Gavin Lamb); Helena Bonham Carter (Minerva Munday); Peter Cook (Mr. Adrian); John Gielgud (Sir Gordon Munday); Jane Horrocks (Jenny); Lynn Redgrave (Joan); Shirley Anne Field (Anne); Judy Parfitt (Lady Stella Munday); Richard Huw (Harry); Kevin Drinkwater (Winthrop); Pat Heywood (Mrs. Lamb); Bryan Pringle (Mr. Lamb); Nan Munro (Lady Blackwater); Ian Redford (Bill); Ben Miles (Spiro); Cyril Conway (Manservant); Noriko Aida (Maid); Richard Strange (Sheila's Friend); Irene Marot (Sheila); Janet Amsden (Mrs. Blake); Aimee Delamain (Mrs. Arbuthnot); Rupert Holliday Evans (Peter); June Ellis (Mrs. Wagstaffe); Pauline Quirke (Muriel Sutton); Anne-Marie Owens, Vivien Tierney and John Cashmore (Opera Singers); Richard MacDonald (Man at Opera); Lula Ioannou and Sarah Morgan (Salon Juniors); Elizabeth Jane Howard (Woman at Party); Cut Double (Rock Band).

LOS ANGELES TIMES, 5/5/89, Calendar/p. 14, Michael Wilmington

In "Getting It Right", a sprightly new comedy based on the Elizabeth Jane Howard novel, Jesse Birdsall plays a punctilious young London hairdresser named Gavin Lamb who lives at home, still a virgin at 31.

Gavin, a lamb with shears, keeps talking himself out of a sex life, though customers swoon over him and dazzling young women give him the eye. And he's locked in one of those quasi-incestuous home tangles with a domineering mother (Pat Heywood), a quiet father and a roomful of books, records and reproductions of Degas.

You'd suspect from all this that Lamb had homosexual tendencies—and indeed, in the film, he has a bewigged,bitchy boss (Peter Cook) and his best friend is a gay makeup man, Harry (Richard Huw).

But, instead, Gavin's a volcano of raging heterosexuality about to explode, just as the movie itself, superficially descended from the anti-Establishment British comedies of the '60s— "Morgan!" "Georgy Girl," "The Knack" and others—has by its climax turned into a conformist parable.

You keep getting the idea that director Randal Kleiser ("Grease") wanted to make a wilder picture, wanted to think himself back to the the heyday of youth and rebellion, the swinging '60s, but that the '80s kept getting in his way, bringing him down.

It's not an unmixed curse, or blessing. Writer Howard, whose dialogue is often spring-fresh, delicately satiric and balletically graceful and swift, writes Gavin as a sensible, decent, highly moral young man, suddenly cast adrift in a sea of sex and temptation.

At a posh party held by a designer's mistress (Lynn Redgrave), he is half-seduced by his hostess and then stumbles into a bedroom where a naked aristocrat (Helena Bonham Carter of "A Room with a View") lies flirtatiously in bed, while Harry's butch lover Winthrop cavorts with a Greek pickup in the bathroom.

There's a triple wish-fulfillment here. Naughtily stylish Joan deflowers him and madcap rich ditz Minerva wants to marry him, dragging him home to starchy daddy John Gielgud and her drunken mum. There's a third pull, sunny normality. Gavin surprises his hair-shop helper and shampoo girl Jenny (Jane Horrocks) feeding swans, and joins her on a sweet, slow courtship full of flowers, music and lilting long-take strolls. An unwed mother, Jenny lives at home too, but, next to her rivals, she is a working-class madonna, closer to Lillian Gish than Judy Geeson.

The first part of "Getting It Right" has an easygoing wit and casual humanism, especially all the scenes involving Redgrave, and Gielgud's fierce turn as a rich, fragile bully. (In his old age, Gielgud has turned into a Paganini of archly delicate comic effects.)

But in the second half, there's an almost tangible slackening. The story skitters perfunctorily from scene to scene: Lady Minerva in drugged-out squalor, sudden romances and marriages. Birdsall is too young and confident for his part, and when the movie starts slipping and drifting, you notice it more.

It's as if Kleiser and Howard had lost their grip or were trying to cram in too much, or as if Kleiser wanted to make something like "My Beautiful Laundrette" and had to switch it into "The Secret of My Success."

There are some delightful moments in "Getting It Right," but the film isn't right at all. It suggests that you should have your fun but play it safe, and then it makes safeness banal, over-bright.

It's a shorn lamb, fleeced of its chance for either true love or crazy glee.

MONTHLY FILM BULLETIN, 10/89, p. 301, Kim Newman

London. Gavin Lamb, a virginal thirty-one-year-old hairdresser who still lives with his parents, accompanies his best friend Harry to a party thrown by Joan, a rich eccentric with whom Gavin strikes up an immediate rapport. At the party, Gavin also meets Lady Minerva Munday, a neurotic aristocrat who has just been thrown out of her half-sister's flat. Gavin refuses to have sex with Minerva, but does take her home to sleep on his frontroom couch. At first appalled at Minerva's presence, Gavin's mother relents when she discovers their guest is titled. At the opera, Gavin meets Joan and she seduces him. Certain that the married Joan is not the right woman for him, Gavin starts to see Jenny, his assistant in Mr. Adrian's salon, a single mother who lives with her own mother, Anne, and her young son. Minerva invites Gavin to her parents' estate in an attempt to impress her father into keeping up her allowance by presenting a respectable fiancé. Sir Gordon Munday, a parvenu seatbelt tycoon, offers Gavin a directorship if he will marry Minerva, but Gavin refuses. Gavin and Jenny become close, and he learns that she is worried Anne will move to Germany with her soldier boyfriend Bill and that she will have to give up her job to look after her child. Minerva has a breakdown, and Gavin sees her to the hospital. Later, she calls Gavin and tells him she has just married a fortune hunter. Harry's boyfriend Winthrop leaves him for Joan, and Gavin pleads unsuccessfully with her to let him go. Anne tells Gavin that she does intend to move but asks him not to tell Jenny. When Jenny finds out, she angrily declares that she will move to Germany too. Gavin persuades her to stay by admitting that he is in love with her.

The bizarre matching of director Randal Kleiser, still best known for *Grease* and *The Blue Lagoon,* and novelist Elizabeth Jane Howard yields a contemporary London romance that vacillates between the relishable and the acutely embarrassing. Kleiser's declared approach to *Getting It Right* has been to strengthen the material's similarities to *Morgan, Alfie, Darling* and *Georgy Girl,* recruiting veterans (Lynn Redgrave, Shirley Anne Field, Bryan Pringle) of that particular mid-60s cycle of swinging British comedy-drama to mingle with up-and-comers like Helena Bonham Carter and new faces Jesse Birdsall and Jane Horrocks. While Kleiser is reasonably adept at Howard's broadly comic sequences—particularly the painful meals Gavin and Minerva share with their respective sets of parents—representing the awful life style the hero wisely manages to isolate himself from, he is less handy when it comes to presenting a positive side. Jenny is so evidently the decent girl with whom Gavin will end up that all the screen time wasted on the predatory Joan and the cracked Minerva seems so much meandering. The couple's courtship—he has her up to his room to listen to classical music and pore through art books—is as coyly unbelievable as the hero's escapades with the other women, but without their deliberate comic thrust.

While the production design manages to catch the nuances of such different locales as the Lambs' New Barnet semi, Harry and Winthrop's minimalist flat, and Joan's docklands conversion, the characters are less well defined than their surroundings. Pat Heywood and Bryan Pringle as Gavin's parents could have stepped out of any ITV sit-com of the past twenty-five years, John Gielgud contributes another of the absurd accents he tends to use for his film cameos, Peter Cook sneakily adjusts his wig and twitches like a hamster as the villainous salon owner, Lynn Redgrave hides behind empty spectacle frames and red wig as the vampirish older woman, and Shirley Anne Field merely has to radiate sensible good humour. Even the leading characters, despite generally fine work from Birdsall, Horrocks and Carter, are disturbingly thin, and whenever genuine feeling tries to creep into the performances the movie turns mawkish. Elizabeth Jane Howard, whose delicacy of approach would suggest that her works might best be adapted into politely barbed BBC-TV serials, is perhaps less well served by the shoehorning of her novel into an attempt to make London swing again than she was when her short story "Mr. Wrong" was turned in New Zealand into a feminist ghost-slasher picture.

NEW YORK POST, 5/5/89, p. 34, Jami Bernard

Gavin Lamb is a shy London hairdresser who at 31 is still living with his overbearing mom and milquetoast dad, is still a virgin, can't relate to women, likes opera, has a best friend who is gay, but is not—NO HE IS NOT—himself gay. Nevertheless, he is going to get it right, in "Getting It Right." Whatever "it" is.

"It" turns out to be sex, confidence, clothes sense and social grace, and Gavin doesn't tackle these areas so much as they are foisted upon him. An older woman takes him under her wing and between her legs, a crazy woman teaches him resourcefulness and the limits of friendship, a naive hairdressing apprentice brings out the protective and the traditional in him. By the end, Gavin is a man of principle, a real go-getter, and a snappy dresser. This is all accompanied by glib voice-over; Gavin's transformation is a bit suspect since he seems to have had the social polish all along but has been too unmotivated to apply it.

"Getting it Right" owes a lot to "Georgy Girl," and as if to drive home the point, Lynn Redgrave is on hand as the older woman who seduces Gavin after a party at her lavish home. At least Georgy, although also a young London misfit, managed to find a life that would accommodate her specialness. Gavin buys into the mainstream lock, stock and hairdryer.

Redgrave plays Joan, rich, bored and unloved. Done up like Dustin Hoffman in "Tootsie," with a flamboyant red wig and overbearing glasses that give her a grotesque, mannish look, Joan is drawn to Gavin, mostly, it seems, because he is an easy mark.

She first introduces Gavin to something far more personal than sex: a game of secrets in which they reveal obvertations about one another that are so embarrassing that if Gavin really were as socially terrifed as he claimed, he would have been out the door in two crimps of a curling iron.

Instead, he unblinkingly admits to Joan that he's a virgin, is attracted to her even though he thinks at first that she's a female impersonator (but hey, he's not gay), and then turns out to be a quick study in the bedroom. (Weight Watchers has done well by Redgrave; though she was 180 pounds when she made "Georgy Girl," she now proudly bares her breasts.)

A second woman has meanwhile come into his life—when it rains, it pours—and this one is

Minerva (Helena Bonham Carter of "A Room With a View"), a neurotic mess who looks like Elvira and who doesn't eat food but "likes to gnaw." (Sir John Gielgud has a small part as Minerva's rich daddy). Even if Gavin is not gay, who would blame him for wanting to be after mixing it up with these women whose eccentricities are displayed without comment like peacock feathers—their *mishegas* isn't funny and does nothing to further either the story or the comedy, such as it is.

Once Joan and Minerva have introduced the subject of females into his life, Gavin looks with new eyes on his assistant, Jenny (Jane Horrocks), who is cute in a rabbity kind of way. Though she is a single mother, she is sexually naive (it only takes a minute, girl)—and, better yet, she is naive in almost every other area as will. She is a lump of clay in Gavin's suddenly steady hands as he teaches her about art and music and refines her sensibilities to coincide with his own, like shaping the teeth of a spare key. By the time she is an unthreatening mirror image, she is perfect for Gavin.

Director Randal Kleiser, who has heretofore mostly made teen comedies like "Grease" and the awful "North Shore," does not seem at home in working-class London. "Getting It Right" is amiable but as bland as Gavin's mother's cooking. The hilarious Peter Cook is straitjacketed into a minor and unprepossessing role as the owner of Gavin's hair salon, and Gielgud livens things up for about 10 minutes as the neurotic Minerva's daddy.

Jesse Birdsall, who was Emily Lloyd's lecherous boyfriend in "Wish You Were Here," brings a nervous tentativeness to the early part of the film as Gavin Lamb, the lamb to the social slaughter. "I've changed from someone to whom nothing happens to someone to whom things never stop happening," he smugly narrates later. The movie itself, unfortunately, shows less sign of movement.

NEWSDAY, 5/5/89, Part III/p. 5, Lynn Darling

"I just want to get it right, that's all," says Gavin Lamb, the hero of this modest little comedy. "Right girl, right place," His pursuit of perfection has left Lamb a 31-year-old virgin still living at home, unable to get on with life, meekly accepting the benign tyranny of his overprotective mother at home and his high-handed boss at the West End hair salon where he works.

"Getting It Right" means to be a character study, drawing deliberate comparisons with such quintessential British examples of the form as "Morgan!" "Georgy Girl" and "Darling." "I made a conscious decision to strengthen these similarities," director Randal Kleiser says in the production notes.

You have to admire his cheek, comparing this bit of mealymouthed ephemeral to the biting wit, trenchant social observation and bedeviled protagonists of such daunting competition: It's like putting Herman's Hermits in the same league as The Beatles.

Gavin (Jesse Birdsall) is an innocent who doesn't stay innocent for long: When his best friend, Harry (Richard Huw), takes him to a raucous party in a fashionable penthouse apartment, his initiation into the mysteries of life and love begins forthwith.

His education is in the hands of three very different women. A glamorously eccentiric older woman (Lynn Redgrave) relieves him of his virginity, an anorexic waif (Helena Bonham Carter) teaches him about responsibility to others, and his pretty, uneducated assistant Jenny (Jane Horrocks) guides him inadvertently into love. All of this is accomplished in more or less tiresome and predictable fashion, with a few self-consciously didactic speeches thrown in along the way.

"Don't worry about being loved, worry about loving. It's far more important," Joan, the older woman, tells Gavin. He in turn has wisdom of his own to impart. "What's art for?" Jenny asks Gavin, who is established as an expert on the subject because he owns a few art books and listens to opera and to Mozart. "For recognizing things, I guess," Gavin says. It's hard to know which is more tedious—the dull-witted attempts at meaningful dialogue between the characters, or the insipid voiceover monologue in which Gavin informs us of his innermost—and most insipid—thoughts. A character study isn't worth much when it focuses on so relentlessly uninteresting a character.

The surprising thing here is that quite a good cast has been wasted on this vacuity. Redgrave has a good time in her vamp role, Carter is winning as the dizzy lost child of unbearably *nouveau riche* parents, Peter Cook is wonderfully odious as the owner of a hair-dressing salon dependent on an increasingly doddering clientele, and John Gielgud tosses off his role as a recently knighted seat belt manufacturer with his accustomed insouciance. Too bad their efforts are wasted on a movie that has nothing to say and says it dully.

VILLAGE VOICE, 5/9/89, p. 68, Stuart Klawans

Signs of Life has one more virtue I haven't yet mentioned: The characters don't learn anything. [See Klawans review.] In *Getting It Right,* Randal Kleiser's terminally dumb comedy, the main character not only learns an important lesson, but tells the audience about it in relentless voiceover.

Gavin (Jesse Birdsall) is a 31-year-old Londoner who works as a hairdresser, lives with his parents, has never laid hands on a woman below the scalp, and adores opera. He is not gay. His best friend is gay, but Gavin himself is absolutely not. He's merely afraid of people, as he explains on the soundtrack. Not that he seems timid in any of his screens, but we are nevertheless to understand that he is shy—and heterosexual.

Taken to a party one night at the home of the wealthy Joan (Lynn Redgrave), Gavin is waylaid by his hostess, who has terrifying red hair and grotesque eyeglasses and insists on giving him a personality reading that would make a Scientologist blush. Gavin feels at ease with her. A few scenes later, she relieves him of his virginity. Before that happens, though, Gavin becomes entangled with the equally reassuring Minerva (Helena Bonham Carter), the mythomaniacal daughter of a merchant baron. Decked out in vampire drag, making unwelcome sexual advances as fast as she can talk, Minerva functions in the plot as the puppy dog character. Gavin strokes her occasinally to show how kind he is. Her opposite number is Jenny (Jane Horrocks), Gavin's assistant at the hair salon. She is a working-class girl who has had sex exactly once, at age 17, received a child for her effort, and has not been with a man since. She and Gavin therefore marry, after he's given her a quick education in the arts. Gavin says this proves he's finally found the right woman; I say he was looking for somebody with a nose just like his. Birdsall has a longish one, with a bump at the end. Horrocks has the same, with a few freckles added. The lesson of *Getting It Right*—no matter what Elizabeth Jane Howard's screenplay seems to be saying—is that people should mate only with the like-nosed.

You might notice, in ads for the film, that John Gielgud and Peter Cook appear in the credits. Don't get excited. They, like Lynn Redgrave, are thrown away like used Kleenex.

Also reviewed in:
NEW YORK TIMES, 5/5/89, p. C15, Vincent Canby
VARIETY, 5/10-16/89, p. 19
WASHINGTON POST, 6/9/89, p. C7, Hal Hinson

GHOSTBUSTERS II

A Columbia Pictures release. *Executive Producer:* Bernie Brillstein, Joe Medjuck, and Michael C. Gross. *Producer:* Ivan Reitman. *Director:* Ivan Reitman. *Screenplay:* Harold Ramis and Dan Aykroyd. *Director of Photography:* Michael Chapman. *Editor:* Sheldon Kahn and Donn Cambern. *Music:* Randy Edelman; *Music Editor:* Kathy Durning. *Sound:* Gene Cantamessa and (music) Bobby Fernandez. *Sound Editor:* Tom McCarthy and Fred Judkins. *Production Designer:* Bo Welch. *Visual Effects:* Dennis Muren. *Art Director:* Tom Duffield. *Set Designer:* Nick Navarro, Gregory Papalia, and Rick Heinrichs. *Set Decorator:* Cheryl Carasik; *Special Effects:* Chuck Gaspar, Joe Day, and Dick Wood. *Costumes:* Gloria Gresham. *Make-up:* Stephen Abrums, John Elliott, and Robert Arrollo. *Stunt Coordinator:* Joel Kramer. *Running time:* 102 minutes. *MPAA Rating:* PG.

CAST: Bill Murray (Dr. Peter Venkman); Dan Aykroyd (Dr. Raymond Stantz); Sigourney Weaver (Dana Barrett); Harold Ramis (Dr. Egon Spengler); Rick Moranis (Louis Tully); Ernie Hudson (Winston Zeddemore); Annie Potts (Janine Melnitz); Peter MacNicol (Janosz Poha); Harris Yulin (The Judge); David Margulies (The Mayor of NY); Kurt Fuller (Hardemeyer); Janet Margolin (The Prosecutor); Wilhelm Von Homburg (Vigo); William T. Deutschendorf and Henry J. Deutschendorf II (Baby Oscar); Michael P. Moran (Frank the Doorman); Olivia Ward (Meter Maid); Mordecai Lawner (Man with a Ticket); Susan Boehm (Young Woman on Crutches); Mary Ellen Trainor (Brownstone Mother); Christopher Villaseñor (Brownstone Boy #1); Jason Reitman (Brownstone Boy #2); Aaron Lustig (Norman the Producer); Page Leong (Spengler's Assistant); Mark Schneider and Valery Pappas (Arguing Couple); Catherine Reitman (Girl with Puppy); Dave Florek (First Cop); Richard Foronjy (Con Ed Supervisor); George Wilbur (Bailiff); Sharon Kramer (Stenographer); Walter Flanagan (Rudy the Museum Guard); Bobby Baresford Brown (Mayor's Doorman); Christopher Neame (Maître d'); Judy Ovitz (Slimed Restaurant Patron); Tom Dugan (Restaurant Cop #1) Angelo Di Mascio (Restaurant Cop #2); Robert Alan Beuth (Store Manager); Ralph Monaco (Police Sergeant); Ron Cummins (Police Lieutenant); Cheech Marin (Dock Supervisor); Yvette Cruise (Maria, Dana's Maid); John Hammil (Detective #1); Ray Glanzmann (Detective #2); Alex Zimmerman (Detective #3); Brian Doyle Murray (Psychiatrist); Louise Troy (Woman with Fur Coat); Douglas Seale (Plaza Hotel Man); Ben Stein (Public Works Official); Erik Holland (Fire Commissioner); Phillip Baker Hall (Police Commissioner).

FILMS IN REVIEW, 10/89, p. 487, Edmond Grant

Slick packaging is what *Ghostbusters II* is all about. Another unnecessary sequel to an entertaining popular success, this item features special effects galore, a pack of familiar faces repeating what they've done better in the past, some witty dialogue for the adult set, and lots of slime and animated ghosties for the kiddie market.

The plot, for what it's worth (some quick millions, to be sure) has our old quartet of pals fighting against the spirit of a Medieval warrior bent on world domination; he intends to start his domination by first inhabiting the body of Sigourney Weaver's baby. Other developments include Weaver and Bill Murray starting up their quippy romance once again, and the GB secretary (played briefly but zestfully by Annie Potts) coming on to Rick Moranis, the perennial nerd.

All the participants are such seasoned veterans of this kind of nonsense that some sequences do come off well, particularly those involving the above mentioned romantic entanglements. But certain very key elements prevent the film from ever attaining the sustained comic atmosphere of the first *Ghostbusters*. The first element is the choppy direction by Ivan Reitman and even choppier scripting by resident GBs Dan Aykroyd and Harold Ramis. At some points, the film simply degenerates into music-video territory, and at others it simply trades in on our memories of its predecessor.

The second factor dragging the film down in the lackluster turns by the GBs themselves. This is not meant to malign Ernie Hudson (the poor soul, a competent performer who is forever condemned to being a trivia question—"Who was the fourth Ghostbuster?") or Harold Ramis (whose brilliance with SCTV and *The National Lampoon* haven't been equalled in his recent incarnation as actor-producer-director). No, the troublesome performers here are the two *Saturday Night Live* alumni, Murray and Aykroyd. Bill Murray surely has his own way with a line of dialogue. He can banter with the best of them, and does so here in his scenes with Weaver. If only it weren't so apparent that the only reason he sardonically sleepwalks (a trait pioneered by the ultimate in disinterested performers, Chevy Chase) through the film is to help out an old *SNL* buddy and make a few million dollars in the process. And Dan Aykroyd, who possesses no comic persona at all when he simply plays himself (as he has done in so much of his post-*SNL* film work), registers here as a complete void who happens to be having a good time with his friends.

Then again, the film can't be torn apart to any large degree precisely because it *is* such a self-conscious piece of merchandising. From its doll like villains to the sometimes excruciatingly loud soundtrack packed with indistinguishable dance music, the film plugs away at being a complete entertainment package, one that fulfills every audience expectation, and doesn't bother treading on any new territory.

And there is some very smooth supporting work by Moranis, Potts, and Weaver (who seems to try to maintain an earnest expression throughout). In fact, the supporting cast is so endearing that one's eye keeps shifting to the periphery of the screen, hoping for some additional familiar faces to take some time away from the extravagant special effects, which include one New York based national monument coming to life. (Incidentally, only one brief celebrity cameo is in the film proper; however such surprise celebrities as Donald Trump, Malcolm Forbes, and the Ramones all show up in the Bobby Brown tie-in music video for the song "We're Back.")

To date, the film has done well for itself at the box office, so it seems likely that some more, even thinner, installments may soon be on the way.

LOS ANGELES TIMES, 6/16/89, Calendar/p. 1, Sheila Benson

Fans of "Ghostbusters" can breathe a little easier. It's slimebusting time again and The Boys are back in ferocious form. One-line zingers ricochet around "Ghostbusters II" like ectoplasmic ghoulies, contained in a production that builds to a grand finale even funnier than the guys' classic duel with the Stay-Puft Marshmallow Man.

And so, during our descent into the Valley of the Sequels, it's nice to discover that the makers of "Ghostbusters II" have worked hard to keep their movie's edge sharp. There is a certain amount of probability here; we can be pretty sure that the Ghostbusters, with their clunky homemade critter-zapping packs, *will* continue to suck all the spectral badness into their little cosmic Roach Motels.

Nevertheless, the movie's style is meticulous, beginning with Ivan Reitman's producing and directing; the script by performers Harold Ramis and Dan Aykroyd; a buoyant musical score, and inspired production details and special effects.

The original cast is all present and accounted for. Bill Murray's Dr. Peter Venkman, who mooned over Sigourney Weaver's efficient Dana Barrett, can do it again, since in the five elapsed years she's found and shed the man of her dreams and father of her baby, Oscar. (Blond, pink-cheeked Oscar, in the person of 8-month-old twins William T. and Henry J. Deutschendorf, is a major heartbreaker.)

Ramis, Aykroyd and Ernie Hudson again play varying degrees of serious and semiserious scientists. And kids, who love this sort of thing, will probably glom onto Peter MacNicol's brilliantly performed Janosz Poha, a smarmy would-be seducer whose gleefully off-center accent will give them something to twist their tongues around in imitation.

The movie's premise seems not at all impossible: There is a repository for all the negative energy exuded by New Yorkers in the course of an ordinary day as they rise, suit up and prepare to annihilate their fellow Manhattanites by thought, word or deed.

This accumulated vituperation has become a river of nastiness flowing just beneath the city streets. Because this is a comedy, the slime is pink-ish and pretty and when it seeps through a pavement crack, it looks no more threatening than thin Smucker's jelly, oozing out of a peanut butter sandwich. However "Ghostbusters" fans know better.

New York has produced such an abundance of vileness that it has nourished a malevolent presence—Vigo (Wilhelm von Homburg), a centuries-old fiend, primed to rule the city before you can say his full name—"Vigo, the Scourge of Carpathia, the Sorrow of Moldavia"—unless something is done.

A looming painting of this broad-browed, piercing-eyed tyrant is at the "Manhattan Museum of Art," where Weaver works as an apprentice art restorer. It seems that Janosz Poha is Vigo's man in Manhattan, and in a faintly "Rosemary's Baby" touch, Vigo needs a baby in whose body to return and conquer. By now, no one can be unaware of the story's drift.

Fortunately, the movie isn't only Adorable Oscar in Jeopardy. The writers have crafted a perfectly sensible opening: They see the city fathers as elected scolds, still royally teed-off at the condition in which The Boys left New York at the close of the last movie. Accordingly, they've been forbidden to bust a single ghost, even with pink slime bubbling away as cheerfully as the Maxwell House percolator.

It's clear that it will take a whale of a manifestation to put our heroes back at the wheel of Ectomobile-1, and sure enough, one explodes, enough to stand even Ramis' Dr. Egon Spengler's jaunty pompadour on end. When ghostbusting is finally legitimate again, the kids in the audience will have a field day with all the swooping, diving apparitions who are rounded up, while the adults may notice their nice details, the ghostly jogger, for example, streaking around the Central Park reservoir, taking his pulse at his throat.

What gives the movie its sense of comic free-fall is its total lack of in-jokiness, that stultifying sense of actors playing for each other's pockets that we've been plagued with lately. To be sure, there's a nice familiarity to the interplay of Aykroyd, Murray, Ramis and Hudson, and of all four with Rick Moranis as their super-dweeb accountant now promoted to tax lawyer, but it's a coziness that works to include, not alienate, the audience. Strangely enough, the pair who seem entirely unconnected are the movie's uneasy lovers, Weaver and Murray, who circle each other with all the warmth of rival real-estate brokers.

Somehow; that doesn't gum things up irreparably. "Ghostbusters II" (MPAA-rated PG) also doesn't seem to be pushing as hard as its predecessor, which of course makes it even more fun. There's an old-shoeishness to the proceedings; even Murray's owlish put-downs seem a little less snide—they're almost affectionate, if that's not too outrageous a word in this context.

Over on the hardware side, this is one of those times when the Industrial Light and Magic crew succeeded totally. Leaving aside the fantastically realized heroine of the film's last sequence, you might consider the Vigo painting, that face that's part Klaus Kinski with a soupçon of Frank Morgan's fearful floating Wizard in "The Wizard of Oz."

In the welter of credits, along with "Bathtub trainers" and "Bathtub wranglers," you'll find "Vigo painting supervisor" Glen Eytchison who should be saluted along with the film's more than 400 other artists and technicians. That would include more regularly recognized jobs: the production designer (Bo Welch); the editors (Sheldon Kahn and Donn Cambern); the cinematographer (Michael Chapman); the costume designer (Gloria Gresham); the visual-effects supervisor (Dennis Muren); creator of the musical score (Randy Edelman) and whoever located the unforgettable Oscar(s), presumably casting maven Michael Chinich.

MONTHLY FILM BULLETIN, 12/89, p. 366, Verina Glaessner

Five years later. While divorcée Dana Barrett's attention is diverted, the pram containing her eight-month-old son Oscar rolls away on to a busy road. Discovering the baby miraculously unharmed, and sensing something supernatural about the incident, Dana enlists the aid of her friends, Peter Venkman (an ex-lover), Raymond Stantz, Egon Spengler and Winston Zeddemore, otherwise known as the Ghostbusters. Legally prevented from operating following the havoc wreaked on New York by their previous adventures, Ray now runs a bookshop and works as a children's entertainer with Winston, while Egon is researching the effects of human emotions on the psychic magnetic field and Venkman hosts a television show entitled "World of the Psychic". Despite Dana's plea that Venkman not be involved, he goes with the others to investigate the possibility of psychic disturbance at her apartment. Finding nothing, they search the street, where they discover increased electrical activity. Ray descends down a manhole and finds a river of slime running through the old underground railroad system. After causing a blackout, the Ghostbusters are taken to court, where they meet their old adversaries the Mayor and his assistant Hardemeyer. But their restraining order is lifted when the court is engulfed by odd psychic manifestations. Dana, who works in the museum's conservation department, is increasingly disturbed by a painting of Vigo the Carpathian which her boss, Janosz Poha, has just finished restoring, and with which he appears to be obsessed. Vigo materialises through his portrait and entrusts Janosz with procuring Oscar so that through him he may return to earth. However, the wary Dana refuses to let Janosz into her apartment. After she and her baby are attacked by slime penetrating her bathtub, she flees with Oscar to Venkman's apartment. While Venkman and Dana go out to dinner, the other Ghostbusters explore the underground system, where they are assailed by various manifestations and emerge drenched in slime. When they and Venkman attempt to inform the Mayor of the city's danger from the slime, which not only displays aggression but causes it in others, Hardemeyer has them incarcerated in a mental hospital. Meanwhile, Dana, returning to the apartment, sees Oscar swept off a ledge by a ghost. At the museum, she finds Janosz about to offer the child to Vigo. With New York terrorised by a rising tide of slime, the Ghostbusters are released, and decide to mobilise mass positive emotions to defeat the slime and Vigo. They hijack the Statue of Liberty, using the slime, rendered harmless by music, to make it move. As Vigo is about to possess the baby, the New Year's Eve crowd begins to sing and the Ghostbusters ride through the streets on the Statue of Liberty. Vigo is overcome by the power of positive emotions and disappears. Janosz is exorcised and Oscar is saved.

The publicity material for *Ghostbusters II* makes some play with the freedom to improvise which Ivan Reitman afforded his cast and writers Harold Ramis and Dan Aykroyd. The result is a film that proceeds by fits and starts, displaying a singularly cavalier attitude to the old-fashioned virtues of the tightly scripted narrative. The business with the slime (confusingly, both product and instigator of human malevolence) seems to have not a lot to do with the rather more conventional excursion into the supernatural provided by the tale of Vigo the Carpathian, while the ghosts, familiar from the televised cartoon as well as the previous film, appear to materialise solely in response to audience expectations.

Reitman's early film, *Cannibal Girls* (showing at the cinema from which slime-threatened patrons flee), was visually sophisticated and assured. Though dogged, as indeed is this one, by a certain literal quality, it had both coherence and the courage of its convictions. Here, his refusal to play the sequel game straight by producing a rattling good yarn plus bursts of the theme tune suggests he may be prey to a certain *ennui* with his quirky band, who superficially seem such a safe bet for serialisation. This said, the film has some grandly conceived set-pieces—baby Oscar teetering on a ledge high above the city before being rescued by a malignant Mary Poppins look-alike, or the Statue of Liberty striding through New York like a benevolent colossus—which recall the very best of strip-cartoon art. But these, in the end, like the Capra-esque finale, with evil vanquished by popular goodwill, go for considerably less than they should.

NEW YORK, 7/17/89, p. 46, David Denby

Ghostbusters II is a flirtatiously self-conscious sequel, a movie playing happily with the spectacle of its own inconsequence. The movie asks, Can anything as flimsy as this material rise off the ground more than once? Five years have passed, and the men who once saved New York from Evil are now faded pop celebrities, thrown on the junk heap by a city that no longer needs them. The solemn Egon (Harold Ramis, of the long, high forehead) has gone back to his research at Columbia, and Peter (Bill Murray) has become a cynically abusive cable talk-show host, goosing psychics and frauds. Ray (Dan Aykroyd) and Winston (Ernie Hudson) strap themselves into their Ghostbusters uniforms—and then run off to entertain at children's birthday parties. "Who you gonna call?" they shout. "He-Man!" shriek the kids derisively.

The beastie spirits return, and the Ghostbusters are needed once again. Poltroonish poltergeists shove Sigourney Weaver's baby carriage (with her baby in it) all over the East Side. It seems a certain medieval Carpathian ruler—a notorious sadist whose portrait hangs in a museum—wants to be reincarnated in Sigourney's child so he can jump to the head of the fish-counter line at Zabar's. (Or is it that he wants to rule the world? Anyway, he wants *something*.) The Evil One, whose name is Vigo, is also in control of a river of pink slime that courses deep below the city streets. The slime—and here's the confusing part—seems at the same time to have been produced by the accumulated bad vibes in New York; it's a river of ill will, a miasma of rudeness and envy, a cloaca of contempt, a....Soon enough, chinchillas arise from rich ladies' coats and go running down the sidewalks with a squeal. All hell is breaking loose in New York.

Ghostbusters II is a clear case of dedicated silliness. The special effects are clunky and ugly, but the movie is amiable and companionable and it delivers the goods. Still, I miss a few things this time around—the ghost lore, with its smells and winds and learned parapsychology gibberish, and the original's awed sense of discovering a strangeness too wild to be entirely laughed off. This movie is not as scary or as funny. Now that Sigourney Weaver is a mommy (the husband has split), the filmmakers won't let her be sexy anymore, which is a shame, since her rising in heat off her bed was the original's giddiest moment.

Director Ivan Reitman doesn't always follow through on his ideas. For instance, he gets the Statue of Liberty to walk all the way to the museum and then doesn't do anything with it. And Reitman is handicapped by setting up a baby as victim—the movie rightly respects our feelings on the vulnerability of infants, but it also suffers from inhibition. The funniest thing in *Ghostbusters II* is Peter MacNicol, who plays the timid little Carpathian art restorer whom Vigo has chosen as the instrument of his purpose. MacNicol has a thing for Sigourney Weaver and promises her dominion over the world if she accedes to the Evil One's plan for her baby. The tiny art restorer thinks he's a winner. An eternally hopeful smile fixed on his face, MacNicol makes vague stabs at the English language, a wanderer in alien thickets who gratefully hangs on to a familiar tree now and then. His Anglo-Carpathian speech is more delicately fantastic—more imaginative, more inventive—than any of the special-effects thrills in *Ghostbusters II*.

NEW YORK POST, 6/16/89, p. 23, David Edelstein

In "Ghostbusters II," Bill Murray bats eyes as femininely suggestive as Bugs Bunny's, and when he stretches out on a couch and beckons his ex-squeeze (Sigourney Weaver) hither, he has the impudent slinkiness of Mae West. No one shrugs out a punch line with such majesty; no deadpan in movies can seem more mischievously alive.

In a way, Murray is the real ghost of this sequel. He's the Ghost of Murray Past, of the ironic put-down artist that the actor—in such sincere projects as "The Razor's Edge" and "Scrooged"—tried to outgrow. But there's no shame in reliving your youth, especially for a hefty percentage of the gross. For that kind of money, I'd go through puberty again.

"Ghostbusters II" turns out to be a pleasantly ramshackle comedy—relaxed and goosey, with consistent stretches of laughs. The film was made quickly, after director Ivan Reitman finished "Twins," and it has some of the rough-and-tumble quality of "Saturday Night Live" and "SCTV."

It isn't an exciting or memorable comedy, a "Bull Durham" or "Beetlejuice." But the performers are on the ball, and there's more team spirit than in the last one—which largely consisted or people floating big, fat pitches over the strike zone and Murray serenely hitting them out of the park.

The plot? There isn't much of one—some strung-together skits, slime gags, tacky commercials and music videos. The guys reunite after going out of business; the guys kick some more ghost butt; the guys save Weaver, her baby and the rest of Manhattan from assorted poltergeists and from the spirit of a 17th century Moldavian tyrant.

The tyrant is the subject of a huge canvas being restored in the wing of the museum where Weaver—a musician last time—now works. She left Murray for "Mr. Right," we're told, when he began to introduce her at parties as "the old ball-and-chain." Then Mr. Right packed up, the child was born and she traded the bow for the brush. Clearly a woman of expandable talents.

The ghost, meanwhile, wants her baby—he wants to grow up in a human body and eventually conquer the world. Nothing like aiming high. So he takes control of the smitten geek (Peter MacNicol) who's her boss; the geek goes after her kid; a river of slime surges through the sewers; sundry spooks disrupt New York life; so who ya gonna call?

The original "Ghostbusters" was a square, clunky, Grand Guignol monster flick with Murray walking through it and sending it up, letting us know it was all a scuzzy con. "Ghostbusters II" is in many ways a better movie, but I miss the subversive element in Murray's performance—the way he dismantled that film as it went along. They've warmed him up here—he even flirts with daddyhood.

There's nothing in the sequel to match the elation of seeing Murray get bombed by a kamikaze blob, rise from the floor and announce, matter-of-factly, "He slimed me." The surprises this time are in the demented shticks—the places where Reitman lets his actors cut loose.

Except for the wide-open mouth, you'd never recognize MacNicol as Stingo from "Sophie's Choice"; his glassy eyes, frozen smile and strangled Slavic accent give him the poignant creepiness of something abandoned by exasperated space aliens.

Rick Moranis returns as the hapless accountant, who's now also a lawyer but remains a thoroughbred nerd—his thick glasses welded to his nose, his hair pasted down on his skull, his words getting tangled as they tumble self-consciously from his mouth.

He and Annie Potts (as the Ghostbusters' secretary) have an improbably sexy rapport; they're both hopelessly nearsighted, and her lackadaisical honking meshes with his anxious bleating—they fill each other's verbal crevices. Their exchanges are transcendent, the apotheosis of nerd humor.

True, Dan Aykroyd is bland and doughy and Ernie Hudson a puzzling appendage. But Weaver continues to be a witty straight man (straight person?) for Murray, and Harold Ramis makes Egon an increasingly tender wonk, a man whose elongated forehead speaks volumes—none of them in English.

"Ghostbusters II" is all riffs, unfortunately. The gags don't build on one another—they're just strung along like beads. So most of the scenes have no punch line, no capper, and even the great ideas come to little.

When the Ghostbusters animate the Statue of Liberty to help dispel Manhattan's bad vibes, the movie doesn't know what to do with her. (For all the film makers tell you, she's still in Midtown.) And a plunge into the river of slime leads nowhere very funny.

A word about that slime: Although there's lots more of it, it's not of the same quality. It lacks a certain elan, a certain eclat, a certain je ne sais quoi, this slime. We "Ghostbusters" fans expect more from our slime. This slime makes people surly, argumentative. But why must slime this time have a plot function? Why can't slime just be slime?

NEWSDAY, 6/16/89, Part III/p. 3, Mike McGrady

First, some catching up. Much has transpired during the five years separating the original "Ghostbusters" and the not-quite-as-original "Ghostbusters II."

Since municipal pressure and lawsuits have forced the Ghostbusters out of business, Bill Murray ("He was borderline for a while and then he crossed the line") is hosting a very funny psychic TV show. Dan Aykroyd and Harold Ramis are back at the lab, only occasionally breaking out their old ghostbusting uniforms, and then only to perform song-and-dance routines at children's birthday parties. Sigourney Weaver has married, had a baby, separated. Rick Moranis has gone from accountant to lawyer without losing any of his essential nerdiness.

Those are the differences. Unfortunately, there are also some samenesses to report. One might wish that director-producer Ivan Reitman had given our intrepid Ghostbusters a different sort of challenge or even a different locale, but the first film was so astoundingly profitable that no one dared tamper with the basics.

Once again the story is set in a New York City haunted by cute, gluttenous and/or vicious ghosts;

once again our heroes are entangled in bureaucratic red tape; once again a skyscraper-sized figure strides through the streets of Manhattan (not the original marshallow boy but, this time, the Statue of Liberty); once again huge crowds gather to cheer on the Ghostbusters as they attack a huge building under psychic siege by the forces of evil; once again Rick Moranis, brutally rejected by a woman, tosses out the same gagline at her retreating form: "Well, I'll give you a raincheck."

The primary difference this time: pink slime. Rivers of pinkness ooze through deserted subway tunnels, seep up through sidewalks, eventually swallow mammoth buildings. Technicians Ramis and Aykroyd analyze the material and announce that it is a psychoreactive substance, a liquid form of negative energy, a concentrate of evil feeding on the bad vibes so readily available in New York City.

The pink slime can be directly linked to an oil painting of a "17th-Century Mudlavian tyrant," a portrait that comes to life periodically to demand the sacrifice of a human baby—Weaver's baby, to be precise: "Now is the season of evil; find me a child that I might live again."

No, no, no—it is not the season of evil, it is the season of sequel, summer. As long as one is in a pleasant summer-weight mood, willing to settle for a few laughs along with the air-conditioning, "Ghostbusters II," just like the original, is an amiable diversion until it starts to take its ghosts seriously, something no one else is apt to do.

When the old pros on hand—call them the gutbusters—are relaxed and winging it, the movie borders on the hilarious. When they turn to scariness and special effects, things slow down. For many, the presence of Bill Murray will be reason enough to see the flick. Once again, he brings insouciance to a high comic pitch as he pleads with us to take nothing seriously, least of all himself.

Nor can I fault any of the other performers. Dan Aykroyd has come up with some splendidly inappropriate new similes: "This whole place is going to blow like a frog on a hot plate." Is Harold Ramis still deadly serious in a scientific sort of way? Hey, is the atomic weight of cobalt 58.9? Sigourney Weaver is on hand to offer an unobtrusive touch of adult intelligence where none might otherwise exist. And Rick Moranis, ah, Rick Moranis—once again he demonstrates, repeatedly, that he is the funniest not-yet-fully-recognized comic in all of moviedom.

NEWSWEEK, 6/26/89, p. 68, David Ansen

The most interesting question about *Ghostbusters II* is not "how good is it?" (not very) but "can it possibly fail?" The delightful 1984 "Ghostbusters" was no ordinary hit—it was the biggest grossing comedy of all time. Given the public's proven appetite for the tried and true and Bill Murray's enormous appeal, it would be miraculous for this sequel to fall on its face. The depressing fact is that some sequels don't have to be any good to "work." Audiences today seem so hungry to recreate their cinematic highs that they may convince themselves they're having a great time watching "Ghostbusters II." The preview audience was cheering when the first title appeared: "5 Years Later," and they let out a victory hoot every time one of the flying specters got zapped by Our Boys. But what you didn't hear much of was precisely what made the first movie a smash: the honest, steady sound of laughter.

In Harold Ramis and Dan Aykroyd's new script the gang of four (Murray, Aykroyd, Ramis and Ernie Hudson) come out of an enforced retirement—they've been banned by the city of New York from parcticing their supernatural craft—to combat a new spectral threat. This time the slime oozing under the city streets has been burdened with sociological weight. The idea is that the slime is psycho-reactive: all the bad vibes of New York have unleashed forces of evil, and unless the Ghostbusters can get some good feelings going destruction is nigh.

Having set up this conceit, with its host of satirical possibilities, the movie amazingly neglects to flesh it out. Where are the jokes showing the legendary incivility of the Big Apple? There are none. Nothing *builds* in director Ivan Reitman's movie, nothing pays off. Why isn't Sigourney Weaver, a juicy comedienne, given anything funny to do? Why is there no tension in her romance with Murray? The filmmakers seem so cocky about the appeal of the Ghostbusters that they forgot to notice their script didn't add up. Basically what you have is an enormous, special-effects-laden movie resting on Bill Murray's ability to toss off a few low-key improvisational ironies. Sure, Murray is funny. You laugh when, under interrogation in a witness stand, he calls the female prosecutor "kitten." But he could do that in any movie. The other standout is Peter MacNicol as the creepy art restorer Janosz Poha. MacNicol invents a strangled middle European accent that is the funniest tongue since Bronson Pinchot's similar bit in "Beverly Hills Cop."

"Ghostbusters II" has its incidental pleasures, but it feels aimless and unnecessary. It short-shrifts the talents of Aykroyd and Ramis and once again gives all the worst material to poor Ernie Hudson. Reitman doesn't even try to build a decent sight gag. But will any of this matter? Maybe "Ghostbusters II," like the pink slime, is a psycho-reactive phenomenon. The good vibes of the audience, earned by the first movie, may save this sequel from itself.

TIME, 6/26/89, p. 89, Richard Schickel

The best kind of bright early summer's day spoiled by the worst kind of dark imaginings: Is it possible that in this season, otherwise so full of innocent promise, Hollywood executives banish all thought of us as audience—discerning, judicious, culturally literate? Does the solstice induce in them some Kafkaesque mental process by which we are converted, for purposes of contemptuous calculation, into some lower life-form? Do moviegoers suddenly seem to them to be, say, a vast colony of ants mindlessly munching through forests of Roman numerals, unconcerned about the taste, good or bad, of anything placed in our path? (Yum—*Indiana Jones III;* slurp—*Star Trek V: The Final Frontier;* burp—*Ghostbusters II.*)

This grim fantasy is engendered by exposure, in rapid succession, to the films underlying those last two presold titles and by the prospect of *The Karate Kid III, Lethal Weapon II, Nightmare on Elm Street V* and, heaven forfend, *Friday the 13th VIII.* Not to mention James Bond umpty-ump. The basic criticism of sequels is as familiar as it is correct: they represent the triumph of commercial caution over creative daring.

Take *Ghostbusters II,* for example. Once again the psychomagnotheric slime is flowing in Manhattan. Once again spooks are aloft among the other pollutants in its atmosphere. Once again paranormal phenomena (this time in the service of Vigo, a sometime Carpathian tyrant, whose spirit inhabits an antique portrait) have singled out Dana (Sigourney Weaver) for special attention. Once again the old team of exorcists—wisecracking Venkman (Bill Murray), absentminded Egon (Harold Ramis), earnest Ray (Dan Aykroyd) and stouthearted Winston (Ernie Hudson)—is ready to deploy its pseudo science in the service of exorcism.

But that pileup of "onceagains" finally undoes this sequel. For if writers Ramis and Aykroyd have slightly altered the circumstances of their central figures, they have not bothered to develop their characters any further. Dana, for example, has a baby and a tangle-tongued boss—marvelously played by Peter MacNicol—who is madly in love with her. The ghostbusters themselves are suffering, to good comic effects, from celebrity burnout and municipal ire over their failure to clean up the mess that they made the last time they saved the city.

But the movie and everyone in it remain, under Ivan Reitman's determinedly casual direction, very loosely organized. They amble agreeably, but not necessarily hilariously, from one special-effects sequence to the next. These are not better, worse or even different from the original's trick work, and their lack of punctuating surprise is the film's largest problem, especially at the shamelessly repetitive climax.

Still, it has moments of wayward life, especially in contrast to the smug torpor of *Star Trek V,* which William Shatner directed from a script by David Loughery. That "final frontier" mentioned in its title is nothing more than your standard black hole, through which the starship *Enterprise* is commanded to navigate by a not very menacing religious fanatic named Sybok (Laurence Luckinbill). He imagines he will find God lurking back of this particular beyond. What he finds instead is, of course, a false deity manifested in the form of an unpersuasive special effect.

This story is treated pretty much as an obligation, a formal requisite of big-budget sci-fi. What really interests the creators of this movie is the middle-aging process as it affects Captain Kirk, Mr. Spock and "Bones" McCoy (respectively, need we say, Shatner, Leonard Nimoy and DeForest Kelley). Good of them, on the one hand, to acknowledge that the boys aren't getting any younger. Bad of them, on the other, not to acknowledge the possibility that after being cooped up on a spaceship for almost a quarter-century, they might be a trifle tired of one another's company. A little scratchy, say, over Spock's unending reasonableness, Kirk's sententious habit of summing up the moral of every adventure. But no, the atmosphere on this voyage is a lot like a late night at an Elks' smoker, all bleary sentimentality and nostalgia for the past. Maybe we will never find God, Kirk suggests at the end, but, by golly, male bonding is a swell substitute.

This is a thought only a Trekkie could love. But it does get one to wondering what these boring guys see in one another. And, even more subversively, what did we ever see in them? It is, one suspects, a notion that may recur as we glumly chomp our way across the bleak summer-movie landscape. Anybody up for a consumer revolt? come on, folks. What are we, men or...ants?

VILLAGE VOICE, 6/27/89, p. 65, J. Hoberman

What goes around comes around, bigger than ever. Like the mindless, autostimulating "waves" that course through the stands at American ballparks, product familiarity celebrates itself: The record weekend grosses racked up by *Indiana Jones and the Last Crusade* are echoed by the spontaneous rhythmic applause greeting the appearance of that unmistakable ambulance-cum-smogmobile 10 minutes into Ivan Reitman's *Ghostbusters II.*

Truly, no value in America is more sacred than a trademark, nothing more comforting than the assembly line production of Mom's Apple Pie. It scarcely matters whether *Ghostbusters II* strokes or satirizes the viewing public—this film will gross a zillion. The nostalgia mode has become a permanent fixture of our cultural economy. What goes around comes around, as often as it can: *Ghostbusters II* isn't a sequel so much as a fond remake, a simulation of the original (and its epoch). Scarcely half a decade after the actual event, we're treated to a partial replay of the summer of 1984, that fabuous New Morning which saw the Olympics staged in Los Angeles (83 gold medals), Ronald Reagan out on the hustings (525 electoral votes), *Born in the U.S.A.* topping the charts (10 million units sold), Indiana J. rocking the Temple of Doom (109,000,000 simoleons), and the Ghostbusters exorcising Central Park West (21,000,000 more than that).

It *was* a heady moment. And, the highest-grossing movie perpetrated by anyone other than George Lucas or Steven Spielberg, the original *Ghostbusters* is the most popular film comedy ever made—as well as one of the most ideologically intriguing. (What's it all about? The movie wasn't all that funny. Many reviewers considered it sub-Abbott and Costello.) Hardly pre-sold, the original *Ghostbusters* was a cult run amok. During the '84 campaign, Democrats and Republicans alike realized that the party that controlled the summer's smash hit (or at least its logo—you may remember the rival Ron- and Fritzbuster T-shirts) would win the election, and the Dems had about as much chance of that as carrying Orange County. More than *Star Wars* or *Rocky, E.T.* or *Rambo, Ghostbusters* was the perfect embodiment of Reaganism—and not simply because, like the president, it celebrated "the indispensable defense science of the next decade."

At once cynical and idealistic, *Ghostbusters* was hailed by *The Wall Street Journal* for its glorification of the free enterprise system. The movie was business school perfect—celebrating the creation and exploitation of a false need. *Ghostbusters* brilliantly inscribed its own advertisements within its text (as Bill Murray exulted after the first successful exorcism, "The franchise rights alone will make us rich beyond our wildest dreams"). Taking the supernatural as a given and then satirizing not belief in the occult but rather the special effects movies that appeal to it, *Ghostbusters* approximated the psychic sleight of hand by which our residential *Zeitgeistmeister* conjured crises and victories to save us from our psychosomatic ills. (Not the least of the movie's tricks was preempting this very analysis by attributing it to the film's ridiculous Environmental Protection Agency agent—the designated "pencil-dick"—who accused the Ghostbusters of fabricating apparitions to dispel them.)

So, *Was geht herein, kommt herein.* In virtually every regard, *Ghostbusters II* is more of the same—perhaps a bit kinder and gentler. That K-G feeling is ubiquitous: In the current *Premiere,* Spielberg explains that he made *The Last Crusade* in part "to apologize" for *The Temple of Doom,* which "was too dark, too subterranean, and much too horrific." (Are these his euphemisms for too racist, too sexist, and much too successful?) There is a kind of pallid new New Morning in America (partly because the old Z-meister is gone and partly because he's not around to make it happen anymore), and, a number of thrilling sewer scenes aside, what *Ghostbusters II* and *The Last Crusade* have in common is their concern for establishing family ties. In *The Last Crusade,* the search for the absent father is identified with nothing less than the quest for the Holy Grail—"I didn't come for the Cup of Christ, I came to find my Pop!" Less Oedipal in its conflicts and less reverential in its worldview, *Ghostbusters II* provides its protagonists with offspring rather than parents.

"Five years later," the film begins. There's a suggestive close-up of organic slime oozing from a crack in the sidewalk and—presto!—Sigourney Weaver is perambulating an eight-month-old infant, jokingly called Oscar. The opening sequence, which sends the tot's carriage careening off into heavy traffic, crosses the central heartclutcher in *Potemkin's* "Odessa Steps" with the trajectory of that venerable, one-gag kiddie classic, *The Slant Book.* Thus, as heavily dependent on baby F/X as it is on animation and miniatures, *Ghostbusters II* is part of the boomer boom that, in movie terms, encompasses everything from *The Wonder Years* to *Pink Cadillac* (Clint Eastwood's answer to *Raising Arizona*) to Max Spielberg (the most influential four-year-old on planet Earth).

In keeping with this downhill coast into adult responsibility, there aren't as many cigarettes consumed here as in the original *Ghostbusters*—not to mention the persistent alienation effect of Murray and Aykroyd's rampant middle-age spread. Still, children will be pleased to find the same abundance of ecto-mucus and hyper-goo. (If anything, the intervening triumph of the Garbage Pail Kids and the marketing of play Slime has significantly enhanced the yuck quotient.) While initially the Ghostbusters are has-beens, reduced to doing birthday parties for "ungrateful little yuppie larvae," the movie's whole agenda is to render Bill Murray patriarchal—or at least, good-with-kids. Indeed, *Ghostbusters II* is so suffused with socially channeled testosterone that the climactic pissing contest will even establish archnerd Rick Moranis as potent. (The token black member of the team, Ernie Hudson, is no less marginalized than in the original.)

This is important because the 'busters are, after all, public servants—affable disaster specialists with a selective sense of wonder. A billion-dollar logo aside, their trademark is a juicy contempt for those literal-minded bureaucrats who are constrained by the reality principle. Thus, *Ghostbusters II* hews to the original pattern of free-market catastrophe, misguided state intervention, and the triumphant rehabilitation of the entrepreneurial spirit (here somewhat inflected by a halfhearted populism). Having inadvertently caused a third New York blackout, the 'busters are put on trial—redeeming themselves when they save the judge from the familiar squadron of blobby, toothless apparitions.

Like its model, *Ghostbusters II* grounds its fantasy in Manhattan local color. Indeed, in the absence of a surefire hit single, the movie's most persistent leitmotiv is its insistence on the city's negative aura. "Being miserable and treating other people like dirt is every New Yorker's God-given right," the Kochoid mayor proclaims in a line that deserves to haunt the upcoming mayoral campaign. "Only a Carpathian would come back to life now and choose New York," Murray smirks. (That's not the only weird lifestyle decision. It's even harder to figure why Sigourney Weaver would return to dating and choose Murray. The city's deterioration matches his own.)

The Last Crusade may have the hottest sex scene in any Spielberg film (albeit played for laffs largely below the frame-line) and a Nazi rally where Hitler gives Indy his autograph, but, as relentlessly overdetermined as it is, it's far less entertaining than *Ghostbusters II*. Reitman's bad taste is as irrepressible as the blob beneath the city: The dread pink slime violates Weaver's apartment as she fills Oscar's bath, erupting out of the tub in the form of a giant penis, which sends her scampering for the relative safety of Murray's boudoir. More frequently, however, the ooze is associated with afterbirth. As the film's resident geek couple, Moranis and the Ghostbusters' gumsnapping secretary (Annie Potts), broach the possibility of having a child, Reitman cuts to a trio of mega-slimed 'busters emerging from a manhole in front of the Metropolitan Museum of Art.

One can appreciate Reitman's Dada gesture in locating the center of evil in New York's preeminent cultural citadel; his movie is frequently so disjointed as to seem virtually avant-garde. Even allowing for its supernatural premise, *Ghostbusters II* makes little narrative sense. The two cosmic threats—the malign painting of the Carpathian potentate, Vigo, which bids to manifest itself in little Oscar and take over the world, and the viscous river of gunk that courses beneath Manhattan, feeding on the city's bad vibes—are only tangentially related. At best, *Ghostbusters II* is a free-associative semiotic barrage, studiously evoking the original even as it giddily addresses all manner of contemporary anxieties. This psychic spritz is the film's central pleasure. The topicality of some images is positively uncanny—the phantom jogger rounding the Central Park reservoir, the totemic use of the Statue of Liberty.

In the Ghostbusters saga, no less than in the legend of Indiana Jones, evil invariably has a foreign accent. But where Spielberg has a taste for villainous Nazis, Reitman—a child refugee from the People's Republic of Czechoslovakia—is, understandably, more taken with the specter that once haunted Europe. Nothing overt, of course. As his green-card jokes suggest, ther's just a vestigial insecurity. Reitman remains an outsider, having grown up in Canada—it was, perhaps, with a double dip of alienation that he orchestrated an American invasion of his birthplace in the underrated *Stripes*. Still, the satire of East European malevolence is the most heartfelt thing in *Ghostbusters II*. (The parody goes well beyond standard Bela Lugosi stuff. The monstrous Vigo may be an excessive stand-in for Gorbie, but the opening send-up of *Potemkin* is unmistakable— Peter MacNicol, who plays the depraved nudnik Janosz, strongly suggests a puny Eisenstein.)

What Reitman can't quite muster is the appropriate nationalist fervor. It's an odd feeling watching *Ghostbusters II* in the aftermath of Communism's well-publicized collapse, particularly as the movie ends with a mad cacophony of patriotic symbols. The film's one element of social realism is the Balkanization of New York. Compelled to rally the city, the 'busters are at a loss, ultimately brainstorming Liberty as a positive version of the Stay-Puft Marshmallow Man (only in Czechoslovakia or Tiananmen Square would the Statue of Liberty have such clout). Brought to life by a combination of cosmic ick and Jackie Wilson, the Lady, as they were calling her back in the centennial summer of '86, strides across the bay and marches up Fifth Avenue. (There's a last, wonderfully anarchic moment when she squashes a cop car as heedlessly as King Kong trampling a native hut.)

Here, along with the energy beams of Ghostbuster's patented proton packs, the movie's various trademarks converge. Like a mob of revelers transported from Times Square, the crowd outside the Metropolitan starts singing "Auld Lang Syne." (Which new year is it?) In the world of Ivan Reitman, this could be considered sentimentality—I think.

Also reviewed in:
NEW YORK TIMES, 6/16/89, p. C5, Vincent Canby
NEW YORKER, 7/10/89, p. 85, Pauline Kael
VARIETY, 6/21/–27/89, p. 24
WASHINGTON POST, 6/16/89, p. B1, Hal Hinson
WASHINGTON POST, 6/16/89, Weekend/p. 41, Desson Howe

GIRL IN A SWING, THE

A Millimeter Films release of a Panorama Film International production. *Producer:* Just Betzer. *Director:* Gordon Hessler. *Screenplay:* Gordon Hessler. *Based on the novel by:* Richard Adams. *Director of Photography:* Claus Loof. *Editor:* Robert Gordon. *Music:* Carl Davis. *Sound:* Preben Mortensen. *Production Designer:* Rob Schilling. *Costumes:* Betina Betzer and Marjorie Lavelly. *Running time:* 112 minutes. *MPAA Rating:* Not Rated.

CAST: Meg Tilly (Karin); Rupert Fraser (Alan); Nicholas Le Prevost (Tony); Elspet Gray (Mrs. Desland); Lorna Heilbron (Flick); Claire Shepherd (Angela); Jean Boht (Mrs. Taswell); Sophie Thursfield (Deirdre); Lynsey Baxter (Barbara); Duke (Mr. Steinbeck).

LOS ANGELES TIMES, 9/29/89, Calendar/p. 8, Sheila Benson

Some films—"Wuthering Heights," "Out of Africa" and more—must be entered into utterly or not all, and "The Girl in a Swing" is certainly one of that number. With two impassioned performances and a soaring musical score that heightens its mood of doomed romanticism, "The Girl in a Swing" is an uncommon spellbinder. It's also an all-or-nothing movie experience.

Like the original novel by "Watership Down's" Richard Adams, "The Girl in a Swing" is a contemporary love story that darkens and deepens as it unfolds. In its opening, Alan Desland, a bright, repressed Englishman in his early 30s, becomes aware of life's erotic possibilities for the very first time. Meeting a beautiful, bold, enigmatic young German girl working in Copenhagen, he falls in love—as wildly and completely as she does. They marry in a matter of weeks and begin a closely shared life in England's Berkshire, idyllic until Karin begins to have mounting visions of menace and dread, portents he starts to share.

It's not a story that condenses without sounding predictable or absurd, and it's neither. Nothing about "The Girl in a Swing" is predictable, especially its supernatural elements. Novelist Adams' power comes from his sure mixing of the commonplace, the sensual and the magical in a seemingly ordinary world. His hints about the consequences of repression have more in common with "The Turn of the Screw" than with films teeming with ectoplasmic manifestation.

Gordon Hessler, a veteran director and the film's adapter, is strongest in his casting and his rapport with actors; in other areas he's sometimes overcautious and pedantic. There's nothing cautious about his two stars' performances, however. You may remember Rupert Fraser from "The Shooting Party" or as the long-separated father in "Empire of the Sun." His Alan Desland manages to suggest reserve without priggishness and the deepening pleasure of a man in the grips of full-tilt infatuation.

As Karin, the German-born enchantress, accent and all, the sloe-eyed Meg Tilly is something of a revelation, even after the surprises of her performance in "Masquerade." Physically, Tilly may look more like Denmark's Little Mermaid than the goddess-like woman of the book with her aura of almost primal sensuality, but Tilly's direct, provocative gaze is enticing in another way and her conviction is absolute.

There's a nice, confident level of civility to the production too: matters of art direction and production design like Desland's upper-echelon country house, his antiques and porcelain shop and the crucial detailing of the porcelain figure of the title. Only the costume design feels timid, off-the-rack or at worst, designed with no discernible flair. (You might question the strange, overheavy cuts to the pianist at the recital the lovers go to, but who knows what promises are made in exchange for an appearance in a film.)

Finally, there is the film's sumptuous Carl Davis music. An American who has lived in England for years, Davis has written music for "The French Lieutenant's Woman," "The Rainbow" and "Scandal," as well as the bittersweet themes for Thames television's "The Unknown Chaplin" and its series on Buster Keaton. All of it is lovely stuff, yet this score seems his finest yet. His work unifies the film, carries it as powerfully as Bernard Herrmann's scores carried Alfred Hitchcock's or Brian DePalma's thrillers.

The care and taste of the production can be laid at the door of Just Betzer, who also produced "Babette's Feast." The book's fans will be relieved to know that Betzer and company have steered away from every lurking pitfall in matters of taste and judgment. Since Adams' story is about the deep-reaching power of unfettered, almost pagan love, with a heroine who drops her clothing as naturally as other women drop their inhibitions, those pitfalls may have been considerable. (The film is Times-rated Mature for its love scenes, frank language and occasional, decorous nudity.)

Yet if the film has a flaw, it may be this very civility. Its restraint is admirable, but in dealing with so much modulation it necessarily loses ferocity. Possibly, this is a story whose telling needs to rip out all the stops—something this production isn't prepared to do. It may be that film itself can't do what's needed here, that these are visions and demons better left to the printed page and the unbounded imagination. Maybe there's really no technique that could take this story to new levels of expressiveness. It's just that "The Girl in the Swing" is good enough that it makes you wish it could.

NEW YORK POST, 9/29/89, p. 21, Jami Bernard

There is an argument to be made against rushing into marriage with someone you don't know well. Is your beloved a devil's disciple? An ax murderer? A liar? An apparition? "The Girl in a Swing," a moody love story as indebted to Hitchcock as to "9½ Weeks," proves that marriage should not be taken lightly, and certainly not quickly.

Alan (Rupert Fraser) is a reserved, repressed British ceramics dealer who falls kaboom for the charms of translator Karin (Meg Tilly), an arresting German woman living a coyly mysterious life in Copenhagen. Alan likes his women the way he likes his porcelain figurines: perfect, delicate, fragile and unchanging, so even when the obviously troubled Karin tries to tell Alan about her past—after their hurried wedding, that is—he puts finger to those lovely trembling lips and hushes her. Life is grand.

But Karin is a strange puppy. Chaste and naive before their marriage, she has sudden bouts of lust that are making Alan a little unbalanced. "I love you to distraction," he is fond of saying, and indeed, finding Karin nude on a garden swing or stripping on a "From Here to Eternity" shoreline has gotten Alan extremely distracted. There is something unholy about all this unbridled passion, accompanied by blackouts, bad dreams and apparitions of a stuffed tortoise and a crumbling ceramic figure.

Whenever there's a sudden high wind, one can suspect the presence of the supernatural, although part of Karin's dread secret is really on the banal side; how she chooses before the marriage to handle that dread secret is not banal but is easily guessed at. The only one in the dark, really, is poor, dull Alan, who doesn't think that Karin's hysteria over stuffed tortoises or her obsession over Macbethian themes of sin and forgiveness are anything to get excited about.

"The Girl in a Swing," based on a novel by Richard Adams, is erotically moody and succeeds in building a creepy felling that will cling to you long after you leave the theater. It is also, unfortunately, clumsily portentous and relies in part for its sense of mystery on extreme and constant close-ups of Meg Tilly's face. Tilly is sexy and appealing, but her face, though open and other-worldly, is not porcelain, nor does it hold the key the movie is searching for.

Tilly's honey-sweet voice affects an endearing accent, a liquid gurgle that lacks the precision of a Streep ("I had a farm in Africa"), but takes on a life of its own, like another character to which attention must be paid.

Director Gordon Hessler gives "Girl" a quick, episodic pace, although the episodes themselves are so similar the effect is of variations on a theme. "I'm tired out with your kindnesses and generosity," says Karin to Alan, and frankly, so are we—Fraser is an eager milquetoast, in contrast to Tilly, who gives an exhaustingly emotional performance.

In case you are thinking of running off with someone you hardly know, here are the warning signs you should look for, courtesy of "The Girl in a Swing". Do they wring the necks of wounded birds? Do they hear children crying from inside locked cabinets? Do they cry at Chopin? Do they hang around the house after they are dead? Do they not have enough money for the bus home? Do they go nutzoid when you mention stuffed tortoises? Do they pray to pagan gods?

If so, have a few more dates before taking the plunge.

NEWSDAY, 9/29/89, Part III/p. 5, Bill Kaufman

"The Girl in a Swing" abounds with simmering eroticism, excellent cinematography and a high level of acting by its stars, Meg Tilly and Rupert Fraser. However, it is seriously flawed by a plot that's confusing and unclearly presented.

This rather peculiar picture, on the art-film circuit, deals with a young couple so distracted by their passioin for each other that untoward things occur. The often vague story line is narrow—the movie is built around the intense love-and-sex relationship that erupts between Alan (Fraser), an inhibited and repressed upper-class British antiques dealer, and Karin (Tilly), a German secretary working in Copenhagen.

Tilly's portrayal of the young woman, who vacillates between being a doe-eyed coquette and a sensuous tigress, is excellent. She exudes a crisp, youthful sexuality. Fraser is equally fine as the young man discovering his own sexuality, a chap so proper (or repressed?) that he declines premarital sex with Foster when she becomes his wife-to-be. The movie has been filmed lushly in beautiful locations here and abroad by director Gordon Hessler, who also wrote the screenplay.

But alas, throughout the film, the pair are subjected to a series of unsettling incidents that are tossed on screen in a totally confusing fashion, often in brief flashes. For example, it's difficult to understand whether the characters are experiencing dreams or real events in the choppy on-screen intrusions that portend some great evil. The movie leaves a feeling of puzzlement rather than resolving the plot.

However, those who can disregard that not-so-small problem may be pleased by "The Girl in a Swing," particularly if they like a challenge—and don't mind leaving the theater asking themselves what really happened.

VILLAGE VOICE, 10/10/89, p. 95, Julie Phillips

While women in the movies often stand for something else—male fear or desire, or some more abstract concept like nature or sex—few movies are as obvious about it as *the Girl in a Swing*. This film has its love interest working overtime: She's Venus moonlighting as Mary Magdalene moonlighting as Eve with the bitten apple in her hand. Like Betty Blue, say, or the women in certain kinds of thrillers, she's as mentally fragile and emotionally distanced as she is physically available.

On a trip to Copenhagen, Alan (Rupert Fraser), wealthy, British, a dealer in antique porcelain, falls into open-mouthed, eyeball-glazing love with Karin (Meg Tilly), a woman with a nice smile, a mysterious past, and a strange relationship to water. He marries her, no questions asked, and takes her back to England, where for a while things are fine: She's charming, likes sex a lot, and inquires politely about pagan cults and the story of Mary Magdalene. But Alan is having strange dreams and hearing the ghostly cries of a child, and when Karin tries to take communion, she passes out at the altar. When she attempts to explain these things to Alan, he insists he doesn't want to know. He says he loves her as she is—meaning as he imagines her to be.

Based on the novel by Richard (*Watership Down*) Adams, *the Girl in a Swing* offers two possible interpretations for its tragic ending: a prosaic one—in which the visions are all just Alan's imagination, and the bad end a result of his delusions or his callousness—and a supernatural or magic one, in which Karin is a mystical being who came from and must return to the sea. It's hard to forgive the film for favoring the supernatural one. This makes the ending happier but also lets the rather caddish Alan off the hook and suggests that Karin's desirability—her sex-goddess qualities—may be dependent on the death of her child.

On the other hand, though well acted and pleasant to look at, *the Girl in a Swing* isn't really convincing enough to take much offense at. B-movie-maker Gordon Hessler directs this international coproduction with a heavy hand. The soft-focus, slow-motion dream sequences are too artificial, the sex scenes too unappealing, Tilly's Germanic accent too fake, and the attempt to make a short movie out of a thick book too obviously difficult. In some ways, it's like watching a period piece, a curiosity from a time when men thought they could still get away with this kind of thing by calling it romance or magic.

Also reviewed in:
NEW YORK TIMES, 9/30/89, p. 14, Caryn James
VARIETY, 12/28/88–1/3/89, p. 13
WASHINGTON POST, 9/29/89, p. D7, Rita Kempley
WASHINGTON POST, 9/29/89, Weekend/p. 37, Joe Brown

GLEAMING THE CUBE

A Twentieth Century Fox Film Corporation release of a Gladden Entertainment presentation. *Producer:* Lawrence Turman and David Foster. *Director:* Graeme Clifford. *Screenplay:* Michael Tolkin. *Director of Photography:* Reed Smoot. *Editor:* John Wright. *Music:* Jay Ferguson. *Music Editor:* Tom Carlson. *Sound:* Donald Summer. *Sound Editor:* John Leveque. *Production Designer:* John Muto. *Art Director:* Dan Webster. *Set Decorator:* Susan Emshwiller. *Special Effects:* Phil Cory. *Costumes:* Ann Somers Major. *Makeup:* Annie D'Angelo. *Stunt Coordinator:* Buddy Joe Hooker. *Running time:* 104 minutes. *MPAA Rating:* PG-13.

CAST: Christian Slater (Brian Kelly); Steven Bauer (Al Lucero); Richard Herd (Ed Lawndale); Le Tuan (Colonel Trac); Min Luong (Tina Trac); Art Chudabala (Vinh Kelly); Ed Lauter (Mr. Kelly); Micole Mercurio (Mrs. Kelly); Peter Kwong (Bobby Nguyen); Charles Cyphers (Harvey McGill); Max Perlich (Yabbo); Tony Hawk (Buddy); Tommy Guerrero (Sam); Christian Jacobs (Gremic); Joe Gosha (Nick Oliver); Andy Nguyen (Tran Thanh); Kieu Chinh (Madame Trac); Joshua Ravetch (Student Pilot); Jack Riley (Homeowner); Angela Moya (Housekeeper); F. William Parker (Motel Manager); J. Jay Saunders (Medical Examiner); Chi-Muoi Lo (Tough #1); Vien Hong (Tough #2); Ngo Van Quy (Billiards Manager); Hao "Howie" Pham (Pool Player #1); Phong Thien Nguyen (Pool Player #2); Khiem Tran (Mr. Phong); Rita Rudner (Mrs. Yabbo); Arsenio "Sonny" Trinidad (Other Nguyen); Lauree Berger (Mrs. Lawndale); Buddy Joe Hooker (Corvette Driver).

LOS ANGELES TIMES, 1/14/89, Calendar/p. 7, Kevin Thomas

There's a genuine attempt in "Gleaming the Cube" to deal with the impact the loss of a brother has upon a likable, footloose teen-ager. Unfortunately, the conventions of the action-adventure/youth-flick genres prevail. The result is an exploitation picture with a little something extra—lots of awesome skateboard wizardry, culminating in a speed-of-lightning chase sequence, in which skateboards are pitted against cars.

The film is geared ruthlessly to teen audiences. In fact, how many people beyond their teens know that its title refers to that exalted state a skateboarder attains at the top of his form?

Christian Slater stars as Orange County teen Brian Kelly, spiky-haired and sloppy, for whom skateboarding has a far greater priority than his studies. But no problem: He has an adopted Vietnamese brother named Vinh (Art Chudabala), a studious and orderly youth, who'll do his homework for him. Then, shockingly, Vinh is found hanged to death in a motel room.

Incredibly, only Brian suspects murder. He does get a local cop (Steven Bauer) to listen, but after a series of contrived macho clashes between the two, Brian takes matters into his own hands.

"Gleaming the Cube" is not the first movie to be set in part against Orange County's large Southeact Asian community. However, as in "Steele Justice," the film makers are interested in it primarily as an exotic backdrop for crime and violence. Surely, the majority of Vietnamese and Cambodian refugees building new lives in America are not involved in gang warfare and other illicit ventures, but that's not the impression you get here.

Writer Michael Tolkin provides only Slater with a role of much dimension, and this nervy, bright young actor, who played Jeff Bridges' eldest son in "Tucker" and Sean Connery's apprentice in "The Name of the Rose" involves us in Brian and his quest. Slater shows us Brian discovering how much brotherly love he actually felt for Vinh, love that had been repressed by resentment.

We get precious few glimpses of Brian's parents (Ed Lauter, Nicole Mercurio)—why, for example, wouldn't they have also suspected foul play in Vinh's death? Slater and Lauter have one good scene in which the father admits he failed to realize the impact upon Brian of his efforts to make his adopted son feel special. There's also an initially wary friendship between Vinh's demure girlfriend (Min Luong) and Brian, but action is the main attraction in this fantasy.

Director Graeme Clifford gets full value from the script (which allows Bauer and others little latitude). The action sequences do dazzle, and Clifford makes the most of the few quieter moments. The film's flashy finish smashes credibility to smithereens, but "Gleaming the Cube" (rated PG-13 for violence) has the feel of a film that turned out exactly as intended.

MONTHLY FILM BULLETIN, 11/89, p. 333, Verina Glaessner

Brian Kelly, a teenage skateboard fanatic, who spends his time hanging out with fellow enthusiasts Yabbo, Buddy, Sam and Gremic, is an embarrassment to his insurance salesman father, and in every way the opposite of his adoptive Vietnamese brother Vinh. A computer whizz kid, Vinh works for Colonel Trac, a leading member of the Vietnamese community who owns the local video store and runs a charity which supplies medical aid to Vietnam. But Vinh is summarily dismissed when he discovers a discrepancy in a bill of lading while doing the charity's accounts, and when he later investigates the warehouse at night he is caught by Trac's henchmen, Vietnam veteran Ed Lawndale and Bobby Nguyen. He is taken to a motel for questioning, suspected of being a Communist sympathiser, and is accidentally killed by Nguyen. His death is made to look like suicide, but Brian, finding the bill of lading and learning that it refers to drugs, begins his own investigation. While hidden in the back of Nguyen's car, he overhears the latter being killed by Lawndale. He takes his story to Detective Lucero who, in the absence of a body and because of his own brushes with Brian, disbelieves him. But when Brian locates Nguyen's apartment, he finds Lucero (who has become increasingly suspicious of Vinh's "suicide") there ahead of him. A police officer who is a Vietnam veteran interprets the bill of lading and reveals that the drugs listed are legally available medical ones. Brian then approaches Tina, Trac's daughter and Vinh's girlfriend, and after overhauling his appearance to convince her to talk to him, is able to connect Lawndale with the voice of Nguyen's killer. He breaks into the warehouse, dodges electronic detection devices, and discovers a cache of arms (intended to carry on the fight in Vietnam) hidden in a crate. He sets fire to the warehouse and attempts to implicate Trac by leaving a cap (which he had earlier purloined from his house) on the scene. He escapes from three Vietnamese bike boys who are hired by Lawndale to run him down (two of whom are caught by Lucero), and armed with a specially strong and speedy skateboard leaves with his friends for a confrontation with Lawndale. The latter kills Trac and escapes with Tina in a police car, pursued by Brian on his board and his friends in their pizza delivery van. After a prolonged chase, Brian is injured, Lawndale is captured and Tina released; she later visits Brian in hospital and the two cement their friendship.

Gleaming the Cube (the title is a skateboarding term for achieving the ultimate) starts out with the not inconsiderable handicap of having to put its protagonists on skateboards. No amount of visual ingenuity or editing skill—and in a vigorous finale Graeme Clifford demonstrates that he has plenty of both—can disguise the awkwardness of the sport of the fact that for the most part the boards hamper rather than enhance movement. Any residual grace displayed is limited to very special terrain, like sections of piping or the drained pool used in one sequence. Another handicap is the cumbersome and not fully thought-out plot, involving Vietnam verterans and the Vietnamese community in Orange County. As anti-Communists refusing to give up the war as lost, Trac and his colleagues would—within the ideological parameters of the action movie—have quite a sympathetic role, and *Gleaming the Cube* seems uncertain how to 'place' them.

The film is also not quite the straightforward revenge saga which one might expect from such set-pieces as Brian arriving late at his brother's funeral, skateboard tucked under his arm, shambling forward to place a lone chess piece on Vinh's coffin. Its heart seems to belong more to the cause of the disaffected teenager, distrustful of adults in general and families in particular (Brian's is pictured in particularly grotesque light, with his father compulsively running videos which speel out Vinh's success and Brian's failures). The film is pushed further in this direction by Christian Slater's performance, with its James Dean-like vocal delivery and askance gaze ("What did we ever do for you?" his parents ask in an orgy of belated self-recrimination; "You took me to Disneyland and I peed on Donald Duck"). It is a pity in the end that the film was not edged further away from formula action and Enid Blytonesque kids' caper towards a more wholehearted treatment of the theme.

NEW YORK POST, 2/18/89, p. 21, Jami Bernard

An airport tarmac, an empty swimming pool, a multi-lane highway with concrete dividers— what do these suggest to you? To Brian Kelly and his punked-out high school buddies, these are places to do crazy things on skateboards: somersaults, backflips all kinds of derring-do. And, most important, these are places where a gook skateboarder can gleam the cube.

I don't know what "gleaming the cube" means, and evidently neither does Brian until his friend tells him the cube is "the place you skate where you let go."

Brian, in fact, lets go several times in the course of this movie, and he has the bruises and scabs to prove it. But what his friend means is that a good skateboarder can experience a zen-like pleasure, given the right tarmac, empty pool or crowded highway.

Indeed, the skateboarding stunts are terrific. Kids fly through the air, gently lapping the top edge of one kidney-shaped pool before flipping and twisting and doing wheelies and all kinds of athletic, graceful maneuvers on their way to the deep end.

The plot, however, is less like this cube business than like the average square-headed teens-solve-a-murder mystery. Brian (Christian Slater) can't believe his Vietnamese adopted brother Vinh (Art Chudabala) has committed suicide, so he sets out to investigate and unleashes the fury of some local businessmen who Have Something to Hide.

The audience is in on the murder from the beginning: Vinh has been checking into suspicious medical relief supplies being shipped to Vietnam in crates that are awfully heavy to be holding gauze bandages. Caught while nosing around the warehouse, Vinh is strangled and his death made to look like a suicide.

Since Vinh is a guy whose biggest sin so far is having smoked his first cigarette, Brian decides to flush out the killers himself. With a little begrudging help from a kindred-spirit detective (an edgy Steven Bauer) and Vinh's old girlfriend (Min Luong), Brian is soon poking his skateboard into things that shouldn't concern him.

"No one knows anything," says a Bad Guy smugly, "except a kid on a skateboard!"

That is definitely the cue for a predictable finale with all the skateboarders appearing over the rise like the kids on bikes in "E.T.," only now their boards are souped up to resemble high-speed manhole covers.

Slater, who was Sean Connery's odd-looking sidekick in another mystery, "The Name of the Rose," is convincing as a recalcitrant youth, even speaking reluctantly as if he's just inhaled a lungful of marijuana. His relationship to the like-minded cop could have been developed more, instead of having Bauer constantly smack the kid upside the head for interfering with the police investigation.

"Gleaming the Cube" is far from unwatchable, though. The skateboard chase scenes are lively and well-edited, the stuntskaters hardly noticeable. It's the "Endless Summer" of skateboarding.

Also reviewed in:
NEW YORK TIMES, 2/18/89, p. 18, Janet Maslin
VARIETY, 1/25-31/89, p. 14
WASHINGTON POST, 1/16/89, p. D3, Richard Harrington

GLORY

A Tri-Star Pictures release. *Producer:* Freddie Fields. *Director:* Edward Zwick. *Screenplay:* Kevin Jarre. *Based on the books "Lay This Laurel"by:* Lincoln Kirstein, *"One Gallant Rush" by:* Peter Burchard, *and the letters of:* Robert Gould Shaw. *Director of Photography:* Freddie Francis. *Editor:* Steven Rosenblum. *Music:* James Horner. *Music Editor:* Jim Henrikson. *Sound:* Lon E. Bender and (music) Shawn Murphy. *Sound Editor:*

Soundelux. *Production Designer:* Norman Garwood. *Art Director:* Keith Pain. *Set Decorator:* Garrett Lewis. *Special Effects:* Phil Cory. *Costumes:* Francine Jamison-Tanchuck. *Make up:* Carl Fullerton *Stunt Coordinator:* Bob Minor. *Running time:* 122 minutes. *MPAA Rating:* R.

CAST: Matthew Broderick (Robert Gould Shaw); Denzel Washington (Trip); Cary Elwes (Cabot Forbes); Morgan Freeman (Rawlins); Jihmi Kennedy (Sharts); Andre Braugher (Searles); John Finn (Mulcahy); Donovan Leitch (Morse); John David Cullum (Russell); Alan North (Governor Andrew); Bob Gunton (General Harker); Cliff DeYoung (Colonel Montgomery); Christian Baskous (Pierce); RonReaco Lee (Mute Drummer Boy); Jay O. Sanders (General Strong); Richard Riehle (Quartermaster); Daniel Jenkins ("A" Company Officer); Michael Smith Guess and Abdul Salaam El Razzac ("A" Company Soldiers); Peter Michael Goetz (Francis Shaw); Pete Munro (Surgeon); Benji Wilhoite (Young Soldier); Ethan Phillips (Hospital Steward); Mark A. Levy (Bigoted Soldier); Randell Haynes (Paymaster); Afemo Omilami (Tall Contraband); Keith Noble (Short Contraband); Dan Biggers (Minister); Marc Gowan (Dr. Rogers); Raymond Godshall Jr. (Dr. Thorpe); Bob Minor (Contraband Soldier); Joan Riordan (White Woman); Saundra Franks (Black Woman); Mark A. Jones (54th Soldier).

CHRISTIAN SCIENCE MONITOR, 1/10/90, p. 10, David Sterritt

[*Glory* was reviewed jointly with *Driving Miss Daisy*; see Sterritt's review of that film.]

LOS ANGELES TIMES, 12/14/89, Calendar/p. 1, Kevin Thomas

"Glory" is an eloquent, heart-tugging Civil War epic about the first black infantry regiment to march off to battle for the Union. And epic *is* the word. Not since John Ford has a film maker created such dramatic large-scale Civil War battle scenes in a major theatrical film.

However, without its fresh focus on the role of the black soldiers in the Civil War, "Glory" would seem old-fashioned in its unabashedly sentimental conflict between good and evil. What makes it as rousing as it is is our awareness that the Civil War was far from a decisive victory for blacks; it was more like the first round in a struggle for freedom and equality that continues more than a century later.

"Glory," which is a touch self-congratulatory, eschews the ironic for the heroic, even though much of what it depicts is inherently, even cruelly ironic, expecially in the spectacle of men who, among their first acts as free men, volunteered to pay for their freedom with their lives.

Written with fervor by Kevin Jarre from various sources and directed passionately by "thirtysomething" co-creator Edward Zwick, "Glory" proceeds confidently in straight-ahead fashion with some astute observations along the way.

Matthew Broderick stars as an actual Boston Brahmin abolitionist, Col. Robert Gould Shaw who, though wet behind the ears, doesn't flinch when he is asked to lead the 600-man 54th Massachusetts Voluntary Infantry, the first black Civil War unit. Broderick gives a flawless performance as this quintessential Victorian idealist, a prim, diminutive man with a Van Dyke beard, who has to dig into himself to find the reserves of courage and leadership.

Broderick shows us Shaw's growth, his learning how to temper his reflexive severity as he gains self-confidence. Keeping him in perspective is his less serious, less focused—but no less decent— friend, Maj. Cabot Forbes, played by a very likable Cary Elwes.

The film makers wisely devote the first of the film's two hours to the regiment's training in a camp in Massachusetts. As the irate Shaw finds he must combat racism that delays uniforms, rifles and even shoes for his black soldiers, we learn to know a group of them. They are: Trip (Denzel Washington), a bitter, cynical young field hand from Tennessee; Rawlins (Morgan Freeman), a quiet, older man, a natural leader and peace-keeper; Sharts (Jihmi Kennedy), a sweet-natured, sharp-shooting innocent from South Carolina; and Thomas Searles (Andre Braugher), a Boston intellectual and freed man who is best friends with Shaw and Forbes.

Shaping the men up is their Irish sergeant-major (John Finn) who insists, not quite convincingly, that he is tough on blacks not because he is a racist but because he wants them to have a chance at surviving. There are unbilled appearances by Jane Alexander as Shaw's mother, the recipient of many of his letters, and Raymond St. Jacques, a dignified Frederick Douglass.

These actors, starting with Washington and Freeman, are distinctive and involving. Braugher's Searles, however, is one of the film's primary strengths, as he tries desperately to meet the psychological as well as physical rigors of his predicament. Braugher's Searles is nicely balanced by Cliff DeYoung's nasty, corrupt Union colonel, a racist who exploits the war for profit.

As it proceeds to its magnificent climactic battle sequence in Charleston harbor, "Glory" reminds us that the Civil War was fought for many reasons. At the same time the film, like "Cry Freedom" and "A Dry, White Season," feels it must tell of a black struggle from the perspective of a sympathetic and noble white. For all that is commendable about "Glory," you nevertheless wish you were experiencing it from the perspective of Trip, a man who gets put down constantly for telling the truth, but who is obliged by the script to shape up and get swept up in the film's selfless heroism, just like everyone else.

Denzel Washington, a born star still waiting for that breakthrough part, brings an anguish to Trip that seems to go beyond the role itself. At times Trip seems a bit too contemporary in his militance, but then he is not as focal, not as developed as he might be.

Remarkable as a period piece and for Freddie Francis's vivid cinematography, "Glory" (rated R for battlefield violence) is an impressive accomplishment for a director whose only previous theatrical film was the yuppie comedy "About Last Night..." Although "Glory" is splendid for what it is, it does leave us wanting more.

MONTHLY FILM BULLETIN, 4/90, p. 105, Richard Combs

1862. Fired by the idealism for the anti-slavery cause he has inherited from his patrician Boston family, young Robert Gould Shaw fights at the Battle of Antietam Creek, and is shaken by the horror of war (wounded, he is found on the battlefield by a black gravedigger, Rawlins). But on his return home, he is overwhelmed at being offered the command, as colonel, of the first black regiment, the 54th Massachusetts, in the Northern army. Shaw persuades his sceptical friend Cabot Forbes to join him as second-in-command, and his educated black friend Thomas Searles eagerly joins up. But at Readville training camp, Thomas is dismayed to find himself sharing a tent with Rawlins, field hand Sharts and the embittered runaway slave Trip. Aware that prejudice may still relegate his men to nothing more than manual labourers, Shaw begins to drive them hard, coming into conflict with Forbes, who believes real training pointless. Trip is whipped for supposed desertion, but Shaw later learns from Rawlins that he was merely trying to replace his ill-fitting, crippling boots; a furious Shaw then forces the quartermaster general to release proper boots and uniforms to all his men, and joins them in ripping up their pay slips when they learn they are to be paid less than white soldiers. In 1863, in South Carolina, the regiment is attached to the "contraband" army (untrained, recently freed slaves) of Colonel Montgomery, a "Jayhawker" intent on vengeful burning and looting. Dismayed that his men are still not considered fit for real combat, Shaw eventually secures their release by threatening to expose the freebooting of Montgomery and his commander, General Hunter. The 54th distinguish themselves in their first action against the Confederates (during which Thomas is wounded), and Rawlins finally quiets the discontent of Trip by declaring it is time they took their turn in the fighting and dying alongside white soldiers. Shaw volunteers his men to lead the assault on Fort Wagner, a heavily defended position guarding the city of Charleston. Despite their bravery, Shaw and a large part of his command (including Trip, Searles and Forbes) are wiped out and the attack fails. Subsequently, some 180,000 blacks joined the Northern army and were credited by Lincoln with playing a large part in the Union's ultimate victory.

Not just the story of the first black regiment to fight in the Northern army in the American Civil War, but the full panoply of the war itself is here. Director Edward Zwick has talked of *Glory* being one of the few films not to use the war simply as background ("We have not had to bend history in order to create drama"), and the production evidently picked up on the enthusiasm and fetishism of the thousands of Civil War buffs who regularly re-enact its battles. Associate producer Ray Herbeck Jnr. is one of them; 1,500 "re-enactors" helped to ensure historical accuracy in the training and equipping of extras for the battle scenes; and a re-enactment of Gettysburg provided the film with some second-unit footage. Colonel Robert Gould Shaw's "original silver candlesticks appear in one scene and even the underside of the bill of [Matthew] Broderick's cap is dyed the perfect Massachusetts medium green, though it is not visible in the film".

This undeniably lends *Glory* a certain vividness and even an appealing novelty value, given that the Civil War—now that Hollywood has ended its silence on Vietnam in a great clamour—might once more be the conflict most conspicuously underrepresented in its country's cinema. But it's a novelty that in the end tells against the film, because it prevents the makers getting very close to their subject, either visually or dramatically. The vividness goes with something over-bright and cleaned-up in Freddie Francis' photography, the air of an overproduced TV mini-series, which misses both the immediacy and the internal sense of authenticity in the more casual, even scrappy, deliberately parched look of the reproduction in Huston's *Red Badge of Courage*. The film (which seems epic in length, but isn't) also moves at an uncertain episodic pace, as if it had been roughly truncated and compressed from a longer series.

Not bending history perhaps demands episodic drama, except that some of the episodes—a party at Shaw's family home, after the opening battle of Antietam, where he is introduced to black abolitionist Frederick Douglass and given command of the 54th Massachusetts regiment—seem unnecessarily elaborate and even redundant. The point might have been to sketch in more of Shaw's background, the peculiarity of his patrician roots which went with the family's dedication to the anti-slavery cause (and their involvement in the Utopian artistic/social experiment of Brook Farm). But this is suggested more succinctly in an opening quotation from Gould's own letters home ("We fight for men and women whose poetry is not yet written, but which will be as enviable and as renowned as any"), as are his subsequent doubts about his novel command ("Try as I may, I don't know these men . . . their music, their camaraderie, which is so different from ours. I am in a position where if I had real strength, I could do a great deal . . . I don't want to hinder them because of my weakness"). Kevin Jarre's script and Matthew Broderick's performance leave these hesitations ill-defined, or dramatise them only as the conventional crisis of a commander torn between sympathy for his men and the need to be cruel to be kind, to teach them both to survive and overcome the sneers of other Northerners that they will never make real soldiers. Again, Huston's use of voice-over quotation from Stephen Crane gave fuller measure to the play-off of interior and exterior drama. And if Shaw is skimped as a character, so too is his relationship with his friend and second-in-command Cabot Forbes, who is initially scornful of the idea of a black regiment, then takes the apparently more liberal line—as Shaw becomes more ruthlessly disciplinarian—that the recruits should not be pushed into aspiring to be what they will never be allowed to become. What also frustrates the potentially fascinating interplay of half-racist, half-liberated attitudes between the two men is the fact that Zwick's writing is never comfortably in period nor outside it.

Something similar, perhaps, undermines the treatment of the black recruits themselves, or ensures that they are never more than half-liberated from certain clichés. The play-off between Denzel Washington's rebellious Trip, who perceives that emancipation might not mean what it says, and Morgan Freeman's Rawlins, a conventionally noble figure, a kind of universal soldier in the Fordian mould, who begins as a gravedigger and rises to sergeant major, tends to neutralise rather than sharpen any cut and thrust of attitudes. *Glory*, in the end, can find no way round the *echt* Fordian scene where Trip, having refused Shaw's offer to carry the regimental colours, will pick them up in the heat of battle, while Ford's feeling for this kind of adventure, for "universal" sentiment and a kind of integration through action, always eludes the film.

NEW YORK, 1/8/90, p. 61, David Denby

In Edward Zwick's *Glory*—a sturdily mediocre, sometimes moving spectacle film about the first black regiment raised in the North during the Civil War—the roles are a series of stock characters borrowed from World War II platoon movies. Matthew Broderick is the scion of an aristocratic Massachusetts family who winds up in command of the unit (he has to prove that he's capable of command). Denzel Washington is a cynical escaped slave who has to be taken down a peg, Morgan Freeman a wise old man who holds everything together, Andre Braugher an effete black intellectual who needs to find his manhood, and so on. Zwick, the TV whiz responsible for *thirtysomething*, doesn't rise to the imaginative level required by his noble subject. The movie is stiffly staged and written, and could use a little more basic exposition to explain such things as why the opposing armies drew within 30 paces of each other before shooting. The actors, however, manage to make the most of their restricted roles.

NEW YORK POST, 12/14/89, p. 37, Jami Bernard

"Glory" is a somber and noble tribute to the generally overlooked contributions by black soldiers in the Civil War, but Matthew Broderick, looking as young as an embryo and sporting a wispy and unconvincing goatee, is not up to leading the charge.

Based on the real-life exploits of the North's showcase 54th Regiment, the first to enlist black men, and on the actual letters home from their young white commander, Robert Gould Shaw, this epistolary movie does everything it can to tell it like it was—except to tell it from the black soldiers' point of view.

In addition to the insult of that, Shaw is less interesting a character than some of the men he leads into the final vainglorious battle. He's stiff, condescending, cowardly and confused. And young. The real Shaw was only 25 when he died, but historical accuracy can backfire. In this thankless role, Broderick looks like his whiskers are about to fly off his face in a gust of wind, while his troops have life writ large on their weary but hopeful faces.

Even the casting of the bigger-name Broderick draws attention away from the strong black cast, which includes Morgan Freeman and Denzel Washington, two actors who don't need any help and who do an outstanding job here, considering the parameters. It is hard to believe that these soldiers would muster anything more than bemused tolerance of Shaw, even if he did eventually go out on a limb to get his men the shoes, uniforms and meaningful work details they needed.

The movie opens with Shaw's sobering experience at bloody Antietam. A couple of grisly hours in a "Gone With the Wind"-inspired medical tent, and Shaw is shaken to his roots.

Back home in Boston with his well-heeled, abolitionist parents (Frederick Douglass is a party guest), Shaw is initially ambivalent about an offer to take command of the North's first black regiment, a rag-tag collection including farm boy Sharts (Jihmi Kennedy), who has dead aim with a rifle; a wise and patient gravedigger named Rawlins (Morgan Freeman), and the angry runaway slave Trip (Washington), who gets the most fireworks with his spit-in-yer-eye temper tantrums and a stoic whipping scene in which a single, angry tear rolls down his cheek

Since the 54th went a long time without any real fighting, the bulk of the movie is a sort of slice of Civil War army life. These scenes are generally to good effect—though staged with the plodding precision of an extra-long march—showing hierarchy struggles, camaraderie, the ebb and flow of hope and loyalty, and how the chance to show their stuff gave the men a sense of self.

It is all narrated in a voice-over by Shaw as he filters the black experience through his disingenuous letters home.

The movie is also about dignity and what it takes to be a man. Shaw eventually volunteers his regiment for the honor of storming the ultimately impenetrable Fort Wagner, the gateway to Charleston. That suicide mission, which took the lives of half the 54th (including Shaw), helped change the North's perception of blacks, so at least the men did not die in vain.

Though he has his heart in the right place, director Edward Zwick ("thirtysomething," "About Last Night...") doesn't always have his camera in same. He indulges in maudlin symbolism to the accompaniment of swelling music. Even scenes that are genuinely moving, like the doomed men's night-before gospel meeting, have problems—in that scene, Freeman's stirring words are undercut by a camera that cannot contain him.

"Glory" looks technically authentic, but rings hollow, its fragile costume-department whiskers flapping dangerously in the breeze.

NEWSDAY, 12/14/89, Part II/p. 7, Terry Kelleher

Are you aware that an estimated 180,000 blacks fought in the Union army during the Civil War, and that Abraham Lincoln credited them with a key role in the defeat of the Confederacy?

If only because many will answer "vaguely"or "not at all," this is a motion picture of importance. At times it may seem more monument than movie, but "Glory" deserves credit for giving honor where it's due.

Indeed, the film makers' accomplishment goes beyond the correction of historical oversight, beyond educational value, to emotional power. "Glory" is undeniably stirring, even when its lofty intent is only too obvious.

"Glory" tells the story of the 54th Regiment of Massachusetts Volunteer Infantry, the first black unit to wear the Union blue. The 54th was led by Col. Robert Gould Shaw, a 25-year-old child of privilege whose military rank stemmed from his Boston family's political clout. Shaw's correspondence is among the sources for Kevin Jarre's screenplay.

The movie opens in 1862, before the Emancipation Proclamation and the raising of the 54th. Shaw (Matthew Broderick) is off to do his heroic bit in combat—"just like the old fellows in the Revolution," he says rather jauntily in a letter to his mother (Jane Alexander). The Battle of Antietam explodes his illusions. Director Edward Zwick does a superb job of re-enacting this horrific engagement, which left some 23,000 casualties. It begins ceremonially, like a mass duel, but soon degenerates into free-form slaughter.

Back up in Boston, somewhat sheepishly bearing a neck wound as his badge of courage, Shaw hesitates before accepting command of the newly formed "colored" regiment. He prevails on Cabot Forbes (Cary Elwes), a friend and Harvard classmate, to serve at his right hand.

Cutting an unimposing figure on horseback, Shaw greets his ragged but eager recruits with a short speech of shaky eloquence. It's clear he's in well over his head, but it's equally clear he's spurred by a genuine sense of duty and abolitionist principle. Despite an unfortunate attempt at an accent, and a tendency to bite his lip too often, Broderick offers a credible, sympathetic portrait of a young man struggling to appear authoritative while he learns the meaning of authority.

Meantime, "Glory" follows three soldiers of the 54th, all patently intended to serve as types: steady, responsible Rawlins (Morgan Freeman), a unifier who rises from gravedigger to sergeant major; Trip (Denzel Washington), an impudent runaway slave who has felt the lash of white power but remains contemptuous of it; and Thomas (Andre Braugher), an educated freeman from Boston who can't help appearing overrefined and condescending to his comrades.

In developing these characters, Zwick and Jarre add a few touches that may be described as cornball: After suffering his abuse, Thomas saves Trip from a Confederate bayonet; on the eve of a major battle, the troops gather around the campfire for gospel songs and heartfelt speeches. But the performances are so strong and true that "Glory" never loses its hold. Freeman is flawless as a natural-born leader who inspires confidence by being himself, and Washington penetrates to the core of a headstrong man waging a personal war of racial retribution. Washington has one long closeup, as Trip is flogged for a disciplinary offense, that's absolutely stunning.

Painstakingly authentic in its period detail, the movie occasionally gets carried away with the "Rally 'Round the Flag, Boys" spirit and revels in patriotic gore. But the white boys in blue are hardly depicted as moral crusaders in a "good war" against slavery. Racism is seen at every level of the Union army—from the "grunts" who revile black soldiers, to the supply officers who deny them decent equipment, to the generals who would cheat the 54th of the chance to prove its mettle in the field.

Zwick, co-creator of TV's "thirtysomething," shows impressive skill in working on a far larger scale. The climax of "Glory" is another prodigious battle scene: the Union assault, spearheaded by the 54th, on Fort Wagner at Charleston harbor. The last, lingering shot is an indelible image of equal-opportunity sacrifice. Cynics may sneer, but with a lump in the throat.

NEWSWEEK, 12/18/89, p. 73, David Ansen

In "Glory," screenwriter Kevin Jarre and director Edward Zwick have got hold of a fascinating and little-explored corner of American history. Set during the Civil War, it's about the first regiment of black soldiers to fight for the Union. Trained under the leadership of a young Boston Brahmin, Col. Robert Gould Shaw (Matthew Broderick), and comprising both free Northern blacks and runaway slaves, the regiment's first obstacle was the racism of the Army they were serving. Deemed unworthy for combat, they were at first denied uniforms, proper boots, equal pay or access to weapons. But Shaw and his men, once they traveled south from Massachusetts, ultimately proved their skill and courage in the bloody assault on Fort Wagner in South Carolina—a near-suicidal charge that earned them a place in history.

Zwick has made an engrossing, sometimes stirring, sometimes wobbly film. The cocreator of "thirtysomething," Zwick seems more concerned with "feelings" than with history, though some of his battle scenes have a stark, intimate power. There are an awful lot of long, meaningful glances between brave men on the brink of battle and an overreliance on James Horner's massive score to pump up our emotions. The usually assured Broderick seems oddly tentative in his role. But the charismatic Denzel Washington, oozing angry defiance, is extraordinary, as are Morgan Freeman as a gravedigger/officer and Andre Braugher as Shaw's erudite black friend turned soldier. But if the sensibilities behind "Glory" sometimes seem anachronistic, this handsome, intelligent movie demands attention: it opens our eyes to a war within a war most of us never knew about.

SIGHT & SOUND, Spring 1990, p. 135, John Pym

Still shaky from his experiences at Antietam, the Civil War's bloodiest battle, Major Shaw covers his pride and misgivings at being offered the colonelcy of the 54th Massachusetts Infantry, the Union Army's first black regiment, by blurting his acceptance and then hurrying from the room. The assembled dignitaries, including the whiskery Frederick Douglass, look distinctly relieved. The formation of the regiment was to be a strategic psychological blow to the Confederacy; no one, however, expected the 54th to see action—but then no one reckoned with the patrician Robert Gould Shaw.

Glory is on one level a straightforward regimental record candied-up by Hollywood. Consider the climax, the suicidal assault on Fort Wagner, upon which the defence of Charleston depends. Who will carry the colours if the standard-bearer falls, Shaw asks. A young man steps forward, the colonel's boyhood friend, an enlisted man from whom Shaw felt obliged to keep his distance. They are as they were before. "I'll see you in the fort, Thomas."

John Ford might have cast the young Henry Fonda as Shaw. Edward Zwick, a TV director (the chic *thirtysomething*) with only one previous feature to his credit (*About Last Night*), cast Matthew Broderick, who shares with Fonda a deceptively slight build and an ability to stand still and act with his eyes. Which is not to suggest that *Glory* is a homage to Ford; far from it, its purpose is to redeem a key moment of black history.

It does, however, share one telling attribute of Ford at his best: it is not ashamed of its sentiments or its Americanism, its pride in Lincoln rather than Reagan. And here lies its significance as a straw in the wind for popular studio entertainment in the 90s: it vaults clean over the shame of Vietnam, to reaffirm the almost prehistoric notion of the value of gallantry in a just cause. And the gallantry is given an edge by a hint that Shaw lost his nerve at Antietam.

Aside from its motives, the film's chief virtue is its spectacular choreography. The final battle, in which Shaw and most of his regiment perish without taking the fort, is a striking combination of dynamism and clarity. The preliminaries are hackneyed, and the director makes a sustained effort to soften the hardest heart, but they work, not least because Zwick and his cast convince us that they genuinely believe in them.

The battle's intensity sucks in the spectator and quickens the blood. The pace gathers as the focus twists in on Shaw and his rush up a dune to the enemy's forward position. Then after more desperate hand-to-hand fighting (it doesn't really matter at this stage who is carrying the colours), the action is halted with a symbolic frozen tableau. It has been some time since one saw a full-dress military engagement recreated with so few showy effects and edited with such assurance.

The black players, notably Morgan Freeman, a one-time gravedigger who becomes the regiment's Sergeant-Major, and Denzel Washington, a runaway slave who finally curbs his self-destructive hatred and embraces his destiny, perform with a notable reined-in dignity. These are repressed, disenfranchised men on the verge of a kind of equality with their white officers: and there is nothing in them of that old demeaning stereotype, the dignified slave. In this particular battle, they are all, black and white, in it together. (To see how far the world has changed, one might compare the performances of these black actors with that of Woody Strode, the cavalry sergeant in Ford's *Sergeant Rutledge* of thirty years ago.)

A soldier in front of Shaw at Antietam has his head blown off; and there is, too, a histrionic amputation scene in the gory surgical tent. On the whole, however, Zwick avoids attention-seeking effects: his subject is not the individual in battle, and what bullets and shrapnel do to him, but the fused, spiritually indestructible regiment; the great simplicities, before the knotted realities of racial prejudice had to be addressed in detail.

TIME, 12/18/89, p. 91, Richard Schickel

It just slips under the wire as the first large-scale Civil War Film of the decade. And it may be the last of the millennium, so far out of favor (and economic viability) have historical epics of all kinds fallen. Maybe one's good response to *Glory* derives from the sheer novelty of the thing and from admiration for the producer's gumption in flinging it in the face of the movie audience's indifference to the pretelevised past.

But not entirely. For the specific historical events the film narrates—the formation, training and terrible blooding in battle of the 54th Massachusetts Regiment, the first black fighting unit enlisted in the Union cause—are little known yet resonant with high symbolic significance. The 54th, led by an idealistic 25-year-old white man, Colonel Robert Gould Shaw (Matthew Broderick skillfully blending shyness and tenacity), had to fight to fight. Their white comrades-in-arms were full of contemptuous prejudice against them, and the high command was afraid to arm black men who had their own bitter racial grievances (many were runaway slaves).

Yet precisely because of their lowly status, these men had a more than usually powerful need to assert their manhood through deadly exertion. *Glory* is at its best when it shows their proud embrace of 19th century warfare at its most brutal. Director Edward Zwick graphically demonstrates the absurdity of lines of soldiers slowly advancing across open ground, shoulder to shoulder, in the face of withering rifle volleys and horrendous cannonade. The fact that the 54th finally achieves respect (and opens the way for other black soldiers) only by losing half its number in a foredoomed assault on an impregnable fortress underscores this terrible and brutal irony.

Kevin Jarre's script makes no direct comment on these matters, and a squad of fine actors ground the film in felt reality: Denzel Washington is a proud and badly misused troublemaker; *Driving Miss Daisy*'s Morgan Freeman a steadying influence; Andre Braugher a Harvard student who finds Emersonian idealism of small help in mastering the bayonet. It is the movie's often awesome imagery and a bravely soaring choral score by James Horner that transfigure the reality, granting it the status of necessary myth. Broad, bold, blunt, *Glory* is everything that a film like *Miss Daisy* [see Schickel's review], all nuance and implication, is not. But arriving together, they somehow hearten: they widen the range of our responses to what remains the central issue of our past, our present, our future.

VILLAGE VOICE, 12/19/89, p. 98, Gary Giddins

When Colonel Robert Gould Shaw and much of his Massachusettes 54th regiment was wiped out in the 1863 charge on an impregnable sand dune called Fort Wagner, he immediately took pride of place among abolitionist martyrs. He was turned into a metaphor by a century of Brahmin poets, from Emerson to Robert Lowell ("Their monument sticks like a fishbone/in the city's throat"), and bronzed by Saint-Gaudens for the Boston Common. The futile assault was historic because the 54th was the first Negro regiment of the Civil War, and it fought valiantly; as a result, 180,000 blacks were made Union soldiers—Lincoln called their participation decisive. A journalist predicted that Fort Wagner would come to represent to blacks what Bunker Hill meant to whites. It didn't turn out that way, perhaps for the same reason the Japanese don't celebrate their kamikazes. The 54th didn't have a chance; the white regiments they were ostensibly advancing didn't show up in time.

In many respects, *Glory*, a flawed but often stirring account of the 54th, does justice to an anecdote that encapsulated not only the barbarism of the war, but the politics that prefers dead saints to live victors. Kevin Jarre's screenplay orders the basic facts into single file, beginning with Shaw's survival at Antietam, and the homecoming party where a mute Frederick Douglass (the actor isn't even listed in the credits) and philanthropist Francis Shaw stand by as Shaw's son is offered the command of the first black troops. Most of the film is taken up with training them, and, as usual in army movies, the regiment is deconstructed into one tentful of representative blacks: Trip, the escaped slave who hates whites and just about everyone else; Rawlins, the wise middle-aged volunteer; Thomas, the educated free black who was a childhood friend of Shaw; and Sharts a field hand who stutters for comic relief. You don't need a weathervane to tell you Trip will come around and distinguish himself as a martyr for all seasons.

The clichés would be deadly if the actors didn't transcend them. To his credit, director Edward Zwick doesn't allow his passion for the surfaces of historical accuracy (the Boston parade in celebration of the 54th's impending glory and the assault on Fort Wagner are especially convincing) to impede the development of his characters. When Denzel Washington, whose Trip is the film's most hair-raising performance, intimidates Thomas (Andre Braugher, all glasses and teeth) simply by moving in on his space, nose to nose, the tension is fairly electrifying. One of the most tautly executed scenes is the most elemental—a ritualistic campfire round of prayerful testimony before battle. Sharts (Jihmy Kennedy, genuinely funny as the stuttering innocent), Trip, and Rawlins take turns as the soldiers clap in time to a spiritual, and for once glory is almost palpable.

Rawlins is played by Morgan Freeman, who, having played a pimp in *Street Smart*, an inner-city principal in *Lean on Me*, and now a good servant in *Driving Miss Daisy* and an ex-slave in *Glory*, has rapidly exhausted the panoply of Negro roles (though he has yet to turn up as a police chief). That he is an astonishing actors who disappears into every role can be lost on no one, but it remains to be seen whether he'll get to play parts that aren't earmarked for the hot black actor of the moment. The range suggested by the knife-threatening scene in *Street Smart* and the solemn dignity of his handclapping by the campfire in *Glory* is extraordinary. And if handclapping seems something less than as opportunity for a leap of actorly imagination, you may want to see *Glory* simply to watch Freeman's face light up with spiritual composure.

With Washington setting off firecrackers and Freeman holding the emotional fort, Matthew Broderick's effectiveness as Shaw comes as something of a surprise. But it's one of the film's more touching conceits to recall that Shaw was an innocent himself, though his age is needlessly fudged: Shaw was 25 or 26, not 23 as he says in *Glory*. When Thomas, who's been having a rough time, stops him to say "Merry Christmas," Broderick's relief at the avoidance of a confrontation is that of a lost adolescent trying dauntlessly to be a martinet, grateful for a few seconds to remember who he is and where he comes from. There are scenes in which Broderick chews over his line readings, eyes growing limpid, self-conscious soulfulness spreading like a stain, but on balance he humanizes Shaw more than the poets did.

The battle scenes are some of the best ever filmed. These are not the soldiers of Griffith or Huston, swarming over hills and ducking behind trees, but nakedly vulnerable opposing flanks, armed chiefly with one-shot rifles, and backed by mortars. The assault on Fort Wagner faithfully reproduces a famous print, but it's the apprentice skirmish at James Island that curls your hair, a scrimmage played over a few yards, men on both sides dutifully trying to reload without cover, bodies dropping up and down the lines. *Glory* is good at depicting the racism on the Union side, and doesn't fudge the burning of Darien by Colonel James Montgomery, in which Shaw was forced to participate. But the rebels don't exist in *Glory*, except as a faceless evil. Hollywood abolitionists have come a long way since *Santa Fe Trail*, in which Raymond Massey played John Brown as though he were a mad doctor from the Universal horror cycle; still, the dehumanization of Confederate soldiers rather mutes the issue of barbarism.

For that matter *Glory* has little to say about the politics of martyrdom. Shaw is shown volunteering his regiment to lead the attack on Fort Wagner, and in fact his troops were hungry to prove their mettle when the offer was made; but the question as to whether they were set up by white commanders is ignored. The smarmy expression worn by Peter Michael Goetz as Shaw's father ably suggests the superior strain of a man who, rather than pressing for the return of his son's body, made propaganda of his interment in a ditch with his men. That's another issue the film avoids.

Sadly, *Glory*'s effectiveness is undercut by Zwick's tendency to telegraph most of the key events, as though he feared the audience wouldn't get them if the music didn't swell to signal the significance. James Horner's score, notwithstanding borrowings from Dvorák, is atrocious: The juice is pumped to the max when Shaw discovers his men haven't deserted, yet the audience knows full well they won't; when Shaw falls in battle, the voices (the Boys Choir of Harlem, no less) and strings sound like emissaries form *The Omen*. Sounds of explosives and the screams of dying men are all the soundtrack needs for the final assault. No less distressing is a centrally placed confrontation between Shaw and Trip, who, expounding 1989 politics, argues that the war is pointless. It's as though a slave in *The Ten Commandments* asked, "What's the point, Moses? Even if we get out of Egypt, we'll never get in their country clubs."

Also reviewed in:
NEW REPUBLIC, 1/8 & 15/90, p. 28, Stanley Kauffmann
NEW YORK TIMES, 12/14/89, p. C15, Vincent Canby
NEW YORKER, 2/5/90, p. 109, Pauline Kael
VARIETY, 12/13/89, p. 30
WASHINGTON POST, 1/12/90, p. D1, Rita Kempley
WASHINGTON POST, 1/12/90, Weekend/p. 39, Desson Howe

GREAT BALLS OF FIRE!

An Orion Pictures release. *Executive Producer:* Michael Grais and Mark Victor. *Producer:* Adam Fields. *Director:* Jim McBride. *Screenplay:* Jack Baran and Jim McBride. *Based upon the book by:* Myra Lewis with Murray Silver. *Director of Photography:* Affonso Beato. *Editor:* Lisa Day, Pembroke Herring, and Bert Lovitt. *Choreographer:* Bill Landrum and Jacqui Landrum. *Music Editor:* Scott Grusin. *Sound:* Petur Hliddal. *Sound Editor:* Julia Evershade. *Production Designer:* David Nichols. *Art Director:* Jon Spirson. *Set Designer:* Kathleen McKernin and Lauren Polizzi. *Set Decorator:* Lisa Fischer. *Special Effects:* Phil Corey. *Costumes:* Tracy Tynan. *Make-up:* Richard Arrington. *Stunt Coordinator:* Steve Davison. *Running time:* 102 minutes. *MPAA Rating:* PG-13.

CAST: Joe Bob Briggs (Dewey "Daddy-O" Phillips); Dennis Quaid (Jerry Lee Lewis); Winona Ryder (Myra Gale Lewis); John Doe (J.W. Brown); Stephen Tobolowsky (John Phillips); Trey Wilson (Sam Phillips); Alec Baldwin (Jimmy Swaggart); Steve Allen (Steve Allen); Lisa Blount (Lois Brown); Joshua Sheffield (Rusty

Brown); Mojo Nixon (James Van Eaton); Jimmie Vaughn (Roland James); David Ferguson (Jack Clement); Robert Lesser (Alan Freed); Lisa Jane Persky (Babe); Paula Person (Marilyn); Valerie Wellington (Big Maybelle); Booker T. Laury (Piano Slim); Michael St. Gerard (Elvis); Carol Russell (Mamie Lewis); Crystal Robbins (Frankie Jean); Tav Falco (New Bass Player); Ryan Rushton (Young Jimmy); Bert Dedman (Young Jerry); David Penhale (Reporter #1); Carl Bogan (Reporter #2); Richard Crowe (Reporter #3); Melisa J. Levine, Cassie Pollard, Mary Yeargin (Kreme Kup Girls); Bruce Stuart (Bank Teller); W.W. Painter (Onlooker); Mark Johnson (Sheriff); Jody Lynne (Party Doll); Joseph Woodward Jr. (Wedding Preacher); Linn Sitler (Realty Agent); Ashley Paige Cook (Mona); Sara Van Horn (Minnie Belle); Juliette Claire Spirson (Lewis Infant); John Mulrooney (Talk Show Host); Peter Cook (First English Reporter); Kim Smith (Second English Reporter); David Sibley (Third English Reporter); Jamila Massey (Bystander); Ryan Ward (Heckler #1); Stephen O'Donnell (Heckler #2); Bejay Baddin (Teenage Girl #1); Kelly Marcel (Teenage Girl #2); Julie Balloo (Female Fan); Ruth Kettlewell (Dowager); John Tordoff (Cockney Porter); Priscilla Harris (Honky-Tonk Angel).

FILMS IN REVIEW, 10/89, p. 491, Kevin Sweeney

Has *Spy* magazine take up film producing? You might have thought so from watching *Great Balls Of Fire!*. This cheeky musical/comedy/virtual fantasy is a slightly cynical hipster's look back at the roots of rock 'n' roll in the manner of a tall tale. Combining exciting musical numbers with a patently campy attitude toward '50s culture, the film turns the bitter life of Jerry Lee Lewis, one of rock's more haunted characters, into a cartoonish summer popcorn movie. It's phony from start to finish, but also a lot of fun, and its commercial failure earlier this year owes less to its entertainment qualities than a glut of other, equally cartoonish but better promoted movies (*Batman, Indiana Jones* and *Ghostbusters II, Lethal Weapon 2*).

A swaggering Lousiana-born piano pounder who could write and sing, Jerry Lee Lewis was probably the most talented of all the rockers looking to dethrone Elvis Presley in the mid-'50s. Lewis began playing the piano at eight, and made his first public appearance at 14 singing "Hadacol Boogie" at the 1949 Ford Auto Show in Natchez. In 1956 he cut a demo tape for Memphis-based Sun Records, Presley's former label, and a month later the self-styled "Killer" followed the King into Sun, where he became the #1 recording artist.

At one time Lewis thought about becoming a minister, and he even studied at the Assembly of God Bible Institute in Waxahatchie, Texas. His early chart busting songs are loaded with barely veiled sexual lyrics and grafted onto fundamentalist imagery. His life struggle, as perceived in this film by the director Jim McBride, is mirrored in the music—a battle of the id over the ego, of the "Devil's Music" over the straight and narrow, of bucking convention in his work and life. "My road was chosen long ago," the movie Lewis triumphantly says at one point. "And if I'm going to hell, I'm going playing the piano."

The film is a weird patchwork: Ostensibly based on a conventional memoir by Lewis' first wife, Myra Lewis, McBride and coscripter Jack Baran also lift several incidents from Nick Tosches' definitive biography *Hellfire*. But McBride clearly has little interest in telling the real story. *Great Balls Of Fire!* is a parody of the *legend* of Jerry Lee Lewis (although it even scrimps on that). Set in the years 1956-58, the film covers his stunning rise with the successive hits "Whole Lotta Shakin' Going on," "Great Balls Of Fire," "Breathless" and "High School Confidential"; his moral tug of war with fire and brimstone cousin Jimmy Swaggart; and a controversial marriage to his 13-year-old second cousin, Myra, which nearly destroyed his career and made him persona non grata within the industry.

Stylized, near-surrealistic scenes abound: School kids bebop on the lawn when Lewis drives by singing "High School Confidential;" Myra flings $20 bills in the air when picking out the furniture for her suburban dream house. When Lewis makes his television debut on Steve Allen's show singing "Whole Lotta Shakin' Going On," the montage of viewers include June and Ward Cleaver and Elvis himself, who curls his lip in derision while a bedmate ignores him and begins moving to the beat. The King, in fact, turns up in a couple of scenes, most memorably after he's been drafted. A solitary Lewis is practicing the piano in the studio when Elvis, in uniform and carrying a duffel bag, walks in. "Just take it. Take it all," he mumbles forlornly.

McBride's last film was the sleeper success *The Big Easy*; he has a talent for rhythm and pacing, and *Great Balls Of Fire!* never slows down—even when turning "serious" (a relative term) when Lewis is deported from scandalized England because of the marriage and his career careens on the rocks. The picture is well cast: Dennis Quaid (the star of *The Big Easy*) is sensational both at capturing the rocker's pomposity and arrogance and duplicating his concert performances (Lewis himself dubbed his original songs for the film). Young Winona Ryder is very funny as Myra, both vulnerable and vulgar. In smaller parts, Alec Baldwin (as Swaggart) and John Doe (as Myra's father and Lewis' partner) have some good moments, and Michael St. Gerard (Rikki Lake's boyfriend "Linc Larkin" in *Hairspray*) gives a dead accurate interpretation of Presley.

While *Great Balls Of Fire!* is undeniably entertaining on its own terms, it's liable to leave a somewhat sour aftertaste with anyone looking for anything beyond the legend. Theres much more to Jerry Lee Lewis than depicted here. His two previous, failed marriages are referred to only very briefly. His relationship with Myra is treated sympathetically, but the film pointedly makes no mention of the fact that Myra was raped a year before she met Lewis. She was a psychological basket case, and considered herself "damaged goods." Lewis' bout with alcohol is portrayed briefly, but only as a reaction to his ostracization by the industry. The film ends in 1958 on relentlessly upbeat tone; there's no real reference to Lewis' self-destructive impulses, his subsequent marriages (including one to woman who died under very questionable circumstances) or his later popularity as a country recording artist in the '60s. There's even a corny title before the credits, assuring audiences that somewhere, tonight, Jerry Lee Lewis is entertaining an audience.

Probably McBride figured younger film audiences wouldn't care much anyway for a straight biopic of a guy who never was very likeable. That seems to be the only rationalization for throwing out practically everything true to Jerry Lee Lewis' life but the music. The music *is* great. Along with Dennis Quaid, the soundtrack was probably considered the film's real allure—a box office miscalculation you can bet some Orion executive has already paid for with his head.

LOS ANGELES TIMES, 6/30/89, Calendar/p. 1, Michael Wilmington

One of the most startling sights and sounds in all American popular music was the young Jerry Lee Lewis, the self-taught country howler and piano virtuoso from Ferriday, La.: blond waves flopping and flying as he savagely blistered the keys, leaped onto his bench or sent it flying and screamed out the lyrics to sexual anthems like "Whole Lotta Shakin' Goin' On"—sometimes capping off the astonishing performance by throwing a lighted match into his piano and setting it ablaze.

In "Great Balls of Fire" director-writer Jim McBride and producer Adam Fields try to reincarnate that fine frenzy by portraying the pivotal two years (1956-1958) of Lewis' life. This was the time when the self-dubbed "Killer" became known as the devil's rockin' emissary, the baddest of pop music's bad boys; when, in rapid succession, he shot to the pinnacle of world stardom and then, through scandal and censorship, came crashing down.

But McBride and Fields, unlike Lewis himself, or his cousin and childhood friend, TV evangelist Jimmie Lee Swaggart (Alec Baldwin), don't seem to believe very strongly in the devil and his power, the war between heaven and hell. They've made a cartoon of Lewis' history, and a musical comedy of his dizzying, anguished, half-crazed rise and fall. They've bleached some of the danger out of his music, most of darkness out of his soul.

That doesn't mean they haven't made a good movie. "Great Balls of Fire" would be an entertaining evening even if it preserved nothing more than Lewis' songs—rerecorded by Lewis with all the soul and groin-stirring fury that he has preserved during three decades.

It also has an often-dazzling comic impersonation of Lewis by Dennis Quaid, a goofy ballet of awesomely confident struts and brags. It has the late Trey Wilson as Sun's Sam Phillips, mixing red-dirt strength with gentle satire. And it has Winona Ryder's delicate portrait of Lewis' 13-year-old bride (and second cousin) Myra Gale Brown, a performance that suggests less innocence despoiled than a sturdy little kid thrust unknowingly into the inferno.

The movie makers probably aren't trying for anything deeper. They've used the actual events of Lewis' life, mostly drawn from Myra's co-written memoir: his meteoric rise, the censorship by radio programmers and booking agents after the child-bride scandal. They've recreated the surface of things conscientiously. Even some of the least likely events in this movie, such as Elvis Presley's wraith-like appearence on induction eve to cede his crown to Lewis, or the gun-waving assault on Sun Studio by Myra's infuriated father (and Lewis' bassist) J.W. Brown (played by John Doe of the rock band X), come straight from Myra's book.

They have toned down Lewis' Homeric drinking and drug-abuse, possibly on the curious rationale that it would be a bad example for youth, as if the rest of his offstage behavior isn't.

The performances are dances, too: as in McBride's "Big Easy," they sometimes resemble choreography. As Bogey and Bacall expressed their passion by lighting cigarettes, Jerry Lee and Myra express theirs by popping bubble gum and twirling the threads. The songs propel the action along in dance-like montages. when Lewis drives his car past the local high school or civil rights protest march, the kids, the marchers, even the cops, rock with him in unison. (Later, they give him a universal "shame on you" high sign.) The events are mostly factual, but what determines our reactions is this tone: a bright, distancing device that celebrates Lewis's talent while it softens his demonic spontaneity.

McBride leaves out something important. He doesn't evade the racial dichotomy in Lewis' culture. We see the singer symbolically joining rock's black and white hands on his piano, in a duet with the salty old blues pianist Booker T. Laury. But, except for the opening scene, when little Jerry and Jimmy Lee race across the tracks to kibitz at a smoky all-black roadhouse, the movie avoids the hard times of the Lewises, so poor they had to mortgage their home to give their child-prodigy an upright piano. It's a crucial gap. Lewis' "flaw" stems partially from the fact that he was a poor boy made suddenly rich, indulging red-neck manners that would have been ignored if he would have stayed poor.

That's the irony of the famous mannerisms that Quaid recreates with such wizardly accuracy: the gestures of a parodied prince. They suggest a teen-age kid trying to be regal, project his "specialness." And it's also the irony of the good-and-evil battle that Swaggart wages with Lewis. The evangelist argues for sobriety and sexual reason, but also for propriety, the middle-class mores that princely Lewis, with his peasant background, tramples on with violently erotic music, drawn from poor black and white roots.

Another irony: The 21-year-old Lewis is being played by an actor in his mid-30s and dubbed by the 53-year-old "Killer himself." Isn't the fire largely gone? Strangely, it isn't. The stand-up rockers still have ecstatic force and Lewis does a tear-jerker like "That Lucky Old Sun" as rarely before, with the power Ray Charles also gives it, a golden melancholy seeping through the hard edges, the piano trills dropping like a weary, heart-torn rainfall.

In life, Lewis' main charm was that he believed himself to be dancing on hell's mouth, believed rock 'n' roll was the devil's music—and, damn it, played and lived it anyway. But, in life and even in "Great Balls of Fire" (MPAA rated PG-13, despite some sexual activity and dialogue), it's that devil's music that saves his soul, sung and played with a power that might make angels boogie.

MONTHLY FILM BULLETIN, 12/89, p. 368, Philip Strick

Ferriday, Louisiana, 1944. Nine-year-old Jerry Lee Lewis and his cousin Jimmy Lee Swaggart sneak across the tracks to Haney's Big House, a black night-club, to spy on the awesome performances of blues players like Piano Slim. The experience shapes their lives: warning against "the devil's music", Jimmy Lee becomes a piano-playing preacher while Jerry Lee, certain that his talent is God-given, dedicates himself to boogie-woogie. Two marriages later, he auditions in November 1956 at Sun Studios in Memphis, Tennessee, for Sam Phillips, the record producer who discovered Elvis, sold him too soon, and is hoping for an encore. Sam and his brother Jud are enthusiastic about the Lewis sound, and with help of disc jockey Dewey Phillips they launch a major promotion to support a Jerry Lee Lewis tour. Much to Swaggart's disapproval, Jerry performs in bar-rooms and night-clubs supported by his elder cousin J.W. Brown on guitar, finding that a song already rejected by Sam, "Whole Lotta Shakin' Goin' On", is a huge crowd-pleaser. After a performance on *The Steve Allen Show* on July 28, 1957, the song becomes a nationwide hit, replacing the latest Elvis release in all the charts. Jerry's greatest fan is J.W.'s thirteen-year-old daughter Myra, and to her parents' concern, their relationship grows increasingly warm. Returning from a tour in which he has triumphantly outshone Chuck Berry, Jerry finally sweeps the startled Myra off to a secret marriage. J.W. comes after him with a gun when he finds out, but with Sam's help they are soon reconciled and Myra finds herself setting up house on limitless funds and total lack of experience in wifely matters. Acknowledged even by Elvis as the "King of Rock 'n' Roll', Jerry Lee is invited to England; Sam and Jud suggest he leaves Myra behind, but he insists that she accompany him. The British press quickly discovers that the "child bride" is Jerry's second cousin and that he is apparently a bigamist. There is a national outcry, his audiences reject him, and within five days the tour has been cancelled. Returning ignominiously to the states, Jerry Lee finds that his career is in ruins and he is doomed to grim years of drink, drugs and disaster in the long hard climb back to the top. Recruited by Swaggart, Myra accepts the comforts of religious commitment, but Jerry Lee unrepentantly takes his own path, continuing to play "the devil's music" as only he knows how.

Great Balls of Fire! is an unreliable memoir, the legend which the Jim McBride-Jack Baran screenplay has decided to print being "a story we essentially invented, based on the facts we knew". The weakness of this approach is that the startling two-year rise and fall of Jerry Lee

Lewis has actually been copiously documented, both musically and in the howling headlines in 1958. The wild Louisiana rock 'n' roller who set fire to pianos on stage, played them with his feet, toppled Elvis briefly from the charts and promptly toppled himself, a bright Lucifer engulfed in unimaginable debauchery, is a familiar figure from the fragile 50s, setting the pattern for innumerable burn-outs to follow. What we don't know so well is the "why" of Jerry Lee. The McBride-Baran version, under the Killer's guidance (he is credited as "production adviser"), omits all reference to first piano lessons from Jerry Lee's bootleg-brewer father, sets the blame squarely on fashionable blacks and blues (overlooking the equally vital Prices, Mullicans and Williams), and pays no mind to the two wives and a son preceding Myra, to whom Jerry Lee simply boasts of past conquests as if inviting disbelief.

This clears the way conveniently for the Killer's preferred account, with discreet additions from Myra's own published recollections of life with Jerry Lee (or, more accurately, without him: the disastrous London visit ironically appears to have been one of the few occasions when they spent some time together). In this light, the charismatic piano player, while admittedly inclined to arrogance, is smitten by the kind of passion that renders age and family ties irrelevant, and stands loyally by his marriage despite the demands and pressures of his career. You might guess from the film's closing sequence, in which Jerry Lee's joyous performance of "Real Wild Child" appears to celebrate the birth of his daughter Phoebe in 1959, that everyone lived happily ever after, especially rock 'n' roll, but of course you'd be wrong. Some other kind of film, based on future and even more erratic memories, would have to tackle the deaths, the near-deaths and the resurrections of Jerry Lee's subsequent thirty years in which, with magisterial dignity, he has maintained a form of musical isolation by endless self-plagiarisation. So what McBride and Baran have "essentially invented" as an intervening compromise is musical fantasy, a rock 'n' roll version of, say, *Oklahoma!*, with Peter Cook as Rod Steiger and the Killer as both Rodgers and Hammerstein.

As a musical, *Great Balls of Fire!* has a resounding package of ready-made hits, belted out in magnificent fresh recordings only a touch less raw than the bargain-basement Sun originals. McBride's visual choreography for these explosions of delight and lust contrives to avoid the rock-concert clichés: the first radio broadcast of "Crazy Arms", for example, is heard over Jerry Lee's triumphantly chaotic drive home, oblivious to his gathering escort of police cars, while "High School Confidential" is staged on the college steps, with cartwheeling students signalling homage to a genre that was already being parodied by the time of *Bye Bye Birdie*. Unexpectedly in the style of John Ford, McBride brings the plot to a halt for the sake of the music, the ritual courtship patterns of the dance counterpointing the restrictive formality of a community otherwise unable to find full expression for its feelings. Quite apart from the *Liberty Valance* aspects of *Great Balls of Fire!*, it turns smartly into a tale of Fordian companionship, even of conspiracy, exemplified by the Phillips brothers and by the Killer's limitless supply of supportive cousins who steer their wild child, sacred or profane, through his persistent and stubborn errors until there's no further hope of rescue.

The McBride twists, however, is that while a home was always waiting for Ford's loners, even if they sometimes turned from its doors, McBride's central characters inhabit a fickle universe in which their "family" are the ultimate betrayers. The surprise about *Great Balls of Fire!*, in fact, is that there was ever any doubt about it becoming a McBride project: the last time McBride filmed the Lewis story, it was called *Breathless*, with Richard Gere, singing along with Jerry Lee's hits, self-regardingly headed for perdition; and at least one encounter in *The Big Easy* directly anticipated *Great Balls of Fire!* by showing Dennis Quaid (again) wooing his girl with a song. Punctuated by Cajun music, *the Big Easy* orchestrated a romantic struggle with a despairing tenderness that would have been maintained intact for *Great Balls of Fire!* were it not that Quaid, reasonably enough, this time lampoons his role, making of Jerry Lee more clown than lover. In consequence, despite all the piano-bashing histrionics, it is Winona Ryder's beautiful performance as Myra that seduces the story, and the "lost soul" rescued at the film's close is not Jerry Lee's but that of his now wiser partner, reinforcing an interpretation of McBride's previous texts as duologues rather than the flashy monologues which Gere and Quaid were encouraged to make of them. Whichever, lost souls have stalked through McBride's work ever since *David Holzman's Diary* and his skill as their guide has now become a real pleasure to behold.

NEW LEADER, 8/7-21/89, p. 21, John Morrone

For months Jim McBride's Jerry Lee Lewis story, *Great Balls of Fire!*, starring Dennie Quaid, has been hyped by Orion Pictures as a major contender in the summer sweeps. The movie, cowritten with Jack Baran, is based on the memoirs of Jerry Lee's "child bride," Myra Lewis. Although it offers another of McBride's tantalizing treatments of a self-conceived, larger-than-life personality, it has, alas, largely been a bust at the box office. McBride has perhaps done himself no favor in attempting to graft his own thematic preoccupations onto the most difficult pop-movie genre, the popular singer biography.

Most such films have failed miserably. The honorable failures—in other words, where the character is exploited for a nobler end than is usual—include Luis Valdez' *La Bamba* (the story of short-lived Chicano teen idol Richie Valens, retold as a tale of triumph over ethnic prejudice) and Karel Reisz' *Sweet Dreams* (about country singer Patsy Cline, whose success is depicted as her reward for suffering a sexist husband). Filmmakers are all too aware that a commercially successful movie is an upbeat one, but forget that the lives of singers (or, for that matter, of most entertainers) tend not to be very cheery. When a rapid inspection of the life they intend to document reminds them of this, they have as a rule chosen simply to sidestep the hard work, grasping ambitions, and down-and-dirty career moves that made all but the most virginal overnight successes (if indeed they have ever existed). Such ugly details as bad marriages, drug addiction, alcoholism and sudden death do inevitably appear in these films, but their treatment is devoid of candor and invariably infused with a revivalist-like hysteria and melodrama.

McBride is not so madly visionary an artist that he would deliberately court commercial failure: His film ignores whatever it actually took to put over Jerry Lee as Sun Records' honkytonkying sensation of 1957-58. This concession to convention, though, sits uncertainly with what it was about Lewis that attracted him to the project in the first place. By concentrating on Lewis' confusion of his self-image as a reg'lar fella with his public image as an invulnerable rock-'n'-roll devil who leers at little girls and tells them a "Whole Lotta Shakin' Goin' On" and ain't it gonna be fun!, McBride has produced a weird and novel hybrid.

This approach is useful and provocative. The creation of a hero in terms of his pictorial impact and kinetic appeal helps keep a subject lively. Yet McBride takes the characterization a step further by making Jerry Lee into a kind of tragic comic-book figure—as he did Jesse, the drifter wanted for manslaughter in *Breathless,* and Remy, the iconoclastic New Orleans detective in *The Big Easy* (also played by Quaid). All are men whose fantasy selves are set on a crash course with the limitations of real life.

Like Jesse, Jerry Lee reads comics and identifies with Superman: Indeed, his flamboyant '50s rockstar outfits make him *look* the part of a superhero. Like Remy he is cocksure of his ability to prevail by bending law and public opinion his way. As it happened, Jerry Lee appalled the nation by his marriage to his 13-year-old cousin, and his career was flattened. The three films are, in the end, tales of comeuppance.

Great Balls of Fire! is not altogether worthless as a chronicle of a musician's life. It is canny on the subject of Jerry Lee's distaste for Southern sanctimony (his cousin is Jimmy Swaggart), and on his recognition that the hip-grinding, sex-and-grits drive in black rhythm-and-blues had the vitality the tamer white kids' rock-'n'-roll lacked. But for this kind of insight one would do better to turn to *Rolling Stone.* You don't watch a Jim McBride film for diluted cultural commentary but for the extreme stylization of his pulsating production design (the only technical asset *Great Balls* lacks is CinemaScope), and to observe his protagonists trying to come to terms with their daydreams.

Winona Ryder, as the barely teen-aged Myra, reveals her emotional range when she tearfully tells Jerry Lee her vision of them together in "a pink house with a blue door and a baby in a highchair." She is sure all of this will be blown up by a "big fat hydrogen bomb." Jerry Lee comforts her, with naïve grandiloquence, in a beautifully composed series of shots by a highway overpass. Yet it is cartoon anguish and cartoon comfort and it is where *Great Balls of Fire!* breaks down. We do not once in the film glimpse a feeling befitting a life-size human being (its second half veers toward outright burlesque); we are presented only with broad strokes of photogenic pop-art desire, akin to the ballon captions in a Roy Lichtenstein canvas.

Quaid, playing a man pumped up in order to fill his own public persona, is better than any other leading man at conveying the fury and barbarity of a no-stops country hellion. It is a pity that no matter how he juts out his jaw and scrunches his eyebrows while lip-syncing Lewis' recordings, he cannot conceal the powerful innocence of his wide eyes and big smile. He never makes himself look quite as sneaky or as downright white trash ignorant as the real Jerry Lee Lewis, who demanded cash payment for his recordings, not knowing what to do with a check.

NEW YORK POST, 6/30/89, p. 25, David Edelstein

Even after his stinkeroo performance in the hydrogen bomb called (appropriately) "Great Balls of Fire!," Dennis Quaid would still be my first choice to play the lead in a film about Jerry Lee Lewis.

Quaid's acting doesn't have the surly, violent streak the part calls for, but both performers throw caution to the wind, and both have an infectious, cock-of-the-walk self-regard. Quaid, who also sings and writes songs, should have had an intuitive rapport with this devil's revivalist, whose soulful baritone and lyrical hiccup lured a generation into sin.

Lewis, the cousin to Jimmy Swaggart who said he'd go to hell playing the piano and who managed also to go to hell doing several hundred other things, would seem the perfect subject for a killer movie bio. (About 50 scenes jump off the page of Nick Tosches' "Hellfire.")

But if you're going to do justice to a story of a man who was considered the antichrist of his era and who married (and abused) his 13-year-old cousin Myra, it behooves you to aim a little lower than a PG-13 rating. Theoretically, you'd want this to be a movie that a Myra couldn't get into.

To say there are no erotic sparks between Quaid and young Winona Ryder is putting it blandly—Jimmy Swaggart would take his kids to see this film. For all it tells you, their rapport consisted of blowing big bubblegum bubbles at each other—they just have this bubblegum thang, know what I mean?

The central problem is that the picture can't decide what it wants to be. A rags-to-riches-to-rags story set in the early days of rock 'n' roll? A swooningly romantic portrait of forbidden love? A satire of a swooningly romantic portrait of forbidden love? How 'bout a campy, kitsch-laden parody of a typical movie-musical biography? How 'bout all of the above?

It's a feat to elicit a 100 percent inauthentic performance from an actor like Quaid, but Jim McBride has pulled it off. A colleague who has spent time with Lewis says Quaid's mannerisms have their source in the Killer, but the actor has whirled them up and mashed them together with no understanding of where they come from.

He constantly throws you out of the movie. After almost every line he pulls back his head and bulges his eyes, like David Letterman doing a rooster impression. Quaid is certainly "on" in "Great Balls of Fire!"—the question is, "on what?"

NEWSDAY, 6/30/89, Part III/p. 3, Terry Kelleher

"Great Balls of Fire," the musical biography of rocker Jerry Lee Lewis, concentrates on his early 20's. Those were the years of his biggest hits—"I'm on Fire" and "Whole Lotta Shakin' Goin' On" and, of course, "Great Balls of Fire." Also the years when he scandalized two continents by marrying his 13-year-old cousin (his third marriage, her first), getting booted out of England and going through enough career ups and downs to satisfy any biographer in Tinseltown.

This was Jerry Lee's early career, before he matured into a legend, long before he first tried his hand as a movie critic. What? You didn't know that Jerry Lee Lewis was a movie critic? And a pretty tough one at that. In fact, the first time Lewis read the script to "Great Balls of Fire!," he reached for a writing implement and scrawled this critique across the title page: "Lies! Lies! Lies!" Not for nothing is he known as The Killer.

That is what the trade calls a capsule review, and it does what a capsule review should do: It gets right to the point. He might also have scrawled "Trite! Trite! Trite!" Or, if he were of a more literary bent, "Unintentionally hilarious! Unintentionally hilarious! Unintentionally hilarious!"

On somber reflection, it seems somewhat redundant to charge a musical biography with lies. The point is not whether lies are being told—of course they are—but are the lies fanciful, diverting, entertaining? And does the music have a good beat and can you dance to it? Yes to all of the above.

While there is no suspense to the film, some tension does exist between bad little Jerry Lee and his cousin, goody-good Jimmy Swaggart (Lies! Lies! Lies!), who are first seen as little boys in Louisiana sneaking over to "the chocolate quarter" and peering into a saloon where sexy ladies in red dresses kick their legs up into the air while a piano player with a heavy left hand entertains. Says Jimmy: "C'm'on, Jerry Lee, let's get out of here. It's *devil* music. I can feel it."

The cousins' lives continue to intersect throughout the film. Almost always, Swaggart (Alec Baldwin) is praying while Jerry Lee (Dennis Quaid) is playing that old devil music. The remainder of the film consists of milestones in the turbulent early years of bubble-gum blowing, piano-destroying, comic book-reading, child-marrying Jerry Lee Lewis.

We meet the recording executive who changed Lewis' whole piano style by noting that girls liked guitar players because "they like to watch 'em wiggle around; you can't do that behind a piano." His brother, who enjoyed "that hot piece of wax you cats cut." The exec who complains, "We can't put out a song like that, it's too...suggestive." The always lurking groupies: "I want you to play me like you play that piano." The bride (Winona Ryder) on her way to the ceremony: "Jerry, I'm only thirteen years old." And, every now and then, back to Jimmy Swaggart: "I'm of the opinion that a God-given talent like yours ought to be for the glory of God."

I would have guessed that director Jim McBride ("The Big Easy") would have been too smart to get involved in cliches of this magnitude. Possibly "Great Balls of Fire!" is intended as a subtle spoof on bad musicals of the past but, if so, it's new proof that you can't have it both ways. Dennis Quaid struts and frets his nearly two hours on the screen, lip-synching to The Killer's music, with an overdone performance that falls just short of being camp. Which is too bad. Seen as comedy, the flick is tolerable. Seen as serious biography, its laughable. Or, as critic Jerry Lee would surely put it: Laughable! Laughable! Laughable!

NEWSWEEK, 7/10/89, p. 72, David Ansen

Brash, bold and broad, *Great Balls of Fire!* holds up a fun-house mirror to the life of Jerry Lee Lewis, the rock-and-roll wild man whose meteoric career in the mid-'50s crashed and burned when word got out he'd married his 13-year-old cousin (while still married to a previous wife). Concentrating on these few hyperbolic years, director Jim McBride ("The Big Easy") and co-writer Jack Baran have chosen to focus on the legend, not the man. What they're after is the raucous, rebellious spirit of rock and roll itself, spelled out in the primary colors of a 1950s musical. Anyone expecting a psychological exposé of Lewis's scandal-ridden life—his six wives, his alcoholism, his troubles with the IRS and reports of violence—should look elsewhere. Dennis Quaid's cocky, flamboyant Lewis, played with a preening audaciousness so broad he sometimes resembles a cartoon character, is no saint, but the movie celebrates him as an exuberant sinner who gave 150 percent of himself to his music. Like his God-fearing cousin Jimmy Swaggart (Alec Baldwin), he's an evangelical performer, but instead of praising Jesus he sings secular hosannas to raging teen hormones.

The advantage of McBride's stylized, movie-movie approach is that he's able for the most part to avoid the dutiful biographical approach of a "La Bamba" or "Buddy Holly Story." There may not be much going on under the surface, but "Great Galls of Fire" is never drab. The musical set pieces really cook (Lewis rerecorded his old hits for the movie), especially Valerie Wellington's and Lewis's versions of "Whole Lotta Shakin' Goin' On." What the movie can't do is bring the story to a satisfying conclusion. McBride tries to keep the upbeat tone, but he's stuck with downbeat facts, and the tale just breaks off at an arbitrary point.

The movie's most delicate accomplishment is its funny, sympathetic depiction of Lewis's love affair with the schoolgirl Myra (on whose memoirs the film is based). Winona Ryder again proves herself the most gifted and endearing teen actress around. She plays off Quaid's manic romantic assault with breathtaking spontaneity, her fresh, wide-eyed face running the scale of adolescent emotions, from glazed puppy love to pop-eyed bewilderment.

TIME 7/10/89, p. 67, Richard Schickel

"If I'm going to hell, I'm going there playing the piano."
—Jerry Lee Lewis

At the time *Great Balls of Fire* alleges the demon rocker made that remark, plenty of people argued that for him the trip represented no more than a return to his roots, a visit with the home folks.

Strange, though, are the ways of fate and fame. The movie shows Lewis' bravado being directed at his cousin, revivalist Jimmy Swaggart, who is portrayed at more or less regular intervals denouncing rock 'n' roll as the "devil music" and praying for the redemption of Jerry Lee's blighted soul. But the real-life Swaggart has since been brought low by the revelation of particularly tacky sexual practices. Lewis' music, manner and morality now seem almost innocent in comparison with what has followed him up the charts and into the hearts of adolescents during the past three decades. Even the act that shattered his career—marriage to his 13-year-old second cousin Myra (the script is based on her as-told-to memoir)—is something we now feel compelled to "understand," if not endorse.

The people who worked on this movie are not without a certain sophistication. They know that the heroic, tragic and farcical modes, all of which they briefly lurch toward in the course of the film, are not really appropriate to their story. They are also aware of how rapidly the world has spun since their protagonist was burning pianos and churning up teenage hormones. Accelerated change of that sort produces the kind of broad fundamental irony that moviemakers who take themselves seriously always love. How dumb we were. And so recently. How easy it is to encourage the audience to join in a superior snicker at simpler times, simpler souls.

The trouble is that rude realism keeps raising its voice, breaking in on the fun. The sound track naturally resounds with the orgasmic hammering of the Lewis beat, wails with the simple, not to say crude, sexual metaphors of his lyrics. Dennis Quaid very successfully re-creates his dervish-like stage presence (he made Elvis' Pelvis look as if it were stuck in the mud) in a portrayal that goes over the top in nicely calculated measure. And Winona Ryder contributes a hypnotically enigmatic performance—articulate innocence and inarticulate knowingness all mixed up—as the singer's nymphet bride. All these authenticities fitfully but forcefully remind us that back in the enervated '50s, there were certain unspeakably raunchy things in life and fantasy that Jerry Lee Lewis put us in touch with while Johnny Mathis and Jerry Vale were otherwise engaged.

Fundamentalist opinion to the contrary, Lewis was not Satan's satrap. Anxious middleclass parents, who saw him as an emissary from a netherworld that was nearer at hand—trailer-park American—were possibly a little closer to the truth. Like Presley, Dean and Brando, he was a figure partially shaped by a popular culture that in the '50s was learning to cater almost exclusively to kids and their need for rebel figures. But there was also an element of discomfiting truth in the message he sent. The thing about the young Jerry Lee was that he was all fecklessness and recklessness, without a shrewd thought in his head—and without a Colonel Parker to cover up his skid marks. There is a certain irony in that, but it is of an altogether more subtle and interesting kind than anything *Great Balls of Fire* has to offer.

VILLAGE VOICE, 7/11/89, p. 66, Georgia Brown

What I wanted to know: Could the movie possibly be as silly-looking as those ads and photos of Dennis Quaid looking like he's been repeatedly goosed? Answer: Yes, it truly can be.

Great Balls of Fire! is a manic, sanitized, goofball version of a turbulent period in what couldn't have been a light-hearted life. Jerry Lee Lewis, from all accounts, is a violent, shameless, hard-assed, tormented s.o.b., whereas this movie, directed by Jim McBride and based loosely on Myra Gale Brown Lewis's account of her marriage to The Killer, comes close to being a musical comedy. It probably should have gone all the way and become one. McBride, who used Quaid so effectively in *The Big Easy*—the sexiest genre movie of '87—now sets him loose to render the wizened redneck Lewis as something like a lovable dim-witted spastic, a great ball of tics. Quaid's performance is so wired and effervescent, and so full of bugs, quirks, and smirks, he looks like he might have been in the county fair's sideshow tent instead of on its main stage. And then at moments the hyped-up actor comes through rather winningly in a way that has something, but not much, to do with Jerry Lee.

There are a few good reasons to be fascinated with Lewis's story, and someone as savvy as McBride is obviously aware of what these are. A whole school of redneck anthropology could be founded on the fact that Lewis is cousin to Jimmy ("I have sinned!") Swaggart. Jerry Lee sings about being possessed as if bent on converting souls; Swaggart preaches about great balls of fire while doing a whole lot of shakin'. Although Swaggart (played by Alec Baldwin) appears in the narrative, the movie has only the most obvious sort of fun with the relationship.

Great Balls opens with the two cousins as small boys in Louisiana, 1944, sneaking down to the wrong side of the train tracks to watch some real down-dirty dancing. What looks for a second like an orgy is jus' black folks having a night out. One of the boys is terrified. "It's the devil's music, I can feel it." I anticipated a little joke here—making Jimmy be the daring one, or at least both or them—but the movie plays the roles straight. Jimmy runs back home while little Jerry can't tear himself away.

McBride takes this and a couple of other early opportunities to make a statement about the origins of rock and roll—namely, that whites stole the beat as well as whole songs (like "Whole Lotta Shakin' Goin' On," which one of the band later refers to when he says, "We can't play that nigger music here or they might lynch us") from African-Americans. In this instance, the piano player's black hands (belonging to Booker T. Laury as Piano Slim) disslove into the white ones of the adult Jerry Lee in Memphis, 1956.

Lewis is practicing at the home of his cousin and bass player, J.W. Brown (John Doe), while readying himself to pay a visit to Elvis's agent at Sun Records. As Jerry Lee blows bubble gum at the piano, so does 13-year-old Myra Gale Brown (Winona Ryder) who is, just this moment, descending from her school bus. The age difference between Jerry Lee at 21 and Myra seems slight, in fact. Ryder at the ripe old age of 16 (when *Great Balls* was filmed) is not more mature-looking than a good many 12- or 13-year-old girls. (If you've ever watched a sixth grade graduation, where the girls are women and the boys are boys, you'll know that I mean.) What she does look here, wearing a ponytail so that her cute little ears stick out, is more middle-class prim and squeaky clean than I imagine the real Myra. Ryder has recently done a wicked all-American teen queen in *Heathers*, but McBride and Jack Baran's script doesn't give her much to tease around with.

Quaid's Jerry Lee acts so immature and silly, he's just a little boy himself—and not really a bad one. Myra admires him; the H-bomb helps out by driving her into his arms to be comforted whenever the subject comes up on TV ("That's the apocalypse," he informs her. "I don't even know what hydrogen is," she confides.) The movie sexiest scene to my mind is one where the smitten Jerry Lee directs his song at a fairgrounds gig to the gaping, lovesick Myra, surrounded by screaming fans. Mom (Lisa Blount) is happy to overlook her suspicions since she's so busy buying the new outfits and appliances Jerry Lee's new success affords. Dad, to his credit, starts sniffing around.

Meanwhile, the legendary Sam Phillips (Trey Wilson) has invited Jerry Lee to become a "member of the Sun family" after offering up some sage observations; "You take a white right hand and a black left hand, and what do you get? You get rock 'n' roll." Sam also puts a bug into Jerry Lee's ear: "Girls like guitar players; they like to see them wiggle around. You can't wiggle behind a piano."

This is enough, presumably, to make a wiggling piano player out of the less-than-graceful Jerry Lee. (I guess Quaid is doing an imitation, but frankly, I don't remember Lewis with all these contortions, grimaces, grotesque sneers, and ungainly struts. Quaid has him walking like someone with his back thrown out.) Performing on the Steve Allen show, he kicks away his chair and Steverino (himself), always a game host, tosses it out of reach.

McBride indulges in some odd visual silliness at this point by showing various TV families (like the Beaver's) sit up and take notice of Jerry Lee's national debut. The scene's kicker comes when, in a bed with red satin sheets, the woman with Elvis Presley gets up as if mesmerized by Lewis on the screen. Later one dark night, the specter of Elvis stops by on his way to the army (shouldering his duffle) to pass Jerry Lee the baton: "Take it!" On a double bill with Chuck Berry at New York's Paramount Theater, Lewis tries to impress a cool, disdainful Berry by setting his piano on fire and playing on amid the flames. So do mighty shows out of little insecurities grow?

McBride's irony toward Lewis flares high at certain points (such as this one), although it's never clear what his larger purpose or point of view is. Jerry Lee's a patheic, infantile clown and a two-bit performer who ripped off black music? Jerry Lee's a psychopath who can't possibly be accurately portrayed while alive, so this will do for now? Best to emasculate the macho bastard? In deciding not to fill in the dark or wild side, what McBride offers up is so goofy it's incoherent, not only psychologically but aesthetically. The movie's attitude made me feel I must be some kind of fool for letting Lewis's sultry, insinuating singing get to me. The has-been's low-down music happens to be the best thing *Great Balls* has going for it.

Apparently (if I'm to trust those TV movie preview shows), McBride's original ending was deemed too downbeat by market research surveys of people who get waylaid in shopping malls and have nothing to do but subject themselves to extensive quizzes and even seminars on the studio's product. Reports had it that, following this lowest-common-denominator approach to filmmaking, a new ending was shot that might or might not be used. Well, it obviously has been used. I can't think that this makes any difference at all.

Also reviewed in:
NEW YORK TIMES, 6/30/89, P. C8, Caryn James
VARIETY, 7/5-11/89, p. 18
WASHINGTON POST, 6/30/89, p. B1, Hal Hinson
WASHINGTON POST, 6/30/89, Weekend/p. 29, Eve Zibart

GROSS ANATOMY

A Touchstone Pictures release in association with Silver Screen Partners IV. *Executive Producer:* Sandy Gallin and Carol Baum. *Producer:* Howard Rosenman and Debra Hill. *Director:* Thom Eberhardt. *Screenplay:* Ron Nyswaner and Mark Spragg. *Story:* Mark Spragg and Howard Rosenman. *Director of Photography:* Steve Yaconelli. *Editor:* Bud Smith and Scott Smith. *Music:* David Newman. *Music Editor:* Craig Pettigrew and Tom Villano. *Sound:* Jim Tanenbaum and (music) Tim Boyle. *Sound Editor:* Mike Dobie. *Production Designer:* William F. Matthews. *Art Director:* P. Michael Johnston. *Set Designer:* Lauren Polizzi. *Set Decorator:* Catherine Mann. *Special Effects:* Calvin Joe Acord. *Costumes:* Gale Parker. *Make-up:* Edouard F. Henriques III. *Running time:* 107 minutes. *MPAA Rating:* PG-13.

CAST: Matthew Modine (Joe Slovak); Daphne Zuniga (Laurie Rorbach); Christine Lahti (Dr. Rachel Woodruff); Todd Field (David Schreiner); John Scott Clough (Miles Reed); Alice Carter (Kim McCauley); Robert Desiderio (Dr. Banks); Zakes Mokae (Dr. Banumbra); Clyde Kusatsu, John Petlock, J. Patrick McNamara, and Jan Munroe (Interviewing Professors); J.C. Quinn (Papa Slovak); Rutanya Alda (Mama Slovak); Brandis Kemp (Aunt Rose); Ryan Cash (Frankie Slovak); Angus MacInnes (Dean Torrence); Lisa Zand (Luann); Alison Taylor (Cynthia Wilkes); Michael Stoyanov (Joel Cleaver); Max Perlich (Ethan Cleaver); Bruce Beatty (Kelly); John Short (Resident); Steven Culp (Jerry Fanning Forrester); Scott Allan Campbell (Ed McCauley); Elizabeth Gilliam (Nina McCauley); Gordon Clapp (Doctor); Jack Murdock (Old Man Patient); Kimberly Scott (Nurse Louise); Diane Robin (Waitress); Rick Goldman (Truck Driver); Tom Kurlander and Susanne Goldstein (Students); Beth Hogan (Marie); O. LaRon Clark (Food Server); Russell Bobbitt (Gunshot Victim); Frank Torres (Gang Member); Bill Rogers and Frank Foti Jr. (Cops); Pola Del Mar (Gang Member's Mother); Jesse Anthony Gonzalez (Gang Member's Brother).

FILMS IN REVIEW, 3/90, p. 172, Frank Scheck

What *The Paper Chase* did for the first year of law school, *Gross Anatomy* would like to do for the first year of medical school. But this film settles for the conventional. Its comedy, like its title, is crass and unsubtle, and its drama never strays far from the predictable. It even has a beautiful but hard as nails female doctor/teacher who dies of a horrible disease by the final reel.

Joe Slovak (Matthew Modine) is a poor but irrepressible young student who shows up at school cocky, full of himself, and without any real desire to practice medicine. Relying on his "excellent retention," he finds his studies relatively easy, and he is more interested in pursuing his beautiful study group member Laurie (Daphne Zuniga). The other group members are not so cavalier: David (Todd Field), Joe's compulsively neat roommate, pops pills to cope with the pressure; Miles (John Scott Clough) spends most of his time sucking up to the teachers; and Kim (Alice Carter) strives wearily to cope with the conflicting demands of husband, daughter, and pregnancy.

The film centers around a "gross human anatomy" class, affording the film both its title and numerous opportunities for black humor as the students huddle over their cadavers. They are presided over by the jovial Dr. Banumbra (Zakes Moake) and Dr. Rachel Woodruff (Christine Lahti), who develops an adverserial relationship with Joe and makes it her mission to turn him into a dedicated doctor. She gives him an unidentified patient's history and asks him for a diagnosis. He comes up with a fatal one. It, of course, turns out to be hers. A consistent limp is the tip-off.

Although the film succeeds occasionally with its dramatic and comic elements, the balance is off, and it never achieves a consistent whole. Matthew Modine exerts all of his considerable charm in what is a fairly ordinary role, and he almost lifts the film out of its mediocrity. Too much of the time the screenplay, by Ron Nyswaner and Mark Spragg, and the direction, by Thom Eberhardt, resemble television movie quality.

LOS ANGELES TIMES, 10/20/89, Calendar/p. 12, Michael Wilmington

The young medical students in "Gross Anatomy"—five hopeful surgeons sharing the same dissection table during a punishing first med-school year—aren't the kind you'd want pawing around your pancreas in some emergency.

Self-centered, callous, shallow, they don't express much desire to help people beyond the formula rote idealism you'd expect from students-on-the-make. Except for pregnant young Kim (Alice Carter), they seem low on sensitivity, as well. These are kids, and a movie, with tunnel vision: yuppie-doctors-in-embryo. One of them (Todd Field) pops pills and hides biochemistry textbooks near his cadaver. Another (John Scott Clough) is a silk-shirted apple-polisher. They're privileged kids for whom success is a touchstone. The major seeming exception, fisherman's son Joe Slovak (Matthew Modine), is slotted as the group's sexy rebel. He bounces a basketball on the way to his class locker.

This sounds like good meat for a satire of the medical profession—a movie that might cheerfully savage its mercenary tendencies—and "MASH" and "The Paper Chase" are the obvious inspirations, along with the real-life experiences of co-producer and ex-med student Howard Rosenman.

But"Gross Anatomy" isn't really geared for satire or humorous realism. There's a charismatic mentor here, like "Paper Chase's" Prof. Kingsfield, plus some of "MASH's" jock irreverence and a pale carbon of its hip, funny attitude toward gore. Mostly, though, the five writters who've pawed over this story in three shifts have shot it full of '80s raw pragmatism and sentimental tomfoolery and left it anesthetized on the table, full of cheerless twitches and spasmodic eruptions of programmed mirth.

There's another deodorant-ad notion of a love affair: Novak and Laurie (Daphne Zuniga) do much of their wooing on a jogging track and, when Laurie succumbs, she says simply "You got me!" Novak's rebellion, meanwhile, is limited to helping his roommate cheat on exams and cheerfully telling his examiners that he's in it for the money. (So, apparently, is the movie.)

Christine Lahti is cast in the John Houseman-type role and, though she is a brilliant actress, she is used badly here.The script suggests that Lahti's Dr. Woodruff sees Joe as a kindred spirit: a rebel, an outsider, a born doctor. Instead, she seems another movie fairy godmother, inexplicably hung up on a self-absorbed goof-off. When, in the movie's big passing-the-torch scene, Joe finds her wasting away from lupus and begins screaming "What do you want from me?," you want to set him right back to his fisherman dad, perhaps to be used as bait.

Is this any way for a potential surgeon to act toward an obviously dying woman? You'd like to think the writers are being sarcastic with Dr. Woodruff's response—she gives him a be-all-that-you-can-be speech—but no such luck. Fifty years ago, Joe would have been wafted with a heavenly choir out of this benediction from his female Dr. Chips straight to worldwide surgical fame. Here, we know we're heading toward the '80s equivalent: a climactic sexy clinch with Daphne Zuniga and soft-rock under the credits.

The director of "Gross Anatomy" (MPAA-rated PG-13 for sex and language), Thom Eberhardt ("Night of the Comet"), shows occasional verve and a lively touch with the actors—especially Modine and Field, surprisingly good as Joe's amphetamine-crazed roommate. But there's a no-exit shallowness to this '80s sentimentalism where people scream, rage and insult each other, cheat, strive ruthlessly for success, and go warm and gooey after they pass the final exam. Who needs heavenly choirs? "Gross," in this case, describes the anatomy class and the movie itself.

NEW YORK POST, 10/20/89, p. 29, Jami Bernard

The misleadingly titled "Gross Anatomy" (no, it's not a teen sequel to "Hardbodies") is a fairly pleasing, unambitious, predictable comedy about the pains and gains experienced by first-year med students, who endure a grueling boot-camp education designed to make doctor material out of only the hardiest souls.

Matthew Modine, a sort of timid person's Crispin Glover, is the mysteriously irreverent student Joe Slovak, a fisherman's son who is almost too smart for his own good. Unafraid of carving up cadavers, Joe is a slippery jokester among anal retentives who apportion their study time down to how many minutes it tales to brush their teeth. Joe, meanwhile, dribbles a basketball on his way to class and only crams for tests at the last minute.

When he is, in fact, tested, it is a different sort of test, one that is designed to bring about humility and caring and other things more doctors could use for their bedside manner. This test of character is gradually administered by his attractive lab partner (Daphne Zuniga, the actress with the Maria Shriver hair) and by his severe but kind-hearted professor (Christine Lahti, whose overdrive talents are left to idle by the confines of her role).

The humor is not gross, but neither is it particularly witty, revolving as it does around formaldehyde jokes and the uptightness of med-school nerds. It is probably safe to say that "Gross Anatomy" would be stiff as a cadaver without the goosey Modine in the lead role.

Still, it is perfectly acceptable as mild entertainment, the kind you might crave during a study break or if you're a high school student exhausted by your first Career Night. A companion was queasy over the cadaver shots, but those are just the thing teen-agers roar over. I only hope the chuckles aren't from our future doctors.

NEWSDAY, 10/20/89, Part III/p. 5, Mike McGrady

First-year medical student Joe Slovak (Matthew Modine), central character in "Gross

Anatomy,'' is able to breeze through medical school playing basketball, chasing girls, having fun—all because of one little trick. Instead of reading entire medical text books, Joe skims texts, reading and memorizing only the information printed in boldface type. Interesting concept. And since many of our readers don't have time to give this review the attention it merits, I'm tempted to adopt the Slovak system, making my most salient points in heavy print. Those in a rush, then, would need only to read—and, of course, memorize—those items in boldface type.

The title, "Gross Anatomy," refers to a required course taken by all first-year medical students. The students meet regularly in a lab filled with cadavers that have been pickled in formaldehyde. During the first year (and the movie) the students dissect those cadavers, study body parts and occasionally use the corpses for small japeries. This may strike sensitive sorts as **disgusting**, especially when the teacher provides such advice as, "Keep your cadavers moist; if they dry up, they're useless."

The title might lead some to believe that "Gross Anatomy" is a spoofy portrait of future surgeons as young cut-ups, but comedy makes up but a small percentage of the film. Distantly related to "Young Doctors in Love," it is a more **direct descendant of soggier sagas** such as, oh, "The Interns" and "The New Interns."

When he is not arriving late to class or shooting baskets or just plain goofing off, young doctor Joe is chasing fellow-student Laurie (Daphne Zuniga) who is **pretty but has a speech impediment**. Her speech impediment is that she speaks only Soaperaese. For example, medical school "is not a game for me. This has to be the most important thing right now. I am just telling you this so that you know why I have to work so hard and why I can't get distracted." Later, she stalls for time, saying,"I just need to sort things out."

Incidentally, she is not the only one with that same speech impediment. That **ordinarily marvelous actress Christine Lahti** is on hand as the anatomy professor, who "worked so hard for so many years trying to turn my best students into perfect doctors" and is now trying to get Joe to shape up: "I want you to be more than you ever wanted to be yourself, and I can't tell you how to be it."

Director Thom Eberhardt, who fared better—funnier, anyhow—with last year's "Without a Clue," is directing a story credited to four writers, **always an ominous sign**. Perhaps it required the services of four writers to get all this in: young love, unexpected sex, students taking speed, pregnancy, emergency-room catastrophes, delivery of a baby in a diner, dropouts, sudden death and five or six workable jokes. **The problem is this: "Gross Anatomy" is not silly enough to qualify as comedy, not serious enough to measure up as drama.**

VILLAGE VOICE, 10/31/89, p. 78, Georgia Brown

The audience for *Gross Anatomy*, a silly comedy about med school directed by Thom Eberhardt, is probably unaccompanied-by-adult 11-year-olds. They'd think the anatomy lab cadaver is gross, and shriek at the cut from the scalpel dissecting the skull to Matthew Modine sawing a drumstick off his roast chicken. They'd even get to see the birth (simulated) of a baby.

They probably could take the cocky character Modine (usually an engaging actor) plays: He's Joe Slovak, a Southern California fisherman's son who makes it into med school but doesn't know what he's doing there. Slovak's thing is to make a show of arriving late at lectures and bouncing his basketball in the halls. Superior "retention" (brain, not sphincter) relieves him from having to hit the books like the others. Significant others include his nerdy roommate David (Todd Field), who hides speed tablets under the mattress, and Laurie (Daphne Zuniga), the young woman he's trying to make but who's determined not to "get distracted."

Joe comes up against a no-nonsense lab professor and assistant dean, Dr. Rachel Woodruff (Christine Lahti). She senses Joe's potential and chides him for being "satisfied with being average." (Somehow she seems not to find him above-average obnoxious.) "Tomorrow is tomorrow," is Joe's motto. Eleven-year-olds might not realize that when Dr. Woodruff lends Joe a case (which he's picked off her desk to browse in) to diagnose for extra credit, the seriously ill patient is herself. Correct that. They'd know, because they watch sitcoms, but they think fiction comes that way.

Also reviewed in:
NEW YORK TIMES, 10/20/89, p. C17, Janet Maslin
VARIETY, 10/25-31/89, p. 29
WASHINGTON POST, 10/20/89, p. B7, Rita Kempley

GROWING UP IN AMERICA

A Cinephile Pictures release of a Morley Markson and Associates Ltd. film. *Executive Producer:* Don Haig. *Producer:* Morley Markson. *Director:* Morley Markson. *Based on a theme by:* Don Haig and George Miller. *Director of Photography:* Morley Markson. *Editor:* Morley Markson. *Music:* Marty Simon. *Sound:* Tom Burger, Anthony Hall, and James Plaxton. *Running time:* 90 minutes. *MPAA Rating:* Not Rated.

WITH: Allen Ginsberg, Jerry Rubin, Abbie Hoffman, William Kunstler, Fred Hampton, Deborah Johnson, Fred Hampton Jr., John Sinclair, Don Cox, Timothy Leary.

NEW YORK POST, 5/3/89, p. 29, V.A. Musetto

There's no mistaking the long-haired, bearded, headbanded young man in the '60s footage. It's Jerry Rubin and he's preaching the overthrow of America: "We're permanent adolescents. We don't want to grow up because we know what growing up in America means."

Cut to a clean-cut, middle-aged chap in dark suit, tie and button-down white shirt. If you weren't told, you would have trouble guessing that he's the grown-up, 1980s edition of Jerry Rubin, who, with his Vanna White-lookalike wife, now devotes his time to making money through theme parties at his New York nightclub.

His change from yippie to yuppie is the most rude and, depending on your point of view, most disturbing revelation in "Growing Up in America," Canadian filmmaker Morley Markson's intriguing and entertaining update on the radicals he chronicled in his 1969 documentary, "Breathing Together: Revolution of the Electric Family."

Rubin's transformation is even more startling when compared with fellow Chicago 7 defendant Abbie Hoffman, who in the '80s continued to fight for the causes he believed in. "I don't wake up each morning saying this is a good day to die," says Hoffman in a comment that takes on new meaning with his sucide last month. "I don't have to change."

William Kunstler and Allen Ginsberg also have stayed true to their '60s beliefs. "My anger is the same today," says Kunstler, the Chicago 7 lawyer who continues to take up the cause of radicals. Beat poet Ginsberg has a shorter and grayer beard and looks more like a rabbi than a revolutionary, but watching him chant and sing in a park, you realize that underneath he's the same old Ginsberg.

LSD guru Timothy Leary, Black Panther chief Don Cox and White Panther leader Jim Sinclair, on the other hand, have comfortably eased themselves into mellow, non-confrontational middle age. Leary markets New Age software from his well-appointed home in suburban Los Angeles. Cox lives in Paris and still dreams of "a revolution to provide everybody with a good life," but he admits that he just wants to be left alone. Sinclair looks at clips of his wild-haired, pot-smoking youth and, with a chuckle, says: "When you see this guy all you want to do is arrest him,"

On the surface, Markson treats all his subjects evenly. He lets his '60s icons speak for themselves. Most come across sympathetically. The one exception is Jerry Rubin; nothing could be more damning than his own words.

Also reviewed in:
NEW YORK TIMES, 5/3/89, p. C20, Vincent Canby
VARIETY, 9/14/88, p. 27

HALLOWEEN 5: THE REVENGE OF MICHAEL MYERS

A Galaxy International release. *Producer:* Ramsey Thomas. *Director:* Dominique Othenin-Girard. *Screenplay:* Michael Jacobs, Dominique Othenin-Girard, and Shem Bitterman. *Director of Photography:* Robert Draper. *Music:* Alan Howarth and John Carpenter. *Running time:* 90 minutes. *MPAA Rating:* R.

CAST: Donald Pleasence (Dr. Loomis); Danielle Harris (Jamie Lloyd); Donald L. Shanks (Michael Myers); Wendy Kaplan (Tian).

LOS ANGELES TIMES, 10/16/89, Calendar/p. 5, Michael Wilmington

After four "Halloweens" of numbingly similar carnage we know what to expect from

"Halloween 5:" nubile teen-agers clutching one another lasciviously and getting slashed to death by a white-masked fiend.

This is the same infinitely repeated plot of "Halloweens" 1, 2 and 4 (3 took a slightly deviant turn), with the same unkillable bogyman Michael Myers, wreaking the same programmed havoc, and Donald Pleasence as the same distraught psychiatrist, repeating the same dire warnings to no avail.

Is everyone in this small town a hopeless moron? At one point, a squadron of police have Michael trapped in the woods; they immediately leave to set up a trap in a deserted house somewhere else.

At the end of "Halloween 4," poor little Jamie (Danielle Harris) was apparently cast as the new bogyman. Now, through some quick double-shuffling, she's once again a victim and Michael, apparently destroyed, is back for another night of slaughter. Danielle is a great screamer, but you quickly get tired of watching her trance out and psychically link with the rampaging Mike: a talent, which, naturally, fails her at crucial moments. You also get quickly tired of "Halloween 5" (MPAA rated R: for sex and violence), even though director/co-writer Dominique Othenin-Girard tries to wake you up by pushing the series' subjective camera strategy to hand-held, quasi-Polanski extremes.

NEW YORK POST, 10/14/89, p. 15, V.A. Musetto

There are lots of tricks but few treats in "Halloween 5: The Revenge of Michael Myers."

The latest entry in the series that started back in 1978 begins where the last one left off, with nut case Myers being pulverized by police bullets and presumably killed (we should be so lucky).

Flash-forward a year. It's Halloween once again in the all-American town of Haddonfield and the masked Myers is—surprise! surprise!—still with us. Being a guy who holds a grudge, he's once again stalking his poor, little niece Jamie, whose now-deceased mommy was the subject of Myers' wrath in the first "Halloween" (got that?).

Along the way, Myers slices and dices his way through Haddonfield's teen-age population and Keystone Kops-like police force (unofficial body count: 13). There's the obligatory teeny-bopper-in-the-shower scene and a final gore-fest that is about as scary as the kids in costume who come to your door on Halloween.

The special effects are routine as these things go (without notes I'd be hard-pressed to remember how Myers offs any of his victims); the acting is adequate at best; and the direction, by someone named Dominique Othenin-Girard, is of the paint-by-numbers variety. What a comedown from John Carpenter's innovative, blood-curdling work in the original "Halloween"!

In this one, everybody seems to be content to just go through the motions, secure in the belief that they have a pre-sold market that doesn't care how good or bad the movie might be.

The only redeeming quality in the unpleasantness is Donald Pleasence, who is back for another go-round as Dr. Loomis, the shrink with the bum leg, scarred hand and face and a single-minded determination to rid Myers of "the rage inside." Pleasence's campy, scenery-chewing performance is what earns "Halloween 5" its half-star. (But why must he wear the same trench coat in each and every scene?)

The movie ends with Myers bound for prison, where, says one cop, he'll stay "until his dying day." Replies little Jamie: "He'll *never* die." Neither, I'm afraid, will this dim-witted series.

Also reviewed in:
NEW YORK TIMES, 10/14/89, p. 13, Stephen Holden
VARIETY, 10/18–24/89, p. 32
WASHINGTON POST, 10/16/89, p. B2, Richard Harrington

HANUSSEN

A Columbia Pictures release of an objektiv Filmstudio/Mafilm (Budapest)/CCC Filmkunst (West Berlin) coproduction in association with ZDF. *Producer:* Arthur Brauner. *Director:* István Szabó. *Screenplay (German with English subtitles):* István Szabó and Péter Dobai. *Director of Photography:* Lajos Koltai. *Editor:* Zsuzsa Csákány. *Music:* György Vukán. *Choreographer:* Péter László. *Sound:* Gyorgy Fék. *Art Director:* Jozef Romvari, László Makai, and Gyula Tóth. *Costumes:* Nelly Vagó. *Make-up:* János Németh. *Running time:* 140 minutes. *MPAA Rating:* R.

CAST: Klaus Maria Brandauer (Klaus Schneider, "Erik-Jan Hanussen"); Erland Josephson (Dr. Bettelheim); Ildikó Bánsági (Sister Betty); Walter Schmidinger (Propaganda Chief); Károly Eperjes (Captain Nowotny); Grazyna Szapolowska (Valery de la Meer); Colette Pilz-Warren (Dagma); Adriana Biedrzynska (Martha, "Wally"); György Cserhalmi (Count Trantow-Waldbach).

CHRISTIAN SCIENCE MONITOR, 4/18/89, p. 11, David Sterritt

Klaus Maria Brandauer became a Hollywood star in the Oscar-sweeping "Out of Africa" a few seasons ago. But some of his most celebrated work has been done with Hungarian filmmaker István Szabó, who shares with Mr. Brandauer a special interest in Central Europe at the time when Nazism was rising to power. Together they made "Mephisto," an Oscar winner featuring Brandauer as an actor who collaborates with the Nazis, and then "Colonel Redl," an Oscar nominee with Brandauer as an Army officer who betrays his commanders.

In their new picture, "Hanussen," the energetic Brandauer plays his most exotic character yet: a stage hypnotist and clairvoyant who really lived in Europe during the '20s and '30s, and earned his greatest fame by foretelling the triumph of Hitler and his party. The picture earned yet another Academy Award nomination for its makers this year, in the "best foreign-language film" category, although it lost to Bille August's long Danish drama, "Pelle the Conqueror."

Like its title character, "Hanussen" can be approached in different ways. On one level, it's a supernatural story, about a man with strange powers to control others and predict the future.

Looked at another way, it's a story of show business, as Hanussen turns his bizarre talent into a passport to fame and riches—until he makes one political prophecy too many and finds himself in a lot of trouble. And it's definitely a tale of politics and history, tracing the fall of the Austro-Hungarian Empire and the rise of Hitler's fascism in starkly dramatic terms.

What weaves the story together, despite its many different facets, is the close rapport of star Brandauer and director Szabó, who are on exactly the same wavelength.

Brandauer is excellent in "Hanussen," running a gamut of emotions from childish anger and fear—especially near the beginning, when he's been wounded in combat—to the egotism of an entertainer who thinks the world is right to worship at his feet. He also does a skillful job of reminding us that Hanussen doesn't really understand his own strange talent. Even as he performs wonders and basks in the applause of all Berlin, you can tell he's ill-at-ease because he simply doesn't know how he does it. Brandauer's remarkable performance, supported by Mr. Szabó's sensitive directing, makes this feeling come alive.

As much as I like "Hanussen" in this respect, I must say it could have been a better film if it had been written and edited with a stronger sense of control.

The movie has at least two fascinating subjects going for it: the rise of Nazism and the hero's supernatural powers. Yet it seems colorless and poorly focused at times, and some of its secondary characters are two-dimensional clichés. Perhaps the blame lies partly with trimming inflicted on the film to suit the allegedly meager attention span of American audiences; a version shown at last spring's Cannes Film Festival was almost a half-hour longer.

Despite its flaws, though, "Hanussen" is a vivid look at an always-gripping period of modern history. And its main performances—by Brandauer and by Swedish actor Erland Josephson as a doctor who tries to understand Hanussen—are marvelous to behold.

LOS ANGELES TIMES, 3/8/89, Calendar/p. 1, Sheila Benson

"Hanussen" is the third of director-co-writer István Szabó's meditations on influence, free will and corruptibility, and possibly the most mature and subtle of the trio. The first two, "Mephisto" and "Colonel Redl" served to introduce the mercurial Klaus Maria Brandauer to American audiences, who would finally appreciate his gift for energizing a scene after "Out of Africa."

As the telepathic "Erik-Jan Hanussen," born somewhat less mellifluously as Klaus Schneider, Brandauer will eventually hold pre-Hitler Berlin in his card-palmer's hand. But first, he has to learn the extent, if not the source, of his talents himself.

Szabó stages that moment in a World War I military hospital, which has brought Erland Josephson's Dr. Bettelheim together with Brandauer's Austrian sergeant. Ill and disoriented as the sergeant is, he and the senior physician recognize a bond of power and sensitivity.

In a scene that is almost a match in intensity for Richard Lester's bomb-defusing sequence of "Juggernaut," Brandauer faces an enraged soldier who threatens to annihilate the whole hospital ward with a smuggled hand grenade. It becomes an exchange of will that leaves Brandauer limp, sweat pouring from him.

But he has had an inkling of his power, which Bettelheim urges him to refine and use along medical and psychiatric lines. Instead, with an old army friend, Nowotny (the distinctive Károly Eperjes), and a beautiful assistant he chooses to call Wally (Adriana Biedrzynska), the newly christened Hanussen goes on the stage and into a spiraling exercise of power. His most flippant predictions come true; his direst ones are echoed in the next morning's newspapers. Tried for fraud, he demonstrates his ability to plug into the yearnings of a whole courtroom of people.

Like "Mephisto," it's an actor's dream role, and increasingly Brandauer is a dream of an actor. Unlike that first collaboration, "Hanussen" is less brash, less flamboyant, less close to the edge of melodrama. You have the sense that Brandauer can take his own powers a little more for granted; he doesn't have to top himself in scene after glittering-eyed scene and it's more restful for an audience.

Hanussen himself is a more complex man; almost an automatic womanizer, his deepest attachment occurs after more than three-quarters of the story is past. It's also in this last third that the most provocative political maneuvering arises, as the seer falls into the hands of a Leni Riefenstahl-like photographer.

White-blond, invariably wearing a dress suit and tie, she announces she's had it with decadence. Instead, she's busy posing naked young Aryan gods and goddesses into "Joy Through Strength" pyramids for the greater glory of the rising Adolf Hitler. Fascinated by Hanussen, she works with him too, advising him on the best lighting, studying and photographing his charismatic poses of authority.

But Hanussen develops a living shadow: Each of his poses, his most successful theatrical devices, turns up a day or so later in the speeches and political appearances of Hitler. He must decide what to do with this juggernaut of his own. It's another Szabó comment on the theatricality of politics, not exactly an unknown element west of Budapest.

Like every film Szabó touches, "Hanussen" (Times-rated Mature for nudity, adult themes) glows with a delicate, soft-edge light, the particular result of the director's longtime collaboration with cinematographer Lajos Koltai, It is also impeccably performed, by Brandauer, by Eperjes and the great Josephson in particular. It is stocked with a staggering and seemingly endless supply of exquisite actresses, a not-uncommon occurrence in a Szabó film. All told, it forms a thoughtful conclusion to a singular and memorable trio of stories.

MONTHLY FILM BULLETIN, 6/89, p. 181, Richard Combs

Towards the end of World War I, Austrian corporal Klaus Schneider suffers a head wound and is treated at a military hospital under the Jewish Doctor Bettelheim. The doctor, who has his own apocalyptic memories/nightmares of pogroms in the past (centred on a boy trapped in a burning tree), is impressed by the presentiments about the future that haunt Schneider. When the latter manages to talk one wounded soldier out of committing suicide with a hand grenade, Bettelheim is convinced that he has considerable hypnotic and even clairvoyant powers. Schneider, who is soon enjoying the favours of Bettelheim's nurse Betty, puts on a mind-reading show in the hospital, which is interrupted by the announcement that the war is over. Subsequently, at dinner parties, Schneider finds his talents called on by businessmen, nervous to know what the future holds for them if the old institutions are swept away. An old army friend, Tibor Nowotny, becomes his impresario; he takes the stage name Erik-Jan Hanussen, and in Vienna is introduced to the curious press (one journalist, Martha, becomes his lover/"medium", calling herself Wally). Hanussen's fame spreads as his casual predictions come true, and the German Under-Secretary of State, Rottinger, invites him to Berlin to try his skills in the political arena. In Karlsbad, he is arrested and tried for charlatanism, but clears himself with an impassioned speech about his empathy with people's needs in hard times. In Berlin, he begins a liaison with Valery de la Meer, an old friend and renowned dancer, but also finds himself coming under the suspicious eye of police chief Trantow-Waldbach. Though he disdains any political allegiances, Hanussen's predictions about the rise of the Nazis begin to associate him with their cause. He is manipulated by the film-maker/photographer Hanni Stahl into "modelling" for her pictures of Hitler, and Nowotny angrily breaks off with him. With the assassination of Rottinger, his position becomes more vulnerable: the Nazis suspect that his predictions may be dangerous. After one of his stag acts involving hypnotism "foretells" the Reichstag fire, Hanussen is taken out by Trantow-Waldbach's adjutant Becker (whom he once made crow like a rooster when he came to heckle his stage act), and is forced to climb a tree and crow in his turn, before being shot along with Valery.

Hanussen is such a close replay of István Szabó's *Mephisto*—apparently based on a real magician/clairvoyant of the inter-war years, as the earlier film took its inspiration from the actor Gustav Grundgens—that an immediate question must be why it was necessary to make it. The irony of Erik-Jan Hanussen's fate is that, however clearly he can see into the future, he ignores the lessons of history—which are the particular burden of the man who first recognises his talents, the Jewish Bettelheim—failing to quit the "burning house" which the latter has seen in his past, and forced to act out another of his nightmares/memories, that of a boy trapped in a tree by his fascist persecutors. But if Hanussen's dying question, "Warum?" voices the perplexity of the theatrical clairvoyant with no profounder insight or sense of responsibility, it echoes rather hollowly as a challenge in any more general sense.

It indicts the indifference, the wilful blindness, the fiddling while the house begins to catch light, of the rest of Europe. But it remains rather beside the point because Hanussen himself is such a peripheral figure. He is a self-made-up man, linked to the Nazis by no specific ambitions (compared to his counterpart in *Mephisto*), whose talent for "realising" the future comes from nowhere and goes nowhere. Of course, Hanussen's lack of connection might *be* the point, since he is not from Germany but its shadow, a casualty and a survivor of the collapse of the Austro-Hungarian empire. His consequent lack of identity, his deliberate confusion of his origins in creating a stage persona for himself (as does everyone in his entourage), becomes a small rehearsal for the elaborate national fictions and theatrical ideology which the Nazis will translate into real tyranny (from one Austrian corporal to another. . .). The revelation that Hanussen shares Hitler's birthday, April 20, is the coincidence that in people's minds seems to turn this prophet of the world to come into one of its active instigators.

Perhaps the best scene in the film is Hanussen's introduction to the studio of photographer/film-maker Hanni Stahl—Leni Riefenstahl?—who is busily composing a tableau of heroic Aryan youth, and who finds an equally mythological use for Hanussen's infinitely adaptable persona. But Hanussen remains a theatrical accident in the Nazi ascendancy rather than, as in *Mephisto*, a theatrical reflection of it and eventually fellow performer in it. *Hanussen* also follows the earlier film in featuring three women with whom the protagonist becomes involved, but whose separate fates there revealed something about the political processes at work, while here they remain rather indistinguishable adjuncts of the magician/charlatan himself. In between Hanussen's function as an extraordinary seer, and his claim in court that he empathises with and hence represents the needs of ordinary people in parlous times—in between, say, the foreboding melodrama of *The Serpent's Egg* (or *Mephisto*) and the whimsical charlatanism of *Mr. North—Hanussen* never locates the theme or the style that will give its hero a proper role.

NEW YORK POST, 3/10/89, p. 30, Jami Bernard

The great Hanussen, who can predict the future with unerring accuracy, was not always thus. He was once Klaus Schneider, an Austrian sergeant in World War I who, while being treated for a head wound and complaining of feeling a great void within him, discovered his prescient and hupnotic powers.

"Hanussen," by Hungarian director István Szabó, is up for an Academy Award for best foreign film. It reunites director, actors and themes from the Oscar-winning "Mephisto" and "Colonel Redl," and while not technically a trilogy, the three are unmistakably companion pieces. All three involve one man's lonely and tormented rise to power within his field—actor, soldier and now actor/seer/soldier—inadvertently betraying himself and his friends as he politics harmlessly toward his goal and gets swept up into the vortex of history.

The lead, again, is expertly played by Klaus Maria Brandauer, the superb Austrian actor who can convey layers and depths of a character with his fleshily mobile face and haunted, taunting eyes.

Dr. Bettelheim (Erland Josephson), while treating Schneider's head wound with hypnotic suggestion, somehow awakens in his patient a similar talent. At first, Schneider's hypnotic gaze comes in handy for mentally, and then actually, undressing pretty women. He looks deep into their eyes, and—cut to the bedroom. But after he reluctantly talks a desperate soldier out of blowing the hospital to kingdom come. Schneider's reputation grows, and with it, an uneasy responsibility.

After the war (which ends just as Schneider is trying out his clairvoyant routine in a hospital revue), he and his impresario pick the stage name Erik-Jan Hanussen and take the show on the road. Along the way, he picks up an addition to his act—a "medium," who is a reporter so mesmerized by Hanussen's talents (mostly in bed) that she is putty in his hands. "You can do what you like with me," she says. In one age, he's a hypnotist, in another, he'd be a ladies' man.

Right after the war is a time of fear and uncertainty, when inflation and Hitler's storm troopers are elbowing aside the old order. The last stages of elegance have given way to decadence—directior Szabó has nude barmaids serving up dripping slabs of cake at an after-threater party—and bizarre sideshows are proliferating on the streets.

In a way, the great Hanussen is just another sideshow. Better dressed and more famous than the street mimes and jugglers, Hanussen still shares the bill with an all-midget opera. It is implied that the public's taste for foreseeing the future, however grim, is a product of the times, and Hanussen's success is itself subject to the vagaries of local politics. He is tried for fraud in Czechoslovakia, but sways the jury less by his psychic powers than by his understanding of their psychology. ("The masses behave like frustrated women," he confides bitterly to friends, seeing himself as the reluctant rapist of their dreams.)

Blindfolded with a luxurious sash, Hanussen is himself blind. His knack for prediction is as random a gift to him as a parrot's mimicry. "Your secret is that you awaken fear," an Indian psychic tells him. He is a cipher for history, and a victim of it. He sees with alarm the ascendency of Hitler, and is punished for his vision.

In fact, in one droll scene, a film director who is the Teutonic ideal of womanhood photographs Hanussen in an attempt to capture "the secret of charisma" and somehow pass it along to Hitler.

"Hanussen," like "Mephisto" and "Colonel Redl," is photographed by Lajos Koltai, with bluish and ghostly backgrounds. The players stand out in relief, naked and unprotected. Just like Hanussen's palm, which the Indian fortuneteller warns him not to show to anyone—"it reveals everything."

Szabó ties up the "burning house" theme—as a child, young Klaus Schneider used his gift to save a little girl from a burning pharmacy. But he is helpless to save Europe from the conflagration to come, symbolized by the fire at the Reichstag.

"Hanussen" is a gripping, engrossing and intricate film, although perhaps the story was better told (and better left?) with the actor's soul sacrifice in "Mephisto."

NEWSDAY, 3/10/89, Part III/p. 5, Mike McGrady

Clairvoyance is not necessarily a gift. Consider the case of Hanussen (Klaus Maria Brandauer), a clairvoyant who has the misfortune of attaining his full power at the same time Adolf Hitler is attaining his. What he forecasts—a terrible inflation, the election of Hitler, the burning of the Reichstag, a time of destruction—is not the kind of vision one particularly enjoys.

In small ways, Hanussen's life seems to parallel Hitler's. He is Austrian by birth and, like Hitler, he has changed his name. And coincidentally (or is it really coincidence?) he even shares the same birth date as Hitler.

Clearly, Hungarian film maker István Szabó is not making a movie about interesting little coincidences. In fact, what he is attempting to do with "Hanussen" is to explain the rise of Hitler. One of five films nominated for the upcoming foreign-film Oscar, "Hanussen" involves the same triumvirate of talents—actor Brandauer, director Szabó, cinematographer Lajos Koltai—who earlier filmed the Oscar-nominated "Colonel Redl" and the Oscar-winning "Mephisto."

Hanussen, a severely injured war veteran, is treated by a kindly Freudian professor who cradles his patient in his arms and effects a "transference of will" followed by tranquilizing hypnosis sessions. Quickly absorbing the doctor's techniques, Hanussen is able to use them himself—at one point heroically stopping another despondent veteran in mid-suicide.

Hanussen's uncanny ability to enter the minds of others guarantees spectacular success with women; it also helps him launch a theatrical career. What is seen as clairvoyance is often nothing more than a special sensitivity: "I can see the human soul. I sense forces, thoughts, longings, wishes." And it may well be his awareness of hidden desires that leads to the prediction that makes him famous: "Adolf Hitler will be chancellor."

Both men are gaining their fame in a Germany beset by poverty, inflation, depression and open immorality. What Hanussen sees—as does Hitler—is the nation's overwhelming need for order, for structure at any cost. Sensing the public's desire to burn the old regime to the ground, Hanussen predicts the Reichstag fire and Nazi leaders echo his prognostications in their oratory: "Now each of us must pick up a torch."

The suggestion is that Hitler's skills were not unlike Hanussen's—a certain showbiz charisma, a talent for reading minds, an ability to detect the need for order at any price. Even the techniques are the same, transference and hypnosis, only on a vast scale. One possible conclusion: Under slightly altered circumstances, Hitler might have been just another small-time entertainer, a mind reader, a clairvoyant. A more jarring possibility: If Hitler was accurately reading the minds of his countrymen, he was their mirror and all must share in his blame.

Klaus Maria Brandauer, best known in this country for "Out of Africa," brilliantly captures the ambivalence of modern man so occupied with his own pursuits and pleasures that he doesn't react properly to catastrophe and may even, unwittingly, contribute to it. Brandauer calls Hanussen "the most complicated film role of my life." Complicated roles are the actor's speciality and his work in "Hanussen" is mesmerizing.

VILLAGE VOICE, 3/21/89, p. 60, Georgia Brown

Men in these Makk films tend to be not only peripheral but crucially wounded. [The reference is to *A Very Moral Night, Love, Cat's Play* and *Another Way*.] In his compatriot Istvan Szabó's films—at least in the *Mephisto-Colonel Redl-Hanussen* trilogy—men are central and wounded. Szabó, born in '39, nearly a generation after Makk—and, like him, a brilliant technician—has had much more international success, but that doesn't make him the better filmmaker. *Hanussen*, yet another collaboration with Klaus Maria Brandauer, and again with screenwriter Péter Dobai, cinematographer Lajos Koltai, and many of the same supporting actors, is easily the weakest of his three variations on the man-in-the-mask theme.

Portent is Szabó's mood. As in *Mephisto*, the hero's fortunes again have some creepy relation to Hitler's rise. Here the film insists on a mystical connection between Hanussen's powers—he performs as a clairvoyant and hypnotist in the theaters of Central Europe—and Hitler's. They're both crowd seducers practicing "transference of the will." Intuiting people's needs and desires, they're looked on as mind readers. But, ludicrously, the connection gets spelled out: They both have the same birthday! And they're both Austrian!

Szabó's previous movies have been more allegorical than psychological, but in this case, the character of Klaus Schneider, a battle-traumatized Austrian foot soldier who takes a cure in Dr. Bettelheim's clinic and becomes Hanussen-the-psychic (he coulda been a psychiatrist), is so opaque that there's no entry into the movie, no way to follow into any ideological connections. (Szabó gets whimsical with names here: Besides the Jewish psychiatrist Bettelheim—played by Erland Josephson—there's a cinematic joke where Jancsó, Wajda, and Menzel are named as "magicians, illusionists," then the brassy "Henni Stahl" appears sculpting from naked models. She also makes heroic documentaries—one called *Triumph of the Pill*, maybe?)

All three of these movies begin and end in helplessness and humiliation. All revolve around sadomasochistic games where roles may get inverted but the antihero always ends up the willing (suicidal) victim. Despite all the mirror images and doppelgänger, Szabó's studies in the pathology of collaboration manage to make collaborating look like something other people, real sickos, do. *Mephisto* was such a popular smash probably because Brandauer's hysterical, misogynistic Everyman was so thankfully alienating. *Redl*, also about a pathetic man protecting secrets, happened to be more subtle and powerful, but now *Hanussen* is so implausible, it mystifies. The rise of Hitler looks like science fiction.

Also reviewed in:
NEW REPUBLIC, 4/10/89, p. 22, Stanley Kauffmann
NEW YORK TIMES, 3/10/89, p. C15, Vincent Canby
VARIETY, 7/13/88, p. 12

HARLEM NIGHTS

A Paramount Pictures release in association with Eddie Murphy Productions. *Executive Producer:* Eddie Murphy. *Producer:* Robert D. Wachs and Mark Lipsky. *Director:* Eddie Murphy. *Screenplay:* Eddie Murphy. *Director of Photography:* Woody Omens. *Editor:* George Bowers. *Music:* Herbie Hancock. *Music Editor:* Bunny Andrews. *Sound:* Gene Cantamessa. *Sound Editor:* John Benson and Cecelia Hall. *Production*

Designer: Lawrence G. Paull. *Art Director:* Martin G. Hubbard and Russell B. Crone. *Set Designer:* Robert Maddy and Alan S. Kaye. *Set Decorator:* George R. Nelson. *Special Effects:* Chuck Gaspar. *Costumes:* Joe I. Tompkins. *Make-up:* Bernadine M. Anderson. *Stunt Coordinator:* Alan Oliney. *Running time:* 115 minutes. *MPAA Rating:* R.

CAST: Eddie Murphy (Quick); Richard Pryor (Sugar Ray); Redd Foxx (Bennie Wilson); Danny Aiello (Phil Cantone); Michael Lerner (Bugsby Calhoune); Della Reese (Vera); Berlinda Tolbert (Annie); Stan Shaw (Jack Jenkins); Jasmine Guy (Dominique LaRue); Vic Polizos (Richie Vento); Lela Rochon (Sunshine); David Marciano (Tony); Arsenio Hall (Crying Man); Tommy Ford (Tommy Smalls); Uncle Ray (Willie); Michael Goldfinger (Max); Joe Pecoraro (Joe Leoni); Robin Harris (Jerome); Charles Q. Murphy (Jimmy); Miguel Nunez (Man with Broken Nose); Desi Arnez Hines II (Young Quick); Ji-Tu Cumbuka (Toothless Gambler); Johnny Smith (Huge Man); Robin Lynn Reed (Woman Employee); Bill Bateman (Orderly); Kathleen Bradley (Lady); Clarence Landry (Old Man); Carmen Filpi (Doorman); Alvin Silver (Headwaiter); Clifford Strong (Man in Front Seat); Margaret Wheeler (Elderly Woman); Joe Littlefield (Elderly Man); Rick Aiello (Man #1); Donald Nardini (Man #2); Robert Vento (Bartender); Mike Genovese (Desk Sergeant); Dennis Lee Kelly and William Utay (Cops); Michael Buffer (Announcer); Marc Figueroa (One of Calhoune's Boys); George Kyle (Man at Bugsy's); Eugene R. Glazer (Detective Hogan); Michael Stroka (Detective Simms); Eddie Smith (Driver); Gene Hartline (Michael Kirkpatrick); Karen Armstead (Bennie's Girlfriend); Lezley Price (Nurse); Randy Harris (Todo La Noche); Woody Omens (Ringside Announcer); Don Familton (Referee); Dennis Kemper (Bathroom Attendant); Larry L. Johnson (King Blue); Prince C. Spencer (Prince Spencer); Roberto Duran (Roberto).

FILMS IN REVIEW, 3/90, p. 166, Kevin Sweeney

The biggest laughs in *Harlem Nights* occur during the opening credits, when Eddie Murphy's name appears five times: In Association with Eddie Murphy Productions; A Film by Eddie Murphy; Eddie Murphy in . . .; Executive Producer Eddie Murphy; Written and Directed by Eddie Murphy. They might as well call the movie "Money in the Bank: Eddie Murphy."

Or maybe "Eddie Murphy: Bulletproof," since nothing any rational person could say can hold back the hordes of fans who'll turn out. For this amiable, amoral comedy about the black proprietors of a speakeasy battling gangsters in 1938, Paramount gave Murphy everything money can buy—and I mean *everything*, including a top supporting cast, big sets, hundreds of vintage autos and several thousand period costumes. The trouble is, Murphy himself insisted on writing the script, which is mostly slack and vulgar, as well as racist and sexist. (Homophobia, Murphy's usual schtick in trade, is surprisingly absent.)

Is there a funnier comedy actor who makes such consistently lazy comedies? *Harlem Nights* starts with an amusing prologue, set in 1918, and you think maybe Murphy can make something out of material that would've seemed pretty corny even in '38. But the ensuing plot is drab and unimaginative, and—oddly enough—Richard Pryor and Murphy (as the speakeasy owner and his adopted son) both underplay to such an absurd degree that they make almost no impression.

Ironically, it's the white bad guys, played by Danny Aiello (in a tense performance as a crooked cop) and Michael Lerner, who give the film even a modicum of snap and style. Murphy's idea of an uproarious scene is a fistfight between himself and gargantuan Della Reese, as a madam working for Pryor. His idea of witty dialogue runs along the lines of "Dad, it's not how many people you shoot, it's who you shoot."

The film isn't unbearable. Herbie Hancock's score is pleasant, if too derivative of *The Sting.* There's some clever throwaway stuff, such as the weird accent of Stan Shaw, as a prizefighter. Arsenio Hall comes out of nowhere in a hilarious cameo as a crybaby gangster. And decrepit Redd Foxx, as Pryor's half-blind croupier, can't help but provide a few laughs with his nonstop catalog of obscenities. But these stopgap good moments can't save *Harlem Nights* from bland dullness.

LOS ANGELES TIMES, 11/17/89, Calendar/p. 8, Michael Wilmington

"Harlem Nights" opens with something shocking for an Eddie Murphy movie: unintentional humor. In glamorous script, the credits announce that this is a Paramount presentation, in association with Eddie Murphy Productions . . . of an Eddie Murphy film, starring . . . Eddie Murphy. The old Murphy—the devilish kid who once disrupted a TV awards show by stealing Lionel Richie's Grammy—might have quashed this crushed-silk canonization with a raucous, honking laugh.

Instead, he has left the audience to do his honking while he eases himself into a stiff-waxy superstar persona as a 1930s Harlem ladykiller, club host, gambler and gunman *extraordinaire* named Quick.

The movie that follows—in which Quick and his mentor Sugar Ray (Richard Pryor) lead a retinue of high-rollers, "hos" and hangers-on in a turf war with the mob—isn't totally barren of humor. But it's certainly barren. It's shot like a lesser '30s movie, full of empty streets, bare rooms and mostly empty and obvious movie sets. And Murphy, who also wrote and directed, keeps shuttling us between them as if his real name were Slow.

If the inspirations are obvious—"The Cotton Club" strained through "The Sting"—the execution sometimes suggests Walter Hill, on a bad day, trying to imitate Mervyn LeRoy. Against this drowsy, drab background—full of vendettas and long-winded sadism, with people crushing each others' hands, slitting throats, torching clubs and gunning each other down—all the elegance is ersatz and all the sex is mean and conniving. The actors supply the only energy, but their badinage often sounds like comics ragging each other to pad out an improvised sketch.

The movie is full of phallic gags about little-bitty guns and crude jokes at physical or emotional infirmities: Stan Shaw's bizarrely punchy heavyweight champ, Arsenio Hall's hysterical gunman who can't stop crying, and Della Reese as the rotund madam Vera, whose barrelhouse contours and posterior supply a stream of gags, especially after Quick shoots off one of her toes. Sadism mixes with sentimentality. In his only love scene, Quick shoots his partner (Jasmine Guy) and poor, waddling nine-toed Vera is later made to pathetically bawl out her love for him.

In this buddy-buddy-buddy movie—with three generations of great stand-up comics (Murphy, Pryor and Redd Foxx) together—two buddies always melt into the background. Pryor grays over into a grinning paterfamilias, popping up occasionally to give Quick a sidekick. Foxx, at first funny as a cantankerous craps croupier too blind to read the dice, turns from instigator of jokes to the butt of them. Some fine comics—like Robin Harris, great in the street chorus of Spike Lee's "Do the Right Thing"—are hardly used. Others, like Della Reese, are abused.

Laurence Paull's production design lacks glitter. The movie also lacks the Harlem outside the gaudy gangland environs, the poverty, filth, pain, humanity, humor and danger that feed these mobster fantasies.

Maybe that enclosure within a world of sex, style and might at the top hints at the problem. Like many superstars, Eddie Murphy may have gotten so tangled up in the myths and myopia of highpower movie making that he can't get back to the gritty, pungent, kick-in-the-throat awareness earlier audiences loved. Since 1984, in popular mausoleum efforts like "The Golden Child," "Coming to America" or the second "Beverly Hills Cop," he's mostly stopped doing what he does best—the quick-witted, generous outsider in a recognizably corrupt urban landscape—while entombing himself in glossed-up, borrowed movie-movie images, like Harrison Ford in "The Golden Child" or some mix of Gable and Redford here.

If he's going to confine himself to bad movies like "Harlem Nights" (rated R for sex, violence and language), it's probably better that he writes and directs them himself. At least he's learning new skills. But he needs, probably, to forget that he's E★D★D★I★E★M★U★R★P★H★Y. Maybe he needs a fresh young kid to run up and steal a Grammy from him.

NEW YORK, 12/11/89, p. 116, David Denby

[*Harlem Nights* was reviewed jointly with *Back to the Future, Part II*; see Denby's review of that film.]

NEW YORK POST, 11/17/89, p. 27, David Edelstein

When stars have so much power that they can do whatever they want without a whisper of interference, they often—quite unintentionally—give you scary insight into what's really on their minds (and what has been allowed to fester on their minds by virtue of their being stars). This is what happens, alas, in "Harlem Nights," directed, written by and starring Eddie Murphy.

"Harlem Nights" is a comic shoot-'em-up about a couple of good black guys, Sugar Ray (Richard Pryor) and his adopted son Quick (Murphy), who run a clean, elegant after-hours gambling joint and whorehouse in the Harlem of 1938.

Pretty soon, a white gangster (Michael Lerner) notices that the "jigs" are cleaning up and he's not. So he sends a cop (Danny Aiello) to extort money from them. When they resist, he tightens the screws—he dispatches gorgeous black women to seduce and then murder them, pits soul brother against soul brother and finally forces the wily pair to mount an elaborate sting in self-defense.

Juvenile, smutty and glacially paced, it is nevertheless an amazing piece of work—a definitive catalog of Murphy's preoccupations.

Admittedly, some of those preoccupations are noble, such as doing well by his spiritual mentor, Richard Pryor. Pryor's Sugar Ray is not a great character, but it's the first time in years that one of America's most brilliant comic artists has looked comfortable on the big screen.

Simply working with energetic black artists has galvanized Pryor. His readings are crisp and alert, and even his wide-eyed double-takes (so appalling in films such as "Moving") suggest a brain at work, nervously calculating its options. As the thoughtful, temperate Sugar Ray, he's both dignified and funny (a rare combination), and Murphy's deference to him both as actor and director becomes the younger man.

Otherwise, Murphy the writer-director-star runs the gamut from unabashed self-worship to psychosis. Cool and sleek in his white dinner jacket, Murphy saunters across the club, the camera close behind him. Kissing the hand of a boa-ed beauty (Jasmine Guy), he speaks in a deep, toasty voice—the kind that says, "I'm catnip to the ladies."

The rest of the time, he slides into his usual falsetto (or his obnoxious, gurgling laugh) and utters lines that all seem to be variations of "Take yo' big, fat, greasy, smelly, fat, ugly, disgusting fat, crusty, gnarled, mother. . . .ing ass outta here."

On the basis of this script, Murphy knows only a handful of words, few of which are printable here but that recur in the movie like mantras. His catalog of gags is similarly constricted. Redd Foxx, as the club's head croupier, is the butt of endless jokes about his near-blindness. (Too bad Murphy forgot to write him comebacks.) And while Stan Shaw is quite funny as a stuttering prizefighter, after a while the let's-yuck-it-up-over-some-one's-handicap humor palls.

Murphy's spectacular insensitivity does generate bizarre and audacious scenes, among them a brutal fistfight between him and Della Reese as the woman who runs Sugar Ray's bordello.

Accused by Quick of stealing, the rotund madam pummels him excruciatingly until he bashes her over the head with a garbage can, pulls a gun and makes quick work of her little toe, It's such an incredible bit (only Murphy would feel entitled to mutilate an older woman on screen) that it's sort of a hoot. If you're into women getting shot, that is.

Murphy's film making is clunky and his staging awkward (and never have sound stages looked more like sound stages), but "Harlem Nights" has its share of belly laughs and lunatic bits—especially a gun battle between Murphy and Arsenio Hall's gang. (Hall turns in a weeping, screeching cameo as the distraught brother of a murder victim, but doesn't have the vocal cords to pull it off entirely.)

The most serious problem with the movie isn't its ineptitude but its ugly, paranoid subtext. In Murphy's universe, white people don't think it's right that a black man should dress in beautiful, expensive clothes and make more money than they do.

When he won't work for them, they have to get him—by going after him themselves, setting him up so that other blacks go after him or sending beautiful black women to seduce and destroy him. (Women being women, it's relatively easy to get them to turn against their own.)

It's no surprise after "Raw" that Murphy thinks most women are out to fleece him, but to see them presented as either slinky psychos (Guy), devious whores (Lela Rochon), fawning sex-kittens (Berlinda Tolbert) or big mamas (Reese) whose every line is a variation on "Kiss my ass" or "I'll kick yo' ass" is to marvel at how little empathy he has.

On that level, "Harlem Nights" isn't simply a bad movie but a kind of tragedy. Early success and freedom have only nourished Murphy's demons; the upshot—the creative plunge of one of the 1980s' most promising artists—has robbed us all.

NEWSDAY, 11/17/89, Part III/p. 3, Terry Kelleher

"Leaving New York should be the last thing we do," says Eddie Murphy's character in "Harlem Nights," and some will detect the irony.

But Murphy didn't deserve the flak he caught for shooting his new movie on Paramount's Hollywood lot rather than in the city of his birth. There's nothing else genuine about the picture—why should the locations be a distracting exception?

Eddie Murphy is the executive producer, director, writer and, of course, star of "Harlem Nights" His name appears in the credits almost as often as a 12-letter Oedipal obscenity is heard in the dialogue.

So what has Murphy wrought? A glossy throwback that revives a "blaxploitation" formula, dresses it up with high production values and adds low comedy.

Richard Pryor is remarkably restrained—not to say inhibited—in the role of Sugar Ray, owner of a thriving after-hours nightclub in 1938 Harlem. Perhaps saving energy for his supervisory responsibilities, Murphy gives a casual performance as Quick, Sugar Ray's troubleshooter and adopted son. Michael Lerner as syndicate kingpin Bugsy Calhoune (the final "e" is an endearing affectation) and Danny Aiello as Phil Cantone, his paid police enforcer, take their nasty roles more seriously. Too seriously, given the surrounding nonsense.

Those are the major players, and by now you've got the game figured. White mobsters make black independents an offer they can't refuse, but the blacks are tough and resourceful while the whites are stupid and incompetently cruel. The better men win.

Strictly speaking, Sugar Ray's side settles for partial victory and profitable retreat. The outcome's essentially the same, however. The key plot element is a scam involving an ostensibly fixed prize fight, but "Harlem Nights" is so slow to get to the sting, and so perfunctory in carrying it out, that you may wish they'd dispensed with the subterfuge and settled the dispute with a traditional gun battle.

Not that there isn't enough rough stuff as it is. "Harlem Nights" offers shootings, bombings, slugfests *and* more exotic bodily harm. Quick and Dominique (Jasmine Guy), Bugsy's slinky mistress, engage in boudoir gunplay after strenuous intercourse. (At least Quick describes it as strenuous; Dominique neither breaks a sweat nor removes her negligee.)

"Harlem Nights" probably will be classified as an action comedy, but "action" connotes movement as well as violence, and this movie is Quick in name only. Murphy's ever ready to take time off from plot development for scenes of pure comedy. There's nothing purer than Redd Foxx (as Bennie, the myopic croupier) and Della Reese (as Vera, the enormous madam) shouting vulgarities at each other, or Stan Shaw (as heavyweight champ Jack Jenkins) proving once again that speech impediments can be fun. True, some of the humor is more inventive, but Murphy has a tendency to spoil his best gags through repetition. Obviously he's too important to obey Johnny Carson's "comedy rule of three."

The sound in "Harlem Nights" is noteworthy for some of the loudest punches in screen history. When Quick and Vera duke it out in the alley, each punch lands with an incredible thud. Fortunately, this man-woman brawl is on the comedy portion of the program, and thus the combatants are left without a scratch.

Lawrence Paull's production design and Joe I. Tompkins' period costumes have just the right look of showy luxury. Take the rerouted "A" train and ride far, far west to the city of make-believe.

NEWSWEEK, 11/27/89, p. 92, David Ansen

Judged strictly as entertainment, *Harlem Nights* is, at best, marginally diverting. A sluggish comic caper, it pits the gambling and prostitution operation run by Richard Pryor and his adopted son, Eddie Murphy, against the big-time gangsters who want to muscle in on their action. It's a poorly paced, unimaginatively written genre piece that has absolutely no feel for its era (the late '30s) or its locale (Harlem). With its nightclub settings, you might hope for some great music and spectacle, but this doesn't seem to interest Murphy, who as the film's executive producer, writer, director and star can take full responsibility for the movie's listless tone, as well as his own oddly disengaged performance.

Murphy's notion of comedy can best be described as infantile: his idea of wit is frequently repeated four-letter words. Much more intriguing is "Harlem Nights's" vengeful subtext. What are we to make of the role Murphy has written for himself, and in which we are supposed to find him as endearingly irrepressible as ever? We first meet Quick as a little boy, when he shoots a man point blank in the head. Before the movie is over, the lovable Murphy gets to (1) slug an elderly woman in the stomach and shoot off her toe; (2) shoot a gangster's moll through the head after sleeping with her; (3) murder three pursuers (one of them Arsenio Hall); (4) blow up a roomful of gangsters. It's nice the world's most popular screen comic wnnts to share his colorful fantasy life with us, but perhaps he should have saved it for his shrink.

TIME, 11/27/89, p. 88, Richard Schickel

The star gets what may be his best laugh in *Harlem Nights* before he appears. The moment occurs when Eddie Murphy's name flashes in the credits for the fifth time. This may represent the new Hollywood record for authorial egotism. It is, in any case, three more mentions than Woody Allen requires to state his creative credentials for a truly imaginative comedy and two more than Orson Welles took for his film directorial debut, which was—let's see, oh, yes—*Citizen Kane*.

Can Murphy be kidding? One would certainly like to think so. But the film that follows is so self-destructively primitive in tone and development that it quickly dismisses the possibility that its superstar proprietor may retain any capacity for self-satire. Or, for that matter, self-control or self-criticism.

An attractive idea lurks at the center of this movie: evoke the glamorous, dangerous spirit of after-hours Harlem in the 1930s and do it in the style of a studio-bound gangster film of the time, in which sets, costumes, lighting all impart a dreamily enhancing air to reality. Implicit in this notion is an even better one: bring blacks in from the fringe of the movie's frame, where they were segregated in the old Hollywood, and make them the story's movers and shakers. To that end, Murphy recruited performers he obviously, and justifiably, admires—Richard Pryor, Redd Foxx, Della Reese—and cast them as the management of a club too prosperous for its own good. A powerful white mob is trying to move in on them.

There, however, useful invention ends. The narrative Murphy develops out of this situation is less a homage to a vanished genre than a knock-off of two more recent successes—*The Sting* and *Prizzi's Honor*—that were funny, but in antithetical, unblendable ways. The movie veers uneasily from not-funny comedy to not-persuasive melodrama. Murphy forgets that the dialogue in old-fashioned crime pictures was as highly stylized as the settings. In place of sharply polished wisecracks, he gives us the steady mutter of the witless, unfelt obscenities that are the argot of our modern mean streets.

But it may be that Murphy's worst idea is his own character. His box-office power having brought Paramount groveling to its knees, offering him any indulgence he wants, Murphy has come to fancy himself a killer, and that is the role he tries to play here: a psychopathic hit man. He is not a good enough actor for this particular assignment, nor has he the skill as writer and director to use coldblooded murder (three times) as the topper for gag sequences. Once or twice his former sweet hipness glimmers through, and he has written a funny bit for his pal Arsenio Hall, playing a man on a murderous crying jag. But mostly *Harlem Nights* offers a depressing answer to that not entirely pressing question, "Will success spoil Eddie Murphy?" It looks as if it has.

VILLAGE VOICE, 11/28/89, p. 97, J. Hoberman

Overproduced and underwritten, *Harlem Nights* is tepid even by the standard of Eddie Murphy's last few films. This abstract period piece is as blandly staged as the pseudoragtime fanfare and soundstage New York that set the scene. *Harlem Nights* is a cut above a vanity project like Frank Sinatra's thematically similar *Robin and the Seven Hoods*, but it feels just as superflous. Murphy's name may be all over the credits, but there's an overriding sense that the star feels he only has to show his face on camera to bring down the house.

On paper. *Harlem Nights* might sound like a corrective to *The Cotton Club*, but, if anything, it feels even more denatured. Set in 1938, this last and most ambitious movie in the five-picture, $15-million deal Murphy made with Paramount in 1983 revolves around a fancy after-hours club that, as a barely sketched black utopia, suggests the African kingdom in *Coming to America*. The benign ruler is Richard Pryor; his suavely willful prince is writer/director/executive producer Murphy, so elegantly turned out he might be posing for *GQ*. Murphy wears his dapperness like a straitjacket; he's so boringly cool he relies on his co-stars for comic relief.

Given the movie's indifference to history, what's most satisfying is the show biz genealogy it offers. There are three generations of dirty-mouthed comics: Murphy, Pryor, and the indestructible (if underutilized) Redd Foxx—plus Murphy's designated sidekick, Arsenio Hall, making a pleasingly manic appearance as a distraught younger brother. The problem is, the movie isn't particularly funny. If the wide-eyed Pryor still seems to be held together with spit and tissue paper, the script, such as it is, affords him the best lines—his nervous delivery giving a spin to the most outrageous of understatements.

Harlem Nights derives the bulk of its drama from the duo of gross white men (Michael Lerner, Danny Aiello) who are trying to close down Pryor's funhouse, and virtually all of its humor from the mildly baroque and heavily repetitive use of the seven words you can't use on network TV. The language is as dirty as the set is clean. Everyone has his or her trademark obscentiy. Della Reese, who plays the formidable madam working out of Pryor's club, can't make an entrance without inviting half the on-camera actors to smooch her butt.

The movie is set during the heyday of the Savoy Ballroom, when Harlem was the jitterbug capital of the universe, but there's no energy on the screen. The camera stolidly positioned for each dull setup, the scenes feel distended; everything takes twice as long as it should. This lethargic pacing is the exact opposite of Murphy's cute, off-tempo asides. (Although the degree of self-assertion is infinitely greater, Murphy's trademark delivery—reactive wordplay tailing off into random gibberish—is eerily reminiscent of Stepin Fetchit's.) *Harlem Nights* is anything but brash; the too-tasteful Herbie Hancock score, synthesizing the most famous Ellington motifs, bathes the action like embalming fluid.

Although this is the first movie that Murphy is credited with writing and directing, it's dauntingly impersonal. The film carries subliminal traces of *Do the Right Thing*, which was in simultaneous development at Paramount—in *Harlem Nights*, Stan Shaw plays a boxer with a severe stutter; Robin Harris (Sweet Dick Willie in Spike Lee's film) has a minor role, Aiello a major one—but, although purposefully demonstrating a successful black enterprise, it scarcely engages the Lee movie. If anything, *Harlem Nights* lends itself to reading as psychodrama, particularly as the two most resonant and extreme scenes involve Murphy's physical attacks on women.

In the more humorous of these battles, Murphy squares off against the awesomely belligerent Reese in a back-alley brawl that escalates from amplified fisticuffs to assault with a deadly weapon. The second, involving a Creole femme fatale (Jasmine Guy), essentially replays the hand-to-hand combat between silken sheets. This even more jaw-dropped tussle involves one of the most brutal examples of a postcoital kiss-off on celluloid—what's the story? The misogyny is such that when Reese subsequently brags that one of her whores has a "pussy so good if you threw it in the air it would turn to sunshine," you have to wonder if this is why *Harlem Nights* was shot under the lights of a studio set.

Murphy's hostility might conceivably work in a comic context. What's nutty is that he seems to be positioning himself to play romantic leads. There's a definite failure to connect here. Although more convincing as a lover than a fighter, Murphy's most convincing as a lover enamored of himself.

Also reviewed in:
NEW YORK TIMES, 11/17/89, p. C19, Vincent Canby
NEW REPUBLIC, 12/18/89, p. 24, Stanley Kauffmann
VARIETY, 11/22/89, p. 19
WASHINGTON POST, 11/17/89, p. D1, Hal Hinson

HAUNTED SUMMER

A Cannon Group release. *Executive Producer:* Menahem Golan and Yoram Globus. *Producer:* Martin Poll. *Director:* Ivan Passer. *Screenplay:* Lewis John Carlino. *Based on the novel by:* Anne Edwards. *Director of Photography:* Giuseppe Rotunno. *Editor:* Cesare D'Amico and Richard Fields. *Music:* Christopher Young. *Music Editor:* Virginia S. Ellsworth. *Sound:* Drew Kunin and (music) Jeff Vaughn. *Sound Editor:* Martin Maryska. *Production Designer:* Stephen Grimes. *Art Director:* Francesco Chianese. *Set Dresser:* Nello Giorgetti. *Special Effects:* Ditta Corridori and Gino De Rossi. *Costumes:* Gabriella Pescucci. *Make-up:* Vittorio Biseo. *Special Effects Make-up:* Manlio Rocchetti. *Stunt Coordinator:* Franco Fantasia. *Running time:* 115 minutes. *MPAA Rating:* Not Rated.

CAST: Eric Stoltz (Percy Shelley); Philip Anglim (Lord Byron); Alice Krige (Mary Godwin); Laura Dern (Claire Clairmont); Alex Winter (John Polidori); Giusto Lo Pipero (Berger); Don Hodson (Rushton); Terry Richards (Fletcher); Peter Berling (Maurice); Antoinette McLain (Elise).

LOS ANGELES TIMES, 12/16/89, Calendar/p. 21, Michael Wilmington

In Ivan Passer's "Haunted Summer," five youthful, life-intoxicated aesthetes, afire with rebellion and revelry, spend an idyllic summer in a lakeside mansion: the Villa Diodati of George Gordon, Lord Byron.

Besides Byron (Philip Anglim) there are Percy and Mary Shelley (Eric Stoltz and Alice Krige) and Dr. John Polidori (Alex Winter). It's an exceptional group, for its radical political and sexual views, its extreme youth (three men in their 20s, two women in their teens) and its extraordinary literary gifts. Extraordinary, too, is their sexual omnivorousness. In the film's perspective, based on Anne Edwards' 1972 novel and research by scenarist Lewis John Carlino, it's a summer of free love, with a dash of polymorphous perversity.

Shelley shares amorous romps with his still unwed Mary and her half-sister, Claire Clairmont (Laura Dern), who is pregnant by Byron. Byron, 28-year-old senior of the group, has made conquests of Claire and Polidori and casts fiery glances at everyone else as well.

Outside, waves gently lap the banks, the sun bathes the hillside and breezes waft through the still, perfect trees. The quintet, dabbling in the occult and drugs (laudanum and opium), read poetry aloud, argue politics, flash erotic signals and drift through lake and landscapes that would have bewitched John Turner, sights exquisitely caught by Fellini's frequent cameraman, Giuseppe Rotunno.

Their relationships are an overfertile seedbed of ideas and literary fancies and a curious tangle of Eros and morality: Byron believes evil is innate, Shelley that man is good and evil is imposed on him. But this is no unfettered paradise. Within eight years, all three men will meet untimely deaths, Polidori by suicide, Shelley in a boating accident and Byron of fever, on a Greek military adventure. The women will survive for decades.

"Haunted Summer" tells the same story Ken Russell used for his 1986 film "Gothic." But "Gothic" was a nightmare Arabesque, preoccupied with the night on which Mary's "Frankenstein" and Polidori's "The Vampyre" were composed or dreamed—and its characters behaved less like poets than denizens of a Hammer Horror film, conceiving not "Frankenstein" but "Nightmare on Elm Street."

Carlino has given us exactly what Russell's scenarist, Stephen Volk didn't: a sense of Shelley and Byron as poets, of Mary and Polidori as novelists, a real delight in the kind of language they used and their own relish in using it. The flamboyant Russell dragged the nightmares up and waved them around. Passer keeps them buried, teasing them almost to the light.

Czech émigré Passer has made at least two masterpieces, the Czech "Intimate Lighting" and "Cutter's Way." He's a director who rarely forces his material on you; it blooms slowly, urged on by a quietly lyrical, realist style. It's a key to Passer's intentions that he's cast young American performers, plus the lovely South African Alice Krige, the cast's standout, instead of Britishers. The Americans, especially Stoltz' sweetly smiling Shelly, Dern's gangly and insecure Claire and Anglim's urbane Byron, seem more youthful and playful, and, in a special way, more innocent.

Working with "Haunted Summer," a project developed for John Huston, and for which Huston's longtime art director, Stephen Grimes, has prepared sumptuous designs and found stunning Lake Como locations, Passer abandons himself to soft, rapt, amused wonder. Barring one stilted scene of soap operatic revelations, his film has a bewitching smoothness, quiet affection.

Ultimately, it's about the artist-as-rebel. But it's less psychological vivisection than elegant romance, a sweet-tempered comedy of manners and morals. The poets are not sacred beasts but holy fools. And the anachronistic cast gives us some of that poetry, that holiness, that foolishness. "Haunted Summer" (MPAA-rated R for nudity and sex) is not a film for everyone. Some audiences, jazzed up to the point where they take no pleasure in poetic language and poetic scenery, may not enjoy it at all. Your reviewer confesses that he can and does; you may as well.

MONTHLY FILM BULLETIN, 5/89, p. 136, Tom Milne

1816. Anxious to resume her intimacy with Lord Byron, who abandoned her in London, Claire Clairmont engineers an encounter in the company of Shelley and his mistress Mary Godwin, her half-sister, with whom she is travelling in Switzerland. Although Mary disapproves of Byron's cynical attitude to Claire, the two poets are mutually admiring; and it is arranged that the trio, along with Dr. Polidori—an aspiring writer sexually in thrall to Byron, who treats him with cruel contempt—shall visit Byron at the Villa Diodati, by Lake Geneva. There, angered by Byron's treatment of Polidori, by his disparagement of Shelley's nature as "too good", and by his mockery of her own feminist beliefs, Mary becomes increasingly hostile; and Byron, attracted to her but rebuffed, persuades Shelley to try opium as being more effective than the laudanum he is using to expand his consciousness. Staging the opium-smoking in a dungeon at Chillon Castle, Byron hopes that the power of suggestion, abetted by his acquisition of Fuseli's painting "The Nightmare", will shake Shelley's faith in human nature by inducing a vision of Mary as a hideous incubus. Shelley collapses, but his serenity is unaltered. Mary accuses Byron of trying to drive a wedge between her and Shelley; and Byron admits that he would like her to love him as she loves Shelley. Struck when Shelley suggests that Byron must himself be frightened of something he thinks will frighten other people, Mary challenges Byron to undergo the same opium experiment. Meanwhile, having confessed her pregnancy to Byron, the distraught Claire faces an ultimatum (to stay with him, she must give the child up, to be cared for by his half-sister Augusta); and Polidori, after admitting to Byron that a publisher has offered £500 for his "secrets", is summarily banished. Duly smoking opium in the Chillon dungeon, Byron screams in terror when a hideous monster appears and kisses him on the lips. Subsequently told by Mary that the "monster" was Polidori in disguise, Byron ruefully confesses that, as much as terror, what he experienced was the sadness of seeing himself. Moved, Mary makes love with him. The next day, taking affectionate leave of Byron, Shelley and Mary depart with the forlorn Claire.

For the space of a few scenes it looks as though, following in the wake of Ken Russell's *Gothic* with this account of what happened that haunted summer at the Villa Diodati in 1816, Ivan Passer may also be going to employ Russell's hard-sell tactics. A coach travels a perilous mountain trail, its trio of passengers displaying a smiling English *sang-froid* to shame their volubly panicky native coachmen; at an inn, miming hysterical nocturnal fears, Claire is calmly welcomed into bed ("You don't have to go through all this to be with us") between Shelley and Mary for a cosy threesome; on the road again, halted by a waterfall and watched by the bemused coachmen, Shelley capers stark naked in the spray, exultantly shouting "I am *alive*!"

Like Byron's first appearance—haughty and demonically unrelenting as Claire humbles herself before him, symbolically juxtaposed with the cold marble statuary of a male nude—these scenes, whether intentionally or not, are slightly over-pitched, as though representing not so much the reality as the absurd notoriety of these subjects for scandal in a society shocked by their disregard for conventional morality. That this emphasis is deliberate is perhaps confirmed by a brief scene in the hotel dining-room, just prior to Byron's arrival, in which Mary and Claire giggle like schoolgirls as Shelley, no longer poet or rebel but a small boy, spits cherry pips at the unsuspecting neck of a weighty dowager.

At all events, starting from the point when Byron and Shelley actually meet and proceed to cement their relationship in an exchange of ideas over the dinner-table, *Haunted Summer* abandons the image to go in quest of the "reality" of the two poets. That first exchange of ideas sets Shelley's faith in the innate goodness of people in opposition to Byron's belief that evil is an essential, ineradicable element of human nature. While Shelley blithely discourses on "rebellion, revolution and then anarchy" in his vision humanity set free of privilege and oppression, Byron cynically counters by remarking of England that the "inhabitants of that dark island" are unlikely ever to rise.

As Mary's increasing agitation implies—hostile to Byron, protective of Shelley—the contest between pragmatist and dreamer is an uneven one. Yet Byron is at a disadvantage in his conviction that, although both poets have scandalised society, Shelley has achieved the more radical impact. Revealingly, he reads Shelley a review of one of the latter's books, in which the critic praised him as "a metaphysical revolutionary" before adding, "behind this, a little boy is what we see". No doubt the qualification was intended as disparagement, but Byron makes no mistake; and the unshakeable armature of innocence that protects Shelley, a serenity born of his credo that love answers love, becomes for Byron a sort of Holy Grail. At first convinced that Shelly needs to be protected *from* his innocence (hence the opium experiment, designed to open Shelley's eyes to his misplaced faith in Mary), he gradually comes to seek the secret of innocence for himself (through the mysterious, magical medium of Mary's love).

It's a fascinating thesis, consistent with the character of each poet as expressed in his work, perfectly orchestrated through excellent performances, but encompassed in Lewis John Carlino's script only at the cost of some clumsy scenes of exposition. Thus, Polidori is required to go out of his way to explain Byron to Mary, through the story of the childhood trauma of the club-foot which prompted the good folk of Aberdeen to dub him "the crooked devil". Byron, similarly, spells out for Mary's sake the rationale behind his treatment of Polidori: "People like him live for humiliation, would die without it". Passer's images, on the other hand, are effortless in their expressive grasp of the complex interactions. In the penultimate sequence, for example, Passer cuts from Mary and Byron making love to a bird planing in the sky. Shelley sits on the lake shore watching it, a book forgotten in his hand, his attitude redolent of rejection. With Byron's hesitant entry into frame, the angles, attitudes and movements all imply a pending scene of recrimination. Instead, the two men smile at each other, say nothing.

"Teach me this game of love for love, lady", Byron had pleaded; oddly, and indescribably movingly, the sense of harmony established between the two poets in this lake shore scene intimates a game well taught and well learned. So in the final sequence of hurried farewells, Byron's parting cry that he may now go to Greece is not merely a knowing gesture to historical hindsight, but Byron's acknowledgment that he still has to put into practice what he has learned. Although the two films could not be more different, *Haunted Summer* finds a surprising echo of *Cutter's Way* in its triangular central relationship. One woman sandwiched between two men: in the earlier film, unable to draw the strength she needs to live from either; here, lending her strength to both.

Also reviewed in:

NEW YORK TIMES, 7/5/89, p. C14, Caryn James
VARIETY, 9/14/88, p. 23

HAWKS

A Skouras Pictures release. *Executive Producer:* Morrie Eisenman and Richard Becker. *Producer:* Stephen Lanning and Keith Cavele. *Director:* Robert Ellis Miller. *Screenplay:* Roy Clarke. *Based on an idea by:* Barry Gibb and David English. *Director of Photography:* Doug Milsome. *Editor:* Malcolm Cooke. *Music:* Barry Gibb and John Cameron. *Sound:* Brian Simmons and (music) Dick Lewzey. *Sound Editor:* Colin Miller. *Production Designer:* Peter Howitt. *Costumes:* Catherine Cook. *Make-up:* Naomi Donne. *Stunt Coordinator:* Marc Boyle, Jim Dowdall, and Val Musetti. *Running time:* 110 minutes. *MPAA Rating:* R.

CAST: Timothy Dalton (Bancroft); Anthony Edwards (Deckermensky, "Decker"); Janet McTeer (Hazel); Camille Coduri (Maureen); Jill Bennett (Vivian Bancroft); Robert Lang (Walter Bancroft); Pat Starr (Millie Deckermensky); Bruce Boa (Byron Deckermensky); Sheila Hancock (Regina); Geoffrey Palmer (SAAB Salesman); Caroline Langrishe (Carol); Benjamin Whitrow (Mr. Grainger); Robyn Moore (2nd Bridesmaid); Connie Booth (Nurse Jarvis); Julie T. Wallace (Ward Sister); Saul Jephcott (Hospital Porter); Roger Sloman (Car Park Attendant); Dafydd Havard (Senile Patient); Keith Buckley (Dutch Doctor); Alan Foss (Church Sidesman); Scott Chisholm (Disco Bouncer); Anthony O'Donnell (Motel Nightman); Menno Van Beekum (Rolf); Kris Emmerson and Kim Teoh (Oriental Bicyclists); Imogen Claire (Paradise Madam).

LOS ANGELES TIMES, 11/10/89, Calendar/p. 8, Michael Wilmington

There's a surprising verbal energy in "Hawks". Though it's about male bonding and life-affirmation in a ward for people suffering from terminal bone-marrow disease, director Robert Ellis Miller and his actors play it mostly blithe and light.

Roy Clarke is a gifted writer (the British TV comedy "Flickers") but his premise here is peculiar, more dreamed-up than felt-out. The movie's central notion—facing death by going on boy's-night-out sprees—mixes up the dolorous and the frolicsome in skittering, over-bright ways.

The main characters are a rakish British solicitor (Timothy Dalton) and an American football player (Anthony Edwards). When they meet in the ward, the solicitor's lines have the fragrant bravura and plummy extravagance of a Shakespearean player on bank holiday.

Stocking hat jammed to his eyes, like Jack Nicholson in "One Flew Over the Cuckoo's Nest," Dalton's Bancroft is a McMurphy who can't find his Nurse Ratched—he's made the world his Ratched instead. He's always busting out for a jaunt to a disco or brothel. When his friend, played with nice understatement by Edwards, moons about suicide attempts, he's ready to wheel him up to the roof and help push him off—all in fun, of course.

This dark-joke binge atmosphere carries into the film's last act, an expedition to Amsterdam where the buddies, disguised as doctors and driving an ambulance, are joined by two plain Janes from England (Janet McTeer and Camille Coduri). And the edginess of the premise, which works well in its first scene—a spectacular suicide attempt in a rock quarry tends to thicken up later on.

The theme is the reverse of Kurosawa's great "Ikiru," where Takashi Shimura's Watanabe faced his mortality with self-sacrifice and good works. In this movie's world, Shimura instead would have taken Toshiro Mifune on long toots through the Tokyo brothels.

"Hawks" is a movie full of balloons and picnics, big prostitutes and romps in bordellos. Often, the movie makers seem to be shaking the characters—and the audience—by the lapels, shouting, "Live, damn you, live!"

There's a weird after-bite to this strategy: Bancroft's suggestion that the way to face death is to put on a red rubber clown-nose, wallow in graveyard humor and go on wild sprees. It all seems less the conviction of a man facing death than of a man pretending to face it. And, apparently, Clarke's script is based on an idea by Bee Gee Barry Gibb (who helps supply an ear-nudging score) and writer David English, who decided to test it out on a romp though Amsterdam.

Perhaps because of this jollyboys genesis, the ambulance spree lacks conviction; if these characters weren't sick, they'd be the self-indulgent chums of one buddy-buddy comedy after another—and the movie's title, which suggests that they're free-flying birds of prey, would get different nuances.

Even with these unjelled, dubious ideas, there's some warmth and feeling in "Hawks" (rated R for sex and language): in the acting of Edwards, McTeer and Dalton, in the sometimes rich language they've been given and in the bright, sympathetic textures of Miller's direction. If the idea men had seen as much strength in life's doves, pigeons or even gulls, this movie's balloons might not have popped so early on.

MONTHLY FILM BULLETIN, 8/88, p. 233, Nigel Floyd

In a London hospital ward for terminal bone cancer patients, sometime lawyer Bancroft wears a red clown's nose and cracks black jokes in an effort to cheer up fellow patient Decker, an American ex-football player. Also in the room is a vegetable-like patient, the screens around whose bed are always drawn. Bancroft and Decker receive visits from their respective parents. Elsewhere, Hazel tells her cousin and confidante Maureen that she is pregnant by a Dutch businessman. The wheelchair-bound Decker fantasises about returning to an Amsterdam brothel, the Hotel Paradise; but terrified by cards which foretell more suffering, he solicits Bancroft's help in throwing himself off the hospital roof. He survives, however, because Bancroft selects a ledge with a short drop. When they return to the ward, the vegetable's bed is empty. In the hospital morgue, the pair swear on the dead man's body to kick and struggle before they die, and then steal an ambulance to gatecrash a wedding at which Bancroft's former girlfriend Carol is a bridesmaid. She refuses to talk to him, and when Bancroft slumps into a depression, Decker adopts the joker's role. The pair take the ferry for Holland, where they encounter Maureen and Hazel and spend the day with them. Decker cannot go through with his visit to the Hotel Paradise, and Bancroft is later rude about Hazel's plan to seek out the father of her child. Decker reveals the truth about their ill-health in order to explain his behaviour. That night, Decker and Maureen sleep together, and Hazel is banished to Bancroft's room, where he is writing a series of abortive letters to Carol. The next day, all four of them drive to Hazel's boyfriend's house; but when she sees his wife and children she decides not to confront him. The women leave for England, and Bancroft takes the stricken Decker to a luxury hotel where he later dies. Back in England, Bancroft and Hazel are married.

While this black comic drama is confined to the terminal ward, it has a bleak incisiveness which is immediately defused once the ill-fated pair leave the hospital. In these early scenes, Bancroft's edgy humour, and the clown's nose which he wears as a "red badge of courage", are at once funny and unsettling, his jaundiced humour cutting to the bone. The mute patient with whom they share a room manifests minimal signs of life by, as Bancroft puts it, "blowing the last post on his anal sphincter". Within this context, the patients' brief forays into the outside world are, if not entirely credible, at least an acceptable comic device. Once these "Black Knights of the Sick Joke" escape into the outside world, however, the drama becomes diffuse and episodic—a problem exacerbated by some sloppy scene transitions. After the gatecrashing of the wedding, the men change places: Bancroft's confrontation with his ex-fiancée induces depression, while the ex-sportsman Decker seems to become much happier in the open air.

Unfortunately, this whole middle section drags interminably, as if Bancroft's maudlin moodiness had begun to infect the film itself. The idyllic picnic scene is simply tedious, the projected trip to the Hotel Paradise fizzles out into nothing, and only when the two couples are once again trapped in the claustrophobic interior of the hotel does any semblance of order return.

The night of lovemaking is sensitively handled, Hazel's gawky charm finally breaking down Bancroft's wall of self-pity, and the ensuing communion is effaced by a discreet cut. Decker's death scene, too, is moving rather than manipulative, though the up-beat ending is simply superfluous. The disparity between director Robert Ellis Miller's sympathetic handling of the actors and his failure to make anything of the exterior scenes suggests that the material might have been better suited to the small screen, where he and début screenplay writer Roy Clarke have hitherto done most of their work.

NEW YORK POST, 11/10/89, p. 29, David Edelstein

Based on a conception by Barry Gibb (of the Bee Gees) about life-affirming patients in a terminal ward, "Hawks" is the laboriously wacky tale of two bone-cancer victims, Bancroft (Timothy Dalton) and Decker (Anthony Edwards), who go AWOL from their English hospital, steal an ambulance and head for a five-floor whorehouse in Amsterdam.

At the start, the slack Edwards—peculiarly cast as an American football player travelling in Europe—hears the news he's dying and tries to drive himself into a quarry. Unable to end his life, Decker is next seen in a hospital with an IV tube running into his hand.

From the opposite bed he's regaled by solicitor Bancroft, an acerbic force of life who makes passes at a hefty nurse and dons a big, red clown nose for laughs. He derides Decker for the latter's attempts at sucide: "All suicides are sulky. It's the ultimate sulk."

Bancroft encourages Decker to wear the clown nose and adopt a healthier attitude toward what remains of his life, but Decker tries to take a swing at his irksome fellow patient. When the ex-jock collapses on the floor and wets his pants, Bancroft holds up the clown nose and hisses gravely: "On the floor in your own urine. See why you need this?"

Er, no.

In the second half of "Hawks" (so named because Bancroft fancies himself and his mate soaring high above the pigeons), the pair encounters two eccentric-looking women—tall and skinny Hazel (Janet McTeer) and short and peppery Maureen (Camille Coduri), who are themselves in Holland to track down the father of Hazel's unborn child.

After chafing at Hazel's idiosyncratic appearance, Bancroft settles down with her and hints at the source of his erratic behavior. Against a background of windmills, he explains, "The most terrifying thing in the world is how beautiful things are…"

It will later turn out Decker is the real force of life and Bancroft—who won't let anyone get close to him—is the real nihilist. Thus, in true buddy-movie fashion, each man has a chance to deliver a tough-but-nourishing lecture to the other.

"Hawks," which resembles a lot of English nonconformist comedies of the '60s, seems terribly quaint. Directed with dull sincerity by Robert Ellis Miller (and leavened with Barry Gibb pop songs), it's appalling not because it's in bad taste but because its bad taste has been infused with the most icky kind of sentimentality.

Dalton, out from his Bondian straitjacket, toils to show us what a zany he can be, squinching up his face, bulging his eyes and hopping around like a leprechaun wannabe. "Terminal tours!" he crows, wheeling Edwards to freedom. "Lazy days! Dying somewhere exotic!" Because sooner or later, "your bowels turn to moosh."

"Hawks" speeds things along.

NEWSDAY, 11/10/89, Part III/p. 9, Terry Kelleher

No one's saying, "Go gentle into that good night," but even Dylan Thomas would tell Bancroft to cool it a little.

Bancroft (Timothy Dalton), a British lawyer with a fatal illness, is one of the two main characters in "Hawks." The other is Decker (Anthony Edwards), an American athlete suffering from the same unnamed "condition" (presumably cancer). They share a hospital room in England.

The moment we meet Bancroft, we can tell he's playing Randall Patrick McMurphy in "One Flew Over the Terminal Ward." He makes salacious suggestions to the stern Nurse Ratched type (Connie Booth), groping her for emphasis. He ogles a skin magazine while eating a banana. He regularly dons a red clown's nose emblematic of his irreverent attitude.

Bancroft wants his new roommate to get the spirit, too. At first Decker feels too sick and depressed to soar like a hawk above the pigeons of the world, so Bancroft has to fire him up with taunts and pranks. (Judging from his energy level, Bancroft must be in full remission.) Bancroft's so obnoxiously life-affirming that Decker grows almost angry enough to kill. It's all part of the plan.

"Way to go, kid," Bancroft says. "It beats feeling pathetic."

There's never a doubt which way "Hawks" will go from here—comedy tinged with tragedy, followed by tragedy tinged with comedy, followed by an "up" ending. The mode of transportation is a stolen ambulance. We never see exactly how Bancroft and Decker got their hands on the vehicle, but like everything else in the movie, it must have been easily arranged.

Headed for a legendary brothel in Amsterdam, the boys pick up two young British women. Hazel (Janet MeTeer) is shy, clumsy, pregnant and very tall. Her cousin Maureen (Camille Coduri) is short and sort of saucy. Initially, Bancroft and Decker pronounce them "unattractive." Inevitably, they find them life-affirming, though Bancroft requires some convincing.

As expected, the buddies eventually reverse roles, with Bancroft wallowing in bitterness and regret and Decker snapping him out of his funk with a shot of the truth.

"That eight-foot girl offers you more warmth than you can handle," Decker says. Way to tell him, kid.

Roy Clarke's screenplay, which offers occasional wit to go with the mawkishness, is based on an idea by singer-composer-producer Barry Gibb and his associate, David English. Gibb wrote the score and several original songs. Director Robert Ellis Miller helped the music along by throwing in a bicycling-and-rowboating idyll suitable for use as a soft-rock video.

The performances are generally competent, and McTeer's talked-about warmth is genuine. To his credit, perhaps, Dalton seems a bit uncomfortable with Bancroft's boorish tendencies. We might be willing to like these characters if they weren't so hard to believe.

Take Decker, supposedly stricken while touring Europe with a football team from the United States. Teammates, club executives, family, friends? Nowhere to be found. (There's a father mentioned in the production notes, but missing from the film.) The fact is, this patient is simply here by arrangment.

VILLAGE VOICE, 11/14/89, p. 199, Gary Giddins

Given a movie menu of two unintentionally unfunny comedies and one unintentionally funny psy-fi, it was a good week to stay home and read. [The reference is to *Communion* and *Second Sight*. See Giddins' reviews.] *Hawks*, at least, has intermittent moment—agreeable shots of the Dutch countryside, a cameo by Sheila Hancock as an ancient hooker—that are moderately more interesting than the face of one's watch. The hilarious idea behind *Hawks* is the product of Bee Gee Barry Gibb and "associate" David English. As English and Gibb drove to a recording studio one week, they discussed good movie themes: "On this particular day we toyed with the idea of what you would do if you were given no time to live." *Hawks* explores the fun you can get yourself into when you're dying from a debilitating nervous disorder.

In Roy Clarke's script, the principals are Decker (Anthony Edwards), an American football player who, for unexplained reasons, is waiting to die in a British hospital ward, and Bancroft (Timothy Dalton), an English solicitor with a sardonic wit who's determined to cheer him up. They share a room with a curtained-off vegetable who represents the final stages of the disease they're all suffering from and whose flatulence is all to characteristic of the film's humor. The first hour is *One Flew Over the Cuckoo's Nest* versus *Whose Life is it Anyway?*. Dalton, who may have accepted the role as penance for his James Bond loot, even wears a knit cap like Jack Nicholson, but he does a meager job of being irrepressible. Edwards, who is confined to a wheelchair, makes several farcical attempts at suicide. They sneak in and out of hospital when they like, visiting a disco and a posh restaurant in their pajamas, since the humorless Nurse Jarvis has confiscated their clothes.

Meanwhile, a homely and awkward girl named Hazel (Janet McTeer) has been knocked up by a visiting Dutch businessman, and together with her bimbo cousin, Maureen (Camille Coduri), resolves to search him out in Holland. By extraordinary coincidence, at that very moment, Bancroft and Decker steal an ambulance with the intention of driving to a whorehouse in Amsterdam. You fill in the rest of the plot—you're bound to do as well as Clarke. What you might not expect is the ingenuousness with which the whole thing suddenly turns into a replay of *Marty*: If you care, Decker dies so that Bancroft may renounce his cynicism and wed the bumbling Hazel. This is a film that suggests the only thing worse than a humiliating, imminent death is being a homely, awkward woman. The gangly McTeer is forced, in Robert Ellis Miller's ham-fisted direction, to trip over herself at every turn. That she emerges with any allure at all is a tribute to her powers of concentration and expressive eyes. Miller photographs Holland as though it were all windmills and pasture; his Amsterdam is the usual neon street of picture windows and overweight whores.

What makes *Hawks* even more disagreeable than its subject or execution is its blithe unconcern for the rudimentary cause and effect of plot. Perhaps the problem was in the editing. The production notes go on about the "revered" Jill Bennett in the role of Bancroft's mother, and Bruce Boa as Byron, "the loudmouthed father of Decker." In the film I saw, Bennett's role is a walk-on, her only line a murmured hello; Boa doesn't appear at all. Maybe they edited out the tissue that would explain why an American was left to die in a British ward; why a man as wealthy as Bancroft would subject himself to the same ward, especially when his only symptom thus far is hair loss; and how it is they managed to drive a stolen ambulance all over Europe without attracting the interest of the police. I wondered also where Bancroft kept his wallet (in his pajamas or robe?), Why that mode of dress caused no undue attention anywhere they went, and why they didn't buy themselves some clothes. Perhaps they were under the influence of aliens...

Also reviewed in:
NEW YORK TIMES, 11/10/89, p. C13, Janet Maslin
VARIETY, 6/1/88, p. 13
WASHINGTON POST, 11/10/89, p. D7, Hal Hinson

HEART OF DIXIE

An Orion Pictures release. *Executive Producer:* Martin Davidson. *Producer:* Steve Tisch. *Director:* Martin Davidson. *Screenplay:* Tom McCown. *Based on novel "Heartbreak Hotel" by:* Anne Rivers Siddons. *Director of Photography:* Robert Elswit. *Editor:* Bonnie Koehler. *Music:* Kenny Vance. *Music Editor:* Adam Milo Smalley. *Sound:* Glenn Berkovitz. *Sound Editor:* Robert Grieve. *Production Designer:* Glenda Ganis. *Art Director:* Sharon Seymour. *Set Decorator:* Sarah Burdick and Douglas A. Mowat. *Set Dresser:* Mark Anderson and E. Scott Ratliff. *Special Effects:* Bob Cooper and Kevin Harris. *Costumes:* Sandy Davidson. *Make-up:* Annie Maniscalco. *Stunt Coordinator:* Danny Aiello III. *Running time:* 101 Minutes. *MPAA Rating:* PG.

CAST: Ally Sheedy (Maggie); Virginia Madsen (Delia); Phoebe Cates (Aiken); Treat Williams (Hoyt); Don Michael Paul (Boots); Kyle Secor (Tuck); Francesca Roberts (Keefi); Peter Berg (Jenks); Jenny Robertson (Sister); Lisa Zane (M.A.); Ashley Gardner (Jean); Kurtwood Smith (Professor Flournoy); Richard Bradford (Judge Claiborne); Barbara Babcock (Coralee Claiborne); Hazen Gifford (Dean Howard); I.M. Hobson (The Governor); Johnnie A. Jones (Cleveland); M.J. Etua (Integration Student); Tom Wright (Black Man at Concert); Ruby Wilson (Clarice); Susan Swindell (Sue Ellen); Anne Dye (Cornelia); Sherry Collins (Peggy Sue); Lois Swaney (Fraternity Housemother); Beverly Eaby (Cherry Delight); Jonathan Faulkner (Spud); Gary Tacon (Greaser in Bar); Darrell B. Crawford (Frat Boy); Michael St. Gerard (Elvis); Johnny Cowan and Rebecca Russell (Fraternity Band Singers).

LOS ANGELES TIMES, 9/18/89, Calendar/p. 2, Kevin Thomas

"Heart of Dixie" has nailed down its time and place right to the last detail, as anyone who was attending a college in 1957 within shouting distance of the Mason-Dixon Line can attest.

It was a time when fraternities and sororities maintained an iron rule over campus social life and were a primary force in shaping values, for better or worse. It was an era when most women felt a trememdous pressure to be engaged to be married by the time they were graduated.

Yet we were responding to Elvis Presley, even if it wasn't cool to admit it in your fraternity house, and we were aware that this young black woman, Autherine Lucy, had stirred up a tremendous ruckus when she became the first black to register at the University of Alabama in 1956.

Adapted by Tom McCown from Anne Rivers Siddons' novel "Heartbreak Hotel," "Heart of Dixie" is set at the fictional Randolph University in Alabama, and it centers on Maggie Deloach (Ally Sheedy), a sorority girl pinned to a handsome scion (Don Michael Paul) of a rich old plantation family. Although outwardly conforming, Maggie, a journalism major, is more questioning, more reflective than her friends. Her life is transformed when she witnesses, during a Presley concert, an unprovoked, brutal police attack on a black man.

"Heart of Dixie" (rated PG) opened without press previews, probably because it's an old-fashioned, unabashed heart-tugger with an all-stops-out ending. Perversely, director Martin Davidson, of two other period pieces, "Lords of Discipline" and "Eddie and the Cruisers," was perhaps too straight on. Youthful audiences today may well find it hard to believe that many people who were their age 30 years ago did act and think the way the young people in this film do. As with the 1987 Matt Dillon film "The Big Town," you may have to be over 50 to connect with "Heart of Dixie."

In any event, the cast is terrific and includes Treat Williams as an AP photographer who tries to raise Maggie's consciousness and Virginia Madsen as Maggie's sorority sister, who has Kim Novak looks and Scarlett O'Hara dreams. You have to have a soft spot for a picture that has Diana Dors (presumably in "The Unholy Wife") on the local theater marquee and has the kids take off to the notorious Ma Beechie's, a reference to Phil Karlson's 1955 classic Alabama "Sin City" exposé, "The Phenix City Story,".

NEW YORK POST, 9/16/89, p. 17, David Edelstein

Maggie (Ally Sheedy), the heroine of "Heart of Dixie," is a traditional Southern debutante in a traditional 1957 Southern college sorority that's powerfully committed upholding the traditional Southern conventions of beauty queenships, motherhood and white supremacy.

There's much talk here (as you no doubt have gathered) of the importance of tradition. And because this is an utterly traditional political-coming-of-age movie, the protagonist must have her eyes opened traditionally wide to the racial and sexual injustices of her time and place and must go on to defy (traditionally) those hallowed traditions and get herself (traditionally) ostracized from her Alabama community.

"Heart of Dixie," directed by Martin Davidson, should be called "The Bigger Easy" since there's nothing remotely new or challenging about it. Blacks, it suggests, should not be brutalized merely for standing around, forced to drink from separate water fountains or prevented from enrolling in white universities.

Know what? I couldn't agree more. But unless the intended audience is elementary and junior high school students (a possibility, it must be admitted), the movie seems ludicrously backward. Haven't we moved beyond the stage where black women are all hearty Aunt Jemimas and black men all martyred Uncle Toms?

Sheedy is actually quite compelling, refusing to indulge in her usual head-cocking and chin-wagging. But she can't rise above the conventional, morality-play structure.

On one side of Maggie is Virginia Madsen as Delia, a platinum blonde swathed in lavender. Delia not only sees women as subordinate and dreams of living on a plantation but also likes to provoke fights between men. She actually gets someone killed—which doesn't stop her from becoming "Honeysuckle Queen."

On the other side, there's Phoebe Cates in the small role of a peppy nonconformist who always talks about moving to Greenwich Village. She's so elfin-cute in her short hair and black leotards that the rebelliousness doesn't come through very distinctly—she's like an All-American cheerleader for the counterculture.

Maggie meets an AP photographer called Hoyt (Treat Williams, in a bland role), whose interest in Civil Rights forces her to open her eyes. No longer can she accept the status quo.

Her boyfriend's father is a filthy rich plantation owner and judge who, when she brings up the unrest among blacks, actually says to her (I swear), "Don't worry your pretty little head about that. Nobody on this river treats his niggers better than I do. Ain't that right, Cleveland?" (Cleveland: "Yazzir!")

As Maggie and her boyfriend drive away, she sees a black sharecropper in the fields holding a small child, and the woman's eyes burn into hers.

There's a lot of that burning-eye stuff. When the cops pummel a black man for doing nothing but showing up at an Elvis Presley concert, she reaches out to touch him and his eyes burn into hers. And he knows she cares.

Why? she asks Hoyt, later, did he just stand there taking pictures instead of trying to help the man? Softly, the photographer invites her into his darkroom, where he plunges a negative into the water and into focus comes the stricken face of the black man being hauled away by cops. The victim's eyes burn into hers. She understands. She hugs the crusading photographer.

Although the black mammies tell her not to get involved, that it isn't her fight, this relentlessly upbeat movie is about Maggie's decision that *it is her fight*. And we watch and congratulate ourselves for our sensitivity—our certainty that if we were there, we'd decide it was our fight, too. (But how many of us marched through Bensonhurst?)

"Heart of Dixie" functions on a kind of trashy, TV movie level—you can laugh at it, enjoy the performances of some of the twittering debs and have an easy cry. Davidson does make the antebellum South alluring: all these lovely girls in their ravishing gowns, these manly men, these smartly-dressed Negroes in their place. And in their place is exactly where "Heart of Dixie" keeps them.

NEWSDAY, 9/16/89, Part II/p. 17, Bill Kaufman

The process of personal and social change, circa 1957, is what "Heart of Dixie" tries to take on.

While it gets the period right, with a nicely recreated backdrop of finned autos, drive-ins and pom-pom sweaters, the deeper theme overwhelms the film as it moves along as sluggishly as molasses flowing uphill.

It aims to deal with one of the major events of the time—the racial integration of southern colleges and the sparks that ignited the civil rights movement—yet the first half is unremittingly tedious.

Far too much of the script is devoted to tediously establishing the characters through full chatter scenes—at the expense of the story.

Set at a tradition-bound fictitious Alabama University, the main characters are three sorority sisters whose lives are mainly concerned with getting "pinned" by boys, marrying right and avoiding "going all the way."

Virginia Madsen plays a flirtatious blonde and Phoebe Cates is a free-spirited ditz. But Maggie DeLoach (Ally Sheedy), a jorunalism major, has increasing doubts about all she has been taught as a well-bred southern belle.

No trumpet flourish, but it's obvious she's on the frontier of something yet unnamed.

The big change in Maggie's life comes in the form of Hoyt Cunningham, a photojournalist played with a sort of square-jawed over-confidence by Treat Williams.

When Hoyt predicts blacks will soon be integrated into southern colleges, one of the girls pipes up, "Are you a Communist?"

Sheedy does a fine job playing the young woman who questions her values, and to her credit, Sheedy is the only performer who appears to have paid attention to the dialogue coach and managed to affect a southern accent that's consistent throughout the movie.

Also reviewed in:
NEW YORK TIMES, 9/16/89, p. 17, Vincent Canby
VARIETY, 9/20-26/89, p. 28
WASHINGTON POST, 9/15/89, p. C7. Rita Kempley

HEART OF MIDNIGHT

A Samuel Goldwyn Company release. *Executive Producer:* James Geallis. *Producer:* Andrew Gaty. *Director:* Matthew Chapman. *Screenplay:* Matthew Chapman. *Director of Photography:* Ray Rivas. *Editor:* Penelope Shaw. *Music:* Yanni. *Sound:* Alan Selk and (music) Yanni. *Sound Editor:* Douglas Murray. *Production Designer:* Gene Rudolf. *Art Designer:* Christa Munro. *Set Decorator:* Stephanie Waldron. *Set Dresser:* Donna Walls, Maggie Durback, and Georgett Carr. *Special Effects:* Guy H. Tuttle. *Costumes:* Linda Fisher. *Make up:* Hiram Ortiz. *Running time:* 96 minutes. *MPAA Rating:* R.

CAST: Jennifer Jason Leigh (Carol Rivers); Peter Coyote (Sharpe/Larry); Gale Mayron (Sonny); Sam Schacht (Fletcher); Denise Dummont (Mariana); Frank Stallone (Ledray); James Rebhorn (Richard); Nick Love (Tom); Steve Buscemi (Eddy); Tico Wells (Henry); Brenda Vaccaro (Betty); Jim Geallis (Lt. Sharpe); Jack Hallett (George); Ken Moser (Cop); Richard Futch (Other Man); Lou white (Blue Rinse); Barry Clark (Reality Man); Janet Mannino (Other Woman); Nina Lora (Carol as a Child); Trey Greene (Sonny as a Child); Marilyn McCann (Ledray's Wife); Michael Flippo (Paramedic); Daniel McCormick (Carol's Boyfriend); Robert

Czarkowski (Sailor); Gretchen Holz (Murder Victim); Nicholas Cimino (Boy No. 1 in Club); Drew Taylor (Boy No. 2 in Club); Mark Peper (Boy No. 1 Outside); Nathan Smith (Boy No. 2 Outside); Melanie Lora (Girl Chased); Carolyn Torlay (Apple Lady); Samuel Colston (Store Keeper).

LOS ANGELES TIMES, 3/3/89, Calendar/p. 10, Michael Wilmington

The air is always a little heavy, the light a little blurry in Matthew Chapman's new thriller, "Heart of Midnight". Watching it is like trying to peer through contact lenses that have gotten clotted with tears, smoke, even fogged with a little imitation Roman Polanski.

Chapman, who made the clever, little romantic thriller, "Strangers Kiss" back in 1984, is trying something more lurid and primal here. And he's stumbling. This is another movie psycho-thriller about sex, the dark past and a lady-in-distress and it takes place in Polanski-land: a deserted old city edifice, full of shadowy corridors, repulsion and cul-de-sacs. The wind hums, the night reeks. And as Ray Rivas' cinematography gets smearier and softer, bluer and more velvety, the eyes blink, frantically.

We're in a nightclub called Mid-night, honeycombed with strange attics, crawl-spaces and locked-up rooms where evil breaks out like an oily sweat. Wandering bemusedly through it all, with an expression of vague curiosity, is Chapman's distressed lady: Jennifer Jason Leigh as Carol Rivers, a girl apparently scarred forever by obscure childhood memories involving a leering uncle who kept offering her apples.

Carol's attempt at recuperation seems dubious; she seeks to exorcise the past by accepting her uncle's legacy, taking up residence in his club, "Midnight," and undergoing several days of increasingly escalating, and thoroughly predictable, psychological hell.

Unsurprisingly, she is soon deluged with apples, locked rooms, bad dreams, skulking transsexuals, prowlers, police and things going bonkers in the night. Apparently, this vile old ex-bordello—warehouse was designed by the lecherous Uncle Fletcher to cater to innumerable vices and depravities. There's a room for everything: pedophilia in the teddy bear bedroom, bondage and discipline in the whip-and-rack-room.

For a neurotic homebody, Carol proves pretty resilient. Nothing fazes her: a rape by two leather-jacketed creeps, insubordination from surly carpenters, Peter Coyote popping up and claiming to be a policeman, and a set of "Nightmare on Elm Street" dreams hurling her from one fantasy to the next. Grisly or improbable, she takes it all remarkably in stride.

Here, Chapman gets lost in Polanski, strangles himself in "Blue Velvet," hoists himself by his own Hitchcock.

Not even Coyote—good as usual as the ambivalent pseude-cop—can save things. Chapman copies from the past without enlivening the present and the result is faintly queasy and sordid, a formula thriller that lacks even the creepy power of an above-ground kink-melodrama like "Kinjite." "Heart of Midnight" (rated R for sex, violence, language) is a set of variations without a theme, a hell with too many exit signs, an apple without a core.

MONTHLY FILM BULLETIN, 2/89, p. 50, Richard Combs

Carol Rivers, emotionally frail because of some past trauma, lives with her domineering mother Betty, and longs for escape. When a lawyer unexpectedly arrives with the news that her Uncle Fletcher has died and bequethed her the downtown night-club, The Midnight, which he was in the process of renovating, Carol insists on taking over the place, despite her mother's dark warnings about both Fletcher and her health. Carol finds three workmen (foreman Richard, the black Henry, and Tom) sort of engaged on the renovations, and her own upstairs living quarters next to other rooms decked out to serve the various sexual fantasies of past clientele. Lonely and unsure of herself, Carol is attacked one night by the drunken Tom, his friend Eddy and a reluctant Henry; when she sets off the alarm, Tom and Eddy are seemingly frustrated in their escape by the club itself, and Henry is shot by a patrolman. Carol is counselled by Mariana from a rape crisis centre, but Detective Ledray, looking at her psychiatric history, disbelieves her story. Further upset as bizarre events suggest that she is not alone in the club, Carol is suddenly confronted by a man, whom she takes to be Lieutenant Sharpe, sent to investigate Henry's shooting, and who is well acquainted with Fletcher's perverse practices. The real Sharpe later comes to call and, unknown to Carol, is murdered in the club's food locker. Carol seeks Mariana's help when she is increasingly beset by nightmares and evidence of another presence in the club; they find a strange shrine in the attic, before being driven out, but Ledray remains sceptical. The supposed Sharpe comes to cook Carol a meal, and she wakes from a drugged sleep to more horrific discoveries.

Her mother is still unable to persuade her to leave, but when she berates"Sharpe" (in fact Larry) at their next meeting, he tells her that he was once Fletcher's partner, that he was sent to jail at the latter's instigation, and that he is anxious to find his sister, who was in Fletcher's control. Alone, Carol stumbles on a labyrinth that gives secret access to all the sex rooms, and is finally captured and manacled by the club's mysterious denizen, Larry's sister Sonny, driven mad by her violation as a child by Fletcher and induction into his sick world (he had similarly approached, and thus traumatised, Carol). When Larry appears, he is shot (apparently fatally) by Sonny, and Carol is only saved by the arrival of Ledray and Mariana. Later, at the club's reopening, Carol makes a dream-like entrance and dances with an adoring Larry.

Matthew Chapman, whose *Strangers Kiss* so amusingly reframed Stanley Kubrick's *Killer's Kiss*, now seems to have leapfrogged over Kubrick's career to arrive at something like a remake of *The Shining*. *Heart of Midnight* is another "the house is the monster" horror movie, in which Jennifer Jason Leigh's fragile heroine attempts to stand on her own two feet (even with one permanently encased in plaster) by taking over a family property, her dead uncle's disused night-club and sex parlour, only to find it becoming the site of all her demons. "There's no logic to this place—it's been so many things that it doesn't know what it is any more", explains one of the sinister-cum-pathetic trio of workmen who are renovating The Midnight when Carol Rivers moves in, giving a brief rundown of its history since it began life as a 30s speakeasy.

The film does a splendid job of setting this up, rhyming the whole dream-nightmare-fairy-tale generated by The Midnight with the fantasy potential of movies themselves. The opening titles are played over grainy images of a woman (an early Marilyn Monroe) exciting herself with an apple, one of the erotic offerings in Uncle Fletcher's wonderland that is also reminiscent of some "innocent" example of primitive cinima (the 1986 *The Kiss*, perhaps). Carol is then briefly seen at home with her mother, a prisoner of this suburban house, of her neurotic past and the dependence created by some unexamined horror; she whispers, "Please get me out of here" as a stranger walks up the drive, and lo and behold he proves to be a lawyer bearing the news of Fletcher's bequest. He tells her that The Midnight is situated in the most run-down part of the city, but the few street scenes there have the permanently deserted, unlived-in look of any movie set, or even of a movie lot itself. Capping this theme, the not-what-he-appears policeman played by Peter Coyote (director Stanley in *Stranger Kiss*) prowls round The Midnight, with which he proves suspiciously familiar, and says, when Carol asks what her uncle was up to, "Having fun, making money, doing what came naturally—entertainment".

A limiting factor is that The Midnight, tawdry sex club that it remains, is not as rich a source of these games of desire and control, simulations of love and death, as either the B-movie set of *Strangers Kiss* or the creative chaos unleashed in *The Shining*'s Overlook Hotel. Nor are characters as ambivalent in relation to them. Everyone, even Peter Coyote's one-time partner in The Midnight, turns out to be a straightforward victim of Uncle Fletcher's arch manipulator and alltime pervert, who leers through a few flashbacks while twirling one of the apples that spill through the film in symbolic overabundance. The exorcism of this demon also proves a rather straightforward matter (compare the more ambivalent roles played by the gangster/financier and the director/manipulator in *Strangers Kiss*), despite the elaborate rhyming games, the "double" structure, which the film conjures up. This provides a double self—a good one and a bad one, or a real one and a reflected one—for just about everybody, beginning with The Midnight itself, in which a fantasy world is surrounded by a labyrinth, and extending through the real cop and the fake cop, the crippled herione and her even more twisted "sister", the overbearing mother and the guardian angel from a rape crisis centre, even the black interloper who is shot by a black partolman.

This aspect is cued by a joke at the outset, when Carol's mother is heard on the phone lamenting the fact that no two apple pies can be made to come out alike. The creation of doubles and the fear of doubles is, of course, a significant element in any Kubrick film, from the *doppelgänger* games in *Lolita* to the projections of *The Shining*, the fear in the latter being that of the would-be novelist hero that he is out-gifted by his son with the power of second sight. *Heart of Midnight* sets up a similar power struggle, and family melodrama, in another environment with the capacity to make fantasies come to life. But it stereotypes them in the story of an evil uncle, a guilty sibling, and the unlocking of a secret in the past. The film turns out to have its own double, a more plainly cautionary tale about incest and child abuse, something akin to the TV movies which have appeared on the subject in the last couple of years. From this perspective, all the elaborate twinning (the role of the rape crisis counsellor, for instance) just looks narratively clumsy, and the shock revelations (Carol's sexual panic grotesquely reflected in Sonny's gender confusion) overstated. One might suspect that the film is having too much of a good thing anyway when it produces another cop, Sylvester's brother Frank Stallone, who also yearns to go into show-business, to turn himself into an "other".

It might also be too much to expect that the film could tie together all its conceptual riddles about gender confusion and identity loss, fantasising, projecting and performing, in a drama that is psychologically satisfying, and liberating for its heroine. In this, it recalls something of the conceptual twists and dramatic problems of Roman Polanski's *The Tenant,* and *Heart of Midnight* is most successful when it is working in an area (a genre?) where Kubrick and Polanski meet—an area where *doppelgängers,* domestic surrealism and repetition compulsions are all symptoms of some unassuageable identity ache. Particularly Polanski is the trio of workmen whom Carol finds in residence at The Midnight, and who seem to have their own sinister plans for the club while not making much headway with the renovations, and the scene in which she tries to track her demon under the floorboards, tip-tapping along with a revolver and her plaster cast. With its coda, the film turns, in both its décor and its drama, on as airy a puzzle as *The Shinning,* as a liberated and glamorised Carol makes her entrance into the luxuriously refurbished pleasure palace. She is swept on to the dance floor by Larry, who had seemed mortally shot just previously, and who declares his love in a phrase—"No one ever said there was any logic to it"— that exactly echoes the workman's comment about the unfathomability of The Midnight.

NEW YORK POST, 3/3/89, p. 25, David Edelstein

As Carol, a disturbed young woman who inherits her uncle's seedy nightclub, Jennifer Jason Leigh is on her own fluttery wavelength; she blurts insults into the mirror and then briskly charges ahead, buoyed by the act of putting herself down. The plot of the Gothic thriller "Heart of Midnight" calls for Leigh to be molested, drugged, shackled and kicked around, but she seems so damaged to begin with that each hellish crisis is just another drop in the swamp of her neuroses—she's peculiarly impervious.

The performance, with its dreamy, disconnected rhythms, recalls Jessica Lange's in "Frances," but it's wonderfully eccentric and seductive in its own right, and it holds this rambling funhouse together. The dissipated former sex club—haunted by something or someone—provides a neat thriller-play-pen setting, and Leigh's jumpiness (she can't stand, for some reason, being touched) makes every creak seem thunderous. This is the first Antsy Drew mystery.

For director and writer Matthew Chapman, the club (called Midnight) is a modern Gothic castle. It's got locked doors, secret passageways and hidden torture chambers; it's a place for his heroine to explore a horrifying past and come face to face with the key to her own repressed sexuality.

It's all fairly clunky, but "Heart of Midnight" has an irresistible look, and Leigh is a sight, her hair bobbed and bleached-blonde, her eyes ringed with black, her sultry mouth red; in seconds she can go from looking sleek and glamorous to tremulous and naked, like an abashed butterfly trying to squeeze back into its cocoon.

She's shot against the garish primary colors of Gene Rudolph's set—crimson walls, blue lights—and as she travels from one kinky high-concept room to the next, her late Uncle Fletcher looms increasingly large as a sadist and pederast. (Uncles in thrillers are usually perverts and occasionally murderers, especially when they wear Hawaiian shirts in flashbacks and lean salaciously into the cameras.) Peter Coyote plays a detective who's even weirder and more distracted than the young woman he's supposed to be protecting, and he harbors an intense resentment of Uncle Fletcher's memory. Coyote and Leigh engage in what passes for sexy banter; to prove he feels things as deeply as she does, he puts a gun with a single bullet in the chamber to his temple and pulls the trigger. (OK, we believe you feel things deeply.)

"Heart of Midnight" is a more pretentious version of a Dario Argento hack-'em-up like "Suspiria". What's missing is the eruption; the climax is slow-motion and arty, as if Chapman decided he was making an "exercise in suspense" instead of of a thriller. And he's on shaky ground morally, denouncing sexual perversion but catering to our prurience. One of the picture's bonuses—I kid you not—is Frank Stallone as a cop. Exploring the stage of the club, he breaks into an Elvis impersonation, and at the station he's more interested in warbling and strumming than in dashing off to catch the murderer. Like his brother, Stallone radiates narcissism, but he has a sense of humor about it. He's wandered into this Gothic horror movie, but no psycho on earth could keep him from plugging his record.

NEWSDAY, 3/3/89, Part III/p. 9, Terry Kelleher

"Heart of Midnight" is aiming for sordid surrealism of the "Blue Velvet" stripe. If you find that repellent, you need no further information about the movie. If you find it intriguing, be advised that your expectations will go largely unfulfilled.

Carol Rivers (Jennifer Jason Leigh) is a young woman with a past. "I nearly blinded a man for making a pass at me," she says. "And then I went deaf. And then I went crazy." Not good. The thing is, did she stay crazy?

Suitcase in hand and an unexplained cast on her leg, Carol arrives in a seedy part of a southern city to take over the Midnight, a dilapidated nightclub she inherited from her uncle. The place is closed for remodeling, and the workmen greet her with an air of salacious curiosity. Carol establishes residence on the second floor, though it's creepy as hell—child's room with toys and teddy bear; S & M room with all the torture equipment; 24-hour (or so it seems) porn video on the omnipresent TV screens.

The first night, three would-be rapists attack Carol. How did they gain entry to the club? An unseen force opened the front door. After getting sympathy from a rape counselor (Denise Dummont) and skepticism from a cop (Frank Stallone), zombie-like Carol goes right back to her chamber of horrors, where the strange occurrences start multiplying. The shower turns on and off by itself. A riderless bicycle whizzes down the hall. A bloody fish head pops up in the water cooler. Apples, some of them wormy, are everywhere.

You wonder why Carol doesn't abandon the club owner's life and return to the family home, but a brief flashback to her nagging mother (Brenda Vaccaro in a "special appearance") is enough to indicate the unattractiveness of that option. A stopgap measure, such as checking into a quiet motel, is never considered.

Obviously Carol is imagining at least some of the rampant weirdness at the Midnight. By leaving open the question of how much, writer-director Matthew Chapman ("Strangers Kiss") keeps us on the hook for quite a while. The huge eyeball crashing through the bedroom door? Pure phantasm. The medicine cabinet with a mind of its own? Debatable. The murder of a visitor? That had to be legit—the audience saw it but the heroine didn't.

And what of the men in Carol's life? Her uncle (Sam Schacht) must have been fairly depraved, but in her childhood memories he seems no worse than raffish (unless the sight of loud shirts and gold chains makes your flesh crawl). Then there's that stranger (Peter Coyote) who may be a detective, a friend, or neither. "Number one," he says, "you're not crazy. Number two, trust me. Number three is a secret."

As long as Chapman has us off-balance, we can't be sure if it's safe to laugh at dialogue like that. Occasionally a line comes from so deep in left field that an elaborate put-on seems a distinct possibility: Carol describes her ideal man as "charming but injured, sad—like he could've been a physicist."

Eventually, when the perils of Carol and the tricks of the director have grown repetitive, the movie must come up with some answers. The ultimate explanation for the Midnight horror show—natural causes in the present stemming from unnatural sex in the past—will be unconvincing to those who prefer plots that make sense and disappointing to those who had hoped Chapman might just be crazy enough to play mind games for keeps. "Heart of Midnight" would be more "real" if it remained inside the heroine's head.

VILLAGE VOICE, 3/7/89, p. 64, Elliott Stein

In one of his last interviews, Ted Bundy claimed that pornography made him do it. Too bad they fried him—it would have been interesting to invite Teddy Boy up to do a guest review of *Heart of Midnight,* a moralizing, no-frills-no-thrills "suspense thriller."

Confused young Carol (Jennifer Jason Leigh) inherits her Uncle Fletcher's nightclub, sets up housekeeping therein, and attempts to renovate the place. The movie is of the house-that-has-a-life-of-its-own subspecies, and, before you can say *The Shining,* there are inexplicable gurglings, sounds of whips and chains, and TV sets blinking off and on, relaying naughty videos in every room. Seems Uncle Fletch had been quite a card; he'd been running a sex club, not a nightclub, and what is more, molesting every young thing in sight, of every persuasion, some of whom return to the joint as wacko grownups to molest his niece in turn. Although Fletch (Sam Schacht) died of AIDS for his sins, we do get to see him smirking sleazily in slo-mo flashbacks and dream sequences.

There are a couple of shower scenes and a clip from *The 39 Steps* on a TV set to give the impression that writer/director Matthew Chapman is Hitchcockian. The goosey payoff, when it finally comes, is actually more reminiscent of one of William Castle's lesser climaxes. What is most dispiriting is the company name presenting this inept wad of tripe. The Samuel Goldwyn moniker has always evoked magic titles for me: *The Hurricane, The Little Foxes, The Best Years of Our Lives.* If they put a VCR in the old man's grave and let him take a gander at what they're putting his name on these days, he'd sit bolt upright and change it back to Goldfish.

Also reviewed in:
NEW YORK TIMES, 3/3/89, p. C8, Vincent Canby
VARIETY, 5/25/88, p. 19
WASHINGTON POST, 3/6/89, p. C1, Hal Hinson

HEAT AND SUNLIGHT

A Snowball Production and New Front Alliance Films release. *Producer:* Steve Burns and Hildy Burns. *Director:* Rob Nilsson. *Director of Photography:* Thomas Tucker. *Editor:* Henk van Eeghen. *Music:* David Byrne and Brian Eno. *Choreographer:* Consuelo Faust. *Production Designer:* Hildy Burns and Steve Burns. *Running time:* 98 minutes. *MPAA Rating:* Not Rated.

CAST: Rob Nilsson (Mel Hurley); Consuelo Faust (Carmen); Don Bajema (Mitch); Ernie Fosselius (Bobby); Bill Bailey (Barney).

NEW YORK POST, 3/31/89, p. 30, David Edelstein

Rob Nilsson's "Heat and Sunlight," which chronicles the excruciating end of an obsessive relationship between a photographer (Nilsson) and a dancer (Consuelo Faust), was wholly improvised by its cast—and Lord, can you tell.

Nilsson, who works out of San Francisco, is a spiritual pupil of the late John Cassavetes, and he loves getting so close to his urban actors' mugs that you can count their pores. As they stare dumbly ahead and fumble for words—conscious all the while of the camera in their faces—they seem a lot less natural than actors who've memorized a script.

For reasons of speed and economy, the movie was shot in two days with video cameras and then transferred to black-and-white film. You can sometimes tell it's video, but the nighttime images are surprisingly sharp, and the look of the picture is arresting—it has a restless, jittery style, as if the cameraman had gobbled a handful of amphetamines and filmed for 48 straight hours.

Unlike most films, in which there can be years between conception and execution, "Heat and Sunlight" seems to have been made in one burst of adrenaline. It uses date-and-time cards to enhance the documentary mood, and it plunges you into the maelstrom of its hero's thwarted passion.

Mel made his reputation years earlier by shooting starving Biafran children, whose pictures still cover his loft—alongside naked shots of his girlfriend. In fact, emaciated Biafrans and hot sex with his "black-eyed gypsy" are all scrambled together in his head, underscored by selections from David Byrne and Brian Eno's "My Life in the Bush of Ghosts."

Nilsson certainly succeeds in ushering us into Mel's feverish mind, which pounds him (and us) with memories. The problem is that Nilsson has no distance at all on this self-involved artist, and the juxtaposition of his love life (however intense) and a famine feels monstrously exploitative. Compare this to, say, Martin Scorsese's "Life Lessons," in which Scorsese can evoke his artist-protagonist's tumultuous state of mind and still give us an over-view.

And Nilsson is no Nick Nolte. At his most charismatic he looks like a young, beardless Abe Lincoln, brooding over pictures of black children. But he's alternately self-dramatizing. Nilsson is a runner (he made a movie about that obsession called "Over the Edge"), and when he tells his buddies he's going for a run—leaving them behind to tell stories about him—it's practically a confession of dramatic impotence.

In one prolonged encounter, he messes up his girlfriend's apartment, puts his hand through glass and, when she calls him a fool, replies, "I'd rather be a fool that felt something."

For all his industrial-strength feeling, though—and for all the pulling off of clothes, fornicating against walls and dancing half naked—there seems little to this great passion except overlapping strains of narcissism. Nilsson's Mel emerges as an incredibly manipulative man, but if the filmmaker knows this he doesn't show us through his technique that he knows. He's lost in his private hall of mirrors.

Last year, "Heat and Sunlight" won first prize at the United States Film festival in Park City, Utah, where a jury of filmmakers hailed its gutsy style. Nilsson does put himself on the line, and I don't mean to fault him for risking self-indulgence. There are worse vices a filmmaker can have; some selves, in fact, are so vast that exploring them becomes an adventure. But self-indulgence without a shred of self-insight is an embarrassment.

NEWSDAY, 3/31/89, Part III/p. 3, Mike McGrady

"Sometimes I feel totally boring," the man says, "Sometimes I am, right?" "Sometimes we both are," his lover agrees. Sometimes everyone is. But this little exchange in "Heat and Sunlight" is endearing for several reasons. These are, of course, the kinds of lines that make a critic's heart take flight, ideal openers for any putdown, lines that very few moviemakers—only the extremely amateurish and the extremely gutsy—would leave intact.

But then, "Heat and Sunlight" is both amateurish and gutsy; and the lines fit in quite well, indeed. The film's flaws and virtues are so closely connected with method of manufacture that any discussion of "Heat and Sunlight" must begin by explaining how the film came into being.

First and foremost, it came into being without benefit of a script. Director-star Rob Nilsson, a San Francisco acting teacher who has done similar film work in the past (for example, 1983's "Signal 7"), begins with only the basic situation—the painful last hours in a love affair—and his central characters. From that point on (Nilsson calls it "direct-action cinema"), the actors wing it, improvising the lines and the moods as they go along.

Perhaps its strongest point is that "Heat and Sunlight" differs so from the run-of-the-reel Hollywood product. The basic technique is hardly new with Nilsson; he shares many of the virtues and failings of the late John Cassavetes, whom he sees as "a Promethean figure." Which is to say, "Heat and Sunlight" can be both naked and intensely personal; it's a form of psychological cinema verite that moves along spontaneously. When it works—patience, patience, it will—it fairly explodes. When it doesn't, it seems windy and self-indulgent.

The major technical differences—color video cameras shooting black-and-white tape, hand-held cameras, two-camera setups with 360-degree lighting—are all intended to free up the action, giving it a kind of range and movement not available in more constrained and formal situations.

The film chronicles the final, painful, violent, jealous and passionate 16 hours of a love affair between a photojournalist (Nilsson) who once won awards photographing starving children of Biafra, and an exotic dancer (Consuelo Faust) who has just taken on a new lover. The film explores, in unblinking fashion, jealousy, obsession, hostility, sexuality and violence.

With improvisational moviemaking like this, some of the richest rewards are serendipitous, moments that the moviemaker happened to stumble over while on a sidetrip. I particularly enjoyed shots of a comedian (Ernie Fosselius) trying out his new no-punchline approach to humor and a group of salesmen sharing small talk at a topless bar.

"Heat and Sunlight," winner of the top prize at the recent U. S. Film Festival, is a movie about perspectives. The photogapher's work, huge blowups of starving Biafrans along with dramatic nude studies of his about-to-be-ex-lover, covers his apartment walls, haunting the film the way it haunts the man. They are constant reminders that his current plight must be seen in perspective. As painful as it is and as damaging, it is truly nothing compared to children starving. When he can accept that, when he begins to move from the past into the present, with a little help from his friends, the film takes on its life as well as its meaning.

VILLAGE VOICE, 4/4/89, p. 63, Amy Taubin

Stubborn and raw, *Heat and Sunlight* is a much-too-close-for-comfort look at sexual jealousy, a messy, unattractive emotion to which most of us occasionally succumb, but which we are hardly anxious to contemplate—or even admit—once the misery has passed. Filmmaker and lead actor Rob Nilsson distills a 90-minute psychodrama—just the high points—from 16 hellish hours in the life of a photojournalist whose girlfriend has failed to pick him up at the airport. The movie refuses the cosmetic distractions of plot; it's simply situation and character. What it offers the viewer are the thrills, embarrassments, and catharsis of self-recognition.

In 1970, Mel Hurley (Nilsson) photographed dying children in Biafra. The experience made his career but left him emotionally traumatized. The possibility that his relationship with dancer/choreographer Carmen (Consuelo Faust) may be ending reawakens unbearable memories. In his mind's eye and on the walls of his studio, images of starving children are collaged with erotic photographs of Carmen. Although there's something both naive and repellent in the baldness of the juxtaposition, it's as revealing as it is disturbing. To feel pain and rage because one is powerless to breathe life into dying children is socially and personally acceptable, even admirable. To feel those emotions because one cannot control the desire of one's lover is childish and megalomaniacal. In both instances, however, one goes out of control when faced with the limits of one's control over other people. But jealousy is intensified by selfhatred—one's guilt about envying someone else's freedom. Nilsson doesn't verbalize this stuff very much, but he finds an abundance of visual correlatives for internal chaos and the horror of being paralyzed between fight and flight.

Like Nilsson's earlier *Signal 7, Heat and Sunlight* was shot on videotape and transferred to 35mm film. Nilsson uses two cameras, both hand-held—shooting simultaneously in verité documentary style. There are no master shots and no cutaways. The careening movement and jagged editing are metaphors for Mel's inner turbulence. Shifting between the two cameras does not provide alternative points of view so much as it suggests a schizoid instability. Although Nilsson's reason for shooting on video is to a large extent economic, he uses the particularities of the video image—the absence of spatial clues, the wrong end of the telescope look—for expressive ends. The floor seems about to give way, the walls are collapsing, and objects are burnt black by the sun.

Inevitably, Mel confronts Carmen. The picture lurches rather than builds to that point. The scene opens with a wildly hysterical bit of business involving a banana and concludes with some violent love-making. But the best part is in between—a mutual memory flashback to a soft-shoe routine with Mel and Carmen as Fred and Ginger peculiarly garbed in underpants and boots with their particular fetish object—mouth retainers—clamped into place. Such creativity does not die an easy death.

Heat and Sunlight is Mel's film all the way, and while I have no quarrels with Nilsson's performance (he has presence, takes a lot of acting risks, and looks like a combination of Jack Nicholson and Clint Eastwood—or maybe that's just video magic), the fact that he dominates both sides of the camera gives the project a narcissistic edge that I'd rather have done without. Some of the best moments are bits of comic relief—a bunch of middle-aged insurance salesmen in a bar discuss how, in an age of diminished expectations, anything that provides a sense of security is a growth industry. The fact is that everyone in the picture has more of a sense of humor than Mel. Nilsson goes out of his way to suggest that Mel's failure in this area is not simply a matter of his current emotional condition—it's a permanent flaw. Maybe that's the reason Carmen's looking elsewhere (although why she'd prefer her bimbo dance partner to Mel at his dourest is beyond me). Mel's tunnel-vision intensity is death to laughter.

Despite the fact that *Heat and Sunlight* won first prize at the U.S. Film Festival in 1988, it took a full year to find distribution. The close-up scrutiny of volatile emotions and the craziness of ordinary people is commercially risky, as out-of-fashion as the black-and-white video look. Real men aren't supposed to act the way Mel does, especially not when the cameras are on them. What Nilsson wrote in his recent tribute to John Cassavetes—"his films show us what 'we' are"—applies to his own work as well. *Heat and Sunlight* illuminates what Hollywood rules out-of-frame.

Also reviewed in:
NEW REPUBLIC, 5/1/89, p. 31, Stanley Kauffmann
NEW YORK TIMES, 3/31/89, p. C17, Janet Maslin
VARIETY, 9/30/87, p. 20

HEATHERS

A New World Pictures release in association with Cinemarque Entertainment (USA) Ltd. *Executive Producer:* Christopher Webster. *Production:* Denise Di Novi. *Director:* Michael Lehmann. *Screenplay:* Daniel Waters.

Director of Photography: Francis Kenney. *Editor:* Norman Hollyn. *Music:* David Newman. *Sound:* Douglas Axtell. *Production Designer:* Jon Hutman. *Art Director:* Kara Lindstrom. *Costumes:* Rudy Dillon. *Running time:* 102 minutes. *MPAA Rating:* R.

CAST: Winona Ryder (Veronica); Christian Slater (J.D.); Shannen Doherty (Heather Duke); Lisanne Falk (Heather McNamara); Kim Walker (Heather Chandler); Penelope Milford (Pauline Fleming); Glenn Shadix (Father Ripper); Lance Fenton (Kurt Kelly); Patrick Labyorteau (Ram); Jeremy Applegate (Peter Dawson); Jon Matthews (Rodney); Carrie Lynn (Martha Dunnstock, "Dumptruck"); Phil Lewis (Dennis); Renée Estevez (Betty Finn); John Zarchen (Country Club Keith); Sherrie Wills (Country Club Courtney); Curtiss Marlowe (Geek); Jon Matthews (Geek Squad Leader); Andy David (Fat Cynic); Kevin Hardesty (1st Heavy Metaler in Parking Lot); Josh Richman (2nd Heavy Metaler in Parking Lot); Bill Cort (Veronica's Dad); Larry Cox (David); Kent Stoddard (Brad); John Ingle (Principal Gowan); Stuart Mabray (Counselor Paul Hyde); Betty Ramey (Teacher in Conference Room); Aaron Mendelson (Nerd in Pauline's Class); Kirk Scott (Big Bud Dean); Mark Bringelson (Officer McCord); Chuck Lafont (Officer Milner); Christie Mellor (Squealing Girl in Parking Lot); Mark Carlton (Kurt's Dad); James "Poorman" Trenton ("Hot Probs" DJ); Adrian Drake (Gruff Teacher).

FILMS IN REVIEW, 8–9/89, p. 423, Charles Epstein

As we turn the corner on a decade characterized by greed, ersatz patriotism, and...egads! teenage coming of age flicks, along comes *Heathers,* a cynical, downright vicious satire on that Darwinian battleground, the middle American high school. Scriptwriter Daniel Waters exhibits an uncanny ear for teen lingo and, like David Lynch (*Blue Velvet*) and John Waters (no relation), a gift for the casually bizarre. Who would have imagined teen suicide—a real and disturbing problem-as grist for hijinks and high camp? That director Michael Lehmann is able to conjure up a truly engaging and deliciously funny (albeit macabre) satire from so grim a subject is among the film's surprising delights.

Like all high schools only much more so, Westerberg High is governed by a rigid caste system. Sitting atop the social hierarchy like a well coiffed and expensively dressed junta is a trio of self-styled "bitches" who refer to themselves as "Heather." As the film opens, Veronica, a renegade egghead, auditions for entree into this exclusive sorority, itself a mini-hierarchy tyrannized by the meanest, and most patrician bitch, Heather One. Early into her "hazing" (mixing at a lascivious college party, and performing a number of nasty little pranks), Veronica meets and falls for J. D. (Christian Slater), a mysterious newcomer who speaks in the unaffected, detached cadences of Jack Nicholson and is expelled from school for pulling a gun on two sneering tormentors in the cafeteria. Veronica soon wearies of her comrades' gratuitous cruelty and, in league with J.D., plans to exact revenge on Heather One. While they concoct a drink intended to make Heather experience a measure of chastening intestinal discomfort, J.D. surreptitiously spikes it with a lethal dose of liquid drain cleaner. When Heather One chokes and dies, J.D. espies the Cliff Notes for *The Bell Jar* on the floor; in a flash of inspiration, he convinces Veronica to contrive a suicide note, the unforeseen consequences of which not only makes "a misunderstood" Heather even more popular than she ever was (enforcing their popularity is the Heathers' main occupation), but triggers other killings that the disarmingly psychotic J.D. also makes look like suicides. (By way of justifying the killing of two leering jocks to a horrified Veronica, he coolly insists he was merely keeping the school safe from date rapes and AIDS jokes). Finally, as Veronica laments in her diary, she had no idea that teenage angst could have a body count; she must abandon the homicidal juggernaut.

Other than the disappointing ending (a cop-out) *Heathers* teems with colorful snippets of teen-speak and inventive situations. First time director Michael Lehmann, however seems at times tentative and does not have a sure hand with his actors many of whom are as wooden as tackling dummies. *Heathers* has few if any redeeming characters and some may find the humor occasionally flirts with the tasteless (if there were a well oiled lobby inveighing against teen suicide, *Heathers* doubtless would have been mothballed). But all strong satire unflinchingly engages the dangerous; if *Heathers* fails to in any way inform in its handling of a sensitive subject (hardly high on its agenda), it does produce some of the heartier laughs this filmgoer has enjoyed since escaping high school many a full moon ago.

LOS ANGELES TIMES, 3/31/89, Calendar/p. 1, Sheila Benson

"Heathers" is about the darker impulses that almost everyone feels at least once during the extended hell week that high school can be: that fleeting urge of "I could just *kill* him (or her)." In "Heathers" they do.

It's set in a rich middle-American high school where the ruling clique of Juniors is called the

Heathers, after the names of all three members. In training to become a Heather is Veronica (Winona Ryder), who instead falls under the influence of a dark, disturbing newcomer, J.D. (Christian Slater). Like Veronica, he seems to sneer at the cruelty and consumerism of their classmates, although his methods are hardly usual. First the reigning Heather, Veronica's oppressor/chum (Kim Walker), is slipped a mug filled with paint stripper; next Veronica lures out, then shoots two obnoxious jock classmates dead in their tracks. It may be disingenuous murder at first, but faced with dead bodies she doesn't stop; she helps Slater forge notes so that all three are believed to be suicides, touching off suicide mania at Westerburgh High.

"Heathers" is a film that thinks of itself as black comedy; certainly some of the targets in Daniel Waters' script are overdue for a zinger or two: school cliques, unctuous teachers, parents who won't be parents and want to be hip post-adolescents, and a society with the values of a television sitcom.

But to mount black comedy successfully, you must have a clearly defined point of view. You must also be willing to follow your dangerous outlook to its most outrageous conclusion, as "A Fish Called Wanda" does when it flattens Kevin Kline with a steamroller. Unfortunately, director Michael Lehmann's point of view is swivelmounted: He doesn't have the courage of his cynicism.

If he did, he'd have to go all the way. Having made treacherous comedy out of the death of innocents—the fact that the innocents are dumb, vicious or loathsome is absolutely beside the point—director Lehmann would have to go out on his self-created limb and saw it off behind him. Having threatened to blow up the high school, "Heathers" would have to end with the biggest explosion of consumers and consumer goods since "Zabriskie Point."

Then we might take his brackish malice seriously. We might not like it, but it would be easier to respect full-tilt nihilism instead of a director who wimps out with a cloying "After School Special" ending, completely different in tone and style from the film's other three-quarters.

Having hung out with J.D. until he turns into a real monster, Lehmann has his appealing Veronica turn over a new leaf; she declares herself "the sheriff in the white hat," new leader of the pack. And to the obese girl who's been the victim of a particularly humiliating Heathers trick, Veronica suggests chirpily that they sit out the prom together, at home over a video or two. Three deaths are waved away without weight or guilt. They simply don't count. That is the most profound cynicism of "Heathers."

The few who remember the interesting, uneven "Static" from two years ago may recall that part of its story turned on a busload of elderly, endearing characters who became hostages in an escalating stand-off with police and finally a SWAT team. In a surprise turn, their bus *was* blown up. And sitting there stunned, as the dust of the explosion cleared on the horizon, you were forced to confront death as something real.

You might make a case that Veronica is an unwilling accomplice in all this, a pawn to Slater's drawling J.D., whom she only later sees as a genuine psychopath. But she's supposed to be the film's smart kid, lured by J.D.'s philosophy as much as his off-beatness.

Then, too, by having Slater play him in his best Jack Nicholson voice, as a grinning, Nicholson psycho-thug, Lehmann undercuts J.D.'s value as a voice of opposition. Setting sick dangerous anarchy against sick dangerous conformism isn't much of a choice. When Veronica rejects him at the end, she's just rejecting craziness, not the flaws in his argument.

Lehmann may not yet demonstrate much heart or even taste; he does have considerable technical skill, and he's also not above borrowing from the best of the past. (That arresting croquet game shot with Ryder's head buried in the grass comes from "Repentance" and from Peckinpah and Jodorowsky before that.) And, in addition to his behind-the-camera artists, especially costume designer Rudy Dillon and production designer Jon Hutman, he has been beautifully served by Winona Ryder, an actress of grace and subtlety since her first moments in "Lucas." As for Slater, now that we have seen his nifty Nicholson turn twice, can he please go back to his own voice, and mannerisms?

Screenwriter Waters is hardly uninteresting: He knows the turf he's tearing up, and some of his more scalding moments, the funeral of the two jocks, the college mixer, are dead-on. (In addition to the grisly deaths, "Heathers' " R-rating is for the film's language, which could scrape hulls. Teen-agers may recognize it; it will give timorous adults fits.)

Of course, some may not want to indulge the "Heathers" film makers beyond their first 15 minutes. As Heather No. 1 drains the hull cleaner in one gulp and crashes through her glass-topped table, the idea of using violent death—today—as a jokey grace note may seem so soulless that audiences decamp right there. There's even another possible alternative. . . .

MONTHLY FILM BULLETIN, 1/90, p. 15, Richard Combs

Veronica Sawyer, a junior at Westerburg High School in Sherwood, Ohio, has become a reluctant member of the ultra chic, ultra bitchy clique of three girls all called Heather (the leader, Heather Chandler, whose key colour is red, Heather Duke in green and Heather McNamara in yellow). This has forced Veronica to sever her old, unchic friendships with bespectacled Betty Finn and obese Martha Dunnstock, and she confesses her confusion and underlying hostility to the Heathers in her diary. She is attracted to a new boy in school, the sardonic outsider Jason Dean (who gives short shrift to the bullying of two senior jocks, Kurt and Ram), and their alliance is sealed when they make love after Veronica quits a party Heather Chandler has insisted she attend at Remington University. J.D. suggests putting Veronica's fantasy of revenge against Heather into effect, but the disgusting morning-after potion Veronica delivers to Heather turns out to be a fatal one mixed by J.D. The horrified Veronica agrees to J.D.'s plan to make her death look like suicide, and they are both disgusted to find Heather being virtually canonised in the communal outpouring of emotion "orchestrated" by teacher Miss Fleming. Veronica is disturbed to meet J.D.'s father, a truculent demolition man who was inadvertently responsible for his mother's death, but agrees to J.D.'s plan to embarrass Kurt and Ram (who have made lewd claims about Veronica). They set up a fake double suicide with a gay motive, which again turns into the real thing at J.D.'s instigation. As suicide hysteria begins to sweep the school (Martha Dunnstock makes an unsuccessful attempt), Veronica finds the strength to reject J.D. But he then begins to manipulate Heather Duke (who has assumed Heather Chandler's role), blackmailing her into circulating a petition supposedly calling for the hiring of a group called Big Fun (whose hit record is "Teenage Suicide Don't Do It") at the school prom. He makes veiled threats to Veronica that her own "suicide" can be arranged if she doesn't help him to stage Heather Duke's; Veronica fantasises about the latter, but then tricks J.D. into believing that she has actually killed herself (at which point he reveals the true contents of his petition: a declaration on behalf of the whole school of its intention to self-destruct). Racing to the school gym during another soul-baring session, Veronica finds J.D. planting charges beneath; she stops him with a gun, and then watches as he sets off another charge strapped to his body. Later removing Heather Duke's red ribbon of authority, she announces a new régime of kindliness in school.

If there's anything which the recent high-school/adolescent angst movies have in common, it's one particular joke: the moment when something outrageous happens in the classroom, when the problems of Life begin to intrude on this rarefied atmosphere, and one of the bespectacled types, one of the "geeks" or "nerds", will anxiously ask, "Are we going to be tested on this?" It has recurred, at least, through the punk playfulness (or indeterminate nihilism) of *River's Edge*, the liberal breast-beating of *Dead Poets Society*, and now the hip teen-dreaming of *Heathers*. It might be the kind of line that crystallises a genre, as "classic" and absurd a statement of moral values as the Western's "The next time you say that—smile". The moral values here may not be as Manichean as in a Western, but perhaps the classroom division between those who think it matters to do well in school and those who only want a way out, between those looking for good grades and those looking for life lessons, could translate into small homesteaders vs. ambitious cattle barons (Elisha Cook Jnr. is the nerd who turns, going up against Jack Palance as the school bully).

Michael Lehmann's impressive directorial début toys lightly, jokingly, with the possibility of turning into a Western: a Leone-like harmonica signals the appearances of the enigmatic Jason Dean, and Veronica announces her final triumph over the Heathers with the line, "There's a new sheriff in town". Beneath these throwaways, there's a serious moral drift which it seems less that the film really intends than that it is powerless to resist: Veronica in the end scorns the temptations of power to throw in her lot with her own bespectacled friend Betty Finn and the wheelchair-bound failed suicide Martha "Dumptruck". It's the moral conflict of style over substance—the elegant but evil cool of the Heathers vs. the gauche good-heartedness of the nerds—and *Heathers* is happiest playing this out as a series of stylistic (or stylish) gags, with a slight air of embarrassment about its final moral clincher.

It's hardly a question of the ending being a cop-out, as has been suggested by reports of the ending that Lehmann wanted (the school being blown up, or Veronica blowing herself up) before New World intervened. The film is not seriously a comedy about high school as a metaphor for society—its false values, its power-hungry cliques, its emotional exploitation. When J.D., with his finger on the button, expresses such a sentiment (people will say the school self-destructed "not because society didn't care, but because the school *was* society"), it's done self-mockingly, another modish gag. If this is black comedy, it's not in the apocalyptic vein of any number of teen movies—say, from *Over the Edge* onwards—which have envisaged the end of society as we know it, but more like the wistfully knowing satire of George Axelrod's *Lord Love a Duck*, whose plot (charmingly evil genie offers to make his teen queen's dreams come true) it also resembles. The ending, at any rate, with Veronica's race against time to stop her demon lover-become-mad bomber, is inevitably, rhetorically, anti-climactic. One roots neither for the school to be blown up nor for it to be saved; the school is just a given, like the "land", perhaps, in a Western. It has at most a cartoon reality, and appropriately, as J.D. prepares to blow himself to a better New World, Veronica nonchalantly puts a cigarette between her lips in anticipation of the blast, which leaves her completely blackened but alive (like many a cartoon cat), the cigarette not just lit but reduced to ash. Since the "hero", the Shane figure, in this genre must always be a co-ed composite, J.D. and Veronica make a more ruthless and amusing composite than most, with the justification that she is led inadvertently into murder by her psychotic *alter ego* balanced by the suggestion that she dreamed him up for this purpose. One weakness is that it's never clear why Winona Ryder's self-possessed Veronica would be seduced by the self-preening silliness of the Heathers, compared to Tuesday Weld's empty-headed pursuit of popularity in *Lord Love a Duck* (since it's Veronica who "calls up" J.D., there is already a reversal here, post-feminist or New Teen style, of the relationship of dreamer and dream object).

But Veronica seems beset from the start by other demons, expressed in frantic bouts of diary scribbling. She wants high school to be "nice", and the only way to achieve that turns out to be murder. If there's a weakness of motivation in *Heathers*, it may be because the whole film is rather dream-like, a product of Veronica's fevered writing and imaginings, with a consequent chaos and interchangeability of roles (both Heather Chandler and J.D. are linked to a fire and brimstone motif). Veronica's free-floating adolescent angst is expressed in both the absurdly hard-boiled girl talk of the Heathers ("Fuck me gently with a chainsaw"; "Why are you pulling my dick?") and the psycho machismo of J.D. James Dean allusion aside, Christian Slater seems to have been directed to play the latter as if he were Jack Nicholson, a combination of intellectual bruiser and provocative little devil. The ending may get its moral justification from Veronica plumping for homesteaders over cattle barons, but it gets its charge from the demonology genre, a quieter, wittier version of *The Witches of Eastwick*, perhaps, in which Veronica, having unleashed and expended her destructive (male?) energy can now recoup it for "good".

NEW YORK, 4/3/89, p. 68, David Denby

The title of a startling and ambitious new independent film, *Heathers*, refers to three rich, beautiful, and vicious girls in an Ohio school who caress croquet balls together and dominate the school's social life. All three are named Heather. Generically, they *are* Heather—lacquered and calculating prom queens, with beautifully coiffed hair and heavy makeup, who bully their way to power ("popularity") at their gruesome high school. The movie takes an icy look at them: They could be upperclass suburban housewives who live for golf and adultery. They have never been young.

The trouble is, I don't believe it. Teenagers can be horrid, but they're still socially knock-kneed. Even the most heartlessly competitive adolescent suffers slippage in her drive to be a shallow, empty adult; a roll of baby fat shows up, tenderizing an overexercised frame. I know that *Heathers* is satire, but satire devoid of affection can be offensive. The movie displays no warmth at all for the three girls and, with one exception, none for anyone else at their school, or for the teachers or parents. The exception is the filmmakers' heroine, Veronica (Winona Ryder), also rich and beautiful, who becomes a protégée of the three Heathers, but with many misgivings. Veronica is smart enough to know the other girls are awful, and at night, raging in her diary, she longs to be rid of them. Then she meets a boy who partly fulfills her wish. *Heathers* might be called an apocalyptic sick comedy; the movie plays with the idea that some of the students are so obnoxious they should be killed.

Heathers has the audacity of a first-time effort (conceived before limits are acknowledged; before common sense is acknowledged, too). The director, Michael Lehmann, a former philosophy student, made his "thesis" film at the University of Southern California film school about a student who applies for a scholarship in order to pay back his drug debts; the writer, Daniel Waters (this is his first screenplay), drew on the weekly column he once put together for his high-school newspaper in South Bend, Indiana. These two may be settling a few old scores. In *Heathers*, the jock football heroes are bruisers so gross they perform vile (and incomprehensible) tricks on *cows*; a trembling-with-sensitivity teacher, a veteran of the sixties, is thrilled by a student suicide because she can use it as an excuse to stage squishy touchy-feely sessions at school. Everyone uses everyone.

Unlike most critics of American materialism, Waters and Lehmann are neither liberal nor pious; they razz the school's token black and make fun of homosexuals. These are *bad* boys, nasty entertainers and probably too sarcastic for their own good. Waters has the kids talking in an obscene jargon (a mild example: "Did you have a brain tumor for breakfast?"). The patois is meant to parody the brutal flipness of the MTV generation, but it grates mercilessly—Waters revels in his own unspeakable creation.

At first, a new boy in school, J.D. (Christian Slater), seems a welcome relief. J.D. dresses in black turtlenecks, and his manner is debonair and ironically literate, like Jack Nicholson at his most shamblingly charming. Quickly he takes the confused Veronica in hand. After spending the night with her, he leads her to the house of the most important of the three Heathers, a dreadful blonde bitch who sleeps in a plush silken bed like some Hollywood glamour queen of yesteryear. Veronica thinks they are playing a trick on the girl—giving her a morning-after concoction that will turn her stomach. But J.D. puts "hull cleaner" in the drink, and Heather No. 1 meets a grisly end.

Up to the point of the murder, I was on the side of this risk-taking movie. But murder puts satire on another level, and I think Lehmann and Waters lose control of their material. Earlier, they've established Veronica as a decent girl, so it makes no sense that she'd walk away, as she does now, from the crime; she's supposed to be bright, so she wouldn't trust J.D., as she does here, a second time—a mistake that leads to more deaths. Veronica stops making sense as a character, and the way the filmmakers show the school responding to the deaths (which Veronica and J.D. pass off as teen suicides) suggests that Waters and Lehmann may be even more heartless and glib than the people they are satirizing. The humor turns sick and self-important, and the merriment sours.

Winona Ryder, who was the lugubrious young girl in *Beetlejuice*, is adorable in her confusions—dark, pretty, intelligent, an ideal teenage actress. But Christian Slater's charm is opaque. Who is the smiling charmer supposed to be, anyway? An avenging angel, the devil, a psychopath? Lehmann has considerable talent: From the beginning, he purposely blurs the line between reality and fantasy, using a gliding camera, slow motion, and candied colors, and he may be a new master of violent reverie, a De Palma in the making. But looking for a grand climax, he falls into low-grade schlock. *Heathers* disintegrates into bloody confrontation.

Heathers was conceived in the Reagan era, but released now, a blast at the cant of "niceness" covering greed and opportunism, it becomes the first significant Bush-era movie. Satire is so rare in American movies that there may be a tendency to overpraise it when it appears. I support *Heathers* in a general way: It's the kind of challenging movie that the independent cinema badly needs to make. But I don't really like it. The filmmakers' loathing for American youth seems excessive and, in its own way, humorless. *Heathers* shows us, rather frighteningly, what a black comedy made without much sensibility looks like.

NEWSDAY, 3/31/89, Part III/p. 3, Mike McGrady

One reason I always look forward to films based on high-school students is that they're an opportunity to study new trends in the language used by today's MTV generation. "Heathers," a comic treatment of teenage suicide written by first-time screenwriter Daniel Waters, freely blends current usage with Waters' own linguistic innovations.

The Waters script refers to a nerd as "a pillow case." Leaving is announced this way: "I've gotta motor." A lapse in intelligence is greeted with, "What'd you have, a brain tumor for breakfast?" A temporary bad mood is "a spoke in my menstrual cycle." Making love is "jamming." A beer is "a kegger." An overweight student is known as "Martha Dumptruck." If something is unsatisfactory, it is "really gnarly." A good guy is a "righteous dude" and a bad girl is "a megabitch." A turn-down is somewhat more poetic, "No way, no day."

A typical conversation, printed in its entirety.

"How very!" says Heather.

"Late," says another Heather.

"Definitely," says a third Heather.

This problem of too many girls named Heather in one school is alleviated when two other students give one of the Heathers a "wake-up cup of liquid drainer" and make it look like suicide. One of the Heather-killers (Winona Ryder) suffers a moment of deep concern: "I'm gonna have to send my test scores to San Quentin instead of Stanford." The other is a new student (Christian Slater), a righteous dude who wears an earring and lives by this code: "The extreme always seems to make an impression."

Agreed. But there are several kinds of impressions. "Heathers" is extreme in using teenage suicide as its base for humor, but the impression is something less than favorable. Like so many other contemporary black comedies, the film can't decide whether it wants to be comedy or melodrama, with the unfortunate result that it concludes by being both unbelievable and unfunny.

So let me express this as clearly as possible to first-time director Michael Lehmann, who may well be a righteous dude but has become involved in a project that is gnarly from start to finish. Definitely. To writer Waters I have but one question: What'd you have, a brain tumor for breakfast? Most of the actors are pillowcases, if I am understanding that term properly. The film is simply not very. In sum: No way, no day.

NEWSWEEK, 4/3/89, p. 67, David Ansen

With its teenage cast and high-school setting, "Heathers" runs the risk of being mistaken for yet another adolescent romp. It's anything but. As black as pitch, this twisted comedy of high-school horrors is a work of genuine audacity. First-time screenwriter Daniel Waters conjures up a middle-American high school dominated by a shallow and callow clique called "The Heathers," named after the three perfectly groomed and perfectly nasty snobs who share the same first name. The fourth member of the clique is our heroine Veronica (Winona Ryder), who defies social etiquette by falling for the motorcycle riding outcast J.D. (Christian Slater). More than a little Mephistophelian, J.D. has a way of making Veronica's darkest wishes come true. Is it by accident or design that the first Heather, who Veronica wishes were dead, expires after drinking cleaning fluid? Waters and first-time director Michael Lehmann not only get laughs out of murder, they even dare to make fun of the sensitive issue of teen suicide. As the body count at Westerburg High grows, J.D. and his innocent accomplice disguise the murders as suicide, and the filmmakers flail the hypocrisy of kids and parents alike in their hollow and media-prompted responses to the tragedies.

Satirically trigger-happy, "Heathers" is bound to evoke outrage, but its jaundiced vision of adolescence isn't as cynical as first appears. Lehmann isn't in perfect control—the movie gets off to a flat-footed start, and the conclusion is chaotic—but when "Heathers" hits its stride, it reaches wild and original comic highs. And in Ryder, and actress with subtleties beyond her years, and Slater, whose sly charisma evokes Jack Nicholson, it has two of the freshest young talents around, Teens may resent "Heathers's" scalding irony, but for anyone out of high school this provocative blast of satirical malice is to be relished.

TIME, 4/17/89, p. 83, Richard Corliss

Where are the teenpix of yesterday? Gone with the demographic wind. As the U.S. movie audience ages toward thirtysomething, Hollywood has discarded the teen genre like so many Molly Ringwald paper dolls. What's left? Only caustic satire, as in the new black comedy *Heathers*, or retro fantasy, as in *Sing*.

At suburban Ohio's Westerburg High, a quartet of teen princesses runs the school. They are called the Heathers, because three of the four are named Heather. The fourth, Veronica (Winona Ryder, pallid of face and sharp as Cheddar), is at first pleased to be accepted by this "bunch of Swatch dogs and Diet Coke heads. They're, like, people I work with, and our job is being popular." Still, she is ready for a sinister avenging force in her life, a juvenile delinquent, a James Dean. He turns out to be J.D., a new boy in town who is itching to make trouble (played by Christian Slater, handsomely imitating Jack Nicholson's silky menace). Veronica may want to get back at one of the nasty Heathers by dropping a phlegm glob in her morning coffee, but J.D. has bigger plans. Soon this Heather is dead, though she does reappear in a dream to whine that "my afterlife is so boring! If I have to sing *Kum Ba Yah* one more time . . ." Then J.D. dispatches two boorish jocks who bugged Veronica. No loss, he shrugs: "Football season is over. Kurt and Ram had nothing to offer the school but date rape and AIDS jokes."

The screenplay by Daniel Waters (a find) offers all that and much more. It believes, like J.D., that "the extreme always seems to make an impression." Its language is extreme—a voluptuously precise lexicon of obscene put-downs and dry ironies—and so is its scenerio, which adjusts the teenpix format to accommodate subjects as bleak as copycat suicides and killer peer pressure.

Heathers finds laughs in these maladies without making fun of them because Waters writes from inside teenagers. He knows what makes them miserable and what makes them bad: that they are already adults but can't accept the fact. "Why are you such a megabitch?" Veronica asks a surviving Heather, and the reply is, "Because I *can* be." *Heathers* locates the emotional totalitarianism lurking in a prom queen's heart. If Michael Lehmann's direction were a bit more astute, the movie could be the classic genre mutation it aims to be: Andy Hardy meets *Badlands*.

Sing, written by Dean Pitchford and directed by Richard Baskin, could be called *42nd Street: Duh Motion Pitchuh*. It carts all the clichés of a Broadway backstage story to a decrepit Brooklyn Central High and populates it with *Sesame Street* renegades. Each class puts on a musical skit, or "sing," with groups led by a black, a Greek, an Italian and a Jew—the "rainbow coalition" that exists only in Hollywood musicals. Yes, the tough Italian stud (Peter Dobson) falls for the sweet Jewish girl (Jessica Steen). And, honest, when the star of her skit gets knocked unconscious, the stud takes over and saves the show. You're going out there a punkster, but you've got to come back a star!

The dialogue is all song cues; Pitchford's songs are standard technopop, except for a comic showstopper, called *Life Ain't Worth Livin' (When You're Dead)*, that the suicidal teens of *Heathers* might take to heart. Otherwise, *Sing* is strictly *Gold Diggers* turned to brass. In the latest teenpix class portrait, it's a dropout.

VILLAGE VOICE, 4/4/89, P. 53 J. Hoberman

When it comes to the survival arts, the high school in *Heathers*—a surefire cult film opening here Friday in the unlikely precincts of the Upper East Side—is as epic an arena as the Roman Colosseum. This black comedy of young (blood) lust, semiconscious desire, and rampant antisocial urges is the most audacious of teenpix, as well as one of the most stylish. Articulating an adolescent hyperreality that's more pop and lurid than the teen Kafka of *Sixteen Candles*, the secular humanist verisimilitude of *Fast Times at Ridgemont High*, and the morbid muckraking of *River's Edge, Heathers* is a brazen provocation.

There probably hasn't been as clever a teen cartoon since *Lord Love a Duck* apotheosized Tuesday Weld some 20-odd years ago, but, hilarious and irresponsible, *Heathers* invites adult outrage by satirizing the sensitive subject of teenage suicide. At the same time, it feeds youthful solidarity with a brutally entertaining representation of the high school caste system and sensational use of adolescent patois. The movie resounds with audience echo lines. "Fuck me gently with a chainsaw. Do I look like Mother Teresa?," the rhetorical question delivered with crushing disdain by the school's reigning 16-year-old megabitch, is only the most irresistibly quotable of half a dozen instant classics.

Immediately establishing its métier as the lunchroom theater of cruelty, *Heathers* plunges into the glamour and callousness of adolescence, with Westerburg High's "most powerful clique" patrolling the school cafeteria—three suavely diffident ultrababes named Heather, plus their ambivalent pal Veronica (Winona Ryder), picking their way past the earnest dweebs who collect food for famine victims, pausing to prank the most unfortunate of fat girls, Martha "Dumptruck," while dazzling star jocks and hapless geeks alike with the trick question of their lunchtime poll. (You win $5 million two days before aliens announce they'll blow up the earth—so how do you spend the money?)

The caf in this densely textured, highly choreographed scene is as redolent as a locker room— you can almost smell the mixture of hormones and anxiety, the avid yearning of the Heather-smitten masses (and the Heathers' loathing for the physically unlovely), the visceral embarrassment of a member of the elite encountering a childhood friend outgrown, the ferocious pressure that traps Veronica in her need for Heather acceptance. Fetching 16-year-old Winona Ryder, who plays the conflicted Veronica with deeper-than-method conviction, has the unselfconsciously contorted facial expressions of youth down pat. "These are people I work with, and our job is being popular and shit," she lamely tells J.D. (Christian Slater), the rebellious hipster who catches her eye and seduces her into a clandestine anti-Heather war of attrition.

Irritating at first, Slater's ongoing Jack Nicholson imitation becomes a kabuki representation of high school cool. (It also link *Heathers* to *The Witches of Eastwick* as Americanized *Faust*.) Ostensibly set in Sherwood [sic], Ohio, *Heathers* seems spiritually more attuned to Beverly Hills or the San Fernando Valley. The 26-year-old screenwriter, Daniel Waters, wrote the script while working behind the counter of an L.A. video store. *Heathers*'s protagonists are filthy rich, fearfully sophisticated, and heavily into arcane slang ("Get crucial"). The ridiculously smooth and snottily self-assured Heather Chandler (Kim Walker) even has a Barbara Kruger "I Shop Therefore I Am" postcard pasted up in her locker. These cool, sarcastic creatures are the children of the blessed.

Still, *Heathers* is something like *The Breakfast Club in Hell*. Once J.D. and Veronica send Heather C. to that great prom night in the sky, covering their tracks with a masterfully forged suicide note ("I die knowing nobody knew the real me"), the movie successfully navigates a difficult transition from the realm of John Hughes to that of Alfred Hitchcock. Heather's "suicide" is not without unexpected side effects. Bulimics can suddenly keep down their lunch, while her poignant missive becomes feeling fodder for an aging hippie's English class. ("Are we gonna be tested on this?" one student demands to know.) More popular than ever, Heather becomes the subject of a two-page spread in the yearbook, as well as an ongoing role model. The hapless Dumptruck tapes a note to her chest and walks into traffic—"another case of a geek trying to imitate the cool people and failing miserably."

Michael Lehmann, the 31-year-old neophyte director, handles this material with a modulated De Palma style (caressing crane shots, dramatic overheads, tricky color coordination), drifting in and out of a casual pop surrealism that owes more to MTV than Dali and Bunuel. (Cinematographer Francis Kenney shot "Girls Just Want To Have Fun," among other videos.) The movie is smartly paced and skillfully acted, but what continually astonishes is Waters's stunning dialogue. ("Dan handed me this 200-page tome," Lehmann told *Premiere*, "unreadable, unfilmable, and one of the funniest, strangest scripts I'd ever seen," In the press kit, Waters describes reading *Seventeen* as "science fiction.") In certain venues, *Heathers* should provoke as much live feedback as *The Rocky Horror Picture Show*: "What's your damage, Heather? Did you have a brain tumor for breakfast?"

No teenpic is without its exploitation aspects, and, having prudently softened Veronica's persona, *Heathers* can't quite achieve closure. After flirting with slasherdom, Lehmann and Waters ultimately make a less-than-successful attempt to go genre-realistic. Still, much of *Heathers* is stylized in unpredictable ways. (The screening room in which I saw the film was full of nervous giggling, with individual hysterics for specific bits of business.) Just as the austere use of pop music renders Waters's dialogue all the more crucial, the total absence of mall culture serves to exaggerate the two basic rhythms of adolescent life—namely, the endless, droning repetition of parental injunctions and the exciting, unpredictable torture of school.

Peer pressure rules—and so does impulse behavior. With the exception of J.D.'s appropriately demonic dad, the film's adults are universally brain damaged. ("Grow up" is the most cutting of the movie's many insults.) What gives *Heathers* its particular edge, however, is its identification with adolescent acting out. *Heathers* is a comedy in which urges can't be squelched, the thought is identical to the deed. "You believed [me] because you wanted to believed—your true feelings were too gross and icky to face," J.D. tells Veronica after she has confided in her diary that her "teen angst bullshit has a body count." Conceptually gross and icky almost to the max, *Heathers* invites comparisons with *Carrie*. But it is really more like *Carrie* in reverse—the destructive power resides not in the wretched and the repressed but the privileged and libidinal.

Heather's real precursor is Dutch director Renee Dalder's 1976 drive-in flick, *Massacre at Central High*, a complex political allegory about revolution and authority that, far more alienated than *Zéro de Conduite*, substitutes a high school for George Orwell's barnyard. The American public high school is, after all, the closest institution this society has to a democratic meritocracy—it's virtually the last place where all economic classes have the opportunity to meet and interact on a more or less equal footing. In this sense, *Heathers* is antiutopian for more than just attacking teenage innocence. As the satanic J.D. points out, "The only place different social types can genuinely get along is heaven" Given the demographic preponderance of youthful filmgoers, *Heathers* may be the most socially realistic American movie released this spring.

Also reviewed in:

NATION, 4/17/89, p. 530, Stuart Klawans
NEW YORK TIMES, 3/31/89, p. C8, Janet Maslin
NEW YORKER, 4/17/89, p. 115, Pauline Kael
VARIETY, 1/25-31/89, p. 15
WASHINGTON POST, 4/14/89, p. C1, Rita Kempley
WASHINGTON POST, 4/14/89, Weekend/p. 33, Desson Hawe

HEAVY PETTING

A Skouras Pictures release of a Fossil Films production. *Producer:* Obie Benz and Carol Noblitt. *Director:* Obie Benz and Josh Waletzky. *Director of Photography:* Sandi Sissel. *Editor:* Judith Sobol, Josh Waletzky, and Edith Becker. *Running Time:* 80 minutes. *MPAA Rating:* Not Rated.

WITH: David Byrne, Sandra Bernhard, Allen Ginsberg, William Burroughs, Ann Magnuson, Josh Mostel, Spalding Gray, Laurie Anderson, Abbie Hoffman, Barry Bartkowski, Judith Malina, John Oates, Paula Longendyke, Elizabeth Lahey, Duka, Zoe Tamerlaine Lund, Marshall Turner, Wayne Jobson, Jim Dyer, Jacki Ochs, Frederic Lahey, Frances Fisher, Sandi Sissel.

LOS ANGELES TIMES, 9/23/89, Calendar/p. 5, Michael Wilmington

"Heavy Petting" isn't much of a documentary, but it's probably a terrific make-out movie.

The subject is teen-age sexuality in the postwar era and the film makers take a jocular attitude that shows they think sex is great and sex education a howl. Producer-co-director Obie Benz juxtaposes educational films, archetypal movie sex icons (Presley, Dean, Monroe, Brando, Tuesday Weld) and the unabashed memoirs of 40 "witnesses"—who collectively recall the days of cruising, petting, making out and trying to go all the way.

All this madly clinical, boobishly straight-faced or dizzily confessional material comes swimming at you in a stew of irony and rock 'n' roll. It's a movie about hypocrisy. It shows what society told adolescents to do, and then has 40 ex-teens describe what they actually did—or in most cases, tried to do but didn't quite succeed at. "I wasn't head of the dating team," Josh Mostel relates with a world-weary look—though he claims that, when he finally mastered more solitary vices, "the rest is history."

For 74 minutes, the film makers bombard us with racy snippets from a loopy cornucopia of postwar sex-education films: forgotten schoolroom turkeys with titles like "Dating: Do's and Don'ts," "How to Say No" and "Physical Aspects of Puberty." In these mostly monochrome films—shot with delightfully primitive techniques, stilted dialogue and charmingly inept actors— puzzled teens and their all-knowing elders come to terms with burning topics like pornography, condoms and venereal disease.

In "Perversion for Profit," most riveting of these mini-epics, a beady-eyed announcer, with a curious half-smile, shows us dozens of nudie magazines with strategic black bars covering the models: all, he insists, part of a communist conspiracy to sap and impurify American teen-agers.

Between this deluge, we get interviews with people like Sandra Bernhard, Judith Malina and the late Abbie Hoffman, who laughs and smiles with an air that, in retrospect, suggests a desperate attempt to recapture happiness. Ann Magnuson, looking sweet and pixieish, recalls how no one would dance with her at a school party. Allen Ginsberg laments that no one loves him, while William Burroughs gives him arch glances. Spalding Gray—who looks like someone you couldn't trust in the dark—describes the techniques of groping, while documentarian Jackie Ochs lists the strategies of fending it off.

It's difficult to connect the two halves of the film. The sex films are mostly from the '50s, while most of the "witnesses" seem to have grown up in the '60s or later. But this time warp fits the film. It's a post-Sexual Revolution look at the "quaint" sexual mores of a vanished past. As such, it's a scattershot, AIDS-era assault (Times-rated Mature for language and theme) that misses as often as it hits. But that doesn't mean it won't have an aphrodisiac effect.

NEW YORK POST, 9/22/89, p. 29, Jami Bernard

Comedian Sandra Bernhard allowed a boy to give her "a shot in my butt" while playing "doctor" in return for a popsicle. Performance artist Ann Magnuson recalls that the word "penis" used to make her howl with laughter. The late Abbie Hoffman remembers "the Great Circle Jerk of '51."

Anecdotes about sexual initiation are always good for a laugh, especially when they come mostly from famous people, and when they are put together, documentary-style, in a film as breezily entertaining as "Heavy Petting."

Twenty-three knowns and unknowns give talking-head interviews about such wide-ranging topics as learning to masturbate (Josh Mostel: "By college I got the hang of it") to feeling sexually inadequate (Magnuson: "I had no breasts; all the cheerleaders had breasts, except Sharon Tromley").

These interviews are scattered among footage of laughable '50s educational films, adolescent behavior instructionals and clips from such cinematic intoxicants as Marlon Brando in "The Wild One," Marilyn Monroe in "Bus Stop" and James Dean in "Rebel Without a Cause."

Rock music is used effectively also to demonstrate the age-old adult paranoia about teen-age hormones on the rampage. When a square, old interviewer asks Elvis Presley why he can't just sing without all that hip action, Elvis looks confused and faintly annoyed: "You take the wiggle out of it, it's finished."

With the ol' devil jungle beat so firmly tied in with libido (you know: sex, drugs and rock 'n' roll), there is an ample use of Golden Oldies soundtrack laid tongue-in-cheek style over the arcane footage, providing a sort of lewd commentary on what those pure-of-heart '50s lads and lassies were doing at their weenie roasts.

The resulting movie is a reminder of how painful and wonderful first experiences can be. Hoffman's never-ending search for "bare tit," musician David Byrne's novel use for the Davy Crockett hat, mysterious teen pregnancies and the tyrannies of peer pressure all make for a prurient good time.

William Burroughs looks on in barely concealed disdain as Allen Ginsberg admits he has never felt lovable. Burroughs claims he has never been a love junkie, needing no love from anybody. "Maybe my cat," he adds.

A while ago, there was a "Funny," a similar sort of "documentary" in which a mix of the famous and the ordinary told the funniest joke they had ever heard. That movie didn't work.

"Heavy Petting" *does* work, however. Even the most blatantly humorous anecdote of sexual awakening carries with it an element of personal pain and embarrassment. And, as you'd expect, the wide range of wacky experiences reinforces what we already know—that with society's never-ending war on the libido, it's a wonder any of us grow up to establish and maintain healthy relationships.

There are plenty of cheap shots to be taken with a subject like this, and Obie Benz, who produced and directed, takes enough of them. Imbecilic educational films are always good for a laugh in any context. But Benz does manage to weave the many elements together in a judicious and enlightening way without sacrificing the spirit of fun that is at the heart of "Heavy Petting."

NEWSDAY, 9/22/89, Part III/p. 5, Terry Kelleher

It should be a real hot number, but "Heavy Petting" plays around and leaves you frustrated. Mama told you there'd be movies like this.

The subject of this "docucomedy" is teenage dating and sex (such as it was) between the end of World War II and the start of the "sexual revolution." The central question is: What did kids know and how in heaven's name did they find out?

With its use of now-campy footage from educational films, newsreels and features, "Heavy Petting" should be guaranteed easy laughs—the "Reefer Madness" of making out. So how come it's a disappointment?

The answer may be found in the movie's history. Obie Benz and Pierce Rafferty started research for "Heavy Petting" in 1982, after they'd worked together on a darker docucomedy, "The Atomic Cafe." They assembled a wealth of material but couldn't find a unifying theme, and Embassy Pictures shelved the project.

Benz returned to "Heavy Petting" in 1985, taking charge as producer and director. He decided to supplement the vintage clips with interviews of real people who would reminisce about their teenage groping days. But now that the movie has emerged under the Skouras Pictures banner, it still doesn't hang together.

"Heavy Petting" is downright promiscuous in the way it flits from one theme to another. Hot-rodding, motorcycle gangs, VD, contraception, pregnancy, pornography, rock and roll. Brief remarks from the interviewees don't link the disparate elements; they just add to the jumble. The film lasts only 80 minutes, but you get the feeling the editing process has just begun.

It's not as if the witnesses don't have a few amusing anecdotes to offer. Obviously Josh Mostel could work up a whole stand-up comedy routine on his dating mishaps. David Byrne has an intriguingly shy way of describing a teen orgy, and Spalding Gray provides a nice touch of old-fashioned New England perversity.

The most interesting testimony comes from William Burroughs and Allen Ginsberg, who appear together. Ginsberg confides that he felt unloved as a youth. Burroughs snorts, "Do you *want* to be loved?" The film moves on for a while, then returns to the literary twosome just as Ginsberg is turning the question back on Burroughs. "Not really," says the author of "Naked Lunch," eyes averted from Ginsberg and the camera. It's a moment to remember, though it probably belongs in a different movie.

There are a number of noncelebrities among the interviewees, and their little stories inevitably seem less amusing, because they come to us with no personal context. We probably wouldn't care about Laurie Anderson's square girlhood, either, if we didn't have a fair idea of what it led to.

Some of the old cautionary films look funny, all right, but Benz never stays with any one of them long enough for the audience to get a bona-fide bang out of it. Too often, "Heavy Petting" looks like a trailer for itself. You think you've got to see this movie, then you realize you just did.

VILLAGE VOICE, 10/3/89, p. 72, Georgia Brown

For *Heavy Petting*, their satire on sex in the dark ages of the '50s, Obie Benz and Josh Waletzky have put together a pretty heavy cast, too. Following lead-talking head David Byrne come such high school heroes and nerds as Sandra Bernhard, Spalding Gray, Ann Magnuson, Josh Mostel, and Laurie Anderson. Posed tastefully against *Reds*-style black, most are quite funny about the painful business of adolescent sex—or sexual rites and etiquette, anyway. William Burroughs may be both funniest and truest when he just winces as Allen Ginsberg describes telling a girl, "Boy, you've got big breasts!" and getting smartly hit with her bookbag. In this film homosexuality is just a gleam in the beholder's eye. This cute and coy documentary (from an idea by *The Atomic Cafe*'s Pierce Rafferty) doesn't want to get into anything, well, heavy.

These may be real people (one trusts) but here they're tightly edited performers, deftly turning any ill effects of so much pressure and taboo into amusing anecdote. Byrne describes the mysteries of impregnation ("If we went skinny dipping . . . what if I would leak or something?") and of masturbation ("You had a certain amount in you, and you'd use it and go dry about 18"). Cinematographer Sandi Sissel's perspective on pregnancy was somewhat starker: "Mother said she'd rather me get run over by a car." Judith Malina recalls the night she and Julian Beck saved her mother's life: "Open the windows, turn off the gas, we'll get married!"

Woven between the interviews are quaint clips from instructional films (such as *How To Say No* and *Physical Aspects of Puberty*), period newsreels, and B movies. The soundtrack—songs such as "Annie Had a Baby," "Blueberry Hill"—reinforces a point. Youngsters would be entertained and reassured. *Heavy Petting* makes an entertaining health ed film.

Also reviewed in:
NEW YORK TIMES, 9/22/89, p. C13, Janet Maslin
VARIETY, 2/22-28/89, p. 249
WASHINGTON POST, 9/23/89, p. C11, Hal Hinson

HENRY V

A Samuel Goldwyn Company release. *Executive Producer:* Stephen Evans. *Producer:* Bruce Sharman. *Director:* Kenneth Branagh. *Screenplay/Adaptation:* Kennneth Branagh. *Based on the play by:* William Shakespeare. *Director of Photography:* Kenneth MacMillan. *Editor:* Mike Bradsell. *Music:* Patrick Doyle. *Music Editor:* Graham Sutton. *Sound:* David Crozier and (music) Christopher Dibble. *Sound Editor:* John Poyner. *Production Designer:* Tim Harvey. *Art Director:* Norman Dorme. *Special Effects:* Ian Wingrove. *Costumes:* Phyllis Dalton. *Make-up:* Peter Frampton. *Stunt Coordinator:* Vic Armstrong. *Running time:* 135 minutes. *MPAA Rating:* PG.

CAST: Kenneth Branagh (Henry V); Derek Jacobi (Chorus); Simon Shepherd (Gloucester); James Larkin (Bedford); Brian Blessed (Exeter); James Simmons (York); Paul Gregory (Westmoreland); Charles Kay (Archbishop of Canterbury); Alec McCowen (Ely); Fabian Cartwright (Cambridge); Stephen Simms (Scroop); Jay Villiers (Grey); Edward Jewesbury (Erpingham); Ian Holm (Captain Fluellen); Daniel Webb (Gower); Jimmy Yuill (Jamy); John Sessions (MacMorris), Shaun Prendergast (Bates); Pat Doyle (Court); Michael Williams (Williams); Richard Briers (Bardolph); Geoffrey Hutchings (Nym); Robert Stephens (Pistol); Robbie Coltrane (Sir John Falstaff); Christian Bale (Boy); Judi Dench (Mistress Quickly); Paul Scofield (French King); Michael Maloney (Dauphin); Harold Innocent (Burgundy); Richard Clifford (Orleans); Colin Hurley (Grandpre); Richard Easton (Constable); Christopher Ravenscroft (Mountjoy); Emma Thompson (Katherine);

Geraldine McEwan (Alice); David Lloyd Meredith (Governor of Harfleur); David Parfitt (Messenger); Nicholas Ferguson (Warwick); Tom Whitehouse (Talbot); Nigel Greaves (Berri); Julian Gartside (Bretagne); Mark Inman (1st Soldier); Chris Armstrong (2nd Soldier); Calum Yuill (Child).

CHRISTIAN SCIENCE MONITOR, 11/16/89, p. 11, David Sterritt

Kenneth Branagh is an ambitious young artist. Walking in the footsteps of no less a legend than Laurence Olivier, who tackled the same challege back in 1944, this 28-year-old filmmaker has written, directed, and starred in a new movie version of "Henry V," determined to give Shakespeare's great play a vigorous new interpretation for the '80s.

The result of his effort has dignity, intelligence, and moments of considerable power. But it remains too cautious, too deliberate, too polite for its own good. Those who relish any competent rendering of Shakespeare will surely be pleased with it. Those looking for a new and exciting perspective will just as surely be disappointed.

The most important problem of the new "Henry V" is Mr. Branagh's failure to dig deeply into the hero's psychology. In production notes for the movie, Branaugh compares his vision with Olivier's stressing the idea that Olivier saw the play as a "hymn to England," while he himself sees it as a study of "a young monarch burdened with guilt" because of circumstances arising from his father's seizure of power. That's a promising approach to the drama. Branagh is right that the world of 1944, torn to pieces by World War II, was different from today's world in ways that make Olivier's heroic "Henry V" seem dated in some important respects.

Branagh has not replaced that heroicism with compelling new qualities, however. His wish to explore Henry's mind as well as his deeds and to display a heroism that's "spiritual as well as physical" remains more an aspiration than an accomplishment. Branagh also fails to show judicious detachment from the play's rousing celebration of militarism, an aspect of the drama that's better treated as a historical relic than a vital component of its current worth.

Not that Branagh's movie is lacking in all interest. His performance in the title role has moments of verve and energy. Derek Jacobi, in modern dress to signify a "Brechtian" approach, brings real fire to the Chorus's appearances. And the cast is peppered with experienced Shakespeareans: Paul Scofield as the French King, Ian Holm as Fluellen, and Judi Dench as Mistress Quickly, to name the most prominent. Kenneth MacMillan's cinematography has an effectively dark aura that's daringly different from Olivier's hugely colorful treatment, and Simon Rattle's music score has its moments.

It must also be noted, however, that Branagh has nothing up his sleeve to compete with Olivier's inspiration in giving "Henry V" a creatively cinematic structure, beginning the action at the Globe Theatre and later opening it into the real world. And the battle at the climax of the tale, which clearly took a great deal of Branagh's energy, seems overlong and underinspired-especially in contrast to Orson Welles's chilling battlefield scenes in "Falstaff."

In his notes to the production, Branagh says he wanted to make a "Henry V" that would satisfy Shakespearean scholars *and* filmgoers who admire such lightweight enterainment pictures as "Crocodile Dundee" and its ilk. I suspect both groups will find things to like and dislike in his movie, but that neither will be wholly satisfied by it. It's a respectable attempt, not an exciting one.

LOS ANGELES TIMES, 11/8/89, Calendar/p. 1, Michael Wilmington

Heroism is something the movies have often cheapened; verbal poetry and rhetoric they often ignore altogether. Yet—seemingly on fire with all three—the young British actor-director Kenneth Branagh has brought them, in blazing measures, to his adaptation of William Shakespeare's "Henry V."

At first, it seems a madly audacious endeavor. Branagh—trying to match Laurence Olivier's astonishing triple feat of adapting, directing and starring in a filmed "Henry"—butts heads with an inarguably great movie and the champion British classical actor of the century.

Yet, his skill and passion equal his daring. This thrilling new version of the play complements rather than challenges Olivier's. If Olivier gave us the glint of sunlight on armor and the wind roaring through the pennants and flags, Branagh gives us the rot, the mold, the wounds and the crusted blood underneath.

Olivier, in a conceit dazzling in its wittiness and prettiness, staged "Henry" in a mock-up of the Globe Theater and sets skewed to the style of Renaissance Flemish or Dutch paintings. Branagh's sets are the vast, empty castles of movie epics or horror shows, and his battlefields are plateaus of mud and gore under gray, bristling skies, where men die foully. If Olivier gave us the ultimate poet-warrior king, Branagh gives us a blunt but brave boy, a sawed-off, sandy-haired runt, passing through fire and chaos to manhood. Olivier, with nonpareil irony and grace, told the story from the top down. Branagh tells it from the bottom up—with all its vileness, misery and uncertainty.

This is a dark, savage "Henry"—post-Marx, post-Brecht, post-"Paths of Glory," post-Vietnam—in which the heroism is undercut with bloodshed and in which the Chorus (Derek Jacobi) glides, at first, through a movie sound stage, all in black, his voice scarringly urbane.

Death is stripped of every scrap of nobility. Both sides, British and French, are equally full of heroism and cowardice, sadism and self-sacrifice. In place of Olivier's great showpiece scene—the equestrian French army charging jubilantly right to left in a burst of stallion exhilaration—Branagh gives us a "Chimes of Midnight"-like battle of stabbings and clouts in the mud, capped by a somber, dazzling Wellesian tracking shot on Henry, as he carries the corpse of Falstaff's Boy across a somber, reeking wasteland of broken bodies.

Branagh, only 28—about Henry's age at Agincourt, and almost a decade younger than Olivier when he made his 1944 version—is a current *Wunderkind* of British theater. And his versatility in his only two movie parts, "High Season" and "A Month in the Country," was shocking, as if the same actor could master roles meant for either Monty Python or Montgomery Clift.

In playing Henry V, he's taking one of the great glamour roles in Shakespeare. Yet he deglamorizes it, ripening steadily through the forge of warfare until the burst of fiery rhetoric on his great "St. Crispin's" speech.

"We few, we happy few, we band of brothers," keens the erstwhile Prince Hal, his face shining in the gloom, to his mud-encrusted, outmanned army and, like Churchill's surging wartime oratory during the Blitz, this speech makes the blood run hot, the sinews quiver. That's the force of Branagh's conception. Olivier, working in wartime to arouse national spirit, gave us a hero who surpassed understanding. Branagh roots his in the loam of common character.

The movie is about a different kind of heroism as well: the heroism of the theatrical ensemble. Paul Scofield is an uncharacteristically sage King Charles VI, Ian Holm a dour Fluellen; Robert Stephens a scabrous, cowardly thick Pistol; Charles Kay and Alec McCowen two magnificently conspiratorial church prelates; Emma Thompson a notable non-feather-brained Katherine (playing a deliciously wry courting scene with her husband, Branagh); Robbie Coltrane (in flashback scenes borrowed from the "Henry IV" plays a sad, blubbery dying Falstaff.

Assembling and vivifying this marvelous cast, Branagh has the ultimate justification of his "Henry." Great roles like these should not lie fallow because of the vagaries of studios. We don't need less, more perfect Shakespearean movie adaptations. We need many more.

The British won at Agincourt because of superior technology. The expert Welsh archers mowed the French cavalry down. But in Shakespeare's world, they also won because of gorgeous poetry and heart-stirring eloquence. Branagh's expertly cut and reshaped "Henry V" (Times-rated mature for violence) gives us the grimy face of war, yet he also gives us the guts—and the soul and poetry that animate them both. Egoist and daring scamp Branagh may well be, but so, in ways, were Olivier and Welles. It's a pleasure to welcome this young lion and his company's splendid "Henry" to their ranks.

MONTHLY FILM BULLETIN, 10/89, p. 302, Geoff Brown

1415. Convinced by the Archbishop of Canterbury that he has a legal claim to the French throne, King Henry V prepares for invasion. As his forces gather at Southampton, Henry quashes a conspiracy among his nobility, and sends Exeter with an utimatum to the French Court. At the Boar's Head Tavern, Mistress Quickly, Bardolph, Pistol and Nym mourn the roguish Sir John Falstaff, Henry's former mentor, who has passed away. With war imminent, the men join up, along with Falstaff's young serving boy. Before laying siege to Harfleur, Henry exhorts his troops; after a fierce battle, the town's governor relents and opens the gates. At Rouen, the French Court determines to crush the invader, while the Dauphin's sister Katherine takes tuition in English from her maid, Alice. Henry's army is bedraggled and famished. When Bardolph is caught pillaging and sentenced to hang, Henry ignores their past friendship and allows the execution. The French finally decide to give battle. Nerves are taut in both camps, and Henry wanders in disguise listening to the common soldiers. Williams' questioning of the justice of the English cause sets Henry pondering on the burden of kingship; but by morning—St. Crispin's Day—he recovers confidence and sends his men into battle with a rousing speech. On the field of Agincourt, English archers wreak havoc among the French cavalry, who sustain heavy losses. After giving thanks to God for his victory, the grieving Henry carries the body of Falstaff's serving boy—killed in a massacre of all the army's juveniles—across the muddy battlefield. While peace terms with France are negotiated, Henry sets about wooing Princess Katherine (despite the language difficulties). The treaty is signed and the marriage arranged: England and France and united.

"The more I thought about it", Kenneth Branagh explains in the production notes, "the more convinced I became that here was a play to be reclaimed from jingoism and its World War Two associations". Goodbye, then, to the virile spirit and rich colours of Olivier's imaginative patriotic pageant; hello to a bullying, calculating king, to an Agincourt drenched in mud, to "war is hell". If any war is brought to mind it is now World War One, particularly in scenes where Henry's soldiers lay siege to Harfleur, bogged down in their trenches, while flames and explosions erupt all around.

Branagh's interpretation is certainly justified, both by the text and by recent theatrical tradition. In this first production of his own Renaissance Films, he has taken the opportunity of the larger cinematic canvas to punch home the point with added scenes and business. Flashbacks to Prince Hal, Falstaff and the roisterers in *Henry IV Part One* are injected to show how times, and the king, have changed. Bardolph's execution—an offstage event in Shakespeare—now becomes a prominent set-piece, with Henry glaring imperviously at the gnarled old acquaintance strung up on a tree. Even the Chorus (Derek Jacobi in contemporary coat and scarf) gives the corpse an admonishing glance before launching into the Act IV prologue.

But the dubiousness of the film's style becomes painfully apparent during the Agincourt battle. With grey skies above the mud below, the English and French clank their swords in hoary slow motion, while shots of English arrows raining down are repeated several times too often. After the horrific French death toll is enumerated, and praise given to God for the English victory, Henry slowly carries the body of Falstaff's serving boy across the devastated landscape, while a single voice—followed, of course, by full chorus and fulsome orchestra—intones a tear-yanking setting of the psalm "Non nobis, Domine".

The film's visual tedium, vulgarity and musical mediocrity would be more bearable if Branagh himself were a more persuasive lead actor. At first the omens are good. After a grandiose entrance through a huge doorway's shaft of light, he buckles down to the early scenes' politicking with quiet but threatening intensity. But once battle commences, his high-decibel readings and facial grimaces hardly suit the intense closeups favoured by Branagh the director: as a result, both of Henry's arias of exhortation, before Harfleur and Agincourt, fall fatally flat. Among the rest of the cast, Robbie Coltrane (Falstaff) is absurdly miscast, Brian Blessed huffs and puffs as Exeter, Judi Dench makes a superlative Mistress Quickly, while Emma Thompson and Geraldine McEwan (Katherine and her maid) provide a welcome oasis of fun and high spirits.

NEW YORK, 11/27/89, p. 74, David Denby

There is a moment in the remarkable new *Henry V* that I will never forget. The battle of Agincourt is over, ending in an English victory nearly incredible in its one-sidedness. Henry (Kenneth Branagh), exhausted, bloodied, a very young king only beginning to comprehend the scale of his triumph, picks up the body of a slain English boy and carries him across the battlefield, past the remnants of the filthy struggle we have just seen—past dead bodies caught on stakes, pierced with arrows, lying in muck and water.

As he walks, in a continuous shot lasting minutes, a joyous choral hymn swells on the soundtrack, and Henry's army gathers behind him and follows after; he passses exhausted French nobles too stunned to acknowledge him, and some poor French women robbing corpses. Then, from deep in the frame, other French women—mothers, we realize, of slain young men—rush at Henry in fury. As his men push them aside, Henry walks by without even noticing. All the cruelty and despair of war lies in that fleeting instant. Henry continues on his way, climbing a slight rise, his entire army now around him, and deliberately, ceremoniously, lays the body in a cart. At that moment, his kingship is achieved—he has accepted responsibility for the dead, for the victory, for all of the burdens of leadership.

And Branagh's triumph is completed, too. This 28-year-old Irish-born actor, who directed the movie and stars in it, has gone up against Laurence Olivier's famous 1944 film—and performance—and come out very well indeed. I have some doubts about Branagh's tragic "modern" view of war. I think that Olivier's sunshiny spectacle of battle is more appropriate for this particular play of Shakespeare's; it is even, in some ways, historically more accurate. Still, the entire film, magnificently cast, passionately played, is stirring and deeply humane.

Olivier's movie is a celebration of both theater and cinema. It begins in a mockup of Shakespeare's open-air theater, the Globe, at an actual performance of the play in Elizabethan times. A rowdy audience gets doused by rain for a while and even hears some bad acting—Olivier pays loving tribute to the orotund traditions he is about to leave behind. By degrees, the Globe gives way to open fields, sometimes photographed realistically, sometimes appearing as lovely painted backdrops in pretty, book-of-hours style. The whole movie is conscious pageantry, led by Olivier's ringing, heroic Henry.

Branagh, on the other hand, works close in and ignores theatrical convention. This is cinema, only cinema. At the beginning, the Chorus—played by the fluent Leslie Banks in Olivier's film—is a modern man in an overcoat (Derek Jacobi) walking among the lights of a film set. He thrusts open two gigantic doors, and Henry is revealed, silhouetted in candlelight, entering his throne room. Henry sits down, the camera clinging to him. Through most of the movie, the camera stays in close-up and medium shot. The acting is a little scaled down, sometimes surprisingly intimate for this most public of Shakespeare's plays. Don't misunderstand: These are still British classical actors; they don't go in for sycophantic horsing around, bids for easy public approval. In Olivier's film, however, we are more aware of the beauty of the verse as verse than we are in Branagh's.

Branagh's recently crowned king has courage, but he's still feeling his way. In his first big scene in front of the court, Branagh talks in a near-whisper, as if Henry were checking to see if his authority would flourish in a show of quiet control. Later, when the French herald brings the insulting gift of tennis balls from the Dauphin, Branagh's voice rises, his eyes open wide, and we see what Henry is made of. The sight is startling.

Branagh looks a little like James Cagney: He's unheroic of stature, medium-size, with a stumpy trunk, a rounded jaw, big ears, and rather close-set, pale-blue eyes. He certainly has Cagney's pugnacity and glee. One can believe Henry was a bad boy as a prince—there's a gleam of playful malevolence in him. But he's also shrewd, and hard as nails underneath. Restoring some passages that Olivier cut from the play, Branagh gives us a Henry who threatens the people of Harfleur with atrocities and who orders, however regretfully, the hanging of his old tavern companion Bardolph for stealing. Shakespeare's theme of the maturing of a young man into the bitter realities of leadership has more sting Branagh's way. But Olivier's way has more romance. In the glorious big speeches, Branagh offers simplicity and less variety and rhetorical resourcefulness than Olivier, but power enough. He makes a straight climb to his peaks. Olivier, more calculating but also more daring, ascends to planes of volume and emotion, going up, then down a bit, then up over the top in a series of culminating clarion blasts that are incomparably thrilling.

Reality is Branagh's mode. The movie's coloring is a somber brown, the lighting scheme for the interiors yellowish and sallow, as if candles provided the only illumination. The tavern scenes are roistering and mercifully brief. I admit to being occasionally bored with Shakespeare's commoners and clowns, and was grateful for the pruning of the text. Judi Dench makes a magnificently fleshy and moving Mistress Quickly, and Robert Stephens is heartbreaking as Pistol. Branagh's is rowdy, direct, mud-earthy Shakespeare, though never pillow-fight silly, like Zeffirelli's dreadful burlesques *Taming of the Shrew* and *Romeo and Juliet*. Mindful of war's dreadful toll, Branagh gives his production a sweet gravity, an intimacy with suffering and endurance, that is everywhere noble and fully felt.

But does his view of war completely make sense? In the battle scene, the English longbow archers, staring into fog, fire their arrows blindly into air. There follows a frightening, bone-mashing mêlée that the English, somehow, entirely dominate. The overall impression is of a furious chaos. But at the actual battle of Agincourt, the English seem to have seen the field clearly and known what they were doing. The initial hail of arrows provoked a French charge, which was then halted by the stakes the English had pounded into the ground; the French horses and riders piled up, and many turned around and rode back, only to be struck from the rear. Those who weren't struck ran into their own oncoming men at arms. The panic that followed allowed the English to devastate the French ranks.

For the first time, commoners wielding longbows nullified a charge of armed knights. Agincourt was a turning point in the history of war, as Shakespeare, in his way, knew, and that's the way

Olivier stages it—as the end of medieval knighthood, with the French cavaliers so heavily armed that they have to be hoisted with pulleys onto their horses. In Branagh's version, the English, aiming into the mist, could have hit their own men. Branagh stages a modernist, absurdist-tragic struggle in which everyone is blindly groping in the void, yet, wanting it both ways, he retains the one-sided English victoy. The kind of battle he shows us couldn't possibly have led to that outcome.

I'm not saying that Branagh's depressed view of warfare—the standard contemporary one—is *wrong*, only that here it's ahistorical, an imposed attitude. Until fairly recently—let's say until the Battle of the Somme, in 1916, in which 420,000 British men were sacrificed for a few yards of ground—war was generally thought of as a noble and rational exercise of national spirit, a testing of mettle. Shakespeare thought of it that way. Certainly *Henry V*, written after the English victory over the Spanish Armada, is not an anti-war play. Still, whatever one's quarrel with it, Branagh's film is a thrilling accomplishment.

NEW YORK POST, 11/8/89, p. 37, David Edelstein

With impudence bordering on heresy, 28-year-old Irish-born Kenneth Branagh has adapted, directed and cast himself in the title role of a new film of Shakespeare's "Henry V."

In keeping with his working-class roots, Branagh has shorn the play of pomp and ornamentation; in keeping with the ill repute into which warfare has fallen in the last quarter-century, he has identified and harped on a note of horror and woe that was absent from Laurence Olivier's rally-the-troops rendition (made while Britain fought for its life); in keeping with his precocious agenda, he has fashioned a bloody masterpiece.

To find the equal of this "Henry V" in the vigor of its attack and slyness of its intimacy, you'd have to go back to Olivier's "Richard III." This is a momentous occasion—a production at once passionate and judicious, and one that makes Shakespeare a thing of mounting excitement as cinema.

Branagh has said he wanted Shakespeare to appeal to fans of "Crocodile Dundee"—appalling in prospect, but achieved with finesse. Derek Jacobi's Chorus enters in a trenchcoat, buttonholes the camera and ushers us into a sound stage. He works at a jabbing, Brechtian pitch, inviting the audience to "judge ... OUR PLAY!!!" and pushing open a mighty oak door as the orchestra thunders its approval.

From the start you'll notice the preponderance of close-ups in a play that has usually been thought of as declamatory, public-spirited. Scarlet and gold are replaced by deep browns and dusty greens, fanfares by Pat Doyle's brooding strings.

Branagh has plumbed the work drama rather than spectacle, making Henry less an ideal monarch by temperament than a young man struggling to define how an ideal monarch should be—he is very much the Hal of the two parts of "Henry IV" instead of a finished king.

Branagh's Henry is a youth possessed of somewhat clayish features, prominent ears and imperfect skin. Deliberate in his manner, he works to conceal all traces of the reprobate in him, and Branagh underlines this internal battle through flashbacks from his tavern days with Falstaff (Robbie Coltrane), Bardolph (Richard Briers) and Mistress Quickly (Judi Dench).

He is an isolated figure, aware that he must carry the fate of a nation on his shoulders. When betrayed by three close friends, he hisses "Get thee to your deaths" with the soft fury borne of hurt as well as rage. Branagh can emphasize both the magnificence of what he is attaining and the loss of something precious–his spontaneity and easy affection (which dies when he hangs Bardolph for plundering a church).

In short, this working-class actor-director underscores not the beauty and naturalness of Henry's heroism but the sheer intelligence and will of it.

Which is not to suggest that the formal beauty of the verse has been sacrificed. Branagh trained at the Royal Academy of Dramatic Arts; his readings have the soaring clarity that comes from trusting Shakespeare and respecting the meter. His intoxication with the language is contagious— as is his thrill at playing opposite such actors as Dench, Ian Holm and Robert Stephens.

We have always thought of "Henry V" as Shakespeare at his most warlike. But Branagh reveals a play more modern in spirit, much closer to the two earlier "Henrys," in which each death is terrible and, as Williams puts it, "I am afeard there are few die well that die in a battle."

From the start Henry urges his advisers to weigh their words, lest they "awake our sleeping sword of war," and there is a chilling calm in his warnings to the French messenger—superbly played by Christopher Ravenscroft as a reasonable man embarrassed by his charge. The messenger senses at once the unfrivolous nature of the young king—that he speaks softly but may carry a big stick.

Throughout, Branagh fights Shakespeare's caricatures of the French, most clearly by casting Paul Scofield as their king. Scofield's thickened features and heavy, furrowed brow make him seem a man weighted down by tradition, gravely moored, unable to reposition himself to fight this startling young adversary. So "Henry V" becomes his tragedy as well as Henry's triumph.

But even the triumph is ghastly. Branagh's battle scenes are studies in agony, beginning with the terror in his soldiers' eyes as they behold the French mob. (There for budgetary reasons, the shot is more effective than one of 10,000 extras.) The English archers rear back, their arrows fly with an awful whistle and the camera traces the arc.

The war that follows is somber and dirty—mud and blood in the rain, each death a wrenching waste. When it is over and the English discover their juvenile flag-bearers slaughtered, Henry lifts a dead boy (Christian Bale) and carries him the length of the field—a single shot past fallen, punctured men (old women stripping them, rummaging through the purses) and puddles brackish with gore.

It is amazing that, after this, Branagh can switch gears and end with a courtship scene between Henry and the princess of France (Emma Thompson, Branagh's wife) that is dryly amusing and romantic—climaxing in Henry's fully earned assertion that he may kiss her because, as king and future queen, "We are the makers of manners, Kate."

The scene is earthy and awkward and modern in feel; Branagh is a populist without a trace of vulgarity. This "Henry V" reminds us that Shakespeare's plays endure not because of their beauty as poetry but their overpowering lucidity as drama. In the parlance of Branagh's working-class milieu, this is Shakespeare that gives you a rattling good night out.

NEWSDAY, 11/8/89, Part II/p. 5, Mike McGrady

It seems a most unlikely time for "Henry V" to come back to life. Past revivals of Shakespeare's final historical drama have almost always been for the delectation and inspiration of a country involved in war, threatened by war or contemplating war. The young Henry's tremendous David-and-Goliath victory over France's superior armies is capable of setting an audience's blood aboil with patriotic fervor, and it was no accident that Laurence Olivier's rousing film version came out in 1944, when the world was engulfed by war. Depending on one's prejudices and the mood of the moment, "Henry V" is usually reckoned either a stirring crowd-pleaser or a "puerile appeal to patriotism." Whatever the response, there's no doubt that the play tends to sacrifice poetry for politics, personality for pageantry. Few through the years would quarrel with the critic who observed that "No one bored by war will be interested in 'Henry V.'"

But today, in this era of glasnost, young English actor-director Kenneth Branagh—frequently dubbed "the new Olivier" in the British press—has been prompted to change the play's emphasis and shape, making his film less a paean to war and more a story of a king putting his youth behind him and getting on with the business of being a man.

While Henry has been described variously as "Shakespeare's only hero" and "the hero-king of England," Branagh's close-up cameras focus in on a man in conflict, a post-Falstaffian Henry just learning to take control of his armies, his world and himself.

Control is the theme of "Henry V," with the "temperate winds of grace" battling against "the filthy and contagious clouds." This is a king who must maintain control as his youthful boozing companions are led to the gallows, as young boys in his charge are slaughtered by the French, as bedraggled troops must be sent out against a superior foe.

By doing away with the customary costuming and pageantry, Branagh brings the sometimes dry material to a personal level. As Henry strolls unrecognized among his troops on the eve of battle, it becomes a deeply moving moment when he defends his own humanity to his men: "I think the King is but a man, as I am: The violet smells to him as it does to me; the element shows to him as it does to me, all his senses have but human conditions." Branagh manages these quiet moments beautifully, without sacrificing any of the fervor as Henry extolls his soldiers—"We few, we happy few, we band of brothers"—on to an unlikely victory brilliantly filmed with close-up cameras and slow-motion highlights.

At 28 the extravagantly gifted Branagh is the exact age of the man he brings to life. He is aided mightily by the addition of many performers drawn from the Royal Shakespeare Company's 1984 production. Derek Jacobi, Paul Scofield and Robert Stephens, as the lowlife Pistol, are standouts.

Branagh's goal was a film "that will satisfy the Shakespearean scholar as well as those who like 'Crocodile Dundee'." Well, the action-lover may find the whole slow-going, "unrivaled for tediousness" as one early critic put it, but it does remain one of the few Shakespearean plays where actions speak louder than words.

I can't imagine a treatment of "Henry V" that could match this one for imagination, quiet strength and—here's the surprise—humanity.

NEWSWEEK, 11/20/89, p. 80, Jack Kroll

Who would have the chutzpah to challenge Laurence Olivier, who directed and starred in the most celebrated of all Shakespearean films? The brash lad is Kenneth Branagh, who at 28 has matched Olivier's double feat with his own production of *Henry V*. At that tender age Branagh already runs his own stage group, the Renaissance Theatre Company; has written his autobiography, "Beginning"; and has nettled many in Britain's cultural establishment who see him as more pushy than precocious. But Branagh's film is a splendid piece of work, a "Henry V" for our time. Olivier's 1944 movie was a thrilling trumpet call that made the 15th-century warrior-king a symbol of the World War II spirit of Dunkirk. Branagh's film is more psychologically complex, exposing the mixed motives in Henry's decision to invade and conquer France. The mood of this "Henry V" echoes not the just war against Hilter but the ignoble adventure of the Falkland Islands.

Branagh, who had never directed a film before, scraped up $9 million to make the movie (mostly through the efforts of Stephen Evans, a stockbroker and theater buff who's also the executive producer). And he rounded up an elite cast of classical Brits: Derek Jacobi as the Chorus, Paul Scofield as the French King, Ian Holm as the Welsh captain Fluellen, Judi Dench as the bawd Mistress Quickly, Robert Stephens as the braggart Pistol, Emma Thompson (Branagh's wife) as the French princess Katherine and many more. Branagh wants and gets a gritty realism rather than the romantic mythography of Olivier's film. Scofield's face is haunted by a fatalistic wisdom as he foresees the havoc that the audacious Henry will bring. The lowlife rogues Pistol, Bardolph, Nym and Quickly, former cronies of Henry's wastrel youth, are played not for laughs but for chilling truth: Kenneth MacMillan's camera mercilessly scours their faces, ravaged with drink, disease and mortality. The battle of Agincourt, where the English annihilated the French, is no chivalric, picture-book clash but a bloody, muddy, throat-cutting, gut-slashing killing field.

Olivier delivers Henry's big arias—"Once more into the breach" and the St. Crispin's Day speech with an exultant musicality that makes your heart leap. Branagh's more desperate eloquence has its own poignant power. When Olivier's victorious Henry woos Katherine, you don't believe him for a moment when he protests that he's just an ordinary Hank ("such a plain king that thou wouldst think I had sold my farm to buy my crown"). But when Branagh speaks those words you believe him. Indeed the Belfast-born Branagh has an appealing, tough-jawed Jimmy Cagney quality. This boyish toughness adds savor to his outstanding performance and helps to explain his astonishing success at an early age.

Although some English critics were miffed that Branagh would dare to go up against Olivier, Branagh sees his film not as competing but complementary. "Olivier's performance is incomparable," he says. "I can't speak like that. No one can. When I was doing those great speeches I was hearing two voices simultaneously—mine and his." But Branagh depicts a morally ambiguous Henry, a Henry capable of threatening the French with the violation of their women and the spiking of their babies. "That speech was cut out of Olivier's film," he points out, "along with the scene in which he deals with the traitors. I gather Olivier made those cuts at the behest of Winston Churchill, who didn't want any wartime mention of the possibility of English savagery or treachery."

When he first played Henry onstage, Branagh got an interview with the Prince of Wales, who he felt could give him a key to the king's character. Branagh-bashers regard this as another self-aggrandizing maneuver on the actor's part. Not true, he says. "I wanted some insight into Henry's mind. There were spiritual qualities that I wanted to bring out in my Henry that I saw in Prince Charles just by talking to him. People say he's reactionary or not very bright. My impression was that he is a genuinely visionary man, with that sense of regality, melancholy and responsibility that I felt was central to Henry."

Branagh has also been criticized for putting out a somewhat premature autobiography. "I was offered a large sum of money to do the book," he says. "It all went for offices for the Renaissance company. I don't take a salary. We have no home theater. We get no public subsidy yet. It's a particularly British thing, to assign you hero status very swiftly and then, once a certain point of success has been reached, you're suddenly a vulgar, conspicuously visible whippersnapper.''

Neither in performance nor in conversation does Branagh come through as an egocentered type. He seems to be one of those rare birds who combines exceptional acting talent with an even rarer gift for leadership. When he and Evans were scrounging money for ''Henry V'' he heard the same thing everywhere. ''People said, 'How dare you make this film? Who do you think you are? Don't you know there's another version with a rather remarkable actor?' ''

His bulldog commitment carried him throught; Branagh sees himself as part of a tough new wave of British actors who include Daniel Day-Lewis, Gary Oldman, Natasha Richardson and Fiona Shaw. ''I have a certain kind of roughneck quality,'' he says. ''It comes from my working-class Irish stock.'' He told the actors in his company, ''Don't be afraid of making fools of yourselves. Don't give us that staid, reserved English acting. Give it some bollocks.'' Next May, when the Renaissance company comes to Chicago with new productions of ''King Lear'' and ''A Midsummer Night's Dream,'' Americans will be able to see just how tough Branagh and his gang are.

TIME, 11/13/89, p. 119, Richard Corliss

The great doors swing open to reveal the caped figure of King Henry V, sexily backlighted. His bishops and courtiers gaze at him like apostles at the unseen Jesus in some old biblical epic. And finally the monarch of Britain—and of this robust new movie—shows his face and speaks. It is an entrance angled to register awe for Kenneth Branagh. But how much awe can a 28-year-old actor, little known outside Britain and directing his first film, expect to inspire? Branagh recalls that when Judi Dench, who plays Mistress Quickly, first saw this scene, ''she laughed in my face and said, 'I've never seen an entrance like that! Who do you think you are?' '' He retorted, ''The film is not called *Mistress Quickly the Fourth.*'' No, but it might be called *King Ken.*

He doesn't look like a Shakespearean matinee idol, this thin-lipped Irishman with puddings skin and a huge head piked like a pumpkin on his stocky frame. He lacks conventional star magnetism: the athletic abandon, the flaming sexuality, the audacity of interpretation that risks derision to achieve greatness. Expect no swooning teenagers to queue at his stage door, no desperate fan to write him suicide notes. Anyway, he would reject that form of hero worship, for his personality radiates shopkeeper common sense. He is a model of Thatcherite initiative in a British arts scene of radical distemper.

In short, Branagh seems as remote from Laurence Olivier as, say, Sandra Bernhard is from Sarah Bernhardt. Yet the English press praises him—damns him too—as ''the new Olivier.'' If the label is unfair to both men (at 28, even Olivier was not yet ''Olivier''), it is correct to suggest a family resemblance. For, like Olivier, Branagh has a résumé to match his notoriety.

He is the most accomplished, acclaimed and ambitious performer of his generation. In 1984 he dazzled audiences as the youngest actor ever to play the title role in *Henry V* at the Royal Shakespeare Company (RSC). He starred in the *Masterpiece Theater* mini-series *Fortunes of War.* He built his own repertory company and led it through sold-out seasons in London and the provinces. He has written two plays and an autobiography, *Beginning.* He even married his leading lady, TV star Emma Thompson. No doubt about it: Branagh has conquered Britain.

This week he invades U.S. movie theaters (in New York City and Los Angeles, with a dozen other cities to follow next month). He will buck the odds as he did when making his film—as Henry V did on his French campaign—and with no smaller an appetite for success. Did Olivier make a landmark film of *Henry V* when he played in and directed it in 1944? Then the new Olivier would do it again—bloodier and maybe better—in hopes of luring the unlettered moviegoer for whom Shakespeare is a synonym for Sominex.

Just to make the challenge sporting, Branagh would plan his film while starring in three roles with his Renaissance Theater Company. And he would shoot his *Henry,* for a pinchpenny $7.5 million, in seven weeks, less than a third of the time Olivier took. On the first day, the novice director didn't know to shout ''Action!'' until someone poked him in the ribs. How could he make a decent film under so daunting a shadow?

Well, he's done it: created a *Henry* for a decade poised between belligerence and exhaustion. He found a camera style that illuminates the actors with torch power and Rembrandt lighting. His élite cast reads like a *Burke's Peerage* of British acting: stage eminences Paul Scofield, Ian Holm, Derek Jacobi, Alec McCowen and Robert Stephens; TV comedians Richard Briers and Robbie Coltrane; Brian Blessed and Christopher Ravenscroft from Branagh's RSC *Henry;* most of his own rep company; and his bright bride Emma. This galaxy surrounds a director who, like Henry, can orchestrate a magnificent sally, manipulate diverse talents, bend them to his will. And temper artistry with efficiency: Branagh completed the shooting ahead of schedule and under budget.

Olivier's *Henry V*, commissioned by the wartime British government, was a handsome piece of morale boosting. It said all the war's a stage. And on this stage a tiny band of English heroes defeated the evil French (read German) army at Agincourt. It's Robin Hood vs. the Nazis. Olivier's pageant was sunny and sumptuous, and so was his Henry: resourceful in battle, generous in victory, ever cheery and brimful of confidence. Why, he might be Kenneth Branagh!

But not Branagh's new Henry. This is a headstrong lad evolving into a strong King. He can betray as well as be kind, renouncing old friends like Falstaff and Bardolph even if it means they die heart-broken. He can threaten rape and murder of the innocents, then summon God to provide divine artillery and lead the English "once more unto the breach." The Agincourt battle, which Olivier staged as a fantasy joust, is a muddy, brutal fellowship of death here. It has the acrid tang of World War I carnage and the guilty aftertaste of victory in the Falklands. In its crafty heart, *Henry V* is an antiwar war movie.

Henry knows that at Agincourt he has won a great upset, with all of France as his booty. Yet Branagh has to show the awful cost. In an elaborate, chilling tracking shot that lasts nearly four minutes, the exhausted King staggers across the battlefield, the dead weight of Falstaff's boy page across his shoulders, past a tableau of casualties. Instead of a triumph, then, a requiem—for youthful ideals tested in war and found lacking. Not until film's end, when Henry plays the soldier unsuited to seduction, does the sly dazzle of Branagh's charm break through the heavy clouds of Henry's majesty. He is an earthy Olivier and his worthy avatar.

For the man who would be King, early life did not promise much in the way of spotlights. The Branagh family, working-class Protestants in Belfast, produced craftsmen, not stage stars. Ken's father was a carpenter who moved the family to Reading, England, in 1970, when the Troubles roiled too close to home. Within a year, as Branagh recalls in his breezy autobiography, "I'd managed to become English at school and remain Irish at home." It was his first acting challenge, and it fueled his resolve to perform.

As a student at the Royal Academy of Dramatic Art, Branagh displayed the salesman's knack of charm and fearlessness—the seductive intelligence, so crucial to performing, managing and directing. He wrote to Olivier for advice on the role of Chebutykin in *Three Sisters*. He took notes on playing Hamlet from John Gielgud. He determined to play the Dane at a performance attended by the Queen and Prince Philip. Later, preparing his RSC *Henry*, he won an audience with Prince Charles at Buckingham Palace to discuss the isolation felt by a national leader. Wooed and won by the young actor, Charles became a patron of the Renaissance.

But there was more to Branagh than blond ambition. Says Hugh Cruttwell, then RADA's principal: "He had all the talent and initiative you can see in full flood now." Other people soon saw it too. Just out of RADA he won the plum role of Judd, the cynical Marxist student in *Another Country*—a performance whose laser intelligence and subversive edge announced an actor at the start of a brilliant career. He would fulfill that promise when the RSC's Adrian Noble cast him as Henry V.

"Ken's got the general's gift of being the man you automatically follow," says Richard Briers, who plays Bardolph in the film *Henry* and will assay King Lear in the Renaissance's tour of the U.S. next year. Branagh needed that royal self-assurance to build a major acting company and mount a large film. He will need more of it to sustain his career at its current velocity. "Quite soon," says Terry Hands, the RSC's artistic director, "Ken must decide whether he will be an admin man or a great actor. If a leading actor is also running the whole show, he's worried about the box office, the creaking floorboard, the divorce of his cast member. All these can sap that tunnel vision, and the performance can become too controlled."

Tunnel vision is no problem for Branagh—but in the service of the play, not the perks. "I'm not interested in being rich and famous," he avers, "in smoking a big cigar and driving a big car. I want to stay human-size, just as I wanted to make Henry V as manlike as possible." He plans to shoot two films in 1991: a Shakespeare comedy, perhaps *Much Ado About Nothing*, and a modern story set in Chicago. Meanwhile, he may write a novel. And at night he will read himself to sleep with a good book.

So we ask: What are you reading these days? "*Wuthering Heights*," he replies. Ah, yes. Hollywood made a movie from that one 50 years ago, and made a star of the actor who played Heathcliff. Larry something. What ever happened to him?

VILLAGE VOICE, 11/14/89, p. 113, Georgia Brown

As 28-year-old Henry V, 28-year-old Kenneth Branagh settles onto the throne. He listens as the archbishop confects his bribe on behalf of the church—a baffling, windy, trumped-up justification for Henry to invade France. Cut to the king whose noticeably *filled* crotch now appears just inside the frame. "Now are we well resolved," he mutters.

Intentional or not (how could it not be?), this shot of Harry puts a fancy exclamation point on the hard-to-liven (much abbreviated) Act I of Shakespeare's *Henry V*. Just then, the French ambassadors open their cask of insulting tennis balls—a gift from the jokester Dauphin, meant to remind Henry what a good-for-nothing he'd been as Prince Hal—and the word *balls* bounces around in a lively, fruitful, vulgar Elizabethan way. Balls is what Henry is determined to show he has; Branagh is, too.

What a stunning debut! A British stage and TV actor virtually unknown here, Branagh—starring and directing—takes on none less than Laurence Olivier, whose patriotic, now quaint *Henry V* (made when he was 38) seemed to be the only filmed *Henry V* we'd need, or at any rate, get. This was the wartime movie that inspired James Agee to rhapsodize in *Time*: "I am not a Tory, a monarchist, a Catholic, a medievalist, an Englishman, or, despite all the good that engenders, a lover of war; but the beauty and power of this exercise was such that, watching it, I wished I was, though I was, and was proud of it." Branagh's revision is also a stirring war story—shot in rain and mud, not green fields—but his adaptation emphasizes many of Shakespeare's bleak, subversive ironies and the play's dark, grisly, furious underside that, despite the upbeat last act, doesn't let go.

Henry V tells of a green, untried king, son of a usurper, determined to make people forget both his father's crime and his own slumming with the Boar's Head crew by waging a war with France. Basically, Harry's just following his dying father's advice (*Henry IV*, II): "Be it thy course to busy giddy minds/With foreign quarrels; that action . . . /May waste the memory of the former days." Magnetic and a fast take, he has to improvise and gather advice, then make hard decisions to impress his rivals and constituency.

Mindful perhaps of what his father accomplished, the king decides to execute three would-be traitors just as he embarks for France. As for former lowlife friends who have not, with the king, turned a new leaf, he orders the hanging of the pomegranate-nosed Bardolph (Richard Briers) for pillaging, and (as we watch Bardolph swing) justifies himself, explaining that leniency is the best policy toward French peasants. (Olivier delicately excised traitors, Bardolph's sentencing, as well as memory of Henry IV's crime from his movie. Some of Henry's more bloodthirsty threats are omitted here, too.)

The Irish-born Branagh makes a stolid Henry—squarish, no lips, the stubborn look of a scrapper and a droop of baby fat in the face. When Harry gets revved up, making his rousing into-the-breach and St. Crispin's Day speeches to the troops, he discovers his gift, becoming radiant and dazzling, like his emblem the sun. The Act V scene in which he woos Katherine of France (Emma Thompson, Branagh's wife) extends Henry's mastery over a rhetoric of conquest. You could call this a verbal rape except that the lady, having no choice, consents. As always, this plays as immensely charming.

Visually, *Henry V* may be conventional, but the novice director uses conventions nicely, sometimes brilliantly. Despite a frugal budget, there are some terrific bloody battle scenes (English longbows versus French cavalry), which manage to suggest war's terror and meanness. (Shakespeare's Irish, Scotch, and Welsh soldiers anticipate World War II movies with their corporals from Texas and Brooklyn.) Cinematographer Kenneth MacMillan takes wonderful close looks at a succession of lived-in faces—including those of Paul Scofield as the French king, Judi Dench as Mistress Quickly, and Brian Blessed, a grand, bearlike Exeter.

The heart of the play may be the king's meeting with Michael Williams (played by an actor named Michael Williams). This is when, the night before battle, he disguises himself in a cloak to offer the men his "little touch of Harry in the night." The savvy commoners, it turns out, are skeptical and sarcastic, and Williams especially—tough, resigned—is both more persuasive and more richly eloquent than "Henry LeRoy." Paul Fussell must love Williams's argument:

But if the cause be not good, the King himself hath a heavy reckoning to make when all those legs and arms and heads chopped off in a battle shall join together at the latter day and cry all, "We died at such a place"—some swearing, some crying for a surgeon, some upon their wives left poor behind them, some upon the debts they owe, some upon their children rawly left.

The cause, every audience should know, isn't just. Even if *Henry V* can be performed as if it's about the joy of soldiering, *Henry V* on the page can be read as a melancholy play about the costs of imperialism, chauvinism, and intoxication with heroes. Branagh's choices don't always show this to be his reading (his depiction of the aftermath of Agincourt seems almost agonizingly conflicted), but they often do. Setting the tone is Derek Jacobi's all-in-black Chorus—a solemn, subdued spokesman for history and the theater (in contrast to Leslie Banks's cheerleader in the Olivier version). Another example is Branagh's using William Bird's *Non nobis domine* more like a dirge than a psalm, and returning to it over the closing credits when many directors would stay with lighter notes of peace. The words, "Not unto us, Lord, but to thee be the glory," turn grimly ironic.

Branagh's talent, Shakespeare's genius, is in making us feel that undeniable pull of patriotic rhetoric ("We few, we happy few, we band of brothers"), then undercutting the euphoria. (You may still want your Kennedy back, but you'll distrust the impulse.) This glorious, invigorating, *popular* Shakespeare should definitely be seen by everyone, including young people, who will fall in love with the words. Just be sure to brief them on the first two acts.

Also reviewed in:

NATION, 12/11/89, p. 724, Stuart Klawans
NEW REPUBLIC, 12/4/89, p. 28, Stanley Kauffmann
NEW YORK TIMES, 11/8/89, p. C19, Vincent Canby
NEW YORKER, 11/27/89, p. 104, Pauline Kael
VARIETY, 9/20–26/89, p. 29
WASHINGTON POST, 12/15/89, p. D1, Hal Hinson
WASHINGTON POST, 12/15/89, Weekend/p. 65, Desson Howe

HER ALIBI

A Warner Bros. release. *Executive Producer:* Martin Elfand. *Producer:* Keith Barish. Director: Bruce Beresford. *Screenplay:* Charlie Peters. *Director of Photography:* Freddie Francis. *Editor:* Anne Goursaud. *Music:* Georges Delerue. *Music Editor:* Frank Fitzpatrick. *Sound:* Bruce Bisenz. *Sound Editor:* Julia Evershade. *Production Designer:* Henry Bumstead. *Art Director:* Steve Walker. *Set Decorator:* James W. Payne. *Special Effects:* Guy Faria. *Costumes:* Ann Roth. *Make-up:* Medusah. *Stunt Coordinator:* Ron Rondell. *Running time:* 91 minutes. *MPAA Rating:* PG.

CAST: Tom Selleck (Phil Blackwood); Paulina Porizkova (Nina); William Daniels (Sam); James Farentino (Frank Polito); Hurd Hatfield (Troppa); Ronald Guttman ("Lucy" Comanescu); Victor Argo (Avram); Patrick Wayne (Gary Blackwood); Tess Harper (Sally Blackwood); Bill Smitrovich (Farrell); Bobo Lewis (Rose); Jane Welch (Millie); Austin Hay (Oliver); W. Benson Terry (FX); Joan Copeland (Audrey); Liliana Komorowska (Laura); Alan Mixon (Nina's Father); Barbara Caruso (Nina's Mother); Marlene Bryan (Laurie); William Aylward (Greg); Sara E. Pfaff (Heather Blackwood); Trevor Soponis (Tony Blackwood); David S. Chandler (Eugene Mason); Bill Grimmett, Ted Sutton, Brian Costantini (Cops); Norman Fitz (Judge); Nat Benchley (Prosecutor); T.J. Edwards and John Badila (Defenders); Leonard Auclair (Jack the Author); Dick Harrington (Henry the Neighbor); Corazon Adams (Consuela); Lisa Nicholas (Waitress); Hank deLuca (Ian the Editor); Joann Havrilla (Woman at Lecture); Pankaj Talwar (Dr. Singh); Dick Rizzo (Knife Clerk); Joseph Eubanks (Coctail Man); Patrick McDade and Allen Fitzpatrick (Federal Agents); Gregory A. Fessler (Store Manager); Edward Conery (Bernardini's Lawyer); Brian Desmond (Court Officer); Wilfred Williams (Frank's Partner); Gary Lee Leventhal (Detective); Charles Cotel (Security Guard).

LOS ANGELES TIMES, 2/3/89, Calendar/p. 1, Sheila Benson

Mysteries are supposed to lull before they startle; it's part of the plan. Certainly the credits of "Her Alibi" lull us into thinking that, like them, the movie will be witty, sophisticated and elegant. It is certainly elegant *looking*, but 15 minutes into the action the thrill is gone and director Bruce Beresford seems to have no clue as to how to find it.

Those nifty credits are the jacket illustrations of prolific mystery writer Philip Blackwood (Tom Selleck), who has hit a writing block and can't churn out any more steamy adventures for his hero, Peter Swift. In desperation, he hits a few real courtrooms, looking for inspiration. For a while it seems as though the film's screenwriter, Charlie Peters, is on a charming tack, bringing on a quartet of old courtroom regulars who greet Selleck as one of them, cluing him in to the juicier cases in the building. However, the four remain under-developed, like so many other nice touches in the story.

The courtroom is just a ploy to let Selleck meet Nina Ionescu (Czech-born actress-model Paulina Porizkova), a "Romanian" mystery woman. Before you can say "jurisprudence" Selleck has lied gracefully, providing Porizkova with an alibi at her murder trial, and detective James Farentino has swallowed the obvious lie, allowing this ludicrous plot to inch its way forward. You'd expect more from students in Screenwriting 1A classes.

It's all to get our two stars under one roof, Selleck's country house, probably one of the most ruggedly seductive retreats around. It should be: The production designer is Henry Bumstead, who's done everything from "Vertigo" to "To Kill a Mockingbird" and from "The Sting" to "The Little Drummer Girl." But then producer Keith Barish has assembled a world-class technical slate: England's great Freddie Francis ("The French Lieutenant's Woman," "Dune") was the cinematographer; France's Anne Goursaud ("One From the Hear," "Ironweed") was the editor; Wayne Fitzgerald designed the titles; the music is by Georges Delerue ("Jules and Jim," "Silkwood"), and the splendid Ann Roth ("Klute," "Day of the Locust," "Working Girl") did the costumes.

And all this loving talent is in the service of this loosely crocheted screenplay, studded with tired little ribaldries and action that finds shooting a man in the hip with an arrow hilarious. The waste is enough to make you keen piercingly in the aisles.

The film's fun is supposed to come from the contrast between Selleck's macho Peter Swift dialogue and his own klutzy behavior. He's twitterpated by the very sight of Porizkova who may or may not be a real murderess. Do audiences really want to see Tom Selleck—the closest thing we have to Clark Gable—lurching about like Chevy Chase; hurled onto his car with his face smooshed up against the windshield and the wipers on? Nice that he can take himself so lightly; pity that he has to.

Porizkova, who was delicately ingenuous in "Anna," gives exactly the same reading here. To many it may not even matter. She can also be found riding bareback, bounding on a trampoline or slipping into a bath towel—simply watching her in motion is a jaw-dropping sight. Her lifelong complicity with cameras has relaxed her utterly; put her in front of one and she moves her long, long legs and arms with a floppy doll languor that's enchanting. But after quite a lot of this, even the most undemanding fan may want a bit more: a characterization perhaps.

It's as useless to hope for as the possibility that director Beresford will rouse himself from his torpor and get this movie going somewhere. From the way characters pop onscreen unexpectedly, especially Selleck's family and friends in the last third of the film, there's a hint that crucial scenes may have vanished, but it takes a faith stronger than mine to think they would have helped much.

MONTHLY FILM BULLETIN, 5/89, p. 137, Verina Glaessner

Phil Blackwood, a pulp-thriller writer chided by his agent Sam for his current inability to produce, seeks inspiration in a courtroom. There his attention is caught by Nina, a beautiful Rumanian, who apparently speaks no English, accused of murdering a compatriot. Phil inveigles his way into her cell disguised as a priest, discovers that she can in fact understand English, and offers to provide her with an alibi by claiming that they are lovers and were together at the time of the murder. Despite the scepticism of the DA and Lieutenant Farrell, Nina is released and Phil drives her to his house in Connecticut (her reluctance to go quickly overcome when she glimpses three supposed Rumanian embassy officials, Troppa, Comanescu and Avram, in fact from the KGB). Phil begins to turn his recent adventures into fiction, but after a demonstration of Nina's knifethrowing ability, and a visit from the still suspicious Farrell, begins to doubt her innocence. Deterred from leaving by the constant presence of the KGB men (who also attempt to eliminate her by bombing the house), Nina is taken to meet Phil's family. She is able to rescue a small child who becomes stuck on the barn roof, then cooks a meal for the family but makes an elaborate excuse to absent herself, secretly meeting her sister Laura. When the Blackwoods' cat dies after apparently sampling some of Nina's food, Phil assumes that she has poisioned them all, and the party adjourns to the hospital to have their stomachs pumped. It transpires that the cat was poisoned elsewhere, and Nina, who has meanwhile returned to the house with Laura to say goodbye, learns from Phil's notes that he still harbours suspicions of her guilt and is using their relationship as source material. Declaring herself free of him, she leaves; but Phil and Sam have discovered from a number of clues that she is to meet her family—circus performers who are visiting from Rumania—at a commemoration of the great clown Grimaldi's death. Farrell discloses that the family is in hiding awaiting confirmation that they will be allowed to defect from Rumania. Dressed as clowns themselves, Phil and Sam infiltrate the gathering and confront the similarly disguised KGB men, whom Phil delivers into the hands of the police. The safety of Nina and her family is assured.

Her Alibi is subtitled "A Romantic Comedy". Sadly, what it delivers in the way of comedy tends to play on a single note—the running gag, rendered in voice-over, of readings from the dynamic wish-fulfilment doings of Phil Blackwood's fictional hero played out against the bathos of the author's real life. The romance, such as it is, has a sour and slightly disquieting undertone. Nina conjures mystery (her foreign origin) and fatal sexual allure, but detached from an ambience (e.g., *film noir*) which might allow these anxieties to be explored, she simply personifies a treacherous sexuality for which Blackwood's bumbling is no match. It is—tellingly—only when she loses her own "voice" and approaches him using the sub-pornographic phrases of *Playboy*, or indeed of Blackwood's own pulp fiction, which she takes for acceptable romantic small talk, that any *rapprochement* is possible.

The film is at once a send-up of Tom Selleck's dumb macho persona (irresistibly recalled by the script) crossed with a classic Hollywood screwball comedy of sexual ineptitude. Blackwood at the lectern delivers a talk on his novels to a wholly female and rather fashionable audience. When confronted by a blunt questions as to his hero's failure to get to sexual grips with the girl ("Is he gay?"), he responds by fumbling and upsetting the water jug, while explaining that he "lives by a certain code". This is a set-piece that could have been played by both Jerry Lewis and Cary Grant, but it's a mark of Selleck's insubstantiality that our main response is embarrassment. Part of the problem is that his *Magnum* persona is already too self-conscious and self-guying to stand further deconstruction. Bruce Beresford seems to feel most at home with the light social comedy of the scenes involving Blackwood's family, a reminder that his true abilities perhaps lie more in the exploration of the romantically small scale, as in *Tender Mercies*. As it is, lacking a script able to go beyond the obvious, and direction able to make up for the lack of wit and sophistication, *Her Alibi* tends to rely instead on such diversions as the witless doings of the three notably "unreconstructed" KGB heavies.

NEW YORK, 2/20/89, p. 71, David Denby

Her Alibi, starring Tom Selleck and Paulina Porizkova and directed by Bruce Beresford, is the worst movie I ever saw 40 minutes of. As I made my departure—a life-affirming act if there ever was one—my unhappy colleagues in the daily press, chained to their oars like the galley slaves in *Ben-Hur*, sighed loudly and piteously. Poor devils! My sympathies to their labors. (Liberation awaits a better season.) In the first third of the film, Charlie Peters's script reaches its brightest moment when the hero, a tough-guy mystery writer, is advised by his word-processing program to erase the current draft of his new novel. Peters himself was apparently less fortunate in his choice of software.

Who's responsible for putting this screenplay into production? Director Bruce Beresford, who once seemed a respectable practitioner of his difficult but glorious art? (Beresford joins fellow Australian Roger Donaldson, the *auteur* of *Cocktail*, as the quickest sellout of the decade.) Producer Keith Barish, who opened shop less than ten years ago with so many touching promises of quality? Tom Selleck, who showed signs, in *3 Men and a Baby*, of developing an acceptable light-comedy acting style? Warner Bros., the most erratic of studios? Speak up, somebody. I've made my confession. Now you make yours.

NEW YORK POST, 2/3/89, p. 19, David Edelstein

It was dead—reeking dead, sitting on the screen like a giant platter of lox.

The corpse was called "Her Alibi," and it was supposed to be the story of a detective writer (Tom Selleck) who springs a luscious Romanian (Paulina Porizkova) from jail when she's booked for murder.

Selleck's Phil Blackwood is blocked these days, creatively speaking, and wants to get his juices flowing. Plus he has fantasies about this leggy Slavic stunner, fantasies he translates into prose as hard-boiled as an egg that's been ... boiled till it's ... hard:

"Her breasts squished against him like ripe pomegranates ... "

He carts the doll back to his Connecticut estate, and then—and then—this is where the flick begins to rot on the screen. To add insult to homicide, Porizkova wears clothes. Lots of them. It's more than an hour before they sleep together, and even then you don't see any flesh.

After 40 minutes, two whey-faced colleagues from the slicks fled the scene, dissolved by the cadaver's stench into quivering pools of jelly. But I'm a tabloid kinda guy, and to me it was Estee Lauder. Clutching my pen and notebook I felt like Thomas Noguchi, Coroner of the Stars.

Selleck works on a novel about this perplexing case (even though he doesn't know the ending), but fears the ravishing Romanian might really be a killer and will pierce his heart for keeps.

He tries to move a dresser in front of his door, but she catches him. "Some people ride bicycles," he says, by way of explanation. "Some people jog. I move furniture."

"You are a very odd man," she says.

"Am I to take that as a compliment?"

Even the repartee is pushin' up daisies.

She reads one of his books and tells him, "It's—how you say?—pr-pr-"

"Profound?"

"Predictable."

He is crushed. And curious. For this paragon of pulchritude won't tell him if she really iced the stiff, or what she's actually doing in the U.S. of A.

Here are the clues. Match wits with screenwriter Charlie Peters:

1) Through her window, Selleck spies her seated before the mirror, her face smeared with white greasepaint, drawing a triangle over one eye.

2) She throws knives with stunning accuracy.

3) She escapes from Romanian agents in a department store by jumping on a trampoline, kicking the aforementioned agents, and somersaulting over a tall shelf.

4) When Selleck's nephew gets trapped on top of a barn, she deftly shimmies up a rope, travels along the apex of the roof like a tightrope walker, and rescues the kid.

Is she:

a) The Bionic Woman?

b) The ghost of Ayn Rand?

c) An overpaid fashion model pretending to be an actress?

d) A member of a Romanian circus family trying to defect to the U.S.?

A real brain-teaser, eh?

But there is a larger mystery here, a mystery unlike any I've tackled since "The Strange Case of 'Howard the Duck.'" We're not *really* meant to laugh at Selleck's clumsiness, are we? No, it's too—how you say?—pr-pr-predictable.

My suspicion is that Bruce Beresford, the Australian who made all those high-minded pictures like "Breaker Morant" and "Tender Mercies," directed this film with a gun to his head. But who was holding the gun?

Who killed "Her Alibi"?

Warner Bros., the studio whose name it bears? Keith Barish, the producer, who kicked off his career with pointy-headed art flicks like "Sophie's Choice"? Nah, couldn't be. They wouldn't have gone and shown the picture to a top dick like me. And what would they gain from a stinkola bigger than King Kong, Godzilla and Rodan rolled into one?

Hmm . . . let's chew on this . . . Selleck looks like a pansified wimp . . . Selleck is known for his right-wing political views . . . The KGB are the villains, but the plot is so dated and preposterous that the movie ends up making the Cold Warriors look like morons . . .

Of course! What a chump—it's been staring me in the face:

"Her Alibi" is a KGB plot to sink Tom Selleck's film career!

Case closed, end of story. Or is it?

It's late at night; the moon shimmers in the East River like the eye of a putrefied corpse. Somewhere a projectionist loads a reel of film, and the image of Tom Selleck—one of our nation's manliest men—appears on a screen, tarnished, sissified, upstaged by a Czechoslovakian model. The Soviets sleep well tonight, while Americans quail.

"Who will be next?" they ask. "Arnold? Clint? *Sly??*" I take a belt of whiskey. That's the burden of democracy: Idiot actors have the freedom to choose chowderheaded scripts. She's a battered old babe, our Liberty, but with assets to die for.

NEWSDAY, 2/3/89, Part III/p. 3, Mike McGardy

In "Her Alibi" Tom Selleck plays a mystery writer with a divided personality. Shy and self-conscious, he hasn't been in a fistfight since his sixth birthday and hasn't loved a woman in four years. On the other hand, the hero of his best-selling novels, rough-and-tough detective Peter Swift, manages to do all the things that the author only dreams of doing.

The result, then, is a kind of Walter Mitty duality—while Selleck fumbles and bumbles his way through real life, he is constantly rewriting his biography as it would be lived by the fictitious Peter Swift.

For example, while the author stirs Bosco into his nightly glass of chocolate milk, he is thinking, "Swift poured himself a bourbon." Confronted with a gorgeous murder suspect (Paulina Porizkova), he is blushingly tongue-tied while his Peter Swift alter ego is musing, "She had the face of an angel, ethereal, beautiful. He wondered what her breasts looked like."

This, the film's major running gag, holds up well enough, but, unfortunately, what's transpiring on the screen is every bit as false as Selleck's super-macho inventions. As a result, you can't take either side of the personality seriously and most humor has to be taken seriously before it can work.

But how can we take Selleck seriously in the title role? Can you imagine the big guy playing Walter Mitty? Of course not. While Selleck may not hear this complaint often, his appearance is all wrong. Of what possible use are escapist daydreams and futile fantasies to someone with a weight-lifter's physique and a matinee idol's rugged good looks?

And this is merely one way the film challenges credulity. The opening events are little more than a series of absurdities. Glimpsing the perfect Paulina from a distance, Selleck senses her innocence ("Her? How could *she* kill anyone?"). Next, this shyly modest daydreamer dons a priest's costume so he can visit her in jail where he risks felony charges by offering to give her a bogus alibi. He even persuades his literary agent (William Daniels) to risk prison by backing him up.

And this is but the beginning. Fortunately, the film offers enough comic distractions to keep the unlikelihoods from becoming ruinous. The script by Charlie Peters (a couple of years ago he wrote the awful "Blame it on Rio") has enough comic interludes—usually found well off the main story line—to elevate the film all the way up into the category of time-killer. And director Bruce Beresford ("Breaker Morant," "Tender Mercies") turns flimsy into funny on more than one occasion.

Paulina Porizkova, with the face that has decorated 300 magazine covers, reveals a pleasantly light touch (in her only other film, "Anna," she revealed a pleasantly serious touch). She accepted this role, she says, because it reminded her of "Cary Grant's romantic comedies, which are my alltime favorites." But a Cary Grant movie without a Cary Grant can be pretty silly business.

Let me conclude on a negative note by observing that "Her Alibi" continues the most disturbing trend in Hollywood these days. I'm talking, of course, about critic bashing. It began when "The Dead Pool" featured the slow, gruesome murder of a movie critic. Next, in "Switching Channels," a TV exec says, "Gain some fat, we'll make you a movie critic. From now on, you're our ... Man in the Dark." Selleck here has lost his former wife to a critic ("It must've been *so* humiliating," his agent commiserates) and the title of his new book is "Death of a Critic." Well, critics happen to be human too; we have our feelings. If you prick us, do we not bleed? Sure we do—and then we get even.

VILLAGE VOICE, 2/14/89, p. 70, Bruce Handy

These are the dog days of January and February ...

The less said about *Her Alibi*, an avowed romantic comedy, the better. Except that mention Paulina Porizkova, the weirdly attenuated model, and Tom Selleck, the annoyingly genial actor, done up in full clown regalia: red noses, white grease paint, jiggling pantaloons—the works. By this point in the film, we already know that the two stars have no flair for comedy, and many readers, I think, will share my conditioned prejudice against circus clowns; in all, a miserable aggregation. While a nadir is an impossibility in so bad a movie, this scene comes close. And yet, it does serve to remind us once again of the cinema's terrible power to indiscriminately suck us into whatever vacuum it puts in front of us. As the custard pies begin to fly, you watch the two hapless (yet no doubt well-rewarded) stars stumble through their mortifying paces, and you realize ... *you're watching*. Bruce Beresford, who used to be a real director, is the man responsible—or at least the man who pocketed the paychecks. *Responsible* suggests a more active role than seems likely, given the disinterested ineptitude of *Her Alibi*'s makers.

Also reviewed in:
NEW REPUBLIC, 3/6/89, p. 24, Stanley Kauffmann
NEW YORK TIMES, 2/3/89, p. C13, Vincent Canby
VARIETY, 2/8–14/89, p. 20
WASHINGTON POST, 2/3/89, p. B7, Rita Kempley

HIGH FIDELITY—THE ADVENTURES OF THE GUARNERI STRING QUARTET

A Four Oaks Foundation release. *Producer:* Allan Miller. *Director:* Allan Miller. *Director of Photography:* Dyanna Taylor. *Editor:* Tom Haneke. *Running Time:* 85 minutes. *MPAA Rating:* Not Rated.

WITH: The Guarneri String Quartet: Arnold Steinhardt (Violinist); John Dalley (Violinist); Michael Tree (Violist); David Soyer (Cellist); and Jaime Laredo, Alexander Schneider, Harry Beall, Nancy Pallesen.

CHRISTIAN SCIENCE MONITOR, 9/28/89, p. 11, David Sterritt

"High Fidelity" is billed as a movie about "The Adventures of the Guarneri String Quartet." If you didn't know string quartets have adventures, consider the challenges of playing great music all over the world—not to mention travelling and working with the same colleagues, day in and day out, for a quarter of a century.

Still, the life and work of a classical quartet doesn't sound like the most exciting possible subject for a movie, even when the star of the show is the Guarneri String Quartet, one of the most respected chamber-music groups of our time. It's to the credit of director/producer Allan Miller that his documentary about this foursome is often a sprightly and charming experience. Although it isn't fast-moving and becomes a little dull at times, it's surprisingly funny and has an elegant structure—beginning with an emphasis on talk but ending with the pure eloquence of the ensemble's own playing.

What's special about the Guarneri, aside from the extraordinary skill and musical sensitivity of its four members, is that it's the oldest "original" string quartet in the world. It was formed 25 years ago, in 1964, and consists of the same four men to this very day: violinists Arnold Steinhardt and John Dalley, violist Michael Treem and cellist David Soyer.

They are proud of holding their group together for so long. Still, they make no secret of the tensions that such a long association leads to—tensions that give the movie an important part of its meaning. These guys are brilliant musicians with first-rate technical abilities and musical instincts. Yet they are also four guys—with different personalities, separate private lives, and ideas about music that don't always agree.

Working together (rehearsing, concertizing, giving interviews, even appearing in this movie) has to get a bit wearing once in a while, especially after more than two decades. At times, the members of the Guarneri seem like an old married couple—a *large* old married couple—that's still in love, but can't stand being together every minute. Fortunately, they meet this challenge with goodwill and good humor, even if they sometimes go out of their way (as one amusing scene demonstrated) to get hotel rooms as far apart as possible when arriving in a new city for a recital.

In addition to seeing the Guarneri members interact with each other, "High Fidelity" audiences hear plenty of good music—ranging from Haydn to Dvorak, some of it played in concert and some during rehearsal or recording sessions. There's a particularly fascinating glimpse of the quartet playing a César Franck piece and arguing about whether to include it in their repertoire.

Earlier work by filmmaker Miller includes "From Mao to Mozart: Isaac Stern in China," which picked up an Oscar for "best documentary" eight years ago. His directorial energy in "High Fidelity" isn't always as high as I could wish, and there are some basic questions the film doesn't answer. For example, I was left wondering why the Guarneri members have stayed together as a quartet instead of deciding to pursue solo careers, since all have played as soloists and could surely move in that direction if they wanted.

Despite a few gaps in its information, "High Fidelity" is a likable and entertaining film that makes a fine commercial for top-quality chamber music. It proves, as one quartet member puts it, that string quartets are not only for "the rich and the Viennese" to enjoy.

FILMS IN REVIEW, 12/89, p. 618, Eva H. Kissin

This is a film about four men making music together for 25 years, the remarkable Guaneri String Quartet. It is an explanation and a celebration of their history. Created by the team that made Isaac Stern's musical journey to China so memorable ("From Mao To Mozart"), director and producer Allan Miller and editor Tom Haneke have done it again, but done it differently.

Here we are witness to the daily musical lives of the four men. Arnold Steinhardt (violin), John Dalley (violin), Michael Tree (viola), and David Soyer (cello). All four experimented with other musical careers until the concept of becoming a quartet, doing something they all loved for a living, became a reality. "It's the only life I can imagine for myself. I must be very neurotic," one remarked.

The film doesn't gloss over the difficulties involved. Each man is an individual with his own particular tastes and feelings. For example, Steinhardt proposes a new piece for one of the upcoming programs (four or five must be created annually). The other three reject it. He swears he'll propose it each year until they accept it. They haven't—so far.

At rehearsals, in shirt sleeves literally and figuratively, there are constant tensions—questions of accent, interpretation, and tempo. Who is right? it remains to be seen. Essentially they must respect each other in order to work together. With four strong players, democracy becomes "bulky," Tree remarks ruefully. Rehearsals can be periods of hairsplitting, nit-picking and eventual compromise. Sometimes one can listen and hear in a new way. Compromise and adjustment to one another's needs and feelings are intrinsic to the situation. Short tempers must be kept under control. They have to live and play together.

These men, all very different, spend more time together than they do with their families. To manage this successfully, each attempts to maintain his own privacy. They never room together on their travels, and always requesting accomodations on different floors. Although their journeys take them through the great cultural spots of the world—the Nineteenth Century charms of Baden Baden, the distinctive city-scape of Prague, the watery glories of Venice—they don't always enjoy these visits in the luxury associated with travel. An unexpected storm, a late plane—can necessitate dinner from a styrofoam cup. The concert, after all, is fixed in time and place.

The concert, of course, is the culmination of their efforts. Here, combed and elegant in their dark suits, the players represent civilization at its best—four artists working together to create a mutual product—the music that their efforts have turned into an "alchemy" (their word), a mutual harmony, a common language.

High Fidelity is obviously a rich visual and musical experience, an "open" visit with the oldest and best string quartet in the world. However, it is subtler than an aesthetic triumph. Somewhere, between the tension of rehearsals and the final harmony of the concert, there is a message to individuals and societies about the problems and rewards of making music together.

NEW YORK, 10/2/89, p. 75, David Denby

The four cranky virtuosos of the Guarneri Quartet have been criticizing one another's tastes, grating on one another's nerves, and avoiding one another socially for a full quarter-century. Allan Miller's documentary *High Fidelity* suggests that the longevity of this brilliant four-way partnership depends as much on uninhibited complaining—the music-world equivalent of a marital quarrel in a Laundromat—as it does on an ineffable and heroic communion with the music and one another. A democracy of grumpiness.

Old photos of the men as young longhairs reveal that they may once have been free-spirited and prankish, but those days are long gone. If you regard the quartet as a single entity, the movie is a portrait of the artist as middle-aged bourgeois. First violinist Arnold Steinhardt has the most singular appearance: He's aristocratic-looking, slender, with a high forehead, but he's whiny and pompous—except when he plays, at which time he becomes as graceful as an angel. John Dalley, the second violinist, a Midwesterner, is rather inarticulate and cut off; David Soyer, the wonderful cellist, is grouchy, rotund, and funny; and violist Michael Tree has soulful eyes and an air of exquisite dissatisfaction—he might have been an actor in Chekhov's plays. None of the four says or does anything of much interest. Eager to dispel the slightest whiff of high culture, Miller presents them as regular Joes, tossing Frisbees with their kids, farming, cooking, praising George Burns and Neil Simon.

Yet at the end of *High Fidelity* (awful title, by the way), there is a performance in Albuquerque of the dazzling last movement of Beethoven's Quartet in C Major (Op. 59, No. 3), and near the conclusion of the movement, as one instrument after another makes its entrance, rushing lickety-split through the incomparable *perptuum mobile* music, the quartet takes off into the stratosphere. Something like a miracle happens, and has been happening, in the Guarneri's performances of Beethoven, Schubert, Brahms, Bartók, and others since 1964, *High Fidelity* suggests that though these men may not have been tough enough or egotistical enough for solo careers, their collective brilliance arises from the ordinariness of their temperaments. In rehearsal, their musical skills reach incandescence through friction and mutual criticism and compromise. *High Fidelity* becomes an ironic essay on the banality of greatness in musical performance.

NEW YORK POST, 9/15/89, p. 25, Susan Elliott

The Guarneri Quartet has been together, in its original incarnation, longer than any extant string quartet—25 years, to be exact. Allan Miller, the documentary film's director/producer, is a musician, arts administrator, and filmmaker whose documentary "From Mao to Mozart: Isaac Stern in China" won an Academy Award in 1981. Whether "High Fidelity" will do the same is anyone's guess; for the most part it is a wellpaced, realistic look at the lives—both collective and individual—of four men dedicated to making music together.

The film follows the quartet to Venice, Prague, Albuquerque and points between. Performances and rehearsals are neatly intercut with interviews and travel scenes. On a train leaving Baden-Baden, the group reflects on its performance the night before, which was being taped for television: "That was one of the most uncomfortable concerts we've ever played," says violist Michael Tree. "If I had been in the audience," adds cellist David Soyer, "I would have left."

Some of the rehearsal footage is stunningly candid, and a conversation between Tree and first violinist Arnold Steinhardt, in which the violist argues that he should be allowed to play violin occasionally, becomes almost uncomfortable to witness.

"There has to be that candor to survive," comments Steinhardt after a particularly rowdy rehearsal segment. Much is also made of the foursome's respect for one another's privacy: Checking into a hotel in Tampa, they ask, in all seriousness, for rooms on separate floors.

The film uses excerpts of quartets by Haydn, Schubert and Dvorak, and Bartok, among others, always taking care to balance art with entertainment; a performance of a Mozart Quartet is interspersed with reminiscences of student pranks at the Curtis Institute—where Steinhardt, Tree and violinist John Dalley shared a rooming house.

Coverage of their personal lives seems a bit contrived at times but is nonetheless engaging. Steinhardt plays Frisbee with his son; Soyer drives a tractor and plants seedlings; Tree shares a meal with his family; and Dalley, the elusive one with the puckish grin, shoots baskets—somewhat self-consciously—in the driveway with his son.

There are brief interviews with friend and colleague Jaime Laredo, with Sascha Schneider, who first put the four men together in 1964, and with manager Harry Beall, who complains, ironically, about the group's aversion to publicity.

Despite its occasionally distracting grainy quality, the film's pace, variety, and behind-the-scenes intimacy should make it attractive to both quartet aficionados and casual listeners.

NEWSDAY, 9/15/89, Part III/p. 5, Peter Goodman

How has the Guarneri String Quartet stuck together for 25 years? That's the first question posed to them as "High Fidelity: The Adventures of the Guarneri String Quartet" opens, and it runs like a figured bass throughout this intriguing, if specialized, film.

The Guarneri holds the current record for longevity with the same personnel: violinists Arnold Steinhardt and John Dalley, violist Michael Tree and cellist David Soyer. They have been playing between 100 and 150 concerts a year almost since they first got together in 1964 at Vermont's Marlboro Music Festival at the suggestion of Alexander Schneider, himself a former member of the famed Budapest Quartet.

A few other quartets have been around longer (the Juilliard dates from the '40s) but always with significant personnel changes. The stress of travel, rehearsals and interaction with fans, supporters, managers, stage crews and everyone else in the music business is very wearing: It can be harder than marriage.

And their rehearsals are like four-way wars, full of intense disagreements about every aspect of the music they're playing. So one does wonder about these four men: thin, patrician Steinhardt, placid, jocular Dalley, intense, nervous Tree and bearish, aggressive Soyer.

The question is never entirely answered, but plenty of information is provided by film maker Allan Miller, who won an Oscar for "From Mao to Mozart: Isaac Stern in China." The players joke and muse about it, from Dalley's remark that it's only for the money to Steinhardt's paean to the grandeur of the music.

But violinist Jamie Laredo, who co-directs the Philadelphia Chamber Orchestra with Tree, comes closest when he goes back to their roots. Steinhardt, Dalley and Tree were classmates, roommates and fellow pranksters at the Curtis Institute of Music, forming the kind of deep bonds that can last a lifetime. And Soyer, a World War II veteran much older than the others, has a bluff, straightforward honesty that apparently has fit in well.

It is also apparent, from the care they take not to travel together and to keep their musical and personal lives separate, that the players guard their insides well. One can feel it in a tense but circumspect argument between Tree, who'd like to get a chance to play the violin a little, and Steinhardt, who doesn't want him to. This is the sort of thing that can tear a group apart; Tree finally admits that he holds back because it would be too hurtful to them all.

Music, of course, has a most significant role, but the film is at least as much about the group's dynamics the often harried world in which its members work. An early sequence following them from rehearsal to airport to Baden-Baden to backstage to concert (editor Tom Haneke worked with Miller on "From Mao to Mozart") has a visual and emotional complexity very like a piece of music itself. What one sees often matches what one hears.

The Guarneri is an essentially conservative ensemble: Its repertoire is traditional and it rarely ventures into the 20th Century or away from the mainstream (Steinhardt is defeated in his annual attempt to get Fritz Kerisler's pretty, inoffensive A Minor Quartet onto a program). But they do what they do supremely well. And this film goes as deeply into how it happens as one can without trying full-scale psychoanalysis.

VILLAGE VOICE, 9/19/89. p. 72, Leighton Kerner

It's encounters, rather than adventures, that this warm, funny, serious, and deftly executed film is about. The Guarneri—probably the most widely popular string quartet now operating—is shown over the 1987–88 season in encounter after encounter with audiences, TV cameramen, recording executives, tour impresarios, and reception hosts. What's more important, they repeatedly lock horns and make valuable truces with their music and with one another. If violinists Arnold Steinhardt and John Dalley, violist Michael Tree, and cellist David Soyer were just starting out as a foursome, as they did in 1964, then, yes, they might be called adventurers. But having become the world's oldest quartet without a roster change, they also know their professional territory as few other performers do, and, as this picture shows, they're way ahead of the game.

Also ahead of the game is director/producer Miller, a former conductor and, since 1979, artistic director of Symphony Space. He brings cinematic as well as musical expertise to this project. Those who saw his TV exploration of a Zubin Mehta/Los Angeles Philharmonic performance of Ravel's *Bolero* or his Oscar-winning chronicle of Isaac Stern's 1979 tour to China, *From Mao to Mozart*, should not be surprised at *High Fidelity*'s lively mix of tough rehearsal debates, family gatherings, and travel-time griping. To a music critic who sometimes misses a sense of individual personality in the Guarneri's otherwise amazingly proficient concerts, they constantly enliven *High Fidelity* with personality to burn. Steinhardt, at 52 the youngest of the four, doesn't rule the group as many older-time first violinists have, but just faces frustration when unsuccessfully trying to convince his colleagues that Fritz Kreisler's Quartet in A Minor is really worth playing in public. "Okay," says he in abject defeat, "I'll play it in another life, and I'm taking the parts with me."

Michael Tree also hits an artistic brick wall. He'd like to play the violin instead of viola when programming permits it. No luck. The avuncular Soyer listens sympathetically but asks, like an amateur therapist, "Why is this important to you?" Tree can't explain and merely shrugs. Soon all such dissatisfactions seem buried as the four, at their next concert, tear through the rollercoaster finale of Beethoven's third "Rasumovsky." Dyanna Taylor's camera work and Tom Haneke's editing here are dazzlingly musical.

Rehearsals are tough but not destructive. The musicians themselves tell us bits about their lives before and since the Guarneri was formed and they hint that their quite different personalities meshed luckily but enduringly. An argument about one single note's potential influence over tempo and dynamic may end in sudden compromise and will undoubtedly resurface when that piece comes up in another season, but temperaments and talents remain interlocked. It's one of this film's many virtues that it shows the quartet together in their own special, public world, one that coexists with four separate private ones.

Also reviewed in:
NEW REPUBLIC, 9/18&25/89, p. 34, Stanley Kauffmann
NEW YORK TIMES, 9/15/89, p. C19, Vincent Canby
VARIETY, 8/23-29/89, p. 29

HIGH STAKES

A Vidmark Entertainment release. *Executive Producer:* Michael Steinhardt. *Producer:* Amos Kollek. *Director:* Amos Kollek. *Screenplay:* Amos Kollek. *Director of Photography:* Marc Hirschfeld. *Editor:* Robert Reitano. *Music:* Mira J. Spektor. *Production Designer:* Joan Herder. *Running time:* 102 minutes. *MPAA Rating:* R.

CAST: Sally Kirkland (Melanie Rose, "Bambi"); Robert LuPone (John Stratton); Richard Lynch (Slim); Sarah Gellar (Karen); Kathy Bates (Jill); W.T. Martin (Bob); Eddie Earl Hatch (Earl); Betty Miller (Mother); Maia Danziger (Veronica).

NEW YORK POST, 11/17/89, p. 30, V.A. Musetto

It's been a tough week or so for Sally Kirkland. Last Friday, she opened in "Best of the Best," a simplistic sports movie that should have been labeled "worst of the worst." Today we find her in "High Stakes," a low-rent "thriller" that should never have been made at all.

And to think that just two years ago, Kirkland, a one-time Warhol superstar, appeared on the verge of a renaissance thanks to her award-winning work in "Anna." So much for that!

"High Stakes" begins with Kirkland doing a super-mean striptease in a seedy bar. Bob Dylan sings in the background. She is, we are quick to learn, Bambi, a stripper-hooker in the employ of a nasty fellow named Slim.

One night, after having been tossed from the limousine of a dissatisfied customer, Bambi chances upon John Stratton, a Wall Street type who has been mugged while prowling 42nd Street in search of a prostitute. Ignoring the first commandment of survival in New York City—Thou Shalt Not Befriend Strangers Found Lying in a Pile of Garbage in Times Square—Bambi takes John home "for a glass of water." (Maybe it's the way he screams, "I am not a weirdo!")

Well, one thing leads to another. And by the second gulp of water John has fallen hopelessly in love with Bambi. We know because later that night John will risk his life—three times!—at Russian roulette to save Bambi and her 8-year-old daughter, who by now are the prisoners of Slim and his gang of low-lifes.

You don't want to know any more of the events leading up to John's heroism (stupidity, actually). Nor the events that follow. Suffice it to say that they are improbable. Also suffice it to say that, throughout, the direction is wooden and uninspired and that the acting is laughable and amateurish (except for Kirkland's, which is just laughable).

The blame for this mess goes to its director-writer-producer, Amos Kollek, whose father is Teddy Kollek, longtime mayor of Jerusalem. I saw Amos Kollek's "Goodbye, New York," a disarming 1985 comedy starring Julie Hagerty, so I know that he's capable of doing better. Maybe next time.

NEWSDAY, 11/17/89, Part III/p. 7, Mike McGrady

"High stakes" is the kind of movie where everyone, even the gold-hearted hooker, is a bit of a philosopher. She (Sally Kirkland) is forever saying things like, "Everybody should have somebody."

It's the kind of movie where the hardheaded businessman (Robert LuPone) gambles millions on stocks in the morning, falls head over heels for the hooker at night and cheerfully risks his life for her by dawn. He also happens to be a bit of a philosopher who specializes in cosmic queries: "Doesn't anybody ever care about anybody anymore?"

"High Stakes" is the kind of movie where there's no such thing as a car ride without a chase, where the bad guys wear sunglasses at night, where the businessman-hero plays Russian roulette without so much as a grimace and where his philosophical musings reflect a deep flexibility: "I used to be so sure of everything. Now I don't know."

I refuse to fault Kirkland, LuPone or Richard Lynch because they are clearly much better than their material. However, I have no compunction about citing writer-producer-director Amos Kollek, son of the mayor of Jerusalem, because this is not a first offense (his most recent effort was "Forever Lulu").

Considering the kind of reviews he is certain to get, I only hope that he, too, is a bit of a philosopher.

VILLAGE VOICE, 11/28/89, p. 110, Julie Phillips

The earth tones, the shadows on everyone's faces, the way a woman puts a gun to a man's head and murmurs, "I'm gonna *enjoy* blowin' this *fucker* away"—for the whole first hour, *High Stakes* looks like a throwback to '70s exploitation movies, without the drugs (or like reruns of *Starsky and Hutch*). An aging stripper, single mother, and part-time prostitute named Bambi (Sally Kirkland) comes home one night to find an emotionally impaired Wall Street speculator (Robert LuPone) mugged and bleeding on her Times Square doorstep. They become pals. John's shy at first—when her pimp breaks down the door, Bambi has to disarm the guy pretty much on her own. But later, when the head pimp is holding Bambi and her small daughter hostage, and John is playing Russian roulette for their freedom, the combination of risk and violence opens him up, allowing him to start pushing Bambi around (he's protecting her, you understand) and make drippy remarks about her eyes and hair.

Then the pimps are disposed of and the danger past, and with half an hour to go, writer/director Amos (*Forever Lulu*) Kollek flings *High Stakes* forward a decade into *Working Girl* territory. Bambi reveals her real name to be Melanie Rose (which sounds almost as made-up); she goes straight, cuts her hair, brings her daughter back from Mom's house in Queens, and trades in her tacky scarlet dresses for tacky electric-blue business suits. She's independent now, theoretically— yet the film stubbornly requires that she get her man, as if another, richer violence junkie is what she needs to complete her life. And so *High Stakes* is revealed to be not about thrills after all, but about the importance of family, and the evils of money and the class divide.

Sally Kirkland definitely gets an A for effort here. LuPone ducks out of the contradictions of his role, adopting an allpurpose sardonic smile that makes him look like he knows better, and allows him to preserve a certain charm; Kirkland throws herself into Bambi heart, soul, and silicone. The trouble is, she doesn't look at all like a woman named Bambi. She seems to like playing fallen and over-the-hill women (and she claims to have been a go-go dancer at one time), but what worked for *Anna* doesn't work for *High Stakes*. In the movies, the difference between fallen and *hardened* is one of quality, not just degree, and Kirkland's coy smiles, class looks, and streak of dizzy-blondness don't quite convey a sense of down and out in the sex trades. A social conscience might be part of what drew her to the project (she mentions in the production notes a near rape that galvanized her sympathies, and she did talk Dylan into writing two songs for the soundtrack), but not even Sally Kirkland—maybe she less than anyone—can convince us that between stockbrokers and streetwalkers there's all that deep a chasm. In the land of exploitation movies, haven't they been friends for years?

Also reviewed in:
NEW YORK TIMES, 11/17/89, p. C20, Vincent Canby
VARIETY, 5/31–6/7/89, p. 33

HONEY, I SHRUNK THE KIDS

A Buena Vista Pictures Distribution release in association with Doric Productions. *Executive Producer:* Thomas G. Smith. *Producer:* Penney Finkelman Cox. *Director:* Joe Johnston. *Screenplay:* Ed Naha and Tom Schulman. *Story:* Stuart Gordon, Brian Yuzna, and Ed Naha. *Director of Photography:* Hiro Narita. *Editor:* Michael A. Stevenson. *Music:* James Horner. *Music Editor:* Jim Henrikson. *Sound:* Wylie Stateman and (music) Shawn Murphy. *Sound Editor:* Scott Martin Gershin, Mark La Pointe, and Chris Hogan. *Production Designer:* Gregg Fonseca. *Art Director:* John Iacovelli and Dorree Cooper. *Set Dresser:* Denise Pizzini. *Visual Effects:* Michael Muscal. *Creatures/Miniatures Supervisor:* David Sosalla. *Mechanical Effects:* Peter M. Chesney. *Image Coordinator:* Robin D'Arcy. *Costumes:* Carol Brolaski. *Make-up:* Del Armstrong. *Stunt Coordinator:* Mike Cassidy. *Running time:* 93 minutes. *MPAA Rating:* PG.

CAST: Rick Moranis (Wayne Szalinski); Matt Frewer (Big Russ Thompson); Marcia Strassman (Diane Szalinski); Kristine Sutherland (Mae Thompson); Thomas Brown (Little Russ Thompson); Jared Rushton (Ron Thompson); Amy O'Neill (Amy Szalinski); Robert Oliveri (Nick Szalinski); Carl Steven (Tommy Pervis); Mark L. Taylor (Don Forrester); Kimmy Robertson (Gloria Forrester); Lou Cutell (Dr. Brainard); Laura Waterbury (Female Cop); Trevor Galtress (Male Cop); Martin Aylett (Harold Boorstein); Janet Sunderland (Lauren Boorstein).

LOS ANGELES TIMES, 6/23/89, Calendar/p. 12, Michael Wilmington

"Honey, I Shrunk the Kids," in which shrunken suburbanites are thrust into the ominous jungle of their Gargantuan back yard, is a cautionary comedy about human beings deformed by science, a bright, overloud fable about suburban conformity.

In the movie, four squabbling kids, the Szaslinskis and the Thompsons (Amy O'Neill, Robert Oliveri, Thomas Brown, Jared Rushton), are zapped to sub-insect dimensions by Mr. Szalinski's wacko attic experiments and accidentally tossed out with the trash. They have to trek back to the front porch, evading killer bees and oceans of yuck, while the Szalinskis frantically try to locate them.

In a weird way, what happens to the kids is what happens to the movie. The humans shrivel to crawling piffles or get deformed into caterwauling robots; the super-tall grass and the giant cookies and insects take over. Through this yard prowl gigantic roaches and one compassionate ant, big as a yak, who befriends the quartet after they harness him and feed him cookie crumbs. Befitting the story's frail antic tone, this benevolent pismire is called "Anty."

Even so, there's something delightful about this grotesque perversion of scale—there always has been, from the 1940 "Dr. Cyclops" to the 1957 "Incredible Shrinking Man." "Honey, I Shrunk the Kids" is a prodigy of visuals and special effects, amusing as long as production designer Gregg Fonseca, art directors John Iacovelli and Dorree Cooper, creatures supervisor David Sosalla and mechanical effects coordinator Peter M. Chesney keep yanking out the wonders they've wrought from polyurethane foam and machinery: bees like helicopters, cookies like flying saucers, a bowl of Cheerios like a condo pool filled with crusty inner tubes and a subtropical forest of a back yard with blades of grass, wondrously lit by cinematographer Hiro Narita, towering like palm trees.

Like "Back to the Future," "Honey, I Shrunk the Kids" is a little toy balloon of a TV sitcom episode pumped up to zeppelin proportions. But it lacks "Future's" panache. Director Joe Johnston is a longtime art director for George Lucas' Industrial Light and Magic, but, in the beginning, he hammers the jokes at you as if he were making 40 successive kitchen cleanser commercials.

The actors who play the parents are mostly TV veterans: Rick Moranis (SCTV), Marcia Strassman ("Welcome Back, Kotter") and Matt Frewer ("Max Headroom"). They and the children play their scenes at a deafening rip, screwing up their faces, screaming the lines and larding them up with huge takes and pauses.

The movie was shot on a sound stage in Mexico City, and in the press book, Moranis notes jocularly that the non-bilingual technicians laughed at the movie's slapstick, but couldn't get the verbal humor. I couldn't get it either. The comic timing of the first 15 minutes of the film has the lugubrious, gallumphing hysteria of a mating dance by six jealous blind elephants, without its compensating grace and charm.

It's not just the direction that's at fault. We might ask why it takes the youngsters, even at mite-size, half a day and night to traverse the Big Back Yard. Or why they don't try to whistle for their dog after a first failed attempt. Or why Szalinski doesn't yell out for them to signal him—instead of dementedly crawling around and swinging himself on a Rube Goldberg hoist.

Original director Stuart ("Re-Animator") Gordon wrote the story, with Ed Naha and Brian Yuzna; Naha and Tom ("Dead Poets Society") Schulman finished the script. And, possibly, if Gordon had directed this film, it would have had more edge. It certainly would have had better timing.

You can see his original intentions: burlesque horror and a cheery little post-'60s allegory about neighbors learning to get along. But, since the acting is as overblown as the grass, the story's heart shrinks as the mechanical wizardry gloriously expands.

"Anty" winds up stealing the show, as the only character in "Honey, I Shrunk the Kids" (MPAA rated: PG) capable of arousing human feelings. When that brave arachnid met his fate, my heart felt a little like a 6-foot-tall Cheerio about to sink.

LOS ANGELES TIMES, 6/23/89, Calendar/p. 12, Charles Solomon

Screening with "Honey, I Shrunk the Kids" is "Tummy Trouble," the first installment in the new Disney-Amblin "Maroon Cartoon" series starring Roger Rabbit and Baby Herman.

Director Rob Minkoff and his crew meet the challenge of matching the brilliant opening of "Who Framed Roger Rabbit." Mother once again leaves Roger in charge of Baby Herman, who promptly swallows his favorite rattle. Roger rushes him to the hospital ("St. Nowhere") and pandemonium ensues.

The animators use Roger as a rubbery physical comic. His eyes swell to the size of kettle drums when he is surprised, and his nose, tail, ears and tongue stretch with the Silly Putty elasticity of Daffy Duck in Bob Clampett's wilder "Looney Tunes."

But Roger's personality is closer to that of the monumentally inept Wile E. Coyote of Chuck Jones. His misplaced faith in his ability to solve any problem makes him the architect of his own defeat.

At the end of the film, Roger and Baby Herman walk off a live-action set, repeating the premise of the feature. The device works nicely, although the cartoon would be complete without it.

"Tummy Trouble" is the first Disney animated short to be released in nearly 25 years. Its manic pace and slapstick humor burst with the zaniness of the Warner Bros. cartoons and Tex Avery's MGM shorts, rather than Disney's more restrained "Silly Symphonies."

For decades, animators and fans have prayed for the return of the short films that were once the mainstay of the American animation industry. As audiences rediscover the pleasures of watching a cartoon before a feature, instead of a Coca-Cola commercial, they may start demanding them.

The Disney animators are already at work on a second Roger short, "Roller Coaster Rabbit." "Tummy Trouble" will be a tough act to follow.

MONTHLY FILM BULLETIN, 2/90, p. 41, Kim Newman

Absent-minded inventor Wayne Szalinski has been neglecting his family while he toils in his suburban attic in an attempt to develop a miniaturisation ray which will revolutionise the freight industry. His neighbours, Big Russ and Mae Thompson, feel that Wayne is a dangerous weirdo, his wife Diane is on the point of leaving him, and his children Amy and Nick are shunned by their peers, especially the Thompson kids Little Russ and Ron. While Wayne is trying to present his ideas at a scientific convention, Diane is away from home after an argument, and the Thompsons are preparing for a fishing trip, an accident with the dog and a baseball triggers the shrinking machine. Amy, Nick, Little Russ and Ron are miniaturised, before Wayne returns despondent from the conference and vandalises the machine. He unknowingly sweeps up the children with the debris and dumps them with the garbage at the bottom of the garden. The children escape from the garbage bag, and realise that they have a make a trek equivalent to a walk of several miles through the jungle-like tangle of the Szalinski front lawn to the house. With the aid of an industrious ant, who sacrifices himself in a battle with a scorpion, the children make the trip, with Amy and the unconfident, father-dominated Little Russ forming a tentative romantic relationship along the way. While the Thompsons have had to cancel their trip and are furious with their absent children, Wayne and Diane realise what has happened and overcome their differences to search for the tiny children. After a night in the lawn, the children escape from an automated lawn-mower and find their way to the Szalinski breakfast table, where Wayne discovers them just as he is about to eat his son with a spoonful of cereal. The children are restored to their normal size, and the families are reunited.

Far more successfully than *The Incredible Shrinking Woman* or *InnerSpace*, this turns the perennial s-f miniaturisation gimmick into the material for a broad comedy. Like such recent s-f/horror movies as *Parents, The 'burbs, The Stepfather, Meet the Applegates* and *Life on the Edge*, this returns to the kind of perfect suburban setting of 50s situation comedy, and proceeds to reveal (here,literally) a jungle amid the neatly trimmed lawns and *Dick and Jane* primary colours. However, while the sit-com horror cycle (which includes *Society*, a film by Brian Yuzna, one of the original authors of *Honey, I Shrunk the Kids*) has savagely laid into the resurgent family values of the late 80s, this is essentially a pleasant return to such vintage Disney items as *The Absent-Minded Professor* and *The Love Bug*. The crowed-pleasing special effects and giant sets are seamlessly integrated with a lightly inspirational story-line that brings the misfit kids together and also reunites their squabbling parents as they deal with non-stop dangers.

While the Szalinskis and the Thompsons might start out as troubled families, with the contrasted failings of work-obsessed geek Wayne and macho bully Big Russ contriving to make their kids feel small even before the shrinking ray has cut loose, the ordeals the children undergo in the lawn—and their parents face searching for them—finally bring about a tidy resolution of all their problems. By contrast, Jack Arnold and Richard Matheson's *The Incredible Shrinking Man*—the touchstone of all miniaturisation movies—used the hero's plight to expose the hidden cracks in his apparently perfect ordinary life. The film also goes against *The Incredible Shrinking Man* by suggesting that the small world might not be entirely hostile, with the shrunken children finding miniature allies in the animal kingdom—whizzing about on the backs of bumble-bees or hauled heroically towards the house by a sympathetic worker ant. Of course, the mandatory bugs and creepy-crawlies also serve as an excuse for the film to show off its effects, and certainly the fight between the heroically self-sacrificing Anty the Ant and what looks like an out-of-scale scorpion is a highlight of dimensional animation to match any of Ray Harryhausen's monster battles.

Although colourful and busy, with James Horner peculiarly borrowing a theme from Nino Rota's *Amarcord* score, the film suffers somewhat from the very tidiness of its script. The children and adults are subservient not only to the special effects but to the predictable resolutions of their too-pat problems, as the children overcome their various weaknesses while lost in the lawn and their fathers similarly deal with their character flaws (the mothers, as in most Disney product, are shown to be long-suffering rather than equally instrumental in messing up their kids). Of the personable performers involved, only Amy O'Neill and Thomas Brown make much impression, and then merely in a brief, convincingly gawky almost adolescent, almost-love scene played inside a giant Lego brick.

NEW STATESMAN & SOCIETY, 2/16/90, p. 42, Suzanne Moore

Small-town America was especially created in Mexico City for *Honey I Shrunk the Kids*—the latest film from Disney. And this *is* that rare phenomenon—family entertainment. Despite the hype aimed at young kids around *Batman* for instance, you still had to be 12 to see it. *Honey*, on the other hand, is full of lines like: "We've just got to get this family back together again." It's hardly an original story: eccentric boffin Dad accidentally shrinks his own and his neighbours' kids to a quarter of an inch. He then throws them out with the trash and their mission is to negotiate the backyard, which now appears a sinister jungle, so that they can return home and back to their original size.

Honey works suprisingly well, with special effects for once being humanised by the presence of children. The kids ride on ants and slide down candy wrappers until of course they are eventually reunited with their respective families who have become closer and more understanding as a result of the experience. The humour of the film turns on our identification with the plight of the kids. We all remember what it's like to feel small. The kids' lives are continually threatened by careless adults who might step on them, throw them away or even accidentally eat them. The children are invisible—their pleas inaudible in the big grown-up world.

And, whimsical as this film is, we might remember in our rush back to the family exactly who it is that benefits and who suffers. Women may give up on their men and construct alternative families with their female friends as in *Steel Magnolias*, kids may be unable to make their voices heard, but the new-found family man of the ad men's fantasies—however ecologically deep—continues to be serviced and supported in a way that most women can only dream about. This is the one side of the family business that you won't see in the movies.

NEW YORK, 7/17/89, p. 46, David Denby

In *Honey, I Shrunk the Kids,* four clever and resourceful children, reduced to the size of gnats by scientific error, fight off gigantic ants, nibble at a massive cookie, and are almost eaten themselves in a spoonful of milk and Cheerios. This Disney adventure-comedy about the terrors of scale, directed by Joe Johnston, is cleanly staged, engagingly written, and easily played.

NEW YORK POST, 6/23/89, p. 25, Jami Bernard

There's a word my friends use to describe how they feel when they are feeling low—*weewah.* It is the crestfallen sound of a muted trumpet. That's how the kids in "Honey, I Shrunk the Kids" feel even before nutty scientist Wayne Szalinski's miniaturization machine physically cuts them down to size.

"Honey, I Shrunk the Kids" is a harmless science-fiction adventure for kids, the kind Disney once turned out like soap bubbles. During a search for a stray baseball, Szalinski's two children and the two neighbor kids are zapped down to about a quarter-inch, then inadvertently thrown out with the trash and forced to make their way across the wilds of a suburban back yard. This yard is replete with jungle-high blades of grass, a rogue lawnmower, giant insects, intense sprinkler systems and oversized pollen.

The result is mildly amusing, something kids can get into because they too feel belittled or ignored by their parents, or because they would secretly love to have just such an adventure. The lucky ones really are the four actors who play the tiny tots—they get to slide down twisty grass blades, get soaked in mud pools, climb into oversized Leg-os and ride a mechanized baby ant that looks like one of the monsters from those Japanese B-movies.

One of the kids even gets to swim for his life in a super-bowl of Cheerios (the cereal is played by inner tubes in makeup) while his full-size dad is absent-mindedly spooning up his breakfast.

The search by the two sets of suddenly concerned parents provides a thin connecting tissue—obviously the film makers wanted to temper the special-effects scenes with some family-bonding stuff, but it's pretty wreak. Even the reliable Rick Moranis, who plays the nerdy scientist too preoccupied with his invention to notice his offspring, seems subdued. (There is more and better of him in the concurrent "Ghostbusters II.")

Jared Rushton ("Big") and Amy O'Neill play the two older kids, who get a little romance out of their big adventure. The pintsized actors' skills range from bland to bratty.

For the most part, the special effects are delightful and convincing. The kids are swept into a dustbin by a giant broom, hitch a ride on a bumblebee and make a mascot of a big-pincered insect. Meanwhile, Szalinski hovers over the back yard in a contraption he's rigged out of the clothesline so he won't step on the wee ones.

Director Joe Johnston, a former art director from Industrial Light & Magic, uses his special effects background to cut skillfully enough from the big to the small so that it is not a distraction.

Of course, not for a second do we believe there is any grave danger facing the foursome. Their biggest nemesis is some of the cliched backbiting they engage in at first. And the film's biggest nemesis is that horrible, syrupy patina that kid-adventure movies tend to take on, as if to make up for the unstructured fun the kids have away from home. The Szalinski family, despite the presence of a genius father, is ultimately as dull as any you'd find on TV. It's no wonder that the only time these kids don't feel *wee-wah* is when they're the size of a thumbnail, on their own in an adult-free world.

The movie is preceded in theaters by "Tummy Trouble," a Roger Rabbit cartoon. It harkens back to the days when you got more than just a feature for the price of a ticket. At today's ticket prices, they should throw in a dinette.

NEWSDAY, 6/23/89, Part III/p. 3, Terry Kelleher

This entertainment package from Disney opens with "Tummy Trouble," 7½ minutes of slam-bang-zowee cartoon action featuring Roger Rabbit and Baby Herman of "Who Framed Roger Rabbit" fame.

Then there's the clever animated credit sequence for "Honey, I Shrunk the Kids," in which miniature children run for their lives through a maze of gigantic household objects.

Finally, the feature begins, and you have to ask yourself: Can the humans top, or even equal, the "Toons"?

Not really. "Honey, I Shrunk the Kids" might be more effective as a short subject.

Bear in mind, however, that I'm not a parent constantly seeking acceptable motion picture fare for young children. For the kids, "Honey, I Shrunk the Kids" should be fun. For their adult guardians, it's merely OK.

The incredible shrinking bit has been done before—in "The Incredible Shrinking Man" and "The Incredible Shrinking Woman," not to mention television's "Land of the Giants." But "Honey" does it better, at least from a technical standpoint. First-time director Joe Johnston used to be art director of special effects at Industrial Light & Magic, so you know this movie offers state-of-the-art shrinkage.

But the mischievousness of the title and the presence of Rick Moranis at the head of the cast seem to promise a bent brand of comedy that the movie generally declines to deliver. Moranis is underused as the absentminded physics professor whose electromagnetic shrinking machine goes haywire. For the most part, the focus is on the four youngsters—two belonging to the scientist and two to the jerk next door (Matt Frewer)—who are accidentally scaled way down to a quarter-inch in height, then swept out with the trash and forced to survive in the backyard jungle.

The extra-small fry (teens Amy O'Neill and Thomas Brown and squirts Jared Rushton and Robert Oliveri) have amazing adventures, all right: riding an angry bee, turning an ant into a contented beast of burden, fleeing a killer lawn mower. Danger is never far away for these microscopic survivors. Romance blooms after Brown saves O'Neill's life, but a huge scorpion interrupts their first kiss.

Meanwhile, the grown-ups don't do enough that's funny. Frewer berates Moranis for the children's plight, and blusters to hide his inadequacy as a father. (Big symbolism: Before the kids get shrunk for real, Frewer's wife accuses him of making their older son feel small.) Moranis and his wife (Marcia Strassman) express guilt over the strains in their marriage. "Somehow I feel this is all our fault," she says. Don't blame yourself, honey. The worst parenting in the world couldn't reduce a child to the size of a baked bean.

The chief running gag involves the professor's ingenious but absurd efforts to hunt for the kids without stepping on the grass and crushing them. Anyone would laugh at the sight of Moranis, rigged up to resemble a human helicopter, hovering over his lawn. But he has to come down sometime.

Roger Rabbit and Baby Herman are more fun. They're about the law of gravity.

TIME, 9/18/89, p. 93, Richard Corliss

One dictionary definition of culture is "the propagation of bacteria and other microorganisms in artificial media." For perplexed parents, that comes close to defining today's pop culture— creepy little things that can give their kids the fever and make adults sick. Go figure: as scientists and sociologists toil to prove that just about everything is harmful, pop culture stridently insists that everything is O.K., as long as it's loud, rude or brutal. This makes for a poignant dilemma, especially when a couple of four or eight or twelve wants to go to the movies. In the first few minutes of the PG-rated *Uncle Buck*, a six-year-old blithely discusses the propriety of a fourletter word whose use got a movie banned in New York State in 1962. And this is the mildest of provocations facing parents who want to be cautious without being tyrants. Raise kids today? Naaah, cage'em.

In the '50s, children hid their pop culture under the mattress. Horror comics, B movies and rhythm and blues offered kids safe passage to subversion, while parents dozed off to the official kitsch of crooners and Bible epics. Today, though, mid-cult gentility has been ghettoized in a terrain liberated by the Pied Pipers of rock and schlock. Kid culture is *the* culture. Comicbook films (*Batman*) and TV shows (*ALF*), heavy-metal music clangorous enough to drive parents and dogs wild, all merit solemn consideration in the critical and financial pages. Works that were once intended for grownups and maybe children are now intended for kids and the occasional hip adult. What used to be forbidden to the young is now required watching, listening and reading for all ages. And parents are left fretting that American mass art has become one big piece of Boogers candy.

So if they have toddlers, parents retreat to their local cinema day-care center for the trite and true: nature fables, comic fantasies and Disneyesque cartoons. At the moment, a slew of such pictures beckons to desperate moms and dads. Disney, Hollywood's most reliable baby-sitter, has grossed more than $100 million this summer with *Honey, I Shrunk the Kids*, a lame jape that blends the old *Flubber* formula (Dad as a ditsy scientist) with the ageless theme of children lost in a dark adventure world (in this case, their backyard). Disney is also issuing a return ticket to Never Land with its rerelease of the 1953 cartoon *Peter Pan*. This is a trip that still soars like Darling dreams over the London skyline.

Another 20th century children's classic in cartoon form, *Babar: The Movie*, sets the boy king of Elephantland on a journey to protect his sweet Celeste. Though this Canadian cartoon borrows some gentle wit from Jean de Brunhoff's tales, it lacks Disney's fullbodied animation and narrative gusto. There are endangered pachyderms, a child separated from her mother, comic supporting animals—all the makings of cartoon magic—but unlike *Dumbo, Babar* doesn't fly.

At the head of the kindergarten class is *The Adventures of Milo and Otis*, a 1986 hit in Japan, concocted by author Masanori Hata and director Kon Ichikawa (*Tokyo Olympiad*) and Westernized by screenwriter Mark Saltzman. Filmed in a four-year period on Hata's farm, this liveaction feature tells of Milo, a barnyard kitten who is forever getting into trouble—tangling with ornery bears and lobsters, losing his way in a stream of a swamp—and, thanks to his dogged puppy pal Otis, wriggling out of it.

Milo and Otis requires no Mr. Ed mouth movements, no aerobatic special effects—no human characters either—to fill children and adults with the giddy sense of discovering an innocent new world. Though the beguilements threaten to fray toward the end, the film is constantly buoyed by Dudley Moore, who narrates the story and plays all the voices: a pompous frog, a friendly fox, a Margaret Rutherfordian sea turtle. Without pushing, the film also teaches lessons in sociability. "Otis thought of a word eveyone knew: 'Please.'" To those responsible for *Milo and Otis*, a movie fan with preschool children can only say, "Thank you."

But what is a parent to say to the people in charge of entertaining kids in the years between Pampers and puberty? Perhaps "Help!" These days childern get zapped by the raucous vitality of pop culture before they hit double digits. Too old for cuddly kittens, too young for caped crusaders, elementary-schoolers find few movies that offer the modern equivalent of a Hardy Boys or a Nancy Drew book. Steven Spielberg tries hard, but young teens are the more appropriate target for his *Indiana Jones, Innerspace* and *Goonies* yarns.

So it's back to Disney, whose latest G-rated safari, *Cheetah*, was produced by Walt's nephew Roy. Blending *Born Free* and *3 Men and a Baby,* the film sends teenage siblings Ted (Keith Coogan) and Susan (Lucy Deakins) off to Kenya to befriend a tribal boy (Collin Mothupi) and become surrogate parents of an orphan cub. It's all pretty tame. When Ted declares his yen for jungle adventure, Susan observes, "I think you've been watching too many PBS specials." So has *Cheetah's* director, Jeff Blyth; he may offer his moviegoing students a trip to the wildlife sanctuary, but it still feels like school.

Like school, these films may be valuable in keeping kids off the streets and away from threatening images, both cultural and societal. But soon enough, parents realize that their children cannot be isolated in the plastic bubble of G-rated entertainment. Other, more hazardous wildlife awaits them. If fiendish Freddy or pretty Poison doesn't get to them, the atrocities on the nightly news will. It's an R-rated world out there. And the ultimate danger is not that they will be driven by aggressive movies or music to commit violent acts, but that they will turn emotionally jaded, unable to react to a personal or national tragedy with anything but studied irony. These days, virtually nothing seems sacred, or even serious, to adults. Children can't help getting that message. And Disney can't help them unlearn it.

VILLAGE VOICE, 6/27/89, p. 75, Manohla Dargis

In the '60s Disney produced films my parents tried to protect me from: *Son of Flubber, The Shaggy Dog, The Love Bug*. On the cusp of the '90s the studio returns to its absentminded-professor mode with *Honey, I Shrunk the Kids*, one of the summer's Big Movies, reportedly costing close to $30 million.

Honey's threadbare plot involves a wacky scientist (Rick Moranis in the Fred MacMurray role), whose gizmo zaps his and the neighbors' kids into mitesized morsels. ("We're all the size of boogers!") As with Alice in Wonderland (or more pointedly, children of divorce), it's the familiar that threatens. The movie opens the morning after Mom and Dad have had a fight and Mom has spent the night elsewhere. Miniaturized, the kids are nearly squashed by Dad, who not only sweeps them into the trash, but puts them out for curbside collection. In a fantastic voyage back to safety, they cross a backyard jungle where automatic lawn sprinklers spout monsoons and a dive-bombing bee becomes an airborne bronco (a giddy highlight due to a swooping Steadicam and one of the world's largest blue screens), while a Snapper mower suggests a slice-and-dice finale.

Baby-faced Moranis, looking like a slenderized Wally Shawn (*that* would have been inventive casting), is a gifted physical comedian but absurd as anybody's dad. This drawback dilutes the movie's slim, if intriguing, premise: It's Mom's absence, Dad's carelessness, and the imminent threat of family disintegration that plunges the kids into crisis. Stuart Gordon (*Re-Animator*) was originally slated to direct (he co-wrote the story upon which the screenplay is based), and it's possible he put a nasty spin on the material that scared the studio off. In the Wonderful World of Disney, however, kids learn to care and share, and their disappearance draws the parents closer together as they realize failure and atonement.

This is 1989: The jokes are nastier ("I hope your face ends up on a milk carton") and the effects jazzier, but too much is numbingly familiar. Why the tired adherence to gender clichés? Why couldn't Mom be the absentminded professor this time around? Why isn't Sis the whiz kid? And, in another version of the twisted-ankle syndrome, why must she (whose main concern is to get to the mall) nearly die, only to be rescued by her teen love interest?

Honey, I Shrunk the Kids is neat, clean, bland. (Its ridiculous PG rating is probably due to the credo that G turns off the 10-plus crowd.) If your local multiplex offers kiddie prices, fine. Whether or not it's $7.50 worth of laughs is another matter entirely.

Also reviewed in:
NEW YORK TIMES, 6/23/89, p. C17, Caryn James
VARIETY, 6/20–7/4/89, p. 16
WASHINGTON POST, 6/23/89, p. F1, Rita Kempley

HORROR SHOW, THE

A United Artists release. *Producer:* Sean S. Cunningham. *Director:* James Isaac. *Screenplay:* Alan Smithee and Leslie Bohem. *Director of Photography:* Mac Ahlberg. *Special Photographic Effects:* Peter Kuran. *Editor:* Edward Anton. *Music:* Harry Manfredini. *Sound:* Hans Roland. *Stunt Coordinator:* Kane Hodder. *Running Time:* 94 minutes. *MPAA Rating:* R.

CAST: Lance Henriksen (Lucas McCarthy); Brion James (Max Jenke); Rita Taggart (Donna McCarthy); Dedee Pfeiffer (Bonnie McCarthy); Aron Eisenberg (Scott McCarthy); Matt Clark (Dr. Tower).

NEW YORK POST, 4/29/89, p. 19, Jami Bernard

It's another bad night for Lucas McCarthy. He keeps having these dreams where he ends up in the basement being hacked to death by a cleaver-wielding madman. It's enough to drive a family oriented hero cop insane.

And indeed, people around him are beginning to wonder if Lucas is insane. Ever since he captured the most fiendish mass murderer in history, Lucas hasn't been himself.

"You just tried to strangle me," she points out.

"Don't start with that psychiatry stuff," he snaps at his wife.

"The Horror Show" is a pretty routine fright flick involving a tenacious madman's quest beyond death to terrorize and destroy the cop who put him in the electric chair.

Lance Henriksen, that trustworthy android from "Aliens," is Lucas, wiry and tense and in bad need of a night's sleep. Henrikson brings a lot of intensity to his work, but this is no "Aliens."

Brion James plays his nemesis, Max Jenke, a charismatic ax murderer who French-fries people's fingers and whose last request is to be buried with his cleaver by his side. James seems to relish the role, making Max an enthusiastic, inventive psycho, but the action mostly calls for him to scowl and bellow. He does this very well, but hey—uncage the beast!

"I'm gonna tear your world apart," Max promises even while the electricity is coursing through him in the chair. He's obviously been seeing too many "Hellraiser" movies. "I'm coming back to mess you up!" he swears, using worse language than that. Lucas is duly discomfited.

"The Horror Show" does not waste too much time on character or plot development. Max is furious at being caught, which is maybe not as compelling a reason for his deadly grudge as if, say, he and Lucas had been boyhood chums or in love with the same woman or something.

And to explain why the maniac's spirit continues to thrive even in death, a shlumpy professor is dropped in with some mumbo-jumbo theory about pure evil being a form of electricity.

Safely lodged in the McCarthy basement, Bad Max Jenke could probably decimate the entire family any time he wanted. But, being a maniac, and having about an hour of the movie to go, he simply frightens them a lot, by killing the daughter's boyfriend, skinning the cat (there's more than one way, after all), tying up the lines with obscene phone calls, and doing an "Aliens" chest-buster number on the comely daughter (played by Dedee Pfeiffer, Michelle's comely little sister).

Using a tight camera, director James Isaac telegraphs terror in every scene, but for all that anxiety there are no real surprises. In fact, with the abundance of close-ups, there is something almost static about the action.

The sets seem a little chintzy. Most of the budget must have gone to Max's shape-shifting scenes—he appears as an animated turkey, for example—but the nondescript basement, which serves as the setting for much of the carnage, is decorated almost solely with a garment-center clothing rack and a furnace from Hell.

The frequent scares seem almost mechanically induced, like little electric shocks. When will filmmakers realize that true terror comes from the dark corners of the human heart and not from the special effects or wardrobe departments?

NEWSDAY, 4/29/89, Part II/p. 17, Bill Kaufman

Producer Sean Cunningham, responsible for the original "Friday the 13th" and another chiller, "House," is still plumbing the depths of mayhem with "Horror Show."

Cunningham's latest effort to scare up moviegoers is a film that goes for state-of-the-art shlock value, and hardly offers anything other than a constant string of gruesome scenes held together loosely by a weary plot. Would you believe a decapitated head discovered in a sizzling deep fryer? The main character, detective Lucas McCarthy, played sluggishly by Lance Henriksen, is relentlessly hunted by a maniacal killer, Max Jenke (Brion James) who has murdered—count 'em—116 people.

Jenke is so thoroughly malevolent that he's able to rise smoldering from the electric chair as he's being executed. The AC-DC propels the murderer into, well, let's just call it another dimension. The remainder of "The Horror Show" oozes around supernatural events that occur as Jenke returns to wreak havoc upon McCarthy's family.

It's all been done before, so don't expect any surprises in this very routine thriller.

Also reviewed in:
NEW YORK TIMES, 4/29/89, p. 15, Stephen Holden
VARIETY, 5/3-9/89, p. 16
WASHINGTON POST, 4/29/89, p. C4, Richard Harrington

HOW I GOT INTO COLLEGE

A Twentieth Century Fox Film Corporation production and release. *Producer:* Michael Shamberg. *Director:* Savage Steve Holland. *Screenplay:* Terrel Seltzer. *Director of Photography:* Robert Elswit. *Editor:* Sonya Sones Tramer and Kaja Fehr. *Music:* Joseph Vitarelli. *Music Editor:* Mark Green. *Sound:* Petur Hliddal and (music) Armin Steiner. *Sound Editor:* Tom McCarthy Jr. *Production Designer:* Ida Random. *Art Director:* Richard Reynolds. *Set Decorator:* Kathe Klopp. *Special Effects:* Louis Cooper. *Costumes:* Taryn DeChellis. *Make-up:* Ken Chase. *Stunt Coordinator:* Randy Lamb, Pistol Pete Marquez, and Mike Washlake. *Running time:* 86 minutes. *MPAA Rating:* PG-13.

CAST: Anthony Edwards (Kip); Corey Parker (Marlon); Lara Flynn Boyle (Jessica); Finn Carter (Nina); Charles Rocket (Leo); Christopher Rydell (Oliver); Gary Owens (Sports Announcer); Brian Doyle-Murray (Coach); Tichina Arnold (Vera Cook); Bill Raymond (Flutter); Philip Baker Hall (Dean Patterson); Nicolas Coster (Jellinek Sr.); Micole Mercurio (Betty Kailo); Robert Ridgely (George Kailo); Richard Jenkins (Bill Browne); Bill Henderson (High School Coach); Helen Lloyd Breed (Chancellor Holbrooke); Nora Dunn (Bauer); Phil Hartman (Benedek); Bob Eubanks (Himself); Susan Krebs (Mrs. Wyler); O-Lan Jones (Sally);

Maya Lebenzon (Amy); Annie Oringer (Kelly); "Queen Kong" (Female Wrestler); Diane Franklin (Sharon Browne); Bruce Wagner ("A"); Tom Kenny ("B"); Taylor Negron (Mailman); Fran Bennett (Mrs. Cook); Duane Davis (Ronny Paulson); Adam Silbar (Jellinek Jr.); Marlene Warfield (Librarian); Edward Mehler (Anxious Boy); Daniel William Carter, Marisa Desimone, and Greg Binkley (Eggheads); Lawrence C. Spinak (Startled Boy); Willie Smith (Willie); Phill Lewis (Earnest Boy); Stella E. Hall (Woman with Lasso); Morris Wilkes Jr. (Smart Aleck); Leon Fan (Asian Student); Emily Munson and Sara Munson (Twins); Richard S. Horvitz (Young Enterprizer); Vernetta R. Jenkins (Cassandra); James McIntire (Army Recruiter); Jim Painter (Lonestar State Recruiter); Tara Vessels (Waitress); Ashleigh Harris (Kiddie Korral Girl #1); Juliet Sorcey (Kiddie Korral Girl #2); Davyd McCoy (McDonald's Employee).

LOS ANGELES TIMES, 5/20/89, Calendar/p. 4, Chris Willman

This week's celebrated fine film openings include both "Road House," with the direction credited to one Rowdy Herrington, and now "How I Got Into College," directed by a Mr. Savage Steve Holland. It's an especially good weekend at the nation's movie houses for either auteurs or professional wrestlers.

Holland, of "One Crazy Summer" and "Better Off Dead" wacked-out teen-pic notoriety, isn't exactly known for a light satirical touch. And he was hurriedly brought onto the "College" set after the previous director was fired, purportedly because she was trying to add some small measure of sophistication to what was being positioned by the studio as a sub-low-brow slapstick comedy. None of these omens augur well for a good picture.

"College" *isn't* a good picture by a long stretch, but it's not half as noxious as the personnel changes, the long shelf time and (especially) the commercials would promise. Holland's touch is not as heavyhanded as you might expect; he lets the good, the bad and the ugly gags in Terrel Seltzer's uneven but intermittently amusing script all zip by breezily enough, and doesn't let his zaniness completely eclipse sensitivity to character.

Buying the movie involves buying the idea that waiting to hear back from colleges is a major life trauma on the order of marriage, childbirth or the onset of male pattern baldness. (The kids here keep phoning home for mail updates, screaming at their parents: "Is the envelope *fat* or not?") This limits the target audience pretty much to high school juniors and seniors, who may get a kick out of Holland's overdramatization of the admissions process with occasional horror-movie music and deep-focus photography parodies.

The post-SAT-anxiety set, wearied by the "Porky's" legacy, may manage to find a little consolation in a plot centered around the desperate campaign of one senior (Corey Parker) to be admitted to an exclusive institution of higher education—even if his quest does have more to do with catching up with the girl of his dreams (Lara Flynn Boyle, who looks a cross between Elizabeth McGovern and Brooke Shields, as the prom queen with a heart of gold) than the pursuit of truth. In this genre, you take what nobility you can get.

As it now stands, "How I Got Into College" (MPAA-rated PG-13 for two cuss words) isn't exactly Ivy League material, but bored-of-education high schoolers playing hooky during the teachers' strike could find far less motivational matinees to attend.

NEW YORK POST, 5/20/89, p. 19, Jami Bernard

There is a case to be made for college applications being a time of dread and indecision in a teenager's life—but then, at that age most activities have the same effect. If picking a college is any worse than going on a big date, "How I Got Into College" fails to prove it.

This adolescent comedy follows the travails of several high school seniors as they flunk their SATs, attend a college fair, and argue with their parents over which school to pick. Marlon (Corey Parker) has chosen Ramsey College solely because it is the college of choice for the beautiful class president, Jessica (Brooke Shields look-alike Lara Flynn Boyle).

In the process of applying, interviewing, and writing her essay, Jessica finds that she's not the only cheerleader in the stadium ("I discovered that I'm boring and predictable"). And while Marlon is paying shyster SAT tutors to teach him things like it is better to make a wild guess than to leave a question blank, he discovers that although he is indeed directionless and untalented, lots of people are worse off.

An overlapping story deals with two attractive young recruitment officers who want Ramsey College to put less emphasis on "the numbers" and more in individuality.

The dullness continues apace as our good-looking, white-bread characters go in and out of uninspired fantasy sequences in which they imagine what would happen to the people in those problem-solving questions (how long would it take two men in a leaky boat to bail it, given the parameters) if they got the questions wrong. (The men would drown.)

The token disadvantaged, fatherless black girl works in a McDonalds; it's a pretty demeaning stereotype except that with the way education is going in America today, most college grads wouldn't qualify for minimum wage anyway.

If there is any drama to be had in a picaresque saga about college recruiting. "How I Got Into College" doesn't find it. All it really accomplishes is serving as a product-placement vehicle for Reeboks sneakers.

NEWSDAY, 5/22/89, Part II/p. 5, Lynn Darling

As major traumatic events in the life cycle go, the process of choosing and being chosen by a college is right up there, a time for putting on the line an ego that hasn't even jelled yet. "How I Got Into College" exploits the terror and panic involved amiably enough, though it's better suited to those who have yet to go through the process than to anyone old enough to have survived it.

Marlon Browne (Corey Parker) is a typical suburban high-school senior, short on grades, short on SAT scores, long on potential. He has a novel method for deciding what college he wants to attend—he'll go anywhere that the love of his life, Jessica Cailo (Lara Flynn Boyle), decides to go. Jessica wants to go to Ramsay, a small Pennsylvania college embroiled in its own battle over what kind of students it wants to encourage—the protoyuppies who look good on paper, or the sensitive, wild-card types like, yes, Marlon.

The movie isn't much on plot, but it does have a good time with some of the traditional rites of passage: Marlon's anguish over the SAT exams, for instance, comes to life in fantasy sequences in which characters involved in particularly difficult questions wait desperately for him to come up with the answers. The cupidity of professional advisers chock-full of gimmicks and fast talk and the horror of the official college interview also get a mild, if obvious, send-up.

All this works as well as it does due to the relaxed efforts of Corey Parker, whose laid-back approach to his character keeps the movie from getting as cutesy as it sometimes seems in danger of becoming.

Also reviewed in:
NEW YORK TIMES, 5/20/89, p. 15, Richard Bernstein
VARIETY, 5/24–30/89, p. 34
WASHINGTON POST, 5/22/89, p. B2, Richard Harrington

HOW TO GET AHEAD IN ADVERTISING

A Warner Bros. release of a HandMade Films production. *Executive Producer:* George Harrison and Denis O'Brien. *Producer:* David Wimbury. *Director:* Bruce Robinson. *Screenplay:* Bruce Robinson. *Director of Photography:* Peter Hannan. *Editor:* Alan Strachan. *Music:* David Dundas and Rick Wentworth. *Choreographer:* David Toguri. *Sound:* Clive Winter and David Stephenson. *Sound Editor:* Alan Paley. *Production Designer:* Michael Pickwoad. *Art Director:* Henry Harris. *Set Decorator:* Robyn Hamilton-Doney. *Costumes:* Andrea Galer. *Make-up:* Peter Frampton. *Running time:* 95 minutes. *MPAA Rating:* R.

CAST: Richard E. Grant (Dennis Bagley); Rachel Ward (Julia); Richard Wilson (Bristol); Jacqueline Tong (Penny Wheelstock); John Shrapnel (Psychiatrist); Susan Wooldridge (Monica); Mick Ford (Richard); Jacqueline Pearce (Maud); Roddy Maude-Roxby (Dr. Gatty); Pauline Melville (Mrs. Wallace); Rachel Fielding (Jennifer); Tony Slattery (Basil); Pip Torrens (Jonathan); Donald Hoath and John Levitt (Businessmen); Gordon Gostelow (Priest); Sean Bean (Larry Frisk); Hugh Armstrong (Harry Wax); Francesca Longrigg (Nurse); Tanveer Ghani (Hospital Doctor); Joanna Mays (Phillis Blokey); Vivienne McKone (Receptionist); Victor Lucas (Tweedy Man); Dawn Keeler (Tweedy Woman); Kerryann White (Girl in Elevator); Christopher Simon and Gino Melvazzi (Waiters).

CHRISTIAN SCIENCE MONITOR, 6/30/89, p. 10, David Sterritt

"How to Get Ahead in Advertising" isn't a very wild title; it sounds like an instructional film or a self-help picture.

But the movie behind it is wild indeed. It's a savage attack on the advertising business and on the modern mentality geared toward buying and consuming things that are often useless, and sometimes dangerous—like cigarettes, one of the picture's main targets.

It's also a science-fiction film and a horror movie, all rolled into one fiercely satirical package that went into commercial circulation after appearing in the prestigious New Directors/New Films festival at the Museum of Modern Art here.

If you consider the title literally, you'll have some idea of what "How To Get Ahead in Advertising" is about.

The hero, Dennis Bagley, is a hot young ad man who prides himself on being able to sell anything to anybody.

He has a high-paying job with a powerful firm. He also has a lovely wife and lots of energy—everything he needs for his idea of the good life.

What he *doesn't* have is a bright idea to fit the latest product he has to sell: a new kind of pimple cream. Strain as he might, he can't dream up the right slogan, and the tension grows so strong that he develops a pimple himself.

But it's no ordinary blemish. As it develops, it starts to look like a face.

Then it starts talking, spouting the kind of advertising gobbledygook that Dennis himself is growing sick and tired of.

With growing horror, Dennis realizes that he *has* gotten a head in advertising—a second head growing on his own body, and threatening to take over his life at any minute.

I won't give away more of the story, except to say that it gets even crazier—and so does Dennis. He now hates advertising *and* his new head, and wants to save the world from both of them.

There's nothing subtle about the comedy that flows from this situation.

Dennis has a foul mouth, whichever of his heads is talking, and some scenes are as gross as Monty Python skits gone haywire.

For instance, when Dennis starts destroying all the products in his kitchen, or when the new head turns out to be a glutton that enjoys slugging ketchup straight from the bottle.

As yucky as the film gets, its anti-advertising message doesn't get lost, and it always returns to its basic theme—that we're about to be suffocated by our society's glut of pointless and harmful products.

That's a message worth heeding, and it's hammered out with relentless energy by filmmaker Bruce Robinson and actor Richard E. Grant, the same team that gave us the bizarre comedy "Withnail and I" a couple of years ago.

The cast also includes Rachel Ward, who gives a surprisingly modulated performance in manic circumstances.

"How To Get Ahead in Advertising" is loud, aggressive, and boisterously crude. But it has something serious on its mind, and that's more than can be said about many current films.

LOS ANGELES TIMES, 5/5/89, Calendar/p. 1, Sheila Benson

It must have taken a heap o' advertising to get British writer-director Bruce Robinson as livid as he is in his savage comic satire "How to Get Ahead in Advertising."

He has conceived of all the accumulated horrors of the ad game—seductions for the joy of smoking, lures for pimple creams and toilet-bowl fresheners, warnings against bad breath, denture offensiveness and foot odors—erupting as a boil on the neck of one clever, upper-class v.p. of the ad game, Dennis Dimbleby Bagley.

The nasty pustule appears as Bagley, a 15-year veteran adman with a late-blooming conscience, decides finally that, with his help "brains are being laundered daily," and he is soul-sick about his part in it. Whirling in to see Bristol (Richard Wilson), the acerbic head of his agency, he quits. He is going to turn his talents to warning the world about the fallout from the joint venality of advertising and television, from false claims, from lies about safety, from outright perversions of the truth.

How is he going to reach these masses? Bristol asks blandly. "Walking up and down with a sandwich board? [That's] Advertising, dear boy."

It's also a sample of the wit served up by "How to Get Ahead," a full-scale diatribe written with the passion of a G.B. Shaw and delivered with assault-rifle speed and a zealot's intensity by Richard E. Grant. This is Grant's second collaboration with film maker Robinson; his first was as the unemployed and notable decadent young actor Withnail, in "Withnail and I."

So just as a major player for good seems to be born, Bagley's affliction arrives, this throbbing boil where his neck and shoulder join. What it turns out to be, by nasty stages, is a whole other personality, a minuscule new head which plans a takeover of Bagley's mind and body. The new one is as much a spokesperson for the glories of ads as Bagley has become a crusader against them.

Watching, aghast from the sidelines, is Rachel Ward as Julia, Bagley's wife. If Grant has the showy role, a double one actually, when the small-mustached, false Bagley makes his appearance, then it is Ward who lands the pivotal one. She is, in one body, the most beautiful and compassionate wife imaginable, and the moral center of the piece. And she is radiantly fine.

"How to Get Ahead" (MPAA-rated R for language) is a strange piece, to be sure. It's cruel, funny, knowing, never less than biting and occasionally brilliant. Pure fury seems to have driven Robinson to it; anger he alludes to as Bagley talks about the strong anti-smoking campaign he had created, which eventually was shelved after pressure from above. Her Majesty's government, with its wishy-washy stand on package labeling, like its timid warnings on cigarette packs, is the target of his unleashed venom.

There are problems in creating something as simultaneously funny and unlovely as a talking boil. It's possible that some audiences will lose interest once they learn that the effects are good but minor; the boil, even when grown to full manhood (boilhood?) isn't a patch on The Fly. But then, this isn't that sort of movie.

This is a blistering broadside, a warning for the safety of our souls. When Bagley scornfully decries the advertising double-think in which "oil companies are sold as champions of the environment," Americans might well squirm. And when, on the subject of the rain forest, Bagley predicts that "within 25 years Brazilians will be fixing oxygen prices the same way that Arabs fix oil prices," you may wonder if 25 years is too optimistic a guess.

Bagley is played with a glittering-eyed, diabolical intensity and outrage by Grant. Whether he's giving a withering demonstration of an ad presentation guaranteed to annihilate the competition, or leaping around the gardens of his exquisite country house like Wile E. Coyote on speed, Grant is untouchable.

There is an awful power to Robinson's rhetoric and an irrefutable logic. As one or the other Bagley (not fair to tell) rides up these green and pleasant hills at the end, delivering his credo for the world's future, Robinson pulls out all satiric stops: that is Scarlett O'Hara's speech about starvation and every brave harangue Britons ever listened to during World War II. And It's enough to put a cold hand on your heart.

MONTHLY FILM BULLETIN, 8/89, p. 227, Adam Barker

Advertising executive Dennis Bagley is obsessed with the problem of devising a new way to sell a pimple cream. He reassures his boss Bristol that the campaign will be ready on time, but grows increasingly desperate as the deadline approaches. When he takes his wife Julia out for lunch, he only has spots before his eyes; his behaviour outrages his fellow commuters, and at a dinner party he mortally offends one of his wife's feminist friends by saying she is fat. The next day, Julia finds that Bagley has apparently gone mad and is destroying all the things in the house because he thinks they are infected by advertising. After discovering that he has a repulsive boil growing on his neck, Bagley insists on resigning; soon he believes that the boil is talking to him, and everyone else concludes that he has become schizophrenic. With the boil emitting a stream of advertising slogans and obscenities, Bagley starts to make a videotape explaining the evils of advertising, but he is repeatedly interrupted by the boil arguing with him. He is persuaded to see a psychoanalyst—who asks if he has any sexual problems—and then decides to have the boil surgically removed when he discovers it has sprouted a moustache and is starting to look like him. In hospital, the boil attacks his head and substitutes itself for his head, resulting in the inadvertent removal of his real head. The new Bagley has no trouble devising a pimple cream campaign: he decides to promote boils using a monstrously spotty female singer, which subsequently generates a demand for anti-boil preparations. He also starts to make increasingly bizarre sexual demands on Julia. But Bagley's real head, now a lacerated incision the size of the original boil, tells Julia where the anti-advertising video is hidden, and she realises what has happened to her husband. The next morning, she leaves him. Uncaring, Bagley charges away on a horse, spouting free-market rhetoric to the accompaniment of "Jerusalem".

How to Get Ahead in Advertising follows Bruce Robinson's first film, *Withnail & I*, in trying to epitomise the spirit of an age, with the scene now moved from the late 60s to the late 80s. Richard E. Grant's advertising executive might have stepped straight out of the pages of a style magazine and into a savage satire. Just as in *Withnail & I*, it is really only Grant's performance which holds together a plot which stretches credulity to breaking point, and brings some of the most outlandish yet hilarious lines of dialogue to the screen with conviction. "I've lived with thirteen and a half million housewives for fifteen years!" Bagley proclaims in a pitch for a health food campaign. "She has two point three children, one point six of which will be girls. She uses sixteen feet six inches of toilet tissue a week, and fucks no more than four point two times a month. She's got seven radiators and is worried about her weight, which is why we have her on a diet".

Bagley begins and ends the film as a stereo-typical ad-man who believes in market share and the target consumer. In between, he suffers a period of derangement during which he turns against all the acquisitive instincts which have previously motivated him. More a collection of embittered one-liners against the Thatcher years than a sustained critique, *Advertising* suffers from the extremism applied to every scene. There is hardly any mounting dramatic effect, more a sensation of being shouted at for ninety-four minutes by a brilliant but obsessive rhetorician. There is little to quarrel with in this attack on consumption-led social policy, except for the naivety with which it is mounted. Bagley's attempt to clear his house of useless commodities is as utopian a notion as the communal living of the 60s or the self-sufficiency of the mid-70s. Later, Bagley's counter-blast against advertising takes the form of a monologue to a video camera, relying on a simple, direct address to the viewer which advertising and all its associated media-wise disciplines have not only overtaken but incorporated. Authenticity has become simply another campaign strategy.

Concealed beneath the layers of hectoring polemic is an underlying strand of sexual anxiety which recalls Marwood's discomfort in the presence of Uncle Monty in *Withnail & I*. The rebellious boil is a grotesque manifestation of male anxiety about the body, culminating in the castration nightmare of Bagley's decapitation. Misogyny is also never far from the surface, with the first target of Bagley's abuse being Penny, his wife's feminist friend, and the "boil" Bagley's pro-pimple campaign being fronted by a hideously ugly go-go dancer. Julia, on the other hand, is the very model of tedious housewifely virtue, showing no more signs of personality than the products Bagley advertises. The drama is really confined to a conflict between male characters—Bagley and the boil taking the place of Marwood and Withnail in the earlier film. Robinson is at his best when writing about mental instability and its nonsensical logic: "I'm on the coast of panic" says Bagley, in a phrase which sums up the dominant mood of Robinson's films. But *Advertising* begins to lose its way at the point of Bagley's decapitation—the decisive moment when the boundary of plausibility is crossed. An unwillingness to decide whether it is a surreal fantasy or an allegory with real implications leaves *Advertising* unhappily straddling the generic dividing line.

NEW LEADER, 5/1/89, p. 21, John Morrone

A thrid English entry [the reference is to *Scandal* and *For Queen and Country*.] now making the rounds, Bruce Robinson's *How to Get Ahead in Advertising*, was the highlight of the recent New Director/New Films Festival. In many ways it is the perfect kind of British comedy for the '80s. It exploits that undying breed of English eccentric with a taste for soapbox pontification in language that is no less fruity than rhetorical, yet with a visual elegance quite unlike the often staid proscenium compositions still creeping into British cinema from conventions of theater and television. Writer-director Robinson and star Richard E. Grant romp through this film—recalling their similar performance in its 1986 predecessor, *Withnail and I*—as if they were David Lean and Noel Coward on amphetamines. They tell the story of an ad-man's comic collapse, and with Grant running amok physically and verbally, this movie is all talk *and* all action.

Grant plays Bagley, a rail-thin, livewire account executive who is positively ad-dicted to his work—until the day arrives when the angle he needs to promote an acne cream eludes him, and he resolves never again to manipulate the vulnerable egos of helpless teenage consumers. One discovery ("I have found that brains are being laundered daily, and it shall be no more!") is followed by another even more dire: A boil is growing on his neck, and rather than dissipate, it is quite literally coming to a head. A talkative little head, in fact, with evil, pus-ridden eyes, red gash mouth, and a habit for talking in promotional jargon that reflects the most dastardly capitalist ideals.

Which head will win? The born-again Bagley, who has learned to eschew materialism, or the boil, such a little chatterbox that Bagley plugs its mouth with glue (in perhaps the film's funniest and most disgusting scene) when he can't work its outbursts into his conversations?

Grant plays both head and boil (though not simultaneously—one has to see the film to observe how this works) with more than a bit of Michael Keaton's brand of ferocious quick-change lunacy. As the company man he is a camp villain, as florid as Captain Hook; as the dropout from corporate life he is like Peter Pan in a state of perpetual anxiety. And he lives up to the shape and inventiveness of a comedy whose most flagrant joke is a pun embedded in its very title. *How to Get Ahead in Advertising* leaves most other farces chasing their tails.

NEW STATESMAN & SOCIETY, 8/11/89, p. 34, Suzanne Moore

Not so long ago I was ticked off by a respected left-wing intellectual for being interested in adverts, for thinking that they might be worthwhile and important objects of study. She was, she said, saddened that while she had always looked to utopian novels for her inspiration, I should cling to advertising imagery for mine. Yet it strikes me that though most ads are better and more imaginatively written than these strangely lifeless tomes, they are actually very similar. They are almost the only ways we have of imagining the future—a future perfect that is endlessly deferred. Ads are about "micro utopias", individual futures, the attainment of which depends only upon the attainment of the product.

In these glorious days when lifestyle has replaced living, when the individual rules OK, when ads appear in art galleries and when a word isn't meaningful unless it is prefixed by self—self-referential, self-conscious, self-indulgent—it is severely retro to hark back to the fact that the purpose of advertising is really to *sell* us things. Like seeing an old photograph of yourself in some particularly naff seventies outfit, we would prefer to forget that there was a time when we wanted to *destroy* rather than merely *deconstruct* the advertising system.

As Gladys Knight says: "God, it was all so simple then—the way we were." The way we were involved a lot of talk about Big Brother, the all-consuming power of the media, and how advertising propped up the whole disgusting debacle with lies that made us want things that we shouldn't/didn't want and certainly ought not to have.

It's quite a shock then, to see these naive but passionate views brought to the screen with a vengeance in Bruce Robinson's new film *How to Get Ahead in Advertising*. Robinson's second film (which is quite as idiosyncratic as his first, *Withnail and I*) is little more than a loopy rant fuelled by genuine hatred for the whole advertising industry and held together by Richard E. Grant's hyperactive performance.

The story itself is a surprisingly literal working through of a very simple idea—that advertising is a putrefying growth on the neck of humanity that gradually infects and contaminates the whole body politic. The boil in question appears on the neck of Dennis Bagley, a brilliant young advertising executive who is having problems working up a campaign for a new spot cream. The futility of the whole enterprise gets to him and instead of thinking up lines like "blitz those zits", he jacks in his job and decides to tell the world how awful everything is. Meanwhile, the boil is turning into a head and a talking one at that—a monstrous alter-ego who grunts in adspeak and who cares about no one but himself.

Grant cranked up to the hilt, with a cardboard box on his head arguing with the boil and whispering into a video camera about the "mechanics of the holocaust" is a sight worth seeing. But for a lot of the time *How to Get Ahead in Advertising* is not very good farce, with its satirical targets too wide-ranging to be smashed successfully. It sweeps you along with its adolescent energy yet doesn't know how to channel that energy effectively. But while ranting may sacrifice the finer points of any argument, it is powerfully cathartic and inspirational in its expression of deep hatred of what used to be referred to as "the system".

If you want a subtle critique of the advertising industry you are more likely to find it in all those highly sophisticated advertisements designed to be decoded by the media literate than in this film. And Robinson is quite clearly wrong about a lot of things. Ads may not be completely honest, decent and legal but they are not downright lies. If they were they could simply be replacd with good adverts that tell the truth, a fetishised commodity if ever there was one. The fact that they sell us images of ourselves as we would like to be and we buy them, that we supply the demands— to be more beautiful, more happy, more healthy, means that the whole process is both a lot more fragile and a lot more complex than Robinson allows for us. Ads involve the ultimate insider trading—between our dreams and ourselves.

So it is certainly not the case that these desires can be categorised into false and true needs by some puritanical polemicist. After all what's wrong with wanting? Isn't wanting things to be better the necessary spur of change? Instead Robinson offers us such profundities as "greed out of control" and "we are living in a shop", and veers from suggesting (reasonably) that capitalism is responsible for advertising to advertising is responsible for capitalism (unreasonably).

However, his desperate anger at the way things are is still appealing. The film, with its essentially British humour, is apparently going down well in the States. Yet, perhaps I have seen too many adverts because I want it *all*. I don't want to be forced to choose between the undeniable intensity of the political impulse that rants and raves and screams "no" at the top of its voice and the more fashionable attitude that says "see advertising as a supremely crafted fiction that can tell us more about the orchestration of desire than any political pamphlet". I don't want to have to choose between advertising as the Old Lie of the Old World or the New Truth of New Times.

While Robinson is yelling that the emperor is naked, many of us are busily discussing the witty design not only of the emperor's clothes but of our own.

For if the emperor is naked, then so are we. Whether these clothes are visible or invisible is somehow irrelevant. they are still what we use to get dressed up in. And their function as decoration is every bit as important as keeping us warm.

NEW YORK, 5/22/89. p. 71, David Denby

I usually hate a movie in which an actor delivers a long, blistering tirade, taking us right over the top to the higher glories of egomania. The kind of speech that may provide a scorching big moment in the theater—carefully prepared for and absolutely necessary to bring the play to its required climax—often looks hollow and pompous when magnified and exposed by the intimacy-seeking movie camera.

But James Woods, especially in *True Believer*, has shown us how witty tirade-acting can be, and now here is the young actor Richard E. Grant, who rants and raves and hisses and glares most entertainingly throughout the new British comedy *How to Get Ahead in Advertising*. The movie, which was written and directed by Bruce Robinson—a former actor who certainly knows how to write an expansive part—is a frenzied satire about advertising and greed that turns into a Kafkaesque nightmare. Robinson, who earlier collaborated with Grant on the mannered and garrulous comedy *Withnail & I*, is saying nothing new about the evils of advertising, but the movie is fun anyway as it sends up a mighty wind, a tempest of abuse, invective, and rodomontade.

Grant plays the ace London adman Dennis Bagley, a cynical, driven master of the art of selling antidotes to such woes as piles, dandruff, and bad breath. Bagley is a genius at exploiting the buyers' anxiety. But knowing as he does that his clients' products are largely worthless and his own methods fraudulent, he's developed anxieties of his own. Alone in his office, he acts out ideas for commercials, and Grant, imitating a beautiful actress selling a pimple cream, vamps himself in the mirror, flapping his arms and large hands. Bagley is coming apart. His usual tics and phobias rise and spill over the sides; he turns into a shrieking hysteric obsessed by boils and determined to purify himself and get out of advertising for good. But his unconscious takes revenge, and he raises a boil of his own, a nice big one on his neck. It grows larger and larger; it begins to speak, ridiculing and punishing his new anti-advertising drive. The embodiment of greed, it finally takes over his life. Like James Woods, Grant has a high, tense forehead and a lean, wired-up body—furious thoughts, it appears, have chased all the flesh from his frame (Grant would make a great inquisitor; a great flagellant, too). From the first scene, launching himself into a virtuoso presentation on behalf of poisonously fatty English sausages, he's firing all his engines at once, glowering, crushing syllables, riding over other voices. Grant, like many another hyper-articulate English actor (Dirk Bogarde, Alan Bates), has a talent for disgust: As Bagley, he's fantastically precise about the gross textures of life—the junk in the sausage, the needs and satisfactions of the typical frowsy British housewife who consumes it. In his own life, Bagley, of course, has superb taste; together with his slenderly beautiful wife (Rachel Ward), whom he appears to have selected for her bone structure, he lives in a stone country house with a robin's-egg-blue kitchen. He entertains the local gentry, plays the country squire. His good taste, put at the service of exploiting bad taste, has made him a wailing schizophrenic.

I enjoyed the ranting early passages of the movie best. Bruce Robinson's attacks on product advertising and greed may be familiar, but the blowhard stuff he has written has rarely been delivered with so much gloating, hyperbolic relish. Once Bagley begins wrestling with his talking boil, however, Robinson turns to grotesque comedy, a sort of high-civilization *Alien*, and the movie becomes laborious—*too* grotesque for its super-literate ambience and rather pedantic about its own freakish conceits. Bagley tries to cover the boil, walking around his house swathed at the neck and bent over, but the mischievous thing begins yammering—there are many wearisomely orchestrated social embarrassments before fancy friends.

The boil, which like its master with the addition of an ugly mustache, takes over, extinguishing the real Bagley. But the new Bagley is less complex than the original. He doesn't have doubts or a conscience; he wants only to sell, sell, sell. I hate to rebuke anyone for taking a risk, but I think Robinson's talent is for words, social satire, and Waspish, chic comedy, not for whimsical horror. The movie would have been better if it had remained at the level of exuberant psychological comedy. Certainly, in the person of Richard E. Grant, it boasts one of the most outlandishly entertaining English performers since Charles Laughton last broke all the demure rules of screen acting.

NEW YORK POST, 5/5/89, p. 29, David Edelstein

Dennis Bagley (Richard E. Grant), the hero and villain of the riled-up satiric horror-comedy "How to Get Ahead in Advertising," is the kind of sniggery bully who loves to get drunk and insult feminist vegetarians at dinner parties. An advertising whiz at a large English firm, he browbeats his colleagues for sport; the movie opens with a wild lecture/tirade that packs every paranoid suspicion you've ever had about advertising into five minutes of gloriously irresponsible rant.

His point—nothing novel, but rarely this hilariously articulated—is that products are irrelevant: advertisers package fantasies for a nation of fantasy-junkies. Catering to consumers' vanity and feigning concern for their welfare, Bagley can sell shampoo to a bald man or the same old "suppurating, fat-squirting little heart attack traditionally known as the British sausage" to a country of health nuts.

Bruce Robinson, who also wrote and directed the prickly cult comedy "Withnail and I," makes Bagley the mouthpiece for this amoral business the way Oliver Stone, in "Wall Street," turned Michael Douglas into the voracious capitalist of our nightmares. But unlike Douglas' Gordon Gekko, Bagley is a complicated fellow with pangs of conscience. "How to Get Ahead in Advertising" is the tale of his schizophrenic soul—and body.

Frazzled and despondent over his inability to devise an ad campaign for a routine pimple cream, Bagley has a vision of a society manipulated (without its knowledge) by greedy businessmen—a society where Big Brother isn't watching you but you're watching him (on the television) and obeying his exhortations to buy, buy, buy. So he quits his job and trashes his household, announcing to his horrified wife, Julia (Rachel Ward), that he's going to purge their home of all products acquired under the influence of advertising.

It's at this point that the movie leaves the rational world behind. The crazed ex-adman develops a large boil on his neck, which grows ever more nasty as his resolution to fight his old profession deepens. Then the boil opens a pair of blue eyes. "It's alive! It's alive!" shrieks Bagley in the neurasthenic tones of Colin Clive's Dr. Frankenstein.

Without giving too much away, the evolution of the boil recalls a rather enjoyable Grade-Z horror flick called "The Manster," in which a man slowly grows a second head on his shoulder. But in "The Manster" the extra noggin had no politics, whereas this No. 2 is a reactionary pig, the sum of all Bagley's advertising slogans and near-sexual lust for market-penetration.

Whether the boil (which speaks with a Cockney accent) is real or the product of a madman's fever-dream is beside the point; the carbuncle represents Bagley's dark side, and in its way it's a visionary. It denies categorically that we live in an age of limits—it wants to see the freeways crammed with automobiles and a chemically fattened chicken in every pot.

The radicalized Bagley, on the other hand, is obsessed with the destruction of the Brazilian rain forests, which are being leveled to provide grazing areas for future Big Macs and Whoppers. (Alas, this is not science fiction; our children might have to eat their fast-food hamburgers under oxygen masks.)

In some ways, "How to Get Ahead in Advertising" belongs to the Angry Young Man genre; its heart is more in polemic than drama, and Robinson lets his political outrage swamp his storytelling. When the giddy hysterical Bagley gets replaced by the suavely malevolent boil, the movie's energy level drops. It could have used another twist.

Yet even when the politics are strident and the structure repetitious, Robinson's dialogue is a riotous mixture of highbrow agitprop and infantile toilet humor—his bile is refreshingly unleavened. And if the picture stops dead for a political debate, when was the last time you saw one between a man and his boil?

One thing is certain: You've never seen a performance like the one by Grant—a skinny, ripsnorting marvel. Early on, you can taste his relish in twisting and bullying people into submission—he's like a snotty, sophomoric Harlequin, with a highpitched voice that drips venom. (When he speaks of "large blind fat girls with boils" every syllable jumps out of the screen.) But you can also see the way his acids eat him up, and how quickly his bluster disintegrates into whiny self-pity.

"How to Get Ahead in Advertising" is virtually a oneman show, but Ward has some terrific scenes in which she soothes her babyish husband. She's maturing into one of the screen's great beauties, all bright eyes and starched cheekbones. And Richard Wilson underplays to perfection Bagley's boss—strangely dulcet and unflappable, even when the boil calls him an "anus" in mixed company.

NEWSDAY, 3/30/89, Part II/p. 7, Lynn Darling

"How to Get Ahead in Advertising" wastes no time in foot-dragging subtlety. From the opening scene, this ebullient dissection of the advertising industry in all its heinousness takes off with rocket-like acceleration toward its target.

Dennis Bagley (Richard E. Grant), the ultra-hyper genius behind countless successful media campaigns, is explaining the tricks of the trade to a meeting of openmouthed acolytes. Deceit, lies, hypocrisy and the creation of demand for useless or harmful products are, needless to say, only a few of the weapons he embraces in his harangue.

But despite the conviction ringing in his voice, Bagley is hiding a secret: He is blocked, desperately blocked in his effort to create a campaign for the launching of a new pimple cream. Even the gallons of alcohol and endless stream of cigarettes he's consuming, and the support of his beautiful wife (Rachel Ward) won't provoke the Muse; before long the strain has gotten to Bagley in a literally monstrous way.

"How to Get Ahead in Advertising" is a dramatic change of pace from British director Bruce Robinson's first comedy, "Withnail and I," which was a small, subtly engaging autobiographical look at the end of the '60s in England. This time, he's opted for a bellicose tirade against a very vulnerable subject—the movie takes no prisoners in its send-up of the fiendish influence of advertising and other mass media.

Robinson was also responsible for the screenplay of this movie, and like "Withnail," it is beautifully written; Bagley's almost nonstop invective is wonderful to listen to. The problem is that there's not a whole lot that's new here—the idea that advertising and other forms of mass media are dangerous, manipulative hogwash is not exactly the stuff that stops presses. Bagley's increasing hysteria over this idea requires a certain amount of patience from American audiences who have heard all this before.

In fact, the movie's premise involves a hefty serving of farfetched special effects to put it over the top. But its wildly vengeful, comic spirit finds such a wonderful expression in Richard E. Grant's performance that I was ready to forgive almost anything in the way of obviousness. Watching Bagley act out possible approaches to pimple advertisements in his office, or presiding naked in the kitchen over a mad scheme to put right his life, or scandalizing a couple of fellow commuters on a train is a joy. His role, which involves an extremely schizophrenic approach to character, inspires Grant to dizzying heights of lunacy. I'll wait impatiently for his next collaboration with Robinson.

TIME, 5/22/89, p. 110, Richard Schickel

Take that title literally. Under pressure to come up with an advertising campaign for a new pimple cream, hardcharging Dennis Bagley (Richard E. Grant) develops a nasty little boil on his neck. Ah, yes, a psychosomatic symptom, bound to happen to anyone with a conscience who is trying to sell patent medicine. The viewer settles back comfortably, prepared for some nice English silliness about a chap trying to muddle through a trying situation.

But, no. When the boil comes to a head, it *is* a head. It has eyes, nose and a foul, funnily flapping mouth—Bagley's id made manifest and shouting down his superego like some corporate raider ragging management at a stockholders meeting. Goodbye, Ealing Studios. Hello, Kafka. And for a while, pretty good Kafka. As he showed in *Withnail and I*, director Bruce Robinson has a truly weird sensibility, and Grant is his kind of guy, an actor morosely and ferociously resistant to normalcy and good cheer. In a story in which his wife (a spiritless Rachel Ward), his boss and medical science tell him all he needs to be cured is rest and a more optimistic outlook, Grant's is a presence to be treasured.

But Robinson is after more than black humor. He wants us to see this tormented body as a metaphor for a tormented body politic; the wildly successful British advertising business may be to the Thatcherian age what imperialism was to the Victorian. But here Robinson sets down his hot satirical lance and slaps a soppy poultice of preachment onto the end of his movie. It proves to be a 19th century home remedy for an ailment he has convinced us may be curable only by more up-to-date and radical means.

VILLAGE VOICE, 4/4/89, p. 58, Amy Taubin

Directed by Bruce Robinson (*Withnail and I*), this high-concept horror film decks out a slim insight with some dazzling verbal play. Bagley (Richard E. Grant), a crack advertising executive, becomes blocked while working on a pitch for pimple cream. In the course of his nervous breakdown, he realized that TV is Big Brother, but rather than it watching us, we watch it— voluntarily. Bagley is prepared to unleash this revelation on the world, but he's saved from so self-destructive an impulse by the erection of a giant boil on his neck. The boil grows a head, and the head talks. Its language is the language of television. Sold out, both shows. Warner Bros. is releasing the film in early May.

VILLAGE VOICE, 5/9/89. p. 63, Georgia Brown

There's this vicious boil on the neck of Dennis Bagley (Richard E. Grant), advertising account exec. Not something you would think you want to go to the movies to see. Having squeamishly avoided the boil when it was playing at "New Directors" earlier this spring, I mustered courage only recently. Well, the impish carbuncle is pretty queasy-making, a nifty special effects creation worthy of *Aliens*. As it swells, hair sprouts, and its tiny scrunched features, peering out from the Dijon mustard plaster, gather definition. Then it grows a mustache and begins to talk in slogans about dentures.

How To Get Ahead in Advertising is smashing comedy in the Marxist spirit of *High Hopes*. (Why are the English making terrific subversive cinema and we are not? Wasn't Reagan as effectively provocative as Thatcher?) Written and directed by Bruce Robinson (*Withnail & I*), this is the tale of advertising world hotshot Bagley, blocked in his creative efforts for a pimple-cream account. "Piles and dandruff and bad breath are nothing compared to boils," he rants. A nasty snob, he really can't abide zits. (Which is, of course, the point of the cream's campaign.) No matter that the cream has a "Mother Nature formula," so that "if it doesn't work, you can spread the fucker on toast." Bagley is repelled; a manic in overdrive, he's having a round-the-clock anxiety attack. At lunch with his concerned wife, Julia (Rachel Ward), he explains the industry's finer points: "Nobody in advertising wants to get rid of boils; they only want to offer *hope* of getting rid of them."

What happens next lost me momentarily. (The movie's strong point is not cohesive plot or character motivation, but electrical energy.) In the heat of revulsion, Bagley begins to turn his wrath from boils to advertising itself. (As from a pimple to a suppurating tumor?) He quits his job: "I'm going to cleanse my life." At his handsome country house he insults the dinner guests (I lost the gist here too) and next morning begins his new life by ridding the house of all products tainted by advertising. At this juncture, he discovers the boil.

The boil, you see, is Bagley's voracious advertiser's id, and it wants back its ascendancy. The family doctor refuses to operate. Given the patient's delusion, he says, "I wouldn't be lancing it, I'd be decapitating it." Loyal Julia tries to calm Dennis: "It's all part of this silly, silly stress you're under." (The distractingly beautiful Ward was no doubt cast as an antidote to the ugly boil.) And Dennis himself suffers from having to be constantly alert to the boil's backtalk. "I'm going crazy trying to incorporate it into my conversation." With the boil splitting off Bagley's nasty side, he becomes a rather endearing victim. To keep from waking the boil, he puts his head into a carboard carton in order to videotape a secret message to his wife, his confession that he hopes to save the world. Unfortunately, the repulsive little bugger has a cunning mind of its own.

Publicity notes indicate that Robinson himself is fanatic on never buying anything he's "knowingly seen advertised." I like that in a director. But it isn't refreshing convictions that save *How To Get Ahead* from its incoherences, occasional overenthusiasm, and creaky mechanics (including overbearing score). Robinson has verve and talent, he writes charged dialogue, and, a former actor himself (*The Story of Adèle H*), he chooses performers well. He made me cheer a movie about a boil.

Also reviewed in:
NATION, 5/15/89, p. 676, Stuart Klawans
NEW REPUBLIC, 6/5/89, p. 28, Stanley Kauffmann
NEW YORK TIMES, 5/5/89, p. C8, Vincent Canby
VARIETY, 3/15-21/89, p. 13
WASHINGTON POST, 6/2/89, p. D1, Hal Hinson
WASHINGTON POST, 6/2/89, Weekend/p. 41. Desson Howe

ICE HOUSE

An Upfront Films release. *Producer:* Bo Brinkman. *Director:* Eagle Pennell. *Screenplay (based on his play):* Bo Brinkman. *Director of Photography:* Brown Cooper. *Editor:* John Murray. *Music:* Carmen Yates and Tony Fortuna. *Production Designer:* Lynn Ruth Appel. *Running time:* 86 minutes. *MPAA Rating:* Not Rated.

CAST: Melissa Gilbert (Kay); Bo Brinkman (Pake); Andreas Manolikakis (Vassil); Lynn Muller (Father); Buddy Quaid (Little Pake); Nikki Letts (Little Kay).

NEW YORK POST, 6/16/89, p. 25, Jami Bernard

Remember little sloe-eyed Melissa Gilbert tumbling across the meadows in "Little House on the Prairie"? Now she's tumbling around a slummy Hollywood apartment with a psychotic ex-lover from Texas and a slack-spined fiance from Greece in a different kind of house, "Ice House," written by and co-starring Gilbert's husband, Bo Brinkman.

Adapted from Brinkman's off-off-Broadway play, "Ice House" is about two lovers from a one-horse Texas oil town attempting to come to terms with their pasts and their vitriolic interdependence. The road to enlightenment is a long and dusty one, paved with rambling reminiscences and gradual revelations of sordid deeds past, none of which is particularly surprising, each of which is milked for as much emotional mileage as possible.

Pake (Brinkman) has come banging on the door of Kay (Gilbert), hoping to convince her to come back to Texas and start over. Kay, though declaring she isn't stupid anymore and wouldn't fall for one of Pake's old tricks, quickly proves that she is just as stupid as ever. She opens the door.

Hollywood, despite the symbolism of its name (which is what lured the couple there in the first place), has been a bust for Kay and Pake. Kay has found a new boyfriend, a sleaze who probably wants to marry her so he can get a green card. She has taken to dressing in black leather bustier and skin-tight pants, an attempt to look moneyed, and spends much time killing roaches by drowning them in hair spray.

Pake, meanwhile, looks like he hasn't bathed since the Alamo, and is sleeping in the shrubs "under the H of the Hollywood sign"—one of many romanticized symbols of desperation that this film revels in. (The first part of the movie uses silent-film-type iconography to make bombastic points: Pake looks up from a garbage can where he is foraging for food to see a poster of Charlie Chaplin's Tramp looking down on him; this motivates him to go to beat up Kay's new boyfriend.)

It is unclear how long Kay and Pake have been separated, but when they get back together they deftly resume their routine of "Who's Afraid of Virginia Woolf" squabbling. The camera stays on them long and hard; the play-like structure, with long, wordy scenes taking place in one room, is too constricting for film, even granting that the subject matter is constricted lives.

The dramatic climax is an awkwardly directed scene in which Pake is hog-tied on the floor by the new boyfriend and forced to watch something he'd rather not. Later, Kay threatens to kill Pake in a graphically symbolic way, while the new boyfriend lounges unconcernedly nearby, which is ludicrous in light of the situation. Director Eagle Pennell could have helped out with better staging.

Not to mention better pacing. Long streams of tall-tale memories meander without point, like a child's prattle. "Ice House" is a poor man's "True West," but Brinkman does not have Sam Shepard's ear for the poetry of small-town life. "Can't you get it through your thick skull, it's over between us" and "I thought it was me, but IT WAS YOU" are typical examples of the kind of overwrought, cliche-ridden dialogue. When the occasional interesting phrase does crop up—as when Pake recalls the shiny, crackly oyster-shell parking lot of his youth—it seems out of place.

It's clear the film makers were saddled with a low budget. "Ice House" has the production values of a porn movie, with inadequate lighting and muddy sound. The flashback scenes and lyrical shots of oil machinery clanking away fare better.

Melissa Gilbert at least is better than her material, but that Greek boyfriend, played with exaggerated hand gestures by Andreas Manolikakis, has to go—he seems to have the accent of a "Saturday Night Live" skit, and where he appears, unkind laughter follows.

Brinkman's unwashed, hair-trigger Pake is a character that is indeed recognizable, although not happily so. Brinkman the screen writer has a lot more affection for his Pake than the viewer may be able to muster. Taking small lives to the big screen requires more than earnest intentions.

NEWSDAY, 6/16/89, Part III/p. 3, Lynn Darling

"Ice House" takes off from an easily recognizable formula, sort of ersatz Sam Shepard by way of low-rent William Faulkner: Create two down-and-out characters, throw them in a room together, let them say and do terrible, sweaty things to each other and then Wait for the Truth to Emerge.

In this case, desperate character No. 1 is Pake (Bo Brinkman), a failed young country-western star who we see sighing over Gene Autry's star in front of Mann's Chinese Theater and eating garbage out of a trach can before he turns up at the sleazy hotel room of desperate character No. 2: Kay (Melissa Gilbert), his ex-girlfriend, a young woman given to tight pants and black leather bustiers, who spends her time murdering cockroaches by drowning them in hair spray and holding her dolly while listening to country-western music.

Pake has come to take Kay away from this tawdriness and bring her back to Texas, where their romance began long before. But Kay is having none of this—Pake's unfortunate habit of beating up her current boyfriend and torching his car has gotten on her nerves. A patient man, Pake settles in to rant and rave and make long, boring soliquies so that these two crazy kids can get to the bottom of things.

The trouble is that not much emerges from all the yelling and screaming and squalid acts of vengeance except the sort of dark secret that can too easily masquerade for meaning. In flashbacks and more soliloquies, we learn all about Kay and Pake's childhood, the signal events of which never achieve the slightest degree of reality. It's like listening to summaries of secondhand soap opera plots—the terrible events reveal nothing meaningful beyond the bare bones of their dismal lives.

It's pretty squalid all right: "Ice House" revels in its sleazy atmosphere, romanticizing it without ever making it believable. Pake and Kay spend a lot of time telling each other and Kay's bored Greek boyfriend (Andreas Manolikakis) all about the pain they've suffered, but the characters sound throughout as if they're talking about someone else.

Bo Brinkman based the screenplay for "Ice House" on his own Off-Off Broadway play, "Ice House Heat Waves." Maybe the dialogue rang truer on the stage: "Once you forgot where you're from, you're nowhere," Pake tells Kay. "I'm just trying to find myself, that's all, " she tells him. It's an extremely low-budget production: Most of the action takes place in front of a more-or-less stationary camera in the hotel room, which eliminates the possibility that the tedium might be relieved by any offbeat or interesting angles on the proceedings.

Despite the awkward flailings of her husband's script, Melissa Gilbert does a fine job of letting the sweetness and vulnerability of her character break through her tough-girl veneer. Brinkman's acting provides more insight into his character than the dialogue he's written for him. Pake's passion and his dumb yearning for something better come to life on his face the way they never do in the speeches he gives.

VILLAGE VOICE, 6/20/89, p. 94. Julie Phillips

Melissa Gilbert seems pretty determined—and understandably so—to put some distance between herself and her years of wholesomeness as Laura on *Little House on the Prairie*. And yet, you might think of *Ice House*, the movie she has made with writer/co-star/husband Bo Brinkman, as a similar arrangement. About a family as twisted and bad as Laura's virtuous and good, *Ice House* is a kind of *Little House on the Oil Field*: a far more unpleasant, but equally unreal account of childhood in the Heartland.

A Tennessee Williams in Sam Shepard's clothing, Brinkman packs his script—originally an Off-Off-Broadway play—with dark family secrets. Pake (Brinkman), a rather psychotic drifter, has come to Hollywood to bring his true love, Kay (Gilbert), back to Texas , starting by clobbering her new boyfriend from behind with a baseball bat. Kay, a whorish waif, seems to harbor some affection for the unpalatable Pake, enough to spend the night screaming at him; together, they engage in the long bouts of awkward exposition that uncover the truth about their sordid mutual past.

Outside of a few convincing bits of drama, *Ice House* is basically contrived. The shouting matches seem straight out of a beginning improv class, and the revelations themselves are somehow disappointing: These days, incest is more the stuff of self-help books than theater. And director Eagle Pennell's decision to stick close to the play is unfortunate: The long takes and close quarters only make the film more stiff and stagy. The film's finest moments are its rare flashbacks to Texas and the twisted, oddly beautiful machinery of the oil fields. As Pake remarks, with the cliché juice dripping down his chin, "Once you forget where you're from, man, you're nowhere."

Also reviewed in:
NEW YORK TIMES, 6/16/89, p. 14, Vincent Canby
VARIETY, 6/21-27/89, p. 24

I'M GONNA GIT YOU SUCKA

A United Artists Release of an Ivory Way Production in association with Raymond Katz Productions and Front Films. *Executive Producer:* Raymond Katz and Eric L. Gold. *Producer:* Peter McCarthy and Carl Craig. *Director:* Keenen Ivory Wayans. *Screenplay:* Keenen Ivory Wayans. *Director of Photography:* Tom Richmond. *Editor:* Michael R. Miller. *Music:* David Michael Frank. *Music Editor:* Jeff Charbonneau. *Sound:* Oliver L. Moss. *Sound Editor:* John Kwiatkowski, Dane Davis, and Danetracks. *Production Designer:* Melba Farquhar and Catherine Hardwicke. *Set Decorator:* Kathryn Peters-Hollingsworth. *Set Dresser:* Tom Cortese. *Special Effects:* Fred Cramer. *Costumes:* Ruth Carter. *Make-up:* Laini Thompson. *Stunt Coordinator:* Alan Oliney. *Running time:* 90 minutes. *MPAA Rating:* R.

CAST: Keenen Ivory Wayans (Jack Spade); Bernie Casey (John Slade); Antonio Fargas (Flyguy); Steve James (Kung Fu Joe); Isaac Hayes (Hammer); Jim Brown (Slammer); Ja'Net DuBois (Ma Bell); Dawnn Lewis (Cheryl); John Vernon (Mr. Big); Clu Gulager (Lt. Baker); Kadeem Hardison (Willie); Damon Wayans (Leonard); George James (Bruno); Marc Figueroa (Knuckles); Robert Colbert (Farrell); Marilyn Coleman (Funeral Mourner); Jester Hairston (Pop); Hawthorne James (One Eyed Sam); Anne Marie Johnson (Cherry); Gary Owens (As Himself); Eve Plumb (Kalinga's Wife); Clarence Williams III (Kalinga); Michael Goldfinger (Sergeant); John Witherspoon (Reverend); Homeselle Joy (Mourner); Vickilyn Reynolds (Sadie); Paul Motley (Luther); Charles Cozart (Anchorman); Brian Maguire (Policeman); David Alan Grier (Newsman); Ariana Richards (Little Girl); Ben Ryan Ganger (Little Boy); Carl Craig (Man in Love); Nancy Cheryll Davis (Woman); Kim Wayans (Nightclub Singer); Robin Harris (Bartender at Sam's); Cullen G. Chambers (Brothel Man); Terri Bivalcqua (Brothel Woman); J.W. Alexander (Inmate); Roy Fegan (Dead Pimp); Howard Allen (Coffee Shop Customer); Bee-Be Smith (Coffee Whop Waitress); Bobby Mcgee (Pimp); Dana Mackey (Big Brim Bouncer); Ludie Washington (Big Brim Bartender); Bobby Mardis (June Bug/Big Brim Pimp #1); Wren Brown (Big Brim Pimp #2); Tony Cox (Wayne Evans); Tom Wright (Brothel Man); Eugene R. Glazer and Michael Conn (Officers); Finis Henderson III (Player); Chris Rock (Rib Joint Customer); Terry Christiano and Liza Cruzat (Bimbos); Peter McCarthy (Weasel); Bentley Evans (Crowd Member); Richard McGregor (Gang Member); Tommy Morgan (Referee); Gerald Walker (Man in Audience); Kojo Lewis (Watchman).

LOS ANGELES TIMES, 2/17/89, Calendar/p. 8, Michael Wilmington

In Keenen Ivory Wayans' "I'm Gonna Git You Sucka," there's sometimes a light line between sendup and near-celebration.

The movie is a satire of the early '70s blaxploitation action movies: all the "Shafts," "Black Caesars" and "Superflys" with their natty, super-masculine heroes, flamboyant pimps and murderous drug czars. Its most obvious model is 1980's "Airplane!" But, where the Zucker-Abrahams-Zucker "Airplane!" team probably didn't much like the disaster movies they spoofed, Wayans is satirizing something he's closer to: urban street culture and the black super-heroes of his movie-going youth. On one level, he is having a giggle at the inflated, phony imagery. On another, maybe he misses it.

Wayans, an engaging comic with a sweet smile, casts himself here as returning Army veteran Jack Spade. Machismo is a joke in "Sucka"; Spade is a mama's boy whose 10-year Army hitch won him medals for surfing and good conduct. Returning home to his mama (the formidable Ja'net Dubois), his dead brother's willing widow (Dawnn Lewis), and to a neighborhood despoiled by the vile depredations of vice-lord Mr. Big (John Vernon, once again coming up like thunder), Jack searches somewhere, anywhere, for a hero to model himself after.

He finds, successively, supercop Slade (Bernie Casey of "Hit Man"), superpimp Flyguy (Antonio Fargas of "Cleopatra Jones"), rough-neck soul food titans Slammer and Hammer (Jim Brown of "Slaughter" and Isaac Hayes of "Truck Turner") and karate king Kung Fu Joe (Steve James of "American Ninja"), all of whom do straight-faced "Airplane!"-style sendups of their old or current image—and all of whom, in the end, prove less ferocious than Jack's mama.

Wayans' directing isn't up to his writing, and his writing isn't always up to his acting. And he misses one aspect of the black actioners almost completely: their pace and zonked-out, overheated style. He is also guilty of an occasional gross, tasteless scene, like the "take it all off" encounter with lascivious bar-girl Cherry, a woman of many parts.

There are misfires in "Sucka," (MPAA rated R for language) but there's also some funny stuff. Wayans shows a refreshing taste for self-mockery, something his old "Raw" colleague, Eddie Murphy, might study. In one scene, as a gorgeous cabaret singer gives a shockingly bad rendition of "When the Saints Go Marching In" in pseudo-Sarah Vaughan style, the waiter explains to stunned patrons that she gets away with it because she is the director's sister. As it turns out, she (Kim Wayans) really is.

MONTHLY FILM BULLETIN, 11/89, p. 334, Kim Newman

Any Ghetto, U.S.A. Junebug Spade is dead in the street, having overdosed on gold chains supplied to him by white villian Mr. Big. The latter sends Leonard and Willie, two thugs, to collect Junebug's $5,000 debt by kidnapping his widow Cheryl and forcing her into prostitution. Leonard and Willie arrive just as Junebug's brother Jack returns from a ten-year hitch in the army, but it is the brother's tough mother, Ma Bell, who beats them up and throws them out of the house. Jack, sworn to bring down Mr. Big, tries to persuade John Slade, a black vigilante hero from the 70s who used to go out with Ma Bell, to come out of retirement and throw the chain pushers out of the ghetto. Slade refuses, as does Kalinga, leader of the People's Revolutionary Army. But Slade relents and agrees to join the crusade, recruiting a group of black action heroes—hardmen Hammer and Slammer, former superpimp Flyguy and martial artist Kung Fu Joe—to help. The heroes start to break up Mr. Big's businesses—a gold store, a brothel, the Big Brim Bar—and the gangster fights back by having Leonard and Willie kidnap Cheryl, who has rekindled her old romance with Jack. Kung Fu Joe tries to takes on 57 corrupt policemen and is severely wounded, Hammer is disabled by his excessive armoury when he trips over, Slammer is crippled by a severe wound to his giant bunion, and Slade accidentally blows himself up. Jack, who has suffered all his life because of his mother's reputation as a two-fisted heroine, is about to take on Mr. Big alone when Ma Bell intervenes, and Jack locks her in a closet so he can confront and overcome the bad guys. Accepting the congratulations of his battered comrades, Jack officially becomes a proper black hero when he is given his own signature tune.

Usually, the problem with genre spoofing is that the target is either too large (the Western genre in *Blazing Saddles*) or small (*Star Wars* in *Spaceballs*) to be worth the effort. Like *Airplane!*, on which it was evidently modelled, *I'm Gonna Git You Sucka* gets round the problem by fastening on to a cycle rather than an entire genre, and has the advantage, even fifteen years after the black action movie petered out, of being the first on the scene to poke fun at a tradition that was patently ridiculous in the first place. Like all the best satirists, Keenen Ivory Wayans clearly has a great affection for his subject, and has managed not only to persuade such stalwarts of the bygone genre as Bernie Casey (*Cleopatra Jones, Black Gunn*), Antonio Fargas (*Shaft, Cleopatra Jones*), Issac Hayes (*Truck Turner*), Jim Brown (*Slaughter*), and comparative newcomer Steve James (*American Ninja, Hero and the Terror*) to send themselves up—though

Fred Williamson, Pam Grier, Richard Roundtree, Ron O'Neal, William Marshall, Vonetta McGee and Jeanne Bell are sorely missed—but to get Hayes and Curtis Mayfield to burlesque their soul themes from *Shaft* and *Superfly*.

At the time of the superspade boom, which was inaugurated in 1970 by Ossie Davis' *Cotton Comes to Harlem* and turned into a trend by Gordon Parks Jnr.'s *Shaft*, it was often obvious that players whose talents were mainly comic were being forced to take the action movie too seriously, so here it is a pleasure to see them allowed to cut loose. Antonio Fargas features in a brilliantly sustained gag sequence worthy of Tashlin as he comes out of jail after ten years dressed in his outrageous pimp costume—which features platform shoes with goldfish swimming inside them—and struts proudly down the street, his cool demeanour evaporating as the passersby go from befuddlement to ridicule. When Jack Spade finally confronts Mr. Big, John Vernon steps out of character and gives a speech justifying his appearance as an exploitation villain by pointing out that Shelley Winters and other luminaries found nothing to be ashamed of in their over-the-top performances in the likes of *Cleopatra Jones*. This gag cuts even deeper with audiences familiar with the distinguished Vernon's career, which has slipped from major studio work like *Point Blank* and *Dirty Harry* into the Z-movie mire of *Killer Klowns from Outer Space*, *Chained Heat* and *Invasion of the Body Suckers*.

The film spoofs the makeshift production values of many low-budget action films, for instance when Ma Bell in the fight scene is replaced by a white stuntman with a moustache, but also extends the blacks-in-Hollywood theme of Wayans' work as a writer-performer in *Hollywood Shuffle* by indulging in all the excesses of the early 70s as a gentle way of getting rid of them. The film takes care to cover all the bases of the black action genre by including corrupt white cops, a gratuitous night-club song (a terrible soul version of "When the Saints Go Marchin' In" by the director's sister), one totally pointless nude girl in the brothel sequence (in addition to a feebly screaming extra wearing an "Another Model Turned Actress" T-shirt), incomprehensible jive talk, non-stop music, stupid fashions and a pompous Important Theme, with gold chains replacing heroin as the plague sweeping the ghetto. Finally, the film has the trace elements of a genuinely serious theme in its suggestion that black cinema should move on from the exploitation vogue as Jack Spade's rap replaces John Slade's soul theme at the end, and the hero learns to live without leaning on his bumbling heroes or his action-man mother.

NEW YORK POST, 1/13/89, p. 27, David Edelstein

Keenen Ivory Wayans, the writer, director and star of "I'm Gonna Git You Sucka," grew up on black exploitation movies—"Shaft," "Superfly," "Cleopatra Jones," prison and kung-fu pictures—and always dreamed of making his own version of "Airplane!" out of them.

Wayans, who co-wrote and starred in "Hollywood Shuffle," casts himself as Jack Spade, an Army secretary who returns to "Any Ghetto, U.S.A." to find that his brother has O.G.'ed—that is, died from an overdose of gold chains, supplied to the ghetto by the very bad (and very white) Mr.Big (John Vernon).

When Big's goons (Kadeem Hardison and Damon Wayans) try to shake down the brother's comely widow (Dawnn Lewis) and mama (Ja'net DuBois), Jack tracks down the aging heroes of blaxploitation pictures past—John Slade (Bernie Casey), Flyguy (Antonio Fargas), Kung Fu Joe (Steve James), Hammer (Isaac Hayes) and Slammer (Jim Brown). Their mission is to screw up Mr. Big's operations, and finally put him out of business for keeps.

Along the way, there are scattershot laughs. Wayans devises a Youth Gang competition in which kids race ahead of barking dogs while carrying TV sets, and Flyguy recalls a Pimp of the Year contest in which he won the talent portion with the poem, "My Bitch Better Have My Money."

But Wayans hasn't learned from "Airplane!" that the only way to do this kind of gagfest is with a straight face, with the actors behaving as if they're in a real blaxploitation movie. Here, everyone seems to be in on the joke, and the timing is sledgehammer-obvious. The chief gag is that these super-heroes are too old to be doing what they're doing. They're klutzy instead of cool, and you know what happens to klutzes around guns and dynamite. Kaboom.

What's most disappointing about "I'm Gonna Git You Sucka" is that it's *just* a bunch of jokes—that it tells you so little about what Shaft, Superfly and Cleopatra Jones meant to Wayans. The blaxploitation era came in the decade after the Civil Rights movement, and through these pictures Hollywood shrewdly took advantage of blacks' new sense of entitlement.

I'm not suggesting that Wayans should have made a *scholarly* blaxploitation satire. But watching this movie, you have no idea that John Shaft was the paradigm of black potency—the guy who (as the Isaac Hayes theme song made explicit) could drive all the white chicks crazy in bed, curtly dismiss them in the morning, and go organize an army of ghetto blacks to take out The Man.

The character in Wayans' movie is a community organizer, a sweetie, and while that's a funny idea (Shaft getting tired of all the macho crap), it hasn't been developed. Flyguy (Superfly) is just out of fashion, his absurdly high heels (he affixes his shoes to small aquariums) drawing hoots and jeers instead of applause.

One joke with enormous potential is an interview with the black-power guerilla Kalinga (Clarence Williams III, from "The Mod Squad"), whose lair is draped with "Kill Whitey" posters and slogans. But Kalinga is married to a blue-eyed blonde (Eve Plumb) and has two adorable, fair-haired children.

But the scene, with its bitter satire of black-power impulses, is so lamely acted and directed that you're not even sure what the joke's supposed to be.

United Artists evidently knew this wouldn't be a critics' picture, and opened "I'm Gonna Git You Sucka" in cities like Washington first. It has done well. And the movie has its admirers: some of the audience at its first New York screening laughed on cue. The suckas.

NEWSDAY, 1/13/89, Part III/p. 3, Lynn Darling

You remember black exploitation movies—big, violent super-heroes blasting away at all manner of bad guys and working their way through a legion of nymphomaniacal women to a slick, jazzed-up score.

It was trash, but it wasn't hard to understand the contemporary appeal. The movies were popular in the early '70s when they provided the ultimate escapist fantasy in the aftermath of all the Great Society's broken promises. What's harder to understand is why, 15 years later, it's now time for an exercise in cinematic recycling: "I'm Gonna Git You Sucka" is meant to be a parody of movies like "Shaft" and "Superfly," but most of the time, it merely manages to be as lame in its own right as the originals.

The movie, which takes place in "Any Ghetto, USA," does have a few pretensions to passing cleverness: Keenen Ivory Wayans plays a young hero whose courage and confidence are blunted by a mother (Ja'net DuBois) who fights all his battles for him—it's a nice send up of the ludicrously macho nature of the original heroes.

But mostly this movie is boring—the contemporary references, while obvious, aren't pointed enough to make it more than an exercise in unnecessary nostalgia. Young Jack Spade (Wayans) is back from a 10-year hitch in the peacetime army (he has medals for precision typing and latrine patrol) to avenge the death of his brother Junebug, who has OG'd—that is, died of his addiction to wearing an overabundance of gold chains. Before long, he's enlisted an aging, retired superhero, John Slade (Bernie Casey), and a quartet of his old buddies to help him destroy Mr. Big (John Vernon), the powerful bad guy behind the gold epidemic.

The movie does manage to send up nearly every convention of the genre—John Slade walks around with a small band in his wake, playing his theme music. But even given the alarming news that the '70s are about to become chic again, it's difficult to summon any emotion livelier than total indifference.

"I'm Gonna Git You Sucka" was written and directed by its star, Wayans, who, as the co-writer of Robert Townsend's "Hollywood Shuffle," proved he knew a thing or two about insightful satire. But in his first solo attempt, he has opted for slow-moving inanity: Much is made for instance of one tough guy's throbbing bunion.

For those who wax nostalgic at the mere thought of black exploitation movies, however, "I'm Gonna Git You" is chock-full of references to the old days. Isaac Hayes, who won an Academy Award for the theme to "Shaft," plays one of the old heroes, while Jim Brown, the ex-fullback turned actor, is another. And Curtis Mayfield contributes a parody of the music he wrote for "Superfly."

VILLAGE VOICE, 1/17/89, p. 69, Donald Suggs

The first solo effort by black comedian and *Hollywood Shuffle* cowriter Keenen Ivory Wayans, *I'm Gonna Git You Sucka* purports to send up the inner-city adventure films of the '70s. Set in "Any Ghetto, U.S.A.," the film opens with the death of a small-time dealer named Junebug

Spade. Pulling back the white sheet to reveal a corpse entangled in a Tut's tomb worth of jewelry, the investigator solemnly notes that it wasn't an OD but an OG—death by too much gold.

When Junebug's brother, Jack (played by Wayans himself), returns to investigate the circumstances of Junebug's untimely demise, he discovers that gold addiction has overtaken the town. He enlists the help of three retired black superheroes (played by blaxploitation period pieces Bernie Casey, Jim Brown, and Isaac Hayes) in bringing down the man who's pushing these hubcap-sized medallions and gold-plated bicycle chains, a white villain called Mr. Big.

"The success of this film is more important than its content," Wayans freely admits. It's a way of getting more experience, experience he badly needs. Though he's clearly set out to tell a story, he ends up with a series of vignettes, most of them awkwardly strung together and poorly paced. Still, *Sucka* has haphazard hints of comedy, and they carry the movie. In one scene, Jack goes to talk to black-hero-turned-community-leader Slade (Bernie Casey), only to find him hosting a street-gang Olympics, hoodlums with color televisions on their shoulders racing down a track with police Dobermans in hot pursuit. Antonio Fargas (who most will remember as Huggy Bear from *Starsky and Hutch*) gives a comic performance as a convict daydreaming about the days when he won the Pimp of the Year contest, resplendent in a hot-pink suit as he sweeps the talent section, reading a poem entitled "My Bitch Better Have My Money."

Other veteran comedians who are able to rise above the muddled plot perform admirably, particularly Ja'net DuBois as Jack's overprotective mama, but there's also some embarrassingly poor acting. Dawnn Lewis is supposed to be funny in her lead role as Junebug's widow and Jack's rekindled flame, but her only comic touch is an occasional helpless little sigh that sounds more like the squeal of a frightened pig.

The term "black exploitation" has always referred more to the wide profit margins of these low-budget, black-oriented films than to their social relevance. *Sucka*, which skirts, even mocks, the racial issues that most young black film-makers are fighting to raise, reinforces this distinction. The essential elements of the genre, the up-your-ass attitude and the up-in-your-face sexuality, everything except a few '70s wardrobe flourishes, are absent. What intrigues Wayans most about blaxploitation is its marketability.

"I wanted to make a movie that was as funny as *Hollywood Shuffle* or Spike Lee's *School Daze*," he explains. "But I wanted it to be a movie that could take me out of the art houses and into the mainstream. In the '70s, we proved that we could make all different kinds of films, from *Cooley High* to *Sounder* to *Lady Sings the Blues*. As black filmmakers in the '80s, we have to prove that we're financially viable."

Intent as Wayans claims to be on remaining commercial—he and Robert Townsend have just completed a screenplay about the rise and fall of a Temptations-style singing group—his talent clearly lies on the outer limits of comedy. (Asked how he made the transition between timing a stand-up routine and directing a movie, Wayans shrugs, "I didn't.") And black-oriented comedies may yet prove to be the most effective vehicle for Wayans's chaotic sensibility. When asked about the kind of films he'd ideally like to make if there were no financial constraints, his first reponse is that he'd like to do something dealing with the civil rights era or the black experience in Vietnam. Then he pauses, smiles, and says, "And, of course, a lot more comedies like this one."

Also reviewed in:
NATION, 2/13/89, p. 208, Stuart Klawans
NEW REPUBLIC, 3/6/89, p. 25, Stanley Kauffmann
NEW YORK TIMES, 1/13/89, p. C6, Janet Maslin
VARIETY, 12/21–27/88, p. 14

IMMEDIATE FAMILY

A Columbia Pictures release. *Executive Producer:* Lawrence Kasdan. *Producer:* Sarah Pillsbury and Midge Sanford. *Director:* Jonathan Kaplan. *Screenplay:* Barbara Benedek. *Director of Photography:* John Lindley. *Editor:* Jane Kurson. *Music:* Brad Fiedel. *Music Editor:* Allan K. Rosen. *Sound:* Sandy Berman and (music) Tim Boyle and Bobby Fernandez. *Sound Editor:* Warren Hamilton Jr., Randy Kelley, Marvin Walowitz, Beth Sterner, and Karen G. Wilson. *Production Designer:* Mark Freeborn. *Art Director:* David

Willson. *Set Designer:* Byron Lance King. *Set Decorator:* Kimberley Richardson. *Special Effects:* John Thomas. *Costumes:* April Ferry. *Make-up:* Irene Kent. *Stunts:* Bobby Porter, Jacob Rupp, and Barbara Bruce. *Running time:* 95 minutes. *MPAA Rating:* PG-13.

CAST: Glenn Close (Linda Spector); James Woods (Michael Spector); Mary Stuart Masterson (Lucy Moore); Kevin Dillon (Sam); Linda Darlow (Lawyer Susan Drew); Jane Greer (Michael's Mother); Jessica James (Bessie); Mimi Kennedy (Eli's Mom); Charles Levin (Eli's Dad); Harrison Mohr (Eli); Mattew Moore (Jason); Kristin Sanderson (Kristin/"Picasso"); Merrilyn Gann (Kristin's Mom); Wendy Van Riesen (Pregnant Woman); Ashlee MacMilliam and Nora Kletter (Girls at Puppet Show); Katie Murray (Birthday Girl); Babs Chula (Birthday Girl's Mom); Ben Reeder (Paul); Thor Derksen (Paper Boy); Jonathan Sedman (Kid with Football); Jeff Stanford (Lab Technician); Elinore Then (Dr. Nathanson's Nurse); Walter Marsh (Dr. Nathanson); Ken Lerner (Josh); Deryl Fell (Father at Game); John Kirkconnell (Son at Game); Rebecca Toolan (Real Estate Woman); Donna Peerless (Linda's Client); Pamela Ludwig (Anna); Deborah Offner (Kathy); Lynn Eastman (Phone Operator); Janet Judd (Woman on Bus); Freda Perry (Lawyer's Receptionist); Brenda Crichlow (Doctor's Receptionist); Celine Lockhart (Rich Mother); Anita Kam (Rich Daughter); Bill Croft (Man on Phone); Veena Sood (Admitting Nurse); Tess Brady (Delivery Doctor); Royce Wallace (Nurse); Daniel Roberds (Baby William/Andrew); Benjamin Altschul (One-year-old William); Nora Heflin (Dr. Samuels); Richard White and Darrell Roberds (Anxious Fathers); Gloria Reuben (Maternity Nurse); Blu Mankuma and Andrew Kavadas (Crib Movers); Alma Beltran (Spanish Woman); Andrea Mann, Beatriz Pizano, and Venus Terzo (Spanish Woman's Daughters); Jo-Anne Bates and Rob Roy (Home Buyers); Joyce Erickson (Vet Receptionist); Simone Clelland (Anne Marie); Robyn Simons (Girl in Vet's Office); Liam Ramsey (Lucy's Stepbrother); Maya Saunders (Lucy's Stepsister); Stephen E. Miller (Lucy's Stepfather); Jane Mortifee-Birch (Sam's Mother); Chuck Bennett (Sportscaster); Colleen Darnell (Salon Employee); Christmas (Ellen the Dog); Toothpick the Clown (Himself).

LOS ANGELES TIMES, 10/27/89, Calendar/p. 4, Sheila Benson

What in the sweet name of goodness is "Immediate Family" doing in a movie theater? You expect writing this leaden from the grimmest ghettoes of television: earnest, unbuoyant talk that takes a subject like childlessness and teenage adoption and flattens it into drama that's predictable down to the smallest reference, which in this case is a flowering plum tree.

Obviously, the film's cast of heavy hitters—Glenn Close, James Woods and Mary Stuart Masterson—has boosted it over the fence and into the local 14-plexes. Don't let that sway you. Mush is still mush, even when it's directed by "Heart Like a Wheel's" Jonathan Kaplan.

Cast as the film's warm, loving center, neither Close nor Woods seems comfortable or even ideal for the assignment. You keep waiting for Woods' vet, a specialist in canine microsurgery, to develop a mean streak and to drop that kitty he's holding; instead, he perseveres as the year's most unlikely Mr. Nice Guy. You wait, too, for Close to retire that radiantly artificial smile and those brimming eyes and just *be* for one single moment. It never happens.

The film poses a virtually undebatable question: Where will a baby from an unplanned pregnancy get its best shot in life? Will it be with its birth parents, struggling under-class teenagers (Masterson, Kevin Dillon), or with a pair of have-it-all, childless professionals (Close, Woods).

Given this setup, the answer should be pretty clear-cut, but Barbara Benedek's screenplay turns our feelings around, unintentionally. As we meet Close's rigid realtor, on her way to an upscale child's birthday party, she complains that animals hate her, children don't like her and she always buys the wrong present. We're supposed to feel just the opposite, to see her charm, to get to know her human qualities. Unfortunately, the more we're shown, the more we side with the animals.

Her character is relentless—socially obtuse, self-pitying and preachy. "You're asking me the secret of a happy marriage?" she muses to Masterson, who didn't exactly ask. "Respect, affection, a lot of laughs, a sense of yourself and only one person gets to be crazy at a time." (One friendly component in a marriage doesn't even *place* on that list?)

Not all the performances are so achingly high-minded. Take a look at what Masterson has done with this pregnant waif who choses "open adoption"—in which both adoptive parties meet before the birth—as the best way for her baby. Masterson's teen-ager, the child of a 17-year-old mother herself, is by turns cocky, lost, suspicious, yearning and coming to maturity almost before our eyes. Even her smallest emotion is pure and real.

As the baby's sweet, faintly dim father, another damaged kid, snubnosed Kevin Dillon gives the picture's other solid performance. But the pure likability of these two creates the movie's only real conflict: We have a decent too-young couple who must give up their baby and, as the lucky recipients, a pair of cool, remote adults, two of the last people on earth you could see in mixing in the messy dailyness of parenthood.

Even the music is specious. This isn't a musical score, it's connect-the-titles time—every song asks a musical question that the screen then answers. When Close and Woods go through their infertility regimen, the song is "Creatures of Love." As Masterson slumps in dejection, Ray Charles croons "Young girls do get weary . . . try a little tenderness." The young couple slips away on a lyrical drive to "Motherless Children." And Van Morrison's "Into the Mystic" does double duty, but its most excruciating use comes when Close and Masterson dance to it, in a moment of ineffable bonding.

This, from the usually thoughtful producing team of Midge Sanford and Sarah Pillsbury ("River's Edge," "Eight Men Out"), under Lawrence Kasdan's production banner, and from Kaplan, who has in the past looked at women with such detailed sensitivity ("Heart Like a Wheel," "The Accused"). How does the song go? "Say it isn't so. . . .''

FILMS IN REVIEW, 3/90, p. 174, Edmond Grant

Babies, babies, babies. If the movies produced by Hollywood's major studios are indeed an accurate reflection of our national consciousness, it appears that the primary concern of every American (apart from exploring the scars left by the Vietnam War) is the desire to have and/or care for a cuddly toddler. This latest "baby movie" is a rather somber piece that brings to mind *thirtysomething, The Big Chill*, and those afterschool specials about "babies having babies."

Here the focus is on an infertile couple, played by James Woods and Glenn Close, who are patently obsessive about becoming parents. Close fixates on her friends' snotty offspring, while Woods stares longingly at a father with his young son at a pro football game. After their repeated attempts at artificial insemination fail, they finally hit on a satisfactory alternative, a form of "open adoption" wherein the adopting parents meet the child's real mother and offer her financial and emotional support throughout her birthing experience. In laymen's terms, this procedure has come to be known as "surrogate motherhood;" this phrase is noticeably absent throughout the film, possibly because the final movement of the storyline bears some resemblance to the "Baby M" situation, albeit in a tamer fashion.

The surrogate mom that Woods and Close become linked with is a young woman without direction (Mary Stuart Masterson) who wants to have a child in the future, but feels she can't afford to support one at present. Her decision to give the baby up for adoption is seconded by her boyfriend (Kevin Dillon), a jaunty aspiring heavy metaller who comes to visit her in Seattle (the film, like most others nowadays, is set in an American town, but was shot in Canada) as she prepares to give birth and render her child to the yuppie couple. Things remain casually episodic and awfully subdued until the actual birth occurs, and Masterson decides that, as the title of half-baked 70s TV movie proclaimed, "I want to keep my baby." Once this decision is made, some true dramatic tension is injected into the proceedings, but given the insufferably mellow nature of the characters played by Woods and Close, and America's deepseated need to have a satisfactory (read: happy) ending for every movie, you can be sure that things will surely look brighter before the closing credits.

As for the film's laid back, meandering approach, that can clearly be attributed to screenwriter Barbara Benedek, who co-wrote *The Big Chill* with Lawrence Kasdan (the executive producer of *Immediate Family*); director Jonathan Kaplan, who despite having made films of some depth (*Heart Like A Wheel, The Accused*) and others severely lacking (*Project X*) has never shown an inkling of a coherent style, seems content here to let Benedek's storyline unfold in the manner dictated by Kasdan's film (now utilized weekly on *thirtysomething*): a few instances of sobbing, a picturesque location for the characters' home, terse monologues which reveal a particular character's past and attitudes, and, most importantly, the bonding ritual of enjoying the same pop music. Here, that function is filled by a sequence where Close and the still pregnant Masterson sing and dance around to an old Van Morrison tune (on CD, of course). The scene has a slightly beguiling edge to it because both actresses seem to be having fun, but it does nothing to enlarge upon the mother-daughter connection between the two that had been introduced in the sequences preceding (this idea, that Masterson relates to Woods and Close as *her* surrogate parents, is a subtext that could have stood further development).

And, as in *The Big Chill*, the characters seem to rest solely on the strengths of the actors portraying them. Thus, despite Close having given a flawless performance as perhaps the *über*-mother of them all in *The World According To Garp*, her work here seems weak and facile, mostly because her character exists as nothing more than an obsessive urge to reproduce. And Woods . . . well, the greatest irony of Woods' career is that he is now acquiring a good deal of critical and public recognition for being a talented performer, just as he is giving his weakest performances—first the hyperactive excess of *The Boost*, and now this restrained besweatered veterinarian. He obviously chose this role as a bid for normalcy, attempting to counteract the "volatile psycho" image he's carried so well in the past. But, suffice it to say, he won't be doing his talent justice if he goes on playing namby-pamby individuals like this happily wedded, sensitive yuppie. Woods' character here is *such* a patent niceguy that he becomes believable only at the one instance where he seems on the verge of blowing up—at a hospital check-in desk, as a business-like nurse asks all the proper questions while Masterson is going into labor. Otherwise, he is gentle, accepting, and altogether quite dreary. When Masterson changes her mind, and later at the film's predictable climax, one expects Woods to raise an objection, cause a fuss, and address the situation directly. Instead, he and Close meekly accept, making their characters less than realistic.

But it's not true that all the characters are so undistinguished, as Masterson does quite a lot with her simply constructed role (for all the culture/age gap jokes in the film, Benedek's heavy metal characters are as laid-back and faceless as their elder yuppie counterparts). She has thus far been featured in a few overlooked quality features (*At Close Range, Heaven Help Us*) and was the best thing about some other less-than-adequate releases (*Some Kind Of Wonderful, Chances Are*); here, she does a meticulous job of portraying confused youth in transition. The awkwardness her character feels upon encountering the prosperous yuppie couple, and later, the heart-sick devotion she has for the baby that isn't supposed to be hers, emerge despite the paper-thin dialogue and assorted plot contrivances. Masterson gives the character an air of *believability* that thankfully transcends the subdued approach favored by Benedek and Kaplan. Her efforts distinguish her performance and lend the film the air of poignancy its plotline demands.

There's something definitely wrong, however, when only one character rings true in a drama that purports to be about contemporary domestic realities.

NEW YORK, 11/6/89, p. 102, David Denby

Vietnam vet, long thought dead, returns to wife now married to swell guy. Lesbian couple raises child produced in vitro from sperm donated by swell friend. Man marries tall, swell gal who turns out to have had transsexual operation. (Had enough?) Infertile yuppie couple readies itself to adopt child of poor teenage girl, who, at last minute, decides to. . . .

Two of these premises have just been made into awful movies (the first became *Welcome Home*); the others probably will be any day now. (And what about the tragedy of inter-species marriage? We can't forget that one.) These are subjects, however, not for theatrical features but for sob-sisters-in-arms Oprah and Geraldo, or for TV movies. A TV-movie subject can be defined as something so lurid and painful that you *have* to do it in good taste. But did Orson Welles ever make a Sensitive Movie? Or John Ford or Martin Scorsese or any other good director you can think of? The greatest sensitive movie of all time was Robert Benton's *Kramer vs. Kramer*, and though I liked it in 1979, I can't imagine looking at it again.

What's unusual about a new, terrible example of the genre, *Immediate Family*, is that it stars James Woods and Glenn Close, two actors I expected to bring a certain edge to anything they play. I was wrong. "Having come off *Fatal Attraction* and *Dangerous Liaisons*," says Close, "I wanted to do something on the healing side of life." But healing is something one does in a clinic, not in a film; an actor embracing virtue this way gives himself a flattering reason for boring the audience. Close, playing a suffering, frustrated woman, puts herself in an emotional corset; she hardly even gets angry. And Woods is cast as an even-tempered veterinarian—for God's sake, James *Woods*, the most feral of actors, the great nihilist of the screen, Dr. No himself! How could he do this to us? He keeps his dignity by snarling a few times, but he's grown disgustingly handsome and presentable, like Robert Goulet on the dinner-theater circuit.

Immediate Family is part of the ominous development of shooting movies in Vancouver, a placid Canadian burg that stands in for allegedly idyllic American cities. Close and Woods live in a beautiful Seattle house overlooking the bay, a house perfect except for the absence of. . . . Now, truly, infertility is an agony for any couple that experiences it, but it's a private, intimate kind of burden, and it's an awful subject for movies. The humiliations of the fertility clinic would be dramatically passable only if played for desperate humor, for gallantry at the edge of the specimen jar, but here they're done straight. Close and Woods have nothing to say—nothing, as actors, to do. The characters' problem forces them to be always nice to each other. *Immediate Family* was directed by Jonathan Kaplan (*The Accused*), who in the past has proved himself a crackerjack B-movie talent. I pray that this isn't Kaplan's bid for respectability. He paces the first

40 minutes of *Immediate Family* so somberly that we might begin to get the idea that if the couple had made a few more jokes or shown some temperament, they wouldn't be as deserving of parenthood.

An adoption lawyer puts Woods and Close in touch with a pregnant, working-class teenager (Mary Stuart Masterson) from Ohio. She shows up in Seattle, and they all look one another over and ask awkward questions, and then the father shows up, a lout (Kevin Dillon) who is decent enough underneath, and there are more awkward questions. The young couple aren't ready to marry—they're just kids. Why don't Woods and Close adopt *them*? Wouldn't that solve the problem? (I guess not.) Anyway, the lout goes home; Masterson (who gives a fine performance) has the baby, with Woods and Close taking her through the delivery; and then, and then . . . but I can't go on. Modesty forbids.

"We were referred to as the crying producers," says Sarah Pillsbury of herself and Midge Sandford, who brought forth *Immediate Family*, "because every time [screenwriter] Barbara Benedek showed us a new scene, we cried." I think we can all agree that this sort of thing has to be discouraged. It just might be catching.

NEW YORK POST, 10/27/89, p. 21, David Edelstein

As this "thirtysomething" culture grows increasingly baby-conscious, the longing for a perfect family becomes yet more hallowed; anything that frustrates it, the most hellish form of torture. "Immediate Family," the misbegotten problem drama, confronts two taboo subjects in Hollywood—infertility and the grim realities of class. Confronts, flattens and trivializes.

Glenn Close and James Woods play Linda and Michael Spector, a well-to-do Seattle couple unable to have a child and utterly miserable. Linda tries everything to get pregnant; when she fails, she and Michael arrange to adopt the baby of Lucy (Mary Stuart Masterson), a young woman living in a depressed, Midwestern industrial town who feels that she and her boyfriend, Sam (Kevin Dillon), aren't ready for parenthood.

The central device of the film is poignant and eerie. The Spectors, eager to impress Lucy with their qualifications, bring her to Seattle to have her baby and are so bubbly and excited that they lavish her with care—they treat her as family.

So the punky young mother, whose own home was broken and whose economic circumstances are dire, has a glimpse—for the first time in her life—of how happy a family can be. When the baby is born, she cannot bear to part with it.

If you know any couples who've failed to conceive—or if you've thought much about the Baby M case—you'll appreciate the grim irony of this scenario. Infertile couples, it seems, just can't win. (Lucy's and Sam's lower-class genes are iffy to begin with, but even those prove unattainable.) The story has no heroes or villains and no clear solution. It's a bitter pill.

But in "Immediate Family" it has been sugared. Pop songs underscore key sequences, and the characters signal pain by cracking self-deprecating one-liners. The opening is jokey, as Linda encounters friends with children and babies at every mocking turn. En route to a birthday party, she tells Michael her present is sure to be spurned by the child; when it is, the camera holds on her sardonic yet suffering face.

The tidiness of that moment is an insult, and there are lots of insults. The script, by Barbara Benedek, makes its points heavily, but with grace and occasional wit; the direction, by Jonathan Kaplan, just makes them heavily. Kaplan, who once made the interesting "Over the Edge," has evolved into a blah TV-movie *meister* with a knack for making fools of actors.

Bits that should be thrown away get thunking overemphasis. When Michael glimpses a father and son at a football game, the image becomes archetypal—in silhouette and slow-motion. Dillon (cast with a heavy hand) is encouraged to be aggressively proletarian, and Woods (playing nice) gives a grotesquely overscaled portrait of nervous heartiness.

In the center, Close widens her eyes, presses her lips together, cocks her head and tries to look adorably vulnerable. Clearly, this actress is tired of being hissed. Her face topped with Little Orphan Annie curls, she wears oversized blouses and skirts to make her frumpily demure. And even when she's cute, she's appalling—a mugging pixie.

But the problems of "Immediate Family" go deeper than pop songs and bad acting. The way the script is constructed, the upper classes will inevitably be victimized by the lower, who aren't just going to deprive them of a baby that should be theirs, but who cannot possibly raise a child correctly.

To underscore this point, Lucy and Sam hold their son with cigarettes in their mouths; behind them, factories belch smoke into the gray sky and neglected children squabble. Growing up, in this context, means recognizing that in spite of biology, certain people should have children and others (the lumpen) shouldn't.

Like so much of Hollywood's socially conscious film making, the movie operates out of a bizarre mixture of liberal guilt and condescension. It does squeeze tears, but even if you go with it—aware that, however stereotypical, it has granins of truth—it ends with an amazingly irrelevant, upbeat twist that sends audiences home snickering.

Alone in the cast, Masterson emerges a real human being. As always, the actress is dryly unaffected, without vanity or self-consciousness, superbly right. Having just given birth, her decision not to hold the baby—a plain, soft "no"—is devastating, suggesting a struggle between two thankless options and a lifetime of dreams deferred.

NEWSDAY, 10/27/89, Part III/p. 3, Mike McGrady

"Immediate Family," the chronicle of an affluent married couple's efforts to adopt a baby born to an unmarried poor couple, represents a profound change of pace for almost everyone involved.

Glenn Close, fresh from her brilliantly unsympathetic work in "Fatal Attraction" and "Dangerous Liaisons," has said she wanted a film that was upbeat, positive. Jonathan Kaplan, director of "The Accused," a violent re-creation of a celebrated gang rape, here tries his hand at a relatively gentle domestic drama.

Then, too, James Woods, coming off gut-wrenching work in "The Boost" and "True Believer"—not to mention his stirring Emmy-winning performances in "Promise" and "My Name Is Bill W."—was evidently looking for some time off, or at least a role that would place no undue demands on his talent.

Finally, writer Barbara Benedek, credited with co-writing several scripts including the sparkling screenplay for "The Big Chill," here goes it alone for the first time. Evidently, she needs help.

This pool of high-priced talent has conspired to create what is known in TV-Land as an M.O.W., or: Movie of the Week. And, yes, "Immediate Family" would make a perfectly adequate Movie of the Week.

It has the essential ingredients. Beginning with a typically modern problem: the adoption of a child. It even examines the problem through a particularly current concept known as "open adoption"—that's where the adopting parents come to know the biological mother (and, in this case, the biological father) before the baby is ever born. This enables one concerned party to explore genetic possibilities while the other checks out proposed environment.

The progress of the movie, as with any self-respecting M.O.W., comes from simply connecting banal moments. Would-be mommy Close is surrounded by annoyingly fecund friends who all tend to ask her variations of the same question: "So, Linda, are you pregnant yet?" She and the would-be daddy (Woods) visit medical specialists; collect, concentrate and transmit sperm; hit the bottle in despair; save money, and finally turn to a lawyer who specializes in adoptions.

If one were to judge entirely by the evidence offered in "Immediate Family," the concept of open adoption is more than flawed; it's lousy. As the two would-beadopters hover over the biological parents (Mary Stuart Masterson, Kevin Dillon), one is reminded of other hovering creatures—specifically, vultures. And by the time the would-be parents are assisting at the birth, even ceremoniously snipping the umbilical cord, the image goes beyond hovering to one of swooping.

Although the biological parents love one other and plan marriage followed by other children—presumably, keepers—the movie argues that this first baby will be much better off with more settled parents in more affluent surroundings, in fact in a beautifully furnished nurserey/w/water view.

All that separates this from any other Movie of the Week is the caliber of talent on hand, talent that ensures some of the manipulative efforts will draw a larger-than-small-screen response. But not all that much larger.

TIME, 11/6/89, p. 84, Richard Corliss

The Spectors' car swerves to avoid a boy who has darted out into the road, and nice Michael (James Woods) mutters to his nice wife Linda (Glenn Close), "Some people should not be allowed to have children!" He is voicing a common belief that those who are having the most kids can't raise them, and those who can afford kids aren't having them. O.K. then. Who should raise the first generation of 21st century teenagers? The healthy, efficient yuppies, who just might be able to fit a child into their Filofax schedules? Or the chainsmoking unmarrieds of the underclass, with lives of nosiy desperation awaiting them like so many episodes of *Married . . . With Children*? In a society where childless can still be a near synonym for lifeless, are the "wrong" people having too many kids? Are there any right parents?

Immediate Family touches all these bases lightly, like a gazelle on a home-run trot. Openhearted and canny, the film offers few answers, takes no sides. It paints the yups, Linda and Michael, as decent, attractive people. Their friends' kids may run wild in a toddler road show of *Lord of the Flies*, but the Spectors seem ideal parents-to-be. Yet they can't be biological parents. Every month Linda says, "I spend two weeks whacked out on fertility drugs, two weeks depressed that they don't work." In the bathroom, Michael opens a specimen jar, picks up a wellthumbed copy of *Penthouse* and sighs. There is no joy in their rituals, only emptiness and failure. Time to adopt a baby.

Lucy Moore (Mary Stuart Masterson) has a baby, or will in a few weeks. In the modern fashion of adoption, the Spectors spend time getting to know her. And to like her—Lucy has a lot to like. A blossom growing out of white trash, she teeters between unaffected adolescence and poignant maturity. But perhaps the Spectors are also rehearsing for parenthood; perhaps they are determined to send sweet signals across the barriers of culture, class and age. They realize that their ability to adopt her baby depends finally on Lucy's whim. So, effectively, they adopt Lucy. She is an '80s Eliza Doolittle in the Spectors' pristine palace, getting a tantalizing glimpse of the good life on loan. Should her child live there? She's not sure. Could she live there? In a minute. Forever.

Despite its customized carpeting of a soft-rock score, *Immediate Family* isn't exactly sentimental. It's a fond diagnosis of sentiment, which director Jonathan Kaplan (*Heart Like a Wheel, The Accused*) observes with his usual handsome care. Close and Woods, more familiar playing high-powered candidates for psychosis, are laser-precise as the Spectors. They work hard at appearing comfortable in roles without edges. But the Spectors, who set the film's agenda, cede sympathy to Lucy, as the well-to-do in movies inevitably do to the poor-but-spunky.

The film's admirable trick is to shift the balance without opting for heroes and villains. Kevin Dillon, as Lucy's boyfriend, lists toward the loutish, but he's no jerk. And Masterson's fine, grace-noted performance is like the film: full of wit, skepticism and hope for compromises that won't ruin lives. This is a serious comedy that locates wry smiles in everyone's burdens and opportunities. The tears come at the end.

VILLAGE VOICE, 10/31/89, p. 78, Georgia Brown

Dawn Steele's first baby by Columbia arrives with announcements in double-page spreads in *Vanity Fair* and *The New York Times Mcgazine*. The smoky black-and-white ads for *Immediate Family* (which is in color and an engaging if confused comedy-melodrama with quirky interstices) elide nicely with the Laurens and the Calvins. What's being sold is a handsome, well-dressed pair—Glenn Close and, believe it or not, former sleazeball James Woods—and also, their proprietary interest in another couple's unborn baby. One version of the ad includes the other couple—two teenagers in fringes and leather and obviously from the other side of the tracks—making this half look like a Guess? Spread.

Immediate Family, directed by Jonathan Kaplan, opens inside a Saab convertible tooling down manicured suburban Seattle boulevards. (Seattle residents will laugh; the mountains are wrong, the waterfront's wrong. It's really Vancouver.) On their way to the birthday party of a friend's child, Linda and Michael Spector (Close and Woods) are on edge. She's uncomfortable at these parties where the other grown-ups are focused either on pregnancies or offspring. Suddenly a boy chases a football into the street and Michael has to slam on the brakes. "Some people ought not be allowed to have children," he fumes. The Spectors, he implies, should be allowed. Their problem is that they can't have them.

Actually, it's not quite clear who writer Barbara Benedek thinks ought to be allowed to have children. (Benedek coscripted what could be called the proto-yuppie movie, *The Big Chill*, with Lawrence Kasdan, who's executive producer here.) The lawn party turns out to be a scaled-down Gaefryd-type affair revolving around a bunch of little monsters. One slams a ball off Linda's head and won't apologize; the birthday child is miffed at Linda's gift, a computerized talking bear: "I have that toy already!" The movie's perspective on this collection of budding sociopaths isn't clear. Maybe it's just trying to say kids are a handful? The Spectors, anyway, are not differentiated from their fellow well-to-do professionals, except by their infertility. There's no reason, I mean, to think that a child of theirs would have better values or manners.

Linda sells real estate and Michael is a vet for suburban pets. In their late thirties now, they graduated from Cornell together, so they'd obviously been accumulating for awhile before deciding to multiply. But now Linda finds herself spending "two weeks of the month wacked out on fertility drugs," and the other "two weeks depressed because they didn't work." Michael reads Viking Contemporarys in bed, and in the morning digs up a *Penthouse* to try to make "a baby in a jar." Unsuccessful and plain tuckered out, the Spectors decide to apply to an adoption agency. After the red tape, they're put in touch with a birth mother, one Lucy Moore (Mary Stuart Masterson), a spunky 17-year-old pregnant by her boyfriend Sam (Kevin Dillon).

When Lucy gets on a Greyhound bound for Seattle, where she's to stay until her delivery, the movie's focus shifts. It's a shift consistent with the strong preference Kaplan showed for working-class heroines in *Heart Like a Wheel* and *The Accused*. The eclipse of the Spectors, though, leaves Benedek's screenplay looking rather like an improvisation. As the Spectors turn vague, it's harder to make a case for them—a case that the movie needs to make.

Brave, self-contained Lucy, with her shag haircut and voluminous overalls, quickly establishes herself as more mature, openhearted, and articulate than Linda, who grows cooler and more reticent as the plot develops. (Although Close's part is seriously underwritten, the actress doesn't appear engaged. One scene, à la *The Big Chill*, in which the two women dance to Van Morrison, doesn't look as spontaneous and joyful as it should.) With a good deal made of the fact that Lucy's own mother died when she was seven, *Immediate Family* can't help but hold out the possibility that Linda in some way will adopt Lucy. But who would be the mother? Lucy, who's been housekeeping for her truck-driver stepfather and his kids, is the one with the maternal touch.

When Sam joins them for a visit, his brashness gives the Spectors a bit of a scare. So does the information that his hard-drinking dad killed a co-worker at the factory. Sam asks to borrow the Saab, and as the two kids take off, Michael quips that next thing you know, "We'll end up on Geraldo Rivera as 'the most gullible couple in America.' " (Woods gets the movie's best jokes, but, besides a dose of basketball mania, not much in the way of characterization.) The teenagers, who turn out to be too good to be true, take over as the movie's point-of-view characters. By the time the baby's born, the Spectors have nearly receded into the wallpaper.

In the end, after a few twists—the last a real weepy—we find out that *Immediate Family* does think that the Spectors ought to have children. They deserve a baby precisely because they have a stunning view from the crib, a Saab and a Jeep to drive baby to karate classes, and funds to import au pairs and buy tiny, cunning wardrobes. Perhaps it's Kaplan who succeeds in qualifying this message slightly—suggesting that the deprived will come into their own one day—but he can't erase the specter of so many pampered darlings coming of age in the early 2000s. With the crack babies and the money babies, this should be some place to grow old in.

Also reviewed in:
NEW YORK TIMES, 10/27/89, p. C18, Janet Maslin
VARIETY, 10/18-24/89, p. 25
WASHINGTON POST, 10/27/89, p. B7, Rita Kempley

IN A GLASS CAGE

A Cinevista release of a TEM Productores Asociados production. *Producer:* Teresa Enrich. *Director:* Agustin Villaronga. *Screenplay (Spanish with English subtitles):* Agustin Villaronga. *Director of Photography:* Jaume Peracaula. *Editor:* Raul Román. *Music:* Javier Navarette. *Art Director:* Cesc Candini. *Running time:* 110 minutes. *MPAA Rating:* Not Rated.

CAST: Gunter Meisner (Klaus); David Sust (Angelo); Marisa Paredes (Griselda): Gisella Echavarria (Rena); Imma Colomer (Maid).

LOS ANGELES TIMES, 5/12/89, Calendar/p. 9, Kevin Thomas

At least Spanish writer-director Agustin Villaronga, in his 1982 debut feature "In a Glass

Cage," lets you know what you're in for with his precredit sequence. In the cellar of a remote castle-like structure in Spain, a middle-aged man with strongly Teutonic features (Gunter Meisner) has strung up a naked, badly beaten adolescent boy. Near death, the boy receives a tender kiss from his tormentor before receiving a final blow from a thick piece of lumber.

This compulsive murderer, Klaus, who had been a Nazi concentration camp doctor with a sexual penchant for torturing boys, flees in apparent self-loathing to the parapet of the castle and falls, jumps or is pushed. It leaves him paralyzed and confined to an iron lung in a large, isolated 19th-Century villa. One day an intense pale young man named Angelo (David Sust) turns up at the mansion determined to nurse the helpless Klaus, who has an understandably miserable wife (Marisa Paredes) and a devoted young daughter (Gisella Echavarria). As it turns out, Angelo not only wants revenge but to become Klaus, whom he worships sexually even though he is intent on destroying him. Along the way he will force Klaus to witness two torture deaths of boys.

The point of the depicting this extreme morbidity seems to be to show us how evil, in the form of sexual psychopathology, begets evil. Although Angelo, as an adolescent, had been forced by Klaus to service him sexually, it is hard to accept that this incident, as traumatic and deplorable as it is, would be enough to make Angelo want to assume Klaus' identity in all its hideousness.

As an exploration of the relationship of sex and violence within a homosexual context, "In a Glass Gace" (Times-rated Mature) is so vague that, intentionally or not, it smacks of homophobia. That Villaronga displays considerable skill as a film maker has the effect of making his film seem all the more dangerous. But it is hard to understand why anyone would want to see this film, let alone make it.

NEW YORK POST, 3/24/89, p. 25, Jami Bernard

The glass cage of the title is an iron lung, and in it lies Klaus—or what's left of Klaus—a doctor who during the war performed sadistic experiments on children in the death camps. A stark and forbidding young man, Angelo, comes to care for Klaus, although he has no hospital training and in fact has some very unique ideas about how to amuse his charge.

But wait. Before we go any further, you have to know something about "In a Glass Cage." It is a sick film about sick things, and it has a lot of sicko scenes. Okay, now some of you are interested and are getting ready to go to the theater, and *you* guys I hope I never meet in a dark alley.

On the other hand, if you can stand the subject matter and if you don't eat a full meal before seeing it, you'll have a wonderful surprise—this is a well-made—no, *masterfully* made—movie, a remarkable directing debut by Agustin Villaronga, who also wrote the script. (Maybe I don't want to meet *him* in a dark alley, either.)

The movie's insights into the nature of sadism and the way it is engendered in its victims, plus its terrifyingly slow transmutation of Angelo into Klaus, are powerfully disturbing. Perhaps you don't like to be disturbed at the movies. But how many times does a movie come along that can do that? This is a horror film without special effects; the horror comes from the darkest recesses of human nature.

Klaus (Gunter Meisner) is living in seclusion with his wife, Griselda, (Marisa Paredes) and daughter, Rena, (Gisela Echevarria). Once a sadist, always a sadist; the war is over, but Klaus is still doing a little freelance experimenting on young boys in the area. After one such torture, he falls off a roof (perhaps he is pushed) and ends up imprisoned in the glass lung. It's not too much of an acting stretch for Meisner; mostly he has to gasp for air whenever someone pulls the plug.

Angelo (David Sust) insinuates himself into the family unit, and it is soon clear that he is less a nurse than a disciple of the great Klaus. It's good to have a role model, but the misguided Angelo has found Klaus' wartime notebooks and begins reenacting the old experiments, forcing Klaus to watch, supine, from his machine.

Whoops, I forgot the sex scenes. Well, I didn't forget, but what can you say about iron-lung sex scenes except that there's a surfeit of heavy breathing? "Don't worry, I can do many things for you," says Angelo. Hoo-hah. The link between sadism and sexual stimulation has rarely been so apparent. "I felt his loathing invade me, giving me pleasure," reads Angelo from Klaus' old notes, a recipe book of tortures.

Meanwhile, Angelo has disposed of the wife after he finds her playing around with the fuse box once too often. And the daughter, Rena, has taken a liking to Angelo. The new family unit plays board games—Rena and the disembodied head of her dad, watching though a shaving mirror, against Angelo, whose bloodlust is mounting.

"Angelo is insane," whispers Klaus to his daughter. Hey, look at the pot calling the kettle black! But by now, Angelo has wallpapered the stairwell in wire mesh to simulate the death camp, and the bodies are starting to pile up in the basement.

One of the scariest performances is that of Gisela Echevarria as the daughter, a girl of indeterminate age who with her high forehead and soft curls looks at first like a child out of a '50s family sitcom, later like an old, empty shell in a little body.

The bluish haze over the film, coupled with the incessant, uncomfortable hiss of the lung's respirator, make this film a nightmarish, punishing experience. That hardly sounds like a compliment, but in the case of "In a Glass Cage," it is.

VILLAGE VOICE, 3/28/89, p. 69, Elliott Stein

The joyful shock, the energizing jolt, that accompanies the recognition of an important new talent at home with itself and with the cinema has become increasingly rare. My last such encounter goes back to the first time I was introduced to the work of an unknown named Pedro Almodóvar a few years ago. That sensation is back, its source again Spain, with the release of *In a Glass Cage (Tras el cristal)*, the first feature directed by Agustin Villaronga.

Although period and locale are left unspecified, this disturbing tour de force is set in the Franco era—apparently sometime during the '50s. A Nazi doctor (Günter Meisner) who had enjoyed participating in death-camp experiments has taken refuge with his wife and adolescent daughter in an isolated house in the countryside. An accident puts him in an iron lung. One day, Angelo (David Sust), a strange youth, arrives out of nowhere, claiming to be a trained nurse sent to take care of the invalid. He wins over the daughter, who becomes his doting ally, and soon takes over as master of the house. During scenes of feverish erotic ritual and contagious madness, it becomes clear that the young Angelo had been molested by the doctor as a child, and has returned in search of something far more complex than revenge.

Villaronga doesn't take a false step. *In a Glass Cage* contains some of the most bizarre love scenes ever conceived (anyone for iron-lung sex?) and the best classical suspense-murder sequence anyone has put on screen since the demise of Hitchcock. The film is tinged with grisly humor, deceptive gentleness, and moments of entertaining Grand Guignol; as the cycle of abuse and murder comes full circle, the tone becomes one of stately sadness. This study on the fascination of evil is the only new movie with real fangs I've seen in years, but, despite a few harrowing sadistic moments, of exploitation there is not a trace.

Javier Navarrete's music is insidiously haunting. During the big cat-and-mouse set piece, Jaume Peracaula (a shepherd in the Pyrenees before he became Barcelona's most respected cinematographer) makes the most of the delirious art nouveau gewgaws and noodly shadowed nooks of the Gaudiesque mansion where most of the movie was shot. Sust is remarkable in his first screen role, while veteran German actor Meisner (Bergman's *The Serpent's Egg, Is Paris Burning?*) is superb as the demented doctor. (He appeared not only as Hitler in *The Winds of War*, but as Hitler's sister Angela in Gerard Oury's *L'As des as*.)

In a Glass Cage was made in 1985 and, although critically acclaimed, was violently attacked by Spain's right-wing press. Villaronga has just finished a second feature, *Los chicos de la luna*, an esoteric adventure story shot in Tunisia. We should not have to wait another three years for his next work. Villaronga is what a "new director" should be.

Also reviewed in:
NEW YORK TIMES, 3/24/89, p. C13, Stephen Holden
VARIETY, 3/5/86, p. 16

IN COUNTRY

A Warner Brothers release. *Producer:* Norman Jewison and Richard Roth. *Director:* Norman Jewison. *Screenplay:* Frank Pierson and Cynthia Cidre. *Based on the Novel by:* Bobbie Ann Mason. *Director of Photography:* Russell Boyd. *Editor:* Antony Gibbs and Lou Lombardo. *Music:* James Horner. *Production Designer:* Jackson DeGovia. *Running Time:* 120 minutes. *MPAA Rating:* R.

CAST: Bruce Willis (Emmett Smith); Emily Lloyd (Samantha Hughes); Joan Allen (Irene); Kevin Anderson (Lonnie); John Terry (Tom); Peggy Rea (Mamaw); Judith Ivey (Anita); Dan Jenkins (Dwayne); Stephen Tobolowsky (Pete); Jim Beaver (Earl); Richard Hamilton (Grampaw); Heidi Swedberg (Dawn); Ken Jenkins (Jim Holly); Jonathan Hogan (Larry); Patricia Richardson (Cindy); Kimberly Faith Jones (Donna); Don Young (Speaker); Joe Ross (Principal); Mark Sawyer-Dailey (Drugstore Manager); Linda Kinard (Drugstore Cashier); Reverend W.G. Harvey (Reverend); Rebecca Reynolds (Nurse); Erin Hendley (Irene's Baby); Tyler Cote (Donna's Baby); Gena Colley (Marlene); Belinda Coatley (Belinda); Hazel Elliott (Volunteer); Walter Spann (Hotshot).

CHRISTIAN SCIENCE MONITOR, 10/4/89, p. 11, David Sterritt

"In Country" belongs to the new breed of post-Vietnam films that deal not with the morality of the war, but with the difficulty of healing the scars it left in the American psyche.

It's a dubious practice, I think, to disregard the question of whether this war should have been fought in the first place, much less the question of whether war itself can be justified as a human activity in any but the most desperate of circumstances. Yet the aftermath of Vietnam is a worthy subject in its own right, and some corrective is needed to the idea (implicitly dealt with in "Dog Soldiers" and a few other films) that soldiers who were drafted to fight in Vietnam are best ignored now that the war is history. With much sincerity and a modicum of intelligence—certainly more intelligence than the finale of the current "Casualties of War" show—"In Country" addresses their plight and some issues related to it.

The story takes place mainly in a small Kentucky town called Hopewell, where most folks have done their best to forget about Southeast Asia and the slaughter that took place there. But the aftermath of a war is a lingering thing, and, try as they might to put Vietnam out of their minds, the community finds the upsets of that experience are hard to erase. Eventually, the film's main characters are drawn to the Vietnam War Memorial in Washington, where their emotions come into the daylight and are dealt with openly at last.

"In Country" has two protagonists. One, played by Emily Lloyd, is a teen-age girl named Samantha, whose own father (whom she never knew) died on a Vietnam battlefield. The other is her Uncle Emmett, played by Bruce Willis, a veteran whose amiable personality is marred by some very eccentric behavior. Each of them is troubled by this war that ended years ago: Emmett is haunted by memories of what happened there, Samantha by questions about it. "In Country" is the story of their slow progress toward some kind of understanding—with each other, and with the past that's been a burden for them both.

I saw "In Country" shortly before its United States première, when it was the opening-night attraction at the annual Festival of Festivals here in Toronto. Most of the audience found it shallow and inconvincing. I eventually encountered a handful of people who agreed with me that it raises an important subject—the need to remember and understand a national trauma—and that its performances have a lot to recommend them. Still, even I have to agree that the last half-hour, set at the Vietnam Memorial, is pretty weak, sliding into the weepiest kind of sentimentality.

I hope "In Country" finds a reasonably big audience despite its shortcomings, however, since it treats the effects of Vietnam with seriousness and avoids any hint of sensationalism. The acting in the film also deserves a nod of approval: Mr. Willis shows a subtlety that I haven't seen in his work before, and the gifted Ms. Lloyd can apparently do just about anything, as her work in this picture—following her portrayals of an English girl in "Wish You Were Here" and a Brooklynite in "Cookie"—heartily demonstrates.

Directed by Norman Jewison, a filmmaker with a long (though mixed) track record, "In Country" has its failings. But its sincerity and conviction lift it above much of the instantly disposable cinema now on our movie screens.

FILMS IN REVIEW, 12/89, p. 622, Pat Anderson

At the age of 16, in her very first film , *Wish You Were Here,* Emily Lloyd became an instant star. Now, at the ripe old age of 18, she has proved that that initial performance was no fluke. As Samantha in *In Country*, Lloyd emerges as a superbly accomplished actress. This English youngster, playing a teenager from Hopewell, Kentucky, is perfect: not a syllable, nor a foot, out of place. Her very presence lights up the screen.

And she is ably supported by Bruce Willis (yes, the swashbuckling Bruce Willis of *Die Hard*). He is her uncle Emmett, with whom Sam chooses to live and take care of—consciously trying to be grownup yet youthfully spirited at the same time—rather than move to Lexington when her mother (Joan Allen) remarries. Emmett is an apathetic unemployed Vietnam veteran who hangs around with a handful of returnees: all more or less misfits, still trying to make a place for themselves in the 1980s South of laxer morals and pervasive fast food chains. But Emmett *did* come back, unlike his brother-in-law, Sam's father, who was killed in Vietnam.

Norman Jewison has done a wonderful job of directing this movie of a small southern town with its Sunday home fried chicken with all the trimmings; the excitement of high school graduation ceremonies; girls gossiping, piercing each other's ears, telling their secrets; and the long, lazy summer car rides.

But ultimately the film concerns one family's attempts to come to terms with the most unpopular war in America's history. Sam's questions about the father she never knew stir and disturb Emmett and his buddies: the dichotomy is that they want to remember—to return to the camaraderie of fighting days—but those memories include pain and guilt. She rebuffs her high school sweetheart (Kevin Anderson), and after discovering and reading her father's letters home, castigates her mother for leaving them behind when she remarried. She visits her grandparents, searching for answers about her father's personality: stirring up *their* emotions. She even simulates her own Vietnam by camping alone in a swamp, dressed in fatigues, while re-reading her father's letters by flashlight.

The inevitable climax, a journey to Washington to visit the Vietnam Veterans Memorial, is beautifully handled; neither sentimental nor maudlin but unaffectedly touching. And the location photography there in particular is flawless, but veteran photographer Russell Boyd has also captured the exact flavor of the little Appalachian town—as have the screenwriters Frank Pierson and Cynthia Cidre, as well as the admirable supporting cast.

Films about Vietnam are no longer novelties, but *In Country* is very special.

LOS ANGELES TIMES, 9/15/89, Calendar/p. 1, Michael Wilmington

"In Country" is set in a small Kentucky town called Hopewell. And, in a way, that sums up the movie's sentiments. It's a film of beatific intentions and upbeat goals. It hopes well for America, and it wants—in its portrayal of one average family and the impact made on them by the Vietnam War—to draw its audience together, unite them in a vast, healing flood of sympathy.

Sometimes it does. The ending—with teen-age Samantha (Emily Lloyd), her uncle Emmett (Bruce Willis) and her portly grandmother Mamaw (Peggy Rea) at the Vietnam War Memorial in Washington—is charged with emotion. The sight of the memorial, gleaming and black, stretching out on a verdant lawn, with it seemingly endless roll call of the dead; the visitors searching for the names they love and remember; the almost ritualistic way they find and touch the graven name of Sam's father . . . all this is done with a mixture of intensity and discretion, sunlight and shadow, that becomes disarming and even devastating.

Like "Field of Dreams," this is a movie about reconciliation that tries to become an act of reconciliation itself. Based on a novel by Bobbie Ann Mason, it tries to view Vietnam non-sensationally, to capture the problems of many veterans. "In Country," a phrase that refers to Vietnam from the soldier's viewpoint, tries to connect with the basic, bedrock feelings that many of us associate with the strong inner core of American people. It wants to make its audience a community again.

The director, Norman Jewison, has a plush, silky craftsmanship; he eases us into the scenes effortlessly. His central character, Sam, is a teen-ager who might be defined by the word "spunky." She's full of sass and curiosity, charging around the Hopewell streets, or cruising in a beat-up convertible. Lloyd, a Britisher working on her third accent in as many films, sparks up her scenes.

Sam lives with one Vietnam vet, her morose, sardonic uncle Emmett, and knows plenty of others: Emmett's buddies Pete (Stephen Tobolowsky), a right-wing tattooed lecher; left-wing hothead Earl (Jim Beaver), and Tom (John Terry), a misty-eyed wounded romantic. Sam also has a boyfriend, Lonnie, local basketball hero and macho creep (Kevin Anderson) and grandparents, Mamaw and husband (Richard Hamilton), who may remind you a bit of Ma and Pa Kettle. Sam's mother (Joan Allen) lives in the city. Urbanized, upwardly mobile, she's left rusticity, and Sam, behind.

The movie is constructed like a detective story; it suggests dark depths beneath Hopewell's apple-cheeked surface. Sam, intrigued by Emmett's curious behavior, discovers a bundle of letters and photographs from her father and, suddenly, Vietnam and its meaning begin to obsess her—even causing her to ditch smug Lonnie and take up with misty-eyed vet Tom. If the Southeast Asian war was a "heart of darkness" for Coppola, here it's the guilty town secret. Why does her uncle stay by himself, rail against injustice, howl in the rain? Why is Tom skittish about women? Why do Hopwell's veterans seem ignored or set apart by the town? Most important, why did her father die and leave her?

Jewison is often at his best with comedies or musicals; his natural talent may not quite jibe with the low-key realism that's a major strength of Mason's book. He tends to lyricize the plot, punch up the humor, dig for moments of melodrama or high sentiment. Significantly, the best single performance in the film—Judith Ivey's bawdy nurse, Anita—is a blatantly theatrical star-turn that eschews subtlety or surface naturalism. Anita, who is even deprived of a final scene to wrap up her character, seems almost too broad, too bravura. Yet, even more than the exemplary Emily Lloyd, she seems most in tune with Jewison.

"In Country" is seemingly loose, rambling, anecdotal. Yet, we're always clear—too clear—about where everyone stands, including the film makers. (They're good liberals who want to appeal to a heartland audience.) Each scene has a point; each character is usually being driven toward self-realization, as if by a shuttle bus. And sometimes there are comic sceances that seem too jovial, too cliched.

Jewison, whose direction exudes self-confidence, isn't afriad of seeming corny, and this pays dividends in the wonderful moment when Pete and Earl, brawling at a vet's party, suddenly see each other's eyes, clasp hands and embrace. But Hopewell never really seems completely real. Bathed in honeyed light and a peach glace lusciousness caught by cinematographer Russell Boyd, the movie suggests the lacquered, idealized small towns of musicals such as "Meet Me in St. Louis."

Yet, in a way, none of this really matters. There's a decency about this movie that's almost palpable. It's not trying to pump us up with false jingoism or the sins of the past. Jewison, a Canadian, probably approaches the entire subject with a mediatory mood. If his two best previous social dramas—"In the Heat of the Night" and "A Soldier's Story"—were detective stories with racial themes, there's one buried here too. These white Southern vets—somewhat like the black vets they must have fought with (but whom we mostly don't see here) are a group apart, a group ostracized or discriminated against, carrying their own special bond of brotherhood and freight of pain.

"In Country" may not quite be the healing experience Jewison and his collaborators want it to be. But, though the extremity of Sam's search makes her begin to seem like a Vietnam groupie, there's a fable-like purity to the quest.

When Sam camps out, pores over her dad's journal and envisions the war, this forced scene actually has a symbolic resonance. It suggests the collective dreams of Vietnam that have been coalescing now for a decade, mostly in the movies: Vietnam as tragic myth, as macho rite, as fantasy vindication, as swamp of horror. And it sets us up for the beautiful ending of "In Country" (MPAA rate R for sex and language), where Jewison masterfully tries to turn back toward the few unshakable realities. All the people that died there. All the people that mourn. The earth that swallowed up the bodies and blood. And the sky that covers them, both living and dead, forever.

MONTHLY FILM BULLETIN, 1/90, p. 17, Richard Combs

When Samantha Hughes graduates from high school in Hopewell, Kentucky, she is the same age as her father Dwayne when he left for Vietnam, where he was subsequently killed. Sam's mother Irene now lives with another husband and their family in Lexington, but Sam resists her encouragement to go to college there, preferring to stay with her Uncle Emmett, a Vietnam veteran still deeply affected by his experiences. Sam, in fact, spends a lot of time with Emmett and his variously disaffected or cynical Vietnam buddies, like Pete and Tom, to the annoyance of her boyfriend Lonnie. Sam's curiosity about Vietnam, steadfastly resisted by Emmett, is intensified when she finds a photograph, military ribbons and letters of her father's. Sam turns to Tom (a mechanic from whom she and her friend Donna hope to buy a car to give them more freedom and mobility) in her need to know more about her father and how he died. At a Vietnam veterans' dance, Sam hears of some of the horrors of the war, and later sleeps with Tom. Emmett goes missing and Sam, declaring herslf tired of other people's troubles and chafing at the restrictions of her life, gives Lonnie back his friendship ring. Irene turns up with Emmett (he has drunkenly found his way to Lexington) and buys Sam a VW from Tom. Donna, who is now pregnant, declares to Sam's disbelief that she wants to keep the baby. From Grampaw and Mamaw, Dwayne's parents, Sam obtains a diary of her father's, and spends a night in the nearby swamps (similar to Vietnam) reading what he saw and felt just before he died. In the morning, found by Emmett, she confesses that she's not sure now if she likes her father, and Emmett talks for the first time of his own emotional legacy. They take Mamaw on an unprecedented trip to Lexington, where Sam tells her mother she is willing now to go to college; they then visit the veterans' memorial in Washington, and after finding Dwayne's name, Emmett, Sam and Mamaw leave with a sense of peace.

In her short story "Shiloh", Bobbie Ann Mason describes the break-up of a marriage, in which the catalytic factors are an accident that puts the husband out of work and brings a new and uncomfortable closeness, the wife's taking up body-building and then a night-school course in composition, and her mother's urging them both to repeat her own honeymoon trip to a Civil War memorial, the Shiloh battlefield in Tennessee. There, reflecting in a numbed way on his departing wife and on what once happened in the serene landscape around him, the husband finds it hard to make them both seem real: "Leroy knows he is leaving out a lot. He is leaving out the insides of history. History was always just names and dates to him ... And the real inner workings of a marriage, like most of history, have escaped him". What makes the story so effective is its sense of the intimacy of a national and personal history, and at the same time of great emotional distances to be covered. The emotional somehow becoming physical: the trip to Shiloh is made to seem a once-in-a-lifetime odyssey.

Interestingly enough, *In Country* touches on similar elements: Emmett has been put "out of work", out of touch with normal life, by Vietnam; Sam, his niece and minder, is beginning to chafe at the limitations of her life; and new horizons are opened up after a trip with Sam's grandmother to the Vietnam veterans' memorial in Washington. What prompts doubts about the film is that one never feels the intimacy of the two histories, and the sense of distance, emotional or physical, is confused (possibly these are weaknesses from the novel, though the detail of Mason's writing tends to keep this kind of ground well covered). In the final trip, for instance, which Emmett and Sam take with her grandmother, the latter protests that "I've never been out of my time zone", and the arrival in the city of Lexington is like landing in a new world for both the old woman and her granddaughter. The threesome are then immediately transported with no difficulty to Washington, DC, and the ritual of touching Sam's father's name on the veterans' wall has a similarly magic healing effect. Throughout one feels the yoking of Vietnam as a "big subject", as hard for the film to approach as it is for the war's scarred veterans, to the neutral detail of Sam's growing up, her sweatily jogging nowhere for much of the film, the friendships and family ties and the small-town ethos from which she eventually has to shake loose.

The growing up and the coming to terms with Vietnam themes are linked through Sam's need to know more about her father who died there, and in the process to detach herself from the war-haunted Emmett. As a psychological scenario, however, this is only perfunctorily worked through, and the dramatisation of one scene from Vietnam—the ambush in the swamp where Dwayne Hughes is killed—is not as indicative of "the horror" as it needs to be, despite its repetition in snatches throughout the film. When it is paired with the scene where Sam takes herself off into the Kentucky swamps to read her father's diary, the two actually neutralise rather than illuminate each other. Similarly, when Sam is found in the morning by Emmett, his summation of the war ("In country, you were on your guard every second or you were dead") is another old soldier's tale that effectively closes out the hints of horrors the GIs perpetrated as well as the ones they suffered. In the end, the film spells out the double meaning of its title—to the troops, "in country" was Vietnam and "the world" was everything else, which echoes Sam's coming-of-age plight—without lending it any substance or complexity.

NEW YORK, 9/25/89, p. 129, David Denby

A decade ago, after such thundering disasters as *Fiddler on the Roof, Jesus Christ Superstar, Rollerball*, and the unspeakable ... *And Justice for All*, I would have cited Norman Jewison as one of the least talented—certainly one of the least sensitive—directors in Hollywood. But recently, the Canadian-born Jewison, 63, has cured himself of the sin of overemphasis. Gentleness now abideth in his soul. Resolutely putting aside thoughts of Jane Fonda's spiritual crisis in *Agnes of God* (1985), we can thank Jewison for three enjoyable and accomplished movies—*A Soldier*

Story (1984), *Moonstruck* (1987), and the new *In Country*, an adaptation of Bobbie Ann Mason's 1985 novel.

Jewison is now relaxed and confident enough to work with slightly amorphous material, to hold his moods rather than punch up every scene as if Darryl Zanuck were about to stub out a cigar in his ear. At the center of *In Country* is a girl's noodling around in search of herself after graduating from high school. Sam (Emily Lloyd), of Hopewell, Kentucky, can only be called second-generation Vietnam. She never knew her father, Dwayne, who was killed in battle there when her mother (Joan Allen) was pregnant with her; she lives with her wasted uncle, Emmett (Bruce Willis), who also fought; and she hangs out with Emmett's friends, all of them Vietnam combat vets, bitter, cutoff men angrily stumbling through the fragments of their broken lives.

Trying to understand what her dad went through, Sam reaches out to the vets. She's stirred by their troubles and becomes so empathic that she seems almost goofy to them. She's not a crab or a busybody—she's a vivacious young girl. But she can't stop asking questions about the war (so many questions that you wonder why she doesn't take herself off to the library). Sam is caught between wanting to experience Vietnam for herself and wanting to revive the men's sexual powers, restore the vets to the manhood they've mysteriously lost.

Emily Lloyd, the leggy, blonde eighteen-year-old English actress who starred in *Wish You Were Here*, jumps right into this rural Americana, stretching her vowels like chewing gum, throwing herself down onto beds with a bored sigh. The dissatisfaction she brings to a line like "God, this town is dead without a mall" is lovely. She makes Sam both ordinary and extraordinary—awkward, but bright and willful enough to cast off the mediocrity and defeat of a gossipy small town where people accept failure too easily. Lloyd is touching and true in her increasing indifference to Kevin Anderson, who plays a good-looking high-school basketball star hot for her. Sam goes out with him but remains unawakened. He's cocky but just a boy; the broken-down men mean much more to her, and the way Lloyd is made uneasy by his caressing banter is a wonder. Lloyd is tremendously talented, with great natural instincts. If she has a problem, it's that she's almost too eager to act. She climbs all over the other actors, and at one point I thought she was going to devour Bruce Willis, who is determined to give a quiet and internalized performance.

This is no star trip: Willis comes out of the background and recedes into it, and he stays in character. He's got the ragged-hip look of the burned-out cases among the Vietnam vets—Fu Manchu mustache, stubble, long hair worn either loose or in a tiny pigtail. And he's got the vet's soul right, too. Emmett and his friends have been through the war and drugs and the GI-hippie reaction after the war, and then Ronald Reagan, and they're a mass of contradictory impulses—patriotic yet contemptuous of the government, abashed and angry. Their unhappiness has hardened into pride in being out of it. Emmett won't take a job; he molders in his sister's house, letting Sam look after him, and he cultivates oddity so people will leave him alone. Apart from one moment when he has to deliver a kind of aria of lament on his knees and he's pushing too hard for sensitivity, Willis is execellent. His manner, fogged, fey, spooked, and unreachable, is just short of sinister; he carries a sense of raging affront that he buries under teasing, malign little games.

The war in Vietnam, the way Mason depicts it (Frank Pierson and Cynthia Cidre did the adaptation), is a curse that persists for years and hangs on into the next generation. The men are bereft. Their community never honored them, the Veterans Administration is unresponsive, and some of them are suffering from headaches and weird rashes and other side effects of Agent Orange. They are embarrassed that they didn't win and, in Emmett's case, embarrassed that they're still alive. The movie has a cranky but noble subject—the way personal loss and defeat in the war have fallen on unsophisticated, patriotic people as a sledgehammer blow whose effects are never examined or even acknowledged. Sam's family is all screwed up; that's why she can't do anything with her life until she makes some sense out of Vietnam. She has to lay the Furies to rest for all of them.

Nothing is more dangerous in art than trying to re-create the lives of "ordinary" folk. But if my eyes and ears are to be trusted, Jewison has avoided the usual mistake of patronizing sentimentality and has handled this vulnerable material about damaged lives with tact and spirit. *In Country* was shot in Bobbie Ann Mason territory—western Kentucky—and the sounds and tempo of a gregarious small town seem to have soaked into the production. *In Country* has an unhurried, exploratory, yet always lively and attentive gaze that is very pleasing. The movie draws its strength from the music of Mason's dialogue, especially when people are just sitting around arguing, nagging, or grieving. Jewison has resisted the obvious temptations to inflate the material;

the uncomprehended sense of loss the way a young girl haltingly realizes the need to heal are statement enough.

NEW YORK POST, 9/15/89, p. 21, David Edelstein

It's tempting to think of the culture of the '80s as an immature response to the traumas of the '60s and the Vietnam War. Rather than examining and working through those devastating upheavals, the nation turned to fantasy (through Reaganism) and dissociation (through drugs); no truth seemed too big for people to repress.

The beauty of Norman Jewison's "In Country" (based on the novel by Bobbie Ann Mason) is the gentleness and compassion with which it explores the idea of a traumatized culture—a culture erected on denial. The movie is set in a small Kentucky town where the Vietnam War continues to eat away at the inhabitants, many of whom served "in country" or lost members of their family.

But no one thinks or talks about the war and what it meant, except to say that the government didn't support Our Boys or that we should've paved those rice paddies over and put a McDonald's in the middle. Mostly, everyone goes about his or her business.

Everyone, that is , except Samantha (Emily Lloyd) whose father was killed in Vietnam shortly before she was born. After a brief prologue set in the '60s, we meet Sam as she graduates from high school, waving enthusiastically at her Uncle Emmett (Bruce Willis) in the stands.

She lives with Emmett instead of her mother (Joan Allen), who remarried and moved to the suburbs. Emmett was in country, too, but never talks about the experience or her father. In general, he's friendly and remote; he lets her boyfriend Lonnie (Kevin Anderson) stay over in her room, and at night he goes out drinking with other vets.

When Sam finds a box of letters from her father, she begins to ask questions: how he died, what the war was like, why no one wants to talk about it. She's always bugging her mother, her uncle and another ex-soldier, Tom (John Terry), who fixes cars on the outskirts of town and who eyes her with more than a passing fancy.

And gradually she (and we) realize that the war is still gnawing at people, stunting their growth and the growth of everything else. As Samantha reads her father's letters and pokes around, the film turns into the story of people waking up from a long stupor, gingerly beginning to grapple with their long-repressed anger and grief.

The stupor is slightly contagious, and this is not—let's face it—a new theme. It's a blurry movie, and much of the script is either meandering or overwrought. Sam goes for one too many runs with Bruce Springsteen's "I'm on Fire" on her Walkman—after a while it seemed like a freight train was runnin' through the middle of *my* head.

I could also have done without Willis scrambling up a tree in the middle of a thunderstorm and screaming at God to show His face, or his obsessive excavations under the house, searching for remnants of past cultures. (My Metaphor Meter went off the scale.) James Horner's music elicits only deja vu: a familiar mix of strings (for uplift) plus hollow trumpets (for the bitter sadness of war).

But Jewison's direction is both relaxed and alert, and the movie breathes. The Australian cinematographer Russell Boyd uses a soft country light to give the images a gentle radiance—he neither romanticizes nor condescends. And the editing, by Anthony Gibbs and Lou Lombardo, is exquisitely sensitive.

Jewison gives his actors lots of space, and the supporting cast is perfect down to the smallest bit player. Willis is the big surprise. He wears his long hair brushed back, exposing a lengthening forehead, and he sports an unfashionable mutton-chop mustache and a tuft of hair under his lip. He's hard to recognize, especially without his TV mannerisms. His Emmett is purposefully recessive: Nothing goes out or comes in. It's a modest, likable performance—unilluminating, but so different from anything Willis has done that you can't help admiring it.

The English Lloyd has been cast as the all-American teen-ager:she eats Twinkies, swills diet sodas and complains that "this town is dead without a mall." Her regional American accent is the best you'll ever hear from an English performer, but the words that tumble out of her mouth don't always make sense—she's all over the place.

Lloyd holds nothing back as an actress, which is a strength in exhibitionistic roles like the one that made her a star in "Wish You Were Here." She's engaging here, but maybe she should learn to hold *something* and to stop looking as if she wants to swallow the other actors.

Lloyd does, however, have the film's most moving scene, in which she stares at a photo of her dad (only a year older than she is now) and says, simply, reproachfully, "You missed Watergate, 'E.T.,' you missed everything. And you were just a country boy and you never knew me." If she'd whimpered the speech, we might have steeled ourselves. It's her annoyance that cuts us to the heart.

The movie is an improbable synthesis of "The Best Years of Our Lives" and "Casualties of War." It suggests that the vets' agony has two sources: both the memory of what it felt like to be always in the presence of death, and the horror of what some did as a result—i.e., slaughter Vietnamese civilians.

"In Country" doesn't indict these vets for participating in an unjust war. Its tone is forgiving, but the forgiveness is predicated on remembrance. The daringly protracted finale captures the starkness of the Vietnam Memorial—the descent in which a few names gives way to tens and then hundreds and then thousands of names. The horror is overwhelming, but so is the final blessing.

The movie implies more than it dramatizes, but its vision of a fractured, post-Vietnam white America hits home. More important, the release of two compelling Vietnam films in a single month suggests that the long stupor of the '80s may at last be over. Movies are starting to mean something again.

NEWSDAY, 9/15/89, Part III/p. 3, Mike McGrady

No one can doubt that Vietnam was this era's Civil War, a monumentally divisive event that tore the entire country into two opposing camps. Although the war itself dragged on to its eventual end, the other war, the one at home, was never clearly resolved.

"In Country," based on the acclaimed Bobbie Ann Mason novel, looks at the many ways this unresolved conflict still manifests itself in the small town of Hopewell, Ky. Although well over a decade has passed since the last shot was fired, the trauma lives on, and one family finds itself still mired in that war of long ago.

Seventeen-year-old Samantha (Emily Lloyd) is a high school student whose father was killed in Vietnam a month before her birth. She shares a home with her uncle Emmett (Bruce Willis), a burnt-out veteran who survives on a diet of beer, television and hard-earned cynicism.

Lloyd, the young English actress who sparkled in "Wish You Were Here" and picked up the speech patterns of New York City for "Cookie," switches easily to Samantha's gentle southern accents. What is important is not Lloyd's gift for accents, however, so much as her tremendous emotional honesty, an enviable ability to cut directly to the heart of a character.

By mentioning Lloyd first, it is not my intention to slight Bruce Willis, who does his best work by far here. The actor's physical appearance—he is a solemn, disturbed presence behind a Fu Manchu mustache—is so different that he may not be immediately recognized. Even less recognizable will be his performance as the damaged veteran, a performance that is restrained, sympathetic, serious, real.

The girl and her uncle are sharing Samantha's family home. Her mother (Joan Allen) has left her home with all of its Vietnam memories and started life fresh with a new husband and new baby. Some of those memories are contained in her dead husband's Vietnam diary, others in letters written when he was in country: "The world's a dream now I'm here. Maybe when I'm home, this'll be a dream."

The dream of Vietnam haunts the movie much the way it still haunts this country. It's there in the poorly attended "Vietnam Veteran's Dance" in a gymnasium decorated with miniature helicopters and war mementoes. It's there in the faces of veterans who ceremoniously don their old fatigues on an outing. It's there in the old woman who still can't fully accept her son's death: "He did good for his country and I take comfort in that." Mostly, it's there in the alienation of Emmett who has started to suffer from headaches, strange rashes and a tendency to go haywire in thunderstorms: "I'm just hanging on here with every bit of strength I got...there's something wrong with me, like I got this hole in my heart."

Episodic, disjointed, at times talky, "In Country" assumes a powerful dramatic focus as three generations—Samantha, Emmett and the girl's grandmother—take off on a trek to the Vietnam War Memorial in Washington. Their aim is simple, to find Samantha's father's name and leave a geranium in his honor. What they manage to find, in a deeply affecting finale, is healing and acceptance.

Director Norman Jewison has made 24 feature films, including such movies as "In the Heat of the Night" and "A Soldier's Story." His most recent work, "Moonstruck," caught the comic checks and balances of a modern city family. The rural family in "In Country" brilliantly captures the ordeal of an entire country, and may even be part of the healing that finally seems to be coming our way.

NEWSWEEK, 10/2/89, p. 70, David Ansen

The main characters in *In Country*, the teenager Sam (Emily Lloyd) and her Uncle Emmett (Bruce Willis), are each grappling with the legacy of Vietnam. Emmett fought in the war and hasn't been the same since. A semirecluse with rashes on his body and more nagging wounds in his soul, he's holed up in Hopewell, Ky., looking after Sam and trying to push the war out of his mind. Sam, on the other hand, can't hear enough about it. Her father, whom she never knew, was killed in Vietnam, and she's obsessed with his memory. This summer she's discovered a box of his letters and his combat diary, and she's determined to pump Emmett and his vet pals for any information that might shed light on the war that has cast such a long but indecipherable shadow over her life.

Norman Jewison's film of Bobbie Ann Mason's novel wants to strike a hopeful, healing note two decades after that divisive event. While one can respect its lofty intentions, the movie doesn't seem to have any better sense than its high-school heroine of just what it's looking for. At once underdramatized and faintly stagy, it keeps promising revelations that never quite materialize. Everything leads to a climax at the Vietnam Veterans Memorial: while it's hard not to be moved, the impact may have more to do with the power of that monument than anything the movie has genuinely earned.

Bruce Willis, almost unrecognizable with a Fu Manchu mustache and thinning, slicked-back hair, does an honorable job chucking his TV persona. On the surface, he's got Emmett down. Yet his deep psychic wounds never seem quite real. It may not be Willis's fault: the screenplay by Frank Pierson and Cynthia Cidre lets him declare, but not demonstrate, his crippled nature: he's got no one to play off of.

Jewison seems oddly afraid of his own material. If you want to make a movie about healing, you first have to show the disease. Why blunt Emmett's scars? And why has Jewison softened the contents of Sam's father's Vietnam diaries, which are meant to horrify and disgust the girl? When she declares, after reading his final entries that she doesn't like him, we're puzzled partly because Jewison mistakenly chooses to show us the father's death, which evokes pity, not revulsion.

Because "In Country" is built more on details than plot, the missteps are critical. There are moments that suggest the movie that might have been steeped in Mason's transitional New South, where the K Mart culture collides with backwoods ways. Whenever Joan Allen appears, playing Sam's remarried suburbanite mother, the movie seems to snap to attention. But Emilly Lloyd is a mixed blessing in the central role. This young English actress has no problem with her Southern accent, and she's got vitality to burn, as she showed in "Wish You Were Here" and "Cookie." But she hurls herself into the part with more enthusiasm than comprehension. Her vivacity is appealing, but her inner life remains opaque. Like the movie itself, she rarely gets under the surface.

TIME, 10/2/89, p. 90, Richard Corliss

Viet Nam represents a great jagged gash in the fabric of American history, an ugly tear in a tapestry that people once believed had been woven out of high ideals and simple decency. A few years ago, when it became obvious that it was time to repair that rent, our popular culture took on something of the air of a vast quilting bee, with writers, filmmakers and TV producers bending over their restorative needlework.

Samantha Hughes (Emily Lloyd) of *In Country*, an adaptation of the novel by Bobbie Ann Mason, is a direct, even artless, projection of this healing spirit. There is nothing metaphoric about the empty space left in her life by the war; her father was killed in Viet Nam before she could know him. Her mother having remarried and moved away, Samantha has chosen to stay behind and share the tumbledown family home in Hopewell, Ky., with her uncle Emmett (Bruce Willis), a veteran damaged by the war in some way he refuses to name. Now in the summer after her high school graduation, she comes upon the letters her dad wrote from Nam, and eventually his diary. Using this material to chart her way, she sets out, innocent but determined, to reimagine her father and the long-ago war that took him from her.

Samantha's straight-ahead spirit as evoked by Lloyd is irresistibly winning. Eventually it becomes the wedge that pries Emmett out of his shell and forces the girl's grandmother Mamaw

(Peggy Rea) to face the feelings that she too has denied since her son's death. These are superb performances as well: Willis has never employed his alert reserve to better effect; Rea perfectly catches both the refrigerator-tidying comedy and the unspoken yearnings of an American Everymom.

In its early passages, *In Country's* script perhaps pursues too many banal and inconsequential matters as it portays teen life in a small town. Samantha has a boyfriend who does not match her in wit and spirit. She has a girlfriend contending with an unwelcome pregnancy. But the film starts to gather force and direction when a dance, organized to honor the local Viet vets, works out awkwardly, And when—at Samantha's insistence—Emmett and Mamaw join her on a pilgrimage to the Viet Nam Veterans Memorial in Washington, the movie achieves real power. Director Norman Jewison understates his final sequence with admirable tact. No melodramatic shocks of recognition, no epiphanies—merely simple people silently touching the names of loved ones inscribed on the memorial, tentatively, thoughtfully restoring connections. It is just fine, just right, just enough for now. *In Country* is, finally, a lovely, necessary little stitch in our torn time.

VILLAGE VOICE, 9/19/89, p. 68, Georgia Brown

I guess Emmet sounds like a good ol' boy's name because there's an Emmett at the heart of *In Country*, too. [The reference is to *The Big Picture*.] Bruce Willis does such a terrific job of looking seedy, fortyish, stoic, and solid that I hardly recognized him with his thinning, sun-bleached hair. Willis on *Moonlighting* seemed too smug for my taste, but *Die Hard* was one of my favorite genre movies, and seeing what he achieves here makes me a fan.

But Willis's ease and stature is wasted in this tedious adaptation of Bobbie Ann Mason's novel, directed by Norman Jewison (*Moonstruck*). Publicity has made a mountain of the search for the right actress to play Sam (Samantha) Hughes—telling how the teenage British actress Emily Lloyd beat out 500 competitors and once again (as with Cookie of Bay Ridge) was stuck with a real American family to pick up an accent and the proper way with gum. Well, Lloyd mugs, grimaces, flails her long arms, and is excruciating to watch. She has the mannerisms of a precocious six-year-old. In the way of some idiomatic translations, she gets surface business okay and essentials all wrong.

Frank Pierson and Cynthis Cidre's screenplay turns Sam's obsession with her father—killed in Vietnam around the time she was born—into a literal, overstated quest. Sam talks to her father's photo ("You're just a country boy and you never knew me"), reads his letters aloud ("Seems like we've been in-country forever"), and nags anyone who'll listen ("Tell me!Tell me!"). Having picked up the shame and the anger of the vets and her mother's avoidance, as well as her grandparents' bland patriotism, she doesn't know how to sort it all out.

Willis's Emmett, Sam's uncle, gives not so cryptic answers, and other vets in the small Kentucky town supply more pieces. The wife of one confides that she made her husband put his jar of pickled Vietcong ears out in the garage or someplace. Issues are raised, then skirted. It's not clear whether Emmett's rashes and headaches are due to Agent Orange, but all these men are, one way or another, wounded misfits. Emmett's "You weren't there, so you can't understand it" probably comes closest to the movie's point of view.

Fans of Mason's homespun dialogue will find slim pickings. "Boy, you're in a mood." "God, this town's dull without a mall." "I didn't mean to step on your feelings." A couple of "shit fits." Sam's obese grandmother, called Mamaw (Peggy Rea,) gets the real darling lines. When she goes to stand on a ladder at the Vietnam Veteran's Memorial wall, she worries, "Somebody might see up my dress."

Mason's no Flannery O'Connor, but neither is her work anywhere near this dull or patronizingly quaint. The movie's last 10 minutes use Washington's Vietnam memorial to turn the movie into a sun-drenched, haze-filtered tearjerker. I cried, but it was for something different.

Also reviewed in:

NATION, 10/9/89, p. 396, Stuart Klawans
NEW REPUBLIC, 10/16/89, p. 30, Stanley Kauffmann
NEW YORK TIMES, 9/15/89, p. C6, Caryn James
VARIETY, 9/13-19/89, p. 31
WASHINGTON POST, 9/15/89, p. C1, Rita Kempley

INDIANA JONES AND THE LAST CRUSADE

A Paramount Pictures release of a Lucasfilm Ltd. production. *Executive Producer:* George Lucas and Frank Marshall. *Producer:* Robert Watts. *Director:* Steven Spielberg. *Screenplay:* Jeffrey Boam. *Story:* George Lucas and Menno Meyjes. *Based on characters created by:* George Lucas and Philip Kaufman. *Director of Photography:* Douglas Slocombe. *Editor:* Michael Kahn. *Music:* John Williams. *Music Editor:* Kenneth Wannberg. *Sound:* Ben Burtt, Tony Dawe, and (music) Dan Wallin. *Sound Editor:* Richard Hymns. *Production Designer:* Elliot Scott. *Art Director:* Fred Hole. *Set Decorator:* Peter Howitt. *Mechanical Effects:* George Gibbs. *Visual Effects:* Michael J. McAlister. *Costumes:* Anthony Powell and Joanna Johnston. *Make-up:* Peter Robb-King. *Stunt Coordinator:* Vic Armstrong. *Running time:* 127 minutes. *MPAA Rating:* PG-13.

CAST: Harrison Ford (Indiana Jones); Sean Connery (Professor Henry Jones); Denholm Elliott (Marcus Brody); Alison Doody (Elsa); John Rhys-Davies (Sallah); Julian Glover (Walter Donovan); River Phoenix (Young Indy); Michael Byrne (Vogel); Kevork Malikyan (Kazim); Robert Eddison (Grail Knight); Richard Young (Fedora); Alexei Sayle (Sultan); Alex Hyde-White (Young Henry); Paul Maxwell (Panama Hat); Mrs. Glover (Mrs. Donovan); Vernon Dobtcheff (Butler); J.J. Hardy (Herman); Bradley Gregg (Roscoe); Jeff O'Haco (Half Breed); Vince Deadrick (Rough Rider); Marc Miles (Sheriff); Ted Grossman (Deputy Sheriff); Tim Hiser (Young Panama Hat); Larry Sanders (Scout Master); Will Miles (Scout #1); David Murray (Scout #2); Frederick Jaeger (World War I Ace); Jerry Harte (Professor Stanton); Billy J. Mitchell (Dr. Mulbray); Martin Gordon (Man at Hitler Rally); Paul Humpoletz (German Officer at Hitler Rally); Tom Branch (Hatay Soldier in Temple); Graeme Crowther (Zeppelin Crewman); Luke Hanson (Principal SS Officer at Castle); Chris Jenkinson (Officer at Castle); Louis Sheldon (Young Officer at Castle); Nicola Scott (Female Officer at Castle); Stefan Kalipha (Hatay Tank Gunner); Peter Pacey (Hatay Tank Driver); Pat Roach (Gestapo); Suzanne Roquette (Film Director); Eugene Lipinski (G-Man); George Malpas (Man on Zeppelin); Julie Eccles (Irene); Nina Almond (Flower Girl).

CHRISTIAN SCIENCE MONITOR, 6/13/89, p.11, David Sterritt

"Indiana Jones and the Last Crusade" set a record as soon as it opened—becoming the all-time champion for box office earnings on a single day.

True, the previous champ wasn't exactly distinguished: the impossibly crude "Beverly Hills Cop II," starring Eddie Murphy as a wisecracking policeman. But a winner is a winner, and there's no disputing the built-in popularity of the "Indiana Jones" format that director Steven Spielberg and executive producer George Lucas have so cleverly cooked up. Indy's third offering pulled in more than $10.5 million May 27 and set house records at many theaters, according to Variety, the entertainment newspaper. Looking beyond opening day, its first 12 days reportedly pulled in $70 million—dwarfing even the mountainous earnings of Indy's last outing, "Indiana Jones and the Temple of Doom," not to mention the adventure that started his career, "Raiders of the Lost Ark."

What's causing all the excitement? Nothing very new or different—that's for sure. "The Last Crusade" is just another yarn about Indy Jones, the handsome archaeologist with a taste for risky projects, colorful sidekicks, and exotic locations. This time his father, an archaeologist with a quieter and more scholarly style, has disappeared while researching the Holy Grail and tracking down its centuries-old hiding place. Adding spice to the story is a likable cast including not only the expected Harrison Ford and Denholm Elliott but also Sean Connery, an inspired choice as Indy's feisty pop. The settings of the story range from the Middle East to the heart of Germany in the Nazi years.

Since a zillion moviegoers will see any Indiana Jones film no matter what reviewers say, there's little point in reporting whether "The Last Crusade" thrilled or bored me more or less than its predecessors did.

As it happens, Indy's new escapade seems reasonably fresh and energetic much of the way, although it bogs down in a silly chase (on a military tank) just when it needs a shot of real inventiveness, and the last third has more than its share of heavy-handed and even hackneyed moments. The film's style is a tad more muted than it might have been, as if Mr. Spielberg were tiring of his own visual pyrotechnics, but it maintains the formulas that have made the series so successful.

More important to observe is that Spielberg and Mr. Lucas have toned down some distasteful angles that made their previous collaboration, the "Temple of Doom" adventure, not just frivolous (as Indy's stories invariably are, almost by definition), but downright offensive. True, the main female character of "The Last Crusade," played by Alison Doody, has a nefarious streak that prevents her from being a true heroine and revives old stereotypes of the scheming, two-faced woman who can't distinguish between facts and emotions—and shouldn't be trusted even if she could. Yet she's more resourceful than the woman Kate Capshaw played in "Temple of Doom," a continually helpless damsel who needed rescuing every two minutes and did more hysterical screaming than Fay Wray in the original "King Kong."

Also soft-pedaled in "The Last Crusade" are the racist implications that became uncomfortably strong in "Temple of Doom," where Indy strutted like a Great White Hero among people of color who were consistently helpless, villainous, or both. I don't think Spielberg or Lucas consciously intended any racist or sexist reverberations in that movie, but they should have been far more alert when they decided to base their Indy series on styles borrowed from Hollywood matinee serials of 40 years ago. Unfortunately, they picked up some very dubious baggage along with the appealingly nostalgic nuggets they unearthed and recycled. It's encouraging to see that they mostly avoid this trap in their latest venture.

In other ways, "The Last Crusade" is about what you'd expect from the people who made it. Lucas likes to pull a father-figure out of his hat when he's ending a trilogy; so the senior Mr. Jones makes an appearance here, just as Darth Vader turned out to be Luke Skywalker's benign daddy when the "Star Wars" series drew to a close.

Also predictable is the film's simplistic treatment of themes from religion and myth. In the first Indiana Jones picture, "Raiders of the Lost Ark," the biblical Ark of the Covenant almost fell into the hands of bad guys, who would have used its "awesome power" for evil ends-and "The Last Crusade" follows exactly the same pattern, only with the Holy Grail this time. It's curious that Spielberg and Lucas see these venerated objects not as symbols of divine inspiration but as repositories of a blind, undiscriminating force that can be wielded (like the three wishes from a genie or a magic lamp) by whoever gets their hands on them.

The same way of thinking crops up in other contemporary films, such as "The Seventh Sign," in which the heroine prevents some biblical prophecies from coming true, thereby delaying the end of the world for another millennium or so. This all adds up to a foolishly superstitious view of religious themes—especially disappointing when coming from someone like Lucas, who's allegedly a sincere student of religious and mythical motifs in world culture.

This may be taking "Indiana Jones and the Last Crusade" more solemnly than it deserves, but since so many people will see it, we'd best be aware of the notions it embodies and the messages it delivers.

On the evidence of "Willow" and the Indiana Jones pictures, Lucas seems permanently stuck in a trivializing attitude toward the timeless material he likes to employ. Spielberg has shown a bit more potential for growth, moving toward a more mature world view in "The Color Purple" and "Empire of the Sun" than he showed in his earlier films.

"The Last Crusade" is a step backward for him, but backwardness is an integral part of the Indy series right from its kiddie-matinee origins. Here's hoping its more careful approach to matters of race and gender indicates a new thoughtfulness that will continue to be felt in later Spielberg films.

LOS ANGELES TIMES, 5/24/89, Calendar/p. 1, Sheila Benson

We're told that this is our last romp with ol' Indiana, that after "Indiana Jones and the Last Crusade," the bullwhip will be retired. Well, even if he's considerably more battered than his nearest competitor, Indiana quits at the top of the heap. It's just that the heap isn't what it was eight years ago. It's been almost flattered to death.

You can't roll monstrous boulders straight at audiences any more and have a whole theater-full duck and gasp with fright—and pleasure. We may be plumb gasped out. And although Harrison Ford is still in top form and the movie is truly fun in patches, it's a genre on the wane.

Even the sparks that fly by combining Ford with Sean Connery as his strict, scholarly father, the *first* Prof. Henry Jones, aren't quite enough. What used to be thrilling is beginning to feel mechanical, and it's a shock to find the usually watchful Spielberg and Co. making careless mistakes. (Keep your eye on the "X" that marks the spot and you'll discover what looks like a huge continuity glitz. Uh oh.)

In Jeffrey Boam's script, from a story by George Lucas and Menno Meyjes ("The Color Purple's" screenwriter), this last installment follows a headlong race for the Holy Grail, the life-long obsession of Indy's estranged medievalist-father. It is Papa Jones' exhaustive diary, a marvelously convincing prop, which contains all the clues save one to the location of the Grail. The players are our heroes, on one hand, and those all-purpose villains, the Nazis, on the other. It seems they want the Grail as passionately as they wanted the Ark two movies ago. (Don't Nazis take notes? Compare notes? Learn from electrifying experience?)

But first, a prologue to show us where young Indy (River Phoenix, virtually wasted) got most of his trademarks and his aversion to snakes. It's full-tilt action in this opening quarter hour, and even with the jokey bits, like Indy and the rhinosaurus horn, it's a chase that seems to go on forever.

It's just the first of many. During the enfolding story of the rediscovery of father and son, there are chases by speedboat, by motorcycle, by airplane, horseback and armored tank. The Jones boys, separately or together, are bombed, strafed, chain-choked and menaced by sheets of flame. These slice-and-dice chases begin to feel less like Indiana Jones and more like James Bond.

What the frenetic action constantly breaks up are the growing moments of affection between this remote father and the son who has long felt shut out of his life. Indiana's resourcefulness begins to change his father's faintly patronizing air, and his father's presence gives Indiana at last a chance to vent his feelings of rejection. It makes this quest story an inward one—or it's clearly supposed to.

But the focus is on the sensur-round action. Both Ford and Connery play their I-never-told-him-I-loved-him moments full-out and unabashedly, and they alternate them with good, acerbic, air-clearing bits of accusation and grousing. But then someone strafes or pistolwhips them and the sentiment is diffused. In retrospect, "The Last Crusade" (rated PG-13 for intense action) becomes a blur of activity, not clearly defined peaks of emotion.

And even with more than two hours of running time to tell this story, Spielberg plunges into some scenes with such a perfunctory set-up that he catches his audience unprepared. The whole knight's tomb sequence in Venice is so rushed that there's no sense of real work on Indiana's part to solve this part of the puzzle. It's too easy, too headlong; we're onto a major discovery only minutes after Indy and Denholm Elliott's Marcus Brody have stepped off that gondola. Abruptness like this dazes and almost bewilders an audience; it certainly doesn't let them anticipate, experience and then savor a sequence as elaborate as this one.

Boam's screenplay, which has nice, whimsical moments (like the Venetian librarian's book-stamping joke), needs more of them or more great bits of action that grow from character, such as Connery's inventiveness on the beach with his umbrella and the seagulls. "Raiders" was a plum-pudding of such indelible bits and they are sorely missed.

Back again are John Rhys-Davies' splendidly expansive Sallah and Elliott's quintessentially British Museum curator Brody. The film makers seem to have given up the job of finding a suitable woman for Indiana after they retired Karen Allen's Marion Ravenwood from "Raiders." But that's no excuse for the alliances held by Alison Doody's icy Austrian art historian, Dr. Elsa Schneider.

It's as though, in forging a bond between father and son, the idea of any woman became impossible, so the film makers gave Indiana a clearly impossible choice. It may be in the spirit of the hero-myth, but you can't blame audiences for wondering where the harm would be in one splendid partner to accompany the lads into the sunset, a sort of 1938 Lauren Hutton.

Best on the technical side are the far-ranging production designs of Elliot Scott and the reverberating, many-layered soundtrack by Ben Burtt. Costume designers Anthony Powell and Joanna Johnston seem to have had a field day with Dr. Schneider, who grows more hilariously like something out of "The Night Porter" with every change of clothes. She finishes like someone out of Rommel's Afrika Korps, and whether or not we're supposed to giggle, it's hard not to. John Williams' music is nice, reminiscent and loud, and Douglas Slocombe's camera work is handsome without calling undue attention to itself. While the rest of the hundreds of special effects seem flawless, the blue screen in that smallplane sequence is so far below the quality we expect from this perfectionistic group that it stands out startlingly.

By the end of all this noise and confusion, what have we learned? Possibly something more serviceable than lofty: That Harrison Ford is probably better at a blend of action, soulfulness, churlishness and charisma than any actor of his generation. And that Sean Connery is now certifiably eternal. Didn't we know that going in? Ah well, I suppose there's no harm in underlining it.

MONTHLY FILM BULLETIN, 7/89, p. 198, Ann Billson

Young Indiana Jones daringly makes off with a priceless historical artefact to stop it falling into the hands of private collectors but, after a hectic chase, is forced to give it back to its "legal" owners . . . Many years later, the Grown-up "Indy" is an archaeology professor, and still battling to ensure that such artefacts end up in public museums. When told by wealthy collector Walter Donovan that his father, mediaevalist Dr. Henry Jones, has disappeared in mid-quest for the Holy Grail, Indy agrees to follow the clues in the old man's notebooks in the hope that they will help reveal his whereabouts. He and his colleague, Marcus Brody, travel to Venice, where Dr. Elsa Schneider leads them to a Crusader's tomb. There, Indy finds the missing clue to the Grail's location and, after another hectic chase, narrowly escapes being killed by members of a group dedicated to keeping it concealed; he learns that Dr. Jones is being held captive by the Nazis. He and Elsa bluff their way into a German castle and Indy rescus Dr. Jones, though not before Elsa (who has slept with both father and son) and Donovan reveal themselves to be Nazi sympathisers and the notebooks are sent to Berlin. To recover them, Indy and Dr. Jones infiltrate a Nazi rally, escaping via airship and plane. Brody, meanwhile, has gone to the Middle East and met up with Indy's old ally Sallah (see *Raiders of the Lost Ark*, M.F.B., August 1981), but is captured by the Nazis who, with Elsa and Donovan, head out into the desert. Indy and Dr. Jones arrive on the scene and, after yet another hectic chase, everyone ends up at the temple of the Grail. Only Indy and his father possess the knowledge to survive three potentially lethal obstacles, but Donovan forces Indy to lead him to the Grail by mortally wounding Dr. Jones—whose life can now be saved only by drinking from the Grail. They are greeted by the last surviving Crusader, who invites them to identify the Grail from hundreds of goblets. Elsa purposely selects the wrong one for Donovan, who drinks from it and dies, but gives the true Grail to Indy, who uses it to heal his father. But she and the rest of the Nazis fall to their deaths after ignoring the Crusader's advice by trying to remove the Grail from the temple. Indy and Dr. Jones ride off into the sunset with Brody and Sallah.

Indiana Jones and the Last Crusade is, essentially, *Raiders of the Lost Ark* with an added father-son relationship. Set between *Lost Ark*'s 1936 and the beginning of World War II, it not only brings back some of the same characters (Brody, Sallah), and resurrects Paul Freeman's Belloq in the guise of Julian Glover as Walter Donovan, but also reruns many of the set-pieces: large numbers of everyone's favourite phobia (in this case, rats and snakes), the desert settings and the final melt-down of the too-inquisitive villains, for example. Since Indy has his father as a foil this time around, however, we no longer have any need for a spunky heroine *á la* Karen Allen (or even for a simpering ninny along the lines of *Temple of Doom*'s Kate Capshaw); Elsa is very much a pawn of the plot, required to swap allegiance as the script demands, and she remains a cypher. It is, moreover, highly unlikely that Indy, with his previous experience of Nazis ("I hate those guys!" he snarls as lookalikes for Hitler and his cohorts launch into a full-blown Leni Riefenstahl spectacle), would trust a *German*.

Following in the footsteps of its two predecessors, the film's most enjoyable and inventive sequence comes right at the beginning; here an episodic chase sequence which outlines the origin of Indy's trademarks—whip, hat, scar and fear of snakes. The director can now handle action sequences standing on his head, but there are signs of tiredness in the pow-zap formula: tanks speeding through the desert are too similar to the trucks of the first film, and no match for the careening mine-railway cars of the second. The action needs to be backed up with a corresponding tension within the relationships. And though, with the mild sparring between father and son (initial antagonism turning to gruffness melting into admiration and affection) there is more emphasis on character than in the first two films, one cannot shake off the suspicion that whatever success there is in this department is due as much to the acting skills and public images of Ford and Connery as to anything in the script.

As far as the director's personal input goes, it might be tempting to see Connery as the long-lost father who is absent from *E.T.* With each film that he makes, however, it becomes apparent that Spielberg's most individual statement, and most spectacularly successful work in artistic if not box-office terms, was the unfairly maligned *1941*, watered-down traces of which are now discernible in every film he makes: here a dogfight, there a nightclub brawl. Presumably confused by the relative commercial failure and lack of critical plaudits for *The Color Purple* and *Empire of the Sun*, he now appears to be running on the spot in Boy's Own territory.

NEW STATESMAN & SOCIETY, 6/30/89, p. 46. Suzanne Moore

Prepare to be blockbusted, Indiana Jones is back. Indiana Jones—the reply to all those who complain that they don't make films like they used to—returns for his third adventure *Indiana Jones and the Last Crusade*. And what's more: "This time he's bringing his Dad". Sean Connery, in a remarkably clever move, has been brought in to play Indiana Jones Senior; and who better than a superannuated James Bond in a movie which makes the Bond series look decidedly dated. This might seem strange when you consider that Indiana Jones movies are set in the late thirties. But, while Bond is desperately trying to get modern, *Indiana Jones*, with its heart in some blurry nostalgic time, (a stagey prewar thirties), is thoroughly postmodern.

Indiana Jones is obsessed with museums and their contents. After all, he is an archaeologist and his almost existential quest is to return "artefacts" to their rightful places. "This belongs in a museum" he declares on more than one occasion. He risks life and limb, not for private wealth you understand, but for the collective good of putting these precious objects on public display. In *Raiders of the Lost Ark*, it was the sacred ark of the covenant that he was seeking, and in the *Last Crusade* the lost object is none other than the holy grail.

Steven Spielberg is a different kind of archaeologist. He seeks not to recreate or understand the past, but to recreate feelings about the past through gazing at different kinds of sacred objects. Clearly for Spielberg one of these most sacred objects is cinema itself. The old stories of adventure, of romance and of magic are his gods. Fantasies that you could dissolve into, films that you lived rather than watched. No, they don't make them like they used to. But then nor does Spielberg.

Rummaging through the "imaginary museum" of our past, Spielberg replaces history with what Frederic Jameson calls "libidinal historicism", a jumble of stylistic devices that signal "pastness". The vagueness of period simply adds to the possibilities for fantasy. And Spielberg knows, as every grown-up does, that his past, his childhood, is what has actually been lost. No wonder then that *Indiana Jones* has been so successful—it is not only for children but also for those who want just for a moment to feel childlike. It's a game that we all play from time to time.

And Spielberg plays it better than most. So well in fact that it's hard not to feel even in the middle of a most magical moment—well, just ever so slightly manipulated.

Plot-wise, *The Last Crusade* is a virtual remake of *Raiders of the Lost Ark*. After the hard drinking, wisecracking heroine of the first movie, and the screaming bimbo of the second, we have instead an Austrian temptress, Dr Elsa Schneider, who beds both Indiana's (Junior and Senior) and ends up working with the Nazi's.

This you might have thought would provide a little oedipal tension between father and son but the incident gets lost as the action races on. But then I guess a woman pales into insignificance compared to the holy grail and the battle between good and evil. As we have come to except from all Spielberg projects, the money is right there on the screen in brilliantly huge action sequences. He makes big films and big soundtracks. The score to *The Last Crusade* is as important for dramatic tension as are the visuals, especially when the volume is cranked up to the full as it tends to be in the larger cinemas.

Like the first film in the series, *The Last Crusade* veers both from classic adventure sequences, where goodies and baddies are clearly demarcated and a good right hander will always do the job, to late eighties' special effects. Fog-type stuff rises out of the ark blinding all those who look. Yet Spielberg only used these effects in the presence of the sacred object—the ark/grail to suggest greater cosmic forces.

The meshing of myths—both secular and religious—is something that Spielberg excels in. Both *ET* and *Close Encounters* had strong religious overtones; or rather they keyed-in to the half-remembered stories that are most people's experience of Christianity. The point is not whether we thought of *ET* as a Christ figure or *Close Encounters* as the second coming, but that their vague humanistic, anti-materialist message, seemed almost mystical in a culture that finds itself increasingly embarrassed by anything "spiritual".

The Last Crusade is anything but embarrassed. It uses a mix of Arturian legend, biblical prophesy and striking religious imagery to get its message across. In one scene, Indiana senior lays wounded and bleeding, while Indiana junior goes to get the grail that will save his father's life. After the usual terrors, he returns and as he pours the holy water over the wound it heals and Connery is made whole once more.

This miracle is attributed to the power of god, and yet it can only be achieved through the power of the sophisticated special effects of the 1980s. Spielberg is only able to achieve these sublime moments through complicated technology and all but the most naive of audiences know this.

If Spielberg is trying to make pure cinema, we have to be pure spectators—to deliberately suspend our belief. Spielberg's brand of epic mysticism is decidedly self-conscious and if that approach doesn't work he will bowl you over with his ripping yarns. As Indiana Jones rides off into the sunset, having found and lost the holy grail, we ride home having glimpsed what we have lost. That perfect moment, a long, long time ago when an image on a screen could take your breath away, when images meant something important, that far off time when we could *believe*, when our faith was in something other than fakes.

NEW YORK, 6/5/89, p. 58, David Denby

Violent, gaudy, and pleasingly eccentric, the thrills in Steven Spielberg's Indiana Jones series follow hard one upon another, like the spikes on an old war machine. Yet from the beginning, there has been something hollow in the joke devised by Spielberg and George Lucas (who produced the series). By inflating pulpy/twerpy ideas from thirties serials into huge modern spectacle movies, they have embraced a weird disproportion, staging infantile material with a grandiosity of means way beyond any dramatic or emotional need. The disproportion may be the point of the joke, but it leaves me uneasy, as though I had eaten at a restaurant serving hot dogs and sauerkraut in a silver chafing dish.

The treasures Indy searched for in the earlier movies—the ark of the covenant and the magic rock stolen by child-beating Thuggees—meant nothing apart from their role in firing up the action. In *Indiana Jones and the Last Crusade*, there's another unspeakably important yet somehow meaningless prize—the Holy Grail (oh, *that* ol' thing)—accompanied by much ersatz religious piety about our Lord, our Lord. ... The piety should convince no one. Despite Spielberg's genuflections and some solemn tones from John Williams (Wagner did it better in *Parsifal*), *The Last Crusade* is certainly meant to be all in fun. After the disastrous "dark" trash of the Temple of Doom scenes in the last Indiana Jones film, Spielberg has gone back to the frivolous core of his material, back to his ecstatic-transportation mode: rampaging cars, spinning planes and boats, a horse, a gleaming picture-book dirigible, an outsize, frightening tank, the trouble is, the material isn't exhilarating anymore. The energy level remains high, but the joke of disproportion has worn thin. Cliff-hanging has roughened Spielberg's hands.

Screenwriter Jeffrey Boam (working from a story by Lucas and Menno Meyjes) has devised a prologue setting up the character of Indy as a teenager (River Phoenix), a fearless boy who nevertheless can't win the respect of his father, Professor Henry Jones (Sean Connery), medieval scholar and crank. Twenty-six years later, the professor disappears while searching for the Grail. Indy chases after him, stopping over in a Venetian catacomb in the company of an Austrian blonde (Alison Doody) who may or may not be a Nazi, and many wriggling brown rats.

When he rescues his father from a Nazi fortress in Germany, the movie suddenly finds an emotional center. Sean Connery, his gray-white beard coming to a self-satisfied little point, gives a fine comic performance as a querulous, amazingly competitive old man. Connery, wearing academic tweeds and wire-frame glasses, makes Professor Jones infuriatingly precise and demanding, fussy and full of crotchets; yet Connery still has his bulk, his burly force, and, raising his eyes, he takes on Harrison Ford with fierce pride.

The father-son rivalry is strung through the fights and escapes. In front of his father, Indy feels himself judged and reverts to being a boy (just what his father wants); he has to prove himself by pulling his father out of one scrape after another. Enormously self-pleased, the old man is indifferent to danger yet helpless in the face of it. His arrogance goes so deep that even though Indy keeps saving him, he won't acknowledge that his grown-up son is anything but a bumbling, exasperating kid. The jockeying back and forth between these two stays pretty much on the surface, but the actors make the most of it. Connery brings Ford alive: Finally, Indy wants something besides adventure—his father's love—and Ford, curling his lip in chagrined disbelief that he can't get it, responds to Connery more openly than he has to any of the women in the series.

And what is the emotional center of Spielberg's life? Judging from the Indiana Jones serial, it's a fear of being shut in, crushed, entombed. There's a nifty scene in a Venice lagoon in which Indy races away from pursuers in speedboat. His boat ducks between two large cargo ships that are being pushed together by a tug; he squeezes through, but the other boat gets crunched. Walls are always closing in on Spielberg's hero. Trying to escape a Nazi warplane, Indy and his dad drive into a tunnel. The plane follows, losing both wings, its fuselage sliding through the tunnel alongside Indy's car. The parties look at each other in surprise, placing the seal of absurdity on the joke.

But not everything in *The Last Crusade* has the fizz of originality. There's some routine rassling on top of a tank; a rather sad bit with a revolving secret door in a castle. The chase in the prologue sequence appears to be a reprise of the clichés of the earlier films. It's depressing to see Spielberg pulling out his rats and snakes like some carnival-sideshow entertainer and settling for the implausible, unimaginative second-best in some scenes.

Like *Raiders of the Lost Ark*, this picture offers a climax of overwhelming cheesiness, with pompous special effects and embarrassing religioso junk. The Indiana Jones movies have gone nowhere because they aren't about anything but thrills. Spielberg even depends for excitement on those reliable old demons the Nazis. "If the Nazis get the Grail, the armies of darkness will march across the earth," someone says. But the armies of darkness *did* march across the earth, and without the Grail. I know this is just a comic fantasy film and that the Nazis are meant to be nothing more than *heil*-Hitlering dummies who conveniently represent absolute evil. But Lucas (who worked on the story) and Spielberg, lost in Pop again, seem to forget that history is something that bloodily happened and is not just a set of symbols available to juice up a story.

For Lucas, producer of *Howard the Duck* and *Willow*, there may be no hope. He hasn't touched life since those few lovely scenes in *American Graffiti*, long, long ago. His mind has hardened into "innocent" fantasy. But Spielberg is another matter, and now that he's fulfilled his agreement with Lucas to make three Indy films, he can move on. The serial has begun to pall in us. Judging from his wistful comments about what he would *like* to do with his life, it's begun to pall on him too.

NEW YORK POST, 5/24/89, p.31, David Edelstein

About 15 minutes into "Indiana Jones and the Last Crusade" I stopped thinking that Steven Spielberg was holding back on purpose (starting small, softening us up for the thrills to come) and realized that something was seriously wrong. This was like watching a great ballet star repeatedly land a beat too late.

The props and the setups were all in place, but the action didn't have the snap and hurtling momentum of the second Indiana Jones film or even the breathless innocence of the first. The timing was off, and the picture as a whole seemed bland and muffled—not bad, but not ... Spielberg.

It hurts to write this, because the anticipation most of us bring to a new Indiana Jones adventure is one of the chief pleasures in movies. As the lights go down the child in us is already giddy, primed for thundering chases and hairpin turns, vats of slithering snakes or bugs, torch-lit descents into pitch-black caves lined with crumbling skeletons.

Of course, the adult in us knows that the real thrill isn't Indy cracking his whip but Spielberg cracking his—pushing those fun-but-tacky Saturday-matinee serials into dizzying, undreamt-of realms. To see him nervous and inexpert in his task is like a nasty reminder of our own mortality. Gravity no longer seems conquerable.

On paper it still sounds nifty. Once again, Jones (Harrison Ford) locks horns with the Third Reich, this time over his medieval-scholar dad (Sean Connery), whom they've kidnapped in their quest for the Holy Grail. As with the Ark of the Covenant, the Nazis have this thing about Christian symbols, which they're sure will legitimize their world domination.

Once more, rival archeologists pore over ancient maps and fragments of sacred tablets and face off in a cave in the middle of the desert—with God and Industrial Light and Magic putting on a heckuva show. On the way are boat, tank and blimp chases; an escape from a flaming medieval castle; and a romp in the hay with a blonde, Aryan explorer called Elsa (Alison Doody), whose cheekbones could draw blood.

But "Indiana Jones and the Last Crusade" is really about a son in search of his father and a father in search of his son—that's the true Holy Grail, or, as the script calls it, the "illumination."

See, this turns out to be the core of Indy's combination of machismo and wonkishness—that his father ignored him as a kid. And as Jones Sr. and Jr. flee the Nazis, the pained recriminations fly thick and fast, along with the chastened dad's excuses. ("I respected your privacy.") At bottom, the film is about finally winning your dad's respect—and making the ol' boy suffer a bit for his sins of omission.

Spielberg told Premiere magazine that this third installment is the closest to him: He was (and still is) distant from his father. He also said it was meant to "atone" for "Indiana Jones and the Temple of Doom," the movie that gave us the PG-13 rating (its pull-out-the-throbbing-heart scene irked a few pollyannaish journalists) and that he now blames (good-naturedly) on producer George Lucas.

Too bad, because "Temple of Doom" was by leagues the best directed of the series, even if it was undercut by a moronic script and some tasteless Third World stereotypes. Spielberg compressed so much visual information into so little space that the movie was exhausting, an overload. But no one ever gave us a ride like that.

This time, the director seems afraid to crack the whip too hard. He comes down on the side of sunniness and openness; he avoids claustrophobia as if he himself is claustrophobic (or maybe crito-phobic). Despite his proclaimed involvement with the material, his work is ambivalent, as if Lucas' boys adventure genre can't begin to contain his feelings.

Worse, his staging doesn't have the old slapstick precision: An escape from a flaming sewer is interrupted in midstream (or midscream); a boat chase rivals those of later 007 movies for blandness; and the opening sequence, where River Phoenix plays Indy as a young scout (it shows how he acquired his trademark hat, whip and chin scar), doesn't transmit to the audience the boy's primal terror.

A climatic battle between Jones and a Nazi tank that holds his dad and friend Marcus (Denholm Elliott) has some brio, but even here Spielberg holds his shots too long, as if afraid we'll miss something. That we're impatient is a mark of how great he has been in the past. (That we're appalled by the cheesy, cartoony special effects is testament to how great those have been, too.)

The picture's only novelty is Connery, and teaming up James Bond and Indiana Jones is certainly an inspired idea. Except this ain't Bond—more like Yoda. Casting the magnificent Connery—with his roguish power and ravaged heroism—as a befuddled academic is like dressing a Michelangelo in tweed. I'm all for casting against the grain, but this is a waste of a titanic screen presence.

The script, by Jeffrey Boam, is smart for this kind of film, and it has one classic exchange in which the smitten Jones steals a flower from a Venice street vendor and hands it to the dour Elsa who sadly points out that "tomorrow it will have faded."

"Tomorrow I'll steal you another," says Indy without missing a beat.

What's marvelous about that passage is how it sums up (and celebrates) Indy's cockiness; in the face of death he's sure he can pluck another blossom, steal another blossom, steal another life—and he can.

It drags him (and the adventure) down when he gets into the Arthur Millerish stuff with his father and when each has a turn mourning the other's passing. I'm not sure why it's so flat. It might be because the "illumination" is generic, as is most of the Judeo-Christian awe and the use of Nazis to represent evil. It's generic the way the last episode of the Lucas "Star Wars" trilogy was—with all the ghosts lined up smiling while the little Ewoks gamboled.

Spielberg's movies are often about compensating for a weak father, and he's far more in tune with the sensitive, feminine side of himself than the masculine. That's why his best thriller— indeed, the best thriller of his generation—is "Jaws," which dazzlingly evoked a child's terror of the sea while poking fun at the machismo of Robert Shaw's shark hunter.

That he can't make "Indiana Jones and the Final Crusade" so expressive is a sign of how badly his mannerisms have smothered his once-magical instincts as a storyteller—and how miserable he is about that.

It's no surprise to hear him, in interviews, announce that he wants to abandon the "Spielberg style" and rediscover his direct emotional ties to a piece of material. The master stylist has finally understood that somewhere along the line the style mastered him. Here's to liberation.

NEWSDAY, 5/24/89, Part II/p. 2, Mike McGrady

Back at his university lecture hall, our old friend Indiana Jones, wearing a tweedy three-piece suit, peers out through spectacles and explains that archeology is a dry and precise science, not something glamorous, adventurous or, God forbid, risky.

"Archeology is the search for fact ..." he says. "We do not follow maps to buried treasure, and X never marks the spot."

No sooner are those words uttered than Indiana once again dons his familiar fedora and faded bomber's jacket, once again picks up his bullwhip and traipses the globe. After rescuing his kidnaped father from the Germans ("Nazis—I *hate* these guys!" he mutters), he joins him in a quest for the Holy Grail, a search that of course makes use of a secret map with a sizable "X" indeed marking the spot.

This crusade carries Indiana into fiery caves, through rat-infested sewers, into castles crawling with Nazis. He must wage battles from the back of a horse and from a speeding motorcycle, from the belly of a tank and a huge dirigible, from a single-engine airplane and a motor launch racing through the canals of Venice. Finally, when he does reach the Canyon of the Crescent Moon, the resting place of the Grail, he must sidestep guillotines, trapdoors, poison potions, a treacherous blonde and a 700-year-old Spaniard.

In other words, nothing out of the ordinary for Indiana Jones. All routine, all quite normal, all S.O.P. for Steven Spielberg's great comic-book creation.

Welcome back, Indiana! The daredevil archeologist who first appeared in "Raiders of the Lost Ark" and later popped up in "Indiana Jones and the Temple of Doom" makes a blazingly successful return in "Indiana Jones and the Last Crusade," a roller coaster of a movie that swoops from cliff to cave, from thrill to chill, from peril to laughter.

The two earlier Indiana Jones flicks have been world-beaters (their combined box-officer take exceeds $600 million), but this is the biggest and the best of the lot. If I were to single out the one major improvement, I would have to cite Sean Connery playing Indiana's father—less adventurous but every bit as resourceful as the son. Along with the appearance of Connery comes a massive infusion of humor and humanity.

Director Spielberg is on a rescue mission of his own. With "Indiana Jones and the Last Crusade," Spielberg single-handedly rescues us from the dullest, drabbest movie year in memory. And despite the film's state-of-the-art technology, there is something wonderfully old-fashioned about it all—perhaps because he takes us back to a time when cars had cranks and airplanes had propellers and men had pure values and the guts to back them up.

With "Indiana Jones and the Last Crusade," Spielberg should finally get that long-overdue Best Director Oscar. Nor will his trip to the podium be a lonely one. Look for executive producer George Lucas, cinematographer Douglas Slocombe, film editor Michael Kahn, production designer Elliot Scott, any number of special-effects technicians and perhaps—why not?—Harrison Ford.

Although Ford has starred in more super-blockbusters than any other actor, he has never been granted his artistic due. Possibly because he makes it all look so easy. Once again, Ford's solid and unflashy work keeps the entire enterprise tethered to some kind of reality. But this time, Ford doesn't have to do it all alone. Connery provides abundant charm and wit, not to mention an intriguing father-son relationship—especially when the two men discover they have been sharing the love of the same beautiful woman (Alison Doody). In additon, Connery's presence provides the entire film with a heavy ironical overlay: He was, of course, the first movie-land James Bond and, as such, the true sire of Indiana Jones.

The Spielberg-Lucas team seems to have made nothing but inspired decisions. The role of that great English character actor, Denholm Elliott, again playing Indiana's bumbling academic boss, has been expanded, and Elliott joins Connery in providing an antidote to all the derring-do. The appearance of River Phoenix as a young Indy expands on the character of Indiana Jones. The strongest addition of all may have been Jeffrey Boam ("Innerspace"), a script writer with a consistently light touch. The film will surely have its detractors, those who will point out that Spielberg has made yet another comic-book movie, that it's not remotely realistic, that the characters are drawn broadly and that the humor tends to be obvious. Yes, yes, yes—all valid, all true, all quite perfect!

NEWSWEEK, 5/29/89, p. 69, David Ansen

It's only been eight years since "Raiders of the Lost Ark" took the moviegoing world by storm. What's hard to believe is that in 1981 Steven Spielberg's rousing resurrection of the Saturday-matinee serials seemed so stunningly fresh. Well, as Indy himself said, it's not the years, it's the mileage. Less than a decade later, *Indiana Jones and the Last Crusade,* the third and last of the series, arrives in an altered movie landscape, having to compete not only with the other Indy Jones movies but with dozens of "Raiders" clones, from "Romancing the Stone" on down to "The Further Adventures of Tennessee Buck."

Spielberg still does it best. Only a determined grouch could deny that "The Last Crusade" is a lot of fun. Superbly crafted, it's a much airier romp than the claustrophobic, grisly "Indiana Jones and the Temple of Doom." But only an amnesiac could deny that the original thrill is gone. Spielberg still directs with wide-eyed enthusiasm, but the genre is in its decadent phase. The Indy Jones movies have become as self-knowing as the James Bond series, so effortlessly tongue-in-cheek that any real sense of danger or surprise is obliterated. If "Raiders" was a goof on old movie conventions, "Last Crusade" is a goof on a goof.

The saving grace and freshest moments of the new installment are attributable to Sean Connery's delightful presence as Indiana's archeologist father. Jeffrey Boam's screenplay provides a beguiling, competitive father/son interplay for Connery and Harrison Ford, which they perform with relish. Without this running Oedipal gag, "The Last Crusade" might seem like just a rerun of "Raiders," with the search for the Holy Grail substituting for the ark of the covenant and the Nazis reprised as villains. It seems that Papa Jones, consumed with a lifelong obsession with the Grail, has disappeared in his search for it—sending Indy, bullwhip in hand, on a dual mission to rescue Dad and find the Grail before the Nazis get to it first.

Before Spielberg gets down to his plot—an adventure that takes us from the United States to Venice, Austria, Berlin and the Middle East—he opens with a spectacular 16-minute set piece showing us the teenage Indiana (River Phoenix) in 1912. Pursued by ruffians from whom he has rescued a valuable artifact, the fearless young Indy hops aboard a speeding circus train, where he must elude not only gun-toting villains but a lion, a rhino and the inevitable overloaded vat of squirming snakes. You can almost hear Spielberg cackling with delight off-screen as he conducts this cliffhanger overture into a Rossinian frenzy.

A few of the set pieces fizzle: there's an oddly anticlimactic boat chase, and in the climactic encounter with the Grail, Spielberg disappointingly backs off from the mystical possibilities of the quest and settles for earthbound, literalistic effects. Fortunately, "Indiana Jones" dishes out the action so generously and with such goodhumored confidence you feel like an ingrate for carping. This thrice-told tale gives you your money's worth. Now it's time to hang up the bullwhip and move on.

TIME, 5/29/89, p. 82, Richard Corliss

"Tell me a story, Dad."

So the father tells a story of a modern knight in fedora and leather jacket, a disinterested seeker of treasure and truth who leaps vast crevices, evades killer boulders, outwits nasty Nazis and dodges vengeful spirits while searching for the legendary Ark of the Covenant. The child is beguiled, and Dad is impressed, despite himself. Pretty good yarn ... Raiders of the Lost Ark.

Next night. "Tell me another story ... the same, but different."

This time Dad sends the rogue archaeologist to India to battle child-enslaving thugs, take a roller-coaster ride through lower Hades and narrowly escape the world's first heart surgery performed without benefit of anesthesia ... Indiana Jones and the Temple of Doom.

"Pretty scary, huh, Son?" The child shivers, then shrugs.

Third night. "Tell me another story, Dad—the same, but different ... and better!"

Moviegoers have two surrogate storytelling dads: George Lucas and Steven Spielberg. Lucas, who dreamed up *Star Wars* for a generation of space cadets, is the mastermind of the Indiana Jones series. Spielberg directed the trilogy, which reaches its thrilling climax this week when *Indiana Jones and the Last Crusade* opens on 2,327 movie screens in the U.S. and Canada. The star is Harrison Ford—three times Indy Jones, three times *Star Wars'* Han Solo and the unchallenged hero of a derring-do, me-too movie decade.

And for their newest, most invigorating collaboration, these three godfathers of the '80s action epic have adopted a father of their own. Sean Connery, who as James Bond helped sire the thrill-machine genre, brings his masterly charm to the role of Indiana's estranged dad Henry Jones. Lucas and Spielberg, Ford and Connery prove that a sequel can be as fresh as the face of a teenage Indy confronting his first hairbreadth challenge. *Indy 3* is the same, different and better. It infuses vitality into the action-adventure, a movie staple whose ravenous popularity and endless, predictable permutations have nearly exhausted it.

Something similar might be said of Hollywood this summer—the so-called summer of the sequels. Between now and August, moviegoers will be offered up seconds of *Ghostbusters* and *Lethal Weapon*, a third *Karate Kid*, fifths of *Star Trek* and *A Nightmare on Elm Street*, an eighth *Friday the 13th* and, for the 17th time around, James Bond, in *Licensed to Kill*.

Is this sequel mania evidence of economic health or of creative bankruptcy? Cunningly, the theatrical-film industry has held its ground against the marauding armies of the video revolution. In fact, one format has fed the other, as audiences first view pictures on the big screen, then supplement their cinema appetite at home. Last year saw record grosses both for theatrical films and for videocassettes. But movie budgets have increased as well, and even a gambling man turns cautious with $40 million on the table. Hence the moguls have relied on brand names and roman numerals.

This summer, the experts say, everything old is gold again. "1989 has the makings to break all records," says Larry Gerbrandt of Paul Kagan Associates, a media-research firm. "We're seeing sequels to some of the most successful movies ever. And since no two of the big ones are being released head to head, each of them could hit a home run." Notes producer Laurence Mark: "Sequels aren't necessarily about a failure of the Hollywood imagination. They're about lowering risks." So why, in a business full of expensive risks, shouldn't Hollywood be allowed just one near-sure thing?

In a way, every movie, every work of fiction, is a sequel—the latest chapter in a book of stories as old as once upon a time. The narrative conventions are age-old too: that man defines his nature through action; that the path to wisdom winds through false friends and moral booby traps; that maps lead to buried treasure and X always marks the spot; that manly virtue will be rewarded with a king's garlands and a kiss at the fade-out. The Indy stories are just the most recent link in a chain forged at the first campfire, when an elder spun tales to keep the clan together and the demons at bay.

Tale spinners Spielberg and Lucas (who devised the story with Menno Meyjes) and screenwriter Jeffrey Boam were obviously brimming to work variations on the nearly $700 million-grossing theme. For openers, they toss teenage Indy (River Phoenix) into a nest of cave robbers, a lion's den and a snake pit, thereby explaining, with an economy that Feuillade and Freud might admire, the origins of their hero's hat, his favorite weapon and his fear of serpents. The movie's creators have not grown tired. They keep the action cracking as smartly as Indy's bullwhip.

"I've learned more about movie craft from making the Indiana Jones films than I did from *E.T.* or *Jaws*," says Spielberg, who won't take on Indy a fourth time. "And now I feel as if I've graduated from the college of Cliff-Hanger U. I ought to have paid tuition." Spielberg's camera style neither misses a trick nor reveals how it's done. See how he cues the change of a Zeppelin's course by the shadow scampering across a cocktail glass; watch a motif of cigarette lighters carry complicity from one character to another. Like a fine old haunted castle, his film has secret staircases of suspense, revolving panels of plot.

Indy 3, like *Raiders*, features airplane stunts, a brawl on a careening vehicle and a sacred quest: a search for the Holy Grail, the cup Jesus used at the Last Supper. The film expands the role of Denholm Elliott as a museum curator and tosses in a cameo appearance by Adolf Hitler, who autographs Henry's Grail diary. A new twist is Elsa (capable Alison Doody), a blond sorceress poised between greed and glory. She is an Indy gone wrong, and the series' first indispensable female.

A vamp is standard baggage in the thriller genre, especially in the Bond films, from which the Indy series took some sideways inspiration. In 1977 Spielberg told Lucas he wanted to make a James Bond movie. "I have something better than James Bond," Lucas replied, and sketched the scenario for *Raiders*. The Indy series bears traces of the Bond films in its superhero with an edge of surliness, its globe-girdling itineraries, its villains purring megalomania, its neat blend of macho cynicism and schoolboy pluck. But *The Last Crusade* has something better than James Bond. It has Sean Connery.

Since he eighty-sixed 007 almost two decades ago (with one aimless visit home in 1983 for *Never Say Never Again*), Connery has mothballed his toupee and gained a twilight twinkle. He is the movies' sexiest, most majestic older star. And yet at 58 Connery was thought too young to play Indy's father, who was originally conceived as a crotchety gent like *On Golden Pond's* Henry Fonda. It was Spielberg's idea to cast Connery, a decision that illuminated the film and its filming. "When Sean and Harrison arrived on the set," Spielberg recalls, "everyone got quiet and respectful. The two are like royalty—not the royalty you fear because they can tax you, but the royalty you love because they will make your lives better."

Connery's arrival opened the script up to puckish revisions, as when Henry reveals he has slept with Elsa, with whom Indy has also dallied. At a "Huh?" of disbelief from Indy, Henry preens defensively, protesting, "I'm as human as the next man." Indy growls back, "I *was* the next man!'' Would the Henry Jones character, as originally conceived, have slept with Elsa? ''No,'' says Boam with impeccable movie logic, ''but Sean Connery would.''

''I wanted to play Henry Jones as a kind of Sir Richard Burton,'' Connery says. ''There was so much behind him and so many hidden elements in his life.'' In the beginning Henry speaks to his long-lost son slowly, with wide eyes and grand gestures, as if Indy were a child in need of gentle remedial education. ''I was bound to have fun with the role of a gruff, Victorian Scottish father,'' Connery says of Henry (remember, the Jones family hails from Utah). ''And have fun I did—so much so that I told Harrison, 'If you give me all the jokes, you'll really have to work for your scenes.' ''

Ford, 46, who is married to *E.T.* screenwriter Melissa Mathison, is one of the world's richest actors. But he could have told Connery he's no stranger to hard work: he supported himself in lean times as a carpenter to the stars. He's had lean dreams too. ''George and Steven may be living out their childhood fantasies on film,'' he says, ''but I didn't come from the same crate of oranges.'' Indeed not. ''My first childhood ambition was to be the guy who carried the coal from our house to the coal chute in a wheelbarrow. I remember there was this big pile of coal, and then he did his job, and then there was no coal. I liked the rhythm of his work. It was a job you could see getting done. My dad would come home from *his* job and talk about how unhappy everyone was there. And compared to that, I'd rather have shoveled coal. I was four or five.''

Ford is a man who holds few illusions about star quality. Movie magic may be an aging prostitute under a harsh streetlight for a kid whose grandfather played vaudeville in blackface and whose father produced innovative TV commercials in Chicago. ''One day I met the actor who played Sky King, the aerial ace,'' recalls the actor. ''He turned out to be short, heavyset and unconventional looking. It intrigued me, how different show business was from what people thought. And maybe that disposition gave me a reality register that has been a fixture in my life.''

Ford thinks the way Bogie talked, and he takes an old-fashioned movie star's pleasure in the craft of filmmaking. ''I love to work,'' he says. ''I like doing something difficult and complicated. It's like setting yourself in a maze and learning the maze so you always come out in the right place at the right time. I'm a technical actor. For me, acting is part intellectual, part mechanical. It's being in control of your mind and body at the same time. The emotions you show may be spontaneous, but the bricks have to be carefully laid to fit with the other pieces. You don't fool around with the work.''

You don't fool around with Ford, or Indy. In the film's prologue, young Jones is chased and chastened by a band of scavengers. The gang's leader tells Indy, ''You lost today, kid. But that doesn't mean you have to like it.'' Real-life flashback: when Ford was about young Indy's age, he enteres a junior high school where, he recalls, ''the favorite recess activity was to take me to the edge of a sharply sloping parking lot, throw me off, wait for me to struggle back to the top, then throw me off again. The entire school would gather to watch this display. I don't know why they did it. Maybe because I wouldn't fight the way they wanted me to fight. They wanted a fight they could win. And my way of winning was just to hang in there.'' He refused to be a sissy, so he would be Sisyphus.

''Other people gave up,'' Ford says of his hard-won acting eminence. ''I don't give up. That's all.'' A good man to make a movie with, if you're Lucas and Spielberg and Connery. A great quartet of storytellers to watch riding off into the everlasting sunset at the end of Indiana Jones' last and best crusade.

VILLAGE VOICE, 5/30/89, p. 57, Georgia Brown

So now we may speak of a trilogy. With *The Last Crusade*—seeking the Holy Grail, no less—the team of Steven Spielberg, George Lucas, and Harrison Ford serves up its final Indiana Jones chapter, not with the bang avid fans may be expecting (I duly record my 14-year-old's dissent on this point), but with a rather plaintive, filial whimper. Although another kinetic road comedy, this one's less frenzied than the first two; it's also a Pop-Junior buddy picture where the Jones boys bicker and bait each other—and even share a woman. With the filmmakers in their forties and fathers too, the Oedipal twist is hardly surprising. (Yes, the repressed returns even for those who have made it big. Measured against what the father withholds, even very big can look puny.)

Not long ago in his faraway galaxy, Lucas took the occasion of his final *Star Wars* picture to unmask the fascist father. As the resident Indiana Jones storyteller, he now makes clear that Indy, for all his prowess, is just one more harried, haunted son. In director Spielberg's universe, dads have usually been conspicuous by their absence; they take off on quests of their own, leaving Mom and the kids to fend for themselves. The roving Indiana could be cousin to the Richard Dreyfuss character in *Close Encounters* in his obsession with supernatural, i.e., religious, forces and in his lack of interest in other humans.

As for Ford, whose career caught fire when he played Lucas's space cowboy (fittingly named Solo), he's best when embodying the cynical, wisecracking hero and sexual cad. When Princess Leia admitted she loved Han Solo while he was being lowered into oblivion, he replied, "I know." Poor girl. (Poor little girls loving a generation of boy children formed on this model of the rake.) Ford has played Indy in this same offhanded style, his frown transformed by gold, not flesh. His acquisitive eye is on the prize; women are more duty than pleasure. (In Roman Polanski's *Frantic* or Mike Nichols's *Working Girl*, not allowed to wear his armor, Ford seems at a loss.) Hollywood's three musketeers have a profitable way of meshing.

The Last Crusade opens with a teen-aged Indiana (played by River Phoenix at an awkward age) during a Boy Scout outing on the spectacular plateaus and buttes of the American West. He stumbles onto robbers plundering a cave; they've just found "the cross of Coronado." The head plunderer, in fedora and leather jacket, looks like an eerie blend of Ford and Spielberg himself. When young Indy steals the cross ("That cross is an important artifact and it belongs in a museum!"), a merry Spielbergian chase ensues, continuing on board a circus train.

What's notable at this point is the explicit phallic stuff. Kid Indy is terrified by a huge serpent, and then he falls into a mess of smaller snakes. (The episode explains the genesis of the hero's snake complex in *Raiders*.) Then a rhino horn nearly stabs his groin while a man on top of him is pummeling away. Fear of emasculation or of buggery? The point is that this manhood-in-danger business leads back to dear old Dad: When Indy finally makes it home, still clutching the jeweled cross, Professor Jones doesn't even look up from the illuminated manuscript he's copying. "Count to 10. ... In Greek!" orders the pedant. So aloof is he, his face (like God's or Orson Welles's) isn't even shown. The man in the brown fedora apparently takes over as the boy's imaginative mentor.

From interviews it seems pretty well established that both Lucas and Spielberg grew up with distant, withholding fathers. The two sons appear to have pooled resentments here. Sean Connery's Professor Henry Jones Sr.—who enters the movie late but then proceeds to take over—is a crotchety, twinkle-eyed fogey and (in case you're expecting it) nothing at all like the aging warrior he played in *The Untouchables* or *Robin and Marian*. (Neither Darth Vader nor Obi Wan Kenobe either.) The filmmakers chose Connery but are determined not to let him win much sympathy, although the way he taunts his son does humanize our Indy, who loses his smugness and looks like a whipped puppy. Jones Sr. gives his son a shocking slap for using Jesus Christ as an expletive (an event raw enough, to have come, I suspect, out of *someone's* life). At another point, Dad delivers the ultimate verbal slap: "You left just when you were becoming interesting."

One of the first things Dad reveals to Junior—who hates being called that—is that he too slept with Elsa, Indy's erstwhile girlfriend. *He* knew she was a Nazi. ("You should have listened to your father." Dad may be an ass and a tyrant, but father-son reconciliation is waiting in the wings. Mom, though, rates one cryptic mention. If the faceless Asian masses are back again in all their facelessness (poverty as background color), so is the series's gratuitous sexism.

Would it have made a difference if Steven and Amy had had a girl? I mean, would the Indiana Jones movies have grown less rather than more brazenly antifemale? And what if George and Marcia hadn't gone through that nasty divorce? After all, *they* have a girl. I'm wondering if *The Last Crusade* might have featured a (token) woman who was not a Nazi and a greedy, (literally) grasping blond betrayer. (Granted, she waffles.) Not for the first time does the James Bond ethos come to the kids' picture. (I realize that it may be too late for those guys who prefer their martinis shaken to learn not to fear girls.)

Raiders' Karen Allen, a sassy tiger, had class—even if, after her first scene, her function was to tag along and require rescuing. (Stories from the set that Allen and the men didn't get along aren't surprising; her face looked actually desperate, as if she were fighting for her life.) Kate Capshaw as Willie, *Temple of Doom's* floozy, had uppity moments, but she was basically a screamer. Clearly, she was around to faint over the eyeball soup and the monkey-brains dessert, and to be strapped spread-eagled in a cage (by Indy) and lowered over a boiling lava pit. Game, yes, but a ditzy broad.

Now comes Irish actress Alison Doody in her first screen role. She looks like Cybill Shepherd and, like *Moonlighting's* Maddie, Doody's art historian Elsa Schneider is a smart-mouth. (That's the way scriptwriters create strong women.) At least she finished her doctorate. But to make the movie's single woman outside the crowd scenes—the woman who screws both Pop and Junior, so who else can she be but Mom?—a Nazi (with even a suggestion that she's doing Hitler too), this, jerks, is irresponsible. We're talking here about calculated box-office entertainment, child fare—not the dictates of art. They make it look as if they picked the actress for her last name.

Spielberg told *Premiere* that he was making a final Indiana Jones movie to apologize for the second—which he now disowns as "too horrific" "There's not an ounce of my own personal feeling in *Temple of Doom*." (I confess to finding *Temple of Doom* great fun, a piece of dessert.) He didn't tell what personal feelings went into *Last Crusade*, but what I'm wondering about is the pointed shot of *Das Kapital* being burned in a Nazi bonfire. Is this some message from the mount? Does it have to do with sharing profit points?

As for the Grail quest, sequel to the search for the Ark of the Covenant (in *Raiders*), it's nice of Indiana Jones to have guarded the culture's myths, especially from those bad old Nazis. ("I hate those guys.") When we get to the Grail's inner sanctum, though, for all the millions, the effects look cheesy—as they did when the Ark blasted forth spooks and goblins. (Some things, it is worth noting once again, are resistant to F/X treatment.) The conceit at the end of *Crusade* is that the cup that caught the blood of the crucified son will carry potion to heal the dying father. Every child who has tried to heal a wounded parent—each of us—could be easily drowned in grief at this point, but the film only minimally, briefly touches. Why? Because, I think, the harshness of the father-son business doesn't come near to being resolved. It's always grating underneath the slapstick. As the guys ride into the sunset, Daddy's still putting Junior down.

Also reviewed in:
NATION, 6/19/89, p. 862, Stuart Klawans
NEW REPUBLIC, 6/19/89, p. 28, Stanley Kauffmann
NEW YORK TIMES, 5/24/89, p. C15, Caryn James
NEW YORKER, 6/12/89, p. 103, Pauline Kael
VARIETY, 5/24–30/89, p. 25
WASHINGTON POST, 5/26/89, p. 41, Desson Howe

INNOCENT MAN, AN

A Touchstone Pictures release in association with Silver Screen Partners IV. *Executive Producer:* Scott Kroopf. *Producer:* Ted Field and Robert Cort. *Director:* Peter Yates. *Screenplay:* Larry Brothers. *Director of Photography:* William A. Fraker. *Editor:* Stephen A. Rotter and William S. Scharf. *Music:* Howard Shore. *Music Editor:* Suzana Peric. *Sound:* C. Darin Knight and (music) Michael Farrow. *Sound Editor:* Dan Sable. *Production Designer:* Stuart Wurtzel. *Art Director:* Frank Richwood. *Set Designer:* Sig Tinglof. *Set Decorator:* Chris A. Butler. *Special Effects:* William H. Schirmer. *Costumes:* Rita Ryack. *Make-up:* James L. McCoy. *Stunt Coordinator:* John Moio. *Running time:* 113 minutes. *MPAA Rating:* R.

CAST: Tom Selleck (Jimmie Rainwood); F. Murray Abraham (Virgil Cane); Laila Robins (Kate Rainwood); David Rasche (Mike Parnell); Richard Young (Danny Scalise); Badja Djola (John Fitzgerald); Todd Graff (Robby); M.C. Gainey (Malcolm); Peter Van Norden (Peter Feldman); Bruce A. Young (Jingles); James T. Morris (Junior); Terry Golden (Felix); Dennis Burkley (Butcher); Thomas B. Kackert (Dove); Vito Peterson (Handjob); Charle Landry (Stevie); Tobin Bell (Zeke); Scott Jaeck (Albert); Holly Fulger (Yvonne); Philip Baker Hall (Judge Lavet); J. Kenneth Campbell (Lieutenant Freebery); Jim Ortlieb (Convict, Robby's Death); Ralph O. Benton, Jim Staskel, Brian J. Williams (Men on Tuna Boat); Maggie Baird (Stacy); Alanniss Alldero (Convict Torturer); Bob Maroff (Venucci); Derek Anunciation (Lester); Ben Slack (Woznick); J.J. Johnston (Joseph Donatelli); Brian Brophy (Nate Blitman); Ben Rawnsley (Cop at Jimmie's); Dean Hall (Mike); Gary Matanky (Mechanic at Hanger); Jack R. Orend (Officer at Bust); Ernie Lively (Donatelli's Dealer); David Rhodes Brown (First Convict); Larry Brothers (Basketball Con); Jeffrey Earl Young (First Guard); Lt. Mike Budge (Warden); David Meligan (Correctional Officer); Dave Florek (Court Clerk); Gary Velasco and Robert E. Nichols (Courthouse Guards); Ron Collins (Fritz).

LOS ANGELES TIMES, 10/6/89, Calendar/p. 6, Michael Wilmington

Like the double-tongued lady in "Hamlet," "An Innocent Man" protests too much.

This cautionary thriller about an unjustly imprisoned airline mechanic has a chance to be a canny blend of gutsy melodrama and "J' Accuse" against the prison system. But, by the end, it has gone as slick and corrupt as the crafty old con (F. Murray Abraham) who advises Tom Selleck's framed Jimmie Rainwood on jail survival. On a fundamental moral level, "An Innocent Man" is guilty as hell.

Hell, indeed, is the chasm that seems to be opening here at first. Like Hitchcock's "Wrong Man," Selleck's Rainwood is a luckless bystander: Two wild and crazy narcs, Parnell (David Rasche) and Scalise (Richard Young), get an address wrong, break into his house and shoot him down. The writer, Larry Brothers, obviously hates these gonzo cops: a pair of cocaine-tooting, hedonistic, trigger-happy cowboys who get sexually excited during their raids. When they discover their error, they barely hesitate to cover their tracks, planting drugs and a real gun on the unconscious Rainwood and railroading him into jail.

Brothers had a good design: The innocent, solid Rainwood in the slammer and these rotten cops running wild on the outside, threatening Rainwood's wife (Laila Robins). But then, the movie takes a sharp, incredibly miscalculated turn. Faced with intimidation and rape by a prison gang of blacks, Rainwood is counseled by Abraham's wise old Virgil Cane to kill the ringleader, Jingles (Bruce A. Young). And, after a beating and a gang rape—which looks something like a fraternity hazing—he does, stabbing Jingles with a homemade shiv in the prison urinal after sneaking up on him from behind.

It's a sad, sour moment. How does anyone involved justify a scene where the "hero" murders an unarmed, if obviously dangerous, man with total impunity? It is even worse where there is the implication that killing makes you more of a man, gets you accepted into the jolly jail-yard fraternity, puts a stop to strangers stealing your toothpaste.

In a genuinely realistic movie with recognizable, flawed characters, scenes like this could work. But Rainwood is a standard big-movie-star part: drained of moral flaws, a generic innocent man. Selleck plays him without agony, without reflection, with the stoicism of a born camera subject. He learns the moves of murder and jail-yard *machismo* as if it were another basketball game. We're left to conclude that this is the way life is. You've got to kill or be killed, eat or be eaten. It's an ugly twist and it leads into the movie's vapid last act, with the wild and crazy narcs snared in a ridiculously complex set-up involving Mafiosi, Jewish lawyers and yet another hostage standoff.

Director Peter Yates probably wants some of the gritty, underworld reslism of his 1973 "Friends of Eddie Coyle," but he's hamstrung. The doses of prison argot and atmosphere drain this movie of its rightful outrage—as if the persecuted Yakov Bok in "The Fixer" had been turned into the "Terminator." Instead of making the fairy tale real, they make it a nightmare of sadistic wish fulfillment and penal envy, with situations culled from bad movies and names and titles culled from rock songs.

The good things in "An Innocent Man" can be summed up in four words and one initial: F. Murray Abraham, David Rasche.

Abraham gets some macabre humor out of his oily role and Rasche does something more. With his cheerlessly savage smile, ice-blue eyes and slightly ravaged features, he makes Parnell a chilling narcissist-psychopath, the ultimate golden boy gone wrong. Like the crazy surfer CIA agent Rasche played in "Best Defense," his Parnell magnetizes every scene he's in.

And there's a well-deserved, if obvious, indictment of the current penal system, which the movie draws as a factory for turning out more, and more vicious, criminals. Unfortunately, a similar kind of system seems to be cranking out stuff like "An Innocent Man" (MPAA-rated R for language, sex and violence): a factory for turning out more, and more vicious, movies.

MONTHLY FILM BULLETIN, 6/90, p. 163, Tim Pulleine

Detectives Parnell and Scalise, ostensibly ruthless in pursuit of drug offences, are in fact in thrall to drug boss Donatelli, "busting" only those connected with his competitors and passing on most of the impounded dope to him. One night, however, Parnell mistakes an address given him over the phone, and the two men raid the Long Beach home of aircraft engineer Jimmie Rainwood, whom Parnell shoots when he challenges them. Realising their mistake, they frame the unconscious Rainwood for assault and cocaine possession, subsequently enlisting a perjured witness to say he sold Rainwood drugs. Backed by his wife Kate, Rainwood declines the urgings of his lawyer Feldman to accept a plea bargain; in the upshot, he is found guilty and sentenced to six years' jail. Sent to Orville prison, he is victimised by black convict Jingles and his two cohorts; after being beaten up but refusing to name names to chief officer Freebery, he is given fifteen days in solitary. Subsequently, veteran convict Virgil Cane spells out that only by killing Jingles can he hope to survive. After seeing a homosexual gang rape instigated by Jingles, Rainwood is convinced, and a situation is set up whereby he mortally knifes Jingles with no witnesses. Freebery sends him to "the hole" for ninety days, but he emerges a big man in the prison. He becomes firm friends with Cane, who reveals that Parnell and Scalise were responsible for his own arrest and his girlfriend's death. Kate has meanwhile been putting pressure on the authorities, and has persuaded Fitzgerald, police internal affairs investigator, of the crookedness of Parnell and Scalise. After three years, Rainwood wins parole, but no sooner is he home than the two cops appear, taunting him that he is "state property" and their plaything. In despair, Rainwood and Kate (with guidance from Cane in Orville) devise a plan, to which Fitzgerald is unofficially made privy. With the help of ex-con Malcolm, Rainwood sets up the two cops so that they raid a dealer in Donatelli's employ, then holds them up and takes the "impounded" cocaine. Donatelli gives the two cops an ultimatum for its recovery (though they plan to keep it and make off); Rainwood phones them anonymously to do a deal. A parking-lot rendezvous is set, which Fitzgerald wiretaps. But Parnell shoots Malcolm and Scalise is killed in the ensuing affray; Rainwood pursues Parnell and, after a bruising fight, is narrowly prevented by Kate from killing him. Some time later, as Rainwood resumes his job, Parnell arrives at Orville, to be greeted with relish by Cane.

Apart from the exposé elements in its picture of penal conditions, *An Innocent Man* combines a melodrama of unjust conviction and retribution with an existential study of character under pressure in virtually primordial circumstances ("You didn't know a thing about respect until I taught you", Cane tells Rainwood after the latter has killed Jingles). Neither storyline nor treatment, however, are in any way distinctive enough to plait these strands together. As a consequence, the small element of surprise in the construction, Rainwood's release on parole little more than halfway through the film, signals only a crashing of gears as the revenge plot gets under way; and the implication that Rainwood's remoulding by his prison experience ("You don't know me any more", he tells his wife) has ironically equipped him to deal with his subsequent dilemma becomes no more than an irrelevant platitude.

This underlying lack of cohesion is partly due to the casting in the central role of an actor who is not only physically imposing but whose screen persona is one of ebullience and confidence, and partly due to a failure of imaginative nerve in the depiction of Rainwood's prison ordeal. This is most apparent in the way that his prolonged subjection to solitary confinement is elided by a single cut, while the latter part of his stay in jail is dispensed with altogether. A more basic explanation lies, though, in the succession of false notes struck in the plotting, all the way from the farfetched initial mistake over the address, via the uncommon ease with which Rainwood is able to put paid to Jingles in the inexplicably deserted latrines, and on to the peculiar dealings between the crooked cops and the mobster Donatelli. The unsavoury top-dressing of explicitiness and four-letter language only serves to heighten by default the resemblance elsewhere to the more mechanical species of made-for-TV movie, while the mawkish dialogues between husband and wife do not even stop short of the ringing, "No matter what happens, I love you".

NEW YORK POST, 10/6/89, p. 27, David Edelstein

At the start of "An Innocent Man," upright engineer Tom Selleck tells his pretty new wife (Laila Robins) that the world isn't big enough to hold him—that there's no place on earth he doesn't want to see and experience.

Because we know this is the story of a guy who's framed for a crime he didn't commit, when we see him in a prison shower with only a bar of soap between him and three 250-pound black guys, we think, "Tee-hee, Tom's gonna change his mind now."

But he doesn't change his mind. Faced with the prospect of becoming someone's "kid" in the Big House, Big Tom bares his teeth—this white-bread babycakes turns into one mean mother. Don't be messin' with him in no shower. He'll stick you and do you, and I ain't talkin' outta the side of my neck—I'm tryin' to give you a solid.

Oh, excuse me, the prison lingo is so damn seductive I just can't restrain myself. The studio assures us it's authentic: screenwriter Larry Brothers, the production notes tease, has "first-hand knowledge" of life behind bars after dropping out of Amherst to pursue his chief interests—drugs and crime.

It seems only natural, then, that Brothers should use his second hand to type screenplays in which he teaches fraidy-cat Americans the hard rules of survival.

This slick, racist package (briskly directed by Peter Yates) is engineered to make you ripsnorting mad at the inequities of the criminal-justice system. After all, if this could happen to a white guy with a good job and a pretty wife, it could happen to you, too, sucker.

The chief villains are two cops (David Rasche and Richard Young) who specialize in stealing coke from dealers and then selling it to a local mob boss. There's no way a guy like Selleck would get involved with these sort of greaseballs, except Rasche is so jittery and coked-out he mixes up addresses.

The pair go to Oak Way instead of Oak Lane, and Rasche plugs Selleck when the latter walks out of the bathroom with a hair dryer in his hand. At that point, they have no choice but to plant a real gun on him and several bags of cocaine around his house.

Woe to Selleck and Robins. Their big mistake is having any faith in the system. "What the hell is goin' on when the police can do whatever they feel like?" Selleck ruminates. (If the hero of the movie had been black instead of white, this lament would have had more resonance.)

Sentenced to six years, Selleck reaches out to his wifey and she to him as he'd dragged away, screaming—he wants to hold his wife, all he asks is to hold his wife. And as the music swells, the tears roll down our faces: the American family has been violated. Someone must pay.

And now the hard lessons of prison life begin. Selleck's cellmate, a wise-ass punk (the entertainingly hammy Todd Graff) gets skewered and flambeed; shortly thereafter, Selleck is accosted by the aformentioned blacks.

Is "An Innocent Man" a guilty pleasure? I must admit, I was looking forward to seeing the blockish Selleck play "kid" to a bunch of the brothers. (Who knows? Maybe he'd find himself.) But alas, he remains unsullied; after prissily clinging to civilization, Selleck finally understands that in this world you get tough or you get took.

Tutored by a hardened con, Virgil Cane (F. Murray Abraham, not Levon Helm), he learns that this is "an insane place with insane rules but it ends up being logical." At first we suspect that Virgil has a thing for Selleck, but this isn't that kind of movie. Virgil just has a big heart is all, even though he regularly disembowels people.

Listening to Abraham talk prison jive is one of the film's few pleasures: "You did a piece of work and you held your mud," he tells Selleck, approvingly. Apart from these bits, "An Innocent Man" provides none of the sleazy fun you get from lower-budget prison pictures. It has too many ugly life lessons to teach—it's both brutal and sanctimonious.

Other fine, theater-trained actors hold their own amid the dreck. With Selleck as her co-star, Robins must emote for two; she acquits herself nobly. And Rasche's paranoid, coming-apart-at-the-seams specialty turn hasn't gotten stale—although it is taking its toll on his features.

As always, Selleck only goes through the motions of acting. The poor man's James Garner, his voice is light and inexpressive, his face a mask with a mustache. Prison life is supposed to harden him, but Selleck is so superficial we can't tell the difference. He holds his mud, all right.

NEWSDAY, 10/6/89, Part III/p. 3, Terry Kelleher

A group of hard cons surrounds and threatens the new man in the cellblock.

"Tension in the big house—just like in the movies," cracks an onlooker.

There you have it: the self-defining moment in "An Innocent Man." This one's like a lot of other prison flicks, only they didn't have Tom Selleck.

Let's crawl out on a limb and proclaim "An Innocent Man" Selleck's best action movie yet. That means it's somewhat more entertaining then "High Road to China," "Lassiter" and "Runaway." Credit for this minor accomplishment goes primarily to director Peter Yates. He has always been at his best when toughness and tension are called for, as in "Bullitt" and "The Friends of Eddie Coyle."

The star performance is adequate at best. The original screenplay is only intermittently credible, even though writer Larry Brothers' resume includes an unspecified period of personal experience with penal servitude.

This movie was to be titled "Hard Rain" until "Rain Man" and "Black Rain" oversaturated the marketplace. Actually, "An Innocent Man" is more appropriate. The opening scenes establish that Jimmie Rainwood (Selleck) is not only innocent but well-night perfect—an amazingly expert mechanic for an airline, loving husband to the beautiful Kate (Laila Robins). His sole lapse in life was a marijuana rap at age 18. But he was busted at a *rock concert*, for cryin' out loud.

Jimmie's a poor fit for the drug-pusher profile, but two corrupt narcotics cops (David Rasche and Richard Young) break into his home and put a couple of bullets in him before realizing they've got the wrong address. To cover their backsides, they plant dope on the premises and a gun in Jimmie's hand. The court gives him 6 years.

Intimidated, beaten and threatened with rape early in his term, Jimmie is counseled by a wise old head (F. Murray Abraham) that he can win the inmates' respect only by killing his chief tormentor. (Apparently it's not impressive enough that Jimmie's mustache is always neatly trimmed, even after a stretch in solitary.) Yates gives us a few heart-pounding moments as Jimmie carries out this advice, but then the movie flattens out.

The newly respected Jimmie becomes the toast of the yard, bantering easily with the baddest dudes, dominating the pickup basketball games with his soft jump shot. Out on parole, he goes after revenge by working an unsurprising sting on the cops who set him up. Jimmie tells Kate he's different now, that he "did things" in stir. But Selleck doesn't act all that different, and Jimmie's wife is awfully incurious about those "things."

Abraham gives a special touch to a stereotypical role. He even manages a straight face while uttering this gem of prison argot: "Don't you be talkin' out the side o' your neck when I'm tryin' to do you a solid." Rasche works hard to make his dirty cop both nutty and nasty, but the character winds up resembling Sledge Hammer on speed.

"An Innocent Man" is in no way inferior to "Lock Up," Sylvester Stallone's recent big-house romp. So how come it's getting only two stars? Sorry, but the judges must impose a half-star penalty for the movie's racial content.

It's not because Jimmie is taunted and terrorized by a black gang; surely racial animosity is a fact of prison life. But there's something faintly offensive about the way Kate goads a black police investigator (Badja Djola) into taking action against the cops who victimized Jimmie: She claims—falsely, as it happens—that they called him a "punk nigger." Then she smiles at her cleverness.

Also reviewed in:
NEW YORK TIMES, 10/6/89, p. C15, Janet Maslin
VARIETY, 10/18–24/89, p. 30
WASHINGTON POST, 10/6/89, p. C17, Hal Hinson

INTOLERANCE

A New York Film Festival retrospective. *Producer:* D.W. Griffith. *Director:* D.W. Griffith. *Director of Photography:* G.W. Bitzer and Karl Brown. *Editor:* James Smith and Rose Smith. *Music:* Joseph Carl Breil and (Persian musical themes) Farahanguize and Sidney Sprague. *Set Designer:* Frank "Huck" Wortman. *Reconstruction Supervisor:* Gillian B. Anderson and Peter L. Williamson. *Running time:* 209 minutes. *MPAA Rating:* Not Rated.

CAST: Lillian Gish (The Woman Who Rocks the Cradle); Mae Marsh (The Dear One); Fred Turner (Her Father); Robert Harron (The Boy); Sam De Grasse (Jenkins); Vera Lewis (Mary T. Jenkins); Howard Gaye (The Nazarene); Lillian Langdon (Mary, the Mother); Olga Grey (Mary Magdalene); Gunter von Ritzau and Erich von Stroheim (First Pharisees); Bessie Love (The Bride of Cana); Margery Wilson (Brown Eyes); Eugene Palette (Prosper Latour); Spottiswoode Aitken (Her Father); Ruth Handforth (Her Mother); A.D. Sears (The Foreign Mercenary); Constance Talmadge (The Mountain Girl); Elmer Clifton (The Rhapsode); Alfred Paget (Prince Belshazzar); Seena Owen (Princess Beloved); Carl Stockdale (King Nabonidus).

NEW YORK POST, 10/4/89, p. 25, David Edelstein

Watching D.W. Griffith's "Intolerance"—which has been restored by the Museum of Modern Art and was accompanied Monday at the New York Film Festival by the Brooklyn Philharmonic Orchestra and Chorus—it was easy to itemize this silent 1916 epic's inadequacies.

A study of intolerance and persecution throughout history, the movie takes an age to get going. Of the four interwoven stories, the one about the Huguenot massacre in Reformation France is sketchy; the Christ segment is useful only as a Greatest Hits collection of quotes; and the modern tale is a cornball melodrama with a hilarious car/train chase and a last-minute gallows reprieve. Even the celebrated fall-of-Babylon sequence is little more than spectacle.

As a propagandist, Griffith is akin to a card-carrying ACLU liberal. In his 1916 storyline, ugly female Prohibitionists calling themselves The Uplifters seek only to repress those who are happy; these crones set in motion a chain of events leading to the slaughter of striking workers and to the entry of a decent young man into a life of crime that nearly destroys him.

Griffith believes that the zeal to reform through punishment is in almost all cases hypocritical and, the root of much of the world's evil. (It's what sent Jesus to the cross.) He doesn't prove his point, he simply proclaims it—forcing his characters to behave according to his theories and then editorializing either for or against them.

But this is obviously all beside the point. "Intolerance" remains incomparably magnificent— nutty and visionary, ludicrous and breathtaking.

In his cross-cutting from one era to the next (a source of inspiration to Eisenstein) Griffith bestows more power on cinema as an art form than anyone in modern Hollywood. His tapestry— on which the actions of one era echo those of another and another—envelops you in wonder and horror: You feel in your bones the way history repeats itself and mankind evolves (or doesn't evolve).

Griffith remains one of a handful of directors able to shift easily from eye-popping spectacle to moments of penetrating intimacy. He did, after all, invent the close-up, and what he does with actresses like Mae Marsh and Constance Talmadge is a marvel. And this is dizzyingly expressive spectacle; the titanic sets and teeming, bleeding hordes of Babylon convey the immensity of war's pointlessness and absurdity.

Overreach though it might, the picture as a whole transcends its parts. It's an astonishing weave and still among the greatest of all movies.

The original score resurrected by the festival proved to be a shockingly pedestrian pastiche— albeit redeemed by some fine warbling and playing. The restored print could use even more restoration—in many cases, still frames inserted for continuity (in place of lost footage) compounded the sense of loss. The kineticism of Griffith must be preserved above all else; these freeze-frames are for your VCR when you have to go to the bathroom.

NEWSDAY, 10/3/89, Part III/p. 5, Tim Page

D.W. Griffith's 1916 film "Intolerance" occupies a position of supreme importance in the history of the cinema, but it has been edited and re-edited so often that most of the prints in circulation are notoriously corrupt. And so the Museum of Modern Art deserves our warmest gratitude for its splendid new reconstruction, which received its premiere at Avery Fisher Hall last night as part of the New York Film Festival, complete with atmospheric tints and shadings, and the original musical score by Joseph Carl Breil, played by the Brooklyn Philharmonic Orchestra.

"Intolerance" was Griffith's attempt to provide a worthy successor to his own "Birth of a Nation." It features celebrated stars and what may still be the grandest set ever created, Griffith's evocation of ancient Babylon. "Intolerance" was the most expensive and complicated film that had been made by anybody to that point; its technical innovations alone could be the subject of a book.

Another thing about "Intolerance" is that, for all of its magnificence, it doesn't really *work*. Indeed, it reminds me of the gigantic, experimental airplane to which Howard Hughes devoted so much of his attention. Like the "Spruce Goose," "Intolerance" is clearly the creation of an ambitious, idiosyncratic man of genius. It is deeply calculated, meticulously detailed, endlessly fascinating. But it is also impractical and, ultimately, all but impossible to get off the ground.

The essential problem lies with Griffith's narrative method. "Intolerance" attempts to tell four simultaneous stories—the fall of Babylon, the crucifixion of Christ, the St. Bartholemew Massacre of the Huguenots in medieval France, and a gritty fiction of crime and punishment in a modern (ca. 1914) American city. Griffith crosscuts from story to story, century to century (the late Iris Barry dubbed this "the only film fugue") in an attempt to trace intolerance through the ages. The sole link among the four is a dim, mysterious, timeless shot of Lillian Gish rocking a cradle, an apparent reference to the director's beloved Whitman and "Out of the Cradle Endlessly Rocking."

It is a moot question whether Griffith would have been able to make such narrative disjunction work even if his settings of the four stories were all of the same quality. In any event, they are not. The crucifixion story, by far the shortest of the four, is presented in a series of polite, distanced tableaux. The French massacre is little more than blood "n" guts, with a sketchy love interest tacked on.

This leaves the Babylonian and the modern stories, the one a spectacle of legendary proportions, the other a claustrophobic, Dreiserian study of human beings trapped by social and economic forces they cannot control. Both of these are powerful and (in completely contrasting ways) beautiful, and they feature the only fully developed characters in the entire film—Constance Talmadge's "Mountain Girl" and Mae Marsh's "The Dear One," performances that have lost little of their immediacy over 75 years. But the moment one gets interested in the drama, the scene shifts, Lillian Gish rocks the cradle, and we're back watching bloodied Huguenots.

There are other problems. Griffith concludes the film with an absurd *deus ex machina*—the skies open, prison bars evaporate and soldiers throw down their guns in mid-kill. It seems not only sentimental but half-hearted, as pro forma as "They all lived happily ever after" at the end of a bedtime story. Nor is the film's theme traced in a particularly rigorous manner (the Babylonian story, for example, is about imperialism, not intolerance).

And so "Intolerance" is the less than completely satisfying sum of extraordinary parts. But those parts are so strong and the film is so clearly the work of a great master that one willingly overlooks its inconsistencies. And the best moments of "Intolerance" are unforgettable I'd gladly sit through it again simply to watch Mae Marsh's kaleidoscopic array of conflicting emotions in the courtroom scene.

The new, reconstructed "Intolerance" is a triumph of scholarship and sensitivity; more than a half hour of heretofore "lost" material has been restored. This is as close to a complete "Intolerance" as we are likely to come: every scene that Griffith shot is now represented, one way or another. When actual footage was unavailable, Gillian B. Anderson and Peter L. Williamson, who supervised the reconstruction, used still frames from a book that the director prepared to copyright his film. The effect is surprisingly successful, often haunting, and bogs down only in moments of extreme animation, when it slows the pacing. With all of its imperfections, "Intolerance" is *sui generis*, and I do not anticipate a more moving film experience for a long time.

Also reviewed in:
WASHINGTON POST, 10/1/89, p. B1, Richard Harrington

IRON TRIANGLE, THE

A Scotti Brothers Pictures release of a Eurobrothers film. *Executive Producer:* Ben Scotti and Fred Scotti. *Producer:* Tony Scotti and Anglea Schapiro. *Director:* Eric Weston. *Screenplay (based on the diary of an unknown Vietcong soldier):* Eric Weston, John Bushelman, and Larry Hilbrand. *Director of Photography:* Irv Goodnoff. *Editor:* Roy Watts. *Music:* Michael Loyd, John D'Andrea, and Nick Strimple. *Sound:* Robin Gregory, Mark "Frito" Long, and (music) Carmine Rubino, Johnny Valentino, and Tony Papa. *Sound Editor:* Bill Dannevik, Don Warner, and Bill Young. *Production Designer:* Errol Kelly. *Set Dresser:* Neelawathura Wijewardene. *Special Effects:* Yves De Bono. *Costumes:* Yingnapa Viryasiri. *Make-up:* Gabor Kernayaiszky. *Running time:* 91 minutes. *MPAA Rating:* R.

CAST: Beau Bridges (Captain Keene); Haing S. Ngor (Captain Tuong); Johnny Hallyday (Jacques); Liem Whatley (Ho); James Ishida (Khoi); Ping Wu (Pham); Richard Weygint (Swan); Allan Moore (Murphy); Bobby McGee (Joop); Joseph Seely (Grover); Iilana B'tiste (Khan Ly); François Chau (Captain Duc); Jack Ong (Ṣhen); Sunny Trinidad (Thuy); Sophie Trang (Lai); Glen Chin (Chau).

LOS ANGELES TIMES, 2/3/89, Calendar/p. 12, Kevin Thomas

"The Iron Triangle" is an entirely decent effort to view the Vietnam War through the eyes of a young Viet Cong guerrilla as well as those of a veteran American captain. For all its sincerity and despite the effectiveness of newcomer Liem Whatley and Beau Bridges, it is a grueling and tedious business, not that much different from any routine and bloody B war picture. Somehow, too, the notion that the enemy can be a guy not so different from us comes as scarcely an astounding revelation.

Adapted from an actual Viet Cong soldier's diary by director Eric Weston and co-writers John Bushelman and Larry Hilbrand, the film takes its title from a region northwest of Saigon at the base of the Ho Chi Minh infiltration route where the highest number of enemy troops was concentrated. Although only 17, Ho (Whatley) is a seasoned and resourceful soldier, idealistic and dedicated yet not reveling in bloodshed, an attitude that riles zealous, thick-headed Communist Party official (James Ishida). Bridges is a capable leader, patriotic without being consumed by hatred for the enemy. At one point Bridges' Capt. Keene spares Ho's life. What is Ho to do now that he has captured Keene? Unfortunately, the question proves not to be as trenchant or suspenseful as one would wish.

Complementing Whately and Bridges' solid performances are those of Johny Hallyday as a cynical French mercenary and veteran of Dien Ben Phu and Haing Ngor as Ho's level-headed commander, a man not unlike Keene. "The Iron Triangle" (rated R for standard war movie violence), which was filmed in Sri Lanka, is high-minded but not nearly distinctive enough to be involving.

MONTHLY FILM BULLETIN, 10/89, p. 303, Julian Petley

In 1969, the U.S. and their South Vietnamese allies are engaged in heavy fighting with the North Vietnamese and Vietcong in an area north-west of Saigon known as the Iron Triangle. On one side are Captain Keene, an idealistic young infantry officer; Jacques, a bitter French mercenary and veteran of Dien Ben Phu; Captain Duc, a ruthless ARVN officer whose brutal methods put him in direct conflict with Keene; and Khan Ly, a South Vietnamese propaganda official who is having an affair with Jacques. On the other are Captain Tuong, a regular officer and commander valiantly struggling against the better equipped Americans and South Vietnamese; Ho, an idealistic young guerrilla who takes no pleasure in the killing he has to carry out; his friend Pham who is fighting to avenge the death of his family at the hands of South Vietnamese troops; and Khoi, a Communist Party official with a zeal for killing which is beginning to cloud his military judgment. Khoi displays his ruthlessness by shooting a suspected enemy collaborator while he prays by the roadside. Keene comes into conflict with Duc and Jacques over the torture and killing of prisoners. He is detailed to kill Jacques and Khan Ly, whose bodies are then displayed to the villagers. In the course of an ambush, Keene is captured by Ho and Khoi; the latter wants to kill him but Ho decides to take Keene back to their base camp. During the long and arduous journey, tension mounts between Khoi and Keene. When Keene finally kills his adversary in a fight, Ho lets him escape. Keene returns to his unit in time for the battle of My Thang, in the course of which Ho is wounded. Keene finds him with a hand grenade, ready to blow both of them up. He relents, however, and the two men, who have come to respect each other, survive.

As the spate of Vietnam films continues unabated (*Jacknife, BAT 21, Platoon Leader, 84 Charlie MoPic*), *The Iron Triangle* distinguishes itself as the first American feature which attempts to show the war from the points of view of both sides in the conflict. Although narrated by the Beau Bridges character, the film in fact claims to be based on the diary of an unknown Vietcong guerrilla, and certainly it presents an effective soldier's eye-view of the conflict, largely eschewing the wider political issues. In fact, it's indicative of the film's stance that the most "committed" characters on each side (Khoi on the one hand, Duc and Khan Ly on the other) are also the most negative in a narrative which, for the most part, avoids easy war film schematics. It's also of some significance that both Duc and Khan Ly are South Vietnamese, that it is the South Vietnamese troops who are shown torturing and murdering their prisoners, and that the film's other negative character is French, the cynical Jacques who murders villagers and believes that the Vietnamese should be left to "kill each other off". In other words, the Americans get off relatively lightly . . .

However, the film is not really concerned with blame or analysis but rather, like almost every "anti-war" film from *All Quiet on the Western Front* onwards, to show the human realities beneath the political and strategic issues. In this respect, it works rather well, particularly in the scenes between Ho and Keene: the latter's war-weariness, Ho's idealism mingled with fear and distaste, the gradual forging of a bond between the two men, are all effectively communicated, as are the rigours of guerrilla life. The scenes with the North Vietnamese/Vietcong are also graced by a dignified cameo from Haing Ngor as the highly professional Captain Tuong. Given that Ngor played Dith Pran in *The Killing Fields*, that his own family were wiped out by the Khmer Rouge, and that he has accused the Vienamese government of "killing not only my people but also my culture and my country itself", such a role is more than a little surprising but seems to have been undertaken in the humanist, anti-war spirit that informs the film as a whole. Most at home in small-scale, quotidian scenes, *The Iron Triangle* seems curiously ill-at-ease in the action sequences.

Curiously, because when all is said and done, this *is* a war film and is being sold as such. Whether director Eric Weston has consciously tried to de-dramatise the action scenes (the choral music over the final battle being a case in point), or whether he has been let down by lack of resources and slack editing, must remain a moot point.

NEW YORK POST, 2/3/89, p. 21, Jami Bernard

The Vietnam pictures are still coming fast and furious, and here's one with a twist—"The Iron Triangle" spends as much time documenting the hopes, dreams, terrors and infighting among the enemy camp as it does among the "good guys" (you know, *our* side).

With this device, we are treated to a rare insight: That war is hell, and so is a badly made war movie, no matter whose side you're on.

Handsome Beau Bridges is a captain on the American side whose facility with the Vietnamese language makes him a valuable player in the deadly area known as the Iron Triangle: "It looks like paradise, but it's . . . the bloodiest corner on the Ho Chih Minh Trail," we learn from Bridges' battle-fatigued narration.

Having this Capt. Keene speak Vietnamese also gets around the sticky issue of how to portray the Viet Cong without resorting to subtitles. All the actors speak English, so we can assume that what we are hearing is being filtered through the mind and memory of Keene, who is a wellspring of platitudes like: "On the other side of the barrel of a gun there was a man like me."

The movie unfolds in parallel universes, separated by the usual dense foliage we've come to expect in Vietnam movies (this one was filmed in Sri Lanka). In one camp are the North Vietnamese foot soldiers, living in mazes of underground tunnels, so poorly equipped that they fight over confiscated American weapons while invoking Communism, loyalty and rank.

Mediating these petty disputes is Capt. Tuong, all grace under pressure. He is played with restrained dignity by Haing Ngor, the Cambodian doctor who achieved instant stardom here (and an Oscar for Best Supporting Actor) by playing Dith Pran in "The Killing Fields." This movie is a big step down for him.

Meanwhile, back among the Americans, there's the usual assortment of scared recruits and unfeeling louts, all hoping for a flesh wound so they can be shipped back home. Bridges is a humane father figure, worrying over his men and preventing the South Vietnamese from torturing their prisoners.

In fact, most of the fighting in this movie's Vietnam is over who gets to torture which prisoner.

We learn in the course of the narration that many Viet Cong kept diaries, including one ambitious, sensitive young soldier named Ho (pleasant newcomer Liem Whatley). From this diary, the Americans will later be able to learn all about Ho's hopes and dreams: you know, everything you ever wanted to know about Victor Charlie but didn't know enough of the language to find out.

"Soon this carzy war would bring us together," narrates Bridges, and sure enough, Ho soon takes Keene prisoner.

Now we get a cross-cultural male bonding thing going in the jungle. He teaches Keene to find food, and Keene shows by his liquid-brown puppy eyes that he may be an American, but he's sincere.

There is a very brief subplot involving a beautiful South Vietnamese propagandist. "There are some sights in war you never forget—the sight of a beautiful woman," narrates Bridges, much to the amusement of the preview screening audience.

Director Eric Weston ("Marvin and Tige") co-wrote the script; the idea of showing the war from both sides is laudable. Unfortunately, in the course of personalizing the war, the filmmakers have succeeded in making it petty, as if the whole Vietnam experience could be boiled down to a scuffle between rival gangs whose leaders, under different circumstances, could have been such good friends.

NEWSDAY, 2/3/89, Part III/p. 3, Lynn Darling

You have to give "The Iron Triangle" some credit for good intentions: It does make a conscientious effort to highlight the humanity common to both sides of the Vietnam War. Instead of reducing the Viet Cong to a series of terrifying shadows in the jungle, meting out relentless and anonymous death to the Americans, the movie presents the VC up close and personal. This is a movie in which the fighting members of the National Liberation Front flirt shyly over rice bowls, talk about their hatred of killing, and indulge in comradely oneupsmanship at the evening self-criticism sessions.

The Americans are pretty nice guys as well: They take time out to rescue small babies while liberating the local village, they think twice about shooting an enemy between the eyes, and they maintain a properly cynical attitude toward the pious sentiments for which they are allegedly fighting.

Unfortunately, its carefully egalitarian approach to the sensibilities of both sides is about all that the movie has going for it. There's no edge to the terse but tiresome script, which telegraphs most of its sentimental developments in a stolid voiceover narration. And the two characters who come laboriously around to the conclusion that "on the other side of the barrel of a gun was a man like me" are never drawn in enough detail to become much more than symbols of the brotherhood of man.

"We couldn't have been more different, maybe we couldn't have been more alike," observes Capt. Keene (Beau Bridges) about his NLF counterpart Ho (Liem Whatley). "Soon the war would bring us together. This is our story."

It's not much of one. Capt. Keene is a tired middle-aged career soldier trying to keep his men in one piece while not surrendering totally to the futility he's mired in. Out on patrol, his unit is ambushed by a fierce cadre of Viet Cong and he comes face to face with the idealistic young Ho, whose dedication to the NLF cause must coexist with his reluctance to turn himself into a cold-blooded killing machine. "I've been ordered to kill a woman," he tells the shy young village girl he's taken a fancy to. "It troubles me."

Well, it doesn't trouble him all that much—Ho does end up sticking a knife into the woman in question. To its credit, "The Iron Triangle" doesn't ignore the brutality of the war in its effort to present both sides of the conflict—it's another thing the two sides have in common.

But the movie never advances beyond the easy parallels it draws between its two main characters. Even when Ho and Keene finally spend a good deal of time together, their insights into one another's character are the usual threadbare cliches about men at war—they're like two puppets manipulated by the platitudes they're meant to embody.

Both Bridges and newcomer Whatley look appropriately pained and sincere through all of this. Haing S. Ngor (who won an Oscar for best supporting actor in his film debut in "The Killing Fields") has even less to work with as the wise North Vietnamese Captain Tuong. The only person who seems to have any fun is James Ishida, as an ambitious Party flunky who's had it with Ho's goody-goody comrade bit. At least his character contains the embryo of some recognizable human emotions.

VILLAGE VOICE, 2/14/89, p. 60, J. Hoberman

The least one can say for Lawrence and *Lawrence* is that together they embody the imperial anti-imperialist fantasy of riding with the Indians against the cavalry. [See Hoberman's review.] There's a kindred sort of cultural critique operative in the latest Vietnam flick, *The Iron Triangle*. Stolidly directed by Eric Weston and well-lensed by Irv Goodnoff, this frugal production boasts inviting Sir Lankan scenery and a couple of genre innovations—the most important being the use of a Vietcong hero.

Vietnamese have been virtually invisible in most American films about the war, but for long stretches, *The Iron Triangle* is a crypto-Indian-point-of-view western in which solemn VC melt in and out of the jungle foliage, addressing each other in stilted, accentless English. "Good hunting, Ho?" the 17-year-old guerrilla protagonist (Saigon-born Liem Whatley) is asked when he returns to camp, having ambushed and killed two American grunts and taken their rifles and Chiclets. (The second innovation—also contributing to the B oater feel is the total absence of '60s rock. Instead, VC warriors are entertained by a revolutionary dance recital—a young woman, festooned with red streamers, ceremonially bayoneting a comrade wrapped in the American flag.)

Named for War Zone D, northwest of Saigon, "the bloodiest corner of the Ho Chi Minh trail," as beleaguered Captain Keene (Beau Bridges) quickly informs us, *The Iron Triangle* doesn't lack for conflict. The Americans squabble with their allies, the VC make fun of China, Ho regularly squares off against Khoi (James Ishida), the party official attached to his unit. (Superdignified Haing Ngor is the nominal head.) Although the movie's most lurid interlude concerns a hearts-and-minds battle over a sexbomb propagandist (Iilana B'tiste) guarded by a mad-dog French mercenary (Johnny Hally-day), the usual mode is anxiously humanist. Keene frequently frets about American casualties, telling an arrogant SVA officer, "I'm here to keep my men alive, then get the hell out."

This confusing credo is never exactly explored, but when the captain is taken captive by the 'Cong, the issue of prisoner rights comes to the fore—especially as Ho takes a special interest in Keene. ("We've always been told the ends justify the means, but not this way," Ho scolds bloodthirsty Khoi.) War being war, turnaround is fair play, and, in the climactic conflagration, complete with VC Valkyrie and *Platoon*-style requiem, Ho's unit is overrun. As Captain Keene broods over the fate of the VC who saved his life, the final voiceover can't help seeming bizarre. "After they took Ho, I found his diary. . . . I hear he made it." I'm not sure what *it* means, but something tells me it's not this film.

Also reviewed in:
NEW YORK TIMES, 2/3/89, p. C8 Vincent Canby
VARIETY, 2/8–14/89, p. 24
WASHINGTON POST, 2/3/89, p. B7, Rita Kempley

JACKNIFE

A Cineplex Odeon Films release of a Kings Road Entertainment presentation of a Sandollar/Schaffel production. *Executive Producer:* Sandy Gallin. *Producer:* Robert Schaffel and Carol Baum. *Director:* David Jones. *Screenplay (Based on his play "Strange Snow"):* Stephen Metcalfe. *Director of Photography:* Brian West. *Editor:* John Bloom. *Music:* Bruce Broughton. *Music Editor:* Patricia Peck. *Sound:* Gary Alper, Patrick Rousseau, and (music) Armin Steiner. *Sound Editor:* Don Sharpe. *Production Designer:* Edward Pisoni. *Art Director:* William Barclay and Serge Jacques. *Set Decorator:* Robert J. Franco and Gilles Aird. *Set Dresser:* Russel Berg, Martha Fishkin, Daniel Mahon, Suzanne Labrecque, and Glendon Light. *Special Effects:* Richard Johnson, John Elliott, and Dan Kirshoff. *Costumes:* David Charles. *Make-up:* Joan Isaacson. *Stunt Coordinator:* Everett Creach. *Running time:* 102 minutes. *MPAA Rating:* R.

CAST: Robert De Niro (Megs); Kathy Baker (Martha); Ed Harris (Dave); Sloane Shelton (Shirley); Ivan Brogger (Depot Mechanic); Michael Arkin (Dispatcher); Tom Isbell (Bobby Buckman); Kirk Taylor (Helicopter Gunner); Jordan Lund (Tiny); Charles Dutton (Jake); Bruce Ramsey (Corridor Student); Jessalyn Gilsig (His Girlfriend); George Gerdes (Tony); Josh Pais (Rick); Lois Dellar (Cocktail Waitress); Joel Miller and Irene Rauch (Restaurant Couple); Paul Hoover (Upscale Bartender); Paul Hart (Potbellied Man); Loudon Wainwright III (Ferretti); Brian Delate (Briggs); Walter Massey (Ed Buckman); Elizabeth Franz (Pru Buckman); Sal Dominello (Tuxedo Tailor); Joseph Grillo (Florist); Tim Conover ("Joe College"); Gabrielle Carteris (College Girl in Bar); Madison Arnold (Sam, Bartender); Tom Rack (William Green); John Boylan (Frank, Phys. Ed); Tanya Tree (Tanya, Frank's Wife); Keith Glover (Soldier).

CHRISTIAN SCIENCE MONITOR, 4/14/89, p. 11, David Sterritt

Vietnam-War movies come in two categories: films about the war itself, and films about its aftermath, when soldiers returned home and faced readjustment to ordinary life. That second category includes such pictures as "Coming Home" and parts of "The Deer Hunter."

The latest addition to this group is a small but incisive new film called "Jacknife," about the complicated relationship of two veterans who served in Southeast Asia together. Much of the picture isn't really about Vietnam or the war at all; it's about a friendship, a romance, and the sometimes clashing personalities of the people involved. Vietnam lurks in the background of all the characters' memories, though, giving their relationships an unexpected depth and complexity.

The plot begins when two old vets get together: Robert De Niro as the happy-go-lucky one, dancing through life on the strength of his own high spirits, and Ed Harris as the depressed one, who never quite recovered from the trauma of combat. He drinks a lot, gets little joy out of life, and shows occasional signs of erratic behavior.

He's not alone in seeming mentally unstable at times—even Mr. De Niro's usually cheerful character can fly off the handle and become wildly self-destructive. But he goes to a self-help group for veterans, and he spends time with a counselor, thus keeping his instability under control, if not really cured. The story kicks into high gear when he falls in love with his old buddy's sister, played by Kathy Baker in the movie's third excellent performance. Her brother tries to stop this romance, for reasons that aren't completely clear until we learn about a memory the two veterans share—concerning another buddy who died in combat, and a failure of nerve that's still tormenting one of our heroes after all this time.

There are only a few wartime scenes in "Jacknife," and that's just as well, since these moments are not particularly striking. (The picture's modest budget has something to do with this.) But the love-story aspect and the relationship of the two veterans are handled with commendable sensitivity. De Niro is always convincing, yet always unpredictable in the seemingly cheeful role; Mr. Harris becomes steadily more interesting as the story develops; and Ms. Baker is perfect as his sister—attractive enough to make a believable girlfriend for De Niro, yet shy and plain enough to explain why she's never found anyone before now.

The movie was directed by David Jones, whose other films—"Betrayal," from a Harold Pinter screenplay, and "84 Charing Cross Road," about a long-distance love affair with books—have also been literate, human-scaled dramas. He's the kind of director American films need badly right now: a moviemaker with no interest in action or special effects, but a gift for making the deepest emotions spring to life before our eyes. "Jacknife" is a small movie, but it won't be forgotten in a hurry.

LOS ANGELES TIMES, 3/10/89, Calendar/p. 6, Kevin Thomas

"Jacknife" is a small independent film, more suited to television in its scale and in its clear theatrical roots than the big screen, yet its key roles are so juicy that it attracted a major cast: Robert De Niro, Ed Harris and Kathy Baker. As admirable and affecting as it is, you cannot help but feel it would have more impact as a Hallmark Hall of Fame presentation than as a movie.

Adapted by Stephen Metcalfe from his play "Strange Snow," it illuminates the lingering effects of the Vietnam War on its veterans. De Niro is Megs, a bearded, long-haired mechanic, an uninhibited, exuberant man who has seemingly come out of nowhere to settle in a small New England town, the home of his Vietnam buddy Dave (Harris), who shares the big old family home with his schoolteacher sister Martha (Kathy Baker). Very early on you are made to feel that, had Megs not shown up, Dave and Martha would have probably managed to live out their disappointed lives.

Now that Megs, whose wartime nickname was Jacknife, has arrived it's clear that nothing will ever be the same for this brother and sister; their existence has become precarious. That Dave is far from happy to see him is compounded by the fact that Megs and Martha, unlike as they are, are attracted to each other. Director David Jones effectively creates and sustains an unsettling atmosphere: you're uncertain whether it's Megs or Dave who is most likely to lurch out of control. Clearly, Megs is as desperately in need of connecting with people as Dave is profoundly disturbed by Megs' presence. In this increasingly volatile situation we're made aware of how events in the past can become ticking time bombs.

"Jacknife" is the third film for Jones, a distinguished veteran of British theater and television. ("Betrayal" and "84 Charing Cross Road" were his first and second.) He combines a great gift for directing actors with an efficient, unpretentious style. However, unlike his two previous films, you hunger for images to match the powerhouse performances of his three stars. Megs provides the most marvelous opportunities for De Niro to continually surprise—and often amuse—us with his portrayal of a man who seems to have discovered what he needs to make his life work but who is still scrambling to get a purchase on it.

Megs is as caught up in his quest as Dave is clenched in denial, and as a result, Harris has some absolutely shattering moments. Kathy Baker, whose portrayals in "Street Smart" and "Clean and Sober" have established her as a distinctive and greatly gifted actress, finds countless ways in which to keep Martha from becoming the stereotype of a spinster school-teacher.

Filmed on location primarily in Meriden, Conn., a key 19th-Century manufacturing center, with some interiors shot in Montreal, "Jacknife" (rated R for language and adult situations) is a work of standard kitchen-sink realism that cries for a more boldly cinematic, stylized look and a far more original score that the hearts-and-flowers elegiac composition provided by Bruce Broughton. Thankfully, there's absolutely nothing pedestrian about Robert De Niro, Ed Harris and Kathy Baker.

MONTHLY FILM BULLETIN, 9/89, p. 273, Julian Petley

Joseph Megessey ("Megs"), a garage mechanic in an industrial town in Connecticut, decides to visit fellow Vietnam veteran Dave and invite him on a fishing trip. The two have not seen each other since the end of the war, in which their friend Bobby was killed in a Vietcong ambush, an event which left them both guilt-stricken and traumatised. It was Dave and Bobby who christened Megs "Jacknife" after he told them how he had once wrecked a truck. Dave, a former high-school football star now a truck driver with a drink and drugs problem, lives with his sister Martha, a shy and retiring teacher of biology at the high school. At first Dave and Martha are annoyed by Megs' early morning eruption into their lives, but eventually they both agree to go fishing with him. Over the ensuing weeks, Megs and Martha find themselves drawing closer together—she vistis him at the garage and he takes her to the war memorial on which Bobby's name is inscribed. Dave, who is still suffering nightmares about Bobby's death, feels increasingly threatened by their relationship and, after seeing them together in a bar, has a violent row with his sister. He quits the local Vietnam veterans' group, and becomes increasingly agitated after a visit to Bobby's parents. Martha invites Megs to the highschool prom, which leads to an even more heated argument with Dave; she accuses him of treating her like their mother and plans to move out. While the prom is in full swing, a drunken Dave storms into the school and smaskes the glass cabinets containing the school's sporting trophies, including those he won. Later, filled with remorse, he is reconciled with Megs; he returns to his veterans group and begins to pull himself together. Megs and Martha, who had been on the point of ending their relationship, are reunited.

Jacknife was adapted by Stephen Metcalfe (also responsible for turning *Cousin, Cousine* into *Cousins*) from his 1982 Off-Broadway play *Strange Snow*. If the result seems to cast back further than that, it may have something to do with the intentions of producers Robert Schaffel and Carol Baum, both of whom came to the project with the recreation of 50s classics in mind. In Schaffel's case it was the Paddy Chayevsky-scripted *Marty* and in Baum's *The Rainmaker* and Martin Ritt's *The Long, Hot Summer*. *Jacknife*, clearly, has elements of all three: Robert De Niro recalls Ernest Borgnine's lonely Bronx butcher who suddenly and unexpectedly finds love, while his eruption into Martha's life carries distinct echoes of the other two films, in both of which a stranger comes to town and sweeps a lonely local girl off her feet. More specifically contemporary, of course, is the Vietnam background, although this too has its cinematic antecedents in the numerous late 40s movies featuring traumatised former GIs. This is not to suggest that *Jacknife* is derivative, simply that it is somewhat old-fashioned, which has both its positive and negative aspects.

The film features some magnificent ensemble playing right from the opening scene, in which Robert De Niro virtually breaks into his friend's house and rouses a hungover Dave and an alarmed, then annoyed, Martha. De Niro's coaxing them round with his patter about the delights of "breakfast beer" followed by a gargantuan meal in a diner is a joy to watch. Equally memorable are the first tentative moments in Megs and Martha's developing relationship—De Niro suggesting intense vulnerability beneath the non-stop bluster and banter, and Kathy Baker revealing an increasing degree of determination and sensuality under what at first appears a rather timid, defeated exterior. In a remarkable performance, ranging from near-catatonia to extreme physical violence, Ed Harris' Dave becomes an essentially tragic figure, ruined by forces quite beyond his control and even comprehension. However, as directed by David Jones (*Betrayal, 84 Charing Cross Road*, and numerous productionsfor BBCTV), the film does retain a theatrical quality which no amount of opening out can overcome, and what one regrets finally is the absence of anything as cinematically exciting as the performances themselves.

NEW YORK POST, 3/10/89, p. 29, David Edelstein

As the title character—a brash, caring Vietnam vet—in the soap opera "Jacknife," Robert De Niro gives his liveliest performance in several years. The movie is a drag, but it's fun to see De Niro plugged-in again, even if he's playing an angel—an explosive misfit whose last stage of therapy is bringing his old combat buddy (Ed Harris) back to the land of the living.

De Niro wears his hair recklessly long and sports a thick black beard. Beyond vanity here, he inhabits the role the way he didn't the tempestuous bounty hunter in "Midnight Run." His dark, burning eyes signal the presence of a psychic wound, but the wildness is gone. Bluff, always smiling, this working-class mechanic now holds himself in check.

Dave, the guy De Niro goes back for this time, isn't haunted by 'Nam the way Christopher Walken was in "The Deer Hunter." Fleshy and bleary, with a mutton-chop mustache, the former jock deals with the war (and the loss of his best friend in combat) by denying its importance, by hiding like a trout under a rock—to borrow one of the film's metaphors.

That's your clue that he's going to explode eventually, because the premise of movies like

"Jacknife" is that a man has to let it all out—preferably with his buddies or support groups. (Women are at best ineffectual and at worst harmful to men.)

The woman here is Dave's sister (Kathy Baker), a schoolteacher without a lot of self-confidence in a town with few interesting, eligible men. She takes care of her brother, mostly, and when De Niro's Megs arrives on the scene with his exhortations to go fishing, drink beer in the morning and eat huge breakfasts (he's so life-affirming, he's Zorba the vet), the two take a shine to each other.

Jealous Dave, of course, begins to lose it, gulping down the scotch like a . . . trout heading for the nearest rock. And then there are the flashbacks, as Dave sits bolt upright in bed, sweating, and we hear the sould of helicopter blades on the soundtrack. Suddenly, we're in the chopper as it lifts up; men push Dave, screaming, out the door and he lands hard on his leg. From the bush comes the rat-tat-tat-tat of enemy fire.

I don't wish to trivialize the traumas of Vietnam veterans; the problem is the movie does. With their dependable flashbacks, haunted expressions and predelicton for putting their hands through windows, vets make good fodder for three-character plays and films. But by now these elements are all clichés—there is such a thing as a generic Vietnam vet melodrama.

"Jacknife" feels generic in other ways, too—the hollow trumpets when DeNiro and Baker visit a Vietnam memorial, for example, thoroughly banalize the moment. Directed by David Jones, the man responsible for the unwatchable film of Harold Pinter's play "Betrayal," the movie appears to have been massacred in the editing room. The cutting in the early scenes is grisly—the back-and-forth images leap out at you. If it weren't for these three actors, "Jacknife" would scarcely seem suitable for television.

But the actors are very good. Harris makes Dave a frightening case—wasted, withdrawn, unwilling and unable to face the world. And Kathy Baker is lovely in her first big, non-floozy part. It's a dreadful, passive role, but her conviction shines, and in the fishing scene she's called on to save the film's metaphor—that cowardly trout.

See, the fish she pulls from the water looks about as dead as they come, but gamely Baker wriggles it, nearly equalling Bela Lugosi's heroic effort to make a rubber octopus look as if it was squeezing the life out of him in "Bride of the Monster." If that doesn't merit a Purple Heart, how 'bout at least a Golden Turkey?

NEWSDAY, 3/10/89, Part III/p. 3, Mike McGrady

The basic "Jacknife" story, depicted repeatedly in films and teledramas, has become a dramatic cliche for our time. Surely you know the story by now. Vietnam veterans harboring unresolved conflicts are unable to make connections to this time and this place. They wear fatigue jackets and beards; they guzzle boilermakers and pop pills; they drive trucks and repair cars. And always, waiting in ambush for them at the end of day, are memories, nightmares, flashbacks, emotional explosions.

So familiar has this story become that I have started to think of it as a brand new film genre—the PTSD (Post-Traumatic Stress Disorder) genre.

PTSD movies all seem to follow the same pattern. The film's starting point, inevitably a particularly violent battlefield episode in Vietnam, usually results in the death of a buddy. The veteran returns again and again to the incident until mounting pressure forces a psychotic episode. Only later will he learn to talk about his experiences and air out his guilt feelings, often in a group-therapy session featuring other suffering veterans.

Although "Jacknife" departs from this plot in no significant way. Stephen Metcalfe's script, based on his Off-Broadway play "Strange Snow," tends to be somewhat more literate than prior films and the direction by England's David Jones ("Betrayal," "84 Charing Cross Road") serves to bolster that literacy.

However, there is one vital difference between "Jacknife" and earlier offerings, and that is the difference provided by three performers with strengths that carry them well above the level of cliches.

Robert De Biro and Ed Harris, blue-collar workers raised in the same Connecticut industrial town, saw a close friend killed in Vietnam. This experience has turned Harris into a surly, brooding, civilian zombie who comes to life only when he realizes his school-teaching sister (Kathy Baker) is launching a romance with De Niro, and then he goes beserk. He denies both De Niro's friendship and the reality of Vietnam: "I was never there. It never happened. It's over and done with, you understand?"

The proceedings are slow-paced, predictable and at times mawkish enough to qualify as soap opera. However, the relations between the three central characters are always electric. Harris is slow to emerge but the emergence—"I don't like me very much"—offers a gut wrenching moment that will leave you stunned.

No actor in America wears a blue collar more naturally than De Niro, and once again he offers a subtly shaded portrait. Set against the coarseness and crudity are elements of wit and sensitivity and intelligence. While his courtship of his friend's sister bears more than a few echoes of "Marty," it is moving and funny throughout. But we expect this kind of work from De Niro and Harris. Kathy Baker, who played the ill-fated prostitute in "Street Smart," not only holds her own with these two dramatic superstars, she absolutely shines.

I could have predicted the story before seeing the movie; what I couldn't have foretold was that it would be performed with such intensity and believability. The story remains familiar but the treatment is not.

VILLAGE VOICE, 3/14/89, Renee Tajima

One benefit of an aging population is less flesh and more meat on the big screen. Two new releases—one a working-class drama, the other a romantic farce of the upper middle class—break no new cinematic ground, but skillfully remap movie formulas to reveal something about the human condition.

Jacknife is reminiscent of television's golden age, when stellar acting, direction, and a powerhouse cast—not glittering images—made the drama. Its premise seems like a hundred other postwar stories but is defined by the sharp edges of Vietnam. Ed Harris is Dave, a hard-drinking trucker with the beer-bellied swagger of a former jock, a man hard fast on dismissing Vietnam from memory. "It's like I was never there," he explains, but in fact, he never really came home. Dave, and his schoolteacher sister Martha (Kathy Baker) live an uneasy adulthood alone in the cocoon of their childhood house until it is shaken by the arrival of war buddy Megs (Robert De Niro). Two-thirds of a combat trio, Dave, the brooding one, and Megs, the volatile one, are trapped in an emotional dance set 20 years ago by their friend Bobby's death in combat.

Delivering dialogue marked by striking credibility and ease, Harris and De Niro brilliantly maneuver a balance of machismo and susceptibility. Megs is a garrulous auto mechanic forever in overdrive; he has a penchant for calling Dave "you great swinging dick." Having achieved a tentative peace with himself, Megs tries to do the same for Dave. He also falls in love, a talkative Stallone to Baker's more thoughtful, complicated Talia Shire. And, as in *Rocky*, their relationship threatens the brother's emotional refuge, setting off explosive results.

Also reviewed in:
NEW REPUBLIC, 3/6/89, p. 24, Stanley Kauffmann
NEW YORK TIMES, 3/10/89, p. C10, Janet Maslin
VARIETY, 3/1–7/89, p. 18
WASHINGTON POST, 3/24/89, p. C1, Rita Kempley
WASHINGTON POST, 3/24/89, Weekend/p. 39, Desson Howe

JAN SVANKMAJER: ALCHEMIST OF THE SURREAL

An International Film Exchange release. *Director:* Jan Svankmajer. *Running time:* 99 minutes. *MPAA Rating:* Not Rated.

NEW YORK POST, 5/3/89, p. 28, V.A. Musetto

Animation. The word brings to mind a never-never world of prince charmings, lovable animals and happy endings. If you've seen the works of Jan Svankmajer, the word will also conjure up images of centuries-old human rot, malevolent toys and frightened little girls.

Svankmajer is a 54-year-old Czechoslovakian filmmaker whose "Alice," a surreal updating of the Lewis Carroll tale, won cheers when it premiered at Film Forum 1 last year. Now the always-innovative theater has brought Svankmajer back for an encore. It's called "Jan Svankmajer:

Alchemist of the Surreal" and it consists of eight short films he made from 1964 through 1983. Svankmajer's strange and wonderful world is not an easy one to describe. Perhaps these precis will help.

"The Ossuary" (1970) is a rapidfire, black-and-white tour of an ossuary containing the skeletons of victims—more than 50,000 of them—of the 14th century Black Plague. "The Fall of the House of Usher" (1981), meanwhile, takes us on a tour of the "melancholy house" of Edgar Allan Poe's imagination while a narrator reads from the story of Lady Madoline and Roderick Usher.

In the live-action, black-and-white "The Flat" (1968), a man who is mysteriously locked inside a dank room is thwarted—a bent fork, an egg that refuses to break, a piece of bread hollowed out by rats—in his every attempt to eat. Luis Bunuel's "The Exterminating Angel" and Roman Polanski's "Repulsion" come to mind. "Down to the Cellar" (1983) is a variation on the same theme. This time Svankmajer's protagonist is a young girl, and his photography is in color.

"Jabberwocky" (1971) opens with a hand briefly but repeatedly spanking a naked bottom, then precedes to, in Svankmajer's words, "reveal cruelty and fear right where they are least expected, in the world of toys and childhood dreams." "The Last Trick" (1964), the director's debut film, fuses animation and live action as two rival magicians do battle on a small stage.

There, I've tried. But as I feared there really is no way, after all, that the printed word can do justice to the astonishing technical virtuosity and haunting magic of these films. You're best off going to the Film Forum, where the macabre mind of Svankmajer will be laid bare through May 16.

VILLAGE VOICE, 5/9/89, p. 63, Georgia Brown

Jan Svankmajer could appreciate a pus-packed protagonist. Unsentimental as only Communist-bloc residents can be, the Czech animator is a poet of overripeness, of slime, rot, and mold. The beauty of Svankmajer's work, though, is that while it draws us into a dismal swamp, it also (as in the Jacques Prévert poem recited in one of the films) draws us a bright singing bird. On one level, these eight shorts—between 10 and 15 minutes each—provide an overview of Svankmajer's film career; on another, they create a mesmerizing narrative of their own. Put together smartly by people at the British Film Institute, the program climaxes with the filmmaker's most overtly personal work thus far, the small masterpiece *Down to the Cellar*.

Svankmajer gets directly to the root meaning of animation—literally breathing life (anima) into the lifeless. A crafty alchemist, he takes ordinary inert, motiveless objects—chairs, spoons, vegetables, toys; rocks and stones and tress—and, with the aid of esoteric charms pulled from his bottomless black satchel, illuminates (or betrays) the things' intentional, quite agitated interior life. While Svankmajer's work (which usually employs puppets and trick photography) recalls the strong current of Eastern Europe's earthy, folk-wise surrealism—of the poetry, say, of the Serbian Vasko Popa—specifically he's heir to the rich Czech surrealist tradition, with its genesis in the hyperbolic Mannerism of Rudolf II's court and its literary flowering in the works of Capek, Hasek, and Kafka.

Born in 1934 and living his portion of the 20th century in Prague, Svankmajer has an imagination shaped by totalitarianism. Small wonder that he's obsessed with the mechanics of indifferent, brutal forces, and with helplessness and victimization. But the genesis of his morbidity really is a prior fascism—the one that invades childhood. His main subject could be said to be the effects of stress on the child's imagination.

Svankmajer's first film, *The Last Trick* (1964), and *Punch and Judy* (1966) turn on the same basic situation: Two puppet figures indulge in some cursory civilities before proceeding to an orgy of mutual mutilation. But Svankmajer produces a marvelously mysterious effect by putting in the center of the quarrel a live creature—the artificial context heightening the creature's "liveness," a state that clearly has its pros and cons. In the first film, a black beetle creeps into one of the puppets' nostrils and later makes his way into an ear. (The puppets' body cavities, like Cornell boxes, contain wonders.) By the frenzy's finish, though, the beetle lies dead on its back (shades of Gregor S.)—an innocent explorer, victim of raging titans. (In the other film, a guinea pig eats oats while two puppets kill each other over who owns him.)

In 1968, the year of the Russian invasion of Czechoslovakia, Svankmajer released *The Flat*, a black-and-white Kafkaesque parable with a human actor—a poor soul trapped inside a maliciously appointed one-room apartment. (The stove is flooded with water, the faucet gives out stones, the soup spoon has holes in it, an egg drops through the table and smashes his toe.) Coming two years later, *The Ossuary* (another commentary on grim events) conducts a visual tour of the famous Sedlec Ossuary—where 50,000 to 70,000 skeletons, victims of the Black Death, are used in a bizarre display of "bone art." Removing the tour guide's voiceover from his first version of the film, Svankmajer dubbed in a jazz score and Prévert's peom "Hom To Draw a Bird." ("First, draw a cage with an open door.../Wait for years.../If the bird sings, it is a good omen./You can sign your painting.")

Those who saw Svankmajer's full-length *Alice* last fall can now see his other homage to fantasist Lewis Carroll, *Jaberwocky*. Glimpses of a bare child's bottom being spanked interlace the credits, suggesting among other things that the Victorian nursery in the film becomes furiously activated by a child's vengeful or guilty imagination. Toys come alive in capricious—sometimes bloody or sexually suggestive—ways, and the main drama seems to point to a rite of passage (a slaying of the Jabberwock?). At the end, the small boy's suit in the wardrobe turns into a man's suit. An impish black cat (the only live being) no doubt makes reference to Poe—Svankmajer's other English-language inspiration. The minimal, atmospheric *The Fall of the House of Usher* in black and white is another Svankmajer ode to what Poe called "the sentience of all vegetable things."

Vegetables live, briefly, in the three-part *Dimensions of Dialogue*. In a dazzling opening sequence, Giuseppe Arcimboldi-like heads (one of vegetables, one of kitchen utensils, one of writing tools) fight duels in a savage scissors/paper/stone game. (Arcimboldi was one of the stars in Rudolf II's 16th century Prague circle.) The strongest head chews another one up and vomits out a finer grain—filings, gruel, or mush—until, diversity eliminated, all heads are clay. In the next sequence, a clay man and woman kiss and make love. But when they come apart, a bit of clay is left over, and, like a clinging child, the little blob wants one of them of take care of it. When the man throws the little blob in the woman's face, the shit, so to speak, hits the fan.

The child has been at the center all along, yet it's the exquisite tale *Down to the Cellar* that precedes it. A little girl (Monika Belo-Babanova) with braids and red shoes is sent to the cellar of her apartment house to fetch potatoes from the potato bin. On her way downstairs she meets a leering man who offers her candy, and a sinister woman sloshing soapy water over the hallways. Down in the cellar it's dark, dank, and dripping; the impish black cat joins her, so do the man and woman. What she encounters down there suggests the range of threats to children. The film's glorious final moments sear clean to the blackest unconscious. The infinite despair on the child's face is heartbreaking; what she does next is heart-mending.

Also reviewed in:
NEW YORK TIMES, 5/3/89, p. C19, Caryn James

JANUARY MAN, THE

A Metro-Goldwyn-Mayer release. *Producer:* Norman Jewison and Ezra Swerdlow. *Director:* Pat O'Connor. *Screenplay:* John Patrick Shanley. *Director of Photography:* Jerzy Zielinski. *Editor:* Lou Lombardo. *Music:* Marvin Hamlisch. *Music Editor:* Curitis Roush. *Choreographer:* David Allan. *Sound:* Bruce Carwardine. *Sound Editor:* Michael O'Farrell and Sharon Lackie. *Production Designer:* Philip Rosenberg. *Art Director:* Dan Davis. *Set Decorator:* Gary Brink and Carol Lavoie. *Set Dresser:* John Oates Jr. and Michael Stockton. *Special Effects:* Neil Trifunovich. *Costumes:* Ann Roth and Neil Spisak. *Make-up:* Bernadette Mazur and Patricia Green. *Stunt Coordinator:* Greg Walker. *Running time:* 97 minutes. *MPAA Rating:* R.

CAST: Kevin Kline (Nick Starkey); Susan Sarandon (Christine Starkey); Mary Elizabeth Mastrantonio (Bernadette Flynn); Harvey Keitel (Frank Starkey); Danny Aiello (Vincent Alcoa); Rod Steiger (Eamon Flynn); Alan Rickman (Ed); Faye Grant (Allision Hawkins); Ken Welsh (Roger Culver); Jayne Haynes (Alma); Brian Tarantina (Cone); Bruce MacVittie (Rip); Bill Cobbs (Detective Reilly); Greg Walker (January Man); Tandy Cronyn (Lana); Gerard Parkes (Reverend Drew); Errol Slue (Chief Sunday); William Christian (Tim); Ann Talman (Sarah); Bill Cwikowski (Press Representative); Billie Neal (Gwen); Malachy McCourt (Hob); Paul Geier (Detective Muse); Lazaro Perez (Ramon); Katherine E. Miller (Olympia); Jane Sanders (Mia); Colin Mochrie (Pat); Warren Davis (Bill); Joan Heney (Claire); Maida Rogerson (Mildred); James Mainprize (Harry); J.B. Waters (Police Officer); Harmony Cramp (Girl in Fire); Jack K. Tsirakis (Maitre'd); John Kayton (Emergency Services Leader); Fred Booker (Janitor); Kimberly Glasco and Rex Harrington (Ballet Dancers).

FILMS IN REVIEW, 4/89, p. 234, Michael Buckley

The January Man is a terrible waste of a talented cast and an audience's time.

John Patrick Shanley, whose second screenplay, *Moonstruck,* won him an Oscar (and was enjoyed by this reviewer as much as his first, *Five Corners,* was detested) herein cooks up a muddled stew concerning a serial killer in New York, who strikes once a month, and the eccentric cop assigned to catch him.

Kevin Kline is the cop, Harvey Keitel is his brother, the police commissioner, who's married to Kline's ex-mistress, Susan Sarandon. Rod Steiger gobbles up scenery as the Mayor and has a contest with police captiain Danny Aiello as to who can scream louder. Mary Elizabeth Mastrantonio is the Mayor's daughter, who goes to bed and falls in love with Kline, and Alan Rickman plays an oddball artist who assists Kline. Where *The January Man* (directed by Pat O'Connor) will strike again is determined through astrological signs and musical notes and a precious waste of time.

By the time this is read, *The January Man* will have been apprehended and sentenced to life imprisonment on videocassette. Renters beware.

LOS ANGELES TIMES, 1/13/89, Calendar/p. 6, Sheila Benson

A singular quirkiness has been the most engaging quality of "The January Man's" writer, John Patrick Shanley: characters like Nicolas Cage's in "Moonstruck," who lost one hand because of love—well, love and not paying attention to a bread-slicing machine—or the assortment of Bronx poets and psychopaths in "Five Corners."

There's a very Irish quality to Shanley's work, a wild lyric hand with character and dialogue that makes his pairing with Irish-born director Pat O'Connor all the more understandable. (Thus far O'Connor has made a mad quinella of films: the distinguished "Cal," the delicate introspection of "A Month in the Country" and the truly loony "Stars and Bars.") Unfortunately, this same unpredictability is what makes "The January Man" charming and exasperating at the same time.

Its characters are the Manhattanites whose speech patterns intrigue Shanley so, from an intrepid, utterly unorthodox ex-detective, Nick Starkey (Kevin Kline), to a Tammany-style mayor (Rod Steiger, with an aureole of white hair) and a vindictive police commissioner (Harvey Keitel).

In proper Shanley cat's-cradle style, Keitel is also Kline's brother, and Keitel's now-wife, Susan Sarandon, was the flame who fed Kline's home fires only a few short years before. And to thicken the plot, it is the mayor's 23-year-old daughter, Mary Elizabeth Mastrantonio, who begins an impetuous affair with Kline just as this romantic thriller opens.

Some years earlier, Kline was banished from his slot as the police department's great intuitive master sleuth to the New York Fire Department (?!) on trumped-up allegations of graft. It turns out to be dirty family doings.

However, the amiable Kline has settled as contentedly into the life of a firefighter as he had into the life of a detective—perhaps more so. Putting out fires and saving children seems a little more straightforward to him than dealing with the twisted mentalities of the world of homicide.

But after the serial killings of 11 young women over as many months, from *somewhere* comes the cry to bring hero-firefighter Kline back as special investigator on the case. It's a move made over the reverberating protests of precinct Capt. Danny Aiello. However, it comes at the bellowing request of mayor Steiger, and as any actor can tell you, it is a losing battle to get into a screaming contest with Rod Steiger, "The Last Hurrah" himself.

O'Connor and Shanley give generous texture to Kline's character, to his friendship with Ed-the-artist (the charismatic Alan Rickman, "Die Hard's" saturnine villain), to the torch that Kline still carries for Sarandon and to the setup for his immediate hot-sheet romance with Mastrantonio. Yet, enticing as all this is, it wreaks havoc with the movie's crime-thriller format, which requires that we at least *pretend* to believe Kline's method in fathoming the killer's madness.

Kline begins with the provable theory that the killer has used prime numbers as the dates of each of his previous 11 murders, and thus will strike on a predictable January date. As the unflappable Ed turns into a wizardly sidekick, Kline goes into three-dimensional computer imaging and side trips to the planetarium to flesh out his digram of his quarry's mental processes. It makes us mesmerized by the workings of this psychopath's mind and frustrates us mightily when we learn as little as we do about him at the movie's end.

Kline's leaps of intuition might put even Sherlock Holmes' eyelids at half-staff in disbelief. And if those leaps bother you, don't even think about the jumps in behavior that Sarandon's biting, minkswathed matron must make during the course of the film (rated R for language and brief nudity). It's a tasty but hors d'oeuvre-size role for Sarandon, making her character the second one we leave wanting to know more about.

"The January Man" is nothing to seek out if you want airtight logic. What it offers is charm, blather, the dazzlement of writing and performance that wear thin well before the final, credulity-straining quarter. Kline, Mastrantonio, Sarandon and Rickman carry its charm most effectively; although the Kline-Mastrantonio affair begins precipitously, it is amplified in a way to sweep you away, too. But you know what county you're in when one of the young under-detectives calls Kline admiringly, "a shamus"; it's far closer to Glocca Morra than the County of New York.

MONTHLY FILM BULLETIN, 5/89, p. 138, Anne Billson

New York City. On New Year's morning, Allison Hawkins becomes the eleventh victim of a serial killer when she is strangled in her apartment. Mayor Eamon Flynn, whose daughter Bernadette was a friend of the murdered girl, responds to pressure by persuading police commissioner Frank Starkey to reinstate his brother Nick as a special investigator. Nick, who was forced to resign from the force after allegations of graft and who is now working as a fireman, agrees to help in the case, but only if Frank's wife Christine (who cut short her affair with Nick to marry his brother) will come to see him. They are still attracted to each other, but the visit ends in angry recriminations; it appears that Christine has stolen a cancelled cheque which would have proved that Nick had taken the rap for Frank. Despite antagonism from Captain Vincent Alcoa, Nick installs himself in an office in the 2nd Precinct and puts his friend Ed, an eccentric artist, on the payroll. Nick meets Bernadette at Allison's funeral and promptly takes her to bed, then allows her to stay at his apartment because she feels insecure; Christine finds her there and later infuriates Flynn with news of the affair. Nick, meanwhile, examines the police files and deduces that the killer will strike again on the following night, but the case is apparently closed when another woman is strangled in copycat murder and the culprit commits suicide immediately afterwards. Nick is dismissed, but Alcoa grudgingly agrees to turn a blind eye to his further investigations. Nick, Ed and Bernadette manage to work out the exact location of the next murder. Bernadette acts as a decoy and, after a struggle, Nick overpowers the killer and turns him in to the police. Christine, accepting that Nick has now transferred his affections to Bernadette, presents him with the missing cheque.

The January Man is a mind-boggling hybrid. It initially presents itself as a thriller, is side-tracked via a lot of complicated plotting in which all of the main characters turn out to be linked, either emotionally or by family ties, to one another, and then veers all the way off the rails into knockabout farce. In retrospects, the murders appear to be no more than a means of oiling the wheels of the various relationships. By the time the killer actually puts in an appearance, the action is being almost entirely played for laughs; the life-or-death struggle, in which Bernadette's neck is protected by a surgical collar, is comically protracted and ends with Nick rolling his adversary in a carpet. As in *Manhunter*, the hero is blessed (or cursed) with the ability to get inside the mind of his quarry, but here his deductions are patently absurd: calculating the date of the next murder through prime numbers is halfway credible, fixing on the building via stellar configurations might just about pass muster, but alighting (with the help of a few hummed notes) on the very popular song by which the murderer selects his storey is pushing credibility too far. As if to acknowledge the ludicrousness of it all, John Patrick Shanley's script then has one of the characters say: "We're lucky because there are only two single women living on the sixteenth floor and one of them is currently visiting Disneyworld".

Shanley's other screenplays (*Five Corners* and *Moonstruck*) do suggest that he is rather less interested in the mechanics of genre than in character, dialogue and the construction of family networks, all coloured by the details of specific New York locations. Unfortunately, so much of *The January Man's* running time is taken up with outlining the plot that he hardly has room to develop these elements, and the characters rarely rise above the one-dimensional, despite (or perhaps because of) being saddled with lashings of loveable quirks; Alan Rickman's computer-literate artist, in fact, is nothing *but* quirk. Nick is first seen bursting through the wall of a blazing building with a rescued child in his arms, an impossibly heroic figure who has such seemingly endless reserves of tolerance and humour that he is really too good to the true; this rather neutralises all the business with the cancelled cheque since one cannot believe that he would ever dream of clearing his name by getting his brother into trouble. Despite over-the-title billing, Steiger (looking increasingly like a manic Norman Mailer), Sarandon and Keitel give undeserved weight to what turn out to be little more than glorified cameo roles.

NEW LEADER, 1/23/89, p. 23, John Morrone

In the prologue to *The January Man*, two fashionable young women, dressed to the nines for New Year's Eve, step sleekly into their cars and are driven away. One purrs contentedly to the chauffeur, "Gracie Mansion, please." The other heads home, to a posh but more modest address, and is promptly murdered upon arrival. The identity of the victim goes largely undiscussed throughout the film, other than that she is the best friend of the survivor, who turns out to be the daughter of an Irish-American mayor of New York named Eamon Flynn. Since mayor Flynn is played by Rod Steiger doing his best to look and sound like Carroll O'Connor, and since Mary Elizabeth Mastrantonio plays Bernadette, the daughter, with the off-center urban look of an '80s Anna Maria Alberghetti (the result of a mixed Irish-Italian marriage, perhaps?), we start watching the ethnic bits pile up.

Mayor Flynn and his up-from-the-ranks commissioner of police, Frank Starkey (Harvey Keitel), are facing political heat because the murder of Bernadette's friend has hit too close and is too much before the public. "Miss December," as I'll call her, was the 11th in a series of unsolved "blue-ribbon" strangling murders begun almost a year before. To avoid the possibility of a 12th corpse in January, the Mayor, Frank and a retrothinking, pasta-gutted precinct captain, Alcoa (Danny Aiello), are forced to bite a very hard biscotto: to hire back to the force the Commissioner's gifted brother Nick (Kevin Kline), a "Beatnik" ex-cop marking time in the Fire Department who just might crack the case. Nick isn't exactly thrilled. Flynn once made him the scapegoat in a bribery scandal concocted to protect Frank. Now the brothers are barely on speaking terms, and their working together is further made unpalatable because of a woman they have shared. Christine (Susan Sarandon), a gal with patrician ambitions, ditched Nick for his power-mongering brother and still has the paperwork that could prove Frank actually took the bribe.

British director Pat O'Connor, whose 1984 sleeper *Cal* revealed him as a sensitive observer of ethnic tensions, would seem an apt choice for *The January Man*, yet he is virtually eclipsed by John Patrick Shanley's script. Shanley, a playwright, became last year's most visible new screen writing talent for his disarming treatments of Italian and Irish neighborhood neuroses in *Moonstruck* and *Five Corners*. But trapping a serial killer sits most uneasily upon the volatile social fabric he has created here. His intention, apparently, was to enrich the stale police-procedural plot while setting the characters' personal conflicts in motion, but the result is a dissipation rather than a heightening of suspense. Since Shanley shows little interest in the killer (who at the end is apprehended and dismissed with amazing dispatch), we don't either.

What, however, is he trying to say about this bunch of working-class blokes who have sold out by climbing the political ladder, or have flaked out by becoming the vivacious socialite or the underappreciated genius? As Shanley has it, if you haven't entered public service for personal advancement, you concentrate on private pursuits. (When not grubby from fire fighting, Nick practices a particularly indigestible style of cuisine and talks art and economic injustice with his neighbor, played redeemingly well by Alan Rickman as the crankiest of nonconformists.)

You may be tempted to dismiss the film as *All in the Family* dressed up like *Serpico*. Rarely have I seen the duplicity of civil servants so linked with their middle-class ethnicity. Even Kevin Kline, in the lead, seems to play down to his role, performing athletically when breaking down a door but giving dispirited readings to coy lines uttered in moments of crisis.

Though on the outskirts of the story, the most revealing character is Christine. Dressed waspily in a severe black sheath dress, a plain string of pearls and far too much hairspray—the least flattering persona Sarandon has ever been asked to portray—she looks simply terrible knowing she's wed the wrong man, the wrong class, the wrong way of life. The film telegraphs what a dumb move this was (Nick baldly asks her, "How can you sleep with him after you've been with me?"—and, frankly, we're inclined to agree). How Christine will resolve the frustration induced by her greed, and what she will do with the bribery evidence, are practically the only sparks of suspense in *The January Man*. Of course, both questions are tangential to the plot, but if this is a thriller, so is *Abie's Irish Rose*.

NEW YORK POST, 1/13/89, p. 25, David Edelstein

The writer John Patrick Shanley ("Moonstruck," "Five Corners") has a fondness for characters who get things off their chests. In a big way. They holler, wax poetic, jump into bed with one another; sometimes they even commit murder. People don't just live with their feelings in a Shanley script—they're too busy acting them out, turning them into high drama.

In the comedy "Moonstruck," the way these people overdramatized their emotions—like characters in an Italian opera—gave the film its exhilarating daftness. But when the subject is less frivolous and the director doesn't have a grip on the wildly fluctuating tone, you get something like "The January Man," a pathetically routine comic thriller stuffed with ridiculous plot turns and overripe dialogue.

The movie is lively and fairly easy to watch, but nothing in it gels, and most of the audience I saw it with left muttering darkly. It opens as if it's serious business, as two tipsy young women in short skirts leave a New Year's party. The cab drops the first at her building; her friend (Mary Elizabeth Mastrantonio) yells, "Call me if you're blue," which turns out to be one of the film's best lines, since the woman is subsequently strangled. (For a flashy effect, this is crosscut wiith the dropping of the ball in Times Square.)

Mastrantonio, we learn, is the daughter of the mayor (Rod Steiger) of New York City, and the murder of her friend is but the latest in a series of seemingly random slayings. (Lots of loud New York Post headlines to this effect—it's nice to be appreciated.)

The desperate mayor orders the commissioner, Frank Starkey (Harvey Keitel), to call in Starkey's younger brother Nick (Kevin Kline), an eccentric genius who was chucked off the police force two years earlier for taking, bribes—although it's subsequently clear that Nick took the fall for his sleazy brother.

Nick is now a fireman, and just so you'll know he's a heroic kinda guy, you see him run out of a burning building with a small child in his arms. And just so you'll know he's a heroic, hip kinda guy, he promptly calls for "a cup o' cawfee, preferably an espresso." What you don't quite know is how to take this outlandish introduction, and it's a fair sign of things to come.

As in "Moonstruck," the brothers are involved with a single woman, played by Susan Sarandon. She's married to the rich, stodgy older one, but it's the younger one she really loves—the crazy, passionate, creative one. Shanley is repeating himself very quickly. When Nick and his brother's wife have dinner after two years apart, he ends up making a mad speech about how much he loves her and she ends up slapping him.

It worked better last time, if only because Nicolas Cage was so inventive. As the cop with the flaky soul of an artist, Kline doesn't hold your interest—he lacks variety. He's hugely talented, but perhaps too extroverted for films; he can't relax and let you discover things in his character. Maybe as a result, no matter what he's playing, he always seems like an actor.

Nick, who keeps weird hours and orders the harried police captain (Danny Aiello) to hire his rumpled artist-neighbor (Alan Rickman) to paint birds and clouds on the walls of his office, does his police work the way Shanley probably writes—by wandering around, free-associating and drinking lots of coffee.

Instead of just calling in the mayor's daughter for questioning, he tails her from her friend's funeral, and when she cries to him about how little people say to each other in conversation (death has changed the way she views the world), Nick rises to the occasion and makes a pass at her. The nice thing about a Shanley script is that people don't beat around the bush.

The not-so-nice thing about this script is that it can't keep its mind on the murderer. "The January Man" is structured like a thriller but neither Shanley nor the director, Pat O'Connor, pays attention to the plot. The movie has almost no suspense or atmosphere. Nick solves the case by staring into a computer and managing to discern the psycho's ingenious pattern. (It's too bad all serial killers don't operate with such artsy logic—they'd be easier to track.)

The picture has some psychological interest, if only for Shanley's mother-bashing. Nick tells his brother that the killer's mom had a big effect on his life (big surprise), and that their own problems have a lot to do with *their* mom. Nick took the bribery rap for his brother, he says, because mother loved him more, and he felt he owed his brother something. You're meant to speculate on the similarities between Frank and the psycho.

O'Connor makes the leaps from serious drama to dumb comedy with no style; he seems to have shot the script as he found it, and the film lurches haphazardly from one tone to the next. Watching "The January Man," one realizes how much Norman Jewison contributed to making "Moonstruck" all of a piece. Shanley needs smart directors.

He needs smart editors, too—to chop out all his terrible lines. "I'm a fireman," Nick explains to his brother. "I run into these f---ing buildings when they're on fire." And then, when Nick has refused his brother's plea to return to the force: "Go, Frank. Go. There's a lot between us. None of it is good."

Of course, there's an element of deliberate self-parody in Shanley's writing, and what he's trying to do here is obvious: take a typically cliched killer-on-the-loose movie and give it some goofy texture. But "The January Man" is Quirky and Offbeat in ways that make me loathe those particular adjectives. Shanley doesn't toy with clichés—he mauls you with them. And the cast is full of veteran scenery-chewers who seize you by the collar and roar.

In his return to films, Rod Steiger spends his time either shrieking or looking distracted, as if checking the door for his bookie. He doesn't act his big speeches so much as conduct them, drawing out the words like a lunatic maestro. I spent a while trying to decide if the performance was really, really terrible or the work of genius. The answer is probably in the middle somewhere—terrible but so weird that it's bearable. Like "The January Man."

NEWSDAY, 1/13/89, Part III/p. 3, Mike McGrady

Why can't moviemakers be consistent? If the highly praised writer of "The January Man," John Patrick Shanley, were at top form, we'd doubtless be talking today about charm and offbeat warmth. If director Pat O'Connor were working at his peak, "The January Man" would be described as sensitive and deeply touching. And if the celebrated cast of character actors were operating at full capacity, "The January Man" would be an electric experience for us all ...

But, alas, moviemakers *do* have their off-days. And the only reason I can imagine seeing "The January Man" is to watch a collection of top talents suffering career lows.

Out of left field, screenwriter Shanley, highly praised for "Moonstruck," has made a literary specialty of eccentricity. That this can be a prescription for disaster was made clear in the recent "Five Corners"—a cloyingly cute movie where a madman strangled zoo penguins and an urban vigilante stalked killers with bow and arrow. While both that film and this one drew audience laughter, it was seldom where intended. Once again Shanley finds himself on the wrong side of the chasm separating the offbeat from the outlandish.

Similarly, director O'Connor scored highly last year with a delicate, little film entitled "A Month in the Country." It's hard to believe that same talent could later fashion the horrendous Daniel Day-Lewis comedy, "Stars and Bars." There O'Connor revealed a monumental unfamiliarity with things American—speech, rhythm, humor. The tin ear and heavy hand are back in full force for "The January Man."

In fact, I'll wager we won't see more overacting in a single movie this year. What should have been casual asides come out as screams underlined by waving arms. When in doubt, shout. However, when actors as diversely talented as Harvey Keitel, Danny Aiello, Susan Sarandon and Mary Elizabeth Mastrantonio are guilty of such flagrancy, you begin to sense it may not be their fault.

How bad is the overacting? It's so bad that the explosively emotive Rod Steiger comes close to blending in with the rest of the cast. And Steiger, who chews more scenery than a full battalion of backstage rats, behaves as though he's being directed with a cattle prod.

"January Man" would have us believe that the corrupt mayor of New York (Steiger) and the corrupt police commissioner (Keitel) rehire Keitel's ex-cop brother (Kevin Kline) because he's the only one on Earth who can solve the serial murders plaguing the city. Brother Kevin agrees to come back and solve the crime, but only if allowed to cook dinner privately for brother Harvey's pretty wife (Susan Sarandon). And if the police department will hire his artistic nextdoor neighbor (Alan Rickman) who paints birds on squad-room walls.

Kevin then meets the mayor's daughter (Mary Elizabeth Mastrantonio) and says, "This restaurant is a five-minute walk from seven hotels. And I'd like to get a room in one of them." Which they do. However, it's not until they get to solving the crime with the assistance of computers and planetariums and musical scores that the film reaches its crescendo of implausibility.

One final positive word. Kevin Kline, who was so good in "A Fish Called Wanda," retains a measure of charm and also creates one hilarious wobbly-kneed ice-skating routine. Any actor who can emerge unscathed from a fiasco like this is better than merely good.

TIME, 1/23/89, p. 59, Richard Schickel

There are mysteries, and then again there are mysteries. Those that involve capital crimes oblige a movie to solve the puzzle clearly, neatly and, one hopes, surprisingly before the final fade-out. There is, however, a better class of enigma that involves less deadly, even comical, forms of human behavior. And there is a better class of film that is wisely content to set forth such shadowy dilemmas and leave them unresolved, resonating in our minds.

The January Man is modestly, ingratiatingly, a movie of the latter sort. To be sure, it begins with a serial killer claiming a victim, and it ends with the guilty party being taken into custody. But the deductive process that normally leads to this conventionally ordained conclusion is perfunctory and even somewhat implausible. What interests writer John Patrick Shanley, who won an Academy Award last year for *Moonstruck*, is the infinite and usually inexplicable capacity of ordinary people to turn flaky without warning or change of expression. The prime example here is Nick Starkey (Kevin Kline), a former New York City cop and now a fireman. As Starkey, Kline has the best entrance in recent movie memory: bursting spectacularly out of a burning building, cradling the child he has rescued in his arms, he collapses to the sidewalk and calls for a cup of coffee, "preferably espresso."

Besides being brave, Nick is something of an ironist. This quality, if nothing else, is a sign of intelligence. Before taking up fire fighting, Nick was a cop falsely tainted by corruption. Now the very people who secretly profited by victimizing him—the crooked, volcanic mayor (Rod Steiger) and the bland, bureaucratic police commissioner (Harvey Keitel)—need him to lead the hunt for a maniacal killer.

It is an offer the ironist cannot refuse. Not only is the commissioner his longloathed brother, he is also the man who married Christine (Susan Sarandon), a haughty socialite for whom Nick still yearns. His price for cooperation? One tête-à-tête with that ambiguous lady. In Shanley's world, it is inevitable that this does not go awfully well. Nick asks her to listen to the wine breathe, serves octopus for the main course and generally comes on too strong. It is also inevitable that a perfect substitute for Christine will soon turn up. And it does, in the form of the mayor's daughter (Mary Elizabeth Mastrantonio). This is not love as usual; this is the need for sexual revenge.

What prevents *The January Man* from turning into a downscale *Dangerous Liaisons* is the movie's refusal to let the characters acknowledge this edgy subtext. Shanley instead provides a funny, melodramatic hubbub to distract our attention. His busy plotting may require a suspension of incredulity, but he is well served by good actors; by a director, Pat O'Connor, with a taste for the acrid flavors of big-city life; and by his own delight in human eccentricity.

VILLAGE VOICE, 1/17/89, p. 65, Katherine Dieckmann

John Patrick Shanley has been criticized for sticking to Italian-American family dramas, so maybe he wrote *The January Man* as a stretch. But as a follow-up to the shamelessly enjoyable *Moonstruck*, it's a complete bust. The assemblage of New York actors (Kevin Kline, Harvey Keitel, Susan Sarandon, Danny Aiello, Mary Elizabeth Mastrantonio, Rod Steiger) is a casting agent's wet dream, but they're wasted in a script that stabs at thriller-cop-romance-comedy-melodrama genres, only to miss them all. This mishmash is only accentuated by the direction of Pat O'Connor, who has proven he does very well making moody dramas on his bonny home turf (*Cal, A Month in the Country*), but bombs in the States, since he apparently has no ear for American speech (the painful *Stars and Bars*, which largely lampooned Southern white trash, and now this.)

At least the movie's timely: it's January, right after New Year's. A serial killer who's been murdering a single woman every month for 11 months has just made the mistake of knocking off the mayor's daughter's best friend. So Mayor Eamon Flynn (Steiger) leans on police commissioner Frank Starkey (Keitel) to hire Starkey's estranged brother, Nick (Kline), to crack the case, a decision that enrages precinct captain Alcoa (Aiello), who can't stand Nick's eccentricities. Every dialogue in this chain of command is embarrassingly strident, as well as overmic'd: O'Connor has all his male actors, save Kline (who's too busy perfecting his ingratiating moustachioed charmbag mode from *A Fish Called Wanda*), shouting into each other's faces, veins bulging and spittle flying, to get their points across. The results are disastrous, especially in Steiger's case.

Nick isn't all that eager to get involved, since he was dumped from the force by his jealous brother and has made the obvious career move by becoming a bohemian fireman. When he's not in his classic Village pad hanging out with his nextdoor neighbor, who's (whatta twist) a moody painter (Alan Rickman, of course), he's hurling himself through steel doors to save little girls, recovering with the memorable line, "Wonder if I could get a cup of coffee? Preferably espresso?" The situation is further complicated by the fact that Frank stole Nick's girl, Christine (Sarandon, in what has got to be the most unflattering hairstyle ever foisted on an actress). Nick wants her back, but then he meets the mayor's feisty daughter, Bernadette (Mastrantonio).

The January Man is neither suspenseful nor funny. When Nick confronts Christine on her betrayal, he cries, "How do you get wet? Do you think about the money?" She responds by slapping him three times, the sound amplification and pauses struggling to create a laugh that never comes. The film also borrows from *Moonstruck* with its wrong-brother romance and its use of Lincoln Center as a signifier of high culture. There are flickers of Shanley's biting urban wit (also a pleasure in his script for *Five Corners*), such as when the mayor blurts out, "That prick with the scarlet cape, the cardinal" midsentence, and we register amusement without elaborate cueing. But *The January Man* is the clearest possible case of what happens when screenwriters become hot properties, and whatever they've got is salable. Shanley broke through on the quality of his work. Here it's no longer the writing but the name that's the thing.

Also reviewed in:
NEW REPUBLIC, 2/6/89, p. 24, Stanley Kauffmann
NEW YORK TIMES, 1/13/89, p. C8, Vincent Canby
VARIETY, 1/11–17/89, p. 44
WASHINGTON POST, 1/13/89, p. B7 Rita Kempley

JIMI PLAYS MONTEREY

A Movie Visions release. *Producer:* Alan Douglas. *Director:* D.A. Pennebaker and Chris Hegedus. *Running time:* 50 minutes. *MPAA Rating:* Not Rated.

WITH: Jimi Hendrix (Guitar); Noel Redding (Bass); Mitch Mitchell (Drums).

LOS ANGELES TIMES, 9/16/89, Calendar/p. 4, Chris Willman

Watching Jimi Hendrix bob back and forth behind his guitar with alternating grace and aggression in "Jimi Hendrix Live," (at selected theaters), it's easy to feel that this was the first and very possibly the last time that heavy metal was ever really sexy.

After he picks wondrous solos from every unnatural position (and with his teeth), and by the time he sets his instrument down on the stage floor at the climax and picks at it from above, finally setting it afire, the interchange is almost too obvious: This isn't music about lovemaking, it's music *as* lovemaking.

The beauty of "Hendrix Live," directed by rock documentarian D.A. Pennebaker (the early Dylan chronicle "Don't Look Back," "Depeche Mode 101"), is that even two jaded decades after Hendrix's death it is able to remind you just how dangerous all this was—not just Hendrix's wild showmanship, but his revolutionary approach to whacking new, beautifully distorted sounds out of the instrument, a la Miles Davis.

The stereo sound track is much sharper than the quality of the film itself, unreleased and mostly elementary concert footage shot at the 1967 Monterey Pop Festival. (Pennebaker worked on "Monterey Pop," the 1969 film of that festival, and the title credits bill this film as "Jimi Plays Monterey.") The brief introduction, narrated by "Papa" John Philips, is just right in tone and length and helps set the scene with such tidbits as the fact that Hendrix was in such a fiery mood at Monterey because he had to follow the Who, whose own showman tendencies he felt compelled to compete with.

NEW YORK POST, 7/12/89, p. 23, David Edelstein

In 1967, at the height of the "Summer of Love," two black performers crashed the white San

Francisco rock scene in the big-deal Monterey Pop festival. Otis Redding would die six months later in a plane accident; Jimi Hendrix would burn for another three years before succumbing to drugs.

Their June 18 performances, which made them legends even in their own lifetimes, are the highlight of D.A. Pennebaker's feature "Monterey Pop." Now Pennebaker and Chris Hegedus have assembled the rest of each artist's Monterey set. The two films, "Jimi Plays Monterey" (50 minutes) and "Shake" (20 minutes), aren't especially vivid as cinema, but they're rock-'n-roll seances—they mesmerize you with their life force.

Hendrix gets the royal treatment—narration (by "Papa" John Phillips), archival footage (from the Hendrix estate) and an overture (in which a bedraggled artist, Denny Dent, attacks a brick wall with brushes and creates a remarkable Hendrix before your eyes).

After years as a back-up man and cult figure, Hendrix went to England, formed "The Jimi Hendrix Experience" (with Noel Redding on bass and Mitch Mitchell on drums) and returned to America for his debut at Monterey. According to Phillips, neither Hendrix nor The Who's Pete Townshend wanted to follow the other. Phillips flipped a coin, Townshend won and Hendrix jumped on a chair and announced that if he had to follow The Who, he'd pull out all the stops.

In concert, he's orange-ruffled, plumed and endearingly stage-struck. Clearly stoned, he breaks into eerie, private laughter and babbles about how groovy it is to come back here and really play, wow, mmmmm, look at those beautiful people out there. Tongue and teeth don't w-w-work together with the same synergistic power as fingers and guitar strings, teeth and guitar strings, even crotch and guitar strings.

The strings, in short, are an extension of him—and of the atmosphere. On "Wind Cried Mary," Dylan's "Like a Rolling Stone" and "Wild Thing," his Stratocaster seems to pick up transmissions—all the era's bad vibes—and distill them into, like, music, wow. The noise and reverb can be unbearable and then suddenly gorgeous; he makes feedback sing the blues.

The crowd is hushed, and Pennebaker and his editing crew seem afraid to cut away from him, to show anything except his torso in the frame. That's OK: Watching Hendrix wave that guitar through the air like a wand, you'll be struck by the judiciousness of his playing—there isn't a single wasted chord or squeal in the entire set.

In his famous finale of "Wild Thing," Hendrix surrenders to his orgiastic urges. He plays with his crotch, then kneels over the supine Stratocaster and plucks a single string until, unable to contain himself, he lets loose with a stream of lighter fluid from between his legs and then torches the guitar. Finally he obliterates it, its purpose served.

It's Otis who has a tough act to follow, but "Shake" is marvelous fun—less a razor's-edge performance and more of a party. Out he bounds in his blue suit, spritzing good cheer, a polymorphously perverse soul raver.

In fast numbers like "Shake" and "Respect," he oohs and ahs and can't stop his feet. He's always rocking and dipping out of the frame—the camera can't hold him. And that's true in the slow songs, too, those caressive ballads "I've Been Loving You Too Long" and "Try a Little Tenderness."

In the latter, Pennebaker surrenders to his sentimental impulses and concocts his sole crowd sequence—a huggy montage of beautiful, groovy chicks and their beautiful babies, lovers and pets. It's shameless, but like most of this program, it works beautifully.

NEWSDAY, 7/14/89, Part III/p. 3, Stephen Williams

In the annals of pop culture history, the Woodstock festival ranks as one of the touchstones of the contemporary rock era. Fact is, Woodstock was the sequel to the Monterey Pop Festival.

Peace and love flowed like wine in the summer of 1967, when hippies, straights, adults, babies and all manner of music fans gathered on the California coast to celebrate, in one day, a muscial form that was on the verge of turning itself inside out.

Among the rock and rollers on stage that day in June—Janis Joplin, the Who, Jefferson Airplane, Country Joe and the Fish—were Otis Redding, who would not live to shake it up at Woodstock, and Jimi Hendrix, who died 13 months after the big do at Max Yasgur's farm.

Cinema verite film maker Donn Pennebaker filmed Redding's short set and all of Hendrix' groundbreaking performance, the guitarist's first in the United States with his band, the Experience. The clips have recently been compiled and released as two films, the 50-minute "Jimi Plays Monterey" and "Shake (Otis Redding)," an exhilarating 20-minute short featuring Redding ripping up on five songs.

There is, of course, a sense of history about both these films, and a poignant sense of tragedy as well. Redding was killed six months after Monterey in the crash of a chartered plane. Hendrix, supported by drummer Mitch Mitchell and Noel Redding on bass, was a sensation in Great Britain in 1966 and 1967. His appearance at Monterey, which was orchestrated by Paul McCartney, cemented his ascendency to superstardom. But tensions in his organization, as well as Hendrix' growing dependence on drugs, foreshadowed his death at the age of 27.

The Monterey set is prefaced by some archival shots of Hendrix when he was performing at Greenwich Village's Cafe Wha? as a member of Jimmy Jones and the Blue Flames. Ex-Papa John Phillips (of the Mamas and the Papas) adds a minimal commentary to the film, and he sums up Hendrix' mysterious guitar style. "You could watch him like a hawk," Phillips says, "but you could not figure out how he did it."

Prancing in a purple feather boa, Hendrix struts his stuff before Pennebaker's rather staid cameras. Compared to today's technology, the videotaping and audio recording methods were positively primitive 22 years ago, and Pennebakers's 16mm camera view was by necessity restricted.

But the fire in this case comes from the artist, not the production tools. The left-handed Hendrix coaxes the most delicious licks out of "Foxy Lady" and the slower "The Wind Cries Mary." He plays the Stratocaster with his teeth and flutters his tongue—the audience looks thoroughly confused at several points in the show—and, in a classic rock exorcism, sets his guitar on fire during "Wild Thing." Hendrix promised to outdo the Who and Pete Townshend, who smashed his guitar on stage just before Hendrix came on. It isn't recorded whether Townshend ever *burned* his guitar.

Redding's forceful, propulsive performance in "Shake" is minus his classic "(Sittin' on) The Dock of the Bay," because Redding and bandmate Steve Cropper (Redding's backing band here is Booker T. and the MGs) wrote it after the Monterey Festival. Redding died before his biggest hit was released.

But Redding delivers a powerful version of his own "Respect," which Aretha Franklin later adopted as one of her anthems, as well as the Rolling Stones' "Satisfaction," a song with which Redding hit the Top 40 pop charts in 1966. Throughout the film, Redding's act is breathless and exuberant, enough proof of why he ranked as one of the country's greatest black singers, and had the potential for enormous crossover success among pop audiences as well.

The third part of this Pennebaker "trilogy" package at the Film Forum is a nifty little five-minute "subway ride" though New York called "Daybreak Express," filmed to the music of Duke Ellington.

VILLAGE VOICE, 7/18/89, p. 73, Robert Christgau

Never too taken with cinema verité's low-rent perks, D.A. Pennebaker has been a reluctantly ineluctable rockumentarist since *Don't Look Back* caught Bob Dylan in the act and *Monterey Pop* prepared the way for both Woodstock and *Woodstock*. In 1969 he took less than a week to organize production on *Toronto Pop* (later *Keep on Rockin'*, still later *Sweet Toronto*); just last year he contracted to shoot a Depeche Mode feature, group unheard. Outtakes from *Monterey Pop*, a more carefully conceived and realized project, found their way into version two of the Toronto movie. Now he's recycled *Monterey's* two most undeniable performances into a 20-minute Otis Redding short, *Shake*, and a 50-minute Jimi Hendrix doc, *Jimi Plays Monterey*. Can Janis Joplin, who gigged twice at the festival, be far behind?

The Hendrix movie, plumped up with non-Pennebaker footage from swingin'era London and accounts of the guitarist's Village days by Monterey honchoturned-cocaine-survivor John Phillips, is the featured attraction. But *Shake* is the prize. Well-shot vintage soul performances are as scarce as chitlins on Wall Street, and though these 20,000 white protobohemians weren't exactly Redding's hippest audience, he was definitely out to prove something to "the love crowd." Clad in a memorable forest-green suit, the most country of the great soul men trundled his oversized body all over the stage in a condensed set of surefire material. The glaring spotlight effects that spoiled Redding's segment of the original film are mostly gone; except for the girls-of-Monterey montage accompanying "Try a Little Tenderness," Pennebaker honors the visual facts, most notably Redding's bighearted face. In the best verité traditon, Pennebaker is drawn to interesting faces—even his tribute to the ladies doesn't settle for pretty.

By my count, *Jimi Plays Monterey* is the fifth concert documentary devoted solely to Hendrix, and while it may be the best, no one would claim it's definitive. Sure beats *Rainbow Bridge*, say, but the music can't match that sorry film's "Train Kept A-Rollin'," or *Woodstock*'s "Star-Spangled Banner." Music was a given for a Hendrix stuck with topping the Who's guitar-smashing tour de force. It's great sport to watch this outrageous scene-stealer wiggle his tongue, pick with his teeth, and set his ax on fire, but the showboating does distract from the history made that night—the dawning of an instrumental technique so effortlessly fecund and febrile that rock has yet to equal it, though hundreds of metal bands have gotten rich trying.

Admittedly, nowhere else will you witness a Hendrix still uncertain of his divinity. Dead at 27, he was never not young, but he didn't stay this innocent for long. Redding, who would die sooner and younger, was always a little naïve, and never so innocent. Maybe that's the difference between soul and rock.

Also reviewed in:
NEW YORK TIMES, 7/12/89, p. C14, Stephen Holden
WASHINGTON POST, 3/17/89, p. D7, Richard Harrington

JOE LEAHY'S NEIGHBORS

An Arundell Productions film. *Producer:* Robin Anderson and Bob Connolly. *Director:* Robin Anderson and Bob Connolly. *Director of Photography:* Bob Connolly. *Editor:* Ray Thomas and Bob Connolly. *Sound:* Robin Anderson. *Running time:* 90 minutes. *MPAA Rating:* Not Rated.

VILLAGE VOICE, 4/4/89, p. 58, J. Hoberman

In the follow-up to their 1983 *First Contact*, documentarians Robin Anderson and Bob Connolly focus on the fruits of that epochal meeting between New Guinea tribespeople and Australian settlers. Dapper Joe Leahy, son of a tribal woman and the expedition leader, has built a coffee plantation on aborigine land—and thus introduced his less developed half-brethren to the wonders of capitalism. This account of their education is meandering, serendipitous, and sometimes very funny. It also requires a fair amount of concentration—which is why you have to wonder that ND/NF decided to punish the audience by tacking on the aptly titled *A Day and a Half*, 23 minutes of third-rate, ersatz Mike Leigh.

Also reviewed in:
NEW YORK TIMES, 4/1/89, p. 14, Richard Bernstein
VARIETY, 3/15–21/89, p. 13

JOHNNY HANDSOME

A Tri-Star Pictures release of a Guber-Peters Company production. *Executive Producer:* Mario Kassar and Andrew Vajna. *Producer:* Charles Roven. *Director:* Walter Hill. *Screenplay:* Ken Friedman. *Based upon "The Three Worlds of Johnny Handsome" by:* John Godey. *Director of Photography:* Matthew F. Leonetti. *Editor:* Freeman Davies, Carmel Davies, and Donn Aron. *Music:* Ry Cooder. *Music Editor:* Jim Weidman. *Sound:* Richard Goodman. *Sound Editor:* Jerry Ross. *Production Designer:* Gene Rudolf. *Art Director:* Christa Munro. *Set Decorator:* Ernie Bishop. *Set Dresser:* John Kaufman. *Special Effects:* Joseph Mercurio. *Costumes:* Dan Moore. *Special Make-up:* Michael Westmore and Zoltan Elek. *Make-up:* Michael Germain and Ken Diaz. *Running time:* 93 minutes. *MPAA Rating:* R.

CAST: Mickey Rourke (John Sedley); Ellen Barkin (Sunny Boyd); Elizabeth McGovern (Donna McCarty); Morgan Freeman (Lt. A.Z. Drones); Forest Whitaker (Dr. Steven Resher); Lance Henriksen (Rafe Garrett); Scott Wilson (Mikey Chalmette); David Schramm (Vic Dumask); Yvonne Bryceland (Sister Luke); Peter Jason (Mr. Bonet); J.W. Smith (Larry); Jeffrey Meek (Earl); Allan Graf (Bob Lemoyne); Ed Zang (Prestige Manager);

John Fertitta (Prestige Salesman); Raynor Scheine (Gun Dealer); Ed Walsh (Judge); Jim Burk (Prison Guard); Ken Medlock (Shipyard Accountant); Gie-G Duncombe (Accounting Secretary); Dick Butler (Shipyard Security Guard); Blake Clark (Sheriff); Eugenia Ives (Nurse); Tulla Cove and Connie Lemoine (Dancers).

FILMS IN REVIEW, 1–2/90, p. 44, Edmond Grant

The characters in films directed by Walter Hill have no need for names. Their proper names are usually supplied somewhere along the line, but as their adventures proceed, it's just as well to think of them as "the crook," "the cop," "the good girl," "the bad girl"—all the standard types found in the classic Hollywood action feature.

This play with the myths and clichés of the action film has been a consistent thread in Hill's work, from his experiment in European minimalism, *The Driver*, to the rock fable, *Streets Of Fire* (with time out for commerical fodder like *Brewster's Millions* and *Red Heat*). His latest, *Johnny Handsome*, follows in that tradition by presenting a protagonist whose seamy circumstances and obsessive need for revenge seem quite familiar, an echo of the classic film noirs (like *The Big Heat*) where vengeance could become a character's only reason to keep living.

But as steeped in filmdom's past myths as they are, Hill's better films also put a decidedly modern twist on things. The twist here is that the seamy crook protagonist has a rather nasty form of facial elephantitis; hence his ironic moniker, and the film's title. Looking as he does, Johnny (Mickey Rourke) has very few friends, and the one close friend he does have, Mikey (Scott Wilson) is killed in a badly handled rare coin store heist. Once Johnny is apprehended by the police (his cohorts having split the scene of the crime after disposing of Mikey), an option appears that he never before thought possible: to have his face surgically altered, so that he can look "normal." All this is the result of a vaguely described criminal reform program (not one of the film's better plot points), that is intended to prove that if a criminals self-image is improved, his attitude toward society will change.

Fat chance. Johnny's only thought upon receiving his new identity is how to give a little payback to the ruthless couple (Lance Henriksen and Ellen Barkin) who killed his friend. He gets the idea of pulling a heist at the shipyard where he works, and recruiting the cutthroat couple, looking to first humiliate them by stealing the haul from the job, and then kill them. All that stands in his way is conscience incarnate—the sweet attractive young woman he works with and starts seeing socially (Elizabeth McGovern), who doesn't want him to slide back into the gutter.

This last named aspect, the "good girl" character, comes straight out of the film character, comes straight out of the film noir mythos—the virginal female who could change the hero's life around if only he would let her (he won't). Hill uses characters like this as the stock figures they are; his impeccable casting of the principal roles does bring some added depth to the characterizations, but, Elizabeth McGovern's beautous presence aside, how much can actually be done with this kind of role?

And so, as in all stories of good and evil, the bad guys end up capturing the brunt of our interest. The objects of Johnny's obsessive hatred are portrayed as the ultimate in leather-clad menace; Lance Henriksen just exudes evil in his time on screen, and his counterpart, Ellen Barkin, is even more fearsome, combining as she does a flagrant sexuality with a cruel temperament, best exemplified by her pistol whipping her victims at every possible convenience.

Certainly, some of the film just doesn't quite click—for instance, the frequent loss of New Orleans accents (Rourke and McGovern trade off on this), a silly British nun character who teaches Johnny the rigors of speaking clearly once his harelip is removed, and the facile way that the "Cop" character (Morgan Freeman) pieces together the various strands of Johnny's change in identity. Even the one aspect that makes the film so especially unique seems troublesome in retrospect—namely, the way in which Johnny's condition is displayed. Rourke does a good job of creating a vivid characterization behind the *Mask*-like makeup, but throughout these sequences, one can't help but think that Hill may have been better served by a technique used in the noir classic *Dark Passage* (1947), wherein the audience views everything from the protagonist's point of view up until he gets his face operated on. Perhaps a contemporary audience may not sit still for such an esoteric presentation, but the clear views of Johnny's deformity make the film seem as if it is shifting gears when, after the hospital sequences, it changes back into a simple tale of revenge. With the focus given for some time to the treatment of Johnny's condition, it can be believed that the film will be a tale of rebirth, or coping with change. But *Johnny* is not a film chronicling the treatment of a handicap; it's a straightforward action picture that attempts to show the never changing status of human nature by having a group of familiar characters go through their particularly fate ridden paces.

LOS ANGELES TIMES, 9/29/89, Calendar/p. 4, Michael Wilmington

"Johnny Handsome"—the new Walter Hill thriller about a deformed sociopath and his second chance at life—has a temperament like a three-time loser.

This action movie works fine in its hard-bitten, gutty first half, when it's locked up in the jail or the hospital. But when it's sprung into the open air in the payoff sections, "Handsome" can't handle freedom. It gets sucked back into the bad habits of most '80s Hollywood revenge thrillers. It wanders, falls into memory lapses and jumps in logic. To cover up, it starts screaming and picking fights. Finally, it blows its cool completely, hurling around crashed cars and gunfights, wild profanity and empty sleaze.

By the climax—a gunfight in a graveyard with a hostage and a lot of yelling—we may have forgotten how good "Johnny" was in the beginning: in the scenes with sensitive doctor Forest Whitaker and cynical cop Morgan Freeman, or when Mickey Rourke sees his new face for the first time and the tears streamed down in it. Isn't there some kind of support group for movies like this? Car-Chase Anonymous?

Rourke is the movie's Johnny Handsome, another of his recent gallery of gamy outsiders. And if parts of the role seem ripe for parody—the Elephant Man Without a Cause—he still manages to connect with it. A petty street criminal with a heroic soul underneath a misshapen face, Johnny has one friend—a fatherly heist man played with bruised heart and wounded smile by Scott Wilson—and two deadly enemies: wild, evil street scum played by Lance Henriksen and Ellen Barkin.

After these depraved enemies kill his friend during a torpedoed jewelry heist, Johnny takes the fall and gets his chance. A warmhearted doctor (Whitaker) offers to change him completely: remove his harelip, get therapy for his cleft palate and operate away the ridges of facial bone, the frontal encephlocele that gave him his nickname.

Most actors give you the impression they're living out other people's fantasies; Mickey Rourke is one of a handful who always seem to be living out his own. That may be why he's a cult star in Europe, where he's seen as part of a direct line from Dyonysian '50s hoods like Brando and Dean. And, here, when he first gets his new face, all of his usual wary, evasive, pulled-in mannerisms work for the character. Rourke's Johnny seems to be discovering the world in a new way, smiling to himself at people's changed reactions, though later he gets too comfortable, goes from bruised outsider to swaggering stud too easily.

The doctor believes he's giving Johnny a new life. The cop on the case, Drones (Freeman), seems convinced that he's a recidivist, a backslider. Torn between these two, the bleeding heart and the misanthrope, the movie gets its best moments. Whitaker has a wonderful, self-righteous touchiness, and Freeman gives his part that unshakable concentration and cold, teasing malice that made his Fast Black in "Street Smart" one of the great movie villains of the '80s.

Hill must realize that he has pure gold whenever Rourke, Whitaker and Freeman are together in any combination. He's obviously cast the last two against type, even against the script: A.Z. Drones and Steven Resher are names that suggest white Southerners or urban Jews, not blacks. Making both authority figures black—and making Johnny an outcast because of his physical characteristics—temporarily gives "Handsome" an ironic edge, which it then loses completely in the second half, when the sense of evil gets halting, corny, boobish.

Walter Hill's best '70s work had real nerve and gristle, an interesting balance between a love of movie machismo and a tendency to subvert it, but he also had a tendency to schematize every thing, reduce his stories to fable and formula. Here, perhaps because he's adapting a novel (by John Godey) and working with a different writer—Ken Friedman, who's written several Jonathan Kaplan films, including "Heart Like a Wheel"—there's initially more attention to character. All these people live on the cusp. Even the heroine, Elizabeth McGovern as a sweet secretary named Donna, isn't part of conventional society. At best, she's a slummer.

Film noir is an overused term but, at the beginning, that's what Hill, Friedman and the cast and crew reach for and get. "Handsome," shot by Matthew Leonetti, has a hard, cool veneer. The rhythm of the scenes, the smack and drive of the editing—separated by the credits, and later by fadouts—suggests a dangerous lassitude, chopped up ruthlessly.

Hill sticks to that deliberate pace at first, but it begins to go awry in the gauzily romantic scenes with Johnny and Donna, and it vanishes in the lower-depths bouts with Barkin's sneering slut, Sunny, and Henriksen's junkyard-dog-mean Rafe: two characters so unrelievedly vicious that they become comic. Barkin obviously likes to play bad girls, but here she indulges herself. Her performance doesn't have the perfectly judged knife-edge of provocation, sexuality and terror she puts into "Sea of Love."

It's a shame, because when you watch the the Johnny-Sunny scenes, you realize that if Sunny played them sweeter, showed a "nice" side beneath the icy venom, she's immediately become much scarier. But that kind of ambivalence is probably beyond "Johnny Handsome" (MPAA-rated R for sex, language and violence). This movie can spot the handsome face that lies beneath an ugly exterior, but it seems to get fooled by the rot that sometimes lurks beneath the sweet and the safe, the formula and the sure-fire.

MONTHLY FILM BULLETIN, 5/90, p. 130, Tom Milne

New Orleans. Anxious to avoid a second term in jail, John Sedley—known as Johnny Handsome because a congenital deformity has left him hideously ugly and semi-articulate—reluctantly agrees to help his friend Mikey, who urgently needs cash to retain ownership of his night-club, by planning the robbery of a rare coin shop which Mikey has set up with two acquaintances, Rafe Garrett and Sunny Boyd. Johnny's plan works well, but Rafe and Sunny pull a double-cross and get away with the loot, leaving Mikey dead and Johnny under arrest. Refusing a deal offered by cynical black police lieutenant Drones in return for shopping his accomplices, Johnny is sentenced to five years, but soon lands in the prison hospital, victim of a knife attack arranged by Rafe and Sunny (who have taken over Mikey's club and are afraid Johnny will inform on them). There Johnny attracts the attention of Dr. Resher: given a new face through plastic surgery, and a new voice through speech therapy, Johnny wins a parole after submitting to psychological re-evaluation tests, and is found a job under an assumed name in a shipyard. He meets nice girl Donna, who works in the accountancy department, and a mutual attraction develops. But Drones is still hounding Johnny, refusing to believe he has changed inside, certain that he will be out for revenge. Discovering that Donna is being sexually harassed by her superior Earl—in effect blackmailing her because she helped him out of a jam by altering some invoices—Johnny resorts to strong-arm tactics to frighten Earl off. Then, deciding that he and Donna belong in different worlds, he breaks off their relationship and sets out to avenge Mikey. Approaching Rafe and Sunny (who don't recognise him), Johnny enlists their aid in robbing the shipyard, intending to use Sunny's infatuation with him to engineer their downfall. But visiting Johnny's room to plead her love, Donna is found by Sunny looking at photographs of Johnny's face before and after surgery. Taking Donna as a hostage to the cemetery where Johnny has arranged a meeting, Sunny tells Rafe who Johnny really is. Rafe vindictively carves Johnny's new face with a knife before he, Johnny and Sunny gun each other down, leaving Donna to mourn and Drones to close the case.

This must have seemed like a good idea at the time: a role tailor-made for Mickey Rourke as a sleazy small-time crook whose seemingly hardcore shell conceals untapped wells of tenderness, and whose monster-movie ugliness, heart-rendingly misinterpreted by a cruelly cynical world, would hopefully tap the same source of fairy-tale sentimentality as TV's highly successful *Beauty and the Beast* series. In the event, what emerges is a faintly risible mess, torn between a dozen stools and never managing to settle squarely on any of them.

The action quota is taken care of by matching robbery sequences, one at the beginning and one at the end, effectively staged but remarkable only in that most of the viciousness and the nastiest violence is credited to the account of a pretty girl (the Ellen Barkin character). In between times, a magic wand is waved (no very good reason is put forward for the VIP treatment meted out to Johnny Handsome), and within the space of a shot or two of operating theatre and speech therapy exercises, a be-latexed monster is transformed into Mickey Rourke. Around this, reaching out tendrils towards romance and social concern, a busy plot weaves what is presumably intended as a panoramic view of the corrupt and cynical world through which the new-born soul must make its innocent way.

"Real sad story", Lieutenant Drones comments drily, unmoved when the doctor in charge of the case, pleading that Johnny surely deserves a break, accounts for his congenital malformation by explaining that his mother was a junkie whore. Drones' obstinate adherence to the old adage of "once a thief, always a thief", as he prods and nags Johnny towards his fate, may well be a deciding factor in the latter's behaviour; so may the fact that his first encounter with purity is to find it being victimised, as Donna—having bent the law purely out of the kindness of her heart—is blackmailed by the man on whose behalf she sinned.

The trouble is that, with Rourke wandering expressionlessly through the film while the script forces its jigsaw pieces together without regard to whether they fit or make a pattern, the end result is no more than the meaningless sum of its parts. A film-maker like Bresson would undoubtedly have excavated the torments and conflicts behind the mask. In Walter Hill's hands, Johnny Handsome sees his trust betrayed and his best friend murdered; pause, Hamlet-like, for indecision and the acquisition of a new face from a *deus ex machina*; then, with new face making the job easier, he exacts his revenge. Some calculatedly nasty violence and energetic performances apart, so what?

NEW YORK, 10/9/89, p. 83, David Denby

Perhaps the most salient critical question raised by *Johnny Handsome*, a big-studio job all the way, is this one: Can a good film be made by a director with a second-rate mind? Walter Hill, the foundering brain in question, has made some very good movies in the past (*The Warriors, The Long Riders, 48 HRS.*), but the way his career has been evolving recently suggests that he has given in to some sort of primal action-director's crud. *Johnny Handsome* features the kind of underworld-revenge plot much favored in the B-movies of the forties, with the additon of a near-sick-joke disfigurement theme: Mickey Rourke, born deformed, and a lifetime criminal, undergoes reconstructive plastic surgery and returns, pretty and thus unrecognizable, to get back at a ruthless gang of thieves who did him dirt years before.

The movie is wonderfully made-satisfyingly lurid in camera style, with terrifically shot heist sequences and plenty of nasty fun at every moment. And it is generally well acted. Forest Whitaker, Morgan Freeman, and Elizabeth McGovern turn up in small but important roles; Mickey Rourke is quietly bitter and physically impressive as the man with the face. Ellen Barkin, on the other hand, seems to need to demonstrate she can get real down-and-dirty. Playing a murdering slut who enjoys pistol-whipping men across the face, Barkin may think her obvious lip-chewing is a lot more amusing than it actually is. And despite the movie's strengths, Hill's tin-pot fatalism takes its toll. Can a man remake himself by getting a new face? Or will he be spiritually deformed for life? The awful thing is that Hill's gaudily sadomasochistic final scene—a real lulu—gives a definitivie answer to these ridiculous questions.

NEW YORK POST, 9/27/89, p. 19, David Edelstein

The hero (Mickey Rourke) of the brutal, sardonic "Johnny Handsome" combines the nightmare worst of the Elephant Man and the Beast on TV's "Beauty and the Beast." His leonine face is cleft in twain, and blobby protuberances of flesh disfigure every inch of what's left.

It's a face only a mother could love—but even his mother, he says, couldn't deal with it. And that can make a fella mean. The point of the movie is that Johnny is twisted to the core; even after plastic surgery has miraculously given him a GQ puss he can't leave behind the world of robbery and revenge.

The thriller, directed by Walter Hill, has been executed so cleanly and potently that you can't help being riveted—even while protesting that, at heart, the thing is a crock, crippled by its simple-minded script and its boneheaded macho fatalism.

Can this director shoot an action sequence! In the dynamite opening, Johnny and his gang blow into a rare-coin emporium; hard shards of glass explode into the camera as it sweeps from side to side and the robbers (in milky, Mummenschanz-like masks) roar at each other to move faster, faster. The scene is all smash and jangle, with lightning views from the black-and-white surveillance camera and sickening, funhouse-mirror shots down the barrel of guns about to blaze.

Not all goes according to plan, however: Johnny is betrayed in mid-heist by two snarling nasties (Ellen Barkin and Lance Henriksen) who shoot up his buddy (Scott Wilson) and try to take him out, too. Arrested, he's stabbed in prison and ends up in a hospital under the care of a kindly, liberal fat-boy called Dr. Steven Resher (Forest Whitaker), who says things like, "Surgery is a deterrent to criminal recidivism."

He believes he can make Johnny a better person by correcting his disfigurement, but Lt. A.Z. Drones (Morgan Freeman) thinks differently; the lawman knows Johnny is a bad 'un no matter how pretty his features. And when the remodeled Johnny gets paroled and goes to work as a hardhat, Drones is sure it won't be long before the ex-freak starts thinking about settling old scores.

Hill, a stunning action stylist in "Hard Times," "The Warriors" and "The Long Riders," got bored and self-parodic during the last half of the '80s, knocking off hollow Sam Peckinpah imitations and hack jobs like "Red Heat." But he's all there in "Johnny Handsome."

True, his idea of character is (to put it kindly) elemental, and the movie has a sizable dead spot in the center. But for the first time in years you can taste Hill's pleasure in telling a story and his actors' pleasure in playing their parts to the hilt.

Between scenes, the film fades to black; rumbling thunder suggests the iron hand of destiny at work. The pacing is controlled, stately, with lots of witty shots from Johnny's point of view as characters stare into the camera and tell him what an ugly or beautiful sumbitch he is.

Rourke's Johnny, struggling with a speech impediment even when healed, has a muffled voice and moist, wounded eyes; the actor hasn't been this striking since "Diner." There's a muzzy softness in everything he does; even when he pulls a knife on a man who insults him, he pokes the flesh gently with its point, sliding it lightly, caressively around the jugular, the nose, the eyes.

The script, by Ken Friedman, doesn't break the skin, either. The suggestion that Johnny's afraid to be normal isn't explored; he seems to gravitate toward vengeance because the movie gets tired of hard work, clean living and the love of a nice, working-class girl (Elizabeth McGovern). His fatalism is the opportunistic refuge of a blowhard who doesn't quite know what to do with himself when the shooting stops.

But what an amazing cast he has assembled. Freeman, chewing gum and smiling broadly under his Stetson, brings a jaunty bonhomie to Drones' wearying moralism—he sees the whole set-up as a huge joke. ("Well bless my ass," he purrs, staring into the camera at Johnny's new face.) Whitaker, in an even dumber part, suggests the lonely, overweight wonk that gave birth to the do-good surgeon. The rosy McGovern has such a good time with her New Orleans accent that she infuses these saintly clichés with life.

You want villains? Barkin and Henriksen are live wires, the sort of scummy thugs who'd kill you as soon as look at you. They're neon-lit vipers, and in private they don't converse, they hiss imprecations—they're always on the verge of sinking their fangs into each other. Henriksen, his flesh skeleton-tight, is hilariously coiled; Barkin, for the second time in a month, is a smoking wonder.

Under a mop of yellow hair and sporting a tattoo like a welt on her cheekbone, Barkin twists her little mouth into the cruelest of smiles and sashays off in her micro-mini to seduce her latest mark. Her voice is cracked and shrill, with an accent so trashy it makes mean words even meaner. ("Geek" comes out "gake.") I've never seen an actress deliver pistol-whippings with so much relish; she sees a head and she can't wait to bash it in.

NEWSDAY, 9/29/89, Part III/p. 3, Mike McGrady

"Johnny Handsome" is one of those movies where everything—*everything!*—is overstated. One of those movies where gates never click shut when they can clang. Cars don't simply pull away from curbs, they *screech* away. Trucks don't rumble, they roar. Why settle for an ordinary bar when you can have a topless bar? Background music? No, "Johnny Handsome" leaves nothing in the background, not even the music.

When the little things are out of proportion, the big things will be at least equally misshaped. The bad guy (Lance Henriksen) is not merely bad, he wears black leather trousers and slices up faces. His female partner (Ellen Barkin) is more than simply evil: When she's not gut-shooting her criminal cohorts, she's beating up grown men with Tysonic uppercuts. The tough cop (Morgan Freeman) is so tough he can take in a hideously deformed criminal and comment, "You probably got a lotta people feelin' sorry for you . . . Not me." And the good guy (Forest Whitaker), a plastic surgeon who straightens out criminals' features, is not merely good; one more authenticated miracle and he's a cinch for sainthood.

I hold director Walter Hill directly responsible for all this nonsense, this visual shouting. Many years ago, Hill directed the very successful "48HRS.," a Nick Nolte-Eddie Murphy movie with enough solid humor to counterbalance any excesses. Since then, Hill has been involved in—no, responsible for—one dismal absurdity after another: "Brewster's Millions" and "Crossroads" and "Extreme Prejudice" and "Red Heat." The man is proving to be a terrible director, bad enough to drag some genuine talents down with him.

Mickey Rourke is an actor who deserves better. If Rourke's career decisions matched his natural gifts, life would be a succession of movies like "Diner" and "Barfly." Instead, the way things now stand, it's mostly "Angel Heart" and "9½ Weeks" and "A Prayer for the Dying." While Rourke, as Johnny Handsome, provides the film with its few genuinely moving moments, these are entirely too few and too far between.

Handsome is a criminal with deformed features. No, not just deformed; initially, he would seem to be a relative of TV's Alf. During the course of a robbery, Johnny sees his only close friend gunned down by their fellow thieves. While in prison, Johnny runs into the saintly surgeon who gives him his new set of features and he comes out of prison with his new natural disguise, determined to avenge his friend's murder by killing the killers.

The newly prettified Johnny finds employment as a metal worker, wins the love of a beautiful co-worker (Elizabeth McGovern), then throws it all away as he seeks his revenge in a bloody massacre that would surely qualify as depressing if it carried even a hint of reality.

Of all the flick's depressing aspects, none is more downhearted than the caricature created by Barkin, who has been so effective in such movies as "The Big Easy" and "Sea of Love." Here Barkin is presented as the meanest of the mean, the kind of woman who takes one look at the pre-operation Johnny and observes, "Talk about hiring the handicapped!"

And what's the end result of all the exaggeration? "Johnny Handsome" never engaged my mind or my heart; however, the endless shrillness did manage to clear my sinuses.

VILLAGE VOICE, 10/3/89, p. 71, Georgia Brown

Once upon a time (in *The Warriors, The Long Riders, Southern Comfort*, even *48 Hours*) Walter Hill, like Scott, made films that seemed to reflect personal obsessions. *His* featured Odyssean heroes, who have absented themselves from felicity awhile to perform necessary, dirty missions, then wearily fight their way back to home and hearth. It was tense, manly business, occasionally gratifying in the way of Peckinpah. Now, though, Hill settles for ghoulish villains, macho posturing, and flurries of brutality.

In *Johnny Handsome*, Hill's taste for grotesquerie (fulfilled in *Red Heat* by Arnold Schwarzenegger) gets a special workout in Ken Friedman's adaptation of a John Godey novel. Johnny (Mickey Rourke) is a New Orleans drifter born with features no more delicate than the Elephant Man's. Raised in an institution, he excuses his prostitute mother's rejection of him: "I wasn't exactly her dream come true." Johnny's one friend, Mikey (Scott Wilson), gets doublecrossed in a holdup by a really trashy couple, Rafe (Lance Henriksen) and Sunny (Ellen Barkin). While Johnny serves time for the robbery, he aches for revenge.

He also becomes the beneficiary of state-of-the-art surgical procedures when a prison doctor (Forest Whitaker with glasses) sees a perfect chance to test theories about the relation of social rejection to criminal behavior. If Johnny will have a new face, the gentle doctor will get him paroled. The road to rehabilitation is not short, however. Surgery and speech therapy take months, and the movie's momentum bogs down.

The liberal doctor's ideological antagonist is Lieutenant Drones (Morgan Freeman), a hard-bitten detective working on the initial robbery. A patient vulture, Drones swoops in and out of the film flashing a tight smile and reminding Johnny, "I know who you are on the inside." Even Drones, though, has to pronounce the operation's results "fucking amazing." Johnny, now as handsome as Mickey Rourke, gets a job and dates a sweet office worker (Elizabeth McGovern).

Hill works with tight closeups and elegant compositions, but he's unable to maintain tension, and when the ending finally limps into view, it's a real downer without any cathartic power. Rourke generates sympathy enough, but the sluggish script fails to give Johnny potency. Rafe and Sunny's sheer nastiness is comicbook stuff, yet Hill seems riveted by it. Here is a strong cast wasted.

Also reviewed in:
NEW YORK TIMES, 9/29/89, p. C10, Janet Maslin
NEW YORKER, 10/16/89, p. 110, Pauline Kael
VARIETY, 9/13-19/89, p. 39
WASHINGTON POST, 9/29/89, Weekend/p. 37, Roger Piantadosi

KARATE KID PART III, THE

A Columbia Pictures release. *Executive Producer:* Sheldon Schrager. *Producer:* Jerry Weintraub. *Director:* John G. Avildsen. *Screenplay:* Robert Mark Kamen. *Director of Photography:* Steve Yaconelli. *Editor:* John

Carter and John G. Avildsen. *Music:* Bill Conti. *Music Editor:* Stephen A. Hope. *Sound:* Barry Thomas and (music) Dan Wallin. *Sound Editor:* Scott A. Hecker. *Production Designer:* William F. Matthews. *Art Director:* Christopher Burian-Mohr. *Set Designer:* Carl Stensel. *Set Decorator:* Catherine Mann. *Special Effects:* Dennis Dion. *Costumes:* Tom Johnson. *Make-up:* Del Acevedo. *Stunt Coordinator:* Pat E. Johnson. *Running time:* 111 minutes. *MPAA Rating:* PG.

CAST: Ralph Macchio (Daniel La Russo); Noriyuki "Pat" Morita (Mr. Miyagi); Robyn Lively (Jessica); Thomas Ian Griffith (Terry); Martin L. Kove (Kresse); Sean Kanan (Mike Barnes); Jonathan Avildsen (Snake); Christopher Paul Ford (Dennis); Randee Heller (Lucille); Pat E. Johnson (Referee); Rick Hurst (Announcer); Frances Bay (Mrs. Milo); Joseph V. Perry (Uncle Louie); Jan Triska (Milos); Diana Webster (Margaret); Patrick Posada (Man #1); C. Darnell Rose (Delivery Man); Glenn Medeiros (Himself); Gabe Jarret (Rudy); Doc Duhame (Security Guard); Randell Widner (Sparring Partner #1); Raymond S. Sua (Sparring Partner #2); Garth Johnson (Spectator #1); E. David Tetro (Spectator #2); Helen Lin (Tahitian Girl #1); Meilani Figalan (Tahitian Girl #2);

LOS ANGELES TIMES, 6/30/89, Calendar/p. 10, Kevin Thomas

"The Karate Kid Part III" is one film too many. The fresh and inspired 1984 sleeper, a stirring, worthy crowd-pleaser, starred little Ralph Macchio as the new kid in Reseda who defeats the high school bullies when coached in karate by Noriyuki (Pat) Morita, his apartment house handyman. It did cry out for a sequel, which took us to Okinawa for new and reasonably enjoyable adventures. Part III, however, is not merely a disaster of the most uninspired contrivances but is actually unsuitable for youngsters, the series' natural audience. The Karate Kid has gone the way of Rocky (whose series was also launched by director John Avildsen).

Macchio's Danny La Russo and Morita's Mr. Miyagi are back from Okinawa and learn that Martin Kove's Kreese, the nasty proprietor of a karate studio where all those bullies are trained, has gone bankrupt because Danny defeated them all and became a karate champion. Leaving town, Kreese pays a farewell visit to his old Vietnam buddy Silver (a smirky, steely Thomas Ian Griffith), an industrialist who lives in a Frank Lloyd Wright mansion in the Hollywood Hills. Silver, whose life Kreese saved in the war, is inexplicably a raging, ultra-sadistic psychopath. You'd think Silver would merely offer Kreese a job, but no, he sends him off to a Tahiti vacation while he plots revenge against Danny with the relish of Ming the Merciless.

Danny has reluctantly agreed with Mr. Miyagi that he should not defend his title—that the use of karate is to defend one's honor and not to win trophies. Sure enough, after some of the most labored and improbable plot maneuvering ever devised, Danny has to defend his title against a Silver clone (Sean Kanan).

Two things make Part III objectionable for impressionable kids. First, it's absurd that as highly a principled a man as Mr. Miyagi would, after only the slightest protest, allow Danny to spend his college education savings on launching him in a bonsai tree nursery (which never, by the way, seems to attract a single customer). Wouldn't Mr. Miyagi at least want Danny to consult his mother (Randee Heller), who is away the entire film caring for a sick uncle? In short, the film gives the impression that if you're a whiz at karate you don't need a college education. Second, the monstrous Silver offers to coach the unsuspecting Danny in a manner that does serious harm to the youth. Do we really need this protracted display of sadism, which just might give some youngsters some dangerous ideas.

So ridiculous is Part III that Danny doesn't actually expect Mr. Miyagi to understand that he agreed only to defend his title because the bad guys had him and his girlfriend (Robyn Lively) dangling over a cliff. The film defeats Macchio, now nearly down, and Mortia, as skilled as they are, and Kove isn't able to be amusingly villainous in such glum circumstances. In short, writer Robert Mark Kamen gave director Avildsen and his cast too little to work with for "The Karate Kid Part III" (rated a lenient PG) to have gone into production in the first place.

MONTHLY FILM BULLETIN, 9/89, p. 274, Kim Newman

Upon returning from Okinawa (see *The Karate Kid: Part II,* M.F.B., August 1986), under-eighteen karate champion Daniel LaRusso and his mentor Mr. Miyagi decide to set up a bonsai shop. Karate instructor Kreese, whose dojo has gone out of business since Daniel defeated his champion fighter and Miyagi humiliated him in a car-park brawl, appeals to his Vietnam buddy Terry, a toxic waste millionaire, and he agrees to help Kreese get his revenge. Terry hires Mike Barnes, a thuggish young martial artist, and plans to have him brutalise Daniel in this year's championship contest. Miyagi, who doesn't approve of karate being treated as a sport, persuades Daniel not to enter the competition, but Mike begins to put on pressure. He and his thugs steal all the bonsai trees, and when Daniel and his girlfriend Jessica descend into a chasm to find a rare tree Miyagi has brought from Okinawa, Mike hauls up their ropes and refuses to help them up until Daniel signs for the contest. Miyagi refuses to train him, but Terry—posing as a humble instructor—takes him on and educates him in his philosophy of extreme violence, hoping to get at Miyagi by perverting his disciple. Terry hires a thug to pick on Daniel at a night-club, and Daniel breaks the latter's nose. He then rejects Terry, who reveals himself to be in league with Kreese and Mike. Miyagi finally agrees to coach Daniel and, in the championship bout, the Karate Kid takes gruelling punishment from Mike, but ultimately triumphs.

Like such diverse parts three as *A Nightmare on Elm Street* and *Porky's Revenge*, this instalment ignores most of the narrative amendments made in the first sequel and reintroduces major characters from the inital film left out of the follow-up. With Ralph Macchio rather plumply leaving adolescence in the lead and "Pat" Morita reduced to Charlie Chan-isms ("For a person with no forgiveness in heart, losing even worse punishment than death"), the star of this picture, by default, is Thomas Ian Griffith as the Mephistophelean millionaire who amuses himself torturing his best friend's enemies: "I'm gonna make them suffer and suffer and suffer, and when I think they've suffered enough I'm gonna start with the pain". He brings some genuinely nasty villainy to a series that is otherwise overwhelmingly good-natured to the point of tedium. However, the plot devices needed to get Miyagi to agree to coach Daniel for the big fight become extraordinarily dull, and young love, meanwhile, has rarely been shown so boringly on screen. The unfortunately named Robyn Lively replaces the equally bland heroines of the first two parts as the weak third corner of the triangle mainly propped up by Macchio and Morita.

NEW YORK POST, 6/30/89, p. 27, Jami Bernard

It's time to enter Ralph Macchio into the "Picture of Dorian Gray" sweepstakes of celebrities whose faces stay young while their gigs get older and older. Macchio is back, sputtering and fuming over whether to defend his championship title, in "The Karate Kid III." In real life, Macchio is ready for his second mortgage, but in this sequel to the successful karate kickfests, he is still the eager yong grasshopper learning at the knee of mentor Pat Morita.

Home from Japan (see "Karate Kid II"), diminutive Daniel LaRusso (Macchio) decides to blow his college money on opening a bonsai shop for Mr. Miyagi (Morita). Aside from a phone call from his mom early in the movie, no one ever bothers to check on how that education is progressing, so Daniel and Mr. Miyagi are free to set up shop, cultivating the dainty bonsai trees and living a life of Zenlike tranquility.

The bonsai tree serves as a metaphor for Daniel's inner strength ("Like tree has strong root, now so do you, Daniel-san"). But really, the constant pruning and nursing of the delicate trees is more reminiscent of how the film makers have milked as many greenback offshoots as possible from the original, refreshing "Karate Kid." This is one of those sequels that eloquently proves the point that people are more comfortable seeing again what they've seen before.

Martin Kove is back, briefly, as the bonsai boys' nemesis, the one who gives karate a bad name. Kove turns over the reins of revenge to his friend, the evil Terry Silver (Thomas Ian Griffith), a smooth character with long, slicked-back hair, a millionaire black belt who is equally at home dealing in plutonium futures as snapping someone's kneecap.

Terry wants to get Daniel back in the ring to defend his title against Terry's protege, dubbed "The Bad Boy of Karate," so you can imagine it's going to be a tough fight. But Mr. Miyagi refuses to help Daniel train, because karate must serve a higher and nobler purpose. Also, it would make the movie end too soon.

The drama revolves around Daniel's sneaking out on his mentor to train with Terry, who has tricked him into thinking he's a good guy. This new kind of training has Daniel bashing his bare feet and knuckles into slabs of hard wood, making them bleed and swell. Daniel may be strong of root, but he is weak of brain and doesn't see it's a trap.

But don't think for a moment that "Karate Kid III" is out to cheat its audience of some bang-up fight sequences. Griffith is tall, lean and mean and has great form; compared to him, Macchio's little crane-dance "kata" exercise doesn't look all that imposing. The movie is sprinkled with enough martial arts altercations to please the fans, although the Rockyesque finish (remember, director John Avildsen is a "Rocky" alumnus) doesn't quite add up and some of the confrontations seem rushed, as if the actors were in the path of an oncoming train.

Griffith is more than adequate as the vengeful meanie. "I'm gonna make them suffer, and suffer, and suffer, and when I think they've suffered enough, *then I'll start with the pain!*" he promises.

Sleepy-lidded Morita is great, as usual, as the omniscient mentor with the sly sense of humor. Maybe they should dump the kid and do a "Karate Old Guy" series, as the audience reserves its biggest cheers for Mr. Miyagi. Macchio seems to be overcompensating for his age by acting like an exasperated hothead. Neither the discipline of karate nor a love interest (Robyn Lively) can make him fly right.

As amiable as the "Karate Kid" movies are, they glorify pain and sadism. You know something's wrong when the heartstrings are tugged not by human accomplishment, but by the kidnapping of a bonsai tree.

NEWSDAY, 6/30/89, Part III/p. 3, Mike McGrady

Five years have passed since "The Karate Kid" earned its Black Belt at the box office, but the characters are only one year older in "The Karate Kid Part III."

Again, teenage Daniel LaRusso (Ralph Macchio, now 27) must match kicks and chops with a bigger, stronger, meaner opponent. Again, Mr. Miyagi (Noriyuki "Pat" Morita), saves Daniel's butt when the bad guys gang up on him. Again, Daniel has a new girlfriend (Robin Lively succeeds Tamlyn Tomita and Elisabeth Shue).

Tired of the same old formula? You'll be happy to learn that the second "Karate Kid" sequel contains a welcome, even if unintentional, element of selfparody. We've gone from the rudimentary "Rocky" dramatics of the original to the Okinawan feuds and face-saving of "Part II" to the sort of cartoon villainy that should be sanctioned by the World Wrestling Federation.

Kindly recall Kreese (Martin Kove), the evil Viet vet who coached the dirty Cobras in "The Karate Kid." Ever since Mr. Miyagi brought him to his knees at the start of "Part II," Kreese has been on the skids. Who wants to learn karate from a blowhard who can't lick a semi-elderly Oriental philosopher half his size? As "Part III" opens, Kreese close his dojo and slinks away from L.A.

Enter Kreese's patron, Terry Silver (Thomas Ian Griffith), super-evil karate master and super-rich trafficker in chemical waste. Kreese saved Silver's life in 'Nam; now Terry returns the favor by setting in motion an elaborate plot to destroy Daniel and Mr. Miyagi and review his war buddy's career in karate education.

"'I'm gonna make 'em suffer and suffer and suffer," Silver vows. "And when they've suffered enough, I'll start with the pain." Jesse "The Body" Ventura couldn't have said it better.

First, Terry handpicks a challenger for Daniel's All-Valley championship—Mike Barnes (Sean Kanan), the notorious "Bad Boy of Karate." Next, Barnes coerces Daniel into defending the title, against the sage advice of his instructor. (Mr. Miyagi say: "If karate used to defend plastic metal trophy, karate no mean nothing.")

Next, Silver poses as a nice fellow, supplants Mr. Miyagi as Daniel's coach and puts the impressionable lad on a training regimen designed to make him suffer and suffer and suffer. Poor Daniel doesn't realize he's been bamboozled till Barnes, Silver and the long-absent Kreese surround the kid and say, in effect, "booga-booga."

The climax of "Part III" closely resembles that of the original, with Daniel overmatched in the tournament final and Mr. Miyagi worrying on the sidelines. But the Bad Boy's handlers, Silver and Kreese, steal the show with their taunting, gloating, raging and scheming. If Bobby "The Brain" Heenan ever retires from professional wrestling management, either Griffith or Kove could fill his role admirably.

Some of us prefer to think director John G. Avildsen and writer Robert Mark Kamen chose to have a bit of fun with "The Karate Kid" before Daniel LaRusso finally retires. But as Mr. Miyagi might say: "If 'Part III' rake in another hundred million, 'Part IV' would be matter of honor."

Also reviewed in:
NEW YORK TIMES, 6/30/89, p. C17, Caryn James
VARIETY, 7/5-11/89, p. 18
WASHINGTON POST, 6/30/89, p. B9, Rita Kempley

KICKBOXER

A Kings Road Entertainment release. *Producer:* Mark DiSalle. *Director:* Mark DiSalle and David Worth. *Screenplay:* Glenn Bruce. *Story:* Mark DiSalle and Jean-Claude Van Damme. *Director of Photography:* Jon Kranhouse. *Editor:* Wayne Wahrman. *Music:* Paul Hertzog. *Music Editor:* Cliff Kohlweck. *Sound:* Ara Ashjian, Greg Cheever, Art Schiro, Grant Roberts, and (music) Barry Keenan. *Sound Editor:* Mike Le Mare. *Producation Designer:* Shay Austin. *Art Director:* Sita Yeung and Chaiyan Chunsuttiwat. *Set Dresser:* Lai Yuk. *Special Effects:* Tuffy Lau, Samrit Sripaitakkulvilai, Bang, and Daeng. *Costumes:* Ella Yu and Mutita Na Songkla. *Make-up:* Earl Ellis, Mable Fung, and Tommy Chan. *Stunt Coordinator:* John Cheung. *Fight Scenes:* Jean Claude Van Damme. *Running time:* 97 minutes. *MPAA Rating:* R.

CAST: Jean-Claude Van Damme (Kurt Sloane); Dennis Alexio (Eric Sloane); Dennis Chan (Xian); Tong Po (Tong Po); Haskell Anderson (Winston Taylor); Rochelle Ashana (Mylee); Steve Lee (Freddy Li); Richard Foo (Tao Liu); Ricky Liu (Big Thai Man); Sin Ho Ying and Tony Chan (Huge Village Men); Brad Kerner and Dean Harrington (U.S. Announcers); Mark DiSalle, Richard Santoro, Louis Roth, and Nickolas James (U.S. Reporters); John Ladalski (U.S. Referee); Matthew Cheung (Surgeon); Wong Wing Shun (Lo); Joann Wong (Tao Liu's Wife); Michael Lee (Old Man in Village); Africa Chu (Messenger); Zennie Reynolds (U.S. Fighter); Montri Vongbuter and Amnart Komolthorn (Ancient Warriors); Pairat Lavilard (Gym Officer); Kanthima Vutti (Eric's Girl); Ong Soo Han (Tong Po's Opponent); Priwan Sriharajmontri (Kurt's Opponent).

LOS ANGELES TIMES, 9/11/89, Calendar/p. 6, Chris Willman

In lieu of John Cusack mastering the art of kickboxing over in England in "Say Anything II," which may not be forthcoming for a while, alas, fans of the brutal sport have to make do for now with Jean-Claude Van Damme kicking some nasty Thailand booty in the egregiously dull "Kickboxer."

This may not be the dumbest action picture of the year, but it's not for lack of trying. Insurmountable plot implausibilities, rampant racial stereotyping, superfluous nudity and inhuman amounts of comically exaggerated violence—"Kickboxer" has it all. But the real kicker to all this, so to speak, is the use of jarring shifts in tone, perhaps to suggest the moral rootlessness of its characters, or maybe to suggest that its writers and directors got kicked upside the head themselves by accident during the production.

First it's a *vengeance-is-mine-sayeth-the-action-hero* flick, as Jean-Claude witnesses his brother (Dennis Alexio) getting his spinal cord cracked in the ring by a Thai champion/bully. To avenge his sibling's paralysis, he trains with a witty 'n' wise martial-arts master (Dennis Chen), and suddenly it's "The Karate Kid" redux. The tone gets lighter, and Van Damme engages in pratfall humor and smooches with his new Thai sweetie in the rain, and brother cheers them on from his wheelchair.

Lest audiences think the training hero is losing the eye o' the tiger amid all that sweetness, though, the evil Thai champ kidnaps the brother, rapes the girlfriend and—get this—*seriously injures Jean-Claude's dog.* Thus the stakes are high when the big kickoff comes and the mortal enemies fight "the ancient way," by dipping their bandaged hands in resin and broken cola bottles. (Way back in those days there were no national kickboxing commissioners to spoil all the fun.)

Come picture's end, the bad guy has had his ugly mug wupped halfway to kingdom come—which hardly seems like ample karmic comeuppance for the rape of the love interest, which never would have happened if Van Damme hadn't pursued his grudge. But what's a little female sexual violation when a man's man is busy setting the record straight?

In this cartoon world, Jean-Claude's gal can recover from that rape just as easily as his dog recovers from its critical wound. Somebody here could use a good swift kick in the seat, and it's not the Thai villain.

MONTHLY FILM BULLETIN, 9/89, p. 274, Verina Glaessner

Eric Sloane, American kickboxing exponent, wins the national championship in California and then tells his brother Kurt that he intends to go to Bangkok, the home of kickboxing, to take on the best there is. This turns out to be Tong Po, whom Kurt tries to dissuade his brother from fighting (having seen him attacking a concrete column before the bout) and who quickly finishes the challenger off with several crippling blows to his back. Kurt is helped to get him to the hospital by one of the spectators, Winston Taylor, an American burdened by the guilt of having been unable to save a buddy in Vietnam. When he is told that Eric will never walk again, Kurt declares that he will confront Tong Po in the ring and defeat him; unable to find a teacher in Bangkok willing to train him, Kurt is directed by Taylor to Xian, a Muay Thai master who lives in retreat in the jungle. Making his way there, Kurt is first caught in a trap and then sent by Xian on an errand which leads him into a fight with gangsters in the employ of Freddy Li, Tong Po's manager. Xian then accepts him as a pupil and puts him through a rigorous training schedule, while Kurt also makes friends with Xain's niece, Mylee, who runs the village store. Kurt wins a bout with Li's number two kickboxing champion, and a fight is set up with Tong Po. Eric, now out of hospital, tries unsuccessfully to dissuade his brother, but Li has his men kidnap Eric and Mylee, and the lattter is raped by Tong Po. Released, she asks Winston not to reveal to Kurt what happened. In the bout—fought with fists bound with hemp and dipped in resin and broken glass—Kurt initially comes off worse, and is told by Li that if he does not stay the set number of rounds his brother will die slowly. But Xian, with the help of Winston, who overcomes his fear that he is a coward, rescues Eric, and they arrive at the fight with Mylee. They begin the chant of "White warrior" with which Kurt's victory over his previous foe had been greeted. Seething now with righteous anger (Tong Po has told him of the rape), Kurt throws aside all restraint and defeats his opponent.

Kickboxer plays a number of its cards absolutely correctly. It sticks closely to the *données* of the genre, for one thing. There is the revenge motif, the scenes of gangster intimidation of the innocent (here Mylee), the prolonged training sessions carried out with increasingly *recherché* equipment under the instruction of a discriminating recluse rather than in a workaday gymnasium, and there is the climactic bout with spectacular weaponry (the glass-spiled gloves finally thrown off in favour of burning poles). There are also moral tests of courage, fortitude and ingenuity. A semblance of street credibility is lent by location shooting unglossy enough to recall Bruce Lee's *Big Boss* some fifteen years ago, although *Kickboxer* carries none of the wider implications of Lee's balletic streetfighting adventure. For one thing, the racial terrain has been changed, and it is a very European Jean Claude Van Damme who avenges the defeat of his ugly American brother, Dennis Alexio. European articulateness and charm are allowed to win through where a red-neck propensity for "kickin' ass" has signally failed. Whatever the political implications, the fights are persuasively mounted and Van Damme, with an eye perhaps to Schwarzenegger's mantle, exhibits some of the latter's goofy charm if not his over-blown physique.

NEW YORK POST, 9/9/89, p. 17, Jami Bernard

Before we discuss the merits of "Kickboxer"—and that won't take long—let's cut to the chase. Movies in which grown men beat each other up real good need a special hook, like a comedian's schtick, something to set it apart from other movies in which grown men beat each other up real good. In "Kickboxer," that hook is a way of fighting called the "ancient style."

The ancients must have been some fun bunch. They wrapped their fists in hemp (ancient burlap), dipped them in honey and then rolled them in crushed glass. The film makers must have figured that by the time the big climactic finale rolls around, the audience will have grown restless with the simple art of kickboxing and will need more incentive to sit it out. There are just so many variations on the kick to the head, after all.

Anyway, hemp and honey and cut glass can't be so bad, else why would the bad guy lick his knuckles with such obvious relish?

Well, maybe the ancient style isn't for everyone. Neither is "Kickboxer." Neither is its handsome star, Jean-Claude Van Damme, who wants so desperately to drink with the big boys—Schwarzenegger, Stallone, Norris—that he has made several genre homages in a row ("Bloodsport" and "Cyborg" preceded this one).

Van Damme plays Kurt Sloane, younger brother of Eric (Dennis Alexio), the U.S. heavyweight kickbox champion. Kickboxing, by the way, is like boxing, only the guy does a split while standing up so that his toe goes up your nose. Despite the violence, it's really very graceful.

Eric is pretty cocky and decides to take on the champion of Thailand, where the kids kickbox before they can walk. Eric takes along Kurt as his waterboy, although he hopes Kurt will grow up to be a lawyer.

Incidentally, Kurt has an impenetrable Belgian accent, and his brother Eric sounds like a street kid; they explain this plot hole by saying that one brother was raised by dad in America, the other by mom in Europe.

Well, Eric gets his head kicked 'round the block by the Thai champ, Tong Po (playing himself; a scary thought), and gets his spinal cord snapped as well. Kurt, after going off on a crying jag, vows revenge. Visions of the bar exam go right out of his head; now he wants to train in the ways of the martial art called Muay Thai and lick big ugly Tong Po (who will be busy at that point licking his glass-coated fists).

Now it's time for the generic sensei, or martial arts master, the kind that we know so well from movies like "The Karate Kid." Xian (Dennis Chan) has all the traits we have come to expect from a wise old teacher: an inscrutable sense of humor, unusual aphorisms ("Never make decision on empty stomach") and a Machiavellian system of educating his pupil. Exercise regimens include dropping boulders on Kurt's chest from great heights, forcing his legs into a split with a system of hemp and pulleys (no glass shards, though) and telling a barful of meanies that Kurt says their mothers have sex with mules. Don't try these maneuvers at home, kids.

There's also a love interest who is treated with far more macho unfairness than any movie warrants, and a Vietnam veteran who chauffeurs Kurt around Bangkok in his love van.

Certain training secenes were filmed in Thailand's Ancient City, an atomospheric open-air shrine/museum that makes a beautiful backdrop. The final punch-out is set in a kind of Roman gladiator dungeon, also atmospheric.

Van Damme, a former karate champion himself, choreographed the fight scenes, and some of the moves are spectacular and inventive (choppy editing detracts from the effect). The one-star rating is for the quality of the movie as a whole, but those who enjoy watching feet being pushed up people's noses will come away satiated (at least I hope so; we don't want poeple like that roaming the streets unless it's out of their system).

Van Damme is physically graceful, great material for low-budget action films. But his acting is stiff and his accent is too thick to be charming; it sounds like the script provided more of a challenge than the biggest, meanest, hairiest kickboxer alive.

NEWSDAY, 9/9/89, Part II/p. 15, Terry Kelleher

Wonder no more whether there'll be another "Karate Kid" sequel after the box-office flop of "The Karate Kid: Part III."

"Karate Kid IV" is already here.

Oh, the names and a few details have been changed. This picture is called "Kickboxer," and its star is Belgian bruiser Jean-Claude Van Damme, who looks a good deal more formidable than Ralph Macchio and has the martial-arts trophies to prove it. The setting is Thailand, not L.A. or Okinawa.

But if you've seen any "Karate Kid" movie—or any "Rocky," for that matter—you can recite this plot in your sleep. Eric Sloane (karate champ Dennis Alexio), the cocky American kickboxing titlist, blows into Bangkok and promptly gets his clock cleaned by the toughest Thai of them all— the massive, brutal, thoroughly reprehensible Tong Po. (Since Tong Po plays himself, he probably sees the character as a swell fellow.) Eric is left paralyzed and his kid brother Kurt (Van Damme) vows to gain revenge by vanquishing Tong Po in the ring.

First, however, he must study the ancient form of combat known as "Muay Thai," roughly translated as "really dirty kickboxing." Kurt, knowing that a droll Pat Morita type makes the perfect mentor under these circumstances, asks Xian (Dennis Chan) to train him. Xian, also familiar with movie ritual, puts his new protege on a regimen that combines punishing exercises, menial chores and romance with his beautiful niece Mylee (Rochelle Ashana).

Kurt has one tuneup bout in which he blitzes his opponent Mike Tyson-style and earns the nickname "Bak Shung" (which means—no kidding—"White Warrior"). Tong Po's backers grant Kurt a shot at the big guy, but are willing to use any means—foul or fouler—to insure an unfair fight. It takes a Bak Shung to beat these odds.

Mark DiSalle, the producer and co-director (with David Worth), boasts that his was the first film company permitted to shoot in the Ancient City, a remarkable outdoor museum outside Bangkok. Unfortunately, the story of "Kickboxer" is such a museum piece that everything about the movie looks ancient.

Van Damme, who also starred for DiSalle in last year's "Bloodsport," does more than beat on people in "Kickboxer." He sheds a few tears, even shows off his disco dance moves. There's no need to work on his accent, because the script claims his character was raised in Belgium.

Hey, this acting's a snap.

Also reviewed in:
VARIETY, 8/30–9/5/89, p. 28

KINJITE: FORBIDDEN SUBJECTS

A Cannon Films release of a Golan-Globus production. *Executive Producer:* Menahem Golan and Yoram Globus. *Producer:* Pancho Kohner. *Director:* J. Lee Thompson. *Screenplay:* Harold Nebenzal. *Director of Photography:* Gideon Porath. *Editor:* Peter Lee Thompson and Mary E. Jochem. *Music:* Greg DeBelles. *Music Editor:* Virginia S. Ellsworth and John LaSalandra. *Sound:* Craig Felburg. *Sound Editor:* Tony Garber. *Art Director:* W. Brooke Wheeler. *Set Decorator:* Margaret C. Fischer. *Set Dresser:* Lance Clarke, Craig Gadsby, and Neil B. Wolfson. *Special Effects:* Burt C. Dalton. *Costumes:* Michael Hoffman. *Make-up:* Carla Fabrizi. *Stunt Coordinator:* Ernie Orsatti. *Running time:* 97 minutes. *MPAA Rating:* R.

CAST: Charles Bronson (Lieutenant Crowe); Perry Lopez (Eddie Rios); Juan Fernandez (Duke); Peggy Lipton (Kathleen Crowe); James Pax (Hiroshi Hada); Sy Richardson (Lavonne); Marion Kodama Yue (Mr. Kazuko Hada); Bill McKinney (Father Burke); Gerald Castillo (Captain Tovar); Nicole Eggert (DeeDee); Amy Hathaway (Rita Crowe); Kumiko Hayakawa (Fumiko Hada); Michelle Wong (Setsuko Hada); Sam Chew Jr. (McLane); Sumant (Pakistani Hotel Clerk); Alex Hyde-White (English Instructor); Jim Ishida (Nakata); Jill Ito (Japanese Hostess, Tokyo); Leila Hee Olsen (Nobu-Chan); Richard Egan Jr. (Vince); Deonca Brown (Louise); Sheila Gale Kandlbinder (Simming Coach); Chris Bennett (School Photographer); George Van Noy (Race Starter); Helen Lin (Tokyo Subway Girl); Richard E. Butler (Joey, Deli Owner); James Ogawa (Kokuden Representative); Bill Cho Lee (Ota); Cynthia Gouw (Japanese Hostess, L.A.); Veronica Carothers (Blonde Hostess); Alonzo Brown Jr. (Mugger); Michael Chong (Lieutenant Lim); Yung Sun (Grey Haired Japanese); Shaun Shimoda (Japanese Calligraphy Teacher); Mindy Simon (Schooligirl); Samuel E. Woods (Hot Dog Vendor); Rob Narita (Japanese School Principal); Yuri Ogawa (Mrs. Ota); Shelli Rae and Jessica Younger (Duke's Girls); William Brochtrup (Hairdresser); Laura Crosson (Officer Petrini); Tom Morga (Krieger); Kim Lee (Porno Actress); Marilyn Frank (Lesbian Pedophile); John F. McCarthy (Porno Theater Manger); Jerome Thor (Perverted Gentleman); Erez Yaoz (Rosario); Robert Axelrod (Security Guard); Elisabeth Chavez (Marie Rios); Simon Maldonado (Eddie Rios Jr.); Don Morton (Turnkey); Jay S. York (Duke's Cellmate); Lane Leavitt (Crane Operator); Jophery Brown and Clifford Strong (Duke's Thugs).

LOS ANGELES TIMES, 2/3/89, Calendar/p. 11, Michael Wilmington

From one angle, "Kinjite: Forbidden Subjects" is just another Charles Bronson action thriller—a bit sleazier and more repellent than most—in which Bronson is put through his patented paces and car chases by director J. Lee Thompson, a brazen old pro who apparently doesn't care any more whom he offends.

Child prostitution, pornography, cocaine, rape, public masturbation, sadism, extreme violence, racial stereotyping: The unsavory scenes pile up thick and fast. On one hand, we have a villain, an elegant, amoral pimp named Duke (Juan Fernandez, the pretty-boy sadist of Stone's "Salvador") who hooks children on drugs. On the other, we have a hero, Bronson's Lt. Crowe, who's pathologically protective of his teenage daughter, brutalizes suspects mercilessly and explodes in racist tantrums.

Trapped between them is a "respectable" Japanese businessman (James Pax) who fondles a teenage girl—Crowe's daughter, no less—on a bus and whose own daughter is kidnaped by the pimp. Who is there to choose among this deviant trio, as Thompson keeps crisscrossing back and forth, driving them to mutual release or perdition? Isn't this the same sordid farrago we get served again and again, usually over the sleek, vacant machismo of a Stallone or a Schwarzenegger?

Maybe. Maybe not. Bronson and the 75-year-old Thompson have made nine movies together, starting with 1976's "St. Ives." This is the strangest, most intense of the lot.

The movie's unusual scenario, by Harold Nebenzal, is desperately symmetrical. It keeps sabotaging any moral frame of reference. Most of the time, Crowe is a man possessed, off-kilter, exorcising his own sexual demons in increasingly grotesque, and almost gratuitous, explosions of violence.

Unlike the Stallone-Schwarzenegger specials, the violence is rarely justified. It just keeps accumulating, insanely, driving Crowe and Duke to greater feats of deviance and sadism, culminating in a lurid, appalling climax. After every outburst, Bronson usually has a shamed, naughty expression—after he advances on a sado-masochist, or forces a $25,000 Rolex watch down the pimp's throat. These are his own "Kinjite" or forbidden subjects, just as Pax's are the public molestations.

"Kinjite" is a pretty odd, murky stew. If you think you might be offended by it, don't go. You will be. Thompson has always had an evil sense of humor, and the movie repeatedly crosses the line between dramatizing a situation and exploiting it, exposing racism or moral rot and almost indulging in it.

But the disturbance you feel in watching "Kinjite" doesn't just come because it has a sordid subject, some bad scenes or a heavy cargo of shock and sleaze, but because it leaves us, much of the time, with no moral anchor. "Kinjite" (MPAA rated R for sex, violence, nudity, drug use, abuse of children and language) is a hard genre movie with something different...though not everyone will have stomachs strong enough to look for it.

NEW YORK POST, 2/3/89, p. 23, Jami Bernard

Charles Bronson is back, and he's mad. He's mad because he's doing yet another action *cum* vigilante flick, and even *he* is getting bored.

This time he's a cop, Lt. Crowe, who has arrested one too many pimps. The work is getting to him. One day, he even gives a john a taste of his own medicine, by using a plastic implement on the guy where the sun don't shine. Is Lt. Crowe turning gay? Or is he just in need of a vacation?

He turns to his wife for sympathy. She is more sympathetic than most, because she is Peggy Lipton, who used to be in "The Mod Squad." Not only has Lipton been demoted to housewife, but in their one kissing scene—and come on, it's just a smooch—Bronson screws up his face with absolute distaste. Bring on the sick revenge scenes, he seems to be saying.

But I digress, and so does "Kinjite," a rambling, disjointed movie about Crowe's efforts to stop a pimp called Duke from specializing in young girls. "Kinjite" is the Japanese word for "forbidden subjects," although nothing seems to be forbidden in this movie.

When a Japanese businessman's daughter is abducted, Crowe is called in. Crowe doesn't give a flying plastic implement about this guy's daughter, because Crowe's own daughter was once molested—well, touched—by an Asian, and now Crowe hates all Asians with a passion.

It happens that the kidnapped girl's dad is the same guy who once made a pass at Crowe's daughter. That's the beauty of Hollywood.

Now, who are we to like in this movie? In an effort perhaps to humanize Bronson, he has been allowed heart (he brings deli sandwiches to the local priest) and opinions ("California nouvelle cuisine is finished"). But oddly enough, director J. Lee Thompson allows Bronson to appear to be certifiably insane, not only to his Mod Squad alumnus wife, but to his tried-&-true movie audience as well.

Shall we like the Japanese businessman then? Much time is spent showing Mr. Hada (James Pax) foolishly pawing the geisha girls back home, and then telling his wife, "Your sexual gifts are few and bitter." Once in America, Hada tries to feel up the first teenager he sees.

So naturally, the audience is going to turn to Duke the pimp (an oily Juan Fernandez). Duke dresses nice, has dreamy eyes, and is not in the least perturbed by having no morals. To prevent us from siding with the pimp, Lt. Crowe qualifies all references to him ("that sleazebag Duke," "that...head Duke," etc.).

So there's no one on screen to root for, and even though things blow up real good at the end, there's not much action for the action fans. "Nothing for anyone" seems to be the motto at work here. Bronson looks annoyed and distracted, and his typically wooden delivery has gotten so much more wooden that you'd have to count his rings to see how old he is.

"Kinjite" delights in suggesting tortures beyond the imagination. There are shots of briefcases full of sex implements; a gang rape scene is shot by showing a door opening and closing as various men come out pulling up their zippers. It is a profoundly sleazy movie that manages at the same time to be dull.

Also reviewed in:
NEW YORK TIMES, 2/4/89, p.17, Janet Maslin,
VARIETY, 2/1–7/89, p.20
WASHINGTON POST, 3/6/89, p. C2, Richard Harrington

K-9

A Universal Pictures release. *Executive Producer:* Donna Smith. *Producer:* Lawrence Gordon and Charles Gordon. *Director:* Rod Daniel. *Screenplay:* Steven Siegel and Scott Myers. *Director of Photography:* Dean Semler. *Editor:* Lois Freeman-Fox. *Music:* Miles Goodman. *Music Editor:* Nancy Fogarty. *Sound:* Donald Summer. *Sound Editor:* Richard L. Anderson. *Production Designer:* George Costello. *Art Director:* Jay

Burkhardt. *Set Designer:* Rance Barela. *Set Decorator:* Maria Caso. *Set Dresser:* Cindy Rebman. *Special Effects:* Bob Ahmanson. *Costumes:* Eileen Kennedy. *Make-up:* Charles Balazs. *Stunt Coordinator:* Gary Combs. *Running time:* 105 minutes. *MPAA Rating:* PG-13.

CAST: James Belushi (Dooley); Mel Harris (Tracy); Kevin Tighe (Lyman); Ed O'Neill (Brannigan); Jerry Lee (K-9); James Handy (Byers); Daniel Davis (Halstead); Cotter Smith (Gilliam); John Snyder (Freddie); Pruitt Taylor Vince (Benny the Mule); Sherman Howard (Dillon); Jeff Allin (Chad); Bob Ari (Dr. Saunders); Alan Blumenfeld (Rental Salesman); Bill Sadler (Salesman Don); Marjorie Bransfield (Hostess); Mark Mooring (Cop); Jerry Levine (Ernie); Rick Cicetti (Waiter); Dan Castellaneta (Maitre d'); Wendel Meldrum (Pretty Girl with Dog); Coleen Morris (Woman in Rolls Royce); John Castellanos (Man in Rolls Royce); McKeiver Jones III (Sergeant); J.W. Smith (Pimp); Dean Hill (Butler); Gary Combs (Sculley); Steve Artiaga (Latino Employee); Lela Ivey (Nurse); Vic Cuccia (Security Guard); Ralph Elias (Officer); Richard Landus Kent (Pedestrian); Michael Dean Wise (Burt).

LOS ANGELES TIMES, 4/28/89, Calendar/p. 17, Kevin Thomas

"K-9" is a buddy movie with a difference: one of the guys is a dog. That's just fine because James Belushi and his handsome co-star, a German shepherd named Jerry Lee (on screen and off), are as spiffy a team as Butch Cassidy and the Sundance Kid. Jerry Lee, named for Mr. Lewis, is a real killer, too.

Cast as a member of the San Diego Police Department K-9 Corps, Jerry Lee can go for the throat (and other vulnerable parts of the body) if you're one of the bad guys. At other times, Jerry Lee is the complete charmer, albeit always independent and unpredictable. He never cottons to the notion that Belushi's Detective Tom Dooley is the senior partner of the team just because he is the human.

Actually, Jerry Lee is just what Dooley needs. Dooley is a headstrong, corner-cutting chance taker, the kind of cop forever in hot water and who has always resisted working with a partner. (You've met the type a million times before on the screen and on the tube; thankfully, Belushi is able to play Dooley deftly for laughs.) In helping the detective go after a drug kingpin (Kevin Tighe, gleefully nasty), Jerry Lee proves he is far more valuable to Dooley than for his ability to sniff out narcotics.

In Steven Siegel and Scott Myers' serviceable rather than inspired script, the plot is standard, even stale cops-and-robbers fantasy, a throwaway device setting up the funny and touching relationship between Dooley and the German shepherd. Jerry Lee may be an exceptionally bright animal, but his trainer Karl Lewis Miller deserves much credit for making him seem so human. There is a warm, robust, good-natured quality to Belushi that makes his Detective Dooley easy to take. Mel Harris certainly is a good sport as Dooley's rich, elegant lady who clearly adores Dooley for his love-making abilities rather than his intellect. (She was, Dooley recalls, reading Celine on the beach at La Jolla when he first noticed her.)

That the plot is never developed beyond the routine and that the jokes are not all thigh-slappers, although there are a few, keeps "K-9" (PG-13 for some violence and raunchiness) from being more than a minor effort. But as such, it's enjoyable, thanks not only to its charismatic duo, but also to the skilled comedy direction of Rod Daniel, whose strong sense of pacing is enhanced by Miles Goodman's driving but not overpowering score.

MONTHLY FILM BULLETIN, 10/89, p. 304, Philip Strick

On the trail of Lyman, a major drug dealer, narcotics cop Thomas Dooley narrowly avoids an ambush which leaves his car a write-off. Trying unsuccessfully to appease the girlfriend, Tracy, with whom he was supposed to be spending the evening, he goes out after Freddie, a small-time crook he suspects of having set him up for the attack. Beaten into atonement, Freddie reveals that a large consignment of drugs is being stored at one of Lyman's warehouses. Now all Dooley needs is a new car, which his superiors refuse to supply, and a partner, which they insist he accepts, and he has Lyman cornered. Coolly sorting out an armed siege for a colleague, Brannigan, who is impatient to catch a plane, he strikes a bargain for as replacement vehicle and goes to the San Diego Police K-9 Training Facility to select the one kind of partner he feels he can tolerate—a dog. He is assigned an Alsatian called Jerry Lee, intelligent to the point of eccentricity and said to have the best nose in the business for drug detection. Together they raid Lyman's warehouse, but the dog traces nothing more than a joint being smoked in a cupboard. Dooley's confidence in his new partner is restored, however, when Jerry Lee rescues him from a gang of thugs in a bar-room. He takes the dog home to meet Tracy, but the night is constantly interrupted by Jerry Lee's apparently jealous behaviour. Next day, after tracking Lyman, Dooley is again ambushed in his car but after a chase and a struggle his assailant is killed. Jerry Lee sniffs out a drug cache hidden in the man's car, and Dooley realises that Lyman stores his drug shipments inside vehicles with the help of a car dealer, Halstead. Learning that Tracy has been kidnapped, he bursts in on a lavish dinner party hosted by Lyman and creates chaos until dragged away by the police. He hopes that this will convince Lyman it is now safe to shift a major delivery, and Halstead is seen leaving with a laden transporter-lorry, which Jerry Lee brings to a halt. At the rendezvous revealed by Halstead, a confrontation leaves Lyman dead and Jerry Lee wounded. The dog is rushed to hospital where Dooley, reunited with Tracy, agonises over his partner. When the cop declares his loyalty the dog makes a prompt recovery, and the three of them drive off on vacation.

Chiefly providing the excuse for James Belushi to experiment with a wisecracking role to call his own, amid a patchwork of thefts from the Chevy Chase school of deadpan one-liners and the Robin Williams society of agitated improvisations, *K-9* grabs at any straw that drifts by in the hope of keeping comedy afloat. When this fails, as it often does, the film resorts to a fusillade of action—fights, pursuits, killings and gunplay—to convey the illusion of excitement and drama. Bewildering changes of mood from scene to scene effectively undermine the supposedly developing relationship between the slobbish cop and his Alsatian partner: despite the useful plot premise of a "rebel" police dog with above-average intelligence, the animal performs some routine law-enforcement tricks but remains reassuringly normal apart from the indignity of being dubbed with a hollow vocabulary of grunts and growls.

The main weakness of Rod Daniel's approach, consistent with his *Teenwolf* début, is this eagerness to anthropomorphise the canine character, as if a dog became funnier in direct ratio to its resemblance to the red-blooded American male. Jerry Lee is accordingly required to drool over his partner's girl and gets rewarded in one scene with ten minutes in the back of a car with a pedigree poodle, after which the soundtrack, already a heavily polluted area, explodes with gloating rock vocals even Fritz the Cat would have disdained. Worst of all, during the appallingly coy hospital sequence at the end, the wounded Jerry Lee is shown as just pretending to be near death in order to trick his untrained minder into an emotional commitment previously beyond the man's capabilities. Ironically, the closest Belushi comes in *K-9* to finding an authentic purpose is when, in tentative imitation of the other Belushi's powers of excess, he interrupts an extravagant dinner party to bestride the tables and shatter the décor. Having tried, with ingratiating industry, the possibilities of supercop, stud, and straight man, he may after all be more comfortable as mere psychotic.

NEW YORK POST, 4/28/89, p. 32, David Edelstein

K-9'' is one of the weirdest movies of the year, a formula buddy picture that has been photographed and edited in the vague, floating, affectless style of an arty TV commercial.

The plot, dialogue and performances are trashy and routine, but the camera work (by Dean Semler) gives the action a dreamy, ominous buzz; the movie's zonked rhythms are so at odds with the idiot material that you stare at the screen and go, "Where the hell am I?"

See, this is a picture about a messy, unorthodox cop (James Belushi) and his partner, a vicious, dope-sniffing German shepherd called Jerry Lee (Jerry Lee). They don't get along: like most mismatched cop-film partners, they spend a lot of time snarling at each other—only in this case they actually do snarl. But they're both determined to get their man, a murderous, dark-suited shipping magnate (Kevin Tighe) whose fortune comes form cocaine.

The script borrows liberally from "48 Hrs.," "Beverly Hills Cop" and every other comedy-thriller-buddy movie of the last few years. It has its bright patches, but it's basically a junk heap. Belushi has contempt for search warrants and civil rights—he's very clever at pressuring slimeballs into ratting on their bosses (especially in one scene, when he handcuffs a guy to the sideview mirror of his car and then drives onto the San Diego freeway).

Belushi might be the shallowest actor in movies; everything he does feels secondhand. But in "K-9" he has moments of jaw-dropping oddness. When his upscale girlfriend (Mel Harris) gets kidnapped, he makes a speech to Jerry Lee about how they met on a beach, how she was coating her mouth with lip gloss and reading Celine, "the original French person." It goes on and on, this reminiscence, dribbling away to nothing while the dog and the audience stare blankly.

The director, Rod Daniel ("Teen Wolf"), clearly didn't want to make a slob comedy. He wanted something classy, with an edge, and he let Semler (who specializes in offbeat pictures like "The Road Warrior," "The Coca Cola Kid" and "Dead Calm") lay on the hallucinatory, bleached-out visuals.

The style is wrong for the script, but had it been right this would still be a piece of swill. At least this way there are surprises. Although "K-9" has no suspense and a lot of mistimed gags (it probably won't work for the kind of audiences that normally go to a picture like this), it's the dammedest thing, and it kept me watching.

When the dog saves Belushi in a roughneck bar, the camera plunges right into the melee with swerving, hand-held shots of Jerry Lee tearing into assorted scummy thugs. Even when he's playing cute, this is a frightening creature. In fact, the movie's best moments are when you think (hope?) he's going to rip Belushi's throat out.

NEWSDAY, 4/28/89, Part III/p. 5, Terry Kelleher

Sometimes it seems every other American movie or television show is about mismatched police partners.

Nah, couldn't be more than 30 percent.

Last summer, James Belushi and Arnold Schwarzenegger co-starred in "Red Heat" as police partners mismatched by nationality and ideology. The next logical vehicle for Belushi would have been a story about police partners from different planets, but he wasn't cast in either the movie "Alien Nation" or the TV series "Something Is Out There."

Now here he is in a film about police partners mismatched by species. Dooley (Belushi) is yet another lone-wolf narcotics cop who's always in dutch with his superiors: Jerry Lee (Jerry Lee) is a "stressed-out" German shepherd with a nose for drugs, an aversion to discipline and an appetite for chili. They're both black sheep, though only one walks on four feet. They have some fun, they have some scrapes and narrow escapes, and they come as close to male bonding as circumstances allow. After all, as Dooley observes, they're "both members of the animal kingdom."

Producer Charles Gordon likens "K-9" to 48 HRS." Director Rod Daniel calls it "sort of the ultimate extension of the buddy film." The choice of animals aside, what we have here is a formula picture. Of course, that doesn't mean the formula isn't competently executed. Daniel keeps the camera and the action moving nicely. Belushi is energetic and aggressive in pursuit of the lowbrow laughs in Steven Siegel and Scott Myers' script. Jerry Lee can be quite personable when he's not baring his fangs or engaging in Rin-Tin-Tinish heroics.

But therein lies the problem with "K-9," as with many other "action comedies." Even if you howl at the sight of Jerry Lee going through a car wash or invading Dooley's bed or panting after a sexy poodle, you may feel a bit uncomfortable when the wild and crazy canine snarls, lunges and actually takes a bite out of crime. Granted, they don't call them "attack dogs" for nothing, but realism has its place and it's not here.

The same goes for the overall level of violence and unpleasantness. It's OK for Kevin Tighe to be sinister as the druglord Dooley's dogging, but does he have to shoot an underling in the head at close range? Must he inspire a sadistic henchman by encouraging him to make a murder "as messy and painful as you want"? In the climactic hail of gunfire, when Dooley lets out a primal scream as he squeezes off round after round, just keep telling yourself it's only a comedy, only a comedy.

The most thankless role in "K-9" belongs to Mel Harris as Dooley's neglected lover. Early in the movie, she decries his attitude. "Making a bust is more important than making time for me," she complains. It's bad enough having to deliver such a line, but Harris is called upon to argue in her underwear. Near the end, when she becomes the latest in a long line of cops' women to be taken hostage, both Dooley and the bad guy refer to her as "the girl." This is Harris' bigscreen reward for all that good work on "thirtysomething"?

James Handy has the second-most-thankless role—the detective lieutenant who orders the free-wheeling cop to play it by the book. But now we're all so sick of this character that few will mind when Dooley threatens to sic the dog on him.

Also reviewed in:

NEW YORK TIMES, 4/28/89, p. C19, Stephen Holden
VARIETY, 5/3-9/89, p. 12
WASHINGTON POST, 4/28/89, p. D7, Rita kempley

KOMITAS

A Margarita Woskanjan Filmproduktion in collaboration with WDR, SFB, Channel Four, RTSR, RTBF, FFA, FKT, K.j.d.F, and the Alex Manogian Cultural Fund. *Producer:* Margarita Woskanjan. *Director:* Don Asharian. *Screenplay (Armenian and German with English subtitles):* Don Askarian. *Director of Photography:* Jorgos Arvanitis and Martin Gressmann. *Editor:* René Perraudin and Marion Regentrop. *Music:* Komitas, Donizetti, and Teyra. *Sound:* Michael Bootz. *Art Director:* Jürgen Kiebach and Michael Poladian. *Costumes:* Bernhard Muhl. *Running time:* 96 minutes. *MPAA Rating:* Not Rated.

CAST: Samuel Ovasapian (Komitas); Onig Saadetian (Terlemesian); Margarita Woskanjan (Pupil); Rev. Yegishe Mangikian (Katholikos); Rev. Gegham Khatcherian (Armenian Monk); Sybille Vogelsang (Nurse); Mohammad Tahmasebi, Eskander Abadii, and F. Teyra (Musicians); Kaweh Jaryani and Sonja Askarian (Angels).

VILLAGE VOICE, 3/28/89, p. 64, Georgia Brown

The Armenian monk and composer Komitas (1869–1935) spent his last 20 years in mental institutions, "victim of a nervous disorder," following Turkish extermination of two million Armenians in 1915. Russian-born Don Askarian composes a dense, compelling meditation on Komitas's silence that has some of the flavor of Tarkovsky or Paradjanov. Sections with headings such as "Hospital," "Childhood," "Journey," open onto stunning, enigmatic tableaux that evolve gradually by means of slow pans and reverse tracking shots. Events of erosion, dissolution, spilling, and staining dominate.

Also reviewed in:
NEW YORK TIMES, 3/23/89, p.C16, Vincent Canby
VARIETY, 9/14/88, p. 31

KUNG FU MASTER

An Expanded Entertainment release of a Chiné-Tamaris/Sept coproduction. *Producer:* Agnès Varda. *Director:* Agnès Varda. *Screenplay:* Agnès Varda. *Based on a short story by:* Jane Birkin. *Director of Photography:* Pierre-Laurent Chenieux. *Editor:* Marie-Josée Audiard. *Music:* Joanna Brudowicz and Les Rita Mitsouko. *Sound:* Oliver Schwob. *Running Time:* 80 minutes. *MPAA Rating:* R.

CAST: Jane Birkin (Mary Jane); Mathieu Demy (Julien); Charlotte Gainsbourg (Lucy); Lou Doillon (Lou); Eva Simonet (The Friend); Judy Campbell (The Mother); David Birkin (The Father); Andrew Birkin (The Brother).

LOS ANGELES TIMES, 6/22/89, Calendar/p. 3, Sheila Benson

Ah, the French. Up to their old tricks of making crazy Americans feel out of step with what these cosmopolites take so comfortably in stride. Take Agnès Varda's "Kung Fu Master" a movie devoted to the absolute denial of psychological effect.

French to the core, it is about truly "crazy love," an affair between divorcée Mary Jane (Jane Birkin)—who is 40 and lives with her two daughters, ages 6 and 15—and 15-year-old Julien (Mathieu Demy), a schoolmate of her daughter Lucy's.

Birkin herself wrote the original story, which Varda altered slightly and which is cast within the family and shot at Birkin's pretty comfortable Paris house. Varda's own son, Mathieu, is the boy; Birkin's two daughters, 6-year-old Lou Doillon and 16-year-old Charlotte Gainsbourg, play her girls, Lou and Lucy. It doesn't help the creepy quality one bit.

No one who saw the French "Devil in the Flesh" of 1947 could fail to understand the young married woman's fascination with that 17-year-old schoolboy. Director Autant-Lara made that absolutely clear, particularly when he cast Gérard Philipe as Raymond Radiguet's auto-biographical adolescent, a boy struggling to manhood in the context of the First World War.

That was youth; this is sub-adolescence. Indulge this movie to the hilt, and you still come back to the question of what is lacking in this adult woman's life that would make her rush to re-create the dopiness of an adolescent's first crush. Or why she is so quick to sacrifice the psychological well-being of the two children she already has for this particularly blank sweet kid. With a Gallic shrug, the film makers make no effort to tell us. It's a given. *You* know. Well, try my damnedest, I don't know.

Mary Jane, profession unstated, is struck by Julien after helping him throw up, since he has indulged in nasty vodka-beer-wine mixture at Lucy's outdoor party. Mary Jane's younger daughter has a fever and, singing gently to her upstairs a little later, Mary Jane catches Julien studying her. She decides that he is "superb."

After she runs into him, literally and only semi-accidentally, at the school, they share a Coca-Cola and she watches him, wrapped up in his favorite video game, Kung Fu Master, which he plays "with such skill and such passion." In it, the maiden on the top floor must be rescued by the little pajama-clad hero, after he vanquishes demons of every kind.

Now, almost any woman will tell you that there is a powerful aphrodisiac in watching a man absorbed in something he does well, from messing with a car motor to putting a mathematical equation on a blackboard, to turning out an omelet. And there are qualities about adolescence that have their own undeniable appeal; a stray curl at the nape of a neck, an endearing bravado that covers inexperience.

But watching a man, who may have a few more things in his head, and fixating on an absorbed child are two quite different matters. Except, perhaps, to the French. Beyond Julien's passion for his game, Varda doesn't tell us anything about him, except that he may want mothering. (Both his parents are a convenient continent away.) Actor Mathieu is big-eyed and grave and obviously the apple of his own mother's eye. But he is not terribly interesting and, rather than 15, he looks two or three years younger, which makes the movie feel really pathologic. (It is MPAA-rated R for the relative discretion of their nuzzling love scenes.)

So when he begins to turn up with daffodils for Mary Jane, and she, our narrator, begins to talk about his phone calls, which "thrilled" her, the non-French mind may reel.

Presumably this is shy, pure romance. A respite from "grown-up" behavior. An unpressured process of learning to love. Well, if Mary Jane lived by herself, that might be one thing. But she's responsible for two other young lives. And when she and Julien take off for her family's island— taking 6-year-old Lou with them, abruptly leaving Lucy behind with her maternal grandparents— where are our sympathies supposed to lie? Varda cares so little about anyone but this pathetic little couple that we're never even shown Lucy's reaction, as though her feelings were beside the point.

And how are we supposed to feel aobut this semi-*triste* island idyll, just momma, her baby and her baby-love? What do we make of the moment when Mary Jane confesses shyly, "I'm too old for you. . . . I know I won't be around when you start shaving." The closest thing to comment about little Lou's presence here is one shot of her, wailing, unattended, at the water's edge.

The movie makes much of French adolescent's understandable preoccupation with AIDS. The bottom line of AIDS is responsibility for those one cares about. Perhaps it is only the French who worry about sexual responsibility yet behave as though psychological responsibility was something only the unsophisticated troubled about. The unsophisticated and those crazy Americans.

NEW YORK, 7/17/89, p. 46, David Denby

Mary Jane (Jane Birkin), the fortyish divorcée who is the heroine and narrator of Agnès Varda's *Kung Fu Master*, falls in love with a boy—the fifteen-year-old Julien (Mathieu Demy), a school chum of Mary Jane's daughter. Julien is small for his age; he's feline and smooth-faced, and if he has some imperious quality that a grown woman might respond to sexually, we can't see it. Yet Mary Jane, a great big beautiful woman, curls up with this runt and drones on about her obsessive love. Varda presents this material not as a ludicrous indiscretion of early middle age but as a grand *amour*, right up there with madame de la Mole's passion for Julien Sorel.

NEW YORK POST, 6/23/89, p. 27, Jami Bernard

French films have a way of making sore subjects seem cute and harmless—the lighthearted infidelity of "Cousin, Cousine," the compassionate incest of Louis Malle's "Murmur of the Heart." Now, similar to "Murmur of the Heart," there is "Kung Fu Master," a movie that takes the sting out of an affair between a 40-year-old divorcée and her daughter's teen-age schoolmate.

The movie's ad phrase, "Love is where you find it," might lead you to think mom is frustrated or lazy when it comes to dating, but neither is the case. Mary Jane (Jane Birkin) espies gawky young Julien (Mathieu Demy) throwing up at her daughter's party, and the two take a shine to each other.

It's true that Julien's parents are out of town and that watching Mary Jane sing her younger daughter to sleep is probably then a selling point for a homesick 15-year-old. After all, most kids look longingly at their friends' parents and imagine a better life under a different roof.

It is less understandable why this easygoing, tomboyish, self-sufficient woman would tumble for a kid whose only interest in life is in a video arcade game called Kung Fu Master—hence the misleading title only one week before the opening of "Karate Kid III."

The video game requires the player to advance through five levels of highkicking aggressors to rescue a fair maiden. Along with the the movie's references to AIDS, condoms and the game Dungeons and Dragons, it is implied that the younger generation is coming of age under a new confusion of rules, where at every level of the game the stakes are higher.

"Are you ready to die for love?" asks a woman handing out AIDS leaflets on the street. Julien is learning to rescue the fair maiden before he knows properly what, if anything, to do with her.

The older-woman, younger-man initiation is usually a male fantasy, but in this case, director Agnés Varda ("Vagabond") adapted a short story by actress Birkin. There is less of Mrs. Robinson in Mary Jane than Cloris Leachman as the high school coach's wife of "The Last Picture Show." Although there is none of the bitterness of that character, it is Mary Jane who does the pining and who is just a little bit out of her mind over this kid.

In fact, the first time she realizes she's drawn to the boy ("He couldn't have looked more pathetic, yet I found him superb"), she sets out to find him after school and nearly mows him down with her car.

Birkin's original short story may have left out a few details, which the movie also does not fill in and maybe doesn't mean to. Why the attraction? What are the psychological effects on the lovers and on Mary Jane's adolescent daughter? Is the mother's obsession an out-growth of her competition with her daughter, or of the lack of communication between them?

Instead of exploring questions the audience will undoubtedly have, "Kung Fu Master" blithely sends the mismatched couple off to a deserted island idyll. How the boy makes it through without any video games we'll never know.

Adding to the confusion of the romance itself and the almost merry way in which Varda presents it (less merry, on the other hand, than in "Murmur of the Heart") is the casting of Varda's and Birkin's kin in all the key roles. Varda's son plays Julien, and virtually Birkin's entire family plays Mary Jane's daughters and parents. It is a provocative casting decision, maybe a funny one. Maybe a cruel one.

"Kung Fu Master" has a bittersweet taste, but without the tang that would make it memorable.

NEWSDAY, 6/23/89, Part III/p. 5, Lynn Darling

Mary Jane, the protagonist of French director Agnès Varda's latest movie, meets the love of her life under rather trying circumstances—she discovers him drunk and throwing up in her bathroom, as a matter of fact—but she realizes right away that something very special is happening to her. Sure, as a romantic item, they have a few differences to contend with—he's 15, she's 40, for starters—but no one ever said the road to great romance isn't rocky.

Before long, Mary Jane (Jane Birkin) is getting all fluttery inside just standing next to her intended as he devotes himself to his favorite video game, "Kung Fu Master." And Julien (Mathieu Demy) is soon mustering his pubescent charm, such as it is, in an all-out attempt to seduce her. In the end, the amazing thing is not that he succeeds, but that Varda attempts to portray this cockeyed relationship as if it were even remotely within the bounds of the marginally believable.

All right, so plot isn't everything. Credibility isn't even everything. This is the sort of movie in which theme and symbolism is everything, and "Kung Fu Master" has a lot to say on that score. About the arid emotional wasteland in which young people must come of age these days. About the end of romance. About the perilous frontiers of sex, where AIDS haunts even the most casual, bantering conversation. About the forms of escape that people embrace to deliver themselves from a meaningless world.

But all this hifalutin' stuff doesn't have a chance in the teeth of the absurd relationship at the heart of this movie. There's nothing about these two characters that clues you in for an instant as to what they could possibly see in each other—there's no logic, twisted or otherwise, to the attraction, as there was in, for example, both the novel and the movie version of "Lolita." She's a boring housewife and he's a boring kid, and between the two of them they generate all the fatal attraction of dishwater.

Stripped of the warmth, humor, humanity and insight that enabled Louis Malle to make a glorious movie out of incest in "Murmur of the Heart," Varda's movie has to settle for moments of unintentionally ludicrous humor. During the lovers' first quarrel, for instance, he insults her by calling her "Mommy," and she tells him he's too young to smoke. At another, more plaintive moment, Mary Jane sadly tells Julien that she knows she won't be around by the time he starts shaving. Ah, the ephemeral nature of love.

At least that sort of thing is better than contemplating the two of them in bed together, discreet as those scenes are. While Varda clearly means us to contemplate the existential ramifications of her obviously mismatched pair, it's not metaphysics in which we're forced to wander, but the unsavory neighborhood of child abuse.

VILLAGE VOICE, 6/27/89, p. 70, Georgia Brown

How worldly are the French. Tales of ripening seeds and tender shoots leave us feeling so parochial and prudish. Look at our Mrs. Robinson—that hunched, brooding bird of prey—and *her* liaison was with a big boy, a graduate of college, not grade school. Leave it to Americans to cast the older woman relationship in its worst light. In France, older women are tender and acquiescent, simply easing the adolescent on his way, (wistfully) sending him out into the world of his peers. And when he thinks of her—and he does—he's not exactly kind, but he's appreciative. (Or maybe the impervious boy is just more brutal in getting up and going.)

Further edifying us on this subject, Agnès Varda's *Kung Fu Master* has a light, decorative surface that gives it the look of a fable, or an antipsychological tease. The film opens with a droll pan of 14-year-old Julien imitating a video game karate kid, hopping along the street, chopping and kicking at the villains he meets. In the game Kung Fu Master, the video boy must advance upward five stages, knocking off monsters until he saves the fair Silvia, who's tied to a chair. It's a game of chivalry.

Julien is an appealing, big-eyed boy, smaller than many kids his age, but shorter by a lot than lanky Mary Jane, the mother of his already full-grown classmate, Lucy. Mary Jane is played by the tomboyish, gap-toothed Jane Birkin, who is, as always, great fun to watch. (She also wrote the story on which the film is based.) In her forties now, Birkin very much resembles her fellow countryman Mick Jagger. (This sounds grotesque but it isn't.) She wear jeans and unbuttoned shirts with her chemise showing.

Varda, who always leans heavily on decor, on diverting the eye (the better, you might say, to detach it from the brain), uses Birkin's personal style, including the actress's actual Paris house—a riot of wallpaper and taxidermy—for its ornamental value. Birkin's two daughters, Charlotte Gainsbourg (by actor/composer Serge Gainsbourg) and Lou Doillon (by director Jacques Doillon), play Mary Jane's daughters, Lucy and Lou, in the film. When the plot moves to London, Birkin's parents (her mother is the actress Judy Campbell) appear in their own house and garden—as do other Birkin family members. To complete the elaborate incestuous joke, Julien turns out to be played by Mathieu Demy, Varda's son by director Jacques Demy.

Varda's blends of documentary and fiction may sound interesting theoretically, but in practice they've amounted to gimmick more than substance. In this case, the director lays claim to "a pure truth which comes out of people acting together with their close family or friends." (Press materials come with three pages of Varda quotes.) Pure truth evidently is brittle and so slight you could miss it.

In the movie's first scene, Lucy, who seems like a regular kid, gives a party in the family garden. The teenagers tell AIDS jokes and fool around with a condom that comes in a magazine ad. When Julien, perhaps less mature than the others, gets drunk and goes inside to find a place to throw up, Mary Jane teaches him the trick of putting his finger down his throat; she even puts hers in for him. Then, as she tends to Lou, the younger daughter, who's ill and feverish, Julien watches longingly from the doorway. It turns out that his parents are off in Africa and he's living with grandparents. The boy needs his *maman*.

But it's Mary Jane—divorced, a freelance designer of some sort, and generally at loose ends—who's really nooked. A few days later, fantasizing about running into Julien, she literally runs him down—hits him with her car outside the lycée. She takes him to a café, where he demonstrates his skill at Kung Fu Master and she gazes, smitten. "Boys are curious and vulnerable," she says somewhere along the way.

The film, which is curious and invulnerable, is from the older woman's point of view. The boy is more or less a cipher—an object of obsession—though at times (improbably) a pursuer in his own right. Mary Jane's passion is mysterious and irrational (in the way of passions); it's also hard not to find it unbelievable. I'll buy infatuation—but when she acts on her feelings (after Lucy catches the two kissing), and goes off with Julien to an island, with Lou along (apparently sleeping in the same room), the movie becomes quite bizarre. Mary Jane doesn't grow tired of Julien (who seems singularly uninteresting), or have second thoughts. Concern for Lucy seems nonexistent. All the while, Varda pretends the whole business is so natural, so understandable, really, that you'd be a fool for doubting. On the other hand, she also makes anyone look like a fool for taking any of the proceedings seriously.

Varda's trick, masked sometimes as artistic, sometimes as philosophical, strategy, is to show human beings behaving as if they're denatured or inhuman—like another form of animal life. In *Le Bonheur* (1965), a handsome young carpenter in the provinces, happy with his wife and children, begins an affair; when his wife finds out and drowns herself, he marries the other and goes on in his happiness. (The entire first family was played by members of one real-life family.) All this is presented without moralizing, and in its prettiness and evenness of tone, it's hollow and most irritating. Happy is as happy does. *Que será, será. Kung Fu Master* has a somewhat different ending—sentimental in a more predictable way—but it's the same blithe nonsense.

Also reviewed in:
NEW REPUBLIC, 6/26/89, p. 27, Stanley Kauffmann
NEW YORK TIMES, 6/23/89, p. C12, Caryn James
VARIETY, 2/24/88, p. 404

LA BOCA DEL LOBO

A Cinevista Inc. release of a Producciones Inca Films/Tornasol Films/Televisión Española production *Producer:* Gerardo Herrero and Francisco J. Lombardi. *Director:* Francisco J. Lombardi. *Screenplay (Spanish with English subtitles):* Augusto Cabada, Giovanna Pollarolo, and Gerardo Herrero. *Director of Photography:* José Luis López Linares. *Editor:* Juan San Mateo. *Music:* Bernardo Bonezzi. *Sound:* Daniel Padilla. *Art Director:* Marta Méndez. *Special Effects:* Fernando Vásquez de Velasco. *Costumes:* Luzmila Ferrand. *Make-up:* Florentino Point, Narda Aguinaga, and Veronica Oliart. *Running time:* 122 minutes. *MPAA Rating:* Not Rated.

CAST: Gustavo Bueno (Lieutenant Ivan Roca); Antonio Vega (Vitin Luna); José Tejada (Gallardo) Gilberto Torres (Sergeant Moncada); Bertha Pagaza (Julia)

MONTHLY FILM BULLETIN, 6/89, p. 171, David Wilson

1983. A platoon of government soldiers is despatched to a remote village in the mountainous Ayacucho region of Peru. The area has been heavily infiltrated by Communist guerrillas of the "Sendero Luminoso" movement, and the local peasants are uncooperative. On their first morning there, the soldiers find a Communist flag flying over their headquarters. Privates Luna and Gallardo arrest a villager found with an incriminating document and torture him, but their lieutenant intervenes and decides to take the man over the mountains for interrogation by military intelligence. Next day, the bodies of the lieutenant and two other soldiers are found on the mountain track. A new lieutenant, Roca, arrives and immediately institutes a tougher régime. Despite some misgivings about his uncompromising methods in dealing with the villagers, morale among the soldiers improves until, with Roca away on patrol, the post is attacked by guerrillas. On his return, Roca assembles the villagers and warns them that he requires their co-operation. Luna discovers that Gallardo has brutally raped an Indian woman, but he remains silent when her father lodges a complaint with Roca. When Gallardo is forcibly ejected from a wedding party he tries to invade, Roca orders mass arrests and beats up one of the villagers so severely that the man dies. Realising that the other prisoners—who include women and children—know about the beating, Roca herds them together and takes them to the mountains, where he orders his men to shoot them. Only Luna refuses to open fire. He is arrested. Now utterly disillusioned, he challenges Roca to Russian roulette. But given the chance to kill the lieutenant, Luna deliberately fires wide. He leaves the village, discarding his army uniform.

The Lion's Den is based on an actual event, the massacre by para-military police of a group of Andean peasants accused of belonging to the "Sendero Luminoso" (Shining Path) revolutionary Communist organisation who since 1980 have operated in the Ayacucho region of Peru. It is not, however, a historical reconstruction of that event, on the model of earlier Latin American films like Jorge Sanjines' *Courage of the People*, but a fictional drama which accommodates one moment of historical reality. The film's rhetoric is theatrical rather than political: its politics are those of psychological motivation, and at a fairly basic level. The central conflict is not between the army and the revolutionary guerrillas (who are an unseen enemy, melting into the barren mountain landscape), but within the army platoon itself. Raw recruit Luna looks to tough lieutenant Roca as his role model, and is disillusioned when his hero proves to be a psychotic coward. The massacre of the Indian peasants is channelled into a pretext for a simple morality tale about the loss of innocence.

This theme is schematically signalled in framing shots of a child herding sheep, which have the effect of implying that the mountain villagers are merely the innocent bystanders and occasional victims of both an external and an internal conflict. In the film's reality (the infiltration of the guerrillas) and in its fiction, they simply get in the way. When some thirty of them are herded together on the mountain slope and shot, the significant point for the film appears to be not the massacre itself but the fact that Private Luna refuses to open fire. And his refusal is not so much a matter of personal morality—even less of a political awakening—as of disenchantment with the model soldier who has previously justified his uncompromising methods (like shooting a farmer's cow to teach him a lesson in discipline) with the comment that "You must do what you must do if you're a man". The credibility of Luna's progress from innocent awe to contempt for the father figure who has inspired it is somewhat undermined by the film's representation of Roca, who from the start is clearly a man obsessed. His fanaticism is explained with some soap-opera psychoanalysis: the generals in Lima have denied him promotion because of his involvement in a game of Russian roulette which ended fatally. And for that, the film seems to be saying, peasants are massacred. Atrocities are the work of psychopaths with a grudge.

Another game of Russian roulette, melodramatically orchestrated, brings the film to its uncertain conclusion. Luna runs away, turning his back on the army after discovering that his hero is not only a murderer but (worse, it seems) a coward. The only other character developed beyond a background figure is the soldier who tortures a suspect, rapes an Indian woman, and sneers villainously. The film's primary-coloured theatricals are only enhanced by Francisco Lombardi's relentlessly television-style direction, all mid-shots and darkly lit, cluttered interiors.

NEW YORK POST, 8/18/89, p. 25, V.A. Musetto

The "other" war movie [the reference is to "Casualties of War"] opening today is called "La Boca del Lobo," a Peruvian import tucked away at the always-innovative Public Theater down on Lafayette Street. I vigorously recommend a visit.

The setting is Peru, and the antagonists are government troops and the pro-Mao Shining Path guerrillas, who have been locked in a "dirty war" that has claimed upward of 15,000 lives—mostly innocent peasants—since 1980.

Francisco Lombardi's "Boca," a prize winner at last year's San Sebastian Film Festival in Spain, is based on an appalling true event: the 1963 army massacre of 47 men, women and children who were rounded up at a wedding party, accused of being terrorists, then marched to a canyon and shot.

Around this slaughter, which is recreated with understated but compelling frankness, Lombardi masterfully weaves the fictional story of a group of homesick young recruits who have been sent to a remote Andean village to battle the guerrillas. The pivotal character is Vitin Luna (Antonio Vega), a well-connected soldier who has volunteered for the assignment—"The sacrifice isn't too great," he tells a buddy—as a way of helping his military career.

The unseen (by us and the troops) guerrillas methodically go about their work, sneaking down from the mountains, replacing the government flag with their own and leaving their mutilated victims bedecked with propaganda graffiti. One casualty is the troops' sympathetic, by-the-books commander. He is replaced by the hard-nosed Lt. Roca (Gustavo Bueno), who seeks to rouse the troops with a tough "it's either them or us" speech.

Luna is at first impressed with Roca. But his fellow troops grow increasingly cruel toward the Indians. Then a native storekeeper is raped by a soldier and the chain of events that leads to the massacre is set in motion. So, too, is Luna's disillusionment with his commander and the brutal, irrational war.

Lombardi skillfully and logically builds his case, not so much in favor of the Shining Path but against the army, which comes off as a sadistic gang of liars, thieves, rapists and killers. You don't necessarily have to agree with him. But there is no denying that "La Boca del Lobo" is bold, unflinching filmmaking.

VILLAGE VOICE, 8/22/89, p. 85, Manohla Dargis

In the bright, hard sunlight of the Andean Sierras, a small platoon sets up a base in the tiny hamlet of Chuspi. These young tenderfoots, led by a paper-pushing lieutenant, are ripe prey for the unnerving tactics of the Sendero Luminoso, Peru's notorious Shining Path guerrillas.

While Hollywood periodically reinvents Vietnam as the Fall, *The Lion's Den* is as chilling and topical as the November '88 Americas Watch report on Peru. Hundreds of its civilians have been "disappeared," with reportedly up to 15,000 dead in the last decade. The U.S. press often links Peru's woes directly to the Shining Path, historical amnesia that conveniently neglects the circumstances of their origin. You don't have to apologize for the guerrillas to understand them, that their emergence from the Andean province of Ayacucho in 1980 was predicated on centuries of Spanish colonialism, years of despotic military, rule, and unflagging racism.

Director Francisco J. Lombardi, though emphatically not supportive of the Shining Path, focuses his attention on the atrocities committed by the government's military, who are responsible for far more deaths than the Maoist-inspired group. Brutal and disturbing, *The Lion's Den* is based on events that occurred in 1983, soon after an Emergency Zone was established in the Andes by an armed forces command. Set up to combat the Shining Path (which has since reasserted its control over the region), the zone became a killing field, with military and police squads carrying out widespread extrajudicial executions and massacres of peasants even rumored to be rebel sympathizers.

Vitin Luna (Antonio Vega) is a young, baby-faced soldier who has volunteered for service in the zone. He's eager for action, hoping the experience will land him a spot at a military academy. The others are less enthusiastic and loll about the dusty, empty town drinking, and damning the Indians. While Luna and the others sleep, the guerrillas stay busy, sneaking down from the mountains and into the village, covering its whitewashed adobe walls with threats and rhetoric, running up their hammer-and-sickle flag at the army post. The lieutenant, along with two other soldiers, is ambushed, leaving the unit temporarily stranded without leadership or supplies. (A request for reinforcements is met with the news that the military is sending them magazines to keep them "happy.")

The soldiers are jolted from their desultory state with the appearance of Roca, the replacement lieutenant, played with restrained intensity by Gustavo Bueno. Roca has an approach to soldiering that at first merely seems a harsher take on the Lou Gossett Jr. school of cadet training. Driven by his ugly, violent past, he takes the offensive with the Shining Path, pushing his men out on patrols and terrorizing the peasants into cooperation—he even leads the entire village in an enforced sing-along of the national anthem. Roca's hypermilitarism is deftly linked to his overripe sense of machismo, the connection between war and feverish masculinity made explicit in his paranoid rants against "queer" journalists and judges.

Lombardi wisely never shows any of the guerrillas, only their work. The tedium of the soldiers' lives is punctuated by occasional visits from the enemy, who, nothing if not effective propagandists, tend to drape their mutilated victims with graffiti'd tear sheets, leaving them on the church steps as if they were gifts. The Shining Path remains out of reach and, fueled by Roca's gung-ho ravings ("This is war, we can't fall into moral traps!"), the soldiers' frustrated boredom is transformed into ever increasing brutality against the Indians.

The film's horrendous denouement is based on a real incident in which dozens of men, women, and children, members of Andean village wedding party, were slaughtered by members of the Civil Guard. The violence is devastating, a damning indictment of an official policy taken to its grotesque, inevitable conclusion. Afterward, there's a superfluous scene in which Luna and Roca face off, but to his credit, Lombardi doesn't tack on the neat resolution of standard-issue drama. *The Lion's Den* remains unsparing.

Also reviewed in:
NEW YORK TIMES, 8/18/89, p. C17, Vincent Canby
VARIETY, 10/5/88, p. 155

LA BOHEME

A New Yorker Films release of an Erato Films/La Sept/SFPC/Generale d'Images, Travelling Productions/ Videoschermo coproduction. *Executive Producer:* Jean-Claude Bourlat. *Producer:* Daniel Toscan du Plantier and Claude Abeille. *Director:* Luigi Comencini. *Screenplay (adapted from Henri Murger's novel "Scènes de la Vie de Bohème):* Luigi Comencini. *Libretto:* Giuseppe Giacoso and Luigi Illica. *Director of Photography:* Armando Nannuzzi. *Editor:* Sergio Buzi and Reine Wekstein. *Music:* Giacomo Puccini. *Music Editor:* Jean-Michel Bernot. *Choreographer:* Adriano Sinivia. *Sound:* Guy Level. *Art Director:* Paolo Comencini. *Costumes:* Carolina Ferrara. *Make-up:* Tamani Berkani. *Running time:* 106 minutes. *MPAA Rating:* Not Rated.

CAST: Barbara Hendricks (Mimi); José Carreras (Rodolfo's Voice); Luca Canonici (Rodolfo); Angela Maria Blasi (Musetta); Gino Quilico (Marcello); Richard Cowan (Schaunard); Francesco Ellero D'Artegna (Colline); Federico Davia (Benoit/Voice of Alcindor); Ciccio Ingrassia (Parpignol); Michel Senechal (Voice of Parpignol); Mario Maranzana (Alcindoro); Michel Beal (Inn Keeper); Massimo Girotti (Old Suitor).

LOS ANGELES TIMES, 6/8/89, Calendar/p. 1, Martin Bernheimer

Last year, Franco Zeffirelli's "Otello." Now, Luigi Comencini's "La Boheme." The two, thank goodness, have little in common. Zeffirelli thought nothing of second-guessing Verdi, mutilating an operatic masterpiece in the name of cinematic art. Comencini has the good sense to trust Puccini.

Trust, in this case, should not imply slavish devotion. Comencini's sensitive little film does take a few narrative liberties.

The action is pushed forward, gently, from 1830 to 1910. It does no harm.

Some muted dramatic innovations are permitted. Mimi overhears the bohemians' horseplay and exit before she plots her own entrance. She also plants her "lost" key at Rodolfo's feet.

Musetta acquires a wealthy suitor, suavely delineated by Massimo Girotti. Silently, if intrusively, he stalks much of Act III.

The cameras follow the protagonists as they are allowed to move, logically, from room to rrom and from interior to exterior. The music is occasionally—and discreetly—embellished with the whistle of wind on the Latin Quarter rooftops.

This is hardly the stuff of revolution. Comencini respects his source too much to permit gimmickry. He contents himself with illuminating detail.

The translation from opera house to movie house does pose some obvious problems, and the director does not attempt to solve them all. The characters on the screen open their mouths wide and pretend to sing, even though the score has been prerecorded. The milieu remains realistic, even though the emotive scale is stylized.

It doesn't take long to get used to the contradiction. Disbelief is willingly suspended.

Essentially, this is a thoughtful representation of a lofty sentimental indulgence. Comencini goes about this challenge with surprising modesty. He has described his task simply: "dressing up a pre-established sound track with pictures."

The sound track in this case is a splendid facsimile of Puccini's *verismo* potboiler. It is conducted with equal brio and delicacy by James Conlon.

The pictures sometimes suggest in-jokes. A solitary beggar strolls by to fiddle the postlude to "Ah, Mimi, tu piu non torni." The band at the Café Momus literally accompanies Musetta's Waltz.

At the end of the love duet, we suddenly see Mimi through Rodolfo's eyes; she is framed by glitzy carnival lights. Marcello may curse his paintbrush at the beginning of Act III, but we see the erstwhile Cubist reduced here to sketching kitsch madonnas in chalk on the sidewalk.

It can be argued that such inspirations detract more than they add. Fortunately, Comencini resolutely keeps his eyes, and ours, in the right place at every crucial juncture.

The right place, much of the time, is the expressive face of Barbara Hendricks, who plays Mimi. No simpering soubrette, she makes the heroine warmhearted, resolute, mildly aggressive, all the more vulnerable for her generosity of spirit.

Her sweet, bell-like tones might prove inadequate for the strenuous cantilena in a big opera house. She sings with uncommon sweep, purity and pathos, however, for the microphones.

Her Rodolfo turns out to be less effective for several reasons. His singing is tender, poetic, ardent. His acting is earnest and stilted.

The dichotomy is easy to explain. Jose Carreras completed the recording in July, 1987, shortly before he was stricken with leukemia. At short notice, he was replaced in front of the cameras by Luca Canonici, a baby-faced Tuscan tenor on the brink of his own career.

Angela Maria Blasi, formerly of Los Angeles, introduces an earthy Musetta who gratefully and gracefully evades the usual sex-bomb traps. Gino Quilico complements her as a lyrical, somewhat self-conscious Marcello. Francesco Ellero d'Artegna (Colline) and Richard Cowan (Schaunard) provide properly youthful, agreeably sympathetic counterpoint.

The Parisian vistas convey bleak storybook charm. The colors are muted, sometimes patently artificial. Though arguably over-amplified, the Orchestre National de France plays *con brio* and, it would seem, *con amore.*

Mimi dies prettily—in her own bed, for a change. Fade-out time is still handkerchief time. Some things never change.

Comencini may adjust Puccini's focus for the new medium. But he never alters the basic structure, never compromises the fundamental impact.

He is musical. It is reassuring.

MONTHLY FILM BULLETIN, 1/89, p. 11, Anne Billson

Christmas Eve in the Latin Quarter of turn-of-the century Paris. Rodolfo, a penniless poet, burns his latest manuscript in a futile attempt to warm the attic where he lives with his friends: the painter Marcello, the philosopher Colline, and the musician Schaunard (who has earned enough money to buy some food and drink). Benoit, the landlord, comes to collect the rent, but the friends ply him with drink and, pretending to be outraged when he boasts about his extra-marital affairs, send him away empty-handed. While the others go out to the Café Momus, Rodolfo stays behind to finish a magazine article and encounters Mimi, a seamstress who lives next door. She faints, and then pretends to lose her door key. They exchange life stories, and fall in love. Together, they join the others at the café. Musetta, Marcello's old flame, turns up with Alcindoro, her latest sugar-daddy. The ex-lovers taunt each other for a while before being reconciled; all the friends depart together, leaving Alcindoro to pick up their tab. A month or so later, upset by Rodolfo's persistent jealousy, Mimi visits Marcello at the tavern where he is painting signs, and breaks down in tears when she overhears her lover explaining that his jealousy is really a mask to hide concern for her poor health, which is exacerbated by the cold and damp of the attic where they live. Marcello squabbles with Musetta, who goes off with a wealthy admirer, while Mimi and Rodolfo sadly agree to part company. Some months later, Mimi's condition has deteriorated and Musetta brings her back to the attic so she can be with Rodolfo. Colline sells his coat to buy medicine, and Musetta pawns her earrings to buy a muff for the sick girl. After reminiscing with Rodolfo about happier times, Mimi dies.

For the most part, this is a straightforward rendering of Puccini's most popular opera, shot on sets wich might almost have come straight from a stage production, although the camera is occasionally allowed to meander across snow-covered rooftops or to move from exterior to interior locations in mid-act. This proves rather distracting in the Café Momus scene, when the bustling goings-on indoors fail to mesh smoothly with seemingly irrelevant action (the toy merchant and the children) in the street outside. Luigi Comencini's sole stab at reinterpretation comes in his attempt to give Mimi more of an active role in her first meeting with Rodolfo: she is shown, in numerous visual asides, listening intrigued as the loud banter of her next-door neighbours carries through the thin walls, and eventually decides to take matters into her own hands by approaching Rodolfo on the slimmest of pretexts. Thereafter, the character reverts to her usual slide into passive sweetness, spasms of coughing and death, though Barbara Hendrick manages to be pathetically affecting rather than cloying. The fact that the soprano is black has apparently proved distracting to some critics, but there is no reason why she should not be, and this would quite likely make her even more attractive to a self-styled Bohemian poet (think of Baudelaire and Jeanne Duval).

As ever, the secondary twosome of Marcello and Musetta provides a more lively example of a romantic relationship than that of Rodolfo and Mimi: lovers concealing their true emotions by flirting or bickering or feigning lack of interest in each other. (Marcello's paintings, incidentally, seem excessively avant-garde—verging on cubism—for the period of the libretto; no wonder he has not sold any.) The orchestra, at times, comes perilously close to being swamped by the vocal track, but the performances are convincing, even if the faces seem a little mature in close-up. Italian tenor Luca Canonici, who stepped in at the thirteenth hour to mime to José Carreras' prerecorded vocals after the latter was taken ill, offers such a credible portrait of Rodolfo (immersing himself so totally in the romance of his own life story that he fails to notice his audience has left the room) that one wishes he'd been able to sing it himself. Ultimately, while this is a solid piece of transposed theatre rather than an inspired cinematic visualisation, the success of any production of *La Bohème* hinges on its ability to trigger the tear ducts; this one manages to generate a satisfactorily substantial clutch of sodden Kleenex.

NEW YORK POST, 6/9/89, p. 25, Jami Bernard

The sentimental Puccini opera about the flower maker who coughs herself to death and the starving poet who loves her is brought to the screen in "La Boheme," a film by Luigi Comencini that is just the teensiest bit afflicted with a wasting disease of its own.

Look, operas are operas. They make no apology for themselves. They are their own event, their own kind of theater, inimitable and grand. With few exceptions—"Carmen" comes to mind—operas that are transferred bodily onto film tend to look like a wax museum charmed by moonlight.

Given this, "La Boheme" is a good-looking, well-produced entry in the opera-film genre, but it suffers from the usual stiffness (opera singers are not the most fluid of actors). And the choice of Puccini's cry-fest is perhaps not the most muscular vehicle for cinema.

It's turn-of-the-century Paris, and two artist pals are starving in a garret. Rodolfo, the poet, flings his latest manuscript into the grate to provide a short-lived Christmas Eve fire for himself and the painter Marcello. "What are you doing?" is one of the first lines of dialogue; you can see right away how opera loses something in the translation.

Rodolfo is charmed by a neighbor, the diminutive Mimi, who has come for a light for her lamp; their story overlaps with that of Marcello and the flirtatious Musetta. The men are violently jealous and possessive of the ladies, and these romances alternately kindle and die. It just goes to show that there were men who were afraid of commitment even in olden times.

While Marcello is both attracted and repelled by Musetta, who appears to use men like dishrags, Rodolfo is thoroughly smitten by the fragile Mimi. Why he starts suspecting her of a cheating heart when all she has is a wracking cough is a mystery; anyway, his jealousies break them up and they are reunited only at the end, when she dies a protracted and aria-filled death. I hope I am not giving anything away by this; if you know nothing about opera at least you know that someone usually dies nobly through the full course of the final act.

What you really want to know is how much does "La Boheme" contribute to the body of Name-That-Tune opera songs, you know, the ones you hum in the shower but can't recall later?

Well, "La Boheme" has one really magnificent aria, the kind of swelling music that bespeaks passion supreme. Unfortunately, with the subtitles, we find that Musetta is taunting Marcello with something like, "Nyah, nyah, nyah, I'm the greatest thing since sliced bread . . ."

The pivtal role of Mimi is played by Barbara Hendricks, a native of Arkansas. Hendricks makes up for the gusto with which she sings by looking timid; still, it is not timidity that should ail her character, but weakness. The director's choice to have Mimi make the first move on Rodolfo creates some confusion: Is she a flirt or isn't she? (She is also saddled with the ugliest clothes, including a pillbox-pink sheath that looks like something out of Barbie's castoffs.)

Luca Canonici lip-syncs Rodolfo to the gorgeous strains of José Carreras, who is not known for his acting skills (neither, apparently, is Canonici) but who probably doesn't appear in the movie because of his recent battle with leukemia.

The lip-syncing is flawless, but Canonici still needs a fire lighted under him. Who has the consumption here, anyway? And if that big sound is really coming from his mouth, shouldn't his chest be heaving in sync as well?

"Love's a fire which consumes a lot of fuel," complains Marcello (believe me, it sounds better in Italian). But the only ones really breathing fire are the artists' landlord, who makes a brief appearance to collect the rent and complain about skinny women ("nothing but trouble"), and Angela Maria Blasi as Musetta. Blasi's Carol Burnett-like grimaces and physicality lend some spark to the artists' turgid love lives.

In this movie, she *is* the greatest thing since sliced bread.

NEWSDAY, 6/9/89, Part III/p. 5, Lynn Darling

The marriage of grand opera to film can be a daunting match: The opera's larger-than-life situations derive their energy from score and libretto, not plot or character, and the visual elements, which are shaped by the requirements of the stage, are intrinsically at odds with the fluid, intrusive character of the camera. When it works, as Franco Zeffirelli's version of "La Traviata" did six years ago, the result is exhilarating, the exalted passions of one form liberated by the visual expansiveness of the other. When it doesn't, the film maker's art becomes just an annoying set of tricks superfluous to and distracting from the opera's own ornate beauty.

Director Luigi Comencini works hard to do right by "La Boheme," and some of his ideas do help to open up Puccini's lyric vision of the artist's life and make it more at home on the screen. He gives an imaginative twist to the introduction of Rodolfo, the poet living in romantic poverty in his garret, and Mimi, the fragile young flower maker. In this version, it is Mimi who engineers their first meeting. Comencini intercuts Rodolfo's boisterous goings-on with shots of Mimi listening to them in her own small room and then using a spent candle as a pretext to get to know her neighbor.

But other innovations come across as fussy, overly decorative touches, making the opera look like a parlor filled to the brim with lace doilies and fringed lamps. At one point, as Rodolfo (Luca Canonici with the voice of José Carreras) sings to Mimi (Barbara Hendricks) in his bare studio, we see her surrounded by a trellis of blinking pastel lights. It's a startling and inadvertently funny moment—Mimi looks frozen, as if she's been transformed into a dime store religious icon.

In an effort to satisfy the camera's love of action, Comencini also introduces an unnecessary subsidiary character—a flirtatious elderly nobleman shows up at one point to be a silent witness to the simultaneous quarrels of Mimi and Rodolfo and the other pair of lovers, the fickle Musetta (Angela Maria Blasi) and the painter Marcello (Gino Quilico).

None of these ideas bring the opera to cinematic life—it maintains a stuffy, airless quality throughout, and the characters remain gauzy, distant apparitions. With the exception of Barbara Hendricks, the acting is stiff and unconvincing. The music, of course, is still glorious—though you don't need to go to the movies to find that out.

VILLAGE VOICE, 6/13/89, p. 68, Leighton Kerner

Luigi Comencini's 1988 film of Puccini's *La Boheme* has a visual lyricism that often comes near to matching the music's lyricism, which, of course, says a lot about the director's sensibilities. Shooting to the already finished Erato recording, Comencini had to march to the paces, the expansive phrasing, the liberal and quite appropriate *rubati* of James Conlon. Since Conlon is one of the world's best opera conductors—here he elicits untypically lustrous and lively playing from the National Orchestra of France—the collaboration works most of the time.

More specifically, it works beautifully once we're past the first, deadly 20 minutes or so, until Mimi, the tubercular seamstress, knocks on the door of Rodolfo, the penniless poet. Up to then, and during a couple of brief lapses later on, Comencini seems too shy to show how, or even if, this evergreen score may have inspired him. The joking among Rodolfo, painter Marcello, philosopher Colline, and musician Schaunard and their scam against the landlord are played out as if the actors are under sedation. The soundtrack bubbles with vigorous voices, but there's no vigor to be seen. If the singers had been made to sing full out on camera, rather than merely mouthing their syllables to match the recording's playback, the sheer energy of that singing would have filled the gap.

But Mimi, in the sweet, true soprano and occasionally sparkling, always touching presence of Barbara Hendricks, comes to the rescue, and the camera comes to life. In this version, we actually meet her right at the start, as she overhears in her flat the rumpus created by her neighbors, then decides to set up a meeting with the unsuspecting poet.

Comencini also adds a non-Puccini character in the person of an elegant old roué, who pursues Marcello's girlfriend, Musetta, and inadvertently, but sympathetically, observes the Act III emotional crisis among the two pairs of lovers. Massimo Girotti's tactful performance surely justifies the old gentleman's presence. In fact, *Bohème* as a spectator sport becomes a subtheme of the movie. Perhaps the director was indulging in movie nostalgia, but when passersby stop in their tracks in a snowy street to register sympathy with the almost reconciled Mimi and Rodolfo, and when a carriageful of ladies becomes absorbed in Rodolfo and Marcello's where-is-she-now duet, memories arise of those '30s movie operettas where some chevalier or other sets a blockful of Parisians to smiling, singing, and dancing. Puccini has been treated a lot worse at the Met. And sung a lot worse, too.

Hendricks is a joy. José Carreras, the first Rodolfo of Franco Zeffirelli's extravaganza version at the Met back in 1982, takes the role on the Erato recording, but leukemia prevented his film appearance, and another tenor, Luca Canonici, is the Rodolfo you see. Once past that first 20 minutes, he acts in plausible rapport with Hendricks, although the production calls for still more fire. Carreras sounds as well as he ever did after abandoning his uniquely sweet and light singing in midcareer for a bigger, coarser sound. But the high emotion remains in his voice, and once in a while you hear a tantalizing pianissimo to remind you of what might have been. Gino Quilico brings his accustomed dash, solid baritone, and good looks to Marcello, and Richard Cowan, Francesco Ellero d'Artegna, and the great veteran, Michel Sénéchal (a cameo as the voice of Parpignol) are part of a fine ensemble. But it's the Musetta of Angela Maria Blasi, vocally ideal in a world of bawling-bawd Musettas, and confidently scrumptious in the film's 1910 updating, who walks away with the whole movie.

Also reviewed in:
NEW YORK TIMES, 6/9/89, p. C14, Vincent Canby
VARIETY, 2/24/88, p. 467

LA LECTRICE

An Orion Classics release of an Élefilm/AAA Productions/TSF Productions/Ciné 5/Sofimage coproduction. *Producer:* Rosalinde Deville. *Director:* Michel Deville. *Screenplay (French with English subtitles):* Rosalinde Deville and Michel Deville. *Based on "La Lectrice" and "Un fastasme de Bella B. et autres récits" by:* Raymond Jean. *Director of Photography:* Dominique Le Rigoleur. *Editor:* Raymonde Guyot. *Music:* Ludwig Van Beethoven. *Sound:* Guy Level. *Sound Editor:* Philippe Lioret. *Production Designer:* Thierry Leproust. *Artistic Director:* Ysabelle Van Wersch-Cot. *Set Decorator:* Max Legardeur, Roseanna Sacco, and Marion Griffoulière. *Costumes:* Cécile Balme. *Make-up:* Joel Lavau. *Running Time:* 98 minutes. *MPAA Rating:* R.

CAST: Miou-Miou (Constance/Marie); Christian Ruché (Jean/Philippe); Sylvie Laporte (François); Michel Raskine (The Agency Man); Brigitte Catillon (Eric's Mother/Jocelyne); Régis Royer (Eric); Simon Eine (The Hospital Professor); Christian Blanc (The Old Teacher); Marianne Denicourt (Bella); Maria Casarès (The General's Widow); André Wilms (Jocelyne's Lover in Rue Saint-Landry); Patrick Chesnais (The Businessman); Clotilde de Bayser (Coralie's Mother); Jean-Luc Boutté (The Police Inspector); Bérangère Bonvoisin (Joël's Mother/The Hotel Waitress); Pierre Dux (The Judge); Léo Campion (Eric's Grandfather); Charlotte Farran (Coralie); Hito Jaulmes (Joël); Maria de Medeiros (The Silent Nurse); Isabelle Janier (The Talkative Nurse); Sylvie Jean (The Agency Secretary); Gabriel Barakian (Jocelyne's Husband).

FILMS IN REVIEW, 10/89, p. 488, Eva H. Kissin

A beautiful young woman, Miou-Miou, with her short blond hair and delightful self-effacing manner, something of a soft yellow kitten, lives with a too-busy young scholar. Bored and somewhat lonely, she decides to use her lovely speaking voice to read aloud to others. In addition, the young lady appears to have a working knowledge of literature.

She places an ad in the Classifieds against the specific advice of the editor, and receives a series of responses that connect her to the world. Her first client is a fifteen-year-old boy, the victim of an accident, in a wheel chair. Taken by Miou-Miou's gentle manner and implicit sexuality, he soon has her reading Baudelaire. Only the presence of Maman in the next room keeps the weekly visit within bounds.

Another student, a Hungarian general's wife, is a spirited bedridden older lady who is in love with the heroes of the Russian Revolution. She supplies the reading here. The endless repetition of the works of Marx and Lenin are literally *her* bedtime stories. However, our reader is so good at what she does that Madame gets out of bed to celebrate Lenin's birthday. Madame's maid, a beautiful frustrated Balthus type, has her own problems. She fantasizes spiders crawling up her legs and has the welts to prove it. Miou-Miou helps her with some practical advice about underwear.

An aged judge who can no longer read wants to hear a young female voice reading de Sade. And impotent business man regains some of his sexual magic through Miou-Miou's weekly "Lecture lessons." To all of her clients, she is caring and motherly, adjusting her particular breed of feminity to their special needs. Each home changes because of her presence.

The film moves well. Visually, Miou-Miou's daily walk to work through the curving French streets lined with turn of the century stone buildings, is very satisfying. The absolutely suitable music of Beethoven supplies the same gentle suggestive background as her presence.

It's all quite charming and somewhat light, perhaps a continental breakfast of a film rather than a whole meal, but a nice beginning nevertheless.

LOS ANGELES TIMES, 5/12/89, Calendar/p. 4, Sheila Benson

"Reading is fine," says the police inspector in "La Lectrice," "but look where it leads." In Michel Deville's arch and exhaustingly clever film it leads a reader-for-hire, the exquisitely droll Miou-Miou, into playing teacher, parent, sex-therapist and revolutionary, all at a reader's wages.

Considering the passions that reading can unleash, "La Lectrice" (The Reader) is without a trace of any passion, especially one for movie making. A series of boxes within boxes, stories within stories, it begins in bed, as Constance (Miou-Miou) begins reading a novel to her work-obsessed lover Jean (Christian Ruché). But lest anyone become aroused by that setting, Deville makes the high, intellectual level of his intentions stultifyingly clear from the beginning.

The novel she reads is Raymond Jean's "La Lectrice," the story of Marie, who, like Constance, lives in Arles and decides one day to capitalize on her passion for literature by hiring herself out as a professional reader. As she begins, Constance becomes Marie, who goes about the depopulated city streets with a springywalk, wearing a series of perky, multicolored knit hats, perhaps to underline her playful nature.

Her first client is 14-year-old Eric, in a wheelchair as he recovers from a serious accident. He wants the poetry of Baudelaire, the stories of De Maupassant. When he also gets the inch of thigh showing between Marie's black cotton stockings and her skirt, the erotic intensity of the moment propels Eric into a seizure. It does not, however, end things between Marie and Eric or even between Marie and Eric's mother, who knits her a bed jacket.

Next is the nearly blind widow of a Hungarian general who gets a "marvelous text on precious metals" by Karl Marx, among other political subjects. (She's played by Maria Casarès, that great icon from Cocteau's "Orpheus.") Later, it's a flustered and sexually stunted businessman, whom the eternally obliging Marie obliges with a bit of Marguerite Duras' "The Lover," never losing her place even when seated atop her client in her underwear.

Deville, who a few years ago gave us the suffocatingly precious "Peril," a mystery-romance in which the actress Anémone affected a cane and a mock limp as a sort of *frisson*, outdoes himself here with his whimsies. "La Lectrice" (rated R for sexual situations and texts) is a movie that almost hugs itself with self-congratulation at its literacy. Mostly, that comes from elaborate film and literary references.

Thus Bella, the widow's maid, who believes that spiders are attacking her, is a reference to Jorge Luis Borges and Manuel Puig: Borges because his story "Theme of the Traitor and the Hero" was the basis for Bertolucci's "The Spider's Strategem"; Puig for "The Kiss of the Spider Woman."

Lose anyone yet? It's possible that the average, or even the superior moviegoer might not catch this cunning insider tidbit. Reviewers have it a little easier; it's laid out for us in the press kit. Some of the rest of the jokes are simpler, like the results when Marie reads "Alice in Wonderland" to the precocious 6-year-old Coralie.

The problem with "La Lectrice" is that it's an entire film based on conceits like this, and, amusing as a few of them are, not long into the film they begin to pall. Then there is the distaste factor, whose very existence might astound the French. Presumably, we are men and women of the world, so why should the sight of a lovely young woman obediently giving each client exactly what he needs, sex, a groping feel, a look at her seminaked body—because he has employed her as a reader—strike us as soulless, even outrageous, rather than a comment on Marie's sweet earnestness? Perhaps because watching impersonal sex is entirely different from reading about it.

Besides, isn't Deville working against himself? Reading *should* inspire, seize, arouse its audience, especially the person reading. Where's the fun in the passionless reader? Not in "La Lectrice," you can be sure.

MONTHLY FILM BULLETIN, 3/89, p. 81, Sylvis Paskin

Arles in winter. In bed one night with her boyfriend Jean, Constance reads to him from a novel called *La Lectrice*, whose heroine, Marie, like Constance, enjoys reading ... Marie is persuaded by a friend to offer her services as a reader to people who are in some way incapacitated, and she places an advertisement although she is warned that it could lead to misunderstandings. Her first client is Eric, a young man confined to a wheelchair who lives with his mother and eccentric grandfather. She also visits an elderly general's widow who is blind but lives in some splendour with her cat and maid Bella, and a little girl, Coralie, whose busy mother wants someone to entertain her. Her last response is from a tense and repressed company director who is too busy to read for himself. At Marie's first session with Eric, he becomes so agitated by the sight of her stocking top that he has to be taken to hospital. Coralie interrupts their first reading by asking to visit the local funfair, where she reveals that she is wearing all her mother's jewellery. They rush back but Coralie's mother has phoned the police believing her daughter to have been kidnapped by Marie and all her jewels stolen. On her second visit to the general's widow, Marie talks to Bella, whose legs are covered with red blotches and who claims that they are caused by spiders living inside her. The widow wants to celebrate Lenin's birthday, and she and Marie hang red flags from a balcony and throw red roses over passers-by. Later, called to the local police station, Marie is questioned about what happened with Coralie and is shown a photograph of her rose-scattering. At Eric's birthday party, Marie meets his friend Joël, and is presented by Eric's mother with a beautiful bed-jacket to wear while she reads. The company director, with whom Marie has begun an affair, feels released by his new-found sexual potency and tells Marie that he is leaving for Africa. When Marie next visits the widow, she finds that Bella has left; in a postcard she tells how her forehead had been pierced with scissors while having her hair cut, releasing the spiders, and that now she is free. Asked to read the Marquis de Sade to a retired judge, Marie reluctantly complies, but when she finds that he has invited other men to attend their next session, she runs back to her boyfriend Philippe, sure that she is now out of a job . . . Her own enthusiasm fired by her "reading", Constance wonders about offering her services for hire.

Taken from Raymond Jean's 1986 novel, and some short stories from his 1983 anthology, *Un fantasme de Bella. B. et autres récits*, Michel Deville's *La Lectrice* is also something of an anthology of his own previous films. It deals in voyeurism, game-playing of a perverse and fantastic nature ("Each one of my films is a *jeu*"), the doubling of characters (the real and the dream woman in *La Femme en bleu*, the two neighbours in *Péril en la demeure*), and questions about manipulation and exploitation. Like the hero of *Péril en la demeure*, Marie/Constance enters a new and possibly threatening world with each domestic threshold she crosses. She serenely assumes that she has chosen the appropriate text for each of her listeners: Marguerite Duras' *L'Amant* for the frustrated entrepreneur, *Alice in Wonderland* for the charming runaway Coralie, *War and Peace* for the Eastern European general's widow, and Baudelaire's *Les Fleurs du mal* for the tumescent adolescent Eric.

But their responses prove to be not what she expected. The pleasure she provides is, in most cases, of an erotic and troubling nature, driving her clients to aberration and anarchy. Marie's love of language spurs her on, wending her way through the pale glowing city of Arles in winter. But it is the language of love that her listeners want to hear. Her clients' pleasure in these texts is more in line with Barthes' precepts about narrative being an Oedipal quest, an unveiling of truth, highlighted by the scene where, after reading to Eric, Marie raises her skirt above her head to satisfy his curiosity. He asks if she will repeat the gesture on her next visit, only this time "*sans culottes*". Marie is on the whole indulgent of and undisturbed by her clients' sexual vagaries, until confronted with the judge and the coterie he has assembled to hear de Sade's *Justine*.

In his elegant and delicate *mise en scène*, Deville employs a careful colour symbolism. Marie herself always wears blue, consistent with her dreamy and imaginative nature. Eric's home is decorated the green of a forbidden Eden, and the general's widow is surrounded by red—roses, flags, red-bound books on revolutionary politics, the blotches on her maid Bella's legs. The curious and inventive Coralie and her abstracted *maman* live in a black-and-white décor reminiscent of the chessboard setting of *Alice Through the Looking-Glass*. Within all this measured artifice, Deville also supplies some characteristic ruptures in emotional tone. There are moments of poignancy: Marie reads the myth of *Jason and the Golden Fleece* to the wheelchair-bound Eric, who asks when she thinks he will leave on such a journey. Marie's innocent enjoyment of the funfair is rudely dispelled when Coralie reveals that she is wearing all her mother's jewellery, and the edgy scenes with the company director culminate in an encounter of vaudevillian vulgarity when he and Marie finally reach the bedchamber.

Deville's balletic narrative inventiveness is reminiscent of the eighteenth-century play-wright Marivaux, who also liked to put his characters in a setting where realism counts for little and games of love and chance are played with subterfuge and finesse. But for all its cinematic *"marivaudage"*, its visual ingenuity, formal *audace* and witty Gallic cultural references, *La Lectrice* has a hollow heart. Voltaire remarked of Marivaux that he had spent his life weighing flies' eggs in cobweb scales, and the same gibe could be levelled at Deville. *La Lectrice* is a frothy conceit, a true *jeu d'esprit*, but when it has said all that it has to say, albeit with panache, it has said nothing. Deville uses several of Beethoven's sonatas as accompaniment, but perhaps some Mozart "Divertissements" would have been more apt.

NEW LEADER, 4/3–17/89, p. 21, John Morrone

What you might forget after seeing Michel Deville's *La Lectrice* (literally, "The Reader") is that it is a comedy. For despite a fleet, feathery tone, this film is hardly a featherweight affair. It is, rather, an uncommonly literary movie about a decidedly serious person who enjoys reading aloud—not the most obviously cinematic subject—but its high spirits never flag, even if the ending is bittersweet.

Set in Provence, *La Lectrice* (based on a novel and stories by Raymond Jean) recounts the experiences of Marie, a woman "gifted with a pretty voice," after she decides to hire herself out as a professional reader. At first merely a visitor in a series of strange houses, she has little idea how her role as storyteller and communicator will be subtly altered when her respective charges transform her into friend, confidante, mother, lover. Marie is played with poise, generosity and good humor by Miou-Miou, who in keeping the character open and ebullient throughout prevents the necessarily episodic film from seeming choppy.

Marie's initial client is a young man, Eric (Régis Royer), watched over by his mother since he was crippled in a traffic accident. Unwillingly celibate, Eric listens to Marie read Guy de Maupassant's "The Hair" while watching the slit of her skirt idle up her thigh. The preoccupations of a seconed client, a Hungarian general's widow (Maria Casarès), are entirely different. To her, Marie reads from Marx on the form and usages of precious metals. Marguerite Duras' *L'Amante* is chosen for a torpid, anxiety-ridden executive (Patrick Chesnais), who craves Marie's affections. And to a neglected six-year-old (Charlotte Farran) Marie recites Lewis Carroll.

Deville, co-writer of the script with his wife Rosalinde, defines each situation not only through characterization but by image and music. Leitmotifs, taken from Beethoven sonatas, are established for most of the principals, and domestic settings for the reading appointments are assigned a distinctive color, omnisciently underlining the mood struck between Marie and her listener. All this would be confining or overdetermined were it not for the element of inquiry, the expeditionary flavor, Deville attaches to *La Lectrice*. He bids us to consider the act of storytelling, and suggests that the heart of communication is less in what is actually said or written than in what is felt or interpreted. Beyond the power of words used to relate a story there is the unpredictable tension created by the listener, who identifies—sometimes even confuses—the tale with the teller.

It dawns on Marie, too, that her associations with her clients have begun to influence the texts she selects, and that she is no longer an impersonal conduit for literature but a living medium with extraliterary functions. Thus, she helps the general's widow hang politically provocative banners from a townhouse window, agrees to lift her dress before the smitten Eric, sleeps with the businessman, and mothers the child whose own parent becomes jealous of Marie's charms.

Rumors about Marie eventually come to the attention of the police, who are suspicious of her unusual profession. ("Reading is fine," they say, "but look where it leads!") Then the demand of a sly magistrate (Pierre Dux), anxious to undo Marie by proving she is a kind of literary panderer, succeeds. Requested to dispassionately read a brutally erotic passage from the Marquis de Sade's *120 Days of Sodom*, Marie falters and, saddened by her inability to dissociate herself from the embarrassing, explicit text, realizes she must discontinue her service.

Although the ending is downbeat, *La Lectrice* remains a gentle, hospitable film, elegantly observant of the pleasures and pitfalls of communication. Only David Mamet's *House of Games* (with its multilayered plot and incantatory dialogue, forcing us to listen not to words as they are said but to the deceptions beneath them) springs to mind as an equivalent achievement, sensitive to the netherworld of language and action. Where Mamet's approach is dry and mysterious, however, Deville's is wry and sportive.

Admired in France but underrecognized in the United States, Deville failed to attract an American audience with his stylish 1984 thriller *Death in a French Garden* (*Péril en la demeure*). Perhaps he will do better this time around. For he has given us that rare thing, a deft symbolic comedy.

NEW YORK POST, 4/21/89, p. 31, Jami Bernard

Constance reads in bed to her distracted boyfriend. It is a novel about a young woman, much like Constance, who reads books to people for a living . In fantasy while reading aloud, Constance becomes the reader, *La Lectrice,* of the novel, and in fact the movie is based on an actual book. Yes, it's the old book within a movie within a book wthin a movie routine (have I got that right?)

With Miou-Miou's soft, reassuring voice doing the reading, the movie practically emits that musty aroma of libraries that makes you want to be in one—which, you can imagine, is both a blessing and curse for a film, a product of a different medium.

The gamine Miou-Miou is Constance and then doubles as Marie, the *lectrice* of the novel. Marie places an ad for her literary services in a newspaper, hoping for handsome men and great adventure, and closes her eyes tightly before meeting her first client, like a child anticipating a gift.

As it turns out, no handsome men, but a bevy of broken people as disparate as a paraplegic teen who is more interested in his reader's thighs than in words, and a nervous businessman who is also interested in Marie's things but can't overcome his inhibitions without the help of his reader's astute choice of racy material.

Marie takes the place in their lives of a bartender or hairdresser—a wise but professional confidant who can soothe and advise. As she warms to her calling, she sizes up her clients and chooses just the text that will bring them to life.

For a neglected child, she reads *Alice in Wonderland,* then takes the girl off to a wonderland of her own, a carnival. For a blind but jolly old widow of a Hungarian general—"I am 100 years old and I am bored"—she reads Marx and Tolstoy, then whisks her off for a street demonstration.

Sometimes the assignments get out of hand. A retired, respectable-looking judge has his pals over for a deadpan reading of the Marquis de Sade. "Reading is fine, but look where it leads," warns a nevertheless intrigued cop when Marie keeps finding herself in trouble for her literal and figurative literary seductions.

The streets and apartments of Arles are brightly, cleanly lit, providing the best kind of visual backdrop for Miou-Miou, winningly impish with her blond pixie hair and ultra-blue woolen hat framing that serious little face.

Also of interest is Maria Casarès ("Children of Paradise") as the passionate centenarian.

Director Michel Deville weaves the film's components together in scraps and echoes (some of the actors play dual roles), and the result is light, and yes, a bit slight.

"La Lectrice" is a charming picaresque, although it seems to drag a bit after the novelty wears off. Still, it is a pleasure to watch and listen to Miou-Miou, chapter and verse.

NEWSDAY, 4/21/89, Part III/p. 3, Mike McGrady

"La Lectrice" is *not* just another sexy French movie. I want to be crystal clear on this point because some less sophisticated viewers may be confused by the fact that the central figure (Miou-Miou) tends to run around in a state of undress while offering a variety of clients a variety of love experiences.

Although some may harbor doubts about the film's seriousness of intent, "La Lectrice" could do more to stamp out international illiteracy than any number of well-intentioned governmental programs. This tale of a professional reader who visits the very old, the very young and the very ill, satisfying *all* their needs much the way a good book might, illustrates the joy of reading as well as any movie in memory.

For a teenage boy (Régis Royer) confined to a wheelchair, the reader selects romantic poetry by Baudelaire and Maupassant while occasionally . . .um . . . exposing herself. To a businessman suffering from insecurity, she reads Marguerite Duras' "The Lover" even while engaged in acts of intercourse. For an aging judge (Pierre Dux), she chooses selections from the Marquis de Sade.

Still, you say this sounds like "La Lectrice" is just another sexy French movie? *Au contraire!* Every effort has been made to keep the film respectable. For example, the action, and I do mean action, all takes place in the mind of a woman reading a book to her husband, a woman with an obvious gift for fantasy, a woman able to throw herself into her work with rare passion. Sexy? *Mais non!* Writer-director Michael Deville absolutely—*absolument!*—insists on the film's essentially intellectual nature. There is all that literature being read aloud. Lest anyone still remain unconvinced, Deville has thrown in many high-brow cinematic extras. The music, all courtesy of Beethoven, provides a different sonata for each character. Moreover, each character is color-coded, given a color scheme that matches personality and music.

Still suspicious? *Incroyable!* The film is based on two books by Raymond Jean, an author of impeccable intellectual credentials, and echoes countless other works. A maid attacked by spiders has a symbolic connection to "Theme of the Traitor and the Hero" by Jorge Luis Borges, Bernardo Bertolucci's "The Spider's Stratagem" and "The Kiss of the Spider Woman." That's according to the publicity notes. Let me confess that one or two of these symbolic tie-ins may have escaped my attention at first, but it's difficult to concentrate fully when a lovely woman keeps dressing and undressing in front of you.

I have but one fear about "La Lectrice." Hollowood has an unfortunate tendency to remake French movies in its own image. We saw this recently when the lighter-than-air "Cousin, Cousine" was so poorly translated into "Cousins." The way we tend to remake French movies is to first neuter them, then add huge amounts of lead. If there were anything heavy-handed about "La Lectrice," anything even slightly self-conscious, people might get the impression they were watching, well, a sexy movie instead of a challenging exercise for the intellect, which is what this is. *Vraiment!*

VILLAGE VOICE, 4/25/89, p. 71, Georgia Brown

The use of literary text in film stimulates an emotional effect that French New Wave directors understood well. Who can forget the reading of Poe's "The Oval Portrait" in *Vivre sa vie*, the rehearsal of *Bérénice* at the ending of *Une Femme mariée*, Oscar Werner spelling out the title page of *David Copperfield* in *Farenheit 451*? As far as I can tell, Michel Deville—whose birthdate lies between Godard's in 1930 and Truffaut's in '32—has no interest whatever in this transaction between forms. Deville's *La Lectrice* is a sex comedy using books and reading the way it uses wallpaper and designer bedsheets. Sets by production designer Thierry Leproust give the film the look of a series of Martex spreads. Cute, if that's how you like your movies.

A woman reading becomes the woman read about (both played by Miou-Miou). Constance, the first woman, has an irritable boyfriend Jean—"My eyes hurt...read to me"—who turns into fictional Marie's tepid boyfriend Phillipe (Christian Ruché). The book Constance reads aloud to Jean is a Raymond Jean novel, *La Lectrice*, about a woman who—out of desire for a profession that will engage her passion—places an ad offering herself as a reader to those unable to read.

The clients Marie elicits are an incapacitated bunch: a crippled 14-year-old boy who wants a glimpse of what's under her skirt; a near-blind Communist widow of a Hungarian general (Maria Casarès of *Les Enfants du paradis* and *Orphée*); a rich businessman and premature ejaculator (Patrick Chesnais) who also wants to get under her skirt; a six-year-old whose fashionable mother has no time for her; a retired judge with a library of leather-bound first editions who wants to hear Marie read about rude things that can be done to what is under her skirt.

Reading is the least of what this Dr. Ruth cum babysiter is required to do. None of her clients is listening anyway. Well, except the creepy judge. (Marie's reading to him of a buggery passage from de Sade's *The 120 Days of Sodom* is the movie's only affecting use of a text.) But the others find every excuse to keep her from her intended purpose—the widow hears a sentence from Marx and begs to join a street demonstration; the child doesn't even get a word from *Alice in Wonderland* before she takes off for a street fair; the boy hears mention of a golden fleece and asks Marie to pull up her skirt; the businessman listens to a snatch of Duras's *The Lover* and wants to lick Marie's quite nice behind—and Marie, in her smart red hat or her smart blue hat, in her white underwear or without, is happy to oblige. Well, except for the creepy judge.

Deville intersperses Leproust's color-coordinated interiors (sets built in a Paris warehouse) with whimsical shots of the pert Miou-Miou making her rounds up and down the streets of old Arles. (The movie was so clearly shot in discreet phases—interiors and exteriors—that the concept of "location," as with all those American movies transposed to Canada these days, loses credibility.) I should mention that each character, having his or her own color scheme and style of decor, gets a theme from a Beethoven sonata besides.

Also reviewed in:
NEW YORK TIMES, 4/21/89, p. C10, Vincent Canby
VARIETY, 8/24/88, p. 86
WASHINGTON POST, 5/19/89, p. D7, Hal Hinson
WASHINGTON POST, 5/19/89, Weekend/p. 41, Desson Howe

LAST WARRIOR, THE

A SVS Films release. *Producer:* Keith Watkins. *Director:* Martin Wragge. *Screenplay:* Martin Wragge. *Director of Photography:* Fred Tammes. *Editor:* Jacqueline Le Cordeur. *Music:* Adrian Strijdom. *Running time:* 94 minutes. *MPAA Rating:* R.

CAST: Gary Graham (Bartholomew Gibb); Maria Holvoe (Katherine); Cary-Hiroyuki Tagawa (Lieutenant Homma); John Carson (Priest); Steven Ito and Al Karaki (Imperial Marines).

NEW YORK POST, 10/20/89, p. 27, V.A. Musetto

"The Last Warrior" is the most hilarious new movie in town. Problem is, it's supposed to be deadly serious.

The pic belongs to the Macho Guy and Beautiful Innocent Woman Stranded on an Island genre. He's Bartholomew Gibb, a hunky Marine stationed on a jungle isle to keep tabs on the Japanese fleet toward the end of World War II. She's Kate, a beautiful nun-to-be, who gets left behind with Gibb (don't ask why) when Japanese troops haul off the island's natives and church missionaries.

Enter Imperial marine Lt. Homma, a beefy Japanese soldier with pulsating nostrils and a ceremonial sword who (again, don't ask) decides he can't just kill Gibb and get on with the war. No, the death must take place "with honor" or somesuch. (If you're wondering where the rest of the Japanese army is, so am I.)

This silly premise allows Gibb to bare his muscular chest, tumble off cliffs and plunge through windows, looking none the worse for wear. It also allows Kate to run hysterically through the jungle in a white gown that, when the light catches her just right, becomes transparent.

"This is war, sister," screams Gibb. "You're an arrogant, conceited man," Kate screams back. Yes, love at first sight.

"How long are we going to stay here," Kate inquires over the campfire one night. "Until they quit," snarls Gibb. Rambo couldn't have put it better.

Gibb is no match for the barrel-chested Homma. But is the Japanese content to finish off Gibb when the chance arises? Of course not. "It wasn't meant to end like this," Homma proclaims, standing over his foe after a hand-to-hand battle on the beach. Yeah, they have another 30 minutes worth of film to fill.

"The Last Warrior" is the directing debut of Martin Wragge, who in better times made his living in real estate. I'll have to admit that he has a knack for eyecatching visual (if you ignore the cliched slow-motion fight scenes). But the script (by Wragge) is so trite, disjointed, unbelievable and unitentionally funny that it doesn't much matter.

Gibb is played by Gary Graham, who was Tom Cruise's brother in "All the Right Moves." Here he looks like someone suffering from terminal Stallone Syndrome. The Swedish-born Maria Holvoe is Kate. The script doesn't give her much to work with, but I have a feeling that with decent material she could be a fine actress.

Homma is portrayed by Cary-Hiroyuki Tagawa, last seen as the "chief eunuch" in "The Last Emperor." The press notes quote Tagawa: "Working with director (Bernardo) Bertolucci was quite a career break." Well, fellow, "The Last Warior" is no way to take advantage of it.

VILLAGE VOICE, 10/31/89, p. 83, Manohla Dargis

As Michael Douglas proves to us in *Black Rain*, America may be losing the trade war, but hell, we can still kick some serious (Japanese) butt. In *The Last Warrior*, director/writer/ex-realtor Martin Wragge proves that for true satisfaction, it's back to WW II, the war we *won*. Delirious hyperschlock, *Warrior* takes place during the spring of '45. On a Pacific island a U.S. marine, Bartholomew Gibb (Gary Graham), with an '80s pumped-up chest and limited word count, is a one-man radio unit feeding info to intelligence, sleeping with Polynesian maidens on his off-hours.

A Japanese warship invades and abducts the natives (it's a small island), along with a white priest and his flock of nuns. Gibb hurls himself through the mission's stained glass and escapes to find company with Kate, a winsome Swedish beauty with ski-slope cheekbones (Maria Holvoe), who just happens to be a novice nun. (This makes for lines of pure, terse beauty like "This is war, Sister" and "Why a nun?") The two join together against three imperial soldiers left behind to kill Gibb. Luckily the Japanese prefer swordsmanship, and Gibb rapidly dispatches two of them in fights shot almost exclusively in loving slow motion—arcing spurts of gore intercut with fetishistic close-ups of weaponry and tortured flesh.

The other last warrior is Imperial Marine Lieutenant Homma (Cary-Hiroyuki Tagawa), who, when he's not staring balefully at *Life* pictorials on Pearl Harbor, plays cat and mouse with Gibb. Homma easily captures his foe, but then embarks on a crash course to teach the ignoble Yank the art of battle. The lessons climax in epiphany on the beach. Gibb lies hog-tied one evening at Homma's feet as the lieutenant lectures him. "One on one you are no match for us, except when you fight us with one of your *machines*." Homma then winds up Gibb's Victrola and in one stroke intimates the glorious electronic future of Japan (not to mention that of Sony, whose subsidiary, SVS, is distributing *Warrior*).

This ideological hash, however, never allows us to forget who the enemy is. Most of the close-ups of Homma (including an ugly scene with a cobra) are cropped to frame only his eyes. The requisite defilement of the white vestal virgin forces Kate to bare her breast—crucifix dangling next to a pink nipple—for her Asian captor. As with most action flicks, however, the sister is peripheral to *Warrior's* central romance, a sweaty affair that finds Gibb and Homma continuously sticking pointed objects into each other's bodies.

Also reviewed in:
NEW YORK TIMES, 10/21/89, p. 16, Stephen Holden
VARIETY, 5/31-6/7/89, p. 36

LAWRENCE OF ARABIA

A Columbia Pictures release of a reconstructed and restored version of the 1962 film. *Producer:* Sam Spiegel. *Producer (restoration):* Robert A. Harris and Jim Painten. *Director:* David Lean. *Reconstruction/Restoration:* Robert A. Harris. *Screenplay:* Robert Bolt. *Director of Photography:* F.A. "Freddie" Young. *Editor:* Anne V. Coates. *Music:* Maurice Jarre. *Rerecording Mixer:* Gregg Landaker. *Sound Editor:* Winston Ryder. *Production Designer:* John Box. *Art Director:* John Stoll. *Set Decorator:* Dario Simoni. *Costumes:* Phyllis Dalton. *Running time:* 216 minutes. *MPAA Rating:* PG.

CAST: Peter O'Toole (Lawrence); Alec Guiness (Prince Faisal); Anthony Quinn (Auda Abu Tayi); Jack Hawkins (General Allenby); Jose Ferrer (Turkish Bey); Anthony Quayle (Colonel Harry Brighton); Claude Raines (Mr. Dryden); Arthur Kennedy (Jackson Bentley); Donald Wolfit (General Murray); Omar Sharif (Sherif Ali Ibn el Kharish); I.S. Johar (Gasim); Gamil Ratib (Majid); Michael Ray (Faraj).

LOS ANGELES TIMES, 2/15/89, Calendar/p. 1, Sheila Benson

From the suppressed excitement in its overture to the last moments as that prophetic motorcyclist overtakes Lawrence's open car in the desert, David Lean's "Lawrence of Arabia," restored to its full clarity and magnificence, is one of the Seven Wonders of the cinematic world.

Nothing to come along since "Lawrence's" release in 1962 has diminished the power of cameraman F.A. (Freddie) Young's desert vistas. Stretched out in 70-millimeter Super Panavision vastness, the movie's most pungent memory has lost nothing to time as a shimmering pin point in the center of the screen becomes clearer and clearer and can finally be read as a man, all in black, on camelback, riding straight toward the camera. It's still the greatest actor's entrance in movies, the one that launched Omar Sharif into American movie-going consciousness.

But Lean never makes haunting pictures for their own sake; he uses scale to sculpt character, and as our themes shrink along with our screens, the joy of storytelling on this epic scale is thrilling. It couldn't have been an easy story to shape. Thomas Edward Lawrence was a scholar, a soldier, a hero with notable flaws and a man whom Lowell Thomas said had "a genius for backing into the limelight."

In his literate, subtle screenplay from Lawrence's autobiography, "The Seven Pillars of Wisdom," Robert Bolt has kept all of Lawrence's complexities: his reticences and his flair for bravura; his compassion and the blood lust that came on him after his capture by a Turkish Bey at Deraa. And in fleshing out the man, Peter O'Toole has fatally colored our vision of Lawrence; the 5-foot-4 "El Aurens" will forever live as a 6-foot 2 gold-blond demigod.

What has changed? We're finally able to take O'Toole's unwavering charisma for granted and look beyond him to the film's uncommonly compassionate and shaded portrayal of these Arab leaders. They emerge as proud, brave, ancient, honorable: Alec Guinness' elegantly ironic Prince Feisal or Sharif's firebrand Sherif Ali, fascinating alternatives to the all-purpose villainy that has been the Arabs' lot on screen for so long. The intensity of Lawrence's exchanges with these sinuous, seductive men make us forget completely that it is a film without women.

Bolt has been only moderately successful in explaining what was taking place historically: a revolt by the Arabs against the occupying Turks during World War I. Bolt is better at laying out Lawrence's passion to create an Arab nation.

Bolt and Lean are best at change-ups, at shifting down from scenic vastness to intimate, highly charged moments between two or three characters. Wonderful vignettes emerge: Claude Raines at his Cheshire-cat best as the foreign office politician Dryden; Jack Hawkins' shrewdly manipulative Gen. Allenby, and Jose Ferrer's indelible Turkish Bey, whose beating of Lawrence reveals to the Englishman two sides to himself that he finds unendurable: a human side and a streak of masochism.

That last trait, of pleasure in punishing his body, has been hinted at in a reinstated early, crucial scene between Lawrence and his fellow soldier-cartographers in Cairo. Sliding his fingers up a match to put it out, Lawrence says: "Of course it hurts. The trick is not minding that it hurts."

There's a slyness to the film makers' presentation of Lawrence; twice, they set off his superhuman accomplishments with scenes in which a detached observer catches him when he believes himself utterly alone. As he runs to float his silken sheik's robes, given by Sharif as a measure of homate, and to catch his reflection in his dagger, we move sideways to see his preening, mortifyingly, from the point of view of Anthony Quinn, as Auda Abu Tayi, sardonic leader of an opposing tribe.

The film, now 3 hours and 36 minutes long (rated PG, because its language is pure although its scenes are sometimes bloody), is in two unequal halves. The action before the intermission is the upward arc of Lawrence's life, the second half is his tragic unraveling, documented by Arthur Kennedy's Jackson Bentley, a correspondent and resident ugly American.

The first half ends after Lawrence has pulled off a seeming military impossibility, crossing the oven-like Nefud desert and capturing the Turkish stronghold of Aqaba. Lawrence's return is a moment of unabashed theater—Gen. Allenby conferring with his filthy, burnoose-clad lieutenant, equal to equal. It's a little embarrassing to discover how deeply satisfying the scene is.

The shorter second half, as Lawrence's illusions are stripped from him, is almost unendurably painful and oddly unsatisfying. Here, the great visual moments are invariably connected with suffering, like the scene in Allenby's quarters when Lawrence's wounds at the hands of the Turks bleed through his jacket. This stigmata is an eerie, almost Shakespearean, device, a bloody witness to his "weakness."

In the year after its debut, "Lawrence's" overwhelming authority collared seven Academy Awards—best picture, director, (color) cinematography, (color) art direction, sound, editing and music. Although it seems shocking that O'Toole and Sharif were omitted, now we can also be grateful for its artful and resourceful restorers, Robert Harris and Jim Painten, to Columbia Pictures and the quartet of Martin Scorsese, Steven Spielberg, Jon Davison and Dawn Steel, who supported the complex restoration.

NEW YORK, 2/13/89, p. 78, David Denby

In the age of the VCR, as millions of viewers molder before big pictures haplessly vibrating on tiny screens—Mahler symphonies played on a pocket comb—we could all use some reminding of what the movies can do. The reissue of *Lawrence of Arabia* and, for the zillionth time, *Gone With the Wind*, both arrayed on huge screens, restores a little grandeur to the moviegoing experience. Our movies may never recover the ambition they once had, but at the Ziegfeld, with hundreds of Bedouins, swords upraised, thundering across the desert, their women in black howling on distant cliffs, we'll at least know we're not sitting in bed listening to the faucet drip between lines of dialogue.

Columbia Pictures restored the 1962 *Lawrence* to its original length and presented it last spring to Sir David Lean, now 80, who reedited and cut it slightly. A few dialogue scenes have been extended, some transitions improved and details added, the effect of which is to make *Lawrence* seem even grander than before—and also better paced (Lean tightened the whole movie.)

For the uninitiated: This great and strange film, a colossally flamboyant mixture of pomp and neurosis, celebrates and deplores T.E. Lawrence (Pete O'Toole), the tremulous classical scholar and Arabist from Oxford, translator of Homer, author of the beautiful, rapturously egotistical autobiography *The Seven Pillars of Wisdom*. Lawrence, no more than an obscure junior officer on the British general staff, wandered into the desert in 1916, made contact with a variety of mutually hostile Arab tribes, and led them on a series of devastating raids against the Turks, whom both the British and the Arabs wanted thrown out of the Middle East. Lawrence imposed himself on the imagination of an alien culture, turning himself into a lurid desert savior—great military hero, endurer of privations, beyond measure, seeker of the Arab soul.

With the restored passages, we get more of a sense of arrival and departure: Lawrence sweeping with Bedouin tribesmen into the camp of a rival tribe, Lawrence reentering his life as a British officer in Cairo. The joinings and partings that mark the stages of the journey across the desert are now clearer. Everything is clearer. Looking at the movie, you feel as if your eyesight had suddenly improved. New prints have been struck from the rebuilt 65-mm. negative, and the superfine grain structure yields stunning detail, all of it rendered in an accurate, slightly dry color palette.

Lean and his cinematographer, Freddie Young, shot *Lawrence* in such intimidatingly alien places as Jordan's Jebel Tubeiq—a desolate area of reddish-brown sand dunes and huge rock formations from whose heights gigantic vistas appear in the endless expanse of desert. The movie is an opening up to depths, and depths within depths. In two of the most famous sequences, black specks in the distance resolve themselves into heroic matter—riders emerging from steaming lakes of heat. We're constantly pulled deeper into the frame. *Lawrence* is about conquering space; its great crossings and journeys become spiritual as much as physical feats. At one point, Lawrence mentions Moses in the Sinai, and it's amusing to think of *Lawrence* as a biblical spectacular—only with the psyche of its hero worn on the sleeves of his robes.

Back in 1962, critics complained that Lawrence's character wasn't coherent enough to hold the movie together. But the dramatic arc of his development seems clear enough to me. A would-be Nietzschean superman, Lawrence, consciously theatrical, wills himself into greatness and becomes an inspirational leader, collapsing in the end when the harshness of the desert brings out in him a horrifying, addictive love of pain and slaughter. For the modern hero, willing to explore the depths of his own character, physical glory pursued to the ultimate leads inevitable to its opposite—degradation and self-annihilation. Lawrence was that kind of modern man and was shocked at what he found in himself. The movie dramatizes a rapid rise and a sudden, mortifying fall—a withdrawal, really, into a state of willed nonexistence. In the person of the volatile, extraordinarily handsome young Peter O'Toole, Lawrence becomes an actor exuding glamour and mystery who abruptly absents himself from the state—a Garbo of history, done in by self-disgust.

At the moment, Lean and screenwriter Robert Bolt are preparing a movie version of Joseph Conrad's *Nostromo*, but they already made their Conrad novel on film in *Lawrence*. *Lawrence of Arabia* is their *Heart of Darkness*. It is surely the greatest epic of the postwar Anglo-American cinema, and one of the few made for adults. Lean doesn't plunge into the middle fo the action the way Kurosawa or Peckinpah does. He holds back and makes a majestically composed movie in which space becomes spiritual distance: We are thrilled by the size of foreground, middeground, and background, all held in balance. On the big screen, we can finally see all three and lose ourselves blissfully in the clarified vastness of the image.

NEW YORK POST, 2/8/89, p. 23, David Edelstein

Early in "Lawrence of Arabia"—before we've seen much of Arabia—British Lieutenant T.E. Lawrence (Peter O'Toole) is an impudent secretary in Cairo. After receiving new orders, he announces to his colleagues that he's going to the desert to see Prince Faisal (Alec Guinness), whom he hopes to assist in the Arab revolt against Turkish rule. Lawrence blows out a match, and there's a startling cut to the sun rising hot on the vast, orange desert horizon, which reaches from one end of the wide screen to the other.

The cut, complete with crashing cymbals and thundering orchestra, is showy and heavyhanded, but this is beside the point. Confronted with that huge, empty, satiny desert—in Super Panavision 70—the heart leaps. This, dear reader, is the widest of wide-screen motion pictures. If you've only seen "Lawrence" on TV, you haven't really seen it; you might as well listen to Beethoven's Ninth over the phone.

Trimmed by its producer in early 1962 (after three weeks of release), "Lawrence" has now been meticulously restored, color-corrected, dubbed (by many in the original cast) and re-edited by director David Lean himself, who never had the chance to do his "fine cut." Thanks to Robert A. Harris, who spent two years on the reconstruction, there is finally a clear, definitive "Lawrence," both enlarged and sharpened.

At the Ziegfeld, one of the country's great theaters, the images are lustrous and stark against a pale, titanic canvas. The landscape is integral, and Lean and his cinematographer (Freddie Young) immerse you in it completely. When, on their camels, Lawrence and his guide trudge past a mightly rock face, the desert opens up, vertiginous and sublime. Man is but a speck in this gorgeous abyss.

The scale of the film discourages intimacy, and Lawrence isn't an easy hero to read. In 1962, reviewers criticized O'Toole for being mannered and neurasthenic, preferring Omar Sharif's simpler, more accessible Sherif Ali. But today Sharif seems blockish—a mere foil—while O'Toole's performance, in all its capriciousness, gels.

He is beautiful, first of all, a slim, straw-haired boy with full lips and shining blue eyes. O'Toole's Lawrence isn't campy, but he has a schoolgirl's giddiness—a subversive delicacy—and a penchant for self-dramatization. Lawrence knows that part of the secret of inspiring the Arabs is the creation of a myth around himself, and he comes to believe in that myth; galloping exuberantly around the camps in his flowing, silken sheik's robes, he seems tipsy with his own exoticism.

Yet O'Toole also conveys Lawrence's deep respect for the Arab mind and temperament, and he struggles valiantly to reconcile the aims of the Arabs with those of the British government—which would love to divide Arabia with France at the close of the First World War.

Proudly insisting that "nothing is written," that man creates his own destiny, Lawrence's triumphs in the field embolden him while the deaths of those he loves turn him reckless and nihilistic. His sense of invincibility is cruelly shattered when, on a secret expedition to Der'a, he is beaten and sexually assaulted by a Turkish commander (Jose Ferrer)—a sequence that is longer and more harrowing in the restored version.

This golden boy becomes a hero for the modern age: a man debased instead of ennobled by bloodshed; a master strategist who, in the midst of carnage, is overcome by the human tragedy in general, and by his own capacity for sadism (and masochism) in particular. His integrity irrevocably lost, he hurls himself into the killing. Once Damascus has been taken he returns to England, exhausted and ashamed, longing only to obliterate the self he has so dramatically inflated.

The film's Lawrence has been described by critics as enigmatic; others, notably John Mack in his penetrating 1976 study "A Prince of Our Disorder," complain the movie turns him into a cartoon sadist. (Mack's criticisms seem odd after seeing the film again—his and Lean's Lawrence aren't that far apart.)

The restorations help to counter both charges. In the truncated version, when Lawrence and his army come upon a column of retreating Turks, his hysterical command to take no prisoners seems a tad . . . excessive. Now we see what motivates the subsequent Tafas massacre — the Turks have just slaughtered scores of Arab women and children. (This in no way justifies the murder of 5,000 men, but it does explain the depth of the Arabs' fury.)

What is certainly true—even in the restored version—is that at no point does Lawrence crystallize into a *character*, a finished thing. Lean and screenwriter Robert Bolt respect his contradictory nature too much to pin down his motives. They are also, as artists, impersonal by temperament—more interested in the public than the private man.

The impersonality isn't always intentional, and at times "Lawrence" seems ponderous and elephantine. There are none of the ragingly kinetic battle scenes we associate with modern directors—no release. Unlike most war films, "Lawrence of Arabia" doesn't accelerate in its battles; it sustains its flat, stately, detached tempo for nearly four hours.

Yet this, too, works for its subject. Distances in the desert are so vast and travel so arduous that the pace of the film is itself expressive. When Lawrence's army at last reaches a destination—when it surges into the coastal city of Aqaba, for instance, in a single, high-angle shot—one feels a rare exhilaration at the sight of their sudden swiftness. They were moving this quickly all along—except the desert's immensity made it seem as if they were standing still.

Similarly, "Lawrence of Arabia" might not always look like it's moving, but it shifts effortlessly from sweeping historical to knotty psychological forces. The stasis is deceptive—a mirage.

NEWSWEEK, 2/6/89, p. 75, David Ansen with Constance Guthrie

Perhaps you were one of the lucky ones who saw "Lawrence of Arabia" in December 1962, when it ran 222 minutes in glorious 70-mm splendor. Or perhaps you saw it a month later, when 20 minutes had been lopped off by producer Sam Spiegel to allow more showings. By the time it was released again in 1971, even more footage had been cut, making T.E. Lawrence, an enigmatic figure to begin with, an all but incomprehensible one. And if you were really unlucky, you saw it only on TV or home video, where its spellbinding desert vistas are chopped into postage-stamp images of sand.

None of these versions—even the first, which won seven Oscars and is considered by many to be the most intelligent epic ever turned out by Hollywood—was precisely the one director David Lean intended. Rushed into release in '62, the film didn't get the fine-tuning that Lean wanted. Now, 27 years later, after an arduous restoration overseen by producer-archivist Robert A. Harris and his partner, Jim Painten, Lean's vast and intimate masterwork will be unveiled in its definitive form—216 minutes of some of the most ravishing movie images you'll ever dream of, shot by cinematographer Freddie Young. Lean himself did the final cut, taking Harris and Painten's 223 minutes and trimming seven minutes from it.

Lean's extravaganza, which cost a whopping $15 million back then, is the rare proof of the usually dubious bigger-is-better esthetic. We are enveloped in the immensity of Lawrence's passionate ambition to become a warrior/savior who will unite the Arab tribes against their common enemy, the Turks. But though the movie encompasses the global implications of World War I and British colonial ambitions in the Middle East, it never loses its intimate focus on Peter O'Toole's delicate, dashing Lawrence. There's a haunting irony in the sheer scale of the movie— all this blood, all this glory, rests on the slight, elegant shoulders of a self-invented English adventurer who ultimately recoils from the savagery he finds inside his own contradictory soul. In retrospect, it's the pivotal Hollywood epic: its stately, classical style looks back to the heroic adventure movies of the past, while its ambivalent, subversive content anticipates such future, antiheroic spectacles as "Apocalypse Now."

When Harris first got his hands on the camera negative of the original print, not only was it warped and badly scratched, it, too, had been cut. Even more daunting, the audio for the 20 excised minutes had been thrown away. "There was no surviving print," Harris recalls, "and there was no written continuity of the film. So when we started we didn't even know what it was we were trying to restore."

In all, it took more than two years and over $600,000 to reconstruct the movie. Columbia delivered about 4,000 pounds of material to Harris's office. Months of screening time were spent finding the missing footage, which was all in unmarked boxes. But even when the film was reassembled, with some new material added, "we still had more than 10 minutes that had no dialogue surviving, no music and no effects," recalls Harris. The sound track had to be re-created from scratch. Since what was on screen didn't always follow Robert Bolt's script, a hearing-impaired couple were hired to lip-read certain scenes in order to reconstruct the dialogue. Peter O'Toole and Alec Guinness re-recorded their lines in London, Anthony Quinn did his in New York and Arthur Kennedy was tracked down living in Savannah, Ga. Their voices had changed over the years, so Gregg Landaker, a master sound mixer, altered the harmonics electronically to match the original tones of the actors.

At one point, Columbia Pictures, during David Puttnam's tumultuous last months as studio chief, dropped the restoration project. It took the passionate lobbying of Steven Spielberg and Martin Scorsese to save the film: they persuaded Puttnam's successor, Dawn Steel, to back it again. "The negative was absolutely crumbling," Harris says. "Had they not acted when they did, right now we would not be able to see the film. It would not be restorable, ever."

The result is the happiest news for movie lovers in a long time. In February this mesmerizing spectacle will open in New York, Washington and Los Angeles. If audiences respond favorably— and they'd be crazy not to—it will open all across the country. They really don't make 'em like this anymore: for almost four hours, the new "Lawrence of Arabia" reminds us of the transcendent power of the movies.

TIME, 2/6/89, p. 62, Richard Corliss

It seemed a mad gamble: a $12 million epic about an eccentric English adventurer on the fringe of World War I, set in the sere deserts of the Middle East. It was hell to shoot: 18 months in the singeing sun of Jordan, Morocco and Spain. It had an obscure actor in the title role and no speaking parts for women. When it opened in New York City during the 1962 newspaper strike, one of the film's few reviewers, Andrew Sarris, called it "dull, overlong and coldly impersonal ... hatefully calculating and condescending."

How sweet the balm of history. Like its half-mad hero, *Lawrence*, in its pristine splendor. One more movie hero, film archivist Robert A. Harris, spent years sifting through 3½ tons of film to reconstruct Lean's film, which, like the stone monuments of the Sahara, had been eroded by time. On this gorgeous *Lawrence*, with its sparkling 65-mm prints and crisp Dolby sound, Harris was the producer and the chief surgeon. Next week the film has gala premieres before opening in New York City, Washington and Los Angeles.

Robert Bolt's eloquent, epigrammatic script traces Lawrence's career from mapmaking in the British army's Cairo headquarters to masterminding Arab nationalism. In Peter O'Toole's pensive, swashbuckling incarnation, Lawrence makes for a curious messiah. With his skin like a mandarin orange dipped in sand, his voice intimate and cryptic, his haunted eyes staring from inside his burnoose, O'Toole creates a towering, tragic, high-camp sheik of Araby.

In 1962 *Lawrence* was the ultimate epic—cinema at the apex of its ambition and intelligence. Lavish in visual beauty, the film also boasts economy of style: it knows how much can be shown in a shot, how much can be said in a few words. But the picture was a harbinger too. If Lawrence was the last colonial God-man, he was also the movie epic's first moody hero, father to countless sacred screen madmen. And in the picture's political wrangling and massacre scenes, we see hints of American history in the late '60s and American movies today: a preview of Viet Nam and a prequel to *Platoon*.

This was the first of Lean's three elemental dramas—*Lawrence* (sand), *Doctor Zhivago* (snow), *Ryan's Daughter* (sea)—and the most spectacular, a feast for smart eyes. Two camels negotiate the swollen dunes like ants moving across a sleeping woman's legs. "The desert," says Lawrence, "is an ocean in which no oar is dipped." Lean and cinematographer Freddie Young translated that simile of the Saharan sea into screen poetry. They caught the wash of sand curling off the crest of a dune, the seaside effect of light shimmering over the parched expanse. When Lawrence finally treads in the surf of Aqaba, he can celebrate more than a military victory; he is primed to savor a mirage come true. The sand is now water, and this miracle man can walk on both.

But what miracle could save *Lawrence* from Hollywood's corrosive carelessness? Producer Sam Spiegel had shaved 20 minutes from the film's original 217, and 20 more were cut upon the film's 1970 rerelease. "It was as though some little rodent was nibbling at the healthy body of the film," O'Toole says. "And not even a tasteful rodent." Harris soon discovered that the negative was warped and scratched; splices were falling apart. The distributor, Columbia Pictures, had also junked more than 600,000 feet of dialogue and music tracks. Not only would the film have to be pieced together, but also ten minutes of the dialogue demanded redubbing.

"I like to take on things that I can't do easily," Harris says. Here was a worthy challenge. He imported prints from England, Germany and the Netherlands and married bits of them to snippets from Long Island City, N.Y., and Hollywood. Aided by Lean and film editor Anne V. Coates, he determined the sequence and duration of each shot. Parts of the dialogue track had been lost, so Harris lured some of the stars back into studios, using electronic tricks to lighten the aging voices. Arthur Kennedy, whom Harris located by calling every "Kennedy, A." in Savannah, recorded his lines there. Anthony Quinn did his dubbing in New York City. And Lean, 80, directed O'Toole and Alec Guinness (Prince Faisal) in London. "When I was sitting there," the director says, "there was hardly a line of dialogue that I couldn't finish." Finally, Lean and Harris supervised the mix in Hollywood. "They did a magical job there," he says. "It was a work of love."

So love conquers all, even the ravages of time. As Spielberg says, "*Lawrence of Arabia* 25 years later looks better and sounds better than any film that has been in theaters since *Lawrence of Arabia*." Now only three tasks remain. Lean should keep working with Bolt on their new film, *Nostromo*. Hollywood should get cracking on other overdue restoration work. And moviegoers should hie out to some triplex or googolplex and see how ravishing movies used to be.

VILLAGE VOICE, 2/14/89, p. 59, J. Hoberman

Old elephants never die, nor are they allowed to quietly fade away. Over at Radio City, the ever-ponderous *Gone With the Wind* celebrates its 50th anniversary with what feels like its 100th rerelease. A few blocks uptown, the restored *Lawrence of Arabia* lumbers into the Ziegfeld to a chorus of awe-struck hosannas. (Meanwhile, I've applied to the New York State Council on the Arts for a grant to reconstruct the Roxy as the right venue for the uncut *Call Me Bwana*.)

Lawrence of Arabia, which first materialized here in 1962 during a newspaper strike and is making up for lost ink, has enjoyed a reputation as the thinking person's epic, and that's part of its canny showmanship. There are more "ideas" per se in any John Ford western, but now more than ever, *Lawrence* seems the culmination of a certain imperial style—assured, nudgy, and spectacularly produced, if not divinely inspired. Although ostensibly English, the film marks the acme of American aspiration. There's more than a hint of delirious New Frontiermanship in its representation of a handsome, quixotic molder of Third World aspiration.

Dramatizing its own sense of entitlement, the movie opens with a fanfare of rhapsodic corniness: a ceremonial drum roll, a pre-screening overture played with the lights up, then the first insinuating burst of Maurice Jarre's "Slave Girl of Bagdad" theme. The hero's fatal motorcycle mishap, which leaves his goggles gently dangling on a branch, segues to funereal harrumphing ("He was the most extrah-ordinary man I ever knew"), then socks you with the great orange sky, bombastic Jarre resounding o'er the Arabian dunes. There's a Barnum & Bailey lyricism to *Lawrence's* first 20 minutes, but director David Lean and scenarist Robert Bolt can't sustain the clichés—although Bolt's most flaccid lines are characteristically delivered with the flourish of an engraved invitation on a silver plate. (Lawrence to guide, after many hours slogging through the desert: "You do not drink?" Guide to Lawrence, after suitable pause: "I am ... bedouin.")

At four hours, the movie is more tolerable than thrilling—although it's hard to deny the planetarium vistas, the vast expanse with a soupçon of sand blowing in one corner. (That the desert is a superb special effect is known to anyone who's ever seen Bill Viola's video, *Chott El-Djerid*.) For this, perhaps, we should thank producer Sam Spiegel—who lived in Palestine for eight years during the '20s, at one point supporting himself as a Jerusalem tour guide—and his crony, King Hussein of Jordan.

Under circumstances that would doubtless make an interesting movie in themselves, *Lawrence* was filmed on location in the kingdom Hussein's clan received for helping the British. Hussein had an understandable interest in supporting a project that so glowingly portrays his great-grand uncle, Faisal. But if *Lawrence* is likely the most Arab-a-philic Hollywood production since Valentio's last movie, *The Son of the Sheik*, it's not exactly a treasure trove of positive imagery. Omar Sharif's stellar entrance notwithstanding, the film doesn't stint with the burnt cork: As Faisal, Sir Alec Guinness appears in lisping Semitic mode, while Anthony Quinn plays desert warrior Auda Abu Tayi from behind a putty schnoz worthy of *Der Stürmer*. (It's especially terrifying in 70mm.)

In re-releasing this stirring postcolonial spectacle, Columbia is practicing a form of Puttnamism without the inconvenience of deposed production chief David Puttnam. *Lawrence* offers the kick of empire—it's a profoundly conservative movie that will doubtless be upvalued in the current cultural climate. Released at the moment that Godard, Resnais, and Ron Rice were challenging official pieties, *Lawrence* was, as David Denby puts it in the current *Premiere*, "regarded in higher critical circles as ... square and irrelevant." (As passé as *Lawrence* may have seemed in the winter of '62–'63, it was not without impact: The blistering desert scenes in *The Good, the Bad, and the Ugly* seem one result, while Lean's influence on recent Spielberg and Scorsese is alluded to by the "special thanks" they receive in *Lawrence's* new credits.)

Still, *Lawrence's* is not altogether square. The most compelling aspect of the film remains "El Aurens" himself. Lawrence's image was initially created by Lowell Thomas (played, under another name, by Arthur Kennedy); albeit more a complex individual, he belongs, with Rupert Brooke and Ernst Jünger, among those civilized men who found a perverse freedom and elemental purity in the course of fighting World War I. In *Lawrence*, perhaps, this attitude reaches its apogee—the hero is attracted to the desert because it's "clean." Lawrence's autobiographical *The Seven Pillars of Wisdom*, privately published in 1926 (the same year Valentino scored in his swan song) presented war as romantic adventure, fought by noble savages far from the trenches of Flanders Field, infused with desert mysticism and an undercurrent of sexual fantasy.

There's an aspect of *Lawrence* that is *Boy's Life* writ large. Exhibiting a toughness bordering on masochism, the actual Lawrence was small, hyperactive, and foppish, while Faisal, 31 at the time of their meeting, embodied for him another masculine ideal: "tall, graceful, and vigorous. ... His nature grudged thinking, for it crippled his speed in action." If this fails to evoke the calculating Guinness, it scarcely matters; the movie's ambiguous ideal is Lawrence himself. Peter O'Toole was far from Spiegel's first choice, but he appears in retrospect as a stroke of casting genius. Lean and intense, O'Toole dominates the film, his blue eyes blazing out of his burnoose or shimmering in the desert like twin oases, An emotional dervish, he can be fiercely gaunt or inappropriately flighty, waxing vixenish when devious General Allenby (Jack Hawkins) anticipates *The Last Temptation of Christ* by playing a resolute Judas to his wavering Jesus.

Teetering on the brink of a nervous breakdown or gruffly running his desert cult ("My friends, who will walk on water with me?"), O'Toole plays Lawrence as a magnificent cipher—a tormented, madcap adventurer with a fondness for Arab boys and desert gear. His joy at going native is worthy of *Glen or Glenda*. Presented with a royal burnoose, O'Toole launches into a full-scale preenfest. Small wonder that both actress Arlene Dahl and Harry Cohn's widow attended the Oscar ceremonies at which *Lawrence* carried off seven trophies (virtually acing *Mutiny on the Bounty* and *The Longest Day*) wearing dresses inspired by the film. Mooning over his charges, Lawrence is the virgin bridge of the desert. In the intermission closer, he arrives at British headquarters in full bedouin regalia, tenderly guiding an Arab boy into the officers' bar despite frantic cries of "Get the little wog out!" (At the end of the movie, the question of identification comes full circle—the hysterical Lawrence is finally taken for a wog and knocked down by a British soldier.)

Surrounding himself with rough trade, O'Toole's Lawrence wages war in a trembling snit, presiding over the massacre of an entire troop. This is not John Wayne, nor does the film shy away from the infamous incident at Dera'a. By Lawrence's disputed account, he was taken prisoner by an amorous bey and, having protected his honor by slugging the Turkish official, was consequently beaten and gang-raped by the bey's men. ("He now rejected me in haste, as a thing too torn and bloody for his bed.") Ripely played by José Ferrer, the bey rips off Lawrence's shirt, fondles his chest, takes a punch in the mouth, and orders a beating, leaving the rest to the viewer's imagination. "Perhaps *Lawrence of Arabia* is one brutal queer film too many," a *Voice* critic mused back in '62, winding up with a request for more movies with girls. Indeed, *Lawrence* is a virtually womanless show and O'Toole, running about in bedouin drag for hours at a time, functions like David Bowie in *Merry Christmas, Mr. Lawrence* (another descendant) as the universal object of desire.

Lawrence is certainly the most oddball of epics, marred by the strain of enforced normalcy. Shortly before the movie's release, Irving Howe wrote an essay characterizing *The Seven Pillars of Wisdom* as a self-conscious literary performance ("fierce . . . shocking . . . agitated") and its author as a genuinely modern (that is to say, neurotic) hero: introspective and ambivalent, half self-flagellating overachiever, half tawdry press hype. O'Toole's performance aside, *Lawrence* never turns against itself. Proudly, and often ponderously, linear, it could be the work of a kinky Kipling. Still, it seems appropriate that the movie should thunder back into view during the trial of our own debased equivalent, Oliver North. Ollie is to Lawrence what sitcom is to grand opera.

Also reviewed in:
NEW REPUBLIC, 2/20/89, p. 26, Stanley Kauffmann
WASHINGTON POST, 2/3/89, Weekend/p. 31, Desson Howe
WASHINGTON POST, 2/8/89, p. B1, Rita Kempley

LEAN ON ME

A Warner Brothers release. *Executive Producer:* John G. Avildsen. *Producer:* Norman Twain. *Director:* John G. Avildsen. *Screenplay:* Michael Schiffer. *Director of Photography:* Victor Hammer. *Editor:* John Carter and John G. Avildsen. *Music:* Bill Conti. *Music Editor:* Stephen A. Hope and George Craig. *Sound:* Alan Beyer. *Sound Editor:* Tom McCarthy and Burton M. Weinstein. *Production Designer:* Doug Kraner. *Art Director:* Tim Galvin. *Set Decorator:* Caryl Heller. *Special Effect: Costumes:* Jennifer von Mayrhauser. *Make-up:* Toy Russel-Van Lierop. *Stunt Coordinator:* Harry Madsen. *Running Time:* 108 minutes. *MPAA Rating:* PG-13.

CAST: Morgan Freeman (Joe Clark); Beverly Todd (Ms. Levias); Robert Gillaume (Dr. Frank Napier); Alan North (Mayor Don Bottman); Lynne Thigpen (Leona Barrett); Robin Bartlett (Mrs. Elliott); Michael Beach (Mr. Darnell); Ethan Phillips (Mr. Rosenberg); Sandra Reaves-Phillips (Mrs. Powers); Sloane Shelton (Mrs. Hamilton); Jermaine Hopkins (Thomas Sams); Karen Malina White (Kaneesha Carter); Karina Arroyave

(Maria); Ivonne Coll (Mrs. Santos); Regina Taylor (Mrs. Carter); Michael P. Moran (Mr. O'Malley); John Ring (Fire Chief Gaines); Tyrone Jackson (Clarence); Alex Romaguera (Kid Ray); Tony Todd (Mr. Wright); Mike Starr (Mr. Zirella); Michael Best, Stephen Capers Jr., Anthony Fuller, Dwayne Jones, and Kenneth Kelly (The Eastside "Songbirds"); Yvette Hawkins (Mrs. Arthur); Nicole Quinn (Lillian); Elsie Hilario (Louisa); Steven Lee (Richard Armand); Michael A. Joseph (Brian Banes); Richard Grusin (Mr. Danley); Jim Moody (Mr. Lott); Veniece Ross (Sally); Raul Gonzalez (Ramon); Luz Tolentino (Conchita); André Howell (Reggie); Nancy Gathers (Tanya); Corey Ginn (Charles Yale); Marina Durrel (Miss Ruiz); Nathalee Fairmon (Nathalee); Rev. Hershel Slappy (Rev. Slappy); Todd Alexander (Derrick); Anthony Figueroa (Hoodlum at Microphone); Delilah Cotto (Chita); Frances Sousa (Francesca); Lynda LaVergne (Student); Robert Kamlot (Photographer); Linda M. Salgado (Linda); Marcus Toure Boddie (Markus); Ashon Curvy (Ashon); Michael Imperioli (George); Marcella Lowery (Mrs. Richards); Frank Napier (School Board Member #1); Robert Rosenberg (School Board Member #2); Jennifer McComb (Ellen); Knowl Johnson (Tommy); Anthony G. Avildsen (Anthony); Pat McNamara (Police Officer); Harry Madsen (Teacher in Cafeteria); Heather Rose Dominic (Stacey); Mario Biazzo (Student in Cafeteria); Kisean Blount (Girl in Cafeteria); Bruce Malmuth (Burger Joint Manager); Frank Firrito, Manuel Carneiro, and Steve Adrianzen (White Boys/Singers).

FILMS IN REVIEW, 6-7/89, p. 361, Charles Epstein

In the tradition of Rambo, Dirty Harry, et al, comes Joe Clark, the maverick principal of *Lean On Me*. As the opening disclaimer states, what we are about to see is "based on a true story"— allowing John Avildsen (director of *Rocky*) some liberties with the celebrated saga of one of the more embattled principals in the annals of pedagogy. As the film opens, a dashikied Joe Clark presides over an animated classroom of eager junior high students.

The film jumps ahead twenty years to the graffitied corridors of New Jersey's Paterson Eastside High, lorded over by thugs, drug dealers—or, in Joe Clark's favorite word—miscreants. Cut to the mayor's office where Dr. Napier, the school superintendant, lobbies for the installation of his buddy, Joe Clark insisting that the no-nonsense Clark is just the man for the job. The mayor, needing results, accedes (if the school's average score on the basic skills test doesn't come up to snuff the state takes over the school).

Clark takes over the school as if leading a palace coup, rounding up the school's most notorious trouble makers, and in front of all those assembled in the auditorium expels them from school grounds—permanently. Clark, an equal opportunity dictator, tyrannizes his faculty at their first meeting, demanding absolute silence as he barks marching orders. Following the first day of Clark's reign, he is introduced at a contentious school board meeting where he faces down his opposition with a cascade of characteristically verbose rhetoric; his fiercest critic, a radical black woman whose son was among those "incorrigibles" Clark expelled earlier in the day, vows to have him removed and for the balance of the film schemes to do just that.

Roaming the halls with his trademark bullhorn, Clark orchestrates (or bullies) wholesale change: the walls are repainted, learning the school song is mandated, the doors are chained to keep out drug dealers, and in general, a semblance of order is restored.

Similar to the urgent training scenes in *Rocky*, the entire school, underdogs girding for the fight of a lifetime, gears up for the upcoming basic skills test. Meanwhile, Clark's nemesis, made a member of the school board after cutting a deal with the opportunistic mayor, presses him to dispatch the fire chief to the school and have Clark arrested for fire code violations.

As evinced by *Rocky*, director John Avildsen is very adept at pressing the right buttons. Almost on command he elicits tears, laughs, sighs, tension. Indeed Joe Clark lends himself to the kind of simple, almost fail-safe formula that is Avildsen's metier. Clark combats injustice and corruption with a basic moral code that puts a premium on results. His "unconventional" tactics, brutal in any other context, are made acceptable, even heroic, by the nightmarish universe he attempts to subdue, affording us ample opportunity to let loose with a few cathartic cheers—and to suspend judgment. But questions persist. Clark's methods did producer shortterm results, but the ends, as they say, don't invariably justify the means, especially if those means border on the fascistic. Morgan Freeman presents both Clark's attractive larger-than life "heroic" side and his less attractive dogmatism. But Freeman is such a soulful presence, he can't help imbuing Clark with many more endearing than repulsive qualities. Robert Guillaume, the principled, conservative-minded superintendent, is typically warm and sober. The balance of the cast, especially the spirited teenagers in the parts of the students, is just fine.

LOS ANGELES TIMES, 3/3/89, Calendar/p. 4, Sheila Benson

After its prologue, "Lean on Me" opens on a maelstrom of choreographed violence at Eastside

High School in Paterson, N.J., which practically guarantees that no one will glance at the credits below. As the camera prowls hallways and bathrooms of this predominantly black and low-income school, a sea of kids are picking fights or buying dope at the school door, and a teacher is being beaten into insensibility.

This, the film assures us, was standard behavior until the arrival of tough new principal Joe Clark, who would turn the place around through flamboyantly radical behavior. Clark is played by Morgan Freeman, possibly the most formidable actor on the American scene.

As anyone who has seen him on stage in "Driving Miss Daisy" knows, he is boundlessly gentle. He can also suggest menace so dangerous that you shiver ("Street Smart"). He has a seemingly limitless range, quicksilver modulation, surprise, a dry humor and a watchful intelligence. Using words alone, he can pound another actor right into the ground. Mrogan Freeman is not an actor to mess with.

It wasn't for his gentle side that he was chosen as Joe Clark. If the bullhorn-and-baseball-wielding educator was going to have his inning on the screen, he couldn't have prayed for better casting than Morgan Freeman.

And it is Freeman who will give thoughtful audiences their thorniest problems in "Lean on Me." When director John Avildsen ("Rocky," "The Karate Kid") turns up the heat, staging scenes like that high-school-from-hell opener, or a massive rally at the close, or the many moments of confrontation that dot the film, and then sends Freeman in, against the action, to impose his strength by sheer force of will, it's thrilling. If ever an actor needed a bullhorn less, it's Freeman.

He makes you forget—want to foreget—the words that Michael Schiffer's script puts so clearly in the mouth of a music teacher: that Clark is a bully, a despicable man, and one who seems to be threatened by any opinion that runs counter to his own.

The problem with "Lean on Me" is a stripped-down script with no room left in it for complexities, and revved-up direction that makes it move anyway. Schiffer trots out some of the arguments of Clark's opponents, then drops them. But even more crucially, he doesn't suggest that there is any educational alternative to invective, to the expulsion of 300 students Clark characterized as "hoodlums," and to the baseball bat.

The choral music teacher, played feelingly by Robin Bartlett, is fired before the film is a third over. Every person who opposes Clark is either power-hungry, like Lynne Thigpen's leader of the parents group, or corrupt, like the fictionalized mayor. There's no middle ground to take.

As in "Stand and Deliver," everything is geared to previously unmotivated students taking a test crucial to the survival of the school. And the producers have chosen cannily; Avildsen is masterly at mounting a slow-building school-wide frenzy leading up to a minimum basic skills exam.

Clark's only ally is his friend of more than 20 years, Frank Napier (Robert Guillaume), now Paterson's superintendent of schools. (Guillaume has a sympathetic presence, but years of television have left him no match for Freeman's crackle and authority, and scenes in which he must dominate Freeman are awkward.)

Clark's vice principal, Joan Levias (Beverly Todd), hates his methods but not his objectives. A few of the students are characterized: stocky young Thomas Sams (winning newcomer Jermaine Hopkins), and Kaneesha Carter (Karen Malina White), as the daughter of a young welfare mother whose upward progress is marred by a sudden personal crisis.

You may remember none of the actors, because almost no meat has been put on their characters' bones. Then, in the middle of all this forgettability, there is Regina Taylor as Mrs. Carter, that young welfare mother, explaining why she has seemingly turned her back on her daughter. It is a scene of such power, variety and observation as to send you away shaken. This is an actress to watch.

The real Joe Clark has very nearly created more problems than he has solved. True, his students work in graffiti-free and drug-free halls, prowled tirelessly by Clark himself. But, glossed over by the film makers are some of the statistics of his administration: Reading scores among his seniors are still in the bottom third of the country, and the overall dropout rate has risen from 13% to 21%.

Those details are not on the screen, which rocks with positive messages of uplift and self-pride. Those are marvelous qualities, not reinforced often enough in massaudience films with nearly allblack casts. But should it be too much to ask that a film with this much of a lock on its audience's emotions also challenge their minds? Clark's way or anarchy: It's not much of a choice.

NEW YORK, 3/20/89, p. 73, David Denby

Military-style discipline combined with leader worship is the only force that can save the black and Hispanic youth of America's urban schools. At least that's the unmistakable import of *Lean on Me,* John G. Avildsen's whipped-up, fraudulent movie about New Jersey high-school principal Joe Clark, whose bullhorn-and-baseball-bat swaggering so thoroughly charmed President Reagan and former secretary of education William Bennett. The picture, as if made by these ideologues themselves, finds the answers to excruciating problems in wish fulfillment and bad old movies.

In the film, when Clark takes over in 1987, Paterson's Eastside High is in desperate shape. Once a decent school, it has degenerated into a hellish war zone of drugs, beatings, and chaos. Enter Joe Clark, a longtime teacher in Paterson. Clark (Morgan Freeman) is the last hope: If he can't raise the students' test scores significantly inside a year, the state will take over the school. Within days, Clark summarily throws out 300 troublemakers—miscreants, he calls them—on the basis of lists compiled by teachers. The movie quickly glides over this controversial practice, which has so enraged parents, educators, and civil libertarians. In the movie, Clark doesn't interview the accused kids; nor does he check the names against police records or distinguish between repeat and first-time offenders.

But already we're in Fakesville. The actual Joe Clark, who took over in 1982, not in 1987, kicked out failing and habitually tardy students as well as thugs; he "expurgated" (his word) students who may have had learning difficulties or terrible problems at home. The rationale Clark offers in the movie is that these screwups aren't going to graduate anyway, so why not separate them from the students who are still salvageable? He *Knows* they won't pull themselves together. The movie doesn't attempt to prove the correctness of his judgment; it celebrates a man taking extreme steps—any steps, so long as they are drastic. He throws the bums *out.*

The metaphor here is war. Clark's discarding the rotten apples is the equivalent of an army field doctor's giving up on the seriously wounded. And structurally, the movie follows the pattern of an old platoon genre film. Clark, like John Wayne, Jack Webb, or Lou Gossett Jr. whipping the recruits into shape, first insults the students, breaking down their individuality, and then builds them back up, instilling discipline and group pride. The main instrument is the school song, which everyone must learn. In the corridors, working his bullhorn, Clark is a hands-on boss, screaming abuse and encouragement, high-fiving everyone, charging into students' personal lives. He is everywhere at once: No one takes a pee without his knowing about it. Morgan Freeman is a dominating performer with a great voice that could cut through steel, but he mostly works on one level, without the shading I had hoped for. Shouting his way through the role, he makes Clark a stiff, surly, unlovable, and egotistical man. But Avildsen builds an atmosphere of hero worship around him.

The students in this movie are all demoralized—hapless ninnies and clowns. After their initial shock, they fall in love with Clark and defend him during his troubles with the school board (this did happen at Eastside). The movie suggests that the students respond to him because Clark is the father they never had; his harsh attention is better than no attention at all. But rather than develop this insight, Avildsen (*Rocky, The Karate Kid*) turns on the juice of power uplift: The movie's climax, hyped like the big game of the football season, is the basic-skills test. Passing the test becomes a group effort. Try harder, and *sing!* Clark in his holy rage cleans up the corridors and heals the students; the music turns into inspirational soul.

Some of this communal spirit is touching, but what does it mean? After all, if you don't know vocabulary and algebra, you can't score high in reading and math skills. In *Lean on Me,* education is somehow merged into the eighties celebration of winning—a collective Rockyism. Just when things are looking bad—Clark in jail, the students raising their fists in union outside the courthouse (all fabricated)—the fabulous test scores come in, miraculously vindicating Clark's methods. But in reality, there was only a tiny improvement in the scores. On March 3, the Washington *Post* reported that "Eastside's standardized proficiency tests are still among the lowest in the state." The small improvement may have been caused by Clark's pitching out the troublesome low achievers.

Lean on Me exudes a merry spirit of victory, and anyone who doesn't climb aboard is presented as corrupt, envious, or irrationally hostile. Yet Joe Clark created little besides law and order at Eastside High School. The movie, a true product of the hallucinatory Reagan era, cherishes symbols rather than achievement, the show of force rather than the result of force. In other cities, principals of formerly "hopeless" schools have produced startling records of academic success. But it's the man with the baseball bat who becomes the media star. In the glare of Clark's triumph, on one in the movie even says that his trampling on individualism and liberty is regrettable. A show of getting tough with black kids is enough to exite conservatives (who rarely demonstrate much concern with the education of minorities). Order is celebrated as an end in itself. Hungry for solutions, neoconservatism, in this demagogic movie anthem, blunders into neo-Fascism.

NEW YORK POST, 3/3/89, p. 23, David Edelstein

Given the desperate shape of most inner-city schools, it's no wonder that people in this country have long hungered for a powerful father figure, a man with the guts and tenacity to clean up our filthy urban cesspool. They hear about families in which dads vanish, teenage moms live on welfare and kids show up for classes packing automatic wespons, and they say, "Someone ought to discipline those animals."

Then they read about a new breed of principal, a black man who unceremoniously exiles the vermin, maintains martial law in the classroom and poses for the press with a baseball bat. And they say, "It's about time."

These are the emotions—many of them understandable—that have helped make a hero of Joe Clark, principal of East Side High School in Paterson, N.J., and the inspiration for the lead character in "Lean on Me." To the complex, tragic problem of minority education, the movie provides a tidy, Reagan-era solution: fascism mixed with Hollywood uplift.

The strategy is to take Clark, a man who emerges in TV and print interviews as a self-styled blowhard and gleeful provocateur of humanists and liberals, and turn him into the Father of Us All.

Written by Michael Schiffer and directed by Avildsen, "Lean on Me" is as glibly dishonest a piece of moviemaking as any I have seen. It's also reasonably skillful, and audiences in search of that Rockyesque rush of good feeling—which comes from seeing messy issues made kindergarten-simple, so that all you have to do is clap and cheer—will flock to it.

In the pre-credit sequence, set in 1965, Clark (Morgan Freeman), a dedicated but bellicose teacher, is bounced from East Side by his union in a puling concession to management. Clark knows that the ejection of so potent an instructor is an invitation to chaos. "This place," he says portentously, "deserves exactly what it gets."

What follows is a visual master-stroke. Clark leaves the union meeting, walks down the hall and turns the corner. Pause. Fade to the same corridor, from the same angle, 20 years later, except the walls are now covered with graffiti and students conduct dope deals in full view. Boys paw girls; fights erupt; a teacher's head is dashed against the floor. The throbbing, heavy-metal music shrieks, "Welcome to the jungle."

Clark, you understand, was prophetic, and now that his warning has come to pass and the heat is on the mayor and superintendent of schools (Robert Guillaume), this reckless visionary is summoned like Patton back to the front; he's the only SOB who can get the job done.

The Patton comparison isn't casual. Clark is the renegade general who must whip these raw recruits into shape, banish miscreants and snuff out dissent. "This is not a damned democracy," he tells his teachers. "We are in a state of emergency, and my word is law."

The teachers and students fight Clark at first—they don't understand that he's a *benevolent* dictator, that they should be grateful to be taken in hand because it's only way out of so miserable a situation. But we, in the audience, are meant to appreciate that the means, in this instance, jusitfy the ends.

Freeman is a fluid, unfussy performer, and he's a pleasure to watch. He's as centered as a dancer, and his speech and movements are measured, supple.

Everything about him is different from his actual counterpart, which wouldn't be a problem if "Lean on Me" didn't so explicitly glorify a real man and an increasingly popular philosophy of education (which has been endorsed by William Bennett, former secretary of education under Ronald Reagan).

The movie's Joe Clark holds the hand of pregnant young girl instead of barring her from school, and follows children home to counsel their single mothers instead of referring to them as bastards over the P.A. system. Clark allegedly did both.

The movie's Clark gets those achievement test scores up—triumphant proof that his methods pay off—instead of failing to raise the school's average.

But let's be realistic: "Lean on Me" is not about education. Its real subject is how well its director, John Avildsen, can manipulate an audience. Avildsen has made reactionary hits ("Joe"), Capraesque-humanist hits ("Rocky"), and pacifist-liberal hits ("The Karate Kid"). Clearly, politics mean little to him; all he cares about is that—in the evocative blurbspeak of Joel Siegel— "you're up on your feet and cheering" an underdog winner.

He does smooth work, but if you think movies are about more than being jerked around by unscrupulous people, "Lean on Me" may get you steamed. There isn't a shred of tension or ambiguity because the film has only one point of view: Big Daddy's.

The movie raises the traditional objections to Clark only to show how wrongheaded they are. Even the fire chief's charge that chaining every fire exit in the school could, in the event of a blaze, result in catastrophe is brushed aside. The chief, a man who's just doing his job, must be shown to be a racist who's itching to topple this uppity black man. Everyone except Clark has an ulterior motive.

As it happens, Clark and the filmmakers are the only ones who do have ulterior motives. With its sleazy distortion of fact, daddy-worship and cornball Hollywood climax (adoring East Side students marching on City Hall yelling, "Free Joe Clark!"), this could turn out to be a profitable myth for all concerned. A TV series seems inevitable, and the rights to Clark's continuing adventures will not come cheap.

Looks like America has a brand-new superstar.

NEWSDAY, 3/3/89, Part III/p. 7, Mike McGrady

Here's Eastside High in Paterson, N.J., before the arrival of the new principal. Security guards read girlie magazines while there's rioting in the auditorium, terror in the cafeteria, mugging in the girl's lavatory. The school corridors are teeming with screaming, brawling, gun-toting, pill-popping, window-breaking, spray-painting, high-fiving, knifefighting, drug-dealing students who tear sweaters off girls, beat teachers bloody and shut the fat boy in his locker.

"Somebody, help!" the fat boy screams repeatedly. "Somebody help!"

Enter "Crazy Joe" Clark (Morgan Freeman), a principal who carries a baseball bat in one hand and a bullhorn in the other, an educator who uses "tough love" to inspire his students to achieve higher scores on the state's basic skills test (though specific statistical results are never presented).

A statistic or, for that matter, anything approaching a fact, would violate the entire spirit of "Lean on Me." Where many films open with a solemn declaration of truth, "Lean on Me" opens with: "The following *is based on* a true story." (Italics mine). The obvious care in wording provides a neat out for moviemakers who have no interest in truth or anything approaching it.

"Lean on Me" has the same outline, though nowhere near the same effect, as the recent "Stand and Deliver." In each instance, a school with a minority population is rescued from academic indifference by a charismatic individual willing to battle lethargy and inspire discipline. The difference in title seems highly significant. "Stand and Deliver" insists students are responsible for their own success while "Lean on Me" is an open invitation to let a strong figure handle all the problems.

Incidentally, while I think the film is hogwash, I'm not claiming that it's ineffective hogwash. The sneak-preview audience surrounding me shouted back at the screen, produced tears on cue and applauded the gloriously hokey windup.

Here, full credit must go to director John G. Avildsen who directed not only "Rocky" but also the first two "Karate Kid" epics. We are in the hands, then, of a world-class manipulator, a director who knows just what strings to pull and just when to pull them. He is helped in his chores by the highly effective Morgan Freeman as Clark.

And what are the secrets of Joe Clark's success? Well, he refuses to listen to the teachers in his school ("No one talks at my meetings; you take out your pencils and write!"); he summarily discharges 300 students ("You are out of here forever!"); he explains the dismissal to angry parents through a heavenly visitation ("I gave my word to God, and that's why I threw those bastards out"); he insists all surviving students learn one thing ("You will sing the school song on demand or you will suffer dire consequences"); when the music teacher tries to teach Mozart, he disagrees ("You're fired!"); his plan for drug control ("I want every door in the school chained and locked") violates fire laws and common sense.

The film's educational prescription calls for browbeating, bullying, fascism and slogans shouted through a bullhorn. If thoughtful people took any of this seriously, it might be dangerous. Fortunately, there's little danger of that.

TIME, 3/13/89, p. 82, Richard Schickel

The belief that tough guys are really decent guys at heart may be, as Norman Mailer once remarked, "one of the sweetest thoughts in all the world." And a necessary one. For, as the novelist also observed, "there's nothing more depressing than finding a guy as tough as nails and as mean as dirt."

Since John Avildsen, who directed *Rocky* and *The Karate Kid*, is obviously not attracted to depressing subjects, you know up front that *Lean on Me* will lean heavily on Mailer's theorem in telling the Joe Clark story. The estimable Morgan Freeman plays the man who became the last-hope principal of crime-ridden, drugsoaked, graffiti-infested Eastside High in Paterson, N.J.

Clark gained national attention—including a TIME cover—by bullying students and faculty into a state of moral grace and academic excellence. His wellpublicized symbols of rule were a bullhorn and a baseball bat. His lessons included expelling 300 of the worst troublemakers en masses, chaining the school's doors to bar drug dealers and—whooping audience delight here—inveighing colorfully against laziness, incompetence and any politician or community leader who questioned his ways. But underneath all that, as the movie points out, were sweetness and caring: Clark redeeming a crack addict (Jermaine Hopkins), mending a mother-daughter conflict, nursing a comic obsession with getting the kids to sing the school song with gusto.

The movie finds nothing ambiguous in this tale. No student rebels, reform is achieved at miracle speed, all opposition is seen as opportunistic. In short, complexity is sacrificed to fast-food inspirationalism. After the cheers die and the tears dry comes the realization that *Lean on Me* is serving up empty emotional calories. They don't leave you sick, just hungry for an honest meal.

VILLAGE VOICE, 3/14/89, p. 63, Lisa Kennedy

Morgan Freeman, in John Avildsen's *Lean on Me*, plays a man who wants so be a star (or is that czar?), principal Joe Clark.

Freeman's performance must be good: Clark remains a bully. Against a narrative hell-bent on constructing a hero, Clark is no such thing. What a relief. Films based on "true stories" that are unfolding even as we sleep seem dangerous, wavering between just another plot line and propaganda. Anyone who's had a verbally abusive, physically intimidating father knows that Clark's triumph at Eastside High is a tribute to tough love.

The devices on which *Lean on Me* are built are often cheap but sometimes affecting. The film opens with the clear lilt of an alma mater and a shot of stately Eastside High. The year: 1967. Dashiki-clad Clark is just a teacher who enthusiastically runs a game show-like class where the boys vie with the girls over points of Western civ. All but one of his students are white, and they're all '60s squares. "Crazy Joe" gets traded to another school, and, 20 years later, it's back to Eastside High, which has become a holding pen, or, according to the soundtrack, a "jungle."

To underscore a movie about a predominantly black urban high school with a song by Guns N' Roses attests to the fact that, even more than rap, heavy metal is the sound most folks fear. Avildsen (*Rocky*) is not very subtle in his manipulations, and the movie doesn't really settle down into being watchable until a defined outsider threatens the sanctity of Clark's school. Once that happens, and the bureaucrats become the dangerous Other, you can sit back and watch some sweet-looking kids use a lot of energy to buoy this tired narrative. Give me *To Sir With Love*.

Also reviewed in:
NEW YORK TIMES, 3/3/89, p. C16, Janet Maslin
VARIETY, 2/1-7/89, p. 18
WASHINGTON POST, 3/3/89, p. D4, Hal Hinson

LET IT RIDE

A Paramount Pictures release. *Executive Producer:* Richard Stenta. *Producer:* David Giler. *Director:* Joe Pytka. *Screenplay:* Ernest Morton. *Based on the book "Good Vibes" by:* Jay Cronley. *Director of Photography:* Curtis J. Wehr. *Editor:* Dede Allen and Jim Miller. *Music:* Giorgio Moroder. *Music Editor:* Curt Sobel. *Sound:* Les Lazarowitz and Bernard Blynder. *Sound Editor:* Cecelia Hall. *Production Designer:* Wolf Kroeger. *Art Director:* Frederick C. Weiler. *Set Decorator:* William D. McLane. *Set Dresser:* Michael Calabrese and Amy Shaff. *Costumes:* Wendy Keller. *Make-up:* Elizabeth M. Lambert. *Stunt Coordinator:* Arthur Edwards and Bobby Foxworth. *Running time:* 85 minutes. *MPAA Rating:* PG-13.

CAST: Richard Dreyfuss (Trotter); David Johansen (Looney); Teri Garr (Pam); Jennifer Tilly (Vicki); Allen Garfield (Greenberg); Ed Walsh (Marty); Richard Edson (Johnny Casino); David Schramm (Lufkin); John Roselius (Reardon); Joseph Walsh (Vibes); Ralph Seymour (Sid); Cynthia Nixon (Evangeline); Richard Dimitri

(Tony Cheeseburger); Robert Towers (Mickey Jax); Michelle Phillips (Mrs. Davis); Robbie Coltrane (Ticket Seller); Tony Longo (Simpson); Mary Woronov (Quinella); Trevor R. Denman (Race Track Announcer); Tony Fraietta (Louie Kidder); Sid Raymond (Solly Friedman); Darci Osiecky (Sheila); Joe Petrullo (Maitre 'd); S.A. Griffin (Trainer); Lee Sandman (Businessman); Ron Max (Man in Looney's Cab); Rosanne Covy (Woman in Looney's Cab); Dee Dee Deering (Woman with cane); Rachel Rogers (Woman at Paddock Rail); Geraldine Dreyfuss (Woman during Chase); Robert Baron (Hugh Sipes); Tom Kouchalakos and W. Paul Bodie (Customers); Martin Garner (Rudy); Kenneth Russell (Shoeshine Man); Larry Litt (Waiter in Jockey Club); Omar Caraballo (Police Officer with Reardon); Robert Hoelscher and Nelson Oramas (Police Officers); Lorin Dreyfuss (Grandstand Person); Jiji Connolly (Nurse at Bloodbank); Ann E. Gilliam-Martin (Mrs. Slade); Phil Philbin (Track Official).

LOS ANGELES TIMES, 8/21/89, Calendar/p. 1, Kevin Thomas

"Let It Ride" has the makings of a real sleeper. In addition to its nonstop hilarity, it has a feel-good, send-'em-home-happy quality that has become one of the rarest of screen commodities.

It really is the kind of movie they don't make anymore, on several counts. First of all, it's Runyonesque race-track comedy, a genre one might well have thought past reviving. Second, its humor is gentle and unpretentious: There's no going for hard, slam-bang yocks or elaborate set-piece catastrophes requiring a legion of stunt people. Believe it or not, the abundant humor in the sterling screenplay Ernest Morton adapted from Jay Cronley's "Good Vibes" actually derives from the foibles of human nature and not from special effects.

Richard Dreyfuss may have won an Oscar for his amusingly high-minded New York actor in "The Goodbye Girl" and given us plenty of laughs in "Moon Over Parador," "Tin Men" and "Down and Out in Beverly Hills," but it's just possible he surpasses himself as Trotter, a Miamian who just can't stay away from the horses. He is onscreen practically the entire film, and there is a terrific momentum he sustains as he roller-coasts between despair and elation. Determinedly jaunty—he prances when he's ecstatic—he has the kinetic energy and fast retorts of James Cagney.

Resolutions are often made to be broken. When, over a Chinese dinner, Trotter vows to give up gambling while his adored wife, Pam (Teri Garr), promises to make no more scenes, you know this truce isn't going to last beyond the fortune cookies.

"Let It Ride" gets under way—and never lets up—once Trotter's taxi-driving pal Looney (David Johansen) tapes a back-seat conversation between two passengers discussing a fixed race at Hialeah. Trotter goes for it, rationalizing that a sure thing doesn't constitute gambling. A couple of plot twists and turns later, he seems to be on an incredible winning streak. But what if it runs out?

There's a terrific throwaway quality to the gags and the jokes that gives the film its blitheness. You're reminded of vintage Hawks and Wilder and Sturges, of the Hollywood Golden Era comedies that sparkle timelessly because their makers didn't take themselves too seriously, didn't press too hard for laughs, but did cook up great lines for their wonderful supporting players.

"Let It Ride" has its own glorious character people. In addition to Garr's loving but distraught wife and Johansen's goofy loser, there is, most important, Allen Garfield's Jockey Club rich guy with the pneumatic baby-voiced mistress (Jennifer Tilly); Robbie Coltrane's sour ticket seller, whose view of Trotter moves from contempt to awe, and Michelle Phillips' delicious blonde society tramp. (Accepting the offer of a drink from Trotter, she says breezily, "Why not? I'm on the pill.") "Let It Ride" looks good in a low-key way, and Giorgio Moroder's eclectic, funky mood-setting score is crucial in helping maintain tone as well as pace.

In an instance of saving the best for the last, "Let It Ride's" special hero is its director, Joe Pytka, making his feature debut after years in documentaries, music videos and innovative, prize-winning commercials. He never lets archetypes slide into stereotypes or good nature drift into sentimentality, and he's never afraid to let Dreyfuss and Garr seem anything less than the very bright people they are. "Let It Ride" (rated a rather severe PG-13) plays like an All-American, nose-thumbing, warm-hearted yet undeniably dark-tinged comedy classic.

NEW YORK POST, 8/19/89, p. 17, David Edelstein

The gambling comedy "Let It Ride" has a high-flying story: A scrappy loser named Trotter (Richard Dreyfuss) has the day of his dreams at the race track—the day all of us wish we could have just once in our lives, when Lady Luck won't detach herself from our arm.

Based on Jay Cronley's breezy novel "Good Vibes," it's a wish-fulfillment movie, a tall tale, with everyone at the track, from the poorest to the swells at the Jockey Club, coming alive and opening up to this blessed human being—a reformed gambler who suddenly can do no wrong.

And probably the reason the movie doesn't work—despite some intensity and a lot of talent—is that the race track isn't populated by real people but by character actors given the big green light. They're more juiced-up than the horses, without the horses' precision.

The director, Joe Pytka, has never made a feature, and it shows. He comes from rock videos and commercials, among them the dandy ones with Micheal J. Fox ducking out his fire escape in the rain for a Pepsi.

Throughout, he uses the "Guys and Dolls" overture "Fugue for Tinhorns," but he hasn't learned from composer Frank Loesser, who makes those voices fluid, overlapping. Pytka fractures the action, giving you oodles of fast, teensy close-ups—he lets nothing ride. What should be a loose ensemble comedy becomes a Cuisinart comedy.

The movie features scores of faces poring over Racing Forms and praying for divine intervention, but at its center is Dreyfuss' Trotter, a man who promises his wife (Teri Garr) he won't gamble anymore and will move back in with her but gets a sure-fire tip from two gangsters in the back of his buddy's cab and decides to risk $50 on a 40-to-1 shot.

Dreyfuss has a hurtling energy, and you can understand what draws people to him—he exudes invulnerability. Echoes of early conversations give him tips on which horses to bet; everything clicks; the world seems an orderly place.

Dreyfuss, however, should stop behaving as if he's blessed as an actor, as if he can do no wrong, because that's what got him into trouble in the first round of his career. Trim and alert as he is, he's lost the modesty and self-discipline he had in "Down and Out in Beverly Hills," his triumphant return to acting. He's winking at the audience again.

As Trotter's cabbie buddy Looney, musician David Johansen tries to hold his own with Dreyfuss and gives a grotesquely overscaled performance—you don't discover anything in Johansen becasue it's all on the surface. He makes the character seem braindamaged.

But "Let It Ride" is elsewhere full of tender mercies, notably Jennifer Tilly's short, absurdly low-cut red dress, which squeezes her like a tube of toothpaste. (Too bad her role, a big-hearted bimbo, is such a cliché.) Garr is messy-haried and messy-voiced and overflowing with messy emotions. She's a lovable mess, but her role's an insult. (It's not messy enough.)

Other actors register strongly: Michelle Phillips as a high-class nympho; Robbie Coltrane as a ticket seller carried away with Trotter's winning streak; Cynthia Nixon (always lovely and believable) as a 19-year-old on a nervous betting binge.

What's refreshing about "Let It Ride" is that it doesn't get moralistic and dash its hero against the pavement for longing to be a winner. But it sweats so hard to win the box-office derby that it leaves you feeling parched. It's a comedy of dehydration.

NEWSDAY, 8/19/89, Part II/p. 15, Terry Kelleher

Before betting the price of a ticket on "Let It Ride," figure the odds on enjoyment.

First, gauge your fascination with gambling and the racetrack scene. Then look deep into your soul and estimate your tolerance for Richard Dreyfuss at his most manic.

If you like the ponies and Dreyfuss, this picture's a lock. If you favor one of two, it's a toss-up. If you're dubious about both setting and star, put your dough in savings bonds.

Dreyfuss portrays a Miami cab driver (somehow he doesn't seem the type) whose gambling problem is threatening his marriage. Trotter (note funny name) swears to the wife (Teri Garr) that his wagering days are over, but hours later a fellow hackie (David Johansen) gives him a sure thing in the first race at Hialeah. Faster than you can say "they're off," Trotter's at the track and on an incredible, positively mystical lucky streak.

The opening music, "Fugue for Tinhorns" from "Guys and Dolls," announces that "Let It Ride" has Runyonesque aspirations, and in the early going director Joe Pytka appears capable of fulfilling them. In his first feature, Pytka shows a good eye for the levels of horseplaying society—from the seedy railbirds in their shot-and-a-beer saloon (though Dreyfuss is never quite seedy enough to blend in) to the pseudo-classy patrons of the jockey club, including the crass tycoon (Allen Garfield) and his cute bimbo (Jennifer Tilly). Pytka evidently appreciates the irony of Hialeah's beauty; the park looks too nice to lose your shirt in.

Ernest Morton's script, from a book by Jay Cronley, display a degree of insight into the gambler's psychology, particularly the idea that there's something courageous and noble about risking instant destitution. As "Let It Ride" rounds the track, however, addiction seems less amusing. It's hard to force a chuckle when Johansen's character sells his blood to raise betting money.

But if "Let It Ride" starts losing ground at the far turn, the acting bears much of the blame. Even in farcical circumstances, Dreyfuss is at his best under control. Pytka allows him too much room for screaming and gesticulating. As Garr's style is not dissimilar to her co-star's, the effect can be overwhelming when they share the screen.

"Let It Ride" has a difficult time finding the finish line. After all, there's really nothing for Trotter to do but keep returning to the $50 window (manned engagingly by Robbie Coltrane). Moviegoers may prefer to play this one safe—say, two bucks to place.

Also reviewed in:
NEW YORK TIMES, 8/19/89, p. 14, Stephen Holden
VARIETY, 8/23–29/89, p. 30.

LETHAL WEAPON 2

A Warner Bros. release of a Silver Pictures production. *Producer:* Richard Donner and Joel Silver. *Director:* Richard Donner. *Screenplay:* Jeffrey Boam. *Story:* Shane Black and Warren Murphy. *Based on characters created by:* Shane Black. *Director of Photography:* Stephen Goldblatt. *Editor:* Stuart Baird. *Music:* Michael Kamen, Eric Clapton, and David Sanborn. *Music Editor:* Chirstopher Brooks. *Sound:* Willie Burton and (orchestral) Bobby Fernandez. *Sound Editor:* Robert Henderson. *Production Designer:* J. Michael Riva. *Art Director:* Virginia Randolph and Richard Berger. *Set Designer:* Dianne Wager. *Set Decorator:* Marvin March. *Special Effects:* Matt Sweeney. *Costumes:* Barry Delaney. *Make-up:* Scott Eddo. *Stunt Coordinator:* Charles Picerni and Mic Rodgers. *Running time:* 112 minutes. *MPAA Rating:* R.

CAST: Mel Gibson (Martin Riggs); Danny Glover (Roger Murtaugh); Joe Pesci (Leo Getz); Joss Ackland (Arjen Rudd); Derrick O'Connor (Pieter Vorstedt); Patsy Kensit (Rika Van Den Haas); Darlene Love (Trish); Traci Wolfe (Rianne); Damon Hines (Nick); Ebonie Smith (Carrie); Mary Ellen Trainor (Police Department Psychiatrist); Steve Kahan (Captain Murphy); Mark Rolston (Hans); Jenette Goldstein (Meagan Shapiro); Dean Norris (Tim Cavanaugh); Juney Smith (Tom Wyler); Nestor Serrano (Eddie Estaban); Philip Suriano (Joseph Ragucci); Grand L. Bush (Jerry Collins); Tony Carreiro (Marcelli); Allan Dean Moore (George); Jack McGee (Carpenter); Robert Fol (Consulate Guard); Virginia Shannon (Consulate Office Worker); Danny Ondrejko (Consulate Clerk); Jim Piddock (Consulate Envoy); Kenneth Tigar (Bomb Squad Leader); Jim Birge and Patrick Cameron (Bomb Squad Cops); David Marciano and Tommy Hinkley (Cops); Norm Wilson (Detective in Squad Room); Jeanne McGuire and Catherine Guel (Computer Operators); Lionel Douglass (Officer Friesen); James Oliver (Officer Moss); Salim Jadid (Policeman); Orlando Bonner (Tow Truck Driver); Cynthia Burr (Owner of Honda).

FILMS IN REVIEW, 10/89, p. 483, C.M. Fiorillo

Martin Riggs isn't suicidal anymore, but he's as crazy as ever in *Lethal Weapon* 2. This sequel is every bit as explosive as its brilliant original. The film opens in the middle of a car chase and slyly reestablishes the characters of the two leads—in case anyone forgot them. Unfortunately, the script is seriously flawed.

To start the action, detectives Riggs (Mel Gibson) and Roger Murtaugh (Danny Glover) discover a trunk full of Krugerrands. This discovery is linked to the wimp they are assigned to protect: a nerdy accountant named Leo (Joe Pesci). Leo has been laundering dirty money for a group of South African diplomats-cum murderers, who happen to own a lot of Krugerrands. It's hard to tell who is more excited about harrassing the diplomats, Riggs or Leo. Both are thrilled to be in the action. Unfortunately for Riggs, diplomats are immune from arrest. This fact, of course, doesn't stop him from pursuing these bad guys. And that is what mars an otherwise fine film.

Gibson's Riggs is funnier this time around—less psychotic, but still wild. Sanity, it seems, can slow you down. Gibson gives a solid performance. His emotional breakdown comes after the poignant realization that the South Africans are responsible for his wife's death four years earlier. Again, Gibson's range allows him the luxury of fully realizing and displaying tragic emotions. Glover's Murtaugh is as cautious as ever. He carries the same standard police six-shooter, but is equally adept at handling a carpenter's nail gun. Glover offers an easy-going performance to counteract against both Gibson's and Pesci's manic antics. Riggs and Murtaugh are completely meshed—they even bicker like two old men.

Pesci (*Once Upon A Time In America*) is a certified scene stealer as cop-wanna-be Leo. [Pesci received kudos from the National Board of Review for his work as Jake LaMotta's brother in *Raging Bull*.] His performance is hilarious. (Another scene stealer is Sam, the dog, as himself.) Darlene Love and Traci Wolfe reprise their roles as Trish and Rianne Murtaugh, but serve only as decorative set pieces.

Patsy Kensit (*Absolute Beginners*) is the major female lead. She plays Gibson's doomed love interest, and assistant to the villainous South African diplomat Arjen Rudd. As played by Joss Ackland (*White Mischief*), Rudd suavely represents the essence of the evildoer who knows he can't be caught. But neither Ackland nor Derrick O'Connor (*Hope And Glory*) as Rudd's ruthless right-hand henchman Pieter Vorstedt equal the cold charisma of Gary Busey's "blond, albino jackrabbit," Mr. Joshua, from *Lethal Weapon*.

Jeffrey Boam (*Indiana Jones And The Last Crusade*), who wrote the screenplay, dutifully follows the recipe originated by Shane Black (who, with Warren Murphy, is given story credit on 2) for a successful, if marred, sequel. (I'll deal with that later, but was it really necessary to kill off Riggs' new leading lady? Doesn't that constitute cruel and unusual punishment for a guy who already lost his wife to the same bunch of idiots?)

If you can overlook the potholed plot, Richard Donner's slick direction and non-stop action sequences and Stephen Goldblatt's vibrant photography join forces to help make *Lethal Weapon 2* come alive.

On the whole, *Lethal Weapon 2* is a terrific Hollywood summer package. It's got style, action, humor and Mel Gibson. Cars give chase, explosions abound, and people die in uniquely vicious and bloody ways.

Unfortunately, the powers-that-be on this picture ruined what could have been a great death scene for a romantic hero by letting Riggs live. Both the photography and music for the powerful closing scene are stunning. (No one dies in movies like they used to anymore—look what they did to Mr. Spock.) This, of course, leaves the door wide open for a *Lethal Weapon 3*.

Or perhaps not. Lack of a dynamite death scene is not the major problem with this picture. Riggs would probably be better off dead because no matter how you slice it, he and Murtaugh were renegade cops during their final confrontation with Rudd and Vorstedt. Laws were lanced. Diplomats were done in. (Even Sonny Crockett of *Miami Vice* backed off from a legally protected diplomat.) For the two vigilante detectives, it may be along time before their next assignment.

LOS ANGELES TIMES, 7/7/89, Calendar/p. 1, Michael Wilmington

"We're back! We're bad! You're black! I'm mad!"

That's the kind of dialogue we get in the new car-crash, heavy-artillery thriller, "Lethal Weapon 2." And, if it suggests a movie poster catch-phrase instead of human speech, it's probably intentional.

In 1987's "Lethal Weapon," a quasi-suicidal cop named Martin Riggs, who didn't care if he lived or died, was partnered with a steady, cautious black family man, Roger Murtaugh. It was another male-bonding cop movie, with gimmicks out of "48 HRS." and "Magnum Force," a relationship out of "The Defiant Ones," and an incredibly silly kung fu showdown climax.

Still, the Riggs-Murtaugh friendship touched a nerve, partly because two superb actors, Mel Gibson and Danny Glover, were playing the parts, and partly because the director (Richard Donner), cinematographer (Stephen Goldblatt) and composers (Michael Kamen and Eric Clapton)—all of whom repeat their chores here—gave it a hard, bright, whirling surface that suggested chrome on fire, with a backbeat.

The key scene in this new "Lethal Weapon" occurs early on, when Riggs switches on his TV set and immediately finds the Three Stooges and with manic abandon, tosses the channel-changer over his head—no need to look for anything better than *this*—and begins wildly laughing.

But there's something wrong. The Stooges haven't done anything funny yet; they're just standing there. Riggs is cued to break up at the thought of what he knows is about to come. The scene signals how this whole movie plays: it reacts to things almost before they happen, as if Riggs, Murtaugh and Leo Getz (Joe Pesci), the embezzling gang accountant who tags along with them, were a lethal form of Three Stooges.

The movie is keyed up, hyper. The action scenes are outrageously overscaled, with 10 times more firepower than seems necessary. If there's a car-chase through downtown Los Angeles, Riggs will chase the car up a freeway ramp on foot. (The only wonder is if he doesn't catch it.)

"Lethal Weapon 2" has the brain-rattling pace of a terminal speed freak going the wrong way down an expressway. When people get angry at each other, they don't swear or fight. They drop a dumpster on somebody, or blow up their house at a poker game, or hitch up a truck and chain and pull their house off a hillside. (The film makers are no pikers; they've obviously built a real house and then pulled it down.)

In the first "Lethal Weapon," events were keyed around Riggs' Russian Roulette life style. In Part 2, he's supposedly cured and everyone else acts crazy—including Murtaugh, who shoots killers with a nail-gun and then remarks, apparently to the atmosphere, "I nailed'em!"

There are no lag spaces. If Murtaugh settles down for a quiet evening of TV, the very first thing he sees will be a condom ad starring his own daughter. Love is fast here—except for Murtaugh and wife Darlene Love, who act like a sexless TV sitcom family out of the '50s. There's a grand romance between Riggs and a secretary (Patsy Kensit), which goes by so speedily, it seems to be on fast-forward: it takes about 15 speeches for them to wind up in bed, even less for a full-scale catastrophe.

Some of this gives the film a sophisticated cachet that the first "Lethal Weapon" didn't have. On a very simple level, Jeffrey Boam's script, taken from a story cowritten by the first movie's scenarist, Shane Black, is clever. The dialogue tries to give us the punchy inside banter of pros on the run. Donner and Boam include knowing little touches: the Murtaugh daughters chide their dad about eating tuna, because of the dragnet techniques that kill dolphins. And these villains aren't just villains. They're diplomats and staff from the South African consulate; when one of them is caught on shipboard surrounded by corpses and drug money, he pulls out a card and says: "Diplomatic immunity."

Boam also includes scenes where Riggs and Murtaugh kid each other about being in love; they're in each other's arms after Murtaugh's toilet, wired by the mob, blows up. The end of this movie is like pop Wagner—or maybe the Wagner in Chuck Jones' "What's Opera, Doc?" This kind of hip riff on the homoerotic undercurrents of malebonding cop movies doesn't make the relationship any less superficial. It's more like a guy who comes on and tells jokes you've heard before, and then winks and says he knows they're bad; *he's* heard them before, too.

And, though it's nice to have a big-audience action movie attacking apartheid and the slaughter of sea mammals, instead of acting as an enlistment poster for the Army Air Corps, local vigilante groups or the reopening of the Vietnam War, the sentiments don't really transcend the car crashes.

It's no good saying that "Lethal Weapon 2" (MPAA rated R for language, partial nudity, violence and sex) isn't a highly professional, super-craftsmanlike job, or that actors like Gibson, Glover and Pesci—and Joss Ackland and Derrick O'Connor (the bad guys)—aren't doing excellent work in a rigid, overspecialized format. Or that this movie won't please the majority of its intended audience. It is. They are. And it will.

But there's a sense in which all these recent one-against-a-hundred cop and war thrillers represent the gaudy degeneration of the great tradition of the American action movie: substituting hardware for atmosphere, exaggeration for suspense, sadism for humor, shtick for character, blood and guts for body and soul. It's ironic, because it seems obvious that what the public liked most about "Lethal Weapon"—and what Donner and Boam want to give them more of—were the scenes with Mel Gibson and Danny Glover acting together. It's a tribute to both actors that they keep their cool and charisma here, even when they're locked in each other's arms and a toilet is flying out the window.

MONTHLY FILM BULLETIN, 10/89, p. 305, Kim Newman

After a violent chase through downtown Los Angeles, cops Martin Riggs and Roger Murtaugh find a fortune in Krugerrands in the boot of the car they have been pursuing, but the drug connection they were after escapes. As a punishment, their boss assigns family man Murtaugh and semi-psychotic widower Riggs to look after Leo Getz, an accountant who has embezzled large sums from a drugs cartel and is offering to turn state's evidence. Realising that the cases are linked, Riggs and Murtaugh allow Getz to lead them to the house from which the drugs business is being run. However, after a shoot-out and another chase, it transpires that the house is occupied by South African diplomat Arjen Rudd, and that his team of drug-dealing hit men all have diplomatic immunity. Riggs does his best to harass Rudd, whereupon the diplomat has his murderous sidekick Vorstedt set a bomb on Murtaugh's toilet. Riggs helps Murtaugh escape the blast, and they continue their unofficial war on Rudd. Riggs has been pursuing Rika Van Den Haas, Rudd's secretary, and while they are making love in his trailer, Vorstedt's men launch an all-out assault on their police department colleagues. Murtaugh overpowers the two men sent to kill him, but cannot prevent Getz's abduction. Two helicopters attack Riggs' trailer, and he is captured by Vorstedt, who admits that he killed Riggs' wife before throwing him off a pier. Underwater, Riggs discovers that Vorstedt has had Rika drowned and uses an escapology trick to survive. Riggs and Murtaugh attack Rudd's house and rescue Getz, then head for the docks, where Rudd is loading the vast profits of his drug deal aboard a South African freighter. In a battle, Riggs and Murtaugh destroy the money, and Riggs kills Vorstedt before being riddled with bullets by Rudd. The diplomat claims immunity, but Murtaugh kills him anyway. Murtaugh comforts his wounded friend, who proves too tough to die.

If *Lethal Weapon* was a prime example of the machine-made action-man movie of the 80s, then this is a model of sequelcraft. Without repeating too much of the plot of the original movie, it brings back the main characters and their tics—Riggs' unpredictable semipsycho outbursts, Murtaugh's family man concerns—intact, and transposes them into a plot that frequently threatens to move them away from their familiar mean streets into a super-Bondian world of bizarre master villains, mass destruction and over-the-top stunts. Richard Donner pulls out all the stops in the set-pieces, as when Riggs pulls away the foundations of Rudd's stilt-built Hollywood Hills headquarters and drags the whole structure off the side of the hill, but remembers to give his personable stars enough quiet moments to exchange jokes or half-choked admissions of manly love. If Murtaugh's ordeal on the toilet (he has to sit still with his trousers down for twenty hours before help comes) is engagingly absurd, then the final sequence—will Riggs shot full of enough bullets to kill the Terminator still cracking jokes and suggesting to his partner that he will be back on the job in the morning—moves on to an almost surreal level of action-movie lunacy.

Between Mel Gibson and Danny Glover and the stunts, no one else gets much of a look-in. Patsy Kensit is called upon to be charmed by Gibson's doggy nuttiness, express some token reservations about her government's home policies and peel off her conservative attaché's secretary suit for some jokey sex with Riggs before she is unceremoniously drowned. The whole film tries to adopt Gibson's half-crazy, half-funny tone, juxtaposing slapstick schtick of the Three Stooges variety with non-stop squib-exploding gunfire, gimmicky deaths worthy of a slasher picture (one car chase winds up with a villain's head being removed by a flying surfboard and the BBFC have looked especially askance at Murtaugh's unorthodox use of a nailgun when attacked by two assassins in his half-finished garage conversion), vehicular carnage and dollops of political anger.

The South African angle allows for one amusing moment when Getz and Murtaugh try to get a consular official to explain why the hulking black cop shouldn't emigrate to the land of the Cape, but it mainly smacks of an opportunist way of not further offending Latin Americans upset by cinema's identification—in films from *Scarface* to *Licence* to *Kill*—of Central America with the heroin business. While it would be churlish to dislike a product so brimful of energy, it is disturbing that the underlying callousness of the Stooges should be applied to the psycho cop genre, and that Danny Glover's straightarrow regular-guy cop should be so smoothly and easily aligned with Mel Gibson's vindictive vigilante in the finale. While Dirty Harry was forced to throw away his badge after gunning down his man, it is obvious here that, even though they have effectively waged war on a foreign country and killed off twenty or thirty diplomats, Riggs and Murtaugh will be welcomed back to the force with open arms for *Lethal Weapon* 3.

NEW YORK, 8/7/89, p. 43, David Denby

Lethal Weapon 2 is much more entertaining than its lethally boring predecessor. The new villains—South African drug-dealers hiding behind diplomatic immunity—are bizarrely vicious (the great Joss Ackland is their chief) and have wonderfully musical nasty accents. Mel Gibson, in and out of the buff, gives his loosest, goosiest performance yet, though I still find Danny Glover, in the harder role of the square, a trial to watch. In the next sequel, Glover should be liberated and Gibson turned into a sobersides.

NEW YORK POST, 7/7/89, p. 21, David Edelstein

Last week, Spike Lee changed the way we think and talk about movies (and violence) in this country; now it's back to the same old rat-tat-tat. "Lethal Weapon 2" is the lowest form of film making, and I don't know whether to laugh or cry over the fact that I had a good time at it—that as bloodthirsty swill goes, it's kind of fun.

The original "Lethal Weapon" did something unusually well: It made you primitively mad. You didn't just want the bad guys to die, you wanted them to hurt while they died. The movie engorged you with anger, then made the killing orgasmic—it gave surges of pleasure with each broken neck and body-spattering shooting.

"Lethal Weapon 2" is a smoother, better-crafted picture than the first, and Mel Gibson, with his hair swept back and his eyes piercingly blue, remains a spectacularly wired action hero. The movie has a porny-violent kick that's hard to resist—it aims low and blows its target to smithereens. But Lord, how low it aims.

The sequel begins in mid-car chase; our heroes can't even wait for the bell before they're screeching through traffic and swerving to avoid submachine gun blasts.

The driver is Murtaugh (Danny Glover), the family man; his partner, Vietnam vet and loner Riggs (Gibson), wants to get his paws on the wheel so he can rocket the vermin off the road. We don't know who the vermin are or why they're being chased, but we know Mel wants them bad: He's so gung-ho that when he loses his car, he tears after them on foot—onto the highway.

The blond guy they're pursuing gets away in a chopper but leaves behind a million in gold bars—Krugerrands. Soothingly, his boss (Joss Ackland) tells him not to worry about the mishap, then shoots him (splat!) in the head. At least the man's a diplomat.

Actually, he is a diplomat. Ackland, whose lordly wattles and purring lisp suggest a cross between Alec Guinness and Boris Karloff, turns out to be the South African minister of diplomatic affairs. Trumpeting his immunity to arrest and prosecution, he runs drugs out of his embassy and sneers at the blacks (among them Glover) on the L.A. police force.

The South Africans have become the Nazis of late '80s action flicks; there's nothing like white supremacists to get an audience righteously drooling for blood. Mind you, I've no objection to a mainstream thriller taking potshots at that government, but it's a little weird to see a movie this gore-hungry go out of its way to be Politically Correct.

In addition to swiping at apartheid, for instance, "Lethal Weapon 2" suggests that you boycott tuna because of all those dolphins getting tangled in the tuna nets. (Switch to albacore, the movie counsels. And, oh yes, if someone grabs you by the throat from behind, try a power drill in the middle of the forehead—he'll drop like a sack of bricks.)

Despite the choppy, slam-bam overture, the first part of the picture is loose and silly, with some charm. The script, by Jeffrey Boam, goes in heavily for one-liners—jokes on Glover's conservativism and Gibson's impulsiveness. Many of the gags are funny; all are pitched to the peanut gallery.

Glover's up-tight because his daughter's in a sexually frank TV commercial. Gibson shows how much excruciating pain he can take when he gets out of a straitjacket by dislocating his shoulder. (He cleans up on bets in the squad room.) They're as different as can be, these guys, but the point of the film is that they're buddies unto death.

There's another buddy this time: Joe Pesci, who was Robert De Niro's brother in "Raging Bull." He plays an accountant for the South Africans who skimmed from the top and ratted on them when they put out a contract on him. Gibson and Glover get assigned to guard the little con man, and that's lucky for him and us: With his jabbing delivery and duck-whistle voice, Pesci gives the picture some comic energy and some class.

There's a jolt of sex this time, too. Gibson's love interest is the minister's secretary, Rika Van Den Haas (Patsy Kensit), who assures him she dislikes her racist country but took the job so she could live in the United States. (It's important that she's Politically Correct if Gibson's going to sleep with her.)

Kensit's a blonde, blue-eyed number with a flat face—cheekbones so high and wide you think God was having Silly-Putty fun stretching her out. She wears one of these cute little black dresses that's perfect for all occasions: taking dictation, getting seduced, getting asphyxiated.

The movie's first hour is foreplay, marking time agreeably until it can make Gibson mad—beat him bloody, waste people he cares about, then unleash him, a bug-eyed psycho, to blow the hell out of a lot of insolent Afrikaners.

If this were a TV show, superdad Glover would teach Gibson that vigilantism solves nothing. Gibson would probably get killed and Glover would return, saddened but strengthened in his essential pacifism, to the bosom of his family.

"Lethal Weapon 2," however, lives for its climactic orgy of violence, and Glover's only sane response is to become a killing machine himself. By the end, the movie turns us all into revenge fiends, grooving to the massacre beat. We leave feeling sated, plug-ugly, asking our companions, "Was it good for you too?"

NEWSDAY, 7/7/89, Part III/p. 3, Mike McGrady

By this time we pretty much know what to expect from a buddy-action-adventure-danger (B.A.A.D.) movie. We can count on the following ingredients:

1. Two cops who, though absolute opposites, love each other deeply. Flaky, unpredictable, wisecracking, white Mel Gibson and steady, strong, slow-on-the-uptake, black Danny Glover are ideal B.A.A.D. buddies.

2. A merciless and thoroughly unlikable villain (Joss Ackland) with a heavy foreign accent from a despised, totalitarian government. South Africa? Yes, South Africa should do rather nicely.

3. A beautiful, young woman whose burning love for one of the B.A.A.D. buddies is destined to cause her no end of difficulties.

4. Car chases, fisticuffs, gun duels, surprise explosions, massive building demolitions.

5. A terribly bloody shoot-em-out between the too-good-to-be-believed buddies and the too-evil-to-live villains.

OK, that's the basic B.A.A.D. movie recipe. What distinguishes one B.A.A.D. movie from another are the little extras, the way the movie functions within the limits of the form. "Lethal Weapon 2" has enough added ingredients to rise above other B.A.A.D. movies and easily surpass the hugely successful original.

The first thing it has going for it is a script by Jeffrey Boam ("Indiana Jones and the Last Crusade," "Innerspace") whose strength is clearly humor. This explains why the film's high spots are not the fireworks but the funny stuff that goes on between shoot-'em-ups.

Its second great unexpected additive is a sterling bit by supporting actor Joe Pesci, who portrays a state witness being protected by Glover and Gibson. Pesci, who was unforgettable as the kid brother in "Raging Bull," is a Mafia banker ("All I did was I laundered a half-billion dollars in drug money, OK?"), also a perfect nebbish who wants only to man the sirens as his two guardians are diverted into endless games of cops-and-tyrants.

A word here about Patsy Kensit, the obligatory love interest and token female. The word: attractive. Women in a B.A.A.D. movie typically have little to do other than look cheerful despite having a life expectancy that is, at best, limited. Kensit, who is currently lead singer for the rock group Eighth Wonder, starred at the age of 4 as Mia Farrow's daughter in "The Great Gatsby," and she has grown up very nicely.

"Lethal Weapon 2" is the kind of high-voltage entertainment this country has the patent on and despite the fact that he must honor all the form's conventions, director Richard Donner ("Superman," "Scrooged") is the slickest of pros. Even the most familiar action sequences—even the obligatory explosions and gunfights—are done with a degree of freshness. Donner's pacing is swift, and he's as good at timing punchlines as punches.

Yes, it all ties together too neatly. Agreed, it's meant to be enjoyed, not believed. Sure, it treats violent death as the highest form of entertainment. But some things are unavoidable, simply part of the genre. And with all of its flaws, "Lethal Weapon 2" remains one of the best of a B.A.A.D. lot.

NEWSWEEK, 7/17/89, p. 53, David Ansen

Lethal Weapon 2 starts with such a bang you might suspect it's the first movie on steroids. Dispensing with opening credits, it plunges us unprepared into the midst of a car chase that takes superhuman effort to follow. Not being a fan of the popular "Lethal Weapon"—a slick buddy action comedy so generic it put me in a funk—I grumpily resigned myself to another two hours of alienation from the *vox populi*.

Then, 30 minutes into Richard Donner's sequel, I got hooked. The moment was easy to pinpoint: Riggs (Mel Gibson) and Murtaugh (Danny Glover) are sent to protect a pint-size accountant named Leo Getz, who's testified that he laundered half a billion dollars for a drug-dealing mob. Getz is played by Joe Pesci (Robert De Niro's brother in "Raging Bull"), and his nudgy, motor-mouthed, petulant Leo sends "Lethal Weapon 2" into comic orbit. Excitedly tagging along on our heroes' adventures, he runs through the slam-bang action sequences like a barking terrier, his wagging tail threatening to get in the way of his bodyguards' deadly business.

The new "Lethal Weapon" plays a cinematic version of good cop/bad cop: it pummels the audience with the one-two punch of comedy and violence. It's the extremity of the juxtaposition of grisly and jaunty that gives this movie its distinctive, pop Jacobean tone. Screenwriter Jeffrey Boam (working from a story by Shane Black and Warren Murphy) justifies the heroes's trigger-happy impulses by coming up with a gang of villains no one could forgive. Not only are they world-class drug dealers, they are also glowering racists who work for the South African government. As if this weren't enough, we later learn that one of these creeps was responsible for the car-crash death of Riggs's wife described in the first "Lethal Weapon." Having made sure that Riggs and Murtaugh are, to say the least, properly motivated, the movie rolls up its sleeves and indulges in some extravagant mayhem, executed by director Donner with lip-smacking expertise.

Subtlety is not the draw here: condom jokes and toilet humor alternate with car crashes and machine-gun killings. Yet the movie has a bouncy, comic-book appeal: sadism has rarely been so good-natured. The secret, in addition to Pesci's bravura turn, is in the interplay between the volatile Gibson and the kinder, gentler Glover, who are more fun to watch together now that they don't have to pretend not to get along. The real love story here is between the cops—the subsidiary romance between Gibson and Patsy Kensit, playing a wan "good" South African, feels halfhearted: the filmmakers don't even try to create a full-scale female character. They have no such problem with the bad guys, robustly played by Joss Ackland and Derrick O'Connor: you anticipate their demise with great glee. But the pressure is now on the screenwriters: how are they going to up the ante of villainy for "Lethal Weapon 3"? Perhaps opium-dealing Chinese communists killed Riggs's *mother*.

TIME, 7/24/89, p. 53, Richard Corliss

It's an *oid-y* world out there. Tabloids run factoids about humanoids on steroids. In a world gone synthetic, why should movies offer something as organic as a hero? Welcome, then, to the age of the heroid. In the old days, a hero like Bogart had brains and guts but also a nagging heart and the seductive scowl of obsession. Often he failed; sometimes he died. He was real: us, with muscles. A heroid, though, is just the muscles. He owes more to comic strips than to romantic or detective fiction. Never really alive, a heroid cannot die; he must be available for the next assembly-line sequel. He is the cyborg chauffeur of mechanical movies.

You can hear the clockwork sputtering inside the brawny breastplate of this week's heroids: Los Angeles supercop Martin Riggs (Mel Gibson) in *Lethal Weapon 2* and Her Majesty's secret servant James Bond (Timothy Dalton) in *Licence to Kill*. Both men are rogue avengers, out for bloody justice against cartels that have killed or threatened their partners and spouses. Both pictures, with their suavely depraved drug lords and curt disregard for constitutional safeguards, play like extended episodes of *Miami Vice*. Both scenarios choose their villains from the current list of least favored nations: South Africa in *LW2*, a thinly disguised Panama in *Licence*. "Remember," Bond's nemesis (Robert Davi) warns the film's Noriega, "you're only President for Life."

That dealer-diplomats in *LW2* are just your ordinary bad guys. They keep zillions of Krugerrands on hand to finance their chicanery. They have a getaway helicopter conveniently waiting in downtown Los Angeles at the end of a car chase that totals dozens of innocent drivers. Now if only this gang could shoot straight, they might rid the world of Detectives Riggs and Murtaugh (Danny Glover)—and spare moviegoers further sequels to the loathable smash hit of 1987.

The first movie raised the craft of torture to a low art. Expect no less in *LW2*, directed by Richard Donner and written by Jeffrey Boam. This installment features a surfboard decapitation, death by carpenter's nail gun, a bomb wired to a very sensitive seat (plot device lifted from Elmore Leonard's novel *Freaky Deaky*), and reduction of the Afrikaaner diaspora by about one-half. As Riggs tells Murtaugh, "We're back! We're bad! You're black! I'm mad!" Mad to the max. Riggs may not know how to spell *apartheid*, but he knows whom he hates. He even knows how to strike a blow for American property values. When the Boers perforate his beachside shack, Riggs finds appropriate recourse. He kills their house.

In *Licence to Kill*, the bad guys' hideaway blows up real good too. And there are some great truck stunts. A pity nobody—not writers Michael G. Wilson and Richard Maibaum nor director John Glen—thought to give the humans anything very clever to do. The Bond women are pallid mannequins, and so is the misused Dalton—a moving target in a Savile Row suit. For every plausible reason, he looks as bored in his second Bond film as Sean Connery did in his sixth.

Licence's only innovation comes in the closing credits. To atone for Bond's use of cigarettes, the producers print the Surgeon General's caveat on the evils of tobacco. Another warning would have been welcome: CAUTION: EXPOSURE TO HEROIDS MAY CAUSE SUMMERMOVIE BURNOUT.

VILLAGE VOICE, 7/11/89, p. 72 Stuart Klawans

Forget *Batman*. If you're looking for cartoon-like ultraviolence on a brain-dead summer's day, then *Lethal Weapon 2* is your best value for money—and it's even politically correct. The studio that once celebrated our Soviet allies in *Gremlin From the Kremlin* now gives us its latest live-action "Looney Tune": an exercise in mayhem and vulgar humor, with nothing on its mind except being faster and louder than the first *Lethal Weapon*, and maybe ending apartheid, and promoting the tuna boycott, and presenting a positive image of interracial male love.

All this, and you don't have to wait for the action. By the time the Warner Bros. logo has faded from the screen, a car chase is already in progress, with Mel Gibson and Danny Glover frantically miming their characters. I say miming because the dialogue, which is largely unintelligible, is dispensable as well. You're already supposed to know that the blue-eyed one is a borderline psychotic named Riggs, who might have killed himself years ago, except that, being a cop, he gets to kill other people instead. The tall, dark, and handsome one is his partner Murtaugh, a middle-aged family man who dreams of a peaceful retirement but keeps letting Riggs drag him into trouble. If you don't already have this information, the film will eventually supply it, but not before taking care of really important business, such as destroying cars, shop windows, and large chunks of the Los Angeles freeways.

The villain who instigates this carnage—the Elmer Fudd character—is Rudd (Joss Ackland), head of the South African consulate. Not only is he evil, but he also enjoys diplomatic immunity. Our heroes, Daffy and Sylvester, must therefore turn vigilante in order to punish him. Is it inaccurate to portray L.A. cops as freedom fighters? Is it morally questionable to show them breaking the law? Sure—but then, as the payoff, you get to see Gibson parading with an antiapartheid placard, an image that might do as much good as Bishop Tutu's next three interviews with Bush.

Granted, the politics are only an excuse for the rest of the movie. But then, filmmakers will always need excuses to justify the way they appeal to our baser instincts. Richard Donner has picked a worthy justification and makes sure the instincts are fully satisfied. Good for him; good for Joe Pesci, who is outstanding in the Bugs Bunny role (as a federal informer); and good for Glover and Gibson, who are willing to play the buddy premise to its logical conclusion. When the shooting is over and the squad cars are on their way, Gibson looks into Glover's eyes and says, "You really are a beautiful man. Give us a kiss before they come."

Top that, Caped Crusader.

Also reviewed in:

NEW YORK TIMES, 7/7/89, p. C18, Caryn James
VARIETY, 7/5–11/89, p. 18
WASHINGTON POST, 7/7/89, p. D1, Rita Kempley
WASHINGTON POST, 7/7/89, Weekend/p. 33, Roger Piantadosi

LET'S GET LOST

A Zeitgeist Films release of a Little Bear Film. *Executive Producer:* Nan Bush. *Producer:* Bruce Weber. *Director:* Bruce Weber. *Director of Photography:* Jeff Preiss. *Editor:* Angelo Corrao. *Sound Editor:* Maurice Schell. *Running time:* 119 minutes. *MPAA Rating:* Not Rated.

WITH: Chet Baker, Carol Baker, Vera Baker, Paul, Dean and Missy Baker, Dick Bock, William Claxton, Flea, Hersh Hamel, Chris Isaak, Lisa Marie, Andy Minsker, Jack Sheldon, Lawrence Trimble, Joyce Night Tucker, Cherry Vanilla, Diane Vavra, and Ruth Young.
MUSICIANS: Frank Strazzeri (Piano); John Leftwich (Bass); Ralph Penland (Drums); Nicola Stilo (Guitar).

CHRISTIAN SCIENCE MONITOR, 4/28/89, p. 11, David Sterritt

"Let's Get Lost," a documentary about the late jazz musician Chet Baker, was nominated in the recent Academy Award race and has played major film festivals, including New York's prestigious New Directors/New Films series. Now it's finally heading for theaters: Its première engagement is in progress at New York's enterprising Film Forum, and its national release commences next month.

And not a moment too soon. This is easily the best documentary, and the best all-around movie, I've seen in a long while—although its subject has sad and unsavory aspects that may disturb people with no special interest in jazz or biographical film.

Even by jazz-musician standards, the late Chet Baker was something of an odd man out. Check the notes to his currently available albums, and where you expect to see unvarnished hype you'll find excuses for his shortcomings. One speaks of his "ups and downs" and "extremely uneven" work; another mentions the "somewhat erratic" period it dates from; a third describes the "rollercoaster extremes and musical paradoxes" of his early career. With press agents like this, who needs critics?

Even his admirers found Baker a hard musician to pin down. During the 1950s, he built his reputation on the "cool" sound of the West Coast school.

Yet he also recorded with members of the hard-driving East Coast contingent, and didn't shrink from playing a Miles Davis number now and then—as if inviting, rather than repelling, the charge that he borrowed too heavily from Davis's patented style. On top of these musical matters, Baker led a tormented personal life, with unsuccessful marriages and persistent drug problems. He died last year while still in his 50s.

Why must attention be paid to such a man? The answer lies in his music, which was simply gorgeous. It's not to every taste, of course. His trumpet playing and singing are so unassuming— almost relentlessly so—that they veer closer to pop than to jazz at times. And there's no question that Baker was always at his best in the ballad form, giving some of his albums a consistency that's almost too much of a good thing. His most successful music was so exquisitely conceived and controlled, however, that it must have reflected a core of dignity and decency within the man himself. Such beauty can't have been an accident.

In addition to his musical accomplishments, Baker summed up much that was best and worst in the culture of his time. This was especially true during his rise to fame in the 1950s, when his moody handsomeness and relaxed demeanor made him an epitome of "beat generation" charm. Later he sank into a more laid-back and even lethargic manner related to the excesses that dogged him. Yet his music stayed uncannily smooth and expressive, as his sessions in the late '80s attest.

To film "Let's Get Lost," director Bruce Weber and cinematographer Jeff Preiss took their crew on the road with Baker, accompanying him across the United States and to Europe during the last year of his life. The movie shows him in candid moments, in music sessions, and in interviews before the camera. Sometimes he struggles to remember and speak through some kind of mental fog; at other times, especially when he plays and sings, he's alert and engaging. But he's always fascinating, in a way that's cautionary and exemplary by turns.

Rounding out the portrait, the film includes interviews with Baker associates and clips from his occasional feature-film ventures, including a Robert Wagner-Natalie Wood epic based on his early life and a couple of productions in which he acted.

"Let's Get Lost" is a movie drenched in atmosphere, reflecting both the '80s, when it was made, and the '50s, which it were Baker's good (and bad) old days. It casts a welcome spotlight on the crystal clarity of Baker's best musical achievements, and for this alone it's a welcome arrival.

LOS ANGELES TIMES, 5/25/89, Calendar/p. 3, Sheila Benson

"There's a lot of [deleted] attitude's goin' on here," Chet Baker growls, annoyed, during a late-night, late-in-his-life recording session. Amen. "Let Get Lost" runs on attitude, on surface, on an adoration of beauty and a horrified fascination with the loss of that beauty. It's a phoney Valentine, an exploitation of the ruined old junkie that Baker had become, done with the complete complicity of Baker himself.

Why wouldn't Baker be an accomplice? Here was Bruce Weber, heavyweight fashion photographer and fledgling film maker, Mr. Calvin Klein Ads himself, clearly a worshipful fan. He was able to pour almost unlimited amounts of money—reportedly $1 million—into a documentary portrait whose focus was entirely Baker. Since's Weber's entourage apparently includes the young boxers from his first film, "Broken Noses," as well as nymphet actress-models, there would be a constant, adoring audience to listen to all the old stories all over again. Why hesitate?

Baker didn't. And so we have this gorgeous-looking, creepy portrait: Baker nodding in and out of consciousness, answering these dim interviewers ("Do you find life boring?") or smothered happily between two beautiful women in a 1950s convertible, driving up the Pacific Coast Highway as Weber makes his delirious homage to the cool '50s.

The film *is* gorgeous; cameraman Jeff Preiss's rich, contrasty black-and-white turns the thick palm trees silver as the wind hits them; you think you've never seen them so beautiful before and you're right. Beauty and banality, arm in arm.

We are spared nothing. Baker on the bumper cars. Santa Monica beach at twilight, where the boxers, would-be Baker look-alikes, bop, somersault and preen in white socks and pompadours, yearning for a scintilla of Baker's aura. The long-haired model whirls round and round, as instructed by someone off-camera. It's as vapid and as pointless as it sounds and probably only someone in Baker's state could stand much of it.

And his music? There is that, of course. But in a world centered around image, music takes a back seat to cutting-edge cheekbones. Weber has such little respect for Baker's music that he muscles in on the end of a phrase to have one of Baker's ex-old-ladies rag on another one, a wife or another ex-girl friend. Or Weber overrides the music so we can hear his precious questioner prod: "Maybe you can tell me about your unfortunate encounter and how you got your teeth knocked out. ..."

A few of the old gang elude this stultifying approach: musician Jack Sheldon, as drily hilarious as he ever was, tells outrageous stories from the bad old days, and tall, sandy-haired photographer Bill Claxton describes the camera's affinity for Baker: "He had charisma. This was a new word in the mid-'50s."

Claxton was almost Baker's own age when he took the photographs that cemented Baker into everybody's memory book as *the* icon of jazz, at 22. The Claxton eye is extraordinary; a riffle through his contact sheets makes it clear that the young man with the camera was as arresting a talent as the young man with a horn. (And, shot for shot, a more dynamic artist than Weber, at least in Weber's Greek-god ad work.)

Weber's chloroformed presentation seems to regard the loss of his crazy good looks as the real tragedy of Baker's life. Over and over Weber cuts from footage of Baker at 57 in the most merciless light possible, looking like a seamy con man or a raddled Oklahoma cowboy who's been out in the weather too long, to the blank, undeniable beauty of Baker in his early 20s. He's the perfect idol, whispy, whispery, enigmatic, someone you could project everything onto because there was so little *there* there.

"Let's Get Lost" is a three-layer exercise in betrayal: Baker's casual lifetime habit of letting down anyone near him. As ex-love Diane Vavra says, "You can't really rely on Chet. Once you know that you're OK."

There is Weber and his crew, in Stillwater, Okla., softly coaxing damning admissions out of Baker's mother, Vera, his wife and the kids, having first gotten their trust. Elsewhere, without a touch of empathy, Weber eggs on Baker's other women to bad-mouth one another. He gets Vavra to pose—again in harsh outdoor light—with a huge picture of her loveless love.

Finally in Europe, after the Cannes Film Festival, and a notable performance of "Almost Blue" for the festival goers—"the worst possible crowd"—Baker is his frailest, his very joints seem to grate. In their hotel room, Weber purrs on camera, "I know you're without your methadone, Chet, you're feeling sick and desperate...it's been so painful to see you like this." Even the unflappable Baker seems stunned. "This is a big drag and completely unnecessary," he says softly.

Audiences may agree.

MONTHLY FILM BULLETIN, 2/90, p. 42, Adam Barker

The story of legendary jazz trumpeter Chet Baker is traced from his lowly birthplace in Oklahoma to the golden years of jamming with the likes of Charlie Parker in Los Angeles in the 50s, and into a slow decline from the 60s onwards, largely precipitated by drugs. Interviews with Baker and his entourage shot in 1987 are intercut with archive footage. William Caxton, the photographer, and Dick Bock, the record producer, recall the sudden impact of his angelic looks and demonic talent, and stories of Baker's youthful mischief-making are laid over recent footage of his disciplinarian attitude in the recording studio. Fellow trumpeters complain about the ease with which Baker played phrases which took them hours to perfect. The adulation is tempered when Baker's former wives and lovers recollect how he came and went at will, leaving behind a trail of children. His mother admits that, however impressive his achievements, he has been a disappointment as a son. The singer Ruth Young, one of Baker's more recent lovers, claims that he has lied about one of the crucial events of his career, a beating he claimed to have received from a gang of young blacks which stopped him from playing for three years. Young says it was a single person who had had enough of Baker's treacherous ways. Baker's account of the drug-related events which led to his imprisonment in Italy in 1960 also differs from the official version. The climax of the film is a performance by Baker of Elvis Costello's "Almost Blue" to a sadly unmoved audience at the Cannes Film Festival in 1987. Baker died in Amsterdam in May 1988.

"Not all good things come to an end/It's only a chosen few" ("Almost Blue", Elvis Costello). Bruce Weber, one of the most influential fashion photographers of the 80s, began his film-making career with *Broken Noses*, a documentary about a young boxer. *Let's Get Lost*, his account of jazz trumpeter Chet Baker, takes another beautiful male image and peels away the layers to reveal the messy and sometimes tragic reality underneath. "Everybody's got a story about Chet Baker", recalls one of his fellow musicians. Baker took the 50s jazz world by storm with his boyish good looks and attachment to melody in an age of be-bop discordance; along with Art Pepper, Baker defined the sound of West Coast jazz in this period. But *Let's Get Lost*, which starts out looking like a piece of hero-worship,with black-and-white (in the present-day as well as archive footage) lending its subject iconic status, and his ultra-cool jazz flowing under every scene, gradually allows a different picture to emerge.

Baker is revealed as not just a traditionally evasive ageing jazz musician, but as a pathological liar throughout his life. The exclusive rights to his life story were granted first to Ruth Young—and then to Bruce Weber. "It's a no-win situation with a junkie", acknowledges his long-term lover Diane Vavra. Much of the poignancy of the film derives from the contrast between the young, Matt Dillon-esque Baker and his appearance in the 80s, his face pitted and cracked by a lifetime's drug use. Baker frequently appeared on television at the height of his career, and also in feature films (he was to have starred in a 1960 film version of his life, *All the Fine Young Cannibals*, but he was arrested, and his part was taken by Robert Wagner). Even in old age (he was fifty-seven during the making of the film), Baker preserved much of the vocal and instrumental freshness of his youth, producing an uncanny disjuncture between sound and image.

Andy Minsker, the boxer at the centre of *Broken Noses*, puts in an appearance, and his uncanny resemblance to the young Baker reinforces the sense of the latter's rapid decline. *Let's Get Lost* shares with *Broken Noses* a casual, elliptical construction making use of many different sources— interviews, archive footage, and home-movie sequences—while the stylised use of black-and-white seductively counterbalances a disturbing story of personal manipulation and deception. Weber, in fact, remains caught in much the same contradiction he revealed in *Broken Noses*, between the aesthetic sensibilities of a stylist and the investigative instincts of a documentarist. It remains to be seen which path he will choose.

NEW YORK, 4/17/89, p. 62, David Denby

In Bruce Weber's documentary *Let's Get Lost* the late jazz trumpeter Chet Baker, shown as a young man, has stunning high cheekbones and deep-socket eyes; photographed by Weber's crew in 1987 (Baker died last May), his flesh is withered and scarred, with the dried-out hollows of a lifelong junkie. The fabulous bones, however, are still there, and women caress Baker's face tenderly, nostalgically, in homage to the extraordinary-looking man he once was. On camera, Baker is courtly and remote and very quiet. The incredibly talented jazz musicians like Baker or Charlie Parker who destroy themselves with drugs remain elusive to filmmakers, too subtle and guarded and manipulative to let anyone pluck out the heart of their mystery. They fascinate and betray and fascinate again. The subject of *Let's Get Lost* is as much the people obsessed with Chet Baker—especially the tough, beautiful women pushing one another out of the way—as Baker himself.

Bruce Weber is a fashion photographer; he has a vested interest in making the erotic momentous. He uses high-contrast black-and-white film here, which flatters Baker's Greek-god, sculptured look. There's something in Baker's distant beauty that mesmerizes him, too. Awestruck, the movie goes on and on, repeating itself, stuck, an endless monument to a frozen, distant artist. Chet Baker played cool jazz; in the movie he sings soft, slow ballads in the lightest, tenderest voice you've ever heard. His rarefied art remained secure. Even at the end, at Cannes in 1987, his singing was something sinuous and delicate whispered into your ear—music to cuddle to.

NEW YORK POST, 4/21/89, p. 27, David Edelstein

"Let's Get Lost," Bruce Weber's portrait of Chet Baker near the end of his life, has a twisty lyricism you don't find in slow, reverential art films about jazz greats—perhaps because its subject barely seems to exist. Shot with a hand-held camera in high-contrast black-and-white, the movie swirls around the elusive jazz trumpeter as it might around some floating apparition, moving quickly for fear that the specter will melt into air.

The *image* of Baker is vivid, as always—the razor-cut cheekbones, slicked-back hair and sunken eyes, which with age sank even deeper into his wizened, mummy-like face. But the point to be inferred from Weber's layered collage—which mixes modern footage with glamorous '50s stills and film clips—is that the "coo," self-absorbed junkie was an emotional black hole, unplumbable if never silent.

Weber, who made his fortune as a fashion photographer (he did the Calvin Klein underwear ads), began the project as a short film about his idol and then couldn't tear himself away. Shooting was, by all accounts, a logistical horror, the director and crew never certain if Baker would show up and in what condition he'd be in if he did. (Baker's preferred high, as he confesses in the picture's final minutes, is the speedball, a heady mixture of cocaine and heroin.)

It's no wonder that Weber, who financed "Let's Get Lost" with his own money, dwells—in interviews with what might laughingly be called Baker's extended family (wife, girlfriends, neglected children)—on the artist's reliability. "Chet cons people," says one lover, who goes on to describe the trumpeter wheedling drug money out of casual acquaintances. His old mother, when asked if Chet was a disappointment as a son, smiles and says, slowly, "Yes. But let's not go into that."

What emerges is a portrait of a drifter, a man who wanders in and out of people's lives without notice, always managing to convince them of his sincerity and always letting them down. He leaves a bittersweet taste. Asked if there's anything she'd like to tell her father, Baker's daughter peers into the camera and calls, with acid geniality, "Don't be such a stranger."

In "Let's Get Lost," Baker might be the most lovingly photographed stranger in history, his James-Dean-with-chops image clearly more important to Weber than his music. Weber's failure to scrutinize Baker in the context of jazz is, I think, a major flaw, and one which leaves the movie lopsided. (It might, to be fair, have something to do with the 57-year-old junkie's frailness—the performances in the film don't do him justice.)

Baker's lightness, his lack of roots, his dreamy self-absorption enabled him to let down his guard as a performer. When he played he was alone with his trumpet; when he sang—in a thin tenor that issued from his head and not his chest—he seemed to be squeezing the sound painfully through a tiny hole into the microphone. Baker's solos often drift in tentatively from the fog, grow in brightness and intensity, and then recede.

Weber, in his ardor, does attempt to penetrate surfaces, and even when he fails he entertains. He shoots Baker on the beach in Santa Monica with assorted young musicians and models—this to suggest the trumpeter's eternal sense of his own youthfulness. And when cinematographer Jeff Preiss swings his camera in the direction of some frolicking dogs, the shot seems meant as an allusion to our hero, the quintessential aimless, skittery West Coast jazzman.

Nothing in Chet Baker's life had weight, but there's a kind of beauty in that: Baker could be Salina in a jazz version of "The Unbearable Lightness of Being"—without apology or explanation, content to be observed, living only in the moment. "Let's Get Lost," can be viewed (as J. Hoberman suggests in the Village Voice) as a study of cool—bloodied by life but unbowed. The shell might have crumbled, but the attitude stands tall.

NEWSDAY, 4/21/89, Part III/p. 5, Stuart Troup

Chet Baker's trumpet sound was much like his singing voice—subdued, plaintive, stunning. But his career, which had held so much promise, stumbled through drug-related interruptions, disability and erratic behavior.

Like Baker, "Let's Get Lost," is stunning when it offers his haunting sound, and it stumbles by interfering with it often. Photographer Bruce Weber has nonetheless packaged an often-poetic profile, buoyed by Baker's presence and commentary during the last year of his life. (Baker was found dead last May, at age 58, after apparently falling from his Amsterdam hotel window.)

The film, in black and white, is filled with riveting contrasts. The photos by William Claxton show a virile and handsome Baker of the 1950s, lookin much like James Dean, and the later clips parade a debilitated and gaunt victim, his face a reflection of chemical ravages. And some of his explanations of his actions are contradicted by those who knew him best.

Two things go unchallenged, however: (1) The skill and warmth of his musicianship, and (2) the way he apparently manipulated the women in his life. Of the former, trumpeter Jack Sheldon notes that Baker was "a natural"; that while everyone else had to practice long and often, Baker could walk in cold, after a hiatus, and be perfect. Of the latter, his ex-lovers and ex-wives seem unified about how he used women. It was part of his charm.

Producer/director Weber surrounds much of this footage with scenes of youngsters on the beach in Venice, Calif.; which appear to have little connection to the film. And a scene with Baker driving a bumper car at a crowded carnival rink seems out of place, unless Weber saw it as a metaphor for Baker's life.

The film's redemption, however, comes from Baker himself, singing and playing trumpet, explaining, lying—charming to the end. But the music is often interrupted by cutaways or voice-overs. Weber even gets to Baker's mother and his children—including a son who looks more like James Dean than his father did—to enrich the portrait.

He was a tragic figure. In Paris, he once told writer Mike Zwerin how he was embarrassed in the 1950s when he had placed higher in the polls than Dizzy Gillespie and Clifford Brown, "both of whom he adored," because he was "the great white hope" with the pretty face. He wasn't in their league then, and he knew it. But in the 1980s, when he was capable of playing jazz as well as anyone, he was dismissed as a has-been; a junkie who often didn't appear at scheduled engagements, and who more than once fell off his chair on stage.

But when he played or sang, Baker could still break your heart.

NEWSWEEK, 5/29/89, p. 69, David Ansen

Bruce Weber's mesmerizing, collage-like documentary about the jazz trumpeter Chet Baker, *Let's Get Lost*, is fixated on the two faces of its subject. One face is ravishing, the other ravaged. The first is the treacherously angelic face of the golden-boy musician of the '50s, when he was discovering his own lyrical, languidly romantic horn style molded by the cool hedonism of the Los Angeles jazz scene. It's the face of a matinee-idol heartbreaker. The second is the hollow-cheeked death mask of the 57-year-old man, a year before he died in 1988. It's the face of a con artist and ex-con, blasted by decades of speedballs (Baker's preferred mixture of heroin and cocaine). When he speaks, the zombie pauses say more about the toll of his life than his inarticulate words. But when he sings you can see that the musician in him never died. Eyes closed in a reverie, he launches into Elvis Costello's "Almost Blue" in a performance at Cannes, and though the voice is just a reedy shadow of itself, he casts a magician's spell.

For the acclaimed photographer Weber, who made his name idealizing male beauty in fashion spreads, the physical transfiguration of Baker, his longtime idol, must cut to the quick. Interviewing Baker's girl friends and one of his three wives, who bitterly recall their no-win relationships, Weber obviously shares their hopeless infatuation. "Let's Get Lost," is about addiction, and not just to drugs. It's also about love junkies, doomed to fall for incorrigible bad boys like Baker, hooked on the glamour of self-destruction. "You really can't rely on Chet," says Diane Vavra. "If you know that, you can pull through." Vavra fell for Baker after he'd had his teeth knocked out in a fight—halting his career for years until he learned to play with dentures.

Weber doesn't pretend to give us a definitive view of the man's music. It's sometimes frustrating when he cuts away from a tune, and it's more annoying when Weber surrounds Baker with his own claque of models and hangers-on, cavorting in staged scenes of enforced "fun." But in the end, Weber's self-indulgences don't really matter; they may even help make "Let's Get Lost," one of the most hauntingly personal jazz movies ever made. Weber's seductive eye perfectly matches his obsession: his black-and-white images, at once dreamy and tinged with dread, seem to get to the heart of Baker's music, which up until the end still held out the plaintive promise of romance. Weber's film is a mash note that turns into a *memento mori*.

VILLAGE VOICE, 3/28/89, p. 64, J. Hoberman

Bruce Weber's portrait of jazzman Chet Baker is a romantic, poisonous valentine to the '50s, with the doomed Baker presented as something like James Dean, Elvis, and Jack Kerouac all rolled into one genius junkie hipster. Drifting back and forth in time, *Let's Get Lost* is sensationally shot in rich, grainy black-and-white—it's at least as much about photography as it is about music, or the nature of cool, or the corrosive lifestyle that transformed the astonishingly beautiful, uncannily vacant young Baker into a cowboy derelict cum singing corpse.

VILLAGE VOICE, 4/25/89, p. 59, J. Hoberman

The epitome of cool, jazzman Chet Baker has a haunting vacancy: listening to his forlorn trumpet or his ethereal, constricted singing is like being sweet-talked by the void. There's an inviting absence of affect that attracts the psyche like a vacuum. It's grimly appropriate that Baker met death in a mysterious fall from an Amsterdam hotel window last May. A longtime heroin addict, his was the romance of oblivion—something acknowledged by the title of master fashion photographer Bruce Weber's documentary-portrait, *Let's Get Lost*.

Weber's film, which had its local premiere at last month's "New Directors" series and opens Friday for a three-week run at Film Forum 2, presents the doomed Baker as something like James Dean, Elvis, and Jack Kerouac all rolled into one genius junkie hipster. The movie is shamelessly in love with its subject: the ferociously photogenic young Baker had the face of a butch Greta Garbo, or maybe Steve Canyon gone AWOL—impossible cheekbones set off by a sleek pompadour and a provocatively focused blankness. Even old Baker, a seamy looking drugstore cowboy cum derelict, retains his streamlined profile and incongruously gentle voice. Q: What planet did he come from? (A: Oklahoma, 1929, where, according to his mother, he learned the trumpet in two weeks.)

If Baker is Weber's fetish, the filmmaker is scarcely alone. *Let's Get Lost* is populated by a collection of spellbound Baker fans—ranging from ex-associates and young lookalikes to former wives, old girlfriends, and abandoned children. The movie is a dense mix of voiceover interviews, interpolated archive shots, and lyrical self-dramatizations. Elegantly informal, it fugues back in time—as when the camera spins over the old contact sheets of some 1953 session. Weber's love for these old photographs is palpable; it rivals his passion for Baker. *Let's Get Lost* is one of the most photo-mad movies ever made. (Weber even includes an *hommage* to his low-rent precursor Andre De Dienes, the '50s poet of Amazon nudes in appropriately curvaceous Western landscapes.)

The beefcake parade in Weber's 1987 documentary *Broken Noses*—which is not only dedicated to Baker but portrays a young Portland boxer who could be the musician's teenage self—seems closer to Weber's photography than the less physical *Let's Get Lost*. Still, the languid, chlorinated *Scorpio Rising* effect produced by *Broken Noses*'s incongruous juxtapositions of hot fighting and cool jazz points the way to the second movie's swoonier evocation of some echt American masculine ideal. (It also suggests Baker's vocal knack for delivering heavy lyrics with the lightest possible touch.) *Let's Get Lost* is a paean to '50s glamour in which Baker is simultaneously foreground and background.

Thus, totally infatuated with its own surfaces, *Let's Get Lost* skims over the jazz scene. The talking often steps on the sounds, although there are some indelible instances of old (and young) Baker shaping his thin voice around a song—not so much crooning as wincing in his concentration. (The suggestion is always that Baker's music provided moments of crystalline order in a frantic, chaotic existence.) Still, Baker's music provided moments of crystalline order in a frantic, chaotic existence.) Still, Baker's image is Weber's subject, and *Let's Get Lost* is nothing if not voluptuous imagemaking. There's a jagged fluidity and a maximum of texture that allows for the interpolation of all manner of amateur, paparazzi, or studio filmmaking—including a heartfelt, ridiculous clip of Natalie Wood being blown away by Robert Wagner's trumpet in the Baker-inspired *All the Fine Young Cannibals*.

Let's Get Lost was shot by Jeff Preiss, in rich, grainy black-and-white, and although the camerawork is jaunty and hand-held—tilted compostions, breathless pans—the look is as lush as it is quirky. (Preiss's own unpretentious 8mm celebrations of Lower Manhattan have the same stylistic signature of skewed angles, abundant shadows, and precise lateral pans.) The documentary keeps breaking into impressionistic home-movie shards. The film's moody impasto is swirled with digressions: Chet in some Cadillac convertible bombing through the night, a gaggle of kids bebopping on the beach at Santa Monica like beatniks out of a time warp.

Like ethno-aesthete Robert Gardner, Weber is one documentary filmmaker with the means to indulge his tastes. He spent something like a million dollars on this production, much of it visible on the screen. There's sensational Euro-footage—images of the Left Bank in the late '50s, an impromptu scat session in a Paris hotel room, a montage of celebs at the Cannes Film Festival (accompanied by Chet singing an uncharacteristically expressive "Just Friends"). Extraneous to the main narrative, the Cannes sequence is Weber at his most life-affirming—it suggests the high-style hedonism of his Obsession ads or Rio book, with sub-jet set hunks and disheveled babes voguing in all degrees of expansive undress.

Some purists may be unhappy, but the movie is a pleasingly dense mix, with old Baker playing behind young Baker's vocalizing, or the young Chet reproachfully singing "You Don't Know What Love Is," while an old lover contradicts his story of getting his teeth knocked out (and embouchure temporarily destroyed) by vengeful drug dealers. The most barbed of these musical comments is the slow pan over Baker's wife, mother, and children—"all his victims," as one colleague puts it—as we hear him sing "Blame It on My Youth." As the young Baker was something like a cornfed Adonis, the notion of blaming indiscretion on his youth seems tantamount to cursing the Arctic for an abundance of snow.

Let's Get Lost opens with the less sublime sounds of old Chet in a recording studio, mumbling something about there being "a lot of fucking attitude here,"—and, indeed, there is. Life, in this dark carnival, is a succession of frozen, fleeting gestures. Perhaps it takes a fashion photographer to fully grasp the pathos of film as moment-by-moment memento mori. Long before he offers his final, almost lilting "Arrivederci," well before his final leap into the void, Chet appears to be a singing corpse.

Also reviewed in:
NEW YORK TIMES, 4/21/89, p. C8, Janet Maslin
NEW YORKER, 5/1/89, p. 75, Pauline Kael
VARIETY, 9/14/88, p. 26
WASHINGTON POST, 6/2/89, p. D2, Hal Hinson

LETTERS FROM A DEAD MAN

A New Yorker Films release of a Lenfilm Studio film. *Executive Producer:* Raisa Proskuryakova and Yuri Golinchik. *Director:* Konstantin Lopushansky. *Screenplay (Russian with English subtitles):* Konstantin Lopushansky, Vyacheslav Rybakov, and Boris Strugatsky. *Director of Photography:* Nikolai Prokoptsev. *Editor:* T. Filanovsky. *Music:* Alexander Zhurbin. *Sound:* Leonid Gavrichenko. *Set Designer:* Elena Amshinskaya and Viktor Ivanov. *Special Effects:* A. Filaretov and I. Krinsky. *Costumes:* A. Sapunova and E. Shapkaits. *Make-up:* V. Savelyev. *Running time:* 86 minutes. *MPAA Rating:* Not Rated.

CAST: Rolan Bykov (Professor Larsen).

MONTHLY FILM BULLETIN, 10/87, p. 311, Tom Milne

Following a nuclear holocaust triggered by accident, a military curfew is enforced in a devastated city, and groups of survivors are screened by a medical commission: only the young and healthy are welcome in the already overcrowded central bunker where they are scheduled to remain for thirty to fifty years until the atmosphere becomes radiation-free. In the ruins of a museum, remnants of the staff form one such group. With them is Professor Larsen, a Nobel Prize-winning scientist, who had left the central bunker to look for his wife Anna and son Eric: he found Anna, now dying of radiation sickness, but not Eric, to whom he mentally addresses letters detailing his experiences while attempting to prove scientifically (without sufficient data) that the devastation was not global, and that the planet is not now uninhabitable. Braving the brutally enforced curfew to try to barter tinned meat against painkilling drugs for Anna, Larsen comes upon another group: some traumatised orphanage children in the care of an aged pastor and a girl who refuses to leave for the central bunker when the children are rejected. Anna dies; the elderly museum director commits suicide; and the group decides that there is nothing now to prevent them from going to the central bunker. But with the aged pastor dead, the girl delivers the traumatised children into Larsen's care, and he refuses to abandon them. Alone with the children on Christmas Eve, still convinced that going underground is not the answer, Larsen constructs an artificial tree for the children to decorate in the hope that the traditional celebration will awaken their will to survive, then leads them out into the unknown.

It takes a long time to get there, but a small flame of imagination begins to burn in the final sequence of Lopushansky's film. Watched expressionlessly yet trustingly by the children, Larsen constructs his futuristic Christmas tree of metal and paper while his voice-over, drafting yet another never-to-be-sent letter to his son, recalls the traditional celebration as a time "when people tried to make each other happy, gave presents, met and chatted in warm rooms, then went out to welcome the first star in the sky". The children obediently light the candles on the tree. Larsen sets the hands of a clock to midnight. A bell tolls. Then as the children set out into the darkness and desolation, blindly clinging to each other in single file like a string of circus elephants, one realises that the voiceover is now that of a child, recapitulating this whole preceding sequence (there was no star that night, we learn, and Larsen the saviour died) as a tribal memory handed down through generations from some unimaginable yet reassuringly human future. Instead of being left with the prosaic humanism of Larsen's last words ("As long as a person walks there is hope"), we are suddenly transported, much more enticingly, into areas of legend.

For all its stabs at Tarkovsky mysticism, the rest of the film is, alas, fairly prosaically humanist, with the museum setting and its litter of broken books and damaged artefacts providing an all-too-convenient cue for much speechifying about mankind striving to outdo itself scientifically and creating masterpieces of art while knowing they were short-lived and useless: "Art recorded our search for an ideal, our despair, the cry of a lonely creature". One attempt to visualise the immediate effects of nuclear destruction tends to be much like another, mainly a matter of hunks of rubble, people bundled up in ragbag assortments of clothing, and a prevailing absence of light which means that you can't see too much. Shot in monochrome or sickly sepia tint, evidently on a very limited budget, the film is nothing much to look at. And the fact that the characters (Larsen excepted) are tedious cyphers puffed up with rhetoric doesn't make it any more palatable despite its patent sincerity.

NEW YORK POST, 1/27/89, p. 27, Jami Bernard

This Russian version of "The Day After" must have cleaned up at the box office over there after Chernobyl.

Set in subterranean fallout shelters after a misfired nuclear missile (whoops!) has turned the city, maybe the world, into a gray-green hell, we follow a Nobel Prize-winning scientist as he struggles to survive and understand.

He and several others are existing in the hollows of a museum—how fitting, for they too are now relics of a vanished world on display. As they all begin to rot from radiation, they go about a daily routine that includes group dinners of meticulously apportioned rations, like three olives or something per plate.

Everyone tries to find a way to cope. Someone recites a decorous message of condolence every time someone dies. Someone else decides that exposing the skin would be healthier, or at least more human, and so appears bare-breasted at the dinner table.

The scientist tries to use his scientific skills to carve order from chaos. "I must pose a logical problem and reach a hypothesis," he says, studying seismographs and collecting charts.

In his head, or in reality—maybe a little of both—the scientist writes letters to his son, who is most likely dead. "Dear Eric," he writes, and proposes an end to the distinction between day and night, "because the world has lost its variety."

Indeed, infrequent forays in gas masks to the streets above reveal a monochrome world full of brackish puddles, endless litter and shadowy figures of black marketeers who peddle pain-killers for tinned food.

In another sanctuary are a dozen silent orphans, who represent the only hope in this bleakest of bleak films. The next generation, and all that. The professor builds them a rag-tag Christmas tree of wire and junk in one of the movie's several sympathetic moments.

"Letters from a Dead Man" does all right when it's not being sanctimonious and heavy-handed. The scientist notes drily that he has solved the Cooper Equation, something that sounds like it has been bugging mathematicians for centuries. You see, at the end of the world, none of this matters.

"The history of mankind is creating more successful ways of suicide," remarks another guy. Next time, tell us something we don't know. Like what the hell is the Cooper Equation?

VILLAGE VOICE, 1/31/89, p. 62, Elliott Stein

If you hanker for a Soviet *The Day After*, make a beeline for *Letters From a Dead Man*, a postnuclear holocaust movie completed before Chernobyl and released just after to record business at Moscow wickets. It is set in the ruins of a town that had once been a missile site. A fatal button has been pushed by accident; nuclear winter now seems to have settled over the entire world. Much of the action takes place in the bomb shelter of a ruined museum, where as elderly Nobel Prize-winning professor writes letters in his mind to a son missing since the explosion. He occasionally ventures outdoors—there everything is a sickly greenish blue—where other survivors barter canned goods and painkillers. Encountering a group of orphans living in a ruined church, the old man fashions a Christmas tree out of debris for them. Before he dies, he urges the children to attempt an escape from what may be merely an area of limited radiation. With their departure in the dirty snow, the film ends on a note of ambiguous hope.

Letters marks the feature debut of director Konstantin Lopushansky, who once worked as Andrei Tarkovsky's assistant. There are a few scenes which bear some superficial resemblance to *Stalker*, although *Letters*'s style bears no trace of Tarkovsky's fervid lyricism. As the professor, the veteran Rolan Bykov delivers a solid performance of the old school—he's a Lionel Barrymore of the Steppes.

Also reviewed in:
NEW YORK TIMES, 1/27/89, p. C11, Richard Bernstein
VARIETY, 11/12/86, p. 15

LEVIATHAN

A Metro-Goldwyn-Mayer Pictures release. *Executive Producer:* Lawrence Gordon and Charles Gordon. *Producer:* Luigi De Laurentiis and Aurelio De Laurentiis. *Director:* George P. Cosmatos. *Screenplay:* David Peoples and Jeb Stuart. *Story:* David Peoples. *Director of Photography:* Alex Thomson. *Editor:* Roberto Silvi and John F. Burnett. *Music:* Jerry Goldsmith. *Music Editor:* Kenneth Hall. *Sound:* Robin Gregory. *Sound Editor:* Mike Le Mare. *Production Designer:* Ron Cobb. *Art Director:* William Ladd Skinner and Pier Luigi Basile. *Set Designer:* Craig Edgar, Jim Teegarden, Maria T. Barbasso, Alessandro Alberti, and Daniela Giovannoni. *Set Decorator:* Robert Gould and Bruno Cesari. *Visual Effects:* Barry Nolan. *Creature Effects:* Stan Winston. *Mechanical Effects:* Nick Allder. *Costumes:* April Ferry. *Make-up:* Zoltan Elek. *Stunt Coordinator:* Randell Widner and Rocco Lerro. *Running time:* 103 minutes. *MPAA Rating:* R.

CAST: Peter Weller (Beck); Richard Crenna (Doc); Amanda Pays (Willie); Daniel Stern (Sixpack); Ernie Hudson (Jones); Michael Carmine (DeJesus); Lisa Eilbacher (Bowman); Hector Elizondo (Cobb); Meg Foster (Martin); Eugene Lipinski (Russian Ship Captain); Larry Dolgin (Helicopter Pilot); Pascal Druant (Winch Operator); Steve Pelot (Winch Operator).

FILMS IN REVIEW, 6–7/89, p. 368, Ken Hanke

"Your worst nightmare come true," claims the newspaper ad, and, if your worst nightmare centers around a big budget, bloated beached-whale of a movie that washed ashore for no apparent reason to terrorize theater patrons with new lows in tedium and unoriginality, *Leviathan* lives up to that claim. It doesn't matter so much that the film is a brazen theft of Ridley Scott's *Alien*, since that overrated space opera was in itself a pretty straightforward pilfering of an Edward L. Cahn "B" picture from 1958 called *It! The Terror From Beyond Space*, decked out in state of the art effects work and Scott's oddly stylized direction. What matters is *Leviathan*'s complete lack of substance, style (despite director George P. Cosmatos' damndest efforts at aping Ridley Scott), coherence, construction, or a single surprise—pleasant or otherwise. The picture should have been called *A Clockwork Rip-Off*, so mechanical is the whole soggy mess.

Just how *Leviathan*'s producers have managed to escape a nice plagiarism suit is open to question. Not only is the difference between deep space and the deep blue sea marginal in terms of look (cramped and dark—the entire picture is like being trapped in a cave), but the film manages to only slightly vary the development of the story. The substitution of a genetic experiment (via tainted Russian vodka—a weird combination of Russophobia and some extreme "just say no" object lesson) for a parasitic alien life form isn't much of a stretch, since the resultant creature (in its various muting stages) behaves in an identical manner to its "inspirational" parent. That the fiendish beastie first looks like an oversized garden slug with chrome teeth as opposed to a phallus with chrome choppers hardly qualifies as an exercise in original thought. Holding out the "monster-out-of-chest" bit for a late effect doesn't make it fresh—just later. And so it goes.

Even *Leviathan*'s characters (if that they can be called) are straight out of *Alien*, worked around as if designed by the advertising department from TV's old *Mod Squad* ("Three cops—one black, one white, one blonde"), or ordered up from Screenwriting 101's Chinese Take-out menu ("One stalwart hero from column A, one plucky heroine from column B, assorted subgum fried ethnic types from column C, etc."). And despite this firmly established guidelines, the motivations of the types range from the vague to the nonexistent. Why, for instance, does Peter Weller (giving an impossible performance in an impossible role) have one glassy-eyed scene in which he appears to be under some sort of hypnotic influence from the Evil Big Business forces that control the undersea mining operation he's in charge of? What earthly reasoning could lie behind Amanda Pays' shock-effect leap into the frame—apart from the effect itself? Why, for that matter, was this thing even made?

By far the most impressive aspect of *Leviathan* is its amazing ability to stretch time. While this may be an achievement of limited practical value, it's hard to deny that not every film can make 103 minutes of screen time seem at least twice that long. Thank goodness.

LOS ANGELES TIMES, 3/17/89, Calendar/p. 4, Kevin Thomas

"Leviathan" is "Alien" under water. It's not nearly as sophisticated or as terrifying as the Ridley Scott film, but it looks good and moves fast. It's elementary fun with a couple of scary moments along the way.

Off the coast of Florida a crew of six men and two women are nearing the end of a 90-day stint 10,000 feet beneath the ocean's surface. Headquartered in Shack 7, a huge octagon of spun-molded steel, the crew dons cumbersome motorized suits to mine the ocean floor of precious metals for Trans-Oceanic, a multinational corporation represented via a TV monitor by an icy executive (Meg Foster), whose interest in profits rather than the welfare of her undersea employees is not exactly disguised.

Headed by a geologist (Peter Weller), the crew is already experiencing understandable cabin fever when it discovers the hulk of a huge Soviet ship. Sixpack (Daniel Stern), the least serious, most stir-crazy member of the crew, hides a flask of vodka he finds on the vessel, and shares it later with one of the women (Lisa Eilbacher). Naturally, or unnaturally, as it turns out, a couple of slugs of the stuff produces the most horrifying results.

Written by David Peoples and Jeb Stuart from a story by Peoples, "Leviathan" (rated R for language, standard horror movie violence) is the old monster-of-the-deep movie slicked up to play as a cautionary tale about the perils of genetic engineering. Creature effects specialist Stan Winston and his studio have come up with the usual gelatinous monsters that mutate before our very eyes.

Playing against his "RoboCop" image, Weller comes on as the most hesitant and reluctant of leaders who, of course, matures in crisis. Only Richard Crenna, as the crew's doctor, a scientist with a tragic incident in his past, has a role with any dimension to it. Other crew members are played capably by Amanda Pays, Ernie Hudson, Michael Carmine and Hector Elizondo. Along with Crenna, resourceful cameraman Alex Thomson and production designer Ron Cobb, whose technically intricate settings at once striking and convincingly functional, the film's strongest asset is the crisp, punchy direction fo George P. Cosmatos, best known for his two Stallone blockbusters, "Rambo" and "Cobra," but more fondly remembered for the sly 1982 horror allegory "Of Unknown Origin," which also starred Weller.

MONTHLY FILM BULLETIN, 5/90, p. 132, Kim Newman

Off the coast of Florida, the Tri-Oceanic Corporation has a deepsea mining base, currently commanded by geologist Beck. Nearing the end of a lengthy spell underwater, the miners are getting fidgety. Sixpack, the most anarchic of the group, and Willie, a would-be astronaut, discover the wreck of the "Leviathan", a Russian ship which is not officially missing. Sixpack retrieves the ship's safe from which he takes a hipflask of vodka, sharing it with Bowman, a female comrade. The next day, Sixpack has a severe rash, from which he seems to die, while the rig's highly qualified but disgraced medic, Doc, makes a tentative diagnosis of massive cellular mutation. Martin, the surface liaison woman from Tri-Oceanic, refuses to bring the miners up early, claiming that there is a hurricane raging on the surface. When Bowman sees Sixpack's corpse turning into a monster, she commits suicide rather than go the same way. The mutating corpses are disposed of, but a severed limb from Six-pack's body remains inside the rig, and regenerates into a new monster. Doc reasons that the "Leviathan" was part of a Soviet genetic experiment, and that the ship was sunk when the programme got out of hand. The monster attacks two miners, DeJesus and Cobb, and they also begin to transform. Doc destroys the escape pods to limit the monstrosity to the rig, and is bitten and infected by Cobb. Beck and Willie discover that Martin's hurricane story is a sham, and that the corporation has already announced their deaths. The monsters, which retain some human intelligence but can live underwater, breach the hull of the rig, and it begins to collapse. Beck, Willie and Jones, the survivors, escape to the surface in their deepsea diving suits, but one of the monsters bursts out of the sea and kills Jones before Beck disposes of it with a distress flare. Rescued by the coast guard, Back and Willie are enthusiastically greeted by Martin, and Beck punches her in the face.

In terms of production values, *Leviathan* comes at the expensive end of the current cycle of underwater science fiction films, but like the more cheapskate entries (*DeepStar Six*) takes its plot cues slavishly from *Alien*. Among the carry-overs from Ridley Scott's film are production designer Ron Cobb's sets and a Jerry Goldsmith score; a grouchy mixed-sex, mixed-race crew of blue-collar types who keep up a constant stream of nervous patter to punctuate the script's sillier stretches; a monster found in a wrecked ship that grows inside its discoverer; a treacherous and coolly feminine representative of the evil corporation (there, a computer; here, Meg Foster with a severe hair style); a scientist whose motives turn out to override his commitment to his crew mates; a two-fisted heroine whose sexuality is only apparent in the number of excuses the film finds to strip her down to her underwear; and a multifunctioned monstrosity, designed by Stan Winston of *Aliens*, that bloodily rampages through the supporting cast.

Given the familiarity of it all, *Leviathan* is at least an enjoyable rip-off, with a crew of straight-faced victims who give their stereotyped roles enough tics to make them welcome. Peter Weller, in particular, reuniting with George Pan Cosmatos after the bizarre terror-by-rat picture *Of Unknown Origin*, makes a credible he-man hero as a geologist who wins the shaky loyalty of his crew by doing a mining shift to help them meet their quota but who is still nervous about his command, while Lisa Eilbacher and Daniel Stern, as the first victims, do well by the traditional roles of the doomed cut-ups whose wisecracks disappear under special effects make-up. *Alien* was itself highly derivative of 50s monster movies, and the current screenwriters have taken the trouble to go back to Roger Corman's *Attack of the Crab Monsters* for a plot twist about the monster absorbing the memories of its victims. Which lends the whole genre a pleasing circularity, since the next glub-glub-glub picture due for British release is Corman's very own rip-off of *The Abyss, Lords of the Deep*.

NEW YORK POST, 3/17/89, p. 25, David Edelstein

We moviegoers don't ask for much; every so often we just wanna see a bunch of tough-looking dudes get royally wasted. And Lord, the swill we have to sit through for a few cheap jolts. For instance, "Leviathan." "Alien" at the bottom of the sea. Multiracial mining crew stumbles on botched genetic experiment and gets mutated, slimed and eviscerated by marauding fishwich. Yum.

George Cosmatos, who made "Rambo," directs "Leviathan" as if he's the guy in the diving suit—it's one 10-ton step at a time. The picture manages to be both plodding and incoherent; to figure out what's going on—why, for example, the company doesn't seem in any hurry to pick these people up once they start getting chomped—you'd have to have seen "Alien."

Peter Weller is the joyless commander, Richard Crenna the disillusioned doc, Daniel Stern the horny alcoholic who (natch) gets contaminated first. There are a couple of good sight gags involving Stern's festering, reanimated corpse, and Ernie Hudson gets some great wisecracks, especially when the frosty-eyed company rep (Meg Foster) tells the crew (on a video link) that she knows they must have gone through hell. "Gone?" he exclaims. "Bitch, we're still *here*."

The "girl" is the insolently pretty Amanda Pays, who played a reporter on the short-lived network "Max Headroom" series. The strategy is amusing: She's a strong, liberated woman but the filmmakers ensure that she strips to her undies as often as possible. She's going to take the astronaut training test in a couple of days, so she keeps in shape by jiggling—er, jogging around the ship with her Walkman on. Real smart with a hungry monster around.

Apart from Pays' physique, "Leviathan" is low on thrills: The false scares (when you think it's the monster 'cause the music goes BONG!!! but it's just one of the crew saying, "What's happenin', guys?") are better than the real ones. To maintain an atmosphere of spine-tingling suspense, the director cuts to slimy pieces of the creature—a couple of frames at a time—as if to remind you why you're there.

The monster, by Stan Winston, is one of these generic shape-shifters that snaps at people and burrows into their bodies. We have no idea if there's one or several creatures, or even what the rules are—it's able to regenerate from a severed limb, so clearly blowing it up isn't going to do much good. We're told it absorbs people's intelligence along with their bodies, but it's no rocket scientist; it gobbles down a flair and calmly waits to explode.

"Leviathan" is gorgeously photographed in deep acquatic greens (by Alex Thomson) and cleverly designed (by Ron Cobb). But the fact is, folks, *it doesn't need to be this good*. It doesn't need the Dolby Spectral sound or the Afga XT color negative. It needs some pulp imagination and a sense of play. Most of the shocks are achieved by volume, by head-splitting rumbling and hissing and screeching.

As a strategy, this might be ingenious. In "Leviathan," no one can hear you snicker.

NEWSDAY, 3/17/89, Part III/p. 5, Mike McGrady

The best line in "Leviathan" is given to Jones (Ernie Hudson), the black member of the ethnically balanced crew mining the ocean floor three miles beneath the surface.

You have to understand, Jones has just witnessed all the following: the contamination of the group's spunsteel housing unit by "organisms of unknown origin"; the death of a wise-cracking, skirt-chasing shipmate (Daniel Stern) who develops black boils that erupt like miniature pus-packed volcanoes; the suicide of a female crew member who has come down with the same space-age ailment; the strangulation of the Puerto Rican crew member by what is either a large snake or a tentacle of an even larger monster; the sight of corpses melting down into a pulsating green slime, then reforming themselves as snakes; the cold-hearted company executives up above cutting off all possible escape routes; the explosion of the entire undersea housing unit; a harrowing escape to the surface trailed by angry monsters and then at the last moment—oh, no!— being greeted by a convoy of hungry sharks.

That's when Jones delivers his big line.

"Talk about having a bad day!" he says.

In fact, the entire plot can be outlined through a series of familiar lines. Beginning with "Oh, God, they're alive!" and "It's growing!" and "This company's commitment is to the almighty dollar" and "I've seen this disease, and it's no day at the beach" and "We're losin' air faster than I thought" and "Eight minutes to implosion!"

A second way of describing the plot is to point out that it is identical to "Alien" in everything except specific setting and quality. Not only does "Leviathan" retell the story of both "Alien" and "Aliens," it *looks* very much like those earlier pictures—undoubtedly because the resident special-effects geniuses, Nick Alder ("Alien") and Stan Winston ("Aliens"), won their Oscars for creating identically monstrous effects in the recent past.

The most significant difference between both "Alien" movies and "Leviathan" is that the earlier films attempted to deal with human beings as well as monsters. At this juncture, I feel compelled to point out that director George P. Cosmatos, also put together such movies as "Rambo II" and "Cobra."

Also reviewed in:

NEW YORK TIMES, 3/17/89, p. C18, Janet Maslin
VARIETY, 3/22–28/89, p. 22
WASHINGTON POST, 3/20/89, p. B2, Richard Harrington

LICENCE TO KILL

An MGM/United Artists release. *Producer:* Albert Broccoli and Michael G. Wilson. *Director:* John Glen.

Screenplay: Michael G. Wilson and Richard Maibaum. *Director of Photography:* Alec Mills. *Editor:* John Grover. *Music:* Michael Kamen. *Music Editor:* Andrew Glen. *Sound:* Edward Tise and (music) Dick Lewzey. *Sound Editor:* Vernon Messenger. *Production Designer:* Peter Lamont. *Art Director:* Michael Lamont. *Set Decorator:* Michael Ford. *Special Effects:* Laurencio Cordero, Sergio Jara, and Neil Corbould. *Special Visual Effects:* John Richardson. *Costumes:* Jodie Tillen. *Make-up:* George Frost and Naomi Donne. *Stunt Coordinator:* Paul Weston. *Running time:* 135 minutes. *MPAA Rating:* PG-13.

CAST: Timothy Dalton (James Bond); Carey Lowell (Pam Bouvier); Robert Davi (Franz Sanchez); Talisa Soto (Lupe Lamora); Anthony Zerbe (Milton Krest); Frank McRae (Sharkey); Everett McGill (Killifer); Wayne Newton (Professor Joe Butcher); Benicio del Toro (Dario); Anthony Starke (Truman-Lodge); Pedro Armendariz (President Hector Lopez); Desmond Llewelyn (Q); David Hedison (Felix Leiter); Priscilla Barnes (Della Churchill); Robert Brown (M); Caroline Bliss (Miss Moneypenny); Don Stroud (Heller); Grand L. Bush (Hawkins); Cary-Hiroyuki Tagawa (Kwang); Alejandro Bracho (Perez). Guy de Saint Cyr (Braun); Rafer Johnson (Mullens); Diana Lee-Hsu (Loti); Christopher Neame (Fallon); Jeannine Bisignano (Stripper); Claudio Brook (Montelongo); Cynthia Fallon (Consuelo); Enrique Novi (Rasmussen); Osami Kawawo (Oriental); George Belanger (Doctor); Roger Cudney ("Wavekrest" Captain); Honorato Magaloni (Chief Chemist); Jorge Russek (Pit Boss); Sergio Corona (Bellboy); Stuart Kwan (Ninja); José Abdala (Tanker Driver); Teresa Blake (Ticket Agent); Samuel Benjamin Lancaster (Della's Uncle); Juan Pelaez (Casino Manager); Mark Kelty (Coast Guard Radio Operator); Umberto Elizondo (Hotel Assistant Manager); Fidel Carriga (Sanchez's Driver); Edna Bolkan (Barrelhead Waitress); Eddie Enderfield (Clive); Jeff Moldovan and Carl Ciarfalio (Warehouse Guards).

CHRISTIAN SCIENCE MONITOR, 7/18/89, p. 11, David Sterritt

Hollywood movies are usually geared to be popular and uncontroversial, so they can provide clues to what's going on in the American consciousness. A look at the new James Bond picture, "Licence To Kill," shows a development worth noticing: the Contras of Nicaragua no longer have the respectability they enjoyed during the Reagan years.

Bond's main adversary is a Latin American criminal who purchases Stinger missiles from the Contras so he can threaten to down an American airliner if the Feds don't lay off his drug-running operation. The film assumes that the Contras would sell their weapons to any high bidder, and that they wouldn't care if the bidder happened to be a psychotic criminal.

The bad guy only uses his Stingers during the final shootout with Agent 007, but the other key ingredients of his crookedness—drugs and money—are practically the stars of the movie.

This is another sign of the times, also visible in "Lethal Weapon 2," a midsummer hit that arrived slightly earlier. In that picture, two Los Angeles cops chase a South African who uses diplomatic immunity to shelter his narcotics dealing.

South African officials and Contra-supplied Latins may be new on Hollywood's roster of stock villains, but as characters they're just facile variations on the Nazis, Commies, and other politically aligned antagonists who plagued heroes in bygone melodramas.

Like them, the new breed of heavy serves not only as a foil for the good guy but, more significantly, as a reflection of American xenophobia—a trait that plagues all manner of movies from Indiana Jones epics to backalley exploitation flicks.

Bond is a "foreigner" himself, of course, but "Licence To Kill" minimizes Britishness by transplanting him to the Florida Keys and other locations near the United States, and by teaming him with a former CIA operative. He even resigns from Her Majesty's Secret Service at one point, becoming (just like the "Lethal Weapon 2" heroes) a vigilante on a purely personal vendetta. The movie also flaunts its America-first leanings with pointless inside jokes, including plays on the names of former President Kennedy and Jacqueline Kennedy.

The other hallmark of "Licence To Kill" is its violence, which is surprisingly vicious for a warm-weather entertainment with a PG-13 rating. Bond has always been a casual killer, of course, even in the days when Sean Connery played him with a *savoir faire* that hasn't been equalled. But his nastiness has been escalating, and it reaches an awful height in his new adventure.

One example is a moment when 007 has his antagonist completely subdued and dangling helplessly over a hungry shark. Instead of tempering law enforcement with mercy, Bond cheerfully tosses a heavy suitcase (stuffed with the villain's ill-gotten cash) at the bad guy, deliberately plunging him to a horrible death. All of which gives a chuckle to Bond's sidekick, who promptly remarks, "What a waste—of money!"

Violence and xenophobia apart, "Licence To Kill" is at least as lively as most other current movies. One comparison is with "Batman," which—according to one of my teenage children— doesn't have enough "bat-traps" in it (a bat-trap being a fiendish device found in the "Batman" comic books for killing the hero). By contrast, "Licence To Kill" has plenty of Bond-traps, from the aforementioned shark to that old favorite, a conveyor belt leading to a deadly machine.

None of them work, of course, and 007 is sure to return for plenty more sequels. They may well feature Timothy Dalton; so I'm happy to report he's more human and less wooden in "Licence To Kill" than in "The Living Daylights," his last outing. As unlikely as it seems, Mr. Dalton actually appears to be growing in the Bond role, which is potentially stifling because its own popularity has so rigidly defined it.

John Glen has directed "Licence To Kill" with the same dogged energy he brought to four earlier Bond epics.

The supporting cast includes such veterans as Desmond Llewelyn, who has played the character called Q in all but two of the Bond pictures, and Robert Brown, who's played M since "Octopussy" in 1983. Also on board, in his film-acting debut, is singer Wayne Newton as an evangelist who's as oily as he is phony.

Footnote: In one more sign of the times, "Licence to Kill" is the first movie I know of with a Surgeon General's Warning at the end because of the on-screen use of tobacco products.

While this is a step in the right direction, I have two further suggestions: Leave those tobacco products on the cutting-room floor in the first place, and slap a Surgeon General's Warning on the whole movie—since its eager violence pollutes the filmgoing atmosphere at least as much as James Bond's cigarettes!

LOS ANGELES TIMES, 7/14/89, Calendar/p. 1, Michael Wilmington

Time marches, age withers and everything falls into decay...except James Bond, still spruce and deadly after all these years.

The series has been with us since 1962 and, like many another old timer, tends to repeat itself. Yet, every once in a while, it pulls in its stomach, pops the gun from its cummerbund, arches its eyebrow and gets off another bull's-eye. The newest, "Licence to Kill," is probably one of the five or six best of Bond.

At first, it's hard to suggest why. "Licence" (the title is deliberately anglicized) milks the formulas as before: a mix of sex, violence and exotic scenery, with Bond on a one-man raid against an archetype of evil, while seducing women and taking in sights. Here, the locales include the seaspray expanses of Key West and the garish palaces of Mexico City disguised as a fictitious "Isthmus City."

Yet the overall tone has gotten more burnished, somber. The new movie sends the new Bond, Timothy Dalton, on a desperate one-man vendetta against an apparently omnipotent South American cocaine czar. And it isolates him, kills or maims three of his best friends, strips him of his rank, his government, his very license to kill. It leaves him with almost nothing but his wits—and dear old chic-weapons expert Q (Desmond Llewelyn), who pops up ex officio with another bag of lethal cameras and exploding toilet accessories.

It even strips away a little libido. As Timothy Dalton plays the role—with wolfishly sad eyes—this is a more wounded and sensitive Bond than we've ever seen, the sort of Bond the late Laurence Olivier might have imagined. (The look is there, but not the lines.) Bond's appetite for sex seems more distracted, tentative. His women—Carey Lowell as a helicopter pilot and double agent, Talisa Soto as the drug czar's faithless mistress—are more self-sufficient. His armor has sprung a leak.

Where Sean Connery was wry and self-confident and Roger Moore natty and self-mocking, Dalton projects something strange for a hero identified with impeccable sadism: inner torment. The walk is tense; cigarettes pour out fumes of *Angst*; the smile carries a hint of pain.

Connery always seemed to be enjoying the world hugely—and he carried the audience along with him, made them enjoy it as much as he did. Roger Moore didn't seem to be enjoying the world so much as ignoring it and, instead, enjoying himself—or perhaps some internal reflection. Dalton, by extreme contrast, doesn't project much enjoyment at all. He projects pain. And pain, obsession and revenge are what "Licence to Kill" is all about.

It's not a film about an urbane adventurer, moving with eerie confidence through a violent, chaotic world. It's a film about a bereaved friend, half-crazed with grief, relying on his instincts and professionalism to carry him through a situation rotten with peril. Like Stallone's Rambo or Eastwood's Dirty Harry, this Bond has been stiffed by the world and abandoned by his government. He is a loner, driven by overwhelming personal hurts—confronted with a cool, sexy foe who, in some curious way, almost recalls the old Bond.

Previous villains in the series tended to be older, more urbance, wicked paterfamilias figures. Instead, Robert Davi, a heavy in "Die Hard," makes Franz Sanchez—who's modeled on modern drug kings like Carlos Lehder of Colombia's Medellin cartel—a sexy adventurer who metes out rough justice with style and merciless sarcasm. And he has a code: loyalty matters to him more than money. Against this new-style villain, Bond, the dark angel, twists what seems to be Sanchez's only good quality—his insistence on loyalty—against him, trying to strip away his friends one by one and convince him of their treachery.

It seems to isolate Bond as well as Sanchez. Yet it leaves him with everything that counts: the gimmicks, the archetypes, the formulas, the old jokes of a full 27-year and 16-film tour of duty. Like all Bond movies it has its set-pieces, chief among them a roaring, rousing Mad Max-style climactic, exploding chase involving three Kenworth trucks, jeeps and a small plane set on a desolately beautiful Mexican mountain road. It's planned and staged with the exquisite carnage of a silent comedy car chase, with gags topping gags, and surprises leaping over each other—just as one flaming truck leaps over the plane.

Produced and co-written by old hands Albert Broccoli and Richard Maibaum (whose tour dates back to 1962's "Dr. No"), directed and co-written by new veterans John Glen and Michael G. Wilson, the movie whips up a combustible brew of old and new. Is it just updating the new cliches: the incessant car crashes, gruesome sadism, heavy hardware, feistier heroines? (Just as there used to be obligatory sexpots-in-distress, Carey Lowell almost seems an obligatory lone wolf.) Perhaps—but all those movies stole from the Bond films, too, often draining out the crucial elements that make them fun: self-kidding humor and exotic locales.

"Licence to Kill" (MPAA-rated PG-13, despite extreme violence and suggestions of sex) has the usual bursts of illogic, the gratuitous sex or violence. But gratuitious sex or violence have always been fixtures of Bond's world. Often the formulas grate on you. Here, they ignite. This is a guilt-edged Bond; there's a core of darkness and pain in the glittery world exploding around it.

MONTHLY FILM BULLETIN, 7/89, p. 207, Julian Petley

James Bond is on leave in Florida, where he is about to be best man at the wedding of his friend Felix Leiter, head of the Drug Enforcement Agency. On their way to the ceremony, Leiter, Bond and his friend Sharkey discover that drugs baron Sanchez is nearby in the Bahamas. They capture him, but he is freed by one of his henchmen, Milton Krest, who operates behind the cover of a marine biology laboratory. Sanchez's men kill Leiter's new wife and Sharkey, and Sanchez himself feeds Leiter to a shark. Leiter survives, though badly mutilated. Bond pursues Sanchez via Krest, but is warned by M that Sanchez is the Americans' responsibility. When Bond refuses to obey, he is suspended from the service. Taking matters into his own hands, he manages to enter Krest's research vessel, the "Wavekrest", and ruins his cargo of drugs before making off with the proceeds from his deals. Learning of Sanchez's whereabouts in Isthmus city, where he owns a bank and a casino, Bond poses as a gambler, enlisting the aid of Pam Bouvier, a charter pilot who pretends to be his secretary. Sanchez is setting up a deal with a group of Oriental drug barons, one of whom, unbeknownst to bond or Sanchez, is in fact Kwang, an undercover narcotics agent from Hong Kong. Bond's gambling brings him to the attention of Sanchez, and he offers his services, but Sanchez declines. Bond is about to kill Sanchez when he is captured by Kwang and taken to his hideout, where he is handed over to the British secret service as a 'rogue agent'. On Sanchez's orders, the Isthmus City army blows up the hideout. Discovering Bond tied up in the wreckage, Sanchez decides he was sincere, and takes him to his home to recover. Persuaded by Bond that Krest has double-crossed him, Sanchez kills him and takes Bond and the Oriental dealers to his drug factory, which is disguised as a meditation centre. Pam enters the centre posing as a candidate for a meditation course. When one of Sanchez's men recognises him, Bond starts a fire. Sanchez orders the tankers which transport his drugs to leave the centre, and a chase ensues. Bond finally kills Sanchez by igniting his petrol soaked clothes with Leiter's lighter.

This is the fifth Bond to be directed by John Glen, and continues the process which he initiated of turning the films back into "straightforward thrillers", of emphasising the characters as much as the gadgets and sets, and keeping the humour wry and laconic rather than allowing it to become simply jokey and camp. In this he has been greatly aided by the casting of Timothy Dalton, whose Bond is more in the style of the young Sean Connery than the dandified Roger Moore. As Umberto Eco has pointed out, the pleasures of the Bond film, like the pleasure to be gained from other kinds of thriller, lie as much in repetition as variation ("The reader finds himself immersed in a game of which he knows the pieces and the rules—and perhaps the outcome—and draws pleasure simply from following the minimal variations by which the victor realises his objective"). Foremost of those, of course, are the action sequences, of which *Licence to Kill* contains three exemplary specimens.

The first is the statutory pre-credits sequence which, as usual, combines daredevil stunting with a degree of outrageous humour, as Bond, dangling from a helicopter, literally "reels in" Sanchez's aircraft before he and Leiter parachute in to the latter's wedding. The second begins with an underwater battle and proceeds with Bond firing a harpoon gun at the floats of a seaplane taxiing on the surface, waterskiing along behind the plane, then pulling himself aboard and throwing out the pilot. The climactic action sequence is an extraordinary chase down mountain roads involving petrol tankers, a crop-dusting aircraft and a villain armed with Stinger guided missiles. Q is allowed to take on more than his usual role as inventor of outlandish gadgets for Bond and actually helps him as a 'field operative', while the film marks another stage in the process whereby the Bond women have come to enjoy an existence as something other than the hero's playthings or as the seductive embodiment of evil. Romantic interest, though present, is quite low-key, and when Bond asks the resourceful Pam to pretend that she is his executive secretary, she comes back with, "Why can't *you* be *my* executive secretary?"

One of the most surprising and drastic shifts in the Bond mythology, however, concerns his relationship with M and the rest of the service. The scene in which Bond is disciplined by M and ends up assaulting both his boss and his fellow agents must be as outrageous to Fleming purists as Marlowe's shooting of Terry Lennox in Robert Altman's *The Long Goodbye* was to Chandler disciples. From this point on, in fact, *Licence to Kill* is really a story of personal revenge and it is this, aided by Robert Davi's performance as a convincingly nasty criminal as opposed to the cypher-like super-villains of some previous Bonds, that provides the story with its narrative drive. It has to be said, though, that the drive flags from time to time, that the film is too long, and that the sub-plot involving Stinger missiles and the contras is barely comprehensible, since the relevant information is gabbled out by Pam when attention is focused primarily on a scene of action.

The fact that the villains on this occasion are tied up with extreme right-wing forces, however, does show that the Bond myth is fairly flexible in an ideological sense. On the whole, the films have served as a rather good barometer of East-West relations, and it would be difficult to imagine an anti-Soviet Bond in this era of *glasnost*. Instead, the universally reviled figure of the drug baron provides a much more effective target, and the film abounds with scenes in which dealers get their just deserts: most striking of all is that in which Krest explodes all over his ill-gotten gains. But however moral its message, it and about half a dozen other scenes have fallen foul of the censors both here and in the U.S. and have been trimmed to qualify for 15 and PG13 certificates respectively, with the American version being slightly less cut than the British. This is one of the few Bonds to suffer in this way, a difficulty which the producers seems to have failed to anticipate when changing the Bond image for the 90s.

NEW STATESMAN & SOCIETY, 6/23/89, p. 44, Suzanne Moore

It's not really surprising, when you think about it, that James Bond movies are a key text in the study of popular culture. With the aid of Open University notes on Ian Fleming's fabulous creation, most of us could trot off some sort of essay about how the character, James Bond, reflects certain attitudes about class, gender and nationality. It's almost as if Bond was written for the purpose of being read for his ideological incorrectness by angsty academics who felt decidedly uncomfortable that they actually enjoyed these unsound films.

Where could you find a better example of xenophobic, chauvinistic behaviour? Whether as a fantasy of post-colonial or masculine power, James Bond films are rampantly reactionary. So how do you explain their popularity? Of course you can't without recourse to words like "pleasure" and "fantasy", words which these days can at least be spoken out loud rather than slipped in as a footnote in the analysis of culture.

This overall lightening up, this acceptance of old-fashioned virtues like entertainment and escapism means that James Bond fans can sleep sound in the knowledge that they no longer have to feel embarrassed about getting off on the cunning stunts of this most British of macho men. After all having a rape fantasy doesn't actually mean that you want to be raped and watching a Bond movie doesn't necessarily mean that you want to be James Bond. Or does it?

It takes a dour feminist indeed—a part I cetainly don't relish—to insist that the fantasies that films like this engender are unacceptable. Yet reaction to the latest Bond movie. *Licence to Kill,* is interesting in that it points to a kind of *critical paralysis* (what Meaghan Morris has described recently as banality) in left cultural analysis. It's a sign of the times that Sally Hibbin, writing about the film in *Marxism Today*, is ultimately less censorious about the film than many articles that have appeared in the press and in commercial women's magazines such as *Elle.*

While I wholeheartedly embrace the move towards accepting the complex and fascinating thrills and spills of pop culture, it's not enough to say of a Bond movie it's a "fantasy world" and leave it at that. Without some idea of how these fantasies intersect with the "real" world, we might as well pack our bags and go home.

But then if the postmodern condition means the negation of critical distance, why bother in the first place? There will always be more of where that came from which we, in our incredibly smug postmodern way, can remain knowingly immersed in. It doesn't matter whether you switch on or off, it doesn't matter whether you like it or not, and it doesn't really matter if *Licence to Kill* bored the arse off me. Because, as they say, it's just a "fantasy world". I guess it's just not mine.

What is really curious though, is that while we have downed our critical tools, exploring rather than castigating popular pleasures, those pleasures have themselves changed. Even fantasies like James Bond have to reflect changes in the "real" world. Several components of the Bond formula have been revamped in the new movie. (*Licence to Kill* was incidentally called "Licence Revoked", a title considered too difficult for the American market.)

Glasnost has meant that it's no longer plausible to have Bond battling against an evil empire of nasty Russians. Instead, a new stereotype has to be found. This time it's slimy South American drug barons and, as in so many recent action movies, drug dealing has become the crime *par excellence*, that is quite literally, the root of all evil.

Organised crime mirrors organised capital—its multinational, global nature requires villains who can transcend national boundaries, both in terms of plot and audience. It also has that tinge of morality that shifts Bond's character out of the world of espionage and into the realms of the more traditional hero. In the film, dollar bills are forever being strewn around and yet Bond wants none of it, presumably his mind being on higher things.

Bond himself—the second outing for Timothy Dalton—is more realistic, more human (he bleeds), more caring (he nearly cries), less of a bastard than he used to be and consequently less charming. Yet the move towards realism pulls against the essential fantasy of the film. Those Bond hallmarks such as the stunts and the gadgets also seem less amazing and the stuff of any one of a thousand cop films. There is the obligatory mid-air stunt, the underwater fight and the car chase where Bond hangs on to various moving vechicles and then kicks out the driver. The gadgets, a hangover from the sixties obsession with technology, are even more disappointing. In days when 11 year olds are already expert hackers, exploding toothpaste just won't do.

But the biggest, and most publicised, change is in the treatment of women. *The Living Daylights*, the last Bond movie, was described as a safe sex film which seemed to mean that it had no sex in it. *Licence to Kill* follows on from this, with a "liberated" heroine and remarkably few sex scenes.

Carey Lowell plays Pam Bouvier as a tough modern, but modelly, woman, She gets to make a couple of secretary jokes and wants to be called Ms, which seems to generate laughter in itself. As a token feminist she is, I suppose, better than nothing, though naturally she succumbs to Bond's charms in the end.

As the fantasy has altered to accommodate reality, the fantasy has become less *fantastic*. Heralded by many critics as a return to the original essence of the Fleming novels, the new James Bond seems to be a combination of what Raymond Williams called the residual and emergent aspects of cultural life. To ignore the distasteful elements in our rush to celebrate its popularity, its power as fantasy, is as bad as the older, left position of dismissing much popular culture on the grounds that it was popular. Just as this film rethinks its old formulas, substituting realism for wishful thinking, we must rethink ours.

NEW YORK, 7/24/89, p. 52, David Denby

In the new Bond, *Licence to Kill* (yeah, sic), a South American drug lord flies to Key West and takes a whip to his girlfriend, who has escaped from him and gone to bed with someone else. The drug lord, Sanchez (Robert Davi), carries out the punishment without any particular glee, as if scarring his girlfriend were a requirement of his high position in the world. *Licence to Kill* is frequently sadistic (Sanchez drops people into shark tanks, explodes them in pressure cabins, and so on), yet the sadism doesn't have the mocking, just-for-laughs outrageousness of, say, Gert Frobe's theatening 007's crotch with a laser in *Goldfinger*. As the Cold War has faded and Bond's original identity as jaunty knight of the West has faded with it, the material has lost its debonair edge and its sense of the ludicrous.

But it's gained something else. This new Bond is a grimly purposeful action film. Sanchez is intelligent, dangerous, violent; he's a genuine threat, and the menacing Davi plays him with a subdued malevolence that gets more impressive as it goes along. Even though Sanchez kills people in movieish ways, we know that men like him actually exist, men with private armies who send thousands of pounds of cocaine into this country every year. He's only a slight exaggeration of the truth. Bond is given a private motive for wanting to bring him down—Sanchez has killed his friend Felix Leiter's wife and shark-tortured Leiter on their wedding night. If I'm not mistaken, the audience sat forward in its seats, especially eager to see the defeat of this monster, a far more serious opponent for Bond than Blofeld or Drax or any of the other purring, hissing, cat-stroking villains of the past.

The movie is not just the usual string of wilder and wilder stunts; it has an up-to-the-minute plot (devised by the regulars, Michael G. Wilson and Richard Maibaum) featuring drug-smugglers, Stinger missiles, and the *contras*, and it comes to something like a genuine climax. After many exciting clashes, the movie ends with a sustained chase down a mountain road with huge Kenworth trucks rearing their heads like motorcycles as they pass through flames. Director John Glen has given up the deliberately absurd style of action moviemaking he had mastered for pictures like *Octopussy*. The action in this movie is more plausible, more exciting, more violent. Bond, it's true, still hangs from airplanes and clings to tiny submarines, but when he does so, he seems to be showing off, indulging his nostalgia for those carefree days when he was merely saving the free world; the presence of M and Q and Moneypenny is nostalgic, too. Like other action heroes, Bond fights, scrambles, shoots, and gets knocked out; he seems quite vulnerable, even a little desperate at times.

Timothy Dalton's heavy-browed, frowning face fits this dour movie much better than it did the awful *Living Daylights*, where he seemed not to get the joke. Dalton doesn't have much personality and is not going to loosen, and the audience will probably never really take to him. Playing the role straight, Dalton doesn't carry himself with an amused sense of who Bond is. But he's serviceable; he'll do. As for the ladies, the model/actress Talisa Soto tries, and fails, to play Lupe Lamora, a masochistic, lying, double-crossing olive-skinned beauty (Pussy Galore redux). Soto's perfect skin gleams, but she can't read a line. Carey Lowell, however, is one of the more appealing Bond women—not a slithering murderess but a sexy can-do girl with a sparkle of pleasure in her eyes. She's eager, not languorous, the first feminist Bond heroine I can think of. Lowell, an ex-model, carries small deadly pistols hidden about her person; when Dalton disarms her, it's the sexiest moment in the movie.

NEW YORK POST, 7/14/89, p. 23, David Edelstein

The latest Bond film, "Licence to Kill," has the preening vigor of a slimmed-down fatty. On he bounds, displaying his old, voluminous trousers, then executes a cartwheel. He does it jerkily, with little style, but let's face it, you're impressed. After more than a decade of bloated, campy 007 adventures, you don't expect to see anything this close to a lean, mean fighting machine.

The Bond producers, as attentive to their audiences as soap opera writers, feared their secret agent was losing touch with the masses. Because the masses love vigilante movies (among them "Die Hard" and "Lethal Weapon"), the strategy here is to make Bond mad—mess up or kill people he cares about and then, when he won't give up the fight, get him booted (unconvincingly) from Her Majesty's Secret Service.

To provoke his wrath, they've provided a "Miami Vice"-style villain, Sanchez (Robert Davi) a sadistic cocaine lord with a pitted face. Snared in Key West by Bond and CIA agent Felix Leiter (David Hedison), Sanchez escapes with the aid of greedy traitors, then mutilates Leiter and murders his new bride (Priscilla Barnes).

Bond, who was Leiter's best man, isn't suavely out to save the world, cruising through exotic locations with his state-of-the-art gewgaws. The script takes pains to show how driven he is to avenge his buddy, protocol be damned. He's down and dirty, this Bond. He's nobody's organization man. He's a lethal weapon, a diehard. Don't mess with him.

In the course of 007's vendetta, "Licence" director John Glen engineers some taut action sequences; Bond gets bounced from one tight spot to another even tighter one, ending up (in a nice twist, reminiscent of TV's "Wiseguy") as Sanchez's employee and confidant. For the climax, the film makers ape the truck chases in "Raiders of the Lost Ark" and "The Road Warrior." (The stunt driving is, as always, wizardly.) The upshot is that "Licence to Kill" has suspense and an edge, which puts it well ahead of its immediate predecessors. What it lacks is savoir-faire, the wit and dash of most of the Sean Connery Bonds and the lone Roger Moore surprise, "The Spy Who Loved Me." Most of all, it lacks a Bond—any Bond.

In his second outing, Timothy Dalton has fluffier hair and a more insistent smile. He's certainly wiry, and Glen takes pains to show him wriggling up ladders and doing a few of his own stunts. But there's also something finicky and impatient about him—you feel as if you're taking up his time, keeping him from Stratford-on-Avon and "Coriolanus" or "Macbeth."

Dalton is a thespian, after all, and the producers make much of the fact that this Bond can grieve. They've written him a grieving scene. He finds Leiter's new bride murdered; he grieves. He finds Felix chewed up by a shark; he grieves some more.

When he's finished grieving, he gets teed off. But Dalton has limits—he can't grieve and get teed off at the same time. Only one emotion per scene. When people tell Bond that he's acting foolishly and risking the lives of other agents, Dalton looks at them blankly, unable even to register their quibble. He doesn't strike you as obsessed; he strikes you as a boob, a weenie—smaller than life.

The problem is that Dalton has no style—he's too literal-minded to grasp the surreal elegance of 007's universe. Who needs a grieving Bond, anyway? Connery, a better actor, didn't worry about realism—he knew that style was all. Moore confused style with attitude: The look on his face wasn't "I can handle anything" but "My stand-in can handle anything." He turned the Bond pictures into camp.

Reacting to Moore, Dalton substitutes a dry, peevish narcissism that shuts us out. He doesn't even seem to realize he's in the same movie with the best Bond dame in years—Carey Lowell as a peppy agent who more than once saves 007's hide.

A prickly feminist who bristles when Bond refers to her as "Miss," she still manages to strip down to her scanties with little provocation and hike her dress above her thighs in mid-chase. The conception of her part is flagrantly sexist, but the film makers have at least realized that a woman who does something else besides slink, scream and swoon is a much bigger turn-on. She's a progressive bimbo.

Glen isn't an actor's director. Apart from Lowell, Davi and Anthony Starke (as a yuppie whiz kid who targets Sanchez's cocaine markets by age and socioeconomic group), the cast stinks up the screen. A couple of supermodel Talisa Soto's readings are classics. My heart went out to her, reciting her histrionic lines as if she'd learned them phonetically, never dreaming she'd have such power over audiences—driving women to shudder, grown men to weep with laughter.

NEWSDAY, 7/14/89, Part III/p. 3, Mike McGrady

Quoth the villain, just before feeding a federal narcotics agent to his pet shark: "I want you to know this is nothing personal. It's purely business." Nothing personal...purely business—that's about as accurate a capsule description of the latest James Bond flick, "Licence to Kill," as one is apt to encounter.

Twenty-seven years ago, when James Bond first exploded on movie screens in "Dr. No," it was much more than just an explosion of gunpowder. With Sean Connery as 007, it also happened to be an explosion of roguish charm and humor. Connery's natural warmth was never restricted by the role; the actor was never bottled in Bond. Movieland's first 007 had humor, charm, humanity, even an occasional moment of vulnerability—all of which served to counterbalance the preposterous array of guns, girls and gadgets.

Connery's personality is precisely what is missing from "Licence to Kill," the 16th Bond outing starring the fourth James Bond. Timothy Dalton, back for his second tour of duty, continues to handle the physical chores with comparative ease. He looks fit in a tuxedo, and his stage background has more than adequately prepared him to deliver the series of wisecracks that compose the greater portion of his script. But Dalton shows no more warmth or charm than Q's latest concealed weapon, which is, incidentally, a bullet-firing camera, a "signature gun" with an "optical palm-print reader"—making it, in effect, a distinctly personal gun-camera or camera-gun, depending on whether you're shooting snapshots or druglords.

When James Bond is every bit as plastic as the explosive Q has packed in his toothpaste tube, one is left with no recourse other than to sit back and watch the aerial stunts and explosions, the underwater stunts and explosions, along with the occasional women of unnatural construct and even less natural motivations.

For those who insist on some connection, no matter how remote, to real life or real emotion, be forewarned that the story line consists of litter more than people being killed and/or maimed in varied state-of-the-art ways—by pet shark, by swordfish nose, by flame, by speargun, by submersible vehicles, by monster Kenworth W 900 B trucks, by Aerospatiale helicopters. After each slaying, a lame wisecrack. Bond, studying a just-impaled corpse, quips, "Looks like he came to a dead end."

Dalton seems an island in this sea of gore, unable to connect with anyone else on the screen—not the men bearing such truncated names as M and Q, not the beautiful women forever forcing their attention on him. He brings to mind a Shakespearean actor (which he was) strolling through material for which he is eminently overqualified (which he is). Although his women-playthings are sufficiently attractive, Talisa Soto may be the least accomplished actress ever to grace a Bond flick, a lineup that includes Ursula Andress and Britt Ekland.

Just for the record, the story has something to do with 007's being disarmed. As M breaks it to him, "Effective immediately, your license to kill is hereby revoked. I order you to hand over your weapon now!" Why this demotion? Why the loss of his precious Walther PPK? Well, Bond is charged with trying to avenge the brutal maiming of a friend, specifically with waging "a personal vendetta." Needless to say, he's innocent. Nothing about this James Bond is remotely personal, not even a vendetta.

NEWSWEEK, 7/17/89, p. 52, Jack Kroll

So you think the James Bond stories are simple spy-sex-shoot-'em-up stuff? Well, they've long been fertile ground for heavy-headed critical types, one of whom has applied to the Bond works "a Lévi-Straussian analysis of a series of binary oppositions which...provides the structural coordinates for the system of ideological meanings..." Such academic gobbledygook makes you wish you had a *Licence to Kill*, which happens to be the title of the new Bond movie. This, the 16th Bond, is a pure, rousingly entertaining action movie which makes it clear that "Binary oppositions" are good guys vs. bad guys and "ideological meanings" are us vs. them.

In this Gorbachev-era Bond, commies have been replaced by druggies. The villain, Sanchez (Robert Davi), is a cold-eyed, pockmarked Noriega look-alike who knows that profit is the reigning ideology and that cocaine has truly become the opiate of the people. Screenwriters Michael G. Wilson and Richard Maibaum turn Bond into a killing machine, out to avenge his buddy Leiter (David Hedison), whose honeymoon has been bloodily curtailed by Sanchez's sadistic thugs. When Bond's superiors won't allow him to muscle in on the U.S. agents' pursuit of Sanchez, 007 refuses to turn in his precious Walther PPK semiautomatic and zooms off on his own.

From that point on it's ka-boom, ka-bam, ka-Bond. Director John Glen is the Busby Berkeley of action flicks, and his chorus line is the legendary team of Bond stuntpersons who are at their death-defying best here. Unlike the grungy, mean-spirited violence of the Rambo movies, there's something almost soothing about the gorgeous precision of these action sequences. To give away only one: there's an amazing stunt in which a flaming car goes off a cliff, blazing scarily *above* a low-flying plane.

It may be that this almost total reliance on action is a sign that the Bondmakers are still nervous about Timothy Dalton. In Dalton's Jamesian debut, "The Living Daylights," the producers tried to "humanize" 007, even flirting with monogamy, which was exactly what they did with poor George Lazenby, who played Bond in one film, the 1969 "On Her Majesty's Secret. Service." Happily, such heresy has been abandoned; in this movie Bond is back leching and lusting and macho as ever. The Bond producers, the world's classiest procurers, have come up with two splendid Bond girls, Talisa Soto, a smoky Latin beauty, and Carey Lowell, a stunning Wasp type. Lowell's character is just about the most intrepid of all Bond girls, a CIA pilot who snaps at the chauvinist 007: "I've flown to the toughest hellholes in South America."

As for Dalton, he's a fine actor who hasn't yet stamped Bond with his own personality. For one thing, he's got an eyebrow problem. Sean Connery was a master at the single-eyebrow lift; Roger Moore excelled at lifting both eyebrows. Caught in this bind, Dalton has gone beneath his brows, specializing in the double eye-twinkle. A twinkly James Bond? Needs some work.

TIME, 7/24/89, p. 53, Richard Corliss

[*Licence to Kill* was reviewed jointly with *Lethal Weapon 2*; see Corliss' review of that film.]

VILLAGE VOICE, 7/18/89, p. 73, Amy Taubin

"Let's hear this again," says skeptical drug lord Franz Sanchez—head honcho of (ho-ho) Isthmus City—to his trembling minion. "He water-skied behind the plane, jumped on it, threw the pilot out, and flew away?"

"Would I make something like that up?" the minion quavers.

Of course not. We, too, saw 007's sea-and-sky routine, and 90 action-packed minutes later (with no closure in sight), we vaguely remember it. One of the notable aspects of *Licence To Kill* (the original and more suggestive title was *Licence Revoked*) is its two hours-plus running time, though happily the 16th James Bond saga doesn't feel a smidgin longer than it actually is.

Licence To Kill has, as they say, "all the elements"—specifically earth, air, fire, water. With principal locations in the Florida Keys and the Bahamas, most of the action takes place under or over the Atlantic, the Gulf, and the Caribbean. And the finale features a drag race between gasoline tanker trucks that burns up the side of a mountain.

Like the final episode of *Miami Vice* or *Shannon's Deal*, John Sayles's pilot for NBC, *Licence To Kill* casually takes as common knowledge the connection between the three C's—contras, CIA, and cocaine. (Did the government win immunity by granting Hollywood rights to the ongoing story?)

When on the first night of their honeymoon, Bond's pal Felix Leiter (formerly of the CIA, now of the Florida Drug Enforcement Agency) gets partially chewed by a shark and his new bride is shot to death, Bond is determined to take revenge. No matter that M forbids his agent to meddle in U.S. affairs, and revokes his license to kill (cautioning that Bond is, of course, still bound by the Official Secrets Act). Realizing that government agencies are too corrupt, cowed, or ideologically bankrupt for the task at hand, the consummate company man takes it upon himself to destroy the world's cocaine supply. He gets some help from Q, who risks M's wrath to supply James with the usual array of lethal gizmos, and from Pam Bouvier, a spritely ex-CIA operative turned freelance pilot.

In his second outing as Bond, Timothy Dalton is agile, well-spoken, emotionally noncommittal, with a good body for clothes and a hairstyle vaguely reminiscent of Olivier in *Wuthering Heights*. Dalton's an immeasurable improvement over Roger Moore—it's not his fault that Sean Connery is an impossible act to follow. As the fearless pilot, former Ford model Carey Lowell seems in splendid health, but is a bit too wholesome to have been knocking around with the company she claims to keep.

Director John Glen keeps the action wet 'n' wild, preferring pretty shots to careful continuity (a wise choice given the baroque turns of the plot). This is the first Bond film that owes neither title nor story line to Ian Fleming. It could have been worse.

Also reviewed in:
NEW REPUBLIC, 8/7&14/89, p. 27, Stanley Kauffmann
NEW YORK TIMES, 7/14/89, p. C8, Caryn James
VARIETY, 6/14–20/89, p. 7

LIFE AND NOTHING BUT

A Hachette Pemiere et Cie/Groupe Europe 1 Communications-AB Films/Little Bear-Films A2 co-production. *Executive Producer:* Frédéric Bourboulon and Albert Prévost. *Producer:* René Cleitman. *Director:* Bertrand Tavernier. *Screenplay (French with English subtitles):* Jean Cosmos and Bertrand Tavernier. *Director of Photography:* Bruno de Keyzer. *Editor.* Armand Psenny. *Music:* Oswald d'Andrea. *Sound:* Michel Desrois. *Art Director:* Guy-Claude François. *Costumes:* Jacqueline Moreau. *Running time:* 135 minutes. *MPAA Rating:* Not Rated.

CAST: Philippe Noiret (Dellaplanne); Sabine Azéma (Irène); Pascale Vignal (Alice); Maurice Barrier

(Mercadot); François Perrot (Perrin); Jean-Pol Dubois (André); Daniel Russo (Lieutenant Trévise); Michel Duchaussoy (Général Villerieux).

MONTHLY FILM BULLETIN, 11/89, p. 347, Tom Milne

October, 1920. Trying to cope with the desperate legacy of the First World War as head of a military unit assigned to trace those still officially listed as missing, Major Dellaplanne balks when General Villerieux relays a request for an "unknown" soldier to be interred under the Arc de Triomphe at a commemorative ceremony. With Dellaplanne arguing the absurdity, since his mission is to *identify* unknown soldiers, Villerieux assigns the task to an aide. Meanwhile, working with amnesiacs at a remote military hospital, Dellaplanne is less than courteous when a beautiful young woman—Irène de Courtil, chauffeur-driven, trailing the wealth and influence of an industrialist father-in-law who is also a member of the Senate—descends in the belief that one of the amnesiacs may be her missing husband. Nevertheless, after making it clear that none of his 350,000 cases is special to his mind, Dellaplanne agrees to do what he can. Approached by Alice, a young teacher scraping a living as a waitress while trying to trace her missing sweetheart, Dellaplanne makes her the same promise. Irène, Alice and Dellaplanne meet again, along with hundreds of people anxiously seeking confirmation of the fates of their loved ones, at the newly excavated site of a wartime disaster: a railway tunnel, mined by the Germans, which blew up as a French military convoy was passing through. Miserably bivouacked in a factory while bodies are exhumed and identified—and Dellaplanne distinguishes himself by rescuing tunnel workers threatened by poisonous gases—the two women befriend each other, and Dellaplanne realises that they are looking for the same man: Irène's husband, whom she never really loved, ran away from his privileged background to work in a factory, where he met and fell in love with Alice. A young sculptor (working on one of the many war monuments in progress) is attracted to Alice; and to force her to face life again, Dellaplanne deliberately disillusions her by revealing that the man she loved was already married. Gradually coming to understand Dellaplanne, Irène intimates that her love is his for the asking; but still haunted by his mission, further inhibited by the social and age differences between them, Dellaplanne finds himself unable to ask. In due course, the "Unknown Soldier" is selected by lot from eight candidates and ceremonially interred. In 1922, corresponding with Irène, who has emigrated to America and plans to settle in Wisconsin, Dellaplanne at last feels free to declare his love.

True to the pre-Nouvelle Vague principles on which Tavernier has predicated his career, *La Vie et rien d'autre* has a faint and not unpleasing tang of antiquarianism about it, as though it might have been adapted from some forgotten Jean Giraudoux novel (first cousin to *Siegfried et le Limousin*, perhaps), served up through a script with a flavour of witty interwar cynicism, a seasoning of Popular Front class antagonisms, and as topping a heady romance to keep the customers happy. Not for the first time in a Tavernier film, the result of his determination to administer a pill while simultaneously offering the traditional sugar coating is a tendency to fly off in several directions at once.

The basic idea is the beguiling one of a man condemned to keep the past alive by ferreting around in memories for the half-forgotten clues which help to bring the dead back again, so to speak, by attaching memories to names, names to bodies; a task which has become for him an unending voyage into darkness and despair. Not just because success almost invariably means presenting irrefutable proof to people of the death or mutilation of their loved ones, but because he is accompanied in his task by an increasing awareness of a social conspiracy of silence. Hampered in his work on the one hand by official reluctance to acknowledge his estimate that some 350,000 bodies still await identification, and on the other by official refusal to inform him as newly unearthed caches of corpses are hastily consigned to oblivion before he can investigate, he is hemmed in on all sides by plans for war memorials, resonant symbols like the Tomb of the Unknown Soldier, purportedly designed to preserve the memory of the horrors and the sacrifices of war, but in fact calculated to bury them under a placid weight of stone. Remember the abstraction, forget the reality.

Much of this aspect of the film is quietly and acidly funny, especially as the guidelines laid for the selection of the Unknown Soldier—"No English or Boches under the Arc de Triomphe"—lead to all sorts of problems, with the General's aide wandering helplessly in a literal fog, like Alice in No Man's Land, assured by a peasant woman that *nobody* knows the troops who died defending her land ("I knew every one of them by name"), and narrowly avoiding unmentionable gaffes (like selecting a candidate from a battlefield where colonial troops, almost certainly black, fought and fell). Pleasantly abrasive, too, are the inevitable rip-off artists at work at the scene of the tunnel disaster, scavenging on misery by offering to locate missing relatives for a consideration; the local elder busily plotting to get the village boundary lines changed, because his has no dead sons, their neighbours have so many that they wouldn't miss a few, and the compensation which could be claimed looms enticingly; the suggestion that Irène de Courtil's father-in-law, industrialist and politician, had negotiated a gentleman's agreement with his Boche counterparts, safeguarding each other's factories from destruction during the war.

Thrown out in a conversation between Dellaplanne and Irène, occasioned by the fact that their temporary billet at the tunnel site is one of her father-in-law's (undamaged) factories, this implication of an unholy alliance between business interests remains otherwise undeveloped. Instead, the film expends far too much of its time and energy on fleshing out the central romance, which proceeds along predictable lines, with class distinctions disappearing and Irène gradually melting into loving acquiescence as Dellaplanne increasingly demonstrates his dedication to the cause of humanity. Sabine Azéma is little more than blandly adequate, although Philippe Noiret, affectingly, lends his special brand of hangdog quirkiness. But neither Noiret nor the beautifully chosen locations (resplendent in bleak and wintry desolation) can do much to counteract the air of contrivance that begins to take hold with the revelation that the two women, conveniently complementing each other socially and emotionally, just happen to be searching for the same man.

NEW LEADER, 1/8/90, p. 23, John Morrone

One of the festival's [New York Film Festival] biggest surprises was Bertrand Tavernier's long (135 minutes) *Life and Nothing But*. Free of the director's usual labored style and affected pessimism, it is astonishingly moving. Set in 1920 near the Atlantic French coast, its main figure is a martinetish officer in charge of indentifying nameless men killed in the Great War and matching up grieving families with shelf upon shelf of abandoned belongings.

Dellaplanne (Phillipe Noiret) is the military man who has to make sure that the ledgers tally and the number of unclaimed bodies decreases daily. But what appears at first to be an insanely impossible task becomes a personal crusade when Dellaplane encounters two women—the wealthy, haughty Irene (Sabine Azema) and the working-class Alice (Pascale Vignal)—unknowingly seeking the same dead soldier. Dellaplane unravels the triangle, and it is finally this unlikely idealist's bureaucratic punctiliousness, as he insists each body be named, each memento be sent home, that connects him to life in the face of war's oblivion. Shot in gray widescreen expanses, *Life and Nothing But* is austere but deeply felt, hidden moments plucked from an epic canvas of postwar European sorrow.

NEW YORK, 10/16/89, p. 75, David Denby

War itself, and the moment just before war breaks out, has been dramatized repeatedly in novels and movies. But one of the great, ignored subjects is the moment immediately *after*—the time of echoes and aftershocks and halfhearted improvisations, when survivors gather numbly around the holes in the ground. Bertrand Tavernier's *Life and Nothing But*, recently shown at the New York Film Festival (and at this writing without a distributor), is filled with aftershocks of the most dangerous sort—the time is 1920, in France (in the area of the Verdun battlefield), and buried shells, lying about everywhere, explode when nudged the wrong way. In this gloomy, bitter time, widows and parents, caught between grief and rage, scour the countryside looking for a scarf, a diary, anything that could identify their loved ones. These families and lovers still wait to bury their dead: 350,000 of France's 1.5 million casualties remained unidentified at the end of the war.

The great Philippe Noiret, thinner in middle age but still in magnificent voice, stars as the French-army major in charge of searching for and identifying "missing" soldiers. The major, obsessed with his bizarre and tragic job, has become a ghoulishly witty man. The number of dead seems like an absurd joke to him, and so do the official hypocrisies of the French leaders, who demand the production of a single "unknown soldier" for a public-relations march to the Arc de Triomphe. The major finds a soul mate for his ironies in a beautiful, veiled, rather haughty Parisienne widow (Sabine Azéma) who is looking for her husband; the two fight each other and hesitate at the edge of a love affair. Though somber in color and death-shadowed, *Life and Nothing But* turns into a passionate and funny movie—large-scaled, panoramic, and strikingly odd. Tavernier has thrown light into many of the strange corners of life after war.

NEWSDAY, 10/3/89, Part III/p. 5, Terry Kelleher

Statistics are commonly thought of as cold and impersonal, but in Bertrand Tavernier's new movie, one man strives to keep hope and humanity alive through fanatical attention to numerical accuracy. The central character in "Life and Nothing But" is Maj. Dellaplanne (Philippe Noiret), a French army officer assigned to account for the dead and missing of World War I. The time is the fall of 1920, almost two years after the armistice, but Dellaplanne's task remains awesome—there are missing soldiers and unidentified bodies in the hundreds of thousands.

It sounds incredible until you consider that of the 5 million Allied combatants who gave their lives in the "Great War" of 1914–1918, almost 1.5 million came from France or its colonies. Tavernier has a sardonic Frenchman boast, "We beat Napoleon's record in only four years."

There's an elegiac tone to much of "Life and Nothing But," but the movie also has humor, and the humor has bite. A sculptor credits the war with ushering in an artistic "golden age": Every village needs a monument for its dead. The powers that be call for an "unknown" soldier to be interred beneath the Arc de Triomphe—"an anonymous holy relic," as Dellaplanne says—and a harried officer named Perrin (François Perrot) combs the ravaged countryside for suitable candidates. Dead colonials need not apply.

Dellaplanne goes about his job with determination and indignation, resisting pressure to close the books on the war and proceed as if "a million and a half dead only *appear* dead." Alice (Pascale Vignal), a young woman of the working class, tries to find her fiance, while Irène (Sabine Azéma), a senator's privileged daughter-in-law, searches for her husband. Stirred by his compassion for Alice and his growing attraction to Irène, Dellaplanne gives both cases special attention.

The story progresses deliberately toward a coincidence whose symbolism is all too obvious. But even as Bruno de Keyzer's photography captures the fading light and disheartening chill of late autumn, Noiret's superb performance conveys Dellaplanne's (and Tavernier's) commitment to life in all its seasons.

VILLAGE VOICE, 9/26/89, P. 66, J. Hoberman

Somber yet chic, a sentimental love story masquerading as a major statement, Bertrand Tavernier's latest is quintessential bourgievision. Although the background search for World War I's MIAs suggests a metaphor for current French cinema, *Life and Nothing But* is really a middle-aged dating film, featuring much country French cuisine and Philippe Noiret at his most lovably gruff. There's no distributor. (How much can they be asking?)

Also reviewed in:
NEW YORK TIMES, 10/3/89, p. C15, Janet Maslin
VARIETY, 8/30-9/5/89, p. 29

LIGHTNING OVER BRADDOCK: A RUSTBOWL FANTASY

A Zeitgeist release. *Producer:* Tony Buba. *Director:* Tony Buba. *Director of Photography:* Brady Lewis. *Editor:* Tony Buba. *Music:* Stephen Pellegrino. *Runing Time:* 80 minutes. *MPAA Rating:* Not Rated.

LOS ANGELES TIMES, 10/7/89, Calendar/p. 8, Michael Wilmington

"Lightning Over Braddock: A Rustbowl Fantasy" is a movie with flesh, sweat and a warm grip. You can sense a human being behind it. As you watch, you begin to see as he sees, hear as he hears.

Shot over four years on a budget of about $40,000, "Lightning" is the first feature of Tony Buba, a 44-year-old quirk documentarian. Buba sets it in his hometown, a once-thriving Pittsburgh suburb called Braddock. Over the last 15 years, he has made a dozen short films about its people: a smoothly engaging macho bantam street hustler named Sal Caru, a union organizer-rock accordionist named Steve Pellegrino and a constantly failing but eternally buoyant local entrepreneur named Jim Roy. All of them are in this film too.

And now, since his town, along with the rest of the area, is dying—its population down by almost 75% the nearby Dorothy Six mill about to be closed, businesses and movie theaters shuttered, the school gone—Buba's become a chronicler of the disintegration of the American Dream.

The movie is reflexive. We see "Lightning" being shot, dreams of Tony and Sal, parodies of "Gandhi" and "Rambo," wildly enthusiastic reviews on TV. But it's clear that this collaboration will fall apart, that an anticipated Hollywood contract will never arrive. Meanwhile, outside, the mills close, the streets empty, the ex-workers demonstrate. Life subverts the macho fantasies of the movie: pipe-dreams incarnated in the smooth, goombah-goombah Sinatra-inflected badinage of Sweet Sal, the way his baritone drags on "yeaaah," the profanity and braggadocio that rolls off his tongue like honeyed cough drops.

As Buba shows us a parade of clowns and victims, marchers and kvetchers, he makes it clear that he does not stand apart from them. Like his neighbors, he is watching a world and a way of life collapse. Like them, he tries whatever he can, in some small way, to prevent the inevitable. And like them, he dreams foolish, glamorous, violent dreams of success, romance and revenge.

Unlike them, he can record those dreams, play them back. A recurrent image of "Lightning" is the mustachioed Buba—looking something like a cheerful, sloppy Pittsburgh Zapata—hunched over his movieola, contemplating the film he's shot, trying to make sense of it. But he can't. The order he finds is the one he's imposed. The region that is dying will die whatever he does.

"Lightning's" major flaw is the fantasy sequences, too tacky for the overall vision. And there are substantial elements to that vision. "Lightning Over Braddock" is about dreaming as your world dies around you. It's a central theme of American literature, but Buba jokes it up, concentrates on these three dreamers whose wild energy and bounding hope survive even the most ridiculous context.

The ex-student radical Buba ruminates on the possibility that, when he dies, he will be greeted at the gate not by Peter but by Sacco and Vanzetti. Sal rages in his room at the stardom and wealth being denied him. Pellegrino sings "Jumpin' Jack Flash" on his accordion—without sound, since there was no money for music rights. "Braddock, city of magic, where have you gone?" croons Jimmy Roy, in a melancholy lounge-lizard voice, against a backdrop of dying urban glitter. That is the core of this modestly immodest, expansively humble, objectively subjective, gigantic little film: lost magic.

In its ragged perfection and wise silliness, "Lightning Over Braddock" (Times-rated: Mature for language) invites us to dream and wake up at the same time.

NEW YORK POST, 3/8/89, p. 25, V.A. Musetto

The man with the accordion is leading a rousing rendition of "Jumpin' Jack Flash." Only we don't hear the music. It seems that the people who own the song wanted $15,000 to allow Tony Buba to use it in his latest film, "Lightning Over Braddock: A Rustbowl Fantasy."

Fifteen thousand dollars! That's three times the per capita income of Braddock, Pa., Buba's dying hometown. "I told them, I don't want Mick Jagger to come to Braddock to sing it. I have a friend who plays it on the accordion," Buba tells us in a voiceover as Stephen Pellegrino belts out the song we can't hear. And anyway, it wouldn't "be politically correct to pay that kind of money," Buba continues. "What if, when I die and get to heaven, it isn't St. Peter at the gate, but Sacco and Vanzetti?"

Acutally, the music company did Buba a nice favor. Pellegrino's soundless performance provides one of the movie's funniest sequences and more importantly, a pointed commentary on the plight of Braddock, a blue-collar town six miles from Pittsburgh along the Monongahela River.

Once, when the steel mills were working overtime, Braddock thrived. There were 20,000 people, seven movie houses and a bustling 200-store shopping district. Today, with the darkening of many of the factories, the unemployment rate is 37 percent and the town has lost 14,000 people, all its public school and theaters, and five of its churches.

It is the decline of Braddock that Buba chronicles in "Lightning"—playing today through March 21 at Film Forum 1—and in most of the 14 short documentaries that preceded it over the past 15 years. His latest effort, made for a mere $40,000, is billed as his first work of fiction. But that's a bit of a misnomer. Actually, "Lightning" is a fascinating and entertaining hybrid of home movie, documentary, autobiography, cinema verite, even some ego massage.

The "story" concerns a 50-ish street hustler named Sal Caru, star of Buba's award-winning "Sweet Sal" (1979); convinced that he made Buba's career and isn't getting credit, Sal seeks revenge.

This sort-of plot provides the basis for the 44-year-old Buba to take stock of his career to this point—some autobiographical detail, parts of his previous movies. And to update the further decline of Braddock. USX is closing down the old Dorothy Six mill, and Buba—"the Boswell of Braddock"—has his cameras there for the protests: an old man urging his younger union brothers to "take to the streets;" USX chief David Roderick being hustled into his limo on a cold Sunday morning, oblivious to the shivering pickets surrounging him outside church; a Jesse Jackson rally; and a Walk for Peace.

Buba intersperses the serious with patches of humor. Like the day "Mahatma Gandhi," also known as Sweet Sal, came to Braddock and rode down the main drag in an open convertible, accompanied by a bimbo blonde in white fishnets, black mini and leopardskin top. Or the day Buba went to a priest for his first confession in 20 years and admitted that his "most grievous" sin in all that time was wanting to make a Hollywood musical.

Through it all, the dedication and concern of Tony Buba comes through loud and clear. When asked why he doesn't forsake Braddock for the lure of Hollywood big bucks, Buba replies: "I like being a big fish in a small town. And besides, we need more films like "Lightning Over Braddock."

NEWSDAY, 3/8/89, Part II/p. 5, Lynn Darling

For 15 years, independent film maker Tony Buba has been chronicling the slow death of Braddock, Pa., the flinty, hardshelled milltown where he grew up and continues to live.

He's quite content, he admits in his affably candid way in this wacko film, to be a big fish in a small, nearly nonexistent pond. Buba's self-deprecation is disarming; it also belies the affection, respect and insight he brings to the people who inhabit this sad, failed pocket of what used to be thought of as the American Dream.

For years, the steel towns near Pittsburgh were tough, strong, vital independent enclaves, inhabited by working-class people who fashioned a living for themselves and a future for their children out of the steel mills. When the mills began to shut down, victims of corporate greed and union miscalculation, there was talk that a brave new world would take the place of the hulking, rusting dinosaurs hard by the Monongahela River. It didn't work out that way, of course: The men who made their living in the mills found they had no place in these high-tech dreams. Unemployment skyrocketed and so did suicide, divorces, alcoholism and infant mortality. Little towns were forced to play the state lottery in a desperate attempt to stay alive.

Buba deftly lays out the nature of the slow-leaching disaster that hit these towns in "Lightning Over Braddock." His movie is an affable jumble of documentary fantasy and autobiography, held together by his quirky, dedicated sensibility. He mixes statistics, history and his own commitment to activist social politics into his movie, but his primary focus is on the wiry, often outrageous humanity that infuses the people who still live there, clinging to their sense of themselves like survivors to a scrap of wood in a shipwreck.

Principal among these characters is Sal Caru, or Sweet Sal, as he likes to refer to himself, a bantam-weight street hustler who starred in one of Buba's earlier films and has since become the bane of his existence. It is Sweet Sal's contention that the modest fame Buba has won for his films belongs to Sal himself: Buba intercuts his own commentary on Braddock and the travails of its people with Caru's profane excoriation of Buba and all his works. The relationship between the film maker and his subject becomes the engine that drives this gritty piece of whimsy along its erratic path.

Not that there aren't a lot of detours: "Lightning Over Braddock." includes a surreal scene in which Sweet Sal, dressed as Gandhi, is assassinated, in a manner reminiscent of JFK, during a parade down Braddock's main street; clips of local TV interviews with Buba himself, and scenes from Buba's other films, complete with Buba's voiceover commentary. Buba defines his politics in that commentary with clarity and good humor. Noting that a scene of an accordion player playing "Jumpin' Jack Flash" has no soundtrack, he tell us that he would have had to pay $15,000 for the rights to the song, three times the per-capita income in his home town. "What if, when I get to heaven, instead of St. Peter at the gate, it's Sacco and Vanzetti?" he says. "And they say, 'You paid fifteen thousand for a song instead of spending that money for political organzing?' I wouldn't get in.''

Shot in grainy black and white, "Lightning Over Braddock." has the rough edges of a particularly daft home movie; like a home movie it trails off without developing much of an ending. But there's nothing amateurish about Buba's vision: He shows us his characters' eccentricities and the fissures in their sanity without condescending to them or simplifying the frighteningly harsh future they face.

Also reviewed in:
VARIETY, 9/14/88, p. 27

LISTEN TO ME

A Weintraub Entertainment Group release. *Producer:* Marykay Powell. *Director:* Douglas Day Stewart. *Screenplay:* Douglas Day Stewart. *Director of Photography:* Fred J. Koenekamp. *Editor:* Anne V. Coates. *Music:* David Foster. *Sound:* Tom Causey. *Production Designer:* Gregory Pickrell. *Set Designer:* Joe Hubbard. *Set Decorator:* Kim Samson. *Costumes:* Durinda Rice Wood. *Running time:* 107 minutes. *MPAA Rating:* PG-13.

CAST: Kirk Cameron (Tucker Muldowney); Jami Gertz (Monica Tomanski); Roy Scheider (Charlie Nichols); Amanda Peterson (Donna Lumis); Tim Quill (Garson McKellar); George Wyner (Dean Schwimmer); Anthony Zerbe (Senator McKellar); Christopher Atkins (Bruce Arlington); Quinn Cummings (Susan Hooper); Jason Gould (Hinkelstein).

LOS ANGELES TIMES, 5/5/89, Calendar/p. 15, Kevin Thomas

"Listen to Me" is not a typical youth film. It takes us to a sun-drenched, ultra-modern Southern California college campus, but instead of the usual jocks and bikini-clad women we meet a bunch of bright, squeaky-clean super-achievers. They are all members of the small institution's high-ranking debating team, coached by hard-driving professor Charlie Nichols (Roy Scheider). "Listen to Me" is admirably off-beat, quite engaging, but its finish is disturbing in ways writer-director Douglas Day Stewart had surely not intended.

In a sense "Listen to Me" seems an old-fashioned movie: the film's young people actually have other things on their minds besides, but not excluding, sex. It's very contemporary, however, in that it shows us persuasively that college can be a real pressure cooker for anyone with any degree of seriousness, especially in the sharply competitive arena of debate. Making it even more timely is Nichols' announcement that the big subject of the national intercollegiate competition will be abortion.

Here's where writer-director Douglas Day Stewart gets into trouble with his anti-abortion bias. Indeed, instead of making the case against abortion, his film serves to show how much emotion anti-abortionists can stir up without addressing the realities that the pro-choicers outline, not to mention the matter of women's rights. Stewart seems to realize this, when after the climactic debate before members of the Supreme Court, the one woman (not called Sandra Day O'Connor) on the bench reveals she believes in upholding Roe vs. Wade but gives the anti-abortionists her vote in the debate because of their skill. The bothersome implication here is that in debate what counts is effectiveness of presentation—which in this instance is shameless grandstanding—rather than the substance of the argument.

If the conclusion of "Listen to Me," with all the thorny questions it raises in a highly loaded context, overshadows all that has gone before, the getting-there is involving. The film's young stars couldn't be more likable. They are also so articulate that they wouldn't be believable if they weren't playing gifted debaters.

Kirk Cameron's Tucker and Jami Gertz's Monica are freshman on scholarships. He is an Oklahoma farm boy; she is from a blue-collar Chicago family. In contrast, Tucker's roommate, Garson (Tim Quill), is a rich and powerful senator's kid who seems to have everything but is miserable because he is expected to follow in his father's footsteps. There is a great deal of contrivance and even more manipulation in "Listen to Me," but Garson's anguish rings true. Also life-like are the flaws in the character of Charlie Nichols, to whom Scheider brings energy as well as qualities of ruthlessness and regretfulness.

So much of "Listen to Me" is so far more stirring and thought-provoking than most Hollywood films of any genre that it's a shame that Stewart, who received an Oscar nomination for his script for "An Officer and a Gentleman," didn't take a step back and let us decide for ourselves how we should feel about the issues it raises.

NEW YORK POST, 5/5/89, p. 34, Jami Bernard

Hot on the heels of "Criminal Law," a suspense thriller that attempted to legitimize the brutal murders and mutilations of young women by tying the killer's motives to an indignation over abortion, comes "Listen to Me, " where a debate team of eager young students wins kudos for its college by arguing against abortion in a national competition. Whatever happened to the notion of a liberal Hollywood?

Of course, having these struggling kids argue the majority pro-choice view would stack the deck. But really, having a teenager who was raped by her father's friend fretting that maybe she shouldn't have had an abortion shows an amazing insensitivity on the part of the filmmakers to rape victims and to the teen-age audience at which this movie is aimed.

It is refreshing that the blood sport of choice at Kenmont College is debating, where scholarship students work their butts off to learn how to maim with the power of words, thoughts and logic, instead of fists, guns and arsenals of special effects. Tucker (puppy-dog Kirk Cameron) and Monica (lovely, sensitive Jami Gertz) are the tyros on the team, lowly born and high-minded and intent on knocking senior debater Garson McKellar from his perch.

Garson is a senator's son, a troubled charmer being groomed for a career in politics that he doesn't want. Actor Tim Quill is perfect for the role—he looks like a young Warren Beatty, except in the scenes with his demanding father, during which he looks suspiciously like Joe Kennedy.

Roy Scheider is the tough debate coach, tougher even than those cinematic football coaches. To underscore the intensity of debate as sport, the practices take place in sloped Coliseum-type arenas.

Amanda Peterson ("Can't Buy Me Love") plays a physically handicapped debater whose sense of self is restored by a little extracurricular elocution with Christopher ("Blue Lagoon") Atkins.

The personable cast is rounded out by the children of the famous, including Jason Gould, Peter De Luise, Christopher Rydell and Moon Zappa.

It's good that "Listen to Me" aspires to something more than showing teen-agers acting out their feelings of invincibility through prowess in a sport. But there is something creepy and inflammatory about cashing in on the current Supreme Court debate on Roe vs. Wade. If women's rights are going to be decided, as the movie implies, based on which side gives the more polished performance, then we're in a pretty sorry state.

NEWSDAY, 5/5/89, Part III/p. 3, Terry Kelleher

Doesn't a movie about college students deserve some credit for focusing on the debate team rather than the football team or the drinking team or the panty-raid team?

Not if the movie is to debating what TV's "Nightingales" is to nursing.

Douglas Day Stewart, writer-director of "Listen to Me," says this is a film about the leaders of tomorrow, their idealism and serious-mindedness. You want to believe him, though the pictures in his past—"Thief of Hearts," "An Officer and a Gentleman," "The Blue Lagoon"—can't be said to have intelligence as their common denominator.

But "Listen to Me" quickly shows itself to be a no-brainer. It wants to be manipulative, but it's too inept. It wants to be melodramatic, but it's too ridiculous. The movie isn't even educational, because we learn surprisingly little about how debate works. Here it looks pretty much like "The Morton Downey Jr. Show."

Kirk Cameron, the teen idol from TV's "Growing Pains," plays Tucker Muldowney, an Oklahoma farm boy who's one of only two freshmen to land a debate scholarship to fictive Kenmont College of California. The other is Monica Tomanski (Jami Gertz), a working-class Chicagoan who shuns romance because of a dark secret in her past. It goes without saying that Tucker will win over Monica, whom he calls by the name of her home city. The line that does the trick is: "How 'bout just a simple hug, Chicago?"

"Listen to Me" would be more tolerable if Tucker and Monica were all we had to worry about. Unfortunately, we also get to know Kenmont senior Garson McKellar (Tim Quill), the tortured son of a rich and powerful senator (Anthony Zerbe). Handsome Gar, the school's No. 1 debater, is under family pressure to become president of the United States, but he'd really rather be a playwright. (You know literature is his true calling when he threatens to quit both debate *and* tennis to concentrate on his writing.) This conflict, along with his unfulfilled need for true love, causes Gar to take a high-speed, death-wish drive that ends with his hot sports car on the edge of a cliff. Whew, that Stewart sure knows how to rev up a talky movie.

The climax is a forensic "42nd Street," a rhetorical "Rocky." When the script sidelines Gar the star, it's up to Kenmont's freshman phenoms to outtalk the arrogant easterners from Harvard in the national collegiate championship—which, for purposes of this movie, is contested before five Supreme Court justices and a national television audience. (Wonder if ESPN outbid C-SPAN for the rights.) The Harvard men argue from logic and evidence, as Harvard men tend to do. Tucker and Monica, urged by their coach (Roy Scheider) to "win this thing on drama," carry the day with tears and true confessions.

The question under debate, by the way, concerns the morality of abortion. Ads for "Listen to Me" are emphasizing this angle, suggesting that the film "may anger and disturb you." In fact, Stewart merely fuzzes up the issue, hoping you'll stand up and cheer no matter where you stand.

The proper response to "Listen to Me" is "Aw, shut up."

VILLAGE VOICE, 5/16/89, p. 73, Elliott Stein

For a while, *Listen to Me* lulls you pleasantly. Ths cast is full of bright, fresh faces. Although set at a posh California college, the film seems to be steering clear of the clichés of most "youth" movies—jocks and nerds do not occupy the foreground, and students are not concerned with partying or spring-break mayhem. A standard but agreeably written and portrayed romance between two freshmen—city girl and country boy—is obviously in the offing. Then, bit by bit, its real agenda emerges, and in the final reels, *Listen to Me* turns into a glibly demagogic antiabortion diatribe.

Tucker (TV *Growing Pains* teen-idol Kirk Cameron), a wide-eyed and babyfaced farm boy from Oklahoma, and Monica (Jami Gertz), a saloon-keeper's daughter from Chicago's South Side, attend Kenmont College on debating scholarships. After their team wins a number of awards around the country, Kenmont is pitched against Harvard at the national tournament, which takes place in an anteroom of the Supreme Court building in the presence of five justices. The subject is nothing less than "choice" versus "right to life."

At first the Harvard team, debating for choice, seems to be getting the upper hand—they argue that abolishing the *Roe v. Wade* decision would oblige women to return to back-alley abortions. The Harvard team is all-male smug, impeccably groomed, articulate, snotty, and self-confident, with Ivy League elitism written all over. At half time, *our* side, the side we've been programmed to be on—the lovable farm boy and the barkeep's daughter—is seriously in need of a verbal touchdown. Kenmore's coach (Roy Scheider) urges them, "Don't go for philosophy; you'll have to find your arguments within yourselves."

At this point, David Foster's treacly music swells mightily as Jami (who has manifestly been holding back from Tucker during the entire film, in spite of the affection he inspires) rises and tells the captivated throng how she had been raped by a drunk at age 14, found herself pregnant, and had an abortion. Ever since then, she hasn't really been able to trust men. "But it wasn't their fault. It was because of what I did. ...*Roe v. Wade* gave us women a cross too heavy for us to bear." Then Tucker gets up and follows with an impassioned speech about how decisions like Roe have led to the breakdown and decadence of our "quickie divorce" consumer-culture society. Agape with admiration for this brilliant youth, one of the justices mutters, "This national-character approach is a fresh new way of looking at the matter!"

Kenmore triumphs, natch. Monica and Tucker come tumbling out of the Supreme Court building, romp on the Mall, and, in the film's final shot, embrace in front of the Capitol. They presumably go off to graduate and breed happily ever after.

Listen to Me was written and directed by Douglas Day Stewart, best known as the perpetrator of the screenplay for that egregious glorification of militarism, *An Officer and a Gentleman*. His newly born film will most likely also do well at the wickets, thanks to Cameron's large teenage following. More's the pity—it's the most manipulative sty of hogwash released by any major studio within memory.

Also reviewed in:
NEW YORK TIMES, 5/5/89, p. C10, Caryn James
VARIETY, 5/10–16/89, p. 19
WASHINGTON POST, 5/6/89, p. C3, Rita Kempley

LITTLE MERMAID, THE

A Walt Disney Pictures release in association with Silver Screen Partners IV. *Producer:* Howard Ashman and John Musker. *Director:* John Musker and Ron Clements. *Screenplay:* John Musker and Ron Clements. *Based on the fairy tale by:* Hans Christian Andersen. *Director of Animation:* Mark Henn, Glen Keane, Duncan Marjoribanks, Ruben Aquino, Andreas Deja, and Matthew O'Callaghan. *Editor:* John Carnochan. *Music:* Alan Menken. *Songs:* Howard Ashman, Alan Menken, and Robert Kraft. *Music Editor:* Kathleen Bennett. *Sound:* Carolyn Tapp and (music) John Richards. *Sound Editor:* Richard C. Franklin Jr. and Louis L. Edemann. *Art Director:* Michael A. Peraza Jr. and Donald A. Towns. *Visual Effects:* Mark Dindal. *Layout Supervisor:* David A. Dunnet. *Backgrounds Supervisor:* Donald A. Towns. *Running time:* 82 minutes. *MPAA Rating:* G.

VOICES: Rene Auberjonois (Louis); Christopher Daniel Barnes (Eric); Jodi Benson (Ariel); Pat Carroll (Ursula); Paddi Edwards (Flotsam and Jetsam); Buddy Hackett (Scuttle); Jason Marin (Flounder); Kenneth Mars (Triton); Edie McClurg (Carlotta); Will Ryan (Seahorse); Ben Wright (Grimsby); Samuel E. Wright (Sebastian).

LOS ANGELES TIMES, 11/15/89, Calendar/p. 1, Michael Wilmington

Midway through The Disney Studio's "The Little Mermaid," there's a calypso number called "Under the Sea," led by a hypersensitive crab named Sebastian, with his "hot crustacean band." It's a no-place-like-home number, with Sebastian trying to persuade the title character, tawny-tressed Ariel, not to think that "the seaweed's greener...undah somebody else's lake," not to leave her ocean home in seemingly foredoomed pursuit of the handsome, human prince she has saved from shipwreck.

Ariel won't listen. She's a sturdy, headstrong girl, nubile prey for the evil seawitch Ursula, who wants to steal her voice and soul. But, especially after this infectious showstopper by "Little Shop of Horror" songwriters Howard Ashman and Alan Menken, the audience will probably open right up. "The Little Mermaid"—impudent, grandiose, a multilevel crowd-pleaser—almost returns the Disney animated features to their glory traditions of the '30s and '40s.

It's a different kind of film than the old classics. Coming after four decades of limited animation and MTV, it looks more hyper-active than "Snow White" or "Pinocchio." There's a heightened element of sexual sophistication in the story—partial nudity and double entendres, despite a "G" rating—and it shows off new wrinkles like computer animation, used for three-dimensional movement on the ships and shipwrecks.

But this movie, directed and written by John Musker and Ron Clements, with a yeoman team of animators, designers and craftspeople, shares with the classics a sense of over-reaching, of grabbing every snazzy effect possible within old-line narrative forms. Perhaps the literary source inspired everybody: director Jean Renoir, who adapted two Hans Christian Andersen tales himself, was among many who considered him a great writer.

It may be the setting. "The Little Mermaid," with its largely subaqueous backgrounds, doesn't have that flat, dry, overly crisp look which came over cartoons in the '50s. It looks wet and dense. The animators fill the water with shimmers and sparkles, wraiths of weed and shiny crops of coral, and they create amazing illusions of underwater movement.

"Mermaid's" saucy heroine, Ariel, isn't much like Andersen's sad, noble sea-maid. She's a sexy little honey-bunch with a double-scallop-shell bra and a mane of red hair tossed in tumble-out-of-bed Southern California salon style. She has no gills, but, when she smiles, she shows an acre of Farrah Fawcett teeth.

The movie lacks Andersen's exquisite poignance. There is nothing here to match his sea-foam coda or his annihilating line: "But mermaids have no tears and so they suffer all the more." Andersen's story was really a Christian parable: the poor or disinherited, defeated on Earth, will gain, through love and suffering, their chance to rise to heaven. The Disney version is, instead, about the shopping-mall generation gap: Ariel winning over tyrannical dad King Triton and beating the dirty-minded wiles of her bad benefactress, witch-with-a-B Ursula.

Although there is a primal power to this story that most recent Disney cartoons lack—a sense of desperate striving, the pain of worlds out of reach, life-or-death determination—it still sometimes seems nothing vital is at stake here: just hunk dreamboat Prince Eric, a Tom Cruise clone and the movie's weakest character. With his romance-comic features, golly-gee voice and strange no kissing fetish, he's a someday prince you may wish wouldn't come around at all.

It was the villains and the comical cuties who always dominated the Disney cartoon features. That's what happens here. Wright's Sebastian has every scene in his pincers, Buddy Hackett gives the goofy gull Scuttle his usual slobbery panache and Rene Auberjonois voices a wonderful Looney Tunes-style maniac French chef.

Actress Pat Carroll and the Ursula animators pump astonishing gobs of rotten-flirty menace and perversity into Witch Ursula, who looks a bit like the late actor Divine pasted over with an evil Jack Nicholson leer and squeezed into a cleavage-popping black evening gown, tailing off startlingly into eight squiggling black octopus tentacles. With her pet moray eels, she is a genuine nightmare, an obese lavender voluptuary peeling off lines like "Life's full of hard choices...I'n't it?" with blowzy relish or erupting from the ocean like Moby Dick on bonbons.

"The Little Mermaid" is a big leap over the Disney Studio's last two cartoon features, but though it gets its special distinction from the complex water-world effects, it's probably Pat Carroll, the Ashman-Menken songs and Wright's Sebastian who will make it a hit with audiences. That rousing calypso "Under the Sea" is the key scene. Starting like a little joke ballad scored to bone-bouncy steel drums, it quickly builds into a fine frenzy, the background whipped up with scads of sea-creatures singing, pounding and tail-flipping against shifting backgrounds of green, blue, purple and sizzling red.

Over it all is the exuberant vocal rendition by Sam Wright. Wright, who played Dizzy Gillespie in "Bird," here earns himself a place of honor beside Cliff Edwards' Jiminy Cricket, Edward Brophy's Timothy, Clarence Nash's Donald Duck—and Walt's own Mickey Mouse—in the top-cel gallery of Disney vocalizations. He does Sebastian with a gravelly Caribbean patois that has a touch of Irish brogue and a hint of "Ninotchka's" Sig Ruman.

When he hits the protracted climax with its tricky inner rhymes—"Everything's bettah down where it's wettah," "Each little clam here knows to jam here" *"Each little snail here knows how to wail here!"*— he should have any audience in his pocket. And so, with its dreamy, coruscating ocean kingdom, robust songs and fairy-pop pizazz, should the Disney Studio's new triumph, "The Little Mermaid" (MPAA rated G).

NEW YORK, 12/4/89, p. 143, David Denby

The great news about Disney's new animated feature, *The Little Mermaid*, is that it's consistently funny. Disney put two teams together: the animation veterans Ron Clements and John Musker, who wrote and directed (earlier they did *The Great Mouse Detective*), and Alan Menken (composer) and Howard Ashman (lyricist), who wrote the songs and are best known for *Little Shop of Horrors*. This movie, roughly based on the Hans Christian Andersen fairy tale, doesn't have the blooming, fluttering sweetness that marred the Disney films of the fifties and that made one want to run to the nearest meadow and stomp on butterflies and daffodils. The good humor is clean.

An animated feature needs to create a whole new world, and this one certainly does that—an underwater kingdom ruled by a bare-chested, bearded Triton, carrying a huge, phallic pitchfork whose prongs send out lightning flashes. Triton has a rebellious sixteen-year-old daughter, a mermaid, Ariel, who collects man-made objects from wrecked galleons and longs for human contact. Ariel is restless: Fish, crustaceans, and birds are just not enough for her (poor thing). She reasons that the men who made the beautiful things she collects can't be all bad, even though everyone below the waves says they are.

Ariel sings, and her voice is a benign lure, a siren song promising love rather than destruction. She saves a young prince named Eric from drowning, and he falls for her. But Ariel runs afoul of the sea witch, Ursula, who, in refreshing break from the slinky, black-haired dames skulking through past Disney films, is a fat, raucous vamp, with a teasing basso voice. Ursula has white hair and red lips and six legs. She's a shortchanged octopus. Pat Carroll, who does her voice, sounds more like a female impersonator than like a woman, which is a bit confusing, though not necessarily for children. Perhaps low camp works best underwater. Carroll is elemental, uncontrollable, uproarious.

The animation is a great success. I often get sleepy at live-action underwater films. The slow-moving heaviness and greenish-blue tints leave me depressed; the exotic beauty wears thin quickly. Here Disney's palette is somewhat somber but still vibrant, with a lot of creatures rushing about in graceful rocking, swirling motions—movement that is smoother and easier to take than the constant zip-zip-zip of most animated action. Yet it's not *slow*. In the calypso song "Under the Sea," a celebration of life at full fathoms five, the animation reaches a giddy peak of inventiveness, with oysters and snails plonking their shells like steel drums.

Ariel is meant to be a typical American-mermaid teenager, with spunk and enough drive to go after what she wants. Jodi Benson, who does her voice, sounds like every ambitious young performer we've ever heard in musicals; she's a bit shiny for my taste, but the voice is ardent and pure-sounding. Eric is boringly drawn as a sort of stupid seafaring hunk, and he's followed around by an Eager Dog, the one unfortunate concession to kiddie-movie formula. But the minor characters are true inventions. Ariel is accompanied in her adventures by a court composer and general adviser to the king named Sebastian, a crab of exquisite civility. In a stroke of genius, the filmmakers got the actor Samuel E. Wright to speak Sebastian's lines in a haughty Jamaican accent whose formal contours and suave modulations caress the words. Sebastian is highly intelligent, though put-upon, and desperately tries to hold on to his dignity when chased across a kitchen by a French chef with a cleaver. His particular nemesis, however, is Scuttle, Ariel's sea-gull friend, who is full of fluent misinformation and whose delirious verbal convolutions (Buddy Hackett, at his funniest, does the voice) cause Sebastian to drum his claws on the rocks in irritation.

Ariel makes a deal with Ursula. She attains human form, but only for three days and without her beautiful voice. If she can't get Eric to kiss her within that time, she belongs to Ursula forever. The resolution of *The Little Mermaid* sweetens Andersen's ending considerably, but the movie holds its comic edge. Trying to get the prince to come across, Sebastian composes another calypso number, "Kiss the Girl," and the whole above-ground animal kingdom sings and smooches in what could almost be a parody of the old honeyed Disney tone. If one judges by the kids sitting around me, children are completely engaged by *The Little Mermaid*. It doesn't settle for easy laughs, or easy scares; the violence is minimal and mostly of the storms-at-sea, purple-foam variety. The movie offers wit and honest delight, both rarities in children's entertainment. The best of animation has combined with show-business savvy, making *The Little Mermaid* the most entertaining animated feature since *Yellow Submarine*.

NEW YORK POST, 11/15/89, p. 27, Jami Bernard

With "The Little Mermaid," Disney returns to its yester-year habit of adapting fairy tales with staying power. And with a happy confluence of lively, witty animation, distinct voices matched perfectly to character, and a timeless-sounding Broadwayish score, Disney has created a minor classic. Maybe a major one.

The mermaid herself, with flaming red hair aswirl as she searches for sunken human treasures, has much more spunk and character than the prettily passive Snow White; so much for nostalgia.

But comparing "Mermaid" to Disney's treasure trove of animated greats is unnecessary because after much experimentation (including last year's ho-hum "Oliver & Company"), the studio has gotten it right—an old-fashioned story, a modern sensibility, slier humor and less dorky sentimentality. "The Little Mermaid" is funny and swell, liltingly animated and full of songs you can come away singing.

Very loosely based on a Hans Christian Andersen fable, the story is about the pangs of father-daughter separation, about accepting strangers and about having to make a Hobson's choice.

Ariel, a beautiful 16-year-old mermaid, the sea-grape of her mighty father's eye, falls in love with a human prince she spies through the porthole of the prince's ship. Consumed with longing to join him on land, she trades her magnificent, haunting voice to the evil sea witch Ursula in exchange for a pair of legs.

The contract has strings, of course, and the now voiceless Ariel must get Prince Eric to kiss her before sundown on the third day or she will become Ursula's shriveled, miserable pet, like so many sea creatures before her.

Ariel is accompanied to the surface by her pal, Flounder, and by a calypso crab named Sebastian, a sort of funky Jiminy Cricket who tries to convince Ariel of the wisdom of staying home by leading all the fish and plant life in a rousing Jamaican chorus of "Under the Sea," full of Dr. Seuss-like sight gags ("Blow, blowfish, blow! . . . Each little slug here cutting a rug here") and splashy color.

Ariel, with a wonderful, clear voice by Jodi Benson, is all hair and big, big eyes; the prince is not as fortunate, but then, animation has never done too well by princes. His dog Max is better animated, with his slobbering affection and paws-akimbo excitement.

Ursula, a great, ominous, oozing black-&-purple squid, is a delicious villain, aided immeasurably by the throaty, unctuous sarcasm of Pat Carroll's voice.

And right up there with Carroll is Samuel E. Wright's excitable little crab, Sebastian. Wright gets the most laughs, along with Buddy Hackett's unmistakable voice and timing as a bird-brained bird.

The songs, by Howard Ashman and Alan Menken, have a show-tune sensibility that will ensure they're remembered.

It's funny, romantic, and—OK—scary, just as it should be. This kind of terror is enthralling, stimulating. Just as yesterday's kids cowered at "Bambi" and "Pinocchio," films they remember now with great affection, let today's kids see how powerful animation can be.

NEWSDAY, 11/15/89, Part II/p. 7, Drew Fetherston

Have you seen any Disney favorites of your youth lately?

If you were a child when you first made their acquaintance, don't be tempted to see one again, unless duty requires that you bring a child to see it. Like anyone over age 10, you will most certainly be more impressed by their implausibility than by their childish charms.

Similar problems attend "The Little Mermaid," the Disney organization's first feature-length animated fairy tale since 1959's "Sleeping Beauty." This tale of a young mermaid seduced by the glamor of life above the tide line, tailor-made for tykes, may well have the charm of seasickness for someone richer in years. For an adult, "The Little Mermaid" is much like a first-grader's school desk: awkward, confining, not a little uncomfortable.

Some of the film's failings are no doubt apparent only to a jaded adult eye.

The colors in the animation are too exuberant for the mature viewer; the ocean is a fizzy aqua, the fish come in such unlikely shades as cerise, magenta and puce. The mermaid's hair is a brick-red blob.

Devices too familiar from earlier works, such as cute animal sidekicks for major characters, may well seem fresh to clean-slate imaginations. "The Little Mermaid" has several of these: A blue-and-yellow fish named Flounder accompanies the title character; her father (here Triton himself) relies on a badly drawn crab named Sebastian.

The introduction of a buffoonish seagull with the voice and manner of Buddy Hackett, so distressing to ears long since weary of Hackett's imbecilities, no doubt enriches the film wonderfully for those of tender years. The streamlined story, no longer cluttered with a melancholy ending, is fit for tots accustomed to the uncomplicated world of the half-hour sitcom.

Those youngsters may not notice that the animation in "The Little Mermaid" lacks the more-than-realistic clarity of earlier Disney epics. This is particularly noticeable in the faces and mouths of the characters, which have the odd movements of a dubbed film. The eyes, too, have little that is human (or even fishlike) about them; they are drawn absurdly large.

The sole character drawn with characteristic Disney verve, the witch Ursula, may resonate best in older viewers familiar with the film work of Divine, the late transvestite diva. The top half of Ursula is substantially Divine; the lower half is all octopus. But creators of "The Little Mermaid" were careful to make Ursula accessible to younger folks as well; she at one point says to the finny heroine, "You've got it, sweetcakes."

"The Little Mermaid" is musically different from but almost equal to other Disney animated features. There is no single song to match, say, "When You Wish Upon a Star" or "Whistle While You Work," but several of the seven songs supplied by Howard Ashman and Alan Menken (whose past work includes "Little Shop of Horrors") are good.

And, too, there are moments when the animation literally soars, when it gives one a gulls-eye view of a seaside town or a mermaid's perspective of a storm-tossed sailing ship. At these moments, one might wish to be of an age better able to appreciate the modest charms of "The Little Mermaid.''

TIME, 11/20/89, p. 91, Richard Corliss

[*The Little Mermaid* was reviewed jointly with *All Dogs Go to Heaven;* see Corliss' review of that film.]

VILLAGE VOICE, 11/21/89, p. 96, Elliott Stein

Attention should be paid to the simultaneous release of two animated features that will be vying for the kiddie trade from now through the holidays: Disney's *The Little Mermaid* and MGM/UA's *All Dogs go to Heaven* [see Stein's review], directed by Disney refugee Don Bluth.

Mermaid co-director Ron Clements has stated that fairy tales are great movie sources because of their ability "to instill hope." Of course, if they don't, he might have added, you can always pervert them to blunt their true poetry and make them over into merchandised musical lollipops. In Hans Christian Andersen's subtle and marvelous tale, the charming prince does not marry the little mermaid who has saved his life—the ungrateful wretch (shades of reality!) weds the high-toned daughter of a neighboring king instead. The mermaid, devoid of hope, maddened and about to stab the prince, drops the knife, jumps back into the sea, and is destroyed—she turns to foam.

This said, the Disney version is an occasionally entertaining job, even if it does have trouble padding its thin story line to feature length. There is one showstopper, dangerously early in the film: "Under the Sea," an elaborate production number led by the mermaid's comic sidekick, Sebastian the Crab (voice of Samuel E. Wright). This catchy calypso ditty (music by Alan Menken) sets hundreds of dancing fish into amusing Busby Berkeleyish gyrations. Sebastian is the film's Jiminy Cricket, its saving grace and only memorable character. The heroine (voice of Jodi Benson) is a simpering implausibility. Although the picture is set in fairy-tale days of yore (Disney medieval revival), she sports a Miss Clairol coiffure and brays Valley Girl slang. Andersen's mermaid yearns to become human as much to attain an immortal soul as to marry the prince. This movie doesn't know from souls.

Also reviewed in:

NEW REPUBLIC, 12/25/89, p. 26, Stanley Kauffmann
NEW YORK TIMES, 11/15/89, p. C17, Janet Maslin
NEW YORKER, 12/11/89, p. 140, Pauline Kael
VARIETY, 11/8/89, p. 32
WASHINGTON POST, 11/17/89, p. D7, Hal Hinson
WASHINGTON POST, 11/17/89, Weekend/p. 51, Desson Howe

LITTLE THIEF, THE

A Miramax Films release of an Orly Films/Renn Productions/Ciné Cinq/Les Films du Carrosse/SEDIF co-production with the participation of the Centre National de la Cinématographie. *Producer:* Jean-José Richer. *Director:* Claude Miller. *Screenplay (French with English subtitles):* Annie Miller, Claude Miller, and Luc Béraud. *Based on an original screen treatment by:* François Truffaut and Claude de Givray. *Director of Photography:* Dominique Chapuis. *Editor:* Albert Jurgenson. *Music:* Alain Jomy. *Sound:* Gerard Lamps and Paul Laine. *Sound Editor:* Nadine Muse. *Art Director:* Jean-Pierre Kohut-Svelko. *Set Decorator:* Jean-Pierre Svelko. *Special Effects:* Jean-François Cousson and Guy Trielli. *Costumes:* Jacqueline Bouchard. *Make-up:* Joel Lavau. *Running time:* 109 minutes. *MPAA Rating:* Not Rated.

CAST: Charlotte Gainsbourg (Janine Castang); Didier Bézace (Michel Davenne); Simon de la Brosse (Raoul); Raoul Billerey (Uncle André Rouleau); Chantal Banlier (Aunt Léa); Nathalie Cardone (Mauricette); Clotilde de Bayser (Séverine Longuet); Philippe Deplanche (Jacques Longuet); Marion Grimault (Kebadian); Erik Deshors (Raymond); Rémy Kirch (Pascouette); Renée Faure (Mother Busato); Claude Guyonnet (Young Priest); Jacques Herlin (Sacristan); Gilbert Bahon (Police Sergeant); Catherine Arditi (School Teacher); Pierre

Maguelon (Mr. Fauvel); Marie-Thérèse Orain (Ms. Pigier); Sherif Scouri (Cohen); Joëlle Bruyas (Sister Marie-Odile); Clothilde Baudon (Bonnin); Jacky Nercessian (Theatre Genre Director); Annie Legrand (Hotel Receptionist); Chantal Neuwirth (Farmer's Wife); Denise Chiabaut (Doctor); Florent Gibassier (Carpenter).

LOS ANGELES TIMES, 9/1/89, Calendar/p. 1, Sheila Benson

When he made "The 400 Blows" in 1959, François Truffaut wanted the film to contain a parallel story of a girl delinquent a few years older than his autobiographical 13-year-old hero, Antoine Doinel. Although he eventually erased her from "The 400 Blows," Truffaut apparently never obliterated the girl from his mind.

Over the years, he accumulated more material for the character of Janine, who was, according to letters in his recently published "Correspondence," based partly on the first woman he lived with when he was 17. A year before his death, Truffaut asked his close friend and co-scriptwriter, Claude de Givray, to work with him on the material, and at Truffaut's death, in 1984, a 35-page treatment existed.

That passed to producer-director Claude Berri ("Manon of the Spring"), who chose director Claude Miller ("The Best Way," "Garde à Vue")—in his earlier years an assistant to Truffaut as well as to Jean-Luc Godard—to adapt the final screenplay and to direct it. (Miller's fellow screenwriters were his wife Annie Miller and Luc Béraud.)

All this is prologue to "The Little Thief," a fine, beautiful film, deceptively simple and marvelously subtle, which bears traces of both film makers' sensibilities. If it is a closing of the circle that began with Antoine Doinel, it may also be a first step down the road traveled with Janine Castang.

Perhaps, to Truffaut's Doinel films, we will someday add one or two more in the Castang series by director Miller. He has already made one earlier feature with "The Little Thief's" remarkable star, Charlotte Gainsbourg, the 1985 "L'Effrontée" ("Charlotte and Lulu").

A great deal of "The Little Thief" depends on your reaction to Gainsbourg, since the narrative rests entirely with her. Flat-nosed and thick-maned, with a look that is sullen or lost by turns, she also possesses a shy smile whose unfolding can twist the heart. Frankly, it took seeing the film twice to appreciate completely the delicacy and bruised sensibilities with which Gainsbourg invests Janine, a waif whose life is spent making excuses for the mother who abandoned her.

We meet Janine in 1950. The postwar era is conjured up in a few seconds of newsreels: the giddy celebration after the liberation of Paris, the shaved heads of pretty Nazi collaborators, even now smiling defiantly for the cameras. Janine's missing mother was possibly one of those. Having "fooled around" with Nazi officers during the war, she has lit out, leaving her little daughter with an older uncle and his shrill younger wife in a poor provincial town that might be straight out of "Small Change."

As though it were her due, Janine begins by stealing cash from schoolmates' lockers and graduates to boosting real silk panties, fox stoles and cigarette cases from unwary shopkeepers. It is, as we see poignantly enough, a clumsy attempt at badges of adulthood: All around her she sees Yanks and compliant French girls; what she sees in the mirror is not reassuring. For moral instruction, she has the local movie screen and a rudderless existence at home with her adulterous aunt and belittled uncle. (A nice detail is her rough uncle's skill at drawing, his real passion. He's a rich character, richly played by Raoul Billerey.)

Caught after a brazen theft from the village church, she is given a chance: a job as a maid in a neighboring city. While working for this earnest, well-to-do young couple, the Longuets, she meets someone Truffaut may have intended as a harsh self-portrait: Michel Davenne (Didier Bézace), a 43-year-old married man who cloaks his pleasure in having a 17-year-old mistress in his virtue in being her teacher and "protector."

One of "The Little Thief's" intricacies is in its even-handedness with so many of its characters: Janine's uncle; young Mme. Longuet; Michel. Simultaneously we see how Janine could charm this bookish provincial, how she would genuinely try to turn herself into his vision of her as a modest, accomplished secretary, and how a moment of real lust could blow this whole mentor/mistress game apart in a second. (The film is MPAA-rated R for adult themes.)

It happens soon enough: Janine falls for the worst type. Do they not always—didn't we all, at 17? The ferrety Raoul (Simon de la Brosse), roughly her age, is a would-be motocross competitor and a worse crook than she; he hasn't even mastered his movie shtick, flipping a cigarette into his mouth. And he brazenly blames his brief impotence on the fact that he *needs* two sheets, top and bottom, and a real bed, for a proper setting.

But she invests all her starved feelings in his vision of grand passion; soon she's parroting his contempt for the straight life and a straight job and stealing for him on a grand scale. With what unfolds next, this could be as bleak a story as Agnes Varda's "Vagabond," yet it's not.

Miller, with a delicate and magical touch, introduces cameras and photography into the equation, his own addition to Truffaut's text. if you wish, the "photography" that lured Truffaut into the world of cinema. Janine stumbles into it in the least likely place—a Catholic-run girl's reformatory—from a kindred, defiant soul, Mauricette (Nathalie Cardone, in the film's one searing performance).

The freeze-frame conclusion of "The 400 Blows" was intentionally ambiguous but not promising. You cannot help but take heart as the road lifts at the end of "The Little Thief," and that amazing a cappella chorus that framed the opening credits reappears again with its cheeky marching song. (We know now it is the choral group Michel directs.)

Things did not go swimmingly for Truffaut's first mistress; somehow Miller allows us to hope for more for Janine. We want to *believe* the film's text, that with her camera—and in spite of her encumbrances—Janine would steal nothing more than images in the futrue.

MONTHLY FILM BULLETIN, 8/89, p. 246, Philip Strick

1950. In a small town in central France, sixteen-year-old Janine Castang is reluctantly housed with her Aunt Léa and Uncle André. Convinced that the mother who abandoned her will return some day, but meanwhile eager for adulthood, she steals clothes and make-up from shops and classmates. Caught in the act of stealing funds from the local church, she narrowly avoids prosecution and is encouraged by André to find her first job, becoming housemaid at the home of a young couple, the Longuets. Visiting a cinema, she falls asleep on the shoulder of Michel Davenne, a forty-year-old married man, who treats her kindly but, to her frustration, resists her immediate advances. Disposing of her virginity with the help of a workman at the Longuet house, Janine firmly steers Michel into making her his mistress, and in return he pays for her fees at a secretarial college during her time off work and for a room of her own, while introducing her to the pleasures of music and literature. Janine protects a young thief, Raoul, she finds robbing the college office and, much smitten, begins to share her time between him and Michel. As she and Raoul become involved in fullscale theft, Michel is ditched entirely. When the Longuets hold a house party, Janine ransacks their guests' belongings and goes on the run with Raoul; for a while they hide out among sand dunes on the coast, but soom the police catch up with her and Janine is sent to a remand centre. She becomes friendly with Mauricette, who has a camera and teaches her some of the basics of photography; together they escape from the centre with the help of Mauricette's boyfriend, Raymond. Janine realises that she is pregnant by Raoul and decides to go back to her home town, where she knows of an abortionist. Mauricette gives her the camera as a parting gift. Back home, Janine finds Léa and André despondent about their future. Her mother has written at last, to say she has a new boyfriend and won't be coming back. At the local cinema, Janine sees Raoul in a newsreel, among troops embarking for Indochina. She visits the abortionist, who accepts the camera as payment in advance. Changing her mind, Janine defiantly steals back the camera and sets out to face whatever the world may have in store for her and her unborn child.

According to Truffaut's collaborator Claude de Givray, *Les quatre cents coups* was originally about two young outcasts, Antoine Doinel and Janine Castang, whose part-comical, part-perilous escapades on the edge of disaster would be shown in parallel. As it turned out, of course, there was more than enough to the Doinel story for several screenplays and the Janine character took a differenct route through Truffaut's work. If Doinel was more directly autobiographical (with extra input from Léaud), Janine became the Woolrichian *femme fatale* of Truffaut's other stories, careering just beyond his grasp all the way from Bernadette Lafont on her bicycle to Fanny Ardant as the lethal woman next door. Every rogue male and wild child in the Truffaut bestiary was copiously outnumbered by his Adèles and Anglaises, his brides in black, his Mississippi mermaids—and in apparent recognition at last that Janine was no longer to be denied her explanatory opening chapter, Truffaut, after making notes about her throughout his life, had planned *La Petite Voleuse* to be his next project after *Vivement Dimanche*.

He left a thirty-page synopsis which Claude Miller, previously Truffaut's assistant on eight films, was by general agreement the ideal director for. "All the themes thrown into those thirty pages attracted me", says Miller, "and seemed to be part of my 'family' of topics. I felt totally at at home with the subject". In turning *La Petite Voleuse* into a screenplay, however, Miller's intervention inevitably makes a new woman of Janine: instead of being the "final" Truffaut film, presented as faithfully as possible (actually an assignment unlikely to please the Truffaut purists or to concern the average audience), the identity of the piece has shifted to a less easily defined area, somewhere between *Une belle fille comme moi* (Truffaut) and *L'Effrontée* (Miller), a context in which whatever the critical loyalties, it appears more realistic to consider ignoring Truffaut's contribution altogether. Some of the few lines of dialogue in Truffaut's synopsis appear in the film ("I kept all those that were to do with sexuality", reveals Miller), some of Truffaut's events have been omitted entirely ("because I didn't have the time or the inspiration"), and at least one section, dealing with the remand centre, has been substantially expanded because "I wanted, out of personal interest, to spend a week filming a group of hard, violent, delinquent girls". Since it is unimaginable that Doinel's female counterpart would *not* spend a considerable time on remand, Truffaut's purpose becomes even more elusive at this point.

The identity problem is also compounded by Miller's own range of films which, inspired by writers as different as Highsmith, McCullers, and the dazzling Marc Behm, would seem only accidentally to have anything to do with Truffaut's universe, were it not that Truffaut also wanted to make Highsmith's *This Sweet Sickness* (filmed by Miller in 1977 as *Dites-lui que je l'aime*) and that elements of the Hitchcock/Graham story *Marnie* clearly influenced both directors and turn up once again in *La Petite Voleuse*. The only safe critical standpoint, it seems; must be to interpret her story not by supposition, of what Miller thought that Truffaut might have had in mind, but more simply and accurately as another of what can be termed Miller's "emotional travelogues", those explorations of crimes and choices that lead all his characters, male or female, to an equivocally open (but not very optimistic) conclusion. Future Janines in Miller's work will doubtless clarify the issue. Meanwhile, the surface of his Truffaut tribute is compiled from a miscellany of the fine and the awkward, the clumsy and the delicate. No mistaking the nod to *Quatre cents coups* in Janine's first encounter with the sea, or the Bazin reference in her introduction to Victor Hugo, or the Truffaut/Vigo inspiration for the tramping column of remand kids and the children's songs on the soundtrack. Janine, too, is a child of the movies, meeting one love and losing another as the newsreels slip by, and finding at last that she and the camera might have a special affinity.

There are the wipes, iris shots, and elisions of pace and plot that were Truffaut's hallmarks, but with a warmth of eccentricity among the lesser characters that one associates more with Miller. He says he aimed for a nostalgic sepia, but Miller's colours (and lighting) are often startlingly harsh and his décor stiflingly intricate as though he had too much to say (and no other way of saying it) about the separate lives of, for instance, Janine's aunt and uncle, her bourgeois employers the Longuets, or even the grim lineliness of the abortionist with her store-cupboard of pathetic relics. An unappealing waif despite the undeniable charm of Gainsbourg's performance, Janine plays war-babe hell-bent on independence with a ferocity unexpectedly evocative of her British equivalent in *Wish You Were Here*, opting like her for a seaside prospect of single parenthood which seems unlikely, in the long run, to save her from the fate of the previous generation she has so unscrupulously plundered. "We're losers!" say boyfriend and uncle alike, and they show every probability of being right. At least, it is to her credit, and Miller's, that Janine is not yet ready to capitulate.

NEW YORK POST, 8/25/89, p. 26, V.A. Musetto

If it were up to me I'd knock out 10 seconds of "The Little Thief," the French import that marks François Truffaut's final contribution to the screen. Ten seconds may not seem like much when you're talking about a film of nearly two hours. But in this case it makes all the difference between a fully realized work and a flawed one.

Those precious moments come at the very end: A two-sentence denouement concerning the future of our protagonist—a 16-year-old petty thief and liar. Intended to avoid what would otherwise be a cryptic fadeout—will she or won't she mend her ways?—the ending jars us and breaks the mood that the picture has painstakingly built up. Why must we have everything spelled out, all the loose ends neatly tied up? Some things are better left to the imagination of the individual viewer.

Now that I've gotten that off my chest, I must tell you that "The Little Thief"—directed by long-time Truffaut assistant Claude Miller from a story idea by his mentor (who died before he could film it)—is otherwise superior filmmaking.

Charlotte Gainsbourg (last seen here in Agnès Varda's "Kung Fu Master") portrays the title character, Janine Castang. Her mother, a Nazi collaborator, deserted her after World War II. So she lives on a dairy farm with her aunt and uncle, who are unable to control her thievery—a carton of Luckies here, a piece of lingerie there.

When she's caught stealing from the church, Janine drops out of school and takes a job as maid to a bourgeois couple. On a night out at the movies, she picks up Michel, a 43-year-old married man who leads the church choir and likens her to Esmeralda of "The Hunchback of Notre Dame." When Michel refuses to help her lose her virginity, Janine finds a workman who is more than willing to do the job.

From Michel, who by then has given in to lust, she moves on to Raoul, a brash young man who shares the girl's passion for crime. They loot her employers' home and flee to the sea (as did Antoine Doinel in "The 400 Blows"). But Janine soon finds herself pregnant and in reform school, and the film's final crisis is set in motion.

Miller has said that his only condition for making "The Little Thief" was that Gainsbourg, whom he had directed previously, play the lead. With her childish voice and intense, womanish pout, the daughter of British actress Jane Birkin and French musician Serge Gainsbourg is, indeed, the perfect choice for the precocious Janine. (You may be reminded of Isabelle Huppert's portrayal of the bad girl in Claude Chabrol's "Violette.")

Didier Bézace is effective as the bookish Michel, although Simon de la Brosse, as Raoul, may be trying too hard to live up to his reputation as "the French James Dean."

The script, by Miller and his wife, Annie, is economical and to the point. As is his direction, complete with little Truffaut-like idiosyncrasies. The Master would be pleased. Now if only we could do something about those 10 seconds.

NEWSDAY, 8/25/89, Part III/p. 3, Mike McGrady

The French have always been ethical alchemists, taking the rest of the world's vices and magically transforming them—well, if not into virtues, at least into something human and tolerable. What we think of as sin often becomes romance on the French movie screen, and what we consider immorality is upgraded, at the very least, to amorality. We should not be unduly surprised, then, by the warm and understanding treatment accorded the schoolgirl heroine of Claude Miller's "The Little Thief."

Sixteen-year-old Janine (Charlotte Gainsbourg) would be classified as an incorrigible guttersnipe in most other parts of the world. Especially in any small town in the year 1950. Among her activities: casual seductions, an affair with a married man, carelessness leading to pregnancy, arranging for an abortion and random acts of physical violence.

And that is not even to consider her major hobby—thievery. She steals valuables from boarding-school classmates, furs from the department store, cigarettes from parked cars, valuables from her employer and a husband from a wife.

The miracle is , while busily stealing everything not nailed down, she also manages to steal your heart.

Some will credit this to the story itself. (The movie's screen treatment was written by François Truffaut just before his death; if he had lived, this was to be his next project as a director.) Much credit must also go to actress Charlotte Gainsbourg, the 17-year-old daughter of English actress-singer Jane Birkin and French singer-director Serge Gainsbourg. Young Gainsbourg lights up the screen with a heartbreakingly plaintive quality, a seductive blend of shyness and courage, that wins us over no matter what casual crime she's contemplating at the moment.

Originally, Janine was to be a central figure in Truffaut's first film, "The 400 Blows," but the director came to feel she merited a film of her own. Like Janine, Truffaut was also in his mid-teens in 1950, a school dropout who lost himself in movie theaters. Also like Janine, he was a petty thief who spent time in reform school.

Ties to Truffaut are strengthened by his selection of Claude Miller to direct "The Little Thief." Miller was for many years Truffaut's apprentice, and while he doesn't imitate his mentor, there are unmissable stylistic echoes of mood and pacing.

Janine's story, of course, is more than the case study of a cute kleptomaniac. In one sense, it describes any young person's search for something worth having in a world where there seems to be no room for her. The people in Janine's life—an aunt and an uncle scraping out a brutish existence on a farm, a bourgeois couple who hire her as a maid, the married man who uses her four hours a week—add nothing of value to her life.

In fact, she feels no sense of self-worth until she runs into a boy her own age who also happens to be a thief. Both are lost souls, but at last she finds a place to belong and someone who appreciates her precisely the way she is. Ironically, while in prison she learns to do something she enjoys—to operate a camera and take photographs. Thus, Janine's happy ending parallels Truffaut's destiny. Thereafter, "...she would steal nothing more than images."

NEWSWEEK, 4/11/89, p. 55, David Ansen

When François Truffaut died in 1984 he left behind a project that he had been meditating on since the days of "The 400 Blows." Knowing that he would not live to film it, he passed the story on to producer Claude Berri, and it has been directed by a man who was Truffaut's assistant for many years, Claude Miller. *The Little Thief* is compelling in its own right, but it carries an extra load of meaning for anyone who grew up cherishing Truffaut's wounded lyricism, his effervescent *tristesse*.

Miller's film reminds you of Truffaut at every turn, filled as it is with echoes of the late director's work. But Miller is his own man, with his own more sedate, less quirky rhythms. In telling the story of the teenage thief Janine Castang (Charlotte Gainsbourg)—a female counterpart to Antoine Doinel in "The 400 Blows"—he remains true to Truffaut in two significant ways: his sympathy for Janine never succumbs to sentimentality, and he never moralizes.

Janine, deserted by her parents, is raised by her aunt and uncle in a French provincial village. It's 1950, and the schoolgirl is already a confirmed thief, raiding the local stores for luxury items—silk lingerie, expensive furs—that remind her of the glossy romantic fantasies she devours at the local cinema. Though Janine's compulsion is never "explained," we can see that she's stealing an identity for herself, escaping into a double life of petty crime.

Caught filching from the church collection box, she leaves town to take a job as a maid, and begins to live out her amorous fantasies, first with a married 43-year-old (Didier Bézace) who encourages her to go to secretarial school, then with a lean young criminal (Simon de la Brosse) who takes her again outside the law. Like Doinel, her rebellion lands her in a reformatory, from which she escapes. But the open-ended conclusion leaves room for hope: perhaps she will stop living borrowed fantasies and begin to live her own.

Though the events in "The Little Thief" are often bleak and violent, Miller's movie has a benign glow: it's adolescence recollected in tranquillity. The beguiling Gainsbourg is an astonishingly subtle, honest young actress. Truffaut's "last testament" has been left in good hands: he would have recognized Janine as one of his true children, a bruised, plucky survivor.

VILLAGE VOICE, 8/29/89, p. 66, Stuart Klawans

To begin with some hype-disposal: *The Little Thief* comes to our screens bearing a reputation as François Truffaut's final legacy, which is rather a large claim. I would estimate it to be about a quarter true. Though the screenplay is not Truffaut's it does derive from a story that was partially his and has been directed in copycat fashion—excuse me, as an homage—by Claude Miller, who was Truffaut's assistant fro 10 years. So it would be stretching things to call *The Little Thief* a posthumous work. What seems most characteristic of Truffaut in the film is its bare subject—but that, as it turns out, is saying a lot.

Every comfortably right-thinking citizen of France would despise the protagonist of *The Little Thief*, whom the film depicts with unsentimental sympathy. Set in the years just after the occupation, this is the story of a 16-year-old girl whose mother was a Nazi collaborator (and, no doubt, a black marketeer). Janine (Charlotte Gainsbourg) evidently feels no shame about this blot on the family history; she merely regrets that her mother had to run away, leaving her to a grubby life in her aunt and uncle's dairy. A muddle of romantic notions, class resentment, and sheer cussedness, Janine soon drops out of school, tries to steal the collection money from the church, hangs out in the movies like a real Truffaut character, and more or less spits in the eye of the moneyed liberals who want to bring her up in the world (though not, of course, too high). Perhaps the American equivalent of this character would be a white girl with Klan affiliations in some third-rate Southern city—a girl who isn't really dirt-poor, but who feels her poverty desperately and is willing to do anything to escape it; anything, that is, except educate herself or work. That's the sort of person our heroine represents—and, to improve the insult to middle-class values, at the end of the film she is pregnant with another one just like herself.

This much of the film, at least, seems genuinely to belong to Truffaut, whose image as a charmer takes a well-deserved beating from *The Little Thief*. Though it's easy enough to caricature him as a cinematic St. Francis—a gentle, whimsical, warmhearted little man who liked children and probably would have preached to the birds, had they shown an interest in Howard Hawks—Truffaut could be as acerbic, as confrontational, as flat-out mean as any of his New Wave colleagues, whether in the pages of *Cahiers du Cinéma* or in his films. (Think of the delight with which he killed off the crook's mother in *Shoot the Piano Player*, or the gratuitious insult he flung at Marcel Carné in *Small Change*, or any of his other throwaway gags—they seem light-fingered, but might better be called high-handed.) In the story for *The Little Thief*, he left us another of his improprieties, disarming on the surface, infuriating underneath.

With admirable speed and economy, the film begins by putting Janine in context: She is eager for pleasure, and pleasure is just what postwar France offers her. The problem is, she can't afford the goods. Moreover, she is sufficiently young and brash to accuse everybody else of wanting the same things she wants; and she's right, too, up to a point. Caught at home with a cache of shoplifted goods, she avoids arrest only because the irate store manager sees a chance to repossess a few items more than he'd lost—as Janine is quick to point out. Found stealing from the church—she is almost always caught in her thefts—she looks the young curate in the eye and offers him "anything' if he'll let her go. His reaction makes it obvious that she's hit his weak spot—though, having feelings more complex than Janine will credit, the priest both turns down her bargain and also refuses to press charges.

From the curate, she proceeds to Michel (Didier Bézace), a married man in his forties whom she picks up at the movies. Again, she's right in thinking he'll want to sleep with her. She's somewhat less clear-sighted in predicting that, once she's no longer a virgin, people will treat her properly, as an adult. Nor does Janine fully understand Michel's motives. He invites her to choir practice and talks about Victor Hugo—thus introducing her to the culture of a provincial bureaucrat—and tries to help her get ahead in the world by enrolling her in a secretarial school. She doesn't seem to recognize her guilt, or his fantasies of being a patron; she just understands his desire and his sense of superiority. And so she is ripe for the bad boy in the drama, Raoul (Simon de la Brosse), who drops in—literally—to provide Janine with her first real boyfriend and set in motion the somewhat creaky mechanism of her final crisis.

Perhaps some of the flesh for this story was suggested by Truffaut, along with the bones; but I have to credit the Millers for all the details that could not have been worked out in a scenario—the way Janine and her captor are eerily silent when she's caught robbing the church, the way she and Michel abruptly fling themselves together at the start of their affair, the way her uncle, on a visit to the city, slowly unfolds his money when treating her at a restaurant. But the Millers also have a few shortcomings, most notably their casting of the inert Charlotte Gainsbourg as Janine.

With her flat, blunt-featured face and ungainly body, Gainsbourg might seem an ideal choice for the role—a *jolie laide* who is remarkably at ease in her imagined social class. That's the good part about Gainsbourg. The bad is that she has approximately two facial expressions; I know, because she recently used them both in Agnès Varda's *Kung Fu Master!*, in which she played a hip young girl in present-day Paris. She also favors a wispy little voice, which she seems to have inherited from her mother, Jane Birkin (also on view in *Kung Fu Master!*), and which can be intensely irritating, since it is supposed to be coming from a girl whose emotional ground zero is truculence. When Gainsbourg is on screen with a live actor, she isn't so bad—by being inert, she at least gets carried along with the flow. That's the case when she appears opposite Bézace, for example, whose Michel is all swallowed emotions and sputtered self-justifications and the sort of kindness that might as well be extended to a stray dog as to Janine.

But Gainsbourg also spends a lot of time acting with de la Brosse, a kid who imitates his betters in the manner of Sean Penn aping De Niro. He even does a cigarette-flipping trick after the style of Jean-Pierre Léaud; and the Millers don't interfere. In fact, I have the uneasy feeling they encouraged him. With Gainsbourg and de la Brosse together, the film takes on the emotional vacuity of any brat-pack picture. Too bad nobody thought to give the lead to Nathalie Cardone, a dark, ferocious young woman who is sensational as Janine's closest buddy in reform school.

But neither Gainsbourg nor the occasional heavy-handed touch by the Millers can ruin the film. They just make it a bit more earthbound than a Truffaut film would have been, a bit more insistent on hammering home its points, a bit less open to human oddity. For all that, *The Little Thief* is still worth seeing for the way it neatly combines an individual case study and a social critique, with the latter explaining the character and eliciting sympathy without ever cheating her into being likable. That's a kind of subtlety you don't get in many movies, especially the current crop of American ones; and on top of that, *The Little Thief* tells its story with an efficiency that would have been very welcome in *Batman*.

Also reviewed in:
NEW YORK TIMES, 8/25/89, p. C13, Caryn James
NEW YORKER, 9/4/89, p. 89, Terrence Rafferty
VARIETY, 1/25–31/89, p. 15
WASHINGTON POST, 9/29/89, p. D7, Hal Hinson

LITTLE VERA

An International Film Exchange release of a Gorky Studios film. *Director:* Vasily Pichul. *Screenplay (Russian with English subtitles):* Maria Khmelik. *Director of Photography:* Yefim Reznikov. *Editor:* Yelena Zabolotskaya. *Music:* Vladimir Matetsky. *Sound:* P. Drosvev. *Sound Editor:* Pavel Drozdov. *Art Director:* Vladimir Pasternak. *Costumes:* Natalya Polyakh. *Make-up:* Valentina Zakharchenko. *Stunt Coordinator:* N. Sysoyev. *Running time:* 130 minutes. *MPAA Rating:* Not Rated.

CAST: Natalya Negoda (Vera); Andrei Sokolov (Sergei); Yuri Nazarov (The Father); Liudmila Zaitseva (The Mother); Andrei Fomin (Andrei); Alexander Alexeyev-Negreba (Viktor); Alexander Mironov (Tolik); Alexandra Tabakova (Christyakova); Alexandra Linkov (Mikhail Petrovich).

FILM QUARTERLY, SUMMER 1989, p. 18, Andrew Horton

Vasily Pichul's *Little Vera* (1988) has emerged as a new Soviet film that has found a home audience and an enthusiatic one abroad wherever it has been shown. On the most immediate level, the film can be seen as a clear example of Gorbachev's *glasnost* (new openness) policy as applied to film. But it is much more.

While not a "woman's film" *per se*, this recent Soviet work set in a drab Ukranian industrial town is written by a woman (Pichul's wife, Maria Khmelik) and is centered around Vera (Natalia Negoda), an eighteen-year-old Russian woman whose disjointed emotional life suggests significant questions of gender as well as of *glasnost*. As Teresa de Lauretis notes in *Technologies of Gender*, "Although the meanings vary with each culture, a sex-gender system is always intimately interconnected with political and economic factors in each society." The raw edges of *Little Vera*'s narrative are thus those of an oedipal and patriarchal system (political/economic/cultural) of signification and representation that is showing serious signs of disruption and change.

Three early shots set the tone and direction for the rest of the film. The opening establishing shot before dawn is of a bleak industrial town on the banks of a large body of water. The second is a morning scene on the balcony of a cheaply built apartment house as Vera is told in a brusque and unsympathetic manner by her mother to "make something of your life...as your brother has done." And shortly thereafter, again on the balcony, her working-class father quietly tells her in a comforting voice, "Cherish your youth."

What Maria Khmelik captures in her script, which she wrote in 1983 after visiting her husband's native town and family (the script found no sympathetic producer for four years, in other words until *glasnost* had come into being), is the "on-edge" existence Vera lives out. The film chronicles a few brief weeks in Vera's life. The driving force of the narrative is her romance with an engineering student, Sergei—a Dionysian free spirit. We observe their engagement, separation and eventual reunion, tentative though it may be, on the evening that Vera verges on suicide.

American reviewers will surely capitalize on the many "firsts" in this low-budget Soviet feature by a young husband and wife team: first Soviet film with a sense of sexual candor (the actress Natalya Negoda has contracted to grace the pages of *Playboy*), the first mention of AIDS in a feature film (a passing joke about government warning pamphlets), and the first direct suggestion of non-white children as offspring from white mothers. Yet I am more interested in the strength of the film as a refreshingly straightforward contemporary portrait of a provincial Soviet young woman and her relationships. And among these, it is her close tie to her "nurturing" father that holds a special interest.

The intensity of the father-daughter tie alone gives *Little Vera* a curious urgency unusual to traditional Western narrative patterns. But it is also important to view the film in relation to the changes being wrought under *glasnost* since film-makers began to replace bureaucrats in the hierarchy of the Soviet film industry in 1985. From this perspective Pichŭl's film is notable on at least four counts: it is made by a director who came from the working-class provincial background he treats on the screen (he is of Russian origin from Zhdanov, a Ukranian industrial town on the Sea of Azov); it was produced by Gorky Studios (Moscow), one of the smaller studios, thus suggesting the emerging importance of studios other than the mammoth Mosfilm in Moscow and Lenfilm in Leningrad; it dares to show rough edges in terms of cinematic style—a direct alternative to the long tradition of "well-made" Soviet films, including even the auteuristic and lyrical works of a director such as Andrei Tarkovsky, the folk/mythic surrealism of a Paradzhanov, the sense of robust humor of Georgian comedies and satire (Abuladze's *Repentance*), or the imaginative mixed-media films (drama and documentary) of someone like the Film-makers' Union president, Elim Klimov; and it is an important contribution to a growing number of films that honestly capture a "no win" mood of many Soviet young people today as opposed to the forced optimism of so many Socialist Realism films of the past.

Khmelik depicts the edge of a life without spiritual or even passionate materialistic values. Vera is at the same time empty and cramped. She is cramped by the drabness of her town, her job as a switchboard operator, the lack of physical and psychological space in her family's apartment, and by a general absence of alternatives to the roles that appear laid out for her. And she is empty of clues as to how to break out of her environment. Her name, of course, is emblematic. "Vera" means both "faith" and "verdict" and thus "little Vera" reflects both her age/position and her lack of hope or, conversely,the glimmer that hope may exist. Both readings make sense.

More specifically, Vera is on the edge of a perception of how her life is defined by the men who surround her. There is her successful doctor brother, Viktor, who has even managed to move to Moscow. Andrei is the ineffectual young man, "calm and polite," who pursues her like a puppy dog and who thus offers her a traditional romance, marriage, social status which she rejects. More important, however, Vera exists between the sympathetic acceptance of her quietly desperate father and the antisocial freedom represented in Sergei and their tempestuous affair. Neither wholly modern (despite her streaked hair and mod clothes) nor traditional, Vera is squarely caught in the middle with little hope of escape.

Little Vera does, however, chart this young Soviet woman's development as a movement away from her father and towards her lover-fiancé. While much of feminist theory details the importance of the mother-daughter relationship in its reevaluation of Freudian psychology (the Demeter-Persephone pattern, as Carol Gilligan and others note), little work has updated Freud's brief exploration of the Electra Complex (a daughter's adoration for her father). And while there is much in literature and film about daughters under the spell and shadow of domineering and/or impressive "successful" fathers, there has, to my count, been relatively scant attention given to the possibility of nurturing relationships between an "unsuccessful" and nondomineering father figure and daughter. *Little Vera* in part explores this terrain.

Because of the distance her mother places between her husband and Vera , the daughter must also play wife and mother to her father. Thus while the father urges Vera to "cherish her youth," Vera is, in fact, the one who takes his complaints about his heart trouble seriously and who then undresses him and tucks him in bed early in the film.

The developing conflict of roles and values within Vera comes to a crisis once Sergei is officially her fiancé. A birthday party for her father becomes the climax for her confusion. Pichul and Khmelik use an effective structuring device within the film according to which almost every scene starts on a seemingly congenial note and then proceeds to break down. The birthday party is no exception. Vera is caught in the middle once more as the two main forces in her life suddenly quarrel and come to blows. Sergei, who operates on spontaneous passion, beats up the father and tosses him into the bathroom, locking him in. The scene ends as the father frees himself and stabs Sergei—sending him to the hospital in critical condition.

Afterwards, as Vera attempts to cope with her divided feelings, the family plans a picnic by the sea. That moment disolves into bitter antagonism as her mother shouts to Vera, "I never wanted to have you anyway." Denied maternal friendship and support, Vera retreats to the edge of the sea in a rain storm only to be followed by her father. He gently holds her as he quietly says, "My little daughter." Pichul holds the moment long enough for us to feel the mutual understanding and shared loneliness these two feel for each other. And he manages to do so without pushing the scene into traditional melodramatic forms (even foregoing underscoring music).

Vera is unable to negotiate her emotional/psychological life between her father and Sergei. If her father had been the traditional patriarch, the separation would have been easier. But though Vera herself never communicates her confusion on a verbal level, we sense she glimpses the limiting realities of life with either man and has not yet reached a level of consciousness in which she would consider life alone. (Compare the strong ending of Abram Room's *Bed and Sofa* [1927] in which the young heroine, caught between her life with her husband and lover, walks out on both, claiming "Neither of you is worthy to be the father of my child.")

The suicide scene in her family's apartment follows soon thereafter. In a terrifying depression involving booze and pills, she clasps a childhood photograph of herself to her chest. Soon after her brother and Sergei (who has escaped from the hospital) reach Vera before she loses consciousness, she and Sergei are shown together again in Vera's bed, exhausted, frightened, quiet. "Do you love me?" she asks Sergei, as she has throughout their relationship. "I was afraid," he replies. They are not yet married, have no apartment to go to, no careers unrolling before them. And Vera still has little faith in her own identity. However, they are together...alone. A little hope, therefore.

But the film closes with two final images: that of the father keeling over in the kitchen, followed by that of a longshot of the small city similar to the opening image. The mother has no role in this resolution. And whether her father is dead or simply having another attack, it is clear that Vera has already begun the difficult task of "growing up" and leaving her childhood behind. As comforting as her father's affection has been, it was not enough, could *never* be enough. Pichul ends as he began, with another dawn shot. Hope or life repeating itself? Vera and we, the spectators who have lived (vicariously) through her experiences, are free to decide.

In the spaces created by such "unfinalizedness" (Mikhail Bakhtin's term) the Sphinx has a chance to set an alternative agenda in the Oedipus tale without the need for suicide and self-sacrifice.

If the British phase of neorealism in cinema in the late fifties and early sixties was characterized as "kitchen-sink" realism, *Little Vera* might be dubbed "kitchen-table" cinema, a "novi realism." For Pichul's unflinching camera grounds Vera in a literally cramped familiar environment (the apartment) centered further around the kitchen table and the different functions it serves for the family—work/meals and conversation. Even in the finely etched scene between Vera and her girlfriend at her apartment, the scene is cast around the kitchen table as Christyakova, her friend and the mother of a black child, announces she is content to settle for a relationship with a boring but well-meaning middle-aged man. In the same scene, shortly before what is to be Vera's wedding, Vera, who has been on edge throughout the film, suddenly breaks into tears: "This is the happiest time of my life but I want to cry all the time."

Such a scene—and the film is chock full of revealing "everyday" moments—suggests how far contemporary Soviet cinema has now been allowed to move from the false enthusiasms and wooden idealism of Socialist Realism in its most rigid forms. There is an engaging offhandedness about many of the sequences that suggests a blend of improvisation and keen writing paired at a conceptual level. Again, such a disjoined approach to narrative not only reflects "youth" but also Vera's perspective as a woman, unhappy with her lot, but not yet articulate enough to determine her own destiny. And of course some of the images/lines/contexts may be striking but not completely intelligible to the non-Soviet audience.

In a beach scene, for instance, restless youths tattoo large images of St. Basil's cathedral on their backs. A sign of protest or of religious belief or of some level of joking? Perhaps a blend of all three. Also on the beach, Sergei asks Vera, "What is our common goal?" and she replies with "Communism" in a voice that is tinged with irony, parody, but also, we sense, with the leftover response of years of conditioning that has lost all meaning. "The challenge today," Pichul explained to me in Montreal (August 1988) during his first trip with his wife out of the Soviet Union, "is to find osme *spiritual* values in this life."

Pichul is more modest than some Soviet critics who have already dubbed *Little Vera* "the first honest Soviet film." "What's great is that we actually made it," the 28-year-old director explained in Montreal, where the film was awarded Best First Feature. Thus his answer to those who felt the overall impression of the film was one of a crushing hopelessness was revealing: "The film is an attempt to come close to the abyss of our life today. Actually our real life is even darker, and yet I remain an optimist. Making a film is an exercise in hope!"

FILMS IN REVIEW, 10/89, p. 488, Frank Scheck

This sexually frank Russian film, is more interesting for its Glasnost sociological implications than for its dramatic content. But it does offer a stark portrait of a depressed industrial city in modern Russia, and an excellent performance by Natalya Negoda (also the star of a recent *Playboy* pictorial) as a disaffected Soviet youth.

The film covers familiar territory for Western audiences in its account of Vera, a rebellious teenager with streaked hair who fights with her parents, drinks, takes drugs, listens to rock and roll, and sleeps around. Her parents, an overweight, nagging mother, and an alcoholic, truck driver father, don't know what to do with her, and they are totally confounded when she brings home her latest boyfriend, a college student named Sergei, to live with her.

Sergei is less than deferential. In fact, he is openly contemptuous, and he and Vera's rebellious sexuality creates a tension that finally leads to violence. These scenes of family cruelty have a psychological intensity that give the film a power and universality that erase geographic borders.

Director Vasily Pichul's filmmaking is often crude and rudimentary, and the visuals suffer from the low budget and often cramped locations, but he and screenwriter Maria Khmelik have succeeded in making a new kind of Russian film. A monster hit there, seen by over fifty million people, *Little Vera* is a signal that we may soon have a reliable new source, besides France and Italy, for art house films.

LOS ANGELES TIMES, 4/28/89, Calendar/p. 1, Sheila Benson

Little Vera, unhappy at last. And at first. And in between. But how else is a bored, nervy 18-year-old supposed to feel, living at home, nagged at every turn?

Sassy, sensual Vera is the second thing the camera lingers upon as the startling Soviet film "Little Vera" opens. The first shot is a long appraising pan along the depressing seaport city of Zhdanov, smoggy, industrial, grim. Across its polluted river is the cramped cement-blockhouse apartment Vera shares with her parents, indistinguishable from every other apartment building in their row.

Next, director Vasily Pichul shifts our attention to leggy Vera, pensively eating cherries on the apartment's ratty balcony. She's streaked her dark hair herself; when it's combed out, teased and sprayed, the peroxided wisps look like feathers around her face, heightening the slightly predatory cast to her features.

Just out of high school, Vera is currently in limbo. Her truck driver father asks every single day—and at least twice at night, when the gin or vodka that are his nightly release have dulled his memory—whether her admission to college has come through. Her mother, a foreman in a fabrics plant, spends all *her* time shrilling about the unwholesomeness of Vera's friends. And when her parents get tired, they put Vera's successful older brother Viktor, who lives in Moscow, on the phone to read her the riot act.

A lot of good it does. Wearing fishnet stockings and a leather miniskirt, Vera goes to the public park with other aimless kids every night. When fights break out, the sight of patroling police with their German shepherds seems to deter no one.

It's when one of these brawls turns into a full-scale riot that Vera meets Sergei, a college student whose cool is even greater than her own. Almost instantly they become lovers, giving audiences plenty of time to savor Vera's casual attitude about semi-nudity, or whatever they care to savor during the couple's private moments.

They're not private enough for Vera, who gets tired of Sergei's classmates dropping in on them. By telling her parents the lie that she is pregnant, she moves Sergei under their roof, a living situation doomed from Meal One.

With this first, autobiographical feature, 28-year-old director Pichul's strengths seem not to lie in construction or even in storytelling. The screenplay, by his wife Maria Khmelik, repeats scenes without particularly expanding on them. But there's a power that comes from making what you know about, and Pichul grew up in Zhdanov; his parents live, even now, in an apartment that could double for Vera's.

And Pichul is also on firm ground with his actors and downright canny about his casting. For the parents in this flagrantly controversial film, he buffered himself by using two veritable icons of Soviet cinema: handsome, silver-haired Yuri Nazarov as the powerful blue-collar father, pathetic during his nightly drunks, and Liudmila Zaitseva as Vera's worried, small-minded mother, who has the worst pin-curls in life.

Then, of course, there is Vera, played by the ferociously assured newcomer Natalya Negoda, a 24-year-old actress with such feral intensity and compound-complex shifts of mood that we're lulled into overlooking the fact that, as a film, "Little Vera" is raw about the knuckles. (It's Times-rated Mature for its sexual situations and partial nudity.)

It doesn't have the elegant, theatrical style of Russian soul-baring that we're used to from Nikita Mikhalkov ("Slave of Love," "Unfinished Piece for a Player Piano"). On the other hand, it's lightyears away from a sudsy weeper like the interminable "Moscow Doesn't Believe in Tears." (No, its Academy Award, collected over "Kagemusha" and "The Last Metro" has not gone unremembered. Or understood.)

"Little Vera" has a few tragi-comic truths to get off its chest and, whether one lives in "the workers' paradise" or far, far away from it, these truths are as frightening as an unexpected glimpse into hell.

A few bouncing moments of nudity aren't "Little Vera's " shockers, it's the film's gray-on-gray portrait of daily Soviet life, in boxes made out of ticky-tacky, bounded on four sides by boredom, alcoholism, pollution and repetition, and on the top and bottom by hopelessness and bureaucratic indifference. The family is in ruin; the prospects of the next generation are dismal. And there is no strength to cling to anywhere: God has been lost and the Party has proved bankrupt.

Only the hopelessly romantic can believe that Vera's cheeky spirit will, somehow, prevail. If that were true, Vera might be the Soviet Alice Adams (Booth Tarkington's Alice, not George Stevens' with that awful uplift-finish), climbing the stairs to that dulling secretarial school with the same bravery that Vera may adopt in her job at the telephone exchange. The two young women have the same fire. But Alice at least had a world waiting for her when she finished the hated school. Vera has only the example of her parents, and that's enough to quench the most intense fire.

MONTHLY FILM BULLETIN, 7/89, p. 195, Verina Glaessner

Vera, who lives in an industrial town with her parents, is one of a group of young people waiting for their papers for higher education to arrive. She is scornful of Andrei, a boy from her class in high school who is in love with her, and at a local open-air dance is attracted to a youth, Sergei, whom she has not seen before. When the dance threatens to turn into a brawl and is broken up by the police, Vera returns with Sergei to his hostel and they make love. The next day, Vera meets her friend Christyakova (whom Vera's parents disapprove of) in a café; when Sergei arrives, Christyakova makes advances to him but he sits with Vera. Andrei receives his call-up papers for the navy and Vera attends his farewell party, but despite his protestations of love she leaves to go to Sergei's hostel. Vera and her father go to the airport to collect his son Viktor, a doctor living in Moscow whose marriage is breaking up. Some embarrassment ensues when Viktor turns up at the hostel with a girlfriend and finds Vera there with Sergei, who is an old acquaintance of his. Vera tells her shocked family that she is pregnant and is going to marry Sergei; at the engagement party, Sergei turns up late and inappropriately dressed, and peremptorily leaves with Vera when Viktor gets angry. When Viktor returns to Moscow, Sergei moves in with Vera but finds her father's drinking and mother's intrusiveness hard to bear. During a miserable drinking session, Christyakova tells Vera of her affair with Mikhail Petrovich, who is teaching her yoga. During another family meal, Vera's father begins drinking and abusing Sergei; the boy attacks him and locks him in the toilet. When he is released, he grabs a kitchen knife and stabs Sergei. The latter is hospitalised, and when Viktor returns he prescribes tranquillisers for Vera. Her mother persuades her to tell the police the stabbing was an accident: they cannot afford to have her husband in prison. Sergei releases himself from hospital and returns with Viktor to the house, where they find that Vera has attempted to kill herself with an overdose of pills and alcohol. Viktor saves her, and after she is put to bed leaves for Moscow. Sergei stays with her while her father drinks himself into oblivion and collapses on the floor.

Little Vera arrives in this country trailing a reputation as an unprecedented "exposé" of the socialist paradise of the U.S.S.R. We are as far here from a cinema of positive protagonists as we are, in the opening and closing pan around the industrial townscape, from the fervour of Constructivism. What is more arresting, however, is the extent to which the film refrains from giving a simple naturalistic account of its characters' blighted lives. The conventions of realism certainly determine the treatment of Vera's family: her mother, whose weary rituals of food preparation no longer provide a viable focus for family life, and her father, disillusioned and alcoholic. Yuri Nazarov's performance suggests a lifetime of small defeats and limitless self-disgust, and in his relationship with his daughter (she is the one who puts him to bed after his drinking bouts), the skeleton of a more traditional tale of family relationships is adumbrated. When the camera pans at one point across the bleak domestic interior to the accompaniment of the Soviet national anthem announcing the radio station's closedown, we might well be watching a kitchen-sink television drama.

But it is around the character of Vera and her friend Christyakova that the film becomes both less comfortable and less predictable. To some extent, it appears a sour *hommage* to the Czech New Wave, with the two girls as depressed second cousins to Vera Chytilová's larky heroines in *Daisies*, their whimsical, though far from lighthearted, anomie providing ironic comment on the world in which they live. Natalya Negoda's twitchy and unfocused performance is almost Brechtian in its refusal to engage "sincerely" with her dialogue—she speaks as though quoting from an alien text—or indeed with the camera. She is given remarkably few close-ups, which leaves the impression of an object under investigation that is somehow refusing that role. It is typical that when Vera visits the police station to give the version of Sergei's stabbing in which she has been coached by her mother, she, and we, are distracted to such an extent by the lurid tale of domestic strife unfolding at an adjacent desk that we never do get to hear her explanation. In a scene on the beach, Sergei ironically takes the role of a socially concerned investigator and quizzes Vera about her "goals in life". "We have one shared goal", she replies, "Communism".

The social documentary, in effect, is contemptuously dismissed as a tool for investigating contemporary issues. But if it was Vasili Pichul's intention to depict the old characters in the "old" way and the new in a "new" way, he has ultimately reckoned without the power of realism (with which we feel so comfortable) to cancel whatever subversive charge Negoda's performance contains. Romanticism, it seems, must win out and Vera's "lost" relationship with her father cannot help being seen in some sense as the cause of all the distress. Taking his cue perhaps from the references to Pushkin and Christyakova's beatnik versifying, Pichul has recourse to a series of rhetorical gestures—Andrei leaping from a boat into the sea at one point—of which Vera's father's collapse is only the last and most dramatic. These do nothing to dispel, in fact only underscore, the impression of a film finally too eclectic and ill-assorted to do more than register its own disgust at the plight of its characters.

NEW YORK, 4/17/89, p. 61, David Denby

Little Vera, the breakthrough Soviet film (explicit sex and much drunken unhappiness), is not, I'm sorry to say, a very good movie. Still, as a cinematic event, it has a few things going for it—not just our enjoyment of the pretty young lovers bundling on their grimy bed but our equally prurient curiosity about everyday life in the Soviet Union. *Little Vera* is a portrait of a boozing working-class family in which the daughter, Vera (Natalya Negoda), a coarse, vital girl just out of high school, streaks her hair and sleeps around, a Russian rebel without a cause. When she falls in love with a handsome student, she brings him home, and the movie becomes a vodka-soaked *All in the Family*.

Little Vera has been seen by some 50 million Soviet citizens. This is a staggering number of people to line up for a messy little picture, however erotic, made in a style of slaphappy kitchen-sink realism. what they're seeing is a spectacle a lot more shocking than a man and woman in bed. *Little Vera* is a revelation of deep and apparently endless despair at the heart of what used to be known (not always ironically) as "the workers' paradise." Some of the millions plunking down rubles must have taken derisive pleasure in seeing such misery acted out—in a spirit of hapless, hopeless comedy, too.

The movie was shot in Zhdanov, a port city on the Sea of Azov that was named (or rather renamed) after Andrey Aleksandrovich Zhdanov, Stalin's murderous postwar scourge of the nation's cultural and intellectual life. The 28-year old director, Vasily Pichul, was born there and grew up in an apartment very much like the cramped, boxy little place Vera's family lives in. An industrial center, Zhdanov looks gray and polluted; there's a beach to escape to, but it turns out to be rocky and uncomfortable. On summer nights, the girls put on lipstick and meet the boys, who wear sixties long hair, at a kind of open-air disco where they dance to Soviet rock. For some unexplained reason, a fight breaks out between rival groups of boys, and policemen with dogs break up the party.

Vera meets Sergei (Andrei Sokolov), a male dish with floppy blond hair, and they go off together, finding privacy in Sergei's dormitory room. But the single-sex building has the cement walls of a prison cell, so Vera takes Sergei home, with disastrous results. Her mother, heavyset, a worrier, labors as the comptroller of a fabric factory; at home, she cooks, pickles things, and shouts aimlessly at everyone. She has long given up on her truck-driver husband, a fine-looking man who degenerates every night into a sodden clown. There's plenty to eat, and a bottle of good English gin, as well as the inevitable vodka, sits on the kitchen table. But the family is sunk in nonstop bickering. The parents shout at Vera and call her a whore, but she just ignores them, and Sergei coolly narcissistic and indifferent to everything, sponges off them and gets up from the table without saying a word.

Natalya Negoda, a slender, beautful woman with a perfect figure and a slightly blank sullenness, is a good actress—her face can look pouty and dumb one minute and sharp and malicious the next. She's like Natalie Wood with a sense of humor. But Marie Khmelik, who wrote the screenplay, doesn't give her enough to work with. We can see that Vera, slowly drifting into a dulll life as a telephone operator, is lost, that she's gone numb with fear and resentment. She hates hypocrisy and blurts out the truth, but she's not an interesting girl; she has no *words*.

The movie resembles a British working-class drama of 30 years ago (around the time of *A Taste of Honey*) but without the eloquent rage, the poetry of bitterness. Pichul, trying for spontaneity (a fallacy imported from Western movies), produces lots of incoherent noise and mulling around. The movie is awkwardly staged and shot. Half the time, Pichul can't get his equipment into the tiny rooms, so he has to peek at the characters from behind a doorway; at key moments, the camera winds up in the wrong place. Here and there he gets a tone of black-comedy dismalness, like John Cassavetes at his shaggiest, but his fondness for grog and grovel and mess almost shuts out our interest in the characters. The loutish Sergei, glamorous in his naked blond handsomeness, never does say much of anything.

The funny thing is that this radical Soviet movie is shaped like a neo-Victorian morality tale: Both Vera and Sergei undergo severe punishment for their little fling. Their rebellion leads nowhere, and perhaps, for a Soviet audience, that's the point. What seems punitive and draggy to us might ring true in Moscow: There *is* no way out, not even for the young and sensually arrogant. Though not overtly political in any way, *Little Vera*, depicting as it does the Soviet family as a crumbling wreck, is unmistakably a political act, a stinging rebuff to a state that once promised to satisfy all of its citizens' needs. Zhdanov would have hated the movie and packed off the entire cast and crew to a labor camp.

In the West, *Little Vera* means something else. The media's delight in Soviet cultural liberation has recently developed a peculiarly lubricious tone: The Russians may be tasting forbidden pleasures, but it's the West that is licking its chops. In the May *Playboy*, Natalya Negoda ("that *glasnost* girl") is spread out in the magazine's usual lacquered, amber style—topless, her back arched, breasts thrust out. The capitalist photo session (black lingerie, leopard skins, a little water sprinkled on her chest) seems to have made her fleshier, more abandoned, more conventionally lewd. *Playboy*, of course, makes merry with the idea of screen eroticism behind the Iron Curtain, though the magazine's attitude is just a driveling exaggeration of what's heard elsewhere. It's almost as if the West were pimping for the Soviets—or, a little more precisely, as if we were a dirty-minded uncle enjoying his niece's losing her virginity. Look, they *drink!* They *fornicate!* Wow!

I feel no nostalgia whatsoever for Stalinist puritanism, but I don't think rock and roll or explicit sex scenes are going to save the Soviet soul. Still, Soviet citizens may now be enjoying life a little more than in the past. From the evidence of this movie, they couldn't enjoy it much less.

NEW YORK POST, 4/14/89, p. 35, David Edelstein

Fifty million Soviets have seen "Little Vera," the grim coming-of-age story in which Natalya Negoda appears semi-nude and takes part in a brief sex scene. Such monkey business could never have slipped past the censors pre-Gorbachev, and watching the topless young actress as she straddles her boyfriend, I could not help exclaiming, "What a perestroika!"

Now that I've satisfied your prurient little minds on the subject of "That *Glasnost* Girl"

(Playboy's phrase), it's time to address the movie itself—a dreary piece of kitchen-sink realism. Politically, "Little Vera" is said to be a milestone because it boasts no Commie sloganeering, although not many Stand By Your Tractor pictures have ever made it to the West. Soviets, sated with propaganda, clearly welcome this breath of foul air; we, on the other hand, have been hearing what a dump the place is for years.

"Little Vera" opens expressively with a shot of smokestacks, gray buildings and battered factories. This is meant as a metaphor for the spiritual state of the Soviet working class. A teen-age girl with a frosted mop of hair in her face and garish sunglasses turns out to be Vera, who for most of the movie slinks around in a black leather miniskirt and fishnet stockings while various authority figures scream at her.

When we see her eyes they're frosted, too. Negoda, whose performance has been mysteriously acclaimed, has a habit of striking cool, alienated poses and staring off into the distance. She comes alive only when she lusts. After a rock 'n' roll dance turns into a riot, she winds up in a tiny cot with a feckless, sinewy student named Sergei (Andrei Sokolov). Thereafter, she can't get enough of him. Although they drink and take pills, sex is their drug of choice, youth and beauty their all-too-temporary succor.

The film, directed by the 28-year-old Vasily Pichul, has scary, crazy-comic rhythms in its scenes in Vera's cramped, rundown apartment. Pichul switches to a hand-held camera, which dizzily jerks and swerves as Vera's drunken father (Yuri Nazarov) lumbers around in his T-shirt, railing against his "sailor's whore" of a daughter while smashing lights (many things are smashed in this movie) and swilling vodka (much vodka is swilled in this movie).

When Vera brings Andrei home for a special dinner, the ne'er-do-well shows up in red flowered shorts and with a major attitude. The scene at the table—in which the entire family compulsively pours and belts down shots of vodka—is deftly staged, and the screenplay by Maria Khmelik (Pichul's wife) makes fine, wry points about each character.

But the central point of "Little Vera" overwhelms everything else. The Soviet Union, it says, is one bleak place. And it says this relentlessly, piling misery upon misery as if trying to make up for all those lost years. Yet never, through its technique, does it suggest a larger vision of human possibilities. It's too busy trafficking in counter-propaganda: Bleak! Empty! Hopeless!

The "Little Vera" press release inadvertently suggests the problem when it cites the film's "uncensored look at the seamier side of working class Soviet life: alcoholism, drug abuse, vandalism, rock 'n' roll, promiscuous sex and nudity." Now, I've never considered nudity particularly seamy, and in this country, rock 'n' roll sells a lot of Nikes and Pepsi. Someone's getting carried away.

But everything is seamy in "Little Vera." Even eating: the proles in their T-shirts loom over their plates, cramming food into their maws without ever looking up. And the camera is cuckoo for squalor. If Vera visits a hospital, it must promptly circle the room to reveal the human wreckage.

These sights might be liberating to Soviet audiences, but there's an element of self-congratulation in the hosannas for "Little Vera" over here—our Capitalist hearts leap at hearing the Communists' slogans turned against them. Their despair strengthens our sense of righteousness.

Is there anything else to this movie? One rave newspaper review of "Little Vera" features the word "anomie" three times (once preceded by "hopeless"), while "bleak" and "futility" appear twice. The critic also speaks of Vera's "boredom," "vacant, uncomprehending eyes" and "dull will to survive" in this "barren emotional landscape"—this "vacuum" in which the characters conduct thir "empty wrangling" as a diversion from the "emptiness of their lives."

Not bad—in less than 500 words this reviewer captures the movie's bleak, barren, hopeless, empty, dull, futile anomie quite nicely. If "Little Vera" is a harbinger of the new Soviet cinema, we critics are going to have to start hitting our thesauruses.

NEWSDAY, 3/31/89, Part III/p. 5, Lynn Darling

There's a lot about the 18-year-old protagonist of this fascinating film that will look familiar to Americans who maintain even a nodding acquaintance with contemporary adolescence. Vera is in some ways the quintessential teenage time bomb, alternately surly and catatonic with her parents, her streaked unruly hair crowning a face masked by a glaze of studied boredom, her lithe body harboring a sexuality over which she exercises the kind of control normally associated with a runaway truck.

Set against the usual cinematic verities about life in the Soviet Union, however, "Little Vera" is also an amazing study of working-class anomie in a country that until recently was exporting films that emphasized the heroism of politically correct tractor drivers.

Vera (Natalya Negoda) is a restless young woman in whom the ripeness of youth is already about to be overtaken by the hopeless anomie in which her parents have long been mired. Her mother is a weak, ineffectual factory worker, her father a self-pitying drunk. "What's going to become of her?" they wail, as Vera stares off into the distance, heedless of their emotional storms.

In fact, it's easy to see what will become of Vera—her own life will reflect the futility of her parents'. Though she spends her days and nights in restless procession, drinking and dancing and exploring all the things her body can do, it's only the quick flame of youth that sparks her: Her fate is already written in her vacant, uncomprehending eyes.

Director Vasily Pichul follows Vera through the course of her passion for Sergei, a handsome, irresponsible, disdainful lout who eventually moves into the claustrophobic apartment she shares with her parents. As the tension between her parents and her lover grows, Vera is torn between them; the camera captures their empty wrangling from the tight confines of corridor and kitchen.

There is no love here, no values beyond the dull will to survive. The barren emotional landscape is reflected outside in the shots of bleak factories and vacant lots and deserted shipyards.

The vacuum in which Pichul's characters live makes a mockery of the old slogans and rhetoric: "So do you have a goal in life!" Sergei asks Vera as she sprawls langorously in her bikini "We have a common goal, Sergei, communism," She answers, her voice drenched in sarcasm.

Pichul poses no alternatives to the emptiness of the lives he studies, but he knows where the answer won't be found: There is a shot of Vera waiting by the side of a road, her face set in the opposite direction from the heroic statue that towers above her. His sharp, revealing dissection of these lives, however, is devastating. "Little Vera" is a bleak, surprisingly funny film that reveals an unexpected universality—neither capitalism or communism, it seems, has cornered the market on the futility that afflicts so much of contemporary urban life.

NEWSWEEK, 4/17/89, p. 71, Jack Kroll

Any doubts about the seriousness of *glasnost* have been swept away: the Soviets have signed a treaty with Hugh Hefner. The figure wearing half a T shirt that graces the cover of the current Playboy is that of Natalya Negoda, headlined as "the Soviets' first sex star." But Negoda is nobody's bimbo. She's an extraordinary young actress who is the star of *Little Vera*, a new Soviet film that has sold more than 50 million tickets in the U.S.S.R., generated great controversy, had worldwide success at film festivals (winning Best Film and Best Actress at the Chicago Film Festival) and is now moving into national release.

Soviet cinema is celebrating its 70th anniversary this year, and "Little Vera" is the first Soviet film in all those years with an explicit love scene. But the real shock waves have come from its unblinking look at the bleak quality of life among ordinary Soviet people. Shot in Zhdanov, an industrial port city whose skies are fouled by smokestacks and whose people are smogged by hopeless inertia and an aimless life that has broken their spirit, the film makes an archetype out of the teenage Vera. She frosts her punk-style hair, stokes herself with gin and pills, fights with her alcoholic truck-driver father and her hapless, overeating mother. Vera falls in love with Sergei, a nihilistic student who moves in with her family, treating them with a contempt that leads to violence.

"Little Vera" (the title also means "little faith") is a deeply pessimistic film, but it has a fierce energy, a buried anger, that goes right to your gut. Soviet guts have been hard hit. At one performance a woman in the audience cried out: "Aren't you ashamed to show lives like that?" Another shouted back: "Aren't you ashamed to live like that?" Reaction has split along generational lines, with younger people defending the movie against their more conservative parents. "Little Vera" is the first film for director Vasily Pichul, 27, screenwriter Maria Khmelik (his wife), 27, and the second for their star Natalya Negoda, 25. They signal a Soviet new wave determined to speak for itself. The script gathered dust for three years until Gorbachev eased restrictions in the movie industry. "Without glasnost," says Khmelik, "our film could not have been made." In Pichul's words: "The moment has come to show what we think."

So what's Negoda doing in Playboy, with a cover plus a 10-page spread? Well, as she put it (through an interpreter) on a recent visit to New York: "You want glasnost? OK, you got glasnost!" She is well aware of the ironies involved in a repressed Soviet culture's wish to break into the open air of a more Western-style freedom (and Western-style commercialism). Negoda agreed to pose for Playboy (an idea suggested by the film's U.S. distributor) despite her reservations, which are still unresolved: "On the one hand, the pictures correct the stereotype of a Soviet woman, on the other hand they turn me into an American stereotype. Americans keep asking me, 'Are you a sex symbol?' I ask them, 'Do you have a sexual problem in this country?' "

Her riveting performance as Vera—catatonic, hysterical, sensual, suicidal—has made her an instant star. The noted director Elem Klimov went up to Pichul and said, "You made a fabulous movie and I understand you got this girl right off the street." This left-handed compliment at first offended Negoda, who worked hard to create Vera, a character not at all like her. The daughter of parents who are both directors, Negoda trained at the Moscow Art Theater School. She joined a youth theater, where among her roles she played Holden Caulfield's sister Phoebe in a stage version of J.D. Salinger's "The Catcher in the Rye." Now Negoda has become a heroine to young Soviet women. "We get a lot of mail from girls who say, "I'm 17 and you've just played my entire life." They mob me for autographs, many symbolically want me to write on their identity cards, which is a crime in the Soviet Union."

Negoda gives a great deal of credit to the superb actors in "Little Vera," including Alexandra Tabakova as Vera's impudent friend Lena and above all Yuri Nazarov and Ludmila Zaitseva as Vera's parents. "Unfortunately, our parents' generation is the one that's been taught to lie all the time. They love their kids, but they don't know how to speak the truth. That's why they can't be spiritually close to their children." Negoda is aware that in a real sense she is a child of glasnost: "I don't want the new spirit to stop. I don't want things to go back to what they were. Our country has suffered enough. We're very tired of not having just an ordinary life." Meanwhile her extraordinary life continues. She's finishing a new film, "The Nights are Dark in Sochi," with Pichul and Khmelik, which will open the Venice Film Festival in August. "It's about problems that apply not only to us," she says, "but to people all over the world."

VILLAGE VOICE, 4/4/89, p. 58, J. Hoberman

As much a news item as a movie, Vasily Pichul's third feature comes on like epic Norman Lear. This funny, if overlong, saga of a sullenly willful teenager's enthusiastically botched love affair and cramped, clamorous home life is fascinating both for the chaos it shows and the stridency with which it shows it. The southern port city of Zhdanov—Pichul's hometown—appears as a ruined landscape of grim factories and blasted housing tracts. Meanwhile, human nature is treated like the return of the repressed. *Playboy* cover girl Natalya Negoda is memorably mercurial as Vera, a sharp-featured number with two-tone hair, and the ensemble acting is often uncanny, particularly once Dad puts the Beefeater's on the table and everyone begins hitting the bottle.

VILLAGE VOICE, 4/18/89, p. 63, Georgia Brown

Every Soviet citizen is allocated by the state landlord a minimum of nine square meters of living space—a statistic gathered from Joseph Brodsky's memoir, titled after his family's 40 square meters in Leningrad, "In a Room and a Half." "For us," he writes, "an apartment is for life. . . ."—floor space in the psyche. In one of last year's memorable gallery shows, Ilya Kabakov reconstructed, and reimagined, the 10-room communal apartment of his Moscow childhood. "Life as we live it here is dominated by a general, archetypal feeling of extremely closed spaces," writes Kabakov on the effect of real estate on the Soviet spirit.

Little Vera's unhappy family, living in the provinces, is fortunate to have its own kitchen and bathroom to be unhappy in. According to Gerald Peary in the *Los Angeles Times*, director Vasily Pichul (born 1961) returned to his hometown of Zhdanov (a seaport in the Ukraine); found an apartment like the one he grew up in and where his parents still live; and filmed a script written by his wife, Maria Khmelik—itself based on visits to her in-laws. The film's memorable scenes are not those with the newsmaking nude and sex shots, but rather ones recorded by a camera stationed in a narrow hallway, trained into a sliver of tiny, cramped kitchen where the movie's main action takes place. Pichul's selective topoanalysis creates claustrophobia extending beyond the strictly spatial.

As this grim comedy opens, Daddy comes home, screeching his big red truck to a halt (he's a truck driver), and his not-so-little Vera is waiting on a tiny terrace that opens off the kitchen. Vera (Natalya Negoda) nibbles on something small and stares off into the trees as Mom (Liudmila Zaitseva), and then Dad (Yuri Nazarov), complain about her inertia ("Have you got your college acceptance yet?'') and make a good deal of a $20 bill found in her pocket ("Since when do we have dollars?''). They even call elder brother Viktor, a Moscow doctor, to get his arbiter's opinion on the matter. Defiant, Vera tears up the bill and flushes it down the toilet. The bathroom, with its broken light switch, also opens onto the hallway, just beyond the kitchen, and is the home's second most important room—the place to go to for privacy, or punishment.

"Why don't you say something?" asks exasperated Dad. "What's there to say?" Vera wants to know. Vera and her father, a maudlin alcoholic, have a special relationship; she's the one who puts him to bed when he's drunk and feigning his heart attack, while Mom stubbornly ignores him.

But with friend Christyakova and other teens hanging out in a local park, Vera, who aspires to be a telephone operator, has a lot to say. At night, Vera takes off her shmatte, teases her frosted hair, and puts on makeup, her red-and-white striped sweater, black leather miniskirt, net hose, and heels. (Alternating the two outfits for most of the film, Vera inexplicably appears later in a new wardrobe.) At an outdoor dance, patrolled by police with German shepherds, Vera meets Sergei (Andrei Sokolov), a university student and a new face in the crowd.

Before long, Vera and Sergei are sleeping together in his dorm room and even talking marriage. When Vera appeals to her bitter, withholding mother, telling her she's pregnant, Mom asks which she prefers, a boy or girl. Vera unhesitatingly replies, "A boy!" Her mother regards the answer as indicative of Vera's fatal impracticality: "*I* wanted a girl so she could give me a hand." In a later scene, a fed-up Viktor reminds his parents, in his sister's presence, that they had wanted a second child only to qualify for a larger apartment.

Sergei, as surly as Vera in his way, appears at a dressy family dinner in his honor wearing shorts and a T-shirt. He refuses to play by the family rules, and when he moves into Vera's room— following the conventions for Soviet newlyweds—the balance of power in the little apartment is threatened. Cornered, Dad fights for his territory, aided by Mom, a mobilized Viktor, and finally by Vera.

Pichul's intentionally rough direction, at times with conspicuous hand-held camera, gives *Little Vera* an appropriately crude, cinema-vérité look—complemented by raw, and noisy, sound. The movie has plenty of flaws; it could use much tighter editing, for one. But its strongest point may be Khmelik's knowing screenplay, which overcomes early show-and-tell, next-news-bulletin tendencies to stick valiantly with the characters' grim destinies. Khmelik demonstrates impressive insight into cycles of rage and need, children's fear of expulsion even from suffocating environments.

I happened not to be wild about Vera. Negoda—who's managed to appear as *Playboy*'s May cover girl while going with an economist back in the USSR (a feat that may or may not contain internal contradictions)—seems only a passable actress, pouting on cue and looking a bit too mature for an 18-year-old. As Vera's parents, veterans Zaitseva and Nazarov are much more convincing as sad personalities further warped by degrading circumstances. Nazarov's confused father may be the movie's most sympathetic character. It's to *Little Vera*'s credit that each of its people emerges with a measure of dignity intact.

Also reviewed in:

NATION, 5/15/89, p. 675, Stuart Klawans
NEW REPUBLIC, 5/1/89, p. 30, Stanley Kauffmann
NEW YORK TIMES, 3/31/89, p. C18, Vincent Canby
VARIETY, 7/20/88, p. 14
WASHINGTON POST, 5/5/89, p. D1, Hal Hinson
WASHINGTON POST, 5/5/89, Weekend/p. 41, Desson Howe

LOCK UP

A Tri-Star Pictures release of a White Eagle Productions/Carolco Pictures presentation of a Gordon Company production. *Executive Producer:* Michael S. Glick. *Producer:* Lawrence Gordon and Charles Gordon. *Director:* John Flynn. *Screenplay:* Richard Smith, Jeb Stuart, and Henry Rosenbaum. *Director of Photography:* Donald

E. Thorin. *Editor:* Michael N. Knue and Donald Brochu. *Music:* Bill Conti. *Music Editor:* Stephen A. Hope. *Sound:* Charles Wilborn. *Sound Editor:* David B. Cohn. *Production Designer:* Bill Kenney. *Art Director:* William Ladd Skinner and Bill Groom. *Set Decorator:* Jerry Adams and George DeTitta Sr. *Special Effects:* Joe Digaetano. *Costumes:* Bernie Pollack. *Make-up:* Gary Liddiard. *Stunt Coordinator:* Frank Orsatti. *Running time:* 100 minutes. *MPAA Rating:* R.

CAST: Sylvester Stallone (Frank Leone); Donald Sutherland (Warden Drumgoole); John Amos (Meissner); Sonny Landham (Chink), Tom Sizemore (Dallas); Frank McCrae (Eclipse); Darlanne Fluegel (Melissa); William Allen Young (Braden); Larry Romano (First Base); Jordan Lund (Manly); John Lilla (Wiley); Dean Duval (Ernie); Jerry Strivelli (Louie Munafo); David Anthony Marshall (Mastrone); Robert Vazquez (Officer Vazquez); Tony Munafo (Prisoner); Frank Pesce (Johnson); Troy Curvey Jr. (Prison Receptionist).

LOS ANGELES TIMES, 8/4/89, Calendar/p. 14, Kevin Thomas

"Lock Up" is yet another Syvester Stallone macho fantasy in which he plays an underdog of superhuman endurance. Once again, his ability to survive extreme brutality is used to justify equally savage acts of revenge. As experienced a rabble-rouser as Stallone is, he by now defies credibility to the point of inviting unintended laughter.

As a convict at the mercy of Donald Sutherland's crazy prison warden and his equally sadistic goons, Stallone survives one horrific physical and psychological assault after another, yet emerges after each hideous session as smiling and relaxed as if he had spent a weekend in Palm Springs. Increasingly, Stallone has become the hero of live-action cartoons.

In his own view, Stallone's Frank Leone ought never have gone to prison in the first place. He was only avenging his foster father, an auto mechanic, after the old man had been attacked by thugs with "connections" that enabled them to get Leone sent up. When Sutherland's hateful Warden Drumgoole refuses to allow Leone a deathbed visit to his foster father, he breaks out, even though his sentence has only two weeks to run. The incident draws Leone additional time at a "country club" facility, but it also generates bad publicity for the warden, who is transferred to the notorious old Gateway penitentiary, a vast pile with an immense copper Beaux Arts dome. (All this has happened before the picture starts—and thus requires a heavy dose of exposition.)

In the darkness of night, the warden somehow manages to have Leone moved to Gateway, where he will have six months in which to destroy the convict. The warden may be a man obsessed, but Stallone's writers make sure their star has plenty of scenes in which he can display his good-natured camaraderie with the nicer convicts. Consequently, "Lock Up" veers constantly between unabashed sentimentality and unspeakable violence, all of it underlined broadly by Bill Conti's score.

As supremely silly as "Lock Up" (rated R) essentially is, it is the work of filmmakers who know exactly what they want and how to get it. Lean and tough, Stallone looks great, and so does this film. Although at 100 minutes it's overly long, it moves well under John Flynn's slam-bam, pumped-up direction. Much of the time Stallone is laid-back and humorous, confident enough in his star power to allow his supporting players showy turns: John Amos (as the Warden's adamantine but reflective second-in-command), Sonny Landham (as a looming, vicious con who does the warden's bidding), Tom Sizemore (as the garrulous prisoner Dallas), Frank McCrae (the hulking, kindly Eclipse) and Larry Romano (as the doomed, 20-year-old First Base).

Sutherland seems to have tongue firmly in cheek, and Darlanne Fluegel has precious few moments as Leone's rather dim-seeming fiancée. (Why doesn't she get the press to investigate Leone's transfer, for example?). As for Stallone, he's overdue in stretching his talent, not just his muscles.

MONTHLY FILM BULLETIN, 2/90, p. 44, Kim Newman

Frank Leone, a low-risk prisoner in Norwood Jail, has only six months to serve on a jailbreaking sentence and is planning for a future with his girlfriend Melissa. In the middle of the night, Leone is rousted by Meissner, a guard from the maximum security Gateway facility, and transferred to the rougher prison. Warden Drumgoole of Gateway, who has arranged the transfer, hates Leone because his career has been stalled since the prisoner's earlier escape, which was prompted by the warden's refusal to allow Leone, six days before his release on a trumped-up charge of aggravated assault, to visit his dying surrogate father. Drumgoole vows to break Leone, and encourages brutal guard Manly and convict Chink, the 'yard boss', to make life hard for him. Leone is befriended by the fast-talking Dallas, and in turn takes young lifer First Base under his wing. When First Base outrages Drumgoole by driving a car, which Leone and his friends have restored, around the yard, it is Leone who is taken into solitary and brutalised. Meissner disapproves and reprimands Manly for continually beating Leone, but Drumgoole pushes further. Chink murders First Base and Leone beats up the killer in the yard, winding up in hospital when one of Chink's gang stabs him in the back. An apparent psychopath visits Leone and tells him that when he is released next day he has been paid by Drumgoole to rape and murder Melissa. Leone enlists Dallas' aid in an escape attempt, but Dallas has sold out to Drumgoole to set him up and Leone is beaten by Manly and the guards, including the officer who posed as the psycho convict. Dallas, also beaten and betrayed, kills Manly and himself, and Leone seems to escape. However, while Meissner's guards are searching the area, Leone confronts Drumgoole and straps him into an obsolete but functional electric chair. Drumgoole confesses to Meissner that he wanted to force Leone to attempt an escape, and thereby receive a further ten-year sentence. Meissner has Drumgoole arrested, and Leone is released on schedule.

Given the premise of "Sylvester Stallone in jail", *Lock Up* is precisely what one would expect, with the regulation elements from previous prison movies—a bird fancier, a megalomaniac warden, flabbily sadistic guards, mind-cracking spells in solitary, mess hall shiv-stabbings, a likeable martyr to spur the hero to action, muddy rough-housing with a football in the yard, a gruelling escape attempt—thrown into a plot structured around Stallone's usual hymn to the indomitability of the blue-collar spirit ("Your body has to be in here, but your brain doesn't"). With an impeccable rationale for his initial incarceration, Stallone is every sinewy inch the uncompromised hero, while Donald Sutherland's leering Warden Drumgoole, quite the nastiest screen officer in a men's prison since Hume Cronyn in *Brute Force*, has had an antique electric chair restored and gloats over the opportunity to give his nemesis a guided tour of Hell.

As usual in Stallone movies, the lines are quickly and irrevocably drawn and, aside from the characters who are obvious psychotics (Drumgoole, Chink, Manly), everybody (even in "the worst shithole in this system") instinctively admires, likes and respects the star. The promised endless torment relaxes to allow for a lyrical fixing-the-car sequence scored with a song by the inappropriate Bill Conti, and Leone is soon surrounded by buddies among the cons and gaining the grudging respect of the good guards. Typical of the star's muscular liberalism is the film's refusal to cast a black actor in an unsympathetic role: both the guards who stand against Drumgoole and Manly are black, as is the cheerful head of the auto shop where Leone works, and even the one-scene cameo character who turns up to give the hero the bad news about First Base. Unlike most action movie stars, Stallone has yet to cast himself as a professional criminal hero, and too much time here is taken up with elaborations on his essential decency (looking after the vulnerable First Base) and modest ambitions (he wants to open a garage). When Clint Eastwood (*Escape from Alcatraz*) or Burt Reynolds (*The Longest Yard*) were sent to jail, their personae were rather more interestingly stretched by the genre.

NEW STATESMAN & SOCIETY, 2/9/90, p. 44, Suzanna Moore

I have never met a woman who fancied Sylvester Stallone. Evidently his ex-wife found it difficult too, but let's not get into that ... Nonetheless, Stallone, grunting and sweating like a pig, is thought to provide a suitably heroic role model for the masses. He is after all a man's man. And, most importantly, he always wins. But every dog has its day, and as we move into the caring, sharing nineties the Rambo mentality looks decidedly dated if not actually dead. So Sly is getting thoughtful and, in his new movie *Lock Up*, directed by John Flynn, he is getting positively philosophical.

He plays a "model prisoner", Leone, who has Paul Klee posters on his cell wall and talks a lot of ill-conceived psychobabble about mindsets and "up attitudes". He certainly needs an up attitude when he gets transferred to a maximum security hell-hole run by the very nasty Warden Drumgoole. Donald Sutherland, as Drumgoole, has a good time being thoroughly evil and trying to break Leone. Prison cliché is heaped on prison cliché and we get to see Stallone being endlessly beaten up, humiliated and being physical in his vest. Until, of course, he tries to break out.

Lock Up is at such pains to stress that Leone is a hero that it becomes positively nauseating—he can literally do no wrong. Quite why he is in prison in the first place is glossed over. Presumably he was in the wrong mindset. But in between the long stretches of Stallone's martyred body—the fetishisation of the wounded male is a staple of this genre and Stallone exploits it to the full—we have a wonderfully daft male bonding sequence. Led by Stallone, and with an appropriately soulful lovesong playing in the background, a gang of the nicer inmates restores a red Mustang in the garage. Men and engines and horseplay with hosepipes? Is it any wonder that we need to be continually reminded that Leone has got a suitably virginal blonde girlfriend waiting on the outside for him? As the homo-erotic subtexts of Stallone's and Schwarzenegger's films are pushed to the forefront, I'm still waiting for the day when they can discuss homosexuality explicitly—but I guess that would take a *real* hero.

NEW YORK, 8/4/89, p. 25, Jami Bernard

Muscular, sad-eyed Frank Leone and his girlfriend have a little hand thing they like to do, a symbol for "everything's OK," a wavy motion like something you'd expect from a girl-group's backup singers. But everything is not OK. You see, Frank is a convict, and he's about to be incarcerated in hell.

At least that's what the fiendish, vengeful warden promises him when Frank returns from furlough to his country-club prison, only to be removed abruptly in the middle of the night to Gateway, ostensibly the worst prison in the universe (and filmed at Rahway State Prison in New Jersey, itself not such a pleasant place).

There Frank is beset by sadisto guards, ugly galoomphs, a big guy who wants to steal his good-luck locket and other types to whom exercise hour means time to lift weights and break heads.

The warden is punishing Frank because Frank once made a fool of him. Does Frank deserve such bad treatment? No, he does not. He is Syvester Stallone, and he is the proverbial prisoner with the heart of gold. Whatever he was originally jailed for, you can bet it was something that was in the public interest, because Frank is the kind of stand-up guy who shares his rations, who saves bread crumbs for the Birdman of Gateway, who teaches a raw kid how to drive a car even though it gets Frank six weeks in solitary.

For its genre, and for a Sly Stallone movie, "Lock Up" isn't so bad. It has everything a prison movie should have: needless torture, mind-bending solitary confinement, odd moments of male bonding, constant threats of rape, plentiful stabbings.

There's a mudbath of a football game with overmiked body blows and lots of foul play. There's Stallone steaming under all this unfairness until his goat is finally gotten, and then it's action city, with plenty of opportunity for the audience to go crazy-nuts and make fools of themselves.

What more could you possibly want in a Stallone flick?

And don't say dialogue. Stallone doesn't need more than a heavy-lidded stare to convey all that he has on his mind. And when he does have his big speech, about how the warden owns them all and everything is no use, he says a whole lotta words, and then everyone is exhausted from the effort, so it's good that we can get back to the exercise yard where Frank is groaning in slow-motion.

Donald Sutherland plays a warden with a funny name, Drumgoole, and I don't know how he can keep a straight face quoting as he does from the Handbook for Heavies. But if someone must do it, it may as well be Sutherland, with his psychotic brush-cut hairdo. This is a warden whose hobby is restoring electric chairs, "This is hell—I'm going to give you the guided tour," he says, alluding to the House of Pain, which, forgive me, I thought was from "The Island of Lost Souls."

Sutherland palpitates with pleasure in his vainglorious attempts to break Frank's spirit—and he tries, he really does. Frank gets everything from a mouthful of fumigant to a knife in the kidney.

John Amos— remember Gordy the Weatherman?—is another sadisto guard whose facade cracks early; he turns into a softie just about the time Prisoner No. 510 needs a pal.

The violence here isn't gleefully over the top, as in the "Lethal Weapon" series, but for a certain type of fan, "Lock Up" is as good an entertainment as, say, mudbath football in a prison yard. Yo! To each his own.

NEWSDAY, 8/4/89, Part III/p. 5, Terry Kelleher

Boys, it doesn't get any better than this.

We're not talking about beer commercials. The subject is a slightly higher art form—Sylvester Stallone movies.

"My films are always about the lone man rising above his oppressors," the star declares in the production notes for "Lock Up," his latest. "It's a formula that I believe in because I think that life is a formula."

OK, if Stallone's going to stick with the formula, and he can't be Rocky or Rambo every time out, what other parts can he handle? His supercop in "Cobra" was *too* venomous. The arm-wrestling truck driver of "Over the Top" was more amiable but didn't deliver enough action.

In "Lock Up," Stallone has found an answer. His character is Frank Leone, an innocent convict (his only crime was taking the law into his own capable hands) tormented by the hateful Warden Drumgoole. No progressive penologist would have a name like that.

Frank is tough without being obnoxious about it. He's not boringly indestructible like Rambo, but he's blessed with Rocky's amazing recuperative powers. This hombre can dish it out, but he also has to take it. In fact, the more he takes it, the more you long to see him dish it out. How's that for a beautiful formula?

Going for an authentically grim look, director John Flynn shot a number of scenes at New Jersey's Rahway State Prison. Otherwise, realism is strictly beside the point. "Lock Up" positively revels in its use of Big House cliches.

"This is hell," announces Drumgoole, played by Donald Sutherland with his patented touch of supercilious evil. "You won't break me," Frank vows. "You'll never get away with it," warns the warden when a fed-up Frank finally makes his break. The plot and dialogue (except for the dirty words) could have come from any number of past prison movies. The bone-crushing football game is lifted from one in particular, "The Longest Yard."

The cons are fairly decent chaps once you get to know them—except for the inmates who form Drumgoole's hand-picked goon squad, led by the tirelessly menacing Chink (Sonny Landham). It's the brutal guards who really belong behind bars, though their captain (John Amos) eventually develops conscience pangs.

Yes, "Lock Up" is the kind of picture that requires you to check your brain at the ticket booth and load up on popcorn in the lobby. But Flynn has a sure hand with action (if not thought), as he proved in "Rolling Thunder" and last year's "Best Seller." Rooting interest grows as the hero takes a licking and keeps on ticking. and Tom Sizemore provides a dash of humor as a motor-mouth who insinuates himself into Frank's confidence.

Two factors keep "Lock Up" from receiving a full critical pardon. The first is Flynn's weakness for excessive violence. Even is a correctional institution, there should be a limit on shivs in the gut and kicks to the groin. The second problem is Frank's chronic gullibility, which might not be so annoying if he didn't espouse a sensible, self-protective philosophy: "DTA— Don't Trust Anybody."

Frank Leone is a lone man rising above his oppressors. He's also no Einstein. In other words, he's Sly Stallone's kind of guy.

VILLAGE VOICE, 8/15/89, p. 61, Amy Taubin

Lock Up, this summer's Sylvester Stallone vehicle, is a jail-house version of the Christians-to-the-lions story. The noble one (looking ever more like Victor Mature) endures repeated physical abuse but emerges unscarred and unbroken. With big burnished production values, *Lock Up* is probably his best film since *Rocky,* Whether out of genuine conviction, astute analysis of the demographics, or as a penance for the Rambo series, the film exhibits surprisingly good racial politics, though it's a trifle suspicious that one of the major bad guys (who, like all the other bad guys has blue eyes and pasty white skin) is nicknamed "Chink."

Also reviewed in:
NEW YORK TIMES, 8/4/89, p. C10, Stephen Holden
VARIETY, 8/9-15/89, p. 21
WASHINGTON POST, 8/4/89, p. B1, Hal Hinson

LODZ GHETTO

A Jewish Heritage Project film produced with a grant from the National Endowment for the Humanities and the Corporation for Public Broadcasting. *Executive Producer:* Stephen Samuels. *Producer:* Alan Adelson. *Director:* Kathryn Taverna and Alan Adelson. *Screenplay:* Alan Adelson. *Director of Photography:* Jozef Piwkowski and Eugene Squires. *Editor:* Kathryn Taverna. *Still Photography:* Gary Becker and Kathryn Taverna. *Music:* Wendy Blackstone. *Running Time:* 103 minutes. *MPAA Rating:* Not Rated.

VOICES: Jerzy Kosinsi (as Mordechai Chaim Rumkowski); Theodore Bikel, Nicholas Kepros, Barbara Rosenblat, David Warrilow.

LOS ANGELES TIMES, 11/29/89, Calendar/p. 5, Michael Wilmington

The textile center of Łódź in Poland once housed the second largest concentration of Jewry in Europe. Like many ghettos, it was a center of intense religious, intellectual and artistic activity, as well as the myriad joys and tribulations of day-to-day life. But, from 1940 to 1945, Łódź and its ghetto changed, terrifyingly. It became, successively, a prison, a wartime factory area and, finally, a way station for the charnel house.

In 1940, 200,000 of the city's Jews were forced into the 4½-square-mile ghetto. Penned in by barbed wire and German edicts, they were eventually joined by more than 20,000 refugees from neighboring countries. By the time Łódź was liberated in January, 1945, only about 800 survivors were left. The rest either died of starvation or illness or were herded off to Auschwitz and other camps during the frenzied slaughter ordered by Heinrich Himmler in his Reich's twilight.

Words can't do justice to tragedy and suffering on this scale. Neither, unfortunately, can "Łódź Ghetto," an often admirable documentary that falls into the trap of overdramatizing material that never needs it.

Faced with nearly unimaginable horror— hospitals emptied of the sick by ghetto police, chidren shot before their parents' eyes—only the simplest, purest eloquence is needed. Yet co-directors Alan Adelson and Kathryn Taverna push so hard for tragedy, trying to elaborate these cries of grief into a filmic Bach chorale, that they lose some force and anquish.

The script is developed from testimony preserved in journals and the speeches of the ghetto's controversial "elder," Mordechai Chaim Rumkowski. In their excellent source book for the movie, published by Viking, Adelson and Robert Lapides arrange these segments chronologically, with the speakers identified. But, in the film, since no voice is identified until the closing credits, they merge into one universal, almost abstracted chorus—which distances us.

So does the diction of the narrators, who include actors David Warrilow and Theodore Bikel. It's a bit too crisp, the shadings of hurt too expertly calculated. Sometimes, it sounds as incongruous as Orson Welles or William Conrad, in sonorous tones of pear-shaped passsion, lamenting about their imminent starvation.

Least convincing is novelist Jerzy Kosinski— an irony, since he was born in Łódź and lost his parents there. Kosinski plays Rumkowski with a strident, staccato Nazi-villain voice. Yet is it likely that this self-conscious leader would have revealed himself so unequivocally in public oratory? In Adelson's book, Oskar Rosenfeld (voiced here by several actors, including Bikel) describes Rumkowski's demeanor as "well-mannered, clean, calm, benevolent." Instead, Kosinski gives us the inner man—"cunning, spiteful, treacherous, predatory"—with no counterpoint between appearance and reality.

There was a horrible schism in Rumkowski. A Zionist who devoted his later life to charity work for orphans, he wound up sending children off to be murdered. Unlike the elders of the Warsaw Ghetto, he didn't take poison rather than aid the deportations. And unlike Warsaw, Łódź didn't rise up in futile but glorious revolt. That's the core of this story's terror.

To the extent that this flawed but compassionate documentary reveals that terror, it remains valuable. The words of the Łódź inhabitants—the poetic journalists Rosenfeld and Josef Zelkowicz, both of whom died in Auschwitz (along with Rumkowski); the pragmatic survivor Jakub Poznanski; the idealistic student Dawid Sierakowiak, who died at 19 of tuberculosis, and the earthy Irena Liebman, who survives to this day—all are the most powerful demonstration possible of something we often characterize too glibly as the human spirit.

That spitit can be pure and courageous, like the words that are its weapons here. It can be foul and murderous, like the Nazi tyrants. Or it can be simple and ingenuous, like most of the victims. "This tragedy has no heroes," Rosenfeld wrote. "And why call it a tragedy? Because the pain does not touch upon something human, on another's heart, but rather is something incomprehensible, linked with the cosmos. ...In the beginning, God created the Ghetto. ...."

Whatever their failings here—and there are more than a few—in re-creating that ghetto, Adelson and Taverna help rekindle an indispensable flame.

NEW YORK POST, 3/22/89, V.A. Musetto

Lodz is a city in central Poland. It was occupied by the Nazis starting in September 1939. From

1940 until their removal to death camps, more than 200,000 Jews—mostly Poles but also including 1,000 Czechs after the "de-Jewing" of Prague—were herded into the city's ghetto and used by Nazis as slave labor. Only 800 of the 200,000 would be alive for the liberation.

"Lodz Ghetto," opening today at Film Forum 1, is the chilling story of those atrocities. The soundtrack contains firsthand accounts of the terror, taken from diaries, letters and official pronouncements. It is woven together with extraordinary visuals—still photos taken (at extreme risk) by the victims themselves, color slides snapped by an unknown German, six minutes of film made by the Nazis, and footage of the ghetto as it looks today.

Most disturbing are the accounts of Mordechai Chaim Rumkowski, the Nazi-appointed leader of the ghetto, his voice recreated by writer Jerzy Kosinski, who was born in Lodz and lost his family there.

As the "eldest of the Jews" in the ghetto, Rumkowski offered to supply Jewish labor to the Nazis in return for food and other supplies. Factories to make guns and uniforms were set up, and the Jews were forced to work 12-hour days to further the German war effort.

Rumkowski pleaded with his fellow Jews to work hard and obey the Germans. "Work protects us from annihilation," he told them. "Nothing bad will happen to people of good will."

Many of the Jews believed Rumkowski would protect them from death. They were wrong, of course. And in the end, even Rumkowski and his family would be put aboard a train for the ride to Auschwitz.

Ironically, the trick used by the Germans to get Lodz Jews on the trains was an offer to protect them from the advancing Russian army which, the Jews were told, would not look favorably on those who cooperated with the Nazis. Most were taken in by the trick, but some went into hiding rather than go.

We hear one account of 40 people who hid for months in a 30-foot-deep ice cellar. "Our nerves are shattered, but we're not sorry we defied the Germans," one wrote in his diary after nine weeks. "He who hides, survives."

"Lodz Ghetto," directed by Kathryn Taverna and Alan Adelson, is first-rate filmmaking. It isn't always easy to watch, but it should be seen.

NEWSDAY, 3/22/89, Part II/p. 10, Leo Seligsohn

Forty-nine years ago this month—six months after they marched into Poland—the Germans began the methodical destruction of 200,000 Jews in Lodz, Poland.

"Lodz Ghetto" is a powerful telling of that story, distilling all talk to the words left behind in diaries, letters and official pronouncements by the doomed inhabitants.

The result is an elegy of sorts—a dark, wide-ranging cinematic poem, richly dramatized and scrupulously illustrated. Some of the footage and still photos are rare. Rarer still is the cumulative voice the documentary builds as it unwinds through months and years in the ghetto. The victims didn't know their fate when these pictures were being taken or what was in store when they wrote the words we hear. We know, of course.

"Lodz Ghetto" taps into that notion of timelessness, of then-and-now, of not-knowing-and-knowing. It is captured in the opening quote: "Listen, and believe this, even though it happened here. Even though it sounds so old, so distant, and so foreign." The movie begins with shots of Lodz streets today. It fades to the same intersections, the same buildings—circa 1940-45. Soon, old images are overpowering the new and the story begins.

The Germans had a scenario. They enclosed the ghetto behind barbed wire and then brought in 1,000 more Jews, Czechs, refugees from the "de-Jewing" of Prague. They put the able-bodied to work in ghetto factories, making uniforms for the Germans. At the same time, they started sending inhabitants out on "the transports" in ever greater numbers. Told they were being relocated, they died at Auschwitz.

While much of the nightmare is familiar, the Lodz story differs from other Holocaust accounts in one respect. It thrusts a man named Mordechai Chaim Rumkowski into a role for which a parallel in human history would be hard to find. Statesmanlike, wearing a Homburg and horn-rimmed glasses, Rumkowski was the ghetto's Jewish fuhrer. What his Nazi handlers asked him to do, he did. He was the ultimate appeaser. Novelist-actor Jerzy Kosinski, born in Lodz, speaks the words Rumkowski once uttered:

"Dictatorship is not an ugly word. With it, I earn the German's respect." And: "Work protects us from annihilation." Then: "I give you my word of honor...Nothing bad will happen to people of good will." Finally: "If we deliver our victims by ourselves, there will be peace. . . Jews of the ghetto, come to your senses! Volunteer for the transports." Under orders, he implored parents to part with their children. The Germans were demanding 20,000 under the age of 10. They threatened take 24,000 if they were rebuked.

Jews who resisted were shot or hanged. One segment captures the horror of one multiple execution. Rumkowski, at the same time, was warning the ghetto about a prison he had built for demonstrators and troublemakers. Ultimately, the Germans sent him to a death camp. There were 800 ghetto inhabitants who hid and survived till the end of the war—one group of 340 in a 30-foot-deep ice cellar, which is shown, toward the end of the documentary, as it looks today.

My only small quibble with the film is the occasional use of the motif of the kneading of dough and baking of bread in a large Lodz bakery today. As the loaves are shoveled into fiery ovens, the life-death symbolism seems superfluous, if not intrusive. Moving background music and simple words from the past are better: "Henushi, my golden child, I think of you constantly. I'm alone and in my pain. Are you as gray as I am now? I see you."

Words such as these, gleaned from among the thousands that were researched, are ultimately what sets "Lodz Ghetto" far apart from the ordinary.

VILLAGE VOICE, 3/28/89, p. 57, J. Hoberman

Europe has its phantom geography—part of which is mapped by Kathryn Taverna and Alan Adelson's *Lodz Ghetto*, currently at Film Forum. The Manchester of Poland, Lodz had a prewar population of some 250,000 Jews. After the Nazi invasion, the city was renamed Litzmannstadt and incorporated into the Reich, its Poles were dispersed, its Germans augmented by "colonists," and its Jews imprisoned in a squalid ghetto—the first to be established in Poland and the last to be liquidated, in part because of the maneuvering of a mad Jewish politician named Mordechai Chaim Rumkowski.

The story of the Lodz ghetto crystalizes the Jewish dilemma under Nazi rule. Systematically starved, brutalized, and isolated from the gentile population, Jews were left to cut a deal with the conquerors as best they could; continually hoping the worst was over, many saw no choice but to follow leaders offering short-term solutions. The 62-year-old Rumkowski, a failed textile manufacturer and minor community activist, became the head of the *Judenrat* (Jewish council) or, in the quasi-medieval jargon favored by the Nazis, the "eldest" of the Jews. Turning the entire ghetto into a giant slave-labor sewing factory, Rumkowski bought time for many Jews by feeding the Nazi deportation quotas with those too sick, too old, or too young to work—including, inevitably, the parents and children of his captive constituents.

There is an Old Testament quality to Rumkowski's terrible self-deception. On the eve of annihilation, he set up his own "perfect" Jewish community, complete with social welfare programs, security police, and a bureau of statistics that chronicled every aspect of ghetto life. This abundance of written and photographic documentary material is one aspect of Lodz's uniqueness, as was Rumkowski's personality. The "king" had his portrait printed on the worthless ghetto money and postage stamps, commissioned poets and artists to celebrate his reign. One might say that Rumkowski reproduced Nazi rule as farce, except that, when the deportations to the death camps began in earnest, he held the power of life and death over his subjects.

A horrifying and pathetic figure attempting to make sense of unresolvable moral questions, Rumkowski holds considerable fascination for students of the Holocaust. He is cited at some length by Saul Bellow in *Mr. Sammler's Planet*; served as the inspiration for Leslie Epstein's problematic 1979 novel, *The King of the Jews*; and appears in at least two English-language plays and a number of works by the Lodz-born Yiddish writer Rachmil Bryks, who was deported to Auschwitz for reciting a poem that mocked the king. The literature on Lodz is extensive as well. Lucjan Dobroszycki, another survivor of the ghetto, recently edited a 500-plus-page volume of documents; the archival photographs formed the basis for *The Story of Chaim Rumkowski and the Jews of Lodz*, an exemplary documentary made for Swedish television in 1982 by Peter Cohen and Bo Kuritzen.

Painfully unsentimental, *The Story of Chaim Rumkowski* presents this material with stark, relentless understatement. *Lodz Ghetto*,, which draws on many of the same images, is painful both to watch and to write about—albeit for different reasons. Whereas the Swedish documentary is distanced, the American one is an impressionistic narrative that opens with a trolley ride through contemporary Lodz, then a match-cut back to the German occupation in 1939. The effect is startling, but, in the worst tradition of the movies, *Lodz Ghetto* seems driven by no necessity beyond the momentary shock. Rushing desperately at its subject, it is at best a movie of lacerating fragments and jagged details.

Devoid of all but the simplest visual rhetoric, *The Story of Chaim Rumkowski* could almost be a slide show. *Lodz Ghetto*, by contrast, is fearfully overwrought—understandably, if unfortunately, suffused with a kind of nervous hysteria. Taverna and Adelson search for movement everywhere they can, cutting and tracking, fashioning a busy soundtrack in which the testimony of victims is dramatized over a musical hodgepodge, by turns sentimental and atonal. (As a friend of mine who has been working with Holocaust material for a dozen years, and living with it all his life, said, "The movie does your crying for you.")

In its use of Auschwitz documentation, Harun Farocki's recent *Images of the World and the Inscription of War* suggests that each photograph is in itself the subject for a movie; Adelson and Taverna, however, crop and zoom with abandon, mitigating the power of their archival material with interpolated modern shots (and vice versa), bombarding the viewer with grotesquely "emotional" readings of anonymous quotes. The filmmakers seem never to have considered the problem of these callow performances or reckoned with the audience's having to filter the words through the distraction of actors acting. (The shrill, Lodz-accented exhortations of Jerzy Kosinski, who "plays" Rumkowski, is a partial exception; Rumkowski is at least part of Kosinski's childhood memory.)

Part of the greatness of Claude Lanzmann's *Shoah* lies in its evocation of absence, its powerful restraint, and its utter scrupulousness in questioning the conventions of cinematic representation. The Holocaust is now so bound up with (Ashkenazi) Jewish identity that one is tempted to connect this principled refusal to illustrate that which cannot even be imagined with the Hebrew injunction against graven images, or speaking the name of God—although it is also a strategy that compels the viewer to experience the remains of the remains. The irony is that *Lodz Ghetto*'s frontal assault drives spectators to seek refuge in programmed responses. One can only approach such devastating subject matter obliquely, as in the awful tenderness of Christian Boltanski's piles of discarded clothing or his wall pieces constructed from blurry photographs of forgotten children.

Lodz Ghetto never acknowledges its own impossibility, the paradox of representing what can only be trivialized by representation. "We read books on Auschwitz," Maurice Blanchot explains in *The Writing of the Disaster*. "The wish of all, in the camps, the last wish: know what has happened, do not forget, and at the same time never will you know."

Also reviewed in:
NEW YORK TIMES, 3/22/89, p. C19, Stephen Holden
VARIETY, 12/28/88–1/3/89, p. 12

LOOK WHO'S TALKING

A Tri-Star Pictures release of an M.C.E.G. production. *Producer:* Jonathan D. Krane. *Director:* Amy Heckerling. *Screenplay:* Amy Heckerling. *Director of Photography:* Thomas Del Ruth. *Editor:* Debra Chiate. *Music:* David Kitay. *Music Editor:* Frank McKelvey. *Choreographer:* Mary Ann Kellogg. *Sound:* Ralph Parker. *Art Director:* Reuben Freed and Graeme Murray. *Set Decorator:* Barry W. Brolly. *Set Dresser:* Dan Hanen, Herb Noseworthy, Al Schedler, Faye Thorp, John G. Kennedy, Nancy Ford, and Geordie Tocher. *Special Effects:* Bill Orr. *Costumes:* Molly Maginnis. *Make-up:* Todd McIntosh. *Stunt Coordinator:* Rick Avery. *Running time:* 93 minutes. *MPAA Rating:* PG-13.

CAST. John Travolta (James); Kirstie Alley (Mollie); Olympia Dukakis (Rosie); George Segal (Albert); Abe Vigoda (Grandpa); Bruce Willis (Voice of Mikey); Twink Caplan (Rona); Jason Schaller, Jaryd Waterhouse, Jacob Haines, and Christopher Aydon (Mikey); Joy Boushel (Melissa); Don S. Davis (Dr. Fleisher); Louis Heckerling (Lou); Brenda Crichlow (Secretary); Andrea Mann (Salesgirl); Douglas Tuck (Cab Stealer); Alex Bruhanski (Street Worker); B. Casey Grant (Admitting Clerk); Oscar B. Ramos (Hospital Worker); Aurelio DiNunzio (Orderly); Jeff Irvine (Admitting Doctor); Shirley Barclay (Nurse); William B. Davis (Drug Doctor); David Berner (Mr. Impatience); Jerry Wasserman (Mr. Anal); Daliah Novak (Carrie); Zena Darawalla (Lupe); Nicholas Rice (Harry); Neal Israel (Mr. Ross); Blu Mankuma (Director); William Britos (Home Orderly); Deejay Jackson (Burly Orderly); Ida Berner, Bea Cartmell, and Eleanor Maines (Ladies); Mollie Israel (Little

Girl); Ryan McIntosh (Little Boy); Gerry Bean and Deryl Hayes (Pilot Friends); Enid Saunders (Ester); Nicole Stevens (Silly Baby); Christy Smith (Baby Megan); Sabrina Bailey (Sand Box Baby); Farah Abassi (Chatting Baby); Amber Brownmiller (Blowing Kiss Baby).

FILMS IN REVIEW, 1–2/90, p. 39, Edmond Grant

It's astounding. It's amazing. To think that an awful-scripted, resolutely dumb gimmick movie could set a new boxoffice record and then remain number one in ticket sales nationwide for more than a month. It's unthinkable.

But, it should come as no surprise, it's all true. *Look Who's Talking* had the highest grossing first weekend *ever* for a picture released on a non-holiday weekend (remember, Spielberg and Lucas debut their releases around the holidays). Then, despite the fact that the first audiences should have spread the word of mouth that, yes, the kid is cute, but the movie is *bad*, it went on to stay in the number one box office slot for a number of weeks afterward, earning over $50 million in the process.

That first weekend statistic isn't surprising. A TV advertising blitz nicely encapsulated the film's concept (about all that could be accentuated), while print ads that were a solid echo of *Raising Arizona* (baby in sunglasses over block lettering) began cropping up in the newspapers. The concept seemed promising to the millions of movie-goers who had made hits out of *Baby Boom* and *Three Men And A Baby* (this is putting aside the audiences who stayed away in droves from the "baby" cycle's last two gasps, *For Keeps* and *She's Having A Baby*).

Well, the concept is a cute one. In fact, it could be the premise for a very entertaining skit on a variety show or the subject of a silly TV movie. As the entire *raison d'etre* of a feature film, though, it's decidedly skimpy, and as executed here by writer-director Amy Heckerling, it's often pathetic. In case you've missed the publicity blitz, the surprisingly good reviews given by critics reputed to have some form of taste, or (gasp) the film itself, here's the gimmick/concept: Single mother Kirstie Alley gives birth to a baby who does numerous precocious things, and, unbeknownst to her, comments on them (and everything else around him) in the voice of Bruce Willis, the hip-for-fifteen-minutes star of that quickly obsolete 80s' hit, *Moonlighting*, who somehow acquired a legitimate film career despite a noticeable lack of any true charm or versatility.

What an idea. A baby that thinks with the voice of Bruce Willis (and, even more frightening, the movie opens with a *sperm* who speaks with the voice of Bruce Willis). While they were at it, Ms. Heckerling and the producers decided to make the film even more of an oddball item by casting in the somewhat pathetic role of the Mr. Right cabbie who courts Kirstie a somewhat bloated John Travolta, the hip-for-fifteen-minutes star of the 70s, whose last feature was something called *The Experts* that was of such dubious merit that it was never given a U.S. theatrical release.

And to further the freakishness, why not add some well recognized character actors? How about Olympia Dukakis as the concerned mother, pleasant and talented George Segal in the thankless role of the slimy businessman who jilts Kirstie (and is the Willis-speak baby's biological father), and poor old Abe Vigoda (who acts *sans* dentures throughout his scenes here) as Travolta's grandfather?

But putting all questions of taste, form, and hapless casting aside for a moment, let us confront the movie's central issue, the question that supersedes all others: what will the baby say next, and will it be as funny as the quips featured in the creatively edited ads that have been showing on television? Well, it's apparent that the filmmakers had no idea what the baby would say when the movie was being shot, because at points the baby's remarks seem like a justification for whatever the kid on screen chose to do—at one particularly sad moment, the child actor reaches to tug at Vigoda's eyebrow's, as the Willis voice says, "Hey, what's these big furry things here. I'll give them a tug." Give us a break.

These remarks, incidentally, were not the work of Ms. Heckerling. The true source was revealed when John Travolta came on the "Joan Rivers Show" to plug the movie. Yes. Joan and her writing partner concocted the dazzling repartee that Mikey (the child's character name) enacts with ease. The creative process for this bit of scripting involved watching footage of the child actor's antics and supplying humorous dialogue to fit the given situation.

The child actor (actually there are four boys who play Mikey at different ages, the last one being clearly old enough to speak for himself) may have been improvising, but the rest of the cast simply phoned in their work. Kirstie Alley makes occasional attempts at performance; in fact much of the film is centered around her efforts to find Mikey a suitable father. Travolta, however, plays his cabbie character as an older, paunchier Vinnie Barbarino. Everyone else is just along for the ride, except Willis who manages to overact without even being seen.

During its running time, *Look Who's Talking* does earn one special distinction; it is the hands-down best example ever of a film set in the U.S., but shot in Canada, that *never for one moment* appears to be taking place in an American city. Heckerling and her producers should have realized that the sloping , skyscraper-less streets of Vancouver make a very poor substitute for the real thing, the cluttered, filthy streets of New York. Other films have done quite nicely substituting a Canadian city for an American one, but here further attention is drawn to the disparity by the fact that two (count 'em, two) speeding car chases figure prominently in the plot. One would think that by making a baby the star attraction, the producers had already done enough to lure in their audience, but evidently they had so little confidence in the insipid script that they felt these chase sequences were needed. (Perhaps they could have also used Jim Belushi's *K-9* co-star to pick up the slack that still remains.)

Ms. Heckerling has directed one great film, *Fast Times At Ridgemont High;* hopefully the talent that she evidenced there will return at some future date. For now, we can only be grateful that the film's final joke, Mikey's newborn baby sister speaking with the voice of Joan Rivers, didn't become a gruesome reality (better Bruce's verbal swagger than Joan's infernal whining). But then again, there's always the possibility of a sequel. . . .

LOS ANGELES TIMES, 10/13/89, Calendar/p. 12, Chris Willman

Filmgoers fed up with the plethora of cute movie toddlers may want to steer clear of "Look Who's Talking," the opening minutes of which offer a special-effects look at the process of conception, taking precociousness to its most utter and horrifying extreme: Bruce Willis as a talking, smart-aleck sperm.

"Come on, guys! This way!" says Willis in voice-over, leading a brigade of tadpole-like swimmers toward the mecca that is the ovum of unexpectedly expectant mother Kirstie Alley, who has just been impregnated by a married man weaselly caricatured by George Segal. It's a resolutely cute opener.

So is the rest of the movie but, rather surprisingly, given the gimmicky premise, it's not gag-me-with-a-pacifier cute nearly as often as it is genuinely charming. Movies in which animals, babies or other voiceless beings speak their thoughts rarely work, but part of the strength of "Look Who's Talking" is that Willis, as the sperm/fetus/baby, isn't *always* talking. There's enough fairly witty interplay between Alley, suitor John Travolta and the other grown-ups that the picture could conceivably work even without the baby talk.

Another unexpected strength is that it's as much from the woman's point of view as it is from the infant's, thanks to writer-director Amy Heckerling, whose own mothering experiences account for much of the casual insight of the script. It doesn't skimp on its unwed, 35-ish mother's *Angst:* "You have no idea how hard it is to love someone so much who looks like someone you hate," Alley tells her son, whose teary missing-in-action daddy has yet to meet him.

One mistake Heckerling does make is in painting her bright mother-to-be as such a sap when it comes to married men. A woman like Alley might stay indefinitely with a smarmy toad like Segal, sure, but to really, really believe all those excuses he makes for not leaving his wife? Not likely.

In any case, Alley has been predictably abandoned in favor of a less rotund mistress by the time she goes into contractions. At this point, she's lucky enough to flag down New York's foolhardiest taxi driver, Travolta, who also has enough of a sweet streak that he abandons his cab to assist in the delivery.

Travolta eventually ends up baby-sitting, and the kid is much quicker to identify him as a primo daddy candidate than his mom is. It's been set up early on that Alley fantasizes her dates as prospective stepfathers, so once she and Travolta fall into bed, her amorous impulses are immediately stifled by an amusing fantasy of her future life as a blue-collar housefrau playing barefoot baby-maker to a portly, beer-popping Travolta.

Heckerling's feminist tendencies don't prevent her from writing her share of crass dialogue, like the "needle-removal" scene here, with Olympia Dukakis overhearing and misunderstanding an innocent exchange.

Yet by and large, after bottoming out with the John Hughes script of "European Vacation," this is Heckerling's chance to prove herself again as a director and for the first time as a writer;

the sensitivity that informed the best moments of her first feature, "Fast Times at Ridgemont High," is rampant here. And if the desire for fast comic timing causes her to skirt the more painful issues she has dredged up, at least there's a sense of timing here, which is a lot to ask for these days.

Hackerling's revival is also the ideal comeback for Travolta, who—after the annoying aerobics of "Staying Alive," "Perfect" and "The Experts"—was badly in need of a role requiring little physicality and maximum gentleness. He's every bit as charming and vulnerable as we've all forgotten he could be, and Alley, too, is little short of perfect in her most appealing part to date.

As for the baby's-eye view of the affair, about half of Willis' lines in "Look Who's Talking" (MPAA-rated PG-13 for language and sexuality) are as cloying as you might expect, but the other half actually make a decently funny stab at approximating an infant's singleminded mindset. Never mind that the animatronic doll that stands in for the fetus looks suspiciously like the Chucky of "Child's Play." At least they haven't tried to make the baby a cynic; in fact, there's very little that's cynical about this surprisingly smart, sweet-tempered movie. W.C. Fields and his philosophical kin need not apply, of course.

MONTHLY FILM BULLETIN, 4/90, p. 113, John Pym

New York. Mollie, a thirty-three-year-old unmarried accountant, becomes pregnant by Albert, one of her firm's clients, a childishly selfish businessman incapable of leaving his wife and two daughters. She tells her parents, Rosie and Lou, both also accountants, that she has been artificially inseminated by an anonymous medical student. Mollie's hopes of marriage evaporate when she catches Albert in a dress shop grappling with Melissa, his office decorator. Albert declares he is in love, whereupon Mollie's waters break; she hurtles to St. Jerome's Hospital in a taxi driven by the kindly James. Unknown to Mollie, James attends the birth of baby Mikey. Later, James becomes Mikey's regular babysitter in exchange for Mollie turning a blind eye to his use of her address as a means of getting his grandfather Vincent into a residential home. A bond grows between James and Mikey, a normal child, but like all other babies, the owner of a grown-up interior voice and a full set of laid-back adult emotions. After three disastrous dates, the last deliberately sabotaged by the babysitter, Mollie allows herself to be taken up in a twin-engine airplane by James (a part-time flying instructor). That evening, however, as they make love, she is incapacitated by a vision of slobbish family life with the beer-bellied James. Albert attempts a reconciliation, but is violently rebuffed by James on his first visit to Mikey and is later baffled as a furious Mollie defiles his expensive new desk. Mollie defuses a crisis over Vincent at the residential home, but is uncertain how to approach the still-offended James. Mikey, meanwhile, toddles off and is carried away inside a broken-down car on the back of a towtruck. James saves the baby from a pile-up and is rewarded with his first word ... Later, James takes Mikey to hospital to meet his new sister Julie.

There is no great novely in this relaxed and agreeable comedy—it begins with a school of tadpole sperm, one of which must surely be young Woody Allen, feverishly wriggling towards its goal with many a whoop of encouragement from the leader—except for the device of the talking babies. Mikey, who seems to have been affected by the analgesic given Mollie during his birth, is a very cool customer indeed; he goes with the flow, like any self-respecting hippy, and is happiest in the company of James, a character who, apart from a sense of responsibility to his grandfather, now in his second childhood, is very much the freeloading baby himself. "Don't start with me, kid", says Mikey's wrinkled sister, clearly a future accountant. "I've had a day you wouldn't believe. Can we talk ...?"

Amy Heckerling's script favours the ladies. Despite a curious weakness for the unashamedly selfish Albert, Mollie is that modern heroine, a capable, uncomplaining, but sentimentally soft-centred single thirtysomething-year-old; and she has in Olympia Dukakis's Rosie a mother to match. The men, by comparison, are frail plants: toothless Grandpa; spineless, irksome Albert (an ingratiating George Segal), a dismal file of single men who take Mollie out on excruciating dates, and one of whom she has to pay for herself. What prevents the comedy from being an entirely one-sided contest, however, is John Travolta, who has developed into an accomplished straight-man. In this instance, he carries off that dangerous quality, throwaway wholesomeness, with practised and surprising geniality. The film should probably carry a warning that it is not for spectators with an aversion to babies (a soiled nappy is triumphantly upturned on Albert's desk, and there are, perhaps, too many cute messy meals). But this is effervescent, well-acted comedy, and satisfyingly delivers a happy ending that is visible well in advance (Mikey's first word is, of course, "Dada"). An enterprising exhibitor might consider playing *Look Who's Talking* with writer-director Amy Heckerling's first film, *Getting It Over With* (1977), an engagingly innocent short comedy about a college girl's determination to lose her virginity.

NEW STATESMAN & SOCIETY, 4/13/90, p. 45, Suzanne Moore

Whoever would have thought that when the original medallion man himself was practising his disco moves in front of the mirror, this vain creature would be reincarnated some 12 years later as a caring, sharing new man? But John Travolta has done just that. He has made it from snake-hipped Tony Manero in *Saturday Night Fever* to lovable cabbie and surrogate daddy in *Look Who's Talking*. You've come a long way, baby, as they used to say in those horrible American cigarette ads. And there days you can't go a long way without a baby tucked under your arm somewhere.

The premise of *Look Who's Talking*—a baby that comments on every situation—might at first sound radical. But, when you hear that the baby's innermost thoughts are to be conveyed with a voice-over from Bruce Willis your heart sinks. Written and directed by Amy Heckerling, *Look Who's Talking* is as yucky as babyfood. It works best as an advert for anti-abortionists and that awful organisation Families Need Fathers. So you'll no doubt be pleased to hear that it has already spawned a spin-off TV series and a sequel.

Its pre-credit sequence is quite astonishing. An army of manic spermatozoa, led by the Bruce Willis sperm, shouting "Come on boys, it's this way" swim towards the silent, waiting egg. Like many women, I find it impossible to conceive (pardon the pun) of sperm as sweet little things. Giving them "personalities" merely adds insult to injury.

Predictably enough, in *Look Who's Talking*, the Bruce Willis sperm gets there first, turning into a Bruce Willis embryo. (Didn't anyone tell the filmmakers that embryos look more like something out of *Alien* rather than cute plastic dolls?). Mollie (Kirstie Alley from *Cheers*) is the receptacle that all this is taking place inside of an uptight accountant who has been impregnated by one of her married clients Albert (George Segal). Unfortunately, Albert explains "I'm going through a selfish phase right now." Mollie ends up a single mother, but not before she has met Our John who plays a sweeter than sweet taxi driver.

The baby is born. It wisecracks continually in Bruce Willis's voice, which makes you wonder why it wasn't strangled at birth. Travolta, all goofy smiles and stupid remarks, babysits regularly while Mollie looks for a suitable father for her offspring. We know, of course, that the man she needs is at home playing *Saturday Night Fever* with the baby who wants him to be his daddy. But he is poor and working-class and she is looking for something more upmarket.

There is very little difference between Travolta's character and that of the baby: they are both cute in that infantile way that seems to go down such a storm in the States. The best kind of new man, it would appear, has the mind of a one-year-old. Or, perhaps more optimistically, one-year-olds are new men in the making.

A nice contrast to all this completely uncalled-for gooeyness is some real goo. It's served up to sublime effect in Brian Yuzna's *Society*—a horror movie that is more hilarious than horrific.

Yuzna himself describes *Society* as "psychofiction" rather than pure horror, and if anything, one of the problems of the film is that it is a little too knowing in what it is doing, its message superimposed instead of integral to the story. Sometimes repression has provided the richest material for horror films. Indeed, the themes of this movie have been the staple of much horror, resting as they do on giving teenage alienation a physical reality and locating the monstrous aspects of our culture firmly within what has become known as "the underclass".

Society reverses this: teenage hero Bill starts to get paranoid about his own super-rich, super-normal Beverly Hills family. Not only does his family look like neo-Nazis, but his sister was involved in ritual sex with her parents and with most of polite society. Meanwhile, members of Bill's peer group are being bumped off one by one as he dumps his cheerleader girlfriend in favour of the flirty Clarissa. It is Clarissa's mutant mother—a sort of Divine-like zombie who steals the show.

It all ends with an orgy of silme and special effects, and apart from *Society's* cynical attitude to the family, the last ten minutes alone make the film worth seeing. Most of all though, while everyone is falling over themselves to deny such feelings existed, it's a joy to see a film that reinstates both a thoroughly proper class hatred and a thoroughly necessary class war.

NEW YORK, 11/13/89, p. 110, David Denby

I was surprised by something in Amy Heckerling's first film as director, *Fast Times at Ridgemont High*—a scene of sexual initiation, shot from a teenage girl's point of view, in which the camera took in the underside of a baseball-dugout roof as the girl lay on the bench below. Heckerling has had her troubles recently, but she still has the gift of empathy—and she puts her camera in the strangest places. Her new, surprise hit, *Look Who's Talking,* is often dumb and obvious, but the comic ideas keep flowing,one after another, and some of them are charming. I enjoyed the spermatozoa swimming upstream for their meeting with destiny, and the babies talking to themselves, rational creatures marveling at grown-ups' obtuseness. Kirstie Alley is pleasant but uninspired as a woman with poor taste in men, but John Travolta—puffy-looking, yet still handsome—is extremely charming as an unaggressive young man born to be a father. I can't recall audiences' yearning so openly for two characters to get together in marriage.

NEW YORK POST, 10/13/89, p. 28, Jami Bernard

Well, it was a long shot, and it didn't work.

Having the voice of Bruce Willis fill in for the possible thoughts of a fetus in Kirstie Alley's womb is such a bizarre concept that—who knows? Maybe it could have gestated into something. And having single mom Alley fall in love with the taxi driver (John Travolta, no less) who rushes her to the hospital when she goes into labor is so...New York. Or at least the New York that Hollywood probably envisioned when some bonehead gave this a green light.

Nobody wanted this movie to succeed more than I did (except, perhaps, the people who put money or reputations into it). Falling in love with your taxi driver? The guy who speaks just enough English to tell you he's never heard of Manhattan? This oughta be rich.

Alley plays Mollie, an uptight accountant who is having an affair with a married heel (a whiny George Segal). She decides to keep the love child, if you call that love, and then interview a succession of dates as to their daddy eligibility.

She does not realize, as we do just as soon as the meter drops, that handsome cabbie James (Travolta) has been in love with Mollie ever since he watched her giving birth to little Mikey. Since then, he has been babysitting Mikey for free, because you know how sensitive and family-oriented New York cabbies can be.

Listen, we could forgive all that, really we could, were it not that "Look Who's Talking" is utterly, painfully embarrassing, to the actors and the audience. Olympia Dukakis as Mollie's plain-speaking mom is encouraged to be lewd and obvious. The beautiful Alley is made as unattractive and scheming and silly a woman as ever tried to snare a man for the wrong reasons. Willis' sarcastic voice-overs for this exceptionally unmotivated baby-actor looks like a bad dub of a foreign movie, and his funny lines hit their mark only about one in five.

Worst of all, Travolta, who has been in cinematic hibernation for years, is forced to play off his "Saturday Night Fever" memories, showing how right he is for Mikey by doing the hustle around Mollie's kitchen. This dance step is a little outdated in a movie in which a single woman brings a baby into the world with less thought than she'd give to organizing her Filofax.

Like Dukakis, Travolta is encouraged to mug playfully. In a movie with a baby, let the baby be cute! At least once!

The wretched excess and missed comedic opportunities (and there were not many to start with) are the province of writer and director Amy Heckerling ("Fast Times at Ridgemont High," "National Lampoon's European Vacation"). Her idea of humor is endless shots of the baby spitting up food, or gramps spitting up food, or Travolta inadvertently administering breast milk to his coffee.

The one good thing about the movie are the fluid pink shots of sperm scurrying to make their appointed rounds to soundtrack accompaniment of "I Get Around" and excited male voices yelling, "Yee-hah!" The special-effects embryo is also very encouraging. Once the baby is born, though, he is an ill-used prop who is more likely to arouse fear of parenthood in the audience than any goo-goo sympathy.

Funny line: George Segal explaining why he can't leave his wife for the pregnant Mollie—"I'm going through a selfish phase right now."

Unfunny line: When Mollie tells her cab driver that she was artificially inseminated, he responds: "Are you a lesbo?"

Funny bit: Willis' voice-over as the baby feels the effects of mom's Demerol injection.

Unfunny bit: To show that Mollie's dates are not right for her, the script has them talk about things like barium enemas. In detail.

Travolta, sloppily amiable as the camera pokes itself into his face with regularity, at least looks like he's happy to be back on film.

The baby, however, looks troubled. One of the first things the baby says, courtesy of Willis, upon being born, is, "Put me back!" If only the film reel could have said that as it left its canister to be projected in theaters near you.

NEWSDAY, 10/13/89, Part III/p. 5, Terry Kelleher

If a baby could talk, what would a baby say? "Gimme some milk." "Change my diaper." "Don't drop me, stupid." Things like that.

They sound funny in the voice of an adult. Sid Caesar has been doing the routine for decades. Just imagine he's an infant in a crib and he'll have you laughing for 10 minutes.

Now here's a whole movie with the same concept. It lasts 10 times as long and requires no imagination. This is not progress.

The ads say the baby in "Look Who's Talking" has "John Travolta's smile, Kirstie Alley's eyes and the voice of Bruce Willis." That's a mite misleading. Alley is the unwed mother. George Segal is the married philanderer who fathers her child. John Travolta is the handsome cabbie who wants to be the permanent man in Alley's life.

But forget the smile and the eyes. It's the voice—rather, the voice-over—that counts. Willis starts speaking for Baby Mikey from the time he's a mere spermatozoon. As a fetus, Mikey calls for apple juice and wonders aloud at the development of his male organ. Soon he's out in the world, and his quips (which only the audience and, apparently, other babies can hear) range in cleverness from "I got something cold and wet in my shorts" all the way to "Who's this yutz?"

In fairness, the words are only part of the gag. Out of the mouth of an adorable babe (four cutie-pies play Mikey at various stages of his first year) seemingly comes the unmistakable sound of a former "Moonlighting" star and wine-cooler spokesman. Thanks to Brucie, Mikey's an infant with an attitude, even when he's saying nothing hipper than "Holy cow."

To those who think this gimmick alone is worth the price of admission, have a ball. To those who expect a decent comedy along with it, take a pass. With "Johnny Dangerously," "National Lampoon's European Vacation" and now "Look Who's Talking," writer-director Amy Heckerling appears determined to prove that her first film, "Fast Times at Ridgemont High," was uncharacteristically cerebral.

Heckerling knocks us over the head with the idea that Mikey loves Travolta for his *childlike* charm. Meanwhile, Alley knocks Travolta and Segal over the head when they get out of line. One time she floors Travolta with a punch to the face—all in good fun. (He recovers in time to teach Mikey his "Saturday Night Fever" disco steps, in case you didn't realize he was *that* John Travolta.) Segal later knocks Travolta over the head with a telephone receiver and doesn't hurt him a bit.

As if they weren't dumb enough by themselves, these people have relatives. Travolta removes a splinter from Alley's finger while her mother (Olympia Dukakis) stands outside the door listening. From the sound of things, Mom thinks they're having sex! Travolta's senile grandfather (Abe Vigoda) is on hand to lend poignancy to the proceedings—when he's not reaching for laughs by taking out his teeth.

In closing, let us ponder Mikey's words upon emerging from the womb: "Put me back in." some baby talk makes perfect sense.

Also reviewed in:
NEW YORK TIMES, 10/13/89, p. C12, Vincent Canby
VARIETY, 10/18–24/89, p. 28
WASHINGTON POST, 10/13/89, p. C7, Hal Hinson
WASHINGTON POST, 10/13/89, Weekend/p. 43, Roger Piantadosi

LOOKING FOR LANGSTON

A Sankofa Film and Video/British Film Institute production. *Producer:* Nadine Marsh-Edwards. *Director:* Isaac Julien. *Director of Photography:* Nina Kellgren. *Editor:* Robert Hargreaves. *Art Director:* Derek Brown. *Running Time:* 40 minutes. *MPAA Rating:* Not Rated.

CAST: Ben Ellison (Alex); Matthew Baidoo (Beauty); John Wilson (Gary); Akim Mogaji (James); Dencil Williams (Marcus); Guy Burgess (Dean); Simon Fogg (Jez); James Dublin (Carlos); Harry Donaldson (Lederjunge).

LOS ANGELES TIMES, 1/26/90, Calendar/p. 10, Kevin Thomas

British film maker Isaac Julien's elegant meditation on black gay sexuality, "Looking for Langston," has outraged the estate of Langston Hughes because it depicts the late poet as being homosexual.

The Hughes estate succeeded in preventing the film from being shown at the Los Angeles International Gay and Lesbian Film and Video Festival last July, even though it had aired on the BBC, and forced Julien to remove a fragment of a Hughes poem.

At the beginning of the black-and-white, 42-minute film, the voice of writer Toni Morrison, speaking at the funeral of James Baldwin, is heard saying: "Homosexuality was a sin against the race and had to be kept a secret, even if a widely shared one."

Set primarily to the words of another poet, Essex Hemphill, and the music of Blackberri, "Looking for Langston" intercuts archival material, mainly of the Harlem Renaissance of the '20s, with poetic vignettes dramatizing a range of black gay experience up to the present.

The key setting is a gay nightclub that looks like a corner of an ancient Gothic church where tuxedo-clad men—mostly blacks—pursue each other. Among them is Alex (Ben Ellison), who bears a striking resemblance to the young Hughes and who zeroes in on a tall, spectacularly-muscled man (Matthew Baidoo). Their subsequent scenes in the nude are as chaste as George Platt Lynes photographs, their bodies sculpted in light and shadow.

Julien treats Hughes as an icon, as a point of departure to consider the oppressed state of black gays through the decades, of their exploitation by white gays, and of the specter of AIDS and of the bitter aftermath of the Harlem Renaissance when black artists and writers "went out of style" with white sophisticates and intellectuals. The film is as much a celebration of James Baldwin as it is of Langston Hughes, and by extension, all creative black people. "Looking for Langston" is exceptionally poignant and imaginative.

That description doesn't quite fit Sandy Daley's Warhol-like half-hour "Mapplethorpe: Robert Having His Nipple Pierced" (1970), which, as the title spells out, depicts the late photographer undergoing the procedure while cradled by his lover.

Visually, the film is actually as discreet as "Looking for Langston," but it is accompanied on the sound track by Patti Smith rambling on and on about her own sex life, sexual attitudes and bodily functions in unrelenting crudeness and even ignorance. Regardless of what point Daley was trying to make by way of contrast, the effect is to suggest a gratuitous misogyny. Both films are Times-rated Mature.

MONTHLY FILM BULLETIN, 2/90, p. 45, Kobena Mercer

In Isaac Julien's short film, Langston Hughes is not the subject of a biographical documentary so much as an evanescent presence invoked by a dream-like montage of poetry, music and cultural history. Hughes is widely remembered as the key poet of the black American artistic movement in the 1920s known as the Harlem Renaissance, but here his public persona is secondary to the enigma of his private life—his sexuality. In an age when homosexuality was regarded as a "sin against the race", the idea of "coming out" was unthinkable. *Looking for Langston* imaginatively reconstructs a world previously hidden from history and reflects on "the beauty of the people with freakish ways."

Its languid monochrome texture and stylised art direction evoke an ambiguous sense of time and place. Characters inhabit the fictional milieu of a 20s speakeasy, in which tuxedoed couples dance and drink champagne, celebrating hedonistic pleasure in defiance of the hostile world outside, which intrudes at the end as thugs and police raid the club and 80s house music plays on the soundtrack, almost like a music video. Archival film and sound recordings combine with contemporary poetry and music by Essex Hemphill and Blackberri, both black gay American artists. In its mosaic of visual and literary quotation—from James Baldwin and Toni Morrison to Jean Cocteau and Kenneth Anger—the film unravels complex themes of sexual repression and racial transgression. For example, an exchange of looks between Langston (Ben Ellison) and his mythic object of desire, "Beauty" (Matthew Baidoo), provokes a hostile, competitive glare from Beauty's white male partner (John Wilson), who in turn contemptuously rejects the inquiring look of a young black man. Allusions to pornography and Robert Mapplethorpe's black nudes similarly underline the question of who has the "right to look", without oversimplifying the erotic fascination with "difference" that gives a volatile edge to inter-racial sexuality.

Like other young black British independent film-makers, Julien is motivated by a concern with the past in order to throw new light on contemporary issues. The contributions of black artists to modernism have been consistently written out of official versions of history—or, as Stuart Hall conveys in the film's commentary, after the 20s the "primitive" Negro was no longer in vogue and wealthy white patrons found other uses for their money. In this sense, *Looking for Langston* is an archaeological project, reconstructing the historical continuum in which black aesthetic expression has been an integral part of modernism. And it points out that the contributions of black women and gay men have been rendered even more invisible by conservative notions about a homogeneous and undifferentiated black "community".

This critical interest in history suggests that Julien is attempting a dialogue (or its visual equivalent) with the different traditions from which he has invented his own artistic identity as a black gay "auteur". Black people have historically been the objects of representation, rather than its subjects and creators, as racism often determines who gets access to the means of representation in the first place. Julien overturns this double-bind as the black subject "looks back". Certain motifs, such as the "direct look" whereby black characters seem to ask the audience what *they* are looking for, appeared in the first film by Julien and the Sankofa workshop, *Territories* (1984). With a new degree of self-confidence (and a considerably larger budget), *Looking for Langston* continues and develops this artistic project, deepening the critique of racial representation by extending it into the domain of fantasy. At times, the seductive quality of the film's preoccupation with its own stylishness risks a degree of cliché, but this is a risk worth taking if a wider audience is thereby invited into the dialogue about the "politics of difference".

VILLAGE VOICE, 9/26/89, p. 64, Amy Taubin

Limned with desire, Isaac Julien's meditation on the life and work of Langston Hughes not only brings the Harlem Renaissance out of the closet but also redefines its significance for both black history and modernist art.

VILLAGE VOICE, 11/7/89, p. 67, J. Hoberman

Isaac Julien's controversial *Looking for Langston* had its local premiere at the New York Film Festival. This 40-minute free-associative "meditation" on Langston Hughes will never be mistaken for Bourne's recent PBS portrait. As Lisa Kennedy reported in the *Voice* several weeks ago, *Looking for Langston* is under attack by the Hughes estate. Still, although framed by a kinescope of the poet reading "Ballad of a Fortuneteller" on TV, the film's romantic, sinuous mixture of refilmed newsreels, clips from old "race" movies, and sultry beefcake has less to do with Hughes's ambiguous sexuality (let alone his life) than a desire to freeze a historical moment and illuminate it with the white heat of desire.

Looking for Langston is nothing if not studied. There's a hint of Derek Jarman in the dream encounter between the tuxedoed poet and his naked ideal, the artfully posed cherubs holding personality posters (of James Baldwin, among others). The statuesque bods, languorously entwined in bed, suggest a more exotic Calvin Klein ad. In *The City Sun,* Armond White made a suggestive comparison to the aestheticism of Prince's much-maligned *Under the Cherry Moon;* the vein of neo-hi-de-ho mined by August Darnell seems another corollary. What's most impressive is the British-born Julien's capacity to conjure a fabulous, lost Harlem. As in an Oscar Micheaux film, a nightclub serves as fantasy central—a shimmering speakeasy beneath a church where elegant black men dance cheek-to-cheek to subcultural anthems ranging from George Hannah's 1930 "Freakish Blues" to the disco-ecstasy of Royal House's "Can You Party?"

Toward the end of the movie, this subterranean paradise is stormed by a mob of white skinheads. The room spins, the champagne glasses smash. Then it's back to the middle-aged Hughes: "I could be blue, but I've been blue all night long." It's a measure of Julien's own ambiguity that the word *blue* carries three meanings (at least), and a measure of his success that he connects this lost Renaissance to another that's poised to happen.

Also reviewed in:
NEW YORK TIMES, 10/1/89, p. 61, Caryn James

LOST ANGELS

An Orion Pictures release. *Producer:* Howard Rosenman and Thomas Baer. *Director:* Hugh Hudson. *Screenplay:* Michael Weller. *Director of Photography:* Juan Ruiz-Anchia. *Editor:* David Gladwell. *Music:* Philippe Sarde. *Sound:* Edward Tise. *Sound Editor:* Winston Ryder. *Production Designer:* Assheton Gorton. *Art Director:* Alex Tavoularis. *Set Decorator:* Robert Kensinger. *Set Dresser:* Lisa Lopez. *Special Effects:* Dale L. Martin. *Costumes:* Judianna Makovsky and Milena Canonero. *Make-up:* Karen Bradley. *Stunt Coordinator:* Rick Barker. *Running time:* 117 minutes. *MPAA Rating:* R.

CAST: Donald Sutherland (Dr. Charles Loftis); Adam Horovitz (Tim Doolan); Amy Locane (Cheryl Anderson); Don Bloomfield (Andy Doolan); Celia Weston (Felicia Marks); Graham Beckel (Richard Doolan); Patricia Richardson (Mrs. Anderson); Ron Frazier (Barton Marks); Joseph d'Angerio (Sweeney); William O'Leary (Link); Kevin Corrigan (Gata); Gary Riley (Spooky); Michael Cunningham (DAB Kid); Leonard Portar Salazar (Paco); Jonathan Del Arco (Angel); Eddie Hernandez II (10th St Boy); Cehlia Barnum Newman (Paco's Girl); David Herman (Carlo); Max Perlich (Frankie); Gino De Mauro (Barry); Nina Siemaszko (Merilee); Shana O'Neil (Jenny); Dana Behr (Anita); Mary Greening (Mary); Kevin Tighe (Dr. Gaeyl); John C. McGinley (Dr. Farmer); Jane Hallaren (Grace Willig); Peter Maloney (Dr. Peter Ames); Lee Wilkof (Ted Bingham); James N. Harrell (Shelby); Constance Shulman (Beautician); Marjie Rynearson (Receptionist); Frances Fisher (Judith Loftis); Jack Gold (Judge); Keone Young (Victor Eng); Park Overall (Richard Doolan's Girlfriend); Henry R. Harris (Juvenile Hall Policeman); Fredric Arnold (Mr. Shay); Diane Perella and Babetta George (Women at Felicia and Barton's Party); Sharmon Anciola (Charles Loftis' Daughter); Brian Beary (Kid #1); Matt Chapman (Kid #2); Pauley Shore (Kid #3); James Raddin (Kid on Phone); Jason Tirado (Field Policeman); William Steis (Field Policeman); Tom Patton (Field Policeman); Gordon Michaels (Bartender); Andrew J. Bley (Student); John Dichter (Policeman); Maribel Lizarraga (Student); Larry Gregory Nelson (District Attorney).

LOS ANGELES TIMES, 5/5/89, Calendar/p. 12, Sheila Benson

You've seen the soothing ads on television: If your teen-ager has a drug or a drinking problem, this shady-acred estate with its licensed staff is just the place to have your troubles taken off your hands. The backdrop for the overheated "Lost Angels" is one of these private psychiatric facilities that specialize in treating affluent kids who have taken a bad turn.

As he begins his story of Valley boy Tim Doolan (Beastie Boy Adam Horovitz), who has good reason to feel unwanted since his parents' divorce, director Hugh Hudson walks a tightrope between a fascinating demonstration of the inner workings of such places, and the increasing melodrama of Michael Weller's screenplay.

By the film's end, the tightrope is gone, Hudson—and we—are wallowing in fevered, nightmarish stagings, camera movements from hell and a loss of all common sense. It's in moments like this that you remember that Hudson is not only the director of "Chariots of Fire," but he was also the director of "Revolution," and it's that movie's jaw-dropping silliness that he is up to here.

It's pity, because both Horovitz, in a nicely played debut performance, and , especially, Donald Sutherland, as Tim's white-bearded, compassionate psychiatrist, are fine.

Tim has been put in the insurance-funded facility, where Sutherland's Dr. Charles Loftis works, primarily because Tim's newly remarried mother doesn't want his wild behavior to complicate her life. But Loftis is not without complications himself. His wife seems tired of heading a family that plays second fiddle to any one of his cases, and Loftis' escape for some years has been alcohol.

Although the conclusion is the purest nonsense, the growing scenes of trust between Tim and Loftis are nicely drawn, as are many of the school sequences. But it's never a good sign when a writer resorts to first-person narration to tell us feelings and reactions that would be better left unsaid, or performed. Then with the subplot about Tim's influential, older stepbrother Andy (Don

Bloomfield) and the gang both boys belong to—the DABs, white Valley kids who hate but emulate black and Chicano gangs—Hudson begins to hyperventilate cinematically. He is helped, unfortunately, by the excesses of the usually poetic cinematographer Juan Ruiz-Anchia.

Comfortably well-off but neglected kids have been the fodder for films from the hypnotic ("On the Edge" and "Suburbia"), to the vacuous ("Less Than Zero"). It's not hard to see why: These casts absorb dozens of the seemingly endless supply of shiny-faced teen-age actors who flood both coasts, and the roles have sure-fire empathy with their peers who buy the tickets. (This one, however, is MPAA rated R for language and sex.)

Unfortunately, *these* lost angels are an uneven assortment. As Cheryl, the pivotal mixed-up siren, 17-year-old Amy Locane, who comes from television, seems to have been taught that every word needs a change of expression. Every single word. It makes her time on screen exhausting.

Almost worse is Bloomfield as Tim's loco brother, who seems to have patterned his performance after Willem Dafoe's in "Streets of Fire." It's too bad that these and other excesses of style whittle away at the affection audiences would otherwise have for these tormented kids.

NEW YORK, 5/22/89, p. 72, David Denby

Given the events of recent weeks, this isn't the best moment for a movie about teenagers who go bad because their parents don't love them enough. The children who are loved and watched but still go bad haunt us much more. Yet that's hardly the only reason that Hugh Hudson's *Lost Angels* looks like something ABC's *Movie of the Week* left out on the back stoop in 1974.

Hudson and Michael Weller, who wrote the screenplay, don't even get into the freshest part of their subject. In *Lost Angels*, a group of white, middle-class boys in the San Fernando Valley, bored and restless, imitate the style of the local Hispanic street gangs. The white gang, called Dead at Birth (the initials, spelled backward, are BAD), seem like haplessly mixed-up losers, and the Latinos are puzzled by them. So are we: What are they doing? The gang is said to be based on an actual group, but their existence still feels like an aberration, and Weller doesn't investigate the oddity of it—or even take much notice of the irony that the white kids wind up in deadly brawls with the Chicanos they're imitating.

Weller has something else on his mind—parental betrayal. The hero of *Lost Angels,* a silent piece of sheepish self-consciousness named Tim Doolan (Adam Horovitz), skulks about sadly, looking for someone to talk to. Tim's dad, a violent lout, won't oblige him; his mom, sweet enough but vague and selfish, has lost touch with who he is. Q.E.D.: The kid is messed up. (What brilliance at diagnosis!) Horovitz, a member of the mock-tough rap group the Beastie Boys, has foxy eyes and an unfortunate Richard Gere smirk. To his credit, Horovitz lacks the narcissism of the Brat Pack actors, but he lacks the interest that some young narcissists possess, too. He seems passive and rather nice, as if he had been loved too much rather than too little.

Hugh Hudson, trying to touch ground after swinging through jungle trees (*Greystoke*) and choking on musket smoke (*Revolution*), shows little talent for this kind of suburban earnestness about sons and brothers and teen dating and therapy sessions. Weller writes astonishingly clumpy dialogue for the teens, and Hudson doesn't allow them any grace, any cool; he makes them mostly loud and stupid, which gives us no reason to watch them. (In the movies, a bad kid can be violent, but he'd better be beautiful or expressive or he's hopeless.) *Lost Angels* is alternately glum and lurid; in some confusing scenes set at a private psychiatric facility, the filmmakers expose the place as a snake pit, yet at the same time they show Tim finding a doctor there who saves his life. As the doctor, Donald Sutherland, half asleep, is the only watchable thing in the movie. Wisps of disgust gather around Sutherland's humane attentiveness—touches of vanity that save the performance from the goody-goody boringness of Judd Hirsch. Sutherland's doctor has our admiration. The movie makes the kids so tiresome that we think of him as a true hero for wanting to talk to them at all.

NEW YORK POST, 5/5/89, p. 33, Jami Bernard

Assuming that the features of a movie could be rearranged like a Mr. Potato Head, there are two casting changes that could have given "Lost Angels" the kind of ironic edge it lacks.

One would be to keep Donald Sutherland in the role of the weary shrink who ministers to juvenile delinquents in a private mental institution where middle-class kids are dumped by uncaring parents, but to give the role of Tim, a disruptive youth rebelling against authority, to Sutherland's own devilish-looking son, Kiefer.

The other option would be to keep the bad boy role in the hands of Adam Horovitz, that middle-class kid from the Village who drives the establishment insane with his obscenity-swilling rap group The Beastie Boys, but give the role of the father-figure shrink to Horovitz's own dad, Israel, the noted playwright.

Even without these casting changes it is clear that middle-class kids who have access to material things can end up just as angry and alienated as children from the slums. That is not exactly news. It is what a movie makes of this theme that can set it apart from the usual run of stories about teen angst. "Lost Angels," directed by Hugh Hudson, gets off to a good start but bogs down; for a metaphor, think of Hudson's famous slo-mo shot of runners on the beach in his "Chariots of Fire."

In the city of Los Angeles, in the city of lost angels (get it?), Tim—dubbed "Chino" by his white-bread home boys, a gang called Dead At Birth—is surrounded by jerks. (He uses a different word, but it boils down to the same thing.) His new stepfather is a jerk. His mother is on the cusp of jerk-dom. His natural father is a vicious, vindictive jerk, and when Tim is arrested because he's hanging out with a girl who's just driven her alcoholic mom's car into the pool, his jerk father tosses in a complaint about Tim's gun and drug possession.

Now Tim is in jail and soon, through the kind of trickery only an adolescent can expect of his parents, he is in a falsely cheery lockup for non-conformist teens (aren't they all?). And he's surrounded by another circle of jerks.

The story is the same all over. The girl who drove her mom's car off the deep end (Amy Locane) is also in the detention center, along with every other teen who ever had jerky parents who drink, divorce, deceive. Aside from the girl who smears crud on her naked body or the guy who laughs too loudly, these are normal, healthy teen-agers with a lot of unfocused anger who are packed off to detention the way some kids go to sleep-away camp.

Of them, our Beastie Boy—in his film debut—is probably the most sane and upstanding. He adjusts to life in the impossibly stratified and rigid life of the detention center with more ease than you'd expect; in fact, the saner you are, the more likely you'd rebel against the arbitrary, exaggerated, Kafkaesque version of Robert's Rules of Order which governs group therapy sessions. Inmates put their name tags on a tote board and move up and down the levels of privilege, losing points and incurring childish punishments like "quiet corner" for arcane infractions.

Tim gradually learns, with the help of the grizzled, kindly shrink Dr. Loftis (Donald Sutherland), that his pals over at the Dead At Birth society are not the stand-up guys he thought they were. In record time (the insurance that covers the clinic stay usually runs out in three months) Tim learns all the important things about love, responsibility and identity.

Maybe if more kids formed rap groups that specialize in blowing up gigantic rubber phalluses, they might get all those growing pains out of their system.

Horovitz is quite good in the kind of role that Sean Penn and Matt Dillon began their careers with. He has a laconic ease in front of the camera and is equally at home with a self-possessed sneer as with the concern that marks his emergence as an adult of the non-jerk variety.

It is the intrusion of some derivative, badly photographed gang-war activity (a la "West Side Story") and a sub-plot involving a sweaty-faced, desperate half brother that detract from "Lost Angels" just when it was getting interesting.

The movie is dedicated to two tots who bear the last names of the director and the screen writer (Michael Weller). May they not grow up to drive the car into a pool, and if they do, may they write plays, make movies, blow up giant phalluses and otherwise channel their creativity so they don't end up in the kind of clinic "Lost Angels" depicts. That sort of place could make a jerk of anyone.

NEWSDAY, 5/5/89, Part III/p. 5, Lynn Darling

Children grow up fast these days, discarding their innocence like a worn-out toy and with it what little protection innocence can give: The most dangerous shards of these splintered times seem to find teenagers first. Making their way through the maze is hard to do, harder still when parents abandon their responsibilities in favor of their own selfish searches. The results can be frightening: As the makers of "Lost Angels" point out, private psychiatric hospitals catering exclusively to adolescents have become something of a growth industry in the affluent havens of Southern California.

Director Henry Hudson ("Chariots of Fire") finds a harsh Orwellian world in these places—in "Lost Angels" such institutions function as little more than profit-oriented factories where parents can park their children in lieu of going through the bother of raising them.

"They can't do this to us," says young Timothy (Adam Horovitz) when he finds himself in the Valley Acres Psychiatric Hospital surrounded by dozens of other kids like himself. "It's got to be illegal or something."

Tim is in Valley Acres by mistake: After a rumble between Dead at Birth, the gang of middle-class white kids to which he belongs, and a much tougher Latino group, Tim drops in on Cheryl (Amy Locane), a pretty, stoned-out blonde whose idea of washing her mom's car that particular night is to drive it into the family swimming pool. Mom gets a little upset and has Cheryl and Tim arrested. Eventually Tim ends up bound and sedated and staring up into the kindly eyes of Dr. Charles Loftis (Donald Sutherland), the shrink who wants to save him from his life of errant anomie.

For Tim, life at Valley Acres consists of figuring out a way to play along until he can escape or until the family insurance runs out, at which point, Cheryl assures him, he will be considered cured.

It's not hard to understand Tim's desire to leave Valley Acres. Other than the heroic Dr. Loftis, the staff members are a particularly hardboiled lot: One therapist interrupts a young woman's tearful account of the sexual abuse she sustained as a child when his beeper goes off. "Hold that thought," he says briskly as he leaves.

It's less easy to figure out Tim. "What is the matter with you people?" Loftis yells as a family therapy session degenerates into a bout of vicious name-calling by Tim's parents as their son sits silently on the side. Hudson doesn't have much of an answer to that question beyond the usual heavy-handed cliches: aimless youth; broken home; indulgent, irresponsible mother; violent, repressed father. The screenplay (by playwright Michael Weller) is equally simplistic: "Why do you want to cause trouble?" the poor Latino gang leader asks the middle-class white gang leader. "Because it's something to do," he replies.

Adam Horovitz (a k a King Ad-Rock of The Beastie Boys) does a fine job as Tim; his nervous, tensile energy and unpredictability play well off Sutherland's smoothly professional performance as Loftis, the '60s veteran with a few demons of his own. But their characters are overwhelmed by a movie that expects you to get angry about the plight of its young characters without bothering to build up much compassion for them.

It's too bad, because there are some nice touches in "Lost Angels." When Tim returns home unexpectedly, he finds his mother throwing a large party—the adults are gathered around a piano singing "Mellow Yellow" and "Mr. Tambourine Man" in tipsy voices. Cheryl, wandering around a glitzy shopping mall in a drug-induced stupor, slumps down next to a pianist playing "Anything Goes." The details add texture and social context, enriching the otherwise unrelenting indignation in which "Lost Angels" is steeped.

VILLAGE VOICE, 5/9/89, p. 68, Stuart Klawans

And now, a spot quiz for aspiring filmmakers. Suppose you are shooting a scene in which a wild-eyed youth with a pistol confronts a surprised crowd on the street. The youth dashes forward into the frightened spectators. How do you film the action?

A: You show everybody diving for cover.

B: You plow a hand-held camera into a double line of extras, pushing them aside while they stare at the lens.

If you picked A, then congratulations—you are too smart to have directed *Lost Angels*. Hugh Hudson got the job. In fact, if you can read this sentence, you are too smart to watch the film. Stay home and catch up with *A Current Affair*.

The story, as spun out in Michael Weller's screenplay, is something like *Rebel Without a Cause* as reimagined by Tipper Gore. Tim (Adam Horovitz), the misunderstood son of middle-class fools, has run slightly afoul of the law, mostly through the agency of Cheryl (Amy Locane), a girl he hardly knows. Confined for a period to juvenile hall, Tim is released to the custody of his mother, provided she checks him into a psychiatric center for antisocial teenagers. There, Tim meets up again with Cheryl and comes under the care of the humane Dr. Loftis (Donald Sutherland).

Since Tim has been a pure victim till this point, even having been drugged by the psychiatrists and trussed to a bed, the audience might well be rooting for his escape. But, like *Getting It Right* [see Klawans' review], *Lost Angels* is a film with a dumb voiceover, which in this case reveals that Tim wants to be evil. Yes, he needs to be locked up in the loony bin, because he is under the influence of nasty rock 'n' roll songs and Satanic imagery. While Dr. Loftis tries to lead him to the light, Tim's half-brother, Andy (Don Bloomfield), is dragging him down into the teenage inferno.

Shot with no irony, little attention to continuity, and only the slightest leavening of unintentional humor, *Lost Angels* will be remembered in the history of cinema for a single distinction: It is the film that made *Getting It Right* look good.

Also reviewed in:
NEW YORK TIMES, 5/5/89, p. C13, Vincent Canby
VARIETY, 5/10–16/89, p. 18
WASHINGTON POST, 5/5/89, p. D1, Rita Kempley
WASHINGTON POST, 5/5/89, Weekend/p. 41, Desson Howe

LOVERBOY

A Tri-Star Pictures release. *Executive Producer:* Leslie Dixon and Tom Ropelewski. *Producer:* Gary Foster and Willie Hunt. *Director:* Joan Micklin Silver. *Screenplay:* Robin Schiff and Tom Ropelewski and Leslie Dixon. *Story:* Robin Schiff. *Director of Photography:* John Hora. *Editor:* Rick Shaine. *Music:* Michel Colombier. *Music Editor:* Jeff Carson. *Sound:* Peter Hliddal. *Sound Editor:* Jerry Ross. *Production Designer:* Dan Leigh. *Art Director:* Ann Champion. *Set Decorator:* Ethel Robins Richards. *Set Dresser:* David Lanning, Jorge A. Lynch, Edson Moreno, and Richard Cline. *Special Effects:* Howard Jensen and James Hart. *Costumes:* Rosanna Norton. *Make-up:* Bruce Hutchinson. *Stunt Coordinator:* M. James Arnett. *Running time:* 98 minutes. *MPAA Rating:* PG-13.

CAST: Patrick Dempsey (Randy Bodek); Kate Jackson (Diane Bodek); Robert Ginty (Joe Bodek); Nancy Valen (Jenny Gordon); Charles Hunter Walsh (Jory Talbot); Barbara Carrera (Alex Barnett); Bernie Coulson (Sal); Ray Girardin (Henry); Robert Camilletti (Tony); Vic Tayback (Harry Bruckner); Kim Miyori (Kyoko Bruckner); Robert Picardo (Reed Palmer); Kirstie Alley (Joyce Palmer); Peter Koch (Claude Delancy); Carrie Fisher (Monica Delancy); E.G. Daily (Linda). Christopher Cohill and Wayne Collins Jr. (Little Leaguers); Kathy Spitz (Blonde at Señor Pizza); Elizabeth Scherrer (Brunette at Señor Pizza); Sandra Beall (Robin); Faith Burton (Champagne Woman); Laurie Brown (Intellectual Woman); Anne Lavezzi (Lion's Mane Woman); Alexandra More (Fudge Sundae Woman); Marilou Miller (Lovers Lane Woman); Rebecca Holden (Anchovy Woman); Sir Lamont Rodeheaver (Boy); Bonnie Rodeheaver (Little Sister); Alisa Wilson (Nurse Darlene); Bill Kalmenson (Male Patient); Irene Olga Lopez (Spanish Maid); H. Hunt Burdick (Hotel Manager); Cheryl Rhoads (Mom at Pool); Anne Silverman (Girl at Pool); Tony Schwartz (Guest at Tiki Joe's); Katie Regan (Health Spa Woman); Roberto Martin Marquez (Juan); Bryce G. Williams (Parking Valet); Robert Petkoff, Stacey Hughes and Tonia George (Waiters at Tiki Joe's); Richard Brestoff (Robot Voice); William H. Valdez, Gil Combs, and Benny Moore (Policeman).

LOS ANGELES TIMES, 5/1/89, Calendar/p. 10, Sheila Benson

When bad things happen to good people, the result is "Loverboy," which opened citywide Friday with no press previews. In it, Patrick Dempsey plays a disingenuous college boy who, instead of working for $4.80 an hour delivering pizzas on his summer vacation, makes $200 an afternoon delivering warmth, understanding, tenderness and wildly unsafe sex to every unhappily married woman in greater Los Angeles. The password? Extra anchovies on the pizza.

A good many talents crashed and burned on this project, most notably Joan Micklin Silver, the credited director. It is possible to imagine that in really brutish hands, the gamy qualities of this script by Robin Schiff and Tom Ropelewski & Leslie Dixon could have been made worse. That scene, for example, in which the customer for Dempsey's last "delivery" turns out to be his own mother (Kate Jackson). Shaken but undetected, Dempsey makes a second-story getaway, then sends over the pizza parlor's one real Italian stud in his place. How about *that* for an understanding son?

Director Silver is also generous toward Dempsey's assorted ladyloves, including Barbara

Carrera as the perceptive tycoon who puts him onto his true calling, and married ladies Kirstie Alley and Carrie Fisher, among others. But the director has been able to do nothing with this wheezing script, one of the subplots of which involves Dempsey's dad believing that his son is gay. And the movie's moments of physical farce are mortifying.

What makes "Loverboy" (rated PG-13 for sexual situations) such a pitiful waste is that Dempsey has so much potential charm. Learning ballroom dancing by following Fred Astaire videos, learning about the world from his matinees, he remains the class of the picture. However, if you crave Dempsey in a role worthy of him, you'll want "Some Girls." And if you're already one of "Loverboy's" victims, "Some Girls" is mandatory to get the taste out of your mouth, where it lingers like too many anchovies.

MONTHLY FILM BULLETIN, 6/90, p. 166, Tim Pulleine

Los Angeles. Randy Bodek, completing his second year at college, has aroused the resentment of his girlfriend Jenny by his subordination to others and his inability to tell his parents of their relationship. Moreover, his mediocre scholastic performance causes his father Joe, boss of a small construction company, to threaten to cut off his funds. Impulsively, Randy opts to make his own way in the world, but gets no further than a delivery man's job at the Señor Pizza shop. Then a chance meeting with wealthy Alex Barnett changes his situation. She enlists him as a lover and insists on paying for his attentions, and after she moves on, she recommends his services to several friends, who summon him via coded delivery requests to the store. Prominent among these clients are Dr. Joyce Palmer, Monica Delancy (whose husband is a bodybuilder), and Kyoko Bruckner (married to one of Joe's business associates). Randy now aims to pay his way through a further year at college, though problems have arisen at home because of his mother Diane's unfounded suspicion that Joe is having an affair with his secretary Linda, and Joe's supposition (on the basis of misunderstanding overheard remarks) that Randy is homosexual. Meanwhile, Jory, an erstwhile fellow student of Randy's and a rival for Jenny, tells her what is going on. Randy has almost acquired sufficient capital when he finds to his horror that his next assignation is with his mother (a patient of Dr. Palmer), but he contrives to avoid her at the appointed motel and sends his workmate Tony as a substitute. Diane gets cold feet, but Tony is so smitten by her that he gives chase when she makes off for the party being held to mark her twentieth wedding anniversary. In the meantime, a chain of events started by Harry Bruckner's almost discovering his wife in flagrante and his erroneous supposition that she is having an affair with her doctor (none other than Joyce Palmer's husband) leads eventually to Bruckner, Palmer and Delancy forging an alliance to trace the man who is cuckolding them. They at first take this to be Jory, whom they beat up before discovering the truth; then they, too, converge on the Bodeks' party, bent on revenge. Chaos ensues, but eventually the assorted misunderstandings are cleared up; the three husbands are arrested for disturbing the peace; Tony strikes up a friendship with Linda; Joe and Diane patch things up; and Randy and Jenny come to a new understanding.

Where a comedy like *Look Who's Talking* manages, if in a rather slapdash way, to connect suggestively with contemporary attitudes, *Loverboy* purveys a brand of wish-fulfilment which seems curiously adrift in time. The opening animated credits sequence proves, in fact, to be all too appropriate in its frenzied redolence of 60s comedies, and the material often suggests a crude and juvenile variation on *The Graduate*. Some of the humour might well be considered dubious as well as dated, though the prurience ("Your name could be on the wall of every ladies' room for miles", enthuses Sal over Randy's revelations) is rather negated by the unlikely supposition that the well-heeled women whom Randy services would be driven to the attentions of a teenage delivery boy. Similarly, the sub-plot about Joe's belief that his son is homosexual, treated in sit-com style ("Wait till he wants to borrow your make-up", he warns his wife), is chiefly distinguished by the flimsy contrivance on which the father's assumption is based.

The plot might be read as a comic fable in the "frog prince" manner, with Alex functioning as a kind of fairy-godmother, and with the notion of Randy undergoing a magical transformation underlined by the use of swooning 30s pop standards to accompany the fanticated montage of his becoming an ideal ladies' man. But this is never more than an incidental conceit, and while Randy's dalliances throw up a few snappy asides on affluent Californian life styles (such as Monica's dismissive view of the tastes of her husband's female acolytes: "All they want to do is eat kelp and drink spritzer"), these are so few and far between that the film for its first half seems to be doing no more than marking time.

When the action later shifts into something nearer a knockabout mode, even honouring the tenets of bedroom farce to the extent of having Randy hide beneath the foam of Kyoko's bath when her husband almost interrupts their liaison, the pattern of misunderstandings and complications is quite ingeniously and divertingly knitted together. Even in this register, though, the climactic mêlée at the anniversary party is slackly staged. That physical comedy of this sort is not really the director's forte is all the more obvious if one sets the mechanical stratagems of *Loverboy* alongside the affectionate character-drawing of *Crossing Delancey*.

NEW YORK POST, 4/29/89, p. 17, Jami Bernard

The most astonishing thing about "Loverboy," a comedy about a youth who spends his summer as a hired stud to raise cash for his tuition, is how it sidesteps such issues as AIDS, social responsibility and feminism. And please, none of that "but it's directed by a woman" to imply that if it's OK with her, it surely must have its heart in the right place.

Even if that woman is Joan Micklin Silver, who seemed to care about affairs of the heart in "Crossing Delancey." On second thought, she did create in that movie a New York full of lonely, desperate women who haunt salad bars like sad, skinny wraiths.

"Loverboy" has the kind of laconic, breezy self-assurance of a partygoer with a lampshade on his head who doesn't realize the joke isn't necessarily going over well. A personable cast headed by the ingratiating Patrick Dempsey wears the lampshade well.

Dempsey plays Randy Bodek, a personable college sophomore whose lack of sensitivity to his live-in girlfriend, Jenny (Nancy Valen), is endangering their relationship. Meanwhile, his grades are failing, causing his father to cut off the funds.

During summer break, Randy gets a job as a pizza delivery boy, and though he's young and gawky, the lovely, lonely ladies of Beverly Hills find him so irresistible that soon there is a whole network of them calling for special afternoon deliveries.

The women are all frustrated by Neanderthal husbands who don't know how to romance a lady. Randy soon catches on that the way to a woman's heart is through such novelties as listening to her, dancing with her and being nice to her. This might have been funnier if it were played broadly, but Silver seems to find the humor in Randy's sexual exhaustion.

Meanwhile, his dad thinks Randy is gay, his mom thinks his dad is having an affair and vice versa. Randy still loves Jenny (although he doesn't see any conflict in taking $200 a pop from his clients) and some of the husbands are getting suspicious. Naturally, there is a big, bang-up finale, where everyone in the cast gets to beat up everyone else in the cast for various reasons.

Barbara Carrera, Carrie Fisher and Kirstie Alley play some of the neglected wives with a hankering for extra anchovies. As a point of interest, Cher's boyfriend, Rob Camilletti, plays a pizza slinger with a bad Italian accent. He seems to enjoy his moment in the spotlight, but Cher doesn't have to worry about finding shelf space for an extra Oscar.

The movie has a lot of nerve indulging in gay-bashing when its heterosexual hero is such a jerk. Beyond that, consider that everyone finds Randy's professional sideline harmlessly amusing, from his girlfriend (maybe he's cheating on her but at least he notices her new dress) to his mother (who narrowly avoids having a special delivery from sonny boy herself).

Now, even if you can believe that all these lusty, intelligent women have no choice but to pay in order to relieve their tedium, you still have to deal with the comedy's dearth of humor. A typical line from the pen of Leslie Dixon ("Outrageous Fortune"): "I come on to every girl that walks, and they throw up," complains Randy's envious pal.

Dempsey was tapped for the role most likely because he attracted older women in "In the Mood" as the unabashed "woo-woo kid." He seems very easy with the physical comedy the movie calls for, and his boyish charm does deflect some of the nastiness of the situations he finds himself in.

Still, if it's a choice between "Loverboy" or a pizza with extra anchovies, I'd...well, I'd probable order in Chinese.

NEWSDAY, 4/29/89, Part II/p. 15, Lynn Darling

A very good question is asked at the end of "Loverboy." Young Randy Bodek has just finished explaining to his girlfriend Jenny that he has spent the summer charging a whole lot of women in Beverly Hills $200 each to satisfy whatever desires they wanted satisfied. He tells her that he did this not only to earn the money for his college tuition but to find a way to repair the rift between them.

"How would you feel," asks Jenny, "if I said I slept with all these guys this summer and I did it for you?"

"I'd hate you," Randy replies. And while hate may be too strong a word to apply to this addlepated, ill-conceived bit of irritating fluff, the idea of turning the tables isn't a bad one. How would we feel about a comedy that's about a teenaged girl who figures out that the only way she can earn another semester of higher education is to service approximately 40 middle-aged men?

That's the premise that's meant to be so hysterically funny in "Loverboy." Informed by his father (Robert Ginty) that he will no longer pay for a college career that has yielded nothing better than a crop of failing grades, Young Randy (Patrick Dempsey) begins the summer by working as a pizza delivery boy. Through a complicated series of events, he falls into another line of work—women with considerably more than mozzarella on their minds have only to phone for a pizza with extra anchovies to get an apparently tireless teenage boy.

"I just couldn't say no," Randy (of course his name would have to be Randy) explains to one of his co-workers when asked how he got into this line of work. Besides, as he tells Jenny (Nancy Valen), he didn't sleep with all of them. Some of the women just wanted him to make them feel special, to show them a little romance and respect. Sure.

It's OK though, really. By the end of the movie, all is forgiven. Dad is so glad to find out that his son isn't gay that he just forgets all about the fact that the kid is a hooker. Mom, who came awfully close to employing the busy little entrepreneur herself, is delighted that he has a nice girlfriend. And the cuckolded husbands get to experience a little male bonding, as they sing along to a Jerry Lee Lewis song while they make plans to tear the young gigolo to pieces.

Joan Micklin Silver directed this movie from a script cowritten by Robin Schiff, who came up with the idea for this thing. "Loverboy" is described in the production notes as a marked departure for Silver. You bet it is. Silver's other pictures, like "Hester Street" and "Crossing Delancey" showed wit, charm and sensitivity. Here's hoping she makes a speedy recovery.

Also reviewed in:
NEW YORK TIMES, 4/29/89, p.15, Caryn James
VARIETY, 5/3–9/89, p. 12
WASHINGTON POST, 4/29/89, p. C2, Hal Hinson

LUCKIEST MAN IN THE WORLD, THE

A Second Effort Company release of a McLaughlin, Piven, Vogel Inc. presentation. *Producer:* Norman I. Cohen. *Director:* Frank D. Gilroy. *Screenplay:* Frank D. Gilroy. *Director of Photography:* Jeri Sopanen. *Editor:* John Gilroy. *Music:* Warren Vaché and Jack Gale. *Sound:* Lee Orloff. *Production Designer:* Nick Romanac. *Running Time:* 84 minutes. *MPAA Rating:* Not Rated.

CAST: Philip Bosco (Sam Posner); Doris Belack (Mrs. Posner); Joanne Camp (Laura); Matthew Gottlieb (Sheldon); Arthur French (Cleveland); Stan Lachow (Schwartz); Yamil Borges (Mrs. Gonzalez); J.D. Clarke (Robert Whitley); Moses Gunn (Voice); Joel Friedman (Sam's Partner).

LOS ANGELES TIMES, 5/5/89, Calendar/p. 14, Kevin Thomas

Only a born storyteller as sincere and inventive as Frank Gilroy and an actor's actor like Philip Bosco could get away with "The Luckiest Man in the World," making its twist seem fresh, funny and poignant instead of a gimmick.

This fine little film is roughly a reverse take on "It's a Wonderful Life." In the beloved Capra classic an angel shows a despairing James Stewart all the bad things that would have happened to his family and his friends had he never been born. In writer-director Gilroy's film almost everybody wishes apoplectic, ruthless New York garment manufacturer Sam Posner (Bosco) were dead. They almost get their wish; Sam barely misses a plane for Miami which crashes on takeoff, killing all aboard. Nudged by a sepulchral voice (Moses Gunn), Sam is confronted with what a monster he is and becomes eager to make amends.

The challenge, of course, is in sustaining Sam's odyssey, which is where Gilroy and Bosco shine. (Bosco is best known to moviegoers as the financier in "Working Girl.") The responses of Sam's family, employees and colleagues are consistently inaginative, as full of humor as they are of pain, and Bosco is as convincing as the newly warm Sam as he is as the cold jerk of the past. Some encounters are a little more persuasive than others, and there are a few moments of hesitancy on Gilroy's part as to how to wrap everything up. However, it's quite easy to be beguiled by this wise and rueful fable.

This a very New York film, with its emphasis on characterization rather than style, with its cast composed of actors rather than movie stars. The wonderful Bosco, stocky, open-faced and expansive, is well supported by Doris Belack as his understandably cynical wife; Joanne Camp as his perplexed mistress; Matthew Gottlieb as his confounded transvestite son and Yamil Borges as the beautiful young widow of the man who took Sam's plane seat on standby. They and many others, including Joel Friedman as Sam's paralyzed ex-business partner, are a constant pleasure. "The Luckiest Man in the World" is the kind of film that many people would enjoy; it has more substance than chic, and its sensibility and perspective are comfortably middle-aged. Gilroy still remains best-known for his 1964 Pulitzer prize-winning play "The Subject Is Roses" and for its 1968 adaptation to the screen. He also wrote and directed such satisfying and intimate films as "Desperate Characters," "From Noon Till Three," "Once in Paris" and "The Gig."

NEW YORK POST, 2/22/89, p. 27, David Edelstein

Frank D. Gilroy, who wrote and directed the low-budget comedy "The Luckiest Man in the World," must be the pluckiest man in the world. A successful playwright in the '60s (he won a Pulitzer Prize for "The Subject Was Roses"), Gilroy now taps a regular group of investors to fund modest, well-intentioned movies about adult relationships and mid-life crises. They don't make a dime, but on he goes, making his nice, unexceptional pictures for an audience that—on the evidence—no longer exists.

The latest film tells the story of Sam Posner (Philip Bosco), a Scrooge-like garment manufacturer who misses a plane that subsequently crashes, killing everyone on board. Seated on a toilet in the airport men's room, asking God why he has been spared, Posner hears a voice (Moses Gunn) from the next stall: He has been spared because he is a jerk, the voice explains, and has much to set right in this world.

Posner decides to make amends for a life of exploitation, greed and emotional fascism, but that isn't as simple as it sounds. The central (and only) joke of "The Luckiest Man in the World" is that the people to whom he apologizes won't have any part of him; the damage, they tell him, has been done.

His wife (Doris Belack) doesn't trust his urge to reconcile, and can't forgive him for lost time; his doting mistress (Joanne Camp), whom he has dangled for years, decides to reject him when he finally pops the question; and his son (Matthew Gottlieb), a transvestite, has too much invested in hating the old man.

Even the partner (Joel Friedman) Posner ruined—now on his deathbed and paralyzed— miraculously summons up the energy to spurn the repentant businessman.

Much of Gilroy's dialogue has push and wit, and he can certainly shape a scene. But he's a woefully pedestrian filmmaker. There's no beauty in his technique, no life in his camera; he brings out everything stagey and hamhanded in his own writing. (Gilroy the writer deserves better than Gilroy the director.)

And that writing is hamhanded, even when it's clever.

Gilroy boasts in interviews that he resisted the urge to make "The Luckiest Man in the World" a farce—he wanted the humor "edged with feeling." But a farce rhythm and some satire would do wonders for this extreemly repetitious parable, with its wet, humanist uplift. (Whenever you see a movie in which a rich, guilty Jewish guy heads up to Harlem with money in his pocket and a song in his heart, it's time to check out the Pac-Man machine in the lobby.)

As Posner, Bosco doesn't have much intimacy with the camera (all those years of middlebrow Shakespeare have left him terminally bluff), but at least he isn't a slob. And Gilroy shows some skill with the other actors, even if he doesn't know how to shoot them.

Doris Belack, in the Elaine Stritch role, does the salty, suffering broad bit with taste and restraint. As the gay son, Matthew Gottlieb could be a summa graduate of the Harvey Fierstein School of Wisecracking Through Mascara-Stained Tears. And Joanne Camp has an attractive, tremulous simplicity as Posner's mistress.

The movie is diverting enough, but watching it, I couldn't help feeling sad for Gilroy—a playwright without a country. He writes for the kind of theater that was long ago snuffed out by the insane economics of Broadway. Off-Broadway, meanwhile, features well-made plays about the problems of upper-middle-class New York executives—but only if those executives are 30 something and ultra-trendy. These days, Gilroy's work might not even be steamy or hip enough for television.

His last film, "The Gig"—about an amateur jazz group that treks up to the Catskills for their first and last professional booking—had some texture, and apart from a bad, downbeat ending, it was honestly observed. "The Luckiest Man in the World," however, seems embarrassingly out of touch.

In one scene, a bum asks Posner for a dollar to buy (he truthfully admits) some booze, and the now-generous businessman responds by peeling off a 20. This knocks the beggar for a loop: "What're ya' tryin' to do, kill me?" he moans, and staggers off without the money.

That's the level of "The Luckiest Man in the World." The gag is mildly amusing, but anyone who lives in the real world knows that no such derelict would leave empty-handed. It's only in the glib, dated, boulevard-comedy universe of Frank D. Gilroy that a homeless alcoholic would pass up $20 for the sake of a punchline.

VILLAGE VOICE, 2/28/89, p. 61, Renee Tajima

It's a typical day for Sam Posner, irascible king of the rag trade with John Gotti's fashion sense and a similar regard for humankind. Using the phone as a weapon and lethal wit as ammunition, Sam puts the screws on everyone: a smart wife, a dumb mistress, the union, and business associates alike. All this earns him a wealth of disposable income and even more animosity. Posted on the factory wall is a tribute from his employees: "Happiness is seeing your boss's picture on a milk carton."

Frank D. Gilroy's *The Luckiest Man in the World* is a delightful, Capraesque tale of a Seventh Avenue Scrooge who, even when sudden tragedy moves him to redeem his evil ways, continues to reap what he's sown. Sam's reckoning comes when he arrives late at the airport. (He reminds his chauffeur to wait a few minutes, so he can fire him in case he's missed the plane.) It seems Sam has been spared by crosstown traffic: Flight 6 crashed on take-off. Stunned by his fate, Sam hightails it to the john, where he ponders the inevitable question, "Why spare me?" The answer emanates from a pair of two-toned wingtips in the next stall. It's a second chance, the other-worldly voice tells him. Thus enlightened, Sam sets out to make amends.

Philip Bosco as Sam is the consummate character actor—a lovable villain who discovers there are no Tiny Tims in the world. This is New York City, 1989, baby, and nobody wants to be a Christmas turkey. When Sam promises to love and cherish his much-abused wife, she eyes him warily, "What's the angle?" His son, Sheldon the queen, is furious at his father's new leaf: "The one thing that keeps me going is my hate for you. Would you deprive me of that?" At points, the story treads in predictable territory. Sam's woes become belabored—even a drunk in Central Park gives him grief—but Gilroy manages to take a few left turns toward a fresher narrative course.

Gilroy, who won the Pulitzer for *The Subject Was Roses*, writes his women characters fuller and with even more complexity than he does the men. As Mrs. Posner, Doris Belack is absolutely brittle—a woman vulnerable to her husband's romancing, but whose protective armor rises on automatic. Joanne Camp's Laura, the sweet-tempered mistress, is no bimbo, but a thirtyish romantic who realizes that she just wanted to be asked. There are no visual pyrotechnics or profound moral sketches in this movie. *Luckiest Man* is simple and fun. Its a writer's film with minimal production values and a pace set by dialogue and wit. The only thing keeping it out of a larger venue is a budget that deprives it of bigger stars and slicker looks.

Also reviewed in:

NEW YORK TIMES, 2/22/89, p. C18, Walter Goodman

VARIETY, 2/22–28/89, p. 233

MACHINE DREAMS

A First Run Features release of a Barfuss Film Production. *Director:* Peter Krieg. *Screenplay:* Peter Krieg. *Director of Photography:* Peter Krieg. *Editor:* Peter Krieg. *Music:* Rolf Riehm. *Running time:* 87 minutes. *MPAA Rating:* Not Rated.

NEW YORK POST, 8/9/89, p. 26, David Edelstein

The German documentary "Machine Dreams" has a lucid, nonjudgmental tone; it gives itself up to its subject—the fantasies and anxieties of men about machines.

The films by Peter Krieg meditates on machines throughout history, machines in myth; it studies machines in places we might otherwise not look—in religion and in the military, where human individuality is systematically quashed. It asks why man continues to fabricate ever more complicated machines, in hopes, perhaps, of one day merging with them himself.

Literally, it presents itself as a dream: A young man with snowy white hair lies on a table surrounded by TV monitors on which interviews flash. Sometimes we enter those screens; at other times we watch him dream. A cool-voiced narrator carries us from interview to interview; the tone is bland, but you might find yourself getting lost in increasingly anxious reverie.

For Krieg makes connections that chill the soul. He suggests that ritual is the oldest thinking machine, that man fears disorder so much that he works to find order—and out of that primal terror comes our obsession with machines, which represent our deepest wishes and most crippling anxieties.

Preying on that longing for order, he shows us a church that is interested primarily in forcing man to conform, spelling out the idea that self-realization comes through labor to encourage both more machine dreams and (by implication) the survival of capitalism.

And from there he makes a leap to the killing of beggars and cripples; the creation of labor camps; the imprisoning of men in hivelike structures where boot camp instructors work intensely to break down a man's sense of self—so that he can be part of a flawless machine.

In the last part, Krieg ruminated on cybernetic evolution, especially seen through the eyes of Marvin Minsky (MIT's "father of artificial intelligence"). Minsky is convinced that machines could be "human" in years to come; that emotion is merely the result of anxiety produced by switching modes of thought; that when machines can be taught to fantasize and fear, they will be just like us—by which time our brains may be implanted with small computers to speed up our own thought processes.

This merging of man and machine is neither mourned nor exalted. But the absence of emotion and of comfortable natural settings suggests that man is increasingly being cut off from his essential self—by a technology evolving faster than the humans whose desires it's meant to serve. It's a technology that, in a sense, has a life and will of its own.

NEWSDAY, 8/9/89, Part II/p. 5, Janice Berman

Peter Krieg, who's been dissecting elements of the age of enlightenment for the last few years, has turned his attention to technology. His new documentary, "Machine Dreams," which follows "Father's Land" and 'The Soul of Money," attempts to explain technology as an outlet for our fondest hopes and deepest fears. How else, Krieg asks, can we account for the fact that technology is driven forward by space exploration and the military?

His is not the only explanation, of course; the most logical one is that space and the military, spiritually poles apart, are technologically symbiotic and, in the world of Star Wars, quite inseparable, much as we would wish it otherwise.

The military alert is struck from the outset, as the auteur, supine in his jammies and wired with sensors, rests before several TV monitors, on one of which a Marine drill instructor is explaining the need to dehumanize recruits so as to transform them into fighting machines. Later the director, who is also a jorunalist and inventor, will lie similarly abed in a factory, surrounded by giant turbines, as his voiced-over musings continue.

"In my dream, I see a man who perceives himself as just a mechanism," he says. . . "I am, for I think." And we watch an old automaton—a mechanical man from an earlier century—write "cogito ergo sum"—I think, therefore I am.

Only when man can dream a machine, says Krieg, can he build it, and only when he has built it can he recognize that he is more than a mechanical puppet. that observation leads to footage of mechanical puppets—robots—of every description. There's film of them riveting cars like busy yellow spiders, assisting in brain surgery, clattering aimlessly around on the floor of machine-artist Jim Whiting's loft, following a shopper through a Japanese department store and playing Japanese music. The robot musicians look human; their "skin" is pliant. The scene of the two robots *in flagrante delicto* is particularly weird and funny.

This assortment of images, a cybernetic "Mondo Cane," far outstrips the commentary, a numbing soup of every theory Krieg can come up with on his own or from experts. The scientific experts, the film's talking heads, are obviously wizards, but it's but it's irritating, nobody is identified until the credits.

VILLAGE VOICE, 8/15/89, p. 69, J. Hoberman

The attempt to give advanced technology a human face is also [the reference is to *Young Einstein*] the subject of *Machine Dreams*, a feature documentary by West German filmmaker Peter Krieg that opens today for two weeks at Film Forum 1. As much an essay as a piece of reportage, Krieg's film uses the science of robotics as a pretext to meditate on the emotional aspect of mankind's ambivalemt feelings for its mechanical servants.

Krieg, whose *September Wheat* (a polemical documentary on world hunger) was shown at the Film Forum back in 1981, celebrates the love that barely knows its own name but underlies commerical movies as disparate as *Robocop, Making Mr. Right*, and everything featuring bodybuilder Arnold Schwarzenegger. The film opens with a provocatively alienated montage—a creaking factory, a gigantic shopping mall, a prone man hooked up to a television set—and goes on to profile a galaxy of androids ranging from friendly robot gnomes pouring tea or schlepping groceries to a mobile security-vehicle as sinister and implacable as any golem. There's nothing more uncanny than the visual joke of seeing a monkey robot's clockwork innards, unless it's the maniacal crablike twitching of a disembodied nervous system.

Perhaps in defiance of its own subject matter, *Machine Dreams* is a lot less didactic than it might be. Krieg's use of the TV monitor is vaguely reminiscent of Godard's in *Numero Deux*. Television in *Machine Dreams* functions as a sort of internal thought balloon or dream machine: A video sergeant explains how basic training makes men into automatons, a TV savant provides a rap on Jeremy Bentham and his extremely contemporary notion of redemption through the mechanical. When Krieg defines astronauts as cyborgs or *pachinko* parlors as temples of machine worship, *Machine Dreams* seems like a more prosaic version of Chris Marker's sci-fi-inflected account of Japanese animism, *Sans Soleil*. (Indeed, there's a Japanese scientist on hand to explain that machines are not only metallic and soulless but "tender and erotic" as well.) And when MIT professor Marvin Minsky, the so-called "father of artificial intelligence," genially defines *consciousness* as "a small amount of memory," the movie becomes provocatively materialist.

Bracingly unsentimental, Minsky characterizes law and religion as "teaching machines" (by which he means, practical means for maintaining order), and political radical that he is, Krieg keeps returning to images of the army and the church. Still, *Machine Dreams* suffers a bit for the director's aesthetic naiveté and genderized blinders. Although Krieg seems oblivious to the lively machine worship that has been a theme in the 20th century avant-garde from Marinetti's Futurists through Stalin's first Five Year Plan to Andy Warhol's Factory, he does at one point use the analogy of Marcel Duchamp's *Great Glass (The Bride Stripped Bare by her Bachelors, Even)* to make the point that "all machines are female for they represent—first of all—the fantasies of men." Tell it to your blow-drier, Mr. Clean.

Also reviewed in:
NEW YORK TIMES, 8/9/89, p. C17, Stephen Holden

MAGIC TOYSHOP, THE

A Roxie Releasing Company release of a Granada Television film. *Producer:* Steve Morrison. *Director:* David Wheatley. *Screenplay (based on her novel):* Angela Carter. *Director of Photography:* Ken Morgan. *Editor:* Anthony Ham. *Music:* Bill Connor. *Choreographer:* Stephen Jeffries. *Sound:* Nick Steer. *Production Designer:*

Stephen Fineren. *Special Effects:* Aardman Anderson Lyons. *Costumes:* Hilary Buckley. *Make-up:* Julie McNeil. *Running time:* 104 minutes. *MPAA Rating:* Not Rated.

CAST: Tom Bell (Uncle Philip); Caroline Milmoe (Melanie); Kilian McKenna (Finn); Patricia Kerrigan (Aunt Margaret); Lorcan Cranitch (Francie); Gareth Bushill (Jonathon); Marlene Sidaway (Mrs. Rundle); Georgina Hulme (Victoria). *DANCERS:* Marguerite Porter (Coppelia/Nymph); Lloyd Newson (Artist); Jeremy Kerridge (Chinaman); Jayne Regan (Blank Puppet), Marina Stevenson (Cleopatra).

MONTHLY FILM BULLETIN, 7/87, p. 210, Jill Forbes

While Melanie, Jonathon and Victoria's parents are on a trip to America, the children are being looked after by Mrs. Rundle. One night, Melanie tries on her mother's wedding dress, goes into the garden wearing it, and locks herself out of the house. She climbs a tree to reach a first-floor window, and in so doing ruins the dress. She is therefore not surprised when, as though in punishment, a telegram arrives the following morning announcing that her parents have been killed in a plane crash. Kindly Mrs. Rundle takes a position elsewhere, the house and its contents are sold, and the children are packed off to live with their mother's sinister brother Philip, who keeps a toyshop in South London. They find him living with his Irish wife Margaret, who has not spoken since their marriage, and her two brothers Finn and Francie. All three are mobilised to help Philip perform plays with the puppets he makes. The children are disturbed and upset by their new surroundings. Victoria becomes very attached to Margaret; Jonathon tries hard to ingratiate himself with Philip and attempts to learn the puppet-making trade; Melanie, meanwhile, is simultaneously leered at and humiliated by her uncle and forced to play the central role in a production of *Leda and the Swan* enacted with puppets. This infuriates Finn who has fallen in love with Melanie, and he destroys the swan puppet, afterwards seeking comfort in Melanie's arms. The next day, while Philip is away, the entire family revolts against his authority, beginning with Finn who usurps the master's chair at table. Francie and Margaret are discovered by Melanie to be lovers, and Melanie herself climbs into bed with Finn. On his return, Philip finds his order challenged everywhere, and tries to murder Francie. But the puppets revolt against him, and Francie escapes, carrying a huge wooden puppet of Philip to the park where he throws it on a bonfire built for Guy Fawkes night. Margaret and Victoria disappear leaving Finn and Melanie alone.

This is a film more for Angela Carter fans than for uninitiated filmgoers. It has the, by now, recognisably "Carter" ingredients: the critique of patriarchy, the genesis of female sexuality, the fascination with the themes of children's literature and with the fantastic, the taste for the grotesque. *The Magic Toyshop* draws on classic fairy-tales (the toys which "come alive") and themes of Victorian literature (the orphans who are badly treated), but is ambiguous about location in time, implying a half-modern, half-historical setting. Philip's toyshop, for example, appears Victorian, as does his occupation (for who, in the era of *Spitting Image*, makes lifesize puppets that give such grotesquely unconvincing performances?). Moreover, his attitudes are so anachronistic that he seems to have survived beyond his own time and into one in which it has become possible for people to die in air crashes.

Much of our uncertainty on this score must be attributed to Tom Bell's highly credible portrait of the cold sadist whose authoritarian impulses transcend diachronic considerations. However, the viewer's uncertainties in this regard also render the interpretation of the other characters more difficult. Finn and Francie would appear to be a couple of Irish wild boys whose slightly gauche demeanour has more to do with their national origin than their dependence on sister and brother-in-law, while Melanie, Jonathon and Victoria, though very much Babes in the Wood, have none of the ingenuousness that one might have expected—particularly not Melanie, who is only too aware of her own sexual impulses.

The Magic Toyshop is adapted from a short story and wears its literary origins on its sleeve. Angela Carter's themes and characters presuppose a knowing audience—one which takes for granted that we're living in an *après*-Freud world and that the post-war approaches to textual analysis have been incorporated in our psychic mechanisms. It is obviously fine for the happy few to assume a self-conscious reader or viewer, *au fait* with structuralism, post-structuralism, feminism, Marxism, and so on, but less rewarding for the broader audience that may require educating to conform to what is supposedly immanent in its mind. It is easy to accept—indeed, it is accepted—that a fantasy film should be located outside time, but harder, as is the case here, to cope with two, coterminous but different times, the nineteenth-century and the twentieth, and even harder when at last one of them, the nineteenth, is not, as it were, real time but time as filtered through the nineteenth-century novel. The illumination that each period brings to the other makes a sociological point about tradition and convention very tellingly, but is not particularly rewarding from a fictional and narrative point of view. Such trade-offs are perhaps more profitable on the printed page than on celluloid, so that *The Magic Toyshop* is probably fine for those who are willing and able to play the Carter game, but merely puzzling for those who do not have the wherewithal.

NEW YORK POST, 7/26/89, p. 21, David Edelstein

In interviews, the brainy English writer Angela Carter—who wrote the 1968 novel and screenplay of "The Magic Toyshop"—speaks of weaving Freud and Marx in a necromantic, fairy-tale tapestry. In plain English, that means her big bad wolves aren't just lecherous, they're also fascist, capitalist patriarchs—three words that, in leftist-feminist literature, spell T-R-O-U-B-L-E.

In his surreal, radiantly moody adaptation, director David Wheatley orchestrates Carter's heavy symbolism with a light hand. Its heroine, Melanie (Caroline Milmoe), is a wealthy 15-year-old who dances before a mirror and then regards her naked body in bloom. As shots of blossoming pink flowers suggest, she's beginning to exude that young-woman aroma that drives boys (and movie cameras) wild.

Her parents on holiday in America, Melanie sneaks up to her parents' room, dons her mother's wedding gown and wanders into the yard under the moonlight—through a jungle-like garden that conjures up William Blake.

The door of the house slams shut and Melanie must climb a tree to her window—a journey fraught with psycho-sexual terror. The wedding dress tears, she pricks her finger and drops crimson blood on its lacy folds, and when she finally makes it to her window (half scrambling, half floating), an apple falls from the tree.

OK, kiddies, let's translate roughly: Melanie has come of age, lost her innocence, soiled her mother's wedding dress. After cleaning the blood from her parents' bed, she's handed a telegram by a black-clad motorcyclist; without opening it, she knows her parents have been killed and that she, metaphorically, has killed them.

The young woman and her two siblings (bespectacled, 12-year-old Jonathon and tiny Victoria), must now move in with their father's estranged brother, Philip (Tom Bell), who owns a toyshop in London.

Despite his passsion for puppets, Uncle Philip isn't a Gepetto kinda guy—he's an icy, tyrannical patriarch.

No need to play "What's My Symbol?": women, the Irish, little kids—you name it, the nasty English Capitalist patriarch represses it. Uncle Philip treats his marionettes with more respect than people, whom he regards as his true puppets. Eventually, he commands Melanie to dance in a puppet-show ballet of 'Leda and the Swan," menacing her from on high with the most phallic-looking swan ever made.

Philip's symbolic rape of Melanie drives the young artist Finn (who has been making awkward, vaguely twisted overtures to the receptive girl) to take an ax to the swan—an act that sets the stage for revolution, conflagration.

What saves "The Magic Toyshop" from tedious allgory is the buoyancy and ripeness of its images—its habit of drifting from a dreary, crabbed reality into the dreamy fantastic. The trouble is that Carter's plumbing is all on the outside; this fairytale would have been far less pretentious if its dreamlike elements were fully integrated into the narrative.

But young Caroline Milmoe keeps the movie alive. She's terrified by her freedom, yet she's teasingly nubile, intoxicated by her burgeoning sexuality. For such young women do patriarchs overstep their bounds, ensuring their overthrow. And film critics have to be careful, too.

NEWSDAY, 7/26/89, Part II/P. 5, Terry Kelleher

If you relish the challenge of interpreting dreams and symbols, you may resist the temptation to snicker, or snore, through "The Magic Toyshop."

But if you're a literal-minded, naturalistically inclined moviegoer with a comparatively low tolerance for the weird, you'll probably conclude that writer Angela Carter and director David Wheatley suffer from bats in the belfry—or toys in the attic.

"The Magic Toyshop," which Carter adapted from her 1967 novel, starts by introducing us to

Melanie (Caroline Milmoe), a pretty 15-year-old experiencing sexual stirrings. With her parents away in America, Melanie decides to put on Mother's wedding gown and take a nighttime stroll in the garden of her English country home. The front door blows shut, locking Melanie out. The girl tries to get back into her bedroom by climbing an apple tree. She cuts herself, and the white dress is stained with blood. A single apple falls from the tree. Bill Connor's lush music score calls attention to the crashing symbols.

Next morning, a black-clad motorcyclist delivers a fateful telegram (deep, rumbling chord on the soundtrack): The parents have been killed in a plane crash. Along with her younger brother and little sister, Melanie is packed off to London, where the children are to live with their mysterious Uncle Philip (Tom Bell).

Philip owns a toy shop, but he isn't too much fun. His beautiful Irish wife, Margaret (Patricia Kerrigan), was struck mute on their wedding day. Margaret's younger brothers, the artist Finn (Kilian McKenna) and the fiddler Francie (Lorcan Cranitch), are thoroughly tyrannized by Philip, who requires all members of the household to witness or participate in his "marionette microcosm"—large-size puppets in perverse playlets presented regularly in the basement.

There are touching moments as the lonely Melanie adjusts to her new life, and gently humorous ones as she alternately rebuffs and encourages the male forwardness of Finn. (No slouch in the symbolism department, he's surreptitiously painting her as Eve in the Garden of Eden.) A couple of the surrealistic touches are delightful, particularly a Spuds McKenzie-like terrier who jumps in and out of a painting on the wall.

But the dog is the only thing in the movie that moves quickly. Uncle Philip goes about his wickedness so deliberately that he inspires more impatience than fear.

When he drafts Melanie to play the virgin in his marionette production of "Leda and the Swan"—pointedly inquiring whether she's begun to menstruate—"The Magic Toyshop" crosses the line between strangeness and silliness.

"The swan was so ridiculous," Melanie says after her stage encounter with the flapping, featured puppet. "But all the same it did scare me." Presumably, the audience should concur with her entire statement, not just the first half.

Soon it's anything-can-happen time in toyland. Incest rears its head. Bell contorts his face. People start vanishing into thin air. Aware that the element of surrealism gives the film makers a way out, we half-expect to find Melanie yawning and stretching in her warm bed back home. "And then I woke up," she might say. It would be a cheat, but at least it would be a finish.

"The Magic Toyshop," however, is not an adolescent's dream. First shown on British television, it comes billed as an "adult fairytale." In other words, it's the kind of show Uncle Philip might put on in his basement, if only he had the budget.

VILLAGE VOICE, 8/1/89, P. 61, J. Hoberman

Adapted by Angela Carter from her 1967 novel, *The Magic Toyshop* resembles her hothouse prose, at once delicate and overwrought, innocent and knowing. Although it's as self-conscious a yarn as any Indiana Jones flick, *The Magic Toyshop* is less serenely confident, more secretively bright-eyed and flushed in its particular cleverness. As an adventure, the film is a pageant of introversion. Even more than Carter's stories, this grown-up fairy tale, opening today for a two-week run at Film Forum 1, explicates itself.

Richly cluttered with special effects and wind-up dolls, *The Magic Toyshop* looks right for kids but, obsessed as it is with the pangs of adolescent sexual awakening, it's a treat that's intended for mature audiences. The movie looks like domesticated Cocteau, or an inebriated pastiche of a '40s Hollywood gothic. (As in *The Spiral Staircase*, every other scene seems to begin with a cloud of steam or a swirl of goose down.) As enjoyably creaky as a carnival carousel, the plot immediately turns mysterious—a red-haired woman gazing out a shop window into the rainy dusk, a seedy-looking musician rushing inside to play violin for the peculiar ritual that unfolds in the cellar. A life-sized marionette begins to twirl, and the image shifts to the 15-year-old Melanie (Caroline Milmoe) pirouetting before the mirror.

The Magic Toyshop, which was directed by David Wheatley for British TV in 1988, is elaborately dreamy. The film's time frame is obscure, the pacing is fluid, and every incident encrusts itself with free-floating symbols. Left home with two younger siblings while her parents travel abroad, the gravely ripening, surprisingly snaggletoothed Melanie pulls down mother's wedding dress from the closet, puts it on, and inadvertently locks herself out of the house. It's night, there's a garden, but you can't call this wish fulfillment—all she wants to do is get back inside. (With impeccable dream logic, Melanie climbs a tree, pricks her finger, and bloodies the gown.) By now the objective world is half dissolved in fantasy. When a goggled motorcyclist brings the news of her parents' death, the photograph of her sinister Uncle Philip breaks into a smile.

In Victorian fairy tale tradition, the orphaned Melanie and her sibs are packed off to South London to stay with dour Uncle Philip and mute Aunt Margaret (Patricia Kerrigan) in their digs above the toy shop. In addiion to a mad assortment of puppets and marionettes, a gaudy parrot and a supernatural bull terrier, this dingy land of make-believe is inhabited by Margaret's two picturesque brothers, Francie (Lorcan Cranitch) and Finn (Kilian McKenna). The latter, who is not much older than Melanie, immediately fixates on the girl. After watching her unpack, he insists on undoing her braids, an advance to which she responds by tartly observing, "Don't you ever wash your neck?"

Adolescent impulses will win out, but in this dismal landscape, everything takes on metaphoric weight: the Irish jigs the brothers perform after midnight, the scuzzy bathroom (a glass holding Uncle Philip's dentures dominating the foreground) with its deliquescent soap. Uncle Philip, played by Tom Bell, the nasty movie projectionist who seduced jailbait Emily Lloyd in *Wish You Were Here*, is no less creepy in this manifestation. He's a tormented, priggish magician who doesn't allow the kids to play with his toys. (His only thought for children is how to molest them.) It's suggested that Uncle Philip carries an incestuous torch for Melanie's mother, and he lowers over the movie like a dark cloud. "He used to send us toys, but Mommy burnt them because they were so frightening," Melanie telld Finn. (It's a pity we don't get to see them. The most memorable of Philip's creations is a cuckoo clock inhabited by a taxidermically stuffed bird.)

Although Philip is monstrously oppressive, he's also weirdly sympathetic. Twisted as he is, he's an artist who, for lack of any other audience, compels his family to witness the playlets he presents under the rubric "Flower's Marionette Microcosm." Typically, these puppet shows are all about him. In "An Artist's Passion," accompanied by fiddler Francie's lugubrious rendition of "Dance of the Sugar-Plum Fairy," an artist paints a statue's face and brings it to life—too much so, it would seem. As Philip intones that "each man kills the thing he loves," the marionettes themselves start to come unglued, flailing blindly away at each other. Finn, cackling with laughter, plunges facedown onto the stage; Philip, of course, runs to check on the discombobulated puppet.

More linear and less flamboyant than *The Company of Wolves*, the 1984 film Neil Jordan directed from Carter's scripts, *The Magic Toyshop* resolves itself as a straightforward coming-of-age film and rebellion against Philip's patriarchal regime. Events come to a head when the puppet master informs Melanie that his next production will be "Leda and the Swan", with Melanie herself playing Leda opposite his most cherished (and phallic) puppet. "Big swan, little Leda," he smirks, and, ridiculous as it is, this dramatization of interspecies rape becomes grotesquely discomfiting. Even more than "An Artist's Passion," this piece illustrates the failure of art. Because we see Melanie first as a woman, admiring herself naked in the mirror, and only then watch her assume her social role as a child, Philip's lust seems less inappropriate than it does clumsily sublimated.

This is why, as rich, funny, and resonant as it is, *The Magic Toyshop* appears to end a bit abruptly. Events spin into a postmodernist, Pre-Raphaelite delirium on the eve of Guy Fawkes Day, with Philip's temporary absence liberating family and puppets alike. There's an appropriate showdown, but, for all the concluding fireworks, *The Magic Toyshop* is quieter than *The Company of Wolves*—and also less of a movie. (Although Carter supposedly disowns the earlier film, it clearly belongs to her. Certainly, nothing Jordan directed before, or has done since, has been nearly so intelligent or so excessive.) *The Magic Toyshop* suffers for lacking *The Company of Wolves*'s show biz élan. The heroine may be less airbrushed, but her arena is more constricted. When the family falls away and only Melanie and Finn are left, you realize that what the *Toyshop* is selling is a version of *When Harry Met Sully*...—a fable on what it takes to make a couple in this world.

Also reviewed in:
NEW YORK TIMES, 7/26/89, p. C17, Caryn James
VARIETY, 12/17/86, p. 20

MAHABHARATA

A Chanel Four Television company/Les Productions du 3ème Etage/Brooklyn Academy of Music co-production. *Executive Producer:* Michael Birkett, Michael Kustow, and Harvey Lichenstein. *Producer:* Michel Propper. *Director:* Peter Brook. *Screenplay:* Jean-Claude Carrière, Peter Brook, and Marie-Hélène Estienne. *Director of Photography:* William Lubtchansky. *Editor:* Nicholas Gaster. *Sound:* Daniel Brisseau and Dominique Delmasso. *Production Designer:* Chloé Obolensky. *Running time:* 171 minutes. *MPAA Rating:* Not Rated.

CAST: Robert Langdon-Lloyd (Vyasa); Antonin Stahly-Viswanadhan (The Boy); Bruce Myers (Ganesha/Krishna); Vittorio Mezzogiorno (Arjuna); Andrzej Seweryn (Yudhishthira); Mamadou Dioume (Bhima); Jean Paul Denizon (Nakula); Mahmoud Tabrizi-Zadeh (Sahadeva); Mallika Sarabhai (Draupadi); Myriam Goldschmidt (Kunti); Erika Alexander (Madri/Hidimbi); Ryszard Cieslak (Dritharashtra); Hélène Patarot (Gandhari); Georges Corraface (Duryodhana); Urs Bihler (Dushassana); Sotigui Kouyate (Bhishma/Parashurama); Yoshi Oida (Drona); Tapa Sudana (Shiva).

CHRISTIAN SCIENCE MONITOR, 4/30/90, p. 10, David Sterritt

Before it became a movie, "The Mahabharata" was the theater event of the last decade: a nine-hour extravaganza based on an ancient Indian epic of enormous length and scope. Adapted for the stage by director Peter Brook and writer Jean-Claude Carrière, it had its first performances in a French rock quarry, then toured Europe and visited the United States about three years ago.

Since it was greeted with excitement wherever it went, talk about a film version didn't take long to develop. Never one to do things halfway, Mr. Brook has assembled two editions of "The Mahabharata" on film—one about six hours long, intended mainly for television, and one just under three hours long. The shorter edition is now on-screen in the United States, traveling to one city at a time in "special event" showings.

As a literary work, "The Mahabharata" is profoundly Indian, written in Sanskrit more than 2,000 years ago and said to be the basis of Hindu culture. Yet the movie, like the play before it, is a very international production—directed by Brook, an Englishman, from a screenplay he wrote with Carrière and Marie-Hélène Estienne, both French authors. The main performers come from Brook's theater group, the International Center of Theater Research, which is based in Paris but has members from 36 different countries.

The story of "The Mahabharata" also transcends any particular place or time. The portions included in the film represent just a tiny fraction of the entire Hindu poem, which—the movie's distributor helpfully informs us—is 10 to 15 times as long as the Bible, or eight times longer than the "Iliad" and the "Odyssey" put together.

Not surprisingly, this enormous epic has a long and complicated plot even in its condensed motion-picture form. It's narrated by two individuals: a storyteller who also takes part in the action, and a scribe who has an elephant's head on a human body. Their tale, on the most basic level, is about two rival families struggling for control of the known world over a very long period of time.

I first saw "The Mahabharata" onstage at the Brooklyn Academy of Music in New York, all nine hours of it in one marathon session. I was very impressed by its ambition and scale, but I can't say it moved me the way a true masterpiece does. In some important ways, "The Mahabharata" is very similar to Indian music: Just as an Indian raga is all melody, with little in the way of harmony or modulation, "The Mahabharata" is all story—moving endlessly from one incident to another, but rarely pausing to develop themes or characters in depth.

This is an ancient and valid form of narrative art, with precedents (such as "The Thousand Nights and a Night," perhaps the most famous example) stretching back for centuries. But it requires that a modern Western audience adjust its expectations in radical ways, especially with regard to the expanded use of time and the comparative lack of a familiar psychological dimension.

Every individual spectator will have to decide whether "The Mahabharata" offers aesthetic and intellectual dividends great enough to reward this effort. For me, the answer is only a partial yes.

The movie, like the play, has moments of great beauty and drama. Yet it often failed to engage me as its episodes succeeded one another like grains of sand through an ancient Indian hourglass.

The film version is certainly more compact than its stage counterpart, however, and portions of it are strikingly effective as they express the story's mixture of human and supernatural elements with their own combination of vivid performances and elaborate studio settings. I'll add that all the moments I remember most clearly from the theatrical production are included in the three-hour film version—which has passages of rich and compelling artistry, even if it doesn't have the high level of multicultural excitement for which one might have hoped.

NEW YORK POST , 4/27/90, p. 41, David Edelstein

The excitement of "The Mahabharata" on stage was watching Peter Brook and his multiracial cast distill this national epic—the rock of Indian religion, at 10 times the length of our own Bible—into a sort of campfire epic on a largely bare stage. It was theater as ritual, both rough and sacred, and the primitive magic was at times overwhelming: You felt you were witnessing the invention of the wheel.

A filmed version is, inevitably, a compromise, but Brook and French dramatist Jean-Claude Carriere have managed to create a compelling hybrid, with the fluidity of a stage production and some of the intimacy and sensuality of a movie. It is, however, an arm's-length experience: Brook has retained the objectivity of a stage director and what should be a pipe dream of the beginning of the world often seems cold, formal and distant.

Compressed to 6½ hours for television "The Mahabharata" has been further distilled into three for the big screen. You don't make the same kind of investment now or have a chance to live with characters (and the program that reminds you who they are); the uninitiated might experience the tale as one long blur—men with spears hurrying into and out of pools of light on a burlap-colored desert.

There isn't enough variety in Brook's technique: He seems to have taken to heart the Bhagavad-Ghita's exhortation to see different things with the same eye.

However, his blend of alertness and detachment can result in scenes of extraordinary vividness and horror. In essence, "The Mahabharata" concerns two clans, the Pandavas and the Kauravas, both descended from the gods and more related than either suspects. They wage a bitter, pointless war, and each comes by the weapon of ultimate destruction—a thinly veiled metaphor for the Bomb.

Brook, a pacifist, lingers on the atrocities and oaths of vengeance with the eyes of a sorrowful god, underlining the conviction that the pain of victory comes close to the pain of defeat.

The climax is gravely magnificent: Karna's inability to invoke the ultimate weapon and his death by arrow, Dushassana's killing and disembowelment, Duryodhana's emergence from his hiding place under the ice to meet his destiny. Even dimmed by translation, "The Mahabarata" sends out bolts of enlightenment.

NEWSDAY, 4/27/90, Part II/p. 5, Joseph Koenenn

In the beginning was the Sanskrit version, 18 volumes of myth and legend called "The Mahabharata." Westerners by the thousands were introduced to "The Mahabharata" by British director Peter Brook, who, with the dramatist Jean-Claude Carriere, lifted it off the page and onto the stage. Their nine-hour production has played around the globe, including a fall, 1987, visit to the Brooklyn Academy of Music's Majestic Theater.

In the move from stage to film, "Mahabharata," a three-hour distillation of the 5½-hour TV version, has lost a few of its subplots, much of its limited supply of humor and hardly any of its wordiness.

As in the stage play, its sporadic bits of action are separated by long, sometimes rambling discourses on weighty topics, such as the meaning of life and the basis of Hindu philosophy. The action centers on competing members of two half-divine families from whom all of India is descended. In ecumenical moments, the epic shares features of other religions—a virgin birth, an infant boy abandoned in a basket on the riverside.

But the film's major message comes from the inevitable and brutal combat between the two sides. And, in the hands of Brook and Carriere, it becomes as contemporary as the latest antiwar protest.

Brook, designer Chloe Obolensky (a longtime Brook stage collaborator making her movie debut) and cinematographer William Lubtchansky have produced a product that is dazzling, even in its talkative periods.

Brook said he sought diversity rather than uniformity in his cast. If there was an opening, he tried to find someone as unlike the others as possible.

The result is a multinational, multiracial cast that has varying degrees of fluency in English (and only one Indian, Mallika Sarabhai). Some actors' lines can barely be deciphered by even the careful listener. But they all have faced of great character, and Lubtchansky loves to fill a whole frame with one, dwelling on its strength as well as its imperfections.

VILLAGE VOICE, 5/1/90, p. 78, Georgia Brown

At the *Voice*, we drew straws to see who got to review *The Mahabharata* and I lost. Actually, the earnest one volunteered. Now I'm Lazarus come back to tell you that although this is not a movie movie, it's fun, worth seeing, and too short at a speedy 170 minutes—although given the numbers who walked out on the screening, it's obvious that others weren't having as good a time as I was. Profound? No. But you might get intimations.

For the culturally illiterate, and for those who didn't absorb the message when Peter Brook's big-top came to BAM, *The Mahabharata* is one of two great epics of ancient India—a huge Sanskrit poem and vast compendium of Hindu culture. For the screen, Brook has pared down his first, theatrical, paring-down to what I can only assume are central stories. Or maybe they are the ones he and fellow screenwriters, Jean-Claude Carriére and Marie-Helene Estienne, liked best.

Brook begins with the storyteller, Vyasa (Robert Langdon-Lloyd), and a tall, appealing boy (Antonin Stahly-Viswanadhan). "I've composed a great poem. ... It's about you," Vyasa tells the boy. "If you listen carefully, at the end you'll be someone else." Listening carefully, even with the promise of a new personality, is a difficult assignment until you begin to get the main characters straight. It doesn't help that these aren't named Kareem, Judy, or Accattone, or that stories about Bhishma, Yudhishthira, and Dhritharashtra fly past like so many springtime sparrows. Patience. *The Mahabharata* is a great soap opera.

The center of the narrative becomes the war between two rival families, the Pandavas and the Kauravas. The Pandavas are five brothers born of two mothers and Pandu, "king of the known world." All five marry a single woman and appear ecstatic with the arrangement. One day in a dice game, they literally lose their shirts to the jealous, power-hungry Kauravas (whose mother gave birth to a large metal ball that obligingly split into a hundred sons) and are sent into exile. At the end of 13 years, a world war or battle of titans breaks out, with the philosophical Krishna (Bruce Myers) fighting on the side of the Pandavas. "When chaos threatens, as it does now, Krishna takes on a human form and comes down." Good to know.

As for Brook's production, it's not naturalistic, but suggestive in the way of his theater work. Indoor sets make use of bamboo curtains and oriental rugs; for out-door scenes, mud and bushes are hauled in. Most of the actors—from 36 countries—speak English as a second language. Acting is rhetorical, directly out of the theater. Little attempt is made to use the cinematic medium and the feel of synopsis is very strong. Yet, speaking as someone who can barely sit through anything with live actors, including the New York Film Critics Circle awards, I was entertained.

Also reviewed in:
NEW REPUBLIC, 5/7/90, p. 28, Stanley Kauffmann
NEW YORK TIMES, 4/27/90, p. C16, Stephen Holden
VARIETY, 9/13-19/89, p. 32

MAJOR LEAGUE

A Paramount Pictures release of a Morgan Creek/Mirage production. *Executive Producer:* Mark Rosenberg. *Producer:* Chris Chesser and Irby Smith. *Director:* Davis S. Ward. *Screenplay:* David S. Ward. *Director of Photography:* Reynaldo Villalobos. *Editor:* Dennis M. Hill. *Music:* James Newton Howard. *Music Editor:* Ellen Siegel. *Sound:* Susumu Tokunow. Sound Editor: J. Paul Huntsman. *Production Designer:* Jeffrey Howard. *Art Director:* John Reinhart. *Set Designer:* Bill Rea. *Set Decorator:* Celeste Lee. *Set Dresser:* Adam Silverman. *Special Effects:* Dieter Sturm. *Costumes:* Erica Edell Phillips. *Make-up:* Joann Wabisca. *Stunt Coordinator:* Rick Le Fevour. *Running time:* 89 minutes. *MPAA Rating:* R.

CAST: Tom Berenger (Jake Taylor); Charlie Sheen (Ricky Vaughn); Corbin Bernsen (Roger Dorn); Margaret Whitton (Rachel Phelps); James Gammon (Lou Brown); Rene Russo (Lynn Wells); Wesley Snipes (Willie Mays Hayes); Charles Cyphers (Charlie Donovan); Chelcie Ross (Eddie Harris); Dennis Haysbert (Pedro Cerrano);

Andy Romano (Pepper Leach); Bob Uecker (Harry Doyle); Steve Yeager (Duke Temple); Peter Vuckovich (Haywood); Stacy Carroll (Suzanne Dorn), Richard Pickren (Tom). Kevin Crowley (Vic Bolito); Mary Seibel (Thelma); Bill Leff (Bobby James); Mike Bacarella (Johnny Wynn); Skip Griparis (Colorman); Gary Houston (Ross Farmer); Ward Ohrman (Arthur Holloway); Marge Kotlisky (Claire Holloway); Tony Mockus Jr. (Brent Bowden); Deborah Wakeman (Janice Bowden); Neil Flynn (Longshoreman); Keith Uchima (Groundskeeper #1); Kurt Uchima (Groundskeeper #2); William M. Sinacore (Coleman); Richard Baird (Hal Charles); Julia Milaris (Arlene); Roger Unice (Rexman); Michael Thoma (Gentry); Patrick Dollymore (French Waiter); Joseph Liss (Guy in Bar); Gregory Alan Williams (Bull Pen Guard); Peter Ruskin (Gateman); Michael Hart (Burton); James Deuter (Phil Butler); Jack McLaughlin-Gray (Jerry Simmons); Tim Bell (Body Building Assistant); Joe Soto (Security); Ted Noose (Lyle (Matthews); Lenny Rubin (Clubhouse Man); Thomas P. Purdoff (Umpire #1); Jeffrey J. Edwards (Umpire #2); Alexandra Villa (Hostess); Michelle Minyon (Working Class Bar Patron).

FILMS IN REVIEW, 8–9/89, p. 419, Pat Anderson

In Spring, all through the land, umpires yell "Play ball!" And now not only in parks and stadiums, but in theatres too. *Major League* is a lighthearted, funny look at yet another bumbling team: this time the Cleveland Indians, though this team is *not* made up of the real life perennial American League basement Tribe.

The owner Rachel Phelps (Margaret Whitton), who has inherited the club from her husband, hates Cleveland and wants a team so inept that the attendance will drop and she can move the franchise to Miami. So all these misfits are brought in to further her scheme. They are called in from the Mexican circuit, veteran catcher Jake Taylor (Tom Berenger); paroled from prison, Charlie Sheen as rookie pitcher Ricky Vaughn (shades of Billy Martin having Ron LeFlore paroled from Jackson State Prison to play with the Detroit Tigers); from used-car salesmen to unemployed loafers, come mediocre players and religious freaks (including Dennis Haysbert as a first baseman who uses an elaborate voodoo set up to enhance his hitting); Willy Mays Hayes (Wesley Snipes) who electrifies his cohorts by running like Roger Bannister and proves *if* he can get on base, he can steal at will. Corbin Bernsen, the only holdover from the regular team, is a third baseman who is too concerned with mussing his hair and possibly scratching his face to go after hard chances.

But surprise, surprise, new manager Lou Brown (James Gammon) not only wants no part of Rachel Phelps' machinations, but also convinces his unenthusiastic team this is their only chance to make good. So they bumble, fight, practice—and start winning games. The owner gets mean, and players meaner. And the fans love it. Especially Charlie Sheen, whom the teeny-boppers nickname "Wild Thing" and sing to every time he goes to the mound. Guess what? Come September which team is down to the wire with the New York Yankees? Yup. Really down to the wire, and the last game of the series also contains one of the most amusing baseball sequences on film.

All the actors seem to be having a ball in this movie, and Charlie Sheen even looks as though he could have made a baseball player if he hadn't opted for the family business. What an enjoyable film this is: predictable, but a great deal of fun.

LOS ANGELES TIMES, 4/7/89, Calendar/p. 10, Kevin Thomas

"Major League," an amiable and amusing hot weather diversion, trusts mightily that the Cleveland Indians and their fans are blessed with a good sense of humor.

Taking note of the fact that the Indians haven't won a pennant since 1954, writer-director David Ward imagines that the team has been inherited by a hard-hearted ex-Vegas show girl (Margaret Whitton). Her notion is to hire such a bunch of losers that attendance will plummet and she"ll be able to move the franchise to Miami, a city with a climate much more to her liking. (There will also be a Palm Beach mansion for her as part of the deal).

You don't have to be Sherlock Holmes to deduce that the recruits won't turn out to be the deadbeats Whitton expects them to be. Ward, who won an Oscar for his script for "The Sting" and more recently adapted "The Milagro Beanfield War," deflects predictability with admirable deftness. He does this with generous doses of humor and affection, a clear love and extensive knowledge of baseball and the Indians—who he says he's rooted for since he was 5 years old—and a starry cast that gets into the good ol' boy spirit of the story.

Tom Berenger's Jake Taylor is a playboy now in his 30s with such bad knees he hopes for just "one more season in the sun." Charlie Sheen's Ricky Vaughn is a punker, just finishing doing time for car theft, a kid with a fast ball but no control. Corbin Bernsen's Roger Dorn is a talented third baseman whose mind is more on money than baseball; he's more interested in preserving his profile for TV commercials than with exerting himself. Burly, seen-it-all manager Lou Brown (James Gammon, always a pleasure), recruited reluctantly from his tire business—and unaware of his employer's true intentions—has his work cut out for him in shaping up a team that also includes Wesley Snipes as a rookie with the wonderful name of Willie Mays Hayes and Dennis Haysbert as a voodoo-practicing Cuban émigré. Bob Uecker, a canny, witty standout, is the Indians' jaded but game radio announcer, and elegant newcomer Rene Russo is the beauty that Jake let get away and is determined to win back.

Ward directs his actors as adroitly as he has written for them, and the vulnerability that he allows his three stars to reveal is really what makes the movie work. No one, not even baseball fans, should go to "Major League" hoping for "Bull Durham's" sex, raunch and sophistication. But "Major League" (R-rated for language) has its own ingratiating charm.

MONTHLY FILM BULLETIN, 11/89, p. 336, Philip Strick

Following the death of the owner of the Cleveland Indians baseball team, his widow, former showgirl Rachel Phelps, takes over their management. The Indians have been notorious failures for thirty-four years, but Mrs. Phelps plans to ensure that this is their worst year yet so that she can transfer the franchise to Miami where the weather is better. She instructs general manager Donovan and training manager Brown to begin trials with a group of lacklustre athletes guaranteed to produce disaster. These include veteran catcher Jake Taylor, nearly worn out and on the point of retirement; pitcher Ricky "Wild Thing" Vaughn, a young hellraiser on parole for car theft; third baseman Roger Dorn, a wealthy professional no longer inclined to make any effort; outfielder Willie Hayes, a newcomer with a remarkable turn of speed; and baseman Pedro Cerrano, a Cuban exile inspired by voodoo. Although each has his skills, they form a chaotic partnership on the field and despairingly begin a losing season, much to Mrs. Phelps' delight. Jake takes the opportunity of his return to Cleveland after a season in Mexico to renew his relationship with Lynn Wells, a local librarian, now expecting to marry Tom, a snobbish yuppie. She tries to avoid Jake, but his persistence begins to win her round. He also bullies the Indians into taking themselves more seriously; despite every effort by Mrs. Phelps to make life difficult they show signs of playing a reasonable game occasionally. When at last they learn that Mrs. Phelps actually wants them to fail, they are galvanised into a series of victories making them the season's most popular team; their final challenge will be a play-off against the New York Yankees. As the big day approaches, Jake is upset by Lynn's move to live with Tom, while Dorn's wife decides to avenge herself on her unfaithful husband by seducing Ricky, who only finds out who she is when about to partner Dorn on the field. A suspenseful game against the Yankees leaves the Indians jubilant, Mrs. Phelps thwarted, Ricky and Dorn reconciled, and Jake and Lynn reunited.

A raucous and unlikely celebration of American-style gamesmanship, rendered peculiar enough by the mysteries of the sport itself but more so by the team owner's inflexible eagerness for failure (surely she would profit as much from victory?), *Major League* offers a potentially uncongenial prospect among the current crop of baseball movies, at least for British audiences. As well as revealing some dubious tricks of the trade, such as a resumé of the lotions that might be applied to a ball before its flight, the film besieges us with such broad humour in the locker room and beyond—a raspberry here, a urination there—that the uninitiated must be tempted to regard the whole venture as slapstick fantasy in which the ultimate triumph is as pointless as the preceding defeats. Curiously, however, it is in dealing with fantasy that *Major League* manages within reason to redeem itself. Like a domesticated *Dirty Dozen*, it assembles a pack of wearily disillusioned no-hopers and transforms them with a magical wave of the montage into slightly bashful super-heroes. What matters on this route from ignominy to outrageous fortune is not so much that the players discover that their combined skills have transcended their individuality, but that they are largely unchanged by the process, ending up as gullible—even as juvenile—as they started.

Delighted with the enduring skill of human nature at fooling itself, David Ward's story distantly recalls his Oscar-winning script for *The Sting* by exploring a series of deceptions and reversals. The basic premise is that one deceit (by the baseball team's owner) is countered by another (the team's secret determination to win), and this is embroidered with such appropriate bits of narrative as the scenes of the player's wife getting back at her husband by deceiving him with another player, who is also conned in that he doesn't know who she is. The other central relationship, between the dogged sportsman and the evasive librarian (played with calculated charm by Tom Berenger and newcomer of René Russo), is similarly a brittle contest of appearances. He tricks her into renewing their relationship, she misleads him into confronting his rival (presented as a probable phoney), he tricks her by reading *Moby Dick* as promised but only in comicbook form, and she has the last trick by appearing unexpectedly (and unmarried) out of the cheering crowds at the end.

A parallel accordingly emerges between the vacuous rituals of the baseball business (complete with masonic semaphore and bubble reputations) and the hopes of its participants, two of whom find physical effort finally more reliable than faith, while another makes his dreams come true by literally running after them. The wish-fulfilment aspects of the story reach their climax with the concluding game, but are also apparent in the punctuating shots of Cleveland itself, its industrial vistas ravishingly filmed by Reynaldo Villalobos in sunlit hues of nostalgia. This is the director's home town, and it hasn't had a baseball triumph, says Ward, in a good thirty-five years. But his hopes remain high...

NEW YORK, 4/24/89, p. 98, David Denby

David Ward's *Major League*, which brings us down to earth with a belch, is a very familiar type of lowbrow comedy about a bunch of jerk-offs, meatballs, weirdos, and bums who wind up in the starting lineup of the Cleveland Indians and manage to amaze everyone by putting together a magnificent season. As obvious as a burlesque show and as amiable as a profane old bullpen coach, *Major League* ia pretty consistently funny and sometimes uproarious. Tom Berenger gets stuck with a soulful straight role, but Charlie Sheen, Corbin Bernsen, James Gammon, and a young actor named Wesley Snipes throw, run, slide, spit, and fumble like the incomparable 1962 Mets.

NEW YORK POST, 4/7/89, p. 31, Jami Bernard

"Major League" is minor league entertainment about a baseball team of misfits who manage to pull themselves together for the playoffs and become hometown heroes, much to the chagrin of the club's ex-showgirl owner, who wanted them desperately to fail.

The jokes mostly consist of endless shots of fumbled balls, teammates who start out as polar opposites but who learn to work together, players who are hired on the strength of one ability but who lack every other skill in the book.

Listless direction and a wandering script (both by the same person, David Ward, who wrote the scripts for "The Milagro Beanfield War" and "The Sting") have trouble keeping even this most straightforward of movie conceits—losers into winners—from striking out.

All this despite the pairing of Charlie Sheen and Tom Berenger, who were last together in "Platoon." This movie provides more bad fodder for the endless and endlessly boring controversy over whether there can be a good baseball movie. Anyway, here's the pitch:

"Major League" is set in Cleveland, where the Indians haven't won a pennant since '54. Rachel Phelps (Margaret Whitton) inherits the ball club from her deceased husband and hopes to move it to Florida, where the social climate is as hot as the weather. Only she can't break her lease with Cleveland unless she can get attendance down, which she can't do unless the team really stinks.

So she presents her dream lineup, which includes a voodoo worshiper, a penal colony rookie, an old-timer with bad knees and a dead person ("OK, cross him off the list").

The bulk of the movie's laughs come early, as the rag-tag team arrives for spring training. These are generally visual gags, guys looking like mean machines or effete snobs (one player brings a set of golf clubs with knitted booties on the ends; a menacing teammate steals a bootie to keep his bat warm).

Sheen, who is lately making a specialty of baseball movies ("Eight Men Out"), plays Ricky, known as "The Wild Thing" and introduced with appropriate musical accompaniment. Ricky has been sprung from jail for this career opportunity. He has a good arm, but his aim is off; he's more likely to kill a batter than pitch to him

For the role, Sheen has razored his hair into sharp little pennants behind his ears. Bizarre. Nice earring, though.

Corbin Bernsen plays Roger Dorn, a prissy, preppie player who would rather protect his handsome looks than win a game.

Dennis Haysbert is Pedro, a voodoo worshiper who keeps incense and sacrificial totems in his locker. He's a big mother; laughs are squeezed out of the audience by placing the camera directly in front of his face and having him growl. It's the Mr. T school of filmmaking.

Berenger has the most appealing role, that of Jake Taylor, a womanizer whose stint in the

Mexican leagues has taught him that he should have held onto his old girlfriend (the lovely, nicely coiffed Rene Russo). Much screen time is spent watching the wickedly handsome Berenger try to lure her away from her new beau, a nerdy, yuppie lawyer. The decks are too stacked to make this very interesting.

Wesley Snipes comes out best as Willie Mays Hayes ("I play like Mays and I run like Hayes"). While Berenger and Sheen are playing it straight and hoping humor will find its way to home plate, Snipes is the one character who actually makes jokes. He should have run like Hayes from this movie.

The other bright spot is former ballplayer Bob Uecker as the occasionally sloshed radio announcer, whose between-innings happy talk runs to telling the folks back home that Sheen's character "is a juvenile delinquent in the off-season."

Tension is so lacking during the predicatable and interminable finale that writer/director (and former Cleveland resident) Ward resorts to a soundtrack of ear-splitting cheers from the stands. It is the sports-film equivalent of canned laughter, a noise that is meant to dictate the audience's response. Things must be pretty dull in Cleveland to warrant such hysterics.

NEWSDAY, 4/7/89, Part III/p. 3, Mike McGrady

Baseball and laughter, which blended so deftly in last season's "Bull Durham," are back again in "Major League," a low-level laffer with an appealing cast and the kind of go-for-the-gut humor that made "Police Academy"all that it is today.

While it can often be difficult to determine when broad comedy slips over to farce, "Major League" presents no such problem. When a movie depicts the Cleveland Indians as pennant contenders, farce is the word. Although the flick delivers more pleasure than any real-life Cleveland game in memory, it suffers from a severely split personality.

For fully half the movie, while the players are being introduced, it provides raucous, thoroughly unchallenging, crotch-grabbing humor. However, during the latter stages, the humor turns into inspiration as the low-flying Indians make a run for the pennant against the Yankees.

The movie opens on a somewhat more truthful note with headlines outlining the Indians' past achievements: "Indians' Slump Reaches 34 Years." A brand new owner ("Can Vegas Beauty Turn Tribe Around?") is determined to move the team to Miami, but the only way she can manage this contractually is to force attendance down. And the way to do that, she decides, is to hire a collection of has-beens, misfits, ex-cons, Cuban defectors and flakes. In other words, a not untypical Cleveland team.

Unfortunately, much of this lineup turns out to be a carbon copy of the "Bull Durham" lineup. We have the wild young fireballer (Charlie Sheen); the veteran catcher (Tom Berenger); the veteran catcher's veteran girlfriend who also happens to be a baseball expert ("You ought to open your stance a little—they're pitching you inside"); and, the superstitious Cuban who sacrifices chickens, kisses snakes and lists his religion as "voodoo."

Welcome additions include an aging spitballer who stores jalapeno peppers in his nostrils to provide a reliable supply of moisture and a womanizing third baseman (Corbin Bernsen) who has trouble with grounders: "It was out of my reach. What'd you want me to do—*dive* for it?" Finally, "Major League" comes with its own play-by-play announcer, played by Bob Uecker in fine form: "He leads the league in most offensive categories, including nose hair."

So far, so good. Then writer-director David. S. Ward decides to have it both ways. He wants us to laugh at these stumblebums, and then he wants us to take them seriously as they pull ever closer to the Yankees in a pennant race that, of course, goes down to the last out of the last inning of the last game, a "Rocky"-type windup complete with "Rocky"-type music, that will carry credibility only with Little Leaguers who still sleep with their baseball mitts.

Tom Berenger is steady and likable, and Corbin Bernsen—that's right, Arnie Becker from "L.A. Law"— is a delight. This is Charlie Sheen's second season in the bigs (last year he debuted in "Eight Men Out"), and he may be the most gifted baseball player ever to pursue an acting career (as a high school pitcher in Santa Monica, he was promising enough to be offered a baseball scholarship). While he makes a nice comic contribution here, the movie must ultimately be considered Hollywood's equivalent of the sophomore jinx.

TIME, 4/24/89, p. 78, Richard Corliss

A boy's sport, a man's game. Baseball lodges in the American male heart because the fundamentals look easy enough for any Little Leaguer to master. Too soon, men realize that pro ball demands a genius for grace, concentration and magnificent egotism. They may agonize over the career path not closen, the debt too steep, the woman so close but just beyond their reach. For many, though, a dream of athletic stardom is the one that got away. So they stick with baseball, living and dying with their team, analyzing stats with the rapt anguish of a rabbinical student cramming for a final. To their favorite players they are both sons and fathers—part hero worshipers, part child psychologists. They become a collective, possessive lover of their idols. Baseball fever: boys catch it, men can't shake it.

Not even movie men are immune, as witness last summer's *Bull Durham, Eight Men Out* and *Stealing Home*. And here come two more films, both directed by their writers, that play games with baseball. David S. Ward's *Major League* is a rowdy, genially cynical comedy about jocks and Jills. Its fanciful Cleveland Indians team is a bunch of rejects from the Mexican, minor and California Penal leagues. Now coming to bat: the veteran catcher on his last legs (Tom Berenger), the Willie Mays wanna-be (Wesley Snipes), the pampered third baseman (Corbin Bernsen). And on the mound, a fastballer (Charlie Sheen) with control problems on and off the field. With this gang, in this comic fantasy, the Tribe can't lose.

Major League doesn't try too hard or aim too high, but it is pretty funny. With its stock characters, breezy dialogue, dense ambience and instinct for easy emotions, it could serve as the pilot for a pay-cable sitcom. The film's tone is acerb, but its climax is as predictably uplifting as *Rocky*'s and as surefire effective as *Damn Yankees'*.

The hero of *Damn Yankees* was a pennant-winning natural named Shoeless Joe Hardy. The hero of Phil Alden Robinson's *Field of Dreams* is a farmer (Kevin Costner) who dreams of bringing Shoeless Joe Jackson back to earth for one more game. The great outfielder may have helped throw the 1919 World Series, but the farmer idolizes him and his Black Sox teammates for their innocence! So with the help of his trusting wife (Amy Madigan) and a crusty blacky author (James Earl Jones) who doesn't mind that all the old major-leaguers were white, he plows down his cornfield to erect a ball park and populate it with phantoms.

Despite a lovely cameo turn by Burt Lancaster, *Field of Dreams* is the male weepie at its wussiest. There is poetry in baseball, sure, but it is not shaggy doggerel of the Joyce Kilmer stripe: "I think that I shall ne'er remark/A cornfield green as Fenway Park." It comes in the concrete poetry of a Bill James statistical analysis, or in the sprung rhythm of a Roger Angell paragraph. Or in the flight of a ball from the pitcher's hand toward the catcher's glove, with a million delicious options at stake.

VILLAGE VOICE, 4/18/89, p. 72, Richard Regen

If you're the type of person who likes baseball movies (like me), you've already seen *Major League*—it's every baseball pic ever made. (One might have expected better from writer/director David S. Ward, who won an Academy Award for his screenplay for *The Sting* and wrote and directed *Cannery Row*.) An evil owner wants the team to lose so he/she can take over/move the franchise, but the noble players foil the plot by overcoming their ineptitude to vie for the pennant (*The Natural*); haphazardly collected misfits, rejects, and weirdos who initially hate each other grow to love and respect one another while building themselves into a fine-tuned baseball machine under the tutelage of a grizzled but lovable manager (*The Bad News Bears*); the main character, a beat-up but wordly veteran catcher, has one year of glory left and a sexy woman to woo (*Bull Durham*); and the home team, a perennial loser, overcomes its traditional nemesis, the hated Yankees, to win it all (*Damn Yankees*).

The fictional Cleveland Indians in *Major League* are a potpourri of rookies, has-beens, and one-dimensional players (not unlike the real Tribe), featuring Roger Dorn (Corbin Bernsen), a prissy, overpriced third baseman; Ricky Vaughn (Charlie Sheen), a rookie fireballing punk pitcher fresh from prison; and Jake Taylor (Tom Berenger), an over-the-hill catcher playing out a drunken string in the Mexican League. Throw in a Cuban slugger who's into voodoo but can't hit a curveball (Dennis Haysbert), a sassy streetwise outfielder with blinding speed but no bat (Wesley Snipes), and a veteran God Squad right-hander (Chelcie Ross), and the result is *Police Academy meets Casey at the Bat*.

The film has its comic moments, expecially when Bob Uecker, making his screen debut as the Indians' radio announcer, does his shtick behind the mike, with gems like "This guy threw at his own son in a father-son game," but on the whole, the comedy is uneven and hackneyed.

Berenger's Jake is Sybil in double knit: One scene he's cooing, "I'm just a guy trying to put his life back together"; the next he's growling, "I'll cut your balls off and stuff them down your throat."

In terms of baseball, *Major League* is science fiction. Besides the Indians actually winning games, men get bunted home from second base, and big league players ride buses on road trips and sleep in army barracks during spring training. Picture Keith and Darryl discussing who gets the top bunk.

Also reviewed in:
NEW REPUBLIC, 5/8/89, p. 26, Stanley Kauffmann
NEW YORK TIMES, 4/7/89, p. C19, Caryn James
VARIETY, 4/12–18/89, p. 20
WASHINGTON POST, 4/7/89, p. C1, Hal Hinson

MAKING "DO THE RIGHT THING"

A First Run Features release of a Chamba Organization and 40 Acres and a Mule Filmworks production. *Producer:* St. Clair Bourne. *Director:* St. Clair Bourne. *Screenplay:* St. Clair Bourne. *Director of Photography:* Juan Cobo and Joseph Friedman. *Editor:* Susan Fanshel. *Music:* Steve Coleman. *Sound:* Nelson Funk. *Sound Editor:* Donald Klocek. *Running time:* 58 minutes. *MPAA Rating Rating:* Not Rated.

WITH: Spike Lee, Danny Aiello, Ossie Davis, Ruby Dee, Giancarlo Esposito, Bill Nunn, Richard Edson, John Turturro, Melvin Van Peebles.

NEWSDAY, 11/3/89, Part III/p. 7, Janice Berman

It's the feeling of empowerment that's the best part of St. Clair Bourne's documentary, "Making 'Do the Right Thing,' " which focuses on the impact of Spike Lee's film on the Bedford-Stuyvesant neighborhood where it was made.

Working there was no easy task, even for a crew as professional as Lee's. Although it took eight weeks to shoot, "Do the Right Thing" had to look as though it happened in a single day. Sets had to be constructed and then protected; the community, inconvenienced as much as intrigued by the film maker's constant presence, had to be courted.

But as we see in the documentary, which was partially funded by Lee, there's no sense of noblesse oblige. Lee's Forty Acres and a Mule company, almost entirely black, wanted the community to participate in everything from working as extras to taking out the trash. It paid off. "Do the Right Thing" drew its power as much from its sense of place as from its controversial storyline.

Scenes from the aftermath of the Howard Beach murder, on which Lee's film was based, are intercut in the documentary, and in interviews the cast addresses questions about racism and its effects not just on the movie but on their lives.

Lee himself offers what he considers one of the keys to his film's success: that he doesn't make value judgments about the way things ought to be, but focuses on life as it is. Life as it is, or was the day the film wrapped, seems to be pretty good, and we see the neighbors' pride that Lee's movie was made on their block. And from one community leader, we hear the hope that the positive energy would endure after life returned to normal.

The emphasis on "reality," one gathers from "Joe's Bed-Stuy Barbershop: We Cut Heads," has been with the film maker throughout his brief and blazing career, beginning as early as New York University Film School. The film—his graduate thesis—is not without its flaws. Lee's script, about a barbershop the Mob has subverted to the numbers racket, leaves us dangling, although there are predictions that everything will work out.

Yet here, before "Do the Right Thing" or even "She's Gotta Have It"—and packed into one hour—are all the elements that make Lee's movies so interesting. For instance: people and sets that look as though they might exist even when the cameras aren't running. A weighing of the good and bad aspects of vice, in this case the numbers racket. And a powerful sense of good people trapped in a situation that's as much a product of society as it is of individual evildoers.

VILLAGE VOICE, 11/7/89, p. 67, J. Hoberman

Speaking of babes in the woods [the reference is to *Sidewalk Stories*], Spike Lee is anything but one. Thus, albeit directed by veteran documentarist St. Clair Bourne, *Making "Do the Right Thing"*—which opens Friday at the Bleecker on a bill with Lee's 1982 NYU dissertation film, *Joe's Bed-Stuy Barbershop: We Cut Heads*—has to be seen as an ancillary product, one more part of Lee's burgeoning image empire.

Do the Right Thing doubtless has its secret history, but don't expect to learn exactly why Paramount put the movie in turnaround (and what, if anything, studio asset Eddie Murphy had to say about that). Bourne restricts his gaze to the Bed-Stuy street where Lee built Sal's Famous, and, although one member of the crew refers to the "tense, hostile environment around us," there's even more racial solidarity here than in *Do the Right Thing*. The Fruit of Islam guards who protected the set never let down their guard. Bourne is left to interview the actors—only a few of whom, notably Giancarlo Esposito and Danny Aiello, get past the familiar platitudes. *Making "Do"* is exactly that: It doesn't go beyond workmanlike.

Also reviewed in:
NEW YORK TIMES, 11/3/89, p. C17, Vincent Canby
VARIETY, 9/6–12/89, p. 29

MEMORIES OF PRISON

A Produçoes Cinematograficas L.C. Barreto production. *Executive Producer:* Mario de Salete. *Producer:* Lucy Barreto and Luiz Carlos Barreto. *Director:* Nelson Pereira dos Santos. *Screenplay (Portuguese with English subtitles:* Nelson Pereira dos Santos. *Based on the novel by:* Graciliano Ramos. *Director of Photography:* José Medeiros and Antonio L. Soares. *Editor:* Carlos Alberto Camuyrano. *Sound:* Jorge Saldanhà. *Production Designer:* Jose Oliosi. *Art Director:* Irênio Maia. *Set Designer:* Adilho Athos and Emily Pirmez. *Costumes:* Ligia Medeiros. *Running time:* 174 minutes. *MPAA Rating:* Not Rated.

CAST: Carlos Vereza (Braciliano Ramos); Glória Pires (Heloisa Ramos); Paulo Porto (Dr. Cabral); David Pinheiro (Captain Lobo); Jofre Soares (Soares); Nildo Parente (Manoel); José Dumont (Mario Pinto); Wilson Grey (Gaucho); Waldyr Onofre (Cubano); Jackson De Souza (Arruda); Tonico Pereira (Desiderio); Jorge Cherques (Goldberg); Antonio Almeijeiras (Leonardo).

CINEASTE, VOL. XIV, No. 2, 1985, p. 21, Robert Stam & Ismail Xavier

Ever since his first fiction features in the Fifties, the work of Nelson Pereira dos Santos has been marked by a generously critical spirit and by one overriding preoccupation—the ways in which the progressive filmmaker can express the values and concerns of the *"povo,"* the marginalized masses of the Brazilian people. This preoccupation has taken diverse forms over the years—from the sympathetic portrait of Rio Slumdwellers in *Rio 40 Graus* (*Rio 40 Degrees,* 1955), to the unsentimental depiction of peasant life in *Vidas Secas* (*Barren Lives,* 1963), to the critique of middle-class intellectuals in *Fome de Amor* (*Hunger for Love,* 1968), through the enthusiastic endorsement of Afro-Brazilian culture in *O Amuleto de Ogum* (*The Amulet of Ogum,* 1974) and *Tenda dos Milagres* (*Tent of Miracles,* 1977). *Memories of Prison* represents the mature and fulfilled realization of this ongoing commitment to the Brazilian people.

Based on the prison memoirs of Brazilian novelist Graciliano Ramos, the film charts Ramos' descent in the hell of the prisons of the Thirties fascist-populist dictator Getulio Vargas. More specifically, the film chronicles Ramos' imprisonment between March 1936 and January 1937. Arrested without explanation as part of an anti-leftist sweep aimed at Communists, Trotskyists, anarchists and liberal critics of the regime, Ramos at first resigns himself to incarceration because he is tired of a jealous wife (Heloisa), of public service, and of the pettiness of provincial life. He does not realize that he is about to be conducted on a forced tour of diverse forms of incarceration: ordinary jail, correctional facility, penal colony. Dos Santos slightly tampers with the actual chronology of events in order to emphasize a downward spiral into degradation, so that Ramos begins as a relatively pampered political prisoner and ends as the abused victim of the aptly-named "Colonia," a kind of concentration camp on the Atlantic coast, where he is informed that he has no rights and that his destiny is not to be rehabilitated but to die.

This summary of events is somewhat misleading, however, for the film simultaneously displays a very different movement. With each successive attempt at systematic dehumanization, Ramos paradoxically gains character and humanity through resistance. Ramos, whom we have seen from the beginning as a complex, proud and somewhat solitary man with an intense interior life, turns incarceration into a springboard for liberation. He gradually becomes a more committed human being at the same time that he comes to truly appreciate his vocation as a writer. Within the abject promiscuity of the "Colonia," he discovers what separated him, the progressive bourgeois intellectual, from the people. The terrible and useless violence of his third world gulag becomes, for him, the scene of a purificatory rite, a platform for human development.

Despite the director's claim (see accompanying interview) that he follows the novel "quite closely," the film is in fact creatively unfaithful to the source memoirs. The film insinuates that Ramos' manuscript is saved by the collectivity for imminent publication; in actual fact Ramos lost his prison manuscript and his memories only became transformed into written text over a decade later. While the book is quite dispassionate in its presentation of events, the film arranges all the dramatic situations around a central crescendo—the writer's increasing participation in the life of the prison and the prisoners' increasing collaboration in the work of the writer. A whole network of accomplices helps Ramos write, not only by providing anecdotes and information but also by physically protecting the manuscript. (In the source memoir, for example, it was not the manuscript but money that was hidden behind a bush). One prison comrade brings him a notebook and pencil, while another brings stolen paper. But the other prisoners also need the writer; a once reticent worker asks Ramos to correct the text of a manifesto, and even the warden, in a memorably comic sequence, asks him for his stylistic advice. What emerges is a remarkable portrait of collaboration between the writer and the people. The climax comes with the collective defense of the manuscript, which has become a group patrimony. And now the author's "witness" can turn the common experience into remembered history.

While Graciliano Ramos was dry and deliberately undramatic in his presentation of events, the film is more emotionally overwhelming; the spectator is led, thanks to the director's masterful *mise-en-scène* and effective ensemble acting, to a climax quite absent from the book. What the film loses in fidelity to Ramos it gains in faithfulness to the director's central vision of the role of the progressive artist. The film offers a ringing endorsement of the vocation of literature—and by analogy of the cinema—as critical register of the general experience. Despite political repression, the artist, in creative communion with the people, manages to construct his oeuvre, and both artist and people benefit.

Nelson Pereira dos Santos' films, even when set in the past, almost invariably speak to the present as well. *Vidas Secas* (1963), although set in the '40s, really addressed the question of agrarian reform in the '60s. *How Tasty Was My Little Frenchman* (1971), set in the 16th century, also speaks indirectly of ongoing genocide in the '70s. Despite Vincent Canby's claim, in his largely negative *New York Times* review, that *Memories of Prison* is politically irrelevant and self-indulgent, in fact the film has everything to do with the present moment in Brazil. The prison's "Freedom Radio" speaks of foreign debt and bankers' agreements, and a soldier tells the writer, in a transparent allusion to the twenty years of military rule dating from the 1964 coup: "It will take you civilians a good while to get rid of us." The eagerness of the prisoners to come to decisions by vote also evokes, for the Brazilian, the recent energetic campaign for direct presidential elections. The films begins and ends, furthermore, with the Brazilian national anthem, at a time when patriotism is back in style in Brazil, not because of feats in space or Olympic victories, but because of popular militancy and the end of military rule. The anthem is sung in a hesitant rather than a jingoistic manner, and the films's final freeze frame is accompanied by the variations that the 19th Century American composer Louis Gottschalk embroidered around the themes of the Brazilian anthem. The anthem marks the space of the film as a Brazilian space, suggesting that Brazil itself has the aspect of a prison—a lively and colorful prison, but a prison nonetheless.

Within the prison, we encounter a splendid gallery of characters, all based on real-life prototypes: the seasoned militants (Leninists and Trotskyists), the rebellious soldier, the Jewish doctor, the worker, the northeasterner. On the other side, the figures of authority—police, guards, warden, high military officials—are treated without Manichaeism or dogmatism: dos Santos, like Ramos, can see the human being behind the uniform. The prison represents not only Brazil under the Vargas dictatorship, and not only Brazil after the 1964 coup, but also what the director himself calls the "chain of social and political relations which imprison the Brazilian people." Thus the prison becomes the image of a national condition. But this condition also allows space for struggle. In one cell, the prisoners study English, in another, mathematics. In the central courtyard, discussion of Marxism. One prisoner writes poetry; another takes down notes for a novel. The speaker for "Freedom Radio" tries to raise morale. And an anarchist mocks them all. All play their role in the collective construction of freedom, just as all play their role in the collective elaboration of Ramos' book. Thanks to the writer and the filmmaker, the rest of us can remember as well.

LOS ANGELES TIMES, 8/2/85, Calendar/p. 12, Michael Wilmington

In the mid-'30s, a Brazilian writer, educator and leftist named Graciliano Ramos was arrested during a crackdown by one of his country's most repressive regimes: the dictatorship of Getulio Vargas. Ramos spent months in a high-security jail with other political prisoners. Eventually he was transferred to a worse jail, an island hell, whose commandant calmly informed his charges that they had not been sent there to be punished or rehabilitated—but to die.

Ramos survived. And his account of this incarceration has been made into a great Brazilian film, "Memories of Prison," a masterly blend of political protest and cinematic realism. At its best, this film gives what you feel must be the essence of prison life: the sweat, the pain, the agonizing day-to-day torpor and defeat, the absurdity, the tense, shifting camaraderie, the brief triumphs of defiance or perseverance and, over all, an ultimate slow grinding and wearing-down of the spirit, like a blade dulled and cracked against a wall.

The scenarist and director of the film, Nelson Pereira dos Santos, seems uniquely suited to the material. Long considered Brazil's foremost director (the late Glauber Rocha dubbed him the "conscience" of *cinema novo*), he previously adapted Ramos' novel of itinerant northeastern peasant farmers. "Vidas Secas" ("Barren Lives"). This film, modeled on the postwar Italian classics of Rossellini and De Sica, intimately involves you in the bleak lives it documents: creating a view of human misery that, because of its clarity and avoidance of sentimentality, becomes poetic, even exalting.

Similarly, in "Memories of Prison," Ramos avoids sentimentalizing himself. The actor who plays Ramos, Carlos Vereza, is a small man with kindly, mousy eyes and a weak chin: the antithesis of the movie hero. His Ramos behaves badly at many points—toward his wife, toward his fellow prisoners. As a well-known writer, he occupies a privileged position. The other prisoners curry his favor, bring him gifts and ask, with naive hesitancy, if they will be included in the book. So fallible and non-charismatic is this Ramos that some audiences (perhaps expecting the stubborn nobility of "The Fixer") may think it a failure of the film.

But Ramos is not intended to be a hero, a saint, an exemplary sufferer—or even an effective spokesman. He is, simply a witness. And it is as a witness, one who scrupulously records the facts, that he achieves his greatness. Having experienced what he does here (and, by extension, what millions of others have suffered under dictatorships of the right and left throughout the world) he acts, through his literary skills, as the unchosen soul of them all—something the prisoners, in a striking penultimate scene, intuitively recognize.

"Vidas Secas" is usually regarded as the summit of Brazilian *cinema novo*. (It may also be the most moving neo-realist film made outside Italy.) But, since he shot it in 1963 before another military crackdown, dos Santos has evolved his style considerably, experimenting in many forms and modes, from *cinema verite* to pastiches of Resnais and Fellini, to experiments in such popular genres as gangster thrillers, fantasies and musicals. In "Memories of Prison," he seems to subsume all this eclecticism yet also to hearken back to the earlier film's purity. It's made with enormous assurance, in a luminously simple, clear style. If it doesn't have all the rigor and stark beauty of "Vidas Secas" or the intense imagination of another coming Brazilian prison film, Hector Babenco's "Kiss of the Spider Woman," it achieves, in its final hour, a harrowing integrity and emotional stature. (This last section remained almost intact, when dos Santos shortened the film from 3 hours, 7 minutes, to 2¼ hours for its American release.)

As in the greatest prison films, Renoir's "Grand Illusion" and Bresson's "A Man Escaped," dos Santos doesn't have to illustrate oppression by personalizing it, by showing vicious guards or sadistic warders. But what he does show stands as testimony to the power of the word (and, by extension, the image) to attack and reveal injustice. Dos Santos, in telling the story of Graciliano Ramos, becomes, like him, a witness to injustice, a voice of the persecuted, raising the sort of eternal and eloquent plea which, over and over again, often outlasts the persecutors it decries.

VILLAGE VOICE, 1/24/89, p. 55, Amy Taubin

Despite the fact that Nélson Pereira dos Santos's *Memories of Prison* took the Critics' Prize at Cannes in 1984 and comes equipped with a set of rave reviews from the West Coast (*The Hollywood Reporter* dubbed it "the thinking man's *Great Escape*"), it's taken five years to open in New York. The timing has only enhanced its relevance. Based on an autobiographical novel by Graciliano Ramos, *Memories* opens with the arrest of its protagonist, a writer who earns his living as a civil servant in the department of education. Though the charges are unspecified, he believes they have something to do with his refusal to force his staff to sing the national anthem. It is 1936, and Brazil's new military government has suspended civil liberties.

While not as markedly innovative as Pereira dos Santos's earlier *Vidas Secas* or *How Tasty Was My Little Frenchman*, *Memories* combines a 19th century operatic framework (it actually begins with a five-minute musical overture played over a single static image) with a modernist reflexive narrative—most of the time, we watch the leading character, Ramos (Carlos Vereza), steadfastly writing the novel that becomes the basis of the film. At first, he is confined to a jail for political prisoners. The company is lively, morale is high; the inmates, most of them activists and guerrilla soldiers, plan collective strategy, organize classes, and pool their resources to buy cigarettes and other small luxuries. Ramos chain-smokes, drinks coffee, and writes continuously. Just when things are looking up—his novel is about to be published, and he's made a rapprochement with his wife, who's a frequent visitor—he is transferred to a forced labor camp for thieves and murderers, where political prisoners are the minority. "You are not here to make good, you are here to die," the warden jeers at his charges. Near starvation, Ramos is relieved from work detail. He keeps writing, on paper the others steal for him. His Buddha-like dedication shields him from the worst abuse of the guards and attracts even the most vicious criminals to his cause: They realize that he is their witness. His writing is their link to the outside; it assures their place in history.

Memories is rich in characterizations, deftly and often flamboyantly defined with a few lines and gestures. Vereza's seemingly effortless, implosive performance carries most of the film. By the end, his face is burnt clean, leaving only his eyes, which, like lasers, never falter. Ramos is one of Brazil's most political writers, but his position here is far from doctrinaire. Indeed, he balks when an attempt to enforce collectivity interferes with his work. *Memories of Prison* affirms the individual creative act—specifically the act of writing—grounded in social consciousness, as the basis of freedom.

Also reviewed in:
NEW YORK TIMES, 1/20/89, p. C6, Vincent Canby
VARIETY, 5/16/84, p. 131

METHOD, THE

A Pacific Star Productions release. *Producer:* Joseph Destein. *Director:* Joseph Destein. *Screenplay:* Rob Nilsson, Joel Adelman, and Joseph Destein. *Director of photography:* Stephen Lighthill. *Editor:* Jay Boekelheide and Victoria Lewis. *Music:* Ray Obiedo. *Sound:* Ann Evans. *Art Director:* Gary Frutkoff. *Running time:* 105 minutes. *MPAA Rating:* Not Rated.

CAST: Melanie Dreisbach (Anna Beringer); Richard Arnold (Nick); Deborah Swisher (Monique); Anthony Cistaro (Tony); Robert Elross (Vincenzo); Jack Rikess (Greg); Kathryn Knotts (Demi); Rob Reece (Michael).

NEW YORK POST, 10/20/89, p. 27, Jami Bernard

Anna is a middle-aged mother and housewife starting afresh as an acting student in "The Method," an uneven but engaging low-budget film that is a sort of "Fame" for a slightly older crowd.

Although highlighting Anna's painful progress from a stilted Lady Macbeth monologue to landing her first bit part in a real movie, "The Method" spends a lot of time lovingly cataloguing the Stanislavsky-inspired acting exercises that bring members of Anna's acting class to heightened self-awareness, better stage presence, and sometimes great humiliation.

Produced, directed, and co-written by Joseph Destein, "The Method" has distracting and numerous lapses of editing, story and character continuity, and spends far too much time showing acting students making like zoo animals or reliving old sensory experiences. But Melanie Dreisbach does a creditable job as Anna, with a Blair Brown-ish sincerity and an unaffected style amidst so much Method posing.

Robert Elross also provides a nice touch as the crusty, trusty old acting teacher who is able to take his students down a peg without shattering them. Richard Arnold as the teacher's grandson, who takes an interest in Anna and teaches her the fundamentals of playing with tactile food and enjoying the mess of it, is also good, although his character, like many of the others, is left largely undeveloped. By the way, Arnold looks like a cross between Bert Lahr and Walter Matthau; you just wait for him to do something clever (he doesn't).

As Anna learns rather too quickly to deal with jealous roommates, hostile scene partners, and suppressed emotions, she reaches a skill level that seems unlikely, given her early "Macbeth" solo. And yet she is never too ridiculous.

Whether you feel the others are ridiculous will depend largely on your feelings about Method acting, in which past memory and sensation are called upon to inhabit an actor's roles. Mickey Rourke and Kim Basinger played with their food too, in "9½ Weeks," and it didn't exactly win them Oscars.

NEWSDAY, 10/20/89, Part III/p. 5, Janice Berman

In "The Method" a woman, 41, breaks up with her husband in Seattle, jumps into the family Volvo and drives to San Francisco, there to undertake the acting lessons she abandoned 20 years earlier in favor of marriage and family.

It is, in short, her last chance at fulfillment. Anna Beringer (Melanie Dreisbach) wants to be an actress in the worst way, and "The Method," a low-budget, amateurish-looking film that premiered at Cannes in 1987, often chooses the worst way to go about telling the story.

But a life in the theater has never been without its charms, and even when the hackneyed elements—the jealous roommate, the lecherous leading man—are brought in, something keeps you watching, and it's more than horrified fascination.

To begin with, Dreisbach is a good actress. Her Anna Beringer evolves from a mouse (it's hard to watch her first acting lessons) to a figure of strength and sass. If there weren't already a Diane Keaton, whom Dreisbach closely resembles, she'd be a New Face shoo-in.

The quest not just for the good but for the new is one of the many unhappy truths of the acting business, and these things do not go unexamined. For instance, the director was able to cast his film with 30 Method acting students culled from 500. That is a clue as to how many actors are, as they say, at liberty.

So what is The Method? And well you might ask. The film's vignettes of actors imitating animals, shivering, faking orgasms and talking like children—no matter how well-rendered—are not very enlightening. We have no idea why Beringer was so drawn to The Method as opposed to one of the many other dramatic disciplines, nor why it worked well for her.

That's just one flaw of a script—by Rob Nilsson, Joel Adelman and director Destein—that presents its characters one-dimensionally, at best.

The script sounds as if it were written by three people who have let their wishful thinking run wild. Beringer seems to exist in a vacuum. Her children, who she says are in college, are never heard from.

Her relationships with men, as with her world at large, ring false. Her avoidance of and then carnal interest in Tony (the James Deanish Anthony Cistaro) rings hollow, but so does the naivete of her friendship with Nick (Richard Arnold), nephew of her acting teacher Vincenzo (Robert Elross), whose approach is much like that of a Freudian therapist.

When Anna, most predictably, gets her big break, it's to play a hooker. We see Anna going before the cameras with her nose bashed in, playing the victim of an awful beating, as a singer warbles a sugary song in the background about the realization of one's dreams.

The final scene, at the film's premiere, is simply incredible, forcing one to believe that "The Method" is not without its madness.

VILLAGE VOICE 10/31/89, p. 84, Amy Taubin

Although it makes some tired, rudimentary gestures toward fictional narrative, *The Method* is basically a documentary about an acting class, shown from an acolyte's (producer, director, co-writer Joseph Destein's) engrossed point of view.

Nearing 40, but with ingenue looks still intact, Anna Beringer (Melanie Dreisbach) leaves husband and children and moves to San Francisco (hardly a center of theatrical activity) to fulfill her long-delayed ambition to become an actress. She enrolls in the class of a famed teacher of "the method," Vincenzo DiMatteo (Robert Elross). Under his tutelage, she learns various techniques such as "sense memory" and "emotional recall," which, because they result in hyperventilation, allow the most boring people to seem momentarily arresting. Her initial strangled-voice attempts at Lady Macbeth win the derision of her fellow students, but after an unspecified period of study, she's able to mark her nonetheless singsong delivery with frequent gasps and choked-back sobs. Better yet, the reward for total immersion in her craft is a three-line part—as a banged-up hooker—in a SAG (i.e., professional, regardless of how seedy) movie.

Although Vincenzo would probably disagree, no one should encourage any of the students in his class—most of the actors in the film—to pursue anything more demanding than a career in sitcoms. And while the film is (unintentionally) devastating in its portrayal of students of the method, the last shot is a bit much. Anna gazes with rapt approval at her own image on the screen. No actress is either that narcissistic or that much a fool.

Also reviewed in:
NEW YORK TIMES, 10/20/89, P. C18, Vincent Canby
VARIETY, 5/20/87, p. 106

MIGHTY QUINN, THE

A Metro-Goldwyn-Mayer release in association with Star Partners II of an A & M Films production. *Executive Producer:* Dale Pollock and Gil Friesen. *Producer:* Sandy Lieberson, Marion Hunt, and Ed Elbert. *Director:* Carl Schenkel. *Screenplay:* Hampton Fancher. *Based on the novel "Finding Maubee" by:* A.H.Z. Carr. *Director of Photography:* Jacques Steyn. *Editor:* John Jympson. *Music:* David Anderle and Anne Dudley. *Music Editor:* Dina Eaton. *Choreographer:* Vincent Paterson. *Sound:* John Pritchett. *Sound Editor:* Jonathan Bates. *Production Designer:* Roger Murray-Leach. *Art Director:* Greg Keen. *Set Dresser:* Brian Read. *Special Effects:* Giorgio Ferrari. *Costumes:* Dana Lyman. *Make-up:* A. Medusah Aulenta. *Stunt Coordinator:* Dean Ferrandini and Dan Bradley. *Running time:* 99 minutes. *MPAA Rating:* R.

CAST: Denzel Washington (Xavier Quinn); James Fox (Elgin); Mimi Rogers (Hadley); M. Emmet Walsh (Miller); Sheryl Lee Ralph (Lola); Art Evans (Jump); Esther Rolle (Ubu Pearl); Norman Beaton (Governor Chalk); Alex Colon (Patina); Robert Townsend (Maubee); Tyra Ferrell (Isola); Carl Bradshaw (Cocodick), Maria McDonald (Jax); Fitz Weir (Athens); Baldwin Howe (Bim); David McFarlane (Henry); Bernie McInerney (Dr. Stuhlberg); Keye Luke (Dr. Raj); Ron Taylor (McKeon); Oliver Samuels (Rupert); David Ellis (Jersey); Ronald Goshop (Fudge); Kenneth Casey (Phylo); Henry Judd Baker (Nicotine); Fred Lloyd (Pilot); Cathi Levy (Secretary); Renee Menzies McCallum (The Maid); Charles Hyatt (Security Guard); Sharon Marley Prendergast (Jody); Cedella Marley (Eliza); Clive Walker (Bartender); Dallas Anderson (Francis); Calvin Michell (Apollo); Rowan Byfield (Blizzard); Nabbie Natural (Turtle); Bob Andy (Raisen); Dennis Titus (Percy); Peter Lloyd (Groom); Bobby Ghisays (Pater); Deon Silvera (Beautician); Erica Aquart (Bride); Michael London (Preacher); Michael Rose and Rita Marley (Wedding Singers).

FILMS IN REVIEW, 6–7/89, p. 364, Charles Epstein

The Mighty Quinn is a hodge-podge of intrigue, lifted from the mundane by its lush tropical backdrop, assortment of local eccentrics and sinuous reggae soundtrack. Xavier Quinn (Denzel Washington), the earnest police chief of an unnamed Caribbean island, gets word that a prominent, well connected businessman has been murdered at the island's toniest resort. Quinn speeds away on his jeep/police car, and as he takes a blind turn, just avoids hitting the motorcycle and side car of boyhood friend and local legend, Maubee (Robert Townsend), whose fame rests on, among other things, petty thievery and his Houdini-like ability to elude the cops. Although they've pursued separate and opposite paths and don't often meet, the straight arrow Quinn and the roguish Maubee share an affinity and genuine affection. Quinn suspiciously eyes the suitcase that was thrown from Maubee's motorcycle, but pressed for time, hops into his jeep and heads for the murder scene.

Quinn arrives as the head of the decapitated corpse is fished out of a boiling Jaccuzzi. Maubee, he is told, is the leading suspect. He questions the businessman's widow (Mimi Rogers), tries tracking his Cheshire-like "friend', and is soon joined by a dubiously nondescript man named Miller (M. Emmet Walsh) who, under false pretenses, tags along as he continues his probe.

A number of subplots are soon introduced: Quinn's wife, leader of an all-woman reggae trio, is hostile and aloof because of his lack of attention; Hadley, the beautiful and promiscuous widow, tries seducing him, so does a woman we meet in the film's opening scenes. Meanwhile, we learn that Miller was dispatched by some shadowy cabal in Washington to retrieve a sum of money targeted for a group of "rebels" taken from the country by the murdered businessman and now in the hands of Maubee.

As Miller stalks the island, Quinn begins fitting the pieces into place. Although he doesn't quite know how Maubee came into possession of the suitcase of $10,000 bills, Quinn learns that the businessman died of a snakebite which clears Maubee. Quinn finally gets him to explain his involvement.

Not only is this a muddled, and highly unlikely tale of intrigue, *The Mighty Quinn* also wastes its two talented and charismatic stars. Maubee, a sort of black leprechaun abruptly appearing and disappearing simply doesn't stay on screen long enough for us to get the full measure of his character. Only Robert Townsend's immense charm keeps us interested. Denzel Washington, an actor of cool intelligence and controlled passion, seems bored with an unchallenging role. Once he's got the Caribbean cadences down, he's not called on to do much more than look suave in his crisp white uniform, perform a handful of roundhouse kicks, and display the mental agility that earned him the post of police chief and keeps him one step ahead of everybody except Maubee. The two stars enjoy a good chemistry, and would make for a dynamic pairing in a more plausible film. The direction is pedestrian as is the photography, considering the rich setting. The script's subplots, more pointless than pointed, would be more of a distraction if the mean story, stripped of its exotic trappings, weren't so transparent and derivative. If nothing else Iran-Contra has and will continue to furnish many a lazy writer with a ready-made plot contrivance: the clandestine diversion of funds orchestrated by some shadowy cabal in the recesses of the White house...and variations on the scheme.

LOS ANGELES TIMES, 3/17/89, Calendar/p. 6, Michael Wilmington

The best Hollywood mystery thrillers of the '40s and '50s emphasized character, atmosphere and style. In the '80s, they went in another direction, zeroing in on blood, guts and car-crashes, a lot of high-speed catastrophes glued together with rock 'n' roll and smirking co-stars.

That's why "The Mighty Quinn" is fun. Though based on a novel, "Finding Maubee," by a writer, A.H.Z. Carr, whose work hails back to the Ellery Queen-Raymond Chandler era, it's definitely a new style of thriller. The car crash, blood spurts, sex and helicopters explode—but "Quinn" goes for the old-line virtues, too. The movie sparkles with playful tension, bubbles with amiability. The plot is formula, unsurprising, but the film makers and cast seem to be enjoying themselves; their sheer ribald exhilaration becomes infectious.

Set in Jamaica, "Quinn" focuses on Xavier Quinn (Denzel Washington), a cop with family troubles, and his relentless pursuit of his boyhood buddy, the elusive ganja-puffing island idol Maubee (Robert Townsend), for a dubious murder involving snakes and scandals in high places. Hanging on the sidelines, while the two twist their way through all the sinuous alleys, collapsible houses, tropical streets and crystalline beaches are a gallery of suspects: M. Emmet Walsh in another of his sneaky-mean, smile-while-I-kill-ya-buddy roles; James Fox as a plastic priglet; Mimi Rogers as seductive but bored wife of a wealthy resort manager; Norman Beaton as a timid blowhard of a governor; Esther Rolle as a wheelchaired voodoo mama; and Sheryl Lee Ralph as Xavier's furiously sexy ex.

The characterizations are relatively shallow; compare Beaton's cheeky histrionics here, for example, with his magnificent performance as cricketer Willie Boy in "Playing Away." But they're done with exhilaration and dash. The exaggerations always seem tongue-in-cheek, and Washington has the right presence to anchor this kind of comic thriller: charged, quiet, charismatic, a lot like the young Sidney Poiter.

At the core of the movie is the relationship between the straitlaced Quinn and his scapegrace lothario buddy Maubee. And perhaps it is a weakness of "Quinn" that we don't see Townsend that often; he is basically doing an extended cameo, skittering around the edges of the film like an antic ghost. Over both of them, in the darkness, are the real killers, playing dangerous games of money, war and conquest.

Maubee seems to incarnate temptation and irresponsibility, especially for the broken-up family man, Quinn. Maubee symbolizes the life he could have lived, the easy road he could have boogied down—as Quinn gets more and more trapped in bureaucracy and alienated from his roots, his woman and child, his island ties. The scene where the two fall asleep in an ocean-side convertible, the wanderer and the cop manacled together, is one of the movie's emotional nerve-ends. But it's far too short.

The director and the writer, Carl Schenkel and Hampton Fancher, don't dig down very deep. But they blow everything to hell very stylishly and they get some of the often-lost thriller virtues: An idiosyncratic, pungent milieu, robust characters, a patina of cynical political observation.

With cinematographer Jacques Steyn, Fancher uses a flashy, breezy, deep-focus look that seems to mix "Touch of Evil" tracks with "Kiss Me Deadly" angles, while soaking up a lot of lemony Jamaican sunlight and reviving that atmosphere of deep corruption and rain-soaked night life that characterized classic film noir. Whether as thriller or carnival, reggae romp or killer comedy, "The Mighty Quinn" is fun in a minor key, blood sport with a beat.

MONTHLY FILM BULLETIN, 7/89, P. 210, Tim Pulleine

A Caribbean island. When the decapitated body of U.S. businessman Donald Pater is found in a jacuzzi at a luxury hotel, the proprietor, Elgin, tells the local police chief, ex-FBI agent Quinn, that his boyhood friend Maubee, a petty crook, was seen running from the scene. The governor, fearing damage to the tourist industry, pressures Quinn to treat the case as open-and-shut. But an autopsy reveals that death was in fact caused by snake venom, and Quinn (who is estranged from his singer wife Lola and lives apart from her and their young son) decides to pursue enquiries. He learns that Elgin's badly treated wife Hadley has been intimate with both Pater and Maubee, and that the now vanished Maubee has been having an affair with Isola, niece of crippled Ubu Pearl, a supposed witch or exponent of obeah black magic. Meanwhile, an enigmatic American, Miller, arrives on the scene, claiming to represent Pater's interests. Quinn is tailed by a Latin American gunman, Patina, whom he subsequently arrests, though the latter is rapidly freed on the governor's orders. Patina is then killed by Miller; it transpires that both were involved, along with Pater, in an aborted covert U.S. operation to fund a Central American contra movement with "special issue" currency, and that the money, due to be returned to safe custody, has been stolen by Maubee. Quinn locates Maubee's hideout, and deduces from what he finds there something of what is going on. Miller's pursuit of Maubee leads him to Ubu Pearl, whom he burns alive in her shack after she refuses to help him. Quinn tracks down Isola and through her finds Maubee, who reveals that Pater was the father of Isola's baby. When Pearl found out, she persuaded Isola to leave a deadly snake in his hotel room; Maubee had followed her, and on finding Pater dead, beheaded his corpse and put it in the jacuzzi to confuse the evidence. Miller arrives and after a face-off with Quinn appears ready to depart peacefully with the money, turned over by Maubee. When helicopter takes off, Maubee tries to hang on to it, and is shot by Miller. But Maubee has put a snake in the money bag; after it bites the pilot, the helicopter crashes, killing Miller and destroying the money. Later, Quinn and Lola are reconciled.

The Mighty Quinn attempts to amplify a *policier* plot by highlighting its Caribbean locale, using the well-worn device of boyhood friendship between hero and antagonist as a link. Unfortunately, even in simple dramatic terms, the two elements never gell. The mystery thriller narrative is perfunctory to the point of near incoherence (with Quinn's eventual elucidation of the conspiracy largely a matter of off-screen guesswork). More deleteriously, though, the social background is never explored in any depth. Quinn's professional and matrimonial difficulties are wholly statutory, such figures as the pusillanimous governor are one-dimensional and most of the scene-setting—including the black-magic element—remains stock local colour.

The air of commercial package-making is emphasised by the contrived nature of the musical interpolations, including not only song numbers by Lola (whose fellow performers are played by Bob Marley's daughters) but even a bizarre scene in which Quinn himself, seeking respite in a saloon, sings and plays the piano. The direction, taking its cue from the early shock-cut from the discovery of Pater's corpse to a close-up of a singer in full cry, is at once over-emphatic and anonymous. Denzel Washington as Quinn, cutting a markedly American figure, appears displaced from his surroundings, while M. Emmet Walsh is dispiritingly cast to type as the degenerate Miller.

NEW YORK, 3/6/89, p. 56, David Denby

In *The Mighty Quinn*, Denzel Washington is Xavier Quinn, the ambitious young police chief of a small Caribbean resort island, and Robert Townsend is Quinn's old friend Maubee, a happy small-time hustler in dreadlocks who is the principal suspect in a murder case. As a police thriller, *The Mighty Quinn* is only a step or two above television, but at least the setting is fresh and the atmosphere ripe. The American actors, who learned Jamaican accents for their parts, roll their vowels around like coconuts on a table. Away from America, they seem to be having an unconstrained good time. Playing a local legend—a great lover and free spirit—Robert Townsend exudes a physical pleasure in his rascally role.

The Mighty Quinn was shot in and around the shabby but beautiful town of Port Antonio, on Jamaica's northeast coast. As I looked at the fullness of the light from the wide-open skies, the sweat forming on the actors' brows, the dark greens and blues, I had one of those naively gratifying only-at-the-movies experiences: I felt I was actually there, actually feeling the heat and light on my skin. In the middle of a chase, I would lose myself in the ocean and the banana trees. All it takes is a few loops in the same old rope to convince and enslaved moviegoer that he's a free man.

The producers, hoping for a soundtrack hit, have worked as much music into the picture as possible. People are always breaking into song—even Denzel Washington sits down at a piano and does a blues number. There are also slithery poisonous snakes, a witch who casts spells, and some of the trashiest island whites ever to be found clutching a gin and tonic: James Fox as a weak but vicious hotel manager; Mimi Rogers, jaw hanging loose, as his wife, a masochist who seems to have nothing to do but get slapped around and throw herself at men; and gut-heavy, sinister M. Emmet Walsh, a CIA man running a covert operation. (Walsh looks amusingly like Eugene Hasenfus, the American pilot shot down while delivering supplies to the *contras*.) The rottenness of the whites suggests that the movie was conceived as an exotic new variety of black-exploitation picture.

A Caribbean native, Xavier completed his education in the U.S. Marines and the FBI, and is caught, as they say, between two worlds—the results-oriented demands of his training and the more easy-going life at home. His old friends and his wife admire his sparkling-white police uniform, but they also razz him because he can't relax and enjoy himself anymore. When a white businessman is murdered at a resort hotel, almost everyone, including the governor of the island, insists that Xavier simply arrest his black friend Maubee.

The Mighty Quinn, which Hampton Fancher adapted from a novel by A.H.Z. Carr (Carl Schenkel directed), doesn't give Denzel Washington quite enough to chew on. If he was to transcend the clichés of a TV-series dilemma, his character should have become either a very angry or very funny man. Neither happens. Held back by the script, Washington can't decide whether to play Quinn as a tormented guy or as a straight hero with problems. Mostly he does the latter. The performance isn't as big as one would like. But sooner or later, Denzel Washington will become a great movie star. He has a quick, fluid intelligence, fierce concentration, a beautiful voice, and a graceful way of taking the obvious macho emphasis out of an action role. Maybe next time.

NEW YORK POST, 2/17/89, p. 25, Jami Bernard

Seeing Robert Townsend all gotten up in dreadlocks, speaking in unconvincing sing-song and grinning from here to there, you can't help expecting a vignette out of Townsend's own "Hollywood Shuffle," maybe something from his "school for black acting" about how to become a Bob Marley or a Jimmy Cliff.

Unfortunately, "The Mighty Quinn" is not a comedy—although with a little editing it could well have been.

The plot pits a murder and some lackluster international intrigue against the idyllic setting of a generic Caribbean country, all steel drums and white-foamed surf (it was shot in Jamaica).

Townsend plays Maubee, an Errol Flynn-type pirate of a local hero wanted in the murder of a white businessman, who was found decapitated and boiled in his hotel Jacuzzi. Denzel Washington ("Cry Freedom") is Quinn, the stuffed-shirt police chief who, with his mainland FBI training and crisp white uniform, is considered something of a sellout. He must bring in Maubee, his childhood chum, even though he's certain that Maubee couldn't have committed the crime. As Quinn's estranged wife (Sheryl Lee Ralph) paraphrases Michael Jackson, "He's a lover, not a killer."

The muddy plot involves variations on the usual: a suitcase full of $10,000-bills; a poisonous snake that is more metaphor than reptile; the sensuous wife (a dewy-eyed Mimi Rogers) of a man (James Fox) who seems more of a snake than the snake; a cackling island witch (Esther Rolle in a wheelchair) who has curses and imprecations to spare. Evidently Sheryl Lee Ralph's purpose in the film is to lead two of Bob Marley's daughters in a Supremes-like trio who are trying to break into island showbiz with a personalized version of Dylan's "The Mighty Quinn."

The movie opens with a scream. There are lots of screams to come, but this primary, primal scream belongs to the lyrics of a song ("Guess who's coming to dinner tonight—de dreadlocks"). That kind of thing, plus Townsend's sporadic, impish appearances, his dreadlocks bobbing into the frame, make you think you're in for something topsy-turvy. No such luck. "Mighty Quinn" is very staid, respectable, somewhat tedious entertainment.

The movie that might be hiding is this island prison is one in which Quinn, all messed up in de head from that FBI training, finds that crime-solving in the Caribbean requires a fresh approach. With everyone knowing everyone else on this island, and nobody talking, maybe Quinn could finally come into his own by using his native knowledge of the island and its psychology.

"Quinn" seems to be headed in that direction in one scene: "Maybe you saw him?" asks the police chief while hunting for Maubee. "Not exactly," "Well, where exactly didn't you see him?"

Washington, a fine actor, is stiff and unmotivated in his starchy good-cop role. The only scene is which he opens up is when he sits down at the piano to sing a bluesy "Cakewalk into Town," his Rasta accent momentarily discarded like the parasol in a rum punch.

Townsend is a pleasurable distraction from all the trumped-up intrigue; his Maubee is a pleasure-seeking, ganja-smoking ladies' man, a small-time scoundrel with whom no one can stay angry for long, the kind of man for whom they wrote the song "Don't Worry Be Happy." Since he consistently and mysteriously eludes capture, we don't see nearly enough of him.

Switzerland's Carl Schenkel directs with what perhaps is a Swiss idea of what a Caribbean country is like Hey, mon! You need more than a dreadlock-wig to give a movie a flavor of de islands.

NEWSDAY, 2/17/89, Part III/p. 5, Bill Kaufman

"The Mighty Quinn" is a straightforward caper that's a couple of hoots-and-a-half for the most part, mainly because it has a decent story and cast and, like the pretty Jamaican locale and reggae soundtrack, it's easy on the eyes and ears.

No new ground is broken by the movie, but if nothing else, it's a bit of a change to see some good guy-bad guy chases away from weary urban settings. Denzel Washington is Xavier Quinn, police chief of a tiny resort island. He has been nicknamed "Mighty" by the villagers because of his enthusiasm for the job, which from time to time includes a little tough stuff. Just back from a stateside FBI training course, Quinn quite literally bumps into a childhood pal when his official Jeep collides with a motorcycle driven by Maubee (Robert Townsend), the island's con artist.

After a wealthy executive is murdered, Maubee, a charming but conniving ne'er-do-well, becomes the leading suspect—at least for a while—as Quinn sets out to solve the case. Some action is provided by a slinky Mimi Rogers, who does a nice job of playing the restless wife of a resort operator.

One of the best things about the film is that Quinn is portrayed as a savvy, intelligent sleuth with a mile-wide streak of warmth and sensitivity. He's the type of guy who finds time to visit his estranged wife's home to take his young son out.

Washington, who won an Oscar nomination for his role as Steven Biko in "Cry Freedom" and was on TV in "St. Elsewhere," puts a good spin on his portrayal of the Mighty Quinn. Faced with a bungling island bureaucracy and some other shady dealings, he sets off on a chase and beats up an assortment of bad guys. "The Mighty Quinn" also provides moviegoers with a quickie tour of Port Antonio, an off-the-beaten track paradise on the northeast coast of Jamaica. It's worth noting that the film's musical consultant was Rita Marley, wife of the late reggae king, Bob Marley.

VILLAGE VOICE, 2/12/89, p. 67, Renee Tajima

If he ever made *Hollywood Shuffle, The Sequel*, Robert Townsend might face cinematic atrocities of African-American themes on a more sophisticated level. Take *The Mighty Quinn*, in which the talents of Townsend and Denzel Washington, as well as a provocative premise of neocolonial racism and international intrigue, are all wasted. The film doesn't know if it's *The Harder They Come* or *Club Paradise*.

Washington plays the title character, Xavier Quinn, an upstanding, take-no-shit police chief on an idyllic Caribbean island. Fresh from FBI training in the U.S., Quinn combines the cool demeanor of Virgil Tibbs with the territoriality of a southern sheriff. He knows it's a new day and the Europeans are only guests. Making all too brief appearances, Townsend plays Maubee, the chief's boyhood friend and an elusive rogue, whose reputation on the island achieves mythic proportions in the Jimmy Cliff vein.

The friendship is tested when Quinn goes after Maubee for the murder of a right-wing capitalist, leading to a promising tale of Contragate machinations. But Swiss-born director Carl Schenkel turns this meaty premise to mush. The standoff between Quinn and the pompous British resort manager, Elgin (James Fox)—over race, machismo, and the delectable Mrs. Elgin (Mimi Rogers)—is half-hearted, even laughable. Finding Quinn and his wife in conversation, Elgin fumes, "If I had waited another minute before I came here, would I have found you both on the floor?" The story follows a weak trail of Maubee's exploits, which at times looks decidedly B-movie, replete with Townsend performing some outright Bruce Lee leaps. Even the clever insinuation of laundered gun money and CIA-backed mercenaries into the plot is only fodder for a few random murders and a fiery helicopter crash. With Rita Marley as musical consultant, *The Mighty Quinn* is a movie more worth listening to than watching.

Also reviewed in:
NEW YORK TIMES, 2/17/89, p. C14, Vincent Canby
VARIETY, 2/15-21/89, p. 20
WASHINGTON POST, 2/17/89, p. C7, Rita Kempley

MILK AND HONEY

A Castle Hill release of an Independent Pictures/Zenith Productions Ltd. production. *Producer:* Peter O'Brian. *Director:* Rebecca Yates and Glen Salzman. *Screenplay:* Glen Salzman and Trevor Rhone. *Director of Photography:* Guy Dufaux. *Editor:* Bruce Nyznik. *Music:* Micky Erbe and Maribeth Solomon. *Sound:* Bruce Nyznik. *Art Director:* François Seguin. *Running time:* 90 minutes. *MPAA Rating:* Not Rated.

CAST: Josette Simon (Joanna Bell); Lyman Ward (Adam Bernardi); Richard Mills (David); Djanet Sears (Del); Leonie Forbes (Miss Emma); Jane Dingle (Maureen); Errol Slue (Gordon).

LOS ANGELES TIMES, 8/11/89, Calendar/p. 15, Sheila Benson

The agonizing plight of Jamaican immigrants to Canada is the subject of "Milk and Honey," a well-intentioned, particularly well-acted film that falls apart before its midpoint and finishes with soap opera flourishes. A pity, because its star, Josette Simon, is as much a find as "Mona Lisa's" Cathy Tyson.

Like Joanna Bell (Simon), many of the women who emigrate have been lured by promises of comfortable money as nannies and instead find themselves virtual indentured servants. Joanna has powerful reasons for leaving her small Jamaican town; a single mother, she doesn't want to see her 6-year-old son, David (Richard Mills), raised in rural poverty. In a wrenching parting, Joanna leaves him with her mother, and in one day makes the jump from the tropics to a Toronto with snowdrifts in the streets

The cultural differences are almost as severe, and directors Rebecca Yates and Glen Salzman make those absolutely clear in the first sequences. To Joanna, this gleaming clean nanny's room with its own bath seems amazing; we may notice that the heating duct runs right through it, and it seems to be a conduit for the family's television sound, but this and a salary of $225 each week seems like heaven.

But her first paycheck, minus all the allowable deductions—her air fare, paid off in installments, a pension plan, the $70 per week *they* charge *her* for room and board—is $20. And, talking to other nannies in the park, she finds that she's as caught as they all are. Until she gets papers as a "landed immigrant," which can be years, she is a "foreign domestic," earning a fixed $126.40 per week and forbidden to do any other kind of work.

And so we skip two years. Joanna, whose hair is now handsomely cropped close to her head, is still working for the same unfeeling middle-class couple who now have two babies, and she is savvy, isolated and desperately lonely, her church her only bulwark. The screenplay, by Trevor Rhone and Salzman, makes superficial attempts to characterize her other friends: the warm and pious Miss Emma (Leonie Forbes), bosomy Maureen (Jane Dingle) the Liverpudlian, and the lively Del (Djanet Sears) clearly heading down the primrose path with her con-man boyfriend (Errol Slue), known as Mr. Fix-It for his way with immigration scams.

Joanna has also had an almost disastrous encounter with a night-school teacher, Adam Bernardi (Lyman Ward), who makes a clumsy pass at her. All these story threads will come together when Joanna brings her son, now 8, up for Christmas holidays, then impulsively, decides she cannot bear to send him back and will try to keep him in the country illegally.

"Milk and Honey" may be a bit flat-footed and didactic in its opening; at least that section tracks and the material is interesting. By the second half, contrivance is all, and it feels as though gaping chunks had been left out, particularly in the relationship between Joanna and Adam, who resurfaces as principal of the school in which she registers the truant David.

It goes now from drama to melodrama to semi-love story to seeming tragedy with an atrocious upbeat ending in Jamaica that solves nothing and makes you wonder for the sanity of the people involved. Salvageable are the performances of Djanet Sears as the unexpectedly malevolent Del, and Ward, whom you may remember as the sought-after senior executive fox-trotting his way to success in "Ray's Male Heterosexual Dance Hall." And, of course Simon, a member of London's Royal Shakespeare Company, who will some day have material worthy of her.

NEW YORK POST, 6/16/89, p. 25, David Edelstein

Jo (Josette Simon), the beautiful Jamaican heroine of the Canadian drama "Milk and Honey" is tall, reedy, almost foolishly chipper. She's one of those people who are often described as "lit from within," the sort who survives the slings and arrows of an unjust society because she knows in her heart that God loves her.

As the movie opens—in a rural Jamaican village—Jo tells her 7-year-old son, David, that she's going off to Canada to be a live-in housekeeper and nanny to earn money for him. In the next scene, her ramshackle cab gets stuck behind a bus on the way to the airport, and Jo frets that she'll miss her plane. When it finally passes the bus, there's a surge of elation; everyone in the cab squeals to heaven.

There's something about this moment that suggests "Milk and Honey" won't just be the story of a good immigrant whose illusions are dashed by a cruel and unfeeling society.

It will be partly that, of course, but it's also going to be about that surge of joy and freedom when you finally pass the bus—that moment when the world is suddenly full of possibilities.

On paper, "Milk and Honey" sounds like everything one dreads about earnest, politically correct movies, but its openness and humanism take the weight off its message. It's often very funny and its actors transcend ideology.

It doesn't feel overdetermined, even when Jo's yuppie employers (on cue) withhold wages from her unfairly; when Immigration won't allow her son to remain in the country; and when a night-school teacher (Lyman Ward) attempts to make love to her while they're stuck in a snowstorm in his car.

The film, directed and co-produced by the husband-wife team of Rebecca Yates and Glen Salzman, stays light and quirky even when its subject is downbeat and predictable. The teacher in the above scene isn't an exploitive white chauvinist but a shy and lonely bachelor who truly thinks Jo's lovely; the movie gives this endearing bumbler a chance to redeem himself, and he does.

Simon, a member of London's Royal Shakespeare Company, is too busy living the part of Jo to strike martyred poses. And there's an extraordinary performance by a charismatic, 12-year-old actor named Richard Mills, who plays David with wary intelligence. When, two years after Jo has left, he arrives in Canada to visit her, the expression on his face is proud and embarrassed and slightly defiant. (Seeing him wander out of Customs, she remarks that "he's so black.")

The resentment David feels toward his mother for leaving can't help but erupt. In a harrowing scene, he lets a baby carriage—containing one of the white children for whom his mother left him—roll down a hill; you don't know whether to cry harder for the infant, who is undamaged, or the adolescent, who is extremely damaged.

Yates and Salzman got the idea for "Milk and Honey" from Salzman's brother's nanny; then they contacted the Jamaican playwright Trevor Rhone ("The Harder They Come") to co-write the script.

It's their first feature, and it has lapses. There's some confusion in the film over a friend of Jo's who dies and leaves her money, and there's a bad, caricatured performance by her white male employer. Yates and Salzman don't always probe the messier implications of their story—they skip along the surface rather tastefully. But it's a lively surface, and the climax is unexpectedly suspenseful—the second half of the film actually works as a thriller.

You have to admire these two white directors, who one day looked at the black nannies minding the white kids in a Toronto park and decided to tell these women's stories as simply and unsensationally as possible—to dramatize their expectations, their disillusionments and the ways in which they'd managed (or not managed) to cope with their alienation.

NEWSDAY, 6/16/89, Part III/p. 3, Lynn Darling

It isn't easy for film makers to re-create a world as intricate as the one that immigrants must fashion out of shared pain, disillusion and bittersweet memories. It's built of small threads and tenuous connections, and it can fly apart at the smallest vibration of the hostile bureaucracy that looms constantly overhead. "Milk and Honey," a quietly intense drama by Canadian film makers Rebecca Yates and Glen Salzman, succeeds in conveying with fine-tuned perception the hope and desperation that can haunt that world, and the long odds that threaten the lives within it.

Joanna Bell (Josette Simon) is a beautiful young Jamaican woman, determined to provide a better life for her young son David than the one she can manage in her native country. She comes to Toronto to work as a nanny for a young professional couple with an infant son, and finds herself caught up in a life very different from the one she imagined in Jamaica. Lonely and isolated by the benign indifference of her employers, she finds companionship with three other nannies who share her burden of futility and frustration as she waits for the "landed papers" that will permit her son to join her.

The directors deftly juxtapose the frosty middle-class comfort of Joanna's days in her employers' house with her life outside their home. At one point, to cope with the disappointment and shock over just how much of an indentured servant she has become, Joanna seeks relief in a Pentecostal church service, where her anguish turns to abandon amid the emotional frenzy of the service. The little church is bathed in a warm, amber light that emphasizes its importance to Joanna as a haven from coldness and intransigence.

Things begin to fall apart for Joanna after a Christmas visit with her son (Richard Mills). David is angry with her for having left him, and jealous of her attention to her employers' children. Realizing she's going to lose him, Joanna arranges to keep David with her illegally. Soon, she is living in a fear-haunted world where no one is who she thinks they are—not Del (Djanet Sears), one of the nannies who first befriended her; not Adam (Lyman Ward), the principal of David's school; or Gordon (Errol Slue) the street-smart operator to whom she turns for help.

Josette Simon conveys her character's indomitability without resorting to Little-Eva-on-the-ice-floe heroics. There's a charismatic quickness and an intensity to her acting that plays off Lyman Ward's lumbering decency in an effective counterpoint.

As Joanna's troubles deepen, "Milk and Honey" begins to rely too heavily on coincidence and melodrama as it heads toward an ending that takes a real sweet tooth to accept. But the relationships that have been established between Joanna, her son and Adam sustain the movie—they're warm and quirky and heartwarming in the way that characters who rise above their own fallibility often are.

VILLAGE VOICE, 6/20/89, p. 94, Julie Phillips

Domestic service is arguably not the stuff or movies. It's messy, repetitive, boring. Living in a house not your own, taking care of children not your own, doing the dirty work of someone else's country, waiting for the citizenship that might or might not come through—it's an undramatic kind of frustration, and it's not polite and Bergmanesque, either. Changing diapers is no one's idea of existential despair.

Still, *Milk and Honey* gets across some of the hopelessness of housework in Babylon. The Land of Milk and Honey is in this case Canada, where young Jamaican mother Joanna Bell (Josette Simon) goes to be a poorly paid nanny for a snotty white couple. If she works hard enough and waits long enough, she might get her "landed papers"—a Canadian green card—and be allowed to bring her young son, David, to Toronto. Losing hope and patience, she tries to keep David with her after a visit and discovers that, as a non-person, she is not permitted to have anything of her own.

Jo is no doormat, no permanent victim: It may take her three years to get around to calling her boss "bitch," but when she does it, she good and means it. But in Canada her only options are variations on the domestic. The only live-out job she can get is as a fast-food waitress. Of her three nanny friends, one dies, worn out by years of waiting, and another marries her employer. The third, Del, liberated from housework by the arrival of her landed papers, becomes the mistress of the morally greasy "Mr. Fixit" (his specialty is selling forged immigration papers). Given David to keep for Joanna, Del beats and starves him, revenge for her own years of nanny work.

Cowritten by Trevor Rhone (the Jamaican playwright who also helped write *The Harder They Come*), *Milk and Honey* is not quite so earnest as your average social injustice movie. There is room for moral ambiguity, and by the end it even tightens into a kind of thriller, with the immigration office tracking Jo and David down. What it lacks in didacticism, though, it partly makes up for in conventionality. Minor characters are drawn straight from stock: lecherous male teachers; venal, upwardly mobile employers; dumb cops. The white grade school principal (Lyman Ward) who first tries to get Joanna into bed and then helps her try to keep her son is the Basically Nice Guy who recovers his humanity through good deeds, but it's never quite clear why we should care about the state of his soul. In these rather ordinary terms, directors Rebecca Yates and Glen Salzman do what they can: *Milk and Honey* is a fine, honest movie, approaching the heart of an uncinematic frustration.

Also reviewed in:

NEW REPUBLIC, 7/31/89, p. 25, Stanley Kauffmann
NEW YORK TIMES, 6/16/89, p. C10, Caryn James
VARIETY, 9/7/88, p. 27
WASHINGTON POST, 9/19/89, p. D10, Hal Hinson

MILLENNIUM

A Twentieth Century Fox Film Corporation release of a Gladden Entertainment Corporation film. *Executive Producer:* John Foreman, Freddie Fields, Louis M. Silverstein, and P. Gael Mourant. *Producer:* Douglas Leiterman. *Director:* Michael Anderson. *Screenplay based on his short story, "Air Raid":* John Varley. *Director of Photography:* Rene Ohashi. *Editor:* Ron Wisman. *Music:* Eric N. Robertson. *Robot Choreographer:* Glen Kotyk. *Sound:* Douglas Ganton and (music) Hayward Parrott. *Sound Editor:* Jim Hopkins. *Production Designer:* Gene Rudolf. *Art Director:* Charles Dunlop. *Set Designer:* Jeffrey Ginn. *Set Decorator:* Jacques Bradette. *Set Dresser:* Caroline George and Dan Conley. *Special Effects:* Nick Fischer. *Special Visual Effects:* Sam Nicholson. *Costumes:* Olga Dimitrov. *Make-up:* Barbara Palmer. *Special Prosthetic Make-up:* Bob Laden. *Stunt Coordinator:* Shane Cardwell. *Running time:* 106 minutes. *MPAA Rating:* PG-13.

CAST: Kris Kristofferson (Bill Smith); Cheryl Ladd (Louise Baltimore); Daniel J. Travanti (Arnold Mayer); Robert Joy (Sherman); Lloyd Bochner (Walters); Brent Carver (Coventry); David McIlwraith (Tom Stanley); Maury Chaykin (Roger Keane); Al Waxman (Dr. Brindle); Lawrence Dane (Vern Rockwell); Thomas Hauff (Ron Kennedy); Peter Dvorsky (Janz); Raymond O'Neill (Harold Davis); Philip Akin (Briley); David Calderisi (Leacock); Gary Reineke (Carpenter); Eugene Clark (Craig Ashby); Cedric Smith (Eli Seibel); Michael J. Reynolds (Jerry Bannister); Victoria Snow (Pinky Djakarta); Susannah Hoffman (Susan Melbourne); Claudette Roach (Inez Manila); Barry Meier (Helicopter Pilot); James Kirchner (Foreman); Bill MacDonald (FBI Agent, Morgue); Jamie Shannon (Young Bill Smith); Timothy Webber (Audio Technician); THE COUNCIL CHAMBER: Chapelle Jaffe (Stockholm); Christopher Britton (Buffalo); Gerry Quigley (Khartoum); Leonard Chow (Beijing); Scott Thompson (Controller); John Kozak (Investigator); James Mainprize (Investigator); Bob Bainborough (Investigator); Daryl Shuttleworth (T.V. Reporter, Crash Site); Gerard Theoret (Time Scan Operator); Edward Roy (Gantry Controller); Debbie Kirby (Stewardess); John Stoneham (Hijacker); Linda Goranson (Hostage); Syd Libman (Passenger); Patrick Young (Reporter #1); Paula Barrett (Reporter #2);

Richard Fitzpatrick (Reporter #3); Reg Dreger (Reporter #4); Cordelia Strube (Reporter #5); Marvin Caron (Reporter #6); David Bolt (1st Board Member); Maida Rogerson (2nd Board Member); Mark Terene (Waiter); Jank Azman (Evacuation Worker); Kevin Fullam (TUA Worker).

LOS ANGELES TIMES, 8/26/89, Calendar/p. 10, Kevin Thomas

"Millennium" is a hopelessly tedious time-travel fantasy that represents the all-too-typical mediocrity of the commercial Canadian cinema.

John Varley may be a prize-winning science-fiction writer, but his screenplay, which he adapted from his short story "Air Raid," is altogether unpersuasive. Add conscientious yet plodding direction by Michael Anderson, cut-rate special effects and production design, and you've got a big bore. "Millennium" has little to distract you from the obvious phony hair coloring of its stars.

They are Kris Kristofferson and Cheryl Ladd and, to their credit, they are game. Kristofferson plays a burned-out air-disaster investigator who encounters the slightly mysterious Ladd while attempting to find out what caused a midair collision between a DC-10 and a 747 somewhere in the Midwest.

When, after a night of love making, Ladd says gratefully, "You're the best thing in a thousand years," Kristofferson understandably doesn't pick up the clue, but we soon learn that she has come from the future on a mission most improbable. Ladd and especially Kristofferson are convincing lovers, but their romance hasn't a prayer in overcoming its leaden circumstances. Third-billed Daniel J. Travanti is stuck playing a smug physicist with a strong interest in time-travel.

Despite its title, "Millennium" (rated PG-13 for adult situations) should have a short life span.

MONTHLY FILM BULLETIN, 11/89, p. 338, Philip Strick

Crash specialist Bill Smith heads the investigation into a mid-air collision between a 747 and a DC-10. Computer error is implicated, but there are puzzling details which Bill keeps to himself at the press conference despite pressure from an eccentric enquirer, Dr. Arnold Mayer. One of the airline staff, Louise, takes Bill's mind off his problems; but after they spend the night together, Bill is mystified to find that Louise has disappeared and is unknown to the airline. Among the plane relics he finds a strange gadget which immobilises him; Louise appears, grabs it, and vanishes in a blaze of light. She is a commando from the far future where a desperate rescue programme is under way among the dying remnants of the human race; with the help of the Gate, a device which enables them to monitor and visit the past, they are plucking hundreds of people from imminent disaster and preparing to send them millions of years ahead to create a new civilisation. Any mistakes in this perilous scheme can set off a "timequake" which would alter history, destroy Louise's world, and wipe out all hope of human survival. Bill's discovery of the "stunner", accidentally dropped during the seizure of passengers from the doomed 747, is an error that Louise had been sent back to correct. Now obsessed with tracing both her and the stunner, Bill is fired by his employers but tracks down Mayer, the only person likely to listen to his story; he finds that Mayer was the survivor of another intervention from the future, a 1963 plane crash, and still has the stunner he picked up then. Now a specialist in time theory, Mayer guesses that the stunner holds the secrets of future technology—but at this point Louise intervenes once more to remove the evidence. Mayer is accidentally killed in the struggle, Bill insists on returning with Louise through the Gate, and back in the future a massive timequake caused by Mayer's death begins the final disintegration of Louise's world. Her surviving colleagues reverse the Gate in time for throngs of "rescued" fugitives to escape into an unknown future century, and Louise and Bill go with them.

John Varley's short story "Air Raid" (first published in 1977), in which the passengers of a doomed airliner are hoisted from certain death for recruitment on a five-year space flight to colonise Centauri Three, is an impressive concentration of ideas, implications, and pure writing energy. Yielding to the temptation of being expanded for potential screenplay purposes, it became the novel *Millennium* in 1983, successfully incorporating some spectacular additional material including a salute in each chapter heading to the (relatively few) classics of time-travel fiction, by Wells, Bradbury, Kuttner, Moorcock and others, and concluding with a wry postscript from God. Varley's novel parallels the "testimony" of two protagonists, the investigator in the present and the "commando" from the future; intriguingly similar in their disenchantments, they are steered into partnership by an intricate master plan intended to correct the environmental damage currently rendering the planet uninhabitable. While not particularly convincing, this project provides the opportunity for some fine pyrotechnics of writing and construction, forming a hard-boiled detective tale with a wide range of soft-boiled sub-plots.

Translating these to the screen, Varley's script seems to have been forced into exposing their weaknesses rather than their rewarding complexity. Images and incidents have been plucked piecemeal from the book for conventional visual effect, and left stranded without adequate purpose or explanation. Chief victim of this process is the robot, Sherman, gradually revealed in the novel as a prime architect of the whole adventure but left here as a freakish piece of furniture resembling the Tin Man (the link is deliberate in Varley's text but merely distracting on screen). In the book, the terminal pollution of the distant future is the careful context for the governing Council, its members tenuously held together with prosthetics and transplants for their brief and ugly life spans. On film, Coventry and his colleagues are mystifying hellraisers, horror-movie images laughably at odds with the sophisticated technology of the Gate and its purposes.

It is exasperatingly difficult to understand their predicament when "normal" bodies are shuttling to and fro through the Gate by the hundred under the supervision of the immaculate Cheryl Ladd. Varley's words stitched it all together (revealing up front that his heroine, too, is a patchwork of decay), but the film, with a smug incongruity, simply forges dismissively ahead, relying on Albert Whitlock's magnificent artwork to paint over the cracks and chasms at the end. With a wearying predictability, Michael Anderson's grip on his futuristic fable strangles most of the life out of it by concentrating on the star-crossed lovers who, as in *Logan's Run*, find instruction and liberty against a background of general collapse. This girl from the future needs guidance in the mechanics of passion, prompting a sequence of erotic initiation echoing the contrivances of *My Stepmother Is an Alien* and tipping the whole thing into what would be romantic melodrama if the central performances permitted. As it is, a mood of polite interest is generated but Kris Kristofferson has such difficulty with outbursts like "All I wanna do is find her!" that anything of an intensity sufficient to span the centuries is seriously unsubstantiated.

NEW YORK POST, 8/26/89, p. 21. Jami Bernard

They won't be showing "Millennium" on in-flight screens any time in the near future. It opens with a spooky, well-executed crash, in which one plane sort of skims the top of another. The ways in which the movie skimps on showing apocryphal special effects (lots of close-ups, for example, so you can't see the background) are not important—the movie is an intriguing sci-fi mystery with a strong, human story and enough light moments to make those stabs at Higher Meaning more palatable.

The basic premise is about time travelers who make a living visiting fatal airplane crashes of the 20th century for a do-good mission that would only confuse you if I tried to explain it. One of these travelers, a futuristic babe named Louise (Cheryl Ladd), journeys back to the present to seduce a government air disaster investigator (a grizzled-looking Kris Kristofferson) and retrieve a little stun gun she dropped during one of her missions.

The investigator, Bill Smith, falls for the mysterious stranger who, unbeknownst to him, comes from a future where the slightest "paradox"—conundrums caused when a time traveler alters the course of history—rocks their world like an earthquake. "You're the best thing in a thousand years," purrs Louise after she is introduced to the old-fashioned pleasures of sex. "I was, wasn't I?" says Bill.

Past, present and future tenses get a little confusing, and a sequence in which a second look at the past from a different point of view is not as sharp as it should be, but the plot puzzle is as entertaining as watching Louise try to learn how to seduce a man with the transmitted aid of her personal robot back home, a wise-cracking droid who sighs, "Well, this seems to be my day for spelling out the obvious." Louise's culture clash is done with much more finesse than the usual alien-learns-manners movies.

Kristofferson is fine; Ladd is on the bland side; Daniel J. Travanti is amusing as a physics professor who's on to something. Definitely for science-fiction lovers, but acrophobics might want to stay home.

NEWSDAY, 8/26/89, Part II/p. 17, Terry Kelleher

Bill Smith (Kris Kristofferson) of the National Transportation Safety Board realizes there was something strange about the mid-air collision of a DC-10 and a 747 when he examines two digital watches found in the wreckage: Incredibly, both are running backwards.

And you, moviegoer, will realize there's something strange about "Millennium" when you check your watch, which you're bound to do frequently in the course of this science-fiction exercise. Though "Millennium" is a movie about time travel, time seems to stand stock-still while you're watching it. Now *that's* incredible.

Yet dullness is not the film's most salient quality. It's risibility. The serious parts of "Millennium" are so laughable that the attempts at intentional humor blend in only too well.

One thing's certain: Nothing in "Millennium" is worth seeing twice. That's why it's such a drag being subjected to a rerun in the middle of the movie.

While Bill's investigating early on, he keeps running into Louise Baltimore (Cheryl Ladd), who appears to be a stewardess. Fabulous eye contact right away, followed by "unforgettable" sex. Then the lady vanishes.

Turns out Louise was a time traveler from a thousand years ahead, assigned to charm Bill for reasons not worth explaining. When she gets back to the future, her boss says she bungled her assignment and must return to the past and do it over. So here she comes again.

In the repeated scenes, the camera angles are changed in a feeble effort to reduce the boredom factor, but the inane dialogue proves as unforgettable as the passion. We also share some moments with Bill and Louise that we didn't see the first time they got together, and these are played primarily for chuckles. The gag here is that a woman of the distant future doesn't know how to drive a car, eat an apple, etc. Funny thing, though: Louise has managed to learn '80s catch phrases such as "open up emotionally."

Right now you're probably wondering how the Earth of the future shapes up in "Millennium." The air quality stinks. The inhabitants are infertile. And most of the men have a severe hair-loss problem. On the plus side, Louise has the trendiest coiffure on the planet. You can tell Ladd's character is operating in the future when she sports her angular Brigitte Nielsen hairdo. For the past she favors a softer, shampoo-commercial style.

The principal supporting players are Daniel J. Travanti, as a Nobel Prize-winning physicist and plane-crash buff, and Robert Joy, as a "humanoid" who serves as Louise's personal robot and wit. Joy's make-up serves as a handy disguise in case he wants to deny involvement, but Travanti can't hide behind those prominent spectacles. As for Kristofferson, a humanoid would have brought more life to the part.

"Millennium" was written by science-ficton author John Varley and directed by Michael Anderson, whose credits include "Around the World in 80 days" and "Logan's Run," a futuristic film with something of a following. This project may seem like a waste of their valuable time, but they can always hawk the home-video version at Trekkie conventions.

Also reviewed in:
NEW YORK TIMES, 8/26/89, p. 15, Stephen Holden
VARIETY, 8/23–29/89, p. 28

MIRACLE MILE

A Hemdale Releasing Corporation presentation. *Producer:* John Daly and Derek Gibson. *Director:* Steve DeJarnatt. *Screenplay:* Steve DeJarnatt. *Director of Photography:* Theo Van de Sande. *Editor:* Stephen Semel and Kathie Weaver. *Music:* Tangerine Dream. *Music Editor:* Kenneth Hall. *Sound:* Morteza Rezvani. and (music) Rick Kline. *Sound Editor:* Michael Redbourn. *Production Designer:* Christopher Horner. *Art Director:* Richard Hoover. *Set Dresser:* Christine Bonnem, Paige Augustine, and Kara Hayak. *Special Effects:* Robbie Knott. *Visual Effects:* Jena Holman and Marty Sadoff. *Costumes:* Shay Cunliffe. *Make-up:* Robert Arrollo. *Stunt Coordinator:* Gary Jensen. *Running time:* 87 minutes. *MPAA Rating:* R.

CAST: Anthony Edwards (Harry Washello); Mare Winningham (Julie Peters); John Agar (Ivan Peters); Lou Hancock (Lucy Peters); Mykel T. Williamson (Wilson); Kelly Minter (Charlotta); Kurt Fuller (Gerstead); Denise Crosby (Landa); Robert Doqui (Cook); O-Lan Jones (Waitress); Claude Earl Jones (Harlan); Alan Rosenberg (Mike); Danny De La Paz (Transvestite); Earl Boen (Drunk Man in Diner); Diane Delano (Stewardess); Jose Mercado (Busboy from Diner); Alan Berger (New Person in Catering Truck); Howard Swain (Babbler); Raphael Sbarge (Voice of Chip); Lucille Bliss (Old Woman in Diner); Cynthia Phillips (Female Cop); Chad Taylor (Male Cop); Edward Bunker (Nightwatchman); Brian Thompson (Power Lifter); Herbert Fair (Leslie); Tina Webster (Girl in Aerobics Class); Kirby Tepper (Yuppie at Heliport); Jenette Goldstein (Beverly Hills Chick #1); Victoria

Powells (Beverly Hills Chick #2); Jordana Capra (TV Anchorwoman); Bruce Hayes (TV Anchorman); Rickie Biggs (Brian Jones); Peter Berg (Band Member); Chloe Amateau (Schoolteacher); Alan Dillard (Lobster Man).

LOS ANGELES TIMES, 5/19/89, Calendar/p. 13, Michael Wilmington

"Miracle Mile" is about the end of the world on Wilshire Boulevard. If that sounds absurd, it's an intentional riff. Writer-director Steve DeJarnatt tries to bring home the grisly horrors of the post-nuclear age by slamming it into an unlikely environment: Los Angeles from 4 a.m. to 5 a.m. when hardly anyone is awake except for an assortment of loners, night people, crooks and cops.

DeJarnatt is after contrasts and he's selected his background brilliantly. Most of the movie takes places in a small area defined by Fairfax Avenue, Wilshire Boulevard and Park La Brea, with the La Brea Tar Pits as a final swampy symbol of time's inexorable passage, man's impermanence. The milieu reeks of money and an almost lunar alienation: banks and corporations tower above empty streets in a lonely thin strip, sitting targets about to be smashed by a cosmic bowling ball.

It's a metaphor for the paranoid dilemma of the hero, jazz trombonist Harry Washello (Anthony Edwards), who—already desperate after accidentally breaking a date—mistakenly receives a call on an outdoor pay-phone from a missile silo worker, frantically trying to warn his dad that World War II has just been triggered.

Is it a hoax? A joke? For the next hour, as pale light drips down, Washello races around trying to beat the Apocalypse, find his girl Julie (Mare Winningham), and make it to a helicopter-rendezvous point on the Mutual Benefit Life Building. The movie is like a berserk West Coast version of "After Hours" or "Into the Night" on fail-safe: a romantic chase comedy turned meltdown nightmare.

Even assuming that fear had addled Harry's wits, he acts in an unusually crazed manner: scouring the empty streets and an exercise clinic for a copter pilot, pushing the drugged Julie along Wilshire in a shopping cart instead of getting a lift from her parents, hooking up with a street booster who's accidentally caused the death of two cops, and wandering quizzically into the gutted remnants of the old Ohrbach's building to check out a smashed-up police car—with barely 20 mununtes left to Zero Hour.

DeJarnatt, who wrote the script more than 10 years ago, is a highly talented young film maker with a great sense of mood, tension and pace. But he's also got the '80's movie weakness for dreaming up big moments and then not tying them sufficiently to inner reality, not thinking out his scenes enough from the inside. Too often the drama seems to be on automatic pilot. The symbols take over: L.A. as callous yuppie playground, the electronic media wilderness, the deserted city of night. In this movie, nuclear apocalypse is like the *deus ex machina* of a fantasy play: the fairy godmother who's going to swoop down and straighten out all the plot twists.

Parts of "Mile" have a weird, goofball penetration into L.A. night culture, like the comic coffee-shop scene, probably inspired by Hitchcock's "The Birds." There are other things in the movie that freeze you stiff, things that touch you or make you laugh. And some it's almost impossible to accept.

There's something self-indulgent about this pop-Wagnerian notion of two lovers daring everything to be together, though they've only just met that day at the Page Museum. If I were around on the morning of the apocalypse, I like to think I'd grab a pocketful of quarters and try to call all the other people I love best or respect most and warn them. This never seems to occur to Harry; he doesn't even ring up his parents.

It's the usual me-decade movie romance: the boy and girl racing alone in the night, the crazy, dopey people trying to keep them apart. At its best, "Miracle Mile" is a strong, idealistic modern thriller that seethes and pounds with excitement. At its weakest, it's another "You-and-me-against-the-world-babe" movie—with the kicker being that the world is about to end.

NEW YORK, 6/5/89, p. 59, David Denby

In Steve DeJarnatt's *Miracle Mile*, named after the famous strip of commercial real estate along Los Angeles's Wilshire Boulevard, the rumors of an impending nuclear-missile exchange, arriving in the dead of night, produce at first a few terrified escapees in the neonized streets—people rattling out of town with all their possessions in their cars—and then, at sunrise, with the strike only minutes away, a violent chaos crushing the entire neighborhood. It may be a sign of creative perversity in DeJarnatt that he finds much that is bizarrely funny in the gruesome mess; he also exhibits a fondness for outré L.A. types, an appreciation of the antic desperation of final encounters, and a young man's general love of going over the top.

Working with cinematographer Theo Van de Sande, DeJarnatt has a terrifically alive camera style, which makes up for some of the cruder bits of dialogue. Certainly the frenzied plot, in which the hero (Anthony Edwards) and the girl he's just met and fallen in love with (Mare Winningham) try to reach the airport and head south, is crassly conceived—one wonders at their selfishness and emptiness (where are they going?). There's something nuttily amoral in a filmmaker's turning the end of the world into an against-the-clock thriller. Still, DeJarnatt has a volatile talent. One awaits his post-apocalypse work.

NEW YORK POST, 5/19/89, p. 27, David Edelstein

Steve DeJarnatt's "Miracle Mile" is an entrancing piece of movie making—an adolescent daydream of first love, an adolescent nighmare of nuclear holocaust.

No one has thought to show how one can be an extension of the other, but DeJarnatt (who has nurtured the movie for a decade) is a haunted man. Immersed in his vision, you feel at first as if you're a guest in a crackpot's fever-dream; then you suspect that you've dreamed it already yourself and had the good sense to forget it.

DeJarnatt's alter ego is Harry Washello (Anthony Edwards), a goofy, self-conscious trombonist who wants to be Glenn Miller. Performing in Los Angeles, he visits a museum of natural history and catches sight of a colorfully dressed young woman named Julie (Mare Winningham).

It took millions of years for God to create the worlds, says Harry, in a voice-over, while the camera floats past murals of the primordial stew; "It took 30 years for Harry to find the right girl." The two meet formally over the La Brea tar pits—a setting that enraptures many death-obsessed Hollywood outcasts.

"Miracle Mile" is bracketed by teeming swamps and tar pits, by the beginning of life and the all-consuming end. Harry makes a date to pick up Julie at midnight when her waitress shift expires and then goes back to his hotel to take a nap. (She has promised to give him the night of his life.) He tosses away a cigarette; there's a quick shot of a bird fluttering with a butt in its mouth; a piece of shrubbery smokes.

We see Harry as he sleeps deeply, secure that his alarm is going to wake him, while fragments of flame can be viewed in the distance. Fire trucks come, the hotel's power goes off and on and the full moon rises. And Julie waits outside her coffee shop as the revolving digital clock ticks off the increments of her woe.

When Harry's alarm goes off, it's not 11:30 but 3:30 a.m. and he arrives at the coffee shop to find her gone. He leaves a message on her machine; then the pay phone rings, he answers, and it's a frantic young man who thinks he's talking to his father, who says he works in a North Dakota missile silo and that the missiles are set to fire in 50 minutes. And then we hear machine-gun fire.

We in the audience know that the call is some sort of prank—except, increasingly, we don't know. Then we know it's just Harry's dream except, increasingly, we don't know that either.

And while we argue with ourselves about what we're seeing, the people in the diner—led by an officious businesswoman (the tight-featured Denise Crosby)—charter a helicopter to the airport and a plane to Antarctica, to a valley with no rainfall where generations could be sustained. Harry tears off to find Julie and bring her along. Dawn creeps in.

The picture's deficiencies are obvious: DeJarnatt can't write full-fledged characters; he's not sure how humans actually talk to one another. And while the Tangerine Dream's shimmering organ and choral music works fine, it's the only part of the movie that's overly familiar: If this is the end of the world, how come we've heard it before?

But the cool, clean look of the picture and its Lego colors are a marvel—at $6 million of $7 million, this looks to have cost twice that. And the tidy, urban shopping-mall landscape is just the right unreal setting for the last hours of life.

Mare Winningham, with her broad, flat nose, gives Harry's obsession some weight. Winningham isn't a gorgeous bimbo; she's eccentric-looking and smart. To be smitten with her you need a rich imagination, and Edwards has that. The actor's blandness works well here; he's not fully there, he's nine-tenths in fantasyland.

"Miracle Mile" resembles our nightmares in that there's a clear destination—the helicopter pad on top of the Mutual Benefit building—but it can never be reached. The building looms over everything, so near and so far, but just when we think we're about to reach it, we have to go somewhere else for something.

Harry has to get Julie. He has to get gas. The thief (Mykel T. Williamson) whose car he shanghais has to get his nuclear-activist sister. Harry crashes into a busy health club at five in the morning to look for a helicopter pilot.

The absurdities in "Miracle Mile" have a way of making it feel even more real—it hits you on a different level than "The Day After," and it continues to buzz in your synapses after the initial, pit-of-the-stomach dread has worn off.

I went from thinking of the film as a sickening downer to something oddly sunny. That the world will explode is a given—but hey, Harry's met a wonderful girl. The final images are womblike in their comfort. This demented reverie is nihilist's idea of rapturous escapism.

NEWSDAY, 5/19/89, Part III/p. 5, Mike McGrady

Not many moviemakers would have the temerity to end an otherwise pleasant little movie romance with a nuclear holocaust that obliterates everything and everyone in sight. However, in the case of "Miracle Mile,"that final blinding explosion comes close to qualifying as a happy ending.

For much of "Miracle Mile" you may be under the misapprehension that you're watching a not-untypical boy-meets-girl movie. Sensitive, lonely Anthony Edwards discovers pretty, pug-nosed Mare Winningham in a museum and immediately feels deep stirrings: "I think I've always been a romantic kind of guy. But I never had anyone to feel romantic with before."

As romantic and sensitive an Edwards is, Mare is more than his match. I produce as evidence their dinner that very night, a trip to a seafood restaurant where live lobsters are displayed in an aquarium. Well, these crazy-in-love kids buy those lobsters, snatch them right off death row and take them down to the ocean, where they can be set free. Ah, love! Ah, Hollywood!

That first day is sheer bliss, right up to the very moment Edwards gets a wrong number and inadvertently learns that a major nuclear exchange is about to commence: "Fifty minutes and counting." Talk about poor timing. That gives Edwards about an hour to seek out his new lover, find a helicopter and get out of town. Only an hour? Seems like days.

Throughout, one wonders what writer-director Steve DeJarnatt seeks to say. Something about the relative strengths of young love and the hydrogen bomb? Another antiwar statement? A ban-the-bomb message? No matter. When an audience begins to look forward to a nuclear holocaust, seeing it as some kind of a mercy killing that will put a film out of its misery, the point is moot.

VILLAGE VOICE, 5/23/89, p. 61, Georgia Brown

Now that apocalypse plays nightly in the neighborhoods, offering itself in so many garden varieties, the great nuclear disaster theme has faded from screen memory. It's telling that Steve DeJarnatt's pre-*glasnost* script was conceived nine years ago—practically in another age. But his low-tech *Miracle Mile* is droll, splendidly twisty, and offbeat; and the nuclear risk, of course, has never gone away.

Harry Washello is a tall, gangly, trombone-playing geek (he's played by Anthony Edwards, *Revenge of the Nerds's* Gilbert) who has his eye out for "the right girl." In an L.A. natural history museum—during a video presentation of the original Big Bang and what that wrought—Harry spots pert, intelligent-looking Julie (Mare Winningham, who, with her pale skin and modified crew cut, looks a bit like Miou-Miou). A cute chase sequence (scored by Tangerine Dream) has Harry pursuing Julie through exhibits depicting the evolution of life on earth. They finally come together, as in as fit of regression, on a ledge overlooking plaster mammoths emerging from the burbling La Brea Tar Pits. (*Miracle Mile* is titled after the stretch of Wilshire Boulevard that links the primordial tar pits with contemporary skyscrapers.)

DeJarnatt's style threads between naive and savvy. Casual non sequiturs and weird, off-the-wall details keep viewers alert and sorting out what's important and what's throwaway—e.g., Harry bumps his car into a palm, and rats tumble onto his hood. (Dutch cinematographer Theo Van de Sande, of *The Pointsman* and *The Assault*, avoids slick effects for a definitive B look.) Then there's a ricocheting sequence reminiscent of the opening gag from Richard Rush's *The Stuntman*: Harry flicks a cigarette off his balcony; the butt is picked up by a pigeon who applies it to its nest resting on the building's electrical wires; fire ensues, causing Harry's alarm clock to conk out, which makes him three hours late picking up Julie from her night shift at Johnnie's diner; this puts him outside a corner phone booth just in time to pick up a fatal wrong number. But the sequence is more than a gag—it's a foreshadowing of dangerous chain reactions, a sample of what happens when humans carelessly interact with their habitat.

The hysterical phone call comes from someone named Chip, who works in a North Dakota missile silo. He's phoning his dad (but has dialed the wrong area code) to tell him the base's warheads are locked into a countdown: "We shoot our wad in 50 minutes." (On what was to have been Harry's big sex night, the little death turns into the great big one. But who's to say which he's most afraid of?) For his part, Chip gets shot by some big daddy who instructs Harry, "Forget everything you just heard and go back to sleep."

Harry returns to the diner, where he tries unsuccessfully to forget what he heard, then to share the message with a motley assortment of 4 a.m. coffee-drinkers—among them, a dim-witted young woman posing as a stewardess (wearing her sister's uniform); a skeptical young man in drag; two workers vainly trying to make time with Landa (Denise Crosby), a sveltely suited stockbroker who's speedreading the Cliff Notes edition of *Gravity's Rainbow*. (Now there's a touch.) The unlikely crew finally responds to Harry's alarm and mobilizes for a bail-out charter flight to the South Pole. What famous people shall we wake up and take with us? Pat Riley's name comes up first.

Harry, though, wants to take Julie, and to that purpose he alone turns back into the doomed city—an Orpheus after his Eurydice, who's taken a Valium and is so deep under that he puts her in a grocery cart. Julie lives with her grandmother, Lucy (Lou Hancock), who hasn't spoken to her husband, Ivan (John Agar), for 15 years. The two have vowed not to speak until the day they die. From all appearances, this'll be the day.

The escalating violence of the movie is notable for a nightmarish zaniness, with nuclear dread unleashing an almost whimsical havoc. Once massive gridlock takes over—and civic decency flies out the window—violence becomes more conventional, and the movie grows somewhat heavy-handed about human rapaciousness. But *Miracle Mile* is most intriguing when the ostensibly gentle, nonviolent Harry—who's the type to buy up lobsters from a seafood restaurant in order to return them to the ocean—begins to seem like the catalyst for all the flaming destruction in his wake. (Harry has a black counterpart named Wilson, who also seems both harmless and charming while wreaking chaos.)

I'm not sure, though, if DeJarnatt even intends this monster-is-ourselves reading. (He tells us much less about Harry and his curious isolation than he does about Julie and her feuding grandparents.) In the end, it's clear that the director means Harry to be a hero—for keeping his head, for caring about Julie more than escape—but moral lessons are, as usual, less engaging than unintended subtexts. It's more interesting noting that for Harry to get a girl to himself requires taking the whole world down with him.

Conventional sci-fi formula dictates a last-minute reprieve—in this case, that resourceful Harry will find some way to avert impending disaster, or wake from his dream. *Miracle Mile*, though, doesn't cheat once having set in motion its perfectly plausible scenario for doom. My problem with this is that it's perfectly consistent with the horrid New Fatalism.

Also reviewed in:
NEW YORK TIMES, 5/19/89, p. C16, Stephen Holden
VARIETY, 9/7/88, p. 34
WASHINGTON POST, 6/14/89, p. B11, Rita Kempley

MISS FIRECRACKER

A Corsair Pictures release. *Executive Producer:* Lewis Allen and Ross E. Milloy. *Producer:* Fred Berner. *Director:* Thomas Schlamme. *Screenplay: (based on her play "The Miss Firecracker Contest")* Beth Henley. *Director of Photography:* Arthur Albert. *Editor:* Peter C. Frank. *Music:* David Mansfield. *Sound:* Glenn Berkovitz. *Production Designer:* Kristi Zea. *Art Director:* Maher Ahmad. *Set Decorator:* Debra Schutt. *Costumes:* Molly Maginnis. *Running Time:* 102 minutes. *MPAA Rating:* PG.

CAST: Holly Hunter (Carnelle Scott); Mary Steenburgen (Elain Rutledge); Tim Robbins (Delmount Williams); Alfre Woodard (Popeye Jackson); Scott Glenn (Mac Sam); Veanne Cox (Tessy Mahoney); Ann Wedgeworth

(Miss Blue); Trey Wilson (Benjamin Drapper); Amy Wright (Missy Mahoney); Kathleen Chalfant (Miss Lily); Robert Fieldsteel (Tommy Turner); Greg Germann (Ronnie Wayne); Avril Gentles (Mrs. Biggs); Bert Remsen (Mr. Morton); Angela Turner (Caroline Jefferson); Lori Hayes (Sally Chin); Barbara Welch (Joe Ann Jacobs); Billy Nichols (Auctioneer); Mitch Saxton (Mitch); John Burgess (William); Christine Lahti (Clara Archer); Wilson Lahti Schlamme (Baby Willie Archer); Brent Spiner (Preacher Mann); Bronwen Sennish (Mrs. Mann); Gene Caldwell (Old Man); Jewell N. Guion (Old Woman); Cham Trotter (Franklin Rutledge); Christiana Throne (Little Carnelle); Jody Lovett (Little Delmount); Murray L. Cain (Judge, Bobby Potato); Earle Ingram (Judge, Dude P. Jones); Joyce Murrah (Ruby Kay).

CHRISTIAN SCIENCE MONITOR, 5/16/89, p. 11, David Sterritt

Beth Henley is a respected playwright: She's written several major productions, and her "Crimes of the Heart" won the Pulitzer Prize for drama, even though it was her first full-length play.

Something unfortunate happens when Ms. Henley decides to do a movie, though. The film version of "Crimes of the Heart" won Oscar nominations for her and Sissy Spacek, but it didn't quite work as a comedy or a drama.

Ditto for "True Stories," which she wrote with David Byrne of the Talking Heads rock group. Her other original screenplay, "Nobody's Fool," with Rosanna Arquette, was a disaster—not funny, not convincing, not anything.

Henley's new movie, "Miss Firecracker," is based on the play she wrote right after "Crimes of the Heart," and there are a lot of similarities between them. Again the setting is the Deep South; the most important characters are women; and the story might seem sad—even tragic—if there weren't so much goofiness in so many of the situations.

A less welcome similarity runs through the performances in the two movies. There's a quality in Henley's dialogue that seems to encourage overacting by just about everyone.

It happened to good actresses like Jessica Lange, Diane Keaton, and Ms. Spacek in "Crimes of the Heart," and in "Miss Firecracker" it happens once more.

Holly Hunter, who was so excellent in "Broadcast News," overdoes her role here. So do Mary Steenburgen and Alfre Woodard, although to a lesser extent.

One woman in a bit part actually overacts with her teeth, which the makeup department has covered with some kind of yellow film. It's hard to appreciate the movie's virtues when each performance is scrambling so much for attention.

This is too bad, because the story has potential. The heroine (Ms. Hunter) is a young woman who used to have a bad reputation, but thinks she can gain respect by winning the local beauty-and-talent contest.

Ms. Steenburgen plays an older sister who did win it, years ago, and Ms. Woodard plays a friend who wants to help.

Other characters include the heroine's crazy cousin—I mean *really* crazy, as played by Tim Robbins in the film's best performance—and a colorful assortment of friends and neighbors.

The plot follows all the steps in preparing for the contest and going through it, and the bittersweet moments right after it's over.

Why does "Miss Firecracker" seem overcooked much of the time?

Maybe speaking Henley's brand of eccentric, even zany dialogue is just too stimulating for most performers, and they don't realize they're pushing their roles too hard—especially when the characters have flamboyant natures to begin with, as you can tell just from their names: Carnelle, Delmount, Popeye.

Whatever the cause, "Miss Firecracker" is a movie that tries too hard. You want to like it, but in the end it just tires you out.

LOS ANGELES TIMES, 4/28/89, Calendar/p. 16, Michael Wilmington

Mississippi playwright Beth Henley specializes in dippy, small-town Southern Gothic; black humor with polka dots. In her 1981 Pulitzer-Prize winner "Crimes of the Heart," she gave us three oddball small-town Southern sisters united in catastrophe. The new Henley play-into-film, "Miss Firecracker," has three more relatives coming together for another disaster: Yazoo City's annual Fourth of July beauty contest.

It's a low-budget production with major-league acting by Mary Steenburgen, Holly Hunter and Alfre Woodard. It's not directed sharply enough; Thomas Schlamme is particularly weak on the fight scenes. The humor is as arch as arch can be: One character sews little uniforms for pet bullfrogs.

But Henley's special style and viewpoint come through: a bittersweet comic world of defiant oddballs, highfalutin phonies and passionate, half-crazy dreamers.

The tacky little beauty competition has awesome significance for two characters: ugly-duckling Carnelle Scott (Hunter), who idolizes her beautiful cousin, Elain, and cherishes the dream of winning her old title, and Elain Rutledge herself (Steenburgen), who, beneath a mask of honey-chile seduction and gracious wiles, would probably rather faint than see her title demeaned by scruffy little Carnelle.

Carnelle has two friends to sustain her foolish fancies: her alcoholic carny boyfriend, Mac Sam (Scott Glenn), and her wide-eyed, radiantly enthusiastic seamstress Popeye, (Alfre Woodard). But she's caught between her cousins: Elain and crazy poet Delmount, whom Tim Robbins turns into the image of an NBA-size Michael J. Pollard after an all-night drunk. Carnelle is besotted on Elain's fancy lies, torn up by Delmount's rude outbursts. All she wants is one thing: to be a beauty. But can she?

When her dialogue is working right, Henley gets the audience laughing and snorting by turns. What usually saves her is the innate theatricality of her main subject, Southern women, and of her approach. She is an ex-actress who knows the kind of emotions and lines actors like to play and she filters her characters through all the Southern or Midwestern Gothic plays she remembers from the '50s on: Williams, Faulkner, Inge, McCullers. Her plays are actors' showcases; that's why they attract such good actors.

There are a lot of good ones here: Holly Hunter, who originated the part of determined little Carnelle; Robbins; Glenn; Ann Wedgeworth, and the late Trey Wilson. Most of all, there's Woodard, who makes Popeye a giddily wonderful goofball romantic, and Steenburgen, who is absolutely deadly as Elain. Steenburgen plays all of her lines with two levels: the preening syrupy top; the curdled, resentful vinegary underpinning. And she keeps them in a dizzy comic balance. She shows us what makes this pretty, silky little witch tick.

Henley likes to play with the simmering, pathological underside of small-town Southern life, the hatreds, the jealousies, the obsessions, madness, even murders, but she usually leaves it all spinning clownishly from one joke to the next. There's a whiff of condescension in her portrayals; after all, she's a city girl from Jackson.

But the high point in "Miss Firecracker" is probably Carnelle's crack-brained patriotic tap-dancing routine at the contest, and there the condescension works comically. Hunter catches the scattered, fierce concentration and crazy glee of the inept performer. There is ridicule there, but there is also affection. And in our last flashback image of Carnelle as a little girl, beaming, full of love, infatuated with the wonderful, sweet cousin who throws her a rose, there is compassion as well.

MONTHLY FILM BULLETIN, 6/90, p. 168, Tim Pulleine

In the small town of Yazoo City, Mississippi, orphaned Carnelle Scott has grown up in her (now dead) aunt's home with her older cousins Elain and Delmount, and her most vivid childhood memory is of seeing Elain crowned as Miss Firecracker at the annual 4th of July carnival. In the summer of 1988, the last year in which she is eligible by age, Carnelle herself enters for the contest, at the finals of which Elain, who has made a rich marriage and now lives in Atlanta, is to give the keynote address. Carnelle's chances appear none too good: her hair is dyed scarlet, and her "standing" is impaired not only by her unskilled job at a fish plant (from which she has anyway just been fired) and the tumbledown state of her aunt's home, but by her past reputation as a flirt, which has led to her being nicknamed "Miss Hot Tamale". Now, however, she sees herself as reformed, though she continues a friendly dalliance with Mac Sam, a carnival hand whose easygoing beliefs co-exist with his being both consumptive and alcoholic. Elain returns, confiding to Carnelle that she is on the point of leaving her husband Franklin, but to Carnelle's dismay proves not to have brought with her the red dress in which she won the contest and which Carnelle hoped to wear in turn for good luck. Delmount, who proves to have spent some time in a mental hospital, also turns up, intent on selling his mother's home (bequeathed to him alone) and becoming a philosophy student on the proceeds, though in the upshot the property's decrepitude renders it unmarketable. Against the odds, Carnelle, aided by the dressmaking efforts of the apprentice milliner "Popeye" Jackson, qualifies as one of the five finalists; but the competition itself proves a humiliation, in which she ends up in fifth place. Back home she discovers that Elain had brought the dress after all but out of jealousy had declined to part with it. This knowledge, together with the valedictory encouragement of Mac Sam, allows Carnelle to see herself in a new light, and she resolves to leave Yazoo City. Amid the 4th of July fireworks, she climbs on to the dome of the town observatory, and when a passer-by asks if she is all right, she declares that she is.

Like Beth Henley's earlier stage adaptation, *Crimes of the Heart, Miss Firecracker* offers a comic-cum-"poetic" look at emotional dilemmas and identity crises in a small southern community. But in moving somewhat down the social ladder, the writer seems not only to be striving more obviously for effect, but—at least in this transposition—to have lost any clear sense of focus. In particular, this concerns the absence from the exposition of "back story", as regards Carnelle's position vis-à-vis her cousins, her earlier reputation for "loose" morals, and the nature of her relationship with Mac Sam. That the latter is so poorly integrated is all the more regrettable since, brief as it is, his is the most distinctively written characterisation. His laconic, good-humoured equilibrium ("This life of mine is strictly on the house") and the sense that in his down-at-heel way he controls his own destiny, symbolically intimated via his job as a carousel operator, contrast with everybody else's disorientation, which is variously shaded farcically, as in Delmount's ambitions to embrace philosophy and penetrate the meaning of life, or satirically, as in Elain's vanity and social climbing.

But this still leaves Carnelle herslef as an arbitrarily conceived figure whose desire to transcend her surroundings never really convinces at either a literal or a more heightened level. The histrionic performance of Holly Hunter, who created the role in the theatre, only tends to underline the problem. For a while, the film's surface is brisk and lively enough to conceal the split in treatment between theatrical convention and an attempt at opening-out. But by the time the contest itself is reached, the discrepancy is increasingly evident, along with the inconclusiveness of the various sub-plots, like the failure of Elain's marriage and the abortiveness of Delmount's efforts to sell the homestead. Even the ultimate revelation about the red dress registers more as an afterthought than as a moment of truth, leaving Carnelle's subsequent ascent to the observatory dome to pronounce her new-found self-belief as a gesture which is hollowly theatrical in more ways than one.

NEW YORK, 5/15/89, p. 101, David Denby

Miss Firecracker, which Beth Henley has adapted from her 1984 play *The Miss Firecracker Contest*, is theatrical and obvious in ways that this theaterphobe normally enjoys less than the rest of the world, but after a while I stopped fighting the movie, and I *did* enjoy it. So there. Holly Hunter plays a southern girl so desperate for attention that she dyes her hair the color of a ruby-red sofa in an old whorehouse. Eager to make us feel the courage and nobility of an untalented girl, Hunter writhes, trembles, hyperventilates, and does everything but turn herself inside out. She does too much. But she redeems herself when she calms down and looks at a man. No one looks at a man as intently as Holly Hunter.

I can't take the dramatic material of *Miss Firecracker* very seriously, but Henley writes juicy roles for actors, and first-time movie director Thomas Schlamme, who has made cable-TV specials with Sandra Bernhard, Whoopi Goldberg, Spalding Gray, and Bette Midler, gets the maximum fun and color out of a great group of performers. This is an inconsequential but entertaining and affecting movie (and far better than the two earlier movies made from Henley's work, the fussy, nattering *Crimes of the Heart* and the vapid *Nobody's Fool*).

Henley writes about the comedy—or perhaps the comic myth—of the South, an area of America still blessed with a richer cast of personal eccentricity and a wilder loneliness than the rest of the country. As in so many southern novels and plays, there's a dark, dowdy old house, which represents both a powerful tradition and the stifling weight of the past, and a variety of loopy and ravaged characters—a pair of ugly sisters used for comic relief; a lover of Hunter's (Scott Glenn), dying of TB, who croons erotic blandishments between coughing fits; a black seamstress (Alfre Woodard) who tells long, wandering stories and then laughs at her own conversational fecklessness. The many characters are part of a web of affection and support; they are all slightly hapless, but in Henley's world they cheer one another up.

Hunter plays Carnelle Scott, who lives in the house of her late aunt, where she was dumped many years earlier after her father died, a miserable little girl dressed in rags with ringworm in her hair. Brought up by the aunt, Carnelle is tiny compared with her two cousins, the tall and handsome Rutledges, Elain (Mary Steenburgen), who married well and moved away, and the wild, poetry-writing Delmount (Tim Robbins), who has just spent some time in an insane asylum. As a girl, Carnelle had to shave her mangy hair and wear a wig, and as she grew up, trying to prove to herself that she was attractive, she made out with half the boys in town, earning the name "Miss Hot Tamale." *Miss Firecracker* is about Carnelle's insatiable desire to win the town's annual Fourth of July talent contest—a victory that would finally end her miserable youth and demonstrate once and for all that everyone liked her.

Even when she wears tight little tops, there's nothing in the least sluttish about the strenuously earnest Hunter, so she really isn't credible as the former Miss Hot Tamale of Yazoo City. Her desperation to win the contest is more than convincing, though. Carnelle does a marching tap dance to "The Star-Spangled Banner," a pathetically square idea (though not as square—or as funny—as the reading from *Gone With the Wind* that wins the contest). Hunter, who performed this role onstage, goes so deep into the heroic indomitability of mediocrity, spinning and flinging a wooden gun like a baton, doing the splits, that she almost seems like Sally Field blackmailing an audience for love. If there were only that awful contest going on in the movie, *Miss Firecracker* would be insufferable, because Henley writes relentlessly about a desire that has no particular resonance. With one look at Carnelle, we take her in completely; there are no twists and turns, no buried revelations.

Fortunately, the movie has more. Carnelle's cousins show up—first Elain, now a prim rich lady running away from her boring husband, and then anarchic Delmount, a wildly romantic charlatan, half-Mississippi Heathcliff, half-clown, who knocks down furniture every time he enters a room. Elain, who has always condescended to her ragamuffin little cousin, likes to shut out everything ugly and disorderly, and her wild brother, tormented by visions, is always trying to make her face up to life. For years these two have been torturing each other—their relationship is funnier and more volatile than anything else in the movie. (Perhaps Henley should return to it in another play.)

Steenburgen has the stature and the southern graciousness to pull off the studiously refined manner of a would-be great lady, and she's an accomplished comedienne—a wiggle of the shoulders and her way of going dark and mean around the mouth let us see the selfishness and vanity in Elain's act. Robbins, the gangly young pitcher Nuke LaLoosh in *Bull Durham*, is very tall, with comically brooding heavy jowls and a big, shapeless nose—he looks like the beetle-browed Beethoven in his rage-over-a-lost-penny phase—and he brings great satirical bravado to the role of a blowhard with literary pretensions. And when Robbins finally links up with the story-telling Alfre Woodard, a new, fumbling tenderness comes out in him.

Both Elain and Delmount condescend to Carnelle, and yet they get caught up in her drive to win the stupid contest, experiencing it as a chance to achieve the transcendence they have missed. Schlamme keeps the volume up high, but there's no way of playing such obvious material quietly. He pushes actors further than one expects—and the movie becomes a vivid tribute to Henley's theatricality, her affectionate and comical indulgence for the inept, the shameless, the dissatisfied.

NEW YORK POST, 4/28/89, p. 29, David Edelstein

Carnelle Scott (Holly Hunter), the heroine of the comedy "Miss Firecracker," is a spunky, eccentric young woman who plans to leave her small Mississippi town and go out with a bang—she's determined to win the local Fourth of July beauty pageant, the Miss Firecracker Contest.

She's familiar, Carnelle is. This vulnerable woman—who aches for acceptance (but on her own terms), who survives through a mixture of craziness and stubbornness, who "can take it on the chin" and still emerge with her sense of self-worth intact—is the generic Beth Henley heroine. The problem is that Carnelle, her fellow firecrackers and her zany Southern milieu are starting to wear out their welcome. Big time.

At her best, in "Crimes of the Heart," author Henley rides the crest of self-parody. What's sad is how often everywhere else she pitches over. On stage, her characters can be entertaining—ribald exhibitionists, parading their quirks like majorettes in a marching band—and you can overlook the gooey sentimentality. But the medium of film exposes her mannerisms. Her people lack a private dimension.

Carnelle has curled her hair and dyed it hideously scarlet; a pint-sized ball o' fire, she strides around in short skirts and pumps. Known throughout the town as "Miss Hot Tamale," she longs to class up her act, to be a certified queen like her cousin, Elain (Mary Steenburgen), who wore the Miss Firecracker crown many years ago, married a wealthy man and left town.

In addition to Elain, who shows up at Carnelle's crumbling manse to contemplate leaving her stodgy spouse, Henley provides a male misfit, Elain's brother Delmount (Tim Robbins), who's fresh out of a sanitarium. Robbins, so masterful in "Bull Durham," makes a speech in his first scene that goes something like this: "I'm tired of hiding from philosophical calling. I have destiny! I have resources! Destiny is mine!"

Robbins slouches seductively and bulges his eyes, but there's no way to recover from an introduction like that. He's supposed to fall for Carnelle's friend Popeye (Alfre Woodard), a dazed loon who claims to hear with her eyes, and their courtship scenes are almost unwatchable—they look like a pair of village idiots.

I have no idea why the film is so uninvolving—why a playwright and director whose only purpose is to charm and entertain should so repel an audience. The director, Thomas Schlammme, likes actors enough to put his camera smack-dab in their faces. He has made some grand commercials for shows like "Cats" and a few good comedy specials; the problem might be that he's used to selling his material hard, and Henley's plays are oversold to begin with. If anything, a director needs to de-escalate them—to let them breathe a little, to get them out of the audience's face.

Hunter, who played the role on stage, is giving a stage performance. She fumbles with her lines to make them sound more natural, but her face is a mask of eagerness and there's too much of her grasping, hurting, quivering vulnerability.

There's too much of everything—primary colors, syrupy music, a talent show that could have come straight out of "True Stories" (which Henley co-wrote). Steeburgen mixes a few Valley Girl inflections into her Southern drawl and gets a few laughs, but it's a measure of how overbearing the picture becomes that this supercilious phoney is so much easier to take than the heroine. At least she doesn't keep clawing at our heartstrings.

As a carnie and Carnelle's sometime lover, Scott Glenn greets Hunter and then explodes in one of the worst bronchial spasms I've ever heard. "You still got the cough?" asks Carnelle. *No. I'm totally cured.* The scene points up what's wrong with "Miss Firecracker"—its heroine wonders if he's still got the cough while the audience is ducking phlegm.

NEWSDAY, 4/28/89, Part III/p. 3, Lynn Darling

There are many routes to redemption in this world—we take our salvation wherever we can find it—but few of them are as gratifyingly eccentric as the one chosen by the heroine of Beth Henley's "Miss Firecracker." Carnelle Scott, a bad girl gone good in the small town of Yazoo City, Miss., has chosen a beauty pageant as the outward sign, the visible proof, of her inward grace—if she can only win the town's annual Miss Firecracker contest, why then she can leave her hometown in "a blaze of glory."

The wonderful thing about Beth Henley's characters is the way in which the quirky comedy and bizarre circumstances of their lives cloak deeply felt, poetic yearnings. Carnelle (Holly Hunter) is not the only seeker in Henley's screen adaptation of her play "The Miss Firecracker Contest." Carnelle's friend, the seamstress Popeye Jackson (Alfre Woodard), wants to find the Elysian Fields—she's pretty sure it's a place to which you can buy a bus ticket. And Delmount (Tim Robbins), Carnelle's haunted, crazy cousin, decides to quit his job scraping dead dogs off the side of the road because he's tired of hiding from his "philosophical calling."

None of which is easy in the stagnant social pond of Yazoo City, where the question of who your daddy was and what your reputation is determines your chances in life. As an orphan whose reputation is best summed up by her nickname, "Miss Hot Tamale," Carnelle should be stalled in the starting gate. But, as her friend and sometime lover Mac Sam (Scott Glenn) puts it, she's someone who knows how to take it on the chin—how she learns as well to cut her own path to "what you can reasonably expect out of life" is at the heart of Henley's engaging, sharp-eyed story.

But "Miss Firecracker" loses a lot of its bite and much of its manic pace under the direction of first-timer Thomas Schlamme, who steeps the story in its sentimental side. The movie opens and closes with a shot of the child Carnelle in her moth-eaten hat waving at a passing parade—the bookended pathos takes away the tartness of Henley's vision of her world. Schlamme also lets his attention wander during scenes that depend on an unerring sense of timing and focus—one of Carnelle's big moments during the Independence Day pageant, for instance, drifts away from the movie like a lost child.

Holly Hunter earned rave reviews as Carnelle Scott on the stage, and luckily her performance survives that transfer to the screen—she's a desperately vulnerable, yearning bundle of fire and energy and heart, a girl with dreams so big they make her a wide-open target for the petty meanness of the world.

This time around she works in buoyant counterpoint with Tim Robbins' crazily noble Delmount and Mary Steenburgen as Carnelle's pretty, prissy cousin Elain, trapped in her role as the sort of quintessential Southern belle that even she realizes is a pathetic anachronism. Alfre Woodward as the dreamy seamstress Popeye is a wonder, stealing every scene she's in with her sweetly dizzy charm.

NEWSWEEK, 5/1/89, p. 75, Jack Kroll

Hasn't the South as a cornucopia of Lovable Eccentrics worn out its welcome? After Tennessee Williams? After Carson McCullers? After—what, you say your appetite for L.E.'s is insatiable? Then *Miss Firecracker*, which Beth Henley has adapted from her 1984 play, is your heaping platter of that delicacy. #1: Carnelle Scott (Holly Hunter) dyes her hair a poisonous red and yearns to win the Yazoo City Miss Firecracker pageant, at which she does a desperate dance, turning cartwheels with an American flag in her mouth. #2: Her cousin Elain (Mary Steenburgen), who insists her marriage is a success because "we have such beautiful clocks," has put her wacko but nice brother Delmount in a "clean, cheerful asylum." #3: Delmount (Tim Robbins) leaves the asylum, gets a job picking up car-flattened dogs from the highway but quits because "I'm tired of hiding from my philosophical calling." #4: Popeye (Alfre Woodard), the black seamstress, hears voices through her ears and sews clothing for bullfrogs.

There are others, all sloshed with the molasses of sentimentality, ladled on by director Thomas Schlamme. In the play, Popeye was white; here she's back so she can have an L.E. interracial affair with Delmount. This switch of races seems gratuitous—an example of what Yeats called "the will doing the work of the imagination." The cast is gallantry itself.

TIME, 5/1/89, p. 68, Richard Corliss

Movies are show, plays are tell. Here's one difference. In Beth Henley's 1984 off-Broadway hit *The Miss Firecracker Contest*, a seamstress named Popeye Jackson explained that as a child she "used to make little outfits for the bullfrogs that lived out around our yard." In this expansive adaptation, Popeye (Alfre Woodard) displays one such frog, cunningly coutured in a nurse's gown with matching stethoscope. Ah, the glamorous realism of the cinema! It's cute too.

As screenwriter, Henley has dramatized elements only hinted at in her play, but the story is the same. Sweet, just slightly trampy Carnelle (Holly Hunter) determines to win the Miss Firecracker Contest as a way of standing up to the mocking townspeople and claiming some of the limelight that illuminates her chic, snooty cousin Elain (Mary Steenburgen). Two men, Carnelle's sometime lover Mac Sam (Scott Glenn) and Elain's wild brother Delmount (Tim Robbins), act as a geek chorus to the drama, but, typically in a Henley play, the real conflict is between young women clawing each other for respect, attention and love.

The movie's tone is high-pitched and precise. Everybody plays to the max, especially Steenburgen, sweet magnolia condescension dripping from every elongated syllable, and Hunter, crazy for acceptance, clinging to Delmount, desperately fanning the summer heat off Elain's body. They serve well this fable about the need to realize that some dreams are better off not coming true, at least in a town where the local tramp is the wisest soul around and the pouting princess is revealed as a frog who needs to put a stethoscope to her own porcelain heart.

VILLAGE VOICE, 5/2/89, p. 70 Renee Tajima

Miss Firecracker plays close to home for me, since I've known the vagaries of being small-town royalty in a place where—for women with few other options—a beauty crown means achievement. For those of us who grew up just shy of the postfeminist march of institutional "herstory," our best role models were the adored, elder girl-women who seemed to be born to the secrets of belonging.

Writer Beth Henley plumbs these secrets in her funny, backwater tale of Carnelle Scott (Holly Hunter), the inevitable outsider and beauty queen wannabe who works in the meantime as a fish-gut sucker. Like the dreamy, awkward southern girlhood understood by Carson McCullers, Henley's characters know the pain of being out of synch in a place where conformity is king.

Carnelle is a girl who has never quite figured it out. Her attempt at glamour is a red fright-wig hairstyle that virtually screams "henna." And, striving to be popular with the boys, she only manages to earn the title "Miss Hot Tamale" of Yazoo City, the kind of Mississippi town that, at quick glance, could still be locked in time, circa 1962. Now in her last year of eligibility, Carnelle wants to fulfill a lifelong dream of winning the Miss Firecracker crown, still worn in her childhood memory by an older, idolized cousin, the "perfectly perfect" Elain (Mary Steenburgen).

True to its theatrical origins, director Thomas Schlamme's adaptation of Henley's play is a vehicle for the rollicking cast that populates Carnelle's world. Even the long-departed are colorfully wrought, like the unseen Aunt Ronelle, whose pituitary gland was replaced by that of a monkey, making for "an extremely furry individual." Ronelle had adopted eight-year-old Carnelle, a little troll of an orphan, to be raised with her own children Elain and Delmount (Tim Robbins), a raucous would-be poet. In the days leading up to the contest, Elain, now the well-heeled wife of an adoring Atlanta businessman, once again graces Yazoo City, this time to deliver the Firecracker contest's keynote speech, "My Life as a Beauty." Delmount also returns, fresh from recent employment collecting dog carcasses, and a previous stint as a mental patient.

In the movie, Henley's memorable parade of small-town types is rendered with varying degrees of success. Holly Hunter plays another spunky firebrand à la *Broadcast News*, but she seems too old and a touch too savvy to be convincing as the gum-chewing, starry-eyed Carnelle. She is at her most wildly comic when she endows the send-ups with a touching vulnerability, as in the climactic contest sequence in which she dejectedly pulls cotton balls from her bra and bemoans certain ruin. (Meanwhile Elain tries to comfort her: "Oh, Carnelle, I don't think anyone noticed when you tripped.")

But the movie falls flat when it tries too hard. Hunter's tap-dance scene should be a comic tour de force, but the effort is as forced as Carnelle's own longings. Alfre Woodward, who plays Popeye, a near-blind seamstress and Carnelle's bosom buddy, verges dangerously close to a variation on Butterfly McQueen. Consistently good are Steenburgen and Robbins as the quirky but goodhearted elder cousins. Steenburgen plays deliciously to type: a coy, almost squirming modernday Scarlett who has it all figured out. Robbins, hilarious as a half-witted felon in *Raising Arizona* (also with Hunter), looks here like a hulking, giant-sized Michael J. Pollard, but he plays a certain chemistry to both Hunter and Steenburgen.

Henley is a master of the written world, but her stories are filled with imagery that comes alive through her characters. When Schlamme allows whimsy to rule—Delmount and Elain in a gossipy tango, Popeye gazing at the moon from a gingerbread house of an observatory—he leavens the excesses of acting with the magic that informs Henley's tales.

Also reviewed in:

NATION, 5/15/89, p. 677, Stuart Klawans
NEW REPUBLIC, 6/12/89, p. 26, Stanley Kauffmann
NEW YORK TIMES, 4/28/89, p. C12, Caryn James
NEW YORKER, 5/29/89, p. 103, Pauline Kael
VARIETY, 4/19–25/89, p. 22
WASHINGTON POST, 5/12/89, p. D7, Hal Hinson
WASHINGTON POST, 5/12/89, Weekend/p. 39, Desson Howe

MR. UNIVERSE

A Hunnia Filmstudio/Cine Universe Corporation film. *Executive Producer:* Miklos Kollo. *Producer:* Andras Ozorai, Gabe Von Dettre, and Kathi Gati. *Director:* Gyorgy Szomjas. *Screenplay: (Hungarian with English subtitles):* Ibolya Fekete, Ferenc Grunwalsky, and Gyorgy Szomjas. *Director of Photography:* Ferenc Grunwalsky. *Editor:* Anna Korniss. *Sound:* Gyorgy Kovacs. *Running time:* 96 minutes. *MPAA Rating:* Not Rated.

CAST: Laszlo Szabo (Laszlo); George Pinter (Lord); Mickey Hargitay (Himself).

NEW YORK POST, 3/9/90, p. 27, Martin Burden

Laszlo, a man fo no discernible profession, is watching a TV show in a Budapest cafe, and sees a documentary about Mickey Hargitay, a Hungarian muscleman who became Mr. Universe, part of the biceps brigade in Mae West's cafe act, a film actor and husband of Jayne Mansfield.

Idea! Make a movie about Mickey and Jayne. All he has to do is get permission from Hargitay, whom he hasn't seen in 25 years, and then only fleetingly. Laszlo doesn't know much, if anything, about film-making, but he has a friend in New York, known only as Lord, who has made films and will direct this epic, for which he has grandiose plans.

"Everybody knows who Mickey Hargitay is," he assures his cafe pals. "He's Mr. Universe. Arnold Schwarzenegger played him in "The Jayne Mansfield Story." Mickey and Jayne are the dream couple! Everybody in America knows them."

In his euphoria there is no mention of the fact that the dream couple was divorced in 1963 and Jayne died in an accident in '67. And while Hargitay may still be a well-known name in Hungary, he's a trivia question in the U.S.

"Mr. Universe" is the off-beat, funny story of the odyssey of Laszlo and Lord across America to see Hargitay. Directed by Gyorgy Szomas, the movie (dialogue in Hungarian, with English subtitles) drew praise when it was shown as part of last year's New Directors /New Films series. It gets its first theatrical engagement starting today at the Public Theater in the East Village.

When Laszlo gets to New York he is surprised to find Lord is a cabbie. "But he is a film-maker!" he exclaims. "That is his dream."

"Well," says a friend, "he's on his way to his dream—by taxi."

Laszlo convinces Lord to join him in the movie effort, to emulate Hargitay's becoming part of the American dream: "Mickey is rich, famous and Hungarian. Just a guy from Budapest, like us."

"Yes," says Lord, pragmatically, "but he made it. That's the difference."

And so, without ever contacting Hargitay, without knowing if he'll agree to see them, the two hopefuls set out from New York to Hollywood—in Lord's yellow cab, by way of Nashville, Graceland, Dallas. With the meter running.

And in this on-the-road film, director Szomas shows us glimpses and sounds of the U.S. that many travelers often do not see and hear, or those they disregard. It's a colorful chunk of Americana, and Szomas pins it down with a foreigner's eye—backroads and highways, the small-town streets, stores and people, the signs, the unending radio commercials for real estate and cemeteries, restaurants and hotels, the country songs, the announcers—from twangy to unctuous.

The director is fascinated with camera angles—high overhead, angled or tilted, close-up and zoom shots. It might not always be effective, but it's certainly different.

Finally the traveling duo reach Hollywood (the meter reads $2,921) and make an appointment with Hargitay.

The former Mr. Universe, now 60ish and a successful businessman, still ruggedly good-looking, greets them at his big home in the Hollywood hills. He listens to their suggestion—and his answer is the climax of the story.

Laszlo and Lord find that the American dream may still be out there—but not for everyone. Still, it's entertaining to see how they learn this lesson.

NEWSDAY, 3/24/89, Part III/p.3, Mike McGrady

Ever since the pioneering days of moviemaking, there has been a solid Hollywood-Hungary hookup. In fact, during the era of Michael Curtiz, Alexander Korda and Bela Lugosi, this declaration of policy suddenly appeared on the walls at MGM: "It's not enough to he Hungarian. You have to have talent, too."

The feeling among Hungarian moviemakers, then and now, can be boiled down to this: If you have a camera and some film, you're a moviemaker. The Hungarian moviemakers who put together this chaotic, sometimes hilarious, intentionally pointless "Mr. Universe" have something more than just the basics. They also happen to have a personal connection to former Mr. Universe, Mickey Hargitay. That's right, the muscular husband of the late star, Jayne Mansfield, the fellow impersonated by Arnold Schwarzenegger a few years ago on television.

"Mr. Universe" details the strenuous efforts of two Hungarian moviemakers to reach Hargitay in his home in the hills of Hollywood. The trail actually begins in a Budapest bar where Laszlo (Laszlo Szabo) is watching a television interview with Hargitay recalling the day he first stepped onto American soil, penniless but optimistic: "I knew everything was up to me. The plane landed, I was happy, I knew the world was mine."

Immediately recognizing the dramatic potential here, Laszlo launches into a chorus of, I'm Beginning to See the Light'' and then hops a plane to New York where he tracks down another former Hungarian moviemaker (George Pinter), a taxi driver who once actually knew Hargitay. The fact that Lord now drives a cab doesn't disturb Laszlo in the least: "An auto is like a sponge—he soaks up everything, like a sponge, then lets it out. Everybody drives a cab in his life. Even I did."

Laszlo announces to the dubious cabbie: "We're rich. I've got an idea," and he explains that the movie project won't require much of an investment: "Two to three million will be enough. Low budget!" And, after all, they have an unbeatable subject, Hungary's leading export: "Mickey's name is as good as gold."

To find Hargitay, now a prosperous businessman, the two would-be moviemakers journey across America by Yellow Cab. During this comic odyssey—think of a Hungarian Tom Sawyer and Huck Finn—they are exposed to great varieties of landscape and people, and they work out the final details for their movie, to be entitled, naturally, "Mr. Universe." An example of their thinking: "It will be 'a movie of hard times, not the glitz and the gorgeousness.'"

What makes "Mr. Universe"—this film, not the one they're planning—is a spirit of chaotic fun. To call it uneven is to be overly charitable; to call it funny is to understate the case. Much of the film is shot off-kilter, which somehow seems appropriate. The sound track is punctuated by American radio tidbits—news flashes, Cadillac commercials, country music refrains, get-rich-quick land schemes. Audible artifacts of modern America. Nothing seems out of place. But then, when you're telling a shaggy-dog story—and that is exactly what "Mr. Universe" is—anything goes.

VILLAGE VOICE, 3/28/89, p. 64, J. Hoberman

Cheap, eccentric, and extremely funny, this discombobulated road film has the cinephilic feel of a Lower East Side super-8 epic or vintage nouvelle vague: Two Hungarians drive a yellow cab from New York to Los Angeles with grandiose, if vague, plans for a spectacular movie starring Miklós "Mickey" Hargitay, onetime consort to Jayne Mansfield and the Arnold Schwarzenegger of his day. Mr. Universe not only satirizes the Magyar version of the American Dream, it reeks of subtext. The three principal actors are all expatriates; Hargitay playing himself as a living, breathing hunk of Hollywood, dazzling proof that America works.

VILLAGE VOICE, 3/13/90, p. 76, Georgia Brown

For a real vision of America, go see Mr. Universe, one of the hits of last year's "New Directors," now opening at the Public Theater. Hungarian director György Szomjas begins his disarmingly light movie (two wild and crazy guys go cross country) with a TV interview: Former muscle-man Mickey Hargitay is describing his first impression of the New World, of flying when he was a 14-year-old from a Hungary torn by war and bombs, to the United States where, incredibly, "nothing had happened!" To be from a place where everything has happened and come to one where nothing has provides a fruitful way of looking at the American dream.

Watching this interview in a Budapest café is sometime actor Laszlo (Laszlo Szabo), who determines on the spot to go to the States and put together a movie about Hargitay, a Hungarian national legend. Not only did the big guy succeed in being crowned Mr. Universe, but he married Jayne Mansfield. Together the couple used to visit the old country and wow the populace. (Photos of Jayne and a haystack, Jayne on a pig farm.) On one of her visits, reports the cabbie driving Laszlo to the Budapest airport, Mansfield had occasion to bend down and pick up something: "I had never seen such a cleavage like that before." Hungarians also recall that she was reported to have an IQ of 185.

In New York Laszlo tracks down his talented countryman known as the Lord (George Pinter, no relation to Harold), who'd earlier come to the U.S. to make his fortune as a film director. He's found driving a cab. "This is America. You're a cabdriver one day, a filmmaker the next," explains one of his minions. Eventually Laszlo and the Lord decide to drive the cab to L.A. and present their project of Hargitay, now a retired real estate developer living on a hill that overlooks Hollywood and the Pacific. "He's just a guy from Budapest, like us," they reason.

The Lord maps out the route, with stops in Virginia ("backyard of the Founding Fathers"), Nashville ("Dollywood"), Memphis's Graceland, and Texas, where, he reports, a man named Zapruder bought a roll of film one morning and sold it that night for $1,000,000. He wants to soak up the ambience of the land he's going to portray. Along the way, as the country passes, they talk of Mickey and Jayne. The meter, when they reach the other ocean, reads $2921. Laszlo, feeling a twinge of guilt, decides he may drop in on the son he hasn't seen for four years. ("How's your wife?" he asks the Lord. "Which one?" comes the answer. This is no country for settling down.) They find Hargitay (he plays himself) on his hill, looking like a trim, handsome cowboy and living in a splendor that might have been decorated by Czech emigré Ivana.

Szomjas is neither a naïf nor a "new director," but a veteran filmmaker in a sophisticated national cinema. His New Wave stylistics and handheld camera here look both fresh and intentionally seedy, droll and suitably disreputable. He's a connoisseur of off-beat artifacts and piquant fragments—the messages of signs (like the painted city wall proclaiming "No Air") and of the country's ubiquitous, manic AM radio. As if two alternate movies are being made (which, he means us to ask, is true?), he breaks into color footage with stretches of black-and-white and switches back and forth from English to subtitled Hungarian. Godard-like, Szomjas punctuates his narrative with aphorisms from the already arrived—some of whom (Bela Lugosi, Zsa Zsa Gabor) are Hungarian, some (Bruce Lee, Andy Warhol, Jonas Mekas, Judy Garland) not.

One quote is taken from a sign once posted on the wall at MGM studios: "It's not enough to be Hungarian. You have to have talent, too." The Hungarian/Hollywood connection continues unbroken. Szomjas knows that talent is not as important as being from a country where everything has already happened.

Also reviewed in:
NEW YORK TIMES, 3/9/90, p. C14, Vincent Canby
VARIETY, 3/2/88, p. 30

MONEY JUGGLER, THE

An Archer Films production. *Producer:* Constance Marks. *Director:* Leo Rubinfein. *Screenplay:* Leo Rubinfein and Constance Marks. *Based on a story by:* Louis Auchincloss. *Director of Photography:* Michael Mayers. *Editor:* Constance Marks and Mia de Bethune. *Music:* Joshua Selman. *Running time:* 56 minutes. *MPAA Rating:* Not Rated.

CAST: John Cunningham (John Grau); Roxanne Hart (Elly Drayton); Pirie MacDonald (Roger Jordan); Remak Ramsey (Hilary Knowles); Robert Stattle (Townie Drayton).

VILLAGE VOICE, 3/21/89, p. 64, Renee Tajima

In Leo Rubinfien's *The Money Juggler*, four patrician Columbia alums gather over g&t's and their ambiguous obsession for the unseen protaganist. This Boeskian figure is an amalgam of the decade's Jewish tycoons who raid the WASP business sanctums, then presume to enter its social sanctuaries. The movie would be little more than an immaculately produced picture of snob anthropology except for its story by Louis Auchincloss, with his wry insider knowledge of upper-class struggle.

Also reviewed in:

NEW YORK TIMES, 3/19/89, p. 60, Vincent Canby

MONSIEUR HIRE

An Orion Classics release of a Cinea/Hachette Première et Cie/Europe 1 Communication/F.R. 3 Films Productions film. *Producer:* Philippe Carcassonne and René Cleitman. *Director:* Patrice Leconte. *Screenplay (French with English subtitles):* Patrice Leconte and Patrick Dewolf. *Based on the novel "Les Fiancailles de M. Hire" by:* Georges Simenon. *Director of Photography:* Denis Lenoir. *Editor:* Joëlle Hache. *Music:* Michael Nyman. *Sound:* Pierre Lenoir. *Set Designer:* Ivan Maussion. *Costumes:* Elisabeth Tavernier. *Running time:* 81 minutes. *MPAA Rating:* Not Rated.

CAST: Michel Blanc (Monsieur Hire); Sandrine Bonnaire (Alice); Luc Thuillier (Emile); André Wilms (Police Inspector).

CHRISTIAN SCIENCE MONITOR, 4/23/90, p. 11, David Sterritt

When it comes to mystery stories, Americans and Europeans have very different approaches.

Americans like movies that *move*; their talent for making that kind of picture is envied in many other parts of the world. So their mysteries, like their other films, often put the emphasis on action and violence. Europeans, by contrast—particularly the French—tend to be fascinated more by character and atmosphere, a taste that gives their dramatic films a very different flavor.

"Monsieur Hire" is an excellent example of this difference. A new psychological mystery from France, it's an absorbing picture, with a mood unlike that of any American film I've seen in a long time. But it doesn't move very much, at least until the climax, so you'd better be prepared to sink into it—on its own slow, almost meditative terms—if you're going to enjoy it.

The plot centers on Monsieur Hire, a man so quiet and mild-mannered that you might wonder if he's still breathing. He lives alone; his greatest passion appears to be bowling; and there's nothing about him to attract the slightest attention. He has his secrets, thought, including the unpleasant fact that he's a voyeur, and that he has an obsession with a beautiful woman in a nearby apartment. She's no innocent herself—when she realizes there's a peeping tom in the neighborhood, she plays along with him and encourages him.

Events switch into high gear when they finally meet, and when he learns a secret about her life (or rather, her boyfriend) that puts their strange relationship on a very different level.

"Monsieur Hire" is one of those movies that have press agents pleading with critics: Please don't give away the ending, or even too much of the story!

That's fair, since this is a mystery, and part of the fun is wondering what's going to happen next. On the other hand, the plot of "Monsieur Hire" may already be familiar to some Francophiles, since it's taken from a Georges Simenon novel and was filmed by French filmmaker Julien Duvivier, under the title "Panique," back in 1946.

In any case, I'll only mention that while the story is involving, the ending struck me as a bit of let-down, not bold or original enough to cap the buildup that leads to it.

Still, the movie as a whole has an odd fascination that makes it worth seeing if you like a brooding psychological tale now and then. Michel Blanc gives a superb performance in the title role; he's as quiet and recessive as his character demands, yet he holds the screen as strongly as a movie star should. This is his fifth movie with director Patrice Leconte, and you'd never guess that all the others have been comedies. This collaboration is as intense as it is gripping.

Alice, the object of Monsieur Hire's twisted affection, is marvelously played by Sandrine Bonnaire, who's known to Americans for such highly praised French movies as "A Nos amours" and especially Agnès Varda's memorable "Vagabond," in which she played a tragically rootless young drifter. She has a mixture of charm and vulnerability that's just right for the ambiguous foil who brings out the best and worst in Monsieur Hire's murky personality.

"Monsieur Hire" is not a masterpiece of French cinema, and I think it was overpraised in early reviews that appeared after its showings in the Cannes, Toronto, and New York filmfests. But it's put together with great skill by director Leconte and such gifted collaborators as cinematographer Denis Lenoir and British composer Michael Nyman, who has done the music for all of Peter Greenaway's films. In all, it's a picture that gets under your skin, in a sly and insinuating way that French filmmakers seem to have mastered more thoroughly than any others.

LOS ANGELES TIMES, 5/4/90, Calendar/p. 6, Sheila Benson

With his round black hat, pale face and black coat, Monsieur Hire, from the splendid movie of the same name, might have stepped straight out of a painting by Magritte; you half expect to be able to see blue sky and clouds straight throught him.

Instead, this small, mysterious bachelor is at the heart of a luminous and hypnotic new film made from one of the novels by the always-reliable Georges Simenon. Michel Blanc plays Hire and Sandrine Bonnaire plays his prey, the sensual young woman he watches every night from his window opposite hers in their old Paris apartment building.

Bonnaire and Blanc are an extraordinary pairing: the warm, carelessly seductive Alice and the reclusive, amost universally disliked Monsieur Hire, who spends most of his nights in the dark, listening to Brahms and staring at the yellow rectangle of light that is her apartment. What makes it creepy is that after the startling night when Alice catches Monsieur Hire at his compulsion, she doesn't report him to the police. Instead, she uses her power over him to draw him into her life until they are both held by a delicately manipulated bond of eroticism.

It's frightening for us, since we know that the milky-skinned, deeply emotional Hire is a suspect in the murder of the 22-year-old girl from the apartment next to his. An almost fatherly inspector (the craggy-faced Andre Wilms) is on the case, dropping in at odd moments to hound Hire, while at the same time director Patrice Leconte drops visual hints—a white mark on Hire's black suit—that recall "M" and Peter Lorre's psychopathic killer.

The film's last major character is the thuggish Emile (Luc Thuillier), plainly less in love with Alice than she is with him. And that is enough about the story, which is a skein of subtleties played with the utmost deliberation and intelligence. (The film is rated PG-13, since its eroticism is almost entirely suggested, not shown.)

The actors are fascinating. Blanc's work has so many different levels and layers as he builds first sympathy for Hire, then fear about his motives, that it needs to be seen more than once to appreciate the depth involved.

Alice is one of Bonnaire's rare sunny characters, a country girl from Provence with predictably lousy judgment about big-city men, but one who's comfortable with her sexuality and blessedly unneurotic. Bonnaire has now shed every ounce of the puppy fat she had in "A Nos Amours" and in "Vagabond"; with the contours of her face defined this way, she's become even more interesting to watch and she's always been a compelling actress.

"Monsieur Hire" is marvelously all-of-a-piece. Denis Lenoir's lighting camera work sets a mood that's cool and detached; as a result, in retrospect this seems to be a film played out in bluish moonlight. The atmosphere is further deepened by the faintly ominous musical score of British avant-gardist Michael Nyman, known also for his music for the films of Peter Greenaway.

Director Leconte, who was also co-adapter with Patrick Dewolf, has deliberately made the period and even the location undefinable, an interesting idea that connects his film subliminally to French *policiers* of the '30s and '40s, to the Polanski of "The Tenant" or to early Hitchcock. Leconte also seems to like visual puns, like the one in which Hire, eating a soft-boiled egg, is shot from above and behind, the top of the egg and the top of his perfectly rounded balding head making an exact match.

MONTHLY FILM BULLETIN, 4/90, p. 114, Tom Milne

A girl, Pierrette, is found murdered. Chief suspect is Monsieur Hire, a bald, pallid, middle-aged tailor, whose strange and solitary habits have made him an object of fear and loathing in the neighbourhood. Although the taxi driver who saw the killer running towards the apartments where Hire lives cannot make positive identification, the police inspector in charge of the case continues to harass his suspect vindictively. Hire meanwhile continues watching, from his apartment where he never switches on the lights, pretty young Alice in the apartment opposite. One night, in the light of an electrical storm, Alice is terrified to catch a glimpse of Hire's face at the window. She nevertheless pays the embarrassed Hire a visit, hastily retreating before his anger when she provocatively asks what he most enjoys about what he sees. Realising the extent of Hire's interest after he turns up at the skating-rink where she has been taken by her boyfriend Emile, Alice arranges to meet Hire in a restaurant for dinner. There, after telling Alice of the house he owns in Switzerland and offering her a rail ticket should she wish to join him there, Hire reveals that he knows she is not dining with him for the pleasure of his company, but because she is wondering if he knows that Emile killed Pierrette (it was an accident; Emile fled in panic to Alice's room; and Hire saw what they did with Emile's bloodstained raincoat). Subsequently, encouraged by Alice's response to his confession of unbearable loneliness and assurance that he loves her too much ever to go to the police, Hire is emboldened—especially after Emile runs out on her to save his own skin when the police become suspicious—to make arrangements for them to leave for Switzerland together, assuring her it doesn't matter whether she loves him in return. Alice fails to turn up at the station, and Hire returns home to find the police waiting for him: Alice has framed him for the murder. Contriving to escape, Hire falls to his death from the roof. But the police receive a letter from Hire revealing the truth, posted when he thought Alice would be safe with him in Switzerland . . .

Unlike Julien Duvivier's earlier adaptation of Simenon's novel (as *Panique* in 1946), which tended to stress the ready public assumption of guilt in an innocent but unprepossessing bystander, the present version is more concerned with the private mechanisms which set a sordid little tragedy in motion. Accordingly, where one might perhaps have expected the more conventional hypnotic spell of long takes, Patrice Leconte assembles his film, mosaic-style, out of a crossword puzzle selection of brief, sometimes tantalisingly elliptical scenes.

The method, peculiarly apt anyway in a film whose central image is of the half-hidden voyeur at a window trying to grasp as much as possible of the object of his desire half-hidden behind another window, brings manifold rewards. Not least is the way it stresses the essential isolation of all the characters (except for the anonymously gregarious crowd), each locked away within his or her own preconceptions and preoccupations; or the way in which it persuades the viewer to probe into the obscurer areas of human behaviour.

There is, for example, the question of the cageful of white mice glimpsed in Monsieur Hire's workshop, one of which dies, is carefully shrouded in a square of sample cloth, then carelessly tossed away into a canal: are they kept as companions by a lonely man, or do they serve some more sinister purpose? There is the enigma of the two Monsieur Hires: in his own neighbourhood, an object of mistrust and cruel childish malice; at the bowling alley where he is evidently paid to demonstrate his sure-shot skills, a cheerful extrovert responding to public adulation of his prowess. Above all, there is the constantly shifting spectre of what, exactly, Monsieur Hire is looking for.

The opening scenes introduce him in the conventional voyeur image, seeking vicarious or vicious pleasures from arenas where he himself dare not appear. "How long since you came inside a woman?" sneers the police inspector convinced of his guilt. Hire does not reply, and we cut to a scene in which he is innocently feeding some pigeons; but later, as if in answer to that question, comes a sequence in which, clearly enjoying more than the advertised tariff in a massage parlour, he breaks away in distress, crying, "You're just whores ... I'm tired of screwing you!"

Later yet, however, in one of the two remarkably intense love scenes in which Alice seems to be as firmly gripped by *amour fou* as Monsieur Hire, he launches into a moving (and like much of the film, surprisingly erotic) description of the tenderness and joy he once experienced in those same massage parlours. The implication, of course, is that what Monsieur Hire so desperately seeks is a love not bought but given. Yet, for all that the film gradually persuades one to modify contempt and extend understanding, the mind and the heart of Monsieur still retain their darker recesses. Having faced the object of his unending love and desire, Hire nevertheless assures her that it doesn't matter if she still loves Emile: "No one will ever love you as I do". A dark note of perversion still casts its shadow, and one can't help wondering what would have happened had Alice reached Switzerland in the enigmatic company of Monsieur Hire.

The first of Patrice Leconte's nine features to be released in this country, replete with a bizarre, sardonic humour that underlines his primary reputation as a director of comedy, *Monsieur Hire* may not be to everyone's taste—start pulling at loose threads ,and the whole edifice tends to fall apart—but it is brilliantly conceived, admirably acted, and staged with stunning confidence.

NEW YORK, 5/14/90, p. 106, David Denby

The French film *Monsieur Hire* may be exactly the kind of European art that some Europeans would like to get away from. The title character, a balding, wraithlike Parisian tailor with the black clothes of an undertaker, stands at his window every night listening to Brahms and spying on a young woman across the alley. Monsieur Hire (Michel Blanc), with his whited-sepulcher face, is of course meant to be a kind of toothless vampire; the girl (Sandrine Bonnaire) is the force of life. The movie is based on the same Georges Simenon novel that Julien Duvivier made into the classic *Panique*, with Michel Simon and Viviane Romance, in 1946. I've never seen *Panique*, but it must have more blood in it than *Monsieur Hire*.

The situation is promising. Monsieur Hire has seen enought through the window to know that the girl's handsome young lout of a boyfriend has committed a murder. And she doesn't mind Monsieur Hire's peeping; she even visits him in his apartment, encouraging his advances. Is she merely trying to protect her boyfriend? Or is she excited by his attention? *Monsieur Hire*, alas, is a case of perversity without dramatic interest. The movie is terminally languid. Patrice Leconte's direction, dreamlike in a stiff, uninvolving way, produces on scene after another in which one, and only one, thing is allowed to happen; the actors, hampered by Leconte's rigidity, never get a chance to explore and open up their characters.

NEW YORK POST, 4/20/90, p. 23, Jami Bernard

A general rule of thumb is that love affairs with the Peeping Tom across the way don't enjoy a high rate of success. But you know the French when it comes to *amour*—even the unlikeliest of couples give it their best shot.

In the last few weeks we had "Too Beautiful for You," in which Gérard Depardieu abandoned his angelic wife for his plain but passionate secretary. And in "Mama, There's a Man in Your Bed," Daniel Auteuil did the same for his black cleaning lady.

Now Sandrine Bonnaire is crawling around on all fours, provocatively retrieving a bag of spilled tomatoes from betwixt the legs of the ashen-faced voyeur across the way, in "Monsieur Hire."

Of course, she has an ulterior motive, as does he, in this creepy romantic mystery, one part Hitchcock and two parts Fritz Lang.

Michel Blanc, more known for comedy—he was the object of *mon dieu*, Gérard Depardieu's affections in "Menage"—is the strange, solitary, "M"-like little man who comes and goes to the taunts of neighborhood children. He sits in the dark of his spare apartment, watching Alice (Bonnaire) across the way as she makes love with her no-goodnik boyfriend.

Hire is a meticulous tailor and keeper of pet mice by day, voyeur by night, and he is under suspicion by an equally strange police inspector for the murder of a young woman. The inspector has his own problems—in fact, he at first appears to be the dead girl's father, such an interest does he take in her murder.

Obviously this inspector has not read interviews with the neighbors of killers who say the guy was the last person they's ever suspect. Hire, a wan, unpopular figure, is the first person anyone suspects, and he seems sadly aware of but indifferent to this.

Hire has other fish to fry. He'll do anything to have that girl across the way. It takes a literal lightning flash for her to discover she is being watched; her subsequent meetings with her watcher are poignant and strangely touching, especially—in addition to the tomato scene—a slow-motion sexual exploration at a boxing match.

Based on a novel by Georges Simenon, "Monsieur Hire" is a delicately suspenseful film by director Patrice Leconte. I have no idea why he opted to use Cinemascope for so claustrophobic a subject; it seems like a strange choice.

Both Blanc and Bonnaire play slightly against type. Bonnaire, who was adrift and melancholy in "Vagabond," is a lively, sensual object of scrutiny. And Blanc is as mysterious as the sinister Peter Lorre of Lang's "M", as courtly and lonely as Burt Lancaster in "Atlantic City" watching Susan Sarandon rub lemon on her breasts.

He watches impassively, his pallid face hanging disembodied against his window, as across the way Alice irons, writes letters, or throws him a glance while making love with her fiance.

Peeping Toms have a way of knowing a little this and that about their subjects, and Alice, once she is over the shock of finding she is being watched, teasingly attempts to find out just how much of this and that Monsieur Hire really knows.

Plot twists and a viscerally stunning ending give the movie a lovely, creepy poetry.

NEWSDAY, 10/6/89, Part III/p. 5, Mike McGrady

Avid moviegoers already know quite a bit about France, but "Monsieur Hire," screening at the festival Sunday, will reinforce that knowledge. Monsieur Hire (Michel Blanc) is a Peeping Tom who has spent months spying on lovely young Alice (Sandrine Bonnaire) as she bathes, dresses, makes love and lives her life in an apartment across the courtyard from him. When a bolt of lightning reveals his presence to the young woman, she seems at first shocked. In time, however, she softens and makes efforts to reach out to him sympathetically and even lovingly.

Only later do we learn that Monsieur Hire may have seen evidence linking the young woman to a murder he himself is suspected of committing. As the two become entangled emotionally, the plot twists become profound without ever straining credulity.

Perhaps only the French would cast a Peeping Tom (with one past arrest for indecent exposure) in such a sympathetic light. The fact that he is an unregenerate misanthrope is also allowable. They even permit a romance with the object of his afflictions.

"Don't you want to love me a little?" she asks.

"Could you love two men?"

"Why not?"

What does all this tell us about France? Oh, perhaps nothing too novel. Moviegoers have long known that the French are worldly in matters of the heart, far more accepting of sexual...ah ...idiosyncrasies than other nations. Also, that they are sophisticated, complicated and appreciative of a director like Patrice Leconte, who can mix murder with a touch of sexual depravity and come up with a stunning psychological thriller like "Monsieur Hire."

NEWSDAY, 4/20/90, Part III/p. 3, Mike McGrady

Monsieur Hire (Michel Blanc) is a voyeur who has spent months spying on lovely young Alice (Sandrine Bonnaire) as she bathes, dresses, makes love and lives her life in an apartment directly across the courtyard from his own. When a bolt of lightning reveals his presence to the young woman, she seems at first shocked. In time, however, she softens and makes efforts to reach out to him sympathetically and even lovingly.

Only later do we learn that Monsieur Hire may have seen evidence linking the young woman to a murder he himself is suspected of committing. As the two become entangled emotionally, the plot twists become profound without ever straining credulity.

Perhaps only the French would cast a Peeping Tom with a past arrest for indecent exposure in such a sympathetic light. But moviegoers have long known that the French are more worldly in matters of the heart, far more accepting of sexual idiosyncracies. Also that they are sophisticated, complicated and appreciative of a director like Patrice Leconte, who is able to mix murder with a touch of sexual depravity and come up with a stunning psychological thriller.

VILLAGE VOICE, 9/26/89, p. 66, J. Hoberman

Not Chabrol but not half bad either, this moody romantic thriller is exactly the sort of French noir Richard Roud used to round out his lineups. (The more things change...) Although *Monsieur Hire*'s Peeping Tom premise likely eliminated Kieślowski's far superior *Short Film About Love*, a witty bit of programming matches this Patrice Leconte feature with Sharon Sandusky's short *C'mon Babe (Danke Schoen)*—a kindred yet nonnarrative exercise in behavioral compulsion, musical repetition, and cute li'l rodents. One hopes that the joke (not apparent until you've seen both movies) won't be lost.

VILLAGE VOICE, 4/24/90, p. 66, Julie Phillips

Early on in *Monsieur Hire*, after a girl's body has been found and the prime suspect questioned, we see that suspect eating, in loving close-up, a soft-boiled egg. Balding, pasty, a child-murderer type in the best Peter Lorre tradition, M. Hire (Michel Blanc) is as repulsive as the runny yolk—which is, of course, the point. A tailor by trade, a voyeur by disposition, he spends his evenings in the dark, listening to Brahms and watching his neighbor, Alice (cute, pragmatic Sandrine Bonnaire), mess around with her boyfriend in the apartment across the street. He keeps pet mice, which he may or may not be killing off slowly; he tells a pointed story about a sweet old lady who used to feed the pigeons poisoned birdseed. He goes to a whorehouse, where he can take out his frustrations by yelling at the women. An attempt to participate in life, by following Alice and the boyfriend to a skating rink, ends in a bloody fall. For some unexplained reason, he moonlights as an exhibition bowler.

When Alice discovers M. Hire watching, she starts to watch back. She waits for him in his building, attracting his attention by dropping a bag of tomatoes down the stairs. As subject rather than object, she's threatening (a stray bit of feminism here?), and he backs off; but she gets him to take her on a date, and the film edges incongruously toward romance. He hangs around while she's with her shiftless cutie, asks her to run away with him, makes her the working-class Seberg to his shapeless, reclusive Belmondo.

Thematically, *Monsieur Hire* is a mess. Based on a novel by Georges Simenon, it starts out to be about how kindness and cruelty are just different aspects of love. Blanc—best known as a comedian—is wonderfully amorphous, misunderstood nice guy one second and nasty sex offender the next. But by the end, his character is so diffuse as to be almost random, and the film falls apart into sentimentality and a gratuitous act of selflessness that undercuts everything that's gone before. Director Patrice Leconte takes a sophomoric pleasure in loose ends and red herrings, so that whole scenes, including a potentially powerful one in which the police ask Hire to reenact the night of the crime—and another where he gets a tattoo—vanish without a trace. Besides, the question of whether or not M. Hire could be an object of love just doesn't seem worth asking. If he's not a pervert, what's interesting about him? (As an object of desire, he's another story. When he puts his hand in Alice's blouse at a boxing match, he becomes startlingly, morbidly attractive—the kind of person you'd sleep with but you'd be grossed out by after.)

It's a great film to look at, stylish and inventive, full of the standard stuff—a lot of profiles in shadow—but also smart framing and some lurid greens and purples. Some recurring images, like the egg, help give the film a needed coherence; some are corny, other enjoyable for their own sake. Most of *Monsieur Hire* is enjoyable for its own sake: It playswith some interesting ideas (not that voyeurism hasn't been done to death on film—it's so neatly cinematic), and Bonnaire makes the thinly sketched Alice sexily hard-edged and tough. But you just can't respect a film that so completely backs out of all its commitments. It's a tour de force in a vacuum: all dressed up and no place to go.

Also reviewed in:
NEW REPUBLIC, 4/23/90, p. 26, Stanley Kauffmann
NEW YORK TIMES, 4/20/90, p. C15, Vincent Canby
VARIETY, 5/24–30/89, p. 26

MORGAN'S CAKE

An L.L. production. *Executive Producer:* Jim Newman, Judy Newman, and Lura Janda. *Producer:* Rick Schmidt. *Director:* Rick Schmidt. *Screenplay:* Rick Schmidt. *Director of Photography:* Kathleen Beeler. *Editor:* Rick Schmidt. *Music:* Gary Thorp. *Sound:* Nick Bertoni and John Claudio. *Video:* Rick Schmidt and Morgan Schmidt-Feng. *Running Times:* 87 minutes. *MPAA Rating:* Not Rated.

CAST: Morgan Schmidt-Feng (Morgan); Willie Boy Walker (Morgan's Dad); M. Louise Stanley (Morgans' Mom); Rachel Pond (Rachel); Aaron Leon Kenin (Leon); Eliot Kenin (Leon's Dad); John Claudio (John); Lee Chapman (Painter); Nick Bertoni (Nick); Rick Reynolds (Mover).

NEWSDAY, 3/24/89, Part III/p. 5, Bill Kaufman

Morgan is an about-to-be-18-year-old with adolescent problems that appear to be somewhat overwhelming—for instance, he has wacky divorced parents, no job and it's time to register for the draft. And oh yes, Morgan's girlfriend is pregnant.

Despite its laundry list of grief, "Morgan's Cake" is for the most part a cheerful film about the durability of youth. Or perhaps, the thick-headedness of youth. Either way, director Rick Schmidt has managed to insert a lot of humor into this little film that at times has the deliberate feel of a home movie cranked out with a hand-held camera.

Near the beginning of the film, for no reason, a stranger hands Morgan a videocamera and tells the youth to use it. The black-and-white movie is intercut with a series of what looks like aimless vignettes videotaped by Morgan, and they appear on screen in color.

Much of "Morgan's Cake" is rambling and disjointed, but perhaps that's what director Schmidt intended as a metaphor for life. His son, Morgan Schmidt-Feng, who plays Morgan, is quite good as the befuddled youngster trying to bungle his way through a mountain of trials and tribulations. There's a hilarious scene where Morgan's dad, played by Willie Boy Walker, spouts a lengthy monologue on how he himself avoided the draft during the Korean War. Though the film has its limits, "Morgan's Cake" does indeed have its choice moments.

VILLAGE VOICE, 3/28/89, p. 64, Renee Tajima

Morgan is an 18-year-old coming of age in idyllic, surfside poverty on the California coast. Director Rick Schmidt's son, Morgan Schmidt-Feng, is the film's main attraction as the sweet-faced teen who's striving to be a mature, responsible adult in the face of his girlfriend's pregnancy, the draft, and post-Aquarian Age parents. Although its production values are spare, the movie is full of quintessential California characters who send up hilarious monologues that perhaps only someone who's worn puka shells could truly appreciate.

Also reviewed in:
NEW YORK TIMES, 3/25/89, p. 13, Janet Maslin
VARIETY, 2/8–14/89, p.28

MURMUR OF THE HEART

An Orion Classics release of a co-production of Nouvelles Editions de Films; Marianne Productions (Paris)/Vides Cinematographica (Rome)/Franz Seitz Filmproduktion (Munich). *Producer:* Vincent Malle and Claude Nedjar. *Director:* Louis Malle. *Screenplay (French with English Subtitles):* Louis Malle. *Director of Photography:* Ricardo Aronovich. *Editor:* Suzanne Baron. *Music:* Charlie Parker, Sidney Bechet, Gaston Freche, and Henri Renaud. *Sound:* Jean-Claude Laureux and Michel Vionnet. *Art Director:* Jean-Jacques Caziot and Philippe Turlure. *Costumes:* Ghislain Uhry. *Running Time:* 118 minutes. *MPAA Rating:* R.

CAST: Léa Massari (Clara); Benoit Ferreux (Laurent); Daniel Gélin (Dr. Chevalier); Marc Winocourt (Marc); Fabien Ferreux (Thomas); Michel Lonsdale).

LOS ANGELES TIMES, 4/6/89, Calendar/p. 3, Sheila Benson

Young Laurent Chevalier, hero of Louis Malle's sunnily sensual reissued "Murmur of the Heart" has a wide, droll mouth that curls up at the ends like a Picasso line drawing and ears almost like a faun's. Something about that look, combined with his skinny skittishness, lets us tolerate 14-year-old Laurent even when he behaves like a consummate brat; when, for example, in an agony of jealousy he deliberately drops a bottle of milk for their aging family maid to clean up.

Also, it's 1954. Horrific manners are the mark of the lordly young Frenchman, these three particularly; sons of a well-off Dijon gynecologist and his free-spirited Italian wife. Their world would change soon enough; it is already changing: the French are losing at Dien Bien Phu; in a little more than a decade, kids this age from the bourgeoisie would became radicalized.

Writer-director Malle, who wrote the film in one firestorm week in the spring of 1970 and finished it the following year, conjures up that family, that time, that insular smugness with a notable mixture of affection and observation. It's his family, something we recognize even more clearly after "Au Revoir Les Enfants."

Malle, too, had the two older brothers, the love for Charlie Parker and Jelly Roll Morton, the heart murmur and the summer at the spa that his young Laurent shares. Even the hilarious game of spinach tennis is from memory. But the funny, earthy, faintly unhappy Italian mother, Clara, a wild bird untamed by her 20 years stifled in the bosom of the French bourgeoisie, is Malle's creation.

She has been given indelible life by Léa Massari, an apricot-colored goddess whose charm lies in her exuberance, her physicality, her very *un*-Frenchness, and in an utterly disarming sprinkling of freckles. Clara, the daughter of a radical political exile, was a 16-year-old visitor to France when Charles Chevalier (Daniel Gélin) became her first lover and then her husband, to the consternation of his moneyed parents.

Of their three sons, Laurent (Benoit Ferreux), the youngest, is her favorite. She adores and babies him; (somehow) he sees her spirit for what it is. His older brothers, Marc (Marc Winocourt) and Thomas (Fabien Ferreux, Benoit's own brother) have fallen into the habit of putting her down, telling her that she couldn't even pass their exams.

When scarlet fever leaves Laurent with a heart murmur, Clara goes with him to a health spa up in the mountains. The two are like one closed fist against the young prigs and Royalists Laurent encounters, these children of the stuffy, social French families who populate the spa. Clara, by being herself—playing her first game of tennis in sneakers and street clothes—seems marvelous to these 16-and 17-year-olds.

It's at the spa, triggered by an evening of Bastille Day celebration, that the scene that made the film a *cause célèbre* occurs. It's a subdued, nuzzling moment between boy-child and intensely affectionate mother, when all his impacted jealousy, fascination, adoration and curiosity carry Laurent across the line into incest.

Eighteen years ago, some of us were so busy priding ourselves on being shockproof that we didn't really think to question Malle further: to wonder at how firmly he denied the moment its reverberations—to both parties. If *this* was incest, tasteful, "open," utterly without consequence, then what was all the fuss about? Actually, what today's audiences may wonder is what the *movie* is about if this moment, toward which the film is so insistently pointed, is so without effect.

From today's vantage point, "Murmur of the Heart's" strongest memory becomes its climate: political, familial, full of warmth, family jokes and indulged bad manners, brotherly acts of rivalry and support. This may be just what Malle was aiming for: in his words, "a contemporary comedy of French bourgeois education." (The film is MPAA-rated R.) What we see now is elegant detail, sharp observation, perfect performances (especially by Benoit Ferreux and the sublime Massari). And a possibly far-reaching moment that becomes simply one of those enigmatic Gallic shrugs.

Could it really be as weightless as all that? Perhaps. Possibly. One wonders.

NEW YORK POST, 3/17/89, p. 23, V.A. Musetto

The year 1989 may well go down in cinema history as the Year of the Revival, in which great old films were rereleased in sparkling new prints, not necessarily in revival houses but in first-run theaters as if they had been made today.

"Lawrence of Arabia" and "Gone With the Wind" have already reopened with great fanfare, and "Wuthering Heights" is about to be, on what seems to be an unofficial admission by moviemakers that new isn't necessarily better.

But that's grist for another story. My purpose today is to sing the praises of a rerelease, "Murmur of the Heart," the enticing and invigorating Oedipal comedy that the venerable Louis Malle made in 1971 and which is being brought back starting today at the Lincoln Plaza.

The time is the spring of 1954, the setting is the French city of Dijon. Our first encounter with the bourgeois Chevalier family is surprisingly uneventful.

The three teenaged brothers are caught up in the usual juvenile pranks (wine, women, cigars and petty thefts from Mom's purse). Dad (Daniel Gélin) is a successful, matter-of-fact gynecologist who shows little concern for his boys and even less for his beautiful, younger Italian wife, Clara (Léa Massari). But then our attention is drawn to Laurent (Benoit Ferreux), at 14 the youngest and most introspective of the three boys. He reads Camus, muses about suicide and, most importantly to our story, is a virgin. It is the sexual education of Laurent that is at the soul of "Murmur of the Heart."

Lesson No. 1 comes with the discovery that his free-spirited and sensual mother is having an affair, and a quite open one at that: She meets her lover in the middle of the day, in front of her family's comfortable home. Lesson No. 2 involves a visit to the neon-lit brothel presided over by Madame Madeleine. Laurent's initiation with an understanding *fille de nuit* is going according to schedule until his brothers burst into the bedroom, abruptly terminating the encounter.

And so Laurent's coming of age must wait for a visit to a spa (he has a heart murmur and a doctor orders his mother to take him there for a rest). Through a mixup, they get a suite with one bedroom instead of two. Laurent accidentally sees his mother in the tub, and earns a slap for not diverting his eyes. She runs off for two days in Paris with her lover and returns distressed. Mother and son become confidantes and she reveals how at age 16 she met his father and became pregnant.

Then, one night after a party at the hotel, with too much red wine consumed, Laurent and Clara wind up in bed together, and the young man is deflowered.

A touchy subject, incest. Not one normally suited to comedy. But Malle's semiautobiographical scenario deals with it delicately and maturely (see Bertrand Tavernier's "The Passion of Beatrice" for a vastly different approach). Malle makes it perfectly clear that neither Laurent nor Clara will suffer any long-lasting ill effects of what comes across as indiscretion rather than depravity. It was, Clara assures the boy immediately afterward, "a beautiful moment...one that will never be repeated." And we have no cause not to believe her. Indeed, by morning they—and the audience—are able to laugh off the entire matter. Normal family life has resumed.

"Murmur of the Heart" is, rest assured, solid and intelligent throughout, filled with knowing wit and subtle jibes at bourgeois life—the juxtaposition of a stuffy aunt and uncle with the carefree mother, for example. The acting is first-rate, especially that of Massari and Ferreux. And Malle, as he has so often shown, has an exceptional eye and ear for the fine detail, from the music of Charlie Parker to a radio broadcast of the Tour de France to debate over French involvement in Indochina.

Vive "Murmur of the Heart"!

NEWSDAY, 3/17/89, Part III/p. 3, Lynn Darling

It was a little daunting to think of seeing "Murmer of the Heart" for the first time since it was released in 1971. It was a wonderful and charming film 17 years ago; but then a lot of what was charming and wonderful 17 years ago has turned to dust since then. There are only so many items in one's nostalgic repertoire that should be willingly exposed to the harsher light that the present can cast on the past.

It was, after all, a different world when "Murmur of the Heart" first opened in a limited release. The Vietnam War and the protests it engendered, the free-spirited rejection of stuffy bourgeois values promoted by the counterculture, all found a bold and blithely exuberant echo in Louis Malle's rare and surprising domestic comedy that derives a certain amount of its substance from a question of incest. Would the movie stand up once those cultural underpinnings had been taken away?

In fact it stands up wonderfully well, a testament to Malle's talents as a film maker and his loving appreciation for the eternal verities of growing up. "Murmur of the Heart" is a timeless piece of moviemaking, anchored in qualities that never go out of style: a sensitive understanding of the human heart and a wise eye that finds a surprising and unexpected humor in the unlikeliest of places.

Set in a staunchly bourgeois household in Dijon in 1954, as France began the painful process of its withdrawal from Indochina, the movie focuses on the coming of age of 15-year-old Laurent Chevalier (Benoit Ferreux). Sensitive, intelligent, possessed of the usual hormone-driven demons that beset adolescence, he is the youngest child of a stuffy middle-aged gynecologist (Daniel Gélin) and his irrepressible Italian wife (Léa Massari).

Malle explores Laurent's ripening perspective on the world at an age when life's inconsistencies, its ironies and its bewildering passions seem to strike home with the force of a blow. His growing up is both aided and exacerbated by his two older brothers—their attempts to initiate him into life's mysteries include a trip to a local prostitute whose efforts on Laurent's behalf they drunkenly interrupt.

But the boy's most important ally in his efforts to understand the world is his mother, whose own youth and uninhibited free spirits have placed her at odds with her husband's hidebound temperament. When a bout of scarlet fever leaves Laurent with a heart murmur, mother and son go off to a health spa together. There Laurent's impatience to storm the world of men and women comes to an unexpected and decidedly offbeat conclusion.

Malle brings a sophisticated and worldly understanding to the events that transpire in his film, and yet there's nothing jaded or cynical about his approach. His characters explore, with the quarrelsome provocativeness of youth, every piece of cant and convention they come across, and it was this boisterous energy that was part of the movie's initial charm. That's still there. But what also comes across this time is Malle's patience with human fallibility and his confidence in the ability of people to find their way in the world with their benevolence and guilelessness intact. That's a tricky proposition at any age and one that's as necessary to contemplate now as it was 17 years ago, when the world seemed a less impossible place.

VILLAGE VOICE, 6/27/89, p. 70, Georgia Brown

Murmur of the Heart, a somewhat notorious 1971 semiautobiographical comedy in which a mother and son have a one-night fling, has been rereleased, and I recently saw the film at the Quad, where it is playing after a very respectable uptown run; the audience laughed lustily throughout, and some people applauded at the end. Even without its moment of incest, *Murmur of the Heart* appears to be a crowd-pleaser.

Laurent (Benoit Ferreux), a 14-year-old whose legs are three quarters of his body, is the youngest of three sons in a well-to-do Dijon family, back in a liberated 1954. We see Laurent and his two older brothers fooling around with Italian-born Maman (Léa Massari) as she dresses in her bedroom. (The French view Italians as their free spirits.) She shoos away one son who is pissing in her sink, then merrily chases the other to get back some money he's taken, only to turn around and give it back because he says he needs it. What a mom! Laurent gets teased because he's her pet. Papa (Daniel Gélin), a dour gynecologist, even seems jealous—an emotion explained (later) when Laurent discovers that his mother refuses to sleep with his father, and that she has a lover.

This is the sort of freewheeling family where three brothers (one dressed up as Mother) gaily measure penises and then, when the faithful, long-suffering housemaid walks in, they turn and try to get her to judge. Laurent's brothers decide to treat him to a night at the local brothel, then barge into the room where he's just been initiated and drag him off his new lover. What brothers!

In a movie overstuffed with daring details, some are wonderful and, unlike the ones above, ring true. When Laurent is left alone at a spa (where he's being treated for his heart murmur) because his mother has gone off with her lover for a couple of days, he lovingly spreads her underwear on her bed, making the pattern of her body. He puts on her makeup and imitates her voice.

Whereas a whole film might have led up to a moment like this, *Murmur of the Heart* always has to go further. And further, as if on a dare. Then it runs from the implications of its choices. The movie's pace is frantic, almost hysterical; the tone is off. If you're not with the film, you'll find it excruciatingly grating. The main performances are forced and tense. The gawky Ferreux begins to resemble a windup toy. After a while, all the furiously accumulated detail begins to look exhibitionistic (look at this! and this!). Malle's movie is better than Varda's [the reference is to *Kung Fu Master*; see Brown's review of that film] but it's similar in using cuteness to make incest (real or approximate) look easy.

Also reviewed in:
NEW YORK TIMES, 11/7/71, p. B1, Vincent Canby
WASHINGTON POST, 4/21/89, Weekend/p. 31, Desson Howe

MUSIC BOX

A Tri-Star Pictures release. *Executive Producer:* Joe Eszterhas and Hal W. Polaire. *Producer:* Irwin Winkler. *Director:* Costa-Gavras. *Screenplay:* Joe Eszterhas. *Director of Photography:* Patrick Blossier. *Editor:* Joele Van Effenterre. *Music:* Philippe Sarde. *Choreographer:* Eva Nemeth and Karoly Nemeth. *Music Editor:* Joele Van Effenterre. *Sound:* Pierre Gamet, Gerard Lamps, and William Flageollet. *Production Designer:* Jeannine Oppewall. *Art Director:* Bill Arnold. *Set Designer:* William B. Fosser. *Set Decorator:* Erica Rogalla. *Special Effects:* Sam Barkan. *Costumes:* Rita Salazar. *Make-up:* Steve LaPorte. *Running time:* 124 minutes. *MPAA Rating:* PG-13.

CAST: Jessica Lange (Ann Talbot); Armin Mueller-Stahl (Mike Laszlo); Frederic Forrest (Jack Burke); Donald Moffat (Harry Talbot); Lukas Haas (Mikey Talbot); Cheryl Lynn Bruce (Georgine Wheeler); Mari Torocsik (Magda Zoldan); J.S. Block (Judge Silver); Sol Frieder (Istvan Boday); Michael Rooker (Karchy Laszlo); Elzbieta Czyzewska (Melinda Kkalman); Magda Szekely Marbury (Judit Hollo); Felix Shuman (James Nathanson); Michael Shillo (Geza Vamos); George Pusep (Vladimir Kostav); Mitchell Litrofsky (Sandy Lehman); Albert Hall (Mack Jones); Ned Schmidtke (Dean Talbot); Joe Guzaldo (Joe Dinofrio); Tibor Kenderesi (Pal Horvath); Christiana Nicola (Maria); Kevin White (Clerk); Gyorgy Emod (Andras Nagy); Ralph Foody (Pawn Broker); Magda Sass (Translator #1); Owen Rice (Courtroom Reporter #1); Margo Winkler (Irma Kiss); Larry Brandenburg (John Szalay); Pauline Kaner (Reporter); Mark Steggerda, Leonard E. Boswell and Douglas Marcinek (Courtroom Guards); Agnes Gallwitz (Translator #2); Zoltan Gern (Man in Budapest); Jane MacIver and Megan Warner (Secretaries); Erica Heit M.D. (Doctor); Tracy Grant (Servant); Toni Fleming (Housekeeper); Ed Blatchford (Young Man); Andy Avalos and Tim Skilling (Weathermen); Tom Stienke (Sports Announcer); Donnez Harris (Security Guard); Gabor Koncz (Limo Driver); Nicholas Christianson (Boy with Mikey); Richard D'Angelo (Violent Protester); George Carson (Boy #2); Rocky Finlay (Boy #3).

CHRISTIAN SCIENCE MONITOR, 2/7/90, p. 10, David Sterritt
[*Music Box* was reviewed jointly with *Enemies, A Love Story*; see Sterritt's review of that film.]

CINEASTE, Vol. XVII, No. 3, 1990, p. 45, Gary Crowdus
Wouldn't it be shocking to discover all of a sudden that the neighbor who lives just a few doors down the block—the elderly, always courteous gentleman with the wife and two grown kids, the guy who always keeps his lawn so neatly mowed—was actually a Nazi war criminal? No matter how surprised you'd be, however, it wouldn't be difficult to join the general condemnation of him that would be sure to follow. How would you respond, though, if the man accused of crimes against humanity was your own father? That's the provocative premise of Joe Esterhaz's script for the new Costa-Gavras film *Music Box*.

The story centers on Ann Talbot (Jessica Lange), a Chicago criminal lawyer, who is summoned one day to the suburban home of her father. Michael Laszlo (Armin Mueller-Stahl), to learn that the Justice Department has notified him that he is to be tried for lying about his war-time activities when he applied for American citizenship upon entering the U.S. nearly forty years ago. If convicted, he will be stripped of his citizenship and deported to his native Hungary where he will stand trial for war crimes. Following a hostile confrontation with the government's prosecuting attorney. Jack Burke (Frederic Forrest), from the Justice Department's Office of Special Investigations. Talbot decides to defend her father in court because she is sure he is simply the victim of mistaken identity.

Familiarizing herself with the government's case—which includes affidavits of eyewitnesses to atrocities allegedly committed by her father and incriminating documents such as a Special Section (*Einsatzkommando*) ID card indicating his membership in the Arrow Cross, a Hungarian fascist party which collaborated with the Nazi SS—she is at first unnerved by the enormity of the charges against him. She pursues a defense against him. She pursues a defense strategy which attempts to prove the Hungarian government's persecution of her father for his anticommunist protest activities in the U.S. With the assistance of her former father-in-law, Harry Talbot (Donald Moffat), she ultimately succeeds in having the charges against her father dismissed. Her legal victory becomes personally meaningless, however, when she accidentally discovers proof of her father's guilt and she must confront the horrible truth.

In this regard. *Music Box* is less interested in detailing the horrors of the Holocaust or in dramatically meting out punishment to one of its perpetrators, than it is in remembrance, in bearing moral witness to those cataclysmic historical events. Thrust into a family crisis of truly nightmarish proportions, the viewer experiences the dilemma from the daughter's perspective, sharing her long, tortured process of repeated denial and final, begrudging admission of the truth. Jessica Lange's Ann Talbot serves as the dramatic and moral linchpin for this politicized family drama in much the same way that Jack Lemmon's Charles Horman did for Costa-Gavras's *Missing*.

As a defense attorney, it's not important for Ann Talbot to believe in the innocence of her client, but, in this case, as a daughter, it's of crucial importance to her. By attempting to disprove the testimony of eyewitness accusers as, at best, mistaken identifications made involving events that occurred more than forty years ago, or, at worst, Jewish or communist vindictiveness, she is able momentarily to rationalize away—in her own mind, at least—the charges against her father. Even as her investigator, Georgine (Cheryl Lynn Bruce), discovers evidence suggesting attempts to cover up his past. Ann steadfastly refuses to believe that her father, a widower who raised her and her brother from infancy after their mother died, is a man who could be capable of such inhuman acts. In her heart, she knows he is innocent: "I'm his daughter. I know him better than anyone. He is *not* a monster!"

Given the enormity of the crimes involved, though, and the fact that the defendant is her father, it becomes increasingly difficult for Talbot to separate her own sense of morality from her professional role in the strictly legal pursuit of due process. Although she is shown to be a street-smart criminal lawyer (in a brief opening scene she is seen preparing to defend a drug dealer whom she nevertheless addresses as "scumbag"), Talbot can get only so much mileage out of her professionally cultivated cynicism. Listening to some of the horrendous courtroom testimony against her father, she is visibly shaken and must struggle to regain her composure.

In this regard, the emotionally restrained accounts of brutal acts of rape, torture, and murder as heard in the official atmosphere of a federal courtroom are more dramatically powerful than flashback reenactments of the crimes could ever be. An elderly Hungarian man identifies Mike Laszlo as "Mishka," an Arrow Cross leader who on a December evening in 1944 bound him and other members of his family together with baling wire, fired bullets into the heads of his father and wife, and pushed them all into the icy Danube River. Speaking in Hungarian translated for the court, another eyewitness describes how in January 1945 this same "Mishka" stopped a woman and her seven year-old son, and, after accusing them of being Jews, shot the woman in the head and then killed the boy as he threw himself on his mother's body. Other witnesses recount horrifying acts of rape and torture committed by "Mishka" at a Budapest interrogation center.

When Ann's red-baiting and Jew-baiting defense strategy yields only intermittent success, and she fears losing the case, she solicits the legal assistance of her former father-in-law. Although he plays one of the smaller roles in the film, Harry Talbot is one of its most intriguing characters. It is through the characterization of this OSS veteran and unregenerate Cold Warrior that *Music Box* broaches some of the recent revelations of U.S. government complicity in the postwar evasion of justice by Nazi war criminals and their Eastern European collaborators. The rumors that Harry Talbot "sipped bourbon with Klaus Barbie," for example, refers to the immediate postwar recruitment by the Office of Strategic Services (OSS, the wartime precursor to the CIA) of leading

Nazis and other fascists as counterintelligence operatives against the Soviet Union in the initial stages of the Cold War. In exchange for providing sensitive information on the Soviet military, many Nazis who were subject to prosecution for war crimes were either protected by their U.S. spymasters or, like Klaus Barbie, the notorious "Butcher of Lyon," were provided with escape routes to Latin America.

In addition, thousands of lower level Nazi thugs and murderers and Eastern European fascists were allowed to enter the U.S. after the war. A thinly-disguised anti-Semitism which then prevailed in the U.S. Congress led to the framing of the Displaced Persons Acts and other postwar immigration policies which hindered the entry of Jews and other Holocaust victims while establishing quotas which actually facilitated the entry of Nazis and other fascists, including those who served in the extermination camps and those who, like Mike Laszlo, assisted in the slaughter of Jews and other "social undesirables" in countries throughout the Eastern Front.

Music Box casts even darker aspersions on Harry Talbot's character by suggesting that he shares more than just a fervent anti-communism with the former Nazis he recruited. At several points, the film reveals a discernible strain of anti-Semitism in his politics, such as his having explained to his grandson, Mikey (Lukas Haas), that the Holocaust is all "lies and exaggeration." As such, Harry Talbot is a disturbing reminder of the sometimes pathological nature of anti-communist ideology and how it has often been used—whether in Nazi Germany, in other European countries, or in the U.S.—as a conveniently patriotic smoke-screen for the expression of anti-Semitism and other bigotries. Catholic clerics and nuns, for example, are seen among Mike Laszlo's supporters at his trial.

It is at the suggestion of Harry Talbot that Ann calls a KGB defector to testify about Operation Harlequin, an intelligence operation whereby the Soviets allegedly falsified Nazi ID documents in order to discredit Western enemies of socialism. The film's "Operation Harlequin" is actually based on the Czech-Soviet Operation Neptune of the mid-Sixties and other Soviet disinformation campaigns designed to extend the statute of limitations on the prosecution of Nazi war criminals. Although this "KGB defense" has often been utilized in such trials, the evidence has consistently been denied. The manner in which this information is presented in the film, however, leaves ambiguous the question of its validity. Jack Burke appears completely surprised by this new defense tactic and requests an immediate adjournment.

Mike Laszlo is shown to have even shadier friends in his homeland when the judge and both attorneys travel to Budapest to hear the testimony of a terminally ill prosecution witness who has identified Laszlo as a member of the Special Section. The evening before the testimony, Talbot is visited in her hotel room by an elderly man who simply identifies himself as a Hungarian who believes in the innocence of her father. Secreted into the gift box of chocolates he leaves her are documents which undermine the testimony of the prosecution's new witness, although it remains unclear whether the documents are authentic or forgeries. Unfortunately, the rats' nest of international political intrigue to which *Music Box* occasionally refers may make for little more than murky plotting for less historically informed viewers.

Music Box is arguably the most substantial script yet written by Joe Esterhaz, currently one of Hollywood's most commercially successful screenwriters, who is best known for his scripts for *F.I.S.T.* (1978). *Flashdance* (1983), and *Jagged Edge* (1985). After the implausibilities of plot and characterization that fatally flawed *Betrayed*—the immediately preceding Esterhaz/Costa-Gavras collaboration which unsuccessfully attempted to blend a political expose about racist paramilitary organizations in America with a clichéd romantic triangle melodrama—*Music Box* represents a distinct improvement for both writer and director.

Unlike *Betrayed*, the family situations and characters in *Music Box* seem much more authentic and personally observed, which is understandable since Esterhaz, the son of a Hungarian novelist, is himself an immigrant who as a youngster spent several years in Displaced Persons camps after the war. Although some may note surface similarities between the plot of Esterhaz's *Jagged Edge* and that of *Music Box*, the attorney/client relationship in the latter film is used for purposes beyond merely suspenseful entertainment. Esterhaz's dialog still unfortunately displays a tendency for the Big Dramatic Line and excessive irony, although there is thankfully nothing so obvious here as the repeated references in *Betrayed* to the racist main character's fondness for "white cake."

Although *Music Box* is one of Costa-Cavras's most emotionally compelling films, he has succeeded in this regard without relying on what most critics and many moviegoers have come to regard as his sole stock-in-trade—flashy cinematic technique, especially heart-pounding action sequences, for which he has shown such an obvious flair in films such as Z, *State of Siege*, and *Missing*. Indeed, *Music Box* qualifies as that most deadly of all genres, the courtroom drama, since most of the film consists of courtroom and other dialog scenes, with few exteriors and virtually no action sequences. Nonetheless, the courtroom testimony scenes—filmed in the sparest, simplest, and most straightforward manner—are among the most dramatically powerful in the entire film. The fundamental human emotions at the center of this drama do not require underlining by cinematic pyrotechnics, and the film's one cinematic flourish, coming at a dramatically significant moment, functions in this context like a grace note in a musical composition.

In a film filled with fine performances, Jessica Lange, in the film's central role, stands out. A middle class professional with working class roots, Ann Talbot exudes a self-assured, emotionally controlled manner which occasionally gives way to sudden flashes of anger. Throughout the long trial, despite mounting evidence against her father, she remains resolute in her heartfelt conviction of his innocence. Her emotional resolve visibly shatters, though, when she unexpectedly discovers conclusive evidence of his guilt, and she reels as if from a physical blow. The final confrontation with her father is heartrending, as we see her being torn, from one second to the next, between love for her father and a repulsion over the acts he has committed.

Ann Talbot's final, difficult decision confirms the only morally responsible course of action. By portraying the issue in such powerful dramatic terms. *Music Box* reminds us of a historical lesson that—as recent revelations of some of the actions of our own government, all too ready to sacrifice moral principle for political expediency, demonstrate—cannot be taught too often. As Justice Robert Jackson, Chief Prosecutor at the Nuremberg War Crimes Trial explained: "The wrongs which we seek to condemn and punish have been so calculated, so malignant and so devastating that civilization cannot tolerate their being ignored because it cannot survive their being repeated."

FILMS IN REVIEW, 4/90, p. 232, Herbert G. Luft

Music Box, a motion picture directed by Costa-Gavras, is a sharply edged indictment of war crimes. As written by Joe Eszterhas, it is an expose of an Hungarian Nazi who has lived in America for more than forty years with his background carefully disguised. Set into the frame of a court room hearing in Chicago, the story explores the possible guilt of a jovial, elderly father and grandfather, who is a retired blue collar worker in suburban Illinois. Was he a member of the Hungarian Special Forces unit during WWII assigned to ferret out Jews and anti-Nazi elements in Budapest?

The accused, throughout the whole proceedings, proclaims his innocence, insisting that the U.S. authorities must have picked the wrong man. At last, his past is revealed through a faded set of photographs by chance popping out from the hidden chamber of a music box.

The daughter, a lawyer, is the defense attorney who cannot believe the devastating evidence that her beloved father had been a sadistic monster, who, for his own pleasure, tortured innocent victims before killing them. World War II photos prove that the "decent" Mike Laszlo had thrown children, with their hands tied behind their backs, into the icy waters of the Danube and watched them drown.

Jessica Lange gives a performance of great intensity as the daughter torn between love and admiration for her father (who had cared for her and her younger brother after the untimely death of their mother) and disgust at the atrocities committed by the same man during the war years. Herself a mother, the attorney feels compelled to protect her 11-year-old boy from the evil influence of the old man by reporting the evidence to the authorities.

Armin Mueller-Stahl (currently in the German-language epic, *Spider's Web*, as a bullying Prussian aristocrat of the early 1920s) gives a fine double-faced characterization of a devoted family man and a disgusting brute. He portrays the character with such skill that American audiences will love to hate him.

Before preparing his scenario, screen writer Joe Eszterhas studied the trial record of John Demjanjuk, the Ukrainian-born Cleveland autoworker, indicted in Israel for crimes against humanity. Eszterhas is also the author of Costa-Gavras' film *Betrayed*, dealing in psychological depth with para-military organizations in America.

Costa-Gavras said of *The Music Box:* "The film is not about vengeance, it is about remembering. I don't think it is necessary to hunt down old men to punish them. It seems somehow meaningless to do that now. They should have been punished years ago. The important thing is to discover how, as human beings, they could have committed such acts.''

LOS ANGELES TIMES, 12/25/89, Calendar/p. 2, Michael Wilmington

Perhaps, in our movies, we've grown too accustomed to the slick, the violent and the ersatz. When great pure dramatic subjects come up—evil in our century, brutality vs. conscience—do we know how to handle them anymore?

Costa-Gavras' ''Music Box'' focuses on a crisis of conscience within a young Chicago lawyer (Jessica Lange) defending her father (Armin Mueller-Stahl) at a deportation hearing where he is accused of Holocaust-era crimes. It's an intelligent, ambitious work, with a deep, resonant political subject.

Costa-Gavras, who can be a master film maker, directs with his usual fluid yet steely expertise. Whether he's staging shocking revelations in a courtroom, the jockeying between lawyers outside in hallways or bars, or the draining confrontations of the defendant and his family, he never over-tips into bathos or hysteria. His rhythms are inexorable; his mood, alert and intense.

There are flashes of brilliance throughout the entire cast, in the minor roles of the courtroom witnesses (Elzbieta Czyzewska, Magda Szekely Marburg, Felix Shulman, Michael Cillo) and particularly in the lead performances of Lange as lawyer Ann Talbot and Mueller-Stahl as her father, Mike Laszlo.

Yet there's something missing in the movie, a spark that would ignite that conscience into a blaze of outrage, a jolt that would plunge us more viscerally into the plight of the characters: the father who sees his world crumbling into Kafkaesque persecution, the daughter who suspects he may be a monster.

''Music Box'' isn't muddy or irresolute. It certainly isn't cheap or oversensational. But it may oscillate too much between the urge to present complex material fairly and to resolve everything in a movie form as mechanically perfect and repetitive as the film's music box itself—where, as it runs out, all the secrets are hidden.

As in ''Betrayed,'' the strategy of Costa-Gavras and writer Joe Eszterhas is to show fascistic excess from a conservative perspective. Ann's blue-collar family and her stalwart, *lumpen* brother (Michael Rooker) are juxtaposed with the silken North Shore world of her ex-husband's father, a corporate lawyer (Donald Moffat) who tells his grandson that the Holocaust is a myth. From outside comes the threat, the man goading her conscience—Frederic Forrest as prosecutor Jack Burke—who has such a sour, badgering demeanor that he's almost like an unsuccessful nuisance suitor.

As Ann faces the victims who accuse her father, each one shatters her sense of certitude. Eszterhas, who also wrote ''Jagged Edge,'' may be at his best with impassioned polemic and courtroom scenes like these. Here, he obviously wants to persuade everyone that the Holocaust and its revelation of mass evil reverberates within our souls still. He's not universally eloquent. There's not much spontaneity in his dialogue, and his characters talk as though they're giving testimony even when they're outside the court. But that's not necessarily a drawback; most of them are lawyers, judges or paralegals.

But though Costa-Gavras and his writer share this gutsy, tell-it-all-and-damn-the-consequences approach, ''Music Box'' is, at bottom, a conventional trial melodrama with revelations that come too easily and glibly—and a final confrontation that lacks the high pain, horror and grief the actors seem more than ready to give it.

It's a disappointment. It was Costa-Gavras—in movies like ''Z,'' ''The Confession'' and ''State of Siege''—who, two decades ago, redefined the world's conception of political melodrama. In these hellishly exciting or punishingly intense movies—as in Gillo Pontecorvo's 1966 ''Battle of Algiers''—truth seemed to emerge with battering force.

But in recent years, it's Oliver Stone, obviously influenced by Costa-Gavras' classics, who seems to have seized more surely those old qualities of muckraking fury, bravura action pyrotechnics and passionate attack. Costa-Gavras may be making the mistake of keeping his voice too muted, too reasonable. ''Music Box'' is ultimately too slow, too measured, too careful a film. It needs more imbalance and recklessness.

What does triumph here are the actors. As Laszlo, Mueller-Stahl—the East German emigré actor who became famous in his work for Fassbinder and Agniezka Holland—has an unforgettably swallowed-in look. His Laszlo speaks with a gravelly whisper that suggests a soul drying up inside him, an extreme reticence that could belong to a dutiful immigrant steelworker or perhaps a cunning man of violent temper carefully disguising himself. It's part of the film's strategy, and Mueller-Stahl's, to keep us constantly swinging between these two possibilities.

As Ann, Lange has a marvelously open, healthy gaze. Costa-Gavras, a master of melodrama, locks her into tight compositions and long takes and surrounds her with a collection of mildly hot-headed or self-convinced characters that throw that healthiness into relief. He makes the atmosphere around her thrum with an understated menace. In the icy, overcast Chicago cityscapes, Lange's face is like a Midwestern blossom, grainy and sweet. Costa-Gavras uses it as a kind of emblem of American idealism, American courage.

"Music Box" (rated R for language and mature themes) doesn't excite the senses, as even the most vacuous big studio products sometimes do. It also doesn't excite the audience in deeper ways: It doesn't imbue the drama with passion, doesn't expose the psychological or political issues in any but the most obvious ways.

Given its ground rules, could we expect it to? Costa-Gavras may be playing a doomed game, trying to squeeze truth and idealism into the new super-melodramatic forms of the '80s. Still, even if "Music Box" doesn't work on every level, it's an honorable attempt. We should never undervalue idealism and courage. In movies, as in life, we will always need them.

MONTHLY FILM BULLETIN, 5/90, p. 135, Philip Strick

Mike Laszlo, respectable retired Chicago blue-collar worker, is suddenly summoned to face extradition charges. Eye-witness reports of Hungarian atrocities during the war, at last released by the UN, implicate him as Mishka, feared leader of an SS-organised death squad. Laszlo reassures his daughter, Ann, and his beloved grandson Mikey that the claim is untrue; a criminal attorney, Ann decides to defend her father in court, although warned by her former father-in-law, wealthy lawyer Harry Talbot, that her personal involvement in the case could be risky. The prosecution, headed by Jack Burke, has a copy of a war-time identity card in the name of Laszlo; a succession of witnesses identify the photo on the card as the face of Mishka and recall his crimes. Ann throws doubt on their stories by establishing Communist bias in the witnesses and collusion between them, suggesting they are part of "Operation Harlequin", designed to destroy the reputations of former Eastern Europeans. Following the account by one witness of her torture at Mishka's hands, Laszlo collapses in revulsion and has to be briefly hospitalised. But despite herself, Ann has growing suspicions: the identity card has been authenticated, and her research assistant has found that Laszlo was blackmailed in the past by fellow Hungarian Tibor Zoldan, now dead. A vital witness, Pal Horvath, is discovered in Budapest and the case is convened at his bedside as he is too ill to travel. His evidence only reveals a plot to get Laszlo back to Hungary, and Ann promptly moves for dismissal of all charges against her father. Being in Budapest enables her to trace Magda, Zoldan's sister, who gives her a pawn ticket, all that remains of her brother's effects. Back in Chicago, the ticket redeems a music box which, when Ann sets it to play, yields up a sheaf of photographs of Mishka and his victims. Clearly Zoldan had been in no doubt that Mishka and Laszlo were the same man. Ann confronts her father privately at the press reception celebrating his release, but he shrugs her off. She sends a report with the photographs to Burke, and they are published in the *Chicago Tribune*. Clasping her son, Ann sadly waits to see if justice will yet be done in the case she has all-too-successfully defended.

At face value, *Music Box* is the account of a woman's realisation of her father's true nature. Fiercely resisting all that is claimed about him until the evidence she uncovers for herself is irrefutable, she declares him a nonperson ("You don't exist") and leaves him presumably to find himself another defence lawyer. While this looks like the basis for a good story, it can only properly function as a preface: the single career woman now has to raise her young son (who adores his grandfather) amid crippling disillusionment. How can she function as a mother and a lawyer in this moral wilderness? Evidently this is not the concern of Costa-Gavras and his writer-producer Joe Eszterhas; staying close to the courtroom-detective format (*Jagged Edge*, for example), they confine themselves to the intricacies of revelation, not rehabilitation, and on this moderately provocative level simply keep us guessing as to whether father or daughter has got the right story. This leads tidily to the final showdown between culprit and accuser, an opportunity for Oscar-contending displays of passion from Jessica Lange. Significantly, the scene is awkward and rather lifeless.

This has to be because Costa-Gavras and his plot have something else in mind. He seems, for this crucial scene, to be far more interested in his setting, an elegant room of mirrors, than in his cast, and where he should be moving in for close-ups he stands well back from his heroine and leaves her to rant until the words have been used up. The mirrors can be usefully justified as reflections of deceit and the insubstantial, but they are also part of another message, in which the daughter's anguish is of lesser concern. Having selected the full 'scope screen for his subject, Costa-Gavras fills *Music Box* with opulent panoramas of Chicago architecture, sudden overhead shots of marble halls and glass arcades, generous warm interiors of casual wealth and good taste. Within this cocoon of spectacular comfort, the sordid and unreliable details of a disposable past seem irrelevant, an inconvenient fiction against which to celebrate the triumphant present. As if embarrassed by its fakery of authentic trials, *Music Box* favours a cool and indifferent distance: there is an eerie moment when the camera comes forward from the back of the courtroom to stare down in fascination at the remote drama being staged below, its geometry more vital than its topic of debate. Even when the lawyer finds herself by the Danube at the spot where blood once flowed, the sunlit innocence of the location, with children at play, is like a dismissive cancellation. Could it be that the director of *Z* has given us, in this visual code about materialism worth killing for, his version of *The War of the Roses*?

More to the point, *Music Box* resounds with variations on the Eszterhas/Costa-Gavras plot for *Betrayed*, in which endless conspiracies were uncovered by a sleuthing heroine finally unable to trust anybody. This may be the inevitable result of fusion between the writers of *Flashdance* (Eszterhas) and *Missing* (Costa-Gavras), but it consigns *Music Box* to something like Paul Wendkos territory, where secret and profane brotherhoods prey habitually on sacrificial innocents. So many strings are being pulled to get the influential criminal back to Hungary, to keep him in the States, and to win a legal victory irrespective of guilt, that his daughter can hardly avoid entanglement. The most insidious claim upon him, of course, is that of the family; a masculine hierarchy controls all the rituals in *Music Box* just as it did in *Betrayed*, and leaving the war-crime references in parenthesis (although these too are largely centred on the loss of parents and children), the "real" story of the film is chillingly one of a struggle between father and daughter for possession of the boy, Mikey.

With the help of his other, equally cynical grandfather, Mikey is being smoothly groomed as a recruit to the merciless, mercenary male line of the family, and his mother's recapture of him at the end seems likely to be no more than temporary. When Costa-Gavras, filming through a maze of crystal and mellow furniture, reveals one grandfather manipulating the press while the other firmly controls the boy on his pony as they ride in obedient circles, the perpetual helplessness of the merely female seems beyond remedy. On the other hand, it is with the help of other women (particularly her industrious assistant, Georgine, who uncovers most of the vital information) that the lawyer gets hold of the unlikely music box that confirms the extent of her problem. And a case could be made that while the grandfathers represent the ruthless standards of the past (those of the present are conspicuously low-key in the form of the absent father), there is still a chance for the future to be shaped by the mother. Costa-Gavras' heroines may suffer every kind of loss, but they do have a knack for survival . . .

NEW YORK, 1/15/90, p. 56, David Denby

If writer Joe Eszterhas and director Costa-Gavras had anything profound in mind when they set out to make *Music Box,* they managed to conceal it. The picture is essentially a courtroom drama about a dour Hungarian American who may or may not have been a war criminal during Hungary's Fascist period and his American-born daughter (Jessica Lange), a lawyer who defends him when the United States tries to strip him of his citizenship. Was he or wasn't he? And will she continue to love and support him if he was? Taut, decently acted, but no more interesting than a TV movie.

NEW YORK POST, 12/26/89, p. 29, Jami Bernard

The savvy, needling question at the heart of "Musix Box" the one which makes the political personal, is: How well do you really know your parents? Few can imagine their parents having sex, let alone committing atrocities (other than the ones they committed on us.)

So when lawyer Ann Talbot (Jessica Lange) agrees to defend her Hungarian immigrant father against charges that he was a Nazi war criminal, she does it because, as her brother says, "Blood is thicker than spilled blood," and because, after all, it's only Daddy. As the case progresses, Ann asks the question we all ask as we truly grow up—who is this man really?

Costa-Gavras, the director who gave us "Missing" and other movies in which individuals are forced by political realities to take a stand, is concerned in "Music Box" with personal awakening and the responsibility we all have (even film makers) to future generations to throw light on what is more comfortably left in shadow.

Brave stuff, although at times he shows an alarming naivete, as he did in "Betrayal," in which Debra Winger falls in love with the white supremacist she is investigating. In "Musix Box" the daughter's defense of the father (Armin Mueller-Stahl) is too pat, almost wildly unbelievable. For a parking violation, yes, but for deportation hearings hinging on whether her father initiated gang-rapes, bayonet tortures and mass murders, no. She would be hard-pressed to sit through such a trial, let alone defend it.

The story bears resemblance to what recently happened to John Demjanjuk, who was deported and tried as "Ivan the Terrible," the sicko responsible for pushing the controls at the Treblinka gas chamber. His poor, blinkered family was supportive right up to his conviction. But then, at every murderer's trial, a mother claims that her son was raised with discipline and religion (the warning signs right there).

I won't tell you whether Ann Talbot's father really did those awful things, although the evidence against him is peculiarly weighted (screenwriter Joe Eszterhas is also responsible for the jarringly similar "Jagged Edge"). It is Ann's growing suspicions, and how they force upon her a larger responsibility, that is at issue. An unglamorous Jessica Lange, her eyebrows thickly furred and puzzled, is terrific, visibly struggling with a personal, moral, legal, emotional, even career dilemma.

Steely eyed German actor Mueller-Stahl plays the father, a rough role since it must strike a balance between the family man (he does push-ups with his grandson, well played by Lukas Haas), and the possible monster (who raped a girl and then forced her to do push-ups over an upended bayonet).

A more obvious villain is Ann's father-in-law, a distinguished government operative whose job it had been to "turn" Nazis into U.S. agents. To some, evil is relative.

The movie drags a bit; it's not taut. The music box, a Pandora's box, is a late, lovely prop that has seemingly nothing to do with anything except perhaps the opening credits.

Still, "Music Box" is a suspenseful human drama that poses interesting questions about the ability of humans to reinvent themselves, and about the universal need to believe in goodness. See if for Lange, in any case.

NEWSDAY, 12/26/89, Part II/p. 5, Mike McGrady

The last time director Costa-Gavras sat down to make a movie with writer Joe Eszterhas and producer Irwin Winkler, the result was "Betrayed," an expose of right-wing extremism that was so simplistic, so propagandistic, so essentially foolish that it proved only one thing: Extremism in the depiction of extremism is no virtue.

Since one cannot readily imagine why these three would want to associate with one another again, it is something of a pleasure to report that their new joint venture, "Music Box" is a step up. However, in all candor, it's difficult to imagine the film that would *not* be a step up.

"Music Box" is a psychological study of what happens to a middle-class American family when it is learned that the grandfather, a Hungarian immigrant, may have been a butcher-torturer working with the Nazis.

The fine German actor Armin Mueller-Stahl, outstanding in such movies as "Colonel Redl" and "Angry Harvest," is totally credible as Michael J. Laszlo, the hard-working immigrant who is the very model of a family man, proud father of a promising attorney (Jessica Lange) and doting grandfather to her young son (Lukas Haas).

When papers are served charging him with war crimes, his lawyer-daughter is not overly perturbed: "It's not you, Papa. They made a mistake. Don't worry we'll get this all cleared up." However, when she informs the government prosecutor (Frederic Forrest) that they've got the wrong man, he seems less than convinced: "Like hell we do."

Laszlo persuades his daughter to represent him in court—after all, she knows more about him than anyone else. Well...yes and no. She knows he's hard-working and clean-living, a generous and supportive family man. What she doesn't know, on the other hand, would fill a courtroom. Which it does as witness after witness testifies that Michael J. Laszlo was, indeed, a Nazi who specialized in torture, rape and cold-blooded murder. Finally, his daughter can stand it no more: "Stop it! He is not a monster! I'm his daughter. I know him better than anyone."

Through clever tactics, the daughter wins fine legal points and quite possibly the case. But this is not an issue she would like to see decided on technicalities. Finally, a trip back to her father's native Hungary reveals that we don't always know others, even loved ones who share our daily lives. And, further, that the line separating man from monster can be a thin one.

While many of the details are intriguing (the answer to the riddle lies concealed in an ornate antique music box), the telling of the story is so straightforward and predictable as to be just a bit pedestrian. Details are spelled out, repeated, then repeated again.

Jessica Lange is one of those rare actresses who seem able to find characters somewhere deep within themselves. What she brings to the surface is natural and unforced. Armin Mueller-Stahl, given the more difficult task of merging the appearance of integrity with the possibility of evilness, is up to the task. Director Costa-Gavras, the most effective political propagandist ("Z," "Missing," etc.) in all of movieland, is not intent on delivering a message this time out. However, he does have a point and that point ("It's too late to change what happened," one character tells another , "but it's not too late to remember") is a point that surely bears repetition.

TIME, 1/8/90, p. 76, Richard Corliss

[*Music Box* was reviewed jointly with *Triumph of the Spirit*; see Corliss' review of the film.]

VILLAGE VOICE, 12/26/89, p. 99, J. Hoberman

Not just a seasonal bouquet of unspeakable atrocities, *Music Box* gives you domestic drama through the roof. This Costa-Gavras package (opening Christmas Day) is an Electrafied variation of the John Demjanjuk story in which the accused war criminal's defense attorney is his very own daughter.

Mainly a courtroom drama, *Music Box* is distinguished by some robust performances—Armin Mueller-Stahl as a gruff Hungarian immigrant charged with the mass murder of Budapest Jews during the winter of 1944, Frederic Forrest as the aggressively befuddled prosecuting attorney, and Jessica Lange as the sturdy defender of her father's innocence. (Lange, an exciting actress despite unfortunate taste in material, plugs into this family romance so directly she takes on an almost-dangerous glow.)

Costa-Gavras is onto a great theme. As Mueller-Stahl is forever pointing out, the accused criminal in dock is not the same person as the perpetrator. This takes on additional resonance as amplified by a child's natural ignorance of a parent's prior life. But staggering under the weight of history, *Music Box* can't afford ambiguity. People and incidents appear and disappear as quickly as items on the Bush agenda, and no one ever escapes their type. The explicitly Jewish judge bends backwards to give Lange the benefit of every doubt; of course, if he seemed biased toward the prosecution that would be another shallow cliché. (Only an abstraction, he can never be permitted his own dark night of the soul.)

Class lines are drawn with European distinctness. While Mueller-Stahl isn't exactly lovable, the archvillain is Lange's ex-father-in-law (Donald Moffat)—a cynical Cold Warrior cum operative. When Lange asks if he knew any old Nazis, he winks and tells her, "They were all salt-of-the-earth types, like your old man." This bastard hats everyone. Ranting against *glasnost*, he fastidiously ignores Lange's crude steelworker brother who, in a typically ponderous irony, is roaming around a suite proffering salami sandwiches—the proletarian version of a power lunch.

Also reviewed in:

NATION, 1/1/90, p. 30 Stuart Klawans
NEW REPUBLIC, 2/5/90, p. 27, Stanley Kauffmann
NEW YORK TIMES, 12/25/89, p. 49, Caryn James
NEW YORKER, 1/8/90, p. 90, Pauline Kael
VARIETY, 12/27/89, p. 10
WASHINGTON POST, 1/19/90, p. B1, Rita Kempley
WASHINGTON POST, 1/26/90, Weekend/p. 35, Desson Howe

MUSIC TEACHER, THE

An Orion Classics release of RTBF/K2-One film. *Executive Producer:* Jacqueline Pierreux. *Director:* Gérard Corbiau. *Screenplay (French with English subtitles):* Gérard Corbiau, Andree Corbiau, Patrick Iratni, Jacqueline Pierreux, and Christian Watton. *Story:* Luc Jabon and Gérard Corbiau. *Director of Photography:* Walther Van Den Ende. *Editor:* Denise Vindevogel. *Music:* Ronald Zollman. *Sound:* André Defossez. *Production Designer:* Zouc Lanc. *Costumes:* Catherine Frognier. *Make-up:* Nicole Demeulder. *Running Time:* 100 minutes. *MPAA Rating:* PG.

CAST: José Van Dam (Joachim Dallayrac); Anne Roussel (Sophia Maurier); Philippe Volter (Jean Nilson); Sylvie Fennec (Estelle Fischer); Patrick Bauchau (Prince Scotti); Johan Leysen (François Manssaux, Sophie's Uncle); Marc Schreiber (Arcas, Prince Scotti's Protégé); Jeannette Bakker (The Diva); Yvette Merlin (Louise); Jean Musin (Lhomond, Dallayrac's Manager); Alain Carre (Attendant to Prince Scotti); Ulysse Waterlot (Orchestra Conductor at Competition); José Van Dam (Bass-Baritone for the role of Joachim); Dinah Bryant (Soprano for the role of Sophie); Jerome Pruett (Tenor for the role of Jean and Acras).

LOS ANGELES TIMES, 7/19/89, Calendar/p. 3, Michael Wilmington

José Van Dam, who plays a tragic baritone in the Belgian movie "The Music Teacher" has a face full of magnetic pain, sad eyes brooding over an imperious chin. And the movie, directed by Gérard Corbiau, surrounds him with period decor so chill and lovely it looks as if the frames would shatter if you touched them.

"The Music Teacher" was designed as a vehicle for Van Dam, Belgium's finest opera singer, and Corbiau gives his star a lustrous backdrop. It's full of spacious country chateaus, lakes at sunset and shiny floors on which every footstep makes a great, echoing, metallic click. In the midst of this pre-World War I splendor, Van Dam's Joachim Dallayrac—suffering saint, unspoken lover and musical martinet—languishes stoically. Occasionally, he breaks into poignant song, generally Mahler's mournful "Ruckert Lieder."

But if it's a sumptuous-looking display, it's also a shallow one: a gleaming Cognac glacé laid over steaming cornball kitsch. Wonderful as it looks and as Van Dam sounds, it's a campy pastiche of a story, the sort of thing that might have been imagined by someone listening to Deutsche Grammophon lieder records while staring rapturously at the album covers.

People are introduced as "the greatest baritone of the age" (Dallayrac), "the would-be greatest tenor and soprano"—Dallayrac's protégés Sophie (Anne Roussel) and Jean (Philippe Volter)— and the plot revolves around a contest to determine the next great tenor. It's almost a classical music "Rocky."

There are also scraps of soap opera: touches of terminal disease and unspoken love, an ambiance of the chic and excruciating. When people die, their teacups shatter on the floor, and veil-like white window curtains whip picturesquely inward. If the name of the villain, Dallayrac's arch-nemesis Prince Scotti, suggests a classy old vampire, that's exactly how Patrick Bauchau plays him. His Scotti reeks of elegantly perverted menace and malice and he has a smirking protégé for the greatest-tenor title, Arcas (Marc Schreiber), who looks a bit like a *Hitler-jugend* cast by Luchino Visconti.

Scotti himself was once up for greatest-baritone-of-his age laurels, which he lost when his voice cracked in mano-a-mano competition with Dallayrac. Now he has to content himself with being the age's greatest musical impresario, patron of the age's greatest recital, where reputations are made or broken instantly. There, history may repeat. On the schedule: a dueling-tenors battle between Jean and Arcas, staged in matching white masks and "Amadeus" tricorns.

Where have all these unrivaled voices come from? Sophie happens to be the niece of Joachim's best friend, François (Johan Leysen); Jean is a petty thief whom he spots picking pockets at the city square. What sheer operatic density! Jean's sturdy tenor happens to be exactly the same voice possessed by Scotti's sour little protégé, Arcas. It's even dubbed by the same singer, Jerome Pruett. Amazements never cease.

Corbiau deserves every credit for the splendiferous look of the film, done on a modest budget, and for building it around Van Dam—as promising an actor as he is superb a baritone. The Leporello of Joseph Losey's 1978 film "Don Giovanni," Van Dam, along with cinematographer Walther Vanden Ende and production designer Zouc Lanc, brings elegance and taste to a movie hovering constantly on the edge of the cloying and silly.

But how much better would it have been if Corbiau had forgotten all these Verdi vendettas?

If he had simply focused on the poignant relationship between Dallayrac and Sophie? On the last autumn of a virtuoso, desire repressed into song? We'll never know. Mahler and repressed passion may be more evocative, but dueling tenors are undoubtedly a sexier sell.

NEW YORK POST, 7/7/89, p. 23, David Edelstein

"The Music Teacher" is a laughably obvious middlebrow Belgian art picture with an irresistible hook: Its hero, Joachim Dallayrac (José Van Dam)—a great, aging opera star—withdraws from performing and takes on two young disciples, training them in his chateau to be the finest singers in the world.

It's a rocky process—or, rather, a "Rocky" process, since there's all sorts of strenuous discipline involved, and since the training culminates in a recital/competition in the palace of Dallayrac's archrival, the unscrupulous creepo Prince Scotti (Patrick Bachau).

The movie, which was nominated for an Oscar for Best Foreign Film, is actually a shameless mix of "Pygmalion" and "The Karate Kid." Luckily, it's also swamped with the music of Mahler, Mozart and Verdi, much of it sung by the thrilling Van Dam or by Dinah Bryant and Jerome Pruett, who dub the ingenues playing Dallayrac's students. Even at its kitschiest, "The Music Teacher" is infinitely more pleasurable than another round with Daniel and Mr. Miyagi.

Directed by Gérard Corbiau, who once made a profile of Van Dam for Belgian televison, the picture is blandly plush and high-toned, with faces bathed in rose and umber, as if it's always sunset.

There are shots of pale green plants receiving rain from the heavens, and the sapling Sophie (Anne Roussel) receives rain from the heavens, too—the haunting bass-baritone of her teacher, whose voice moves her to tears. Her face puckers winsomely when she's transported, and in this movie, she's often transported.

"The Music Teacher" introduces the first picturesque singer-ruffian I've seen in at least a decade—Jean (Philippe Volter), who strolls around the village square warbling brightly and picking people's pockets. (Advice to pickpockets-in-training: Singing Puccini might not be the best strategy if you don't want to be conspicuous.)

But the movie has to establish a stroke that Jean is 1) a no-goodnik and 2) immensely gifted—the best tenor in the world in 10 years, according to Dallayrac, who rescues the young man from an angry village mob and whisks him to the chateau for a couple of years of music lessons. "He sings as well as he steals," pronounces the music teacher in his oily, lubricious voice, leaning back from his chin.

Van Dam isn't the world's most animated actor, but he does open up in song, and the lines the writers give him are actor-proof, anyway. He rows ahead of Jean in a boat, commanding the young swain to swim hard and build up his stamina; he rattles around the studio opening and closing curtains while Sophie sings, forcing her to concentrate on the music and nothing else.

Corbiau suggests in these scenes that the music has isolated Dallayrac even as it has enriched him—that perfection as a performer has meant learning to love his loneliness. Doted on by his companion and pianist Estelle (Sylvie Fennec), the music teacher struggles with his feelings toward Sophie; he broods on his mortality while Mahler fills the soundtrack.

The script of the movie is shallow, but the music fills it up, exalts it. Dallayrac, who won't record his voice for posterity on the brand-new phonograph, comes to terms with his life in the most eloquent way imaginable—in Mahler's "*Ich bin der Welt abhanden gekommen.*"

You don't really mind the soap-opera banality of Sophie and Jean or the fact that the movie cheats on its "you must love your loneliness" message and lets them sleep together. Besides, when the pair journey to the palace of Prince Scotti, "The Music Teacher" junks the tony angst and turns into a trashy, entertaining melodrama.

The Prince, who "broke his voice" in a singing duel with Dallayrac several decades earlier, had nursed a grudge ever since, and has fanatically trained his own protégé, Arcas (Marc Schreiber), to go lungs-to-lungs with Jean.

The movie climaxes in their duel, which isn't exactly edge-of-your-seat but is certainly fun—especially since Bachau can make his ears twitch alarmingly when he hears his rivals in song. Jealous to the end of Dallayrac's power, he hisses to Sophie: "I want to know why music submits to him. I want to know his secret."

Alas, it isn't enough that Prince Scotti is a blackguard; he appears to be a homosexual as well, and very likely is the lover of his disciple, Arcas. The inescapable suggestion is that the heterosexual purity of Dallayrac, Sophie and Jean will always triumph over the twisted perversities of Scotti and company. As anyone who knows the music world can attest, that's a sentiment as stupid as it is bigoted.

NEWSDAY, 7/7/89, Part III/p. 3, Mike McGrady

What would you get if you crossed "The Red Shoes" and "Rocky"? If you were extremely fortunate, you might come up with an approximation of the new Belgian film, "The Music Teacher."

A surpassingly romantic tale (a la "Red Shoes"), one that culminates in a high-pressure international singing contest (well, "Rocky" may be stretching it), "The Music Teacher" is an evocative and beautiful film with the ability to draw applause from music lovers and tears from turnips.

The film begins with an ending of sorts, as an aging opera great, movingly played by aging opera great José Van Dam, completes a concert with this announcement: "Ladies and gentlemen, that was my last performance. You'll never hear me again. I thank you for everything. God bless you."

Among those who are shaken in different ways by the singer's sudden retirement are his accompanist and constant companion Estelle (Sylvie Fennec), a lovely 18-year-old protégé Sophie (Anne Roussel), and his lifelong vocal competitor and enemy, Prince Scotti (Patrick Bauchau).

Accompanied by the two women—his new student and his life's companion—the teacher retreats to a lavish country estate. Although the student is openly infatuated with him and he less openly with her, the teacher stoically retains a stern professionalism and seeks to redirect her love into the music they share: "You must concentrate to the point where you no longer see me . . . Nothing exists but your voice and the song . . . The music is invading you; let it penetrate you."

When her infatuation shows no signs of diminishing, the music teacher takes on a second student, a petty thief (Philippe Volter) with a natural voice and an appealingly rough demeanor. In Van Dam's moving performance, we feel the full pathos of age stepping aside for youth. Because of their teacher's tireless efforts, the two students are finally ready for their first international competition against the protégés of the evil Prince Scotti.

The clear danger in all this is the lurking possibility of kitsch, of slipping over from the nakedly romantic to the melodramatic, and what saves the movie more than once is the brilliance of the music. Director Gérard Corbiau's love of music (his early television films examined the lives of Igor Stravinsky and saxophone inventor Adolphe Sax) grants it co-starring prominence. Works by Mahler, Verdi, Bellini and Mozart are given superb renditions by Van Dam, along with the voices of Dinah Bryant and Jerome Pruett.

The importance of the music—at times it replaces script as the prime storytelling medium—gives "The Music Teacher" an entirely different feel from the established movie equations, as words and plot take a back seat to music and image. The lush camera work by Walther Vanden Ende is a perfect accompaniment, and the performances, too, seem passionate, emotionally revealing.

"The Music Teacher" may not be for all palates, certainly not for those who would choose a "Rocky" over a "Red Shoes," but those others—are there any pure romantics left out there?—will find it highly fulfilling. A popular success in its native Belgium and on the festival circuit, it was one of five films nominated for last year's best foreign-film Oscar.

VILLAGE VOICE, 7/11/89, p. 72, Amy Taubin

José Van Dam is a rarity—an opera star who sings onscreen with restrained passion and manages to deliver lines without embarrassment. *The Music Teacher* (the nominee from Belgium for the 1989 Academy Award for Best Foreign Film) is a vehicle for Van Dam, but that's not enough of reason to make a movie. Aspiring to Bergmanesque simplicity, the script ends up slogging through cliché. The only surprise is how few of the possible plot complications are ever explored.

Van Dam plays Joachim Dallayrac, a singer who retires at the height of his career and devotes himself to training a single pupil, Sophie Maurier, a pretty 18-year-old lyric soprano who looks fetching in Edwardian high collars. As Estelle Fischer (Sylvie Fennec), his longtime lover and accompanist, predicts, Joachim and Sophie fall in love, but Joachim maintains a hands-off policy.

Enter Jean Nilson (Philippe Volter), a petty thief with a brazen tenor voice that promises future greatness. Jean plans to exploit Joachim—he starts by pocketing the silver—but he becomes enthralled with music and bonds with his teacher in an Oedipal struggle for Sophie's affections.

Besides the vaguely sadistic manipulations that take place during the singing lessons (basic training for grand opera), emotional exchanges between the characters are so perfunctory that to call the atmosphere in Joachim's luxurious country house repressed is overly suggestive.

The climax of the film is Sophie's first public appearance. Joachim delivers his babes to a competition hosted by his arch rival, Prince Scotti (the smilingly villainous Patrick Bauchau), and leaves them to fend for themselves. Panicked, Sophie falls into Jean's arms and finally is allowed to lose her virginity. A few hours later, with Jean smiling encouragement from the wings, Sophie walks onstage, trembling, launches into "Sempre Libera" from *La Traviata*, and instantly discovers herself as a performer. She (or rather Dinah Bryant, who dubbed her voice) sings with an all-or-nothing defiance, intoxicated with her own accomplishment, goading herself to greater and greater risks.

The moment is colored by a notable irony, of which director/writer Gérard Corbiau is, I suspect, totally unaware. Sophie sings with dazzling conviction about a desire for total freedom, forgetting in the thrill of the moment that, like Violetta, the character she plays, she's more dependent on her mentor's approval than she can afford to admit.

Also reviewed in:
NEW REPUBLIC, 7/31/89, p. 24, Stanley Kauffmann
NEW YORK TIMES, 7/7/89, p. C14, Caryn James
VARIETY, 9/14/88, p. 30
WASHINGTON POST, 8/18/89, p. D7, Joseph McLellan

MY LEFT FOOT

A Miramax Films release of a Ferndale Films/Granada Television International production in association with Radio Telefís Eireann. *Executive Producer:* Paul Heller and Steve Morrison. *Producer:* Noel Pearson. *Director:* Jim Sheridan. *Screenplay:* Jim Sheridan and Shane Connaughton. *Director of Photography:* Jack Conroy. *Editor:* J. Patrick Duffner. *Music:* Elmer Bernstein. *Music Editor:* Kathy Durning. *Sound:* Kieran Horgan and (music) Brian Masterson. *Sound Editor:* Ron Davis. *Production Designer:* Austen Spriggs. *Art Director:* Austen Spriggs. *Set Decorator:* Shirley Lynch. *Special Effects:* Gerry Johnson. *Costumes:* Joan Bergin. *Make-up:* Ken Jennings. *Stunt Coordinator:* Peter Brayham. *Running time:* 103 minutes. *MPAA Rating:* Not Rated.

CAST: Daniel Day-Lewis (Christy); Ray McAnally (Mr. Brown); Brenda Fricker (Mrs. Brown); Ruth McCabe (Mary); Fiona Shaw (Dr. Eileen Cole); Eanna McLiam (Older Benny); Alison Whelan (Older Sheila); Declan Croghan (Older Tom); Hugh O'Conor (Younger Christy); Cyril Cusack (Lord Castlewelland); Owen Sharp (Younger Tom); Darren McHugh (Younger Benny); Keith O'Conor (Younger Brian); Marie Conmee (Magso); Adrian Dunbar (Peter); Kirsten Sheridan (Younger Sharon); Jacinta Whyte (Jenny); Julie Hale (Rachel); Tom Hickey (Priest); Ulick O'Connor (Critic); Lucy Vigne-Welsh (Petra); Daniel Reardon (Tony); Phelim Drew (Brian); Patrick Laffan (Barman); Derry Power (Customer in Bar); Eileen Colgan (Nan); Sara Cronin (Girlfriend); Jean Doyle (Woman with Pram); Britta Smith (Nurse); Conor Lambert (Punch and Judy Puppeteer); Martin Dunne (Waiter); Charlie Roberts, Ger O'Leary, and Mil Fleming (Mourners); Simon Kelly (Liam).

CHRISTIAN SCIENCE MONITOR, 12/5/89, p. 10, David Sterritt

"My Left Foot" must be one of the year's least-promising movie titles, but the film behind it is surprisingly memorable. This is partly because of its subject, and partly because of a remarkable performance by Daniel Day-Lewis, whose foot—and yes, the rest of him—is as eloquent as anything a movie has shown us in quite a while.

The hero of "My Left Foot" is Christy Brown, a real-life writer and painter whose autobiography is the basis for the movie. In the film, as in his life, Mr. Brown is almost completely paralyzed, able to move only his left foot. But it's quite a foot, the way Brown has trained it—capable of typing, painting, and accomplishing many of life's daily tasks. The movie follows him from his birth in 1932, in Dublin, until he's in his late 20s and meets a young nurse who will later marry him. Along the way it shows his progress from an extraordinarily difficult childhood to adulthood, and to success as the very thing he wasn't supposed to be capable of becoming: a communicator and artist with an international reputation.

"My Left Foot" is not always a pleasant film to watch. It shows Brown's disabilities in agonizing detail and, just as important, Brown himself turns out to have a far-from-perfect personality. But the imperfections of his all-too-human nature are exactly what makes the picture different from the common run of inspirational movies about people with handicaps, which often tend to idealize their disabled heroes.

By contrast, Brown is often a nervy, irascible, and downright insufferable fellow. What's more, the film makes no excuses for him. It simply puts him on the screen for us to judge however we will—as a heroic man who triumphs over a disability, and as a volatile, often cranky character who could make life miserable for the people around him.

"My Left Foot" is also generous in recognizing the sources of Brown's accomplishments: It pays quiet tribute not only to him but to his mother, who refused to accept the idea that physical limitations must lead to mental limitations. She had an enormous number of children—Christy had 13 surviving brothers and sisters—but she managed to give her most troubled child the love and help he needed to become someone who's special by any measure.

"My Left Foot" has been directed in a rather ordinary way by Jim Sheridan, an experienced theater director making his feature-film debut. There's nothing ordinary about Daniel Day-Lewis's performance as Christy Brown, however. True, he's not the only skilled performer in the cast, which also includes Cyril Cusack, the later Ray McAnally, and Brenda Fricker as Brown's mother, as well as Hugh O'Conor playing Brown as a child. Yet it's Day-Lewis who lights up the screen most brilliantly. He has already won praise for his vivid acting in "My Beautiful Laundrette" and "A Room With a View," and for his less exciting work in "The Unbearable Lightness of Being" last year. His portrayal of Christy Brown is sure to earn him more raves than ever. And if the Oscars don't take notice of him, I'll be amazed.

FILMS IN REVIEW, 12/89, p. 616, Kevin Lewis

My Left Foot, the autobiography of Christy Brown, born with cerebral palsy, has been a classic in Ireland since its publication in 1955. As much as the foredoomed Brown succeeded against great odds, this motion picture is truly an unexpected surprise: Ireland doesn't produce many motion pictures and, in fact, has no significant indigenous film industry; the film's producer, Noel Pearson, is a stage producer and Jim Sheridan a stage director. Sheridan wrote the script with Shane Connaughton on commission from Pearson, who was a close friend of Brown. Brown choked to death on food in 1981 at the age of 49. Movies about the handicapped traditionally win awards and articles in medical magazines, but rarely are boffo at the box office. This unsentimental, slyly humorous movie may or may not catch on with the public, but it will be a revival house and video staple for many years.

As the twisted and paralyzed Christy, born into a large and poor Dublin family in the Depression years, Daniel Day-Lewis gives the performance of his young but already spectacular career. He creates a multi-layered character who doesn't plead for love or audience sympathy, but who is alternately reclusive, moody, depressed and angry when he is thwarted. As young Christy, the thirteen-year-old Hugh O'Conor is equally remarkable. Viewers will not soon forget the boy's blazing eyes, determined mouth and focused intelligence, already fully aware that he is expendable to the world and that he will have to find a creative way to make a living and gain respect. Sheridan, Day-Lewis and O'Conor have created what amounts to that often abused term, a docu-drama. The viewer believes that he is seeing not a recreation but the real thing. Brown could only use his left foot, but he amazingly became a prolific writer and painter. Exhibitions of his paintings were held and his expressionist art was widely appreciated. He wooed unsuccessfully his doctor, Eileen Cole (played in Vanessa Redgrave fashion by Fiona Shaw), who was responsible for his recognition as a painter and writer, but married his nurse who reluctantly found herself falling for Christy's blunt but charming wit. At one point, Mary (played by Ruth McCabe) refuses to fetch another item for Christy—in this case, a match. "I'm not your mother," she patiently explains. "I don't need a f——g psychiatry lesson. I just need a f——g match," he snaps back.

As Mrs. Brown, the devoutly Catholic mother who encourages Christy to the point where she starves her family to provide Christy with a wheelchair, Brenda Fricker is unforgettable. She is constantly pregnant (there were thirteen surviving children in the brood out of twenty-two) but she concentrates on her crippled son. Mr. Brown, played by the late Ray McAnally, is gruff and strikes anyone who criticizes the Browns for not putting Christy in a home. What is remarkable about this true story is the level of support Christy received from his parents and siblings, most of whom had to sleep in the same bed in litter fashion.

The film does not explore any element outside of the family. Though the Church comes in for some ribbing in a sequence where a priest chastises the paralyzed child for having a sexually explicit book, the plight of the handicapped in a poor society where able-bodied people are unemployed is self-evident.

Sheridan's directorial style is reminiscent of John Ford. The prototype for *My Left Foot* could be *How Green Was My Valley*. The relationship between mother and son, and the relationship between Christy and his brothers is remarkably similar. One scene of the family gathered at the round kitchen table with the mother gazing at them from behind a sheer white curtain is pure John Ford. The brawl in the pub after the funeral of Mr. Brown is another Ford-type scene, as is the sequence where the family builds the studio for Christy.

My Left Foot is a perfect example of that phrase "a film that proclaims the dignity of the human spirit" without being preachy and by being thoroughly entertaining and moving.

LOS ANGELES TIMES, 11/10/89, Calendar/p. 1, Sheila Benson

Who goes to the movies for moral uplift? You want moral uplift, go to the Ice Capades. So don't think that seeing "My Left Foot" wins you some kind of spiritual merit badge. This one you see for the pure love of great movie making. Its tough-minded, unsentimental writing and ferociously brilliant acting—across the board and especially at the top—manage to give a pretty good idea of what Christy Brown, the Dublin-born writer, poet and painter, was all about.

As Brown began the autobiography he called "My Left Foot," in honor of the only limb he could control enough to write with: "There were nine children before me and 12 after me. Of this total of 22, 13 lived." None, however, quite like Christy. This son of an impoverished bricklayer was born with cerebral palsy and, in the fashion of the day in 1932, was called a "dunce" and a "poor half-wit" for the first nine years of his life. *Out* of his mother's earshot.

Probably because co-writer and director Jim Sheridan, a Dubliner, is from a huge and poor family himself, the film sneers at heart-tugging exactly the way Christy would, and with very nearly his same blunt Anglo-Saxionisms. Neither poverty nor Christy's condition is the subject here; they are the givens.

Instead, 13-year-old Hugh O'Conor, who plays young Christy, and Daniel Day-Lewis, who picks up at Christy's 17th birthday, meld to create an extraordinary portrait of a wild, difficult, far-ranging mind, a man unsparing of himself and of others, full of rage and despair, for years full of untapped sexuality, who at last achieves some modicum of heart's ease. It is a spellbinding journey.

In his first film, director Sheridan frames the story with a fundraising ceremony outside Dublin on the estate of Lord Castlewelland (the splendid Cyril Cusack), at which 21-year old Christy is being honored after publication of his autobiography.

The wheelchair-bound, blackbearded writer is put into a drawing room with a nurse to look after him, until his appearance. Drinking his whiskey from a straw-and-flask arrangement in his tuxedo jacket, Christy casts a satyr's eye over this lively, open woman, Mary Carr (Ruth McCabe) and begins his assault, using his book as an opening wedge. And as she starts to read, raptly, and to see his paintings illustrating its pages, we move into his childhood.

O'Conor's young Christy has the baleful look, the fierceness, the clamped-down mouth that Day-Lewis will have; it seems entirely likely that one could grow up into the other. But O'Conor's performance is nearly all mime and sound, the boy is like a furious projectile. Speech will come later.

Sheridan (and co-writer Shane Connaughton) tips us off to what is boiling inside this wild-eyed boy two years before the family sees it. When the breakthrough finally comes, the scene is a real killer. As O'Conor lies, exhausted, after spelling his first word in chalk with his foot, the energy he's used to do this seems to pour off him in waves. (The scene is framed as a visual reference to another later on, as father and son lie beside each other, close as these opposites will ever be.)

The older Christy will be reached through a crop-haired, luminous-eyed teacher, Dr. Eileen Cole (Fiona Shaw). He is now Day-Lewis, a late teen-ager and young man, torn by his sexuality, his loneliness, the depths of what he needs to say. Speech therapy will help him say it; particularly some of his crisper Anglo-Saxonisms (the reason for the film's R rating). This is a portrait of the hero as a socially almost-impossible young man: randy, uncontrollable, barely redeemed by the swiftness of his wit.

Day-Lewis seizes the role, and almost immediately gets us to look beyond the man in the chair to the soul inside. It's a performance with a fantastic trajectory; he is sly, funny, as swift as he can be with these squash-shaped syllables, wicked, mordant and openly romantic;

But he's not all charm. Cross him or, as it happens, let him fall in love and be left, and his rages are horrible. This is the tyrannical side of Christy's disablement, and the film makers don't avert their eyes to its unpleasantness.

They also don't avert their eyes to the realities of poor Irish life, but it's treated as throwaway stuff, details too familiar to single out, like the single stunning fact of 22 children in one woman's lifetime. There's the meanness of this poverty; the children four in a bed upstairs, even when they are in their late teens and one in that bed is the uncontrollable Christy. There's also the enveloping warmth, always; an unspoken family-first unity, even when it means rallying around a bullying, empty shell of a father (the late Ray McAnally in a fine, last performance). And there's the pure, boundless love that radiates from the maginficent Brenda Fricker as Christy's mother.

She plays her like the rock she must have been, without a jot of martyrdom or a flicker of complaint and without an actressy moment. And in keeping with her self-effacing power, Sheridan keeps his ensemble up and together, so that even Day-Lewis' incandescence never runs away with the film. It can't have been easy, since this is one of film's definitive performances, with a subtlety and physicality of almost eerie accomplishment.

MONTHLY FILM BULLETIN, 9/89, p. 278, Geoff Brown

1959. While waiting to appear at a fundraising gala, Christy Brown, the Irish writer and painter severely crippled at birth by cerebral palsy, is attended by a nurse, Mary Carr, who begins reading his newly published autobiography, *My Left Foot*. Christy is born in 1932 to a Dublin bricklayer's wife. He lives at home and, encouraged by Mrs. Brown, struggles to communicate using his left foot—the only part of his body whose movements he can control. At the age of seven, he manages to scrawl the letter "A" with a piece of chalk. Mr. Brown remains doubtful about his handicapped son's potential until he scrawls a complete word—"mother"—on the floor. As a teenager, Christy feels the pangs of first love, and begins to express himself through painting. When Mrs. Brown enquires about a wheelchair at the local hospital, she is referred to Dr. Eileen Cole, a therapist, who invites Christy to attend her clinic. After he refuses to stay in a class of crippled children, Dr. Cole visits him at home, improving his speech and mobility, introducing him to Shakespeare, and arranging for a gallery exhibition of his paintings. Christy falls blindly in love with her, only to discover she is due to marry the gallery owner, Peter. Devastated, Christy attempts suicide, and begins drinking. To help him shake off his depression, the family build him his own room in the back yard. Mr. Brown dies suddenly in 1957. In the midst of another depression, Christy is stimulated to write his autobiography, tapping out the words on a typewriter letter by letter. The book earns him £800, which he gives to his disbelieving mother. At the gala, hosted by Lord Castlewelland, patron of Dr. Cole's clinic, Christy badgers Mary Carr into spending the evening with him. Struck by his indomitable spirit and wicked sense of humour, she agrees; the two launch their lives together with champagne, watching the dawn break over Dublin.

We open, impressively, with Christy Brown's bare left foot strenuously battling to draw out a record and plop in on to a gramophone turntable. We end, horrendously, with a freeze frame of Christy and his future wife, nurse Mary Carr, joyously opening a bottle of champagne early in the morning on the hills overlooking Dublin. There is every reason for this true-life account of triumph over adversity to end on an upbeat, of course, though one could wish that director Jim Sheridan—making his first feature after extensive theatrical experience in Dublin and New York—had not plumped so readily for the handiest visual cliché. In between these framing images, Christy Brown's early life is relayed through a conventional flashback structure, which darts back and forth between Mary Carr at the fund-raising gala, turning the autobiography's pages, and the recreated scenes of Christy's youth. Both Daniel Day-Lewis (as the mature Christy) and Hugh O'Conor (as the young, mute lad) give immensely skilled, physically strenuous performances, which never teeter over into heart-tugging tactics.

Indeed, Sheridan and co-writer Shane Connaughton (scriptwriter of another film about a struggling Irish artist, James Scott's *Every Picture Tells a Story*) go out of their way to avoid pools of tears, continually stressing young Christy's impish sense of fun and lively participation in neighbourhood games. The ploy works well in the scene where Christy's home-made wooden "chariot" is used to steal from a delivery lorry, though the sudden eruption of a John Ford pub brawl after Mr. Brown's funeral seems an unnecessary display of forced jollity. Throughout, Sheridan shoots in a clean, functional manner, leaving his fine actors to carry the burden of Brown's remarkable story. And he manages at least one haunting image, when Christy—his head at ground level—struggles through the blocked parlour door to find his dead father's head lying eerily alongside.

NEW YORK, 11/13/89, p. 109, David Denby

At one of the most stirring moments in *My Left Foot*, the bluff, hard-drinking Irish paterfamilias Paddy Brown (Ray McAnally) picks up the bent form of his crippled son—a boy who (to Paddy's eyes) has just shown his first signs of intelligence. Like Robin Hood carrying a stag on his shoulders, he bears him aloft to the local pub, where he bursts through the front door and announces to the assembled drinkers, "This is my son, Christy Brown. GENIUS."

My Left Foot, which climbs to glory on the strength of Daniel Day-Lewis's astounding performance as Christy, is an old-fashioned great movie. So much emotion combined with so little self-consciousness now seems a rarity in art, a gift from an earlier, less knowing age. The greatness of *My Left Foot* is all the more startling for having come out of a subject that seems hopeless—the development of a terrified child with cerebral palsy into a strongly egotistical, remarkably accomplished man, the real-life Irish artist and writer Christy Brown. The film transcends questions of taste. Christy's fierce temperament, emerging from the harsh Irish millieu, burns like raw whiskey, which, taken neat, washes away doubt, self-pity, embarrassment. This movie about a diseased man is one of the least sickly films ever made.

Christy Brown was born in Dublin in 1932 and died in 1981; he won fame as both painter and memoirist. When we first see him, he's a grown man in his late twenties, and he's untamable—flirtatious, aggressive, and dangerously witty. The disease still has a hold on him. His head jerks up and back, his mouth opens only at one corner, and he talks in quick gasps (though quite clearly). He's a commanding presence, but the only part of his body that his brain can control smoothly is his left foot, a large foot with a strong big toe. With that foot, he grasps his brush, he types, he turns the pages of a book. Christy has been summoned for a fund-raising affair at a palatial house, and as he waits upstairs to make an appearanace, he comes on to the nurse hired to watch over him. She sits there, pretending to ignore him, and as she reads his published memoir, we see his life from the beginning.

Playing Christy as a boy, a young actor named Hugh O'Conor does an amazing matchup job with Day-Lewis. When he's about eight, Christy lies under the stairs, his mouth locked, his whole body quivering in fear as his dad thumps up and down. The late Ray McAnally—beefy, red-faced, menacing—makes the bricklayer Paddy Brown unshakable in his parental authority. Paddy is narrow and bullying, often jealous of independence and strength in his sons, yet with a force of prideful life in him that fills Christy, who often hates him, with rage and ambition. It's the old lionlike masculinity, restored and refined in the spirit of a crippled boy who refuses to give up a single one of his desires. Christy's mother, played by the fine Brenda Fricker, is his support and champion; she alone realizes when he's still very young that he has great intelligence. The relationship between them is delicately detailed through all its stages of mutual solace, trust, dependence.

The Irish theater director Jim Sheridan, making his first film (he also wrote the screenplay, with Shane Connaughton), works cleanly, with strength, simplicity, and fullness of emotion. Sheridan dramatizes everything we need to know, yet he doesn't prolong scenes for that extra moment of pathos that turns sentiment into sentimentality; the curtness of the editing, the absence of obvious lyricism or emphasis, keeps the movie swift and dry. Sheridan doesn't exaggerate the brutality of Irish working-class life; he just presents it plainly (no fuss in made over the fact that the Brown family grows and grows—13 of the 22 children survived—and that Mrs. Brown is chained to her kitchen).

Christy gets wheeled around in a cart by his brothers and other neighborhood boys—wheeled around *hard*, without concern for danger; he becomes the centerpiece of their revels. In a soccer game, when he's a teenager, he sits at the goal and uses his head to stop the ball; later, carried into place to take a penalty shot, he smashes the ball with his all-powerful left foot. We get the point: The crowded family life and the rough but affectionate street play are more effective therapy than the most meticulous isolated care and softest protection. Insensitive, ignorant, but humane Ireland saves Christy from passivity and melancholy.

There seems to be no way of getting an easy grip on Daniel Day-Lewis's prodigal talent—or appearance. As the young upper-class exquisite with pince-nez in *A Room With a View*, he was dried-up and prissy; he wore a white streak in his hair as the ardent gay punk in *My Beautiful Laundrette*; he was lithe and handsome, with a high forehead and thick, dark hair, in *The Unbearable Lightness of Being*. In the very first shot of the movie, we see the left foot placing a needle, with great difficulty, on a record, and as the music begins—an aria from *Cosi fan tutte*— the camera travels to Day-Lewis's face. He pulls his head up and away from us. He might be a music lover in transport—until he jerks back, glaring at the camera. That glare is a surprise. It presents a challenge: "You can't look away, can you?" Much of what he does with the physical side of the performance is shocking in its directness and power. And later, with his long neck extended as he leans over to read a book lying on the floor, he's almost beautiful, like a folded Buddhist at prayer.

Day-Lewis takes over when Christy is seventeen and his talent as a painter is beginning to emerge. His mother finds him a doctor who can teach him to speak clearly—a young woman (Fiona Shaw) who believes in his genius—and then Christy begins to suffer. The doctor not only teachers him to speak but opens up many things for him, and he falls in love with her. Some years later, after a triumphant gallery show of his paintings, she takes him out to dinner with friends and announces her engagement to the gallery owner, a pleasant chap also at the table. Christy's rage is frightening and grotesque. Drunkenly, he explodes and repeatedly bangs his head on the table as if to bash his brains out before all of them. In Christy, the erotic fire never goes out. *My Left Foot* is possessed by an almost Old Testament fervency. Everything in the movie—the large, overburdened family, the downtrodden mother, the bullheaded father, the disease, the art that comes of it—says that this life in all its sullenness and misery, this life is good.

NEW YORK POST, 11/10/89, p. 27, David Edelstein

In the first shot of "My Left Foot," a bare foot sets a record on a turntable and places the needle in the groove. It looks like work, but that's the only option Christy Brown (played by Daniel Day-Lewis) has: he was born with cerebral palsy, and while his intellect is fierce (often, in fact, too fierce), he has motor control over just that one limb.

Brown's palsy is only the starting point for Jim Sheridan's riveting film, which towers above the usual inspirational, overcoming-one's-handicap picture—thanks, in large part, to Day-Lewis' furious and physically miraculous performance.

Even in the early scenes, with the superb Hugh O'Connor as the young and inarticulate Christy, you can see the human being trapped beneath the contorted body—terrified and maddened by a world where self-expression seems impossible and where he's forced to endure the patronizing exhortations of clergymen and fools.

The key to the movie's fascination is that the Dublin-born Brown—who, before his death from choking on a piece of meat in 1981, painted hundreds of pictures and typed several books with that left foot—isn't a particularly agreeable person.

Spoiled by his plump, tireless mum (Brenda Fricker) and ignored by his blowhard dad (the late Ray McAnally), he was regarded as an idiot until he finally exercised those toes and (in an overwhelming scene) wrote the word "mother" on the floor with a piece of chalk. What Brown communicated thereafter was often cranky and subversive, especially when he started hitting the whiskey.

And what a difference it makes when a handicapped hero isn't aggrandized—when he's fierce and moody instead of a martyr. On that score alone, the film is leagues ahead of "Gaby," in which the palsied heroine was thoroughly nice and the movie, as a result, thoroughly blah. "My Left Foot" is wrenching because Brown copes the way most humans would—immaturely, imperfectly.

It also benefits from its hero's unsentimental point of view. As a writer (the film is based on his first book), Christy Brown was more interested in the dynamics of his huge family than in his disability.

Through his eyes, we see the devoted mother, who—as her son begins to be accepted by the outside world—becomes increasingly jealous and unhappy. In part she resents the intrusion of others, and in part she fears her son will get his hopes for a happy life up too high. The beauty of this scheme is that at this point, Christy's bluff father becomes as much of a moderating influence on her as he had been on him.

Sheridan also explores Christy's adoration for Dr. Eileen Cole (Fiona Shaw), who taught him how to speak and then brought him to the world's attention.

His unrequited love for her—the first woman outside his mother to show him affection—triggers the film's most squirmy and painful scene, in which Christy, fresh from a triumphant gallery opening, becomes progressively more drunk in a fancy restaurant and bellows the most terrible words he can conceive: "You're—not—my—mother. NEVER forget that."

Day-Lewis, whose eyes are huge, dark and burning, plays the rage above all else. And as he speaks (in words that grow increasingly—although never perfectly—clear) you can see that each contortion of his mouth is a spasm produced in anger. Longing for physical love and companionship, Day-Lewis' Brown is incessantly wracked by what Christy called, "My own isolation, even in the midst of people."

"My Left Foot" takes its tone from Christy's isolation and never brings him too close to us—it respects his private hell. But it's funny and exhilarating in spots, especially when the incorrigible Brown puts the moves on a nurse (Ruth McCabe) looking after him before a benefit. (The movie is told in flashbacks as the nurse peruses the book "My Left Foot.")

Sheridan and his co-writer, Shane Connaughton, don't spend much time with Brown's painting or writing—signposts to his inner world. But Day-Lewis' performance reaches out to us, a signal through the flames. He makes us ponder the miracle of communication—and of acting.

NEWSDAY, 11/10/89, Part III/p. 7, Mike McGrady

"My Left Foot," the film biography of Irish author Christy Brown, was noted here during its recent New York Film Festival debut as one of the most wrenching movies in years. It's one of those films ("The Elephant Man" and "The Mask" come to mind as others) that make it difficult at times to look at the screen. However, the rewards of doing so far outweigh any momentary discomforts.

What makes the film grim (in a strangely joyous way) is the fact that Christy Brown is condemned to wage a lifelong war against crippling cerebral palsy, unable through much of his life to make himself understood or to move beyond a crawl.

And what makes the movie joyous (in a strangely grim way) is the fact that Christy Brown was able to overcome these unimaginable disabilities and communicate with the world using only the toes of his left foot. Despite the glaring limitations, Brown managed to author a series of well regarded books and even established himself as something of a watercolorist.

What makes all this work, both the grimness and the joyousness, is a performance by Daniel Day-Lewis that is close to miraculous. Day-Lewis is not just credible, he's out-and-out inspiring as the man who, though barely able to speak a word or climb a stair, is able to swear with wit and power, drink, proposition a nurse, launch a barroom brawl and, in time, win the heart of his lady love. He is seen as a man who loved life too much not to live in.

Added bonuses: Ray McAnally, in his last role, plays Christy's loud-mouthed blustering father with strength and humanity. Irish actress Brenda Fricker as his mother is both a tower of maternal strength and the voice of reason. The fact that there is no let-up, no false notes, reflects most favorably on first-time director Jim Sheridan.

NEWSWEEK, 11/27/89, p. 90, David Ansen

There are usually good reasons to shy away from movies about disabled heroes triumphing over adversity: aside from their sentimentality, they usually turn their protagonists into bland receptacles for the audience's pity. My Left Foot, about the Irish writer and painter Christy Brown, a victim of cerebral palsy, takes this potentially maudlin genre and gives it a swift, rude kick in the pants. Director Jim Sheridan, his co-writer, Shane Connaughton, and a remarkable cast led by Daniel Day-Lewis aren't interested in softening up the audience with old clichés. They've honed in on a very particular man: a nervy, naughty, brilliantly prickly character who, written off as a moron as a child and trapped in a twisted body with a spastic life of its own, clawed his way out of a childhood of poverty into a career as a man of letters, demanding the same earthly pleasures that any man might.

Played as a boy by the terrific Hugh O'Conor, and from age 17 on by Day-Lewis, Brown is presented with all his messy contradictions intact. Angry, lustful, witty, a boozer who lashes out vindictively when his romantic dreams are dashed, he's a Rabelaisian figure encased in a body fit for an ascetic. We see how, with only his left foot under his control, he learns first ot write the alphabet, convincing the world that he's not mentally defective, and then goes on to conquer painting and literature. But these breakthrough moments are not what the film emphasizes: his handicap is the subject only insofar as it forms his ferociously courageous character.

"My Left Foot" takes its swift, blunt tempo from Brown himself, an acerbic spirit quick to banish notions of self-pity. Sheridan coaxes from his entire cast performances of bracing freshness. Brenda Fricker as the stalwart mother whom Brown adores shows us a strong, good woman without a trace of stickiness. As her bricklayer husband, the late Ray McAnally lets us see under the bluster of this patriarch who sired 22 children (only 13 survived). Fiona Shaw is crisply radiant as the doctor whom Brown falls in love with. (For a harrowing emotional experience, it's hard to top the scene in a restaurant when he discovers she's going to marry another man, and publicly acts out his rage.) But it's the sly, greedy-for-life performance of Day-Lewis that anchors "My Left Foot" indelibly in our memories. There's more than great technique on display here: you feel you've been taken inside Christy Brown's proud, biting, embattled soul.

TIME, 11/6/89, p. 84, Richard Corliss

The Irish will put up a good fight, even when they're shadowboxing. So Christy Brown had a head start in his battle against petrifying cerebral palsy. There were other crippling odds to buck. He was the tenth of 22 children born to a sod-poor Dublin bricklayer. For the first nine years of Christy's life, his siblings tended him as they would a houseplant: feed it, water it and keep it out of the way. Only his mother dared nurture him with her fierce, uncompromising love, and one day Christy stuck a piece of chalk in his left foot and made his mark on the floor: MOTHER.

My Left Foot, Brown's autobiography about his hard-won emergence as a painter and author, could be meat for good drama or the sap in a TV-movie treacle pudding. This Irish film is mostly meat. Knowing that the audience will embrace Christy, the filmmakers are free to make him as stubborn as he is courageous. For Christy everything begins with will: the will to be understood, to do well things he would not be thought able to do at all and, later, to be loved by the pretty doctor who would only admire and inspire him.

At the end the picture goes soft—say, from the rigorous humanism of *The Elephant Man* to the emotional sops of *Life Goes On*. But that is no crucial flaw in what is at heart a love story written in pain. As Christy's parents, Brenda Fricker and Ray McAnally are flinty, unrouged, splendid. And Daniel Day-Lewis' triumph is nearly as spectacular as Christy's: to reveal the blind fury in his eyes and stunted gestures, to play him with a streak of fierce, black-Irish humor. Brilliantly, Day-Lewis shows a mind, and then a man, exploding from the slag heap of Christy's body.

VILLAGE VOICE, 11/14/89, p. 113, Georgia Brown

Another ferocious performer [the reference is to Kenneth Branagh in Henry V] is Daniel Day-Lewis in *My Left Foot*, Jim Sheridan and Shane Connaughton's adaptation of Irish writer Christy Brown's life story. The working title for his autobiography, jokes Christy in the movie, was "Reminiscences of a Mental Defective." Born with cerebral palsy, he was treated as a "vegetable" and a "poor, unfortunate half-wit" until the day he took a piece of chalk between his toes and wrote the word *mother* on the floor.

I wouldn't want to steer anyone away from a movie containing a scene (the one in the restaurant) that Pauline Kael says "may be the most emotionally wrenching scene I've ever experienced in the movies," but I was more *interested* in Day-Lewis's performance as the physically twisted, rage-choked, affection-starved Christy than I was emotionally caught up. Different *gouts*, I guess. The childhood section of the narrative, where Christy is played (fiercely, too) by Hugh O'Conor, affected me more than the adult one, in part because I was less distracted by performance.

Christy's father (Ray McAnally) is a Dublin bricklayer who spends his money in the pub and Mrs. Brown (Brenda Fricker) is a gentle, courageous breeder. In real life she gave birth 22 times although only 13 children survived. Here she is depicted as an exceptionally nurturing, ruddy-cheeked mother despite the family's grinding poverty; you're allowed the sense that she was able to devote herself to her 10th, Christy, who has his place on the floor under the stairs and a crude wooden barrow to be wheeled around in. (Other family babies poke in and out occasionally.)

A late coming-into-language is always moving. The boy Christy, mouth excruciatingly locked and black eyes flashing, looks like he's bursting with words. All he can manage is animal-like grunts. Until he ekes out that first word, only his mother credits him with intelligence or sensitivity. When he's 19 (played now by Day-Lewis), a specialist (Fiona Shaw) begins training his speech and coordination. Ever lovesick, he falls for the doctor and is devastated when she tells him she's getting married.

Locked into a spastic, drooling, largely helpless body, he continues to fight against pity an avoidance. Day-Lewis's incarnation indicates that Christy Brown was wickedly funny and lusty— a typically and untypically tormented Irishman. The movie ends with his courtship of Mary (Ruth McCabe), a spunky, no-nonsense woman assigned to look after him, whom he married. (Brown had success as a novelist and died, choking on dinner, in 1981 at age 49.)

Crisp and clean as Sheridan's (first-time) direction is, the screenplay turns the life into a series of highlights and lowlights: how Christy summons help for his mother who's collapsed; how Christy the goalie makes a save with his chin; how Christy rescues the family from the cold. As a realistic fiction, this needs more of the mundane—such as the scene showing the brothers sleeping in the same bed, heads to feet. A highly unusual life becomes too much of a traditionally inspirational story. I can't help being reminded of what the Taviani brothers, in *Padre Padrone*, wrought from similar special material.

Also reviewed in:
NEW REPUBLIC, 11/27/89, p. 24, Stanley Kauffmann
NEW YORK TIMES, 11/10/89, p. C10, Vincent Canby
NEW YORKER, 10/2/89, p. 98, Pauline Kael
VARIETY, 8/23–29/89, p. 31
WASHINGTON POST, 12/20/89, p. B1 Hal Hinson
WASHINGTON POST, 12/22/89, Weekend/p. 51, Desson Howe

MYSTERY TRAIN

An Orion Classics release of a JVC presentation of an MTI production. *Executive Producer:* Kunijiro Hirata and Hideaki Suda. *Producer:* Jim Stark. *Director:* Jim Jarmusch. *Screenplay:* Jim Jarmusch. *Director of Photography:* Robby Müller. *Editor:* Melody London. *Music:* John Lurie. *Sound:* Drew Kunin and (music) Tom Lazarus. *Sound Editor:* Robert Hein. *Production Designer:* Dan Bishop. *Set Decorator:* Dianna Freas. *Special Effects:* Gary King. *Costumes:* Carol Wood. *Make-up:* Meredith Soupios. *Running time:* 110 minutes. *MPAA Rating:* Not Rated.

CAST: Masatoshi Nagase (Jun); Youki Kudoh (Mitzuko); Screamin Jay Hawkins (Night Clerk); Cinqué Lee (Bellboy); Nicoletta Braschi (Luisa); Elizabeth Bracco (DeeDee); Joe Strummer (Johnny); Rick Aviles (Will Robinson); Steve Buscemi (Charlie); Rufus Thomas (Man in Station); Jodie Markell (Sun Studio Guide); William Hoch, Pat Hoch, Joshua Elvis Hoch (Tourist Family); Reginald Freeman (Conductor); Beverly Prye (Streetwalker); Sy Richardson (Newsvendor); Tom Noonan (Man in Diner); Stephen Jones (The Ghost); Lowell Roberts (Lester); Sara Driver (Airport Clerk); Richard Boes (Second Man in Diner); Darryl Daniel (Waitress); Calvin Brown (Pedestrian); Jim Stark and Elan Yaari (Pall Bearers); Vondie Curtis-Hall (Ed); Royale Johnson (Earl); Winston Hoffman (Wilbur); Rockets Redglare (Liquor Store Clerk); Marvell Thomas (Pool Player 1, Dave); Charles Ponder (Pool Player 2); D'Army Bailey (Pool Player 3); Tom Waits (Radio D.J.).

CHRISTIAN SCIENCE MONITOR, 12/1/89, p. 11, David Sterritt

If the title of "Mystery Train" seems familiar, it's because that was also the title of a classic song by Elvis Presley back in the '50s, when he was still a down-home singer with a new-fangled rockabilly style. The spirit of Elvis runs through the "Mystery Train" movie just as it ran through that great old record. It's a quirky, surprising, funny, sad picture—and easily one of the 10 best films I've seen this year.

One of the unexpected things about "Mystery Train" is that it gives us three stories for the price of one. All take place on one night in Memphis, Tenn., where Elvis got his start. And all center on one seedy hotel, an incredibly run-down place where just about anyone might drop in (the ghost of Elvis appears at one point!) and the desk clerk is played by none other than Screamin' Jay Hawkins, another legendary rocker who has blazed a trail or two in his time.

The first part of the movie is about a teen-age couple from Japan, who've come all the way to Tennessee to see the famous Sun Records studio where Elvis made his first classic recordings. What's amusing and poignant here is how different Memphis turns out to be — how drab and unexotic — compared with what these travelers must have expected. Then again, they're not very exotic themselves: The young man's idea of self-expression is to operate his cigarette lighter with a flourish, and the woman spends a lot of her time trying to make her boyfriend crack an occasional smile. They're not exactly extroverted people. Yet the more we get to know them, the more we can't help liking them.

Part 2 is about another foreigner in Memphis: a strong and likable Italian woman, stopping over en route to her husband's funeral. She finds herself in the run-down hotel, sharing a room with a stranger who won't stop chattering about her boyfriend problems. The movie turns darker when that boyfriend is introduced in the third section; he's an Englishman living in Memphis, and he's about to get in serious trouble with the law. At the end, all three storylines come neatly and unexpectedly together in a finale that can only be called bittersweet.

"Mystery Train" has a quiet, slightly absurd mood that will give you a *deja vu* feeling if you've seen earlier movies that filmmaker Jim Jarmusch has directed: the brilliant "Stranger Than Paradise," the less dazzling "Down by Law," and "Permanent Vacation," his impressive debut film. They're all about outsiders, and the most recent ones anticipate "Mystery Train" by centering on rootless people traveling in threes, making strange and humorous odysseys across an American landscape.

"Mystery Train" is most similar to "Stranger Than Paradise" in atmosphere and tone, yet it carries Mr. Jarmusch into a bit of new territory. Unlike his last couple of pictures, it's photographed (by Robby Müller) in expressive color. There's a fairly explicit sex scene, opening up a highly emotional area that Jarmusch has never explored before. And there's a peculiar scene wherein the Japanese woman does everything she can to make her boyfriend smile, while the man keeps insisting he's happy even when he doesn't look it. A friend of mine suggests this is Jarmusch talking to his critics—saying that his *movies* are happy and funny even when they wear their straightest faces.

I think that's true, and that "Mystery Train" is as entertaining as it is offbeat. It's also inventive and imaginative enough to stand as one of the most original movie excursions in recent memory.

LOS ANGELES TIMES, 12/20/89, Calendar/p. 4, Michael Wilmington

The great American originals, from Poor Richard and his Almanack to Little Richard and "Tutti Frutti," often show a genius for mixing up the mundane with the spiritual, the everyday with the ecstatic. That's Jim Jarmusch's strategy in his beautiful new movie, "Mystery Train," one of the year's best. It's a jewel-like, minimalist film about a group of crisscrossing wanderers and outlaws on one lyrically strange day and night in Memphis—where haphazard-seeming events slowly merge into entrancingly complex figures and patterns.

Three times, in separate but interlocking tales, we pass through the same time period and streets, with characters who rarely meet but whose destinies intertwine like overdubbed tracks in a blues record. Always, in our triple voyage through the end of the night to dawn, we seem on the brink of a revelation, a peek at the inner workings of some incomprehensible machine. Perhaps it's a Swiss watch, ticking toward doom. Perhaps it's a mystery train tunneling through to Graceland with a weird cargo of coincidence, careless love and Memphis blues.

The movie's crossroads is the Arcade Hotel, a dingy, other-side-of-the-tracks establishment filled with gauche oil paintings of Elvis, manned by a huge, somnolent night clerk in an electric red suit (Screamin' Jay Hawkins) and his half-pint butt of a bellboy (Cinqué Lee, Spike's younger brother).

Through its doors pass in succession Mitzuko and Jun, a barely bilingual and feuding Japanese couple (Youki Kudoh and Masatoshi Nagase); a rich Italian widow, Luisa (Nicoletta Braschi) and a speed-rapping transplanted New Jerseyite, DeeDee (Lorraine Bracco), bunking together by chance; and three gassed fugitives, on the lam from a jam. The latter include Dee Dee's brother, Charlie (Steve Buscemi), her jilted boyfriend, Johnny (Joe Strummer), and their running buddy, Will (Rick Aviles).

None of these three roomfuls—down the hall from each other in rooms 27, 25 and 22—are aware of each other's presence, though they're linked by the same recurring moments: a radio rendition of Elvis' plaintive "Blue Moon," an early morning gunshot. But their stories, haunting in isolation, explode with new meanings when they're juxtaposed.

Graceland and the quasi-religious myth of Elvis are the touchstones of this "Train," which was partially inspired by Chaucer's "The Canterbury Tales"; Jarmusch shows us Memphis' own Chaucer Street to gently reinforce the point. But Jarmusch, like his great cinematic teachers, Nicholas Ray and Wim Wenders, is more a poet of isolation than of community. In "Mystery Train," as in his masterpiece, "Stranger Than Paradise," he's making melancholy comic riffs on Virginia Woolf's theme: "Disparate are we." Friendship and love both seem founded on illusion.

The joyless liaison of the Japanese couple—enthusiastic Mitzuko and grumpy Jun, who disagree about everything, including Elvis' superiority over Carl Perkins—is echoed in the mismatch of Dee Dee and Johnny. The three fugitive buddies are united only by desperation and false family bonds. And generous Luisa is tricked by everyone around her, from DeeDee to a glib news vendor (Sy Richardson) to the sleazy hustler (Tom Noonan) who tells her about Elvis' hitchhiking ghost and then tries to sell her the King's alleged comb.

All this might seem to imply a deeply misanthropic view, but Jarmusch doesn't glory in his characters' disunions. His comedy, painfully hip, is also full of compassion. Perhaps no one since Harold Pinter has been as effective at creating conversations between people basically talking to themselves, but just because Jarmusch shows so many missed connections doesn't mean he banishes the possibility. Even the movie's most catastrophic act, the one that makes outlaws of the three buddies, stems from a generous, though insanely exaggerated, impulse.

Its cruelest act happens so offhandedly many may miss it. Callous Jun explains that he's photographing the hotel fixtures because he only records what he knows he'll forget; immediately afterward, he snaps a shot of his radiant little girlfriend, who stares at him uncomprehendingly.

Together with cinematographer Robby Müller, shooting in color this time, Jarmusch makes sure we'll never forget Memphis. With his trademark sideways traveling car shots, he catches eerie blues hanging over distant housing projects or neon rhinestone patterns in dusky windows. John Lurie contributes a piercing Sun Studio-style guitar score and the cast makes a near-perfect ensemble. If anyone deserves to be singled out, it may be the effulgent Kudoh (star of the Japanese dark comedy "The Crazy Family") or night clerk Hawkins, for his great slow-burn comeback to a fast-food commercial for the vile-sounding "Jiffy Squid."

There's something sad and sweet, fragile and strong, about "Mystery Train," luminous as pearl, dark and deep as night. It shows us America through a kind of triple screen; it's hard to believe Jarmusch isn't at least subconsciously uniting his triple stylistic influences of Japanese and European cinema and American "outlaw" movies. And, like Norman Mailer, he is fascinated by the urban prototype of the "White Negro."

It's a comic poem of American alienation from someone who can hate its meanness, love its soul and laugh at it clownishness. Perhaps it's fitting that the movie's lodestar, Elvis, shows up only once, as a wraith or a dream: a gentle, polite, confused boy in a gold lamé suit, apologizing for being in the wrong place. Like everyone else in "Mystery Train" (rated R for sex, nudity and language), he's just a stranger there himself, passing through to God knows where, in a land where grace may be long gone.

MONTHLY FILM BULLETIN, 12/89, p. 372, Mark Nash

FAR FROM YOKOHAMA: Two Japanese tourists, Jun (a Carl Perkins fan) and Mitzuko (an Elvis Presley addict), arrive by train in Memphis, Tennessee, intending to visit Presley's home, Graceland. After trekking across the deserted town with their single suitcase, they check into the Arcade Hotel, with its night clerk resplendent in red suit and younger bellboy. There are Elvis portraits in every room, and Mitzuko plays with a scrapbook in which she is documenting Elvis' influence on Western art. Jun takes photos of the fixtures and gazes out the window; a train passes; they make love and argue. "Domino" is followed by "Blue Moon" on the radio. In the morning, packing to leave, they hear a gunshot; "This is America", says Jun, unsurprised. A GHOST: Luisa, waiting for a flight from Memphis back to Rome with her husband's coffin, wanders dazedly round town. In a diner, she is approached by a disturbed-looking man with a story: travelling to Memphis, he kept passing what seemed to be the same hitch-hiker; the latter turned out to be Elvis, who asked him to find a girl from Rome and give her his comb. The man asks ten dollars for the comb, and Luisa gives him another ten to go away. When she sees him waiting outside, she checks into the Arcade Hotel and offers to share her room with the distraught Dee Dee, who explains that she's leaving town after breaking up with her English boyfriend and without saying goodbye to her brother Charlie. They go to sleep as "Blue Moon" plays on the radio; in the middle of the night, Luisa wakes to see Elvis' ghost, which vanishes when she wakes Dee Dee. As they leave in the morning, they hear a shot; "A 35", says Luisa matter-of-factly. LOST IN SPACE: In a bar, Johnny (called "Elvis" because of his quiff and sideburns) is complaining to his friend Ed about losing his job and his girlfriend walking out on him. When he starts brandishing a gun, Ed calls Johnny's friend Will who summons his girlfriend's brother Charlie. In a liquor store, an argument leads to Johnny shooting the owner; he and Charlie drive drunkenly around town (a train passes over the bridge; "Blue Moon" plays on the radio) before checking into the Arcade Hotel. In the morning, Charlie prevents Johnny from committing suicide but is himself shot in the leg; Johnny and Will put him in their truck then leave to avoid the police. At the airport, Luisa runs to catch her flight, while Mitzuko and Jun leave Memphis by train, in the same carriage as Dee Dee.

With its three interconnected episodes, *Mystery Train* has the structure of an elegant puzzle. A few characters in the different stories are related to one another (e.g., Dee Dee in *A Ghost* and Johnny in *Lost in Space*) and they all end up in the Arcade Hotel on the same night without realising it. It only gradually becomes apparent that the episodes are connected, and that the second story is taking place at the same time as the first. There are overlaps of incidents between all three (the same tunes on the radio; the bored actions of the bellboy and the night clerk; the gunshot which terminates each episode), while we are teased into working out, or supposing, other connections for ourselves (is that the same train we saw in the previous episode?).

It's impossible to say that the characters' drives and desires motivate the film. Rather, as one would expect from Jarmusch, his narrative is carefully de-dramatised. Incidents unroll at a leisurely, quasi-realist pace: for instance, Lisa's encounter with the newsvendor, who sells her a dozen or so magazines which she then carries around but doesn't read (she already has a novel, *Orlando Furioso*). They say a little about her—she appreciates a good sell—and they become the source of further incidents or gags (examined by others in a restaurant, dropped in the hotel foyer, given away). Character is played down and objects almost come to take its place: the cumbersome suitcase that Jun and Mitzuko carry around, the Elvis comb in the second episode, the gun in the third.

By creating stories which happen simultaneously, Jarmusch reinforces the sense from his earlier films of characters blocked, trapped, or just standing still. There is no analysis of U.S. society, just a presentation: these people, this night, Memphis, as existential at Sartre's *Nausea*. *Mystery Train* is a film about time in several senses: the repetitions of the stories and the differing personal experiences of time. The two foreigners, Jun and Mitzuko, wait becalmed in "a different time zone"; the two white American characters seem jumpy and nervous to no purpose; the background to the stories, the night-town of Memphis, is static, enduring (it is also the world of a black underclass), which the film reinforces with references to Edward Hopper. Deserted streets and decaying buildings; shabby hotel rooms with neon flashing outside: Robby Müller's superb photography at times approximates Hopper's faded Technicolor palette.

The film is dominated by the ghost of Elvis Presley: his portrait, his ghost in the hotel room, Johnny's nickname, his music on the radio. But this is not a referential film. It doesn't enshrine Elvis—the paintings are shabby, the Japanese tourists appear not to visit Graceland, the ghost ends up in the wrong room. Elvis' presence serves in a way to heighten the film's other non-references. Screamin's Jay Hawkins and Joe Strummer are there not as musicians but as actors. Hawkins, as the night clerk, is impressive; Strummer, still the rock star refusing to act, is somewhat embarrassing and given some laughable lines to deliver: "It's not our fault we're white", vintage Rock Against Racism, sticks out. The non-referentiality perhaps points to what Jarmusch feels is an absence of history—or what is usually termed postmodernism: Memphis has no past, only the present of representations.

Mystery Train feels like Jarmusch's earliest New York experimental work, with a Warholian emphasis on duration and the everyday: anti-narrative, anti-action, anti-psychology, anti-cinematic in a sense, where the pleasure lies in appreciating difference within a repetitive structure. Unlike, say, the emptiness of Antonioni, which says something about (usually) Italian character and society, the emptiness of a Jarmusch film seems arbitrary and throwaway. Perhaps this reflects the lack of a political vocabulary; the lack of a desire to say anything "significant" (the opposite, for instance, of Spike Lee, whose brother Cinqué appears here as the bellboy). Or maybe the mix of avant-garde and mainstream pleasures is too unstable to bear repeating too often.

NEW STATESMAN & SOCIETY, 12/15/89, p. 48, Suzanne Moore

Jim Jarmusch makes modern-day ghost stories. His ghosts are not the headless ghouls of tradition, but the ghosts that all of us glimpse from time to time—those fleeting visions of other times, other places, other cultures that connect us both to the past and to each other. Yet Jarmusch is still regarded as an ultra-hip minimalist whose earlier *Stranger than Paradise* and *Down by Law* were stylish black-and-white explorations of alienation.

With his stranger's eye and quirky observation of what it means to be a "foreigner",

Jarmusch's films have found cult audiences everywhere, though he remains one of the few American directors not tempted into the mainstream. *Mystery Train* is financed with Japanese money and the first story in the three tales he relates centres on a pair of Japanese teenagers. The director denies that there was any pressure from his producers but it doesn't matter anyway as "Far from Yokohama" is the finest of the three episodes.

The three stories are woven together by their location—a seedy hotel in Memphis run by the magnificent Screamin' Jay Hawkins (sic). But soon other links become apparent as we realise that three stories take place simultaneously. The innocent Japanese couple have come to Memphis on a rock'n'roll pilgrimage to see Graceland and the Sun Studios. The same afternoon, but in the next story, Luisa arrives in town, awaiting a flight to take her husband's body back to Rome. She ends up in the same hotel, sharing a room with Dee Dee who has just left her boyfriend. He, meanwhile, has got drunk and shot a liquor store owner, and is also lying low in the hotel.

With his usual cool, Jarmusch creates these parallel universes and lets us make the connections—the ever present Elvis, the sound of a gun going off, the DJ on the radio, the noise of love-making. This is film-making of immense complexity that shatters the usual linear narrative into little pieces, all of which reflect something different, and yet Jarmusch still manages the laid-back, effortless feel he is renowned for, aided by Robby Müller's cinematography which gives Memphis an ultra-violet glow.

Unlike so many of his contemporaries whose characters talk constantly, Jarmusch writes scripts about what people don't say or can't say.

In *Mystery Train* these gaps, or absences, are where ghosts from other stories congregate, where we begin to remember things long forgotten, where the story becomes genuinely haunting.

NEW YORK, 11/20/89, p. 120, David Denby

Jim Jarmusch's highly praised new comedy, *Mystery Train*, is not a movie to see after a poor night's sleep. Yes, I know that Jarmusch's drawling pace is integral to his style—in *Stranger Than Paradise* and *Down by Law* he created some nifty comic effects with it. Jarmusch is a master of nagging noncommunication: A girl in this new film who prattles nonstop stands out hilariously, a sea gull among dead fish. The funk that envelops Jarmusch's characters has an eccentric richness, like the sour-mash fumes thickening the corner of a neighbourhood bar.

So one can't dismiss his use of sullenness and dumbstruck attenuation as a mere minimalist trick. Nor does one wish for this hero of the independent cinema to acquire the conventional slick skills of a hack Hollywood operator. Still, a director who depends on people talking past one another can never develop much momentum. In *Mystery Train*, Jarmusch comes close to crawling in place.

Mystery Train is set in Memphis, where rockers like Elvis and Jerry Lee Lewis synthesized elements out of the blues and country and western more than 30 years ago. Such settings as a shabby old hotel and bar and the Sun Records recording studio, where Elvis and others made their early hits, are the very places where legendary blues and rock artists once walked. There's nothing obvious or overinsistent in the movie's atmosphere: Robby Müller's daylight cinematography is clear-textured, with a steady or gently moving frame; the night scenes have Müller's wonderful luminosity—everything seems to glow, even the streets. Just by being photographed in this way, the dilapidation is turned into poetry. Neglected and scarred, the heroic old places have become, once again, the spiritual home of the blues.

There are echoes of the fifties on the radio, and Elvis, like the Holy Ghost, is everywhere, hovering, always hovering. Screamin' Jay Hawkins, an authentic wild man from early rock days, appears as a night clerk at the seedy Arcade Hotel, where a good part of the movie is set. A large, florid swell with jet-black hair and a red suit, he sits in nearly complete silence through the early hours, accompanied by a tiny sidekick (Cinqué Lee, Spike's brother) in chimpanzee-bellboy attire. We never find out why a broken-down old hotel needs a bellhop, but these two, a noiseless Mutt-and-Jeff comedy act, are the glue holding Jarmusch's three sets of characters in place.

Although the three stories take place at the same time and all end up at the hotel, Jarmusch tells them one after another—end to end—rather than intercutting them. In the first episode, two Japanese tourists show up in Memphis. Mitzuko (Youki Kudoh), a breathless little rag doll with wax lipstick, is thrilled by any scrap of Elvisiana. She's an idolater, but her boyfriend, Jun (Masatoshi Nagase), impassive and disconnected, has pretensions to cool. They drag themselves around, light cigarettes, debate whether they should go to Graceland or Sun Records; they visit both, but they don't actually see anything in Memphis, which turns out to be a blank for mere tourists. The episode is amusing, but it feels, almost fatally, like a lazily satirical theater sketch. It's thin and overcontrolled. One can almost hear the dead air in an Off-Off Broadway room and the giggles of the knowing.

The second story is an extended joke about contrasting types—a young Italian, Luisa (Nicoletta Braschi), whose husband has died and who is waiting to return to Rome, and a talkative American woman, DeeDee (Elizabeth Bracco), running away from her boyfriend. Luisa, set upon by con artists, is another of Jarmusch's Europeans wandering amid the cultural detritus of America. In the third story—the most developed and the funniest—a morose Brit, Johnny (Joe Strummer), whom the local blacks call Elvis, loses his job and his girlfriend (DeeDee, from the previous episode) in a single day. With DeeDee's anxious brother (the comic Steve Buscemi) and a black friend (Rick Aviles) in tow, Johnny stumbles into a liquor store and shoots a clerk who makes a racist remark. Dead drunk, the three finally collapse at the hotel.

This segment has the contours of a classic absurdist fable. Johnny shoots a man for no real reason, and there's not much beyond inertia holding the three men together—the other two get caught up in the nightmare without much liking Johnny. Strummer (formerly of the Clash) makes Johnny appallingly stupid, and the pasty-faced Buscemi is painfully funny as the sap who realizes that his whole life has been changed just by his tagging along.

By telling the stories the way he does, Jarmusch takes editing back before D. W. Griffith, who developed the technique of simultaneous narrative, which subsequently became one of the principal definitions of the cinema. Yet it's amazing how little in the way of aesthetic shock Jarmusch's daring produces. He plays mild, teasing games with our expectations. In each of the first two stories we hear pistol shots, but only in the third do we find out who fired the shots and why. Jun and Mitzuko make love in the first story; the sounds of their lovemaking come through the wall in the second story, 45 minutes later. And so on. At the end, as a train pulls out of town, the three sets of characters pass one another, heading off in different directions. They are all lost, floating among the driftwood and candy wrappers. Yet they are too small—skiffs passing in the night—for any of these connections to matter except at the level of whimsy.

Jarmusch is trying to bring rhythm and something like closure to material that's essentially rambling and anecdotal—a pseudo-solution to the problem of weak narrative. It's odd, too, that he makes such a fuss over Elvis, since the orgiastic spirit that Elvis unleashed in the mid-fifties seems utterly foreign to Jarmusch's temperament. *Mystery Train* is a blues movie without the suffering and pleasure that make the blues emotionally overwhelming. Seeing it, one feels Jarmusch has pushed hipsterism and cool about as far as they can go, and that isn't nearly far enough.

NEW YORK POST, 9/29/89, p. 25, David Edelstein

Set in Memphis, Jim Jarmusch's insubstantial new comedy "Mystery Train" consists of three vaguely interlocking stories. The key word is "vaguely," for Jarmusch is loathe to tie things up in a neat package.

The characters inhabit the same crumbing downtown hotel (presided over by a riotously sober Screamin Jay Hawkins and Spike Lee's charming brother Cinqué), breathe the same air and listen to the same Elvis Presley songs on the radio, but Jarmusch seems to take pride in the fact that their paths never cross and their stories remain open-ended.

He should. Although "Mystery Train" is the least formally satisfying of his three features (I'm not counting the thing he did before "Stranger Than Paradise," "Meeting with Remarkably Bad Actors" or whatever it was called), it's a daring attempt to break out of his straitjacket of cool. The steps are tiny (as are all of Jarmusch's steps), but they're important. The deadpan breathes.

In the first segment, two Japanese tourists, the ultra-cool (Masatoshi Nagase) and sprightly Mitzuko (Youki Kudoh) explore the drab environs—including Sun Studios and Graceland—make love with a portrait of Elvis staring on and head for New Orleans.

In the next, a sad Italian widow (Nicoletta Braschi) ends up spending the night in the hotel with a garrulous, impoverished woman (Elizabeth Bracco) fleeing her hot-tempered boyfriend. In the third, that boyfriend (Joe Strummer), drunk, shoots a racist liquor-store manager and high-tails it to Memphis with his buddies (Rick Aviles and Steve Buscemi).

Brilliantly shot (in color) by Robby Müller, the movie's images come back to haunt you. The joke seems to be that everyone who visits Memphis gets spooked — Elvis and the ghosts of other dead musicians penetrate people's consciousness. Beyond that, the meanings are anyone's guess, but this minimalist triptych is like Jarmusch's "The Love Boat" — it's suggestive even when you're not quite sure what it's suggesting.

NEW YORK POST, 11/17/89, p. 29, Jami Bernard

If there is any American film maker as consistently hip as Jim Jarmusch, he has yet to be found. Jarmusch now turns his sights on Memphis, and just as he did in previous movies ("Down by Law," "Stranger Than Paradise"), defines and refines his slice of retro-cool Americana through the eyes of visitors.

In this case, he does it with three separate, concurrent vignettes about foreigners who, in the course of an overnight at a seedy hotel, are touched by the ghost-of-Elvis aura that hangs over the depressed landscape like overripe fruit ready to drop.

In the first vignette, two Japanese tourists (Masatoshi Nagase and Youki Kudoh) come to the birthplace of Elvis to absorb the atmosphere and see Graceland and Sun Studios, where the great musicians once recorded. As alien to the landscape of his downtrodden Memphis as Elvis would be in Tokyo, they nonetheless seem to soak up and thrive on the hallowed atmosphere.

They spend the night at the Arcade Hotel, where each room is adorned with a cheesy portrait of The King.

The second story involves an Italian woman who, while waiting to accompany her husband's casket back home on the next day's plane, shares a room at the Arcade with a chatty-cathy on the run who is strapped for cash. The Italian, Luisa (Nicoletta Braschi), has already been approached in a diner by a strange man who claims to have waited many years to deliver unto her Elvis' pocket comb. Luisa has had it to here with Elvis stories, yet she has an epiphanal experience in her hotel room.

The third story involves three pals who drive and drink the night away after one of them (Joe Strummer), depressed at losing his job and his girl and annoyed that everyone calls him Elvis because of his pompadoured 'do, shoots a liquor store owner. The three sack out at the Arcade.

Certain moments in the course of the three stories overlap with one another, providing a loose sort of continuity—the idle chitchat of the hotel's night clerk (a funny, restrained Screamin' Jay Hawkins) and the bellhop (Cinqué Lee, Spike's younger brother); the sounds of a late-night DJ (the voice of Tom Waits); a couple making love; an early-morning gunshot.

But don't expect a neat bundle of reunited couples and "Big Business"-type group revelations and a big finish with brass bands. Jarmusch's sly, mild, meandering structure superimposes one vignette atop another, like the layers of a dream whose symbols can align or stand alone as they wish.

The movie is full of Jarmuschisms. The Japanese tourists' red suitcase is laden with T-shirts and trinkets, as if they had planned to barter their way through Memphis. The three men on the lam from the liquor store incident argue over whether "Lost in Space" was a good TV series or not. A street is named Chaucer Street, as if this were a modern Canterbury trilogy about pilgrims penetrating the heart of America.

While funny and quirky, "Mystery Train" lacks the unfettered joy of "Down by Law" but seems to show more concentration on the part of the film maker. The film is dedicated to Sara, who is Sara Driver, Jarmusch's main squeeze and a film maker in her own right; she has a small part as an airline clerk.

NEWSDAY, 11/17/89, Part III/p. 5, Terry Kelleher

This is Jim Jarmusch's first movie in color, and his first to co-star the ghost of Elvis Presley. But don't get the idea he's out to make a big commercial splash and land on the cover of People.

"Mystery Train," seen in late September at the New York Film Festival, has the whole package of Jarmusch idiosyncrasies: long takes, long silences, fractured English, seedy locations, a cast of characters going nowhere slowly, a soundtrack that's got the blues. There are more people here than in "Stranger Than Paradise" or "Down by Law." That doesn't mean there's more action.

Jarmusch describes "Mystery Train" as a "minimalist 'Canterbury Tales.'" The movie tells three stories, all taking place on the same day and involving guests at a Memphis hotel notably short on amenities, unless your idea of an amenity is a portrait of Elvis in every room.

Tale 1 features a young Japanese couple (Masatoshi Nagase and Youki Kudoh) who check into the Arcade after a somewhat disappointing day of rock-and-roll sightseeing. In Tale 2, Nicoletta

Braschi (from "Down by Law") plays a just-widowed Italian stranded in Memphis by plane trouble while trying to transport her late husband's body back to Rome. She shares a room at the Arcade with a garrulous New Jersey native (Elizabeth Bracco) who's leaving her boyfriend, a "crazy" Briton nicknamed "Elvis" for his hairdo and sneer. In Tale No. 3, "Elvis" (Joe Strummer) gets his girlfriend's brother (Steve Buscemi) and another man (Rick Aviles) mixed up in a drunken spree that leads to a liquor-store robbery. The three fugitives lie low at the Arcade, where the desk clerk (Screamin' Jay Hawkins) and bellhop (Cinqué Lee) uphold the night-shift standard of benign neglect.

The first two stories end with the sound of a gunshot; the third reveals who fired and why. But the movie's sense of mystery comes from atmosphere, not plot. Once again, Jarmusch's camera follows strangers in a strange land—or, rather, a land that seems strange when seen through the stranger's eyes. The presence of foreigners permits the film maker to enjoy a favorite pastime: playing with language and cultural differences. You hear a burst of Japanese and the subtitle reads, "Yeah, but Elvis is still the King." If you find something intrinsically funny in this, you're on the Jarmusch wavelength.

"Mystery Train" offers a couple of guaranteed laughs (the Japanese couple gets a bewildering tour of Sun Studios; the spirit of Elvis converses ever so politely with the Italian widow), but the humor is mostly the sort that brings a chuckle after a moment's consideration. Maybe the boring stretches make Jarmusch's admirers more grateful for the jokes. Whatever he's up to, it's still working.

NEWSWEEK, 12/4/89, p. 78, David Ansen

Jim Jarmusch's *Mystery Train* is as minimal and underground as Zemeckis's sequel, *Back to the Future Part II*, is overstuffed and mainstream. But in his own offbeat way, Jarmusch seems in danger of becoming as formulaic as the most commercial Hollywood director. From "Stranger Than Paradise" to "Down By Law" to his latest ode to marginal Americana, Jarmusch has been mining the same esthetic turf, with diminishing returns.

Once again we're given a droll, deadpan view of America—here Memphis, home of the King, Elvis Presley—as refracted through foreign eyes. "Mystery Train" tells three stories in order, but each is happening simultaneously. In the first, a pair of teenage Japanese lovers make a pilgrimage to Sun Studios and check into the seedy Arcade Hotel for the night. In the second, an Italian widow spends the night at the same hotel with a young chatterbox who's just left her boyfriend. In the third, the boyfriend, a surly Brit nicknamed Elvis, commits a murder and holes up at the Arcade with his two buddies. Though the stories barely overlap, there are suggestive links between the tales, like the gunshot, heard in the first two stories, that gets explained at the third. This novel structure is the movie's most intriguing device, and Jarmusch continues to have a great eye for moody lowlife settings. But his minimalist dramaturgy, so resonant in "Stranger Than Paradise," just doesn't give you enough to chew on. His iconoclasm is beginning to look like complacency. It's time this talented filmmaker put more matter in his mannerism.

SIGHT & SOUND, Winter 1989/90, p. 64, John Pym

The two Japanese tourists get down from their train at the start of Jim Jarmusch's new film like self-confident African explorers. They carry a red suitcase on a bamboo pole between them, and the girl, Mitzuko (Youki Kudoh), totes a child's leopard rucksack containing that modern first-aid kit a Walkman and two headsets. They have come from modern Yokohama to flyblown Memphis, Tennessee, to see for themselves the shrines of Graceland and Sun Studios. They are quite without fear, being young; and he, Jun (Masatoshi Nagase), like a latter-day greenhorn gunslinger, is ready to take on all-comers with his quickdraw cigarette lighter.

The tone of this, the first of the three episodes of *Mystery Train*, is fresh and agreeably playful. Jun, forlorn and resolutely unimpressable, is the quintessence of teenage sophistication: in fact, he knows nothing—the train arrives in Memphis, by his reckoning, two days early—and is wholly dependent on his girlfriend. Mitzuko, on the other hand, is a bubble of enthusiasm, boldly practising her English on the bemused natives and refusing to let Jun's gloom infect her, at one point smooching his face with vivid lipstick in a vain attempt to make him smile.

They spend the night at the Arcade Hotel. The timid bellboy waits and waits for his tip. Mitzuko finally notices him and, rummaging through her treasure-laden suitcase, proudly presents him with some wampum, a Japanese plum. It sits on the reception desk until the by now thoroughly confused boy announces he's not going to eat it, whereupon his resplendent boss (Screamin' Jay

Hawkins) pops it into his mouth, with the air of a chameleon swallowing a particularly delicious fly.

What follows is less lively, though it goes down as easily as Mitzuko's plum. An Italian widow, Luisa (Nicoletta Braschi), is stranded in Memphis while waiting for a connecting flight to Rome where she is taking her husband's remains; she also spends the night at the Arcade, sharing a room with a talkative young woman, Dee Dee, who has just split up with her boyfriend. The joke here is that the Italian never mentions her problem. Luisa is visited by the spirit of Elvis (having earlier been duped by Memphis' standard "ghost of Elvis" tall story); at which point one begins to wonder if whimsy is not in danger of overwhelming the proceedings.

Both episodes end with a pistol shot. "It's America", Jun knowingly observes; "It's a .38," says Luisa, with what one imagines is more authority. The third episode, the longest and most laboured, reveals the cause of the shot. An Englishman, Johnny (Joe Strummer), the man with whom Dee Dee has broken up, a lager lout far from home, shoots the owner of a liquor store and then spends the night, with two nervous companions, holed up at the Arcade.

The weapon goes off a second time during a scuffle as Johnny melodramatically tries to blow his brains out. The three stories then come together, after a fashion, with the Japanese heading by train for New Orleans and the shrine of Fats Domino, Luisa running for her plane and the three low-lifes making what they take to be a getaway from the cops and in the process crossing beneath the tracks of the train. Moral: What do we know of the dramas occurring in the next room?

Mystery Train, evocatively photographed by the clear-eyed outsider Robby Müller, is occasionally touched with comic inspiration. The guide on Jun and Mitzuko's visit to the tiny Sun Studios, for instance, edges her party step by step along the wall as if she was an orchestra conductor. There are, too, some cherishable performances, notably by the deadpan Screamin' Jay Hawkins, with his fastidious insistence on the $22 room charge and his delicate emendations of the guest ledger. Like many fairground rides, however, one disembarks from this one with the slight feeling one might have had just a bit more for one's money.

VILLAGE VOICE, 11/21/89, p. 87, J. Hoberman

History may ultimately judge Jim Jarmusch to be the hipster's Frank Capra—a canny sentimentalist with an "aw-shucks" hammerlock on the national dreamlife—but there's a reason why he remains the hottest young filmmaker on the international circuit. While Spielberg and company produce hyperbolic simulations of Hollywood B-movies, Jarmusch reinvented the Bs' no-frills aesthetic. His minimalist vaudevilles (complete with dialect humor) are irreducibly, confidently American. They have the musical repetition and abstract vernacular of black-and-white sitcoms, '50s doo-wop, and pre-Vietnam comic strips.

Still, Jarmusch is not a simple celebrant of retro stylistics. His obsessive running gag is the representation of America through alien eyes. More and more, this seems to have been a particularly '80s trope, informing everything from the mega-hit *E.T.* and the indie triumph *Liquid Sky*, through the disposable comedy of *Splash*, its ideological cousin *Moscow on the Hudson*, and Eddie Murphy's *Coming to America*, to a subtitled sleeper like *Bagdad Café* and the eccentric post-Wenders excursion of *Mitteleuropa* wiseguys Péter Góthar, György Szomjas, and Aki Kaurismäki. It is as if that wondrous New Morning in America could only be confirmed from the uncritical, born-again perspective of a mermaid, Martian, or Hungarian immigrant.

Mystery Train—the new Jarmusch, shown to great acclaim at the last New York Film Festival and opening theatrically at the Cinema Studio on Friday—goes down this road one more time. The movie consists of three successive, albeit simultaneous, stories, each set in Memphis and involving foreign protagonists (who inevitably wind up spending the night at the same sleazy fleabag, the Arcade Hotel). The credit sequence introduces the most endearing of these outlanders—a young Japanese couple, stolid Jun (Masatoshi Nagase) and perky Mitzuko (Youki Kuduh), as they Amtrak through Tennessee, Elvis singing the title song, and a succession of automobile graveyards whizzing past the window.

Celebrant of this sort of entropic Americanarama, Jarmusch is the postmod Walker Evans, a cartoon Robert Frank, for whom the whole roadside United States is a vast moldering museum. (Call it Desolation Row.) No less than the Cleveland of *Stranger Than Paradise* or the New Orleans of *Down By Law*, his Memphis is a stage set—empty, rundown, ineffably cool—through which Jun and Mitzuko wander, carrying their bright red suitcase peasant-style on a bamboo pole, as uncomprehending as they are appreciative of the native life forms they encounter. *Mystery Train*'s first third would make an apposite short subject on a bill with one of Nagisa Oshima's early '60s youth films, set as they are in a stridently Americanized Japan. Even so, Jun and Mitzuko represent something of the director's own point-of-view.

Although *Mystery Train* is his first movie with black speaking subjects, Jarmusch has long been recognized as an apostle of White Negroism. (Self-consciously hip as he is, how could it be otherwise?) In the Jarmusch cosmos, oldtimey Negroes—as opposed to militant blacks or self-defined African Americans—are the essential Americans. Jun and Mitzuko know that they've arrived when one thanks them in Japanese. The teenage immigrant in *Stranger Than Paradise* signaled her a priori love of America through her allegiance to Screamin' Jay Hawkins's "I Put a Spell on You," and Screamin' Jay himself turns up here as the Arcade's nightclerk. (Resplendent in crimson jacket and matching tie on black shirt, he's hilariously restrained—as proud and skittish as a tethered race horse.)

Always adept at characterizing his movies, Jarmusch has described *Mystery Train* as a minimalist *Canterbury Tales*, the stories of religious pilgrimages made to the shrine of Sun Studio. This is most explicit when Jun and Mitzuko gaze up at a statue of Elvis the way an earlier generation of Americans might have gawked at Michelangelo's Pietà; like the Greil Marcus book of the same title, *Mystery Train* is consecrated to the enigma of the greatest White Negro of them all. Thus, the movie provides a comic counterpoint to the mortician splendor of William Eggleston's sarcophagal Graceland studies. The Arcade offers no TV, but provides an icon of Elvis in every dank room.

Indeed, *Mystery Train* is the most ironically ethereal of posthumous Elvis movies—celebrating the deity whose "disappearing body," as Canadian "panic" theorists have it, is "a flashing event-horizon at the edge of the black hole that is America today." Mitzuko recognizes the face of Elvis on both the Buddha and the Statue of Liberty, and it is precisely because Luisa (Nicoletta Braschi), the Italian protagonist of the movie's central (and weakest) episode repeatedly misunderstands the Elvis references dogging her 12-hour Memphis layover that He reveals Himself to her in an appropriately ridiculous mystical vision.

Ultimately, the King is made physically manifest in the form of onetime punk idol Joe Strummer, here playing the pugnacious and pompadoured Englishman dubbed "Elvis" by his black buddies. In the course of the film's final episode, this pseudo-Presley demonstrates that he can be as feckless and violent as any real American. Embarking on a drunken spree, he shoots an unpleasant liquor store owner with the same sodden *esprit* his namesake might have used to plug a TV, dragging along two cronies (performance artist Steve Buscemi and former TV host Rick Aviles) on an absurd journey to the end of the night that, perhaps too loosely, knots the movie's separate narrative strands.

Easier to enjoy than champion, *Mystery Train* builds up enough momentum in its first half-hour to sustain the ride. *Stranger Than Paradise* was the near-seamless synthesis of a quarter-century of underground movies, and Jarmusch may never again achieve its swallowed-up perfection. *Down By Law*, a tactical retreat from this one-shot classicism, seemed a glossy gloss on the previous film. (Serving mainly to establish the director's commercial credentials, *Down By Law* narcissically reveled in its own capacity to embody a self-proclaimed "sad and beautiful world.") Now, having lowered expectations all around, Jarmusch returns with a more realistic display of his strengths and weaknesses: *Mystery Train* is never so slight that it lacks charm. Invention may flag, but not so much as to distract from the inspired comedy of its best moments or the clarity of its conception.

Like each of his films, *Mystery Train* is a confessional in which Jarmusch tells all that he knows about America. What's new about this installment is that the foreigners are tourists rather than immigrants. Their investment in this country is passionate but transitory, and, for that reason, *Mystery Train* seems the most melancholy of Jarmusch films—and perhaps the most self-reflexive. It's suggestive that it was bankrolled by JVC, the Japanese electronics giant that pioneered the VHS video format. First Columbia Pictures, then Radio City, Ronald Reagan, and now this. No wonder Jarmusch's worldview seems preserved in amber. Unlike his forebears, he may never go Hollywood or grapple with the echt-American dilemma of selling out; his innocence can remain intact, his "independence" has already been bought.

Also reviewed in:

NATION, 12/11/89, p. 726, Stuart Klawans
NEW REPUBLIC, 12/11/89, p. 24, Stanley Kauffmann
NEW YORK TIMES, 11/17/89, p. C16, Vincent Canby
VARIETY, 5/17-23/89, p. 33
WASHINGTON POST, 2/2/90, p. C1, Hal Hinson
WASHINGTON POST, 2/2/90, Weekend/p. 33, Desson Howe

NATIONAL LAMPOON'S CHRISTMAS VACATION

A Warner Bros. release of a Hughes Entertainment production. *Executive Producer:* Matty Simmons. *Producer:* John Hughes and Tom Jacobson. *Director:* Jeremiah S. Chechik. *Screenplay:* John Hughes. *Director of Photography:* Thomas Ackerman. *Editor:* Jerry Greenberg. *Music:* Angelo Badalamenti. *Production Designer:* Stephen Marsh. *Running time:* 97 minutes. *MPAA Rating: PG-13.*

CAST: Chevy Chase (Clark W. Griswold Jr.); Beverly D'Angelo (Ellen); Randy Quaid (Eddie); Diane Ladd (Nora); John Randolph (Clark Sr.); E.G. Marshall (Art); Doris Roberts (Francis); Julia Louis-Dreyfus (Margo Chester); Mae Questel (Aunt Bethany); William Hickey (Uncle Lewis); Brian Doyle Murray (Frank Shirley); Juliette Lewis (Audrey); Johnny Galecki (Rusty); Nicholas Guest (Todd Chester); Miriam Flynn (Catherine); Nicolette Scorsese (Mary); Ellen Hamilton Latzen (Ruby Sue); Cody Burger (Rocky).

LOS ANGELES TIMES, 12/1/89, Calendar/p. 9, Michael Wilmington

John Hughes, Hollywood's resident humorist of the terrors beneath suburbia's halcyon surfaces, has at them again in the sometimes funny, sometimes tasteless "National Lampoon's Christmas Vacation."

Hughes' typical all-American family of previous Vacations, the Griswolds—headed by Clark (Chevy Chase) and Ellen (Beverly D'Angelo)—have only to hunt for Christmas trees or settle down to dinner for something awful to happen. The Christmas turkey dries up. Thousands of house lights refuse to glow. The Christmas tree explodes and sets Grandpa (William Hickey) on fire.

Every ladder Clark climbs up collapses. Every yuletide decoration clunks him on the head. Hordes of relatives keep pouring through the door, a parade of undesirables that includes lushes, addle-brains and a matriarch (Mae Questel) who ties up her cat in Christmas packages and bumbles into the Pledge of Allegiance when called on to say Grace. Worst of all is the sudden arrival of Clark's belching bucko of a country cousin, indigent Eddie (Randy Quaid), who shows up in an RV with a full chemical toilet and plops himself and his family of four down for the duration, leering and handing over his gift list.

This hideous vision of a suburban Christmas gone totally amok is, typical of Hughes, encased in a sentimental overview—like a Norman Rockwell portrait with a punk rock backbeat, and spiders nibbling through the frame.

In Hughes' movies, the teen-agers are usually realists, even when they're romantics, and their parents are usually crazy—maybe because they'd rather be teen-agers. But, here, Chase's Clark is a mixture: a crazy romantic. There's such a fiery obsessiveness behind his desire, constantly thwarted, to construct the ideal Christmas that, in a way, he's like Terry O'Quinn's homicidal dad in the "Stepfather" movies. Hughes and director Jeremiah Chechik, must know this; they deliberately mix up horror movies and sentimental family comedies in their imagery.

Chevy Chase has not been on a roll lately, and to say that in "National Lampoon's Christmas Vacation" he's funnier than in his last six movies combined may sound like high praise, until you remember those six movies. "Caddyshack II" alone almost throws them into the "minus" laugh range. But here, he does what he does best: flat-out slapstick and subversive tear-downs of his own smooth image. This sweet, goofball, manic middle-class daddy brings out his sharpest reflexes and he gets good support from D'Angelo, the bulging-eyed slob-in-excelsis Quaid, and from Questel and Hickey as his dottiest relations.

Chechik, making his feature debut is a TV commercial-music video specialist; he's done the glitzy-romantic "Night belongs to Michelob" spots. And the incongruous elegance of his style—the grandiose frames, loaded with squeaky-clean suburban iconography—makes a good setting for Hughes' flatulent grotesques.

On the crass side there is some failed "Fish Called Wanda" style vicious animal slapstick, the usual loose multi-sketch Hughes construction and sophomoric badinage and so much bathroom-level humor that it's no surprise when the sewer blows sky high.

That's the oddest thing about Hughes' satiric slant on suburbia: his commingled desire to celebrate it and blow it up. Throughout the film, there's a suggestion that Clark wants desperately to be free of his family, like the childless swingers next door—which may be why those two are the most horrifically abused people in the entire movie. There's also a suggestion that, behind this modern, wired-up insanity, there's an ideal holiday gathering, which the characters are trying, and failing, to reach.

Hughes' demolitions of middleclass Midwestern suburbia have a weird schizoid intensity, as if he were fighting his way through to dreams he's rejected, while his satiric knife gets encrusted with chocolate globs. Sometimes sentimentality and sadism are reverse sides of the same coin—which may be why one scene of "Christmas Vacation" (MPAA rated PG-13, despite raw humor and innuendo) fuses imagery from "It's a Wonderful Life" and "The Texas Chain Saw Massacre" in a single visual gag. At the end, this cruel and foolish suburban Yule twists into a happy, sappy grin. It's a fusion of Rockwell and Capra with the age of mass murder and media overkill, but it's really too slick to be soft, too cool to be warm.

NEW YORK POST, 12/1/89, p. 25, David Edelstein

The biggest gut-buster in "National Lampoon's Christmas Vacation" involves a cat that gnaws too hard on a Christmas-lights wire and turns into Crisp-Fried Fur-Ball. Otherwise, the third instalment of this blah series is in pretty good taste—meaning pretty dull. Its inoffensiveness offended me.

In 1983, John Hughes had a neat idea—to take the kind of mild, shambling family comedy that he and other baby-boomers grew up with in the late '50s and early '60s (something like "Mr. Hobbs Takes a Vacation" with James Stewart) and give it a jolt of post-"Animal House," gross-out black humor.

"National Lampoon's Vacation" sent up those old films while playing on our nostalgia for them and the orderly, sitcom world they represented; it gave you the movie and the Mad Magazine parody of the movie simultaneously.

The joke is that Clark Griswold (Chevy Chase) wants to be the kind of dad who exists only on TV and in Norman Rockwell paintings—the kind of Superdad portrayed by Ronald Reagan for eight years. But unlike Reagan, the Griswolds lived in a world of poverty and crime and incest and kids already jaded by the time they reached kindergarten.

This time out, Clark resolves to give his wife and kids an old-fashioned family Christmas with a tree cut down from the forest and a pre-energy-crisis house that's covered with golden bulbs. He wants to sing carols and go sledding and have the grandparents in residence for the week. He plans to break ground on a pool with his Christmas bonus.

As you might predict, Clark screws up from the outset. He gets into a drag race with a couple of cretins in a pick-up on his way to find the perfect tree. He's oblivious when, in the frigid woods, his daughter's lips turn blue and her eyes milky. Installing his 2,500 strings of bulbs on the house, he wackily mishandles the ladder. And the boss (Brian Doyle Murray), ever mindful of his stockholders, has other ideas about this year's bonuses.

Clark is potentially a great character. He's so desperate to give his wife and kids a great *family* experience—to be the good provider and the all-American patriarch—that it ties him up in knots and makes everyone miserable. And his clumsiness could be a metaphor for his mixed motives.

For Clark, despite his touching idealism, is in many ways a monster. He doesn't care much about his wife—he has routine fantasies about big-breasted young women. And his kids roll their eyes and ask to be excused when he tries to get them to play along with his daddy schtick. It's his own ego that's on the line, not their happiness. (His last words, appropriately, are "I did it.")

But whatever subversive ideas there are in Hughes' script are muffled by his assembly line approach to gags. Chevy Chase, who used to be able to take a pretty good fall on live TV, needs an army of stunt men nowadays, and a runaway sled scene is just a jumble of rear-screen projections and shots of stunt men sailing through trees and sides of barns.

Watching Buster Keaton's "Our Hospitality" recently, I was reminded how exhilarating and poetic slapstick can be when it's unedited—when a performer functions as a kind of anti-ballerina, losing gracefully to the forces of gravity. Here the slapstick leaves no residue. There's nothing to think back on—no brilliantly staged bits or socko moments. There's one gag and then there's another and then you go home.

As usual, most of Hughes's best jokes are body-oriented. The grandparents show up and launch into discussions of their hemorrhoids or discolored moles. The country cousins led by Randy Quaid (who had the best scenes in the original "Vacation") bring a trailer-home with an overflowing toilet and some unidentified fungus on their toddler's upper lip.

Like last year's "Scrooged," "Christmas Vacation" is torn between being a tasteless hoot and a family Christmas movie with soaring carols and a wet, smiley finale. Clark assures his little niece that yes, there is a Santa Claus, and it's the same conversation you've heard a hundred times except the lass uses language that would make a quarterback blush.

You can't have it both ways, though, and I doubt much of anyone will be pleased. There's no reference to Jesus in this movie—presumably the Griswolds' Christmas vacation has nothing to do with religion. That would require some conviction, and conviction might jeopardize that big Christmas bonus.

NEWSDAY, 12/1/89, Part III/p. 5, Terry Kelleher

Right up front, "National Lampoon's Christmas Vacation" lets you know exactly what sort of holiday cheer is in store.

Look at the title. In fact, Clark Griswold (Chevy Chase) and his family are not off on another vacation trip. They're at home in their Chicago suburb, celebrating the holiday with a pack of visiting relatives. But the word "vacation" is necessary to alert moviegoers that this is a comedy in the profitable tradition of "National Lampoon's Vacation" (1983) and "National Lampoon's European Vacation" (1985).

Consider the animated credit sequence, in which a series of accidents befalls clumsy old St. Nick. It's the perfect warm-up for a movie that stays in the cartoon mode even after switching to live action. No matter how nasty the fall, collision or other mishap, Clark recovers instantly and miraculously. Wrecked repeatedly, his house somehow cleans and repairs itself between scenes.

Observe the Griswolds' first adventure. They're speeding along a country highway in search of the perfect Christmas tree, and Clark somehow gets the station wagon trapped between the wheels of a giant logging truck. Presumably, Clark is scared, but Chase looks *mock*-scared. His mug may say, "Oh, no," but there's "hee-hee" in his eyes. This is your signal that Chase isn't actually portraying the blundering, gullible family man. He's playing himself playing the character. Comedy once removed.

Study the surroundings when the Griswolds are out on the open road. Have they reached some mountainous part of the Midwest, hitherto unexplored? No, "National Lampoon's Christmas Vacation" was shot in Colorado. Try to ignore the topography and concentrate on Clark's Chicago Bears cap. Besides, Chicago's own John Hughes did the script, and everyone knows he's got a thing about setting movies in his hometown.

Hughes, who wrote "National Lampoon's Vacation" before turning out his trademark teen flicks of the mid-'80s, can be counted on to provide a few laughs even in his less distinguished efforts. "Christmas Vacation" has its goodies: the turkey that's more than a tad overcooked, the grandiose light display on the Griswold property that nearly causes an area-wide power outage.

But when Clark's aged aunt (Mae Questel) enters bearing gifts and Clark's wife (Beverly D'Angelo) says, "Oh, you shouldn't have," the old lady responds, "Did I break wind again?" And when a police SWAT team bursts into the Griswold home and the cop in charge orders everybody to "freeze," Mrs. Griswold keeps her hand right where it was—on Clark's crotch. These are the more typical moments, and the awesome responsibility for them must be shared by Hughes and first-time director Jeremiah Chechik.

Considering the material, the supporting cast is oversupplied with talent: John Randolph as Clark's father, E.G. Marshall as his father-in-law, William Hickey as a senile uncle, Randy Quaid as the gross country cousin (a reprise from the first film). Clark's kids are still called Audrey and Rusty, but they're now portrayed by Juliette Lewis and Johnny Galecki (succeeding Dana Hill and Jason Lively of "European Vacation" and Dana Barron and Anthony Michael Hall of "Vacation").

The funny thing is, Rusty's gotten younger and shorter in the past four years. Guess that's what happens when your dad's so immature.

Also reviewed in:

NEW YORK TIMES, 12/1/89, p. C12, Janet Maslin
VARIETY, 12/16/89, p. 32
WASHINGTON POST, 12/1/89, p. B1, Rita Kempley

NAVIGATOR, THE: AN ODYSSEY ACROSS TIME

A Circle Films release of an Arena Film presentation in association with the Film Investment Corporation of New Zealand. *Executive Producer:* Gary Hannam. *Producer:* John Maynard. *Director:* Vincent Ward. *Screenplay:* Vincent Ward, Kely Lyons, and Geoff Chapple. *Director of Photography:* Geoffrey Simpson. *Editor:* John Scott. *Music:* Davood A. Tabrizi. *Sound:* Dick Reade and (music) Richard Lush. *Sound Editor:* Liz Goldfinch. *Production Designer:* Sally Campbell. *Art Director:* Mike Becroft. *Special Effects:* Paul Nichola. *Costumes:* Glenys Jackson. *Make-up:* Marjory Hamlin. *Stunt Coordinator:* Timothy Lee. *Running time:* 92 minutes. *MPAA Rating:* PG.

CAST: Bruce Lyons (Connor); Chris Haywood (Arno); Hamish McFarlane (Griffin); Marshall Napier (Searle); Noel Appleby (Ulf); Paul Livingston (Martin); Sarah Pierse (Linnet); Mark Wheatley (Tog #1); Tony Herbert (Tog #2); Jessica Cardiff-Smith (Esme); Roy Wesney (Grandpa); Kathleen-Elizabeth Kelly (Grandma); Jay Saussey (Griffin's Girlfriend); Charles Walker (Old Chrissie); Desmond Kelly (Smithy); Bill Le Marquand (Tom); Jay Lavea Laga'aia (Jay); Norman Fairley (Submarine Captain); Alister Babbage (Grigor).

CHRISTIAN SCIENCE MONITOR, 7/21/89, p. 10, David Sterritt

"There's a myth in New Zealand that if you dig hard enough, you'll end up in England," says Vincent Ward, a young New Zealand filmmaker. Artists enjoy myths, and Mr. Ward decided to take this one literally—by concocting an offbeat fantasy called "The Navigator," which opened recently to good reviews in the United States.

"The Navigator" begins in a medieval English village that lives in fear of an approaching plague. A nine-year-old boy named Griffin has been haunted by dreams and visions involving a journey to some unknown city where a tribute to God will avert the impending disaster.

A small band of men sets out to find this mysterious city, starting their quest by traveling through a deep mine shaft. They emerge on the other side of the world—in New Zealand of 1988, some 700 years and 10,000 miles from home. Bewildered but unbowed, they travel through this bizarre new land in search of the right place to complete their task.

Ward sees both pathos and humor in the idea of people traveling through an unfamiliar land. In a Monitor interview at the Cannes Film Festival, where "The Navigator" aroused a good deal of international interest before its American première, he said it was partly inspired by a published account of visitors from New Guinea arriving in Australia and spending a long time figuring out how to get across a crowded highway.

But making fun of people was never part of Ward's plan. "I looked for things that would give [the story] a strange sort of truth," he says. "And always I looked for different sorts of relationships between the two periods that would give it a thematic spine. ...I was interested in the discrepancy between a naive [14th-century] view of the world, and what we know [today] interfacing with that." He also looked for "humorous, often ironic comparisons" between medieval and modern times, seeking ways in which "one period would comment on the other."

More specifically, Ward continues, "the film is also about faith. I don't really mean religious faith, although these people are...strongly religious. It's more how in terms of despair, a belief that you can control your own fate — and clinging on to that — is the only way you can finally *do* anything. If you don't have some belief or faith, and if you don't *act*, it's very difficult to change things."

Too many of today's films have "pessimistic, post-apocalyptic" attitudes, Ward says. "There's a feeling that technology...speeds up to such a pace that it's hard for human beings to keep abreast of it. Yet it's *not* impossible to change things."

Ward spent more than two years preparing the screenplay of "The Navigator," collaborating with several writers along the way. "It took a lot of time to bring such an odd idea into the shape I wanted it to have," he recalls. "I also did massive visual research, even to the extent of sending people up copper mines [in Cumbria, England] that people hadn't gone into for maybe 100 years."

The richly colorful style of "The Navigator" grew from Ward's artistic background. "I've worked [in cinema] as an art director," he says, "but mainly I've trained as a painter. I'm a filmmaker by accident. I never intended to be one!"

This happy "accident" started when Ward decided to trade his active participation in sports for an involvement with the arts. "I became a painter...and went to art school," he says. "I started using camera equipment because I had ideas about film, but it was always with the thought of going back to painting. One film kind of leads you to another, though, and it's very hard to go back."

Ward considers two very different filmmakers—American comedian Buster Keaton and Danish dramatist Carl Dreyer—to be his chief cinematic inspirations. "I also tend to be interested in perception," he says, "and in characters that live on the perimeters and have their own peculiar view of the world. My films are generally representations of...how [such] people see reality."

This interest in outsiders and people with marginal lives is rooted "in my own sense of self," Ward explains. "I grew up on a farm and spent a lot of time on my own, quite isolated. When people spend a lot of time on their own, they tend to dwell a lot in their own imaginations. I suppose that's affected the concerns of my characters."

This doesn't mean "The Navigator" is an inward-looking film, however. It has social and even political ideas on its mind. Ward is very much a native of New Zealand, which has aroused international controversy by keeping nuclear weapons away from its territory. He says his film "is not driven from end to end with a political intention." But he points out that "it has a nuclear submarine that the medievals see as a sea monster. ...There's also a speech on a television set by a nuclear-submarine captain about 'pockets of refuge,' and there is an analogy drawn [in the story] about one tiny place trying to remove itself from the rest of the world. The film isn't conclusive about what it says, but it raises these issues. ...There are also analogies drawn with AIDS."

By concerning itself with these subjects, Ward hopes his movie will serve as part of a "dialogue" with his audience. "It talks about things," he muses, "and it says one can fight against what appears to be inevitable. So it's an optimistic film!"

One reason for widespread curiosity about "The Navigator" in the movie world is its unusual nationality. While other New Zealand productions have opened in American theaters, such as "Sleeping Dogs" and "Smash Palace," that country produces only six or seven films each year. In addition, "The Navigator" has the distinction of being the first coproduction between New Zealand and Australia, its down under neighbor.

"I was lucky enough to be able to use the resources of both countries," Ward reports, adding that the Australian and New Zealand sensibilities are in some ways an odd couple. "To crudely characterize Australian films," he says, "they often use simple stories told very directly. New Zealand films are quite different—it's the difference between a continent and two small islands. The sense of self is different.

"New Zealanders tend to be more introspective," he continues. "Their stories are often darker. The country itself is cold and dark—that's the feeling you get looking at it—whereas in Australia there's an openness, a brightness, and an enormous expansiveness. ...The cinema of New Zealand is often about isolation, more so than Australia, and that has affected me.

"But I make my own films, and they're often quite personal. ...They're often cool in color, and dark. ...I like things that are harsh, and environments that are quite strong. ...Always in New Zealand you're very aware of the land...being a palpable force.

"Those are characteristics I can draw on in common with other New Zealand films. ..."

LOS ANGELES TIMES, 4/5/89, Calendar/p. 5, Kevin Thomas

Vincent Ward's "The Navigator" transports us to as remote a time and place imaginable, a snowcovered copper-mining village in Cumbria, in March of 1348. The rapidly advancing Black Plague has not yet arrived along the Scottish border, and the villagers, trusting in the psychic dreams of a 9-year-old youth, Griffin (Hamish McFarlane), believe that if the miners make a pilgrimage to a distant city, erecting a cross of copper on its spire, God may spare the village from the epidemic.

With "The Navigator," Ward, the gifted young New Zealand film maker, has fashioned a beguiling fable, suprising and original, the kind of film that is fully realized visually. We associate the medieval with harshness, and while Ward's imagery contains much that is starkly dramatic, "The Navigator" is a film of great warmth and camaraderie. Ward's pilgrims are hearty, good-natured fellows, devout without being fanatic and genuinely caring of each other's welfare. The film exudes a sense of community, rooted in a closeness to nature as well as God, that's enough to make you grow wistful in envy.

Even though Griffin's visions instruct the men to burrow their way to the other side of the earth, using only the most primitive of machinery, you may be as surprised as they are when they surface in an unnamed modern city (actually a composite of Auckland and Wellington). Ward misses no opportunity to show us the pilgrims awed and terrified by having traveled so abruptly into the present. Ward, however, has more in mind than a simple time-travel fantasy, although he does not overlook its potential for humor or wonderment; "The Navigator" is finally a fable of faith and sacrifice.

The film is energized by a remorseless sense of forging ahead, a determination on the part of both the film maker and his people to see a task through—and in doing so—to arrive at the truth of a matter, consciously or otherwise. Like Werner Herzog, Ward is drawn to people who reach out for the outer limits of human experience.

Geoffrey Simpson's alternating high contrast black-and-white and muted color sequences are a key asset. Davood A. Tabrizi's score is at once fresh and timeless, a good summary for "The Navigator" (Times-rated Mature, appropriate for older children) itself.

MONTHLY FILM BULLETIN, 5/89, p. 144, Tim Pulleine

A mining village in Cumbria, 1348. Connor, whose wife Linnet is pregnant, returns from a foray into the outside world to confirm rumours of the devastation caused by the Black Death. The villagers hatch a scheme, inspired by a dream experienced by Connor's young brother Griffin, to make a pilgrimage to a far-off cathedral, taking local copper to cast a crucifix for the spire as an atonement. Connor is initially reluctant to act as leader, but eventually the expedition (comprising Connor, Griffin, one-armed boatman Arno, the gentle Martin, the pragmatic Searle, and his brother, the childlike giant Ulf) sets off. They proceed by way of one of the mine shafts above the village, which according to legend reaches to the other side of the world; and acting on Griffin's dream, they tunnel forwards, emerging on the edge of a huge city in the present-day Antipodes. Exhilarated but bewildered, they press on, first negotiating a main road, a task from which Ulf retires defeated. Connor goes to locate the cathedral and start the rigging, while the others search for a foundry to cast the copper. They find one, on the verge of being closed down, and the workers agree to help them. They direct the pilgrims to the cathedral on the far side of the harbour; the party appropriates a boat and a horse, and cross the harbour despite being nearly capsized by a submarine. Meanwhile, Connor, despite straying into a railway yard and being carried away by an engine, has reached the cathedral; the others have difficulty finding their way through the city. Eventually, they all forgather, and the dangerous task (which according to the dream must be accomplished by daybreak) gets under way. At its conclusion, Griffin, whose dream has shown an unidentified figure falling to its death, realises that he is the victim...In Cumbria, the party, including Griffin and Ulf (who has spent the time tunnelling under the road), returns to rejoicing that the threat has been averted. But then Griffin realises that Connor has earlier been infected by the plague, and that though he has apparently recovered, Griffin himself now carries it. Griffin exiles himself from the village. The dream image of a coffin (presumably Griffin's) is seen floating away on a lake.

Imagistic in method and visionary not only in form (given the basis in Griffin's dream, which opens and then punctuates the action) but in aspiration, *The Navigator* throws up some difficulties in ascribing meaning to its strange concatenation of events. In some respects, the film's procedures—signalled by the divide between the fantasticated black-and-white of the mediaeval sequences and the more or less realistic colour of the contemporary ones—appear rather schematic. An example would be the episode in which Griffin ventures into a video showroom: a bank of screens replaying identical images from a wild-life documentary, succeeded by snatches of hortatory commentary about both nuclear weapons and the spread of AIDS, explicitly signifies modern malaise. Hardly more oblique is the allusion to post-industrial decline in the sequences involving the redundant foundrymen.

But this sequence also indicates a capacity to deflect ready-made meanings. While the process of the casting of the crucifix itself is ritualistically elevated by the visuals and by choral and percussive effects on the soundtrack, the episode also contains some robust humour ("Can you understand these buggers?" one of the foundrymen asks his mates, and another remarks that the interlopers look as if they have "been in the bush for a while"). A humorous ambiguity complicates matters generally, notably in the sequence of the voyagers' attempts to negotiate the traffic on the highway, where the absurdity of the situation may point up the terrors of modern machinery, but serves more potently to offset and heighten the visitors' earlier wonderment at the beauty of a modern city. Certain passages, however—in particular, the harbour crossing with the white horse in the rowing boat—register as little more than exercises in picturesque surrealism.

The characterisations, though not developed, in their quick-sketch fashion achieve an unaffected individuality, especially the subsidiary figures of Ulf and Martin. The latter's disbelieving question in the foundry sequence, "The church is poor?", helps to diminish the grandiloquence surrounding the theme of religion and the decline of faith. Analogous with this is the combination of narrative urgency and matter-of-factness which distinguishes the Cumbrian episodes, with the fantastic journey met head-on by the script, yet transmogrified visually by the extraordinary, patently real, rock-bound settings (redolent of the locales of Vincent Ward's earlier *Vigil*), into which at one point there flaps a giant bird which might have come out of Méliès.

The concluding passage, in which the travellers (including the ostensibly "dead" Griffin) return to the Middle Ages, is certainly somewhat bewildering, but this also contributes to its effect. There's the possible symbolism of Griffin's infection by the plague representing a legacy of "future" decay, and his implied self-sacrificial death becoming an act of atonement which, like the recurring fire and water imagery, seems to echo Tarkovsky. But such an interpretation remains a matter of conjecture: it is the rhythmic and visceral qualities of the film which command attention.

NEW YORK POST, 6/28/89, p. 24, Jami Bernard

It is the time of the Black Death, and young Griffin is having bad dreams. He sees a torch falling into an abyss, a body falling from a church steeple, a fantastical city ashimmer with light. Certainly nothing in Griffin's world—a poor 14th century English mining village—has prepared him for this.

Griffin's prophetic visions lead him and a band of fellow villagers, including his idolized older brother, on a quest to the other side of the world, where they must erect a cross as an offering to God and thus save their village from the Plague. And all this by day break.

"The Navigator" is a simple, beautifully etched fable of faith and perseverance by New Zealander Vincent Ward. Although the story sounds ridiculous, it is told with elegant conviction.

The look of the movie is mystical and threatening. The medieval scenes are shot in foreboding, high-contrast black and white, with rolling skies and a fathomless icy countryside, like picture postcards from the Gulag, accompanied by a haunting Celtic soundtrack.

When the hardy travelers emerge, miraculously, on the other side of the world, it is Ward's artistry that makes this new world—bustling, 20th century Auckland—just as alien a place.

Here a superhighway is a macro-organism of maximum danger. A ride on the front end of a train is as nightmarish as your first time on the Cyclone. A submarine surfaces like a mythological serpent.

Ward finds the humor of the culture clash without ever losing sight of his human-scale wanderers. In fact, the first glimpse of the city is so breathtaking you'd think the shock alone would kill them. At another point, the miners are hopelessly stranded, although they are standing near a 911 call box. Their skills are about as useful now as Club Med bar beads at a Las Vegas gaming table.

Hamish McFarlane is earnest and delightful as the prescient 9-year-old, right down to his tongue-twisting accent.

Director Ward's connection of the Plague to AIDS is a bit much, but his grasp of and devotion to his otherwise enigmatic material makes "The Navigator" a great and charismatic adventure.

NEWSDAY, 6/28/89, Part II/p. 5, Terry Kelleher

Some dreams haunt our waking hours, beckoning us to bed for the next weird and wondrous installment.

That's the approximate effect of "The Navigator," a dreamlike movie about a 9-year-old boy whose prophetic visions take him and five adult companions on an awesome, frightening trip through time. Long after you emerge from the darkness of the theater, you'll feel yourself being pulled back to the mysterious world created by director Vincent Ward. It's not a sweet dream, but it is an enthralling one.

"The Navigator" opens in 1348. We're in a remote mining village in northwest England, and we see its bleakness in black and white. Returning from a fact-finding mission to "the outside world," heroic Connor (Bruce Lyons) reports that plague is on the way.

Meanwhile, Connor's young brother, Griffin (Hamish McFarlane), dreams in color: a falling torch, a mine shaft, a cathedral, a falling man. What does it all mean? Before dawn breaks, an underground journey must be made to the far side of the world, and a copper cross must be placed atop the tallest spire in Christendom. Do this and the village will be spared from the Black Death.

In a scene that can only be described as nightmarish, the inhabitants repulse a boatload of diseased refugees. But they can't ward off the epidemic much longer. The boy's visionary prescription, at first greeted with skepticism, looks more and more like the village's only hope. Griffin, Connor and four comrades set out on an impossible quest to appease the Lord, guided by nothing but pieces of a child's dream.

Far side of the world, indeed. The pilgrims' destination turns out to be a large city in New Zealand, 640 years into the future. The night lights dazzle them. The traffic terrifies them—and us, because we see it through their eyes. Clutching a religious carving, the timid oaf Ulf (Noel Appleby) is paralyzed at the prospect of crossing a busy highway. Connor winds up pinned to a speeding locomotive, his cheeks billowing in the ferocious wind.

There are moments of humor and harmony on the far side. Though they initially mistake them for "Hare-bloody-Krishnas," some foundry workers agree to help the time travelers fulfill their mission. For the most part, however, the medievals find the modern world alien and ever-threatening. This is the kind of trip we take in dreams—the kind that can end with a free fall at any second.

Ward's vision depends not on special effects but on his often inspired selection of images, as well as on the extraordinary photography of Geoffrey Simpson. If the editing by John Scott sometimes promotes confusion, it may be presumed to do so on purpose. None of us must know where "The Navigator" is going until it gets there.

The twist at the end, while not without a certain logic, will leave many puzzled and unsatisfied. But those who share the dream of "The Navigator" are bound to return to it, perhaps before the next dawn breaks.

NEWSWEEK, 4/17/89, p. 72, David Ansen

The Navigator begins, darkly and mysteriously, in ominous back-and-while images, in 14th-century England, at the time of the Black Death. In a harsh, remote mining village, a small band of hooded men sets off on a spiritual quest to ward off the plague. Among them is a 9-year-old boy, Griffin (Hamish McFarlane), who has been receiving strange visions. Before dawn breaks, they must find the great cathedral Griffin has seen in his dreams, and mount a cross on its steeple as a tribute to God. To reach the celestial city of his vision they tunnel through the center of the earth. When they emerge, these medieval pilgrims find themselves in a city in New Zealand—in 1988.

From the ominous black-and-white images that open the film to the rich nighttime colors that greet the startled eyes of these 14th-century adventurers, "The Navigator" announces itself as the work of a fresh and unusual talent. Thirty-three-year-old New Zealand filmmaker Vincent Ward has an uncanny gift of photographing the present through medieval eyes, so that the objects we take for granted become magical and strange. Crossing the city's harbor in a rowboat, the villagers are terrified by the sudden emergence of a submarine, which looks to us, as it does to them, like a giant sea dragon. They try to harpoon it.

There is humor in Ward's vision, but he doesn't play the time-travel motif for jokes: "The Navigator" is a tense fable about faith, community and sacrifice. Though its visual style is very sophisticated, it *feels* medieval. Ward is attempting to show the parallels between the two distant centuries, but he may have overreached when he explicitly equates the Black Death and AIDS. Having raised such a loaded metaphor, he doesn't follow through in any coherent, thematic way. "The Navigator" is a bit too cryptic to be fully satisfying: emotionally, it leaves you feeling oddly suspended. But Ward, who combines Werner Herzog's dogged visionary zeal with some of George Lucas's showmanship, is a filmmaker with a big future. Nothing he does in this haunting, original film is run-of-the-mill.

VILLAGE VOICE, 7/4/89, p. 72, Georgia Brown

Vincent Ward's *The Navigator: An Odyssey Across Time* is another award-winner—taking Australian Oscars for best feature, director, cinematography, and editing—about obsession, albeit of a spiritual nature. The 33-year-old Ward, a New Zealander, has been touted as "the anti-podean Werner Herzog" for his apocalyptic sensibility and propensity for remote locations, as well as for rigors he's prone to put a crew through. Filming this, his third full-length feature, Ward helicoptered actors, including a pregnant woman and four children, up to a frozen volcanic lake—a deserted, snowbound, subzero site inaccessible by roads. Actor Bruce Lyons compares filming with Ward to "joining a medieval craft guild where you signed your apprenticeship in blood."

The Navigator opens on a small mining village in Cumbria, England, 1348. Outside, the Black Death rages, but the remote village has so far been spared. This information arrives in titles; what we see, accompanied by medieval chants, are cryptic images—a torch thrown into a mine shaft; a church steeple and someone climbing, perhaps falling; a cross submerged underwater—visions, it turns out, seen by nine-year-old Griffin (Hamish McFarlane), who's waded out into a freezing lake. These ominous, if essentially bland, images occur so often in the film one gets to know them well.

The portentous mood is kept up for most of the movie's duration. Pitched at high seriousness, the film is edited for mystification. It's not that the plot is particularly difficult to follow, but this Christian fable has frustratingly little resonance outside sheer oddness. Ward favors ostentatious shots of his actors—chosen apparently for expressive features—from underneath, so they're silhouetted against the sky. The cinematography (by Geoffrey Simpson) is sometimes impressive, but it's ungrounded.

Griffin's older brother, Connor (Bruce Lyons), returns from an information-gathering foray into civilization, only to consent—under the influence of Griffin's hallucinations—to lead a small expedition, including the boy, out again. The object of the quest: to place a cross on top of a particular steeple before dawn. This is supposed to save the village from the plague. It turns out that the steeple is on a church in 20th century Auckland and that the miners must tunnel through the earth as well as over time. Well, if you say so.

Once these time-travelers break through the far crust, *The Navigator* turns from silvery black-and-white to color, particularly dreamy nighttime blues. "It must be God's city, there's so much light," observes one of the men, wide-eyed at the distant sight of Auckland. Their first major task is crossing a freeway. One of the group, a fat man in a leather helmet, is so terrified he has to be left behind. The others promise to pick him up on the way back. The slightly reduced band—in their 14th century helmets, hoods, and robes—encounters civilization in a series of incidents chosen for visual effects. Connor finds himself pinned on the front of a moving train; the men cross a bay in a small boat with a white horse when a nuclear submarine surfaces like an iron whale; Griffin is transfixed by a bank of TV sets in a shop window. It is at this point that we hear an announcer give a bulletin on AIDS.

That some analogy between AIDS and the black death might be made isn't surprising. The wonder is that it seems, in the movie's context, so inapt. In *The Navigator*'s Christian allegory, the sacrifice of one innocent is supposed to save the entire community—not exactly how plagues have worked, then or now.

Also reviewed in:
NEW YORK TIMES, 6/28/89, p. C17, Caryn James
VARIETY, 5/11/88, p. 28
WASHINGTON POST, 7/29/89, p. C1, Hal Hinson

NEAR DEATH

A Zipporah Films release of an Exit Films production. *Producer:* Frederick Wiseman. *Director:* Frederick Wiseman. *Director of Photography:* John Davey. *Editor:* Frederick Wiseman. *Sound:* Frederick Wiseman. *Running time:* 350 minutes. *MPAA Rating:* Not Rated.

NEW YORK POST, 10/7/89, p. 19, David Edelstein

For the first hour of Fred Wiseman's six-hour documentary "Near Death," I could not see the screen for a mask of tears; it was impossible to watch the living hooked up to respirators, lacerated by tubes and surrounded by edgy, stricken families. Lifetimes come to an end, not with a whimper but with thrashing and agony. I couldn't imagine who could take a camera here, to the medical intensive-care unit of Boston's Beth Israel, or why so invasive a procedure would be necessary.

The reasons are clear quickly. The doctors and nurses who minister to these people don't have the luxury of tears. And they haven't enough—they go through this grueling process every day. Wiseman's camera stands back and watches them struggle among themselves with the most difficult question in the world: When to admit it's over, withdraw care and end the pain.

In "Near Death," which will be shown in January on public TV, the film maker focuses on four patients, three of them elderly, one a young man. Even raising the issue of death is monstrously difficult. The word "dying" is never used with patients or their families; dispatched to break the news of what's inevitable, one doctor, Taylor, cannot keep from adding that there's always hope, always a chance for a miracle.

Dr. Weiss, the head of the unit, emerges an immensely complicated figure. At first, he's Dr. Death to Taylor's Kildare—the morbid one, the one who's first to venture an opinion that a patient won't survive.

But his callousness is a mask for genuine despair. Disheveled and depressed, he speaks compulsively of working so hard to keep people going, pushing that boulder up the hill again and again to have it roll back down. You can't blame him for not wanting to be crushed by it: you can only marvel at his lucidity—and stature—amid such anguish.

We hear of the old days, when a carcinoma would kill a man and that would be that. Now, thanks to chemotherapy, many recover, but the doctors in this unit see the ones chemo mortally wounds, whose hearts and lungs and kidneys give out under the strain. At what point, Weiss asks, do they decide if they're managing someone's death or their chance to live? As both families and doctors tiptoe around the issue, the ICU becomes a torturous limbo.

Six hours is a long time, but not when you realize how much is at stake. This is a heroic piece of film making.

Also reviewed in:
NEW YORK TIMES, 10/7/89, p. 11, Janet Maslin
VARIETY, 10/11–17/89, p. 33

NEW YORK SHORTS: FIVE NEW FILMS FROM N.Y.U.

WILD SOUND (15 minutes). *Director:* Lee Sachs. STRAY DOGS (23 minutes). *Director:* Mark Richardson. PART VII (24 minutes). *Director:* Thomas Wallin. KING'S ROAD (26 minutes). *Director:* Joseph Rosato. HANG 'EM REALLY HIGH (22 minutes). *Director:* Danniel Baron. *Running time:* 110 minutes. *MPAA Rating:* Not Rated.

NEWSDAY, 11/3/89, Part III/p. 7, Janice Berman

Give the show two-and-a-half stars for overall, 110-minute impact. But a couple of these student films, which used to be seeable only at festivals and the like and now are on view for anyone willing to plunk down seven bucks, are terribly impressive, and none isn't worth a look. Pretty clever of the Angelika Film Center, a sleek new multiplex, both to acknowledge the presence of the neighboring Tisch School of the Arts and to court the student community.

Best in show has to go to director Joseph Rosato's "King's Road," a 26-minute, savage/sweet drama about two brothers battling for their dreams. The rural setting is wonderfully rendered by camera operator Donna Lennard. Michael Saint Gerard ("Hair Spray") and Vinny Cassa, as the older and younger siblings respectively, turn in sensitive performances.

Lawyer-turned-film maker Thomas Wallin makes a great case against sequential horror flicks with "Part VII." In 24 minutes of fast-paced, deliberately cliché-ridden and extremely funny blood and guts, the heroine rebels. "You are my sixth boyfriend, and you'll be dead meat before the end of the first reel!" she screams in the movie-within-the-movie before wreaking vengeance on the hack writer who created her.

The 15 minutes devoted to "Wild Sound" highlights the talents of Lee Sachs, film maker and performer, as a maker of wild sound. That's the film term for random noise on a sound track, but it's the descriptive term for the noises Sachs makes, which seem to enchant passengers in his Checker cab. One guy even tries to steal his sounds. Fifteen minutes of these noises, even when they're joined in a romance with a woman who also makes weird noises, seems about enough. Yet "Wild Sound," shot in and around the city, has a fanciful innocence about it. The credits, with voiced-over cooing and crowing, are a stitch.

Director Danniel Baron's "Hang 'Em Really High," a spoof of Westerns of every stripe, is set in New York City—a clue as to the wildness of his humor. A little more control would have been nice, but then we might have missed the spectacle of a shootout on a landfill, with a fake saguaro cactus as a prop, or a line like, "Hasidim, but who are they?"

Mark Richardson's "Stray Dogs," in which a white child is kidnaped by a black teenager, is ambitious in the scope of its chase sequences through the swamps of Florida. But it has a disappointingly flat script, and its actors leave much to be desired.

VILLAGE VOICE, 11/7/89, p. 77, Manohla Dargis

Like the other films in "Apparatus Presents," *Big Character Poster* has a creative edge. Now, if only NYU would inspire the same in its student productions. Nonetheless, Angelika Film Center should be commended for showcasing five of them for a regular commercial run; let's hope this starts a trend.

"New York Shorts," which begins on a flat note with a limp parody, soon picks up with Thomas Wallin's *Part VII*, a film that feels like something from Stephen King, but mercifully shorter. (King's latest novel actually shares a similar conceit.) A successful slice 'n' dice screenwriter is set upon by one of his own creations. Tired of being tormented in countless bloody sequels the teenage heroine seizes control of the script she's being written into and wreaks revenge. ("You're my sixth boyfriend," she wails à la Jamie Lee Curtis, "and you'll be dead by the end of the first reel.")

Lee Sachs's *Wild Sound* is a series of scenes strung together to highlight its creator's amazing vocal pyrotechnics. Sachs's trilling, sputtering scat singing and talented impersonations (he does an outstanding dog cough) are almost enough to make up for the fact that this is really a filmed performance, and not much of a movie.

Also reviewed in:
NEW YORK TIMES, 11/3/89, p. C4, Stephen Holden

NEW YORK STORIES

A Touchstone Pictures release. *Executive Producer:* Jack Rollins and Charles H. Joffe. *Running time:* 130 minutes. *MPAA Rating:* PG.

LIFE LESSONS—*Producer:* Barbara DeFina. *Director:* Martin Scorsese. *Screenplay:* Richard Price. *Director of Photography:* Nestor Almendros. *Editor:* Thelma Schoonmaker. *Sound:* James Sabat. *Sound Editor:* Skip Lievsay. *Production Designer:* Kristi Zea. *Art Director:* W. Steven Graham. *Set Decorator:* Nina Ramsey. *Set Dresser:* Dave Weinman. *Costumes:* John Dunn. *Make-up:* Allen Weisinger. *Stunt Coordinator:* Danny Aiello III.

CAST: Nick Nolte (Lionel Dobie); Patrick O'Neal (Phillip Fowler); Rosanna Arquette (Paulette); Phil Harper (Businessman); Kenneth J. McGregor, David Cryer and Paul Geier (Suits); Jesse Borrego (Reuben Toro); Gregorij von Leitis (Kurt Bloom); Steve Buscemi (Gregory Stark); LoNardo (Woman at Blind Alley); Peter Gabrial (Himself); Mark Boone Jr. (Hank); Illeana Douglas (Paulette's Friend); Paul Mougey (Guy at Blind Alley); Deborah Harry (Girl at Blind Alley); Paul Herman and Victor Argo (Cops); Victor Trull (Maitre d'); Richard Price (Artist at Opening); Brigitte Bako (Young Woman).

LIFE WITHOUT ZOE—*Producer:* Fred Roos and Fred Fuchs. *Director:* Francis Coppola. *Screenplay:* Francis Coppola and Sofia Coppola. *Director of Photography:* Vittorio Storaro. *Editor:* Barry Malkin. *Music:* Carmine Coppola and Kid Creole and the Coconuts. *Music Editor:* Thomas Drescher. *Sound:* James Sabat. *Sound Editor:* Michael Kirchberger and Dan Sable. *Production Designer:* Dean Tavoularis. *Art Director:* Speed Hopkins. *Set Decorator:* George DeTitta Jr. *Set Dresser:* Dave Weinman. *Costumes:* Sofia Coppola. *Make-up:* Richard Dean.

CAST: Heather McComb (Zoe); Talia Shire (Charlotte); Gia Coppola (Baby Zoe); Giancarlo Giannini (Claudio); Paul Herman (Clifford, the Doorman); James Keane (Jimmy); Don Novello (Hector); Bill Moor (Mr. Lilly); Tom Mardirosian (Hasid); Jenny Nichols (Lundy); Gina Scianni (Devo); Diane Lin Cosman (Margit); Selim Tlili (Abu); Robin Wood-Chappelle (Gel); Celia Nestell (Hillary); Alexandra Becker (Andrea); Adrien Brody (Mel); Michael Higgins and Chris Elliot (Robbers); Thelma Carpenter (Maid); Carmine Coppola (Street Musician); Jo Jo Starbuck (Ice Skater).

OEDIPUS WRECKS—*Producer:* Robert Greenhut. *Director:* Woody Allen. *Screenplay:* Woody Allen. *Director of Photography:* Sven Nykvist. *Editor:* Susan E. Morse. *Sound:* James Sabat. *Sound Editor:* Dan Sable. *Production Designer:* Santo Loquasto. *Art Director:* Speed Hopkins. *Set Decorator:* Susan Bode. *Set Dresser:* Dave Weinman. *Special Visual Effects:* Stuart Robertson and Joel Hynek. *Costumes:* Jeffrey Kurland. *Make-up:* Fern Buchner.

CAST: Woody Allen (Sheldon); Marvin Chatinover (Psychiatrist); Mae Questel (Mother); Mia Farrow (Lisa); Molly Regan (Sheldon's Secretary); Ira Wheeler (Mr. Bates); Joan Bud (Board Member); Jessie Keosian (Aunt Ceil); Michael Rizzo (Waiter); George Schindler (Shandu, the Magician); Bridgit Ryan (Rita); Larry David (Theatre Manager); Paul Herman (Detective Flynn); Herschel Rosen (Store Clerk); Andrew MacMillan

(Newscaster); Jodi Long and Nancy Giles (T.V. Interviewers); Mayor Edward I. Koch (Himself); Mike Starr and Richard Grund (Hardhats); Julie Kavner (Treva).

CHRISTIAN SCIENCE MONITOR, 3/8/89, p. 10, David Sterritt

Who needs Hollywood, when New York can serve up the tastiest movie treats of the season?

"New York Stories" is a new example of an old breed: the anthology film, in which different filmmakers take individual approaches to a common topic. The subject here is simply New York City, and the movie's three chapters have little in common except a deep affection for that great place—and an eagerness to express that affection in the most colorful terms imaginable.

Woody Allen and Martin Scorsese are mavericks who have avoided Hollywood—and Hollywood formulas—throughout their careers, basing themselves proudly in the East Coast filmmaking scene. Francis Coppola is a similarly ornery character, rooted less definitively in New York but always fascinated by the idea of an alternative to Hollywood's studio establishment. The three join forces in "New York Stories," and although their main purpose is obviously to have a whale of a good time as storytellers and *cinéastes*, the excellence of their work makes a terrific case against Hollywood as the movie capital of the late '80s and beyond. Since all three chapters are winners, I'll deal with them in the order they take on-screen.

"Life lessons" starts off the picture with an excursion to downtown Manhattan, courtesy of Martin Scorsese, who covered some of the same turf in "After Hours" a few seasons ago.

Our heroes are Lionel, a burly artist, and Paulette, an insecure painter who shares Lionel's messy loft. Lionel is a bundle of energy that's barely held in check by two things. One is his love for the woman in his life. The other is a perilously dim recognition that the real world has rules less free-wheeling than the passions that surge through his art. He's used to grabbing what he wants as impulsively as he spatters paint on his canvases. Paulette won't be grabbed that easily, though. She's fallen for a "performance artist" who's younger and hipper than Lionel, and, although she still lives in Lionel's spare room, her thoughts are elsewhere. Which is driving Lionel crazy.

Nick Nolte gives a powerhouse performance as Lionel, and Rosanna Arquette isn't far behind as Paulette, a tantalizing mixture of vulnerability, charm, and hidden strength. Both of them are precisely in tune with Mr. Scorsese's over-the-top filmmaking, which uses a supercharged collection of cinematic devices to evoke the supercharged feelings of Lionel and the not-quite-suppressed chaos of his self-centered world. The best portions of the film don't have characters at all, in the usual sense—they're goofily poetic interludes in which the screen fills with Lionel's flying paints, and the sound track wails with classic rock-and-roll, perhaps the only other art that could echo Lionel's seething emotions.

If you had to label "Life Lessons," you'd probably call it a comedy. But its most successful moments go beyond the usual movie categories, soaring into a world that belongs only to Scorsese and the latest addition to his gallery of indelible characters, which already includes such amazing figures as Travis Bickle of "Taxi Driver" and Rupert Pupkin of "The King of Comedy."

"Life Without Zoe," the second episode of "New York Stories," announces its childlike intentions in its opening credits: Directed by Francis; photographed by Vittorio; music by Carmine; and so forth, without a last name in sight. It's as if the filmmakers were as young as the main characters, who are still in their early school years. In fact, those filmmakers are veterans: filmmaker Francis Coppola, cinematographer Vittorio Storaro, composer Carmine Coppola.

The tale is as youthful as its characters, and as exuberant. Zoe is a poor little rich girl, living in a Manhattan hotel with every luxury except loving parents—since her mom and dad are overachieving artists who find little time for home. Zoe isn't lonely, though. She has lots of friends, from her loyal butler to her latest new schoolmate, the richest boy in the whole world. With them at her side, she gets involved in a wacky intrigue, returning a fabulous jewel to the queen of an exotic land.

The story doesn't make a bit of sense, and often it's hard to tell whether Mr. Coppola is kidding or just fooling around. The movie holds together by virtue of sheer energy and color, though, barreling past its own plot-holes with unstoppable momentum. It's not the most controlled picture you ever saw, but it's certainly a change of pace from everything else around, and it shows the unpredictable Coppola in a refreshingly buoyant mood.

"Oedipus Wrecks," which caps the "New York Stories" trilogy, is a quintessential Woody Allen fable—which means his admirers will adore it and his detractors will do the opposite. But even the anti-Allen faction will probably be glad to see him go back to comedy after the somberness of "September" and "Another Woman," two of his least successful outings.

The modern, middle-aged Oedipus of his new movie is named Sheldon—and, while he isn't married to his mother, he's certainly obsessed with her. Or rather, with her nagging. She just won't let him alone. And if there's a willing listener, including his own fiancée, she's still more eager to give her critical view of his faults, failings, and frustrations.

The plot thickens when Sheldon's mother disappears, in a manner so hilarious I won't give it away here. Then she reappears, in an unexpected way that makes our hero's life more wretched—and more henpecked—than ever. It all comes out fine in the end, but not before Sheldon's dignity has met some mighty harrowing challenges. Allen's performance is vintage Woody material, and there's marvelous supporting work by Mia Farrow as Sheldon's fiancée, Julie Kavner as a sort of Manhattan witch doctor, and Mae Questel as the notorious mom. (If you feel a sense of *déjà vu* when you hear Ms. Questel, by the way, it's because she used to supply Betty Boop's squeaky voice in movie cartoons of yore.)

All the "New York Stories" have a couple of things in common. For one, they're photographed by masters of the cinematographic art: Nestor Almendros in Scorsese's episode, Vittorio Storaro in Coppola's, and Sven Nykvist in Allen's. They also make a canny use of just the right music at just the right moment—especially when rock-and-roll breaks out in "Life Lessons," and when Allen uses classic jazz and standards to punctuate his story. Only the Coppola chapter seems a little slack in the music department, relying less on Carmine Coppola's composing skills than on the uninspired sounds of Kid Creole and the Coconuts, who keep popping up on the sound track.

"New York Stories" is the latest in a long line of anthology films, from the French "Paris vu par..." to the Italian "Boccaccio '70" and many more. They've been a rare breed in recent years, but this colorful outing may put them back in style again. Three cheers for producer Robert Greenhut, who put the package together. Here's hoping it's the beginning of a trend.

The film is rated PG, reflecting a bit of rough language and a few sexy moments, particularly in the "Life Lessons" segment.

FILMS IN REVIEW, 6–7/89, p. 362, Edmond Grant

It's very rare occasion indeed when noted directors decide to pool their efforts and produce a feature length "anthology" film. These sorts of features really flourished only in the early to mid-60's, when the French and Italian cinemas were literally bursting at the seams with talented visionaries who worked quite well within the shorter format required by these anthologies, which were usually organized around a central theme (*The Seven Deadly Sins*) or a locale (*Love In The City, Paris Vu Par...*).

A few American anthologies were produced decades ago (*Flesh And Fantasy, O. Henry's Full House*), but the format is rarely given consideration under current conditions (Last year's *Aria*, though backed in part by American producers, contained the work of only one American director). And so, *New York Stories* emerges as a true curiosity piece. A conglomerate-era *Tales Of Manhattan*, the film is the product of three contemporary masters—Martin Scorsese, Francis Coppola, and Woody Allen. The results, unfortunately, show some of these filmmakers' strengths and, in certain cases, more than a few weaknesses.

The lengthiest of the three tales is Martin Scorsese's "Life Lessons." Though the plotline—detailing the eventual dissolution of the relationship between an uninhibited artist (Nick Nolte) and his live-in associate (Rosanna Arquette)—is decidedly skimpy, Scorsese does his peerless best with it; combining the kinetic visual style that enlivened *The Color of Money* with the satiric view of lower Manhattan's "underground" present in *After Hours*.

By focusing their attention on these two characters, Scorsese and scripter Richard Price are able to take a number of deliciously on-target swipes at the pretentions of the artistic ego (a feat attempted, but not at all successfully achieved, in *Slaves of New York*, reviewed elsewhere in this issue). And as the bickering couple, both Nolte and Arquette do a splendid job, aptly rendering subtle emotions amidst all the self-involved tirades—Arquette should be especially grateful for the way that Scorsese and cinematographer Nestor Almendros fixate the camera on her, transforming her at one point into another of Scorsese's slow motion blonde goddesses.

Though essentially a satire, "Life Lessons" is also an ode to creativity. Scorsese and Almendros' smooth camerawork and use of an inventory of visual devices (including the anachronistic iris shot) slyly reproduces Nolte's character's artistic intensity; as the camera follows the artist's stroke, we get the definite impression that Scorsese is once again using the screen as his own canvas, rendering complex emotions with the flourishes of a grand master.

Francis Coppola's "Life With Zoe," the slightest of the three entries, is little more than an exercise in nepotism. Coppola's daughter Sofia is billed as the co-scripter (one wonders which family member produced the incredibly flat and artificial-sounding dialogue) of this silly tale of a poor little rich girl who would like to spend more time with her parents, a virtuoso flautist (Giancarlo Giannini) and an uptight businesswoman (played by Francis's sister, Talia Shire).

At times visually stylish, "Zoe" has considerably less substance than the average after-school special. The adult performers play along amiably, particularly Don Novello who almost steals the show in his brief turn as a peppy butler. But this is essentially a little girl's fantasy, and so Heather McComb, who plays Zoe, gets to dominate the proceedings. A sad choice of material for the man who has worked superbly on both the large scale (*The Godfather*), and the small (*The Conversation*).

The third story comes from a director who, much like Scorsese, has done much to celebrate New York in many of his previous films: Woody Allen. "Oedipus Wrecks," Allen's contribution, is a welcome return to comedy after his last two Bergmanlike angst fests, yet it remains a marginal Allen creation because it is entirely predicated on one joke.

The joke concerns Woody's nagging mother (Mae Questel) who dominates his entire existence. Without giving away the premise, it can be said that "Oedipus" relies on the sort of comedy with a surreal twist that Allen has previously confined only to his short stories, and to brief "fantasy" sequences in his comedies (The only film to contain a large dose of surrealism was the unpleasant, and largely uncomic, *Stardust Memories*). What can be revealed is that this time Woody's character is a lawyer, whose lovemate is played by a very pregnant-looking (guess who) Mia Farrow.

Though the premise is silly and comes off like a Jewish version of an Ionesco play, "Oedipus" does have its rewards. For one, Allen's return to speaking right to the camera, a wonderfully endearing form of first person narration and the best way ever conceived of incorporating a lot of quick "standup" one liners. Also, Allen's beautifully evocative facial reactions—his response to a magician's announcement that Questel will be placed in a box to be stuck with sharp blades, is priceless.

Thus *New York Stories* is an odd amalgam, a mixed bag of styles that doesn't show all three directors off to good advantage, but does make clear the fact that, as regards form *and* content, Scorsese knows exactly where he's going, Coppola doesn't appear to have a clue, and Allen is thankfully getting back on the right track.

LOS ANGELES TIMES, 3/3/89, Calendar/p. 1, Sheila Benson

Three New York-savvy directors take aim at the Big Apple in "New York Stories" and give it their best shot. In the overview of these tender craftsmen, the city emerges as the nurturing ground for passion, for privilege and as no place whatever for a little privacy.

For Martin Scorsese and Woody Allen, whose short films concern the essential nature of an artist and the essential nature of a family, respectively, this is classic stuff. For Francis Coppola, who's made a jet-set fairy tale from a trifle co-written with his 17-year-old daughter, Sofia, it's a breathtakingly pretty embarrassment. Eh, two like this out of three is still great odds.

We open in the rich tones of Scorsese's "Life Lessons," and the vast loft inhabited by one of the giants of the New York painting scene, Lionel Dobie (Nick Nolte)—not called "The Lion" for nothing. He's well aware of the voltage he generates, sexually and commercially; he dispenses it as he does his talent, prodigiously, and with full knowledge of its impact.

But now, with a show due in three weeks, he's in the exquisite agony of the artist-procrastinator. It's a state given an even keener edge by the defection of his lover-assistant-pupil Paulette (Rosanna Arquette), who's wandered off to be trifled with by a *performance artist* (!). It has left Lionel a basket case and, on her return, uncharacteristically pliant.

Richard Price's screenplay, the film's notes explain, was inspired by the elements of Dostoevsky's short novel "The Gambler," as well as by the diary of his protégée and one-time mistress, Apollinaria Suslova, with the art world substituted for the literary one. It's a terrific script. Not only does it sound the way we imagine real artists talk, but there's hardly a nuance of obsessive behavior in it that doesn't ring true: Price might be reworking the classic Jackson Pollock story about the full year he had to complete a mural for Peggy Guggenheim, and the all-night frenzy of creation he went through the night before it was due, beginning at midnight and ending at sunrise, with one of his major works pulsating from her wall.

That same intensity infuses "Life Lessons," making it a delight on every level. There's Nolte's full-out power as the loving Lion, agonized, authentic, demoniac, funny and smothering by turns. (Actually, Nolte's creation is so strong that to end the piece on the note that it does feels almost like a trivializing of the character.) There's the restless, prowling camera of Nestor Almendros, irising in, Truffaut-like, on a warmly remembered detail of Paulette's person, or peering over the top of a canvas at the slashing, brooding Lion at work.

There is also the maddening look-but-don't-touch attitude of Arquette as a pupil who's grown out of her role. There is Kristi Zea's production design, which sings in its every detail of the New York art scene, and Thelma Schoonmaker's lovely editing. Finally, there's the music: the Lion pulls his inspiration from the "masters," Procol Harum, Django Reinhardt, the "Nessun Dorma" of Puccini, all played at lease-breaking levels.

We are pitched from this density to the weightlessness of "Life Without Zoe," a Coppola family conceit of calculated disingenuousness. However, that's only one of the problems facing this pretty piffle. Lodged somewhere on "Fairy Tale Theater," or as an example of how one half of 1% of New York lives, it might still be cloying, but sandwiched between two solid stories it's in terrible trouble.

The screenplay is like a variation of De Maupassant's "The Necklace" written by the precocious Eloise of the Plaza. This time it's bossy 12-year-old Zoe of the Sherry Netherland (Heather McComb), a true creature of New York, who wears Chanel hats to school and bullies room service into rounds of strawberry daiquiries for her classmates while they pore over the latest Paris Vogue.

Pop (Giancarlo Giannini) is a world-class flutist, therefore gone a lot; writer-photographer mom (Talia Shire) roams the globe, leaving Zoe to be clucked over by the Sherry's staff and to yearn for a *real* family. "Zoe" seems to want to say something about loneliness amid surfeit and a child's cleverness in reconciling her family, but it has a hard time with a script this flimsy and erratic, and moments like the one when Zoe breaks up her parents' reconciliation kiss with "Cut!" do little to cement her charm. The Sherry is the Coppola compound, East; does he have nothing deeper to convey about the ironies of life de luxe in today's New York than this Fabergé egg of a film?

Fortunately, through the lenses of Vittoria Storaro and the production design of Dean Tavoularis the segment is meltingly lovely, reaching some sort of peak at a costume ball for kids given by the richest boy in the world. Here, the Cirque de Soleil is an entr'acte and, in the quarters of a sheik's wife, silver helium pillows float like shining punctuation marks. The sequence just doesn't have a brain—or a heart.

It bottoms out as Zoe drops off a promised second batch of Hershey's kisses to an (unseen) homeless man living in a cardboard box in front of the Plaza, prompting him to mutter, "*She's* why I love New York!" To quote from Mr. Nolte's character only minutes before, it's enough to make you go up on the roof and howl like a gut-shot dog.

There'll be no howling over "Oedipus Wrecks," the jewel of the piece. Can you remember how long it's been since we've seen Woody Allen *run*? Or wear funny hats? Even more than Allen's other films, this one, which is a perfect balance of length, story and atmosphere, should be seen, not read.

Seems fair enough to tell you that Mia Farrow is safely on board again, as is cinematographer Sven Nykvist, editor Susan Morse and production designer Santo Loquasto. But you'll have to see it to find out what happens to his mother. Know, however, that in another of Allen's triumphs of casting, she is played by Mae Questel, the silvery little voice of Betty Boop and Olive Oyl. And that she is absolutely marvelous, an assessment she would probably accept with aplomb.

Also to be unearthed, like the treasure that she is, is Julie Kavner, whom Allen secreted slightly off center-screen in both "Hannah and Her Sisters" and "Radio Days." She comes into her own here as a medium who has a crystal as big as the Ritz and a little difficulty fitting the earpieces of her sensible glasses under her somewhat occult headband. Don't waste time reading—drop the paper. Go. Go.

MONTHLY FILM BULLETIN, 11/89, p. 339, Louise Sweet

LIFE LESSONS: After a tense meeting with his agent, Phillip Fowler, about work in progress for his new show in three weeks' time, middle-aged artist Lionel Dobie hurries to the airport to meet his young protégée/lover Paulette. She angrily insists that she didn't want to see him again, and tells him that she wasn't on holiday with a girlfriend (as she had claimed) but with performance artist Gregory Stark, who then left her. Dobie insists on taking her back to their studio loft, and when she expresses doubt about her work, and talks of returning home, he tells her she will be lost if she leaves New York. She agrees to stay temporarily on a platonic basis, but Dobie finds it hard to overcome his erotic fixation and carry on with his work. At a party she picks up young artist Reuben Toro, and while they make love in the loft Lionel attacks his canvases in wild frustration. Paulette insists on attending a performance by Gregory Stark, and Lionel tells her to approach him afterwards, knowing she will be rebuffed and hoping she will accept his own declaration of love. But Paulette is not mollified, and when Lionel later starts a brawl with Stark, she calls her brother to take her home. Lionel fiercely returns to his painting; a little later he is seen at the opening, offering another young admirer a course in "life lessons" if she becomes his assistant. LIFE WITHOUT ZOE: Twelve-year-old Zoe, whose father Claudio, a world-renowned flautist (in legend, a seductive calling), and mother Charlotte, a photo-journalist, are estranged and rarely at home, lives in the Sherry-Netherland Hotel and every day is packed off to school, stylishly if breathlessly clad, by a butler. Zoe and her friends are intrigued by a new boy at school, Abu, lonely scion of a fabulously wealthy Eastern family. Later, during a robbery of the security boxes at the Sherry-Netherland, Zoe manages to retain a package of her father's, which turns out to contain a "tear of Shiraz", one of a pair of earrings given Claudio by the Princess Soroya under the spell of his music. With the help of Abu (who is the princess' nephew), Zoe plans to return the earring to her in time for a forthcoming party where she is expected by her husband, Sheik Omar, to be wearing the earrings. The children arrange their own costume party, during which Zoe is able to slip the earring back to the grateful princess. In the process, she helps her parents to cement a reconciliation, and they all take off to hear Claudio play beneath the Acropolis in Greece. OEDIPUS WRECKS: To his psychiatrist, anxious attorney Sheldon Mills confesses that, although he has changed his name from Millstein and been accepted by a top-flight WASP law firm, he cannot escape the influence of his archetypal Jewish mother Sadie. Mother is particularly unhappy about Sheldon's current fiancée, Lisa, a divorcée with three children; she goes with all of them, however, to a magic show where she is volunteered for a disappearing act and promptly disappears for real. At first horrified, Sheldon soon experiences a new sense of release and sexual freedom, and calls off the search for Sadie. But she then rematerialises as an apparition in the skies above Manhattan, hectoring Sheldon as before and discussing his little foibles with the whole city. Desperate, Sheldon consults Treva, a Jewish girl and would-be occultist, whose efforts to exorcise mother have no effect. After an evening of commiseration with Treva, and a meal like his mother used to make, Sheldon returns home to a farewell note from Lisa. He then has a revelation: on a rooftop, he introduces Treva as his new fiancée to mother, who promptly descends from the skies, settling down to discuss her son with Treva.

Three slices of the same city by three directors—the films of two of whom at least have always been umbilically attached to New York—seems as promising a basis for a portmanteau film as any of the collections assembled in the past around particular authors (Somerset Maugham) or themes (the Italian sex reports). In this kind of scene-painting, though, where the landscape and the characters are meant to represent one another, problems of size and scale, in the short-story format, predominate. Working to roughly the same length and format, the three have not found it a consistently comfortable container. Martin Scorsese's tale of the tortured relationship between a middleaged artist and his protégée/love object—derived from the diaries of Dostoevsky's mistress—spirals off emotionally in more directions than the canvas (Scorsese's or his hero's) can contain. Francis Coppola's sketch, a designer *Arabian Nights*, on the other hand, seems to contain too little, and just goes on doodling and decorating. And Woody Allen, whose films have tended to break down into fragments and anecdotes anyway, gets it just about right with a tale that nicely, comically toys with problems of size and perspective.

Life Lessons, which involves a typically Scorsese duo and their tango of incompatible needs and desires, runs aground first of all on the old problem of representing an artist and his art on screen. Nick Nolte, who plays the fêted but anxious Lionel Dobie as a kind of bruised bear, stumbles about his studio, adding curls and dashes of oil paint to enormous, clotted canvases (by Manhattan artist Chuck Connelly), driven more by sexual frustration and rejection than inspiration, working always to loud music. But the rhythm of the music seems to have little to do with the tone and scale of the paintings, which are room-size, dark and overpainted, while

Dobie's efforts on top are smaller, merely repetitive swirls. If the episode never seems to get at anything essential in Dobie's relationship to his art, it sketches even less satisfactorily his ambiguous, disingenuous teacher-pupil relationship with Paulette and her unhappy feelings about her own art (by Susan Hambleton, in various undeveloped styles of figurative painting). Part of the problem may be that Nolte and Rosanna Arquette have a limited range in their roles, but Scorsese always seems to be sliding away from them into a more conventional satire on artistic pretensions and the New York art world (flashbulbs exploding, à la *Raging Bull*, and all).

If Scorsese is reaching for more than he can accomplish in this truncated format, Coppola seems to be playing down to less than he can do. What he has attempted is to lend himself to the smart-set fairy-tale world of his daughter Sofia, who co-wrote the script and designed the costumes and the decorative licorice-twist credits. The attempt to create a children's world with the dash and style of 40s Noel Coward is still burdened with a sense of false naivety, however, and the children's apeing of grown-up fashion makes them appear not so much sophisticated as prematurely aged and knowing. The reunion that precocious Zoe engineers between her unlikeable parents seems as false and impermanent as the glitzy props, and like Lionel Dobie's artistic calling, the magic seductiveness of her flute-playing father has to be taken on trust.

The beguilement of art, characters heeding variations on the siren song of the city, might be one link between the three stories. More than that, however, they are alternately whimsical and bitter-sweet tales of emotional control—a more necessary defence than art, perhaps, against urban anomie. In this respect, Allen's *Oedipus Wrecks* manages to be both the most extreme fantasy—as Arnold Mills discovers the mother he may indeed have magically wished out of his system returning to haunt the skies of his city—and the most rooted in urban reality. Or at least in that sense of comic reality which, in his *New Yorker* sketches and retold chassidic tales, Allen has always been able to lend the stereotypes of the city, the family, the Jewish mother and the son who, in frozen alarm and resignation, watches his wife-to-be about to pick up from his de-etherealised mother. Allen's ending seems almost too quiet, too woebegone, even for a short story, but it makes its point about the ties that bind and control more effectively than the drive towards a "twist" ending, or the fantasy flourish, of its stablemates.

NEW LEADER, 3/6/89, p. 20, John Morrone

New York Stories is high-powered revival of a narrative format that has been largely passé since the mid-'60s: the sequence film, with one or more directors contributing featurettes built around a unifying theme, star, author, or prop. Anyone who recalls *Dead of Night*, the famous British horror anthology, or De Sica's *Yesterday, Today, and Tomorrow*, or Woody Allen's *Everything You Always Wanted to Know About Sex*, has enjoyed what often was an appealing kind of storytelling that several generations of episode television have, alas, eclipsed. But sequence films also let the storyteller "off the hook," since the unifying factor is the focus, not the director, whose chief concern is maintaining his own voice among the ensemble.

New York Stories assumes—and expects the audience to assume—that "only in New York" could the tales it tells unfold. They are: "Life Lessons," directed by Martin Scorsese and written by Richard Price; "Life Without Zoe," directed and co-written (with his daughter Sofia) by Francis Coppola; and "Oedipus Wrecks," directed, written and starring Woody Allen. It is almost a moot point who or what gets the worst deal in these stories, the audience that has been led to expect familiar urban eccentricities gently satirized, or the City, presented as an arena for artists, children and lovers to indulge themselves at the expense of others. The theme linking sequences is Manipulation—of people, circumstances and one's own past.

In "Life Lessons," the fleshy and powerfully-built Nick Nolte plays Lionel, a famous, middle-aged, grizzly-in-a-tux Soho artist stuck midway in the creation of a huge canvas that sits accusingly uncompleted in a loft strewn with a paint and Brillo-pad compost. Its unfinished state makes Lionel anxious.

He's lovesick, too. His live-in assistant, Paulette (Rosanna Arquette), wants out because she is too worried about her own career as an artist, and too uninspired romantically to return Lionel's affections. Throughout most of "Life Lessons," the two circle each other like a pair of unevenly matched erotic gamesters, he whining, she declining.

Both are pretty well connected to external worlds of fellow painters, exhibitors and performance artists—the whole downtown, "Slaves of New York" scene. Still, Lionel harangues her as if no one else existed.

Price's script is heartlessly savvy, revealing the way these gifted, ruthless New Yorkers get it on and get ahead. It also allows Scorsese to side with Lionel and stack the deck against Paulette, who remains underdeveloped. The angst being explored here is clearly Lionel's. He begs for sexual attention and yet whimpers, "I just wanted to kiss your foot. It was nothing personal." Indeed, for the hardly satirical remark is symptomatic of this would-be lover's objectification of his love.

Nothing seems very "personal" to these people. They're too busy by-passing each other to ever really connect. While he works, Lionel fills his loft with a constant rock-and-roll blare, and what aids creativity snuffs out communication. He's happiest (though for a hang-dog like him the term is entirely relative) when he is slapping and smearing on paint, attacking his canvas with an aggressive frenzy. Once exhausted, he switches from Procol Harum's "A Whiter Shade of Pale" to something classical—yes, "Nessun Dorma" from *Turandot*, the movies' most overused bit of operatic shorthand for moments of male heterosexual yearning. (To emphasize this, the recording used is by Mario del Monaco, who possessed the butchest tenor of the last 30 years.) All of these scenes of Lionel at work demonstrate that his career is far more fulfilling than his romantic relationship, despite his protesting otherwise.

Similarly, the lessons in life that Lionel claims to be teaching Paulette—how not to use and be used—are shown to be contradictory, and the trick ending is of course that once Paulette walks, she's effortlessly replaced. A curvaceous new candidate vamps Lionel for the job at the gallery opening where he finally exhibits his now-finished canvas: a mural-sized panorama that seems to depict a city in flames. Scorsese makes no attempt to reconcile this sad and unnerving image, Lionel's vision of a city in distress, with his own casual and off-handed portrait of New York as the playground of emotional deadbeats. The tone of "Life Lessons" is ultimately at odds with the cautionary tale about self-deception it apparently wants to tell. The social climbing and career net-working of Manhattan's art parasites are enacted with shameless bravura. Cards on the table, and no apologies.

Francis Coppola's tasteless "Life Without Zoe," set in an arid and even higher-rent district than "Life Lessons," could arguably be titled "Life Without Life." Much like the storybook Eloise who lived at the Plaza, Zoe (Heather McComb) is a little rich girl who lives at the Sherry Netherland Hotel, where she is attended by a manservant and left to her own devices by her globetrotting parents. Along with her similarly wealthy friends at the Fieldston School, she is confident, sophisticated and unbearably shallow. She cozies up to visiting Middle Eastern princes, hails taxis with aplomb, and has access to a vast allowance that is 100 per cent disposable, unearned income. It's *her* tool for manipulating her surroundings, and she works at that without complaint.

Although the plot has something to do with the 12-year-old's scheme to reunite her farflung parents, the details that stick are the Hershey's Kisses she throws at the homeless man who lives in a box on Fifth Avenue. Zoe's life flaunts itself carelessly, and the girl in all her pint-sized shrillness comes to resemble the overstuffed society matron whose perfume is too heavy and whose voice is too loud. Money buys happiness for Zoe, not for us: There's not a bit of *joie de vivre* in "Life Without Zoe."

One waits an eternity for Woody Allen to show up, but "Oedipus Wrecks" turns out to be about yet another kind of manipulation. Allen plays Sheldon Mills, an executive engaged to be married to Lisa (Mia Farrow, again standing in for Allen's idea of an attractively de-ethnicized, vanilla WASP temperament). Sheldon is still being brutalized, however, by his monumentally vulgar, outspoken mother, Mrs. Millstein (Mae Questel). Justifiably, he would like his mother to "just disappear," and his wish seems to come true during a stage magician's act when Mrs. Millstein, "chosen at random from our audience," vanishes from inside a streamer trunk that's been pierced with swords. (Such images of phallic vengeance are scattered throughout "Oedipus Wrecks.") Momentarily relieved of Mother, the son's mood clears and his sex life improves, but she returns as a disembodied head floating over Manhattan, spewing abuse at her son and making the whole City privy to her version of Sheldon's life story, from bed-wetting boy to hapless bachelor.

Hoping to manipulate his own past by suppressing it, Sheldon is instead punished by a virago who cannot be controlled. The mother-vs.-son jokes are funny but uncommonly vicious, and Allen has never written so self-punishing, in fact masochistic, a role for himself. (One exchange made me gasp. Lisa complains that Mrs. Millstein-in-the-sky is "saying horrible things about me in foreign words, like '*courveh*.'" She asks Sheldon what it means. "Oh, something Jewish," he mutters—"whore.").

The ultimate joke in "Oedipus Wrecks" is how Sheldon gets Mother to descend from on high and leave her public life. She'll only cooperate when Sheldon, now dumped by his WASP fiancée, falls for earthy, possessive, zaftig Treva (Julie Kavner), a phony psychic he originally hired to exorcise Mrs. Millstein. Thus, the man who sought to rid himself of one Jewish mother ends up with two, and anticipates spending his life henpecked by both mother and wife. This only in New York, Woody Allen? "Oedipus Wrecks" is *New York Stories*' ninth circle of metropolitan hell, and I walked away from the film convinced I had spent two hours-plus in an inferno characterized by gridlock, bad white wine, and exact-change fares—a less-than-divine comedy.

NEW STATESMAN & SOCIETY, 11/17/89, p. 44, Suzanne Moore

London, it is often said, is getting more like New York every day. Central London is now too expensive to live in except for those who sleep overnight in their offices. But while residents of Manhattan are emotionally immune to the bundles of rags sleeping rough, *we* are still surprised at the increasing homelessness on our streets.

But New York is much more than the sum of its homeless. We know this because we have seen it in the movies. New York *is* the movies in a way that London never will be. London films are never quite right. They are always someone else's London, while New York, a city no older than movies themselves, belongs to all of us.

New York Stories, then, is an intriguing concept; three "filmlets" by three directors who have continually used the city as source and inspiration—Francis Ford Coppola who recreated turn-of-the-century New York in *The Godfather* and 1920s Harlem in *The Cotton Club*, Martin Scorsese who made the seminal *Mean Streets* and *Taxi Driver*, and Woody Allen who sets nearly all his films in Manhattan.

This chance to play, to sketch out ideas or to turn in a crisp short story has resulted in three very different films that in reality have little connection with each other. You can't help feeling that a tighter brief would have provided a more satisfactory whole, but then these are the Big Boys in the Big Apple.

The biggest, of course, is Coppola (both Allen and Scorsese are notably little men). His filmlet "Life without Zoe" is one of the biggest embarrassments that I've seen for a long time.

Co-written with his daughter Sofia, it is a tale about an incredibly rich 12 year old who lives in the very expensive Sherry-Netherland Hotel, attended by a butler while her parents travel the world. It really doesn't have a single redeeming factor, and if the sight of 12 year olds with carefully ripped jeans and Chanel hats doesn't make you sick, then clearly you are as out of touch as Coppola must be.

"Life without Zoe" also contains a scene that is more vomit-inducing than anything *Halloween 4* could dream of. When Zoe, in Lady Bountiful mode, distributes "Silver Kisses" (a kind of chocolate) to a bum living in a box, he mutters, "That's why I love New York." Thank God, then, that both the first and last contributions are worth catching.

The last, "Oedipus Wrecks", is such perfect Woody Allen that it is almost a parody of itself. From the first shot of him monologising to the camera about his mother during a therapy session, we know exactly what we are in for. He takes full advantage of having only a short time. Basically this is just a one-joke filmlet, but even though it's an old joke it is still very funny. When Allen's archetypal Jewish domineering mother mysteriously disappears, Allen is at last free. When she reappears as some giant TV image hovering over the Chrysler building discussing with the whole city his premature baldness, bedwetting and how he doesn't eat properly, his life is made hell again—until he meets a nice Jewish girl.

I don't share the much-expressed opinion that Allen should go back to making comedies instead of all those miserable films of late. It is not the seriousness I object to, but the stultifying tastefulness of it all that I don't like. He certainly manages to make more "serious points" in a film like this than he ever does by having the middle classes dissect each other's neuroses in coffee-and-beige living rooms. The fantasy of "Oedipus Wrecks"—of having your parent not die but simply disappear out of your life—is one that I'm sure most of us can get into.

The first, and I think the best, of the three *New York Stories* is Scorsese's "Life Lessons". Nick Nolte is a Grizzly Adams-lookalike and an artist of some repute. Rosanna Arquette is his assistant, one-time lover, and herself an aspiring painter. He wants her, she no longer wants him. He paints brilliantly and she wants to know if he likes her works rather than just her body.

Scorsese has explored the theme of the impossibility of a relationship between two creative people—there was no happy ending for Liza Minnelli and Robert De Niro in *New York, New*

York. As a portrait of the end of a relationship, "Life Lessons" manages a wry sympathy for both characters. Nolte wildly splashes on the paint to the sounds of Dylan and Procul Harum and is, like Scorsese, unembarrassed by the romanticism or unfashionableness of the music.

Scorsese layers on his themes—creativity, middle age, infatuation, dependency—with a slithery double edge that means that Nolte's outbursts about great art being about having no choice are always punctured by Arquette's pissed-off expression. Scorsese, with remarkably few brush strokes, paints a "genius" who is talented despite his shallowness, immaturity and impossible ego.

In Faber and Faber's new book *Scorsese on Scorsese*, the man himself contrasts what he does with the ultra-cool Jim Jarmusch who has said that in his films he doesn't want to tell people where to look: "Well, I *do* want them to see the way I see. Walking down the street, looking quickly about, tracking, panning, zooming, cutting and all that sort of thing." Scorsese does it in "Life Lessons", pulling back from artwork to paint-spattered cassette player. It is hard to say which image is more beautiful, which is more important—the artistic process or the product.

"Life Lessons" is also the most New York of the *New York Stories* in that it is clear that Arquette only puts up with Nolte because she has nowhere else to live. Like the characters in Tama Janovitz's *Slaves of New York*, relationships have to be orchestrated around housing situations rather than vice versa. For all three *Stories* occupy a supremely privileged space in the city. They may not have to deal with what Kathy Acker recently described as a city "writhing in pain", they may not deal with homelessness, race riots or the causal violence of the place, but because of that they don't conjure up its vibrancy, the properly acute stroppiness of its citizens. For this you still need to see Spike Lee's *Do the Right Thing*—a New York story of a very different kind.

NEW YORK, 3/13/89, p. 63, David Denby

Driven, obsessive people are everywhere, but New York seems to specialize in them. In this city, a man muttering to himself may be a genius or merely one of the star-crossed or pixilated millions. *New York Stories*, an omnibus film with separate episodes directed by three famous filmmakers, doesn't offer an overarching vision of life in the city. But it must mean something about the relentlessness of existence here that the two good stories, the ones directed by Martin Scorsese and Woody Allen, are about obsessional personalities. On the other hand, Francis Coppola, the director of the third section (and a non-New Yorker), tries merely to charm and winds up nowhere.

Scorsese's episode, "Life Lessons," is dominated by a famous painter named Lionel Dobie, an institution of the New York art world. A big, heavy man, shaggy, with matted beard and hair, Dobie may behave badly, make a fool of himself, but it doesn't really matter. He's Lionel Dobie, "the Lion"—and everyone indulges him. His work is his defense. Nick Nolte, one of the few grown-up American actors, does a wonderful job with this sacred monster. In such films as *Who'll Stop the Rain* and *North Dallas Forty*, Nolte's thick, heavy body and cigarette-scarred voice seemed the very oak of experience. Nolte doesn't sweat the small stuff; he gets to the essence of things. Profane, independent, a shambling and and rugged man's man, he's a hero in a contemporary style, without the self-mythologizing posturing of a Gary Cooper or John Wayne.

Padding around his huge loft, Lionel falls into periods of doubt and disgust, but eventually he rouses himself, attacking his monster canvases, creating the work for his next big show. He's the kind of artist who needs a certain amount of conflict and mess in his life. The current mess is his Punch-and-Judy relationship with the screechy, complaining 22-year-old Paulette (Rosanna Arquette), his "assistant," who lives with him in the loft and plays at her painting. Paulette is meant to be a good-looking girl who is ordinary in all other ways, the contemporary equivalent of a model who possesses some feature (in this case, her little angel's feet) that arouses the erotic imagination of a great man who doesn't want, or need, a wife or a "complete" relationship. In fact, Lionel is not much concerned with who his mistress is. As far as Lionel can see, Paulette doesn't exist by herself. He's creating her, teaching her the rough glories of "life," and she should be grateful.

The joke is that Paulette is exasperated, even oppressed, by Lionel's egotistical devotion. He talks a high line about inspiration but doesn't respect her enough to give her a straight answer about her own work, which she suspects is lousy. She screams at him, but still, slavishly adoring, he persists, suffering her abuse at parties, agreeing to her demand that he stay out of her bed. Scorsese and writer Richard Price, drawing on Dostoevski's *The Gambler* and the diary of Dostoevski's young mistress, have created a complex irony: Lionel Dobie is a bastard and deserves what he gets, but, at the same time, his arrogant assumption that he's the most exciting thing that will ever happen to Paulette is probably right.

This little movie has drive and temperament and wit. Price, the novelist turned screenwriter (he wrote *The Color of Money* for Scorsese), is blessed with a peculiarly harsh and comic New York vivacity. He writes scenes of sudden rage better than anyone (it's one of Scorsese's specialties, too). He does the art-world stuff—parties, performance garages, painters' small talk—with a more authentic flair and emotion than any screenwriter before him. And Price is generous to minor characters—the downtown types lounging at an art opening, two cops sitting in a patrol car. His New York is the most worldly and articulate of cities.

The filmmakers' conception of Dobie goes back to the heroic Abstract Expressionist period of New York painting. As rock music blasts in the background, Dobie slabs thick swatches of paint on the canvas; he's what used to be called an action painter (Chuck Connelly did the principal canvas used in the movie). Scorsese, pushing the narrative along hard, works in analogous ways as a director, with a harsh, abrupt attack, lots of discontinuous "jump" cutting, and lens irises opening and closing in D.W. Griffith style. The rough, moment-by-moment intensity that Dobie brings to his painting is there in the movie.

"Life Lessons" might have been a vibrant small classic were it not for Rosanna Arquette. What does Scorsese see in her? He used her once before, in *After Hours*, and she's grown worse as an actress. (He may be suffering from obsession, too.) She's got that teenagey come hither look—the upturned nose, downy upper lip, and golden skin—but she's so limited in emotional range that even her looks begin to sour after a while. As Paulette, she lacks the pliancy, the ambiguous seductiveness of a young woman being flattered and adored by a fmaous man. She's shrill and flat—shrewish, almost. We know the point is that Lionel can't really see who Paulette is, but Arquette is downright unpleasant, and Lionel at times seems merely nuts for bothering with her. Her one-dimensional acting throws the story out of balance; we stop viewing her complaints with sympathy. But Nolte—proud, vulnerable, just rolling along no matter how many obstacles lie in the way—gives an enduring performance. His strength fuels the ironic joke that brings "Life Lessons" to its abrupt but satisfying conclusion.

Woody Allen's "Oedipus Wrecks" isn't great—it's really rather thin, without the texture of *Hannah and Her Sisters* or the energy of his earlier anarchic films. The conclusion feels limp, almost lazy. But "Oedipus Wrecks" is certainly funny, and halfway through it I realized I was so relieved that Allen was working in comedy again that I didn't much care that the episode wasn't great.

The premise is simple: A successful 50-year-old Jewish corporate lawyer, Sheldon Mills (né Millstein), is still plagued by his mother (Mae Questel). There she is, his nemesis—tiny, implacable, always *talking*. She corrects, she criticizes, she tells him he looks terrible, she reminisces about his childhood, practically wiping his little tushie is front of his refined Gentile girlfriend, Lisa (Mia Farrow). Woody plays Sheldon himself, and seems to be offering some personal testimony. Mom embodies what the lawyer (and perhaps Woody Allen too) hates most about Jewishness—the demonstrativeness, the smothering affection and oversolicitude. He loves her, but when he thinks of life without her, a silly grin comes over his face.

Woody Allen is tough enough to understand that power, not just love, is the issue. Mom keeps coming back to Shelly's baby years in order to retain the importance in his life that she once had. The movie is a fable of filial impotence, and like many fables, it leaves realism behind. At one moment, a voice emerges from a coffin. My heart sank. Another Bergman imitation? But all was well: The sequence is hilarious; Woody Allen is in control of his art once again.

Francis Coppola's "Life Without Zoe" is a neo-*Eloise* bit of whimsy about a rich girl living in the Sherry Netherland. Coppola wrote it with his seventeen-year-old daughter, Sofia, and I'm sorry to say that the movie reflects the wish fulfillment of an adolescent girl—that she be the center of everything—without the charm that would absolve the story of its narcissism. But two out of three episodes that take the city's measure isn't a bad ratio.

NEW YORK POST, 3/1/89, p. 25, David Edelstein

What a package: three short New York City-based films by three of America's nerviest directors, Martin Scorsese, Francis Coppola and Woody Allen—artists whose works have, in radically different ways, helped to shape our understanding of life in the '70s and '80s. There's probably no way "New York Stories" could live up to our hopes, but there are riches here: as omnibus films go, it's a Mercedes.

Apart from the setting, there's no link between each short, and Scorsese's Soho, Coppola's Fifth Avenue and Allen's Upper East Side are worlds apart. Maybe that's the point—the Big Apple is big (and wormy) enough to accommodate each man's vision.

In the first and most striking film, "Life Lessons," Scorsese plunges us into the dying throes of an affair between Lionel (Nick Nolte), a bigwig abstract painter, and Paulette (Rosanna Arquette), his live-in assistant. As the young woman attempts to wriggle out of Lionel's grasp, the artist labors mightily to hang onto her—pleading, wheedling, howling "like a gunshot dog."

Romantic obsession is no stranger to Scorsese or writer Richard Price (in such harrowing comic novels as "Ladies Man"). Nolte, in a marvelous performance, functions as their alterego, a galvanic mixture of genius infantilism, and bearishness—Soho's Grizzly Adams.

It soon becomes clear that Lionel thrives on pain. With an exhibition looming, the blocked painter snaps to work as soon as Paulette announces, coldly, that she doesn't love him. His tape deck blasting. Lionel spills his guts across the huge canvases.

Scorsese paints, too, with his camera, gliding along the canvases and dabbing at his characters. We feel in both director and character the *attack*, the titanic compulsion to translate these longings into a higher, immortal realm. (Scorsese, an asthmatic, has a style both muscular and fluid; he's an Olympian director.)

Price's script is pure, incendiary conflict—two animals tearing at each other in an attempt to seize control. Late in the film, Arquette has a great moment when she orders Lionel to prove his love by kissing a policeman; the curl of her lip is so sadistic that we search her eyes for a clue to what she's really feeling.

It's too bad she's so petulant the rest of the time. Arquette is better here than in her last few, insecure performances, but she no longer seems comfortable just being observed. Her face is tense and mask-like—all wounded eyes and bleating, thrust-out lips.

As a result, it's hard to care about her when she utters the movie's key line: "Sometimes I feel like a human sacrifice." Lionel doesn't love her, he desires her—he wants to consume her, to use her as kindling for his art.

That's the surprise of "Life Lessons"—that a story presented from a man's perspective finally rebounds on that man, exposing the limits of his point of view. Lionel's feelings are both volcanic and disposable. It's unclear if Scorsese and Price think his exploitation of young women is justified, given his stature. They're probably still trying to puzzle that out in their own lives.

Woody Allen's "Oedipus Wrecks," the third in the trilogy, also verges on self-criticism. Allen plays an uptight Jewish lawyer who changes his name, moves in WASP circles (his fiance is played by Mia Farrow) and labors to downplay his Jewishness—which erupts into his life in the form of a vulgar, dominating mother (Mae Questel).

Allen has never made a film about Jewish self-hatred. He has *exhibited* it—it's the subtext of much of his work, and "Hannah and Her Sisters" is in some ways the ultimate fantasy of Jewish assimilation. This time, however, he confronts it directly, and the results are often liberating.

This is a comedy, so Allen must think it's less consequential than "September" or "Another Woman." But it's amazing how vital the movie feels, and how emotionally connected he seems to the material; the voice is his own—not Bergman's or Chekhov's. (He's back to laundry jokes.)

Comedy can accommodate anger, and that's the prevailing tone. Confronted with a mother who infantilizes him in public—who seems bent on making the world aware of her son's ethnicity and bodily functions—he feels a rage that borders on the existential. Reconciling her presence with his longing for WASPiness is no small problem.

When Fate (or the hero's unconscious) disposes of this demon, he is euphoric. I won't spoil for you the manner in which she returns—even more powerful in the afterlife than in the flesh—but it's a superbly nightmarish idea.

Alas, the filmmaking in the last third of "Oedipus Wrecks" is flat; Allen is looser here than he has been lately, but also less expressive. And the windup is jokey and tentative—he doesn't explore the implications of despising your mother and yet longing to marry her. (Surprise.)

However sketchy (this is, after all, a sketch), the film is a breakthrough: Allen is toying with a problem that's been murderously difficult for him to acknowledge, even when it has dominated his work. Now: Does he have the *chutzpah* to go even further?

Coppola's "Life Without Zoe" is harder to get a grip on. It's not unpleasant—just bewildering.

The film is a collaboration between Coppola and his 17-year-old daughter, Sofia (who also designed the splashy costumes), and it's a gloss on the book "Eloise at the Plaza."

The heroine, Zoe (Heather McComb), lives at the Sherry-Netherland off Central Park. Mostly, she's alone with her butler (Don Novello). Daddy (Giancarlo Giannini) is a famous flutist who's always on tour, and Mommy (Talia Shire) is a basket-case.

Yet the movie isn't about what's missing from her life but what's there: glamour, money, intrigue, exotic meetings with billionaire Arab boys and opulent parties with adolescent girls who are worldly beyond their years.

Vittorio Storaro basks the nymphets in rosy light, his camera drunk on plushness. But Coppola doesn't have a clear attitude toward these people. His tone is serenely indulgent bordering on fatuous, especially when he has to advance the (dumb) plot.

The gist of it is that Zoe, through her connections, comes through for her dad. And maybe that's what "Life Without Zoe" is about, too: Sofia Coppola coming through for her globetrotting father—and Coppola basking in her glow. How else to explain the title? The only character without Zoe is the famous dad; the audience gets more than a full dose.

NEWSDAY, 3/1/89, Part II/p. 2, Mike McGrady

The basic idea behind "'New York Stories" is a beauty: Take three of our top film directors—Martin Scorsese, Francis Coppola, Woody Allen—and invite them to each make a short film set in Manhattan.

The virtues of the idea are immediately apparent. There is the pleasure of watching large talents adjust to shorter-than-usual lengths. Then, too, there is a competitive aspect: If you're mixing it up with champions, you want to be seen at your best, possibly as *the* best. While the results don't quite live up to expectations, any buff should be entertained by "New York Stories." It *is* fun, and only one of the contributions qualifies as a turkey.

Scorsese and Allen are, unsurprisingly, very much at home in New York. So much of their best work has been done here that the city often seems to dictate its shape. The shapes dictated here are similar—lightweight but entertaining pictures of neurotic relationships.

In "Life Lessons," Scorsese explores the tension between a New York artist (Nick Nolte, in a nice change of pace) and a young woman (Rosanna Arquette) willing to share his loft but not his love. Writer Richard Price (he also scripted "The Color of Money" for Scorsese) comically probes some of the ironies built into a modern New York affair.

With his girlfriend away and his big show only three weeks off, Nolte is stymied, a victim of artist's block. Arquette storms back into his studio, teasing him, cuckolding him, torturing him and somehow inspiring him to pick up his brushes and start creating his wall-to-wall modern masterpieces again. Is angst essential to creativity? If so, and that's the film's stance, then New York is the ideal environment for an artist.

"It's an expensive city," someone says.

"It's the *only* city," Nolte replies.

Woody Allen's segment, "Oedipus Wrecks," offers welcome comic relief to all those fans who've been suffering through Woody Allen's Blue Period. Here's the Allen of old, the Manhattan shnook with an analyst, a dominating mother (Mae Questel), a *shiksa* girlfriend (Mia Farrow), a more acceptable (to Mom) alternative (Julie Kavner) and a problem: "I'm fifty years old, I'm the partner in a big law firm, and I still haven't resolved my relationship with my mother."

During the movie "Manhattan," Allen's alter ego claims to be writing a book about his mother: "The Castrating Zionist." Well, here she is in full flower—dominating, funny and larger than life (at times, literally so.)

Coppola's "Life Without Zoe" makes the mistake of concentrating on a thoroughly spoiled rich girl (Heather McComb) who lives in the Sherry Netherland Hotel while her parents (Talia Shire, Giancarlo Giannini) are usually traveling abroad separately. Not only is Zoe rich, she's condescending, patronizing, materialistic and thoroughly unappealing. When her mother makes a surprise visit home, interrupting an ice-cream party, Zoe is put out: "You should have given me a fair warning that you were coming home; I would've reserved a room at the Plaza." Where the little brat could doubtless look up her buddy, Eloise.

Zoe has hotel staffers bowing and scraping; her idea of an after-school activity is shopping by limo; she treats her mother to a flight to Paris, first-class; she slips candy kisses to a homeless man who lives in a box and who is simply thrilled by the girl's largesse: "Geez, that's why I love New York! Have a nice day! See you soon, I hope!"

Never a stickler for reality, Coppola is seldom this far off base. He shares the writing credit with his daughter, Sofia, and the film co-features his sister, Talia Shire; the best that can be said for it is that it has provided employment for the family.

NEWSWEEK, 3/6/89, p. 58, David Ansen

Anthology movies, the cinematic equivalent of grazing, tend to be more exciting in anticipation than in execution. From "7 Capital Sins" to last year's "Aria," these compendiums of short films from star directors rarely bat better than .333. That's great for a ballplayer but bad for a movie. *New York Stories*—a trio of unrelated tales of Manhattan from Martin Scorsese, Francis Coppola and Woody Allen—hits a happy two out of three. The one strikeout—Coppola's contriubtion—is tucked into the middle, so you can't avoid it, but the passionate Scorsese and the hilarious Allen should not be missed.

Scorsese's "Life Lessons," written by Richard Price, is a tautly strung tale of obsession set in the downtown art scene. Inspired in part by the diary of Dostoevski's mistress and protégée Apollinaria Suslova, it stars Nick Nolte as a lionized but isolated painter who develops a fixation on his young assistant (Rosanna Arquette) as he feverishly works on a new show. She shares her mentor's loft but spurns his sexual advances, which only feeds his obsession. Nolte's Lionel Dobie is a smothering, egotistical bear of a man, but Scorsese obviously identifies with his creative pain. Nolte makes this ambiguous hero—is he an emotional con artist or a man in the grips of a genuine romantic agony?—a powerfully touching figure. This darkly funny dance of deflected desire is filmed with slashing, unsettling lyricism and pumped up with an inspired score that ranges from Procol Harum to Puccini. As in all Scorsese movies, the erotic is flecked with dread, and love, possessiveness and power intermingle ambiguously. Only the ironic coda disappoints—it's too facile a resolution, but it's easily forgiven. From first to last edgy frame, "Life Lessons" vibrates with life.

Woody Allen is back in peak comic form in "Oedipus Wrecks," playing a 50-year-old lawyer whose lifelong struggle with his tiny, overbearing Jewish mother (Mae Questel) reaches a crisis as his marriage to a shiksa (Mia Farrow, of course) approaches. It would be a shame to reveal too much else. Suffice it to say that Allen's tall tale, like many of his best short stories, takes a breathtaking leap into the supernatural, and that Julie Kavner makes a delicious appearance as a decidedly eclectic Manhattan spiritualist. Woody's recent forays into solemnity haven't dimmed his comic timing a bit, and his acting seems to have acquired new subtleties. One long take, in which he discovers his heart's true desire while gazing at a chicken leg, achieves Chaplinesque grace. The ultimate Jewish-mama joke, "Oedipus Wrecks" takes that tired old riff to cosmically humiliating heights.

Coppola's "Life Without Zoe" is an "Eloise"-like fable about a spoiled little rich girl (Heather McComb) who lives in the Sherry Netherland hotel while her famous flutist father (Giancarlo Giannini) is off giving concerts and her photojournalist mother (Talia Shire) trots around the globe. Meant to be a heartwarming fantasy complete with costume ball, Oriental princess and stolen jewels, it's crammed with lavish production values and little else. Written by Coppola with his 17-year-old daughter Sofia, who's obviously working out her ambivalent feelings about being a famous movie director's daughter, "Life Without Zoe" makes neither emotional nor narrative sense, and it seriously misjudges our affection for its brattish heroine. The opening credits of this all-in-the-family effort are all on a first-name-only basis (Music by Carmine, Cinematography by Vittorio, and so forth). You could get away with that in a home movie; on a work this overproduced and incoherent it just looks like hubris.

SIGHT & SOUND, Autumn 1989, p. 279, Richard Combs

In filming literature, it's most axiomatic that the short story is a better source than the novel. It allows for expansion and elaboration, making a spectacle of the point; a great deal of effort does not have to go into finding short cuts to the point. When the movies themselves go in for short stories, the problems of compression and shortcutting return, perhaps because the cinema is naturally discursive, depending on a build-up of evidence, of images, rather than a whittling away to a single image, irony or emotion. The problems are variously manifest in *New York Stories*, and it's no surprise that the most successful of the three tales ('Oedipus Wrecks') is directed by Woody Allen. This may have something to do with the fact that Allen has become less cinematic the more accomplished he has become as a film-maker, determinedly preserving his roots not only in New York, but in the *New Yorker* sketch form in which he began.

His title conjures the classic Jewish mother joke ('Oedipus Schmoedipus'), and what follows is that joke infused with Allen's personal iconography. The sketch begins with a psychiatrist, to whom Arnold Mills (Allen) is confessing that, although he has successfully passed into an *echt* WASP law firm, and tried to detach himself from his background by truncating his name (from Millstein), he is still plagued by his mother's smothering ways. When mother mysteriously disappears during a magic show, guilt gives way to a sense of release; until the day she reappears, funnier and more awesome than anything in *Ghostbusters*, as a nagging apparition in the skies of Manhattan.

If this is classic *New Yorker* Allen, it might seem dismayingly old-fashioned in terms of his film career, a return to the skits of *Everything You Always Wanted to Know About Sex*. But the "mother in the sky" is also akin to the movie conceits of the later Allen, to the absconding screen hero of *The Purple Rose of Cairo* or the compulsively assimilating one of *Zelig*. Into these sophisticated effects, the movies themselves disappear, leaving in their place their creator's elemental fears of non-existence, non-acceptance. Arnold having his childhood bedwetting discussed on the evening news is the ultimate nightmare of public exposure, worse than the dinner guest who turns into a rabbi in *Annie Hall*.

The city as a personal, thoroughly internalised landscape of the author/hero's fears is the one thing the Allen sketch has in common with Martin Scorsese's opening story "Life Lessons", in which painter Lionel Dobie (Nick Nolte) seems, in his vitality and despair, so plugged into the energy circuits of New York that disconnection would mean death. In fact, so much does Lionel insist on this, particularly when his protégée Paulette (Rosanna Arquette) starts making angry noises about quitting him and the city, that one suspects the vignette is partly a parody of the Big Apple love story.

It might be truer, however, to say that "Life Lessons" is inevitably a parody of a Scorsese movie, mainly because so much of past Scorsese is jostling for entry. The way the story chooses to exist, with an iris shot closing on Lionel as he goes into his pitch about offering "lie lessons" to another admirer at another opening, certainly has the ironic neatness of O. Henry. But that is not the same as the spiralling conclusion of a truer Scorsese: those tales of heroes convinced of damnation relentlessly pursuing redemption. "Life Lessons", in a sense, gives us too much Scorsese for the piece to work on its own terms: something of *Raging Bull* in the way Lionel attacks his giant canvases, and just as fiercely attacks whatever his gaze fixes on (another iris shot as he contemplates Paulette's bare foot); something of *The Color of Money* (also scripted by Richard Price) in the agonies of the older man trying to hold his own against the competition ("Are you a graffiti artist?" he warily asks one pick-up of Paulette's); and touches of the comedy of frustration of *After Hours* in the pixillated menace of the details of New York night life.

The middle episode, "Life Without Zoe", on the other hand, gives us rather less than we might expect of Francis Coppola. It has been set up on a premise true enough to the film-maker—creating a project that is then allowed an evolution of its own, to go where it will, the resulting film to some extent being about how it got there—which on this occasion does not take us very far. "Life Without Zoe" was written with Coppola's 17-year-old daughter Sofia, who designed the costumes as well, while Coppola's actress sister Talia Shire and composer father Carmine also take part: the generosity and the "family" context being further true elements. But the resulting fantasy—about children playing semi-adults in a world from which the real adults have abdicated—involves a degree of feigned naivety, of willed frivolity, that is fatal to this kind of project.

From her cosseted isolation in the Sherry Netherland hotel, Zoe (Heather McComb) conceives two fairy-tale schemes: to reconcile her estranged, globetrotting parents, and to restore a fabulous jewel to an Eastern princess, who gave it to Zoe's father, a renowned and dangerously seductive flautist, and must have it back before her husband, the king, finds out. Coppola has abetted his daughter in dressing New York for a cod *Arabian Nights* fable, but the result is not one from the heart, and if a Coppola film, even in miniature, is not that it is little else.

"New York is almost an unnamed character in the story," Coppola is quoted in the production notes, giving the predictable rationale for this three-way urban cross-section. Producer Robert Greenhut—who was originally approached by Woody Allen with the idea of his doing three short stories himself—echoes the notion that all the film-makers have in common is the city. "We originally talked about having three different approaches with a theme running through them all, but I thought it would be more interesting not to have this, since we didn't want to pre-empt any ideas that the directors might offer us.''

On the contrary, all three seem to have found their way to a common theme—love's labours lost, or strangely diverted—and might be judged more by what they have done with that than by what they have shown of New York. Coppola ends with a quaintly qualified fairy-tale tag, ''And we all lived happily—so far—ever after,'' Scorsese with a picture of the romantic artist as helpless victim of his own impulses, and Allen on the most bitter-sweet note of all, as Arnold finds that race, boiled chicken, and mother hovering over the Chrysler building will inevitably shape his heart's desire.

TIME, 3/6/89, p. 68, Richard Schickel

Invidious comparisons being the curse of the creative class (and the perverse joy of the critical community), the first thing one must say to Martin Scorsese, Francis Coppola and Woody Allen is ''Brave lads!''

They have each contributed a short film to *New York Stories*, probably knowing as they signed their contracts that their work, when combined, would not be judged for its total effect, which is delightful, but scored like some unlikely Olympic event. One imagines reviewers grouped around the pool, holding up flash cards (9.5, 7.0 or whatever) as these men, possibly the best American directors of their generation, paddle back up to the surface after their plunge into the unfamiliar depths of the anthology film.

The dive into the short-movie form is highly difficult, especially when confronted from the platform of a lofty reputation. It requires the same concentration of effort and narrative skills needed for a full-length feature but, without the distractions of spectacle or subplot, makes flaws more obvious. In these circumstances. Scorsese and Allen have a natural advantage. Their core following is not big enough to support the grand movie gesture, and they have learned the art of compression that seems to bore, if not actually depress, their ever thrashing colleague.

Scorsese is hardly a highly verbal filmmaker. His gift is to pack the equivalent of a thousand words of dialogue into a single elegant image. *Life Lessons* is about a bearish artist (Nick Nolte) whose reputation is currently bullish in chic circles but is distinctly on the decline as far as his lover assistant (Rosanna Arquette) is concerned. Both actors are excellent, as is Richard Price's script, which is taken from a passage in Dostoyevsky's life. But it is from the observation of simple things—a slo-mo close-up of a cigarette being discarded, a brush slathering gobs of paint on a canvas—and from the way he establishes the counterrhythms of artistic creation and emotional destruction that Scorsese sidles slyly up to the highest truths of his tale.

Allen's method is different. In *Oedipus Wrecks*, his efficiency is that of the perfectly practiced anecdotalist, not wasting a moment on irrelevant detail, yet knowing when to linger over the important ones. In this brisk vignette, Allen himself plays Sheldon, victim of a kind of transcendental Jewish-mother joke. It would spoil the fun to say how he transforms a stock figure, a yammering, smothering mom (Mae Questel, who is splendid), from a private torment into a public menace, but it is literally magical to behold.

Coppola's *Life Without Zoe*, a sort of *Eloise* story set at the Sherry Netherland Hotel instead of the Plaza, is the weakest entry. It occasionally says something mildly amusing about the overprivileged children of New York City's rich and famous. But Coppola and his co-writer, who happens to be his 17-year-old daughter Sofia, cannot settle on a tone for their overplotted yarn of a Junior Ms. Fixit, working simultaneously on the cases of a poor little rich boy and her parents' wavering marriage. The Coppola team tries satire and sentiment, but the story is not so much concluded as abandoned in a muddled rush. Give it a 5.5, and be grateful for the 10.0s on either side of it.

VILLAGE VOICE, 3/7/89, p. 59, Amy Taubin

Inspired by the French *Paris vu par...* and the Italian *Boccaccio 70*, three auteur heavy hitters—Martin Scorsese, Francis Coppola, and Woody Allen—have made short comedy films about ''this hell of a town.'' Predictably uneven, *New York Stories* opens with a world beater (the Scorsese section), follows with a mess (the Coppola), and concludes with a riotous retread of a sour one-liner (the Allen)—it actually made me sick with laughter. The fact that all three are set in high-rent districts is probably more than coincidental, but I doubt that a conscious desire to preserve the dramatic unities figured in the massive overdetermination.

Scorsese's "Life Lessons" starts out dreamy and hyperbolic and, over the course of 45-plus minutes, milks the incongruities of these two tonalities for wildy poignant, edge-of-hysteria humor. To the tugging organ strains of Procol Harum ("Whiter Shade of Pale"), a succession of iris shots alternately tunnels toward or opens out from ludicrously clichéd images of an artist's studio—paint-smeared palette, encrusted brushes casually arranged like flowers in a tin can, half-empty brandy bottle. If not for the muted luminescence of the cinematography (Nestor Almendros), we'd be in George Kuchar-land. (And we are, to the extent that the act of painting is revealed as exuberantly scatological). But the quality of the filmed image speaks a more controlled and self-conscious language of fetishism—very *Vertigo*esque. (And where has there been a more marked reference to the iris than in that film's Hitchcock/Bass title sequence?)

Strikingly archaic, the iris not only isolates a detail from a broad visual field, it also calls attention to the act of seeing (in the way a conventional close-up would not). Which is appropriate, since the subjects of this seemingly light-touch throwaway are nothing less than how painting and film are meshed in visual fetishism, and, to a lesser degree, how the interplay of '50s pictures (still and moving) yielded the '80s art world.

Bumbling, bearish Lionel Dobie (Nick Nolte) probably attained manhood in the Cedar Bar, but had to wait 30 years for Neo-Expressionism to propel him to art world glory. (He's a kind of Julian Schnabel, but with a past.) Protected by limited intelligence and an excess of physical energy, he hasn't a clue—as he bounds around his studio, hurling paint and basketballs with equal abandon to rhythms of vintage Bob Dylan and Puccini's *Turandot*—that the ego-obliterating risk-taking of Abstract Expressionism has ossified into a cult of personality. And that the second time around, the myth of authenticity repeats itself as farce. Buoyed by his self-image as life force incarnate and by the recent infusion of big bucks, he's engaged in an affair with a polished Golden Delicious apple of young womanhood, Paulette (Rosanna Arquette).

Life Lessons begins with the relationship ended but not yet over. Paulette (no surname!), who wants Dobie to recognize her for her painting, not her sexuality, has decided to move out. Her refusal of his attentions transforms his infatuation into full-blown obsession. Imagining himself still in control of the situation, Dobie magnanimously offers to let her stay on rent free and free of her sexual obligations. Of course, his calculations fall prey to his uncontrollable emotions, especially when she brings a series of young usurpers (Steve Buscemi and Jesse Borrego) into the picture. The comedy is in the split between mind and gut, and Nolte plays it with rare delicacy and wit. He can't keep himself from barging into her bedroom on the pretext of rescuing misplaced brushes and basketballs flung out of bounds. Standing dazedly at the foot of her bed, he fixates (iris in) on her bracelet-adorned ankle. (He: "I had this impulse. . . I wanted to kiss your foot. It's nothing personal.")

Dobie's the kind of guy who flirts with humiliation but stops short of suicide (or murder), and the film's most startling scene shows us exactly where that line is drawn. It's his massive sense of self-preservation that makes Dobie a prolific artist and a fun guy to have around—at a distance. The reason that "Life Lessons" is a comedy of obsession (rather than a tragedy like *Vertigo*) is that we know from the beginning that this affair is far from a once-in-a-lifetime thing. The artist with "fire-power" can risk (psychic) castration because there'll always be another adoring art student in whom he can restore his damaged cock.

But what of the young artist herself? In order to function as an object of desire, a fantasy projection, she must remain a glowing enigma, the pure embodiment of denial. Which is a pity. Because if this film is really about what art is at the end of the 20th century (as opposed to an amusing depiction of male megalomania), then surely the reasons she cannot succeed as an artist are as interesting as the reasons he can. The script makes a few superficial gestures in this direction, but, for the most part, her failure is written off as lack of talent (whatever that may be). I'm not saying that it's Scorsese's responsibility to give her an equal share (and especially not in a 45-minute film), only that "Life Lessons" would seem even richer if it were set in a film culture that acknowledged sexual dialectics.

This omission is even more an issue in Woody Allen's "Oedipus Wrecks," the ne plus ultra of Jewish Mother jokes. Returning to the center of his own picture (tenderly lit by Sven Nykvist), Allen plays Sheldon Mills, né Millstein, a 50-year-old attorney at a very conservative (read WASP) firm, engaged to a radiantly Rubenesque Mia Farrow, but still agonizingly in the grip of his overprotective, overcritical, relentlessly infantilizing Ma. Couched extremely skillfully at the edge of fantasy (with a first scene set in a psychoanalytic session), the film grants Mills-Millstein the fulfillment of his deepest wish—his mother disappears—and then plunges him into his worst nightmare. She returns as a giant projection floating above the city—a cross between Dreyer's head "vampyr" and the beneficent, high-flying grandmother of De Sica's *Miracle in Milan*—and exposing the secret of his origins, as well as his bed-wetting proclivities, to an attentive audience of eight million. Although Allen is dazzlingly and ruthlessly on the mark when he defines her image literally as his projection, he shows us nothing about either character that we haven't seen before. But the film becomes mildly unsettling when, with a flourish of a chicken leg, Allen takes a 180-degree turn from what seemed like unvarnished autobiography. What? Can midlife crisis be really resolved by "the girl just like the girl that married dear old Dad"? Should we keep our eye on Page Six?

Imagine a whimsical tale about a slightly older (say 11-years-old), much richer Eloise, who lives alone in the Sherry-Netherland, and gets her kicks bestowing Hershey's Kisses on grateful homeless people and going to costume balls thrown by even richer preteens in the Metropolitan Museum. In the end, she leaves New York to be reunited with Mom and Dad in the shadow of the Acropolis. Incongruously shot like a Michelob commercial (by Vittorio Storaro, who was probably only following the boss's orders), it was directed by Francis Coppola from a script cowritten with his daughter Sofia. I don't want to think about their relationship.

Also reviewed in:
NATION, 3/27/89, p. 426, Stuart Klawans
NEW REPUBLIC, 3/27/89, p. 24, Stanley Kauffmann
NEW YORK TIMES, 3/1/89, p. C17, Janet Maslin
NEW YORKER, 3/20/89, p. 93, Pauline Kael
VARIETY, 3/1–7/89, p. 16
WASHINGTON POST, 3/3/89, p. D1, Hal Hinson

NEWS FROM HOME

A World Artists release of a Unité 3/INA (Paris)/Paradise Films (Brussels) production. *Producer:* Alain Dahan. *Director:* Chantal Akerman. *Screenplay:* Chantal Akerman. *Director of Photography:* Babette Mangolte. *Editor:* Francine Sandberg. *Sound:* Dominique Dalmasso and Larry Haas. *Sound Editor:* Dominique Dalmasso. *Narrator:* Chantal Akerman. *Running time:* 90 minutes. *MPAA Rating:* Not Rated.

MONTHLY FILM BULLETIN, 7/79, p. 150, Jan Dawson

Images of Manhattan—fixed-camera shots, panning shots, travelling shots—are sporadically accompanied by the texts of letters to the director from her mother back home in Europe, letters recited, in English, in a heavily accented monotone.

The news from home which provides Chantal Akerman's film with its title in fact travels in two directions. While the letters from Belgium, with their catalogue of minor illness, domestic routine, betrothals and financial anxieties, paint a picture of claustrophobic family life, the images build a no less eloquent picture of alien urban life, initially as isolated and claustrophobic as anything the director has left behind her. Unlike most formalist films, this one is elegiacally emotional ("constructed according to my feelings" is Akerman's description of it); and cumulatively, its images build up a "narrative" element at least as strong as that contained within the spoken texts. The counterpoint proves complex: while the mainspring of the film's tension lies in the lack of any direct connection between images and words, the latter—with their endless litanies of love and anxiety all minor variations on a single theme—explain the presence of the film-maker in this most alien of cities. Although Akerman appears nowhere in the film (unless one counts a reflection on a subway window that is arguably hers), her own motivations for leaving the over-protective, uneventful home are communicated obliquely but with an abundant clarity. As, too, are her shifting feelings for her home away from home. Babette Mangolte's extraordinary camera-work, most of it carried out in the penumbral light which evokes a wistful solitude, flattens the city streets, suggesting a hermetic world of impenetrable surfaces: if there is a life beyond them, it is one into which the film-maker, casting herself as the eternal outside observer, can never enter. New York appears alternatively as a domain of high walls and closed doors, or as a gigantic goldfish bowl. The only words one hears in the course of the film are the mother's, and even they are distanced from themselves by both the deliberately literal English translation and the dull monotone in which they are rattled off; they are also drowned out for whole phrases and paragraphs by the sounds of the city's traffic and its transportation systems—but never by the voice of its inhabitants. For the solitude the film-maker expresses is mirrored in her subject—both city and inhabitants alike. The normal proportions of narrative cinema are reversed—people become expressions of a landscape on which even their graffiti fail to produce a humanising effect.

The film's opening shot provides an elementary example of the technique it will employ with advancing complexity: the camera, positioned some way down a street walled in by high brick buildings on either side, is pointed up the road towards a lateral street. A car crosses the first street, passes out of frame; another car makes a right turn, hesitantly, slowly passes the camera; a group of children carrying cardboard boxes appear from the horizon, etc.: the permanence and solidity of the street, rather than the ephemeral movements of cars or people, emerge as the camera's "real" subject—an effect heightened by the fixed focus, by the fact that the camera makes none of the customary concessions to movements within the frame. Gradually, as the film progresses, the shots grow longer, even accommodating movement within them, and the streets of this New York ghost town (curiously evocative of *Paris qui dort*) become more crowded. The feelings of shyness and strangeness reflected in the construction of the film's first minutes gradually give way to a bolder curiosity: the first time the director takes her camera down into the subway, it is to observe only the graffiti-sprayed door of a compartment; later, she plants it firmly at the end of an aisle, observing her fellow travellers and their reactions, to it more than to one another. The people who fall within its field of vision remain curiously separate from one another, their lives the antithesis of that family warmth which punctuates the soundtrack. The letters from home, even if the news remains the same, also start to tell a different story. At first spaced out, they later merge together (two weeks between subway stops), conveying the effect that time is compressed by the very repetitiveness of events—on both sides of the Atlantic. Though there's also a point, about three-quarters of the way through the film, where time itself seems to become the subject, where the film slackens and the spectator grows exhausted from the effort of so many fresh starts and returns to zero, from watching people watching people, waiting for human contact or meaningful experience with the same weary resignation they, and we, wait for the subway train to draw into the early-morning platform. But then the film soars triumphantly into motion: first a long travelling shot from a car moving downtown to the port; then a fixed shot from the stern of a slowly departing boat. As camera and boat pull away from Manhattan, the city becomes a whole rather than a maze, the science-fiction skyline exerts its old mythical power before its sharp outlines are swathed in a rising mist, and seagulls lend their voices to the soundtrack. The final sequence-shot has all the mysterious poetry of a landscape by Monet or Turner. The film-maker departs, more confident, but still irrevocably alien.

VILLAGE VOICE, 7/18/89, p. 65, J. Hoberman

Film Forum 2's Chantal Akerman retro continues apace with her 1976 *News From Home* (today only). Most simply described, the film is a portrait of Manhattan, in which a generally static camera presents a succession of geometrically framed streetscapes—it's a spare and ravishing "city symphony" that takes its cues from Manhattan's own relentless grid.

Although Akerman's New York is largely a city of non-sites—empty Tribeca alleys, dingy Midtown parking lots, an abandoned gas station tucked into the crook of another building's wall—the symmetry of her compositions gives it the classical aura of ancient Rome. If New York isn't exactly transfigured, it certainly is defamiliarized. (A long stare at Veselka's flourescence and chrome makes that humble luncheonette seem as machine-tooled as a Harley Davidson.)

The movie has its own mysterious logic. Akerman travels from neighborhood to neighborhood, varying her rhythm with a few long pans. There's a sequence shot from a car traveling up Tenth Avenue that unfurls like an endless, rundown Mondrian, but the strongest sequences are those filmed in the underworld. Akerman plants her camera in the middle of the Seventh Avenue local and lets it ride three stations, the doors opening and closing with majestic indifference.

The camera's imperturbable gaze is similarly bracing. Akerman and cinematographer Babette Mangolte are connoisseurs of harsh urban forms. As in Ernie Gehr's *Still* or Ken Jacobs's *Sky Socialist*, New York is at once monumental and ethereal—its gray mass eroded by unseen forces and phantom tears. Akerman, however, is more interested than they in the city's human presence (or rather absence). Her cool, visceral images are accompanied by occasional readings of letters from her mother back home in Belgium. Barely audible over the ambient street noise, these naive, repetitive expressions of maternal concern underscore New York's strangeness, its distance from Europe, and the impossibility of describing the city's affect. Albeit reversing the archetypal greenhorn view of harbor and skyline, *News From Home* is the tale of a belated immigrant. (The movie could be called *A Brivele der Mamen* [A Little Letter to Mama], after the ferociously popular turn-of-the-century Yiddish ballad.)

Even though *News From Home* was obviously filmed during the summer, there's almost no nature here. It's a world of iron and stone—the only natural element is human. (Each one of us is that tree grown in Brooklyn.) Bathed in harsh green light, surrounded by graffiti and cigarette ads, subway riders are stolidly indifferent to noise and camera alike. This movie should always be playing in New York, not once every six years in a sadly beat-up print.

Also reviewed in:
NEW YORK TIMES, 7/11/89, p. C16, Stephen Holden

NEXT OF KIN

A Lorimar Film Entertainment release. *Executive Producer:* Larry De Waay. *Producer:* Les Alexander and Don Enright. *Director:* John Irvin. *Screenplay:* Michael Jenning. *Director of Photography:* Steven Poster. *Editor:* Peter Honess. *Music:* Jack Nitzsche. *Music Editor:* Richard Whitfield. *Sound:* Glenn Williams and (music) Michael Hoenig. *Sound Editor:* Martin Maryska. *Production Designer:* Jack T. Collis. *Set Designer:* John Warnke. *Set Decorator:* Jim Duffy. *Set Dresser:* Michael Gianneschi and David Gianneschi. *Special Effects:* Joe Lombardi. *Costumes:* Donfeld. *Make-up:* Art Anthony. *Stunt Coordinator:* Walter Scott. *Running time:* 111 minutes. *MPAA Rating:* R.

CAST: Patrick Swayze (Truman); Liam Neeson (Briar); Adam Baldwin (Joey); Helen Hunt (Jessie); Andreas Katsulas (Isabella); Bill Paxton (Gerald); Ben Stiller (Lawrence); Michael J. Pollard (Harold); Ted Levine (Willy); Del Close (Frank); Valentino Cimo (Rhino); Paul Greco (Leo); Vincent Guastaferro (Paulie); Paul Herman (Antonelli); Don Herion (Zimmer); Don James (David); Brett Hadley (De Witt); Rodney Hatfield (Hollis); Richard Wharton (Selkirk); Kelly Blair (Tolbert); Charlie Williams (Pierce); Michael Wise (Snakeman); Joseph Ryan (Grandpa); Anndrena Belcher (Patsy-Ruth); Jean Ritchie (Charlene); Nancy Jeffrey (Aunt Peg); Tina Engle (Rosalie); Kim Cole (Hollis' Wife); Starla Fugate (Gerald's Girlfriend); Michael Sassone (Melvin); Neil Giuntoli (Shorty); Fred Crowther (Old Hillbilly); Billy Branch (Preacher); Celene Evans (Lady Bartender); Michael Dizonno (Vinny); Tim Quill (T.V. Reporter); Jack Kandel (Hillbilly Bartender); Sally Murphy (Hooker); Mark Roberts (Furniture Mover); Patrick Balch (Young Boy, Kentucky); Relioues Webb (Young Boy, Chicago); Arlene Lencioni (Mrs. Isabella); Lew Way Chin and Morgan Biscomb Melto (Violin Students); Elizabeth Ruf (Woman in Bar); Al Neal (Man in Bar); Joelle Pasquale (Daughter #1); Mia Ferro (Daughter #2); Keela Gootee (Daughter #3); Pamela Prater (Selkirk's Wife); Mary Ann Berkhart (De Witt's Wife).

LOS ANGELES TIMES, 10/23/89, Calendar/p. 8, Michael Wilmington

In "Next of Kin," Patrick Swayze plays Truman Gates, hillbilly cop in Chicago, hunting for the big-city Mafia varmint who killed his kin and trying to ward off the even more dangerous vendettas of his other backwoods brother, Briar (Liam Neeson).

It's the Mafia vs. the Mountain Boys, with Fish out of Water, Feudin' and Fussin'. This collection of marketing hooks was strung together by two writers, Michael Jenning and Jeb Stuart, who seem to have done most of their research on rural America and big city crime by watching old Walter Hill movies, or maybe just watching the trailers from old Walter Hill movies.

To call this story a collection of hackneyed stereotypes would be complimenting it. "Next of Kin" doesn't have the logic of a good cliché. After a fairly good, tense opening, it keeps rolling up one preposterous scene after another: wild man Briar's one-against-a-dozen antics as he challenges the Cosa Nostra on their own stomping grounds; lone studs swaggering into dangerous locales and challenging everybody; Michael J. Pollard's cuddly grimaces as an inexplicably friendly hotel clerk; the Three Stooges antics of a clownish Mafia hit man; bizarrely loose-mouthed killers confessing everything over vino and tape recorders, and Truman's unusual relationship with his classical violinist wife, Jessie—who plays fiddle in the hills and leaves the country folk rapt with wonderment.

In the long-suffering but competent cast, Baldwin is memorably nasty as the chief killer and

Neeson has appropriated a set of vocal inflections that, on closer inspection, seem to be Ben Johnson's. Director John Irvin gives it all a patina of quality, including smoky Steven Poster cinematography that suggests Vilmos Szigmond with his glasses fogged, and a pump-them-up score by Jack Nitzsche.

If this machismo-tipsy movie were a little sillier, it might qualify as a classic of dumb camp. By the end, when we discover that the feudin cousins and the fussin' Cosa Nostra are all basically good old boys—or maybe "good old, good olds"—and also that you can blow away half of Chicago and stage a massacre in a graveyard without even waking up the neighbors, you may be ready to break out the moonshine or break out of the movie theater. Either one is preferable to watching "Next of Kin" (MPAA rated R for violence).

MONTHLY FILM BULLETIN, 6/90, p. 169, Kim Newman

Truman Gates has moved from the Appalachian backwoods to Chicago, made a career for himself as a cop, and married Jessie, a violinist. Back home, his brother Briar resents his "selling out" to the city life style. Gerald, Truman's other brother, works as a truck driver in the city, but plans to return to his roots as soon as he has earned enough money. John Isabella, a mob boss, has just promoted his own son Lawrence over the boy's unstable half-brother Joey Rossellini, and is trying to take over a slot-machine business. Lawrence and Joey put pressure on the owners of the business by running one of their trucks, which is being driven by Gerald and his friend David Wilkins, off the road. Gerald fights back, and is murdered by Joey. Truman takes Gerald's body home for burial, insisting that Briar should not take the traditional hillbilly vengeance and that the Chicago police can handle the case. However, while Truman searches for David Wilkins, Briar terrorises Joey and his gang, who try to assassinate him. The brothers reach an uneasy truce and find Wilkins, who tells them that Lawrence was also a witness, leading Truman to put pressure on the young man. Joey, who doesn't trust Lawrence, kills his half-brother and tells his father that Briar committed the murder, and then shoots Briar dead after luring him into a trap. The entire Gates clan descends on Chicago, while Truman, finally stepping outside the law, arranges a shoot-out with the mobsters in a cemetery. The battle is stopped by the arrival of John, who has discovered the truth about Lawrence's murder, and the mafioso shoots Joey dead. Truman goes home to Jessie.

A glum action-man movie, very similar in tone to John Irvin's previous work on *Raw Deal*, albeit with a pony-tailed, hillbilly-hatted Patrick Swayze as a slow-to-burn revenge hero rather than the casually genocidal Arnold Schwarzenegger. Given that the film's potential appeal is predicated on the theme of violent revenge, it seems to take an eternity for the Hamlet-like hero to come round to the cause. The plot builds very slowly towards its formulaic shoot-out finale, with secondary hero Briar (the oddly cast, oddly accented Liam Neeson) handling far more of the action (terrorising the mobsters by shooting at pinball machines, leaping from train to train on the elevated railway) than the sulky Truman. In the end, Truman comes off as something of a get-in-the-way spoilsport, suggesting that the film might have been more enjoyable on a thick-ear level if it had junked all its discussion of the ethics of revenge and eye-for-an-eye family feuds (the backwoods mountain men and the Sicilian mafiosi are crudely paralleled) and concentrated instead on Briar's *Death Wish*-cum-*Crocodile Dundee* crusade against the anachronistic slot-machine tycoons. Despite a fine supporting cast, who are mainly wasted, and a distinctive score from the still-underrated Jack Nitzsche, this fails to match the free-for-all feel of Swayze's last action picture, the ebullient *Road House*.

NEW YORK POST, 10/21/89, p. 17, Jami Bernard

"Next of Kin" is one of those movies that desperately wants the audience to come out armed with some new catch-phrases, like Clint Eastwood's "Make my day" and Arnold Schwarzenegger's "Let's party." Afraid, however, that audience members will not recognize the new war cry when they hear it, "Next of Kin" provides an ample selection from which to choose.

Now it is time for our Saturday movie quiz. If you were not lucky enough to have seen "Next of Kin" at the theater I did, where members of the audience went beyond that annoying habit of talking out loud as if they were in their living rooms and talked instead AS IF THEY WERE BEING DROWNED OUT BY A HELICOPTER, then you will have to guess the answers.

1. If you were Patrick Swayze, a Chicago lawman whose brother had been killed by gangsters, you would:

a) Initially appear to be too refined for bloody revenge because you have a wife (Helen Hunt) who plays classy classical violin;

b) Show considerable anxiety by having your face twitch in tight closeup;

c) Announce to the Mafia don, one of whose two sons may have done the killing: "I got three counties worth of kin who're gonna settle this!"

2. If you were Liam Neeson, playing one of Swayze's hillbilly brothers in the same wardrobe he wore as a homeless person in "Suspect," you would:

a) Kill time after the third brother's funeral with the time-honored hillbilly tradition of throwing machetes at logs;

b) Leave the head of a deer you recently caught to chill in the refrigerator until you have fully grasped the meaning of your brother's death;

c) Track down the gangster brothers, point a gun at them and say: "You ain't seen bad yet, but it's a-comin'."

3. You are Swayze again, the hero lawman, and you want to do your hillbilly relatives proud. You:

a) Speak in a backwoods accent that is the only comprehensible one in the entire cast, but not by much;

b) Beat up your one remaining brother while the two of you are handcuffed together because this makes for a very macho fight scene;

c) Announce: "You mess with my brother, you mess with me!"

4. You are John Irvin, director of "Next of Kin." You want to make an action movie with a subtheme of sibling rivalry. You:

a) Shoot everything really dark so no one can tell who's who, especially in the final graveyard shoot-out scene, reminiscent of the anonymous deaths in your previous "Hamburger Hill";

b) Think you're pretty clever by setting up opposing sets of brothers who each have a different agenda;

c) Throw in lines like: "It's not what ya coulda done...it's what's gotta be done!"

5. You are three counties' worth of Patrick Swayze's kin, and boy, are you ticked off about losing that brother. You believe in the theory of an eye for an eye, so you:

a) Pack picnic hampers, rattle-snakes, dogs, bows and arrows and drive to Chicago to settle old scores;

b) Take along Michael J. Pollard, in an obscure role as Neeson's temporary landlord, because he looks like he could be an awful lot of help in a shootout;

c) Look thoughtful while the soundtrack plays a tender ballad whose lyrics go something like: *"Anyone wants to get to you, they have to go through me first."*

6. You are Patrick Swayze. You are very handsome, agile and bankable. You are starring in duds such as "Tiger Warsaw," "Steel Dawn," "Road House" and "Next of Kin." You should:

a) Fire your manager.

b) Fire your agent.

c) Go to the Catskills and brush up on your mambo. Maybe Jennifer Grey will come by and take you away from all this.

NEWSDAY, 10/21/89, Part II/p. 15, Janice Berman

If Patrick Swayze, whose act has faltered since the surprise smash "Dirty Dancing," can't pick good scripts, he'd better quit picking good co-stars. Swayze, playing a Chicago policeman named Truman Gates, comes across as the weakest actor in this tedious, would-be action thriller.

In "Next of Kin," Gerald Gates (Bill Paxton), Truman's kid brother, is rubbed out as the mob tries to take over the vending-machine business where he works.

The family, Kentucky hill folk, wants revenge, especially Truman's other brother, Briar (Liam Neeson), who heads to the Windy City, shotguns loaded. This is a modest role, but Neeson, who was so striking in "The Good Mother," again manages to convey a sense of explosiveness.

Other standouts in the cast are Michael J. Pollard, who plays a wimpy flophouse manager to fine effect, and Adam Baldwin, leading a fairly impressive roster of mobster meanies. Too bad for Swayze, who walks, stalks and fights his way through the role in a workmanlike, but charmless, fashion.

Briar wants to uphold the down-home ethic of an eye for an eye. But Truman, so citified he's even married to a violinist—not a fiddler—wants to let the police find the murderer. At first, that is; this would not be an action thriller if there weren't relatives headed for Chicago, bent on satisfaction and armed with things like snakes, cleavers and bows and arrows.

If only it had taken some real police work to find the suspects. If only we'd been surprised at the final moment of the story. If only Swayze didn't walk around in that dopey felt hat.

Also reviewed in:
NEW YORK TIMES, 10/21/89, p. 16, Janet Maslin
VARIETY, 10/25–31/89, p. 30
WASHINGTON POST, 10/21/89, p. C2, Rita Kempley

NIGHT GAME

An Epic Productions release. *Producer:* George Litto. *Director:* Peter Masterson. *Screenplay:* Spencer Eastman and Anthony Palmer. *Story:* Spencer Eastman. *Director of Photography:* Fred Murphy. *Editor:* Robert Barrere. *Music:* Pino Donaggio. *Production Designer:* Neil Spisak. *Running Time:* 93 minutes. *MPAA Rating:* R.

CAST: Roy Scheider (Mike Seaver); Karen Young (Roxy); Lane Smith (Witty); Richard Bradford (Nelson); Paul Gleason (Broussard); Carlin Glynn (Alma); Anthony Palmer (Mendoza); Alex Morris (Gries); Matt Carlson (Bibbee); Rex Linn (Epps); Alex Garcia (Sil Baretto).

LOS ANGELES TIMES, 9/16/89, Calendar/p. 4, Michael Wilmington

Four years after directing Geraldine Page to an Oscar in the poignant Horton Foote drama "A Trip to Bountiful," director Peter Masterson crashes out of type with a slasher movie set in Galveston, Tex., about a maniacal hook-handed stalker who kills beautiful blondes on a lonely, deserted stretch of beach immediately after Houston Astros victories.

In "Night Game," helicopters relentlessly circle skyscrapers. The police—regular guys with gamy home lives—are puzzled, angry. They scream, bash each other on the noggin in frustration. Every time they arrive on the scene to investigate, two or three of them have to be pulled apart from strangling each other in a wild melee.

Small wonder they're frustrated. The crazed killer has so little respect for their intelligence that he sends messages of apology to local sportswriters whenever he botches up his own serial pattern. And, meanwhile, beautiful young blondes—including the petulant fiancee (Karen Young) of investigating police Lt. Mike Seaver (Roy Scheider)—keep trotting down that lonely beach like lemmings, or wandering down dark streets, or disappearing into the crazy house—always in oblivious ignorance that the Houston Astros are about to win another one.

There's no way to make this work—short of finding a new Ed Wood Jr. ("Plan 9 From Outer Space") to mess it up amusingly.

"Night Game" answers the burning question: Would bad, improbably plotted slasher movies be any better if they had humor, strong characters and pungent dialogue instead of incessant car-crashes and blood-letting? The answer, surprisingly, is no.

There's one near-excellent performance, though: Richard Bradford's sly, sodden, dyspeptic old police chief. It's a shame that directors like Masterson and actors like Bradford have to get hornswoggled into nonsense like "Night Game" (MPAA-rated R for sex, language and violence), when there's wonderful Texas material lying around just aching to be made.

NEW YORK POST, 9/16/89, p. 19, Jami Bernard

Before getting to the movie at hand, "Night Game," let's take a moment to consider the serial killer, since he is the topic of so many movies of late, including last week's "Relentless," which handled him poorly, and this week's "Sea of Love," which handles him well.

The serial killer, like the soap opera addict, is someone who thrives on the familiar yet never feels sated. In this way, the serial killer lends himself to film portrayal, since he is Old Faithful, guaranteed to kill again and leave a bounty of notes and clues for the detectives. And when the detectives slow down, the responsible serial killer will even drop a dime (or a quarter) in an attempt to get the ball of justice rolling.

I suspect that much of the appeal of the serial killer for today's undemanding movie audiences is that a fresh killing every 10 minutes is more satisfying a clue than a measly fingerprint.

Finding a serial killer usually comes down to solving a mathematical puzzle—why does he murder every other day of the week? Or only when Mercury is in retrograde? Or, in "Night Game," only when a certain baseball pitcher wins a game?

As you'll see in this movie, figuring out when the killer will strike may lead to finding out who he is, but it doesn't necessarily lead to good drama. The serial killer, alas, is becoming old hat. He is just too predictable. Perhaps it is time for him to hang up his meat cleaver.

A craggy-looking Roy Scheider play Mike Seaver (a name that continues the baseball theme), a police lieutenant in Galveston, Texas, who is plagued by a string of murders in which women's throats are slit ear to ear as if by a large meat hook. The murders are tied in with the baseball season, but the link—even after it is explained and the murderer revealed—is a dramatically weak one. It is as implausible as the final scene, in which a Houston Astros game is held up for a highly unlikely reason.

It is the fundamentally weak premise of why the killer kills that gives rise to a smokescreen of folksy subplots: Seaver's ongoing jurisdictional dispute with fellow lawmen; Seaver's impending marriage to a girl half his age (Karen Young); Seaver's baseball past.

Tentatively directed by writer-actor Peter Masterson (his wife, Carlin Glynn, plays Scheider's cranky future mother-in-law), "Night Game" is set in a Galveston that is more like a small town where everyone knows everyone else—which, if that were the case, would make it pretty hard for a hook-wielding maniac to hang out. Most of the action takes place in the parking lot outside a carnival; you'd think cute young girls would steer clear of the place after all those chalk outlines on the concrete.

The clues are in the form of autographed napkins. "He's got a taste for blondes and he's got nice handwriting," is how one cop sums up the killer.

Considering this is a *policier*, there's not much action. The murders are special-effects gory, and the rest of the time Seaver and company leisurely discuss, cruise, question, and pop aspirin. It's a talky, scaled-down thriller, slow-paced and full of insignificant asides, muddled like a pitcher who can't keep his mind on the game. Masterson is more at home with personalities and relationships than blood and gore.

When we finally meet him, the killer's brief, weary explanation for his deeds is barely satisfying. I guess that means the serial killer will be back, in yet another form, in yet another movie, next week.

NEWSDAY, 9/16/89, Part II/p. 17, Terry Kelleher

There's action at the Astrodome, as we see a member of the Houston Astros knock the ball a long way.

Cut to a rabid Astros fan listening to the game on his car radio. He pounds the steering wheel and prays for the ball to go foul.

Charge an error to editor Robert Barrere, but it's really not fair to single him out. The quality of play in "Night Game" is sloppy all around.

Roy Scheider plays Mike Seaver (no relation to Tom), a Galveston cop on the trail of a homicidal maniac who's been butchering blond women with some kind of hook. It's mentioned briefly, without explanation, that Seaver once played professional baseball. It's mentioned briefly, without explanation, that he left the Dallas police under a cloud. It's established that he's a native of Galveston, yet Scheider makes no attempt at a Texas accent. In fact, Seaver tweaks the police department's secretary for her twang. Galveston's police chief (Richard Bradford) sure talks Texan. He says stuff like, "Don't be throwin' me no bones, ol' hoss, cuz this ol' dog can still hunt." He keeps warning Seaver not to tangle with a corrupt rival from the country sheriff's department (Paul Gleason). Seaver's blond girlfriend (Karen Young) talks Texan, too. Though he's old enough to be her father, she wants to marry him in the worst way. Maybe she doesn't know what happened in Dallas. But then neither do we.

Since the movie spends a lot of time following the Astros' progress in the pennant race, it eventually dawns on Seaver that the murders have a baseball tie-in. It's about as plausible as a Pete Rose alibi.

So Seaver jumps in the car, tunes in the Astros and races off to stop the psycho before he kills again. Regardless of his record in Dallas, this cop has seen enough thrillers to know that the next designated victim can be none other than the young blond in *his* life.

Were it not for a little comic relief here and there, "Night Game" would be duller than a late-season clash between the Braves and the Phillies. Give some credit to producer George Litto and director Peter Masterson. They've got cheek.

Seaver drops off his girlfriend at a theater offering a double feature of "Kansas" (a 1988 flop produced by Litto) and "Full Moon in Blue Water" (a 1988 flop directed by Masterson). "It's supposed to be a cute movie," she says, urging Seaver to join her. "The newspaper gave it three-and-a-half stars."

The smart cop prefers to save his money, knowing some pictures turn up at the video store in practically no time.

Also reviewed in:
NEW YORK TIMES, 9/16/89, p. 15, Caryn James
VARIETY, 9/20–26/89, p. 29

NIGHT IN HAVANA, A: DIZZY GILLESPIE IN CUBA

A Cinephile USA release of a Chisma production. *Producer:* Nim Polanetska. *Director:* John Holland. *Screenplay:* Alan Honigberg. *Director of Photography:* Bill Megalos. *Editor:* Vincent Stenerson. *Sound:* Larry Provost. *Interviewer:* Alan Honigberg. *Running Time:* 84 minutes. *MPAA Rating:* Not Rated.

LOS ANGELES TIMES, 9/18/89, Calendar/p. 9, Kevin Thomas

There's an unasked question hovering over Don Holland's "A Night in Havana: Dizzy Gillespie in Cuba" that casts an unfortunate shadow over an otherwise infectious documentary on the great jazz trumpeter's 1985 trip to Cuba to headline the fifth International Jazz Festival of Havana.

Gillespie himself provides the perfect opening for that question when, at the beginning of the film, he offers that he is the only member of his contingent who feels comfortable visiting Cuba in the light of so much long-held American hostility toward Castro. Why didn't off-screen interviewer Allen Honigberg ask him why he felt this way? Why didn't Honigberg then proceed to the heart of the matter, which would have been to ask Gillespie what he thinks about Cuba's sorry history in regard to human rights, and those of minorities in particular? The question really is pertinent because Gillespie does bring up the oppression of blacks in America and because he is made to look naive when he remarks that in contrast to Cuba during the corrupt Batista regime, "Havana now looks so peaceful."

You have to believe Dizzy Gillespie is too sophisticated not to know the score about the history of freedom of expression under Castro and not to take too seriously the dictator's expansive personal welcome. Gillespie in fact emerges as an extremely shrewd, warm and wise man who enjoys an enviable harmony with himself that is reflected in his wonderfully mellow music.

He is clearly an ambassador of good will par excellence who takes great pleasure in connecting with his musical roots, explaining that the drum, which is at the heart of African music and culture, was forbidden to slaves in the United States while blacks transported to Cuba were allowed to keep theirs. The entire film depicts Gillespie enthusiastically making cross-cultural connections, bringing pleasure to thousands of Cubans with his music, famed for its innovative Afro-Cuban motifs, and discovering in a performance of the Folklorico Nacional an exuberant preservation of African traditions.

"A Night in Havana" (Times-rated Family) concludes with Gillespie bringing his remarkable band together with that of a contingent of Cuban musicians, including pianist Gonzalo Rubalcaba. It is a joyous, thrilling synthesis, one that Gillespie hoped to repeat in New York only last month. But Rubalcaba and his band sadly were denied visas by the State Department.

NEW YORK POST, 5/19/89, p. 29, Lee Jeske

This cheerful little documentary about a Dizzy Gillespie trip to Cuba is the antithesis of "Let's Get Lost," Bruce Weber's grim portrait of Chet Baker. No drugs, no self-destruction, none of the usual jazz documentary descent-into-hell business—a more avuncular, optimistic subject than Gillespie could not be hoped for.

But a documentary should illuminate its subject. There are three subjects here—Gillespie, Cuba and Afro-Cuban music—but his film only skims their surfaces. We hear some good music, laugh at a few well-worn Gillespie anecdotes and see travelogue shots of a crumbling Havana. Feature film material? Uh-uh.

Gillespie, best known as a co-creator (with Charlie Parker) of bebop, was a primary force in the fusing of jazz and Afro-Cuban music in the 1940s. Under the guidance of trumpeter/composer Mario Bauza (who's just mentioned here), Gillespie delved deeply into the sounds emanating from the Palladium, Broadway's "Home of the Mambo," just a hop, skip and rhumba from 52nd Street.

Bauza, whose brother-in-law Machito was a pioneering Afro-Cuban bandleader, introduced Gillespie to Chano Pozo, the brilliant conga player who was an important part of the Gillespie big band before he was killed, mysteriously, two years after emigrating from Cuba.

Decades after his first involvement with Afro-Cuban music—which continues to color his music and is the basis for some of his most famous compositions—Gillespie finally got the chance to travel to Cuba. This is not the record of that trip. This visit took place a couple of years later, diminishing the drama of the great Gillespie venturing to the source of much of his musical inspiration.

The seeds of an enlightening documentary are here: Gillespie discusses Afro-Cuban rhythms and why African customs remained particularly strong in Cuba; he interacts with Cuban musicians and pays a rather odd visit to the home of Chano Pozo (where he quizzes Pozo's stone-faced sister as to whether Pozo was murdered for stealing money before leaving Cuba).

But director John Holland never delves too deeply into Afro-Cuban music. Instead he takes us to a Gillespie meeting with Fidel Castro, shows us his band on stage (Gillespie plays very sharply, as does Cuban trumpeter Arturo Sandoval), plops him down in front of a touristy folkloric show and has him discuss some of his usual topics (his cheeks, his relationship with Charlie Parker).

The film's funniest moment—as Gillespie explains that the source of a trumpeter's strength is not from the diaphragm, but from a much more southerly muscle—has nothing to do with Cuba at all.

And there's a disturbing aspect here. Gillespie notes how peaceful Havana's streets are, as opposed to the gambling- and prostitution-filled Havana streets of yore. Castro's notorious repression of artists (including jazz musicians) does not come up.

There are worse ways to pass an hour and a half than zipping around Cuba (or anyplace else) with Dizzy Gillespie. But "A Night in Havana: Dizzy Gillespie In Cuba" never does much more than that.

NEWSDAY, 5/19/89, Part III/p. 5, Stuart Troup

Dizzy Gillespie talks with infectious charm, weaving stories much the way he builds awesome musical solos. Put a microphone in front of him and get out of the way. He rarely disappoints.

Add a movie camera and you have a study of an expressive man—with or without his trumpet. In "A Night in Havana," John Holland and Nim Polanetska have captured a pretty slice of Gillespie's charm—walking, talking, singing, mugging, playing.

The focus of the music and the talk are the Afro-Cuban ties to jazz, a connection that Gillespie helped foster more than 40 years ago. But Gillespie transcends the subject matter because his presence alone is fascinating. The result is an often amusing portrait of a musical genius. We see him interacting with children, dancing with *Conjunto Folklorico*, meeting Fidel Castro and talking about musical relationships.

The film's setting is Gillespie's trip to the 1985 Havana Jazz Festival. Along the way he meets the sister of Chano Pozo, the Cuban drummer with whom Gillespie played and composed in the late '40s.

"He was a master of the drums and dance," Gillespie says. "he was putting Afro-Cuban music into jazz, and I was attempting to put jazz into Afro-Cuban music." They both succeeded.

Gillespie performs with a number of Cuban players, including Arturo Sandoval and Gonzalo Rubalcaba. Some of the music is strong, especially from trumpeter Sandoval, who infuses Gillespie's "Night in Tunisia" with rippling, adventurous passages. And Gillespie says as much with his eyes as with his voice when he sings, "Gee, Baby, Ain't I Good to You."

His commentary is a special treat, whether he's delivering another of the 25 or so versions about how the bell of his trumpet first became bent, or the humorous, questionable source of a trumpeter's wind.

The photography is especially powerful in the closeups of Gillespie's face, whether he's telling an anecdote or inflating his lung-like cheeks in a trumpet chorus. At one point, the camera moves from him to the open horn case in which his trumpet lies in plush red velvet.

"The trumpet just sits there, surrounded in luxury," he says slowly. "It just sits there. . . waiting to mess someone up."

VILLAGE VOICE, 5/23/89, p. 64, Amy Taubin

Dizzy Gillespie's bebop style was distinguished by its Afro-Cuban rhythms. In *A Night in Havana*, director John Holland follows Gillespie on a long overdue visit to Cuba, where he jokes around with Fidel, plays piano with Cuban trumpeter Arturo Sandoval, does some impromptu dancing with Folklorico Nacional, and jams at the Fifth International Jazz Festival of Havana. Although Gillespie may be past his trumpet-playing prime, he's an amazing showman, especially when he's dancing. Holland probably shouldn't have stretched 30 minutes of good material into a feature-length film; nevertheless *A Night in Havana* has some star-crossed moments.

Also reviewed in:
NEW YORK TIMES, 5/19/89, p. C14, Stephen Holden
VARIETY, 5/25/88, p. 19

NIGHTMARE ON ELM STREET 5, A: THE DREAM CHILD

A New Line Cinema release. *Executive Producer:* Sara Risher and John Turtle. *Producer:* Robert Shaye and Rupert Harvey. *Director:* Stephen Hopkins. *Screenplay:* John Skip, Craig Spector, and Leslie Bohem. *Based on characters created by:* Wes Craven. *Director of Photography:* Peter Levy. *Editor:* Chuck Weiss and Brent Schoenfeld. *Music:* Jay Ferguson. *Production Designer:* C.J. Strawn. *Mechanical Effects:* Andre Ellingson. *Visual Effects:* Alan Munro. *Special Visual Effects:* Peter Kurran and Phillip Downey. *Optical Special Effects:* Ted Rae and Doug Beswick. *Make-up Effects:* Chris Biggs, Todd Masters, and Greg Nicotero. *Freddy Krueger Make-up:* David Miller. *Running time:* 90 minutes. *MPAA Rating:* R.

CAST: Robert Englund (Freddy Krueger); Lisa Wilcox (Alice); Danny Hassel (Dan); Whitby Hertford (Jacob); Kelly Jo Minter (Yvonne); Erika Anderson (Greta); Nick Mele (Alice's Father); Beatrice Boepple (Amanda Krueger); Joe Seely (Mark); Valorie Armstrong (Dan's Mother); Burr DeBenning (Dan's Father); Pat Surges (Racine Gibson); Clarence Felder (Mark's Father); Matt Borlenghi (Jock); Beth Depatie (Anne); E.R. Davies (Delivery Doctor); Bill Dunnam (Truck Driver); Don Maxwell (Coach Ostrow); Cameron Perry (Guest); Stacey Elliott (Girl in Locker); Marc Siegler (Thirty Something); Andre Ellingson (Orderly #1); Steven Grives (Doctor Moore).

FILMS IN REVIEW, 11/89, p. 550, Ken Hanke

"Faster than a bastard madman! More powerful than a speeding loco-maniac! It's Super-Freddy!" Maybe so, but it looked awfully like more of the same old Freddy to me, despite this extravagant claim from everybody's favorite undead child molester cum demonic teen-slasher cum standup comic in the course of his latest screen adventure. Okay, for the record, the film is better than *Part IV* and streets ahead of *Part II*, but it fails to measure up to the fulltilt ditsiness of *Part III*, and is many blocks removed from Wes Craven's original film. This isn't to say that *The Dream Child* is an especially bad series entry, but neither is it any great shakes—and therein lies the problem not just with this film, but with the entire *Elm Street* series. For a horror film to work it either has to be extraordinarily good (I'd put Craven's film in this category) or stupefyingly bad. Middle of the road doesn't quite make it, and so a not bad film like *The Dream Child* really isn't as much fun as, say, *Friday the 13th VIII—Jason Takes Manhattan* (next thing we know, Jason will be putting on a musical with Mickey Rooney and Judy Garland in a disused glue factory as a benefit for wayward girls). Simply, *The Dream Child* isn't good enough to be good, nor bad enough to laugh at.

The plot this round centers on Freddy getting to his meat-on-the-hoof victims through the mind of an unborn child. Neat enough, I suppose, and the idea *does* offer room for some weightier than usual thoughts in these abortion-conscious days, which the film proceeds to mangle into incomprehensibility. Is the film's "Save This Fetus" attitude a pro-life stance? Maybe. But if it is, the point undermines itself by the very fact that any number of people have to meet untimely ends all because the main character insists on carrying the child full-term. This *might* be a satirical thrust at the more wigged-out pro-lifers, but that probably awards the film more intelligence than it possesses. In any cases, the point isn't pursued with great fervour.

As two or three viewers may recall, Freddy (Robert Englund) was last seen being ripped to pieces by the souls of his previous victims at the end of *Part IV*, making his resurrection a bit of a problem for lesser mortals than screenwriters. However, ever since someone figured out that Frankenstein's Monster only fell through the burning windmill floor into a convenient cistern to emerge singed and soggy (and understandably testy) for the sequel, no problem of this sort has been insurmountable. And it sure isn't here. For one reason or another, Freddy manages to make his return by going through his birth again in nightmare fashion. Freddy's origins were pretty thoroughly mapped-out in *Part III*—the results of the multiple rape of a nun accidentally locked in a room with a hundred violent madmen ("the bastard son of a hundred maniacs"). Regardless of the biological impossibility of this fanciful notion (and the fact that in this entry Robert Englund—sans Freddy make-up—appears as one of the lustful lunatics), it has become part of the series myth and is here used to handily eat up screen time by acting the event out. Alas, the best the film can come up with is a bunch of stock madhouse cliches and a rather tasteless birth scene in which the infant Freddy behaves very like the Alien after it hops out of John Hurt's chest. Oh, well.

The *Alien* echo is part of the problem with the film, too. There is a basic derivative quality to most of the proceedings. Freddy's bathtub attack from the first film is here "transformed" into a shower attack that is far more elaborate and far less effective. One lengthy sequence (and one of the better ones, too) is brazenly ripped-off from—of all things—an a-Ha music video, which itself was pilfered from Ken Russell's *Altered States!* Only at the end does the film truly spring to creative life via the use of some extremely complex process work that jumbles the perspective of the images, producing an almost Escher-like effect. It's not enough to propel the film into greatness or even near greatness, but it is a stunning few moments in a film generally marked by Stephen Hopkins' rather uninvolved direction.

Quite the most bizarre thing about *The Dream Child* is the unintentional furor it has spawned with a group of "concerned" citizens, whose apparent abundance of spare time might be better used in the cause of the homeless, AIDS, or preventing Televangelists from becoming president. For one reason or another, these folks have jumped on this film on a "violence begets violence" outrage. Despite the fact that *The Dream Child*'s fantasticated violence is much less bloody (and far more improbable) than that shown in more mainstream films like *Die Hard* or *Lethal Weapon*, the very strange thing about all this is the fact that so much of the outcry is based on a sequence in which a motorcycle turns nasty, and thanks to special effects "murders" its rider—hardly an act of violence that even the most ambitious copy cat could hope to emulate. I'd not worry overmuch about your teenage children seeing this, but, just to be on the safe side, leave your motorcycle at home.

MONTHLY FILM BULLETIN, 6/90, p. 169, Kim Newman

Springwood, U.S.A. Newly graduated high-school student Alice Johnson, whose control over her dreams enabled her to defeat ghostly mass-murderer Freddy Krueger (see *A Nightmare on Elm Street 4: The Dream Master*, M.F.B., May 1989), has just become pregnant by her football-hero boyfriend Danny. She has also started to dream again of Freddy, and of Amanda Krueger—Freddy's raped-by-madmen nun mother—and of a mysterious child called Jacob. Alice, after a spell in the dreamworld, calls Danny, who is at a graduation party, and explains that Freddy has returned. While speeding to meet Alice, Danny is attacked by Freddy—who takes the form of a van and a motorcycle—and dies in what is taken for a road accident. Alice can't convince her friends—model Greta, comics artist Mark and nurse Yvonne—that the menace is real, and can't understand how Freddy, who only exists in her dreams, can appear while she is awake. Greta and Mark are killed—diet-conscious Greta being stuffed with food and choked by a chef Freddy, and Mark turned to paper and cut up by a superheroic Freddy—and Yvonne is dragged into a dream and convinced of the danger. Alice realises, thanks to some help from Amanda, that Freddy is appearing through the dreams of her unborn child, whom he is trying to possess so he can be reborn into the real world. Jacob is the image of the child Alice would naturally have, and is the focus of the ghost's schemes. Alice confronts Freddy in Jacob's dream, and defeats him again, banishing him to the nether world so that her son can be born normally.

While the *Elm Street* films get more and more impressive visually, their scripts make less and less sense, resulting in projects as incoherent, flashy and uninteresting as this. There are the usual excellent effects/dream scenes—Freddy as a motorbike engulfing a speeding teen, Freddy as a comic-book superhero cutting apart a paper man—and the obtuse humour has been toned down. But the story advances through disorienting lapses and leaps, another uninteresting selection of teenagers are brought on and killed off, the mainly junior performers are mainly inept, and bits and pieces of the earlier films are rehashed in an attempt to keep up the continuity. Stephen Hopkins, recruited thanks to his work on an interesting Australian psycho movie *Dangerous Game*, does an astonishing job of making the film visually engaging, especially in the dark and dripping asylum setting of the major dream scenes, with an unsettling use of such typical genre images as the broken and bleeding doll, the womb-like tunnel of dreams, and the scuttling, *It's Alive*-style Freddy baby monster.

But this over-drive style is constantly undercut by the screenplay, which was originated by novelists John Skipp and Craig Spector, written by Leslie Bohem and extensively rewritten by the uncredited David J. Schow, otherwise a talented writer of short horror stories. The problem is that all these capable authors have been required to shoehorn their own ideas around the givens of an increasingly cannibalistic series, and that nothing really convinces even on the trash level of *A Nightmare on Elm Street III: Dream Warriors*, the best of the sequels. Just about the only new angle this movie comes up with, apart from the intermittent pro-life propaganda discussions about teenage pregnancy, is the attempt to underline Wes Craven's original thesis that it's all the parents' fault for killing Freddy in the first place by outfitting the teens with a succession of feckless, drunken and grotesque fathers and mothers.

Nastiest of these is Greta's mom, whose "networking" party and attempts to shove her daughter into a cover-girl career are trashed in a set-piece (Freddy stuffs the girl to the point of bursting) that is very uncertain and distasteful in its cartoonish humour. Like New Line's *Leatherface: Texas Chainsaw Massacre III*, also scripted and disowned by Schow, this has the feeling of a story that comes from nowhere and goes nowhere, marking time between sequels, keeping its options open and refusing to make any narrative advances. The scariest idea in the film, underlined by yet another open ending, is the possibility that this nightmare will never end, the non-existent story spinning out forever, with occasional Freddy wisecracks, until the profits stop coming in.

LOS ANGELES TIMES, 8/11/89, Calendar/p. 16, Kevin Thomas

"A Nightmare on Elm Street 5: The Dream Child" has the effect of a relentless undertow, trapping its young people in a grisly fantasy of supernatural terror masterminded by the unconquerable Freddy Krueger. In only his second feature, Australian director Stephen Hopkins, whose background includes comic illustration and set design, has created a dynamic, fully visually realized experience. It's every bit as gory as "Batman" but more cohesive and its struggle between good and evil more tightly integrated.

Lisa Wilcox's blonde, tenacious Alice returns from the fourth film to do battle with Freddy all over again. As virtually every teen-ager could tell you, Freddy Krueger was a crazed child-killer who was burned alive by the parents of his victims but who returned in the dreams of a fresh crop of young people to wreak more deadly havoc. The way he returns this time is ingenious: in the dreams of the Alice's unborn child, which finally involves a confrontation with Freddy's own mother. The film works its way through some splendidly scary nightmares to achieve an aura of redemption more spiritual than you would think possible in a no-holds-barred exploitation picture.

Right from the start the film, written by Leslie Bohem and rightly R-rated, announces it originality: Just as we think we're being asked to watch yet another homage to "Psycho's" shower scene, the sequence takes off in an entirely unexpected direction. One of Alice's friends is a gifted cartoonist (Joe Seely), which allows for some inspired art direction and use of animation and also serves to underline the notion that no comic-book hero stands a chance in the face of true evil.

In creating a film that has images reminiscent of "The Cabinet of Dr. Caligari" as well as "Metropolis," Hopkins and Bohem have had a major assist from production designer C.J. Strawn, whose work in the fantasy sequences has much the witty and stylized quality of Michael

Riva's complex and whimsical constructions for "The Adventures of Buckaroo Banzai," and from visual effects supervisor Alan Munro. Cinematographer Peter Levy and editors Chuck Weiss and Brent Schoenfeld, and surely many others as well, have contributed virtuoso work.

Robert Englund is a gleeful Freddy, that mass of scar tissue with five mini-scythes in place of fingers on his right hand. Wilcox, Seely, Kelly Joe Minter and other young actors do well playing roles in which they must constantly despair of trying to get their elders to believe in the seemingly impossible. More and more, Freddy emerges as a symbol of the irrational world that awaits youngsters, who must find within themselves the courage to conquer it. Clearly, we haven't seen the last of Krueger.

NEW YORK POST, 8/11/89, p. 25, V. A. Musetto

Nobody has ever mistaken the "Nightmare on Elm Street" movies for "Citizen Kane." But they could always be counted on for eye-popping, slick special effects and a couple of snappy one-liners from Freddy Krueger, the gentleman with the shriveled face, gravelly voice and six-inch steel fingernails.

Who cared if it was the same old plot over and over—child-molester Freddy, the illegitimate son of a nun and a hundred maniacs, takes revenge on the vigilante parents who burned him to death by entering their teen-age children's dreams and slaughtering them until one intrepid girl sends the demented fellow to what seems like his final reward but isn't?

Young audiences loved to shriek as Freddy (Robert Englund) dispatched victim after victim in all sorts of gooey but ingenious ways. And it paid off for the producers, New Line Cinema. The first four "Nightmare" movies have netted the small company more than $25 million. And that doesn't count the millions raked in from Freddy products—a board game, key chains, pajamas, even bubble gum—as well as videocassettes and cable TV. Quite a gold mine.

But, judging by the latest venture, "Nightmare on Elm Street 5: The Dream Child," New Line had better start looking elsewhere for easy dollars. This one is so wimpy and tired that even the most die-hard "Nightmare" fans are bound to be disappointed.

I saw it in a theater filled with young people, just the audience the series is aimed at. And were they restless! The movie had trouble dredging up even one good scream, and the only laughs came at spots that the director, an Australian named Stephen Hopkins, never intended. There weren't any boos at the end, but there wasn't much applause, either.

The special effects? Sure, but they're uninspired and instantly forgettable. Only one sequence stands out. And for the wrong reason. It has to do with a fetus—sweet young Alice (Lisa Wilcox) is pregnant by her recently murdered boyfriend, and Freddy wants to steal the unborn baby's soul in order to be born again. (Don't yell at me, I didn't write the script.) With the nation divided on the abortion issue, the repellent shots of a fetus cavorting inside Alice couldn't be more untimely and unfortunate. No matter what side of the abortion controversy you're on, you're bound to be offended.

The piece de resistance in the earlier movies was the final special-effects orgy—a blowout between Freddy and his prey. Not this time. The finale is so tame and anticlimactic, and arrives so quickly and unexpectedly, that you might think the projectionist mislaid a reel or two.

"Nightmare 5" looks as if its creators were just going through the motions, so sure that the picture would be a hit that they didn't have to try any more. If the comments by the two teen-agers behind me on the way out of the screening are any barometer, they may have overestimated fans' loyalty. No. 1: "It just fell apart." No. 2: "Yeah, *that* was no nightmare."

NEWSDAY, 8/11/89, Part III/p. 3, Terry Kelleher

Freddy Krueger spelled it out in the previous sequel. "I am eternal," declared everybody's favorite sleep-disturber in "A Nightmare on Elm Street 4: The Dream Master."

Now he's back on the big screen in "A Nightmare on Elm Street 5: The Dream Child," proving once again that he and the profit motive will be with us forever.

Admittedly, I'm not a typical "Nightmare" fan. Some get off on the terror and suspense, as Freddy finds ever more fiendish ways to control teenagers' dreams and make them die before they wake. I go for the comedy. To me the series reached its peak in No. 3, when a teen's talk-show dream was hosted by Freddy in the gentlemanly guise of Dick Cavett. But if you think any "Elm Street" entry owes you more than a token amount of originality or wit to go with the expected special-effects demonstration, you'll likely be disappointed in No. 5.

Lisa Wilcox returns as Alice, the "dream master" who vanquished Freddy—temporarily—at the end of No. 4. (Alice is just graduating from Springwood High, though she looks old enough to be the guidance counselor.) Apparently Freddy can't re-enter Alice's dreams directly, but he's able to wreak his usual havoc through the dreams of her unborn child, fathered by her wooden-hunk boyfriend, Dan (Danny Hassel). In another strained plot line, Alice communes with Freddy's dead mother (Beatrice Boepple), a nun who conceived our steel-clawed antihero after she was raped by lunatics in the friendly neighborhood asylum.

Robert Englund's Freddy hasn't lost his panache, though his one-liners are sounding more and more like Henny Youngman rejects. But the supporting cast, except for the still-appealing Wilcox, is notably weak. Joe Seely gives such a blah performance as Alice's classmate Mark, an aspiring comic-book artist, that we can't fully enjoy the creative way Freddy nips his career in the bud.

The movie offers one other wedding of horror and warped humor: Freddy subjects a lissome young beauty (Erika Anderson) to fatal force-feeding. The rest of the special effects may be described as numbingly impressive. Great technique, guys, but so much of this gore we've seen before. Wake me when the shrunken heads of Freddy's victms emerge from his oozing guts—again.

Australia-based director Stephen Hopkins does hardly anything interesting with the down time between killer dreams. With "A Nightmare on Elm Street 5," there's no longer the slightest necessity to develop character or make a modicum of sense. Even the set-up for the next sequel is vague and perfunctory.

"All right, Krueger, this is for keeps," warns Alice before the latest climatic showdown. Is there anyone left in America who doesn't know she's just blowing smoke?

Also reviewed in:
NEW YORK TIMES, 8/11/89, p. C10, Caryn James
VARIETY, 8/9–15/89, p. 25
WASHINGTON POST, 8/12/89, p. C9, Richard Harrington

976-EVIL

A New Line Cinema release of a CineTel film. *Executive Producer:* Paul Hertzberg. *Producer:* Lisa M. Hansen. *Director:* Robert Englund. *Screenplay:* Rhet Topham and Brian Helgeland. *Director of Photography:* Paul Elliott. *Editor:* Stephen Myers. *Music:* Thomas Chase and Steve Rucker. *Music Editor:* Jeff Charbonneau. *Sound:* Beau Franklin and (music) Chase-Rucker Studios. *Sound Editor:* John Post and David Lewis Yewdall. *Art Director:* David Brian Miller. *Set Decorator:* Nancy Booth. *Set Dresser:* Michael Warga, Clair Bear Gaul, and Michelle Turnbull. *Special Effects:* Kevin McCarthy and Sandra McCarthy. *Costumes:* Elizabeth Gower-Gruzinski. *Make-up:* Susan Reiner. *Stunt coordinator:* John Michael Stewart. *Running time:* 92 minutes. *MPAA Rating:* R.

CAST: Stephen Geoffreys (Hoax); Patrick O'Bryan (Spike); Sandy Dennis (Aunt Lucy); Jim Metzler (Marty Palmer); Maria Rubell (Angella Martinez); Robert Picardo (Mark Dark); Lezlie Deane (Suzie); J.J. Cohen (Marcus); Paul Wilson (Mr. Michaels); Greg Collins (Mr. Selby); Darren Burrows (Jeff); Joanna Keyes (Suzie's Mother); Gunther Jensen (Airhead); J.J. Johnston (Virgil); Joe Slade (John Doe); Demetre Phillips (Sergeant Bell); Don Bajema (Deputy); Jim Thiebaud (Rags); Wendy Cooke (Gang Girl); Thom McFadden (Minister); Larry Turk (1st Operator); Cynthia Szigeti (Female Operator); Christopher Metas (Cashier); Roxanne Rogers (Waitress); Bert Hinchman (Coroner); Nay Dorsey (1st Paramedic); Jim Landis (2nd Paramedic); Ed Corbett (Santa Claus); Quigley (Aunt Lucy's Parrot).

LOS ANGELES TIMES, 3/27/89, Calendar/p. 12, Kevin Thomas

"976-EVIL is a stylish, imaginative variation on "Carrie" that marks the promising directorial debut of actor Robert Englund, famed as Freddy Krueger in the "Nightmare on Elm Street" series. The horror picture is also sparked by the presence of Sandy Dennis in an amusingly flamboyant pivotal role.

Dennis plays the blowsy Bible-banging mother of a repressed, bullied high-school student nick-named Hoax (Stephen Geoffreys), who gets his grisly revenge on his many tormentors when he dials a "Horrorscope" service which seems to be run by Satan himself.

If writers Rhet Topham and Brian Helgeland don't provide much in the way of fresh scares for Englund, they do develop the psychology of their people to a greater extent than is usual for such genre fare. As a result, for all its gory forays into the supernatural, "976-EVIL" is of most interest for its wry portrait of seedy small-town America, a place where the kids are dangerously bored, where "a guy can't make a buck anymore" but where the local Foursquare Church still announces a sermon on how "Jesus Loved the Devil Out of Me." The irony here is that the strictly raised Hoax is far more vulnerable to the temptations of the Devil than his older cousin Spike (Patrick O'Bryan), a good-looking, likeable dude with a bright girlfriend (Lezlie Deane).

Clearly, Englund has put his experience in front of the camera to good use behind it. He draws performances more varied and dimensional than is usual for horror pictures, and his controlled direction of Dennis is especially adroit. Dennis appears only briefly throughout the film, just enough to be appropriately vivid and fun but not long enough to seem over the top or merely campy.

"976-EVIL" is essentially a mood piece with a *film-noir* look created by cameraman Paul Elliott and art director David Brian Miller. The drab, cluttered settings created by Miller and set decorator Nancy Booth are meticulous in their apt details, and "976-EVIL" has a better look than many far more expensive pictures. The violence is standard Grand Guignol, but is of a sufficiently brooding and graphic nature that the film's R-rating—given also for language and sex—should be observed in regard to children.

MONTHLY FILM BULLETIN, 1/89, p. 22, Tim Pulleine

Garden City, a small town in California. The orphaned Spike, a high-school senior, lives under the nominal guardianship of his eccentric Aunt Lucy, who has a houseful of cats and is obsessively devoted to TV evangelism, making her own son, the younger Hoax, introverted and lonely. Spike loses heavily in a poker game with fellow members of a school gang, the Barracudas, and risks losing his motorcycle. Idly dialling an advertised "Horrorscope" phone number (976-Evil), he hears from "the Master" an exhortation to self-help and on impulse steals the required sum from Lucy's cache of money. He is caught in the act but matters are disrupted by an apparent "miracle" involving fish falling from the sky. Lucy contacts *Modern Miracle* magazine, which sends reporter Marty Palmer to interview her. At school, Hoax is rescued by Spike from being tormented by the Barracudas; Spike makes a date for that evening with a classmate, Suzie, and subsequently Hoax spies jealously on their lovemaking. Hoax dials the Horrorscope number and receives a message which encourages him to make a play for Suzie, who by now has had a row with Spike. He is unsuccessful and the Barracudas intervene to compound his humiliation. Inspired by a further phone message, Hoax schemes to revenge himself on Suzie by casting an evil spell which causes spiders (about which she is phobic) to appear before her; this leads, however, to Suzie's death. Meanwhile, intrigued by the situation, Marty has talked to Hoax's teacher, Angella Martinez, and subsequently locates the premises of Horrorscope, only to learn from the sinister proprietor, Mark Dark, that the service was discontinued some months before; when Marty returns and enters secretly, he is amazed to see the equipment seeming to work of its own accord. Hoax has a further run-in with the bullies, and finds he is able to wreak lethal vengeance on one of them; that evening, by now distorted in outward appearance, he intervenes in the gang's poker game and causes the gruesome deaths of his remaining tormentors. Returning home, he confronts his mother, and after an altercation does her to death. He is followed by Marty and Angella, and the latter enters the (mysteriously changed) house to find the cats feasting on Lucy's corpse, before being confronted by the now totally deranged Hoax. Spike arrives and grapples with Hoax, who falls into a bottomless pit which his imprecations have opened up outside the house. But later, at the Horrorscope headquarters, another caller is unaccountably answered...

Robert Englund, the fearsome Freddy of *Nightmare on Elm Street*, makes his directing début with a horror film possessed of some of the same qualities of bizarre invention and technical adroitness. *976-Evil* confidently puts its restricted scale to claustrophobic use, and both settings and characterisations (most obviously that of the crazed Aunt Lucy with her menagerie of cats) combine tongue-in-cheek exaggeration with the authentically rebarbative. The toilet block in which most of the high-school scenes seem to take place is hyperbolically squalid, and is matched in more traditional pop-Gothic terms by the cobwebbed environs of the supposedly defunct "Horrorscope" studio. The misanthropy and grotesquerie, moreover, find humorous expression in sundry incidentals, whether it is the stomach-churning glimpse of a biology bisection exercise

("Hurry back, we're cutting the gonads next", says the sinisterly beaming teacher), or Palmer handing over a previous customer's meagre tip to the surly waitress at the diner (slyly named Dante's) with the remark, "I guess somebody left this by mistake". Englund shows, too, some real flair in orchestrating the show-piece sequences, even to the extent of persuading the viewer at the climax that Angella would pursue her investigation of the ravaged house rather than dash off in the opposite direction.

But what makes the film enjoyable in parts rather than satisfying as a whole is not just the narrative incoherence—not least as regards the hocus-pocus over the spiders—or the intermittent recourse to a gory explicitness that is juvenile rather than neo-Jacobean, but more basic failures of construction. Neither Spike, initially presented as if he is to be the central character, nor the inquiring journalist Palmer, who moves rather arbitrarily to the centre of the action after starting out like a source of comic relief, are dramatically integrated. Partly in consequence, the viewer is not properly "placed" *vis-à-vis* the victimised Hoax and his quest for revenge. These short-comings tend to rob the film of cumulative effect, but one remains curious to see what Englund might make of more integrated material.

NEW STATESMAN & SOCIETY, 12/16/88, p. 43, Suzanne Moore

There are a few laughs to be had [the reference is to *High Spirits*] but nothing like so many as in *976-Evil*, a horror film directed by Robert Englund, Freddy of *A Nightmare on Elm Street* fame. Basically another wimp's revenge movie, it's a perfect example of how contemporary horror has become what Philip Brophy describes as "a saturated genre". The pleasure of a movie like *976-Evil* depends precisely on its ability to embrace the clichés and conventions of other horror films—on this genre's amazing capacity to eat itself alive.

Like so many of these teen horror flicks, it is set in a small American town conjured up as usual by a diner, a church and a school, in some indefinable time that may be the present but could be the fifties. Somehow, this hazy conception of time and place serves to intensify the events in the film—it seems enough to simply suggest "normality" at the beginning of the movie, as we know that by the end this will be overturned. Since the audience is already complicit in the knowledge that everything is not what it seems, then it doesn't matter if things never seem too real or too accurate in the first place.

In this way the tackiness of the film-making is in itself a source of pleasure that gets reabsorbed by the text. While other genres strive for flawlessness, horror is often able to turn its flaws into virtues by overplaying them—by actively inviting the audience to recognise them.

This is why the most horrific sequences can be the most hilarious while the humorous scenes can be so sick that they leave the nastiest after-taste. The wimp in *976-Evil* is Hoax, a fumbling no-hope adolescent who gets picked on by the local high-school gang. He idolises his cousin Spike who is cool enough to have a pony-tail, a motorbike and a girlfriend. They both live in a house dominated by Hoax's weirdo mother "Aunt Lucy"—a monstrous mother in the long line of maternal madwomen from *Psycho* to *Carrie*. Aunt Lucy is a religious nut with a penchant for ridiculous wigs.

While she witnesses a modern-day miracle—fish pouring out of the sky—Hoax has been getting up to other things. By dialling a telephone answering service he has been talking to the devil who promises him special powers. And sure enough the quietly odd Hoax soon turns into a reptile with extended finger nails and is slashing faces in the boys' toilets. As his body changes into something completely different, he extracts revenge on everyone including, of course, his mother.

This link between adolescent sexuality—the feeling of a body changing, growing, being out of control—and its grotesque exaggeration in horror movies has often been discussed but this element may explain the genre's continuing fascination for young audiences. What is disturbing is that in so many of these films the responsibility for unleashing these horrific powers is laid squarely at the feet of the female characters.

Hoax's inability to break free from his mother's grip (in all these films the father is always absent) as well as his rejection at the hands of Spike's girlfriend is what finally turns him into the devil incarnate.

The only thing that appears to be able to save him is Spike's rendering of the American Dream—"We'll drive cross country on our bikes, on the open road, get a couple of babes..." But, alas, the devil has got his hooks in and anyway the family home has literally turned into hell with the kitchen covered in ice and a gaping fiery abyss appearing in the living room. It's reassuring to know that Hoax is not impressed: "Once you've been to hell, everything else pales in comparison".

What remains the most shocking thing about these kind of movies is that although hell is loosely bound to vaguely religious imagery, they make it abundantly clear that it is actually located in the heart of the family and in the minds of its young men.

NEW YORK POST, 3/25/89, p. 19, Jami Bernard

Robert Englund, the guy who plays Freddie in the "Nightmare on Elm Street" series, has directed his first feature film, and yes, there are some long fingernails in it. If only the movie had teeth as well.

This mild horror/slasher pic, aimed at the high school crowd, uses the device of a call-in "horrorscope," a sort of hot line to Hell, where you dial the number, receive some unearthly advice, and then not only do you pay with your soul, but you run up a big telephone bill too. Callers get tips on how to pay back gambling debts or get a hot date, but the more times they call in, the more indebted they are to the disembodied voice on the other end of the line. The most persistent callers start sprouting long black fingernails.

Filled with obvious sight gags (the local cafe is called Dante's, there are posters of hoof-prints on the walls of the gym), "976-EVIL" has a sort of complacent good humor that seems to have lulled its actors into not trying very hard. Even when the very jaws of Hell open beneath their feet, no one looks too surprised.

Eventually, it turns into a typical revenge-of-the-nerd movie, wherein the dufus whose head is always getting pushed down a toilet finally sprouts his nails and gets even, courtesy of Dial-a-Devil.

The only performance of any interest is by the increasingly bizarre Sandy Dennis as a blowzy religious fanatic who keeps lots of cats (as in real life) and falls to her knees in ecstasy during a shower of dead fish.

Dennis plays the mother of Hoax (Stephen Geoffreys), a hopeless nerd who wears his bookbag around his neck and gawks at pretty girls. He adores his good-looking, Harley-riding cousin, Spike (Patrick O'Bryan), who lives in the house across the way; as children they must have been close, because there's still a pneumatic tube hookup between their bedroom windows, through which Hoax sends such inspired messages as "Hi, Spike!"

Sipke discovers the power of the mysterious phone number and gets a hint on how to pay off a poker debt. He steals the money from his crazy aunt across the way, and she pitches a fit until it starts raining fish.

The aunt, impressed with the fish-fall, notifies a reporter from Modern Miracle Magazine. "The skies began to r-r-rumble," purrs Dennis. Sporadically during the course of the movie, the reporter tries to get to the heart of things.

Meanwhile, in other unrelated sideshows, we see how other folks who decide to hang up on the Devil are hounded to death by a ringing in their ears. All the phones in the world start to jangle sickly, or is that your nerves?

When the local hoodlums rub pizza all over Hoax's face, who's he gonna call? He dials 976-EVIL, and soon he's killing and maiming and tearing living hearts out.

During the predictable and protracted showdown, in which all attempts at story and character are tossed into the abyss of special effects, Hoax tells his cousin, "Once you've been to Hell everything else pales by comparison." You see, hell can be in your own back yard or in your neighborhood movie theater.

Also reviewed in:
NEW YORK TIMES, 3/25/89, p. 12, Richard Bernstein
VARIETY, 3/29–4/4/89, p. 16
WASHINGTON POST, 3/25/89, p. D7, Richard Harrington

NO HOLDS BARRED

A New Line Cinema release of a Shane Productions film. *Executive Producer:* Vincent K. McMahon. *Producer:* Michael Rachmil. *Director:* Thomas J. Wright. *Screenplay:* Dennis Hackin. *Director of Photography:* Frank Beascoechea. *Editor:* Tom Pryor. *Music:* Jim Johnston. *Sound:* Scott Smith. *Production Designer:* James

Shanahan. *Set Decorator:* Lynn Wolverton. *Stunt Coordinator:* Buck McDancer. *Running time:* 92 minutes. *MPAA Rating:* PG-13.

CAST: Hulk Hogan (Rip); Kurt Fuller (Tom Brell); Joan Severance (Samantha Moore); Tom "Tiny" Lister (Zeus); Mark Pellegrino (Randy); Bill Henderson (Charlie); Charles Levin (Ordway); David Palmer (Unger); Stan "The Lariat" Hansen (Neanderthal); Armelia McQueen (Sadie).

LOS ANGELES TIMES, 6/5/89, Calendar/p. 3, Michael Wilmington

Pro wrestling phenomenon Hulk Hogan is the main attraction of the garish, sub-"Rocky" action-satire, "No Holds Barred," and he has a peculiar Jekyll-Hyde persona during the movie. Outside the ring, he's quiet, gentlemanly and deferential. While wrestling, his face becomes distorted and maniacal: eyes bulging, neck muscles taut, mouth stretched into a silent but leonine scream.

It's the beast unleashed, the hulk unbuckled. The movie itself is about the war of nerves between a gentle but heroic wrestler and a raving madman who runs a national TV network. And, if you've labored under the delusion all these years that there was something phony about TV wrestling, "No Holds Barred" will set you straight. In the film's world, every ludicrous chokehold, every laughable belly-flop, every preposterous rope-slam is totally legitimate.

Instead, it's TV that's phony. Here, it's run by greedy, dangerous lunatics and sniveling toadies who, in the pursuit of higher ratings, will stop at nothing: including prostitution, murder or screaming and hollering until their faces turn blue.

Hogan plays Rip, good-natured wrestling superstar and benign blond behemoth; the movie's ingenuity has not extended to finding him a last name (Rip Rogan? Rip Roxoff?). Kurt Fuller plays his demented nemesis: the upspeakable network executive Tom Brell.

Brell first tries to woo soft-spoken Rip to his lineup with the gentle approach (for him): waving money in his face, shoving and pummeling him. When these restrained tactics fail, Brell turns to kidnaping, extortion, assault and attempted murder. He enlists the services of a homicidal maniac named Zeus (Tiny Lister) who challenges the champ to a match with no rules. Zeus also beats Rip's brother to a bloody pulp. (Lest critics accuse the movie of veiled racism—Zeus is black— other blacks are always included, hiding behind Rip or cheering him on at fights, whenever Zeus appears.)

Obviously Brell is not rational. There must be easier ways to win good ratings than this. But Rip and his friends are irrational too; they never call the police to complain that a maniac is threatening them and committing violent crimes. Instead, Rip fights it out as he always has: alone, indomitable, in the ring, *mano-a-mano*. Will he win? Will he smash, bash and thrash the obstreperous Zeus? Will he rescue the lissome Samantha (Joan Severance)? Will his little brother walk again? Will the vile Brell get his comeuppance? Will the sun rise tomorrow?

"No Holds Barred" gets no points for originality. It's written with the subtlety of a body-slam and directed with the finesse of a hammerlock. But the movie never takes itself seriously and director Tom Wright (TV's "Beauty and the Beast") has fun with the wrestling montages. Hogan himself has an appealing screen presence—like a gallant teddy bear who goes berserk every 10 minutes or so. Kurt Fuller, last seen gibbering insanely in "Miracle Mile," comes up with the kind of congenitally sneering wild-man bully who might have harassed Abbott and Costello.

And if you still think TV wrestling is mostly phony, consider this: "No Holds Barred" was produced by Shane Productions, which is, according to the press book, run by the "executive brain trust" behind the World Wrestling Foundation of which Hulk Hogan is currently world champion. What group would know better whether pro wrestling is just a big show?

NEW YORK POST, 6/3/89, p. 19, Jami Bernard

If it is possible that one movie can signify the end of civilization as we know it, then that movie is "No Holds Barred," a paean to the pea-brained entertainment known as wrestling.

You're probably wondering who am I to talk, since there is evidence that the Three Stooges were my "imaginary playmates" as a child. Yes, we all have something to hide.

Still, it does not bode well for humanity, decency, society or even the rest of the afternoon that the pre-teen audience at the first showing of the movie yesterday bounced joyously in their seats as the super-blond Hulk Hogan gruntingly smashed his coincidentally black opponent into sour mash.

No only do we have a new generation of kids completely entranced by the marvels of stupidity, and willing to spend their parents' money on making the World Wrestling "We're Not Fake"

Federation into a veritable Fort Knox. Now we also have punch-'em-up movies that violate that one last code of chivalry—the ostensible protection of women. In "No Holds Barred," several females get punched or whacked in the face. Joan Severance is kidnapped and nearly raped, much to the evident satisfaction of an audience that shares the same vocabulary as the movie villain (Tiny Lister), whose only lines are grunts.

Two wrestlers have managed, through savvy public relations maneuvers, to enter the consciousness of the thinking public—Andre the Giant and Hulk Hogan. Andre managed to pull his considerable weight in "The Princess Bride," where he was typecast as a giant. Now Hogan, who is genuinely attempting to present himself as a role model for kids, has a starring role as a wrestler who is more interested in charity work than in marketing his image (his role in this movie notwithstanding).

An unscrupulous TV network honcho, Brell (Kurt Fuller), wants to sign up "Rip" (Hogan) in order to boost the ratings, but Rip can't be bought, no siree bob. So Brell goes to the most hellish bar in the world, the kind where the urinals are spilling over like the Fontana de Trevi, and signs on as many toothless, nose-picking, drooling hulks (no offense, Mr. Hogan) for a "Battle of the Tough Guys."

"These people would cheer at a hanging," protests one of Brell's cohorts.

"That's the beauty of it," he replies.

The winning Tough Guy is Zeus (Lister), a black behemoth with half an eyebrow who has a nervous habit of clanging his wrist manacles together the way grasshoppers rub their hind legs.

Through a series of taunts and intimidations and by kidnapping Rip's girlfriend (Severance, poor thing) and mutilating Rip's little brother, Brell goads Rip into taking on Zeus. From then on it's a punchfest, the human equivalent of a car chase.

Hogan, accustomed to the theatrics of wrestling (no, it's not "fake," it's just "entertainment," ha ha), does not embarrass himself, considering that he has a crying scene and a sex scene (including an annoying ripoff of the "Wall of Jericho" episode from "It Happened One Night," a *real* movie). He also inflicts damage on some Nautilus machines, and has to say the word "doody."

The beautiful, clear-eyed Severance should think of this role as just a bad dream. (If you want to see her in something, try "See No Evil, Hear No Evil.")

For protection, I banded together in the theater with a fellow film critic, who likened the escalation of opponents in "No Holds Barred" to the structure of the Iliad—but you see, that's the trouble with film critics, always reading into things. Yes, this movie represents the decline of Western Civilization. But The Iliad? That's going too far.

NEWSDAY, 6/3/89, Part II/p. 17, Bill Kaufman

Hulkamania: An affliction of the mainly young, characterized by an insatiable desire for Hulk Hogan movable figures, records, T-shirts, records, posters and other curios, all marketed and promoted for the express purpose of enriching the World Wrestling Federation by more than $300 million annually.

Hogan has generated an incredibly well-orchestrated merchandising campaign, and this furiously paced movie, aimed at young grunt-and-groan fans, is part of it.

"No Holds Barred" can't be taken any more seriously than, well, televised wrestling matches. Hogan, a relatively dapper beefcake as far as ring musclemen go, plays—what else—a popular TV wrestler named Rip. All you need to know about the all-brawn-and-no-brains script is that Tom Brell, a hyped-up television network president, played as a sweeping caricature by Kurt Fuller, wants to lure Rip away from the competition. Spurned, Brell and his staff of yes-men embark on a campaign to degrade Rip. Want to bet they can't do it?

Some Hogan fans may feel somewhat distressed when they see their hero in the throes of love, making goo-goo eyes at a female marketing whiz vapidly played by former fashion model Joan Severance. Happily, there's much more crush than mush. A few funny lines get tossed off here and there. The beautiful exec takes Rip to a posh restaurant and the snooty waiter, reading the menu in French, glares at the tieless wrestler: 'Perhaps monsieur, a hamburger or a foot-long hot dog for you?''

Somewhat at a loss for acting, but never at a loss for action, "No Holds Barred" gives buffs a full wrestling card. Among the assorted animal-like opponents Hogan faces on the streets and on the canvas is a monstrous wrestler named Zeus (Tiny Lister) who has "Z's" shaved into his hair. Hogan's followers will also get to see him face off against inanimate opponents like the door of a speeding limousine. The automobile loses.

Also reviewed in:
NEW YORK TIMES, 6/3/89, p. 12, Stephen Holden
VARIETY, 5/24–30/89, p. 32
WASHINGTON POST, 6/8/89, p. B6, Richard Harrington

OLD GRINGO

A Columbia Pictures release of a Fonda Films production. *Executive Producer:* David Wisnievitz. *Producer:* Lois Bonfiglio. *Director:* Luis Puenzo. *Screenplay:* Aida Bortnik and Luis Puenzo. *Based on the novel "Gringo Viejo" by:* Carlos Fuentes. *Director of Photography:* Felix Monti. *Editor:* Juan Carlos Macias, William Anderson, and Glenn Farr. *Music:* Lee Holdridge. *Music Editor:* Tom Carlson. *Choreographer:* Ana Merida. *Sound:* Simon Kaye and (music) Bobby Fernandez. *Sound Editor:* Tom McCarthy. *Production Designer:* Stuart Wurtzel and Bruno Rubeo. *Art Director:* Scott Ritenour. *Set Designer:* Steve Saklad and Tom Warren. *Set Decorator:* Tessa Davies. *Special Effects:* Jesus Duran Galvan, Fermin Duran Martinez, Adrian Duran Martinez, and Alejandro Duran Velazquez. *Costumes:* Enrico Sabbatini. *Make-up:* Lee Harman, Peg Schierholz, and Alberto Lopez. *Stunt Coordinator:* Mickey Gilbert. *Running time:* 119 minutes. *MPAA Rating:* R.

CAST: Jane Fonda (Harriet Winslow); Gregory Peck (Bitter/Ambrose Bierce); Jimmy Smits (Arroyo); Patricio Contreras (Col. Frutos Garcia); Jenny Gago (La Garduna); Gabriela Roel (La Luna); Sergio Calderon (Zacarias); Guillermo Rios (Monsalvo); Jim Metzler (Ron); Samuel Valadez "de la Torre" (Pedrito); Anne Pitoniak (Mrs. Winslow); Pedro Armendariz Jr. (Pancho Villa); Stanley Grover (Consul Saunders); Josefina Echanove (Clementina); Pedro Damian (Captain Ovando); Maya Zapata (Dolores); Jose Olivares (Trinidad); Alicia Del Lago (Trinidad's Wife); Carlos Cardan (Matias Salazar); Evangelina Sosa Martinez (Guadalupe); Hector Rivera (Ataulfo); Victor Carpinteiro (Hilario); Salvador Sanchez (Floreal); Maria Victoria Mondragon (Old Woman); Jose Juan Rodriguez (Old Man); Mario Arevalo (Casimiro); Laurel Lyle (Librarian); Richardson Morse (Editor); Jose Jorge Zepeda (Administrator of Hacienda); Roberto Sosa Martinez (Lucio); Maria Luisa Coronel (Maria); Amelia Zapata (Juana); Mark Kelty (Journalist #1); John Williams (Journalist #2); Arturo Rodriguez Doring (Mexican Journalist); Fernando Moya (Hotel Clerk); Juan Antonio Llanes (Assistant Hotel Clerk); Abel Woolrich (Tall Soldier); René Pereyra (Short Soldier); Martin Palomares (Wounded Man); Roberto Ortiz (Federal Officer); Stewart Smith (Journalist with Glasses); Paul Williams (Cinematographer); Steven Spencer (Assistant Consul).

FILMS IN REVIEW, 1–2/90, p. 45, Kevin Sweeney

Most of us gringos have a pretty simplified view of the Mexican Revolution; the wonderful "rightness" of heroic, white clad campesinos waging a noble struggle for social and economic justice against the rich has always held a romantic, almost fairy tale fascination—which has always made the revolution a natural for movies. In the last 20 years, recall such memorable Westerns as Sam Peckinpah's *The Wild Bunch* and Sergio Leone's *Duck You Sucker*. Like these, the recent *Old Gringo* attempts to simultaneously mythologize and explode American and European notions of "romantic" Third World revolution.

Set in 1916, the year before the Mexican constitution was signed and the bloody struggle began to wind down, *Old Gringo* is about two very different Americans who find themselves, for a few days, on the side of the angels. The title character is aging author and journalist Ambrose Bierce (Gregory Peck), who, disgusted with the United States—he tells people his name is "Bitter"—has come to Mexico to fight with the peasants, meet Pancho Villa and, inevitably, die. (The real Bierce disappeared and presumably died in Mexico.) The other is Harriet Winslow (Jane Fonda), a middle-aged, unmarried schoolteacher who's come down to work for a wealthy landowner. Convinced that her life has been a sham, Harriet sees this trip as a last chance to become passionate about something in life.

That something is Arroyo (Jimmy Smits), a dashing young revolutionary general who leads an attack on the landowner's hacienda. Arroyo is the bastard son of the rich man, and the revolution is a way of exorcising his guilt of being born half gentry. But after capturing the hacienda, Arroyo finds himself spiritually paralyzed by his past; he begins acting more and more like the strutting patron, and ignores orders to rejoin the main army under Pancho Villa.

Based on a complex, multi-layered novel by leading Mexican writer Carlos Fuentes, *Old Gringo* loses something in the translation from book to film. Like its source, the movie wants to be both a romance and an anti-romance—sweeping music and gorgeous vistas juxtaposed with violent cruelty. What worked in the novel doesn't really come off here because the motivations and inner feelings of the two men have been inpossibly garbled in the transition.

At some confused level Arroyo and Bitter are supposed to be hazy mirror images of each other (one young, one old; one idealist, one cynic), and their love-hate relationship obviously represent the fragile border between Mexico and the United States, the Third World and the First World. Obviously, the danger of conceiving characters as symbols rather than real people is that things tend to become overblown and contrived. This is a problem that has defeated filmmakers, even ones more talented than director/co-scripter Luis Puenzo, an Argentinian who came to fame with *Official Story* in 1984.

Even granted its flaws, this still represents a worthwhile and original attempt on the part of Hollywood to do something different, and certainly didn't deserve the almost universal critical panning it received. In terms of physically portraying the time and place, *Old Gringo* is an often powerful piece of filmmaking. Shooting on magnificent location north of Mexico City. Puenzo displays a sure hand with both large scale action scenes and intimate drama.

A great deal of the film's appeal comes from Gregory Peck, who at 73 goes full blast with a vigorous, lyrical portrayal of a crotchety old bon vivant looking to recapture lost love and sense of idealism. In his scenes with Fonda's adoring Harriet especially, Peck is at once grandfatherly-wise and unabashedly sexy, representing old-fashioned star power at its best.

LOS ANGELES TIMES, 10/6/89, Calendar/p. 1, Sheila Benson

If you've ever yearned for the big movies of the '40s, lush and improbable, bolstered by the star turns of real movie stars, then just possibly "The Old Gringo" is your meat. Although its setting is the Mexican Revolution, in some ways it's like one of those swaggering pirate epics where an unpredictable, reekingly macho brigand takes possession of his chaste woman captive, changing both their lives forever.

It does have a nicely unsentimental performance by one of its two certified movie stars, Gregory Peck, as the title character, the caustic and brilliant journalist Ambrose Bierce—who calls himself "Bitter" here. But somehow "Old Gringo" emerges, naive and pulsing, as a sexual fantasy of the Mexican Revolution, all sunsets and sumptuousness with a peculiarly split focus.

Things have been knocked out of whack by the fact that it was Jane Fonda who bought the rights to Carlos Fuentes' novel and labored to get the film made, taking on the (then) subsidiary role of the novel's 31-year-old spinster, Harriet Winslow. Fonda has called her "Old Gringo" "a movie about a woman who takes responsibility." At any rate, she takes center stage. It might also be seen as "The Loves of the Not-So-Old Gringa," torn between the young revolutionary general Arroyo (Jimmy Smits), who deflowers her, and the graceful, brilliant Bierce, who yearns to.

Harriet (age unspecified) impulsively leaves her tepid life in Washington, D.C., with her widowed mother for Mexico. She's been hired as teacher to the children of the aristocratic Miranda family at their baronial hacienda. But the revolution arrives at the Mirandas' doorstep before Harriet does. One of Pancho Villa's regiments, headed by Gen. Arroyo, takes possession of the hacienda, forcing the Mirandas out and leaving Harriet stranded there, not a prisoner but a curious onlooker, attracted and repelled by the excesses of the upheaval around—and eventually within—her.

The Mirandas' mirrored and parqueted palace is a magnet: for Harriet; for Arroyo, who is actually a Miranda himself, the bastard son of the landowner and a servant at the hacienda, and for the dry and witty Bierce, witnessing the final fire with knowing cynicism. (Every fire: the revolution's, Harriet's, Arroyo's and his own.)

Arroyo becomes becalmed at the mansion in whose kitchens and servant's quarters he was raised. Now virtually lord of the place himself, he finds it harder and harder to leave, to take his troops to Villa at the front. In this equation, Bierce, reluctantly, becomes sounding board and father figure to Arroyo and more of a father figure than he'd like to be to Harriet.

Bierce takes a little explaining to most modern audiences, who may have their curiosity raised and not quite answered by the film. He was an incisive writer with ideas well ahead of his time. He was a complicated man who rode alone into Mexico in 1913, when he was 71, to see the revolution for himself and disappeared without a trace. His fiction, with its overtones of the supernatural and of dreams (including "Occurrence at Owl Creek Bridge") captivated Fuentes, who put the old gringo at the heart of his story.

While the book is a parable, an intellectual game, the movie is about the birth of Harriet's passion. The film doesn't *need* Fuentes' literary convolutions—these references are excess baggage here, properly stowed away by director-writer Luis Puenzo and his collaborator, Aida Bortnik. But what the film gives us instead is a stale romantic triangle of the '40s: Locked in the arms of her revolutionary leader, stoked and stroked by her elderly American journalist, Harriet will return to America a better person. It's as if all that patting and prodding were an infusion of consciousness, not simple romantic and sexual fun.

Using Puenzo, the Argentine director who made "Official Story," as director and co-writer presumably assured the film of a properly Latin feeling. Actually, in terms of the cultural differences between Argentina and Mexico, it was a little like hiring a New Yorker to write about New Mexico. But like a good researcher, Puenzo immersed himself in Mexican history, and the result, to these foreign eyes, seems at least respectful. It is certainly an elegant production (MPAA-rated R).

The performance of the film is Peck's, probably one of the best of his career. If he seems more an elegant rider than a hell-for-leather adventurer, so be it; he certainly conjures up the mysterious complex Bierce. And for an embodiment of a romantic revolutionary leader, you probably couldn't do better than Smits, either. (You might ask for clearer writing and editing near the film's end to prepare us for his fate, however.) Jenny Gago seems a great find as La Garduna, the cheerful camp follower. Ironically Fonda, whose strength was what carried the film to the screen, seems at all times too strong a personality for the innocent Harriet, or even her later incarnation as Harriet La Passionara.

MONTHLY FILM BULLETIN, 10/89, p. 307, Tom Milne

Washington D.C., 1913. Harriet Winslow, a spinster schoolteacher, happens to be present at a ceremony honouring the septuagenarian writer Ambrose Bierce. Impressed by the honesty with which Bierce repudiates his own writing, and the society which misused it, Harriet—having already broken off a conventional engagement contracted to please her mother—refuses to go on countenancing the pretence that her father is a Cuban War hero buried in Arlington Cemetery (actually, tired of a loveless marriage, he simply failed to come home), and leaves for Mexico to take up a position as governess. In Chihuahua, undaunted by news that the revolution has spread, Harriet hires a peasant guide to take her to the Miranda hacienda, unaware that he is in fact General Tomás Arroyo, a youthful aide to Pancho Villa. Accompanied by Bierce, who has come to Mexico to die, Arroyo uses Harriet to trick his way into the hacienda, routs the Federal troops guarding it (the wealthy landowners, Harriet's employers, have fled), and occupies it on behalf of the revolution. In the skirmishing, Bierce distinguishes himself by his reckless courage; while Harriet, horrified by the bloodshed, busies herself with educating the women and children to build for the future. Mockery of the old gringo and the gringa turns to grudging respect; while sexual attraction ripens to a kind of loving between Arroyo and Harriet, and love of another sort blooms between Bierce (grieved by his estrangement from his daughter) and Harriet (haunted by the loss of her father). But Arroyo, under orders to move on in support of Villa, seems unable to tear himself away from the hacienda: the bastard son of the landowner, who raped his peasant mother, Arroyo becomes increasingly autocratic, like the father he hated, as he broods over ancient documents proving his (and the people's) title to the land. Despairing of persuading Arroyo that words on paper are worthless, Bierce burns the documents as a deliberate provocation, and is shot dead by Arroyo. Allowed to return to Chihuahua and reporting the death of a U.S. citizen to the consulate, Harriet—respecting Bierce's desire for anonymity—identifies the victim as her father. Arriving to claim the body for burial at Arlington, Harriet is stunned to find that Villa has decreed that Bierce, like Arroyo, deserved execution for disobeying orders (though not to be shot in the back); and that her signature is required as witness to a double execution, with Bierce's exhumed body propped up alongside Arroyo to face the firing squad.

True to the Hollywood habit of tailoring literary conceptions for painless consumption, this adaptation of Carlos Fuentes' novel opens, after a credit sequence anticipating the exhumation of Ambrose Bierce's body, with a scene in a bookshop where Harriet overhears, from a distance, Bierce's bitter denunciation of himself, his readers, the worlds of publishing and journalism The idea of bringing this "meeting" up front, instead of leaving Harriet quietly to deduce Bierce's identity shortly before he dies as the novel does, is presumably to suggest that Bierce served as an example to Harriet; and indeed, Fonda's Harriet duly muses on the "courage" which led Bierce, like her father fifteen years before, to abandon their worlds. The use of the word courage is singularly unfortunate in the context, since it permanently obscures the irony with which Fuentes pinpoints the old gringo's "courage" as a fear of almost everything except the merciful oblivion of death, and Harriet's as that of the holy fool protected by a sense of cultural superiority (though both, movingly, are reborn in the course of their odyssey).

A more valid purpose of this opening sequence is of course to alert the audience to the old gringo's identity. But for all the film tells one about Ambrose Bierce, presumably just a name to most people nowadays, remembered if at all for the enduring mystery of his disappearance off the face of the earth one day in 1914, he might just as well have been left anonymous. The one piece of tangible information supplied by the script is that Bierce is haunted by his daughter's estrangement from him; and this is used as a somewhat obvious pointer to the nature of the relationship (non-sexual, despite a playful pretence of carnality) between Bierce and Harriet which counterpoints the relationship (purely sexual, despite yearnings for it to become otherwise) between Arroyo and Harriet.

In the novel, on the other hand, Fuentes' imaginative reconstruction of Bierce's state of mind, lent detail and shading by oblique references to his stories and other writings, posits the despair of a man who has come to see the misanthropic melancholy of his literary output—cruelly, even macabrely sardonic in its satirical assessment of human nature—as literally destructive. Holding his "failure" as a writer directly responsible for the actual or figurative annihilation of his wife and family through indifference and neglect—"My own son died twice... first as an alcoholic and then as a suicide, after reading me and telling me, Old man, you have written the blueprint for my death, oh, beloved old man"—Bierce goes to Mexico, "crosses the frontier" as Fuentes has it, in search of a dream of humanity.

Fuentes uses his frontier metaphor with extraordinary richness. "Each of us has a secret frontier within him", he writes in describing Bierce's immediate sense of liberation on crossing the border into a Mexico on the move, "and that is the most difficult frontier to cross because each of us hopes to find himself alone there, but finds only that he is more than ever in the company of others". Locked tightly into the company of Harriet (whose frontier is one of the mind) and Arroyo (faced with a frontier of the heart) as he crosses his frontier into death, Bierce undergoes change along with them as the revolution brings change to Mexico. Their three-way relationship, little more than a brief romantic encounter and a father/daughter substitution in the film, is infinitely more complex in the novel. Not only does Fuentes document their evolving attitudes within a panoramic perspective that acknowledges a wealth of contributory factors (ranging from the history of Mexico, by way of the aspirations of Manifest Destiny, to the tenets of Catholic and Protestant faith), he also peoples the dreams of his three protagonists with an inexhaustible system of haunting surrogate relationships.

Thus, Arroyo becomes the son(s) Bierce has lost; Bierce becomes the hated father who sired a bastard Arroyo; Harriet becomes Arroyo's hapless peasant mother, victim of arrogant "foreign intervention"; and the system even extends to fleeting *correspondances*, like the enigmatic coincidence between Bierce's morbid fear of dogs and the tale of Arroyo's fraught encounter with two savage mastiffs as he hides out in a landowner's cellar on the eve of the revolution. All this, providing the book with its elusively reverberating emotional overtones, is pruned away in the film, leaving a conventional romantic adventure that misfires on most cylinders, further hampered by direction which stages the action sequences (far too predominant anyway) in sub-Peckinpah style filtered through the Spaghetti Western mode.

NEW YORK POST, 10/6/89, p. 25, Jami Bernard

In the first project with her new production company, Fonda Films, Jane Fonda plays a frustrated spinster—the script's words, not mine—who livens up considerably when she becomes embroiled in a spicy love triangle during the Mexican Revolution.

A subject that is obviously dear to Fonda and the film makers—it is based on a book by Carlos

Fuentes—"Old Gringo" seems meticulous in its attention to period detail and accuracy, almost smothered in it. And yet, when Fonda's Harriet Winslow points to a group of Mexicans making merry in their festive native garb and burbles: "Just look at them!," the camera unfortunately catches a washerwoman who looks about as pleased with her lot as a McDonald's cashier.

Harriet Winslow, a schoolteacher, wants to change her life. "I'm not a girl, mother, I'm a SPINSTER!" she spits at her mom, as if she were the French lieutenant's WHORE or something.

Fired up when she overhears a stomping tirade by the irascible old writer and adventurer Ambrose Bierce (a real-life figure used fictionally), Harriet accepts a governess job for a wealthy family and heads down Me-hee-co way.

She arrives just as her new employers are being blown away by the revolutionaries, led by the charismatic Gen. Arroyo (Jimmy Smits of "LA. Law"). There is much bloodshed and horses falling over (a disclaimer at the end of the film assures that none of the animals were ill-treated, although there haven't been such stunt horses since the wire-trippers of Westerns).

Also caught up in the fray is an elderly gent, who turns out to be none other than Bierce (Gregory Peck), the cynical muckraker who, historically, disappeared in his later years in the thick of the revolution and whose final days are accounted for in the movie by his involvement with Pancho Villa's troops.

Harriet, like the movie, treads cautiously in the midst of all this Mexican nationalism, and though she eventually embraces, if not the cause, then the man fighting for it, she is still, for all practical purposes, a *gringa*, and the black-clad old writer is the Old Gringo, and the Mexicans use these words so often that if they were product placements someone would be rich.

Both the general and the Old Gringo develop a fascination for the *gringa*, enhanced no doubt by the lack of other availabe females aside from the battalion's spitfire of a prostitute.

With a flowery voiceover narrative by Fonda ("How could I not remember...The story began before I knew it was a story"), "Old Gringo" veers off occasionally into the land of the romance novel, complete with bodice and the kind of desperately sensual sweeping off of the feet that supposedly appeals to, you know, SPINSTERS. While certainly a woman's budding sexuality is cause for joy and film making, it also trivializes the freedom struggle with which the movie seems seriously concerned.

Peck, a national treasure, still looks like a guy who can make women sigh, as his character here claims. He does the dignity-with-humor bit as few others can.

Fonda is a thornier problem. Her Harriet arrives South of the Border with an appropriately up-tight bearing, but even when her eyes soften and become pools of liquid, which happens often, Fonda never seems to invest Harriet with the free-spiritedness that SPINSTERS are supposed to have when dark-skinned seducers unwrap them from their tightly coiled tortilla shells.

In the trailer for the movie, letters 10-foot-high roll across the screen with the last names of the stars: FONDA ... PECK ... SMITS!

Smits?

Not of the same caliber, Smits gives a sexually charged and emotionally vacillating performance as the charismatic general who gets sidetracked from his revolution by his horse, his hacienda and the *gringa*. "This hacienda is driving you crazy!" warns the Old Gringo. Evidenced perhaps by the comment from the general to the *gringa:* "You will tell your grandchildren you once ate tortillas, but you will forget the smell!"

Is another country's political turmoil ultimately about giving Americans a new lease on life? Will Harriet forget the smell of the tortillas? Will the handsome general shoot his horse or the Old Gringo? Find out, if you're up to it.

NEWSDAY, 10/6/89, Part III/p. 3, Mike McGrady

"Old Gringo" is clearly a project very close to Jane Fonda's heart. She has, in fact, for eight years been developing the idea of a movie centered on American writer Ambrose Bierce's adventures in the Mexican Revolution.

As far back as 1980, Fonda approached Mexico's foremost novelist, Carlos Fuentes, and told him of her "dream to make a movie that was about my country and his and the relationship between them." She then sought out Argentina's top director, Luis Puenzo ("The Official Story"), and he spent many months researching the subject, seeking locations and polishing the script based on Fuentes' 1985 novel, "Gringo Viejo."

This was but the beginning. The costly epic, shot on location in Mexico, required millions of dollars, hundreds of extras, two imported horses trained to crash through windows and 10 Italian tailors overseeing a small army of Mexican seamstresses who made the peasant clothing that was then aged, at still more expense, by using sandpaper, dust, fat and bleach.

The results of all this monumental planning and effort? "Old Gringo" recalls Bierce's definition of "achievement" in "The Devil's Dictionary": "The death of endeavor and the birth of disgust."

All that effort—for what? For a dreary script, a muddy philosophy, a routine, old-fashioned historical epic in which noble intentions get lost in the dust of galloping horses, the explosion of gunpowder, the pitter-patting of lovers' hearts. In point of fact, it's hard to determine what those noble intentions ever were.

What appears on the screen is a series of commonplace fabrications involving an attractive American spinster (Jane Fonda) who signs on to be the governess for a wealthy Mexican family. But the year is 1913 and by the time Fonda arrives in Mexico, Pancho Villa's armies have made wealthy families an endangered species.

The suddenly unemployed Fonda finds herself in the company of curmudgeonly old Ambrose Bierce (Gregory Peck) and a fiery young general (Jimmy Smits). The several ongoing stories—the spinster-governess finding passion in the arms of the soldier, the aging writer searching for a meaningful death, the freedom-fighting Mexican conquering the grand hacienda where he was raised as a servant—overlap but never mesh. The movie expresses nothing more than a vaguely defined anti-Americanism that here seems to fall under Bierce's definition of "prejudice": "a vagrant opinion without visible means of support."

While the appearance of Gregory Peck is guaranteed to inspire affection in the heart of any moviegoer, this is no more than a pale reminder of his great past roles. At that, he fares better than either Fonda or Smits, who are both earnest and serious-minded in doomed efforts to make caricatures come alive.

The presence of director Luis Puenzo is barely noticeable. In the past, his political points were perfectly clear. Here his message is ambiguous enough to invite no reaction stronger than ambivalence. He can't seem to decide whether to film a routine historical fiction or a movie with something to say; he opts for the former, and it is, of course, at the expense of the latter.

VILLAGE VOICE, 10/17/89, p. 90, Georgia Brown

Old Gringo's palette looks like it has been coordinated with Jane Fonda's hair. It's all chestnut, ocher, sienna, and a range of beiges—except for black and white to distinguish its two important men. Primary colors are filtered out; even sky and cactus are pale and wan. These gold and sepia tones, I guess, are to make one think back to days when men were men and women were either ladies or whores.

The movie is adapted from Carlos Fuentes's novel, which Jane Fonda optioned before it was published because Fuentes, a friend, assured her it contained a part for her. Perhaps in Spanish the book is not as silly as it reads in translation. That "the old gringo came to Mexico to die" is repeated many times, sometimes in one-sentence paragraphs. The plot involves an imagined meeting of writer-eccentric Ambrose Bierce—the old gringo—with one of Pancho Villa's generals and an American lady; it's ostensibly about the clash of cultures. The lady is properly awed.

In Chihuahua, Bierce (Gregory Peck) runs into Harriet Winslow (Fonda), who's come to be a governess to the wealthy Miranda family. Brave Harriet has thrown off her mother's yoke ("I'm not a girl, Mother, I'm a *spinster!*") for a spiritual (i.e., sexual) quest involving her supposedly dead father—actually he never came back from the war in Cuba because he'd found a woman. Together gringo and gringuita wander in and out of a lot of fighting. Both become infatuated with the tall young General Arroyo (Jimmy Smits (from *L.A. Law*). Arroyo too has father troubles, since his was Miranda and he's now busy overthrowing landowners.

The movie stalls while actors deliver windy set speeches adapted from the novel by Argentinian director Luis Puenzo and co-writer Aida Bortnik (both from *The Official Story*). I say *stalls*, but it was hard to tell where it was heading. As the codger, Peck delivers his monologues quite charmingly and shows himself a game trouper. As the spinister (31 years old in the novel), Fonda plays shy and virginal (at moments fierce old Hanoi Jane peeks through). In romantic scenes with Peck, she's photographed to show age (not 51 exactly), and with Smits she looks about 10 years younger. Harriet's father fixation gets worked out on the live body of one man and with the dead body of the other. Gentle music comes up each time Harriet learns something new.

Columbia held back *Old Gringo* in a way that showed its own opinion, but the screening audience seemed to get some giggles from the picture. And, don't forget, the Hollywood-size location fees contributed to the Mexican economy.

Also reviewed in:
NEW YORK TIMES, 10/6/89, p. C8, Janet Maslin
VARIETY, 5/24–30/89, p. 6
WASHINGTON POST, 10/6/89, p. C1, Hal Hinson

ON THE MAKE

A Taurus Entertainment Company release of a Rayfield Company presentation. *Producer:* Fred Carpenter. *Director:* Samuel Hurwitz. *Screenplay:* Fred Carpenter and James McTernan. *Story:* Fred Carpenter. *Director of Photography:* Gerard Hughes. *Editor:* Ross Gelosi. *Music:* Phil Caradonna, Don Kehr, Michael Stein, and Kirk Fisher. *Sound:* Cathy Calderon. *Running Time:* 77 minutes. *MPAA Rating:* R.

CAST: Steve Irlen (Bobby); Mark McKelvey (Kurt); Teresina (Lori); Kirk Baltz (Richard); Tara Leigh (Jane); Jennifer Dempster (Vivian); Michael Ross (Danny); Don Alexander (Paul); Laura Grady (Tina).

VILLAGE VOICE, 10/3/89, p. 72, Renee Tajima

Imagine a celluloid skull and cross-bones dancing to a teen beat. Variously anti-AIDs and promonogamy, *On the Make* warns (straight) teenagers just how lethal today's rites of passage can be. Most of the movie takes place during the long disco nights of two youths: sentimental Bobby, on the rebound from a high school romance, and philandering Kurt, just a dance away— what will be his last dance, so it seems—from his hundredth conquest.

With voluminous energy and a thinly constructed plot, the film shows how Kurt got as good as he gave. Actor Mark McKelvey as the adolescent Mr. Goodbar has the pretty looks of a small-time Rob Lowe but cheeks sunken enough to suggest malaise. Even alter ego Bobby (Steve Irlen) probably wouldn't trust him alone with his own sister (neither would she, referring to Kurt as "that walking hard-on") and ultimately refuses to follow him down the same road to moussed, mini-skirted ecstasy.

Made on a minuscule budget by two young filmmakers, *On the Make* has the feel of an elongated, if risqué, public service announcement, with a little *Saturday Night Fever* thrown in. Perhaps because of their own youth, the filmmakers seem to know this world well. The cast of club-lifers that swirl around Kurt and Bobby performs with unaffected ease. They're full of small gestures that make adolescent ardor so refreshing—like pulling gum out of a girl's mouth before you kiss her. Although the requisite sequence of pickup lines doesn't come close to the hilarity of Spike Lee's "dog" montage in *She's Gotta Have It*, the dialogue is real, with little of the pseudo-hip-talk you get when old people make films about young people.

Above all, *On the Make* is a morality tale: Illicit sex equals death. But the film doesn't offer many alternatives—safer sex, for example. When teenagers are in question, raging hormones have got to be a factor. But *On the Make* may, at the very least, contribute to the chorus of little voices you hope your kid will strain to hear in a clinch.

Also reviewed in:
NEW YORK TIMES, 9/29/89, p. C18, Caryn James
VARIETY, 6/28–7/4/89, p. 18

ONE WAY TICKET, A

A Producciones Testimonio film. *Producer:* Agliberto Meléndez. *Director:* Agliberto Meléndez. *Screenplay (Spanish with English subtitles):* Agliberto Meléndez, Danilo Taveras, and Adelso Cass. *Director of Photography:* Pedro Guzman Cordero. *Editor:* Pericles Mejia. *Music:* Rafael Solano. *Sound:* Miguel Heded. *Art Director:* Orlando Menicucci. *Running time:* 92 minutes. *MPAA Rating:* Not Rated.

CAST: Angel Muñiz (René); Carlos Alfredo (Isidro); Horacio Veloz (Payano); Miguel Buccarelli (Turin); Victor Checo (Angel); Nini Germán (Elpidio); Felix Germán (Belarminio); Angel Hache (Piro); Pepito Guerra (Valerio); Rafael Villalona (Quimo); Juan Maria Almonte (Goyo); Frank Lendor (Captain); Danilo Taveras (Lawyer); Giovanny Cruz (Rufino); Delat Soto (Maria); Juan Karlos Mañon (Tony).

NEWSDAY, 3/21/89, Part II/p. 5, Lynn Darling

"A One Way Ticket" is an angry film, a passionate, searing examination of the horrifying consequences of human misery and the corruption that feeds on it.

A first feature film from the Dominican Republic, "A One Way Ticket" lays out the hopelessness and futility that confront a group of working people trying to make a life for themselves in the teeth of the poverty that controls them.

They are young men, working in a bakery, with families to support; life is a bare grovel for subsistence sustained only by the energy of their youth.

America is the dream that dazzles them, keeps them from sinking. While they fear the danger, the expense and the consequences of a decision to make their way there, they find themselves with no other alternatives.

"We belong here, there has to be a way of improving the country," says a young pregnant woman to her husband after he says he plans to leave that night, smuggled away on a freighter.

It's an idea mentioned several times in "A One Way Ticket," but these are not the people who will make a revolution or dedicate themselves to the process of orderly reform. While their lives are sketched only sparingly, the haplessness of their fates is easy enough to grasp: These are the victims of history, not its manipulators.

And as victims, they come under the heel of those who have cut their own deal with the opportunities that desperation affords. Everyone looks the other way while the traffic in human misery goes on.

The corrupt minister and the guards down at the docks have their own anthem—as one of them says, "crooks get rich overnight while an honest man dies working." They know on what side of that dichotomy they care to be.

Director Agliberto Meléndez lets nothing distract him from the brutal forces that impinge upon the ordinary men whose fate he examines; his movie maintains the simple driving inevitability of the tragedy it documents.

Meléndez used a number of non-professional actors in his film; they come across as voices of the common man, rather than carefully detailed characters. Sitting in the hold of a ship bound for Miami, they tell stories about their pasts and trade fears of the future. Not even those most vigilant about the dangers they face can predict the fate that ultimately engulfs them.

Based on a true story, "A One Way Ticket" is a harrowing movie that survives an often stilted plot and uneven pace on the strength of its moral outrage. There have been few movies that have tried to put a human face to the vast waves of migration and the forces that propel them, and fewer still that try to show the cold perversions of character that flourish in their midst.

VILLAGE VOICE, 3/21/89, p. 64, Elliott Stein

In 1981, a group of men that had paid a high price to be smuggled into the U.S. aboard a ship bound for Miami were drowned when their hiding place, a ballast tank, was deliberately flooded. This shocking story is debased and reduced to dull melodrama in what ND/NF is presenting as the first feature film made in the Dominican Republic. Its director, Agliberto Meléndez, is active in Dominican politics, and the film's sense of outrage is strong—corruption on all levels is detailed at length. Unfortunately, its bungled execution sends all good intentions up the spout.

Also reviewed in:
NEW YORK TIMES, 3/21/89, p. C20, Stephen Holden
VARIETY, 10/19/88, p. 14

OUT COLD

A Hemdale Releasing Corporation release. *Executive Producer:* John Daly and Derek Gibson. *Producer:* George G. Braunstein and Ron Hamady. *Director:* Malcolm Mowbray. *Screenplay:* Leonard Glasser and George Malko. *Director of Photography:* Tony Pierce-Roberts. *Editor:* Dennis M. Hill. *Music:* Michel

Colombier. *Sound:* Robert Eber. *Production Designer:* Linda Pearl. *Art Director:* Lisa Fischer. *Costumes:* Linda Bass. *Ernie Dummy/Special Make-up Effects:* Andy Schoneberg. *Running Time:* 87 minutes. *MPAA Rating:* R.

CAST: John Lithgow (Dave); Teri Garr (Sunny); Randy Quaid (Lester Atlas); Bruce McGill (Ernie Cannald); Lisa Blount (Phyllis); Alan Blumenfeld (Lew).

LOS ANGELES TIMES, 3/3/89, Calendar/p. 6, Sheila Benson

To watch nifty actors try to breathe a little life into torpid, tacky material is bad enough. When, in the case of "Out Cold," the talents squandered are those of John Lithgow, Teri Garr and Randy Quaid, it feels like a criminal offense.

"Old Cold" clearly sees itself as black comedy of the "Blood Simple" vein, when it's really only misfired situation comedy with a little dirt under its fingernails. From the stylishness of the titles comes a note of hope that this may be something promising—a photo collage it's telling us that Garr, Lithgow and his buddy, Bruce McGill, have been pals since high school, through the Army and back into civilian life; that Garr and McGill have married and that the men have opened a modest butcher shop together.

Alas, that's it for the charm. Picking them up a decade or more later, Lithgow is a wimp, McGill a bully and Garr a ditzy version of a James M. Cain dangerous dame. When McGill slaps her around, Garr hires Quaid, the lowest rent detective on the San Pedro docks, to document her husband's philandering. The inept Quaid gets something more; photos of what he thinks is a liaison, but is actually evidence of a murder, involving Lithgow, Garr and McGill, only one of them innocently.

A lot of the humor in the George Malko, Leonard Glasser script comes from the appearance and disappearance of the corpse, frozen—in the butcher shop locker—into a sort of permanent Highland fling. It's about this time you realize that this enterprise (rated R for language and grisly situations) has not a single character to care about. And also that, thanks to Malcolm Mowbray's flaccid direction, the corpse isn't the only one around to seem trapped forever.

Ah, but audiences can be out, in the twinkling of an eye, an escape you might devoutly wish for this cast. Incidentally, this is the second film to mix Quaid and raw meat of very dubious origin. If this is a trend, it should be nipped in the bud, *now*.

NEW YORK POST, 3/3/89, p. 27, Jami Bernard

This is the second film in as many months in which Randy Quaid plays opposite a mound of raw meat. Like "Parents," in which Quaid played a cannibalistic '50s dad, "Out Cold" is a black comedy—only this one doesn't work. Even the raw meat isn't right for the part.

There's a good cast on hand, though. The ever-versatile John Lithgow is a partner in a small-town butcher shop. His partner (Bruce McGill), a boyhood chum who married the woman Lithgow loved and has turned into a leering, beefy, overbearing womanizer, uses his position behind the counter to convince female customers to get under the counter with him. And while he's off catting around, Lithgow is left to dutifully strain yucky chopped meat through the grinder and clean up things in the meat locker, which is, luckily for the plot, equipped with a faulty lock.

The suffering wife is played by a not so suffering Teri Garr, a beautiful, bored housewife who hires seedy private detective Quaid to spy on her husband and collect evidence for a divorce.

As you'd expect, the faulty door comes into play soon enough. The partners have a fight and the next day, McGill is found in the meat locker, frozen to death. Lithgow thinks he did it, but really it was Garr who came along after the fight and locked her husband in. The rest of the movie involves some vaguely slapstick attempts to cover up the murder and hide the body and get the bumbling Quaid off the trail.

The term "black" is perhaps too dark a word to describe the comedy here. The funniest moment is when a half-eaten ice cream bar is frozen solidly to the dead man's face, and adheres to it no matter what.

McGill's fleshy wife-beater and -cheater has some life in him, but obviously not for long. Why he agreed to that nude scene is beyond me, but then many of the scenes drag uncomfortably as the actors try frantically to find something funny, funnier, squeezing blood from a turnip.

Quaid, whose enormously malevolent comic potential was tapped in "Parents," is on his own here most of the time, stumbling onto things he shouldn't and misreading what he sees.

As for his old co-star, the meat, it was filmed in "Parents" in a comically subversive way. Here, the meat is shot to maximize its resemblance to human waste, very funny to 3-year-olds.

NEWSDAY, 3/3/89, Part III/p. 9, Mike McGrady

"Out Cold," a film that tries very hard to be black comedy, never quite makes it beyond bleak comedy. The difference between bleak and black? Well bleak comedy has all the requisite sickness of black comedy but none of the laughter.

John Lithgow plays a shy, small-town butcher who mistakenly believes he has killed his womanizing partner (Bruce McGill). The real murderer, the victim's widow (Teri Garr), encourages this misunderstanding so that Lithgow will help her dispose of the body, which is currently hanging from a hook in the frozen meat locker at the butcher shop. The disposal becomes complicated when an incompetent private eye (Randy Quaid) bumbles onto the scene. Before long there are two bodies requiring disposal. If you include the film itself, we're talking about a grand total of three stiffs.

"Out Cold" is the kind of film that finds its humor by having people constantly trip over frozen bodies. Another main source of humor is guns going off accidentally. So much for humor. There is, I will concede, one major mystery connected with the film, which is: What on earth are John Lithgow, Teri Garr and Randy Quaid doing in this amateurish little mess?

VILLAGE VOICE, 3/7/89, p. 64, Bruce Handy

You wouldn't think you could dislike a film that has a scene built around an ice cream bar frozen to the side of a corpse's face. Yet the laws of probability are shattered by *Out Cold*, a stunningly lame and amateurish comedy that ought to embarrass Randy Quaid, Teri Garr, and especially director Malcolm Mowbray (who was previously responsible for the crisp, stylish, and very funny *A Private Affair*). The only principal not likely to be embarrassed by this not-very-black comedy about a love triangle and a dumb detective is John Lithgow, who always overacts. The man can't stand stillness. Watch him here staring dolefully at a departing lover: a beat, another beat, then *bam*—he starts wiggling his eye brows and scrunching up his forehead, milking the moment like a man possessed.

Also reviewed in:
NEW YORK TIMES, 3/3/89, p. C14, Janet Maslin
NEW YORKER, 3/6/89, p. 95, Pauline Kael
VARIETY, 2/15–21/89, p. 20

OUT OF THE DARK

A CineTel Films release of a Zel Films production. *Executive Producer:* Paul Bartel. *Producer:* Zane W. Levitt. *Director:* Michael Schroeder. *Screenplay:* J. Gregory De Felice and Zane W. Levitt. *Director of Photography:* Julio Macat. *Editor:* Mark Manos. *Music:* Paul F.Antonelli and David Wheatley. *Music Editor:* Adam Smalley. *Sound:* Trevor Black and (music) Wayne Cook. *Sound Editor:* John Post and David Lewis Yewdall. *Production Designer:* Robert Schulenberg. *Art Director:* Jess Moreno. *Set Decorator:* Margaret Goldsmith. *Set Dresser:* Jane Smith. *Special Effects:* Kevin McCarthy. *Costumes:* Elisabeth Scott. *Make-up:* Angela and Elizabeth Levitt. *Special Make-up Effects:* Tony Gardner and Lisa Schulze. *Stunt Coordinator:* Mike Cassidy. *Running time:* 90 minutes. *MPAA Rating:* R.

CAST: Cameron Dye (Kevin/Bobo); Karen Black (Ruth); Lynn Danielson (Kristi); Karen Witter (Jo Ann); Starr Andreeff (Camille); Karen Mayo-Chandler (Barbara); Angela Robinson (Vanessa); Teresa Crespo (Debbie); Tracey Walter (Lieutenant Frank Meyers); Silvana Gallardo (Lieutenant Sophie McDonald); Bud Cort (Stringer); Geoffrey Lewis (Dennis); Divine (Detective Langella); Paul Bartel (Motel Clerk); Hector M. Morales (Mexican Man); Irene Olga Lopez (Mexican Woman); John Debello, Richard Embardo, and Sandra Ramsdell (Policemen); Joanna Hemmerling (Woman in Garage); Larry Robb (Russ, Janitor); Tab Hunter (Driver); Jim Katz (Langella's Assistant); Charles Champion (Young Cop); Marcie Leeds (Claudine); Lainie Kazan (Hooker Nancy); Bond Bradigan (Hooker Lee); Camille Marie and Kathleen Grant (Hookers); Zane W. Levitt (Coroner); J. Gregory De Felice (Police Photographer); Brent Haleen (Dead Cop); Shiner (Asberry the Dog).

LOS ANGELES TIMES, 5/5/89, Calendar/p. 13, Michael Wilmington

"Out of the Dark" has a surface like Day-Glo on chrome, even though its heart is pure slime. It's a tongue-in-cheek, slasher thriller about a psychotic killer in a clown outfit, slaughtering the women who work in a telephone sex service called "Suite Nothings." It reeks of low intentions and sleazy pretensions.

Bobo, the movie's killer, looks like a cross between Bozo the Clown and The Joker of Batman comics. Bobo slays his victims in ways that are supposed to be surprising or droll: bopping them with baseball bats, strangling them with telephone cords or prowling around with a huge, serrated knife that practically screams *phallic symbol*. Since the cops—including the late Divine—suspect a hunky professional photographer (Cameron Dye), we also seem to be getting another Hitchcockian "wrong man" thriller, with another couple-on-the-run.

Director Michael Schroeder and cinematographer Julio Macat are trying for some of the voluptuous, overheated stylishness of a Brian De Palma thriller. But if the film suggests De Palma, it's a De Palma who has forgotten how to create suspense.

The movie is paralyzingly shallow; the only feeling you can detect behind it is the desire to make a movie. And though it's trying for a certain cold, nasty, hyper-stylized chic, the lines are so dumb and the acting so mannered or vacuous that the effect is like a clammy-handed massage. Even good actors like Karen Black, Bud Cort, Tracey Walter or Geoffrey Lewis are used as if they were big plastic cutouts of themselves. It's stultifying. Watching "Out of the Dark" is like staring at a strobe light while someone keeps screaming and dirty jokes are droned in your ear.

The acting and writing—which are, respectively, erratic and bad beyond belief—suggest a porno movie, but when Schroeder shoots a sex scene, he does it in chi-chi fragments. Virtually every sequence is borrowed from something else: "Body Double" or "Dressed to Kill," "Stripped to Kill," "Jagged Edge" or "Psycho." When the film makers feel classy, they stage a scene with a faceless crowd and a street accident victim who seems lifted from Buñuel's "Un Chien Andalou"; as a camp touch, they throw in Tab Hunter as the man driving the car. That's what the whole movie is: clammy-handed camp. "Out of the Dark" (MPAA rated R for sex, violence and language) should probably be kept out of the light as well.

MONTHLY FILM BULLETIN, 5/89, p. 148, Julian Petley

When Jo Ann, who works for the telephone-sex operation Suite Nothings, is beaten to death by a man wearing a clown mask, Lieutenant Frank Meyers, Lieutenant Sophie McDonald and Detective Langella are called in to investigate. At the scene of the crime, they find a business card belonging to Kevin, a freelance photographer, who proves to have been doing a photo-spread on Suite Nothings, where his girlfriend Kristi also works. Barbara, another employee, is followed home by the clown figure, who murders both her and a Mexican passer-by. Meyers and McDonald set a trap for the killer, using Camille as bait, but the killer outwits them, strangling her and killing and injuring members of her police guard. Kristi believes that Stringer, the firm's accountant, is the murderer, and she and Kevin break into his office where they find a collection of pornography and sado-masochistic equipment. But Stringer arrives, and Kevin and Kristi flee to a sleazy motel where, that night, two prostitutes are murdered. Meyers, McDonald and Langella arrive to investigate, Kevin and Kristi escape, but shortly afterwards Meyers and McDonald arrest Kevin at his studio for murder. Kevin calls Kristi and asks her to break into Stringer's office again in the hope of finding incriminating evidence. This she does, and discovers what appears to be a pair of breasts in a filing cabinet. Stringer arrives, vehemently denies that he is the killer, and after a running fight with Kristi is knocked down and killed by a car. Meyers is suspended and Kevin released. He and Kristi leave for his cabin in the country, but once there, Kristi finds a clown mask in Kevin's luggage. She shoots him when he tries to kill her, but fails to realise that he is still alive. Just as he is about to kill her, Meyers arrives and finally despatches him.

Kevin's remark to Kristi, as they book into a particularly sordid motel, that "It's an adventure in sleaze", perfectly sums up the garish, gleefully tacky tone of *Out of the Dark*. Executive producer Paul Bartel (who plays a decidedly strange motel clerk) has described it as a film that "glows in the dark with sex, violence, telephones, and all the other things that are dear to the hearts of American people. *Out of the Dark* is about the beast within, denial, misogyny, Hollywood, Los Angeles by night—and about $2m!". As in Bartel's own films, there's a strong vein of playfulness and parody, and a distinctly quirky humour co-exists alongside the more violent and occasionally horrific elements. Producer/writer Zane W. Levitt worked for some time as Bartel's personal assistant (he also studied at the San Francisco Art Institute under Mike and George Kuchar, whose influence can be perceived here), and director Michael Schroeder worked as first assistant director on Bartel's *Lust in the Dust* and *Longshot*. In addition, Bartel was the executive producer on Schroeder's first feature, *Mortuary Academy*, which was produced by Levitt (typically, a cinema in *Out of the Dark* can be glimpsed playing the film).

Small wonder, then, that Bartel refers to *Out of the Dark* as a "family reunion". Its jokier elements are established right from the start in the Suite Nothings office, where the girls answering the phones play their expected roles to the hilt and thereby send up the whole business (this hasn't, however, stopped the BBFC from excising some of the raunchier exchanges, as in the case of *Call Me*). Such elements are also present in the would-be hard-boiled dialogue ("He probably gets more ass than a toilet seat"), deliberately ridiculous lines like Meyers' repeated question to the Suite Nothings girls, "Have you had any strange calls?", Divine's characterisation as Detective Langella, Stringer being run over by a car driven by Tab Hunter, and the Mexican woman who seems less upset about the murder of her husband than her mistake in thinking that Kevin and Kristi are "from television".

The tougher elements obviously include the numerous killings, of which the first is the most striking. As Jo Ann jogs round a park, she encounters a clown who engages her in an imaginary game of baseball (shades of the climax of *Blow-Up*) before beating her to death with his bat. This tense, ambivalent scene is excellently choreographed and nicely utilises the sinister ambience which so often attaches to clowns. Ominous, floor-level shots abound throughout the film, along with such tropes as the wildly swinging lamp in the scene of Kevin's police interrogation. Such devices might have seemed forced and self-consciously "stylish", but achieve overall a nice sense of contemporary *noir*. Whether the humour sits comfortably with what is still, in the last analysis, a stalk 'n' slash movie, is another matter.

NEW YORK POST, 5/5/89, p. 34, V.A. Musetto

Things aren't so sweet for the women who work at Suite Nothings, a phone-sex outfit specializing in $4-a-minute dirty talk. Some nut case in a clown mask is killing them faster than they can dial 911, and the cops are thwarted in every attempt to grab him. Even a police trap goes awry, claiming not only another beautiful victim but the cop who was guarding her as well.

If you're wondering why there was just *one* cop watching over the potential victim of a crazed serial killer, you're not alone. The same question popped into my mind as I watched "Out of the Dark." The only answer I could come up with was that the people responsible for this mess couldn't care less about credibility—or about most of the other subtleties of moviemaking.

"Out of the Dark" looks as if director Michael Schroeder (his only previous try was something called "Mortuary Academy") shot more film than he could use, then randomly cut out parts without any concern for how the remaining bits fit together. Characters are introduced, then immediately forgotten. A potentially interesting subplot involving the sex-agency boss (Karen Black) and her young daughter seems to have ended up on the cutting room floor. Add this incoherence to a pedestrian murder story already lacking believability and you have a disaster.

It didn't have to be this bad. Schroeder had at his disposal some quirky cult actors who could have made a difference, but he chose to throw them away in minor parts.

Divine is prominently listed in the credits, but you have to wait nearly an hour before the out-of-drag actor, in what turned out to be his final screen role, shows up as a mustachioed detective named Langella. His mere presence momentarily shakes the movie out of its doldrums, but he is quickly gone and forgotten.

Another bright spot is provided by Paul Bartel ("Eating Raoul"). Decked out in a ghastly wig and a smirk, he adds a fleeting touch of sardonic humor as the manager of a hot-sheets motel. (Come to think of it, he's the best thing "Out of the Dark" has to offer.) Black, Tab Hunter (as a motorist) and Bud Cort (as a kinky accountant) have their moments, too, but there aren't enough of them to make a difference.

The movie closes with this dedication: "In loving memory of Divine." What a way to go.

NEWSDAY, 5/5/89, Part III/p. 5, Drew Fetherston

WHACK. The shovel blade goes about a third of the way through the guy's head, stopping just above the eyebrow.

ULP. The motel clerk finds that the hooker has been carved into messy pieces in the bathtub.

WHEN. Sometimes these humor-horror films get a little hard to take.

One suspects that the makers of "Out of the Dark" realized that their story—madman slays phone-sex beauties—was likely to be faulted for a dearth of redeeming social content, and decided to graft a few gag lines onto scenes otherwise designed to make you gag. Presto! Respectability.

Well, not quite. This is a sleazy film whose pretensions to humor and camp ring hollow.

Karen Black plays Ruth, the owner of a Los Angeles firm called Suite Nothings, a phone-sex service that employs a gaggle of young women. One caller, a bit sicker than the rest, makes veiled threats to some of the employees, whose bloody murders follow.

Suspicion falls on a lusty young photog rapher who has been helping the young women, uh, well, assemble their portfolios. To free himself from the suspicions of a loutish cop, the photog hatches a scheme to find the real killer.

WHACK. ARRGH. ULP. Things don't go too well; the killer — who wears a clown face while he goes about his ugly business—is too tricky. The usual suspects—the nerd next door, the good-guy photographer, his vicious drunk of a former boss—are rounded up and paraded.

Each of the murders is lovingly set up: We see the victim, unaware, and her stalker. He closes the gap slowly, delaying his pounce, his every move caressed by the music track. The victim senses that something is wrong, reacts too late. . . This is sorry and creepy stuff, foreplay for those who find a thrill in consummate violence. Such sick stroking fills "Out of the Dark."

So when a coroner says that he's worked up a big lunchtime appetite putting the hooker's corpse back together, persons of refinement may be forgiven for not laughing. And those endless shots of young women yawning with boredom as they whisper lurid nothings to slavering geeks don't seem funny when they're being bashed, slashed and strangled.

Even the common murder-mystery courtesies that a film maker owes the audience—continuity, fair clues, no red herrings—aren't honored. The script abounds in contradictions, misleading clues and outright deceptions, all tossed together to maintain a bogus sort of suspense.

The unevenness of both cast and script are never synchronized: When the acting isn't bad, the script is terrible; when the plot gets rolling, the acting stalls. Most of the weight falls on Black, Cameron Dye (as the photographer) and Lynn Danielson (as Ruth's employee, the photographer's steady); while they aren't terrible, they can't make much good from something so bad. Tab Hunter and Divine (the late transvestite star of John Waters' films) have cameos.

The only saving grace in "Out of the Dark" is some interesting camerawork. It isn't anything revolutionary—some extreme closeups, some slow-motion and some interesting lighting and framing—but in so flawed a context, it looks good.

VILLAGE VOICE, 5/16/89, p. 73, Elliott Stein

Michael Schroeder's *Out of the Dark* is a spoofy, low-budget whodunit set in the milieu of a sleazy L.A. phone-sex business. Someone is killing the ladies who work for Ruth (Karen Black), proprietress of Suite Nothings, Inc. Is it Stringer (Bud Cort), the fidgety accountant with a desk full of s&m toys? Or Kevin (Cameron Dye), the fetching fashion photographer?—"Look at that guy," a woman detective investigating the case remarks. "He probably gets more ass than a toilet seat."

The movie's blasé erotic folderol is moderately amusing—up to a point. ("Nobody can handle nipples like Bobo," phones in the killer, who wears a clown's mask, as he squashes a fly in closeup, then nicks his own nipples with a knife.) Before long, *Dark* becomes a routine slasher opus, a tad more pretentiously directed than most. Divine can be seen—it's his final role—as a cop, in a cameo, in male attire, sporting a badly glued moustache.

Also reviewed in:
NEW YORK TIMES, 5/5/89, p. C9, Stephen Holden
VARIETY, 5/3-9/89, p. 12

OUTRAGEOUS ANIMATION

An Expanded Entertainment release of 22 animated shorts by various directors. *Producer:* Terry Thoren. *Running time:* 88 minutes. *MPAA Rating:* Not Rated.

NEW YORK POST, 1/27/89, p. 30, Jami Bernard

There is a famous 90-second animated short by Marv Newland called "Bambi Meets Godzilla" that is hysterically funny the first time around. It still bears up after multiple viewings, but there's nothing like the first time you see that brief, historic encounter between the Bamb-ster and the behemoth.

That cartoon was made back in the early '70s, and much of its appeal was in how unexpected it was, how unlike the roseate, wholesome Disney tradition. "Outrageous Animation" is dedicated to Newland's creation, and kicks off with it.

Then it's all downhill.

Which is not to say there is not some fine and funny work here. It's just that the shock value of bird-droppings, rude noises, toilets flushing and "boogers" wears thin over the course of 22 shorts and 88 minutes.

On the bright side, there is "Lupo the Butcher," by Danny Antonucci, about a fed-up, foulmouthed butcher (*"Buncha peegs!"* he yells at the camera audience) who gets as good as he gives with the cleaver.

"One of Those Days," by Bill Plympton—who was nominated for an Oscar for his hilarious "Your Face"—uses his quavering, scratchy-line drawing style to depict a day where everything goes wrong, from the point of view of the guy who is about to get electrocuted, bitten, punched out, even steamrolled flat.

"Late Night with Myron," by Bob Scott, shows a guy glued to an evening of channel-switching.

"An Inside Job," by Aiden Hickey, is a dentist's-office nightmare. An insane practitioner reenacts, in a hapless patient's mouth, the Frank Norris novel "McTeague," about a dentist's descent into greed and loathing.

Norwegian Thor Sivertsen weighs in with "Zwisch," boiling a man's life down to 90 seconds. It bears a certain resemblance to Bruno Bozzetto's "Life in a Box."

And Csaba Szorady's "Rondino," about a graphically cheerful and complete torture session, is probably the most remarkably shocking.

If only George Griffin's "The Club," about a stuffy members-only club for penises, had been included. Irreverence for its own sake, without humor, can get pretty ordinary.

VILLAGE VOICE, 1/31/89, p. 67, Katherine Dieckmann

The best cartoons, no matter how loud and wild, send messages through subliminal suggestion rather than the brand of BOING! head-pounding their hapless animals and dopey humans go through. Take *Horton Hatches the Egg*, a Warner Bros. short about Dr. Seuss's nurturing male elephant, that recently preceded *The 5000 Fingers of Dr. T* at Film Forum: The biggest (knowing) laughs came from the animator's rendering of Horton's trunk, which in no small way resembled a swinging dick.

"Outrageous Animation," a compilation of 22 international shorts too nasty for the mainstream (or just the kids), pushes the genre's garish tendencies to mostly pointless effect. The series is "dedicated" to its opening entry, *Bambi Meets Godzilla*, where a cute baby deer nibbles at grass until a gigantic monster foot descends into frame to crush it. This is the visual equivalent of those buttons and truckers' caps that read "Shit Happens" or "Life's a Bitch and Then You Marry One." Penis humor, bird shit, and farts abound—the compilation is a little like a long visit with your vulgar uncle.

An exception to the stupid sex jokes is Michel Ocelot's *Four Wishes*, a disturbing look at sexual repulsion, filtered through the bequest of four wishes by a saintly figure to a miserable peasant couple—who soon find themselves covered with an excess of reproductive organs. Disgust is always most effective when it's elevated from the groin to the head. Thus Aidan Hickey's *An Inside Job*, drawn in that hideous airbrushed '70s poster style, wreaks an inventive sadism less from the presence of dental tools in a champed-open mouth than from its literate psycho-periodontist voiceover.

A couple of darkly cynical Eastern European entries break away from the simpleminded gross-out numbers: Csaba Szorady's *Rondino* comments on genocide, as two black-cloaked figures torture a man, only to remove their cloaks and reveal they're exactly like him. In Dragutin Vunak's 54-second *Dialog*, one line-drawn head addresses another, his "speech" taking the form of a Merz-like collage of fragments. Suddenly, his listener's mouth disgorges a gun that promptly halts this inarticulate confab.

But the real standouts here are Bob Scott's *Late Night With Myron*, a beautifully animated black-and-white play on channel-switchers' show-biz stereotypes (as cunning as Roger Rabbit), and Wes Archer's hyperkinetic *Jac Mac and Rad Boy. . .Go!*, about two gnarly L.A. dudes whose joyride winds up making their nihilistic fantasies come true. *Jac Mac* is a speedy fusion of thrash metal, apocalyptic possibility, and a RAW comics aesthetic. It gives its flamboyant violence and pervasive ickiness a decided context—an agenda that most of the animations here could put to good use.

PACKAGE, THE

An Orion Pictures release. *Executive Producer:* Arne L. Schmidt. *Producer:* Beverly J. Camhe and Tobie Haggerty. *Director:* Andrew Davis. *Screenplay:* John Bishop. *Director of Photography:* Frank Tidy. *Editor:* Don Zimmerman and Billy Weber. *Music:* James Newton Howard. *Music Editor:* Nancy Fogarty. *Sound:* Scott Smith. *Sound Editor:* Richard L. Anderson. *Production Designer:* Michael Levesque. *Art Director:* Colleen Kennedy and Wynn Thomas. *Set Designer:* William B. Fosser and Bundy Trinz. *Set Decorator:* Rick T. Gentz. *Special Effects:* Tom Ryba. *Costumes:* Marilyn Vance-Straker. *Make-up:* Rodger Jacobs. *Stunt Coordinator:* Terry Leonard. *Running time:* 107 minutes. *MPAA Rating:* R.

CAST: Gene Hackman (Johnny Gallagher); Joanna Cassidy (Eileen Gallagher); Tommy Lee Jones (Thomas Boyette); John Heard (Colonel Glen Whitacre); Dennis Franz (Milan Delich); Pam Grier (Ruth Butler); Kevin Crowley (Walter Henke); Ron Dean (Karl Richards); Nathan Davis (Soviet Press Secretary); Chelcie Ross (General Hopkins); Joe Greco (General Carlson); Ike Pappas (Himself); Marco St. John (Marth); Reni Santoni (Chicago Police Lieutenant); Michael Skewes and Johnny Lee Davenport (M.P.'s); Thalmus Rasulala (Secret Service Commander); Joe Guzaldo (Press Secretary Rogers); Dianne Timmerman (Female Backpacker); Charles Mueller (Male Backpacker); Wilhelm Von Homburg (West Berlin Police Lieutenant); Anatoly Davydov (Soviet Colonel); William Musyka and Gary Berkovich (Soviet Generals); Allen Hamilton (American General); Greg Noonan (Command Post Commander); Kate Lynch (Henke's Wife); Mary Seibel (Henke's Mother); Joe D. Lauck (Senator Bruce); Dick Cusak (Secretary of State); Boris Leskin (Soviet Foreign Minister); Danny Goldring (Undercover Bum); Gregory Alan-Williams (Colonel Woods); Jack Kandel (Soldier with Orders); Nick Kusenko (General Carlson's Aide); Tina Gloschenko (Henke's Girlfriend); John Hardy (Sky Cap); Henry Godinez (Lockup Police Officer); Kathryn Joosten (Waitress); Oksana Fedunszyn (Eileen's Secretary); Ralph Foody (Building Manager); Mike Bacarella (Paramedic); Steve Barbo (Hotel Police Officer); Eddie Bo Smith Jr. (Ft. Belvoir Duty M.P.); Greg Goossen (Soldier in Provost Marshall's Office); Dennis Cockrum (Computer Technician); Ivory Ocean (Washington, D.C. Police Officer); Metta Davis (Washington, D.C. Witness); Alex Ross (Liquor Store Clerk); Will Zahrn and Michael Gaylord James (Nazi Goons); Nancy Baird (Milan's Wife); Gene Barge and Walter Markley (Secret Service Agents); Otto Von Wernherr (East German Army Lieutenant); Hilda McLean (Old German Woman); Leon Samoilovich (Soviet Security Agent); Dmitri Polytnsev and Lana Berkovich (Translators); John D'Amico (Soviet General Secretary); Ray Allen (United States President); Dr. Christine Cassel (Speaker at Governors Conference); Billy Bosco and Chad Smith (Milan's Sons); Phillip Prevost (Hospital Police Officer); Jack Gold (Governor).

FILMS IN REVIEW, 12/89, p. 618, Edmond Grant

Seasoned solider Johnny Gallagher has a problem: his name keeps being linked to security projects that fail, through no fault of his own. Gallagher's devotion to duty hasn't gotten him very far in the armed forces, but his bad reputation makes him the perfect scapegoat for an incredibly risky covert operation. The operation, planned in tandem by renegade factions of the Pentagon and the Kremlin, involves the upcoming meeting between the President and the Soviet Secretary General. Gallagher's job, unbeknownst to him, is to hand deliver an assassin into Chicago, the city where the event is to take place.

Gallagher is a strong willed and resourceful character, to put it mildly. He is also, in certain parties' opinion, the perfect candidate for the role of dupe. To be able to play such a character, who battles against impossible odds with only his own innate ingenuity and a few good friends to help him, you need a strong actor. This requirement *The Package* has met in the person of Gene Hackman, who makes Johnny Gallagher seem realistic even amidst the most fantastic of circumstances.

True, Hackman isn't the only virtue possessed by *The Package*. Despite certain foolish plot twists, the storyline moves at a good clip, and at points even calls to mind the great paranoia thrillers of the past, from the classic Richard Condon assassination scenarios (*The Manchurian Candidate*, *Winter Kills*) to the ultimate military coup, *Seven Days In May*.

As the movie proceeds, it becomes apparent that the assassin ("the package" that Gallagher has been assigned to transport into the U.S.) is a sort of mirror image for Gallagher—the skilled mercenary he could have become had he valued money and excitement above all else. As played by Tommy Lee Jones, the character has a peculiar resonance that prevents us from ever hating him—as he makes clear to Johnny, he's merely a superb marksman hired to do a job.

The supporting players in the drama all do their best to help or hinder Gallagher in his quest to stop the assassination. Joanna Cassidy, as Gallagher's ex-wife, falls short of the mark as a female counterpart for Hackman; Dennis Franz (*Hill Street Blues*) is his grubby old self as a helpful cop acquaintance; and the talented but underused John Heard, in a change of pace, plays the sneering, despicable Colonel who sets the whole mechanism in motion.

The taut direction by Andrew Davis never misses a beat; although the final chase sequence does go slightly off the track when it places Hackman in a speeding car, and brings to mind visions of the classic El-train chase in *The French Connection*.

All in all, fans of suspenseful political thrillers aren't likely to find a better *Package* for another few years.

LOS ANGELES TIMES, 8/25/89, Calendar/p. 10, Michael Wilmington

There's no wasted motion in "The Package," a post-*glasnost* political thriller in which an Army sergeant, wrongly wanted for murder, stumbles onto an international anti-disarmament conspiracy. The movie races from scene to scene, moment to moment, country to country, with the breakneck velocity of a motorcycle crashing through a computer room.

Director Andy Davis ("Code of Silence") keeps his scenes jumping with pungent details, banter, edge-of-the-frame business sliding past fast. The editors, Don Zimmerman and Billy Weber, never let the film linger. They keep it blasting along, intercutting several planes of action, lucidly knotting up mutiple plot strands—right from a brisk Berlin peace conference opener to a widly improbable finale. Gene Hackman's Sgt. Gallagher racing under the El, wearing a pop-eyed grimace that's homage to "The French Connection."

Hackman races practically everywhere in this movie, even when a phone call might suffice. The movie stays in overdrive: It can't give us any breathers or its mix of ultra-realistic surface detail and barmy plot formulas might collapse. "The Package" is like a bad dream culled out of TV newscasts and gussied up with *film noir* plot shtick. The writer, John Bishop, mixes up the old love-on-the-run plot—Hackman and wife Joanna Cassidy on the lam—with the ultra-paranoid form of "The Parallax View" and a stop-the-assassin premise that recalls "The Day of the Jackal."

We knew Charles de Gaulle wasn't going to be assassinated by the Jackal, and we can guess nothing bad is going to happen to the Soviet premier and American President here—especially when we see that they're being played by actors who are ringers for Gorbachev and Bush. Instead, the suspense boils out of Gallagher's predicament and the scheme's complexity—the patsy deliberately reminiscent of Lee Harvey Oswald set up as the fall guy for the real killer: Tommy Lee Jones as a mercenary commando.

Jones plays psychopaths with a burnt-out gaze and a mirthless smile that suggests that the only real sensual kick he gets anymore is from a well-executed murder. This snaky sensuality bounces interestingly off Hackman's fine work as Gallagher the good soldier and the third military archetype played by John Heard: a tight-lipped, tight-bottomed bureaucrat and Cold War lover.

"The Package" (MPAA-rated R for violence) tries to tackle interesting issues rather than hook into another revenge fantasy—though it doesn't have the baroque nuttiness of a Richard Condon-derived political thriller like "The Manchurian Candidate." Hackman, Jones, Heard, Cassidy, Pam Grier and Dennis Franz—in another of his greaseball cop roles—are always interesting to watch. And Davis still suggests he might evolve into an action specialist in the Don Siegel-Phil Karlson class—if he chooses less apocalyptic scenarios.

MONTHLY FILM BULLETIN, 6/90, p. 171, Philip Strick

Among the preparations for a historic disarmament conference in Berlin, young serviceman Walter Henke is arrested on the orders of Colonel Glen Whitacre. Outside the conference building, a patrol headed by Sergeant Johnny Gallagher challenges two young hikers who have lost their way; released, they turn out to be terrorists whose target is an American general as he leaves the conference. Reprimanded for not having foiled this attack, Gallagher is given a new assignment: he is to escort a "package", the court-martialled Henke, back to the U.S. to serve a prison sentence. On reaching Chicago, however, the "package" is rescued from custody by waiting thugs who beat Gallagher unconscious. As soon as he has recovered, he heads for Henke's home, only to learn from family photographs that his lost "package" was not Henke at all. Gallagher turns to his ex-wife Eileen, an army personnel officer, for clues from Henke's service record; they deduce that the "package" was in fact a Vietnam veteran, Thomas Boyette. Unknown killers dispose of Henke's wife and one of Eileen's colleagues. Eileen is the next target but with the help of Gallagher and his friend Delich, a former Vietnam colleague now on the Chicago police force, she narrowly escapes. Meanwhile, the real Henke is guided by Colonel Whitacre into infiltrating a neo-Nazi group, under the impression that he is now working for the CIA. Gallagher traces the neo-Nazis as well, and raises the suspicions of their leader, Karl Richards, who sets a trap in which Delich is injured and Gallagher is arrested. Bundled into a "police car", Gallagher is taken to a hideout where Boyette is preparing for an assignment. Next morning, when Boyette has left, Gallagher breaks free and rushes back into Chicago where crowds are awaiting the arrival of the American and Soviet leaders to celebrate the end of the Cold War. In the building overlooking the hotel chosen for this meeting, Delich and Gallagher find the dead Henke, shot by Boyette so that his body will be taken for that of an assassin. As Delich shoots down Richards, Gallagher searches for Boyette, finding and shooting him just as he is about to kill the Soviet leader. When Whitacre arrives, moments later, Gallagher realises he masterminded the whole plan, convinced that the nuclear deterrent is the only guarantee of global security. Making his getaway, Whitacre is killed by his own chauffeur.

The first screenplay by theatre actor-writer John Bishop is a piecemeal construction from which it appears all the best bits have been filched and all the explanatory text has been ditched. This is possibly because no amount of explaining can justify the blatantly convenient coincidences whereby everybody arrives in the right place at the right time—such as the intervention by a seriously wounded cop in a duel between two men who have just run several streets away, or the thwarting of the assassination attempt at the very moment that the trigger is being squeezed. There is also an engaging lack of concern about motivation: Gene Hackman does another marathon in the *French Connection II* manner (although mostly by car, as befits his now senior status) simply in order to mingle distractedly with the crowds through whom, a little later, his ex-wife also ploughs an ineffectual path, breathing heavily over she knows not what. Lesser characters are disposed of with casual disdain (we are never clear about what makes the luckless Mrs. Henke or the nervous secretary Ruth so dangerous to the conspiracy), and even the villain is finally despatched—with a silent and unknown companion—by a sudden gunman who could be working for anybody. Distant memories are to be evoked, perhaps, of such shadowy melodramas, heavy with anxiety, as *The Parallax View* or even the original *Man Who Knew Too Much*, but while the socio-political context for *The Package* is neatly guessed (complete with splendid Gorbachev lookalike), this is nothing like the sign of the times it pretends to be.

What director Andrew Davis rather obviously has in mind is action, not polemic. After Chuck Norris (*Code of Silence*) and Steven Seagal (*Above the Law*), he has graduated to heavyweight Hackman and aims to make the most of him. Interestingly, while the actor charges about with convincing ferocity at every opportunity, he also makes a solid presence felt in the conversation pieces as if determined to elevate the story by his own bootstraps. His exchanges with Tommy Lee Jones, the lethal "package" he is escorting back to the States, extract a genuine warmth and respect (as well as an excellent performance by Jones) from the relationship between two professionals who recognise each other's strengths and capabilities. And the same sense of hazardous partnership emerges from his early scenes with Joanna Cassidy (later sadly wasted). Given that this air of amiable collusion under fire continues in the friendship with the Chicago cop, we might guess that Hackman at least is a Hawks fan, as signalled by the genial lope of his first authoritative appearance, all Wayne-ish affability and instruction. If so, neither Davis nor Bishop has yet learned how to accommodate such an allegiance—but they and their cast between them have nevertheless, with much industrious pursuit and gunplay, contrived to chop out an entertaining enough thriller.

NEW YORK POST, 8/25/89, p. 23, David Edelstein

The paranoid-conspiracy thriller "The Package" has a plot no murkier than many in its genre and some agreeable barbs at CIA covert ops, Ollie North types and the lunatic Right. It also has first-class actors, among them Gene Hackman and Joanna Cassidy, and one of those climaxes in which the hero races across town to prevent an assassination—a sure-fire nail-biter.

So why, oh why, is the picture such a dud?

To reveal the plot in its entirety would spoil the—not suspense, exactly. Not fun, either. It would actually spoil this review, because it would take too long and you'd get as lost as the audience watching the movie.

Let's just say that Hackman plays Johnny Gallagher, a dependable army sergeant who's assigned to transport a soldier (Tommy Lee Jones) to America to be court-martialed. This "package" isn't what he seems, however, and it soon becomes clear that our hero is a patsy.

Somehow, everyone ends up in Chicago, where the president and Soviet premier intend to announce a treaty that will mean the end of all nuclear arms—a treaty that certain spooky military hard-liners on both sides will do anything to keep from being signed, even if it means starting World War III. I'm prepared to buy the part about the hard-liners and World War III. But CHICAGO?

The director, Andrew Davis, works out of the Windy City, where he set his last two films, "Code of Silence" (with Chuck Norris) and "Above the Law" (with Steven Seagal). They were smoothly crafted martial arts and artillery jobs, uninspired but far above the ordinary. Now he has an A cast and a script that mixes elements of "The Day of the Jackal" and Kennedy-assassination conspiracy theories. And he blows it big-time.

Davis and his writer, John Bishop, remined me of guys who start to tell a joke and keep remembering stuff they've forgotten. They have all these pieces and they don't know where to put them; they turn into blithering idiots.

There's so much cross-cutting that *you* have to supply the momentum—you keep leaning forward and pumping your fists, as if to say, "Come on, get back on track, forget about this other stuff, come on . . ." It gives new meaning to the phrase "edge of your seat."

Davis cross-cuts in the middle of a car chase to Gallagher's ex-wife (Cassidy) babysitting a couple of kids. In the final agonizing seconds, they cut to her dashing through a hotel lobby—you have no idea where she's going (and she never does get anywhere). If you come out of this movie mopping your brow and saying "Whew!" then you should think about doing something more exciting with your life.

Doing "French Connection" stuff in a thriller this flabby makes Hackman look bad—this is the first time in a film that he has shown his age. Cassidy gets one good scene, in which she tries to dodge her ex-husband's question about whether she's sleeping with anyone, but then she becomes an appendage.

There is some fun here, if you just want an excuse to visit an air-conditioned theater. Jones, who never caught on as a romantic lead, makes an entertaining hit-man—a moral burnout with a streak of gallows humor. And as the covert-ops commander, John Heard is a hoot, as always; blank and dead-voiced, he's like something under a rock, a slug. He seems to shrink from even the light of the camera.

NEWSDAY, 8/25/89, Part III/p. 3, Terry Kelleher

Gene Hackman has this strange weakness for assassination plots. Twelve years ago he starred in Stanley Kramer's "The Domino Principle" as a convict recruited by right-wing conspirators to murder a politician. It turned out to be one of the worst movies of his career.

Nevertheless, here he is now in "The Package," a thriller revolving around a plot by American and Soviet military hardliners to torpedo a nuclear disarmament treaty by assassinating the president of the United States and/or the leader of the USSR.

Make no mistake: "The Package" is much more competently done than "The Domino Principle." Director Andrew Davis handled Chuck Norris in "Code of Silence" and "the next Chuck Norris," Steven Seagal, in "Above the Law. " Fast-paced action is Davis' forte, and Chicago is his hometown.

Like the Norris and Seagal chop-'em-ups, "The Package" is set primarily in the weathered but photogenic Windy City, though the locale is a bit of a reach in this case. John Bishop's script has the George Bush and Mikhail Gorbachev look-alikes choosing Chicago as a meeting place for its symbolic value as the site of the first controlled atomic reaction in 1942.

Davis gets the expected solid performance from Hackman as a determined Army sergeant pitted against the forces of darkness, plus interesting work by Tommy Lee Jones as the sardonic hit man and John Heard in an atypical role as the cold-blooded colonel who gives him his orders. It's not the cast's fault that the intriguing premise is developed without even a modicum of complexity or originality.

Instead, "the Package" is tied together with cliches and conveniences. When Hackman needs to check on Jones' identity, he has only to turn to his former wife (Joanna Cassidy), a lieutenant colonel in personnel. Naturally, they resume the verbal sparring they enjoyed in their married days. "You're still a pain in the ———," she observes affectionately. Right then you know she's in this thing all the way to its exciting conclusion.

Hackman enters an Army base in Virginia, and immediately he's slapped on the back by an old chum who says, "Remember that time you saved my———at Fort Bragg?" What do you want to bet that Hackman will call in that I.O.U. minutes later when he needs to escape from house arrest?

With the story about to shift to Chicago, Cassidy wonders what she and the ex-hubby will do for allies on that unfamiliar turf. Don't worry, Hackman says. "I know a guy in Chicago I can trust." Wouldn't you know it's a Vietnam buddy turned tough cop, and wouldn't you know "Hill Street Blues" veteran Dennis Franz is on the force in yet another movie? Give him a serious bullet wound and Franz responds by running faster and shooting straighter. Hospitalize him and he busts out. He's the kind of guy who's got to suck it up and go where the action is.

At the end, of course, it's squarely up to Hackman to save the world. Fortunately for the world, the conspirators don't do the wise thing and kill Hackman as soon as they capture him. No, they chain him to a post and feed him milk and cookies. He takes to the snack the way Popeye turns on to spinach,.

"The Package" is watchable throughout, but it can't carry the weight of superpower politics. The idea had potential—too bad it's in a movie with such limited aspirations.

NEWSWEEK, 9/4/89, p. 68, David Ansen

This political thriller is a nifty summer sleeper, not always plausible but far more exciting than many of its overhyped competitors. The intrigue starts at a historic disarmament conference in East Berlin when terrorists kill an American general. Career Army sergeant Johnny Gallagher (Gene Hackman), unjustly blamed for bungling his security duties, is handed the thankless task of escorting a court-martialed serviceman (Tommy Lee Jones) back to the States to serve time. That assignment goes lethally awry, too, and Gallagher begins to realize he's up to his neck in a global conspiracy. Director Andrew Davis ("Above the Law") and writer John Bishop keep one step ahead of the audience as this mile-a-minute, *glasnost*-era cliffhanger zips from Berlin to Washington to a race-against-the-clock finale in Chicago. Hackman is the loner who, aided only by his ex-wife (Joanna Cassidy) and an old Vietnam pal (Dennis Franz), must single-handedly foil an international cabal. You may not swallow every coincidental encounter and hair's-breadth escape, but this crisp, complex thriller makes you care what happens every moment; Hackman brings such road-worn humanity to his part you may not realize until the end that this Everyman is a Superman in middle-age disguise.

VILLAGE VOICE, 8/29/89, p. 66, Stuart Klawans

Batman is not the only example of a lumbering Hollywood production. *The Package*, a guns-and-conspiracies thriller, is so slow to set forth its premise that the filmmakers hired newsman Ike Pappas to show up periodically, microphone in hand, and explain the plot—though the story hardly bears much examination.

It seems that the U.S. and USSR have concluded a nuclear disarmament treaty that is so darn good, the generals and the spies will be driven out of business. Some of the bad guys on both sides have therefore decided to revive the Cold War, hiring an assassin (Tommy Lee Jones) to do in one or more of the national leaders. The hit is planned for Christmas in Chicago. Nobody with an ounce of sense goes to Chicago in December; nevertheless, that's where the president and the Soviet premier will be, and that's where Jones is going, too, thanks to a little trick played on Sergeant Johnny Gallagher (Gene Hackman).

Gallagher, who is serving in Germany, is told he's supposed to escort a courtmartialed soldier back to the U.S. to stand trial. The soldier, of course, is Jones, who has been supplied with fake military ID and a few fellow conspirators to help him escape once he lands stateside. Jones thus enters the country without a trace, and Gallagher is left with the uneasy feeling that he's been set up. So he runs for help to his ex-wife, Eileen (Joanna Cassidy), who happens to be a lieutenant colonel.

And yet, here's how the finale goes: Hackman escapes the bad guys, with a lot of bludgeoning of faces and squealing of tires. Cross-cut to Cassidy, who is cooking breakfast for some children. Hackman drives like crazy to get to the intended scene of the assassination. Cross-cut to Cassidy, who is packing the children off to safety. Hackman and Cassidy meet; he says he will pursue Jones, while she should forward a message to the Secret Service. Off she goes on her secretary's job; off goes Hackman to do what a man must do. He races toward Jones's lair. Cross-cut to Cassidy, who is running through a department store. No, I'm not kidding—she seems to have found time to go shopping. Cross-cut to Hackman, who is involved in some gunplay. Cross-cut to Cassidy, who is left standing in a crowd of mothers with babies.

For unintentional humor, this is even better than Andrew Davis's previous film, *Above the Law*, which you might recall as the world's first Mafia/cop/martial-art master picture. I'm still not kidding. But it's no joke when Cassidy, who is one of the strongest women on the screen today, has to fry eggs while her man tends to the heroics. According to the plot of *The Package*, Hackman is the conspiracy's first victim. But, the way I see it, Cassidy is the one who really got set up.

Also reviewed in:
NEW YORK TIMES, 8/25/89, p. C12, Vincent Canby
VARIETY, 8/23-29/89, p. 28
WASHINGTON POST, 8/25/89, p. D1, Rita Kempley

PAPERHOUSE

A Vestron Pictures release of a Working Title film. *Executive Producer:* MJ Peckos and Dan Ireland. *Producer:* Tim Bevan and Sarah Radclyffe. *Director:* Bernard Rose. *Screenplay:* Matthew Jacobs. *Based on the novel "Marianne Dreams" by:* Catherine Storr. *Director of Photography:* Mike Southon. *Editor:* Dan Rae. *Music:* Hans Zimmer and Stanley Myers. *Sound:* Peter Glossop. *Sound Editor:* Mark Auguste. *Production Designer:* Gemma Jackson. *Art Director:* Frank Walsh and Ann Tilby. *Special Effects:* Alan Whibley. *Costumes:* Nick Ede. *Make-up:* Jenny Shircore. *Stunt Coordinator:* Gareth Milne. *Running time:* 94 minutes. *MPAA Rating:* PG-13.

CAST: Charlotte Burke (Anna); Elliott Spiers (Marc); Glenne Headly (Kate); Ben Cross (Dad); Gemma Jones (Dr. Sarah Nichols); Sarah Newbold (Karen); Samantha Cahill (Sharon); Jane Bertish (Miss Vanstone); Gary Bleasdale (Policeman); Stephen O'Donnell (Dustman); Barbara Keogh (Hotel Receptionist); Karen Gledhill (Nurse).

LOS ANGELES TIMES, 3/17/89, Calendar/p. 6, Michael Wilmington

Fever dreams, daydreams, nightmares, the world of art and imagination: These are the subjects of Bernard Rose's "Paperhouse." But the film isn't shot in that languorous, soft-focus style we associate with movies about reverie. The vision here is laceratingly sharp. Ultimately, "Paperhouse" becomes a film about how dreams can subvert or attack the real world, open it up to fear, loathing and maybe rebirth.

In "Paperhouse's" dream world, the light is pitiless, pouring down on a doppelganger land of eerily isolated fields and trashed houses, full of harsh surfaces, hidden monsters and keen, knife-like edges—a world ready to crack open over a hellish, fiery core. Much of the movie is set in the mind of a sick, bedridden little girl, creating her own territory on paper, with paints or crayons, and in the inner chambers of her mind—in dreams and delirium. And it becomes grindingly intense, a visually and aurally sophisticated little shocker, shivery and ripe with childhood terrors.

"Paperhouse" is based on a Catherine Storr novel called "Marianne Dreams." Here, the renamed Anna (Charlotte Burke) is a little girl who makes childish pictures and then dreams herself into a world where they become real. The tilted house of her drawings stands huge and abandoned in a vast, deserted field of endlessly waving gray-green grass, its rooms occupied by another of her creations: a little, legless, stick-figure boy called Marc (Elliott Spiers).

Is he also real? Anna's doctor has another patient, another Marc: suffering from muscular dystrophy. And, gradually, Anna becomes convinced that the fates of the dream Marc, the drawn Marc and the real Marc are inextricably joined, and that her drawings are changing all their lives, perhaps destroying them. Every personal and psychic horror she can imagine, including the conversion of her own father into a mad, dark stalker, is dredged up as she seeks to save her friend: the boy she never meets in the waking world.

There's nothing boring about "Paperhouse." The sound track and images keep working you up, squeezing out cold sweat. Obviously, director Bernard Rose saw the novel's central conceit, that dreams come true, as a visual springboard. And, though he and script writer Matthew Jacobs haven't delved far into the psychology—haven't really made Anna's dilemma real—thery've had a field day with the dreams, the crazy surfaces, the hallucinatory edges.

These dreams—the horrific paternal assault, the mysterious bicycles, helicopters and ice-cream machines—are like Andrew Wyeth under ether, like crisp, deep TV-ad visions out of Dali and de Chirico. The photographic style, by Rose and cinematographer Mike Southon (Ken Russell's "Gothic") probably owes as much to Rose's career in rock videos, as Southon's taste for Hammer horror movies. In their eyes, both nightmare and real world have a diamond-hard brightness, sliding into the terrifying, skewed emptiness of the dream fields surrounding Anna's paper house and a huge phallic lighthouse.

The child actress who plays Anna, Charlotte Burke, may be too old for the part. She is 13, perhaps playing 11, but the drawings she has supposedly made look like the work of a 6- or 7-year-old. Still, Burke has an admirable resilience and energy; so does Spiers. And the adults around her have a scarily equivocal quality: Glenne Headly, the corrupt ingenue of "Dirty Rotten Scoundrels" as her too-rational mother, Ben Cross of "Chariots of Fire" as her night-and-day father, Gemma Jones as her skeptical doctor.

The ideas here aren't new. Postwar '40s British films often took us into these dream worlds and childhood realms. But the technology is, as recent dream-films like "Time Bandits" or "Dreamchild" have already shown. The movie all but attacks you, largely through its lethally sharp images, and a music score by Hans Zimmer ("Rain Man") and Stanley Myers that is full of dark jags, edges and harsh screams too. "Paperhouse" (PG-13, despite intense, nightmarish scenes) puts up an impeccable surface, rips it up, reveals a hell underneath; an incongruous paper world of flesh and paint, blood and fire, oceans of tears.

MONTHLY FILM BULLETIN, 6/89, p. 186, Philip Strick

At school on her birthday, eleven-year-old Anna suddenly passes out, seeming to find herself on flat heathland resembling one of her own drawings with a house in the distance. When she wakes, she refuses to allow her anxious mother Kate to take her home, and promptly plays truant instead. Playing hide-and-seek with her friend Karen at a disused railway station, Anna faints again; the house reappears but there is no reply to her knock. Police and tracker dogs, summoned by Karen, trace the missing girl and her mother calls in their doctor, Sarah Nichols. Anna draws a face at one of the windows of her house picture, and when she falls asleep a boy materialises at the window of her dream house. Realising that whatever she draws will influence her 'vision', she feverishly designs a house interior enabling her to reach the boy in his room; when they meet, he says that his name is Marc and that he is trapped, unable to walk. During the doctor's next visit, she diagnoses glandular fever and tells Anna about another patient, a boy called Marc, who spends all his time in bed. Drifting in and out of sleep, Anna adds other furnishings to the dream house; she also tries to draw her father, who has been away for months, in the hope that he can carry Marc to freedom. But the drawing comes out badly, and when a figure does appear outside the house it is dark and menacing. Anna's condition worsens, and although she tries to burn her picture she becomes trapped in the dream house as her "father" breaks in and takes her away. Rescued with Marc's help, she drags her friend to the safety of a nearby lighthouse as "father" and dream house go up in flames. She wakes in hospital where she has been taken during a crisis in her illness, and while she convalesces she designs the interiors for Marc's new home. But at their next meeting he sadly withdraws from her, and soon she hears that the real Marc has died. Reunited with the family thanks to a job reassignment, her father takes them for a seaside holiday to complete Anna's recovery. From her hotel window the girl sees "her" lighthouse, and she rushes to the cliffs to see if Marc is there. She finds a note from him, promising to return, and a helicopter lowers a rope ladder to carry her away. But Marc's voice warns her to stay back from the cliff edge, and in the embrace of her mother and father she remains earth-bound as she tells them that she knows her friend is safe.

Arguably credible as the fever-dream of a pubescent schoolgirl whose primitive artworks both reflect and influence her subconscious, *Paperhouse* plays some confusing tricks in order to intensify what might otherwise have been a rather trivial *faux-naif* narrative. Granting the unlikely event—contrary to the experiences of, say, Alice (in Wonderland) and Dorothy (in Oz)—that the *only* images colouring a troubled girl's fantasy would be her own drawings (which acquire remarkably sophisticated detail and dimension in their hallucinated detail and dimension in their hallucinated form), the story then links her imaginary companion with the reported case history of a boy she has never met. Dodging confirmation that the boy of her dream and the real child are one and the same (a simple snapshot of his face could have substantiated the suggestion of paranormal empathy between them), the film wilfully subverts its own subjectivity in the final sequences by introducing a "real" lighthouse (the exact copy of Anna's drawing) with a note beside it and, worse, a "real" helicopter by which her friend may or may not have been lifted into the beyond.

It's possible, of course, to interpret each of these apparitions as continuing visions in a disturbed mind (Anna may have seen the lighthouse during a previous visit, the note may be for somebody else entirely, it may be a stiff breeze that buffets her parents, not a helicopter, and so on), but the ambiguities are unhelpful. If Anna, supposedly rational after her serious illness, has received positive evidence that "Marc is alright now, I know he is!", we are surely entitled to share in this reassurance. Equally distracting in *Paperhouse* is the girl's relationship with her parents. Her mother, speaking at all times in the crisply careful tones of a dentist's receptionist, appears incapable of relaxation, warmth or sympathy ("You fainted? So you're *not* ill", she keenly diagnoses at one point), while the missing father, whose only image around the home is a beach shot from last summer, has an awesome anonymity even when he suddenly materialises as Ben Cross. We might expect, in light of the innocently phallic details of the girl's preliminary sketches, that the primary glitch in her psychological welfare relates to this absent man in her life, who does indeed come bursting in when she gets too closely attached to his young rival and has to be despatched in a pit of fire.

As an analysis of family tensions, the film's only clear illustration is that it takes more than a few dropped hints to create a thesis. Whatever it fails to prove, however, *Paperhouse* offers a modest triumph in the production design by Gemma Jackson (who contributed much of the atmosphere to Neil Jordan's *Mona Lisa*). The dream house is a strikingly gaunt structure on a perilously bleak landscape, its interiors opening out with uneasy perspectives and cruel shadows worthy of *Caligari*. As they slowly accumulate furniture and clumsy, inoperable toys and gadgets, the rooms become suitably eerie metaphors of disorder, a bizarre mental parallel to the girl's own cluttered home where, by contrast, the colours are deceptively luxurious. Filmed with some appealing swoops and glides by Mike Southon's camera, the haunted residence grows increasingly forbidding under siege, finally sinking Usher-like into a splendid inferno of flame. An adventurous choice as a first feature for rock-video director Bernard Rose, *Paperhouse* compensates for hesitations in all other departments by such gratifyingly frequent displays of visual panache.

NEW YORK POST, 2/17/89, p. 28, David Edelstein

Anna (Charlotte Burke), the young English protagonist of the nightmare-fantasy "Paperhouse," is not your usual cute-kid heroine. She's actually a pain—a surly little girl who frequently gets booted out of class and who routinely defies her harried mother (Glenne Headly). Something's eating her, and it comes literally to life in this strange and voluptuous dream-film, a journey into the seething unconscious of a troubled child.

The movie, based on "Marianne Dreams" by Catherine Stoor, doesn't break new ground—many children's stories, among, them "Alice in Wonderland" and "The Wizard of Oz," suggest the ways in which a child's anxieties can in dreams be translated into dark, surrealistic settings and violent characters. But "Paperhouse" fleshes out the connections. Watching it, I was reminded of something vital that I'd long ago forgotten—how concrete, to a child, a fantasy can be.

Anna's dreams are intensified by mononucleosis, marked by a high fever and delirium. In school she passes out, and as she leaves one world, she rises up in another, out of the high grass in a wind-swept moor. In the distance she sees a tall, charcoal-colored house, which looks as one-dimensional as something on a sketch pad. It has come from her own, in fact—somehow, Anna's drawings have begun to spring to life in her dreams.

When the girl's doctor (Gemma Jones) tells her about another of her patients, a bed-ridden little boy, she draws him in the window of her paperhouse, and the next time she dreams she finds Marc (Elliott Spiers) in residence.

Marc, who is lonely and cannot walk, doesn't know about the real world—he thinks this house is all there is—but the more she learns about the actual boy, the more she realizes it's him in her paperhouse. He's the friend she's always longed for, and he's slipping away from his own world.

The director, Bernard Rose, has made a lot of music videos, and "Paperhouse" is almost a full-length one. The camera rises and falls to the lush, often choral music of Hans Zimmer and Stanley Myers, and drifts around this play world full of monochromatic colors and oversized props—all of which Anna draws in with her pencil. But as Anna's fever rises and waking up becomes a struggle, her dreamscape grows more menacing—it's a place where her deepest fears are palpable, and where her absent father (whom she has introduced into the drawing to help her stricken chum) appears in the form of a hammer-wielding bogeyman.

"Paperhouse" doesn't quite gel. It lacks the visionary texture of the best Surrealist films, and there are places where the symbolism feels too pat. It could use more psychological detail, more grounding. (The adults, in particular, are ciphers.) Worse, the finale is maddeningly grandiose, a mawkish ascent-to-the-heavens that would give E.T. the dry-heaves. It's a good thing that Burke is such an ingratiatingly surly heroine—a relief from all the cinema's saccharine Alices.

At its most vivid the movie immerses you in the teeming cauldron of adolescent fantasy, where bodily fluids and mythical dreads and the threat of the outside world all blur together. And it has one primal image—the blind, mottled father (Ben Cross) in silhouette on a distant hill, beginning his slow journey toward the house that protects his daughter. As he pounds on the door and calls her name—while Anna tries desperately to wake up and rip him out of her drawing—he's more terrifying than the Big Bad Wolf, Darth Vader and Freddy Krueger put together.

When he finally catches up to her—the landscape crumbling, molten-lava erupting from the earth—and begins to pound sickeningly hard on the little girl's chest, you might have an inkling of what's actually going on, of what in the real world could trigger so violent an action. And all your fever-dreams may come flooding back to you—those moments when the real and the imagined coalesced into a single, indelible image.

NEWSDAY, 2/17/89, Part III/p. 3, Mike McGrady

"I'm having dreams, mom," the 11-year-old girl says, "but they're real; I *know* they are."

"Dreams can't be real, sweetie," her mother comforts her. "They can frighten you but they can never hurt you."

"Paperhouse," a new English film that sometimes seems half case study and half horror movie, suggests perhaps dreams do have the power to hurt. In so doing, it avoids the failure that makes most horror films unfit for adult consumption; it doesn't make a practice of insisting we believe the unbelievable. There are no scaly monsters slithering from slime, no fangsprouting werewolves, no furry toothsome creatures gnawing through the front door.

"Paperhouse" asks only that we accept the proposition that dreams can seem real and who would quarrel with that? Of course, when dreams become real and reality becomes dreamlike, we are looking at the beginnings of madness—and what in real life is more frightening than that? Since the horror-movie staples in "Paperhouse"—a strange haunted house, a hammer-wielding killer, fiery crevices slicing open the earth—are all parts of a nightmare, the horror becomes logical, explainable, believable and, of course, all the more horrific.

Anna (Charlotte Burke) is a lonely girl whose world—school, boys, teachers, parents—is changing, unreliable. Unable to find stability, Anna begins retreating into her dreams. She draws a crude square house on her sketch pad and that very night comes upon that same house sitting in the middle of a vast field. Since her paper house is empty, she then sketches in the essentials—ice cream machine, bicycle, outsized radio and—why not?—a playmate, a pale and sickly boy (Elliott Spiers) unable to walk.

When she decides to add a rough sketch of her father (all we know of him is that he was a heavy drinker who now lives in another town), she has second thoughts and angrily scratches out his face. That night the faceless father (Ben Cross) appears in her dreams as a monster, a huge figure who brutally attacks her and her self-designed playmate.

Frequent fainting spells accompanied by high fevers force Anna to spend more and more time in her dreams. No longer is she sure where the dream ends and reality begins. Will the two worlds become one? When she can no longer force herself awake—even though we all hear a distant alarm clock clanging—the source of real terror becomes the fragility of her sanity, of life itself . . . When she is seen wandering on the very rim of a towering cliff, eyes closed, there's no longer any way of determining what is real; I don't recall a horror movie provoking a more powerful response.

My only serious quarrel with the film is prompted by rare lapses into traditional trickery. When Anna receives a real note from an imaginary friend, the film stoops beneath itself. However, for the most part, 28-year-old director Bernard Rose, a music-video veteran, makes marvelous use of unexpected rhythms and shows a surprisingly sure hand with both visual and audio effects.

Although the four principal performers—Burke, Spiers, Cross and Glenne Headly as the mother—are fine, this is not an actor's picture so much as it is a movie of ideas. The central idea, that our everyday world is such stuff as nightmares are made on, may not be terribly new to either psychologists or movie makers but the treatment makes it seem fresh.

NEWSWEEK, 2/20/89, p. 65, David Ansen

"I am not a drawing!" protests sickly young Marc to 11-year-old Anna, a troubled girl who's certain Marc exists because she drew him with crayons. In the chilling, illusory world of *Paperhouse*, one cannot be absolutely certain of what is flesh and blood and what's a figment of Anna's fevered imagination. Little Anna (Charlotte Burke), a willful and lonely child, is subject to fainting spells, and when she blacks out, or sleeps, she finds herself on a wind-swept heath approaching a three-dimensional house exactly like the one she's drawn on paper. Marc (Elliott Spiers) appears in the house after she's drawn a sad face in the window. But Marc can't walk. Is it, as Anna believes, because she's forgotten to draw his legs? Or is Marc the boy her doctor has told her about who is hospitalized with muscular dystrophy and has only a little time to live? Perhaps Anna can save him, just as she created him ...

Produced by Tim Bevan and Sarah Radclyffe, the team responsible for such ambitious films as "My Beautiful Laundrette," "Wish You Were Here" and "A World Apart," and directed by newcomer Bernard Rose, who comes out of music videos, "Paperhouse" is a small, spine-tingling English gem. Fear has fallen on crude times: with a few exceptions (David Cronenberg, George Romero) horror films have become the province of butcher-boy directors, who boast big body counts and leave nothing to the imagination. This simple but resonant fantasy film doesn't require much gore to produce goose bumps—it knows that the most fertile soil for horror is in the dreamscapes of childhood, booby-trapped with primal Oedipal terrors. Rose's film—written by Matthew Jacobs from Catherine Storrs novel called "Marianne Dreams"—can be interpreted in a straightforward psychological vein as the sickbed nightmares of a girl troubled by an absent, alcoholic father (Ben Cross) and a young mother (Glenne Headley) with whom she fights. Or you can take it as an ambiguous exploration of the landscape where dreams and reality intermingle.

Rose directs with a confidence remarkable in a first film: he gets the tone right and never oversells the material. He takes his cue from the childlike simplicity of Gemma Jackson's production design with its Magritte-like fantasy world. Equally important is the chilling Hans Zimmer score, with additional music by Stanley Myers (plus Fauré's "Requiem"). This talented team makes fright respectable again.

VILLAGE VOICE, 2/21/89, p. 67, Renee Tajima

Paperhouse is a visually stunning, 20-minute *Twilight Zone* segment stretched to a feature-length movie. Even the interior setting—a sickly boy's window out to his neverworld—resembles the opening graphics in NBC's revived version of the series. Like the television show, *Paperhouse* attempts to explore the frightening world of the human psyche—in this case, of childhood—our fears deepened by blurring the line between reality and the subconscious. Anna (Charlotte Burke) is a lonely and impressionable schoolgirl whose fantasy life comes alive in her drawings. She falls ill and, as a raging fever builds, so does her otherworldly relationship with an ailing boy named Marc (Elliott Spiers), who's trapped by useless legs in the house of Anna's mind.

Located on a stark, Andrew Wyeth plain, the mysterious house is also the setting for Anna's confused relationship to her absent father. In reality a nice guy who drinks a little too much, and whose work takes him away from home, in Anna's dreams he's a stalking figure, a blind Oedipus whose black Reeboks loom closer and closer as he threatens a horrible fate. Here, the movie takes a disturbing turn. Whereas the power of horror-suspense is in its subtleties, director Bernard Rose has Anna's dream father inexplicably beating the holy shit out of the little girl.

Paperhouse is a disappointing change of pace for Working Title, makers of socially charged films like *Sammie & Rosie Get Laid* and *A World Apart*. Rose, previously a music video director, builds tension with pounding music rather than dramatic turns. And the emotional interior life of a young girl's coming-of-age, implicit to the story, is lost in the forest of visual gimmickry and an overpowering soundtrack.

Also reviewed in:
NEW YORK TIMES, 2/17/89, p. C16, Janet Maslin
VARIETY, 9/21/88, p. 30
WASHINGTON POST, 3/24/89, p. C1, Hal Hinson

PARENTHOOD

A Universal Pictures release of an Imagine Entertainment film. *Executive Producer:* Joseph M. Caracciolo. *Producer:* Brian Grazer. *Director:* Ron Howard. *Screenplay:* Lowell Ganz and Babaloo Mandel. *Story:* Lowell Ganz, Babaloo Mandel, and Ron Howard. *Director of Photography:* Donald McAlpine. *Editor:* Michael Hill and Daniel Hanley. *Music:* Randy Newman. *Music Editor:* Dan Carlin Sr. *Sound:* Richard S. Church. *Sound Editor:* Anthony J. Ciccolini III. *Production Designer:* Todd Hallowell. *Art Director:* Christopher Nowak. *Set Decorator:* Nina Ramsey. *Set Dresser:* William A. Cimino, Linda Marais, and Nicklas Farrentello. *Special Effects:* Kevin Harris and Bob Cooper. *Costumes:* Ruth Morley. *Make-up:* Fern Buchner and Peter Wrona Jr. *Stunt Coordinator:* Artie Malesci. *Running time:* 120 minutes. *MPAA Rating:* PG-13.

CAST: Steve Martin (Gil); Mary Steenburgen (Karen); Dianne Wiest (Helen); Jason Robards (Frank); Rick Moranis (Nathan); Tom Hulce (Larry); Martha Plimpton (Julie); Keanu Reeves (Tod); Harley Kozak (Susan); Dennis Dugan (David Brodsky); Leaf Phoenix (Garry); Eileen Ryan (Marilyn); Helen Shaw (Grandma); Jasen Fisher (Kevin); Paul Linke (George Bowman); Alisan Porter (Taylor); Zachary Lavoy (Justin); Ivyann Schwan (Patty); Alex Burrall (Cool); Lowell Ganz (Stan); Rance Howard (Dean at College); Max Elliott Slade (Young Gil); Clint Howard (Lou); Lamont Lofton (Fotomat Clerk); Erika Rafuls (Amy); Jordan Kessler (Matt); Bill Cohen (Eddie); Isabel Cooley (Barbara Rice); Greg Gerard (Doctor Lucas); Paul Keeley (Kevin, Age 21); Walter Von (Opposing Coach); W. Bruce O'Donoghue (Umpire); Claudio Jacobells (Student #1 at College); Hilary Matthews (Student #2 at College); Sherry Ferguson (Screaming Co-ed); Todd Hallowell (Track Official); Maxie Pontius (Safety Man at Track); Richard Kuhlman (Young Frank); Lloyd Cleek (Miles); Dana Mark (Audrey); Louisa Marie (Woman Teacher #1); Cyndi Vicino (Woman Teacher #2); Steve Zurk (Highway Policeman); Emil Felski (Doctor at Hospital); Charmin Talbert (Nurse at Hospital); Julie Lander (Student in Hallway); Janet Moore (Irate Woman in Audience); Connie Adams (Cindy).

FILMS IN REVIEW, 11/89, p. 549, Edmond Grant

Conceived as some kind of ultimate statement on the current condition of the American family, *Parenthood* is a very busy comic drama which is both highly engaging and shamelessly manipulative.

The highly structured plotline centers around a rather large family that seems to be experiencing nearly every possible parenting dilemma, all at the exact same time. Particular emphasis is placed upon a middle-aged couple (Steve Martin and Mary Steenburgen) who are primarily troubled by their overly sensitive son's difficulties in school, but who also have to cope with the husband's job troubles, the various distractions thrown at them by their relatives, and the fact that (as the old country hit went) another one's on the way.

The other archetypal situations gone through by their relatives include: a father (Tom Hulce) who expresses a complete disinterest in his offspring; a single mother's problems dealing with her teenage daughter's sudden marriage and pregnancy (the mom, Dianne Wiest; the daughter, Martha Plimpton); a couple (Rick Moranis, in his third film role this summer, and Harley Kozak) who are set on turning their young daughter into a whizkid; and the understanding grandparents (Jason Robards and Eileen Ryan) who are supposed to grin and bear it while their progeny go through parenting hell.

The multiplicity of storylines gives the film episodic quality which is good in one respect, as it allows each situation to play itself out and each character to get his or her say, but which also unfortunately serves to obscure some of the film's better moments. For at certain points in the film, one gets the distinct impression that particular characters are present only for the purpose of "completing the picture"—it's as if scripters Lowell Ganz and Babaloo Mandel wouldn't have been satisifed exploring only one or two of these problems, and somehow felt that they had to find a possible identification figure for *every* parent (or potential parent) in the audience (those too old to be parents of the newborn—why, their surrogates are the irascible old grandfolk). This identification is blunted, though, when one considers that this brood (like the ones in *Ordinary People* and *Terms Of Endearment*) are hardly "average" as regards financial status—they are a quite comfortable white family whose only non-house owning member is Hulce the wanderer. However, considering the broad-based box office reception the film has achieved thus far, it appears that most Americans do indeed identify with financially comfortable WASPy white Americans.

The film's cornerstone is clearly its rather large and impeccably chosen cast. In the central role, Steve Martin does some fine comic work, though his dramatic scenes have a peculiarly strained quality to them. Several other casting decisions seem perfectly natural: Dianne Wiest's sobbing, squinty-eyed mother role here seems a casual extension of her last few film performances; Rick Moranis has done the egghead bit to perfection elsewhere, and Martha Plimpton has made a specialty of playing the gangly teenager. And rounding out the family portrait gallery is Jason Robards who delivers the film's strongest performance as the Buckman clan's understanding patriarch.

Though the screenplay has a schematic quality to it, there are some singularly touching sequences, such as the scene where Robards tells Martin about the true, unending nature of a parent's commitment to a child, or when the family's always-silent great grandmother finally speaks up to deliver an odd but charming metaphor for Martin and Steenburgen's troubles.

The touching quality of these moments does much to erase the bad taste left by director Ron Howard's Spielbergian attempts to manipulate the viewer's emotions (which reach an abysmal level in the hyper-tearjerking finale) and the film's peculiar endorsement of irresponsible teenage pregnancy—though Wiest is sure that Plimpton's marriage won't last more than six months, she encourages her daughter to have her baby because "what she wants, I want."

Essentially, *Parenthood* delivers some way-out domestic humor (Martin engages in a number of fantasy sequences that are quite funny) and an occasional truth about the way that parents view their children, and vice versa. Howard's mawkish handling of the film's sentimental side, however, only goes to show that American attitudes about the nuclear family might have changed, but Hollywood's depiction of it still hasn't.

LOS ANGELES TIMES, 8/2/89, Calendar/p. 1, Sheila Benson

"The thing about being a parent," snarls Jason Robards' patriarch in "Parenthood," an irascible, near-failure at the job himself,"is that it never, *never* ends." How many sighs will float through the audience at that moment, validating a sentiment that seems to come from one parent's very corpuscles.

Then, because this is a screenplay by the team of Lowell Ganz and Babaloo Mandel ("Splash," "Night Shift"), Robards adds a kicker to his sentence. It's one of the pungent jabs to the funny bone that sets the movie's tempo, an unrelenting one-two rhythm that eventually overwhelms any demurrers about sticky-sweet patches in the face of this much wit, nerve and insight.

Parenthood never does end, of course, and neither does being a son or daughter, which is the beauty of this movie's across-the-board appeal. This may be one family, but as it spreads over four generations and four separate households, no special-interest group is left unscathed.

Baby boomers may feel it's aimed directly at them, with its excruciatingly funny portrait of a father (Rick Moranis) who is going to see to it that his daughter has a nodding acquaintance with Kafka, square roots and karate, well before she's 4. Parents of school-dubbed "hyperactive" or clenchingly tense 8- to 10-year-olds will be certain the movie makers were eavesdropping on their last parents' conference.

Those with "impossible" neon-haired teen-agers whose every sentence is punctuated by a slammed door, might swear that "Parenthood" was *their* group portrait. And adult children of alcoholics (are they the largest growing subculture right now or does it only seem so?) might claim the movie as *their* own after watching the emotional fallout from Robards' boozy, indifferent attempts at fathering, four decades later.

Doesn't sound like a comedy? Ah, but that's exactly what gives this very real comic delight its backbone. Director Ron Howard, who also created the film's original story with Ganz and Mandel, uses these bittersweet elements like smelling salts, to bring us around after the laughing-gas effect of the jokes. His fine touch with ensembles ("Cocoon") reaches real maturity here, as he pulls together the script's tendency to skitter between sociology and sitcom, making it into one perceptive, delicious whole.

A family tree may be in order. Robards and a vastly put-upon Eileen Ryan are parents of two sons—Steve Martin and young black sheep Tom Hulce—as well as two daughters—Dianne Wiest, whose husband has left her, and lovely newcomer Harley Kozak, whose husband (Moranis), alas, has not. There are what seem to be 142 assorted children parceled out to these parents, although it may only be seven. And there is Helen Shaw's Grandma, who is actually great-grandma.

Over at Steve Martin's house, we get a heartfelt portrait of a father trying wildly to juggle increased pressure from work and his need to give his three children what he never had, a father figure. Martin may be a touch anxious as he goes about it, however, and that tenseness has transferred itself to his 8-year-old son Kevin (Jasen Fisher), whose face has all the relaxation of a barnacle clinging to its rock. Mercifully, Martin has had the good sense to have married Mary Steenburgen, the ballast to his every wild gyration. If you were going to choose a single person to represent serene faith in the future, you could do no better than Steenburgen.

Wiest, still furious about her ex-husband's abandonment of their two children in favor of his "new" family, is trying to be the cool, unshockable modern mom. It won't be easy. She has to arrange her face around a teen-age daughter (Martha Plimpton) with a live-in boyfriend (Keanu Reeves) who lives only to drag-race, and a young son (Leaf Phoenix) whose video tastes run to the X-rated. Wiest has the movie's tartest lines and most spirited character and she does them both proud.

Hulce, along with Robards, gets "Parenthood's" unsympathetic character, a compulsive gambler and absent-minded father (to a winning, half-black little son, the result of a fleeting liaison with an "Elvis on Ice" chorine) who, if not stopped, would sell the family house and every stick in it to stay ahead of his gambling debts. Best line: As he is dumped out of a gambler's moving car onto the pavement Hulce explains quickly that "friends" dropped him off. "Friends slow down," Robards observes dourly. "They even stop." Yet it's the interaction between these two that makes the film's greatest poignancy. (That and a brilliantly written scene as Martin says good night to his sweet, troubled son.)

Battles and boners; lost retainers and lost virginity; first marriages, last marriages and marriages that may not last. The film makers seem to know it all intimately and are able to laugh nevertheless.

The quibbles come from a couple of points: The almost hysterically pro-parenthood ending, so broad some of the careful tone is sloshed away. The cheap-shot lines thrown (mostly) to Grandma. The character of Robards' extremely long-suffering wife, butt of his every disparaging remark. Was she the victim of the script's dropped stitch? Seems as though she deserves to get a bit of her own back. Finally, isn't it time for a moratorium on Rick Moranis' unvarying character, the nerdy lover/husband who, in picture after picture but especially here, attracts perfectly dazzling women for unfathomable reasons. He has become as irritating a bit of movie shorthand as Wallace Shawn.

The remaining cast, young, old and in-between, is lovely. Among the standouts are Keanu Reeves' jangly-limbed lover who proves to have unexpected facets; Harley Kozak's luscious, level-headed wife and both Jasen Fisher's and Leaf Phoenix's distressed young sons.

As you might imagine, Randy Newman's songs on the score are particularly apt and, along with Donald McAlpine's splendid cinematography, Ruth Morley's costumes seem exceptionally inventive, especially Martin's improvised bathmat chaps when he is called upon to be Cowboy Gil, a children's party entertainer.

MONTHLY FILM BULLETIN, 1/90, p. 21, John Pym

The Buckmans attempt to be good parents. Gil and his wife Karen agonise over Kevin, their oldest child, who is threatened with consignment to a special school. Gil's sister Susan wants a second child to normalise a family dominated by husband Nathan's obsessive "education" of three-year-old Patty. Gil's other sister, the divorced Helen, puzzles over her secretive son Garry and capitulates to her tearaway daughter Julie who sets up in her mother's house with oafish husband Tod. Meanwhile, the itinerant Larry, the youngest of the four siblings, comes home with his son Cool hoping that his indulgent father Frank will settle his debts preparatory to a new money-making venture. Gil triumphs at Kevin's ninth birthday party by substituting for the absent cowboy entertainer. Having failed to sell Frank's prized vintage automobile, Larry begs for $26,000 to save him from murderous gangsters. Susan uses flashcards to inform Nathan that she is leaving him. Relieved that Garry has found a dutch uncle in Tod, Helen begins a relationship with George Bowman, her son's homely biology teacher. Gil resigns his job when he is not made a partner; Karen, to her husband's fury, announces that she is pregnant. Later, however, Kevin delights his father by taking a winning baseball catch. Frank agrees to finance's Larry's flight to Chile and to take on the permanent care of Cool. Susan, who has returned to teaching, yields before her class to an off-key serenade by the contrite Nathan. Helen compels the pregnant Julie to stand by the irresponsible Tod after he narrowly escapes injury in a drag-race crash. Gil, who has withdrawn his resignation, is reconciled with Karen. Justin, their youngest, wrecks a school production of *Snow White* while trying to "rescue" his sister Taylor. The Buckmans gather for the birth of Helen and George's baby girl.

In the extended closing scene of this sentimental portrait of a St. Louis family, five generations—from Frank's mother to Julie's child—mill about a maternity ward exuding the sort of dewy benevolence brought on the world over by the birth of a baby. *Parenthood*, from the director of *Splash* and *Cocoon*, is not, however, *Fanny and Alexander*: no genuinely terrifying demons lurk in the corners of these childen's lives; and the gangsters menacing Larry are very much off-screen. There is, to be sure, Garry's inarticulate sense of the betrayal of his dentist father (on whose surgery he takes his revenge) and his sister Julie's childish contempt for their mother (she sneers at Helen for taking sexual pleasure from a machine). In the end, however, a wand is waved over these misfortunes and we leave, as so often, feeling that it is, indeed, a wonderful life.

As sentimental portraits go, however, and barring one or two over-caramelised scenes (such as Nathan's interminable rendition of "Close to You": "He sang it at our wedding", Susan informs the class), *Parenthood* has enough spritely moments to keep it running smoothly. Mary Steenburgen and Dianne Wiest, as the sisters-in-law Karen and Helen (both so to speak having trained for their roles with Woody Allen), bring a sympathetic seriousness to the proceedings which at times anchors the more crackerbarrel tendencies of the men (the four principals—crusty Jason Robards, scampish Tom Hulce, serious but idiotic Rick Moranis, and look-at-me Steve Martin—here very much true to form).

Parenthood is composed of vignettes which build to the unexceptional moral that parenthood is for life. A few of these, such as Steve Martin's performance as Cowboy Gil with his chaps made from a halved bathmat, have an irresistible silliness and most, such as grim-faced Patty giving her father a knock-out smack during a martial-arts lesson, sidestep the pitfall of indulging the habits of very small children. The one unabashedly indulgent sequence—the performance of *Snow White* in which little Justin battles for the honour of his abused sister Dopey—is somewhat redeemed by a pan across the audience all of whom are, of course, indulgently videoing their offspring: a shot, on reflection, which might stand for the film as a whole.

NEW STATESMAN & SOCIETY, 1/5/90, p. 44, Angela McRobbie

When an American blockbuster film with an unprepossessing title like *Parenthood* is released to great acclaim, it is clear that something is going on in the world of cinema culture, which can neither be explained simply by reference to Aids nor to the creeping success of the moral majority. Nor are demographic factors life the gradual ageing of the population sufficient to explain the appeal of a film where the hero, Gil, (Steve Martin) is silver-haired and 40 something, and its sexiest moment occurs after an exhausting Saturday spent with the children at a baseball match when tired Gil falls into bed with the even-more-tired Karen and after approximately 30 seconds of love-making says: "Oh, have I got there already?" At which point he is distracted by the failings of the teachers at his son's local school and loses interest entirely in wherever it was that he had got to.

The deep social fears and anxieties which are reflected in *Parenthood* evolve entirely round the question of family life. The film recognises that irreversible changes have taken place in the family. Couples split up when there are children and when there are none. From now on children can expect to grow up in anything but the nuclear family.

Different types of household have developed to take this factor into account. New ways of living have given rise to new familial relations, half-sisters live with half-brothers. Children move from one household to the other, week-days, weekends, holidays. *Parenthood* doesn't try to role back the carpet. Instead it pokes gentle fun at these new combinations and suggests that, for the good of the child, we adults lower our expectations. Family love is better than single sex, and who cares if the earth doesn't always move. This is a film where everybody is ordinary, nobody is fabulously good-looking, where the family is not romanticised or even celebrated, but is simply asserted as the framework within which people live out their lives and bring home their failures as well as their, mostly small, successes.

In *Parenthood* the world of work, so seductively portrayed only three years ago in another blockbuster *Wall Street*, is at best a means of earning a living and at worst somewhere that men only get promotion if they manage to set their visiting clients up with call girls, or "prostitutes" as Gil spells it out, to emphasise his disapproval, when he tries to explain to his wife why he handed in his resignation. For her part Karen (Mary Steenburgen) is thinking vaguely (but only vaguely) of getting back to work as her youngest child approaches school age. That thought is put paid to when, presumably as a result of one of their less interrupted sexy moments ("Have I got *there* already?") she gets pregnant with her fourth child.

Gil and his family are at the heart of *Parenthood*. Gil feels deeply that his own father did not give his children the attention they deserved. He is determined to get it right this time and, as a result, spends more time with his kids than his colleagues in the company. His son is labelled emotionally disturbed by his teachers who want him placed in a special school. Karen and Gil see him as gifted and sensitive. He is a "special" child who needs as much parental attention as they can give. As a result Gil gives up his leisure time to coach him in baseball and to entertain him and his friends at his birthday party dressed as Cowboy Bob.

Karen "glows" periodically with maternal fulfilment and in these moments Gil tells her how much he loves her.

Gil's sister Helen (Dianne Wiest) is a divorcee struggling to bring up her children alone, and his other sister is married to a man who is obsessed by education, and tutors his three-year-old daughter as though she was preparing for her finals. The youngest brother of the family, the black sheep, has returned to this white, lower-middle-class community with a mixed-race child. There are raised eyebrows round the table, but happily not for long.

In the end everyone that is female has a baby. And if the men could, they would. Even Helen who eventually goes out with her son's biology teacher has one, and thus brings love, men and sex to what had been a celibate single family set up. Baseball, children's parties, TV dinners, toddlers, babies, more babies. Who in their right mind could find pleasure in this pre-John Updike version of small town America? Who could allow themselves to be overwhelmed by these good old values barely disguised in the language of the "new"?

I for one was. Not just because the humour was infective and the soundtrack was by Randy Newman. *Parenthood* succeeds for three quite simple reasons. First, its real subject matter, apart from those other moments that would appeal to the average member of the moral majority, is that huge unending space of time which we give over to our children. The long waits in the playground, the hours in the supermarket, the "activities", the treats, the anxieties. To call this "domestic labour" or "reproduction" was never quite right. It remains not good or bad but simply life, around which work, sex, achievement, and disappointment wind their own inevitable paths.

Second *Parenthood* puts sex back in its place. Twenty years of the sexualisation of culture have taken their toll. The pressure on men to perform in the sexual olympics of the body beautiful are here replaced by other kinds of performance. For some of the time at least it is sufficient simply to be a "dad". Finally, the film works because delinquent-looking boyfriends turn out to be nice guys, women in their late forties end up giving birth, and decent men who don't get laid by prostitutes get offered their jobs back. It's a long way from *Klute*.

NEW YORK. 8/14/89, p. 79, David Denby

The ads for Ron Howard's *Parenthood* set us up for another slapstick comedy. You know the type: kids wiping chocolate hands on the drapes, shoving toys cars into the VCR, while Steve Martin, as the movies' latest Mr. Mom, tries desperately to get everybody into the tub before dinner. Well, that's not it at all. *Parenthood* is certainly a comedy, but it's also surprisingly ambitious. The movie's subject is nothing less than the emotional condition of middleclass parenthood, the commonplace confusion—desperation even—of men and women convinced that no matter how hard they try to do things right, they are always, somehow, getting them wrong.

Even on the best of days, parents stagger across the decks of their rolling ships, semi-helpless captains steering without instruments through fog and lashing rain. Haunted by child-rearing theories they only half understand, vaguely resentful and vaguely guilty, mortifyingly self-conscious, they hang on to the tiller with baffled determination. When they finally do straggle into port, it's usually not the port they were aiming for, and they have no idea how they got there. Did they just drift in, or were they steering straight after all? *Parenthood* suggests that in the end it doesn't much matter.

The movie was put together by the same team that did *Splash:* producer Brian Grazer, writers Babaloo Mandel and Lowell Ganz, director Ron Howard. Among them, these worthy citizens have so far produced sixteen children. Not startlingly, *Parenthood* is thickly populated, with some of the maddening, buzzing busyness of large families—another person, another problem always there to think about, never any peace. There's a patriarch of sorts (Jason Robards) who has four grown children, all with children of their own. *Parenthood* tracks the romantic ups and downs within each marriage, but it always comes back to the parent-child connection as it flourishes or wanes through the generations. For parents, its the obligation that never ends, the much longed-for, welcomed, and never-cast-away millstone around one's neck.

Parenthood has the bouncing energy of some of the kaleidoscopic Robert Altman movies of fifteen years ago, though without Altman's thicket of cross-references, without the richness and eccentricity of his atmosphere or anything like his bitter humor. Howard punches out the scenes emphatically, each making its point and then ending. The movie is supposed to be set in a suburb near St. Louis, but it was actually shot in Universal's new production facility in Orlando, and it has that TV-sitcom, Nowheresville feeling, bright, scrubbed, and anonymous. *Parenthood*, I suppose, is only a superior example of commercial product. Still, it's the kind of fast, light, big-Hollywood movie that has gratifying reserves of emotion.

At its center is Steve Martin, giving the most emotionally committed performance of his career. as Gil, pressured, unwilling corporate employee and roaringly energetic father. Gil's own dad (Robards) was gruff and remote—he still is—and Gil is determined to give his kids everything he didn't get. He wants his three little ones to grow up (it's his litany) "confident, well adjusted, and happy." He's relentlessly driving them to be confident, well adjusted, etc., and of course he's mainly making them tense and crazy. Kevin, his oldest, eight going on nine yet infantile in many ways, is a high-strung boy who falls apart easily, understandably panicking under a fly ball when his dad is coaching the Little League team.

Steve Martin has often used his explosive clown's skills to suggest pent-up hostility; it's fascinating to see him do it to express love, twisting himself into a pretzel as he tries to drive away the little boy's unhappiness. At the same time, he brings out the deeply foolish narcissism in Gil's drive. In the movie's loveliest moments, Gil dreams of his son's future gratitude to him (we see the reveries): *He* is going to be the hero of his son's life. But in the present, when Kevin doesn't immediately shape up, Gil goes stiff with disappointment, as if every effort he makes should instantly be answered by an improvement in the kid's mood (this, I can tell you, is a common delusion). Gil's brother-in-law, Nathan (Rick Moranis), is in thrall to another kind of parental madness. Nathan stuffs his little daughter—a pie-face of three—with letters, words formulas, every bit of information she can take in. "They're sponges!" Nathan exults, sending the tiny child spinning along some mythical fast track (in Manhattan, he'd fit right in).

Gil and Nathan, demanding results all the time, are more infantile than their children. But the women are sane. Gil's wife (Mary Steenburgen) and Nathan's (Harley Kozak) don't bother with theories; they simply do what's necessary, resisting their husband's more foolish ideas, holding things together. Both actresses are touching, but Dianne Wiest is outright marvelous in the juicier role of Helen (Gil's sister), a lonely and anxious divorced mother who invests all her emotions in her children. Sensing her need, her teenage daughter and son have disgustedly pulled away from her. But a rejected mommy is not the same as a rejected lover; she always has some leverage and some strength. Wiest has those crinkled eyes, her clipped, harried look, and her nervous smile, greeting each outrage from the kids with a beseeching grin. The way she plays Helen, she's a mother whose every instinct tells her, despite much hurt feelings, to stay available, stay open—they'll come back. Wiest's soft hopefulness, combined with anger underneath (which comes bursting out in weird, almost unconscious little jokes), gives the performance its pathos and its comic tension.

Suddenly, at the end, all the problems between parents and children, and between parent and parent, are resolved too neatly and quickly. The message that life is a roller coaster, with its ups and downs, is spelled out for us—unnecessarily, since the whole movie says as much. *Parenthood* is glib. Ron Howard is an entertainer with roots so deep in commercial television and movies that the artist in him can't quite come out. But he's a man of feeling, and he certainly gets onscreen, as no moviemaker before him has, the teasing, taunting complexity of child-rearing, the perversity of a job that flummoxes even the most intelligent and self-composed people. Jason Robards's patriarch has been too distant from one son, too indulgent of another. The children in the movie who are overmonitored are going crazy; the ones neglected have become withdrawn. Steve Martin's Gil fights off his sense of failure with heroic bursts of energy—when he finally relaxes and learns to float, it's a fine moment, a well-earned release. There is, of course, no answer for parents. But it often doesn't matter, which is the final joke. Most kids come through no matter how badly Mom and Dad screw up.

NEW YORK POST, 8/2/89, p. 19, David Edelstein

The new comedy "Parenthood" has a resonant, bittersweet subject—parents' terror of screwing up their kids—and a dream ensemble. The elements are in place for a brutally funny psychodrama, but the film makers move gingerly, like parents plying a potentially explosive child with Gummi Bears.

Steve Martin plays Gil, a man whose father (Jason Robards) paid no attention to him as a child, often leaving him at ball games in the care of hot-dog vendors. In the opening, young Gil tells a vendor that when he's a dad, he'll stay with his own kids if it kills him. But it turns out he's a dad already: The vendor is part of a fantasy, which snaps to an end when his wife, Karen (Mary Steenburgen) tells him the ball game is over and it's time to go home.

It's a seductive overture—wacky yet painful—and as the credits roll, Randy Newman's theme song "I Love to See You Smile" is ironically harmonious: Gil, still working through his own childhood miseries, seems destined to pass them on to his kids.

The problem with "Parenthood" is that it doesn't maintain that level of irony. Slickly directed by Ron Howard, it's a maddeningly schizoid work: now hip and tough and funny, now drearily wholesome, full of hopeless conflicts and sitcom reprives. It's also mistitled: the subject isn't parenthood but fatherhood. Mothers have little to do with what's really going on.

The picture throws its net wide, portraying four related families, each with a different kind of dad. Nathan (Rick Moranis) thinks kids are capable of absorbing tremendous amounts of information, so he's filling his toddler's head with languages, books, assorted disciplines—much to the horror of his wife, Susan (Harley Kozak).

On the other hand, Gil's divorced sister Helen (Dianne Wiest) must raise her kids without any father at all: 16-year-old Julie (Martha Plimpton) spends nights in her room with a burnout drag-racer (Keanu Reeves), while adolescent Garry (Leaf Phoenix) is a virtual recluse, pining for a daddy to give him discipline and direction.

Everywhere you look there are children damaged by dads who are either too attentive or not attentive enough. Gil's brother Larry (Tom Hulce), on whom their father lavished attention, is now an irresponsible gambler with a neglected mulatto son (named "Cool"). Too much indulgence finished Larry; too little will finish his son.

In the center is our hero, Gil, trying to walk a tightrope between authority figure and chum—all while dreaming of a future in which his jittery eldest son is either valedictorian or a sniper in a bell-tower. The most horrifying paradox is that the better he is as a dad, the less he can provide for his family: promotions at his advertising firm go to guys who put in 12-hour days.

Through all the sub-plots, raising a family is shown to be a messy, bumptious business, fraught with hairpin turns. So why is the picture itself so candied, so high-toned, so smooth? Why isn't it looser and shaggier, with some bustle in the margins?

Howard is one of those directors who was better before he learned his craft—now he squeegees the life out of his subjects. The overly tidy script might have been penned in the intervals between family therapy sessions and power lunches; it throws kisses to the audience.

Fortunately, the cast is never glib, and the movie often swells with honest feeling. Martin is stunningly good: eyes full of pain, he has the naked yearning of a clown who has sweated off his makeup. And the clowning has a dramatic point—when he entertains his wife and kids, he's laboring to hold chaos at bay.

Wiest does her specialty turn—teary self-loathing—and no one does it better. Her Helen is a scary portrait: a mother so crippled by insecurity that she's always undermining her own authority, choking on her orders a second after she issues them. No wonder her kids are screwed up.

Wiest has a great rapport with Plimpton, a nervy young actress who seems incapable of registering a false emotion. Her Julie is one of those teens who's always demonstrating her independence by flouncing out of one dependent relationship and into another.

There's so much insight here that it's a shame the film goes soft. But let's not kid ourselves— that's what will make it a hit. In the end, irony gets its comeuppance: the old grandmother (Helen Shaw) makes a speech about how marvelous rollercoasters are and isn't being a parent learning to love the crazy ride?

Gil, the ironist, makes fun of her attempt to sum things up, but our laughter is cut short by his wife, who screams that the old woman is brilliant. Gil makes a joke about grandma's senility, but it's all over; during the next crisis, the camera shakes, screams fill the sound track and Gil realizes that parenthood—full of lovely moments and bloody awful moments—is indeed a roller-coaster. So's "Parenthood."

NEWSDAY, 8/2/89, Part II/p. 3, Mike McGrady

With "Parenthood," Ron Howard returns to his roots, that familiar terrain known as Sitcomland, but he makes some interesting alterations in the landscape. Howard, of course, is the original sitcom kid—he started out as Opie in Andy Griffith's Mayberry and came of age as the carrot-topped Richie in "Happy Days." All grown up now and directing movies ("Splash," "Coccoon," "Willow"), Ron Howard has filmed his first family situation comedy, but "Parenthood" is definitely not designed with small screen in mind.

The extended family in "Parenthood" is not worried about niggling little concerns like kids' pre-prom complexion problems or someone stealing nickels from mommy's purse. The aging family patriarch (Jason Robards) is concerned because one grown son (Tom Hulce) has just returned home with an illegitimate son and a gambling debt of $26,000. Robards' other son (Steve Martin) has fathered a Little Leaguer who sees a psychiatrist regularly.

Then there's Rick Moranis, who has started his 3-year-old daughter in the fast lane—taking karate lessons, studying Spanish, learning square roots. Dianne Wiest's 13-year-old son smuggles pornographic videocassettes into his bedroom while her daughter (Martha Plimpton) uses her own bedroom to stage X-rated photos with her boyfriend-lover (Keanu Reeves).

These are the kind of problems that were never hinted at on "Father Knows Best"—followed by reactions that are equally different. When Wiest picks up the wrong pictures, getting her daughter's do-it-yourself porno packet, she selects one of the overexposures and says, calmly, "I think this one is my favorite." Her daughter's angry reaction: "I thought someone in the family ought to be having sex with something that didn't require batteries."

From mommy's vibrator and daughter's do-it-yourself pornography, "Parenthood" proceeds to take on premarital sex, postmarital abortion, contraception, cruelty, neglect, abandonment, sex in a moving car, smother love, party strippers for hire and children who chant every revolting verse to a childhood ditty entitled "Diarrhea." While this kind of thing may seem more appropriate to the "Movie of the Week" than family dramedy, it does add a nice bite to the sweetness that is normally such a constant in Sitcomland.

What also saves the film is an all-star lineup in fine fettle. Steve Martin would, of course, by any kid's favorite dad. When the balloon twister fails to show up for the big birthday party, Martin steps in and fills the bill, putting on a dazzling entertainment that delights the young partygoers and the wider audience as well.

"Dad, when I grow up, can I work where you work?" his son asks.

"Why?"

"That way, I can still see you every day."

Ah, the rewards of parenthood—they're also there, mixed in freely with the failures and outright disasters, with the funny moments and sad ones. Howard, rebounding nicely from last year's "Willow," expertly juggles clashing elements. Of course, no parent has to be told that the job can be thankless, but it's nice to be reminded that it's also rewarding. And necessary.

"It never, ever ends," Robards says. "You never cross the end zone and spike the ball."

NEWSWEEK, 8/7/89, p. 61, David Ansen

At its best, Ron Howard's *Parenthood* captures better than most contemporary American movies the sheer messiness and tumult of middle-class family life. Written by Lowell Ganz and Babaloo Mandel from a story they concocted with Howard, this crowded, inventive movie is both an update of—and a far cry from—the child-raising comedies and sitcoms of the '50s. Father doesn't know best anymore; Mom's cute 8-year-old may be emotionally disturbed; Grandpa is a drunk and his 27-year-old son is a compulsive gambler with a contract out on his life, and single mothers have to cope with teenage daughters sleeping with drag-racing boyfriends in the next bedroom while angry 13-year-old sons smuggle porno tapes into their VCR's. "Parenthood" *is* a comedy, but its laughs are rooted in pain, disappointment and exasperation. Steve Martin fans expecting "The Jerk Raises a Family" may be startled to discover a movie whose emotional range is closer to "Terms of Endearment."

Howard's movie encompasses four families and four generations. Steve Martin, married to Mary Steenburgen, is the overanxious father of three, determined not to make the mistakes his distant, alcoholic father (Jason Robards) made with him; he is also consumed with guilt over his eldest son's emotional problems. His sister (Dianne Wiest), abandoned by her husband, is pathetically trying to be the perfectly liberal mother to her rebellious daughter (Martha Plimpton) and sullen son (Leaf Phoenix), her open arms willing to absorb the myriad shocks that come her way. Taking a far different approach to parenting are Rick Moranis and Harley Kozak, grimly determined to raise a Super-baby daughter, who at 3 is reading Kafka and practicing karate. Meanwhile, Martin's lost younger brother (Tom Hulce) shows up at Robards's house with his half-black son (the result of a fling with a Vegas showgirl) and his latest frantic get-rich-quick scheme to fend off his debtors, forcing Grandma (Helen Shaw) over to Wiest's expanding household, where Plimpton's flaky new teen husband (Keanu Reeves) has moved in.

Part soap opera and part satire, "Parenthood" reaches its comic peaks in its blackest moments (Martin has an uproarious paranoid day dream that his troubled Little Leaguer son will become a Charlie Whitman-style psychopath). Even when the movie is straining for uplift, there's an underlying bleakness: in the never-ending struggle of raising kids, the moments of peace and reconciliation can only be fleeting. But because the comedy is so embattled, the sentiment has an extra punch, as in the lovely, funny kitchen scene when Wiest discovers that her dumb, punk son-in-law is an oddly benign role model for her unhappy son. The scene could be a paradigm for the movie: you laugh, then find you have a lump in your throat.

Howard's touch hasn't been this sure since "Splash"; he's woven this enormous cast into a wonderful ensemble. Touching and muted, Martin shows that even under severe restraints he can still be funny. Steenburgen's comic touch is delicately precise. Robards is in top form as a man who late in life has to face up to his parental responsibilities. Wiest is superb as a mother with surprising residues of strength: she's the movie's richest character, alternately annoying and admirable, and she plays it for all it's worth. The less familiar Kozak, bridling under her husband's humorlessly scientific approach to child rearing, has a wonderfully unaffected charm. Hulce, in an unsympathetic part, shines as he seldom does playing good guys. The youngsters are no less fine, particularly Phoenix and little Jasen Fisher, the anxiety-ridden problem child.

If the late '50s was the "Blame Mom" era in pop culture, the later '80s is eager to reverse the equation. Perhaps "Parenthood" indulges in fashionable sexual politics (or male filmmaker's guilt) by making *all* the mothers such nurturing and resilient figures (while the men tend toward foolish rigidity). Now and then, it stoops to cheap laughs and sappiness (Grandma has some of the phoniest laugh lines). But in a movie so teeming with smart observation and well-earned emotion, the lapses seem negligible. Let's hope the bittersweet pleasures of "Parenthood" don't get lost amid the more primal screams of summer.

TIME, 8/7/89, p. 54, Richard Schickel

Life, alas, is not a football game. It does not provide a goal line we can cross with cheers ringing in our ears, an end zone where we can spike the ball and do a victory dance. What it provides, in dizzying abundance, is one damned thing after another. This vividly expressed thought comes to us courtesy of *Parenthood*'s Jason Robards, who plays Frank, the grandpaterfamilias of a clan he has considerable reason to wish he had not extended quite so extensively back when he was young and frisky.

It's not that the family's troubles are so terrible; it is that they are so terribly typical. Eldest son Gil (Steve Martin) is a perfectionist who wants to be the ideal husband, father, provider and Little League manager that Frank never was. Gil's wise and patient wife (Mary Steenburgen) can deal with the pressure his anxious idealism generates, but his eight-year-old son cannot. The boy's school is insisting that special education is his only hope. His ball team is down on him because he keeps muffing easy pop-ups. Which, of course, makes Gil try even more unnervingly to be Superdad.

Still, Gil's household is a sea of tranquillity compared with those of his siblings. One sister is single-parenting a potential juvenile delinquent. Another is married to a character played by this summer's one-man nerd fest, Rick Moranis (*Ghostbusters II* and *Honey, I Shrunk the Kids*), who has their two-year-old memorizing square roots and reading Kafka. Then there's a brother, who drifts back home looking for a new way to get rich without working, help with his gambling debts and a place to park his illegitimate child, whose name is Cool, whose skin is black and whose mother is about to do a jail term. Didn't Tolstoy say that each unhappy family is funny in its own way?

There is something brave and original about piling up most of our worst parental nightmares in one movie and then daring to make a midsummer comedy out of them. It really shouldn't work, but it does. The movie does not linger too long over any moment or mood, and it permits characters to transcend type, offering a more surprising range of response to events. Martin, for example, gets to do distraction as well as obsession, and Robards is allowed sentiment as well as cynicism. Because Ron Howard, who was responsible for *Cocoon*, has a talent for ensemble hubbub, there may be more good, solid performances in this unlikely context than in any other movie this year.

Maybe *Parenthood* should have toughed out more of its stories or left a couple of them dangling ambiguously. And the baby boomlet at the end, to which all branches of the family contribute, may strike viewers as a little too resounding a triumph of hope over experience. It can be argued, however, that a picture that confronts the ordinary bedevilments of middle-class life as honorably as this one does has earned the right to a little happiness. Besides, it's always better to change a diaper than to curse the darkness.

VILLAGE VOICE, 8/8/89, p. 63, Renee Tajima

I don't know how it is for city people, but if you grew up like I did, *Parenthood* seems a veritable anthem to the suburban family. Four generations of Buckmans live in an anonymous green-lawned town. This ensemble of characters, all effectively played, ranges from a hyperactive toddler, Justin (Zachary Lavoy), to the unsentimental Frank (Jason Robards), a failed patriarch in the tradition of Willy Loman. Frank's clan only looks like the American ideal (two boys, two girls). Gil (Steve Martin) is the painfully responsible eldest son, raising three kids with wife Karen (Mary Steenburgen); there's Helen (Dianne Wiest), a divorced mother; Susan (Harley Kozak), married to consummate fast-track father Nathan (Rick Moranis), who feeds three-year-old Patty a diet of vegetarian food and Kafka; and finally Frank's favorite, Larry (Tom Hulce), a charming scoundrel, who's fathered a son named Cool by a black Vegas showgirl and former star of "Elvis on Ice."

The story's structure, as in '80s television dramas like *Hill Street Blues* or *L.A. Law* , shifts in and out of the four households. *Parenthood* is full of small moments with larger meaning—things we've either seen at home or heard about at a family barbecue. From that realism emerges the same touch of whimsy found in director Ron Howard's *Splash* and *Cocoon*. In those movies, the characters chose to forego the mundane for the unknown, a symbolic death. But *Parenthood* is about regeneration, the struggle to improve life here in Caldor-land, through our children.

This spirit is no better embodied than in Helen's household. Wiest is superbly funny and heartbreaking as the single mother of a pair of typically troubled children. Teenage daughter Julie (Martha Plimpton) and boyfriend Tod (Keanu Reeves) could have been plucked out of any American mini-mall. he's a *Fast Times at Ridgemont High* Sean Penn who's gotten lucky with a babe: the boyfriend-scourge we've all brought home at one time or another that parents tolerate rather than welcome. Plimpton is at that uncertain age between womanhood and girlhood, vulnerability and cruelty. In one screaming match sparked by Wiest's hilarious discovery of a roll of prurient photos that Tod shot "to record our love," Julie screams, "Well, I think someone in this house should be having sex with something that doesn't require batteries." Wiest endows her role with a vulnerability and wry humor that give us a sense of how single mothers keep it together. Even while facing her own loneliness and advancing age (to the prospect of being a grandmother, Wiest exclaims, "I was at Woodstock, for Chrissakes!"), she tries hard to fathom the children's uncertainties about growing up, father or not.

Gil's family is more functional, almost by decree: Gil consciously molds himself as the antithesis of his own neglectful father. Here Martin, a comedian who has the capacity to zoom out of control, is less *Three Amigos* and more *Roxanne*—believably funny, like the dad on the block who always makes you laugh. Gil and Karen's current worry is Kevin, the oldest child (with an oldest-child complex), who seems to have a brow permanently knitted in despair. Howard handles the relationship beautifully, grounding Gil's hopes and fears in Kevin's Little League career. This is where a father first sees his kid in sometimes painful comparison to other children. Gil reverts to a fantasy life to play out his anxieties. In parallel scenes, he first imagines Kevin's college graduation, where the now-confident young valedictorian honors his dad. But in another vision, the grown Kevin, never having resolved his childhood conflicts, is a mad sniper ensconced in a college bell tower.

It won't be difficult to identify with any point in the configuration of relationships and personalities in *Parenthood*. Only in the yuppie extremes of Moranis's Nathan—who's raising his toddler by a book that must have been cowritten by Michael Milken and Bernie Siegel—does the comedy get strained: His is a one-joke family. Otherwise, *Parenthood* is a tribute to the director's skill at expressing middle-class existence without the angst of a Cheever or the preciousness of a Spielberg.

Also reviewed in:
NEW YORK TIMES, 8/2/89, p. C15, Stephen Holden
NEW YORKER, 8/7/89, p. 75, Terrence Rafferty
VARIETY, 8/2–8/89, p. 18
WASHINGTON POST, 8/2/89, p. D1, Rita Kempley

PARENTS

A Vestron Pictures release in association with Great American Films, Limited Partnership. *Executive Producer:* Mitchell Cannold and Steven Reuther. *Producer:* Bonnie Palef. *Director:* Bob Balaban. *Screenplay:* Christopher Hawthorne. *Director of Photography:* Ernest Day and Robin Vidgeon. *Editor:* Bill Pankow. *Music:* Jonathan Elias. *Music Editor:* Thomas Drescher. *Sound:* Douglas Thane Stewart. *Sound Editor:* Skip Lievsay. *Art Director:* Andris Hausmanis. *Set Decorator:* Michael Harris. *Set Dresser:* Michael Richard. *Special Effects:* Gord Smith. *Costumes:* Arthur Rowsell. *Make-up:* Linda Gill. *Stunt Coordinator:* Rick Forsyth. *Running Time:* 83 minutes. *MPAA Rating:* R.

CAST: Randy Quaid (Nick Laemle); Mary Beth Hurt (Lily Laemle); Sandy Dennis (Millie Dew); Bryan Madorsky (Michael Laemle); Juno Mills-Cockell (Sheila Zellner); Kathryn Grody (Miss Baxter); Deborah Rush (Mrs. Zellner); Graham Jarvis (Mr. Zellner); Helen Carscallen (Grandmother); Warren Van Evera (Grandfather); Wayne Robson (Lab Attendant); Uriel Byfield (Little Boy); Mariah Balaban (Little Girl); Larry Palef (Announcer).

FILMS IN REVIEW, 2/89, p. 105, Michael Buckley

Parents, the first feature directed by actor Bob Balaban, is a cerebral horror film that well may turn viewers into vegetarians.

Set in the 1950s, Christopher Hawthorne's screenplay presents a typical suburban family—Dad (Randy Quaid), Mom (Mary Beth Hurt), and Junior (Bryan Madorsky)—who move into a new community. While *Hit Parade* tunes play in the background, Dad practices golf, Mom decorates cakes, and Junior suffers from nightmares. At school, he draws a picture of his family that disturbs the teacher (Katherine Grody) and the social worker (Sandy Dennis). The boy also meets a new girl in town (Juno Mills-Cockell), who claims that she's from the moon. What bothers the lad the most, however, is the main course at dinner. "What are we eating?" he asks Mom, who replies, "Leftovers." "Leftover from *what*?" And thereby hangs the tale.

Mostly seen from the youngster's viewpoint, the movie maintains an eerie quality throughout and there are some great images (e.g. the boy, in slow motion, dives into his bed—which becomes an ocean of blood). The pace never slows and Balaban's direction is assured and astute.

The performances are quite good. Randy Quaid is properly mysterious and mysteriously proper. Mary Beth Hurt masterfully portrays the giddy side of gothic and non-pro Bryan Madorsky is completely convincing in his wide-eyed wonder. Looking remarkable like Shelley Winters, Sandy Dennis makes a very nervous counselor and reminds one of Judy Garland's high strung helper in

A Child Is Waiting (1963); both women seem highly unlikely to be able to put a child at ease.

The final confrontation will strike some as too gruesome, but fans of the genre shouldn't be disturbed. *Parents* is far more intelligent than the many lesser schlock horrors that have made fortunes and it deserves some just desserts.

LOS ANGELES TIMES, 1/27/89, Calendar/p. 7, Michael Wilmington

In "Parents" Randy Quaid and Mary Beth Hurt make a perfect pair of all-American '50s gargoyles: the suburban mom and dad from hell.

They play Nick and Lily Laemle, two Indiana suburbanites whose distraught tot (Bryan Madorsky) watches the murderously sunny facade of his home life crumble into bloody madness. The movie crumbles too, into narrative anemia. But the surreally ordinary Quaid and Hurt help keep the facade sunny and murderous, chirpy and loathsome.

They also keep the lawns clipped, the kitchen sparkling, the dining tale bounteously heaped with mysterious leftovers. Everything is shiny, shiny...except at night, when Michael hears sinister chompings and gurglings.

What goes on in the dark? Quaid, immaculately dull, waggling a golf club, has the supercilious smirk of a secretly naughty football coach, the menacingly modulated charm of "Leave It to Beaver's" Ward with a bloody cleaver. Hurt looks a bit like a Celeste Holm-Betty White clone on perky pills. She has stiff skirts that flounce and bounce and the stiffer white smiles of a Frigidaire saleswoman with a body in the freezer.

You don't really need the collection of '50s oldies on the sound track, from "Cherry Pink and Apple Blossom White" to "Moments to Remember," to set the period. These two actors, plus art director Andris Hausmanis and costume designer Arthur Rowsell, nail the '50s to the wall immediately.

Unfortunately, screenwriter Christopher Hawthorne hasn't nailed down anything. He's just flung another high-concept dart into space, one more marketing hook in search of a movie. The concept has promise. These evilly immaculate parents are symbols of the greed and immorality that can lurk beneath a middle-class facade, the cancer cells of the Eisenhower era, the rot beneath the frozen smile. There's also the shaggy corpse of a psychological drama about troubled childhoods buried in here somewhere.

The script makes sense only on its own symbolic level; strip away the symbols and the story becomes scatterbrained. Why hasn't Michael suspected his parents before? Why are they so careless now? Why does the consummate opportunist Nick forbid his son to play with the daughter of his boss? Why does Sandy Dennis' nosy, blowzy social worker march into the Laemle's home and go prowling around upstairs and down? Why is Michael so careless with a telltale stolen scissors?

First-time director Bob Balaban gives "Parents" an attractively flashy surface and voluptuously askew camera angles; it was Balaban who dreamed up the idea of setting it in the late '50s. But "Parents" looks like the work of bright, well-intentioned people who've seen a lot of vacuous, predictable horror movies and become convinced that they could makes a vacuous, predictable horror movie, too—with a sociological point.

Unhappily enough, they've succeeded...completely. Those who prefer their sociological points without vacuous horror movies attached, may walk out famished. "Parents" (MPAA rated R for mature theme and violence) is all leftovers, despite the tasty little tidbits that Quaid and Hurt keep sporadically cooking up: Dad's spotless collars and loopy grin, Mom's brittle Cutex-lacquered claws.

MONTHLY FILM BULLETIN, 6/89, p. 187, Philip Strick

1958. Moving with his parents to their new home in an Indiana town, little Michael Laemle is increasingly aware of the oddity of adults. Dedicated to keeping up appearances, Nick and Lily Laemle are an aggresively fashionable couple, but with a secret passion their son is not yet old enough to understand. Half-asleep one night, Michael interrupts them in an inexplicable embrace, of which he recalls brief disturbing details in the days that follow. They also seem excessively interested in food, which they set before him in copious quantities. At his new school, Michael is befriended by another newcomer, Sheila Zellner, whose claim to be an alien greatly appeals to him; their teacher, Miss Baxter, thinks them both eccentric and becomes alarmed when a picture Michael draws of his home life is heavily crayoned in red. She brings it to the attention of the school psychiatrist, Millie Dew, who interviews Michael, suspecting his growing sexual awareness;

his nightmares, however, are more to do with the kitchen than the bedroom. Puzzled at the vast amounts of red meat that always seem to be available in his home, Michael secretly visits his father's office, a laboratory where the effect of new chemicals is tested on human bodies. He narrowly escapes discovery by hiding under a dissecting trolley while his father works on a corpse. That night, when his parents are asleep, Michael explores the cellar and finds a human leg suspended from a butcher's hook. He tells Miss Dew at school next day, and she rushes back to the house with him; she finds a corpse but before she can leave she is attacked and felled. As Nick and Lily prepare a barbecue of juicy steaks that night, Michael declares war; his father tries to explain that he'll soon get a taste for human flesh, as his mother did, but Michael stabs him with a steak knife. Protecting her son, Lily is accidentally killed, and Nick, staggering after the boy, sets off a gas explosion that burns the house down as Michael gets away. Safe with his doting grandparents, he is settled down at bedtime beside a late-night snack: a glass of milk and a sandwich bursting with succulent red meat.

Full of good things, *Parents* first catches the eye for its wonderful evocation of suburban America in the late 50s, an era of earnest respectability whose styles and fears are preserved and familiar on film through the enormous output of science-fiction "quickies" for which 1958 was a peak year, and equally hasty (and, as a result, revealing) rock 'n' roll movies of the time. Both genres, as we can interpret them now, signalled a growing turbulence beneath the brittle American façade in that ominous interlude when the dimly anticipated traumas of the 60s seemed to be kept at bay solely by golf clubs, resolute hair styles and Perry Como. Whether under threat from alien invaders or, even worse, from over-heated teenagers, consumerism defended itself by the strenuous championing of decency and decorum, a mood of militant goodwill which *Parents* captures perfectly for its glossy surface (even the friendly small-town school-crossing attendant gets a cosy wave as the Laemle family drive to their new home). Posing its characters like the folksiest of Rockwell images against a pristine array of domestic gadgets, soap powders, and television-commercial furniture, the film draws deliberately and accurately from the bold, emblematic colours of *Invaders from Mars* at one end of the spectrum and *The Girl Can't Help It* at the other to tell a matchingly subversive tale of unreliable adulthood, its masks, its secrets, its sudden uncontrollable hungers.

Although the soundtrack only strays musically as far as Big Bopper and the ruder notes of Perez Prado (the melancholy of Orbison would have inflicted too dark a mood in this context), *Parents* is also an exploration on the margins of *Blue Velvet* territory, where dreams form a precarious bridge between people as they wish to appear and as they really are. On the evidence of his first feature, however, Bob Balaban's humour is less baleful than that of Paul Bartel, whose *Eating Raoul* was surely a point of stimulus. The horror-film aspects of *Parents* are even rather conventional, apart from a striking early nightmare when the boy hurls himself on to his bed and promptly sinks into a tide of blood. The scene of a victim being knifed through the slats of a cupboard door borrows from *Halloween*, and the venture into the cellar where a human leg hangs from a hook is an echo, as Balaban acknowledges, of *The Texas Chain Saw Massacre*. While hardly allowing the attention to wander, these macabre events are actually less interesting than the many details which would be mere trivia were it not for the impressive visual style that Balaban has adopted in order to reveal them.

The boy's parents lean over him (and us) in crushing, slightly distorted close-up, their bland reassurance (the father favours the Gatsby-esque term "sport", with all its uneasy associations) emerging like pronouncements of dire warning. A simple shot of the boy in foreground and the adults apparently miles away at just the other end of the room with their jigsaw defines with spectacular precision his many forms of isolation, while innocent moments at the barbecue with its mountain of smoking offal, or the kitchen with its containers of minced meat and glutinous mixed grill, need only a bass tone for accompaniment (the sounds recall the unnerving compositions of Lynch's collaborator, Alan Splet) to convey a gut-wrenching distaste. There is a beautiful moment when the boy arrives home unexpectedly early from school and his parents stand looking at him as if stunned, wine glasses abstractedly in their grasp, the whole tableau frozen with a collective and inexplicable guilt. More flashily, the discovery of a corpse at the cellar window (unclear why it's there, but no matter) prompts the shrieking retreat of the camera at high speed through the house and up the chimney to the roof in time to see an ominous car pulling into the drive.

Another attraction of *Parents* is its sly transition from coming-of-age comedy, a *Burning Secret* filmed in the manner of John Waters, to the revelation that a quite different appetite is what motivates the grown-ups. Glimpsed and seemingly misunderstood in orgiastic embrace by their sleepy son (who has been warned: "The only time you get nightmares is when you take your pyjamas off"), the couple turn out to have been misunderstood by *us* when later recollections of the scene confirm that they were in fact rolling in the family's next meal. The film avoids sharp focus on the reasons for this indulgence, which adds to the fun and, in a sense, to the child's valid perplexity at the parasitical humours of adult existence.

While evidently not intended as urban vampires of the *Near Dark* breed, the husband and wife seem able to enjoy gargantuan bouts of cannibalism without undue strain (he's chunky, but she's as thin as a rake). This would substantiate some gentle hints of his alien origin were it not for the delightful concluding illustration of an all-American-boy upbringing. Another suggestion, linked with the husband's research work at a chemicals factory ("defoliants are a growth industry", he says proudly, reducing a tankful of plants to a rotten pulp), is that their toxic diet is gradually eroding their sanity. This vagueness possibly leaves the plot a touch undernourished, but the performances are so good (Balaban's own experience as an actor seems to have drawn the best out of his cast, particularly from Sandy Dennis as a self-parodying weirdo) that the result is completely refreshing.

NEW YORK, 2/13/89, p. 79, David Denby

In Bob Balaban's first feature film as director, *Parents,* a little boy (Bryan Madorsky) can't eat the food his mom lays out before him—cooked meats, even at breakfast, and much larger than bacon strips, too. At night, wandering into the living room, he sees his parents rolling around on the floor with blood on their jaws. But then, when his mother comes into his room, the blood has become merely lipstick, smeared in passion. *Parents* is an example of the art-horror film. Psychology and dreamy ambiguity and even a patina of satire surround a core of grisly terror. The movie is set in the fifties and decorated in pastel plastics, yet the satire of the fifties blandness doesn't quite mesh with the theme of parental cannibalism. I wish the movie were funnier and that Sandy Dennis, who can't walk across a room without tripping, were not locked in a closet and menaced with knives. Randy Quaid (as the daddy) isn't ambiguous enough for art horror—he seems vicious from the opening shot. But Mary Beth Hurt, her hair ironed in a flat wave, is unnervingly perky as Mom. A boy could follow her to hell itself.

NEW YORK POST, 1/27/89, p. 27, David Edelstein

In the '80s, filmmakers have crystallized our view of the '50s as the antiseptic decade—the Clean Decade—in which rows of identical split-levels went up, designs were sparkling and futuristic, and everything tasted better out of a can. The satiric horror movie "Parents" lingers over this vision; queasily funny and dreamlike, it's rooted in a child's tormented response to a life of conformity and repression.

Specifically, young Michael (Bryan Madorsky) becomes convinced that his immaculately chipper parents are monsters; that they are killing, cooking and eating people; and that they want him to eat people, too.

The film, written by Christopher Hawthorne and directed by Bob Balaban, is a sort of tidy, kindergarten version of "Blue Velvet," with hints of "Invaders From Mars," "The Stepfather" and David Cronenberg's "They Came From Within," It's a plodding, one-joke movie, but the joke is layered and unnerving, and Balaban serves up some squirm-inducing images.

From the start, Michael is profoundly alienated from his oppressively hearty father (Randy Quaid) and brittle, chirpy mother (Mary Beth Hurt). Dad, a defoliant expert at a company called Toxico, builds the future by poisoning the planet; Mom, in her spotless kitchen, massages bloody meat and wet, shiny organs. In close-up. To the tune of cheerful '50s pop songs.

The chasm between parents and child widens when the nightmare-riddled Michael comes upon them having sex—although that isn't necessarily what he thinks they're doing. In the clinch, their faces are smeared with either lipstick or blood, and in the boy's mind—where fantasy and reality are meshed and interwoven—it's certainly the latter.

Are the parents cannibals? I ain't tellin', but in a sense the question is irrelevant—it's too literal-minded. "Parents" blooms from the brain of a child, a brain that turns wrenching, irresolveable conflicts into metaphors. In a culture in which repression rules—in which everything is "de-bodyized" (as Cronenberg might put it)—sex and flesh and the eating of flesh get all swirled together.

The tone is eerily flat and poker-faced—surreal but never cartoonish; the audience laughs more out of nervousness than anything else. The sight of a boy piping "I'm home!" plays differently when in place of the Cleaver household is a cavernous white space webbed with shadows and strewn with blue plastic lamps and amoeba tables. Actual cleavers too.

Balaban makes good use of close-ups, as if scrutinizing the parents' faces for signs of life. But there are few chinks in their blandness, few links between their sunny masks and inner hunger.

As the mother, Hurt wears her hair shellacked to one side, keeps a tiny smile on her face and speaks in an airy sing-song. This woman treats emotions the way '50s moms treated vegetables (keep them canned and in the cupboard); yet underneath her mask—an insane placidity—Hurt manages to suggest real love and conviction, the belief that anything messy is best left unsaid. It's a superb turn.

Balaban, an actor, gets consistently terrific performances. Randy Quaid makes the father a malevolent jack-o'-lantern, hissing awful stories ("When little boys tell lies, their jaws starts to tighten and their lips get stuck together permanently") and smiling as he slices up corpses in his lab. (Note to sound crew: great squishy scalpel noises.) Quaid is a dad who seems frighteningly close to giving up on his reclusive son—tossing the kid away and starting all over again.

As Michael, Madorsky is a find. He's one of those kids with big, round eyes and huge ears—picturesquely hypersensitive. But what's special is his delicate, stammering intelligence; his lines really sound as if he's thinking them up.

Madorsky has lovely scenes with Juno Mills-Cockell as a tall girl in his class who says she's from the moon, and who attempts to seduce Michael (or what passes for it) by reclining in his parents' meat locker and splashing his naked chest with red wine. As Bill Murray put it in "Tootsie," "We're getting into a weird area here."

Maybe best of all is Sandy Dennis as Miss Dew, the socialworker assigned to Michael's case. Fidgety and bloated—a real mess—Dennis makes the woman so poetically discombobulated that we know just what Michael means when he says that she doesn't belong in the world of grownups.

With all these nifty ingredients, it's a shame that "Parents" doesn't have more impact. Although brief (83 minutes), it's a bit monotonous, and it could use another twist, a change of gears. Maybe the problem is that it's not quite irrational enough—that it's as well-groomed as the surface of the culture it depicts. But enough complaining: Why roast this savory morsel any further; "Parents" gives you lots to chew on. (Oh, yuck.)

NEWSDAY, 1/27/89, Part III/p. 7, Mike McGrady

Sometimes, this job can be simplicity itself. With some movies, such as this new one, "Parents," it requires not so much the preparation of a lengthy analysis as the posting of a simple warning. *Warning: Avoid "Parents" at all cost.*

If, through some miscalculation, you should find yourself in a theater showing "Parents," don't blame yourself. Every effort is being made to keep you from knowing what this film is like and what it's about.

Warning: Don't be taken in by the advertising and promotion that suggest "Parents" is a cute little spoof of the 1950s—"Golf is the sport of the day and every young mother is frantically decorating her new split-level with the sleek space-aged furniture of the atomic age," reads the early ads.

Warning: Don't be misled by lofty self-serving statements from character actor and first-time director Bob Balaban, who claims his film is exploring such serious themes as, "How hard it is to be a child, particularly when you realize that your parents are not perfect, how a veneer of politeness can be used to disguise any problems a family may have."

Warning: Don't be lured by a cast topped by the talented Randy Quaid and Mary Beth Hurt as the picture-perfect suburban couple. And don't be seduced into the theater if you hear about the excellent and quirky little performance by Sandy Dennis as the school psychologist.

Warning: Finally, if you' re in the movie theater, don't be fooled by the mildness of the film's beginnings. Get up and leave at once. Otherwise you may be suckered into thinking you're watching an innocuous satire of the Eisenhower-era mentality. Quaid—hubby, golfer, amateur wine maven—works as a chemist specializing in the promising new field of defoliation at the nearby Toxico plant. Perky, peppy Mary Beth Hurt in her uplift bra and stiletto heels is all enthusiasm as she moves her little family into a brand-new suburban split-level complete with fake stone walls, fake fireplaces, palette-shaped cocktail tables, colorful throw pillows.

New house," she says to her little boy (Bryan Madorsky). "New friends. Oh, Michael, things are really going to change for you now that we're here. We'll have more time to spend together."

The film's backdrop—cars, songs, innocence—provoke smiles, nostalgia, a feeling of warmth. *Warning*: Get out now, while you still can. The housewife, surrounded by a magazine-inspired kitchen, makes a large production number out of every new meat loaf. Only the boy seems unhappy with a diet composed exclusively of leftovers.

"We've had leftovers every night since we got here," he complains. "I'd like to know what they're leftovers from."

"From leftovers-to-be," Quaid explains.

Hmmmmm, not exactly. You see, Quaid spends an inordinate amount of time in Toxico's "Division of Human Testing" studying corpses, cutting them up and occasionally taking his work home with him. The school psychologist (Sandy Dennis) doesn't believe the boy's reports and follows him home one day where she duly notes a large rat, a human corpse and a maniac trying to kill her with a baseball bat.

Final Warning: At this point, close your eyes. The film becomes pure bucket-o'-blood cinema—intrafamilial stabbings, human limbs hanging from meathooks, additional corpses and rats, unkillable villains and rooms filled with blood.

Well, never say you weren't warned.

NEWSWEEK, 2/13/89, p. 79, David Ansen

[*Parents* was reviewed jointly with *Three Fugitives*; see Ansen's review of that film.]

VILLAGE VOICE, 2/7/89, p. 57, Katherine Dieckmann

Newspaper ads for *Parents* sport a Ken Russell blurb declaring "Takes over where *Blue Velvet* left off." Whoa, Nelly. If anything, *Parents*'s vintage '50s decors and sexual hysteria precede *Velvet*'s unsettling time warp—but there *is* a creepy surrealism at play in this flawed, but wickedly smart, black comedy. Too bad it falls to pieces (so to speak) in its literal-minded, effects-ridden final half hour.

Meet the Laemle family. They've just moved into a spanking new, sitcom-ready house. There's Dad (Randy Quaid, meshing stolid middle-agedom and latent insanity), who works as a researcher for a chemical corporation called Toxico. Mom (Mary Beth Hurt) is Donna Reed-ready with her tight blond coif, sleeveless blouses, and commitment to the kitchen. This couple would be perfectly happy in their fussy kitschscape were it not for their sober, wide-eyed son, Michael (Bryan Madorsky). He picks at dinner, it afraid of the dark, and has vile nightmares involving a lot of blood (and, sadly for such a pleasurable art-directed movie, loads of slo-mo and grainy black and white). When asked to draw a portrait of his family in his "very own" workbook at school, little Michael does an Art Brut number with heavy red crayon slashes.

So his teacher calls in the school shrink, Miss Millie Dew (a puffy, slovenly, chain-smoking, scene-stealing Sandy Dennis), to unravel the enigma of the child's tortured subconscious. But the clues have already been laid out in the editing and the heavily arty, but nonetheless knockout, cinematography by Ernest Day and Robin Vidgeon. With a postcard mise-en-scène, wild panoply of camera angles, exaggerated point-of-view shots, and propensity for objects looming in the front of the frame, *Parents* makes good on Mr. Laemle's prebedtime chiding to Michael: "You can be yourself in the dark," he grins, tapping his temple. So can we. The movie's rich visuals work on our brain synapses to link up sex, repression, bourgeois perfectionism, and, above all, the vast consumption of red meat among Americans in the '50s. Details are inspired, from the period food cans and products, to the careful attention to dinner prep (chopping and mincing), to the scene where Michael's mom offhandedly chews on her son's fingernail just before she tucks him in for the night.

Despite this stacking up of information, midway through *Parents* I had no real idea where it was going (though word of mouth and reviews mean that most audiences will). That excites me.

But screenwriter Christopher Hawthorne, who has a keen ear for stereotypical '50s diction and deadpan dialogue, is working with a no-win premise. Eventually, the sparkle and shine of the Laemles' domestic life have to fully reveal its fissures, its seamy underside (hence the *Velvet* parallel), and that's when the movie becomes a bloody mess. The *Eating Raoul* denouement is better left a suggestion than a spelled-out resolution. It forces Balaban (a character actor who's been in *Midnight Cowbay*, *Catch-22*, *Close Encounters of the Third Kind*, *Absence of Malice*, and *Prince of the City*, and is directing for the first time here) to go for the worst kind of psycho-slasher tropes to drive home the setup—which turns out to be nothing less than a cannibalistic implosion of the nuclear family. Faulty as it is, however, *Parents* offers sociological proof of why '50s kids turned into '60s vegetarians. There's no more convincing connection than this movie between keeping up with the Joneses, perverse practives hidden beneath the sheets, and meat loaf.

Also reviewed in:
NATION, 2/13/89, p. 206, Stuart Klawans
NEW YORK TIMES, 1/27/89, p. C10, Caryn James
NEW YORKER, 3/6/89, P. 95, Pauline Kael
VARIETY, 1/25–31/89, p. 14
WASHINGTON POST, 3/17/89, p. D1, Hal Hinson
WASHINGTON POST, 3/17/89, Weekend/p. 37, Desson Howe

PARTY LINE

An SVS release of a Westwood production. *Producer:* Tom Byrnes, Kurt Anderson, and William Webb. *Director:* William Webb. *Screenplay:* Richard Brandes. *Based on a story by:* Tom Byrnes. *Director of Photography:* John Huneck. *Editor:* Paul Koval. *Music:* Sam Winans. *Sound:* Glen Berkovitz. *Art Director:* Mark Simon. *Stunt Coordinator:* Jeff Smolek. *Running time:* 91 minutes. *MPAA Rating:* R.

CAST: Richard Hatch (Dan); Shawn Weatherly (Stacy); Leif Garrett (Seth); Greta Blackburn (Angelina); Richard Roundtree (Capt. Barnes); James O'Sullivan (Henry); Terrence McGovern (Simmons); Shelli Place (Mrs. Simmons); Tara Hutchins (Alice); Marty Dudek (Butch).

NEW YORK POST, 2/11/89, p. 19, Jami Bernard

This tepid slasher thriller attempts to cash in on the "party line" phenomenon, that safe-sex way for lonely yuppies to "meet" people without leaving the reach of their cellular phones.

In "Party Line," Leif Garrett plays a wealthy psycho killer who chats up girls on the party line, meets them, and slashes their throats. Likewise, his sexy sister (Greta Blackburn) brings home guys for baby brother to kill.

This role ought to relieve Garrett of the heavy mantle of teen idol. He dresses in his dead mother's wedding gown and gets all sniffly when his sister calls him a mama's boy. He plays lugubrious dirges on the piano while Sis improves her pecs on the Nautilus.

Only when the corpses are stacked so high at the local disco that it's becoming a fire hazard does the investigating team of a beautiful deputy district attorney (Shawn Weatherly) and an unconventional cop (Richard Hatch) begin to get cracking.

Before you can say, "Sorry, your call cannot be completed as dialed," the beautiful deputy DA is posing as a party-line girl to trap the suspect. Will her line go dead? Or worse, will she be rescued by her partner and spend the rest of her days running up phone bills?

Some gratuitous makeout scenes and a minor subplot involving a curious baby-sitter make this about as exciting as dialing for the correct time.

Also reviewed in:
VARIETY, 11/2/88, p. 23

PATTES BLANCHES

An Interama release of a Majestic Film production. *Director:* Jean Grémillon. *Screenplay (French with English subtitles):* Jean Anouilh and Jean Bernard-Luc. *Director of Photography:* Philippe Agostini. *Editor:* Louisette Hautecoeur. *Music:* Elsa Barraine. *Set Designer:* Léon Barsacq. *Running time:* 92 minutes. *MPAA Rating:* Not Rated.

CAST: Suzy Delair (Odette); Arlette Thomas (Mimi); Fernand Ledoux (Jock Le Guen); Paul Bernard (Julien de Keriadec); Louise Sylvie (Maurice's Mother); Michel Bouquet (Maurice); Betty Daussmond (Julien's Aunt); Edmond Beauchamp (Policeman); Geneviève Morel (Marguerite).

NEW YORK POST, 5/26/89, p. 37, David Edelstein

Commercially unreleased in this country, the 1949 French film "Pattes Blanches" ("White Shanks") is one of those rich, chewy melodramas in which each character burns with some fierce hidden objective and lust forces all buried resentments to the surface—resentments based on class, money or sexual privilege. People act recklessly, with tunnel vision and tumultuous results.

Playing at the Public Theater, "Pattes Blanches" is one of the most entertaining pictures in town—a find. Directed by Jean Grémillon (from a play by Jean Anouilh), it's a marvel of compression, a thing of mounting horror.

Set in a fishing village on the coast of France, the film takes its title from a pale aristocrat, Julien de Keriadec (Paul Bernard) who lives in a chateau by the cliffs.

He's called "White Shanks" by the local children because of his leggings, which are worn outside his trousers to signal his impoverishment: Apart from his manor and its furnishings, he lives "like a savage." His only defender is Mimi (Arlette Thomas), the hunchbacked young servant of the local inn, who sees in Julien a figure of romance and mystery.

The people of the village resent Julien through no fault of his. It was his father they remember, a man of unbridled lust who'd pounce on almost every woman he met, and who had the money to get away with it. Among the bastards left in his wake is Julien's half-brother Maurice (Michel Bouquet), a gaunt brooding little rat whom Julien threw out of the chateau when his father died.

Now Maurice lives to destroy his half-brother, and in "Pattes Blanches," he gets his chance—but by accident, not design. The innkeeper, Jock (Fernand Ledoux) imports a curvy mistress, Odette (Suzy Delair), from the city, and Maurice is instantly enthralled.

The plush Odette, who had worked as a seamstress for Jock's rich aunt, is repulsed by the middle-aged fisherman and innkeeper, but she desperately craves those silk dresses and pearl necklaces he lavishes on her. When Mimi returns from the chateau with a silken gift from Julien, Odette follows her back the next day and, merely to prove her superiority to the hunchback, seduces the pale, reticent aristocrat.

Then she allows herself to be seduced by—and to fall in love with—Maurice, who sees in her the instrument of his half-brother's undoing.

On screen, these machinations play out easily, naturally, with little confusion: every action has an inexplicable logic. And underneath the movie's soap-opera plotting is a mind haunted by unresolvable issues: how great wealth and the unnatural power it bestows can warp human impulses; how injustices committed generations earlier can explode into violence in the present.

"Pattes Blanches" develops some of the power of a Hardy novel or an Ibsen drama—what keeps it out of that league is that its characters have less stature. But Grémillon's ominous, deepfocus compositions are marvelously suggestive; without relying on close-ups, he ushers you totally into his characters' minds.

The film peaks during the wedding of Odette and Jock, when Maurice, seething with jealousy, creeps to a window and summons the bride to her destiny. Odette wants no more part of his plot against Julien, but nothing can stop Maurice now. There's an eerie, almost subliminal shot of the twisted brother's breath misting up the window, and the editing is startling: It builds up speed as if plugged into Maurice's heartbeat.

The climax on the moor is a bit abrupt and the denouement confusing, but no resolution could really do this story justice. The pleasure (and pain) of "Pattes Blanches" is in watching its ingredients come inexorably to a boil, and from feeling not only that its characters are acting stupidly but that we—in their place—would act exactly the same way.

VILLAGE VOICE, 5/30/89, p. 64, Julie Phillips

It's always dark in the little fishing village in *Pattes Blanches*, a starkly lit, expressionistic, Transylvanian night where the moon glints harshly on the sea and the cliffs were just made to have people thrown over them. Director Jean Grémillon, working from a script by Jean Anouilh, trowels on the plot convolutions and the extravagant gestures of high soap opera: the cheap mistress, the aging cuckold, jealousy, lust, mother love, the voyeuristic stare of the disinherited son. Made in postwar France (1949), *Pattes Blanches* is a kind of extrastrength Marxist Gothic, a stern lesson in the econmics of fornication.

In this little Breton village live haves and have-nots. Named for the gaiters that make him look half mummified or paraplegic, Pattes Blanches (Paul Bernard) is the son of the old count: He has a title and a château, but no money and no sex. Children throw rocks at him. Maurice (Michel Bouquet) is Pattes Blanches's handsome, consumptive, illegitimate half-brother: part Heathcliff, part Iago, part Norman Bates, he wears torn shirts and has only sex. (Maurice loves his mother; Pattes Blanches has a fetish about his dead mother's bed.) Jock (Fernand Ledoux), the innkepper and fish dealer, has no sex and not much hair, but he's got all the money. Mimi (Arlette Thomas), Jock's hunchbacked servant, is pure of heart and has nothing.

When Jock goes to town for his aunt's funeral and brings back her gold-digging servant, Odette (Suzy Delair), as his new mistress, he upsets the town's fragile system of exchange. She's got hard currency, sex, more sex than anyone knows what to do with; in return, she demands luxuries—a new dress, a bathtub, a piano—that the town can barely supply. (When she complains that Jock smells of fish, he rips the pendant off her neck and yells, "Where do you think this came from?") Impatient and greedy, she outflanks the humble Mimi to seduce Pattes Blanches, and is seduced in turn by Maurice, who sees in her the instrument of his revenge. On the day of the wedding—the only scene in the whole movie, just about, that was filmed in broad daylight—Maurice glares down from the high cliffs, cursing the entire happy town. That night, as the wedding guests dance and polka music plays, the four lovers search frantically for each other across the moor, in an elegantly choreographed fit of sexual jealousy that ends with a brief, exquisite murder.

A not wholly unhappy resolution invokes the Law and the redemptive power of True Love; it's not very believable. The ending is tacked-on satisfaction in the *Fatal Attraction* mode: The film has an internal logic that is resistant to the usual justice and morality. Grémillon gives a surprisingly ambiguous cast to his overwrought material; set designer Léon Barsacq's spare, whitewashed, low-ceilinged village helps suggest the moral and economic poverty that underlies the lurid plot mechanics.

Almost unknown here, Grémillon is regarded in France as a near equal of Jean Renoir and René Clair. He began his career making silent documentaries, with titles like "The Electrification of the Paris-Vierzon Line" and "The Manufacture of Light Bulbs"; in the '30s, he moved on to features and began making the noir melodramas that were considered his best work. Never released theatrically in the U.A., *Pattes Blanches* has acquired cult status in France in recent years. It's not hard to see why: With its combination of high-minded sentiment, class consciousness, and sleazy pleasure, it delivers a wicked satisfaction.

Also reviewed in:
NEW YORK TIMES, 5/26/89, p. C10, Stephen Holden
VARIETY, 9/28/89, p. 15

PEDDLER, THE

An Arts Bureau of the Organization for the Propagation of Islamic Thought production. *Director:* Mohsen Makhmalbaf. *Screenplay (Persian with English subtitles):* Mohsen Makhmalbaf. *First episode adapted from a story by:* Alberto Moravia. *Director of Photography:* Homayun Payvar (first episode), Mehrdad Fakhimi (second episode), and Ali R. Zarindast (third episode). *Music:* Majid Antezami. *Running time:* 95 minutes. *MPAA Rating:* Not Rated.

WITH: Zohreh Saramadi, Esmail Saramadian, Behzad Behzadpour, Faridkashan Fallah, Morteza Zarrabi.

LOS ANGELES TIMES, 3/28/90, Calendar/p. 3, Kevin Thomas

"The Peddler" takes its title from the the the final vignette in this dynamic, earthy, three-part film, which in its concerns and gritty style resembles the films of Italian Neo-Realism. Part I in fact is a pitch-dark satire in the manner of the most macabre of Italian filmmakers, Marco Fereri, and concerns a couple living in a Tehran shantytown who have four severely crippled children, and not realizing that their new baby is most likely normal, struggle mightily to avoid keeping it.

Even more bizarre is the second episode, which plays like a baroque homage to "Psycho" with its weird mother-and-son relationship. The third part deals with the paranoia a petty crook experiences in regard to a ring of smugglers. As in "Salaam Bombay!," you can all but smell the stench of noisy, congested street life; the director's images are dense and heady, and his exuberance overwhelms.

NEWSDAY, 3/25/89, Part II/p. 17, Mike McGrady

"The Peddler," one of the surprise hits of this year's New Directors/New Films series at the Museum of Modern Art, is an unlikely film from an unlikely source. It's actually three short films—call it "Teheran Stories" and you won't be far off—directed by Mohsen Makhmalbaf, one of the leading moviemakers in modern Iran.

But perhaps the phrase "modern Iran" is an oxymoron, if we are to believe the evidence offered in "The Peddler," the first Irani movie ever invited to participate in the New Director/New Films series and one of the few modern Irani movies to be seen over here.

Of course, one of the great rewards of New Directors/New Films is the fact that we are allowed glimpses of many societies. This year's Soviet films, for example, point up an interesting array of problems—the growth of nihilism, increasing bureaucracy and corruption, the spread of an aimless rock-and-roll culture. Offerings from France point up a societal angst stretching from middle-class adults to urban teenagers who will seem remarkably familiar to us.

If one were to measure Iran on the basis of "The Peddler," one would conclude that the country is impoverished, ugly, brutal, violent. But first I should begin by explaining "The Peddler" is not intended to be a critical picture (by now we can all appreciate why criticism is not exactly a flourishing trade in Iran). Moviemaker Makhmalbaf, 37, a militant who served five years in prison for battling the Shah's police, was one of the founders of the Organization for the Propagation of Islamic Thought, the group that produced this film among others.

Although his intent is not to offer a critical picture of the society, that is the inevitable result. His aim is to show man in his three stages of existence—birth, life and death. However, a summary of each segment will show why realism in Iran can easily be taken for criticism.

In the first short film, a slum-dwelling family in Teheran is awaiting the birth of a new baby. Since the other children in the family are all deformed, crippled and malnourished, the parents intend to abandon the baby, thus giving her a better shot at life. Along with the horror of their situation, a touch of humor. ("Why did you have to marry your cousin?" the welfare nurse asks. "Whose cousin should I have married then? he replies.)

The second short film deals with a young man going insane as he cares for his ancient mother while trying to survive on inadequate welfare checks. The third film opens at the marketplace with the slitting of a sheep's throat followed by slow bleeding and the spasms of the animal in its death throes. Then it gets...rough. A peddler, witness to a murder, is taken for a ride by gangsters; along the way he dies a thousand imaginary deaths before facing the real one.

The Iran that emerges from the films is a country of ugliness unrelieved, of harrowing poverty, of enormous cruelty. The fact that the films are technically superb, both honest and imaginative, does not make them any easier to watch.

VILLAGE VOICE, 3/28/89, p. 64, Elliott Stein

This is a genuine oddity, all the odder for having been produced under an authoritarian regime. Its individual characters are idiots, retards, and psychos; when they form groups, these are generally mindless vigilantes or lynch mobs. Director Mohsen Makhmalbaf, who has made eight films, tells three tales here: a poverty-stricken couple, inbred cousins whose children are all cripples, abandons a newborn daughter; an "effeminate," crazed man attempts to get his mother's corpse to take a shit; and a smuggler informant is brutally killed. Much of *The Peddler* is bargain-basement Buñuel, although it is marked by a wildly undisciplined directorial style of some interest.

Also reviewed in:
NEW YORK TIMES, 3/26/89, p. 45, Janet Maslin
VARIETY, 11/30/88, p. 16

PEKING OPERA BLUES

A Gordon's Films International release of a Cinema City production. *Executive Producer:* Claudie Chung. *Producer:* Tsui Hark. *Director:* Tsui Hark. *Screenplay (Cantonese with English subtitles):* To Kwok Wai. *Director of Photography:* Poon Hung Seng. *Editor:* David Wu. *Music:* James Wong. *Art Director:* Vincent Wai, Ho Kim Sing, and Leung Chi Hing. *Costumes:* Ng Po Ling. *Running time:* 104 minutes. *MPAA Rating:* Not Rated.

CAST: Lin Ching Hsia (Tso Wan); Sally Yeh (Pak Neil); Cherie Chung (Sheung Hung); Mark Cheng (Ling Pak Hoi).

NEW YORK, 2/6/89, p. 66, David Denby

Year after year, the Film Forum brilliantly goes about its job of programming new documentaries, new animation, premieres of American, European, and Asian features, as well as the most interesting revivals in the city. I don't get to the elegant twin theater on Watts Street nearly as often as I want to, but whenever I go, I see something good—most recently the astounding *Peking Opera Blues.*

Peking Opera Blues, made in 1986, has already received critical support (during earlier showings at the Asia Society) from J. Hoberman of the *Voice* and David Edelstein of the *Post* and should receive more. In addition to its two weeks at the Film Forum, the movie played in Chinatown, which is great for Chinatown, a loss for everyone else. Really, I don't see why some enterprising theater on the arthouse circuit doesn't book the movie and built it into a specialty event. It could become the movie sensation of the season.

The first thing to be said about the teeming Hong Kong school of filmmaking—of which this movie, from most accounts, is the masterpiece—is that the directors and the audience have a completely different idea about action than we do. Action, in Hong Kong, has nothing to do with realism; action is rhythm and color—exuberant shenanigans, raised to the highest degree of excitment. It's as if the filmmakers had decided, "The cinema is all illusion anyway, so why not make it as spectacular and crazy as possible?" People die in Hong Kong movies, but no one gets hurt or suffers—the escapism is "pure." Tsui Hark, the Vietnamese-born, Texas-educated director of *Peking Opera Blues*, is a whirling master of pop filmmaking. In the Indiana Jones series, Steven Spielberg sends Indy up against rolling boulders, a savage helicopter propeller, snakes, a cliffside. One man tries to avoid a surging mass of perils. But Tsui Hark sends multiple bodies flying through the air in perfect formation; he causes entire roomfuls of thugs to duck or jump in unison; he choreographs tumultuous fights in the midst or around the sides of people performing onstage. Simultaneity is the principle of his action. He orchestrates the most outrageous stunts, one after another, and his rushing, indefatigable inventiveness is riotous. In Hong Kong movies, action drives out the other elements of filmmaking. Unhindered by any obligation to realism or character, action becomes extravagant, even decorative, and turns, inevitably, into comedy.

The movie is set in Peking in 1913, a chaotic time just after the fall of the imperial dynasty and the establishment of the republic, and it features no fewer than *three* heroines—beautiful young girls fighting for liberation. One, the daughter of a warlord, is a stern revolutionary; the second wants to perform in the all-male Peking Opera, even though her father, the head of the company, won't break tradition and allow a woman onstage; the third, a servant, is a greedy little opportunist and thief. The hustling ambition of these three doll-dynamos drives a plot that offers every kind of scramble, rout, escape, and confrontation as well as a surprising amount of good-natured satire (at times, the movie even appears to be satirizing itself). The action is centered around the opera house, with its two tiered and trapdoored stage, but it also bursts out to a candy-land Peking composed of immaculate streets, lavish "decadent" houses, and treacherous rooftops. At times this Peking resembles a gigantic maze, with new toys located in every corner. *Peking Opera Blues* is a sensational piece of frivolous moviemaking—wild buffoonery carried to the borders of art. Since it's entirely devoted to the pleasure principle, you would be crazy to miss it.

NEW YORK POST, 1/25/89, p. 27, Jami Bernard

The face of a man in full, vibrant theatrical make-up and a wicked scowl fills and holds the screen at the start of "Peking Opera Blues"; it's as still an image as the movie offers, a delicious tease, like balancing at the top of the steepest loop of a roller coaster. You'll need to strap yourself in as you go over the edge for this deliriously exuberant piece of action cinema from Hong Kong, playing for only two weeks at Film Forum 1.

The setting is 1913 Peking, a period of warlords jockeying for position following the revolution that established the Republic of China. Three women, each after their own ends, join forces by happenstance to expose a deposed warlord. The leader of the trio suspects this guy is in cahoots with foreign banks; if she exposes him, Democracy will rule.

The triumvirate is played by Hong Kong's three leading ladies, but the film suffers not at all by playing where these actresses are unknown.

Tso Wan (Lin Ching Hsia) is a general's daughter whose contact with the West has snared her sympathies. Dressed in mannish attire and allied with the local revolutionaries, it is she who marshals the others to steal the evidence she needs from her own father's safe.

Pak Neil (Sally Yeh) is the daughter of the manager of the Peking Opera, where she desperately wants to perform. Unfortunately, that colorful form of theater is tradition-bound not to allow women on stage. Her fondest dream is "to be reincarnated as a man so I can play a woman."

Sheung Hung (Cherie Chung) is a maid who takes advantage of a palace revolt to make off with a box of jewels. The box goes astray and remains just out of frantic arm's reach for the rest of the movie.

Each of the women has a dominant male figure in her life who must be overthrown to make way for the new social structure—Chung's is the corrupt warlord who already has 28 wives, but still has time for the maid.

Using the code phrase "Peking Duck," the trio reconnoiter at the Opera House, their base of operations. To get the document they need from the safe, they need the key—which is firmly attached to the general's belt. Plans to relieve him of his belt come fast and furious, and are just as quickly foiled. For example, a poisoned dim sung meant for the general is eaten by his mistress instead.

Several seduction scenes also go hilariously wrong, including one where the object of seduction goes limp, not from lack of desire but from a bullet through his head.

Though saddled with the worst example of English subtitles in recent history ("It get crowdy in here"), "Peking Opera Blues" is a visual treat, a rambunctious, fast-paced tightly edited spree that has been compared, often, to the Indiana Jones adventures.

Directed by the popular Vietnamese-born Tsui Hark, it alternates martial arts chop-outs and balletic Errol Flynn stunts with farce and slapstick. In one beautifully choreographed scene, a sleepy foursome under the same blanket manage to elude the notice of the opera manager when he comes to rouse his daughter.

There are hair-raising near-misses and a line-up of opera actors in full regalia swinging as one from the rafters on colored streamers.

There is even a slow-mo Peckinpah shootout and an extended rooftop battle royale with shingles a-breaking, soldiers a-leaping, and a-dying, too.

If you're familiar with the action comedies of Jackie Chan, who is probably Hong Kong's most popular export here, you'll recognize the kinetic, acrobatic style of what is being touted as the most appealingly commercial new kind of cinema today. "Peking Opera Blues" played last year at the Hong Kong Film Festival at the Asia Society; Film Forum 1 gives you a second chance to catch the new wave.

VILLAGE VOICE, 1/31/89, p. 59, J. Hoberman

The power-pop triumph of the past few years, *Peking Opera Blues* lures you in with its pounding, crazy beat. The very first image is a close-up of an elaborately made-up Chinese opera performer staring down the camera and howling with laughter. His stylized gaiety is infectious; it dares the viewer to remain aloof. This action comedy by Hong Kong director Tsui Hark—a movie which delighted the international festival circuit (and has enjoyed two runs at the Sun Sing) before opening, semilegitimately, at Film Forum—is a breathlessly choreographed jape that's almost irresistible.

Like much recent HK fare, *Peking Opera Blues* is a period piece that reflects the Crown

Colony's anxiety vis-à-vis reunification with the People's Republic. Hark has described the movie as a satire on the Chinese "ignorance of democracy," but it seems equally a fantasy about the breakdown of an established social order. Set in 1913, two years after the fall of the last emperor, the film is the sort of tangled narrative thicket in which unscrupulous warlords engage in sinister conspiracies, while adventurous gold diggers search for hidden jewels amid frequent bouts of stylized make-believe. As the title suggests, theater rules: Hark's cubistic backstage is a vortex of entertainment, greed, and intrigue wherein three attractive heroines—a comic gold digger, a would-be actress, and a general's daughter, who for no particular reason (and not very convincingly), has disguised herself as a boy—join forces to pursue their separate agendas. Typically, the aspiring actress is the most "sincere" character.

Peking Opera Blues is like an action film built around the Bangles—a glitzy ironic pajama party in which the stars almost never stop role-playing, their antics punctuated by all manner of reversals, sight gags, and subversively genderbending pratfalls. (Women were not permitted to appear in the Peking Opera, something addressed here with a vengeance.) The whole movie has a knowing quality that hovers over, and ultimately supersedes, the perfunctory plot. With its kick fights and chases egged on by the gongs and clicks of James Wong's keening, twanging score, the film is a continual coming attraction for itself—the action as accelerated in Hark's bang-bang editing as it is amplified by his performers' exaggerated reactions, continual hide-and-seek, and frequent disguises. (The most fequently asked question: "How come you are here?")

In its insouciant, breakneck pace, *Peking Opera Blues* owes something to the Spielberg/Lucas *Indiana Jones* films, but it's less overweening and more deliberately flimsy (not to mention wholly immune from ethnocentric Indy-imperialism). The mode is self-aware rather than self-conscious. As blatantly two-dimensional as the movie is, it engages the entire spectrum of popular amusement East and West. When Hark travesties a traditional opera by having a pair of (disguised) characters turn up onstage in identical costumes, he combines the consternation of two of the most celebrated Marx Brothers routines. But at the same time that *Peking Opera Blues* parodies its source, it derives the most spectacular acrobatic stunts organically, from the rich soil of the opera's form.

How does one get to be the world's wittiest action director? Born in Vietnam, transplanted to Hong Kong during the war, Hark attended film school in Texas, codirected a documentary (with Third World Newsreel's Chris Choy) in New York's Chinatown, then returned to HK to make his reputation in television. Clearly this 37-year-old director/producer/sometime actor, who has been twisting local genres since his thriller, *The Butterfly Murders*, appeared in 1979, knows something about the relative nature of cultural values and the instability of ruling forms.

Hark suggests a comic Eisenstein. It's not just his machine-gun editing, but his use of typage, his analysis of circus attractions, his fascination with signs, and his interest in political upheaval that link him to the Soviet master. If Hark belongs to the Internationale of commercial entertainment, it may be because the era of revolutionary heroism is long since over. Like Eisenstein's, Hark's movies seem to flow from some preideological wellspring: For all its pow, *Peking Opera Blues* has an unexpected backbeat of melancholy and loss—it's the Boat Person's *Battleship Potemkin*.

Also reviewed in:
NEW YORK TIMES, 1/25/89, p. C15, Richard F. Shepard
VARIETY, 9/17/86, p. 24

PENN & TELLER GET KILLED

A Lorimar Film Entertainment release. *Producer:* Arthur Penn. *Director:* Arthur Penn. *Screenplay:* Penn Jillette and Teller. *Director of Photography:* Jan Weincke. *Editor:* Jeffrey Wolf. *Music:* Paul Chihara. *Music Editor:* Suzana Peric. *Sound.* John Sutton III. *Sound Editor:* Skip Lievsay. *Production Designer:* John Arnone. *Set Decorator:* Beth Kushnick. *Set Dresser:* Scott Rosenstock. *Special Effects:* Steve Kirshoff. *Costumes:* Rita Ryack. *Make-up:* Carla White. *Stunt Coordinator:* Jery Hewitt. *Running time:* 89 minutes. *MPAA Rating:* R.

CAST: Penn Jillette (Penn); Teller (Teller); Bill Randolph (Floor Director); John Miller (Steve, the Bandleader); Ellen Whyte (Make-up Woman); Caitlin Clarke (Carlotta); Ted Neustadt (Bob, the Host); Tudor Sherrard (Frat

Boy #1); Billy Morrissette (Frat Boy #2); Jon Cryer (Frat Boy #3); David Patrick Kelly (Fan); Leonard Parker (Porter); Christopher Durang (Jesus Freak); Camille Saviola (Airport Security Guard); Gwen Shepherd (Mother); Avanti Taylor (Little Girl); Madison Arnold (Slot Player); Jamie Tirelli (Maitre d'); Millie Tirelli (Waitress); Leonardo Cimino (Ernesto); Joe Milazzo (Ernesto's Guest); Paul Calderon (Juan); Eddie Gorodetsky (Big Guy); Lum Chang Pang (Muscular One); Maria Laboy (Woman Timekeeper); Ben Lin (Rope Holder #1); Jimmy Carr (Rope Holder #2); James Randi (Rope Holder #3); Rob Elk (Heckler); Nancy Giles (TV Interviewer); Marilyn Cooper (Woman in Parking Lot); Patrick Whitney (Taxi Pusher); Beth Woods (Screaming Showgirl); Anne Connors (Laughing Showgirl); Celia McGuire (Officer McNamara); Caitlin Clarke (Celia McGuire); Robert LaSardo (Mugger #1); Tom Sizemore (Mugger #2); Reg E. Cathey (Fan's Friend); Alan North (Old Cop); Matthew Penn (Young Cop).

LOS ANGELES TIMES, 10/21/89, Calendar/p. 3, Kevin Thomas

On stage and on TV, Penn & Teller turn magic upside down and inside out with a surreal wit and formidable ingenuity, poking fun at old-fashioned sleight-of-hand, yet seeming always to go familiar sure-fire, crowd-pleasing tricks one dazzling step better..

However, if you're seeing them for the first time in "Penn & Teller Get Killed," you might well wonder what all the fuss is about.

Their screen debut is so disappointing that their film lives up to its title all too closely—and, as the writers of the screenplay, they have only themselves to blame. In the manner of venerable vaudeville teams making the switch to movies, they play themselves. While promoting their upcoming engagement in Atlantic City (where the entire film was shot), Penn, in response to criticism that their humor and trickery are sometimes too violent, irrepressibly tells a TV audience how exciting it would be if someone actually tried to kill him. Of course, it soon seems as if somebody really is trying to do him in.

This proves to be a comic premise with a quite literal death wish. To their credit, Penn & Teller come up with a macabre finish, but the getting there is a real chore. Very little of their tricks are on view along the way, and even fewer laughs. If Penn & Teller are going to be this conventional on the screen, they're going to need gag writers, just like Bob Hope.

But there's no reason that big, burly Penn Jillette, with his curly forelock, booming voice and trademark three-piece suits and the diminutive, mute, acrobatic Teller have to be like other entertainers. Considering that their producer-director was Arthur Penn, there was reason to hope their collaboration with him would result in a film as venturesome as Penn's "Mickey One." What we get, however, are an R-rated Penn & Jillette who aren't as much fun as Abbott & Costello.

NEW YORK POST, 9/22/89, p. 27, David Edelstein

Both unctuous and sneering, magicians Penn & Teller belong to a bracing new class of performers who make a joke of their show-biz insincerity. They're first-rate Houdinis, but what really sparks them is confrontation: They love to taunt us suckers with how easily we're hoodwinked and goaded—and with how much we want to be.

Penn & Teller live for punky shocks. They pretend to cut a snake in half and get drenched in blood; uh oh, says a grim Penn, we really killed it. Teller fails to escape from some contraption and is drowned or gorily dismembered. As he floats or as blood spurts out, the moment hangs...and hangs...while part of the audience shifts uncomfortably and the other half screams with glee at the outrageousness.

That hanging moment is the core of "Penn & Teller Get Killed," their amazingly misbegotten new movie, written by the pair and directed by Arthur Penn ("Bonnie and Clyde"). I couldn't wait to see what masters of one medium could do with another, and rumblings that the studio hated the film made me want to see it even more. It sounded dangerous.

Well, it is dangerous, and it's also a fiasco. In the movie, Penn & Teller play themselves: a pair of magicians—one large and obnoxious, the other short and enigmatically silent—who can't help getting on people's nerves.

On a talk show, Penn announces (in a reading so unnatural you're not sure if he's supposed to have just thought of it or if it's a put-on—or both) that he'd love it if someone were trying to kill him. It would give focus to his life.

Thereafter, he's accosted by morally indignant viewers. How can he be so casual about something as sacred as life? Isn't he aware that there are nuts out in TV land who are obsessed with celebrities and who could take his words to heart?

Penn doesn't care; he and Teller are too busy playing elaborate tricks on each other. Teller slips a steel ball into Penn's pocket at the airport, making the metal-detector go off and driving Penn into an anti-fascist rage against a guard; Penn, to get his revenge, chains Teller to an airport pay phone with a toy gun hooked to his hands.

In Atlantic City, Penn gets shot in the arm by an assassin hiding in a billlboard. Is this a charade or for real? A female cop called McNamara shows up to protect Penn. Why is her fridge stocked with Diet Coke (for Penn) and Yoohoos (for Teller)? Why does she, too, love to listen to the Velvet Underground and Milo while watching Three Stooges films? Coincidence? Absurdism? Or part of a larger plot?

Are we watching a wretchedly acted and directed movie, or is the badness a put-on, designed to make us edgy, unsure of what's real and what's phony? And what does it mean to call the picture irritating when it's working so hard to irritate? Has it therefore fulfilled its ambitions? Is its very unwatchability a mark of Penn & Teller's triumph?

We're lost in layer upon layer of irony. (Doubtless Penn & Teller are, too, which might be the spur for all this.) Under pressure to ingratiate themselves to a mass audience, they must see this squirm-inducing B-movie as proof of their punk integrity, their refusal to sell out to Hollywood the way, as magicians, they refused to go the Doug Henning route.

But on stage Penn & Teller can get away with their boorish attitude because they're virtuosos. They grew up with magic and for years worked the carnival circuit; they can hold their own with any magician alive.

As screenwriters, on the other hand, they're rank amateurs, and what's meant to be ironically bad looks sincerely inept. The poor taste isn't liberating in "Penn & Teller Get Killed." It's just obvious and dull-witted—it makes you claustrophobic.

Arthur Penn (no relation to Penn Jillette) has directed some great American movies, but his realism feels lackluster in this setting. The picture needed a lively showman, a modern William Castle. (Stuart Gordon or even Frank Henenlotter spring to mind.) Why didn't Penn & Teller go with their strengths and talk to the audience? Why did they shy away from cinematic gimmicks?

They have the late Andy Kaufman's instincts: Kaufman, too, might have made a comedy without a single laugh in the last 15 minutes, but his routines were (at least in retrospect) a riot. The end of "Penn & Teller Get Killed" just seems like a dull remake of "The Maltese Bippy." Could there be a cult audience for this? Will anyone out there think self-conscious clunkiness is hip?

NEWSDAY, 9/22/89, Part III/p. 3. Terry Kelleher

Last year, Penn & Teller put out a home video titled "Cruel Tricks for Dear Friends." Now comes the first feature film for this "new vaudeville" team, and it's chockfull of cruel tricks.

Will it expand their circle of friends? Maybe they just don't care.

"Penn & Teller Get Killed" is certainly one of the most off-putting movies of the year. It has an attitude that fairly shouts, "If you're not hip to what we're doing, tough." And the ending adds an exclamation point.

The picture opens with Penn Jillette and his silent partner, Teller, doing their comedy-in-magic act on a national television show whose host looks and dresses like David Letterman. "I wish someone were trying to kill me," Penn declares. A little fake throat-slitting follows for your amusement.

At the airport en route to a gig in Atlantic City, Penn & Teller begin a tit-for-tat round of practical jokes that escalates through the rest of the movie. Teller keeps slipping objects into Penn's pockets, frustrating his efforts to clear the metal detector. Penn responds by cuffing Teller's thumbs to a reasonable facsimile of a gun, then alerting security.

This is the time to stop and consider: Are these the kind of guys you want to spend an hour and a half with? If you're in doubt, you're probably some kind of yokel. In the car bound for Trump Plaza, the boys' manager (Caitlin Clarke) reports: "The 'I wish someone were trying to kill me' bit is not playing in the Midwest."

In sophisticated coastal New Jersey, Penn & Teller while away their offstage hours with one elaborate ruse after another. Teller tries to make Penn think someone really is trying to kill Penn. Penn tries to make Teller think someone is really, really trying to kill Penn.

It's not completely clear what Penn & Teller are trying to make the viewer think. The hoaxes, which feature transparent disguises and inside jokes, are neither very puzzling nor very funny. If you're a midwesterner or the equivalent, the puzzlement will come in trying to determine what's supposed to be funny.

Admirers of the duo may see "Penn & Teller Get Killed" as the cinematic extension of their stage act, in which the tricks are obviously tricks, not "illusions." But different media have different requirements, and successful illusion is usually what "movie magic" is all about. Penn can't compel audience involvement by stepping down off the screen and dragging "volunteers" out of their seats.

Arthur Penn, who got more laughs 22 year ago out of the violent team known as "Bonnie and Clyde," largely fails to draw the black comedy from his co-stars' original screenplay. Directorial artistry notwithstanding, of course, a demented fan stalking a celebrity with homicidal intent will never be some folks' idea of a hoot.

If certain scenes move with irritating slowness—particularly the one filmed partly in black and white—the irritation is probably intentional. And if you don't like it, Penn & Teller dare you to make yourself disappear from the theater.

VILLAGE VOICE, 10/3/89, p. 72, Manohla Dargis

Penn & Teller are renegades. These self-proclaimed "bad boys of magic" gleefully spill trade secrets and despise musty stage trickery, preferring power drills, sharp instruments, and buckets of blood to colored silks, capes, and canes. Not for the easily offended, their gallows humor is for people who find the combination of tripe, psychic surgery, and suicide funny.

Since the film's title, *Penn & Teller Get Killed*, gives away its ending, what counts is not what happens, but how, On a late-night TV talkshow Penn Jillette, with pre-Salman Rushdie recklessness, announces that he wishes someone were trying to kill him. One murder attempt leads to another as bullets and ninja stars fly. The act moves to Atlantic City and ends up in a tenement near the boardwalk.

Penn & Teller Get Killed doesn't push the duo's most intriguing ideas—suckering audience volunteers into acts of violence—far enough. A likable film, it's really only a series of skits strung together. Two of their best scenes are Penn's call to revolution while being dragged from the Trump Plaza, and a genuinely moving parody of *Death Wish*, with Teller as an erstwhile equalizer.

Dressed in identical gray suits and red ties, Penn & Teller are brazenly affected, and the movie is crammed with their cooler-than-thou bits of business that often work (a Three Stooges "all Shemp" film marathon) and sometimes bomb (the Velvet Underground hasn't been a secret for a while). The biggest surprise of the film, however, isn't a Penn & Teller illusion but Caitlin Clarke, who, as the duo's manager and Penn's sometime girlfriend Carlotta, does Dietrich's *Witness for the Prosecution* performance one better. (Christopher Durang has a superb cameo as a Jesus freak.)

Penn & Teller Get Killed isn't much of an argument for the auteur theory. Aside from its dark edge, there isn't much of the film's other Penn, director Arthur (*Bonnie and Clyde*), in evidence. The cinematography is cheesy, and tighter editing could have glossed over the dead spots.

I have one major complaint about the film: the number of plugs for Diet Coke and Yoo-hoo. (There are too many Trump Plaza signs as well.) So many product shots are offensive—and, presumably, profitable.

Also reviewed in:

NEW REPUBLIC, 10/30/89, p. 25, Stanley Kauffmann
NEW YORK TIMES, 9/22/89, p. C10, Janet Maslin
NEW YORKER, 10/2/89, p. 100, Pauline Kael
VARIETY, 9/13-19/89, p. 36
WASHINGTON POST, 11/18/89, p. C3, Hal Hinson

PET SEMATARY

A Paramount Pictures release. *Executive Producer:* Tim Zinnemann. *Producer:* Richard P. Rubinstein. *Director:* Mary Lambert. *Screenplay (based on his own novel):* Stephen King. *Director of Photography:* Peter Stein. *Editor:* Michael Hill and Daniel Hanley. *Music:* Elliot Goldenthal. *Music Editor:* Charles Martin Inouye.

Sound: Mark Ulano and (music) Phil Bulla. *Sound Editor:* Larry Mann. *Production Designer:* Michael Hanan. *Art Director:* Dins Danielsen. *Set Designer:* Michael Reidy and Patricia Klawonn. *Set Decorator:* Katharin Briggs. *Set Dresser:* Cathy L. McKenney. *Special Visual Effects:* Gene Warren Jr. *Costumes:* Marlene Stewart. *Make-up:* Lance Anderson. *Running time:* 105 minutes. *MPAA Rating:* R.

CAST: Dale Midkiff (Dr. Louis Creed); Fred Gwynne (Jud Crandall); Denise Crosby (Rachel Creed); Blaze Berdahl (Ellie Creed); Miko Hughes (Gage Creed); Brad Greenquist (Victor Pascow); Susan J. Blommaert (Missy Dandridge); Michael Lombard (Irwin Goldman); Mara Clark (Marcy Charlton); Kavi Raz (Steve Masterton); Mary Louise Wilson (Dory Goldman); Andrew Hubatsek (Zelda); Liz Davies (Girl at Infirmary); Kara Dalke (Candystriper); Matthew August Ferrell (Jud as a Child); Lisa Stathoplos (Jud's Mother); Stephen King (Minister); Elizabeth Ureneck (Rachel as a Child); Chuck Courtney (Bill Baterman); Peter Stader (Timmy Baterman); Richard Collier (Young Jud); Chuck Shaw (Cop); Eleanor Grace Courtemanche (Logan Gate Agent); Donnie Green (Orinco Driver); Lila Duffy (Budget Clerk); John David Moore (Hitchhike Driver); Beau Berdahl (Ellie Creed II).

LOS ANGELES TIMES, 4/24/89, Calendar/p. 5, Kevin Thomas

"Pet Sematary" finds Stephen King at his farthest out, never more simultaneously compelling and repelling, but there's no denying that in Mary Lambert he has a director who can go the distance and make the contradiction work. No doubt King's multitudinous fans will have flocked to the film on opening weekend, but it's going to be fascinating to see if—or how soon—backlash sets in.

There's a big difference between that which is depicted on the printed page and on the big screen, and movies—so far—haven't gotten much more gruesome or disturbing than "Pet Sematary."

The film is Americana at its most Gothic, a depiction of a normal family made vulnerable by the eternal yearning to cheat death. It cuts to the deepest human emotions, and there certainly are going to be many people who aren't going to be willing or able to take it. "Pet Sematary" is one of the most numbing mainstream American movies since "The Exorcist."

The Creeds and their new home, a warmly decorated simple Victorian in rural Maine, seem straight off the pages of Better Homes and Gardens. The father, Louis (Dale Midkiff), is a Chicago doctor who has taken a position at the nearby college. He has a devoted wife, Rachel (Denise Crosby), and the requisite two children, Ellie (Blaze Berdahl) and Gage (Miko Hughes), still a toddler.

Their picture isn't quite magazine-perfect right from the start. Although the Creeds' house is nicely situated on a rise with a lovely lake to its back, it's awfully close to the highway, which gets a great deal of noisy and dangerous truck traffic. The Creeds' elderly neighbor Jud (Fred Gwynne), who has lived his entire life in a seedy house directly across the way, tells them that the trucks have over the years exacted a terrible toll of animals, especially dogs and cats. Jud shows them a hidden, nearby burial ground, a ramshackle, slightly sinister area with home-made gravestones and crosses bearing a rickety sign reading "Pet Sematary." But what about that old Indian burial ground that lies beyond the pet cemetery?

With only one feature under her belt—and a much-maligned one at that, "Siesta"—but various commercials and key music videos behind her, Lambert goes for strong, succinct images and never stops to worry whether there's a lack of credibility or motivation.

The actors, mainly from TV and none of them possessed with a sexy, glamorous movie-star aura, couldn't be more aptly cast. As in the recent "Disorganized Crime," Gwynne is the anchoring presence as a classically dry, laconic New Englander who seems to know some terrible secret. Elliot Goldenthal has composed a helpfully ominous score, as moody as vintage Bernard Herrmann, and Peter Stein's cinematography is superbly varied, from the bright hues of a glossy magazine to the dark shadows of the charnel house. No question about it, "Pet Sematary" (rated R for extreme violence) is a handsomely produced film.

You could say facetiously the moral of the story is to avoid buying a house too close to the highway. In a very real way that is King's point, which is that all it takes is a simple misjudgment to unleash the forses of destruction.

MONTHLY FILM BULLETIN, 11/89, p. 341, Philip Strick

Dr. Louis Creed, his wife Rachel, their children Ellie and Gage, and their cat "Church", move from Chicago to the small country town of Ludlow in Maine. Their nearest neighbour, Jud Crandall, warns them about an adjoining road used by massive tanker trucks; he shows them the animal graveyard where many pets killed on the road have been buried. Louis takes up his duties as Head of Medical Services at the local university, where one day a dying student, Victor Pascow, is brought in after a road accident. That night, Louis dreams that Pascow leads him to the pet cemetery and warns him not to pass the barrier of fallen trees just beyond it; Louis wakes next morning to find his feet covered in dry mud. While Rachel and the children are visiting her parents in Chicago for Thanksgiving, Church is killed on the road; when Louis sets out to bury the cat, Jud guides him over the barrier on a perilous climb to the ancient burial ground of the Micmac Indians. Next day, the cat has revived and returns home to await Rachel and the children; Ellie has dreamed of her pet's accident and now complains of his strange smell and sinister behaviour. The death of Miss Dandridge, Jud's home help, prompts Rachel to reveal how she was forced by her parents to look after her dying sister, Zelda, a memory that has haunted her ever since. In a horrific accident, their son Gage is killed by a truck, and Louis begins to wonder if the child, like the cat, can be resurrected, despite warnings from Jud about the tragic results of previous such attempts. Sending Rachel and Ellie back to Chicago, Louis transfers Gage's body to the Micmac burial ground and waits for a miracle; meanwhile, Rachel has been alerted by Ellie's dreams of Pascow that something is wrong and hurries back to avert disaster. Pascow, unseen, helps her to overcome obstacles in her path. While Louis is asleep, Gage returns from the grave, takes a scalpel from his father's bag, and uses it first to kill Jud and then Rachel (who at first mistakes the child for Zelda). Summoned by Gage on the telephone next morning, Louis goes to Jud's house, destroys both Church and Gage, sets the place alight, and carries his wife's corpse to the Micmac ground. He reasons that she has a chance, thanks to his prompt action, of reviving to near-normality. But when her mutilated form indeed returns to his embrace, Rachel is carrying a knife...

The first of Stephen King's screenplays to be adapted from one of his own novels, *Pet Sematary* was filmed in his home state of Maine where, says King, he did once have a country house beside an animal graveyard and a busy road. In all other respects (it seems reasonable to assume), the story avoids the autobiographical resonances of another *Stand by Me* except in its few homespun glimpses of rural life and its continuation of King's customary concern (partly as novelist, partly as parent) with the precocious behaviour of pets and children. "What was interesting in writing the script", he comments, "was that there were things not in the book I realised I could add". In fact, given that the book derives most of its weight from descriptive detail, woven around a relatively uncomplicated storyline which leaves plenty of room for supplementary action, he has added remarkably little. Much to the film's advangtage, visual ambiguity replaces and enriches King's often strident vocabulary; with such simplicities as a fallen swing, a speeding truck, the close-up of an eerie neighbour, or the peculiar difficulty of lifting a dead animal from a frozen lawn, the camera works more wonders than the scenario.

What King *has* chosen to develop does little to repair the main weaknesses of his best-seller. Setting aside the minor irritation that the "pet sematary" of his title is nothing more than a detour from the plot's main path, the motivation of the force controlling the ancient burial ground remains unconfronted. This malignant power evidently substantiates the admirably concise warning in W.W. Jacob's classic story "The Monkey's Paw" (to which King's novel refers) that to summon a loved one back from the grave can be a serious mistake—but it confusingly has little to do with the unfortunate Micmacs whose territory is now afflicted. The family feuds and loyalties which lend some coherence to the novel and justify its punchline (Zelda's repellent death, for instance, or the fight which chillingly dislodges her coffin at the funeral) are simply plundered for their shock effect en route to the final bloodletting. Emaciated, then, rather than enhanced by its adaptation, *Pet Sematary* as a movie is nevertheless strikingly well told.

No stranger to the living dead, following her pop videos and the fascinatingly overheated *Siesta*, Mary Lambert falls on King's story with an enjoyable ferocity. She has the knack of defining gulfs between her characters by simple glances and stances, so that the Creed family (note the encircling spaces between husband and wife) contrives to be a battleground of brittle misapprehension, encompassing kids and in-laws, before a word is spoken. Greatly assisted by Fred Gwynne's performance as the folksy, haunted hermit who recalls too many bad times past and fears too many to come, Lambert expands the formulaic horror into something modestly more substantial by maintaining a furious pace and a grip that knows when to relax. The scene, for example, of the toddler's inevitable collision with a truck is constructed with a cruel precision, and if all the usual excesses of the genre are well exercised, King's old darkhouse clichés have come up with far more edge and shine than he deserved. Usefully odd, frustratingly uneven, *Pet Sematary* resembles *Siesta* in suggesting more than it can reasonably deliver, but conveys some surprisingly genuine anguish from time to time.

NEW YORK POST, 4/22/89, p. 19, David Edelstein

The ideal film adaptation of a Stephen King horror novel would feature King himself (or an actor stand-in) wandering around the set like the Stage Manager in Thornton Wilder's "Our Town."

"Ayah," he would say in his folksy Maine singsong, "there's Rachel. Pretty girl. She's gonna get her entrails ripped out in a coupla minutes, but let's not get aheada our story."

And between the scenes of carnage and hysteria he'd wag his head and say things like, "Ayah, it's prob'ly wrong to believe there can be any limit to the horror which the human mind can experience. No sir, no limit. Horror spawns horror, one coincidental evil begets another...." And then it's on to more mayhem.

The reason movies such as "Pet Sematary" rarely reflect King's work is that they almost never give you that ruminative flavor. They dish up just the routine, secondhand shocks, with none of the tour-guide-in-hell relish that holds them together on paper. (Brian De Palma gave "Carrie"— by miles the best King adaptation—his own voice, a mixture of lyricism and ghoulish wit.)

"Pet Sematary," based on one of King's better novels, is smoothly made and watchable, but it's totally impersonal. The story itself is almost unbearably traumatic—the horror-spawning-horror stuff I quoted above is from the middle of the book, and it's a fair harbinger of what follows. But the movie (from a screenplay by King) bobs along the surface with cheap, pop-up scares and zombielike acting. It leaves no residue in your mind.

From the overture the tone is off. The camera prowls around the bleak, loamy "pet sematary" (the misspelling is from a sign drawn by children) while the music shrieks "Be afraid! There's scary stuff here!"

Cut to a truck roaring into the frame. We're in Ludlow, Maine, where Dr. Louis Creed (Dale Midkiff), the new head of health services at the university, has just moved into an attractive colonial with his wife Rachel (Denise Crosby) and two children. Problem is, it's right on the major route to Bangor, and the tankers that thunder by (in Dolby stereo) leave a lot of dead animals in their wake.

The pet cemetery sits about a mile in back of the Creeds' house, on the edge of a deep forest that was once inhabited by MicMac Indians. Its presence upsets Rachel, who lost a sister to spinal meningitis when she was a kid and doesn't like to think about mortality. In fact, she doesn't believe children should ever be exposed to the idea of dying—which is the audience's big hint that there are lots of juicy deaths on the way.

When Rachel and the kids leave town for a few days, the family cat, Church, is squashed by a truck, and Louis is frantic at the thought that he'll have to break the news to his daughter, Ellie (Blaze Berdahl). But the kindly old neighbor, Jud Crandall (Fred Gwynne) has an alternative plan. He takes Louis out past the cemetery to the MicMac burial ground and directs the doctor to bury it in a sacred circle.

I don't want to give away any surprises, but obviously either the cat comes back to life or it doesn't. If it doesn't there's no story, so it obviously does. And if it comes back and it's OK then there's no story either. And if nothing else dies and gets buried in the MicMac graveyard then we're only talking about pets—and King is after bigger game.

What he's trying to evoke is a primal terror—a daddy's perception of his children's mortality and how fragile their ties to the world really are. With borrowings from "The Monkey's Paw" he runs with that fear, showing how one honest mistake begets another begets another begets another, the whole becoming, as King puts it, a Rube Goldberg absurdity—you have to laugh to keep your sanity.

Mary Lambert, a rock-video director who made the fractured art-film "Siesta," has a lot of energy, and she isn't afraid of messiness and jarring tones. She handles the youngest child, Gage (Miko Hughes), with grisly wit in the final confrontation, and she does well by the reanimated cat, which has luminous gray fur, eyes like yellow coal and a slurry walk.

But she's too solemn and overexplicit for this story, which needs much fewer literal-minded shocks, and she's bad with the actors. Midkiff is strictly a TV pretty boy (he looks a little like James Darren), and he can't pull you into his dementia—his face becomes frozen, catatonic.

Denise Crosby is tight and humorless, with the least convincing smile I've ever seen on an actress. Only Fred Gwynne—warm, folksy, yet with a grave, doomy edge—holds the camera.

King should never write his own screenplays. He doesn't know how to conceal the wheels and pulleys of his plotting, and he relies too much on boring flashbacks and little kids with second sight. His one weird stroke is the friendly, campy ghost of a college student (Brad Greenquist) flattened by a truck. The guy keeps popping up to warn the family of danger—the top of his head gone, his eyes milky, the capillaries gray on his face. He makes the afterlife look much jollier than the dreary here-and-now.

NEWSDAY, 4/22/89, Part II/p. 15, Bill Kaufman

Stephen King has in recent years earned a reputation as one of the most successful tellers of ghost stories.

Perhaps one of King's better novel was "Pet Sematary," a nightmarish story about evil and malevolent entities that rode the best-seller lists for more than six months a half-dozen years ago. Here, for the first time, chillmaster King has turned his own book into a screenplay—which in this case might be akin to being unable to see the forest for the trees.

The film stars Dale Midkiff as Louis Creed, a young physician who, with his wife (Denise Crosby) and child, relocate from a big city to a rural Maine village. There he takes charge of the local college's hospital. Fred Gwynne, an actor enjoying a resurgence of popularity, does a competent job as elderly neighbor Jud Crandall, who becomes a father figure and catalyst of sorts when the family faces unholy terrors. And his authentic Down East twang adds realism to the role.

The movie starts off sluggishly—one of its main problems—with unnecessary build-ups to establish the premise. And there are a number of extraneous attempts to shock moviegoers with scare devices—for instance, the family's toddler runs into the road as a speeding truck approaches, only to be saved at the last moment by Crandall.

When the family's beloved pet is run down and taken to the weird little cemetery behind the house, we know strange things are going to occur. (The misspelled title comes from the homemade sign made by children and placed at the cemetery for their departed animals,)

As far as macabre motion pictures go, "Pet Sematary" can be logged as still another tale of the living dead come back to spook those on the other side of darkness. That old standby, the haunted house, remains as a centerpiece. As for the ugly creepie-crawlers, "Pet Sematary" is state-of-the-art, but breaks no new ground in the horror thriller realm.

Also reviewed in:
NEW YORK TIMES, 4/22/89, p. 16, Vincent Canby
VARIETY, 4/26–5/2/89, p. 26
WASHINGTON POST, 4/22/89, p. C1, Richard Harrington

PETER PAN

A Walt Disney Classic release. *Directors:* Hamilton Luske, Clyde Geronimi, and Wilfred Jackson. *Directing Animators:* Milt Kahl, Frank Thomas, Wolfgang Reitherman, Ward Kimball, Ollie Johnston, Marc Davis, Eric Larson, John Lounsbery, Les Clark, and Norm Ferguson. *Story (based on the play "Peter Pan") by:* Sir James M. Barrie. *Film Editor:* Donald Halliday. *Music:* Oliver Wallace. *Music Editor:* Al Teeter. *Songs:* Sammy Fain, Sammy Cahn, Oliver Wallace, Frank Churchill, Erdman Penner, Winston Hibler, and Ted Sears. *Sound:* Harold J. Steck and Robert O. Cook. *Special Processes:* Ub Iwerks. *Running time:* 77 minutes. *MPAA Rating:* G.

VOICES: Boddy Driscoll (Peter Pan); Kathryn Beaumont (Wendy); Hans Conried (Hook/Mr. Darling); Bill Thompson (Smee and Other Pirates); Heather Angel (Mrs. Darling); Paul Collins (John); Tommy Luske (Michael); Candy Candido (Indian Chief); Tom Conway (Narrator).

LOS ANGELES TIMES, 7/14/89, Calendar/p. 8, Charles Solomon

For children who grew up during the Baby Boom era, there were always two "Peter Pan": the TV version with Mary Martin and the animated feature by Walt Disney. Each had its special charms, and the cartoon "Peter Pan" remains one of the most exciting and colorful films in the Disney canon.

Disney discarded the wistful nostalgia for the illusory innocence of childhood that pervaded Sir James Barrie's original play and replaced it with brash Yankee energy. This Peter Pan is a cocky, all-American boy, more like Tom Sawyer than the smug British popinjay Barrie envisioned.

The Disney artists also changed or discarded much of the traditional stage business. For the first time, Peter was voiced by an actor (Bobby Driscoll), rather than portrayed by an actress. The Crocodile, who had always been an offstage sound effect, appeared on the screen. The artists eliminated Peter's impassioned plea to the audience to clap their hands to prove they believe in fairies and save Tinker Bell's life as a theatrical effect, rather than a cinematic one.

When the film was first released, critics complained about the portrayal of Tinker Bell as a human pixie rather than as a beam of light. This depiction is actually very close to Barrie's descriptions of her as feminine, vain and slighty vulgar. Watch her monumental self-pity as she collapses into tears while Captain Hook bewails her abandonment by Peter.

The Disney crew made even greater changes in the Captain. Barrie's elegant pirate who had "something of the *grand seigneur*" about him was transformed into a volatile comic villain. Captain Hook's battle with the ravenous Crocodile include some of the wildest, funniest scenes in any Disney cartoon. They represent a near-perfect marriage of slapstick animation and a deliciously overplayed vocal performance by the late Hans Conried.

Made in 1953 when the artists were still at the height of their powers, "Peter Pan" features some genuinely magic moments that expand the original play. No stage wiring could duplicate the freedom of movement Wendy, John and Michael experience when they discover they can fly. The sequence in which Peter turns the pirate ship to gold and sails it over the London skyline stands out as an example of a fantasy that can be realized only in animation.

The film carries its years very lightly, with one regrettable exception: its depiction of the Indians, including the "What Made the Red Man Red?" number. Although Disney treated them more respectfully than Barrie had, these characters are '50s movie *Injuns*, whose dialogue runs to "heap big" this and "do-um" that. The sequence is too long and too important to the story to cut. (Parts of it are also beautifully animated, especially Tiger Lily's graceful dance.) For better or worse—probably worse—it remains a testament to Hollywood's ethnic sensibilities during the '50s.

This complaint aside, "Peter Pan" is a wonderfully upbeat family entertainment that offers a welcome respite from the summer glut of fistfights, shoot-outs and car chases.

NEW YORK POST, 7/14/89, p. 28, Jami Bernard

You said you'd never grow up, and look what happened to you. But that doesn't mean you can't relive the pleasures of childhood fantasy with "Peter Pan," Disney's 1953 animated adaptation of Sir James M. Barrie's swashbuckling fairy tale.

Disney returns its "classics" to the theaters—where they deserve to be shown—on a complicated seven-year schedule, something like the Vulcan mating cycle. "Peter Pan" has been seen in many incarnations, including the original Broadway version (also aired on television) that starred Mary Martin swinging from the rafters as Peter and its current re-creation as a segment of "Jerome Robbins' Broadway."

In some versions, the sprightly boy returns to visit Wendy after she is grown and winds up entertaining the next generation, which is what Disney movies return to do today.

The story (and it will all come back to you) starts with Wendy, John and Michael in the nursery, where Wendy's tall tales have her brothers enthralled. Mom and Dad are off to whatever dull event it is that adults attend; when they're safely out of the way, Peter Pan swoops in the window, looking for his shadow. He's accompanied by Tinker Bell, a very womanly little pixie with Barbie Doll proportions.

With a sprinkling of pixie dust (from an unwilling Tinker Bell), the children are able to fly about and join Peter Pan for a trip to Never Never Land, a place where children don't grow old, although they do face a certain amount of menace from the local pirate ship, led by the dread Capt. Hook (with an excellently fiendish voice supplied by Hans Conried).

"Peter Pan" is big on adventure and intrigue, filling its 77 minutes with such plot developments as the kidnapping of Tinker Bell, the kidnapping of Tiger Lily, an Indian princess in Never Land, the kidnapping of Wendy and some other assorted run-ins between Peter's band of Lost Boys and the Indians, Peter and Capt. Hook, and Capt. Hook and his nemesis, a snapping crocodile. Lotsa action for little tots, most of whom in a preview screening were either moaning with anxiety or asking really loud questions, like "Where's he going? Is he dead?"

If you ever wonder what forces create the annoyance of today's happy-talk audiences who think they're in their living rooms, you have only to hear today's "modern" parents who, instead of teaching their children to, uh, SHUT UP, feel compelled to answer every question elaborately and loudly. Why can't the discussion wait until Quality Time later in the day?

Oh, yeah, back to the story. The humor of this cartoon resides in some wonderful animated sight gags, such as when a grizzly hoping to take a swipe at young Michael is perplexed by the kid's stuffed bear.

The funniest character is the crocodile, pulsating with devilish hunger for the rest of Capt. Hook (he's already made a hook of the captain's hand; now he's ready for the main course).

Music is cleverly integrated into the story, enhancing words and gestures and containing as many character themes as that other Peter's story, "Peter and the Wolf."

Unfortunately, growing up means more than just giving up on the idea of flying—it also means seeing things in a cartoon that you didn't notice the first time around. "Peter Pan" is not what you'd call a feminist work. The females, whose job it is to be either "mother" or "fun time" for the males, are so insanely jealous of one another that they're constantly trying to bump each other off. Tinker Bell tells the Lost Boys to shoot down the Wendy Bird, the mermaids try to drown her.

There's a mother-in-law joke. Tinker Bell's first disillusionment in life comes when she notices in a mirror that she has adult hips and thighs, surely making her a candidate for anorexia in the sequel.

Still, you don't have to be of any particular age to enjoy the animation and adventure of "Peter Pan." You can only hope that, just as full-scale wonderments like this one belong in a big public theater, so does silence on the part of the audience—whether they're children or those adults who once claimed they'd never grow up, and who, in a way, never did.

NEWSDAY, 7/14/89, Part III/p. 3, Terry Kelleher

After 36 years and five re-releases, you start to see Walt Disney's "Peter Pan" in a slightly different light.

Ever notice, for example, that when Father says Wendy is old enough to have a room of her own, he's unquestionably right? She looks old enough for all sorts of things.

Ever notice the skimpiness of Tinker Bell's outfit? This pixie looks like an extremely diminutive cousin of Li'l Abner's Daisy Mae, and she's not averse to shaking her booty.

Ever notice that Never Land is a regular hotbed of jealousy? Tink is steamed over Peter's attentions toward Wendy—enough to want her put out of the way by any means necessary. And Wendy's plenty peeved when Peter dallies with those mermaids (also scantily clad, by the way).

Ever notice that Peter has a Bryant Gumbel-size ego to go with those Mr. Spock ears?

Ever notice how *prissy* Wendy is?

OK, we're talking about a 1953 cartoon here, but didn't somebody notice that the depiction of Indians was a teeny bit racist? There's a word for the song "What Made the Red Man Red?": Ugh.

All that said, the family entertainment value of "Peter Pan" remains high. The music is markedly inferior to that in the Broadway and TV version starring Mary Martin; the sappy choral arrangements don't help. But when Peter flies the Disney way, you can't see the wires no matter how hard you look. Kids of all ages—excuse the expression—will get a lift when he and the Darling children first take to the skies.

The animation is often marvelous, not only in action but in characterization. There's never been a funnier villain than Captain Hook, whether he's caught in the jaws of a speeding crocodile or slipping a golden ring onto his famous prosthesis. Of course, a good deal of the credit goes to Hans Conried, who gave perfect voice to such Hookisms as "You blithering blockhead." And the blockhead in question, the blithering Mr. Smee, is the cutest henchman you ever did see. In fact, he looks like a refugee from Disney's "Snow White and the Seven Dwarfs."

For children, "Peter Pan" holds up nicely. For adults, it holds the attention by raising intriguing questions overlooked in 1953: Do Peter and the "lost boys" really look upon Wendy as a mother figure? How about a hot date down by Mermaid Lagoon?

TIME, 9/18/89, p. 93, Richard Corliss

[*Peter Pan* was reviewed jointly with *Honey, I Shrunk the Kids*; see Corliss' review of that film.]

PHANTOM OF THE OPERA

A 21st Century Productions release. *Producer:* Harry Alan Towers. *Director:* Dwight H. Little. *Screenplay:* Duke Sandefur. *Based on a screenplay by:* Gerry O'Hara. *Director of Photography:* Elemer Ragalyi. *Editor:* Charles Bornstein. *Music:* Misha Segal. *Sound:* Cyril Collick. *Art Director:* Tivadar Bertalan. *Special Effects Make-up:* Kevin Yagher. *Costumes:* John Bloomfield. *Running time:* 95 minutes. *MPAA Rating:* R.

CAST: Robert Englund (The Phantom); Jill Schoelen (Christine Day); Alex Hyde-White (Richard); Bill Nighy (Barton); Stephanie Lawrence (Carlotta); Terence Harvey (Hawking); Nathan Lewis (Davies); Molly Shannon (Meg, New York); Emma Rawson (Meg, London); Peter Clapham (Harrison); Mark Ryan (Mott); Yehuda Efroni (Ratcatcher); Terence Beesley (Joseph); Ray Jewers (Kline); Robin Hunter (Roland); Virginia Fiol (Sarah); Cathy Murphy (Esther); André Thornton Grimes (Bartender); Jaclyn Mendoza (Maddie); John Ghavan (Dwarf).

LOS ANGELES TIMES, 11/6/89, Calendar/p. 4, Kevin Thomas

Freddy Kreuger as the Phantom of the Opera?

That's pretty much the way it turns out in the latest film version of the durable Gaston Leroux tale when Robert Englund, who plays the hideous, terrifying madman in the "Nightmare on Elm Street" series, assumes the role of the phantom. But this new "Phantom of the Opera" which has no connection with either of the current stage versions—is a film at odds with itself.

Both director Dwight H. Little and Englund himself reveal strong romantic impulses in keeping with the timeless story of the disfigured, deranged composer who terrorizes the Paris Opera in order to promote the career of a young singer (played this time by pretty Jill Schoelen with appropriate sweetness and naivete) with whom he has fallen hopelessly in love.

However, because they are working within the exploitation genre, they are required to lay on the gore, with the result that horror effects overwhelm the tragic love story. The irony is that the great unmasking scene, still so potent in both the 1925 and 1943 film versions, has little impact because so much blood and guts has gone before it.

In essence, this "Phantom" is a queasy blend of Grand Guignol and Max Ophuls. Writer Duke Sandefur has come up with an effective modern framing story, set in New York, to provide an intriguing supernatural dimension to the Phantom. The bulk of the film is set in London (rather than Paris) a century ago, yet it was shot in Hungary amid many opulent period Mittel Europa locales. It would seem that the lush settings inspired Little and cameraman Peter Collister to go for baroque quite literally.

Little, who directed "Halloween 4," displays plenty of panache only to confront us with a Phantom who, instead of wearing the usual mask, has created an overlay of human skin to cover his scar tissue, and then applied a layer of makeup to cover the sutures. In this guise Englund's head looks like a piece of sculpture painted over in flesh tones, a suitably macabre effect. The trouble is that we're asked to watch this Phantom putting on and taking off all this stuff several times, and that's a total, fantasy-destroying turn-off which undercuts the considerable pathos Englund attempts to bring to this most tormented of men.

It's too bad that Little and Englund didn't—or weren't permitted—to aim higher, because clearly both possess that talent to have done justice to "The Phantom of the Opera," which has received an altogether appropriate R-rating.

MONTHLY FILM BULLETIN, 6/90, p. 172, Kim Newman

New York, Christine Day auditions for the leading role in a Broadway musical, choosing for her demonstration piece "Don Juan Triumphant", an obscure work by Erik Destler, a Victorian composer reputed to have been a murderer. After doing her piece, Christine is struck on the head by a falling sandbag, and wakes up in the person of a nineteenth-century understudy for the famous diva Carlotta in a London production of Gounod's *Faust*. Christine is being coached by Erik, who has been hiding in the sewers beneath the opera house since striking a deal with the Devil whereby he gave his face in exchange for musical genius. Erik commits murders, flaying his victims and sewing their skin over his deformities. Carlotta discovers a corpse in her dressing-room and is unable to perform on opening night, whereupon Christine gives a successful performance. Barton, the manager of the opera house, influences Harrison, a powerful critic, to give Christine a bad review, in order to placate Carlotta, and Erik murders Harrison. Inspector Hawking

investigates, and tells Richard, Barton's partner and Christine's boyfriend, about Erik's crimes. Christine is disturbed that Erik, who gradually reveals himself to her, is a monster, and tries to break with him. But he kidnaps her from a masked ball, where he has killed Carlotta, and takes her to his underground lair. Hawking, Richard and two policemen follow the Phantom and are killed in the process. They manage, however, to set fire to his lair and shoot him, and the apparently dying Erik tries to pull Christine into the flames. But she is whisked back through time to the present, and on waking up is told by the producer that she has won the leading role. Realising that he is the Phantom reborn, she stabs him to death, destroying his music in the hope that it will keep him dead. Later, Christine encounters a street magician who is the image of Erik
. . .

This is the first of several competing Phantom-related projects to reach the screen—beating the lavish Tony Richardson-Arthur Kopit-Charles Dance TV production and the modernised quickie *Erik's Revenge* (filmed as *Phantom of the Mall*)—in an attempt to cash in one the stage success of Andrew Lloyd Webber's romantic musical interpretation of the Gaston Leroux standard. The "high concept" of casting Robert Englund, Freddy Krueger from the *Elm Street* series, as one of the classic movie monsters, brings with it a reliance on make-up effects for shock value—as when the Phantom sews on his new face in painful close-up using an array of nineteenth-century dressmaking and surgical implements—and a few of Englund's trademark sick wisecracks ("You're suspended", he tells a stagehand as he hangs him). Whereas Lon Chaney used mime and Claude Rains his expressive voice to create a character even under the mask and the make-up, Englund is buried under thick make-up even when trying to pass for normal and is unable to do much with the role.

This Eastern European-shot film occasionally has a pleasantly Hammer Films/Gothic feel, even if the supposedly extensive sewers ("There must be hundreds of miles of tunnels down here") and the Phantom's lair are very obviously cramped sets. Haphazardly scripted on the model of the *Elm Street* sequels, where every incident seems designed simply to keep the pot boiling and to keep plot options open for the next movie, it uses bits and pieces of Leroux's original, plus touches here and there from all the films (especially the London setting and rat-infested sewer from Terence Fisher's version). The film stumbles badly over the origin of the Phantom, an issue ignored by Leroux and the 1925 Lon Chaney movie, in which Erik is a simple freak, and elaborated at length by the 1943 Claude Rains, 1963 Herbert Lom and 1983 Maximilian Schell versions, not to mention Brian De Palma's *Phantom of the Paradise*, all of which devise elaborate reasons for the Phantom's scarring. Here, in an incoherent flashback prompted by the performance of *Faust*, Englund sells his soul to a midget Devil in a Victorian brothel, and gets the facial scars as part of the bargain (wishing to be loved for his music, this Phantom is mutilated so that he will not be loved for anything else).

This *Phantom of the Opera* still fails to make any sense as a story, kicking off with a back-to-the-past contrivance, taking time out from Christine's story to include some Victorian hell-raising, and winding up with at least three false endings that serve only to set up an already announced sequel, *The Phantom of Manhattan*, in which Erik continues his ravages in a less expensive present day. Further afflicted with a wooden supporting cast of divas, London bobbies and impresarios—not to mention the usually excellent Jill Schoelen (*The Stepfather*) as a heroine whose shallow careerism makes her impossible to like—this doesn't even manage to rise to the occasion with the story's set-pieces, leaving out altogether the crucial chandelier-dropping sequence and fumbling by having revealed too much too early when it gets around to the unmasking scene that is the emotional, dramatic and horrific high spot of all the earlier *Phantom* films.

NEW YORK POST, 11/4/89, p. 15, Jami Bernard

Gaston Leroux's scary classic novel "The Phantom of the Opera" is transformed into something more hideous than the deformed Phantom himself—a ghastly slasher movie (that takes liberties with the story) in which the man who plays Freddie in the "Nightmare on Elm Street" series slices and dices his way through the London opera community of 1889, looking for that high note.

All you blue-rinsed Broadway veterans, take heed: this is *not* the film version of the show, the one with the cute half-mask to signify the Phantom's disfigurement. This is a horror movie, with blood and entrails and pieces of face falling off in leprous gumbo.

Christine Day (Jill Schoelen) is a modern young woman, a Juilliard student who has chosen an obscure piece by composer Erik Destler with which to audition for a musical. She could have picked "Send in the Clowns," but no, she's fixed on a haunting melody that, when sung, makes blood drip through the notes on the manuscript page.

During the audition, a stagehand drops a sandbag on her. When she wakes up, it is 1889 London, and she is the opera singer on whom composer Destler has a big, fat crush.

Destler has sold his soul to the devil and sports a ravaged face that needs constant stitching up with swaths of dead people's skin. Destler haunts the opera house as the Phantom, visiting Christine only in shadows and giving her career a boost by seeing to it that the lead soprano gets a bad case of laryngitis on opening night.

In fact, the Phantom kills off the theater critic who pans Christine's debut, then he kills off anyone who looks at him cross-eyed.

Christine in her own way is as ambitious as Destler, but her ambivalence seems more the fault of the inept direction by Dwight H. Little ("Halloween 4").

Robert Englund, a Shakespearean actor before he lent his talons to the role of Freddie, is not bad as the Phantom, a composer who sold his soul that his music may live. Englund's bitterly regal bearing and aquiline profile, and that arch way he has of cracking wise, make him a reasonable choice as long as this story of obsession and ambition is going the horror-pic route.

Englund is surrounded, however, by resounding ineptness. Jill Schoelen, the fresh-faced actress who played the daughter in "The Stepfather," is not up to 19th century costume drama.

Kevin Yagher's special-effects makeup is suitably disgusto, especially when the Phantom is stitching himself up for a big night on the town or goppily tearing his ear and nose off for bedtime.

This movie is from Menahem Golan's new 21st Century Film Corp., and its production values far exceed the script and acting. The sets are lavishly intricate and gloomy, and onto them stumble mystified actors whose passionless performances tear the skin off a story that should have been a classy natural for the horror film genre.

NEWSDAY, 11/4/89, Part II/p. 17, Terry Kelleher

Come to think of it, Freddy Krueger and the Phantom of the Opera could be considered brothers under the skin. Both are killers with ugly faces.

So there's no compelling reason why Robert Englund shouldn't have a shot at playing the Gaston Leroux character who dwells in a cave beneath an opera house and promotes the career of his pretty protégé by bumping off anyone who stands between her and stardom.

Sure, we've already had at least four "Phantom of the Opera" films. Sure, there are two musical theater versions currently on the boards. Sure, NBC has a mini-series coming up. The more the scarier.

What sets this "Phantom" apart from the pack? Nothing much really, except more gore. Like his predecessors, Englund's Phantom is hideously disfigured, but he seldom wears a mask. Instead, he periodically performs a crude form of plastic surgery on himself. That means lots of close-up stitching and flesh peeling—even an instance of ear removal.

When the latest Phantom commits murder, he does it up brown. Two victims are beheaded. One is quite thoroughly skinned. "This is the work of an artist," says the investigating officer.

The story opens in contemporary New York, where young Christine (Jill Schoelen) is auditioning for a stage musical. A falling prop bops Christine on the head and knocks her back a hundred years. Now she find herself the only American in a London opera company, understudying a temperamental diva (Stephanie Lawrence), romancing one of the managers (Alex Hyde-White) and benefiting from the advice of a ghostly voice coach (your servant, the Phantom). From here, director Dwight Little guides the movie along a wellworn, corpse-strewn path.

Except for the grisly makeup effects by Kevin Yagher (who left his mark on Englund's last three "Nightmare on Elm Street" films), this "Phantom of the Opera" is rather old-fashioned. The acting and dialogue are distinctly on the fustian side. After trying one prehomicide pun in the early going, Englund's Phantom generally eschews the sort of wisecracks Freddy Krueger is so fond of. He's all business, and the business is melodrama.

Fans of the Broadway show should be warned that the new "Phantom" movie is not a musical—although when Englund declares, "I am the music," one fears he'll launch into a selection from Barry Manilow's greatest hits. And all customers should be warned that the ending of this Menahem Golan production raises the familiar specter of a sequel. That would be taking superfluity to extremes.

Also reviewed in:
NEW YORK TIMES, 11/4/89, p. 12, Caryn James
VARIETY, 11/8/89, p. 36
WASHINGTON POST, 11/4/89, p. G7, Richard Harrington

PHYSICAL EVIDENCE

A Columbia Pictures release. *Executive Producer:* Don Carmody. *Producer:* Martin Ransohoff. *Director:* Michael Crichton. *Screenplay:* Bill Phillips. *Story:* Steve Ransohoff and Bill Phillips. *Director of Photography:* John A. Alonzo. *Editor:* Glenn Farr. *Music:* Henry Mancini. *Music Editor:* Stephen A. Hope. *Sound:* David Lee. *Sound Editor:* Michael O'Farrell and Sharon Lackie. *Production Designer:* Dan Yarhi. *Art Decorator:* Dennis Davenport. *Set Decorator:* Jacques Bradette. *Special Effects:* Rory Cutler and Kaz Kobielski. *Costumes:* Betsy Cox. *Make-up:* Katherine Southern. *Stunt Coordinator:* Stan Barrett. *Running time:* 99 minutes. *MPAA Rating:* R.

CAST: Burt Reynolds (Joe Paris); Theresa Russell (Jenny Hudson); Ned Beatty (James Nicks); Kay Lenz (Deborah Quinn); Ted McGinley (Kyle); Tom O'Brien (Matt Farley); Kenneth Welsh (Harry Norton); Ray Baker (Strickler); Ken James (Hank Carruth); Michael P. Moran (Tony Reugger); Angelo Rizacos (Tony Sklar); Lamar Jackson (Delmar Fraser); Paul Hubbard (Burt Knight); Larry Reynolds (Trial Judge); Peter MacNeill (Brannigan); Laurie Paton (Mabel); Don Granbery (Vincent Quinn); Barry Flatman (Brody); Malcolm Stewart (Ames); Richard Fitzpatrick (Kravitz); J.W. Carroll (Samson); Kathy Michael McGlynn (Gladys); Djanet Sears (Sheila); Claire Cellucci (Tanya); Michael Donaghue (Frank Stella); Anthony Sherwood (Lou); Angie McNab (Amy Farley); Laurie Holden (Matt's Girl); David Clement (Warden Debilis); Steve Whistance Smith (Lee); Dave Efron (Buddy); Stan Barrett (Tiny); Ken Bates (Jumper); Matt Cooke (Arraignment Officer); Michael Rothery (Doctor); Gene Mack (Brawny Guard); Chris Thomas and Norm Henderson (Nick's Cops); Stewart Arnott (Nick's Assistant); Eddie Driscoll (Jenny's Assistant); David Ferry (1st Cop); Victor Ertmanis (2nd Cop); Michael Copeman (Potential Juror); Diane Douglas (Woman Juror); Allan Aarons (Bastianelli); Steven Hunter (Bailiff); Jennifer Inch (Waitress); François Klanfner (Louis); Terry Tweed (Arraignment Judge); Louis Negin (Jake Farley).

FILMS IN REVIEW, 5/89, p. 302, Edmond Grant

In recent years, the plotlines of Burt Reynold's films have become as thin as his ever shifting hairline. This, his most recent outing, has a confusing storyline, listless direction and some dismally drab acting.

True, the first scene—wherein a suicidal man poised to jump off a bridge has a close encounter with a corpse—promises better things to come. But as soon as Burt enters the picture, and we find out that he's a gritty, hard edged ex-cop who's been framed for murder, we're back in painfully familiar territory.

The film does provide one unfortunate surprise. That has to do with Reynold's costar, the dazzlingly attractive Theresa Russell. Ms. Russell has distinguished herself playing troubled women in quartet of films with her husband, director Nicolas Roeg, and Bob Rafelson's *Black Widow.* Here, playing a "normal" individual—the yuppie lawyer who's bent on getting Burt acquitted—she seems woefully inadequate, and uncharacteristically stiff.

The strained relationship between lawyer and client fails to strike any sparks, and the numerous red herrings that are introduced do little to heighten the tension level. Various other parties, on both sides of the law, are shown as having motivations for the killing Reynolds is accused of, and the only person who can provide him with an alibi for the time of the murder (gangster's wife Kay Lenz) is too scared to speak on his behalf.

It used to be that Reynold's off-handed charm was sufficient enough to keep skimpy material like this afloat. But, times have changed, and so, apparently, has Reynolds, who seems bored and disinterested in his latest efforts. With the charm factor absent, it's no surprise that *Physical Evidence* is already well on its way to joining Burt's last three "tough cop" pictures (*Heat, Malone,* and *Rent-a-Cop*) on video store shelves and constant cable replays.

LOS ANGELES TIMES, 1/27/89, Calendar/p. 6, Michael Wilmington

Something seems to have gone dead inside "Physical Evidence." It's a cold, bright, thick movie without any life or passion. Yet passion, both moral and romantic, is its subject. It's a thriller about a lawyer (Theresa Russell) defending a brutal ex-cop accused of murder (Burt Reynolds), and the story plays up their class and cultural differences, the corrupt society around them, the byzantine quirks and crannies of jurisprudence.

How did it go so flat and empty? Director Michael Crichton and writer Bill Phillips seem to be frantically recycling bits and scraps of every recent upscale thriller-romance, pushing all the buttons in a doomed attempt to make something, anything, light up the scoreboard.

The parts seem interchangeable. There's a sexy lawyer battling public prejudices in a tangled legal system. (Isn't that "The Accused"?) There are backstage finaglings at a sensational trial ("The Verdict," "Suspect"); three-cornered romance with undercurrents of murder and obsession ("Fatal Attraction"); a disgraced cop trying to clear his name ("Witness"). Phillips and Crichton are like a pair who walk into a casino and try to win by playing every game in the house. Everything in "Physical Evidence" has an antecedent; there's scarcely a moment that seems real or honest.

The most obvious influence of all is "Jagged Edge," the 1985 hit by "Evidence" producer Martin Ransohoff—whose son Steve is credited here with part of the original story.

Original?

The movie begins with a preposterous set-piece: A hapless would-be suicide tries to hang himself from a bridge over Boston Harbor. When he discovers a corpse in the girders, the two get tangled up in the rope and fall, dangling over water. The scene is staged with such a bouncy rhythm, it's obviously intended to tickle and shock. But why would a suicide victim pick a hugh, well-travelled bridge to *hang* himself from? Isn't that a bit like like walking out on a skyscraper ledge and slitting your wrists?

It's best not to ask questions like that about "Physical Evidence"; you'll never stop. Halfway through the trial, lawyer Jenny Hudson calls a witness, a gangster's wife (Kay Lenz), who's going to give Reynolds' Joe Paris an alibi, by admitting they were together, alone—until the nasty prosecutor (Ned Beatty) brings her murderous gangster husband into the courtroom, intimidating her into silence. Did this woman believe her spouse wouldn't find out about her confession unless he actually heard it in the courtroom?

So it goes. Michael Crichton is a writer-director whose movies, even at their best, seem a little disengaged and remote. They revolve around gimmickry, scientific extrapolation, clockwork robberies, robots—and they're usually weak on character. Here, working with a story that's an illogical patchwork of other movies, his style seems even more remote; empty of physical beauty, though John Alonzo shot it; devoid of humanity, despite a fine cast. Only when the movie focuses on its plethora of sleazy villains, a Crichton specialty, does it come briefly alive. The sleaze sweepstakes is won, hands down, by Angelo Rizacos as a cotton-mouthed contract killer and snitch.

But, even though everything in "Physical Evidence" seems to collapse, star Burt Reynolds doesn't. Reynolds has had such bad luck with his projects recently, that critics sometimes react as if his movies were high-wire acts. Will he make it? Will he fall?

But the emptiness of "Physical Evidence" doesn't muffle Reynolds. He exudes dark, glowering authority and plays against his own charm. It's a nice performance—along with Rizacos' Tony Sklar, Larry Reynolds as the trial judge and Laurie Paton as a lewd receptionist. It's not enough.

Reynolds' Paris can't save "Physical Evidence" because the movie is built around Russell's Jenny: a role that doesn't have the range of her Nicolas Roeg films. It leaves her stuck in legal absurdity, erupting in soft-minded yuppie spats with her jealous screen roommate Ted McGinley.

"Physical Evidence" is a thriller that doesn't ignite, a mystery that doesn't mystify and barely makes sense. Like the corpse and the suicide in the movie's opening scene, this movie leaves us dangling over dark water, supposedly in Death's embrace but feeling silly.

MONTHLY FILM BULLETIN, 9/89, p. 279, Philip Strick

Former Boston cop Joe Paris, now an embittered down-and-out, is accused of the murder of Jake Farley, an underground figure he openly despised. Joe has no alibi and was dead drunk on the night of the murder; his seemingly hopeless case is assigned to ambitious defence attorney Jenny Hudson. They dislike each other, but Jenny's first achievement is to get Joe released on bail against the objections of District Attorney Nicks. Following threats from the murdered man's son, Matt Farley, Joe studies police records of his past arrests to find who might have a grudge against him; he is assisted by a sympathetic officer, Strickler. Unexpectedly, Jenny is informed by Deborah, wife of crime boss Vincent Quinn, that Joe was with her on the night of the murder. To the fury of her fiancé Kyle, Jenny insists on hearing about Joe's relationship with Deborah, despite Joe's certainty that the doubtful alibi puts Deborah's life at risk. Joe suspects the involvement of Harry Norton, a crook he once jailed, but finds that Norton is only just arriving back from Rio. When the trial begins, Jenny is warned by her employers that she is handling the case badly; her confidence is further shaken by the burglary of her home and an attack by Matt Farley. Quinn insists that Deborah was with him on the night of the murder, and Joe "fires" Jenny for putting Deborah in danger; after walking out on Kyle, the attorney is isolated and in despair. Finding Strickler destroying apparently incriminating tapes he has stolen from Farley, Joe decides that he and Jenny must after all work as a team and they are reconciled. A phone call from a convict, Tony Sklar, suggests that Norton hired him to kill Jake Farley, who stole Norton's former girl friend when Norton was imprisoned. Sklar is murdered before this can be substantiated, but Joe and Jenny manage to keep his death secret while Joe compiles a tape from the phone call that makes it sound as if Sklar is still alive and threatening revenge. Joe then plays the message over the phone to three main suspects, Quinn, Farley and Norton, as police patrols wait to see which one of them makes a move. Confusion is caused by Strickler's renewed intervention until both he and the Quinns are killed, and Jenny finds herself in lone confrontation with Norton. After a desperate struggle, she shoots him down.

In theory, the rambling structure of the Elmore Leonard stories much favoured by Burt Reynolds as context for his recent portrayals of jaded tough guys should have integrated profitably with novelist/filmmaker Michael Crichton's more precise (but equally intricate) plotting to yield a sharply appealing comedy-thriller. In practice, as written by Bill Phillips, *Physical Evidence* seems only to have drained the interest and inspiration from everybody concerned: the story wanders with tenacious but bewildering logic among a mass of motivations and interventions, and depends on at least three convenient informational inserts in order to function at all. Crichton's interest in manipulative technology is confined here to the unremarkable notion that one convincing telephone message can be constructed from another. Never much of a stylist, he has opted this time for what he terms "an updated *film noir* look", resulting in largely inoffensive anonymity but with occasional and revealing clumsy lapses like the crudely staged and rather despairing freeze frame at the end. The theme of lady lawyer under stress is already a bit of a cliché after *Jagged Edge, Suspect* and *The Accused,* and Theresa Russell, distractingly weighed down by heavymetal jewellery, is unable to create anything memorable from this glum, waspish version except when venomously detaching herself from her repellent fiancé. There is some attempt at feisty badinage in response to Reynolds' ruminative wisecracks, but in general the protagonists contemplate each other in such apathy that without even a decent villain (to match, say, Charles Durning in *Stick*, Vittorio Gassman in *Sharky's Machine*, or Gene Simmons in *Runaway*) the whole exercise, while never quite collapsing, contrives to look and sound peculiarly futile.

NEW YORK, 2/13/89, p. 79, David Denby

Listening to Theresa Russell rattle through her lines in *Physical Evidence*, I contracted the vague anxiety I used to feel when Jimmy Carter gave a speech. Carter never seemed to know where he wanted the emphasis to fall in a sentence—the beginning, the middle, the end, nowhere? The affect Carter displayed rarely linked up with the meaning of the words he uttered. (He was an unconvincing actor, and the country, alas, wanted a persuasive one—a man who at least seemed to mean what he said.) As a chic Boston public defender, Russell is so vague and tentative, she appears to be a bit player rehearsing the part until the star shows up. Her character is menaced by thugs and lied to by her own client; everyone suspects that she's not up to the job of defending a man accused of murder, and Russell does little to dispel the thought. Burt Reynolds, who gives a good, serious performance as the defendant—a down-at-the-heels cop—gets insultingly shunted to the side, while Russell, petulant when she should be angry, huffy when she should be aggressive, holds the screen for eons, furling and unfurling her beautiful streaked hair like some legendary glamour queen of the past. *Physical Evidence*, directed by Michael Crichton, is an embarrassment—one of those script-conference disasters in which little-seen minor characters assume greater plot value than the people constantly in front of us on the screen. Crichton doesn't give the material any tension. After a nifty opening sequence, the movie seems geared to Russell's floundering and vapid performance.

NEW YORK POST, 1/27/89, p. 29, David Edelstein

You're going to be reading a lot of cruel reviews of the new thriller "Physical Evidence," in which Theresa Russell defends ex-cop Burt Reynolds from a murder rap. Many will be accurate, but there is something too easy about laughing at this movie, the way one might laugh at a very stupid person or a man who has forgotten to zip up his fly.

A short time ago, many critics received a letter from Martin Ransohoff, producer of "Jagged Edge" and "Physical Evidence."

"Dear David" my copy began. "A few years ago Linda Ronstadt and Nelson Riddle teamed up to create a trio of albums reviving the songs of the '40s. . . Its recent revival has been rewarding to those of us who remember with fondness that rich music and slower pace. . ."

Ransohoff goes on to say that he and director Michael Crichton wanted "Physical Evidence" to recall that slower '40's pace. It "attempts to explore whether it is feasible, in 1989, to do a love story without sex, handle murder and suspense without gratuitous violence. . ." etc.

What Ransohoff is asking us is to respect his intentions, his refusal to pander to the barbarism of the '80s. In deference to this producer's values (and taste in music), and because I—unlike many critics—take no pleasure in savagery—I shall attempt to discharge the obligation of reviewing his film in a restrained and gentlemanly fashion:

IN "Physical Evidence," the incredibly stinkeroo new thriller—

No. That is the wrong tone. I am not a sadist, and, as I have said, I respect Mr. Ransohoff's intentions too much to go for easy laughs. Perhaps the review should begin with an account of the leading performance:

AS the attorney defending Burt Reynolds's suspended policeman from a charge of murder, Theresa Russell acts like a centerfold on quaaludes walking through a screen test—

No, that is unchivalrous. It would be better to describe the performance nonjudgmentally:

Early on, Russell announces to Reynolds that her expensive clothes are not her, that she goes deeper than that. "This is me, brains and guts," she says, pointing, inexplicably, to her shoulder, and eliciting gales of laughter—

Stop it. This is like laughing at someone with a lobotomy. Perhaps a formal, New York Times-style description would lighten things up.

In the role of the lawyer, Russell speaks in a husky, inexpressive voice and reels off her long speeches as if she'd learned them phonetically. To suggest thinking, she furrows her brow, but cannot help seeming like an unbelievable bimbo—

Enough. Perhaps we should table our Russell discussion. After all, a performance of this caliber is partially the fault of the director.

Director Michael Crichton has lately been absorbed in the study of out-of-body experiences. Perhaps this would explain why there is no one at the helm of "Physical Evidence." Come back, Michael—

Quit it, jerk. Don't make fun of people's metaphysical beliefs. Maybe I better just say something nice and have done with it. I am not a sadist.

Burt Reynolds, who has looked in his last few pictures like something out of Madame Tussaud's, should act with Russell more often; beside her, he appears almost human—

Oh forget it.

Sorry, Martin. You don't expose your throat to a critic and expect him not to chomp. It's our nature. And besides, when I get nostalgic, I listen to the Sex Pistols and the Buzzcocks.

NEWSDAY, 1/27/89, Part III/p. 5, Mike McGrady

There was a time in Joe Louis' career when the champ kept in shape by regularly climbing into the ring with second-raters—his famous "Bum of the Month Club." Anyone forced to attend Burt Reynolds' movies will surely understand the concept since it's so similar to Reynolds' own Bummer of the Month Club. The only significant difference between the two men's planned battles with mediocrity is that Louis won his bouts.

Last year it was "Rent-a-Cop" and "Switching Channels." This year, so far, it's "Physical Evidence." If Burt Reynolds were, indeed, a fighter, next year he'd be opening the card in Scranton, Pa.

The central character in "Physical Evidence" will prove an overly familiar creation, to both Reynolds and his followers. Unshaven and unsteady, Reynolds is a cadger of cigarettes and a belligerent boozer subject to sudden blackouts and painful hangovers (strangely, despite all these personal failings, his frequently displayed musculature evidences an abiding devotion to physical fitness).

Drunk or sober, he can still demolish hired goons with a single blow and fracture the hearts of secretaries with a single crooked grin. He talks dirty, sneers at yuppies, wisecracks his way through disaster, wins the woman, etc. etc. So what else is new? Nothing. . . .

Acting opposite Reynolds is the lovely Theresa Russell (the blond killer in "Black Widow") as the young attorney who defends Reynolds when he is charged with murder. The kittenish Russell brings about as much credibility to the role of lawyer as she would to, oh, say the role of Thurgood Marshall. She puts no stamp on the part at all, does nothing to individualize it and, worse, seems awkward with the most familiar of lines.

The familiarity of those lines and characters and notions must be attributed to writer Bill Phillips, but director Michael Crichton has failed to add an ounce of creativity. Oh, maybe just one ounce. In fact, the opening sequence wherein the corpse is discovered is highly charged moviemaking that only serves to accentuate the flatness of what follows.

One of the surest indications of a bad movie are unbroken patterns, familiar patterns that don't make room for surprises or unusual details or, as a result, humanity.

Since toughness is Reynolds' main characteristic, it soon becomes his only characteristic and then there is no limit to that toughness—even when it's incomprehensible. A uniformed cop comes up to offer his support stammeringly and Reynolds snaps, "You got something to say, say it." That response makes no sense at all unless the cop is a villain, and if the cop turns out to be a villain, it also make no sense since there's no way Reynolds could guess that fact at first meeting.

Consider, too, how the film treats its token yuppie, a broker who has the effrontery to live with the attorney earmarked for Reynolds. The yuppie (Ted McGinley) wears bright red suspenders and hair cream; he bathes in a hot tub and refers to lovemaking as "sharing quality time." Finally, when he's beaten up by a hood, he whines, "He broke my *Rolex!*" All of a pattern, all phony, all catering to familiar attitudes.

But the film itself is nothing more than a compilation of familiar patterns. The too-tough Burt and his too-sexy lover; the too-villainous villain; the too-weasely weasels. As the too-violent violence mounts and the too-red blood flows, you will surely be forgiven for leaving before the too-predictable ending.

VILLAGE VOICE, 2/7/89, p. 68, Manohla Dargis

Producer Martin Ransohoff and Columbia Pictures must be praying that lightning strikes twice. *Physical Evidence*, their new release, is advertised as "from the producer of *Jagged Edge*," and it bears more than a casual resemblance to the '85 thriller from the same team. This time, however, it's Theresa Russell, not Glenn Close, who plays the idealistic attorney defending a client (Burt Reynolds) who may be a sadistic killer.

Did he or didn't he? Reynolds plays Joe Paris, a hot-tempered, liberal cop who's been arrested for the murder of a nefarious underworld associate. Paris, fulfilling the requisite hard-boiled profile, is a hard-drinking widower on suspension for assaulting another officer. Russell's the green public defender, Jenny Hudson, who lives with her boyfriend, a junk-bond broker (an excuse for a quick lecture on the evils of white-collar crime), and wields power shoulders—she's the kind of Hollywood professional whose unhappiness is signaled by how tightly her hair is coiffed.

Sluggishly directed by Michael Crichton (*Coma, The Great Train Robbery*), *Physical Evidence* is 99 minuites of lowrent bathos. The supporting cast does what it can with the creakily recycled script by Bill Phillips (Tom O'Brien as the murdered man's son is a particular standout), but Russell and Reynolds fare less well. The major problem is that both leads are stranded without the benefit of clear direction and saddled with some of the movie's worst lines. (Who could do anything with bedroom repartee like "No ways, José." "I ain't José"?) But Reynolds, in an apparent effort to (again) shed his hee-haw persona, is remarkably low-key, and it's a mistake that he has not been given more screen time. Although his three-day growth and flared slacks don't make him a down-and-out regular Joe, Reynolds is one of the film's less painful features.

Russell, on the other hand, is a disaster. In danger of becoming the Sondra Locke of art-house movies, she's taken on another role meant to prove her versatility. In *Physical Evidence*, she reprises a characterization—a moist prepubescent trapped in the body of an adult—familiar from husband Nicolas Roeg's film. Along with her kittenish physicality and flat baby-voice delivery, this creates an enormous credibility problem. (It doesn't help that she tends to thrust her chest forward whenever the script flounders.)

Courtroom dramas (*Marie, Suspect, The Accused*—and especially the subgenre of Woman-Lawyer films—function as a symbolic female rite of passage. Gray flannel, briefcases, and legalese are supposed to give actresses (and, by extension, women in general) a veneer of seriousness, as if battling inside the judicial system (like the corporate world) were the ultimate triumph of liberation. Perhaps even more disturbing, however, is the recent spectacle of women wreaking bloody vengeance. The shameless finale of *Physical Evidence* finds Russell with hair flowing and gun blazing. For Hollywood, postfeminism means that women have earned the right to shoot-to-kill as guiltlessly as men; they just get to dress better.

Also reviewed in:
NEW YORK TIMES, 1/27/89, p. C10, Janet Maslin
VARIETY, 1/25–31/89, p. 14
WASHINGTON POST, 1/27/89, p. D7, Rita Kempley

PINK CADILLAC

A Warner Bros. release of a Malpaso production. *Executive Producer:* Michael Gruskoff. *Producer:* David Valdes. *Director:* Buddy Van Horn. *Screenplay:* John Eskow. *Director of Photography:* Jack Green. *Editor:* Joel Cox. *Music:* Steve Dorff. *Production Designer:* Edward C. Carfagno. *Running time:* 122 minutes. *MPAA Rating:* PG-13.

CAST: Clint Eastwood (Tommy Nowak); Bernadette Peters (Lou Ann McGuinn); Timothy Carhart (Roy); Michael Des Barres (Alex); John Dennis Johnston (Waycross); Geoffrey Lewis (Ricky Z)

LOS ANGELES TIMES, 5/26/89, Calendar/p. 1, Michael Wilmington

"You shouldn't mess with a man's vehicle," someone remarks during the course of "Pink Cadillac." He's referring to the splendiferously tail-finned, precious-pink 1959 Caddy of the title, but it might also be a veiled reference to the movie itself. It's the latest in a long line of Clint Eastwood Saturday night action specials, full of salty violence and cool humor.

In this one, Eastwood plays Tommy Nowak, a wry, T-shirted skip tracer (he tracks down bail-jumpers) with a penchant for fey impersonations and a weakness for ditzo blondes in tight pants. It's Eastwood's vehicle: his hand on the wheel, his lips peeled for the quips, his pedal to the metal. The movie was conceived for no other reason than to give him something to drive. But, as long as he's at top speed, with Bernadette Peters, snuggling up, bombarding his ear with pert, wise-acre badinage, it's a fairly amusing cruise.

The movie zips along amiably between Sacramento and Reno, out through the Sierras and the Nevada highways, racing through a mythical terrain Eastwood seems to have defined for himself since the mid-'70s. It's open, clear uncluttered, threaded with highways, gas stops and edge-of-the-town taverns, populated with nymphs, squares, salty old geezers, bartenders, eccentrics, maniacs and oddballs.

Eastwood's Nowak, as with his old Sergio Leone characters, is a kind of bounty hunter: a skip tracer working for a madly mugging Sacramento bail bondsman. But Nowak isn't a lonely outsider. John Eskow's script is really a love-on-the run thriller. In this case, Norwak falls for his prisoner: lamb-on-the-lam Lou Ann McGuinn (Peters), wrongfully arrested because of the idiotic counterfeiting activities of her dodo husband, Roy (Timothy Carhart), who is mixed up with a band of half-witted white supremacists and ex-convicts called the Birthright. The pink Cadillac, which passes from hand to hand during the ensuing melee, is Roy's; its trunk is crammed with money from the Birthright's war chest.

It's a sign of the movie's tone that although these are trademark villains for an Eastwood movie—surly fanatics and backwoods imbeciles on a macho trip—they're eventually played less for menace than clownishness. They're a pack of bigoted nincompoops, and though they commit arson and kidnaping and snort amphetamines off hunting knives, they're less like the street scum of "Sudden Impact" than the looney-tune bikers in "Every Which Way But Loose."

"Pink Cadillac" has a strong visual design and lots of juicy, self-confident acting. But it doesn't transcend its star vehicle trappings or chemistry. The construction of the story is so soft, you get the impression that if the driver and navigator were replaced, the movie might turn rattletrap and fall apart.

That wouldn't seem as disappointing if it didn't come right after Eastwood's last directorial effort, "Bird," the intricately jazzy ode to bop great Charlie Parker, which vaulted Eastwood, surprisingly for some, to the front row of current American directors. "Bird" deserved all its praise. It was a passionate piece of tight-lipped romanticism, beautifully acted and articulated.

"Pink Cadillac," conversely, wasn't directed by Eastwood, though it's clearly his movie. It was handled by key Malpaso associated Buddy Van Horn, who did "Any Which Way You Can" and "The Dead Pool" and usually directs Eastwood's action sequences. Van Horn is an amiable director—an ace at action, obviously—but he doesn't seem able to transform material that is inherently this thin and unimaginative.

When he has scenes with Eastwood, Peters, William Hickey (as a shy, shambling trailer park manager), John Dennis Johnston as a maniac or Geoffrey Lewis doing a little sitcom aria as a brain-burned '60s-era ID forger, Van Horn lays back and doesn't seem to interfere. But he is too amiable and laissez faire in the dialogue scenes. He doesn't seem to have dropped down a dramatic through-line. You may find the shifts of Lou Ann's husband, from bozo to villain to stumblebum to sidekick, bewilderingly unconnected. Or fail to understand why Tommy and Lou Ann are so lazily laconic and jokey just after they've run a gauntlet of killers with automatic rifles.

In a way, Eskow's "Pink Cadillac" script has the same construction as all those buddies-in-love-on-the-road movies of last year, "Rain Man," "Twins" "Things Change" and "Midnight Run." But Eastwood tries to mix up road action movie with screwball romance.

He is also consciously creating a new kind of character for himself. Nowak is a "master of disguise," who successfully impersonates a starchy chauffeur, a rodeo clown, a sleazy "hey-bro" promoter with pencil-thin pimp mustache and, finally a redneck nerd. And Eastwood doesn't play these roles for pyrotechnic brilliance, as Robin Williams might have; he gives them a sly, draggy, antic quality.

He acts as though he were having a great time subverting his own image, like Bogart as the swishy bibliophile in "The Big Sleep." Eastwood's interaction with Bernadette Peters also has a different swing than usual. Peters' Lou Ann is a goad and a tease, a scrumptious little honeybunch out to wilt his whiskers; she's such a snazzy actress, she brings it off. Eastwood's bemused reactions to her high jinks are the spice of the whole movie. He seems to be saying: Mess with my vehicle all you want.

NEW YORK, 6/12/89, p. 78, David Denby

Bernadette Peters loosens up Clint Eastwood a little and entertains herself as well in the pleasantly ramshackle shaggy-dog story *Pink Cadillac*.

NEW YORK POST, 5/26/89, p. 37, David Edelstein

A funny thing happens during the mousy, amiable road picture, "Pink Cadillac": Clint Eastwood tries to give a genuine comic performance. What's funny isn't his acting; it's the mere sight of this stone-faced super hero putting out.

"See the monolith mug!" the posters should exclaim. "See the monolith talk in a falsetto! See the monolith disguise himself as a lisping hick! See the monolith give those granite features a workout!"

He's often embarrassing, but he sure works up a sweat. And that by itself is impressive. Eastwood is like Guy Lombardo doing "Sympathy for the Devil": You don't buy it, but you appreciate the difficulties involved.

Eastwood plays Tom Nowak, a skip-tracer who sometimes traps his quarries by phoning them, announcing that they've won a radio contest and showing up at their door with a limo and a pair of handcuffs. Quite a card. (However, it's hard to see how anyone could accept Eastwood's timbreless effusions as those of a deejay.)

Nowak has been hired by a bail-bondsman (Gerry Bamman) to track down Lou Ann McGuinn (Bernadette Peters), a pale young mother who'd been arrested for being too close to her ne'er-do-well husband Roy's sack of counterfeit money when the police busted into their mobile home.

On impulse, she'd jumped bond and driven away in Roy's pink Cadillac, unaware it held $253,000 belonging to a white-supremacist paramilitary group.

The Aryan army is pretty p.o.'ed; you can tell because the psycho leader, Alex (heavy-metal rocker Michael Des Barres), stands Roy up against a poster of his wife and traces his silhouette with machine-gun bullets. (He's the sort of villain who says, "We will deal with the female.")

As the female, Peters makes a wonderful screwball heroine, both dazed and iron-willed. She's more than a foot shorter than Clint, and when they converse—she in that strangled little voice, he in his toneless rasp—you wonder how the hell they can hear each other. They're like mysterious forest creatures, and their rapport is likably weird.

It's no surprise that when Nowak finds Lou Ann in Reno, he can't bring himself to turn her over to the cops. He's no "Dirty Harry" Callahan; he's a stumblebum who doesn't want any trouble. Yet he can't suppress his finer instincts. When the goons steal Lou Ann's baby, he rises to the occasion as, alas, we always knew he would.

That's the problem—you always know what's next. Although the dialogue (by John Eskow) has a lot of comic spin and the actors are in there pitching, the plotting is slack and the picture weighs in at 122 minutes. It's also drab looking. Malpaso, Eastwood's production company, is famous for making movies cheap, fast and dark, and claustrophobia does nothing for a thriller-comedy set in the Sierras.

Too bad Eastwood didn't direct the picture himself instead of turning it over to the anonymous Buddy Van Horn. Maybe he was preoccupied with his performance, with getting his eyebrows to curl just right for that look of disgusted incredulity.

"Pink Cadillac" is bound to anger audiences expecting either a junky comedy like "Any Which Way but Loose" or a junky shoot-'em-up like the "Dirty Harry" sequels. It's better than those orangutan and Harry pictures, but nowhere near as charming as Eastwood's "Bronco Billy," which bombed.

At the climax, part of me was thinking it would be a shame if he turned into Clint Eastwood and wasted everyone because up till now it had been a sweet little picture with not that much violence.

The other part of me was thinking it would be a shame if he didn't turn into Clint Eastwood and waste everyone because up till now it hadn't been lively enough to compensate for the relative lack of violence.

That's the kind of debased thinking you get into if you see a lot of trash vigilante movies— primitive, irresponsible and utterly reasonable. Now that he's cleaned up his act, Eastwood may suffer the rejection of the yahoo audience whose taste he helped to nurture. There's justice in that somehow.

NEWSDAY, 5/26/89, Part III/p. 3, Lynn Darling

All the usual elements are in place in this latest Clint Eastwood vehicle: the upright loner with a code of his own, out there doing his job, being a man in a man's world; the bad guys out there doing *their* job, pillaging and plundering and violating, in relentless fashion, the usual standards of decency. But this being the late '80s, when even Rambo got around to showing a nurturing side in his last guts and glory epic, there's also a baby thrown into the mix, just so we know what a kind and caring guy Tommy Nowak, Eastwood's character, really is.

Nowak is a "skip tracer," a guy who makes his living tracking fugitives who have jumped bail on a wide variety of sleazeball crimes. He likes his work: He gets to wear a lot of disguises to surprise his prey, he doesn't have to talk much, and he doesn't have to answer to anyone except his obnoxious but malleable boss.

Nowak has no complaints until he comes up against a pert, little housewife on the lam from counterfeiting charges. Lou Ann McGuinn (Bernadette Peters) is by her account a woman who hasn't gotten much of a break in life—she thought she was marrying James Dean, she tells Nowak, and ended up with a hapless, two-bit amphetamine freak (Timothy Carhart) who has got himself mixed up with a bunch of racist psychotics banded together under the name of The Birthright.

Of course Lou Ann had nothing to do with the counterfeiting—she has stolen her husband's big, beautiful Cadillac to rescue her baby and herself from the life they're living. Pretty soon not only Nowak but a crew of maniacs in pickup trucks is looking for her.

It's not hard to figure out where "Pink Cadillac" is going from here—the relationship between Eastwood and Peters is pretty formulaic, built along standard romantic comedy lines. But the two stars generate none of the chemistry needed to give this vehicle a much needed jump start.

As a romantic couple, Eastwood and Peters seem particularly mismatched: Eastwood's showing his age in this one, but he's still Eastwood, easygoing, laid back, paying a state visit to a role he's done many, many times before. Peters, meanwhile, is a melange of acting shticks, va-va-voom sexy one moment, innocent madonna the next, ditzy blonde right after that. Only rarely do the two stars seem to be inhabiting the same movie.

NEWSWEEK, 6/12/89, p. 67, David Ansen

On the Clint Eastwood Toughness Index, *Pink Cadillac* ranks somewhere in his middle range, alongside such amiable action adventures as "The Gauntlet" and "Thunderbolt and Lightfoot." His new character, Tommy Nowak, a "skip tracer" who chases bail-jumpers, isn't a hardboiled obsessive like Dirty Harry, nor is he as soft as Bronco Billy. In a sense, this is Eastwood's "Fletch," in which he gets to do impersonations—like donning a gold lamé jacket as a Las Vegas smoothie—that show off his endearing talents as a mimic.

A relatively laid-back Eastwood effort, "Pink Cadillac" finds him chasing Bernadette Peters, the Kewpie doll wife of an ex-con. Hubby's involved with a nasty gang of white supremacists, whose counterfeit money she's absconded with in his '59 Caddy convertible. Eastwood teams up with her in an unlikely but genial effort to bring these miscreants to their knees. John Eskow's script rarely strays from formula, but it's peppered with witty potshots. Posing as a racist rube to gain entry to the villains' hideaway, Eastwood asks one of the supremacists in mock innocence, "If we get rid of all the Jews and blacks, man, what are we going to do for entertainers?" The creep brightens with an answer: "We'll still have David Letterman."

Peters is pretty cute, but this wonderful stage actress never quite seems a real person on screen; she's more an idea of a character than the thing itself. Under Buddy Van Horn's nonchalant direction, the Eastwood/Peters romantic chemistry is rather low voltage, but they both seem to be enjoying themselves. Keep your expectations modest, and you will, too.

TIME, 6/5/89, p. 78, John Skow

Under the right circumstances—temperature in three digits, air conditioner broken, the tube showing tractor-pull-contest reruns, the dog under the bed with an attack of chiggers, marriage teetering, car defunct with black-lung disease and only one movie within walking distance—*Pink Cadillac* is a tolerable summer-weight flick. Clint Eastwood and Bernadette Peters have a somewhat better time than the viewer, but they probably do in real life too.

Eastwood plays a fun-loving hard guy who captures fugitives who have skipped out on their bail money; cons a villain into believing he has won a date with Dolly Parton, then shows up in a limousine and arrests him; dresses up as a rodeo clown and nabs a bad-guy bull rider on first bounce, just as the bull has tossed him. Peters plays—but you knew this, didn't you?—a gorgeous, daffy bail jumper. She isn't really a villain, of course. Her dopey husband is involved with a crew of gun-fondling white supremacists, and they need to hide $250,000 in counterfeit bills, which he stows under the folded-up top of his pink 1959 Cadillac convertible.

That leads to a lovely shot of dingbat Peters wheeling down a dirt road, radio blasting, with funny money blowing out of the back of the car. She has one foot on the dashboard, and bubble-gum bubbles are popping out of her funny little rosebud mouth, right there in the middle of her funny big custard-pie face.

That's pretty much the movie. Peters is cute and irresistible, Eastwood is cute and irresistible, and then the two of them, like ballet dancers, are cute together. Peters' character has a baby, who is cute too, but the kid still has a lot to learn. Everyone plays off stereotypes of stereotypes, so Peters does a send-up of Eastwood's middle-aged machismo, and Eastwood, eyelids fluttering prettily in that fine Mount Rushmore face, takes off Peters' little-girl-lost act. Eastwood wins.

These two, in fact, are surprisingly funny, and they belong in a movie with a real plot; say, one on the level of *The Cannonball Run*. Here the white supremacists snarl and shoot off a lot of George Bush firearms, but the only dramatic tension comes from worrying about that lovely Cadillac. They wouldn't really hurt it, would they? Don't bet on it.

VILLAGE VOICE, 6/6/89, p. 62, Georgia Brown

Pink Cadillac is throwaway Clint, but for those who'll take the lean, squinty, grizzled one any which way they can get him, it will probably tide them over. Eastwood's long-time associate (since TV's *Rawhide*) Buddy Van Horn directs, and John Eskow is credited with the screenplay (his first outside of two shorts for *Saturday Night Live*), but the show is Eastwood's and the attitudes are, too. In this meandering movie, he's a bit of a one-man-band, doing imitations and getting off quips on the law, gun control, and sexism. ("I have a firm policy on gun control: If there's a gun around, I want to control it.") I'm not sure what it means when a guy in a deli orders a "Chief Justice Warren Burger." ("Gimme a Warren," sounds the waitress. "Burn it.") But I got that the movie's subject has to do with the conflict of authority and personal imperatives.

Eastwood plays Tommy Nowak, a "skip-tracer" for an enterprising sleazeball bail bondsman. As a version of the bounty hunter Eastwood once was, the occupation is a mythic comedown, but it's in line with all the two-bit drifters the man obviously feels kin to. Eastwood sometimes looks like he aspires to be the Bobbie Ann Mason, or even the Barry Hannah, of screenland—poet of the boondocks and good ol' boys. I like the ambience, the man's affinities. I just wish this vehicle had some juice.

To bring his man in, Tommy adopts disguises. (Chevy Chase could do this part.) He puts on the red nose of a rodeo clown, or he slicks his hair, glues on a pencil mustache, and wears a gold jacket to pose as a huckster in a Reno club. (He comes out looking like Michael Caine doing David Niven in *Dirty Rotten Scoundrels*—only this is chintzy Reno rather than the Riviera.) The movie opens with Tommy screaming like a radio disc jockey as he phones a burly creature named Capshaw holed up in a trailer, informing him he's won a date with Dolly Parton. (The film has a country soundtrack coordinated by Eastwood and producer David Valdes.)

That night, dressed as a limousine chauffeur, Tommy arrests the hulk, though he also is required to rough him up a bit. The next day, in the town luncheonette (the one with the Warren Burger specials), Tommy runs into Capshaw's yuppie lawyer, who insults him, telling him "There's a thin line between what you and some outlaws do." Clint's parting shot, "May be a thin line, but it isn't invisible," sounds like mellow Dirty Harry.

One of Tommy Nowak's assignments is to bring back another trailer park denizen, Lou Ann McGuinn (Bernadette Peters), who has jumped her $25,000 bond (she's been arraigned for passing counterfeit money) and is reported heading toward Reno in her furious husband's 1959 pink Cadillac convertible. (A line the movie reprises with innuendo goes, "Didn't anybody ever tell you not to mess with a man's vehicle?") Not only does she have her husband's prize possession, but she has their eight-month-old baby girl and a quarter of a million dollars in either counterfeit or real cash. (The baby isn't usually on board but stored at her sister's.)

Lou Ann's husband, Roy (Timothy Carhart), is a ne'er-do-well, a chronic screw-up, involved with a disgusting white supremacy group known as the Birthright. Alex (Michael Des Barres), the group's head scum, is determined to get the money back to build "the arsenal of my dreams." The Birthright's headquarters in the woods already resembles a theme park where psychos can practice with their semiautomatic assault weapons. (Some of these warriors are women.)

In the course of their car travels and motel nights together, Tommy and Lou Ann share confidences about their marriages (he's had two and is woman-shy, while she thought she "was marrying James Dean") and begin to become a duo. Tommy mimics her "little girl lost" routine (watch Clint bat his eyes) but sees her predicament. "That's one thing we have in common," he tells her; "I'm through taking shit from men, too." She teases him about his pose as "an American wildcat"—that endangered species. In aiding Lou Ann, Tommy makes it clear that he's willing to follow *his* law, not "*their* law," although he is trying hard to reconcile the two.

For all this, the chemistry doesn't really cook. The ghost-pale, pouty Peters has spunk, but the film is too slackly paced for it to be more than a string of episodes; action tends to devolve into oneliners. One of the more memorable comes when, minding her business, Lou Ann is accosted by a flasher; she takes a good close appraising look before observing coolly, "Looks like a penis— only smaller." Messing with a man's vehicle is given the green light.

Also reviewed in:

NEW YORK TIMES, 5/26/89, p. C.11 Caryn James
VARIETY, 5/31–6/7/89, p. 26
WASHINGTON POST, 5/26/89, p. C1, Hal Hinson

PLAFF!

An ICAIC (Instituto Cubano de Artes e Indústrias Cinematográficas) production. *Producer:* Ricardo Avila. *Director:* Juan Carlos Tabio. *Screenplay (Spanish with English subtitles):* Daniel Echevarria and Juan Carlos Tabío. *Director of Photography:* Julio Valdes. *Editor:* Roberto Bravo. *Music:* Nicolas Reynoso. *Sound:* Raúl Garcia. *Running time:* 90 minutes. *MPAA Rating:* Not Rated.

CAST: Daisy Granados (Concha); Thais Valdés (Clarita); Raúl Pomares (Tomás); Luis Alberto Garcia (José Ramón); Alicia Bustamante (Asunción); Jorge Cao (Contreras).

VILLAGE VOICE, 4/4/89, p. 58, Coco Fusco

She is the new Cuban white woman—uppity and scientifically inclined. He is the new Cuban mulatto, a smart and sensitive baseball player who has just dumped his first wife for her. His mom is so freaked out by her new daughter-in-law that she drives herself crazy trying to find out who has put a *santería* spell on her. Juan Carlos Tabio's screwball socialist comedy is full of Cuban idiosyncrasies, but plays it safe on its social critique. Nonetheless, few at the Cuban film school ICAIC these days match this director's ability to make revolutionary rhetoric sound as funny—on purpose.

Also reviewed in:
NEW YORK TIMES, 3/31/89, p. C18, Vincent Canby
VARIETY, 1/4–10/89, p. 74

PLOT AGAINST HARRY, THE

A New Yorker Films release of a King Screen production. *Producer:* Robert Young and Michael Roemer. *Director:* Michael Roemer. *Screenplay:* Michael Roemer. *Director of Photography:* Robert Young. *Editor:* Terry Lewis and Georges Klotz. *Music:* Frank Lewin. *Sound:* Peter Vollstadt and Paul Jaeger. *Art Director:* Howard Mandel. *Costumes:* Lily Partridge. *Running time:* 81 minutes. *MPAA Rating:* Not Rated.

CAST: Martin Priest (Harry Plotnik); Ben Lang (Leo Perlmutter); Maxine Woods (Kay Plotnick); Henry Nemo (Max); Jacques Taylor (Jack); Jean Leslie (Irene); Ellen Herbert (Mae); Sandra Kazan (Margie); Ronald Coralian (Mel); Max Ulman (Sidney); Margo Solin (Millie).

CHRISTIAN SCIENCE MONITOR, 2/2/90, p. 11, David Sterritt

Every moviegoer knows about "The Godfather" and the other Italian-American gangsters who've paraded across the screen in decades of Hollywood moviemaking—from the notorious Rico of "Little Caesar" in the '30s to Al Capone of "The Untouchables" in the '80s, to mention just a couple of the famous rogues.

But as a welcome contrast to this screen stereotype of mobsters, a new comedy called "The Plot Against Harry" looks at a numbers racketeer who happens to be Jewish.

At the beginning of the film, Harry is back in New York City after nine months in jail. This scene sets the story's tone, since the first thing Harry has to do is bawl out his henchman, Max, for picking him up late at the prison. Max explains that he couldn't find a parking space, and he had to pick up Harry's shirts at the cleaner's. "It figures, Max," says Harry." "All you had was nine months."

Not long afterward, Harry rams somebody's car when he's out driving, and finds himself in a reunion with his family—his ex-wife, his pregnant daughter, and a grandchild he never knew he had. He goes through various adventures with these and other characters, including an attempt to go straight by buying a catering business, and a party at a TV telethon that ends up costing him a lot of money. The mood is wryly amusing throughout the story, rarely becoming particularly serious (except when illness enters the picture) but never stooping to broad comic effects, either.

With its unusual characters and atmosphere, "The Plot Against Harry" is one of the season's most offbeat movies. Nothing in it is more unexpected, however, than the history of the movie itself. It was filmed in 1969 by director Michael Roemer, whose best-known movie is "Nothing But a Man," a gentle 1964 drama about the problems of a Southern black family. (That picture was codirected by Robert M. Young, who photographed "Harry" and has since directed a number of good movies, including "Alambrista!" and "One Trick Pony," on his own.)

When he finished shooting "Harry," nobody Mr. Roemer showed it to thought it was funny, or even interesting. So he put it on the shelf, where it lay ignored for 20 years—until last year, when Roemer decided to make a videotape of all his movies as a gift for his family. People saw "The Plot Against Harry" for the first time and found it hilarious.

With this encouragement, Roemer submitted it to film festivals in New York and Toronto, where it was shown to great laughter and applause. It's now going out to theaters as the first great discovery of the 1990s, two decades after it was made.

This said, it must be emphasized that "The Plot Against Harry" is a modest film. The laughs are subtle, coming not from physical action or slapstick, but entirely from situations and characters.

While some of the actors are professional—including Martin Priest, who plays the title role—others are gifted amateurs, discovered by the filmmaker in all kinds of places, including Jewish drama groups.

"The Plot Against Harry" isn't likely to be a smash hit; it will be most successful in large cities, with audiences who want something different from slam-bang Hollywood comedies. But it has the special kind of charm that comes from watching believable characters behaving in real, if eccentric, ways.

It's so long since "The Plot Against Harry" was made, incidentally, that the filmmakers have been busily tracking down members of the cast—some of whom had practically forgotten the whole thing—to tell them about the new success of their movie. None of them dreamed they'd be earning their first laughs this long after the cameras stopped turning.

FILMS IN REVIEW, 6–7/90, p. 368, Edmond Grant

There's no trouble at all with this *Harry*, although it took more than two decades for this uniquely comic slice of life to reach the light of day, via the dark of film festival auditoriums in Toronto and New York. Completed in 1969, the film was shelved for lack of interest from those who counted in the industry, and now, due to shifting critical perspective and more than a handful of stray luck, the film is finally getting the audience it so richly deserves.

The story behind the film's delayed twenty-one-year release is as curious as the picture itself. Director Michael Roemer, having just come out with the critically acclaimed *Nothing But a Man*, was given carte blanche by an independent producer to make exactly the kind of film he wanted, with no corporate supervision of any kind. With a slight budget and a little imagination, Roemer produced *Harry*, a deadpan comedy that takes place in several locations in and around New York City. After a series of less-than-successful screenings, including one for the head of Columbia Pictures, Roemer put the film away and went on to make documentaries and features for PBS' *American Playhouse*, and teach at Yale; his co-producer and director of photography, Robert M. Young, went on to make a number of higher budget pictures, among them *The Ballad Of Gregorio Cortez* and *Dominick And Eugene*. In the process of making a video transfer of *Harry* as a present for his children, Roemer decided to send the film to the Toronto and New York film festivals on a lark. Both festivals accepted, showing *Harry* to glowing critical notices and causing New Yorker to pick it up for distribution. So what is the fuss all about?

The film is a sixties' film, a bona fide sxties' film, one that neither mentions Vietnam nor the sexual, political, and chemical revolutions that marked that period. But like certain dramas of that time (*Midnight Cowboy, The Pawnbroker*) and a few comedies (*Bye Bye Braverman, A Thousand Clowns*), *Harry* captures the essence of day-to-day urban living during that era, showing the attitudes, institutions, and fashions that are by now considered exceptionally hip because they have become "retro." *Harry is* "retro" without even trying; Roemer's documentary filmmaking experience gave him an eye for peculiar detail that makes the film a wonderfully ironic record of its time. Its central character may lament the way that things have changed since he went into prison, but the audience finds itself lamenting the way things have changed since *Harry*'s era.

The plot is simple: Harry (Martin Priest), a stonefaced criminal, exits prison only to disover that he has been gradually cut out of his "business" by his partner. Suffering from an enlarged heart and eager to go legit, he invests in a catering business with his ex-brother-in-law. But his worries are far from over, for now he is forced to cope with the family he ignored when he was a criminal bigshot, and must honor a subpoena to appear before a government committee investigating his former mob boss. As the obstacles pile up, Harry's plight seems a great deal like that of the victim-heroes written about by Bruce Jay Friedman, Joseph Heller, and company. In fact, the film often seems like the perfect cinematic equivalent for the neurotic, often surreal, prose written by the Jewish wing of the Black Humor movement of the sixties.

Much like those writers did with their schlemiel protagonists, Roemer defines the world that Harry inhabits by placing him in odd locales, and having him attend some memorably odd events. True, Harry breezes his way through some settings common to regular gangster movies (the backs of plush limousines, health clubs, a seamy hotel) and others that exemplify the suburban life he longs to lead (a barbecue, a large wedding, a golf course). But the scenes that remain with one long after viewing *Harry* are those that occur in places that kitschophiles would die to visit, like the lobby of the hotel where Harry stays, wherein an exotic dancer is always present on a platform in the corner, strutting her stuff underneath a neon "Go-Go" sign. Or the sequences that take place during a bizarre ceremony of some sort: the lingerie fashion show where Harry is reunited with the daughter he hasn't seen in over a decade, a dog training class, the initiation rites of a men's "secret society" that he is forced to join, the impeccably gauche party held in a speeding NYC subway car (the hostess wants her friends to experience the subway as it really is, replete with decorations, champagne, and formal attire), and, in a final bit of delicious satire, the no-budget "Have a Heart" telethon, at which Harry is both a donor and one of the afflicted.

Throughout this off-the-well odyssey, the cast members are truly impressive, particularly as there are no recognizable faces among them—Roemer cast friends of friends and professionals he found in small theater groups. Martin Priest, whose only other notable film role was in *Nothing But a Man*, underplays Harry to the point of perfection. His nonplussed responses to the craziness around him—including a chance car crash where Harry runs into (literally) his ex-wife and her family, and the dilettante party hostess' following him around as research for her thesis on crime—possess all the eloquence of silence and the pathos of a major comic actor. Everyone else in the cast comes across as equally genuine, especially Ben Lang as Harry's perpetually smiling ex-in-law who consistently puts down Harry's crooked past, while readily accepting the money he made off of it.

The fact that this joy of a movie has been recovered from oblivion should be an inspiration to other non-studio-backed, but resourceful, filmmakers everywhere. Let's just hope that the next film on *Harry*'s level doesn't take 21 years to get around to a theatrical release.

LOS ANGELES TIMES, 1/31/90, Calendar/p. 3, Michael Wilmington

In the 1960s, Michael Roemer—who made the trail-blazing racial drama "Nothing But a Man" with partner Robert M. Young in 1965—was one of the nation's most promising independent film makers. But, in the '70s, he faded into the fringes of film and academia—teaching at Yale, writing occasional essays and emerging infrequently as a film maker for PBS and "American Playhouse."

Now, in a delightful storybook reversal, Roemer is back in the critics' spotlight, thanks to "The Plot Against Harry," the very film that drove him away 20 years ago. Back in 1969, early screening audiences found it unfunny and off-putting, studios rejected it for distribution, and Roemer, exhausted and disappointed, put it on the shelf.

While we can only speculate on the films Roemer might have made if "The Plot Against Harry" had found its audience in 1969, it is here to appreciate now: a balmy, deliciously deadpan Jewish gangster comedy that takes a wry, sneaky peek into the seamier sides of urban Jewish culture.

Its milieu of hectic bar mitzvahs, dotty middle-class clans, Mafioso suburban barbecues, secret pseudo-Masonic ceremonies, daft heart telethons and brassiere models studying the ballet is exposed with a sly mix of affection and lacerating satire.

Martin Priest is the Harry Plotnik of the title, a *schlemiel* of a gangster who's run afoul of both his clientele and his one-time Mafia protectors. Plotnik's motor has run down: a weary old businessman with an apparently bum heart, fresh out of jail, who worked his way up through the rackets, he now finds his empire crumbling—at the same time a chance reunion with his divorced family prompts him to go legit. There is nothing malicious about Harry. He may have been a bad husband, but he is nice to his *kvetch* of a sister, Mae (Ellen Herbert) and his corpulent *klutz* of a bookkeeper-gofer (songwriter Henry Nemo).

Roemer is very careful to show us, three years before Coppola's "The Godfather," that there's not much moral or social difference between Harry and the straight businessmen whose world he wants to crash: His rival, Big Julie (Julius Harris), is merely obeying the laws of commerce and the changing neighborhood. In this world, paranoia, business, crime and family are all weirdly intertwined.

Made originally during a minor American Jewish movie renaissance, when Woody Allen, Mel Brooks and Paul Mazursky were all directing their first films, "Harry" lacks their overtly fantastic-comic edge. It buries its comic knives under a seemingly conventional, right off-the-rack surface. Roemer is a documentary maker and social realist and his closely detailed, low-key approach may have worked against the humor back in 1969: the era of psychedelia, jumpcuts and wild, snazzy, sometimes elliptic film making.

Here, the photography of Robert M. Young—who went on to a strong solo directorial career himself ("Triumph of the Spirit")—is black-and-white, the compositions are flat, functional and unflashy. The strength of "Harry" lies almost entirely in its unusual humanity, the depth of its social observations and its determination to draw everything—even the comic exaggerations—from life.

In the opening scene, Priest plays his character—who's going to suffer a seizure shortly through—with such enervated, exhausted rhythms, it's easy to see what may have failed to connect with screening audiences in 1969. But you'd be wise to wait this time for the appearance of Ben Lang, as Harry's seraphically smiling brother-in-law and catering partner, Leo Perlmutter.

When Lang comes on, his unctuous nonstop grin lights up the screen. The comic rhythms suddenly take hold. Ebullient Leo becomes the perfect contrast for haggard Harry. The whole film suddenly seems more confident and bubbly, though Lang—who made this one film before moving back to an auditor's job at the New York Department of Labor, may have been the main casualty of the movie's non-release. It's hard to imagine he wouldn't have won more roles if "Harry" had been seen in 1969.

"The Plot Against Harry" was not exactly ahead of its time. One of the reasons it looks good now, in fact, may be that it's so resolutely *of* that time. It doesn't succumb to the 1980s vices of weak stories and characters, scrubbed-up milieus and archetypal conflicts. It's a movie that's *about* something: the collision of old and new values, the thin line that separates crime and organized business, the wary complex bonds between families.

That engagement keeps it fresh now. In 1969, Roemer might have been accused of airing dirty laundry—something Spike Lee or even Mazursky and Allen are sometimes accused of today. Now the laundry itself carries a whiff of nostalgia. In "The Plot Against Harry" (Times-rated Mature for language and sex), Harry the sad-eyed, failing gangster is just one more victim of urban change, kitsch culture and modern business methods. Life Joseph K in "The Trial," the plot against him is life itself.

NEW YORK, 10/9/89, p. 82, David Denby

Twenty years ago, Michael Roemer, the director of the highly praised independent feature *Nothing but a Man* (1964), shot a comedy about a Jewish gambler in the Bronx—Harry Plotnik, king of the concourse numbers rackets—and then ran out of money before he could finish it. Exhausted by the production, which he shot with a tiny crew, and depressed by the general indifference of the people he showed the footage to, Roemer let the film languish and retreated to his teaching position at Yale (he subsequently made, for PBS, some fiction films and the excellent documentary *Dying).*

Recently, Roemer pulled his movie out of mothballs and completed postproduction work on it, whereupon it was accepted by the Toronto and New York film festivals. *The Plot Against Harry* is not a great film—it's not as sharply defined as it should be—but it's consistently witty and enjoyable, a labor of love that should find its own loving audience. It's also one of the best and most comprehensive satires of Jewish American life ever put on film.

Harry, played by Martin Priest (physically a cross between Roy Cohn and Lenny Bruce), gets out of jail and discovers he's no longer a big deal. His neighborhood is changing; his black lieutenant is taking over his turf, and Harry doesn't have enough clout with the mob to take it back. Even worse, Harry is unable to resist the powerful forces of upward mobility in the Jewish community. His ambitious family gets its hooks into him, and he falls among caterers and do-gooders—the twin menaces of Jewish American life—who turn out to be more predatory than the gangsters he normally associates with. Quickly, they bring him to his knees.

Roemer gooses the milieu—the bar mitzvahs and telethons, the charity parties, the cabbagy Concourse hotel with its solarium—more gently than he should, but still with remarkable energy and detail. Harry, I suppose, isn't much of a crook to begin with, and in the end, the relentless, interfering solicitude of his friends and family overwhelms his instinctively sleazy habits. His rehabilitation may be a triumph for virtue, but for him it can only be a defeat. The movie is a fascinating time capsule and a satire worthy of the young Philip Roth.

NEW YORK, 1/15/90, p. 54, David Denby

Poor Harry Plotnik! At home in his Grand Concourse hotel, he can't even bed down with a blonde hooker for the night without his elderly sister, Mae, barging in on him, bearing a vaporizer for his cold. Harry (Martin Priest), the disconsolate small-time gangster in *The Plot Against Harry*, doesn't know what's hit him. He emerges from nine months in the slammer (the time is 1969), only to discover that his prosperous little numbers racket in the Bronx has fallen apart. Even worse, his upwardly mobile family seems determined to shame him into virtue. They don't take him seriously enough to be afraid of him. He's in deep trouble.

The Plot Against Harry teases the implacably respectable and right-minded spirit of middle-class American Jewish life. Amelioration dogs Harry's steps; his family and friends are too ambitious and too sentimental to simply let him be a bum. They walk in on him, walk all over him, and remake his life. He's bullied by charity organizers, coaxed into the catering business by a benevolent but manipulative man who never stops smiling and is in cahoots with Harry's formidable ex-wife. These improvers and do-gooders and caterers never leave hime alone.

Martin Priest, a theater and TV actor who should be better known, gives Harry some slit-eyed menace in the early scenes. Working the phone in his black Cadillac, Harry tries to get his business going again, and Priest's baleful, disgusted stare is all acid. Later on, his face goes bland, and petulance creeps into his voice. Suddenly the snake turns into a ewe—like Roy Cohn crossed with a sheep. In this suffocatingly virtuous milieu, Harry is merely a curiosity, a minor celebrity with a notorious past. He goes on the radio and appears at fund-raising events as a reformed "gambler." The people around him are so solicitous and helpful (always raising money), they destroy him. He may become a success as a family man, but he's a pathetic failure as a gangster; rehabilitation robs him of his identity.

The Plot Against Harry is both a wonderful and original satirical comedy and an unwitting time capsule recovered from its shadow life on the shelf. The movie was shot 21 years ago by writer-director Michael Roemer and his partner then, producer and cinematographer Robert M. Young. Roemer, 62, a German Jew born in Berlin, came here after spending the war in an English school for refugee children. For years he worked in documentary filmmaking, but he's best known for the dignified feature he made in 1964, *Nothing but a Man*, the first film to take a plain, open look at black life in the South. *Harry* was cast both with professional actors and with amateurs from Jewish theatrical groups. The aura of brilliant amateurism—in the positive sense of the word—is part of the movie's wistful and homely charm.

Roemer works in loosely constructed, tableaulike scenes, with odd characters running in and out and pushing Harry to the margins of his own life. The black-and-white cinematography is excellent, and the sound recording is clear, but *Harry* doesn't offer conventionally effective dramatic emphasis and shaping. The story is there, and the jokes are certainly there, but to fully enjoy the movie, the audience has to share Roemer's love of close observation. The movie doesn't do all the work for us. When Roemer showed it to friends in 1969, nobody laughed. Depressed, and exhausted from the production, he dropped the film and retreated to Yale, where he has taught for the past two decades. (His most important work in that time was the fine 1975 PBS documentary *Dying*.) When he got some money for postproduction work last year, Roemer finished the film and took it to the Toronto and New York film festivals (with great success).

From the detailed, crowded opening scenes set in prison and in the New York streets, one understands how good a documentary-maker Roemer is—and also how much fiction attracts him. His risk-taking technique is in its own way sternly exacting; the story is just central enough to be felt, while the free, exuberant activity pours in around the edges. Harry attends many "Affairs" (the menace of my own youth). Bar mitzvahs, weddings, charity telethons . . . Roemer shoots them in an entirely deadpan way, without exaggeration and without embarrassment, too, capturing the mixture of beneficence and jaw-dropping boredom. The details of the human comedy are all in place—the kosher hot dogs next to the surgical instruments at a *bris*; the peculiar clammy atmosphere of the hotel, with its "solarium" and bewigged prostitutes elbowing someone's aunt out of the way. That up-from-the-Bronx era of American Jewish life has all but vanished; *Harry* brings it back.

Some of the fifties Italian comedies, like Mario Monicelli's *The Big Deal on Madonna Street*, with Marcello Mastroianni, displayed a similar spirit of baffled harassment, with life's daily routines hampering and then overwhelming a man's mulish criminal instinct. But *The Plot Against Harry* is also a peculiarly Jewish satire. In *Portnoy's Complaint*, completed the same year (1969), Philip Roth insisted that the hardest thing for Jewish boys was not to be good but to be *bad* (this was before Ivan Boesky and some of the other recent Jewish boys made their mark). The amateur actors Roemer has cast around Priest show us what Harry is up against. There's the big-bellied, gentle Henry Nemo (in real life, a songwriter) as Max, Harry's sweet, shuffling "henchman"; Ben Lang (an accountant) as the always smiling, always positive, but extremely cagey caterer Leo; Maxine Woods (a psychoanalyst) as Harry's ex-wife, Kay, her face drawn tightly in disgust for the husband she long ago gave up on. These performers don't do much of anything, but they are unerringly perfect in appearance and manner. The goodness of these people is a curse on Harry.

If Harry himself had been conceived as a stronger character, the movie might have been a classic. He hardly struggles against his strange fate, so his defeat isn't as poignantly ironic as it should be. And the movie stays pretty much on the same emotional level. It doesn't grow and develop, working through tensions and crises; it's not a dramatic work. But if it's all on the same plane of tender satire, that's a good place to be. Discovering *The Plot Against Harry* was an unanticipated joy; the picture should find its own loving and devoted audience. Imagine: a cult movie you could take you mother to see.

NEW YORK POST, 1/12/90, p. 24, David Edelstein

In 1969, Michael Roemer showed "The Plot Against Harry" to a few audiences and distributors. Nobody laughed. Roemer handled rejection gracefully. He put the film in a drawer and never took it out again. He went into a funk. He started teaching (the kiss of death).

What happened next is the stuff of myth. Last year, Roemer wanted to give the film to his children and decided to have it transferred to videotape. Watching the print, the man doing the transfer laughed. Roemer, his confidence restored, struck 35-millimeter prints and sent them off to the New York and Toronto film festivals, which instantly accepted "The Plot Against Harry."

Small wonder. Everything that must have seemed pointless in the late '60s now seems poignantly funny and rare. The movie is like a message in a bottle, dropped 20 years ago into rough seas. Only now can it be read and savored.

Harry (Martin Priest) is a Jewish hood, a numbers man, who emerges from a nine-month prison sentence to find his world has changed. Former employees have moved in on his territory; allegiances have shifted; and when, out of spite, he rams a car that has swerved in front of him, he nearly kills his ex-wife, Kay (Maxine Woods), whom he hasn't seen in years, his brother-in-law, Leo (Ben Lang) and his pregnant daughter (Sandra Kazan).

The slender joke of the movie is that Harry, thrust by fate back into his middle-class Jewish community, is not allowed to remain a small-time gangster—in this world, the push toward respectability borders on the fanatical. Some Jews can be manipulative—relying on guilt trips or scare tactics—and poor Harry, the straightforward racketeer, isn't in most of their league.

Mischievously, Roemer telegraphs Harry's mortality early on. As the gangster leaves prison in a limo, the camera follows some mini-skirted young women crossing the street past a coffin being loaded into a hearse; later, it lingers on the pale, dissipated Harry (a Type A personality) eating a filet mignon as a prostitute arrives.

Behind "Harry" is a longing for days of simpler indulgence without all the worries about butter, cholesterol, stress, AIDS, the IRS. And what fear won't kill, high-mindedness will. His brother-in-law and ex-wife run a kosher catering business. Sudden exposure to them plus a bout of what might be angina seals Harry's fate. He'll pump money into their outfit, meet the rabbi and Jewish philanthropists—go legit.

What seems modern about the film—the reason it plays better now—is its ironic attitude toward kitsch. The catering halls and bar mitzvah parlors seem outrageously tacky, and the camera surveys them deadpan, amused and appalled by the milieu.

Roemer captures, as few ever have, the peculiar mixture of vulgar materialism and social conscience that characterized, in particular, the middle-class Jewish community in the late '60s.

The best audience for "The Plot Against Harry" isn't just oldsters nostalgic for more shameless days but baby-boomers who were bar-mitzvahed at the time and remember their coming-of-age as Theater of the Absurd.

Whom does Martin Priest resemble? One colleague suggested Marcel Dalio, star of "The Rules of the Game", I though of an older and more dissipated Billy Joel.

Whichever he resembles, he has small eyes, heavy lids and a witty poker face—he regards his new surroundings with the blinking incredulity of something that has just crawled out from under a rock.

The second joke of "Harry" is that every time he's shamed or compelled to do the right thing, he digs his grave a little deeper. Testifying before a congressional hearing, he protests his legitimacy and winds up having his books subpenaed. "They can't put me in jail now," he bellows. "I'm trying to change my life!"

Alas, Harry's predicament doesn't have much emotional heft, and that's what keeps the movie small. Roemer's film making is both alienated and sentimental—it tugs at our heart even as it shuts us out. He could use less Jarmusch and more Mazursky. And he's no storyteller. Even the simplest plot machinations play confusingly and at the wrong speed.

But the black-and-white photography (by Robert M. Young, who went on to become a director) is marvelously fresh—a reminder of how much street-life routinely came through in the documentry-style movies of the '60s.

And the actors, many from Jewish drama groups, are priceless. I'll mention two: the stoop-shouldered Ben Lang (new a retired auditor), whose sleepy delivery masks a cagey intelligence; and Maxine Woods (now an Upper East Side psychoanalyst), who can suggest in a single look at Harry both affection and deep skepticism (a useful talent for a shrink, methinks).

NEWSDAY, 1/12/90, Part III/p. 3, Terry Kelleher

A guy's locked up nine months and the outside world can change for the worse.

Harry Plotnik, central character in "The Plot Against Harry," gets out of prison and finds his Bronx numbers operation is going to hell. Revenue down sharply, runners quitting right and left, syndicate support wavering.

A movie's locked up 20 years and the outside world can change for the better. Michael Roemer, writer-director of "The Plot Against Harry," finally gets his picture off the shelf and discovers that what had been deemed unreleasable is now called sensational.

Part of the film community's enthusiasm for "The Plot Against Harry" may be overcompensation for past neglect. But Roemer's straight-faced (often glum-faced) comedy, generously praised last fall at the New York Film Festival, deserves to be seen for its quality as well as its history.

What made "The Plot Against Harry" so puzzling to studio executives two decades ago is precisely what makes it so interesting today. The story is offbeat enough: Lower-echelon racketeer finds himself swept up in Jewish bourgeois respectability. But oh, how Roemer tells it.

Photographed in black and white by Robert M. Young (director of the current "Triumph of the Spirit") and edited with minimal concern for transitions and such amenities, "The Plot Against Harry" follows this Plotnik (Martin Priest) from one faintly absurd situation to another, never pausing for exposition, explanation or justification. There's a sense of gradualness to Harry's transformation from minor-league criminal to apprentice burgher, yet the film is over in only an hour and 20 minutes. At the end the protagonist doesn't seem too sure exactly what's happened to him. The same goes for the viewer.

It's the small laughs that make "The Plot Against Harry" an unexpected pleasure: the apron-clad Mafia don hosting a thoroughly suburban cookout; a charity cocktail party held on a subway train for the right touch of urban atmosphere; a bemused Harry being inducted into an unwittingly wacky fraternal order, or making peace overtures to his ex-wife (Maxine Woods) during a canine obedience class. In fact, Roemer elects not to bid for the big laughs, except perhaps when Harry's smothering sister (Ellen Herbert) brings him a vaporizer and finds he's in bed with a hooker instead of a cold. The movie is so determinedly deadpan that it consciously stops short of its comic potential.

The Bronx-born Priest, who played a Southern bigot in Roemer's "Nothing But a Man" (1964), is wonderful at the head of this no-star cast. His Harry continually shows signs of confusion and nervous indigestion, but once it's clear the world has pulled a fast one on him, there's an admirable calm in the way he goes with the flow. Henry Nemo, better known for songwriting than for acting, is consistently funny as his sweaty aide-de-camp. Woods, a psychoanalyst by profession, seems comfortable in the role of Harry's ladylike ex-. Ben Lang, an auditor in New York State government at the time Roemer chose him, is a nice fit for the part of Harry's former brother-in-law, a caterer who sponsors him for membership in the law-abiding middle-class.

The truth is that "The Plot Against Harry" would have profited from the presence of a few more professionals in front of the camera. So it's not perfect, OK? But 20 years in the lockup was a gross miscarriage of justice.

VILLAGE VOICE, 1/16/90, p. 72, Georgia Brown

"Half the kids on the block, they went to jail. Not Harry." At least that's what aging Mae Klepper (Ellen Herbert) tells the ladies at the pool about her sainted younger brother. Little does Mae know that the dour, frazzled Harry (Martin Priest) has just been released after serving nine months for a charge related to the small-time numbers racket he runs. And if nine months is too short a time for his slow-moving henchman, Max (Henry Nemo), to get Harry's shirts back from the cleaners, it's a long time to be absented from the teeming, dog-eat-dog world of petty criminals.

The Plot Against Harry opens with Harry back on the street of the Bronx—phoning from the back seat of his black Cadillac with faithful, thick-headed Max at the wheel. It doesn't take long to discover that his operation isn't taking what is used to take, that his former flunkies have branched out on their own, and that commissions investigating organized crime are busy serving subpoenas. Back at his luxurious residence hotel, he finds his sister installed in a neighboring room—the better to tend Harry with chicken soup and vaporizers—and his usual call girl unavailable. ("Lois couldn't make it. I'm Sherrie, remember?")

One dark night, Harry's past comes back with a jolt. Taking the wheel from Max, he swerves into a car that turns out to be carrying his former wife, Kay (Maxine Woods), his former brother-in-law, Leo (Ben Lang), a nine-months-pregnant daughter he hasn't seen since she was three, her husband, and even a granddaughter. "I coulda killed you," marvels Harry, who was in fact trying to force their car off the road. Now he becomes tantalized by the "normal" life he might have led.

Michael Roemer's gentle, wistful, thoroughly charming comedy scored hits at last fall's Toronto and New York film festivals because it is engagingly acted—mostly by well-directed amateurs— and studded with flaky, *haimish* details, many showing what it was like to grow up Jewish at a certain time in the city. Its black-and-white cinéma vérité style (Robert M. Young, Roemer's collaborator on *Nothing But a Man* and recently director of *Triumph of the Spirit*, is the cameraman) places the film in the late '60s as firmly as do the actresses' miniskirts and princess-of-the-Nile eyeliner. What was not '60s, according to its maker, is the film's wry, self-mocking, deadpan humor. Harry has the feel of picaresque tales from Eastern Europe featuring schlemiels or holy fools—and so does the poignant (true-life) story of how *The Plot Against Harry* got lost and found again.

Roemer says that when he previewed a finished print of *Harry* in 1970, the audiences—even his dearest friends—didn't laugh, didn't "get it." Despairing of ever finding a distributor, he put the film away. He took a teaching job and made a few films for PBS. Nearly 20 years later, he was overseeing the process of putting all his films on videotape as a gift for his children, when, lo and behold, the guy who was doing the transfer of Harry began to laugh!

This has the ring of a Hasidic or zen parable, an extended black joke: Success is foiled for want of a cosmic guffaw and arrives only after another life is lived, another journey taken. The Plot Against Michael Roemer has, as I say, a certain familial resemblance to the story of Harry by the same author.

The agent for Harry's renewal is not so much Kay, the handsome wife Harry obviously will always desire and always manage to infuriate, or his newly found daughters, but the toothsome Leo, who acts as a sort of fairy godbrother-in-law. Leo is one of those people whose pasted-on sunny smile (and unusual denture formation) has become circuited to his brain, determining his view of the world. This asset provides him with a natural calling—head caterer in a firm that services temple functions.

In contrast, Priest's thin, pale, wincing Harry looks chronically preoccupied (one might say, harried) and chronically constipated. (Harry is either redeemed or doomed, depending how you want to see it, for want of a decent bowel movement.) His art of the deal will always find him screwed. "I thought Jewish people suppose' ta be smart," says a Mafia boss with whom Harry's trying to strike a bargain. But Harry's will to remain small-time is stronger than his criminal acumen. Fortunately, he's now back among people who forgive him practically anything because he's family. Yes, well, someone does tell him that he's "a disgrace to the Jewish people."

Lang's hunched, beaming Leo—who runs off with the picture whenever he appears—will never get royally screwed. He will never win big either. Licking his fingers to put the finishing touches on the chopped liver shaped like a chicken for a *bris*, or sponsoring Harry's initiation into his lodge, the Mystic Knights of the Sojourners, Leo—more joiner than sojourner—eagerly throws himself into ritual and ceremony. A parade of relatives at a bar mitzvah reception, each holding a lighted candle (his innovation), can make his weekend.

As a parody of things Jewish, Roemer's movie is much more affectionate than savage. *The Plot Against Harry*, despite its title, made me believe that to be Jewish in America means never to be left out alone in the cold.

Also reviewed in:
NATION, 2/5/90, p. 178, Stuart Klawans
NEW YORK TIMES, 1/12/90, p. C13, Janet Maslin
VARIETY, 9/13-19/89, p. 37
WASHINGTON POST, 3/9/90, p. D1, Hal Hinson

POLICE ACADEMY 6: CITY UNDER SIEGE

A Warner Bros. release. *Producer:* Paul Maslansky. *Director:* Peter Bonerz. *Screenplay:* Stephen J. Curwick. *Based on characters created by:* Neal Israel and Pat Proft. *Director of Photography:* Charles Rosher Jr. *Editor:* Hubert de la Bouillerie. *Music:* Robert Folk. *Music Editor:* Doug Lackey. *Sound:* Steve Nelson. *Sound Editor:* Jeff Clark. *Production Designer:* Tho E. Azzari. *Set Designer:* Richard Fernandez and Eric Orbom. *Set Decorator:* Tom Bugenhagen. *Special Effects:* Gene Grigg. *Costumes:* Peter Flaherty. *Make-up:* Bernadine M. Anderson. *Running time:* 87 minutes. *MPAA Rating:* PG.

CAST: Bubba Smith (Hightower); David Graf (Tackleberry); Michael Winslow (Jones); Leslie Easterbrook (Callahan); Marion Ramsey (Hooks); Lance Kinsey (Proctor); Matt McCoy (Nick) Bruce Mahler (Fackler); G.W. Bailey (Harris); George Gaynes (Lassard); Kenneth Mars (Mayor); Gerrit Graham (Ace); George R. Robertson (Hurst); Brian Seeman (Flash); Darwyn Swalve (Ox); Billie Bird (Mrs. Stanwyck); Arthur Batanides (Mr. Kirkland); Beans Morocco (Bank President); Alexander Folk (Well Dressed Man); Michael Fosberg (Friend #1); Fritz Bronner (Friend #2); Alan Hunter (Business Man #1); Mark Jay Goodman (Business Man #2); Daniel Ben Wilson (Tackleberry Jr.); Greg Collins (SWAT Team Leader); Christopher Wolf (Gym Officer); Angelo Tiffe (Cop #1); Tony Montes (Cop #2); Anna Mathias (Bank Teller); Melvin Glover (Rap Man #1); Ralph Blandshaw (Rap Man #2); Starr Gilliard (Officer); Dennis Ott (Looter); Susan Hegarty (Saleswoman); Peter Elbling (Store Manager); Carlos Cervantes (Hustler); Darryl Henriques (Man in a Hurry); Allison Mack (Little Girl); Michael Leopard (Gym Officer); Rusdi Lane (Yuppie with Squeaky Shoes); Peder Melhuse (Cop Who Sighs); Kort Falkenberg (Old Man); Gerry Lock (Old Lady); Gary P. Smith (Police Officer); Roger Reid (Xeroxed Policeman); Lou Butera (Pool Shooter); Roberta Haynes (Bus Passenger); Tom Lawrence (Cop Who Eats Chili).

LOS ANGELES TIMES, 3/14/89, Calendar/p. 4, Chris Willman

The official title is "Police Academy 6: City Under Siege," but the conspiracy theorists among us and those who remember "The Omen" can surmise just what *that's* short for—"Police Academy 666" is more like it.

The mild PG rating is hardly indicative of the horrors within. There are no stars to replace the long-departed Steve Guttenberg, just a dizzying stream of supporting players left over from previous manifestations of the "P.A." series.

In lieu of much plot to speak of, these revolving pratfalls make up the movie. To wit (so to speak): Ditzy George Gaynes does his senile shtick. Wacky Michael Winslow does his vocal sound effects. Dainty Leslie Easterbrook does her squeaky voice. Sultry Marion Ramsey heaves the bosom that makes men fall down. Trigger-happy David Graf sets off the big ammo. Bossy G.W. Bailey gets his comeuppance by sitting on chairs with unscrewed legs. Klutzy Bruce Mahler knocks over everything in sight....

Directing this episode is Peter Bonerz, whom many will remember as a likable '70s sitcom actor with the same fondness with which they remember the former Cat Stevens. ("Bob Newhart Show" rerun-boycott, anyone?)

MONTHLY FILM BULLETIN, 9/89, p. 280, Philip Strick

A daredevil trio known as the Wilson Heights Gang unleashes the worst crime wave the city has ever experienced. In desperation, the Mayor demands that Police Commissioner Hurst assemble his best team to combat the crooks, and a special unit is summoned under the direction of Commandant Lassard together with his abrasive rival Captain Harris. Investigating a bank robbery, Lassard's nephew Nick deduces that the gang is controlled by a mysterious mastermind with inside knowledge that could only have come from the police department. Harris promptly conveys this theory to the Mayor and is delighted to be asked to find proof that Lassard himself is the villain. His first effort to gather evidence, however, while disguised as a window cleaner, ends in humiliating failure. Setting a trap for the gang, the entire unit is on hand to protect the much-publicised Zimbazwi diamond as it is transported by security van, but the incompetence of Harris and his amiable assistant Proctor ensures that the jewel is stolen. The gang is nearly cornered after another jewel robbery, escaping thanks to Harris' bungling intervention, and when some of the stolen jewellery is found in Lassard's office, the commandant is suspended and his team assigned to routine patrol duties. Resolutely continuing their hunt for the gang in secret, Lassard's regulars discover that the crimes have all been committed in an area scheduled for redevelopment for a new rail link. The gang sabotages the city's power supply, and amid the chaos that follows they are identified and pursured by the Lassard team; the crooks are finally cornered near the mastermind's hideout, and despite his attempt to deter the cops with poison gas, he is soon on the run. A wild chase through the city traffic leads at last to Commissioner Hurst's office, where two identical commissioners accuse each other of being the miscreant. Unmasked, one of them turns out to be the Mayor, who admits to having planned the crime wave in order to buy cheap property that will soon escalate in value. Hurst reinstates Commandant Lassard and his team, and during a jubilant public ceremony of congratulation the glowering Captain Harris is carried aloft under a festive column of balloons.

That the easily derided *Police Academy* concept should have reached its sixth incarnation is surprise enough, but even more remarkable is that, with nothing to lose, the whole routine is beginning to show pleasantly redeeming signs of life. This is not to deny that the interminable feud between the seraphic Lassard and the malevolent Captain Harris has become painfully uninteresting, but with the disappearance of heavyweights from the series (both Steve Guttenberg and Bobcat Goldthwait in their opposite extremes had become too overpowering), the lesser characters now have the opportunity to explore their own possibilities in more detail. Some of them, of course, have nowhere to go: the sycophantic Proctor merely pops his eyes at greater length, while Jones (the specialist in strange noises) fills in some time with a puzzling impersonation of Jimi Hendrix. But the Amazonian blonde cop Callahan (who, as plainclothed jogger, addresses the microphone in her copious cleavage with a terse "Nothing unusual here") and the belligerent Tackleberry (who, as plainclothed taxi driver, ejects an unwanted fare by pointing a hand grenade at him) are developing nicely, even if Hightower (the gentle giant) and Hooks (the little squeaky one) still seem to be floundering in search of a suitable context.

The amiable Fackler, who unknowingly spreads swathes of catastrophe by his very presence, is a wonderful invention, while the Mayor for this episode, played with genial zest by Kenneth Mars, keeps losing his words and substituting wild paraphrases ("justice" becomes "that, you know, court thing"), another nice idea that sparkles briefly but is gone too soon. Efficiently hustled along by former actor-writer Peter Bonerz (star, twenty years ago, of John Korty's comic fantasy *Funnyman*), Stephen J. Curwick's meandering follow-up to his début script for *Police Academy 5* enterprisingly aspires to a combination of *The Getaway, The Naked Gun* and *Batman*. At its worst, like the final gag with the balloons, the film has a juvenile silliness, much as any *Police Academy* fan has the right to expect. But at its best, as when the three crooks ignore their droning mastermind hidden behind his pretentious screen and fight each other with water pistols, or when Harris, ignominiously glued to a chair, makes his seated progress down a crowded corridor pretending that nothing's wrong, it is spasmodically and blissfully hilarious.

NEW YORK POST, 3/11/89, p. 19, Jami Bernard

Like something out of a slasher movie, the "Police Academy" series keeps hobbling along even after all its limbs have been severed. The series has become so predictable and stale that if you do chuckle, it's just one of those involuntary spasms that occur after death.

However, even within the vacuum of filmmaking that is the "Police Academy" phenomenon, it is possible to detect that No. 6, "City Under Siege," is slightly better than No. 4. (I missed No. 5—sorry, I'm not a completist.)

That some of the jokes are funnier, or maybe just less offensive, than they used to be is owed to the direction of Peter Bonerz, who once played the pilot on the old "Bob Newhart" show, one of the funniest TV series ever.

The regular misfit members of the Academy are back, except, of course, for anyone who had the talent or agent to get them out of there—namely, Steve Guttenberg and Bobcat Goldthwait.

Here's who is left: the big bruiser (Bubba Smith), the little lady with the shrill "I don't know nothin' 'bout birthin' babies" voice (Marion Ramsey), the guy who can imitate kitchen appliances (Michael Winslow), the klutz (Bruce Mahler), the psycho (David Graf), the female bodybuilder (Leslie Easterbrook), and some others—all under the command of the ingenuous commandant (George Gaynes).

The team is called upon to break the Wilson Heights Gang, a thieving trio who take their orders from a never-seen "Charlie's Angels"-type boss known as the Mastermind. I certainly don't want to spoil the ending for you—dramatic tension like this you don't get every day—but it's a rule of thumb in an ensemblecast picture that the bad guy (or the one who buys the farm) is the one who is not a regular on the series. That rules out everyone except. . .well, I'll keep it under my hat, or under my seat with the leftover popcorn.

In fact, the most exciting part of the movie was when the final reel got caught in the projector at a Times Square movie house and a member of the audience yelled to the projectionist, "Hey, stop smoking crack!"

When the final 10 minutes were finally shown, the projector was pitched too high and cut off all the heads. So anyone who could not figure out who The Mastermind was by the aforememtioned rule is probably still wandering around Times Square, wondering whodunnit.

But the question, as always with the "Police Academy" series, is not whodunnit, by why see it.

NEWSDAY, 3/13/89. Part II/p. 7, John Anderson

Saturday afternoon's audience of kids watching "Police Academy 6" was like a meeting of Mensa compared to what was happening on screen.

In the great Hollywood tradition of never letting taste get in the way of a quick buck—and of bleeding any successful idea to a point far beyond anemia—Warner Bros. has coughed up another in its series of adventures of a group of police officers for whom "inept" is a fawning compliment. The Peter Bonerz-directed epic is subtitled "City Under Siege." At the risk of stating the obvious, the only thing under siege is our intelligence.

But being obvious is what this film is all about. The jokes are obvious, the plot is obvious, it's obvious there'll be a "Police Academy 7." It's obvious, too, that any kids reared according to the Stooge theory of pediatric comedy (developed by Drs. Howard, Fine and Howard in the 1930s) will know what's coming along before it gets there, which is too bad. There aren't enough movies for kids. But "PA 6" is what happens when people just don't care.

To summarize, a trio of hold-up men hired by a criminal mastermind is terrorizing the city and the Police Department's investigating officer, Captain Harris (G.W. Bailey) is getting nowhere, mainly because he's an incompetent, toadying buffoon. Enter his former colleagues, and our heroes, who are assigned to the case, setting the stage for Harris' petty maneuverings to steal all the credit and stymie the investigation. Harris makes the bad guys look good, but then again, in this movie, the good guys make the bad guys look good. In fact, the bad guys are the most charming thing about "Police Academy 6." Police Benevolent Associations should be up in arms. The plot is really just a thread on which to hang some tired slapstick routines and lowbrow antics that were done better by the aforementioned Howard, Fine and Howard.

Bubba Smith is in his sixth "PA" and through seniority, has achieved top billing. He does what little he does fairly well. Previous "Academy" costars have taken early retirement, or perhaps they became detectives. More likely, they're working as department store security guards.

Bailey and George Gaynes as Commandant Lassard give their usual good performances. Matt McCoy, whose supercilious Nick Lassard is the gifted child in this group of slow-witted delinquents, gets to deliver those "Dragnet"-style zingers—"It's one of us," he says, when a leak is discovered to be thwarting the team's probe. Just one question, Lassard—if you're so smart, what are you doing in this movie?

Also reviewed in:
NEW YORK TIMES, 3/11/89, p. 17, Richard Bernstein
VARIETY, 3/15–21/89, p. 13
WASHINGTON POST, 3/11/89, p. C6, Richard Harrington

POWWOW HIGHWAY

A Warner Bros. release of a HandMade Films presentation. *Executive Producer:* George Harrison and Denis O'Brien. *Producer:* Jan Wieringa. *Director:* Jonathan Wacks. *Screenplay:* Janet Heaney and Jean Stawarz. *Based on the novel by:* David Seals. *Director of Photography:* Toyomichi Kurita. *Editor:* James Stewart. *Music:* Barry Goldberg. *Production Designer:* Cynthia Sowder.*Costumes:* Isis Mussenden. *Running time:* 91 minutes. *MPAA Rating:* R.

CAST: A Martinez (Buddy Red Bow); Gary Farmer (Philbert Bono); Amanda Wyss (Rabbit Layton); Joanelle Nadine Romero (Bonnie Red Bow); Sam Vlahos (Chief Joseph); Wayne Waterman (Wolf Tooth); Margo Kane (Imogene); Geoff Rivas (Sandy Youngblood); Roscoe Born (Agent Jack Novall); John Trudell (Louie Short Hair); Wes Studi (Bull); Tony Frank (Captain Roberts); Chrissie McDonald (Jane Red Bow); Sky Seals (Sky Red Bow); Maria Antoinette Rogers (Aunt Harriot); Nicholas Anthony (Condo Man); Kandi Brooks (Lucinda Sanchez, Hi-Fi Hut Cashier); Rodney Grant (Brave on Horse); Graham Greene (Vietnam Vet); Irene Handren-Seals (Jail Guard); Lafayette J. Harris (Stockyard Foreman); Bill T. Head (Sioux Driver); Ron Holstrom (Police Officer); Mike Means (Young Buddy); Marc Miles (Patrolman); Nuchie Nashoba (Condo Woman); Rogene Not Afraid (Floozy); Leigh Opitz (Waitress); Randal Patrick (Hi-Fi & Car Salesman); Stephanie Roberts (Secretary); Ariane Rowland (Young Bonnie); Chris Rowland (Light Cloud); Keith Shoulder Blade (Young Philbert); Titus Shoulder Blade (Manny); Anam Taylor (Bull Miller); Pat Van Ingen (Pueblo Woman); Floyd Westerman (CB Radio Voice); Del Zamora (Fidel de Baca).

LOS ANGELES TIMES, 3/17/89, Calendar/p. 1, Sheila Benson

Very rarely, an actor's presence casts a shadow almost larger than the production that shelters him—or her. You saw it with Chief Dan George in "Little Big Man." With Louise Fletcher in "One Flew Over the Cuckoo's Nest." And you'll discover it again in "Powwow Highway," a little zinger of a comedy with a rare backbone of intelligence; unsurprising when you learn that the debuting director is "Repo Man" co-producer, Jonathan Wacks.

As it follows the careening path of a pair of buddies, heading on a rescue mission with diametrically different ideas of how to get there—and how quickly—it's a pretty irresistible movie. But for pure lovability, it's given a run for its money by the amazing young Canadian actor it presents, Gary Farmer, who co-stars with A Martinez.

Farmer plays Philbert Bono, a gentle, mammoth Cheyenne from Lame Deer, Mont., who gets it into his head to follow the spiritual path. It's harder to find that path now than it was in simpler times. Now your pony is a junkyard Buick Wildcat, circa 1964, and the Old Ones, who could answer questions about the way of a warrior, are fed up with being sages and would rather let television play across their faces, undisturbed.

But there is never a doubt that Philbert, a more-than-6 foot, 280-pound seeker, will make it to warriorhood. For one thing, who could stop him? For another, who would want to? Pure goodness emanates from Farmer's Philbert—a kind of sweetness that an audience reads instantly. The only time in recent movie memory that I can recall such sweetness returned in equal waves of affection toward a character was the furor that greeted. E.T....and Farmer is as far from mechanical as you can be.

"Powwow Highway" quietly camouflages its serious concerns about American Indians, letting us absorb them cumulatively during this pell-mell odyssey. Disillusioned activist Buddy Red Bow (Martinez) and Philbert Bono trek together from Montana to Santa Fe, in the car Philbert has named "Protector." Buddy has gotten a desperate call from his estranged sister, Bonnie (Joanelle

Romero). She's apparently been framed, then jailed with her two young daughters, in Santa Fe for possession of marijuana.

The men were at high school together, but Buddy's intense political concerns and Philbert's lifelong low-key flair have kept their paths separate. Apparently, his work has kept Buddy out of touch with his family too, since his sister's phone call is the first news he'd had that he's an uncle. Twice.

Wack's direction of the screenplay, by Janet Heaney and Jean Stawarz, from the novel by David Seals, has a way of conveying hard facts obliquely but surely. As Toyomichi Kurita's eloquent camera sweeps the mean, littered face of the Northern Cheyenne reservation, even the dog seems to be limping. "Powwow Highway" is full of such snapshots and panoramas, mute instruction for those who will see.

The film's inspired comedy comes as Buddy's unvented fury collides with Philbert's quiet imperturbability. Philbert meanders, Buddy makes tracks; Philbert has spiritual stops to make on the way, Buddy may explode before he makes them all. It's the set-up for every road comedy worth its octane, from "It Happened One Night" to "Midnight Run," and already we know that the qualities of each man will rub off on the other.

One of Philbert's most important stops is the yearly powwow at Billings, Mont., an event Buddy sneers at. Indoors, in a *gym*, to him it's a joke: "As though a few lousy beads was a culture or something." Yet there's an exchange here with a damaged Indian Vietnam vet, and the pull of the dancing itself that begins to speak to Buddy. (A beautiful moment by Martinez, this is one of the scenes that needs to play out longer, to really build and soar, and either Wacks or the independently made film's budget held back at this point.)

Meanwhile, in Santa Fe, Bonnie's self-reliant girls have found a way out of their detention home at the same time a feisty, lifelong friend Rabbit Layton (Amanda Wyss) arrives to make bail for Bonnie. The boys arrive at about the same time, only to run up against the bossy belligerence of the Santa Fe policewomen. It's what makes Philbert's solution to all their problems—and his cherubic deadpan as he goes about it—all the more satisfactory.

But it's not amiable mix of characters at the end nor even the deeply satisfying action that fixes "Powwow Highway" (MPAA-rated R) permanently in our affections, although it has the sort of ending that makes kids at matinees split nearby eardrums with their delight.

It's the sight of Philbert, leaving a token sacred to *him* at a sacred spot, or, the real power of Philbert, the storyteller, or best of all, Philbert at the break of dawn, the film's most awesome memory.

MONTHLY FILM BULLETIN, 5/90, p. 136, Farrah Anwar

Buddy Red Bow, a politically active member of the Northern Cheyenne Reservation, is contacted by his sister Bonnie (now living in Santa Fe and estranged from her brother for many years) with the news that she and her two young daughters are being held on a drugs charge with a $2,000 bail. Torn between family and tribal loyalties (Buddy is engaged in current negotiations with a mining company, represented by fellow Cheyenne Sandy Youngblood), he decides to leave for Santa Fe after being entrusted with $2,000 by Chief Joseph Mahtasooma for an upcoming cattle deal. He hitches a ride with Philbert Bono, a childhood friend, in his newly acquired '64 Buick, unaware that Philbert (who treats his car as his pony "Protector") is undertaking a spiritual odyssey—a Powwow Highway—to various Red Indian landmarks. The detours and delays cause friction between the friends, though Buddy helps Philbert to move an old friend (and fellow Vietnam veteran) Wolf Tooth and his wife away from the violent harassment of a rival businessman. Arriving in Santa Fe on Christmas Eve, Buddy and Philbert are denied access to Bonnie, who has also been denied release over the holiday period although a childhood friend, Rabbit Layton, has offered to put up the bail. (It transpires that the drugs were planted on Bonnie by the FBI in order to distract Buddy from negotiations with the mining company, of which Sandy Youngblood is aware.) While Buddy is arguing with the guards, Philbert helps himself to just over $4,000 from an unguarded safe room. A bar-room fight with Youngblood confirms Buddy's suspicions about the charges, and Philbert then uses "Protector" to help break Bonnie out of jail. She is reunited with her children, and a police chase ensues as Philbert also picks up Buddy and Rabbit. Chief Mahtasooma, having grown suspicious of Buddy's absence with the cattle money, arrives in Santa Fe, and attempts to hinder the police pursuit with a herd of cattle. But as the Buick finally gives in to the rigours of its journey, Philbert pushes Bonnie, Rabbit and the children out before crashing over a mountain top. Buddy is thrown clear, but just as Philbert's friends are mourning his demise, he emerges unscathed from the bushes ...

The production notes to *Powwow Highway* allude to months of scholarly research to ensure historical accuracy, with the cast participating in real-life powwows and other sacred rituals. In the event, the MOR soundtrack, car chases and sassy (and narratively redundant) heroine take precedence, and the potentially intriguing notion of a spiritual road (Powwow Highway) between ancient tradition and modern reality is effectively squandered. After a promising start, in which Buddy and Philbert are convincingly placed in a blue-collar environment of "shootin' pool and chasin' pussy", the film annexes them glibly to odd-couple comedy, with Buddy's volatility (a product of his political impotence) clashing with the easy charm of the mentally slow but emotionally sturdier Philbert. The film's real track should have been to explore the tragedy of its "heroes", as both Buddy, always relying on a right hook rather than reason to make his point (psychotic?), and Philbert, inspired by the "voices" of dead religious figures (schizophrenic?), fit criteria that would safely explain them in terms of modern-day psychiatric disorders.

In that sense, they are not such distant relatives of Will Sampson's Chief Bromden in *One Flew Over the Cuckoo's Nest*, whose response to the conforming forces of White America was self-induced catatonia. But instead of exploring how racial discrimination results in this personal effacement, *Powwow Highway* settles for the affirmations of the buddy movie, without achieving either a consistently manic tone or a convincing balance between character, humour and suspense. (Casting further back, none of Philbert's visions of Indian grandeur and glory match the eerie mood conjured by the Crow burial ground sequence in *Jeremiah Johnson*.) The film's death knell is probably sounded by its attempt to pass off plot weaknesses (Philbert's chance entry into the police-station vaults) as a kind of mystical "kismet", and its sentimentality (the childhood flashbacks) as tenderness.

NEW YORK POST, 3/24/89, p. 23, David Edelstein

The makers of the Cheyenne Indian drama "Powwow Highway" have learned from their ancestors' mistakes. Their ancestors aren't American Indians but scores of American independent filmmakers—renegades who, over the years, have told depressing tales of Appalachia and other remote regions of the country and have, in the process, bored us silly. Or rather, bored us Politically Correct.

"Powwow Highway" is no dreary, realistic tract about the miseries of life on an Indian reservation. It's a funny, botched, often disturbing pulp odyssey—a buddy-buddy car-chase picture with a political charge. Maybe half of it is formula, shoddily done. You spend the movie shaking off cliches the way a pitcher shakes off really dumb signals from his catcher. And then you get a signal you like.

The movie, directed by Jonathan Wacks (producer of "Repo Man") begins with a vision of the Northern Cheyenne Indians in their prime: headdresses, splendid horses, golden plains. This tableau melts into crumbling tin shacks, broken-down cars and packs of hungry curs—the landscape of today's Cheyenne. It's a thuddingly obvious cross-fade, but we take the filmmakers' point: This ain't no powwow.

One Cheyenne, however, sees beauty in all this: Philbert (Gary Farmer), a big lug who dreams of the magic and wildness and glory of his heritage. He trades some whiskey and baubles for a rusted, rattletrap '64 Buick, which he refers to thereafter as his "Pony," and to the audience's amazement its engine turns over.

Philbert is a sentimental figure, and in another context he'd be idiotic. But he's paired here with Buddy Red Bow (A Martinez), a Native American activist with a violent temper and an impatience with Cheyenne ritual. They're your classic buddy-buddy combination, and when Red Bow's sister, Bonnie (Joanelle Romero), gets busted in Santa Fe on a trumped-up drug-possession charge, the young hotshot waylays Philbert and orders him to drive from Montana to New Mexico.

The formula is familiar from scores of B movies, and the villain, as usual, is the law. See, the feds arrested Bonnie because they wanted Red Bow out of Montana—they're trying to convince the tribe to sell their rights to the Indians' land, which is rich in coal and uranium.

We get the usual grim statistics hurled in our faces: "Seventy-five percent of our people live below the poverty line," rails Red Bow. "This ain't the American dream we're livin'—this is the Third World!" But the director's real purpose is to get these two On The Road, where he can hilariously contrast the angry activist and the serene philosopher.

When Red Bow trashes a car-stereo store after the manager condescends to him, simple Philbert counsels him on the power of the great spirit. And when Philbert drives off the road, wades into a lake and chants a prayer to the setting sun, Red Bow regards him as a madman. Eventually, of course, Philbert will rouse himself to political action, and Red Bow will be softened by forces larger and more mysterious than any individual's wrath.

Whenever possible, the screenwriters, Janet Heaney and Jean Stawarz (working from a novel by David Seals), nudge their story into myth. When Philbert uses his CB, he makes contact with a trucker called "Light Cloud"—the name of a Cheyenne God. And it really could be that god— the voice directs Philbert to a sacred Black Hills mountain, where the gluttonous, moon-faced Indian leaves a Hershey bar behind as a gift to the great spirit.

Farmer is a wonderfully deadpan comedian, and although his features are heavy and clay-like, when he sings or chants they're transformed—they fit. The mythical aspects of "Powwow Highway" work so well that we're let down when the movie doesn't get bigger and crazier and more chancy. Wacks' timing actually gets flabbier, and when the pair arrives in Santa Fe much of the air goes out of the picture. He brings in Amanda Wyss as Bonnie's feisty friend from Texas—who tries to bail her out and ends up arguing and making bedroom-eyes at Red Bow—and he can't seem to position the camera so that we see anything much except her long, blue-jeaned thighs. The scenes between them are an embarrassment.

The movie is just good enough to make you hate it for not being better—for blowing the climax and not coming up with a real ending (what's there resolves nothing). But the power and charm of "Powwow Highway" are undeniable. The actors are inventive and compelling, and when Red Bow and Philbert visit a violent, rundown reservation and meet up with an old buddy—so traumatized by Vietnam and the horror he sees around him that he can't get any words out—the image is unspeakably moving.

The Red Bow-Philbert combination is so likable you'll wish you could see them again. They'd made a great pair of Cheyenne crime-solvers. Or they could take on Washington, D.C. Messed-up as it is, "Powwow Highway" leaves you hungry for more.

NEWSDAY, 3/24/89, Part III/p. 3, Terry Kelleher

The road picture is an equal-opportunity formula.

Arriving today is "Powwow Highway," another in a long line of films about mismatched companions who learn from each other en route to wherever. But this time the traveling buddies are a couple of contemporary Cheyenne Indians from Montana, and it's the different cultural background that gives the movie a special claim on our attention.

The script by Janet Heaney and Jean Stawarz, based on David Seals' novel, has to stretch a bit to get the duo movin' on down the highway. Buddy Red Bow (A Martinez from the "Santa Barbara" soap opera) is a wiry, angry activist, an embittered veteran of wars foreign (Vietnam) and domestic (Wounded Knee, 1973). Philbert Bono (Gary Farmer) is a gentle 300-pounder whose inclinations are spiritual rather than political: He fancies himself on a quest to become a latter-day mystic warrior.

Buddy has been opposing a strip-mining project on the reservation, so an evil bureaucrat at the Bureau of Indian Affairs arranges to have the troublemaker's sister (Joanelle Romero) arrested down in New Mexico, figuring he'll run to her aid and forget his crusade. Buddy takes the bait, all right, but apparently has neither car nor money. So he misappropriates $2,000 from the tribal council and cadges a ride with Philbert in that '64 Buick clunker the big fellow just bought at a junkyard. Philbert dubs the vehicle "Protector, the War Pony" and seems to think Santa Fe's as good a destination as any.

Now, a road picture wouldn't be a road picture without aerial shots of the protagonists' auto cruising along the scenic interstate. And at one point we even get Creedence Clearwater Revival on the soundtrack. If "Powwow Highway" is worth taking, however, it's for the side trips. While Buddy snoozes, Philbert steers Protector toward the Black Hills of South Dakota, where the movie has its best seriocomic moments. After huffing and puffing his way up a sacred mountain, Philbert offers the gods a chocolate bar, which he has abstained from devouring in an act of heroic self-denial. Later, Buddy joins Philbert for some ritual chanting in a stream—and obviously can't believe what he's waded into.

The Buddy-Philbert relationship is not unlike that of the impatient auto salesman and his autistic brother in "Rain Man." In fact, Farmer stresses his character's childlike qualities almost to the point of suggesting mild retardation. But how his sojourn with Philbert changes Buddy is unclear, or at least unconvincing. Is Philbert's "blissed-out" attitude, his simple faith in the wisdom of the ancients, relevant to the condition of today's Native Americans? Will his experiences on the road make Buddy more patient, more philosophical, less confrontational? "Powwow Highway" raises these questions—especially when Buddy hooks up with an old American Indian Movement comrade (Wayne Waterman) who has grown tired of the struggle—but it never comes to grips with them.

Director Jonathan Wacks seemingly can't decide whether "Powwow Highway" is a feel-good movie or a think-hard movie. The ending comes down on the feel-good side, as Buddy and Philbert—joined by Buddy's sister, her two kids and her best friend (Amanda Wyss)—walk away laughing after eluding the long arm of the lawless law. Who knows where they're going or how they plan to get there?

NEWSWEEK, 4/3/89, p. 70, David Ansen

Mainstream Hollywood, which generally employs ethnic characters for comic or criminal relief, has left open to the independents vast unexplored cultural terrain. "Powwow Highway," a comic road movie about two Northern Cheyenne Indians, benefits mightily from the freshness of its subject matter. If director Jonathan Wack's enjoyable but facile movie only scratches the surface of its tale, we're still grateful for the attempt. Janet Heaney and Jean Stawarz's script retools the buddy-movie formula by creating an Indian odd couple. Red Bow (A Martinez) is a Hollywood-handsome political activist bursting with unproductive rage; his unlikely partner is the huge, junk-food-devouring, sweet-natured Philbert (the delightful Gary Farmer), who is following a vision of his spiritual heritage. Taking off from their Montana reservation in Philbert's wreck of a car, they begin a roundabout odyssey that culminates in Santa Fe, N.M., where Red Bow's sister has been jailed on a trumped-up drug charge by villainous Feds. Unfortunately the jerrybuilt plot doesn't do justice to the characters, and the pat, crowd-pleasing finale leaves too many issues unresolved. "Powwow Highway" keeps you hooked into its energy, but it seems torn between wanting to explore its theme of politics and spirituality and wanting to follow commercial fashion. It's a perfect example of the schizoid state of the independent film scene: one eye's on art, the other's on Variety.

VILLAGE VOICE, 3/28/89, p. 57, J. Hoberman

Few setups seem more endemic to movies than the tale of two guys on the road, but *Powwow Highway*, in which the peripatetic pals are impoverished, young Cheyenne Indians, has its own loopy vibe. Pitched somewhere between magic realism and earnest regionalism, this is the first American movie with the feel of certain Australian ones—a sense of the national landscape as pulverized alternate universe. Pushing their rusted-out '64 Buick from a reservation in Lame Deer, Montana, to a prison outside Santa Fe, New Mexico, Buddy Red Bow and Philbert Bono travel through a terrain of invisible ruins. Theirs is a primordial planet glimpsed through the fissures of the white world.

Like Buddy and Philbert, *Powwow Highway*—which opens Friday at the 57th Street Playhouse—rides roughshod over limitation. This flawed, likable movie can be schematic, with crudely drawn conflicts and a few scenes out of a Native American *thirtysomething*, but, as realized by first-time director Jonathan Wacks from a novel by David Seals, it's loose and breezy, casually vivid in a way that few well-meaning independent films allow themselves to be. Even when Wacks stumbles, he's clearly onto something. The material here is so rich, it extends off the frame. (Indeed, certain unexplained actions and lapses in continuity suggest the existence of a longer version than the present 91-minute one.)

Powwow Highway is hardly a humanistic idyll. Albeit steeped in Indian politics, it's basically an audience film. Still, when not being a buddy movie or a chase comedy or a muckraking tract, *Powwow Highway* is a debate on the nature of Native American identity. The radical activist Buddy (part-Blackfoot A Martinez), a bitter, wiry veteran of Wounded Knee, drafts the romantic would-be traditionalist Philbert (Canadian-Mohawk Gary Farmer) to help rescue his estranged sister Bonnie from the New Mexico pen, where she's been unjustly imprisoned in order to lure troublesome Buddy off the reservation. Their meandering trip takes the pair through frontier towns and Denver condos, with detours to various sacred or historical sites and a powwow held in a high school gym.

This is a small movie,but it has a glossier look than most indies; in some ways it's overproduced. One might have wished for a funkier, less rollicking pace. That the film's tone oscillates between Jonathan Demme sweetness and the sort of dogged Dudley Dorightism one associates with the more high-minded products of the Sundance Institute or American Playhouse seems built into the conception. Handsome Buddy is given all the p.c. lines. "This ain't the American dream we're living," he tells the tribal council when a citified Cheyenne renegade tries to sell off the reservation's mineral rights. "This is the Third World." But Philbert has the movie's soul.

A massive, imperturbable mooncalf who thinks it's time for "gathering medicine," Philbert is the irascible Buddy's opposite—although their characterizations are fraught with ironies. For all his talk of community, Buddy is an ornery, perhaps anachronistic, loner—"You'd think a few lousy beads and a couple of feathers were a culture or something," he grumbles at the powwow—while the placidly mystical, junk food-eating Philbert seems strangely in tune with the modern world: He talks Cheyenne religion over his CB radio, leaves a Hershey bar as an offering on a holy mountain, and gets half his visions from TV. (A used car salesmen in s Sioux headdress inspires him to visit the junkyard to buy his "pony.")

Powwow Highway was bankrolled by George Harrison's HandMade Productions and directed by the coproducer of *Repo Man*, and there probably hasn't been so countercultural a western since Dustin Hoffman went Cheyenne in *Little Big Man. (Powwow Highway* is nearly as moralizing as the Arthur Penn film, but it's less smugly sentimental.) Buddy and Philbert are both inveterate potheads—Philbert buys his jalopy for a lid—and the cops are tools of the capitalist pigs. The epiphanies even trigger bursts of pseudo-Crosby, Stills, and Nash; one of the most ecstatic road shots is scored to "Who'll Stop the Rain?"

The movie's narrative invention flags when the guys reach Santa Fe. Still, *Powwow Highway* is fashioned from the stuff of legends. And if Wacks doesn't always have the confidence of his own lyricism, every once in a while he gets off a zinger. Philbert and Buddy drive their moving death-rattle past a Mount Rushmore that's less camp joke than desecration, less idiotic desecration than a joke on the white man that cuts deeper than camp.

Also reviewed in:
NEW REPUBLIC, 4/24/89, p. 24, Stanley Kauffmann
NEW YORK TIMES, 3/24/89, p. C11 Janet Maslin
VARIETY, 8/31/88, p. 38

PRANCER

An Orion Pictures release of a Nelson Entertainment presentation in association with Cineplex Odeon Films of a Raffaella production. *Producer:* Raffaella De Laurentiis. *Director:* John Hancock. *Screenplay:* Greg Taylor. *Director of Photography:* Misha Suslov. *Editor:* Dennis O'Connor. *Music:* Maurice Jarre. *Music Editor:* Dan Carlin Sr. *Sound:* James Thornton and (music) Sean Murphy. *Sound Editor:* David McMoyler. *Production Designer:* Chester Kaczenski. *Art Director:* Marc Dabe. *Set Designer:* Thomas Wilkins. *Set Decorator:* Judi Sandin. *Set Dresser:* Naomi Slodki. *Special Effects:* Mike Menzel. *Costumes:* Denny Burt. *Make-up:* Lance Anderson. *Stunt Coordinator:* Bobby Porter. *Running Time:* 103 minutes. *MPAA Rating:* G.

CAST: Sam Elliott (John Riggs); Rebecca Harrell (Jessica Riggs); Cloris Leachman (Mrs. McFarland); Rutanya Alda (Aunt Sarah); John Joseph Duda (Steve Riggs); Abe Vigoda (Orel Benton); Michael Constantine (Mr. Stewart/Santa); Ariana Richards (Carol Wetherby); Mark Rolston (Herb Drier); Johnny Galecki (Billy Quinn); Walter Charles (Minister); Victor Truro (Mr. Young); Marcia Porter (Mrs. Fairburn); Loren Janes (Mrs. Soot); Robert Zimmerman (Wagnall); Shirley Starnes (Mrs. Hofsetter); Michael Luciano (Bert); Jesse Bradford (Boy #1); Eric Sardeson (Boy #2); Joseph Morano (Boy with Santa); Belinda Bremner (Miss Bedelia); Terry Jayjack (Mrs. Wetherby); Steven Pressler (Hank); Dale Balsbaugh (Mr. Wood); Sandra Olson (Town Woman); Dan Atherton (Town Man).

LOS ANGELES TIMES, 11/17/89, Calendar/p. 6, Kevin Thomas

"Prancer" is the perfect Christmas gift for the whole family, but it's arriving awfully early. Couldn't they have waited at least until after Thanksgiving?

Anyway, Christmas is fast approaching in the film's Grandma Moses-like setting, a quaint snowcovered Midwestern farming community. At the grade school, a teacher is rehearsing her students in the songs they will sing in the Christmas pageant, and she is having no luck in getting 8-year-old Jessica Riggs (Rebecca Harrell) to sing softer.

It's shrewd introduction to our little heroine in that we're not asked to find her adorable. She is a bright, headstrong child, pretty rather than beautiful, with auburn pigtails and no-nonsense clothes. She has the appearance of a girl who lacks a mother's touch. She is going to win our hearts, not by conquettishness, but by her faith and courage.

There is considerable strain in the Riggs household. Jessica's father John (Sam Elliott), a widower, is a struggling apple farmer. He's an overburdened, decent man of few words, not much imagination and considerable irascibility, much of it provoked by his daughter. Jessica's older brother, Steve, (John Joseph Duda) gives her a hard time, as older brothers will. There may be love in the shabby Riggs household, but it remains beneath the surface.

In this hardly unusual but rather tense family situation, Jessica comes upon a beautiful, wounded reindeer, which she becomes convinced is really one of Santa's reindeer. She's determined to heal him and return him to Santa Claus in time for Christmas.

Written by Greg Taylor, "Prancer," which has a shimmering Maurice Jarre score, is the story of how an innocent but strong-willed child's belief in God (and Santa Claus) transforms her family and her community. Director John Hancock is ideally cast for this material, for in films from "Bang the Drum Slowly" to the recent "Weeds" he has revealed an ability to deal with highly charged emotions with directness and without apology. Of course, "Prancer" (rated G) is a sentimental Christmas season heart-tugger, but it's not ashamed to be so, and it is not unduly manipulative.

Harrell carries the film with an impressive performance for a child whose only previous experience was as a singing litterbug in a school play. Her Jessica, a fully developed portrayal, expresses a wide range of emotions as she meets one challenge after another. Elliott's underplaying pays off in a splendid climactic scene. Duda is just right as the brother, and so is Rutanya Alda as Jessica's concerned aunt. Cloris Leachman is fun as a witch-like reclusive neighbor, but her part has been either trimmed or was underwritten in the first place.

Occasionally, the dialogue for Jessica is not merely precocious but adult. What 8-year-old, however smart, would say "History is going to like you for this"? You could wish, too, that the world of Jessica was not so absolutely WASP. Even Abe Vigoda, cast as the overworked local vet, plays a character named Orel Benton.

NEW YORK POST, 11/17/89, p. 31, V.A. Musetto

"Prancer" is a no-frills but heartwarming little story of a young girl in a quiet all-American town who nurses a reindeer back to health because, in her words, "He's one of Santa's. Prancer, actually."

At the center of the story and of the movie's winning charm is Rebecca Harrell, who makes her acting debut as the heroine, 8-year-old Jessica. She gives the picture a sweetness and earnestness that goes a long way toward making up for its static direction and derivative story.

The screenwriter, Greg Taylor, says he was influenced by Steven Spielberg's "E.T. The Extra-Terrestrial." The similarities are quite evident: Jessica finds the injured reindeer in the woods, hides it on the apple farm owned by her widower father, suffers when it is sold to a mercenary store owner, then frees it in an everything's-okay-now finale. Frequent shots of a full moon remind you further of the Spielberg classic.

"Prancer" is directed by John Hancock, who previously has done nice work with the very different "Bang the Drum Slowly" and "Let's Scare Jessica to Death." Unfortunately, he doesn't have the Spielberg touch when it comes to children's fantasy.

That's where the well-chosen cast of "Prancer" comes to the rescue. Young Harrell gets fine support from the quietly authoritative Sam Elliott as her financially pressed father and, in minor roles, Abe Vigoda as a veterinarian who, rather reluctantly, helps the injured reindeer, and Michael Constantine as a shopping-mall Santa to whom Jessica turns when she wants to find the "real" one.

Best of the supporting cast, though, is Cloris Leachman as an eccentric neighbor—"Terrorist! Terrorist!" she rants when Jessica accidentally ruins her prized plants—whose heart is melted by the young girl. Too bad we never learn more about what in the first place turned her into a wild-haired recluse hiding away in a big house.

NEWSDAY, 11/18/89, Part II/p. 15, Bill Kaufman

There's something rather symbolic near the beginning of "Prancer" when a wooden reindeer, part of a Christmas display being strung across a street, falls off and breaks as a shocked little girl watches.

Little Jessica (newcomer Rebecca Harrell), the 8-year-old who witnesses the mishap, is feeling insecure. Her mother recently died, and she's also coping with her father, a basically loving but outwardly sour man (Sam Elliott) who runs a struggling apple farm that's facing imminent foreclosure. When the child asks whether they'll still be able to eat, Dad tells her, "Sure, we'll have applesauce, apple pie, apple fritters, baked apples..."

When Jessica wanders across an injured reindeer in the woods just before Christmas, she becomes convinced that the creature is Prancer—you know, the one who, along with Dasher and Dancer, et al., is part of Santa's famous team. Since she's afraid of her father's reaction, Jessica hides the animal on her farm, hoping to nurse it back to health in time for the Christmas Eve sled-pulling job.

In keeping with a tenet of most children's fantasies, "Prancer" has a cast filled with oddball characters. Cloris Leachman is excellent as Mrs. McFarland, the eccentric recluse who lives on the adjacent farm. Veteran actor Abe Vigoda drops grumpy platitudes by the bucket, playing a cautious but well-meaning veterinarian who ministers to the injured reindeer. Harrell, who makes her acting bow in this picture, is a winsome little performer who, happily, is able to avoid being cutesy. She has a talent for conveying real emotion.

And as one might expect in a family movie like this, there are moments of grief. Jessica's broken heart seems in pretty poor condition when her dad discovers the recovering animal and it is sold to a shopkeeper. But while a tear or two may be shed, we all intuitively know that in family films of this type, everything's going to come up roses in about 89 minutes.

Also reviewed in:
NEW YORK TIMES, 11/17/89, p. C22, Caryn James
VARIETY, 11/15/89, p. 24
WASHINGTON POST, 11/17/89, p. D7, Rita Kempley

PRINCESS TAM TAM

A Kino International release presented in association with the George Eastman House Film Archive. *Executive Producer:* Arys Nissotti. *Director:* Edmond Gréville. *Screenplay (French with English·Subtitles):* Pepito Abatino. *Adaptation and Dialogue:* Yves Mirande. *Director of Photography:* Georges Benoit. *Music:* Exlixo Grenet and Jacques Dallin. *Choreographer:* Floyd Dupont. *Sound:* Antoine Archimbeaud. *Set Designer:* Lazare Meerson. *Costumes:* Phillipe et Gaston. *Running time:* 82 minutes. *MPAA Rating:* Not Rated.

CAST: Josephine Baker (Alwina); Albert Préjean (Max de Mirecourt); Germaine Aussey (Lucie de Mirecourt); Robert Arnoux (M. Coton); Viviane Romance (Odette); Georges Péclet (Dar); Jean Galland (The Maharajah of Datane).

NEWSDAY, 2/10/89, Part III/p. 5, Bruce Eder

Movie buffs—even serious ones with long memories—can be forgiven for never having seen "Zou Zou" (1934) or "Princess Tam Tam" (1935). The last time either of these two French films starring Josephine Baker ran in New York (or anywhere else in America) was back in 1951 at the old Fifth Avenue Theater.

Both films, representing Baker's best screen work, open a two-week run today at Film Forum 2 in newly made, newly subtitled prints. (Baker's adopted son, Jean-Claude Baker, will be on hand to introduce tonight's 7:10 show of "Princess Tam Tam.") These films' very obscurity reflects the larger paradoxes in Baker's life and career.

Josephine Baker (1906–1975) was born in St. Louis, Mo., into an impoverished childhood. By her teens, however, she discovered that she was a natural performer, a dancer and singer, and began a career as a chorus girl that took her to Paris at 19 to appear in a stage production called "La Revue Negre."

For Baker, as for other black American performers of the period, including Paul Robeson, leaving the United States proved a liberating experience, both personally and professionally. Away from institutionalized racism, Baker became a star in the 1925 production. She later moved to the "Folies Bergere" and became renowned as the "Ebony Venus," the toast of Paris between the wars. With her sensual, uninhibited stage presence, her startling, exotic appearance, and costumes that Grace Jones could only dream of today, Baker was a natural for motion pictures.

Her screen debut came in Paris in 1934 with "Zou Zou," directed by Marc Allégret, a semi-biographical story of an impoverished laundress who gets a break and becomes a stage star, all while carrying a torch for sailor Jean Gabin. A year later, under director Edmond Gréville, Baker starred in the more ambitious "Princess Tam Tam," a Pygmalion-like fantasy shot in Tunisia, about an author (Albert Préjean) who goes to North Africa for inspiration and instead finds Baker, a wild, gypsy-like girl whom he transforms into a social butterfly.

What's surprising about both movies is just how "American" they look and feel. Indeed, the subtitles are almost superfluous. Both resemble the kind of personally tailored, cleverly made vehicles that Warner Bros. created for James Cagney, Barbara Stanwyck, William Powell and Al Jolson during this era. And each contains production numbers reminiscent of Busby Berkeley's work.

There were differences, of course, at least one of which may account for neither film's being released in America. Baker's leading men in both pictures are white, which prompted one British film trade weekly to speculate on negative audience reaction, and probably kept them out of this country altogether.

Each film also has elements of purely cinematic interest. "Zou Zou" was directed by Marc Allégret (1900–1973), a nephew of author André Gide. Allegret began his career in 1925 with a documentary about his uncle's African journey entitled "Voyage to the Congo." He directed the 1932 version of Marcel Pagnol's "Fanny," and became known for finding future stars—Simone Simon, Michele Morgan, Raimu, Jean-Paul Belmondo, Alain Delon and Brigitte Bardot did their earliest screen work in his pictures. "Princess Tam Tam" director Edmond Gréville (1906–1966) worked with celebrated film maker Abel Gance early in his career, and later did films in England including "Noose" (1948) and "Beat Girl" (1960).

VILLAGE VOICE, 2/14/89, p. 64, Amy Taubin

Princes Tam Tam (1934) and *Zou Zou* (1935), two French vehicles for Josephine Baker—the great music hall performer who truly merits the overused adjective *insouciant*—have been reissued by Kino in glistening 35mm subtitled prints, now on view at the Film Forum. Both films allow Baker to let loose her full acting range—from clowning, gawky wild child to stylish, knowingly sexual woman of the world—and to explore, however warily, the kind of interracial love story forbidden to her in America. Although *Princess Tam Tam* is probably the more coheent of the two (it throws in some documentary footage of Tunisia along with the fake palm trees), *Zou Zou* has the legendary "Haiti" number, with Baker, clad in a few strategically placed feathers, imprisoned in a bird cage, singing in her unexpectedly delicate, trilling voice about her lost Caribbean home. *Zou Zou*'s extra attraction is the young Jean Gabin, who, it now appears, began his career as a hoofer. See both of them for Baker, whose presence cannot becontained by either the films or her own reputation.

Also reviewed in;
NEW YORK TIMES, 2/10/89, p.C13, Vincent Canby

PURGATORY

A New Star Entertainment release in association with International Media Exchange, Filmco, and Kingsway Communications. *Executive Producer:* Dimitri Villard and Robby Wald. *Producer:* Ami Artzi. *Director:* Ami Artzi. *Screenplay:* Felix Kroll and Paul Aratow. *Director of Photography:* Tom Fraser. *Editor:* Ettie Feldman. *Music:* Julian Laxton. *Sound:* Philip Key. *Production Designer:* Robert van der Coolwijk. *Set Decorator:* Eva Strack. *Stunt Coordinator:* Mark Myron. *Running Time:* 92 minutes. *MPAA Rating:* R.

CAST: Tanya Roberts (Carly Arnold); Julie Pop (Melanie Davis). Hal Orlandini (Bledsoe); Rufus Swart (Paul Cricks); Adrienne Pearce (Janine); Marie Human (Kirsten); David Sherwood (Stern); Clare Marshall (Ruth Arnold); Hugh Rouse (Rivers); John Newland (Ambassador Whitney).

NEW YORK POST, 1/7/89, p. 20, Jami Bernard

Here's the question the folks at New Star Entertainment were probably asking themselves: What sort of plot device can we use as an excuse to get Tanya Roberts out of her clothing, forced to have sex with loathsome men, and unable to escape?

Suddenly, their eyes lit up; the answer was simple. Have her be in the Peace Corps during a military coup in some fictional African nation, throw her in the slammer on a trumped-up drug charge, and have the warden be a pimp. Yeah, that's the ticket!

"Purgatory" is not a scary movie, but the audience at yesterday's screening sure was. Grunts of approval could be heard throughout the theater as the lovely Miss Roberts was forced to endure countless humiliations while wearing prison-issue silk teddies.

If "Purgatory" has higher-than-average production values for an exploitation movie of its kind, that's the only good thing that can be said for it. The plot is ridiculous, the acting atrocious the sex scenes as salaciously debasing as possible. To add insult to injury, the dialogue is full of such time-killers as, "But don't you *see*? and "Don't cry—that's what they *want* us to do!"

Roberts is thrown into this nightmare prison with another pure-as-driven-snow American girl, only this one has the good sense to commit suicide early in the picture—she'd seen the rushes.

This "Midnight Express" meets "Charlie's Angels" gives new meaning to the concept of penal reform as the prison warden—who, incidentally, was educated at Harvard Business School—explains to a tearful Tanya that the only way to survive at the euphimistically named Purgatory Prison is to, um, be *nice* to the men he'll introduce her to.

First he introduces her to himself. *Quelle surprise*! Roberts squeals in indignation. In fact, Roberts squeals a lot of her lines. If a movie like this can't even have convincing screaming from its semi-nude actresses, what on earth is it trying to offer?

But yesterday's audience didn't mind. They sat as attentively as if this were the opening night of the New York Film Festival.

"Purgatory" goes for maximum titillation; artistic concerns were not in the budget. Therefore, plenty of ersatz sex, gang rapes, disrobing and crying scenes.

Tanya Roberts seems oddly modest during her gratuitous nude scenes. Did she have an inkling that there'd be no early Oscar chatter about her performance?

Here's a hint for her character: don't wear revealing midriff cotton blouses during military coups in obscure African nations. It can only lead to no good.

Also reviewed in:
VARIETY, 1/18-24/89, p. 22

QUEEN OF HEARTS

A Cinecom Entertainment Group release of a Nelson Entertainment presentation of an Enterprise/TVS Films production. *Executive Producer:* Graham Benson. *Producer:* John Hardy. *Director:* Jon Amiel. *Screenplay:* Tony Grisoni. *Director of Photography:* Mike Southon. *Editor:* Peter Boyle. *Music:* Michael Convertino. *Sound:* Peter Glossop and (music) Dick Lewzey. *Sound Editor:* Peter Pennell. *Production Designer:* Jim Clay. *Art Director:* Philip Elton. *Costumes:* Lindy Hemming. *Make-up:* Magdalen Gaffney. *Stunt Coordinator:* Gareth Milne. *Running time:* 103 minutes. *MPAA Rating:* Not Rated.

CAST: Vittorio Duse (Nonno); Joseph Long (Danilo); Anita Zagaria (Rosa); Eileen Way (Mama Sibilla); Vittorio Amandola (Barbariccia); Roberto Scateni (Falco); Stefano Spagnoli (Young Eddie); Alec Bregonzi (Headwaiter); Ronan Vibert (Man in Pig Scene); Matilda Thorpe (Woman in Pig Scene); Anthony Manzoni (Doorman); Sydney Kean (Pepe); Ray Marioni (Mario); Sarah Hadaway (Teresa); Anna Pernicci (Angelica); Ian Hawkes (Eddie); Jimmy Lambert (Bruno); Frank Rozelaar-Green (Gino); Lee Simpson (Maurice); Jason Rush (Jason); Frank Coda (Gennaro); Lino Omoboni (Barber); Michael Mears (Father Anthony); Tat Whalley (Beetle); Nicola Kimber (Club Hostess); Paul Casimir (Car Mechanic); Jane Hollowood (Postwoman); Henry Goodman (Taxi Driver); Cliff Parisi (Manager); Melena Noia (Nonno's Mother); Rhys Brock (Young Nonno).

FILMS IN REVIEW, 11/89, p. 556, Pat Anderson

It is not in Padua but San Gimignano where these delightful contemporary Montagues and Capulets spit on each other. Rosa (Anita Zagaria) loves Danilo Lucca (Joseph Long), spurns Barbariccia (Vittorio Amandola) whom her stern Mama Sibilla (Eileen Way) has picked for her, and in a wacky chase scene elopes to England with her beloved—only to find Mama on the same boat.

We know all this because the Lucca's youngest son Eddie (Ian Hawkes), the movie's narrator, tells us: "That's how Mum and Dad got married. It was incredibly romantic—or so it was the way Dad told it."

In 1985, Cannes' Palme D'Or winner was the Yugoslav *When Father Was Away On Business*, and *Queen Of Hearts* has much in common with that excellent picture. Both are narrated by the families' youngest, innocent, rather naive sons. Both deal with family vicissitudes: the joys, the sorrows, sibling jealousies, grandparental animosities and fathers' adversities.

The basis of the conflicts in the Yugoslav film was the political climate. Here it is hurt pride and passion. Barbariccia's quest for revenge and his jealousy of the Luccas with their love for each other and their children, their successful family cafe in London's Italian quarter, is like an Italian opera plot with all emotions worn on all sleeves.

So while Barbariccia schemes against Danilo, tight-lipped Mama Sibilla, after 20 years in London, still disapproves of her somewhat lazy, gambling prone son-in-law. But by this time it is a rather comfortable habitual irritation. It is now her eldest grandson, go-getter Bruno (Jimmy Lambert) who really needles his easy going father. And besides, when Nonno Lucca (Vittorio Duse) comes over to join his son's family, Mama Sibilla has somebody she can really vent her spleen on. The minute he arrives and starts talking, she fixes him with a look of utter contempt, draws herself up to her full height and haughtily hisses in her very thick accent "Here, we speak English. Only English." But later, when she reminds him once again, *he* suddenly draws *himself* up, looks her right in the eye and confounds her with "How do you do, old chum."

Eddie, our hero, is a real child: happy, sad, troubled, joyous. With his best friend Beetle (Tat Whalley) ("Beetle didn't have a family so we lent him ours, sort of") roams the streets, gets up to mischief, tries to help in his father's fights with Barbariccia and makes every day an adventure.

Director Jon Amiel, renowned for *The Singing Detective*, himself the son of immigrants, gives Tony Grisoni's screenplay depth, warmth and understanding. All the actors *are* their characters. You don't see any wheels turning. And it is good occasionally to be spared the ubiquitous dazzling special effects and car or jet chases for humor and the genuine feelings of this splendid film.

LOS ANGELES TIMES, 9/29/89, Calendar/p. 8, Sheila Benson

For some time now, American films have become less and less hospitable to whimsy or fantasy. Once the truffles of the film world, fantasy has come to mean hardware, generally so over-produced that it sinks of its own weight, while whimsy perished for lack of nourishment years ago.

So it's particularly nice to see that the imported "Queen of Hearts," a thoroughly inventive and rewarding comedy-fantasy, is unafraid of either of these delicacies.

Opening among the towers and spires of Gimignano, a medieval town near Florence, "Queen of Hearts" soon flies, like its desperate lovers, to London's present-day Italian quarter. That's where our 10-year-old hero, Eddie Lucca, and his sprawling family live, up over the Lucky Cafe, their pride as well as their livelihood.

But first, in Gimignano, we meet Eddie's parents, Danilo (Joseph Long) and Rosa (Anita Zagaria), our faithful, fateful lovers. In this prologue, Rosa's fierce little mama has betrothed her to Barbariccia, the town's richest bachelor, but Rosa, who loves Danilo, will have none of it. Hounded by the entire village, the two lovers make a suicidal leap after deciding they cannot live without each other. Somehow, magically, they—and we—are flying to London where, over the course of the film's 20 years, their family and their little cafe will become part of the heartbeat of the Quarter.

Newcomer Tony Grisoni's screenplay is a delight: fresh, charming, not infrequently poignant. The Luccas are at the movie's center and director Jon Amiel has filled in around them with a sketchbook's worth of faces: grandfathers, grandmothers, aunts, uncles, cousins and might-as-well-be family members. Small, big-eyed, dark-haired Eddie (Ian Hawkes), youngest of the four Lucca children, is our omnipresent narrator and resident mischief maker. (Imagine an Italian Lukas Haas and you have a fair idea of Eddie's charm).

Eddie's best friend, red-haired Beetle (Tat Whalley), is a whiz at anything electric. We watch as a vast family wedding is enlivened by the boys' talents at generating small electric shocks, while Amiel sets up the whole event to look like some squirming corner of a Hieronymus Bosch canvas. (Amiel has already had noteworthy experience in signature scenes; his most famous previous credit is Dennis Potter's "The Singing Detective," one of television's finest and most inventively staged dramatic fantasies.)

Years whiz by, as they have a way of doing. Danilo's visiting father, Nonno (Vittorio Duse), becomes as much of a fixture as Rosa's grandmother, Mama Sibilla (Eileen Way), who never smiles. Children grow up, break their parents' hearts, then break their own. Suddenly, with the force of an entrance in opera, the vengeful Barbariccia (Vittorio Amandola) appears back on the scene. He has mellowed not one small bit, and the still-beautiful Rosa has never left his thoughts.

Luckily, "Queen of Hearts," an English production of an Italian family's saga, complete with a magical talking pig's head and a miraculous hearing aid, is as long on inventiveness as it is on charm; it's almost impossible to predict which way the story will jump. (Not even when one of its pivotal scams is as familiar as one from "The Sting.")

Although the film is beautifully photographed by Mike Southon ("Paperhouse"), a few of grandfather Nonno's recurring dream sequences don't completely work; not enough to get disturbed about. Every one of its actors works superbly; most of them, who come from British or Italian theater, are making their English film debuts. (Not Vittorio Duse: In 1942 he was the lead in Visconti's "Ossessione"; he's 72 now and still arresting.) They are an enchanting lot.

MONTHLY FILM BULLETIN, 10/89, p. 309, Whedbee Mullen

In a small town in Italy, lovers Danilo and Rosa flee from their parents and Rosa's enforced engagement to Barbariccia. They are miraculously saved from a suicidal leap, and set sail for London's Italian quarter, where they are joined by Rosa's mother, Mama Sibilla. One Christmas, prompted by a vision of a talking pig's head, Danilo wins enough at cards to purchase the Lucky Café, where he and Rosa raise four children (events being largely seen through the eyes of ten-year-old Eddie, the youngest of the four). Bruno, the oldest son, frets over his father's impracticality, while Theresa, their unmarried sister, becomes pregnant. Danilo's father, Nonno, arrives from Italy for a visit and is soon at loggerheads with Rosa's pious mother. Barbariccia, still intent on reclaiming Rosa and destroying Danilo's livelihood, is now a club owner and restaurant retailer. He forecloses on Danilo's espresso machine and assumes control of a neighbouring establishment, Gennaro's betting shop, displacing its previous proprietor and his son, Eddie's best friend Beetle. Eddie learns from Beetle that Bruno is actually working as a debt collector for Barbariccia. Faced with ruin and betrayed by his family, Danilo takes up Barbariccia's challenge to gamble for his lost goods, and he forfeits his café, home and wife. While Nonno lies dying, Danilo unsuccessfully attempts suicide. Eddie retrieves his dead grandfather's gun and tries to shoot Barbariccia, passing out after apparently wounding Bruno. But his magically unscathed brother carries Eddie home, rejecting Barbariccia in favour of his father. Danilo, Bruno and Eddie decide to try their luck once again at Barbariccia's establishment. With some practical help from Beetle and divine intervention from Nonno, Danilo wins at the dog races and Barbariccia is ruined. Danilo, however, offers to tear up his betting ticket if Barbariccia will relinquish his claim to Rosa. Barbariccia agrees and the family is reunited.

With *Queen of Hearts*, former TV director Jon Amiel (responsible for the award-winning BBC series *The Singing Detective*) rehearses a now familiar litany on the vicissitudes of life and love in Britain. In the style of *Hope and Glory* and *Wish You Were Here*, *Queen of Hearts* combines a dreamy mythologising of Britain's past with a peculiar brand of not-quite-social-realism (generally distinguished by its obsession with the unwed teenage mother). This reverie on growing up British/Italian fails to blend fantasy and reality, nostalgia and propaganda, and although the disparity is obviously deliberate—Italy as land of romance, magic and adventure is contrasted with Britain, home of the condom ad—it is no less unfortunate. Ultimately, we are meant to accept Amiel's "Italy" where love triumphs and luck runs true as the counterpoint to quotidian life for immigrants in the U.K. The impossibility (not to mention social irresponsibility) of this emerges clearly from the various contrivances to which the film resorts in order to reach its happy ending.

Hoping to restore Danilo's café, and break Barbariccia's bank, Eddie's friend Beetle rigs up an elaborate betting scam involving a complex, mechanical apparatus—emblems of his street-wise "check" and British practicality. In the final draw, Barbariccia's henchmen discover Beetle's taping machine, leaving Eddie, the pensive Italian, to save the day when he receives a hot tip over his dead grandfather's hearing aid. Although several supernatural events occur prior to the closing scene (the lover's leap, the prophetic pig's head), these episodes clearly represent Eddie's subjective musings on his parents' past. With ghostly hearing aid, however, Amiel asserts Eddie's fable as the privileged, and somewhat preposterous, version of events.

Only through the intermediary of an imaginary "Italy" can Amiel approach, or perhaps avoid, the questions typically raised by mainstream British cinema about the exact nature of British experience. Indeed, *Queen of Hearts* is riddled with contradictions. For instance, it is impossible to determine when the film takes place; the programme notes suggest the 1950s, but the prominently displayed Kit-Kat bars and aforementioned billboard promoting "safe sex" hint otherwise. Set in the past, the film inevitably returns us to the present, as it vacillates over contemporary issues, only to slip again into soothing melodrama. An already mythologised social commentary succumbs to a second varnish of Italianate cliché; we are left with a film suspended between fantasy and realism, unable to commit to one or the other or even to open a fruitful dialogue between the two.

NEW LEADER, 10/2-16/89, p. 21, John Morrone

A colleague at a well-known film magazine once told me with conviction that the British can only make little pictures. "Small country, small films," he said. David Lean and Michael Powell apparently slipped his mind, along with the gifted phantasmagorist Jon Amiel, director of the seven-hour *Singing Detective* and other television films. Now Amiel has done *Queen of Hearts*, his first theatrical feature, a satisfying fable about faith and fortune that places Amiel alongside Stephen Frears, Neil Jordan and Philip Saville as one of the most lyrical British filmmakers of the '80s.

Written by Tony Grisoni, *Queen of Hearts* effectively employs the conventions of kitchen-sink drama the British cinema has always excelled in. The film has sense of extravagance that is strikingly un-British, though, perhaps because its characters are Italian.

Danilo and Rosa (played by Nottingham-born Joseph Long and the exquisite Italian actress Anita Zagaria) are star-crossed lovers in a small southern Italian town. In a moment that is so grandly melodramatic it might have been taken from a libretto, the two run up a church tower to escape the butcher Barbariccia (Vittorio Amandola), to whom Rosa has been unwillingly betrothed. Then they make a stunning leap into the void, expecting to die, but instead land safely in a haytruck. Soon they board a ship headed for England, accompanied by Rosa's sharp-tongued grandmother (Eileen Way) as chaperone.

Danilo's surname is Lucca. Although it does not mean "lucky" in Italian, Grisoni uses the sound of the word to suggest chance and felicitous coincidence. These are the determining forces in the family's life, not the whiskey and the dole that shape the drab existence of so many characters in British films.

The London where Danilo and Rosa settle down in the 1950s is a hard place to make a living. But while waiting tables in a Soho eatery Danilo has a miraculous vision that leads the family to prosperity—a roast pig's head comes to life and warns him to "fear the man with the knife" and "trust the coin." The man, of course, is Barbariccia, who is still in pursuit of Rosa and has followed the Luccas to London to cause as much trouble for them as he can. The coin is a five-pound note that Danilo gets as a tip and gambles into a wad large enough to buy the Lucky Cafe. With the loan from friend Mario's appliance shop of a coffee machine—lovingly dubbed *la bella macchina*—the Luccas' star is soon rising.

Much of the film's mood of enchantment derives from the voiceover narration by Danilo's son Eduardo, or Eddie the dreamer (Ian Hawkes). He adores dispensing espresso alongside his brother Bruno (Jimmy Lambert), his sisters and his grandmother. Most of all, though, he favors Nonno (Vittorio Duse), the grandfather known in the family for his fantastic anecdotes whom Eddie models himself after once Nonno arrives in London.

Like the old storyteller, Eddie loves to spin a good yarn. Having received the tales of the flight from Italy and the talking pig with a wonderment usually reserved for Biblical legends, he is the natural chronicler of the Luccas's fortunes.

Eddie's voice guides us through the family's colorful, eccentric lives and prepares us for the sad turn of events that overtakes them. When Barbariccia becomes a wealthy nightclub nabob, he purchases Mario's store and repossesses the *bella macchina* that had been lent out to the Luccas.

Gradually, he exacts his elaborate revenge, partly by alienating the ambitious Bruno from his unsophisticated parents with the promise of women and cash.

Throughout the involved and charmingly improbable plot twists in the second half of the film, Eddie's faith in true love that never dies and in the wisdom of one's parents is affirmed. Hope and love are what redeem the Luccas and thwart Barbariccia, making him at the end the victim of his own selfish dream. Even he, we learn, has the feelings of a credulous child—"But you were *promised* to me," he weeps helplessly to Rosa, who will never be his. The movie redeems the villain, too.

Queen of Hearts is unabashedly a fairy tale (and it is photographed as such by Mike Southon, distilled onto the screen in the brown and gold colors of a Sienese painting). All the scenes you want and expect to see in a film of this kind—conflicts between rivals, siblings, lovers, schemers— take place in good old-fashioned style.

Yet the work is hardly predictable, in large part because we are unused to portraits of family solidarity. A harmonious family is nowadays more a tarnished ideal than a reality, and as an artistic subject it is often treated so dully in grubby films of domestic realism that most audiences welcome an offbeat, big-hearted handling with open arms. *Moonstruck*, for instance, is one box-office hit that succeeded marvelously at persuading us to believe its concluding toast, *"Alla famiglia!"*

In *Queen of Hearts* (is it a coincidence that both movies are about people of Italian descent?) Amiel's daringly nonrealistic approach plays out its home truths in a passionate *dramma giocoso*. The result is as deeply gratifying as a well-sung aria, or a bedtime story about a faraway place told in a magically foreign accent.

NEW YORK POST, 9/20/89, p. 25, David Edelstein

When "The Singing Detective" ran on television, Jon Amiel must have been the most ignored director on earth: All the attention for that fabulous vision went to writer Dennis Potter. In recent interviews, Amiel said it bothered him to be slighted, but that really, when you think about it, not noticing a director's presence is the highest compliment you can pay him.

It's a compliment that no one will pay him for "Queen of Hearts," the most self-consciously directed film I've seen in years. Amiel, no doubt eager to get his due this time (and who can blame him?), has taken this sweet, simple tall tale of an Italian family in England coping with strife and temptation and thoroughly swamped it. It's hard to see the characters through all the moving camera shots, ominous low angles and twisty points of view.

Considered in a vacuum, Amiel's work is marvelously fluid, and his overture conjures up the most entertaining of silent melodramas. In the opening a pair of young Italian lovers, Rosa (Anita Zagaria) and Danilo (Joseph Long) flee the rich man, Barbariccia (Vittorio Amandola), to whom the girl has been promised. Chased to the top of a tower, they clasp hands, stare into each other's eyes and leap to their deaths—to be saved by a passing cart full of straw.

The narrator announces that this is how his parents met, and we giggle at the hyperbolic intensity of the boy's fantasy life. Prepared for a gear change as the film joins the Lucca family in London, we find, however, that "Queen of Hearts" stays pretty much on that remote, stylized level.

Amiel must have wanted to create tension between the way the boy, Eddie (Ian Hawkes), sees the kingdom into which he has been born and the way it actually is. But all we can see is flashy (albeit heartfelt) technique and preciousness.

Working as a waiter in England, Danilo hears words of wisdom from the head of a roast pig, which directs him to save his money. He does and buys the Lucky Cafe—one of those cozy, bustling places where the regulars banter with the owners and the focal point is an ornate espresso machine. No wonder Eddie thinks he's blessed.

The dark cloud is Barbariccia, who swore revenge when his beloved Rosa was carried off. Now, 20 years later, he arrives in England, buys up several businesses and begins to gnaw at Danilo, first by hiring his son, Bruno (the slick, exuberantly physical Jimmy Lambert) as a debt collector, then by repossessing the prized espresso-maker.

Inevitably, Danilo pushes into Barbariccia's gambling parlor and wagers everything he has (including his wedding ring) against this self-made monster. What happens, the film asks, when the Luccas' fairy-tale love is tested, and the blessed atmosphere of the early scenes gives way to ones of desperation, insanity and death?

Perhaps if Amiel's style weren't so sweeping and operatic, we could relax and get a bead on the characters. But this is one of those movies that does all the work for you—the images don't breathe by themselves because the director's always pumping them up.

A film this rich, however, is bound to offer pleasures. The cinematographer, Mike Southon, gives the images a warm, brown hue that's never obnoxiously quaint. Southon's most riveting subject is Zagaria, whose movements are bewitchingly sculpted; she does most of her acting through her large, opalescent eyes.

The whole cast is evocative—huge but never cartoonish. Amandola in particular shines: he makes the villainous Barbariccia poignant, emotionally arrested, ridiculous in his own eyes. Out of such crippled self-esteem are the most barbarous cruelties justified. Also the most strenuous film direction.

NEWSDAY, 9/20/89, Part II/p. 7, Mike McGrady

"Queen of Hearts" opens in the timeless setting of a medieval Italian hill town, and closes 20 years later in a London abustle with cutthroat businessmen and gamblers. It opens on a classic note, with a lovely young bride fleeing an arranged marriage to elope with her true love—and it ends with her now middle-aged husband risking his business, his home and even his marriage on the turn of a card.

It begins with an epic theme, true love triumphing over all obstacles, and ends with a fixed horse race.

Although one cannot help preferring the epic beginnings of "Queen of Hearts" to its hectic endings, director Jon Amiel's clear talent for blending so many divergent viewpoints and storytelling styles into a pleasant little heartwarmer of a movie is wholly admirable.

Much honored for "The Singing Detective"—an equally complicated mix of fantasy, dreams and reality—Amiel has assembled four generations of warm, earthy characters and provided them with the kind of romantic travail and ethnic overstatement that qualifies the film as a kind of "Moonstruck" with an English-Italian accent.

The events depicted in "Queen of Hearts" come from the memories of a middle-aged man who was the youngest son in his family; his boy-man split vision gives Amiel an opportunity to vary styles. The story of the original elopement of the man's parents, a legend embellished and polished as it was handed down through generations, merits every bit of the epic quality Amiel brings it.

And it also makes sense that the early years in London, the story of the boy's father's moving up from waiter to cafe proprietor, be told in precisely the way it must have been presented to the young boy—drudgery brightened by an occasional miracle. For example, a talking pig that offers magical gambling advice ("Trust the coins but beware the King of Swords") that leads his father to a London gambling hall where he wins the stake that enables him to open his own business.

And, finally, the movie takes on a more modern feel—faster paced, more realistic, grounded in the first-hand observations of the boy weaving together his own memories of love and money and death, the stuff of any family saga.

Throughout, screenwriter Tony Grisoni has larded his script with nuggets of familial wisdom. As the boy's grandfather lies in his sickbed, the ancient grandmother strives to put the boy's mind at ease: "It's all right. Nothing strange. He's only dying."

While Amiel has apparently filled his cast with every Italian actor available in England, the most memorable performance comes from English actress Eileen Way as the terminally grim grandmother. Joseph Long as the boy's father and Italy's Anita Zagaria as his mother are both outstanding.

On the surface, "Queen of Hearts" seems to be a straightforward rendition of a complicated story. Although its concerns—love, marriage, family, revenge, death—are basic, the means of bringing them together is enormously complex, and Amiel must be congratulated for making it all seem so simple.

TIME, 10/2/89, p. 90, Richard Corliss

Hollywood wants to paint an anecdote on a $40 million canvas. The Brits, in their strapped-for-quid, post-David Lean days, toil to see how many angels can dance on the head of a penny. For perhaps a tenth of *Black Rain*'s budget, *Queen of Hearts* lays out a beguiling panorama of romance and revenge, coming of age and coming to terms. Oh, and the niftiest talking pig since Porky.

In the cloistered Italian village of San Gimignano, bold Rosa (Anita Zagaria) is engaged to a town big shot but loves Danilo Lucca (Joseph Long). In a suicidal swoon, the lovers leap from the cathedral tower—and land, in a flick of Tony Grisoni's supple narrative, in London's Italian quarter. Ten-year-old Eddie Lucca (Ian Hawkes) tells the story with a child's wily innocence as filtered through the memory of a wistful adult.

Jon Amiel has catered this sort of phantasmagoric feast before; he directed Dennis Potter's magnificent TV serial *The Singing Detective*. Once or twice Amiel is hobbled by the conflicting demands of a sprawling vision and a thin wallet. The movie starts out of breath and keeps on running. But that's O.K.; in fact, for a couple of hours it's criminally enjoyable. Who would have thought that you could transport three roiling generations of Italians and get *Moonstruck* in Britain?

VILLAGE VOICE, 9/26/89, p. 70, Amy Taubin

Hands are as often tipped in endings as in beginnings. Over the final image of *Queen of Hearts* we hear the following little speech: "My name is Eddie Lucca and that's my story. You can believe it or not, but that's the way I remember it. ..." Then the prepubescent soprano that we've been hearing for the preceding two hours dissolves into a mellow baritone, and the grown-up Eddie Lucca natters on about how sometimes when he turns the corner, he expects to see the Lucky Café and the little street where he grew up, but he never does. Well, Eddie, you and I know that this speech, like what's come before it, is an attempt to let us have our nostalgia and laugh at ourselves for indulging it—without ever asking why, at this moment, we want to do that. Frankly, though, it also suggested to me that you, or your director, suspected that something just hadn't jelled and you wanted to cover your asses by offering a possibly confused audience what seems like a choice—I mean, is this *I Remember Mama* or what? Such vacillation, on top of a heavy dose of whimsy, cancels what little suspension of disbelief was still operating within me, and I want to scream things at the screen like, "Of course you'll never find it, you idiot, because it was a set built specifically for this picture."

As in operetta or melodrama (again, dear reader, the choice is yours), Rosa (Anita Zagaria) loves Danilo (Joseph Long) but has been promised to Barbariccia, the butcher (Vittorio Amandola). The lovers flee their tiny Italian village and settle in London (in the aforementioned set), where they have four children, buy a restaurant, and are joined, in time, by Rosa's mother, Mama Sibilla (Eileen Way), and Danilo's father, Nonno (Vittorio Duse). Then Barbariccia arrives to claim the woman he still regards as his property (and his passion), Danilo makes a terrible mistake, and it's up to Eddie (Ian Hawkes) to save his family.

Despite Amiel's attempt to give the film a look by bathing it with golden light, *Queen of Hearts* owes much to television—its set to *EastEnders* (though it lacks that program's pungent topicality), and its memory structure and flashes of fantasy to Dennis Potter's *Singing Detective*, which Amiel directed. Unlike the rampaging return of the repressed in the latter, the id is markedly absent from *Queen of Hearts*'s treacly visions—although at one point a talking pig makes a brief appearance.

Also reviewed in:
NEW YORK TIMES, 9/20/89, p. C19, Caryn James
VARIETY, 9/6–12/89, p. 23
WASHINGTON POST, 10/11/89, p. B2, Hal Hinson
WASHINGTON POST, 10/13/89, Weekend/p. 43, Joe Brown

RACHEL RIVER

A Taurus Entertainment release of an American Playhouse theatrical film presentation. *Executive Producer:* Lindsay Law. *Producer:* Timothy Marx. *Director:* Sandy Smolan. *Screenplay:* Judith Guest. *Based on the stories of:* Carol Bly. *Director of Photography:* Paul Elliott. *Editor:* Susan Crutcher. *Music:* Arvo Part. *Production Designer:* David Wasco. *Costumes:* Linda Fisher. *Running time:* 90 minutes. *MPAA Rating:* PG-13.

CAST: Pamela Reed (Mary Graving); Viveca Lindfors (Harriet White); Craig T. Nelson (Marlyn); Zeljko Ivanek (Momo); James Olson (Jack Canon); Ailene Cole (Svea); Jo Henderson (Estona); Jon De Vries (Baker).

LOS ANGELES TIMES, 2/24/89, Calendar/p. 8, Kevin Thomas

Our first glimpses of the remote Minnesota town called "Rachel River" give an inviting tug, even though it's late fall and on the verge of a clearly harsh winter.

Here, at last, is an American community that looks untouched by the garishness of ubiquitous modern roadside culture, a town that looks the way it might have 25 or even 50 years ago. Yet by the time this film, which possesses a Shaker-like simplicity, is over, we realize that it takes as much resilience to live here as it does almost any place else. Yes, there is a kindly sense of community but also loneliness and frustration.

"Rachel River," which Judith Guest, author of "Ordinary People," adapted from the stories of Minnesota writer Carol Bly, brings to mind Sherwood Anderson's "Winesburg, Ohio," but is not as despairing. The citizens of Rachel River, all of whom come to such full life on the screen, are hardy souls. They may suffer, but they don't give up.

We meet them, one by one, as the news spreads of the death of the reclusive Svea, a widow who lived in a cluttered shack on the outskirts of town and is rumored to have left a small fortune. Svea will inevitably become the subject of a radio sketch by Mary Graving (Pamela Reed), a gifted writer who realizes she knows little about the dead woman. Mary is clearly talented and admired by her neighbors, but as a divorcee with two small children and an irresponsible ex-husband, she worries constantly about making ends meet.

Two very different but equally awkward men are attracted to her: James Olson's Jack, a well-educated mortician, who has an intellectual bond with Mary but is too self-conscious and repressed to be an effective suitor, and Craig T. Nelson's Marlyn, a hard-drinking good ol' boy deputy sheriff, often obnoxious but confidently sexy and not nearly as stupid as the mortician insists he is. (Of Jack, Marlyn remarks shrewdly, "How could he go off to college and come back an undertaker?")

As splendid as Olson and Nelson are—as is everyone, including Zeljko Ivanet, subtle as a wistful retarded youth—the film is dominated by Reed and by Viveca Lindfors, who offer contrasting portraits of youth and old age, of a woman coping with the middle of her life and of a woman, herself still healthy and strong, confronted with the loss of all that she has cherished. Reed and Lindfors are actresses of distinction rather than celebrity, and of different generations, yet "Rachel River" may well represent the best opportunity each has ever had on the screen. Reed's Mary finds herself wondering whether she can continue on alone, both emotionally and financially; Lindfors' Harriet, her features worn yet durably handsome, wonders how she will ever be able to let go emotionally, in the face of cruel circumstance, of all that has sustained her.

What distinguishes "Rachel River" from most other independent American films is not only its ensemble portrayals under the spare and rigorous direction of Sandy Smolan, a documentary film maker in his feature debut. It also boasts appropriately austere images, captured by cinematographer Paul Elliott and its exceptionally rich and evocative score, composed by the distinctive New Age composer Arvo Part. The contrast between the way "Rachel River" (rated PG-13 for language and adult themes and situations) looks and the way its sounds expresses perfectly the difference between the faces its people try to present to the world and what's going on behind them.

NEW LEADER, 2/20/89, p. 23, John Morrone

An American effort to raise film standards through linkage with public television, *Rachel River*, is painful. The film takes its name from a fictional town in North Minnesota, the kind of place where you can't sneeze without someone offering you a handkerchief. People there aren't just related by blood or marriage but by the cold, aloof winter landscape. It keeps them bundled up against the chill and makes them intensely interdependent. An elderly Norwegian matron tends her dying husband while she recalls warmer, gayer days in both their lives. A young writer—a divorcee raising a family while in financial straits, who is being courted by the deputy sheriff and the village undertaker—reflects on the community's heritage in her weekly radio broadcast. And a reclusive old woman dies in her poky, unheated cottage, with a rumored fortune hidden somewhere on the property, stirring up the overlapping suspicions of the townspeople.

The mosaic quality of *Rachel River* is probably the result of novelist Judith Guest's stitched-together adaptation of several stories by Carol Bly. Both Minnesotans, Guest and Bly no doubt have a feeling for the wistful, eccentric, tradition-loving locals—mostly Scandinavian-Americans—that populate these stories. But Guest fails to develop the characters beyond the size of literary miniatures. Constructs that may offer poignant epiphanies of country life within the parameters of a short story look pale and underwritten on screen. Director Sandy Smolan doesn't help matters by concentrating on what seem to be the sluggish, bewildering antics of self-absorbed rustics. You don't want to patronize these people—some of the performances, by Pamela Reed and Viveca Lindfors, among others, aren't bad—but they keep heaving sighs and they keep saying things like, "This is one strange and dismal world we're living in." Can that possibly be the best country wisdom available nowadays? The whole tone is too tasteful and too enervated.

The folks in Rachel River suffer the burdens of personal and elemental duress. Audiences may have a bigger problem. Like other features funded or partially supported by public broadcasting's American Playhouse and Robert Redford's Sundance Institute (a developmental think-tank for liberal filmmakers), this one pumps up its subjects with respectability but then drains it of vitality and punch. The film bids us think Big Thoughts—spiritual uplift, social concern, rural dignity. The words that came to my mind were: airless, stagnant, unfailingly well-meaning. We are not inspired, we're deadened. The filmmakers turn Rachel River into Dullsville.

It remains a curiosity why so many American Playhouse theatrical films (*Stacking, Stand and Deliver*, and *Waiting for the Moon* are other notables) aren't very much better. In trying to offer American moviegoers an up-market alternative to the kiss-kiss-bang-bang that is the major studios' bread and butter, these filmmakers, many of them young and emerging from extensive television experience, tend to be more concerned with giving movies a good name than with invigorating their material with style and movement. Perhaps because they have an eye cast toward their films' eventual broadcast on PBS, they become victims to the self-censorship of "good taste" gently imposed by public television. (TV audiences will be able to judge *Rachel River* for themselves in June.) It is gratifying when they are attracted to literary subjects otherwise ignored by the mainstream, such as the violent gothic meditations of James Purdy's *In a Shallow Grave*, but frustrating when the quirkiest and most provocative of them all, Joyce Chopra, is met with controversy over *Smooth Talk* because of its danger-ridden erotic tension.

All of which, I suspect, bodes poorly for the subvention of American theatrical films by public television. For all its good intentions, *Rachel River* is symptomatic of its producers' failure to create vital films from the small, initmate subjects it chooses to focus on. I found it ironic indeed that *Rachel River* received a Sundance/Panavision grant, in the form of Panaflex cameras that permitted filming in difficult Minnesota temperatures of 20 below zero—ironic because *Rachel River* is deep freeze cinema.

NEW YORK POST, 2/17/89, p. 27, David Edelstein

Immense gray clouds drift across the chill skies in "Rachel River," and the trees aren't just bare—they seem to have been eaten away by heartache. You can hear it in the string quartet on the soundtrack, that heartache. The town is in northern Minnesota—Lake Wobegone country—but there's no Garrison Keillor to liven up these woebegone days and nights. The only radio host in town is Mary (Pamela Reed), a divorced woman sunk in loneliness.

Mary does a weekly spot for a country station; she reads community notices and advertisements, and then goes on to tell stories about Norwegian saints and other gentle personages. Modest as she is, she's the only one who attempts to put the town's happenings into some kind of perspective; when an elderly recluse named Svea dies, it's up to Mary to deliver a truthful obituary about a woman for whom no one much cared.

"Rachel River" doesn't have a lot of whoopee. It's one of these earnest, arty pieces of regional filmmaking that for a period dominated the American "independent" scene, the kind of picture that gets funding from Robert Redford's Sundance Institute and ends up on American Playhouse. But it exemplifies the valuable aspects of that genre, too. It's gracefully acted, and the cold settings produce some crystalline images. The movie is never dead; it flickers with warmth.

The action unfolds over the week between the discovery of Svea's body and the funeral. Trudging through the town and talking to people who knew her, Mary comes to regard Rachel River as a ship of lost souls—drunken, despairing, aimless. Her only interludes are several slow-motion fantases of bliss, after which the present looks even bleaker.

Mary's children are off with an ex who won't support her, and her most active suitor is Jack (James Olsen), an undertaker who's clearly smitten but too shy and worshipful to hold her interest. Her only soul-mate is Harriet (Viveca Lindfors), an elderly Swedish-American who still talks to and sleeps with her husband, a glassy-eyed stroke victim. (Lindfors is very moving but mostly unintelligible; for the longest time I thought she was murmuring in Swedish.)

Sandy Smolan, directing his first feature, had the right idea by casting Reed, one of cinema's besk-kept secrets. (It was the right idea in other respects, too; he married her a couple of months later.) Reed has a great sexy-gurgle laugh, and she keeps the picture grounded. Her Mary is earthy and quietly subversive, with a keen sense of irony about herself. (When she's doing dumb things, you know she's watching herself and thinking how dumb they are.)

The movie takes tentative steps toward waggishness: Jack gets a lecture from a colleague in how to be a craftier undertaker; Svea's nephew Marlyn (Craig T. Nelson), a drunken deputy, tries to bully his sister into buying the cheapest coffin; and the town simpleton, Momo (Zeljko Ivanek) drifts in and out of people's consciousness. (According to the press notes, he's supposed to represent a higher form of wisdom.)

But Smolan doesn't wander too far from his lucid-stupor tone; he must think that shaking off the depression would be a betrayal of his subject. The message of "Rachel River" isn't how to make your life less glum by finding new friends, putting on a show, moving away, whatever. It's about reconciling yourself to the glumness of a worst-case scenario. When a potential Mr. Right pops up—a baker with a hint of poetry—Mary beats a hasty retreat, and he only reappears in her pipe dreams.

A romance with this nice man would spoil the dark-night-of-the-soul climax, in which both Mary and Harriet seek relief in fantasy—the former by drinking too much and going to bed with an alcoholic lout, the latter by wandering out to the now-empty farmhouse in which she spent her life. Harriet's walk down the long road is so achingly beautiful that it makes you shiver, but the movie's resolution, in which both women experience a flood of self-sufficiency, feels contrived.

Nelson's Marlyn is the brightest spot, the loosest cannon. An underacter by temperament, he plays this belligerent dunce in a high-decibel monotone, and his directness is hilariously winning.

When Mary reaches bottom, she ends up next to Marlyn on a bar stool, throwing down the scotches. Carried away with his good fortune, he sticks his face in her face and asks if she wants to hear him sing a couple of Tammy Wynette songs.

"No I don't, Marlyn, Really, I don't. Please."

It's a very funny bit, but what an opportunity was missed: no one seems to have realized that a couple of Tammy Wynette songs might be just what the doctor ordered. Beats a string quartet, anyway.

NEWSDAY, 2/17/89, Part III/p. 5, Bill Kaufman

With the barren, wintry Northern Minnesota landscape as a backdrop, the self-sufficient characters whose lives intermix in "Rachel River" are, in sense, all spiritual pioneers on a journey of self-discovery.

This vivid, realistic character study of farm folks offers an honest and thoughtful glimpse at the tapestry of daily life in the small, tightly knit community of Rachel River. Here, human foibles are quietly brought to the surface until they appear to be overwhelming. Despite their trials, the characters manage to prevail.

Pamela Reed, as Mary Graving, plays a young woman who broadcasts a weekly gossip program over the local radio station from a makeshift studio in her home. Graving becomes fascinated with the life of an old farm woman, a recluse who has died amid rumors that a fortune is hidden somewhere on her property.

As Graving, a divorced mother of two, examines the old woman's life, her own dreary existence is amplified. Her loneliness can not be quelled by the pair of suitors vying for her attention: Jack Canon, the local undertaker, a sensitive but secure man played wonderfully by veteran actor James Olson, and Marlyn, the town's yokel deputy sheriff (Craig T. Nelson), a loutish nephew of the dead, old lady who constantly argues with his equally oafish sister.

As the strong-willed Harriet White, Viveca Lindfors is looked up to by many because of her seeming strength. Dispirited because her son has sold her homestead out from under her, she patiently bides her time as a dutiful wife, taking up residence in an old age home where her crippled husband languishes. Lindfors, with her etched face still beautiful, is thoroughly suited for the role.

The film is not without its gently humorous moments. There's the brief scene, for instance, when the mildly retarded village wanderer, Momo (Zeljko Ivanek), plucks a crumpled newspaper out of a garbage can on the street, folds it neatly and innocently offers it for sale as the sheriff walks past. Without missing a beat, the officer knowingly hands Momo a coin and promptly tosses the newspaper back into the basket.

Director Sandy Smolan chose well by filming the picture on location during the fall and winter months. The gray, harsh locales set an evocative mood for the slowly building movie, which, incidentally, won the prize for Best Cinematography at last year's United States Film Festival.

VILLAGE VOICE, 2/28/89, p. 61, Amy Taubin

Were it not for Paul Elliott's exquisite ciematography, *Rachel River* would be just your average American Playhouse product—kinder, gentler, and more literary than a Hollywood slice of white-bread life. I can't remember a U.S.-made film this luminous—indoors and out—since *Days of Heaven*. Catch the theatrical run; don't wait until TV transmission (scheduled for June) mangles its precise framing and muddies its subtle palette.

Set in the frigid wilds of Minnesota, the film describes the effect of the death of Svea, an elderly (and possibly wealthy) widow, on the inhabitants of a one-store, one-bar, one-old-age-home town. Mary Graving (Pamela Reed), divorced with two small children, identifies with the dead woman and fears she will come to a similarly lonely end. Mary has her own radio program; for a half hour every week, she talks about life in Rachel River. She spends the rest of her time dodging clumsy suitors, quarrelling with her ex, and trying to make ends meet.

As Mary, Reed is tough, smart, and likable. She manages to make lines like "sometimes you just get lost in the dumbness of it all" sound witty, incisive, and even moving. With barely three minutes of screen time, Jon De Vries scores as Mary's dream lover—a quirkily romantic presence, well worth fantasizing about on long winter evenings. Unfortunately, the acting in several other crucial supporting roles is a tad overemphatic.

Too often in *Rachel River*, less does not seem like more. At these moments, however, there's still the image to fall back on. What I never expected is that, just as Svea haunted Mary, there's something about Mary that, days after the screening, refuses to let me write her off.

Also reviewed in:
NEW YORK TIMES, 2/17/89, p. C18, Caryn James
VARIETY, 9/23/87, p. 28
WASHINGTON POST, 5/12/89, p. D1, Hal Hinson
WASHINGTON POST, 5/12/89, Weekend/p. 39, Desson Howe

RAINBOW, THE

A Vestron Pictures release. *Executive Producer:* William J. Quigley and Dan Ireland. *Producer:* Ken Russell. *Director:* Ken Russell. *Screenplay:* Ken Russell and Vivian Russell. *Adapted from the novel by:* D.H. Lawrence. *Director of Photography:* Billy Williams. *Editor:* Peter Davies. *Music:* Carl Davis. *Music Editor:* Joe Illing. *Choreographer:* Imogen Claire. *Sound:* John Murphy. *Sound Editor:* Nigel Galt. *Production Designer:* Luciana Arrighi. *Art Director:* Ian Whittaker. *Set Dresser:* Peter Walpole. *Costumes:* Stephen Miles. *Make-up:* Ken Lintott and Lindy Shaw. *Running time:* 104 minutes. *MPAA Rating:* R.

CAST: Sammi Davis (Ursula Brangwen); Paul McGann (Anton Skrebensky); Amanda Donohoe (Winifred Inger); Christopher Gable (Will Brangwen); David Hemmings (Uncle Henry); Glenda Jackson (Anna Brangwen); Dudley Sutton (MacAllister); Jim Carter (Mr. Harby); Judith Paris (Miss Harby); Ken Colley (Mr. Brunt); Glenda McKay (Gudrun Brangwen); Mark Owen (Jim Richards); Ralph Nossek (Vicar); Nicola Stephenson (Ethel); Molly Russell (Molly Brangwen); Alan Edmondson (Billy Brangwen); Rupert Russell (Rupert Brangwen); Richard Platt (Chauffeur); Bernard Latham (Uncle Alfred); John Tams (Uncle Frank); Zoe Brown (Ursula, Aged 3); Amy Evans (Baby Gudrun); Sam McMullen (Winifred's Baby).

CHRISTIAN SCIENCE MONITOR, 5/9/89, p. 11, David Sterritt

At a time when many filmmakers like to play it safe, Ken Russell likes to do the opposite. Early in his career, he showed a knack for popular, mainstream pictures like "Billion Dollar Brain" and "Women in Love," which earned Glenda Jackson an Oscar as 1970's best actress.

But such conventional projects were too tame for Mr. Russell. Soon he was flabbergasting audiences with kinky scenes from "The Devils" and turning his love for music into streams of bizarre images in films like "Tommy." In recent years, Russell has poked his toe into the mainstream once or twice—his "Altered States" was an *almost* conventional horror movie—but movies like "Salome's Last Dance" and "Gothic" were closer to hallucinations than entertainments.

His last picture, "The Lair of the White Worm," told a recognizable story, but its style was right out of nightmareland.

So it's quite a surprise to find Russell back in the world of conventional moviemaking (in style, if not always in content) this year. With one notable exception, "The Rainbow" is almost old-fashioned—in its story, the way it's made, and even its characters, a number of whom are from the same family that "Women in Love," adapted from the D.H. Lawrence novel, focused on almost 20 years ago. However, that exception—Russell's graphic fascination with sexual passions—will put "The Rainbow" firmly off-limits for many filmgoers.

The main character of the film is Ursula Brangwen, a young woman coming of age in rural England at the turn of the century. Like many of Lawrence's characters, she has too much energy and imagination to accept a time-honored way of life that her family and neighbors never question. She becomes a teacher and tries to fit in with the British educational system, but feels tortured by it.

More controversially, she also has a couple of stormy love affairs—one of them with another woman—in her search for physical and emotional freedom. Although she never quite finds this freedom, the movie ends on a note of hope. Russell has never been known for his good taste, and "The Rainbow" finds him true to form at times, especially when Ursula gets sexually involved with a female schoolteacher, in scenes explicit enough to deserve the movie's R rating and then some.

Other aspects of the film are uncharacteristically traditional, however, including the bright-eyed performance of Sammi Davis as Ursula and the sturdy acting of Glenda Jackson as her mother.

Unlike the sprawling and uneven Lawrence novel, Russell's movie is less a family saga than the story of one young woman, set against an increasingly modern and unpleasant English countryside that Lawrence and Russell criticize (much like Dickens before them) for losing its humanity in the name of progress. Despite limitations and excesses, "The Rainbow" does a convincing job of capturing England as it moves into a challenging, and in some ways frightening, new century.

FILMS IN REVIEW, 10/89, p. 490, Eva H. Kissin

D.H. Lawrence, the writer who unbuttoned *all* the buttons of post Victorian England, had trouble writing and editing *The Rainbow*. He worked hard at it, eight versions in three years. "Whatever else it is, it is a voyage of discovery toward the real and eternal land", he said. It attempts to reach "a deeper stratum than I think anyone has ever gone in the novel."

Lawrence, the coal miner's son, was doing some pretty heavy exploring himself in a rapidly changing world. When Lawrence persuaded Frieda von Richthofen, the German aristocrat, to leave her husband and children to marry him, he was making his own grand gesture toward freedom, the first step in his personal voyage. Frieda brought the openess of European thinking (Sigmund Freud, etc.) to the young Englishman who was trying to escape the insularity and repression of his own life.

In a changing England, where Victoria had finally become an adjective (after sixty-four years on the throne), where modern industrialism was destroying the pastoral landscape, and rapid transportation brought ideas as well as individuals across great distances, Lawrence was concerned with the individual and his spirit. His sense that the only remaining value was the individual and his particular passion (sexual or political), is the essential statement of *The Rainbow*. Lawrence felt the mystery of life, and stressed living and experiencing it as the primary means of self discovery. If this all sounds very 1960's, it's because it was.

The book, suppressed and burned in 1915, describes the two generations of Brangwen women who precede Ursula, and carefully delineates their relationships. Ursula's mentor, her Polish grandmother, Lydia, had brought a new refined sensibility into the family of heavy, land oriented farmers. She had sought relating as an individual to her emotionally repressed but physically passionate husband. Their daughter, Anna, Ursula's mother, had further problems with her husband, but was carried away by a grand sexual passion that resulted in a household filled with wet and hungry babies. Both women were locked in an undeniable Laurentian power struggle proportionate to the strength of their characters.

The film, beginning essentially with Ursula, the third generation, lacks the book's personal familial background for her particular drive toward rewarding relationships and consequent self-fulfillment. To the degree that Ursula is a product of her times, 1915, as opposed to her grandmother and mother's generation, the film does suggest historical reasons for her feelings. Furthermore, she is better educated that the two women who preceded her. Although she battles with her father to free herself by earning her own living—teaching—she is a source of embarrassment to his pride as a proper provider. In addition, her character is not defined enough for us to believe she could ever make her ultimate decision to take on the conventions of society itself. She doesn't appear bright or deep enough to have thought it all through. We are not even surprised that she failed her college examination.

In the film, Ursula, considered "the first modern woman in literature", and the "first Twentieth Century free spirit", simply doesn't seem strong enough to reject the attractive Skrebensky with whom she has been having a passionate love affair—laced with its daily struggle for individual power. Like so many others, she's all for sexual freedom and its pleasures until she finds herself pregnant. Then her choice to marry reflects that of all the women behind her, no choice at all, only the protective convention of marriage itself.

Even though the heroine's characterization, in both the book and the film, is not thoroughly satisfying, twenty-four year old Sammi Davis, a product of the Midlands herself, who left home and a convent school at seventeen, and struggled with starvation in order to act, says she identified strongly with the character. While she has considerable charm and catches the spirit of the age quite well, she does not seem suited to the role. Amanda Donohoe, who plays her literal first love, a Phys-Ed teacher, is far more credible as the "advanced," emancipated woman who makes a conscious choice for marriage as the best female solution in an imperfect world. Anton Skrebensky, the red-coated soldier on leave from the Boer War, played by Paul McGann, is well cast as the handsome charmer who found Ursula more than he bargained for. David Hemming, Christopher Gable and Glenda Jackson (back in the same family for which she won an Oscar in *Women In Love*) are all thoroughly good in their roles.

Perhaps the outstanding contribution to what could be a disappointing film, is its cinematography by Billy Williams of *Gandhi* fame. The very textures of the period clothing, the light through the plaster dust in the local church, the glow of the family scenes (you can almost smell the freshly washed babies), and above all, the deep appreciation of the pastoral landscape and its full sensuous pleasure suggest the real magic of filmmaking. Lawrence himself, the originator of all this, free spirit that he sought to be, would have been truly impressed by the magic of the camera and the eye of the artist behind it.

The *pre*-quel to his prize winning *Women In Love*, Ken Russell has been involved in efforts to bring *The Rainbow* to the screen for years. We owe him a vote of thanks for a visually beautiful and always interesting film.

LOS ANGELES TIMES, 5/18/89, Calendar/p. 1, Michael Wilmington

> ...There was a faint vast rainbow...its pedestals luminous in the corruption of new houses on the low hill, its arch the top of heaven.
>
> —D.H. Lawrence, "The Rainbow"

The rainbow that arches away from the muddy, mundane colliery town toward the vaults of heaven at the end of D.H. Lawrence's great 1915 novel is, for his heroine Ursula Brangwen, a symbol of the exaltation that drives her on, makes her dissatisfied with town, family, friends and lovers.

But for Ken Russell, in his movie of "The Rainbow," this vision of sun and rain is slighter, sweeter. It's a candy-colored little arc, bright as jam, that Ursula first sees in childhood. It lies over an enchanted rural dell that might be the gateway to Oz or Wonderland.

Perhaps those rainbows signal the difference between book and film. The novel gouges and bites, leaves bloody marks and the salt of tears in its havoc-strewn wake. The movie is emerald-green and pretty to a fault, a lovely little bauble that gleams in your hand like an ice crystal about to melt.

In Lawrence's "Rainbow," we see what happened to the Brangwen sisters, Ursula and Gudrun, before his later novel "Women in Love" began. It's a long family saga in which Ursula's revolt is fed by three generations of frustration and buried dreams; Russell's movie only covers the last six of its 16 chapters.

Russell's "Rainbow," done with the sure-handed expertise of a born film maker, mostly details six years in the life of Ursula (Sammi Davis). The film takes her from virginity to her first great love, Anton Skrebensky (Paul McGann), through a rhapsodic lesbian interlude with her teacher Winifred (Amanda Donohoe), through the scalding experience of her first job, as elementary teacher in a school, bedeviled by a brutal headmaster (Jim Carter's Harby) and snot-faced, sneering delinquents.

The movie's Ursula, like Lawrence's, is in rebellion against dead forms and stale proprieties. Passionate, selfish and anti-democratic, she's determined to flee the repetitions and traps of her existence, to live clean, free and whole. For Lawrence, there's a desperation to this flight, but Russell takes a lustier tone. His style doesn't reflect Lawrence's, but complements it. It's warmer and writtier, more artificial and unnatural.

When Russell adapted "Women in Love" two decades ago, he was like a brawny magician with a hot poker for a wand. He knew how explosive the material was and he used Lawrence's Edwardian sexual memoir-fable like a grenade, blasting the screen with passionate images. Yet he also played the material lyrically, lightly, turned it into a near-musical.

In Russell's "Rainbow," the lyricism predominates, fittingly since it's a film about rural roots and a young girl's coming-of age—but also, perhaps because, with a limited budget and the whole glacial process of movie-making these days, he has to play it safe. His movie celebrates Ursula's rebellion, but it shows a reverence for the land and countryside that wasn't as present in "Women."

Much of the darkness has gone out of the story, the black rages of Ursula, her lovers and parents. It's been transferred to more obvious villains: headmaster Harby, turned here into a Dickensian bully, and the Russell-created sadist-Sunday painter, MacAllister (Dudley Sutton). Even Winifred, her role much expanded, is played with some of the demonic edge of her vampire-princess in Russell's "Lair of the White Worm."

Perhaps Russell, in his 60s, doesn't feel as much like throwing grenades. For D.H. Lawrence, heaven and hell could both be encompassed in the lusts and loves of the body, but for Ken Russell, sexuality is just as often horrific or comic. Though he hasn't stinted on the story's sexual frankness or social abrasiveness, Russell has taken a softer, gentler tone, so much so that Sammi Davis' Ursula, played with the physicality and raw force of the earlier film, often seems out of place, like a strident chalk squeak against the story's glassy surface.

Russell deliberately brings back many of his "Women in Love" collaborators, giving the project an air of reverie and reunion: cinematographer Billy Williams, designer Luciana Arrighi. Glenda Jackson, who earlier played Gudrun, the icy aesthete, here appears as Gudrun's mother, Anna. Once again, she gives the finest performance in the movie. And Christopher Gable, who, in "Women in Love," played the young drowned aristocrat, is here the ever-grinning father Will Brangwen.

Because of all this—the nostalgia and sentiment—"The Rainbow" has been hailed by some as Russell's return to form, his best film since "Women in Love." I disagree, but only because I think Russell's form never left him. Excellent as this movie is, his most exciting and creative cinematic work tends to be in his musical films and composer biographies, from the BBC's "Song of Summer" onward.

He is often at his best when he seems most outrageous and unfettered. Yet in "The Rainbow," he proves he can wear his fetters well. Just as Ursula's rainbow shoots up to heaven from the dark, corrupted ground, Russell's "Rainbow" (MPAA rated R for nudity, sex and language) carries the glint of passion, revolt, art: jewels of the spirit shining through the flood as it regenerates and renews the earth.

MONTHLY FILM BULLETIN, 1/90, p. 22, Jill Forbes

Ursula, daughter of Will and Anna Brangwen, is the eldest child of prosperous Midlands farmers. Even as a youngster she aspires to a world beyond the confines of the farm, a world which is symbolised by the rainbow she tries to seize hold of. As an adolescent, she becomes convinced that a life like that of her parents, and her mother especially, is too constricting. She comes under the influence of Winifred, her gym teacher, with whom she goes tramping the dales and swimming in rivers. However, for all her professed independence, Winifred rapidly agrees to marry Ursula's wealthy Uncle Henry, owner of the local colliery. Henry has meanwhile introduced Ursula to Anton Skrebensky, a guardsman about to be sent to the Boer War. At Winifred's wedding, Ursula and Anton make love but Ursula is not sure she wants a life as Anton's wife. When she learns that she has been successful in her matriculation exam, Ursula announces her intention of getting a job. Her father is horrified that a daughter of his should go out to work, but Ursula finally overcomes his prejudices and begins life as an apprentice teacher in an elementary school. She is unable to keep order and is dismayed by her colleagues' cynicism, but she perseveres until she is finally admitted to University College Nottingham. She fails her degree, however, and learns almost at the same time of Anton's marriage to another woman. Her independence, it seems, has not paid off, yet she retains the image of the rainbow to inspire her to further achievements.

When *The Rainbow*, Lawrence's fourth novel, published in 1915, was prosecuted by the police, he was prompted to leave England for Italy and thus bring to an end a chapter in his life. *The Rainbow* does, however, adumbrate many of the themes later developed in *Women in Love*, which can be seen not so much as a sequel as a more highly elaborated version of it. These facts are relevant to *The Rainbow*'s adaptation to the screen, not only because Ken Russell himself made the film version of *Women in Love*, and to some degree repeats his earlier film here, but because *The Rainbow* does not offer a conventional narrative but serves as a vehicle for the exploration of some of Lawrence's obsessions (although not in the mature form in which they are to be found in *Women in Love*).

All of this presents considerable difficulties which have not been altogether successfully overcome. Russell, who coauthored the adaptation as well, chooses to centre the narrative on Ursula, eliminating at a stroke the multi-layered portrait of three generations of the Brangwen family contained in the novel. In so simplifying the passage of time, he poses some problems to the viewer who is given little indication that *any* time has elapsed, for example in Ursula's relationship with Anton. In focusing on Ursula, Russell has not distorted the Lawrentian message: Ursula's career is, after all, very similar to that of Lawrence himself and she is a good representative of his ideas. But the yearning for self-fulfilment—or, better, self-realisation—which is Lawrence's theme *par excellence*, is occasionally interpreted here as incipient feminism. Ursula, who is far from being a proto-suffragette (her longings are far too apolitical for that), runs the risk of being anachronistically seen as such due to the simplifications of the narrative. Furthermore, while Sammi Davis is convincing as a rebellious adolescent, she gives too shallow a performance to hint at the murky depths which Lawrence seems to require (the film of *Women in Love* suffered from the same shallowness).

In concentrating on Ursula's biography, the film also loses a crucial dimension of the novel: its critique of English culture and civilisation. The colliery owner here is merely a benign host and husband; the miners are never seen and are only referred to once. The film does have an eye for landscape which gives some sense of Lawrence's Englishness; the period details of costume and furniture are lovingly reproduced, the portrait of the elementary school could have come straight out of a Victorian painting, and Glenda Jackson and Christopher Gable give excellent cameo performances as Ursula's parents. But *The Rainbow* falls far short of the impact of the original, and without that it is not clear what Russell sought to add to his adaptation of *Women in Love*.

NEW YORK, 5/29/89, p. 65, David Denby

Watching *The Rainbow*, Ken Russell's adaption of D.H. Lawrence's great novel of 1915, I felt a measure of sympathy for a director I've always despised. For the movie is a sincere effort—not very good, or even interesting, but at least not ludicrous in Russell's usual volcanic-spasmodic style nor lurid in the manner of his earlier Lawrence adaption, *Women in Love*. The movie illustrates passages from the magnificently written later sections of *The Rainbow*, offering episodes from the girlhood and young womanhood of the soulful Ursula Brangwen (one of the Brangwen sisters Lawrence returned to in *Wowen in Love*). Russell, who wrote the screenplay with his wife, Vivian, gives us Ursula's love affairs with both the class mistress Winifred Inger (Amanda Donohoe) and the young officer Anton Skrebensky (Paul McGann); her trials as a teacher in a shabby school culminating in her humiliating discovery that she can master the unruly, hostile children by using the cane. At the end, there's an appearance by the famous stampeding horses, much loved by academic explicators, and a big rainbow, seemingly painted in the sky in Disneyish candy colors.

The Russells have taken Ursula (Sammi Davis) out of the generational family history Lawrence rooted her in and made her a seeker of fulfillment—nearly a contemporary feminist (which will astound the feminists who have long attacked Lawrence as a sexual reactionary). *The Rainbow* is composed of highlights from Ursula's struggle for selfhood. But Lawrence's genius for moment-to-moment emotional definition, his awkward, astonishingly powerful inwardness, gets lost in the mere outward representation of the events—Ursula is now just a dissatisfied girl with a wonderful face and lots of fire. Davis, not a beauty but with a provocative upturned curl to her mouth, is more angry than passionate, more mischievous than questioning. She has spirit, but she's not the powerfully yearning performer that the role needs.

Russell is an impatient director, incapable of working novelistically with a slow, subtle development of themes, a slow ripening of moods. He lurches from one big scene to another, from one climax to another. The thorny, painful teaching scenes, for instance, are excellent, yet what they mean in Ursula's overall life remains a blank. Ursula's lesbian affair occurs without any resistance or reflection, though Russell gives us plenty of golden nakedness, with the tall, slender women racing through misty vales and jumping into water. He squeezes more dampness out of Sammi Davis and Paul McGann's making love, uncomfortably, near a waterfall. Russell takes his sensual liberation very literally; he doesn't seem to realize that the revolution Lawrence initiated has long been won, and that what we need now is an understanding of the characters' interior dilemmas, without which Lawrence is turned into the earnest sensationalist his contemporaries mistakenly accused him of being.

NEW YORK POST, 5/5/89, p. 31, Jami Bernard

The Brangwen sisters are back, and so is Ken Russell, the playful, psychosexual director who put D.H. Lawrence's "Women in Love" on the screen 19 years ago. Now we go back in time to the girlhood of one of the sisters, Ursula, in Lawrence's "The Rainbow," or a portion of it, anyway. It ends where "Women" picked up; in today's jargon, "The Rainbow" is a prequel.

Although sometimes sly and sometimes fevered, "The Rainbow" is a relatively restrained piece of Russell-mania. It begins with a determined little Ursula toddling along after a big, phony-baloney rainbow, the first in Russell's series of little jokes. You can't grasp a rainbow, certainly not one as impossible looking as this, but you can certainly run after it all your life. It's as if to say that the glory of the chase is what sets dreamers apart from slugs.

Ursula is a dreamer. Her well-meaning but shortsighted father (Christopher Gable) is a slug. In fact, turn-of-the-century English mining country is littered with slugs. Will Brangwen tackles young Ursula in mid-quest and returns her to the fold, something he will try to do all her life.

Home is a place of noisy, traditional domesticity, overseen by Glenda Jackson, who played Ursula's sister in "Women in Love." Now she plays the mother, a measured woman constantly striking a balance between duty to her family and to herself.

Dad may be satisfied by a piece of bread slathered with a rainbow of jams, but little Ursula is not—without so much as glance at the bread, her gaze continues onward and upward. After the opening credits, she is all grown up, nearly matriculated, still driven by a longing for the unattainable.

Sammi Davis ("Lair of the White Worm," "Mona Lisa") is Ursula, headstrong, inquisitive, outspoken. Intelligent, too, but that's not as important to her as courage—really, the courage to chase rainbows when all around her are eating bread and jam.

But first, a little preparatory hanky-panky with the gym teacher, a bony, confident Amanda Donohoe. Ursula develops a schoolgirl crush on Donohoe's Winifred, who strips down to her Medusa crimped hair at the toss of a croquet mallet. The most you'll ever get from men, according to the brazenly touchy-feely Winifred, is passion. She explains this to Ursula over lingering kisses, much nudity and a gentle massage that is Russell's female version of the nude wrestle between Alan Bates and Oliver Reed in "Women in Love."

"Relax, you're in the hands of a qualified osteopath," is Winifred's reassurance to her nervous student. As another alumna of Russell's campy "Lair of the White Worm," Donohoe has just the right bearing and inflection for the role; the same line, with the same wink to the audience, occurs later when Winifred loses points with Ursula by selling out for a more acceptable life with Ursula's piggishly coal-rich Uncle Henry (David Hemmings).

Ursula has more disapointments in store as she chases her rainbow down. While it's not true that men just want one thing from a girl—actually, they want several things, each nastier than the next—Ursula's first sexual experience with a man, a banal soldier named Anton (Paul McGann), causes neither the earth to move nor the rainbow to brighten. (And her ensuing romance with him follows the same pattern.)

After fighting her family for the privilege of working outside the home, she gets a position as a teacher where she is terrorized by her students and leered at by her lecher boss. No one said a dreamer's life would be all restful REM sleep.

The sex scenes have Russell written all over them. A seduction that in another director's hands would be erotic and slow is accompanied by loud, disturbing music. A harmless game on a swing is similarly disturbing, portentous. Images get fragmented, senses are heightened; Russell and his wife, Vivian, who co-wrote the screenplay together, must have some hoo-hah sex life.

Davis has a hard, Carly Simonish jawline and a sullen look that save her from being just another spitfire of a heroine. Hemmings is also very good as the rich uncle she rails against.

The road to this rainbow—and it is just a road, after all, there is no pot of gold waiting—is paved equally with disappointments and passion. If it is less compelling than "Women in Love," it is also more reasonable.

NEWSDAY, 5/5/89, Part III/p. 3, Lynn Darling

There was a wonderful to-the-barricades quality to director Ken Russell's first bout with D.H. Lawrence. In 1970, when "Women in Love" was released, Lawrence's ideas about Man and Woman and the exaltive power of sex proved irresistible to a generation dizzied by the heady mixture of liberation and lust. Russell did a good thing bringing Lawrence's novel of ideas to the screen—he ditched a lot of the talk, concentrated on the two love stories and gloried in the sensuality of it all, up to and including a naked homoerotic wrestling match. Sex and love and polymorphous perversity! Lawrence, by way of Russell, became an eloquent spokesman for the carnal explorations of the '60s.

This time around, Russell is the victim of changing times—Lawrence's ideas no longer mesh so perfectly with the prevailing cultural climate. The novelist's preachy discourses on a woman's need for freedom, on the tyranny of domestic servitude, on the clash between familial ties and individual self-expression, no longer have the force of revolutionary aphorisms. Now it all sounds a little old hat.

Russell's version of "The Rainbow" concentrates on the last third of Lawrence's novel (to which "Women in Love" was something of a sequel). It is the story of the coming-of-age of young Ursula Bragwen (Sammi Davis), a headstrong young woman bent on discovering her own capacity for passion and on claiming her own measure of independence. Ursula combines a strongly sensual nature with an endless appetite for indignation. She isn't about to step meekly into the claustrophobic role of domestic subservience laid out for her in the coal-mining country of turn-of-the-century England.

Instead she embarks on a voyage of self-discovery that includes a passion for her beautiful, blond schoolmistress (Amanda Donohoe) and an equally strong desire for a young army officer (Paul McGann). Mostly, however, she storms around the countryside spouting off about everything and everyone under the sun. "I want to be a lion, not a lamb," Ursula says. Mostly, she ends up being just a brat.

By cutting out all of Lawrence's account of the preceding generations of the Bragwen clan, and the traditions and the toil that had rooted them to the land, Russell presents Ursula out of context; we're given only shorthand versions of what she's rebelling against and how powerful a force her family is in her life. Instead Russell opts for heavy-handed symbolism—the movie begins with the child Ursula running after a rainbow in the sky only to be snatched up by her father. "I want it," says baby Ursula. "You can't have it," says her father.

The problems inherent in so truncated a version of the novel are exacerbated by Sammi Davis' performance. An actress who showed a light, winning touch as the teenager in love with an American soldier in "Hope and Glory," Davis develops only one note here, and it's a relentlessly shrill one. As she begins to lecture querulously on yet another subject that offends her, one begins to wish that someone will send this young woman to her room.

Davis' performance seems overstated in part because everyone else in the movie is so muted. Paul McGann seems barely to occupy his half of the love scenes, even when he's entwined in naked embrace near a waterfall. Amanda Donohoe, as the other love of Ursula's life, is more successful, but her character flickers in and out of the movie so willfully that her relationship to Ursula is left irritatingly murky.

Even Glenda Jackson, as Ursula's domestically enslaved mother, is vague and unconvincing. Jackson's role is note a large one, but her presence is a sad reminder of just how good "Women in Love" was—she won an Oscar for her performance as the stormy, passionate Gudrun in that film.

NEWSWEEK, 5/8/89, p. 69, Jack Kroll

Obviously to adapt D.H. Lawrence for the screen is to ask for a great deal of trouble. The universe of his novels lies so deep inside his characters that there's a kind of madness in attempting to capture it on camera. But the specter of madness has never stopped Ken Russell. His 1969 "Women in Love" was controversial—in some ways it played fast and loose with the novel—but it had power and beauty and an incandescent sincerity. Now, 20 years later, Russell has taken on an even tougher task with his film version of *The Rainbow*, the predecessor to "Women in Love." The new film has the sincerity and the high intelligence of the earlier one, it too has great visual beauty, but it doesn't have that flaming incandescence.

Lawrence's novel dealt with three generations of the Brangwens, a farming family near the coal mines of Nottinghamshire. Russell has wisely gone right to the last part, the story of Ursula Brangwen (Sammi Davis) and her struggle to find personal freedom in imperial, turn-of-the-century England. When the book was published in 1915, it was banned for its sexual explicitness. Part of the story deals with the strong emotional and sexual feeling between the schoolgirl Ursula and one of her teachers, Winifred (Amanda Donohoe).

This was hot stuff in Edwardian England; one of Russell's problems is to make a modern audience feel the shock of this relationship. He comes close to succeeding, helped by the intensity of the two performances. Winifred is a kind of false start of modern feminism; her anti-macho, libertarian credo is compromised when she marries Ursula's uncle Henry (David Hemmings), who owns the local coal mine, which he runs with disregard for the plight of the miners. Hemmings's suavely chilling performance is part of a fine ensemble, including Glenda Jackson (who won an Oscar for "Women in Love") as Ursula's mother. Sammi Davis, with her wise-child face and erupting sensuality, evokes the rainbow of emotion in a character who spoke for Lawrence himself.

Russell isn't always totally faithful to Lawrence. When Ursula becomes a teacher in the local school, Russell makes the despotic headmaster Mr. Harby (Jim Carter) even more awful by having him make a pass at her. This is gratuitous in a sequence otherwise memorable in its evocation of the school's Dickensian atmosphere that turns Ursula into a child-whipping tyrant. And Russell reverts to his incorrigible ways when he has Ursula pose nude for a creepy old artist who tries to initiate her into the merrily English joys of spanking.

It's shenanigans like this that have blinded many critics to the remarkable talents of Ken Russell. Those talents are often on display here, for example in the wonderfully scary scene, complete with Lawrentian erotic overtones, in which Ursula encounters a troop of huge horses thundering through the woods. Equally eloquent are the painfully sweet love scenes in which Ursula discovers that the young soldier Anton (Paul McGann) is not the man who can satisfy both her passion and idealism. Lawrence drenches the reader in that idealistic passion; Russell's appealing film can only suggest its disturbing force.

TIME, 5/15/89, p. 75, Richard Schickel

There is a time in every young reader's life when the works of D.H. Lawrence strike with the force of revelation. His novels can leave you transformed (at least temporarily) by his visionary social criticism and his earnest reflections on the endless struggle for a transfiguring sexuality. Ken Russell's adaptation of *The Rainbow* is faithful not only to Lawrence's spirit but also to the naive idealism he was (one hopes still is) capable of animating in eager, youthful hearts.

The Rainbow is a coming-of-age story set in turn-of-the-century Britain, when the modern world was also coming of age. In its first sequence, little Ursula Brangwen (who will grow up to be played by an intense Sammi Davis) races dangerously close to the water, reaching out for the title symbol. As she leaves home in the final sequence, another rainbow arches above her, beckoning her onward. In between, she experiments with lesbian and heterosexual lovers (Amanda Donohoe and Paul McGann, respectively), endures a bleak passage as a teacher in a working-class school and witnesses the end of an Edenesque England. All these experiences test her, stir her questing spirit and lead her finally to feminist independence, which was never more attractively stated than it was in these early, innocent days.

Certainly the challenge of recapturing that spirit on film seems to have tranquilized Russell. His imagery is more confident, less feverish, but no less potent than it has been in years. Perhaps that is because it is once again enlisted in the service of a story worth telling, ideas worth thinking about and a life worth caring about.

VILLAGE VOICE, 5/9/89, p. 70, Lisa Kennedy

One of the first questions you may ask after seeing Ken Russell's adaptation of D.H. Lawrence's *The Rainbow* is, "What took him so long?" Never mind that it comes 19 years after the acclaimed *Women in Love*; and never mind that his is something of an inverse sequel—*Women in Love* followed the Brangwen sisters, Glenda Jackson's Gudrun and Jennie Linden's Ursula, while *The Rainbow* (the movie, not the novel) is completely Ursula's story.

But what kind of story exactly? The worry is that it's another one of those protofeminist (sometimes they are feminist) stories. Films that a few years ago were a blessing (*My Brilliant Career*) are now either retro or worse, rendered slightly neocon by the very fact that they present a peculiar coming-of-age saga as an archetype without a history—or with only a family history. *The Rainbow* could easily have been the latest comer to the genre set in coal country: nice, although nothing special. But a toned-down Ken Russell, by *Lair of the White Worm* and *Gothic* standards, puts just enough odd touches in the movie to make it off-color.

Russell's *Rainbow* begins in the final third of Lawrence's book. Here a very young Ursula (a fourth-generation Brangwen) sees a rainbow and does what most little children are wont to do on spying something they must have: She makes a break for it, out of the house and beyond the yard, down a grassy hill and nearly to the embankment of a river, before she is swept up by her rather hysterical father, Will, who'd come home in time from work to avert what he clearly thought would be a drowning. Again and again Ursula's adventures are complicated by male anxiety: first with her father, then her suitor, a young arrogant soldier, Anton Skrebensky (Paul McGann).

After Will lifts up his little daughter, Russell cuts to the house where Glenda Jackson reappears—this time as his wife, Anna—bathing an infant. To go from tiny Ursula's breakneck sprint to the naked vulva of her little sister, Gudrun, is too amusing: What, after all, is desire created out of but lack? Offensive? Not really. This is one of Russell's many visual puns—there are a couple of verbal ones, too—that make the movie at times a humorous outing. Russell holds his usual wacky visual digressions to a minimum, instead locating the bizarre in the quotidian: A swing ride becomes a little too delirious; a roast beef fills up the screen as Will Brangwen carves it badly (which in itself is funny because he's an ecclesiastical sculptor); a banal swim class becomes the scene of a seduction.

The Brangwen family is an Everyfamily, in which just enough parental silences and stutters create a very particular brood. Christopher Gable plays Ursula's magnanimous, artisan, somewhat feminized father. The bottom line is that this tentative, loving, somewhat awkward, ultimately foolish father wants his way. (How fitting that his name is Will.) Jackson's Anna is the stolid head of the household. Hers is a small part, but Jackson is compelling, all silences and stares and short retorts meant to right husband or daughter. Her two or three do-as-I-say-not-as-I-do asides to Ursula (Sammi Davis) clearly feed her daughter's desire to, as Ursula says, "want some other kind of life."

Whatever there is for Ursula lies beyond her family. Often she is shown returning home to what looks like a family photo without her: her mother in the vortex of giggling children. When Ursula first tells Will that she wants to work, to teach, he coaxes her, then loses his temper. Ursula shouts back, "There's a place for me, and I want to go." That the place has no name, and that its marker is an optical illusion, make for a convincing representation of what really can't be represented: desire.

Having desire as an object of the film makes for some libertine moments. At times, the film seems likely to lunge into an English *Philosophy in the Bedroom*: first, with the initiatory seduction of Ursula by Winifred (Amanda Donohoe), and twice more with the suggestion of sodomy. These latter odd moments of a different kind of male power occur once when Winifred introduces Ursula to a letch who feels even more used and indignant than Ursula as his advances are rejected, and a second time when she meets the headmaster of her school, who tricks her into bending her ass his way.

But the moments that mark *The Rainbow* as truly interesting have less to do with sexual awakening and seduction than with class. After the upright Ursula—who often calls her terribly wealthy Uncle Henry (David Hemmings) on his blood money—beats a child in her classroom so hard that her cane breaks, she finally, figuratively, comes into her own class. And—this is a remarkable touch, since the miners' children are blackened—she then finishes the word she'd been trying to write on the blackboard before all the commotion: *Pretoria*.

Yes, it's nice that the rainbow, the completely artifical splay of color that Russell begins and ends the film with—so unnatural as to be rather festive—marks Ursula's convenant with her own desire. What lies beyond it, though, is what makes Russell's *Rainbow* sometimes familiar and sometimes clever.

Also reviewed in:
NEW REPUBLIC, 5/15/89, p. 28, Stanley Kauffmann
NEW YORK TIMES, 5/5/89, p. C8, Caryn James
NEW YORKER, 5/29/89, p. 102, Pauline Kael
VARIETY, 5/3–9/89, p. 12
WASHINGTON POST, 6/9/89, p. C7, Hal Hinson

RED SCORPION

A Shapiro Glickenhaus Entertainment release. *Producer:* Jack Abramoff. *Director:* Joseph Zito. *Screenplay:* Arne Olsen. *Story:* Robert Abramoff, Jack Abramoff, and Arne Olsen. *Director of Photography:* João Fernandes. *Editor:* Dan Loewenthal. *Production Designer:* Ladislav Wilheim. *Running Time:* 102 minutes. *MPAA Rating:* R.

CAST: Dolph Lundgren (Nikolai, "Red Scorpion"); M. Emmet Walsh (Dewey Ferguson); Brion James (Krasnov); Carmen Argenziano (Zayas); Al White (Kallunda).

LOS ANGELES TIMES, 4/24/89, Calendar/p. 5, Kevin Thomas

"Red Scorpion" is a numbskull live-action comic book designed to show off a stolid Dolph Lundgren as a superhero.

Writer Arne Olsen and director Joseph Zito would have us believe that Lundgren is a Soviet assassin dispatched to an Angolalike African nation to kill the leader of a rebellion against oppressive Soviet-led Cuban forces. (The leader, played by South African actor Ruben Nthodi, is reportedly based on Jonas Savimbi, a pro-Western leader of an Angolan guerrilla movement and ally of South Africa.)

It scarcely requires a crystal ball to predict that Lundgren's Nikolai, "the perfect killing machine," will undergo a change of heart and realize who the true oppressors are.

The film makers aren't actually all that interested in the plight of the citizens of the fictional Mombaka. (They, in fact, weathered much adverse publicity from anti-apartheid groups for filming in Namibia and for obtaining from South Africa the military equipment seen in the picture.)

Lundgren is not without humor, and he reveals a surprisingly engaging smile. However, films like "Red Scorpion" (rated R for language and heavy violence) are in the long run likely to hinder rather than further his career.

NEWSDAY, 4/20/89, Part II/p. 11, Bill Kaufman

Ever since Rambo did it, seems like some film makers assume there's an audience-building cachet to having brawny heroes pick up enormous machine guns and spray the landscape.

Dolph Lundgren, who comes to the screen straight from the Glistening Triceps School of Drama, spends much of "Red Scorpion" fighting the enemy with what looks like a small piece of field artillery jammed against his overly developed shoulder.

And when he's not doing that, he saunters around making grotesque faces and intimidating anything that gets in his way.

As the hero of this predictable action film aimed at young audiences, Nikolai (Lundgren) is ostensibly a Soviet-trained special assassin, a platinum-haired war machine assigned to murder the dissident rebel leader of a small African country.

Moviegoers, of course, will recall Lundgren's other excursions playing Russians: He was the

Soviet boxer in "Rocky IV," a part that gave him far more credibility than he earns in this tedious picture. And he also was a KGB agent in "A View to a Kill."

An example of how unintentionally laughable a character he plays in "Red Scorpion" comes when Lundgren takes a swig of vodka, then enters a noisy barroom. As he stands at the door, a sudden silence comes over the room. He commands attention by burping.

A few moments later, perhaps to keep the sullen group's attention even longer, he sprays the place with that awfully big machine gun.

Also reviewed in:
NEW YORK TIMES, 4/21/89, p. C17, Stephen Holden
VARIETY, 4/26-5/2/89, p. 26
WASHINGTON POST, 4/22/89, p. C3, Richard Harrington

RELENTLESS

A New Line Cinema release of a CineTel Films presentation. *Executive Producer:* Paul Hertzberg and Lisa M. Hansen. *Producer:* Howard Smith. *Director:* William Lustig. *Screenplay:* Jack T.D. Robinson. *Director of Photography:* James Lemmo. *Editor:* David Kern. *Music:* Jay Chattaway. *Music Editor:* Jack Tillar. *Sound:* Craig Felburg. *Sound Editor:* John Post and Steve Williams. *Set Decorator:* Ann Job. *Set Dresser:* Dara Waxman. *Special Effects:* Guy Faria. *Costumes:* Verkina Flower. *Make-up:* Bill Miller-Jones. *Stunt Coordinator:* Spiro Razatos. *Running time:* 90 minutes. *MPAA Rating:* R.

CAST: Judd Nelson (Buck Taylor); Robert Loggia (Bill Malloy); Leo Rossi (Sam Dietz); Meg Foster (Carol Dietz); Patrick O'Bryan (Todd Arthur); Ken Lerner (Arthur); Mindy Seeger (Francine); Angel Tompkins (Carmen); Beau Starr (Ike Taylor); Harriet Hall (Angela Taylor); Ron Taylor (Captain Blakely); Roy Brocksmith (Coroner); G. Smokey Cambell (Terrell); Frank Pesce (Marra); Matt Bolduc (Young Buck, 7 years); Lou Bonacki (Desk Sergeant); Edward Bunker (Cardoza); Michael Francis Clark (Ernie); Nay Dorsey (Elevator Man); Joe Flood (Art Wicker); Buck Flower (Old Man); George Gallo (Medical Examiner); John F. Goff (Doctor Park); Jon Greene (Detective Captain); Paul Hertzberg (Police Photographer); John Homa (Spencer); Locky Lambert (Rene); Michael Leopard (Chubby Cop); Jason Lustig (Computer Operator); William Lustig (Cop #2); Robert Madrid (Swarthy Cop); Vic Manni (Detective); Armand Mastroianni (Cop); Brendan Ryan (Corey Dietz); Laura Tracy (Young Mother); Ingrid Van Dorn (Lab Technician); Dan Vogel (Furillo); Michael Weiner (Young Buck, 12 years); Michael Keith Woods (Black Cop).

LOS ANGELES TIMES, 8/30/89, Calendar/p. 7, Michael Wilmington

As you watch "Relentless," a relentlessly bad new killer-creep thriller with Judd Nelson as a kid with a cop complex, you may start to ruminate on what the movies say about Los Angeles.

Think about it. Anyone watching the average L.A. location thriller might come to believe this city is populated entirely with crazed sex killers, wise-cracking cops, flashy drug-dealers, corrupt politicians, slick Hollywood agents and lawyers, joggers, fantastically sexy models cavorting in condo bedrooms and maniacs chasing and shooting each other on the freeways. Everybody has a telephone answering machine, personalized license plates and old movie posters on the walls.

"Relentless" doesn't quite have all of that, but it does have a crazed slasher: Nelson as Buck, distraught son of a disciplinarian cop and brooding police academy reject. There are also plenty of wise-cracking police, notably Leo Rossi as a brash young dick who thinks he knows it all and Robert Loggia as a grizzled old pro who probably does. And there are numerous victims accumulating around town, while television remote crews wander around shoving their microphones into people's faces.

The cliches here are bicoastal. Rossi's Sam Dietz is a transplanted New Yorker, a Son of Sam-case vet who despises the plastic West; Loggia's Bill Malloy is a buddy of Tommy Lasorda. Down at the various precinct houses are a lot of disgruntled superiors who keep screaming incoherently and threatening them in various unconvincing ways. Dietz also has a cute family, including a New Age Wife (Meg Foster), who encourages him to take out his hostility on plants.

Nelson's weird performance—a *sotto voce* psycho, moodily muttering while staring into mirrors—suggests he's still in a semi-funk over his last movie thriller, the mind-boggling "Blue City." Loggia and Rossi often seem to be auditioning for Barry Levinson. William Lustig directs furtively, with a lot of sneaky little camera moves and sideways sidles through smoggy exteriors and interors. The snap-crackle-and-poop dialogue is credited to the possibly mythical Jack T.D. Robinson.

Does "Relentless" (MPAA-rated R for sex and violence) derive any of its L.A. images as much from life as from bad movies? Well, it does have realistic-sounding street noises. It also suggests that the police are sometimes slow to answer private distress calls—though, in this movie, it's probably because they're rehearsing wisecracks. ("Take my magnum...please!")

NEW YORK POST, 8/30/89, p. 25, Jami Bernard

As we all know from the typical psycho personality profile, boys who have strict, disciplinarian fathers grow up to become deranged serial killers.

Sometimes you don't have to delve into their past to figure out that these boys are trouble. Often you can pick up the telltale signs: a strange, half-shaved haircut; no visible means of support; a complete arsenal in their closets; a habit of addressing random comments to the air or to framed photos of those strict, disciplinarian fathers of yore.

Buck Taylor is one such child of discipline who is tearing pages from the Los Angeles phone book, circling names and killing seemingly at random. He makes the victims participate in their own murders.

Two police detectives are on the case, one of them a streetwise ex-New Yorker (Leo Rossi) whose one claim to fame was having helped track down the Son of Sam killer through zealous paper work. The other one is an easygoing L.A. department veteran (Robert Loggia) of the doughnut-eating school of cops who hang out until someone else types up the report.

Had they looked in Buck Taylor's closet, or even noticed his strange haircut, they could have wrapped up the case in an instant. Instead, "Relentless" is indeed relentless in stretching out a thin, unimaginative plot that is totally lacking in dramatic tension. We know from frame one that Buck's our man, but first we must wade through the requisite scenes of the cop partners learning to male-bond, which is mostly accomplished by the streetwise cop cursing and the other one laughing at everything like a hyena.

Meg Foster, the actress with the extra-worldly eyes, plays Rossi's prissy wife, uttering such retro lines as "How is the roast?" and instructing her husband to talk to potted plants to relieve his tension. None of this is for laughs.

Judd Nelson certainly seems perturbed enough to be a psycho killer. Even the camera shies away from him, rarely getting a clear close-up, as if the entire movie were ashamed of him. Because young Buck's torture-training is told in flashback with a child actor, Nelson doesn't have much of a role; it's the cop duo who are the stars. Even there, the ever-reliable Loggia looks like a contender for the psycho ward himself, what with all that chuckling and chortling over nothing at all.

Rossi, who played the lead rapist in "The Accused," has a smirky self-confidence that is not at all unappealing, just inappropriate, as is most everything else in this sad mess of a movie.

NEWSDAY, 8/30/89, Part II/p. 5, Mike McGrady

Once it is noted that "Relentless" is another psychopathic murderer movie, serial killer division, we've pretty much said all that need be said. In Hollywood, once you label both species and subspecies, you can guess, with a fair measure of accuracy, which characteristics will thereafter be observed.

For starters, we can assume that the psychopathic serial killer (Judd Nelson) will be moody, a loner, a gun collector living in a drab rented room. We can also be fairly certain that he is the victim of an unhappy childhood, quite likely a bullying father, and that, further, we will be exposed to that childhood unhappiness in flashback form.

But enough of this clinical pscyhology—the killer must be stopped. By a cop. Usually, in fact, by two cops, law enforcers who share nothing in common other than their squad car. Once we hear that Robert Loggia is in the cast, we can be absolutely certain that one of the detectives will be tough, grizzled, world-weary, jaded—a cynical old vet whose hard outer shell doesn't quite cover a soft core of basic human decency.

The second cop, of course, will be an exact opposite, a provider of counterpoint. The youngster (Leo Rossi) will surely be idealistic, bushy of tail and bright of eye, impatient with his partner's cynicism and deeply dedicated to the rapid apprehension of serial killers: "I really want to do my job, but this guy [Loggia] won't let me."

Of course, whenever we have buddies in blue, we also have enormous interference from above, from a police bureaucracy bound in red tape and usually personified by a hard-nosed, publicity-sensitive, loud-voiced, by-the-books captain (Ron Taylor).

Since this is a serial-killer movie, we also know there will be several gory murders, each committed with as much flair as can be mustered. Therefore, we should not be surprised to see one victim stabbed in the throat with one of those compressed-air cork removers usually applied to the opening of wine bottles. So much for creativity. The other slayings—stabbings, chokings, shootings—are varied but familiar, graphically depicted with great emphasis on gruesome details. Moreover, since this is a serial-killer movie, we should anticipate that several of the victims will be female, vulnerable, attractive and, from time to time, only partially clothed.

Finally, once we know that one of the cops is young, happily married to an attractive wife and the father of a small child, we may even be able to guess at the serial killer's final target, or targets. And we might also sense that the only one in a position to rescue them will be...yes...the cop himself.

The fact that the flick makes use of professional actors and fairly slick direction by William Lustig in no way obviates the fact that not only is it predictable, it is *intensely* predictable. It is, in fact, "Relentless."

VILLAGE VOICE, 9/5/89, p. 80, Georgia Brown

Relentless is a creepy little thriller starring Judd Nelson as Buck Taylor, a young serial killer. In my press materials, names of director and writer were nowhere to be found, but you can't hide so easily, William Lustig and Jack T.D. Robinson, respectively.

This movie's lighter side takes off from the fact that Sam Dietz (Leo Rossi) has left the New York City Police Department to become a detective in L.A., where cops are so mellow they hardly know how to follow up leads. Sam's wife, Carol (Meg Foster), who had wanted to leave New York for a more serene life, is one of those wisecracking, sad-eyed, good-natured sorts become very familiar to the *policier*. She zips up Sam's fly in the morning and over dinner asks about his "first day as a dick." "What's a dick?" his son wants to know.

Buck, who does lots of push-ups and jogs along the cornice of his seedy tenement, is the son of a cop, too. Ike Taylor, killed in a shootout, is seen in hazy, bleached flashbacks putting his young son through the paces of some sort of survival training in the desert. The aim of this course is unclear. There're no nuances about authoritarian fatherhood here; to call Ike mean and nasty would be an understatement. You missed the target with your first shot, you little chicken—whack, whack.

Now Buck looks like a zombie as he addresses his father's sullen photo: "Was all of it for nothing? What now?" The young basket case takes Dad's unheard orders to commit a series of grisly murders—all of which are spelled out in the movie as forms of suicide, or infanticide. Buck picks strangers out of the phone book because their names resemble his. Once he gets the police aroused, he engages Sam and partner Bill Malloy (Robert Loggia) in an "If I'm so sick, why can't you catch me?" contest. Demented or not, he's a match for the slow-witted L.A. force.

Closing credits come up over a Norman Rockwell illustration that Buck, or Ike, has torn from a magazine and pinned to a wall. A cop sits at a soda fountain next to an adoring kid. Lustig and Robinson would like to put a comparatively fine (ironic? didactic?) point on very crude material.

Also reviewed in:
NEW YORK TIMES, 8/30/89, p. C20, Vincent Canby
VARIETY, 5/24–30/89, p. 33

RENEGADES

A Universal Pictures release of a Morgan Creek Productions presentation of an Interscope Communications film. *Executive Producer:* James G. Robinson, Joe Roth, Ted Field, and Robert Cort. *Producer:* David Madden. *Director:* Jack Sholder. *Screenplay:* David Rich. *Director of Photography:* Phil Meheux. *Editor:* Caroline Biggerstaff. *Music:* Michael Kamen. *Music Editor:* Jim Harrison and Christopher Brooks. *Sound:* Bryan Day. *Sound Editor:* Larry Kemp and Wylie Stateman. *Production Designer:* Carol Spier. *Art Director:*

James McAteer. *Set Decorator:* Elinor Rose Galbraith. *Set Dresser:* Michael J. Meade. *Special Effects:* Tim Fisher. *Costumes:* Gina Kiellerman. *Make-up:* Christine Hart. *Stunt Coordinator:* Mickey Gibert. *Running time:* 107 minutes. *MPAA Rating:* R.

CAST: Kiefer Sutherland (Buster); Lou Diamond Phillips (Hank); Jami Gertz (Barbara); Rob Knepper (Marino); Bill Smitrovich (Finch); Floyd Westerman (Red Crow); Joe Griffin (Matt); Clark Johnson (JJ); Peter MacNeill (Denny Ramson); John Di Benedetto (Corvo); Gary Farmer (George); Kyra Harper (Nema); Joseph Hieu (Gang Leader); Dee McCafferty (Cop Outside Bar); Heide Von Palleske (Hooker in Bar); Tom Butler (Detective Geddies); Jack Blum (Keith Weinstock); Paul Butler (Captain Blalock); Big Yank (Dealer); Robert La Sardo (Skinhead); Alar Aedma (Big Ponytail); Michael Rhoades (Small Ponytail); Joyce Gordon (Receptionist); Kay Tremblay (Old Woman); Justin Louis (Rookie Cop); Steve Whistance-Smith (Store Detective); Jackie Samuda (Woman Cop); Andy Knott (Hotel Clerk); Zoey Adams (Saleswoman); Jack Newman (Bookkeeper); Marcelle Griffith (Hooker in Motel); Tom Christopher (Hooker's John); Dick Callahan (Bartender); Janelle Hutchison (Annette); Steve Wayne Lederman (Detective); Garfield Andrews (Thug Knife); Gene Mack (Cop in Alley); Richard Gira (Cullen); Richard Sali (Cop By Salon); Von Flores, David Lee, and Gaston Poon (Gangbangers); Paul Hill and Kyle Anderson (Nema's Kids); Richard Acheampong (Teen on Train); Matt Birman (Yuppie with Corvette); Robert Latimer (Chauffeur); Real Andrews (Cop).

LOS ANGELES TIMES, 6/2/89, Calendar/p. 4, Kevin Thomas

"Renegades," a shamelessly contrived, ultraviolent macho fantasy, stars Kiefer Sutherland and Lou Diamond Phillips, who are too talented and too successful to be wasting themselves on such trash.

Sutherland plays a maverick undercover Philadelphia cop who has infiltrated a ring of jewel thieves. For absolutely no discernible reason except to further the plot, its icily lethal ringleader (Rob Knepper), while making his escape, steals a lance sacred to the Lakota Sioux on display as part of a gallery exhibition of Lakota arts and crafts. This allows Phillips, a tribe member, to team up (warily) with Sutherland in his pursuit of the bad guys.

David Rich's script provides for maximum bloodshed and destruction of property and minimal common sense. Director Jack Sholder can at least be credited for maintaining a high level of energy in deploying the film's rampant foolishness, which includes Sutherland's miraculously rapid recovery from a gunshot wound to his abdomen.

It's a real shame that Gary Farmer, the hilarious co-star of "Powwow Highway," is gunned down early on, because his massively humorous and sweet-natured presence would have been a welcome comic relief.

As it is, the only laughs that occur in "Renegades" (rated R for extreme violence) are in its final scene, when Phillips, not once but twice, mispronounces "cavalry" as "calvary."

MONTHLY FILM BULLETIN, 3/90, p. 73, Kim Newman

Philadelphia. Buster McHenry, an undercover cop, has been working on his own time, infiltrating a gang run by the psychotic Marino, in the hope that he will be led to a crooked policeman in the department who let Buster's father take the blame for a scam he was also involved in. However, Marino drags Buster along on a jewel heist which turns sour when the crook shoots dead the book-keeper who leaked a safe combination to him, and a violent and destructive chase takes place. Detouring through a museum, Marino shoots dead a Lakota Sioux Indian and steals a sacred spear which is being exhibited. Buster tries to stop Marino, but is forced to drive the getaway car, and is then shot in the stomach. Hank Storm, brother of the dead Indian, has Red Crow, his witch-doctor father, nurse Buster—who has publicly been declared a rogue cop and is being sought by his colleagues—back to health, and forces the cop to help him track down Marino and the spear. Buster and Hank abduct Marino's girlfriend Barbara, and are pursued by the crook's hit men. Marino and Lieutenant Finch, the crooked cop, try to get to the pair via Red Crow, but the old Indian resists and is killed. Barbara is shot by Marino to slow down his pursuers, and Buster, trying to help the dying girl, is forced to allow Finch to arrest him. He realises that Finch is the man he has been after, and the lieutenant turns the cop and the Indian loose, knowing they will follow him to Marino's ranch, where they can be killed. But Buster and Hank overcome Marino's assassins, Finch is killed by the gangster, and Buster saves Hank by impaling Marino with the sacred spear. Buster is vindicated, and Hank returns the spear to his people.

Having demonstrated his mastery of carcrashing and bullet-squibbing with *The Hidden*, Jack

Sholder here tackles the slightly thornier field of the star-vehicle action movie and is required to show his junior action men—Kiefer Sutherland as a childish urban Lone Ranger and Lou Diamond Phillips as a smugly superior Tonto—in a good light while still destroying as much property and as many minor thugs as possible. But with two unbelievable contrivances in the first reel—that Buster would go through with a jewel heist apparently on the off-chance that Marino will mention the name of his cop associate, and that Marino would pause during a breakneck chase to steal a rather unimpressive looking sacred spear—the film piles plot idiocies upon themselves with dizzying speed, usually while the heroes are dashing around so energetically that they don't have time to think. Even more damaging to the basic premises of the film is that Marino and police lieutenant Finch don't take many pains to conceal their relationship from Marino's huge gang, and that Buster and Hank spend so much time trying to find out a piece of information—where Marino lives—that everyone else appears to have. The upshot is that, for all its non-stop action and violence, *Renegades* is a wearying, rather dull little picture.

The casting of Sutherland and Phillips reunites two of the Young Guns, but while their boyish cowboys were at least credible as syntheses of Brat Pack posing and traditional movie heroics, their attempts here to slot into parts that might have made sense played by elders like Stallone or Chuck Norris are just inept. Sutherland is introduced in typical *Dirty Harry* fashion, stumbling out of a bar into a hostage situation and using a fake drunk act to outsmart a perpetrator who is holding off dozens of heavily armed stooge cops, but never suggests the kind of world-weary presence necessary for the rogue-cop genre. Phillips, who is burdened with mystical Indian music burbling on the sound-track whenever he considers anything spiritual or does supernatural Sioux tricks like tracking a car through ESP or leaping from one elevated train to another, is a wooden Indian, whose devotion to tribal lore—he seems more upset by the theft of the spear than by the deaths of his father and brother—borders on the psychotically insensitive. With Jami Gertz as a token woman who is shot out of hand, the film is obviously supposed to centre on the initial hostility/ultimate bond of Buster and Hank, but the stars never really strike sparks off each other, suggesting that the current generation of Brats really do need to hang out in a Pack (*Young Guns, The Breakfast Club, St. Elmo's Fire*, etc.) rather than strike out on their own or try to pair off.

NEW YORK POST, 6/2/89, p. 23, Jami Bernard

The Lakota lance, according to the legend that precedes the opening credits of the new buddy action movie "Renegades," is an ancient Indian spear that is rumored to be able to kill three buffalo with one throw. I don't know about the buffalo, but the Lakota lance does manage to kill about 10 minutes of screen time in a movie rife with McGuffins (that's filmese for "red herrings"). When the carnage is done—and this includes a car chase, a barn afire, a beauty salon under siege, a stampede and a motorcycle out of nowhere—it seems that every plot device along the way was really beside the point.

Kiefer Sutherland and Lou Diamond Phillips are the targets of both a band of diamond-stealing thugs and a corruption-ridden Philadelphia (via Toronto locations) police department. Sutherland is Buster, an offbeat, rule-defying undercover cop in the tradition of everyone from Dirty Harry to Dennis Quaid in "The Big Easy." Buster joins the diamond heist in hopes of nailing a dirty cop, but gets a high-speed car chase and a big fat bullet wound for his troubles.

Phillips is Hank, a Lakota Sioux who is out to avenge the death of his brother and retrieve the lance, which was stolen by the diamond thugs in a moment of sheer, arbitrary nastiness. Hank kidnaps the wounded Buster to find that old gang of his.

But first, there's that bullet wound to attend to. Hank's medicine-man dad shakes a feather and chants *hey-a hey-a* over the bloody mess that is Buster, and soon Buster is up and spoiling for a fight. He doesn't yet realize that this is a buddy movie, that he will be required to develop a love and respect for his Indian nemesis, and that this bond between the two young men can only be realized once they have engaged in fisticuffs.

Until then, Buster acts like he's going to run away and right all wrongs by his lonesome, which would never do. Although the young Sutherland does seem to have the stuff to carry a movie, and has one of the most outlandishly interesting faces and demeanors of the younger breed of actors, this is not the sort of movie you'd want to park on just one person's shoulders. There's no *there* there, as they say.

And so, he begins to trust Hank, whose good-luck medicine rock succeeds where trail markers and plot fail.

Attention Lou Diamond Phillips: You have got to steer clear of these stolid-Indian roles. And enough already with the hollow-woodwind sound and tinkling wind chimes to denote "proud, mystical Indian" on the sound track.

The plot is just a peg on which to hang several special-effects adventure extravaganzas. Sorry to say, these are misconceived and misdirected (by Jack Sholder, of "The Hidden"). But scenes that should have bristled with excitement contain too many faux pas.

For example, the ramp that enables a car stunt is clearly visible; reactions are ill-timed or inappropriate. At the end of one chase, a police car with ample time to parallel park for donuts makes like a lemming and plows purposefully into a bunch of overturned squad cars.

The movie curiously changes its mind early on about Buster. When we first see him he is bad-boy incarnate. Slovenly and irreverent, he knows just how to defuse a hostage situation and make ordinary cops look like fools. "I'll tell you what you are—you're a menace!" shouts one cop, with just a trace of affection. You can practically hear the entire force break into a chorus of "How Do You Solve a Problem Like Buster."

Later, Buster proves to be a bit of a whiner, insisting on taking charge and doing the driving, and proving himself more pleasantly mortal. Sutherland brings a lot of zest to his role as a young cop in over his head, but the puppy-dog camaraderie between the two buddies is done in by a ludicrous, unfocused story, manhandled action sequences, central-casting bad guys and assorted boners, like Jami Gertz's slow-motion "Flashdance" death scene.

If you're wondering where Gertz fits into the story, well, she gets her 10 minutes along with the Lakota lance—may it find its three buffalo in greener pastures.

NEWSDAY, 6/2/89, Part III/p. 5, Mike McGrady

What separates "Renegades" from all the other cop-action-buddy movies? Other than a perceptible lack of intelligence, that is. Well the difference here, the gimmick, if you will, is that one of the action-buddies is an American Indian.

Lou Diamond Phillips gives that role the full Noble Redman treatment. As an Indian, Phillips has many mysterious talents, all of which come in handy, let me assure you. He can track a car down a paved highway. He can leap from the roof of one speeding train to one heading in the opposite direction. He can cure grievous bullet wounds by filling a room with smoke and having his father chant the following, repeatedly, "Hey-ya-vee-hey-hey-ya." By simply rubbing his magic medicine stone, he can tell when his father is in deep trouble. And, finally, he has exemplary posture.

His new buddy (Kiefer Sutherland) is a police officer who is in such deep undercover that other cops are hunting him down for crimes (grand larceny, murder, etc.) that he did, in fact, have a hand in committing. Though not an Indian, Sutherland has some mysterious powers all his own. For example, he's in danger of death from a bullet that tears a gaping hole in his stomach. Despite that, he's immediately involved in fisticuffs that would leave a Tyson tuckered out, also a 20-foot leap from a rooftop that might prove fatal to anyone not in a movie.

As implausibilities make way for impossibilities, one will wonder why this unlikely duo is involved in so many unlikely things. Well, Phillips is searching for the crook who stole his tribe's sacred lance, which has been handed down from one generation to the next, because "legend has it that the lance could kill three buffaloes with a single thrust." Coincidentally, Sutherland is searching for the same man. And so they join forces, with entirely predictable results.

What is not predictable is the degree of technical expertise that went into the making of this tripe. There's no such thing as a buddy movie without a car-chase scene; however, this car-chase scene is a knockout. Unfortunately, the ace technical work is glaringly at odds with the woeful dramaturgy. But perhaps this shouldn't surprise us. Jack Sholder made his reputation directing "Nightmare on Elm Street, Part II."

VILLAGE VOICE, 6/13/89, p. 68, Stuart Klawans

Another relationship forged in hell [the reference is to *Vampire's Kiss*] figures in *Renegades*, a buddy picture starring Kiefer Sutherland and Lou Diamond Phillips. The former is a tough young Philadelphia cop going undercover to expose police corruption; the latter, a Lakota Sioux who becomes the cop's unwilling partner in order to recover a tribal artifact. I have now expended more thought in explaining the premise than David Rich did in writing the script. For your part, you can imagine a lot of airborne cars and automatic weapon fire, and there you have it—seven bucks saved.

If you insist on seeing *Renegades*, though, prepare yourself for an experience slightly less in touch with physical law than a Looney Tune. This is a picture in which Sutherland takes a bullet clean through the gut, bleeds for about half an hour, and then recovers sufficiently overnight to pick fights and run across rooftops (the secret: Native American medicine and a full moon). His recuperation is somewhat more believable, though, than the conduct that got him into the jam in the first place. His undercover investigation having gone wrong, Sutherland does not simply surrender to the police—he threatens the lives of half of downtown Philadelphia and then goes fugitive. This, in turn, is more believable than the friendship developing between the runaway cop and the noble Lakota. Sutherland's little escapade costs Phillips not only his tribal artifact, but also the lives of his father and brother. But what's a little bloodshed between two idols of the mall matinee?

I think the movie would have been better if the buddies had been a Lakota Sioux and a female vampire. Certainly Sutherland would not have been miscast any more severely. Despite an honest effort, he looks 10 years too young for his role and not terribly street-smart; so, if he was going to make an improbable stretch, why didn't they let him have some fun? Give the lad a miniskirt and fangs, then he could have tracked the bad guys using supernatural powers, thereby saving Phillips the indignity of sniffing the air and intoning, "Right. They went right." Maybe there could even be some kinky sex between the two. That would wake them up at the mall.

Also reviewed in:
NEW YORK TIMES, 6/2/89, p. C13, Caryn James
VARIETY, 6/7–13/89, p. 31
WASHINGTON POST, 6/2/89, p. D7, Hal Hinson

RETURN OF SWAMP THING, THE

A Millimeter Films release of a Lightyear Entertainment production. *Executive Producer:* Tom Kuhn and Charles Mitchell. *Producer:* Ben Melniker and Michael Uslan. *Director:* Jim Wynorski. *Screenplay:* Derek Spencer and Grant Morris. *Director of Photography:* Zoran Hochstatter. *Editor:* Leslie Rosenthal. *Music:* Chuck Cirino. *Sound:* Blake Wilcox. *Production Designer:* Robb Wilson King. *Set Decorator:* Frank Galline. *Swamp Thing Creator:* Len Wein and Berni Wrightson. *Running Time:* 86 minutes. *MPAA RAting:* PG-13.

CAST: Louis Jourdan (Dr. Anton Arcane); Heather Locklear (Abby Arcane); Sarah Douglas (Dr. Lana Zurrell); Dick Durock (Swamp Thing); Joey Sagal (Gunn); Ace Mask (Dr. Rochelle); Chris Doyle (Leechman).

LOS ANGELES TIMES, 5/12/89, Calendar/p. 7, Michael Wilmington

In "The Return of Swamp Thing," the film makers strike a historic blow against censorship: the first instance ever of sex between humans and vegetables in a PG-rated movie. Their audacity knows no bounds.

"Dynasty's" Heather Locklear, looking pouty, blond and busty, stares at Dick Durock in his full "Swamp Thing" regalia—an outfit full of squiggly green growths and bulging, broccoli-like deltoids—and gives him her best come-Heather smirk. Startled, the Thing protests: "It wouldn't work. I'm a plant." The darling girl pooh-poohs his qualms: "That's OK. I'm a vegetarian."

Not content with this attempt to nudge its way into the Hall of Fame of Dumb Camp, "The Return of Swamp Thing" also offers Louis Jourdan, as the evil Dr. Arcane, doing a bored recitative of "Gigi's" title song to a parrot; a sleaze-ball seduction scene when two near-psychotic mercenaries woo each other by showing off their battle scars ("Grenada!" "Haight-Ashbury!"), and another where chortling mad scientists mutate human victims into cockroachheaded freaks.

The movie's source is the much-praised Len Wein-Bernie Wrightson horror-adventure comic and Wes Craven's 1982 movie adaptation, where Jourdan and Durock also appeared. Its strategy: special effects, ham and wisecracks. The plot: The heroic Swampy, victim of a ghastly accident that turned him from a mild-mannered research scientist into a walking vegetable stir-fry, stalks the swamp. He battles baddies, mercenaries and rampaging mutants and kills the icks, and eventually falls for the stepdaughter (Locklear) of his depraved archenemy.

But though the producers (Michael Uslan and Ben Melniker, also of the forthcoming "Batman") and director (Jim Wynorksi, of "Big Bad Mama II") try to keep the old zap-zap comic-book mood and style, they lose all the original's intensity.

This Swamp Thing is not a wounded, tragic romantic, a combination of the Phantom of the Opera and a Caesar salad. He's a Jolly Green Giant, fighting for truth, justice and Heather Locklear; goofing off with cunning little kiddies; popping up like the Lone Asparagus whenever danger threatens.

The producers and script writers had a lot of good material to work from in the Wein-Wrightson comics and the later ones written by the brilliant Alan ("Watchmen") Moore. But they've run aground. This is the same dopey save-the-princess-and-kill-everybody revenge plot we always get.

"The Return of Swamp Thing" (MPAA rated PG-despite violence, ickiness and intra-species activity) is enough to drive you back to the comic book stand. Or even the swamp.

MONTHLY FILM BULLETIN, 2/90, p. 48, Verina Glaessner

From California, Abigail Arcane sets out to visit her stepfather, Dr. Anton Arcane, who lives in a lavish mansion in bayou country protected by his own paramilitary force, in order to learn more about her mother's mysterious death years before. In fact, with his assistants Dr. Lana Zurrell and Dr. Rochelle, Arcane is engaged in a series of bizarre experiments in genetic mutation in an effort to find the secret of eternal youth. In Abby (as in her mother before her), he sees a source of near-perfect genetic material. At a nearby resort, two children, Darryl and Omar, are threatened by one of the mutants produced by Arcane's experiments, but are saved by another mysterious denizen, the Swamp Thing. Wandering into the swamp and accosted by two moonshiners, Abby is also rescued by the hideous creature (to whom she is strangely drawn despite his appearance). He explains that he is Alec Holland, a scientist who was working on a series of genetic experiments intended to help double world food production; the formula was stolen by Arcane and Holland's body was consumed in a fire, but then reconstituted from tissue in the swamp. Arcane's guards (headed by Gunn and Pointsettia) capture Abby, and Swamp Thing is again blasted to pieces. Arcane discovers that he needs a sample of Holland's flesh as well to continue his experiments, but decides to sacrifice Dr. Zurrell instead. Realising this, she helps Abby to escape, and the latter is rescued from Arcane's guards by Swamp Thing, materialising through a bathroom tap. A magic vegetable enables Abby to "see" Holland as he once was, and they consummate their relationship. When Darryl and Omar are threatened by some of Arcane's men, Swamp Thing again comes to the rescue, but in his absence Abby is recaptured. As Arcane is about to begin his experiments, Abby learns from Zurrell that her mother died at the hands of Rochelle (on whom Zurrell has already taken her own revenge). At the end of Arcane's experiment (intended to transfer Abby's energy to him), stigmata appear on his hands and he realises that Zurrell has double-crossed him. He shoots her, but in a fight with Swamp Thing his mansion catches fire. Arcane is left to burn as Abby and Swamp Thing walk off into the bayou, a solitary flower blossoming on her foot in a sign that her genetic make-up has been altered.

Scriptwriters Derek Spencer and Grant Morris adopt a relentlessly "wise-guy" approach to these further adventures of DC Comics' archetypally "green" protagonist (launched on screen by Wes Craven in 1982). It's an approach sadly backed to the hilt by director and Roger Corman protégé Jim Wynorski, who doesn't miss an opportunity to nudge each gag home with cranking obviousness. Without any sense of belief in the mythic possibilities of its *House of Wax/Beauty and the Beast* theme (Arcane's laboratory is a macabre zoo of failed experiments), the film becomes a string of ill-motivated shoot-outs and conflagrations. The material itself may be credulity-stretching, but it's not helped by the more or less comic "turns" which bear little relationship to one another or to the film as a whole.

NEW YORK POST, 5/12/89, p. 27, Jami Bernard

True beauty lies beneath the surface. Admittedly, you have to dig deep to find such beauty in a creature that is half man, half plant-life, an entity that was once the brilliant scientist Alec Holland, before the evil Dr. Anton Arcane and a nasty laboratory explosion put an end to Holland's quest to cure world hunger. But for that special woman who can appreciate Swamp Thing for his good qualities, there are rewards—like a roll in the hay, or the grass, or the swamp.

That's what lies in store for lovely Heather Locklear in "The Return of Swamp Thing," a sequel to Wes Craven's cult hit, in turn based on the DC Comics creature invented by Len Wein and Berni Wrightson. "Return" lifts its sex scene straight from Alan Moore's more modern story "Rite of Spring."

Swamp Thing is a lonely superhero, too hideous for the company of mere mortals but not content to vegetate all his life; he battles his nemesis Dr. Arcane and other lesser evils from his home base in the swamp, an eerie, overgrown world of foliage, muck, and things that go *squish* in the night.

This sequel brings us back to the swamp, where Dr. Arcane is still trolling for Swamp Thing when he is not tending to his devilish genetic experiments in the laboratory of his mansion. There, various mutations writhe and moan in pain—one is half human, half roach (dismissed by Arcane as "another disappointment"), one is half human, half elephant. (The special effects makeup on Swampy and the mutants is really wonderful; less goo, more personality.)

Meanwhile, in another part of the country—California, to be precise—Abigail (Heather Locklear) is talking to her potted plants. "Why can't men be more like plants?" is her plaint. She sets out to visit her evil stepfather—Dr. Arcane—to find out whatever happened to her dear dead mother.

Abigail arrives on Arcane's doorstep, and pretty soon she is out for a lonely walk wearing a powder-blue chemise. She is menaced by two yokel moonshiners whose idea of fun up until now was running over dogs. Swampy to the rescue, pistils and stamen poised for action. Instead of turning away in disgust, flower-loving Abigail greets her rescuer warmly. "Why you're...you're a *plant*, aren't you?" she inquires kindly. Romance blossoms.

But their love is hindered by Arcane's fiendish experiments; evidently he needs both Abigail and Swamp Thing as lab rats. Hence some chase scenes and shoot-em-ups and some annoying interludes with a couple of neighboring boys.

"Return of Swamp Thing" is deliberately campy, shooting out tendrils of self-deprecating humor whenever possible; some of the dialogue is subtle enough to amuse without hitting you over the head with the brute force of, say, Leach Man (a phallus-trunked slime who puts in a couple of appearances, mostly to prove that, by comparison, Swamp Things is a good guy).

Dick Durock reprises the role of Swampy. "Where did you come from?" someone asks him. "The bog," he answers, matter-of-factly, in that sort of affable voice of the Professor on "Gilligan's Island." "They call me Swamp Thing," he explains without rancor.

And that's the tone the rest of the movie takes. The travails of Abby and Swamp Thing are not all that pressing amidst the flurry of jokes (an opening sequence in which some feds are menaced in the swamp is more atmospheric).

Locklear, mostly known for her TV work on "Dynasty" and "T.J. Hooker," is cute as a muffin, and speaks her spunky lines as if unaware that this is not Noel Coward. "*Enchante*," a hoodlum security guard greets her. "On parole is more like it," she quips.

Louis Jourdan returns as Dr. Arcane. Dropping a couple of references to "Gigi" may be a mistake; those who remember Jourdan in the charming, suave roles of yore will only be saddened to see him examining serums and playing lugubrious tunes on the organ. He looks either completely in character as the remorseless doctor, or bored and annoyed with everything in his path—camera, crew, sets.

Now for the make-out scene. "I'm a bachelor," Swamp Thing admits, offering Abigail a taste of something plucked from his body. Okay, now we're cooking with gas—or are we steaming with vegetables? Abby hallucinates that Swamp Thing is back to his old Alec Holland self, and they have great sex, a real garden of earthly delights.

In Alan Moore's "Swamp Thing" comic, this episode is moving and lyrical. "Where we touch, the fibers merge and intertangle. I am no longer certain where I end...where he begins...I feel my own hand as he feels it, a warm bird caged within my strong green fingers, pulse hammering in its breast..." Well, you get the picture. In the movie, the scene is played for laughs, with the smitten couple playing house in the swamp.

A campy self-confidence, coupled with seamless special effects makeup, give "The Return of Swamp Thing" a kind of charm that compensates for many flaws—but not all of them. Only those with the IQ of a plant are really going to love this little shop of horrors.

NEWSDAY, 5/12/89, Part III/p. 3, Lynn Darling

Any movie that starts with a Creedence Clearwater Revival song is all right by me, and "The Return of Swamp Thing" has the good sense to get things going with "Born on the Bayou." So what if the movie ends up kitsching itself out in the effort not to be taken too seriously?

At least the film recalls all of its quaintly dumb predecessors, the monster movies of yesteryear, with a good-natured fondness. Swamp Thing himself has the same look of tacky fakery that now endows movies like "Creature From the Black Lagoon" with creaky nostalgia. He's a humanoid in need of a good pruning, a victim of man's inhumanity to vegetable. Once a research scientist dedicated to noble causes, Swamp Thing finds himself again under attack by the villainous Dr. Arcane (Louis Jourdan), the man who first turned him into walking kudzu.

This time around, however, Swamp Thing (played with just the right touch of terminal sincerity by Dick Durock) is not alone in his boggy abode. Before long he's developed a deep, meaningful relationship with the blond and beautiful Abigail (Heather Locklear), Arcane's stepdaughter.

"Is there a Mrs. Swamp Thing?" she asks coyly. "I'm a plant," he says. "I'm a vegetarian," she says, which, when you think about it, doesn't bode well for him at dinnertime.

Based on a D.C. Comics character, and the subject of a 1980 film to which this is the sequel, Swamp Thing has had a good deal more than his allotted 15 minutes of fame. But everyone seems to be having a good time in this movie, from the ones who can act (Jourdan, reprising his role from the original movie), to the ones who can't (Locklear, who bounces around in a series of ridiculously sexy outfits). Besides, it's not every movie that has a bad guy threatening the good guy by telling him, "You're coleslaw."

VILLAGE VOICE, 5/16/89, p. 73, Elliott Stein

Nineteen eighty-nine may go down as the year of comic book movies. We're in for: Warren Beatty's *Dick Tracy*, Tim Burton's *Batman*, Cannon's *Spiderman*, and Brooke Shields as Brenda Starr. (In 1990 will *all* films be produced for 12-year-old boys?) For now, we'll have to settle for Jim Wynorski's *The Return of Swamp Thing*. Wynorski seems to be the crown prince of sequeldom—he's directed *Big Bad Mama II*, *Death Stalker II*, the remake of *Not of This Earth*, and this current follow-up to Wes Craven's original 1982 *Swamp Thing*, based on the popular DC Comics series.

Return was shot at photogenic locations in and near Savannah. Its eponymous hero, Swampie (Dick Durock), formerly the brilliant scientist Dr. Alec Holland, had been set on fire but had the presence of mind to jump into a convenient swamp to douse the blaze. When he emerged, the poor man found he had been transformed into a muck-encrusted, semivegetable thing, half-human, half-plant. In this film's best scene, the precredit sequence, he does battle with Leechman (Chris Doyle), who looks quite a bit like a Creature From the Black Lagoon with a giant foreskin for a head.

The main action is largely a series of dull confrontations between Swampie and his nemesis, evil Dr. Anton Arcane (Louis Jourdan)—a Dr. Phibesish character wont to play the organ in his antebellum mansion when he is not in the lab conducting fiendish experiments on the locals in order to discover genetic secrets that will reverse the aging process. The sight of the elderly Jourdan in this role is more than a bit discomfiting, as it's difficult not to recall the uncommon good looks that accounted for the actor's early international career as a young continental heartthrob.

If memory serves, *Swamp Thing*, the comic strip, was dank, gruesome, often poetic. This film opts for facile camp and comes a-cropper. It could have been exciting *and* moving as a Beauty and the Beast tale, with Swampie as a sort of male Daphne. Instead, a wan romantic interest is simperingly supplied by Arcane's daughter, Abby (the dreary Heather Locklear). It's love at first sight when she meets Swampie—she's from California, you see, and has always talked to plants. Although their chaste love scene is botched by Wynorski, Swampie does seem to give good branch—by the end of the film her foot is sprouting leaves. The creature makeup and costume by Carl Fullerton is excellent—it deserves a better movie. At the very least, *The Return of Swamp Thing* had the makings of good silly fun. It's pretty silly, but not much fun.

Also reviewed in:
NEW YORK TIMES, 5/12/89, p. C17, Vincent Canby
VARIETY, 5/3-9/89, p. 13

ROAD HOUSE

A United Artists release of a Silver Pictures production. *Executive Producer:* Steve Perry and Tim Moore. *Producer:* Joel Silver. *Director:* Rowdy Herrington. *Screenplay:* David Lee Henry and Hilary Henkin. *Story:*

David Lee Henry. *Director of Photography:* Dean Cundey. *Music:* Michael Kamen. *Music Editor:* Chris Brooks. *Sound:* Bud Maffett and (music) Bobby Fernandez. *Set Designer:* Mark Fabus. *Set Decorator:* Phil M. Leonard. *Set Dresser:* Howard J. Fannon, William Fannon Sr., Gus Feederle, and Donald Kaeding. *Special Effects:* Al Di Sarro. *Costumes:* Marilyn Vance-Straker. *Make-up:* Scott H. Eddo. *Stunt Coordinator:* Charles Picerni. *Running Time:* 108 minutes. *MPAA Rating:* R.

CAST: Patrick Swayze (Dalton); Kelly Lynch (Doc); Sam Elliott (Wade Garrett); Ben Gazzara (Brad Wesley); Marshall Teague (Jimmy); Julie Michaels (Denise); Red West (Red Webster); Sunshine Parker (Emmett); Jeff Healy (Cody); Kevin Tighe (Tilghman); John Doe (Pat McGurn); Kathleen Wilhoite (Carrie); Travis McKenna (Jack); Roger Hewlett (Younger); Kurt James Stefka (Hank); Gary Hudson (Steve); Terry Funk (Morgan); Michael Rider (O'Connor); John Young (Tinker); Anthony DeLongis (Ketchum); Joe Unger (Karpis); Tiny Ron (Mountain); Sheila Caan (Judy); Jon Paul Jones (Stroudenmire); Lauri Crossman (Stella); Keith David (Ernie Bass); Ed DeFusco (Oscar); Joseph Rockman and Thomas Stephen (Cody's Band); John Oldach and Joey Plewa (Bandstand Tough Guys); Susan Lentini and Patricia Tallman (Bandstand Babes); Mike Fisher and Bob A. Jennings (Bandstand Bouncers); Dawn Ciccone and Julie Royer (Steve's Girls); Frank Noon (Barfly); Christopher Collins (Sharing Husband); Cheryl Baker (Well-Endowed Wife); Michael Wise (Gawker); Charles Hawke (Heckler); Tom Finnegan (Chief of Police); Darly Sandy Marsh (Strip Joint Bartender); Laura Lee Kasten (Nurse); Bill Dunnam (Car Salesman); Terrance Scott (Loudmouth); Sylvia Baker (Table Dancer); Dennis Ott (Bar Character); Ancel Cook (Grillman); Chino "Fats" Williams (Derelict); Mike Tamburro (Pilot).

LOS ANGELES TIMES, 5/19/89, Calendar/p. 1, Sheila Benson

In "Road House," 1989's comic high point so far, Patrick Swayze plays Dalton, a man at the Zen peak of his profession. In the world of power drinkers, Dalton's single, ringing name is legendary. He's a numero uno "cooler," a saloon bouncer.

He's also a graduate in philosophy from NYU, a fan of the novels of Jim Harrison, the owner of a 560 Mercedes-Benz and a man with a whole lotta pain behind those steely eyes.

In a trade heavy with built-in hazards, Dalton travels with a medical road map of his injuries: the precise placement of the steel pins, cross-hatched scars and undetonated land mines he has picked up.

Called in to shape up the Double Deuce, a decrepit Missouri roadhouse, Dalton already suffers from a nasty knife slash, which lands him at the town's emergency hospital. Shirtless, he poses, arm up behind his head, so that the audience can't help but notice his resemblance, torso-wise, to Michelangelo's David. Also, so this beautiful, sensitive doctor (Kelly Lynch) can close the wound with her medical staple gun. He may need a local anesthetic, she warns. "Pain don't hurt," he reassures her confidently.

Not the way stupidity does. And the crushing assault that "Road House" delivers to fun at the movies is enough to send you crawling out of the theater on hands and knees, bloody and bowed.

First, there is the dreadful compendium script by David Lee Henry and Hilary Henkin, who already has Whoopi Goldberg's "Fatal Beauty" and "Lost Angels" on her rap sheet. In this story of consummate evil (sleekly villainous town boss Ben (Gazzara) pitted against blow-dried, Tefloned good, the dialogue wavers from countrified quaint to hyper-macho, without a single believable moment on its way. It's a screenplay with a dozen antecedents, from the hallowed Western to martial-arts sagas to those '50s movies where one man with his shirt off wreaks havoc in a steamy Southern town. The writers have added a soupçon of Stallone, a pinch of Chuck Norris and a few "Mississippi Burning" fire-bombings for effect.

Most to be pitied among the actors is Sam Elliott, playing Dalton's grizzled best friend and mentor. Elliott is a man of genuine authority, lending his wry and indelible presence to goings-on that are simply not in his league. Swayze genuinely doesn't seem to know the trouble he is in, and Gazzara is too busy smirking at his own villainy. Besides, he is allowed to *sing*.

Then there's the thudding direction by Rowdy Herrington, known previously as the writer-director of "Jack's Back." Melodramatic at best, Herrington is in his element in fight scenes, and out of it the rest of the time. At first that doesn't much matter, since two-thirds of "Road House" *is* fights or explosions, or men howling,, "Waaallll, (blank) you," at one another. "Road House" probably has more (blanks), pound for pound, less inventively employed, than "Platoon."

But it's supposed to have more delicate moments, too, as the doctor shows up at Dalton's place for staple inventory and to murmur admiringly, "You live some kinda life, Dalton. . . ." Here, a light touch might have helped, a sense of humor, a bit of irony. *Nada*.

Obviously, the hope is that the presence of Swayze will bring the "Dirty Dancing" crowd running. Unfortunately, these film makers, including producer Joel Silver, have no clue what made "Dirty Dancing" the hit that it was; they seem to believe it was the *dirty* half. Consequently, if they slavishly copy the lighting and even the setting from the first Swayze hit, and this time have Swayze and the lady in question fill in the gaps that "Dirty Dancing" left to our imagination, it would presumably be enough to send audiences into a ticket-buying frenzy.

Wrong, wrong, wrong.

Fourteen-year-olds could have told them that. It wasn't sex that "Dirty Dancing" delivered, it was romance. But in deep "Road House" country, with (blank) on everyone's lips, (it's MPAA-rated R for language and violence), and the undefined made crassly visible, there isn't a whiff of romance anywhere, any more than there's a single jot of common sense.

MONTHLY FILM BULLETIN, 11/89, p. 344, Kim Newman

Dalton, a renowned "cooler" (a security expert who specialises in bars), is approached by Tilghman, the owner of the rowdy Double Deuce saloon in Jasper, Missouri, and asked to clean the place up. Dalton arrives in Jasper, a town more or less run by racketeer Brad Wesley, fires several criminals and incompetents on the Double Deuce's staff, and instructs the bouncers in his special customer-control techniques. With his kung-fu skills, he defuses several violent incidents, and the saloon turns into a profitable business. He rents a barn-cum-apartment from farmer Emmett, befriends put-upon auto store owner Red Webster, and begins a relationship with Dr. Elizabeth Clay ("Doc"), an intern who treats the various wounds he sustains in the course of his work. When Dalton fires Wesley's nephew, a bartender who has been embezzling, he incurs the gangster's enmity but resists his attempts to buy him off or pressure him with threats. When Dalton continues his stand against Wesley, the local businessmen who are paying the latter protection begin to rebel, and Wesley increases his strong-arm tactics. Wesley has his sidekick Jimmy blow up Red's store and Emmett's house, and Dalton overcomes his reluctance to use a lethal blow in a fight with the bomber, whom he kills. Doc, who witnesses the killing, is revolted and leaves Dalton, and Wesley retaliates by murdering Wade Garrett, the ageing cooler who taught Dalton his trade. Dalton launches a one-man assault on Wesley's estate, and kills most of his hired guns before taking on Wesley himself. The oppressed businessmen of Jasper intervene and shoot Wesley when he is about to kill Dalton, and stand together to save Dalton from prosecution. Dalton is reconciled with Doc.

With enough echoes in the character names (Dalton, Garrett, Younger, Doc, Cody, Tilghman, Bass, Ketchum, etc.) and dialogue ("I hear you're the new marshal in town") to qualify as a latterday Western, *Road House* is very nearly a perfect exploitation movie and, in its blending of the lurid, the silly and the ambitious, is pleasantly reminiscent of the New World rural action movies (*Fighting Back, The Black Oak Conspiracy, Moving Violation*) of the 70s. Patrick Swayze's Dalton is a philosophy graduate martial artist who sets about bringing respectability to The Double Deuce—described as "the kind of place where they sweep up the eyeballs after closing"—with the zeal that Errol Flynn once brought to keeping the outlaws out of *Dodge City*. Swayze, who gets the chance to display his body in energetic kung fu, nude bedroom wanderings and while being stitched up in hospital, has enough self-awareness to be a superior action hero, and slyly sends himself up through extravagant gestures like refusing an anaesthetic as Doc takes a stapler to his side, or putting down an impeccably intellectual tome to gaze with Nick Carraway-like abstraction at the raucous partying taking place at Wesley's mansion on the other side of the lake.

Although there is some attempt to show the workings of Dalton's highly paid profession—he drives a Mercedes but buys a clunker to leave in the parking-lot of the Double Deuce to serve as the butt of the anger of those he has evicted from the place—we learn very little about the art of "cooling". The film is also more interested in exploiting its Western parallels to add mythic resonance to a standard storyline than in any serious examination of how the bar business works. To the casual viewer, the old Double Deuce, with the band performing behind chickenwire and non-stop brawling in the *Dodge City* tradition, might even seem more appealing than the bland night spot, with uniformed bouncers and dayglo décor, it becomes when the bad element has been kicked out.

Sam Elliott adds to his recent run of amiable, whiskery action men as Dalton's ironical mentor, functioning as a cross between Obi-Wan Kenobi and Gabby Hayes. Ben Gazzara has also been allowed to have fun as the thoroughly rotten Wesley, who is introduced as he weaves inconsiderately all over the road in time to the song—"Sh-Boom"—he is singing at the wheel of his gas-guzzler. Otherwise, this is the sort of film where the stuntmen are more vital than the speaking performers. Director Rowdy Herrington, following up his interesting Jack the Ripper movie *Jack's Back*, has some trouble with the awkward scenes between Dalton and Doc towards the end, when the latter is serving too well her traditional generic role of trying in vain to dissuade the hero from taking the violent stand necessary to bring the film to a climax. But otherwise he stages an exemplary series of kung-fu battles, barroom brawls, G-string dance contests, explosions, car crashes, rock "n" roll numbers, shoot-outs, knife fights and macho dialogue exchanges.

NEW YORK, 5/29/89, p. 64, David Denby

A critic who enjoys a piece of trash should say so rather than clamber up the high towers of taste. I had a fine time at the crude new action movie *Road House*, which stars Patrick Swayze as a philosophical but inexorably violent bar bouncer. (That's right, a bouncer.) A good time, that is, until the end when the fistfights and karate chops gave way to explosions and shotgun blasts. It's part of the logic of violent trash that the filmmakers must keep leapfrogging themselves, upping the ante. But *Road House* blows its cool when it gives up on whirling feet.

Our violent pop myths may be in need of a little refurbishing. In recent years, Rambo has been neutered by *glasnost* and Dirty Harry swamped by the sheer nickel-and-dime proliferation of street crime; Arnold Schwarzenegger threatens to grow too sophisticated for his own body. Who is to be the next action hero? After Patrick Swayze's success two years ago in *Dirty Dancing*, a lot of people must have been wondering what to do with him. Swayze is a handsome ex-ballet dancer who moves with speed and grace. He may be a minimal actor, but the glint in his foxy eyes promises something, and he's gentle with women—softly romantic in an age of nonromantic leading men. In *Road House*, the shrewdly popularizing producer Joel Silver (*48 HRS., Lethal Weapon, Die Hard*) and a new director named Rowdy Herrington have made Swayze into a fighting, bare-chested pop icon, a sort of Occidental Bruce Lee crossed with Billy Jack and Buford Pusser (the real-life sheriff played by Joe Don Baker in *Walking Tall*), not to mention every Western hero who walked into a no-good town and cleaned the place up. Swayze is a bouncer who can't be licked.

It's a running joke in *Road House* that he's rather small for his job. But he's meant to be a barroom aristocrat, a svelte smoothy in a profession of lunks. His name is Dalton, just Dalton—a loner, quiet, a guy who doesn't fly off the handle (we're told, in awed tones, that he "studied philosophy at NYU"). Dalton carries many scars on his much-exposed torso, but, like Lawrence of Arabia and Gordon Liddy, he doesn't allow pain to bother him, refusing a local anesthetic when his side has to be sewn back together. (On another bloody occasion, he does his own sewing. The compleat action hero.)

Ridiculous? Maybe not. As the movie conceives them, bouncers are similar in temperament not only to gunslingers but also to movie stuntmen. Specialists in violence, spiritual dandies in a crude trade, they are forever policing sloshed, infantile troublemakers and girls who like to peel off their dresses. Once they've pacified one bar, they move on to another. (What do they believe in— orderly bars? No, like most action heroes, they believe in the perfection of their own style.) Dalton is a legend in the halls of bouncerism second only to the famous Wade Garrett, Dalton's mentor, who shows up to help him out when things get really rough; a mystic brotherhood exists between these two elegant toughs. Wade is played by Sam Elliott, an actor who has never become a star and who turns this defeat into the essence of bottom-dog cool. Elliott has flowing gray hair and a wearily knowing manner (*he's* seen some drunks, the manner says); he makes an exceptionally charming and funny grizzled old rat.

In the beginning of the movie, Dalton moves to a fictional Missouri town just outside Kansas City, and takes over management of a rowdy place called the Double Deuce, flushing out unreliable employees, establishing morale. It turns out that there's a method to being a bouncer— something I'd never thought about, I admit, but nice to know. We hear an enlightening professional lecture from Dalton. Be nice, he says. Walk troublemakers to the door. Get tough only when you have to. Well, at the Double Deuce, which also has live music, fights break out as regularly as sexual encounters in an adolescent fantasy, and all the worst guys—the drunken meatballs—want to take on the bouncer. But Dalton waits, waits until the last minute. His mystique is that he fights only when things are truly out of control (like the Westerner who draws his gun last). Then he uses karate and kick boxing to subdue guys twice his size.

Road House is mostly exploitation junk, but it isn't slick and pretentious, like last summer's

Cocktail. It's true Saturday-night entertainment, corrupt on the surface, sexy as well as violent, and full of raffish good cheer. The screenplay was written by David Lee Henry and Hilary Henkin, who provide some wit and moments of relaxation and atmosphere. Ben Gazzara has the role Rip Torn might have had a few years ago—the movie's wild card, the kind of malicious jokester who sings "Sh-Boom" while driving on the wrong side of the road. Gazzara is the town's leading businessman; he built the shopping mall, and now, surrounded by private goons, he extorts money from the local merchants. The plot in *Road House* is just an excuse for the fights: Swayze runs afoul of Gazzara's thugs; there's a series of challenges and provocations until everyone is dead or defeated. As a director, Herrington offers little in the way of reality, but he has the juice for exploitation. The fights are emotionally satisfying.

And Patrick Swayze holds the movie together. He has an alertness and reserve—and a touch of feminine delicacy, even—that make his action hero almost hip. The moviemakers give him a girl, a willowy blonde, Kelly Lynch, who's elegantly elongated, like Alice in Wonderland, and Swayze and Lynch are hot together. She's there for sex appeal, but in deference to the times, she's made a doctor in a white coat, gazing at X-rays. Having a profession, however, doesn't prevent her from serving the traditional role of women in Westerns. She says the modern equivalent of "Why does this violence have to go on and on?" Well, we know why.

NEW YORK POST, 5/19/89, p. 27, Jami Bernard

Dalton is a guy who is so confident about his skills as *bouncer di tutti bouncers* that he wears white to work at the Double Deuce, "the kind of place where they sweep up the eyeballs after closing."

"Road House" is a movie so exuberantly violent, sadistic, macho, lowdown and ugly that it gives off its own kind of malevolent, psychosexual euphoria. We've seen this before in such films as "Action Jackson," "Lethal Weapon" and "Die Hard"—all, coincidentally, from producer Joel Silver. These gleefully punishing movies take their genre to the limit with just enough humor to distance viewers from the carnage, thus making them feel less guilty about enjoying themselves.

Patrick Swayze is Dalton, a man who women want to bed and who other men want to fight in that homoerotic way of the terminally pugnacious. "I've always wanted to try you—I think I can take you," says the first comer. Another antagonist will later get Dalton in a headlock and announce: "I used to [have] guys like you in prison!"

Dalton is All Man in movieland parlance. He sews up his own wounds with nary a wince. He doesn't need anesthesia; in fact, he refuses it. "Do you like pain?" asks the pretty doctor he will fall for (Kelly Lynch in that new film-fantasy version of the Good Girl: body of a whore and mind of a brain surgeon). "Pain don't hurt," he replies.

In the peculiar, neon-misted world of "Road House," there is an understood fraternity of bouncers. Small towns from here to Missouri (where the movie takes place) have heard of him, the modern version of the Western gunslinger. When the mythical Dalton bursts through the saloon doors of the Double Deuce, people make way. In the hierarchy of bouncers, Dalton is the best, although, as people keep mentioning in a pointless running gag, he's small for the job.

"Road House" doesn't skimp on exaggerating every cliche to the nth degree. Dalton is not only a sensitive guy, he has—get this!—a philosophy degree from NYU. And they say you can't get a job with a liberal arts degree.

Dalton is hired to clean up the Double Deuce. When he arrives, it is a place with chicken-wire protecting the musicians on stage, drug deals, prostitutes, "power drinkers," under-agers. "It was a good night, no one died tonight," says the owner (bright-eyed Kevin Tighe).

Before long, it is as safe as a disco in a Long Island mall. Delton's method? Why, three simple rules—never underestimate the enemy, take the fights outside and play nice. "It's my way...or the highway!" he announces. (The script is a morass of cliches as thick as Swayze's left bicep.)

As the Double Deuce goes upscale, it begins to resemble something out of "Cocktail," all gleaming glass and neon. The only thing holding up the transition is Brad Wesley (Ben Gazzara), a cigar-chomping, sadistic son of a gun who, with his gang of goons, is bleeding the town dry. They come after Dalton's old buddy Wade Garrett (a more dissipated than usual Sam Elliott), and threaten Dalton's new girlfriend, the doctor who seems so bemused that Dalton can do without pain killers that she shows up at the roadhouse in a slinky dress.

If it were a fair world, women would boycott "Road House." It is a movie that simply does not like women. The females here are tarts who seem entranced by the kind of flaccid-faced yokel who in reality could only dream of being in the same room with a woman who looks like that.

Even Dalton's educated ladyfriend must suffer an altogether inappropriately close dance with his best buddy. Real men share, don't they?

But the world is not a fair place, and women will flock to "Road House" because heartthrob Patrick Swayze is shown in all his glory—yes, ladies, buns as well—and does a creditable job as the stolid but tender-hearted bouncer with a shady past. The fight scenes are beautifully, lyrically choreographed; in fact, you can hardly tell the difference between a high-kicking fight or a solitary tai chi practice and a mambo from "Dirty Dancing."

Swayze has a beautiful, limber torso and wide-set eyes that the camera loves. His muscles ripple on cue. And unlike other macho-movie heroes, his character *likes* sex. Except that when the sex scene arrives, there is something off about it. The doc (he even calls her "Doc") looks stricken instead of fired up as Dalton picks up her dress and presses her against a stone wall, on their second date. (Aren't doctors aware of birth control?)

The music in "Road House" is great, mostly supplied by the Jeff Healey Band. Lead singer and guitarist Healey is blind and is incorporated into the story as a character in his own right—a nice move you wouldn't expect from a project like this.

Meanwhile, back at the ranch: "You know, the biggest guy in the world, you smash his knee, he'll drop like a stone," says our philosophy graduate in one of many male-bonding interludes.

The movie, intoxicated with its own sadism, syncopated with a jungle-thump of thrown punches, builds to such a crescendo of pummeling that I actually began to have—no kidding—a twitch in one eye. It's the kind of movie the critics hate and the public loves—both camps having good reason. It's cruel to women, heavy on cliché, slickly and sickeningly violent, awash in two-dimensional characters.

And—call the clinic—I enjoyed it.

NEWSDAY, 5/19/89, Part III/p. 3, Bill Kaufman

You get an idea of what to expect right at the beginning of "Road House" when a handsome bouncer suffers a stab wound while evicting a couple of troublemakers from a disco: He calmly pulls out a surgical kit and sews up his own injury.

Patrick Swayze plays Dalton, king of the bouncers, a guy so good at giving riffraff the old heave-ho he's hired to clean up a worse-than-sleazebag joint in Missouri. How bad is the Double Deuce? It is so bad the owner admits each night "we sweep up the eyeballs," and the rock band performs behind a protective shield of beer bottle-deflecting Plexiglas.

Swayze, whose career got a big boost from "Dirty Dancing," seems to have done himself a disservice by taking on this one-dimensional role. Through most of the poorly written film he gets to mouth dim-witted dialogue, like his admonishment to the club's Neanderthal-ish staff: "It's my way or the highway." Veteran actor Ben Gazzara, who also should have known better, wanders through the movie as Brad Wesley, a corrupt wheeler-dealer. Dalton's pal, a bouncer emeritus who taught him all the gut-wrenching moves required for barroom warfare, is played by Sam Elliott, who, if nothing else, gets to inflict a few decent kidney punches.

Dalton's love interest in this fight-a-minute flick, which might have set some sort of noggin-bashing record, is newcomer Kelly Lynch, a talented young actress who, like all the others in this picture, is hamstrung by the poor script. Of course, on the way to kicking the undesirable elements out of the Double Deuce, there's a climactic riverbank slugfest between Dalton and a bad guy, not to mention a few spectacular automobile crashes.

VILLAGE VOICE, 5/30/89, p. 68, Lisa Kennedy

One of the earliest shots of *Road House* is a tip of the hat to MTV (not a good sign): Music's already throbbing; a low-slung angle reveals a sleek little car; then its door opens, and two feet touch down on the pavement; the camera begins to pan up the calves, the thighs, what a nice miniskirted...Too much of the film is this familiar; and this pandering to the adolescent male—whether he be 14 or 35—makes it a B-movie. B as in bad; B as in boy.

The camera continues into the people-filled bar, following Kevin Tighe's Tilghman, who's come to contract Dalton (Patrick Swayze) to relocate to Jasper and clean up his bar, the Double Deuce. When he finally gets to barter with our man, Dalton is suturing up his arm, having just been slashed by an angry customer. We get the feeling that everyone wants a piece of Dalton—and that he's used to it. And his piece is mentioned often enough: Whenever someone meets him they say, "I thought you'd be bigger." (Somehow I thought Jasper, Missouri, would be bigger too. The size of the town seems kinda indeterminate, big enough for Tilghman to pay Dalton $5000 up front and $500 a night. But small enough for Brad Wesley [Ben Gazzara] to control all of its businesses with an ugly pack of bullies—what they lack in brains they make up for in testosterone.)

Road House's fable of a drifter is pretty safe and sentimental territory for movies. And, of course, Dalton's own enigmatic history gets worked out in the process. It's the type of plot that says real men tend to be loners and respect others—men or women. That they aren't entirely at home with the spoils of the boy war. When Dalton arrives, the Double Deuce is, of course, a hellhole: They're drugdealing, skimming from the kitty, raising hell. After enough fights confirm his legendary status as the nation's best bouncer (this is by far the funniest assertion of the film: the bouncer as cult hero), the Deuce becomes a viable business. But, as Dalton promised one of his crew, "Things are going to get worse before they get better." And the bar turns out to be a microcosm of a town gone sour.

You know to be wary when the film has more stuntman than actors. If 90 per cent of the movie is choreographed violence, and another 9 per cent is male posturing, there's just not much room for women. Just enough in fact for tarts, a nice girl, and a love interest. Patrick Swayze, and Kelly Lynch, as Doc, bring new meaning to the term "significant other." He's a bouncer with a philosophy degree, she's a doctor. Much of his activity goes against the letter of her Hippocratic oath. But one decent but flattened-out female character cannot rescue this film from itself.

Sam Elliott, as Wade Garrett, is one of the best things about the movie. But even his hippie/shaggy dog/bouncer/guru character starts to refer to a woman as a cunt in a moment of passion. And Wesley's beautiful henchman, Jimmy, right before he almost kills Dalton for the fifth time in a drawn-out fight, tells him, "I fucked guys like you in prison." Of course he dies moments after that revelation. Not because he's a rapist, since, hey, this movie is firmly embedded in that culture, but because it suggest queerness. These slips are telling. *Road House* proves that (usually) you can't send a man out to do a girl's job: that is, taking on male culture.

Also reviewed in:
NEW YORK TIMES, 5/19/89, p. C17, Caryn James
VARIETY, 5/24–30/89, p. 34
WASHINGTON POST, 5/19/89, p. D7, Hal Hinson

ROGER & ME

A Warner Bros. release of a Dog Eat Dog Films production. *Producer:* Michael Moore. *Director:* Michael Moore. *Screenplay:* Michael Moore. *Director of Photography:* Christopher Beaver, John Prusak, Kevin Rafferty, and Bruce Schermer. *Editor:* Wendey Stanzler and Jennifer Beman. *Sound:* Judy Irving. *Narrator:* Michael Moore. *Running Time:* 87 minutes. *MPAA Rating:* R.

WITH: Roger Smith, Ronald Reagan, Miss America, Pat Boone, Anita Bryant, Rev. Robert Schuller, Bob Eubanks, Deputy Fred Ross, Rhonda Britton (The Bunny Lady); Steve Wilson (The Tourism Chief); James Blanchard (The Governor); Janet Rauch (The Amway Woman).

CHRISTIAN SCIENCE MONITOR, 1/16/90, p. 10, David Sterritt

It almost never happens, but there's no denying it: One of the season's most talked-about movies is a documentary. It was made, moreover, by a person who usually has no fondness for nonfiction movies.

"Generally speaking," says Michael Moore, "I don't like documentaries. I don't like PBS. I think that stuff is pretty boring. We should have more documentaries made by people who don't like them. They might be a little more interesting."

Most observers agree that Mr. Moore's film, "Roger & Me," is uncommonly interesting. In the movie, "Roger" is Roger Smith, chief executive of General Motors (GM), and "Me" is Moore himself—seeking an audience with Mr. Smith to voice his disapproval of factory closings and layoffs in his home town of Flint, Mich.

The film's humor comes from Moore's dogged hunt for the GM executive, and from ironic glimpses of Flint's municipal efforts to raise its spirits in the face of economic disaster. Its seriousness comes from Moore's obvious concern for the city and his depictions of human hardship.

The movie is flawed. It sometimes has a mocking tone, aiming cheap shots at ordinary Flint citizens as well as government and corporate officials. Moore is also slippery about the sequence of some events in the picture—a fact brought out by Harlan Jacobson's recent interview with the filmmaker in Film Comment.

Despite such problems, "Roger & Me" has captured the attention and affection of more moviegoers than ordinary documentaries ever dream of. I caught up with Moore for an interview during the last New York Film Festival, before his film had been sold to a distributor. He started our conversation by telling me what a movie fan he was.

"I go to everything," Moore says, "and I think it's important that movies be entertaining—that, especially when you have a serious subject, you allow people to laugh a little bit and not beat them over the head with a serious political message. I have very strong political values . . . and I want to see things happen. But I don't want to do it by paralyzing people to the point where they walk out of the theater numb, thinking everything's hopeless."

It was part of Moore's political strategy to make "Roger & Me" a highly personal film. "I think it's very important to put a human face on a corporation," he says. "We talk of them as cold, isolated entities, but they're not. They're run by human beings like you and me, except they have a little more money . . . and we need to know who they are. We live in a democracy. [Executives] control large companies that control our daily lives. . . . Do you know who the president of IBM is? Do you know who the president of AT&T is? I don't know who they are. I should know! I'm a citizen in this country! I should know who's in charge!"

Was there a danger the film might be so funny that people would get its humor *instead* of its message?

"Yes," Moore admits. "That was a real problem in editing it, because at no time did I want the humor to be [excessively] flip."

Yet laughs were another part of Moore's basic strategy. He notes that he and other Flint residents "have seen our family and friends laid off, lose their jobs, and many of their lives destroyed. . . . But you have to figure out a way to communicate that to the rest of the world, because the rest of the world really doesn't care." The way to make this connection with a wide audience, he decided, was to leaven the message with laughter.

"Roger & Me" raises a perenially important question about the relationship between films and audiences: Can a movie make a difference in the way people think and behave?

"It's not going to change things tomorrow," Moore concedes. "But it's a small piece of what I hope is a much larger mosaic of people becoming active in the 1990s. That's something I would really like to see happen. And if I or this film can play a small part in that, it would be great."

Moore's movie has been accused of unfairness toward General Motors and its executives. The filmmaker disputes this charge, but he adds that evenhanded treatment wasn't part of his game plan.

"The thing about 'objective' journalism is a myth," he asserts. "You watch the nightly news every night [and] it's one-sided. On Christmas Eve . . . you don't see families evicted from their homes as you see in this movie, with the sheriff hauling the Christmas tree out the front door."

What TV news does show, Moore continues, is "the same story year after year: The Pope is having midnight mass; some community has a human nativity scene; or another community is battling the [American Civil Liberties Union] over the nativity scene. Maybe you see do-gooders handing out turkeys to poor people. But the story is on the wealthy people who are *doing* these good deeds. . . . The camera rarely follows the person taking the turkey home, to see the person living with plastic on the windows and using the stove as a furnace."

Moore sees the hunt for Roger Smith, which provides the basic framework of "Roger & Me," as only a "hook" on which he hangs the social and economic issues that really interest him.

"The larger issue is that we have an economic system in this country that is not very fair," he says. "We say we live in a democracy. . . . But if we have [democracy] in our government, why don't we have it in the workplace, in our economy? . . .

"We're already seeing the various social ills massively on the rise—in terms of drug abuse, teenage pregnancy, divorce, suicide, alcoholism. . . . I think we're going to see even more chaos among those who used to be the haves and are quickly becoming the have-nots."

Since such problems are of over-whelming importance to American society, why don't films focus on them more often? Moore feels it's because the big-money atmosphere of the movie world mitigates against seriousness nad selflessness.

"They reward you with lots of money," he says with a rueful smile, admitting that his own movie has drawn such rewards. "I will not make that money," he says of profits from the picture. "It will go to the nonprofit group that produced the film. I'll be paid a salary equal to the other crew members."

This doesn't mean he wants to be a martyr, he adds. "I want to live a comfortable life," he says. "I want to live in a nice place in a nice neighborhood. . . . I'm no different from anybody else. But how much is enough? That's the question I really asked General Motors."

LOS ANGELES TIMES, 12/20/89, Calendar/p. 1, Peter Rainer

Documentaries have such a terrible reputation with audiences for being boring and "good for you" that the pesky folk humor of Michael Moore's "Roger & Me" is almost startling. This movie about the effect of auto plant closures in Flint, Mich., the birthplace of General Motors, is being touted as a documentary for people who don't like documentaries, and that's not far wrong.

More to the point, it's a documentary for people who are unaccustomed to how entertaining documentaries can be. All the best ones are.

The jokiness in "Roger & Me" isn't simply in the movie to relieve boredom. The film is a piece of cockeyed outrage, and the black comedy arises naturally, inevitably, from the seriousness of the situation.

In late 1986, General Motors, under its current president Roger Smith, shut down 11 auto plants, which brought to about 30,000 the total number of jobs eliminated in Flint since 1974. (Flint's population is about 150,000.) Moore, who lives in Flint, began filming in early 1988; originally he wanted Smith to accompany him for a day to survey the havoc wreaked by GM's policies in his hometown.

Snubbed in a series of attempts to reach Smith, Moore turns the quest into loopy skulduggery. He includes on the soundtrack the "William Tell Overture" theme music from "The Lone Ranger" during one of his periodic forays to ambush Smith; he poses as a stockholder at the annual GM shareholders meeting and has his microphone cut off moments before posing a question to the prez.

It's apparent early on that Moore isn't going to be granted entry into Smith's inner sanctum, and Moore milks the rejection—makes it politically symbolic. Chunky, rumpled, dressed in his standard working-class uniform of down jacket and cap, Moore stands in clear contrast to Smith's sleek yachting-club gentility. It looks like paint-by-the-numbers Marxism, but Moore wants us to recognize it as a true picture.

This may be Moore's first movie, but he has an extensive left-wing political activist background. In 1976, he founded the well-regarded alternative newspaper Flint Voice; appeared as a commentator on National Public Radio, and was briefly the editor of Mother Jones magazine in 1986. (The $50,000 he was awarded in a wrongful dismissal suit against Mother Jones contributed to "Roger & Me's" $200,000 budget.)

Moore may present himself as an indefatigable bumpkin—did he *really* expect to get in to see Roger Smith dressed in such a rumply fashion?—but there's righteous guile in his film making. He doesn't approach the Flint closures with the kind of documentary gravity that one would expect of a crusading journalist. Instead, he selects incidents for their power to rile you up while making you laugh, by-passing such obvious insertions as shots of long unemployment lines. Moore has a wicked gift for fulfilling audience expectation that many a veteran director might envy; he dispenses with statistics in favor of the "found" humor that is seemingly all around him in Flint.

Some examples: An annual Great Gatsby party put on by the town's upper-crusters, where unemployed auto workers are hired to grace the lawns as "living sculptures"; an opening-night fund raiser in a newly constructed Flint jail, to which moneyed locals, many of them in party costumes, pay $100 to spend the night behind bars; a live "Nightline" telecast on Flint's plight that is unexpectedly aborted when the show's TV transmission truck is stolen.

Moore's rage is spiced by a nostalgia for the boomtown days of his childhood. (Virtually all of his extended family worked for GM; his uncle took part in the 44-day sit-down strike in 1937 that gave rise to the United Auto Workers.) He opens his film with promotional documentary footage from GM's better days in Flint—town parades, Pat Boone and Dinah Shore crooning

Chevrolet's praises. The intended irony here is only partial. Moore tells us that these movies show Flint as he remembers it, and, judging from the honeyed tone in his voice-overs for his section, he must really revel in those days. He accepts the boosterism of boomtown Flint as a populist artifact. It's a mythology that he chooses to believe in.

In present-day Flint, the same boostered spirit is portrayed by Moore as a vast and corrupting lie. Pat Boone is brought back to Flint and, in an interview with Moore, praises Roger Smith as a "can-do kind of guy." Anita Bryant is trundled onstage to sing "Put Your Hand in the Hand." Ronald Reagan takes 12 unemployed auto workers out for a pizza and informs them that there are jobs to be had in Texas. The Rev. Robert Schuller, hired for $20,000, lectures his dispossessed audience to "turn your hurt into a halo." Bob Eubanks, a Flint escapee, returns home to host a stage version of "The Newlywed Game." (He also, while being interviewed by Moore, spouts in what was presumably an off moment a vile anti-Semitic AIDS joke.)

Flint's sky-high crime-rate, a direct result of the rampant unemployment, spurs the city fathers to action. To attract tourism (!), a $13-million Hyatt Regency Hotel and a $100-million AutoWorld theme park are constructed, with disastrous results.

Moore doesn't point up the chronology of these events, many of which predate the 1986 closures by at least several years. For example, Reagan's appearance was in 1980, as a candidate for President; the Hyatt Regency opened in 1982, AutoWorld in mid-1984. But the fuzzy ordering of events doesn't negate Moore's general point—that, instead of jobs and a helping hand, GM fed its workers homilies and condescension. They're informed of the promising careers to be had in the fast-food business, or as Amway salesmen.

Moore's sympathies are resolutely class-based, and at times that makes the film seem too simple-mindedly doctrinaire. The moneyed classes in Flint are portrayed as modern-day Marie Antoinettes.

The working class, many of whom we see in the process of being evicted, are all victims of GM. Even the chief evictor, the black sheriff's deputy Fred Ross, is regarded somewhat sympathetically, because his own roots are working class. Moore doesn't portray any principled civic regard among the well-to-do; he doesn't bring up blue-collar racism toward the Japanese.

Even in the areas where he is on more solid ground, such as the sequence where he mentions GM's move to Mexico in search of cheap non-union labor, and the company's resultant investment in weapons manufacture, Moore breezes through without much analysis. Clearly he is not interested in a deep-dish political treatise here, but the way these issues are skimped and glossed carries its own element of condescension toward the audience. Moore sees the movies as his arena to reach the masses, and he doesn't want to blow his chance, or presumably his own investment, by putting everyone to sleep. Outrage brings out the political cartoonist in him, and he is content to leave the drawings sketchy. He may even feel that that sketchiness best represents the bare, unadulterated truth about capitalism.

If he were an even finer film maker, Moore might have found a way to make more complex political points and *still* hold his audience. He sees what he is doing here as the only credible alternative to the dour documentary approach to urban misery, but his approach isn't comprehensive enough to take in the full tragicomedy of Flint, which is, after all, representative of working-class woes throughout America. When he inserts actual footage of a crazed criminal being gunned downed by Flint police, the images jar with the movie's rollicky nihilism. They seem "too real" for the rest of the film. "Roger & Me" is a terrific movie, but if it were a great one, those images would reverberate with the shareholders' meetings and the AutoWorlds and the Gatsby parties.

MONTHLY FILM BULLETIN, 4/90, p. 116, David Wilson

When General Motors chairman Roger Smith announces factory closures in Flint, Michigan—the company's birthplace—unemployed journalist Michael Moore, who was born and raised in Flint, tries to arrange a filmed interview with Smith to give him the chance to explain his decision to put 30,000 people out of work. Moore and his crew are denied an audience, but continue to pursue Chairman Smith. Meanwhile, they interview a number of Flint citizens, including several former GM employees who are trying to find new ways of making a living. Another former employee, now a deputy sheriff, is filmed evicting Flint citizens who have fallen behind with their rent. There is footage of a union parade; interviews with union officials, with Miss Michigan 88, and with tourist industry workers after the city fathers resolve to turn Flint into a tourist attraction with a luxury hotel and an industrial theme park. Moore attends the General Motors Annual

General Meeting, which is adjourned when he tries to put a question. He finally manages to approach Smith at the company's Christmas party. Smith says he has no plans to visit Flint.

Michael Moore's documentary aspires to make a joke out of the ravages of American capitalism. The joke, which has barbs, was occasioned by General Motors' decision to close down its plants in Flint, Michigan, and move them to Mexico, where labour is cheaper. Since Flint was a Chevrolet town, indeed the birthplace of General Motors, this had unfortunate consequences for its citizens. But this is not a film about unemployment (or, as Moore puts it, "another 'Dying Steeltown' documentary with all the clichés about how horrible it is to be unemployed"). It takes the form of a personal quest, a film-maker's quixotic journey in search of the villain of the piece.

Moore's odyssey takes him on some curious detours. But although the itinerary is picaresque, from the start there is no doubting the identity of the hero. Not many film-makers would choose to begin with their own home movies. Moore tells us that he was born in Flint, moved to San Francisco as a journalist, and returned to his home town unemployed. Introductions over, via black-and-white footage of Pat Boone (who sang for the Chevvy) and an Olympian view of a General Motors anniversary parade, and Moore is disguising himself as the interviewer with a TV crew from Toledo filming the last Chevrolet truck off the assembly line. The unabashed self-indulgence of this opening is matched in all that follows. An attempt to contact Roger Smith by telephone is cut in with a 1930s film montage of switchboards and radiating wires. Ronald Reagan came to Flint and "took a dozen workers out for a pizza". There is film of a fat cats' garden party, with leaner locals hired to play human statues. Asked for his identity card at the General Motors head office, Moore produces a discount card for a cheese company. A TV evangelist is summoned to exorcise the town's scourge ("You can turn your hurt into a halo"). Miss Michigan 88 asks the Flint people to keep their fingers crossed—when she tries for Miss America. One citizen even invokes Margaret Thatcher ("Cheer up, America").

There is an avowedly serious purpose to all this rib-digging jokeyness. In between the gags, we are allowed occasional glimpses of what being out of work means in earnest for the people of Flint: boarded-up shops, a street of abandoned houses, evictions, an escalating crime rate. Yet it is entirely characteristic of the film's determination to be funny at all costs that when he does choose to interview people who have lost their jobs, Moore opts for the eccentric case: a woman who breeds rabbits, for pets or food as you wish; another woman who has started her own line in individually appropriate dress colour by divining her clients' natural season (when the woman telephones Moore to confess a mistake in her own seasonal tone, her obvious embarrassment provides another cue for a laugh).

In terms of structure and argument, *Roger & Me* appears to have been made up as it was filmed. Its polemic-through-gags approach has been received in some quarters as innovative, though in fact it follows—uncertainly—in a tradition that goes back to Emile de Antonio via documentaries like *Atomic Café* and *Rosie the Riveter*. Understandably, it has ruffled feathers nearer home, though as a final caption informs us, the citizens of Flint can't see it in their own town because all the cinemas have been closed. They might, however, have mixed feelings about being exploited for other people's entertainment. Losing your job is no laughing matter.

NEW STATESMAN & SOCIETY, 4/27/90, p. 48, Suzanne Moore

Question: When is a documentary not a documentary? Answer: When people enjoy it. Or so it would seem in the strange case of *Roger and Me*. Michael Moore's film has been a hit with the American public, raking in over six million dollars, and scotching the myth that documentaries automatically mean box-office death. It has secured a distribution deal with Warner Bros, which no one thought would take on this kind of film, and has appeared on scores of critics' top ten movies of last year.

The Roger of the film's title is Roger Smith, chairman of General Motors. The "Me" is Moore himself who, for three years, pursues Roger Smith in order to ask him why he is closing down car plants in Moore's home town of Flint, Michigan. He wants him to visit Flint to see firsthand the consequences of mass redundancies—poverty, evictions, rising crime and general desperation that have hit the town.

Moore never gets that interview but instead uses this device to weave together a series of quirky, acute and funny observations about what happens when the American Dream "goes down the toilet".

But the tide of acclaim for the film turned when Harlan Jacobson, then editor of *Film Comment*, claimed that Moore had juggled with the truth—that the film was not chronologically accurate. Since then the debate has raged not only over the validity of Moore's film but implicitly over the role of documentary itself.

Moore uses archive material full of images of a happy and prosperous working class, interviews with local residents, and offers his own, idiosyncratic version of events. Though he presents himself as a bumbling but good-hearted smalltown boy in a baseball cap who only wants to bring Roger Smith to justice, Moore was in fact a political journalist for over ten years—you can't help feeling he could have got the interview if he had really wanted it. When asked for accreditation he proffers his Chuck E Cheese fastfood discount card. This is exactly the kind of thing that has offended some critics because Moore is playing to the audience when documentaries are supposed to record events rather than manipulate them for easy laughs.

Yet this ploy of the little man up against corporate America does work because however self-indulgent Moore can be accused of being, he is so obviously on the side of the little man. And he unearths a series of bizarre interviews with local people such as the Bunny Lady—a woman who breeds rabbits for "pets or meat" and skins them with amazing dexterity in front of the camera. He charts the decline of the town through its desperate measures to set itself up as a tourist attraction by building an indoor theme park, Auto-World, just as it is closing down its real car factories.

The local sheriff's brutal pragmatism as he evicts mothers and children is as hard-hitting as the interviews with the well-to-do, who hire local people to be "human statues" at their Great Gatsby party. As houses are boarded up a new jail is built. Celebrities such as Pat Boone and the terrifying Anita Bryant are brought in to mouth inanities about "attitude" in a town that has just been named in *Money* magazine as the worst place to live in America.

That all these things happened is not in dispute but the charges that have been levelled against Moore is that they did not happen in the time-span or order he presents them in this film. Events which took place over a ten-year period have been telescoped into three-years. Reagan visited Flint before the plant closures, not after them. The ridiculous drive to promote Flint as a tourist centre also took place before the major lay-offs.

This tampering with chronology in the name of entertainment, combined with the influential Pauline Kael's proclamation that *Roger and Me* was nothing more than "a piece of gonzo demagoguery", have put Moore on the defensive. He claims that his intention was to make "a movie" not a documentary, something that would be seen in shopping malls as well as art houses. Even more controversially he has argued that all journalism re-arranges sequences of events for its own ends.

The popularity of the film compared with the prissiness of the critics again puts Moore on the side of the "man in the street". Yet however naive Moore may appear in his film, *Roger and Me* is ultimately a very sharp piece of filmmaking. His manipulation of events manages to make some very heartfelt and sophisticated points about the workings of contemporary capitalism. You may be able to name another film that encompasses the end of the manufacturing base, the rise of service industries, the relocation of corporate capital in less developed countries, the creation of themed environments that shut out the poor. But I doubt if you can honestly say it makes you laugh too.

What Moore achieves is an essential truth, a reality that is recognisable however this film is viewed. What he has done is simply to reverse the processes of modern capitalism for his own ends. Giant industries personalise their products through personal endorsements, so Moore goes after Roger Smith as personally responsible for the devastation of Flint. He puts a face on to this huge unwieldy process. He may simplify it but he makes us care—he makes himself an innocent in order to show who is guilty. In making Roger Smith a villain, he inevitably makes himself a hero. This is a fundamentally populist strategy but one that I think he gets away with.

Indeed, the most interesting of recent documentaries such as Errol Morris's *A Thin Blue Line* are bending the rules of documentary making. They deny that there is an incorruptible version of truth out there that merely has to be recorded. Instead they make their own truth in the telling, no longer separating the medium from the message. If Moore is to be held accountable for this then to whom? To other journalists, to the people of Flint, or to General Motors? Are some truths so great that they can afford to dispense with smaller ones? If fact is stranger than fiction, Moore's only crime is that he has made it even stranger. He has described his film as "docucomedy" but there is already a word for it: info-tainment—the dramatising of real-life events by some American news networks. It has been regarded universally as a "bad thing". Go and see *Roger and Me* and think again.

NEW YORK, 12/18/89, p. 102, David Denby

Sixty years ago, Singlair Lewis and H.L. Mencken lampooned our amiably philistine business civilization, its mix of hard-nosed realism and honeyed evangelical uplift. In his celebrated *Roger & Me*, first-time documentary filmmaker Michael Moore proves himself a satirist of the Reagan period equal in talent to Mencken and Lewis. Moore, however, has a direct political purpose: He wants to expose the illusions that capitalism employs in the media age to disguise its more damaging operations. His wit has a cutting political anger behind it.

As Moore, who is in his early thirties, tells us in a voice-over narration, he was born into a family of automobile workers in Flint, Michigan, where General Motors was founded. For ten years he edited an alternative weekly newspaper in Flint, and then, in 1986, he was summoned to San Francisco to take over the left-wing monthly *Mother Jones*. Fired after a few months, he returned to Flint just as Roger Smith, chairman of the board of General Motors, was announcing a new round of plant closings. GM, eager to make cars at lower cost in Mexico, abruptly put thousands of people out of work. Once a thriving metropolis, Flint developed the highest crime rate in the nation; stores were shuttered, houses abandoned.

Roger & Me is nothing like the usual Rust Belt documentary. It has the shape and expressive freedom of fiction (and some of Moore's editing of events is closer to fiction than fact). The centerpiece is Moore himself as he attempts to confront Roger Smith and haul the great man off to Flint in order to see the effects of GM's actions. Large, with a big head and a heavy gut, Moore wears jeans and an engineer's hat, a toothpick dangling from his mouth. His getup is as stylized as Woody Allen's urban-man tweeds and corduroys. What it says is "I'm just a rube who loves the people of Flint."

Some rube. Actually, he's a cranky, obsessive, maliciously inventive radical journalist who knows exactly how to use irony and blandness for comic effect. In his pursuit of Smith, Moore, a stolidly polite and persistent figure, shows up with his camera crew at GM headquarters in Detroit or at some swank club in Grosse Pointe, as if guys like him walked in on the chairman of General Motors every day. Of course, he knew he would never get close to Smith; the pursuit is just a conceit, a workable metaphor for the distance any dismissed employee must feel from the boss. Smith, meanwhile, with his round baby face and sharpened tiger teeth, his orotund public clichés, makes a perfect target for populist scorn. Taunting him isn't quite fair, but then massive job lay-offs aren't fair, either.

Lech Walesa and other Eastern European reformers have repeatedly spoken of the "stupidity" of Communism; *Roger & Me* is about the stupidity of American capitalism in the eighties. Rather than adopt polices that would put people to work, the Flint city administration, as Moore shows, escaped into fantasy. In a mad attempt to turn the shuttered downtown ruins into a tourist haven, Flint put up three ambitious projects (built, according to Moore, by laborers brought in from out of state): a Hyatt Regency hotel, consuming millions of taxpayers' dollars; a theme park called AutoWorld, complete with a scale model of Flint's downtown streets in their glory days; a shopping mall in the style of the South Street Seaport. Illusion took over as an economic system.

All three projects quickly failed. Meanwhile, the city imported celebrities of uplift—Anita Bryant and the Reverend Robert Schuller—who urged cheerfulness and self-reliance. Yet the only man in town who had a secure job was Deputy Sheriff Fred Ross, whom Moore follows around as he evicts people from their houses when they have failed to pay the rent. Inexorable yet oddly sympathetic, Ross is a companionable figure out of Dickens.

A new city jail, built to hold the increased criminal population, throws an opening-night party in which yuppie couples, some dressed as prisoners, spend the evening in cells. This is true media-age insanity, the dark side of Reaganism: Having failed at manufacture, America turns to ghastly self-parody. When he was in power, Reagan frustrated liberals. How do you attack a Dr. Feelgood when millions of people are indeed feeling good? Michael Moore has found a voice that isn't priggish or vindictive. Everything in the movie falls into place.

A little too neatly, it turns out. As I learned from Harlan Jacobson's brilliant interview with Moore in the November-December issue of *Film Comment*, Moore moved events around in the editing process. He doesn't tell us, for instance, that the layoffs in 1986 came at the end of a long series of plant-closings in Flint. He implies that the three urban projects failed while he was pursuing Smith, from 1987 to 1989, but actually the projects had all failed before the 1986 layoffs. Moore violated the unwritten law that filmmakers will not misrepresent the sequence of events in a documentary. Still, everything he shows us actually happened in Flint in the eighties as a response to GM's ruthless elimination of jobs. The movie stands as a brilliant portrait of corporate heartlessness and urban folly.

NEW YORK 1/29/90, p. 58, David Denby

Attempting to unseat Michael Moore and everyone who has admired *Roger & Me* (including *moi*, whose review she razzed), Pauline Kael ended her pan in the January 8 *New Yorker* with the following: "*Roger & Me* uses its leftism as a superior attitude. Members of the audience can laugh at ordinary working people and still feel they're taking a politically correct position." This sounds devastating, and I suppose I should be mortified. There's only one thing wrong with it: *Roger & Me* isn't about "ordinary working people." Most of it is about the Reaganite illusion-makers, the shuck-and-jive media types who came to the fore in Flint, Michigan, in the eighties and tried to distract the city and themselves from the city's gruesome economic realities. Not "working people" but make-work people—uplifters, boosters, urban renewalists. Many films have chronicled the problems of the unemployed. *Roger & Me* is the first to chronicle the doings of those who tried to convince us that the unemployed weren't there.

NEW YORK POST, 9/27/89, p. 23, Jami Bernard

Michael Moore's deliriously effective "Roger & Me" is a documentary on the seemingly dull topic of the closing of General Motors' Flint, Mich., plants, which put 30,000 out of work and squeezed most of the breath out of a town built on the auto industry.

You might expect shots of bread and unemployment lines and dour faces. Instead, Moore—a Flint native and former magazine editor making his first movie—treats us to a wild, personalized take not only on what happened to Flint, but on the incredible, agonizing disparities between the haves and have-nots.

The story is bound by a travelogue of sorts as Moore pursues the ever more elusive Roger Smith, the GM chairman responsible (if one can use that word when referring to Smith, who comes off like an uncaring pig) for shuttering Flint and moving the works down to Mexico, where labor is cheap.

Moore's tenacity in the face of puffed-up "public relations" officers and secretaries and security guards is admirable. When he finally gets to a mike at a stockholders meeting, Moore is recognized and Smith abruptly turns off the juice.

Affectionately citing the misguided attempts by the Flint elders to resuscitate the dying city—they erect a multi-million dollar auto theme park, only to see it go bankrupt in a few months—Moore is a Garrison Keillor of the auto-worker set. (His boyhood role model was Bob Eubanks, the future "Newlywed Game" host, because "if Bob Eubanks could make it out of here, so could I.")

He interviews those in town with the safest jobs: the sheriff's deputy who evicts people from their homes, the ladies who forward mail to families who have fled, and the moving companies. He also shows how some Flintians are making do—one skins bunnies in her back yard for $15 a week; others sell their blood on weekdays, resting up on weekends.

This is a masterful, moving documentary, narrated in chatty Woody Allen style. Moore deserves one of those genius grants so he can take on any subject of his choosing.

NEW YORK POST, 12/20/89, p. 26, David Edelstein

Perhaps the most frustrating thing about living through the Reagan era was the Right's public-relations virtuosity. On the day Reagan slashed the corporate-gains tax—making it possible for CEOs to reap undreamed-of rewards—the lead story on every TV station featured the prez hoisting beers with working stiffs in a Boston bar. One o' the guys, man of the people! Man of tycoons and ward-heelers, actually.

The beauty of "Roger & Me," Michael Moore's boffo comedy about life under Reaganism, is that it exposes the populist rhetoric of the Reagan revolution as a colossal scam.

Made for peanuts and unheralded before its smash receptions in the Toronto New York film festivals, "Roger & Me" turns out to be the great American muckraking documentary of the decade. Instead of the usual left-wing pieties, Moore uses savage irony (and often plain savagery) to go where no mainstream journalist would dare. He's unscrupulous but irresistible; you watch and think, "Attaboy! Nail 'em!"

As most people know by now, the Roger in question is Roger Smith, the head of General

Motors—a man who, in line with many CEOs in the '80s, closed plants in the U.S. and moved them to Mexico, where there are no unions or minimum wage. Despite the guarantees of conservative economists, there was no "trickle-down" in Flint, Michigan. Laying off thousands of workers and virtually destroying the town, Smith proceeded to give himself a $2 million raise.

"Roger & Me" is the story of Moore's attempt to bring the GM chairman to Flint to see the economic devastation that he and his company have wrought. We watch the heavy-set, proudly slobby Moore (former editor of Mother Jones magazine) get turned away from GM's headquarters in Detroit and then try to crash Smith's hoity-toity country and athletic clubs.

These are clearly just stunts for the camera—Moore surely never thought he's penetrate such fortresses of capitalism. But the attempts earn for him an amazing degree of sympathy, and help to invoke our populist wrath against Smith and his class.

When he isn't hunting for Roger, Moore turns his camera on the sheriff's deputy, who spends his days evicting people from their homes in Flint. The director also chronicles the town's hare-brained schemes to boost the economy, especially the construction (at enormous expense to tax-payers) of expositions and convention centers, in an attempt to transform what Money magazine dubbed the worst place to live in the country into a mecca for tourists.

Most of Moore's points he scores off the grotesque hypocrisy of men like Smith. Puckishly, the director cross-cuts between the chairman reading from Charles Dickens (who would have loathed him and all he stands for) at a GM party on Christmas Eve and a family in Flint being kicked out of its home—the direct result of Smith's lay-offs.

Moore treats as theater of the absured the Right's bland exhortations to Dream Your Dream and Go For It in the face of crushing poverty and a skewed economic system. As boobs like Anita Bryant and Pat Boone hold forth about unlimited opportunities in America, laid-off workers flop out in fast-food jobs and flounder in faddish businesses like color-consulting.

Moore isn't the most compassionate of narrators, and there are moments when his instincts seem questionable. An article in Film Comment (which allegedly precipitated the ouster of writer/editor Harlan Jacobson) reveals that Moore fudged his chronology, and the air is filled with ominous rumblings about hidden agendas.

Elements of Moore's populism make me deeply uncomfortable. When, looking for Smith, he shows up at a yacht club and lingers on the snooty guards, he stirs our most primitive anger at being excluded—he makes us want to tear their playhouse down. It turns out that Smith doesn't even belong to this club—Moore had made a goof—but it doesn't seem to matter to our host. "Tear it down anyway!" he'd probably say. "Private clubs shouldn't exist!"

Most of "Roger & Me" is finer than that, however. Events of the last year have driven home the failure of Communism to realize its founders' utopian ideals; what remains is to reform capitalism so that men like Roger Smith aren't allowed to enrich themselves at the expense of millions.

For most of the movie you're cackling and hooting excitedly. Then the realization takes hold that what you're watching is a tragedy of overwhelming dimensions. "Roger & Me" should be seen by every voter in this great, blinkered nation.

NEWSDAY, 9/27/89, Part II/p. 5, Terry Kelleher

The credit crawl at the end of "Roger & Me," Michael Moore's documentary on economic depression in Flint, Mich., includes a notice that the film cannot be seen in Flint.

Followed by the punchline: There are no movie theaters left in the city.

But life is not perfect even in a filmgoer's paradise. "Roger & Me," one of the most entertaining movies of the year, can be seen in our area only by those who hold tickets to one of its sold-out showings at the New York Film Festival—tonight at 9:30 or tomorrow at 6:15 p.m. at Alice Tully Hall.

Fortunately, "Roger & Me" will reach a much wider audience soon. The public voted it most popular picture at the Toronto Film Festival earlier this month and, judging from the reaction at a press screening here, New York viewers should find it equally enjoyable. According to Moore, "three major studios and all the independents" have expressed interest in picking up "Roger & Me." A distribution deal is expected by the end of the weeks.

How can a technically primitive, low-low-budget film about the crushing impact of General Motors plant closings be described in terms of entertainment, enjoyment and suchlike frivolity?

No question Moore aims to clobber a callous GM as personified by its board chairman, Roger

Smith. But ridicule is what knocks the corporate giant silly. This radical fights the power—with humor. A Flint native whose father toiled 33 years on the A.C. Spark Plug line, Moore founded an alternative newspaper called the Flint Voice (later the Michigan Voice) in 1976. Ten years later, he left to become editor of San Francisco-based Mother Jones magazine. California didn't agree with Moore, and neither did Mother Jones boss Adam Hochschild. He was fired in a matter of months.

Black in Flint, the jobless journalist found unemployment was the wave of the future at the birthplace of America's largest auto company. GM had begun shutting down three plants, idling about 30,000 workers. Moore decided to make a movie about this sad situation, and it came out funny as hell.

Even the fund-raising part was funny. For seed money Moore used the $58,000 he won in the settlement of his wrongful-discharge suit against Mother Jones. To scare up the rest of the $160,000 it cost to make "Roger & Me," he sold his four-bedroom house in Flint for $27,000 (think what epic films he could have financed if he'd owned a similar residence in the New York area), ran a weekly bingo game ("Growing up Catholic, I knew that that was the best way to raise money"), held yard sales and hit up foundations and generous individuals.

Moore figured it would be an eye-opener for Smith if the GM poobah accompanied him on a tour of distressed Flint. But Smith proved inaccessible behind a dense human shield of public relations types. So "Roger and Me" became the filmed record of a quest. Populistically attired in baseball cap, well-worn jacket, jeans and sneakers, Moore haunts Smith's haunts—the Detroit Athletic Club, the Grosse Point Yacht Club, the GM world headquarters—and gets tossed out at every turn. It's like David Letterman vs. General Electric, except Moore has a serious beef.

"Roger & Me" is a lot more than "Roger Avoids Me." As if the city fathers were eager to furnish material for a rookie film maker's zany satire, Flint flaunted its folly and decadence before Moore's camera. The swells throw a "Great Gatsby" party and hire lucky members of the hoi polloi to serve as "human statues." Homegrown TV host Bob Eubanks presents a special round of "the Newlywed Game" to lift civic spirits (and unaccountably allows himself to be filmed telling truly tasteless jokes offstage).

Pat Boone, who used to croon "See the USA in Your Chevrolet," advises laid-off GM workers to seek their fortune with Amway. Kaye Lani Rae Rafko, Miss Michigan and future Miss America, lends her beauteous presence to a parade commemorating a sit-down strike. Millions in public funds are squandered on a luxury hotel and the astoundingly ill-conceived AutoWorld theme park as Flint tries to retool as a tourist mecca. Meanwhile, a sheriff's deputy tours the city, evicting lay-off victims from their homes.

"Roger & Me" is hilarious. "Roger & Me" is angry. After the screening, someone asked Moore if "Roger & Me" is also "subversive."

"It's legal," he replied. "Torching GM headquarters is not legal."

But you can bet Roger's feet are feeling the fire.

NEWSDAY, 12/20/89, Part II/p. 5, Terry Kelleher

Michael Moore's "Roger & Me," first seen here three months ago at the New York Film Festival, is a low-low-budget documentary about the crushing impact of General Motors plant closings on Flint, Mich.

Strangely enough, it's also a strong candidate for most entertaining movie of 1989.

Moore, the former editor of Mother Jones and the Michigan Voice, clearly aims to clobber a callous GM as personified by its board chairman, Roger Smith. But ridicule is what knocks the corporate giant silly. This radical fights the power with humor. A Flint native, Moore figured it would be an eye-opener for Smith if the GM poobah accompanied him on a tour of the now-devastated city where the auto company was born. But Smith proved inaccessible behind a dense human shield of public-relations types. So "Roger & Me" became the filmed record of a quest. The paunchy, populistically attired Moore haunts Smith's posh haunts and gets tossed out at every turn. It's like David Letterman vs. General Electric, except Moore has a serious beef.

"Roger & Me" is more than "Roger Avoids Me." As if eager to furnish material for a rookie filmmaker's zany satire, the city fathers of Flint flaunted their folly and decadence before Moore's camera. See their incredibly ill-conceived schemes to revive the town's economy and lift its spirits. Hear visiting celebrities such as Pat Boone and Bob ("Newlywed Game") Eubanks utter remarks of surpassing stupidity. You'll laugh. You'll hoot. And you won't forget to get angry.

Recent revisionist criticism of "Roger & Me" in Film Comment magazine has charged Moore with deceptive editing. Be that as it may, the end product is a gas.

TIME, 1/8/90, p. 77, Richard Schickel

Michael Moore is a funny man—and also an angry one. But when you've seen this movie, you have to wonder: Is he entirely honest? One hates to raise this question, since anyone who is willing to run bingo games to help finance his movie has the makings of a folk hero. Especially when his completed picture becomes the talk of the film-festival circuit and achieves what few documentaries ever do: distribution by a major studio, which is said to have paid $2 million for the privilege.

The metaphor through which Moore explores several serious social, political and economic issues is his hometown, Flint, Mich., a boom-and-bust factory community that hit bottom again in the mid-'80s, when its principal employer, General Motors, began a series of layoffs that, according to Moore, eventually cost the city some 35,000 jobs. This created a ripple effect afflicting, it would seem, almost every other business, almost every citizen.

The Roger of the title is Roger Smith, GM's chairman, and the central conceit of the film is Moore's desire to take Smith on a tour of Flint to show him the havoc he has wrought. To this end, Moore and his film crew stalk Smith, showing up and asking to see him at GM headquarters, at the Detroit Athletic Club and at another club, where Smith is not even a member. This leads to a number of funny-edgy encounters with puzzled receptionists and security personnel. At one point Moore flashes a Chuck E. Cheese card as identification.

The scenes of life in Flint constitute the best part of the movie. Pat Boone and Anita Bryant come through, singing inspirational songs and uttering fatuities for Moore's camera. Game-show host (and Flint native) Bob Eubanks does his weary routine and very possibly kills what is left of a fringe career by telling two disgusting jokes to the inquiring reporter. Kaye Lani Rae Rafko, a Miss Michigan who is soon to be Miss America, flashes false smiles and desperately changes the subject when Moore asks her to comment on local conditions. Meantime, the more substantial citizenry gets behind new construction that is supposed to revitalize Flint—a Hyatt Regency, a mall, an automobile museum. They all fail.

As a tragicomic essay on the powerlessness of traditional American boosterism in the face of true economic cataclysm, *Roger & Me* succeeds hilariously—and sometimes poignantly. But it has a number of bothersome aspects. One is its treatment of the cataclysm itself. GM's layoffs were not as extensive or precipitate as Moore suggests, and many of the failed civic-improvement plans were begun years before the firings. But it may be that Moore's largest untruth involves his own screen persona. He would have us see him as a sort of Rust Belt Garrison Keillor, innocent but natively shrewd.

But wait a minute! Far from being a hick, Moore is an experienced professional journalist who knows perfectly well that getting in to see the chairman of anything without an appointment is virtually impossible. He is thus not simply recording reality but imposing on it a fictional design that proves the predetermined point he wants to make. And that makes the viewer wonder about his smash-and-grab intrusions on other realities throughout the film. It may be that his truth is the truth about his subject. And no doubt he is a smart and cheeky inheritor of the great grumbling populist tradition. Too bad he inherited the demagogic side of that tradition too.

VILLAGE VOICE, 10/3/89, p. 61, J. Hoberman

Roger & Me, Michael Moore's enormously engaging documentary, addresses itself more directly to ways by which history awards some speaking parts and consigns the rest of us to be extras.

The movie's ostensible subject is Flint, Michigan—birthplace not only of Moore but the United Automobile Workers of America. Strategically personalizing his material, Moore briefly evokes his childhood and stormy stint as editor of *Mother Jones*. The loss of the latter position sent him back home just as General Motors shut 11 factories, threw 30,000 workers on the scrap heap, and inspired his attempt to bring GM Chairman Roger Smith to Flint for a documentary film.

Working the same circle of postindustrial hell as Tony Buba, the documentary-celebrant of the equally depressed Braddock PA, Moore makes a disarming Virgil. You can't get more vox populi than this heavyset guy in a baseball cap making one unsuccessful attempt after another to penetrate GM headquarters or the Detroit Athletic Club—the sense of turf-conscious class warfare accentuated by the evictions that serve as the movie's grim running joke.

Funny and demagogic, *Roger & Me* comes closer than any documentary I've seen to offering an overview of the past decade. The film opens by harking back 30-odd years to the golden age of working-class prosperity and, although Ronald Reagan only drops in briefly to share a ceremonial pizza with a group of unemployed auto workers, his surrogates are everywhere. The movie swarms with vapid TV personalities and patriotic cheerleaders, and Moore's metaphors for the class struggle can be effectively mordant. Factories close and Taco Bells proliferate; Flint's proletariat work as human statues, sell their blood, raise bunny rabbits for food. As Flint becomes the most violent city in America, crime control becomes the major growth industry, and the more adaptable of the laid-off find work as jailers for the rest.

In a desperate Reaganite ploy, Flint attempts to reinvent itself as a tourist attraction. The city fathers subsidize a luxury Hyatt hotel and squander $100 million on an indoor theme park where the attractions include a miniaturized version of the old downtown, and an auto worker singing a love song to the robot that has replaced him on the assembly line. Everything fails. Flint finishes last in *Money* magazine's list of America's 300 most desirable places to live, while a *Nightline* exposé is aborted just before airtime when the show's equipment truck is hijacked by an unemployed worker. By the end of the movie, even GM's tireless local lobbyist is laid off.

Roger & Me is everything *Mother Jones* isn't—gutsy, populist, outraged, and outrageous. Still, the critique of Reaganism cuts two ways. Moore makes shameless use of Christmas and frequently lays on irony with a trowel. The Toronto Film Festival audience with whom I saw the movie loved the spectacle of American kooks and American degeneration. Indeed, the only place where they might not appreciate this comic operetta *Kapital* would probably be the Hungary of *The Documentator*.

VILLAGE VOICE, 12/26/89, p. 102, Georgia Brown

Roger & Me was hailed in these pages when it played the New York Film Festival in September, but it is now opening at Cinema 2. The "me" in the title—for those who haven't read any magazine lately—is Michael Moore, who may look like a hulking, sloppy bear, but who has impeccable comic timing and amazing grace when it comes to filmmaking footwork. He also has a documentary subject here that he knows like the back of his hand—his hometown, Flint, Michigan, population 150,000 and shrinking.

"Roger" is Moore's archnemesis, Roger Smith, chairman of General Motors and the man Moore insists—for the purposes of the film—on holding responsible for the gradual demolition of Flint, once proud birthplace of the UAW. As a whimsical narrative device, Moore dogs the well-insulated Smith, trying to coax him down from his 14th-floor penthouse so he can just *see* what the loss of 30,000 jobs has wrought. This fiction gives Moore a narrative to hang his I'm-out-for-Trout hat on, while it reinforces a point about the growing gap during the Reagan reign between haves and have-nots. The quest for Roger is interwoven with a series of poignant evictions by a philosophical city marshal.

The hilarious part of *Roger & Me* (I haven't laughed so hard since *The Naked Gun*) is the tour Moore provides of dear old Flint, which was voted by *Money* magazine next to last on its list of livable cities. Narrating in his nasal, nerdy midwestern twang ("I was kind of a strange child"), Moore weaves old footage (home movies and newsreels) with new, as he and his crew butt into various private and civic outings. These include a downtown parade in which Miss Michigan (soon to be Miss America) does a good deal to discredit the minds of beauty queens, and a county fair where native son Bob Eubanks (*The Newlywed Game*) discredits himself.

Moore's movie is so wonderfully fresh, rich, and passionate, I was sorry to learn that he doctors chronology to "improve" his story. (Harlan Jacobson's contentious interview with Moore in the current *Film Comment* provides details.) It's interesting that in his September *New York Times* rave, Vincent Canby, comparing Moore to Mark Twain and Artemus Ward, had Moore pegged: "Mr. Moore makes no attempt to be fair. Playing fair is for college football; in social criticism anything goes. ..." I don't know what Mr. Canby's reaction is to the new information, but to my mind it's one thing to play fair with Roger Smith and another to play fair with the audience.

Also reviewed in:

NATION, 10/30/89, p. 505, Stuart Klawans
NEW REPUBLIC, 1/22/90, p. 27, Stanley Kauffmann
NEW YORK TIMES, 12/20/89, p. C18, Vincent Canby
NEW YORKER, 1/8/90, p. 91, Pauline Kael
VARIETY, 9/13-19/89, p. 36
WASHINGTON POST, 1/12/90, p. D1, Hal Hinson
WASHINGTON POST, 1/12/90, Weekend/p. 40, Desson Howe

ROMANCE

An Embrafilme/S.B. Porducoes Cinematograficas production. *Director:* Sergio Bianchi. *Screenplay (Portuguese with English subtitles):* Fernando Coni Campos, Mário Carneiro, Caio Fernando de Abreu, Cristina Santeiro, Suzana Semedo, and Claudia Maradei. *Director of Photography:* Marcelo Coutinho. *Editor:* Marilia Alvim. *Music:* Chance. *Running Time:* 103 minutes. *MPAA Rating:* Not Rated.

WITH: Rodrigo Santiago, Imara Reis, Hugo Della Santa, Isa Kopelman, Cristina Mutarelli, Sergio Mamberti, and Beatriz Segall.

VILLAGE VOICE, 3/28/89, p. 64, Manohla Dargis

In Sergio Bianchi's bleak portrait of contemporary Brazil, political impotence is signaled by unchecked state corruption, racism, poverty, and AIDS. Three friends of a prominent activist try to find meaning in their lives after he unexpectedly dies. But because *Romance* is a allegorical tale of '80s despair in the wake of the unfulfilled promise of the '60s, each friend in turn must eventually self-destruct—a disappointing failure, in a film with some promise, to recognize that suicide is as much a totalizing myth as romatic idealism.

Also reviewed in:
NEW YORK TIMES, 3/23/89, p. C16, Janet Maslin
VARIETY, 10/19/88, p. 239

ROMERO

A Four Seasons Entertainment release of a Paulist Pictures production. *Executive Producer:* Lawrence Mortorff and John Sacret Young. *Producer:* Rev. Ellwood E. Kieser. *Director:* John Duigan. *Screenplay:* John Sacret Young. *Director of Photography:* Geoff Burton. *Editor:* Frans Vandenburg. *Music:* Gabriel Yared. *Production Designer:* Roger Ford. *Stunt Coordinator:* Angel de la Peña. *Running Time:* 105 minutes. *MPAA Rating:* PG-13.

CAST: Raul Julia (Archbishop Oscar Arnulfo Romero); Richard Jordan (Rev. Rutilio Grande); Ana Alicia (Arista Zelada); Eddie Velez (Lieutenant Columa); Alejandro Bracho (Rev. Alfonzo Osuna); Tony Plana (Rev. Manuel Morantes); Harold Gould (Francisco Galedo); Lucy Reina (Lucia); Al Ruscio (Bishop Estrada); Tony Perez (Father Rafael Villez); Robert Viharo (Colonel Ernesto Dorio); Harold Cannon-Lopez (General Humberto); Claudio Brook (Bishop Flores); Martin Lasalle (Bishop Rivera Y Damas); Eduardo Lopez Rojas (Bishop Cordova); Paco Mauri (Salvador Ramos); Ruben Rojo (Archbishop Chavez); Omar Rodriguez (Rafael Zelada); Juan Pelaez (Ernesto Claramount); José Antonio Estrada (Man with Photo Album); Ivan Carbajal Gonzalez (Chavo Ramos); Sandra Carbajal Gonzalez (Virginia Ramos); Hector Herrera (Alvaro Morazon); Guy De Saint Cyr (Master Sergeant); René Pereyra (Cigarette Man); Joaquin Garrido (Presidential Aide); Alfredo Lara (Señor Lemus); Jair De Rubin (Rutilio Lemus); Evangelina Elizondo (Josephina Galedo); José Chavez Trowe (Don Manuel); Isela Diaz (Girl in Trash Dump); David Carbajal Gonzalez (Boy in Trash Dump); Arturo Rodriguez Doring (Juan).

CINEASTE, Vol. XVII, No. 4, 1990, p. 46, Dennis West and Joan West

Romero is the screen biography of Oscar Romero, the martyred Catholic archbishop of El Salvador. The film examines the final three years of Romero's life, 1977–1980, which in El Salvador was a period of increasing government repression and a prelude to civil war. Romero was known as a shy and orthodox clertic when he was named archbishop in 1977; but he soon underwent a conversion and became an outspoken and influential advocate for the Latin American Church's "preferential option for the poor," for social justice, and for an end to the savage repression routinely inflicted on the poor by the oligarchy and an unrestrained military. One day after publicly calling on soldiers to disobey sinful orders to murder their fellow countrymen, the archbishop, while celebrating mass, was shot by a right wing assassin.

To bring Romero's story to the screen, producer Ellwood E. Kieser obtained financing from a number of Catholic organizations, including the Paulist Fathers; and the film is billed as a Paulist Pictures Production. Since *Romero* was made under Catholic auspices, it is not surprising that Father Kieser, screenwriter John Sacret Young, and director John Duigan have tailored their esthetic approach to fit a traditional Catholic literary genre, the saint's life. Indeed, many

Salvadorans were quick to see that Romero's ministry and death represented the makings of sainthood; and popular belief has already unofficially canonized this remarkable figure.

The filmmakers loosely follow the conventional patterns of hagiographical narration by examining the three phases of Romero's life that demonstrate his saintliness: the conditions under which he takes office; his ministry and conversion; and his exemplary death. Romero, dedicated but unexceptional, is called to extraordinary service as archbishop against a backdrop of social discontent and clerical squabbling. The new archbishop's ministry is punctuated by events of escalating violence that increasingly attack not only those dear to him but the Church itself. Raul Julia's finely nuanced performance convincingly captures the intense anguish and spiritual struggle that these incidents provoke in the conscience of this cautious, conservative, and naive priest as he is slowly converted into a determined and eloquent activist. In the final phase of this modern saint's tale, the assassin's bullet arrests the archbishop's life at the instant the communion chalice reaches its zenith. Cup and human body are suspended for an instant in time before both crash, in slow motion, to the ground, thus mingling Romero's blood with the communion wine, the symbolic blood of Christ.

As befits a traditional martyr's tale, the film suggests parallels between the career of the Salvadoran cleric and that of Jesus Christ. Romero preaches to the masses; and he reclaims a church from secular forces (the military) that have invaded it, just as Jesus expelled the money-changers from the Temple. Jesus resisted the devil's temptations, and the archbishop refuses to be tempted by solutions that contradict his fundamental religious beliefs and duties. He refuses to align himself with either the power and money of the military and the oligarchy, or with the violence of those who, like Father Morantes, urge taking up arms in order to achieve justice for the poor.

There is no Garden of Gethsemane in San Salvador to which Romero can retreat. Instead, we see him stumbling along a desolate road to the spot where three crosses commemorate the murder (depicted in harrowing detail early in the film) of his friend and fellow priest, Rutilio Grande. The ensuing monolgoue announces the archbishop's decision to drink the same bitter cup offered Jesus: Romero chooses to serve his faith, even at the cost of his life. The prelate emerges from his desert meditation into the hands of modern centurions from the National Guard, who proceed to mock him and strip him of his cassock.

Although *Romero* is a modern example of hagiography, it does not end with accounts of miracles wrought by the venerated figure, as the traditional tales do. Instead, the film closes with an inspirational citation from one of Romero's homilies that miraculously links his death to a future victory over oppression: "If they kill me, I shall arise in the Salvadoran people. Let my blood be a seed of freedom. ... A bishop will die, but the Church of God, which is the people, will never perish."

Like the writers of traditional saints' lives, the filmmakers have conceived of their protagonist as reflecting Christ's life and God's will. This approach to characterization allows the filmmakers to glorify the individual and bend historical facts, just as traditional hagiography did. A key scene in *Romero* shows the jailed archbishop traumatized by the screams of the tortured, but the historical Romero was never imprisoned in El Salvador. In another important scene, Romero is subjected to machine gun fire as he attempts to collect the host in a church occupied by soldiers. In reality, Romero ordered a subordinate to undertake that mission. *Romero*'s glorification of the individual also means that the sociopolitical context and the struggles of the ordinary flesh-and-blood folk are subordinated to the all-consuming artistic task of creating a mythical image of a modern-day saint.

As a modern saint's life, *Romero* is a success. Although this approach has bent the historical facts, it nevertheless captures the spirit of Romero's actions and a sense of his widespread support amongst the poor. And by centering their dramatic narrative around a single individual and using other traditional features of mainstream cinema, the filmmakers have made an easily accessible feature that brings news of the desperate sociopolitical situation in El Salvador to a wide audience in the United States.

FILMS IN REVIEW, 11/89, p. 552, Eva H. Kissen

Romero is stirring film about the Archbishop of El Salvador, Oscar Romero, who was assassinated in 1980 as he celebrated mass. His was a political murder: the previous day he had preached a sermon against the establishment urging the military to control the raging violence and sadistic repression throughout the country.

The film is the story of the evolution of this "mouse of a man, a deeply flawed, traditional churchman, rigid, frightened and neurotic" according to Paulist Priest, Father Kieser, producer of the film, who went to Salvadore to interview Romero's former colleagues who made these comments about him.

In the wake of a manipulated Central American election, Romero was selected as Archbishop by the local powers precisely because he was the quiet, bookish type who appeared to be a safe choice. As Archbishop, Romero had to deal with the church itself, the government, and the white Spanish upper class who were part of that government. In addition, he was pulled between these conservative forces and the more active radical priests who felt a profound obligation to the starving Indian population. Furthermore, he had to come to grips with his own essentially conservative nature.

The murder of his friend and colleague, Father Grande, a radical priest, the disappearance of other non-conformists, the death of seventy innocent people during a public communion, the discovery of mass graves, the transformation of a church into a barracks, and the deliberate destruction of the Blessed Sacrament served to open the conservative Archbishop to the flagrant injustice around him. Quiet, thoughtful Romero began to sense the People's need. "You are our voice," one ancient battered Indian woman pleaded.

"There he was—at a turning point in history—a flawed, psychologically scarred human being who, faced with great responsibility and evil happenings in his country, decided he could no longer remain silent. He knew he had to stand up—and by doing it, he was seriously risking his life," said Father Kieser. Consequently, the newly aware and outspoken Archbishop became a danger to the establishment—and had to be eradicated along with the rest of the opposition.

The Archbishop is remarkably well played by Raul Julia, an actor of enormous versatility and sensibility, who was, incidentally, educated by the Jesuits in his native Puerto Rico. This role appears to have tapped unexplored depths in him resulting in a resonant and moving performance. Julia himself is convinced of Romero's commitment to man and God. "He saw God everywhere. For him, God was the people, I'm sure he will be canonized by the Roman Catholic Church, whether it's twenty-five or fifty years from now, doesn't matter."

Other strong performances include Richard Jordan and Alejandro Bracho who play the radical priests. Ana Alicia is also convincing as the torn liberal aristocrat who loses her husband through the junta's arrogance but refuses to have her baby baptized with Indians infants.

The film, shot in Mexico, and ably directed by John Duigan, an Australian filmmaker, has something of the quality of a Rivera mural brought to life. It focusses on the scarred and frequently toothless faces of the peasants and their deep religious hunger. The kindly Archbishop, stripped of his vestments by the military, is almost a Christ figure to them. These peasants, as well as the cold green uniformed hit squads of the militia, constantly fingering their machine guns, give substance and texture to the film. Father Kieser, the producer-priest, (a Paulist priest whose missions are to serve those outside the church), has produced spiritual entertainment for television before making this movie. For his first big film, he collected money from various Catholic sources in order to produce what he considered something of a mission. This mission is a success. Whatever your politics or religion, you will be moved by its quality and sincerity.

LOS ANGELES TIMES, 9/8/89, Calendar/p. 1, Kevin Thomas

"Romero" has the good fortune to have Raul Julia in the title role as the martyred Salvadoran archbishop, but his solid portrayal, a work of simplicity and concentration, cannot redeem a film that in too many crucial ways goes wrong.

"Romero" is an especially poignant example of noble intention done in by misguided means, for Julia invests the archbishop with a spirituality that few heroes of conventional films with religious themes possess.

Much to his surprise, mild-mannered Monsignor Oscar Romero in 1977 is named Archbishop of San Salvador. Some of his colleagues, who identify with the country's ultra-conservative ruling class, predict that he will not make waves despite the rapidly escalating oppression and brutality of the new Humberto regime. The mindless savagery unleashed by the military on the helpless and the innocent is too much for Romero to ignore. Drawing upon his faith as a devout man of God, he gradually emerges as an implacable leader of the opposition, having decided that God's law must transcend that of man.

Writer John Sacret Young and Australian director John Duigan, in his American film debut, sketch the outlines of Romero's fate and its implications for the relationship between church and state clearly enough, but with breadth rather than depth. Although the film does unfold with the requisite sense of tragic inevitability, thanks to Julia, nothing else about it rings true, even though what is depicted is depressingly credible, drawn as it is from recent, terrible (and ongoing) events.

The sad truth is that the film is trite in its dialogue as well as in its direction and is seriously marred by the disastrous miscasting of a key role. Underlying all these flaws is the pervading sense that the film, cursed with the synthetic quality that typically characterizes productions with international casts and crews, really has no business being in English in the first place.

This feeling is reinforced by the fact that the film doesn't deal with the role of the American government in El Salvador's plight, beyond a plea from Romero for us to stop sending arms that will be only used against his country's people. The role of the Vatican in El Salvador is soft-pedaled even more. Cultural imperialism, in the form of materialistic U.S. values and life styles, is noted only in passing, and there's no addressing at all of why Latin American political struggles always seem to involve such extreme acts of cruelty.

One has to wonder why its producer, Paulist priest Father Ellwood E. Kieser, didn't let us experience a Salvadoran film maker's vision of the country's seemingly unending tragedy. Surely the audience that is concerned enough with Central America to be attracted to Romero's story is sufficiently sophisticated to sit still for subtitles. Surely, too, the film would be more appealing to Latino audiences were it in Spanish.

Again excepting Julia, the actors are pedestrian or worse. As a fiery activist priest called Father Rutilio Grande, Richard Jordan looks about as Latino as Robert Redford; it's no help that his Spanish accent is so erratic. The dozens of native extras—the film was shot in Mexico—are terribly self-conscious and often seemingly perplexed. Clearly, Duigan, one of the least-known and most gifted of Australian directors, is way out of his element. Such wonderful films as "Mouth to Mouth," "The Winter of Our Dreams" and "The Year My Voice Broke" show him to be a master of the intimate rather than the epic, and his usual rapport with actors fails him here, except with Julia.

Julia, who brings more to Romero than the script does, seems to draw strength and inspiration from the very solitary man he is portraying. "Romero" (rated PG-13 for violence and bloodshed) is of greatest interest as a study of a skilled professional actor going about his business no matter what. When you should be experiencing a sense of universality in the plight of Archbishop Romero, you may instead find yourself being impressed with Julia's ability to bring passion and meaning to clichés.

MONTHLY FILM BULLETIN, 2/90, p. 49, Farrah Anwar

El Salvador, 1977. On the day of what is promised to be a free and democratic election, the scholastic Monsignor Oscar Romero joins his more gregarious and outspoken friend Father Grande, who himself leads voters past a National Guard roadblock, commanded by Lieutenant Columa. Although General Humberto's election as president comes as no surprise, the appointment of Romero as archbishop in San Salvador does. At a ceremony, Romero is congratulated by many of the landowning aristocrats, including Francisco Galedo; also present are Galedo's daughter Arista and her husband Rafael Zelada (Minister of Agriculture), who present Romero with a gift. The celebrations are interrupted by a dishevelled Father Grande, who announces the massacre that has just taken place among crowds outside the cathedral. He also suggests to Romero that his loyalties should lie with the peasants rather than the rich guests. A few days later, Grande is himself shot dead, and a troubled Romero proposes that a funeral mass be held for the dead (which doesn't receive the support of all his fellow bishops). Soon after, Arista tells the archbishop that her husband has been kidnapped and, offering to mediate, Romero is told that Rafael will be released if Humberto frees his political prisoners. But the president denies the existence of such prisoners; Rafael's body is later recovered from the lava beds, and one of Romero's younger colleagues, Father Osuna, is seized and tortured by Columa on suspicion of being involved in the kidnapping. Romero secures his release, and then gatecrashes a presidential lunch party to declare Humberto a liar when he denies the existence of death squads. As a punishment, Father Grande's church is occupied by the army and the altar shot to pieces as Romero tries to rescue the sacrament. Another confrontation with Columa and his men, as they arrest a group of priests and villagers seeking sanctuary in the church, leads to Romero's own arrest. Released soon after with an apology for the "mistake", Romero roams the villages distractedly seeking divine guidance. When he learns of the rape and murder of a human rights activist, he determines to use all his influence to stop the killings, and begins making regular radio broadcasts of his outspoken sermons. Columa volunteers one of his men to eliminate the priest, and on March 24, 1980, Romero is murdered while performing mass in the cathedral.

Opening with an overhead shot of Salvadoreans gathered outside their cathedral as anonymous National Guard cameras snap away at the ringleaders, *Romero* inevitably recalls Oliver Stone's *Salvador*, which began with a black-and-white montage of the massacre outside the cathedral. But in place of the piranha-like fury of *Salvador*'s Richard Boyle, *Romero* has to content itself with a far less dramatic protagonist whose morality is beyond doubt. Which may explain why the makers of *Romero*, Paulist Pictures ("Paulists are a Roman Catholic order devoted to spiritually serving all faiths and the agnostic"), seem to have taken *Gandhi* (or even *Beckett*) as their model rather than the more explicitly political *Salvador* or *Under Fire*. An even more conservative bio-pic tradition soon comes to the fore when the first of the film's many "Spanish" accents is sounded by Richard Jordan, and the peasant community is represented strictly as cannon fodder, at the mercy equally of the death squads and the second unit director. The landowning aristocracy is distinctly of the "let them eat tortillas" class, and the collective evils of the military régime are personified by a single figure, Lieutenant Columa, a perfectly smiling villain in U.S. Air Force sunglasses.

The transformation of Romero from a withdrawn "bookish" man to a committed critic of the Salvadorean dictatorship is clumsily telescoped (the murder of Father Grande is crosscut with a lavish dinner party, lingering significantly on a doll with a noose round its neck). Raul Julia has sufficient screen presence to retain a vestigial dignity, but he cannot escape the puerility of exchanges like: "What should I do?"; "What God wants you to do". *Romero* might have worked better as an intimate drama (there is a surfeit of crowd scenes), concentrating instead on the intrigues within the Catholic church that greeted and followed Romero's inauguration as archbishop. Approved by the military hierarchy, his appointment was initially greeted with hostility by many church officials who saw him as a "spiritual" rather than an "activist" leader. However, the scenes dealing with clerical machinations are insultingly simplistic (bishops whisper malignly in dark corners). Equally, there is no explicit reference to American involvement in El Savador, no ambiguous "advisers" to muddy the political picture. Considering Romero's open letter to Jimmy Carter in 1980, criticising his support of the death squads, this is a staggering omission.

NEW YORK POST, 8/25/89, p. 25, David Edelstein

As Romero, the archbishop of El Salvador who was murdered by a right-wing death squad in 1980 (many say on orders of Roberto D'Aubuisson), Raul Julia uses his hulking form gingerly, as if it's barely connected to him. He pulls in his shoulders and walks with his body pitched forward, eyes on the ground; behind his thick glasses those eyes are dull, ill-at-ease with the world. He's painfully ordinary.

"Romero" is the story of an inauspicious character altered by circumstances—of a timid man suddenly forced into the world by events he can't in good conscience ignore. The film is often windy and didactic; what gives it complexity (and power) is that it's as much a religious story as a political one. It's about a man who gets the call.

A compromise candidate in 1977 to be archbishop, he's chosen because he won't make waves (the Church thinks) and because he moves among the wealthy and powerful. Romero begins his tenure with a sermon suggesting that certain priests (among them his friend Rutilio Grande, played by Richard Jordan) express their radical ideas too glibly.

Later, when those people are attacked, tortured and killed by the government, he knows he has no choice but to join them—even if that means alienating the people who shower him with gifts and protect him.

Romero never embraces liberation theology, and is unsuited by temperament for civil disobedience. That's why he's a compelling figure—he's at war with his own personality. When defying the military he moves slowly, as if in pain, and the film turns him into a Christ-like figure; near the end, he spends a night walking the desert, praying for a sign.

Julia—so fiery an actor that he can often be monotonous on screen (he lacks variety)—is remarkably effective for most of the film. He speaks deliberately, and there's tension in his restraint: his silences and wary posture are eloquently helpless. Only in the last half-hour—when the director moves the camera too close and lets him scream—do his mannerisms return.

It's no surprise "Romero" has its clunky side. There's a stilted, agit-prop discussion group in the first scene that makes you dread the rest of the picture. And when a left-wing priest and some children ride along a dirt road, the camera lingers too long on their smiling faces. You know they're going to be ambushed.

The film is also hurt by the fact that it's in English (and the fact that English doesn't roll naturally off the tongues of its actors, especially in the peasant roles). It's hard to hear dialogue that sounds like bad Robert Bolt delivered as if it has been memorized phonetically.

On balance, though, "Romero" hits home. You don't have to be a Marxist to believe that the United States (under not just Reagan but Carter) helped to finance the murders of thousands of innocent Salvadorans. And you don't have to be a liberation theologist to be inspired by Romero's example. His only text was the New Testament.

NEWSDAY, 8/25/89, Part III/p. 5, Drew Fetherston

In the past, heroic religious martyrs usually ended up as plaster saints.

In "Romero," the medium is celluloid film rather than plaster, but the effect is quite the same: The martyr, drained of humanity, is propped up to deliver a homily.

It is really too bad, because this film about Archbishop Oscar Romero, murdered in 1980 by right-wing gunmen as he said mass in El Salvador, is driven by the most noble intentions. Indeed, as a documentary-drama about the horrifying violence in El Salvador, it is strong and moving. As a homily on the evils of political repression and the seductiveness of temporal power, it is reasonably effective.

But as a drama about a man's struggle against that seduction and repression, as well as his own fear, "Romero" is unimpressive melodrama. The same must be said of its examination of liberation theology, as practiced by several of the secondary characters in the film.

To be sure, it would have been miraculous had the makers been able to capture such social and personal complexity in 105 minutes of film. Romero's political conversion was nothing sudden like that of St. Paul on the road to Damascus; this was a cautious, conservative man who awoke slowly to duty and righteousness. The film's makers (the Rev. Ellwood Kieser, a Roman Catholic priest, organized Paulist Pictures Inc. to produce "Romero") may be congratulated for recognizing the ambiguities in its central character, if not for dealing with them effectively.

Raul Julia has trouble portraying Romero as a morally empty vessel who comes to be filled with outrage at the bestial treatment of poor people. His Romero is merely calm and thoughtful; he hardly seems aware of the horrors about him until they come very close indeed.

Romero's evolution takes so long that the film is left little time to examine other characters or Salvadoran society. The activist priests whose deaths and tortures contribute to his conversion are more symbol than mortal: One is anguished and saintly, another angry and committed to armed struggle. Although they have names, the film has no time to give them full identities.

The suffering masses remain just that; there is no time at all to give them any individuality. The best the film can do is to linger on faces filled with extraordinary character; these portraits are moving, but cannot substitute for real character development. Acts of incredible heroism in the film—men and women stepping forward to face brutal repression, certain torture and likely death—are performed by ciphers.

One attempt is made to individualize the horror; a young woman who works for human rights is raped, tortured and murdered. It is symptomatic of the film's problems that we hardly get to know her, that we never discover more than her first name.

The evil and snakelike oligarchs actually come off a bit better, in that their hatefulness is more memorable than the saintliness of those they persecute.

For all this, "Romero" does not fail in its effort to show the real horror perpetrated by the faceless death squads; real photographs of real young faces ripped apart by bullets are shown. These nightmare images of torn, no-longer-human faces speak with an eloquence otherwise absent in "Romero."

VILLAGE VOICE, 8/29/89, p. 71, Coco Fusco

A few days before I saw *Romero*, Channel 41 (Mexican Univision) broadcast a special news report that featured El Salvador's former president José Napoleon Duarte claiming that he witnessed radical right-winger Roberto D'Aubuisson plot the murder of the martyred archbishop. Funny how it took the ailing ex-leader nine years to remember. Still, no single murder or disappearance in El Salvador's decade-long civil war has had as much impact. Oscar Romero was too prominent, too much a part of El Salvador's public image. Though he remains a pawn in the ruling elite's power struggles, he has become a symbol, in death as in life, of a victimized Salvadoran majority and an embattled church.

The story of how this bookish, traditionally-minded Jesuit became the voice of reason and compassion in a violently divided country might provide the ingredients for a good movie, but not the guarantee. Australian director John Duigan's version is picturesque but disappointingly wooden. Produced by a priest and backed by the Paulist order, *Romero* is long on piety but short on spirit. It's the kind of movie that would like to be a Cecil B. DeMille epic, but comes off instead like a scaled-down version for Sunday morning TV.

The action begins in 1977, just as Romero is appointed archbishop. The political differences dividing the country are also dividing the church—his colleagues dispute the role of the institution in the face of mounting strife. Romero's more progressive associates would like him to take a public stand on state-sponsored attacks against innocent campesinos. The obscenely wealthy elite assumes he is on its side and bears him expensive gifts. A rather predictable cycle develops in which an atrocity occurs, Romero is called on to respond, and with each event he grows more outspoken. Massacres, kidnappings, and the torture and killing of priests take place, all involving people Romero knows personally, but it's a guardsman's open attack on the sacred Eucharist in an army-occupied church that finally tips the scales and transforms Romero into a liberationist, and ultimately a sacrificial lamb.

Raul Julia's valiant effort to create some of Romero's rather lackluster personality is the film's most convincing performance. The rest of the international cast sticks to soap opera-style grandstanding with their belabored, and annoyingly fake, Spanish-accented English (what I'd call a linguistic version of Taco Bell), rivaled in awkwardness only by the Mexican extras' "Lorde haf maircee"'s. But they are all stuck with a didactic and contrived script that allows no character any interiority and plants polemical rhetoric in every mouth.

Even in war, people do occasionally talk about something besides land reform and violence. And though the filmmaker might like us to believe him, not even the most radical priest will carry a rifle. Harsh realities push everyone to extremes, but this heavy-handed drama stretches things past their limits. It will probably lose the most sympathetic followers along the way.

Also reviewed in:
NEW REPUBLIC, 9/11/89, p. 26, Stanley Kauffmann
NEW YORK TIMES, 8/25/89, p. C15, Vincent Canby
VARIETY, 6/7-13/89, p. 30
WASHINGTON POST, 9/8/89, p. B7, Hal Hinson

ROOF TOPS

A New Visions Pictures release of a Koch Company production in association with Mark/Jett Productions. *Executive Producer:* Taylor Hackford and Stuart Benjamin. *Producer:* Howard W. Koch Jr. *Director:* Robert Wise. *Screenplay:* Terence Brennan. *Based on a story by:* Allan Goldstein and Tony Mark. *Director of Photography:* Theo Van de Sande. *Editor:* William Reynolds. *Music:* David A. Stewart and Michael Kamen. *Choreographer:* John Carrafa and Jelon Vieira. *Production Designer:* Jeannine Oppewall. *Costumes:* Kathleen Detoro. *Running time:* 95 minutes. *MPAA Rating:* R.

CAST: Jason Gedrick (T); Troy Beyer (Elana); Eddie Velez (Lobo); Tisha Campbell (Amber); Alexis Cruz (Squeak); Allen Payne (Kadim); Steve Love (Jackie-Sky); Rafael Baez (Raphael): Jamie Tirelli (Officer Rivera); Luis Guzman (Martinez); Millie Tirelli (Squeak's Mom); Robert La Sardo (Blade); Jay M. Boryea (Willie); Rockets Redglare (Carlos); Edouardo De Soto (Angelo Sanjos); John Canada Terrell (Junkie Cop); Bruce Smolanoff (Bones); Edythe Jason (Lois); Paul Herman (Jimmy); Lauren Tom (Audry); Stuart Rudin (Wino); Robert Weil (Hotel Clerk); Coley Wallace (Lester); José Yñoa (Young Cook); Danny O'Shea (Rookie Narc); Herb Kerr III (Jorge, Capoeirista); Kurt Lott (Zit); Peter Lopez (Burn); Jed Jame (X); Woodrow Asai (Yard Foreman); Angelo Florio (Cop at Dance); Imani Parks (Older Sister).

LOS ANGELES TIMES, 3/17/89, Calendar/p. 4, Kevin Thomas

Robert Wise's "Rooftops," a vibrant romantic fable, takes us into Manhattan's Alphabet City, that section of derelict Beaux Arts apartment buildings lining Avenues A, B, C and D and their cross streets on the Lower East Side. It is an area inhabited mainly by improverished minorities, and it is menaced by drug traffic (and also by gentrification, but that's not part of this movie). Writer Terence Brennan tells us of a group of young people, alone in the world, who have made their homes on the roofs of abandoned structures. "Good view, low rent, plenty of light," says one girl of her makeshift home. "Just what everybody in this city wants."

On a nearby rooftop the young man known only as "T" (Jason Gedrick) has made a cozy retreat in an old water tower and supports himself from whatever he can strip from the old structures and sell as scrap. "T" and the young people who surround him are all decent, self-reliant kids who are struggling to survive without succumbing to the quick money of prostitution or drugs. Of course they are constantly endangered, in particular by the cool and deadly dealer Lobo (Eddie Velez). It is his beautiful cousin Elana (Troy Beyer) who attracts "T."

Since Wise was the director of the multi-Oscared "West Side Story" it's tempting to call this his "Lower East Side Story." But "Rooftops" is not quite a musical in the sense that its people break into song, yet Wise shrewdly directs it as if it were a musical. This is a leaner, smaller-scaled film than "West Side Story," but it has the same driving tempo and vitality. Elana and "T" and their friends are essentially figures in a ballet in which the motif is set by the "combat dance." It is derived from the Brazilian martial arts discipline known as Capoeira, a self-defense tactic disguised as a dance and brought by slaves to Brazil in the 16th Century.

"Rooftops" represents a gratifying collaboration between seasoned pros and much younger talent on both sides of the camera. Production designer Jeannine C. Oppewall and cameraman Theo Van de Sande give the film an unsparing natural look, an approach that could easily bulldoze the film's essentially fairy-tale plot. But Wise and his distinguished editor (and frequent collaborator) William Reynolds bring to the story a rigorous sense of structure and pace; indeed, just as the actors seem choreographed rather than directed—even when they're not dancing—the film itself seems shaped, even sculpted, so that tension evolves from a fantasy being played out boldly against urban locales at their grittiest.

Wise's youthful, great-looking cast exudes talent and energy. Gedrick, who has just taken over as leading man in the Broadway revival of "Our Town," is a splendid hero, understated but no more to be messed with than Dirty Harry, and Beyer, who is probably best known for her role as Diahann Carroll's daughter on "Dynasty," is a poised beauty. Tisha Campbell is her dynamic best friend, and Alexis Cruz is the "Artful Dodger" of the plot, a gifted, diminutive graffiti muralist whose own long coat sports some of his best work. With David Stewart and Michael Kamen's intoxicating score and John Carrafa and Jelon Vieira's crisp choreography it's no wonder "Rooftops" (rated R for language, some violence) has such zing.

MONTHLY FILM BULLETIN, 2/90, p. 50, Richard Combs

In the area of New York known as Alphabet City, a number of dispossessed teenagers have made their homes on the roofs of derelict tenements: the orphaned T, one-time prostitute Amber, and the younger Squeak, a graffiti-ist still trying to carve out his own place. At a night-time party in the streets, where the new vogue is non-touch "combat dancing", T is greeted by his other friends, the deaf-mute punk Jackie Sky, and the strong but pacific Kadim (who looks after his broken-down ex-boxer father), and is quickly attracted to Elena Sanjos. But there are also crack dealers on the block, led by the vicious Santiago ("Lobo"), a cousin of Elena's who forces her to work for him as a lookout (she is also caring for an invalid father). Lobo decides to set up his "crack house" in T's tenement, and throws the latter out, wrecking his water-tower home and rooftop garden in the process. When undercover police led by Rivera, who have been keeping an eye on Lobo, raid the house, Lobo assumes T is responsible (the dealers, warned by Elena, manage to flush away their dope in time). T and Elena make their way back to the water tower, and barely escape a fire set by one of Lobo's men. T takes instruction from Brazilian *capoeiristas*, to whom he is introduced by Squeak and whose style of combat dancing was evolved by slaves as a secret form of self-defence. But he is beaten up when Lobo and his men come looking for him and threaten Squeak; recuperating in Amber's "crib", T tells Elena how he lost his parents (his mother was killed accidentally after a quarrel and his father committed suicide). Squeak, meanwhile, having failed to drive his mother's obnoxious lover Martinez out of their house, repairs to the rooftops and is outraged when he finds Lobo setting up another crack house in the adjacent building. In a fight, Squeak is thrown to his death, and T sets out alone to confront the dealers. Elena rounds up Amber, Jackie Sky and Kadim, and together they defeat Lobo's gang. After a bruising fight, T lures Lobo on to a weakened section of roof, and the latter falls through to his death.

"With *West Side Story*, the opening sequence was an attempt to establish a sense of reality, but also to take a look beyond reality". The sequence to which Robert Wise is referring (M.F.B., November 1979) is, of course, the film's introduction to New York, the grid of city streets shot from directly overhead so that, although "real" enough, it is striking mainly because it is simultaneously so geometric and abstract. Which says something about the necessarily perverse and contrary way one establishes a sense of reality in a genre so stylised as the musical—and also about the connection between low-key realism, the story as a narrative "street plan", and stylistic abstraction in Wise's films generally. To which *Rooftops*, coming ten years after Wise's last film, the first and most interesting *Star Trek*, and nearly thirty after *West Side Story*, might have added some novelty, some stylistic after-thoughts or curlicues, even an elegiac note of "finis", since it is actually set far above the streets of New York. It is largely composed of aerial views; it comprises an "aerial" world, the makeshift one its dispossessed characters have created on the tenement roofs of Alphabet City. Abstraction and reality willingly enough rub shoulders here, abetted of course by the abundant graffiti art which decorates the rubble.

But if the film makes the most of its settings, it unfortunately has little to "ground" it in any other department. The story and characters have the sentimental simplicity of a musical: "good" rooftop kids eventually banding together to drive out the crack dealers who try to take over their block. But one or two dance sequences and the busy soundtrack aside, it is not a musical, and there is surprisingly little choreographic flair, or narrative street-planning, in the way the action sequences are laid out, the circling of the kids, the crack dealers and the undercover police keeping tabs on and trying (ineffectually) to bust the latter through this cruelly derelict territory. As well as an unrealised musical, there is a potential science-fiction quality in the setting, where everyone is so assiduously, and naively, without many visible means of support, trying to make a "home" out of such an inhospitable landscape. The two genres, in other words, to which Wise's stylised realism best lends itself meet in the context of the softest teen romance and the hoariest clichés of the deprived-kids-making-our-alone scenario.

The best that can be said of the film in these respects is that they are also spelled out in the barest, not-quite-abstract detail. The reasons why muscular Kadim is so unwilling to help out in a brawl are indicated in one scene with his broken-down ex-boxer father in a flophouse hotel, and the sympathetic social-worker role that would have been *de rigueur* in this kind of film in the 50s (where it often seems to belong) is only taken up in a token way by sympathetic cop Rivera. The "combat dancing" especially invented for the film, by Twyla Tharp alumnus John Carrafa ("We wanted something new, different and unique that would also express what the characters are feeling": producer Howard Koch) is featured in two isolated sequences, and doesn't prove much help when actual combatants are armed with guns and knives. It is given an awkward historical justification when T is taken to a Brazilian night-club and shown the martial-arts dance *capoeira* (the means developed by slaves for defending themselves while seeming not to). Why this should come as a revelation to the hero, when these New York street kids seem to have thought up *capoeira* all by themselves, only adds confusion to the simplifications.

NEW YORK POST, 3/18/89, p.19, Jami Bernard

The kids of New York who have been tossed out by their parents and are now nesting in lean-tos on the rooftops of the Lower East Side have a secret weapon against the drug dealers—it's a Brazilian slave dance that can kick a person's eye out.

Anyway, that is the idea in the stylized world of "Rooftops," a lame-brained but lively looking movie that was filmed on actual rooftops here. It seems doubtful that there's really such a community of good-looking, hard-working teens who live in pigeon coops and water towers and are working to clean up the neighborhood, or surely we would have heard about them by now from New York Magazine.

When the kids have too much pent-up energy, they challenge each other to a dance—a kind of cross between Bruce Lee and the Flying Wallendas, on the parapets high above Alphabet City.

Jason Gedrick ("Stacking," "The Promised Land") plays T, a reluctant hero, the only white kid in the bunch and the natural leader of all the dispossessed. Grafitti artist Squeak looks up to him, ex-hooker Amber (Tisha Campbell) wants a date with him, and Lobo the local pusher wants him dead.

T sells scrap metal for a living, so he has plenty of spare time to hook up with a troupe of Brazilian dancers who teach him to protect himself with *capoeira*, a dance that presumably the slaves invented so they could protect themselves while manacled. The dance looks pretty interesting—too bad there isn't more of it, or more of it used to better effect. The Brazilians are shot in a choppy style that undercuts the grace and choreography of the dance.

Meanwhile, T has fallen in love with the new kid on the block, Elana (Troy Beyer), a slinkfest of a girl who works as a lookout for her cousin Lobo, the evil drug dealer.

The subject of Elana raises that age-old question: Why do cute girls wear midriff blouses when there's heavy action going down? Wouldn't they be more comfortable in sweats when they're running for their lives, escaping flaming water towers, jumping from roof to roof and exploring abandoned buildings?

Something to ponder. Anyway, Elana is Hispanic and T is not, but if any of this sounds like a sort of updated "West Side Story," forget it. Robert Wise, who directed "WSS," must have won the helm of "Rooftops" in a gambling debt or something. Sure, there's music and street toughs and forbidden love, but except for the colorful look and the location shooting, this is an assembly line war-on-pushers story, with bad guys who are so malignant you don't even like their hair.

Jason Gedrick is adorably earnest as the strong, silent, homeless type; he'll probably survive this and still be on covers of teen magazines.

Meanwhile, as athletic as it looks, I don't think the Brazilian slave number is going to stop many of the city's pushers. Folks, do not try these moves at home.

NEWSDAY, 3/18/89, Part II/p. 15, Lynn Darling

There weren't a whole lot of advance screenings for "Rooftops"—that's why this review is appearing the day after the movie opened. That's usually a bad sign in terms of a movie's possibilities, a fact I mentioned to someone involved in the film's publicity. No, no, no, she assured me. It's just that there was this feeling that a bunch of stuffy middle-aged critics can't relate to heartwarming young people's movie like "Rooftops."

Well, of course, I respect that attitude, so, as a public service and in the interest of fairness, I've included the comments of some of the more vociferous guests at the screening I attended. They were all certified Young People, and their comments appear in parentheses.

"Rooftops" is the story of a group of young people trying to make new lives for themselves amid the abandoned buildings of the Lower East Side. Most of them can't live at home. Amber's mother is a prostitute, Squeak's mother lives with a violent lout who beats her, and T's parents are dead—Mom was electrocuted in an alcoholic quarrel with Dad, who subsequently hanged himself.

But the kids are all right—their makeshift digs have a nice, charming, picturesque look to them, and there's always money for food and spray paint. After all, their living arrangements have a "good view, low rent and plenty of light. Just what everybody in this city wants," as Amber (Tisha Campbell) puts it. (*"Where's the heat, whadda ya do for heat?"*) When they get bored they can always go to the parking lot, where there's beer and people to flirt with. There's also a platform on which the young men engage in a form of combat dancing in which they can get out all their aggressions without ever laying a finger on one another or messing up their outfits (*"When's somebody gonna hit somebody?"*) "I wish these night's could last forever," sighs Squeak (Alexis Cruz).

Sure there's crime—one kid lifts a battery out of a parked car. (*"No way man, car in that condition, battery woulda been gone a long time ago."*) And there are bad guys, like the villainous Lobo (Eddie Velez), a drug overlord who likes to beat up on the nice young kids living in the buildings he's turning into crack houses. When beating them up doesn't work, he tries shooting at them, though with a notable lack of success. (*"Only six bullets? Come on, man, how you supposed to feel safe with six bullets?"*)

Well, anyway, T (Jason Gedrick) falls in love with Lobo's cousin, Elana (Troy Beyer) and after many vicissitudes they do enjoy a few romantic moments together. (*"It's about time. I thought she was never gonna take that shirt off."*) After awhile, the kids even manage to band together to fight a tense and climatic battle with Lobo. (*"That guy's suit's so ugly he deserves to die."*)

Despite an engaging cast of attractive young actors, "Rooftops" is drenched in such unrealistic sentimentality and dime-store nobility that it seems to take place in a time machine. The movie was directed by Robert Wise, who won an Academy Award for "West Side Story," and who certainly knows better. Or maybe it's just that you can't romanticize this stuff anymore, especially when you don't have Jerome Robbins and Leonard Bernstein to back you up.

Also reviewed in:
NEW YORK TIMES, 3/18/89, p. 16, Richard Bernstein
VARIETY, 3/22-28/89, p. 22
WASHINGTON POST, 3/18/89, p. C14, Hal Hinson

RORRET

A New Yorker Films release of a Nuova Dimensione production in association with RAI-TV Channel 1. *Director:* Fulvio Wetzl. *Screenplay (Italian with English subtitles):* Fulvio Wetzl and Enzo Capua. *Director of Photography:* Carlo Cerchio. *Editor:* Massimo Palumbo Cardella. *Music:* Florian Schneider and Ferruccio Busoni. *Art Director:* Bruno Rapisarda. *Costumes:* Alessandra Montagna. *Running Time:* 105 minutes. *MPAA Rating:* Not Rated.

CAST: Lou Castel (Rorret); Anna Galiena (Barbara); Massimo Venturiello (Carlo); Enrica Rosso (Sara); Rossana Coggiola (Sheila) Patrizia Punzo (Cecilia).

NEW YORK POST, 2/8/89, p. 25, Jami Bernard

Director Fulvio Wetzl once worked at a movie theater where he would watch the films from behind the screen as he rear-projected them. Wetzl takes this concept one—okay, maybe two—steps further in the wittily macabre "Rorret," about a voyeuristic theater owner who victimizes his female audience.

"Rorret" is an intellectual treat for fans of film noir. Wetzl recreates and embellishes key scenes from such terror classics as "Psycho," "Dail M for Murder," even "Bunny Lake is Missing." For instance, the shower scene from "Psycho" is done in a high-tech dolly shot around the perimeter of the stall, turning the cross-hatch of the titles into the bars of a cage.

Rorret—yes, backwards it spells "terror"—is the iconoclastic owner of the aptly named Peeping Tom Cinema. He communicates with his newly hired projectionist (Massimo Venturiello) only by telephone, secretly living on a theatrical set behind the stage curtain. Not only can he watch the films in reverse image from his side of the screen, he can also peep through the curtains to catch the audience reaction to his favorite scenes of terror.

And terror is the only thing on the bill at the Peeping Tom. "Cinema of Terror," "Terror in a Mirror," "Blood in the Shower" are some of the titles on the marquee.

Once Rorret (Lou Castel) has spied a likely candidate from the audience, he stalks her and strangles her to death—but not before they've had a little date. Like the roller-coaster ride with Sheila (and remember, "Strangers on a Train" also had an amusement-park murder). "It was beautiful to be frightened. Explosive," says Rorret after the ride.

"It's like making love," replies Sheila. "You start by being frightened, and you end up exhausted."

Actually, Sheila ends up more dead than exhausted, her corpse discarded among the other bloody artifacts in the House of Horrors.

There are more fun dates on Rorret's social calendar. He spies a woman in the audience one night taking pictures of the screen. A fellow fear-ophile! Rorret pursues the woman, an artist who uses the photos as models for her work on canvas. This woman introduces Rorret to a game of Let's Scare Each Other to Death. Rorret wins.

Despite its subject matter, "Rorret" is not a slice-&-dice movie, nor is it particularly scary. Lovingly filled with film-noir "in" jokes, it's more of a comment on film as an illusion of reality. In the world of the Peeping Tom Cinema, only the celluloid is real (Rorret even tries to slit his wrists with the stuff at one point).

Film is so real, in fact, that later, when the screen rolls up, and Rorret stages a live and deadly drama, the audience laughs. Reality is too labored and obvious to take seriously. Only an actress, whose profession it is to feign terror, can possibly beat Rorret at his own game.

The movie also pays homage to such film-noir staples as voyeurism and fetishism, and such film-buff staples as the movie theater as holy temple. With its filmic allusions and its leering taste for the macabre, "Rorret" is good, creepy fun.

NEWSDAY, 2/8/89, Part II/p. 7, Lynn Darling

"Rorret" is a deliciously macabre movie that manages a difficult feat—a clever sendup of a genre almost too ubiquitous to be spoofed, the movie is also a visually entertaining and often thought-provoking exploration of the erotic and manipulative qualities of fear.

Director Fulvio Wetzl fills his own movie with loving recreations of some of most famous examples of the horror film—"Psycho," "Dial M for Murder" "Strangers on a Train," among others, and never gets flattened by the competition. He's having too much fun with the rich vein he's tapped to take himself too seriously.

Rorret is an unassuming psychopath who owns the Peeping Tom, a Roman movie theater devoted exclusively to horror films. He lives in an opulent apartment behind the screen and likes to spend his time peering out from the curtain at his audiences—studying the rapt faces in the dark for the one woman who seems most consumed by her fear.

Rorret is obsessed by fear—he likes to talk about it, he likes to provoke it. The women he chooses to pursue like to talk about it too. Being afraid is like making love, says one of them, after an exhilarating ride on a roller coaster. "In the beginning you are afraid and you end up exhausted."

Actually, she ends up dead, strangled in the amusement park's haunted house while Rorret moves on to his next moment of madness. All of his victims, of course, are beautiful women who tend to dress sexily in brilliant silks and to display a little too much curiosity about the erotic possibilities of terror.

Rorret meets his match finally in a loony actress who shares some of his fascinations—unfortunately at that point the movie tends to get a little too clever and to lose its pace in an overdose of Italian style psychobabble and thematic overreaching. But by then, it's possible to spot this movie a bit of patience—Wetzl's recreations of horror's greatest cinematic hits are always engaging and his camera's sense of style and color make up for the occasional overripe enthusiasms of a man clearly drunk on movies.

VILLAGE VOICE, 2/14/89, p. 70, Stuart Klawans

True cinephiles, the ones who get that puzzled look when confronted by anything life-size and three-dimensional, will want to hurry to see Fulvio Wetzl's *Rorret*. To put it simply, this is a film about looking at films—though it does not stay that simple for long.

Joseph Rorret (Lou Castel) is the reclusive proprietor of Rome's Peeping Tom Cinema, a movie house built in the vaulted crypts of a deconsecrated church. Rorret literally lives behind the screen, passing his time either sleeping on a leather sofa or watching, in reverse, whatever classic of suspense is being projected for his customers on the other side. They *always* see a classic of suspense, because that's all Rorret shows: *Psycho*, *Strangers on a Train*, *Dail M for Murder*, and (needless to say) *Peeping Tom*. Whenever one of these films reaches a climax, Rorret—dressed like Peter Lorre in *M*—pokes his head through a curtain and spies on the women in the audience, panting with pleasure at the sight of them squirming in fear.

So, to revise the definition: *Rorret* is a film about you, the audience, looking at a man looking at women looking at films. There are moments when this intricate-sounding premise sends off sparks—not the lightning bolts of Hitchcock, perhaps, but the pleasurable sizzle of a short circuit in the viewer's brain. That's what happens, for example, when a woman in the audience starts photographing the screen during a showing of *Peeping Tom*, just as the murderer in that film is photographing one of his victims.

But, for the most part, the premise of *Rorret*, like its re-creations of famous scenes from movie history, is more interesting to talk about than to sit through. That's because Wetzl, who seems to me a shade more clever than talented, has finally chosen not to make a suspense film. Instead, *Rorret* is a self-conscious commentary on suspense films, or perhaps an obsessive reenactment of them, drained of the feelings of guilt, desire, and fear of exposure that give the genre its life. As narrative, the film seems slack and sometimes clumsy, and, despite Castel's best efforts to put some flesh on his character, the role of Rorret is strangely desexualized. You get the impression that he spies on women not because it gets him hot but because that's what the folks in the Film Studies Program told him a good psychopath should do.

By this point, you may have noticed that Rorret's name is *terror* spelled backward. Sorry to say, all the other reversals in *Rorret* are about as deeply meaningful as the title.

Also reviewed in:
NEW YORK TIMES, 2/8/89, p. C24, Vincent Canby
VARIETY, 3/9/88, p. 11

ROUGE OF THE NORTH

A Central Motion Picture Company film. *Executive Producer:* James Y. Liu. *Producer:* Lin Tung-fei. *Director:* Fred Tan. *Screenplay (Chinese with English subtitles):* Fred Tan. *Based on the novel by:* Eileen Chang. *Director of Photography:* Yang Wei-han. *Editor:* Chen Po-wen. *Music:* Peter Chang. *Sound:* Duh Duu-jy. *Art Director:* Chow Chi-liang. *Costumes:* Lu Shi-chi. *Running Time:* 106 minutes. *MPAA Rating:* Not Rated.

CAST: Hsia Wen-shi (Ying-ti); Hsu Ming (Mr. 3, Ying-ti's Lover); Kao Chieh (Mr. 2, Ying-ti's Husband); Ma Shao-chun (Yu-shi, Ying-ti's Son); Emily Chang (Chi-show, Yu-shi's 1st Wife); Chang Yu-ling (Tung-mei, Yu-shi's 2nd Wife); Hu Shian-ping (Ying-ti's Brother); Ting Yeh-tien (Ying-ti's Sister-in-Law); Kwan Yi (Old Mrs. Yao, Mother of Mr. 1 & 2); Wu Yien (Matchmaker #1); Li Ying (Old Mr. 9, Reader of the Will); Shirley Chen (Mrs. Pu, Ying-ti's Friend); Hsiao Ai (Mrs. 3); Lin Mei-ling (Mrs. 1); Lu Shi-chi (Boy at Chinese Opera).

VILLAGE VOICE, 3/21/89, p. 64, Georgia Brown

No matter that Ying-Ti fancies the druggist's son; Auntie Wu arranges a match with No. 2 son of the rich Yao family. Mr. 2, as he's called, happens to be a blind hunchback with polio and asthma. The by now familiar donnée for Chinese movies—the barbarism of arranged marriages—becomes excruciatingly creaky soap opera in the hands of director Fred Tan. Opening in 1910 Shanghai, the film takes us on into the arranged marriage of Ying-Ti's own son. *His* wife turns out to have TB and, worse fate, thick lips—"thick enough to make pork chops," frets the cross, opium-addicted Ying-Ti.

Also reviewed in:
NEW YORK TIMES, 3/17/89, p. C5, Richard Bernstein
VARIETY, 5/25/88, p. 19

RUDE AWAKENING

An Orion Pictures release of an Aaron Russo Entertainment production. *Producer:* Aaron Russo. *Director:* Aaron Russo and David Greenwalt. *Screenplay:* Neil Levy and Richard LaGravenese. *Story:* Neil Levy. *Director of Photography:* Tim Sigel. *Editor:* Paul Fried. *Music:* Jonathan Elias. *Music Editor:* Greg Sheldon. *Sound:* Bill Daly. *Sound Editor:* Greg Sheldon. *Production Designer:* Mel Bourne. *Art Director:* Dan Davis. *Set Decorator:* Carol Nast. *Special Effects:* Barnaby Jackson and Gary Zeller. *Costumes:* Peggy Farrell. *Make-up:* Leslie Fuller. *Stunt Coordinator:* Jery Hewitt. *Running Time:* 100 minutes. *MPAA Rating:* R.

CAST: Dion Anderson (Dr. Binibon); Peter Boyden (Dr. Childs); Nicholas Wyman (Dr. Albert); Michael Luciano (Merlin); Cheech Marin (Hesus); Eric Roberts (Fred); Robert Carradine (Sammy); Amy Glass (Twin #1); Becky Glass (Twin #2); Julie Hagerty (Petra); Cliff DeYoung (Brubaker); Ed Fry (Agent Drome); Louise Lasser (Ronnie); Aaron Russo (Voice of Fish); Patrick John Hurley and Daniel Chapman (Agents in Jungle); William C. Carraro (Agent on Street); David Peel and Greg Rex (Hippy Singers); Timothy Leary, Jerry Rubin, and Bobby Seale (Diners at Ronnie's); Peter Nevargic (Julian); Elzbieta Czyzewska (Eema); William C. Paulson (Phil); Larry Attile (Agent Blandish); Tom Sizemore (Ian); Frederikke Borge (Mona); Deena Levy (Wanda); Kevin Dornan (Jay); Davidson Thomson (Amos); Cindy Williams (June); Timothy L. Halpern (Lance); Rodney Clark (Cowboy); Andrea Martin (April); Buck Henry (Lloyd); John Rowe and Brad Tatum (Students at School); B.J. Jefferson (Newscaster); Mark Lewis (Faculty Member); Basia McCoy (Woman on Street); Dave King (Yuppie); Edward Hyland (Man at Newsstand); David Eigenberg (Lawrence); Mitchell Riggs (Seth); Hugh Hayes, Michelle Hurd, and Dulcy Rogers (Students on Street).

FILMS IN REVIEW, 11/89, p. 553, Ken Hanke

Nothing about *Rude Awakening* is nearly as rude as the abuse that has unfairly been heaped upon this good-hearted, surprisingly thoughtful little film, which is, I suppose, not unexpected for a film that spells liberal with a capital "L" these days. Despite the widely held (mis)perception—warmly endorsed by those who sport bumper stickers calling them "public enemy no. 1"—that the media are dyed-in-the-wool pinkos, the vast majority are savvy businessmen, quite willing to blow with whatever wind happens to be coming their way. That, however, cannot be said of screenwriters Neil Levy and Richard LaGravenese, nor producer-director Aaron Russo, nor co-director David Greenwalt, who have been fashioned the kind of truly liberal-minded work that lip-service liberals like Steven Spielberg only talk about while churning out the same life-is-just-a-bowl-of-cherries claptrap. That the film they have made is rough-edged and occasionally messy—much like the '60s "Invasion Films" from Britain from which it draws its inspiration—is less significant than the fact that they had the nerve to make it at all. But bluntly, this is one film that will *not* be ordered up for a screening at the White House. In a world where people can be whipped into a frenzy over someone putting a match to a piece of multi-colored cloth, but can't be made to worry a damn over human beings sitting in parking lots holding signs that read, "I will work for food," *Rude Awakening*, whatever its shortcomings, is a work much needed, but little wanted.

Truth to tell, *Rude Awakening* isn't just a film with a heart in the right place. Rather, it is a generally professional looking work that manages to make its points within a nicely paced comedic framework. Twenty years ago that mightn't have seemed like a major accomplishment in and of itself, but today even mindless comic films are rarely well paced, if paced at all, so a comedy with both purpose and pacing in 1989 comes across as an achievement nearly equal to parting the Red Sea. From the opening credit montage of images from the '60s (people like Timothy Leary and Allen Ginsburg hold the screen while Bob Dylan takes the soundtrack) to the ending credits bouncing ball singalong of the Beatles' "Revolution" (going a long way toward removing the bad taste left by copyright holder Michael Jackson selling the rights to a yuppified tennis shoe company for a TV commercial), *Rude Awakening* moves at a good clip in an admirably straight line.

The plot of the film is fairly simplistic—'60s idealistic radicals Eric Roberts and Cheech Marin flee psychotic Mills Brothers worshipping FBI agent Cliff DeYoung for the jungles of Central America where they set up commune life. Into this laidback life 20 years later come the CIA and the secret plans for the US to start a covert war. Armed with this information, the boys head homeward, certain of their ability to stop this with the righteous indignation of the American people when they learn the truth. The idea, of course, is that the humor will arise from the "rude awakening" they have when encountering not only 1989 America on the whole, but their sold out old friends—and humor does arise from this, but, apart from Cheech's drug deliriums (he's the victim of a government administered overdose of LSD in a *Clockwork Orange*ish experiment that left him a sweet tempered flake with occasional flashes of insight, along with a penchant for conversing with non-existent talking fish (given voice by Russo) and Louise Lasser's aging earht mother, the humor is of the creepiest kind because it's just too true to be funny. Julie Hagerty has a marvelous scene where she outlines the events of the past 20 years, while doing battle with the apparently child-proof cap on a container of ice cream, that is quite funny because of her delivery and the comic byplay. The slow realization of the less than glowing "accomplishments" of those passing years, however, makes the scene ultimately as unsettling as it is funny. The same is true of Buck Henry's brief turn as Lloyd Stooles, a co-op approval committee representative, who happens to be in the process of deciding whether or not soldout hippie Robert Carradine and his insanely upwardly mobile wife (Cindy Williams) can buy into his building when our heroes (with a not wholly willing Hagerty in tow) descend upon their old friend to evade the FBI. Henry's absurd notion that they can accomplish their mission by writing their congressman is funny enough until we learn the reason for his belief in the approach: that he once prevented the building of shelter for the homeless in his neighborhood with one phone call to his congressman. "The system works!" he cries joyfully, and the innate nastiness of the whole concept turns the laughter very bitter indeed.

Throughout the film, Roberts and Cheech are presented as almost magical creatures, able to penetrate not just the sold-out shells that have formed around their old friends, but those of virtually anyone they encounter. (Immune to their charms, of course, is the FBI, as well as Lasser's Nouveau Woodstock yuppie restaurant clientele, who bask in fake nostalgia for a fraudulent '60s, but are horrified to the point of nausea by genuine '60s types Cheech and Roberts.) Thankfully, the film has the wit to stop short of being worshipful of them, arriving at the conclusion that by hiding out for 20 years they soldout just as much as did Hagerty and Carradine. Their old friends may have done nothing about AIDS, the homeless, the ozone layer, the erosion of civil rights, etc., but neither have they. Dropping out and staying stoned for 20 years is just as bad as going mainstream, the film wisely says. (Ironically, it is left to the burnt-out Cheech to put them all back on track with the idea that moaning over the past isn't as important as is what they do *now*.) Even so, Roberts' speech to a seemingly uncaring mob of NYU students is a moving plea for a return to active idealism—made more so by the chilling fact that the speech seems to affect no one.

The most disturbing aspect of the film—and the true "rude awakening" of the title (as much for us as the characters)—is the public reaction to the idea of this covert war once the news gets out. A quick series of man-in-the-street interviews says it all. "We haven't won one in so long that I think a war we could win might be nice," volunteers an elderly lady. "I'm a liberal Republican myself," states a man, who goes on to outline his plan for a war fought by the homeless! With the public so behind it the war not only proceeds, but the draft is reinstated, and our heroes must face the fact that they have brought about the very things they wished to prevent. Unfortunately, all this (borrowed to some extent from the 1933 Wheeler and Woolsey film, *Diplomaniacs*) happens just a little too fast to quite work as it should. The unsettling truth beneath it all comes through, but the effect should come as a slap in the face, and instead it's merely a chilly shiver. It's something, but not enough. Surprisingly, the *Meet John Doe*-like ending where a few people from the NYU speech scene show up to rescue Roberts from his near suicidal depression works quite well, being both moving and uplifting. Alas, the uplift is a bittersweet one. Like the reception the film itself has received, the number of believers is so small that the task before them seems hopeless, and the film wisely decides to end with Cheech talking to the fish before heading into its "Revolution" credits. At bottom, *Rude Awakening* is a brave gesture that seems to realize the apparent futility of that gesture. But as brave gestures go, it's a helluva try.

LOS ANGELES TIMES, 8/16/89, Calendar/p. 9, Kevin Thomas

Imagine a movie about a pair of hippie radicals, cut off from the world for 20 years, suddenly being whisked to present-day Manhattan. Former "Saturday Night Live" writer Neil Levy took this idea to producer Aaron Russo, who in turn worked with Levy and Richard LaGravenese to develop the endearing but uneven "Rude Awakening."

Levy and LaGravenese have come up with some of the funniest and most inspired comic moments of any picture released this year, but Russo, in tandem with co-director David Greenwalt, should have resisted making his directorial debut with so highly verbal and complex script. Co-directors Russo (who produced such hits as "The Rose" and "Trading Places") and Greenwalt (a writer with "Secret Admirer" and two Disney Sunday Night Movies as his directorial credits) are unable to give satire the crisp form and sharp pacing it needs to hit the mark squarely. "Rude Awakening" is more enjoyable than many slicker but less ambitious films, yet it could have been so much better.

Eric Roberts and Cheech Marin are Fred and Hesus, a couple of long-haired Greenwich Village anti-war protesters who take flight to the fictional Central American country of Managuador, where they establish a commune, refusing all contact with the outside world. Inevitably, the turmoil in Central America overtakes them, with a dying American agent entrusting to Fred top-secret papers outlining an American plan for invading Managuador. "It's Vietnam all over," exclaims Fred, who immediately departs for Manhattan, where he intends somehow to stop the war. Accompanying him is Hesus, a comical pothead still hallucinating from a long-ago government LSD experiment.

Fred's old girlfriend, Petra (Julie Hagerty), a quintessential flower child, has now become Princess Petra, a shrill, neurasthenic fashion designer with a $2-million co-op. Hagerty is deliciously zany, but the one time the film comes together and really clicks is when Petra, Fred and Hesus descend upon another old friend, Sammy (Robert Carradine), a businessman who makes $300,000 a year with his chain of tanning salons.

It just so happens that Sammy and his wife, June (Cindy Williams), are in the midst of a crucial interview with a couple (Andrea Martin, Buck Henry) who are to pass on their suitability for an apartment in an exclusive co-op. This sequence is high farce, as good as anything in "Arthur." Henry, Martin, Williams and Carradine put a fresh, hilarious spin on, respectively, the smug ultra-conservative, the falling-down drunk, the up-tight wife and the husband who's trying to control the situation while yielding his sympathies to his old hippie pals.

Nothing that precedes or follows has the tightness and punch of this sequence. The terrific actors and the outrageous dialogue would seem to have fired up Russo and Greenwalt to rise to the occasion. If, otherwise, their pacing is slack, they clearly have rapport with actors, who include Louise Lasser as the radicals' laid-back den mother and Cliff De Young as a frenzied fed. The cast is wonderful, though Roberts, for all his charm and humor, is overly mannered, needing far more control than the directors provide him. The ending of "Rude Awakening" (rated R for blunt language) owes a considerable debt to Frank Capra, "Meet John Doe" in particular, and sad to say, is beyond Russo and Greenwalt's abilities to keep it from foundering in undue sentimentality.

MONTHLY FILM BULLETIN, 3/90, p. 75, Tim Pulleine

New York City, 1969: Hippies Fred and the constantly stoned Hesus are sought by agent Brubaker of the Justice Department for draft evasion and subversive activity. Brubaker is stalled by their landlady Ronnie long enough for the two men to bid farewell to fellow spirits Sammy, an aspiring writer, and Petra, a painter, and make a getaway ... Managuador, 1989: Fred and Hesus are members of a remote, self-sufficient commune, growing their own "grass" and largely out of contact with the outside world. Their circumstances suddenly change when a mortally wounded CIA man staggers into their encampment, and they deduce from secret papers in his possession that the U.S. is planning an invasion of the country. Returning to New York in order to thwart this, they are put under surveillance and soon set their old adversary Brubaker is on their trail. After visiting the Nouveau Woodstock restaurant which Ronnie is now successfully operating, they make contact with Petra, now a big name in TV advertising, who is initially reluctant to admit them to her home. Brubaker and associates arrive, and in an affray Petra is assumed to be in league with the others and duly escapes with them to seek refuge with Sammy, who has abandoned writing for a business career. Their arrival coincides, to the dismay of Sammy's snobbish wife June, with the visit of the pompous Lloyd Stoole and his alcoholic wife April; pandemonium ensues, and in the upshot Sammy opts to leave with the other three. They force an entry to New York University, and subsequently stage a demonstration denouncing the alleged invasion plan. But this meets with an apathetic response, and shortly afterwards Brubaker and cohorts arrive to put paid to further protest. Moreover, the notion of invading Managuador sparks a wave of popular support: headlines proclaim congressional backing, reinstatement of the draft, and declaration of war ... The ex-hippy quartet are thoroughly dejected, but take heart when a group of students approach to seek their help in organising an anti-pollution campaign.

The caricature imagery of pot-smoking, placard-waving 60s "radicalism" in the early sequences of *Rude Awakening* stirs forebodings which prove to be only too well founded. The haphazard, revue-sketch character of the screenplay (it comes as no surprise to find that Neil Levy is an alumnus of *Saturday Night Live*) means that the film is thrown back on such incidental inventions as it can muster. In the event, the annotation of culture shock hardly goes beyond inquiries like "What's valium?" or Petra's identification of housing problems with the burden of having to pay a $2,000 a month maintenance charge for her luxury apartment. The thinness of the "plot", culminating in the ludicrous anticlimax of the off-screen declaration of war, is emphasised by plodding pace and charmless playing, with brief appearances by Buck Henry and Louise Lasser prompting melancholy reminders of their past presence in infinitely superior comedies on not unrelated themes.

NEW YORK POST, 8/16/89, p. 29, David Edelstein

It has been a long time since someone made a pothead comedy about how we've all become cynical and lost our idealism since the heady days of the counterculture. But former rock impresario Aaron Russo has not only financed, produced and co-directed one, he has dedicated it to "all the people who care about the planet and each other...Be good."

Gag me with a hash pipe.

The weird thing is that at its best, "Rude Awakening" is flaky and alive in ways that comedies just aren't in these straighter, more jaded times. And at its worst, it's excruciating—a reminder of why people stopped smoking dope and rattling on about the importance of having ideals.

If you think that sounds like a cop-out then, hey, man, this movie made me so high and then turned into such a downer that I almost couldn't bear to write this review. I'm upset, OK??? Get off my case and I'll tell you about it.

"Rude Awakening" features two filthy, pot-smoking hippies, Fred Wouk (Eric Roberts) and

Hesus (Cheech Marin), who return to Manhattan after 20 years in the jungles of Central America, bearing documents that reveal a forthcoming U.S. invasion of the country of "Managuador."

What a difference two decades make! Their Village hangout is a yuppie restaurant; Fred's spacy artist girlfriend Petra (Julie Hagerty) is a reclusive millionaire clothes designer; their radical buddy Sammy (Robert Carradine) now has a square wife (Cindy Williams) and a chain of tanning salons; and the old rock clubs are now gaudy and high-tech and peopled with SoHo types and investment bankers.

Let's not even talk about how inept this movie is as a piece of storytelling—badly structured, bizarrely paced. None of that matters when the script (by "Saturday Night Live" veteran Neil Levy and Richard LaGravenese) hits its stride and the actors start to cook.

As Wouk (pronounced "Woook"), who was once his commune's charismatic leader, Roberts is (as usual) so overbearing that you don't know how to take him. Yet something in his messy egotism connects with the role. Wouk sees these lost '80s souls and attempts to reinfuse them with his counterculture idealism—he doesn't want to talk with you, he wants to rap with you, man, to connect. He's the kind of guy who's always in your face. Excellent casting.

Cheech Marin—whose Hesus is a casualty of the FBI's LSD experiments—is kept too far in the margins of the plot, but he can still make you laugh like a wasted college sophomore. His scruffy, doper's awe is as fresh as ever—he's the eternal virgin pothead. (But Marin's timing is too sharp to be drug-induced.)

The movie's middle hour is blissfully silly, with some bong-sized laughs. Watch Hagerty attempt to reel off every trend and major happening between 1969 and 1989 while struggling to open a frozen-hard Frusen Gladje container. Bug-eyed, she's insanely focused on her task, yet out of her mouth tumble all the era's traumas—Watergate, Iran, New Coke.

Elsewhere, the directors would have enhanced her performance with editing, but it's hard to blame them for holding on her so long: she's one of the best comic ingenues in movies. And the film boasts two more superb comediennes: Louise Lasser, zaftig now and earthily funny; and Andrea Martin, who gets to cut loose in ways she hasn't since "SCTV."

Martin's scene is the movie's comic hurricane. She and Buck Henry play a conservative couple—the Stooles—who come to Carradine's apartment to interview him and his wife for an exclusive condo, shortly before the surprise arrival of Fred, Hesus and Petra. It's like a classic "Saturday Night Live" sketch, with Martin getting so stewed (to Henry's horror) that she passes into a kind of primordial delirium.

Great moments...Carradine when he hears the voice of his old friend on the phone and goes quiet, everything coming back to him... A brief, riotously matter-of-fact monologue by Tom Sizemore as a financial adviser who takes people's money and instead of investing it, buys art or just gives the (expletive deleted) away...

But when I say "Rude Awakening" goes bad, I'm not joking, big daddy. Instead of accelerating and getting crazier, the movie slows down and becomes more earnest, as the reforged '60s quartet takes over an NYU building and attempts to stir up the student body. The last 20 minutes are in odorama. Seconds before the credits, I found myself stumbling over Joel Siegel (who called me a chicken) to get out the theater and breathe. It was worth being called a chicken by Siegel.

I'm glad I didn't see this movie three months ago, because I'd have bought a gun and ordered Russo and David Greenwalt back into the editing room. You think I'm kidding, but I'd have chained them to their Steenbeck editing table and explained that the '80s gave us the gift of irony, which—in the absence of real eloquence, which is very absent here—can accomplish much more than mushy liberal platitudes.

I'd have told them that idealism (and liberalism) isn't a crime in art, but simplemindedness is. Call me a cockeyed optimist, but I think they'd have listened to me. Or I'd have blown their heads off.

NEWSDAY, 8/16/89, PartII/p. 5, Terry Kelleher

Attention, moviegoers who respond favorably to evocations of that era lossely referred to as "the '60s."

Do you still love the music? Are you stirred by memories of campus protest and the antiwar movement? Do you think America is a more selfish, materialistic country nowadays? Do you think it's high time for a new spirit of activism?

Then you're just the kind of sucker the makers of "Rude Awakening" are looking for.

No, you're not a sucker for holding those views. But you are a viewer who'll give this movie more of a break than it deserves, and you'll probably feel taken when it's over.

Might as well warn you up front: "Rude Awakening" concludes with an inflated dedication ("to all the people who care about the planet and each other") and a follow-the-bouncing-ball sing-along to the Beatles' "Revolution" (as covered by Mike and the Mechanics). It would be hard to forgive even a good movie for ending like this. And "Rude Awakening" is more bummer than blast.

In 1969, two hippies (Eric Roberts and Cheech Marin) go on the lam to avoid arrest for vaguely defined subversive activities. They spend the next two decades in a marijuana-fogged commune in "a small Central American country." When they get hold of "secret papers" detailing a planned U.S. invasion, they head back to New York prepared to tell all, only to find that the peace sign is out, the dollar sign is in, and their former countercultural comrades (Julie Hagerty and Robert Carradine) are totally yuppified.

Anytime "Cheech Marin" and "marijuana" appear in the same paragraph, watch out. Cheech smokes copious dope here, but the major gag is his 20-year hangover from a government experiment in which he was given a massive dose of LSD. Whenever "Rude Awakening" needs a cheap laugh, Cheech has a hallucination. Oh, wow. Oh, no.

The fact is, this comedy has a crying need for laughs at any price. Nothing else in the movie is as funny as those patently fake beards Roberts and Marin sport in the jungle. In a long scene that bids strenuously for hilarity, Buck Henry plays the head of a co-op board judging the fitness of Carradine and his wife (Cindy Williams) to buy into a posh new building. The hippies burst in, to Carradine's embarrassment, and Henry's missus (Andrea Martin) is soon enjoying an intoxicated frolic with Cheech. As if all this weren't sufficiently obvious and belabored, the co-op couple is called the Stooles (rhymes with "fools") and the name is repeated over and over.

Hagerty does well with her changeover from spacy '60s artist to uptight '80s fashion designer, but she melts too easily into her old hippie self when ex-boyfriend Roberts reappears at her side. Roberts' physical attractiveness is properly noted by Hagerty's female friends, but his charisma is much harder to discern. Near the end he improvises a serious political speech that moves Hagerty to tears despite its lack of coherence. We must assume that, like so many Americans, she hears what she wants to hear.

Aaron Russo did it all on "Rude Awakening"—produced, supplanted David Greenwalt as director after shooting had begun, even provided the voice of a fish that talks to Cheech when he's tripping out. The result is a movie that's sluggish of pace and erratic of tone. What "Rude Awakening" has going for it is a sense of sloppy good will, which may be enough for us suckers who are starving for a little peace and love.

NEWSWEEK, 9/4/89, p. 68, David Ansen

What if two hard-core hippie radicals from the '60s (Eric Roberts and Cheech Marin), having spent the last 20 years smoking dope in a Central American commune, were to return to Yuppie Manhattan in 1989 on a mission to stop a war? This promising satirical premise, a kind of Rip van Winkle fable, yields wildly erratic results. Codirected by Aaron Russo and David Greenwalt, "Rude Awakening" has some fun with the greedy, narcissistic '80s—there's a hilarious cameo by Andrea Martin, and Cheech is a hoot. But when it gets speechifyingly earnest about saving the planet you may want to crawl under your seat and hide. It doesn't help that Roberts—an actor with the slippery moves of a used-car salesman—is bizarrely misscast as the idealistic avatar of peace and love. Best wait for the video, when you can fast-forward to the good parts.

VILLAGE VOICE, 8/22/89, p. 86, Amy Taubin

An unrepentant pot smokers' movie, *Rude Awakening* features Eric Roberts and Cheech Marin as Fred and Hesus, two former peace 'n' love communards who return to their old St. Marks Place haunts to save the world, and to remind us that even if hippies were more well-meaning than MBAs, they were just as pushy and self-involved. (The last is my take on what I saw; it clearly isn't what director/producer Aaron Russo had in mind.)

Rude Awakening opens with a flashback to 1969. (The dominant reference in the movie is the student uprisings of '68, but the point of view is straight Woodstock nation. Sorry to be picky.) Confident that the revolution is a fait accompli, but nonetheless paranoid about the FBI, Fred and Hesus take off for Central America, where they spend 20 stoned years with nary a contra in sight. (Russo establishes his cosmetic approach to rule-breaking by allowing his middle-aged actors to play 18-year-olds in SCTV-style—with wrinkles and jowls intact.) Their idyll is shattered when they stumble upon some CIA documents proving that the U.S. has moved its Vietnam operation to somewhere south of Acapulco. "We've got to get back to New York; maybe this time we can stop it," says Fred. Cut to Trumpville.

Strangers in a strange land, Fred and Hesus spend most of their time tracking down their old buddies, who, after some initial confusion about the pair's identity ("I ordered Chinese, not Mexican"), see the error of their ways, throw down their yuppie goods, and follow them. Ronnie (Louise Lasser), earth mother and Rice-a-Roni addict, has become the proprietor of an East Village restaurant, Ronnie's Woodstock ("All God's children welcome: Visa, Mastercard, and American Express"). "Who are these people?" Fred plaintively inquires. If he'd looked carefully, he might've spotted Bobby Seale, Jerry Rubin, and Timothy Leary, just another three suits in the crowd. Flowerchild Petra (Julie Hagerty) is now Fashion Avenue's "Princess Petra." Hagerty has a lovely moment of understated irony when, in her earnest, breathy voice, she enumerates what her ex-squatmates have missed: "There was Watergate and Three Mile Island, acid rain, pollution. . . . We blew a hole in the atmosphere. . . Contragate. . . Then crack came along to give marijuana a bad name. . ."

Buck Henry and Andrea Martin, as a circumspect co-op owner and his alcoholic wife, momentarily raise *Rude Awakening*'s one-note nostalgia into a comedy of manners. There are also good bits from Cliff DeYoung as the dogged FBI man, Robert Carradine as a manifesto-writer-turned-tanning-salon-proprietor ("How do you get the sun to shine only on the ones who pay?" puzzles Hesus), and Cindy Williams as his social-climbing wife.

Sweet as it mostly is, *Rude Awakening* is definitely retarded in its sexual politics. When Hagerty explains that AIDS is "a sort of scourge-of-God plague," and then melts at the touch of a real man's hand, rediscovering that nothing beats being someone's old lady, then 20-years-in-the-jungle starts to look like a pretext for keeping machismo intact.

In this classically structured boys-get-revolution, boys-lose-revolution, boys-find-revolution movie, Fred and Hesus discover that while you still can't trust most over-30s, there's a whole generation of 16-year-olds out there ready to have a go at changing the world. Not one for self-criticism, Russo has a sentimental belief that history can repeat itself, which undermines a potentially prescient farce.

Also reviewed in:
NEW YORK TIMES, 8/16/89, p. C19, Vincent Canby
VARIETY, 8/16–22/89, p. 23
WASHINGTON POST, 8/16/89, p. D10, Rita Kempley

SAND AND BLOOD

A New Yorker Films release of a Septembre Productions/Films A2/La Sept co-production in association with Images Investissements with the cooperation of the Centre National de la Cinématographie. *Producer:* Jean Nainchrik. *Director:* Jeanne Labrune. *Screenplay (French with English subtitles):* Jeanne Labrune. *Director of Photography:* André Néau. *Editor:* Nadine Fischer. *Music:* Anne-Marie Fijal and Nina Corti. *Sound:* Eric Devulder and Jacques-Thomas Gérard. *Set Designer:* Patrice Mercier. *Running time:* 101 Minutes. *MPAA Rating:* Not Rated.

CAST: Sami Frey (Manuel Vasquez); Patrick Catalifo (Francisco Almeira); André Dussollier (Emilio); Clémentine Célarié (Marion Vasquez); Maria Casarés (Dolores Vasquez, Manuel's Mother); Catherine Rouvel (Carmina, Francisco's Mother); Stephane Albouy (Marlo); Camille Grandville (Annie), Pierre Forget (Francisco's Father).

NEW YORK POST, 12/20/89, p. 25, Jami Bernard

Several people throw up during the course of "Sand and Blood," and if you have a weak stomach or a love of animals, you'll be tempted to join them. Sand gets short shrift in this sensuous-looking French film, but blood is in huge supply as a succession of bulls are graphically mutilated in close-up.

Bullfighting is a ritual that many equate with proof of masculinity (but then, so is guzzling beer). In "Sand and Blood," the bull appears to symbolize something Larger Than That, don't ask me what.

Manuel Vasquez (Sami Frey) is a cultured, violin-playing doctor who has a morbid aversion to bullfights because his grandfather was slaughtered in a *corrida* by Franco's men. Strange then that he lives in Nimes, one of the only places in France where they practice bullfighting.

Then there's the handsome young toreador Francisco (Patrick Catalifo), who without his bullfighting skills would be just another slave on the assembly line at the slaughterhouse, like his younger brother. The only difference in the work is the level of finesse.

One man is a healer, the other a torturer. The two men meet cute when Manuel treats Francisco for a wound, and they begin a mysteriously compelling friendship that implies homosexuality, mainly because director Jeanne Labrune films the whole thing—even the brutal bullfight scenes—in a wonderfully sensual, provocative way.

All that doesn't make the film one bit more comprehensible. As the doctor confronts his past, the toreador learns humanity, and at the end—I hope this isn't spoiling it for you—the two men idly contemplate an old bull who just happens to be wandering by. But that's European films for you.

Frey and Catalifo are very good, and the film is a visual treat (including quite a bit of Catalifo in the nude, and I mean *very* nude). But some of the bullring scenes are truly sickening. If animals must die so that we may have art films, then they'd better be *great* art films.

NEWSDAY, 12/20/89, Part II/p. 5, Mike McGrady

Bullfighting and movies don't mix—at least they never have, not in this country. The problem: If a movie is going to accurately portray bullfighting, it is unavoidably going to picture a huge beast being slowly hacked to death by men in gaily colored costumes carrying spears, darts and a sword.

It has never been a sport for the American palate. The most notable Hollywood efforts ("The Bullfighter and the Lady," "The Brave Bulls," "The Magnificent Matador") were box-office fizzlers, and I don't expect this new French film, "Sand and Blood," to reverse that trend.

This study (study, as opposed to story) of two men, a doctor (Sami Frey) and a bullfighter (Patrick Catalifo), not only deals with bullfighting, it does so in an artsy way that also seems out of tune with this country's tastes. You know, not just poetic, but Poetic. The kind of film where the continuity is loose, imagistic and left to one's intuition as much as to the more cerebral processes.

What one intuits is that the doctor is a healer who spends his days treating the sick and all his spare time performing in a string quartet. He despises bullfighting, although his hometown of Nimes, close to the Spanish border, is one of the few French towns that allows the sport to exist.

The bullfighter comes from poverty and his training for the job has consisted of long hours working in a slaughterhouse. The bullring is his passport to fame and fortune, and all that stands in his way is a growing friendship with the doctor. The bullfighter's manager is right to be concerned over the alliance; the doctor's disgust with the sport begins to rub off on the young man, and one is left wondering whether he will be able to continue.

French director Jeanne Labrune doesn't shy away from the bloodiness of bullfighting. In fact, her cameras don't shy away from much at all. As the doctor watches the bullfighter reduce a bull to steak tartare, his nausea proves contagious.

The two actors are excellent. Both Sami Frey, long a favorite of French *auteurs* and seen here in "Black Widow," and young Catalifo seems unerringly right.

The trouble most viewers will have is with the mode of telling the story—the leisurely pace, the lingering shots of landscapes and skyscapes, the close-ups of soulful expressions. Much is spelled out through the use of symbols rather than through events. Sometimes the symbols are crystal clear. As when director Labrune quick-cuts from the bullfight to a slaughterhouse where animals are being garroted and hung up to dry. Unfortunately, at times any reality becomes lost in a thicket of symbols.

I found all this tedious and artsy. In fact, the final symbol of the movie—a long lingering shot of a massive bull wandering through rolling fields—doubtless represented something entirely different to the director than it did to me.

VILLAGE VOICE, 12/26/89, p. 107, Elliott Stein

Sand and Blood is not another remake of Blasco Ibañez's *Blood and Sand*, the romantic novel about the loves of a Spanish bullfighter that provided both Rudolph Valentino and Tyrone Power with juicy star vehicles. This new concoction is set in contemporary Nimes, in southern France, where bullfights are still a popular diversion. It recounts the peculiarly closeted love affair that seems to be beckoning a married doctor of Spanish origin and an attractive young matador. They meet when Manuel (Sami Frey) stitches up Francisco (Patrick Catalifo) after a motorcycle accident. Manuel hates bullfighting, because, you see, his dad was shot down by Franco's soldiers in a bullring—nonetheless, he starts attending the corridas and lying to his wife about his activities. Before it's really clear what's what, Francisco leaves his bulls; Manuel leaves his wife. They're last seen in Spain, heading for the sunset together, but not holding hands. This is one of those everything-has-happened, nothing-has-happened movies—in my book, this genre is usually synonymous with So What? movies. The closest things get to a love scene is a short bit when the doctor squeaks out a tune on his violin while the bullfighter provides flamenco accompaniment on the guitar. Bring back vaudeville.

Catalifo is something of a find. With a lean, expressive body that's totally convincing in the bullring, and a craggy, handsome face the camera nearly licks in admiration, he quickens every shot he's in. The only memorable sequence is the ceremonious dressing of the matador before he enters the ring. We've seen it before, but this time it starts where it should—with hunk in buff.

Also reviewed in:
NEW YORK TIMES, 12/20/89, p. C14, Janet Maslin
VARIETY, 5/18/88, p. 42

SAY ANYTHING

A Twentieth Century Fox Film Corporation release of a Gracie Films Production. *Executive Producer:* James L. Brooks. *Producer:* Polly Platt. *Director:* Cameron Crowe. *Screenplay:* Cameron Crowe. *Director of Photography:* Laszlo Kovacs. *Editor:* Richard Marks. *Music:* Richard Gibbs and Anne Dudley. *Music Editor:* Carlton Kaller. *Sound:* Art Rochester and (music) Bob Schaper and Gabe Veltri. *Sound Editor:* Patrick Drummond. *Production Designer:* Mark Mansbridge. *Set Decorator:* Joe Mitchell. *Costumes:* Jane Ruhm. *Make-up:* Cheri Minns. *Running time:* 100 minutes. *MPAA:* PG-13.

CAST: John Cusack (Lloyd Dobler); Ione Skye (Diane Court); John Mahoney (James Court); Lili Taylor (Corey Flood); Amy Brooks (D.C.); Joan Cusack (Lloyd's Sister); Pamela Segall (Rebecca); Jason Gould (Mike Cameron); Loren Dean (Joe); Glenn Walker Harris Jr. (Jason); Charles Walker (Principal); Russel Lunday (Parent); Polly Platt (Mrs. Flood); Gloria Cromwell (Ruth); Jeremy Piven (Mark); Patrick O'Neill (Denny); Gregory Sporleder (Howard); John Green Jr. (Luke); Bebe Neuwirth (Mrs. Evans); Eric Stoltz (Vahlere); Kim Walker (Sheila); Chynna Phillips (Mimi); Allison Roth (Tammy); Lisanne Falk (Sandra); Montrose Hagins (Bess); Kathryn Fuller (Eva); Lenore Woodward (Sabina); Edward A. Wright (Mr. Taylor); Joanna Frank (Mrs. Kerwin); Jay R. Goldenberg (Al Kerwin); Richard Portnow (Agent Stewart); Stephen Shortridge (Ray); Kathleen Layman (Saleswoman); Tom Lawrence (Shop Customer); Annie Waterman (IRS Secretary); Philip Baker Hall (IRS Boss); Jerry Ziesmer (U.S. Attorney); John Hillner (Court's Attorney); Don "The Dragon" Wilson (Sparring Partner); Nicholas Kallsen (Nose-Setter); Thomas Payne (man in Kickboxing Doorway).

FILMS IN REVIEW, 8-9/89, p. 422, C.M. Fiorillo

When free-spirited Lloyd Dobler falls in love with brainy Diane Court, he knows it's going to be an uphill battle. His best friends tell him so. But Lloyd is nothing if not tenacious. This quirky love story, as written and directed by Cameron Crowe (*Fast Times At Ridgemont High*) turns our unambitious recent high school graduate into an unlikely romantic hero.

Lloyd (John Cusack) eventually wins, loses, and regains the affections of Diane (Ione Skye), thanks in part to her dad's (John Mahoney) fall from grace with the I.R.S.

John Cusack (*Eight Men Out*) is brilliant as Lloyd Dobler. His character is likable if a little lost in all but his love for Diane Court. Cusack's open, animated face and bouncy step add zip to the picture. As played by Ione Skye (*A Night In The Life Of Jimmy Reardon*), Diane is a trifle starchy. She manages to conjure up Diane's alienation but doesn't spark the same on-screen heat as Cusack. John Mahoney (*Eight Men Out*) turns in a terrific performances as Diane's loving, overprotective and possibly larcenous dad. Lili Taylor (*Mystic Pizza*) offers a remarkable supporting role as Lloyd's somber, guitar playing pal Corey.

Say Anything marks Cameron Crowe's directorial debut. He handles his own story deftly. There are several stand-out solo scenes for John Cusack and Mahoney. Crowe's party scenes are suitably "bodacious." He has less luck with the love scenes, which play a bit clunky. Laszlo Kovacs (*Little Nikita*) served as director of photography. Peter Gabriel's song "In Your Eyes" underscores a key scene and is a highlight of the movie's soundtrack.

Say Anything stands apart from standard adolescent movie fare. Crowe's script offers a textured glimpse into a special father/daughter relationship and what happens to it when a kick-boxing third party enters the picture. It's a refreshing alternative to the inevitable summer teen flicks.

LOS ANGELES TIMES, 4/14/89, Calendar/p. 1, Sheila Benson

Trust Cameron Crowe, writer of "Fast Times at Ridgemont High," to dig among the slag heaps of an almost mined-out genre—the teen-age movie—and come up with one of the nicest of the species, a film of warmth, insight, humor and surprising originality. "Say Anything," which marks writer Crowe's first direction, isn't perfect, but when it's good, which is every moment John Cusack is on screen, it's a living joy. And when it's not-so-good—earthbound and not inventive enough—it still almost single-handedly redeems the breed.

Cusack's Lloyd Dobler is something special among his fellow 18- and 19-year-olds just graduating from high school. He is trustworthy, the one you would stick with being "keymaster"—the straight, stern, sober keeper of all car keys—at the graduation party blowout. he cares. He is, in his own diffident way, cool. He doesn't just *like* girls; two of the niftiest girls from his class (Lili Taylor and Amy Brooks) are his best friends and life advisers. And when Lloyd falls in love, as he has with the unattainable Diane Court, it's with the pure, single-minded grip of a snapping turtle.

For some of these reasons but especially the last, Lloyd is not the sort of boy that a fiercely protective father such as nursing-home owner James Court (John Mahoney) might cotton to. Diane Court (Ione Skye), biochemistry major, valedictorian, winner of a scholarship that will take her to England in the fall, is a brain, a beauty and the light of her divorced father's life.

Lloyd lives in a crackerbox apartment with his abandoned-and-now-divorced sister (wonderful, real-life sister Joan Cusack) and her little boy. Then in an act of bravery bordering on the heroic, or the clinically insane, Lloyd asks Diane to their graduation-night party. And, in an exactly similar vein, she accepts.

It's as though Crowe really understood those hundreds of stories about models or actresses or spectacularly pretty woman who never went out during high school, simply because boys were afraid they were unapproachable.

Diane, groomed from infancy as a high achiever, also understands that she's been marked as a "priss." What she finds in Lloyd, during their first, hilarious, beautifully observed date, is a funny, tender, unquenchable optimist who is at the same time her passport to the real world.

To the astonishment of everyone, they begin dating, in sequences that are the heart and the high point of the movie. And, even considering the remarkably open and close level of communication between father and daughter, it becomes a relationship that he cannot understand.

Lloyd doesn't give adults the glib answers they want to hear about his college plans, for example, and beyond. If he can avoid the military life that his career-Army father has in mind for him, he would like to become a champion kick-boxer, "the sport of the future." In the meantime, Lloyd knows emphatically that for a career he does not want to buy, sell or process anything. It's sentences like that that make Mr. Court's eyes get very wide indeed.

Crowe, working here for executive producer James L. Brooks and producer Polly Platt, has taken the time with character details that have become a hallmark of Brooks' other Gracie Films such as "Big." The shadings within Court's character, the over-possessive father, the nurturing owner of an immaculate nursing home, are exceptionally interesting, and Mahoney plays him to the end with a beautifully calibrated touch.

Crowe wants us to see what's wonderful about Lloyd, and he and Cusack make it so easy. But although as a writer Crowe has struggled with Diane, she doesn't quite leap off the page in 3-D the way Lloyd does, or, for that matter, Lloyd's great, musician-confidante Corey, brought to brash irrepressible life by Lili Taylor. Diane remains sweet but unarresting, and nothing about Skye's performance or the writing suggests the intellect that Diane must have.

A few times Crowe simply short-changes us: after their first night together, Lloyd writes a letter that any girl (any woman of any age) would kill to get. We need to see her face when she reads it, but the action gets glossed over and missed.

The second time it's deliberate: After a falling-out, Lloyd turns up at dawn to serenade her, 1980s-style. If there is a more poignant image than Lloyd through Laszlo Kovac's lenses, standing doggedly in the early morning, holding his rig above his head, playing Peter Gabriel's soaring "In Your Eyes," for his unseen love, it's hard to think what it might be. Withholding her reaction this time is a purposeful cruelty to the audience; it leaves us as dazed as Lloyd.

But having set us up with quick, light, deft dialogue and action that insures that we will cherish Lloyd for his shining optimism, his damnfool, heartbreaking singularity, Crowe abandons him at the close.

What gave "The Graduate" its ticking bomb quality was that last shot that, clearly as "Rain Man," said "Uh oh." Crowe leaves that awful consideration out here, and we need it. Along with her father, the audience has been so preoccupied with what's best for the exquisite Diane that no one has quite considered Lloyd's future, in two years, or in 10.

What *will* happen when one day Diane grows fretful under his selfless, ceaseless adoration. When she needs to talk about her work. When his reiterated "I love you" loses its magic and begins to irritate her, as surely as a finger, rubbing tenderly back and forth across the same soft wrist.

Uh oh.

NEW YORK, 5/8/89, p. 80, David Denby

Say Anything, the new teen comedy-romance starring the startlingly fresh John Cusack and Ione Skye, is a lovely film that deserves to be a huge hit. Cameron Crowe, who wrote and directed the movie, is a former journalist who earlier wrote the likable and observant *Fast Times at Ridgemont High*; Crowe's approach is both satirical and affectionate, and his *Say Anything*, among other things, turns out to be the necessary answer to the sourly self-important teen cult film *Heathers*. In *Say Anything*, the kids never become generic types; every trait seems newly conceived. The heroine, Diane Court, is a good girl—a beauty and a straight-A student loyal to her divorced dad (John Mahoney), who idolizes her, imprisoning her with his love; the hero, Lloyd Dobler, her admirer and cavalier, is a natural (unconscious) noncomformist, an Army brat who doesn't know what to do with his life and who seizes on loving and protecting the spectacular Diane as his destiny. The two of them would die before putting it this way, but we can see that coming from messed-up homes, they are both too mature and too emotionally needy for routine teen dating. Their love has the astonished, breathless excitement of a climb to the edge of a precipice. Crowe works expertly with counter-rhythms—Cusack's nervous, joking, run-ahead intensity meets Skye's rich emotional candor. The other kids, essentially foils, are consistently funny; the whole movie has the charm of originality and sincerity.

NEW YORK POST, 4/14/89, p. 33, David Edelstein

Lloyd Dobler (John Cusack), the 19-year-old hero of "Say Anything," can't really speak—he can only jabber. Desperately wooing the smart, lovely and very shy Diane Court (Ione Skye), he's like a maniacal pinball player who's terrified that when the last ball drops the game will end and he'll suddenly find he has no clothes on. Keep it in play or stand exposed.

In the past, with his arch, complacent delivery, Cusack seemed like a guy who learned to act from watching TV talk shows. But his Lloyd is flesh and blood—the self-conscious tics are the character's, not the actor's, and his irony comes with a tremor—as if his life were riding on every hip comeback. It's an inspired performance.

The beauty of his giddy, slightly hysterical little love story is that it shares both Cusack's rawness and his comic expertise: every major scene is a triumphant piece of emotional vaudeville.

Written and directed by Cameron Crowe (who wrote "Fast Times at Ridgemont High"), it's about mismatched teen lovers and an overprotective daddy and all the other stuff we've come to dread in movies since Hollywood began studiously courting the Oxy 10 set. But the picture stands apart. It dares to be wiggy, to let the actors' eccentric rhythms take it over.

For starters, Lloyd's ambition in life is to kickbox. It's probably the most outlandish sport that Crowe could come up with, but it also suggests a certain crazed purity. And Lloyd doesn't hang out with guys but with two lovelorn girls, Corey (Lili Taylor) and D.C. (Amy Brooks). Lili has written 65 songs about her ex-love, Joe (Loren Dean), and Lloyd shares her self-dramatizing impulses.

When he somehow talks Diane into going to a graduation party with him, he can hardly contain himself: He whoops, boxes the wall, then scoops up his 3-year-old nephew (who remains still) and strums him like an electric guitar. The bit is transcendently funny—a slapstick affirmation—and the high doesn't fade.

"Say Anything" gets its name from Diane's peculiar relationship with her worshipful dad (John Mahoney), her closest (and in some ways only) friend. She'll tell him anything, even what she does on her dates with this breezy noncomformist, and the audience gasps to hear her happily confide her sexual exploits while her father listens in dumb horror.

Ione Skye, who played one of the misbegotten teens in "River's Edge," can be startlingly voluptuous in still photos, but her charm as an actress is that on screen those full, ripe features don't fit—she doesn't really know what to do with them. Skye doesn't act or move with the calculated poise of a model. She's awkward in her looks, and she has a slight speech impediment that makes her seem even more fragile. She gives an extraordinary performance here—as wide-open as Cusack's, but without the safety net of crack comic timing.

Crowe lets the two of them carry their long scenes, and what blooms between them is a wholly credible love affair. They find a rhythm with each other, and when they finally make love Lloyd is so spent and dazzled that he can't find his voice. "I think I'm happy," he manages to say.

Diane's father, of course, isn't quite as ecstatic, and before "Say Anything" ends his world will come crashing down. The picture threatens now and then to lapse into schmaltz, but it keeps its comic edge; you know that Mahoney won't go soft on his character when you hear him sing "Rikki Don't Lose That Number" in the most toneless, god-awful croak that's ever issued from the screen.

Crowe must have walked his actors through many of these scenes and encouraged them to take chances—even the performers in the smallest parts seem relaxed and confident, ready to contribute. (Mahoney's impromptu serenade is just too lunatic to have been planned.)

Some will complain, no doubt, that "Say Anything" is just another shopping-mall teen movie, and that it isn't sufficiently radical to justify the time and forebearance of grown-ups. But comic rhythms this gutsy and sustained are rare. At its best the actors sound as if they're winging it, babbling in character like a bunch of jazz soloists. They sound as if they might say anything.

NEWSDAY, 4/14/89, Part III/p. 3, Mike McGrady

No one in all of movieland is listened to more attentively, more *reverentially*, than the producer who is thinking about backing your picture. When producer James L. Brooks (the director of "Broadcast News" and "Terms of Endearment" and the creator of TV's "Taxi") speaks, Hollywood listens. Young writer Cameron Crowe happened to be on hand one day when Brooks was talking.

"Let's me share something with you," Brooks was saying. "I was walking in New York, and I saw a beautiful, young girl walking with her father. There was something about the way they walked across the street, the way he guided her with a slight touch of her elbow and the way they looked at each other that was very inspiring. And I thought to myself: "What if that man was a crook?' "

Like any young screenwriter in his right mind, Crowe applauded the boss" concept heartily, then took it and loped with it, coming up a couple of years later with the script for "Say Anything," a warm and engagingly offbeat film about two seemingly mismatched, graduating high schoolers finding love despite her doting and crooked father's disapproval.

But, guess what? That whole business about Daddy being a swindler is little more than a distraction. In fact, every time the story leaves the two young people and follows Daddy's crooked path, it detours into an area that is contrived and less funny. Producer Brooks should have known better. What makes *his* movies work has never been trickiness of plot so much as honest relattionship between real people.

Writer-director Crowe (he wrote "Fast Times at Ridgemont High") not only pays great attention to Brooks when he speaks, he also has studied hs work. What elevates "Say Anything" well above the John Hughes kiddytoons is that all three sides of the untraditional triangle—boy (John Cusack), girl (Ione Skye) and girl's father (John Mahoney)—seem real.

With this movie, John Cusack ("Eight Men Out") comes into his own. Appealing, gangling, not completely formed, Cusack's life centers around the arcane sport of kickboxing. He knows what he doesn't want out of life: "I don't want to sell anything, buy anything or process anything." Other than that? "I'm looking for a dare-to-be-great situation."

His most pressing goal is to win over the class valedictorian (Ione Skye), a beautiful overachiever heading to England on a fellowship. Although this is truly Cusack's movie, Skye ("River's Edge") is enormously appealing and talented enough to articulate complex feelings through glances.

The real beauty of "Say Anything" has nothing whatsoever to do with the way a seemingly respectable businessman runs a nursing home scam, but in the film's more commonplace occurrences—the pride and love a father takes in a daughter, the sincere but stilted quality of a graduation speech, the first telephone call a boy makes to a girl who may or may not know who he is, the feeling of falling in love, the tragedy of breaking up. You've seen these moments a hundred times before, but Crowe makes you feel you're seeing them for the first time.

Above all, you're going to go away from "Say Anything" applauding John Cusack. At one point he laments his sister's lost girlhood with, "You used to be warm, twisted and hilarious—and I mean it in the best way." I understand him precisely because "Say Anything" is warm, twisted and hilarious—and I mean *that* in the best way.

NEWSWEEK, 4/17/89, p. 72, David Ansen

God is in "the details" could be the motto of James L. Brooks. Whether as a writer-director ("Broadcast News") or as producer ("Big") Brooks always embroiders his movies with quirky, specific touches that make familiar genres fresh. Say Anything, written and directed by Cameron Crowe ("Fast Times at Ridgemont High") for Brooks's Gracie Films, attempts to refurbish the teen movie much as "Big" gently revitalized the body-swapping formula. It's warm and generous-spirited, and Crowe's dialogue is light-years ahead of most adolescent sagas. It also features two splendid performances: John Cusack as Lloyd Dobler, a high-school kick-boxer with an innately optimistic outlook on life and a nervous habit of talking uncontrollably, and John Mahoney as the father of the girl Dobler falls madly in love with. She's a beautiful, scholarship-winning overachiever named Diane (Ione Skye) who enjoys an unusually honest and intimate relationship with her father, whose good intentions hide a dark, deceptive side. Both the boy and the father are devoted to the girl: whose love will prevail?

But for all its sweetness and wit, "Say Anything" doesn't add up. Crowe, a first-time director, shows a delicate hand with actors, but he doesn't use the camera expressively: there's no sparkle in his images, no rhythm to his storytelling. More fatally, he is stuck telling the same old teen-romance story: will the lovable outcast get the golden girl? "Say Anything" finally can't transcend a dull formula. You savor the trees; it's the forest that loses you.

VILLAGE VOICE, 4/18/89, p. 63, Georgia Brown

The spacious, freestanding Seattle house in Cameron Crowe's antiseptic Say Anything, where a doting father tries keeping his worshipful daughter to himself, hardly guarantees its two occupants lasting harmony—especially when a rival suitor and the IRS get their respective feet in the door. But this fairytale version of a fouled nest successfully flown turns out to be as faithless to its psychological premises as Vera is true.

Diane Court (Ione Skye, daughter of singer Donovan) is the senior class valedictorian whose bedroom walls are decorated with charts of the brain and a world map. Belatedly (at graduation), she attracts the class flake and whimsical idealist, Lloyd Dobler (John Cusack). Like Vera's Sergei, Lloyd is on his own; he lives with his married sister (played by real sis, Joan), because his parents are stationed in Germany. (Sergei's are off in Mongolia.) Mr. Court (John Mahoney) wants desperately for Diane to take the fellowship she's won to study in England, and he views Lloyd's gallant attentions as threats to "their" plans. ("It's all working out for you, just like we planned.")

At 13, Diane chose her father in a court divorce, although she still occasionally lunches with her sociable mother. Yet Mahoney's Dad is immediately creepy—too smarmy, too crinkly 'round the eyes—and one's suspicions are soon confirmed. Unfortunately, nothing wonderfully perverse happens; all stays on the level of romance—capitalist realism. Crowe, who wrote and directed the movie (his was the novel, then screenplay, for the infinitely more savvy *Fast Times at Ridgemont High*), makes Diane's transfer of affections from Dad to dear old Lloyd a fairly simple, sensible matter of productive sleuthing followed by righteous anger. Although press materials indicate that Crowe sees his as a feminist text—since Lloyd, he says, reverses the gender pattern by being "willing to spend his life celebrating" the talents of "a spectacular girl"—Cusack's fey charm is the movie's only sign of life.

Also reviewed in:
NEW YORK TIMES, 4/14/89, p. C11, Caryn James
NEW YORKER, 5/15/89, p. 122, Pauline Kael
VARIETY, 4/12–18/89, p. 20
WASHINGTON POST, 4/14/89, p. C1, Hal Hinson

SCANDAL

A Miramax Films release of a Palace Pictures production in association with Miramax and British Screen. *Executive Producer:* Nik Powell and Joe Boyd. *Producer:* Stephen Woolley. *Director:* Michael Caton-Jones. *Screenplay:* Michael Thomas. *Based on "Nothing But" by:* Christine Keeler and Sandy Fawkes; *"Mandy" by:* Mandy Rice-Davies and Shirley Flack; *"Stephen Ward Speaks" by:* Warwick Charlton; *"The Profumo Affair: A Summing Up" by:* Judge Sparrow; *"Scandal '63" by:* Clive Irving and Ron Hall. *Director of Photography:* Mike Molloy. *Editor:* Angus Newton. *Music:* Carl Davis. *Sound:* David John and (music) Dick Lewzey. *Sound Editor:* Eddy Joseph. *Production Designer:* Simon Holland. *Art Director:* Chris Townsend. *Set Dresser:* Maria Djurkovic. *Costumes:* Jane Robinson. *Make-up:* Pat Hay. *Running time:* 115 minutes. *MPAA Rating:* R.

CAST: John Hurt (Stephen Ward); Joanne Whalley-Kilmer (Christine Keeler); Bridget Fonda (Mandy Rice-Davies); Ian McKellen (John Profumo); Leslie Phillips (Lord Astor); Britt Ekland (Mariella Novotny); Daniel Massey (Mervyn Griffith-Jones); Roland Gift (Johnnie Edgecombe); Jean Alexander (Mrs. Keeler); Paul Brooke (Detective Sergeant); Ronald Fraser (Justice Marshall); Alex Norton (Detective Inspector); Jeroen Krabbe (Eugene Ivanov); Keith Allen (Kevin); Ralph Brown (Paul Mann); Ken Campbell (Editor of "Pictorial"); Iain Cuthbertson (Lord Hailsham); Susannah Doyle (Jackie); Joanna Dunham (Lady Astor); Trevor Eve (Matinee Idol); Oliver Ford Davies (Mr. Woods); Deborah Grant (Valerie Profumo); Valerie Griffiths (Landlady); Czeslad Grocholski (Polish Gent); Leon Herbert (Lucky Gordon); Chris Humphreys (Clive); Stephen Kalipha (Hanif); Tracy Kneale (Jennifer); Tony Mathews (Press Secretary); Richard Morant (D'Lazlo); Mia Nadasi (Olga); Jeff Nuttall (Percy Murray); Sarah Prince (Mr. Woods' Secretary); Ann Queensberry (Mrs. Hare); Raad Rawi (Aziz); Terence Rigby (James Burge): Jennifer Scott Malden (Jilly); Johnny Shannon (Peter Rachman); Malcolm Terris (Northern Gent); Joan Turner (Plump Neighbor); Doremy Vernon (Head Girl); James Villiers (Conservative MP); Alison Waters (Joanie); Susie Ann Watkins (Redhead); Arkie Whitely (Vicky); Tariq Yunus (Ayub Khan).

FILMS IN REVIEW, 8–9/89, p. 422, Charles Epstein

Wilbur Mills, Ria Jenrette, Gary Hart... Washington has had its share of sex scandals. But you could fill a bedroom with all the players participating in every lurid sexcapade exposed over the last twenty years and you'll still come way short of the havoc wrought by the notorious "Profumo Affair." In 1963, a little over twenty years before London's near disastrous Big Bang (the day the stock exchange was deregulated, opening a flurry of wild speculation), Harold Macmillan's government was shaken by a series of uh, bangs, of another sort: John Profumo, Minister of War, pleaded guilty to cavorting with a "prostitute" named Christine Keeler—who at the same time was rendezvousing with a Russian naval attaché. The affair had all the classic elements: sex, money, and cold war intrigue. Great stuff.

Scandal proceeds with a cold eye cocked on the facts. We first meet Stephen Ward (John Hurt) as he stands on a street corner, eyeing the local "talent." We follow him as he prowls a posh nightclub throbbing with aristocratic libidos. Ward spots the stunning Keeler in the chorus kick-line, and before long, has her to his flat for a make-over (Eliza to his Higgins). Ward doubles as an osteopath to the rich and famous, and its sex broker (the movie paints him as a frivolous voyeur whose services gain him entry into the rarefied world of England's upper crust—contrary to the pimp depicted by the prosecutor and press). *Scandal* gives us a sampling of ruling class sex habits at the birth of the "swinging Sixties"—from the orgies at Lord Astor's "cottage" to high-class slumming in the black districts. Eventually, Ward introduces Keeler to both the fussy Profumo and ambivalent cold warrior, Ivanov. Soon both relationships falter, as they must, and Keeler goes off on a high-profile binge, giving the discreet Ward no choice but to cut her loose. Bitter and vengeful, Keeler spills the beans to an eager reporter, one thing leads to another, and well. . .the rest is newreels and microfilm.

The main problem with an otherwise crisply laid out story, is the dearth of sympathetic characters. Although the film presents Ward as the pathetic fall guy, he is only an eyelash more sympathetic than the self-indulgent old men paraded across the screen. The fine actor Ian McKellan ia wasted on a skimpily drawn part and despite Ms. Whalley-Kilmer's many charms, Keeler's appeal soon wears thin. However, John Hurt plays the insipid Ward with an amused relish, and Bridget Fonda is just right as the opportunistic Mandy Rice-Davies.

LOS ANGELES TIMES, 4/27/89; Calendar/p. 1, Sheila Benson

"Wet your lips" is the murmured phrase that runs through "Scandal"—a whispered hint to make beautiful young women's mouths glisten and pout even more seductively. Think Brigitte Bardot and you get the image.

"Scandal" is the cracklingly well-acted British film about the 1963 sex-and-politics scandal that rocked Great Britain, causing the resignation of War Minister John Profumo and eventually toppling the Tory government. The film has already made its own headlines with its MPAA-appealed ratings change from its original X to an R, after relatively minuscule snips and a few additions.

Wetting one's lips, teetering on 4-inch heels, furthering one's career by "dates" which spiraled headily up the social ladder—these became second nature for girls of voracious ambition and some sense of their own allure in Britain's hypocritical late 1950s. Or, as the snugly Establishment Stephen Ward explains the very upper classes to 17-year-old cabaret showgirl Christine Keeler: "Anyone who can enter that world has to be very clever *or* very beautiful."

As "Scandal" would have it, letting Keeler (Joanne Whalley-Kilmer) take care of the beauty and Ward (John Hurt) handle the clever department made it a dicey partnership from the first.

Ward, whom the tabloids would later delight in calling "the society osteopath," was adjusting the backs of such notables as Averell Harriman, deposed King Peter of Yugoslavia, Ava Gardner and J. Paul Getty when Keeler came under his practiced eye. In no time he had changed her brassy blond hair dark, to set off her brown eyes.

Ward, charming and unattached, was on everyone's guest list. He knew the tastiest-looking girls. He had a weekend cottage on the fringes of Lord Astor's ancestral Cliveden, leased to him for £1 per year from his chum "Bill," Lord Astor. Life was pretty much Ward's oyster and Christine became his black pearl.

But Ward, who had delusions of himself both as a diplomat and as an asset to British secret service, could never keep his mouth shut. And Christine, although canny and a quick study, looked to him for guidance and some sense of the real workings of his world. Unfortunately, he had none.

That becomes "Scandal's" focus: Keeler's love for and loyalty to the wickedly amusing Ward, their falling-out and his eventual undoing at the hands of the aristocracy, who cut him loose without a second thought when lurid stories hit the tabloids. He was, after all, a vicar's son from a minor public school. Not exactly one of them.

The film holds because of the brilliance of Hurt and the fascination of Whalley-Kilmer, as well as the sly, tongue-in-cheek viciousness of Bridget Fonda's Mandy Rice-Davies. If it is spotty in continuity, Michael Thomas' screenplay demonstrates his good ear for talk, above and below stairs, such as Ward's ingrained manners that let him charm Christine's mother with the same offhanded grace that he chats up guests at an orgy. (A naked but notably discreet orgy, as befits the film's R-rating.)

Director Michael Caton-Jones, perceptive with actors, has also caught the fevered, faintly illicit flavor of these tatty Soho clubs where foreign businessmen mixed with English aristos and frisky wide-eyed girls from the country, newly minted as "dancers" and "actresses."

From this launching pad and under Ward's protection, Keeler met the available spectrum of politics and society, including a Soviet naval attaché, Eugene Ivanov (Jeroen Krabbe), and, ultimately, John Profumo, impeccably played by Ian McKellen, down to the war minister's distinctive balding hairline which makes him look like Koko in "The Mikado." Before long, both men were paying court to Keeler, by this time platonically sharing Ward's fashionable mews flat.

Peculiarly, "Scandal" doesn't seem to American audiences to condemn the real villains of the piece. Presumably British audiences know the film's cheerless subtext full well: that the spectacle of the uppermost classes rallying around one of their own, choosing a scapegoat and suppressing the truth has changed not one jot since the seamy days of 1963.

Also, Americans may not be able to draw an immediate bead on the moral climate of that day with the ease of English audiences, and the film does little to fill them in. Part of the scandal touched on the possibility that Keeler was passing British military secrets from her British lover, Profumo, to her Soviet lover, Ivanov. The British remember bitterly what Americans may not; the defections of Burgess and MacLean to the Soviet Union a few years earlier.

If we cannot quite share the film's subtext, it still contains two luscious performances. Hurt makes the enigmatic Ward irresistible. Struck sideways by Keeler's beauty, he becomes at once mentor, best friend, the most inspired gossip and...unassailably platonic.

Whalley-Kilmer, who managed to be interesting even in "Willow," proves that she was made for the lingering appraisal of a camera. She uses stillness and a few measured movements of her enormous brown eyes to suggest Keeler's preternatural appeal; such deliberate aloofness covers the bare spots in Keeler's education and lets her appear mysterious rather than dim.

The film suggests that Ward's plight went unnoticed by his fellow Britain. Not quite so. His funeral may have gone unattended, but, as one of his biographers noted, there were two wreaths, one with 100 carnations from a group including John Osborne, Kenneth Tynan, Joe Orton and Penelope Gilliatt, with a card that read, "To Stephen Ward—Victim of Hypocrisy."

MONTHLY FILM BULLETIN, 3/89, p. 86, Anne Billson

In 1959, Stephen Ward, a London osteopath, meets seventeen-year-old Christine Keeler, a showgirl at Murray's Cabaret Club. He invites her to share his mews house (but refrains from sleeping with her) and introduces her to some of his wealthy friends, including Lord Astor and property tycoon Peter Rachman. Keeler makes friends with sixteen-year-old Mandy Rice-Davies, another showgirl, who is also introduced into Ward's social circle. In 1961, Ward is approached by an official from M15, who suggests he keep an eye on his friend Captain Eugene Ivanov, a Soviet naval attaché who is suspected of being a spy. Keeler meets Ivanov and later, during a party at Astor's Cliveden estate, Ward introduces her to John Profumo, Secretary of State for War in Harold Macmillan's cabinet. She starts affairs with both men, but resists Profumo's attempts to persuade her to leave Ward. In 1962, Keeler flees back to Ward after witnessing a fight between her West Indian lover, Johnnie Edgecombe, and another man. Edgecombe arrives at the mews house and, when Keeler and Rice-Davies refuse to admit him, produces a gun and fires some shots. Alarmed by the consequent bad publicity, Ward abandons Keeler. She relates her story to a reporter, and the implications of her past liaisons gradually filter through to the press and public. Ivanov leaves the country, and Profumo makes a statement in parliament denying any impropriety in his relationship with Keeler. Ward's friends are harassed by the police, and he finds himself ostracised. Profumo resigns, and Ward is arrested on a charge of living on immoral earnings. Both Keeler and Rice-Davies, appearing as witnesses at the trial in July 1963, refute the charges, but Ward, who takes a fatal overdose of barbiturates before the verdict can be announced, is found guilty. End titles reveal the various fates of all the other main characters, and that the Conservative government was voted out the following year.

It always seemed merely a matter of time and, presumably, of negotiating a path through a minefield of libel laws, before the story of "The Minister, the Model and the Russian Spy" would be brought to the screen. The Profumo-Keeler affair has all the credentials to suggest it would fit perfectly into the British film industry's current obsession with the juicier offcuts of recent history, i.e., those involving three or more of the following elements: sex, drugs, class differences, and the untimely death of one or more of the protagonists (*Prick Up Your Ears, Dance with a Stranger, Sid and Nancy, White Mischief,* etc.). *Scandal* adds would-be exposé of establishment hypocrisy, and dresses itself up in painstaking yet chic period recreation (with picturesque Notting Hill lowlife), a suitably retro soundtrack, and a lavish, almost slavish, attention to details such as lipstick and lingerie (particularly in a *Scorpio Rising* 'assumption of the accessories' scene as Keeler and Rice-Davies prepare to go out on the town).

All historically accurate, no doubt, but carefully presented in such a way as to make the era under examination attractive to the style-conscious sensibilities of today's young cinemagoers.

(One suspects that this film could never have been made during the 70s, if only because 60s fashions were then considered so irredeemably infra-dig.) The trouble with this approach is that the result is less the slice of socio-political relevance that its makers claim than a sort of compilation of the case's most notorious events—Keeler and Profumo meeting by the swimming-pool, the "Man in the Mask" party, Rice-Davies' "Well he would, wouldn't he", and so on. The plot-as-foregone conclusion does not necessarily preclude dramatic tension; in some cases, it can go some way towards adding to it (the death of Patsy Cline in *Sweet Dreams*, the failed assassination attempt on De Gaulle in *Day of the Jackal*). But it requires that characters be invested with an emotional life which will make them more than cardboard cut-outs strung together by relationships no deeper than those inflicted on them by newspaper headlines.

The film purports to offer a nondocumentary examination of the personal ties between Keeler and Ward, implying that he was instrumental in making her what she was. But it is not enough to have her simply say, towards the end of the film, "You pull the strings; I'm what you made me", when all we have seen him do is approve her new hair colour or sit on the sidelines while she cavorts with the cabinet minister or goes questing for marijuana in Westbourne Grove. Ward's eventual downfall, which had the potential for pathetic tragedy, ends up as just another dramatisation of the press cuttings. It may be that the film was misconceived from the beginning, but forging art from the raw material of history is largely a matter of interpretation and, whether by choice or through legal necessity, the film-makers here have fought shy of all but the most perfunctory amplification.

NEW LEADER, 5/1/89, p. 20, John Morrone

A provocative thought suggested itself as I watched *Scandal*, Michael Caton-Jones' film about Britain's 1963 Profumo fuss. Wouldn't it be interesting to match up Stephen Ward, the osteopath whose ambiguous relationship to sexual adventuress Christine Keeler resulted in his trial for procuring women, with Valmont, the aristocratic intriguer of *Dangerous Liaisons*? Imagine eavesdropping on their sexual gossip, their revelations of class privileges, and their feelings about being undone by public and private passions that ran wildly beyound their control. It is now widely believed that Ward was scapegoated by the failing Conservative government to protect then Minister of War John Profumo from the uproar over *his* affair with Keeler and the possible breach of British military security it posed. Valmont, the cynical satyr astonished to be tasting love at last, was run through in a duel over honor; Ward committed suicide to avoid imprisonment and the social annihilation he would suffer for life. What chains these ghosts could rattle!

Although *Scandal* is absorbing, it seems to be so for reasons other than those intended by Caton-Jones or screenwriter Michael Thomas. The film meticulously reviews the ascent of Keeler and her protégé Mandy Rice-Davies from Soho nightclub dancers to good time girls with entrée into the upper crust, and it tracks Keeler's progress as human party favor to assorted peers of the realm and West Indian hipsters. Then, just as a reporter from the *Sunday Pictorial* connects the dots between Profumo, Keeler and a Russian attaché named Ivanov to come up with a bedroom spy triangle, *Scandal* backs away.

Thomas' script, while big on Keeler's sex appeal, is frustratingly vague on exactly how the political mess erupted and how it captured the public's imagination. Profumo, played by Ian McKellen, is reduced to a supporting role; Ivanov, entrusted to Dutch actor Jeroen Krabbe, is virtually a bit part. Likewise, the screen time for Mandy Rice-Davies is as scanty as her underwear, even though Bridget Fonda is billed fourth. As Keeler, Joanne Whalley-Kilmer, who bears an odd resemblance to Natalie Wood, is expert at portraying both temptress and victim, but her range cannot be fully put to use because the film does not belong to her.

The personal crisis of Stephen Ward is the real scandal in *Scandal*. Played by John Hurt, Ward has a gravel-voiced sophistication—he is confident, randy, every bit a self-amused libertine. Ward developed his impressive network of social ties by dint of his prodigious charm and judicious cozying-up; the pimping he was accused of was at best indirect. Pocketing social brownie points, not cash, from the men he introduced to Christine, he was simply "doing a friend a favor" (if the friend was in a high place) at a time in England when, it is worth recalling, even to obtain a bootleg copy of *Lady Chatterly's Lover* for a colleague was a yeoman act.

Ward enjoyed his roles as host and facilitator as much as he savored observing the upper class at work and play. Not born to wealth but aspiring to it, he recognized the interlocking manipulations and rapacious behavior of London's power élite, and worked it for his own pleasure. (His was the *White Mischief* crowd, home from the colonies and horny as hell.) A society given to impromptu after-dinner orgies was not, most of the time, a bad place to be. Sex was fun, power was more fun, and living on the edge of this aphrodisiac combination made him greedy. He only dimly accepted the precariousness of his state of social grace and how dependent his career was on the satisfaction of his customers—who were, on paper at least, his "betters."

Ward's position of relative comfort also blinded him to the dangerous fallout from indiscretions by Christine that could be traced back to him. When he sheltered Keeler in his Wimpole Mews flat from the loud, jealous rage of her latest West Indian lover (played by Roland Gift of the rock Group Fine Young Cannibals), he failed to notice that Christine was under observation by the press and the police, and that he, too, would be involved. Though Keeler risked little—her name, albeit glamorous, was already mud—Ward risked his way of life.

Ward gets his first glimpse of Keeler in a Soho dive, where she is performing a dance surrounded by sparklers—an unreal, idealized image. He claims a longing to "liberate" her "untutored" beauty, and he begins to sketch her. No matter what was believed in court, his infatuation (which the script assumes remained platonic to the end) was less that of a ponce for his tart than of an obsessive artist for his largely indifferent model. "Leave Christine to me," he says when he is confronted by the Profumo connection. "I dreamt Christine up. I can make her vanish." We know, of course, he could not.

In ably juggling urbanity, lust, politesse, and exploitation, *Scandal* gives John Hurt his most atypical yet most compelling role to date. Even if you do not care very much about a European political brouhaha of three decades past, the film offers something timeless in the pathetic grandeur of Hurt's rich, sour performance.

Scandal ends with Ward's suicide note, read in voice-over—"I'm sorry to disappoint the vultures." His enervated, bitterly crybaby tone recalls another victim of Britain's sex wars between the classes: Ruth Ellis of *Dance With a Stranger*, a prostitute who shot her erstwhile posh lover and was the last woman to be hanged in Britain. In her goodbye note before she greeted the gallows, she too apologized—"Please forgive my writing, but the pen is shocking." If Ward and Valmont wouldn't mind, she could join them at their table.

NEW STATESMAN & SOCIETY, 3/3/89, p. 49, Suzanne Moore

Christine Keeler, naked, long legs astride a chair; Christine Keeler clutching her patent leather handbag, coyly pushing the hair out of her dark glasses as she leaves the courtroom; Christine Keeler "model" and "show-girl" cavorting with lords and cabinet ministers in country houses. Keeler, the impassive icon of the early 60s, now lives in a council flat and is broken, many say, by the strain of always having to be Christine Keeler.

John Profumo, the then minister for war with whom she had an affair is still rich, still happily married and was awarded an MBE in 1975 for his work for charity. Stephen Ward, the society ostepath who introduced them and the only man Christine says she loved, took his own life during the trial which followed what came to be known as "the Profumo affair" in 1963.

The affair which Christine now more aptly describes as a "very, very, well-mannered screw of convenience" is the subject of a new British film, *Scandal*. It has attracted an enormous amount of pre-release publicity as it opens up once more many of the unresolved questions surrounding the whole episode.

Starring John Hurt in another quintessential victim role as Ward and Joanne Whalley as Keeler, the film belongs to the growing number of movies which re-examine and re-assess recent British history. *Scandal*, with its commercially viable mix of sex, hypocrisy and breaches of security, strikes an oddly contemporary note in the light of the *Spycatcher* episode.

Though adultery, as Lord Hailsham spluttered out in an interview at the time, was neither the prerogative of the Tory party or even the rich, this particular scandal came at a watershed in British history and was, and still is, perceived to have brought down the Tory government. In reality it was simply one factor, but a factor that nonetheless fleshed out a growing sense of anxiety: the economy was in deep trouble, Britain no longer had an empire. And, more crucially, as regards the Profumo affair, its defence and foreign affairs policies were crumbling. Instead of the nuclear independence that Macmillan had promised, there was complete dependence on the Americans.

Supermac, who in his diaries describes himself as "old, incompetent and worn-out", handled the Profumo affair disastrously by simply refusing to handle it at all and expressing an aristocratic disdain for matters involving "personal affairs". In contrast, Wilson cleverly homed in not on matters of personal morality but on the more politically damaging question of national security—

Keeler had been sleeping with a cabinet minister and a Russian called Ivanov—who was thought by M15 to be a spy—at the same time.

To Wilson, who was busy presenting the Labour Party as a party of modernisation, the whole affair was a gift. He was able to exploit the Rachman connection (Rachman, the notorious slum landlord was Mandy Rice-Davies's boyfriend, and sometime lover of Keeler) to suggest that under the Tory party the top echelons of society were decadent beyond belief, while the ordinary people were bullied and cheated by thugs like Rachman.

The film, like so many fictionalised documentaries, prefers to personalise the story into the relationship between Keeler and Ward, keeping the historical context to a few headlines. In capturing the hypocrisy of the British establishment closing rank and baying for blood this works well, but in trying to portray Keeler and Ward as "class rebels", as producer Stephen Woolley describes them, it definitely fails. Using sex to cross class barriers is, after all, hardly new and if it is a revolutionary act, Cinderella would be the greatest class rebel of them all.

Perhaps it's fairer to say that Ward was a great pretender and his crime, like that of Profumo's, was not what he did but the fact he got found out. Voyeuristic, charming and a connoisseur of the perverse, Hurt plays him sympathetically. He discovers Keeler working in a nightclub and, like Pygmalion, he makes her over, introduces her to his upmarket friends with their downmarket sexual preferences.

For my money, Joanne Whalley just doesn't have Keeler's stunning indifference; the enigmatic coolness that stares out from all those black and white photos. Ludovic Kennedy says of her at the trial that she had "a terrifying little face, vacant yet knowing". This may have been helped by the fact that she was doped up to her eyeballs on phenobarbitone—the valium of its day. Nor was she so *ingenue* as the film makes out; she had already had a horribly botched abortion and had stolen a car to get to London.

After Profumo admitted that he had lied in the Commons, Ward was sacrificed, prosecuted for living off immoral earnings. The trial and Denning's whitewashed report, which cleared the security forces and vilified Ward, were little more than a device to make it look as if after all the government was at least doing *something*.

Ward couldn't take it. The film's cry of "It's not fair" is moving, but then the insidiousness of class has never depended on fairness—despite its protestations to the contrary.

Scandal revels in this hypocrisy and is as voyeuristic in its filming of Keeler and Rice-Davies as the lecherous old men they slept with. To think that their beauty could ever be as powerful as the shabby goings on of the men is naive. The girls were very young: their ambition was to be in a Camay commercial, not to bring down a government.

The real interest of this film lies in the unanswered questions. Did M15 set the whole thing up with Ward working for them? Were they trying to get Ivanov to defect? Did they murder Ward as some have suggested? And the biggest question of all, what happens when politicians lose control of their own security services? What happens when "British Intelligence" is responsible to no one but itself?

I'll leave the last word to Mandy Rice-Davies, as astute now as she was then. Those that suppressed the truth about the Profumo affair still hold power in this country. "That group still exists in the shadows. The people who pressed the buttons remain a shadowy group who inhabit the labyrinths of Whitehall. The sheer ego of it drives me crazy."

Well, she would say that, wouldn't she?

NEW YORK, 5/8/89, p. 78, David Denby

Why is sex so dispiriting in British movies? Is it just the dank light and colorless skin, the middle-aged men swallowing their mustaches as they savor girls far too young, the masochists in their costumes waiting patiently to be beaten? Yes, and a whole attitude as well: The scandal of *Scandal* and of such recent films as *Dance With a Stranger, Personal Services,* and *Wish You Were Here* is not the kinky sex but the moviemakes' grimly squalid or giggle-fit treatment of it. And it's not just vice that comes off that way. With the exception of Stephen Frears, British filmmakers treat sex as something coldly disgusting or tickly and naughty.

Scandal, a reconstruction of the Profumo affair of the early sixties—which brought down Harold Macmillan's Conservative government—is yet another attack on British hypocrisy. Whatever the filmmakers may think, this is a very familiar subject (just about every ambitious British movie of the past three decades has attacked the same thing). The real trick would be to ridicule hypocrisy while making something exciting out of the acts people secretly enjoy and hide.

But *Scandal* lacks sensuality, so the smoldering center, the emotional crux of the Profumo affair—which certainly must have been the desire that various powerful men felt for the teenage party girl Christine Keeler and what she gave them in return—is left largely undramatized. Scenes of men leering at girls in clubs or at parties are not drama.

The young BBC-TV actress Joanne Whalley-Kilmer, who plays Christine, is promising. She has big, beautiful features—full lips and luminous eyes that now and then go soft, glazed over with desire. But Whalley-Kilmer gives a rather reticent and dignified performance—so dignified that the whorish things Christine does often make little sense. This probably isn't Whalley-Kilmer's fault. Michael Thomas's screenplay cuts off Christine's encounters just when we think we're going to see something (not nudity; emotional expressiveness). Ian McKellen, as John Profumo, the ambitious Conservative M.P. and war minister who falls for Christine, is all dispatch and vigorous, awkward motion, whipping off his morning coat for sex as if he were settling down to solve a vexing problem in British Guiana. McKellen, a great actor, has a few moments of pathos when things fall apart—the look on his face is heartbreaking—but his part is undeveloped, too.

Thomas and director Michael Caton-Jones, a former TV filmmaker doing his first feature, construct a documentary apparatus around the scandal, with some newsreels thrown in, and although they convey the flavor of a jaded, exhausted society, they fail to make the sequence of events very clear, and they leave unanswered the question of whether Christine Keeler actually slept with the Soviet military attaché who befriended her, Ivanov (Jeroen Krabbe). (The key to the scandal, heavily exploited by the Labour Party, was the possibility of Christine's passing secrets learned from Profumo to a likely Soviet spy. But recently, some journalists have speculated that Christine fabricated the sexual connection with Ivanov in order to get more money from the tabloid press for her story.)

The movie is also pedestrian in a number of garden-variety ways.... But you don't really want to hear about the cinematography, do you? Let's get back to the dirty stuff: Caton-Jones produces some fine scenes of young Christine and the other girls at a nightclub bouncing into their dressing rooms, grabbing for cigarettes as their costumes fall off—there's a crude casualness to their nakedness that's funny. And I enjoyed a moment in which Christine and her shrewd, avid pal Mandy Rice-Davies (Bridget Fonda), another teen party girl/hooker, put on their make-up for the night, standing side by side before mirrors—the episode has the entrancing professional interest of soldiers buckling up before battle. Those few short scenes are the extent of any fresh understanding of an erotic milieu.

The movie is constructed around a vacuum—the strange, nonsexual love affair between Christine and her discoverer and patron, Dr. Stephen Ward (John Hurt). A clergyman's son, educated in the American Midwest in the semi-disreputable skill of osteopathy, Ward was a charming, worldly man, the kind of merrymaker who enjoys introducing powerful people to one another (his dozens of sentimental friendships, promoted by partying and the exchange of favors, evaporated quickly when he got into trouble). Ward took an interest in the young, pretty things who came to London, teaching beautiful girls with sexual skills some social skills as well. He was a voyeur; he liked gossip and intrigue, and it amused him that rich and powerful men took up with his protégés. He never slept with Christine, who lived with him on and off for several years; dressing her up and perfecting her looks was all the sexual conquest he wanted.

Hurt gives Ward superb manners and qualities prized by the powerful—sympathy, usefulness, a boundless devotion to *their* pleasures. Hurt's bafflement as Ward's friends turn on him, looking for a scapegoat, borders on the tragic—he's the social magician fooled by his own tricks, fooled into thinking that good times bind people forever. He provided girls for orgies, but a schoolboy could hardly have been more innocent.

Ward takes care of Christine and comforts her when she's blue, but nothing emotionally interesting—or even comprehensible—develops between them. What does Christine think when he doesn't go to bed with her but promotes her as a mistress to other men? (She never asks Ward why he isn't interested in her.) Thomas and Caton-Jones are so vague about this relationship that we might be misled into thinking Ward was gay. The implication is that Christine and Stephen's sweet nuzzling on the couch made them innocent—babes in the woods—and more sinned against than sinning. At the core of this *Scandal* there is not sex but sentimentality.

NEW YORK POST, 4/28/89, p. 27, David Edelstein

It's a good thing for the producers of "Scandal" that the film needed last-minute editing to remove some "offensive" shots from an orgy scene, since there's otherwise little about the movie to arouse people's interest—unless you still think the idea of middle-aged British Conservatives bouncing half-naked young girls on their laps is a shocker. (Evidently the prudish ratings board did—which is probably the true scandal.)

The film purports to "tell all" about the Profumo affair—the fling between a prominent Cabinet minister and a promiscuous young woman, Christine Keeler. The exposure and subsequent uproar is alleged to have toppled the Conservative government of Harold Macmillan, and to have helped to usher in the let-it-all-hang-out '60s in Great Britain. It also prompted the suicide of one of its principals, Dr. Stephen Ward, who swallowed a handful of Nembutals shortly before a jury convicted him of pimping for the aristocracy.

Ward (played by John Hurt) is the movie's true subject—or, rather, its tragic hero, a martyr to English hypocrisy. Based in part on Keeler's memoirs, "Scandal" ends up so dodgy and self-serving that it might be an application for Ward's posthumous knighthood. He and Keeler , the film suggests, were only trying to Spread a Little Sunshine.

"Scandal" begins with Sinatra's "Witchcraft," an easy, shimmering pop song that evokes a different era. And at first you think that's what the movie will be about—a beautiful young woman's witchy sex appeal, which can cause so many different kinds of men to do so many foolish things.

Hurt's Dr. Ward, an osteopath, ambles happily down the street, his gaze following different lovely women before fixing on Keeler (Joanne Whalley-Kilmer), a scrumptious showgirl. The rich and powerful like him and the female company he keeps—he resides in an immense Tudor "cottage" of Lord Astor's—and he sees Keeler as a prize acquisition, a potential derby winner.

Showing Keeler around his neighborhood, Ward tells her in his toasty voice that most of the people who live in this society are born into it, that anyone else "has to be very clever or very beautiful." It's obvious how his mind works: He is very clever; she is very beautiful; together they can rule the world.

Although he speaks of the "wild, untutored, elemental beauty" in her that he longs to liberate, Ward sounds more than a little daft, since Whalley-Kilmer is pretty in a cartoon, Stepford-wife sort of way, with huge, pop-out eyes on a tiny face. She's the kind of woman Mickey Mouse might spend a night with if he was determined to cheat on Minnie.

The director, Michael Caton-Jones, doesn't help by introducing her with a cinematic cliche, his camera traveling up her leg to the steamy wah-wah of a trumpet. But for all its blandness, the first hour of "Scandal" is smoothly enjoyable: Ward installs Keeler in her own flat and stands back, savoring his usefulness, as diplomats, ministers and sundry aristocrats come sniffing.

When it's about young women slinking among men who are heady with their own power and wealth, the movie is sexy and fun. There's a nice bit where Keeler and her inexperienced-but-game fellow showgirl, Mandy Rice-Davies (Bridget Fonda) hook on their garters and regard themselves like gunfighters—the twangy music sounds like a Sergio Leone Western. Whenever a wealthy suitor approaches, Christine blurts "Wet your lips" to her eager companion.

Although Ward likes being harmlessly whipped by a middle-aged woman (a plush Britt Ekland), the doctor is foremost a voyeur. He likes to watch, and he likes to hear about Christine's activities the next morning—to know the size of her suitors' private parts. Every tryst he arranges enlivens him, makes him feel a part of the gentry, and Hurt's creased face and serene grin give the movie a heart.

The orgy scene is presented without moralizing, and the bland technique is a pleasant surprise with material this loaded. (I don't know what the X-rated version was like, but what's left is definitely a Masterpiece Theater orgy.) But in the end you realize that the tone is so blithe and indulgent because you're being set up for Ward's victimization and Christine's essential innocence.

Although Christine has an affair with a Russian diplomat (Jeroen Krabbe), "Scandal" never stoops to consider the case's implications for national security, or even to ask the kinds of questions that journalists ventured in the face of Gary Hart's (or John Kennedy's) alleged infidelities. It's not interested in probing the connection between personal morality and political behavior.

The movie turns into the story of Ward's martyrdom, and how the sweet-dear-gentle-harmless little man who just wanted to belong was made a scapegoat and abandoned by a gentry eager to disassociate itself from scandal—hypocrites and cowards, all. It's about how, in court, Christine stands up for his honor and he for hers, despite the fact that she implicated him in the first place.

Not that "Scandal" makes her role terribly clear. The way in which the story breaks is kept purposefully murky—it's mentioned only in passing that Keeler sold her story, for a ton of money, to the tabloids, forcing the Conservatives to target Ward, a government outsider.

The filmmakers make Rice-Davies an exploitative bitch to divert attention from Keeler's own shifty morality. (You can see the way their tiny minds work—they want to distinguish a greedy slut from a selfless one, forgetting it was Keeler's decision to sell her tale that triggered the mess.) In any case, I was grateful they turned Rice-Davies into a trollop, because Bridget Fonda blooms. When she's on the stand in court—exhilarated by the attention—she shows the liveliest spirit of anyone in the film.

It's a small pleasure, though. The tone becomes dull and deliberate, with no sense of the public's reaction. We're told that the Profumo case brought down a government, but we're never told why—for all we know it's because Conservatives were forced to stop having sex with young girls. And Profumo himself (played by Ian McKellen) is barely characterized.

In the end, "Scandal" seems meant to absolve not only Ward but Keeler. The movie shows her phoning his apartment after he expires, as if to say, "She blew the whistle on him, but she was his only friend."

The ratings board is said to have had difficulty with a naked, fuzzy bum in the orgy scene. The picture's fuzzy morals are even less savory.

NEWSDAY, 4/28/89, Part III/p. 3, Lynn Darling

The Profumo affair had everything you could want from a major sex scandal—not only was it steeped in the most lurid sort of doings among Britain's high and mighty, but it had just the right touch of allegedly grave political consequence. That Christine Keeler was having simultaneous affairs with Minister of War John Profumo and suspected Soviet spy Eugene Ivanov meant that even the serious newspapers could go bananas dishing the details. Sex and the upper class and national security—as scandals go, the Profumo affair was perfect.

Although it wasn't obvious then, the affair exploded into view at a quintessential moment in British history, just as the Cold War paranoia of the 1950s was beginning to collide with the freewheeling spree of Carnaby Street. The combination of Conservative Party complacency, rising prosperity and the opening guns in a prolonged attack on old morals and values provided fertile ground for the likes of Stephen Ward and Christine Keeler, and it is their story that "Scandal" explores.

Ward (John Hurt) was a social-climbing osteopath made giddy by his association with the rich and powerful, and Keeler (Joanne Whalley-Kilmer) was his creation—a beautiful, untutored 18-year-old showgirl whom he transformed into the sort of glittering fish that could swim in dangerous waters.

And the waters were dangerous indeed. Eager to please the titled pleasure-seekers he counted among his friends, Ward encouraged their attentions to Keeler and Keeler's colleague, Mandy Rice-Davies. In this version of events, he demanded little from the women besides the details of their going-on. He was thrilled when British intelligence evinced an interest in any liaison Ivanov might strike up with Keeler, and almost pathologically naive about the consequences of his own indiscretion. We're all flesh, he tells Keeler after her first orgy. There's no harm in it as long as no one gets hurt.

Of course it didn't work out that way, and "Scandal" has a delicious time with all the salacious absurdities, like the orgy scene in which one masked partygoer serves drinks wearing only a sign that says, "Please beat me if I fail to satisfy." But director Michael Caton-Jones and screenwriter Michael Thomas also keep a keen eye on the harsh undercurrents of the affair. They point up the social hypocrisy that ultimately made Stephen Ward the scapegoat for the sleazy pleasures of his betters, if the current revisionist theory is to be believed. And they do a deft job of providing a complicated portrait of Keeler—not a one-dimensional, panfried party girl, but a young woman in way over her head. In one brief scene she's trapped by several lustful old powermongers around a swimming pool—a moment that reveals the high life in which she participated as having all the glamour of a bullbaiting.

Joanne Whalley-Kilmer does a standout job as Keeler, creating a character whose gossamer appeal plays in counterpoint to the casually brutal way she is tossed about by those for whom she never had an ounce of humanity. Everyone around her succeeds equally well, from John Hurt's foolish, wounded Ward to Ian McKellen's slickly ambitious, ultimately overwhelmed Profumo to Bridget Fonda's saucily brazen Mandy Rice-Davies.

The movie's only misstep comes when it tries to find a little nobility in the relationship between Keeler and Ward, and pathos in the way their reputations were torn apart in court and in the newspapers. "This is not fair!" Ward shouts in court as his lawyer tries to portray Keeler as a monety-grubbing opportunist. But there were no martyrs and no victims in the Profumo affair, only the sort of amoral predators that the guardians of the public's tottering morals would have to invent from time to time if they didn't obligingly fling themselves into the headlines.

NEWSWEEK, 5/1/89, p. 76, Jack Kroll

I will not be brought down by that girl. So vowed Britain's Prime Minister Harold Macmillan in 1963, when the Profumo affair was threatening to tear apart his Conservative government. "That girl" was 21-year-old party girl Christine Keeler, whose liaison with John Profumo, the minister of war, had triggered Britain's sex-and-politics scandal of the century. A tarnished Macmillan did resign, and the Tories were voted out in 1964. The Profumo business still sticks in the craw of the British establishment. Scripts based on the affair were disapproved or abandoned by both the government-run BBC and commercial British television. The new film *Scandal* was planned as a mini-series, but after several years of hot-potato handling by British TV, producer Stephen Woolley gave up and switched to the big screen.

During the filming, the bishop of Stepney, a friend of Profumo's, urged his neighbors to make noise to disturb the shooting on location. Before "Scandal" opened in London last month, to big business and mostly positive reviews, there was a barrage of criticism from politicians and newspapers, deploring the reopening of old wounds, especially since the 74-year-old Profumo lives a quiet life and was decorated for his work in East London slums. London Transport refused to allow posters advertising the movie in buses and subways. In the United States, "Scandal" had rating problems: it was given an X, according to one of the producers, until it earned an R by cutting out some "rocking motion" in an orgy sequence.

Rocking, shmocking, most of the orgy is still there, including the scandal's notorious "man in the mask," who serves drinks wearing nothing but a sign that says, PLEASE BEAT ME IF I FAIL TO SATISFY. "Scandal" is a pretty raunchy movie, but it's a serious piece of work. Australian screenwriter Michael Thomas and 31-year-old director Michael Caton-Jones are in love with this story—not so much with the scandal itself as the seismic cultural shift it marked in postwar Britain. The days of austerity were ending, London started swinging, the Beatles were coming and Macmillan boasted famously that the country "never had it so good." As morals shifted, the sound of snapping garter belts was heard in the land.

"Scandal" centers not on Profumo (Ian McKellen) but on Dr. Stephen Ward (John Hurt) and Christine Keeler (Joanne Whalley-Kilmer), the Pygmalion and Galatea of this profligate myth. When Ward first spots the teenage Keeler in a sequins-and-skin cabaret show, he homes in on her like a heat-seeking missile. Ward, the "society osteopath" (his patients included Churchill, Elizabeth Taylor, Paul Getty), artist (his sitters include members of the royal family) and social-climbing master of the revels (his revelers included Lord Astor, slumlord Peter Rachman, Pakistan President Ayub Khan), transforms the peroxide-blonde Keeler into a dark-haired woman-child who drives chaps bonkers. None bonks more obsessively than Profumo, whose dangerous liaison is made more dangerous by Keeler's concurrent capers with Eugene Ivanov (Jeroen Krabbe), a Soviet naval attaché and spy.

The complex web of events, involving private sex and national security, that spun from this situation can't be dealt with in detail in a two-hour film. But Thomas and Caton-Jones are faithful to the dynamics of the affair. The movie sees Ward, who was convicted of living on the proceeds of prostitution, as the scapegoat victimized by the power elite; he committed suicide before his trial was over. With his warm eyes gleaming in a cold, anguished face, Hurt catches the contradictory man who thought of himself not as a superpimp but as an artist. "When I see wild untutored beauty, I long to liberate it. This is my life's work," he says. McKellen's Profumo, his receding hair skull-scaped to a devilish black point, is all elegant mendacity as he lies to the House of Commons about his relationship with Keeler, setting up his inevitable disgrace and resignation.

Despite the dark elements of the affair, the movie has an almost exultant sense of new energies breaking loose. These are embodied in Keeler and her friend Mandy Rice-Davies (Bridget Fonda). With her lynx eyes and mocking smile, Fonda is an icon of impudence. In court she coolly answers a lawyer who states that Lord Astor has denied any relations with her: "Well, he would, wouldn't he?" Whalley-Kilmer's stunning, sculptured face and simmering expressiveness give Christine a sense of her own dangerous power. These are delicious performances, capturing perfectly the mischievous muses of a new permissiveness.

TIME, 5/1/89, p. 68, Richard Corliss

Britain's Minister of War John Profumo, husband of refined movie star Valerie Hobson, has been sharing the sexual favors of teen tart Christine Keeler with Soviet spy Eugene Ivanov...Keeler's blond pal Mandy Rice-Davies, 18, declared in court that she had bedded Lord Astor and Douglas Fairbanks Jr....Mariella Novotny, who claims John F. Kennedy among her lovers, hosted an all-star orgy where a naked gent, thought to be film director and Prime Minister's son Anthony Asquith, implored guests to beat him...Ostepath and artist Stephen Ward, whose portrait subjects include eight members of the Royal Family, has been charged with pimping Keeler and Rice-Davies to his posh friends. Part of Ward's bail was reportedly posted by young financier Claus von Bülow.

Talk about your dish! In 1963 English gossip columists figured they had died and gone to tabloid heaven. When these peccadilloes hit the front pages, you couldn't tell the players without a *Who's Who* and a *Burke's Peerage*. The scandal, a wild party held at the sunset of imperial Britain, brought down Harold Macmillan's Tory government and ushered in the era of Swinging London: the Beatles, miniskirts, free love and pricey drugs.

Scandal is an express tour of the Profumo affair that moves with a pop historian's revisionist swagger and plays like *News of the World* headlines set to early '60s rock 'n' roll. Taking a cue from Asquith's *Pygmalion*, the film casts Ward (John Hurt) as an aristocratic makeover artist, discovering Keeler (Joanne Whalley-Kilmer) in the fetid anonymity of a Soho strip club and turning her into a star of the jet-set slumming circuit. *Pluck your eyebrows, Christine. Wet your lips. Come over and say hi to Jack Profumo.*

Stephen loves Christine, in his fashion. He pampers his girls and introduces them to his randy friends because he likes being liked. His sin is in assuming, like nearly everyone who jestered near the thrones of power in Britain and Ameria, that the games could be pubic without ever going public. Enter Profumo (Ian McKellen), who in his high-domed hairdo looks like a samurai of probity. Jack is an indiscretion waiting to happen. He has so little furtive pleasure to gain, and so much reputation to put at risk, that his dalliance has the lurid fatalism of a soap opera. Then Christine snitches to the press, and domestic melodrama stokes national tragedy.

Scandal, whose producers had to snip a few naughty bits from the Novotny orgy to avoid an X rating in the U.S., is wonderfully performed by Hurt (pained irony), McKellen (droll reserve) and, as Rice-Davies, Peter Fonda's daughter Bridget (comic acuity). The film names names and gets the tone right. This is a morally exhausted society, where every woman is a whore and every man a pimp or a trick until proved otherwise. It has no hero or heroine, only a victim: Stephen Ward, who loved trashy women and was betrayed by distinguished men.

VILLAGE VOICE, 5/2/89, p. 67, Georgia Brown

If Britain hadn't been rocked by the Profumo scandal—the affair that caused its eponymous war minister to resign in disgrace and threatened the whole Conservative government—sex might have remained an upperclass secret. So goes a theory. All those years that the underclasses were trying hard to live virtuously and get ahead, the rich (hardly tuckered out from work) were just having fun. But with the grisly facts exposed, the sexy '60s followed the frumpy '50s, and paid-for sex turned into free love. (With the advent of groupies, the rich and famous would no longer need prostitutes.) *Scandal* (which, owing to deadlines, I didn't see in its final American release version, although last minute changes were explained to me by Miramax, the film's distributor here), opening on London, 1959, with TV news snippets featuring those two beaming ur-pappies, Ike and Mac, advances a blurred thesis about the times suddenly changing. As the '50s flash by, Sinatra croons "Witchcraft" (as if we were all under a spell); later, the '60s break out with the Beatles "Do You Want To Know a Secret."

And since every movie requires its love story (another theory), *Scandal* conveniently discovers it has one too. Screenwriter Michael Thomas and director Michael Caton-Jones detect a highly romantic, if platonic, love between Dr. Stephen Ward (John Hurt), osteopath and pimp, and Christine Keeler (Joanne Whalley-Kilmer), eager, attractive 18-year-old "model." Keeler, from the film's point of view, is more or less a London career girl in need of a mentor, and Ward a benign, if less rigorous, Henry Higgins.

Ward's appreciation of attractive women is the note on which *Scandal*'s plot opens. The then successful osteopath and amateur artist—voyeur, connoisseur of sorts—liked to arrange matches for men of wealth and power. (Two men who saw the movie with me afterward asked, "Was he gay?" The answer, I think, is that he had what is clinically known as a "homosexual component" to his makeup.) Ward—whose real-life patients included Averell Harriman, Winston Churchill, Danny Kaye, Elizabeth Taylor—fancied himself a Pygmalion, taking young women with figures but without means and molding them into presentable "escorts" for himself and his friends. Real "Ward girls" sometimes went on to marry millionaires—as did the longtime Ward girlfriend who married Jule Styne. What was known as the "Ward setup" figured prominently in the London scene of the late'50s and early '60s. "It was food from Fortnum & Mason...girls from Stephen Ward," is how one of the papers, quoted in Clive Irving's informative *Anatomy of a Scandal*, described the social climate.

As John Hurt plays the good doctor stepping out on a summer day to gaze on bright young things in their summer dresses, he's not sleazy, certainly—just a tad seedy, a touch depressive. (The real Ward had attempted suicide some years earlier when he'd lost a girlfriend.) At night, a blond on each arm, Ward often goes to clubs such as Murray's Cabaret to see scanty-costume skits based on hits of the day such as "Running Bear (Loves Little White Dove)" and "Red Feathers (With Her Huli-huli Skirt)," At Murray's one night, he spots Christine in her huli-huli skirt. Caton-Jones lets us know what a fateful event this is by using slow motion to represent Ward's overcome state.

Ward's pursuit takes him, driving a white Jag, to a shantytown where Christine is visiting her poor, doting mum. ("I was just passing....*Lovely* setting.") Soon Christine is staying overnight at the cottage on the grounds of Lord Astor's Cliveden, which Ward rents for one pound a year from his aristo pal. (As cottage is to manor, so Ward's service exists adjacent to the great life.) Stephen tells Christine she needn't sleep with him, that he merely wants to make her over, starting with her hair. ("It's my vocation, my vice.") When she gets rid of her bleach job and false eyelashes, she's ready to be taken to dinner parties where the table's centerpiece might be a crystal penis from Copenhagen. She can now be introduced to the minister (Ian Mckellen) and to the spy (Jeroen Krabbe).

Captain Ivanov, a Russian naval attaché, crucial to the scandal technically (state secrets were endangered since he and Profumo were sleeping with the same woman), was a peripheral figure at the time. So is Krabbe's Ivanov, who sulks about criticizing capitalist decadence. And no wonder—with war minister Profumo cheating him in a swimming match at Cliveden and then going for the same girl. McKellen's Jack Profumo has the vulerable blue eyes of a man afraid of women and the bizarre Profumo hairline, but he too is barely characterized. This is not his story. We are reminded, however, that Profumo's wife was, and still is, the actress Valerie Hobson.

What the movie will probably owe its box office to are the party scenes—particularly the one (formerly with some X-rated but stylized nude humping) treating us to the sight of a droopy hairy bottom, a couple of soft puds nearly hidden by sagging bellies, and the gold-painted nipples belonging to a woman said to have had a fling with JFK (Britt Ekland playing Mariella Novotny). I think this is called an orgy.

Michael Thomas's dialogue is crisp and at times comical—funniest in mocking those terribly polite English understatements. ("Dr. Ward, I thought you should know there's a black man shooting at your front door," reports the nosy neighbor. "It's very kind of you to call," replies the doctor.) But for insight into either the Profumo affair or changing times, this is very thin stuff. And trying to convince us that Ward/Keeler is a love story, Thomas and Caton-Jones undermine their big picture with the case's unavoidable facts. They insist that Ward and Keeler's relationship constitutes true affection in a false world, but the film can't help indicating the ways the two continually betray each other. In a courtroom scene just before the ending, showing Ward and Keeler locking eyeballs (strings swelling), the movie loses its marbles.

Seeing Ward and Keeler as the scandal's scapegoats is not a novel view. Ward's suicide before the jury's verdict called commentators' attention to both the establishment's ready sacrifice of an outsider and the law's collusion in the process. Making the film mainly from Ward's point of view was logical tactically. But *Scandal*, interesting as a reminder of events, isn't intense or shrewd or skillful. There's an odd sense of visual unreality (a made-for-TV look) to the film, and Caton-Jones's forays into "technique" are out of film school kindergarten. While Hurt's strong presence humanizes Ward to an extent, the doctor's character, and Keeler's as well, continues to be opaque. As far as penetrating depths, the movie's about as effective as M15 was.

I neglected to mention that Bridget Fonda (daughter of Peter) is adorable as Mandy Rice-Davies, a feisty 16-year-old taken up by Christine and Stephen (in the official view, "recruited") who has an on-again, off-again part in the drama. At the end of the film, when epilogues recount the destinies of the surviving players, Rice-Davies gets laughs: The one born entrepreneur in the bunch, she went on to open a chain of nightclubs, called Mandy's, in Israel.

Also reviewed in:
NATION, 6/5/89, p. 787, Stuart Klawans
NEW REPUBLIC, 5/29/89, p. 24, Stanley Kauffmann
NEW YORK TIMES, 4/28/89, p. C10, Vincent Canby
NEW YORKER, 5/15/89, p. 121 Pauline Kael
VARIETY, 3/8–14/89, p. 21
WASHINGTON POST, 4/28/89, p. D1, Rita Kempley
WASHINGTON POST, 4/28/89, Weekend/p. 31, Desson Howe

SCENES FROM THE CLASS STRUGGLE IN BEVERLY HILLS

A Cinecom Entertainment Group release. *Executive Producer:* Amir J. Malin and Ira Deutchman. *Producer:* James C. Katz. *Director:* Paul Bartel. *Screenplay:* Bruce Wagner. *Story:* Paul Bartel and Bruce Wagner. *Director of Photography:* Steven Fierberg. *Editor:* Alan Toomayan. *Music:* Stanley Myers. *Sound:* Trevor Black. *Sound Editor:* Jay Dranch. *Production Designer:* Alex Tavoularis. *Art Director:* Robert Kensinger. *Costumes:* Dona Granata. *Make-up:* Cinzia Zanetti. *Running time:* 102 minutes. *MPAA Rating:* R.

CAST: Jacqueline Bisset (Clare); Ray Sharkey (Frank); Robert Beltran (Juan); Mary Woronov (Lisabeth); Ed Begley Jr., (Peter); Wallace Shawn (Howard); Arnetia Walker (To-bel); Rebecca Schaeffer (Zandra); Barret Oliver (Willie); Edith Diaz (Rosa); Paul Bartel (Mo); Paul Mazursky (Sidney); Jerry Tondo (June-bug); Susan Saiger (Kelly); Michael Feinstein (Michael Feinstein); Debora Babos (The Bride); Robert Gould (The Knight); Robin Menken (Persephone Cohen); Brett Porter (Policeman #1); Johnny Johnson (Policeman #2); Buckley Norris and Mark Lowenthal (Guests at the Wake); Marty Wyle, Allan Glaser, and Bruce Wagner (Dinner Guests); Milford Wayne Kemp (Thug); Linda Doucett (Woman in Window); Zane W. Levitt (Orkin Man); Darren (Bojangles).

FILMS IN REVIEW, 10/89, p. 489, Edmond Grant

Sick humor is the order of the day in *Scenes...*, Paul Bartel's comic view of daily life among the idle rich of Beverly Hills. In the tradition of classical farce, everyone here lusts after someone they're not supposed to; but unlike more traditional farce, *Scenes...* intersperses jokes about murder, race and castration in between the rampant bedhopping indulged in by the characters.

The catalysts for all this commotion are two servants (Ray Sharkey and Robert Beltran) who make a bet to see who can bed down the other's employer first. The women in question (Jacqueline Bisset and Mary Woronov) aren't averse to the come-ons offered them by the hired help, but, in the space of a single weekend, they are also confronted with a number of other amorous entanglements initiated by their ex-husbands (living and dead), Woronov's pretentious playwright brother (Ed Begley, Jr.), and his new Black wife who has a questionable past.

It's readily apparent from the film's outrageous first sequence (wherein the murder of a servant turns out to be something else entirely), that Bartel has grown as a filmmaker since his hit black comedy *Eating Raoul* (the projects in between that film and this being a series of awfully misguided flops). *Scenes...* succeeds in combining the usual plot twists and misunderstandings of the classic bedroom farce with some very inventive, nasty humor bounced off of the character's rather large pretentions (to which they cling with about as much passion as they can muster): Bisset's belief that she is still a saleable acting commodity, Sharkey's that he can seduce *anyone*, regardless of gender, and Begley's that he is the greatest voice in the modern American theater (he suspects the other characters want to get a glimpse of his latest masterwork, *Nocturnal Admissions*).

As is the case with any dialogue-ripe comedy, good casting is essential, and Bartel has made certain that *Scenes*...is filled with a group of familiar, talented faces. The cast is led by a very enthusiastic Bisset, who seems to relish her occasionally tasteless lines of dialogue; after the genteel, dull-edged humor of *High Season*, this comes as quite a change of pace. Bartel's *Raoul* cronies Woronov, Beltran, and Begley each get their own special moments, as do Wallace Shawn (who gets to do some of his patented intellectual whining) and Bartel himself as noted upper crust diet doctor. Putting in the film's best single performance, however, is Ray Sharkey as the Casanova houseman. Sharkey handles both the comic moments and the sentimental tie-up scenes at the film's end with equal charm and style.

This sentimental taint to the film's final sequences does slightly mar the fine sense of comic pacing. This is a small quibble, though, for a film that achieves something rather difficult: it proves that bad taste can be fun, even in the most rarified of social circles.

LOS ANGELES TIMES, 6/7/89, Calendar/p. 5, Sheila Benson

Paul Bartel's "Scenes From the Class Struggle in Beverly Hills" should have the wide-eyed wickedness that seems to seep right through the films of Pedro Almodóvar. It's almost as *bizarro:* a farce turning on the pan-sexual lust of a collection of high- and low-rent characters in and around the manicured hills of Beverly.

They include a sitcom queen (Jacqueline Bisset), just recently widowed; her next-door neighbor (Mary Woronov), only recently divorced; the housemen of both women (Robert Beltran and Ray Sharkey, respectively) who've only recently entered into a large cash bet over which one can score with the other's lady of the house first. And there are auxiliary characters enough to populate the senior class high school play—a showy role for everyone, including the dog.

But although Bruce Wagner's script has individually hilarious characters, such as Bisset's housekeeper (Edith Diaz), in hourly communion with Aztec gods of revenge, and Bartel has gotten one really delectable performance (Arnetia Walker's as To-bel) and a lovely rapport between his above-stairs mistresses and their below-stairs manservants, "Class Struggle" just can't keep from hugging itself at its own naughtiness. And self-congratulation is the sworn enemy of good raunchy fun, making it arch and pert instead of zinging in there, somewhere well below the belt.

Be assured there is a lot in this sex farce to upset the cautious, beginning with its scalding language and moving briskly to the action, which turns on the commingling of the Bisset and Woronov households while Woronov's house is being fumigated. The easily offended will be (the film's R-rating is for language and sexual situations), or Bartel/Wagner have missed their calling.

Bartel has one lovely moment, as piano music played by Woronov's lonely, sickly teen-age son (Barret Oliver) rises like a warm breeze, traveling up through the house, visibly affecting everyone who hears it. If the sexual roundelays of the household could move as effortlessly, the movie would be a bawdy delight.

In a few actors' hands it almost does. Bisset, glowingly beautiful, uses the light comic edge she displayed in "High Season" to lovely advantage, and Sharkey's preternaturally assured hustler takes no prisoners.

But the most consistent tone is hit by Walker's cheeky To-bel, a pneumatic actress with a few roles in her past that don't seem to be listed on her résumé. Resigned to being mistaken for Diahann Carroll, Leslie Uggams or Cecily Tyson, To-bel has impulsively married Ed Begley Jr., Woronov's brother and one of the worst playwrights ever, judging by the bits of scenes we hear from his past and future plays.

Walker has the knack of seeming to be doing something decorous, then splatting out into lasciviousness without pushing the moment or losing the energy behind it. The visual equivalent of a low-down dirty trumpet, Walker, also the voice on the sound-track song, is magnificent.

But the film needs to move to a level of surprise that goes beyond saucy language and tired sociological put-downs. It needs lightning speed and scorching assurance, not herky-jerky smugness and an oddly timorous suburban air. There's the hint that Bartel can do it; he just has to risk everything and plunge in unafraid, without first testing the water with his toe, or looking around to see if everyone is watching.

MONTHLY FILM BULLETIN, 1/90, p. 23, Kim Newman

Beverly Hills. Recently widowed Clare Lipkin, a former actress, plans to make a comeback, under the supervision of "thinologist" Dr. Mo Van de Kamp. Lisabeth Hepburn-Saravian, Clare's best friend and next-door neighbour, is having her house fumigated as a way of celebrating her divorce from the philandering Howard. Lisabeth, plus her sickly son Willie, her playwright brother Peter and Peter's new wife To-Bel, come to stay with Clare for the weekend. Clare is pestered by the ghost of her husband Sidney, and Lisabeth is put out when Howard, who recently had a fling in Hawaii with To-Bel, arrives. Juan, Clare's manservant, needs money to pay off a debt to bookie June-Bug, and makes a bet with Frank, Lisabeth's bisexual houseman. Each will try to seduce the other's mistress; if Juan wins, Frank will pay off June-Bug, and if Frank wins, Juan will have sex with him. Lisabeth does sleep with Juan, mainly to annoy Howard, but Frank fails to seduce Clare, who tries to affront Sidney's ghost by sleeping with Peter, while To-Bel, who is trying to conceal her porno-movie past, has sexual encounters with Howard and Willie. Zandra, Clare's daughter, sleeps with Frank, and decides to go to Africa on a hunger crusade with the lecherous Dr. Van de Kamp. Juan is too emotionally involved with Lisabeth to admit to Frank that they have had sex, and allows Frank to make love to him before leaving with Lisabeth. Frank pays off June-Bug and leaves on his motorcycle. To-Bel and Howard get together, Willie finds solace with Rosa the Aztec maid, and Clare rejects Peter and Sidney to concentrate on herself.

Scenes from the Class Struggle in Beverly Hills was announced long before "Beverly Hills" became a buzz phrase for titles, from *Beverly Hills Cop* and *Down and Out in Beverly Hills* to *Beverly Hills Vamp* and *Beverly Hills Bodysnatchers*. Indeed, the presence of the four stars of Paul Bartel's *Eating Raoul* suggests that, after his dispiriting output since then, this is supposed to be a return to the personal concerns of the earlier film, as if the director were yet again resuming his much-interrupted career. In the interim, Bartel has been mainly visible as a character actor in his friends'' films (appearing with Mary Woronov in *Heartbeeps, Chopping Mall*—in which they recreate their *Raoul* roles as Paul and Mary Bland—and *Mortuary Academy*) and as the producer of Michael Shroeder's *Out of the Dark* and *Mortuary Academy*. Scenarist Bruce Wagner has described the film as "a kind of radicalised version of *Rules of the Game* or *Smiles of a Summer Night*", and it actually comes across as a less deep-frozen version of Woody Allen's recent attempts to remake European serio-comic classics as pristine American drama.

Like *September, Scenes from the Class Struggle in Beverly Hills* is set almost entirely within the confines of one house, and a character works away at the piano to provide apt accompaniments to the action; like *A Midsummer Night's Sex Comedy*, Bergman's Shakespeare-derived lovers-all-change plot is shuffled through with more solemnity than farce; and like *Hannah and Her Sisters*, the film depends on the ensemble performances of a carefully assembled and yet diverse cast of performers, some from the director's stock company and some from further afield, with Jacqueline Bisset unbending as the sit-com queen just as the similarly British Michael Caine did for Allen. Wallace Shawn even turns up at the mid-way point as a genuine refugee from Allen's New York world (his ex-husband is a variant on his role in *Manhattan*), while Rebecca Schaeffer is a refugee from *Radio Days*, and the end credits play, as did those of *Everything You Always Wanted to Know About Sex*, under Cole Porter's "Let's Misbehave". One joke, whereby Howard and Juan both use a dramatic come-on speech they have borrowed from Peter's latest manuscript to attempt to seduce Lisabeth, is particularly in the Allenish tradition, with lovers caught up in the trappings of romance they have learned from film and theatre.

Bartel still retains his old commitment to the kinky and tasteless, and the film only really gets away from Allen's shadow when being callous—"I don't care who you talk to, when you get a bunch of rich fat people who are determined to get thin at any cost, some of them are going to die. It's a rule of thumb", remarks Bartel as the "thinologist"—or crude, as in Frank and To-Bel's sex scene shot just like the porno movie she has starred in. If the film burbles along quite pleasantly, it's because of Bartel's ability to throw in wholly unexpected bits of character business, as when Rosa the maid starts spouting mystical Aztec blather, or nasty-comic plot turns, as when Bojangles the dog is casually killed off to join the ghostly Sidney in limbo. If the film is less satisfying in its perversity than *Eating Raoul*, it may be because the servants who might be expected to provide the same kind of perspective on Beverly Hills life ("The way I see it, he spent three grand on a bathrobe—he deserved to die", remarks Frank of Sidney) that Paul and Mary Bland do on the Hollywood swingers of *Raoul* are too caught up in their own quirks and power games to be a real focus for the film.

The mix of sweetness and sadism that makes the best of Bartel so delicious is slightly unbalanced here, in that the film refuses to follow its characters to their logical extreme, allowing everybody to get out of the plot without suffering any severe emotional or physical damage. The extra-textual fact the Rebecca Schaeffer, who claimed that the role of Zandra was "the story of my life", was murdered in Hollywood by an obsessive fan shortly after completion of the film suggests how soft Bartel and Wagner finally are on their characters. In the end, the moral centre of the movie is Clare, whose funniest scene finds her in a Doris Day wig (associated with her old sit-com role), trying to sweet-talk a journalist over breakfast while the rest of the household compete to trot out disgusting and/or upsetting revelations. However, one suspects that the reason she comes across as the voice of sanity is that Bisset simply can't match the manic attack of players like Mary Woronov (a Bartel veteran), Ed Begley Jnr. and Wallace Shawn. If Woronov were playing Clare, the final moment when the actress rejects her ghostly and corporeal lovers to concentrate on herself would be an ironic triumph for self-absorption over relationships, but Bisset plays it straight, as if it were a moral not a punchline.

NEW LEADER, 8/7–21/89, p. 20, John Morrone

The only class struggle to be found in Beverly Hills lies in interchanges between white masters and (mostly) Hispanic servants. They run the gamut from "yes ma'am" to "no sir," but on both sides there is the opportunity for erotic exploitation, the promise of hanky-panky. In Paul Bartel's latest farce, *Scenes from the Class Struggle in Beverly Hills*, the hanky-panky runs riot; the movie could easily have been subtitled *Sex Games of the Rich and Famous*. Scenes and devices pulled whole from domestic screwball comedies of an earlier age are here given a flip, and played very, very deadpan. It's Bartel's funniest work in years.

Scenes was released with comparatively little fanfare, but it has stayed around by tickling enough moviegoers with its startlingly rude dialogue—which may sound raunchier than it actually is after much of the tepid Hollywood smart-aleckry of the '80s. The plot is a sly variation on an old gambit (most recently used in *Dirty Rotten Scoundrels*).

Two profligate and eccentric households are thrown together when ex-soap star and sex-starved widow Clare (Jacqueline Bisset) takes in the family of her next-door neighbor Lisabeth (Mary Woronov), whose home is being exterminated. Meanwhile housemen/chauffeurs Juan (Robert Beltran) and Frank (Ray Sharkey) have wagered to sleep with each other's bosslady. If Juan wins, he comes away with big bucks; if Frank wins, he gets a night with Juan, whom he fancies. (The bisexual twist appears only in the film's theatrical release. A source close to Cinecom reveals that the producers, in a fit of homophobia, deleted it from the videocassette version.)

Bartel is lazy about setting his libidinous roundelays in motion; members of the two families all too leisurely start bedding down with one another. Propelled by a series of coincidences just shy of Georges Feydeau, *Scenes* might creak were it not for the portly Bartel himself as Doctor Van de Kamp, Clare's "thinologist," strolling like Mr. Belvedere through the action in the company of his "favorite *chien sauvage*."

Offsetting Woronov's underwritten part and the undercast Bisset (who never fills her role with the camp relish of, say, a Joan Collins), newcomer Arnetia Walker steals the show as To-bel, the high-rollin' black ex-porn queen married to Lisabeth's brother (Ed Begley Jr.). To-bel's best lines are too raw to be quoted in these pages, but her parvenu zest is captured in her description of the new hubby: "He spends and spends...*and* he knows Shirley Maclaine!"

Since his initial film, *Private Parts*, Bartel's crass sensibiltiy—while not endearing him to the major studios—has helped him overcome uneven writing and misfit concoctions of erotic confusion and knockabout comedy. What we remember about his films is not their flaccid pacing but the inspired gags no mainstream script hack would attempt: the two halves of the missing map in *Lust in the Dust*, for instance, revealed to be complementary tattoos on Divine's and Lainie Kazan's derrieres.

Even at its best, *Scenes* is not the high drollery to which it aspires. But in a dry year of comedies the likes of *Weekend at Bernie's, Major League,* ant the unbearable *Troop Beverly Hills,* it seems, in To-bel's words, "just a freaky little act of God."

NEW YORK POST, 6/9/89, p. 25, David Edelstein

The title of Paul Bartel's deadly "Scenes From the Class Struggle in Beverly Hills" is satirical—there is, obviously, no class struggle in Beverly Hills, where people's definition of historical inevitability is a II, III and IV after every successful movie.

There is, however, something subversive afoot: Two servants (Robert Beltran and Ray Sharkey) have made a bet to see which of them can seduce the other's employer first. That's about as close to a plot as "Scenes From the Class Struggle" comes; it's also about as close to a good idea as "Scenes from the Class Struggle" comes.

The picture styles itself as a "Restoration comedy," an erotic ensemble roundelay in a Beverly Hills mansion. Lovers sneak in and out of one another's bedrooms at dawn; battles erupt; most everyone gets paired off with someone unexpected at the end.

People don't converse, they toss off epigrams. "Sweetheart, more and more I think abuse is strictly a California concept" is one such gem. There are others, equally lame, although I confess to liking, "A thing ain't over until you can kick the dead body and it won't fart."

Yet "Scenes" feels less like a Restoration comedy than a mock soap opera—campy, but with an embarrassing vein of mawkishness. Ex-sitcom actress Clare (Jacqueline Bisset) has just lost her husband (Paul Mazursky), who comes back as a ghost because now that he can't sleep with her he desperately wants to.

Clare's next-door neighbor (Mary Woronov) is having her mansion fumigated to remove all traces of her gynecologist husband (Wallace Shawn). She moves in with Clare, along with her visiting brother (Ed Begley Jr.), a pretentious playwright who has impulsively married a black porn actress (Arnetia Walker).

Walker, unbeknownst to anyone, has just had an affair with Shawn; Begley is in love with Bisset; Beltran wants to sleep with Woronov, who has second thoughts about kicking out Shawn; Sharkey has a thing about Bisset and Beltran, and also jumps into bed with Walker and Bisset's daughter (Rebecca Schaefer); and Walker sleeps not only with Shawn but with his cancerous teen-aged son (Barret Oliver).

All this sounds rather sexy, but Bartel's style is clinical and flat-footed. The only scene that's even vaguely erotic is the gay one—Sharkey's seduction of Beltran, which is part of their wager. The heterosexual antics are disposable, but his encounter has real weight.

Bartel (who plays a "thinologist" ensconced in Bisset's house) has built a career on making light of humanism. In his midnightmovie universe, he has taken the horror out of running down innocent bystanders ("Death Race 2000") and cooking and eating innocent people ("Eating Raoul").

So it's surprising that parts of "Scenes" should be so heartfelt. He's clearly trying harder to come to grips with his characters' humanity, and he suffers for the young boy (perhaps a stand-in for an AIDS victim), whose plangent piano music connects many of the sequences.

The problem is that Bartel can't settle on a tone. The film begins with an outlandish nightmare—boiling water thrown in a servant's face for breaking an heirloom—but becomes increasingly dewy-eyed. By the time Walker goes to bed with the boy—saying, "You're 'bout the only guy who never wanted anything from me"—the movie has lost whatever edge it had.

Too sentimental to be satire, too arch to arouse much empathy, "Scenes" also wastes its good actors. Bisset is bright-eyed and creamy, but Bartel's direction forces her into too many artificial postures. Walker and Shawn have their moments, and Sharkey who (along with Kevin Spacey) made the first season of "Wiseguy" one for the ages, slithers through his role like a tanned reptile.

Everyone else succumbs to writing so embarrassing that I shudder to recount it. When someone accuses someone else of waltzing in like Ozzie and Harriet, the reply is, "I can waltz in like Ozzie and I can waltz in like Harriet; I can't waltz in like Ozzie and Harriet, it's too taxing."

Try reading that out loud and you'll understand the problem. Some flip one-liner: the beginning and end of the joke are almost in different time zones.

NEWSDAY, 6/9/89. Part III/p. 3, Lynn Darling

"Scenes From the Class Struggle in Beverly Hills" begins with a wacked-out bit of fantasy: At an exclusive dinner party at the home of a bulimic ex-sitcom star, the maid has broken a valuable piece of Steuben glass. One of the guests, the resident diet doctor, responds by shooting her. As she lies dying in the kitchen, the dinner guests pass around the murder weapon, admiring it as if it were a bauble from Tiffany's, while the actress' late husband sits at the table covered in a black shroud.

It's the sort of setup that promises well, a bit of Buñuel black comedy aimed at the terminal vacuity of the Beverly Hills lifestyle and meant to launch the movie into the more raucous reaches of social satire. And director Paul Bartel has proven he knows how to deliver a malicious send-up—his first feature, the low-budget comedy "Eating Raoul," was a wonderfully blackhearted farce.

But as it turns out, the opening scene is only an illusion within an illusion, a mock tragedy staged for the benefit of the houseboy, Juan, who in turn is only dreaming the scenario in the first place. The scene is hollow at the core, and so is much of the movie that follows.

Part satire, part sex farce, part drawing-room comedy, "Scenes From the Class Struggle in Beverly Hills" follows the sexual pecadillos of two wealthy Beverly Hills households. Clare (Jacqueline Bisset), the ex-sitcom star, lives in a vague cloud of discontent, visited by the ghost of her late husband, Sidney (Paul Mazursky), who is a great deal more attentive in death than he ever was in life. Soon she is host to a large weekend house party—her next-door neighbor, Lisabeth (Mary Woronov), is recovering from her divorce by having her house fumigated, and moves in for the duration, followed by her playwright brother (Ed Begley Jr.), his bride (Arnetia Walker), her ailing son (Barret Oliver) and, eventually, her drunken, philandering ex-husband (Wallace Shawn).

Bedroom doors are soon closing on many variations on the original pairings, ringing a set of changes that are complicated by a bet the two families' houseboys have going: Frank (Ray Sharkey) bets Juan (Robert Beltran) that he can seduce Clare before Juan can seduce Lisabeth. In Beverly Hills, sex is the weapon of choice in the struggle, such as it is, between the vulgar rich and the vulgar poor.

This is upscale Bartel: The movie was filmed in real-life mansions studded with real-life status symbols. The movie has a sharp, glitzy look to it, but it loses much of the breezy insouciance that underscored the hard-edged subversiveness of "Eating Raoul."

Some of the scenes that emerge from all the libidinous plotting are sharply focused: Bartel alternates a tete-a-tete between the two rich women with one between the houseboys—the clichéd observations each couple makes about the other's values and sexual habits play off each other nicely. And most of the actors seem to be having a very good time with their deliberately one-dimensional roles. Bartel's gleeful dedication to skewering the decadent ethics and bloated appetites of his characters gives his movie a great deal of energy and style.

But adultery doesn't pull the same satiric punch that upwardly mobile murder did in "Eating Raoul." For all the frenetic comings and goings, there's a lot of down time in this movie: too many undeveloped characters rushing between too many unresolved situations.

From the beginning, the film aims to provoke outrage with its hip, deadpan sexual frankness. But most of the time all that it elicits is a jaded deja vu. "When you have a bunch of rich fat people who want to get thin at any price, some of them are going to die," the diet doctor (played by Bartel himself) observes. "Yesterday I [had sex with] the houseboy," announces one of the guests. "It was so degrading, I felt like some fabulous farm animal."

As examples of upper-middle-class anomie, these characters aren't telling us anything beyond the obvious. While all of them say and do seemingly outrageous things, they're pussycats at heart. Lisabeth, the bored housewife, simply wants to be loved; Clare, the ex-sitcom star, wants a little fulfillment—even Frank turns out eventually to have a soft spot in his acquisitive heart. The movie isn't nearly as outrageous as it thinks it is, and it ends up falling between the cracks—neither edgy satire nor undated restoration comedy.

"All my life I've been crossing that—line," laments Frank, the pansexual opportunistic houseboy. "I'm always amazed that there's nothing on the other side." The same could be said about Bartel's attempts to scandalize us with his freewheeling set of sexual adventurers.

NEWSWEEK, 6/12/89, p. 68, David Ansen

Paul Bartel's outrageous new satire, *Scenes from the Class Struggle in Beverly Hills,* is that rare thing, a truly dirty movie. Its not particularly erotic (it's too farcical for that) and it's certainly not pornographic, but like Bartel's best movie, "Eating Raoul," it means to shock and frequently succeeds. Bruce Wagner's ambitious screenplay (from a story he concocted with Bartel) wants to be a kind of contemporary Restoration comedy, with echoes of Buñuel as well as Beaumarchais. Spinning this sex farce into motion is a wager laid by two servants, played by Ray Sharkey and Robert Beltran, to see who can bed the other's rich employer first. Their targets are two pampered, indolent grand Beverly Hill dames—the recently widowed Clare Lipkin (Jacqueline Bisset) and her next-door neighbor, Lisabeth Hepburn-Saravian (Mary Woronov), who has moved into Clare's home for the weekend while her own house is being exterminated. She wants to banish all traces of her lecherous ex-husband Howard (Wallace Shawn).

Of course Howard reappears, as does the ghost of Clare's husband (Paul Mazursky). Adding to the crowd of libidinous revelers are Lisabeth's playwright brother (Ed Begley Jr.); his new black bride (Arnetia Walker), a former S&M porn performer; a pompous Beverly Hills "thinologist"

(Bartel) and Lisabeth's sickly son (Barret Oliver). The game of musical beds commences, as Bartel and Wagner savage the nouveau riche pretensions of this ghastly gaggle of hypocrites.

Wagner's script has true audacity; some of his rude lines can make you gasp. But watching the comedy unfold, one is increasingly aware of the gap between reach and grasp. In theory this movie seems deliciously naughty; in actuality you laugh less than you want to. Bartel has always been an erratic filmmaker (the hilarious "Raoul" was followed by the excruciating "Not for Publication"). As a director, he tends to impose his own camp acting style on his cast, and not all the performers are comfortable with the broad, arch style. Begley seems to be straining, Woronov (a Bartel regular) is strangely at sea, and though Bisset acquits herself gamely she doesn't have the lightness of spirit the material requires. The scene stealer is the sassy Arnetia Walker, the only one to find the effortless comic timing this farce needs. Still, the movie never bores. You have to admire Bartel and Wagner's malicious impudence. Their satirical scalpel may be blunt, but it still draws blood.

TIME, 6/12/89, p. 73, Richard Corliss

The big machines are parading by—the *Indiana Joneses* and *Star Treks* and *Ghostbusters*—wearing roman numerals like kill counts on their armor plate. In a steamroller summer, what's a low-budget comedy to do? Strut as brightly and bawdily as possible. Anyway, that is the tactic of the new film from Paul Bartel (*Eating Raoul*), which intrudes on the monster-movie scene like a kid blowing a May Day raspberry in Red Square.

There's not much class, but plenty of struggle, at the Lipkin mansion in Beverly Hills. Oh, sure, the rich know brand names: Harry Winston's jewels drape each mandarin wrist, and much Steuben Glass stand about, waiting to be shattered; and at the funeral for the Lipkins' pet pooch, Michael Feinstein plays piano. But the Lipkins and the Hepburn-Saravians, their haughty next-door neighbors, are egalitarians when considering where their next bedmate should come from. By the end of a weekend in the country, two elegant matrons will have been seduced by their former husbands, one of whom is dead. And everybody upstairs will have slept with everybody downstairs.

Clare (Jacqueline Bisset), a onetime sitcom queen keen for a comeback, had buried her swinish husband Sidney (Paul Mazursky), who materializes and pledges his infernal love to her. Clare's neighbor, Lisabeth (Mary Woronov), has just moved in with her daughter Zandra (Rebecca Schaeffer) because the exterminators are at her house, removing every trace of her ex-husband. Now these women and two others must fend off, or hop on, a platoon of randy males: Lisabeth's wormy ex (Wallace Shawn); her playwright brother (Ed Begley Jr.); her invalid prodigy son (Barret Oliver); and two manservants, sleazy, pansexual Frank (Ray Sharkey) and Juan, the sensitive stud (Robert Beltran). "We're from different stratagems of society," Juan croons to Lisabeth. "But I want to cross over. Like Rubén Blades."

The crossing of class and sexual borders is the rule in similar high comedies: Noël Coward's *Hay Fever*, Jean Renoir's *The Rules of the Game*, Ingmar Bergman's *Smiles of a Summer Night*. But those were about flirtation; director Bartel (who also plays Clare's snooty diet doctor) wants to talk about performance. Though set in the right now, *Scenes* is really a nostalgia piece from the swinging '70s, when coupling could be a game without emotional consequence or physical risk.

Scenes is a game too, cunningly constructed, sleekly appointed, exuberantly performed by a cast that picks up where bad taste leaves off. This one is not for the kids. Even adults will need moral shock absorbers; *Scenes* spits out its wit like a *Heathers* for grownups. Its pleasures may seem arid or acid to anyone who couldn't enjoy, say, a Restoration comedy as it might be played on *Dynasty*. But in a season when most movies are remakes of most other movies, *Scenes* is an original. And if you are in the right black mood, you could laugh till your nose bleeds.

VILLAGE VOICE, 6/13/89, p. 59, Georgia Brown

If *Dead Poets* is square [see Brown's review] Paul Bartel's *Scenes From the Class Struggle in Beverly Hills* is an '80s gloss on square. The titles, written on crimson satin wreathed by gold ribbon, may for a few moments bring to mind lush (garish) Technicolor melodramas of the '50s, but how far Bartel (*Eating Raoul, Lust in the Dust*) can go in mangling such expectations is the subject of his latest experiment in tastelessness. He gets right down to business.

At the head of her heavily laden dinner table, Clare (Jacqueline Bisset), the lady of the manor, recites the Lord's Prayer in the direction of the shrouded body of her recently dead husband,

Sidney (who later returns from the dead as Paul Mazursky), while family and guests chatter on and Rosa (Edith Diaz), the Mexican kitchen maid, continues pouring the wine. But when Rosa accidentally breaks something Steuben, furious Clare follows her to the kitchen and throws boiling lobster water into her face (*avec* lobsters). Then she asks her diet doctor—or "thinologist" as he's known to Beverly Hills clients—Dr. Mo Van de Kamp (the tubby Bartel), to finish the job with his cute little pistol. Just as Juan (Robert Beltran), Clare's handsome, simple-hearted houseman, steps in to revenge his fellow underclass Hispanic, family and guests—with the game Rosa, too— break into a chorus of "Happy Birthday, Juan" and a cake is brought out in the shape of a Mayan temple.

This opening scene—looking great, like a cross between soap and Sirk—happens to be a dream (Juan's), but it's only slightly less bizarre than successive "reality." Bartel—a director who would no doubt revel in a review employing words like *tasteless* or *racist*—does his farcical best to shock: "If this material doesn't offend anybody, it isn't working." Yet with the boundaries of offensiveness flexed nightly on TV sitcoms, the real question is, how funny is it? I wanted to laugh, I really did, but the movie, scripted by Bruce Wagner, kept thwarting me.

Clare's next-door neighbor, Lisabeth (Mary Woronov), while fumigating her mansion—draped in billowing red cloth, "our very own Christo"—is staying over at Clare's. So are assorted members of Lisabeth's household: her son Willie (Barret Oliver), in cancer remission, brooding on mortality and masturbation; her own houseman, Frank (Ray Sharkey), a randy painter; her visiting brother, Peter (Ed Begley, Jr.), peddling his latest play, *Nocturnal Admissions*, and his spanking-new bride To-bel (Arnetia Walker).

It takes a while for Lisabeth to realize that black, lusty To-bel is actually her brother's new wife. Then, since she's planning a trip to Africa ("Not *that* Africa, the *good* Africa"), she thinks to inquire whether To-bel knows anyone over there. In Bartel's world, To-bel is hardly a token black—she's here to bear out that "chocolate mamas" are red-hot numbers who are generous with their favors. By the end, To-bel's even able to assure young Willie, "Yo a ho' lot better equipped than yo daddy." (Daddy is pipsqueak Wallace Shawn—Howard of the raging libido.) The class struggle is also engaged when Frank blackmails the ingenuous Juan into a wager over who can bed the other's horny boss first.

Though *Class Struggle* didn't make me laugh much—an annoying omission—during the last half hour, I realized I'd developed an improbable fondness for this extended family. There's good-naturedness to Bartel's vision—tame praise, I realize, for someone dying to be offensive. And anyway, Jacqueline Bisset looks smashing enough to wile away the time.

Also reviewed in:
NATION, 6/19/89, p. 860, Stuart Klawans
NEW REPUBLIC, 7/10/89, p. 26, Stanley Kauffmann
NEW YORK TIMES, 6/9/89, p. C13, Vincent Canby
VARIETY, 5/10–16/89, p. 27
WASHINGTON POST, 6/16/89, Weekend/p. 41, Desson Howe
WASHINGTON POST, 6/17/89, p. D3, Hal Hinson

SEA OF LOVE

A Universal Pictures release. *Producer:* Martin Bregman and Louis A. Stroller. *Director:* Harold Becker. *Screenplay:* Richard Price. *Director of Photography:* Ronnie Taylor. *Editor:* David Bretherton. *Music:* Trevor Jones. *Music Editor:* Dan Carlin Sr. *Sound:* Keith Wester and (music) John Richards. *Sound Editor:* Norval Crutcher and Randle Akerson. *Production Designer:* John Jay Moore. *Set Decorator:* Gordon Sim. *Set Dresser:* Raman Majlath. *Costumes:* Betsy Cox. *Make-up:* Irene Kent. *Stunt Coordinator:* Dick Ziker. *Running time:* 110 minutes. *MPAA Rating:* R.

CAST: Al Pacino (Frank Keller); Ellen Barkin (Helen); John Goodman (Sherman); Michael Rooker (Terry); William Hockey (Frank Sr.) Richard Jenkins (Gruber); Paul Calderon (Serafino); Gene Canfield (Struk); Larry Joshua (Dargan); John Spencer (Lieutenant); Christine Estabrook (Gina Gallagher); Barbara Baxley (Miss Allen); Patricia Barry (Older Woman); Michael Phelan (Second Murdered Man); Michael O'Neill (Raymond Brown); Michael Fischetti (Doorman); Luis Ramos (Omar Maldonado); Rafael Baez (Efram Maldonado);

Samuel L. Jackson (Black Guy); Damien Leake (Ernest Lee); Zachary Michael Simmons (Ernest's Son); John Thaddeus (Tommy); Joshua Nelson (Willie); Christofer De Oni (Supermarket Manager); Dwayne McClary (Supermarket Cashier); Jacqueline Brookes (Helen's Mother); Thom Curley (Toastmaster); Fred Sanders (Cable Supervisor); Larry Mullane (Clipboard Guy #2); Anthony Catanese (Clipboard Guy #3); Thomas Wagner (Bartender); Manny Alfaro (Doorman); Brian Paul (Mackey); Deborah Taylor (Tense Woman); Ferne Downey (Sasha); Gerald Lenton (Second Murdered Man); Anita Rossi Band (Wedding Band); Nancy Beatty (Raymond Brown's Wife); Arun Greenaway and Nicolina Greenaway (Raymond Brown's Kids); Tony DeSantis (Clipboard Guy #1); Jackie Laidlaw (Yuppie Detective #1); Paul Hubbard (Yuppie Detective #2); Bill Haslett and James Kidnie (Surveillance Team); Bridgit O'Sullivan (Sherman's Wife); Delaney Moore-Wickham (Helen's Daughter); Franz Fridal (Criminal Type); James O'Regan and Wayne Best (Hallway Cops); John Bourgeois and Hugh Thompson (Young Cops); Philip Ho (Karate Cop); Igor Stern (Violinist); Miranda DePencier (Bride); Ty Templeton (Groom).

LOS ANGELES TIMES, 9/15/89, Calendar/p. 8, Kevin Thomas

"Sea of Love" is a satisfactory end-of-summer diversion, the kind of film that works as long as you ask nothing of it beyond simple escape. It's a slick, knowing genre film, through and through, a New York cop suspense thriller that we've seen countless times before.

It does, thankfully, have a sense of humor, and it does have Al Pacino, Ellen Barkin and John Goodman, all of whom are a bright, constant pleasure. Pacino and Barkin do scorch the screen, although this doesn't happen until a full hour into the picture; nevertheless, they become helpful in distracting attention from various inplausibilities.

Writer Richard Price and director Harold Becker take more time and pains than necessary to establish that Pacino's Frank Keller, a Manhattan police detective unsettled by reaching 20 years on the force, is a savvy, dedicated pro, earthy, gregarious and volatile yet an achingly lonely man beneath all the bravado. Goodman's sharp, humorous Sherman, a detective in Queens, comes into the picture when he and Frank team up to try to catch a serial killer whose victims are selected in the personals column of a singles magazine. Their one break appears to be that the murderer is attracted to ads employing poetry.

Barkin's Helen, the cool, sexy manager of a chic shoe store, is one of the respondents to an ad placed by Frank as a bait. After a bit of skirmishing, Frank and Helen commence a highly combustible romance. Never mind that this is contrary to orders; Frank is so carried away that he even resists having Helen's water glass checked for prints. Yet a series of incidents and remarks suggest that Frank's life could very well be in great danger. Golly, Helen even has a copy of Phil Phillips' "Sea of Love" in her collection of old 45s, a record that was playing over and over at the scene of the killings.

On its most basic level, "Sea of Love" works because Barkin has the skill to keep us guessing whether she is actually a man-hating crazy or just a wary veteran of the dating wars. There's no question that we are meant to see writ in large the paranoia that cripples so many relationships out there in the urban jungle, but this is to take "Sea of Love" too seriously. (Actually, the film is preferable to the disturbingly muddled seriousness of "Fatal Attraction.")

There's nothing at all profound in Helen or Frank, and Pacino and Barkin are engaged in showy star turns, loaded with attitudes and poses, that are fun in themselves and in fact appropriate for this superficial entertainment. Their duel of personalities is nicely anchored by the presence of Goodman, whose wit is as formidable as his bulk. Patricia Barry is heartbreaking as an elegant, lonely older woman who has answered Frank's ad.

As sleek as "Sea of Love" (rated R for violence, sex and language) is, it can't quite keep us away from wondering how a smart woman like Helen, whose looks would stop traffic and whose work would bring her into constant contact with an array of sophisticated men, would ever resort to the personals—unless, of course, she really is a psychopath.

MONTHLY FILM BULLETIN, 3/90, p. 76, Anne Billson

Detective Frank Keller, a divorcé who has been with the New York City police force for twenty years, is assigned to solve a murder case in which the victim has been found shot through the head, with the song "Sea of Love" on his record player. When another such murder takes place, Keller and fellow detective Sherman Touhey discover that each victim had placed a rhymed message in the lonely hearts column of a local newspaper. The detectives visit a third man who has placed a similar message, but he is married and refuses to co-operate in case his wife should find out; he too is later found murdered. The detectives persuade their sceptical superiors that they should place their own rhyming message in the newspaper and arrange meetings with all the women who respond. In the course of the investigation (the meetings take place in a restaurant, with the detectives alternating as romantic suitor and waiter), Keller finds himself attracted to one of the suspects: Helen, a shoe-shop assistant who is divorced with a small child. Against Touhey's advice, he postpones taking a sample of her fingerprints and becomes romantically involved, though he remains suspicious, particularly when he finds a pistol in her handbag and "Sea of Love" in her record collection. For her part, she is furious when she discovers his true identity, and even more furious when he mistakenly lets slip that their first meeting had been set up as part of the investigation. Keller is about to ask her to move in with him when he finds evidence to suggest that she had dated all the dead men. Convinced by this that she is the killer, he confronts her; but no sooner has she walked out in a huff than he is attacked by the real killer—her ex-husband Terry, a cable TV repairman who has been jealously shadowing her. After a struggle, Terry falls to his death through a window. Some weeks later, it looks as though Keller and Helen will be getting back together.

As a thriller, *Sea of Love* is set firmly in the "intimate jeopardy" territory exploited so successfully by *Jagged Edge* and botched so completely by the likes of *Physical Evidence:* the professional protagonist (lawyer or cop) becoming unprofessionally involved with someone who might or might not turn out to be the killer. As a device, this has the effect of wrapping a veil around one half of the relationship—in order to preserve tension, the suspect's behaviour must always be ambiguous—while loading the weight of the story on to the back of the other character. The plot of *Sea of Love* is riddled with so many holes that its whodunnit aspects scarcely bear examination, while seasoned thriller-watchers will easily be able to surmise the killer's identity by taking note of a scene which introduces the cable repairman as a potential witness while failing to establish a reason for the unusual prominence his character has been given.

The drawbacks of thriller conventions result in the usual proliferation of minor characters whose only function is to act as suspects, though John Goodman does well as Keller's partner—and the film breaks with recent formula by having the two of them be friends from the outset, thus mercifully eschewing the worn-out antagonistic-buddy scenario. The title, based as it is on a popular song, seems somewhat arbitrary; had the rights not been available, one imagines, the film-makers would simply have moved on to another contender. The film does pick up points, though, by ensuring that the character who ends up carrying the weight is played by an actor whose every tic is a feast for the eyeballs.

Like Robert De Niro in recent projects such as *Midnight Run* or *Jacknife*, Al Pacino (whose roles have been thin on the ground in the past decade), appears to be staking his claim to the straight bread-and-butter genre roles. As the streetwise, jaded veteran cop, Pacino brings just the right touch of exaggeration and is eminently successful at suggesting the character's darker urges: in his hands, Keller's incredible—and crucial to the plot—dithering over whether or not to take samples of Helen's fingerprints could almost be a symptom of a deliberate desire to flirt with danger (though it remains utterly incredible). There is a particularly well-judged scene in which he takes Helen back to his apartment and, discovering a gun in her handbag, is unsure whether she will be emerging from the bathroom to make love to him or kill him. On one level, this is simply recycling the old chestnut of equating the love act with death; on another, it might also contain a rough analogy to the way in which AIDS has made a Russian roulette out of even the most short-lived of physical encounters.

NEW STATESMAN & SOCIETY, 2/23/90, p. 46, Suzanne Moore

What is it about lonely hearts ads, apart from the name, that turns people off so much? I've had many a conversation with people who talk about little else but wanting a relationship, but who start spluttering when I make the practical suggestion of putting an ad in a lonely hearts column. It seems that in this sophisticated age we still want to kid ourselves that romance is something entirely "natural". But what could be more artificial than all those sickly valentine cards?

In fact, most of us meet our lovers through everyday situations, whether at work or through friends or, these days, in supermarkets. But then the unwritten rules of romance—especially for women—involve undercover work. We go to enormous lengths to just "bump into them", to accidentally turn up at the same place wearing our best clothes. Acting "naturally" is more difficult in these situations than winning an Oscar, but we all pretend.

To advertise for sex or love or both blows the cover on this collective pretence and makes us decidedly uncomfortable. Or, in the case of Harold Becker's new film *Sea of Love,* decidedly paranoid. *Sea of Love* heralds the return, after four years, of Al Pacino as Frank, the hard-bitten New York cop, going through a mid-life crisis. Frank drinks and discusses the breakdown of his marriage while examining the latest male corpse in a bizarre series of murders. All the victims have been men who advertised in lonely hearts columns so Frank, and his buddy Sherman, start looking for a woman with a penchant for bad poetry and a grudge against men. They eventually cook up the ridiculous scheme of placing an ad themselves, meeting various "ladies" and getting their fingerprints on a wine glass.

If we are to believe that this is what policemen do, then we really shouldn't be suprised at the vast numbers of unsolved crimes. On one of the dates Frank meets Helen (Ellen Barkin) a woman who talks about animal attraction, which is presumably why she ends up with a cop. Inevitably he falls for her, at the same time, suspecting her of the murders and the film proceeds to play this ambiguous relationship for all it's worth.

Much has been made of the sexual chemistry between the two lead players and here Pacino reminds us once more of both what a good actor he is and how short he is. Barkin has to take off her heels for the sex scenes to put her on an equal footing, so to speak. Nevertheless, her ugly duckling transformation continues; she has gone from playing downbeat wives to fully-fledged sex symbol.

That the clothes often look very fortyish—pencil skirts and shoulder pads—seems no coincidence since she is set up from the beginning as a classic *femme fatale*. That the aggressively sexual woman who threatens the very order of things, who emerges out of the shadows to an almost *Jaws*-type soundtrack, should reappear at a time when the image of the family is being revamped in Hollywood, is not a coincidence either. And this film, which has been a smash in the States, has obvious comparisons with *Fatal Attraction*. In the days when sex can kill, active and healthy female sexuality is often portrayed as life-threatening. Frank's fascination for Helen is fuelled by his knowledge that she may be truly dangerous. After all, in Hollywood's eyes women who take any sexual initiative are all regarded as *suspects* . . .

A more accurate comparison for *Sea of Love* would be *Jagged Edge*, another horribly insidious film where a successful and independent lawyer falls for a man she knows may be a killer. Though *Jagged Edge* at least has the benefit of a taut plot compared to *Sea of Love*'s wholly and, at times, ludicrous script: there is a daft, sexy supermarket scene in which Barkin squeezes a yellow pepper suggestively while Pacino follows her around with his tongue hanging out. Apparently supermarkets have replaced singles bars as hotbeds of sexual promise.

But *Sea of Love* is reminiscent of *Fatal Attraction* in that it's very easy to read it against the grain right from the beginning—to willfully identify with the woman who is marked as deviant, as "unnatural". In spite of all the meticulous work done in film studies on the complex and fluid nature of unconscious identification processes, who can deny the pleasure of *consciously* identifying with the villain of the piece? Just like all those women who cheered inside at the scene in *Fatal Attraction* when Glenn Close, after spying on the cosy domesticity of Michael Douglas's home life, throws up on the grass outside, so too in *Sea of Love* it's quite possible to hope that Ellen Barkin is in fact going around blowing men's brains out.

Even Pacino's character admires the directness of his imaginary murderess, acknowledging that maybe women have reason to be angry with the way men treat them. This symmetry, or empathy, between the hunter and the hunted is a device used over and over again in this kind of thriller. And so, in the mire of male banter that is shown in this film, who can resist smiling at the line: "There is some psycho woman out there who is killing guys?" That serial killers are invariably male and not female is yet another bitter distortion of the truth.

But then *Sea of Love* is one more exercise where men's fear and loathing of women doesn't simply distort the facts but manages to overturn them completely. Its sleight of hand lies in its ability to, on the one hand, expose male paranoia and, on the other, deny it. It legitimises Pacino's paranoia because we don't know until the end if the woman he is with is actually the killer or not. Thus, male fears are made flesh, focused on the body of one particular woman. Sex and danger merge into one. "For if a woman is prepared to seek out sex," this film seems to say, "to be honest about what she wants and doesn't want, who knows what else she might do?" Who indeed?

NEW YORK, 9/18/89, p. 70, David Denby

Sea of Love confirms what some of us had begun to suspect after "Life Lessons" (the first section of *New York Stories*)—that the novelist Richard Price has become the best screenwriter in the country. Price, 39, writes with something of the warmth and sweet anguish of Tennessee

Williams, though he's certainly a northern, urban Williams, with a city writer's cruel patter, an appreciation of the derisive jokes of the streets. His characters—shaggy, stumbling types bitten hard by experience—make messes all the time, yet guilty and ravaged as they are, they still demand more and more out of life. Price's writing is so alert to hidden injuries it's like a radar scan directed at doleful hearts, but for all his funk and rue, he's a funny, funny man.

Sea of Love, written by Price and directed by Harold Becker (*The Onion Field, Taps*), is a violent New York thriller set against the background of the lonely, disconsolate city. Men without women, women looking for men, wailing saxophones on the soundtrack. . . . We may think we know this nightshade mood all too well—the solipsizing drinkers in dim bars, the assignations at Korean vegetable markets at three in the morning. But if we love the city, a feeling for New York blues is probably part of our affection. *Sea of Love* is both an exciting murder mystery and a wonderfully grumpy Manhattan love story—all lust and paranoia. It's about New York as a state of feeling, New York as dissatisfaction and longing.

Someone—probably a woman—has been bumping off men who advertise in the personals section of *New York Weekly* (i.e., *New York* Magazine). The killer has specialized tastes: She preys only on men who write their ads in verse. Even though the poems are self-pitying and corny—*swinging light bulbs of my soul, all calling to you* is the general style—they add to the movie's tone of squashed lovelessness, the forlorn lamentations echoing across city canyons.

The cop assigned to the case is also moldering in empty rooms. Frank Keller (Al Pacino), a twenty-year veteran, won't quit and take his pension because he doesn't know what else to do with himself. He's chained to his job; meanwhile, his wife has left him for another cop, and he sits drinking at night in his West Side apartment, sodden and miserable, running down fast. Pacino himself is not so young anymore, and the extra weight he's carrying doesn't flatter a man his height. Like Frank Keller, he badly needs to make a comeback (fourteen years have passed since *Dog Day Afternoon*), and it's fun to watch him use his worn, sagging body as the greatest gift an actor could be given, scoring point after point with a hoarse voice, a shambling walk, a tired, battered face electrified by bright dark eyes—hot circuits to the brain passing through a surrounding deadness. Growling Price's bitter, bottom-of-the-shot-glass lines, Pacino is the soul of the picture.

After fighting with the cop who poached his wife, Frank picks up a partner, the Queens homicide detective Sherman Touhey (John Goodman), who is investigating another death at the hands of the poetry-reading killer. The big, gut-heavy Goodman has become an invaluable actor. That ballooning body and Humpty-Dumpty face—broad at the jaws, narrowing at the temples—is infinitely more expressive than the perfect trim and the regular features of most other actors. Goodman, joyously alive, prevents the movie from sliding into depression—his Sherman, an affectionate man and a good cop, is as powerfully connected to life as Frank is disconnected; his performance says that it's possible to be a whole person, even in New York.

The scenes of the men working the case together are excellent, but *Sea of Love* is not another male-buddy romance. A lady waits in the wings. The two men put a poem in the magazine's personals section, and the poem lures women—among them, perhaps, the killer—to O'Neals' Balloon. Richard Price and Harold Becker put together a classic New York sequence here. Pretending to be a man on the make, Frank interviews the women who show up. They're a brave lot. Whether desperate for companionship or just excited at the possibility of sex with a stranger, they arrive well-armed, bristling, determined not to be on the defensive. Proud of their ability to size up people at first glance (it's the New York art), some of them spot Frank as a fake. Among the women is Ellen Barkin's Helen, with a red leather jacket and golden hair, leaning across the table as if she were ready to devour Frank in one gulp. She's so gutsy and decisive that Frank decides she must be the murderer. But then he violates his professional code and common sense, too, and goes to bed with her, half expecting a gun to come out in the middle of the night aimed at him.

Is Helen the killer? (Or, in the movie's police slang, "the do-er"?) Pacino's Frank Keller, overwhelmed by this hungry woman (she does *him*, all right), feels as though he's slipped into a dream that may be a nightmare. The tall and sinewy Barkin puts on a sensational act as a ravenous good-bad girl. Stalking Pacino in his apartment, she's a descendant of Jane Greer and Gene Tierney and Lana-Rita-Ava, and of every other sultry woman of the forties who dazzled and betrayed men. Yet no matter how many femmes fatales she plays, Barkin will never turn into a humorless dreadnought like the old broadshouldered sex goddesses. With her crooked grin and her jaw tucked in sheepishly, she's too eccentric and likeable an actress for that. The filmmakers tease us by playing with the forties convention that full, long hair and sexual avidity are sure signs of evil, or at least of danger. But then they take the character out of movie myth and return her to reality. Helen likes sex, she likes to devastate men, but she's also a mother, a daughter, and a responsible job holder—not a killer, just a restless woman looking for contact and sensation. A modern city woman. Right?

From *Jagged Edge* and many other movies, we're familiar with the situation of a lead character falling in love with someone who may have committed a murder, but the standard thriller plot works here as an expression of a specific New York craziness. *Sea of Love* has a messy, powerful erotic pull to it. Becker keeps it dark and intimate—furious nights in grottolike West End Avenue apartments, the lovers never trusting each other, slipping on the rocks, righting themselves, slipping again. Price's writing has heart and precision; he doesn't bluster. The movie is held together by an agonized sense of what living in New York can do to people; the characters have become a volatile mix of guilt and aggression. Richard Price is now the voice of New York in movies, the poet of raw, jangled nerves.

NEW YORK POST, 9/15/89, p. 21, David Edelstein

"Sea of Love" is a deliriously creepy mystery-thriller, as seductive and unnerving as the song that carries it in on a wave of desire. The song (by Phil Phillips) promises love everlasting, and, in a manner of speaking, it delivers. In the first scene, a scratchy 45 spins on a turntable and a naked man moves his body up and down on a mattress, as if having sex. Then a gun goes off and thick, blackish blood runs down his face. Still the record plays, serenading him.

The murder, police think, is the work of a psychotic woman, and she could be anyone: The New York of "Sea of Love" is a jungle of pain—an urban sprawl of lonely, disconnected people. Among them, in fact, is the detective assigned to the case, Frank Keller (Al Pacino), a 20-year police veteran and alcoholic in the throes of a nasty mid-life crisis.

Pacino hasn't made a film since "Revolution" (1985), and I'd forgotten how vivid he could be. His face now has a doggy droop, but his eyes are so wide and dark that they jump out of the screen. He's genuinely feverish, manic and stupefied at once, and the movie has the sense to make his monotonic intensity part of the joke. (Everyone tells him how wired he looks.) Pacino's Frank is pure New York, a messy bundle of needs.

Frank has problems, all right. His ex-wife now lives with his prim partner (Richard Jenkins), and the two discuss Frank's recent drunken phone call to her while examining the body on the mattress. Their clinical indifference to the victim is a grisly irony, because Frank, in his way, is part of the same drama that cost this man his life. And he's about to get sucked in deep.

The key to this beautifully crafted script (by novelist Richard Price) is that the murders seem an extension of a universal longing. You don't know who the killer is, but you know in your bones that the motive has something to do with being unloved in a place as brusque and cold as New York City.

There are soon three naked, face-down victims, and the link among them is that each ran a poem in the Personals column of a New York singles magazine. So Frank decides to run his own ad. (Everyone but him knows he wants to meet babes as well as watch a killer.)

He does the blind date thing in O'Neal's Balloon, sitting opposite a succession of women while his new partner, Sherman (John Goodman), pretends to be a waiter and dusts their wine glasses for prints.

As Frank assures these lonely-hearts he'll call them later in the week (fat chance), the movie develops amazing layers of psychosis: You see a dark look of rejection in the eyes of the women who know he's lying; he might catch a killer, but he might also be generating new ones.

Wittily, the movie builds to the appearance of its chief suspect, Helen (Ellen Barkin). Tousled and nervy in her red leather jacket, Barkin's Helen fixes Frank with a knowing look, tells him the chemistry isn't there and leaves without touching her wine glass.

Of course, Frank will bump into her later and fall in love with her—without, of course, getting her prints. Helen lives with her mother and young daughter, and you can tell she's been emotionally brutalized. Her guard never drops, yet she's angry at being forced to keep it up—policing her own emotions makes her miserable. She'd love to swim in the sea of love, but she knows all about the undertow.

Right off the bat she rails against the "manipulators, liars, guys who wait until you're good and deep before you find out who they really are." She could be talking about the heroes of a number of Price novels (among them "Ladies Man" and "The Breaks")—and maybe (who knows?) she could be talking about Frank, who falls in love and wants her to move in with him almost immediately.

What's extraordinary about Barkin's performance—it's her most alluring—is her flickering mixture of desire and defensiveness. She's shockingly touchy, quick to flare up at the first sign of possessiveness, yet she invites possessiveness, too—shedding her blouse, she moves on Frank like a flame.

Is Frank with her because he knows she isn't the killer or because he thinks she might be? Which is the bigger turn-on? And which will he lay on her first: the keys to his apartment in one pocket or the revolver in the other?

The director, Harold Becker, doesn't have as poetic a touch as one might wish, but his work is solid, unobtrusive. Yes, the movie has some holes. The ending is flat and formulaic, and Pacino lurches a shade too mightily in the latter stages. (He was so over-the-top in "Scarface" he must think he's been underacting for most of "Sea of Love.")

But it's a miracle that Price could cram so many of his obsessions into so traditional a cop thriller. Just as you'll never hear "Blue Velvet" the same way after David Lynch injected sadism and bugs, you'll never hear "Sea of Love" without thinking of lonely souls being summoned to their deaths. As Price says in an interview: "It's romantic and beckoning in a very siren-like way ... It's a good song to die to."

And "Sea of Love" is a thriller to die for.

NEWSDAY, 9/15/89, Part III/p. 3, Terry Kelleher

Maybe it's the dialect.

Al Pacino is speaking his native New Yorkese in this picture. He put on accents in his last two—"Scarface" (Cuban) and "Revolution" (indeterminate)—and they didn't turn out so hot.

Maybe it's the occupation.

The Bronx native last played a New York cop in "Serpico," his first non-"Godfather" hit. Now "Sea of Love" finds him back with the N.Y.P.D. (For purposes of this theory, let's forget his unfortunate tour of police duty in "Cruising.")

Whatever the reason, "Sea of Love" represents Pacino's best film work in a decade. His vivid portrayal of a lonely, boozy, desperately confused detective lifts this enterprise above the commonplace. And we're talking about some heavy lifting here.

Richard Price's screenplay employs a highly unoriginal plot line: Cop investigating a string of murders gets romantically involved with a prime suspect. Will he respect her in the morning? Will he live that long?

All three victims were men who sought female companionship by advertising in a singles publication. So Frank Keller (Pacino) and Sherman Touhey (John Goodman), his cheery colleague, place a personal ad and set themselves up as bait. Frank soon goes crazy for a respondent named Helen (Ellen Barkin), who has a body that won't quit and a sexual appetite to match. Unfortunately, she arouses his suspicion as well as his libido.

But Frank's in an incautious frame of mind. His wife divorced him and married a fellow policeman, and Frank gets that burning, cuckolded feeling every time he sees the guy. His 20th anniversary on the force has brought on a serious midlife crisis. He could retire now at a nice pension, but if he gives up the badge, he'll have nothing left but the bottle.

Choosing recklessness over emptiness, Frank has an affair with Helen that must be described as torrid. Of course, he can't let her know the circumstances of their first meeting, so he lies about his occupation. When Helen finds out he's really a cop, Frank lies about why he lied, launching into an impassioned speech on the lawman's burden. Another lie follows, and another, and Price's script is intelligent enough to make each one at least a half-truth.

Pacino looks distracted, disheveled, dangerously close to the end of his tether. (In fact, it's not entirely clear what Helen sees in him besides extreme emotional need and a still-functioning sense of humor.) Frank is afraid to commit himself, afraid of the way Helen makes him feel—and, not incidentally, afraid she'll cut off his life in the middle. Director Harold Becker occasionally finds a feverish kind of comedy in the situation, as when Frank notices a pistol in Helen's purse and his excitation turns to panic.

"Sea of Love" is not as suspenseful as it could have been, but if Becker had tried for more of a thriller he probably would have achieved less of a character study. The mystery plot is eventually resolved in a manner that may surprise Frank more than the audience. After all, if the detective kept his mind on his work, he wouldn't be in this mess.

This is a movie that will remind you of many another, but it's also a welcome reminder that Pacino hasn't lost his power or his nerve. He seems to be over his mid-career crisis.

NEWSWEEK, 9/18/89, p. 81, David Ansen

In *Sea of Love* Al Pacino plays a veteran NYPD detective who, while investigating a series of sex murders, falls dangerously in love with one of his suspects (Ellen Barkin). This isn't exactly a novel premise, but it's a pretty irresistible one: sexual murder mysteries provide the double whammy of prurience and puritanism, toying with both our deepest fears and hidden desires. The commercial success of "Fatal Attraction" testified to our undying fascination with the femme fatale, but director Harold ("The Onion Field") Becker's new movie actually has more in common with such movies as Clint Eastwood's "Tightrope" and even Pacino's misbegotten "Cruising." In these sexual thrillers the cop/hero loses his bearings in a dark, erotic world; the thin line of professionalism gets blurred as the pursuer becomes a participant.

Detective Frank Keller, a 20-year vet, is a man on the verge of a midlife crisis when the case starts. He's been on the job too long, he's got a drinking problem and he can't get over the fact that his wife left him for another cop. Lonely and out of control, how can be resist the sultry Helen, even though he knows he's violating every police commandment by sleeping with a suspect? Someone has been knocking off men who've been answering personal ads. Pacino and a Long Island detective (John Goodman) think they spot a pattern: the victims have all written their ads in verse. They hope to catch the killer by placing their own poetic come-on in the paper, meeting the women who respond and getting their fingerprints. Keller makes the mistake of falling for a siren who may or may not be planning to kill him.

Moment by moment, "Sea of Love" holds you in a tight grip. It's a stylish diversion, though it never gets much below its self-consciously "hot" surface. When it's over (and the wrap-up is its weakest aspect) you may feel as if you've seen nothing more than a well-produced TV movie. Still, if Richard Price's plot ultimately proves a disappointing contrivance, his scenes have a slangy, gritty vitality. Price, the novelist who wrote "The Color of Money," writes terrific street-smart New York dialogue, and he's given Pacino a role that reminds us why he was, back in the era of "Serpico" and "Dog Day Afternoon," one of the treasures of American movies. There's charm and wit and feeling in his performance, and Barkin, oozing carnality, is every bit his match. "Sea of Love" (named after the Phil Phillips single the killer plays during the murders) may not have the resonance of the great *noir* thrillers it emulates, but it wins so many battles along the way you can forgive it if it loses the war.

TIME, 9/25/89, p. 79, Richard Schickel

When did this vast cloud of depression settle over the movies' police force? Possibly when Joseph Wambaugh quit the Los Angeles department and started writing realistic (and highly adaptable) novels about the modern lawman's unhappy lot. In any case, it is now the formula for cop movies: the detective hero is usually divorced, drinking too much and sleeping too little. Often he wonders what it all means—running around, risking your life and not making any discernible dent in the crime rate.

What saves Frank Keller (Al Pacino) from the depths is wit. He is first seen as host of a church baseball brunch at which the Yankees have been announced to appear. They do not. What does appear is a squad of New York City's finest, who bust everyone in the place. For Keller had invited baseball fans who also happen to have made the most-wanted list.

The same imaginative spirit animates his pursuit of a serial killer who is stalking womanizers (nice reversal of expectations there). Keller and his partner (John Goodman) place ads in the personal columns of an alternative newspaper and start dating the respondents. Needless to say, the likeliest suspect (Ellen Barkin) is also the best bet to comfort our hero.

Sex and menace do not synergize as hysteria, the way they did in *Fatal Attraction*. This film is relatively calm. But it is worth taking in because all concerned catch the tone of New York's besieged multitudes. Their weariness is touched with hope, and their hope with irony. Their realism transforms what might have been an item easily overlooked by the moviegoer into something worth collaring.

VILLAGE VOICE, 9/26/89, p. 70, Amy Taubin

On paper, *Sea of Love* looks promising. A cop in a mid-life crisis (Al Pacino) gets a lech for a woman (Ellen Barkin) who may or may not be a serial killer preying on guys who look for love through the personals.

To the slow-grind beat of the title song, the credit sequence opens with a night shot of the East River, and immediately it's like someone's attached a cement block to the picture. (You might expect some novice MTV director to literalize the metaphor "sea of love" with an image of the nearest body of water, but not an almost-auteur like Harold Becker.) Then there's a dissolve to tawdry Times Square, with a couple of extras in hot pants lounging under the neon, and another dissolve to a happening 10th Avenue diner. (None of these locations ever figures in the action, which, aside from a few excursions to 57th and Madison, is solidly grounded in 15 blocks of the Upper West Side.) As the music builds to a climax, the camera cranes into the window of a bedroom where a bare-assed guy, jerking off facedown on the bed, is about to get his head blown off. It's as predictable as a TV movie.

For all its heavyhandedness, Becker's direction can't plug the holes in Richard Price's screenplay. A psychological thriller, Sea of Love depends on the intricacies of character and relationship. Pacino's Frank Keller, divorced and depressed, furtively longs to be in as torturous a situation as he was with his ex-wife. Keller's the kind of guilt-ridden guy who's only turned on when there are lots of "should nots" involved. Helen (Barkin), in a waist-cinching red leather jacket with shoulders out to there (it's going to look dated even before the film hits the video stores), fits his m.o. precisely. The fact that she's a prime suspect in his murder investigation (and therefore he's lying to her about what he does for a living) guarantees his obsession.

Unfortunately, Barkin plays Helen less as a character than as a series of contradictory poses calculated to make the audience wonder whether she's really a psycho killer or just a nice kid who likes to use all her muscles during foreplay. We gather from the morning-after dialogue that this is supposed to be a torrid affair, but what we actually see is less convincing. Basically, Keller gets all hot and bothered about finding the odd starter pistol or toy gun somewhere on Helen's person (this happens on three separate occasions), and then Helen makes him forget by climbing all over him as if he were an exercycle. Becker, who as a rule favors close-ups and tight two-shots, is uncharacteristically discreet about what happens next, and since the acting in the preliminary rounds ranges from strained to laughable, my imagination refused to operate.

His scenes with Barken aside, Pacino's performance is Sea of Love's most notable asset. He gets good-humored support from John Goodman as a sympathetic fellow officer. The film also has a spectacularly choreographed, brutal one-on-one fight scene. For the record: I knew who the killer was after the first 30 minutes, and I'm no expert in the genre.

Also reviewed in:
NEW REPUBLIC, 10/9/89, p. 25, Stanley Kauffmann
NEW YORK TIMES, 9/15/89, p. C12, Vincent Canby
NEW YORKER, 9/18/89. p. 100, Terrence Rafferty
VARIETY, 9/13-19/89, p. 18
WASHINGTON POST, 9/15/89, p. C1, Hal Hinson
WASHINGTON POST, 9/15/89, Weekend/p. 39, Desson Howe

SECOND ANIMATION CELEBRATION, THE: THE MOVIE

An Expanded Entertainment release of an International Tournée of Animation presentation. *Executive Producer:* Steve Gilula, Gary Meyer, and Terry Thoren. *Producer:* Terry Thoren. *Running time:* 105 minutes. *MPAA Rating:* Not Rated.

LOS ANGELES TIMES, 7/27/89, Calendar/p. 9, Charles Solomon

Audiences weary of the recycled humor in many of the summer's comedy hits will find a welcome change of pace in "The Second Animation Celebration: The Movie!"

A bright, upbeat collection of short films from the second and third Los Angeles Animation Celebrations, the show offers a look at some of the humorous work being done in contemporary world animation. (Most of the more serious films will be showcased in the annual Tournée of Animation later this year.)

The exception to the humorous rule—and the outstanding film in the collection—is the dazzling: "Umbabarauma"(U.K./U.S.A.), made by Susan Young and Mike Smith for the multi-faceted David Byrne. Set to the Afro-Brazilian music of Jorge Ben, semi-abstract images of cockfights, fireworks and dancers metamorphose in an opulent collage of color and motion that evokes the excitement of the Carnaval in Rio. "Umbabarauma" should be a strong candidate for the Oscar for animated short next year.

The figures in Chris Casady's "Pencil Dance' (U.S.A.) are purely abstract, but the shapes and lines dance to the Prokofiev score with a gleeful elan that imbues the film with a comedic feel. This handsome, tasteful work marks the debut of a promising young artist.

"Tin Toy" (U.S.A.) by John Lasseter and William Reeves, the first computer-animated short to win an Oscar, is both a charming entertainment and an impressive example of computer graphics, although the artists missed its obvious ending.

Mikhail Tumelya and Alexander Petrov use old-fashioned drawn animation and rotoscoping in "The Marathon" (U.S.S.R), a warmly affectionate tribute to the enduring magic of Mickey Mouse and the medium of animation. Tony Collingwood strikes a balance between comedy and tragedy in "Rarg" (U.K.), an elaborate fantasy that suggests life really is just a dream. Tom Sito shows how music can transcend cultural boundaries and spoofs superpower rivalries in "Propagandance" (U.S.A.).

If Sito celebrates the ultimate triumph of brotherhood, Matt Groening revels in the frictions of daily life in five episodes of "The Simpsons" from "The Tracey Ullman Show." The animation and artwork are minimal at best, but the writing is so sharply evocative of the petty hassles families create around mundane activities—like picture-taking and going to bed—that the results are hilarious.

The one real dud in the show, Bill Plimpton's "Twenty-Five Ways to Quit Smoking" (U.S.A.), re-uses the scribbly drawing style and clumsily metamorphic animation of his popular "Your Face." That film owed much of its appeal to the novelty of its technique, but the novelty has worn off, and the artist needs to find a new shtick.

NEW YORK POST, 9/15/89, p. 23 Jami Bernard

The latest compilation of animated shorts from Expanded Entertainment, a company which treats its movies as traveling animation festivals, is a splendid mix of the witty, the wise, and the wacky, from animators all over the world—including a bunch of grade schoolers who animated the concept of love and a tribute by the Russians to the very American Mickey Mouse.

Interspersed with blackout episodes from Matt Groening's "The Simpsons" (seen on "The Tracy Ullman Show"), about a family that copes about as well with funerals as with their children's burping contests, "The Second Animation Celebration: The Movie" is a well programmed, varied representation of different animation styles and moods.

Freedom and global cooperation are themes that are frequently sounded. The Soviet tribute to Mickey for his 60th anniversary is a case in point—"The Marathon," in which a silhouette of Mickey dances opposite a silhouette of a rapidly aging human who then makes way for another generation, was made without the consent of Disney's ultra-stern anti-copyright infringement enforcers. After seeing what was done with Mickey by a country that has only seen the character in bootleg prints and videos, the suitably impressed company gave its full backing. The four-minute short is preceded by a message from Roy Disney himself.

"Propagandance," from Tom Sito (who worked on "Who Framed Roger Rabbit"), is another dance contest, this time between an urban breakdancer and an old-time soviet *kazatsky* dancer, is a study in overcoming political brainwashing through cultural give-&-take.

At 11 minutes, Gavrilo Gnatovich's "Lazar" is one of the longer pieces, a colorful and pernicious story about one man's attempt to escape a life bounded by a government-sanctioned "wall," a metaphor for political repression.

Computer animation has a strong presence in this collection, including the Oscar-winning "Tin Toy," about a wind-up toy's attempts to elude the grasp of a behemoth baby.

There are also examples of clay animation (think "dancing raisins"), silhouettes (paper cutouts), and traditional hand-drawn cel animation.

Other shorts of note:

Bill Plimpton's "25 Ways to Quit Smoking," in which one suggestion, for self-discipline, requires the smoker to punch himself in the face after each puff.

"ASIFA Children's Film" is made by children from eight countries who animated the concept of love, from first dates to happy families.

The British "Rarg," by Tony Collingwood, is the longest piece at 21 minutes. The cel-animated fable has a Dr. Seuss look; it is about an idyllic community of inventors who discover that they only exist in the dreams of a man whose alarm clock is about to go off. They scurry to invent something that will keep him dreaming and thus preserve their world.

In "Knickknack," a shelf full of odds and ends shimmy to Bobby McFerrin music while a snowman in one of those shake-&-snow plastic bubbles tries to escape his tiny world. Good use of computer animation by John Lasseter and William Reeves.

"Goonight Norma ... Good night Milton ..." is another example of John Schnall's typically dark humor. Two people savage the guests they'd had over that night while stripping themselves truly naked—and horribly so—for the night.

NEWSDAY, 9/15/89, Part III/p. 5, Leo Seligsohn

There's nothing Mickey Mouse about animated film, as this 105-minute showcase proves. Ranging in length from 30 seconds to 21 minutes, these 24 snippets cut brashly across creative as well as geographical boundaries. Funny, grim, political or purely aesthetic, all are defiantly—often brilliantly—unconventional. Selected from more than 1,500 entrees in the Second and Third Los Angeles International Animation Celebrations, the assembled work presents a striking array of styles from a half-dozen countries, including the Soviet Union and Cuba.

Contrasts are immediately apparent: The first piece is a lighthearted short called the "The Simpsons: 'Goodnight,' " which takes less than two very funny minutes to tell its story of parents unwittingly creating anxiety in their children at bedtime. It's followed by the show's second-longest bit, a dark 11-minute nightmare·called "Lazar," about a man trapped within the walls of harsh regime. Both were made in the United States—the first by Matt Groening and the second by Gavrilo Gnatovich.

While fantasy is employed in almost all the films, the movie's truest fairy tale is the beautifully rendered "Rarg," by Tony Collingwood of the United Kingdom. At 21 minutes, it's the longest piece, moving at an appropriately dreamy pace to relate its gentle tale of the happy kingdom of Rarg—which is just a dream inside the head of a sleeping man who's about to wake up. A gem.

For the technologically minded, there is "Tin Toy," the first computer-animated film to win an Academy Award. It was made by John Lasseter and William Reeves of the United States, who took the prize last year. Simple, touching and five minutes long, it's about a windup soldier's encounter with a demonstrative baby.

A number of the films are abstract. These include "Pencil Dance" by American Chris Casady, in which a troupe of black-and-white pencil marks perform a 2½-minute ballet to the music of Prokofiev. "Finger Wave" by Hungary's Gyula Nagy is two minutes of the directors' hands performing to musical accompaniment. An Afro-Brazilian score creates excitement for splashes of throbbing, bobbing colors in England's five-minute "Umbabarauma," commissioned by David Byrne of Talking Heads, its executive producer.

In "Quinoscopia" Cuba's Juan Padron creates a fast, six-minute satirical series that needles everyday folk. But the movie's strongest one-world political message comes from Tom Sito of the United States, in his 4½-minute "Propagandance," in which a Soviet and U.S. dancer challenge Cold War paranoia. Less dated is a Soviet bit, "Marathon," in which Mickey Mouse actually does get into the act. Made by Soviet student animators, it's a clever four-minute tribute to the famous rodent on his 60th birthday.

The movie ends as it begins—with the hilarious "Simpsons" doing another of their dysfunctional family routines. They are the movie's only performers who can be seen in another venue, "The Tracey Ullman Show." And soon, just to prove where high-class animation can get you, they're slated to appear in their own series.

Also reviewed in:
NEW YORK TIMES, 9/15/89, p. C14, Caryn James

SECOND SIGHT

A Warner Bros. release of a Lorimar Film Entertainment presentation of an Ursus Film production. *Executive Producer:* Joe Caracciolo Jr. *Producer:* Mark Tarlov. *Director:* Joel Zwick. *Screenplay:* Tom Schulman and Patricia Resnick. *Direction of Photography:* Dana Christiaansen. *Editor:* David Ray. *Music:* John Morris. *Production Designer:* James L. Schoppe. *Running time:* 83 minutes. *MPAA Rating:* PG.

CAST: John Larroquette (Wills); Bronson Pinchot (Bobby McGee); Bess Armstrong (Sister Elisabeth); Stuart Pankin (Dr. Preston Pickett); John Schuck (Lieutenant Manoogian); James Tolkan (Captain Coolidge); Christine Estabrook (Priscilla); Marisol Massey (The Cardinal's Secretary); William Prince (Cardinal O'Hara); Ron Taylor (Carl); Adam Lefevre (Mike); Andrew Mutnick (Elmore); Michael Lombard (The Bishop); Barbara Meek (Eileen).

LOS ANGELES TIMES, 11/6/89, Calendar/p. 4, Chris Willman

It won't take any supernatural prescience for most folks to know to steer clear of "Second Sight," the new comedy about a wacky psychic detective agency; the ad campaign ought to offer sufficient forecast. Yet it's even more dire than one might have predicted. Forget earthquakes and assassinations: Where were Jeanne Dixon or Criswell when we needed them to warn us about *this?*

The premise has the distinct aura of a buddy comedy: There's the wild-and-crazy eccentric who is liable to do anything at any second—in this case, Bronson Pinchot (of TV's "Perfect Strangers") as the childlike soothsayer who solves cases and is prone to irritating trans-channeling fits and spasms at a moment's notice. Then there's the down-to-earth wiseacre-partner—in this case, John Larroquette (of TV's "Night Court") as the eternally cranky agency head.

Scripters Patricia Resnick and Tom Schulman have incorporated a few cute twists on the psychic premise, as when Larroquette twists the inert limbs of a sleeping Pinchot into a human antenna in order to pick up a blacked-out game, or when Pinchot is able to dodge bullets thanks to his precognitive ability to foresee where they will hit. Most of the humor, though, centers wearily around the fact that Pinchot's "spirit guide" isn't a Ramtha type but rather a frisky, New Yawk-accented thug named Murray, an overmilked idea good for far fewer snickers than anyone seems to have predicted.

The biggest case for these Boston mind-busters comes when they're called to track down the kidnapers of the local cardinal, next in line to be Pope. The offensive improbability of the Catholic church very publicly hiring a ditzy occultist to solve a sticky missing-persons case is the very least of this movie's problems, and despite the fleeting use of a jealous bishop as a red herring, the background of religious hierarchy doesn't even seem to figure in its dull but baffling climax.

The church setting does allow, however, for a "cute meet" between Larroquette and romantic lead Bess Armstrong, an initially adversarial nun. That this character joined the convent out of sexual repression (feeling guilt over the death of a boyfriend, who just happens to be the entity channeled by Pinchot!) and no religious conviction is just one of many Catholic stereotypes dumbly perpetrated by the picture, try as it might to be utterly, mind-bendingly benign.

Using as many static close-ups as fathomable, director Joel Zwick—in his feature debut, after years of "Mork & Mindy," "Laverne & Shirley" and the like—does his best to make "Second Sight" (rated PG) seem like a failed TV sitcom, working with a lowbrow script that pointedly employs the S-word at intervals to helpfully remind patrons their brains are being fat-fired in a theater and not in their living rooms. Zwick and company have achieved what so many thought to be impossible and made "Vibes" look like an underappreciated classic of the genre. The lights are on, but nobody's home—not even Ramtha.

NEW YORK POST, 11/3/89, p. 25, Jami Bernard

The Second Sight Detective Agency ("We're pretty weird" appears to be their slogan) is on the case of the kidnapped Cardinal, with a hyperkinetic psychic tuning in to the spirit world to find out whodunit and why and also what the next day's winning lottery number will be.

But lately, psychic Bobby McGee (no relevance to the Janis Joplin song) is getting things wrong. If you've seen the trailer for "Second Sight," you know that Bronson Pinchot as Bobby rises lotus-legged from a movie theater seat and predicts, "There's a comedy in your future."

Well, not only is that scene not in the movie (and you don't have to be a psychic to predict that), but Bobby's astral-plane sources must be getting feeble—there's not really that much comedy in your future at all, not if you plan to see this movie.

Oh, there's some. Pinchot tries every gyration and fanny-waggle in the book to get laughs out of the childlike Bobby's psychic ruminations. He does more dialects and accents than you'd find at a Meryl Streep retrospective—including an old New York Jew, a jive-talking street criminal, and the kind of fey, meticulous character that made Pinchot famous as the art gallery clerk in "Beverly Hills Cop."

As his handler, Stuart Pankin breathlessly interprets Bobby's strange activities for awed spectators—"He's throwing a shield of hyper-polarized ions over the Cardinal to protect him!" Pankin exclaims, photographing the moment like a proud papa at a graduation.

And John Larroquette ("Night Court") plays exasperated straight man, an ex-cop who runs the detective agency and only tolerates his employees' shenanigans in the interests of earning a fast buck.

With these ingredients, there *could* be a comedy in your future, but this busy busy mishmash of papal and romantic intrigue and physical humor has a surprising number of dead spots, unless you go for adolescent bodily-noise humor and the sight of Pinchot in a floppy "Burn This" wig and dress.

"Second Sight" seems entranced by its own self-proclaimed weirdness at the expense of its moments of genuine humor, which are so well hidden it would take a psychic to locate them.

NEWSDAY, 11/3/89, Part III/p. 5, Terry Kelleher

"Second Sight" has all the earmarks of a TV movie—sitcom stars in the leads; sitcom director at the helm; high-concept, low-intelligence premise.

But no, it's a full-fledged motion picture, and what would look bad enough on the small screen looks horrible on the big one.

John Larroquette of NBC's "Night Court" plays an ex-cop who runs a detective agency in partnership with a wiggy psychic (Bronson Pinchot of ABC's "Perfect Strangers") and the psychic's handler (Stuart Pankin of HBO's "Not Necessarily the News," which, to be fair, is not s sitcom). Supervising their antics is Joel Zwick, making his feature debut after directing numerous episodes of such series as "Laverne and Shirley," "Mork and Mindy" and, of course, "Perfect Strangers."

And oh, the antics. Pinchot shakes violently and emits unintelligible sounds as he channels the psychic energy of a dead guy called Murray. (Everyone knows the name Murray is guaranteed funny.) Pankin hops around taking snapshots of Pinchot and feeding his protégé candy to keep him from going berserk. Larroquette comments tartly, takes falls and looks pained. We can just imagine Zwick behind the camera, gleefully shouting, "Go to it, boys!"

You'll squirm immediately when Pinchot demonstrates his flair for physical comedy by going into "the pee-pee dance," but even the occasional decent gag is milked to the point of embarrassment. Larroquette discovers he can pick up distant television signals by manipulating Pinchot's limbs. Adjusting this human antenna, he picks up the ballgame. Pankin's wife (Christine Estabrook), wielding the remote control, prefers non-sports programing. And so they duel. Fine, only Zwick keeps the bit going and going until Pinchot has his legs wrapped around Larroquette's neck and...let's just say it gets worse.

All this and a plot, too. Murray's soul is restless in the next world because he was hit by a truck one night when his girlfriend sent him out for ice cream. The girlfriend (Bess Armstrong) entered a convent out of guilt. Now the nun gets involved with the psychic sleuths, who are investigating the kidnaping of the cardinal. Pinchot starts feeling the nun's breasts and generally carrying on as Murray would. Meanwhile, the nun falls in love with Larroquette, even though he's alternately smarmy and surly.

One night, in the heat of detective action, the nun kisses Larroquette on the lips. Then she jumps back and nervously blesses herself.

Let's just say it gets worse.

VILLAGE VOICE, 11/14/89, p. 120, Gary Giddins

The aliens who made *Second Sight*, a made-for-movies TV show about a psychic detective saddled with bad gags and played charmlessly by Bronson Pinchot in a fright wig, came from

Prime Time. That may explain why they rush to do the few things they can't get away with on the home screen—like shit and fart jokes. A story line having to do with a kidnapped cardinal (the veteran actor William Prince, no less) comes into focus after an hour, but you could probably reassemble the reels in any order and get an equally intelligible result. John Larroquette, Stuart Pankin, and Bess Armstrong (as a nun who defrocks herself in the end to serve as Larroquette's love interest) are in it; probably not even their agents know why. The direction by Joel Zwick is beyond criticism.

Also reviewed in:
NEW YORK TIMES, 11/3/89, p. C18, Janet Maslin
VARIETY, 11/15/89, p. 22
WASHINGTON POST,11/4/89, p. G9, Hal Hinson

SEDUCTION: THE CRUEL WOMAN

A First Run Features release. *Executive Producer:* Renee Gundelach. *Producer:* Elfi Mikesch and Monika Treut. *Director:* Elfi Mikesch and Monika Treut. *Screenplay (German with English subtitles):* Elfi Mikesch and Monika Treut. *Inspired by "Venus in Furs" by:* Leopold von Sacher-Masoch. *Director of Photography:* Elfi Mikesch. *Editor:* Renate Merck. *Sound:* Frank Soletti and Casar Gremmler-Welgehausen. *Art Director:* Manfred Blosser. *Special Effects:* Reinhard Twardy. *Costumes:* Anne Jud. *Running time:* 84 minutes. *MPAA Rating:* Not Rated.

CAST: Mechthild Grossmann (Wanda/the "Dominatrix"); Udo Kier (Gregor/Wanda's Ex-Lover); Sheila McLaughlin (Justine/Wanda's American Lover); Carola Regnier (Caren/Saleswoman and Shoe Fetishist); Peter Weibel (Herr Mahrsch/The Reporter); Georgette Dee (Friederike/Suffering Artist); Judith Flex (Judith); Barbara Ossenkopp (Leila); John Erdmann (Customer); Daniela Ziegler (Mother); Katorka Taterka (Daughter); Karin Roewer-Nennemann (Salewoman); George Lanann (Old Man); Jurg Schlachter (Young Man).

LOS ANGELES TIMES, 9/1/89, Calendar/p. 14, Kevin Thomas

Wanda, the darkly beautiful, deeply sensual heroine of "Seduction: The Cruel Woman," is the Robert Mapplethorpe of dominatrices. It's not for nothing that she refers to her house of pain and pleasure as a gallery and perceives herself as a performance artist. "To do something really surprising is art," she declares to a male journalist whose intended research has led to his self-discovery as a masochist.

Inspired by by Leopold von Sacher-Masoch's "Venus in Furs," Elfi Mikesch and Monika Treut's ambitious and complex film is constantly surprising. To begin with, it is quite chaste, with the activities of the gallery implied rather than depicted, despite all the standard bondage and domination gear and attitudes in evidence. For Wanda, as with Mapplethorpe, art and sex—especially along its wilder shores—are one and the same. For Mikesch, who is also the film's inventive cinematographer, and Treut, best known for the recent "Virgin Machine," sadomasochism is the starting point for a consideration of the paradoxes at the heart of human nature and desires and of all relationships. "Seduction: The Cruel Woman" is decidedly more philosophical than erotic, for all its tableaux of sexual fantasy.

We would expect Wanda to be a ravishing enigma and her gallery to exist apart from the world. Yet Pina Bausch dancer Mechthild Grossmann's Wanda is a very human figure of fantasy, as seductive and bemused as silent vamp Nita Naldi and sometimes as lewd as Brigitte Helm's False Maria in "Metropolis." Love may be an illusion to Wanda, but it's unquestionably hard work.

"Love is tiring...like working in a salt mine," she says wearily. Exhausted and suffering a headache, she is comforted by the tender lovemaking of her current No. 1 lover, an elegant middle-aged woman who is a shoe-fetishist. Most tiresome to her is a "slave" (Fassbinder star Udo Kier) who breaks the rules and falls in love with her. As for the gallery, situated in an old warehouse on the Hamburg waterfromt, there is enough traffic noise to remind us that all that happens there is actually part of everyday life.

"Seduction: The Cruel Woman" proceeds with the languorous pace and campy tone characteristic of the more *outré* examples of the New German Cinema. These aspects point up the absurdities of obsessive sexual passion since, on one level, the film is a comedy, yet on another level it is deeply compassionate. Finally, the film makers' attempt at integrating sex, no matter how kinky, with all other aspects of our beings succeeds in their creating a film that is the antithesis of pornography.

NEW YORK POST, 11/3/89, p. 27, Jami Bernard

Masochism gets a workout in Monika Treut's decadent and decidedly unerotic new film, "Seduction: The Cruel Woman." It's dedicated "to masochists and Doris." I don't know about Doris, but it definitely takes a masochist to sit through it.

Right away we know it's European, because it's filmed sort of sideways. Cinematographer Elfi Mikesch (who also wrote, produced and directed along with Treut) either had a bad morning or wanted to attract that art-house audience in a big way. The camera angles are tricky and off-center, but then, this is a movie about fantasy and secret desires, most of them having to do with blood and bathrooms.

Wanda (Mechthild Grossmann) is a hard-working dominatrix who has just opened her own avant-garde S&M gallery in Germany. She coordinates a full slate of punishment games, run by her oh-so-willing staff.

Yet she still finds time to torment her ex-lover (a man who wishes to be treated like a farm animal), her live-in lover (a saleswoman who works in a shoe store that only carries particularly high-heeled pumps) and her most recent lover (an American who resents having to wear a nurse's uniform to work, her work consisting of being whipped on the fanny). Oh those decadent Germans!

Meanwhile, there are cold vignettes of torture devices, men licking floors, an androgynous "slave" getting an impromptu tattoo and a reporter—who has come to interview Wanda about her new club—putting pen aside to plead that he be used as Wanda's personal toilet.

Did I mention this movie is not for every taste? Then again, if you liked "Taxi Zum Klo" (those crazy Germans again!), you may pick up a few pointers here about the whys and wherefores of degrading sex acts.

Shot claustrophobically in cold blues at crazy angles, "Seduction" is based on the Ph.D. work Treut did on the writings of the Marquis de Sade and Leopold von Sacher-Masoch, and you know what *they* stand for. Treut's last movie shown here, "Virgin Machine," was also an inquiry into the nature of sexuality and obsession.

But can't obsession be a little more exciting than this? Treut evidently means to shed more light on the phenomenon of masochism, a sexual culture bound by symbolism and ritual and evidently—according to this movie—one without much passion. "Perversions are only misunderstandings," says Wanda in one of several disappointing pronouncements.

Don't go to this movie expecting to be aroused. As shocking as the material may be to some, it's all talk and no action (OK, some floor-licking and a pale, exposed breast or two). Wanda's staff has such noble role models as David of Thessalonica, who spent three years in an olive tree. Pretty tame without the pimento, huh?

"My profession is being cruel," says Wanda. Sadism has been good to her, and it shows. While everyone else looks angry or bored or desperate, Wanda is alive, her lips vibrantly painted, a secret smile of amusement playing over her face. This is a woman who enjoys her work, but it has taken a nasty toll on her personal life. "Hit me like you used to!" wails her neglected ex-boyfriend, to no avail.

"To do something really surprising is art," according to Wanda. Dispassionate and striking, "Seduction" is indeed surprising. Maybe that's art. But is it good?

VILLAGE VOICE, 11/7/89, p. 74, Georgia Brown

As you're probably aware by now, Woody Allen's *Crimes and Misdemeanors* contains a ca-ca scene. Allen's character, Cliff Stern, goes into paroxysms of disgust, spasms of shame, as his distraught sister describes what her blind date did after tying her up. Well, the squeamish Cliff would run screaming out of his beloved Bleecker Street Cinema (playing revivals in the Allen movie) if he wandered, with or without his niece, into Elfi Mikesch and Monika Treut's *Seduction: The Cruel Woman*, a film loosely based on Leopold von Sacher-Masoch's *Venus in Furs*.

"Be proud of your excrement!"admonishes Wanda the dominatrix. "You can offer your slave no greater punishment—that is, no greater pleasure—than your excrement." (No, you don't witness the act.)

But who's to say that Allen's joke about the sister's dating trauma isn't intended to correspond, however subliminally, with Judah the patriarch's disposal of his mistress Delores. Most of his characters' dealings with the opposite sex are pretty shitty. *Seduction,* you might say, further defines what we talk about when we talk about shit.

Dedicated "to masochists and Doris," *Seduction* opens with a stunning, spooky montage with strange amplified sounds. I'd like to single out the man in white nurse's shoes crawling on his belly as he licks the tiles of some endless bathroom. (Labored breathing.) This shot comes sandwiched between a view—to become an eerie recurring image—of a partially flooded, leaky underground tunnel. A sewer, I guess, the interior of the community's toilet. (Dripping noises.) *Seduction* is a fiction, yet like its hermetic, perversely staid source, it's also an essay on the rites and fetishes of masochism. Treut (*The Virgin Machine*) is a Ph.D. who wrote her dissertation on *Venus in Furs* and de Sade's *Juliette*; Mikesch—her co-director and co-writer—was distinguished cinematographer on Werner Schroeter's *The Rose King.*

Wanda (Pina Bausch dancer Mechthild Grossmann), raven-haired, pale, with glossy red lips, is breaking off with Caren (Carola Regnier), a tight, sedate woman who runs a sleek shoe boutique featuring stiletto heels. Wanda's also cooling towards her devoted, languishing male lover, Gregor (Udo Kier), one of the ensemble in her "gallery"—a dockside nightspot featuring live sadomasochistic shows as well as videos. A new member of the troupe arrives, and her name (ha) is Justine (filmmaker Sheila McLaughlin). While Wanda wears white in bed, black on the job, the blond, dowdier, rather undefined Justine—she can't help it, she's American—wears black and white print dresses and is often shot against black and white tiles. "Time will tell which role you'll play," says Wanda welcoming Justine. She lets her watch the evening's show, during which another performer, Friederike (Georgette Dee), gets a bleeding rose (the emblem of slavery) carved on her back.

One day an eager, nervous journalist, Herr Mahrsch (Vienna artist Peter Weibel), arrives at the gallery to interview Wanda on perversions. She offers him a tour, stopping to watch a video in which she recites a short history of obsession. (It started with Sophronious grazing naked beside the Dead Sea.) The reporter, however, has some burning tastes of his own.

Whether Herr Mahrsch is actually a reporter, or whether his may be another role offered by the gallery, is the kind of reality/fantasy ambiguity *Seduction* puts into a viewer's head— underscoring the fineness of the line between work and play, adult and child. (Is Caren playing with shoes or selling them?) It turns out that Herr Mahrsch, more zealous than the ordinary journalist/voyeur, wants more than anything to become his subject's toilet. Who knows whether reporters covering Leona Helmsley haven't quenched a similar urge?

I hope I don't sound as if I don't take masochism seriously, because I certainly do—as a component of (every) personality and as a state of being that fluctuates between dormancy and raging torment. What else is able to break down the truly cold? The beauty of an activated masochism is that, slicing through to suffering's marrow, it contains a remedy. The fall into masochism is a fall into feeling. Its appeal, its shocking necessity, lies in rehearsal, reconstruction, return.

The stated thesis of von Sacher-Masoch's essentially romantic, but hardly erotic, novel is that lovers crave hurt in order to continue loving (feeling). Nothing kills love like devotion and kindness. Even the dominatrix, weary of satisfying other's cravings for punishment, secretly seeks out indifference and cruelty. Sadists, you might say, are masochists in wolves' clothing. "I was a donkey," von Sacher-Masoch's Severin/Gregor learns too late. "If only I had beaten her."

Treut and Mikesch's film is similarly unerotic (at least *I* think so), exploring its subject in a kind of gallery tour like the one Wanda gives Herr Mahrsch. Except that the viewer isn't invited to succumb. The cool, distanced, claustrophobic *Seduction* isn't frightening, funny, or (like *The Rose King*) ecstatic. But it's strong on imagery—especially fluids, with flooded baths, dank puddles, and the sea lapping just outside the door.

Also reviewed in:
NEW YORK TIMES, 11/3/89, p. C17, Caryn James

SEE NO EVIL, HEAR NO EVIL

A Tri Star Pictures release. *Executive Producer:* Burtt Harris, Earl Barret, and Arne Sultan. *Producer:* Marvin Worth. *Director:* Arthur Hiller. *Screenplay:* Earl Barret, Arne Sultan, Eliot Wald, Andrew Kurtzman, and Gene Wilder. *Story:* Earl Barret, Arne Sultan, and Marvin Worth. *Director of Photography:* Victor J. Kemper. *Editor:* Robert C. Jones. *Music:* Stewart Copeland. *Music Editor:* Michael Dittrick. *Sound:* Dennis Maitland Sr. *Sound Editor:* Gordon Ecker and Bruce Stambler. *Production Designer:* Robert Gundlach. *Art Director:* James T. Singelis. *Set Decorator:* George DeTitta Jr. *Special Effects:* Al Griswold. *Costumes:* Ruth Morley. *Make-up:* Tony Russell-Van Lierop, Tony Lloyd (Richard Pryor), and Monty Westmore (Gene Wilder). *Stunt Coordinator:* Conrad Palmisano. *Running time:* 103 minutes. *MPAA Rating:* R.

CAST: Gene Wilder (Dave); Richard Pryor (Wally); Joan Severance (Eve); Kevin Spacey (Kirgo); Alan North (Braddock); Anthony Zerbe (Sutherland); Louis Giambalvo (Gatlin); Kirsten Childs (Adele); Hardy Rawls (Beefy Tourist); Audrie Neenan (Policewoman and Marilyn); Lauren Tom (Mitzie); John Capodice (Scotto); George Bartenieff (Huddleston); Alexandra Neil (Sally); Tonya Pinkins (Leslie); Bernie McInerney (Dr. Cornfeld); Keith Langsdale (Male Doctor); Jamie De Roy (Female Doctor); Mary Kay Adams (Dr. Bennett); Alan Pottinger (Parking Attendant); Bill Luhrs (Herman); Lisby Larson (Reporter); Mark Smaltz and Rico Elias (Policeman); Doug Yasuda (Professor Kasuda); James Pyduck (Businessman); Michael John McGann (Salesman); Edward Hyland (Cabbie); Thom Curley (Laundry Van Driver); John Ring (Teller); George Buck (Security Guard); Phil Goodbody (Blind Man); George Harris (Bartender); Zach Grenier (Jerk); Joe Viviani (Fingerprint Cop); Alice Spivak (Dispatcher); Shiek Mahmud-Bey (Walkie-Talkie Cop); Joel Swetow (Cabbie); Jane Connell (Woman); Pirie MacDonald (Lodge Tourist); Manuel Santiago (Raoul); Harry Madsen (Cop with Bullhorn); Tom Kubiak (Plainclothes (Cop); Cynthia Lopez (Puerto Rican Woman).

FILMS IN REVIEW, 8–9/89, p. 419, Edmond Grant

A pleasant, formulaic comedy, *See No Evil, Hear No Evil* nearly succeeds as a result of the charms of its two stars. Richard Pryor and Gene Wilder have teamed up twice in the past (*Silver Streak, Stir Crazy*) and both times the results were less than hysterical. This time around, we are thankfully given a chance to get to like the characters they play before we are thoroughly immersed in a ridiculous "chase" plotline.

For these characters are very different from the bland figures played by Pryor and Wilder in their previous outings. Their respective handicaps—Pryor is a blind man, Wilder is deaf—supply most of the movie's comedy. Yes, that does mean that there are moments when we are supposed to laugh when Pryor walks into a wall or Wilder misreads someone's rapidly moving lips. But something else, something far more important, is allowed to emerge because of the hokey, double-handicap premise.

By having these two characters rely on each other the way they do, we not only begin to understand how people with different problems can have a lot in common, we also get a glimpse at the genuine respect and admiration that Pryor and Wilder *the performers* have for each other. The two have functioned well as a comedy team before (one need only recall the scene where Wilder is made "black" by Pryor in *Silver Streak*), but here we receive the impression that the buddies we are seeing on screen really do appreciate each other's abilities when they're not in front of a camera.

But then again there's the plot.

And its *awfully* feeble—Wilder plays a deaf man who runs a magazine stand in an office building; he and blind employee Pryor "witness" the murder of Pryor's bookie, their only clues to the identity of the murderer being that Pryor smelt her perfume and Wilder caught a glimpse of her legs. The murderer and her male cohort then pursue our two heroes, and go so far as to kidnap Pryor's sister, until the whole thing reaches a climax in the mansion of the "Mr. Big" (Anthony Zerbe), who's behind it all.

So much for the plot. Suffice to say that Kevin Spacey and Joan Severance (who were so impeccable together as the incestuous brother-and-sister criminal-moguls on television's *Wiseguy*) effect veddy bad British accents as the villains. But, as stated above, the lame plotline is not what really lies at the heart of this movie.

What's important about *See No Evil* is that for the first time two incredibly talented performers, who have made such an impression on their own, finally have merged their talents together in a comfortable way—there's a well handled scene taking place on a bench in Greenwich Village that proves that fact nicely. And since both men have imbued their often ludicrous characters with such unspoken dignity, you do ultimately find yourself laughing at some of the cheap jokes that are bounced off of their handicaps.

LOS ANGELES TIMES, 5/12/89, Calendar/p. 6, Kevin Thomas

"See No Evil, Hear No Evil" is an apt title for this brisk, ingenious and funny comedy that happily reunites Richard Pryor and Gene Wilder. Pryor's Wally is blind, and he is as proudly stubborn about acknowledging his disability as Wilder's Dave is about admitting that he is totally deaf. They skirmish mightily upon meeting each other, but Dave recognizes enough of himself in Wally to hire him as an assistant at his Manhattan lobby newsstand.

Wally doesn't even have a chance to start work before he and his new boss are swept up in non-stop adventure.

A spectacular brunette (Joan Severance) coolly leaves a bullet-riddled corpse in front of the newsstand. Wally and Dave are the prime suspects. Director Arthur Hiller, who first teamed the duo in the 1976 "Silver Streak," and a raft of writers (Wilder among them) not only never let up with a steady stream of comic catastrophes but also manage to have fun with Wally and Dave in a way that makes them seem like heroes, full-fledged participants in the human comedy that engages us all. The crazy gags and predicaments are never at their expense; the film deftly shows how the two men need to accept their limitations before being able to triumph over them. Part of this process is their realization of their need for each other's friendship.

All of these sentiments, be assured, are left to subtext as the film careens merrily along. Pryor has a wonderful comic moment when necessity dictates that he pass himself off as a Swedish authority on geriatric sex, complete with yumpin' yimminy accent. This is just the broad mainstream comedy that both stars need in the wake of recent less-than-terrific pictures. They play off each other better than ever, and the good-looking "See No Evil, Hear No Evil" (rated R for raunchy language, some nudity) leaves us hoping we haven't seen the last of Wally and Dave. Maybe next time around there will be time for them to find girlfriends.

MONTHLY FILM BULLETIN, 9/89, p. 282, Tim Pulleine

Wally, who is blind but determined to preserve his independence, obtains a job as assistant at a lobby news-stand run by Dave, a former actor who is now deaf. Wally is heavily in debt to his bookie, who comes looking for him while also engaged in doublecrossing a big-time crook, Sutherland, over a revolutionary metal-conductor which he has acquired and disguised as a rare coin. He hides this in Dave's cash box on realising that Eve, one of Sutherland's minions, is on to him; she arrives while Dave's back is turned and Wally is absent, shoots the bookie and steals his briefcase. The police, led by Captain Braddock, link the victim with Wally, and he is arrested along with Dave. Meanwhile, Eve and her accomplice Kirgo realise that the "coin" must have been passed on, and masquerade as lawyers in an attempt to get Dave and Wally out of custody. But by dint of Wally's recognising Eve's perfume and Dave remembering the sight of her departing legs, they deduce that she is the killer, and contrive to escape from the police station. They fall into the clutches of Eve and Kirgo, who repossess the "coin", but the pair get away in a purloined police car—driven by Wally as directed by Dave—despite massed police pursuit. Wally makes contact with his sister Adele, and after a narrow squeak with Braddock's men, the trio reach a resort hotel at Great Gorge, which Dave has discovered (by lip-reading Eve) is her and Kirgo's rendezvous with Sutherland. A medical convention is in progress and the two men pretend to be foreign doctors; Dave is able to sneak into Eve's room and reclaim the "coin" while Adele causes a diversion by ramming Kirgo's car. Eve and Kirgo take Adele prisoner to Sutherland's nearby mansion retreat, pursued by Wally and Dave; they are also caught and brought before Sutherland, who himself proves to be blind. Kirgo and Eve both try to double-cross Sutherland; Kirgo is shot but, after a prolonged shoot-out involving Wally and Dave, Eve kills Sutherland and makes for a getaway helicopter with the conductor. As the police close in, Dave and Wally contrive a final burst of ingenuity which literally lays Eve low and clears their names. Later, the two friends agree that the experience has given them a "damn good time".

To concieve a comedy in which one of the two protagonists is blind and the other deaf is, to begin with, a calculated venture into questionable taste. In the event, *See No Evil, Hear No Evil* is not only blandly unrealistic about these handicaps but is hedged about with scenes of maudlin "buddy" sentiment and bombast (the script allows Dave to characterise himself as trying to remain "the loveable asshole I've always been"). Though the basic premise of the murder and its aftermath is not without ingenuity, the narrative is rambling and perfunctory, lacking any precision—most obviously in the implausible set-piece of the car chase—and providing a context not of parody but of mere juvenile inanity. Next to nothing is made of the chief villain's himself proving to be blind, and even if one assumes that the ludicrousness of the false-coin McGuffin is deliberate, it fails to lend the piece any comic style. Such few laughs as the film manages to provoke are on the margins, as in the scene where a policewoman attempting to photograph Dave for a "mug shot" becomes ever more exasperated at her inability to convey what she wants, and finally gives up with a despairing cry of "I'll get you when you're sleeping".

NEW YORK, 5/22/89, p. 71, David Denby

In *See No Evil, Hear No Evil,* Richard Pryor plays a blind man, Wally, who enjoys getting into fistfights, and Gene Wilder is Dave, who is deaf but turns sarcastic when anyone speaks to him too slowly. Each man, unreconciled to his situation, turns out to be a raging egotist, with a block-size chip on his shoulder. Now and then, this slapstick adventure-comedy, directed by Arthur Hiller (who made *Silver Streak,* starring these two), comes close to sentimentality: As the two men tangle with thieves and killers and cops, they realize that however much they fight the world, they need each other, and they become more and more mutually dependent, with many moments of truth. But Wally and Dave's battling orneriness checks our tears, and this drying out saves the movie.

Playing blind, Pryor exaggerates his usual querulous edginess and paranoia. He picks fights with *voices* he doesn't like, even if they aren't directed at him. And Gene Wilder gives up that moony gentleness that was his earlier shtick; he's more concentrated than I remember him, tougher, more acid. Inevitably there will be complaints that the movie is in terrible taste, that it squeezes laughs out of disabilities. But actually, *See No Evil, Hear No Evil,* gimmick concept that it is, doesn't patronize its heroes at all; some of the laughs may be bumping-into-the-walls obvious, but they aren't insulting or sick.

When Pryor gets into a fight in a bar, Wilder holds him from behind, and they scoot left or right, with Wilder sending aerial-dogfight directions—"Ten o'clock! Twelve o'clock!"—to Pryor's flying fists. Hiller lets the fight go on three or four punches too long, but his comic timing has never been any damn good. I could have done without the unavoidable car chase (with first one man, then the other, at the wheel), and Hiller makes too much of an exasperated dumb New York cop who can't deal with the simple facts of blindness and deafness. nor does Hiller have the finesse to turn a scene in which Pryor bluffs some doctors with a Swedish accent into something really funny. But some of the complexly organized scenes turn out beautifully. Wally's blindness and Dave's deafness, meshing bizarrely like a machine with extra wheels and no gears, produce a two-man team that moves through the world in weird rhythms. Neither can do much without the other. Walking, or scrambling through action sequences, or even just sitting around talking, they have to fight to get through to each other. Their spirit moves us even as we know this summer-season movie is setting us up for *See No Evil, Hear No Evil II* and , inevitably, *III.*

NEW YORK POST, 5/12/89, p. 27, Jami Bernard

Wally and Dave are new-found friends who are working together at a newsstand. Wally is blind. Dave is deaf, but can read lips. Wally asks Dave what he wants out of life. "Not to make a fool of myself," says Dave.

It's too late. Both of them, Richard Pryor and Gene Wilder, happily make fools of themselves for all 103 minutes of "See No Evil, Hear No Evil," a bland, good-natured comedy that rarely rises above the limitations of its premise. The result is a movie you can sit through; if that doesn't sound too hilarious, at least it's not the embarrassment that the last few Richard Pryor comedies have been.

There is an early scene in which Pryor (the blind Wally) jumps to his feet in the subway, screaming, "You mean I'm not white?" while clawing at his face. The jokes are generally of this inoffensively silly caliber. Wilder is the deaf Dave, gently misunderstanding the words he reads on people's lips ("Are you serious? *Fuzzy wuzzy was a woman?*").

Wally and Dave witness a murder—that is, one hears the gunshot and the other sees the great gams of the lady who fired it—and are arrested as suspects. They escape in order to track down the killer themselves, but it turns out that the leggy murderer (the beautiful Joan Severance) and her smoothly evil cohort (Kevin Spacey) are after our heroes themselves; something to do with a rare gold coin that's to die for, literally.

Each scrape that Wally and Dave get into requires some double talk and double-action; if someone is to be punched, the seeing Dave must call out instructions to the more pugnacious Wally. If there is a car to drive, the handcuffed Dave yells directions while blind Wally steers. The jokes don't get much better but there are occasional laughs—the look on Pryor's face when he finds out that the doctor he is impersonating on a convention panel is a gynecologist; the fact that Wilder does not have a gun in his pocket pointed at Severance, he is just happy to see her.

There is an interesting twist near the end when Wally and Dave meet Mister Big (Anthony Zerbe, not on screen nearly enough); mostly the movie is filled with words one protagonist cannot hear and sights the other cannot see.

Arthur Hiller, who directed Pryor and Wilder in "Silver Streak" (their other famous pairing was the not dissimilar "Stir Crazy"), is a native of Canada and somehow makes the New York locations look remarkably like Toronto; this is some neat trick since Toronto is often standing in for New York and fooling no one.

Pryor and Wilder do in fact have a special chemistry—they are like puppies at play and they complement each other. Pryor is loud and excitable; Wilder, with his own sort of fluffy 'fro, is gentle and protective. The movie nevertheless moves along at the pace you'd expect from the blind leading the deaf.

NEWSDAY, 5/12/89, Part III/p. 3, Mike McGrady

Deaf Gene Wilder tells blind Richard Pryor that he has but one ambition in life, and that is to avoid seeming foolish: "I have the terrible fear I'm going to make a fool of myself and everyone is going to stand around and laugh at me."

No, no, no—that's not the way it usually works out. First in "Silver Streak," later in "Stir Crazy" and now in "See No Evil, Hear No Evil," frantic and shrill Gene Wilder has strained to make a fool of himself and everyone stands around and laughs at...Richard Pryor.

"See No Evil, Hear No Evil" sets a more difficult challenge for the comic duo than their earlier films; after all, the basic joke is based on the deadly serious subject of human handicaps. The premise is that two severely handicapped people can work together, become friends and, by pooling their limited resources, manage to get along quite nicely, thank you, even when being chased by cops and killers.

The two men complement each other in every way. In this outing, Pryor is as aggressive as Wilder is reserved; when Pryor gets into a barroom brawl, Wilder stands behind him, pointing him in the right direction, telling him where and when to throw punches, helping him duck.

In addition to providing most of the humor, the handicaps also give the flick whatever dramatic tension it possesses. The two men make less than ideal witnesses when a bookie is murdered directly in front of their newspaper stand. Wilder hears nothing and glimpses only the killer's legs; Pryor sees nothing but catches a whiff of her perfume. The cops decide the two partners are the killers; the true killers decide they must be erased. Let the chases begin!

Although no fewer than five writers take credit for the script (*always* a bad omen), it is essentially a one-joke movie. By the time the writers lose their timidity and allow Pryor and Wilder to depart the premise, it is all but too late. When they do finally free-wheel it, the movie comes alive. No surprise there. Pryor is seldom seen to best advantage when constrained by plot; his natural habitat is the comedy concert and his natural talent is for winging it.

The flick's best moments are not only removed from the main story line, they have but a tenuous connection to sanity. When the two buddies, on the run, check into a resort housing a medical convention, the only way to get a room is for Pryor and Wilder to pass as prominent European physicians. However, their suite does not have king-sized beds.

"I saved you a suite with two queens," the desk clerk says.

"Well, get those fellows out of there," Wilder demands.

And off they go. The comedy thickens when it is learned that Pryor must address the convention of doctors. In a heavy Swedish accent. On his specialty, which happens to be gynecology. The moment the bogus expert starts fielding questions from the floor—"Which exercise would you most recommend for geriatric sexuality?"—we know we're going to be in for a time of it.

Pryor's response to that question, and much of what follows, has nothing whatever to do with blindness or deafness. It's pure vaudeville and it happens to be the movie's funniest segment.

All in all, "See No Evil, Hear No Evil" is a notch above earlier efforts and will be a source of joy unrefined to the fans who made the first two films such box-office hits.

VILLAGE VOICE, 5/23/89, p. 70, Michael Musto

The premise of *See No Evil, Hear No Evil*—a blind man and his deaf friend are wrongly accused of a murder they couldn't even see/hear—fills one with a spine-chilling dread of misbegotten handicapped humor. That the characters are played by human torch Richard Pryor and Gene Wilder, who's spent recent years helping his love, Gilda Radner, recover, from cancer, makes it even creepier. Can this combination of bad-luck kids really make disablement funny?

The film, it turns out, does meet all your fears head-on—every possible line from the blind/deaf jokebook is trotted out like gangbusters. But amazingly, there's an underlying sweetness to it that favors the two heroic losers in a way that's hard to argue with ("I'm deaf, but I'm not stupid," says Wilder, hammering the point home). Even though the sweetness is soured by a car chase and far too many "pussy" and "dickhead" jokes, the film ends up being not nearly as deaf, blind, or dumb as you might perversely hope.

Also reviewed in:
NEW REPUBLIC, 6/12/89, p. 27, Stanley Kauffmann
NEW YORK TIMES, 5/12/89, p. C8, Vincent Canby
VARIETY, 5/17–23/89, p. 30
WASHINGTON POST, 5/13/89, p. C1, Hal Hinson

SEE YOU IN THE MORNING

A Warner Bros. release of a Lorimar Film Entertainment presentation. *Producer:* Alan J. Pakula and Susan Solt. *Director:* Alan J. Pakula. *Screenplay:* Alan J. Pakula. *Director of Photography:* Donald McAlpine. *Editor:* Evan Lottman. *Music:* Michael Small. *Music Editor:* Todd Kasow. *Sound:* Chris Newman and (music) Gary Chester. *Sound Editor:* Ron Bochar. *Production Designer:* George Jenkins. *Art Director:* Robert Guerra. *Set Decorator:* Carol Joffe. *Set Dresser:* Barbara Kastner. *Costumes:* John Boxer. *Make-up:* Fern Buchner. *Running time:* 116 minutes. *MPAA Rating:* PG-13.

CAST: Jeff Bridges (Larry); Alice Krige (Beth); Farrah Fawcett (Jo); Drew Barrymore (Cathy); Lukas Haas (Petey); David Dukes (Peter); Frances Sternhagen (Neenie); George Hearn (Martin); Theodore Bikel (Bronie); Linda Lavin (Sidney); Heather Lilly (Robin); Macaulay Culkin (Billy); William LeMassena (Larry's Father); Tom Aldredge (Beth's Father); Dorothy Dean (Larry's Mother); Alixe Gordin (Beth's Mother); Kate Wilkinson (Aunt Matilda); Christopher Curry (Larry's Brother); Betsy Aidem (Larry's Sister-in-Law); Robert Levine (Judge); Patricia E. Murray, Christopher Murray, and Elizabeth Parrish (Group Therapy Patients); Robin Bartlett, Saundra McClain, and Richard Grusin (Group Therapy Patients); Lewis Arlt (Morty); Mark La Mura (Jack); John Rothman (Veterinarian); M'el Dowd (Real Estate Lady); Julie Garfield (Cafeteria Cashier); Bernie McInerney (Policeman #1); John Ottavino (Policeman #2); Irina V. Pasmur (Olga); Barclay DeVeau (Jackie); Alexander Pasmur (Donnie); Shirley J. Hatcher (Policewoman); Corky (George, the Dog).

LOS ANGELES TIMES, 4/21/89, Calendar/p. 12, Sheila Benson

Anyone who has been anywhere near the meltdown of a divorce and the optimistic fusion of remarriage will recognize that "See You in the Morning" comes from a veteran of those campaigns. Writer-director Alan Pakula has given interviews explaining how close this material is to him, to his heart and to his own knowledge.

Mysteriously, with this weight of experience behind him and in spite of fine work he has gotten from his cast, in particular Jeff Bridges, Frances Sternhagen, Alice Krige and Lukas Haas, Pakula has come up with the most real-looking fake movie imaginable.

Even when situations have an ominously true ring to them, like the fatal moment when Jeff Bridges' super-model wife, Farrah Fawcett, pronounces those stomach-churning words, "We need to have a talk," the aura of the Hollywood Movie is everywhere.

First, there is casting. Good as he is at every nuance of fatherhood and stepfatherhood, persuasive as Bridges has been as everything from an alien to a Santa Barbara wastrel, can you *believe* Jeff Bridges as a psychiatrist? Therapist maybe. Radio talk-show shrink, absolutely. Psychiatrist, nah.

What about Bridges' character? Having been unwillingly wrenched away from his own two young children, this latter-day saint cheerfully takes on a pair of stepchildren who idealize their dead father, a dog who still dotes on his dead master and house put together for another husband.

Bridges even has goodness left over, enough to encourage his new wife to go to the Soviet Union within a month of their marriage to further her fledgling career as a photographer. And when his repressed and certainly understandable feelings finally *do* surface, there's not even an explosion, only the most civilized one-night drinking jag. Not even a hangover.

Finally, having been tempted by his certainly tempting ex-wife during a moment when she feels especially vulnerable, he goes home to his second wife to bare all. Setting aside the potential hostility in that bit of sharing, is Rome calling right now, to arrange the time for his canonization?

Mostly, Pakula has left nothing unsaid. Or rehashed. Certainly he has condensed nothing. Think of the flashes of insight that lit up "Petulia," cryptic words, inflections, arrangements that revealed every painful twist to life as a weekend parent. Somehow, in dealing with deeply personal material, Pakula, a usually inventive director, has become bogged down in flat-footed literalness, as though to savor the *Angst* a detail at a time.

There isn't even real *Angst*, except among the sad little kids from Bridges' first marriage, the PG-13-rated movie's real victims. Bridges' second wife, Krige, is a photographer whose pianist-husband has killed himself when a muscle weakness recurs, signaling the end of his concert career. (He leaves behind a note suggesting hollowly that he *could* of course write movie music, but apparently death is preferable. Really?)

As Krige shares the immediate news of her husband's death with best friend Linda Lavin (in a role that redefines thankless), Krige's 10-year-old daughter (Drew Barrymore) and 8-year-old son (Lukas Haas) come home from school. Krige doesn't give a single indication that their father has just died. Even given this wife's mote of perfectionism, her virtuosity at self-blame, this seems so unreal as to be downright eerie.

But it seems to escape Pakula's notice, along with other peculiarities. What, for example, are we to make of his frolicsome opening sequence? The laughing Bridges-Fawcett family is playing a game with their very young children on their grandmother's island: Whose empty liquor bottle, thrown into these pristine waters, will win the race downstream? Has everyone taken leave of common sense? Are we to accept this giving, sharing, caring, toothsome family as . . . polluters?

MONTHLY FILM BULLETIN, 5/90, p. 138, Richard Combs

Enjoying an apparently idyllic family life, New York psychiatrist Larry Livingston makes regular visits with his TV commercial model wife Jo and their two children Robin and Billy to the country home of Jo's mother Neenie. It is during one of these visits, however, that Jo utters the fateful words "We have to talk". Another family of four, the Goodwins, are currently moving into a new home in New York, and are delighted to find New Year's greetings carved on a secret panel by another family in 1900. But Peter Goodwin, a concert pianist, is suffering from increasing paralysis in one of his hands, and after breaking down during a London concert, he commits suicide. Three years later, Larry and Peter's widow Beth have become lovers, a relationship that began tentatively at a party when they were introduced by their match-making friend Sidney, both developed migraines (Larry after meeting Jo with another man, and realising that he still suffers from the jealousy that helped to drive them apart; Beth from her incessant feelings of guilt and insecurity), and they walked home together. It is some time before they see each other again, Larry still being precoccupied with Jo (whom he discusses constantly with Neenie), and Beth anxious about how her children, Cathy and Petey, who were devoted to their father, will be affected by any romantic relationship. Larry's aggressive courtship eventually breaks down Beth's reserve, and he moves into the Goodwin house. She begins to explore her own ambitions as a photographer, and leaves on a trip to Russia with a conductor friend Bronie (inspiring in Larry some of the jealousy he felt over Jo's professional life). During her absence, Larry tries to strike up a rapport with his stepchildren, but Petey goes missing for a day when he discovers that Larry and Beth want to sell the Goodwin home to start afresh, and Cathy, feeling her role as her mother's confidante has been usurped by Larry, is caught shoplifting at Bloomingdale's. On her return, Beth is overwhelmed by guilt and Larry has to leave immediately to visit the now dying Neenie. After her death, Jo tries to rekindle their relationship; Larry later confesses to Beth that he was tempted, but found he was impotent. Furious, Beth throws him out, but equally furious he returns, and as they both succumb again to migraines, they repair upstairs to make love, causing momentary embarrassment when Cathy and Petey suspect untoward violence and call the police . . . Ten years after *Starting Over*, Alan Pakula is starting over again, with another tale of a divorced man for whom his ex-wife remains the tempting "other woman", a nervous new partner whose guilty doubts reinforce his hesitations, and the extra-generational cast this time of four children from two marriages to add every-which-way step-parent-and-child strains. *See You in the Morning* does not exactly repeat *Starting Over*, but neither does it add to it; what it does is to wear into a deeper groove a distressing tendency that has become evident in Pakula's work since he added the role of screenwriter to that of producer and director. This is so evidently "written" a film, intent on being a study of relationships, that it becomes a collection of opinions about relationships, rather than about the characters who are supposedly having them. Dialogue has a painfully thought-out psychological emphasis as the two families, and assorted friends, probe each other's feelings. But it also has a detached, floating quality, as if the opinions expressed could be shuffled at will between them.

The writing never creates much dramatic conviction or interest in the characters themselves, it never leads them towards something unexpected or even inexpressible. Everything here is so expressed that it has a maddening quality, rhetorical rubberiness that makes one aware of how knowing the script is about its characters without being able to put the knowledge, as it were, into action, to push the film forward from a kind of hypnotised jogging on the spot. "Jo's like her father, she's in love with mystery. Marriage isn't very good for that", counsels the hero's dying mother-in-law about his ex-wife; "My impotent little crime has given you the guilt you've been looking for—punishment for being happy", the hero tells his new partner after a failed attempt to make love to his ex-wife.

One consequence of this over-elaborated confessional writing is that whether the dramatic context is benign, denunciatory or enraged, there's a tone of blandly unvarying goodwill to the film. This may be because the context here is not dramatic at all but therapeutic. Pakula's underlying intention is not to embody his characters but to absolve them, hence the curious sense that the more they talk about themselves the more they seem to disappear. All his films have followed some tack of psychological explication/therapeutic explanation, but it's almost as if, while the director has been turning into more of a writer, the film-maker has been becoming more of a therapist, abandoning on the way his resources for making the film come alive in its own right. "It's a real dialogue picture dealing with relationships; it's *not* an action picture", Pakula has proudly declared, as if celebrating his liberation from the action formulas and genres in which he has had to embody relationships in the past.

But between *Starting Over* and *See You in the Morning*, he has been developing a formula of his own, one neither entirely free of certain conventions (romantic "meeting cute", the "new" family picture) nor prepared to engage with them. It's a development that goes along with his own evolving role as a film-maker, and it's one of sadly diminishing returns: from the producer who was *éminence grise* behind the best films of Robert Mulligan (consider the fascinating authorial cross-over of *The Stalking Moon* and *Klute*), to the *éminence noire* of the director who turned action formulas in all sorts of unexpected directions (from *The Parallax View* to *Comes a Horseman*), and now to what can only be called the *éminence blanche* of *See You in the Morning*—a blank sheet of paper on which will be written fine sentiments, but which will themselves pass through the screen leaving it as blank as before.

NEW YORK POST, 4/21/89, p. 31, David Edelstein

Larry (Jeff Bridges), the hero of Alan J. Pakula's "See You in the Morning," is a cheerful Upper East Side psychiatrist who's always—in his sunshiney way—trying to pin down his and other peoples' motives. A lot of writers would have fun with a character so full of twerpy uplift, but Pakula is an earnest healer, so when Larry tells his new wife, Beth (Alice Krige), "Sweetheart, you can't spend your life in bondage to your guilt," he is talking the way Pakula thinks all people should talk.

The polished, genteel "See You in the Morning" is the story of bright, rich, attractive people who spend a lot of time analyzing their feelings—maybe more time than they spend feeling them. That's a cheap shot, but the movie does a good job of provoking cheap shots—although as I write this, I can hear Pakula say, "You're punishing me because you're angry at yourself."

The protagonists ride into the film with a load of emotional baggage. Beth is an attractive photographer whose husband (David Dukes), a famous concert pianist, committed suicide after paralysis forced him from the stage. Larry comes from a tumultuous marriage to an international model (Farrah Fawcett). "Her one great talent was seducing men," Larry explains. "Marriage interfered with her vocation."

After a brief prologue, "See You in the Morning" begins on the couple's wedding day and then flashes back to show significant moments in their relationship: the party at which they Meet Cute (both have migraines and finger their sinuses in simultaneous agony); their wary courtship; and the day they finally decide to tie the knot after Larry dresses up as Cupid (diaper, white face, bow and arrow) and positions himself at the top of Beth's stairway.

Larry's always doing zany things like that to jar Beth out of her glum neuroses—he's a boyish, irrepressible cutup. That the character is insufferable isn't entirely Bridges fault, although he still has that cockeyed-optimist's glow he had in "Tucker." The role cries our for an actor who looks as if he's done some living, but Bridges is more convincing as Cupid.

The subject of "See You in the Morning" is really Larry's sense of strangeness and his attempts to reach a wife and stepchildren (Drew Barrymore and Lukas Haas) still haunted by the memory of his predecessor. This isn't his house, his kids or his wife—it's someone else's And another man occupies the space he used to fill beside his own wife and kids.

Pakula's vision of modern life as a game of musical chairs—or musical families—has real possibilities. (Farce and musical comedy spring to mind.) But Pakula has fashioned his film in the style of late Woody Allen, with immaculate, Upper East Side settings and a score of old standards.

The characters, meanwhile, don't interact so much as hurl epigrams and snatches of psychobabble at each other. "When you lose one parent you wait for the other one to fall," explains Beth as she tries to account for her children's anxiety. "You will do anything to avoid one more rejection—even marry me," she says later. "Life is one enormous pile of faults for you," says Larry . Then: "I'm sorry. I'm punishing you because I'm angry at myself."

I'm taking these lines out of context, and that's a bit unfair. But the context consists of lots more lines like this—and little else. There are no references to money or politics or the real world. Just high-toned settings and high-toned feelings.

Don McAlpine's cinematography is crisp and, yes, hightoned, with lots of white side- and back-lighting. The family dog looks especially magnificent; the Australian McAlpine, who also photographed "Down and Out in Beverly Hills," has no peer when it comes to dog reaction shots. When the previously hostile animal climbs on a footrest and extends a paw to the beleaguered stepfather, it's a magical moment.

McAlpine lights Barrymore and shiny-eyed Haas in the same way, and each has a scene where she or he extends a paw. When the girl is arrested in Bloomingdale's for shoplifting, Larry tells her he knows why she's acting out. After her father died, she was her mother's right arm, Larry says, and now he has taken her place—now, abracadabra, she has to turn back into a child.

That's a pretty good explanation, but Pakula hasn't dramatized the young girl's feelings. In scenes like this, you realize what a disastrous mistake it was to make his alter-ego a shrink. When he tells Beth that she's throwing him out because she feels she isn't entitled to happiness—that she thinks on some level she deserves to be punished for the suicide of her first husband—Beth has no response except to realize that yes, he's right. He's always right.

It's certainly true that people in therapy spend a lot of time analyzing their own motives. But Pakula has no distance on these people and no impatience with their endless self-scrutiny—he lives for it.

He's clearly a sensitive, intelligent man with the best intentions in the world; there's nothing disingenuous about his work. That might be his problem: he has no artist's cunning. There are no layers to this movie—no mystery or ambiguity. For him, drama is about pinning things down, which might be a good strategy in therapy but tends to sandbag art.

Maybe those early films like "Klute," "The Parallax View" and "All the President's Men"—the ones so marvelous at capturing that floating sense of dread—Pakula now sees as signs of juvenile paranoia. Maybe he thinks he's healthy now. But dramatically this searching, grown-up movie makes it seem as if he's gone back to kindergarten.

You never know—some people might go to "See You in the Morning" and say, "That's my life up there." But most, I'll wager, will feel mighty left out. The movie is exasperating—it's like going to group therapy and not getting to talk.

NEWSDAY, 4/21/89, Part III/p. 3, Mike McGrady

At one point in "See You in the Morning," a woman delivers a rambling, sentimental discourse on the joys of adopting five children from five different parts of the world. Finally, her husband stands up and interrupts the speech: "Anyone interested in the soap-opera rights, contact my lawyer, please."

The line seems significant for two reasons. First, it exemplifies the way veteran writer-director Alan J. Pakula undercuts mawkishness with a self-deprecating wit—he acknowledges the danger at the same instant he counters it. Second, it's a reminder that Pakula retained the soap-opera rights to his own life and 10 years ago began taking notes on his second marriage, notes that gradually evolved into the script for "See You in the Morning."

"Human beings these days are playing a lot of musical chairs and musical houses," Larry (Jeff Bridges) discovers. "And musical families."

Larry should know; he's a player. A psychiatrist who has left a sexually restless wife (Farrah Fawcett) and his two children, Larry has taken up with a widow (Alice Krige) and her two children. As a result, he has moved into another man's home and taken on another man's problems—a sensitive cello-playing boy (Lukas Haas), a girl (Drew Barrymore) racing through adolescence toward trouble, and a dog named George (Corky) that greets him with growls.

Alan Pakula ("All the President's Men," "Klute," "Sophie's Choice") understands the built-in perils in this kind of movie. In fact, he spells them out when he notes his film is "all about textures, execution, characters and contact. It's a real dialogue picture dealing with relationships; it's *not* an action picture."

This is as good a definition as one will find for what was once, in preliberation days, called a woman's picture. Judged on its own terms, the film succeeds. It brushes against a full season of afternoon-TV subplots—marriage, love, death, infidelity, divorce, adoption, suicide, troubled children and even a concert pianist losing the use of a hand (What would you do if I could never give another concert?" he asks his wife)—but only rarely lapses into soap opera.

Most of the time, Pakula is able to add enough wit to float above suds level. Jeff Bridges is of enormous help in this regard; he is a down-to-earth actor whom one trusts and accepts instinctively; his evident masculinity is a godsend. At one point, when domestic problems threaten to engulf him, Bridges hides behind a newspaper and mutters, "Thank you, God, for sports," drawing a laugh of recognition from men in the audience. His co-star, Alice Krige ("Barfly") comes up with an intelligent, crisp performance that also helps bypass danger spots.

But by avoiding danger it seems to me that "See You in the Morning" also manages to avoid those soaring or deeply wrenching moments that can catapult a domestic romance ont the higher ground occupied by, say, a "Terms of Endearment." Instead of going all the way with an emotion, Pakula cuts it off at the pass, usually with a laughline or a shot of wry. Still it seems to me this is the toughest kind of movie to make, and I must applaud Pakula for the effort every bit as much as for the results.

VILLAGE VOICE, 5/2/89, p. 80, Katherine Dieckmann

More leaden than real time, *See You in the Morning* is a belabored sociological vanity about fractured WASP family life: Affable shrink (Jeff Bridges) leaves cover-girl wife (Farrah Fawcett) for widowed, would-be photographer (Alice Krige). Basically, he trades one lush mane and great set of cheekbones for another, gaining a couple of stepchildren with big brown eyes—a boy and a girl, who complement the blue-eyed children he already has—in the process.

At first, it's a mystery why this sudsy material should impel Alan J. Pakula, an occasionally intelligent director (*Klute, All the President's Men*), to write his first original screenplay. (He adapted *Sophie's Choice*.) But the press kit clues us in: *Morning* began as "a writing exercise...over ten years ago," after Pakula's second marriage. Ah, the autobiographical impulse. That personal investment drives Pakula to inflated melodrama—he's got no distance on his characters—while the length of gestation explains the movie's weird, leapfrog structure.

Pakula crosscuts wildly between the two families, relying on flashbacks that we recognize only by the way the camera inches in slowly on a tortured, reflective face. First we're with the Livingstons (Bridges and Fawcett) in Maine. Then we're in an extremely well-appointed Chelsea townhouse with the Goodwins (Krige and David Dukes, her suicidal concert-pianist husband with a paralytic hand). But wait, now we're with a new couple: Bridges and Krige. Then we're back in Maine, hearing about the Livingstons' divorce. However, there are some constants: the presence of Evian water (heavy product endorsement) and the incredibly stilted dialogue. Two examples: "How I longed to be full-breasted" (Krige to her daughter, played by pubescent recovered alcoholic Drew Barrymore), and, on the vulnerability of men, "Y'know, sometimes I think all that terrific male equipment just hangs there by a thread" (Linda Lavin, playing a matchmaker, orphan, and adoptive mom to five kids of mixed ethnicity).

Toward the middle of *Morning*, Pakula calms down and focuses on the second Livingston marriage, and the movie flickers with authenticity—especially whenever Lukas Haas, the wide-eyed boy from *Witness*, is on the screen. Just the way he tugs at his pajamas when he meets his new stepfather is more affecting than all *Morning*'s sweeping strings and pregnant pauses put together; it's a strong and unsentimental child's performance. But the adult actors are fatuous, especially the self-righteously patrician Krige (every bit as nauseating as she was playing the literary lioness in *Barfly*). Pakula should know better: This is one family affair that should have remained strictly Dear Diary.

Also reviewed in:
NEW REPUBLIC, 5/15/89, p. 28, Stanley Kauffmann
NEW YORK TIMES, 4/21/89, p. C16, Vincent Canby
VARIETY, 3/8–14/89, p. 20
WASHINGTON POST, 4/21/89, p. C1, Hal Hinson

1789

An Ariane Films (Paris) production. *Producer:* Alexandre Muouchkine and Georges Dancigers. *Director:* Ariane Mnouchkine. *Screenplay (French with English subtitles):* Ariane Mnouchkine and the company of the Théâtre du Coleil. *Director of Photography:* Bernard Zitzermann, Michel Lebon, and Jean-Paul Meurisse. *Editor:* Françoise Belloux, Frédérique Mathieu, and Françoise Clausse. *Music:* Michel Derouin. *Art Director:* Jean-Noël Cordier, Antonio Ferreira, Claude Forget, Guy-Claude François, and Roberto Moscoso. *Running time:* 150 minutes. *MPAA Rating:* Not Rated.

CAST: Théâtre du Soleil: René Patrignani, Jean-Claude Penchenat, Maxime Lombard, Georges Bonnaud, Fabrice Herrero, Jonathan Sutton, Daïna Lavarenne, Frank Poumeyreau, Marie-France Duverger, Gérard Hardy, Anne Demeyer, Joséphine Derenne, Mario Gonzales, Geneviève Penchenat, Philippe Caubère, Louba Guertchikoff, Nicole Félix, Michel Derouin, Myrrha Donzenac, Jean-Claude Rourbault, Alain Salomon, Roland Amstutz, Françoise Jamet, Serge Coursan, Lucia Benasson, Philippe Hottier, Marc Godard.

NEW YORK POST, 7/11/89, p. 27, V.A. Musetto

Director-writer Ariane Mnouchkine is probably best known to American audiences for "Moliere," the four-hour-and-15-minute biopic that played the New York Film Festival in 1979.

Her cult-like renown in her home base of France, however, rests on her leadership of the Theatre du Soleil, the collective troupe that stages its productions in an old factory on the outskirts of Paris.

In December 1970 the company inaugurated its permanent home with "1789," a group creation depicting events of the French Revolution. It ran for 348 performances, the final 13 of which were filmed by Mnouchkine.

The resulting 150-minute movie, also entitled "1789," is being screened tomorrow through Friday at the French Institute/Alliance Française to mark the bicentennial of Bastille Day.

I never saw the stage production, but judging by the film it must have been quite a spectacle. Performed on several bare stages by a manic young cast, many of whose members take on several roles each, it combines storytelling, carnival, mime, theater and puppetry, with the frenzied action often spilling over into the appreciative audience.

High point, both historically and dramatically, is the fall of the Bastille, as recounted by actresses sitting in the audience as if they were kindergarten teachers telling a story to their students. The narration begins as a whisper, then builds slowly and powerfully to a roar as that "symbol of misery and injustive" succumbs to the people.

But as forcefully as that sequence comes across, there is no hiding the fact that the movie is basically a filmed record of a theater piece (Mnouchkine obviously intended it that way). While this allows you to see the dedication and energy that went into the production, it also makes you realize that even this lovingly made movie cannot duplicate the stirring visual and aural stimuli that the real thing must have provided.

Incidentally, the French Institute's Florence Gould Hall, where "1789" is being screened, is one of the most pleasant places in which I've watched a film. Those folks who divide up movie houses into cramped plexes might want to take note.

Also reviewed in:
NEW YORK TMES, 7/12/89, p. C19, Caryn James
VARIETY, 6/26/74, p. 18

SEX, LIES, AND VIDEOTAPE

A Miramax release of an Outlaw production. *Executive Producer:* Nancy Tenebaum, Nick Wechsler, and Morgan Mason. *Producer:* Robert Newmyer and John Hardy. *Director:* Steven Soderbergh. *Screenplay:* Steven Soderbergh. *Director of Photography:* Walt Lloyd. *Editor:* Steven Soderbergh. *Music:* Cliff Martinez. *Sound:* Paul Ledford and (music) Larry Blake. *Sound Editor:* Larry Blake and Steven Soderbergh. *Art Director:* Joanne Schmidt. *Set Decorator:* Victoria Spader. *Costumes:* James Ryder. *Make-up:* James Ryder. *Running time:* 100 minutes. *MPAA Rating:* R.

CAST: James Spader (Graham); Andie MacDowell (Ann); Peter Gallagher (John); Laura San Giacomo (Cynthia); Ron Vawter (Therapist); Steven Brill (Barfly); Alexandra Root (Gril on Tape); Earl Taylor (Landlord).

CINEASTE, Vol. XVII, No. 3, 1990, p. 38, Karen Jaehne

Sex, lies, and videotape sound like the ingredients for a one night stand, not the culmination of a masculine quest for liberation, as debut director Steven Soderbergh would have us believe. (The title lets us know e.e. cummings has met *thirtysomething*.) The two most interesting characters suffer from a sexual alienation prissy enough to preempt "Thanks for the memory" with "Thanks, but no thanks." Ann (Andie MacDowell) can't bring herself to have sex with her husband, while Graham (James Spader), confessing to Ann that he can't get an erection in another person's presence, manages well enough alone by watching videotaped interviews he's made with women about their sex lives.

Sex, lies and videotape reminds one of Cole Porter's lyrics that "Even over-educated fleas do it" in the song "Let's Fall in Love." It is a comedy, although critics are writing very seriously in response to its unnerving clarion call for love, truth, and confessions. Perhaps it is not so much about sexual politics as it is about the negotiations of sexual politics—that is, what people say and how they move and look when they want a very specific kind of sexual dialog with another human being.

Many critics (mostly male) like to ascribe Ann's alienation to frigidity, while sympathizing with Graham as a New Sensitive Male. How could he *not* turn kinky in face of all those sexually voracious New Insensitive Females? They're *bad girls*—their videotaped confessions prove it—and guys like Graham are far too sensitive to make love to them. Masturbation is his only moral option.

The two other principals, by contrast, are sexual athletes. John (Peter Gallagher), Ann's husband, and Cynthia (Laura San Giacomo), her sister, are busily engaged in a fling so hot it's a wonder they haven't thought of videotape themselves. Before you can say Peyton Place, John demonstrates the social and ethical dimensions of the New Sensitive Male, a man who has been scared into being honest with and about women, going so far as to try to be like them.

With the latest pop technology, Soderbergh wants Graham to explode the neo-conservative

Eighties with video the way David Hemmings did the swinging Sixties with photography in *Blowup*. This recalls some popular notion left over from *cinéma-vérité* that psychological honesty can be had on tape. Is this an extension of the myth that "The camera never lies?" Or that women are so narcissistic that only a camera can get to their true selves? The film encourages us to pose such questions, but is equally adept at avoiding answers within its own "text" and context: the young auteur writes a script in eight days driving from the South to Los Angeles, films it on a minuscule budget, only to win the *Palme* d'Or at Cannes and be acclaimed as the new Cassavetes, capable of thrusting us like a hand into a film that fits like a glove.

Deep within this idea of confessing to Graham's camera—which both female protagonists end up doing—there lies the strategy of permitting the (male) photographer to control our perceptions of female sexuality. In short, it's as if Soderbergh read feminist structuralists and decided to goof on them from the p.o.v. of the New Sensitive Male—"Hey girls, what if I'm a eunuch and guarantee mirror-image reflections of you all doin' the fantasizin'?" Soderbergh is also smart enough not to attempt to provide the visual imagery of those female fantasies; he covers his tracks here with footage of talking heads.

He may not be lying, but who is he kidding? Soderbergh almost had us convinced that this video camera was a confession booth instead of a seduction ploy. This was only possible because of the empathetic flirtation, the soulful anti-materialism, the self-effacing self-obsession of Graham, who is one of those men who has invested his entire being in knowing more about himself than about anything or anyone else. This gives him sufficient security to stay laid back and let others display their neuroses so that he can then demonstrate his "understanding." Spader, as directed by Soderbergh, makes this very attractive, but there are moments when his passivity make him little more than an Electrolux vacuum cleaner. Plugged into a bourgeois environment, he sucks up any women who happen to by lying around.

Of course, Graham doesn't ask men to expose themselves to his candid camera, because he's not trying to relate to men, although the obvious possibility that he's hiding from his own homoeroticism is left unexplored. Instead, Soderbergh presents him as exploring a new relationship to women as a fragile male who, after discovering that his previous relations with women had made him a pathological liar, is convinced that the only way to stay honest is to avoid sex "if anyone else is in the room," as he tells Ann.

The very act of telling Ann such a thing is part of his new "honest" monastic code. If Graham's essential male accessory is out of bounds, will women be more honest with him? Or just turned on by the kinkiness of the ploy, as Cynthia clearly is? Does Soderbergh think men would be more honest as eunuchs? Or are we so unaccustomed to seeing men deal with the failures and disaster of their own desire that we simply prefer Graham's candor?

These are the doubts raised by Soderbergh's sincerity. He wants to show us the many ways we wound each other—and can heal each other, not through the traditional laying on of hands, but rather rigidly adhering to a hands-off policy. Graham knows Ann's lying when she tells him that what she like about marriage is its "security," That may be the funniest lie in any movie of the last two decades!

Ann's own brand of self-obsession can go nowhere until Graham awakens her, which is made palpable for us in an unusually touching scene. In the dead of night, Ann creeps upstairs to Graham's room to observe him sleeping, defenseless. Soderbergh has made her a lonely prefeminist housewife, devoid of seams that would connect her to any larger world, and friends. So she pays somebody to listen to her—psychiatry as the capitalist approach to friendship—until she discovers a friend in her husband's reformed fraternity brother. Graham's blank slate of Truth gets her to divulge her impression that sex is overrated, which can't help sounding like a kind of come-on, wrapped in her gentle Southern drawl. Her titillating Truth is responded to in kind: Graham tells her he's impotent. Another lie, as she will discover when she finally comes to join his video gallery—and once he turns off the damn camera.

Soderbergh is suggesting that honesty and sexuality intersect only when we stop being voyeurs. For this film is nothing if not a study in voyeurism. He's careful not to be judgmental about three of the four lives (John's an educated thug), he does weight in with a very strong statement about responsibility, an often neglected aspect of friendship (and sexuality) in American society.

Graham may think he's an island: we may see him as Shane; but Soderbergh succeeds in developing the arc of Ann's character by having her confront Graham with his responsibility in connecting with other people. Just as Graham and Ann are about to admit that they need each other, Graham retreats into his solipsistic routine, with, "I've got a lot of problems, but they belong to me." His jejune philosophizing and loner pose infuriates Ann. She points out that anyone walking in the door becomes a part of his life. "You've had an effect on *my* life," she accuses him, implicitly challenging him to own up to his own feelings.

How often has sensitivity been used as an excuse for people to stroll in, play the nomad prophet on the eve of destruction, and wander away with "Who, me?" Graham seems like a character recalled from the pioneering days of sexual liberation, when it was considered corny to expect sex to lead to commitment. Now that sex has become a dangerous contact sport, guys like Graham may need video for their rogue's gallery, as Jack Nicholson once used slides for his in *Carnal Knowledge*. Carnal-has become self-knowledge, and Graham is the new "self-made man," if only from a sexual point of view—an onanistic hipster understandably alienated from his professional peers like the self-satisfied John. (It's hard to describe any of these characters without using "self" in the adjectives.)

While Ann and Graham often seem to come from a Seventies time-warp, John and Cynthia are materialist Eighties' types, practicing a sexual realpolitik. Her motivation for a rendezvous with John in her sister's bed, for example, is hazily sketched out as a not unjustified exasperation with Ann's dimwitted "security." Screwing John is Cynthia's way of proving that there is no security in the world except ignorance. The film touches on Cynthia's artisitc aspirations only to contrast it to John's philistine philandering, and her drudgery as a bartender points up John's laziness as a legal eagle.

In the relationship between Cynthia and Ann, Soderbergh sketches the antagonisms of sisterhood with a depressing absence of feminist consciousness. Laura San Giacomo plays Cynthia as one of those women who knows how to pour blood in men's shark pools in order to demonstrate her innate superiority. Nevertheless. Cynthia is Feminismo triumphant: she is presented as the superior woman, especially at the conclusion when Ann comes to bury the hatchet with news of her new job, her new life, and, between the lines, her thanks for flushing John out. But Soderbergh has us gasping alternately at Cynthia's perfidy and performance in bed.

One confrontation in the film promises but doesn't deliver the chemistry of the sensitized types we've been watching in what one could call "Alan Movies" (Alan Alda, Alan Pakula, Woody Allen, and filmmakers feigning the New Sensitive Male schtick who are not necessarily named Alan). Cynthia as the New Tough Killer Femme drops in on Graham, whose "sensitivity" has been impressed on her in tales of his displaced sexuality. Looking lethal, she prowls his empty apartment before she gets down to the Truth with his video panoply: she recounts how the first time she saw a penis she was so amazed that she forgot there was a guy attached to it. The penis is, in fact, the primary problem of very character here. If Ann's feminism is so underdeveloped that getting a job is her first gesture of independence, then Cynthia's feminism has merely get her stuck in the groove of sexual conquest. She seems not to realize that you don't have to crawl; you can walk away.

Soderbergh's characters are achingly familiar but not clichéd, because his direction is as interested in ways they don't lie—the truth of their body language—as in the goals of their relationships. They want or do not want sex with each other; a web of lies and videotape turns that desire into art. Soderbergh tries to shade in the difference between the desire to desire as we watch it in Ann and Graham, and desire to deceive as in John and Cynthia. Which brings us back to the way they negotiate the cold war between the sexes. Ann accuses John of sex with her sister and he lies. John accuses Ann of sex with Graham, and her silence however misleading, confirms it.

Graham lies to himself about celibacy in order to expose women telling the truth. And then a testimony is tucked away for his private pleasure until people like John need it for what facts it may offer. whatever may be recorded, men are oblivious to the truth—because they "haven't the slightest idea who I am," as Ann tells Graham when she seizes the camera to turn it on him. The video camera may be the weapon for her own liberation, as the film suggests, and she may be capable of seizing that weapon and making Graham face his own devices. But John interprets the technology of truth as "sick," as he says after seeing his wife's tape. The health of his organism depends on self-deceit. Graham, too, is operating on the self-deceit, even if he's tipped the Richter scale of sensitivity and fallen apart at some undisclosed point before our story. But he comes to life, as he watches Ann break out of her little solipsistic, shrink-conducted symphony. In a happy ending, these Sleeping Beauties wake up and smell the coffee.

The film refuses to be abstract, while pressing upon us a sense of urgency—but about what? Dismantling the barrier of lies? Stopping video, as Soderbergh says, from "distancing us from other people?'' Whether Soderbergh meant Graham to be viewed with skepticism or not, he and James Spader let him turn *sex, lies and videotape* into an exploration of the phoniness and dangers of isolationism, as Men's Lib gathers steam. Is the key to liberation an escape from pathological lying about love and sex? This movie exists to ask that question. Wisely, it's too open-ended to answer it.

FILMS IN REVIEW, 10/89, p. 482, Edmond Grant

Imagine a one act play about a disatisfied husband who cheats on his apparently frigid wife with her sexpot sister, and the way all three of their lives are altered when the husband's spacey old school mate returns to town and introduces the two women to his own peculiar, distanced version of lovemaking. Add on to that simplistic storyline some eye catching camerawork, very competent editing, and a load of dreary dialogue. What you'll get is this year's surprise winner of the Best Film Award at the Cannes Film Festival, *sex, lies, and videotape*.

First time director Steven Soderbergh has put together a simple work that has the appearance of having something profound to say about male-female relationships, but never quite gets around to saying it. Instead what we experience is a confused psychodrama populated by four especially empty individuals. We start out with the very uptight Ann (Andie MacDowell), who, if better written, could be a refugee from the Woody Allen/Paul Mazursky school of urban neurotics. Next we meet her greasy yuppie husband, John (Peter Gallagher), and her sister Cynthia (Laura San Giacomo, making quite an impression in her first film appearance) who seems to be a sexual being first and foremost. The stage is now set for the entrance of Graham (James Spader), an ''artsy'' type (the other characters label him thusly as a result of his black clothing and zoned-out attitude) who has been rambling around since his last ''serious relationship,'' convincing women to let him videotape them answering questions about their intimate sexual life and, occasionally, performing acts of self-gratification. In any other movie, this would ensure a certain degree of sleaziness. But Soderbergh avoids any note of untoward sleaze by not even concentrating on the videotapes themselves. They simply *exist*—we see a minute or two of one woman talking on video, and later witness an undressed Graham ''reacting'' to what he's viewing. The fact that about two dozen women consented to this peculiar documentation (presumably to help Graham with the impotence he so readily mentions to Ann the first time he meets her alone) is never explored—in fact the whole videotape business is nothing but an outrageous plot device, introduced as a way for the characters to make ambiguous statements about their own lives, loves, and romantic difficulties.

Graham himself is little more than a cipher. As played by Cannes' Best Actor winner James Spader, the character seems like a distressingly spiritual sort of pornographer, a space cadet who never quite turns into a flesh-and-blood being with realistic sexual troubles. As for Spader's acting prize, one can only presume the Cannes jury was applauding his casting against type—usually *he* plays the deceitful greasy yuppie part (*Less Than Zero, Wall Street, Baby Boom*).

Admittedly, Soderbergh presents some topflight visuals. The camera is kept constantly in motion, roving across and around the characters, while the editing and sound work draw parallels between disparate events. So, on a technical level, the film deserves the kudos it's received. However, the perceptive eye of a camera cannot convey depth when there is none to be found in the dialogue, or the characters' actions.

LOS ANGELES TIMES, 8/4/89, Calendar/p. 1, Sheila Benson

With enviable single-mindedness, the two handsome couples in Steven Soderbergh's electrifying psycho-sexual comedy occupy themselves with sex, with lies and with videotape, in a film of exactly that name. It's the funniest and saddest American movie since Jim Jarmusch landed straight in the middle of our consciousness, and it's possibly the most compelling.

Beginning in a therapy session, with the deceptively offhanded remark by a beautiful young wife (Andie MacDowell) that everything is fine in her marriage, except that she's, well, ''kinda going through this thing where I don't want him to touch me,'' the secrets that tumble out are commonplace enough. They're the stuff that Dear Abby readers drink in with their morning coffee; they are also a catalog of upscale affliction: infidelity, obsession, jealousy, impotence, sexual repression and a large dollop of voyeurism.

It's Soderbergh's elegant manner of revealing these...contemporary inconveniences, and of pushing his characters into deeper and deeper psychological water, that creates the film's tranquil spell. As writer, director and editor, his control is mesmerizing. It's also more than a little creepy;

as though Soderbergh were drawing us, a step at a time, into a warm pool where intimate secrets flowed back and forth as simply as currents of water. Feel uneasy about what you may hear? Lie back and float, everything will be all right.

Well, although this isn't Brian De Palma voyeurism or David Lynch creepiness, sometimes it feels as though nothing will be all right. With brilliant economy, Soderbergh lets us see that MacDowell's husband (Peter Gallagher) is a creep in a three-piece suit, that her perfect marriage is a hollow disaster and that she is sleepwalking to keep from knowing it.

And that's *before* Gallagher's old college buddy (James Spader) arrives for a visit. The men make unlikely friends today. The ultimate yuppie puppy, Gallagher has the arrogance that comes with being a law partner at 30, and the sexual combativeness that's led him into a volcanic affair with an artist-cum-bartender (Laura San Giacomo), who happens to be his wife's younger sister.

Blond and quiet-spoken, Spader is open, disingenuously inquiring, almost a '60s throwback—the sort who takes pride in his lack of possessions. Although there is every reason to believe that he is a trust-fund bum, he has blown into Baton Rouge with little more than a change of clothes, a beater convertible, his video camera and a couple of boxes of personal videotapes. If there is something intense about him that puts people off-balance, there is an equal quality that makes them trust him. Especially women.

He intrigues MacDowell, volunteered by her husband to help Spader find an apartment. It might be a classic setup, except that, as Spader explains to her over a delicately probing lunch, he is impotent. Or at least he can't get an erection in the presence of another person, which is as good as impotence. If this disclosure widens her lovely eyes, wait until she asks him idly what's on all his tapes, each with a girl's name? And to what use he puts them?

And that is Soderbergh's setup. What is not apparent from a thumbnail description is the film's lacerating wit, its beautiful look and sound, and the bravura quality to each performance. Or the terrible vein of melancholy that Soderbergh touches.

It's also worth mentioning that only one character in four (MacDowell) could be called sympathetic. The perfectly matched Galagher and San Giacomo deserve one another, and isn't Spader's helpless voyeurism pathetic? Weird? Bizarro? Perhaps, but that will become the fulcrum of the story.

It's no wonder that "sex, lies and videotape," as well as Spader, took the Golden Palm at Cannes this spring, although it's sad that MacDowell's supple, shaded brilliance went unrewarded. This is an American movie that feels French. All this low-key unburdening of sexual trauma. All this talk, punctuated by all these bedroom gymnastics, and not a lethal weapon in sight. (Actually, not a lot of nudity, either, for a film as drenched in sex as this one, MPAA-rated R. It's Gallagher's character who is crass; his creator is discreet.)

If "sex, lies" did not go on to crash through a pair of long-standing psychological barriers as definitively as it does, it would be as creepy as Spader appears to be, as impotently teasing and as uselessly intimate. It's Soderbergh's ability to push his story to its furthest limits that makes it so arresting.

Before it burst on Cannes, "sex, lies and videotape" knocked filmgoers into the snowbanks at the U.S. Film Festival in Park City, Utah, coincidentally with a complete retrospective of John Cassavetes' career. It might seem that, in his own distinct way, Soderbergh is the young American director most clearly in the vein of the dark, deeply missed Cassavetes. Both men, from the very first films of their careers, have demanded that we take a real look at our lives behind the "Shadows," or insulated by "sex, lies and videotape."

MONTHLY FILM BULLETIN, 9/89, p. 282, Pam Cook

John and Ann Millaney are apparently happily married: John has been made junior partner in his law firm, and they have a beautiful home. However, without Ann's knowledge, John is having an affair with her sister Cynthia, while Ann confides to her therapist that John and she have not had sex for months. As old college friend of John's, Graham Dalton, comes to visit. He takes an immediate friendly interest in Ann, and when he decides to stay in the area, she helps him to find an apartment. Over lunch, Ann confides to Graham that she thinks sex is over-rated, and he reveals that he is impotent. One day, Ann visits Graham and discovers his collection of videotapes. She is horrified when he tells her they contain his interviews with women about their sexual experiences, and leaves. Meanwhile, Cynthia, intrigued by Graham ofter talking to Ann, decides to visit him herself. When Graham asks if he can interview her, she consents, revealing on tape that she and John are having an affair. Ann, suspecting that John is seeing someone, asks him if it is Cynthia, but he evades the question. When he finds out from Cynthia about her tape, he is angry and jealous. While cleaning the bedroom, Ann finds Cynthia's earring and, deeply hurt, drives over to Graham and tells him about the affair. Discovering that he already knows, she insists that he interview her. Ann returns home to tell John that she wants a divorce. When he hears about her tape, he drives over to Graham and assaults him. Watching Ann's tape, he learns about her dissatisfaction with their sex life, and sees Ann and Graham start to make love. After John leaves, Graham destroys his tapes and camera. John's career begins to go downhill, Cynthia and Ann are reconciled, and Ann and Graham tentatively begin a new relationship.

Steven Soderbergh's first feature is a modest chamber piece in which necessity has given birth to invention. Four main actors, half-a-dozen scene changes and few camera set-ups have resulted in an intimate essay in which an elliptical, observational style, improvisatory performances and perceptive script combine both to entertain and unsettle. Nothing in the approach or theme is startlingly new; what captures the interest is an engaging ingenuousness which implies that honesty in relationships (and in life) is desirable, and that video can help to achieve it.

This is fairy-tale for our times in which the villain is a competitive, thrusting yuppie lawyer, John, who is having an affair with his wife's sister behind her back. His wife, Ann is the princess, languishing in a sexless marriage, in the grip of housewife's neurosis and in therapy. A prince arrives in the form of Graham, an old college friend of John's who is his moral antithesis: gentle, unambitious and impotent. Graham and his videotapes provide the catalyst which explodes hypocrisy and forces each character to face the truth about themselves: in John's case, his failure to understand or satisfy his wife's sexual needs; in Ann's (she has never had an orgasm and claims sex is over-rated), her inability to confront her own needs and John's failure; for Graham, his lack of a relationship with anything except his videotaped interviews; and for Ann's sister Cynthia, the recognition that her competitive and destructive relationship with her sister is not what she wants.

The drama unfolds at a relaxed pace in leisurely sequences which allow maximum opportunity for the performers, all of whom are excellent, to capture the delicate nuances of personal interaction. This is an actor's film in which dialogue is supremely important, playing off what is said against what is revealed by being left unsaid. In a funny and touching scene, Ann describes her anxieties about garbage disposal, pollution and the ozone layer to her analyst, but becomes coy and defensive when he asks her to talk directly about sex. The more earthy Cynthia, on the other hand, enjoys provoking Ann by being open about sex, while acting out sibling rivalry through her secret affair with John. On one level, this is a story of sex and power, in which those who have sexual knowledge, like John and Cynthia, apparently hold sway over innocents like Ann and Grahem. The tables are turned, however, in a neat reversal, by Graham's impotence. This is what first attracts Ann to him, and encourages women, including Ann and Cynthia, to confide their sexual fantasies to him on videotape. Graham has a library of interviews that Shere Hite would envy, but his concern is less sociological than erotic: he masturbates while watching the tapes.

However, Graham's interest in and knowledge of women does not make him powerful; on the contrary, his role in making and viewing the tapes is passive. When he finds out through interviewing Cynthia that she and John are having an affair, he does not tell Ann, even though they are friends. Only when Ann, provoked by her own discovery of the affair, confronts him about his behaviour and insists that he interview her, is he able to exorcise his self-doubt and make (apparently non-penetrative) love to her, participating for the first time in one of his tapes. Later, when John, mortified by watching his wife's video revelations, attacks Graham and humiliates him in return, Graham destroys his camera and tapes in an apocalyptic gesture of disgust.

Soderbergh's obvious sympathy with Graham and Ann's tender, tentative relationship rather than Cynthia and John's rampant thrashing about suggests that he is promoting a polymorphous, non-phallic sexuality which, especially post-AIDS, is laudable. Yet there is a moral ambivalence hovering somewhere. Video, it seems, uniquely placed at the heart of our private lives, tells the truth; at the same time, it is voyeuristic and can take the place of sex, therefore it is corrupt. With this idea that there is an ideal heterosexual relationship, egalitarian and mutually satisfying, *sex, lies and videotape* threatens to tip over into Joy of Sex naiveté. But Soderbergh is still to be credited with putting eroticism on the agenda in a witty and affecting manner, and with devising an original role for video in relationship therapy.

NEW LEADER, 10/2–16/89, p. 20, John Morrone

By turning its low budget into an asset, Steven Soderbergh's *sex, lies, and videotape* ends up being the most substantial minimalist film of many a year. Set in Baton Rouge, with some scenes shot in temperatures of 100+ degrees, its spare look hardly captures any Southern flavor, and the only heat we see on screen is generated by its cast of four principals. But this is not really Louisiana, this is anywhere—a color-drained "anywhere" in which people drink white wine and iced tea from tall, clear tumblers, dress mostly in black and white, and watch videos in a pale yellow, sparsely furnished apartment. The spaces between these people as they make love, manipulate each other or merely talk in immaculate rooms seem vast, and the atmosphere is hypnotic. Viewing the film feels like a dream you might have while floating in a sensory deprivation tank.

The bare-bones plot is on the surface a simple one. Yuppie lawyer John (Peter Gallagher) and meticulous homemaker Ann (Andie MacDowell) are unhappily married; she is sexually inhibited, and he is having an affair with Ann's barmaid sister Cynthia (Laura San Giacomo). Into this mess comes drifter Graham (James Spader), John's old college chum, whose passive, introverted personality expresses itself through the videotapes he makes of women discussing their sex lives with him.

Graham's peculiar obsession changes the lives of the other three, as his prying camera leads them to revise their perceptions of intimacy and betrayal in love and friendship. He is the Rainmaker with a camcorder, or any movie antihero who serves as a plot catalyst, and Spader endows him with an elusive, otherwordly quality, as if he were a visitor from a distant planet. Although he touches your life, you can't touch him back. Portrait of a young videophile as Mr. Spock.

Soderbergh crafts his first film with precocious skill. Both as writer and director he hides his artifice, disclosing the personalities of his characters in a way that tricks us into forgetting that the story we are watching unfold is fiction. By opening with Ann's therapy session, for example, he creates the illusion of eavesdropping and undetected observation that not only has the effect of making us invisible onlookers in his tiny *faux*-documentary but participants as well.

Indeed, the dialogue—almost exclusively sex-talk—would sound like psychobabble were it not for our total absorption in the characters' very familiar problems. Remarks like, "the object of your obsession is something negative over which you have no control" will break up some viewers anyway. Yet because we are told so little about these people's exterior lives, and so much about their interior doubts and desires, we can shape them in our own image. They are like skeletal constructs whose human qualities Soderbergh relies on us to flesh out from our own experience. He did not needs a higher budget for *sex, lies, and videotape*; our imagination supplies what the film doesn't show. Soderbergh would be terrific writing for radio.

Still, there is well-developed plot behind the subtle scheme for securing our involvement. During the first hour, the dreamy, tentative mood of the film intrigues us and toys with our expectations. Then we witness the revelations of each character's secret activities to the others. Ann learns of John's affair with Cynthia. John discovers that Cynthia has let Graham record her and that she was aroused by talking about sex on tape. And Graham, while taping Ann (who shows up at his home on a dare) learns he can speak about himself, too, when Ann seizes the camera and turns it on him.

Soderbergh is finally not ambiguous at all about what his characters stand for—Ann/fear, Graham/truth, Cynthia/defiance, John/deceit. Moreover, given how expertly *sex, lies, and videotape* seduces us with Cool, we are surprised to see it veer toward a moralizing ending that in a moment of epiphany has Ann surrendering to her desire and Graham conquering his impotence. We do not expect a lesson about how important it is for people to make contact with each other from the writer-director of a postmodern movie with a lower-case title.

Can a message this conventional really be Soderbergh's point of view? Must be. Otherwise, the film becomes little more than a party game for the white middle-class cinephiles who are presumably the audience it is primarily attracting.

Soderbergh has called *sex, lies, and videotape* a film about "accountability," and he has said it is highly autobiographical in the emotions it depicts, albeit not the incidents. If he does not entirely convince us that he stands uncynically behind the relatively happy ending his very hip-ness could be to blame. We assume our talented young culture heroes will remain blasé. We don't mind the movie's occasional clichés intruding upon its laid-back style—the wife's discovery of the other woman's pearl earring is the most outrageous. But Soderbergh has steered us toward a Big Theme in his small, modest work, something American features rarely do without fanfare and prestige. Sad to say, this catches us off-guard. We should be relieved, however, to have our disbelief back again after such a rocky emotional ride.

NEW STATESMAN & SOCIETY, 9/15/89, p. 44, Suzanne Moore

Ann, the central character of Steven Soderbergh's celebrated *sex, lies and videotape*, is a beautiful woman who, as Graham (James Spader) observes, is used to being "looked at all the time". She is the woman John Berger described: so aware of being watched that she watches herself even when alone. As the title suggests, this is a movie about the lie of appearance and the appearance of lies. It took the Palme D'or at Cannes and is certainly a stunningly assured piece of film-making. After a summer in which special effects seemed to have taken over from effective scripts it is good to see a movie whose success is largely thanks to an intelligent and funny screenplay

Soderbergh gets away with long, close-up shots of dialogue that in other films might be deemed pretentious, precisely because *sex, lies and videotape* is so well written and, not least, because most of that dialogue centres on everyone's favourite subject—sex. Andie MacDowell is that rare phenomenon, an ex-model who can act, and she plays Ann with jittery intensity. Married to the upwardly obnoxious John, their colour-supplement life in small town Louisiana appears perfect. He is successful at work, they have a beautiful house, and she has nothing to do but clean it. In her therapy, however, she is obsessed about garbage overflowing everywhere and admits that she has never masturbated.

When Graham, an old friend of John's, comes to stay, his strangely intimate yet hesitant manner and his confession of impotency enable Ann to confide in him. "I think sex is so overrated." This is clearly not the case for her sister Cynthia who is vigorously fucking John at every available opportunity. (Actually Ann doesn't like to use the word "fucking"...though she suspects that something is going on.)

She trusts Graham but is appalled when she finds out that his only sexual pleasure comes from watching videos of women he has taped, talking about their sexual experiences. Cynthia, true to form, is desperate to know what has shocked her prudish sister so much, and when she finds out volunteers to be interviewed.

Soderbergh's use of video within the film is terrific, reminding me of Atom Egoyan's *Family Viewing*, which also uses video as a symbol of sexual alienation. Graham needs the *image* of a woman, not a real woman, to get off. The anonymity of pornography, however, is not enough, it has to be a woman he *knows*. Video guarantees both that distance and that unrealness, by turning everything into an image. Yet it is also the technology of intimacy, of homemovies, of promised reciprocity.

Voyeurism is the paradox that lives and dies on that promise. The voyeur's darkest fear is peculiarly double-sided: that the object of desire is not what it seems, in which case he loses control of the fantasy, and that the object is *exactly* what it seems, in which case total separation is hard to maintain.

With these echoes of *Peeping Tom* and its emphasis on the phallic power of the camera, *sex, lies and videotape* shows more insight into its male characters than its female ones. Laura San Giacomo, as the permanently randy little sister, is a little too close to a stereotype at times. Overall though, the film is totally compelling and all the comparisons and clamouring to classify this new talent—Woody Allen, Eric Rohmer and *thirtysomething*—seem as unnecessary as they are unsatisfactory.

The film's sexiness comes from the fact that it is not afraid to deal with its subject. Sexuality is presented as problematic for everyone concerned, and the film cleverly oscillates between sex as the essential emotional truth and sex as the biggest lie of all. John and Cynthia have great sex because they are both lying to someone else about it. In contrast, Graham and Ann are both painfully honest and painfully inadequate.

Soderbergh has said that this is a film about accountability and it is. But it is really moral, rather than sexual, responsibility that is his subject, a rather old-fashioned concept. If finally, after his witty dismissal of therapy, he falls into the trap of using sex as both revelation and cure—a true fantasy if ever there was one—at least he does it through Ann when, for the first time, she starts asserting her desire. She confronts Graham as he is taping her. Object becomes subject.

When she takes the camera from him he says nervously: "I don't find this turning the tables thing interesting." Well, I do. Because we are all voyeurs and here is a film that delivers what we are all looking for. That elusive commodity that is so often promised but rarely materialises—Adult Entertainment.

NEW YORK, 8/7/89, p. 40, David Denby

In *sex, lies, and videotape*, the characters talk softly to one another, about one another, and finally about themselves, and we are drawn gently but insistently into a labyrinth of lust and betrayal. Murmured into our ears, the dialogue reveals the power of lies and also, surprisingly, the greater power of truth. This purring little movie is highly erotic, yet also rather sternly ethical. It says that confession is not only sexy—self-revelation is the true turn-on—but it's also the road to redemption. Can this be true? Perhaps not, but we're willing to be seduced.

To all appearances, Steven Soderbergh's first feature-length film is a very modest production. Apart from the four central characters—a beautiful, frigid wife, her adulterous husband, her vengeful sister, and a wounded but clever outsider who fascinates the women—there's only a well-decorated house and a few other locations in Baton Rouge, and some videotapes. The movie is a triumph for a very young filmmaker (Soderbergh is 26) and also for the much-heralded but frequently negligible independent-cinema movement, which in recent years has wandered unproductively in virtuous hayfields of boredom. *Sex, lies, and videotape* cost a mere $1.2 million. All it takes to make a good movie is talent and drive—and also, perhaps, a good subject and a healthy interest in the mysteries of personality, preferably in the uniquely complicated and dangerous ways that human beings draw closer to each other.

The movie, which is about intimacy of every kind, puts us in a trance. But cunning and disciplined as *sex, lies, and videotape* is, I don't think it's a great film. The minor penalty of Soderbergh's youth is his occasionally gummy sensitivity. He thinks people should tell the truth and not use sex to manipulate one another or to gain revenge—not *use* sex at all. Which is certainly very nice but a bit bald. His moral ideas wouldn't be enough to animate, say, a serious novel. What saves him from obvious banality, however, is his teasing games with videotapes—movies within the movie—and his command over actors; actors can make a theme like lying and sincerity seem profound. Soderbergh has a wonderfully sly sense of humor too.

In the beginning there is Andie MacDowell as Ann, a prudish, seemingly cracked young beauty burbling non sequiturs to her amused shrink. Garbage . . . she says she's obsessed with *garbage;* she also says she gets along fine with her husband, even though he no longer wants to touch her, and she doesn't want to touch him either. MacDowell has soft, soft looks—full, luxurious brown hair, recessed kitten eyes, readied, pouty lips. There's a southern lilt to her voice that gives piquancy to Ann's naiveté. In a few minutes of screen time, MacDowell creates the character of a giggling, self-conscious young neurotic defending herself with long-outdated proprieties, and right away we sense that Soderbergh's touch is deft, because we laugh at Ann's anxieties and evasions without quite laughing at *her*. There's an antic orginality to her mind—and reserves of obstinacy in MacDowell's manner—that suggests unhappiness and fear rather than dullness.

But she causes extraordinary resentment, as prudish people often do. Her husband, John (Peter Gallagher), a handsome young lawyer, successful, with good taste, has completely lost interest in her. Gallagher, best known for his theater work, has a face in which sensuality is the only developed emotion. With his big, overripe lips and rounded cheeks, he's like a prettier Frans Hals subject looking for an apple to bite into. His manner is eager but threadbare; he doesn't offer any depth, but then he doesn't need to. John slides from one thing to another; he's unconsciously selfish, lying so naturally he doesn't hear himself telling whoppers.

He is having an illicit affair with Ann's younger sister, Cynthia (Laura San Giacomo), who is unlike Ann in every way. Tiny and foulmouthed, Cynthia, who works as a bartender, revolts against Ann's feeling that sex is unimportant by making sex everything. Sex defines her identity, and she uses it to destroy Ann, whom she's always despised. San Giacomo, one of Soderbergh's casting coups, has a husky voice thickened with longing and a small face overwhelmed by large, ravenous eyes. She gives a brazenly erotic but essentially comic performance as a coarsely intelligent woman who allows sexual bravado to mess up her life. John and Cynthia, who meet for sex during the day, don't even like each other. They are screwing Ann out of her peace of mind.

Into this situation glides a different kind of sexual performer, John's old college friend Graham (James Spader). A drifter and by conventional standards (i.e., John's) a loser, Graham begins asking Ann questions about herself the minute he meets her. There's something diffident yet penetrating in his manner; he's remarkably polite yet pressing, even importunate. Spader, so memorable as a mean, calculating young sleaze in such films as *Pretty in Pink* and *Baby Boom,* here has the mildest of blue eyes and long, almost girlish blond hair. In this movie, he's the very image of the nonthreatening male, but he pauses briefly before speaking, as if taking nothing for granted, and his deliberation is somehow challenging and sexy. Spader finds a rhythm so original for Graham that he creates a little aura around himself; everything he does—his reacting to one thing and ignoring another—is mesmerizing.

He easily admits to Ann that he's impotent when he's with a woman, and she's intrigued by his candor. His lambent attention to women is a lure; he's good at getting them to talk and confess and take off their clothes for him, while he sits there with a video camera. Later he watches the tape and masturbates. Graham, without doubt, is the unlikeliest moral hero in recent movies, but here he is—the voyeur who brings enlightenment. Cynthia hears about him from Ann, who has befriended him, and, eager to trump her sister again, she races to his apartment; she's so turned on by confessing and performing for his camera that it changes her life. Soon Ann allows herself to be taped, too, and begins talking about her frigidity and her feelings for her husband. Babbling shall set you free.

The women's undressing and talking about sex for this guy who diddles himself is creepy but not *just* creepy. Soderbergh has got hold of a good filmmaker's idea, and a funny one, too (though he doesn't play it for laughs)—the notion that confessing is itself a sexual act and that sexual confession is more erotic than sex itself. He's very solemn about our needing to break through inhibitions and tell the truth, and his earnestness will probably make the movie a hit (his thoughtful tone forbids us to think we're seeing something dirty and low-down). He's canny as well; he holds back the tapes that Cynthia and Ann make, finally releasing them into the narrative just when we most need to understand the women. Describing the first time she saw a penis (at fourteen), Laura San Giacomo's Cynthia, sitting on a couch, gathers her legs under her and leans forward to the video camera, awed by her memory and by the power the moment gave her. And Ann, in her tape, is a changed creature—still puzzled by sex but demanding, imperious, an aroused, determined woman. We can see now that it was living with her husband's bland duplicity that made her so goofy.

Soderbergh has been making films since he was thirteen, but unlike most of the recent young film whizzes, he doesn't dream of spaceships or furry little creatures. My God, a young director who loves actors! What a relief! He brings the characters so close they seem transparent to us, yet he doesn't go in for that wrenching John Cassavetes stuff, pulling out revelations with iron pincers. This movie is mostly somber and quietly observant, like a soap opera written by a genius of the form. As a filmmaker, Soderbergh resembles Graham—uncoercive but still dominating. And he beautifully dramatizes the small social events that plague a young man—all the varieties of tentativeness, for instance, and the charged awkwardness of first meetings.

The weakness of the movie also proceeds from his youth. Graham the video obsessive, doing nothing with his life but recording other people's souls, is a man who holds existence at a distance. One has the impression that Soderbergh is criticizing himself—and idealizing himself at the same time. (I was not surprised to learn that he wrote the script at the end of a troubled time in his life.) Graham is impotent, he tells Ann, because he used to be a pathological liar, and violent. He rejects potency as if it were a state of being beneath the condition of a genuinely feeling man. He offers the most high-minded (and most easily curable) cause for impotence that I've ever heard of. And since both women respond th him and fall away from the shallow, selfish stud John, we might easily gain the impression that impotence is some higher level of male understanding. Nonsense gathers in the recesses of the movie's gravid explorations.

Soderbergh's sentimental mistake was to treat Graham as a saint of sex rather than view him toughly and satirically as an immensely clever new-style hustler. Witty as some of the writing is, the movie, at its core, is humorless. Still, *sex, lies, and videotape* is a fascinating, eccentric first feature—the best debut film in more than a decade.

NEW YORK POST, 8/4/89, p. 21, David Edelstein

Steven Soderbergh, the 26-year-old writer-director of the low-budget comedy "sex, lies, and videotape," has a gift for teasingly ironic repartee: He makes you laugh at the gulf between what people say and what they're concealing. The movie has a cool, vaguely unsavory allure—you're always privy to each character's dirty little secrets.

Soderbergh's alter-ego is Graham (James Spader), a tousled, cryptic, chain-smoking video director who always looks as if he's just finished masturbating or is just about to start. (Graham would agree with the description.)

After a wandering absence, he returns to his hometown, Baton Rouge, where he moves in temporarily with an old chum, John (Peter Gallagher). Now a flushed, self-satisfied law partner with a properly gorgeous wife, Ann (Andie MacDowell), John regards the bohemian, black-clad Graham with smarmy pity. But the repressed, self-conscious Ann is mysteriously drawn to the enigmatic—almost encrusted—young artist.

In the opening, the camera rests fully on Ann's face as she tells her psychiatrist (Cheshire cat Ron Vawter) of her dread of garbage (it's everywhere) and her discomfort with sex. While she speaks, Soderbergh shows Ann's husband tearing the clothes off her sister, Cynthia (Laura San Giacomo)—a hot, brassy little bartender with a lingering resentment of Ann's goody-good demeanor and pristine beauty.

Soderbergh has you giggling from the start at these ironic juxtapositions—at what the characters withhold from one another (but not from the audience). His camera is as nosy as Graham, who also pries into Ann's inner life, subtly drawing her out. Sexually impotent, Graham is meant to be a human camera: He doesn't take part, either physically or emotionally; he just likes to watch.

The center of the film is Graham's stash of eight-millimeter videotapes, in which he asks different women to talk about their sexual experiences—and do whatever else comes naturally. When Ann discovers the tapes, she flees his apartment in disgust; her sister, the extrovert, zooms right over, eager to bare all.

The thing is, "sex, lies, and videotape" is like one of Graham's tapes on a larger scale. You study these attractive people as they purposely misrepresent themselves, keeping their true thoughts and feelings under wraps. And every time you see beneath their masks—catching glimpses of their dishonesty or squirmy distress—you get a naughty thrill. The film is porn for art house Peeping Toms, who hunger for that flash of naked soul.

Slinking into bedrooms in her short black dresses and cowboy boots, the dark, lithe San Giacomo seems slmost 3-D—it's a performance of startling eroticism. Cynthia has built her act on everything her big sister isn't. She's husky-voiced, vulgar and pointed, yet so witchily self-contained she might be part feline.

San Giacomo's vivid features are crowded together, whereas MacDowell's face is spacious, full of plush expanses. A supermodel for the last decade, MacDowell makes Ann a woman who's so aware of being looked at that she's paralyzed with self-consciousness; she shows you the human being cowering under the heavy-lidded, Pre-Raphaelite mask.

The two actresses play excitingly off each other; the men are much less engaging. Gallagher makes John a credible person instead of a yuppie stereotype, but he can't make him interesting. And Spader, whose limp, spider-webby deadpan is very entertaining, turns moldy and actorish in the climax.

It's a moldy climax anyway, recalling Rovert Anderson's play "Tea and Sympathy," in which a young man is rescued from sexual perversion by the purity of a woman's love. (The woman restores both his candor and his potency.) Here, Graham is the twisted pervert, Ann the redeemer and the videotapes the poison that has saturated Graham's soul.

In the last 20 minutes, it's clear that "sex, lies, and videotape" aims to be a profound indictment of the lies people use to anesthetize themselves to the pain of living. But the fun (and, admittedly, the creepiness) of the movie is its porny charge, its appeal to our voyeurism.

If Graham's videos are meant to be lies—symbols of his emotional cowardice—then what does that say about "sex, lies, and videotape" and the impulses that fueled it? Or would Soderbergh pretend that there's no connection between what he's doing and what he's denouncing in his hero?

This horrible, "sincere" finale—in which all the loose ends are tied up—plays uttery false and hypocritical. Of course, it may also guarantee the picture a larger audience: Soderbergh's sudden burst of puritanism sends people home feeling cleansed, off the hook morally for their prurience. Graham destroys his videos, but Soderbergh can have his tape and denounce it, too. The end of "sex, lies, and videotape" is the real lie.

NEWSDAY, 8/4/89, Part III/p. 3, Mike McGrady

Movie titles are usually chosen for one of two reasons. Either they rather neatly sum up the subject matter—say,"The Texas Chain Saw Massacre"—or they simply catch the eye: such as 1965's "Don't Worry, We'll Think of a Title." But what are we to make of the title attached to the new film that won this year's top prize at the Cannes Film Festival: "sex, lies, and videotape"?

While the title is an eye-catcher, the surprise is that it also happens to be a literal summation of the terrain covered by the film.

First, sex. The film, a first feature by Steven Soderbergh, an unknown 26-year-old director, is a deeply personal exploration of four interlocking sex lives. It focuses first on Ann (Andie MacDowell), a wife more concerned about starving Biafrans than with her own love life. When Ann's psychiatrist asks her how things are going at home, she replies, "Oh, they're fine. I'm kinda goin' through this thing where I don't want him to touch me...I've never been that much into sex, I wouldn't miss it kinda thing."

While Ann busies herself with world problems, husband John (Peter Gallagher), a hustling young lawyer, is carrying on a heated affair with Ann's sister Cynthia (Laura San Giacomo), a barmaid who resents her sister's respectability.

Enter Graham (James Spader), once John's closest college friend, but now a mystical, dreamy young man who has chosen to live his life in the slow lane. Since Graham owns a car, he wonders whether he should rent an apartment: "If I get an apartment, that's another key. I just like having one key." Graham's sex life is nothing to write home about; he feels no excitement "in the presence of another person. So, for all practical purposes, I'm impotent."

Thus, the "videotape." It seems that Graham's libido is activated only when he is alone watching videotaped interviews with women friends who have agreed to answer his most intimate questions about their sexual histories and preferences.

And, finally, the "lies." Sisters Ann and Cynthia, separately, volunteer to be interviewed by Graham. What emerges from these interviews, but ever so slowly, is truth, the truth about them, about their shared male and, finally, the truth about Graham. While Graham's videotape machine at first seems to be his linkup to the real world, it is, in reality, a distancing device, a protective shield. Graham's insistence on truth is threatening to all, even himself, but he now can have it no other way: "I was pathological liar. Or I am, I should say. Lying is like alcoholism and you're continually recovering."

In past movies, James Spader has specialized in mild cases of yuppiesque villainy ("Baby Boom," "Less Than Zero," "Wall Street"), and his Graham is a major departure. The role demands a sense of removal, a missed beat in all responses to the outside world. There's a slight pause as he scrupulously avoids saying what the world expects and, instead, opts for truth unvarnished. Sprader's brilliantly intuitive performance won this year's top acting award at Cannes.

Andie MacDowell is touchingly real as the woman emerging from a life of self-delusion. Peter Gallagher as the lying husband and Laura San Giacomo as the cheating sister may have less sympathetic roles, but are no less effective.

But what makes "sex, lies, and videotape" so involving, and surely a prime reason it won the best-picture award at Cannes, is it explores territory most moviemakers wouldn't approach with an overhead boom. One need not be told this is the work of a Hollywood newcomer, and for young writer-director Steven Soderbergh, it must be reckoned the most impressive film debut in many years.

NEWSWEEK, 8/7/89, p. 61, David Ansen

A good hypnotist doesn't need a fancy costume and a gold pendulum. If he wins your trust, it only takes a few soft-spoken words to put you under. Steven Soderbergh, the 26-year-old writer/director, has the gift. As soon as *sex, lies, and videotape* begins, you know you're in the hands of a filmmaker who knows precisely what he's doing, and you hang on every word to see where he's taking you. This mesmerizing $1.2 million first feature, the grand-prize winner at Cannes, consists mostly of talk, and most of the talk is about sex (the title is literally what the movie's about). Yet with little action, and only one thrown punch, this idiosyncratic, disquietingly funny movie holds you breathless with suspense. It's internal; the cliffs from which we hang are the mysteries of character; the fear—and goal—is intimacy.

"Sex, lies, and videotape" is a form of cinematic chamber music, scored for four young instruments, tightly strung. The setting is Baton Rouge, La., though Soderbergh wastes no time with local color. Ann (Andie MacDowell) is the first voice we hear: talking to her psychiatrist in the giggly, repressed, self-conscious tones of a woman who's not willing to give up being a little girl, she claims her marriage is "fine," except she's "going through this thing" where she doesn't want her husband to touch her. Her husband, the self-satisfied young lawyer John (Peter

Gallagher), is going through a thing himself—regular midafternoon trysts with the raspy-voiced, feline barmaid Cynthia (Laura San Giacomo). Cynthia, however, happens to be Ann's sister, and we quickly surmise that her interest in John is mainly fueled by resentment of her popular, oh so proper sibling. Enter the nomadic dropout Graham (James Spader), an old frat brother of John's. Seductive and definitely a little strange, Graham has a soft, pubescent sexual aura about him and a shrink's talent for eliciting women's secrets. Ann is intrigued; she confesses to him that she thinks sex is overrated. He tells her he's impotent. Soon she makes an even more disturbing discovery: Graham's obsession for videotaping women confessing the most intimate sexual details of their lives.

No more "plot" should be revealed, except to say that Graham's volatile presence alters the chemistry of all their lives. And any mere synopsis could not begin to convey Soderbergh's wit, his charged nuances or the hushed eroticism he achieves without showing any explicit sex. What's astonishing in a director so young isn't just his rigorously controlled camera work or his extraordinary rapport with actors, but his instinct for knowing just how much he can leave out. The understatements and ellipses are often as eloquent as what's stated.

The four stars play Soderbergh's dissonant sexual quartet impeccably: you can practically feel the characters slipping in and out of one another's heads. Who knew that under MacDowell's fashion-model beauty lay such a quirky, funny actress? Who knew that Spader, formerly typecast as an arrogant Yuppie brat, has such quiet, insinuating charisma? Newcomer San Giacomo, raunchy and acerbic, is a powerhouse presence. For the two hours of "sex, lies, and videotape," nothing seems more important than peering into the odd, misdirected souls of these four entangled people. Soderbergh has turned intimacy into art.

TIME, 7/31/89, p. 65, Richard Corliss

[*sex, lies, and videotape* was reviewed jointly with *When Harry Met Sally* . . . ; see Corliss' review of that film.]

VILLAGE VOICE, 8/8/89, p. 55, Georgia Brown

Last spring at Cannes, Spike Lee directed bitter comments the jury's way for its preferring a white boy's wet dream over his own implosive *Do the Right Thing*. Steven Soderbergh's Palme d'Or winner *sex, lies, and videotape* may look more comparable in scope and ambition to *She's Gotta Have It,* Lee's own commercial debut. These romantic comedies both rely on performances and flaunt low budgets to work up attractive visual claustrophobia. And both put female sexuality at the centre of the frame—risky business (touch of hubris) for the young male filmmaker.

But if Soderbergh's first feature is circumscribed, it's also almost stunningly polished—a lovely, exhilarating, rare thing. A young man's love story, it exudes uncanny poise. The self-taught Soderbergh at 26 not only writes, directs, and edits, but clearly has a gift for working with actors. His modest, confused *sex, lies, and videotape* is vastly different from Lee's gutty, beautiful, irritating *Do the Right Thing,* but it too (praise be) is a movie that hasn't been made before.

Despite the racy title, *sex, lies* happens to be quite chaste—sexually and intellectually. As a celebration of the innocence and resilience of women—as well as the patience of an exceptional man to beat a path through the briars—it's a fairy tale, having both a childish side and a share of generalized truth. Soderbergh's moralizing—thanks to the fresh, engaging context—is tolerable, if troubling more in the aftertaste. Youthful sincerity ordinarily looks more naive than youthful alienation, but with the filmmaker neither straining nor showing off, it has the potential to hit like a fresh country breeze. Like his heroine, Soderbergh comes off as a virgin, priggish and beguiling.

Sex, lies opens elliptically, with intercuttings and soundtrack layerings. Sorted out, the gist is this: Graham (James Spader) is driving back to sultry Baton Rouge, Louisiana, where he plans to visit his old LSU fraternity brother, John (Peter Gallagher), while looking for a place to settle; Ann (Andie MacDowell), John's wife, explores her discontents in a therapy session ("The last time I was happy, I got really fat; I put on 25 pounds"); corporate lawyer John ducks out of the office for a session in bed with his wife's younger sister, Cynthia (Laura San Giacomo). Ann and Cynthia (one says *fuck,* the other doesn't) are split parts of a self, just as are Graham and John, formerly "identical" buddies.

Ann's funny momologue dominates the movie's opening. Sitting cross-legged on the analytic couch ("I've gotten real conscious of all the garbage"), she's winsome, clean, and buoyant—also, deceived and inexperienced. Again, these are adjectives that apply to the movie. Her therapist (Performing Garage's wonderful Ron Vawter) zeros in on her garbage problem: "How're things with John?"

"Fine. Except I don't want him to touch me." (Said over image of John and Cynthia naked and touching.) "The few times I felt something I was by myself." When the therapist asks if she does anything about her impulses, she giggles something about "it" being "so stupid." Ann's never had an orgasm. (Don't expect a tour de male force on the order of Mailer's "The Time of Her Time" or Brodkey's "Innocence.")

Plot synopsis doesn't do much for Soderbergh's film. Its life is in droll, quirky dialogue (as when Ann informs Graham, "Sorry, we don't let people smoke in the house"), in superb ensemble acting and spare, clean camera work (cinematographer is Walt Lloyd). Subjected to tight close-ups, Spader (moist, soft, open) and MacDowell (brittle, chipper, open) work together as if under a charm. Soderbergh credits rehearsal sessions for the rapport. Shrewdly, he's cast seasoned actors without star identities. Voted best actor at Cannes, Spader, who's had a few marginal screen roles (he was the villian in *Pretty in Pink* and one of Charlie Sheen's contacts in *Wall Street*), commands the movie—even, apparently, causing the director to revise his ending. A model who doesn't look vacuous, the radiant MacDowell is also quite wonderful. (She was Jane in *Greystoke*.) There's a gloriously funny scene where Ann frenziedly cleans a kitchen sink by practically jerking off the faucet. Gallagher and San Giacomo (in her screen debut) have more conventional, one-dimensional roles. Apparently, all of the actors contributed by improvisation. The result says much more about craft than do most movies.

It also says a lot less about movies than one would expect from a film nominally about film—okay, videotape. Graham turns out to be a voyeur ("I can't have an erection in the presence of another person") who has crisscrossed the country (he tacks a highway map on the wall) interviewing women on tape about their sexual histories and proclivities. "What is the most unusual place you've ever masturbated?" "When did you first see a penis?" "My personal project," he calls this has produced a library of tapes alphabetized by women's first names that he can refer to whenever the urge comes up. The project, not to mention Graham's impotence, serves as a means of seduction. See how readily women take to the prospect of confessing rather than doing anything. Compulsive "bad girl" Cynthia can't wait to address Graham's Sony.

The wonder is how little visual use Soderbergh makes of this visual theme. Except on the literal level, he hardly appears bent on contributing to the literature of voyeurism. Almost as soon as the theme of voyeurism gets introduced, the film quickly denounces the craven business. It hardly gets a chance to demonstrate the lure. Graham may still be making and viewing his tapes, but his heart no longer is in it. Once "a pathological liar," he says, he's become a pathological truth-teller. But there's no sense that Graham—or Soderbergh—knows how much truth the camera can tell, or just what its ways of lying are. Or how lies may lead to truth.

"Video is a way of distancing ourselves and cutting ourselves off, anesthetizing our responses; it's very passive." This is a rather amazingly obtuse Soderbergh generalization quoted in the movie's press materials. Video (together with microwave ovens) may be evil, but what about the way Cynthia's video confession liberates her? What about its therapeutic effects on Ann? How did Graham come to his disillusionment if not by means of his camera? And, to put a point on it, what about cinema's obvious appeal and uses for Soderbergh?

Video and John are the film's two evils; both get smashed. (John's professional comeuppance is one of the movie's obtrusively false notes.) The first is too passive, apparently, and the other too active. Nothing in Soderbergh's analysis indicates comprehension of evil. Or of the routes one travels to earn the capacity for good. John's creep from the start; this isn't evil but villainy. Graham's passivity—paired, I guess, with video's—isn't necessarily what it seems. Graham is sexy in his impotence, and stronger in his perversity than his righteousness. His and Ann's "honesty" is a way of separating them off from the sleaze represented by John. (I don't deny our longing for truth-telling that the movie appeals to.) What's attractive about Ann is not only her protected view of the world, but her capacity for mischief.

Graham rides like a lone, weary cowboy into a troubled community carrying the weight of some mysterious suffering. (He evens wears black. Cynthia clearly resembles the western's town whore who craves for and benefits from the hero's sympathy.) He's Shane, or Eastwood's pale rider, whose instincts for violence conflict with his secret shame. Roused (by pity, the chivalric code, and his host's attractive wife) to using (one more time) his powers, the hero's own conflicts are merely revealed, not solved. Herein lies *sex, lies, and videotape*'s appealing subtext. All those moral messages (no more illicit sex, no more lies, no more videotape) are baggage weighing it down.

Intuitively, Soderbergh has created a gem. On the explicit level, though, the movie's something of a monster. (Trust the tale, not the teller?) In imagining scenarios for a young director with a big success, it's hard not to wonder whether someone needing to put a moral face on things wouldn't be overly susceptible to (re)making official versions of fact. I don't mean this as a sentence. The kid is a natural. Maybe he needs a dark lady to shoot him with a silver bullet.

Also reviewed in:
NATION, 9/4–11/89, p. 250, Stuart Klawans
NEW REPUBLIC, 9/4/89, p. 26, Stanley Kauffmann
NEW YORK TIMES, 8/4/89, p. C12, Caryn James
NEW YORKER, 8/7/89, p. 73, Terrence Rafferty
VARIETY, 2/1–7/89, p. 20
WASHINGTON POST, 8/11/89, p. C1, Rita Kempley
WASHINGTON POST, 8/11/89, Weekend/p. 37, Desson Howe

SHAG: THE MOVIE

A Hemdale Releasing Corporation release of a Palace (Myrtle Beach) Ltd. film. *Executive Producer:* John Daly and Derek Gibson. *Producer:* Julia Chasman and Stephen Woolley. *Director:* Zelda Barron. *Screenplay:* Robin Swicord, Lanier Laney, and Terry Sweeney. *Story:* Lanier Laney and Terry Sweeney. *Director of Photography:* Peter MacDonald. *Editor:* Laurence Mery-Clark. *Music Editor:* Peter Krook. *Choreographer:* Kenny Ortega. *Sound:* Ed Novick. *Sound Editor:* Peter Krook. *Production Designer:* Buddy Cone. *Art Director:* Jon Hutman. *Set Decorator:* Kara Lindstrom. *Set Dresser:* Polar Bear, Vernon Harrell, and John Bromell. *Costumes:* Mary E. Vogt. *Make-up:* Kathy Shorkey. *Running time:* 98 minutes. *MPAA Rating:* PG.

CAST: Phoebe Cates (Carson); Scott Coffey (Chip); Bridget Fonda (Melaina); Annabeth Gish (Pudge); Page Hannah (Luanne); Robert Rusler (Buzz); Tyrone Power Jr. (Harley); Jeff Yagher (Jimmy Valentine); Paul Lieber (The Manager); Donald Craig (Senator Clatterbuck); Shirley Anne Field (Mrs. Clatterbuck); Leilani Sarelle (Suette); Carrie Hamilton (Nadine); Jay Baker (Bib Bob); Joe Seely (The Creep); Pearl Jones (Elvira); Bonnie Cook (Mrs. Carmichael); Janelle Cochrane (Mrs. McBride); Barry Thigpen (MC); Walker Owens (Young Man); William Roberts (Dying Cockroach); Ezra Sutton (Gator Boy); Elliott Phillips (Turkey Sandwich); Joey A. McGroarty (Reverend Buller); Linda Weatherly Wellman (Bathing Beauty); Lisa Lang (Car Hop); Jane Aiken (Ettie Stroos); Robert Jacobs (Jack Stroos).

FILMS IN REVIEW, 11/89, p. 555, Edmond Grant

While it is true that the last thing movie audiences need at this point is one more movie about a group of teenagers who are coming of age, *Shag* (actually titled *Shag: The Movie* by its distributor, presumably to avoid confusion with the carpet of the same name) is a pleasant surprise—a curiously restrained teen comedy which has a beguiling sense of period detail.

Set during the summer of 1963, the film tells the story of four Southern girls who decide to spend their last few weeks before starting college at the "wild" summer festival held each year in Myrtle Beach, South Carolina. The girls get so swept up in all the seasonal fun that they each have timid encounters with the opposite sex, throw a wild party as a group, and generally upset the hell out of the two "bad girls" who serve as their rivals.

As plotlines go, *Shag*'s is certainly not new. And, true, the film does seem at times dangerously close to being a revamp of *Where the Boys Are* (an addleheaded but enjoyable beach film which has inspired more than its share of awful contemporary films, included a disastrous remake). But, despite the pedestrian plotting, something about the picture keeps it from being just another teen outing.

This is due to the choice of locale and the time period in which the film takes place. Very few recent major studio teenage comedies have been set in the Southern United States (the main exception being Florida), and even fewer have been period pieces.

As such, *Shag* doesn't stand up against such archetypal coming of age pictures as *American Graffiti* and *The Last Picture Show*, but its colorful settings, costuming, and lively musical soundtrack do help it to capture both the flavor of an era and a certain sort of adolscent innocence that would seem awfullly coy if presented in a contemporary context.

And though they can't be accused of being overly deep, our four fresh faced heroines are quite appealing, as are the actresses who play them. Phoebe Cates gets the lion's share of attention as a prim young thing who's reconsidering her engagement to a dreary young man (Tyrone Power, Jr.); Page Hannah, Bridget Fonda (once again, as in *Scandal*, playing the enterprising female on the lookout for stardom), and Annabeth Gish complete the quartet. The sequences involving Gish's character (nicknamed Pudge for her childhood appearance) do have a special air of poignancy, though it should be noted that even handedness is not one of *Shag*'s best attributes.

For like its teenage protagonists, the film takes a timid view of sexuality—though one of the girls (Fonda) is eager to sleep with any man who can offer her a foothold in show business, the filmmakers have made a point of avoiding any realistic depiction of teenage sexuality. The girls engage in a series of goofy discussions on the topic, but the focus remains on the social events they involve themselves in—a beauty contest, the wild party, and the inevitable "Shag" dance contest—rather than on their very real feelings of sexual inhibition (Fonda) or inadequacy (Gish).

It's a mystery why *Shag*, shot in 1987, took two years to get a release. It may not register as a teenage classic, but it does play as a sentimental evocation of the end of an era, that's decidedly more fun than profound.

LOS ANGELES TIMES, 7/21/89, Calendar/p. 1, Sheila Benson

"Shag: The Movie" is an utterly pleasant surprise. Its dumbness is confined to its ads and its re-titling, from simply "Shag."

"Shag: The Movie"? Did they think we'd expect "Shag: The Carpet?" It's not what the ad campaign would have have you fear. Not 7,000 beer-laced teen-agers let loose to wreak havoc on a stately Southern mansion. Not Myrtle Beach, full of wacky, sex-crazed teen-agers, looking for love in *all* the wrong places. Well, not just.

Named for a particularly Southern dance craze, "Shag" is an artfully directed, frequently funny and carefully observed story about a quartet of Southern girls in 1963. Brought up in the tradition of "friends till death," their lives will go in very different directions only weeks from now. Then Pudge (Annabeth Gish) and Luanne (Page Hannah) will, expectedly, go on to college, Carson (Phoebe Cates) will have "the wedding of her dreams" and Melaina (Bridget Fonda) will, expectedly, hit the pavement to look for a job.

In the hands of director Zelda Barron, "Shag's" cast is a true ensemble: The actresses not only convince us of the supportiveness/rivalries/loyalties of four dearest friends, but the actors playing the boys in their lives are experienced, innocent, hurtful and innocently hurtful by turns, just like life. And lurking a little at the side is Carrie Hamilton, contributing a killer turn as one of Myrtle Beach's certified baaaaad girls, and proud of it.

The script manages in no time at all to bring back the innocence and the horrors that were 1963. "Pudggggge," her vigilant mother calls after her, "yew forgot your Metrecal." On the way to Myrtle Beach, Luanne stops her mother's Cadillac convertible at the Magnolia Arms motel so all four girls can observe a moment of scared silence on the very spot where a classmate got pregnant last year. (The nifty script is by Robin Swicord and Lanier Laney & Terry Sweeney, from a story by Laney and Sweeney. Someone remembers *awfully* well.)

The occasion for the weekend is to give the engaged Carson one last, chaste fling to remember. She's marrying Harley (Tyrone Power Jr.), who seems to have *Future State Senator* monogrammed on his cuffs and possibly on his boxer shorts. What Luanne, sweetly straight in her harlequin glasses, has forgotten—maybe—is that this is Sun Fun weekend, and that Myrtle Beach will be full of the riffraff that all four have been raised to step decorously around.

That includes Chip (Scott Coffey), the sort who would drop a condom balloon on their windshield, and the dangerously assured Buzz (Robert Rusler), more experienced than all four girls together. No matter that one of these boys is headed for Annapolis and the other for Yale, here at Myrtle Beach they are simply Big Trouble.

The crowning of the Sun Fun queen, judged by major imported talent Jimmy Valentine (Jeff Yagher), the Fabian of his day, and the big shag contest are the weekend's highlights. To the wild rhythms of the Voltage Brothers, these shags are danced so fervently you can believe that there are still shag competitions and reunions all over the South, 25 years later.

There's a danger in overappreciating a film as sweet as this one (a terrible danger, actually, in simply calling it that, but sweet it truly is.) It's small scale; it won't cause riots or even, probably, sequels. But lordy, is it tenderly acted, with an unyielding spine of honesty to all its characters. Director Barron cannot be overpraised for her part in this. And fortunately, "Shag" is not all sweetness, although it's rightfully rated PG and makes for lovely family discussions about "the old days."

There is the matter of the Sun Fun queen competition, which bikini-clad Melaina has set her heart and her sights on. Luckily, we're allowed to be present for her private run-through of her routine, in which the Confederate flag becomes an intimate, personal prop. What she does with the Stars and Bars is enough to make George Bush start thinking about a whole new constitutional amendment.

Kenny Ortega, who has already given us "Dirty Dancing," was the choreographer here. It's wicked Ortega, wicked and lethally funny, particularly as "interpreted" by Bridget Fonda, pouts, kissy-lips, burlesque rasps and all.

(Since "Shag" was completed audiences have had time to discover Fonda as Mandy Rice-Davies in "Scandal." Here she's a sort of Southern starlet-in-the-making; in a time warp, it would surprise no one to hear that Melaina was working in Hollywood, having changed her name to Gloria Grahame. Or Marilyn Maxwell. Or Marilyn Monroe.)

Then there are the Sun Queen barracudas, Nadine (Hamilton), an offsides coach to beware of, and Suzette (Leilani Sarelle), her personal protégé. They're heaven on a stick.

While its conclusion may not entirely startle you, "Shag" at times has a nice way of working against expectation. Here (and especially in 1963), years of upbringing still prevail. When a shocked Luanne says "You *cain't* wear that" to Melaina, eyeing her dearest friend in a bikini with a push-up bra, Melaina doesn't. After all, this is an era where Southern girls have to hide their faces behind towels to tell a boy their answers to their own hand-written sex quiz. (Sample: Have you ever been Frenched in the ear?)

It's an impeccable production—with hair, clothes, music and production design that savor the period without camping it up. There is succinct editing and camera work and lovely performances: Page Hannah, giving definition to the lifelong burden of being a senator's upright daughter; Annabeth Gish's Pudge, blossoming out from under that lovingly patronizing nickname, in no small degree because of Scott Coffey's Chop, her equal in sensitivity...sort of. And there is the surprise of Phoebe Cates' evolving Carson, mistress of Southern wiles, who may or may not settle docilely for the career of wife and mother.

MONTHLY FILM BULLETIN, 9/88, p. 275, Kim Newman

Spartanburg, South Carolina, 1963. Luanne Clatterbuck borrows her mother's car and, with her friends Carson McBride, Melaina Buller and Caroline ("Pudge") Carmichael, sets off on a trip. Supposedly, the girls are visiting Fort Sumter, but actually they intend to go to the Sun and Fun Festival in Myrtle Beach as a final fling before Carson marries dull tobacco heir Harley Ralston and Luanne and Pudge depart for college. In Myrtle Beach, Carson tries to resist the advances of the cool, rebellious Buzz Ravenel, while Pudge is befriended by Buzz's sidekick Chip. Melaina, the group's glamour girl, gets into a feud with Suette and Nadine, a pair of chippies, and vows to defeat Suette in a beauty contest to be judged by teen heartthrob Jimmy Valentine. Luanne dissuades Melaina from performing a provocative dance at the contest, and Suette—who bumps and grinds in a bikini—wins. However, Melaina invites Jimmy, who is overly sheltered by his manager, to a wild party at the Clatterbuck summer mansion. At the party, Carson and Buzz retreat to a nearby boat and "go all the way", while Harley, who has turned up in search of Carson, reveals to Luanne, who has a crush on him, that he feels he is being pressured into the marriage. Jimmy's manager rescues his property from Melaina and Chip is despatched to pick up Senator and Mrs. Clatterbuck—who are arriving unexpectedly—and forestall them while the house is cleaned up. Chip and Pudge enter and win the Shag contest which is being judged by Jimmy and the Clatterbucks, Carson and Harley decide not to get married, leaving them free to pair off with Buzz and Luanne, and Melaina successfully transfers her attentions from Jimmy to his star-making manager.

With a fetishistic succession of retro-chic music, cars and fashions, *Shag* is self-evidently the lastest in the line of teen nostalgia films that stretches from *American Grafiti*, which is evoked through roller-skating waitresses, to *Dirty Dancing*, from which choreographer Kenny Oretga has been borrowed to add some pep to the climactic dance contest. However, the direct inspiration for this particular entry in the cycle would seem indisputably to be Glendon Swarthout's twice-filmed (and twice-bungled) novel *Where the Boys Are*. *Shag* goes so far as to resurrect the character types and plot incidentals of the book, mixed in with familiar bits and pieces from other teen movies, with the result that the film seems like a compilation album of the genre. In no particular order, we are presented with a wild party that trashes an elegant mansion, a crucial dance contest in which the underdogs suddenly display amazing footwork, the black maid who is always wandering into rooms where teenagers ae clinching ("You is the horniest bunch of white folks I's ever seen!"), a mean and macho rebel who prods the soon-to-be settled-down teen queen out of her complacency (Buzz recites chunks of dialogue from *The Hustler*), the self-involved teen star who proves a disappointment to his gold-digging fans, and the awkward but touching relationship between two teens who realise that they aren't quite the geeks they think themselves to be.

In the days of the Breen Office, Hollywood screenwrites were instructed to remove the word "shag" from films on the grounds that "It has an offensive connotation in the British Commonwealth", but the British filmmakers here relish every opportunity to make weak jokes along the lines of "Would you shag with me?" This British knowingness about an American past is something of a handicap, and Zelda Barron, previously known for *Secret Places*, is an odd choice for the project. Much of the genre's appeal depends on the meticulous recreation of an era within memory by people who lived through it, as witness George Lucas' carculture California in *American Graffiti*, John Milius' sand and surf for *Big Wednesday*, or Barry Levinson's Baltimore in *Diner*. The Southern milieu here is sustained by some very wobbly accents (Shirley Anne Field's chief among them), and such oddments as Luanne's conviction that Melaina should perform a speech from *Gone with the Wind* in the beauty contest.

Several major false notes are sounded: the girl's willingness to go to clubs where coloured musicians are playing, and their parents' lack of comment on this, are notably out of place, especially when a film as light as *Hairspray* has had to take account of the habitual racism of the period. The young cast—most of whom are related to more famous performers (note the names Gish, Fonda, Power and Hannah)—are generally appealing, if not particularly distinguished in their mainly one-note roles. The only character who really overcomes stereotypes is Annabeth Gish's Pudge, whom everybody thinks of as fat and unattractive long after she has blossomed into a pretty young woman.

NEW YORK POST, 7/21/89, p. 27, David Edelstein

In "Shag," four Southern girls who've just graduated from high school head for a weekend of sun and fun at Myrtle Beach, where they're hoping for one last fling before life intervenes and carries each in her separate direction.

The year is 1963, the dance is the shag; the '50s are over and the '60s haven't erupted and Lord I'm bored writing about this. Aren't you bored reading it? Wouldn't you rather read PAGE SIX or the sports section or your horoscope?

You've seen this movie. You've seen these girls. Each has a different philosophy of life and each ends up with a groovy guy who'll help her come of age.

Pudge (Annabeth Gish) is a former fatty who's beginning to blossom. Belle-of-the-ball Carson (Phoebe Cates) is engaged to the only guy—a prig—she's ever dated. Luanne (Page Hannah), daughter of a Southern Senator, is a protocol-fiend and killjoy. Her opposite, Melaina (Bridget Fonda), is a sexy girl on the make—she knows what she wants and how to get it.

On the plus side, the script doesn't moralize or work you over. But soft-sell clichés are still clichés, and you aren't exactly rocked with surprise when Carson's straitlaced fiance (Tyrone Power, Jr.) shows up or, after a wild party, Luanne awakes to find her daddy's mansion trashed and her parents arriving at noon.

The director, Zelda Barron, gives the picture a tasteful, Technicolor look that's meant to recall the romances of the early '60s. It's a big mistake. "Shag has no immediacy—the images seem mothballed. The script skips from one girl's story to the next, refusing to let a scene play out; there's more continuity on "Days of Our Lives."

The psychedelic title credits lead you to expect at least a whisper of the germinating counterculture. But film makers in the late '80s aren't free to endorse (or even explore) free love or drugs. So "Shag," a movie about the last gasp of one conservative era, resonates with the values of another that's still going strong. What's the point?

The movie evokes the blandest aspects of "Where the Boys Are" and its update, "Mystic Pizza." Choreogrphed by Kenny Ortega, the climactic Shag competition is meant to give you "Dirty Dancing" vibes, but it's "Squeaky-Clean Dancing" all the way.

Gish, who's always pleasant, doesn't rise above her material (she doesn't seem to know she's supposed to), and Hannah has a gruesome role. Cates has some comic charm: confronting a suitor (Robert Rusler), her body pulls away while her eyes scream, "Take me!" After she does surrender (off screen, of course), she announces, deadpan: "Yes ah'm wahld. Ah've been wahld all alawung. Ah am very out of controw-ell."

As the promiscuous minister's daughter, almond-eyed Fonda is the only reason to see the movie. The daughter of Peter and niece of Jane, Fonda has the sense to toss off most of her terrible lines, refusing to give them any weight. Instead she plays the naughty-minded subtext. Even when idling she sends out tidal waves of desire. Confidence this dazzling is more than good genes; Fonda has the hunger.

NEWSDAY, 7/21/89, Part III/p. 5, Mike McGrady

A final fling before going on to college, career and marriage; a summertime town overrun by teens in customized jalopies; a glittering car-hop palace specializing in fast food and fast romance...sound a bit like "American Graffiti"? Well, maybe just a little bit. But "Shag," a teen-time romance with some nice moments and some promising performances, falls much closer in feeling and flavor to last year's "Mystic Pizza."

Four recent high school graduates, girlfriends ranging in temperament from sedate to wild, assure their parents they are taking an historical excursion to nearby Fort Sumter. After patiently listening to 1963 vintage parental advice ("Don't wear dark lipstick. And don't stay up late"), they thereupon scoot off on a weekend jaunt to Myrtle Beach, S.C., where one of the girls has access to her family's oceanfront mansion, complete with moored yacht.

That's Luanne (Page Hannah), the bespectacled always-proper senator's daughter who cautions her less proper companions: "Act like you've got some upbringing . . . we can have a good time but we cannot be wild." Famous last words.

Then there's Carson (Phoebe Cates), the beauty about to marry stodgier-and-richer-than-thou Harley (Tyrone Power Jr.)—that is, until she meets rakish makeout artist Buzz Ravenel (Robert Rusler). First, it's, "Buzz, I can't allow myself to hurt a decent, Godfearing boy like Harley." Later, it's "Buzz, I can't go around sleeping with every boy that likes me." Still later: "Oh, God, I wish Harley'd die. It'd be so much easier." Finally:" Just don't tell anyone, okay?"

Melaina (Bridget Fonda), the flashy daughter of a fundamentalist preacher, is determined to enter a beauty-talent contest judged by pop singer Jimmy Valentine: "I'm as pretty as any of those girls in Hollywood. And this is my big chance. Jimmy Valentine is going to discover me today."

Finally, there's Pudge (Annabeth Gish), normal and well-adjusted, a girl who hasn't yet "gone all the way" and is hoping for both true love and an opportunity to win the beach resort's annual "shag" dance contest. A sensitive performanc by Gish, who starred in "Desert Bloom," saves the character from clichés.

English director Zelda Barron seems to have a nice ear for American rhythms and is able to extract all available humor from some very familiar teen situations—a hilarious beauty contest, a wild housewrecking party, first love followed by first seduction followed by the climactic and strangely moving dance contest. At first "Shag" might seem to be nothing more than a make-work project for relatives of the famous—among others we find Tyrone Power Jr. and Page Hannah (Darryl's sister), Bridget Fonda (Peter's daughter) and Carrie Hamilton (Carol Burnett's daughter)—but the ensemble work is impressive enough so the film utimately seems more a showcase for future stars.

The only problem is that so much will seem so familiar. And surely no figure will be more familiar to students of Hollywoodiana than the black maid who must clean up the debris following the big mansion-destroying party. As she stumbles across young couples necking everywhere from closets to bathtubs, she observes, "You-all is the horniest bunch of white folks I ever did see." Of course they are . If they weren't, who would bother watching this stuff?

VILLAGE VOICE, 7/25/89, p. 75, Manohla Dargis

Filled to the brim with healthy, tanned white faces, *SHAG: The Movie* affects the slick, amnesiac look of a *Life* advertisement—all gloss, no depth. Set during the final party-beach weekend before four young girlfriends go their respective ways, the movie paints a '63 South Carolina summer as the last gasp of American innocence.

Madras shirts, T-Birds, Bermuda shorts, bubble-flip 'dos—everything looks right, yet *Shag* is a movie in search of a genre. It recalls a half dozen teen movies, mechanically plodding through all the requisite teen-pic rituals—humping, blow-out alcohol orgy—while taking abortive turns as a female *American Graffiti*, remodeled *Where the Boys Are*, and Beth Henley sketch.

As Melaina, Bridget Fonda (Peter's kid), doing another take on the knowing sex kitten she so gamely played in the recent *Scandal*, is the naughty daughter of a Holy Roller preacher. (The film is jam-packed with celeb relatives—Carol Burnett's daughter, Tyrone Power's son, Daryl Hannah's sister—pedigree overload.) Equipped with a Barbie Doll figure and Pepsodent smile, Fonda easily has some of the film's best moments—an awkwardly lewd "modern dance" with a Confederate flag, and a dramatic interpretation of Scarlett's "as God is my witness" speech while dressed in a polka-dot bikini—as she prepares for the Miss Sun Fun beauty contest.

If Melaina is the most animated of the four friends, it's because she knows what she wants (Hollywood) and how she's going to get it (sex). Less self-aware, the others flail around in pre-women's lib incoherence, reduced to mooning for or warding off a good *shtup*. Carson (Phoebe Cates, graduate of the superior boffo teen-sex comedy, *Fast Times at Ridgemont High*) lamely struggles to preserve her virginity, Luanne (Page Hannah) plays southern magnolia ("Y'all act like you got some upbringing"), while Pudge (Annabeth Gish) yearns to do the shag with Chip (Scott Coffey) before he heads off to Annapolis.

Occasional bright lines hint at the movie *Shag* might have been, and a rare opportunity is missed by splitting the girls up for robotic reproduction instead of developing their friendships along the lines of *Diner*. Throwaway references to JFK, the armed services, and female emancipation coyly hint at the seismic change afoot, but conspicuously missing in this southern period piece is any reference to the civil rights movement. The few blacks in *Shag*—servants and members of a local band—function merely as background for the real world of everyday white life. That the August of '63 also saw the watershed march on Washington, culminating in Martin Luther King Jr.'s "I have a dream" speech, cuts to the bone of the film's radical myopia.

Also reviewed in:
NEW YORK TIMES, 7/21/89, p. C12, Stephen Holden
VARIETY, 8/24/88, p. 80
WASHINGTON POST, 7/21/89, p. D7, Hal Hinson

SHAKE

A Movie Visions release. *Director:* D.A. Pennebaker, Chris Hegedus, and David Dawkins. *Running time:* 20 minutes. *MPAA Rating:* Not Rated.

WITH: Otis Redding.

NEW YORK POST, 7/12/89, p. 23, David Edelstein

[*Shake* was reviewed jointly with *Jimi Plays Monterey*; see Edelstein's review of that film.]

NEWSDAY, 7/14/89, Part III/p. 3, Stephen Williams

[*Shake* was reviewed jointly with *Jimi Plays Monterey*; see Williams' review of that film.]

VILLAGE VOICE, 7/18/89, p. 73, Robert Christgau

[*Shake* was reviewed jointly with *Jimi Plays Monterey*; see Christgau's review of that film.]

SHE-DEVIL

An Orion Pictures release. *Producer:* Jonathan Brett and Susan Seidelman. *Director:* Susan Seidelman. *Screenplay:* Barry Strugatz and Mark R. Burns. *Based on the novel "The Life and Loves of a She-Devil" by:*

Fay Weldon. *Director of Photography:* Oliver Stapleton. *Editor:* Craig McKay. *Music:* Howard Shore. *Music Editor:* Suzana Peric. *Sound:* Tod A. Maitland and (music) Michael Farrow. *Sound Editor:* Dan Sable. *Production Designer:* Santo Loquasto. *Art Director:* Tom Warren. *Set Decorator:* George Detitta Jr. *Set Dresser:* Daniel K. Grasso and Chris Vogt. *Special Effects:* Efex Specialists. *Costumes:* Albert Wolsky. *Makeup:* Joseph Campayno. *Running time:* 100 minutes. *MPAA Rating:* PG–13.

CAST: Meryl Streep (Mary Fisher); Roseanne Barr (Ruth); Ed Begley Jr. (Bob); Linda Hunt (Hooper); Sylvia Miles (Mrs. Fisher); Elisebeth Peters (Nicolette Patchett); Bryan Larkin (Andy Patchett); A Martinez (Garcia); Maria Pitillo (Olivia Honey); Mary Louise Wilson (Mrs. Trumper); Susan Willis (Ute); Jack Gilpin (Larry); Robin Leach (Himself); Nitchie Barrett (Bob's Secretary); June Gable (Realtor); Jeanine Joyce (Flower Lady); Deborah Rush ("People" Reporter); Sally Jessy Raphael (Herself); Doris Belack (Paula); Max (Fuzzy). Cerius and Cinderella (Juliette); Herbie (Himself); Lori Tan Chinn (Vesta Rose Woman); Joseph Pentangelo (Detective); Mark Steiner (Valet); Rosanna Carter (Judge Brown); George Kodisch (Court Officer); Manny Olmo (Cook); Alain Jarry (Alain); John Richard Reynolds (Book Store Customer); George Trow (Douglas); Cynthia Adler (Vesta Rose Commercial Voice); Sandra Fine, Christopher Collins Lee, Julie Signitzer, and Scott Wyatt Rawls (Roslyn Artists String Quartet); Mack Brandon and Will Ford (The Mack Brandon Duo); Sally Sockwell and Larry Marshall (Guggenheim Party Guests).

FILMS IN REVIEW, 4/90, p. 233, Edmond Grant

With so much media attention being focused on comedienne Roseanne Barr, it almost seems unfair to the rest of the cast and crew of *She-Devil* to devote an entire review to a discussion of Ms. Barr's incredibly bland acting and ungainly appearance. While the film does seem at times like the textbook definition of a vehicle picture, its unique source material and oddball sense of humor should have generated something quite different.

The plot, which has been strategically altered from the original novel by Fay Weldon and the subsequent British miniseries, concerns a frumpy housewife (Barr)whose comfortable world is shaken to its very roots when her husband takes up with an ultra-glamorous romance novelist (Meryl Streep). The wife sheds her dowdy suburban trappings and bares her teeth for revenge, ruining in short order, her husband's domicile, career, and lovelife.

As a book and miniseries there was a letter-perfect storyline, symmetrical as could be, with numerous dark overtones ripe for exploration. The film, however, thanks to the stilted vision of director Susan Seidelman, a simplistic script, and some rather obvious commercial pressures, is a revenge comedy severely lacking in bite. Seidelman, who at this point ranks as America's biggest woman director (we're talking budgets here—Hollywood's only barometer) also has proven to be a sadly uneven filmmaker, who is capable of producing fresh, bouncy comedies (*Desperately Seeking Susan, Cookie*) and projects that seem miscalculated from the word go (*Making Mr. Right,* this film).

Here, the main difficulties seem to stem not only from the timely but ineffective casting of Barr, but also from the sudden shifts in tone that Seidelman has seen fit to impose. Long stretches of the picture are played at full-tilt, with gross images and exaggerated gestures creating a cartoonish atmosphere which robs the proceedings of any glimmer of reality; then at times the pendulum swings back and we are expected to feel genuine sympathy for poor, put-upon Barr. These sudden, badly executed, shifts would test even the talents of an actress with true range, but Seidelman's choice of a novice film start almost dooms the picture from the outset.

Seidelman's concept of black humor has entirely to do with grotesqueness. The storyline provides ample opportunities for gross-out moments, and Seidelman jumps at every chance, particularly in the sequences where Barr disguises herself as a nurse to find out about Streep's vulgar old mother (Sylvia Miles). Instances of sickening food, warts and other deformities, and select bodily functions are thrown in for intended laugh value—the aforementioned being literally tossed in our faces as Barr empties a bedpan directly into the camera. Eccentric, flaky humor, Seidleman has down to a "t;" shock value, she'd best leave to John Waters and other experts of the fine art of sick humor. Even the casting seems geared in this offputting direction. A genuinely talented actress like the diminuitive Linda Hunt, who plays a dedicated nurse, seems cast simply for her unusual looks—to, in effect, serve as the perfect physical counterpart to Barr's girth. Hunt attempts to imbue her role with a sense of dignity, but the tender sentiments that surround her character wind up submerged in a sea of rash abnormality. Sylvia Miles proves ideal for the role of Streep's mother (a skeleton any person would gladly keep in their closet); she has already made vulgarity her stock in trade, and so seems right at home in Seidelman's grotesque universe.

The freakishness that permeates the movie extends even to the pivotal role of the straying husband, played by the amiable but colorless Ed Begley, Jr. Begley has become a familiar face on television, thanks to his boyish looks and quirky personality. On the big screen, in a series of mercilessly tight closeups, Begley proves to be neither boyish nor endearing. So why all this fuss made over a middle-aged accountant? Would two women, one a respectable homemaker, and the other a prosperous writer, really need to dicker over *him?* There's surely some ironic point to this situation, but Seidelman never exploits the possibilities. It is simply to be accepted as a given that Begley is utterly desirable, as a breadwinner or as a lover.

And finally we reach the two leads. Barr has proved a competent comic perfomer in her weekly sitcom, where she is ably supported by a talented cast; here, Seidelman leaves her to fend for herself in a number of solo moments where she is either committing some act of mayhem against Begley and Streep, or making a play for our heart strings, mooning over the loss of her beloved Begley (something, it is presumed, the female section of the audience will relate to). She proves inadequate to the task on more than one occasion, and one begins to wonder exactly why a well known comedy star is given so little comedy to perform in her first starring role in a feature film.

Faring much better is Meryl Streep, who has been given the lion's share of the comedy, and turns in a wickedly overdone turn as the pampered novelist, who "lives in a palace by the sea" (the phrase which opens the film, and is repeated countless times in Barr's voice-over narration). Streep plays the character like a cartoon, perfectly in keeping with Seidelman's exaggerated approach. Though the villain of the piece, Streep attracts more attention, not only because she, along with co-stars (and daytime soap stars) A Martinez and Maria Pitillo, is one of the few attractive people in the cast, but also because one can be certain that when she is on screen, the film will remain a *comedy* and not slip backward into either forced melodrama or hollow preaching about the solidarity of women.

This last theme is driven home through the grand success of Barr's business venture, an employment agency for housewives returning to the work force. What gets sacrificed, though, is the bizarre undertone to the original *Lives And Loves Of A She-Devil* in which Ruth, the wife, tries to physically transform herself into the willowy novelist. With Barr playing the role, though, it's clear that Ruth could never be anything but Ruth, and so once again plot lines in a Hollywood feature are dictated by casting. And a potentially scathing comedy is further reduced to a toothless wreck.

LOS ANGELES TIMES, 12/8/89, Calendar/p. 1, Peter Rainer

In "She-Devil," the feminine mystique meets its match. As Ruth, the dumpy malcontent whose accountant husband Bob (Ed Begley Jr.) leaves her for Mary Fisher (Meryl Streep), a famously frilly authoress of romance novels, Roseanne Barr swaggers into frame and wreaks ungodly revenge. Her mission has rabble-rousing mass appeal. She's intended as a humongous stand-in for all the women who have ever been rejected in favor of someone younger, shapelier, fluffier.

In her TV series "Roseanne," Barr's roly-poly bulk isn't played for vitriol and vengeance the way it is here. Beneath the wisecracking, she's soft and sensual on that show, and her big teddy bear of a husband, played by John Goodman, is a perfect counterpart—his bluster is as transparent as hers.

In "She-Devil," Barr's stridency is unimpeded, and director Susan Seidelman encourages our identification with her solitary fury. But Seidelman also can't resist scoring points against Ruth. She encourages our physical repulsion to the character, and so we're continually subjected to immense, looming close-ups of Ruth jutting her pudgy face at us. (She has a large mole on her upper lip, and more than a hint of mustache.) Her unattractiveness may represent women's worst fears of how their philandering husbands view them, but Seidelman appears to be in on the razzing. As feminist polemic, "She-Devil" is dubious indeed.

Are there two actresses further apart than Roseanne Barr and Meryl Streep? The high anticipation for this movie is largely based on their pairing. But, except for an early sequence where they first meet at a book party at the Guggenheim Museum—Ruth, in her floral print dress, accidentally spills wine on Mary Fisher—they hardly have a moment together.

The gloriously scabrous 1983 novel upon which the film is based, Fay Weldon's "The Life and Loves of a She-Devil," doesn't allow for much interplay, either, and, in literary terms, the separateness works. (It also worked in the 1986 A&E/BBC-TV miniseries of the novel.) Ruth's guerrilla missions require her to be at a distance; they're more fun that way, and more insidious.

But it's a waste to have Barr and Streep in the same movie and then set them to shadow-boxing. We want to revel in the loony clash of opposite acting styles, but Seidelman and her screenwriters, Barry Strugatz and Mark R. Burns, haven't shaped the material accordingly. A few fantasy confrontations might have helped, since the film, even at its most "realistic," is such a hot-pink, high-camp fantasy anyway.

The funniest sequences in the movie take their cue from this camp floridness. Everything about Mary Fisher is flouncy and full of feminine filigree; she has created herself in the self-adoring image of her own romantic heroines. But, of course, it's all just an elaborate act.

Thanks to Ruth, the fantasy bottoms out, and Ruth and Bob's children and Mary's unwanted decrepit mother (Sylvia Miles), intrude on Mary's seaside Long Island estate. Mary's demureness snaps. Her fragile feathery voice begin to bark with annoyance. Meryl Streep may surprise audiences with her comic zing here, although she was funny in her brief, explosive scene as Lillian Hellman's friend in "Julia," and slyly hilarious, too, as the lawyer in "The Seduction of Joe Tynan."

Streep is such a studied, meticulous actress that, at times, her performance here seems like an *impersonation* of funniness rather than true funniness. But she's so adroit that it's tough to tell the difference. Playing high-style knockabout comedy comes naturally to Streep, or at least it comes naturally to her performer's sense of craft. After such films as "A Cry in the Dark" and "Out of Africa," her role in "She-Devil" may seem like a lark, but Streep goes at it with a ferocity that, in itself, is funny to watch.

"She-Devil" (rated PG–13 for strong language) is pitched deliberately shrill, in the manner of the TV shows and true-confession magazines it periodically parades before us. "Lifestyles of the Rich and Famous" makes an appearance here; so does People magazine and TV talk-show host Sally Jessy Raphael (as herself.)

Seidelman is trying to co-opt the trashiness of the pop media to both give her movie a charge and to indict the culture that elevates the false prettiness of the Mary Fishers of this world. But Seidelman's sensibility is much more in line with Robin Leach's than she realizes. That's why Mary Fisher turns out rather well at the end. That's why, when Ruth starts an employment agency for the "unloved and the unwanted," the women who pass before us are viewed without sympathy as drab specimens.

Perhaps that's why Ruth herself isn't given much of a send-off. She discovers her self-esteem in the transforming powers of rage, and it feels like a hollow victory. If Ruth is meant to be some kind of newstyle heroine, what does it say about her that we last see her defiantly alone in the crowd?

MONTHLY FILM BULLETIN, 5/90, p. 139, Pam Cook

Ruth Patchett, loyal wife to accountant Bob and devoted mother of squabbling teenagers Nicolette and Andy, accompanies her husband to a glitzy reception at the Guggenheim Museum. Clumsy as ever, she spills wine over the glamorous Mary Fisher, a successful romantic novelist. Bob and Mary are immediately attracted, and after the reception, Bob drives Mary home to her luxurious mansion by the sea, where he sleeps with her. The affair develops, though Bob denies it to Ruth. When a meal organised by Ruth for Bob's parents is a disaster, Bob turns on his wife, calling her a "she-devil", and moves in with Mary. Overcome with desire for revenge, Ruth burns down their house, leaves the kids with Bob and Mary, and proceeds to destroy Bob's life. As nurse Vesta Rose, she takes a job at the Golden Twilight rest home, where she knows Mary's mother to be a patient. Substituting stimulants for tranquillisers, she rejuvenates the inhabitants and arranges for the foul-mouthed Mrs. Fisher to visit her daughter. Mrs. Fisher embarrasses Mary in front of Bob and the children and reveals her daughter's past promiscuity to reporters from *People* magazine. The nursing home will not have her back, and Ruth is sacked for breaking the rules. Together with her new-found friend Nurse Hooper, who has savings of $35,000, she sets up the Vesta Rose Employment Agency, finding jobs for women with no confidence or skills. She delivers a leaflet to Bob's office, and when he telephones for a secretary, sends him the sexy Olivia Honey. Jaded with Mary, whose glamour has tarnished since she became a wife and mother, Bob starts an affair with Olivia, but dumps her when, at Ruth's instigation, she tells him she loves him. In revenge, Olivia and Ruth break into Bob's office and transfer his clients' funds into his Swiss bank account, whereupon Ruth despatches Olivia to Rio, informs the IRS, and sends photocopies of Bob and Olivia having sex in the office to Mary. Bob is arrested for embezzlement, and with the help of some loyal Vesta Rose clients, Ruth ensures that he is convicted and sent to jail. Having discovered that Bob embezzled money from her account, Mary dumps him, sells her mansion and becomes a serious novelist. The humbled Bob learns to cook in prison, and Ruth, now the head of a successful business empire, relishes her triumph.

With *She-Devil*, Susan Seidelman's work veers slightly from the screwball fantasy formula that was showing signs of wear and tear in *Cookie*. Even the stylish and witty *Making Mr. Right* could not disguise a fatal hesitancy and confusion in the script about what the film was trying to say.

This time, Fay Weldon's respected novel about a housewife's monstrous revenge on an inequitable society and its romantic myths supplies the necessary coherence, plus an added frisson in the rare phenomenon of a truly destructive heroine whose actions are totally justified. But those familiar with Weldon's *The Life and Loves of a She-Devil* will find neither its political acumen nor its celebration of oppressed womankind's revolutionary potential here.

Screenwriters Barry Strugatz and Mark Burns clearly subscribe to the view that in order to get made (and seen) these days, feminist films about feminism must be fun and are bound to deliver positive heroines of the determinedly American "I will survive" variety. In the U.S. film industry's present conservative climate, Seidelman and producer Jonathan Brett seem to agree, stressing: "This is rare story of vengeance in which everyone at the end comes out enhanced, a better person". In Weldon's novel, enhancement, except of minor characters, is hardly the point. Ruth's revenge (synonymous with her politicisation) leaves a trail of death and destruction, and her realisation of her fantasies leads to a deeply ambivalent conclusion in which she, though rich and successful, is also badly damaged. The logic of Weldon's argument, that women's desires are inevitably perverted by being filtered through male power structures, is lost in Seidelman's version, with a corresponding loss of impact which no amount of irony in script and décor can retrieve. Seidelman seems almost afraid of being taken seriously—witness the parody of a serious novelist that her Mary Fisher finally becomes—as if this might lay her open to the dread charge of pretentiousness.

This said, there is still much to enjoy. Meryl Streep relishes her début as a comic actress, approaching her role as the romantic novelist and seductress Mary Fisher with exactly the right degree of exaggeration required by a film in which characters represent stereotypes rather than people. She is also given some of the best lines: interviewed on TV about her new mini-series, she claims to write novels which make men feel important "to let him know that he is the man, so there's no confusion"; and when she first meets the paltry Bob, she gazes into his eyes and breathes, "A stimulated accountant sounds ... very interesting". Conveying Mary's affected mannerisms with consummate skill, she is even more impressive when the crack begin to appear in Mary's elegant façade as a result of her initiation into domestic life. A tense family dinner at which her foul-mouthed mother, sprung from a nursing home by the vengeful Ruth, sets out to embarrass her daughter begins a process of personality disintegration which culminates in the failure of her latest novel, *Love in the Rinse Cycle*, and a hysterical row with Bob in which Mary thrashes about in fury on the satin-sheathed, heart-shaped bed where she first seduced him.

The instigator of Mary's demise, loyal-housewife-and-mother-turned-*femme fatale* Ruth Patchett, is played by Roseanne Barr, stand-up comedienne and sit-com star whose combination of barbed feminist satire and basic good nature would seem to make her a natural for the part. She is certainly convincing as the lumpy, frumpy housewife, incongruously and unsuccessfully trying out all the bad advice purveyed by the glamour and romance industries in an attempt to keep her husband. But, like the film itself, Barr seems unable to make the cross-over from malice to real malevolence. Her transformation into a "she-devil", accompanied by some rather feeble thunderclap sound effects and red glowing eyes, is hardly sufficient to suggest a hatred capable of making her sacrifice everything she holds dear. Most of her activities in destroying Mary Fisher and disposing of her husband's assets (Home, Family, Career and Freedom) have been somewhat cleaned up—notably the relationship with Nurse Hooper (Linda Hunt), here reduced to a distinctly metaphorical cream-cake orgy.

At the end of *She-Devil*, Ruth is not remodelled into the grotesque distortion of Mary Fisher she becomes in Weldon's novel. Instead, she has lost weight, had an unsightly mole removed, become a successful businesswoman, and taught her husband and his mistress a well-deserved, but not fatal, lesson. Mary Fisher, far from fading away under the force of Ruth's revenge, lives on to become a respected novelist desired by handsome French intellectuals ("Your grasp of ze post-modern metaphor is wonderful ..."). Sadly, the promised assault on glamour and romance is diminished by an upbeat *Cosmo*-style ending in which "People can change" is the bland message obscuring the reasons why they don't have to.

NEW STATESMAN & SOCIETY, 5/11/90, p. 47, Suzanne Moore

Judging by the popularity of the TV series *The Life and Love of a She-Devil* and Fay Weldon's 1983 novel on which it was based, Britain is populated by hordes of potential She-Devils. These women, who recite the selfless Litany of the Good Wife, are actually eaten up by jealousy, resentment and anger. They want power and, above all, revenge. Or at least they want the fantasy of it. And Weldon's novel offers just that—a complete antidote to those countless articles that appear in women's magazines telling us how to channel our anger into something more *positive*, like knitting. The She-Devil is relentlessly and gloriously negative, her hatred all-consuming, the living embodiment of an anger that knows no bounds.

Such unhealthy emotions rarely make an appearance in Hollywood movies though they are the stuff of countless blockbusters and miniseries. Which may explain why Susan Seidelman's film *She-Devil* has not done good business in the States. Perhaps She-Devils don't travel well or perhaps having the film open just before Christmas in a week crowded with seven other movie openings didn't help. Who knows exactly why certain films flop? Maybe the message of *She-Devil* is unpalatable to American audiences. Or maybe itt's just not a good film.

Whatever the case, *She-Devil* has the albatross of a feminist label hanging around its neck, which means that it will be criticised on the grounds that it is both too feminist and that it is not feminist enough. Seidelman, one of the few female directors working in Hollywood with big budgets and big stars like Meryl Streep, has already said that this is her most overtly feminist film to date; though all her previous films have dealt in some way with what she describes as "the politics of beauty and femininity". From *Desperately Seeking Susan* to the under-rated *Making Mr Right* and the flimsy *Cookie*, all have had female leads and a distinctly female sensibility about them that is far more interesting than the explicit message of *She-Devil*. They have dealt consistently with the relationship of women to the images of perfection that surround them, managing so well to capture the kind of skewed femininity that absolutely refuses to play the role of the passive consumer.

So it's strange that Seidelman should choose a novel that not only tells an essentially English story but one whose deconstruction of femininity is so uproariously unsubtle. Indeed, a story in which two women destroy each other because of a man can hardly be called feminist in the first place. She optioned the book three years ago, before the British TV series came out, and managed to get self-styled "domestic goddess" Roseanne Barr to play Ruth Patchett (the She-Devil) and Meryl Streep (Mary Fisher), the impossibly perfect romantic novelist who steals Ruth's husband from her.

The presence of such big stars has meant an enormous amount of pre-release publicity for the film, most of it based on unfounded rumours of Barr and Streep fighting on set. That women can work together without clawing one another's eyes out is obviously a novel idea as far as the American pressis concerned.

Seidelman has had to condense and Americanise the book into one 90-minute film. To do this she cuts out the second half of the novel which means that many of the more disturbing aspects of the story have been cosmetically removed. We first see Ruth Patchett wandering around a beauty store and trying to zip herself into a dress that is way too small for her. She is a misfit in this world of images of beautiful, feminine women. And then a beautiful woman, who both creates and embodies such imagery, begins an affair with Ruth's dumb blonde husband, Ed Begley Jr, who describes his character as "a case of testosterone on the loose."

Before you know it, Ruth has transformed herself into a fully fledged She-Devil, burnt the house down, dumped the kids, and made a shopping list of Bob's assets: 1) home 2) family 3) career 4) freedom. These she sets about destroying one by one. In the novel Ruth doesn't stop there. She goes on to fuck her way through the British class system in order to get enough money to pay for plastic surgery and agonising leg-shortening operations to turn her into a replica of the doll-like Mary.

But, because the film does stop there, the central message of the novel has been changed considerably. Everyone in the film ends up a happier, better person. Ruth is transformed from frump into feminist feelgood heroine, which means she gets a new hairstyle and nicer clothes. Mary Fisher, who ends up dead in the book, merely relinquishes her Barbara Cartland-inspired wardrobe and becomes a more serious person, denoted by the wearing of spectacles.

Yet, despite this toning down, the film has still proved too much for some American critics who are clearly upset at seeing unattractive women cast in big roles. "Do we have to watch this beached whale on screen for 90 minutes?" Roseanne, the loveable American Everywoman who fantasises about eating Mel Gibson, is one-dimensional as Ruth, which only serves to highlight the unsympathetic nature of the character. After all, we are talking about a woman who commits the ultimate crime of leaving her children. Streep, on the other hand, plays against her star persona— the immaculate ice maiden—satisfying our collective whim that one day she might make a complete fool of herself. Here she does so for our benefit.

Even so, overall *She-Devil* is a disappointment. Not because it doesn't fulfil the great expectations of feminists, not because it isn't true to the book, but because ultimately it isn't true to itself. Seidelman's quirky direction veers wildly between caricature, satire and realism and steers away from the darker side of the material. For what she has done is to make what is really a fantasy less fantastic—all the supernatural elements are gone—and therefore less powerful. Seidelman has turned Weldon's ambiguously nasty novel into the kind of textbook feminism that Hollywood prefers. Personal growth quells political anxiety. The She-Devil becomes another "find yourself, express your individuality" *Cosmo*-type heroine in the air-brushed world of happy endings. It will prove doubly ironic then if, despite her good intentions, Seidelman's popularising of the story turns out to be less popular with audiences than the original She-Devil with her warts and all.

NEW YORK, 1/8/90, p. 60, David Denby

In the otherwise terrible *She-Devil,* Meryl Streep, playing a fabulously successful romance writer, wears her pink silk dresses off the shoulder and speaks in a queenly purr. Her head on a swivel, gently seesawing back and forth as she talks, Streep is sexy and also physically funny in a way that she's never been in the movies—throwing herself across beds, using her legs and thighs and rump. Her Mary Fisher is a low hypocrite, but as Streep plays her—with a bit of genuine sweetness—she isn't hateful. She's merely a child living in a candied pink palace, a narcissist who wants everything to be perfect. Streep understands that a fantasy writer begins by creating a fantasy of herself. Seeing herself as a heroine, lost, alone, fated to meet a man she can seduce into dominating her, Streep's Mary dreams in rosy-ripe clichés.

NEW YORK POST, 12/8/89, p. 31, David Edelstein

In the gross, rancid comedy "She-Devil," Roseanne Barr plays a housewife, mother and fatty whose husband (Ed Begley Jr.) falls in love with a fabulously rich, slender and beautiful writer of romance novels (Meryl Streep).

To ensure you notice that Barr is obese, the film makers devise a scene in which Ruth attempts to stuff herself into a mini-dress; as the zipper bursts, the camera lingers on her copious rolls of flab.

Often and in tight close-up, Barr crams jelly donuts and cannoli into her maw, leaving cream on her hairy upper lip (which also sports a mole the size of a Hershey's Kiss). Once while she crams she's observed by a homunculan Linda Hunt, who's soon cramming, too.

I apologize for dwelling on these unappetizing images, but its hard to do justice to the movie's coarseness. Directing her fifth film, the smart, wry Susan Seidelman appears to have sold her soul for the sake of some cheap yocks—she's the real "She-Devil." As a director, she makes Danny DeVito seem like Cocteau.

"She-Devil" is based on a novel by Fay Weldon, who manages to find some meaning in all this degradation. The heroine of the book is riddled with self-hatred, but she isn't an exhibitionist, a circus fat lady.

The novel is about *feminine* self-hatred. Ruth ends up undergoing years of plastic surgery, cutting herself down to nothing. Her odyssey is excruciating, but the book taps into something vital about the way women are taught to regard themselves in modern society.

The movie (from a screenplay by Barry Strugatz and Mark R. Burns), has been tidied up into a feminist fable of revenge, and it's set in a kitsch-heavy, cartoon universe—a universe where hurts have no real sting..

The fable is, on its own terms, seductive. Ruth drops out of her life, burning down her house and abandoning her children and husband to Mary Fisher. Incognito and from a distance, she sets about making the novelist's life a living hell—punishing her for all she has that Ruth hasn't, giving her an industrial-strength dose of what it really means to be a woman (and not a woman in romance novels).

The charge in "She-Devil" comes from watching the princess become unglued: in quick succession, Mary is saddled with noisy, dirty kids and a belligerent mother (Sylvia Miles) who's a constant reminder of the pristine novelist's lowly (and scandalous) past. She's cheated on, stolen from, exposed in People magazine and rejected by her readers.

It's hard to find delight in Ruth's triumph, however, since Barr is so robotic and monotonous—Seidelman lets her rot on the screen like a beached whale. At times this seems like the most self-hating feminist movie ever made.

Barr is just the biggest gross-out in a movie that groans with them: a gerbil gets baked in a casserole and a poodle dashed on some rocks; someone vomits front and center; Seidelman cuts from Barr emptying a bedpan of urine to a waiter pouring cream of watercress soup...

"She-Devil" isn't especially cinematic, though, since Streep and Barr have no real scenes together. (Audiences who go in hoping for a slam-bang confrontation between the Queen of Cinema and the Queen of Sitcoms will feel gypped. And I somehow doubt there will be a rematch.)

Swathed in pink satin, Streep perfumes her words with tiny intakes of breath, and her gestures are swooning—she yields exquisitely. Her Mary Fisher behaves like a fairy-tale princess of Gothic love stories; until she gets her comeuppance (and, in a nice touch, becomes a feminist), she draws strength by appealing to male vanity.

Watching Streep in her early scenes—as she overwhelms Begley's self-centred straw-man—I remembered an acquaintance's account of lunch with her while the two were at the Yale School of Drama. Across the table, he said, she could psych you out, reduce you to a jelly with a single inflection or gesture.

I could imagine what he meant. On stage in the mid-'70s, Streep was the most thrilling comic actress I'd ever seen. She had the wit of a great parodist and fearless precision of a Buster Keaton, and there are glimmers of that here.

Watch her glide naked across a swimming pool when confronted with her lover's wife and kids, hysterically attempting to hold the suds in front of her bosom. Watch her stare despondently into a mirror, turning up her nose and stretching the skin over her cheekbone—making her uniquely beautiful face into a blandly-pretty cover-girl's. Elsewhere, Streep gets all of Mary Fisher's self-intoxication and fluffy, poodle-like phoniness.

But there isn't a whole lot more to get, and the performance goes nowhere. However she struggles, she never transcends the caricature or her surroundings; she's working in a vacuum, lost among the amateurs.

NEWSDAY, 12/8/89, Part III/p. 3, Mike McGrady

What kind of a movie could costar such polar opposites as Roseanne Barr and Meryl Streep? Can you imagine the entity that might accommodate such disparate talents? When the cast for "She-Devil" was first announced, anticipation began to build; not since the "Twin"-ing of Arnold Schwarzenegger and Danny DeVito had there been such an unlikely movieland merger.

However, even stranger than the casting itself are the results: Meryl Streep gets all the laughs and Roseanne Barr is asked to generate all the dramatic fireworks. Small wonder, then, that "She-Devil" never quite gels, never manages to succeed as either drama or comedy.

I suspect the root problem may be the fact that some books resist being translated to film. The original Fay Weldon novel, "The Life and Loves of a She-Devil," was a parable, a story designed to convey its truths indirectly. Well, movie cameras do well with adventure novels and romances, with crime stories and cowboys, but the movie camera that can do justice to a parable has yet to be invented.

"She-Devil" centers on beyond-homely Roseanne Barr, who watches her accountant-husband Ed Begley, Jr. fall in love with slim, beautiful, rich Meryl Streep. When Begley dumps his wife, his children and his pets and moves in with the Other Woman, Roseanne sets about to exact her revenge.

No, revenge is too mild a word, too tame a notion. It was Jack Paar who observed, "I don't believe in revenge; I believe in massive retaliation." The first thing she does—this is just for starters—is burn down her own home so she can deposit her children on her husband's new doorstep. Upon learning that her rival's aging mother (Sylvia Miles) is locked out of sight in a nursing home, Roseanne finds work as a nurse and conspires to reunite the unloving mother and daughter. Later, sneaking into her husband's office late at night, she doctors accounts so that he will someday be imprisoned for embezzlement. And so forth and so on.

All this is clearly designed to satisfy any woman's gut-level need for retribution in a man's world. Unfortunately, as drama, it constantly falls short. To begin, there's no one to root for, not one character in the entire film remotely likeable or worth caring about.

Meryl Streep, who can seemingly do no wrong as an actress, provides a welcome comic turn, but her characterization is the beginning and the end of humor (and characterization, for that matter) in the film. The rest of the humor exists on the level of bedpan jokes, vomit jokes, and blow-up-the-house jokes. A typical exchange occurs when a cream of watercress soup is served and Sylvia Miles translates the French name for the dish ("It's French for 'dog puke' ") to general merriment.

At times, director Susan Seidelman seems strangely forgetful. Roseanne has been given a hairy mountain of a mole adjoining what seems to be a mustache (this surely qualifies as the opposite of gilding the lily), and halfway through the movie, both mole and mustache suddenly disappear without a word of explanation.

Nor is there any effort to establish dramatic credibility. Original details from the book have been exaggerated out of all proportion. (Typical example: In the book, the wife serves a soup containing three pet hairs; in the film it contains the floating corpse of a pet guinea pig.) Unbelievable, unfunny, unnecessary—and that roughly sums up my feelings for the film as a whole.

NEWSWEEK, 12/11/89, p. 88, David Ansen

[*She-Devil* was reviewed jointly with *The War of the Roses*; see Ansen's review of that film.]

TIME, 12/11/89, p. 93, Richard Corliss

Watching Meryl Streep as Mary Fisher, romance novelist, is like seeing Margaret Thatcher play the horse in a Christmas pantomime—and with delicious style. The great gray lady of movie drama brings her precise acting tools to a comedy of manners, flouncing wittily onto a couch, exhaling every word in swooning intimacy, switching from fawn to fume in the wink of a lover's indiscretion. She can even speak American English without an accent. Surprise! Inside the Greer Garson roles Streep usually plays, a vixenish Carole Lombard is screaming to be cut loose.

Streep is the one reason to catch (maybe next year on video) this choppy adaptation of Fay Weldon's exemplarily meanspirited novel. The story could serve as a parable of feminist revenge. Mary steals accountant Bob Patchett (Ed Begley Jr.) away from his fat, drab, warty wife Ruth (Roseanne Barr). Then Ruth, with a systematic resourcefulness she has never displayed as a homemaker, destroys everything Bob loves: house, family, career, freedom. The worm turns into a winner.

As a BBC-TV series, *The Life and Loves of a She-Devil* went gleefully over the top, pitying or despising all its characters. But comedy on the American plan can go soft, as Barr proved when she gave her abrasive stand-up-comic persona a sweetie-pie makeover for her hit TV show. *She-Devil* does the same to Weldon, without substituting much style or attitude. The movie is its own sitcom pilot, and only Streep watchers will be laughing.

VILLAGE VOICE, 12/19/89, p. 94, Georgia Brown

When it comes to wreaking revenge on a lecherous husband, *She-Devil* concocts its baroque scheme unencumbered by guilt. What has poor Ruth Patchett to be guilty about? Except her looks. Ruth (Roseanne Barr) weighs 201 pounds, is probably about five foot two, and has a startling mole like a chunk of prune on her upper lip. (Fay Weldon's novel, *The Life and Loves of a She-Devil*, describes Ruth as "lumpish and brutish," six foot two with "jutting jaw," hooked nose, and *four* moles on the chin, three with hairs growing out.) "Unlucky in that great lottery that is a woman's life," Ruth obviously is not equipped to keep a husband such as Bob (Ed Begley Jr.), tall, blond, agile accountant to the creative. (Weldon enlists all her inventive powers to explain how she ever snared him, a task too demanding for the movie.) Once Bob leaves clumsy Ruth and their two children for the ethereal but steamy romance writer, Mary Fisher (Meryl Streep)—who is tended by a houseboy named Garcia in a pink castle by the sea (shades of Paul Bartel)—Ruth discovers her métier in vengeance.

What follows could be gleeful and cathartic. Susan Seidelman adapts Weldon's grim book—written in high ironic style and from a low cynical point of view—as frenzied slapstick farce. Weldon has a devoted following that will probably not take to Seidelman's efforts on its behalf.

The first phase of Ruth's campaign involves blowing up the family home, sending the not-very-well-brought-up children (Ruth's not much of a mother) to live with the two lovebirds by the sea, and then freeing Mary Fisher's feisty mother (the scary Sylvia Miles) from her tranquilized haze in a nursing home, so that she too can drive Mary bonkers and the ever-faithless Bob into other arms. There are further phases to Ruth's scheme, though not as many as in the novel. The mole finally goes (with never a word said about.it).

As the she-devil, Barr maintains an odd, amblin', down-to-earth prosiness, which may explain her appeal on TV, but it pits her against the relentless contortion of the rest of the movie. Streep's Mary, prisoner of pink, generates high comic self-absorption, though she doesn't really come off as wickedly vain. The result is that Mary draws audience sympathy when she starts falling apart. The only performance really that broke into my glazed-over stupor was Linda Hunt's dour, then blithely liberated, Nurse Hooper.

Also reviewed in:
NEW REPUBLIC, 1/22/90, p. 28, Stanley Kauffmann
NEW YORK TIMES, 12/8/89, p. C8, Vincent Canby
VARIETY, 12/6/89, p. 38
WASHINGTON POST, 12/8/89, p. C1, Hal Hinson
WASHINGTON POST, 12/8/89, Weekend/p. 65, Desson Howe

SHELL SHOCK

An Angelika Films release. *Producer:* Yoel Sharon. *Director:* Yoel Sharon. *Screenplay (Hebrew with English subtitles):* Yoel Sharon. *Director of Photography:* Yoav Kosh. *Editor:* Zohar Sela. *Music:* Edwin J. Reyes. *Sound:* Riccardo Levy. *Art Director:* Ariel Glazer. *Costumes:* Tal Amir. *Running time:* 93 minutes. *MPAA Rating:* R.

CAST: Asher Tsarfati (Gideon); Dan Turgeman (Micha); Anat Atzmon (Dana); Gili Ben-Ozilio (Tali); Stanislav Chaplin (Dr. Klein).

NEW YORK POST, 9/29/89, p. 21, Jami Bernard

It's good to see that the psychological ramifications of war are occupying the talents of film makers here and abroad, to offset the more easily cathartic Rambos. From Israel we have "Shell Shock," a small film about the aftermath of the October War for two men, and how as hospital roommates they attempt to help each other over the trauma.

Director Yoel Sharon has his own demons to exorcise—he was partially paralyzed during a raid that wiped out all but two of his comrades, both of whom suffered from "shell shock," an umbrella term coined during World War I to describe the ills that plague vets: night sweats, impotence, mood swings.

Micha (Dan Turgeman) is the director's alter ego, a handsome young soldier who snaps a photo of his platoon just as it is blown to bits. Micha vainly tries to save a comrade; later in the hospital, a shrink attempts to jog his memory with some questionable tactics. A combination of sodium pentothal and war simulations has Micha crawling around the floor.

"One more session and we'll enter the black hole of your memory," promised the doc. Who's the sick one here, anyway?

Gideon (Asher Tsarfati), meanwhile, is a colonel whose dutiful obeyance of orders from above helped wipe out his unit. He suffers from the usual guilt, plus agoraphobia, a fear of going outside.

When Gideon cooks up a goulash in the hospital room, it touches off a Proustian memory rush for Micha; when Gideon gets the shakes, it is Micha to the rescue. But the men soon find that male bonding—urinating together out a window, singing the old songs—is not enough.

"Shell Shock" attempts to grapple with a complex and unpopular subject—after all, it reminds us that war's victims include the victors. However, even such an emotional issue has difficulty sustaining the audience's empathy. Clinically interesting (and well acted), the movie is without a dramatic centre. Gideon's attempts to reintegrate himself into society border on the bizarre, and all that crawling around can't disguise that the final truth about Micha's lost night ultimately fails to provide any breakthrough insight into Micha himself.

NEWSDAY, 9/29/89, Part III/p. 7, Terry Kelleher

Yoel Sharon was wounded on the final day of the 1973 war in the Mideast and remains paralyzed in the lower part of his body. Now the Israeli film maker tells the fictional story of two soldiers left emotionally crippled by that conflict, two men of sharply contrasting backgrounds who turn to each other for understanding and sympathy.

Sharon clearly wants us to care deeply about the characters in "Shell Shock," to share their agony as he does. Unfortunately, the director's execution doesn't measure up to his aims.

Gideon (Asher Tsarfati) is a colonel, committed to an army career, who emerged from the war with a case of agoraphobia and haunting memories of an Israeli air strike that he mistakenly called down on his own unit. Micha (Dan Turgeman) is a reservist, a fashion photographer by trade, who was found in the desert lying next to a dead comrade. His unit was the target of an Egyptian attack on the last night of combat, but Micha has repressed any recollection of how he survived and his fellow soldiers perished.

These two men are brought together as roommates in the psychiatric ward of a military clinic. There are signs of antagonism the first time we see them together, but quickly they're behaving like best friends. Sharon skips over the warming period in between, denying us a chance to become acquainted with the characters as individuals rather than case studies.

Gideon is soon released, after Micha helps him face the outside world. Micha is deemed in need of further treatment, but he bolts from the hospital when his new roommate gets on his nerves. He and Gideon tie one on, then each goes into a period of brooding and raging.

Micha spends much of his time on an isolated beach, where he likes to wander nude. His girlfriend (Gili Ben-Ozilio) tries to help; he pushes her away. Gideon loses his military command—apparently as part of some unexplained cover-up in the higher echelons—and is reduced to serving in the civil guard. Humiliated, he takes out his anger on his family until his wife (Anat Atzmon) banishes him from the house.

We might come to know Gideon and Micha better if they talked more with the clinic psychiatrist (Stanislav Chaplin). As it is, we view their anguish at a certain distance. Micha experiences repeated flashbacks to the Egyptian attack and its aftermath, and Sharon tries to keep us in some suspense about what may be buried in the "black hole of memory." But we're given little indication of what else is going through Micha's mind. The audience can only wish Gideon had flashbacks. Although we're touched at times by his loss of self-esteem, we simply lack enough information to understand either Gideon's guilt or his victimization.

The resolution of "Shell Shock" is especially disappointing. Gideon bids for redemption through a convenient opportunity for heroism; Micha seeks the truth by shooting pictures. The former scene is blatantly melodramatic, the latter slightly absurd.

No doubt Sharon has a special appreciation for the plight of men like Gideon and Micha. Strangely, "Shell Shock" fails to communicate it.

VILLAGE VOICE, 8/22/89, p. 85, Manohla Dargis

Yoel Sharon's *Shell Shock* is also notable for its antiwar sentiment. Dedicated to the casualties and survivors of Sharon's Israeli unit, all but wiped out on the last day of the Yom Kippur War (which left the director—no relation to the former defense minister—paraplegic), this is an earnest, capable film that focuses on two victims of that war who suffer from shell shock.

Micha (Dan Turgeman), a young fashion photographer, is a member of the reserves, Gideon (Asher Tsarfati) a career officer. Roommates at a psychiatric hospital, Gideon suffers from agoraphobia—he can't even make it out the door—and Micha is tormented by a wartime incident so deeply submerged in his unconscious that treatment seems futile. There are few matters more tedious than someone else's therapy, and Micha's visits to the padded room fail to inspire much interest; the film doesn't pick up until he goes AWOL and Gideon is released.

Back at home Gideon simulates sanity and waits for reassignment—drinking too much, shrieking at overhead planes, smacking his wife and kids. Micha, meanwhile, though still traumatized, decides on a course of self-recovery that includes nastiness to his girlfriend, brooding motorcycle trips to the beach, and drinking bouts with Gideon. The film suffers from allegoric inevitability, grinding down inexorably as each man comes to represent something larger than life Overcharged with a historical and emotional burden that overwhelms the simplified premise, this is good politics but deadly drama. For all its emotional tumult, *Shell Shock* falls flat; yes, the actors emote (Tsarfati is especially good), but there's little frisson.

All is lost by the end, when a deus ex machina crushes the film's fragile realism and Sharon goes into narrative hyperspace. Redemption for Gideon involves terrorism and hostages; Micha finds it by way of a stupefying re-creation of his traumatic lost moments. Defying all reason, Sharon has Micha reenact his nightmare while on a fashion shoot, using leather-swathed models as stand-ins for the lost platoon. (The echo of SS leather fetishism is unsettling.) The sheer lunacy of this gesture—Micha endangers the unwitting women by nearly engulfing them in flames—upends the film, making it veer dangerously into parody.

Also reviewed in:
NEW YORK TIMES, 9/30/89, p. 13, Stephen Holden
VARIETY, 4/27/88, p. 18

SHE'S OUT OF CONTROL

A Columbia Pictures release of a Weintraub Entertainment Group presentation. *Executive Producer:* Robert Kaufman. *Producer:* Stephen Deutsch. *Director:* Stan Dragoti. *Screenplay:* Seth Winston and Michael J. Nathanson. *Director of Photography:* Donald Peterman. *Editor:* Dov Hoenig. *Music:* Alan Silvestri. *Sound:* Ronald Cogswell. *Production Designer:* David L. Snyder. *Art Director:* Joe Wood. *Set Designer:* Daniel Maltese and John Warnke. *Set Decorator:* Bruce Gibeson. *Costumes:* Marie France. *Running time:* 97 minutes. *MPAA Rating:* PG.

CAST: Tony Danza (Doug Simpson); Catherine Hicks (Janet Pearson); Wallace Shawn (Dr. Fishbinder); Dick O'Neill (Mr. Pearson); Ami Dolenz (Katie Simpson); Laura Mooney (Bonnie Simpson); Derek McGrath (Jeff); Dana Ashbrook (Joey); Matthew L. Perry (Timothy).

LOS ANGELES TIMES, 4/14/89, Calendar/p. 6, Michael Wilmington

The main trouble with "She's Out of Control" is that it's never out of control. It's a comedy about rampaging paranoia—about a widowed general manager at a failing rock radio station (Doug Simpson, played by "Taxi's" stud, Tony Danza) who goes bonkers when his 15-year-old daughter starts dating. And the whole movie stays on greased, slick tracks right to the end. Instead of building toward a comic paroxysm, it turns into a polyethylene grenade, made to explode Barbie Dolls.

The movie, which has an ultraprofessional technical sheen, comes on like a rock video version of every piece of TV-or-movie father-daughter-dating shtick since "Take Her, She's Mine." Bespectacled, awkward Katie (Ami Dolenz) takes off her glasses, gets a permanent, a facial and a new wardrobe, and—*voila!*—idiotically grinning boys with glazed, lecherous eyes start tumbling across the Simpson porch like clowns out of a circus Volkswagen.

There's the punk black-leather rebel (Dana Ashbrook), the rich voluptuary with a sneaky grin (Matthew L. Perry), the dumped, heart-stricken boy next door (Derek McGrath) and a half-dozen or so other clichés, loitering around, sweating and shuffling their heels. Inside, Katie's little sister (Laura Mooney) makes dry wisecracks, and a frantic Simpson colleague shows up every 20 minutes to tell him his station's ratings are falling.

The central joke of the movie is that though the daughter has gone overboard—her new-found popularity is driving her wild—her erstwhile '60s rebel father has gone crazier, egged on by his sadistic puppet master: gnomic psychiatrist and best-selling author Dr. Herman Fishbinder (Wally Shawn). Fishbinder is a piercing-eyed troll who seems to enjoy tormenting Doug and feeding his anxieties. He's one of the film's few contemporary notions, and Shawn, as always, does his nasal little bully routine and livens up his scenes. But this doctor-patient relationship is almost senseless. The demented father calls up night and day, and Fishbinder, yanked out of bed or a party, then impatiently reads him something out of the book. (Is this a commentary on radio executives? Does panic make Simpson illiterate?)

The script is another one of those high-concept specials that sound like they were midwifed by an agent. It never swerves to the left or right; it never sneaks up on you. And even though you can always see the jokes coming—like the orgiastic prom or the crunched Jaguar—you can't duck.

In the midst of all this, Tony Danza is rather good. He's willing to throw himself into the part, try to bench-press all these recycled, glitzed-up gags. But, after a while the weight gets too heavy; he seems to be working too hard. The actors who have the cornier, emptier roles, like Shawn, or who play down, like Catherine Hicks (as Doug's nervous sweetie-pie fiancee), fare better. Of the two daughters, Ami Dolenz is a cool charmer, and Laura Mooney, as her little sister, has snappy timing and a great, raucous laugh. (She still won't make you forget Diana Lynn.)

Director Stan Dragoti, cinematographer Don Peterman, editor Dov Hoenig and composer Alan Silvestri are like super-couturiers working on a Plain Jane. They give this empty movie pace and sheen, style and visual zonk; when Dragoti shoots a drag race, he winds up copying, frame for frame, the chicken run in "Rebel Without a Cause." But they've made a sometimes funny, mostly media-referential movie without much real life; a high-tech, high-pro job that has a glamor-robot feel. In the film, Fishbinder has a vanity license plate that reads "I SHRINK." If this production team had a car pool, they ought to get plates that read "WE DEAL."

NEW YORK POST, 4/14/89, p. 39, Jami Bernard

Every girl knows what it's like to be at that awkward age when you pray for the day that the braces come off and the "training bra" finishes its training and the phone starts ringing with dreamboats dying for a date. Of course, life doesn't always turn out that way, but it does for Katie Simpson. One day, she's a dorky kid with thick glasses trying to imitate Jennifer Beals in "Flashdance"; the next day she's a beauty out of control.

If "She's Out of Control" had been a comedy merely about Katie's transition to teen temptress, it could have been a dud. But the one who's out of control is really Katie's widowed dad, Doug (Tony Danza), who cannot cope emotionally with having a hot tamale for a daughter. Every boy on the beach is an imagined threat; every time the doorbell rings it is a potential rapist.

"You can't stop life from happening," says Doug's girlfriend (Catherine Hicks) after she has aided and abetted Katie's transition to babe-dom.

"But I can slow it down a lot," fumes Doug, resolving to have "total control," enlisting the help of his younger daughter (competent brat Laura Mooney) in tracking Katie's every move and screening every unsuitable suitor.

After slamming the door on a succession of candidates, including twins who arrive together, Doug finds to his horror that Katie (Ami Dolenz, daughter of Monkee Mickey) has chosen a guy with one earring and a love van. Doug needs help—his preoccupation with Katie's sex life is taking its toll on the radio station where he works so he turns to a shrink, played to exasperated perfection by Wallace Shawn.

This Dr. Fishbinder has written a book—chapter and verse—advising fathers to spy on their daughters, to befriend the boyfriend as a tactical maneuver (even if it means giving the kid the keys to the Jaguar), to do everything short of locking the girl in a turret.

The shrink frightens Doug by giving him statistics on how many times teen-age boys think of sex, and when he hears that Doug has allowed Katie to go to the prom, he's incredulous. *"Prom? Prom!"* she explodes, as if it were Purgatory with a corsage. "Did you know that 87.3 percent of teen-age girls lose their virginity at the *prom?"*

Yes, three stars is a generous rating. The hilarity is far from non-stop, and Ami Dolenz as Katie is beautiful but unprepossessing. The movie's trailer, in fact, is funnier, and if it were just five minutes longer would render it unnecessary to see the movie at all.

Still, it is an amiable comedy, something fun for teenagers without being gross or inane, and Tony Danza ("Who's the Boss," "Taxi") makes the most of it. He has a priceless look of awe and dismay when he first sees his little girl descend the stairs in a tiny white party dress and thighhigh garterless stockings. His attempts to befriend the thug who's possibly deflowering his darling are funny and dear.

Wallace Shawn in small doses livens up any movie he's in, like hot sauce at a barbecue. "Didn't you read the next chapter, 'Surveillance'?" he spits at his patient after ascertaining that Katie's latest beau is "too good to be true," or the Warren Beatty Syndrome.

Director Stan Dragoti has pulled off similar stunts before with "Mr. Mom" and "Love at First Bite," comedies that skillfully avoided the TV-movie abyss. Part of his success may be due to his background in TV commercials. "She's Out of Control" has that sort of high-tech, quick-cutting look of an ad for a delicious soft drink. In this case, Katie is photographed like the soft drink, and it works.

NEWSDAY, 4/14/89, Part III/p. 3, Drew Fetherston

"She Out of Control" demonstrates, to its detriment, that out of control is not necessarily a bad—or good—way to be.

If this trite and predictable tale had courage enough to get really crazy—or if it lost its head in ways that were not mindless—it might have become something other than a tediously extended episode of a second-rate sitcom.

Instead, "She's Out of Control" exhibits the flaws of the very groups it attempts to satirize: It is as stodgy and predictable as any adult, as uncertain and erratic as any adolescent.

The situation is old enough to have been used by comedists from the dawn of humor, often to much better effect: Doug Simpson (Tony Danza), a widower dad, grows nervous when his 15-year-old daughter sheds her braces, horn-rims, dumpy clothing and, possibly, some inhibitions that are beloved of parents but little esteemed by hormone-fueled teenagers.

If it surprises you that Katie (played by Ami Dolenz, daughter of the former Monkee, Mickey) is soon breaking hearts and creeping in her window at 4 a.m., by all means see the film; it will provide you with a rough outline of what everyone else on Earth already knows.

These characters, worried dad and impatient daughter, are as rigidly defined as anything in classical Japanese theater. It takes a deft hand to make fresh comedy from such, and no such skill is evident in "She's Out of Control." The film uses standard sitcom plotting: Set up a gag, deliver the punchline; set up the next gag, get to the next punchline.

"She's Out of Control" gets up to cruising speed fairly quickly—Katie blooms while Dad's away on a brief business trip; by the time he gets back the boys are baying under her window—but never accelerates thereafter: Suitors—suitable and unsuitable—appear at the door, play out their predictable roles, and disappear.

A couple of interesting possibilities loom but get quickly left behind. In one, Doug wins the heart and trust of Katie's first boyfriend, a lad whose leather garb and stand-up hair put off most adults. When Katie dumps him, the lonely freak turns to Doug for friendship and consolation.

The menage thus created might have been a source of some real fun, even with a cast that shows no particular aptitude for comedy. But it is dumped as quickly as any of Katie's conquests.

When the film does go overboard, it does so in the stale ways so dear to the Hollywood heart—with status-symbol cars and human stereotypes. Thus we have a Jaguar hit by a train; Corvettes, Rolls-Royces and BMWs also get key roles.

Among the stereotypes is a dithering daughterless psychiatrist (Wallace Shawn) whose vanity plate is I SHRINK.

When Doug does swerve out of control, he does it in illogical ways—stealing a car (the worst sort of craziness in California), snapping infrared photos of one of Katie's two-timing beaux, dumping his would-be in-laws to shadow his offspring.

This nonsense produces sour disbelief rather than the pleasant giddiness that accompanies good screwball comedy or farce. The lesson of "She's Out of Control" is that losing control is something best done with care.

VILLAGE VOICE, 4/25/89, p. 71, Katherine Dieckmann

She's Out of Control just might be the first Bush-league morality tale. This advertisement for family values equates retro rock-and-roll with safety (not unlike the electric guitar strapped on our President at his inauguration, and used TV actors to deliver its homilies about trust and father-knows-best. Stan Dragoti's shiny teenflick seems destined to join the other fluff currently dominating *Variety*'s Top Ten—one of the bleakest in recent memory—and you almost have to credit this veteran manipulator (*Mr. Mom, Love at First Bite*) for cashing in on the kindly mood of our nation, where not even the Kinks are safe from usurpation.

A NutraSweet *Smooth Talk, Control* traces the sexual awakening of a good girl—except that, tragically enough, this good girl never turns even remotely bad. Katie (played by chirpy Ami Dolenz, daughter of ex-Monkee Mickey) is a gawky 15-year-old given to copping *Flashdance* moves in her bedroom and chastely dating the red-haired nerd next door. But then her single-parent dad, a rock radio station manager named Doug Simpson (droopy-eyed Neanderthal Tony Danza), goes off on a business trip. His girlfriend, Janet (Catherine Hicks), encourages Katie to indulge in some image transformation. With makeup on, braces off, teased tresses, and thick glasses traded for contacts, Katie becomes a bona fide babe. Doug returns to see his little princess floating downstairs in frilly whites (and slo-mo), headed out on what has become a constant stream of dates.

What ensues is so simplistic it wouldn't interest even a beginning analyst—and, of course, there *is* an analyst in *Control*, a crackpot irritatingly played by Wallace Shawn. Doug freaks, begins obsessing that his daughter is going to lose her virginity (and that the moment won't be "beautiful"), and begins meddling in her life, screaming things like "Total control." The shrink advises him to befriend Katie's most promisingly delinquent boyfriend, a leather-and-studs type with a Mohawk named Joey (Dana Ashbrook). So Doug wows Katie and her friends with his 45 collection, impresses Joey by bragging about how he met Mick Jagger, and lends the youth his red convertible for a *Rebel Without a Cause*-inspired drag race. Of course, in the end, the promisingly monosyllabic Joey goes as gushy as the rest of this good-hearted gang.

She's *Out of Control* stakes the three tried-and-true ingredients for rebellion and neutralizes all of them. There's lots of talk about sex, but no action (and, incidentally, nary a mention of AIDS). Not one cigarette dangles with provocation from a surly lip. The rock-and-roll soundtrack—from '50s classics to '60s grunge to '80s dance music—is used strictly for pumping up Dragoti's vacuous, hyperstylized images. It's tough growing up in a world where Daddy hogs all the pleasure in being bad.

Also reviewed in:
NEW YORK TIMES, 4/14/89, p. C13, Caryn James
VARIETY, 4/19–25/89, p. 24
WASHINGTON POST, 4/15/89, p. C3, Rita Kempley

SHIRLEY VALENTINE

A Paramount Pictures release. *Executive Producer:* John Dark. *Producer:* Lewis Gilbert. *Director:* Lewis Gilbert. *Screenplay (based on his own play):* Willy Russell. *Director of Photography:* Alan Hume. *Editor:* Lesley Walker. *Music:* Willy Russell and (Greek music) George Hatzinassios. *Sound:* Roy Charman and (music) Keith Grant. *Sound Editor:* Jonathan Bates. *Production Designer:* John Stoll. *Set Decorator:* Amanda Ackland-Snow. *Costumes:* Candy Paterson. *Make-up:* Basil Newall. *Running time:* 107 minutes. *MPAA Rating:* R.

CAST: Pauline Collins (Shirley Valentine); Tom Conti (Costas); Julia McKenzie (Gillian); Alison Steadman (Jane); Joanna Lumley (Marjorie); Sylvia Syms (Headmistress); Bernard Hill (Joe); George Costigan (Dougie); Anna Keaveney (Jeanette); Tracie Bennett (Millandra); Ken Sharrock (Sydney); Karen Craig (Thelma); Gareth Jefferson (Brian); Gillian Kearney (Young Shirley); Catherine Duncan (Young Marjorie); Cardew Robinson (Londoner); Honora Burke (Londoner's Wife); Marc Zuber (Renos); Deborah Yhip (Sharon-Louise); Ray Armstrong (Executive Type); John Hartley (German Tourist); Marlene Morley (German Tourist); Annee Blott (Chambermaid); Matthew Long (Male Teacher); Ruth Russell (Veronica); Sarah Nolan (Maureen); Diane Whitley (Liz); Joanne Zorian (Carol); Geraldine Griffiths (Sally); Elaine Boisseau (Woman in Taverna); Giorgos Xidakis (Spiro); Shelia Aza (Cooking Teacher); Alex Wright (Kid in Car); Ged McKenna (Van Driver).

FILMS IN REVIEW, 11/89, p. 556, Kevin Lewis

A film about a Liverpool housewife who becomes a waitress in a Greek tavern would appear to be a kitchen-sink version of *Madame X,* but in Shirley Valentine's case it becomes a comedy about women's lib. And it works in the most delightful way possible. Pauline Collins, best known as Sarah in the television series *Upstairs, Downstairs,* may win an Oscar for this film. She won the Tony and the Olivier Award for playing the part in its stage version.

Willy Russell, who is best known for adapting his play *Educating Rita* into a hit film a few years ago, has accomplished a different task this time. *Shirley Valentine* in its stage version is a one-woman play in which the woman relates the other characters' conversations. In the film version we see all the other characters.

Tom Conti, in particular, is charming and expert at low key humor as the Greek waiter who beds Shirley, the runaway housewife, in his boat. As Shirley's oafish husband Joe, Bernard Hill makes the viewer understand why Shirley would leave her attractive suburban home to live in the Greek Islands as a waitress. Julia McKenzie as the braggart neighbor who is sympathetic to Shirley, Joanna Lumley as the former "top girl" schoolmate of Shirley's who is now a jet-setting hooker, and Alison Steadman as Shirley's feminist girlfriend who wins the ticket that takes Shirley and her to Greece are outstanding in small roles.

Lewis Gilbert has done an outstanding directorial job in combining the elements of the play and film together. Most of what remains of Shirley's monologues are said by Collins to the camera, creating an intimate feeling for the audience. *Tom Jones* tried this approach in a limited way, but it takes courage to sustain this throughout a whole film. Because Collins is not only brilliant and sharp in her timing, but charming, sincere and genuinely humorous, the film works. *Shirley Valentine* is light entertainment, expertly performed. The flaw in the play is, unlike *Educating Rita, Shirley Valentine* is not quite believable. Rita tranformed herself into a thinking person, making it impossible for her to return to her former life. Russell skips too lightly over what lies ahead for Shirley. What remains is not really a wellrounded film but a music hall turn, though it is a richly rewarding and funny turn.

LOS ANGELES TIMES, 8/30/89, Calendar/p. 1, Sheila Benson

Awfully smart of the adapters of "Shirley Valentine" to hang on to big-eyed Pauline Collins, the authentic jewel in their gaudy crown. Without Collins' waves of honesty, her enveloping warmth and the unhurried, confiding way about her delivery, we might well be left to wonder what all the fuss was about in this comedy-drama about a salty Liverpool housewife who, to her own astonishment, does something about the dead-end shape to her life.

In Liverpool and then London's West End, Collins created Shirley Valentine and every other character in Willy Russell's play, which at that time was a full evening's entertainment with a single performer, the indefatigable Collins herself. After collecting England's Olivier Award for her pains, she moved with the play to New York where she won a Tony and, from all accounts, Manhattanites' hearts.

That was still no insurance that she'd be the one to make the movie, however. As film deals are put together these days, it's a wonder that "Shirley Valentine" doesn't star Goldie Hawn, Elizabeth Taylor or Shirley MacLaine—and that is without the slightest disrespect to the singular moxie of any of these women. But it would be as unthinkable as separating Judy Holliday from "Born Yesterday" or, for that matter, "Alfie" from Michael Caine.

So the powers that are—notably producer-director Lewis Gilbert and playwright-screenwriter Russell, the team behind "Educating Rita," and executive producer John Dark—are owed a considerable debt of gratitude for letting Collins, who looks a bit like Joanna Cassidy's unpretentious English cousin, re-create her personal triumph.

But honestly, Collins' vehicle is a creaky old donkey cart. (Husband Joe, in unbelieving astonishment that supper isn't on the table at 6 sharp one night: "You're going 'round the bend!" Shirley, with equanimity, "'Ope so, I've always wanted to travel.") It's also been whittled down to something less of a tour de force now that each of her supporting characters is embodied by other actors, notably Tom Conti as Greek taverna owner Costas, Bernard Hill as her bluff "oppressor" Joe, and Joanna Lumley as her grade-school nemesis Marjorie.

Still, there is plenty left for Collins to get her back into. While frying up steak and eggs for husband Joe's supper, and ruminating on her situation, 42-year old Shirley has the habit of chatting to her kitchen wall or, in other situations, to an Aegean rock. Then, with a roll of those enormous blue eyes, she lets us know *she* knows exactly how daft that may seem.

Soliloquy isn't actually what feels baffling about "Shirley Valentine," it's timing. Are the English really just discovering that many women who hit 40 find their lives unrewarding, their kids unappreciative and their husbands selectively deaf? Or is it just in these well-manicured vehicle-plays, as carefully balanced as Pritikin to be titillating but not too salty, bold but not too brassy. You can agree with Shirley's every complaint, and perhaps add a few of your own, and still feel an odd sense of time warp about these proceedings.

What separates Shirley from her masses of fellow-sufferers is her edge of self-knowledge and her bravery. When her best friend—now divorced—wins a two-week vacation in Greece and inpulsively suggests that Shirley come too, the yearning Liverpudlian cooks two weeks of frozen dinners for Joe, sticks a note on her "Come to Sunny Greece" kitchen calendar and is off. Not without trepidation, or a sense of the giddy impossibility of it all, but truly, safely off (Of course, the film makers have loaded the dice slightly by casting "Bellman and True's" many-layered Hill as Joe.)

Being Shirley, she is able to appreciate everything she encounters: the quality of light, the unfamiliar food, the cautiously friendly Costas, reassuring her at every step of the propriety of his invitation to take her sightseeing around the island on his brother's boat. (The film's R rating comes primarily from Costas' unbridled English, which savors one particular word too many times for the MPAA, and from fleeting nudity.)

And being no fools, Gilbert and Russell pull out every stop in sketching Shirley's fellow-travelers. Her best buddy deserts her; her picky, boisterous Manchester hotel mates, Jeanette and Dougie, mortify her. (If you saw "Rita, Sue and Bob Too," you'll recognize George Costigan, the gap-toothed randy Bob, as this smotheringly friendly Dougie.)

Does Shirley find herself appreciated at last? You betcha. No one with any shred of soul could wish her any less. Alas, the film makers' method of informing us of this is to have Costas' boat rock tellingly at anchor, while the sea ebbs and flows onto the shore and climactic moments from "The Firebird" fill the sound track. And *those* are the moments that blight this film at every turn.

And still actress Collins prevails. Should she go back? Why should she go back? Why, indeed, shouldn't she stay? None of this seems unimportant, in Collins' hands.

Even when Shirley makes announcements—"I used to be the mother. I used to be the wife. Now I'm Shirley Valentine again"—you want to tuck your arm in hers, get her talking about other things and have a good long walk up that beach with her, in the setting Mediterranean sun.

MONTHLY FILM BULLETIN, 11/89, p. 345, Philip Strick

Liverpool housewife Shirley Valentine-Bradshaw leads a domestic existence of routine dullness. The children have left home and her husband Joe, once so much fun, has turned monosyllabic except when she attempts to alter his eating habits. Occasionally she trades insults with her neighbour Gillian or visits with her best friend Jane. The latter wins a fortnight's holiday for two in Greece and asks Shirley to join her, but Shirley is nervous about Joe's possible reaction. Recalling her school days, she likes to think she was a natural rebel: she would smoke and curse, her cakes never rose, and the headmistress was openly eager to be rid of her. A bright future was anticipated instead for the school favourite, her classmate Marjorie. Coming home with her shopping in the rain, Shirley gets splashed by a passing limousine and Marjorie, poised and elegant as ever, jumps out to apologise. They have tea in her suite at a luxury hotel, and Shirley learns that Marjorie is now a hooker, internationally in demand. Back home, Joe loses his temper at being given the wrong supper, and Shirley no longer has doubts about the holiday. She flies with Jane to the island of Mykonos, where Jane goes off with a man she met on the plane and Shirley, after lying on the beach alone, talking to a rock, meets a sympathetic waiter, Costas. Invited on a boat trip with him, during which they make love, Shirley realises she has found a renewed zest for living. She duly makes her farewells when the fortnight is over, but at the airport she decides at the last minute not to leave. Returning to Costas, she gets a job at the taverna, cooking contentedly for the tourists. After phoning repeatedly, Joe arrives to take her back. Shirley invites him to join her for a drink beside the sea. A new life for them both is waiting to be discussed.

Another Willy Russell recital of innocence and experience, the educating of Shirley, while less bookish than Rita's, is similarly soft-hearted rather than hard-headed. Once again the story leaps casually across chasms of unexplored implication to alight precariously on several bright peaks of observation which illuminate the heroine's progress from household subservience to worldly independence. And once again she is left to her own devices just when we most need to know whether the great gamble has paid off: where Rita's schooling left her wandering alone down an airport corridor, Shirley sits in the dusk beside the sea with no clear future in prospect. Must she await the Aegean awakening of her husband (whose grudging loyalty is still something of a mystery) so that henceforth they can provide fry-ups together for the tourists? Or will they revert to those merry courtship days of paint-flicking and shared baths back home in a soggy British suburb, tethered to triviality by sneering neighbours and an enervating inertia?

We have no way of judging—because Shirley's past, too, is without form or logic. Her wit and passion appear to have sprung fully fledged from forty-six hermetic years of inner solitude, unaffected by childhood, marriage or parenthood other than in the acquisition of a vague discontent. She could have been the energetic practitioner of any number of causes of she could, like Rita, have taken a swing at Blake and Chekhov; she would certainly have been to Greece before, and known the reasons why. If she had done all this and *still* been talking to the walls we would probably understand her better. But Russell's portrait of Shirley is disastrously belittling in its suggestion that, for her sort (whatever and wherever they may be), a high season in lotus territory is enough to set her up for life.

What makes it work at all, of course, is Russell's skill with one-liners and Pauline Collins' confident confidentiality in sharing them with us (a trick which works less well in the cinema than in the theatre in that it situates us in mid-air in the most unlikely locations). Her absurd retinue of friends and neigbours provides easy excuse for crowd-pleasing put-downs, the kind that gurantee an uproarious night at the show, but since these characters have simply been fleshed out for the screen from what was scathingly subjective in Shirley's stage monologue, they don't get much of a chance to exist in their own right. An exception is Joanna Lumley's high-class hooker, who serves much the same function as the Maureen Lipman character (the flat-mate who attempts suicide) in *Educating Rita* in that the immense gulf between appearance and fact, control and catastrophe, is what leads the heroine to recognise the tightrope she's walking.

There is a similar evasion from the mundane by Tom Conti, despite his usual repertoire of wearily aggrieved expressions, who goes Greek under a shambles of hair and accent with remarkable plausibility. "I've had such a little life—and it'll be over soon", mourns the mid-life mutineer, her very surname a tribute to mass-manipulated sentimentalism, her outcry hitting a not very elusive target dead centre. Lewis Gilbert, whose skill with cast and décor is reasonable compensation for a carefree hit-and-miss style (which for some reason frequently shuts us on the wrong side of doors), rises both to the manipulation and to the sentiments with such unquestioning loyalty that it seems perverse to ask what, if anything, he thinks the film has valuably demonstrated.

NEW YORK, 9/18/89, p. 71, David Denby

Moviegoers impatient at the slow pace of *Shirley Valentine* are advised to wait until Shirley (Pauline Collins), the bored lower-middle-class housewife from Liverpool, decamps from her stale kitchen and her sullen, unimaginative husband and makes her way to the far side of Mykonos, where she meets a sexy mustache played by Tom Conti. This sleepy-eyed Greek, a very fine mustache indeed, invites her to spend a day on his brother's boat, and reassuringly says something like "I no make fook with you. No. Boat is boat, and fook is fook." Dear God. And the scene in which he does make fook with her, not failing to kiss her stretch marks—the clever dog—is something to relish, too. *Shirley Valentine* is dedicated to the proposition that people should live as much as they can. No one, I imagine, will be actively opposed to this idea. The movie is pleasant and harmless and thoroughly mediocre. But see it if you relish outrageous seducers working their magic during long, long Ionian sunsets.

NEWSDAY, 8/30/89, Part II/p. 2, Terry Kelleher

Sometimes the main character inspires such affection and sympathy that we can overlook a movie's faults.

Frankly, there's a good deal to overlook in "Shirley Valentine." Its theatrical origins are all too apparent. Its insights are mostly old news.

But the performance of Pauline Collins rates a banner headline. Reprising her stage role as an unappreciated Liverpool housewife determined to break out and live, Collins is positively luminous. Last year in London, she won an Olivier Award. This year in New York, she took a Tony. Next year in Hollywood, her name should be on the list of Oscar nominees.

Playwright Willy Russell had some "opening up" to do in adapting his two-character, one-set "Educating Rita" for the screen, but the translation of "Shirley Valentine" presented more of a challenge. Russell's original play (now starring Ellen Burstyn at the Booth Theater) is a monologue by Shirley on her stultifying marriage and her liberating holiday in Greece. The other characters are described and quoted, but never seen.

In the movie, the word pictures are made flesh: the insensitive, befuddled husband (Bernard Hill), the ditzy, selfish daughter (Tracie Bennett), the la-dee-dah neighbor (Julia McKenzie), the "feminist" friend (Alison Steadman), the teacher's pet turned high-class hooker (Joanna Lumley). There's a supporting cast now, and a capable one.

Most important, we get to meet Costas, the Greek tavern owner who gives Shirley a taste of romance and a heady sense of her own possibilities. This role belongs to the estimable Tom Conti, who makes him both sly and ingenuous, both soulful and sheepish. And when we see Costas' home island of Mykonos—ah, the sunsets—we understand why Shirley is loath to leave.

"Shirley Valentine" would be an even better movie if it were more fully a movie. Russell and director Lewis Gilbert, who also did "Educating Rita," still have Shirley talking to the audience part of the time, and the device is at best a necessary burden. (The film opens with Collins addressing the camera at such length that viewers may fear she's leading up to a fund-raising pitch for the Will Rogers Institute.) Granted, some of Shirley's most revealing and affecting observations are confided directly to us, and it's understandable that Russell would want to build on the structure of his play rather than rework it from the ground up. But in a movie we'd rather *overhear* what the characters are saying. It's a tribute to Collins' acting that we appreciate Shirley's frustrations and longings even though we can't help wondering what planet she's been living on. Thank heaven she discovers that a 42-year-old mother of two is not too superannuated for sex and adventure—but where did she get such a foolish idea in the first place?

Such quibbles are cast aside when Shirley laments the "little life" she's led, or defends the honor of Greece against the slanders of boorish British tourists. By the end we're rather glad Pauline Collins has been looking us straight in the eye, because we admire the honesty in her gaze.

VILLAGE VOICE, 9/5/89, p. 75, Georgia Brown

One way of viewing marriage may be as the institutionalized collaboration of two people to perpetuate their own infantilizations. The difficulty of breaking this pact can be enormous. *Shirley Valentine*—written by Willy Russell, adapted from his comedy still perking along on Broadway— endeavors to speak (*chatter* might be a better word) of the woe that is in marriage, but blithely and in oneliners.

Russell's critique of a marriage at a certain stage—a couple in their forties, children "grown," being thrown back on their discontents and disillusionments—isn't profound, but as a shorthand sitcom portrait it's recognizable enough. Specifics pertain to a suburban English working-class couple, but the characters' general situation is universal, so that most people will squirm, and, initially anyway, be affectionately disposed toward Shirley Bradshaw, née Valentine, a plumpish, fresh-mouthed housewife (Tony-winner Pauline Collins) who babbles to the wall while guzzling jug wine and frying potatoes for husband Joe's Thursday steak and chips—except that Joe (Bernard Hill) isn't getting his customary red meat because Shirley has given it to a vegetarian neighbor's muesli-fed bloodhound. Apparently, she empathized with the dolorous hound's deprivation.

Russell's one-character play used only kitchen walls and Aegean rocks as Shirley's interlocutors, but the movie, thank heavens, has fleshed-out dialogue, fellow human presences, and numerous locations. Russell previously did the same sort of screen adaptation of his successful two-character *Educating Rita*. (Just reading about such plays is enough to keep me out of the theater for another 20 years.) This movie, like the previous one, is directed serviceably by Lewis Gilbert.

Vestiges of the old monologue form are still apparent, though. Shirley addresses the camera lens (insinuating that we're all conspirators) and coaxes laughs by winks, eye-rolls, and other mugging, and by serving up a slew of mock definitions and aphorisms—quotables widely quoted when the play arrived (and included in the film's press kit). "...Sex is like the supermarket...just a lot of pushin' and shovin' and you still come out with very little in the end." "Marriage is like the Middle East...There's no solution." While on the subject of terrorists, she moves to her husband's dependency: "If I go to the bathroom for five minutes, he thinks I've been hijacked." On the selfabsorption of a neighbor: "If you've got a headache, she's got a brain tumor."

Shirley mentions often the long-lost Shirley Valentine, today "just another name on the missing persons list." "The Girl Who Used To Be Me" is sung over the titles. We're shown the development of this remembered girl, not within the Valentine family (barely mentioned), but as the victim of a schoolgirl rivalry with a bright, blond thing named Marjorie. A sadistic schoolmarm creates a rebel out of Shirley, thwarting nascent academic ambitions, while sending Marjorie on to O levels. Women beware women.

Where does Shirley go with her rebellion? Into marriage and motherhood. When Shirley and Marjorie bump into each other, now in their early forties, it turns out that the chic Marjorie (Joanna Lumley) has become—not a don or a journalist, and not a stewardess on the Concorde (which Shirley inexplicably expects her to be)—but a "top-class hooker." Revelation: "I wanted to be like you." "*I* wanted to be like *you*." Now they exchange what Shirley calls "the sweetest kiss I've known in years."

Shirley and Joe, born before the generation that "discovered the clitoris," have not had much of a sex life. Joe, to his credit, was once a fun-loving fellow. (A scene with the newlyweds painting a room and ending up kissing while covering themselves with white paint is gruesome.) By now, however, Joe's reduced to fury when he has to eat later than six o'clock ("Picture the headlines," mocks Shirley, "JOE EATS LATE", or be served chips and egg on Thursday. No wonder Shirley is determined to accept an invitation from her mate Jane (Alison Steadman) to go off to Mykonos for a fortnight. From grease to Greece.

"I'm not a feminist like Jane," Shirley makes a point of informing us. Jane, who only became a feminist on the day she found her husband in bed with the milkman ("Honest to God! With the milkman!"), goes around proclaiming that "all men are potential rapists." She also refused milk in her tea. Wouldn't you know that Jane deserts Shirley even before the plane lands, having met a lecher at a villa while queueing for the loo?

But our "Shirley the Brave, Shirley the Marvelous" shows she's made of sterner stuff and can make it fine "on me own." Well, with a little assist from the local Zorba. Tom Conti (who makes a nice latter-day Alan Bates) sports a droopy mustache to play Costas, a benign creature who waits tables at a seaside taverna, strums guitar, dances of course, and takes single ladies for picnic cruises on his brother's trawler. Giving them what they came for. Gallantly, he makes a point of kissing their stretch marks.

It isn't that men can't write about the liberation of women; one of them wrote *A Doll's House*. But Russell's stance begins to look like pandering. SV's chirping banalities ("I haven't fallen in love, I've fallen in love with the idea of living," "We don't do what we want to do, we do what we have to do," "The only romance I've had is with myself") rattle on, and on, until I was looking for a tidal wave to engulf marvelous SV's brave little table by the sea. Collins's Liverpudlian accent and locutions begins by sounding sassy and authentic (she's like a stand-up comic), but they clatter into coyness (and become a bitch to get out of the head the night after). None of Russell's clichés or punch lines can obscure the fact that this housewife's *non servitum* takes the form of hiring out as a waitress.

Also reviewed in:
NEW YORK TIMES, 8/30/89, p. C15, Caryn James
NEW YORKER, 9/4/89, p. 90, Terrence Rafferty
VARIETY, 8/23–29/89, p. 29
WASHINGTON POST, 9/15/89, p. C1, Rita Kempley
WASHINGTON POST, 9/15/89, Weekend/p. 39, Desson Howe

SHOCKER

A Universal Pictures release of an Alive Films presentation. *Executive producer:* Shep Gordon and Wes Craven. *Producer:* Marianne Maddalena and Barin Kumar. *Director:* Wes Craven. *Screenplay:* Wes Craven. *Director of Photography:* Jacques Haitkin. *Editor:* Andy Blumenthal. *Music:* William Goldstein. *Music Editor:* Richard Shorr and Laura Pearlman. *Sound:* Robert Janiger. *Sound Editor:* Michael Redbourn and Richard Shorr. *Production Designer:* Cynthia Kay Charette. *Art Director:* Randy Moore. *Set Designer:* Keith Burns. *Set Decorator:* Naomi Shohan. *Set Dresser:* Mark C. Haskins. *Special Effects:* Bob Phillips. *Costumes:* Isis Mussenden. Make-up: Suzanne Parker Sanders. *Special Make-up:* Lance Anderson. *Stunt Coordinator:* Tony Cecere. *Running time:* 107 minutes. *MPAA Rating:* R.

CAST: Mitch Pileggi (Horace Pinker); John Tesh (TV Newscaster); Heather Langenkamp (Victim); Peter Berg (Jonathan Parker); Jessica Craven (Counterperson); Cami Cooper (Alison); Richard Brooks (Rhino); Sam Scarber (Cooper); Theodore Raimi (Pac Man); Keith Anthony Lubow-Bellamy (Football Player); Virginia Morris (Diane); Emily Samuel (Sally); Michael Murphy (Lt. Don Parker); Peter Tilden (Reporter); Bingham Ray (Bartender); Sue Ann Harris (Waitress); Eugene Chadbourne (Man in Bar); Jack Hoar (Sergeant); Stephen Held (Rookie); Richard J. Gasparian (Cop #1); Joyce Guy (Cop #2); Joseph Roy O'Flynn (Priest #2); Linda Kaye (Woman at Stairs); Vincent Guastaferro (Pastori); Janne K. Peters (Doctor); Bruce Wagner (Executioner); Marvin Elkins (Guard #1); Christopher Kriesa (Guard #2); Bobby Lee Swain (Priest #1); Michael Matthews (Evil Mouth); Ricardo Gutierrez (Guard Sergeant); Ernie Lively (Warden); John Mueller (Fireman); Jonathan Christian Craven (Jogger); Lindsay Parker (Little Girl); Deirdre Allyn Taylor (Young Mother); Kane Roberts (Road Worker); Stephen R. Hudis (Officer Robinson); Gary Michael Davies (Cameraman); Christopher Keyes (Bruno); Timothy Leary (TV Evangelist); Marji Martin (Woman Couch Potato); Ray Bickel (Man Couch Potato); Mark Slama (Kid with Crow Bar); Karl Vincent (Kid with Mask); Wes Craven (Man Neighbor); Holly Kaplan (Woman Neighbor).

FILMS IN REVIEW, 1–2/90, p. 43, Kevin Sweeney

Shocker, from the master of schlock, Wes Craven, is one of the most entertaining bad movies of the year. Coming after the serious and sophisticated (well, for him) *Serpent And The Rainbow*,

Craven is firmly back in the territory of his original *Nightmare On Elm Street*—resourceful teen heroes, high-tech special effects and a script that obeys no known laws of screenwriting, character or logic. It's a campy comic book thriller: junk food filmmaking with some style and a sense of humor.

The story has the feel of a scary bedtime story told by a particularly fiendish babysitter. A California town is terrorized by a mass murderer who wipes out whole families at a time. After colliding with a goalpost, cleancut Jonathan, a star college football player and apparent kick boxing expert, begins having nightmares about the murders. In his dreams he sees the killer, an evil TV repairman named Horace Pinker who, while more animated than Jason, doesn't have quite the pizzazz to make him another Freddy.

Even though Jonathan's scoffed at by his remarkably dense fop father (portrayed by Michael Murphy, a good actor who presumably collected a big paycheck for playing the film's token imbecilic adult), he leads police to Pinker's repair ship—"a hellhole full of evil instruments"— where the limping brute uses dozens of TV sets to practice witchcraft. Pinker manages to kill more people, including Berg's blond-babe girlfriend, before he's captured and sent to the electric chair. And that's where the nightmare just begins.

To attempt to summarize this lunacy any more would be pointless. Just know that highlights of the ensuing mayhem include: ex-drug guru Timothy Leary as a TV evangelist; a scene where the jocks on Jonathan's football team dress up in matching black-leather dusters to knock out the town's satellite dish; and a scene where Pinker possesses an angelic little girl, who proceeds to go psycho with a bulldozer.

Shocker doesn't have any purpose except to be dumb, fast paced and spectacular (though Craven can't resist getting in some infantile potshots at today's TV culture). The film's climax is a brilliantly edited montage sequence where Pinker chases the hero inside a television set and they run, *Zelig*-like, through footage of Hiroshima, KKK rallies, Beaver Cleaver and Boris Karloff as the Frankenstein monster.

The good natured preview audience of mostly young metalheads seemed to enjoy the movie— and its music, which included choice cuts from such titans of the sub-species as Iggy Pop and Megadeath, who pound out "No More Mr. Nice Guy" as Pinker is led to the chair.

"*Ragin*'!" cheered one youthful headbanger as Megadeath blasted on the soundtrack. Heahhh.

LOS ANGELES TIMES, 10/27/89, Calendar/p. 6, Michael Wilmington

Wes Craven's "Shocker" is a horror thriller about media technology infiltrated by a hellish maniac, an insane TV repairman named Horace Pinker (Mitch Pileggi), who converts himself into the phantom of the airwaves, leaping from TV to TV, program to program, body to body.

Pinker—like Craven's earlier villain, Freddy Krueger of the "Nightmare on Elm Street" series—is a monster you can't get away from. In his human incarnation, he uses his job to gain entry to houses—his repair van is emblazoned "We Do It in Your Home"—and slaughters whole families. After he's caught and electrocuted, two events that barely faze him, he becomes something worse: the devil that steals souls and rides in electrical currents, the monster that hides in your TV, the demon of the media.

Obviously this is a symbolic, satiric idea, and a good one. Craven is working over our paranoia of the media and especially TV: the way it manipulates us, takes over our lives, and the endless cornucopia of horrors—wars, crimes, disasters—that pour through its receivers. When we first see Pinker, he's a pair of disembodied hands working over some TV innards. The sets in his horror-gallery of a shop are always turned to riots, war or nuclear blasts. And when the movie's hero, quarterback Jonathan Parker (Peter Berg), fights him, he sometimes uses TV aerials, like a vampire hunter waving a cross. The movie sugggests that the devil controls television and it also hints, bemusedly, that the only way to fight this scourge is with dreams, purity, love—and a handy channel-changer.

Craven, like David Cronenberg or George Romero, is a real virtuoso of lower-case horror, and "Shocker" is crammed with dazzling bursts of macabre technique. There's that couch-potato's nightmare: the moment when a reclining chair suddenly comes alive, possessed with Pinker, and tries to strangle Jon as he watches TV, or the shots of hero and villain diving in and out of sets, or the "Vertigo"—style chase on the station tower. Eeriest of all is one dream sequence where Jonathan passes a TV with a still shot of gray, endless rain and enters a bathroom where one wall has become a shower curtain concealing grisly secrets.

However, it's in those dreams, strung through the entire movie, where "Shocker" goes wrong. Ever since he directed the first "Nightmare on Elm Street" in 1984, abandoning the sequels to others, Craven may be haunted by the fact that he made what many regard as the single scariest genre horror movie of the decade.

Since then, he keeps brewing up new bad dreams in different films, but he's never put them into as taut and compelling a structure as "Nightmare." "Shocker" is so diffusely organized it's almost three separate movies. The first: a fairly standard if stylish and over-gruesome slasher movie. The second: a dubious if hair-raisingly funny reprise of Jack Sholder's "The Hidden"—with Pinker taking over one body after another. The third, the best and most imaginative, mixes up multi-plane nightmares with a modern variation on Buster Keaton's man-into-movie farce "Sherlock Jr." It's in the midsection that the symbolism breaks up completely. Pinker becomes a different kind of monster: controller of bodies and no electronics.

As in most horror movies, the gore—suggested more than emphasized—and dark, raw jokes may drive away sensitive audiences. And the visuals tend to swallow up the actors, though Pileggi has moments of horrific hamminess, Timothy Leary pops up as a greedcrazed televangelist and the usually impeccable Michael Murphy gets a rare chance to roll his eyes and go berserk. But there's already a genre horror classic on TV paranoia, Cronenberg's "Videodrome," and "Shocker" (MPAA-rated R, for sex, language and violence) neither matches it nor Craven's own best. Maybe it's time he forgot about telling us his dreams, or simply took over the "Nightmare" series again, and let them run wild.

MONTHLY FILM BULLETIN, 5/90, p. 141, Kim Newman

A Mid-Western small town is being terrorised by an unknown mass murderer, who slaughters entire families, and Detective Lieutenant Don Parker is heading the investigation. His adopted son Jonathan has a dream in which he witnesses the slaying of his mother and siblings by a bald, limping TV repairman, Horace Pinker, and, when the murders are revealed to have taken place in reality, he is able to convince the lieutenant to arrest Pinker. The murderer kills several of the cops who come to his junkyard hide-out, and vindictively murders Jonathan's girlfriend Alison before he is finally apprehended. Sentenced to death, he conducts black magic ceremonies while awaiting execution and attacks the guards as he is being led to the electric chair. Jonathan and Don, in the audience, are upset when Pinker reveals that he is Jonathan's real father, and when the killer is executed, his spirit takes over that of a doctor in attendance. The latter causes a car crash, and Pinker slips into the body of a cop, using that identity to pursue Jonathan through a park, hopping from person to person now that he is free. Alison's ghost appears and explains to Jonathan that Pinker is able to live on in electrical impulses, and that he can only be defeated if he is tackled on his own plane. With the help of Don, Jonathan lures Pinker into a duel through a television world where he is able to exercise some control by using a channel-switching device. Finally, by trapping Pinker in a television set and cutting the town's power, Jonathan is able to dispel the monster, at least for the moment ...

Having lost creative control of the *Elm Street* series, which he inaugurated, and, more particularly, of psycho superstar/moneymaking franchise Freddy Krueger, Wes Craven is now attempting to kick-start a new splatter series to life and to introduce, in Horace Pinker, a new movie monster for the 90s. While it has some interesting ideas—a few of which have already featured in the coincidentally similar *The Horror Show*, produced by Craven's old partner Sean S. Cunningham—the baneful spectre of razor-fingered Freddy loiters in the background, a not-so-tactful reminder that this is very obviously patterned on the initial *Elm Street* movie. Again, there is a ghostly murderer haunting a small American town, and again the hero, helped by a fatherly cop, has to enter a dreamworld to face the supernaturally powered monster. There is even an in-joke cameo from Heather Langenkamp, heroine of the earlier film, as a barely glimpsed victim of Pinker's.

Perhaps conscious from the outset this time of sequels to come, Craven pays more attention to the origins and background of his monster, demonstrating Pinker's pre-death bad habits in an edgily staged suspense sequence in his TV wasteland hide-out, and in the horrid moment when he bites away the lip of the prison guard called upon to give him mouth-to-mouth resuscitation when he fakes a heart attack during the walk to the electric chair. The execution itself, scored to Alice Cooper's "No More Mr. Nice Guy", is a fine bit of melodrama—with some extra plot tie-ups as it is revealed that the traumatised hero was the one who gave the villain his trade-mark limp—and the subsequent body-hopping business is at least a new wrinkle, even if it is a variation on the monster from *The Hidden* (directed by Jack Sholder, who was responsible for the first *Elm Street* sequel).

However, Pinker still blatantly occupies the same section of the after-life as Freddy, and keeps popping up to make trouble. He can not only appear in dreams, but zip from place to place via TV signals (which Freddy did in the third *Elm Street*), possess innocent people and make bad jokes. Craven's self-plagiaristic script is all over the place—the last act, which features a Pythonesque trip through TV-land, is almost impossible to follow—but he can still stage individual suspense sequences with perfect flair. The body-swapping sequence in a sunny park, which has Pinker inhabiting a succession of stooges including an angelic little girl whose mother abuses the hero for fighting back even as the child is piloting a bulldozer after him, is a neatly orchestrated chase. But all the characters, especially the dumb-hunk hero and his dead but chatty girlfriend, are cardboard, and none of the connective tissue makes any sense. Asked to turn out "another *Nightmare on Elm Street*", Craven has sadly resorted to facile self-imitation rather than coming up with something as fiercely original as his biggest hit movie.

NEW YORK POST, 10/27/89, p. 23, V.A. Musetto

We're in for it now! Bad enough we have to put up with periodic visitations by Freddy Krueger. Now there's Horace Pinker, who, I'll wager, will be returning with the same frequency as old Freddy.

Pinker is the demonic, supernatural madman in "Shocker," the new movie written and directed by schlockmaster Wes Craven. As you most likely know, Craven is the gentleman who started Freddy on his blood-soaked ways with the first "A Nightmare on Elm Street" in 1984 (he has had little to do with the four sequels, but that hasn't meant much difference either way).

Pinker and Freddy have lots in common (besides being homicidal maniacs, that is). Both haunt people in their dreams, both speak with gravelly voices, and both like to treat their victims to a little bon mot before dispatching them ("Eat your heart out, sucker," is par for the course in this one).

But while Freddy is mostly content to slaughter a few teen-agers here and there, Pinker thinks big: He murders whole families (eight or nine by my count). Not to mention cops galore.

Among the victims are the wife and two foster children of the local police lieutenant. But another foster kid, college football hero Jonathan, survives. Luckily for him, he was in bed—fully clothed—with his All-American girlfriend at the time.

But what's this? Jonathan saw the murders in a dream and he knows where Pinker, complete with shaved head and limp leg, hangs out and is going to strike next. But how? Well, fans, it turns out that Pinker is Jonathan's real *dad*. Imagine that!

Anyway, despite the local cops' worst efforts, Pinker is captured. He even fries in the electric chair. But he doesn't die. For, it seems, he has the power to transport his spirit into other people's bodies (you can tell who they are because they drag their leg just like he does). Which, of course, allows him to go about his murderous ways once again.

"Shocker" has a bright moment now and then. The best is a little girl, her body commandeered by Pinker, dragging her leg as she scampers through a park. Pretty funny. And the finale finds Pinker and Jonathan trapped inside a TV set, in which they cross paths with the Beaver and his family and with an evangelist imploring his flock to send "more cash for Christ. More, more, more, more." Again, pretty funny.

On the whole, though, "Shocker" is second-rate, ugly, predictable exploitation, sadly lacking in logic or even in zippy special effects. Who needs it! But here's the worst news: Craven has set the stage for a sequel. No, make that sequels, Now that's scary.

NEWSDAY, 10/27/89, Part III/p. 5, Janice Berman

People who have seen many horror movies have offered this advice: Realize that the blood is just ketchup, they say, and concentrate on how all the victims meet their doom, and it will be interesting and scary and fun.

From their mouths to Wes Craven's ear.

Writer/director Craven, the father of Freddy Krueger ("A Nightmare on Elm Street") has created a mass murderer named Horace Pinker (Mitch Pileggi), who makes his rounds in a TV repair truck. Horace is a modern-day Frankenstein, drawing his energy not only from his victims' blood but from television.

How fortunate he is that we like to watch TV. When Horace is in prison, awaiting execution, he turns on the tube. It sends a shock wave out to him. "You got it, baby!" crows the box. With its energy he's able to reach out and bite—gruesomely, need one add—a couple of his guards, and then wreak truly unbelievable havoc after his visit to the electric chair, which to him is like a blood transfusion.

To be honest, "Shocker" begins quite promisingly. We see a clean-cut football star, Jonathan Parker (Peter Berg), who's drawn into this hunt for the murderer after his foster mother, brother and sister are killed. It's gory, but you can still admire the way Craven has built suspense. There are quick cuts and the camera wavers a bit; the net effect is sharply frightening.

There's even some art; the screens in the TV repair shop, with their identical shots of massed skulls, look like they might have been thought up by Nam June Paik. And there are suitable performances from Michael Murphy as Jonathan's foster father and Cami Cooper as his girlfriend.

Having taken in the audience, the picture loses its way and gets fuzzy and dull, with occasional detours into attempted humor, gore and irony. (Horace's injunction, "Eat—and die," however, doesn't seem to fit into any of those categories.) We're not just looking at a TV-induced monster, but at nuclear holocaust, Arthurian legend (oh, please), ghouls, and faucets that go drip in the night. People and specters jump head-first into televisions, TV cameras and lakes.

And John Tesh has a small role as a newscaster. Now *that's* scary.

VILLAGE VOICE, 11/7/89, p. 77, Elliott Stein

The splatter epics of Wes Craven have often contained folk and fairy-tale elements. With *Shocker*, he's gone a step further and concocted a cautionary fable in which the real villain is not so much the film's archfiend—a serial slasher TV repairman whose specialty is wiping out entire families in one swoop (the sign on his van reads: "We do it in your home")— but that old devil television.

Horace Pinker (Mitch Pileggi), a crazed hunk, practices black magic and animal sacrifice in his repair shop, surrounded by dozens of TV set eternally tuned in to images of the world's atrocities, on which he seems to feed. Eventually captured and sentenced to the electric chair, he makes one last request: not for a hearty meal, but for a TV set. He attaches the cables to his body, and in an extraordinary shot becomes infused with the "spirit" of television: then, when he's put on the hot seat and fried, although his body dies, this malevolent spirit becomes contagious and oozes around town polymorphously, infecting a cross section of the population of the Ohio burg where this madness takes place—cops, doctors, hard hats, benign young joggers, and little girls—turning them all into raving maniacs.

The fiend's nemesis turns out to be his very own long-lost son, Jonathan (Peter Berg), a college football jock. What is more, Jonathan's fiancée's ghost comes along for the ride. Murdered by Horace, Alison (Cami Cooper) returns as a demure wraith with a mission, a sort of vengeful Tinker Bell.

In résumé, this all may sound too silly for words, but Craven has constructed the escalating mayhem with such craft that disbelief is, if not suspended, at least given pause. The narrative is furiously driven along by bursts of heavy metal on the soundtrack and punctuated by scenes of wicked black humor. *Shocker* really comes into its own with the demented final chase sequence, a horror *Hellzapoppin* during which serial killer and son stalk each other, moving from film to video and back to film as they run in and out of, and actually become part of, a gaggle of TV programs—*Leave It to Beacer*, the 1931 *Frankenstein* with Karloff, and, best of all, *Cash for Christ*, which (inspired casting here) features Dr. Timothy Leary as a white-suited TV evangelist. Effects are often spectacular.

Craven's witty movie demolishes genre expectations and may therefore not go down too well with audiences looking for a Saturday night on the town with a ton of popcorn at a mindless slasher flick. Its highs are freaky and unpredictable enough, however, to endow it with some real potential as a rollicksome midnight cult movie.

Also reviewed in:
NATION 12/11/89, p. 728, Stuart Klawans
NEW YORK TIMES, 10/28/89, p. 16, Stephen Holden
VARIETY, 11/1/89, p. 34
WASHINGTON POST, 11/2/89, p. B15, Richard Harrington

SIDEWALK STORIES

An Island Pictures release. *Executive Producer:* Howard M. Brickner and Vicki Lebenbaum. *Producer:* Charles Lane. *Director:* Charles Lane. *Screenplay:* Charles Lane. *Director of Photography:* Bill Dill. *Editor:* Anne Stein and Charles Lane. *Music:* Marc Marder. *Sound:* Paul Cote. *Production Designer:* Lyn Pinezich. *Art Director:* Ina Mayhew. *Costumes:* Jane Tabachnick. *Make-up:* Lisa A. Johnson. *Running time:* 97 minutes. *MPAA Rating:* R.

CAST: Charles Lane (Artist); Nicole Alysia (Child); Sandye Wilson (Young Woman); Darnell Williams (Father); Trula Hoosier (Mother); Michael Baskin (Doorman); George Riddick (Street Partner); Tom Hoover (Portrait Artist); Luis Ramos and Frank John Trezza (Kidnappers); Olivia Sklar (Librarian); Michael Luciano (Detective Grasso); Ed Kershen (Detective Brooks); Joseph Verhaus (Cab Driver); Ian Klapper (Juggler); Herb Reynolds (Ventriloquist); Jomo Wilson (Magician); Jody O'Neil (Customer #1); Michael Baskin (Street Cop #1); Angel Cappellino (Bully's Mother); Paul James Levin (Bully); Robert Tuftee (Carriage Driver); Bill Sage and Edie Falco (Carriage Couple); Robin McWilliams (Breakdancer); Ellia English (Bag Lady); Edwin Anthony, Lewis Anthony Jordan, and Eric Payne (Penny Pitcher); Goma Sellman (Fine Woman); Gerald Lane (Shelter Director); Robert Clohessy, Franklin Gordon, and Bobby Howard (Alley Toughs); Henry Steen (3-card Monte Man); Chris Kapp (Homeless Mother); Elizabeth Lesser (Pregnant Park Mother); Deena Engle, Mary Anne Orbe, Nell Gutman, and Pier Robinson (Park Mothers); Jeffrey Carpentier (Homeless Native American); Bobby Johnson (Homeless Youth); Ben Schneeberg (Homeless Raver); Luis Garcia (Homeless Spanish Speaker); Michael Baskin, Tom Wallace, Jimmy Clohessy, and Raymond Jenkins (Precinct Cops); Jan Leder, Ronald Jackson, Marcel Smith, and Joe Solomon (Jazz Quartet).

LOS ANGELES TIMES, 11/9/89, Calendar/p. 1, Sheila Benson

The emergence of original, outstanding directing talent is always exciting. It's a hint that film may get a transfusion of lifeblood richer than the anemic reconstituted stuff trickling in from Movie of the Week directors or sleek MTV stylists.

Authentic talents make their mark from the first: Spike Lee was someone to watch after "Joe's Bed-Stuy Barbershop: We Cut Heads," as is Terence Davies after "Distant Voices, Still Lives." Jim Sheridan, of "My Left Foot," is clearly a writer-director of intelligence and bracing unsentimentality and Jane Campion—whose stunner, "Sweetie," will be here before long—has a pure, distinctive vision.

And now, with the magical "Sidewalk Stories," we can add Charles Lane, who has had the audacity to make a black-and-white silent movie and make it, in the face of today's shamelessly callous values, with a brimming heart and an activist's outraged passion.

Lane, the film's producer, writer, director, co-editor and central figure, plays a character Chaplin would recognize. Called only the Artist, he's a bashful, ingenious Greenwich Village street portraitist, scuffling to get by in the breath-defining New York winter.

The physically small Lane is part of a collection of street performers—tap-dancers, jugglers, three-card monte dealers—who seem to dwarf him, particularly his bullying rival (Tom Hoover) who might have migrated in from a basketball team. In true silent-movie fashion, the Artist isn't above a bit of sly retaliation, taking a blowtorch to his competitor's sketchpad.

But in the way Hoover towers over Lane, the city looms over them all, bleak, frightening and bitingly cold. That is the demarcation between "Sidewalk Stories," which cares intensely about its street people and their homeless neighbors, and Chaplin, who used little tramps and hobos as stylized, sentimental figures. There is no shortage of emotion here or sentiment either, but it's built on harsher bedrock.

Unexpectedly, the unfettered Lane finds himself in charge of an adorable 2-year-old (Nicole Alysia), wrested out of the care of both parents. He puts her up at his digs, the last remains of a demolished building that he has jerry-rigged to have lights, although it's without heat or a mattress. Lane's character isn't supposed to be able to resist the big-eyed, pony-tailed Alysia; it would be surprising if anyone *could.*

As he searches for the toddler's mother, Lane re-meets a warm, magically unattached baby-store owner (Sandye Wilson), whom, in a delicately charged scene, he has once sketched. She is also astonishingly compassionate for a New Yorker; watching him shoplift clothes for his little charge, she pretends not to see.

Lane is a master at fending for himself, but like someone seeing the city from wheelchair height for the first time, he suddenly begins to see his surroundings from a 2-year-old's precarious point of view. Pushing a stroller, he can no longer dart across red lights. Picking a bathroom door in a restaurant becomes a dicey choice. Just how fierce can he get with sandbox bullies—and their mink-coated mothers?

Lane relies entirely on mime and Marc Marder's buoyant, brilliantly scored music to carry his story points—he even scorns intertitles. Marder is a wonderful choice: He has themes here as memorable as some that Chaplin did for his "Limelight" score. And Bill Dill, the cinematographer, creates equal atmosphere and presence with his rich black-and-white camera work.

However, not all of his cast have Lane's delicate control of silent storytelling; the picture occasionally wobbles when its mimes are less expert or when the plot gets a little too far-fetched, as in its taxi-kidnap incident.

About its equally unlikely love story you may feel more tender, since Wilson is so glowingly readable and real. Nice to think that this cross-class attraction would hold, even when experience suggests otherwise. Lane even creates a dream love scene that might have popped out of "She's Gotta Have It," one that Chaplin's buttoned-up Tramp would never have allowed himself. (It's Lane's moment of quick nudity that gives the film its unfortunate R-rating.)

Wilson is pushed to shelter these two when Lane comes back to find his makeshift flat bulldozed and everything inside ruined. Now he doesn't even have the luxury of a stroller, and the reality of life with a child during the harsh winter is awful. They try missions, but those fill up on the worst nights. Lane's stated intention—that no one look at the homeless in quite the same way after his film—may be realized more acutely after this gentle fable than after more hard-edged portraits, simply because his characters are so tenderly drawn and his touch is, for the most part, so tactful and restrained.

All the more reason to feel that Lane has underestimated his power in his film's very last scenes, when he shifts techniques abruptly and allows his homeless to speak. It's clearly a mistake that comes from the heart and from inexperience, but he should have trusted the enormous bond he had created with us and kept his final eloquent plea within his own stylistic constraints.

It's a mistake, not a disaster. "Sidewalk Stories" is a bold and utterly enchanting creation, and its appearance is a signal to watch the multifaceted Lane closely. Whatever happens next cannot be commonplace.

NEW YORK POST, 11/3/89, p. 25, Jami Bernard

They cheered this black-&-white silent film at Cannes, and with good reason. Charles Lane's sweetly unique independent feature is timely, funny, thoughtful and enjoyable, and if he did rip off (or pay homage to) Charlie Chaplin's "The Kid," well, at least he picked something worthy. You don't get too many movies about the homeless done in Chaplinesque pantomime these days.

Lane, who produced, directed and wrote "Sidewalk Stories," also stars in it as The Artist, a sidewalk portrait sketch artist in the Village who bunks in an abandoned tenement, at least until it's torn down.

He takes on the care of an abandoned toddler (the adorable Nicole Alysia), his first responsible and compassionate act, and the two begin to bond, as Little Tramps and wide-eyed orphans must. If the idea of yuppies purchasing the child's scribbled drawings is cute, the nightly frustration of them finding a safe place to bed down is not. There is even one morning where The Artist awakens from his pile of newspapers and retrieves the child from a cardboard box on the sidewalk.

The Artist also begins a tentatively amorous relationship with a woman who runs a successful baby clothing store. It is through these two new relationships that The Artist's eyes are gradually opened to the enormity of his plight. So—goes the theory—are ours.

When people do speak at the end of the movie, the message is blunt—these sidewalk stories are sweet yet hardly whimsical. The bluntness, though, is surprisingly effective.

Issues of class and race (Lane and most of the characters are black; Lane is physically small and his nemeses are towering) are dealt with somewhat like the cinematography—in black & white. The rich wear furs. And when The Artist imagines a police lineup, he sees himself dwarfed by two big white men in suits, almost like a Robert Townsend skit.

Not all the physical humor is in the same vein. Wall Street's worker bees are shown fighting for a cab tooth and nail, but the more successful touches are the graceful way The Artist steals a look at the camera when an attractive, rich woman asks him to draw her portrait, or the brief shot of a street ventriloquist whose act goes unheard in this largely silent movie.

Lane is not the smoothest or most evocative physical comedian, but he has a workmanlike enthusiasm. Whether stuffing stolen baby clothes in his jacket with the hangers innocently sticking out or learning to perambulate the baby's stroller, he assiduously gets his point across. Never far from his mind is the Little Tramp of yore or his modern counterparts begging for change from every street corner of this city.

The crisp-looking, unornamented cinematography is by Bill Dill, with a gently pointed musical score by Marc Marder.

The social commentary of "Sidewalk Stories" couldn't be more timely and, considering the budget and production limitations, Lane has done a marvelous job on a subject where others, well-meaning but mired in sticky do-goodism, have failed.

NEWSDAY, 11/3/89, Part III/p. 3, Terry Kelleher

When the lights come up, one hesitates to discuss "Sidewalk Stories" for fear words will break the spell.

"Sidewalk Stories," you see, is a silent movie. Not a parody like Mel Brooks' "Silent Movie," but an honest attempt in living black-and-white to carry on the Charlie Chaplin tradition of a tramp bringing a touch of warmth to a cold world.

At first you won't quite believe what Charles Lane is doing in his debut feature. You'll be waiting for *somebody* to speak up. Then you'll be so wrapped up in the movie you won't notice the silence. Finally, when Lane returns you to the aural assault of real life in New York, you'll find your sense of hearing has grown markedly more acute.

Director-writer Lane plays a character he originated in his 1976 short "A Place in Time": a sketch artist who plies his trade on a Greenwich Village sidewalk and lives in an abandoned building. The artist's street is filled with pass-the-hat performers—juggler, ventriloquist, mime—and Lane begins his film at a stroller's pace, allowing us to sample the wares of each. In a foretaste of the Chaplinesque comedy to come, a very tall portraitist (Tom Hoover) sets up his easel within a few feet of our relatively diminutive hero and tries to gain a competitive edge through physical intimidation.

One frigid night, a gambling man (Darnell Williams) and his wife (Trula Hoosier) ask the artist to sketch their little girl (Nicole Alysia). Soon the couple quarrels and the husband goes off with the child. He ventures into an alley, where the artist sees him mugged and killed. The mother having disappeared, the artist suddenly finds there's a tot depending on him.

A number of funny moments follow—some simple and sweet, some sly and self-aware. It's easy to picture Chaplin's tramp of old teaching the little girl to wink or trying to keep her quiet in a library. But Lane's tramp of today has his own perspective on urban life. The artist considers approaching a beat cop for help in locating the child's mother, but thinks better of it when he imagines himself in a lineup of suspects—outfitted in prison-issue garb for easy identification.

Lane clearly respects the silent form, though he doesn't hold it sacrosanct. Outsized gestures and carefully mouthed phrases are occasionally amusing in themselves, and the artist looks into the camera a couple of times as if to say, "Hey, we're all in on this."

A tentative, touching romance develops between the homeless artist and the lovely owner of a children's clothing store (Sandye Wilson). Except for one cheap laugh when the woman clobbers her doorman for barring the artist's way, Lane has gentle fun with the two-different-worlds aspect of the relationship. After dinner at the woman's apartment, the artist takes a page from Jean Valjean's book and latches onto her candlesticks.

Wilson and Hoosier are especially expressive in their silence, and the 2-year-old Alysia is a bundle of natural charm. Lane eschews title cards, but Marc Marder's eclectic music score communicates where words might have failed.

"Sidewalk Stories" creates its own world and at the same time opens our eyes to the world as it exists. Even in the lighter, more fanciful scenes, the tragedy of homelessness is never far in the background. And when it comes to the forefront, we are moved.

For a movie that requires particular patience from the viewer, "Sidewalk Stories" plays a little long at 97 minutes. The bargain-basement budget is much in evidence. But Charles Lane's work is plainly something of value.

VILLAGE VOICE, 11/7/89, p. 67, J. Hoberman

Sidewalk Stories is both sweet and shameless, a movie as embarrassingly timely as it is audaciously unfashionable. There's almost no talking in this low-budget indie—a first feature written, produced, and directed by Charles Lane, who also stars. The mode is pantomime, with an occasional sound effect and an elaborate, low-key musical accompaniment. *Sidewalk Stories* leads with its chin; it's likely the purest homage to Charlie Chaplin since Gene Kelly directed Jackie Gleason in *Gigot*. But Lane, who is black, has more on his mind than bittersweet pathos. *Sidewalk Stories*, which opens here Friday, is a radical attempt to make Chaplin contemporary.

Taking the workday as its organizing principle, *Sidewalk Stories* immediately evokes *Modern Times* with a montage of alienated wage slaves streaming toward the factory, in this case the brokerage houses of Wall Street. Lane makes his point (overplaying a comic bit with two guys fighting for a cab) and moves on down the economic order to the homeless street performers of Sixth Avenue and West 4th Street. Here are the city's bit players—an inept juggler, an unheard ventriloquist, an eccentric dancer, and the filmmaker himself as an underemployed sidewalk portrait artist.

Small, buck-toothed, elaborately quizzical, Lane might be a refugee from an *Our Gang* comedy, but he fearlessly reinforces the Chaplin connection by picking a fight with an older, larger sidewalk artist who could well represent a resistant audience. There's an opaque, self-sufficient quality to Lane's conviction. (Like making an independent feature is crazy enough, so why not appropriate the world's most famous icon?) Part of the joke is that this innocuous little fellow has the effrontery to play Chaplin at all. The rest is that he's so matter-of-fact about it. Lane keeps his center of gravity low to the ground; there's nothing in the film that can knock him over. As much as Lane's pantomime, Marc Marder's functional, unobtrusive music carries a huge burden by pretending to ignore it.

Lane first created his character in a 1976 short, and his cannily understated performance allows *Sidewalk Stories* to make the obvious palatable: The Artist walking past a Soho realtor's office is irony enough. His fearful fantasy of himself sandwiched between two huge whites in a police lineup is sufficient to underscore the wider world's racism. What Lane's Artist lacks in inner life, he recoups in faux naïf wonder. When a sympathetic Young Woman (Sandye Wilson) invites him up to her apartment for dinner, he looks longingly at the bathtub, steps in fully clothed, and sprinkles cleansing powder on his shoes—it's a gag that grows more satisfyingly inexplicable the more one thinks about it. When the Young Woman invites him to spend the night, he walks over to the camera and peers at us in mock confusion.

No less than Chaplin's Tramp, Lane's Artist has a fastidious side—the abandoned tenement where he lives is a cozy lair—and, like the Tramp, too, he's a living reproach to the workaday world. But Lane allows him to simultaneously embody the reality principle; the movie *Sidewalk Stories* takes as its model is *The Kid*, which, first released in January 1921, was Chaplin's most ambitious to date—a deliberate mix of pathos, slapstick, and social commentary that signaled his intentions as a serious filmmaker. Like Chaplin's Tramp, Lane's Artist is compelled by circumstances to care for a small child—in this case a two-year-old girl whose father is (bloodlessly) murdered in a NoHo back alley.

Nicole Alysia, who plays the Child, is more a trouper than a ham, but she allows Lane to make the equation between art and childishness. The Child tries to imitate his wink, the Artist mimics her ballet dancing. Coming as it does in the midst of the *Three Men and a Baby Boom*, *Sidewalk Stories* is well-designed to showcase the humiliations of parenthood—Lane's initial difficulties managing a stroller (and the ridiculous virtuosity he shows once he's mastered it)—as well as the idiosyncrasies of two-year-old behavior (pathetic stretching for that which is out-of-reach, stubborn dragging of feet, unselfconscious nodding out in public). In one of the most resonant scenes, Lane takes the kid to a public sandbox, a natural paradise of bundled-up toddlers, populated in equal measure by middle-class mothers and grizzled vagrants.

Shot silent on the streets in evident cold (and something like two weeks), *Sidewalk Stories* has a throwaway pragmatism that again suggests Chaplin. Although Bill Dill's black-and-white cinematography is crisp, the compositions are static and head-on. The mise-en-scène is perfunctory. The film's look is minimal but not particularly rigorous; *Sidewalk Stories* doesn't have the deadpan classicism of *Stranger Than Paradise*. (One might stretch a point and call Jarmusch an indie Keaton to Lane's neo-Tramp.) Although Lane makes use of a number of scuzzy locations (several conveniently located around the corner from the *Voice*), the Lower Depths are signaled more than plumbed.

Sidewalk Stories is light on its feet—it skims over the maelstrom. Nevertheless, virtually every routine ends by posing the problem of where Artist and Child will sleep. After their tenement is demolished, they move to a Bowery mission. When the shelter is full, the pair search the subway; when the subway proves unpromising, they take to the street. The horror of this quest is a given.

(In one scene Lane wakes up, throws off his newspaper blanket, then pulls the Child out of a box.) Operating in the gap between innocence and experience, *Sidewalk Stories* derives a haunting pathos by merely suggesting the Child's view of her surroundings. The tinkly music-box melody heard as she and Lane perch, without expression, on a narrow mission bed underscores the unlikely cleanliness of the flop. This is, after all, a fantasy—a world where a harshly lit Burger King is an enchanted palace.

I can't deny that there were moments when I wondered if I were being suckered by some updated *Fantasticks* or new *King of Hearts*. Still, ours is a city where Broadway patrons trip over all manner of wretched refuse en route to extravaganzas like *The Three Penny Opera* and *Les Misérables*, which repackage the lumpen in period drag. Stylized as it is, Lane's film is hardly so schizoid. Indeed, his ending is as blunt in its way as that of *The Great Dictator*, albeit considerably more organic than Chaplin's direct address. When sync-sound finally asserts itself, it's as though someone really has stuck a grimy coffee container in your face. Ultimately, *Sidewalk Stories* is less endearing than it is simply disarming. (It might almost give sentimentality a good name.) The movie is like the kid—you want to protect it.

Also reviewed in:
NEW REPUBLIC, 12/18/89, p. 25, Stanley Kauffmann
NEW YORK TIMES, 11/3/89, p. C14, Janet Maslin
VARIETY, 10/4–10/89, p. 34
WASHINGTON POST, 11/22/89, p. D4, Hal Hinson

SIGNS OF LIFE

An Avenue Pictures release of an American Playhouse Theatrical Film production. *Executive Producer*: Cary Brokaw and Lindsay Law. *Producer*: Marcus Viscidi and Andrew Reichsman. *Director*: John David Coles. *Screenplay:* Mark Malone. *Director of Photography:* Elliot Davis. *Editor:* William Anderson and Angelo Corrao. *Music:* Howard Shore. *Sound:* Rick Waddell. *Production Designer*: Howard Cummings. *Art Director*: Beth Rubino. *Set Decorator*: Jeanette Scott. *Running Time:* 91 minutes. *MPAA Rating:* PG-13.

CAST: Beau Bridges (John Alder); Vincent Phillip D'Onofrio (Daryl Monahan); Arthur Kennedy (Owen Coughlin); Kevin O'Connor (Eddie Johnson); Will Patton (Mr. Coughlin Sr.); Kate Reid (Mrs. Wrangway); Michael Lewis (Joey Monahan); Kathy Bates (Mary Beth Alder); Georgia Engel (Betty); Mary Louise Parker (Charlotte).

LOS ANGELES TIMES, 5/5/89, Calendar/p. 12, Michael Wilmington

"Signs of Life," set in a small coastal Maine village, is deliberately shot with a jewel-like clarity that suggests the paintings of Andrew Wyeth: window curtains billowing in the morning breeze, hills and coastline icily distinct. Director John David Coles and cinematographer Elliot Davis turn the town into an objet d'art: precious, irreplaceable. But they also may want to suggest that sad clarity we get in the moments when something is irrevocably passing, leaving us forever.

The movie takes place on the last day of a local shipyard that has been defeated by modernity and fiberglass. The last boat is about to be launched; the boss (Arthur Kennedy) and his housekeeper (Kate Reid) muddle through the dust and detritus of decades; the foreman (Beau Bridges) awaits the birth of his fifth child while despondently mulling over chances of new employment; the two younger workers (Vincent Phillip D'Onofrio and Kevin J. O'Connor) are about to pull up stakes, to leave their loved ones—a retarded younger brother (Michael Lewis) and a girlfriend (Mary Louise Parker)—and head for Florida and an absurd dream of finding buried treasure.

Writer Mark Malone symbolically compresses the day's events, which include a birth, a marriage and (maybe) a death. And, while Kennedy's Owen Coughlin faces mortality, he is dogged by a beaming, spectral young man: the image of his long-dead father.

"Signs of Life" tries to portray a part of America most recent movies ignore: the old, the nonvictorious. But when Bridges' foreman robs a store, he is the dispossessed outlaw: The wind blows the bills off his chest, like the gold dust in "Treasure of Sierra Madre." And when D'Onofrio's Daryl and O'Connor's Eddie hit the road, they are enacting a goofball parody of thousands of highway quests from "Easy Rider" to "Rain Man."

"Signs of Life" sounds like a wonderful movie. But, instead, it's a wonderful idea. It has all the virtues we've come to expect of American Playhouse productions: artistic and social idealism, literacy, careful production, a sense of the landscape, fine acting—especially by Reid, Lewis and Arthur Kennedy, a great American actor too long absent from the screen. But Malone, like Chris Gerolmo in "Miles from Home," comes from a more affluent milieu than his characters. He may unconsciously condenscend to them—at best, turn them into vessels of poeticized guilt, at worst, into a passel of rustic nincompoops.

"Signs of Life" still has something precious to give us: those delicately etched, Wyethesque landscapes, the mood of melancholy community and generosity in the waning day, and Arthur Kennedy as Owen, raging, raging, against the dying of the light.

NEW YORK POST, 5/5/89, p. 31, David Edelstein

The American Playhouse drama "Signs of Life" is set in the coastal town of Easthasset, Maine, on the day when the boat yard of old Owen Coughlin (Arthur Kennedy) goes out of business. Nowadays folks buy Fiberglas boats—there's no call for the kind of thorough, old-fashioned craftsmanship that Coughlin's represents. It's the end of an era, and don't they know it.

The movie tells four interwoven stories. The wife (Kathy Bates) of John Alder (Beau Bridges) is about to give birth to their fifth child, and the loss of John's job will only exacerbate their poverty. Two workers, Daryl (Vincent Philip D'Onofrio) and Eddie (Kevin J. O'Connor) must break the news that they're leaving for diving jobs in Florida to Daryl's retarded brother Joey (Michael Lewis) and Eddie's feisty waitress-girlfriend Charlotte (Mary Louise Parker)—who has a mean right hook.

Coughlin, meanwhile, coping with the failure of his daddy's business, is haunted by a mysterious, black-hatted stranger (Will Patton) who bears an odd resemblance to...no, it couldn't be. Gulp. Could it?

"Signs of Life" is the sort of small, spirited, life-affirming movie that you know was a labor of love. I picture the writer, Mark Malone, dabbing tears from his eyes as he rescues his characters from the brink of disaster and despair. I picture the actors reading the script and saying, "This is a rare project."

The film is the first feature of John David Coles, who does tender, skillful work. An assistant editor on Francis Ford Coppola's "The Outsiders" and "Rumblefish," Coles has a good eye—he knows how to move the camera and he makes vivid use of foregrounds. Elliot Davis' photography has a foggy lyricism, but it never sentimentalizes the characters. The acting is consistently first-rate.

Yet "Signs of Life" is pretty wet. Malone and Coles spread themselves too thin—they want to tell everyone's story, and as they hop from one subplot to the next, they dissipate the movie's impact. They clearly don't mean it to play like a soap opera, but damned if it doesn't have that patched-together feel of "Days of Our Lives." Pretty soon you sense that each character—in the best TV-drama fashion—will come face to face with some painful illusion and then summon up the strength of carry on, and both the crises and happy endings are telegraphed.

Compassion is a tricky thing. Without it, a drama can curdle and shut an audience out. But too much can make a movie feel processed. In "Signs of Life," everything turns out all right because these are lovable little people who have each other, and what they can't do the friendly ghost can—the film settles down into the same fraudulent genre as "Field of Dreams," which blends the worst of "It's a Wonderful Life" with the worst of "The Natural" and "Close Encounters of the Third Kind."

This has more charm, however. Kennedy, back on screen after a decade, brings some brute force to what might have been a sticky role, and he's quite funny phoning up and cussing at all the customers who've abandoned him. In the soapiest segment, Bridges has big Dukakis eyebrows, so his blockishness, at least, carries extra poignance.

O'Connor who played the beat poet in "Peggy Sue Got Married" and a reporter in the great HBO "Tanner" series, has glassy eyes and a cranky, trembling delivery. He's not lachrymose, though—there's a hint of self-parody in his heaviness, and he's superbly matched with Parker, an ample dark-eyed beauty in a gusty debut.

In her scenes in the local diner, Parker has a lovely rapport with her fellow waitress, Betty, played by a middle-aged woman doing a pretty fair Georgia Engel impersonation. The credits reveal it's—zounds!—Georgia Engel.

NEWSDAY, 5/5/89, Part III/p. 3, Mike McGrady

On the day he must close down the family boatyard, ancient and cantankerous Owen Coughlin (Arthur Kennedy) decides to settle some old scores. Reaching for his Rolodex, he finds the cards layered with dust and the names all but faded away. Undaunted, Owen begins calling the townspeople who have done business with his family for generations, the local fishermen who have stopped ordering their boats from Coughlin's and have turned to the modern fiberglass models manufactured in California.

"*Fiberglass!*" Owen roars into the telephone. "To hell with fiberglass and to hell with you!"

Owen is a captain who refuses to go down with his sinking shipyard. In last-ditch efforts to save his family business, he pleads for orders from such unlikely subjects as a vegetating stroke victim and from the youthful ghost of his father, a spirit that pops in on him at odd moments, "That man that came in, that was my father. It's been him all the time, comin' back to size up his little boy."

Arthur Kennedy's Owen Coughlin is another memorable portrait from one of the screen's fine actors. Five times Kennedy has been nominated for a best-supporting Oscar; at the age of 75, he may finally get his due. From the first vision of Owen Coughlin—he is in bed battling nightmares—one is aware of age. The years have left scars and the mind is wandering: "There's someone that's following me around. ...I'm not even sure he's really there." But the age soon becomes unimportant; what is important is the integrity of the man, his ferocity, his unwillingness to go gentle into that good night.

The venerable Kennedy was lured from long retirement by the quality of the script from young Mark Malone. Indeed, it *is* a quality script—at times funny, at times poignant, at times sad. It also gives rise to the two most hilarious scenes of the year. One is a passionate love-making scene in a parked car, passionate right up until the very instant the young woman's heel punctures a window on the young man's gleaming 1969 Chevelle. The other scene involves fishermen in a riotous lying contest.

Although Owen takes the closing of the family boatyard as a personal affront, more lives are affected than just his. Two young laborers (Vincent Phillip D'Onofrio, Kevin J. O'Connor) are planning to drive to Florida and seek fortunes as deep-sea salvage divers. One laborer must first deposit his retarded brother (Michael Lewis) in an institution, and the other must dump his girlfriend (Mary Louise Parker).

The foreman (Beau Bridges), a lifelong boatbuilder whose wife is in the hospital giving birth to their fifth child, is perhaps the most seriously affected. When he goes, hat in hand, to plead for a clerking job in his brother-in-law's hardware store, your heart will break.

First-time director John David Coles and young screenwriter Mark Malone do a fine juggling act, keeping a dozen stories and moods in constant motion. Although the central situation, ordinary people facing up to changing times, may seem reminiscent of "The Last Picture Show," the Maine backdrop is fresh, as are the individuals who give "Signs of Life" its own identity.

Arthur Kennedy's performance resonates throughout the film, making one willing to overlook lesser flaws, flaws that include an occasional jarring inclusion of magic. "Signs of Life" needs no such trickery; Kennedy's presence is magic enough for any movie.

VILLAGE VOICE, 5/9/89, p. 68, Stuart Klawans

From one of the many states George Bush calls home comes *Signs of Life*, an engaging drama about the neighbors he doesn't know. Set in Maine during America's longest-running unacknowledged depression, it is the story of closing day at the Coughlin boat yard and of roughly a dozen characters who, having tied themselves to the company must now cut loose.

Owen Coughlin, played by Arthur Kennedy with all the crotchety-old-man shtick he can muster, has taken the closing so much to heart that he's begun to hallucinate. A mysterious stranger pops up everywhere, smiling ominously at him. Preoccupied by this figure of doom, Owen can fight in only the most quixotic ways against the ruin of his life's work. He drops in on an old friend to deliver an energetic sales talk, not bothering to note that the man has had a stroke and can't respond. Apparently, though, the stroke victim is his last potential customer. Having pitched him and failed, Owen is reduced to calling all the people in town who ever bought a California-made fiberglass boat, just to curse them. He stops only when his secretary, Mrs. Wrangway (Kate Reid), pulls the plug on his phone.

While Owen is thus engaged with his visions and tantrums, his workers are busily planning for the future, after their fashion. John (Beau Bridges), the yard's foreman, wants to move to Maryland, where he might find another boat-building job. But his wife, Mary Beth (Kathy Bates), has other ideas. She wants him to get work in a franchise hardware store; and, since she's about to deliver their fifth child, her position is fairly strong. From her hospital gurney she decrees, "We need more money, now."

John's young colleagues at the yard are closer to him than to Mary Beth in their level of practicality. Daryl (Vincent Phillip D'Onofrio) and Eddie (Kevin J. O'Connor) have decided to drive to Florida and become salvage divers. Eddie has even fixed his car's muffler in anticipation. Sitting behind the wheel, his eyes shining, he sputters knowingly about the joys of Daytona, until Daryl has to ask, "You ever been there?" "No," Eddie says, "but I read about it in books—uh, magazines."

Eddie's chief impediment to leaving town is his girlfriend, Charlotte (Mary Louise Parker), a waitress at the local diner whose first thought, when she needs to get his attention, is to land a solid right hook to his ear. She is a delectable young woman, though, and has other weapons with which to daze her already stultified boyfriend. Daryl's impediment is more severe. His brother Joey (Michael Lewis), who also works at the yard, is mentally retarded and will have to be put in a home if Daryl leaves. Daryl is too good-hearted to do this lightly, but too smart and ambitious to stay mired in town.

Add to these characters a family of cheerful Portuguese fishermen who have bought the last boat made at the Coughlin yard, and you have the main ingredients for his peculiar stew of a film. Not all the makings are fresh—the crusty old man has been around for a very long time, and the retarded boy seems to be a staple of the American Playhouse kitchens. Nor is the manner of preparation always that assured; humor and symbolism are both doled out with a fairly heavy hand. The pieces of the film seem to bob up at random—chowder is not the most structured of foods—but even so, you start to notice a little too much corn in the mixture. And yet, for all that, *Signs of Life* turns out to be a satisfying picture. It is particularly welcome in a season that has all but starved the serious moviegoer.

Credit begins with the unforced performances of Bridges, D'Onofrio, and O'Connor, who are lively and likable in three decidedly understated roles. Lewis, as the retarded brother, succeeds by playing his character as perfectly normal, except for his attachment to a battered transistor radio and his tendency to imitate whatever behavior he sees. The women's roles are less promising all around, but Bates in particular lives up to her good reputation, conveying Mary Beth's exasperation without once dropping into shrewishness.

The screenplay is the first solo effort by Mark Malone, who was coauthor of *Dead of Winter*, John David Coles makes his debut as a feature film director, having previously directed *Hellfire* for PBS. They both take chances and get away with most of them. It's not only that old Owen has his visions of death. Mary Beth is on the verge of giving birth but "keeps clamping down," as her doctor explains it. Joey, when threatened, puts on a life jacket and hides in an abandoned boat; later, he is literally set adrift. John, looking for a job that will be suitable to the Reagan-Bush era of entrepreneurship, learns he will have to put on a patriotic get-up, complete with three-cornered hat, in order to sell hardware. Later, in a field at night, John lies on his back, as if stunned, while $200 in small bills drifts off his chest into the Maine wind.

Whether you find these images memorably evocative or merely tendentious will be a matter of taste. My own tendency is to run like hell from any picture that comes with a ready-made caption; but, in this case, I thought the final effect of *Signs of Life* was complex and unexpectedly subtle. Here is a film with no fewer than five happy endings, none of which the characters would have foreseen as satisfactory, all of which are convincing. That's not a bad trick.

Also reviewed in:
NEW YORK TIMES, 5/5/89, p. C12, Vincent Canby
VARIETY, 4/19–25/89, p. 22
WASHINGTON POST, 5/12/89, p. D7, Hal Hinson
WASHINGTON POST, 5/12/89, Weekend/p. 39, Desson Howe

SINFUL LIFE, A

A New Line Cinema release of an I.R.S. World Media film. *Executive Producer*: Miles A. Copeland III and Paul Colichman. *Producer*: Daniel Raskov. *Director*: William Schreiner. *Screenplay (based on her play "Just Like the Pom-Pom Girls")*: Melanie Graham. *Director of Photography*: Jonathan West. *Editor*: Jeffrey Reiner. *Music*: Todd Hayen. *Production Designer:* Robert Zentis. *Costumes*: Sylvia Moss. *Running time*: 90 minutes. *MPAA Rating*: R.

CAST: Anita Morris (Claire Vin Blanc); Rick Overton (Janitor Joe); Dennis Christopher (Nathan Flowers); Blair Tefkin (Baby); Mark Rolston (Teresa Tremaine); Cynthia Szigeti (Mrs. Crow); Kirsten Price (Sweetie); David Labiosa (Rafael); Cynthia Songe (Rainbow Smiles); Shelly Desai (Bagdasarian); Rita Gomez (Mrs. Alvarez); Cheryl Francis Harrington (Woman with a Toothache).

LOS ANGELES TIMES, 3/29/89, Calendar/p. 4, Michael Wilmington

Dancer-actress Anita Morris, with her torrid red mane and outrageously voluptuous torso, comes close to being the human equivalent of Roger Rabbit's Jessica. She can turn herself into an incarnation of all-American pneumatic sex. But up to now, Morris, who is terrific in small doses, hasn't really adjusted her stage style to the movies.

In "A Sinful Life," Morris has exactly the right kind of role. She plays a sexy, soused, self-parodying dream-goddess of chintzy lust. The movie is a low-budget version of the recent L.A. Groundlings play "Just Like the Pom-Pom Girls," and Morris has the star role of Claire Vin Blanc, which playwright-scenarist-actress Melanie Graham played on stage. It's a ripe, fruity, delectable role and, in it, Morris' zaftig hamminess billows happily against the movie's other star turn: Blair Tefkin as the surreally arrested, time-warped Baby.

Tefkin's Baby is a weird, fiercely grinning, nasal-compulsive descendant of Lily Tomlin's snuffling tots and Fanny Brice's Baby Snooks. (The 20ish Tefkin's age is never rationalized.) And her mama, Morris' Claire, is the ultimate Hollywood poseur: a "retired" dancer-floozy-hooker living in blowzily cheerful squalor in the Franklin-Cahuenga area.

Drifting along in a semi-alcoholic slothful haze, lazily lapsing into casual affairs with the janitor (Rick Overton), seducing her sanctimonious, Bible-thumping neighbor (Dennis Christopher) to obtain her ideal of aesthetic furnishing—a peach-colored love seat—Claire Vin Blanc somehow incarnates part of the soul of '80s Hollywood. She's the rental queen of that partially gutted little dream ghetto, ringed with cherished landmarks, side streets crammed with drug dealers, prostitutes and wanna-bes.

The villains here are macho slobs, meddling bureaucrats, fatties and religious fanatics. The good guys are retired show-biz types, hookers, bizarrely overgrown children and wisecracking transvestites: eccentrics with style. It's a frivolous piece that plays like a bawdy, opportunistic sitcom. But director William Schreiner, who also staged the Groundlings version, knows where the laughs are. Mostly, he pushes the right buttons. Sometimes, as in one bout of cockroach lust, he pushes too hard.

"A Sinful Life" (MPAA-rated R, for sex and language) is basically sound stage-bound with occasional soft-focus outdoor excursions. It ignores what might have been a wonderful modern location: contemporary central Hollywood. A shame. This area is an untapped resource, a great sleazy, pungently human reservoir for which Claire Vin Blanc would have been a perfect off-centerpiece.

It's another case of life wasted in the movies, in a story, ironically, about how movie dreams can sinfully waste a life.

NEW YORK POST, 6/30/89, p. 27, David Edelstein

No one takes off much clothing (thankfully), but the camp comedy "A Sinful Life" has the production values of a hardcore porn flick—er, not that I'd know.

It's aggressively disreputable: The first-time director, William Schreiner, seems to have studied the camera placement in the early films of John Waters, and the script (by Melanie Graham, from a play) dishes up the scuzz de la scuzz for our delectation.

The slutty Southern heroine, aging former "Sonny and Cher Show" dancer and ex-sperm bank receptionist Claire Vin Blanc (Anita Morris), splashes rum on her underarms, stretches out on her furry bed in her flaming red boudoir and tells the dumb stud Janitor Joe (Rick Overton) to "sit right by me you big old angel baby" while the phonograph plays "Let's Make Love."

It's not enough to show roaches crawling all over them as they go at it; the camera settles on a couple of roaches going at it, too.

Sitting through "A Sinful Life" was hell, but reading back over my notes I've been laughing a good deal, remembering Morris' summer-stock-Tennessee-Williams languor and grown-up actress Blair Tefkin's piercing squeak as her daughter, Baby. (When she does the voice of her doll, it's several octaves higher—around the level at which dogs start to get weird.)

There might be a decent script under there somewhere. True, it has a transsexual neighbor who greets Janitor Joe with the line "Hello, sexy boy" and who boasts that people once said she looked "like a young Pam Dawber." It also has a hefty schoolteacher villain who wants to put Baby in a foster home and has a photo of former President Nixon over her desk.

Pretty obvious, and yet the darn thing has integrity. If "A Sinful Life" weren't so stagy, so visually moribund, so claustrophobic or so dated in its tongue-in-cheek tackiness, I could almost recommend it. On the cable porn station, however, it will be sublime.

NEWSDAY, 6/30/89, Part III/p. 5, Mike McGrady

"A Sinful Life" begins with a dentist's bloody suicide and goes downhill from there.

"Is Daddy never coming back?" the dead man's daughter asks tearfully.

"'Fraid not, sweetie," her mother says comfortingly. "Not a good way to start off your birthday, was it?"

Claire Vin Blanc, a former dancer on "The Sonny and Cher Show," is a woman trying to raise her little daughter, Baby, by herself. School authorities would prefer that Baby be reared in another environment. Quite likely because Baby is growing up in an absolute den of filth and depravity.

Full credit for the unsavoriness of the environment must go to mother Claire (Anita Morris), who begins and ends her days with tumblers of booze. Between bottle bouts, she takes janitors to bed, feeds her daughter the basic cold-frankfurter diet and reads her bedtime stories from the TV Guide listings. Her philosophy of child rearing: "So what if you don't dress in the fanciest of clothes. I got you cable."

The script for "A Sinful Life" was written by Melanie Graham from her Los Angeles stage play, "Just Like the Pom-Pom Girls," and directed by her stage director, William Schreiner. It is both technically lamentable and unutterably amateurish.

Anita Morris, as the promiscuous, hard-drinking mother, must share co-starring credit with her cleavage; costume designer Sylvia Moss has provided her with a dozen changes of costume but no changes of neckline. Her amatory conquests—all for the purposes of maintaining guardianship of her little girl—include unshaven, unwashed Janitor Joe (Rick Overton), Bible-spouting, born-again Nathan (Dennis Christopher) and a kindly, gay, transvestite neighbor (Mark Rolston).

Baby, played by Blair Tefkin, an adult who dresses like a very little girl and speaks in a squeaky thin voice, must be applauded for keeping the act going for the length of the movie, which happens to be interminable.

VILLAGE VOICE, 7/4/89, p. 81, Michael Musto

All over the place though its humor may be, *A Sinful Life* exists in a very thin space between aggressive camp and benign existentialism, John Waters, and a commercialized brand of theater of the absurd. As the film picks from its inspirations, it works best when it's not trying and tries hardest when it's not working. A play—Melanie Graham's *Just Like the Pom-Pom Girls*, which originated with L.A.'s Groundlings Comedy Troupe—held up to the camera's scrutiny, *Sinful's* insanities both grate and beguile on the larger scale only a movie can offer.

In the run-down Chateau Hollywood, Claire Vin Blanc (Anita Morris), a former dancer on *The Sonny and Cher Show*, lives with her seemingly brain-damaged daughter, Baby (Blair Tefkin). Baby's father could be any number of people—on her records, under "father's full name," it says "list available on request."

But Claire and Baby are happy without a man in the house, as they read *TV Guide* to each other, admire the pigeon that smashed into their window, and pack raw wienies for lunch. The plot, such as it is, involves Claire's attempt to marry and get a "peach-colored love sofa" in order to impress Baby's diesel-ish, clearly Divine-inspired teacher (Cynthia Szigeti), who wants to take Baby away. But the plot is just a hanger for scene after scene of ditz, whether it be Claire telling a handyman/potential hubby, "We'll discuss my drains tomorrow. I want you to snake my tub," or Baby serving the same character "rum cake surprise," which she made "with Mom's special candies" (prescription drugs). When their drag queen neighbor (Mark Rolston) reveals his true identity and launches into a possibly lesbian relationship, the film's achieved a lunacy all its own.

Like Paul Bartel's *Scenes From the Class Struggle in Beverly Hills, Sinful*'s humor is often more strained than well-done, but this one has more courage in its over-the-topness and would rather take a chance on being bad than settle. The cast is nothing if not willing. Morris is lustily, adorably game as the overripe sex kitten who's got "class up the butt." As Baby, Tefkin employs a gurgly voice replete with every speech defect known to man, and I guess you have to admire her for sticking to it throughout the entire film (except in bookend scenes in which she's an adult). The other actors—from Rolston, whose character is thrilled to hear he looks like a young Pam Dawber, to Dennis Christopher as a Bible-toting Sears credit supervisor—put up so little resistance to the script's wackiness they force you to do the same.

The film treads just shy of awfulness a lot of the time, but at least it's not the awfulness of the summer's mind-numbing big movies. It can be endearing.

Also reviewed in:
NEW YORK TIMES, 6/30/89, p. C12, Vincent Canby
VARIETY, 3/29–4/4/89, p. 16

SING

A Tri-Star Pictures release of a Craig Zadan production from Storyline Productions. *Executive Producer*: Wolfgang Glattes. *Producer*: Craig Zadan. *Director*: Richard Baskin. *Screenplay:* Dean Pitchford. *Director of Photography*: Peter Sova. *Editor*: Bud Smith, Jere Huggins, and Scott Smith. *Music*: Jay Gruska. *Choreographer*: Otis Sallid and John Carrafa. *Music Editor*: Tom Kramer and Bruce Nyznik. *Sound*: David Lee. *Sound Editor*: Mike Dobie and Craig Clark. *Production Designer*: Carol Spier. *Art Director*: James McAteer. *Set Decorator*: Michael Harris. *Set Dresser*: Robert James, Jaro Dick, Elena Kenney, and Tom Coulter. *Special Effects*: Neil Trifunovich. *Costumes*: John Hay. *Make-up*: Linda Gill. *Stunt Coordinator*: Ted Hanlan. *Running Time*: 98 minutes. *MPAA Rating*: PG-13.

CAST: Lorraine Bracco (Miss Lombardo); Peter Dobson (Dominic); Jessica Steen (Hannah); Louise Lasser (Rosie); George DiCenzo (Mr. Marowitz); Patti LaBelle (Mrs. DeVere); Susan Peretz (Mrs. Tucci); Laurnea Wilkerson (Zena); Rachel Sweet (Cecelia); Jank Azman (Mr. Frye); Jason Blicker (Ari); Cuba Gooding Jr. (Stan); Adam Kositsky (Nathan); Sam Moses (Murray Bloom); Ingrid Veninger (Naomi); Sabrina Boudout, Justine Campbell, Indrani DeSouza, Kiki Moritsugu, and Christine Donato (Cheap Chicks); Leonard Chow (Wilson); Craig Hempsted (Romeo); Lloyd Adams and Michael Lamont Lytle (Black Dudes); Randy Lutterman (Clarissa); Mario Marengo (Cyril); Marilyn Peppiatt (Mrs. Simonides); Corinne Promislow (Janine); Rino Romano (Blade); Phil Jarrett (Stanley); Alan Rosenberg (Greasy Guy); Stacie Scott (Senior Girl); Johanna Specktor (Junior Girl); Bunty Webb (Old Jewish Lady); Gino Marrocco (Mr. Abaldi); Mark Terene (Cab Driver); Reg Dreger (Guard); Elena Kudaba (Grandma); Peter Manierka (Grandpa); Murray Cruchley (Insurance Man); Les Carlson (Suit); Marica Diamond (Jewish Mother); Ellen Horst (Italian Mother); Krista Bridges (Pretty Girl); Lou Pitoscia (Lou the Janitor); Howard Jerome (Cop); Doug Bain (Mr. Tucci); Steve Susskind (Store Owner); Catherine Oppenheimer (Cujette).

LOS ANGELES TIMES, 3/31/89, Calendar/p. 11, Kevin Thomas

"Sing" is a slack and sentimental tale in which a community in a dying section of Brooklyn marshals its forces to stage its traditional end-of-semester high school musical competition one last time. In his directorial debut, composer Richard Baskin reveals none of the style that has marked his film scores and other musical ventures. However, what screenwriter-lyricist Dean Pitchford has provided him is little more than a half-baked, heavily ethnic update of Mickey Rooney and Judy Garland's old "Let's Put on a Show" routines.

Black leather-jacketed street punk Dominic Zametti (Peter Dobson) has been maneuvered into serving as choreographer for Brooklyn Central's final Sing by his canny teacher Miss Lombardo (Lorraine Bracco). She is guiding the project with the help of ace student Hannah Gottschalk (Jessica Steen) and fellow teacher Mrs. DeVere (Patti La Belle, who gets to sing only one song, contributing the film's liveliest moment). It's of little use that Dominic and Hannah acknowledge their feelings for each other in the film's final moments. "Sing" could have used that romance earlier, instead of such protracted skirmishing between them that when Dominic does his hot "Dirty Dancing" number his partner is, oddly enough, Miss Lombardo.

Tall and sexy, Dobson is luckier than the rest of the cast. His Dominic is thrust believably into conflict about following his older brother into a life of crime; he can only be surprised by the decency and commitment represented by Hannah and his teacher. On the other hand, Hannah's conflict with her woebegone widowed mother (Louise Lasser, intense in a thankless role), whom she can never please, is too sketchy; we never learn why the mother oppresses a daughter who is pretty, poised, mature, a good student and a hard worker at the family's seedy diner. Bracco is never able to make anything close to the kind of vivid impression she made as Tom Berenger's down-to-earth wife in "Someone to Watch Over Me."

The Sing is actually a Brooklyn tradition, started in 1947 by music teacher Belle Tillis; although now it's on the wane. Wouldn't you know that in "Sing" (rated PG-13 for language) the musical update on "Romeo and Juliet" staged by the sophomores, and the Atlantis fantasy of the competing seniors are elaborate, hard-edged show biz offerings that exude the glitz and razzmatazz of Broadway? With what these elaborate productions would realistically cost, Brooklyn Central could have stayed open at least another semester.

MONTHLY FILM BULLETIN, 7/89, p. 213, Adam Barker

Pupils at the high school in a run-down Brooklyn neighbourhood keep their spirits up through the annual "Sing" competition which provides a platform for local musical talent. The popular but slightly strait-laced Hannah is elected to organise the event, along with the delinquent and unwilling Dominic, who is talked into it by a plucky new teacher, Miss Lombardo (she suspects that it was Dominic who tried to mug her on her first night in Brooklyn). Dominic is contemptuous of the routines being prepared by Hannah, and insists on importing some dancing talent from the street, which results in a dishevelled line of wild-cat dancers whose provocative performance nevertheless impresses Hannah and Miss Lombardo. At Miss Lombardo's suggestion, Dominic reluctantly escorts Hannah to a local club to check on the latest dancing crazes. He immediately abandons her for a lithe beauty on the dance floor, until Hannah catches sight of her former boyfriend Mickey, which spurs her into begging Dominic to dance with her, and they end in a romantic clinch. The following evening, Dominic's elder brother Freddie takes him out on a robbery, and over Dominic's protests he holds up Hannah's family's diner. Spotted by one of his schoolfriends, Dominic is confronted next day by Hannah, and he storms off the show protesting his innocence. The Board of Education, meanwhile, announces that it is closing down the school and cancelling the Sing event. Dominic tries to apologise to Hannah, but she angrily tells him that her family now needs $4,000 to make up for the robbery. The school decides to go ahead with the Sing in secret, while Dominic takes $4,000 from Freddie and returns it anonymously to Hannah's mother. Later, Miss Lombardo tries to convince Dominic that he should return to help with the sing; Dominic is then given a severe beating by Freddie. As the Sing gets under way the following day, one of the leading dancers is accidentally knocked out. Dominic, who has arrived to make his peace with Hannah, is coerced into taking over despite his unjuries, and successfully takes the lead part in the finale. Hannah announces that the spirit of the Sing lives on despite the decision to close the school, and as she and Dominic embrace, the rest of the cast sing the school anthem.

Sing aspires to be a street-wise *Fame*, harnessing the energies of talented young singers and dancers in the cause of community rejuvenation. The relationship between Dominic and Hannah is a little parable about learning how the other half lives, and the staging of the Sing represents an attempt to reconcile a poverty-stricken community divided by its immigrant roots. Unfortunately, the atmosphere is not nearly tough enough to be convincing: no one mentions the major preoccupation of criminalised New York teenagers—crack—and the attempted mugging of Miss Lombardo is laughably half-hearted (gone are the days of the lone mugger, let alone one who is deterred by a slight nip on the hand). The notion that you can dance your way out of the ghetto has always been a suspect one, especially when the performances on display are not that impressive. Peter Dobson is adequate as Dominic, but he is hampered by the fact that Jessica Steen's Hannah has a non-dancing role, limiting their relationship to merely verbal sentimentality.

Flashes of intentional humour are in desperately short supply, although Hannah's first attempt at directing—consisting of a squeaky version of Madonna's "Like a Voirgin"—is genuinely funny. *Sing* itself is a disappointing directorial début from Richard Baskin, who composed the music for *Nashville* and *Welcome to L.A.*, although his recent background in music videos is more in evidence than any influence from Altman or Rudolph. In many ways, *Sing* is remarkably old-fashioned, from its tired heavy-metal soundtrack and out-dated break-dancing, to its underlying theme of communal unification. Recent youth musicals have followed a trend of increasing specialisation, both ethnic (*Salsa*) and historical (*Dirty Dancing*). *Sing* not only reverses this to return to an earlier format—the myth of the polyglot immigrant community uniting around ideals of popular entertainment—but also seems bizarrely out of tune with the work of other film-makers who now believe this myth has fragmented into a number of different "New York Stories".

NEWSDAY, 3/31/89, Part III/p. 3, Lynn Darling

"Sing" is the kind of movie meant to gladden the heart of Andy Hardy. There they are on the big screen, a swell bunch of kids and their neat teacher and they're gonna put on the best darn singing competition Brooklyn has ever seen, despite the mean ol' bureaucrats who want to close down their school forever.

So what if they're performing in a heartwarming song-and-dance movie in which the songs are boring, the dancing is dull and the heartwarming elements project the same warm glow reflected in cracked linoleum? Nothing's going to stop director Richard Baskin from wringing every cliche he can find from this uninspired piece of formulaic fluff.

Not that there's anything wrong with formulaic fluff—"Dirty Dancing" wasn't exactly a cinematic breakthrough, but it filled the predictable outlines of its plot with energy and verve, helped out by a couple of heatgenerating young actors playing the lead characters.

"Sing," on the other hand, seems determined to do anything it can to derail itself.

This version of the formula involves Miss Lombardo (Lorraine Bracco), a feisty young teacher from the neighborhood, Dominic (Peter Dobson), a hood with a heart of gold, and Hannah (Jessica Steen), whose mousy good-girl exterior hides an even mousier good-girl soul. Miss Lombardo wants to save Vinnie from a life of crime by making him co-captain, along with Hannah, of the senior class in the annual Sing competition—a Brooklyn high school tradition in which the junior and senior classes compete to see who can put on the best musical show. Hannah wants to prove to her mother (Louise Lasser, of all people) that she isn't an imcompetent failure, and Vinnie wants, well, whatever Vinnie wants. By the end of it he wants Hannah, which, of course, is the important thing.

All of which would be just fine if it provided an excuse for a lot of great singing and dancing, but it doesn't (except for the one number by Patti Labelle, who plays the junior-class adviser and makes you realize how airless this movie has been until then). Or if it provided a romantic duet between two particularly engaging characters, but it doesnt't do that either—Dobson and Steen generate all the charisma and charm of the multiplication tables.

What we get instead is empty sentiment—the characters talk a lot about what their school and their neighborhood mean to them, but you never see it, or get a sense of emotions based on even a loosely hinged reality.

Sincerity isn't exactly *de rigueur* in a movie like this, but "Sing" uses a lot of big words like "community" and "tradition." The movie tarts itself up in these ideas, but it's all show, about as credible as the bright, shiny set designs that turn Brooklyn into one big set for an endless rock video.

Andy Hardy would have known better.

TIME, 4/17/89, p. 83, Richard Corliss

[*Sing* was reviewed jointly with *Heathers*; see Corliss' review of that film.]

VILLAGE VOICE, 4/4/89, p. 56, Georgia Brown

Sing comes about as close to representing the spirit of the New York City high school institution "Sing" as *Crusoe* does the actual plight of a marooned man. In my maternal capacity, I have fresh knowledge of two actual Sing productions, both fresher and easily more exciting than the bland numbers we see at the end of the movie. Moreover, Sing's whole point happens to be that students, not teachers, conceive, write, direct, and choreograph—as well as perform—an annual musical show; yet *Sing*-the-movie gives top billing to a very hands-on-teacher/adviser, Miss Lombardo (Lorraine Bracco, Flatbush's Debra Winger), and two of its musical numbers to teachers. In hers,

Patti LaBelle seems to be "demonstrating" how songs ought to be sung. Bracco, who dances as if having a fit or trying to keep her footing on a slippery patch—flailing is the word I'm searching for—should not have been embarrassed this way.

The plot develops mostly outside of school in what is meant to be a disintegrating interracial, interfaith Brooklyn neighborhood. Dominic, an Italian hood (Peter Dobson), tries to mug Miss Lombardo, who then blackmails him into serving as senior Sing cohead with Hannah (Jessica Steen), the wholesome (Jewish? Irish?) daughter of the local luncheonette owner (Louise Lasser). Eventually, of course, the two kids fall for each other, and Dominic turns from petty crime to dancing and dating.

Formula movies such as the three F's—*Fame, Flashdance, Footloose*—are the obvious models for *Sing*, but director Richard Baskin and screenwriter Dean Pitchford (script and lyrics for *Footloose*) seem unable here to follow the dotted lines. In the spirit of Sing, Tri-Star should have offered the money to some vigorous high schoolers and seen what they could come up with.

Also reviewed in:
NEW YORK TIMES, 3/31/89, p. C15, Janet Maslin
VARIETY, 4/5-11/89, p. 20
WASHINGTON POST, 3/31/89, p. D1, Rita Kempley

SKIN DEEP

A Twentieth Century Fox release of a Morgan Creek Productions presentation of a BECO production. *Executive Producer:* Joe Roth and James G. Robinson. *Producer:* Tony Adams. *Director:* Blake Edwards. *Screenplay:* Blake Edwards. *Director of Photography:* Isidore Mankofsky. *Editor:* Robert Pergament. *Music:* Tom Bocci. *Music Editor:* John C. Hammell. *Sound:* Jerry Jost. *Sound Editor:* Milton C. Burrow. *Production Designer:* Rodger Maus. *Set Designer:* Bob Beall. *Set Decorator:* Marvin March. *Special Effects:* Danny Cangemi. *Costumes:* Nolan Miller. *Make-up:* Brad Wilder. *Stunt Coordinator:* Joe Dunne. *Running Time:* 102 minutes. *MPAA Rating:* R.

CAST: John Ritter (Zach); Vincent Gardenia (Barney); Alyson Reed (Alex); Joel Brooks (Jake); Julianne Phillips (Molly); Chelsea Field (Amy); Peter Donat (Sparky); Don Gordon (Curt); Nina Foch (Alex's Mother); Denise Crosby (Angie); Michael Kidd (Dr. Westford); Dee Dee Rescher (Bernice); Bryan Genesse (Rick); Bo Foxworth (Greg); Raye Hollit (Lonnie); Jean Marie McKee (Rebecca); Brenda Swanson (Emily); Heidi Paine (Tina); Diana Barton (Helena); Bobb Hopkins (Jonas); Robert Burleigh (Martin Dunn); Sol Vang Tanney (Hotel Concierge); Karen Haber (Leah); Judy Toll (Dixie); Sheryl Lee Ralph (Receptionist); Arsenio "Sonny" Trinidad (Danny); Toni Attell (Waitress); Ben Hartigan (Blind Man); Robert Arthur (Wedding Minister); Deryl Carroll (Funeral Minister); Robert Dowdell (Traffic Judge); Harlan Arnold (Divorce Judge); John McCann (Howard Simon); William Hubbard Knight (Adam White); Mark Goldstein (TV Director); Sati Jamal (Floor Director); Don Maxwell (Fire Chief); John Curran (Jasper); Scott Kraft (Lucas); Ed DeFusco (Policeman); Richard Domeier (Policeman); Steven Majewicz (Romeo); Diane Dickson (Juliet); Charles David Richards (Party Guest); Larry Coven (Party Guest).

LOS ANGELES TIMES, 3/3/89, Calendar/p. 6, Kevin Thomas

Blake Edwards' "Skin Deep" has a couple of the funniest moments Edwards ever devised; it has John Ritter's easy-to-take charm, but it ends up living up to its title far too closely.

Ritter's Zach has it all. He's a Pulitzer Prize-winning playwright, a novelist and screenwriter. He has a bright, attractive wife (crisply played by Alyson Reed), who's a TV newscaster, a profession that in the movies defines the successful contemporary woman. He lives the Southern California life style at its most sybaritic. You have the feeling that this is a man who hasn't stepped outisde Beverly Hills, Brentwood and Malibu for year, except possibly to escape to other equally luxe locales; by the end of the film you're left feeling that this may be true of Edwards as well.

The film opens with a hilarious double whammy that starts Zach spinning out of control even before the laughter starts fading. From then on it's a downhill slide for Zach. Already plagued by writer's block, he gives in to compulsive womanizing, followed by incipient alcoholism and eventual impotence.

"Skin Deep" is a film of moments, some of which are terrific, others considerably less so. The glamour girls, with their great sheafs of shining hair, are interchangeable, but there are nice turns by Vincent Gardenia as Zach's barkeep pal and by Nina Foch as his chic mother-in-law, perhaps the only woman in the world who has never been charmed by him. There's real sweetness and humor in Raye Hollit's body builder, and once again Edwards proves himself one of the few American film makers able, or willing, to present a gay couple (in this instance played distinctively by Peter Donat and Don Gordon) without a fuss.

As adept as Edwards is at using humor to set off Zach's self-destructiveness, to capture the dark undertow of high living, he ends up letting Zach off the hook shamelessly. It's as if Edwards said to himself: "The poor guy has suffered long enough, and, besides, we're running out of time."

Never has a happy ending been so thoroughly unearned. For all his charm, honesty and intelligence—you have no trouble understanding his appeal to wide variety of women—Zach does nothing to help himself as he gives in to epic self-indulgence. Then in his turnaround, we're given the impression that stopping drinking and turning out a best seller are snaps for Zach. (That his wife would even consider taking him back after his progressively outrageous behavior is also confounding.)

In short, "Skin Deep" is a male sex fantasy that says that if you're sufficiently rich, famous and goodlooking, you can go into the most self-destrictive of tailspins and still land on your feet without any real effort.

It's chilling to imagine "Skin Deep" (rated R for sex and language, adult situations) without Ritter, who through sheer dint of his own likability, never quite loses our sympathy for Zach. (This admittedly may not be true for some women in the audience; NOW is unlikely to choose the film for a benefit premiere.) Ritter and Edwards clearly have a strong rapport and plan to work together again. Perhaps the next time will rate a "10".

MONTHLY FILM BULLETIN, 7/89, p. 214, Kim Newman

Pulitzer Prize-winning author Zach Hutton, an inveterate philanderer with writer's block and a drink problem, is discovered by his mistress Angie in an intimate embrace with her hairdresser. Angie is about to shoot Zach when they are both discovered by Alex, Zach's wife. Angie spares Zach, but Alex divorces him. Zach tells his psychiatrist, Dr. Westford, that he knows he must change his ways, but that he is unable to stop chasing women. He lives for six months with Molly, but she leaves him after burning down his house. In between complaining about his problems to Barney, a bartender, and Jake, his lawyer, Zach picks up body-builder Lonnie. He tries to make it up with Alex but she refuses to see him and when he barges in on a dinner party she and her mother are having with Greg, Alex's son by a previous marriage, and Greg's girlfriend Rebecca, who admires Zach's work, the evening proves embarrassing. When Sparky, Zach's agent, commits suicide rather than face a terminal illness, Zach is traumatised because he never made up after an argument with his friend. Forced by the fire into living in a hotel, Zach makes a play for Amy, the girlfriend of unpredictable rock star Rick, and lands in jail after a fight. Pursuing model Emily, Zach winds up undergoing electro-shock rejuvenation therapy with a vindictive Molly, and still reeling from the effects, he causes a car crash. Tipped off by Jake to a party at which Emily will be a guest, Zach arrives dressed as Aladdin under the misapprehension that it's a costume party and drunkenly fails to impress the girl. Tracking down Alex, Zach interrupts her wedding and halts the ceremony. Having touched bottom, he gives up drinking and writes *Change*, a best-seller. At the launch party, he resists Rebecca's advances and is reunited with Alex. It is becoming increasingly difficult to distinguish Blake Edwards' "personal" projects (*"10"*, *The Man Who Loved Women*, *S.O.B.*, *"That's Life!"*) from his simple light comedies (the Pink Panther series, *Sunset*, *Blind Date*, *A Fine Mess*) in that both have, of late, deteriorated to such an alarming extent that the director-writer's continued productivity is not only mystifying but infuriating. Here, as in *"10"* and *The Man Who Loved Women* (and, in happier times, *Days of Wine and Roses*), Edwards focuses on a protagonist in early middle age whose artistic talents (which we have to take on trust) are being eaten into by compulsive womanising and/or excessive alcohol intake. Quite what the shallow Zach, whose world seems bounded by banal bar-room chat and elementary psychiatry (Dr. Westford trots out the scorpion and the frog anecodote from *Mr. Arkadin* to illustrate his patient's problem), is supposed to have written about is never clear, and we see absolutely nothing in his character to suggest any Pulitzer Prize-winning Right Stuff. Indeed, even his drinking and screwing around is so conventional and unilluminating that it is hard to conceive of him putting them to any artistic use, just as Edwards' undeniable personal obsessions are winding up as bland, uniform, nothing-in-particular films like this.

That Zach Hutton is no less a projection of the director than the William Holden and Jack

Lemmon characters of *S.O.B.* and *"That's Life!"* (who are more in Edwards' age range) is made evident by his espousal of attitudes which are far more in keeping with the sixty-seven-year-old director than the forty-two-year-old character. Zach expresses a preference for tinkling out a Cole Porter tune on the piano over the kind of rock music played by Rick, and rails against the modern world as much as any earlier Edwards protagonist, enabling the film to take passing potshots at such passé modernisms as trendy health programmes, aerobics, heavy metal, traffic and lap dogs. Slightly more subtly wrong is the one lapse in the hero's consistent philandering: throughout the film at least until his momentously significant failure to respond to Rebecca, Zach ogles and makes a pass at every pretty woman he encounters, except one, the attractive *black* receptionist at Molly's health clinic. Aside from one jokey and smug reference to AIDS, the film ignores modern sexual mores and assumes that Zach's promiscuity is of vital interest only to himself and to Alex, his preordained soul mate. Angie and Molly may take revenge on him for his fecklessness, but most of his cast-off women remain adoringly indulgent of him.

The old sense of comic timing that used to spark Edwards' work occasionally returns here, as in the perfect and concise depiction of the end of Zach's relationship with Molly in the cut from her setting fire to the piano at which he is playing to their house in flames, or the revelatory moment when Zach's final realisation of how he must change his life coincides with a tidal wave that throws him against a beach house. The wave gag, however, is repeated within moments, and falls flat the second time around, and the other comic highlights—a duel in a darkened room between two men wearing luminous condoms, Zach causing Clouseauesque chaos after the electro-shock treatment, the hackneyed business about the fancy-dressed drunk at a formal ball— are so laboriously set up that they dwindle instead of build and wind up as dead spots in an already dull movie. Aside from Alex's monstrous mother (Nina Foch in the film's sole fine performance), the entire cast—including the put-upon and abused Jake and Barney—unreasonably insist on supporting, nurturing and admiring Zach. What is worse, we are clearly expected to share their attitudes, even though the smugly reformed best-selling author we see in the final scene hardly seems worth distinguishing from the drunken womaniser of the rest of the film.

NEW STATESMAN & SOCIETY, 7/14/89, p. 49, Suzanne Moore

[*Skin Deep* was reviewed jointly with *Farewell to the King*; see Moore's review of that film.]

NEW YORK POST, 3/3/89, p. 28, Jami Bernard

There's a shaggy-dog joke about a guy who keeps getting flooded and burned and termited out of successively expensive houses. He finally turns to the heavens and asks, "Why me?" And God replies, "I don't know... *it's just something about you.*"

It's easy to feel that way about Blake Edwards movies. He must have an audience for them, because he keeps making them—this is his 36th as a director—and certainly other middle-aged men having life crises can relate to things like "S.O.B.," "That's Life" and "10." But that Blake Edwards... *there's just something about him.*

Maybe it's because he's not very funny. The only real laugh in "Skin Deep" comes from a sight gag involving a glow-in-the-dark condom. The audience at a recent screening also went for the scene where our hero, such as he is, goes stumbling into the street after an ex-lover gives him quite a shock (more about that later).

"Skin Deep" stars John Ritter as Zach, a guy whose twin addictions to alcohol and beautiful, brainless women destroys his marriage in the first scene. There he is, caught in bed with one mistress by a second mistress; then his wife, Alex (Alyson Reed), walks in and tosses them all out. Blake seems to find this hilarious. I wonder how his wife, Julie Andrews, is taking it.

Although he still loves Alex, Zach goes off on a booze-and-broads binge that is progressively pathetic and simply an opportunity for Vincent Gardenia to play a wise bartender-shrink, and an even more ample opportunity to undress a few lissome ladies for the camera.

Julianne Phillips, who made this during her much-publicized troubles with Bruce Springsteen, probably saved a lot of money on therapy by playing one of the traduced lovers. She stomps around cathartically, sets fire to Zach's grand piano while he's playing it and eventually gives Zach an electrifying herbal wrap that throws him into convulsions. This, with the laser-condom scene, got the biggest laughs. The funny part really is watching Phillips hook him up with revenge in her eyes, but the audience, naturally, went for the twitching.

Zach, incidentally, is a Pulitzer Prize-winning playwright who has writer's block. Even his fantasies about making love to "little-boy girls" (time for psychoanalysis) can't unblock him. When Alex threw him out, she did irreparable harm—she also threw out his typewriter.

Before you know it, Zach not only can't write, he can't hold his own during sex (I think it's the brassy bodybuilder who cures him, or maybe it's the rock star groupie). Yes folks, the laffs are coming fast and furious.

There is an assortment of other characters—lawyer, agent, analyst—who are also concerned with Zach's creative and emotional descent. "I'm doomed?" Zach asks Alex. "You're Zach," she replies with a shrug. The leopard can't change his spots. "I'm so miserable, I could shoot myself... but I can't because I'm afraid to die," says Zach at another point.

Ritter, looking suspiciously like Robin Williams with beard and moustache, makes Zach a rather depressing lout. When he is not sloshing around at the bar, he is lying to women. Why they fall for him is a mystery. Each new one in his life is introduced as if she will save Zach from his excesses through her sheer beauty—but beauty is only skin deep, and so is each new character. Just when we're thinking we could get attached to pouty Julianne Phillips, the bodybuilder comes along.

Well, one thing stayed with me from "Skin Deep"—the writer's block. There's just something about Blake Edwards that does that.

NEWSDAY, 3/3/89, Part III/p. 7, Mike McGrady

Zach's tragic problem is clear from the opening segment of Blake Edwards' "Skin Deep." We find Zach (John Ritter) in his natural habitat, bed. He is enjoying the sexual favors provided by his wife's hairdresser when his wife shows up and places a loaded revolver against his temple.

"I don't know what to say," says he.

"How about, 'The Lord is my Shepherd,' " suggests she.

About this time, Zach's mistress also appears, sizes up the situation and urges the wife to complete the task at hand. From this point on, the extraordinarily well-named "Skin Deep" is a series of comic skits chronicling Ritter's attempts to cure himself of various addictions and to win back his wife.

"I'm a compulsive womanizer," Zach says to his psychiatrist. "Can't I be cured?"

"Do you *want* to be cured?"

Tough question. No doubt, womanizing is immoral, piggish and time-consuming—but few ardent practitioners care to consider the alternative. The main problem with Zach's womanizing is it doesn't leave him enough energy or time to maintain either his marriage or his career as a best-selling author.

"Skin Deep" challenges credibility by having TV actor Ritter, cute but less than overwhelming, work his way through an awesome lineup of beauties, including one hilarious mismatch with a female weight lifter who would make Schwarzenegger seem an inadequate partner.

Does all this seem a bit like that earlier Blake Edwards movie, "10"? Indeed it does. Ritter, precisely like Dudley Moore in the earlier film, womanizes, doodles about on pianos, sings shakily, drinks far too much, wrecks expensive cars when a beauty walks by, suffers a temporary attack of impotence, achieves his most significant conquest to the strains of classical music and has considerable trouble dealing with a sober and responsible mate. However, if I were to compare the two films on a level of entertainment or artistic achievement, I think this film would be entitled to, oh, "5" or maybe "6".

Much of the film falls flat, except flat is a sadly inadequate adjective for a film that takes such unbridled joy in the unbridled female figure. While Edwards certainly opens himself up to the charge of male chauvinism, I believe much of the film harks back to old-fashioned vaudeville. There are funny lines and funny moments along with a philosophizing bartender (Vincent Gardenia) who analyzes Zach's problem ("You're scared, just like the rest of us") and a shrink who finally locates a cure: "If an alcoholic wants me to cure him, you know what I say? First, stop drinking."

Blake Edwards, the mastermind behind the "Pink Panther" series, has never been a slouch with visual humor, and some of his gags are hilarious. Several scenes feature condoms "treated with an ancient Chinese herb" that enhances performance and glows in the dark. I will let more skilled wordsmiths describe the results; let me simply assure you at this juncture the film's "R" rating is richly merited.

NEWSWEEK, 3/13/89, p. 69, Jack Kroll

Blake Edwards has gone beyond black comedy; there are secondary hues now like bruise blue and even gangrene purple. The master of philander farce has no illusions. In Skin Deep, a kind of belated sequel to "10," John Ritter as Zach, a Hollywood writer, states his position with stark clarity: 'I want a loving, faithful, caretaking wife and I want to make love to everyone else. I want it all.'' Zach has such a wife, Alex (Alyson Reed), who discovers that "everyone else" is just the slightest exaggeration. After she gives Zach the bum's rush he ricochets frenetically from woman to woman: Molly (Julianne Phillips), who tries to reform Zach by first burning down his house and later giving him her special high-voltage herbal wrap; Lonnie (Raye Hollit), a steel-thewed body builder who, as Zach puts it, "makes me feel like Mrs. Arnold Schwarzenegger," and many others.

Edwards's variations on the theme of compulsive infidelity will be seen by many as cynical and chauvinistic beyond redemption, despite Zach's token reformation. "Skin Deep" is no classic, but it draws healthy laughter with its irreverent deviltry on some heavy matters. Just as he had fun with American anxiety about homosexuality in "Victor/Victoria," Edwards dares to make comedy out of heterosexual safe sex in a scene involving a fluorescent condom (two of them, actually). Outrageous? Must be—all three major TV networks refused to accept the scene in a commercial for the film. In his 36th movie in 34 years, Blake Edwards is still laughing at our hang-ups.

VILLAGE VOICE, 3/14/89, p. 64, Stuart Klawans

Like zombies on a blind date, the brain-dead hulks of two departed Blake Edwards pictures meet in *Skin Deep*, producing through their joyless coupling a would-be inspirational comedy.

First among the undead is *"10,"* which returns from the grave complete with middle-aged skirt-chaser, lovely and mature wife, wise bartender, and shrink. The skirt-chaser's profession has been altered from musician to writer, but this change seems nominal, since he repeatedly proves the depth of his soul by playing cocktail arrangements of Cole Porter tunes. It's unmistakable—this character is really Dudley Moore. And yet, through some horrible alchemy of the grave, he has been given the body and voice of John Ritter, whose lack of charm perfectly matches the ghoul-eaten role.

In fact, the role is twice-chewed, also bearing the toothmarks of Jack Lemmon in *The Days of Wine and Roses*. The writer, it seems, has a drinking problem. He even gets the DTs, though this being a comedy of sorts, we see only the aftermath of the fit, when Vincent Gardenia, as the wise bartender, comes by to shoot vitamin B-12 into Ritter's ass.

One of the film's uplifting messages is that men should prefer smart women to frivolous ones. Yet Edwards doesn't throw much Nobel Prize material across Ritter's path. The average woman in *Skin Deep* has never held a real job, chooses her lovers at random, and has a notable streak of vindictiveness. The exception, of course, is the lovely and mature wife (Alyson Reed)—she reads the news for a local TV station.

Since this is an Edwards film, two of three sequences do work. I laughed at them, yes; but I felt ashamed for having done so. Edwards uses the fear of AIDS among heterosexuals as a set-up for his comedic high point; yet *Skin Deep*'s lone homosexual comes down not with AIDS but with cancer. I hadn't expected such delicacy in the choice of disease—especially in a film that sends Ritter to bed with Raye Hollit, a bodybuilder who looks like Arnold Schwarzenegger with tits. There was a time when Edwards might have made something out of that gender-switch. Here, though, the actress is reduced to a sight-gag. Too bad for Hollit, whose performance is a lot more ingratiating than Ritter's. Maybe next time she'll get lucky and be cast opposite Danny DeVito.

Also reviewed in:
NEW YORK TIMES, 3/3/89, p. C10, Vincent Canby
VARIETY, 3/8–14/89, p. 21
WASHINGTON POST, 3/3/89, p. D7, Hal Hinson

SLAVES OF NEW YORK

A Tri-Star Pictures release. *Producer:* Ismail Merchant and Gary Hendler. *Director:* James Ivory. *Screenplay (based on her own stories):* Tama Janowitz. *Director of Photography:* Tony Pierce-Roberts. *Editor:* Katherine Wenning. *Music:* Richard Robbins. *Sound:* Tom Nelson and (music) Scott Lehrer and Frank Ferrucci. *Sound*

Editor: Dan Sable. *Production Designer:* David Gropman *Art Director:* Karen Schultz. *Set Decorator:* Carol Nast. *Set Dresser:* Victor Zolfo. *Special Effects:* Steve Kirshoff, J.C. Brotherhood, and Matt Vogel. *Costumes:* Carol Ramsey. *Make-up:* Marilyn Carbone. *Stunt Coordinator:* Phil Neilson. *Running time:* 125minutes. MPAA Rating: R.

CAST: Bernadette Peters (Eleanor); Jonas Abry (Mickey); Stephen Bastone (Chauffeur); Denise-Marie Beaumont (Ballerina); Mark Boone Jr. (Mitch); Diane Brill (Jogger); Steve Buscemi (Wilfredo); Michael Butler (Performance Artist); Richy Canatta (Saxophonist); Johann Carlo (Performance Artist); Betty Comden (Mrs. Wheeler); Nick Corri (Marley); Anthony Crivello (Hairdresser); Raye Dowell (Cheerleader); Christine Dunford ("B"); Stash Franklin (Graffiti Artist); Kevin John Gee (Kyoshi); Aaron Goodstone (Graffitti Artist); Adam Green (Max); Tammy Grimes (Georgette); Louis Guss (Vardig); Rick Hara (Tetsu); John Harkins (Chuck Dade Dolger); George Harris (Super); Adam Coleman Howard (Stash); Francine Hunter (Hairdresser); Mary Beth Hurt (Ginger Booth); Paul Jabara (Derelict); Sakina Jaffrey (Wilfredo's Receptionist); Tama Janowitz (Abby); Anna Katarina (Mooshka); Ken Kensei (Kiochi); Freddy Korner (Party Guest); Anthony La Paglia (Henry); Kim Larese (Ballerina); Jennifer Lee (Polly); Joe Leeway (Jonny Jalouse); Philip Lenkowsky (Fritz); Charles McCaughan (Sherman); Maura Moynihan (Mona); Harsh Nayyar (Dr. Pandiya); Suzanne O'Neill (Victor's Receptionist); Lazaro Perez (Bill); Dustin Pittman (Party Guest); Madeleine Potter (Daria); Paul Potter (Simon St. Simon); Paige Powell (Party Guest); Mark Robinson (Derelict); Mercedes Ruehl (Samantha); Stillman Rockefeller (Man Who Points); Chris Sarandon (Victor Okrent); Michael Schoeffling (Jan); Richard Steinmetz (Party Guest); Michael David Tanney (Toddler); Stanley Tucci (Darryl); Fabio Urana (Vandal); Bruce Peter Young (Mikell).

CHRISTIAN SCIENCE MONITOR, 3/21/89, p. 11, David Sterritt

"Slaves of New York" is the second movie of the season to offer multiple views of Manhattan life. Unlike the snappy "New York Stories" that arrived recently, "Slaves of New York" is directed by a single filmmaker and has a fairly consistent point of view on the Big Apple and its inhabitants. What both movies share is a lot of energy, an overabundance of color, and a conviction that no single plot—and no single collection of characters—could do justice to the wildest and wooliest of American cities.

The action in "Slaves of New York" swirls around many places and people, but its focal point is lower Manhattan and its heroine is a woman named Eleanor, played by Bernadette Peters in a wacky yet wonderfully sustained performance. A denizen of the downtown arts community, Eleanor is surrounded by eccentrics and outright weirdos, from her boyfriend (a sort of respectable graffiti artist) to a platoon of friends, acquaintances, and hangers-on who occupy her world as permanently as the lofts and galleries where they all hang out.

What's different about Eleanor is that she sees beyond her immediate surroundings. Unlike her friends, she's aware of being a "slave" to all kinds of dubious habits and behaviors, many of them imposed on her by other people's expectations. More important, she aspires to higher things: finding a sense of purpose, achieving a steady "relationship" with someone she loves, and becoming a contented middle-class person. This mystifies her friends, who regard "middle-class" as a cussword—even though they're up to their necks (unwittingly) in their own weird variations on middleclass values.

Althought the narrative centers on Eleanor and her difficulties, "Slaves of New York" is anything but a case history of one discontented woman. Every time you get a firm grasp on the story, it takes off in a new direction, following the adventures of some other downtowner facing difficulties with money, living space, artistic recognition, or perhaps a "significant other" who's not being attentive enough. The movie seems to fly apart at times, splitting the story into bits and pieces that compete for attention on different parts of the screen—as if a linear plot couldn't hope to contain so many people, places, and problems. And probably it couldn't, if only because the characters of "Slaves" have such astonishingly *crowded* lives: their homes crowded with junk, their bodies crowded with clothing, their hearts and minds crowded with petty ideas and endlessly conflicting emotions.

"Slaves of New York" was directed by James Ivory, who's best known for old-school entertainments like "A Room With a View" and "The Bostonians," among others. He does a surprisingly deft job of motion-picturizing Tama Janowitz's antic screenplay, and part of the secret is his good-natured willingness to treat lower Manhattan as if it were as foreign to his own Pacific Coast background as the locations in India that have graced some of his most popular films. His approach to New York isn't noticeably suave, hip, or possessive. Instead it's bemused, amused, and sometimes amazed. Ditto for the cinematography by Tony Pierce-Roberts, who collaborated with Mr. Ivory on "A Room With a View" and outdoes himself here, filling the screen with goggle-eyed motion and color.

In addition to Ms. Peters, the cast of "Slaves" includes an impressive assortment of performers who seem to be having a ball with their mostly manic characters. If you remember Madeleine Potter from "The Bostonians," you'll hardly recognize her as Daria, one of the downtown crowd's most ambitious (and manhungry) members. Mary Beth Hurt is close to perfect as a trendy gallery owner; John Harkins is equally on-target as her wealthiest art-collecting pigeon; Steve Buscemi, a talented Off-Off-Broadway actor in real life, shines in the small role of a small-time clothing entrepreneur. And that's just mentioning a few.

Ms. Janowitz's screenplay is sometimes overwritten—there are times when the dialogue sounds cleverly concocted instead of freely spoken—but it has the ring of truth often enough to glide past its own artsy spots. The movie was produced by longtime Ivory associate Ismail Merchant in partnership with Gary Hendler; it was edited by Katherine Wenning. Its rating is R, reflecting some vulgar language and a small amount of on-screen sex.

FILMS IN REVIEW, 6-7/89, p. 363, Edmond Grant

Despite its obvious attempt to be "of the moment," *Slaves Of New York* is a slice of petrified pop culture, an awkwardly constructed film that desperately strains to be hip. The unlikely individuals chosen to helm the project were James Ivory and Ismail Merchant, a distinguished filmmaking team, who clearly intended the film to be a flashy portrait of an era and an "attitude." Instead, what they've fashioned is a picture that lacks the appealing garishness of its spiritual predecessors, the wonderfully awful "party" and "head trip" movies of the 60's.

Indeed, the late 60's do seem to exert a palpable influence over the film, from its depiction of the current retro, Warhol-esque look of the lower East side fashion world, to the "pop art" inclinations of the artist characters, to the incompetent way director Ivory makes use of a number of stock 60's visual clichés—the clumsy swaying of the camera during the performance of rock music, the dreadful countercutting during party sequences, and the persistent use of split-screen effects to relate actions that have *no* logical connection. These split screen sequences have a particularly Warhol-esque edge to them, in that Ivory lets both dialogue tracks remain at the same volume (a la Warhol's *Chelsea Girls*) therefore unintentionally producing the same effect that Warhol created on purpose—a peculiar feeling of alienation and nonstop audience irritation.

But the direction is only half the problem; the other half is the incredibly disorganized script, written by ubiquitious media celebrity (and, oh yes, writer) Tama Janowitz. Janowitz has strung together the stories in her trendy bestselling collection quite loosely, with characters from separate plot strands encountering each other by chance at parties, in the street, or (lest we forget) at opposite ends of the split screen.

The plot, such as it is, centers around Eleanor (Bernadette Peters), who lives on the periphery of the East Village/Soho art world amidst preening *artistes* and their victims, the "slaves" who co-habitate with them, and invariably get dumped on in public. Peters' brutish artist lover (Adam Colman Howard) is a pretentious idiot who makes a name for himself doing large works which feature vintage cartoon characters (Popeye, Tom and Jerry, etc.). The rest of the artists in the film do equally ridiculous work; here again, the film misses a beat—the "satire" of contemporary art implied by these works is hopelessly played down. We can be sure, however, that the ludicrous hats that Peters creates are supposed to be laughable, as is the performance piece which features a singer bathing in food (Johann Carlo in an appealing cameo). It's not certain, however, what else in the film is supposed to be funny, thanks to Ivory's leaden sense of comic pacing (the brief instances of slapstick are pathetically rendered), and the totally uneven nature of Janowitz's script, which attempts satire in one scene, and then explores the painful relationships of the characters in the next.

The film's only, slight virtue is the cast, who do try to breathe life into their dimly sketched roles. Bernadette Peters brings her usual energy and beguiling charm to the role of Eleanor, making her the film's only truly sympathetic character. Nick Corri, Charles McCaughan, and Madeleine Potter fill out the roles of irritating artists and art world floozy quite nicely, and Chris Sarandon and Mary Beth Hurt are on hand as the people who have to package and exhibit the hyper-chic, graffiti-like artwork.

But to underline the film's aura of shameless self-promotion, there's also a truly awful supporting performance from Janowitz herself as Peters' best friend, a stint which ranks right up there with Stephen King's bit in *Creepshow* as examples of atrocious acting by bestselling authors.

In the final analysis, Janowitz can't be blamed—she's only making hay while her fifteen minutes in the spotlight seem to stretch on and on. It's a pity, though, that Merchant and Ivory had to be party to it, but one thing's for sure—in a few short years (or perhaps months), *Slaves* the book, the movie on video, and the current line of Janowitz-approved clothing selling at Bloomingdale's, will all be sitting on adjoining tables marked "remainder."

LOS ANGELES TIMES, 3/24/89, Calendar/p. 10, Sheila Benson

Reading "Slaves of New York" by Tama Janowitz, some of whose stories ran first in the New Yorker, it's possible to imagine one or two directors who might make something of their trendy slightness. But James Ivory is not the first name to rush to mind; not even the hundred-and-first.

So brace yourself. The impeccable team of Ismail Merchant and Ivory have turned from such usual sources as Henry James ("The Bostonians," "The Europeans") and E.M. Forster ("A Room With a View," "Maurice"), whose works are as raucous as a furled umbrella, to the messy, unfettered savagery of Janowitz and her clamorous loft-living lowlifes. The result is exactly as peculiar as you might imagine.

First, the film makers have let Janowitz be her own adapter, always a risky business and even more so here since she has taken a steamroller to her already affectless Lower Manhattanites. All of them but Bernadette Peters' Eleanor emerge—to use one of Kurt Vonnegut's more succinct character descriptions—as ugly, stupid and boring. Peters, who can never be boring, is merely waifish and masochistic. And miscast.

Stash Stotz (Adam Coleman Howard), whose precious downtown apartment Eleanor shares, is a surly little creep somewhere in his early 20s. That's a switch from the original stories where all these pop painters, jewelry designers or performance artists *manqué* were hovering around 30, depressed that they weren't yet millionaires. Stash's callowness adds an extra, unneeded layer to Eleanor's masochism, since Bernadette Peters is clearly a grown-up and this kid is clearly a bullying numskull.

When we meet Stash he is holding a flea between his thumb and forefinger, refusing to let Eleanor enter their apartment until she leaves all her "contaminated" clothes in the hall after walking their dog. It would take a heroic amount of charm to overcome an entrance like this, but in his downy first mustache, Howard has no charisma and no discernible acting talent either.

However, in this crowd it's hardly noticeable. In the film's fortune cookie characterizations, *obnoxious* is the one word all of them have in common. These are people who whine endlessly about their poverty but never take anything but cabs. *Obnoxious* covers super-macho painter Marley Mantello (Nick Corri), who yearns to go to Rome to create his Chapel of Jesus Christ as a Woman, or maybe just stay in New York and use Eleanor as his naked model for La Christa. Or Marley's best friend, abstract expressionist Sherman McVittle (Charles McCaughan) and *his* lady love, the poisonous Daria (Madeleine Potter), who spends the movie sniping at Eleanor and sleeping with Stash and every other man south of 34th Street who might get her a gallery show.

Neither explained nor developed, these characters pop up to posture in little frail vignettes, then vanish again. They become a maddening, pointless backdrop for a story as banal as any soap opera, no matter how trendy the surface. Director Ivory doesn't so much ride herd on this scene as float unprotestingly on its surface, finally overwhelmed by hats, sets, shoes, banana curls or any quantity of girls with enameled eyes.

From time to time, Ivory splits his screen or places one scene translucently on top of another, but the effect feels less like inventiveness than a desperate attempt to appear hip. It's like one of those eye-widening flights from common sense when someone like Renata Tebaldi decides to get down and sing boogie-woogie: not a pretty picture.

Against it, Eleanor, who faints at nightclubs and fashions ill-made fantasy hats out of trash-can salvage, totters about, fetchingly cloying and almost mortifying in her self-abasement. The fiercely satisfying Mercedes Ruhl, who appears late and leaves early, is Samantha, a fellow hat designer, someone who will listen to her mewling about her great love for that oaf, Stash.

Janowitz fans will be thrilled to find her, droning on bravely, as a reclusive party-goer. And Mary Beth Hurt, who compressed such a world of observation and satiric wit into her role in "Parents," is again marvelous as gallery owner Ginger Booth, although her moment is over much too soon.

What gave Janowitz's stories their charm—in the eyes of some—was the pointed flipness of her narrative voice commenting on the absurdities at hand. In adapting herself, Janowitz has stripped away that ironic layer, leaving us to take these disagreeable hyper-strivers straight. Meanwhile, Ivory, a man who doesn't know the territory and seems to regard it with chilly disdain, has no editorial comment to add.

"Slaves of New York" (MPAA-rated: R) becomes heaven for the costumer and the makeup artists who have gone about their business, making pretty women grotesque in the prescribed manner of the day and the place. Shirley Temple's mother would swoon at the sight of this many ringlets. They won't keep you from stone boredom, but they do add a certain unhealthy fascination to the proceedings, just enough to keep you awake.

MONTHLY FILM BULLETIN, 8/89, p. 250, Anne Billson

Manhattan. Eleanor, an aspiring hat designer who copy-edits for an East Village newspaper, lives with her boyfriend Stash Stotz, an artist preparing for his forthcoming show at a local gallery. Eleanor goes to lunch with Mikell, a South African writer whom she met at a party, but Stash reacts to her description of the lunch date with an unreasonable display of jealousy and derision. Sherman McVittie, another artist, asks his girlfriend Daria to marry him, but she is more interested in Sherman's best friend, Marley Mantello, especially when she learns that, unlike Sherman, Marley has lined up a show of his paintings, and therefore has contacts which might prove useful in furthering her own career as a sculptress. For the same reasons, she is also attracted to Stash when he attends her birthday party, much to the chagrin of Eleanor, who reacts by getting very drunk. Marley's agent, Ginger Booth, introduces him to a prospective buyer who insists they eat a large breakfast. Some of Stash's paintings are slashed or stolen; Daria offers to help repaint them in time for his show. Eleanor collects a coat, for which Stash has traded a painting, from Wilfredo, a fashion designer who expresses interest in her hats. Daria falls off Marley's fire escape and breaks an arm and a leg. Eleanor faints at a rock 'n' roll gig, and Stash again behaves unreasonably when he finds her talking to Mikell. Eleanor goes to the doctor about her fainting fits; he gives her a bottle of smelling-salts. She suspects Stash is sleeping with Daria but he denies it. During a baseball match, Eleanor encounters Marley, who has already asked her to model nude for him; Stash starts a fight. Eleanor's suspicions about her boyfriend and Daria are confirmed during his private-view party. She leaves him, finds her own apartment, and designs hats for Wilfredo's fashion show, which is a huge success. Marley departs for Italy, leaving Daria to Sherman, who has lined up a show at last. Eleanor throws a party; all the guests turn out to be men, and one of them, Jan (whom she met in the park), takes her out on his motorbike...

Tama Janowitz is the third member of the so-called American Brat-Lit Pack to have had a book adapted for the big screen. But whereas the work of Jay McInerney (*Bright Lights, Big City*) and Bret Easton Ellis (*Less than Zero*, the film, of which has yet to be released in the U.K.) utilised a more or less conventional narrative to convey the nihilism of privileged American youth, *Slaves of New York* lacks an obvious hook on which to hang a celluloid tale, and is resolutely upbeat. Janowitz's collection of short stories is not even that so much as a series of vignettes of trendy Manhattan life, in the course of which some characters crop up more regularly than others. Though the film concentrates on the relationship between Eleanor and Stash, the above synopsis is a necessarily selective catalogue of inconsequential events: galleries, gigs and parties *ad nauseam*. Film rights to some of the stories were originally bought by Andy Warhol, and one imagines that he might have got away with a film about the fashionable underbelly of Manhattan's arty milieu which lacked any narrative drive whatsoever. His preference for non-professional actors would have served the material well, while he, and certainly Paul Morrissey, would have been able to strip away much of the surface cuteness. James Ivory, however, brings to the project all the reverence and painstaking period detail previously accorded E.M. Forster and Henry James, but directed here towards a "contemporary" comedy of manners.

That the fashions and artwork on display *already* look hopelessly dated should not have mattered, but the problem is that there is nothing to knit them together into a whole, either as drama or as a portrayal of an era. John Waters' *Hairspray*—in retrospect, looking more and more the definitive pop-arty period reconstruction film—evoked the early 60s not only through its flamboyant sets and costumes, but also in its awareness of movie conventions. But *Slaves* is like a cultural shopping-list, dropping visual images instead of names. Ivory's sporadic use of the split-screen, for instance, offers no illuminating juxtaposition of complementary viewpoints, but merely provokes irritation by presenting conversations or activities which are impossible to follow simultaneously. Tiresome caricatures flailing around in a plot-free limbo, the film's characters dabble in "art" and "design", but there is no sense of personal philosophy, even of the most rudimentary kind, to prop up their facades. Human failings are not so much viewed with generosity as glossed over entirely; intolerable Stash and predatory Daria are presented in exactly the same one-dimensional way as weak, self-deprecating Eleanor, with whom we are presumably meant to identify.

Janowitz's writing occasionally transcended its studied trendiness with glimpses of genuine Big Apple weirdness: the potential buyer who plies his artist with a *Grande Bouffe* breakfast, for example, or the floodlit ball game under the 59th Street Bridge. Both scenes are in the film, but slotted into the meretricious parade of kooks and curiosities as just another couple of wacky *non sequiturs*. The half-jokey central thesis, that whoever owns the apartment calls the tune (thus making a "slave" of the dependent party), is blown wide apart by the apparent ease with which Eleanor manages to find somewhere to live after her break-up with Stash. As screenwriter, Janowitz's major concession to adaptation for the big screen seems to have involved changing Eleanor from someone who designs earrings into someone who designs hats. Ironically but perhaps predictably, it is the writer herself, in the supporting role of Eleanor's out-of-town friend Abby, who comes closest to incarnating the snappy Manhattanite demeanour, delivering her dialogue with an authentic curl of the lip which seems beyond the capabilities, or more likely the life experience, of the rest of the cast: actors to a T, all of them arrayed in primary-coloured pop-art "life styles".

NEW YORK, 3/27/89, p. 69, David Denby

The central character of *Slaves of New York,* a downtown person named Eleanor (Bernadette Peters), makes tall, softly crumbling hats—plaid powder puffs tilted to one side—and lives with the artist Stash Stotz (Adam Coleman Howard), a self-absorbed nag. Eleanor, whose tenuous existence Tama Janowitz has cobbled together from some of the stories in her 1986 collection (same title), wanders from loft to loft, party to party, talking in a cracked little voice, complaining. She's a poor lost lamb—in standard Hollywood story-conference terms, a harmless kook and masochist. Twenty-five years ago, the part would have been played by Shirley MacLaine, and the movie, however vulgar and false, would have had some life. But *Slaves of New York* has none. Not even a glimmer.

Before he died, Andy Warhol optioned Janowitz's stories for a movie. One can see why: the shrugging, affectless tone, the glazed offhandedness about sex, the notion of art as commerce and hanging out... Janowitz is a chip off the old block, though she writes with a ruefully sweet comic gentleness that Warhol, in his many creative incarnations, did not have. The Eleanor character doesn't do drugs; she's not greedy and selfish and publicity-mad; all she wants is decency and responsibility in her relations with people and a little success in her career. The ironic point is that her commonplace, selfless desires make her an outsider in SoHo (it's a minor point). Thinly amusing, the writing laps too mildly at the edge of one's attention to be called satirical. Janowitz natters on; she's funny, rumpled, and easy to take, like a popular "offbeat" guest on a late-night talk show. She's got her voice.

But Janowitz's screenplay, written for the filmmaking team of Ismail Merchant and James Ivory, has no voice and no center, either: Onscreen, Eleanor isn't a heroine who holds a movie together; she's a bedraggled sad sack looking for someone to be nice to her. The other characters drop in, say a few lines, and leave, making reference to things one only half understands. The whole movie has a flustered, fluttering inconsequence: The characters come dressed in studded leather, with mohawks or thick, tangled masses of hair in stacked layers, but no one has any substance. We can't tell if Eleanor's lover, Stash, is meant to be a dislikably moody young talent or just a pretentious phony; in any case, he's a child. We also get lots of the grinning young painter Marley Mantello (Nick Corri) including scenes with his dealer (Mary Beth Hurt), a gallery owner (Chris Sarandon), and a fat collector who fills him with eggs and sausages, but he seems like nothing more than an eager hustler.

In Janowitz's version of the downtown scene, everyone is obnoxious (perhaps, downtown, this passes for a satirical view). The men are petulant, self-regarding, and infantile, the women hangers-on or sex parasites. On the page, some of this was fun, like gossip about strangers overheard in a Laundromat; but in a movie, acted out, infantilism and parasitism leave a big hole where there should be characters to get interested in. And the triviality rubs off on the actors. Peters prattles on forlornly; the young actors chosen to play the male artists are all lightweights, without much sexual presence (which makes the women appear even sadder for being obsessed with them). James Ivory, never a director with much rhythm, can't find a shape for the limp whimsy Janowitz has written for him, and scenes straggle on aimlessly, like stoned shoppers in

D'Agostino who have forgotten why they came to the store. There's only one episode with any snap—a punk fashion show, with models swinging their arms insolently and throwing themselves down in a pile.

Worst of all, Merchant and Ivory have neglected to give us anything comparable to the side benefits we got years ago from the Warhol movies—the through-the-keyhole peeks at a brazenly sexual, casually nihilistic demimonde. Tauntingly attenuated, the Warhol movies were never quite *dull*; Warhol's people saw themselves as stars, and though lost in the immensity of their cracked self-approbation, they could certainly talk. I can recall things Viva or Ondine said in movies I saw twenty years ago, but I can't remember a single line from *Slaves*, which I saw last week. The movie uses up a lot of downtown people (the comedienne Maura Moynihan, for instance) without getting much out of them. Even the art is thrown away.

What are Merchant and Ivory doing in possession of this material? They don't seem in any way suited for it. Their first E.M. Forster adaptation, *A Room With a View* (1986), was a solid achievement, but apart from the lovely *Shakespeare Wallah*, made a long, long time ago (in 1965), *Room* is their only achievement. Lots of people, hoping for a ride from this media event/fashion show, seem to have forgotten how many genteel, undramatic movies Merchant and Ivory have made, how little sexual tension their productions have, how remote they are from the contours of contemporary life. And now, like those models flopping on the runway, the publicity has come crashing down in a heap.

Slaves of New York is yet another triumph for the unspeakably distinguished film company Tri-Star Pictures, which two weeks ago was folded, a willing pig, into the corporate blanket of Columbia Pictures Entertainment. Last fall, a colleague, David Edelstein of the *Post*, got himself banned from Tri-Star screenings by writing that the company, in its four-plus years of operation, had never made a good movie. This is a vicious slander, grossly unfair. The company made *one* good movie (*Peggy Sue Got Married*).

NEW YORK POST, 3/18/89, p. 17, David Edelstein

For weeks, the word on "Slaves of New York"—the screen adaptation of Tama Janowitz's best-selling short-story collection—has been that it's a colossal dud, and yes, it does smell to heaven. But who could have expected anything better?

The combination of Janowitz's twittering prose and the team of Ismail Merchant and James Ivory—purveyors of stultifying, low-budget literary adaptations—was almost more excruciating in prospect. What they've delivered is merely a wildly overdressed pipsqueak—a movie that says, "Notice me," and you say, "Why?"

The heroine, Eleanor (Bernadette Peters), is just such a pipsqueak. She has a king-sized inferiority complex, but she wears loud hats she designs herself—ashtrays with cigars sticking out, for example—to signal that, although she doesn't look like much, she's an quirkily artistic kinda person.

She lives with Stash (Adam Coleman Howard), an emotional sadist who inserts familiar cartoon characters in splashy, pretentious landscapes. The apartment is Stash's, which gives him the power to browbeat her; she's a virtual slave to his moodiness and jealousy. But for some reason Eleanor adores him—even after he has a fling with Daria (Madeleine Potter), a conniving opportunist who's also having a fling with Marley (Nick Corri), who's the best friend of Simon (Paul Potter), who's been living with Daria.

Most of the scenes involve pretentious (there's that word again!), heavily accessorized people standing around under rococo hairdos in crazily discordant interiors. The director, Ivory, observes this landscape as if it's the surface of Mars—there's no expressiveness in his style, and no indictation that he understands or empathizes with his cooly self-involved characters.

The tone of "Slaves of New York" is one part satire to two parts nothing. When it isn't strenuously quirky, it's sexless, boring and trivial—and there's no indication that the filmmakers wanted it to be otherwise. They seem to loathe those people as much as we do.

There's something about this movie that brings out the Stash in me, and it's probably the hypocrisy. Janowitz's conception of her alter-ego is that of a poor little waif who just wants to lead an ordinary life, but who's forced to live with a sadistic blowhard because of her wretched insecurity and the evils of Manhattan real estate. It's "Portrait of the Artist as a Young Masochist," except the trendiness of the references and self-consciousness of the style betrays her true, celebrity-seeking intentions.

Hey, it's no crime in this culture to want to be a celebrity, and Janowitz is certainly a sellable commodity. She even has some talent. The title story is a neat, absurdist little sketch; I remember reading and admiring it in the "New Yorker."

But her vision can't sustain itself for an entire book, let alone a movie; in the end, she doesn't have much insight or interest in the SoHo art scene. She tells us that it's insular, posturing and narcissistic—qualities the movie shares. Perhaps only John Waters could have brought a demented affection to this trashy kitschscape.

Bernadette Peters, whose tiny, round mouth makes her look as if she swallowed a lemon at birth, gives a teensy-weensy, chirpy performance; her expression suggests she's certain that a grand piano is about to fall on her head. She has nice moments, but Janowitz isn't interested in her artistic process (or in anyone else's). There's no suggestion that any of these people are obsessed with anything higher than money or celebrity.

I'd go on but I'm our of time. The studio, Tri-Star, banned me from its screenings a short while back because I said all their movies stunk (shortly before Coca Cola decided something similar and merged them with its other studio, Columbia.)

Anyway, I had to see the Friday matinee and rush back to write this up. Now they're screaming about deadlines and the first edition and there's no time to do anything except type up my notes:

This movie is about hairdos.

Good scene with rich fat guy cooking breakfast for the starving artist while taunting him about how overpriced his paintings are. First character I can relate to.

Madeline Potter looks like someone smashed an ice-cream cone over her head.

Who would invest money in this script???

Tab. Detergent. Oreo Double-Stuffs. (Oh, sorry, I was making my grocery list.)

When will this be over?

THAT'S IT???

NEWSDAY, 3/17/89, Part III/p. 3, Mike McGrady

The primary problem with "The Slaves of New York" is that Andy Warhol died an untimely death. Maybe that requires a word of explanation. You see, at the time of his demise, Warhol owned the film rights to the original Tama Janowitz short-story collection and was preparing his own version of "Slaves of New York."

If Warhol had lived longer, this would, like so many of his other films, doubtless have been idiosyncratic, offbeat, self-indulgent, experimental. A typical Andy Warhol movie. (As I remember, his epic movie "Sleep" focused on a man sleeping soundly for some six or seven hours.) And moviegoers would have accepted the results with a shrug—"Oh, you know, that's Andy"—and it would have wound up, in due time, at theaters catering to midnight cultists.

However, Warhol died and the film rights to the Janowitz stories shifted over to director James Ivory and producer Ismail Merchant, longtime collaborator whose names have become synonymous with quality. Their two most recent projects, "Room With a View" and "Maurice," were sensitive, beautifully made films of formal construction. If one were to chart the movie-making establishment, Warhol would have been way over here to the left, almost off the paper, and Ivory-Merchant would have been at the very opposite end. Although it's impossible to connect them to the late Andy Warhol, they've come devilishly close to making an Andy Warhol movie.

"Slaves of New York" trails closely after a ditsy young woman as she seeks a new mate and a new apartment. The script seems more a collection of captions than anything so coherent as a story. In fact, the script does little more than provide bridges from one artsy party to another. The parties—at nightclubs, art galleries, fashion showrooms, lofts—are all noisy and noisome. Parties one would not want to attend, filled with people one would not want to meet saying things one would not want to hear.

Watching the movie, I found myself concerned about the original author—how would Tama Janowitz react to his muddle? Her book may have been triumph of faddishness over literature, but it did have a nice moment or two and even an occasional insight, none of which seemed to make the transference to celluloid. But, as I was later to learn, author Janowitz can register no complaints about the script. She wrote it.

Her central character, a hat designer (Bernadette Peters), is living with Stash (Adam Coleman Howard), a self absorbed, insensitive, unintelligent, abusive drawer of oversized cartoons. Milling about in the background: another egocentric artist (Nick Corri), a suave gallery owner (Chris

Sarandon), a hip art dealer (Mary Beth Hurt), a sexually liberated sculptress (Madeleine Potter) and others, all equally unappealing.

Peters ("All I ever wanted was an ordinary life") is cute, brittle and theatrical. I take the theatricality to be an indicator that the actress has no clear idea why she should be concerned with this little airhead adrift in a world of airheads; neither will the audience.

And what's the first thing our hat designer does upon finally achieving a modicum of success? Like everyone else in the movie, she throws a party, of course. At that final party, we learn her new success is making her edgy because people are not only responding to her work, they're responding critically: "I hate value judgments. it makes me nervous." Indeed, indeed. I would suspect everyone connected with "Slaves of New York" would hate value judgments. But here's one anyway: Arrrrgggggghhhhh!

NEWSWEEK, 3/20/89, p. 83, David Ansen

After Henry James and E.M. Forster, director James Ivory ("The Bostonians," "A Room with a View") probably had nowhere to go but down. Still, it's a shock just how far he's descended with Tama Janowitz's feeble adaptation of her tales of the downtown bohemian art scene. Ivory seems totally adrift in the trendy world of artist/hustlers, barracuda dealers and manhunting, fashion-mongering women. Attempting jazziness, he litters his movie with split-screen effects, producing the aural and visual equivalent of gridlock. Janowitz's hapless heroine, Eleanor (Bernadette Peters), a designer of funny hats, is trapped in a masochistic relationship with a cretinous pop artist named Stash (Adam Coleman Howard). Through an eternity of flat, shapeless scenes we wait for her to come to her senses and dump the creep. Meanwhile, Ivory gracelessly serves up further examples of boorish male posturing: the overweening egotist Marley (Nick Corri), a painter who wants to build a Chapel of Jesus Christ as a Woman in Rome; the whiny expressionist Sherman (Charles McCaughan) and his sleep-her-way-to-success girlfriend (Madeleine Potter). Though Janowitz aims her heavy satirical artillery at the men, the movie is tainted with an odd whiff of misogyny, as Ivory's camera dotes on the guys and demeans the girls. Everyone ends up seeming a fool. Worse, they are boring fools "Slaves of New York" makes bohemia seem duller than Dubuque.

SIGHT & SOUND, Summer 1989, p. 208, John Pym

In "The Hustle", the central episode of James Ivory's *Roseland*, a young man (Christopher Walken)—personable, compassionate, and above all understanding—finds himself the object of attention of three purposeful women, each of whom he does his best to satisfy. In *Slaves of New York*, twelve years later, Ivory—though not with his regular scriptwriter Ruth Prawer Jhabvala, but Tama Janowitz, the author of the bestselling collection of stories from which the picture is derived—again explores the suject of willing, and in some ways inexplicable, servitude.

Roseland was chiefly about the old: European exiles dreaming of home in a cavernous magical New York ballroom. *Slaves* is about the young, who have nothing to fear and nothing to remember, but who are nevertheless in their own way dreamers, who inhabit makeshift impermanent lofts and who change partners, it seems, with the ease of taxi-dancers. *Roseland* did not find a wide New York audience, and *Slaves* has not on the whole pleased the city's critics. In both films, Ivory used English cameramen, Ernest Vincze and Tony Pierce-Roberts respectively, and there is in the look of both films something singular and, for a director based for many years in New York, wilfully "un-American", in the Hollywy sense. There is, too, in both films, a languor to which it is necessary to surrender. Ruth Jhabvala once described an MIP project as one dreamed up, characteristically, in the suffusing heat of the Rajasthan Desert.

The plot of *Slaves* is set in motion by a flea which bites Stash (Adam Coleman Howard), an aggressively selfabsorbed artist with the heroic beginnings of a manly beard. The flea, Stash claims, standing at his front door in red Mickey Mouse undershorts, came from Andrew, the pristine dalmatian belonging to his girlfriend Eleanor (Bernadette Peters), a hat designer. Eleanor, an original, is Stash's slave—their apartment belongs to him—and she must therefore accept the ritual abuse heaped on slaves down the ages for misdeeds they did not commit. Andrew, it turns out, will be her one unswervingly loyal friend.

Making liberal use of jaunty optical devices, the film then sets about the breathless interweaving of the lives of a loose group of industrious, fired-up young New York artists and those who favour, but in fact depend on them, the city's patrons and gallery-owners. Eleanor vainly attempts simply 'to make friends' with the compassionate soft-centred writer Mikell, who has hovering at his back the sinister, armourplated 'B'. Stash allows himself to be seduced by the serpentine man-eating vamp Daria (Madeleine Potter, making a meal of a most scornful role). Marley (Nick Corri) relentlessly pursues the reluctant Eleanor with pleas to become the model for his 'Christa', the centrepiece of a grandiose chapel to be built in Rome for which he is seeking a patron. Meanwhile, Sherman (Charles McCaughan), Daria's hobbling slave, is cuckolded by Marley, though, it transpires, all Daria wants of her one-nightstands is a souvenir painting or an intorduction to a gallery-owner...

Ivory observes these youthful shenanigans with a notably engaged sympathy. There is little here of the patrician aesthete (as he cast himself in a passing shot in *The Europeans*) silently gazing at a precious objet d'art. He likes these young people, despite their insufferable egocentricity, and he observes their pastimes—club life in 20s Paris had the unquenchable Armelia McQueen, 80s New York has a farouche singer in a bathtub fiercely crunching a celery stick—with genuine, eye-opening fascination. The climactic fashion show, at which Eleanor finds she need no longer be a slave, that her hats have a market and she can at last afford her own apartment, is an extraordinary earsplitting spectacle: not something, one imagines, easily conceived in the Rajasthan Desert.

When Ivory last set a film in New York—*Jane Austen in Manhattan* (1980)—the world was that of rival theatre groups (again with hovering patrons), but the interweaving was both faster and more elliptical. Here, he relaxes into the milieu, lets it find its own pace, as in a scratch baseball game full of adroit comic asides, or agreeably drift away, as in Eleanor's final, decidedly unwild house-warming party, at which Tama Janowitz herself, the only other woman present, shyly locks herself in the bathroom.

From beginner to grande dame, Merchant Ivory Productions has for twenty-seven years been consistently fortunate with its actresses: they are, indeed, one of its hallmarks, and not just the stars but the secondary players too, the capable platoons of begums, mothers-in-law, aunties and landladies. Bernadette Peters is something of an exception, neither a beginner nor a grande dame, she has for several years been a reliable comedienne, though one whose cookiness is, if encouraged, liable to run away with her. Here, decked out with her startling headgear and, at one point, a hairy, flammable coat trailing a foolish tail, she conveys a bruised, weary but never ridiculous resilience which is attractive in itself and gives the picture a down-to-earth centre.

The theme of *Slaves of New York* is, in a sense, the presumption of artists, the gullibility of patrons and the vanity of gallery-owners. Stash carelessly snaps Polaroids of a TV cartoon; a jolly stout patron (cue for a splendid MIP eating scene) has spent a fortune videoing the year-long ordeal of an artist tethered to a dog; and the gallery-owner who mounts Stash's exhibition prissily smooths his hair for a Japanese video team, breaking off an argument with Stash to allow them to reload. But James Ivory also has time for his characters—is their slave—and records their passing, careless, vivid lives with an unalloyed affection; though one cannot imagine his young artists settling down for an evening with Henry James or E. M. Forster, as yet at any rate.

TIME, 3/20/89, p. 73, Richard Schickel

They should have filmed Tama Janowitz's publicity campaign. It was a lot more entertaining, and possibly more sociologically edifying, than *Slaves of New York*, the collection of short stories about the downtown art scene that book flacks so heedlessly hyped to best-sellerdom. Alas, the movie people got stuck with the book and with its author as screenwriter. And now the public is stuck with a movie that compares rather unfavorably to periodontal work in amusement value.

Sustained, coherent narrative is not, shall we say, Janowitz's great strength, and neither is dramatic characterization. Eleanor (the normally perky, cuddly Bernadette Peters in sadly deflated condition) is a designer of funky hats who suffers from a possibly justifiable weakness of the ego. She lives with a graffiti artist named Stash (Adam Coleman Howard) who has a definitely unjustified air of superioirty. Before they finally break up, this tedious pair go to many noisy parties and performance-art evenings. Along the way, art-world fights, flirtations and fornications are noted but not explored in a script that is always lumbering off up aimlessly false trails. Indeed, many characters are written so dimly that it is often hard to tell one from the other.

The fault is not entirely Janowitz's. Her only hope was to find a director who could either respond avidly to the sexual and creative energies of the avant-garde scene or take a satirical cudgel to it. Instead, she drew distant, enervated James Ivory (*A Room with a View, Heat and Dust, The*

Bostonians), who never seems to engage fully with any subject he has tackled and who has never been more fastidiously withdrawn than he is here. In this case, however, audiences will be well advised to follow his example.

VILLAGE VOICE, 3/21/89, p. 57, J. Hoberman

Before he died, Andy Warhol optioned Tama Janowitz's tales of Stash and Eleanor, neopop painter and hapless concubine, and *Slaves of New York*, which brings these, among other Janowitz creatures, to the screen, is a prime (if pallid) example of what Warhol engagingly termed "business art." Less a movie than a marketing strategy, James Ivory and Ismail Merchant's adaptation offers itself as the chance of a lifestyle.

As movies adapt themselves to malls, their relation to the production-consumption cycle may revert to those halcyon days of the '30s when Bernard Waldman and his Modern Merchandizing Bureau transmuted the gowns worn on the silver screen into $40 knockoffs sold at Saks. Scarcely restricted to the obligatory mass-market paperback and sound-track CD, *Slave*'s ancillary tie-ins include a Downtown exhibit of the prop paintings created for the film and—barely a block from Cinema 1—a special Bloomingdale's boutique stocked with *Slaves of New York* T-shirts, jackets, and "accessories."

As with Bloomie's current cofeature, *Dangerous Liaisons*, it will be possible to read the movie, see the book, and wear the lingerie—*Slaves of New York* is a fitting tribute to the first "serious" writer whose look was more important to her work than her voice. The book *Slaves of New York* is both an account and an example of post-Warholian careerism. If its characters work the '80s artworld the way '49ers mined California, their glamorously flaked-out creator seemed to spring full-blown from a press agent's brow—a raven-tressed literary lioness, and egghead Madonna, hailed in a 1986 *New York* cover story as "the female Jay McInerney." (McInerney, who reviewed *Slaves of New York* the following week for *The New York Times Book Review*, fastidiously bracketed Janowitz with Damon Runyon as the colorful, if vulgar, chronicler of a particular Manhattan demimonde.)

"Too fabulous to waste on the book pages," as her publicist once told *Time*, Janowitz posed for glossy ads and produced an MTV-friendly video to plug *A Cannibal in Manhattan*, her aptly named, recycled second novel. Perhaps Warhol would have allowed her to play Eleanor herself; perhaps he would have found some '80s equivalent of Jane Forth to embody the writer's incongruously timorous alter ego. Ivory (who grants the writer a two-scene cameo) goes immediately inauthentic with the opening image of Brassy Bernadette Peters ditzing up Lafayette Street led by a huge dalmatian, her arms filled with packages, her Kewpie Doll kisser contorted around some Merchant-Ivory equivalent of "Zip-a-Dee-Doo-Dah."

This movie wants so terribly to be liked that it could give the epithet "slavish" a bad name. Even Janowitz's extremely mild brand of irony must be played for uplifting farce. Peters's Eleanor comes on like an overaged teen queen, while New York's infectious kookiness is less a matter of *Breakfast at Tiffany's* than Supremes impersonators under the window, raccoons in the garbage, and madrigal singers strolling through the park.

Allowing that Janowitz doesn't leave her populizers too much room for betrayal, *Slaves of New York* could have been worse; some scenes even show a certain delicacy. Peters's inept networking and inappropriate packaging at a loftwarming party—no door on toilet yet—has a tart piquance exaggerated by the shameless opportunism of her sour hostess (Maura Moynihan). But, as *Slaves* is heavier on scenescape than narrative, Ivory's negative flair for satire comes convulsively to the fore. The artworld is a jungle: A rogue elephant collector tramples the foliage, while baboonlike painters contemplate their armpits, ignoring the fragile blossom of Eleanor's charm.

The artists in this habitat are scarcely individuated and barely human, although Adam Coleman Howard, the aggressively callow Stash, has a good moment showing Peters his Popeye watercolors. (Stash's icons are inspired by the various Woody Woodpeckers painted by Janowitz's erstwhile lover and Warhol's onetime assistant, Ronnie Cutrone.) Bruised babydoll features notwithstanding, Peters doesn't demonstrate much more conviction as the pathologically self-effacing (yet secretly "normal") heroine; she makes exactly the same fuss over her errant Stash and an out-of-control blender; Ivory and Janowitz's idea of a gag is to have this aspiring hat designer duck out for a potential tryst wearing an outsized ashtray on her head.

After an hour (around the time Eleanor begins to think of leaving Stash, Ivory makes a desperate lunge towards the Third World exotica of Demmeland, and Michael Musto puts in an appearance bolting for the door), *Slaves* grinds to a halt and falls apart—a victim of too much bad art and too many broad characterizations, a paucity of narrative drive and a surfeit of collapsing chairs. In vain, Ivory attempts to fluff up the torpor with split screens and kicky transitions. Once Eleanor gets her own apartment (a slave no more!), the movie loses its last residual bit of tension—with half an hour still to go. Can it really be a decade since *An Unmarried Woman* found herself in Soho?

Actually, despite the extended quote from *The Wizard of Oz*, Ivory's New York is no Emerald City—let alone an adequate shopping mall. (Perhaps the movie was made to drive rents down.) Incoherently picturesque throughout, *Slaves* looks discombobulated and feels dispirited. A decade of Downtown indies seems to have drained the life out of Soho streets and Loisaida lots; I'd say there was no more juice left in the material were it not that the Scorsese episode in *New York Stories* works similar territory with such knowing verve.

It's striking that both golden Touchstone and hapless Tri-Star, neither studio known around Hollywood for prestige product, have simultaneously weighed in with art films that underline their seriousness by being about *real* art. The joke is that, souvenir paintings and wash-and-wear collectibles notwithstanding, *Slaves of New York* is practically post-post-modern—less an autonomous creation than a stage in the transmutation of a *New Yorker* story to a Broadway musical or (show biz nirvana!) network sitcom.

Also reviewed in:
NATION, 4/17/89, p. 530, Stuart Klawans
NEW REPUBLIC, 4/10/89, p. 22, Stanley Kauffmann
NEW YORK TIMES, 3/17/89, p. C8, Janet Maslin
VARIETY, 3/8-14/89, p. 20
WASHINGTON POST, 3/31/89, p. D1, Hal Hinson
WASHINGTON POST, 3/31/89, Weekend/p. 31, Desson Howe

SOUND AND FURY

A Les Films du Losange production with Le Centre National de la Cinématographie and Sofica Investimage. *Producer:* Margaret Menegoz. *Director:* Jean-Claude Brisseau. *Screenplay (French with English subtitles):* Jean-Claude Brisseau. *Director of Photography:* Romain Winding. *Editor:* Maria-Luisa Garcia, Jean-Claude Brisseau, and Annick Hurst. *Sound:* Louis Gimel. *Costumes:* Lisa Garcia *Running Time:* 95 minutes. *MPAA Rating:* Not Rated.

CAST: Vincent Gasperitsch (Bruno); Lisa Heredia (Apparition); François Negret (Jean-Roger); Bruno Cremer (Marcel); Thierry Helaine (Thierry); Sandrine Arnault (Marcel's Daughter); Victoire Buff (Thierry's Friend); Françoise Vatel (Jean-Roger's Mother); Albert Montias (Marcel's Brother); Antonio Garcia (Grandfather); Fabienne Babe (The Professor); Antoine Fontaine (Principal); Luc Ponette (Assistant Director); Isabelle Hurtin (Social Worker); Jean Cherlian (Squad Leader); Fejria Deliba (Mina); Aurélie Sterling (Mina's Friend).

NEWSDAY, 3/17/89, Part III/p. 5, Bill Kaufman

If nothing else, one thing becomes abundantly clear at the outset of "Sound and Fury," a Frenchmade film that trails a couple of young idlers around a grimy apartment complex in the Paris suburbs—Gallic teenage angst is no different from the same affliction of passage anywhere.

Writer-director Jean-Claude Brisseau explores some very well-known quantities in this workman-like movie, but herein lies its main fault—there is very little fresh ground covered either artistically or cinematographically. Once again we have two teenage pals, Jean-Roger, a younger, more naive youth than Bruno, an older boy who is already on the path to various anti-social patterns, including street crime.

The old story is here: Jean-Roger is a latchkey kid whose hardworking mother is neglectful. Both boys yearn for affection and emotional stability. The younger boy, deeply immersed in sexual fantasies, is treated to a voyeuristic glimpse of the real thing by his friend. And then, of course, there is the peer group pressure of vicious school gangs.

The production notes explain that the film is based on Brisseau's real-life experiences. "Sound and Fury" does indeed provide a rough-edged portrait of teenagers on the threshold of downscale life, but then again, some lives are far more exciting than others.

VILLAGE VOICE, 3/21/89, p. 64, Renee Tajima

This fascinating, uneven study of adolescent angst is set in a bleak high-rise complex overlooking Paris. Bruno exists in a dream world of oppositions that mirrors his schizophrenic real-life attachment to an incorrigible classmate and his violently eccentric family. Director Jean-Claude Brisseau creates an ambitious canvas of the boy's inner and material worlds, yet it is less tapestry than a series of plot lines reminiscent of '50s-era moody youth stories.

Also reviewed in:
NEW YORK TIMES, 3/17/89, p. C4, Vincent Canby
VARIETY, 1/18–24/89, p. 27

SPEAKING PARTS

A Zeitgeist release of an Ego Film Arts production with the participation of Telefilm Canada, The Ontario Film Development Corporation, Academy Pictures (Rome), and Film Four International (London). *Executive Producer:* Atom Egoyan and Don Ranvaud. *Director:* Atom Egoyan. *Screenplay:* Atom Egoyan. *Director of Photography:* Paul Sarossy. *Editor:* Bruce McDonald. *Music:* Mychael Danna. *Sound:* John Megill. *Sound Editor:* Steven Munro. *Art Director:* Linda Del Rosario. *Set Decorator:* Theresa Santandrea-Cull. *Costumes:* Maureen Del Degan. *Make-up:* Nicole Demers. *Running time:* 93 minutes. *MPAA Rating:* Not Rated.

CAST: Michael McManus (Lance); Arsinée Khanjian (Lisa); Gabrielle Rose (Clara); Tony Nardi (Eddy); David Hemblen (The Producer); Patricia Collins (The Housekeeper); Gerard Parkes (The Father); Jackie Samuda (The Bride); Peter Krantz (The Groom); Frank Tata (Clara's Brother); Patrick Tierney (Clerk); Robert Dodds (Doctor); Leszek Lis (Housekeeper's Pet); Sharon Corder (Voice); David MacKay (Man).

LOS ANGELES TIMES, 4/27/90, Calendar/p. 10, Michael Wilmington

In Atom Egoyan's "Speaking Parts," people don't touch; they watch each other on video.

The ideas suggest Steve Soderbergh's "sex, lies, and videotape," but here, Egoyan carries them further. Lost in a strange metallic world of hotel corridors, universal TV hookups and conference rooms, video stores and empty boudoirs, his characters struggle soporifically in a voyeuristic web. Orgies are filmed; even a local cemetery has a mausoleum stocked with video screens and tapes of the dead.

It's a viscid, gelatinously shiny realm in which all movement is gluey and detached, in which the only on-screen sex occurs through a video-phone hookup. Every scene is darkened, as if to accommodate a TV set. Characters watch each other and themselves on VCRs and, when they dream, they start hallucinating about video images that are watching them back.

For Soderbergh, videotape could filter out lies; for Egoyan, it breeds them. The movie's paragon of evil is a producer-director (David Hemblen) who destroys the genuine emotion in the script he's bought by insisting on a spurious TV talk show scene. He's a malign talking head on huge screen hookups, dictating and destroying by remote control. Through this electronic maze, no one feels or really touches until the very last second—and *that* moment is played more like a melancholy coda to a portrait of a world gone askew.

Faking it is part of the film's subject, also the trap into which it occasionally falls. In interviews, Egoyan—like Soderbergh, a great favorite of Wim Wenders—has criticized the "misuse" of film or video as "instruments to enshrine sentiment," and said: "Nothing is more artificial than traditional realism." Yet enshrining sentiment—sentimentality, actually—is exactly what he's used his instruments for here. And his spare, flashily cryptic dialogue is closer to the artificiality of bad movie naturalism than to the high allusive literacy he probably wants.

Egoyan's style is too cool and detached to appear *overtly* sentimental, but his material is impregnated with a kind of syrupy self-pity: pared-down soap opera. A very bad commercial TV movie could have emerged from "Speaking Parts"'" plot line. The discarded writer is a woman, Clara—played with fine, naked-nerve emotionalism by Gabrielle Rose—whose brother died after saving her life with a lung transplant. Clara replaces him with a young actor, Lance (Michael McManus), whom she hires to play the brother in her teleplay; Lance is a hotel employee adored from afar by a young chambermaid (Egoyan's girlfriend, Arsinée Khanjian), who collects all his non-speaking parts on videotape.

The women feel and respond; the men are cold voyeurs. And all of them—these beautiful youngsters wandering disconsolately through corridors of dread in the post-video emotional holocaust—are ruled by a Big Video Daddy and Mama: the producer and the hotel head housekeeper. This whole idea is deeply sentimental. And since Egoyan seems prey to the same vices he attacks—or, more accurately, nibbles at—one wonders if the manipulative, detached video store owner (played by Tony Nardi, who suggests a younger Peter Coyote) is an ironic self-portrait. In the end, "Parts" seems a narcissistic movie. It may be only partial self-kidding that Egoyan's company is called Ego Film Arts Inc.

Still and all, "Speaking Parts" (Times-rated Mature for partial nudity, video sex and language) is subtle, thoughtful stuff for serious filmgoers. It's full of ideas, disturbing metaphors for today's society, and it's subtly made by a promising filmmaker with an intelligent vision. It's also a drowsy, despairing film, in which we and the characters seem to be viewing everything through the other side of an aquarium wall. Egoyan builds up to a paroxysm in which every kind of film or video stock is intercut wildly together: an orgasm of mixed media. But, though Egoyan's characters may never crystallize into flesh and blood, that's part of his point. Video sex is the crucial coupling in his vague, nightmare world, the deadly climax of the Video Age.

MONTHLY FILM BULLETIN, 9/89, p. 283, Adam Barker

Clara sits in a mausoleum watching a video of her dead brother. Elsewhere, a hotel maid, Lisa, is besotted with Lance, an aloof, highclass gigolo provided for the hotel's female guests, who ignores her. Lisa pursues her obesssion at home by watching videos of Lance as an extra in third-rate movies. When Clara arrives at the hotel, Lance spots a film script in her room and assumes she is casting a movie. He approaches Clara, who agrees to audition him privately because of his resemblance to her brother. The audition culminates in Clara seducing him. The next day, Clara indicates to the producer that Lance should get the lead part. It turns out that Clara is the film's scriptwriter, and she has to leave to discuss some changes with the producer. Lance is dejected by her departure, and is more irritable than usual with Lisa. She consoles herself by going to help her local video dealer, Eddy, record a party. She arrives to discover it is an orgy, and Eddy does not need her help. Clara tells Lance via a video-conference line that she will have to stay away a while longer. She encourages him to break into the hotel room of the film's casting director to find out if he has got the part, and to steal the script, which she believes is being changed without her permission. Lisa and Eddy go to record the wedding of one of the film crew, where Lisa upsets the bride. Lance discovers that he has the part. When he reveals to Clara that the script has indeed been changed, she tearfully explains that it is based on the true story of her brother's death. She begs Lance to use his influence with the producer, and he reluctantly agrees. A suicide is discovered at the hotel, apparently the result of an infatuation with Lance. He tells Clara that the sister's role in the film has been changed into a man. Clara is heartbroken by this news, and by Lance's refusal to stand up to the producer. Eventually, Lance stops returning Clara's calls. During the filming of a talk-show sequence, Clara threatens to kill herself. Lisa experiences the show telepathically, and in a concatenation of video images, senses Lance's unhappiness. When she returns home, he is waiting for her, and they embrace.

The video camera has come of age. Envisaged as a double-edged instrument of communication and alienation, it features in two recent films by young North American directors, Steven Soderbergh and Atom Egoyan. The third—and most accomplished yet—feature by Egoyan, *Speaking Parts* examines the tragdey of characters increasingly dependent on video images, not just for their kicks but also in their everyday lives. Clara, who is obsessed with the video image of her dead brother, masturbates to the almost identical image of Lance on a video-conference screen. Lisa makes up for her frustrating encounters with Lance by watching videos of his old movies. Under Egoyan's dissecting knife, video is revealed to be an essentially solipsistic medium, encouraging self-contemplation rather than social intercourse.

Using an ensemble of actors familiar from *Next of Kin* and *Family Viewing*, Egoyan traces the doomed attempts of three obsessive individuals to establish relationships. The androgynous Lance is desired by both Clara and Lisa, while his main concern is with himself. The wooden acting in *Family Viewing* has been replaced by more subtle characterisations (though David Hemblen as the producer reprises the role of overbearing patriarch). Despite an emphatic modernity in Egoyan's use of electronic media in a collage of film and video imagery, underlying this is the well-worn conceit of the film-within-the-film. In a hall-of mirrors of cross-media play, the final scene is a reconstruction of a TV talk show staged for the film being made. Relationships replicate alarmingly, as Lance takes on the film role of Clara's brother while her own role is excised, reversing the real-life death of her brother. In the latter half, however, much of the interest built up during the suggestive first half is dissipated by an increasing preoccupation with political wrangling on the set of the film-within-the-film.

For Egoyan, it is sex above all else which has come to be mediated by electronic processes, whether it be a video camera or telephone answering machine. The most physical human activity is shown to be inseparable from technical gadgetry. Despite the potential here for social criticism (exposure of what constitutes a 'natural' relationship), the film manifests a surprising conservatism. Video, and other electronic devices, are used merely as metaphors in a humanistic exploration of alienation which leaves many crucial assumptions unchallenged. Women, for example, come off badly as demanding, possessive creatures, with Lisa in particular shown as being completely dependent on Lance. Although their final embrace is partly undermined by its unclear status (Lance appears immediately after Lisa's video visions, and may well be part of them), it still represents a girl-gets-boy happy ending. Egoyan's formal and sexual radicalism is, in the end, only skin-deep.

NEW STATESMAN & SOCIETY, 9/22/89, p. 43, Suzanne Moore

The isolation of modern life amid the proliferation of media images is also [the reference is to *Talk Radio*] Atom Egoyan's subject. His new film *Speaking Parts* follows similar themes to last year's brilliant *Family Viewing* and confirms him as a film-maker of dark originality. Unlike Barry Champlain, Lisa, one of the film's central characters, no longer has any faith in words. "There is nothing special about words." Like everyone else in the film she seems entirely alone, in touch with the world only through video images. Again Egoyan mixes video into the film and plays with textures until recognisable images turn into strange abstractions.

As Lisa does her menial job in a hotel she becomes obsessed with Lance—a hologram of a character, an actor who has never had a speaking part. But Lance is involved with Clara, a writer whose true story about the loss of her brother has been optioned by a producer. The story is being rewritten all the time and she and Lance can now only communicate through satellite link-up. While this might sound like a doomy overdose of alienation it is underpinned with ridiculously funny and disturbing dialogue and you can't help admiring the way that Egoyan manipulates his images in a film *about* the manipulation of images.

The climax of *Speaking Parts* is a virtuoso piece of editing and, unusually, Egoyan makes you care about these weird and empty characters. His message, like that of Steven Soderbergh's *sex, lies and videotape*, is deceptively simple: only connect. Yet, like many young film-makers who have grown up in the media explosion, he understands he is always implicated in what he is criticising. Given this, opposition is impossible. Instead his films are a kind of interference. No one in his films can ever get away from the images that surround them; they reach out to someone only to find a screen.

Somehow, sometimes, in *Speaking Parts*, they reach out to each other. As flesh touches flesh, Egoyan makes us believe that it is still possible to know the difference between what is real and what isn't.

NEW YORK POST, 9/29/89, p. 25, Jami Bernard

Canadian film maker Atom Egoyan's latest movie is also about sex, lies and videotape, but it is quite different from that other film. Its plot would sound like an unlikely soap opera, but plot is not quite the way to look at "Speaking Parts," playing at the New York Film Festival tonight and tomorrow. The movie unfolds in alternately mediated and overlapping layers, drawing you into its Nautilus shell of desire and illusion.

Anyway, the plot, more or less: Lance (Michael McManus) is a movie extra who supports himself by working in a hotel where he makes beds and breaks hearts. One of the hearts that is straining belongs to Lisa (Arsinée Khanjian, whose face is a ghost of Andie MacDowell's of "sex, lies, and videotape"). Lisa folds sheets in the hotel, and is so obsessed with Lance that she rents his videos to study his image and somehow *feel* him better.

Also studying screens is Clara (Gabrielle Rose), a scriptwriter who views the image and memory of her dead brother in a post-modern, video-equipped crypt. Clara confers with the producer of her film via conference-room video monitor; she later has videophone sex with Lance, who is up for a part in the movie. Meanwhile, Lisa is attempting to interview brides while taping their weddings, but her questions about the deeper meaning of relationships ("But what do you *see* in Ronnie?") set them to crying.

Images, reality and fantasy become intertwined as the characters do, with the video monitor serving as supreme communicator, distancer and distorter. The movie is sophisticated but not slick, serious but with humor, a deceptively slow, purposeful movie that offers great rewards if you stick with it.

NEW YORK POST, 2/16/90, p. 27, David Edelstein

"Speaking Parts," the third feature by the 29-year-old Canadian Atom Egoyan, is a wry, lulling, pretentious little movie about the way video depersonalizes our relationships, strengthens corporate control over our lives and strips our existence of integrity.

It's a cool, impressive piece of work—its pieces lock trimly into place. But you might emerge feeling starved for human contact, and not altogether sure if it's our corporatized, video-age lives that are the problem or Egoyan's way of crimping human nature to fit his preconceived ideas about the impact of technology on our souls.

Make no mistake, Egoyan has an arresting sensibility (and not just because his film is sometimes a jail sentence). Cleverly, he has fashioned a two-headed protagonist, a man and a woman whose separate odysseys begin and end in the same place.

Lance (Michael McManus) is a bit-part actor with dreamboat features. He cleans rooms in a large, blank, antiseptic hotel, where he occasionally services female clients along with their rooms. Lisa (Arsinee Khanjian) is a chamber-maid who adores Lance—she rents videos of movies in which he has appeared, staring at him on the TV screen as if hoping to make contact with him through his image.

Since the two resemble each other, there's a narcissistic aspect to their relationship, and each has more than a touch of androgyny. Egoyan has them deliver their lines in a narcotic trance, and part of his skill is that you're never sure if they're giving imaginative performances or just flat, zombie-like performances. Bad soap opera acting? No, *stylization.*

"Speaking Parts" has another central character, Clara (the more personable Gabrielle Rose), writer of an autobiographical script about a brother who donates his lung to save his sister's life. At the start of the film, she strolls into a white, high-tech crypt, presses a button and, trembling with emotion, watches a video of her dead brother, who bears a resemblance to Lance.

Conveniently, her film company has set up shop at the hotel where Lance works. The two have an affair, continued when she leaves town by video-link. (They watch each other masturbate.)

Later, when Lance wins the part, he must choose between Clara and the smug, egocentric producer (David Hemblen) who's bent on trivializing her script—indeed, her life story, her monument to her dead brother. The producer—a totalitarian, as patriarchs tend to be in films like this—is viewed largely on a video screen.

Inevitably (and perhaps unfortunately), each story comes to a head. Lance betrays Clara, agreeing to participate in the butchered film; Lisa, who has fallen in with a video-store manager (Tony Nardi) who tapes weddings and orgies, becomes overly invasive, driving the spouse of a bride she has terrorized to turn her camera around on her and scream, "See what it feels like?"

That's a predictable line, even if you haven't seen "sex, lies, and videotape." And once you crack Egoyan's narrative and figure out what he's up to, the whole movie feels academic—an elaborate cinematic proof, an almost mathematical exercise devoid of discovery or surprise.

Video Lies, Video Controls, Video Subsumes, Egoyan says. Well, so does film, occasionally this one. By withholding information and telling his story in dribs and drabs, he conceals from us how dumb and obvious and contrived his material often is.

What keeps "Speaking Parts" from being insufferably priggish is Egoyan's shrewd manipulation of film and video—the serpentine technique that keeps us at once entranced and at arm's length. His poker-faced style is often witty, and as he hops from film to video and back, he does make us feel how much shallower and spookier the video image can be.

But there's something troubling about Egoyan's virtuosity. Rarely has a non-experimental film so wallowed in video while relentlessly pounding home its distrust of it. Our age has fostered a generation of moralistic young film makers with a visceral horror of the video image. Their own talent seems to fill them with disgust.

NEWSDAY, 2/16/90, Part III/p. 3, Janice Berman

When "Speaking Parts" was screened at last year's New York Film Festival, Wim Wenders thrust his own $5,000 prize for "Wings of Desire" upon Atom Egoyan, the 27-year-old writer/director.

Wenders was justified. "Speaking Parts," cool, clever and off-putting, is a musing on video as a symbol of contemporary alienation.

Plot is not as important as atmosphere—a dreamlike world defined by carefully composed images rather than by language. There is little in the way of dialogue. After all, says one character dismissively, "There is nothing special about words."

Clara (Gabrielle Rose), a TV scriptwriter, visits a white, sterile-looking mortuary where she views a color videotape memorializing her brother, who bears a close resemblance to Lance (Michael McManus), a hotel worker and aspiring actor.

Lance—who bears more than a passing resemblance to Rob Lowe—is dead only spiritually. He makes beds; he also lies in them with women guests like the writer. Clara is so pleased with his performance that she auditions him for her TV movie about her dead brother—she still grieves for him—and his unsuccessful lung transplant. It would be Lance's first speaking part.

One of Lance's co-workers, Lisa (Arsinee Khanjian), a chambermaid, has a crush on Lance and has seen every movie he's been an extra in. She gets a gig helping a video store clerk tape special occasions—like orgies and weddings.

"Speaking Parts" inhabits a world where Lance, doing his laundry, pulls a bouquet of red roses out of a dryer, a peculiar life-from-a-crypt image that calls to mind the memorial video. It's a world where the lives of a TV show's staff are in the hands of an icy-commander producer (David Hemblen), an image from far away, beamed larger-than-life into a claustrophobic conference room. Later, Lance and Clara have teleconferenced sex; just another way of using video to achieve that sense of closeness.

Video, in fact, runs away with any moments of life and reality. Clara, who has given up the story that is central to her life so that Lance can have a life on television, becomes increasingly desperate for his attention. But Lance ignores her. He's becoming a TV star, being swept into what, in a more normal world—or perhaps, in our own bygone days—would be unreality.

Clara's story is now beyond her control. The producer has rewritten it and Lance has run with it. Together, they've sucked the meaning out of her existence, and she cannot recapture its truth, despite a desperate attempt to do so.

One might argue that Clara's last-ditch effort to regain control is a cliche, a grandstand play that knocks this well-calibrated film off center. Even so, Egoyan, like Steven Soderbergh with "sex, lies and videotape," has succeeded in making us think about where truth lies.

VILLAGE VOICE, 10/3/89, p. 61, J. Hoberman

The electronic image is no less omnipresent [the reference is to *The Documentator*] in Atom Egoyan's witty, sinister *Speaking Parts*. The third feature by this talented young Canadian immediately establishes a Cronenbergian sense of dread, crosscutting between a lone mourner in a video-equipped crypt and the ominous impersonality of a hotel laundry room.

For Egoyan, video is at once a phantasm and a commodity, a private hallucination and a nexus of social relations, a doppelgänger and an Other, a form of truth and a source of mistaken identity. A disturbed chambermaid, obsessed with an aspiring movie actor, haunts a video store where the clerk analyses customers on the basis of their rentals and supplements his income making VCR tapes of weddings and orgies. A monstrous TV producer issues instructions or kudos via closed-circuit vidscreen—later, a doomed, mutually manipulative couple usurps his technology for a more advanced version of telephone sex.

Not primarily a narrative filmmaker, Egoyan thrives on urban anxiety and excels in scenes based on the deadpan staging of a single monstrous gag. The lapses in continuity and relative absence of street life or connecting shots subvert *Speaking Part*'s sleek, generic look. Indeed, the film's overall lack of resolution only heightens its intimation of an image underclass breeding in the barrios of the North American metropolis.

VILLAGE VOICE, 2/20/90, p. 75, Georgia Brown

For someone just turning 30, Canadian filmmaker Atom Egoyan may be unforgivably sophisticated. His ideas about sex, lies, and the crucial you-know-what make Steven Soderbergh look like a naïve (American) schoolboy. The elegantly polished, crafty, and highly bizarre *Speaking Parts*—Egoyan's third feature, picked up from last year's New York Film Festival—sits somewhere between highbrow sci-fi and high-tech soap opera.

Despite the film's title, nobody speaks until 10 minutes into the film. ("There's nothing special about words," someone remarks later.) Instead of speaking, people *look*. *Speaking Parts* is above all a meditation on images—the presentation of self in everyday technology.

In an eerie mausoleum where one can view videotapes of the dearly departed, Clara (Gabrielle Rose) watches a tape showing her dead brother walking through a field. Sitting on the floor with her TV, Lisa (Arsinée Khanjian)—who sometimes looks like Clara's brother and sometimes like Tiny Tim—watches a piano recital where Lance (Michael McManus), a movie extra, appears as a member of the audience. (The camera, zeroing in and then freezing on Lance's face in the second row, tips us off that Lisa's tape is subjective—that perhaps there are no objective tapes here.) A transfixed look on the women's faces, the naked desire in their gazes, is what Egoyan himself seems focused on. If looks could animate—bring back the dead—theirs would.

Clara's brother died giving his sister one of his lungs in a transplant operation; writing a script based on their story, then trying to keep a bigwig TV producer faithful to the actual experience, are her ways of keeping her brother alive. The beautiful, long-haired Lance, working as a hotel chambermaid while trying out for speaking parts, seems terminally frozen in narcissism. Lisa, in charge of sheets in the hotel laundry, is determined to deflect Lance's eye from his own image onto her. One Clara lays eyes on Lance, she too becomes a fan, wanting to cast him as her brother while (incestuously) taking him as a lover. (The vague resemblance of each of these characters to the others makes for a kind of prismatic effect.)

In her quest for movies featuring Lance's fleeting appearances as an extra, Lisa attracts the attention of Eddy, a clerk in her local video store who films weddings and orgies in his time off. Impressed that Eddy knows how to capture the glistening (zombielike) tears of a father of the bride, Lisa wants to assist him. It's easy, Eddy says, "You've just got to know what buttons to push." (Pushing buttons is an Egoyan theme.) But when the dogged Lisa begins quizzing a bride named Trish about her husband-to-be—"What do you see in Ronnie? I mean, when you're looking at him, what do you see?"—the bride rushes out in tears.

Egoyan coolly evades ordinary expectations of narrative continuity. Exposition is spare and cryptic, and he keeps spatial and geographical relations to himself. It's impossible to get your bearings or to locate an outside world. (Only Eddy seems to have some sort of independent identity—but then, he's cameraman, not a subject.) Most of the film's action takes place inside the sinister hotel that appears to be something of a byzantine directorate, containing the headquarters of state TV production. Its head manager, a prim, stony-faced blond, fixes up female guests with the boys from housekeeping.

If the manager is nasty, meddling Mommy, Daddy is obviously the (nameless) producer, a grim and lethal talking head. Inside a paneled conference room, he pompously instructs his staff via video monitor from wherever he's on location. The same hookup allows Lance and Clara, while she's out of town, to have sex across the board table. Here, for a change, is a startling sex scene. Acting in *Speaking Parts* is superb—fresh, subtle, and witty.

I may have reservations about the film's chilly sensibility, but there's no doubt that Egoyan is a remarkable talent. And anyway, I have the same reaction to David Cronenberg (to whom Egoyan is often compared) and Margaret Atwood, two other widely admired Canadians. When I heard Egoyan was considering directing Atwood's *Life Before Man*, it seemed a perfect matchup. He may have been born in Egypt to Armenian parents, but he seems to have adapted wonderfully to the northern climate.

Also reviewed in:
NEW YORK TIMES, 2/16/90, p. C10, Janet Maslin
VARIETY, 5/10-16/89, p. 24
WASHINGTON POST, 2/2/90, Weekend/p. 33, Desson Howe
WASHINGTON POST, 2/3/90, p. D3, Rita Kempley

SPEED ZONE

An Orion Pictures release of a Raymond Chow presentation of an Entcorp Communications production. *Executive Producer:* Albert S. Ruddy and Andre Morgan. *Producer:* Murray Shostak. *Director:* Jim Drake. *Screenplay:* Michael Short. *Director of Photography:* François Protat and Robert Saad. *Editor:* Mike Economou. *Music:* David Wheatley. *Music Editor:* Jacqueline Carmody. *Sound:* Daniel Masse, David Weisshaar, and (music) Jamie Sulek. *Sound Editor:* Bruce Nyznik. *Production Designer:* Richard Hudolin. *Art Director:* Richard Hudolin. *Set Decorator:* Gilles Aird and Patti Hall. *Special Effects:* John Thomas. *Costumes:* Paul Andre Guerin. *Make-up:* Jocelyne Bellemare and Valli O'Reilly. *Stunt Coordinator:* Betty Thomas and Minor Mustain. *Running time:* 95 minutes. *MPAA Rating:* PG.

CAST: John Candy (Charlie); Donna Dixon (Tiffany); Matt Frewer (Alec); Joe Flaherty (Vic); Tim Matheson (Jack); Mimi Kuzyk (Heather); Melody Anderson (Lee); Shari Belafonte (Margaret); Brian George (Valentino); Art Hindle (Flash); Dick Smothers (Nelson); Tom Smothers (Randolph); Peter Boyle (Chief Edsel); Don Lake (Whitman); John Schneider (Cannonballer #1); Jamie Farr (Cannonballer #2); Lee Van Cleef (Grandfather); Harvey Atkin (Gus Gold); Eugene Levy (Leo Ross); Michael Spinks (Bachelor); Brooke Shields (Stewardess); Alyssa Milano (Truck Driver); Louis Del Grande (Salesman); Carl Lewis (Jogger).

LOS ANGELES TIMES, 4/28/89, Calendar/p. 20, Chris Willman

Outside of these United States, "Speed Zone" is being marketed under the name "Cannonball Fever," and the executive producers are filmic race veterans Albert S. Ruddy and Andre Morgan—so, yes, try as they might to disguise it: This is indeed, unofficially, the breathlessly awaited "Cannonball Run III." Start your engines, high-octane comedy fans!

Just kidding. Whatever your gullibility-per-gallon level, don't let this installment's talented cast fool you. Come back, Burt, all is forgiven.

The only survivor of the Burt Pack on hand is Jamie Farr, as a sheik who pulls out of the race when he can't stop leering at a squeaky-voiced bimbo's enormous breasts. (Let the convulsions begin!) The pack taking over the proceedings this time includes about half the old "SCTV" crew—cast members John Candy, Eugene Levy and Joe Flaherty, along with writer Michael Short and director Jim Drake—all of whom worked on some of TV comedy's finest half-hours before this blotch on their driving records.

There's something frighteningly wrong when Brooke Shields shows up for a two-minute cameo (as herself) and racks up more giggles than Candy, Levy and Flaherty combined. The only other performer to redeem herself is Donna Dixon who does a dead-on impression of Marilyn Monroe. Otherwise, there's even more wreckage among the cast of "Speed Zone" (rated PG) than among the transport.

NEW YORK POST, 4/22/89, p. 22, Jami Bernard

The cars are back, and what's worse, so are the drivers. "Speed Zone" is another low-gear addition to the "Cannonball Run" *oeuvre* of car-crash-as-plot-device movie. It has a whole new slate of "stars" in cameo roles in what is the disaster-movie approach to casting. And "Speed Zone" is indeed a disaster.

The Cannonball Run is a cross-country, no holds barred auto race, usually spearheaded by Burt

Reynolds, who made what feels like a zillion sequels. Anyway, someone figured there was still enough mileage left on the idea, even if the former cast was not available, so they changed the title and had the police chief (Peter Boyle) throw all the old drivers into jail in a "pre-emptive strike," leaving the course clear for a whole new cast.

This new cast is chiefly composed of "SCTV," alumni, who only prove that you can't go home again. In addition to John Candy, Joe Flaherty and Eugene Levy of "SCTV" there's Donna Dixon (wife of Dan Aykroyd), Shari Belafonte, Tom and Dick Smothers, and cameos by Michael Spinks, Carl Lewis, Alyssa Milano, Jamie Farr, and that recent Princeton graduate who may have a degree in rocket science, for all I know, but who sure didn't learn much about choosing scripts—Brooke Shields.

Actually, the self-spoofing Shields scene is the bright spot in this endless stretch of movie. She plays herself as a stewardess of a low-rent airline, because ever since she took time off for college, she hasn't been able to land a decent role. She snaps at the passengers and smugly tells the Smothers Brothers that *she* does not intend to spend her life taking bit parts in stupid movies. Well, we'll see.

Candy plays a sweet, self-effacing parking attendant. He is paired for the race with Dixon, who does a Marilyn Monroe ingenue impression that is to cringe for. They're in the BMW.

Flaherty is a hit man and Matt Frewer is his target, a guy in debt to loan sharks up to his parking lights. They pair up in the Jaguar XJ-12.

Tim Matheson and Mimi Kuzyk are bland TV reporters who enter the race in order to do a first-person report. They're in the minivan.

Shari Belafonte and Melody Anderson are MIT grads with five Ph.D.s between them. They dress up as hot babes because even today—yes, girls, *even today*—making women smart in movies is usually a set-up for some boob gag. They're in the micro-mini skirts in the Ferrari Daytona Spyder.

There's also a Lamborghini Countach and a Bentley Corniche convertible (believe me, someone helped me figure out these car names because the only vehicle I can flag with any certainty is the Checker cab).

The script, by SCTV alumnus Michael Short, brother of Martin, is simply not funny. Of course, since a "Cannonball" movie probably appeals to the same element as wrestling, its hard to know just what they *would* find funny—cars racing backwards on the wrong side of the road seemed to go over well at yesterday's screening.

There are also little lines from other movies tossed in: "Top o' the world, ma!" and "I love the smell of napalm in the morning." If Short was running short of material, why didn't he give me a call? I hear screenwriters make a lot of bucks for turning out junk like this.

NEWSDAY, 4/22/89, Part II/p. 15, Drew Fetherston

The car is red.

The car is going too fast.

All the cars are going too fast.

The police are mad.

If you had trouble with the above plot outline of "Speed Zone"—if it took more than , say, two minutes to read this far—this is your kind of film.

Perhaps that's a tad harsh. Some of the folks who will gladly spend money on this stinker probably salt their conversation with words of several syllables and pepper listeners with designer phrases in foreign languages.

"Lamborghini," you might hear one say.

"Alfa Romeo," his pal might retort.

"Speed Zone" is yet another film about the Cannonball Run, the cross-country outlaw road race that formed the backbone of such memorable films as "Cannonball," "The Cannonball Run" and "The Cannonball Run II"

Don't let the startlingly original title of this latest entry fool you: It's the same dumb story once again. Don't be deluded by what seems like a decent cast—"SCTV" vets John Candy, Eugene Levy and Joe Flaherty; Peter Boyle and The Smothers Brothers. No comic talent could quicken this script.

It is incoherent to its very core. Remember, this is a film about a race: Several comic characters get into cars and head westward.

Each car has a little story attached to it: Will the British gambler take the prize, pay his debts and thus thwart the loanshark's hitman? Will the cheating rich kids get away with their scheme? Will the TV news team in the souped-up van keep up with the racers and make journalistic history?

Viewers may be forgiven for not caring, because director Jim ("Police Academy IV") Drake clearly didn't. The film is so disordered that it's never clear who's in first and who stands where in the rest of the pack.

The only certainty is that the scream of tortured rubber will echo through the theater, and that vehicles will be reduced to smoking hulks at a pace not seen since Rommel's Panzers battled Monty's tank battalions at El Alamein.

Several celebs make cameo appearances: Carl Lewis plays a runner, Brooke Shields and stock car racer Richard Petty play themselves, and boxer Michael Spinks is an outraged non-participant in the race whose car nonetheless gets wrecked.

They are the feeblest sorts of cameos, patched onto the shoddy fabric of the film in the crudest possible fashion. It says much about the whole effort to note that Shields is as funny as anyone else in the film, and Spinks is far from the worst actor.

Also reviewed in:
NEW YORK TIMES, 4/22/89, p. 15
VARIETY, 5/3-9/89, p. 16
WASHINGTON POST, 4/21/89, p. C7, Hal Hinson

SPICES

A National Film Development Corporation production. *Director:* Ketan Mehta. *Screenplay (Hindi with English subtitles):* Shafi Hakim and Ketan Mehta. *Original Story:* Chunilal Madia. *Director of Photography:* Jahangir Choudhury. *Editor:* Sanjiv Shah. *Music:* Rajat Dholakia. *Running Time:* 98 minutes. *MPAA Rating:* Not Rated.

CAST: Naseeruddin Shah (Subedar); Smita Patil (Sonbai); Om Puri (Abu Mian); Suresh Oberoi (Mukhi); Raj Babbar (Sonbai's Husband); Raghu Nath (Masterji); Deepti Naval (Sarasvati).

LOS ANGELES TIMES, 11/3/89, Calendar/p. 18, Michael Wilmington

The Indian film "Spices"—a simple strong social melodrama that rivets your attention and burns your eyes—is set during recent colonial times, in a small lakeside village where fields of red chiles blaze and wave under an unremitting sun.

Just as the heat oppresses the villagers, so do the practices of the period: the rigid town hierarchy, the castes and social divisions, the patriarchal families and, finally, subjection to the colonial regime and the brutal whims of the local Subedar (tax inspector), who represents it.

When the Subedar (Haseeruddin Shah) decides that he wants to sleep with a local woman, he simply takes her. When one of the women, Sonbai (Smita Patil)—her husband off in Calcutta looking for work—refuses him, he will not accept it, his soldiers pursuing her to the gates of the spice factory where she works. And when those doors are locked to him—through the stubborn intercession of the elderly factory guard, Abu Mian (Om Puri)—the Subedar becomes enraged. At first, he squeezes the leaders economically—especially the spice factory's owner, who has less mettle than his guard. Then he threatens to destroy the town.

The Subedar is a petulant, narcissistic, vicious man. But, though he's a brute, he sees himself as a paragon of taste and an irresistible seducer. Shah plays him with the florid gestures of a silent-movie sheik. When he springs his seductions, his nostrils flare, his eyes bulge and he turns on his prized possession, a Victrola. This silly, preening sadist also commands a small detachment of soldiers. His is the voice of the government. And the village men, slowly, reluctantly, succumb to his will.

Sonbai alone is defiant, along with Abu Mian, the simple, pure man who protects her: a faithful servant who keeps his principles even when his employers abandon them. Puri gives him the slow, firm gestures of an arthritic saint, the glaring eyes of a devil. As the contest of wills stretches out, the heat pours down and the town edges, closer and closer, toward crisis.

"Spices" is something of a feminist "High Noon." Like that classic 1952 Western, it presents an inevitable clash between unshakable wills during which the moral core of an entire population is gradually revealed—and it mostly eschews psychological subtlety for broad social strokes. The villagers tend to act en masse. They're mostly types: the chattering, timid tradesmen; the stern but pragmatic Mukhi (Suresh Oberoi), who cannot understand why his wife will not accept his infidelities; the gossipy smirking layabouts and the outraged but frightened women workers.

Melodrama can always be criticized for crudities and exaggerations; "Spices" has more than a few. The humor is coarse, the colors searingly bright, the acting, Patil excepted, somewhat hammy. But, just as "High Noon" processed essential elements of the Western movie mythos into a progressive cry of outrage against conformity and social cowardice, the young writer-director, Ketan Mehta—an admirer of Brecht and Godard as well as Griffith and Chaplin—manipulates the grossly melodramatic forms of most second-rate Indian movies to nail his villains to the wall. The form of the film (Times-rated Mature for adult themes) is a trap, though it begins in a strange, fanciful mood that seems to mingle low-key naturalism with disturbingly broad farce.

At the end, Mehta abandons all naturalism and his style goes as baroque and overheated as Robert Aldrich in his later action movies. But Mehta's graphic sense is lucid and passsionate. He obviously burns with rage at the thought of the inspector's injustice, and he communicates that rage with driving force.

And in the person of his leading actress, Smita Patil—who died in childbirth in 1986 shortly after making this film and who incarnated in her roles and off-screen life a progressive, idealistic stance—he gets an unexpectedly poignant and potent symbol of rebellion. When Sonbai defies the Subedar, she stands for every proud spirit that says, "No." When the old guard defends her, he stands for every policeman who values justice above compromise. And when the door and hinges begin to shake before them, they stand for the fragile barriers that lie between humanity and license, free will and tyranny, courage and chaos.

NEW YORK POST, 9/6/89, p. 27, David Edelstein

In the Indian melodrama "Spices," rows of chili peppers sway in the wind against the baked, near-Martian landscape, and you can almost smell the capsicum and garam masala—the images make your eyes tingle. Lime-green birds lift off from spice plants, and the women who gather by the river to wash and fetch water are exotic creatures themselves, witchy and darkeyed in multicolored kaftans.

The film is set in Gujarat, western India, in the colonial era, but this could almost be the 17th century or some arid, "Dune"-like planet. It's that strange. Then the movie's musty, feminist parable takes over and you're permanently oriented in the late 20th century. Funny how feminist clichés know no borders.

"Spices" appears in conjunction with an eight-film retrospective at the Asia Society of the works of actress Smita Patil, who died in 1986 at the age of 31. Patil performed in both big-budget Bombay musicals and smaller, regional films, and the series offers a hefty sampling of the socially-conscious "New Indian Cinema" of the late '70s and '80s.

In "Spices," alas, the dumpling-cheeked actress does little but strike noble poses, radiating integrity while everyone else whistles and mutters what a looker she is. It's a platform, all right, but not an attractive one; the movie (Patil's last) never lets us discover her beauty for ourselves.

Her antagonist is the Subedar (Naseeruddin Shah), one of several tax collectors who ride through rural India on horseback with convoys of soldiers, pitching their tents beside rivers. If this verison of history is accurate, the landlords often misused their power, and the Subedar here is a particularly swinish fop—he has been Anglicized.

His clothes are raj-chic (breeches, boots, pith helmet), and his soldiers carry a gramaphone and a crop of 78s, which he uses to dazzle the ignorant villagers. (At first they laugh at the machine, then they can't figure out where the voices are coming from.) More to the point, this Subedar is a horny devil, and his roving eye falls hard on the sassy, defiant Sonbai (Patil).

When she slaps him for his salaciousness (an unprecedented act), he sends his soldiers after her, and the woman takes refuge in a fortress-like spice factory. The second half of "Spices" is the standoff between the Subedar and Sonbai, defended now by the factory's foreman, a mottled giant with long, wavy red hair—the Beast to Patil's Beauty.

The movie has a folkloric boldness, and it sounds as if it might be fun, but nothing very interesting passes between Beauty and the Beast, and what follows are windy debates among the villagers, their wives and the politicians—most of whom loathe the Sudebar but think it would be best if Sonbai gritted her teeth and surrendered. Even the women in the spice factory begin to waver in their loyalty.

The movie is vibrantly directed by Ketan Mehta (lots of pungent close-ups and zoom lenses), but there's no way to pump life into confrontations this stilted and didactic. (There's even a sub-plot involving the wife of the town's leader, who insists, to her husband's horror, on sending her little girl to school.) You feel yourself wilting under all the political righteousness.

At heart, though, this is the crudest kind of melodrama—the Sudebar does everything but tie Sonbai to the railroad tracks. In his first scene, he twirls his mustache in close-up—how is this meant to be taken? It isn't ironic: it's a thoughtful twirl, a meditative twiddle. It means: I'm going to use every vicious authoritarian capitalist trick in the book to sleep with this babe.

The climatic violence is staged with laughable clumsiness—the actors swing their clubs gingerly to avoid hurting their co-stars, and the blood is right out of a Lucite can. But it's the moral crudeness that really undoes "Spices." The title comes from an Indian proverb which says that after God made man he was bored and sprinkled spices on the world to make it more colorful. Too bad this movie makes everything so black and white.

NEWSDAY, 9/6/89, Part II/p. 5, Drew Fetherston

The land baron, backed by his band of murderous gunslingers, lusts after a courageous, virtuous young woman in a dusty little town far beyond the reach of government law and order. She spurns his leering advance, slaps him hard and flees to shelter in the village. The gunslingers cow the townsmen into silence, then go to fetch her. Only one man and her own courage stand between her and degradation and death.

Although the baron here is a *Subedar*, a tax collector in rural India, and the one upright man is Abu Mian, the aged guard of a spice factory, the story in "Spices" is the familiar one often told in the classic American western.

Though the paralled is apt, it is not exact. "Spices" is at once more flawed and more profound than its Occidental counterpart: It deals with far more complex social issues, chiefly feminism, in a much more simplistic, melodramatic fashion.

The story is set in the early 1940s, when the British colonial rulers joined cause with the feudal powers and shared the money collected by the tax collectors. When the *subedar* arrives, the village men—including the *mukhi*, the village chief—grovel and plead. When the *subedar* demands women—"Consider this another sort of tax," he says—the chief brings one to share his opulent tent.

Another woman, Sonbai, an abandoned wife, refuses to submit and flees to the town's spice factory, a walled complex guarded by Abu Mian that employs village women. Most of the factory women urge that Sonbai be handed over to prevent reprisals, but the guard defies the *subedar* and his soldiers, setting the scene for the showdown.

A subplot about the wife of the village chief, who is beaten but not silenced for confronting injustices against women, reinforces the feminist message.

The lessons in "Spices" apply quite nicely here despite the cultural gulf, though they are doubtless more powerful in India, where the murder by fire of unwanted wives is still, frequently, an unpunished crime.

Director and co-author Ketan Mehta deliberately chose traditional melodrama, a form replete with overdrawn characters and manipulative devices: The *subedar* struts, frowns and strokes his mustache to the point of comedy. Three victims of oppression—two peasants and the village teacher, a Gandhi disciple—are able to topple the pole to which they have been lashed only by pulling together.

But the central characters are no less human for having been drawn with such ideological care; their actions, base and noble, are believable. Sonbai is nicely played by Smita Patil in her last role; she died at age 31 in childbirth shortly after it was made. Patil had worked for women's rights and had chosen her roles to help that cause.

The film is competently made after the fashion of American westerns: It moves quickly, uses its locations artfully, relies on stylized characters (such as a mealy-mouthed cleric and a lazy, cheating husband) to fill in the social background while it concentrates on a story in which unsullied good confronts unrepentant evil.

VILLAGE VOICE, 9/12/89, p. 76, J. Hoberman

Lithe and intense, Smita Patil lights up the screen; in *Spices,* she illuminates an entire landscape. The belle of a poor village in western India, Patil plays a peasant with the bearing of a queen— even her querulous moods are regal. As the title of Ketan Mehta's film suggests, she's hot stuff.

Patil, who died in childbirth three years ago at the age of 31, was the preeminent Indian film actress of her generation. The daughter of Maharashtran politician, this intelligent, graceful woman worked with virtually every major Indian director over the course of her abbreviated career (making some 70 movies in a half-dozen languages). Although Patil was initially considered too darkskinned and unglamorous for the commercial cinema, she ultimately crossed over—becoming a national figure while blurring the lines between India's "parallel" art cinema and the wet-sari spectacles of the Bombay movie-wallahs.

In *Spices*—which opens at the Third Avenue Cinema today, two days before the Asia Society inaugurates an eight-film Patil tribute—the actress plays her trademark role, the spunky, sensual village woman. The film, which was Patil's last and is dedicated to her, is the first by the 36-year-old Mehta to get a New York run, and, as a double debut, it's long overdue. (Mehta's *Bhavni Bhavai*, which also featured Patil, was shown in the 1981 edition of "New Directors/New Films.")

Set in the decade before India's independence, *Spices* is less a national epic than a fable of male privilege and female solidarity. The feminist subtext that Patil brought to many of her films is here explicit. One strand pits the town's ineffectual Gandhian schoolteacher against the rigid sexual code of the village headman; another has Patil's honor become a metaphor for that of her village. Soon into the film, her husband gets a job on the railroad and gleefully departs, leaving her prey for the local *subedar* (tax collector) and his soldiers, who are terrorizing the town.

Naseeruddin Shah—who plays the *subedar* and who appeared opposite Patil in scores of Indian art films—is clownish but sinister, a puppet play villain come to life. He personifies the arrogance of power. Shah's a windbag, and it's appropriate that the technology he uses to mystify his subjects is an ancient windup gramophone. When a villager wonders what the machine does, one of his soldiers explains that "a ghost will come out and drag fools like you inside." And when a servant breaks one of his 78s, Shah throws a monstrous tantrum, beating the luckless flunky nearly to death. In the film's funniest scene, Shah uses his magic gramophone to astonish the young village woman who has been served up for his delectation—then the needle gets stuck mid-seduction.

When Patil rebuffs Shah's advances, her virtue becomes a matter of state. Pursued by the *subedar's* men, she takes refuge in the village pepper factory, which is then besieged—thus precipitating debates between the *subedar* and the village headman, the headman and the factory owner, the owner and the factory guard, the factory guard and the women who grind the chili peppers, and, ultimately, the *subedar* and the entire village.

Shot in Mehta's native state of Gujarat, *Spices* cost the equivalent of $100,000 and has proved one of the most successful films in the history of India's National Film Development Corporation. The movie is rough around the edges, but it has terrific visual vibrance—mounds of red chili peppers blaze out of the sandy, semiarid terrain. Mehta handles melodrama as boldly as he does primary colors. Filled with village banter and dramatic poses, *Spices* has elements of a folk pageant. The processions suggest the childlike exuberance of a make-believe film. But these dusty streets and ancient houses have a drama all their own.

Mehta has an urban appreciation for folk tradition, and also a certain bemused detachment. (The ingratiating, saffronrobed holy man who pops into the picture and hopefully tells Patil to give herself up—this is, after all, only an illusion—is typical of his ironies.) Mehta's is a new sensibility; he's an educated *faux naif* who calls *Spices* a "backwards synthesis." The film's mode could be described as populist but arty, and it's anything but Eurocentric. More stylized than Satyajit Ray, lighter in tone than Mrinal Sen, Mehta belongs to a generation of Indian filmmakers—Mani Kaul and Kumar Shahani are two others—whose work is seldom seen in these precincts, but whose engagement with their medium is the equal of anyone's anywhere.

Also reviewed in:
NATION, 10/9/89, p. 399, Stuart Klawans
NEW YORK TIMES, 9/6/89, p. C16, Vincent Canby
WASHINGTON POST, 11/18/89, p. C3, Rita Kempley

STAR TREK V: THE FINAL FRONTIER

A Paramount Pictures release. *Executive Producer:* Ralph Winter. *Producer:* Harve Bennett. *Director:* William Shatner. *Screenplay:* David Loughery. *Story:* William Shatner, Harve Bennett, and David Loughery. *Based on the TV series "Star Trek" created by:* Gene Roddenberry. *Director of Photography:* Andrew Laszlo. *Editor:* Peter Berger. *Music:* Jerry Goldsmith. *Music Editor:* Kenneth Hall. *Sound:* David Ronne and (music) Bruce Botnick. *Production Designer:* Herman Zimmerman. *Art Director:* Nilo Rodis-Jamero. *Set Designer:* Ronald R. Wilkinson, Richard McKenzie, Andrew Neskoromny, and Antoinette Gordon. *Set Decorator:* John M. Dwyer. *Special Effects:* Michael Wood. *Visual Effects:* Bran Ferren. *Costumes:* Nilo Rodis-Jamero. *Make-up:* Wes Dawn and Jeff Dawn. *Special Make-up:* Kenny Myers. *Stunt Coordinator:* Glenn R. Wilder. *Running time:* 105 minutes. *MPAA Rating:* PG.

CAST: William Shatner (Kirk); Leonard Nimoy (Spock); DeForest Kelley (McCoy); James Doohan (Scotty); Walter Koenig (Chekov); Nichelle Nichols (Uhura); George Takei (Sulu); David Warner (St. John Talbot); Laurence Luckinbill (Sybok); Charles Cooper (Korrd); Cynthia Gouw (Caithlin Dar); Todd Bryant (Captain Klaa); Spice Williams (Vixis); Rex Holman (J'onn); George Murdock ("God"); Jonathan Simpson (Young Sarek); Beverly Hart (High Priestess); Steve Susskind (Pitchman); Harve Bennett (Starfleet Chief of Staff); Cynthia Blaise (Amanda); Bill Quinn (McCoy's Father); Melanie Shatner (Yeoman).

CHRISTIAN SCIENCE MONITOR, 6/19/89, p. 15, David Sterritt

Trekkies, rejoice. The world's all-time favorite spacecraft, the Starship Enterprise, is back on the wide screen. And this time captain Kirk is in command twice over, since William Shatner directed the movie in addition to playing the skipper of the Enterprise, a role he's handled for more than 20 years. Also on board are Mr. Spock and other members of the crew, plus a surprising new character we haven't met before.

"Star Trek V: The Final Frontier" starts by introducing the new arrival: Sybok, a Vulcan who turns out to be Spock's long-lost half brother. As soon as we meet him, though, we lose sight of him for quite a while—as the movie whisks us into the company of Spock and Kirk, beginning their latest adventure in a place no less exotic than Yosemite National Park. (Spock is in particularly interesting form here: In the space of a few minutes he saves Kirk's life, learns how to toast marshmallows, and admits he doesn't understand the words of "Row, Row, Row Your Boat.")

The movie kicks into high gear when Sybok comes back into the story, taking hostages and hijacking the Enterprise itself. These evil deeds don't seem very Vulcan, and, sure enough, Sybok is a renegade who believes in emotions rather than pure logic. He thinks he's had a vision telling him to go to the center of the galaxy, where he'll meet God and learn to understand the universe. He's crafty enough to reach the heart of the galaxy, but some big surprises are waiting for him—and our heroes—when they land on the mysterious planet they find there.

At its best moments, "The Final Frontier" reminds me of earlier films in the "Star Trek" series that I really enjoyed. The last one, "Star Trek IV: The Voyage Home," was the best of all, with its down-to-earth story and hilarious dialogue. There are flashes of the same friendly humor in the new movie, especially when Kirk, Spock, and Bones are wandering through Yosemite Park together.

And the climax of the "The Final Frontier" has a kind of daring that recalls the first "Star Trek" movie. It's full of big philosophical issues, all treated with a goofy irrationality that only Hollywood could dream up. This is the second movie of the summer that mixes fantasy with themes borrowed from religion—the other being "Indiana Jones and the Last Crusade," wherein the characters quest for the Holy Grail and the "awesome power" it will supposedly give them.

Of the two new pictures, the "Star Trek" entry is easily the more enlightened. When its heroes come face-to-face with a larger-than-life character who claims to be the Supreme Being, and he announces his intention to use the Enterprise as a vehicle for disseminating his power and wisdom, Kirk unmasks the imposter by interrupting and asking an obvious question: If you're really God, why do you need mere objects—even highly technological ones, like the Enterprise—to carry out your wishes?

This contrasts vividly with the attitude of "Indiana Jones" filmmakers George Lucas and Steven Spielberg, who seem to believe that objects (like the Holy Grail, and the Ark of the Covenant in the original "Raiders of the Lost Ark" movie) can indeed carry divine but utterly blind powers usable by anyone who gets their hands on them—an oddly superstitious notion from supposedly sophisticated storytellers.

But even if the new "Star Trek" venture is smarter then Indy's current crusade, I can't get too excited about it. This is largely because "The Final Frontier" never makes up its mind how it wants to entertain us. It lurches from one concern to another—focusing on Sybok for a while, then mechanical problems on the Enterprise, then the mystery at the heart of the galaxy, then a gang of hostile Klingons, and so forth, never settling down on one thing long enough to involve us fully.

This doesn't mean the movie is no fun. The characters are as wonderful as ever, and there's something kind of charming about Bran Ferren's special effects—they're a bit tacky and cheap-looking, which makes them seem all the more believable. Still, the fact remains that some Treks are better than others, and "The Final Frontier" doesn't have the surprising warmth of the very best. It's diverting, but forgettable.

FILMS IN REVIEW, 10/89, p. 486, Frank Scheck

The Star Trek films seem to have fallen into an odd pattern. Only the even-numbered installments are good. The first film was a leaden and overblown epic that succeeded mainly because of nostalgic reasons; the second, directed by Nicholas Meyer, was a crackling adventure yarn that brought back both Khan, the malicious alien created by Ricardo Montalban, and the spirited fun of the TV series. The third, directed by Leonard Nimoy, was a lugubrious exercise in metaphysics as the crew struggled to bring back Spock from the dead; the fourth (and most successful, also directed by Nimoy) brought back the campy spirit of the show as the Enterprise found itself in modern day San Francisco.

This fifth installment, the first to be directed by William Shatner, Captain Kirk himself, falls victim to the odd numbered curse. The series has resumed its ponderous tone, with the starship in pursuit of nothing less than heaven and God himself. They are forced into this crusade by a Vulcan relative of Spock's played by Laurence Luckinbill. This concept is certainly an intriguing one, and in keeping with the philosophical tone of the series, but the pacing of this journey is way off, and the banter among the principals is particularly tired. Attempts at humor, such as the scene where Bones and Kirk attempt to have Spock join in for a spirited rendition of "Row, Row, Row Your Boat," are less than successful.

When the writing and direction are substandard, it becomes more apparent that the crew of the Enterprise are getting on in years. They seem particularly tired this time out, and the on-screen drama is outmatched by the theatrics of these middle-aged performers struggling to maintain their youthful enthusiasm for the material. Things are not helped by such bizarre scenes as the erotic fan-dance that Nichelle Nichols' Uhura performs to distract some randy aliens.

This installment also suffers from some poor special effects, as if the filmmakers, knowing the Trekkies will show up in droves on opening day, couldn't be bothered to go first class anymore. When Kirk and Spock and the rest finally do meet God, the results are, to say the least, anti-climactic. One can only hope that the disappointing results of this film don't prevent the making of a Stark Trek 6, because that should be one terrific film.

LOS ANGELES TIMES, 6/9/89, Calendar/p. 1, Kevin Thomas

"Star Trek V: The Final Frontier" is as much a spiritual odyssey as a space adventure, and it's all the richer for it. It has high adventure, nifty special effects and much good humor, but it also has a wonderful resonance to it.

That's because William Shatner, in a triple-threat assignment, as director and co-writer as well as actor, turns to full advantage the inescapable fact that the Star Trek family, after 23 years, is well into middle-age.

Shatner's Capt. James Kirk and his colleagues have retained the reflexes and openness of youth but at the same time they possess the perspective that only the passage of time can bring. For all its intergalactic cliff-hanging, "Star Trek V" is a mellow experience, a contemplation of life's possibilities and rewards in maturity, tinged with an awareness of mortality.

It is also a film without a villain in the usual sense of sci-fi adventure. The hooded, priestly-looking Sybok (Laurence Luckinbill, in a full-bodied, mesmerizing Shakespearean turn) may be mad, but he is surely not evil. He is a Vulcan, in fact the half-brother of Leonard Nimoy's deadpan Spock. A lifelong rebel against the resolutely cool logic of his people, Sybok celebrates emotion and possesses the power to heal and to cast spells. His goal is to reach "the place from which creation springs," a mythical, gaseous planet beyond the Great Barrier. In his impiety he wants "to meet God,"

To that end he plots to commandeer the Starship Enterprise. As it happens, the long-banished Sybok has turned up on the arid, desolate Nimbus III. Designated "The Planet of Galactic Peace" by the peoples of three different planets, it has a colony, optimistically called Paradise, which has degenerated into a seedy frontier outpost, a haven for outcasts and a reflection of the failure of the Terran, Romulan and Klingon peoples to live in interplanetary harmony. Indeed, in Sybok's pursuit of his dream the Klingon Captain Klaa (Todd Bryant) sees a chance to seize the Enterprise himself, which he declares would make him "the greatest warrior in the galaxy."

Everything that Sybok stirs up allows writer David Loughery, in adapting a story he wrote with Shatner and producer Harve Bennett, to celebrate warm friendship and camaraderie in the face of danger, and eventually, the unknown. In embracing each other these seasoned, expert professional space travelers embrace us as well.

Never have we been made to feel so much a part of the Star Trek family, which includes, of course, DeForest Kelley's Dr. Leonard (Bones) McCoy, James Doohan's engineer Scotty, Walter Koenig's navigator Chekov, Nichelle Nichols' communications officer Uhura and George Takei's helmsman Sulu. (Nichols gets to perform a fan dance that would do Sally Rand proud.) Along for the ride this time are space federation official David Warner and aliens Cynthia Gouw and Charles Cooper.

Bran Ferren and Michael L. Wood's visual/special effects and Herman Zimmerman's production design are at once dazzling and functional, while Jerry Goldsmith's score soars and enthralls.

A special triumph for Zimmerman is his Paradise, half Sahara village and hell-hole of the Old West, undeniably reminiscent of the similar outpost in "Star Wars" but a success on its own terms as a work of eclectic, ramshackle Art Deco design. (Nice touch: someone has scrawled "Lost" next to the "paradise" sign on its arched entrance.)

Shatner and his colleagues are clearly aware that at heart "Star Trek" is pretty square stuff, and they honor this quality with affection and just the right touch of tongue-in-cheekery. Without humor as well as wisdom, Sybok's big moment of the truth would be hokey rather than affecting. The film's loveliest scenes, however, are those which enclose it so gracefully near its beginning and at its end, with Kirk and McCoy sitting around a campfire, earnestly trying to teach the solemn Spock how to sing "Row, Row, Row Your Boat."

MONTHLY FILM BULLETIN, 11/89, p. 346, Kim Newman

Stardate 8454.1. On Nimbus III, Sybok, a Vulcan mystic who has rediscovered his emotions, takes hostage Terran St. John Talbot, Romulan Caithlin Dar and Klingon General Korrd, consuls whose role is to oversee the backwater's reputation as "The Planet of Galactic Peace". A Klingon warship commanded by Captain Klaa is sent to deal with the crisis, and Captain James T. Kirk, Science Officer Spock and Dr. McCoy are recalled from a vacation on Earth to command the still not quite operational "U.S.S. Enterprise" on a mission to Nimbus to resolve the situation without undue violence. On Nimbus, Kirk discovers that Sybok, who is Spock's half-brother, has won over this hostages and intends to capture a starship to travel through the Great Barrier to the centre of the galaxy in search of Sha Ka Ree, a legendary planet, and to meet God. Sybok does gain control of the ship, and converts most of the crew to his cause by helping them deal with their emotional crises. Spock is reminded of the trauma of his half-breed birth and McCoy of his decision to end the suffering of his terminally sick father, but Kirk refuses to be treated for his neuroses. The "Enterprise" passes through the Great Barrier, with Klaa's ship close behind, and finds Sha Ka Ree. Sybok, Spock, McCoy and Kirk take a shuttle to the surface, and are confronted by "God", a formless alien being who asks to commandeer the ship so he can return to the galaxy at large. Kirk asks why a divine being would need a ship, and is smitten by a lightbeam. God turns out to be a malefic presence who has been imprisoned on Sha Ka Ree, and Sybok sacrifices himself to defeat it. Spock and McCoy are beamed off the planet on Kirk's orders, the transporter not being capable of saving all three, but Spock and General Korrd persuade Klaa to rescue Kirk. Kirk, Spock and McCoy resume their vacation.

Give that the *Star Trek* sequels II through IV are a self-contained trilogy bracketed by the destruction and resurrection not only of Mr. Spock but of the starship "Enterprise" itself, it is hardly surprising that this latest instalment should complete the mirror pattern of the series by returning to the themes of the ambitious and awkward first film outing, *Star Trek The Motion Picture*. Harlan Ellison once reported that *Trek* producer-creator Gene Roddenberry only had one story idea, in which the crew of the "Enterprise" meet God, and that conceit, which was buried in the first film, here comes embarrassingly to the fore. Unfortunately, *The Final Frontier* lacks not only the spectacular and visionary effects that distinguished the by no means satisfactory original, but also its occasionally interesting and ambiguous approach to the question of godhood.

The heavy mysticism that has always been a part of the Vulcan segment of the *Trek* universe is embodied in the character of Sybok, who resembles a cross between Jesus Christ and Werner

Erhard as he takes the characters in bathetic flashbacks to the most traumatic periods of their lives. Kirk, who refuses to be lulled by the self-help therapy, and complains, "I don't want my pain taken away, I need my pain", suffers from what is either a potentially intriguing character quirk or (more likely) a slip in series continuity as his implied and resolvable trauma is suggested to be the temporary loss of his best friend Spock, in *The Wrath of Khan*, rather than the unqualified death of his only son in *The Search for Spock*. The Great Barrier in the centre of the galaxy is a sub-*2001* swirling lava light show, breached with ridiculous ease, which compares very badly with the genuinely awesome encounter with V'ger in *The Motion Picture*. And "God", even if revealed as a fraud, is an especially unimaginative Santa Claus face in a pillar of light who huffs and puffs like the Great and Powerful Oz until Captain Kirk puts his hand up to ask an awkward question the deity cannot answer.

This reductionism is typical of the whole *Star Trek* cycle, from television to cinema and back to television again (via *Star Trek—The New Generation*), whereby ideas of Stapledonian vastness are scaled down to a digestible formula. When Nigel Kneale suggested the Devil was a Martian in *Quatermass and the Pit*, the treatment of the theme emphasised the millennial and awesome aspects of the concept. In *Star Trek*, nothing is ever truly alien or truly divine, and everything— Greek gods, legendary gunslingers, Abraham Lincoln, galaxy-spanning amoebae, universe-threatening monsters—is dragged down to the status of guest star. The occasional smart comic moments and character bits imported by Nicholas Meyer into the second and fourth films are replaced here by hokey jokes about astronavigator Sulu getting lost on a walk in the park or Mr. Spock learning to sing "Row, Row, Row Your Boat" for a round-the-campfire finale. David Warner's promising turn as a seedy Graham Greene-style diplomat in outer space is cut sadly short as he goes through the last two thirds of the picture without anything to do except clutter up the bridge. In 1979, *Star Trek The Motion Picture* was perceived to be in commercial competition with Disney's *The Black Hole*, a hotchpotch which also ended with a trite and ridiculous epiphany. *Star Trek V: The final Frontier* feels far more like a sequel to that than to Robert Wise's film.

NEW STATESMAN & SOCIETY, 10/27/89, p. 40, Suzanne Moore

Captain's Log: Stardate 191089.

My battle with the Federation continues. After all these years of tucking my trousers into my boots and boldly going where no man has gone before, I feel I've earned a rest. Shore leave at least. I just don't feel the same about interstellar travel these days. I look back at all the old episodes when the galaxy was my oyster and life seemed to be an endless adventure and I wonder what happened to us all. Me, Spock, Bones and the rest—what a crew. There was no mission too dangerous, no warp factor high enough, no alien more ludicrous than the ones we encountered.

Now I wonder what happened to all that time all that optimism. I guess we got kind of institutionalised up there on the Enterprise. It's funny if I'm not lost in space. I don't know what to do with myself. Well, I was saying all this to the Admiral, feeling that it was time to lay down my transporter for good when he came up with an offer I just couldn't refuse. "Jim," he said, "how about if we give you a new Starship Enterprise a new wig and a chance to direct? Will you do just one more movie?"

I talked it over with Spock—after all he directed the last film and for a Vulcan he didn't make a bad job of it—and we decided to get the old mob together and make *The Final Frontier*. At first I didn't have much of a story and then I had the brilliant idea of the Star Trek crew meeting God. Back home I've been watching some of those TV evangelists and, you know, we've always prided ourselves on the way we deal with metaphysical questions as well as being socially relevant.

So, in this movie, we have this half-Vulcan, Sybok, a charismatic kind of prophet who persuades his followers and half the crew of the Enterprise to go into the centre of the galaxy to find Sha Ka Ree, which is a kind of multicultural concept—Eden, paradise, Shangri-la or something like that.

As you know, up here in the 23rd century we like to keep ahead of the times so I encourage my crew to talk a lot of New Age twaddle. Sybok derives his power from getting people to "share their pain". This is a "cleansing experience" that helps one "draw strength from within". Even Bones tries to get us to "open up" and I have to explain my personal theory about fear being The Great Barrier. But if this cosmic encounter group gets too much for you there is always the running battle with the Klingons.

To be frank, though, the one problem that no special effect could solve was the fact that we've all aged. I mean it was 1966 when we first started the whole damned enterprise. I don't see why a little middle-aged spread should stop me, though. In *The Final Frontier* I prove what an action man I am by a spot of rock climbing. It's a pity about the huffing and wheezing, but it's the others I'm worried about: Spock, bless him, has always looked half-dead; but Bones looks decidedly unwell. Uhuru is rather matronly so I thought I'd help her recapture her youth by getting her to take her clothes off and express a long-repressed desire for Scottie.

I had thought of renaming the movie "fiftysomething" after I realised that we've been doing for years what these yuppie upstarts aspire to. After all, in our self-enclosed world we explore personal crises with the same verve as we explore new planets.

For years now I've realised the final frontier is the human soul, space is merely the arena in which we investigate it. Yet the great mysteries of the universe remain unsolved. I've never told this to anyone before but, after all this time, I still can't figure out why Uhuru has a screwdriver in her ear, how Scottie can mend the whole of the Enterprise with a pocket torch and a spanner and why we always have to drink blue drinks. Maybe it really is time I retired.

NEW YORK, 6/19/89, p. 68, David Denby

In *Star Trek V: The Final Frontier*, the boys break through the allegedly awesome Great Barrier, a galactic no-man's-land that has the consistency of watercolors swooshing around on a piece of glass, and arrive in what appears to be a pink-filtered Monument Valley without Navaho. There they confront God Himself. At least it's *supposed* to be God. Captain Kirk isn't sure, and demands proof. "Jim," says McCoy indignantly, "you don't ask the Almighty for His I.D." Strange. After many years of hiding His light under a bushel, the Big Guy has been showing up frequently in recent movies. In this one, He looks a great deal like Bert Lahr's Cowardly Lion and speaks in an exceedingly low boom-box voice—so low that patrons of theaters that are playing *Star Trek V* on less than high-end equipment may have trouble making out what He is saying. Or even if He is really He.

William Shatner, the muscular dentist who unaccountably wandered into acting, has now wandered into directing, and despite recourse to divine sanction, he mismanages the climax of what is mostly an amiable movie. (After preparing us for a cataclysmic fight between the *Enterprise* and a Klingon warship, Shatner ends the movie with a hasty reconciliation as thrilling as...as a trip to the next Trekkie convention in Wichita Falls.) Pleasantly cheesy and undistinguished, *Star Trek V* offers little excitement or power—though the Klingons, in their leather-pouch skin and huffy Russo-Swedish language, look and sound great. The crew of the starship *Enterprise* have grown fearfully old, and perhaps it's appropriate that they now spend most of their time sitting around, like members of an unusually trivial and insulated club, discussing their feelings for one another. Shatner's sentimental attachment to the actor he's worked with for 23 profitable years is understandable enough. What's amazing, however, is the Trekkies' usual willingness to accept the coy little bits of banter and emotional interplay as the real thing.

This is the most Californian of the *Star Trek* movies. A renegade Vulcan, Sybok, played with fiery eyes and a fine big voice by Laurence Luckinbill (not an actor from whom I expected grandeur), has the habit of embracing someone, looking deep into his eyes, and saying, "Your pain runs deep. Share your pain." He then separates the person from his pain. Captain Kirk rejects Sybok's way, but this laying on of hands is the only thing in the movie that has any emotional resonance. Here, as in many other ways, *Star Trek* betrays its origins in the sixties. Grabbing people by the shoulders, Sybok says to the crew of the *Enterprise* exactly what my group-therapy leader said to me in Palo Alto, California, in the year of our Trek, 1966.

NEW YORK POST, 6/9/89, p. 23, David Edelstein

In "Star Trek V" Sybok (Laurence Luckinbill), a messianic Vulcan with healing powers, amasses a ragtag army of misfits on Nimbus III in the Neutral Zone and shanghais the starship Enterprise to travel beyond the unnavigable Great Barrier to the center of the universe to meet (Sybok is convinced) the Almighty Himself.

If you think that's trouble, the ship is barely operational—it has a skeleton crew, its transporter's under repair and most of its systems are dysfunctional. That means an iffy computer, rickety shields and photon torpedos and—this is the killer—no beaming up or down. NO BEAMING UP OR DOWN.

Worse (can it get much worse? yes it can), the starship is dogged by a belligerent Klingon (but then, all Klingons are belligerent) who wants to vanquish Kirk (William Shatner) so he'll be acclaimed as the greatest warrior in the universe. (You'd be belligerent too if the inside of your starship looked like a breeding ground for athlete's foot.)

Remember the good old days, when all these guys had to worry about was saving the whales? As something of a closet Trekkie (whee! I'm out!) I think this episode's pretty OK. It's not nearly as solid as "The Wrath of Khan," but it's better than "The Search for Spock" and Save the Whales" (or whatever it was called).

Kirk directed it, and he has a better eye than Spock (or maybe just a better director of photography). He cribs a cool shot from "Lawrence of Arabia" in the beginning—the rider coming out of the desert like a shimmering mirage—and he gets excellent FX, especially the giant rib cage that rises out of the ground and the big entrance of God (or Whoever He is—I'm still not sure).

The picture is overblown and lunbering and incoherent—but I'm nitpicking. I do have several serious problems:

□ The film begins with Kirk and his stunt doubles climbing El Capitan in Yosemite. It's good to see that, in the 23rd century, the Earth still has an ozone layer, and the emphasis on fitness is welcome. But, I'm sorry, the whole point of "Star Trek" is the gewgaws and doohickies and thingamajigs. I've already mentioned the absence of beaming up and down, and I'm further dismayed that Spock takes no tricorder readings.

□ Joshing, mugging, dumb jokes—someone should rein these party animals in. The series was a little poker-faced, but I don't know that I really needed to see Uhura dancing in a loincloth or Scotty doing pratfalls or Kirk, Spock and Bones bickering like a bunch of aging hairdressers. The three seem on the verge of a fullscale Three Stooges routine: "Why you..." BOINK! "I oughta..."

□ Luckinbill brings some passion and intensity to Sybok, although every time someone said his name I thought of those crunchy pieces of toast I used to eat when I was teething.

□ Leonard Nimoy's voice is getting hoarser. Is he smoking too many cigarettes? Perhaps Bones could have a word with him. And while we're on the subject, Bones is beginning to earn his moniker. He gets thinner every episode, while Scotty looks like he's hitting the haggis pretty hard. I'm not complaining; I just want them all to live long and prosper.

OK, let's talk "Star Trek" philosophy. Sybok was thrown off Vulcan because he rejected logical upbringing, believing the path to self-knowledge was through emotion. His gift is helping people to confront their deepest pain and then move beyond it. That's why everyone follows him.

But Kirk thinks that "pain and guilt are the things that make us what we are" and that there's something unnatural about casting them off and getting all smiley and worshipful. In the spell of even well-meaning Syboks, says Kirk, you lose your individuality and can be taken advantage of by all sorts of nefarious entities.

I agree! And I underline this because I'd like Kirk, at some point, to address himself to "Field of Dreams," which is a Sybok kind of movie if ever there was one. All those angels helping people face up to their guilt in a cathedral shaped like a baseball field! All those audiences wiping their eyes and saying, "The pain's gone!"

We don't just need more starship captains like James T. Kirk; we need more film critics like him, too.

NEWSDAY, 6/9/89, Part III/p. 3, Mike McGrady

After 79 television shows and four enormously successful flicks, the newest "Star Trek" film brings us a spanking new Starship Enterprise. larger, sleeker and decidedly higher of tech—it is equipped with a new navigational bridge, new observation deck, 30 new television monitors and a new turbo shaft—it also carries one heartwarming holdover from the old craft, a small plaque: "To Boldly Go Where No One Has Gone Before."

That, of course, has always been the mission. It's also the challenge facing anyone who would sequelize a popular entertainment with one of the most devoted—dare I say fanatical?—of followings.

However, the very dedication of that audience—with its Trekkie conventions, its books devoted to minutiae ("The Klingon Dictionary"), its willingness to shell out $350 million for tickets to the previous four films—poses an artistic conundrum. Movie makers may well desire to go where none of the previous movies have gone, but *boldly?* Do they really dare tamper with a formula that's been such an unqualified success?

"Star Trek V: The Final Frontier," more an occasion for nostalgia than innovation, in no way tampers with that basic formula first seen on television back in 1966. Its aim seems to be not to excite so much as to remind the devotee of past pleasures. And for many, it will doubtless be enough to see the familiar lineup doing familiar things. They're all back: Captain Kirk (William Shatner), Mr. Spock (Leonard Nimoy), Dr. McCoy (DeForest Kelley), Scotty (James Doohan), Chekov (Walter Koenig), Uhura (Nichelle Nichols) and Sulu (George Takei). Older, of course, but all in character, all basically unchanged.

Basically unchanged... that's the problem. Even the aliens, the Vulcans and Romulans and Klingons, seem familiar. The Klingons bring to mind a race of ugly Genghis Khans, and they're accompanied by fullback-sized women with skin problems, and even their spaceship is ugly. But we've seen all this before, and they've become familiar, somehow less than fearsome.

The story: A renegade Vulcan, Spock's half-brother Sybock (Laurence Luckinbill), has rejected his logical upbringing and turned to pure emotion. He is able to win over, or brainwash, anyone he encounters through what seems to be intense empathy: "Each of us hides a secret pain. Share yours with me. And gain strength through the sharing." In short order, Sybock takes over the Starship Enterprise and, hotly pursued by Klingons, goes through something called The Barrier to a planet rumored to house God.

Although Luckinbill's human performance is the highlight of the film, most of "Star Trek V" is predictable. While the humor has always been broad, it has never seemed quite this obvious before. Scotty brags, "I know this ship like the back of my hand," and immediately—clunk!—hits his head against a girder and slumps to the floor unconscious.

Moments like this add an ironic subtext to one of the new starship's warning lights: "System Failure." In truth, this is more a letdown than failure. I suspect the letdown relates to the basic truths underlying the characters of Kirk and Spock. The two best films in the series, "III" and "IV'" were directed by Nimoy (Spock), and they were done with appropriate deftness, wit, intelligence and some surprising twists. This is the first directed by Shatner (Kirk), and it's well-meaning, straighforward, earnest, reliable, occasionally clumsy and just a bit plodding.

NEWSWEEK, 6/19/89, p. 63, David Ansen

Ya gotta love the "Star Trek" movies. No other movie series has quite this mix of bad synthetic fabrics and Great Ideas of Western Thought. In its dowdy ceremonial grandeur, it's sort of the royal family of cinema, at once outmoded and seemingly eternal. Take *Star Trek V: The Final Frontier*, directed by the captain himself, William Shatner. What other summer movie is going to invoke "Paradise Lost," the poet John Masefield, and send its cast on a philosophical excursion in quest of God himself? What other entertainment has the chutzpah to stage its climax in what may or may not be Eden? The fact is, by never forgetting to make fun of itself even as it solemnly preaches the gospel of liberal humanism, "Star Trek V" gets away with murder. Such moral earnestness would be laughed off the screen in any other guise, as would the tacky sets. But in the alternate esthetic universe of "Star Trek," vices become virtues. You can take it as camp, but in fact it's just the opposite: "Star Trek" is endearing and enduring precisely because it is utterly free of cynicism. It actually means what it says.

"The Final Frontier" is not as witty as the last installment, nor as well made as "The Search for Spock." But it has the Trek essence in spades. The Enterprise, in a state of disrepair, is sent out on an emergency hostage-rescue mission to a junkyard planet called Nimbus III, where a messianic figure named Sybok (Laurence Luckinbill) has taken command. Sybok is an intriguingly ambiguous figure, part Werner Erhard, part Lucifer. A touchy-feely priest/therapist, he draws out of people their secret fear, and frees them from shame. This is anathema to the skeptical Captain Kirk, a cranky humanist determined to hold on to the Judeo/Christian legacy of guilt. No New Age easy answers for him.

Sybok, a Vulcan who heretically believes in the primacy of feelings, has staged the insurrection to lure a starship to Nimbus III. He needs it to go on his ultimate voyage...beyond the Great Barrier...to the source of all creation where the riddles of the universe will be answered. But is he a savior or a madman? Even the logical Spock and the loyal Bones waver in their allegiances. David Loughery's screenplay (from a story by Loughery, Shatner and Harve Bennett) keeps you wondering about Sybok, which is the fun of "Star Trek V." (He also tosses in a vengeful Klingon warrior, determined to kill Captain Kirk, for diversionary thrills.)

Shatner is a pretty clunky director of action, and there seem to be scenes missing involving the three hostages of Nimbus. An inordinate amount of the movie's emotional pull is attributable to Jerry Goldsmith's big, hardworking score. But Shatner seems at home—as well he should—with the comic interplay of the Enterprise crew. Like an old vaudeville team, these veterans know each other's moves so well they've found a neat comic shorthand that gets more laughs out of the lines than they deserve. The comic charm of Shatner, DeForest Kelley and Leonard Nimoy singing "Row, Row, Row Your Boat" around a campfire in Yosemite Valley plays on 23 years of cozy familiarity with these characters. It ain't art, but it's peculiarly satisfying.

TIME, 6/26/89, p. 89, Richard Schickel

[*Star Trek V* was reviewed jointly with *Ghostbusters II;* see Schickel's review of that film.]

VILLAGE VOICE, 6/20/89, p. 90, Georgia Brown

If a movie as silly as *Star Trek V: The Final Frontier* ("final," my foot) had unknown characters, it would be laughed out of the galaxy. Trekkies, who once were techies (during the TV run in the '60s anyway), now seem to prefer laughs to hard lore. Anyway, this movie's creators do. The special effects here are a yawn; tension is nonexistent. *Star Trek* movies have turned gradually into something like *Family Ties* in space—a long-running domestic comedy in which family members do their schticks and the audience (thirtysomething now) stokes up nostalgia. And, as the guys (and gal) of the *Enterprise* age—since the 23rd century hasn't solved some cosmetic riddles—the camp factor encroaches.

The Final Frontier, directed—some will say helmed—by the dogged Captain Kirk (William Shatner), opens onto a desert planet called Nimbus III, otherwise known as Planet of Galactic Peace. The joke is that the place—graphically borrowed from *Star Wars*'s Tatooine, even down to a smoke-filled dive where the misshapen chill out—is a desert, a depository of space detritus populated by misfits and outcasts. One such, with no hair and repulsive tooth stumps in expansive gums, is out tilling the sand when a hooded figure gallops out of the shimmering haze.

No, it's not Sean Connery but the poor man's counterpart, Laurence Luckinbill. The character, Sybok, is meant to be charismatic, but he hasn't sufficient aura. He's a guru with a smile about as convincing as Timothy Leary's. Pulling back his burlap hood, Sybok pointedly reveals the Vulcan pointy ears. (According to Spock later on, Sybok is a Vulcan renegade who "believed the key to self-knowledge was emotion.") "Share your pain and gain strength," Sybok dares the gummy farmer, who instantly collapses sobbing into his arms. He then invites the pathetic one to join his quest. When asked what he seeks, Sybok reveals that he's after "the ultimate knowledge"; he just needs a starship to take him there.

Meanwhile, the *Enterprise* crew is enjoying shore leave on Planet Earth. The American West seems to have become a favored area after the *Star Trek IV* experience. Camping in Yosemite, Kirk climbs the sheer granite face of El Capitan while the fussy "Bones" McCoy (DeForest Kelley) keeps an eye on him through binoculars from the campsite. ("I'm a nervous wreck!") It turns out that Spock (Leonard Nimoy) is also along; wearing his levitation boots, he kibitzes with Kirk on technique. Come nightfall these three old space cowboys sit around the campfire eating McCoy's home recipe of bourbon-flavored beans ("an explosive combination"), toasting marshmallows, and singing "Row, row, row your boat" in rounds. "Life is not a dream," observes Spock.

Star Trek V could be said to be explosive in the way of McCoy's doctored can of beans. It putt-putts along, but never develops a coherent or accelerating momentum. Individual scenes have a random. arbitrary feel. David Warner makes an appearance in a totally gratuitous role. The feisty old Klingons are back—with those little spines down their frownlines, manning their dimly lit craft—but as villains they're almost superfluous here. Just carrying on their spoilsport destiny. The real villain, believe it or not, is God—or 'God', as he's listed in the credits.

The Final Frontier subtitle refers to discovering God's home base on a fabled blue-tinted planet—"beyond The Great Barrier," in the center of the galaxy, "the place from which creation sprang." Sybok commandeers the new *Enterprise*—which hasn't properly been broken in yet (Scotty still has his wrenches out)—to fly him there. He quickly convinces most of the crew to turn over their pain to him. In a burst of long-suppressed affection, Commander Uhura (Nichelle Nichols) throws herself onto the prone Scotty. But the three strong guys remain skeptical.

There's an embarrassing scene in which Sybok practices his mystical therapy on McCoy ("Your pain is the deepest of all"), showing him a flashback of his aged father's final illness. McCoy, it turns out, has put his father out of his misery ("All my knowledge and I can't save him"), only to learn a year or so later that a cure has been discovered for the fatal disease. Is this more than a man can stand? Spock, who happens to be Sybok's half-brother, gets a little psyche massage, too, with a flashback to his birth. (Seems odd to me that Vulcan women scream during childbirth.)

The sequence is a small attempt—as when comic books run an origins issue—to give the heroes some traumatized human past. Of the three, Kirk remains the holdout: "I *need* my pain," he protests, as if Shatner doesn't care to give over his everyman character to be shrunk. Later, when God comes on—a giant projected head effect, like the Wizard of Oz—Kirk, a bit like Dorothy from Kansas, sensibly (and comically) holds his ground. Well, it's his movie. *Star Trek V,* like El Capitan, is a soft, laboring, benign bore.

Also reviewed in:
NEW YORK TIMES, 6/9/89, p. C10, Caryn James
VARIETY, 6/14–20/89, p. 22
WASHINGTON POST, 6/9/89, p. C1, Rita Kempley

STAYING TOGETHER

A Hemdale release. *Executive Producer:* John Daly and Derek Gibson. *Producer:* Joseph Feury. *Director:* Lee Grant. *Screenplay:* Monte Merrick. *Director of Photography:* Dick Bush. *Editor:* Katherine Wenning. *Music:* Miles Goodman. *Music Editor:* Thomas Drescher and Michael Dittrick. *Sound:* Jan Erik Brodin and (music) Michael Farrow. *Sound Editor:* Maurice Schell, Lou Cerborino, and Barney Cabral. *Production Designer:* Stuart Wurtzel. *Art Director:* W. Steven Graham. *Set Decorator:* Elaine O'Donnell. *Set Dresser:* Jamie Durden-Arbuckle and John Mark Young. *Special Effects:* Cliff Wenger. *Costumes:* Carol Oditz. *Make-up:* Christa Reusch. *Stunt Coordinator:* Gil Combs and Greg Brickman. *Running Time:* 91 minutes. *MPAA Rating:* R.

CAST: Sean Astin (Duncan McDermott); Stockard Channing (Nancy Trainer); Melinda Dillon (Eileen McDermott); Jim Haynie (Jake McDermott); Levon Helm (Denny Stockton); Dinah Manoff (Lois Cook); Dermot Mulroney (Kit McDermott); Tim Quill (Brian McDermott); Keith Szarabajka (Kevin Burley); Daphne Zuniga (Beverly Young); Sheila Kelley (Beth Harper); Ryan Hill (Demetri Harper); Rick Marshall (Charlie); Michael Burgess (Workman); Leon Joseph Pinner (Newsman); Ed Carter, Susan Aude Fisher, and Jim Gandy (Announcers); Steve Jackson (Contestant); Bonnie Cook (Waitress); Robby Sedgwick (Doctor); Ann Pierce (Nurse); Nathan LeGrand (Husband); Paul Branin (Guitar/Sax/Tenor/Vocals); Jim Weider (Guitar); Frank Campbell (Bass); Randy Ciarlante (Drums/Vocals); Stan Szelest (Keyboard/Vocals); Wayne Coleman (Wedding Photographer); Thelma McNinch (Customer); James R. Barrow (Customer); Frances Arndt (Mrs. Crawford).

LOS ANGELES TIMES, 11/10/89, Calendar/p. 1, Peter Rainer

The small-town atmosphere in "Staying Together," set in Ridgeway, S.C., is humid with metaphorical meaning. The streets are a bit too quaint; the homes too ramshackle; the people too countrified and ornery. If you think you've seen it all before—well, you have. And that's the point. The movie is englobed in the sentimentality of a hundred rural coming-of age dramas, and the familiarity breeds not contempt but boredom.

Monte Merrick's script, directed by Lee Grant, is crammed with little life lessons about the value of family. The McDermott clan takes center stage. (The stage reference is intentional.This is the sort of overliterary script where you can practically hear the commas in the dialogue.) Brian (Tim Quill), the oldest of the three rambunctious McDermott boys, is having an affair with an ambitious mayoral candidate (Stockard Channing). Kit (Dermot Mulroney) is dallying with a woman (Daphne Zuniga) engaged to be married. The youngest, Duncan (Sean Astin), is the family wiseacre. He leaves no quip unturned.

Until their father (Jim Haynie) decides to sell it, all three boys work at the family restaurant, McDermott's Family Chicken. Dad is considerate with his family, but he is also remote, walled-in. He is hidebound by his distaste for playing the role of provider. Mom (Melinda Dillon) looks after her men with the aplomb of a woman who has learned how to anticipate her broods' vagaries. She is woozy with maternal understanding.

"Staying Together" is saddled with a generic-sounding title, but it doesn't misrepresent the movie's dull, cloned sameness. Every scene carries its own echo chamber of prior references. If Lee Grant were a better director, the film might have been more accomplished, perhaps: something along the lines of "Stand By Me," with its heightened, boys' book tableaux. She is a clunky visualist, though; the camera always seems to be wobbling about in search of its subject. To overcompensate, she lets the actors go hog-wild, but the effect is bizarre, as if "Ozzie and Harriet" had suddenly gone Method.

Actors-turned-directors often go in for this sort of hyperindulgence, but the dramatics in "Staying Together" don't have the ballast to support all the ridiculous emoting. The hurts of parenthood and the hesitancies of young love ought to have more emotional sting than they receive in this movie. You don't want to embrace these people. You want to give them noogies.

If you feel like you haven't really been to the movies after you come out of "Staying Together," that's probably because it has the paper-thin texture of a made-for-TV production. None of the characters in this coming-of-age drama really age; they simply pass through one event after another until the final, heartwarming wrap-up. But even if the drama had more heft, it's probably too late for audiences to accept the film makers' sugared view of small-town distress. (David Lynch may have killed it for good.) In the movies, we've moved on to other sentimentalities. As, for example, the current fave: the joys of having a baby, and of being a baby, too. The old-fashionedness of "Staying Together" is unbecoming.

The film makers proffer their banalities before us like trophies. They offer a counterfeit view of small-town life as the one and only all-American mother lode. They push the wisdom that, yes, big souls can reside in small places. Except in the noggins of small-minded dramatists, can this really be news to anyone?

NEW YORK POST, 11/10/89, p. 29, Jami Bernard

Three brothers learn to cope with life, love, and the loss of their fast-food chicken restaurant in Lee Grant's tender-hearted "Staying Together," a family comedy-drama that's one of those laughing-through-the-tears jobs.

Heartwarming but not sappy, the trials and tribulations of the small-town McDermott family relies on the apparent chemistry among the three young actors who play the brothers: Tim Quill as the charismatic and rebellious Brian, Dermot Mulroney as the shyly romantic Kit, and Sean Astin as the wise-cracking half-pint, Duncan.

These three are cocks of the walk—in more ways than one—whether roaming the streets at night drunk and proclaiming the town "McDermottville," or pursuing the various women of their dreams, each of whom is all wrong for that particular McDermott but who represents something lovely in their coming of age.

When the sun rises on the McDermott household, mom (Melinda Dillon) is in the kitchen making breakfast, but only Kit, the long-distance runner, is in bed upstairs. (The woman he adores, played by Daphne Zuniga, is about to marry someone else, and Kit only gets to see her on the running track these days.) Brian is off in the arms of the local mayoral candidate (a determined Stockard Channing), and young Duncan is passed out drunk on a park bench. (He's hoping that a local waitress will one day introduce him to something headier than beer.)

Kit dutifully rounds them up from their various delinquencies, and breakfast begins apace with mom fussing, dad cranky, and the boys having fun at their parents' expense.

This harmless routine is broken when dad sells the chicken restaurant without the preliminary family discussion that today's TV-series mentality has led us to expect. The elder McDermott (Jim Haynie) does things the old-fashioned way—he sells the coop, pockets the cash, and drops the news casually over breakfast, stunning and angering his sons.

How they all deal with this and other family upsets, major and minor, forms the core of the movie.

As a slice of life, "Staying Together" does things the old-fashioned way, too. These boys are good, solid, honest, hard-working kids, and their delinquencies amount to no more than the cutting-up of a '50s adolescence. Though sentimental, at least it's not the disease or tragedy-of-the-week formula. It is particularly apt when Duncan jokingly quotes from "Leave it to Beaver" to introduce a new wrinkle.

The ensemble acting, particularly among the brothers, is efficient and joyful. Grant, who also directed the life-affirming tearjerker about old age and memory, "Tell Me a Riddle," is in touch with the nuances of relationships, both within the McDermott family and within the small southern town.

Tim Quill as Brian, the most readily interesting brother, bears a resemblance to John Travolta, with a cagey, lopsided smile and a puppy enthusiasm. The three brothers have distinct personalities, yet you can see how they could be built of the same McDermott stuff.

The supporting roles are all good, including Levon Helm in a small part as a pharmacist who plays in a local band.

NEWSDAY, 11/10/89, Part III/p. 7, Mike McGrady

Ridgeway, S.C., is a town of 370 people and, yes, there are 370 stories in this naked whistle-stop and every blessed one of them seems to find its way into the new movie, "Staying Together."

This extended-family drama—shuffled, cut and dealt by actress-turned-director Lee Grant—has so many characters, so many elements, so many different stories, it's inevitable some will work better than others. Which, unfortunately but unavoidably, means some *don't* work quite as well as others. Although results are mixed, "Staying Together" has enough positive factors to keep one entertained much of the way.

The three McDermott brothers—young wiseguy Duncan (Sean Astin), sensitive jogger Kit (Dermot Mulroney), rebellious older Brian (Tim Quill)—work in the family chicken restaurant. When their father decides to sell the business, without notifying any of his offspring, the lives of the three sons are thrown into sudden disarray, along with the lives of many other reisdents of Ridgeway.

Brian has been having an affair with an older woman (Stockard Channing) who is running for mayor. Kit, meanwhile, has been lusting after a fellow-jogger (Daphne Zuniga) who, though about to marry the local developer-tycoon (Keith Szarabajka), is not above a little premarital fling. And young Duncan is so busy chasing the waitress (Bonnie Cook) he almost forgets to come of age. Which, in a movie like "Staying Together," would qualify as an out-and-out disaster.

You see, this is one of those movies where *everyone* comes of age. Or, at the very least, goes through comparable sea changes. The father selling the business and buying the motor home. The mother returning to her former life as a band singer. The local pharmacist chasing after the mother. Simply untangling the various story lines of "Staying Together" is a full-time job; there are enough small tales here to keep your average afternoon soap going for a year, maybe two.

Among the film's clearest assets: the relationships among the three brothers who are also business partners and woman-chasing, beer-belting buddies; a wonderful scene where mayoral candidate Stockard Channing must carry on a political phone call while simultaneously carrying on a romantic encounter with Brian; a terribly moving scene as the mother of the three grown sons takes up a microphone at the local saloon and makes her first public appearance in 20 years, singing, "While We're Young"; and, if fact, the entire performance by Melinda Dillon (Oscar-nominated for her work in "Close Encounters of the Third Kind" and "Absence of Malice") as the mother.

On the debit side of the ledger: overly melodramatic scenes involving sons fighting with father, mother or one another; occasional dramatic contrivance (such as an unbelievable boys-driving-the-truck-into-the-lake sequence), and far too many intensely dramatic scenes that seem to spring from other movies rather than real life.

Whether "Staying Together" is reckoned a success or failure, the operative descriptive is apt to be "modest." It's the kind of film that often passes all but unnoticed in the theaters before popping up, in short order, at the local video store where it rings only the most distant bells. In fact, I can almost hear the at-home viewers commenting now: "Hey, this is pretty good" or, more accurately, "You know, this isn't half-bad."

VILLAGE VOICE, 11/21/89, p. 92, Georgia Brown

What happens to a small-town Southern family with the handicap of three sons is the subject of *Staying Together*, a picture of some low-key charm directed by Lee Grant (*Tell Me a Riddle, The Willmar 8*). McDermott's Famous Chicken is a family restaurant, which in recent times has been manned by three nearly grown sons, Brian (Tim Quill), Kit (Dermot Mulroney), and Duncan (Sean Astin, son of Patty Duke and John Astin). Flirting with customers and the maternal, large-breasted waitress (scenes which border on the obnoxious), getting high after closing time, the kids fantasize about improvements and eventual expansions.

One morning, paused over his dry cereal, Dad (Jim Haynie) reveals that he hates chickens ("Have you ever seen me eat an egg?") and has sold the restaurant. He and Mom (Melinda Dillon) are buying a camper and plan to explore some of the surrounding territory. Brian explodes at not being consulted and leaves home; the other two cope with career anxieties from the old base. No one's plans turn out as anticipated.

Monte Merrick has written an old-fashioned, unpretentious screenplay about coming of age (the boys) and middle age (the parents). He neatly juggles a fair number of destinies without blurring them, while keeping his details fresh. Brian, for instance, gets involved with an older woman (Stockard Channing) running for mayor, who dumps him after the election, with his dope supplier who lives in the woods; all the while he's working his way into the construction outfit that's demolishing the old chicken place. Kit runs a marathon and then spends the night with an old flame (Daphne Zuniga) who is planning her wedding to Brian's construction boss.

The hometown is supposed to be Ridgeway, South Carolina, but this is a South without any local color to speak of. (Notes say Merrick is from Portland, Oregon.) No one even tries out an accent. Mom does appear to be something of a steel magnolia, but these men are not exactly weeping willows or clinging vines.

Also reviewed in:
NEW YORK TIMES, 11/10/89, p. C15, Vincent Canby
VARIETY, 9/6–12/89, p. 25
WASHINGTON POST, 11/10/89, p. D7, Rita Kempley

STEALING HEAVEN

A Scotti Brothers Pictures release of an Amy International (London)/Jadran Film (Belgrade) production. *Executive Producer:* Susan George. *Producer:* Simon MacCorkindale and Andros Epaminondas. *Director:* Clive Donner. *Screenplay:* Chris Bryant. *Based on the novel by:* Marion Meade. *Director of Photography:* Mikael Salomon. *Editor:* Michael Ellis. *Music:* Nick Bicat. *Music Editor:* Nick Hosker. *Sound:* Louis Kramer and (music) Toby Alington. *Sound Editor:* Bill Trent. *Production Designer:* Voytek Roman. *Art Director:* Dusko Jericevic. *Set Dresser:* Maria Djurkovic. *Special Effects:* Willy Neuner. *Costumes:* Phyllis Dalton. *Make-up:* Paul Engelen. *Stunt Coordinator:* Petar Buntic. *Running Time:* 116 minutes. *MPAA Rating:* R.

CAST: Derek de Lint (Abelard); Kim Thomson (Heloise); Denholm Elliott (Canon Fullert); Bernard Hepton (Bishiop Martin); Kenneth Cranham (Vice Chancellor Suger); Patsy Byrne (Agnes); Cassie Stuart (Petronilla); Philip Locke (Poussin); Victoria Burgoyne (Prostitute); Antonija Cutic (Landlady); Diana Belinic (Girl in Street); Davor Fejzagic (Boy in Street); Mark Jax (Jourdain); Tim Watson (François); Andrew McLean (Gérard); Thomas Lockyer (Thomas); Mark Audley (Luke); Kai Dominic (Paul); Rachel Kempson (Prioress); Angela Pleasence (Sister Cecilia); Slavica Maras (Marie Duroc); Niki Hewitt (Sister Claire); Zvonimir Ferencic (Bishop); Yvonne Bryceland (Baroness Lamarck); Vjenceslav Kapural (Baron Lamarck); Ivo Husnjak (Gaston Lamarck); Jeremy Hawk (Ancient Priest); Moniek Kraner (Jeanne); Drago Mitrovic (Priest); Eugen Marcelic (Astralabe); Lela Simecki (Sister Thérèse).

LOS ANGELES TIMES, 4/28/89, Calendar/p. 17, Michael Wilmington

There is something fascinatingly retrograde about the movie "Stealing Heaven." Set in 12th-Century France, it's based on the legendary affair of Heloise and Abelard. But instead of the year 1118, or yesterday, the movie suggests the '60s: decade of turbulence, idealism, sex and riot.

The film, shot in Yugoslavia, apes the style of the big '60s costume pictures. And writer Chris- Bryant paints the lovers as a quintessentially '60s pair: longhaired beauties trapped in a cloistered society, battling the hypocrites and meanies, the crooked parents, frigid nuns, cops sneering churchmen, who want to stifle their passion.

"Heaven's" Peter Abelard (Derek de Lint) is a charismatic teacher who drinks with his students and encourages them to question orthodoxy. And Heloise (Kim Thomson) looks like a pseudo-hippie rich girl, Burne-Jones mixed with Haight-Ashbury, blasting convention at every opportunity, twitting her twitching uncle Fulbert (Denholm Elliott) about his phony religious relics.

One thing that doesn't peg this film as a '60s product is the unblinkered sexuality. The eroticism and the ideas get overripe early on. Bryant has the pair getting hot for each other by discussing philosophy; they leer over theological ripostes, as if each juicy premise were a chicken thigh from Tom Jones' banquet seduction. There are more bad ideas: such as the scene where Abelard's rascally students plant a naked prostitute in his bed. And another where a group of nuns is thrown out of the convent by a heartless bishop; as they go struggling up a hillside in the rain, one of them lugs a 6-foot wooden cross. (Couldn't they wait and pick up a cross at the next convent?)

By the time we get to the crucial episode, Abelard's castraton by the hirelings of crazy Canon Fulbert, it's played with incongruous (for here) restraint, as if the mutilation purged him of passion, making him a photogenic male saint, like Gregory Peck in "The Keys of the Kingdom."

All of the characterizations are hard to swallow, but the actors are easy to watch. De Lint glows with dedication, Thompson tosses her great Cosmo cover-girl mane ravishingly. Elliott is a fine, squirrelly, sweating villain; he seems capable not just of castration, but of sneaking in and pulling hairs out of your nose in the dark.

The director of "Stealing Heaven," Clive Donner, may be nostalgic. He made his best known and most admired films in the '60s: "The Caretaker," "Nothing But the Best" and "What's New, Pussycat?"—which, unfortunately, may have typed him as a king of high-style naughty camp. But, here, Donner shows some feeling and style. There is a grating softrock score, but the images look incongruously rich. The clever production designer Voytek Roman, who did Polanski's "Cul De Sac," shows us Notre Dame in mid-construction, and Mikael Salomon's cinematography is crisp, burnished and deep; full of plush interiors, mistdraped forests and hills.

True to '60s type, "Stealing Heaven" (MPAA rated R for copious nudity, sex and strong language) attacks repression as evil. But, what's beautiful about the story is the fruit of repression: the letters the lovers wrote after their passion was frustrated and which the movie rarely bothers to quote. In a different key, made with either the chaste austerity of a Robert Bresson or the flamboyant screwiness of a Ken Russell, the film might have worked. In this middle ground, it becomes over-pretty, comic. The lovers turn into scamp-saints, exiled from a Zeffirelli movie into one by Zinnemann: "The Nun's Story" with an emasculated theologian as suffering swain.

MONTHLY FILM BULLETIN, 5/89, p. 151, Verina Glaessner

Twelfty-century France. As Heloise lies dying in a convent, she tosses aside a proferred crucifix and requests instead one from the chapel; from its base she draws out a white feather. Years earlier, as a mischievously enquiring student at the convent of Argenteuil, she incurs the enmity of the strait-laced Sister Cecilia, though she is indulged by the more far-sighted prioress. She returns to the Paris home of her uncle and guardian, Canon Fulbert, a dealer in 'holy relics' who intends to realise as large a return as possible on the marriage of his ward. When a boy is trampled to death outside Fulbert's house, Heloise, rushing to his aid, makes the acquaintance of Abelard, a radical young philosophy teacher whose lectures challenging the ecclesiastical orthodoxy are enthusiastically attended. Abelard is immediately attracted to Heloise, but has taken the customary vows of chastity incumbent on a teacher of philosophy. When he confronts a naked prostitute in his bed as the result of a student prank, he resists her advances but is evicted from his lodgings. He is put up at Fulbert's house and becomes Heloise's teacher; their intellectual kinship deepens into erotic passion, and though Abelard is racked with guilt, Heloise accepts the preordained nature of their love. When Fulbert discovers their affair, Abelard leaves the house and Heloise is confined to her room. She subsequently learns that she is pregnant, and escapes with the help of Abelard and his student Jourdain to stay with her sister outside Paris. She gives birth to a boy she christens Astralabe, after "the instrument that measures the distance between the stars", and Abelard suggests that they marry, which means breaking his vows, in order to remove her forever from Fulbert's control. Fulbert, however, plots his revenge, and on his return to Paris Abelard is attacked and castrated. When Jourdain tells her of Abelard's fate, Heloise lays a curse on her uncle. Abelard, however, rejects her, suggesting that she follow his example and enter a teaching order. Fulbert is banished from Paris; Heloise returns to Argenteuil, but before her ordination secretes a feather, a memento of her love for Abelard, inside the crucifix that will be used in the service. When an old adversary of Abelard's, Vice Chancellor Suger, has her order evicted from their convent, they seek refuge with Abelard at Paraclete. But no sooner are they reunited than he receives instructions to teach elsewhere. He bequeathes his monastery buildings to Heloise's order, promising to return to consecrate the church they are building. Years later he does, accompanied by Jourdain and Astralabe.

A certain failure of the Anglo-Saxon imagination about the Middle Ages was acknowledged unforgettably by Joyce Carey in *Lucky Jim*. Here, if the makers have at least managed to steer clear of 'period speak', they have not, sadly, solved the problem of the incongruousness of contemporary dialogue and speech rhythms in the mouths of twelfth-century characters. "I don't give a sou!", "You'll hate Argenteuil", or "Every inch of my body aches for his touch" hardly suggest the past as another country, while Heloise's comment following Abelard's castration, "You're in no position to make a decision", ranks as a thumping understatement. One touchstone for the representation of pre-industrial life on film must be Pasolini's Trilogy of Life (rather than the film of *The Name of the Rose*), in which not only the performances but the *mise en scène* acquired a sense of strangeness through the attempt to suggest a pre-bourgeois mode of deportment and expression. But Pasolini's influence here fails to go beyond a few clues picked up in the art direction (the bishop's palanquin, the interior of Fulbert's house), and in the casting.

The British stalwarts in the major roles—Denholm Elliott, Bernard Hepton and Kenneth Cranham—enact the piece as if it were an epic of a few decades back, with just a suggestion of the playing fields of Empire in references to the unreliability of Notre Dame's masons ("Flemish, you know"). The lack of an overall vision—and with his background in fairly conventional television costume dramas, Clive Donner was probably not the man to supply it—is never more obvious than in the depiction of Abelard and Heloise's passion, which here suggests neither elemental drives nor the profound and tantalising refinements of courtly love, but by default the much easier option of softcore lust. Within this context, the notion of moral torment becomes, almost by definition, ridiculous: it is left to Derek de Lint's Abelard to indicate this alien frame of mind through much eye-rolling and leaping on horseback.

It goes without saying that the representation of the life of the intellect proves equally intractable, suggesting no more than an ecclesiastical game of Trivial Pursuit. If Donner is no Rohmer or Bresson, this Abelard is decidedly no *nouvelle philosophe*. Somewhere in Chris Bryant's script—and possibly in the Marion Meade novel on which it is based—there is the beginning of a serious discussion of the part played by the forces of law and custom in shaping individual lives. Heloise struggles through romantic passion towards a notion of self-hood apart from the demands of church or her social function as marriageable property. But this too remains a drama that never quite finds adequate expression.

NEW YORK POST, 4/28/89, p. 32, Jami Bernard

Vying in the "greatest love story ever told" sweepstakes (remember, both "Gone with the Wind" and "Wuthering Heights" have enjoyed recent re-releases) is the star-crossed saga of Abelard and Heloise, brought to the screen in "Stealing Heaven," as unhelpful a title as ever graced a story about pre-ordained, ceaseless, angst-ridden, deliriously impossible love. At the end of the critics' screening, there were both sniffles and derisive snickers, as befits any melodrama.

Abelard was a great, charismatic teacher in 12th century France. Students flocked from all over to learn at his knee. He challenged them, debated them, ate and drank and caroused with them. Devoted to his calling, Abelard was conscientiously celibate, as was the custom back then, until he fell in love with the delicious Heloise.

Heloise, for her part, was quicker and smarter and better educated (and prettier) than any of Abelard's male students. She was too inquisitive to be religious and did not share her enamored's penchant for chastity. Her God wouldn't demand such sacrifice.

In "Stealing Heaven," filmed in Yugoslavia (which doubles as well as anything for 12th century France), Abelard and Heloise are not only the best educated and most modern folks around, they are also the best looking. Not surprisingly, it isn't long before they're shedding vows, clothes and caution, and making whoopee anywhere that will accommodate them (a barn, a bed against the wall of a chapel).

Who can blame them? Heloise is played by Kim Thomson, all round, saucy saucer-eyes and cascading red tresses. Is there a more melting close-up to be had? (Cinematographer Mikael Salomon can't get enough of her face; Heloise seems to fill every other frame.) Thomson makes Heloise a regular little spitfire, so amusing to her elders, such a toss of the head, so clever with logic and the teachings of St. Augustine.

Dutch actor Derek de Lint ("The Assault," "The Unbearable Lightness of Being") similarly makes a passionate Abelard, with dark, rugged features and a permanently tormented look. All the energy that went into goading his loyal, rowdy students suddenly finds new inspiration in a Christmas kiss from young Heloise. Off with the scholar's robes and into the bed for some very steamy, very nude love scenes.

Of course, 12th century France wasn't the greatest time for having a fling. You've got your church elders to think of, your reputation, the girl's avenging uncle (a wonderfully grasping and craven Denholm Elliott) and a little matter of an unsavory castration scene. Still, when Abelard and Heloise murmur sweet nothings in each other's ears, they really mean business, till death do they part.

Director Clive Donner manages to give this old-fashioned story a thoroughly modern sensibility—characters have senses of humor, something that is rare in usually stuffy period pieces. This Abelard and Heloise are truly timeless lovers—not only does the story itself endure, but they could easily be transplanted to today: handsome older teacher and spunky underage student constrained by their respective guardians. It's not like having to imagine Zeus turning into a swan or something foreign like that.

However, when you're dealing with passion this grand-scale—the lovers' sex life is over within a few months, although their passion lasts the rest of their lives and the rest of the movie—it is very difficult to avoid a certain degree of skepticism. If Heloise lived today, would she be reading "Women Who Love Too Much" and taking a wine-tasting course at the New School to get over the guy?

By the time Heloise on her deathbed has come to terms with a sassy question she once asked as a young girl, about the private parts of the Almighty, it was achingly apparent that the biggest audience for this movie would be readers of romance fiction. They won't be disappointed.

NEWSDAY, 4/28/89, Part III/p. 7, Bill Kaufman

The love affair between peripatetic philosopher Peter Abelard and 16-year-old Heloise—a foray that resulted in the older man being castrated and eventually forced in shame to take up a life of repentance in a monastery—is a story that has been ripe for dramatization since around the year 1142.

And "Stealing Heaven," an adaptation of Marion Meade's novel about the 12th-Century French theologian and his free-spirited lover who was far ahead of her time, takes on the famed story in a narrow and mildly satisfying form.

Derek de Lint is well cast as Abelard, a teacher in the schools of Notre Dame during the time the great cathedral was being built. As Heloise, Kim Thomson exudes a simmering, naive sensuality along with a keen, inquiring intellect that women of the time were not expected to exhibit—especially when it came to questioning church doctrine.

Fresh from the convent, this niece of the greedy Parisian church official Fulbert, played wonderfully by veteran British actor Denholm Elliott, meets Abelard, and the two soon are lovers. Abelard, as a church teacher, has pledged to lead a chaste life, and his betrayal of this vow forces him to reconcile the spiritual with the secular, the flesh vs. the soul.

"Stealing Heaven" here and there tends to buckle under the weight of overplayed symbolism. As the couple makes love the sound track swells with ecclesiastic music, then the camera pans up to reveal they are unknowingly beneath a large crucifix. The flames of hell flicker on screen after Abelard watchs a stage performance of a dancing devil.

Despite its shortcomings, the movie, which was filmed in Yugoslavia, has enough scope and production values to please the eye. The picture may not be history as written, but it indeed does offer a competent cast and nearly two hours of entertainment.

Also reviewed in:
NEW YORK TIMES, 4/28/89, p. C14, Caryn James
VARIETY, 6/8/88, p. 12
WASHINGTON POST, 4/28/89, p. D7, Rita Kempley

STEEL MAGNOLIAS

A Tri-Star Pictures release. *Executive Producer:* Victoria White. *Producer:* Ray Stark. *Director:* Herbert Ross. *Screenplay (based on his play):* Robert Harling. *Director of Photography:* John A. Alonzo. *Editor:* Paul Hirsch. *Music:* Georges Delerue. *Music Editor:* Daniel Allan Carlin. *Choreographer:* Spencer Henderson. *Sound:* Al Overton and (music) John Richards. *Sound Editor:* Wylie Stateman and Tom Bellfort. *Production Designer:*

Gene Callahan and Edward Pisoni. *Art Director:* Hub Braden and Michael Okowita. *Set Designer:* Steven Wolff. *Set Decorator:* Lee Poll and Garrett Lewis. *Special Effects:* Kevin Harris. *Costumes:* Julie Weiss. *Make-up:* Christina Smith. *Running time:* 118 minutes. *MPAA Rating:* PG.

CAST: Sally Field (M'Lynn Eatenton); Dolly Parton (Truvy Jones); Shirley MacLaine (Ouiser Boudreaux); Daryl Hannah (Annelle Dupuy Desoto); Olympia Dukakis (Clairee Belcher); Julia Roberts (Shelby Eatenton Latcherie); Tom Skerritt (Drum Eatenton); Sam Shepard (Spud Jones); Dylan McDermott (Jackson Latcherie); Kevin O'Connor (Sammy Desoto); Bill McCutcheon (Owen Jenkins); Ann Wedgeworth (Aunt Fern); Knowl Johnson (Tommy Eatenton); Jonathan Ward (Jonathan Eatenton); Bibi Besch (Belle Marmillion); Janine Turner (Nancy Beth Marmillion); James Wlcek (Marshall Marmillion); Ronald Young (Drew Marmillion); Nancy Parsons (Janice Van Meter); Robert Ginnaven (Mayor Van Meter); Tom Hodges (Louie Jones); Rick Hurst (Bark Boone); Robert Harling (Minister); C. Houser (Jack, Jr., 1-yr-old); Daniel Camp (Jack, Jr; 3-yr-old); Norman Fletcher (Mr. Latcherie Sr.); Lori Tate (Mrs. Latcherie Sr.); Robert Adams (Dr. Judd); Carol Sutton (Nurse Pam); Aja Sansone (Monique); Rodney Alan Fulton (Bobby Ray Ross); Spencer Henderson and Sandra Asbury-Johnson (Dancing Couple); Gale J. Odom (Church Singer); Betsy Widhalm (Church Organist); Oscar J. Bienveu Jr. (Doctor); Teresa Beaudion (Receptionist); Gladys Mallard and Betty J. Dove (Nurses); Travis Harrison (Delivery Boy); James Shapkoff III (Delivery Man); Walker May (Newspaper Boy); Robert R. Morgan (Cook); Roger D. McCann and Debbie McCann (Cook's Helpers).

FILMS IN REVIEW, 3/90, p. 169, Jim Welsh

Three out of the last four times I've been to the movies lately I've seen Olympia Dukakis on the screen in supporting roles—as the grandmother in *Look Who's Talking* and in *Dad*, and then as a strong Southern widow in *Steel Magnolias*. In the first two she was merely a supporting character. In *Steel Magnolias* she enjoys a more significant role in a strong ensemble cast that includes Sally Field, Dolly Parton, Shirley MacLaine, Darryl Hannah, and Julia Roberts. She certainly holds her own, even though the movie belongs mainly to Sally Field.

The movie is based on a play by Robert Harling, who also wrote the screenplay for the film directed by Herbert Ross. All the women have funny names and not much in common, really. They congregate in Truvy's Beauty Parlor. Dolly Parton plays Truvy (Sam Shepard plays her husband Spud, but we don't see much of him, since this is a woman's picture and the men are mainly stick figures). It's the sort of role Dolly Parton was born for, chatty and Southern as all get out. "If I had not gone into the music business," Parton said in a publicity statement, "I probably would have been a beautician. so Truvy was a lot like me—a big hearted country girl trying to keep peace in the neighborhood." Moreover, according to the *Washington Post*, Parton plans to introduce a new cosmetic line called "Dollyface." Perfect!

Darryl Hannah plays Truvy's assistant Annelle and it's a pleasure to watch her find and then remake her character. First, she is a mousey newcomer, unsure of herself, but before long she is wearing her hair like Dolly Parton, and acting like her, too. Finally, she finds Jesus and gets married, which opens the way for still another transformation—and still another hairstyle.

Olympia Dukakis and Shirley MacLaine play the two older gals who hang around the beauty parlor, even though they are obviously in a higher income bracket. Class lines are easily crossed (or ignored) in this play. Dukakis is Clairee, the widow of the late Mayor and, later still, the owner of a local radio station. MacLaine is her sour chum, Ouiser Boudreaux, who is something of a cynic, but ultimately a curmudgeon with a heart of gold.

The movie starts out as a comedy, then takes a decidedly melodramatic turn. The Sally Field character is devoted to her frail daughter Shelby (Julia Roberts), who gets married and then, against all advice, gets pregnant. Doctors have warned her that a pregnancy could ruin her health, but Shelby wants to have a baby, whatever the consequences. This part gets heavy during the latter part of the film, when the movie begins to resemble *Terms Of Endearment*, with Sally Field in the Shirley MacLaine role and Shirley MacLaine as a borderline loon; but Sally Field is typecast for the role of the strong, devoted mother, a role she also played in *Places In The Heart*. Julia Roberts played the lead in the surprise hit movie *Mystic Pizza* and is very good here, despite the strong competition.

Robert Harling's play is partly autobiographical, based on the relationship between his mother and his sister, Susan, in Natchitoches, Louisiana, where the film was shot, though the name of the town in the film is Chinquapin. Sally Field met and talked with Margaret Harling to prepare herself for the role. While the shoot was in progress, Field was also taking care of her newborn son.

Robert Harling's obvious talent is for comedy, but Herbert Ross handles the awkward melodramatic downturn deftly, and the comic lines continue to bubble to the surface, even through the suffering. Finally, the movie is a rather touching (if contrived) tribute to friendship.

LOS ANGELES TIMES, 11/15/89, Calendar/p. 1, Peter Rainer

In the published version of Robert Harling's play "Steel Magnolias," he opens with this cautionary author's note: "The women in this play are witty, intelligent and, above all, real characters. They in no way, shape or form are meant to be portrayed as cartoons or caricatures." In Harling's movie adaptation, directed by Herbert Ross, he must have prefaced his script with the reverse caution. The film's yammering sextet is *relentlessly* cartoonish. They do so much prancing and sashaying and elbowing that the film, set in small-town Louisiana, turns into Southern-fried vaudeville. The knockabout unbelievability is exhausting. You want to run for cover.

M'Lynn (Sally Field) is the well-to-do matron whose pretty-as-a-peach daughter Shelby (Julia Roberts), a severe diabetic, is about to be married. Truvy (Dolly Parton), the owner of her own styling salon, Truvy's Beauty Spot, presides over Shelby's pouffing and perfuming. The Beauty Spot is the town's mission control for gossip, and, in the film's opening minutes, we're introduced to its leading players. Besides M'Lynn, Shelby and Truvy, there are Clairee (Olympia Dukakis), the preening widow of the town's former mayor: Ouiser (Shirley MacLaine), a rich, wildly eccentric scold; and Annelle (Daryl Hannah), the salon's mousy new "born-again" assistant.

In the course of the film, these women are thrown into crises that call upon their deepest reserves of empathy. And are they ever empathic! They stalk about acting curmudgeonly in order—of course—to hide how deeply they care. They go in for heavy-duty bonding. Where trouble hits, weeping and wisecracks are sure to follow. When Truvy says "Laughter through tears is my favorite emotion," she's acting as the writer's mouthpiece.

Harling's play, his first, has been "opened up" as a movie, and, as a result, his dramatic intentions are clearer than they were on the stage. "Steel Magnolias" is a serio-comic yowl about the sustaining powers of sisterhood. It's also, by implication, a retort to all the male-bonding dramas in our midst. The film makers want us to recognize the tensile strength in the filigree of women's lives. These gals may be nurturing but they're also hardscrabble.

By contrast, the wimpification of the men in this movie is fairly amusing to observe. Shelby's husband (Dylan McDermott), her father (Tom Skerrit), Annelle's hubbie (Kevin O'Connor), Truvy's mate (Sam Shepard) are all secondary players. They loiter, dazed, on the fringes of the action. Since few films feature as many women as this one does, their prominence here is a form of pay-back. They've seized the screen from the big boys and they won't let go.

Some of the seizing is artful, some isn't. Parton has a sweet, lilting presence, and a suggestion of hard-won disappointment beneath her wigs and wide smiles. Roberts has such fragile freshness that the scene in which she goes into diabetic shock seems like a violation of nature. Dukakis isn't breaking any new ground with her trademarked snideness, but she gets off a few zingers. (She also seems triumphantly impervious to her sometime Southern accent.) Field is rather bland, though—too teary and noble. And MacLaine is wretched. Her performance is a scenery-gobbling amalgam of her work in films like "Terms of Endearment" and "Madame Sousatzka."

Another of Truvy's sayings is, "There is no such thing as natural beauty," but the entire film stands in opposition to this credo. It is precisely the natural, untrussed beauty of these women that we're meant to recognize. Harling and Ross may be deliberately going for the exaggerated and the overblown. They may be pouffing reality, but only as a heightened contrast to their people's all-too-real sorrows. The trouble is, the pouffing crowds out the pathos. That's not entirely bad. The slapstick camaraderie at least has some energy, while the pathos is shameless, four-hanky stuff.

Obviously, the film makers have higher ambitions. The six women with their different backgrounds and temperaments are intended as a symbolic cross-section of femalehood; their plights are representative of all women. But things have gotten out of hand. Instead of a soul-sister ensemble, what we get is a screenful of ego-pumped actresses clonking each other for the spotlight. These belles should take their act on the road as tag-team wrestlers.

MONTHLY FILM BULLETIN, 2/90, p. 51, Tom Milne

Preparations for a wedding in the Eatenton family home are attended by assorted crises. A minor one with crusty neighbour Ouiser Boudreaux, enraged when Drum Eatenton goes on a pigeon-shoot, determined that guests at his daughter's wedding reception on the lawn will not be shat upon; a major one when Shelby, the prospective bride, succumbs to hysterical doubts while having her hair done at Truvy Jones' beauty parlour. As a diabetic, advised that childbearing would be dangerous, is she right to marry, even though her fiancé Jackson Latcherie is undeterred by the prospect of no children? She is reassured by her mother M'Lynn, with help and sympathy from Truvy and Clairee (a sharp-tongued contemporary of Ouiser's), and prayer from Annelle, a bewildered waif in flight from an unhappy marriage who is taken on as an assistant by Truvy. The wedding takes place, and in due course, to her father's joy but her mother's dismay, Shelby announces that she is pregnant: realising that with her medical record she is unlikely to be granted adoption rights, she has decided to ignore medical advice. A son is born, and everyone is delighted. But the birth puts a strain on Shelby's kidneys; M'Lynn volunteers to become a donor for the transplant needed by the time the child is three years old; and the operation seems to be a success until Shelby collapses while trying to lift her son, goes into a coma, and dies. The tragedy makes Truvy realise how much she has neglected her husband Spud while trying to make a success of her beauty parlour; while Annelle, now contentedly married to electrician Sammy, begins to see that her religious fervour (she even objects to beer drinking) is putting a strain on their relationship. M'Lynn is distraught at the funeral, but is snapped out of her depression by the combined efforts of Truvy, Ouiser and Clairee (usually at loggerheads but reconciled for the occasion), and Annelle. M'Lynn is pleased when the pregnant Annelle announces that she and Sammy would like to name their baby—boy or girl—after Shelby. "I might have known there was something wrong", says Dolly Parton of her surly biker son, "when is imaginary playmates wouldn't play with him". There are plenty of acerbic one-liners, delivered with gusto by Parton, Shirley MacLaine and (especially) Olympia Dukakis, but something seems to have gone sadly awry with this adaptation by Robert Harling of his own play offering a women's-eye slant on life, love, death and tribulation in the Deep South.

To begin with, evidently much tougher in its stage version, the script has been put through a sentimental wringer by Herbert Ross. Starting off as a minor-key variation on Altman's *A Wedding*, it abruptly metamorphoses into a lush, excruciatingly elongated emotional wallow which allows Sally Field to indulge some characteristic carpet-chewing as she runs the tearful gamut of a mother's woes. Palatability is not exactly enhanced by the idealisation of the small-town settings (everything clean, green and sparkling white paint), or by the pointedly festal occasions upon which the action takes place (not just the wedding, but Christmas, Halloween and Easter, with even the child labelled a Yankee Doodle Dandy, apparently born on the Fourth of July). The one-liners, implying that things aren't really so rosy, stand no chance against the cosy sentiment.

Even more damaging is the treatment of the male characters, dragged in as necessary appendages to the female experience under scrutiny, but serving only to make the plotting seem at best arbitrary, at worst broken-backed. On the stage, where the exclusively female sanctum of Truvy's beauty parlour clearly served as a key setting, this relegation of husbands to the sidelines was probably a legitimately effective dramatic device. Here, negated by the opening-out process, it reduces them to awkward supernumeraries. Sam Shepard, for instance, is glimpsed in the background a time or two looking hangdog, and is then trundled on for a climactic reconciliation scene with wife Dolly Parton: both play it with feeling, but deprived of substance, it remains empty. Tom Skerritt comes off a little better as the amiably eccentric paterfamilias, but is noticeably excluded from the emotional Field day over his daughter's death. Kevin O'Connor, playing an almost non-existent role as sounding-board for the tiresome Annelle's problems, is as shamefully wasted as Shepard. The moral, in any case, is probably that any writer who dreams up character names like Ouiser, M'Lynn, Truvy, Clairee, Spud and Drum is to be approached with caution.

NEW STATESMAN & SOCIETY, 2/16/90, p. 41, Suzanne Moore

While the film *Family Business* [see Moore's review] centres on father-son relationships with the female characters as marginal, *Steel Magnolias* is the archetypal "women's movie"—slushy, tearful stuff about tough southern women and the values of female friendship. Set in small town Louisiana, the whole thing is shot in yukky *My Little Pony* pastels which someone somewhere must think are appealing to women. Certainly Shelby, the diabetic daughter at the centre of the drama, loves pink. Her whole wedding is coordinated in shades of pink which she describes as "blush and bashful".

The "steel magnolias" of the title refer to Shelby, her mother and their friends, among them the divine Dolly Parton as a hairdresser and Shirley MacLaine as an old grouch. The plot moves predictably along through weddings, funerals, and christenings. Really it's a re-run of the classic maternal melodrama with Sally Field as the self-sacrificing mother. These soapy emotions are actually based on writer Robert Harling's own experience, but he does what so many men do when they try to celebrate women's friendship and portray the women as endlessly chirpy and supportive.

But if you want a good wallow *Steel Magnolias* provides the mush. Very little happens, but emotion is continually in the foreground. This formula may work well on the small screen as with *thirtysomething*, but on the big screen I found myself longing for a car chase or indeed anything that would shake up the complacency of the small town values.

NEW YORK, 11/27/89, p. 78, David Denby

If one believes that dullness is the worst sin in the movies, then the all-star *Steel Magnolias* deserves no one's charity. (On the other hand, I thought I deserved two weeks' pay just for sitting through it.) I'm told Robert Harling's play is charming onstage. On a single set—a beauty parlor—six women in a small Louisiana town meet regularly to bitch at one another and chew over their lives. Harling did the adaptation himself, opening up the play to take in the menfolk and the hustle-bustle of a small town. One can't be surprised that he writes too much exposition, repeating himself over and over, like a high! -school kid telling a story. Or that he fails to realize that theatrical banter doesn't always work onscreen. But how can one explain the all but incredible indulgence of Harling's garrulousness by two such old pros as Ray Stark (producer) and Herbert Ross (director)?

Julia Roberts, as a young diabetic, marries and, against the advice of her mother, Sally Field, conceives a child. The pregnancy, it seems, could kill her, but all she wants in life is a baby—nothing else matters, nothing else interests her. So she becomes a saint. And her mother becomes a saint for trying to save her by giving her one of her own kidneys. (I can think of a lot more Sally Field organs that could be sacrificed.) All you can do is cry for both of them. This tragedy, more embarrassing than enlightening, is embedded in a thick, goopy meringue of unbelievably tedious gossip and bickering, all of it predicated on the assumption that you will find six brawlin', rasslin', lovin' gals from the South irresistibly funny and adorable. Certainly the movie never would have been made if the ladies had fought and reconciled in New Jersey or Ohio.

The way the six stars chew the scenery is nothing compared to their abuse of one another. As a rich termagant, Shirley MacLaine makes two entrances pulled by a large, sloppy dog; MacLaine, plain and furious and horribly rude, is actually funny here and there, but Olympia Dukakis, as a fashionable and ironic lady, is excruciating, sitting on her southern accent as if each obvious sarcasm were dazzlingly witty. Daryl Hannah does nicely as a literal-minded young dope who takes up religion, but Field, as always, is a lead ball in the middle of the movie. After repeating every joke and personal quirk eight times, the filmmakers reprise all the character tags at the end, as if to draw on the bottomless well of our affection. We're more likely to feel immense relief, as when a group of overbearing, self-absorbed, but implacably mediocre people at last exit from the house.

NEW YORK POST, 11/15/89, p. 27, David Edelstein

Set in a small-town Louisiana beauty parlor, "Steel Magnolias" is a holiday showcase for six of our most aggressive actresses—none of whom you'll ever want to share a stage with—and each is in there plugging, ferociously competing for that golden statuette. It's a film about feminine solidarity, but the message is somewhat undercut by all this "Get the hell out of my spotlight" acting.

Make no mistake: You'll laugh, you'll cry, you'll feel good about life—especially upon returning to it. "Steel Magnolias" didn't flourish on stage for nothing. Part gut-buster, part tear-jerker, Robert Harling's script is quite an engineering feat, taking its tone from the character who declares, "Laughter through tears is my favorite emotion." Let's hope it's yours, too, because this is a long movie.

The six actresses—you know their names—play a bunch of battle-axes who gather on the day of a big wedding. The bride-to-be, Shelby (Julia Roberts), is a sweet thing who has diabetes and is told that having children will put a terrible strain on her kidneys, but who—she can't help it—wants to bring life into the world.

After Shelby has a hair-raising (literally) episode of insulin-shock in the salon, her devoted mother, M'Lynn (Sally Field), looks on with concern, knowing she can't rely on the future husband (Dylan McDermott) to look out for her daughter's welfare. Field creases her brow and seems very eager to hold the movie's dramatic burden on her small (but powerful) shoulders; you just know Shelby's in for trouble.

Actually, none of the women can rely on their menfolk—the males of "Steel Magnolias" are harmless flakes, emotional zombies or ciphers. The women are everything. Although they bicker at one another, they're sisters under the skin—zany, wise-cracking Southerners with goofy names. In a cold, cruel world, thank heaven for bosomy buddies.

Ousier (pronounced "wheezer") Boudreaux (Shirley MacLaine) is an eccentric curmudgeon who has a love-hate relationship with Clairee Belcher (Olympia Dukakis), the mayor's widow. Truvy Jones (Dolly Parton) runs the salon and makes self-deprecating jokes about how little of her beauty is natural. Annelle Dupuy Desoto (Daryl Hannah), Truvy's assistant, goes from timid gawk to luscious party girl to Bible-clutching zealot in less than two hours.

The director, Herbert Ross, is a tasteful old hand, and while he does indulge in a lyrical shot of children running with balloons after someone says, "Life goes on," he keeps his actresses under control and in almost the same movie; it never degenerates into the drag show one might fear.

MacLaine is mildly entertaining—she seems to be sending up her reputation as a flake and foul-mouthed shrew. And after some early self-consciousness, Field doesn't labor as hard as usual for our approval. (She doesn't need to—it's built into the role.) The lissome Hannah, cast against type as a myopic twerp, is pretty funny, although her tics and blinks call attention to themselves and in her brief phase as a glamour-puss she drops the character altogether.

I cringed for Parton, however, who has the most natural presence on screen but who is confined to one joke—the artificiality of her beauty. And Dukakis does an appalling Mae West imitation, huskily slinging her awful one-liners as if expecting the audience to drop dead.

Roberts, who will probably be up for every acting award in sight, is so pink and pearly skinned and shiny-eyed that she seems ready to sprout wings and a halo; I can't remember the last time the screen has held so glowing a baby-machine. She smiles in the face of tragedy, arguing "I would rather have 30 minutes of wonderful than a lifetime of nothing special."

It's a shame there's no middle ground. One can, after all, have a lifetime of wonderful even if physically unsuited to bear children. This option doesn't occur to Harling, who based the character on his late sister. No one can dispute the depth of his pain (or sincerity). It's a shame, however, that he has turned a wrenching personal tragedy into a retro soap opera, where women are alternately bitchy or nurturing or both simultaneously. Bitchiness through nurturing is their true favorite emotion.

NEWSDAY, 11/15/89, Part II/p. 2, Mike McGrady

After we've come through weddings, births and deaths; Christmas, Independence Day and Halloween; labor pains, diabetic seizures and kidney transplants—after all this, there is a funeral in "Steel Magnolias" at which Dolly Parton, the small Louisiana town's foremost beautician, makes a crucial point: "Laughter through tears is my favorite emotion."

For all those who share Dolly's peculiar affection—or is the proper word "affliction"?—this tale of female bonding in the Southland is the kind of flick Hollywood hardly ever makes anymore.

Back in pre-feminist America, in the heyday of Hayward and Hayworth, this kind of film might have been referred to as "a woman's movie" or a "four-handkerchief film." Either phrase would imply that the movie would concentrate on matters emotional, that the background music would be heavy with strings, that one could anticipate lingering illnesses and/or sudden accidents and that it might be just as well to leave the old man at home. One could also be sure that by the end of the film, tragedy would make way for happiness the way clouds can part for a rainbow, the way laughter can break through tears.

The fact that "Steel Magnolias," written by Robert Harling and based on his long-running Off-Broadway play, works as well as it does is a credit to the well-honed skills of the high-powered lineup.

In addition to Dolly Parton as the gabby "glamor technician," we have Sally Field as the heroic mother of an ailing bride, Daryl Hannah as a mousy (believe me, this takes *some* acting) hairdresser, Olympia Dukakis as a wealthy widow, Shirley MacLaine as an acid-tongued misanthrope and relative newcomer Julia Roberts as the bride who decides to have a baby—no matter what "the doctors and specialists" say.

Since Harling is transferring his own play to the screen, he treats his original words with enormous respect. The result is a film that tends to be wordy and a script that constantly tends to balance highly manipulative situations against well-turned phrases.

Unfortunately, the women are all clever and witty in almost precisely the same way, which, one suspects, must be Harling's way as well. Dolly Parton puts down her son's date with, "The nicest thing I can say about her is all her tattoos are spelled correctly." Olympia Dukakis will admire a new outfit with, "The only thing that separates us from animals is our ability to accessorize." Sally Field talks of a neighbor's depression: "When it comes to sufferin', she's right up there with Elizabeth Taylor." Shirley MacLaine notes that, "A dirty mind is a terrible thing to waste." In time one can only applaud the customer who laments the absence of a radio in the beauty shop: "It takes the pressure off people feelin' they have to talk so much."

Unsurprisingly, the women get the good lines. Their menfolk—Sam Shepard, Tom Skerritt, Kevin J. O'Connor—are all-but-useless appendages, evident afterthoughts. Where the women have been granted heart and wit and fortitude, the men have been given... eccentricities.

Herbert Ross—best known for "The Goodbye Girl," "California Suite" and "The Turning Point"—has directed 21 pictures in 21 years, and he has shown considerable wisdom in assembling this particular all-star lineup. While the script tends to guarantee the tears, the cast ensures that some of the laughter will show through.

NEWSWEEK, 11/27/89, p. 90, David Ansen

Watching Ray Stark's star-stuffed, overproduced *Steel Magnolias* it's possible to imagine, with a little effort, the slight, sweet and reportedly endearing stage play from which this swollen movie has been adapted. Robert Harling's off-Broadway hit—a celebration of Southern sisterhood—never left the beauty shop of a small Louisiana town and had a cast of only six women. The densely populated movie, pumped up with unnecessary crowd scenes and a handful of utterly extraneous male characters, is as garish and busy as a TV game show. As directed by Herbert Ross, it is so intent on persuading the audience that it is having a heartwarming emotional experience you almost expect TelePrompTers to flash in the theater, instructing you to laugh and cry. "Steel Magnolias" not only tells you how to feel at every moment, it supplies instant recaps to inform you what you've just felt. "Laughter through tears is my favorite emotion," coos Dolly Parton as Truvy, the beauty-parlor owner, just after the movie has produced its shamelessly show-stopping laughter-through-tears emotional climax. This may be the first movie to come with its own critical quotes already appended.

There's nothing wrong with laughter-through-tears, if either emotion is honestly earned. But this sitcomish movie, which blatantly tries to trigger memories of "Terms of Endearment" (the touchstone of L.T.T. movies), has a purely synthetic heart. It may have been filmed on location, but its vision of Southern life is candycoated, backlot Hollywood kitsch.

Just what is "Steel Magnolias" about? Aside from star packaging, it's hard to say. At the center is a spirited New Southern belle, Shelby (Julia Roberts) who, we discover on the day of her wedding, is a diabetic subject to severe bouts of insulin shock. To the horror of her worried mother (Sally Field) and against doctor's orders, she proceeds to get pregnant. Virtually the only dramatic issue here is whether she'll be able to survive having a baby. Once it becomes clear that the movie is no more than an elaborate death watch—its sole purpose being the mechanical production of pathos and uplift—it's hard to stay interested.

The real draw, of course, is the cast. It's an imposing collection of talent, but never for a moment can you believe these women are lifelong friends and neighbors. The movie has as much sense of genuine community as a celebrity "roast." Dolly Parton, surprisingly ill at ease, relates to her costars with all the intimacy of a computerized phone operator. (In her scenes with her "husband" Sam Shepard, the two actors look as if they'd never been introduced.) She even fails to get laughs from Harling's zippy one-liners. Shirley MacLaine, who's becoming a specialist in angry women, does a lively caricature of a curmudgeon whose cynicism, of course, hides a heart of gold. Olympia Dukakis, as the sardonic widow of the town's mayor, struggles with her accent and tosses off barbs with a sideways slur that sounds like Mae West on Quaaludes. Sally Field as the indomitable, tightly wound mother dutifully restrains her natural exuberance and is rewarded with a big Oscar-mongering third-act explosion, which she milks for all it's worth.

Perhaps because they're less familiar, the younger women make a fresher impression. Daryl Hannah, in the cartoonish role of a gawky beautician who goes gung-ho for Jesus, shows some real comic spirit, and Julia Roberts—who sparkled in "Mystic Pizza"—lights up the screen with her liquid fire.

But you never get to know this doomed girl—or any of these women—in any but the most superficial way. The movie is so busy celebrating their wonderfulness it doesn't have time to stop to get acquainted. These "life affirming" steel magnolias looked like artificial flowers to these eyes.

TIME, 11/20/89, p. 92, Richard Schickel

Men have hunting, ball games and bars—plenty of opportunities to practice the hearty, necessary rituals of male bonding. Feminist theory and common sense tell us that women have a similar need to renew gender loyalties. Their problem, traditionally, has been finding suitable places and occasions to do so.

It was observant of playwright Robert Harling to see that a small-town beauty parlor can function as a little lodge hall for women, a place where they can let their hair down while it is being put up. It was clever of him to stock *Steel Magnolias* with Southern belles, wicked of eye and tongue, though ultimately forgiving of heart. It was shrewd of him to work his successful off-Broadway drama around personal milestones (marriage, birth, death) that everyone shares. His characters may be exotics, but their situations are achingly familiar.

Above all, it was brave of Harling to place at the center of what might otherwise have been an episodic comedy the true, tragic story of his sister, a diabetic who doomed herself to early death in order to bear a child, and his mother's struggle to come to terms with that choice. It gives the piece the dramatic focus and the emotional weight it requires.

The play was a swell show; it had something for everyone. The main thing preventing it from being an equally swell movie is the fact that it *is* a movie. A film must offer us something a little more spectacular than half a dozen white chicks sitting around talking. Accordingly, Harling's adaptation hustles them out of the beauty shop and into the life of the town. Suddenly the people they talked about so amusingly behind their backs must be met face-to-face. The conflicts and confusions that sounded so hilarious in the recounting are spread out realistically. And reality, as we know, is never that amusing when confronted head on.

The stylized bitchiness of Harling's writing requires a stage setting. Failing that, it requires a director willing to let his actors throw good lines away or overlap them in ways that work in the movie's naturalistic context. But Herbert Ross insists on theatricality. His editing even provides awkward little pauses for the audience to fill with laughter, just as if this were still a play. As a result, some very good performers (Shirley MacLaine, Olympia Dukakis, Daryl Hannah, Dolly Parton) function less as full-scale sorority sisters than as chorus members who elbow their way up front in a crowd of even sketchier characters.

The film's center lies in the bond between Julia Roberts as the young woman serenely accepting the risk of childbirth and Sally Field as her tightly wound mother, wanting to scream warnings at her daughter but only able to whisper despairing support for her—right through the final coma. Their characters are fully and finely realized, and their work is supported, not subverted, by the style and mood of a film that cries more easily, and more persuasively, than it laughs.

VILLAGE VOICE, 11/21/89, p. 92, Georgia Brown

Steel Magnolias is more or less 118 minutes of lines dying to be quoted. Robert Harling has reworked his Off-Broadway success for the screen, but dialogue still follows the aphoristic, wise-cracking style of stage comedies:

"The only thing that separates us from animals is our ability to accessorize."

"*There* is a troubled, twisted soul. When it comes to suffering, she's right up there with Elizabeth Taylor."

"Time marches on, and soon you realize it's marching across your face."

I forgot who said this last one, but of the six women at the center of this movie, half could be said to have marched-on faces. Shirley MacLaine is Ouiser (a corruption, I think, of Louisa), the town eccentric who wears Oshkosh overalls and pulls on an ugly dog. ("I'm not crazy, I've just been in a really bad mood for 40 years.") She is affectionately tormented by the mayor's rich widow, Clairee (oh, that southern way of doctoring perfectly good names), played by Olympia

Dukakis. Sally Field is M'Lynn, a psychiatric social worker and harried, clucking mother of three.

Dolly Parton's face may show a few gentle bootprints, but then she plays Truvy, the small town's busy beautician, or "glamour technician." Her business's slogan runs, "There's no such thing as natural beauty." Daryl Hannah strives to illuminate this axiom by disguising herself as Annelle, Truvy's homely, troubled assistant. ("My personal tragedy will not interfere with my ability to do good hair,") Least marched-on is Julia Roberts (*Mystic Pizza*, younger sister of Eric) as Shelby, M'Lynn's beautiful, diabetic daughter. The movie opens with the town being done up for Shelby's wedding.

Harling is a native of Natchitoches, Louisiana, population 20,000 (hometown as well of Rex Reed, who dishes the production in the December *Premiere*, apparently because producer Ray Stark refused him access to the set). When he was 32, Harling wrote his play in 10 days after his sister's death of complications from diabetes. That the plot is based on the Harling family tragedy is a fact most people seem to know before seeing *Steel Magnolias*, yet they still manage a good cry.

The play, I'm informed, was set entirely in the beauty parlor, with the six women—getting hair and nails done, mustaches removed—the only characters. The peppy, pastel-colored film version, directed by Herbert Ross, expands to include various local abodes and oak-shaded avenues, as well as males only talked about in the play. Sam Shepard appears as his usual laconic, don't fence-me-in cowboy (Truvy's mate), and Tom Skerritt is M'Lynn's Peter Pan husband.

The point is reinforced that once a Southern belle marries or reaches a certain age, she forfeits chivalrous protection and must turn herself into ramrod, or steel magnolia. This happens because men, victims of a mysterious incapacitating virus, remain fixated at childish stages, or turn quietly inward (the Ashley-Melanie syndrome) or gay. Harling's comedy-melodrama takes the mother-daughter relation as its emotional focus, with Field raging at the gods and coming to terms with the help of her group. Unfortunately, men aren't the beneficiaries of women's healing capacities.

Also reviewed in:
NEW YORK TIMES, 11/15/89, p. C21, Vincent Canby
VARIETY, 11/15/89, p. 20
WASHINGTON POST, 11/17/89, p. D1, Hal Hinson
WASHINGTON POST, 11/17/89, Weekend/p. 51, Desson Howe

STEPFATHER II

A Millimeter Films release. *Producer:* William Burr and Darin Scott. *Director:* Jeff Burr. *Screenplay:* John Auerbach. *Director of Photography:* Jacek Laskus. *Music:* Jim Manzie. *Running time:* 88 minutes. *MPAA Rating:* R.

CAST: Terry O'Quinn (The Stepfather); Meg Foster (Carol Grayland); Jonathan Brandis (Todd Grayland); Caroline Williams (Matty Crimmins); Henry Brown (Dr. Joseph Danvers); Mitchell Laurance (Phil Grayson).

LOS ANGELES TIMES, 11/16/89, Calendar/p. 4, Michael Wilmington

Joseph Ruben's 1987 "The Stepfather"—written by the novelist Donald Westlake and featuring a remarkable, little-known actor, Terry O'Quinn, as a chameleonic psychotic searching for the perfect family and killing the failures one after another—was a shocker aimed at a genre audience that caught the critics instead.

"The Stepfather 2," on the other hand, is the sort of sequel that shouldn't have been made. Not simply because it repeats so many of the devices of the original—the plot, the theme, O'Quinn's airy post-murder whistling of "Camptown Races"—but because it makes nonsense of its predecessor by existing at all.

At the end of "The Stepfather," O'Quinn's murderous, multi-identitied all-American Dad was shot in the back, stabbed in the arm and stabbed again, apparently near the heart. But here, at the opening, he suddenly thrashes up in a prison bed, none the worse for wear except for some nasty chest scars. Having established his extraordinary recuperative powers—a match for Jason's in "Friday the 13th"—the movie makers then whip up an unlikely way to spring him from maximum security prison, involving a credulous psychiatrist and another of Pop's toy houses.

Then, perhaps dizzy with relief, they switch into low gear and simple repetition for the remainder—with O'Quinn, now a counselor, sporting another of his endless supply of pseudonyms and toupees and courting another single mother, with the same relentlessly mild manner hiding the same psychotic rage at his inability to achieve TV sitcom-family bliss.

For a medium-budget horror feature, Ruben's film had unusually lively camera movements and dialogue that satirically sliced up middle-American family iconography. And O'Quinn—as the crazed father who kept switching identities after each massacre and had a smile as smooth and a voice as friendly as Ward Cleaver's—gave an immensely subtle and defined comic-horrific performance.

But the sequel (rated R for sex, violence and language) doesn't have anything extraordinary besides O'Quinn—just as subtle, just as eerily off-center, now drowned in bluishly evocative cinematography, in suspicious females and more temper tantrums.

Director Jeff Burr and writer John Auerbach show a laudable taste for moody tension over non-stop blood baths. But they can't disguise the fact that they're walking around waving a corpse and trying to make it do tricks.

NEW YORK POST, 11/6/89, p. 31, V.A. Musetto

When last seen (in the closing minutes of "The Stepfather"), our all-American mass killer was sprawled on the floor of his neat, middle-class, suburban house, apparently quite dead after having been shot by his wife and knifed by his stepdaughter (in self-defense, of course).

So, you may ask, how can you have a "Stepfather 2" without a stepfather? Silly question. Don't you know that in the world of slasher sequels, a bullet in the back and a butcher knife in the chest are about as serious as a hangnail?

Thus, as "Stepfather 2" unfolds, we find that our demented friend (again played by Terry O'Quinn) is alive and sort-of well in a mental hospital. But not for long. Before you can down your first handful of popcorn, he kills a guard, a too-trusting shrink and a traveling salesman, and heads off into the outside world. Wanna bet he's going to resume his little game of marrying into fatherless families, then slaughtering them when they don't meet his "Leave It to Beaver" standards?

He sets himself up as a phony psychologist and turns his attention to a newly divorced mom and her 13-year-old son. But first there's the matter of the woman's ex-husband—who wants to come back—and a nosy, suspicious mailwoman. I don't have to tell you how these problems are solved.

"Stepfather 2" aims its sights higher than most other movies of this genre. And, despite some illogical moments, it succeeds. Sure, a copious amount of blood is shed, but the gore is treated as a means, rather than an end. Then there are sly little touches of black humor (the phony doc's speciality is family therapy, for instance) and some interesting visuals. Plus an effectively understated performance by O'Quinn as a killer who goes about this business more in the tradition of Norman Bates than Freddy Krueger.

NEWSDAY, 11/4/89, Part II/p. 17, Bill Kaufman

It's unlikely that The Stepfather will join the infamous ranks of, say, Freddy Krueger or Norman Bates, among other well-known screen psychopaths. That's mainly because he lacks a gimmick: no claws, no cross-dressing, no mad gleam.

But after just a few minutes, there's little doubt we're dealing with a world-class wacko here. The gory sequel picks up with The Stepfather (Terry O'Quinn) locked away in a mental hospital, where he was committed after slaying his last family. Obsessed with family life, The Stepfather constructs model homes in the hospital's hobby shop and fills them with tiny idealized family figurines.

Right away, the film begins to stagger under the weight of its ludicrous script. In a series of bloody and patently ridiculous events, The Stepfather manages to escape and, stealing a name from the obit column, assumes the identity of—get this—a psychiatrist.

He moves into an idyllic suburban community and sets up group therapy sessions with neighborhood women. Just like that. Passing for a charming Dr. Joe Average, he begins to shop for a new family, zeroing in on a pretty real estate saleswoman (Meg Foster) and her teenage son (Jonathan Brandis).

Throughout, "The Stepfather II" makes feeble attempts at black humor. In one scene we see The Stepfather peacefully enjoying a Bob Eubanks television game show that gives away homes and family furnishings. In another, he peruses tapes from a videocassette dating service, clicking it off disdainfully when one mentions she comes equipped with a diaphragm.

For fans of this kind of mindless chiller, there's a certain amount of suspense in the film and, like the original, it's overloaded with mayhem and violence. Beyond that, there's little else to recommend it.

Also reviewed in:
NEW YORK TIMES, 11/4/89, p. 14, Stephen Holden
VARIETY, 11/8/89, p. 35
WASHINGTON POST, 12/6/89, p. D6, Richard Harrington

STONES AND FLIES: RICHARD LONG IN THE SAHARA

Director: Philip Haas. *Director of Photography:* Bernard Zitzermann. *Music:* Marc Wilkinson. *Running time:* 38 minutes. *MPAA Rating:* Not Rated.

NEW YORK POST, 4/5/89, p. 21, Jami Bernard

[*Stones and Flies* was reviewed jointly with *Egg;* see Bernard's review of that film.]

VILLAGE VOICE, 4/11/89, p. 71, Katherine Dieckmann

[*Stones and Flies* was reviewed jointly with *Egg*; see Dieckmann's review of that film.]

Also reviewed in:
NEW YORK TIMES, 4/5/89, p. C19, Caryn James

STORY OF WOMEN

An MK2/New Yorker Films release. *Producer:* Marin Karmitz. *Director:* Claude Chabrol. *Screenplay (French with English subtitles) and adaptation:* Colo Tavernier O'Hagan and Claude Chabrol. *Freely adapted from "Une Affaire de Femmes"* by: Francis Szpiner. *Director of Photography:* Jean Rabier. *Editor:* Monique Fardoulis. *Music:* Matthieu Chabrol. *Sound:* Jean-Bernard Thomasson and Maurice Gilbert. *Set Dresser:* Pierre Galliard. *Special Effects:* Jean-François Cousson. *Costumes:* Corinne Jorry. *Make-up:* Judith Gayo. *Stunt Coordinator:* Pascal Guegan. *Running time:* 110 minutes. *MPAA Rating:* Not Rated.

CAST: Isabelle Huppert (Marie Latour); François Cluzet (Paul Latour); Marie Trintignant (Lulu/Lucie); Nils Tavernier (Lucien); Lolita Chammah (Mouche 2); Aurore Gauvin (Mouche 1); Guillaume Foutrier (Pierrot 1); Nicolas Foutrier (Pierrot 2); Marie Bunel (Ginette); Dominique Blanc (Jasmine); Louis Ducreux (Father Mourier); Michel Blanc (Prosecutor Mourier); Evelyne Didi (Fernande); Dani (Loulou); François Maistre (Lamarre-Coudray); Vincent Gauthier (Attorney Fillon); Myriam David (Rachel); P.T. Dumeniaud (Café Owner); Bernard Houdeville (Peasant); Claire Conty (Hairdresser); Thomas Chabrol (Waiter); Catherine Deville (Yvonne); Sylvie Flepp (Berthe); François Lafont (Grocer); Pierre Martot (German); Jurgen Mash (German Officer); Jean Claude Lecas (Robert); Roland Shon (Old Man); Anne-Marie Etienne (Renee); Valerie Leboutte (Marcelle); Fabienne Chaudat (Patient); Jacques Vincent (Member of the Resistance); Jeannine Hames (Voice Teacher); Bernard Cherboeuf (Inspector); Elizabeth Sender (Francine); Huguette Maillard (Monique); Valerie Soudant (Armelle); Lise Roy (Guard); Jean-Michel Noiret (Bailiff); Madeleine Marie (Albertine); Caroline Berg (Helene Fillon); Colette Charbonneau (Nun); Jacques Brunet (Colonel Chabert); Henri Attal (Policeman #1); Jean-François Klein (Policeman #2); Jean-Marc Roulot (Edouard); Franck Lapersonne (Attorney Martinet).

FILMS IN REVIEW, 3/90, p. 172, Eva H. Kissin

"I prefer the microscope to the telescope," said director Claude Chabrol, who has certainly focused with unerring accuray on *Story Of Women*.

This remarkable film, a true story, prize winning but highly debated in Europe where protestors used tear gas to prevent its screening, arrived here late and was reluctantly released because of its traumatic, controversial and timely subject: abortion.

The heroine, Marie, played with depth and insight by Isabel Huppert, is a no nonsense young mother raising two children in dark, occupied, defeated wartime France. Her consuming desire for a singing career appears impossible in terms of the poverty of her life in a cold water flat, her children sleeping in their clothes and with her in her bed for warmth. "We live like rats," she tells her despised husband who has just returned from the war, physically wounded and barely able to pull himself together psychologically.

However, our heroine is a gutsy young woman out for the main chance, and she is willing to take one to get one. She responds to a pregnant neighbor's desperate cry for help and manages to produce a homemade abortion. After the procedure, she asks if she can keep the left over soap. Her real reward from her grateful "client" comes the next day in the form of a phonograph which brings the only note of pleasure into her dark, rabbit warren of an apartment.

If one service brings music, a second one puts jam on her children's bread, a third brings warm clothes, and a fourth a brighter airy apartment. Her family life improves materially and she has no qualms about "helping" desperate women who are not ready to bear children at this time. One exhausted mother speaks of her seven children whom she cares for but doesn't love, and her never ending sense of animal existence.

Our heroine, who is a good manager in the best bourgeois tradition, realizes still more income by occasionally renting out a room in her apartment on an hourly basis to the local prostitute. In fact, life improves so much that she is able to begin her singing lessons.

However, a love affair with a collaborator and the long arm of the law catch up with her. The guilty, self-righteous mood of wartime France, the emphasis on morality and replenishing the population, eventually silence her singing. Her judges are men who may have impregnated unwilling women in their time and used better organized brothels than her "hot" bedroom. Nevertheless the mood of the era influences both their judgment and their verdict.

This brilliant moving film is filled with disturbing after-images of tortured women who shouldn't be pregnant, who are being punished for the same few minutes of love they shared with a man who comes off scotfree. Their upraised legs on the kitchen table remain in your head long after the film's dramatic finale.

It is a film about a loving mother, a woman, no worse than others in business but in the wrong business, who is victimized by her greed and her times. It is a serious story of all women, involving one of the great questions of our own time.

LOS ANGELES TIMES, 10/26/89, Calendar/p. 10, Kevin Thomas

Claude Chabrol's beguiling yet mordant "Story of Women" takes us into the demoralized heart of Occupied France. In a drab port town near Dieppe, a young mother, Marie Latour (Isabelle Huppert), comes upon a neighbor taking a mustard bath in hope of aborting herself. "You'll never do it that way," says Marie, who, after some basic research, calmly performs the abortion on her friend.

A whole new world of possibilities opens up for the impoverished Marie, who is dazzled by the rewards of her new-found profession. For her, the joy of obtaining such precious commodities as cigarettes for herself and jam for her children is as seductive as Eve taking a bite out of that apple. "When you have money, you always want more," observes Marie's prosititute friend Lulu (Marie Trintignant), to whom she is soon renting a room for assignations as yet another source of income.

"Story of Women," whose French title is "Une Affaire de Femmes" ("Women's Business"), is based on a true story. It represents the culmination of Chabrol's three-decade obsession with bourgeois hypocrisy, and he has never had such rich, complex material with which to express it. Chabrol clearly favors women being in control over their bodies. But timely—and scathing—as "Story of Women" is regarding abortion and women's rights, it is above all a terse, tragic yet exhilarating evocation of the most painful period in modern French history.

Chabrol, co-writer Colo Tavernier O'Hagan and Huppert, who took the best-actress prize at

Venice last year for her portrayal of Marie, show us a shrewd yet fundamentally naive woman who sees herself as no worse—and probably much better—than many of her neighbors, an appraisal that is actually quite accurate yet blinds her to danger.

In peacetime, Marie almost certainly would have lived out a drab, dutiful existence, faithful to a husband she no longer loves, but the Occupation has given her a freedom and opportunity so totally unexpected that she's sent reeling. Even though her perfectly ordinary husband (François Cluzet) has inconveniently been sent home from his interment by the Germans, she takes a dashing younger lover (Nils Tavernier), a cynical collaborator. She's as oblivious to the impact of her new way of life upon her husband as she is to the risk of being an aboritonist at a time when the Vichy government is assuaging the shame of defeat with a fierce embrace of moral rectitude.

Chabrol does not judge Marie but rather sees her as a catalyst for her times, revealing the full extent of their corruption and signaling that nothing will ever be the same in the wake of the war.

As a mature work of a master, "Story of Women" (Times-rated: Mature for adult themes) has a terrific sense of immediacy, an enormous vitality and a deep and broad perspective. It's as if Chabrol is reminding us that social change, inevitably slow and painful as it is, is possible even in the face of seemingly immutable human nature.

You couldn't ask more of a cast—Cluzet's diffident but finally enraged husband, Trintignant's gorgeous, warm-hearted hooker, and on and on—but Huppert's Marie is the film's focus, eliciting widely contradictory emotions as we watch her evolve. We become caught up in her sheer joy in embracing life's pleasures fully, in her steadfast love and affection for her children, in her increasingly cruel and dangerous follies and in her eventual self-awareness and calm courage. Huppert, who a decade ago was Chabrol's "Violette," a frustrated murderer of her own parents, has that rare gift that Garbo had in sublime abundance: She is able to give you a complete woman, yet remain a radiant enigma in her beauty and dignity.

NEW YORK, 10/30/89, p. 70, David Denby

Marie Latour, an amateur abortionist arrested and executed for murder by the Vichy government in 1943, is one of the coldest, most dislikable women ever to appear as the heroine of a movie. This is no mistake on the filmmakers' part—we're not meant to like Marie. Claude Chabrol and screenwriter Colo Tavernier, the creators of *Story of Women*, have challenged us to put saide our distaste and perhaps our prejudice, and to see Marie as a peculiar kind of heroine—wartime woman *in extremis*. Some of us, however, may not want to take up the challenge.

Desperately poor, Marie (Isabelle Huppert) lives with her two children in a small, drab town near Dieppe. Her husband is away at the war, and she takes in knitting; then, without thinking much about it, she begins performing abortions in her kitchen. Happily buying sweets for her kids, Marie never realizes—until she's arrested—that one way of making a living is different from another. *Story of Women* is about a woman's amoral instinct for survival in wartime and the hypocritical judgment that men impose on her.

Chabrol, 59, began as one of the principal creators of the New Wave and then became a suavely expert director of thrillers; he now works with great economy and a kind of freezing emotional chastity. He's not selling us anything (certainly not abortion); nor is he building sympathy for his heroine, based on an actual woman, Marie-Louise Giraud (Chabrol and Tavernier fictionalized certain aspects of the character's situation). Chabrol presents Marie with a clarifying dryness— and with an implacable love of truth that is the only passion to be found in the movie.

In Huppert, Chabrol has the most objective of great actresses. Skilled as she is, Huppert is not easy to warm up to. For her, clarity is a function of distance: She fearlessly analyzes the egotistical motives behind most of her characters' behavior, and she's dazzling at all the varieties of indifference and hard-shelled self-centeredness. I always feel I'm learning something bracing and true from watching her—but never that I'm living with her characters from moment to moment (as I do with Bette Davis's tough tomatoes). I'm speaking not of the simple identification that we moviegoers are often said to crave, which could be soft or cloying, but of our instinctive response to the life in an actor. Except for her bouncing hussy in *Coup de Torchon*, no Huppert character that I can recall has *had* much life in her. Her Marie is a study in impervious narcissism; Huppert seems determined, while showing us the courage and resourcefulness in Marie, to make her as restricted in consciousness as possible.

At first, Marie seems merely hostile to men. She slights her cute little son while fussing over her little daughter, and when her long-absent husband, Paul (François Cluzet), abruptly returns abruptly returns from a military hospital, she rebuffs his insistent and increasingly anguished demands for sex. Paul is neither stupid nor unattractive, but he's a demoralized man, economically useless, and he becomes more and more pathetic as his wife turns him down. She has no pity for him; she doesn't love him, and that's that. We're meant, I believe, to see her cruelty as honorable.

Marie, who says that she has felt like a slave her whole life, falls for a handsome young lout, Lucien (Nils Tavernier), who treats her high-handedly and would certainly enslave her if he got the chance. It's one of the movie's sour ironies that Marie has no sexual feeling for her husband, the beaten soldier, but is turned on by the flamboyant posturing of Lucien, a cynical collaborator and informer. Yet she isn't treated satirically, as a woman with awful taste in men, but admiringly, as a willful heroine. Sometimes I think the Fench love perversity too much.

Marie has will without conscience. When a woman dies after Marie has aborted her child, Marie can't see the death as resulting from anything she has done; she shrugs it off. She befriends a smart, beautiful prostitute (Marie Trintignant, who is great fun to watch) and rents her a room to work in. She's not aware that in the eyes of the law she's pimping. In her ignorance and desperate scrambling, she's meant to embody a special kind of female anger at entrapment. The war is on, and occupied France is cramped and squalid. Marie wants to live a little. A provincial Mildred Pierce, she fights for money and pleasure.

And now and then she feels and instinctive solidarity with others similarly trapped, aborting (for a good fee) the pregnancies of harried women whose men are in prison camp, women made pregnant by Germans, and so on. Marie responds to women in trouble. She's stunned, therefore, when the massive legal and religious machinery of Vichy France comes bearing down on her.The movie is very gray in color, and emotionally neutral in tone, but it approaches anger at the end as the Vichy hypocrites wreak their wills on Marie. The same bastards who betrayed the French Jews go into a pious rage about abortion.

Yet pro-choice activists are not likely to find much solace in *Story of Women*. Nor will anyone else. It's a brilliant but bleak and remorseless movie, which treads the narrowest path of honor and is so determined not to truckle to us that it sometimes forgets to engage us at all. The filmmakers must think that in presenting a woman completely lacking in tenderness they are outraging the conventional-minded. But the true outrage of *Story of Women* is that Marie is crushingly limited. She can't put things together, she can't connect, and that's why I find it hard to accept her as the great representative example of woman in wartime. And Chabrol and Tavernier never let up on her. Marie has a fantasy of becoming a chanteuse, but when she goes for lessons, she emits nothing more than a scratchy little warble. Nothing lyrical or stirring rises from the movie except the desire to tell the truth, and that's not enough.

NEW YORK POST, 10/13/89, p. 25, Jami Bernard

Based on the true case of Marie-Louise Giraud, one of the last women to be executed in France during the Occupation, Claude Chabrol's "Story of Women" is an effectively bleak portrait of a poor and none-too-bright woman's attempts to better her life by performing illegal abortions, and the state's hypocritical retaliation against her.

The movie has caused an uproar in France, but then the German Occupation is still, to some extent, an open wound there. Criticism seems to be leveled mainly at the protagonist's reinterpretation of the "Hail, Mary" prayer once she has discovered that true remorse does not necessarily prevent being made an example of, but then religious zealots love to picket over the littlest things.

The beautiful Isabelle Huppert plays Marie Latour, living in the provinces in squalor and struggling to raise her two young children while her husband (François Cluzet) is imprisoned somewhere. The only joy in her life is in imagining a future as a chanteuse and in hanging out with her best girlfriend, who is soon enough carted away for being Jewish.

Marie reluctantly helps a neighbor through a kitchen abortion, and when the neighbor later rewards her with a phonograph, Marie in her desperation sees a ray of hope. She soon has a thriving abortion business that keeps her children in bread and jam. Going from dowdy to chic, Marie becomes a shrewd little operator, renting out the spare room to a prostitute pal, taking on a handsome young lover, signing up for singing lessons.

Morality is not an issue for Marie. She is hardened by war and deprivation. Huppert's face, in constant, claustrophobic closeups, is cold and almost stupid. Like a lab rat that has learned to press a button for reward, Marie matter-of-factly locks her kids out of the kitchen, draws the hot soapy water that will induce miscarriage, takes money from the poor and spouseless and spends it. As she learns to delight in the fills and vanities that money can buy, and as she rejects the handsome, sad-sack husband who returns home, Marie is not a likable woman. She is not meant to be.

She is, however, a survivor, and she survives in her way as those around her—like her collaborator lover—do in theirs. The title of the movie refers not really to a story, but to "women's business," a phrase that helps mediate and thus semantically legitimize Marie's activities.

Director Chabrol often champions criminals in his movies—not because they are criminals, but because they are individuals acting on a unique set of circumstances. The movie is not a pretty one, and Chabrol even seems to stack the decks against Marie; when an abortion goes wrong, the dead woman's sister comes by with a moralistic in-your-face speech. Nonplussed and defensive, Marie accepts the sister's money for the unpaid debt.

The kitchen table abortion scenes, though not graphic, are uncomfortably suggestive, and a recurring executioner theme is unsettling. The movie itself is unsettling. Marie's heady rise and fall are unsettling.

Nevertheless, her imprisonment and sentencing by a governemnt that has had a hand in illicitly killing thousands is an affront. The movie ends on a cautionary note: "Have pity for the children of those who are condemned." Which explains a scene in which the two now-motherless children back home begin exhibiting stress signs indicating that the future generation, with which the government was supposedly concerned, is in for a bumpy ride.

NEWSDAY, 10/13/89, Part III/p. 5, Terry Kelleher

With the controversial subject of abortion set against the endlessly intriguing (at least to French moviemakers) background of the Occupation, Claude Chabrol's "Story of Women" would seem to have the elements necessary to engage an audience's emotions.

At its center, however, stands a heroine whose ambiguity is unlikely to evoke either sympathy or outrage. She keeps you curious, but leaves you cold.

"Story of Women" is modeled on the case of Marie-Louise Giraud, one of the last women to be executed in France. Called Marie Latour in the film, she is first seen struggling to support her two children early in World War II. France is defeated, her husband is missing and times are hard. Her only apparent pleasure comes in indulging improbable dreams of a singing career.

One night, Marie (Isabelle Huppert) walks in on a neighbor and discovers her taking a mustard bath in the hope of inducing an abortion. Unschooled in such things, but figuring that terminating a pregnancy can't be much more difficult than the rest of life's chores, Marie volunteers to perform and abortion on her friend. The procedure proves effective and gradually Marie turns abortion into a lucrative small business.

When her husband, Paul (François Cluzet), returns enervated from the war, Marie withholds sex and information from him. He minds, but not enough to force the issue. The family moves to larger quarters, and Marie diversifies her operation by renting space to a prostitute friend named Lucie (Marie Trintignant). She even hires a combination housekeeper and surgical assistant, whom she urges to sleep with Paul. Marie, meanwhile, is having an affair with Lucien (Nils Tavernier), an attractive but heartless collaborator.

Does Marie pursue her illegal calling out of protofeminism? She's given some dialogue to this effect, but it's belied by her involvement with the sneering Lucien, a chauvinist when it comes to his sex, if not his country. Does she do it to make ends meet in desperate circumstances? Yes, at first. But later we see ample support for Lucie's observation: "When you make money, you always want more money."

Genuinely devoted to her children, casually cruel to her husband, Marie is a woman of contradiction, but Huppert portrays her every aspect so skillfully that we always believe in the character. What we don't do is feel for her, even when Marie suffers unjustly.

Suffer she does at the hands of Vichy authorities determined to make a show of their moral superiority. What a "monstrous hypocrisy," as her lawyer says, for a state that openly cooperates in Nazi butchery to execute a woman for performing back-room abortions. And no hypocrite could be more monstrous than the colornel, wearing one black glove a la Dr. Strangelove, who likens chopping off Marie's head to chopping off a gangrenous limb from the body politic.

Of course, the victim needn't be pure for the unjustice to be great. Yet the judge, for all his cynicism, is not wrong in discerning "a certain cynicism" on Marie's part. Though Chabrol makes what seems like a last-ditch attempt to enter exculpatory evidence into the record—a late manifestation of Marie's provincial naivete, her angry complaint about male tyranny—the heroine's best defense remains thoughtless opportunism.

Perhaps the best thing to be said for this visually intimate but emotionally detached film is that it doesn't turn Marie Latour into Joan of Arc.

TIME, 1/15/90, p. 52, Richard Corliss

In 1943 the Vichy government condemned Marie-Louise Giraud to the guillotine for the crime of performing abortions. She was one of the last three women executed in France. If her story were made into an American TV movie, Giraud would cut one of two familiar figures. She might be a pioneer battler for reproductive rights, bravely tending to the misery of her countrywomen. Or she could be the cold and soulless predator, robbing a besieged nation of its progeny.

All praise, then, to Claude Chabrol for painting the story in honest shades of gray, for finding sense in a case that could wallow in sensation. His Marie (Isabelle Huppert) is caged in a drab marriage in a dull town in occupied France. The Germans have put hopes on hold; survival is a matter of wily compromise. When Marie finds a neighbor artlessly attempting an abortion, she helps out.Word gets around, and soon she is a successful businesswoman. And the perfect homebody: she performs abortions in the kitchen, rents her spare room to a prostitute and takes her collaborator lover (Nils Tavernier) to the bedroom. Like Charles Chaplin's murderous Monsieur Verdoux, she is a microcosm of her amoral country.

Story of Women, named best foreign-language film by three critics' groups, is an eloquent example of Simenon cinema—the kind of movie that, in the manner of Georges Simenon's novels, treats melodramatic subjects with clinical dispassion. Chabrol never coddles viewers; he trusts them to sort out the evidence. His Marie is too complicated to be either a monster or a savior. And Huppert's beautifully deadpan performance finds the ideal emblem for Marie, a vessel empty of everything but human contradictions.

VILLAGE VOICE, 10/17/89, p. 90, Georgia Brown

Claude Chabrol is back with a film the color of Isabelle Huppert's eyes. Concrete gray, sky blue, then gray again, the stark, passionate *Story of Women* follows vicissitudes in the short, briefly happy life of Marie Latour (Huppert), a Dieppe housewife who would have understood Emma Bovary like a sister. The time is the Occupation—or, as the French often say, "after the war" to mean post-1941 (rather a confusing locution, one imagines, to those who were still fighting). Marie's soldier-husband Paul (François Cluzet), suffering an undefined but critical wound, is in a POW camp, leaving her to somehow feed herself and two small children. Well before Paul returns, Marie's heart has become a stone in regard to defeated men.

Une Affaire de femmes is loosely adapted from a nonfiction book by a lawyer, Francis Szpiner, about the 1943 guillotining of an abortionist. The title translates better as "Women's Business," since that's what Marie is running. First to help out a neighbor, then to put jam and cocoa on the table, then to buy fresh lace curtains and move into an apartment where the kids have separate rooms, Marie performs abortions. Sometimes her method (soapy water injected by syringe) works and sometimes not. One patient dies—although here the movie absolves Marie by making the victim a frazzled mother of nine who's been swallowing poisons because she's overwhelmed by kids and poverty.

Marie's son Pierrot peeks through the keyhole at various women lying on the kitchen table; that's "women's business" he's told. "Women's business" is also Marie's cryptic retort to Paul when, home from the camps, he asks where she gets cigarettes, candy, and meat for dinner. For a time, he suspects Marie of being a hooker like her friend Lucie (Marie Trintignant). (That's another business women have recourse to.) Plying Pierrot with a couple of glasses of wine, he's relieved to learn that his wife gets money from women, not men. (From this point on, he's implicated.)

Men, of course, have never allowed abortion to be "women's business." Passing laws and enforcing punishment, they make it their own. Other men make abortion a religious sin. The ethics of abortion are invariably considered collective and state matters rather than individual and medical ones.

In Vichy France, official pieties about family and motherhood directed women to stay home and breed—rather a hard trick when food had to be scavenged and available men were sent to work in Germany. Demand for abortion inevitably rose, since Frenchmen were unable or unwilling to undertake the burden of marriage, and since many women became pregnant by resident Nazis. Birth control was another Vichy no-no. Pétain (childless himself) blamed France's defeat on women for delivering "too few children."

Huppert's Marie is a pale but tough little nut with a turned-down mouth like Jeanne Moreau's—except that Moreau always, even as the Marquise de Merteuil, projected mysterious depths. Huppert, though, projects a frighteningly pure narcissism in a performance so chilling that empathy comes hard. It's strikingly of a piece with her 14-year-old parricide in Chabrol's 1978 *Violette.*

Alternately seductive and sour as a mother, Marie makes a scapegoat out of Pierrot while cuddling Mouche, the baby and her girl. A long time ago Marie rejected their father, and now she blithely involves the children in her contempt, lies, and sexual rejections. When she takes a lover—a sleek, handsome collaborator (Nils Tavernier)—she brings the kids along. Cluzet's bewildered Paul is a tenderer parent and an accomplice in his own emasculation. The origins of the debilitating, self-perpetuating war between the sexes are so vivid here, you could weep or take notes.

The provincial bourgeois family is Chabrol's special milieu, and his take on pathology leads to brilliant touches—particularly his focus on affection-starved Pierrot, whose story this turns out to be. He's a child who, blowing out a candle, says his wish is to grow up to be an executioner. ("My son, my executioner," goes the Donald Hall poem.) Later, he watches his mother's lover—who brags that he "mops up" for the Nazis—put on a mask and chop off a goose's head.

When Marie, with her entrepreneurial soul, follows the example of those around her (the grocer, the candlestick maker) and prospers, the films shifts from drab confinement to the possibility of bright outdoors. Jean-Marc Rabier's camera briefly lets up its claustrophobic closeups. Out goes the frumpy gray cardigan; when Marie's hair goes up, so do the corners of her mouth. It's as if a long, dreary rainy season gives way to a sunny weekend.

But unlike those who continued to thrive on into the Fourth Republic, Marie with her particular (women's) business comes up against Vichy paternalism. She's denounced and in court the judge accuses her of depriving the state of 23 future citizens. Never mind that the state conspired in the extermination of hundreds of thousands of citizens, or that its beneficent custody didn't extend to childred who were Jews. It's in this austere final section that Chabrol and Huppert get us to care about this hardly likable woman. The executioner makes a difference.

The first time I saw *Story of Women*, I was riveted and very shaken afterwards; the second time left me distanced and aware of flaws. What's so uniquely Chabrolian, though, is how his movie escapes being a tract for anything—except understanding. You could call this ethical filmmaking.

Also reviewed in:
NATION, 11/13/89, p. 576, Stuart Klawans
NEW REPUBLIC, 10/30/89, p. 24, Stanley Kauffmann
NEW YORK TIMES, 10/13/89, p. C17, Janet Maslin
VARIETY, 10/18-24/89, p. 25
WASHINGTON POST, 11/3/89, p. C7, Hal Hinson
WASHINGTON POST 11/3/89, Weekend/p. 37, Desson Howe

STRANGE PLACE TO MEET, A

A Hachette Première et Cie/Hachette Productions/Films A2/DD Productions/Deneuve SA/Orly Films/Editions Sidonie film. *Producer:* Patrick Bordier. *Director:* François Dupeyron. *Screenplay (French with English subtitles):* François Dupeyron and Dominique Faysse. *Director of Photography:* Charlie Van Damme. *Editor:* Françoise Collin. *Sound:* Pierre Gamet. *Sound Editor:* Dominique Faysse. *Art Director:* Carlos Conti. *Costumes:* Caroline de Vivaise and Gil Noir. *Make-up:* Renaldo Ribeiro de Abreu. *Stunt Coordinator:* Rémy Julienne. *Running time:* 93 minutes. *MPAA Rating:* Not Rated.

CAST: Catherine Deneuve (France); Gérard Depardieu (Charles); Nathalie Cardone (Sylvie); André Wilms (Georges); Jean-Pierre Sentier (Pierrot); Alain Rimoux (Vincent); Vincent Martin (Roland); Philippe Faure (M.

Martinet); Dominique Reymond (Mme. Martinet); Thierry Der'ven (Louis); Marie-France Santon (Simone); Roger Souza (M. Richard); Chantal Banlier (Mme. Richard); François Toumarkine (Repair Man); Marc Brunet and Philippe Dormoy (Policemen); Annie Mario (1st Woman in Car); Jean-Michel Matusz (Man in Car); Hélène Sarrazin (2nd Woman in Car); Véronique Kapoyan (Nurse); Jean-Claude Bolle-Redat (René); Joëlle Baland (Mad Woman); Patrick Bordier (Man who Chats Up).

MONTHLY FILM BULLETIN, 10/89, p. 297, Geoff Brown

In the midst of a furious argument as they drive down a motorway one rainy Friday night, France and her husband Vincent narrowly miss a suicidal woman who leaps in front of their car. Pulling into a lay-by, Vincent throws France and her fur coat on to the pavement and drives off. Nearby is Charles, a gruff doctor with a broken-down car, who is methodically stripping the engine in an effort to understand its workings. He tries to get rid of the distraught France with insults, but she determines to stay put in case her husband returns. After failing to persuade a passing motorist to remove her forcibly, Charles unbends and lets France spend the night in the back of his car. Next morning, the police order Charles to tow away his vehicle. They stop for coffee at a service area. Discovering from a young waitress, Sylvie, that Vincent had been there the previous night, France settles down in the cafeteria to wait for her husband's return. Charles—supposedly en route to his brother in Toulon—also waits because, despite himself, he is now in love with his companion. Anxious for France to accept the break-up of her marriage, he manages to phone Vincent at home; Vincent tells France to stay at the service area one more day. At night, long-distance lorry drivers arrive and ogle France, who joins them on a crazy ride up the wrong side of the motorway. Charles, inert and a little drunk, remains at the cafeteria, where the restless Sylvie suggests they run away together; Charles accepts. On Sunday, a lorry driver repairs Charles' engine, while Sylvie waits with her bags. The lorries drive off in the rain. In his car, Charles finds France sleeping; after abandoning Sylvie, he leaves with France still in the back.

François Dupeyron may have helped the box-office chances of his first feature by securing gleaming stars like Gérard Depardieu and Catherine Deneuve (they even participated behind the scenes in the production.) But in every other respect, the thirty-eight-year-old maker of shorts and documentaries has done nothing to court easy success. The scenario is dangerously constructed around inaction: the characters simply wait, first at a motorway lay-by, secondly at a service area cafeteria. France waits in vain for the husband who threw her from his car following a frantic argument; Charles, smitten in spite of himself, waits for France to stop waiting and hitch her wagon to his. Yet despite the focus on two people twiddling their emotional thumbs, Dupeyron refuses to fill out his character with explanatory detail—possibly a hang-over from his disdain for fiction during his student days at IDHEC, the Paris film school ("I was already influenced by '68. I refused to make fiction, fiction was 'bourgeois' ").

France, we assume (mostly from appearance), is simply a middle-class wife wedded to husband and home; when she contacts Vincent by phone, her first question is "Did the frost nip the mimosas?". With Charles, we must also rely on a handful of props and hints: a doctor's bag; a cassette of Richard Strauss' *Four Last Songs*; an air of being burned by life, of fear masquerading as misogyny. Surrounding these bald figures, Dupeyron carefully scatters a cluster of contrasting types: the lewd, roistering lorry drivers, as up-front about sex as the others are uptight; the young waitress Sylvie, whose cynical attitude to love compares with the older couples' almost childlike *amour fou*. To complete the sense of a gloomy minimalist exercise, the waiting game is played out on three successive grey, rainy days, dutifully separated by shots of the moon obscured by clouds.

Dupeyron launches his film with dynamic, intriguing shots of France and her husband gesticulating in silence inside their car (even the argument's cause is denied us). He maintains throughout a firm directorial grip, though it is largely up to Deneuve and Depardieu—*la belle et la bête* of contemporary French cinema—to animate the arid proceedings. Deneuve presents a reasonable portrait of a distraught, abandoned woman struggling to maintain her elegance and status quo; while Depardieu makes his shadowy character as sharp as the script will allow. But as the couple perform their fumbling *pas de deux* among wet tarmac, passing traffic and plastic cafeteria tables, one cannot help wondering why they bother.

NEW STATESMAN & SOCIETY, 9/15/89, p. 44, Suzanne Moore

No one with any real class wears fur coats any more, only the very rich and the very naff, so it is a telling sign that Catherine Deneuve spends most of her new film—*A Strange Place to Meet*—huddled up in one. After a row with her husband, she is left in a motorway layby where she meets Gérard Depardieu, stripping his engine in order to see how it works. As he takes his car apart—a rather lame metaphor for re-examining his life—Deneuve's life falls apart before him.

She gets more unhinged by the minute (though naturally the fur coat and immaculate make-up stay put) as she insists that she must prove her love for her husband by hanging around until he fetches her. Inevitably Depardieu falls in love with her and waits for her to stop waiting. This scenario might have been more exciting had the film used more than two locations. But the tedium induced by motorway cafés infuses the whole movie, shot by François Dupeyron, making his directorial debut on a feature film, with a singular blandness.

The premise of the film rests on the partnering of the French Everyman—Depardieu—with the symbol of French Womanhood Deneuve. Unfortunately they produce less sexual chemistry than a Gold Blend advert. And although Deneuve actually *looks* more interesting the older she gets, it is hard to feel any sympathy for her character—a woman who never initiates anything and is entirely dependent on men and their reaction to her. But then Deneuve has always played roles in which, with minimal effort, she becomes simply a beautiful surface on to which men project their desires.

This special kind of blankness is known as "mystique". It must be tough being an icon, especially a female one, since the purity of the image demands the draining away of any depth of feeling. This gives Deneuve that sometimes wonderful "not quite there" quality and it's no coincidence that her most memorable performances have been as prostitutes.

NEWSDAY, 3/18/89, Part II/p. 17, Mike McGrady

The New Directors/New Films series at the Museum of Modern Art, a showcase for unknown talent, is hardly the place one would expect to find a film starring France's two most well-established movies stars—Catherine Deneuve and Gérard Depardieu. But what's new with "A Strange Place to Meet" is not the cast, but director-writer François Dupeyron.

Although Dupeyron's past work consisted of a few shorts, he clearly knows how to tell an offbeat film story using innovative techniques. In fact, evidence of his movie-making savvy was seen well before this film was ever made. Dupeyron found a way to get his script into the hands of France's two superstars who liked it enough to not only star in it, but co-produce it.

Their positive reaction is easily understood. The two lead characters are crazy in different ways and each role invites the kind of no-holds-barred performance that actors stay awake nights dreaming about. Deneuve is a beautiful beminked blonde dumped by her husband at a turnpike rest stop and Depardieu is a burly antagonistic loner who is there systematcially dismantling his automobile engine.

"A Strange Place to Meet" opens at full speed on the Autoroute de Sud. In the car directly in front of us we see the frenzied gesticulations of a battling couple while we listen to the yowlings and howlings of speeding cars and trucks. Suddenly that car veers over into a rest stop and the man drags the woman forcibly from his car and throws her to the ground. When we note that a man has just discarded the incredibly beautiful Deneuve, we may sense realism is not necessarily the highest priority here.

Depardieu, the only other person at the rest stop, comes over and studies the lovely woman disdainfully: "Get this into your head: You can't stay here...I need to be alone!" No, realism is definitely not the highest priority here.

Since Deneuve feels she can prove her love for her husband by remaining until he has a change of heart and returns for her, she is content with watching Depardieu take apart his car engine.

What we have here would seem to be a lunatic-meets-lunatic love story that broadens a bit when they advance from the rest stop to a service area inhabited by a band of fun-loving truck drivers. The point? Well, who hasn't been turned into a lunatic for love? Isn't love itself a form of lunacy? And in time isn't someone always left stranded at a rest stop waiting for another to return?

"A Strange Place to Meet" *is* a strange movie—static, talky, nutty—but it does hold interest. Part of that is due to the star power; but the rest of the credit should go to Dupeyron who clearly knows what he is doing.

VILLAGE VOICE, 3/21/89, p. 64, Katherine Dieckmann

No way François Dupeyron's film would have made it to ND/NF were it not for the

Francophilic appeal of its blond, iconic duo, coproducers Gérard Depardieu and Catherine Deneuve. One night, her husband kicks her ("the most beautiful woman in the world") out of their car at a rest stop. Depardieu, a doctor, happens to be there, fixing his car. He tells her she smells like chicken; later, softening, "You're a dreamer. That's no disease." If you're curious about French truck stops, this dud's for you.

Also reviewed in:
NEW YORK TIMES, 3/19/89, p. 60, Janet Maslin
VARIETY, 11/9/88, p. 18

STRAPLESS

A Granada Film Productions release in association with Film Four International. *Producer:* Rick McCallum. *Director:* David Hare. *Screenplay:* David Hare. *Director of Photography:* Andrew Dunn. *Editor:* Edward Marnier. *Music:* Nick Bicat. *Sound:* Clive Winter. *Production Designer:* Roger Hall. *Costumes:* Penny Rose and Rebecca Hale. *Running Time:* 97 minutes. *MPAA Rating:* Not Rated.

CAST: Blair Brown (Lillian Hempel); Bruno Ganz (Raymond Forbes); Bridget Fonda (Amy Hempel); Alan Howard (Mr. Cooper); Hugh Laurie (Colin); Alexandra Pigg (Helen); Michael Gough (Douglas Brodie); Suzanne Burden (Romaine Salmon); Rohan McCullough (Annie Rice); Billie Roche (Gerry); Camille Coduri (Mrs. Clark); Gary O'Brien (Mr. Clark); Spencer Leigh (Hus); Julie Foy (Nurse); Jacqui Gordon-Lawrence (Staff Nurse); Cyril Nri (Harold Sabola); Julian Bunster (Carlos); Gedren Heller (Madeleine); Imogen Annesley (Imogen); Constantin Alexandrov (Imre Kovago); Dana Gillespie (Julia Kovago); Stephen Holland (Prisoner); Giselle Glasman (Prisoner's Bride); Edward Lyon (Registrar); Derek Webster (Croupier); Jeremy Gagan (Faulkner); Clive Shilson (Peverill); Francesca Longrigg (Secretary); Helen Lindsay (Neighbor); Ann Firbank (Daphne Brodie); Joe Hare (Richard Forbes); Liam De Staic (Phil); Kirsty Buckland (Mary Hempel); Natasha Brice (Natasha); Andrea Linz (Andrea); Saira Whisker (Saira); Melanie Roe (Girl at Station).

LOS ANGELES TIMES, 5/18/90, Calendar/p. 6, Peter Rainer

"Strapless," written and directed by David Hare, is supposed to be a romantic movie for literate grown-ups. In other words, there's not a whole lot of yelling and hair-pulling and laughter— there's not a whole lot of life.

All this dull anomic melancholy is nevertheless meant to signify the currents of cultured passion. Hare, best known as the play-wright of "Plenty," is indulging in a subtle, snobby high-art game here. By stifling the messiness of romantic emotion, he's aiming for a "higher" truth cleansed of "common" feeling. The educated bourgeois sufferers in "Strapless" indulge their sorrows as if they were expensive pets.

Blair Brown is Lillian, an American working for the past 12 years in London as a hospital physician. Vacationing abroad for a week, nursing the breakup of a long-term relationship with an actor, she finds herself being romanced by Raymond Forbes (Bruno Ganz), a mysterious, well-tailored gent who doesn't blink very much. Her retreat from his advances only sparks his ardor; he traces her back to London and proceeds to court her shamelessly, buying her everything from flowers to horses to BMWs. His hang-dog mooniness finally gets to her, even though she knows precious little about him except that he's some kind of bullion entrepreneur and that he speaks his heavily accented English exceedingly slowly, in complete sentences.

Raymond's otherworldly passion is meant to contrast with Lillian's pinched reserve. Even though she's an able doctor, she doesn't draw much emotional sustenance from her work. Her career has closed off her life; she gives and gives and, in the film's narrow terms, gets nothing back. When Raymond cajoles her with a marriage offer, asking her if she's ever wanted to do something "that didn't entirely make sense," she's primed to respond.

"Strapless" (rated R) has a super-sophisticated veneer but it's really just an artsy variant on the lonely-spinster-on-vacation-finds-love-with-a-mysterious-stranger scenario. It's "Summertime" with British damp. Hare wants us to recognize that, despite Lillian's professional role as healer, she's in need of emotional repair herself. It's too neat a formulation. Lillian's romantic renewal seems preordained; it's like the working out of a theorem. In any case, since she doesn't seem to be banking too many fires, her Raymond-inspired "release" has no heat. She's still the same vaguely happy, vaguely sad woman at the end as she was at the beginning. And Raymond is the same cipher.

No doubt Hare intends all this to be a more modern and adult version of what love is really like. No fireworks, just a few spluttering sparklers. But the cultivated high tone of these quasi-lovers isn't necessarily so realistic; by dampening their passions, Hare is foisting his own version of "Invasion of the Body Snatchers" on us. Lillian and Raymond are such tony sufferers they're practically pod people.

The only member of the cast who creates a stir is Bridget Fonda, playing Lillian's younger sister. Fonda's Amy, an aspiring clothes designer who camps out in Lillian's apartment with an assortment of mod friends, has the life force that Hare denies the rest of his characters. Fonda has a sequence in which she recoils before her sister's wrath, and another when she returns that wrath, that are so finely felt that it's as if we were watching the emergence of a major actress right before our eyes. Amy is in the movie to give the film a classic balance. She and Lillian, so different on the surface, share the same plight. They're "strapless," at large in a world where their faith is not soon repaid.

Fonda's ferocity upsets this too-neat balance. If only the film belonged to her.

MONTHLY FILM BULLETIN, 4/90, p. 118, Philip Strick

Lillian Hempel, an American doctor who has worked for the past fifteen years at a London hospital, takes a short European holiday and meets soft-spoken charmer Raymond Forbes. She is intrigued but avoids involvement and returns to the London flat she shares with her scatterbrained younger sister Amy. At the hospital, she does her best to reassure a new patient, Mr. Clark, who has terminal cancer, and observes the concern of hospital staff at cuts in NHS resources. One evening, a horse is delivered outside the flat, a gift from Raymond. He proposes marriage and on impulse Lillian accepts, changing her mind during a protracted wait at the registry office; she needs time to get to know Raymond, and moves into his flat. During following weekends in the country, she meets his rich friends Imre and Julia Kovago, rides her horse in training sessions, and tries her luck at the roulette wheel; Raymond loses £5,000, which unhesitatingly she loans him to cover his debts. He soon pays in back in cash. At the hospital, Mr. Clark's health deteriorates; at the other flat, Amy becomes cheerfully pregnant, much to Lillian's disgust. Her hospital colleagues want her to lead their campaign against NHS cuts but she refuses to get involved. Suddenly she decides to accept Raymond and they get married. Almost immediately he disappears without warning, only to turn up again one evening with another gift, a limousine. She tries to talk him into settling down, but he leaves once more. Later, two men who have his passport question her at the hospital. Under pressure from all sides, Lillian has a breakdown, admitting to the scornful Amy that all her savings have gone to pay Raymond's creditors. Visiting his former schoolmaster, Douglas Brodie, who feels similarly betrayed, Lillian is also able to trace one of Raymond's previous girlfriends, Annie Rice, who casually reveals that Raymond is the father of her young son Richard, and that they are still married. Back at the hospital, Mr. Clark is dying; at the flat, Amy produces a daughter and shows every sign of getting her life under control. Lillian impulsively accepts the task of heading the hospital campaign. Imre brings her a present from Raymond, a model racehorse. Serenely, Lillian and Amy take part in a charity show to raise funds for the hospital, while on a station platform somewhere, hurrying for a train, Raymond suddenly recalls his first meeting with Lillian and turns back for what could be a fresh start.

"They shouldn't stay up, but they do!" asserts Amy as the two sisters, in hazardous evening dresses, prepare to make their appearance at a spotlit fashion show. The strapless nature of their present predicament, emphatically reflecting a ramshackle life style and precarious prospects, comes as an oddly forced conclusion to David Hare's story, forming a contrived epilogue in which, while Lillian's effulgent lover shows every sign of returning for a fresh bout of doting unreliability, Lillian herself is frozen at the brink of her new, public life. Following the unheralded, vaguely surreal, track among illuminated boxes in which the nurses are clothing themselves, the camera stares at the uncommunicative back of Lillian's head, consistently a point of interest throughout the film. We are then left to consider, without further guidance, whether the divided curtain and the spotlight glare might represent a terminal metaphor (she has, after all, recently drawn a curtain over the face of the luckless Mr. Clark), whether she is now passing out of Raymond's reach even as his encounter with a new girl dropping a new handkerchief has by implication placed him beyond hers, or whether in her new-found resilience she has become, like her sister, a symbol of the modern superwoman, able to stay upright regardless of dwindling emotional elasticity (in which case, will the returning Raymond find himself unexpectedly victorious, free to come and go as irresponsibly as he likes?).

In short, the case that Hare is making in *Strapless* seems, despite the concluding radiance, as trapped in ambivalence as it was in *Wetherby*, where the amorous pursuer of truth impotently blew his brains out; certainly it's far more vague than in *Paris by Night*, where the philandering career woman was rightly shot down for her stupidity. Perhaps Amy's salute to straplessness should be interpreted as expressing not so much a rallying call as the writer's puzzlement that against all inducements his heroines contrive to regain and retain their independence. On the other hand, Hare's generally careful visuals can also sustain a more interesting argument. He begins pompously with classical statues in sunlit gardens and the ornate crucifix that brings the two innocents together as if the artless Raymond had been conjured in direct answer to Lillian's lack of faith. "How can dying represent salvation?" she demands, eventually to learn, from Mr. Clark's inglorious final days, that it probably is better to seize any living opportunity to do what feels right.

Unattached, like the heroine of *Wetherby*, gradually she is converted from social isolation and the excuse of being a "foreigner" and becomes instead a committed campaigner, as idealistic as the bigamist who amiably married her for the sake of romantic principle. In the process, she relinquishes the outdoor images associated with Raymond—the lunch under the awning, the garden walks, the rolling countryside where horses thunder past in breathtaking freedom—and grows reconciled to the sad enclosures of the hospital and the community spirit, all lights and applause, of the city world. In contrast to the weary loner of *Plenty* (interestingly a role played by Blair Brown on stage in New York), whose only final consolation is a dream of undemanding French landscapes, and to the ruthless politician of *Paris by Night*, for whom the city is sheer nemesis, Lillian firmly turns her back on cottages and glades (the final blow is the revelation, amid astonishing meadowlands, that Raymond is stilll married and that his wife and son are content to be without him) and espouses a more concrete cause and context. If, with his impossibly seraphic suitor (played with an inevitably angelic smile by Ganz), Hare has hardly provided the most plausible pretext for Lillian's maturity, *Strapless* is at least unusual in charting a path, against the better nature of romantic melodrama, from sunlight to spotlight, from impassive statues to a poised and enigmatic coiffure.

He does so with the same assurance and occasional signs of haste as for his previous film, not worrying too much about continuity and not averse to using slabs of music for easy atmosphere. If there's nothing in *Strapless* quite to match the farewell shot at the aerodrome in *Wetherby*, Hare's camera continues his Resnais-style probing of rooms and corridors, with at least one superb swoop through swinging doors as Lillian breaks through her reticence to accept the task of campaign leader. At one point, inexplicably, Raymond turns over a soup spoon; at another, like a startled bird, the camera perches us in sudden vulnerability above a school quadrant when the bell sounds and pupils run for cover as from an air-raid. The abortive wait at the registry office is a perfectly observed documentary vignette of disenchantment, but Hare caps it with the second marriage scene, a single shot of entwined black (bridegroom) and yellow (bride). He has the Pinteresque knack of throwing the ordinary into disarray by these abrupt details, inarticulately packed with implication: the gift-horse standing in the street, the photographer (Amy's boyfriend) suddenly grappling with an obscure celebrity in a restaurant, the two grey-suited men who force Lillian into a panicked disloyalty, the helpless encounter with the hospital boss in a broom cupboard. These uneasy dislocations add up to a less coherent case than Hare and Blair might like us to believe, but they offer some hope that the best is yet to come.

NEW LEADER, 1/8/90, p. 22, John Morrone

Strapless is playwright David Hare's first film as writer-director to be shown in this country since *Wetherby* in 1985. The two films are so much alike, however, that you could call the new offering a clone of the earlier one.

Heroine Lillian (Blair Brown) is an American doctor who practices in London because she admires the orderliness of the Socialist medical system. A highly accomplished diagnostician, her respect for facts and procedures masks her dislike of emotionalism—she tends bodies with all the severity that Vanessa Redgrave's schoolteacher educated minds in *Wetherby*. Indeed, Lillian's hospital not only corresponds to Redgrave's classroom, but the elusive, dishonest lover who enters her life also serves the same purpose as the suicidal visitor to Wetherby. In both movies Hare poises his self-possessed protagonist on the brink of a shocking disruption in her life.

Lillian's trouble begin when she meets Raymond (Bruno Ganz) in a Portuguese church while on vacation. Quiet, polite, vaguely romantic, he brings off the feat of jolting her out of her chosen solitude and throwing her clearly ordered mind into a tumult. On the verge of being seduced, Lillian protests that she "doesn't get" this Continental gentleman, yet she is tempted enough to investigate. In love, as in her professional devotion to her patient, she plans to "see it through."

Lillian's sister Amy (Bridget Fonda), is another threat to her tidily arranged existence. Brown and Fonda give arresting performances as sisters who just don't click—one being a tight-lipped WASP, the second a reckless youngster. (The actresses actually do not seem to have much rapport, adding to the tension between their characters). Regrettably, Hare takes this dynamism and makes it schematic and predictable. Lillian gradually finds the nerve to warm up to the mysterious charms of her lover by adopting Amy's style of meeting things head on. Meanwhile,—you guessed it— Amy finds herself pregnant and finally decides to shape up her wanton life and "see the pregnancy through."

Little by little Hare robs Lillian of her defenses as neatly as Hitchcock stripped the jewelry from Tallulah Bankhead in *Lifeboat*. Her surrender to a different personality, the gamble on love she takes, bewilders her when she discovers that a relationship between a man and a woman is not an equal rational exchange of "giving and getting." At the same time, the fallout from her romantic confusion affects her attitude toward her work. She finds she cannot give enough to "see through" a terminal patient gripped by pain, and thus feels robbed of the satisfaction she had always gotten in return for her dedication.

In tracking Lillian's progress toward emotional maturity, *Strapless* can be literate and engrossing. But the viewer often pays dearly for Hare's intelligence. The heroines' parts are cluttered with meticulously cross-referenced Get-and-Give speeches and declarations about Seeing-It-Through that badly try one's patience. And the casting seems perverse. Ganz' Raymond is Germanic gloom personified—a huge distraction in this very Anglo-American drama. His slippery performance makes his character so unknowable that locating Raymond's center ultimately becomes a pointless task. We give up on Lillian's quest to understand him.

Finally, we give up on Blair Brown, too. For just as the labored turmoil felt by *Strapless*' ensemble compares unfavorably to the dour but poignant complexities of *Wetherby*, Brown is unequal to Vanessa Redgrave in both depth of temperament and range of expression. Considering the film's theme of accepting our emotional limitations as well as the unfathomable nature of others, the expression on her face is far too inflexible. She does not even rise to the occasion at the finale, when the two sisters appear in strapless evening gowns at a benefit for medical-care workers striking against hospital cutbacks. "Straplessness" is Hare's metaphor for a woman's courage to be herself without outside help, with "no visible means of support." It is ultimately a lesson Lillian learns in spades (maybe she could tell us if her memory is in *her* shoulders), but Brown's primness dogs her character. The clothes Lillian stands up in remain starched to the end.

NEW YORK POST, 9/23/89, p. 19, Jami Bernard

As, er, uplifting as "Strapless" means to be (the title, referring to strapless gowns, is a metaphor for women's singular strength), it still goes to prove that women are imbeciles around men, and that not even a Nobel Prize can keep a woman from falling for the most hackneyed pick-up line.

"Strapless," a movie by British director David Hare ("Plenty"), is about women—specifically, two American sisters who get stuck holding the bag for their fly-by-night lovers, and who find the inner resources to cope with it.

Blair Brown is warmth personified as a doctor in a London cancer hospital. Approaching the dread middle-age, she is swept off her otherwise sturdy feet by the advances of a mysterious, impetuous, dapper gentleman (Bruno Ganz) who lures her into marriage and then heads for the hills. If Brown had heard the clanging warning signs about this guy instead of "When I Fall in Love," which plays over the opening credits, she could have been spared the agony.

Her little sister, played freshly and precociously by Bridget Fonda ("Scandal"), has to face responsibility for the first time in her life when a wandering Argentine leaves her pregnant.

Although well acted and with more layers to the individuals than the average script, "Strapless" suffers from a slightly outdated idea of feminine independence.

The James Bondian mystery man, plus the symbolic strapless gowns (in which the cleavage is uplifted by what could well be wings) give "Strapless" a certain amount of extra baggage that could well affect liftoff.

NEW YORK POST, 5/19/90, p. 17, Jami Bernard

Wtih the dating situation in the shambles that it's in, movies are springing up that supposedly address the issue of women without men. Actually, in "Men Don't Leave" and "Stanley & Iris," Jessica Lange and Jane Fonda as widowed moms find that the answer to being single is to find a guy. Even illiterates may apply.

David Hare, sophisticated playwright that he is, doesn't make life so simple and socially correct for the two sisters in "Strapless," the British film which he wrote and directed and which opens tomorrow after having played the New York Film Festival last year. The title is a reference to strapless gowns, and a metaphor for women's singular strength.

Despite good intentions, "Strapless" plays like a slightly dated idea of feminine independence, maybe a sequel to "An Unmarried Woman" a decade too late.

As uplifting as "Strapless" means to be, both actually and metaphorically, it still goes to prove that women are imbeciles around men, and that not even a Nobel Prize can keep a woman from falling for the most hackneyed pick-up line.

The warm, wonderful Blair Brown, for whom Hare tailors many of his scripts, plays Lillian Hempel, an American doctor working in a London cancer hospital. She has learned to be a compassionate caretaker without blurring the line between sense and sensibility.

Lillian has given up on passion, certainly on love, until she meets your basic mysterious rich guy during a solitary vacations.

This Raymond Forbes (Bruno Ganz) has so much money and time on his hands that he actually comes a-courting with a horse he has bought for the non-committal Lillian. With gift after gift and attention after attention, he wears her down.

You'd think a smart gal like Lillian would be just a little suspicious, maybe wondering where Raymond gets all that money from. What does he do for a living, anyway? Who is he really?

But Lillian is approaching dreaded middle age, so she is swept off her otherwise sturdy feet by the impetuous, dapper gentleman who lures her into marriage and then heads for the hills. If Lillian had heard the clanging warning signs about this guy instead of "When I Fall in Love," which plays ironically over the opening credits, she could have been spared the agony.

She's not the only one with man troubles. Her irresponsible little sister, played freshly and precociously by Bridget Fonda ("Scandal"), is staying with Lilliam, leeching off her and whooping it up with her many male admirers. She must finallly take control of her life when a wandering Argentine leaves her pregnant.

Brown is warmth and intelligence personified. It's a shame we don't see this actress more often in major roles. In this one, however, her intellect and stability work against her—although we know that many otherwise capable people make jerks of themselves in their love lives, the movie exaggerates the extremes (as movies invariably must), making Lillian's impulsive marriage look all the more improbable. It is easy to lose confidence in the character and never regain it.

The sisters are awakened to their inner resources only after such man trouble. But the James Bondian mystery man is such a centrally unresolved puzzle that the movie never fully moves away from him and on to the sisters' self-realization.

The symbolic strapless gowns, an unpoetic literal device in which the cleavage is uplifted by what could well be wings, also affects the movie's ultimate liftoff.

NEWSDAY, 5/18/90, Part II/p.5, Terry Kelleher

Lillian, the heroine of David Hare's "Strapless," is an American physician who has spent a dozen years is England working for the National Health Service. She is dedicated, competent, responsible. Genuinely concerned but slightly aloof, strong but not invulnerable.

Unmarried and about 40, Lillian (Blair Brown) has just concluded an affair that "grew stale" with time. On vacation in Portugal, she finds herself pursued by Raymond (Bruno Ganz), an enigmatic, ostensibly wealthy "entrepreneur" who professes love at first sight. When Lilian flees Raymond's attentions, he pursues her to London and plies her with presents and proposals. Underneath her fear and annoyance, Lillian feels something stirring.

Because Brown brings her particular brand of naturalness and intelligence to the role, we believe in Lillian at the outset of "Strapless." What becomes of this woman, however, is increasingly difficult to accept. It's as if the writer-director took it upon himself to reorder Lillian's existence without consulting her.

If you've seen "Plenty" or "Wetherby," Hare is probably the last person you'd accuse of obviousness. But his intentions in "Strapless" are all too clear. He wants us to realize that romantic love vivifies the lover, whether the loved one proves faithful or feckless. Spontaneity is good. Risk is good. Non-involvement is bad, as is all-work-no-play.

Life is short, Raymond says. You've got to go after things, Raymond says. (He's too urbane to say "grab for the gusto," but that seems to be the idea.) Lillian sees in Raymond a man with "no cynicism, no defenses." That he turns out to be a deadbeat and a deceiver is not so important, or at least that's the line Hare is selling. One tends to think that Lillian left to her own devices, would have Raymond thrown in jail rather than cover his debts after he skips town. She does probe a bit into Raymond's past, but apparently out of nothing more than benign curiosity (to know thy absent loved one is to know thyself). And it's odd, given Raymond's secretiveness, how Lillian is able to trace his ex-wife and old schoolmaster.

There is another close relationship in Lillian's life, and its development is no more convincing. Her younger sister Amy (engagingly played by Bridget Fonda) is a sponger who flits from boyfriend to boyfriend and entertains vague notions of becoming a couturiere—that is, until one of her lovers makes her pregnant and runs off. Amy, a spontaneous creatures, decides to bear the child against Lillian's stern advice. Lo and behold, her dress designs improve dramatically as delivery day nears. Now, which of these sisters is truly the wiser?

"Strapless" is a quiet film, but seldom a subtle one. Though Hare waits a long time to introduce the metaphor of the title, he manages to overwork it before the final freeze frame. To show he's not dwelling on personalities at the expense of his usual political priorities, he also finds a few minutes for the new Lillian to wave the banner against Tory cuts in the health budget.

Brown invests Lillian with the fundamental credibility to stand on her own. Unfortunately, there are precious few moments in "Strapless" when we don't see Hare pulling her strings.

VILLAGE VOICE, 9/26/89, p. 61, J. Hoberman

Count yourself lucky the tickets for this stinker are gone. David Hare's inside-out *Suspicion* (still without distributor) features Bruno Ganz as a rancid Prince Charming and Blair Brown as a refugee from *St. Elsewhere*. The film is inanely pretentious from opening Christ shot to closing freeze frame. The title, which refers to a dress, really should be *Uplift*.

VILLAGE VOICE, 5/22/90, p. 66, Gary Giddins

We keep paying for the once novel ellipses of Harold Pinter as increasingly dim writers borrow his surfaces, confident that a superfluity of dramatic pauses will disguise the lurking shallows. From Alan Rudolph to Peter Greenaway, we are awash in inscrutable activities and pictorial compositions; such are the tides that blind. David Hare's latest exercise in ennui could use a dash of bitters—Antonioni's style, Coward's wit, all right then, a good gunfight at high noon. I suspect he knows that. If not, I can't imagine why he chose to buttress his latest soap with a peculiarly inappropriate and arch title. In the mid-'60s, when Albee's *Tiny Alice* was lambasted for obscurity, the theater where it played began distributing, with the *Playbill*, an article (by Max Lerner, if I remember correctly) that presumed to explicate its mysteries. Hare's title is in lieu of a handout. *Strapless* is about women learning to survive without men; one of the women is actually a dress designer who triumphs with a species of reinforced gowns that also stand up on their own. When her fashions are revealed at film's end, the effect is like having Hare sitting next to you in the theater, yelling in your ear, "GET IT?"

Yes, I think so. Love is good; excessive self-involvement is bad. Life is short. So take a chance. Go for it. Be your own best frient. Please, sir, may I go now?

The trouble with so many contemporary movies is that they depict people who've never been to the movies. The audience is invariably way ahead of them. Thus Hare has to strain from the beginning to make us accept the notion that Lillian Hempel (Blair Brown), an attractive, efficient American doctor working at a hospital in England, would impulsively marry one of those strange continental charmers who keep their business secret, shun premarital sex, boast of enormous sums of money yet live modestly and have to borrow to cover gambling debts, and—worst of all—smile enigmatically. Bruno Ganz plays Raymond Forbes, with an enigmatic smile so impervious, you wonder why Lillian doesn't try to smack it off. Yet, although he turns out to be a fraud (quite a surprise, that) and a bigamist, Hare wants us to admire the romance in his soul. Raymond is a bit of a naïf, that rarest of creatures—a man who genuinely loves women, as one of his mysterious friends tells Lillian. He has an odd way of showing it, though he's terribly well mannered and hasn't the least propensity toward violence. Among current representations of sexual warfare, bigamy is a relatively benign idiosyncracy.

Brown is an appealing if not quite incandescent presence, and Hare often directs her with stars in his eyes. Yet her role is too symbolic for her to breathe sufficient life into it. As her dissolute and pregnant sister Amy, who designs the symbolic dresses, Bridget Fonda pouts and smirks and sheds tears. At first, she's a sexy plaything, thought of a very different sort than her cheeky and treacherous Mandy Rice-Davies in *Scandal*. Her versatility in those roles is impressive and winning. But as Amy cleans up her act, she too becomes emblematic and stiff.

Lillian encounters Raymond in an old church while on vacation in Europe. Like Elias Canetti, she loathes the idea of Christ dying for mankind's sins. "It's obscure," Raymond sagely agrees. He invites her to his hotel (apparently he forgets that he disdains premarital sex). She demurs and returns to London, where he pursues her with a splendid horse and more oblique dialogue. Most people don't know what they want, he argues, but he does. He wants Lilian. On the other hand, asked what he most relished in life, he responds, "Anticipation." At that point, Lillian might have saved herself much grief by buying him a bottle of Heinz Ketchup. Instead, she offers to live with him, and shortly thereafter they elope—though, strangely, she insists on keeping the marriage a secret from everyone, including Amy.

Various subplots intrude. Personnel at the hospital are trying to organize a protest against layoffs, which Lillian refuses to join. A 26-year-old cancer patient is periodically glimpsed in scenes so unpleasant you might well prefer to have Hare sitting in the next seat, helpfully advising you that life is short, gather your rosebuds while ye may. After Raymond disappears and Lillian has a breakdown, discovers his other wife, and receives from him a sentimental trinket that , she remarks, restores her faith, she becomes her own woman, taking charge of the hospital protest and participating in her sister's fashion show. Even Hare may have found all of that a bit neat. So he closes with Raymond at a train station, enigmatic smile in place, first walking in one direction, then, upon seeing a woman who clearly reminds him of Lillian, turning around.

One note on directorial style. Half a century after *Citizen Kane*, the photographic process known as deep focus may still present difficulties for cameramen. But Andrew Dunn, Hare's director of photography, doesn't appear to recognize it as an option. In scene after scene, he alternates between foreground and background, blurring one or the other. Perhaps blurriness, too, is meant to be symbolic.

Also reviewed in:
NEW REPUBLIC, 5/28/90, p. 24, Stanley Kauffmann
NEW YORK TIMES, 5/20/90, p. 60, Vincent Canby
VARIETY 5/17–23/89, p. 35
WASHINGTON POST, 5/19/90, p. C3, Hal Hinson

SUITORS, THE

A First Run Features release of an Embra Films production. *Producer:* Ghasem Ebrahimian and Coleen Higgins. *Director:* Ghasem Ebrahimian. *Screenplay (Farsi with English subtitles);* Ghasem Ebrahimian. *Director of Photography:* Manfred Reiff. *Editor:* Amir Naderi and Ghasem Ebrahimian. *Music:* Nicholas Kean, F. Shabazian, and A. Veseghi. *Sound:* Tommy Louie. *Running time:* 106 minutes. *MPAA Rating:* Not Rated.

CAST: Pouran Esrafily (Mariyam); Ali Azizian (Ali); Shahab Navab (Reza); Assurbanipal Babila (Haji); Bahman Maghsoudlou (Mr. Amin); Manuchehr Harsini (Mohammed); Bahman Soltani (Ghasem); Mariyam Touzi (Mrs. Amin).

LOS ANGELES TIMES, 5/18/89, Calendar/p. 9, Kevin Thomas

Ghasem Ebrahimian's "The Suitors" is so thoroughly unpredictable that it takes a while to appreciate that its view of the Iranian expatriate experience in America is as tragic as it is comic. It is remarkably accomplished in its shifts of tone for a first feature and is so distinctive that it was the only American film selected out of 50 entries for the Directors Fortnight at Cannes last year.

Iranian-born, American-educated, Ebranhimian sets his story in motion with terrific panache. He opens with a group of macho-looking Iranian men capturing a sheep on a farm in verdant Upstate New York. Cut to Kennedy International, where a middle-aged Iranian named Haji (Assurbanipal Babila) and his beautiful, *chador*-clad wife, Mariyam (Pouran Esrafily), become accidentally separated almost upon arrival, eventually reunited by the same men who went after that sheep. They slaughter the sheep (for a feast) in an apartment bathtub, its blood somehow drips into the apartment below, and a paranoid SWAT team leaves Mariyam an instant widow.

"The Suitors" does not turn into a protect picture but instead starts living up to its title as Haji's friends commence pursuing his stunning young widow, who stands to inherit half a million dollars, not to mention a fortune in Persian rugs. Far from grief-stricken, Mariyam married Haji, long a U.S. resident, only to get to America to continue her eduction. For the first time in her life she is experiencing an unexpected taste of freedom, a sensation that neither the women, let alone the men, among her husband's friends comprehend.

The film's twists and turns prove to be as breathtaking as Esrafily's dark elegance. "The Suitors" (Times-rated Mature for intense adult themes and situations) is a sad reminder of the fate of Iran's women, who were in the process of becoming liberated when the Ayatollah ordered them to resume the veil.

NEW YORK POST, 5/17/89, p. 27, Jami Bernard

You'll never think of your gyro platter quite the same way after watching a soulful-eyed sheep slaughtered in a New York City apartment bathtub in "The Suitor," a low-key Iranian comedy in sheep's clothing playing at Film Forum 1.

This directorial debut by the Iranian-born Ghasem Ebrahimian makes skish kebab of the cultural conflicts faced by a beautiful Moslem woman fresh off the plane from Tehran.

With subtle wit, Ebrahimian unfolds the drama of a stranger in a strange land. Mariyam (Pouran) arrives on these shores fully giftwrapped in the traditional veils that reveal only her eyes. In her homeland, the gift of woman can only be unwrapped by man, which leads to an Iranian standoff with the airport customs inspector who must match Mariyam's hidden face to her passport photo. She gets the word from her impatient husband; now she may reveal an ear.

Mariyam will nervosuly wrap and unwrap herself several times more in the course of "The Suitors"; you can sense her longing to be free of her cultural shackles and her fear and fascination with this land, where to be swathed in anonymity is to be started at and branded.

It is the innocent lamb brought to slaughter in the bathtub—facing Mecca, naturally—that sets the wheels turning for Mariyam's possible liberation. Her husband's Iranian pals sacrifice the sheep in a bloody, unpleasant scene, made all the worse by how the men have heretofore admired the tenderness of the animal's eyes; do we detect a parallel here in the treatment of sheep and women?

But this is New York, not Mecca. The landlord downstairs sees blood dripping from his ceiling and promptly calls in the SWAT team, suspecting Iranian terrorism. The SWAT team kills Mariyam's husband, and so she's a single gal in the city before she's even gotten over her jet lag.

At the funeral, Mariyam's sudden availability awakens a deep desire in the loins of her dead husband's friends; before you could stew up a pot of lamb's head soup, Mariyam is saddled with no less than four persistent suitors. The movie deals with Mariyam's attempts to control her own destiny.

The director, who also wrote and co-produced "The Suitors," is as comfortable around his first-time actors as around his camera. He is deft at handling Mariyam's senses of claustrophiobia and exhilaration, both of which can be seen in a simple, frightening trip to the post office.

The film is governed by its own subtle complexities and rhythms that culminate brilliantly in Mariyam making her own sacrifice, a scene that is both sobering and giddy; it is that particular balance that gives "The Suitors" its disarming self-confidence.

NEWSDAY, 5/17/89, PartII/p. 5, Mike McGrady

"The Suitors," a promising first film written and directed by a young Iranian living in New

York, extracts high comedy from the cultural shock suffered by Iranians transplanted to our soil. If comedy had been the film's sole goal, it would have been a resounding success. But, alas, the film is more ambitious than that. It also strives for serious drama, romance, tragedy—and the results are about as mixed as the ambitions.

An Iranian couple is about to arrive in Manhattan and a group of expatriate countrymen plan a celebration. The first step is to prepare a feast. No, actually, the first step is to steal a lamb from an upstate farm. The profoundly confused animal is taken to a New York apartment, where it is allowed to wander, bleating gently, over Oriental rugs that at night are beds for sleeping Iranians.

A variety of cultural differences greet the arriving couple. For example, it requires many moments of anxious negotiation for the immigration officer to persuade the wife to remove her veil so he can compare her features to her passport photo. When the veil is finally removed, we are confronted by an extraordinarily beautiful young woman (played by an architect using the single name, Pouran) who almost immediately becomes separated from her husband, lost and terrified.

But on to the feast. The lovable lamb, now quite at home in the increasingly crowded apartment, is to be butchered in the bathtub. First, according to custom, the animal must be pointed toward Mecca, a task that necessitates argument and a compass—followed by some disturbingly tentative butchering techniques. An artery is finally severed and the spurting blood douses the participants and even leaks into the apartment below.

The building superintendent, taking note of the dripping blood, goes up to question his tenants. He takes in the blood-spattered men, dials 911 and reports that Iranian terrorists are killing hostages in his building. This leads to an invasion by SWAT teams in gas masks, an evacuation of the building, a plan of attack—"These terrorist organizations, we're lucky if we catch one or two of them"—and a brutal armed raid on the apartment where the residents are doing nothing more sinister than comparing recipes for lamb's head soup.

If "The Suitors" had been able to maintain this pace, it would have been both unqualifiedly hilarious, and it would have made many telling points about the difficulty in bridging cultures that are so different and mutually distrustful. However, when the police manage to kill the newly arrived husband, the film's real story begins—the slow-moving and melodramatic tale of Iranian suitors seeking the hand (and the fortune) of the new widow.

"The Suitors" represents a most promising start by Ghasem Ebrahimian, 35, who came to New York in 1974 to study film making. The natural performances he was able to draw from a cast of novices reveals a sure hand. The film, made on a $250,000 budget was the only one of 50 American nominees selected for showing at last year's "Director's Fortnight" at Cannes. Although Ebrahimian shot his movie on 16mm film, often using skateboards instead of dollies, "The Suitors" has the rich texture and feel of a much more expensive production.

VILLAGE VOICE, 5/23/89, p. 64, Amy Taubin

Lots of films open promisingly, only to fall apart after the first half hour. (*Lots* is a relative term—most films are dreadful, period.) Ghasem Ebrahimian's *The Suitors* is a rarity in that it triumphs over a heavy-handed beginning and a meandering middle by pulling off some truly memorable stuff in the final 20 minutes. In fact, had it followed a less circuitous (meaning a more conventionally plotted) route, its impact probably would have been less powerful.

The film is about cultural displacement and its different effects on women and on men. A well-to-do Iranian comes to New York with his bride. Overcome by nostalgia for the old country, his friends hold a traditional feast that they prepare for by slaughtering a sheep in one of their apartments. The blood seeps through the floor and drips on the head of the downstairs neighbor, who immediately suspects terrorism and calls the police. SWAT teams arrive hurl tear gas, and shoot the bridegroom dead.

A week after the funeral, the widow is reading *Vanity Fair*, listening to rap records, and walking around the Lower East Side without her veil. Discovering that she has inherited half a million dollars in insurance money, the friends, one by one begin to court her. The widow, however, has had a taste of liberation, and she refuses to be treated like chattel. Her problem is that her papers and money are in the hands of her husband's former partner, who wants her to marry one of the four stooges—er, suitors—and can't fathom that a good Moslem woman would even consider doing otherwise.

At this point, what had seemed like a black comedy about a group of men who gain wealth but lose their former social status in racist America turns into a first-person study of a woman who, once she realizes that she's been in a corner all her life, fights to the death for her freedom. The weapon she employs suggests that the director is familiar with *Jeanne Dielman*, but this heroine, unlike Chantal Akerman's, is determined to save her skin. Although two-thirds of *The Suitors* looks laboriously, even compulsively, conventional, Ebrahimian cuts loose with some extraordinary images and visual ploys when he finally hooks into the woman's point of view. Madly logical and claustrophobic, the finale of the *The Suitors* leaves you up in the air, but hopeful about the filmmaker's future.

Also reviewed in:
NEW YORK TIMES, 3/23/90, p. C14, Caryn James
VARIETY, 6/1/88, p. 12
WASHINGTON POST, 9/30/89, p. C9, Hal Hinson

SUMMER VACATION: 1999

A New Yorker Films release. *Director:* Shusuke Kaneko. *Screenplay (Japanese with English Subtitles):* Michiyo Kishida. *Director of Photography:* Takama Kenji. *Editor:* Isao Temita. *Music:* Yuriko Nakamura. *Sound:* Koshiro Jimbo. *Art Director:* Osamu Yamaguchi. *Running Time:* 90 minutes. *MPAA Rating:* Not Rated.

CAST: Eri Miyagima (Kaoru/Yu); Miyiki Nakano (Naoto); Tomoko Otakra (Kazuhiro); Rie Mizuhara (Norio).

VILLAGE VOICE, 3/28/89, p. 64, Elliott Stein

Before the houselights dim, you know you're in trouble when you read in the festival flyer that this film is "set in the pseudo-future and delicately evokes a time of pubescent androgyny and metaphysical perplexity." Four boys study at a country boarding school. Yu seems to have jumped in the river out of unrequited love for Kazuhiro. A new kid turns up—a dead ringer for Yu. He says, "I am not Yu." He is. Both jump in the river and die. Or do they? "New director" Shusuke Kaneko is not so new: Prior to this protracted piffle, he perpetrated a peck of porno pix. But a novelty of sorts is that all four boys are played by girls, who, according to an invaluable press kit, "perform their difficult roles without a hint of the lurking smuttiness that boys might have brought to them." Too bad—a bit of smuttiness might have made *1999* easier to sit through.

Also reviewed in:
NEW YORK TIMES, 3/24/89, p. C16, Vincent Canby
VARIETY, 3/22/89, p. 24

SURNAME VIET GIVEN NAME NAM

A Women Make Movies release. *Producer:* Trinh T. Minh-ha. *Director:* Trinh T. Minh-ha. *Screenplay:* Trinh T. Minh-ha. *Director of Photography:* Kathleen Beeler. *Editor:* Trinh T. Minh-ha. *Sound:* Linda Peckham. *Art Director:* Jean-Paul Bourdier. *Running time:* 108 minutes. *MPAA Rating:* Not Rated.

WITH: Tran Thi Hien, Khien Lai, Ngo Kim Nhuy, Tran Thi Bich Yen; Lan Trinh.

CHRISTIAN SCIENCE MONITOR, 4/3/89, p. 11, David Sterritt

As the violence and confusion of the Vietnam war sink into the past, the memory of that disruptive event is being replaced by something else: images of Vietnam created by American movies according to their usual mass-marketing agenda. This is a slow and complex process, but it amounts to a kind of cultural imperialism that few moviegoers ever think of questioning.

Trinh T. Minh-ha is acutely aware of this situation, and in addition, she has a stake in it—as a Vietnamese, a filmmaker, and a scholar who lives in the United States and teaches at an American university. Her newest film, a poetic documentary called "Surname Viet Given Name Nam," is a many faceted work that apposes the realities of Vietnam to the many myths that have been spun about it. Nor does she confine herself to criticisms of simplistic American perceptions. She also addresses problems in Vietnam itself, especially as these manifest themselves in the oppression and exploitation of women.

Distributed by Women Make Movies, "Surname Viet Given Name Nam" was shown as the closing attraction of the prestigious New Directors/New Films festival at the Museum of Modern Art here over the weekend and is now having a special week-long run (through April 9) at the Collective for Living Cinema, before going on to more widespread showings.

Ms. Trinh is a woman of many interests, holding degrees in both music and comparative literature. Her previous films, the short "Reassemblage" and the feature "Naked Spaces: Living Is Round," were shot in West Africa and explore the relationships between people and the environments they create for themselves.

"Surname Viet Given Name Nam" is less allusive and more specific than those movies, perhaps because it deals with Trinh's own compatriots. It zeroes in on Vietnam, probing the ways in which women there have always been deemed second-class citizens—just as Vietnam itself has been deemed a second-class nation by others with more physical and ideological power. The country's social and religious heritage is seen to be grimly oppressive in many ways: traditionally, as in the "four virtues" and "three submissions" which women are supposed to cultivate, and contemporaneously, as in the atmosphere of suspicion and mistrust that Trinh sees as a byproduct of today's Vietnamese political structure. Ancient gender oppression is seen to have a bitter parallel in Vietnam's own oppression by outsiders, and in new social pressures that have built in the country since its reunification after the long period of war.

As if this weren't enough for a movie to deal with, Trinh has other concerns in mind, as well. Even as her examination of ancient and modern Vietnamese culture is unfolding, she looks with skepticism at the documentary form itself, questioning its so-called objectivity and its ability to uncover truth beyond the limits of built-in structures and motives. She reveals and probes her own filmmaking methods, including the use of reenacted interviews with rehearsed women playing the roles of "authentic" Vietnamese counterparts. And she indicates her doubt that cinema can capture the full complexity of a subject as deep and broad as a national culture.

"Surname Viet Given Name Nam" is a visually striking film, weaving many elements— interviews, archival and news footage, songs and dances, printed words—into a rich tapestry of sights, sounds, and ideas, Scenes of traditional life are artfully juxtaposed with pointedly modern views; words take on new meanings as they appear in different contexts; and nonverbal communication comes delicately into play—as the camera quietly leaves the face of a speaking woman, for instance, and wanders to her gracefully moving hands. Trinh is an expressive filmmaker as well as an eloquent one. Her new film, which is her most personal work to date, deserves a wide and receptive audience.

VILLAGE VOICE, 4/11/89, p. 61, J. Hoberman

Even allowing for revived interest in Indochina, Trinh T. Minh-ha's knotty, elusive *Surname Viet Given Name Nam*, at the Collective for Living Cinema through Sunday, is not to be recommended lightly. Trinh's first two documentaries were as unpretentiously artisanal as home movies and as conceptually sophisticated as a graduate seminar at Yale. "My approach is one which avoids any sureness of signification," the Berkeley-based, French-educated, Vietnamese-born multimedia artist told the editors of *Camera Obscura*, a journal that might have been created to explicate her oeuvre.

The idea of Trinh T. Minh-ha is as powerful as her films—as she well knows. In her forthcoming (and formidable) book *Woman, Native, Other*, she almost singlehandedly relativizes the established canon: "She who 'happens to be' a (non-white) Third World member, a woman, and a writer is bound to go through the ordeal of exposing her work to the abuse of praises and criticisms that either ignore, dispense with, or overemphasize her racial and sexual attributes. ...Have you read the grievances some of our sisters express on being among the few women chosen for a 'Special Third World Women's Issue' or being the only Third World woman at readings, workshops, and meetings? It is as if everywhere we go, we become Someone's private zoo."

Trinh originally dealt with this zoo factor by multiplying it—that it to say, by situating herself in another Third World. Her antiethnographic *Reassemblage* (1982) examined village life in rural Senegal as "an empty subject," while *Naked Spaces: Living Is Round* (1985), a study of West Africa vernacular architecture, placed the term "director" under erasure. With *Surname Viet Given Name Nam*, Trinh turns to her own identity—or rather that of the Vietnamese female other. *Surname Viet* is more "professional" than Trinh's African movies, but it exhibits the same discreetly confrontational taste for eccentric camera placement and accented line readings. Deceptively self-evident, the movie has a circular drift, advancing through and around the gradual accrual of details to plot the coordinates of Vietnamese femininity.

Class seems to be the missing factor in the equation, but, nothing if not self-conscious, *Surname Viet* is a construction about a construction. Trinh matchcuts American-Vietnamese beauty queens with more traditional entertainers, juxtaposes an apparent folk dance (shot down the peninsula in San Jose) with images of "modern" women marching in People's Vietnam. She dramatizes, annotates, and orchestrates monologues by five Vietnamese women. Made in Vietnam in 1982 (not by Trinh) and dramatized in California (by Vietnamese exiles) some five years later, these studied, long take portraits are augmented with all manner of refilmed archival and family footage, as well as an audio track that mixes folk ballads with the culture's traditional admonitions for women.

Deliberately staged and painfully acted, the interviews—grimly meek accounts of rote solidarity and everyday paranoia, official glorification and casual dismissal—include a Vermeer composition of a woman cutting vegetables and explaining that "a foreigner in principle is always a spy"; a doctor overcome by the memory of her husband's term in a prison camp; a lifelong communist bitterly pointing out that, for all the official celebration of patriotic heroines, "there is not a single woman at the political bureau"; and a second, older doctor decrying the absence of any doctor/patient intimacy.

Meanwhile, as if to underscore the incomplete or artifical aspect of their discourse, Trinh fragments her subjects, offering a closeup of a mouth or a pair of hands in lieu of a talking head. She has her subjects speak their lines while pacing on and off camera (or turning their backs on it), and concretizes the notion of women struggling to find their voices by having her performers speak English in "Vietnam" and Vietnamese in America. The mode is willful but democratic: Not only does Trinh discuss her criteria for the interviews she used; two of the actresses explain why they took roles in the film in the first place.

Although Trinh's title suggests that Vietnamese women are married to the state, her movie demonstrates that the vaunted grace and compliance of Vietnamese women are the fruits of a patriarchal order that far predates Communist rule. Nor does the filmmaker entirely escape this regime. Dealing as she does with issues of translation, authorship, and narrativity, Trinh draws heavily on the authority of French poststructuralism. (A hurried paraphrase of Baudrillard's ideas on the Vietnam War appears late in the film, almost as an afterthought).

Still, *Surname Viet Given Name Nam* is one movie well-acquainted with its own contradiction. It is with a deeply exquisite tact and a boundless irony that the final acknowledgment in the end credits thanks the husbands of the women for their "patience."

Also reviewed in:
NATION, 4/17/89, p. 529, Stuart Klawans
NEW YORK TIMES, 4/1/89, p. 14, Vincent Canby
VARIETY, 9/27–10/3/89, p. 47

SWEETIE

An Avenue Pictures release of an Arenafilm production. *Producer:* John Maynard and William MacKinnon. *Director:* Jane Campion. *Screenplay:* Gerard Lee and Jane Campion. *Director of Photography:* Sally Bongers. *Editor:* Veronika Haussler. *Music:* Martin Armiger. *Sound:* Leo Sullivan. *Art Direction:* Peter Harris. *Costumes:* Amanda Lovejoy. *Running Time:* 90 minutes. *MPAA Rating:* Not Rated.

CAST: Genevieve Lemon (Dawn/Sweetie); Karen Colston (Kay); Tom Lycos (Louis); Jon Darling (Gordon); Dorothy Barry (Flo); Michael Lake (Bob); Andre Pataczek (Clayton); Jean Hadgraft (Mrs. Schneller); Paul

Livingston (Teddy Schneller); Louise Fox (Cheryl); Ann Merchant (Paula); Robyn Frank (Ruth); Bronwyn Morgan (Sue); Sean Fennell (Boy Clerk); Sean Callinan (Simboo); Norm Galton (Notary); Warren Hensley (Man Handshakes); Charles Abbott (Meditation Teacher); Diana Armer (Melony); Barbara Middleton (Clayton's Mum); Emma Fowler (Little Sweetie); Irene Curtis (Mandy); Ken Porter (Lead Jackaroo).

CHRISTIAN SCIENCE MONITOR, 1/29/90, p. 11, David Sterritt

"Sweetie" is a new movie that's not as sweet as its title. It was made on a modest million-dollar budget by a New Zealander named Jane Campion, who has never made a full-length film before. It's in the news partly because a tidal wave of innovative, energetic filmmaking from Australia and New Zealand swept up moviegoers around 10 years ago—when pictures like "'Breaker' Morant" and "My Brilliant Career" got glowing reviews and introduced fine stars like Mel Gibson and Judy Davis.

In the past few years, that wave has largely washed itself out: Few movies from Australia or New Zealand have fared well on United States screens. But this could be the season to change that. "Sweetie" has caused quite a row at recent film festivals, from Cannes to New York, and is sure to keep moviegoers talking—or arguing—now that it's arriving in American theaters.

The picture starts with a love affair: A young woman named Kay meets and moves in with a man named Louis, who isn't happy to discover her many eccentricities—including a strange fear of trees, which she's convinced have hidden powers. When he plants a tree himself, to commemorate his relationship with Kay, she has nightmares so intense that she has to yank the tree up by the roots to stop them. (Which is too bad, in a way, since these outlandish visions are darkly fascinating to watch on-screen.)

If the movie seems peculiar so far, there's more of the same in store when the title character shows up. Sweetie is Kay's sister, and it's obvious right away that she has problems. She's loud and overweight. You sympathize with her, realizing that she might not be able to help these things. But it's hard to be patient with some of her other qualities, including her incredible selfishness. Before long, you realize she's not just peculiar; she's downright crazy. And the more her family tries to help and calm her the more insufferable and dangerous she becomes.

Cinematically speaking, "Sweetie" has a strong and original style. Before turning to film, director Campion was a painter, and her strangely unsettling images occasionally recall the work of David Lynch, another former artist; one magazine has already called "Sweetie" a sort of "Blue Velvet," and such comparisons are likely to be heard often. In a conversation I had with Ms. Campion at the Cannes Film Festival, she said her approach to cinema is directly related to her artistic background—an observation that helped me understand why the images of her movie are often more powerful than its story.

I respect the visual aspects of "Sweetie," and I'm pleased to discover a filmmaker who thinks in terms of motion pictures rather than "high concept" marketing ideas. I think some of Campion's family satire is also on target. This said, though, I hasten to add that I'm turned off by the movie as a whole. After a brilliant start, it goes downhill when Sweetie herself arrives on the scene, mostly because the filmmaker takes a surprisingly nasty attitude toward her. Sweetie *is* overbearing, obnoxious, and ugly, and we don't have to like those things about her. Still, it becomes clear that she's not this way by choice, but due to a condition of mental and emotional disturbance. In other words, she's ill, and deserves our compassion rather than the revulsion and laughter the film often encourages. "Sweetie" is imaginatively filmed, but it's sadly mean-spirited, too. For all its cleverness, it left a mighty sour taste in my mouth.

LOS ANGELES TIMES, 2/14/90, Calendar/p. 2, Sheila Benson

We haven't had a movie as profoundly unsettling as "Sweetie" since "Blue Velvet." David Lynch's dark metaphor created the same reactions as Jane Campion's first feature; both of them have been called masterly and disgusting, by turns. But while Campion's vision is no less precise and no less bizarre than Lynch's and while both directors deal in manifestations of the unconscious, the comparisons stop there.

Writer-director Campion has her own powerful identity and a far less ominous affect. "Sweetie" is warm, intense and wickedly funny, with a faint edge of danger that's never quite absent, but it has none of Lynch's psycho-sexual torment. Made with a post-Modernist's eye and a brilliant satiric ear, "Sweetie" is the announcement of a singular, smashing talent.

Campion's subject is families, pressure-cookers with no safety valves. She seems to have total recall for details of jealousy and score-keeping, unquestioned love and resentment as she sketches the pulls between two sisters, Sweetie, "Dad's real girl," who's had life-long, unquestioning love, and her sister Kay, who's never felt loved at all.

The story is set in one of the bleaker suburbs in Sydney, Australia, as a family is pulled off-center by its most demanding member, the outrageous Sweetie (Genevieve Lemon), a sometimes mental patient and decidedly free spirit.

Sad-faced and repressed, Kay (Karen Colston) is at the center of the story. In her late 20s and fleetingly pretty, she's Sweetie's slightly older sister. It's a relationship that has taken its toll. Any number of things unnerve Kay, especially trees, whose roots—like her family's—seem profoundly unstable.

Sex is another disquieting subject, but it doesn't keep Kay from moving in with lightning speed on Louis (Tom Lycos), who seems to fit a psychic's prediction of the man she's destined for. The fact that he's just become engaged is totally irrelevant. Bewildered, vaguely flattered, Louis succumbs and moves in, bag and baggage.

Actually, both sisters are irresistible forces when they set their minds on something. It's just that Sweetie's mind has been set so irrevocably, so mistakenly and for so long. She's been fueled from the cradle by her father's vision of her as a rare and God-given talent. We never quite know when Sweetie began to take this information onto another plane, when expectation became craziness, but the two are fused now.

Sweetie bursts back into Kay's life just as Kay and Louis's 13-month relationship has hit a particularly contemporary snag: they love each other, but at Kay's request they just don't make love. Kay's phobias have had a field day recently and the bombshell of Sweetie's midnight arrival doesn't soothe them.

Sweetie is roughly 60 pounds overweight, add an extra 10 pounds for makeup; the beautiful features of her Kewpie Doll face look as though they'd been inflated with a bicycle pump and her lace mitts probably cover sawed-up wrists. She arrives with Bob (Michael Lake), a drooling druggie she calls her producer and she has stopped her medication. However, success is only inches away. "Bob and I are gonna walk through some doors" she announces triumphantly. As soon as Bob stops nodding off mid-sentence.

What really perturbs Kay is the force of Sweetie's uninhibited sexuality, the other end of the spectrum from her own. It doesn't unclench Kay in the slightest.

Sweetie's fluctuating behavior has very nearly destroyed her parents' marriage. As we meet her mother, Flo (Dorothy Barry) she's calmly taken time off to get a breather from Sweetie and from her husband's sentimental uselessness about her.

Campion may not be sentimental but she's a nutsy romantic. The Outback sequence, where Flo has taken a job happily cooking for an outpost of Aussie cowboys, is pure, saturated longing. Kay, Louie and Gordon drive to this wilderness only to find the seven jackaroos, like something out of Agnes de Mille's "Rodeo," spending yearning nights under the blue-purple skies, brushing up on their two-step. It's absolutely magical.

Deadpan funny as the script can be—to balance its horrific moments—its wit is matched by the director's visual style. Campion, with cinematographer Sally Bongers, uses an accumulation of images to build mood; a blizzard of them at first, slowing down as the film builds. Her character's claustrophobia and depressions are caught by subjective angles within rooms or landscapes, yet there's not an uninteresting image in the film.

The cast is breathtaking. Clearly, there would be no film without Genevieve Lemon's uncanny, unsparing Sweetie, touched with a sort of grandiosity of aberration; hers is an amazing creation. But in less flamboyant ways every actor, down to the maddening little boy next door (Andre Pataczek), is working with an equal measure of skill and delicacy.

Campion and Gerard Lee, her co-writer, regard Sweetie with a sort of detached amazement, refusing to sentimentalize her. She's the film's explosive humor, its sexuality, its pathos, and its reflective energy source. There's no question that she's deeply disturbing, yet it's clear that Campion regards this tyrant who has held her entire family hostage emotionally for nearly 25 years—with equal love and clarity. And if there could be any question that Kay's love matches her fury at her mad sister, watch Kay's action in their closing scene together. It's the summation of their entire impossible relationship.

MONTHLY FILM BULLETIN, 5/90, p. 142, Steve Jenkins

Despite the fact that he has just become engaged to one of her workmates, Kay makes love to Louis in a car park, believing that she is destined to be with him. Thirteen months later, they are living together and Louis plants a tree for them. Kay, who has a fear of trees, uproots it and hides it in their wardrobe. The couple experience sexual problems, with Kay asserting that Louis treats her like a sister. They try meditation and sex-by-appointment, but eventually Kay moves into the spare room. Returning home one night, they find that Kay's sister Dawn, known as "Sweetie" and with aspirations to becoming a singer, and her "producer" Bob have broken into the flat. Despite Sweetie's strange manner (she claims to have been in a coma for a year), Louis is sexually attracted to her. Kay is angry when her sister destroys one of her dresses; Sweetie responds by chewing up one of Kay's collection of china horses. Kay and Dawn's father, Gordon, arrives to stay with them while on a trial separation from their mother Flo. Kay wants him to help get rid of Sweetie, but Gordon's attempt to persuade Bob to go fails to penetrate the latter's drugged stupor. Bob leaves anyway. Tricking the upset Sweetie into staying behind, Kay, Louis and Gordon visit Flo, who is working as camp cook for a group of "jackaroos", or cowboys. Flo, deciding that she and Gordon can begin again, returns home with them; she also thinks that Sweetie has too much influence over Gordon and should leave. Meanwhile, Sweetie has wrecked Louis and Kay's home and is behaving as if she were a dog. Flo and Gordon take Sweetie to their home, while Louis leaves Kay after discovering the remains of the tree. Kay is summoned by Flo when Sweetie, naked and painted blue, climbs into her tree-house and refuses to come down. She is joined by Clayton, a small boy whom Sweetie has befriended who lives next door to Kay. Sweetie is killed when the tree-house collapses. Louis and Kay are reunited. Gordon sees a vision of Sweetie as a child, singing in their backyard.

Sweetie, a first feature by Jane Campion after several acclaimed short films, is at once a self-consciously "original" and striking work, and a rather derivative one. In exploring the relationships in and around a troubled family, Campion presents her characters' behaviour as both bizarre and matter-of-factly "normal". This is simply achieved by plunging the spectator from the start into a world where everyday experience (essentially, routine problems between couples, sisters, parents, children) is constantly entwined with the supernatural and the fatalistic. From the beginning, Kay's narration links her childhood resentment of Sweetie with a subsequent fear of the "hidden powers" of trees, a fear which is then "justified" through the sapling which Louis plants and which she destroys, through the death of Sweetie, and finally through the root which prevents her sister's coffin from entering the grave. Similarly, Kay's relationship with Louis is triggered by a visit to a fortune teller, whose prophecy about a man with a question mark over his face is absurdly and literally fulfilled by Louis (via a convenient mole and an improbable curl of hair).

Thereafter, the film can comfortably embrace virtually any shift of tone, from *Comic Strip*-style humour (the drug-soaked figure of Bob, Sweetie's manager), through more surreal moments (the dancing cowboys for whom Flo works as a cook), to pure physicality (Sweetie urinating by the family car or farting in her father's face). And stylistically, Campion matches this waywardness with determinedly non-naturalistic visual gestures, in which time-lapse photography, off-centre framing, overhead shots and large close-ups conspire to create a feeling of a world made strange.

In the end, however, doubts about *Sweetie* centre on a suspicion that beneath all this flaunted weirdness beats a rather softer humanist heart. Certainly, there are moments when a sentimental emotional truth seems privileged, as when Sweetie cries after being tricked and abandoned by her family as they leave to visit Flo, or when the latter expresses her belief that she and her husband can begin their marriage again. Perhaps unfairly, these moments seem overly telling since the film is being championed as a challenging riposte to the aesthetic and moral values of the 70s Australian "New Wave" (see Harlan Kennedy's article "The New Wizards of Oz", *Film Comment*, October 1989).

Campion's film might more usefully be placed in the context of recent American movies which have celebrated family values. When it is compared to *Parenthood*, for example, *Sweetie*'s singularity is not that pronounced; beneath their very different surfaces, both films rely on an audience enjoying the quirkiness of their characters as they negotiate the troubled waters of family life, some sinking, some swimming. Beyond that, there is also the stylistic debt which *Sweetie* owes to David Lynch and *Blue Velvet*. Certain scenes, such as the cowboy dance, simply have the feel of Lynch, but specific images (time-lapsed plants pushing up through the earth; Kay trying to unravel a hose as the tree-house collapses) are direct echoes. That *Sweetie* should suffer by comparison, offering as it does a kind of nowt-so-queer-as-folks alibi in place of a real faith in the bizarre, is probably inevitable.

NEW LEADER, 1/8/90, p. 23, John Morrone

Sweetie is the first feature film done by that unclassifiable Australian talent Jane Campion, whose short works have been seen previously at the New York Film Festival and New Directors/New Films. Campion sometimes frames her distracted, neurasthenic characters as if the very ground the camera rested on were tilted, and the action tipped accidentally into view. Her style goes far beyond the merely eccentric; she seems to chart a strange parallel universe whose quirky emotional realities intersect only slightly with our own.

In this film, Kay (Karen Colston) and Dawn (Genevieve Lemon) are mythical figures of eternal sibling strife. Kay, an enervated despairing creature, takes meditation classes in her futile search for "quiet." When her fat, loud and wildly oversexed sister, known as Sweetie, makes a surprise visit, Kay's ploddingly comfortable married life is thrown into disarray. Talentless at song and dance, Sweetie fancies herself a charmer whose big break into show business is imminent. Instead, she makes a steady descent into madness that catches the family unprepared to cope with her destructive energy.

Most Australians are skeptical of professional psychological help, and *Sweetie* reflects that cultural trait. To American audiences, therefore, Kay's attempt to keep her sister under control may itself seem dotty. Nevertheless, psychologists who have seen the film have remarked on its vivid, almost clinical representation of schizophrenic behavior.

Campion's real artistic achievement, though, has been to dramatize the mortal conflict between life-draining and life-exploding personalities. Whereas thin, wan Kay is so fragile even her dreams upset her, Sweetie's dream life is plastered all over her oily face. Imagine Mia Farrow and Brenda Vaccaro as sisters and you still haven't grasped the volatile chemistry between these two. Go watch Colston and Lemon slug it out with a sad, surreal desperation, certifiably unlike any battle between sisters ever filmed.

NEW YORK, 1/29/90, p. 58, David Denby

Sweetie (Genevieve Lemon) is a libidinous fat girl with the nasty gaze of a devil doll. In the odd, arresting, but unsatisfying *Sweetie*, the first feature directed by the New Zealand-born Jane Campion, Sweetie shows up at her her sister's house with her depraved boyfriend, eats everything in sight, makes love noisily, and throws panic into the air. Suggestions that she leave or desist are met with feline growls and vamping dirty looks. It's hard to tell whether Sweetie is wildly liberated or insane, or both, but Genevieve Lemon, hugely fleshy, with dark eye shadow and bits of lace at her wrists, is an alarming and hilarious travesty of insatiability.

This Australian film has been hailed as a masterpiece of perversity and suburban surrealism. It does, I admit, have an air of unnerving preoccupation. Campion seizes on oddities—for instance, the way a lock of a man's hair falls into a question mark on his forehead. The movie is built of such signs, and of nightmarish memories, moments of congealed eroticism, a sense of the dislocations of family life. But Campion's is not a lyrical style—*Sweetie* stubbornly refuses to get going and come together. Much of the time we are looking at the rigid brow and prissy mouth of Karen Colston, who plays Sweetie's spooked older sister. The movie's mysteries may interlock as visual metaphors, but they don't interlock emotionally.

NEW YORK POST, 10/6/89, p. 27, David Edelstein

"Sweetie," the first feature by Jane Campion, is a moody, frightening, savagely funny and unclassifiable portrait of a disturbed family—a great film, and one of the peaks of this year's nearly valley-less New York Film Festival.

The Australian movie was roundly booed in Cannes, and on one level it's easy to see why—its artiness combined with the aggressive gross-out antics of its central character, Sweetie (Genevieve Lemon), make for a supremely unnerving experience.

The story also unfolds puzzlingly. The opening suggests a crackbrained love story about the affair of an oversensitive young woman, Kay (Karen Colston), and an ordinary young man (Tom Lycos). But when Kay's disturbed sister Sweetie comes to visit, the movie turns into a study of familial insanity.

"Sweetie" offers the best portrait of a schizophrenic I've ever seen, although the film makers are quick to say that her illness has been left unspecified. Overweight, messy, narcissistic, always trying to draw attention to herself, Sweetie at times resembles a John Waters heroine. But since we see her through the eyes of Kay—revolted by messiness and especially fearful of trees—it's tough to enjoy her shenanigans.

The film has a disquieting look. The light is different Down Under—it's bleaching, and Campion fills the house with boldly colored objects of kitsch. The oranges and greens and purples leap out, as does the attempt to impose some middle-class order on this chaotic existence.

Every detail is planted (every shadow, every hue) and yet, miraculously, the movie is alive— endlessly probing and pushing, alert to the trees (literal or familial) that keep forcing their way in. "Sweetie" also offers a brilliant portrait of the girl's father (Jon Darling)—a man who's utterly useless, yet totally destructive, who loves his deranged daughter not wisely, but too well.

The film has been compared to the work of David Lynch, but that's not quite right. "Sweetie" is only Lynch-like in the way it gets under your skin and drives you batty; it's otherwise more relationship-oriented, less dependent on genre. However, "Kitchen Sink" (written and directed by Alison Maclean), the short that precedes "Sweetie" at the Festival, is a disgustingly lovely, Lynch-like study of the hairy object of a woman's desire.

NEW YORK POST, 1/19/90, p. 19, David Edelstein

Kay (Karen Colston), the protagonist of "Sweetie," has an irrational dread of trees—of roots crawling under the house and into her bed. "It's like they have hidden power...," she explains in the movie's doomy prologue.

The beauty of "Sweetie," the first feature by New Zealand native Jane Campion, is that we come to understand Kay's phobia and how it relates to her garish, perhaps schizophrenic sister, Sweetie (Genevieve Lemon), and her pathetically dependent dad (Jon Darling).

It's a moody, allusive film, often downright puzzling. In its first half hour, "Sweetie" seems like a crack-brained love story about oversensitive, superstitous Kay and the ordinary young man (Tom Lycos) she steals from his fiancé when she recognizes him from a description of her future love in some tea leaves.

But when the overweight, messy and childish Sweetie crashes into the couple's prefab, split-level dwelling, the movie turns into a harrowing, often morbidly funny portrait of familial insanity—of family trees in all their monstrous invasiveness.

Sweetie arrives with her boyfriend, Bob (Michael Lake), a perpetually stoned burn-out she claims to be her manager. Although Sweetie can niether sing or dance, she's convinced she has a career in show-business. Oblivious to (or perhaps defiant of) her sister's disapproval, she makes a mess of the house, throws violent temper tantrums and has noisy, interminable sex with Bob on the couple's living-room sofa.

In another movie, what the camera does to Lemon might be considered a violation: It lingers on her, for example, as she squats to urinate outside a car; and the climax finds her naked, smeared with dirt and breaking wind in a tree house while her parents plead with her to come down.

But Campion forces us to work through our revulsion. The character of Sweetie is based on a relative of Campion's co-screenwriter, Gerard Lee, and it views her with suffering detachment.

She's clearly still a child, with a constant need for attention and sensual gratification, and we see how her and her sister's characters have been formed in response to their needy, helpless dad (Darling), who comes to stay with them when their mother (Dorothy Barry) leaves him for a month to cook for "jackeroos" in Australia's outback.

The theme of incest isn't underlined, but we watch, through Kay's eyes, as Sweetie scrubs her father in his tub and purposely drops her soap between his legs. And the sisterly dynamic gets scarier and scarier—Kay is as repressed and withdrawing as Sweetie is gross and forward. When Kay stops sleeping with her boyfriend, Sweetie's all over him.

Pretty soon we see why the girls' mother had to get away from her husband (leaving behind a meal, wrapped and frozen, for every night of her absence). It's this man—whose need for love and attention is more intense than his daughter's—whose delusions have helped to keep Sweetie a child. He loves her selfishly, not wisely, but too well.

"Sweetie" is about the demands for unconditional love that insane people can make and the impossibility of living up to them—at least while maintaining one's independence. Kay's aversion to trees (and sex, and growth of any kind) keeps her father and sister at bay, but also drives away her lover; she's as cursed, in her way, as Sweetie.

"Sweetie" was roundly booed in Cannes and, on one level, it's easy to see why—it's shot through with arty angles and portentous music, and the camera's stance is often clinical. It has a brutal, tragic climax. It's a hard movie to take.

But there's no doubt that Campion is a visionary. The light is different Down Under—it's bleaching, and Campion fills the house with boldly colored objects of kitsch. The oranges and greens and lavenders leap out, as does the attempt to impose some middleclass order on this chaotic existence. Huge trees loom on the horizon in straight rows, like sentries.

Every detail is planted (every shadow, every hue) and yet, miraculously, the movie is alive—endlessly probing and pushing, alert to the trees (literal or familial) that keep forcing their way in. "Sweetie" is part psychology, part myth, part mystery. It's a work of startling originality.

NEWSDAY, 10/6/89, Part III/p. 5, Terry Kelleher

Jane Campion's "Sweetie" is an eccentric Australian comedy that takes a late turn toward tragedy. The trick is to see the turn coming and make the proper adjustment.

This is a movie about two sisters: thin, uptight, skittish Kay (Karen Colston), and fat, coarse, voracious Dawn (Genevieve Lemon), nicknamed "Sweetie" by her doting father (Jon Darling). It's funny, in an odd sort of way, when Sweetie invades Kay's life and turns it upside down. According to Lemon, however, we're meant to bear in mind early on that Sweetie's "unspecified mental problems" and the family's reluctance to deal with them are not entirely a laughing matter.

"It pleases me when people laugh," Lemon said, "but obviously that has to be undercut at some point, or we're in trouble. They have to be moved by it as well."

By this standard, the movie is troubled—but still worth watching.

NEWSDAY, 1/19/90, Part III/p. 3, Mike McGrady

Young New Zealander Jane Campion first created ripples of interest when a student work, "Peel," took the Palm d'Or for best short film at the 1986 Cannes Film Festival. Early awards convinced Campion to try something weightier, something longer, "a modern low budget feature after my own style. I thought if we didn't ask for a lot of money, people would let us try something unusual."

"Something unusual"—the phrase perfectly describes "Sweetie," the young director's first feature, one of the highlights of the recent New York and Cannes film festivals.

"After my own style"—and that phrase explains why Campion's films have been creating such interest. The former artist's style—a mix of metaphor, stark visual images, cutting dialogue, unpredictable happenings—adds up to an intensely personal vision of the different varieties of love that exist within a family.

The film's primary relationship is between staid, responsible, longing-to-be-respectable Kay (Karen Colston) and her insane sister, Sweetie (Genevieve Lemon), a mountainous creature who is sloppy, dirty, loud, insistent, shrewd, sexually grasping and who at times takes to growling, barking and snarling like a dog. Sweetie is a vision with her heavy rings, her black fingernail polish and ebony lipstick, her great folds of flesh, her animal cunning.

There is no ignoring Sweetie. Nearing the end of the film—by this time she is naked, painted black and howling obscene imprecations from a treetop—she has exhausted every member of her family and, undoubtedly, many in the audience. Still, although Sweetie is, by any normal standards, monstrous, there is also something about her that borders on the...well...likable.

For one thing, she's totally free—free to do whatever she wants, whenever she wants. She is free to approach her sister's lover ("I like your face. It's nice. I like it.") and then proceed to smother him with kisses. Since he has been having trouble making love to staid Kay ("Some animals won't mate in captivity," he explains), he is eminently seducible. As is the small boy next door who becomes Sweetie's fast friend. As, finally, are we.

Perhaps we are won over when we recognize that Sweetie exists in all of us to some extent. She is as much a part of everyone's life as roots are part of a tree. Much as Kay would like to sever all her roots, they are there, crawling metaphorically throughout the film, reminding her of her childhood, of Sweetie's old treehouse: "She was the princess. It was her tree. She wouldn't let me up...I used to imagine the roots of that tree, crawling under the house, crawling right under my bed."

And much as Kay would like to deny sisterhood, or any link to the repulsive Sweetie ("She was just born, I didn't have anything to do with it."), she cannot deny family connections or even those connections that may go beyond family. For director Campion hints that Sweetie is, finally, the part of us all that we would deny or conceal or abandon. She is our childlike, free animal nature, our primitiveness, our roots. Using a first-rate cast of unknowns, Campion connects us to Sweetie with flair, humor and impact.

NEWSWEEK, 1/22/90, p. 60, David Ansen

If Diane Arbus were alive and making movies in Australia, the result might be something like *Sweetie*. This haunting and strange film, the first feature of 34-year-old director Jane Campion, who wrote the script with Gerard Lee, tends to provoke the same impassioned debate that Arbus's photography did. At the Cannes and New York film festivals, "Sweetie" was hailed by its admirers as a true original and attacked by its enemies for its cold perversity. The question about Campion is the same one that raged around Arbus: is the grotesquerie of her style a sign of contempt, or compassion!

"Sweetie" is as eccentric as its characters, a bizarrely dysfunctional Australian family. At the heart of the matter are two sisters, rigid and phobic Kay (Karen Colston), who's terrified of trees, and infantile, out-of-control Sweetie (Genevieve Lemon). Sweetie, who has delusions of being a performer, invades Kay's home with her "producer" boyfriend, an aging punk druggie who's almost as hopeless as she. Sweetie, overweight and grotesquely made up, acts out all her inner chaos, barking like a dog when she doesn't get her way. Kay takes the opposite route, shutting down like a clamp, terrified of vitality. At first these characters may seem gratuitously odd. Why does Kay throw herself at her boyfriend Louis, and then when they are settled in together, refuse to sleep with him? "Some animals won't mate in captivity," she explains.

But the pieces of this familial psychodrama begin to fall into place when we meet the sisters' parents, Flo and Gordon (Dorothy Barry and Jon Darling), just as Mum has decided to flee from her husband. Flo finds temporary respite working at a jackaroo ranch in the middle of nowhere. Poor abandoned Gordon, lost without her, comes to stay with his daughters. As he dotes on the demented, self-destructive Sweetie, we see that he's as deluded about his little darling as she is about herself. But his blind love only encourages her doom. All these people are locked into a deranged Oedipal dance they can't perceive, and are thus helpless to stop.

Campion's mannerist, modernist style—tilted angles, asymmetrical framing, lurid, tacky colors—keeps the viewer off balance and on edge. "Sweetie" is both painful and painfully funny. But her rigorously unsentimental vision is anything but unfeeling. Like David ("Blue Velvet") Lynch, with whom she shares a kind of stone-faced nuttiness, she apprehends the perverse by refusing to stand outside it. We have to stumble our way through the gnarled roots of the family madness just as the damaged characters do. This daring, bracing movie is an antidote to all the paeans to the wonders of the nuclear family. Family love, in Campion's coolly heartbreaking film, is a net from which no one escapes unharmed.

VILLAGE VOICE, 1/23/90, p. 75, Georgia Brown

Fear of trees is not just an odd phobia, but rather a debilitating one if you don't happen to live somewhere like 42nd Street and Seventh Avenue—and even that's a bit close to Bryant Park. Kay (Karen Colston), the glowering heroine (to use the world loosely) of *Sweetie*, says trees scare her because "they have human powers." Meaning that humans scare her. When a cracked sidewalk begins to look like tree roots, Kay knows she's come to the end of the road.

Born in New Zealand, based in Australia, 34-year-old Jane Campion achieves something rare and exciting in this, her first full-length feature. Using raw, quirky imagery, point-of-view camera (off-balance angles, close-ups of off-the-wall details), and, from what I infer, fraught memories of under- and overdevelopment, Campion invents her own visceral, personal cinema. She's quite clearly mining the same territory as David Lynch (*Eraserhead, Blue Velvet*) and artists such as Cindy Sherman and Eric Fischl. *Sweetie* has a similar aura of menace and bafflement, as well as thematic body parts, icky things in the grass (ominous, looming Nature!), delicious irony, and sexual enigma. Campion's cinema of the perverse, of controlled hysteria, may work a minor vein of the magnificently obsessed tradition of Sirk, Fuller, and Fassbinder, but who knows where she'll go from here.

Think trees as in Family Tree: invasive roots, strangling, tangled growth that takes place under and above ground. (Campion comes up with some great shots from the underside—of a car and a bed—and a stunning view of swimmers simultaneously under and above water.) Think trees as in Tree of Life: branches of blood vessels pulsing inside the breakable body.

Wearing an unbecoming uniform and a plastic waitress-type badge with her name on it, Kay goes to work in an office. (Campion has a deft, shorthand way of suggesting the dreary arena of women's work while leaving vague what is accomplished there.) The other young women seem comparatively cheerful and "normal"; one is getting engaged. Normally enough, they mock the grim, grating Kay.

For direction in life, Kay patronizes a psychic whose grown idiot son whines and babbles while his mum reads tea leaves. (Kay appears not to notice, perhaps because her sister Sweetie on bad days resembles the man. Like Sweetie in her mad-dog phases, he grabs the teacup and won't let go. But we only make this connection later.) What's distinctive in the early scenes of Campion's movie is how crazy and sane overlap and fuse. The first quarter of *Sweetie*, seen through Kay's eyes and with her voiceover, may be hard to get engaged in except in a wondering, puzzled, or irritated way. But the rest of the film pulls like an undertow.

The psychic tells Kay to find a man with a question mark on his face. When she spots Lou (Tom Lycos)—with a curl in the middle of his forehead and a mole above his eyebrow—Kay makes a beeline for him even though he's just gotten engaged to her co-worker. Inexplicably and before you know it, Lou (who looks like Richard Gere with a black spot) moves in with sour Kay. In honor of their love, he plants a baby elder (as in elder sib?) in the backyard. He doesn't know the terror trees hold for her. The elder becomes a sore point between them (and she gets furious when he says she seems like his "big sister"), but all this diminishes in importance with the arrival of Kay's disturbed and obese sister, Sweetie (Genevieve Lemon).

Sweetie—real name, Dawn—shows up one day with a stoned boyfriend, Bob ("my producer"), and soon makes a play for Lou by licking his legs. She cuts the sleeves off one of Kay's dresses and dyes it her color, black. Her hands are often black with dye and she paints her large nails black. Quickly, she develops a rapport with Clayton, the little boy next door who plays in the yard, because she's like a child, though a very large one. "She was just *born*! I didn't have anything to do with it!" Kay explains to Lou, who by now has turned into a bewildered bystander. (The film fails Lou, whose motives for staying with Kay, particularly once their sex turns placid, are unfathomable.) When Kay punishes her for destroying the dress, Sweetie retaliates by chewing up a few plaster horses from Kay's precious childhood collection.

About this time, the sisters' parents happen to be separating. Mom (Dorothy Barry, a wonderful singer), who appears the sanest of the four, intends to go off into the desert to keep house for a group of cowboys. Straightaway, Dad (Jon Darling) turns up at Kay's to find solace and to be near his pet, Sweetie. He's anxious to find out if Bob thinks she can make a go in show business. His overriding mission, however (in the service of which he cruelly tricks Sweetie), is to enlist Kay's help in enticing Mom back home.

In most movies family pathology is oblique; it usually has to be inferred or interpreted. Here pathology is so bald, insistent, and extreme, it virtually is the movie. This isn't to say, though, that explicitness of pathology precludes mystery. In one key scene, Kay lies in bed next to her mutilated horses, watching Sweetie scrub Dad in his bath. She watches as Sweetie loses the soap and fishes between his legs to find it. Like the horses, childhood and its wounds are near. Children now bathe parents, but loneliness is the same and desire isn't closer to its source. The Other is always lost. The sisters' rivalry for the same unattainable prizes brings them closer to each other than to the prizes.

A few years ago Campion exhibited a trio of shorts at Cannes that generated a good deal of critical excitement. So many elements in the shorts recur in *Sweetie* that it's hard not to see Campion's work so far as having strong autobiographical roots. *Peel*, which won the Palme d'Or for best film, is subtitled "An Exercise in Discipline," and its narrative follows maybe 10 minutes of a drive in the country with a redheaded man, his dark-haired sister, and the man's redheaded young son. When the child peels an orange and throws the rind out the window, Dad slams on the brakes and demands the kid pick up what he's thrown out. The boy runs away; the sister in the back seat nags her brother; the man retrieves the boy, and, now allied, they light into the sister/aunt ("Pick it up!"), who's also peeling an orange and dropping the peel onto the road. A stunningly simple tale terrifically acted, *Peel* reverberates with cycles of pathogenic behavior, and with hurt and fury. Peel, Campion makes us feel, is skin.

Another of these shorts, the black-and-white *A Girl's Own Story*, could be a companion piece to *Sweetie*. The weird sisters here are high school age—nubile, overweight, homely—living at home with their Barbie collections and cutouts of Beatles on the walls. One comes at the other with a knife in the night, but in lighter moments they practice kissing with the younger one putting on a mask. She's the one whom the warring, sexually obsessed parents use as a go-between ("Tell your mother her dress is gorgeous"; "Ask your father where he was so late last night") because they haven't spoken for years.

Here are some other recurring images: a singing child with glasses (goofy and poignant), groups of mocking girls, seduction by an older man (Campion's 30-minute *After Hours* expands on this theme), as well as many shots of legs lying flat, of feet, of a floral carpet, and of swimming, dancing, and licking. Mom in the earlier work, however, is not a bit saner than the coveted Dad.

I should credit, too, the talented cinematographer on *Sweetie*, as well as on *Peel* and *A Girl's Own Story:* Sally Bongers, the first woman in Australia to have shot a 35mm feature.

Take a sibling to *Sweetie*.

Also reviewed in:
NATION, 2/19/90, p. 252, Stuart Klawans
NEW REPUBLIC, 2/26/90, p. 27, Stanley Kauffmann
NEW YORK TIMES, 1/19/90, p. C8, Vincent Canby
VARIETY, 5/10–16/89, p. 18
WASHINGTON POST, 3/2/90, p. D1, Hal Hinson
WASHINGTON POST, 3/2/90, Weekend/p. 37, Desson Howe

TALE OF THE WIND, A

A Capi Films and La S.E.P.T. production with the participation of the French Ministry of Culture and Communication and Stichting Nederlands Film Fonds. *Executive Producer:* Marceline Loridan. *Director:* Joris Ivens and Marceline Loridan. *Screenplay (French with English subtitles):* Joris Evens and Marceline Loridan with Elizabeth D. *Director of Photography:* Thierry Arbogast and Jacques Loiseleux. *Editor:* Geneviève Louveau. *Music:* Michel Portal. *Sound:* Jean Umansky. *Art Director:* Zhao Jinsheng, Zhang Zebin, and Christian Marti. *Running time:* 80 minutes. *MPAA Rating:* Not Rated.

CAST: Joris Ivens (The Old Man); Liu Guilian (The Witch); Liu Zhuang (Chang E, the Moon Fairy); Han Zenxiang (The Monkey); Old Li (The Old Chinese Man); Wang Hong (The Little Girl); Zou Qiaoyu (The Singer); Wu Jian (The Orator).

NEWSDAY, 9/25/89, Part II/p. 5, Terry Kelleher

We've all had our fill of rain and tales of wind lately, but don't let your understandable antipathy toward these elements prejudice you against the Joris Ivens offerings at the New York Film Festival.

The Dutch documentarian and world citizen died this summer at age 90. His last work, the 80-minute "A Tale of the Wind," will be shown tonight at Alice Tully Hall, preceded by "Rain" (1929), his 15-minute "cinepoem" depicting the effect of a shower on the city of Amsterdam. The Ivens program begins at 9:15.

Ivens tended to take on the large themes—nature, war, social change—in a 60-year career that included such efforts as "Industrial Symphony," "Spanish Earth," "The 17th Parallel" and 14-film cycle called "How Yu-Kong Moved the Mountains." In a sense, "A Tale of the Wind" was his most ambitious undertaking because its topic was most elusive. It's about an old man who travels to China with "a crazy plan to film the invisible wind." This old man is Joris Ivens, playing and being himself.

"A Tale of the Wind" is hard to label—a diary of the imagination, a documentary of the fantastic, a journey of the mind. While pursung his crazy plan, Ivens rambles around China showing us many aspects of that land's history, culture and thought. He also goes places in his dreams—to the moon, for example.

At the end a strong wind comes up in the desert—summoned by magic, of course—and whips the film's disparate pieces into a satisfying whole. Or so the beautiful images, coupled with Michel Portal's music, make it seem.

Marceline Loridan, a diminutive French woman with a head of hair that would qualify her for the "Annie 2" auditions, concluded a quarter-century collaboration with Ivens by serving as co-director and executive producer of "A Tale of the Wind." At a press conference following a preview screening, she acknowledged that the film serves well as "testament" for Ivens, but pointed out that they had a number of other projects planned at the time of his death.

"A Tale of the Wind" had its world premiere at the 1988 Venice Film Festival. The project began life in 1984, when Loridan and Ivens resumed work on an unproduced screenplay they had written several years earlier. After the film makers decided on a drastic change of setting from Italy to China, it dawned on them—"like a bolt of lightning," Loridan said—to integrate a study of Chinese civilization with an attempt by Ivens to capture the wind with a camera. For an added touch of metaphor, there was Ivens' lifelong problem with asthma, which made wind a very personal matter.

To raise funds for the $2-million production, the film makers needed a script to show potential backers. They had 200 pages written before shooting began, but there was room for serendipity between the lines.

"We knew from experience," Loridan said through a translator, "how reality can sometimes make you wonderful gifts."

Sometimes they come wrapped like booby prizes. When local official reneged on a government promise to grant the film crew relatively free rein at a museum, their lack of cooperation caused a 10-day delay in the shooting schedule. Fortunately, however, the camera recorded the protracted negotiations, providing "A Tale of the Wind" with a few unexpectedly funny scenes. The bureaucrats' attitude may have been "*tres stupide*," as Loridan put it, but a gift is a gift. When Ivens fell ill during shooting, Loridan elected to shoot a sequence in the hospital. It is there that the old man dreams his way to the moon. Thus, the film makers used reality to go beyond reality, and that's magic. "Filming the impossible is what's best in life," Ivens enthuses when his crew begins to lose heart in the desert. His attitude lifts their spirits, as it will yours.

VILLAGE VOICE, 9/26/89, p. 64, J. Hoberman

If you have to ask who Joris Ivens was, you may be baffled by his final film. Made mainly in China when this pioneer of politically engaged cinema was 90, *A Tale of the Wind* (directed with Marceline Loridan) is a playful film essay and stark last testament—a movie in the tradition of Dreyers *Gertrud* or Buñuel's *That Obscure Object of Desire*, playing the themes of a lifetime and the ephemera of the medium against the fade-out of death.

Also reviewed in:
NEW YORK TIMES, 9/25/89, p. C15, Caryn James

TALES FROM THE GIMLI HOSPITAL

A Circle/Cinephile release of an Extra Large/Winnipeg Film Group production. *Producer:* Ben Bazenholtz and Andre Bennett. *Director:* Guy Maddin. *Screenplay:* Guy Maddin. *Story Consultant:* George Toles. *Director of Photography:* Guy Maddin. *Editor:* Guy Maddin. *Sound:* Clive Perry. *Art Director:* Jeff Solylo. *Costumes:* Donna Szoke. *Make-up:* Donna Szoke. *Running time:* 72 minutes. *MPAA Rating:* Not Rated.

CAST: Kyle McCulloch (Einar, the Lonely); Michael Gottli (Gunnar); Angela Heck (Snjofridur); Margaret-Anne MacLeod (Amma); Heather Neale (Fjola); Caroline Bonner (Elfa Egilsdottir); Don Hewak (John Ramsay); Chris Johnson (Lord Dufferin); Donna Szoke (Fish Princess); Kyle McColloch (Minstrel); Ian Handford (Gravedigger One); Greg Klymkiw (Gravedigger Two).

LOS ANGELES TIMES, 9/11/89, Calendar/p. 6, Michael Wilmington

"Tales From the Gimli Hospital" is such an oddball little show—a Canadian regional production shot for $22,000 and based, tongue-in-cheek, on the folk history of a small Icelandic fishing community in Manitoba—that some audiences may get weirded out during the credits.

It's a dry, fluky comedy about the perils of immigrant communities and bad health facilities—shot in a style that's a clever pastiche of early '30s experimental talkies. The imagery is purposely deranged and the movie pumps it out in slow, deliberate rhythms that become daffy and excruciating.

Sultry vamp nurses, made up like Valley Girl versions of Louise Brooks, try to heal victims of a mysterious epidemic by rubbing their sores with dead sea gulls. Three angelic little girls vanish hand-in-hand in a sylvan wood and later float back down a river in individual coffins.

The characters have names like Einar the Lonely, Elfa Egilsdottir, Lord Dufferin and the Fish Princess. Einar, the crazed hero, (Kyle McCulloch) pomades his hair with fish grease squeezed right from the fish, violates a corpse on an Indian burial platform and indulges in a bout of nocturnal, buttock-grabbing wrestling while bagpipes wail.

Meanwhile, the whole dolorous history is recounted by an ample nurse, Amma (Margaret-Anne McCleod) to two children on a death watch in their mothers' contemporary Gimli hospital room; here, "contemporary" means the early '30s.

There's a loony concentration to "Gimli" (Times-rated: Mature, for style, theme and sexuality). Much of it revolves around the two epidemic victims, Einar and Gunnar (Michael Gottli), as they lie in the filthy, turn-of-the century Gimli Hospital—a makeshift facility in a hay-strewn barn—staring at each other with increasing hostility from their separate beds.

Winnipeg writer-director-editor-photographer, Guy Maddin—whose grandmother was an Icelandic immigrant—has quite an imagination and a talent for pastiche. Maddin tries to capture the look and feel of the early low-budget experimental talkies or late silents, and he's amazingly good at it.

Also reviewed in:
NEW YORK TIMES, 7/28/89, p. C9, Stephen Holden
VARIETY, 10/19/88, p. 243

TANGO BAR

A Manley Productions release of a Beco Films/Zaga Films production. *Producer:* Juan Carlos Codazzi and Roberto Gandara. *Director:* Marcos Zurinaga. *Screenplay (Spanish with English subtitles):* Marcos Zurinaga, José Pablo Feinman, and Juan Carlos Codazzi. *Editor:* Pablo Mari. *Music:* Atilio Stampone. *Production Designer:* Maria Julia Bertotto. *Running Time:* 90 minutes. *MPAA Rating:* Not Rated.

CAST: Raul Julia (Ricardo); Valeria Lynch (Elena); Rubén Juárez (Antonio).

LOS ANGELES TIMES, 3/10/89, Calendar/p. 6, Michael Wilmington

Carnality on the dance floor is often incarnated, in the movies at least, by the tango. Rudolph Valentino cracking his whip; lovely Dominique Sanda whirling Stefania Sandrelli in a torrid clinch.... That's how we visualize the tango, usually under chandeliers ablaze above a tiled floor, in a night pulsing with tropical winds and sexual heat.

But, in "Tango Bar," a movie that's both history and celebration of the tango, the film makers play the dances and songs lightly. There's an affectionately jokey quality, a wink behind the strut. Director Marcos Zurinaga and his smashing choreographers, emcee (Raul Julia), singers (Valeria Lynch, Ruben Juarez) and dancers (including Nelida y Nelson of "Tango Argentino") approach "Tango Bar" like a romp. They're experts who are going to kid all the silly American or European perversions of the dance, while showing us—slyly, knowingly—the real stuff.

The movie is staged as a double reminiscence, professional and personal, by three longtime friends and cabaret artists who form a crackling tango triangle before Argentina's post-Peron military takeover separates them. Now, 10 years later, they meet again, in a reunion fraught with doubts and tensions: Raul Julia as Ricardo, the pianist-composer; pop star Valeria Lynch as the much-desired Elena, and Rubén Juárez as suave *bandoneon*-squeezer Antonio, the guy who fled the Fascists and left his best friend with his girl.

This story is nothing much, "Holiday Inn" gone Latin, and, until the closing note of tango solidarity, Zurinaga doesn't bring out very many political undercurrents. The little dramatic interludes, with the tormented trio staring at each other somberly, meaningfully, are a drag on the action.

But if the dramatic tableaux are static, the cabaret show is mostly a delight. On a strict naturalistic level, there's something overscaled and inexplicable about it, like Busby Berkeley Broadway numbers in "Footlight Parade." Here, on an even tinier stage, a dot of a platform in a minuscule nightclub, Ricardo or Antonio describe some tango epoch or historical tidbit, and suddenly a dozen dancers appear on a vast set—a bordello or grand ballroom, dripping with decor—only to explode to the habanera-like rhythms and vanish. Is it a reverie? Some mystical vision?

There are also the archival clips (an unseen 16-millimeter projector in back?) showing everything from Julia and Teri Garr's number in "One from the Heart" to a determined, puffy tango between Peter Ustinov and Angela Lansbury to one sequence that softly satirizes the American's love of "La Cumparsita"—with Fred and Wilma Flintstone, Valentino, Chaplin, Laurel and Hardy and Gene Kelly all taking a whack at it.

None of it matters, as long as we're amused. And Lynch has a scarringly passionate voice, while Julia and Juárez, as the narrators, work with the seamless near-telepathy of a team like Hope and Crosby. They have the gently cutthroat one-up-manship down cold, slaying each other with an arched eyebrow, a roguish smirk.

The dances are ravishing and so is much of the original score by Atilio Stampone. Set in this bed of voluptuous self-kidding wit, they're amusing, too; they have to be, because "Tango Bar" (Times-rated: Family) is utterly dependent on its musical numbers. The serious thread is snarled and draggy; the logistics of the show are preposterous, but the dances redeem everything. The sinuous Spanish rhythms, echoes of Africa, whispers of the Argentine ghettoes, the swagger and hauteur, the dips, the bends, the sudden almost delirious swoops.... As long as these tango men and ladies have us in their grip, it's more than enough.

NEW YORK POST, 1/27/89, p. 29, Jami Bernard

This is the sort of movie that probably couldn't have been done around any other dance. Can you imagine sitting through the history, politics and social ramifications of the box-step? But even with the sexy tango as its subject, "Tango Bar" is not very light on its feet.

The setting of this Argentine movie, starring Raul Julia, is a nighclub in Buenos Aires, home of a long-running show—a sort of South American equivalent of "The Fantastiks"—which teaches the history of tango and dispenses chestnuts like, "The tango is a secret danced by two." Actually, this is the story of a secret danced by three: the three stars of the show who are about to be reunited after 10 years.

Ricardo (Julia) and Elena (Valeria Lynch) await the arrival of Elena's ex-husband, Antonio (Rubén Juárez), who left the country 10 years ago when the military began banning tangos. Will they all be friends again? Will Antonio hold a grudge against Ricardo for stealing his wife? Will their reunion show be as good as it was way back when?

Since these concerns can hardly pique our interest, the movie switches (with frequent, overused "wipes," a method of cutting to another scene) to extended flashbacks of the old nightclub act itself. Ricardo and Antonio dazzle their audience with a talky, folksy stage show, Ricardo playing the piano, Antonio the *bandoneon*, a lap accordion that is the signature instrument of the tango.

Their banter is punctuated with "West Side Story"-ish dance-at-the-gym scenes. Even Julia shakes a leg against a stained-glass cathedral setting, appropriate for the reverence tango is accorded. (Julia does a very respectable job, although the camera cuts away demurely from time to time.)

The footwork seems technically proficient, but these illustrative dances seem to lack some of the fire and whimsy that were evident in, say, Broadway's "Tango Argentino"—or in Fred Astaire, for that matter, footage of whom appears all too briefly during a Hollywood-tango retrospective scene.

Some of the choreographed scenes are reminiscent of the Brazilian "Opera do Malandro," and it is no surprise to find that one of the choreographers also worked on that.

The choreography is heavy on lightning-fast kicking between partners' legs; ladies and gentlemen, do not try this at home.

The main problem with "Tango Bar" is that the genial lounge act, in which the two men trade good-natured barbs and roll their eyes at the audience, is not a very extraordinary routine, and yet their movie audience howls with delight, the kind you get when relatives are packing the house. Perhaps there is a problem in the translation? The Spanish "tangero" sounds a lot more evocative than the prosaic "tango-man."

Julia, wearing black-rimmed glasses, chain-smoking, looking relaxed and alert, is his usual hammy self. The banter between the two men is often smarmy, at odds with the essentially passionate story of the tango, "that sad thought made into dance."

Lynch makes a decidedly unglamorous tango partner. Down-to-earth, tsk-tsking at the men's stage and off-stage rivalry, she nevertheless has a deep, sexy singing voice that perks things up whenever she belts out lines like "Tango is the moan of a wounded bandoneon." But she's clearly odd-man-out in the tango that's unfolding between the guys.

The framework of this movie is just too static to contain something as lively and impulsive as the tango. The box-step, maybe.

NEWSDAY, 1/27/89, Part III/p. 5, Lynn Darling

"Tango Bar" isn't much of a movie—the story of three old friends who reunite after an 11-year separation is merely a frame for a vibrant celebration of the glories of the dance. As a passionate duel between a man and a woman, the tango is a drama in itself, and it is to the intricacies and the origins of that drama that "Tango Bar" devotes itself.

The movie takes place in Buenos Aires, where Ricardo (Raul Julia) and Elena (Valeria Lynch) wait for the imminent arrival of their old comrade Antonio (Rubén Juárez). Ten years ago, the three of them had staged a popular tango revue in the old cabaret where Ricardo and Elena still work. But when Antonio left the country in protest over the military takeover of Argentina,—his lover, Elena, decided to stay with Ricardo.

That much of the plot in place, "Tango Bar" plunges unabashedly into flashback mode—long dance sequences depict the evolution of the tango from its lower-class immigrant origins while Antonio and Ricardo deliver chatty little lectures on the tango's relationship to the history and the heart of the Argentinian people.

At times, the dance is also used by both Ricardo and Antonio as a metaphor in their debate about the latter's desire to leave the country. The tango is the people's dance, an expression of the national character. Both friends think Antonio's decision is tied intimately—as the dance is— to the theme of betrayal—but Ricardo feels betrayed by his friend while Antonio feels betrayed by his country. To Ricardo, exile is selfish; to Antonio staying is suicide.

The tension between the two friends in interesting but only sporadic; most of the movie is devoted to long choreographed sequences of the tango. The dancers include members of the troupe that toured in the revue "Tango Argentino" and the dances are magnetic—the feet that whip as dangerously as knives, the backs that arch in paradigms of desire, the stylized exploration of the dangerous side of seduction.

But there's also a lot of down time in "Tango Bar": Director Marcos Zurinaga ("La Gran Fiesta") intercuts his history of the dance and its popularity throughout the world with clips of nearly every tango ever filmed, from Astaire and Rogers to Charlie Chaplin to Rudolph Valentino. He's making a point here—about how upper-class Argentinians changed their attitude toward their own cultural legacy after it had been glamorized by Hollywood—but by the time he includes the Flintstones in his cinematic survey, the whole idea has become overly cute.

Given the structure of "Tango Bar," there isn't a whole lot for the actors to do: Valeria Lynch and Rubén Juárez, both popular singers in Argentina, do what they do best, while Raul Julia, though not invested with much of a character, makes the most of a role that only rarely delves much deeper than that of genial emcee.

VILLAGE VOICE, 1/31/89, p. 62, Elliott Stein

Two years ago, Marcos Zurinaga made a promising first feature, *La Gran Fiesta*, a tight little tale of romance and intrigue set in San Juan during World War II. He's now taken a step backward with the numbingly inconsequential *Tango Bar*, made in Argentina. The plot has political pretensions, but it's actually of less substance than that of any old '40s Fox musical starring Alice Faye and Don Ameche.

Antonio (Rubén Juárez) returns to Buenos Aires after 11 years of self-imposed exile—he left when the military government started censoring tangos. With the return of democracy and uncensored tangos, he is reunited with his old buddy Ricardo (Raul Julia) and old girlfriend Elena (Valeria Lynch) in the cabaret where the three of them used to put on shows. The bulk of the film consists of Antonio and Ricardo's nostalgic chitchat on the history of the tango, a sort of illustrated lecture accompained by a few dance numbers made for *Tango Bar* (the tangos are surprisingly unerotic, the production numbers middling), interspersed with clips from older and better films featuring Carlos Gardel, Rudolph Valentino, Rogers and Astaire, and Laurel and Hardy—all of the clips shown in incorrect aspect ratios.

Julia and Juárez's witless banter on-stage is constantly intercut with closeups of extras in the cabaret audience howling with glee—this movie comes with its own built-in laugh track.

(Evidently, the leader of the claque is the movie's own producer.) But the soundtrack is not a total loss: The *bandoleon* music is tough, wiry, and well-played.

Also reviewed in:
NEW YORK TIMES, 1/27/89, p. C14, Janet Maslin
VARIETY, 5/11/88, p. 32

TANGO & CASH

A Warner Bros. release. *Executive Producer:* Peter MacDonald. *Producer:* Jon Peters and Peter Guber. *Director:* Andrei Konchalovsky. *Screenplay:* Randy Feldman. *Director of Photography:* Donald E. Thorin. *Editor:* Stuart Baird. *Music:* Harold Faltermeyer. *Music Editor:* Carlton Kaller. *Choreographer:* Jeff Hornaday. *Sound:* Charles Wilborn. *Sound Editor:* Robert R. Rutledge and Mark Stoeckinger. *Production Designer:* J. Michael Riva. *Art Director:* David Klassen and Richard Berger. *Set Designer:* Alan S. Kaye and Louis Mann. *Set Decorator:* Marvin March. *Special Effects:* Jon G. Belyeu. *Visual Effects:* Peter Kuran. *Costumes:* Bernie Pollack. *Make-up:* Gary Liddiard and Dennis Liddiard. *Stunt Coordinator:* Gary Hymes. *Running time:* 98 minutes. *MPAA Rating:* R.

CAST: Sylvester Stallone (Tango); Kurt Russell (Cash); Teri Hatcher (Kiki); Jack Palance (Yves Perret); Brion James (Courier/Requin); Geoffrey Lewis (Police Captain); James Hong (Quan); Marc Alaimo (Lopez); Phillip Tan (Gunman/Chinese Guy); Michael J. Pollard (Owen); Robert Z'Dar (Face); Lewis Arquette (Wyler); Eddie Bunker (Capt. Holmes); Leslie Morris (Hendricks); Roy Brocksmith (Federal Agent Davis); Susan Krebs (Prosecutor); David Byrd (Judge); Richard Fancy (Nolan); Jerry Martinez (Santos); Michael Jeter (Skinner); Bing Russell (Van Driver); Alphonse V. Walter (Station Cop); Peter Stensland (Kagan); Phil Rubenstein (Sokowski); Elizabeth Sung (Interpreter); Clint Howard (Slinky); Ed DeFusco, Jack Goode Jr., Geoff Vanderstock, and Larry Humberger (Federal Agents); Mark Wood (Desk Cop); Andre Rosey Brown (Cash's Cellmate); Savely Kramarov (Car Owner); Kristen Hocking (Lynn); Tamara Landry and Anna Joyner (Girls in Bar); Melissa Bremner (Dance Double); Dale Swann (Captain); John Walter Davis (Slobber); Shabba-Doo (Dancer); David Lea (Sonny); Glenn Morshower (Co-Worker); Salvador Espinoza (Weasel); Christopher Wolf (State Tropper); Larry White (Cop); Richard J. Larson, Fred Trombley, and Matt Tufo (Detectives); Martin Valinsky (Bailiff); Donald Zinn and Duane Allen (Guards); Robert David Armstrong (Club Doorman).

FILMS IN REVIEW, 5/90, p. 301, C.M. Fiorillo

Poor Sylvester Stallone. Whenever the actor strays from his best known characters, Rocky and Rambo, he misses his mark. *Tango & Cash* is an apparent attempt to blend the nontypical Stallone character (a spectacled Armani-suited Los Angeles detective), with the typical (an arms bared convict). It doesn't quite work.

Directed by Soviet born filmmaker Andrei Konchalovsky (*Runaway Train*) and produced by *Batman* super-duo Jon Peters and Peter Guber, *Tango & Cash* spares no expense when dishing up explosive action. This cop-buddy action picture even tosses a few goodnatured barbs at the Stallone epics and manages a few funny moments.

Tango (Stallone), an uptown, low-tech cop, meets up with his top dog rival Cash (Russell), a downtown, high-tech cop, during a set up staged by criminal overlord Yves Perret (Jack Palance) to remove both men from the local crime fighting scene. Convicted together, the cops are shipped to a maximum security prison where they are out of Perret's hair. After being tortured by the criminals they had themselves incarcerated, the two escape. (The escape scenes are some of the film's finest.) They gleefully romp through several action packed escapades with their James Bond-like accoutrements while trying to clear their names and dispose of Perret. The spectacle of Kurt Russell in drag and both men's naked butts almost compensates for the fact that the prison electrocution and familial kidnapping sequences were both borrowed from *Lethal Weapon*. (Apparently first time screenwriter Randy Feldman is long on cliché, short on fresh ideas.)

Stallone doesn't wear suits well—he's simply too big. So it's no wonder he seems stiff and awkward when buttoned up and spouting stock prices. Stallone and *Tango & Cash* only really get rolling when he strips down to his muscle-tee and beats up bad guys. This, to his credit, he does extraordinarily well.

Russell (*Tequila Sunrise*) is excellent as Cash. He's an irreverant, likeable tough guy throughout. Russell matches Stallone punch for punch in the fight scenes and gives the bigger man a perfect partner.

Palance is implicitly evil as maze-crazed Perret. The film also stars Brion James as Perret's ponytailed, black clad henchman, Requin. Geoffrey Lewis, James Hong, Michael J. Pollard and Lewis Arquette turn in solid performances. Clint Howard (Ron's brother) is a nice surprise. Bing Russell (Kurt's dad) makes a brief appearance. Teri Hatcher, the token female, is banal.

Tango & Cash was photographed by Donald E. Thorin, designed by J. Michael Riva, and scored by Harold Faltermeyer.

With its juvenile humor detracting from its robust action, *Tango & Cash* is a pale imitation of the more colorful *Lethal Weapon*.

LOS ANGELES TIMES, 12/22/89, Calendar/p. 4, Michael Wilmington

"Tango and Cash" is a movie full of odd couples, and perhaps the oddest of all is star Sylvester Stallone and director Andrei Konchalovsky.

Stallone, who wrote "Rocky I–IV" and "Cobra"; Konchalovsky, who wrote the complex masterpieces "Andrei Roublev" and "Siberiade." Stallone, the balladeer of the underdog and impossible odds, of mano-a-mundo combat with hundreds of foes; Konchalovsky, who specializes in clashes between civilization and primitivism.

Where is their special *glasnost*?

Not in "Tango and Cash," unfortunately, even though both of them and co-star Kurt Russell try their damnedest to ram it across. However gaudy its credits, it is one more—and one of the worst written—in an endless line of clenched-up, crashed-out, buddy-buddy L.A. cop star vehicles.

Once again, dueling cops of dissimilar dispositions are thrown together in a wisecracking hellish melee that explodes into a hostage crisis involving somebody's girlfriend.

Not unexpectedly, "Tango" is obsessed with explosions. People wire cars and jam grenades down each other's pants and, at the end, there is another computerized bomb ticking away. There is a quota of phallic gags. There is a sinister drug czar (Jack Palance, cackling away) and a brutish henchman (Brion James, from "Blade Runner").

The script, by Randy Feldman, appears to have been written by a man under a death order not to include, or even to suggest, an original notion. Feldman begins with a Superman Odd Couple: the two heaviest LAPD narc cops, who have oddly never met, thrown together when they're framed.

Feldman doesn't waste time placing these two in tell-tale environments. They're introduced to us by their wardrobes. Stallone as Tango favors elegant Armani suits; blue-jeaned Russell as Cash is the guy who's called "funky." Nor does the writer fool around with ripening tensions. He just wheels his stars up like a couple of howitzers and has them start blasting wisecracks at each other. *Wise* cracks is a misnomer.

Konchalovsky once offered this excellent critical criteria. Good movies, he said, are "unpredictable but logical." The mediocre are "predictable and logical." The bad are "predictable but illogical." Other than the chance to work with Stallone and Russell, or to do a few more prison sequences in the "Runaway Train" vein, it's hard to guess what attracted him to "Tango and Cash," a predictable, illogical movie if there ever was one.

The director plays it bright and hard, hurling the incongruities right at us. But it's not entirely his fault. Executive producer Peter MacDonald ("Rambo III") did the action sequences, and Albert Magnoli ("Purple Rain") mopped up and reshot several scenes, including the absurd opener where Tango stops a gasoline truck full of drugs by standing in front of it and firing his gun.

Freed from the commemorative coin-style posturings of his recent roles, Stallone gives a quick, lively, likable performance. He plays Tango as a slightly fey dandy, steps on his cues, flirts with the camera. He seems more open, jocular, self-amused. And Russell, brilliant in recent films like "Tequila Sunrise," is a good foil here.

But "Tango and Cash" (rated R, for violence, nudity and language) is a waste of talent and energy on all levels: unworthy to Konchalovsky, unworthy also of Stallone, Russell and every superior technical credit on the film.

MONTHLY FILM BULLETIN, 5/90, p. 143, Kim Newman

Los Angeles. Well-dressed, up-market cop Ray Tango and sloppy, down-market cop Gabe Cash have been waging separate wars on the local crimelords, and have seriously inconvenienced international mob boss Yves Perret. Rather than have the cops murdered, Perret forms a plan to humiliate them. Requin, Perret's English henchman, lures Tango and Cash individually to a warehouse, where they find a dead FBI agent hooked up to a tape recorder. Caught red-handed, the two cops are implicated by a doctored tape-recording in the murder, and convinced by their crooked lawyers to plea-bargain for a minimum security sentence, whereupon they find themselves sent to a hell-hole prison full of their old enemies. Perret and Requin bribe their way into the prison to enjoy the spectacle of Tango and Cash being tortured. Cash makes an escape attempt, which has been set up to get him killed, but Tango helps him out and, during a chase, the pair manage to get out of the prison. Back on the streets, the cops terrorise the crooked FBI agent and wiretapper who helped set them up, and track down Requin, who reveals that Perret is behind the scheme against them. Meanwhile, Cash has met Tango's sister Kiki and they have, against her brother's wishes, started a relationship. Borrowing a state-of-the-art police vehicle from inventor Owen, Tango and Cash launch a two-man assault on Perret's high-tech headquarters. Perret has meanwhile had Kiki kidnapped, and uses her to try to hold off the cops. However, Tango and Cash manage to kill the villain and save the girl before the whole facility explodes. Tango and Cash are restored to the force.

Returning to prison so soon after *Lock-Up*, Sylvester Stallone—here sharing centre screen with fellow macho man Kurt Russell—attempts a change of pace by foregoing the blue-collar machismo of his usual screen persona for a sharp suit, some rimless glasses, and a spectacular mix of cop action and comedy. The comic-bookishness of the enterprise is revealed by Jack Palance's recreation of his *Batman* performance as the fantastical master villain who loiters in his highstyle headquarters, and has usefully installed a self-destruct system which provides some last-minute suspense and a satisfying explosion, while Michael J. Pollard does a goofy American retake on the Q character from the Bond movies. The whole thing is constructed as a sequence of serial-style stunts and escapes, with the location changing every twenty minutes and new pieces of hardware (like the heavily armoured police vehicle, more suited for all-out war than community policing) brought on for each new set of explosions. Stallone and Russell play it like Hope and Crosby, constantly squabbling, jockeying for position, and exchanging macho boasts (one prison-shower scene finds them comparing the size of their genitals), and yet falling more or less in love with one another during their breathless adventure.

Stallone's style-conscious yuppie cop is obviously a façade for his usual bare-chested super-hero, while Russell replays the crumpled, cynical character he has perfected for John Carpenter (venturing into drag for one failed comic sequence). There is a vacuum at the centre of the film because neither star is really able to play off the other as required, while Andrei Konchalovsky, slotting more than ever into the American commercial mainstream, is patently less comfortable with the comedy than the action. But if *Tango & Cash* remains an enjoyable thug entertainment, it has more to do with the supporting cast and the second unit than the principals. Geoffrey Lewis (curiously unbilled) is a friendly presence as the regulation police captain who will bend the rules for his favourite sons but complains while doing so, and Palance's evil associates include such welcome stalwarts as Brion James, here given an outrageous cockney accent ("I don't want to be killed by this limey immigrant jerk-off", complains Cash, "I want to be killed by an *American*") and a red ponytail, the insidious James Hong from *Big Touble in Little China*, and granite-jawed monolith Robert Z'Dar from *Maniac Cop*.

With such a solid array of human fiends, the film can afford to get a little sadistic in its action, as Z'Dar is electrocuted during a rainstorm by falling into a generator while the heroes are making a genuinely thrilling break from prison, and Hong, after refusing to be intimidated by being dangled off a tall building, finally cracks when—in a variation on the *Lethal Weapon* "psycho cop" routine—Tango tapes a hand grenade to his mouth. Konchalovsky contributes a sometimes apt dark visual style, but one gets the feeling that all the car-crashing, villain-battering and building exploding sequences were handled by second unit director/executive producer Peter MacDonald, who has filled in on the action for *Batman* and *Rambo: First Blood, Part 2*, and also been allowed to direct all of *Rambo III*. In this connection, it is worth noticing that the film's biggest wink at the audience comes when an onlooker accuses Tango of thinking that he is Rambo, whereupon Stallone grins and spits, "Rambo is a pussy".

NEW YORK POST, 12/22/89, p. 31, Jami Bernard

"Tango & Cash" is Sylvester Stallone's latest and most desperate bid to lighten up his image. As Tango, an intellectual but gutsy L.A. cop, Stallone wears fancy suits and eyeglasses from the

Rob Lowe-Judd Nelson school of how to look smart through optometry. He also plays the stock market. In this buddy action movie, Stallone is "the smart one." The script is peppered with insults about his Rambo career and his lack of diction.

This effort to clean him up is somewhat like hiding an embarrassing uncle under a lampshade, and yet it is not totally a waste. Although Tango's dabbling in the stock market is not to be confused with character development, and he still uses a machine gun when clearing the throat will do, this is a kinder, gentler Stallone, pleasing to the eye in his GQ suits (and in one scene, in the buff), delivering wisecracks with less stiffness than Schwarzenegger if less technique than his partner, Cash, played by Kurt Russell.

There is something here to play with, but unfortunately, "Tango & Cash" botches it like a bad bank job. This is the last production for Warners by the hot-shot producing team of Guber and Peters; maybe Columbia would have paid these guys a billion or two less had they only known.

And it was directed, for the most part—he evidently walked out at some midway point—by Andrei Konchalovsky, who is more of a thinker than is required by this typical story of two cops with differing methods (see "Lethal Weapon" for instructions). Tango & Cash are framed for murder and sent to a correctional facility totally peopled by criminals they personally put away during their days on the force. They escape in order to track down the evil crimelord (Jack Palance) who did them in. In the process, they learn to like each other.

OK, we've seen this sort of thing 100 times. What makes it work at least on some level is that Stallone and Russell are an amiable team, sauntering through this as if they're at a banquet in their honor. Cash does his Rambo impression and Tango needles his partner about his hotheadedness (remember, Stallone is "the smart one").

Granted that you can possibly make a different kind of action hero our of Stallone, you still can't make a silk purse out of a bad script. Screenwriter Randy Feldman, thinking he is writing for Tracy and Hepburn, heaps on the repartee in scattershot style, hoping something in it will be funny. Some of it is. The rest is distractingly pedestrian, banalities passing for wit, full of the usual homophobia jokes to convince action fans that their heroes aren't gay (while nude together in the prison shower, they make the usual stupid cracks about reaching for the soap).

Plus, the villain is all snarl and no essence. His high-tech bank of video monitors and weird fetish for rodents are, as with Tango's stock market hobby, poor excuses for character development.

Ideas are stolen from other action films, particularly those of Schwarzenegger and James Bond (Michael J. Pollard plays the "Q" role). One stunt—the villains being tossed out the front window of their crashed van—is from a Jackie Chan movie.

The movie is sumptuously produced, with a brooding, atmospheric prison escape, our heroes stymied by knife-edged fan blades, sluiced tunnels, mobs of sadists, and a second-act Tarzan slide down an electrified wire. Water and electricity are the driving imageries; I suppose we're supposed to see Tango and Cash as elementally good while separate but who spark crises when mixed together.

The guy's names were chosen more for the sake of euphony than anything else. And other choices in the film, which result in ludicrous plot holes and unbelievable situations (prisoners housed in the laundry room, an LAPD research & development lab that creates super-tanks armed with cannons), are likewise chosen with little regard to sanity.

The sight of Kurt Russell in drag is not as vomitatious as you'd think, so you see? "Tango & Cash" is not all bad. Just mostly bad.

NEWSDAY, 12/22/89, Part III/p. 3, Mike McGrady

"Tango & Cash," new entry in the Buddy-Action-Adventure-Drama (B.A.A.D.) genre, is noteworthy in that it is intended as a means of introducing a brand-new Sylvester Stallone to the world.

Perhaps you've noticed the new Stallone in the ads—the layered hair, the narrow Armani suit, the designer necktie, the mod spectacles. And wait, there's more. This new Stallone is subdued, something of an intellectual, a police officer heavily in stocks and bonds. Here's the character of Tango as described by the actor himself: "He plots his course with a great deal of deliberation. He's not afraid to use intelligence."

So I'm sitting in the darkened theater, waiting for the arrival of this new refined and intelligent Stallone, and my first vision of him is racing after a wildly careening oil truck down a desert highway. Just like the Stallone of yore, the less intelligent and less refined Stallone, he passes the truck on the shoulder, swerves to a screeching halt, jumps out of his car and grabs his pistol.

The new Stallone, again not unlike the old model, ejects the cartridges from his gun and slaps in a special clip of bullets that appear to be small-sized cannonballs. Posed heroically in front of his car, awaiting the arrival of the speeding truck, he begins firing. The truck driver is forced to slam on his air brakes and, as the huge truck freezes in mid-highway, both he and his passenger crash out through the windshield, landing crumpled and dusty at the new Stallone's well-polished Guccis.

A local cop, arriving seconds later, upset by all this violence on his beat, asks Stallone who-the-expletive he thinks he is and a second cop sneers, "He thinks he's Rambo!"

My thought exactly! Despite the alterations in coiffure and tailoring, despite the addition of a few additional lines of dialogue, I see "Tango & Cash" as proof positive that you may take the boy out of Rambo, but you may never take Rambo out of the boy.

"Tango & Cash" is not just another B.A.A.D. movie, it is a B.A.A.D. movie of such purity that it almost qualifies as a classic of the genre. Which is another way of noting the following. The two cop buddies (Stallone and Kurt Russell) are opposites—fashion-plate vs. slob—an odd couple handy with dukes, guns, various forms of violence. These opposites-who-attract never converse when they can wisecrack. (Typical sample: As the truck they're riding bursts into flame, Buddy Stallone yells: "We're on fire!" Buddy Russell responds: "Yeah, we're cookin' now!")

Moreover, the chief villain has a foreign name, Yves Perrett (Jack Palance), a business in drugs and some repulsive personal habits. Women are strictly afterthoughts, usually topless afterthoughts. And, of course, the dramatic structure consists entirely of a series of explosions.

Surprises? The only surprise is the listing of Andrei Konchalovsky as director. A Russian expatriate credited with such serious efforts as "Runaway Train" and "Maria's Lovers," Konchalovsky has had no known prior association with a B.A.A.D. movie. What's a talent like that doing in a joint like this? One possible answer is: very little. Second-unit director Peter MacDonald, director of "Rambo III," is here credited with responsibility for "the action scenes." By my calculation, therefore, it's quite possible Konchalovsky directed no more than six or seven minutes of the finished movie.

Also reviewed in:
NEW YORK TIMES, 12/22/89, p. C16, Janet Maslin
VARIETY, 12/27/89, p. 10
WASHINGTON POST, 12/22/89, p. D1, Rita Kempley

TAP

A Tri-Star Pictures release. *Executive Producer:* Francine Saperstein. *Producer:* Gary Adelson and Richard Vane. *Director:* Nick Castle. *Screenplay:* Nick Castle. *Director of Photography:* David Gribble. *Editor:* Patrick Kennedy. *Music:* James Newton Howard. *Music Editor:* Curt Sobel. *Choreographer:* Henry LeTang and (improvography) Gregory Hines. *Sound:* Stephan Von Hase. *Sound Editor:* David Stone. *Production Designer:* Patricia Norris. *Set Decorator:* Leslie Morales. *Set Dresser:* Anthony Baldasare, Sonja Roth, James Branigan, and Frank DeCurtis. *Special Effects:* Phil Cory. *Costumes:* Patricia Norris. *Make-up:* Michelle Buhler. *Stunt Coordinator:* Greg Elam. *Running time:* 110 minutes. *MPAA Rating:* PG-13

CAST: Gregory Hines (Max); Suzzanne Douglas (Amy); Sammy Davis Jr. (Little Mo); Savion Glover (Louis); Joe Morton (Nicky); Dick Anthony Williams (Francis); Sandman Sims (Sandman); Bunny Briggs (Bunny); Steve Condos (Steve); Jimmy Slyde (Slim); Pat Rico (Spats); Arthur Duncan (Arthur); Harold Nicholas (Harold); Louis Castle (Anthony); Barbara Perry (Milly); Lloyd Kino (Party Hood); Kevin Guillaume (Piano Player); Randy Brenner (Brian); Joel Weiss (Limo Driver).

CHRISTIAN SCIENCE MONITOR, 2/13/89, p. 10, David Sterritt

If you've been longing for the days of Fred and Ginger to make a comeback, there isn't much hope at the moment. I haven't heard of anyone who thinks ballroom dancing is about to be a hot item at the movies again.

But tap dancing is another story. There's something about it that seems right for today, and it keeps popping up in pictures like "White Nights" and "The Cotton Club." Maybe it's back because tap is thought of as a masculine, almost macho form of dancing, suitable for a time when films are dominated mostly by male actors. Whatever the cause, tap is the heart and soul of one of the better movies to arrive in this generally poor season.

It's called "Tap," and its story is pure Hollywood. Our hero is a guy named Max, who has a number of different talents. One is for dancing, and another is for crime: He's a second-story man whose specialty is breaking and entering tall buildings.

Unfortunately, his knack for burglary isn't quite flawless: When we meet him, he's in the slammer. But some thoughtful person has slipped his tap shoes through the bars and put a wooden surface on the floor of his cell, so he's tapping away in jail before the opening credits have ended. Soon he's back in society again, and, true to an ancient Hollywood tradition, he has to choose between two lives—making it big as a dancer or joining his old gang and returning to the easy money (and high risks) of crime. He doesn't decide until the climax of the story, and you can probably guess which choice he makes. Hint: There's an honest girlfriend in the story, who keeps saying things like, "Dancing is your life! You can make it if you *try!*"

Yes, it's pretty corny. And the other characters are even cornier. There's an old hoofer, for instance, whose doctor says to take it easy, but he just can't help dancing. (He's played by—who else?—Sammy Davis, Jr.) And he's surrounded by a whole roomful of *other* old hoofers, each more crusty than the last. We've seen people like them in a million old movies- -not to mention the girlfriend, and the sleazy Broadway producer, and Max's crooked companions.

If you get into the spirit of "Tap," though, you'll greet these characters not as tired stereotypes but as old Hollywood pals. They seem mighty old-fashioned nowadays, but they're still good for a heart-warming moment or two. I don't mean to recommend "Tap" very strongly. It really is predictable, and some of its scenes are nothing but clichés. Some moviegoers also won't like the sex angle, which gets more steamy than old-time Hollywood would have allowed.

Gregory Hines has a marvelous talent for acting and tapping, and the supporting cast has lots of energy and charm. It's hard to resist Mr. Davis, or Suzzanne Douglas as the girlfriend, or Joe Morton as the meanest crook, or Sandman Sims and Bunny Briggs as dancers like themselves.

"Tap" was directed by Nick Castle, whose father used to dream up dance routines for Fred Astaire and Gene Kelly. He's not a wizard of the screen, but he knows how to flesh out a time-tested plot with flying feet and unabashed emotions.

LOS ANGELES TIMES, 2/10/89, Calendar/p. 1, Michael Wilmington

In the dance routines of "Tap," Gregory Hines has a look of lazily ecstatic glee that's almost irresistible. His every move and gesture seems to sing out: "Ain't this a kick?"

When Hines breaks out into a crisp fusillade of taps, metal heels and toe clicking and ticking out the time patterns on the floor, it's not just virtuosity, it's *casual* virtuosity—seemingly beyond trying, beyond effort. Playing a rebellious hothead torn between the worlds of crime and show business, Hines is sensational.

Whether he's bathed in the metallic blues of the opening jailhouse jive shots or the fiery reds and shimmering blacks of the stylized New York streets (lit MTV-style by Australian cinematographer David Gribble), Hines gives "Tap's" central character, Max Washington, a smoky, simmering self-confidence.

He's a hoofing Lochinvar pinned in an obvious plot. On the one side, there are his hoodlum friends outside: gangsters who want his second-story talents, including a trigger-crazy psycho (Joe Morton) slathering for a fight. On the other: eight sweet old hoofers, led by the obviously dying Little Mo (Sammy Davis Jr.) plus a ready-made wife and child (Suzzanne Douglas and Savion Glover), all of whom want him to put on his legendary tapdancing dad's shoes and re-create the legend.

It's an essentially corny role: a Hoofer Without a Cause. But Hines is a joy to watch, anyway. And so are all his fellow tapsters, from 63-year-old Sammy Davis Jr., as a sort of Walter Brennan of the dance floor, to the defiantly sexy Douglas to 14-year-old Glover (who starred in "The Tap Dance Kid" on Broadway) to a septet of spectacular sexagenarian hoofers who come together with Davis and Hines for an "impromptu" tap battle, giving the movie its highest moment.

The scene is a paean to professionalism and community—and old age and friendship as well. Supposedly the battle is a cutting session, but the dancers—Sandman Sims, Bunny Briggs, Steve Condos (the one white club member), Jimmy Slyde, Pat Rico, Arthur Duncan and Harold

Nicholas (of the Nicholas Brothers)—turn it into a celebration. You feel that, underneath, they're all rooting for one another. And so are we.

"Tap" was obviously conceived as a tribute to the whole mystique and tradition of tap dancing. Like his dad, Max is a dancing natural. He can translate the rhythms of the city around him into steps; he's wired to the city's heartbeat. But the script is constructed in unabashed movie-movie form. It's another heavily archetypal story about stubborn oldsters trying to pass the torch to a somewhat reluctant youngster, a staple plot of Westerns and Army movies in the '40s and '50s. Also, in a way, it's a riff on Coppola's 1984 "The Cotton Club": updating it and combining the old Hines and Richard Gere roles into a single character.

The writer-director, Nick Castle, is son of the Nick Castle who worked as a movie choreographer with, among others, Fred Astaire, Gene Kelly and Bill (Bojangles) Robinson. Perhaps inevitably, Castle Jr. presents tap dancing as a vanishing but precious art form, and tries to show Max as the prodigal son-carrier of that tradition, a nascent super talent who's rejected his heritage but has the feet and soul to bring it back. Unfortunately, "Taps's" climactic fusion of tradition and modernity—hooking Max's shoes up to a synthesizer and amp, having him tap along with a rock group—doesn't click.

But Castle, who showed both an essentially sweet temperament and a sensitivity to color and mood in children's movies like "The Last Starfighter" and "The Boy Who Could Fly," seems really intoxicated by the possibilities here. And, because the film delivers so well in the musical numbers—a touching rooftop Fred-and-Ginger number by Hines and Douglas, a rousing MTV style dancin'-in-the-streets routine—perhaps we can forgive the sentimentality, the obviousness, the lapses in logic. (Many of the best Golden Age musicals have them too.) "Tap" is a movie that tries to put an old-fashioned soul under a glistening, taut modern skin.

Hines has perhaps been limited by roles that made him too sweet and ingratiating, that played up his gentle, moon-eyed face. Here, Max Washington is a divided character, a sexy rogue, a bad-good guy. There's an edge of violence to his scenes and, perhaps, because Hines' features are never threatening in repose, the insolence gives his acting and dancing a liberating snap, ease and tigerish force. You can almost feel his delight to be there.

Maybe Sammy Davis Jr. should have let a little meanness or bitterness creep in too. Perhaps the most gifted movie musical star of the late '50s and '60s, Davis, excepting "Porgy and Bess," never really got the right film vehicles or chances. So, you'd like to see more dancing between him and Hines; it's the major frustration of the film.

But if Davis never really got his moment, Gregory Hines, here and now, gets his. Playing in "Tap," (MPAA rated PG-13 for suggestions of sex and violence, language), he has the look of a performer who's seized that moment, caught the beat, found his time. There's a deftness, a cocky swagger, almost a glow around him. When the spotlight pours down, and his feet begin to fly, he has the vibrant, blessed aura of a dancing man on a roll, alive in the rhythms and talking with his toes.

MONTHLY FILM BULLETIN, 7/89, p. 215, Tom Milne

Max Washington, son of a celebrated tap dancer who ended his days in obscurity as fashions changed and demand dwindled, became disillusioned about his own prospects and turned to crime. Now, just out of jail, he looks up his former girlfriend Amy, a tap dancer like her father Little Mo, and her teenage son Louis. Though Amy is sceptical, especially when Max responds to a summons from Francis, his former underworld sponsor, Little Mo and Louis delightedly assume he intends to dance again. Tricked by Little Mo into a "challenge", Max demonstrates— after his father's ageing friends go through their paces—that he has lost none of his skill. Sheepishly admitting that he took up dancing again in his cell, Max remains non-committal when Little Mo enthuses over his future as a dancer, but is pleased when Amy lands him a job in the chorus of a Broadway tap-dancing show. But when Amy further persuades the producer to audition him for a solo spot and Max improvises a routine, explaining that the show's nostalgic choreography is "bullshit", he is fired. He agrees to execute a burglary planned by Francis—an upper-storey jewel robbery tailored to his athletic skills—but suffers a change of heart, replaces the loot, and rejoins the delighted Amy, Louis and Little Mo to announce his return to the professional fold. His début, in a disco whose owner has devised electronic amplifiers for his taps so that he can be heard over the electronic rock beat, is a huge success with the younger generation.

Tap opens with a touch of genuine electricity that flatters to deceive: a silhouette, black on black in the confines of a darkened cell in the still of the night, is gradually galvanised by a dripping faucet into an escalating tap routine as expressive of frustration and despair as any chain-gang blues. Not that the rest of the film isn't enjoyable. Gregory Hines, clearly having a ball and demonstrating conclusively that he has the ability and the charisma to be another Astaire or Kelly, strikes gold every time he puts tap to ground. Sandman Sims, Bunny Briggs and other old-timers do their stuff in a challenge (a staple in every documentary about tap dancing, but invariably irresistible). And there is a very personable little routine from teenage Savion Glover, "The Tap Dance Kid."

The film itself, unfortunately, leaves much to be desired. The dog-eared script, shopworn even in those 30s days when it seemed that bright young prospects were always being blighted by the lure of quick millions in the underworld or the boxing ring, carries so little conviction that it has to be pumped up with fraudulent threats of disaster (Little Mo has a heart condition; Francis has a trigger-happy associate who resents Max) which eventually wither away from disuse. This would have mattered less had the film not also been tempted (like all those Hollywood movies about "real" jazz that ended up in Carnegie Hall) to improve on the art form it professes to revere. With one sequence modelled on the street dance in *Fame*, and the finale doing its best to present Max Washington as John Travolta in *Saturday Night Fever*, it is clear that the film-makers were more concerned with profitable fashions than with honourable traditions. Gregory Hines nevertheless survives, triumphantly, and his contribution remains worth the price of anybody's admission.

NEW YORK, 2/27/89, p. 143, David Denby

Some of the dancing in *Tap* is above praise, but all of the story is beneath contempt. The movie peaks early, when some great old masters of the lost art of tap do their stuff. See it for that and for some of Gregory Hines's heavy-footed but powerful moves.

NEW YORK POST, 2/10/89, p. 21, Jami Bernard

There is a running gag in "Tap," a moralistic romance about a hoofer torn between the glamor of crime and his love for tapping, in which Gregory Hines is chided about showing a lazy left side in his dancing. And that's the trouble with "Tap" itself—a lazy left side that throws this almost-wonderful movie off balance. What a pity.

Tap-dancing is a thrill to watch—it's hypnotizing, infectious and somewhat inaccessible. Good tap dancers are like members of a secret society in which the steps have been passed down through generations. You can't pick up this kind of stuff at the Learning Annex.

"Tap" preserves that reverence for the art, particularly in its casting of a slew of tap legends who just about steal the picture from underfoot during a marvelous early scene in which the oldsters throw down the trappings of their age (playing cards, watering cans) and take on a reluctant Hines in a gleeful tap "challenge."

This all-too-brief scene is a sort of tap time capsule, as Harold Nicholas (of the Nicholas Brothers), Jimmy Slyde, Sandman Sims and others—why, even Sammy Davis Jr.—each take a rat-a-tat turn around a seedy Times Square studio, evidently the last bastion on earth of pure tap.

If only there were more scenes like the Challenge. The other big-bang tap scenes are of the more typical crowd-pleasing fare, such as the "Fame"-like scene in which Hines and the patrons of a nightclub spill out onto a Times Square construction site, tapping their little hearts out to the sounds and rhythms of the city.

A scene like that is to movies what those time-step chorus lines are to Broadway musicals—and this is one movie that goes to great lengths to ridicule the latter. Hines, in trying out for a part in a musical, is forced to deconstruct his style for an officious director who wants the same smiley pablum his show has been dishing out to the tourists for years.

Well, now for the story, which becomes foot-tapping tedious at times. Hines plays Max Washington, son of the late *tap-o di tutti tap-o's*. Max has just gotten out of stir and is probably going to end up back in it if he pursues another jewel heist. His fancy footwork has made him "the best second-story man in the business."

Tugging at Max's conscience are the old-timers, who all live in the rooming house above that seedy tap studio that his father used to own and which is now run by Little Mo and his daughter Amy, an ex-flame of Max's.

That flame has not died. When Max walks back into Amy's studio, the sparks fly faster than if tap shoes had rubbed against deep-pile carpet. Played by film newcomer Suzanne Douglas,

Amy is all no-nonsense alacrity as she teaches tap by day and tucks in the tap legends upstairs by night; with Max, however, the memories of duets gone by melt her, and eventually they have a little Fred-&-Ginger pas de deux on the roof. Their love story—a rarity for blacks in Hollywood—is one of the best things in the movie.

If Amy has plans for Max, so does her father, Little Mo, played by a refreshingly restrained Sammy Davis Jr., *sans* gold chains. (The role does for Davis what "King of Comedy" did for Jerry Lewis.)

Little Mo sees the future of tap in Max's toes, and wants to get the guy into specially rigged "Tap-Tronics" shoes, so that Max can tap to modern music and still be heard over the speakers. All earnestness, Little Mo talks in whispers about Tap-Tronics as if he were offering Max another heist.

The Tap-Tronics gimmick doesn't do much for "Tap", the rabble-rousing finale has a hollow, thunderous sound, like a million tap dancers trapped in a drum.

Hines, with his great, liquid doe-eyes and his own easy style of dancing—as if each step has just occurred to him and required hardly any energy—is a pleasure to watch.

Someone else to watch is Savion Glover, a kid with talent to burn, who plays Amy's tapping teen-age son in search of a father figure. Glover has a deceptively loose, laconic way about him—sort of like Hines himself. Forget Tap-Tronics; here's where the real future of tap lies.

NEWSDAY. 2/10/89, Part III/p. 3, Janice Berman

The history of tap in the movies is old and honorable, but most of it reaches back into the musicals of the '40s and '50s. As a matter of fact, the most recent memorable incidence of tap on film within a narrative framework was the dazzling challenge dance shared by Gregory Hines and Mikhail Baryshnikov in the otherwise soporific "White Nights," released in 1985.

In "Tap," the challenge dance is even better.

"Challenge!" Lil' Mo (Sammy Davis Jr,) shouts gleefully. A clutch of elderly tap dancers—you saw many of them in the documentary "No Maps on My Taps"—assembles in the shabby Times Square studio. Each proceeds to outdo the other, and, collectively, these artists knock the audience's socks off.

Shim-sham, trenches, buck and wing, fast, fast, fast. It's the kind of virtuosic display that makes you forget about the triteness of the script that brings these men—Bunny Briggs, Steve Condos, Arthur Duncan, Harold Nicholas, Sandman Sims and Jimmy Slyde—to the screen. This is a movie about tap dancing, and visibly a labor of love.

I suppose we've got to at least *mention* the story.

Max Washington (Gregory Hines), a tap dancer since childhood, is out on parole after doing two years in Sing Sing for grand theft. He finds himself drawn to his old neighborhood. The suspense: Will he return to the mob, or to the tap-dance studio run by ex-girlfriend Amy (Suzzanne Douglas) and a life that's tap-happy ever after?

Amy is bitter at Max because he ran out on her and her son Louis (Savion Glover), and her dad, Lil' Mo, the surrogate father figure who taught Max every step he knows. It's Lil' Mo who believes in Max, who encourages him to return to dancing.

As Lil' Mo, Davis rates high marks for returning to his beginnings as a tap dancer—as a kid, he was one of the Will Mastin Trio—and for refraining from chewing the scenery. Here, minus his normal quotient of gold jewelry and sycophancy, he's tremendously appealing.

Sandman Sims, who was Hines' chief mentor when he was half of the Hines Brothers (brother Maurice was the other half), doesn't get to do a sand dance here, but he's wonderful as the group's curmudgeon. "The kid's a quitter!" he grumps of Max.

As Max, Hines delivers a mixture of broody intensity and sudden sunniness that makes him fun to watch; besides, he's a spectacular tap artist, heavy and yet not earth-logged, muscular, spontaneous. He's a sexy man, and he has his match in Suzzanne Douglas, who isn't much of a dancer but doesn't have to be.

The side plot—and source of more good dancing, choreographed by Henry LeTang—rises fron Lil' Mo's attempt to convince Max that there's promise in the idea of combining tap and rock. What we see and hear is the brainchild of Alfred Desio, who calls it tapnology. Hines leads the people in the club out to the street, where he gets them into the rhythm of the sounds of the city and soon sets then dancing in exhilarating fashion.

It's a better way of moving than the style that Max is forced to do when he lands a job in the chorus of a Broadway musical. Max is a hoofer. His steps are intense, weighty, spontaneous, complex. With the Broadway steps superimposed on his feet, Max looks like a pathetic chained dancing bear. The message: The soul of tap has been coopted, exploited and finally stripped away in these lightweight, sanitized and, although it's unspoken, *white* routines.

It's annoying to report that virtually every bit of dancing is shot through a haze of smoke or steam. Far from atmospheric, it's irritating to the eye and tends to fuzz the innate clarity of the tap steps.

There are other quibbles, too—a too-spicy love scene between Max and Amy, for instance. As they grab at each other, you wonder why they didn't just shut the door and let the audience fantasize.

And the script is a mass of cliches. It's well-intentioned (written by Nick Castle Jr. whose father collaborated with Gene Kelly and Fred Astaire), but what it needs is a rewrite. Ooooh, ugghhh. Talking about Max's father, another late great tapper, Lil' Mo says, "they couldn't take away his legs and his pride." He also says, "If I'm gonna die, I'm gonna die with my tap shoes on." He also says—oh, never mind.

Despite its flawed script, the central message of "Tap"—about the sheer joy of the art form—is flawless.

NEWSWEEK, 2/13/89, p. 79, David Ansen

[*Tap* was reviewed jointly with *Three Fugitives*; See Ansen's review of that film.]

VILLAGE VOICE, 2/14/89, p. 64, Amy Taubin

Although *Tap*, starring Gregory Hines, is at the opposite end of the sexual politics and production values spectrum, it's just as dependent on dance for its moments of joy. [The reference is to *Virgin Machine*.] Big family-style entertainment, *Tap* frames virtuoso turns by such legendary hoofers as Harold Nicholas (of the Nicholas Brothers), Jimmy Slyde, Sandman Sims, Steve Condos, Bunny Briggs, Pat Rico, and Arthur Duncan, and glitzy show biz numbers featuring Hines, in a sentimental moral tale conspicuously lacking in the specifics of contemporary urban life. A must-see for dancers (who, at the packed preview I attended, cheered every number as if at a live performance) and of obvious appeal to parents with young children, *Tap* clearly wants to be an inspirational story for young black audiences (and not simply because its box office depends on them). Good intentions notwithstanding, I can't imagine the 15- to 24-year-old city dweller who wouldn't shrug off, or even feel ripped off by, the film's preachy high tone.

A must cherished project of both Hines and director/writer Nick Castle, *Tap* is the story of Max Washington (Hines), son of the greatest hoofer of them all, who, turning his back on his own talent and his father's struggle, used his fleet feet to become "the best second-story man in the business." In prison, Max puts on his tap shoes again. Dancing his time away keeps him sane (although it must have had the opposite effect on his fellow inmates, forced to listen to his pounding rhythms). Once released, he takes up residence in a cheap Times Square hotel across the street from Sonny's, the three-story tap studio that once belonged to his father and is now run by Little Mo (Sammy Davis Jr.) and his daughter, Amy (Suzzanne Douglas), Max's old girlfriend. Sonny's is a kind of tap cathedral, part rooming house for the old-time purists, part dance center for young Broadway-bound gypsies. Inside, all is bathed in golden light. Outside, there is nary a crack vial or wrecking ball in sight. The conflict in *Tap* is purely Oedipal. Will Max have the courage to take up the legacy of his father, or will he succumb to the temptations offered by his former gangster employer? Little Mo has a fantasy about the future of tap, and he needs his surrogate son Max to dance it into reality. Mo wants to couple tap with funk music through the use of electronic shoes. (In the grand finale the film uses a digital version of Alfred Desio's "Tap-Tronics" system.)

The numerous father/son relationships behind the making of *Tap* are far more fascinating than the watered-down narrative on the screen. Hines started tapping at the Apollo when he was three, and his early role models were Sandman Sims and Sammy Davis Jr. *Tap* choreographer Henry LeTang was Hine's first dance teacher, while director/writer Castle's father, Nick Sr., collaborated with Fred Astaire and Gene Kelly.

The dancing more than justifies the film, although it's disappointing that the old-time greats take their brief solos early on and then fade into the background. As proven by the recent short-lived *Off Limits*, Hines is as compelling a screen actor as he is idiosyncratic a dancer. He loves playing with his own physical tensions. Expert at the controlled slow build, he can also spring up tight-coiled out of seemingly total relaxation. In the press notes for *Tap*, Hines explains he didn't want to end the film on the note that everthing is great and that tap is the next big thing. "Realistically," he says, "you still can't make a living as a tap dancer." Would that so basic an ambiguity had found its way into the movie.

Also reviewed in:
NEW REPUBLIC, 3/20/89, p. 32, Stanley Kauffmann
NEW YORK TIMES, 2/10/89, p. C17, Vincent Canby
VARIETY, 2/8–14/89, p. 18
WASHINGTON POST, 2/10/89. p. D7, Hal Hinson

TAPEHEADS

An Avenue Pictures release of an NBC Productions and Pacific Arts presentation of a Peter McCarthy/Front Films production. *Executive Producer:* Michael Nesmith. *Producer:* Peter McCarthy. *Director:* Bill Fishman. *Screenplay:* Bill Fishman and Peter McCarthy. *Story:* Bill Fishman, Peter McCarthy, Jim Herzfeld, and Ryan Rowe. *Director of Photography:* Bojan Bazeli. *Editor:* Mondo Jenkins. *Music:* Fishbone. *Sound:* John Pritchett. *Production Designer:* Catherine Hardwicke. *Art Director:* Don Diers. *Costumes:* Elizabeth McBride. *Running Time:* 93 minutes. *MPAA Rating:* R.

CAST: John Cusack (Ivan Alekseyev); Tim Robbins (Josh Tager); Mary Crosby (Samantha Gregory); Connie Stevens (June Tager); Clu Gulager (Norman Mart); Katy Boyer (Belinda Mart); Jessica Walter/ (Kay Mart); Sam Moore (Billy Diamond); Junior Walker (Lester Diamond); King Cotton (Roscoe); Doug McClure (Sidney Tager); Lyle Alzado (Thor Alekseyev); Don Cornelius (Mo Fuzz).

LOS ANGELES TIMES, 10/21/88, Calendar/p. 10, Chris Willman

As the gleefully funny "Tapeheads" begins, an idealistic John Cusack watches a rock music video with narrowed eyes. It's parading disembodied female flesh like so many chicken wings in a commercial, and its crassness disgusts him. "Inane, mind-rot, stench, Pablum," he stammers.

"You could do that!" his more management-minded partner, Josh, says instantly. It sets in motion a cynical, let's-put-on-a- show-biz odyssey that has would-be director Josh (Tim Robbins) and manager Ivan (Cusack) launching themselves into the rock-video business. Mickey, Judy and a barn it ain't.

It is very 1988. The self-proclaimed Video Aces' manifesto is, "Do what you gotta do so you can do what you wanna do." And though "Tapeheads" is chock full of choice satire of pop culture, their yuppie-sounding motto is not one of the targets of the movie's mockery. Instead, a rather jaded, practical message underlies all the inspired lunacy here: Selling out can buy you the chance to achieve your dreams.

Lest this wisecrack-filled doozy of a farce sound more sophisticated than it is, it should be pointed out that "Tapeheads" isn't all that distantly removed from the teen-sex-comedy genre, and makes its sharp points on commercialism and empty imagery through giddily sophomoric gags, not polite, subtle asides. Director Bill Fishman (who made some of MTV's wittiest clips before moving to this assured feature debut) is not timid about taking a tasteless look at a tasteless culture.

The videos-within-the-film are predictably crass, and more watchable than anything on the tube now. The best one comes in the guise of a fast-food commercial, as Josh and Ivan hilariously turn hickish, silver-haired chicken proprietor Roscoe (King Cotton) into a beat-crazed rap master.

The plot thickens to include a corrupt senator (Clu Gulager) searching for a highly damaging videotape, and a sexpot rock photographer (Mary Crosby) who has it. But even as the bullets and innuendoes fly, Josh and Ivan are more concerned with redeeming themselves by reviving the careers of their childhood heroes, the Swanky Modes (played as a Sam & Dave-style duo by soul legends Sam Moore and Junior Walker).

It's to the credit of Fishman and producer/co-writer Peter McCarthy that they keep terminal wiseacres Ivan and Josh as likable as they are profane. (The movie's R rating was earned.) In a banal way, fast-talking impresario Cusack and the more disheveled Robbins neatly symbolize the symbiotic relationship of commerce and art. But more importantly, they're credible as white baby-boomers who had their middle-class destinies completely usurped during their Wonder years by the divine appearance of black acts like the Swanky Modes. "Tapeheads" has almost as much soul as it does good, cheap laughs.

NEW YORK POST, 3/17/89, p.23, Jami Bernard

It is only fitting that "Tapeheads"spoofs the medium of video, because that is where it will be showing up soon enough—may it do better there.

Video entrepreneur Michael Nesmith—yeah, the one with the hat from The Monkees—has been known to finance and encourage offbeat music and video projects, lately with the backing of his Pacific Arts video company. Nesmith financed Alex Cox's "Repo Man" and created the prototype for the music-clip TV station that eventually became MTV.

"Tapeheads" probably sounded like a good idea on paper, something right up Nesmith's alley. It is a spoof of the music video business—of the clips themselves and of the people who make them. Its "in" jokes include casting various misic personalities in bit parts (Stiv Bator, Jello Biafra, Ted Nugent, Nesmith himself, to name a few), and it has a lively soundtrack that includes the Circle Jerks, the Ramones and Devo.

But aside from a feeling of smug self-satisfaction at spotting the famous, there's not a whole lot to hold the attention. The plot is as thin as the latest calibration of magnetic tape.

John Cusack (with an awkward-looking moustache) and Tim Robbins ("Bull Durham") are pals who start in the music-vid business on the ground floor, as filmmakers-for-hire. At first, they are forced to take whatever they can get, like videotaping a "living will," a dog seance, a fast-food rap commercial and an awful Swedish rock band.

Although they try to bring some artistry even to these endeavors—they tar and glitter the alarmed rock band and try to add some documentary pizazz to the living will—they don't get their lucky break until the plot takes a jolting turn toward what the filmmakers probably thought passed for deliriously madcap lunacy. Like meat extender, this plot lumps in misplaced videos, a political sex scandal, an untimely death, a Ninja catfight and a comeback by soul singers The Swanky Modes (disinterestedly played by Sam Moore of Sam and Dave and Junior Walker of the All Stars).

There is much about "Tapeheads" that is reminiscent of the old "Monkees" TV show: A plot that builds like a house of cards until it tumbles in one manic burst, a lightbulb popping over someone's head, cartoon-style, to signify that an idea has hatched. It's an undemanding vignette style that The Monkees stole from the old Beatles movies in the first place.

But humor needs more than form, and "Tapeheads" doesn't deliver the goods. For all its energy, the result is eye-glazingly dull. Its "messages" about form over content, "prosperity through exploitation" and "Do what you gotta do so you can do what you wanna" don't make much of an impact in a movie that revels in the self-same crimes.

Most of the characters come and go, but "Soul Train" host Don Cornelius is at least a memorable sleaze as Mo Fuzz, manipulative honcho of Fuzzball Records.

The scatter-shot vignette style comes up with one winner—a rap-music ad for a fast-food joint that serves only waffles and chicken. It's a one-note joke, and it's just like the old frog-and-peach routine by Peter Cook and Dudley Moore, but it works. The rest of the movie will have to pray for a midnight-movie cult following to keep it in theaters.

NEWSDAY, 3/17/89, Part III/p. 5, Lynn Darling

"Tapeheads" isn't long on subtley—this is the sort of movie that makes its points with a swagger stick, not a stiletto—but it's an energetic lightheaded froth of a movie that races along on its good humor and short attention span.

Like the music videos it mocks so cleverly, "Tapeheads" believes in the quick take and the fast edit, and after a while the frantic pace is as wearing as a couple of hours of MTV. But along the way there are some sharp and gleefully funny bits and pieces that send up the late '80s emphasis on style over substance and ambition over everything.

Ivan (John Cusack) and Josh (Tim Robbins) are a couple of feckless security guards who share an unfocused ambition for what constitutes the good life these days, an eternal devotion to the legendary R & B duo "The Swanky Modes," and a lifelong friendship that unites their disparate personalities into one crazed, symbiotic whole. Josh is the dreamy techno-whiz who can do seemingly anything with a video camera and a Steenbeck. Ivan is the consummate manipulator, decked out in cheap suits and pencil mustache, always looking for the perfect scam.

When the two of them team up to form the Video Aces, a music video production company, they embark on a wacked-out pilgrim's progress in which everyone, from a wily record producer (Don Cornelius) to a sharky rock journalist (Mary Crosby) seems intent on exploiting them on the way up. Along their way to serendipitous fame and fortune, they take on any job that's offered them and the results are some of the best moments of the movie, even when they're playing off old ideas.

Rap music parodies are ubiquitous in these satire starved times, but the Video Aces' TV ad for a fastfood chicken joint is a blithely successful addition to the genre. Similarly, the Aces' attempts to improve a dying man's performance while he's reading his will for the video camera is effervescent if not all that original. The movie is a cascade of moments: If you don't like the Swedish rock group getting splattered with paint while singing a Devo song, blink twice and wait for the dog seance.

Together, Cusack and Robbins infuse the movie with such youthful high spirits that the movie tumbles along around them. Cusack in particular is a source of freewheeling amoral energy, whether he's talking the Aces into a producer's office, or accidentally drinking a candle while trying to suavely seduce rock journalist Samantha Gregory.

Put together under the eye of executive producer Mike Nesmith, the former Monkee who has long been a pioneer in the art and artifice of music video, "Tapeheads" was directed by Bill Fishman, himself the director of over 30 music videos, and produced by Peter McCarthy ("Repo Man" and "Sid and Nancy").

There's a clean, hard surface to the movie's look, one that is as taut and shiny and resistant to introspection as the frenetic dreams of the industry itself. Fishman and McCarthy share co-writing credits for a screenplay that turns a sharp ear for the cliched banalities that pass for thought these days.

"Tapeheads" looks good and has one of the better soundtracks, one that celebrates every musical genre from '60's soul to heavy metal to late-breaking punk. But it's not as hip as it thinks it is. As satire, the movie doesn't have a whole lot to say—it cheerfully sends up the greed, minuscule attention span and preoccupation with fame at the expense of meaningful accomplishment that characterizes late '80s ambition. But it opts for the blatantly obvious whenever a more elusive target enters its sites. A subplot about a presidential candidate trying to recover a videotape of his kinkier sexual escapades almost disappears within its own lame joke.

Their devotion to the Swanky Modes is meant to be the Aces' saving grace in the middle of all this madness, the redemption from the temptations of a polyester success. The Modes have been the Aces' idols since they were kids; when they discover them playing in some low-rent dive, they determine to rescue them from obscurity.

While it's probably pushing it to expect a whole lot of consistent plot development in a movie this scatterbrained, it would have been nice to get a better sense of the world the Modes represent—one of integrity and devotion to the dictates of the heart—more vividly realized. As the Modes themselves, however, veteran soul singers Junior Walker and Sam Moore bring a nice laid-back nonchalance to the weirdness breaking out all around them.

VILLAGE VOICE, 3/21/89, p. 57, J. Hoberman

You'll find an assortment of eccentric artists, idiot pop stars, cameo'd hipsters, and conniving scenemakers in *Tapeheads*, Bill Fishman and Peter McCarthy's manic, amateurish send-up of the Los Angeles video world. The movie opens Friday at the Quad, not far from Mays—which would have been perfectly suited for an ancillary boutique of appropriately shopworn accessories.

Something of a *film maudit*, *Tapeheads* was shelved by De Laurentiis in 1987, released widely (and disastrously) west of the Hudson last October, then received a new lease on life two months ago with a series of successful midnight screenings at Boston's Nickelodeon III. Like *Repo Man*, which McCarthy coproduced and "presenter" Michael Nesmith bankrolled, *Tapeheads* means to be a comic evisceration of L.A.'s urban underbelly; unlike *Repo Man*, however, *Tapeheads*'s wit doesn't have much of an edge. Committedly adolescent and unrelievedly corny, the movie features smooth John Cusack and fuzzy Tim Robbins as a pair of aspiring videomakers, taping everything from sub-Abba Swedish acts and pet séances to fast-food promos and hospital-bed final testaments: "Josh, the man is dead—you're not going to get a different line reading." Mutatis mutandis, one could say the same for *Tapeheads* after half an hour.

Despite cameos by Martha Quinn and Don Cornelius and the runaway crane that invades the skull-and-flaming-tiki-ridden set of a heavy metal band fronted by Stiv Bator, the movie's most striking aspect, musically speaking, is the rampant soul-band nostalgia. (Given this, and the overall taste for '70s schlock, it's no surprise that McCarthy went on to produce *I'm Gonna Git You Sucka*.) Cusack and Robbins are forever intoning their lines in unison and executing routines cribbed from Sam and Dave, here called the Swanky Modes. The Modes are the movie's raison d'être; once they get rolling, *Tapeheads* suggests last year's *Riders of the Storm*, with Sam Moore and (substituting for Dave Prater) Junior Walker in the Dennis Hopper role. Don't take that for praise: *Tapeheads* offers the most convincing proof since Michael Dukakis that Boston College kids don't know everything.

Also reviewed in:
NEW YORK TIMES, 3/17/89, p. C16, Janet Maslin
VARIETY, 2/3/88, p. 14

TAXING WOMAN RETURNS, A

A New Yorker Films release of an Itami Productions Inc. film. *Producer:* Yasushi Tamaoki and Seigo Hosogoe. *Director:* Juzo Itami. *Screenplay (Japanese with English subtitles):* Juzo Itami. *Director of Photography:* Yonezo Maeda. *Editor:* Akira Suzuki. *Music:* Toshiyuki Honda. *Sound:* Osamu Onodera. *Production Designer:* Shuji Nakamura. *Running time:* 127 minutes. *MPAA Rating:* Not Rated.

CAST: Nobuko Miyamoto (Ryoko Itakura); Rentaro Mikuni (Teppei Onizawa); Toru Masuoka (Inspector Mishima); Masahiko Tsugawa (Assistant Chief Inspector Hanamura); Tetsuro Tanba (Chief Inspector Sadohara); Koichi Ueda (Nekota, Onizawa's Right-Hand man); Mansaku Fuwa (Shorty Masa, Nekota's Henchman); Takeya Nakamura (Dietman Urushibara); Hosei Komatsu (Dietman Saruwatari); Mihoko Shibata (Shigeko Ukeguchi, Onizawa's Mistress); Yoriko Doguchi (Nana, Onizawa's Teenage Mistress); Haruko Kato (Kinu Akaha, Holy Matriarch); Yasuo Daichi (Inspector Ijuin); Kinzo Sakura (Inspector Kaneko); Noriko Murai (Masseur Moeyo); Gentaro Ishida (Photographer Kiyohara); Mieko Yuki (Photographer's Wife); Koji Nanbara (Professor Yoneda); Izumi Hara (Old Woman at Onizawa's Temple); Ryu Chishu (Retired Monk).

CHRISTIAN SCIENCE MONITOR, 7/14/89, p. 11, David Sterritt

Juzo Itami belongs to Japan's new breed of filmmakers. He loves to make people laugh, so all his movies have been comedies. He's also an expert at appealing to people of different backgrounds and nationalities: All his early pictures have found success in the United States as well as Japan, and his new one, "A Taxing Woman's Return," seems to be following the same path.

Above all, Mr. Itami likes to poke fun—mischievous fun—at social customs and foibles. His first picture, "The Funeral," satirized the way people behave when other people die. "Tampopo" was a "noodle western" about a sort of samurai cook who gets involved in the Japanese restaurant business.

His last movie, "A Taxing Woman," aimed its comic arrows at the most tempting target of all: money. Its heroine was a tax collector, and her enemies were tax dodgers who tried to hide the profits of the sleazy businesses they ran, from "adult motels" to pinball parlors.

According to New Yorker Pictures, the American distributor of Itami films, it was so popular in Japan that it made "marusa," a once-obscure term for "tax inspection bureau," into a household word.

In the sequel to this 1987 hit, our heroine is hunting even bigger game: frauds who have wormed their way into the worlds of big business, politics, and organized crime. Her main adversary is a phony evangelist (they have them in Japan, too) who earns extra money by forcing people out of their homes so that high-priced office towers can be built on what used to be their living space.

The preacher's sins go in two directions: He pays off influential politicians, on one hand, and terrorizes helpless tenants on the other.

It's a neat racket, but not when the taxing woman gets on his trail, helped by her new yuppie assistant. Other characters include a young woman who's been given to the preacher as payment of a debt; a so-called "holy matriarch" who loves fur coats and jewelry; and a henchman named Shorty who's not long on stature or intelligence.

Like the original "Taxing Woman," the sequel is stylishly filmed and very fast-moving. Itami is an expert movie technician, and he's also an expert at eliciting lively performances from his actors.

These include his wife, Nobuko Miyamoto, who stars in all his pictures and plays the taxing woman here; and the great Ryu Chishu, a legendary actor who's best known for his starring performances in a long list of classics by Japanese director Yasujiro Ozu.

On the downside, it's an unfortunate fact that Itami's films always go on too long—even "Tampopo," his best picture, should have been trimmed a bit—so that we get tired of the fun long before it's ready to end.

"A Taxing Woman's Return" falls into this trap, and some moviegoers may find its occasional sex scenes too strong for comfort, as well.

But the film certainly has a lot of energy, and its subject—the never-ending war between the government and the greedy—is always good for a few surprises. I won't be surprised if the taxing woman has more than one sequel to spring on us in fiscal years to come.

LOS ANGELES TIMES, 7/20/89, Calendar/ p. 1, Sheila Benson

"The Japanese love scandal, don't they?" one of the persuasive Japanese villains purrs to the tabloid journalist in "A Taxing Woman's Return." "They're all peeping Toms." If you've read a single article about the wave of scandals sweeping Japan for at least the past six months, this angry, focused, funny film plays like the most lively backgrounder imaginable.

There is nothing more stimulating than a director furious about something and in complete control of his arsenal of attack. That would be Juzo Itami and his new work, a splendid film whose sense of outrage about high-level corruption in the Japanese social and political fabric fairly vibrates but in no way diminishes his film's wit or liveliness. It may make Itami the most scathing social satirist working in film today.

Itami's first "Taxing Woman" gave us a freckle-faced, utterly dedicated and fearless tax inspector, ex-housewife Ryoko Itakura (Nobuko Miyamoto, the director's engaging wife). Working against convention, she became part of a task force on the trail of small-fish tax dodgers; pinball-parlor operators and adult-motel owners trying to hang on to unreported cash.

Now Ryoko is sturdily in place in her department and a little less the central focus. She is now, in a way, the film's Miss Marple, pointing the way, uncovering the clues. Ryoko is also now sure enough of herself that when they give her a handsome young university grad assistant (Toru Masuoka), a sort of Tokyo Yalie who likes to drop references to "his school," she tells him to just spit out the name, so they can all be impressed, then get on with things.

Itami's tone is sweepingly broad but darker this time. The tax investigators' focus is Heaven's Path, a bogus religious group and its leader, Teppei Onizawa (Rentaro Mikuni). A kicky sect, its mature Holy Matriarch (Haruko Kato) has a taste for full-length Russian sable coats, and its 70-year-old Chief Elder, Onizawa, blesses his cash flock with water that has just cascaded off the naked body of a nubile acolyte and been caught in golden bowls. (That gold is pure; you might not want to bet on the acolyte.)

It is the rabidly lecherous, callous Onizawa who commands our attention, and given our introduction to his vicious side and the life history that seems written there on his face, Itami's ability to create empathy for him seems almost miraculous. Especially when he turns out to be a front for corrupt businessmen and Diet members.

As played by Mikuni, Onizawa has thick silver hair and a boxer's blocky body. His face is almost rubble now, but in his Glen-plaid suit, worn with a silk scarf of his "religion" around his neck, he is devastating.

A man with samurai command and unrivaled influence with gangsters and senators alike, Onizawa still has nightly dreams of being crushed in a gray, fortress-like granite pit. Not even the tender attentions of his devoted young mistress (Mihoko Shibata), a secretary of the cult, soothe him.

They don't quiet his insatiable lust either. Before long, he's seduced and made pregnant the 16-year-old schoolgirl Nana (Yoriko Doguchi) left in his hands by her father as payment for a debt. Then, well after we have written Onizawa off as exactly what he is, Itami shows us new facets to the man.

Nana's baby is precious to him, his connection to immortality. And she, in turn, loves him. Full of tenderness for her, he offers "to buy you your grave," literally and figuratively to offer his protection to her, lifelong. (Itami's use of the passage of the seasons here, from spring to snow on the elaborate grave sites, is especially poignant.)

And, in the film's most startling scene, as the tax officials interrogate him in a bleak room that seems too small for him, Onizawa turns on them furiously.

"We must open Tokyo as an international center," he rages. "We must build more offices. Where? Government and business will never use eminent domain. Tokyo will be bypassed by Hong Kong and Seoul. Do you want Japan to become a second-rate power? Is that what you want?"

Then, in what might be a moment out of "Raging Bull," he bloodies himself in sheer berserk rage against the office walls.

It's an extraordinary scene. It forces us to riffle wildly through what we thought we knew about this corrupt old man. Could this come from some genuine feeling of patriotism, misguided though it sounds? Is it craziness? Is it an act? Whatever it does indeed turn out to be, it is brilliant movie making and marvelous performance.

Don't be misled; the rest of the film is by no means subtle. It has the barefaced trappings of melodrama, which Itami revels in: a ruby God's eye that Sabu might have stolen in "The Thief of Bagdad"; the delivery of a supposedly real severed hand; heroines who discover secret passageways and are almost themselves discovered.

Some of Itami's signature concerns from "Tampopo" turn up again: a mix of food and sex, gluttony and death. Crabs, we're told, have feasted on a particularly luridly photographed body that has been in the water long before it is discovered by the schoolboys in the opening. Our gangsters are next seen, noisily sucking the meat from steaming crabs. (This corpse and later fleeting, appreciative moments of nudity make the film Times-rated Mature.) As he writes about circles of influence, Itami is not unaware of a larger cycle around all of us.

Almost everyone is a little more knowing than we give them credit for. Onizawa's wife indulges her fur-coat fetishes as her price for letting him bed the cult secretary. The gansters, working hand-in-hand with the bankers, have an ace in the hole when dealing with a muckraking journalist. With the tax people on their trail, Onizawa's church officials concoct a foolproof scheme to bury profits, a sort of geometric regression of donations downward, with proper receipts at every level. Onizawa himself runs up against a force more powerful than his own. And so do the honest, dogged tax investigators.

Against all this, Toshiyuki Honda's jazz score works with almost a bouncy samba beat, orchestrated at the end to weave savage laughter in with the music. It gives the film's conclusion its particularly tart bite.

With all he has had to work with in Japan, can you imagine Itami let loose on the political scene in America? Almost makes your mouth water, doesn't it?

NEW YORK POST, 6/28/89, p. 23, David Edelstein

With her dark bangs and cartoon freckles, the rumpled tax-inspector heroine of the Japanese comedy "A Taxing Woman's Return" seems hopelessly out of place amid her tall, gray-suited male colleagues. But Ryoko (Nobuko Miyamato) has a ferrety persistence. Not for her their candy-assed Japanese protocol: she's out there scaling rooftops with her bugging devices, sneaking around the enemy's lair like Nancy Drew.

The idea of a petite, middle-aged woman bringing down the corrupt bigwigs of Japanese industry and politics must seem wildly subversive in a partriarchy as formal as Japan's'—which is one reason "A Taxing Woman" (released here in 1987) was such a huge hit. (The word "marusa," once professional jargon for "tax-imspector bureau," entered the language as a result.)

But sometimes a movie will capture the public's imagination in its native land and leave a foreign audience respectfully cold; New Yorkers will trudge off to see it because a couple of influential critics say "Go!" and then politely try to ignore the fact (as they think about where to get a good meal in the Lincoln Center area) that they didn't get most of the jokes.

This might be what's happening with the films of Juzo Itami, who had a happy success here with his frisky, gastronomic comedy "Tampopo." Itami's other, more polished works—"The Funeral" and "A Taxing Woman,"which were far more beloved by his countrymen—didn't do as well with Americans. The same fate, I supect, will befall "A Taxing Woman's Return."

The sequel was made in the shadow of the Recruit Co. scandal, which recently forced the resignation of Prime Minister Noboru Takeshita. This time, Inspector Ryoko goes after bigger game than the modest tycoon of her last adventure. Where "A Taxing Woman" confined itself largely to accounting, this one has action—fight scenes, gory gangland hits. What happens is of national consequence.

The villains are members of a fundamentalist religious group with a tax-exempt status that allows it to operate without government scrutiny. Led by the hoary, magnetic Onizawa (Rentaro Mikuni), the corporation boasts a payroll that features senators and low-life gangsters. Most of its profits come from the eviction racket—at the behest of developers, it gets rid of tenants protected by "commie" rent-control.

As in "Columbo," we know from the start who the bad guys are and what they're out to protect (we see them shake down couples, menace small children); the pleasure is in watching the tax inspector inch closer to the truth. It might seem strange to root for an IRS equivalent, but in this case it's like the A-Team—protecting the little guy from the big fish when ordinary police can't or won't.

"A Taxing Woman's Return" has a gleaming surface and crisp pacing. The boisterous rock backbeat makes things seem to be moving along even when they're not; occasionally the acting rumbles majestically to life. The film has an edge—the tension between an activity as focused as bookkeeping and the grand passions it arouses. But with all these strengths, "A Taxing Woman's Return" still had me fighting off sleep. (A writer in back of me wasn't as successful; his thunderous snores nearly halted the screening.)

Itami—who has also been a popular actor, columnist and talk-show host—essentially makes comedies of manners. And it isn't exactly big news that Japanese manners don't bear much resemblance to our own. Over here, his social satire has no sting.

A bigger problem is that he has no gift for storytelling. He doodles inventively on a central theme, but his plots don't develop momentun—he's endlessly distracted. This didn't interfere with "Tampopo," where the sloppy, sketch-comedy structure added to the fun. But here his puzzling shifts and lurches throw the audience out of the film. People are likely to tune out before the picture develops a head.

That's a shame, because Mikuni's Onizawa is a fascinating titan, especially when the animal seeps through his sober, formal facade. He has a teen-age mistress (Yoriko Doguchi), and in one scene he leads her to a cemetery and shows her the grave he has pruchased for her ("I will take care of you for life"); in another, he's mesmerized by the young woman's intense flush after sex. When interrogated by the inspectors, he bashes his head against the wall until a river of blood runs down his face.

Miyamoto, who is Itami's wife (as well as the star of his four movies), does likably unpretentious work. She bugs her prissy, university-trained young partner to go into a massage parlor to gather information; she makes herself up as a battered woman and slips into the religious institute, flirting briefly with "A Taxing Woman and the Temple of Doom"; and when she approaches a vault with the evidence to nail Onizawa she breaks into a jaunty, Fred Astaire dance that's elating.

Unfortunately, such eruptions are few. This is primarily the work of the scrubbed, anal-retentive Itami of "The Funeral" and "A Taxing Woman," the Itami most admired by his countrymen. The messy, oral Itami of "Tampopo" might never come again, but I like him better when he still played with his food.

NEWSDAY, 6/28/89, Part II/p. 5, Mike McGrady

Japan's best known director, Juzo Itami, has made a specialty of studying man's deepest and most profound concerns—death ("The Funeral"), gluttony ("Tampopo") and tax-dodging ("A Taxing Woman"). With his newest, "A Taxing Woman's Return," he goes back again to tax-dodging, but this time on a grand scale, exposing a money-lust that infects Japan's religious, political and business structures.

For the second time in as many outings, Itami focuses on the sometimes heroic and sometimes comic efforts of dedicated tax collector Ryoko Itakura (Nobuko Miyamoto) as she focuses her binoculars, cameras and listening devices on a bigtime religious fraud (Rentaro Mikuni) who is turning a classic yen, undeclared of course, by taking an active role in Japan's eviction rackets.

What rackets? All of this requires a word of explanation—and that, in essence, is what's wrong with "A Taxing Woman's Return" for American audiences. For starters, one must understand that Japan has a land-based currency and, further, that land scarcity has caused acreage to skyrocket in price. Therefore, before any new skyscrapers go up, old tenants must be evicted—by hook or crook. This has led to the aforementioned eviction racket, wherein thuggish evictors are offered cash bounties for all residents either forced or lured from their homes.

The film's other basic concerns—a fundamentalist religious sect dodging taxes, politicians on the take, a corrupt chief elder of a far-out religion who takes a teenaged girl as a lover, businessmen who go to any extreme in pursuit of money—will not require nearly as much explanation.

Miyamoto, writer-director Itami's wife of two decades, is back in the title role, once again playing a resourceful and brazen tax collector whose efforts expose the eviction racket, the bogus religion and the shady politicians. While it will be a definite novelty for most Americans to see tax-collectors in a heroic light, Miyamoto's straightforward, natural appeal makes the concept at least possible.

Itami seems to be saying that a country that has turned money-making into an art form should not be surprised if avarice becomes part of the national lifestyle. Once you accept the concept of the almighty yen, one is better able to understand why Japanese audiences were able to sit still for what is an often arid expose of financial wheeling-dealing. American audiences may well feel that as the tax collectors get mired down in the minutiae of their work, the film gets mired down as well.

Some films, of course, travel better than others, and my hunch is that "A Taxing Woman's Return" lacks sea legs. Itami's fast-paced style masks the slowness of the action, but only for a while. The subject matter is so dry—as the revenuers break through bureaucratic red tape to get at company accounts, locate a hidden cash room, crack the code in double books, interrogate suspects endlessly—it sometimes seems to be shot in slo-mo.

Although Itami borrows more than a few stylistic fillips from "The Godfather," much of the film is about as entertaining as sitting through an audit. And, in the interest of total honesty, let me admit to what is doubless a personal flaw on my part: I know that tax-dodging is base villainy but, try as I might, there was just no way I could bring myself to root wholeheartedly for tax collectors, heroic or not.

VILLAGE VOICE, 7/4/89, p. 72, Georgia Brown

His classy genre send-ups have made Juzo Itami an overnight sensation in American art houses. *Tampopo*—his biggest hit here—is charged with flashy cinematic wit as well as sumptuous close-ups of noodles, greens and pork slices nestled in steaming broth. (A lean samurai/cowboy rides into town on his truck and with his sidekick helps a harried widow turn her languishing hole-in-the-wall into a first-class noddle joint.) Born to the medium as son of veteran director Mansaku Itami, the younger Itami worked as a film actor and didn't begin directing until into his fifties. Clearly he has an eye for fresh comic subjects (and for fancy camera angles), but for all his genre play, Itami doesn't really work the conventions; he's more social essayist than storyteller.

A Taxing Woman, which opened here last year around the April 15 filing deadline, starred Itami's wife Nobuko Miyamoto—who has played the heroine in all four of his films—as Ryoki Itakura, intrepid inspector for the national tax bureau, who tracks down various small cheats and dodgers; now, in *A Taxing Woman Returns*, she spies on bigger fry. We first see Itakura's friendly, freckled face behind a pair of high-tech binoculars. This mock *policier* is denser and darker than the first, and it's harder to follow—for non-Japanese particularly. (Rife with in-jokes, the movie makes one think that cultural difference between Japan and the U.S. are vaster than one suspected.) *TW* and *TW Returns* have been credited with mobilizing public opinion in favor of the recent investigation that uncovered the Recruit scandal, eventually bringing down Prime Minister Noboru Takeshita.

In *A Taxing Woman Returns*, which broke Tokyo box-office records and won major movie prizes, the bureau's target is a fundamentalist religious order headed by Chief Elder Teppei Onizawa (Rentaro Mikuni) and his stern, evil-eyed consort, known as the Holy Matriarch (Haruko Kato). Chief Elder is a lech, and the Holy Matriarch tries to satisfy her insatiable appetite for furs and jewels. But the chief is also engaged in complex, far-ranging real estate swindles, colluding with banks, businesses, politicians, and a range of petty thugs to acquire existing housing in order to build lucrative high-rises.

The first half of the film describes heavy-handed methods used to evict stubborn tenants—

bringing in Dobermans, threatening children, taking a jack-hammer to the apartment overhead. One sore holdout, a muckraking photojournalist who threatens to expose the order, is bribed with 50 million yen. When he accepts, they show him they've recorded the transaction and will ruin him in his own press unless he signs over his property: "The Japanese love scandal.... They're all Peeping Toms," one crook observes. Another desperate man, in order to pay off a debt, turns over his demure 16-year-old daughter to be one more mistress to the Chief Elder. (The girl turns out to be not as innocent as she looks in her school uniform.) As usual, corruption takes refuge in patriotism: "Someone must do the dirty work," argues the Chief Elder when officially confronted, "or Tokyo will be bypassed by Hong Kong and Seoul."

Itami concentrates almost lovingly on the tired brutality of the Chief Elder. The film is more or less framed by the old man's recurring nightmare, in which a sheer stone mountainside begins rumbling and crumbling, as he (a tiny climber) tries to keep a handhold. Around this central figure, characters pop up and then drop into some deep narrative canyon, never to reemerge. Inspector Itakura and her boyish new partner, fresh from Tokyo University (played by Toru Masuoka), seem almost incidental to the plot—instruments not so much of right or justice as of some opposing zeal. The Chaplinesque—or Giulietta Masinaesque—Miyamoto is used here in a perfunctory, almost offhand way.

Close attention to Mikuni's craggy features isn't sufficient to evoke real sympathy for the old warrior—who now wants mothering more than anything—even when he too becomes "expendable" and is targeted by unknown forces. (A pointed shot of the wounded chief cradled in Inspector Itakura's arms seems forced.) Itami keeps emotions at a distance; his films stay cold and dry. *A Taxing Woman Returns* is so abrasive I left it feeling chafed.

Also reviewed in:

NEW REPUBLIC, 8/7 & 14/89, p. 26, Stanley Kauffmann
NEW YORK TIMES, 6/28/89, p. C17, Vincent Canby
VARIETY, 8/31/88, p. 39
WASHINGTON POST, 11/15/89, p. B13, Hal Hinson

TEEN WITCH

A Trans World Entertainment release. *Executive Producer:* Moshe Diamant and Eduard Sarlui. *Producer:* Alana H. Lambros and Rafael Eisenman. *Director:* Dorian Walker. *Screenplay:* Robin Menken and Vernon Zimmerman. *Director of Photography:* Marc Reshovsky. *Editor:* Natan Zahavi. *Music:* Larry Weir and Richard Elliot. *Music Editor:* Ellen Segal. *Choreographer:* Bob Banas. *Sound:* Jim Pilcher. *Production Designer:* Stephen Rice. *Art Director:* Dana Torrey. *Set Decorator:* Anna Rita Raineri. *Set Dresser:* Monique La Perriere, Kai Blomberg, and Sandra Stewart. *Costumes:* Judie Champion. *Make-up:* Jenny Brown, Darri Gocha, and Gail Brubaker. *Stunt Coordinator:* Wally Crowder. *Running time:* 95 minutes. *MPAA Rating:* PG-13.

CAST: Robyn Lively (Louise); Dan Gauthier (Brad); Joshua Miller (Richie); Caren Kaye (Margaret); Dick Sargent (Frank); Lisa Fuller (Randa); Mandy Ingber (Polly); Zelda Rubinstein (Serena); Noah Blake (Rhet); Tina Marie Caspary (Shawn); Megan Gallivan (Kiki); Alssari Al-Shehail (Vincent); Shelly Berman (Mr. Weaver); Marcia Wallace (Ms. Molloy); Dan Carter (Geek); Tona Dodd (Mrs. Crocker); Cherie Franklin (Ms. Lugar); Gary Schwartz (Dean Howell); Wendy Brainard (Girl); Ponti Lambros (Stagehand); Alana M. Lambros (Geena); Kevin Best (Attendant); Brett Clark (Bruiser); Ralph Baker (Cop); Jared Chandler (David); Alexana Lambros (Sally); Cindy Valentine (Shana, Rock Star); Lawrence Raymond Banister (Disc Jockey); *MUSICIANS:* Michael Hartung (Guitar); James Keegan (Drums); Kevin Wyatt (Bass); Matthew Walker (Keyboards); Cathy Car (Singer).

LOS ANGELES TIMES, 5/2/89, Calendar/p. 3, Chris Willman

Try this at home, kids: Watch a really preachy "Afterschool Special," but use the remote to switch channels intermittently, being sure to hit the occasional MTV rap video, a "Bewitched" rerun or two, and plenty of commercials in which pretty young people hold brand names up to the camera.

Congratulations. In less-than-scientific and highly cost-effective conditions, you've just reproduced the exact experience of paying $6 to watch "Teen Witch," complete with teen wish-fulfillment fantasies, condescending moralizing, asinine musical montages, horrifying pop songs, French kissing, blatant product plugs and Dick Sargent (formerly of "Bewitched").

Switch witchcraft for werewolves, and the hackneyed plot of "Teen Witch" could easily be that of "Teen Wolf" or a dozen others like it: Unpopular high-schooler develops magical powers, becomes the most popular kid in school, then decides rather unconvincingly at the end to make a stand as a garden-variety mortal after all.

Robyn Lively is the plain-Jane type whose 16th birthday brings the power to cast spells. High on her list of potential recipients: hunky but unavailable Dan Gauthier, who looks as if he's auditioning for GQ.

Be forewarned that this is a high school where, bewitched or not, the youth occasionally break into song (or white rap) and dance—including a memorably ghastly "I Like Boys" production number in a locker room that might have poor Busby Berkeley doing about 1,600 RPM in his grave.

Among the supernatural vets on hand is Sargent, whose casting as Lively's dad is the movie's one good joke. Its one good line goes to its resident psychic, Zelda Rubinstein (who else?), who advises her teen charge to go ahead and use Love Potion No. 9, explaining, "Falling in love is just a trick anyway—the right hair style, the right music. ..." But Zelda also has the movie's worst line: "The real magic is believing in yourself. If you can do that, you can make *anything* happen!"

Guess the makers of "Teen Witch" (rated PG-13, but aimed at an under-13 audience) just didn't believe in themselves enough.

NEW YORK POST, 5/13/89, p. 19, Jami Bernard

What would you have given back in high school to transform yourself overnight from a geek into the most popular girl in school and suddenly enjoy the attentions of the cutest guy on earth? Louise doesn't even have to sell her soul to the devil, although she probably would have—it happens that she is endowed with witchy powers, which come into full bloom on her 16th birthday.

"Teen Witch" does almost the opposite. Once Louise turns 16 and has the world at her feet, the considerable early charm of the movie begins seeping away. And that's too bad, because the movie starts out as a happy cross between "Sixteen Candles" and a modern "Bye Bye Birdie," with several romping, high-energy musical numbers.

The geeky girls of the school, Louise (Robyn Lively) and Polly (Mandy Ingber) are really just normal, fresh-faced teen-agers, but it's the girls with the party dresses and the moussed-up hair who get the guys. To add to her troubles, Louise is mortified when an entry from her diary is read aloud in English class—a passage in which she imagines that hunky Brad (Dan Gauthier) is kissing her all over. Life just couldn't get much worse.

After a fortuitous meeting with fortuneteller Madame Serena (tinny-voiced Zelda Rubinstein, making a career of playing psychics), Louise discovers that she is descended from a long line of distinguished witches. With the help of her Sweet 16 and a magical amulet that conveniently comes her way, she is soon wishing her little brother (the interesting young actor Joshua Miller) into a dog and her English teacher into a state of undress.

With just a little dose of the delicious black humor of "Heathers," this could have been a likable take on teen omnipotence ("We can even make our own money!" chortles Madame Serena).

Anyway, Louise finds out that beneath her geeky clothes there resided, all along, the body of a cheerleader. Who needs witchcraft when a nice party dress will do?

Also reviewed in:
VARIETY, 5/3–9/89, p. 16

THELONIOUS MONK: STRAIGHT, NO CHASER

A Warner Brothers release of a Malpaso Productions/Monk Film Project/Michael Blackwood Productions, Inc. film. *Executive Producer:* Clint Eastwood. *Producer:* Charlotte Zwerin and Bruce Ricker. *Director:*

Charlotte Zwerin. *Director of Photography:* Christian Blackwood. *Music:* Thelonious Monk. *Music Under Narration:* Dick Hyman. *Running time:* 90 minutes. *MPAA Rating:* PG-13.

WITH: Samuel E. Wright (Narrator); Charlie Rouse (Tenor Saxophone); Phil Woods (Alto Saxophone); Johnny Griffin (Tenor Saxophone); Ray Copeland (Trumpet); Jimmy Cleveland (Trombone); Larry Gales (Bass); Ben Riley (Drums); Tommy Flanagan and Barry Harris (Duo-Piano Performance).

CHRISTIAN SCIENCE MONITOR, 11/15/89, p. 10, David Sterritt

A piano is a complicated piece of equipment: a large box with keys, hammers, strings. It's kind of impersonal, really, and this is why it's so special when someone develops a truly personal style on the instrument.

Yet this does happen. Take Thelonious Monk: Countless millions of people have played the piano over the years, but when he knocked out his first five or ten notes—even on a record or the radio—you knew in a flash who was at the keyboard. That's mastery. And that's class.

"Thelonious Monk: Straight, No Chaser" is a new documentary film about Monk, who died in 1982. He was a strange man, with mood swings that made him exuberant at some times but sadly depressed at others. One of the most amazing things about him was his ability to create great music, with surprising consistency, despite his emotional problems—as if his art allowed him to soar above difficulties that might have weighed other people down.

"Straight, No Chaser" takes its title from one of Monk's most famous pieces. (He also wrote the classic " 'Round Midnight," which another jazz film was named after.) The new film is full of Monk's terrific piano playing, and it gives us unprecedented glimpses of Monk offstage dealing with his colleagues and the challenges of his art. He behaves very strangely now and then, projecting his inner turmoil in ways that are fully visible to the camera. But he always manages to take care of business—music, that is—in his own unmistakable manner.

The movie was photographed largely by Christian Blackwood, a documentary-maker who got Monk to trust him over a period of several months during the late 1960s. Also appearing, in scenes photographed more recently, are Thelonious Monk Jr. and Charlie Rouse, the controversial sax player.

Compared with other jazz films that have come out recently, "Thelonious Monk: Straight, No Chaser" is quite conventional. It doesn't have the smoky, impressionistic atmosphere of "Let's Get Lost," the documentary on trumpeter Chet Baker; and of course it's not a fictionalized account like "Bird," the fine Eastwood movie about Charlie Parker, jazz's all-time-great saxophonist.

Some moviegoers will prefer the orthodox style of "Straight, No Chaser" to the more freewheeling approaches of those films, and that's a legitimate choice. Yet there is one problem with the Monk picture: It doesn't dig deeply enough into the roots of Monk's music. He made fundamental changes in the vocabulary of jazz, after all, opening up a world of quirky melodies and harmonies. Where, deep down in his personality, did these breakthroughs come from? The film never gets around to telling us.

Flaws and all, "Thelonious Monk: Straight, No Chaser" stands as an absorbing, entertaining, and often fascinating look at an artist who was as unconventional as he was brilliant. If you like music, it's a must-see. And if you like bebop, it could be the movie of the year.

LOS ANGELES TIMES, 11/17/89, Calendar/p. 11, Leonard Feather

"Thelonious Monk: Straight, No Chaser" breaks the mold that has long been evident in movies about jazz artists. Unlike the fictional and heavily downbeat "'Round Midnight," or the fictionalized facts of "Bird," or the depressing Chet Baker documentary "Let's Get Lost," this is a superbly crafted mixture of old and new footage. (Monk died in 1982 at 63.) There is virtually no reference to drugs, a common element in all the others, and no apparent objective except that of presenting an honest, audio-visual portrait.

Though Monk seemed too esoteric to reach out to a mass audience, the manner in which he and his music are presented here, sandwiched between narrations by his manager, his saxophonist Charlie Rouse and others, could break through the barrier that limited him in his lifetime.

What manner of man was Thelonious Monk? Part of the answer is supplied in footage acquired from a 1968 German TV documentary. Here he is in a recording studio, or a London theater, alone or with a quartet or octet, playing some of the works that have become standards. He seems preoccupied; now and then he leaves the piano and, while the other continue to play, revolves slowly *in situ*, or performs a dance as quirky as his music.

An off-screen narration by Samuel E. Wright, who played Dizzy Gillespie in "Bird," outlines Monk's early years. The musician's troubles with the police—he lost his right-to-work New York cabaret card for an offense he said he did not commit—are discussed by his manager, Harry Colomby.

As the moment neared for his first chance at mass exposure via a Time magazine cover story, Colomby noticed an increasingly erratic pattern of behavior. Monk's son, Thelonious Jr., offers a poignant analysis: "[There were] tremendous fits of depression and euphoria, very schizophrenic type thing...we had to hospitalize him...it's a startling thing when you look your father in the eye and you know that he doesn't exactly know who you are."

There are light interludes: Monk making small talk in a recording studio, trying half coherently to communicate with a waiter in some airport restaurant, yet coming up with a perceptive reaction to a journalist's foolish question.

Monk's wife, Nellie, is seen only briefly, though the couple's closeness is eloquently recalled by Charlie Rouse. The Baroness Pannonica de Koenigswarter, Monk's patron, discusses her ejection from New York apartments because of her musician friends.

Helped by commendable sound and camera work, such Monk tunes as "Pannonica," "'Round Midnight," "Ruby My Dear" and "Crepuscule With Nellie" are perfectly accessible with their incisive statements, idiosyncratic runs and engaging dissonances. If "Ugly Beauty" seemed like an apt title for one Monk song, a more orthodox beauty is expressed when "Well You Needn't" and "Misterioso " are played exquisitely as piano duets by Tommy Flanagan and Barry Harris.

The final tune, "Sweetheart of All My Dreams," is one of those banal ditties that Monk took delight in playing, perhaps tongue in cheek. What he intended by the use of such material may always remain a mystery, but given the enlightened comments, and the sensitive direction by Charlotte Zwerin, who co-produced "Straight, No Chaser" with Bruce Ricker, we are granted a closer glance behind the veil of this half-hidden, exotically gifted figure than could ever be observed during his sadly aborted career.

NEW YORK POST, 9/30/89, p.17, Lee Jeske

From 14 hours of extraordinary footage of the great jazz pianist and composer Thelonious Monk shot by Christian and Michael Blackwood for German television in 1967-1968, Charlotte Zwerin has fashioned the finest full-length jazz documentary ever made.

"Thelonious Monk: Straight, No Chaser" is an insightful and haunting work that succeeds brilliantly on two levels: as a portrait of a most important, and most unusual, American artist, and as a feast of smashing music-making.

Thelonious Monk, who died in 1982, was one of jazz's great eccentrics. He said strange things, wore funny hats, did weird dances and seemed to live in his own mysterious dream world.

He also invented his own musical language during the be-bop revolution of the 1940s—angular, witty, cubist music that laid the groundwork for much of modern jazz and eventally earned him fame and fortune (and a 1964 Time magazine cover).

We see Monk on and off the bandstand—spellbinding us with his music, making us laugh with his antics. Then, about midway through, Thelonious Monk Jr., in a recent interview, talks about his father's "tremendous fits of depression and euphoria, [a] very schizophrenic type thing" that resulted in frequent hospitalizations.

"It's a startling thing to look your father in the eye and know that he doesn't exactly know who you are."

Suddenly the eccentricities become frightening: Are we laughing at a sick man? And how much did that contribute to Monk's blithe music?

A great documentary illuminates its subject. "Thelonious Monk: Straight, No Chaser" illuminates the enchanting musical world of Thelonious Monk.

Unlike some documentaries, which raise questions they purposely don't resolve, Zwerin's film raises questions it *can't* resolve: Was Monk given proper medical treatment throughout his life? (A friend says that in 1972 Monk "suddenly turned to me and said, 'I'm very seriously ill.' ")

Why did he virtually stop playing in the mid-'70s?

What was the nature of his relationship with Baroness Pannonica de Koenigswarter, a longtime friend and jazz patron in whose New Jersey home he lived for the last decade of his life? (Koenigswarter, who died last year, also figured prominently in "Bird," directed by Clint

Eastwood, executive producer of "Straight, No Chaser,") Monk's wife, Nellie, a constant presence in the '68 footage, is referred to as being "like his right hand," and he died by her side. The two women sit together at his funeral.

Zwerin has surrounded the choice '68 footage—of Monk in performance, in the recording studio, backstage at the Village Vanguard, in airports and hotel rooms, walking the street near his West Side apartment—with other vintage Monk performance footage and enlightening interviews with saxophonist Charlie Rouse, who worked in Monk's quartet for 11 years, Koenigswarter, manager Harry Colomby and several others.

The performance are completely absorbing—Monk's a captivating presence on stage, a whirligig of activity; you can't help getting swept up in the accessible swing of his music, from originals like " 'Round Midnight" to giddy, fresh solo piano versions of vintage chestnuts. And the rich on-stage material is beautifully complemented by the backstage goings on and the recent interviews.

Some will be annoyed that the film opens with a standard-issue documentary narrator—"Born in Rocky Mount, N.C., in 1917..."—who hurries us through Monk's first 20 years and disappears. But it works—important moments in Monk's career are detailed by the various talking heads, and a continued narration would have worked against Blackwood's cinema verite footage, the meat of this film.

The only misstep is the inclusion of two duets by pianists Barry Harris and Tommy Flanagan, unnecessarily redundant amid this treasure trove of Monk himself.

"Thelonious Monk: Straight, No Chaser" is an entertaining and disturbing portrait of an American original. It'll make you laugh, it'll make you uneasy, but more than anything it'll make you tap a hole in the floor of the theater.

NEWSDAY, 9/30/89, Part II/p. 15, Stuart Troup

The jazz community has had a long fascination with Thelonious Monk, and not just because of his remarkable compositional output. He was an enigmatic, taciturn figure whose behavior seemed odd and erratic. Conversation about him always musters more questions than answers.

"Thelonious Monk: Straight, No Chaser," perhaps the best film ever made about a jazz personality, answers some of the questions about his health and his mysterious disappearance from the music scene in 1976. But, more important, it provides a vivid portrait that captures his humor, his seriousness, his moods and his singular approach to music. When it's over, we know much more about Monk through his few words, his cavorting, his impatience, his interaction with others and the deftly interspersed commentary by those who knew him.

But what we learn mostly is that he was complex. More important than explanations, we are left with the beauty of his individuality—sometimes bizarre and unpredictably wonderful. Singular, like his music, which underpins and overlays the entire 90 minutes—"'Round Midnight," "Ruby, My Dear," "Misterioso," "I Mean You," "Pannonica" and many more.

Most of the film, which is in black and white, was taken from 14 hours of footage that was shot and edited by Michael and Christian Blackwood over a six-month period in 1967–'68. During that time, they followed Monk on-and offstage, in a recording studio, on the road, in Europe and in New York. Their footage, however, has surfaced only once since then, in a television special that was broadcast in Germany. Director Charlotte Zwerin selected from the 14 hours to make this portrait.

In the words of Bruce Ricker, who coproduced the film with Zwerin, the most extensive visual/aural record of this musical genius had been "just sitting there like the Dead Sea Scrolls of jazz."

Ricker and Zwerin supplemented the Blackwell footage with interviews from saxophonist Charles Rouse, Thelonious Monk Jr., Monk's managers Bob Jones and Harry Colomby, and the Baroness Pannonica de Koenigswarter, at whose home Monk and his wife, Nellie, spent his last years until his death in 1982. And they added performances by pianists Tommy Flanagan and Barry Harris, along with footage from Monk's funeral.

Ricker, who directed "The Last of the Blue Devils," and Zwerin, whose extensive documentary output includes working with Albert and David Maysles on "Salesman" and "Gimme Shelter," wisely packaged this film around the arch radiance of Monk's music and performance. And that, as it should be, is the centerpiece of this magnificent examination of Monk.

VILLAGE VOICE, 10/10/89, p. 95, Lisa Kennedy

Thelonious Monk is sitting next to his wife, Nellie, on a plane; they both look tired, eyes closed, faces tight, a nap on the wing. Thelonious opens his eyes as if from a dream or disturbing thought. He blinks, blinks again staring; he slowly looks across the aisle and into the camera staring, then he smiles. There is something beautifully unbearable at times about *Thelonious Monk: Straight, No Chaser*, strange proof that the vision of a documentary can surpass pure fiction or at least be frightfully omnipersonal.

Thanks to Michael and Christian Blackwood, who followed jazz pianist/composer extraordinaire Monk around the states and Europe and amassed 14 hours of film, there are innumerable moments of pristine footage from the late '60s. While the additional film from television archives, as well as interviews with Thelonius Monk Jr., manager Harry Colomby, road manager Bob Jones, and Baroness Nica de Koenigswarter, is compelling, the movie becomes a minor miracle when the camera is trained on Monk at work playing or just fooling around. The interviews are telling beyond what they say about Monk; they are less important as testimonials than as awed-witness accounts of a historical moment.

Watching Monk seize the sound is a wonder. What is it exactly? That beautiful swat, a pounce, catlike and playful; it's pure Monk. Anticipate his playing "Just a Gigolo." Monk had this way of eyeing the keys like the sound was fluid, and darting here and there underneath them, needing to be exposed—the symbiosis of style and sound. And fortunately the ratio of interviews to performing shots is balanced in favor of the music.

Though the film is not without darkness (Thelonious Jr. and Harry Colomby touch on Monk's manic depressiveness), it is wonderfully humorous. While touring Europe, a young German reporter asks Monk, "Do you think the piano has enough keys, 88, or do you want more?" Monk laughs, not outright but low, "I mean it's hard enough to play those 88," This is the same reporter who worshipfully queries, "Mr. Monk, you always wear different hats and caps in your concerts. Do they have an influence on your music?"

The film is also merciful. It does not end with the bad news we already know—Monk died in 1982 of a brain hemorrhage—but with his music, "Sweetheart of My Dreams" and "'Round Midnight."

Also reviewed in:

NATION, 10/30/89, p. 506, Stuart Klawans
NEW YORK TIMES, 9/30/89, p. 11, Stephen Holden
VARIETY, 11/30/88, p. 13
WASHINGTON POST, 11/22/89, p. D4, Richard Harrington

THREE FUGITIVES

A Touchstone Pictures release in association with Silver Screen Partners IV. *Executive Producer:* Francis Veber. *Producer:* Lauren Shuler-Donner. *Director:* Francis Veber. *Screenplay:* Francis Veber. *Director of Photography:* Haskell Wexler. *Editor:* Bruce Green. *Music:* David McHugh. *Music Editor:* Daniel Allan Carlin. *Sound:* C. Darin Knight and (music) Greg Townley. *Sound Editor:* Richard L. Anderson. *Production Designer:* Rick Carter. *Art Director:* Marjorie Stone McShirley. *Set Designer:* Lauren Cory. *Set Decorator:* Richard C. Goddard. *Special Effects:* Roland Tantin. *Costumes:* April Ferry. *Make-up:* Tommy Cole. *Stunt Coordinator:* Joe Dunne. *Running time:* 96 minutes. *MPAA Rating:* PG-13.

CAST: Nick Nolte (Daniel Lucas); Martin Short (Ned Perry); Sarah Rowland Doroff (Meg); James Earl Jones (Dugan); Alan Ruck (Tener); Kenneth McMillan (Horvath); David Arnott (Bank Teller); Bruce McGill (Charlie); Lee Garlington (Woman Cop); Sy Richardson (Tucker); Rocky Giordani (Bowles); Rick Hall (Dog Handler); Bill Cross (Guard at Prison); Stanley Brock (Release Sergeant); John Procaccino (Highway Patrolman); Kathy Kinney (Receptionist); Way Ching Yu (Girl in Children's Home); Jack McGee (Fisherman); Albert Henderson (Man in Raincoat); Larry Cox (Orderly One); Jeff Perry (Orderly Two); Rhoda Gemignani (Radio Operator); Clive Rosengren (Desk Sergeant); Maryssa Larose (Woman at Bank); Tim De Zarn (First Officer); Larry Miller (Second Officer); Scott Lincoln (Passenger Cop); John C. Cooke (First Thug); Yahoots Magoondi (Second Thug); Woody Eney (First Cop); John Aylward (Second Cop); George Catalano (Cop One); Gary Armagnac (Cop Two); Steven Zediker (Cop Three); Michael Siegel (Cop Four); Mike MacDonald

(Sergeant); Dinah Lenney (Reporter One); Jeannie Wiest (Reporter Two); Paul Tuerpe (Reporter Three); Bruno Acalinas (Motorcycle Cop One); Lance August (Motorcycle Cop Two); Charles Noland (Bartender); Anthony Frederick (Cop with Phone); Terrence Hollingsworth (Money Quick Customer); Dean Smith (Playboy); Richard E. Butler (Watchman One); R.L. Tolbert (Watchman Two); Karl Wickman (Helicopter Pilot).

FILMS IN REVIEW, 5/89, p. 303, C.M. Fiorillo

Comedy may be the frame on which *Three Fugitives* is draped, but pathos and irony are firmly brush-stroked across the silver canvas of Touchstone's latest hit. *Three Fugitives* is the story of an at-odds relationship between two men and the positive influence a charming six-year-old child has on their growing friendship.

Martin Short plays hapless Ned Perry, a beginner bank robber whose botched holdup brings him nose-to-chest with the solid form of Daniel Lucas, played by Nick Nolte. The frail, flighty Ned takes recently paroled ex-bank robber Lucas hostage. Lucas is none too pleased, but when he concludes that the police would rather shoot him than believe he *didn't* attempt to rob the bank, he decides to help inept Ned escape. He is shot in the leg for his effort—by Ned. Soon the table is turned and Ned must aid Lucas. Like his bungled bank robbery, Ned's idea of help is less than brilliant: senile veterinarian Dr. Horvath (Kenneth McMillan (*Protocol*), in some of the film's funniest scenes). Dr. Horvath mistakes Lucas for a dog but manages to secure the bullet and dress the wound. Lucas falls under the care—and spell—of Ned's silent daughter Meg while Ned fares poorly in the clutches of Lucas' greedy "pals." Soon the mismatched trio set off together for a series of mishaps on their way to felony freedom in Canada. Their travails blaze a path of brilliant sight gags, warmth, and familial bonding.

Nick Nolte (*Weeds*) is a gifted actor whose rugged handsomeness and physical size and strength make him a perfect dramatic player. You would not easily mistake him for a funnyman. When paired with someone as frail and hyperactive as Martin Short, the juxtaposition of Nolte's size is the comedy, not the character he portrays. The difference between Nolte and Short—style as well as size—serve up delightful comic routines. Nolte is best at strong, dramatic roles, but he serves *Three Fugitives* well. Short (*Cross My Heart*) is perfectly cast as Ned. He's small, but he's as physical to his comedy as Nolte is to his drama. The pair mesh. Meg is played with graceful dignity by newcomer Sarah Rowland Doroff. The film pivots on this child's expressive eyes and Mona Lisa smiles. James Earl Jones (*Coming to America*) does a fine turn as wiley Detective Dugan, the cop who put Lucas behind bars once and would love to again clang the doors shut tight behind him.

Writer/director Francis Veber (*Les Comperes*) adapted *Three Fugitives* from his original French screenplay *Les Fugitifs*. This Americanization has proven more successful than the unacclaimed Tom Hanks vehicle *The Man With One Red Shoe* (taken from Veber's *The Tall Blond Man With One Black Shoe*). Veber's comic pace clips right along and his direction is equally fluid, given the diversity of acting talent he had to work with. And when the comedy is interrupted for a dramatic bit, Academy Award-winner Haskell Wexler's (*Colors*) gorgeous photography drives the point home.

Three Fugitives is genuinely funny. The screenplay is delicious, the photography is exceptional and the acting is seamless. I cannot compare this film to the original French version which I didn't see, so I can only say that *Three Fugitives* holds up well in translation and can stand alone as a fine "American" comedy.

LOS ANGELES TIMES, 1/27/89, Calendar/p. 4, Kevin Thomas

In "Three Fugitives," Nick Nolte and Martin Short make a frequently hilarious odd couple, but the film itself is shamelessly sentimental and often slapdash. Nolte is a convicted bank robber fresh out of prison who's taken hostage by Short—in a bank robbery!

Nolte's Lucas, a husky blond professional criminal, a man who keeps his cool even when he's enraged, contrasts beautifully with Short's Perry, a slight, desperate amateur in the throes of gun-waving hysteria. This opening sequence in the bank has some of the joyful lunacy of Laurel and Hardy: When a teller tosses a satchel full of money—only $13,000, alas—it lands in a chandelier, provoking new heights of delirium in Perry.

Once Perry and the very reluctant Lucas have made their getaway, however, the film is never again as funny. Early on Lucas clears himself with the police, represented by James Earl Jones, who's virtually in a permanent state of apoplexy.

The fun starts eroding when we learn that Perry is a struggling widower behind in the rent and unable to continue paying for special schooling for his adorable little daughter Meg (Sarah Rowland Doroff) who hasn't spoken a word in the two years since her mother died. What's Perry to do when Meg looks up at Lucas with her big brown eyes and breaks her long silence by saying "Don't go"? Talk about heart-tugging!

The trouble is that we never learn anything about Lucas beyond the fact that he's been convicted for armed robbery *14* times—wouldn't they have thrown away the key long before this?—and that he apparently grew up in an orphanage. How does it happen that Lucas has such a heart of gold behind the gruff Wallace Beery facade? Nolte is an admirably persuasive actor, but if so much is going to be piled on about Perry, we need to know at least a little more about Lucas. As it is, "Three Fugitives" becomes progressively sillier—and less amusing.

There is a lovely turn by the late Kenneth McMillan as a dotty old veterinarian who mistakes humans for animals, and there are many fresh Tacoma. Wash., locales captured luminously by Haskell Wexler.

"Three Fugitives" marks the American directorial debut of France's prolific and popular comedy specialist, Francis Veber, creator of "La Cage aux Folles."

Three of them have been made into American movies—"The Toy," "Buddy, Buddy" and "The Man With One Red Shoe"—and in each instance critics have compared them unfavorably with the originals. Sure enough, "Three Fugitives" was based on "Les Fugitifs" and starred Gérard Depardieu and Pierre Richard, but Touchstone is taking no chances and not planning to release "Les Fugitifs," a big hit in France. The irony is that Veber, in remaking his own film, has brought to "Three Fugitives" (rated PG-13 for comic strip violence) the same aura of contrivance and heavy-handedness that marred those other adaptations.

MONTHLY FILM BULLETIN, 8/89, p. 252, Geoff Brown

Lucas, a paroled robber endeavouring to go straight, is depositing money earned in prison at a bank in Tacoma, Washington State, when he is taken hostage by an inept amateur in crime, Ned Perry. Detective Dugan refuses to believe Lucas was an innocent bystander, and they are both forced to go into hiding. Perry, an unemployed widower struggling to support his autistic daughter Meg, takes the injured Lucas to a senile veterinarian for treatment. The police soon pick up the trail; Perry rescues Meg from her special school only moments ahead of the cops' arrival. He then pressures Lucas into arranging for fake ID from counterfeiters. When they demand an impossible $50,000, Perry is held captive at their bar headquarters; Lucas comes to the rescue by driving a truck into the building. After extracting a written confession from Perry clearing him of the bank robbery, Lucas prepares to leave his troublesome companion, only to be pulled back by Meg's first words since her mother died—"Don't go!" Lucas clears his name until Meg is picked up and taken into custody, where she retreats into silence. Lucas and Perry kidnap her from her reform school and plan an escape to Canada, with Perry disguised in a woman's wig. After Perry is forced to fake pregnancy at a road block, and the trio is escorted by police to a hospital, they slip across the border. Stepping inside a bank to change money, Perry is promptly taken hostage by another would-be robber...

It is tempting to pigeon-hole this Americanised edition of Francis Veber's 1986 release *Les Fugitifs*—the comic tale of two men and a cute autistic child—as Touchstone's proud successor to *Three Men and a Baby*, the film that momentarily lifted the box-office curse from Hollywood's attempts at remodelling European comedies. But the facts speak differently. Not only was *Three Fugitives* conceived as an American film before Leonard Nimoy's version of Coline Serreau's farce entered production; the remake was even being planned before Francis Veber shot *Les Fugitifs* itself. The project's appeal for Hollywood executives doubtless lay in the basic concept: a grizzled ex-convict trying to go straight, yoked by circumstances to a bungling bank robber, with a fetching little girl thrown in for tears. For Veber, the situation provided one more variation on the odd-couple syndrome he has been exploiting since *1973*'s *L'Emmerdeur*; and, in the French version, one more vehicle for the deliberately mismatched team of Gérard Depardieu and Pierre Richard (previously thrown together in Veber's *La Chèvre* and *Les Compères*, themselves due for Hollywood remakes).

Martin Short—likeable, rubber-faced, with a touch of the forlorn lost child—suits the clumsy neophyte's role like a glove, right from his opening armed flourish in the bank (his gunshots crown him with falling plaster). Nick Nolte has the size and gruff demeanour required for the ex-con, but comic flair is not in his make-up; beside the nimble Short he resembles a lumbering animatronic dinosaur, seriously ill-suited to dainty cries of despair like "You're giving me the willies". The material fits easily into its new geographical setting, and Veber's flair for the absurd is kept intact: the late Kenneth McMillan's senile vet is a particularly engaging creation. As a writer-director, however, Veber fails to give *Three Fugitives* the strong propelling force it needs. The scenes with the autistic daughter too obviously tug at the heart strings; and the trio's final flight to Canada—complete with female impersonation and a phoney pregnancy—signally fails to crown the previous handful of chases. Strange, incidentally, to find Haskell Wexler's name attached to the film: his camerawork is anonymously professional, but this relocated Gallic farce-with-a-heart is hardly his *tasse de thé.*

NEW YORK POST, 1/27/89, p. 25, David Edelstein

Touchstone Pictures, the division of Walt Disney Studios that produced the slapstick comedy "Three Fugitives," is said to have the Midas touch, but that might be overrating Midas, whose kingdom didn't also contain Mickey, Donald and Space Mountain.

The company had the biggest film of 1987, "Three Men and a Baby," and the biggest film of 1988, "Who Framed Roger Rabbit"; its president, Jeff Katzenberg, personally made $300 trillion last year. (Well, I forget the exact figure, but it was more than the largest Lotto jackpot.)

Lord knows, you can't argue with success, but you can certainly bemoan it. Watching "Three Fugitives," I had the depressing feeling that I was reviewing a product instead of a movie. Not a new feeling, by any means, but one that seems to deepen with every high-concept, computer-generated picture this studio turns out.

High concept means Nick Nolte and Martin Short, one burly and gruff and cantankerous, one short and funny and lovable, as mismatched buddies on the lam. The third fugitive is Short's cute little girl (Sarah Rowland Doroff), who hasn't spoken a word since her mother's death two years ago and who, at the movie's end, remains tragically mute.

(If you believe the last sentence, maybe you'll like this picture.)

Presto: a buddy-chase-comedy that tickles your funnybone and steals your heart and blah blah blah—I can already hear the TV critics crowing. This is the sort of film that renders criticism useless and in a way people useless, since it regards the average audience member as a set of buttons to be pushed. And sadly, this wouldn't be taken as an insult in Hollywood. Disney stockholders think it's all just swell.

"Three Fugitives" has eight or nine very big laughs, which is more than "'Twins,'" and in its way it's quite accomplished. The picture starts as if it might be a hoot, with Short bungling a stickup and taking Nolte hostage; the problem is that Nolte has just been released from jail, where he did five years for armed robbery. When the cops see the two of them come out of the bank, they're convinced that Nolte's the mastermind.

Nolte bashes Short around like Moe mangling Curly, except that Moe didn't use any expletives. (Nolte uses only one—something about a donkey and an orifice—but 50 or 60 times.) Because there isn't a real plot here, the ex-con is eventually sensitized to the little man's plight (Short needed money to keep his daughter in a special school) and sends him off to see an old buddy for a fake passport. The buddy turns out to be a meanie and holds Short hostage—this helps to differentiate the sweet armed robbers from the nasty ones.

The rest is chases. The cops chase the two men, who chase the little girl (she runs away), and the movie doesn't really end—it just peters out from exhaustion. The writer and director, Francis Veber, has knocked off a lot of immensely successful French comedies, some of which have been remade as American films, others of which will be. Their gags are hit-or-miss, but in none does Veber transcend his initial gimmick. He churns out laughs with the lazy assurance of an organ grinder, and the movies—even when they're funny—grow monotonous.

Nolte and Short are replacements for Gérard Depardieu and Pierre Richard, and the problem is not in the casting—the two are wonderful performers, easily up to their French counterparts. It's just that they have nothing to perform. Nolte's sea-blue eyes signal wildly to us that he's adrift; he talks in his low, belchy rasp and caricatures his performance in "48 HRS."—a caricature to begin with.

Short is overdue for stardom, but if he uses it the way his SCTV colleague John Candy has—by accepting roles in terrible, overproduced comedies—he would be better off as a cult figure. He's a brilliant actor, with a limber body and an ingratiating wit, and he has something in common with the great movie clowns: a starry-eyed faith in gravity, which is always mashing him down.

But he's in danger of becoming too nauseatingly lovable, and the film degrades him: When he dons women's clothes to cross the border, there's a suggestion that he belongs in them, that the little girl really needs a strong, macho dad like Nolte.

"Three Fugitives" is photographed by one of the best, Haskell Wexler, and there's magic in the way he lights the girl, the beams catching her hair and leaving her face a bit remote. (When you actually see her visage, it expresses nothing.)

Bruce Green's editing is deft, and Veber has a good eye for slapstick. But he writes either one-joke parts—like the senile veterinarian of Kenneth McMillan—or no-joke parts, like the exasperated cops of James Earl Jones and Alan Ruck.

Sporadically, "Three Fugitives" is hilarious, but it never achieves any momentum. The laughs are broken up by moments of pathos, so you don't get the sustained high of a good comedy. Is there something wrong with a film that's just a comedy? Must a movie be all things to 100 million people? The answer lies not in our stars, but in our stock options.

NEWSDAY, 1/27/89, part III/p. 3, Mike McGrady

"Three Fugitives," the first American film from France's Francis Veber, is a throwback to another era—a childlike film that gets its excitement from a never-ending chase, its sentiment from a cute 6-year-old girl mixing it up with bank robbers, and its humor from a series of sight gags, some of which work flawlessly.

As well they should. "Three Fugitives" is, after all, Veber's second go-round with the same story—in France it was a commercially successful Gérard Depardieu comedy titled "Les Fugitifs." And by this time, Veber understands very well what makes a sight gag work—surprise that relies on flawless timing—and his timing is above reproach.

However, when all is said and done, Veber's story is still going to be little more than a lightweight time-killer, an innocently appealing bit of fluff that won't overly tax either one's intellect or capacity for laughter.

In refilming his project, Veber picked a star, Nick Nolte, who is an American approximation of Depardieu in both appearance and technique. A just-paroled convict, Nolte wanders innocently into a bank robbery that's in the process of being bungled by Martin Short and immediately finds himself taken hostage. Naturally, the police assume the robbery is Nolte's idea and the chase commences.

The two, Nolte and Short, are soon joined by Short's 6-year-old daughter (Sarah Rowland Doroff), a child of such extreme cuteness as to provoke a communal intake of breath from the audience. However, she has a little problem, a problem that will seem more than passingly familiar to any veteran moviegoer.

As Short explains it to Nolte, "She doesn't talk. She hasn't opened her mouth in almost two years, since her mother died." Hmmmm, sounds very much like a temporary condition to me.

From this point on, the two men and the girl—the three fugitives—are on the run. Since Nolte has been shot, the first stop is at a doctor. Well, not actually a medical doctor but a senile veterinarian (a nice dotty last turn by the late Kenneth McMillan) who is under the misapprehension that Nolte is a dog wounded by careless hunters; for a brief while, he even considers putting the big guy to sleep.

Martin Short (imagine a cross between Pee-wee Herman and a human being) must be the hardest man in the world to slot in movies. His unique comedic talents, once regularly showcased on "Saturday Night Live," have brightened films like "Innerspace" and "The Three Amigos"; here he offers his best film work to date and Nolte is at his most earnest.

While sentiment occasionally spills over into corniness, there are enough deft moments to keep thing from becoming sloppy.

All the chases, however, finally do prove a bit exhausting, and I could only nod my head in profound agreement when Nolte tries to break up the fugitiveship with, "I've been on the run too long. I just can't take it any more."

NEWSWEEK, 2/13/89, p. 79, David Ansen

Formula is the enemy of art and the best friend of hacks and marketing departments. It's easy enough to see the appeal of formula to a studio executive—like Muzak, formula movies make no waves and can be produced by the yard. An ambitious filmmaker, saddled with a formula, can try to wrestle his material into striking new shapes—as director Bob Balaban attempts to do in

Parents. In the case of *Tap*, a splendid subject—tap dancing—has been squeezed inside a formulaic plot on the theory that this will make it more commercial. In the sentimental farce *Three Fugitives*, the French writer-director Francis Veber executes his formula with such ruthless efficiency there's no life left—it's like watching a blueprint.

"Three Fugitives" is Veber's Hollywood remake of his own "Les Fugitifs," which won't be released here. Nick Nolte plays a gruff bank-robbing convict who, on his first day out of the pen, finds himself held hostage in an inept bank holdup executed by amateur Martin Short. Naturally, he's suspected of masterminding the job; naturally, he and Short, after initial animosity, become pals. Not so naturally, but with numbing predictability, we learn that the hysterical Short is a widower who's turned desperado to support his little daughter (Sarah Rowland Doroff) who hasn't spoken a word since her mother died.

"Three Fugitives" is a slick piece of work, and some of the slapstick—like Short's bungled holdup—is genuinely funny. But as soon as the pathos-grubbing tot appears, the audience can abandon all hope. Veber has written so many French farces ("The Toy," "La Cage aux Folles") he seems to be on automatic pilot; by the time Short gets himself up in drag you feel as though you're watching a compendium of Veber's greatest hits. What he's fatally left out here is any shred of plausible human behavior. "Three Fugitives" is the cinematic equivalent of surimi—you could mistake it for the real thing until you start chewing.

"Tap" is a more likable movie and more disappointing. Writer-director Nick Castle obviously intends his musical melodrama as a tribute to the great black tap dancers of the past, many of whom are in his movie. The highlight comes early, when these amazing old-timers—Harold Nicholas, Sandman Sims, Jimmy Slyde, Arthur Duncan, Steve Condos and Bunny Briggs—rise to the challenge of the young tap-dancing hero (Gregory Hines) and demonstrate their still breathtaking routines. (The venerable Slyde and Briggs are currently showing off their virtuosity on the Broadway stage.) But to get to such rousing moments we have to sit through a tale that would have seemed hackneyed 40 years ago. Hines plays a legendary hoofer's son who traded tap dancing for crime: it landed him in jail and now he's out on probation. There follows two hours of fake suspense: will he return to his bad old ways or put on his dancing shoes? Dramatically, nothing deviates from form. Choreographically, it's full of delights—though the big finale, with Hines bringing tap dancing into the rock-and-roll era, suggests that it belongs anywhere but. Sammy Davis Jr. does a nice, unshowbizzy turn as an old hoofer, and Hines, though he hasn't great depth as an actor, has plenty of contagious charm.

The nice thing about "Parents" is that while it ultimately, in its grisly little heart, reveals itself to be a horror film, it's happy to dawdle in more quirky comic concerns before getting down to the business of shock. Actor-turned-director Bob Balaban sets Christopher Hawthorne's tale in 1958 and, with the expert help of art director Andris Hausmanis, revels in the atomic-age modernity of the Eisenhower era, with its profound faith in progress, conformity and keeping up a spic-and-span appearance. But as in "Blue Velvet," which Balaban has clearly studied, dark deeds lurk under the surface of his suburban family. While Mom (Mary Beth Hurt) seems the perfect perky little housewife, and Dad (Randy Quaid) is a golf-playing defoliant expert for the Toxico chemical company, their moody, 10-year-old son, Michael (Bryan Madorsky), senses something's amiss—he's haunted by nightmares of drowning in blood. He's been served too many meals of odd-looking mystery meat, and his pubescent fantasies of sex and cannibalism get all mixed up together. Wonderfully cast and acted, "Parents" establishes an intriguing comic metaphor about the dark side of the nuclear American family but unfortunately doesn't know where to take it. In the end, the wafer-thin script capitulates to the routine horror-movie conventions it's been battling against. But at least until then it puts a good fight.

VILLAGE VOICE, 2/7/89, p. 57, Katherine Dieckmann

Call it *Two Men and a Little Girl*, call it *Les Compères Plus une petite Fille*, call it what you will, but France's master of the mildly vulgar, low-brow buddy film, Francis Veber, has arrived on our shores, riding the Hollywood tide of backing putrid remakes of not-very-good French movies. (Soon to come: *Cousins*, an American version of *Cousin, Cousine*.) Writer/director and, in this case, executive producer Veber has churned out some of his country's biggest box-office hits—*La Chèvre, Les Compères*—reteaming the comedic pair of Gérard Depardieu and Pierre Richard, whose commercial stature at home stems from the trusty combination of a harried straight man and his pesky sidekick. Aside from this formula, Veber's banal recipe for success is an abuse of the pregnant pause and the quick cutaway.

Three Fugitives is propelled by the intrinsic humor of the mismatched duo (*the* prevailing '80s comedy formula)—in this case brawny, passive Nick Nolte as the Depardieu manqué, a just-sprung con named Lucas, and rubbery, effusvie Martin Short playing a dweeb named Perry (Richard's signature type). On the day Lucas goes to open his first postslammer bank account (he's been nabbed for 14 armed robberies), Perry decides to make his first heist in order to support his angelic daughter, Meg (Sarah Rowland Doroff, dressed in blue and white with a blunt cut to resemble a French schoolgirl, or maybe just a shrunken Isabelle Adjani).

Of course, Perry flubs it. The cops arrive, and he selects Lucas as his hostage, thus implicating the ex-con in a crime he knows only too well. The police (led by a predictably booming James Earl Jones) suspect Lucas. But Perry knows he's the one holding the gun and grenade on the surveillance tapes. So off our mutually antagonistic duo goes on a madcap adventure, fleeing the cops, punching people out, and waiting for taciturn Lucas to turn all goopy and sensitive. See, Meg turned mute when her mother died two years back and hasn't uttered a sound since. Will luggish Lucas melt for the doe-eyed girl in the knee socks? *Bien sûr!*

All is not at a loss, however, because Martin Short is slowly proving himself a presence with real possibilities, and not just for the hyper shenanigans he does so well. (His bank robbery scene reveals a klutzy body humor perfectly refined, and he does a drag turn every bit as funny and revelatory of male insecurity as Dustin Hoffman's in *Tootsie*.) But Short has a goony sensitivity that's getting closer to real acting than shtick. Too bad he's stuck in a movie where we're waiting for a kid to lisp endearingly and Nick "Slab o' Beef" Nolte's face to dethaw in a futile attempt to register emotion—or just consciousness.

Also reviewed in:

NEW REPUBLIC, 3/6/89, p. 24, Stanley Kauffmann
NEW YORK TIMES, 1/27/89, p. C6, Janet Maslin
NEW YORKER, 2/20/89, p. 98, Pauline Kael
VARIETY, 2/1–7/89, p. 18
WASHINGTON POST, 1/27/89, p. D7, Rita Kempley
WASHINGTON POST, 1/27/89, Weekend/p. 29, Desson Howe

TIMES TO COME

A Cinevista release of a Tripiquicios S.C.I. production. *Executive Producer:* Maria Angeles Mira. *Director:* Gustavo Mosquera. *Screenplay (Spanish with English subtitles):* Gustavo Mosquera and Alberto Delorenzini. *Director of Photography:* Javier Miquelez. *Editor:* Oscar Gomez. *Music:* Charly Garcia. *Costumes:* Monica Toschi. *Make-up:* Sergio Avello. *Running time:* 96 minutes. *MPAA Rating:* Not Rated.

CAST: Hugo Soto (Miguel Galvan); Juan Leyrado (Morea); Charly Garcia (The Ambulance Driver); Rosario Blefari (The Girl); Aldo Braga (The Policeman); Osvaldo Flores (The Father); Roxana Randon (Nurse); Luis Minces (The Grandfather); Ines Estevez (The Granddaughter); Cecelia Biagini (The Policeman's Daughter); Nestor Sanchez (The Young Doctor); Juan Carlos Ucello (The Journalist); Isaac Haimovici (The Astronomer); Fausto Collado (Morea's Friend); Sergio De Nadai (The Policeman's Buddy); Juan Godoy (Young Miguel Galvan); Matilde Del Corro (The Hospital Computer); Nora Zinski (Miguel Galvan's Ex-Wife); Mauro Bedendo (Jorge); Laura Masnata (The Punk Woman); Sebastian Poulastrou (The Vendor).

NEW YORK POST, 11/18/89, p. 20, Jami Bernard

It's a pretty bleak time in the South American city where Miguel is heading after a long time away. Things have changed. *Times* have changed, and in times to come, *more* things will change. And that's as much linear sense as you'll get from this spare, stylized, eerie, increasingly tedious movie.

Miguel (Hugo Soto) has barely arrived in this militarized urban zone when he is mistakenly shot by a sadistic cop on a routine crowd-control assignment. The wound leaves him paralyzed, frozen really, seeing but not seeing, hearing but not understanding, evidently much like the citizens who turned a deaf ear to the political developments which made Miguel's shooting possible, and then too symbolic for either camp to leave him alone.

Miguel stares at the ceiling in a bed in an empty hospital whose staff is on strike and which is run seemingly by invisible computers from which emanate the occasional cheerful announcement. He is the target of a resistance movement that wants to use him as campaign fodder and of the cop who shot him and doesn't want any more trouble over the incident. After all, this is a city where things just happen, or don't happen, depending upon prevailing powers.

There's also a vigilant ambulance driver who uses the shooting to blackmail the cop.

Without much dialogue to speak of, the urban graffiti "Lobotomy Now" is echoed in Miguel's sudden blankness; but without dialogue and with Miguel out of action, the movie eventually becomes one long chase down deserted industrial settings.

Director Gustavo Mosquera creates a cold, impersonal world, and Charly Garcia, who plays the ambulance driver, composed a driving, stimulating score. The movie is heavily symbolic— suffocatingly so.

VILLAGE VOICE, 11/28/89, p. 102, Georgia Brown

Times To Come, written and directed by the 27-year-old Gustavo Mosquera, arrives from another Capital of Pain, Buenos Aires, where many things appear only to disappear. The state, in Mosquera's grim fable, is presented as menacing but not entirely faceless.

Miguel (Hugo Soto), the sullen silent driver of a battered American car, returns to the capital after five or so years on the road. He hardly gets out of his car and puts on his Walkman when he's shot (accidentally) by a plainclothes cop named Morea (Juan Leyrado), who has lost his temper while trying to control a fleeing group of demonstrators. *Cerebral damage* reads the diagnosis on a video screen, as Miguel lies comatose in a deserted, litter-strewn hospital. The place appears to be run by computer. Every few minutes a disembodied voice broadcasts bulletins such as, "Two point two per cent will be deducted from strikers' salaries," or, "Every year the state loses 50 per cent of drugs destined for therapeutic use. Enjoyment by a few does not justify the crime."

One of the hospital's few attendants, an anonymous orderly/ambulance driver (played by Argentine rock star Charly Garcia, who composed and performs the film's strong score), happens to be a guardian angel, a whimsical revenger. He begins harassing the sinister Morea, while Miguel lies in bed, hallucinating some visitors (a woman wearing what looks like a cunningly ripped bedsheet and no underwear) and actually receiving others.

A central flashback is triggered by his father's arrival. The child Miguel visits an observatory, and there an astronomer steps down from his telescope to deliver a few reflections on time, space, and romantic agony. He also presents the boy with what looks like a desk toy from the Nature Company—"a device," the man tells him, "used to measure time." It's this tinted glass rectangle that Miguel's father brings to his son's hospital bedside. For a time the gadget is intriguing (seeming to hold surreal possibilities), but it turns out to be no more than a conversation piece.

Topography in *Times To Come* resembles tamer portions of George Miller's antiutopias: There are the roadside refineries, industrial debris, derelict gas stations, extended low shots of a car's front wheels on macadam, gangs of gloating punks in leather. Since the heroes and villains are opaque (symbolic, maybe) and the movie generates little dread or suspense, effects lie mainly in ambience. Mosquera relies heavily on graffiti-covered surfaces, small fires, broken telephone booths, flooded underpasses, and littered corridors. Just your usual walk downtown.

Also reviewed in:
NEW YORK TIMES, 11/17/89, p. C20, Caryn James
VARIETY, 5/25/88, p. 20

TOO BEAUTIFUL FOR YOU

An Orion Classics release of a Cine Valse/D.D. Productions/Orly Films/S.E.D.I.F./T.F.1/Films Productions film. *Director:* Bertrand Blier. *Screenplay (French with English subtitles):* Bertrand Blier. *Director of Photography:* Philippe Rousselot. *Editor:* Claudine Merlin. *Music:* Franz Schubert. *Sound:* Louis Gimel and Paul Bertault. *Sound Editor:* Stephanie Granel. *Set Decorator:* Théobald Meurisse. *Costumes:* Michele Marmande-Cerf. *Make-up:* Joel Lavau. *Running time:* 91 minutes. *MPAA Rating:* Not Rated.

CAST: Gérard Depardieu (Bernard); Josiane Balasko (Colette); Carole Bouquet (Florence); Roland Blanche (Marcello); François Cluzet (Pascal); Didier Benureau (Leonce); Philippe Loffredo (Tanguy); Sylvie Orcier (Marie-Catherine); Myriam Boyer (Genevieve); Flavien Lebarbe (The Son); Juana Marques (The Daughter); Carole Bouquet (Colette's Neighbor); Denise Chalem (Lorene); Jean-Louis Cordina (Gaby); Stéphane Auberghen (Paula); Philippe Faure (Colette's Husband); Jean-Paul Farre (The Pianist); Richard Martin (The Man on the Train); Sylvie Simon (The Receptionist).

CHRISTIAN SCIENCE MONITOR, 3/14/90, p. 11, David Sterritt

"Too Beautiful for You," a new import from France, is an unusual kind of love story.

Gérard Depardieu, one of Europe's most popular stars, plays a businessman who has a successful career, a comfortable home, and a smart, beautiful wife. But one day he walks into his office and meets a new "temp" secretary who just started working for him. One look and he's dizzily in love, for reasons he can't begin to understand—since he's already contented with his wife, and she's easily the more glamorous of the two. His friends are just as baffled as he is. Yet he can't deny his feelings, which lead to so many emotional complications that it takes the whole movie to sort them out.

Known in France as "Trop belle pour toi," the film was written and directed by Bertrand Blier, who has become one of Europe's most respected and talked-about filmmakers. His early films, such as "Calmos" and "Going Places," struck me as wildly offensive, largely because their attitude toward women tended to be nasty and paranoid. I once asked Mr. Blier about this, and he said that he didn't think of himself as a sexist, although he acknowledged that many people have found such an inclination in his work.

In any case, the problem has ebbed in such movies as "Get Out Your Handkerchiefs" and "Menagé," which raise their own issues related to vulgarity and taste.

"Too Beautiful for You" isn't exactly pristine in these areas, but it's far and away the most mature and restrained Blier work I've seen, and points him in a newly productive direction.

Much credit for the film's success comes from the vibrant performances of its actresses, who carry their own integrity with them. The wife is played by Carole Bouquet, whose credits include Luis Buñuel's classic "That Obscure Object of Desire," and the deliciously plain girlfriend is portrayed by Josiane Balasko, who's a writer and filmmaker as well as a gifted comedian.

In the pivotal male role, Mr. Depardieu plays equally well with both women; this is his fifth collaboration with Blier, and he knows how to blend seamlessly into the director's ensemble.

In fact, I give top honors for the movie's excellence to Blier and his filmmaking style. "Too Beautiful for You" is gorgeously photographed—by Philippe Rousellot, a talented cinematographer—and its camera movements have a strange, haunting rhythm that fascinated me from beginning to end. The movie has an offbeat screenplay, as well, which slides between the real and the not-quite-real; you never know what's going to happen next, or whether it will be realistic or dreamlike. There's also an evocative score, unexpectedly dominated by Franz Schubert—whose music plays such a strong part in creating the film's atmosphere that even the characters can't help commenting on it.

Having said all this, I must add that "Too Beautiful for You" is not a picture for every taste. It was the opening-night attraction at the most recent New York Film Festival—considered an honor for any movie—and to my surprise, quite a few people grumbled that they didn't like it at all, but found it slow and even boring at times. It also contains a bit of onscreen sex that may be too explicit for some spectators.

Still, the film has lots of admirers, and I predict it will be one of this season's most popular European visitors. It's also nice to see France making a comeback in American theaters after some comparatively dry years. "Too Beautiful for You" comes right after "Camille Claudel," with Depardieu as the great sculptor Auguste Rodin, and next month will bring "Monsieur Hire," an imaginatively filmed psychological mystery, with Michel Blanc and Sandrine Bonnaire giving first-rate performances.

All of which is good news for Americans seeking alternatives to ordinary Hollywood fare.

LOS ANGELES TIMES, 4/13/90, Calendar/p. 1, Peter Rainer

In Bertrand Blier's "Too Beautiful for You", Gérard Depardieu plays a happily married car dealer with a model-perfect wife (Carole Bouquet) who falls swooningly in love with his frumpy temporary secretary (Josiane Balasko).

This may sound like a marital infidelity farce, but the mood is hypnotic and almost rhapsodically self-obsessed. Blier has often made movies that seem clocked to the metronome of his own dream-time. Films like "Get Out Your Handkerchiefs" and "Menage," to name two of his most popular art-house hits, advance the plot in poetic leaps that make sense only retroactively.

Blier isn't interested in traditional narrative successes, and that can make his movies a little maddening sometimes. Particularly, as in his new film, when the poetic linkages are so vague and "personal" that at times it seems as if the film we're watching is only the residue of Blier's unconscious imaginings.

Still, a residue from Blier is more interesting than the fully aware, fully worked out scenarios of most other filmmakers. Gérard Depardieu, a Blier perennial, is well-cast as the husky, smitten Bernard. When he first sees Colette, his secretary, we can understand his infatuation. Bernard may look like an affable lug but he has surprising emotional depths; it makes sense that he would be attracted to Colette, who proves to be not only his physical but his spiritual counterpart. Her frumpiness is as deceptive as his huskiness. There's a sensual undertone to the dutiful, resigned dailiness of her life. She's poised to be lifted into a lyrical realm of sex and comfort.

By casting the two women in Bernard's life as polar opposites, at least in terms of their looks, Blier is setting up what at first appears to be an almost diagrammatic male fantasy. The fantasy is upended, of course: In the normal scheme of things, Bernard's wife would be the frump, his mistress the goddess. That's what's so potentially humorous about Blier's setup here. After Colette first meets Florence, she fumes at Bernard because she can't understand why he might prefer her to his wife. She thinks he's making weird fun of her.

But Blier doesn't play the situation for laughs, and he doesn't simply provide a standard reversal of fantasy expectations, either. For, as it turns out, Florence isn't just a prettified cipher. She's got depths of her own. She anguishes over her loss, and fights to get Bernard back. The more we see of these two women the harder it is to categorize them. Bernard, who is in love with the unfathomable, is, naturally enough, torn between them. They prove equal mysteries, equally out of reach.

In his earlier movies, Blier was famous for expressing the sort of uncensored male romantic fantasies that most filmmakers have the tact to avoid. The women in his films have almost always been species of the Other: lyrical creatures who confound men with their ultimate unknowability. In his new film, men are the Other too. In that sense, "Too Beautiful for You" (rated R for brief nudity), for all its humorlessness, is the film Blier has been working up to since the beginning of his career. Women and men are linked in the same trance-like continuum.

It's a measure of how far-gone Blier is in this film that, given so many ripe opportunities for comedy, he remains resolutely serious. With Pedro Almodovar and David Lynch, Blier is probably the most original comic talent to come along in the movies in the past decade or so. "Too Beautiful for You" certainly resonates with his earlier work, but in academic ways that don't always excite.

The hallucinatory dourness of what Blier has given us can't quite compensate for the lyric comic highs of his best work. Blier can't, or doesn't want to, separate out his own fantasies from Bernard's. That's why the film seems so involuted and personal in ways that don't always connect with an audience. Blier identifies so strongly with Bernard's spiritual-romantic dilemma that he doesn't recognize the raving narcissism at its core.

The film is really about how Bernard needs both halves of the mystery—Colette and Florence—and how he will never be satisfied. The women's dissatisfactions are not presented with the same heft as Bernard's, and so, at its worst, the movie is like the sanctification of some spoiled pasha who can't decide which concubine to idealize. *Quelle problem!*

As good as Depardieu is in this film, the two actresses are equally fine (particularly Balasko, noted in France for her comic roles). They deserve a few more drafts of Blier's ah-sweet-mystery-of-the-sexes elixir. It's possible to admire this film and still feel cheated.

MONTHLY FILM BULLETIN, 3/90, p. 81, Tom Milne

Bernard Barthélémy, a weathly garage-owner, married with two children, suddenly realises that his temporary secretary—plump, dowdy Colette—appears to be smitten with him. Baffled, all the more so in that his wife Florence is both beautiful and a fashion plate, Bernard finds himself secretly meeting Colette in a motel. The suspicious Florence, arriving at the garage on a tour of inspection and seeing Colette, at once guesses the truth. Confronted by Florence, Bernard haplessly admits to the affair, pleading that it is inexplicable and surely short-lived. He nevertheless continues to see Colette, using a room provided by Marcello, a restaurateur friend, after Florence confronts Colette at the motel in a bid to discover what her husband sees in her. Again trying to explain to Florence, but met with her angry suggestion that perhaps he should try living with Colette for a while, he accepts Colette's proposal of a visit to her family's cottage near Béziers. Florence meanwhile takes (or imagines taking) her revenge by offering herself to Marcello. As Colette sadly foresees, Bernard is soon bored by the rustic life. Worried about his children, Bernard asks (or imagines himself asking) the now possibly pregnant Colette's former boyfriend Pascal (who is overjoyed) to take her back. Berating himself as a coward, Bernard sneaks away to return home. While the indeed pregnant Colette finds another man to shower with love, Florence announces her decisions to walk out on Bernard. Despite his pleas, realising he is still thinking about Colette, she does so, leaving him alone and distraught.

Bertrand Blier, less acidulous than usual, has here turned out a film of some charm and occasional perception, but which adds up to rather less than meets the eye. To get at its heart, you have to wade through a minefield of flashbacks and fantasies, sometimes coalescing with reality, never differentiated from it, eventually to discover that they are really little more than fashionable window-dressing.

The official synopsis accompanying the film, presumably prepared or at least vetted by Blier, begins with the proposition that, "In general, a man first meets his wife, whom he marries, and then his mistress, using the latter to be unfaithful to the former". Bernard Barthélémy, it then goes on to suggest, the victim of a programming error, began by meeting his mistress, only afterwards meeting his wife. "How", Bernard is imagined as asking, "do you expect me to explain that to my lovely mistress with whom I have two children?"

All very neat and sophisticated, but the paradox begins to founder as soon as translated into terms of screen images. Beauty, as the saying goes (and as the cinema has spent its lifetime demonstrating) is in the eye of the beholder. So, even if one subscribes to the film's dubious proposition that the ideal attribute of a wife is loving warmth, and of a mistress a smart façade that looks good paraded on the arm (the reverse is just as likely to be true, but in any case why not both at once?), the confrontation as staged is so loaded as to become no contest. Josiane Balasko, as Colette, endowed with cuddly charm, warmth and good humour, acquires all the beauty in the eye of the beholder; while poor Florence, relegated through no fault of the admirable Carole Bouquet to being a walking *Vogue* design, is glacial enough to freeze even the ardour of an Eskimo.

With the characters conceived to stereotype, constantly struggling against the construction but never contriving to escape, the film is reduced largely to a matter of bits and pieces. But of these by far is a scene in which Depardieu, listening to a tape being used by his son to prepare a thesis on Schubert, while himself trying to rationalise his inexplicable attraction to his secretary, finds himself swept along in a romantic tide of passion by the music. Developing into a running gag, with the same theme casting its spell over assorted critical moments, the music also provides a rousing curtain line when Depardieu, left alone and in despair, turns to camera to cry, "Your Schubert's a pain in the ass!" Good performances, elegant direction and frequent charm notwithstanding, it's difficult to avoid reflecting that Godard covered the whole territory more succinctly, aptly and tellingly in *Pierrot le fou*, not least that brief sequence towards the end involving Raymond Devos as a man driven insane by the influence of a song on his love life.

NEW LEADER, 1/8/90, p. 22, John Morrone

Bertrand Blier's *Too Beautiful for You*, which was the [New York Film] Festival's opening night selection, is a wry comedy with philosophical pretensions that tries to explore the mystery of desire. The camera prowls incessantly, moving toward and backing away from the players to music by Schubert. Blier has once again conceived a triangular tale of erotic tension in the style that has marked most of his work since his 1973 *Going Places*, but here a kind of fuzzy charm rather than logic provides the momentum.

As Bernard, a man so hopelessly smitten with his plain, fleshy secretary that he ignores his ravishing wife, Gérard Depardieu looks doped. He has said that he and the two leading ladies "acted in a hypnotic state" to neutralize their anxiety over roles they found emotionally consuming. That may certainly account for Depardieu's performance. But Josiane Balasko is enrapturing as Colette, the secretary absorbed in the challenge of being Bernard's mistress. And there is nothing stupefied about Carole Bouquet's anguished portrayal of Florence, a wife literally driven into a frenzy by the incomprehensible revelation that she is too beautiful for her husband to want her.

Since Bernard seems numbed by his obsession, we watch the reactions of both wife and mistress to the bizarre shift in the laws of attraction. Balanced on the skateboard of a plot that never arrives at a resolution, Colette and Florence trade Gallic epigrams—in combat and mutual commiseration—about the nature of love and passion. "Love clobbers you" and "The dumb things in life are best" are, unfortunately, two typical examples.

Perhaps, though, the latter *aperçu* accurately reflects Blier's thinking. Unable to write a satisfactory ending for this film—a problem he also had with his 1986 *Menage*—he rewards Bernard for his messy (read "dumb") emotions by granting him an implausible dispensation from reason. Lucky hero: He's off the hook, but his mistress is seduced and his wife is abandoned.

That outcome is not surprising. In Blier's male-dominated universe, men routinely turn women into objects and toss them aside, then discuss it all as if doing some academic *explication de texte*. The sexism, moreover, is blithely exercised. Audiences viewing *Going Places* groaned when Depardieu, then a sexually magnetic newcomer, threw an unwanted Miou-Miou into the river. They may have the last laugh on actor and director when they see *Too Beautiful for You*. Sixteen years later Depardieu appears hapless (surely not Blier's intention), his usually powerful screen presence eclipsed by Balasko and Bouquet.

Balasko, well-known on the French stage as playwright and comedienne, is a particularly adept scene-stealer. At one point in the story she observes, "A woman's memory is in her shoulders." Although I don't have a clue as to what that means in the context of the plot, such as it is, she deserves kudos for the way she delivers the nuttiest of Blier's epigrams.

NEW YORK, 3/12/90, p. 64, David Denby

Bernard (Gérard Depardieu), a wealthy automobile dealer and the bemused hero of Bertrand Blier's *Too Beautiful for You*, is married to the stunning Florence (Carole Bouquet), who has the severe brow and noble bone structure of a goddess of wisdom. But into Bernard's office walks a new secretary, a temp, and he falls in love. Colette (Josiane Balasko) is fortyish, heavy, and earthbound, though she has a crooked little smile, the mark of her secret knowledge that she is attractive to men. In any case, she's not beautiful. Yet Bernard, to his own amazement, is enraptured and begins an affair with her while Florence, whom all other men adore, looks on helplessly.

It's as if Bernard had been sprinkled with fairy dust. He's lost, a quivering mass of ecstatic nerves. The sense of magical happenings is enhanced by the music of Schubert, with its surges of intense and poignant longing. "This music is shattering me!" Bernard exclaims at home, almost indignantly, when his little boy plays a recording of the "Death and the Maiden" quartet. Music of course, has always been used in movies to intensify moods, to sweep us up into passionate emotions, and here it's almost shocking how far music can go; Blier is joking about the movies' coercive use of music, and paying homage to Schubert at the same time.

Florence loves her husband, but her perfect beauty, we see, shuts Bernard out; there's nothing he can add to it, and he is reduced to passive worship. The plain Colette, on the other hand, blossoms under Bernard's gaze. Walking into the subway after one of their afternoons of lovemaking, she glows, and all the men standing on the platform smile at her. "She *gives* love," Bernard says, explaining his infatuation to skeptical friends. All of this is funny as the revenge of soul on beauty, but the trouble with *Too Beautiful for You*—and other Blier movies—is that once the director sets up the terms of his erotic and romantic paradox, he simply states them over and over again without knowing how to resolve them. In the dramatic vacuum, we have time to reject his habits of connoisseurship—the measuring and comparing of women, an old French game, here in new, ironic clothes.

Instead of developing the love affair, Blier plays narrative tricks, making his characters describe their own future or comment on their feelings as they are experiencing them. And finally, *Too Beautiful for You* just lurches toward an unsatisfying conclusion. Yet Blier has a talent for the absurdities of love, the irrationality of passion. Since he loves artifice and also obviously loves music, I suggest he film the two Mozart operas—*The Marriage of Figaro* and *Così fan tutte*—that speak of these matters on a level of sublimity. Mozart and his librettist Da Ponte never had trouble finding their way to the end.

NEW YORK POST, 9/22/89, p. 29, David Edelstein

Bertrand Blier's comedy has a great hook: Bernard (Gérard Depardieu), who's married to a tall, aquiline beauty (Carole Bouquet), falls in love with his dumpy temporary secretary, Colette (Josianne Balasko).

No one, including Bernard, can quite believe this turn of events, but he moves as if in a trance, obsessed with the woman, nourished and aroused in her company by something he can't begin to articulate. Somehow, the woman who should be his wife is his mistress, while the one who should be his mistress is his wife.

The whole movie unfolds in a trance, and Blier's work is relaxed, fluid and open-ended. The humor is irrational: The characters speak their thoughts and fantasies aloud, and you can't always tell if they're actually saying this stuff in mixed company or if Blier has simply made us privy to what's going through their minds. (Often they don't seem to know, either.)

As in all of Blier, they keep nothing back: They're always nuttily overdramatizing, throwing themselves into grand, irresponsible passion and then agonizing over their lack of comprehension. Stony in the presence of his wife, Bernard becomes enraged by the music of Schubert, on whom his son is writing a paper, while his magnificent wife floats through the apartment gaunt, white-faced and stricken, like some kind of Japanese ghost.

"Too Beautiful for You" doesn't go off the rails like Blier's "Menage," but he doesn't build on his premise, and the film peters out into irresolution—it seems, in the end, like a generic midlife crisis movie. It's middle-of-the-road Blier. Still, Depardieu is groggily perfect and Balasko heartbreaking; Bouquet, with her rigid, mask-like beauty, makes a striking camera object.

NEW YORK POST, 3/2/90, p. 17, Jami Bernard

Gérard Depardieu has more woman than he can handle in Bertrand Blier's amiable and well-made comedy "Too Beautiful for You" ("Trop belle pour toi"), although it's hard to sympathize with his plight.

For the same reason that the infidelity-a-deux in "Cousin, Cousine" worked very well in French and didn't translate in the American remake of it ("Cousins"), the Gallic fascination with the male inability to keep his pants on doesn't make for the same sort of high drama and low comedy over here. Luckily, "Too Beautiful for You" has neither highs nor lows, but more of a cerebral sort of humor.

Blier has a facile way of making Depardieu's romantic dilemma interesting, nearly intellectual, quite nearly transcendental—but it still boils down to that some men are never satisfied with perfection, poor dears.

Carole Bouquet plays the perfection—the porcelain-lovely wife of Bernard (Depardieu). She adores her husband, is a consummate mother, keeps a lovely house, all those things that men traditionally find appealing. Tradition is an important concept here, because the lover Bernard falls for is everything a mistress traditionally is not—this mistress is dumpy.

Anyway, she's *supposed* to be dumpy—the concept of the movie is predicated upon that—but actress Josiane Balasko actually has an earthy appeal. Nevertheless, the main joke is that Bernard has married the one who should be his mistress, and is bedding the one who should be his wife.

In press notes, director Blier comments: "In general, a man first meets his wife, whom he marries, and then his mistress, using the latter to be unfaithful to the former. This is the traditional course of events. It goes without saying that the mistress is much more tempting than the wife."

He was speaking, as he did when he introduced the movie at the New York Film Festival last year, with tongue in cheek. Still, excuse me if this sticks in my craw. Blier has also said that this is a movie about women. Actually, it is a movie (oh gosh, like so many others) about men *thinking* about women. Not the same thing.

Well, if we can put the fundamental subject aside for a moment, at least Blier handles it deftly, almost strangely.

Bernard is, by virtue of being played by Depardieu, a bearish man, a large, self-centered center of gravity. He has everything a man supposedly wants. And yet he becomes inexplicably drawn to his new secretary, an unremarkable woman who eyes him through the glass partition separating them. His wife has already checked out the new competition and dismissed her as too unsuitable a threat.

Bernard's newfound passion disturbs and frustrates him; this shouldn't be happening. His pangs are not so much guilt as an inability to figure out where he went wrong. Soon the haunting strains of Schubert are too much for him to bear. He paces his perfect home, distracted.

The most interesting device is the way in which Blier introduces realistic-looking fantasy scenes, suddenly and without comment. It is almost as if he is keying in to a parallel universe where the dinner party is still going on but where people are speaking their minds in ways that people never do. A dinner guest confesses to Bernard's wife what he's always longed to do to her. The mistress wanders in and takes her place at the table, dressed in black.

A flashback to Bernard's wedding has the couple explaining their sexual priorities to the assemblage, as to a press conference.

Depardieu, for all his passivity as a man helpless to make up his mind, is full of energy, a bundle of passion, confusion and despair. Bouquet floats through the movie like an ice sculpture in a parade, which is about what is called for.

Balasko is warm and funny and appealing as the Other Woman—after a typical session with her lover, she is so dizzy with fulfillment she confides the details to a perfect stranger on a Metro platform.

If the premise gnaws at any feminist sensibilities, try repeating to yourself: "It's only a French movie; it's only a French movie." You'll feel a lot better about it.

NEWSDAY, 9/22/89, Part III/p. 3, Mike McGrady

In choosing France's "Too Beautiful for You" as the opening-night film of the 27th New York Film Festival, the program committee has chosen to play it safe. Which is not to imply in any way that the Bertrand Blier film lacks spark or imagination. *Au contraire*. These qualities it has in abundance. Along with other ingredients of guaranteed appeal to festival regulars.

In the first place, it stars the universally popular Gérard Depardieu, best known here for "Jean de Florette," an actor who combines the innocence of a boy in the body of a bear, a combination so appealing that he averages three starring roles every year.

Then, too, it is directed by Bertrand Blier who has been represented at this film festival no fewer than four times, most recently with 1986's "Menage," also starring Depardieu.

Finally, Blier's theme, how sexual love can overwhelm reason, is univeral enough to have made this film ("Trop Belle Pour Toi") a sizable commercial success in his native France. It is Blier's belief that love is not only blind, it can be insane—especially when it afflicts a man going through a mid-life crisis.

At the outset, Depardieu seems to have everything—a successful business, loyal friends, a serene home with two photogenic children and a devastatingly beautiful wife (wonderfully played by Carole Bouquet, who co-starred in "For Your Eyes Only" and who is the current Chanel spokeswoman).

With all of this going for him, with everything nicely in place, Depardieu hires a temporary secretary (played by comedian Josiane Balasko) who is dumpy and frumpy, unbeautiful and uncharming. He takes but a single glance at her and—pow!—begins thinking: "I want to touch her skin."

Working within a few feet of each other, separated only by glass partitions, they are able to fantasize freely. Finally, she decides to take the lead: "It's lovely waiting for a man ... You can't just say to a man I want to be in a bedroom with you. It just isn't done. But why not?"

She picks up the phone, buzzes her boss, suffers misgivings.

"What's you want to tell me?" he asks.

"It's about your eyes. They hurt me."

The affair commences, an affair that is ironic, complicated, torrid, funny and ultimately every bit as sad as the Schubert background music that tinges their every encounter with a touch of doom. The contrast between lovely wife and homely lover is profound enough to carry the film a considerable distance, providing it with both its humor and its drama.

At times it seems more an infernal than eternal triangle, but Blier's always-innovative techniques enable us to wander freely within the mind of each of the players. His cameras find not only what does happen, but what is thought and what is fantasized.

Although one is never quite certain what is real and what is imagined, isn't that a bit like love itself? And as long as the love is growing, the movie is appropriately joyous and funny and giddy. With the affair's unraveling, as reality conquers fantasy, it slows down. While we may wonder why man involves himself in a process of unnatural setection, we will never distrust the truth of the situation.

There may be nothing more familiar to moviegoers than the triangular shape, but Blier has found fresh ways to draw the old form.

NEWSDAY, 3/2/90, Part III/p. 3, Mike McGrady

Bertrand Blier's sparkling "Too Beautiful for You" explores how sexual love can overwhelm reason. The theme is universal enough to have made this film ("Trop belle pour toi") a sizable commercial success in the director's native France. It is Blier's belief that love is not only blind, it can be insane—especially when it afflicts a man (Gérard Depardieu) going through a mid-life crisis.

At the outset, Depardieu seems to have everything—a successful business, loyal friends, a serene home with two photogenic children and a devastatingly beautiful wife (wonderfully played by Carole Bouquet, who co-starred in "For Your Eyes Only" and who is the current Chanel spokeswoman).

With all of this going for him, with everything nicely in place, Depardieu hires a temporary secretary (played by comedian Josiane Balasko) who is dumpy and frumpy, unbeautiful and uncharming. He takes but a single glance at her and—pow!—begins thinking: "I want to touch her skin."

Working within a few feet of each other, separated only by glass partitions, they are able to fantasize freely. Finally, she decides to take the lead: "It's lovely waiting for a man... You can't just say to a man I want to be in a bedroom with you. It just isn't done. But why not?"

The affair commences, an affair that is ironic, complicated, torrid, funny and ultimately every bit as sad as the Schubert background music that tinges their every encounter with a touch of doom. The contrast between lovely wife and homely lover is profound enough to carry the film a considerable distance, providing it with both its humor and its drama.

At times it seems more an infernal than eternal triangle, but Blier's always-innovative techniques enable us to wander freely within the mind of each of the players. Although one is never quite certain what is real and what is imagined, isn't that a bit like love itself? And as long as the love is growing, the movie is appropriately joyous and funny and giddy. With the affair's unraveling, as reality conquers fantasy, it slows down. There may be nothing more familiar to moviegoers than the triangular shape, but Blier has found fresh ways to draw the old form.

VILLAGE VOICE, 9/26/89, p. 61, J. Hoberman

Blier's single theme—the irrationality of erotic attraction—gets a rigorous workout, complete with Resnais-style time shifts, in this stolid adultery farce. Albeit not as delirious as previous Bliers, the movie is a shrink's delight (you never know who's going to articulate whose fantasy). Still, its lack of effervescence may confound the opening night crowd; unlike *Women on the Verge of a Nervous Breakdown*, it's not exactly a party film.

VILLAGE VOICE, 3/6/90, p. 64, Gary Giddins

After seeing Bertrand Blier's subtly ingratiating *Too Beautiful for You*, you may never be able to hear Schubert's G-flat impromptu again without smirking. It steals into the life of Bernard—a philandering husband with a heart of gold and a head of tin—like an elusive memory, underscoring his constant sense of impending perplexity. What organ chords are to soap opera, Schubert is to Bernard's tangled existence. Wherever he turns, he is badgered by one of a dozen of the composer's most romantic themes, creeping in on cat's feet. Eventually, he submits. Pascal, a friend of Bernards to whom the injured wife has turned in retaliation, asks him during a patch of commiseration. "Shall I put on some Schubert?" Bernard: "You got some?" Like Schubert, the movie grows on you.

Putting a whammy on Schubert is a characteristic predilection for Blier in this abundantly whimsical variation on the standard triangle. Bernard, played by Gérard Depardieu—looking more than ever like a heavily sedated Karl Malden—is married to the primly beautiful Florence, played, or at least modeled, by Carole Bouquet. Impossibly, it would seem, he hungers for his secretary, the plain and frumpy Colette, a role attacked by Josiane Balasko with a sexual bravado that will gratify similarly distressed "other women." After she sees Florence, who visits the office to make sure her husband's new assistant poses no threat (she takes one look and leaves reassured). Colette admits to Bernard, "Beauty clobbers you. It hurts."

Yet Colette has an unmistakable moxie of her own, and she knows the way to a man's testosterone. The perpetually dazed Bernard is so smitten, he tells Florence of his affair, without identifying the obscure object of his desire. It's not just that he wants to protect Colette. His conventional side knows that adulter, like business, has its pecking order, and that giving up Florence for Colette would be like abandoning the boardroom for the mailroom. Florence's pain, too, would be aggravated by the inscrutable nature of his lust. And then there are the two small kids, one of whom has suddenly developed a baffling taste for Schubert.

She finds out, of course, as do their friends, in the movie's funniest and most elaborate set piece, a surreal dinner that reverts between pure fantasy (Florence in a white dress) and impure reality (Florence in black). In the former mode, one of their frequent dinner guests casually remarks—to a chorus of napkin folding and eye rolling—that he has always had a ravenous yen for Bernard's neglected wife; specifically, he would like to wake up to find her sitting on his face. The exquisite Florence takes charge, as the table turns into a lavish banquet. She apologizes for being too beautiful (applause), announces with great resolve, "Now I intend to be probed more violently," kisses Bernard passionately, and asks, "Any more questions?" They all wake up to the presence of Colette, and the hermetic strains of Schubert.

Blier is heir to the Buñuelian sensibility, which locates political insinuations in domestic mores. His humor is quiet and cumulative, building through an accretion of peculiar remarks and looks and pauses and actions. *Too Beautiful for You* has the appearance, tempo, and feeling of late Buñuel, *The Discreet Charm of the Bourgeoisie* and especially *That Obscure Object of Desire*, in which the teenage Bouquet, one of two actresses alternating as the Object, made her film debut. His style has an intoxicating clarity, given the befogged story. Virtually every scene is shot straight-on—the camera rarely if ever looks up or down. The sets are as polished as chrome, and the movements of the largely impeccable cast are as carefully blocked as in a dance. Depardieu's congenital resignation provides much of the humor. But Blier's cleverly discursive script allows all three points of view to emerge. Colette's perspective is conveyed with the most sympathy: When Florence confronts her after a tryst, she pulls the covers up, looking overweight and vulnerable. Florence, who observes, "An ice cold hand has me pinned to the wall," is the princess coming to grips. None of them get what they want. As Bernard concludes, "Your Schubert is a pain in the ass"—the film's last line, followed by Schubert's full-screen credit. It's all his fault, or may as well be.

Also reviewed in:
NATION, 4/2/90, p. 467, Stuart Klawans
NEW YORK TIMES, 3/2/90, p. C15, Vincent Canby
VARIETY, 5/17–23/89, p. 32
WASHINGTON POST, 4/11/90, p. D2, Rita Kempley
WASHINGTON POST, 4/13/90, Weekend/p. 39, Desson Howe

TORA-SAN GOES TO VIENNA

A Kino International Corporation release of a Shochiku film. *Producer:* Kiyoshi Shimazu and Kiyo Kurosu. *Director:* Yoji Yamada. *Screenplay: (Japanese with English subtitles):* Yoji Yamada and Yoshitaka Asama. *Director of Photography:* Tetsuo Takaba. *Music:* Naozumi Yamamoto. *Art Director:* Mitsuo Degawa. *Running time:* 111 minutes. *MPAA Rating:* Not Rated.

CAST: Kiyoshi Atsumi (Torajiro Kuruma, "Tora-san"); Chieko Baisho (Sakura Suwa); Gin Maeda (Hiroshi Suwa); Masami Shimojo (Ryozo Kuruma); Chishu Ryu (Gozen-Sama); Akira Emoto (Hyoma Sakaguchi); Keiko Takeshita (Tourist Guide); Martin Loschberger (Young Austrian).

LOS ANGELES TIMES, 12/22/89, Calendar/p, 6, Kevin Thomas

"Tora-san Goes to Vienna" but he doesn't arrive until 45 minutes into this nearly two-hour film, the 41st in the world's longest-running film series. Longtime fans of Tora-san (Kiyoshi Atsumi), that lovable, comical itinerant peddler, wouldn't have it any other way.

First, Tora's creator, Yoji Yamada, has to catch up with him in some charming out-of-the-way locale and then bring him home to his relatives' sweet shop in the equally charming Shibamata, that northernmost neighborhood of Tokyo. That Yamada is leisurely about it is the point: in a rushed, busy world only Tora, as feckless as he is and ever luckless in love, seems to have the time to bother with people and their problems.

As always, Tora crosses paths with someone in crisis. This time it's an exceedingly stressed-out young executive (skinny, rubber-faced comedian Akiro Emoto), whom Tora pulls together at a spa. So grateful is the man that he insists Tora accompany him on a vacation in Vienna, which Tora thinks is some place in Kyushu. Once in the Austrain capital, the executive continues the regimen of wine, women and song—very discreetly suggested, for this is a family film—which Tora introduced him to at the spa. Meanwhile, Tora as usual encounters a pretty young woman (Keiko Takeshita) in distress. She is a hard-working tourist guide, in love with a young Austrian (Martin Loschberger) but desperately homesick.

Of course, the Austrian locales add freshness to the Tora formula, but Yamada amusingly makes the point that Tora might as well have stayed home and in his heart never really left Japan.

The cultural riches and grand architecture of Vienna are entirely lost on this wholly unsophisticated man: all that concerns him is the dilemma of Takeshita, with whom he typically becomes more smitten than he realizes. And although Yamada follows Emoto briefly on a standard sightseeing tour of Vienna, it's the Austrian countryside to which the director responds to the extent that we understand why Tora sometimes forgets he is not in Japan.

"Tora-san Goes to Vienna," which has a delightful appearance by the elegant Keiko Awaji as Takeshita's friend (and, as an inside joke, Harry Lime's widow), is as sentimental and endearing as it predecessors. The Tora-sans can always be counted on as a year-end holiday treat.

NEW YORK POST, 11/15/89, p. 28, Jami Bernard

Japan's "Tora-San" comedies, about a bumbling, good-natured, itinerant peddler, comprise the longest-running film series in the world. With No. 41, the working-class hero goes to Vienna— and to America as well, since the series rarely plays here. It's a treat, although it doesn't translate to a pop-culture icon here as readily as it does in the Far East.

Every move Tora-San makes in his travels and travails was greeted at a screening by howls—and I do mean howls—of laughter by the Japanese in the audience. They even cheered the credits. Though endearing and spirited, the movie really seems to depend on having that sort of personal history with the ongoing story and characters. By the time New Yorkers see this genial loser go to Vienna, he has already been around the block a few times in the Far East.

Shot in Cinemascope and with a color palette that evokes the '60s, "Vienna" gradually gets around to where Tora-San (perpetually played by Kiyoshi Atsumi) heads reluctantly to Vienna to satisfy an urge of his new companion, a depressed businessman who has attempted suicide under the wheels of Tora-San's train.

The cultural lures of Vienna mean nothing to Tora-San, who is aimless and homesick, not to mention fuzzy about geography (he thinks he's at a Japanese spa). He ends up following an attractive Japanese tour guide around, falling in love—platonically and hopelessly, as usual.

"He didn't reject the world, the world rejected him," sigh Tora-San's relatives, at whose Tokyo-suburb doorstep Tora-San usually winds up just when they've given up on him. Pronouncements such as this are gleeful in light of Tora-San's hapless, Chaplinesque history.

The push and pull between regimentation and wanderlust seems to be the main attraction of the series; American audiences can laugh along, too, though perhaps not as hard.

VILLAGE VOICE, 11/21/89/ p. 87, J. Hoberman

New political alignments bring new forms of cultural exchange. Starting today, *Tora-San Goes to Vienna* comes to America, the first feature in Japan's longest-running film series to be set off-island, as well as the first to be commercially released in New York.

Conventionally described as a Japanese Everyman, Tora-san is an itinerant, ferociously beaming peddler who roams Japan in his trademark plaid jacket and porkpie hat selling gewgaws at country fairs. Since beginning his epic career as a character on a TV series, he has been the hero of some 40 films—all evoking a vanished gemeinschaft of cozy neighborhoods and family values.

As the Japanese economy took off for the stratosphere, his latest adventures have been a biannual Japanese ritual.

Ian Buruma, who devotes a chapter to Tora-san in his book on Japanese popular culture, observes that this amiable anachronism, unmarried and a failure, is a source of fascination for being everything ordinary Japanese people are not, and an object of love because his endless wanderings confirm just how lucky they really are. (When, five minutes into *Tora-San Goes to Vienna*, one character professes to envy Tora's freedom from the rat race, another quickly points out that this footloose lifestyle means that the deeply middle-aged Mr. Tora is not yet a full-fledged man.) National self-effacement becomes a form of cultural self-adoration.

Not surprisingly, the Vienna that Tora-san encounters is a succession of moldy clichés, delivered with a good deal less panache than those of Jarmusch's Memphis. While his traveling companion runs shamelessly after Western art and women, Tora simply craves green tea over rice. No foreign trophies for him—nor even foreigners. (He's the Japanese who can say "No.") Drama arises once he tags along with a group of Japanese tourists, then spends the rest of the movie trying to persuade their expatriate guide to return home. Steeped as it is in the sadness of being away from Japan, *Tora-San Goes to Vienna* manages to reinforce all insular values while seeming to parody them—it's *Mystery Train* thrown into reverse.

Also reviewed in:
NEW YORK TIMES, 11/15/89, p. C18, Caryn James
VARIETY, 11/15/89, p. 22

TOUTE UNE NUIT

A World Artists Inc. release of an Avidia Films (Paris)/Paradise Films (Brussels) production. *Executive Producer:* Marilyn Watelet. *Director:* Chantal Akerman. *Screenplay (French with English subtitles):* Chantal Akerman. *Director of Photography:* Caroline Champetier. *Editor:* Luc Barnier. *Sound:* Ricardo Castro, Miguel Rejas, Henri Morelle, and Daniel Deshays. *Production Designer:* Michele Blondeel. *Costumes:* Michele Blondeel. *Make-up:* Thérèse Gilbert and Nicole Mora. *Running time:* 89 minutes. *MPAA Rating:* Not Rated.

CAST: Angelo Abazoglou, Frank Aendenboom, Natalia Akerman, Veronique Alain, Paul Allio, Jacques Bauduin, François Beukalaers, Michele Blondeel, Philippe Bombled, Ignacio Carranza, Gabrielle Claes, Aurore Clement, Christiane Cohendy, Nicole Colchat, Edith De Barcy, Dirk de Batiste, Laurent De Buyl, Jan Declair, Jan Decorte, Ingrid De Vos, Alix Dugauquier, Marie-Ange Dutheil, Luc Koning, Philippe Ekkers, Benedicte Erken, David Errera, Pierre Forget, Herman Gillis, Catherine Graindorge, Brigid Grauman, Lucy Grauman, Michel Karchevsky, Tcheky Karyo, Nadine Keseman, Pierre Lampe, Bernard Yerles, Simon Zaleski, Francine Landraine, Gregoire Lapiower, Jean-Philippe Laroche, Susanna Lastreto, Christine Leboutte, Carmela Locantore, Chris Lomme, Michel Lussan, Sylvie Milhaud, Claire Nelissen, Gisele Oudart, Janine Patrick, Jan Pauwels, Benedicte Paquay, Pietro Pizzutti, Juliette Pirlet, Roberto Plate, Isabelle Pousseur, Benjamin Rawitz, Nellie Rosiers, Vincent Rouche, Fanny Roy, Matthieu Schiffman, Marc Schreiber, Véronique Silver, Pierre Simon, Samy Szlingerbaum, Jean-Paul Trefois, Nicole Valberg, Henri van Lier, Florence Vercheval, Jacques Viala, Pierre Vaernewijck, Hilde Van Mieghem, Nathalie Willame, Sandrine Willems, Peter Woditsch.

MONTHLY FILM BULLETIN, 4/84, p. 103, Susan Barrowclough

Brussels, on a hot summer's night. Alone in her apartment, a woman in a low-cut red dress makes a telephone call, then takes a taxi and walks beneath a man's windows, watching him inside. In a café, two strangers sit drinking; suddenly they fall into each other's arms and dance to a romantic record. In a quiet suburban street, a woman impatiently leaves after waiting outside one of the little white houses; a man then catches up with her and they embrace. Another man puts a letter under a door; it opens and he is invited in. A woman tip-toes from one of the houses only to be grabbed and marched off by a waiting man. A little girl stealthily leaves home with a bag and a cat in her arms. An older woman leaves a sleeping man in bed, packs a suitcase and checks into a hotel; at dawn, she returns to her bed and the still sleeping man. In an empty café, a tiny girl and a big man dance to a record and then go their separate ways. Through the doors of a bar, a man looks at a beautiful woman sitting alone. A woman says goodnight to a man and goes indoors; he bangs at the door, she does not respond, and he remains waiting outside. A man with a suitcase goes into a café and resumes an unfinished lover's dialogue. Later, with a storm brewing and the stray sounds of the city—cars, music, clock chimes—drifting in through open windows, men and women toss sleeplessly in their beds, watching their sleeping companions. A man arrives at the apartment of the woman in the red dress. The storm suddenly breaks, and after a few minutes of torrential rain, peace and sleep descend. In the morning, people wake up, have coffee, wash, dress. Couples part, openly or covertly. A man talks about going to Italy, but the woman leaves before he has paid the hotel bill. Another woman creeps downstairs to leave, but is discovered. The woman in the red dress dances with her lover, and he asks why she loves the other man. Her telephone rings and the intimate sensuality of the night is ruptured. The day has begun.

Toute une nuit is made up entirely of a series of fragments, only some of which are described above. While apparently unconnected, they are all similar in tone. These amorous comings and goings, some happy, some unhappy, are all marked by a sense of urgency and emotional tension. Love, to invoke the cliché, may be eternal, but the stress in this film is on the immediate present—a present made precarious by the storm, the heat, the leaden atmosphere, the threatened arrival of morning. As one would expect from Chantal Akerman, the labyrinth that is spun out of these fragments is precisely organised in space and time. The film is divided into three sections of varying length—night, dawn and morning, marked by changing light and atmosphere—and into three locations, comprising a poor area near the centre of town with bars and Oriental music, a suburban street which might be reminiscent of a Hitchcock movie, and a square in the more venerable part of town with a distinguised old apartment house. While Akerman uses real locations for all the exteriors and most of the interiors, the film looks as if it were shot in a studio. It is as if she were working towards (and beyond) the stylished non-naturalistic look of Coppola's *One from the Heart*, with the movements of characters choreographed in and out of the sets in myriad different ways.

There are precedents for *Toute une nuit*. In the 1920s, the Surrealists made their own delighted discovery of what cinema was "really" about by popping in and out of many cinemas and seeing bits of films, but never staying from beginning to end. The American artist and film-maker Joseph Cornell once took a louche Hollywood melodrama set in the South Seas, edited it down to its climactic high points, laid some sultry Hawaiian-type music over it, and called the result *Rose Hobart*. With *Toute une nuit*, Akerman has recreated the Surrealists' kaleidoscopic experience by juxtaposing numerous emotional tableaux, and in the process has reduced the love story to its bare melodramatic bones. As couples meet and separate, arrive and depart, fall in and out of each other's arms, it is like seeing about thirty films, one after the other, without all the conventional elaboration of plot and character to detract from their cumulative effect.

The film's structure also bears some resemblance to that of the pornographic film in its lack of context. It is as if we always arrive at the point of pre- or post-coital emotion: he looks excitedly at her; she dresses; they lie in bed, together but separate. Melodrama rarely shows consummation; the interest lies in the mounting tension. Akerman understands this perfectly, and in this homage to melodrama she dispenses not only with context, but in large measure with dialogue as well. Like the action, the dialogue is reduced to the essential: "I had to see you", "I love you", "Not tonight", "I don't love you anymore". The real soundtrack is meanwhile provided by the moody sounds of the city at night: cars, planes, footsteps and the music of the café jukeboxes promising love in different languages.

One could describe the importance of *Toute une nuit* in terms of experimentation with narrative. But that would neither be faithful to the spirit in which it was made, nor do justice to its very real pleasures. Akerman, for all that has been written about her, is not a formalist. It is true that stringing together a lot of self-contained extracts does create a new sort of narrative, and that the mood of tension and suffocation is created as much by the precise framing and static shots as by what takes place between the characters. But Akerman's real aim is to take her audience on a trip on Ophuls's roundabout, into the emotional fairy-land of a hot summer night, which becomes a time apart from ordinary life, a time to dream, to feel, to react. "The night is like a big studio" (Akerman), and it is the way this studio can reveal the essential melodrama of people's emotional encounters—particularly when they are set one beside the other, each similar yet unique—that fascinates her. *Toute une nuit* says more about the poignant repetitiveness of our emotional lives than one love story in the naturalist mode could ever do.

NEW YORK POST, 6/30/89, p. 25, Jami Bernard

Some say film maker Chantal Akerman is a structuralist, so right away you know the film snobs are going to rush down to Film Forum 2's retrospective of her work, beginning today with "Toute une nuit." Everyone loves a structuralist, *non*?

Well, paste the labels on as you will (and others say Akerman, best known for her "Jeanne Dielman," is *not* a structuralist), but "Toute une nuit" is one of those annoying films where you could kick yourself for being bored because the movie is so obviously the work of someone with intelligence and talent.

Instead of drowsiness, then, "Toute une nuit" induces that wide-eyed zombie lethargy. You're still with the movie, but on the whole you'd rather be at the beach. Hey, call me a philistine, but with a description of "innumerable erotic encounters on a steamy summer evening in Brussels," I thought I was in for lots of sex scenes. *Structuralist* sex scenes, of course.

Instead, "Toute une nuit" is a series of charged, overheated comings and goings between couples whose histories are a mystery, sort of like a collection of outtakes from every romance in which people fall passionately or limply into or out of each other's arms. Men and women are shown anxiously awaiting someone, leaving someone, finding someone, considering someone, pining for someone.

There is a certain mounting humor to these torrid, out-of-context couplings and uncouplings, and there are certain repetitions that shore up the lack of narrative structure—letters and phone calls begun and aborted, doors closing, high heels clacking down streets and up stairs.

Love looks like a pretty dismal thing from Akerman's point of view. Whose passion can have much meaning when nameless couples all over town are clanging together like charged electromagnets? Individuals sit for many moments, isolated in their own angry, lonely passions, until someone notices them and it's a hugfest all around.

The women's thin, old-fashioned summer dresses sway in the breeze, and the men enfold the women urgently like limp ragdolls—but there's nothing sexy about these clinches. This kind of erotica is better left to the film students, the structuralists and the zombies.

VILLAGE VOICE, 7/4/89, p. 69, J. Hoberman

Chantal Akerman's *Toute une nuit* (All in One Night) is another sort of urban nocturne. The mode is austere, the sensibility sweet, and the violence all conceptual. Set in blandest Brussels some steamy summer night, the film is fashioned from the shards of two dozen pulverized melodramas.

Toute une nuit, which inaugurates an 11-film Akerman retro Friday at Film Forum 2, is the Belgian director's fragmented version of *La Ronde*—or maybe a structural-materialist update of *A Midsummer Night's Dream*. Made in 1982, it suggests a collaboration between Gertrude Stein and Cindy Sherman: The movie is purposefully repetitious, borderline cute, and formally rigorous; it's filled with enigmatic, artfully posing creatures in filmy dresses and linen suits.

Not simply episodic, *Toute une nuit* has an all-over zap-TV format. With camera and characters moving in and out of traffic, it jumps from narrative situation to narrative situation: Activities rhyme; locations crisscross as characters meet and embrace, dance and split up, yank each other into cabs, or simply watch everyone else in the throes of passion. Planes fly overhead. Beaten-up Wurlitzers issue snatches of terrible Euroschlock. Men leave women, women leave men, insomniacs stare at the ceiling. The sparse dialogue is functional and opaque, a matter of deadpan jokes and stylized silences. Akerman meanwhile establishes a choreography of indoors and out, upstairs and down, attraction and rejection. Just before dawn, a thunderstorm passes through. And just after daybreak, one woman comes home and pops into bed beside her sleeping husband—just in time for the alarm to go off.

Given the difficulties in lighting the film, Akerman has expressed disappointment that she had to shoot *Toute une nuit* in 16mm rather than 35mm. (Still, the print at the Film Forum is far better than the one screened five years ago at the Museum of Modern Art.) This may be middling Akerman—it's neither as monumental as *Jeanne Dielman* nor as affecting as *News From Home*, neither as original as *The Golden 80s* nor as challenging as *je tu il elle*—but it's a daring pirouette over some velveted void. "The night is a big studio," Akerman has said. You don't need a set. This movie is alert to the beauty of an ordinary car's headlight scraping the side of a nondescript wall.

Also reviewed in:
NEW YORK TIMES, 6/30/89, p. C12, Vincent Canby
VARIETY, 9/29/82, p. 20

TOXIC AVENGER, THE: PART II

A Troma Team release in association with Lorimar. *Producer:* Lloyd Kaufman and Michael Herz. *Director:* Michael Herz and Lloyd Kaufman. *Screenplay:* Gay Partington Terry and Lloyd Kaufman. *Story:* Lloyd Kaufman. *Additional material:* Pericles Lewnes, Fumiyo Furuyo, Yoshiko Miyamoto, Andrew Wolk, and Phil Rivo. *Director of Photography:* James London. *Editor:* Michael Schweitzer. *Sound:* Sekou Shepard. *Sound Editor:* Joseph McGirr. *Art Director:* Alexis Grey. *Special Effects:* Pericles Lewnes. *Costumes:* Susan Douglas. *Special Make-up Effects:* Arthur Jolly, Joel Harlow, Kelly Gleason, and William L. Decker. *Stunt Coordinator:* Scott Leva. *Running time:* 95 minutes. *MPAA Rating:* R.

CAST: Ron Fazio and John Altamura (Toxic Avenger); Phoebe Legere (Claire); Rick Collins (Apocalypse Inc. Chairman); Rikiya Yasuoka (Big Mac); Tsutomu Sekine (Announcer); Mayako Katsuragi (Masami); Shinoburyu (Shockikuyama); Lisa Gaye (Malfaire); Jessica Dublin (Mrs. Junko); Jack Cooper (Mr. Junko); Erica Schickel (Psychiatrist); Dan Snow (Cigarface); Andrew Wolk (Pus Man); Florence Gummersbach and Eric Alan (Homeless Couple); Felix Cortes (Taxi Driver); Bill Ferris and Irene Scase Summerville (Senior Citizens in Taxi); Alex Cserhart and Theresa Faw (Environmentalists); W.E. Benson (Father O'Reilly); Elliot Weiss (Dog Face); Emmy Meyer (Mrs. Beasley); Bryan Perkins and Keith Allen (Messengers); Michael Leoce and Matt Miller (Police Officers); Phil Rivo (Cookie).

LOS ANGELES TIMES, 3/31/89, Calender/p. 11, Kevin Thomas

The only amazing thing about "The Toxic Avenger: Part II" is that Part I generated enough interest to warrant a sequel. In any event, part II is too silly to be funny, and although good-natured in the low-budget Troma Pictures tradition, it is too violent to recommend for children who would otherwise be the most likely to appreciate it. It's not for nothing that it's been rated R. (Certainly most kids see much stuff as violent as this—or more so—but why numb them further?)

You may recall that the Toxic Avenger started out as nerdy New Jerseyite Melvin Junko, whose tumble into a toxic chemical waste turned him into a tall, smudgy-looking muscleman with a hideously deformed, rubber Halloween mask-like face and head. The Toxic Avenger is a sweet-tempered do-gooder whose chemical bath has left him with a built-in evil detector.

This time, Troma partners and co-directors Lloyd Kaufman and Michael Herz contrive mightily to get the Toxic Avenger (played by Ron Fazio and John Altamura) to Tokyo, possibly to make use of Japanese co-production yen. The pretext is that a conglomerate baddie (Rick Collins) who wants to turn Toxie's hometown Tromaville into the "toxic waste capital of the world" must lure Toxie to Japan, where a formula has been devised to render him powerless. We're told the potion is "too volatile" to be shipped to New Jersey.

As it turns out, Toxie's adventures in Japan are no more worth outlining than those that await him upon his return to Tromaville. Alas, Troma promises us that we haven't seen the last of the Toxic Avenger.

NEW YORK POST, 4/7/89, p. 29, Jami Bernard

Don't be fooled by the retro-clever title or by the idea of a super-hero from New Jersey. "The Toxic Avenger II" is not some enjoyably abominable B movie that will impress your date. It is just another tired exploitation movie from the Troma Team, who make movies with great names ("Surf Nazis Must Die") and no redeeming value.

"Toxic II" does have higher production values than any of Troma's previous fare, plus the kind of jokes that pass in Tromaville for upscale (one character quotes David Mamet). Still, guys, it doesn't work. It may not even work for the hard-core exploitation fans, now that there are fewer running sores and more running gags. It's easy to be sleazy; now the Troma Team will find that the leap from Grade Z to Grade B is wider than a toxic dump is deep.

But wait, here's a little catch-up for those who are new to the Troma a brand of entertainment. Troma is an independent outfit that specializes in deliberately adolescently trashy movies. "The Toxic Avenger" was a hit of sorts for them; in it, Melvin the mild-mannered mop boy at a Tromaville, N.J., health spa got slathered in toxic waste and became a gruesome-looking local hero. "I am the first hideously deformed monster hero of super-human size and strength to come from New Jersey," the Avenger proudly informs us in this sequel.

"Toxic II" starts with our hero suffering from boredom. He's cleaned up Tromaville, and now everyone is free to dance in the streets, get tattooed, and exterminate bugs. Melvin has a buxom, blind girlfriend (performance artist Phoebe Legere), but something is missing from his life, enough bad guys to fuel a sequel to his story.

Enter some convenient bad guys. They want to turn the local home for the blind into a toxic chemical dumpsite (toxic chemicals play a big part in Troma films; they help pave the way for special effects makeup involving oozing pustules).

In this movie, Melvin makes a bizarre sidetrip to Japan. Perhaps this is Troma's way of honoring the Godzilla movies; more likely it was cheaper to film there and helped insure an overseas market for the inevitable video.

In Japan, Melvin takes on his long-lost dad, Big Mac (he is also known as the Big Cheese or the Big Mac with Cheese, yuk yuk). Then he learns some sumo wrestling while people get chopped into sushi. Eventually he returns to Tromaville for some more fight scenes, a car chase, and some explosions.

In addition to fewer pustules, there is also less emphasis on showing women having their blouses ripped off or being gang-raped. "Toxic II" is downright enlightened. Of course, a few of the female Japanese extras are completely naked, but that has to be less offensive than Troma's last movie, "War," in which women are raped by AIDS carriers in order to spread disease.

The screenplay assures us several times that there will be a "Toxic Avenger III," That's just the kind of dangerous talk we don't need.

NEWSDAY, 4/7/89, Part III/p. 5, Mike McGrady

One of the enduring perversities to emerge from the 1960s was "camp." Something was camp, you'll recall, when it was "so bad it was good." "The Toxic Avenger: Part II" exists well beyond camp limits; it's so bad it's just plain horrible.

Lacking the subtlety or wit even to qualify as a comic-book movie, this latest aberration picks up where the original "Toxic Avenger" left off. That was the story of Melvin Junko, an anemic mop boy at a health club, who falls into a vat of toxic waste and becomes hideously deformed but...muscular, New Jersey's only superhero and an enemy of polluters everywhere.

Melvin, now known alternately as Toxic Avenger and Ol' Goo Eyes, has cleaned up his hometown of Tromaville, and the residents are dancing in the streets, literally. Toxic's busty girlfriend (Phoebe Legere) is blind, which in this case would seem to be an absolute necessity.

Whenever he's in the presence of evil, Toxic's "tromatons" act up and he cannot rest until he has eliminated the evil. When big-time polluters move back into Tromaville, blowing up the home for the blind, his tromatons go crazy, causing Toxic to tear limbs off people, chainsaw them to bits, rip their ears off, squeeze them into ball-sized objects, boil them alive, decapitate them and exhibit other anti-social behavior. At all times the screen is filled with severed body parts, rivers of blood, unknown actresses without shirts or any combination of the above.

About halfway through the film, my own tromatons began to shudder and vibrate, a phenomenon that occurs whenever I am in the presence of monumental dumbness. If I could have reached the evildoers responsible for this mess—Michael Herz and Lloyd Kaufman produced and directed—I would have given them the only kind of punishment they seem to understand. That is to say, I would have sat them down, talked to them sternly, then ripped off their ears.

Also reviewed in:
NEW YORK TIMES, 4/17/89, p. C18, Vincent Canby
VARIETY, 3/15–21/89, p. 14
WASHINGTON POST, 4/21/89, p. C7, Richard Harrington

TOXIC AVENGER, THE: PART III: THE LAST TEMPTATION OF TOXIE

A Troma Team release. *Producer:* Lloyd Kaufman and Michael Herz. *Director:* Michael Herz and Lloyd Kaufman. *Screenplay:* Gay Partington Terry and Lloyd Kaufman. *Story:* Lloyd Kaufman. *Additional Material:* Pericles Lewnes, Andrew Wolk, and Phil Rivo. *Director of Photography:* James London. *Editor:* Joseph

McGirr. *Sound:* Sekou Shepard. *Sound Editor:* Abe Nejad. *Art Director:* Alexis Grey. *Special Effects:* Pericles Lewnes. *Costumes:* Susan Douglas. *Make-up:* Kathy Mulshine. *Special Make-up Effects:* Arthur Jolly, Joel Harlow, Kelly Gleason, and William L. Decker. *Stunt Coordinator:* Scott Leva. *Running time:* 100 minutes. *MPAA Rating:* R.

CAST: Ron Fazio and John Altamura (Toxic Avenger); Phoebe Legere (Claire); Rick Collins (Apocalypse Inc. Chairman/The Devil); Lisa Gaye (Malfaire); Jessica Dublin (Mrs. Junko); Tsutomu Sekine (Announcer); Michael J. Kaplan (Little Melvin); Traci Mann (Snake Lady); Pericles Lewnes (Painted Face Villain); Edward Burrows (Doctor Goldberg); Raymond Seiden (Dog Face); Sophia Domoulin (Donkey Woman); Arthur Jolly (Donkey Man); Jim McCluskey (Lawnmower Man); Ichiro Yamanak (Japanese Bald Man); Florence Gummersbach and Eric Alan (Homeless Couple); W.E. Benson (Father O'Reilly); Bryan Perkins and Keith Allen (Messengers); Dan Snow (Cigarface); Michael Leoce and Matt Miller (Police Officers); Phil Rivo (Cookie); Charlotte Kaufman (Toxic Baby); Lisbeth Kaufman and Lily Hayes Kaufman (Toxic Children); Patricia Kaufman (Outraged Tromavillian); Sloane Herz (Tromaville Teeny Bopper).

LOS ANGELES TIMES, 11/10/89, Calendar/p. 8, Chris Willman

Troma Inc.'s no-budget scuzz-ball horror-comedies, like the movies listed on the marquee at any Pussycat Theater from week to week, can be counted on to have all their best creative energies invested in the title alone. "The Toxic Avenger: Part III: The Last Temptation of Toxie" is yet another case in which the agonizingly cretinous script seems to have been a bothersome afterthought to the brainstorming session for the name, which in this case promises Scorsese parody and delivers only sore-sleazy prattle. Death be quick.

A prologue recapping the first two films reminds us that the Toxic Avenger—a nerd who gained superhuman strenth and homeliness in an industrial accident—is "the first super-hero from New Jersey." No doubt he's also the first super-hero ever to reach into a squirming bad guy's guts, pull out his intestines and play jump-rope with them in the opening scene of a motion picture.

Toxie's real battle, though, is with old Beelzebub himself, a wacky marauder who offers the Avenger control of Tromaland, N.J., for his complicity. The monstrous hero briefly falls for this devilish line and turns into an ugly, "babe"-spouting, power-tie-wearing yup—an amusing idea badly bungled by butterfingered director/producers Lloyd Kaufman and Michael Herz, whose idea of satire is stuck somewhere between the Garbage Pail kids and fifth-grade boys'-room sex jokes.

Having the hero of the grade-Z "Toxic Avenger III" (MPAA-rated R) resist selling his soul to the devil is too, too ironic; based on this cynical amateur enterprise, Kaufman and Herz seem like the sort of junior *auteurs* who would gladly gift-wrap and offer points on their souls for Satan, if only he would return their calls.

NEW YORK POST, 11/10/89, p. 31, Jami Bernard

Melvin, the former mop-boy who became a mop & glow boy after a date with a vat of toxic waste in the original "The Toxic Avenger," is back for part three, facing a midlife crisis. Like the other two Toxie movies, this one features oozing pustules aplenty.

The hideously deformed Melvin (played alternately by Ron Fazio and John Altamura, depending on whether he is flashing back to his mopboy self) finds himself out of a job now that he has cleaned up crime and pestilence in Tromaville. The chairman of a nasty chemical company buys Toxie's soul—the chairman is really the Devil as he may appear if he landed in New Jersey—so that Toxie can afford an operation for his blind bimbo wife (Phoebe Legere).

Tame and tedious yuppie jokes fill some space as the superhero goes jogging, reads the Wall Street Journal, and "does" brunch. It is the movie's idea that it is environmentally and socially correct.

"Toxie III" also takes some pointed jabs at a subject dear to the folks at Troma: the video industry's tendency to squeeze out "B" titles from store shelves. Toxie lays low two men who call themselves "the Warner brothers" after they threaten that Tromaville's video store will only carry the top 20 titles.

The version I saw was the unrated one that will eventually go out on video; the R-rated theater version may not have all of the guts and goo. If you don't like guts and goo, you have no business seeing this anyway. (In one typical sequence, Toxie rips the guts out of a Warner brother and then jumps rope with them.)

The movie follows the same Troma formula: adolescent humor, giddily stupid lines and situations, atrocious acting, jiggly girls. The only difference this time is that, with a more lavish than usual budget, "Toxic III" is Troma's "Intolerance," with bigger sets and higher aspirations. They're calling the trilogy the "Toxic Ring." Don't be fooled.

NEWSDAY, 11/10/89, Part III/p. 9, Bill Kaufman

Troma, Inc., the company that made such ultra-low budget films as "The Class of Nuke 'Em High" and "Surf Nazis Must Die," has more or less outdone itself with "The Toxic Avenger III," a movie that could end up a cult favorite—if there's a cult that favors a self-righteous hero with a distorted, puffy head who likes to eviscerate his enemies.

"The Toxic Avenger: Part III: The Last Temptation of Toxie" brims with bargain-basement special effects, and the entire film looks as if it had been shot with an old Super 8 camera hastily unwrapped on Christmas Day, 1958.

Former football player Ron Fazio is the grown-up Toxic Avenger, who two movies back as a teenager plunged into a truckload of vile goop and was transformed into a creature of enormous strength. Toxie, as he's called, now has a sexy pal played by a breathless, giggling Phoebe Legere, who skillfully turns the role into a conglomeration of every stereotyped dumb blonde character ever seen.

Romance buoys Toxie to even greater accomplishments, all for the sake of mankind, it seems.When a gang of toughies invades a video store where he works, he becomes something of an avenging punster. "You know, dude, you don't have any intestinal fortitude," says Toxie, as he rips about five yards of squirting gut from a bad guy's abdomen. And then there are the worms-out-of-the-chest and mangled arm scenes.

Of course, there's nothing in this flick meant to be taken seriously. With that in mind, the entire picture becomes sort of an absurd *Grand Guignol* played for laughs. It should appeal mainly to young audiences and anyone who wants to have a hoot because it's all so silly.

Also reviewed in:
NEW YORK TIMES, 11/10/89, p. C10, Vincent Canby
VARIETY, 11/8/89, p. 36

TRIUMPH OF THE SPIRIT

A Nova International Films release. *Producer:* Arnold Kopelson and Shimon Arama. *Director:* Robert M. Young. *Screenplay:* Andrzej Krakowski and Laurence Heath. *Story by:* Shimon Arama and Zion Haen. *Director of Photography:* Curtis Clark. *Editor:* Arthur Coburn. *Music:* Cliff Eidelman. *Sound:* Eli Yarkoni. *Production Designer:* Jerzy Maslowska. *Art Director:* Krystyna Maslowska. *Set Decorator:* Izabela Paprocka. *Costumes:* Hilary Rosenfeld. *Running time:* 120 minutes. *MPAA Rating:* R.

CAST: Willem Dafoe (Salamo Arouch); Edward James Olmos (Gypsy); Robert Loggia (Papa); Wendy Gazelle (Allegra); Kelly Wolf (Elena); Costas Mandylor (Avram); Kario Salem (Jacko); Edward Zentara (Janush); Harmut Becker (Major Rauscher); Burkhard Heyl (Aide to Rauscher); Sofia Saretok (Momma); Grazyna Kruk-Schejbal (Sister, Julie); Karolina Twardowska (Benuta); Juranda Krol (Sarah); Wiktor Mlynarczyk (Beppo); Jerzy Gralek (Kapo Kyr); Andrzej Wojaczek (Kapo Otto); Sebastian Spandel (Lud); Ewa Lesniak (Kapo Hilda); Anna Chitro (Naomi); Halina Chrobak (Clog Thief); Ireneusz Tomczak (Fratelli); Teddy Atlas (Silber); Andrzej Leszczynski (Referee); Lew Rywin (Announcer); Arthur Coburn (Rabbi); Maria Probosz (Rauscher's Girlfriend); Stefania Zubrowna (Dying Woman); Hanna Pater (Prisoner Nurse); Dorota Bialy-Wieczorek (SS Woman); Michal Juszczakiewicz (Sonderkammando).

CHRISTIAN SCIENCE MONITOR, 2/7/90, p. 10, David Sterritt

[*Triumph of the Spirit* was reviewed jointly with *Enemies, a Love Story*; see Sterritt's review of that film.]

LOS ANGELES TIMES, 12/8/89, Calendar/p. 6, Michael Wilmington

At the heart of "Triumph of the Spirit"—a movie that shows us the horrors of Auschwitz from ground level and ringside—there's a schism: a battleground between drama and melodrama, inspiration and facile uplift. Unlike the many fights in the movie, this one is never truly decided.

The film—based on the real-life experiences of Salamo Arouch, a Greek Jew incarcerated with his family at the Auschwitz-Birkenau camps—keeps swerving between the awesome realities of the camps and something shallower: a prototypal tale of a skinny, indomitable boxer who keeps knocking down opponents as fast as his Nazi persecutors can set them up. This exaggerated, romanticized semi-"Rocky" saga, replete with suffering true love, was probably intended as a commercial hedge. But it's the "unsalable" side of "Triumph of the Spirit," the unflinching recreation of Auschwitz, that gives it some stature and riveting intensity.

In life and the movie, Arouch—a Balkans middleweight champ before his arrest— fought more than 200 times before rowdy, carousing camp officers. He won regularly, often brutally, gaining nothing tangible but slight preferential treatment and days more of life. Yet the movie concentrates more on those meaningless external victories than the crucial internal ones, contrasting Arouch with his poor, tough old stevedore of a father (Robert Loggia), finally condemned to death for being unfit.

In the '30s and '40s, radical screenwriters like Clifford Odets ("Golden Boy") or Abe Polonsky ("Body and Soul") used boxing as a microcosm of exploitation and the boxers as tarnished proletarian knight errants. There's an echo of that approach here, but the scenario is still an obvious patchwork, pawed over by many hands. There's an improbable-looking Auschwitz revolt, sudden underground movements, daredevil bombings. And the writers have given Arouch a wholly fictitious Auschwitz-romance—with the lovers eyeing each other wistfully or exchanging stoic vows during their grim captivity, though Arouch and his wife never met until after the camps were liberated.

Yet, despite all this, "Triumph" moves and holds you. Director Robert M. Young and his cast have approached it with absolute seriousness, high dedication. They seem obviously inspired—if not by the writing, then by the subject itself and the overshadowing presence of Auschwitz, where most of "Triumph" was shot.

This huge camp becomes a dominant character: a factory of death, ringed around with gray stone walls, encompassing vast cavernous barracks, where the inmates sleep all jammed together like rats; barren-looking work fields, and the ominous crematories, where the elderly or youthful are gassed. Young won't show us the actual mass executions. He keeps suggesting them elliptically, with shots of the guards inserting the Zyklon B gas canisters or close-ups of witnesses seeing the bodies. But he doesn't have to. The entire setting reeks of death. The very air around Auschwitz, as he and Curtis Clark photograph it, seems to have a stench of brutality.

In many movies, the backgrounds are important. Here, they're crucial. Without Auschwitz, and our full awareness of its gruesome history, "Triumph" might have only a fraction of its impact, the performances only a small part of their power.

Dafoe suggests Arouch's changes against the lines or between them and, though he doesn't project much physical joy, he catches the quick resilience of a fighter who, in real life, was nicknamed "the ballerina." Loggia plays against his usual strengths by showing machismo frustrated, gusto drained. When he cracks apart, it's a truly piteous spectacle.

And Edward James Olmos—who has such amazing concentration that he can create a fascinating performance out of reaction shots—puts icy, ambivalent undertones into the trustie guard Gypsy. If, at first, Gypsy seems simply another prison rat-fink, Olmos soon brings out his subversive side: the mocking Gypsy song, behind an unctuous smile, that he sings to the Germans, his offhand toast to the invading armies.

There are only a handful of concentration-camp movie dramas (Andrzej Munk's posthumous 1963 "The Passenger" may be the best and Alain Resnais' 1956 "Night and Fog" the best film on the subject in any form). But Young, more than even Munk, gets a convincing sense of Auschwitz's day-to-day routine—not in the events as much as the way he stages them, with huge floating vistas behind the characters, prisoners dwarfed by the galaxy of misery around them.

Young's 1978 "Short Eyes" is one of the most authentic of all prison movies. That's the quality he gets here too, on a more grandiose scale: the gray, deadly routine of the place, the somnolent, wavelike mass movement of the inmates, the quiet sadism of the guards. He's very good at capturing slight eerie details of behavior, like the hair-raising moment when a German officer sends a mother off to die with her child, shooting her a soft sneaky look that she mistakes for benevolence.

Young can't cover up the structural weaknesses of the story and he can't build up to a big climax. The last scene of "Triumph," with its strained romantic coda, is a biographical cheat that also plays phony on the screen.

But, unlike many contemporary American film makers, he can give us an experience. The shudder of revulsion that goes through us here is real. So is our pity and grief for the victims, our shock at the staggering cruelty of their jailers. To the extent that "Triumph of the Spirit" (rated R for violence and language) lets the enormity of Auschwitz and its crimes pour through, the film does manage a victory: compromised but real, flawed but searing.

MONTHLY FILM BULLETIN, 6/90, p. 177, Julian Petley

When the Germans invade Greece during World War II, the Jews of Thessalonica are imprisoned in a ghetto. Among them are the Balkan middleweight boxing champion Salamo Arouch, his family, his girlfriend Allegra and her sister Elena. Eventually the entire ghetto is deported to Auschwitz/Birkenau. On arrival at the camp, many of the Jews, including Salamo's mother and sisters, are sent straight to the gas chambers under guise of being taken to the showers. Salamo, his father Poppa and brother Avram, and his friend and sparring partner Jacko are spared, but put in the charge of a particularly brutal kapo. When Salamo beats up the kapo, the fight is watched with interest by the SS. Salamo is summoned before the camp commandant Major Rauscher, and the kapo is summarily shot. Rauscher is a former boxing champion and keen spectator of the sport, and he arranges a series of fights for the entertainment of his fellow officers. There are no rounds, and the losers are sent to the gas chambers. As Salamo fights for his life, his family and friends are gradually wiped out. His brother is killed for refusing to work in the gas chambers, his father is liquidated on the pretext of being too old to work any more, and Allegra is almost beaten to death by the prison guards for stealing a loaf of bread. However, he does strike up an uneasy friendship with a gypsy kapo, who entertains the SS before the boxing matches and is secretly awaiting the arrival of the Russians. During an air raid on a steelworks in which they are both serving as slave labour, Salamo and Allegra manage a hurried meeting. As the Russians approach, the women are evacuated from the camp, Rauscher goes mad and shoots his aide, and the resistance becomes bolder. The destruction of one of the crematoria incurs horrific reprisals. Salamo just manages to escape with his life, the Russians arrive, and he sets off in search of Allegra.

The major problem facing films with concentration camp settings is that too much realism renders them unwatchable, and too little destroys their credibility, relegating them to what Art Spiegelman has called "holokitsch". *Triumph of the Spirit*, the first major U.S. film to have been made on location in Poland and the first feature ever to have been shot inside Auschwitz itself, treads a middle path, with variable results. In some ways, the most successful scenes are the least overtly shocking; like *Holocaust*, it is at its most effective when the almost ungraspable horror of the camps is revealed at an intimate, personal level—for example, the arrival at Auschwitz, with Salamo's terrified family desperately trying to keep together before being summarily split up by an off-hand SS officer; the scene in which Poppa learns of Avram's death and is comforted by Salamo; or the final leave-taking between father and son. Especially in the arrival, director Robert M. Young manages to strike a balance between the general and the particular, to show the microcosm within the macrocosm, while other scenes gain enormously from a sense of restraint, and from the impressive performances of Willem Dafoe as Salamo and Robert Loggia as his father.

Young solves the problem of the gas chambers by not showing them at all, focusing instead on the faces of those who first catch sight of them. The film's most extreme moments are reserved until the end, with the terrible reprisals after the blowing-up of the crematorium presented in a fragmented, nightmarish fashion. Moments like these, with the soundtrack rent by screams and a series of Francis Bacon-like images flashing across the screen, perhaps begin to approach the real horrors of the camps. The boxing matches are also relentlessly gruelling, while the circus and cabaret acts which precede them are rather more interesting, if bizarrely incongruous.

Triumph of the Spirit takes place in what Primo Levi, in his book *The Drowned and the Saved*, called the "grey zone", in which the victims were forced in various ways to collaborate with their persecutors (though the film fails to examine this in any detail). According to producer Arnold Kopelson, "We're exploring moral dilemmas facing people inside the camps", and certainly the film presents a desperate and brutal struggle for survival at all costs (made slightly more palatable, and dubious, by the fact that Young never shows the fate of Salamo's defeated opponents). By the end, as the barely alive Salamo staggers away from the camp gates, an overwhelming sense of depression leads one to question what it says about contemporary Europe that the concentration camps have become an exploitable commodity for a newly emergent democracy.

NEW YORK POST, 12/8/89, p. 33, Jami Bernard

The Holocaust is a difficult film subject for many reasons, not the least being that it is a piece of history so disturbing and unfathomable that it cannot be approached directly, at least not within the framework of a commercial film. And approaching it indirectly runs the risk of trivializing.

The problem with "Triumph of the Spirit," the true story of a Greek Jew who literally fought for his life in the death camps in a series of grueling boxing matches, is that its own reverence for the subject, and delicacy in handling it, has taken away much of the punch.

In fact, the main selling point artistically and commercially is not the presence of a gaunt, wiry, hard-working Willem Dafoe, replete with all the requisite Gleason's-Gym training, but the fact that the movie was filmed in the remains of Auschwitz itself, a setting which hangs over the production like a shroud. Knowing that the actors are standing on the spot where millions were sent to their deaths is more affecting than these horrors as tactfully reflected in the actors' faces.

The restraint exercised by director Robert M. Young may be admirable aesthetically, but, let's face it—as long as you're shooting a film in an actual death camp, why not go for the jugular?

Salamo Arouch (Dafoe), one-time middleweight boxing champ of the Balkans, uses this talent in some Nazi-orchestrated entertainments in order to survive (similar to the theme of the Vanessa Redgrave TV-movie "Playing for Time"). He went on between a magician and a poodle act. As long as Arouch won—and he did, for about 200 matches—he kept on living, and also received lighter work details and extra bread. The losers in these matches were often sent to the gas chamber, but all we see is the defiance, pride and shame all writ large on Dafoe's face after each bout.

Salamo's stevedore father (Robert Loggia in a very effective performance) and other members of his family, including his girlfriend Allegra (feisty Wendy Gazelle), are all in the camps suffering their own hells, slowly being worked or dehumanized to death (or, of course, gassed). And although Salamo shares his extra bread with the pleading hands that reach toward him in the dark, and although in the women's barracks Allegra sees after her sister as much as she can, the story of "Triumph" is about what it takes to keep above water when all around you are sinking.

Salamo's victories in the ring are empty, Pyrrhic ones. For each of his wins, a confrere dies. The steeling against emotion that such a man must have had to undergo does not translate easily to film, especially when Young's camera spends so much time on Dafoe as the mirror to the soul of the atrocities. It is too much to expect from one actor, even such an interesting looking one as Dafoe.

Edward James Olmos plays a gypsy kapo/entertainer so enigmatic we never learn his name, but the actor does a good job of barely masking desperation and opportunism under a slick disguise.

Arnold Kopelson, the eclectic producer responsible both for "Platoon" and "Porky's," was a driving force behind getting this film made, and it is full of good, honest intentions. Perhaps it is too mush to ask of any film that it be more moving, or more chilling, than the German slogan "Arbeit Macht Frei" ("Work will make you free") over the gates of Auschwitz.

NEWSDAY, 12/8/89, Part III/p. 3, Mike McGrady

When history itself is unbelievable, when the facts of a situation defy all laws of probability, dramatic credibility seems beyond attainment. For this reason, perhaps, movie cameras have been notably reluctant to poke about in the ashes of concentration camps.

Some movies, such as "The Pawnbroker," have sought to capture the horror with occasional documentary flashes. At least one film, "Seven Beauties," has used the death camps as a setting for blackest humor. However, the nightmare has been most effectively captured when kept just out of sight, as the undescribed threat in "The Diary of Anne Frank" or "Au Revoir Les Enfants."

"Triumph of the Spirit," on the other hand, neither avoids specifics nor strives for poetic removal. Nothing—*nothing!*—is left to imagination as we follow a young Jewish boxer from a ghetto in his native Greece into crowded boxcars being shipped to a promised "new life in Poland." We sense that this new life will be brief, as the bewildered families pass beneath the famous legend "Arbeit Macht Frei," which marks the entrance to Auschwitz.

No matter how many times we are exposed to the mechanics of this crime of all crimes—the moving of an entire population; the sifting out and slaughter of the old, the young, the weak, the infirm, the slow to respond; the tattooing of identification numbers; the attack dogs; the herding of naked women and children through the cold ("Soon you will enjoy a hot shower")—it remains all but impossible to believe.

Salamo Arouch (Willem Dafoe), the 1938 middleweight champion of the Balkans, is spotted by a German officer who happens to be a boxing fan. Salamo soon learns that boxing will be his one hope for survival, also his one chance to be given such delicacies as a loaf of bread or a swig of brandy.

"How many rounds?" he asks.

"Rounds? No rounds. You fight until one goes down and can't get up."

As he fights to live, he is thrown in with another survivor (Edward James Olmos), an entertainer who provides his Nazi hosts with banter, song and magic and is likewise rewarded with life. Salamo goes on boxing and winning even though his brother and father (Robert Loggia) face execution, even though all his loved ones seem slated for certain destruction.

A simple presentation of the details might make for absolutely riveting drama. However, nothing about "Triumph of the Spirit" is done simply or directly. It's not enough that people fight for a pair of clogs or a crust of bread; each dramatic incident is amplified, blown up, underscored with blaring foreground music. Only Willem Dafoe's performance seems restrained and controlled, and that is what gives the film the credibility and emotional impact it does have.

The horror is relentless. One sits there, numbed by the atrocities, the killings, the casual brutalities. The question the film finally poses explicitly—"How can we do this to our brothers?"—is not answered, has never been answered, may never be answered. But maybe it's enough that the question be asked from time to time, that we be reminded what human beings are capable of—not merely of inflicting terrible pain on one another, but also of eventually surviving that pain.

NEWSWEEK, 12/11/89, p. 90, Jack Kroll

Triumph of the Spirit is the first major motion picture to be made on location at Auschwitz-Birkenau, the site of the infamous Nazi death camp. It's based on the true story of Salamo Arouch, a young Greek Jew who was middleweight boxing champion of the Balkans. Shipped to Auschwitz with his family after the Nazis overran Greece, Arouch (Willem Dafoe) literally fights for his life in boxing matches with other prisoners, the loser going to the gas chambers. This gruesome updating of the ancient gladiators is the central metaphor in director Robert M. Young's harrowing film about the Nazis' foremost achievement, the creation of hell on earth.

This film's major success lies in its depiction of the small details of that hell: the unceasing barrage of irrational orders ("Off hats! Off hat! Off hats!"); the human beings boxed and shelved in these infernal warehouses; the terrain of endless muck and filth; the litany of gasps, groans, grunts that accompany the unrelenting blows of the guards, the grisly vaudeville that entertains the officers—a dog act, a transvestite dancer, a seedily elegant song and dance by a Gypsy prisoner-trusty (Edward James Olmos).

Some script elements are dubious—a fictional romance between Salamo and a young woman prisoner, another prisoner's false pregnancy. At one point Salamo, having knocked out another wretched opponent, exchanges glances with the Nazi officer who's "patronized" him. The nuance is clear: in other circumstances the two men could have been in each other's shoes. Many viewers will find such an implication unacceptable. Luckily, the film's tragic energy and the acting of a committed cast override such "liberal" ambiguity.

TIME, 1/8/90, p. 76, Richard Corliss

Open any volume of modern history, and the blood of innocents pours onto your hands. From government policies of starvation to countless varieties of religious wars, the 20th century newspaper is one huge Domesday Book, a catalog of horrors so vast that numbers lose human meaning. One death is a tragedy; millions of deaths are statistics, to be deplored, then filed away as nightmares beyond comprehension. The atrocities nag at our conscience, finally numbing it. Amnesia seems the only solace.

So it is therapeutic to be reminded of the small stories of heroism, brutality and survival that restore dimension to the century's signature satanic event, the Nazi extermination of European Jewry. What is unusual is that in this holiday season, no fewer than three Hollywood films deal with the Holocaust. *Triumph of the Spirit* tells the true tale of a Greek-Jewish boxer, Salamo Arouch, who literally fights for his life at Auschwitz. *Music Box* fictionalizes the 1988 trial of John

Demjanjuk, a Ukrainian immigrant to the U.S. who was convicted of war crimes. And *Enemies, a Love Story* adapts Isaac Bashevis Singer's 1966 novel about Holocaust survivors sorting out their guilt and their passions in postwar New York City. Still, for all their ambitions, this trio ends up as two honorable duds and a near miss with plenty to recommend it.

There are many reasons, aside from the persona commitment of Jewish filmmakers, for Hollywood's preoccupation with the Holocaust. It is one act of state terrorism that has been exhaustively detailed. The first images of gas chambers and mass graves in 1945 sickened the world, not just with their charnel power but also with an awareness that the villains were once torchbearers of Western civilization. Hitler upended the cradle that had rocked Beethoven and Goethe, and hell fell out. His murder of millions of people for the crime of being born Jewish is an act worth pondering and mourning.

And here is a maxim worth remembering: good motives do not always make good movies. Too often Hollywood finds in the Holocaust a familiar, convenient parable of sanctified martyrdom and slavering sadism. Thorny issues are begged, compelling stories avoided. The dark psychology of the death-camp administrator, himself captive in a twisted chain of command, is rarely investigated. Neither is the prisoner's natural impulse to survive at any cost, which gave rise to "the Jewish members of the GPU, the Capos, the thieves, speculators, informers," as Singer describes them in *Enemies, a Love Story*. Instead, characters are as reductive as in any old-time western. The good guys wear the Star of David; the bad guys wear swastikas. The real victim in these films is dramatic ambiguity, and the result is what critic Art Spiegelman has called "holokitsch."

Triumph of the Spirit might be expected to transcend this label, if only because of one line in the movie's final credits: "Filmed on location at the Auschwitz-Birkenau concentration camps." Co-producer Arnold Kopelson won permission from Polish authorities to use the huge camps (now museums) as the setting for his story. How chilling it must have been for the actors and especially the extras—many of them Auschwitz survivors—to see the place restored as if in full working order.

Yet how little of that dreadful impact comes across in the film, which is too respectful of its subject to find more in it than noble clichés. Salamo Arouch (Willem Dafoe), formerly the Balkan middleweight champ, is interned with his family at Birkenau and soon ordered to take part in boxing exhibitions in which the loser will almost certainly be killed. This grisly dilemma—each of Arouch's knockouts sends his opponent to the gas chamber—is mostly evaded in Robert M. Young's bland direction. The film's only and considerable virtue lies in its documentation of the desperate strategies people devised to stay alive in the death camps.

Some lived even longer, to bear witness to atrocities and bring the beasts to justice. In *Music Box* the accused is Michael Laszlo (Armin Mueller-Stahl), a Hungarian now living in Illinois. Was he the malefic Miska, who as a member of the Arrow Cross during World War II raped women at gunpoint and tossed bundles of Jews into the Danube? Laszlo's daughter Ann (Jessica Lange), an attorney, believes her father is innocent and fiercely defends him in court. But the weight of survivors' testimony is too heavy, too obscene, to dismiss. Can she believe that her doting father committed such acts? And if she does believe it, can she still love him?

Laszlo must be guilty, of course; otherwise, there is no drama. Screenwriter Joe Eszterhas and director Costa-Gavras want to create that drama, but they do not give Ann a strong case to argue, so the film's only suspense is in how long it will take Lange (who gives a smart, sturdy performance) to face the truth. Nor do they allow Laszlo a chance to justify, however speciously, his rancid past. They are content to dwell on the sins of the fathers, in which humanism stares at bestiality across the generation gap. Even in a genial mood, Laszlo sounds like a Nazi: "A healthy body makes a healthy spirit," he huffs as he completes a maniacal regimen of push-ups. Ann's father-in-law (Donald Moffat), who helped relocate Nazis as a CIA agent after the war, is no more enlightened. He derides the Holocaust as "the world's sacred cow." He's not even sure it happened.

Herman Broder (Ron Silver), the passive hedonist in director Paul Mazursky's film of *Enemies, a Love Story*, is sure. There must have been a Holocaust, or Herman would not have hidden from it for most of the war. Now it is 1949, and he lives in New York with, eventually, three loving women: his Polish Gentile wife Yadwiga (Margaret Sophie Stein), whom he married out of gratitude for protecting him in the old country; his passionate mistress Masha (Lena Olin), whom the Holocaust has driven to a volcanic indecision between childbearing and suicide; and his long-lost first wife Tamara (Anjelica Huston), whom he had thought dead in the camps.

Herman's story could be played as brisk black comedy, an "I Led Three Wives" with memories of death ever kibitzing in his restless sleep. But Mazursky is scrupulously fair to the characters—so fair that *Enemies* lacks his films' customary oomph. When it is not vitalized by the beautiful performances of Olin and Huston, the picture takes on Herman's dithering lassitude. And yet there is a method to this meandering. Novelist and director both know a man is more than the sum of the calamities that have befallen him. Herman is a victim, not just of the Nazis, but of his own demons as well. And he is lucky, or doomed, to find three superior women who want to crush him in the bosom of their devotion.

Singer wrote a Domesday Book in which the blood is bathed in tears of conspiratorial laughter. Mazursky has made it into a movie that sidesteps holokitsch with the spry deftness of a Chagall peasant.

VILLAGE VOICE, 12/12/89, p. 99, J. Hoberman

Hollywood demographics never cease to intrigue. Along with this year's Christmas releases are a few so suited to Hanukkah, you have to wonder if this is a trend (or just an Arts and Leisure piece). Paul Mazursky's *Enemies: A Love Story* is adapted from Isaac Bashevis Singer; Costa-Gavras's *The Music Box* sounds like a version of the John Demjanjuk story; and Robert M. Young's *Triumph of the Spirit*, which opens Friday at the Beekman, is based on the life of Salamo Arouch, a Greek Jew who in 1939 became the Balkan middleweight boxing champ and four years later found himself in Auschwitz.

As brutalized as any Roman gladiator, Arouch survived with his fists, fighting 200 bouts for the entertainment of the SS. This extraordinary story apparently inspired *The Boxer and Death*, a tough little Czech film made in the early '60s that only surfaced here last fall at Film Forum. But where *The Boxer and Death* was a sardonic exploration of one man's existential and moral dilemma in the most extreme environment ever devised, *Triumph of the Spirit* is a metaphor for something larger. (The movie's title tells you as much.) No disconcerting drama of the lone individual in an irrational world, this is a work of collective self-affirmation.

Far more than other religions, Jewish identity (essentially tribal) is determined by history. One will never understand contemporary Jewishness unless one grasps the significance of Auschwitz and Israel as historical events: Hell and Redemption are things that happened here, on earth, this century. As *Triumph of the Spirit* was shot in both sacred places (Israel doubling for Thessaloniki), the movie is almost giddy with its own weightiness. Salamo (Willem Dafoe) speaks in the measured cadences of a Hollywood sword-and-sandal epic; Cliff Eidelman's wailing pseudo-Semitic melodies suggest nothing so much as Miklos Rosza's score for *Sodom and Gomorrah*.

Still, this weird grandiosity—perhaps the desire of the self-promoting coproducer Arnold Kopelson—is deflated by Young's direction which suggests another agenda. At once economical, fastidiously tasteful, and totally foredoomed, *Triumph of the Spirit* offers an introduction to what less sensitive filmmakers might term the Auschwitz "experience." The movie puts you (briefly) inside a cattle car and propels you through the actual gate into the chaos of disembarkation— blinding lights, screamed orders, corpses tumbling out, frantic husbands searching for wives, dazed crowds herded to the showers.

Because *Triumph of the Spirit* was actually shot at Auschwitz, the arrival has the quality of a pageant. (It suggests the ritual Storming of the Winter Palace that was staged in Leningrad for several years after the Russian Revolution.) The space is the star, and Young is intelligent enough to hope the scene will speak for itself. He underplays the selection, arranges the terror, choreographs reactions. His compositions are full of night and fog—studied, painterly friezes. But a painter like Luca Signorelli was imagining the Last Judgment; Young reproduces it from the collective memory. Such simulation is hardly worth a thousand words. On the contrary. Anyone who has seen *Shoah* will recognize how infinitely more powerful it is to hear this nightmare described by one who lived it than to watch it restaged. Two minutes of Salamo Arouch recounting a single incident of his stay in Auschwitz would be stronger than anything shown in *Triumph*'s two hours.

Given Young's intimist strategy, *Triumph* requires faces craggy enough to hold a close-up— Dafoe as Arouch, Edward James Olmos as an unnamed gypsy inmate. But the story demands more than any actor can give (or should be asked to give). When one character is offered a job feeding corpses to the crematorium, the director ostentatiously resists showing piles of bodies. The unfortunate alternative is letting his camera linger on the embarrassing feebleness of the actor's response. (Compare this to Filip Müller's first view of the cremo in *Shoah*: "It was like a blow on the head, as if I'd been stunned. I didn't even know where I was. Above all, I couldn't understand how they managed to kill so many people at once....I was in shock, as if I'd been hypnotized, ready to do whatever I was told.")

There are no thunderclaps in *Triumph*. Having explained the process of extermination, the movie emphasizes the daily routine of slave labor (one day, out of hundreds), then haplessly gropes for some respite. The next transport to reach the camp is shown in discreet long shot—a row of little figures, machine-gunned by Germans and backlit by flames—and intercut with a "decadent" SS party. The Germans in this movie reenact *Cabaret* at every opportunity; thus, the most compelling character is Olmos's. Kapo by day, entertainer by night, he's the warmup act of the evening slugfest, serenading the SS so suggestively that they almost experience the degradation of their absolute power. Arouch simply batters his opponent to the ground and is rewarded with a loaf of bread. Only once does he (or do we) suffer qualms: At night, after a victory, he's beset by his half-starved bunkmates—advancing in the dark, hands outstretched, eyes ferally gleaming, their pleading soft and implacable.

There's no one outside of Auschwitz who can judge Arouch. But what *Triumph* cannot grasp is that the heroism of fighting for your life is not the same as the heroism of sacrificing your life. In pitting the boxer against his fellow inmates, the Nazis engaged in the most gruesome sort of Darwinism. Arouch became their *Überuntermensch*, a superJew. (So, too, in a subliminal way, he beomes a Zionist hero.) Because we're spared the sight of his defeated opponents going to the gas chamber, we're cushioned from the monstrous irony of his tragic fate. To defend its affirmation the film needs an unambiguous hero. No wonder Arouch is shown as the last man in the camp. To have other survivors would suggest the possibility of alternate miracles.

This film is caught in another contradiction. Everyone loves a winner, but you cannot make a feel-good movie about Auschwitz. Still, despite the pathos of a positivist title that bizarrely echoes a celebrated Nazi propaganda film. *Triumph of the Spirit* is scarcely the most exploitative example of what Art Spiegelman has called *holokitsch*. On the other hand, the movie's solemn insistence on an impossible verisimilitude inescapably diminishes its subject. (One can't help pondering what it means that Auschwitz should become a movie set, a natural resource for Poland, and s source of hard currency.)

There is a Gresham's Law of images: The facile ones drive the tougher ones out of circulation. The spurious authenticity of the set, Dafoe's obvious training, and the self-congratulation of the movie's hype are ultimately show-biz distractions that pretend to explain (even as they upstage and obliterate) the mystery of Salamo Arouch. This is one horror film where you don't have to keep telling yourself, "It's only a movie." Young and Kopelson do that for you.

Also reviewed in:
NEW REPUBLIC, 12/25/89, p. 26, Stanley Kauffmann
NEW YORK TIMES, 12/8/89, p. C10, Janet Maslin
VARIETY, 12/8/89, p. 34
WASHINGTON POST, 2/2/90, p. C7, Rita Kempley

TROOP BEVERLY HILLS

A Weintraub Entertainment Group release. *Executive Producer:* Charles Fries. *Producer:* Ava Ostern Fries. *Director:* Jeff Kanew. *Screenplay:* Pamela Norris and Margaret Grieco Oberman. *Based on a story by:* Ava Ostern Fries. *Director of Photography:* Donald E. Thorin. *Editor:* Mark Melnick. *Music:* Randy Edelman. *Music Editor:* Frank Fitzpatrick. *Choreographer:* Dorain Grusman. *Sound:* William B. Kaplan and (music) Dennis S. Sands. *Sound Editor:* Fred Judkins and Tom McCarthy. *Production Designer:* Robert F. Boyle. *Art Director:* Jack G. Taylor Jr. *Set Designer:* Sig Tinglof. *Set Decorator:* Anne McCulley-Reynolds. *Set Dresser:* Oscar Delgadillo and Gary H. Rizzo. *Special Effects:* Fred Z. Gebler. *Costumes:* Theadora Van Runkle. *Makeup:* Del Acevedo. *Stunt Coordinator:* Conrad Palmisano and Gary Morgan. *Running time:* 100 minutes. *MPAA Rating:* PG.

CAST: Shelley Long (Phyllis Nefler); Craig T. Nelson (Freddy Nefler); Betty Thomas (Velda Plendor); Mary Gross (Annie Herman); Stephanie Beacham (Vicki Sprantz); Audra Lindley (Frances Temple); Edd Byrnes

(Ross Coleman); Ami Foster (Claire Sprantz); Carla Gugina (Chica Barnfell); Heather Hopper (Tessa DiBlasio); Kellie Martin (Emily Coleman); Emily Schulman (Tiffany Honigman); Tasha Scott (Jasmine Shakar); Aquilina Soriano (Lily Marcigan); Jenny Lewis (Hannah Nefler); David Gautreaux (DiBlasio); Karen Kopins (Lisa); Dinah Lacey (Cleo); Shelley Morrison (Rosa); David Wohl (Dr. Honigman); Tori Spelling (Jamie); Daniel Ziskie (Authur Barnfell); Kareem Abdul-Jabbar (Himself); Brindo Andrews (Redondo Troop Leader); Monty Ash (Old Duffer); Frankie Avalon (Himself); Jan Bina (Freida); Kathleen Bradley (Mrs. Shakar); Eloise Broady (Starlet at Party); Dr. Joyce Brothers (Herself); Mercy Bubalo (Troop Photographer); George Christy (Himself); Patrika Darbo (Mar Vista Troop Leader); Flo Di Re (Wilderness Official); Nancy Fish (Mrs. Grundman); Annette Funicello (Herself); Pamela Galloway (Mrs. Hongiman); Willie Garson (Bruce); Mary Pat Gleason (Kindly Troop Leader); Theodocia Goodrich (Old Woman); Bitsy Gorman (Pomona Troop Leader); Mary Gregory (Judge); James "Gypsy" Haake (Henri); Alvin Ing (Ho); Doug Laird (Motorcycle Cop); Robin Leach (Himself); Cheech Marin (Himself); Deborah Martin (Housewife); Ted McGinley (Himself); Jomarie Payton-France (Saleswoman); William Pedraza (Latino Bellboy); Ron Perkins (Salesman); Claudia Robinson (Wilderness Official); Deborah Rose (Beauty Salon Attendant); Ann Ryerson (Bitsy Barnfell); Christophe Schatteman (Beauty Salon Owner); Hilary Shepard (Salesgirl); Ramon Sison (Bong Bong); Bob Snead (Phyllis Nefler's Lawyer); R. Sparkle Stillman (Old Woman); J.J. Wall (Jack Sprantz); William Wallace (Officer Bill); Joan Weitzner (Restaurant Patron); Anna Marie Wieder (Agnes Woodcock); Karin Woodward (Wilderness Official); Tom Wright (Shakar); Marion Kodama Yue (Karina Bong); Pia Zadora (Herself).

LOS ANGELES TIMES, 3/23/89, Calendar/p. 3, Michael Wilmington

In "Troop Beverly Hills," Shelley Long plays the Beverly Hills ditz as secular saint. Her hair is a flaming mass of just-out-of-bed baby-doll salon curls, her eyes twinkle with elfin lust. After a while, dipped into one cheerfully grotesque Theodora Van Runkle costume after another, she looks both nutty and scrumptious, like a human fruit fondue.

Long is cast as Phyllis Nefler: a Beverly Hills housewife with a name that vaguely suggests "Double Indemnity" and a mania for Rodeo Drive shopping. Phyllis' muffler-salesman husband (Craig T. Nelson) is leaving her in disgust and her daughter is part of notorious troop of failed scouts, or "Wilderness Girls," whom Phyllis, in another attack of dilettantism—like her former enthusiasms for saving whales or Janes Fonda's workouts—has agreed to head.

If you know the rules of this kind of movie game, you know immediately that:

a) Phyllis' girls will be eccentric but lovable, cutie-pie clichés just like Phyllis herself.

b) Phyllis will take them on eccentric but lovable adventures, shot in pricey locales.

c) Phyllis will have an opposing martinet (Betty Thomas as the insidious butch madwoman Velda Plendor), who will stop at nothing to humiliate her and drive her girls out of the Wilderness. Also:

d) Everybody will wind up loving Phyllis to pieces and loving her girls to pieces, and everyone's family problems—including the dictator's daughter—will get straightened out and, more than likely, Phyllis will wind up back again with her husband, who will love her to pieces too. (Love. Ain't it wonderful!)

e) Hopefully, we in the audience, would-be Wilderness Girls or not, will emerge happier, wiser and, like Phyllis, ready for the next shopping spree.

f) While all this is going on, and while the speedy, gorgeous Shelley is zipping and stripping from one Van Runkle creation to the next (What a mad, whirling little fashion dervish she is!) we will be forced to see and hear more bad jokes than we would have thought humanly possible.

What can you say about a movie that purports to satirize, however gently, the life styles of the rich and jaded, and winds up dragging in Robin Leach, Pia Zadora and a charity fashion show? What about a high concept which wants us to react to these super-rich children as if they were waifs besieged by an evil world of K mart-crazed bullies and sadists? What market researcher dreamed up this mix of lewd slapstick and smarmy sentimentality? Are we really expected to reflect on poignant pauses in the acting career of Edd (Kookie) Byrnes? Wonder what preposterous new gown lissome Long will peel into next?

Part of this movie is like a sermon against greed delivered by a preacher in a snakeskin tuxedo with a diamond-studded cummerbund. Do we believe his oratory or his couturier?

"Troop Beverly Hills" has been very gaudily well-dressed—by Van Runkle and Hitchcock's frequent production designer Robert Boyle—and director Jeff Kanew ("Revenge of the Nerds") gives it a little phony gloss and zip. Kanew is good at grotesque stage business, and he's encouraged Long into a symphony of dizzy ditz-shtick. Long is an actress who can't throw away a line—though this is one case where she should have thrown away the whole script. But she gets points for sheer, daffy energy and rampaging pulchritude.

On the other hand, Mary Gross, who recently has been amusing in movies where almost everyone else seemed to be sinking in a sea of flop sweat ("The Couch Trip," "Feds") has been handed a tailor-made Mary Gross part, but with no jokes. It's a technical challenge you wouldn't wish on Meryl Streep; Gross is finally reduced to showing off her cleavage in a pink tutu, while Long does bellyflops in the swimming pool.

"Troop Beverly Hills" (rated PG, despite much bawdy innuendo) was based partially on the reminiscences of its producer, Ava Ostern Fries, once a chi-chi scoutmaster herself. This revelation gives you pause. Are people in Beverly Hills living in the middle of a badly written movie? Maybe not; maybe they only remember it that way.

MONTHLY FILM BULLETIN, 7/90, p. 207, Kim Newman

Beverly Hills, California. Phyllis Nefler, an over-privileged dilettante whose marriage to Freddy, a wealthy businessman, is disintegrating, volunteers to take charge of her daughter's Wilderness Girls troop. Velda Plendor, the regional leader of the Wilderness Girl movement, has been in favour of discontinuing the tiny and generally useless Beverly Hills troop, but her superior opts to give Phyllis a chance. Taking her daughter Hannah and seven other offspring of the rich and famous out camping, Phyllis abandons the expedition during a shower and relocates to the Beverly Hills Hotel. Unable to make the grade in woodcraft and survival skills, Phyllis hands out badges in jewellery appraisal, shopping and other moneyed leisure pursuits, somehow managing to bring the variously neurotic girls together and give them a sense of their own worth. Velda instals her assistant Annie Herman with Phyllis as a spy, but Annie warms to the rich children and rebels, while even Freddy, who is dating an unsuitable younger woman, has become impressed with his wife's determination. Velda has her own daughter's troop, the Red Feathers, intensively sell cookies in Beverly Hills in an attempt to thwart Phyllis' own charity drive, but the latter's showbiz glitz sells more cookies than ever, and the Beverly Hills troop qualifies for the wilderness jamboree, an orienteering contest which the Red Feathers regularly win. However, through a combination of luck and skill, the Beverly Hills girls get ahead. Velda sprains her ankle, and is abandoned by the Red Feathers, who cross the finish line first but are disqualified for leaving their leader behind, whereupon the Beverly Hills troop wins the event. During the celebration, Phyllis and Freddy decide to give their marriage another chance.

In a hideously ironic way, *Troop Beverly Hills* is the *Lifestyles of the Rich and Famous* answer to *The Beverly Hillbillies*. While the old TV show stressed the virtues of the down-home good sense and directness of the Clampett family set against Beverly Hills phoniness and duplicity, this reverses the situation so that it's the wealthy Phyllis, who declares in a moment of Evian-fuelled despair that she has "lost her will to shop", who gets to make a fool of the practical, country-wise Velda, demonstrating the superiority of wealthy ditziness over proletarian envy. Velda, who screams "I hate kids" when angered, is a spoilsport villainess in the tradition of the *Police Academy* movies, scheming to have the unconventional foul-ups kicked out of the organisation but finally humiliated by them. But there is a bitter after-taste to the coda which finds her working as a checkout girl in K-Mart while Phyllis gets her perfect life, and perfect husband, back. It is impossible to react sympathetically either to the latest of Shelley Long's daffy, talent-frittering performances or to the supposedly put-upon offspring of Asian dictators, champion boxers, high-priced lawyers or movie-brat superstar directors. A bizarre clutch of cameo performers—Frankie Avalon, Annette Funicello, Cheech Marin, Stephanie Beacham, Edd Byrnes, Pia Zadora, Dr. Joyce Brothers, Kareem Abdul-Jabbar—barely make an impression, while the snottily angelic child actors, although balanced in ethnic type, are impossible to tell one from the other.

NEW YORK POST, 3/23/89, p. 43, Jami Bernard

So sue me, I laughed.

There is an argument to be made that formula comedies—or formula anythings—should not be encouraged because they contribute to the general decline of creativity in our society. As Albert Brooks says in "Broadcast News," when the Devil arrives, he will slowly, smilingly, lower our standards *just a little*.

In the meantime, you can go ahead and fiddle while Rome burns—"Troop Beverly Hills" has a bright script, some well-cast leads and a lot more laughs than you'd expect from a one-note joke of a story about a prissy Beverly Hills housewife who pilots some spoiled brats to Scoutdom despite anxiety attacks and shamefully drab uniforms. The art-house crowd may not flock to see it, but there are laughs enough for everyone else.

Shelley Long has flopped like a reeled-in fish in most of her firm ventures, but it's not because she's not funny. She's *very* funny, but only in one kind of role—essentially the one she originated on TV's "Cheers," that of an uptight, self-righteous, stick-up-the-derriere snob. In "Troop," she plays a kissing cousin to that character. Her Phyllis Nefler is a champion shopper and appraiser of the finer things. In the midst of a messy divorce from her muffler-king husband (Craig T. Nelson, looking awfully thick in the middle), Phyllis decides to become a den mother to her daughter's Wilderness Girls troop. This way she can have a "mother-daughter bonding thing" and do something useful with her time. She has "a new meaningful life—and a whole new meaningful wardrobe to go with it."

The movie opens with animated credits that show a likeness of Long doing various den-mother chores the Beverly Hills way, like tending to a bruised finger by applying a press-on nail from a Red Cross kit. These credits pretty much tell the story, but the joy of "Troop Beverly Hills" is Long's careful, persnickety delivery of lines like "I'm sure it's very nice to know how to live in the wilds and eat bark."

Betty Thomas ("Hill Street Blues") plays a fascistic Scout ubermeister named Velda who hates the Beverly Hills brats (they've never even sold a cookie) and is determined to see them stripped of their patches. She especially hates the way Phyllis Nefler has turned the traditional Scout garb into a "cocktail frock."

Mouse-voiced Mary Gross ("Saturday Night Live") rounds out the cast as a former yarn-ball salesgirl from K-Mart, a timid gofer who is sent to spy on the Beverly Hills troop, and who naturally begins to side with them. Her role is rudely disposed of in time for the big finale, but it makes sense that the three women all got their start in Chicago's Second City improv group, a proven spawning ground for talent.

At the first Scout meet, the girls arrive in varying lengths of limos. These are the daughters of very wealthy, vaguely familiar, figures: One's parents are a Philippines-style dictator and his multi-shoed wife; another's mother is a Jackie Collins-type trash writer. You just know that the alienated but big-hearted poor little rich girls will eventually find happiness in the Friendship Circle. Director Jeff Kanew has a tendency to get a little sappy ("Tough Guys"), but he knows how to save an otherwise sagging scene with a laugh ("Revenge of the Nerds").

When an overnight camping trip—complete with chocolate fondue over the campfire—gets rained on, Phyllis ushers the girls into a bungalow at the Beverly Hills Hotel, where they order in capuccino and tell scary stories around the fireplace, like about the time Phyllis' regular hairdresser was out and a mysterious replacement permed her hair.

While other troops weave their own cloth, Phyllis has her girls earn patches in jewelry appraisal and describing fall fashions to the blind. Phyllis herself earns a patch in CPR with an overly obliging Officer Bill.

Meanwhile, Phyllis' ex-husband ("He's going through a phase right now," Phyllis explains to her daughter, "It's called being a big jerk") is getting tired of his new bimbo and is coming to realize the true value of a woman who can make beige work for her (with the proper accessories) and who can organize a telethon to sell Scout cookies.

Craig T. Nelson looks puzzled by his role, and so are we. Also forget the useless cameos by Pia Zadora, Frankie and Annette, Dr. Joyce Brothers and others. The main thing is, Shelley Long, Betty Thomas and Mary Gross earn their patches in "Troop Beverly Hills"; may they rise to Eagle Scout.

NEWSDAY, 3/23/89, Part II/p. 7, Lynn Darling

"Troop Beverly Hills" is a movie that's trying its little heart out to win a merit badge in dizzy warmhearted comedy, only to fall on its funny freckle face in the attempt.

Everything about this film is trying too hard—from Shelley Long, to Shelley Long's costumes to its slap-happy message of personal uplift.

Phyllis Nefler (Long) is a daffy red-headed spendthrift who spends her days shopping on Rodeo Drive and getting divorced from her dullard husband, Freddy the muffler king (Craig T. Nelson).

When her daughter Hannah (Jenny Lewis) convinces her to take over as leader of a troop of bored, spoiled Beverly Hills brats, Phyllis sees the experience as a chance to finally prove to herself that she's something more than the silly twit she appears to be.

Little that takes place in the ensuing two hours would support that idea.

Phyllis takes her troops on a campout to the Beverly Hills Hotel, where she orders rroom service and tells them a scary story about a bad permanent she once received. She helps them to earn merit badges in jewelry appraisal and divorce court.

They also win a badge in international affairs—Phyllis praises one of her charges for her help in explaining money laundering and crushing revolutions to the troop as her parents, Ferdinand and Imelda Marcos look-alikes, watch proudly.

None of this sits well with the regional overlord of the Wilderness Girls, Velda Plendor (Betty Thomas), who thinks that Phyllis has perverted the ideals of the organization in engaging in such activities. It is one of the more confusing assumptions of this movie that it is Phyllis and her value system we're meant to be rooting for.

Nevertheless, by the end of it all we're assured that Phyllis has grown wiser and the girls have grown up and everyone's self esteem is in a lot better shape—no higher gift, apparently, can the gods of Beverly Hills confer.

With her flaming red hair, baroque fashions and enthusiasm for the sort of physical comedy that involves falling into swimming pools, Shelley Long is in Lucille Ball mode here. But she gives a pale imitation of Ball's inspired sense of lunacy in a movie that would generate more sparks if it concentrated on rubbing two sticks together.

VILLAGE VOICE, 4/4/89, p. 53, J. Hoberman

A term of abuse in *Heathers* [see Hoberman's review], "Girl Scout cookie" comes in for mild rehabilitation with *Troop Beverly Hills*. This Touchstone knockoff, directed by Jeff *"Revenge of the Nerds"* Kanew and arriving here in time for spring recess, is a one-joke vehicle for Shelley Long, who, as relentlessly adorable as only a sitcom star can be, plays ditzy den mother (and consumption consultant) to a gaggle of poor little rich girls sporting Giorgio backpacks.

Troop Beverly Hills is actually a less toothless satire of Hollywood lifestyles than, say, *Less Than Zero*—the girls get merit badges for "sushi appreciation" and Brownie points for explaining fall fashions to the blind. Indeed, considering the obtrusive emphasis on family values and the American way, the most surprising thing about the movie is that it's not nearly as egregious as it might have been. Even so, the best laugh is a televised bit with Pee-wee Herman wrapping a pair of giant jockey shorts around his head and chortling, "Look, I'm a nun!" If Shelley Long were another Lucy, she would have done that herself.

Also reviewed in:
NEW YORK TIMES, 3/23/89, p. C12, Janet Maslin
VARIETY, 3/29–4/4/89, p. 14
WASHINGTON POST, 3/23/89, p. D5, Rita Kempley

TRUE BELIEVER

A Columbia Pictures release. *Executive Producer:* Peter Rosten. *Producer:* Walter F. Parkes and Lawrence Lasker. *Director:* Joseph Ruben. *Screenplay:* Wesley Strick. *Director of Photography:* John Lindley. *Editor:* George Bowers. *Music:* Brad Fiedel. *Sound:* Larry Kemp and Lon E. Nader. *Production Designer:* Lawrence Miller. *Costumes:* Erica Edell Phillips. *Stunt Coordinator:* Rocky Capella. *Running Time:* 104 minutes. *MPAA Rating:* R.

CAST: James Woods (Eddie Dodd); Robert Downey Jr. (Roger Baron); Margaret Colin (Kitty Greer); Yuji Okumoto (Shu Kai Kim); Kurtwood Smith (Robert Reynard); Tom Bower (Cecil Skell); Miguel Fernandes (Art Esparza); Charles Hallahan (Vincent Dennehy).

CHRISTIAN SCIENCE MONITOR, 3/15/89, p. 10, David Sterritt

What ever happened to the idealists of the 1960s—the people who fought for "people power" against the government, the schools, and every other institution in sight? Most of them are still around, and some have clung to their old beliefs in one form or another. But the world around them has changed, and adapting to new conditions can be hard.

Take the hero of the new film "True Believer," for instance. His name is Eddie Dodd, and once upon a time he was a fighting radical. He went to law school, and when he graduated he was ready to turn society upside down. It's the late '80s now, though, and the old battles have taken a strange new shape. Eddie still takes on the police and the criminal-justice system, but now his clients are mainly drug dealers—sleazy crooks who, everyone knows, are guilty, guilty, guilty.

Eddie always gets them off, and he tells himself this is all right because he's defending individual rights against the system. But it's obvious that this is idealism at its worst. And even Eddie can't help seeing this when his new assistant arrives on the scene: Roger, a young idealist of the '80s who can't believe what a small-timer Eddie has turned out to be. Prodded by Roger and his own conscience, Eddie decides to take a really tough case—defending an Asian prisoner who killed another inmate in self-defense. Studying the situation, Eddie decides his client was innocent of the charge that originally landed him in jail years ago. And he decides to prove this no matter how unlikely it seems, or how hard it is to dredge up facts that have long been buried.

The story is pretty far-fetched at times, and it doesn't unfold smoothly; it lurches from one incident to another without worrying much about the in-between moments. What glues it all together is James Woods's performance. Ever since "The Onion Field," he has been winning my prize as one of Hollywood's most intense and energetic actors. He can strike out once in a while, as he did in "The Boost" recently. But he doesn't let up for a minute as Eddie Dodd, even when the script gets silly or the director pushes the action and the dialogue too hard. Also convincing is Robert Downey Jr. as Roger, the wide-eyed young attorney who turns out to be no slouch in the intensity department (or the idealism department) himself.

"True Believer" was directed by Joseph Ruben, whose earlier movies include "Dreamscape" and "The Stepfather," a first-rate thriller.

He doesn't quite make "True Believer" believable: The story has more twists than he can handle, and some of the characters aren't fleshed out effectively. It's a movie with a real subject, though—how the aspirations of '60s radicals might not be completely irrelevant in the '80s, after all.

FILMS IN REVIEW, 5/89, p. 300, Edmond Grant

If its script had been a little tighter, and the supporting characterizations a bit more developed, *True Believer* could have made a fine "message" TV.

Instead, it's feature film, and a messy one at that. James Woods stars as a hip, Kunstler-esque attorney who takes on the case of a young Korean man who has been serving time in prison for a murder which he claims he did not commit.

There's a passion and undeniable energy in Woods' performance, but the script plays against him, as plot complications pile up and a massive police corruption scandal winds up being at the root of all the injustice. To the film's detriment, the plot complications that are the most tedious are those dealing with the actual murder case. Some interesting sidebars are introduced, however, including the brief sequences delineating the different ethnic groups (one of them run by Nazis) fighting it out in the Korean's prison, and the fact (that no one but Woods' character seems to consider) that the boy was an aspiring member of a Chinese gang, who may have been the ones to tag him as the fall guy for the murder.

These sidebars, which show the racial discord underscoring the murder case, succeed where the main storyline fails. The chief reason for this being the many clichéd elements introduced into Woods' investigation. Firstly, there's Woods' sidekick, a cardboard yuppie (played by insufferably active brat packer Robert Downey Jr.) who inspires Woods to return to his 60s radical attitudes. The team of aged hipster/yuppie is assisted by a female private eye (played by chipper Margaret Colin) who never emerges as a three dimensional character. The same can be said of the Korean and the many corrupt cops whom Woods encounters.

If this were a strict action film, director Joseph Ruben's fast paced approach would be right on target. As it stands, the film smothers its good intentions with stock characterizations and facile attitudes; leaving Woods' acting at full tilt, albeit in a void.

LOS ANGELES TIMES, 2/17/89, Calendar/p. 6, Sheila Benson

"Eddie Dodd," sneers one of his well-heeled clients in "True Believer." "Everyone should own one." Considering that attorney Dodd has just gotten this scum-sucking cocaine dealer off on a well-deserved drug rap, that's hardly gratitude.

But flamed-out ex-'60s activist Dodd doesn't defend New York's every smack dealer and amphetamine manufacturer for their thank-you notes. The chunky packages of cash they send through the mail will do nicely.

Dodd is another in James Woods' dizzying catalogue of interchangeable characterizations in which only his hairdos vary. (Unsurprisingly, hipster Dodd wears a curly, graying pony-tail.) The sneer, the intensity, the percussive delivery that flattens everything in sight—fellow actors especially—remains the same.

The reason to have hope for "True Believer" was that director Joseph Ruben had shown some style before with "The Stepfather." However "The Stepfather" had Donald Westlake's gorgeous script. This one, by Wesley Strick, piles coincidence onto improbability and cliche onto unlikelihood until all our good will is used up. Ruben's stylistic devices, his high angle shots and his black-and-white recountings of courtroom testimony, become just so much cinematic corpse-rouging.

The story involves Eddie Dodd's redemption through his defense of one single innocent client. He's a young Korean prisoner in Sing Sing, Shu Kai Kim (Yuji Okumoto), whom we see kill a Neo-Nazi fellow-inmate within the prison, in what might be called very well-prepared self-defense. Somehow, certainly not through anything persuasive about his client, Dodd decides that Kim was innocent of the crime which sent him to Sing Sing in the first place. And the scenario decides that freeing Kim will cleanse Dodd's soul.

Robert Downey Jr., as Dodd's wildly idealistic new assistant, is along for a good deal of the cleansing. The characters are a hilarious assortment of tattooed Neo-Nazis, sweaty, corrupt cops and transparently evil lawmen in very high places. Their goings-on are photographed as though the camera, too, was wearing a green eyeshade.

Under Woods' almost felonious assault, there seems to be one point at which Downey throws up his hands and quits, enlisting Margaret Colin, "private detective Kitty Greer," in his defection. They move, they speak, but the stuff that galvanizes them as actors seems to have evaporated. Take their hint.

NEW YORK, 2/20/89, p. 70, David Denby

In the exciting New York thriller *True Believer,* James Woods wears his graying hair very long—so long that the grizzled shag, gathered in a loose ponytail, hangs down his neck like a damp old mop. Woods plays Eddie Dodd, ace radical lawyer of the sixties, who once defended the Black Panthers and anti-war protesters but now uses his considerable skills to get drug-dealers released on technicalities. Not much of the sixties is left in Eddie—just his awful hair, the pot fumes in his office, and his hipster's sense of himself as an outsider, which gives him an angry edge even when he's flat on his back. *True Believer* offers James Woods the best part he's had since *Salvador,* and Woods, having lost his skeletal, dead-eyed pallor (his face is fuller now), gives his richest, most humanly appealing performance yet.

Eddie lives and works in a brownish, dowdy office in Sheridan Square, just above the Village Cigars store. In this moldy refuge, this theater of nostalgia (the walls are filled with newspaper photos from Eddie's glory days), he smokes pot and sleeps alone in masturbatory isolation, like a convict in solitary. Eddie Dodd is a mess, but he's a good man, even a great man, and everyone knows it. He has working for him a fresh-out-of-law-school assistant, Roger (Robert Downey Jr.), and a longtime private investigator, Kitty (Margaret Colin), who are both deeply in love with what he could be; they treat him as if he were Achilles sulking in his tent. Still suspicious of power, Eddie believes he's making a valid constitutional point by insisting on the legal rights of drug-dealers. And so he is. But he's also helping vicious thugs in return for cash on the table. Cynicism and righteous bull cover the collapse of his idealism. "Everybody's guilty. Everybody," he says.

True Believer was written by Wesley Strick, a former rock journalist, and he draws on the temperament of the late sixties and early seventies—not the hedonism and innocence so caressingly celebrated recently in the media but what some of us valued much more at the time, the critical shrewdness, the speed at getting to the dirty heart of things. The premise of *True Believer* is that young Roger, who worships Eddie, rouses him from his bitter funk, persuading him to reopen the case of a young Korean-American who may have been victimized by the legal system. The Korean, Shu Kai Kim (Yuji Okumoto), was convicted eight years earlier of murder; in prison, defending himself against a neo-Nazi gang, he kills another man. When Eddie sees Shu Kai in Sing Sing, something in the man's simple words about his years in the pen—"it's been a long time"—moves him, perhaps because it's been a long time since Eddie himself has felt free. Eddie rediscovers his fighting spirit, using what his experience and gut instincts tell him about the corruptions of power. He and his two assistants become investigators, digging into the dark miasma of New York law enforcement.

If we are to live by movie myths, this is one of the better ones. *True Believer* is a defiant antidote to all those films, plays, and TV shows that look back on the sixties in a spirit of despairing self-pity: "I was free then; I was idealistic and happy. But of course none of that has anything to do with life. Life is working at Goldman Sachs." Actually, there have always been plenty of ways to use what one learned in the sixties and still earn a good living. But no one ever admits as much. Instead, playwrights and sitcom writers harp on the alleged euphoric impracticality of the sixties as a way of justifying a sellout afterward. "I'm trapped; we're all trapped; it's the system." Well, we aren't all trapped, and the system is a lot looser than it looks. Inertia and fear are being dressed up as realism. *True Believer,* perfectly timed for the end of the Reagan administration, shows the way back—not through an exemplary figure (that would be a sanctimonious bore) but through the intuitions of a smart street fighter who knows defeat at first hand.

The movie is about redemption, the squarest of subjects; but Joseph Ruben's direction has pace and verve, and James Woods's passionate and funny performance sweeps all before it. The most obviously intelligent actor of his generation, Woods has occasionally used his flashing verbal dexterity and his love for playing creepy characters to show us what a rough, unyielding bastard he can be. He likes to shock us with his killer eyes and psycho snarl. But here, as in *Salvador*, Woods goes so deep into the character that you feel you are looking right into his soul. This is a complex, self-satirizing performance: Woods plays Eddie as a man of genuine feeling but also as a blowhard and a hambone who works up storms of emotion to pressure people and keep himself revved up. He's not a fake, but he's an actor, a man who *sees* himself winning great victories against the Establishment. Every once in a while, Woods makes Eddie pull back and enjoy the effects of his self-righteous rhetoric; the shifts in consciousness are dazzling.

In the courtroom scenes, Woods puts on a rousing show of bravura, going from thunderous roars to a nearly inaudible whisper—his act could be a parody of some legendary spellbinder's trick. Out of court, Woods races ahead in that neurotically intense way he has of seeming to anticipate the next moment, and the moment after *that*. His mind is exhilarated yet clear, like that of a speed freak who somehow understands more as he gets higher and higher. Eddie galvanizes people, including his enemies, who despise his man-of-the-people rhetoric while fearing his legal skills. He's all heart, fired up by injustice and by his valiant Saint George role in defeating it. The man is both a hero and a tremendous pain in the neck.

True Believer moves at the speed of Woods's mental processes; the plot seems to be jolting along so that Eddie won't get bored. The lighting is dark-toned, the New York atmosphere gritty and violent, the revelations satisfyingly convoluted. I enjoyed *True Believer* more than Ruben's highly praised *The Stepfather* (1987), a movie that never burst its horror-thriller genre conventions. *True Believer,* despite its inspirational plot, opens up the world. In this period of inept moviemaking, Ruben, 38, has skills that are almost astonishing: He likes to tell stories with interesting people in them. If he doesn't ruin himself by directing a $30-million fantasy, he should have a brilliant career.

NEW YORK POST, 2/17/89, p. 23, David Edelstein

As Eddie Dodd, the renegade defense lawyer in the dynamite new thriller "True Believer," James Woods isn't so much directed as unleashed. Tear 'em up, Jimmy! Attaboy, sic'em!

You can only stand back and marvel. With his wolfish face, bulging eyes and stabbing delivery, Woods may be the most ferocious ham in movies—a real party animal. Like his photojournalist in "Salvador," his Eddie Dodd is a cyclonic bull artist who doesn't know where the bull ends and the truth begins. And it's the same with Woods' acting. If there isn't always truth in what he does, there's so much high cunning you can't tell the difference. He's a smart S.O.B.

"True Believer" is cunning, too, but considerably more principled. It's really about something. We first see Eddie through the eyes of Roger Baron (Robert Downey Jr.) a smart, liberal, Ivy League lawyer with dreams of clerking for this legend, who during the '60s was champion of the radicals. Roger, who's just itching to fight the Good Fight, arrives in New York and—to his horror—finds his hero getting coke dealers off the hook on technicalities.

Sucking on a joint in his office, today's Eddie holds forth about the threat posed by unscrupulous drug enforcers to the Sixth Amendment. On one level he believes it—he's sure that trashing the constitution is no way to uphold the constitution. But he also knows that the people he springs from jail are scumbags, and so the Good Fight is anything but. He's lost his way: he's still an adversary, but no longer a true believer. No one, says Eddie, is innocent.

Until now. The story proper begins when a Korean woman pleads with the lawyer to take the case of her son, Shu Kai Kim (Yuji Okumoto), who was sent to jail eight years ago for a Chinatown gang murder she swears he didn't commit. In jail, Shu has killed a neo-Nazi in self-defense. (This is the movie's brutal second sequence, shortly after a spooly, slow-motion rendering of the Chinatown slaying.)

No one knows what really happened in Chinatown or why Shu was framed, but the case has racist—and perhaps political—overtones. And meeting this impassive, cold young man, who hasn't asked for help, Eddie sees a reflection of his own despair. When the unctuous district attorney (Kurtwood Smith, the psycho in "Robocop")—famed for prosecuting immigrants and gangsters and leaving the fat cats alone—decided to prosecute Shu himself, Eddie is nettled, provoked. He tears into the case like a dog worrying a bone.

The script, by former rock critic Wesley Strick, is smart and ironic and full of gung-ho repartee, but it doesn't really cut loose from its courtroom-drama frame. "True Believer" might seem like just a terrific TV movie if it weren't for the fervor of its director, Joseph Ruben, and the high-wattage of its star. Ruben knows that energy is Woods' greatest asset, so he paces the movie at breakneck speed, like one of those Road Runner cartoons in which every exit leaves a trail of flames.

Woods and Downey make a crackerjack comedy team, egging each other on as they pore over files and chase down witnesses. Fluffed-up and bespectacled, Downey's Roger goads and challenges his mentor, trying to break through the layers of cynicism and self-deception. And as a private investigator with a soft spot for idealists, Margaret Colin has bright, mocking eyes and a husky way with an insult. Downey and Colin are little more than foils, but matching Woods' stride keeps them hurtling.

Ruben made the cheerily perverse thriller "The Stepfather," and he uses the camera with Hitchcockian wit. In "True Believer" it's at eye level, so that the action of the film has a jittery immediacy—it could almost be hitched to Woods' ponytail. Because the camera and the hero are connected, you're swept up in his outrage and obsession on a visceral level. Eddie's always plunging headlong into barren, isolated settings, and "True Believer" gets scarier and more dizzing as it goes along.

The conspiracy turns out to be a beaut. More than a whodunit, the film becomes a how-could-it-have-happened, a descent into a moral hell where the guardians of welfare have lost all perspective, where the evil has the force of self-righteousness.

"True Believer" doesn't have the audacity of "The Stepfather"—the story of a frustrated "Father Knows Best" type who marries into existing families and then massacres them. This time, Ruben has tried to make a solid mainstream thriller, to work within the system.

He delivers a knockout, yet the picture still goes bracingly against the grain. Eddie's innocence—his belief that the world could be changed—has gone rancid. But the point of "True Believer" is that the vision is renewable, that even at his sleaziest, Eddie has managed to cling to the wreckage of his ideals.

The picture says that noble ends—busting drug-dealers, for example—do not justify ignoble means: putting innocent people behind bars, freeing killers, or violating civil rights. It's anti-vigilante, at a time when even pretend-liberal movies like "Mississippi Burning" say the only way to deal with hooligans is to throw away those pansy lawbooks and bash heads. In a debased genre, "True Believer" proves that fighting the Good Fight can still be a thrill.

NEWSDAY, 2/17/89, Part III/p.3, Lynn Darling

Not with a bang but a whimper: As a symbol of the way the '60s ended, Eddie Dodd, the character at the center of "True Believer," is terrific. A brilliant radical lawyer who made his reputation and fueled his social conscience by defending high profile rebels and victims of societal injustice, Eddie's made a cynical peace with the greed-charged temper of the times. These days he defends drug dealers, getting paid in big stacks of cash by the coke merchants while defending the marijuana possessors for free. He tells himself that in getting these lowlifes off the hook he's really defending the Constitution, but he's not fooling anybody.

He's not fooling Roger Baron (Robert Downey Jr.) a recent law school gradute who stoked himself on Dodd's idealistic exploits while he was a student and who has come to New York to study at the feet of the master. It's not long before Baron has had enough of the detritus Dodd makes his living defending, so when a Korean woman comes into the office to beg Dodd to take the case of her son, a man who has spent the last eight years in jail for a crime she says he didn't commit, Baron convinces Dodd to take the case.

Dodd is a compelling character, the kind that excites curiosity, providing as he does a way into a question that a lot of '60s survivors ask themselves from time to time, the one that David Byrne put rather succinctly: *How did I get here?*

And James Woods does a bang-up job of conveying Dodd's flamboyant style, the righteous anger that is almost like a drug to him, the self-pity that is the flip side of that anger. He's even got the lean renegade sexiness of a guy like Dodd down, the graying ponytail, the charismatic intensity.

What he doesn't have, however, is a fully drawn character to bring to life.

There's not much attempt to paint on Dodd's background, to bring us up to date with how he ended up losing the faith he once had that energized him to fight the system. (Part of the problem, for that matter, is that the movie assumes that it was faith that fueled the '60s in the first place, a dubious proposition at best for an era that found its symbol in a clenched fist.) It's never really clear what the context of Dodd's life is—how he thinks about the era that made a hero of him, how he deals with the world as it is now. It's hard to care about how Eddie Dodd finds himself when we don't get much of a sense of how he lost himself.

Instead the movie relies on obvious clues, visual and aural triggers that are meant to give us an idea of where Eddie Dodd is coming from. Unfortunately, there's only so much that the Jimi Hendrix version of "All Along the Watchtower" can do in terms of summoning up the '60s.

There's more clarity to the relationship between Dodd and Baron. Robert Downey, Jr. captures the younger lawyer's combination of '80s hip cynicism and youthful idealism nicely; he's a good foil to Wood's occasionally over-amped zealot. The chemistry makes you wish the movie had concentrated on the characters it had created and on what their relationship had to tell us about the ways in which times have changed.

But before long, "True Believer" changes gears; it becomes a fast-paced courtroom drama that concentrates on the question of whether it was indeed Dodd's client who committed a street assassination in Chinatown eight years before. It's not a very believable courtroom drama: A lot of 11th-hour coincidence and other creaky plot devices are needed to bring the muddled story to its twisty conclusion. It's not as interesting a question as the movie asks in the first place, but, at least, it's one that comes with a set of answers.

TIME, 2/20/89, p. 94, Richard Schickel

James Woods is not exactly an obscure actor. The man has actually had an Academy Award nomination, among other show-biz accolades. But compared with every Tom, Jack and Dustin, he is truly one of the unsung actors in movies today.

His cult knows where to find him: playing fringe characters in fringe features like *Videodrome* and, just a couple of months ago, portraying a man succumbing to the twin addictions of ambition and drugs in *The Boost*. His Oscar nomination was for *Salvador,* a feverish performance of *Yanqui* journalism confronting Latin revolution that never found the audience it deserved. The big crowd, catching Woods occasionally on television or doing heavy duty in a mainstream movie, has yet to get his message. Or maybe that message is too clear and the public hates what it is hearing.

For this is the age of the really cute guy, and James Woods is a really scary guy, as he shows in his portrayal of lawyer Eddie Dodd in *True Believer*. At the start of the film he sticks his face into a jury box and yells. It is a demonic face, hollowed out by unfathomable passions, the eyes agleam with an anger that may be authentic, or may be faked for persuasive purposes. Or maybe its roots are in something that happened to Eddie in kindergarten. Who knows?

Only Woods. But he's not telling. He's just behaving, out there on the enigmatic edge of the sociopathic, as the sole ruler of the emotional territory that he has made uniquely his. And what is he screaming about? Why, the violated constitutional rights of his client, who just happens to be a guilty-as-sin drug dealer. Eddie bullies the jury into an acquittal all right, but behavior like this is not calculated to get an audience rooting for him.

Neither is the plot in which writer Wesley Strick and director Joseph Ruben (himself something of a cult figure for *The Stepfather* two years ago) enmesh him. Eddie's main business may be straightforward enough: to free from Sing Sing a Korean American named Shu Kai Kim (Yuji Okumoto), who is doing hard, not to say life-threatening time for a murder he did not commit. But the path to belated justice is a sleazy maze, twisted as a paranoiac's logic. A key witness is a man who believes the telephone company assassinated John F. Kennedy.

Neo-Nazis and a plumbing-supply merchant with sidelines in piety and jealous rage lurk there, along with a mastermind whose ends may justify his means but not his perpetual sneer. Youth gangs, corrupt cops, drug smugglers and, yes, some late-model toilet bowls also have their places in a tale whose complexities would devour most actors.

But Woods'angry energy is clarifying as well as terrifying, and when he unleashes it (usually without warning), the effect is to focus our attention where it belongs, not on a suspense story but on the mysteries of human behavior. Not that there are any comfortable conclusions. Woods' idealistic young associate (Robert Downey Jr.) keeps hoping that Eddie will rediscover his '60s idealism. A private eye (Margaret Colin) is standing by to offer redemptive love. These easy, familiar motivations are avoided. Eddie Dodd is not going to be anybody's exemplary case. He is a marginal one, a hard one, and, like the actor who plays him, proud of it. And proud to do what he does superbly.

VILLAGE VOICE, 2/21/89, p. 67, Renee Tajima

Forget that it's really the African-American political movement that set Mississippi burning 25 years ago, or that Korean-American political prisoner Chol Soo Lee was released from San Quentin largely due to the activism of Asian-American groups nationwide. In Hollywood's (re)vision of history, social change is wrought by fiercely independent white men in suits.

The suit in *True Believer* is radical chic tweed, worn by James Woods as maverick lawyer Eddie Dodd, who has traveled a 20-year ideological road from antiwar firebrand to defender of mid-level drug dealers. This fallen lefty's conscience is confronted by none other than Roger Baron (Robert Downey Jr.), a yuppie vision in tortoise-shell specs, who has made his New York pilgrimage to work with the Dodd of the legendary "Chase Manhattan bombing summation" (shades of Isla Vista). Instead, he finds a ponytailed cynic, who, still sporting the huge personality that marched and roared two decades before, proclaims, "The last struggle for constitutional rights is being waged over drugs, and we are in the ring doing battle with Big Brother," as he rips open a brown paper package of cash from a satisfied client.

Baron convinces Dodd to take on the defense of Shu Kai Kim (Yuji Okumoto), loosely based on the Chol Soo Lee case. A young Korean immigrant is falsely convicted in a Chinatown gang slaying. After eight years in the pen, he's up again for fatally stabbing a neo-Nazi inmate in self-defense during a prison fracas. The real-life Chol Soo was a fighter politicized by his legal battle, and his case became a cause célèbre for Asian Americans. In the movie, Shu Kai is a victim whose last hope lies with the legal strategems of Dodd, a renegade David in Goliath's court. (The production notes acknowledge only that Dodd's character was inspired by J. Tony Serra, the San Francisco criminal attorney who defended Chol Soo in his retrial.)

Shu Kai's case forms the story line of the film, but its main event is the Woods-Downey twosome—perfectly matched in the tradition of mismatched pairs—hot on the trail of murder, mayhem, and political corruption. On the surface, Shu Kai's case seems like a classic picture of injustice. After winning a retrial for his client, Dodd is pummeled in front of his office by a thug named Chucky Loeder, who warns him, "Aryan Army says Chink go to trial, you die." But there's more beneath the surface. In an amusing trip to a Jersey Aryan hangout, not only do Dodd and Baron discover that Nazi's love their children, too, but Loeder turns out to be a pseudo-supremacist, a faker.

The Chinatown frame-up and the prison killing become linked in a plot twist that's so unbelievable that even the most ultra of leftists wouldn't dream it. It's pure, predictable Hollywood—surprise witnesses, 11th-hour confessions—that had me on the edge of my seat. Dodd's character borders on the maudlin and theatrical, and it works because of Woods's manic edgy deliver. His Dodd is an arbitrary personality—one that disregards the facts in the service of a higher truth—set against an understatedly funny performance by Downey and fueled by writer Wesley Strick's quick-fire dialogue. Only Okumoto's Shu Kai suffers—when will screenwriters ever learn that Asian Americans talk like everyone else? Here's a good actor limited to uttering stilted responses to Woods's brilliant theatrics.

Kurtwood Smith is perfectly slimy as District Attorney Robert Reynard: He's got the tight-face look of a Nixon-Haldeman clone, ultimately brought down by his own arrogance and belief in compromising principles "for the greater good." *True Believer* is full of these fun references to'60s politics—the key to an official cover-up is a plumbing store—but ideology is only the backdrop and local color for action-packed suspense. The Asian angle is just that. In Hollywood's eyes, Chinatown is still the shadowy place that mystified J.J. Gittes in *Chinatown*, populated by character actors and rich with plot possibilities.

Also reviewed in:
NEW REPUBLIC, 2/13/89, p. 26, Stanley Kauffmann
NEW YORK TIMES, 2/17/89, p. C10, Janet Maslin
NEW YORKER, 2/20/89, p. 95, Pauline Kael
VARIETY, 2/8–14/89, p. 18

TRUE LOVE

A United Artists release of a Forward Films production. *Producer:* Richard Guay and Shelley Houis. *Director:* Nancy Savoca. *Screenplay:* Nancy Savoca and Richard Guay. *Director of Photography:* Lisa Rinzler. *Editor:* John Tintori. *Sound:* Mathew Price. *Sound Editor:* Tim Squyres. *Production Designer:* Lester W. Cohen. *Art Director:* Pamela Woodbridge. *Set Decorator:* Jessica Lanier. *Set Dresser:* Phillip Schneider and Sermin Kardestuncer. *Costumes:* Deborah Anderko. *Make-up:* Chris Bingham. *Running time:* 100 minutes. *MPAA Rating:* R.

CAST: Annabella Sciorra (Donna); Ron Eldard (Michael); Aida Turturro (Grace); Roger Rignack (Dom); Star Jasper (J.C.); Michael J. Wolfe (Brian); Kelly Cinnante (Yvonne); Rick Shapiro (Kevin); Suzanne Costallos (Fran); Vinny Pastore (Angelo); Marianne Leone (Carmella); Marie Michaels (Chickie); Anna Vergani (Grandma); John Nacco (Benny); Ann Tucker (Barbara); Nanette Werness (Josie); George Russo (Tom); Jennifer Occhino (Jennifer); Bernard Jaffe (Carmine); Frankie Pisacano (Baby); Steven Randazzo (Ernie); Mary Portser (Trudy); Donald Berman (Maitre d'); John Salemmo (Johnny); Saverio Guerra (Frankie); Jack Digiorgio (Photographer); Dale Carman (Father Frank); Charmaine Castelli (Kelly); Filomena Dobbins (Lynn); Joseph Giardino (Nicky); Christopher Shaw (Furniture Salesman); Judy Prianti, David Stepkin, and Marylin Monaco (Deli Customers); William Bastiani (Joe Chicken); Ed Pascal (Pete Cigars); Tracy Lundell (Photographer's Assistant); Barbara Tuffarelli (Lady in Bathroom); Daniel Tuffarelli (Boy in Bathroom); Al Juliano (Stripper); Ray Tintori (Ring Bearer); Angela Walshe (Young Woman); Bobby Guay (Boy on Big Wheel).

LOS ANGELES TIMES, 11/10/89, Calendar/p. 8, Chris Willman

It's not exactly a many-splendored thing, but "True Love" is as funny and fascinating as it is unflorid. This lively portrait of young Italian-Americans falling in and out of love come matrimony season in the Bronx plays like a trenchant cross between a teen sex comedy and an Albert Brooks super-realist nightmare. Or maybe "Moonstruck" in hell.

Its young bride, Donna (Annabella Sciorra), and bridegroom, Michael (Ron Eldard), are none too bright as they spend their last few single days wildly careening toward what increasingly looks to be a significantly miserable marriage. As the arguments start, and buddy-bonding suddenly seems much more meaningful than impending vows, they experience a couple's worst dream come true—discovering their true incompatibility within scant days of the ceremony itself.

To laugh or to squirm? There's abundant humor, but director Nancy Savoca isn't afraid to wipe the smile off the movie's face when the pain cuts too deep. And she will leave it up to you whether or not to find dark comedy in the misguided litany of support from family and friends. "Once you two are on your honeymoon and can relax, you'll be fine" and "You'll see, after the wedding, he'll settle down," they rationalize helpfully, a Bronx chorus of denial.

Early on, it's easy to see what Michael, a Peter Pan who plays at responsibility, and Donna, who wants to drag him kicking into adulthood, see in each other. They're the prettiest and probably spunkiest of their fast-talking circle. It's also easy to identify with the mutual irritations that develop and, if sympathy eventually sidles over toward her nagging efforts to grow him up, that's less a feminist viewpoint being foisted than a realistic one. (The contrast between the boys' drunken spree and the vengeful girls' night out is amusingly clear; the women can't have quite as grand a time, never having been taught how to lose themselves so completely.)

The movie ends with a long take of the trussed-up, shell-shocked newlyweds that echoes the final shot of "The Graduate," but there's far less doubt about what life together for this couple will be like, only how much of a fight they'll put up getting there.

It's a kind of fatalism, the planned obsolescence of affection, that may be hard for some audiences to identify with, but in this tightknit Italian culture, divorce or even calling off the wedding are hardly options. In one candid moment, Donna confesses to a pal that she's considered breaking the engagement, but, now, "I can't live here if I don't marry him."

If none of this sounds like the stuff punchlines are made of, in lieu of easy laughs there are plenty of hard-won, subtle, difficult ones coming right out of character. "True Love" also provides the expected wicked hilarity when it comes to satirizing wedding rituals (like the visit to the family friend who pitches $3,000 "hair-loom' rings).

Yet each time you suspect Savoca is finally setting up the big comic set-piece or a slide into sentimentality, she veers off on an altogether more difficult course. Along with her co-writer and husband, Richard Guay, she's fashioned a brave, astonishingly perceptive comic drama rife with perfect details and engaging subplots. Most likely, it's the debut of a major film maker.

Among the cast of unknowns are easily half a dozen playful performances far more Oscar-worthy than the winter's big-budget Academy bait, with radiant Sciorra the most immediate find, and Eldard and Kelly Cinnante (who co-starred in "Tony N' Tina's Wedding" on the New York stage) also dead-on. They make it feel like real life that's being eavesdropped on, but Savoca and her upstart technical crew make it look and sound like a *movie*, too, one you'd swear must have cost several times what this triumph of low-budget invention actually did.

"True Love" (rated R for ample profanity) is, among so many other things, a classic cautionary tale of co-dependency, almost sure to help bring on the end of more than one troubled engagement out in audienceland. See it with someone you love too much.

NEW YORK POST, 10/20/89, p. 27, Jami Bernard

"True Love" is a movie so remarkably true to its subject that it may have fortfeited its chances at the box office. Those who could best appreciate a movie about the arcane, inbred mating rituals of a certain type of working-class New York Italian neighborhood are those who live that very life themselves, and if they're smart, they'll leave the theater so depressed they'll want to "take the gas," one character's deadly kitchen-wisdom solution for errant husbands.

Bleak and scarily funny—while not all that riveting as a movie story—"True Love" is on one level about the tensions an impending wedding cause in a young couple's by-the-book relationship. On another level, it is about how love and responsibility are defined and made palatable by the rigid, well-meaning social conventions that hold a particular tribe together.

The kind of wedding and marriage that Donna and Mikey can expect come down to them so overrefined by preceding generations that they are unable to stand back and assess themselves. Are they really in love? Can the wedding machinery, once in gear, be altered? Will a marriage license give Donna the license to tell Mikey not to go out with the boys on their wedding night?

When the oily caterer suggests dyeing the mashed potatoes to match the hue of the bridesmaids' dresses—one of the film's funnier bits—Donna is intrigued, Mikey disgusted by the idea of "blue food." Neither one is appalled that weddings have degenerated into issues of color schemes and seating arrangements, where love is measured by the size and price of a ring and how much influence the lovers' opposing sets of friends wield.

The movie takes place in The Bronx, but it could as easily be in parts of other boroughs, or practically the whole of Staten Island. Donna and Mikey have been raised like veal, predestined to stay together despite a future of bitter disappointments. They have no idea what makes each other tick. "She says this is important, *and then I don't know what the f— she's talking about!"* complains Mikey to his pals in typically f-word-laden speech.

Donna and Mikey are the modern Kramden family (they watch "The Honeymooners" for sport). Every detail, from the gum-clacking accents to the over-puffed sleeves of the bridesmaids' gowns, is correct, and surprisingly without malice to the characters. They are who they are *fuhget aboudit.*

The refreshing cast, many of them newcomers, thankfully avoids playing it too broadly, or "True Love" would have had to compete with such as "Working Girl" and "Cookie," in which slices of this sort of life are played only for laughs. "True Love" genuinely yearns for its characters in a way that the audience may not care to. On the other hand, it misses as many opportunities as it seizes, spoiling visual humor with ill-placed tight and medium shots.

Newcomers Annabella Sciorra and Ron Eldard are a believable if well-scrubbed Donna and Mikey.

The script, co-written by director Nancy Savoca and her husband, producer Richard Guay, is perversely on target in its inarticulate borough-speak, covering subjects as important to the culture as women's views on oral sex and men's standards of female desirability. This could almost be a documentary.

Which, of course, does not help the movie's commercial appeal. If Donna and Mikey saw this movie, she'd probably get some decorating tips from it and he'd probably be annoyed that the movie tickets cost so much.

Savoca commendably does not take the easy way out at the end, although the sideshow of Donna and Mikey's friends making romantic headway at their ticky-tacky wedding does provide a kind of optimism. The tribe will continue, for better or worse, for richer or poorer, in sickness and in health, *fuhget aboudit.*

NEWSDAY, 10/20/89, Part III/p. 3, Mike McGrady

"True Love" is as much a depiction of tribal rituals as any issue of National Geographic, as perfect and detailed a study of human customs and practices as any Margaret Mead tome. However, what's being explored in "True Love" are the practices and rites of a modern subculture, Italian-Americans who happen to live in the Bronx during the later years of the 20th Century.

This dazzling first film by Nancy Savoca—and what a year this has been for new moviemaking talents!—centers on that most primary of tribal events, the impending marriage of Michael (Ron Eldard) and Donna (Annabella Sciorra), two attractive young people who have only two things in common: geography (the Bronx) and a certain emotion (love).

One is, in fact, more aware of differences than similarities. Michael is something of a traditionalist—he wants the straight black-and-white tux, not the pastel number, nor will he tolerate the caterer's recommendation for mashed potatoes that match the bridesmaids' pale blue gowns. The more venturesome bride prefers pastel tux and potatoes and is not above joining her friends for a pre-nuptial blast at a male-stripper joint.

Each of these enormously likable youngsters is suffering second thoughts. Donna to a friend: "Just think, in two days, I'll be married! You think I should marry him?" Michael to Donna: "Suddenly, everything becomes very, very complicated. I just don't wanta wind up hating my life."

First-time director-writer Nancy Savoca's picture of two people sacrificing a variety of freedoms for the uncertain joys of marriage is a beauty—hilarious, moving, brilliant, involving. We're with the jeweler for the ring negotiations, we attend the stag party that winds up at dawn on the Atlantic City boardwalk, we eavesdrop as a mother fumbles with strictly redundant wedding-night advice: "I don't know, was there somethin' you wanted to ask me? You know everything there is to know, don't you?" And, finally, there is the wedding itself, that ultimate ritual, that joining together of relatives and friends, tribes and neighborhoods, in a naked display of pain and joy, laughter and despair.

"True Love" is a wonderful movie, unarguable proof that you don't need elaborate story or plot gimmicks if you begin with the truth and stick to it. Not only do the details seem perfect, the dialogue is rich with the flavors of the city. The fact that the angelic young women of the tribe are every bit as scatological as the men represents an added truth.

Almost as heartwarming as what happens on the screen is the behind-the-scenes story of making the film. Savoca, a prize-winning graduate of NYU's film school, is married and the mother of two. To raise money for "True Love," Savoca made a nine-minute promotional trailer that attracted the attention of backers, including Jonathan Demme and John Sayles. Collecting money on a piecemeal basis, Savoca and her producer-husband, Richard Guay, assembled a cast of unknowns—absolutely brilliant unknowns—and shot the movie on location in the Bronx neighborhood where Savoca and Guay grew up. The film was entered in this year's United States Film Festival in Park City, Utah, where it won the Grand Prize. Deservedly.

Also reviewed in:
NEW YORK TIMES, 10/20/89, p. C10, Janet Maslin
VARIETY, 2/15/89, p. 29
WASHINGTON POST, 9/15/89, p. C7, Hal Hinson

TURNER & HOOCH

A Touchstone Pictures release in association with Silver Screen Partners IV. *Executive Producer:* Daniel Petrie Jr. *Producer:* Raymond Wagner. *Director:* Roger Spottiswoode. *Screenplay:* Dennis Shryack, Michael Blodgett, Daniel Petrie Jr., Jim Cash, and Jack Epps Jr. *Story:* Dennis Shryack, Michael Blodgett, and Daniel Petrie Jr. *Director of Photography:* Adam Greenberg. *Editor:* Garth Craven. *Music:* Charles Gross. *Music Editor:* Daniel Allan Carlin. *Sound:* Jim Webb and (music) Rob Eaton. *Sound Editor:* Lon E. Bender. *Production Designer:* John DeCuir Jr. *Art Director:* Sig Tinglof. *Set Decorator:* Cloudia. *Special Effects:* Alan E. Lorimer. *Costumes:* Jean Rosone and Eric H. Sandberg. *Make-up:* Dan C. Striepeke. *Stunt Coordinator:* Conrad E. Palmisano. *Running Time:* 98 minutes. *MPAA Rating:* PG.

CAST: Tom Hanks (Scott Turner); Mare Winningham (Emily Carson); Craig T. Nelson (Chief Hyde); Reginald Veljohnson (David Sutton); Scott Paulin (Zack Gregory); J.C. Quinn (Walter Boyett); John McIntire (Amos Reed); David Knell (Ernie); Ebbe Roe Smith (Harley McCabe); Kevin Scannell (Jeff Foster); Joel Bailey (Ferraday); Mary McCusker (Katie); Ernie Lively (Motel Clerk); Clyde Kusatsu (Kevin Jenkins); Elaine Renee Bush (Store Clerk); Eda Reiss Merin (Mrs. Remington); Victor DiMattia (Sean Boyett); Elden Ratliff (Eric Boyett); Cheryl Anderson (Mrs. Boyett); Ursula Lentine (Bride); Sharon Madden (Mrs. Kathy Harper); Daniel Ben Wilson (Mike Harper); Jenny Drugan (Christine Harper); Madeleine Cowie Klein (Animal Control Woman); Julian Sylvester (Animal Control Man); Nick Dimitri (Casey); Scott Stevens (Cop); Terry Israel (Police Officer); Frederick Ponzlov (Police Officer); Andrew Walker (Police Officer); Linda Eve Miller (Mrs. Pine); Jim Beaver (Plant Manager); Beasley (Hooch).

FILMS IN REVIEW, 11/89, p. 548, Ken Hanke

If you handed me a piece of paper and a pen and told me to make a list of 500 things I'd most like to see on the big screen, neither Tom Hanks trimming his nose hair, nor a dog slobbering for 100 minutes would be on that list. This may come as a shock to director Roger Spottiswoode and the five—count 'em—five writers it took to cook up this TV movie of the week masquerading as a theatrical film. (Come to think of it, there's a nose hair joke in John Hughes' *Uncle Buck*, too. Is Hollywood onto something the rest of us have missed, do you suppose?) The best thing that can be said about *Turner & Hooch* is that it is probably harmless. I don't imagine that any irreparable psychological damage is likely to result from the apparently hysterical spectacle of a monumentally unattractive dog salivating all over the screen—and that's really all there is to the film. At bottom, *Turner & Hooch* is simply a badly constructed comedy-mystery (it doesn't take a rocket scientist to figure out the surprise villain once you see where the film is heading) coated in doggie drool.

There is little point in recounting the film's plot, which is more situational than anything. In essence, Tom Hanks is Scott Turner, a fussy neat-nik policeman in a dinky California coastal town, who just happens to become involved in the town's one and only substantial crime a few days before going to his new job in the Big City (in this case, Sacramento). Alas, this crime—a murder—has only one witness. Now who could that be? Of course—Hooch the dog. And so into Hanks sanitized existence comes Ol' Slobber, who destroys nearly everything he owns. In real life, Hanks—or anyone—would almost certainly murder the beast but movies of this type being movies of this type, he sees the lovable side of these antics. (I don't know about the rest of you, but I always feel very fond of things that eat my furniture, trash my kitchen, and disembowel my stereo. Oh, yes.) Not that Hooch is without his merits, since he paves the way for Hanks' romance with the local veterinarian (Mare Winningham)—something like a canine version of George Arliss playing Cupid to the romantic leads, I guess. All this is merely the framework onto which to drape dog jokes, most of which revolve around this damned thing slobbering. It slobbers all over car windows, Hanks' stereo equipment, and even in his shoes. When it isn't slobbering, it's destroying something. The only variation in this comes when the writers are inspired to construct a dog-breaking-wind scene. We can all agree that this is not only tasteful but original, I'm sure. Naturally, the dog turns out to be a swell animal by the time the film gets around to attempting a shameless piece of manipulation at the end, killing it off for no very good reason other than an assault on the tear ducts and to allow Hanks a Big Moment. Hanks nearly pulls it off, but the film undermines him by virtue of its presentation—you just can't accept Hooch's bright, shiny, focused eyes as belonging to a dying dog.

In fact, Hanks is quite good throughout. Not everyone can hold the screen in competition with a dog, but Hanks generally manages it with pleasant authority and assurance. There is one rather charming (and dogless) scene where he and Winningham paint a room in her house in which

Hanks shows much the same quality one finds in the young Henry Fonda without the sense of calculated awkwardness that mars some of the Fonda performances. Even so, the film seems a pretty strange career move for Hanks, despite its undeniable popularity. Possibly, he wanted to show that he can triumph over a ridiculous project. If so, he largely succeeds, but can he—or anyone—satisfactorily explain why he is required to play about a third of the picture in nothing but a pair of black bikini underwear? I do not foresee much future for Tom Hanks, pin-up boy, but perhaps he plans on introducing a line of gents' underclothing. It can be the only excuse.

LOS ANGELES TIMES, 7/28/89, Calendar/p. 7, Michael Wilmington

When Tom Hanks stares testily or fondly at his co-star in "Turner & Hooch," a dogue de Bordeaux named Beasley, you can sense a real connection. And when Beasley stares back—wattles matted with froth, huge red eyes in a Winston Churchill-ish glower—these two actors seem to have genuine respect for each other's abilities. Hanks shrieks; Beasley cocks his head. Hanks pants; Beasley barks. Hanks kvetches; Beasley sniffs. Hanks flinches; Beasley jumps on him and chomps jovially at his throat.

They work together with the seeming near-telepathic sensitivity of longtime vaudeville partners. It's good that "Turner & Hooch" has this chemistry at its center, due to the actors and to Beasley's ingenious trainer, Clint Rowe, because it's another movie that seems stranded without a script, somewhere south of the last deal and east of the fifth rewrite. Shot mostly on Terminal Island, it's the story of Turner, a small-town pier cop in a coastal city who inherits the obstreperous pooch Hooch after his master (John McIntire) is knifed in the aftermath of a nearby murder, leaving the faithful dog as sole eyewitness.

This catastrophe binds together Turner and Hooch in a variation on "The Odd Couple," with Hanks the equivalent of nippy perfectionist Felix and Beasley as another slob Oscar: guzzling beer, swilling whiskey, expectorating, expelling gas, destroying cars, chasing females and otherwise behaving like Walter Matthau unleashed. There is another love interest in "Turner & Hooch," a beautiful feisty veterinarian (Mare Winningham) who pops up as if by magic; she also, conveniently, has a gorgeous collie. But, basically, Beasley and Hanks are the whole show.

For a while, it's not a bad show at that. One reason "Big" worked well was the unself-conscious way that Hanks projects boyish qualities of enthusiasm, curiosity, petulance, candor, spontaneity. He really looks and acts like a kid at heart, and, in this movie, he looks like a fussbudget of a kid who needs a good, big, sloppy dog to warm him out. The production team behind them, with director Roger Spottiswoode and virtuoso cameraman Adam Greenberg ("Near Dark"), gives "Turner & Hooch" crispness and pace. Spottiswoode's movies are always beautifully edited, and there's a sheen to the images: When Beasley shakes his jowls, slow-motion sweat and drool fly off him like sunlit beads in a beer commercial.

The basic plot of a man-dog team tracking criminals, suspiciously similar to the April release "K-9," with Jim Belushi and German shepherd Jerry Lee, suggests that modern movies don't actually influence each other but somehow break out all at once, like epidemics. Tender relationships like the one between Turner and Hooch, full of delicate interplay, compassion and robust fellowship, aren't really being created for men and women, "When Harry Met Sally . . ." honorably excepted.

But the co-stars can distract you only so much. Three separate screen-writing entities—the teams of Dennis Shryak & Michael Blodgett ("Rent-a-Cop") and the ubiquitous Jim Cash & Jack Epps Jr. ("Top Gun") plus executive producer Daniel Petrie Jr.—seem to have canceled each other out. There are hints of Petrie's talent for zippy badinage, traces of Shryak-Blodgett's Gothic cop clichés. Finally, everything seems to get smoothed over by Cash and Epps, the great homogenizers: two writers who could probably take "Anna Karenina" and flatten it out into "Vronsky and Me."

As a bunch, the film makers have created the sort of mystery story that might well puzzle a 12-year-old who had never read a mystery story before and wasn't paying attention anyway, and the sort of love story that 12-year-olds mights throw away to read the mystery story, along with the sort of dog story many dogs would actually enjoy—if the pages were edible.

Luckily the team of Hanks and Beasley are around to save the show, tell a few snappy stories, dance a few licks, chase a few crooks, make you laugh, make you cry. Who needs writers? Hanks has his charm; Beasley has his barks. Everything else is counterpoint. One thing though: Speaking as an old dog-lover, especially of Samoyed mixes, I don't like the ending of "Turner & Hooch" (MPAA-rated PG, despite violence). Movies may actually be going to the dogs these days, but that entails certain rules and responsibilities.

MONTHLY FILM BULLETIN, 1/90, p. 25, Tim Pulleine

Scott Turner, an obsessively neat and tidy bachelor, is an "investigator" (plainclothes detective) in the small Californian town of Cypress Beach. About to depart for Sacramento, he is showing the ropes to his replacement, David Sutton, which involves visiting elderly Amos Reed, maker of frequent calls to the police, in the waterfront shack he shares with his large and enthusiastically watchful dog Hooch. The next day, Amos is found dead, with Hooch guarding his body; he has in fact been killed by Zack Gregory, strongarm man for Walter Boyett, boss of a nearby fish-packing plant (used for laundering Panamanian drug money), after Amos witnessed a fracas between Gregory and a double-crossing employee, Ferraday. Turner volunteers to stay on until the case is broken, and becomes reluctant custodian to Hooch, whom he takes for treatment to vet Emily Carson, establishing a friendship that is to blossom into a love affair. Hooch wreaks havoc in Turner's house, and causes similar disruption at police headquarters. When Boyett's daughter gets married at a nearby church, Hooch takes off after Gregory, who eludes capture by Turner and Sutton. A search of Boyett's plant proves fruitless, but Turner's suspicions are confirmed when he returns with Hooch, who "sniffs" out the connection with an unexplained sum of money earlier found by children on the beach. Turner traces Gregory to an out-of-town motel, and with Hooch's aid forces him to reveal Boyett's complicity. He arranges to rendezvous at Boyett's plant with police chief Hyde, where the latter proves to be the instigator of the money racket. Hyde shoots Boyett to ensure his silence, but Hooch, though mortally wounded by Boyett, attacks Hyde, enabling Turner to overcome him... Some time later, Turner is the Cypress Beach police chief and married to the now pregnant Emily, whose collie Camille has borne five puppies from her liaison with Hooch—four collies plus one diminutive and ultradestructive replica of Hooch himself.

As the plethora of credited writers perhaps reflects, *Turner & Hooch* is something of a dog's breakfast, spinning out a rather rudimentary cops and robbers plot as the excuse for its eponymous relationship. To some degree, the generic context of small-town comedy serves to yoke the two elements together, but this is rather undercut by the slickness of the film's method, which once past the establishing sequences doesn't go in for much in the way of local colour. The romantic sub-plot strikes an arbitrary and unlikely note, and the transformation of Turner and Hooch into the usual cop-movie duo happens a bit too easily. The passage of arms between them and its attendant comic business (like Hooch's penchant for cans of beer) has little spontaneity—it hardly matters little that the odd couple are of different species—and Tom Hanks' button-down charm comes, as it were, off-the-peg.

The most pointed moments are in fact those in which the canine protagonist becomes germane to the detective process. Calling him "the closest thing we have to a witness", Turner asks the disbelieving vet whether Hooch would be able to identify photographs of suspects; the eccentric manifestation of the inevitable car chase is precipitated by Hooch sniffing out the villain's henchman at a wedding reception; and in a grimly comic sequence, he assists in the latter's capture and (by pinning him down by the neck) in his subsequent interrogation. But the climactic mêlée in the packing plant has a standardised (and in the circumstances, too graphically violent) air about it. And even allowing for the quite deftly managed "happy ever after" coda (Disney, *101 Dalmatians*, and all), the demise of poor Hooch in the shootout seems a miscalculation in a light-hearted venture like this.

NEW YORK, 8/14/89, p. 80, David Denby

Turner & Hooch is about a fuss-budget bachelor policeman (Tom Hanks) and the big, wet, sloppy dog he inherits when a friend is murdered. Amazingly, the movie tells us more about the dog than his master. In fact, it's the dog's *slobber* that director Roger Spottiswood finds especially fascinating. Hanks, wrestling with the animal in his underwear, is as charming and physically adroit as ever, but see the movie only if you are a sucker for heavy jowels and stories about beasts who are all heart.

NEW YORK POST, 7/28/89, p. 27, David Edelstein

It isn't a seminal week for the American cinema: The biggest event is the arrival of Beasley (and his stand-in, Igor) as the canine half of "Turner & Hooch"—perhaps the best guy-with-a-huge-annoying-dog picture since that Dean Jones romp, "The Ugly Dachshund." Oh, let's not carp—it tops the "The Ugly Dachshund."

The movie is formula swill, but with a pedigree; it's much classier than it needs to be. Beasley plays Hooch, a giant mastiff, a junkyard dog. When his grizzled owner gets murdered by smugglers, Hooch is adopted by Scott Turner (Tom Hanks), an obsessively tidy California police inspector who hopes the creature will lead him to the old man's killer.

I'll bet you've guessed that Hooch is sloppy, but you've no idea how very sloppy he is. For one thing, he looks like a bowl of Jell-O on legs. For another, the corners of his mouth dribble gross white viscous froth resembling...never mind.

As he bounds (in slow motion) toward an unwelcome visitor, Hooch's great jowls flap like condor wings, pulling back to reveal a pair of mean yellow fangs. At first, he greets Turner by clamping down on the policeman's throat; later, he confines himself to messing up Turner's life.

Hooch is no end of mischief—barking till all hours, leaving trails of goo. In one scene, he tears up Turner's car. ("You're eating the car!" screams Hanks.) In another (an homage, no doubt, to "The Ugly Dachshund"), Hooch breaks out of the laundry room and annihilates Turner's apartment. Then he hits the fridge for a cold one: It's Miller time.

Hooch's co-star is no less estimable: Hanks is shaping up to be the smoothest light-comedy hero in movies. Amazingly, he manages to play an anal-retentive without stopping himself up or forsaking his trademark irony. He bobs along happily, stylishly—he's genuinely buoyant.

More than that, Hanks has a terrific rapport with the dog. In interviews, he has said he'll miss having co-stars who always read their lines the same way, and that makes sense: He's alert to Beasley, ready for anything. In the picture's best scene he coos, "You're not such a monster dog" and tackles the beast, playfully turning the tables. There's more honest affection here than in most love stories.

But the love story is pretty good, too. As a rabidly single veterinarian, Mare Winningham knows she must compete with Hooch for Hanks' affection, and her readings are peppery, tickling. When he jabbers an introduction she comes right back at him, interjecting her comments in the margins: She knows his name, they use the same bank, she knows what he does, where he lives. They have a true puppy love.

Director Roger Spottiswode once made a stupendous political thriller called "Under Fire," which was set during the last days of the corrupt Somoza regime. It's a little depressing to see him, six years later, at the helm of a dog comedy, but at least he's a hot director now. (Ron Shelton, who wrote "Under Fire," broke through with "Bull Durham.")

Adam Greenberg's superb photography is restless, plugged-in, and the editing is crackerjack. When you consider that the plot is leakier than Hooch (five writers got credit for the blah script), Spottiswode generates a surprising amount of suspense.

But the climax, for reasons I can't reveal without risking your wrath, is beastly, unforgivable. In this kind of movie you don't have to... You don't need a realistic... What's the point of...Grrrrrrr.

NEWSDAY, 7/28/89, Part III/p. 3, Mike McGrady

"The Odd Couple," Neil Simon's inspired union of fussbudget and slob, has enjoyed many lives. First it was a Broadway play, and then a big-budget movie, later a long-running television series and eventually an all-black version ("The New Odd Couple"). At one point, the Broadway edition starred women instead of men. I suppose it was only a matter of time before they got around to doing a dog version—and although Simon is nowhere credited, that is essentially what they've done with "Turner & Hooch."

And what a dog! Beasley as Hooch the pooch (think of Oscar Madison) is not only the ugliest dog ever to appear in films, he may well be the ugliest dog ever to appear on Earth. A huge drooling mastiff, Hooch belongs to a lesser-known French breed called de Bordeaux.

The reason this breed is lesser known and, in fact, downright rare, will be immediately apparent. In the first place, who would choose to own a huge, red-eyed, bewrinkled, jaw-flapping, constantly slobbering creature of gargantuan size and questionable personal habits? Secondly, I can't imagine how they persuade these animals to breed; my best guess would involve the necessity of blindfolds. In fact, when Hooch expresses a brief on-screen interest in a comely Lassielike collie, one's first instinct is to call the ASPCA.

An eyewitness to his master's murder, Hooch is enlisted by a compulsively tidy detective named Turner (Tom Hanks in the Felix Unger role) to aid in the investigation of the crime. Before you can say "Sit, boy!" Hooch has torn apart Turner's bachelor apartment, eaten his car's headrest, rearranged his office furniture, howled through the night, solved the crime, saved Turner's life, disarmed the villains and, in general, done all the things that movie dogs have been able to do ever since Asta dug up his first clues for Nick Charles.

This saga of canine super-accomplishment, certainly nothing new to Hollywood, somehow required the services of five scriptwriters. How might so many writers divide such meager chores? Well, a writer with a Bobbsey Twins background must've written the basic police story, a story that was old when Rin Tin Tin was young. The most innocent writer doubtless handled the love story between Turner and the local veterinarian (Mare Winningham) because he conjures up a model of adult propriety. The least talented writers probably handled the humor. One example: Hanks dismisses the sheriff's investigators because, "They couldn't find shoes in a shoebox."

The best moments in the film—and there are enough of them to delight a very young audience—are the moments of spontaneous combustion between Turner & Hooch. And there are moments—Hanks trying to guide Beasley into his car, Beasley dragging Hanks through a pet door, Hanks undertaking to give Beasley a bath—that border on the uproarious. Although no actor in his right mind wants to share a screen with an animal or an infant, Hanks at times musters up enough charm to hold his own. But then—remember "The Money Pit"? "The 'Burbs"?—this is hardly the first time the very talented Hanks has been involved with a large dog.

NEWSWEEK, 8/14/89, p. 56, David Ansen

Just about everything in *Turner & Hooch* is predictable, and the one thing that isn't is unforgivable. Neither of these facts, it should be noted, prevented this tale of a man and his dog from leaping to the top of the box-office charts its first week of release. Before a constitutional amendment is passed making it illegal to criticize adorable canine movies, may I dare to suggest, Scroogily, that a movie this formulaic can rot your soul with boredom?

That said, it must be conceded that "Turner & Hooch" is expertly executed dreck. Tom Hanks is faultlessly funny as a compulsive small-town investigator who learns to loosen up under the influence of his new roommate, a slobbering, couchchewing dogue de Bordeaux who happens to be the only witness to a murder Hanks is eager to solve. (It took five screenwriters to produce the lame mystery plot.) And the drooling Hooch himself (played by Beasley and a stunt double named Igor) is the Charles Laughton of fourlegged Thespians, next to whom Lassie would seem as inexpressive as a dumb starlet. Nor can it be denied that Roger Spottiswoode, the overqualified director ("Under Fire"), mounts this interspecies buddy movie with clean, clever strokes. Sure it's well done; but was it worth doing? And who was the evil genius who decided that this piece of fluff warranted a tragic finale? What happens to Hooch shouldn't happen to a dog, and it certainly shouldn't happen to an audience. There ought to be a law! Where's Jesse Helms when we really need him?

TIME, 8/7/89, p. 54, Richard Schickel

Scott Turner (Tom Hanks) is a tidy bundle of compulsions, the kind of man who gets off on an improved filing system and looks forward to flossing his teeth. Hooch (a mastiff named Beasley) is a messy bundle of sinew and instinct, the kind of dog who lives to wreck your living room and looks forward to sinking his teeth into the necks of people he doesn't like. Also, he drools a lot.

This is obviously not *Lassie Come Home;* it is the odd couple as crime busters. Turner is a small-town detective, an apt occupation for a man of his temperament. He has placed Hooch, the only witness to his former owner's murder, in protective custody. As the movie's none-too-ambitious mystery plot unfolds, it is Hooch, ferociously loyal to both his former master and his new one, who does most of the protecting. He's obviously never heard of Miranda rights. Not that he is a one-note character: he introduces Turner to romance with the local veterinarian (Mare Winningham), and in moments of repose he has a watchful sobriety that becomes a comment on the human propensity to rush around needlessly. If food, sex or loyalty is not at issue, what's all the excitement about?

Hanks, a wonderfully natural and unpretentious actor, may be the only star capable of holding his own against this competition, even stealing a scene or two from his furry friend. In the end, Turner tames Hooch down, Hooch loosens Turner up, and this little nothing of a movie—sweeter and smarter than it has a right to be—may cheer you on through the, uh, dog days.

VILLAGE VOICE, 8/8/89, p. 64, Renee Tajima

While I was growing up, dog heroes on screen were proud, good-looking animals. But in this age of sensitivity and substance, housepet heros, like humans, have character. E.T., a little creature so ugly he's adorable, might have had something to do with this phenomenon. Or maybe it was Mason Reese.

Director Roger Spottiswoode's comedy-action movie *Turner & Hooch* brings ugly-canine cinema to an entirely new dimension. The title dog is played by a de Bordeaux named Beasely—the breed may sound like a classy French wine, but this dog looks like Nighttrain. The reluctant master is Scott Turner (Tom Hanks), a small-town police inspector who inherits Hooch when the dog turns out to be the only eyewitness to a murder. Houseguest Hooch proceeds to bring wild disorder to the cop's compulsively meticulous world. Turner is a Felix Ungar with the spiritual embodiment of Andy Rooney—the type who dustbusts muffin crumbs off his partner's shirt while *driving*.

Turner & Hooch, an uneven blend of comedy and detective story, is funny for all the wrong reasons: predictable gags that play like banana peel tricks. As he wreaks havoc in Turner's house, Hooch laps up a six-pack and barks at the woofers, and what he doesn't eat, he drools on. Hanks, though, is able to transcend the slapstick with a humorous running dialogue directed at, variously, himself, God, and the impassive Hooch. The movie adds one more notch for comedian Hanks, of whom you could now say, "That guy could play opposite a slobbering dog and still be funny."

Also reviewed in:
NEW REPUBLIC, 9/11/89, p. 27, Stanley Kauffmann
NEW YORK TIMES, 7/28/89, p. C8, Caryn James
NEW YORKER, 10/16/89, p. 110, Pauline Kael
VARIETY, 8/2–8/89, p. 18
WASHINGTON POST, 7/28/89, Weekend/p. 33, Desson Howe
WASHINGTON POST, 7/29/89, p. B7, Rita Kempley

UHF

An Orion Pictures release of a Cinecorp production. *Executive Producer:* Gary Frederickson. *Producer:* Gene Kirkwood and John Hyde. *Director:* Jay Levey. *Screenplay:* Al Yankovic and Jay Levey. *Director of Photography:* David Lewis. *Editor:* Dennis O'Connor. *Music:* John du Prez. *Music Editor:* Katherine Quittner. *Sound:* Bo Harwood. *Sound Editor:* David McMoyler. *Production Designer:* Ward Preston. *Art Director:* Tim Donahue. *Set Designer:* Ron Yates. *Set Decorator:* Robert Zilliox. *Special Effects:* Mike Menzel. *Visual Effects:* Bill Mesa. *Costumes:* Tom McKinley. *Make-up:* Lynne Eagan. *Special Effects Make-Up:* Doug White. *Stunt Coordinator:* George Fisher. *Running Time:* 97 minutes. *MPAA Rating:* PG-13.

CAST: Al Yankovic (George Newman); Victoria Jackson (Teri); Kevin McCarthy (R.J. Fletcher); Michael Richards (Stanley Spadowski); David Bowe (Bob); Stanley Brock (Uncle Harvey); Anthony Geary (Philo); Trinidad Silva (Raul Hernandez); Gedde Watanabe (Kuni); Billy Barty (Noodles); John Paragon (Richard Fletcher); Fran Drescher (Pamela Finklestein); Sue Anne Langdon (Aunt Esther); David Proval (Head Thug); Grant James (Killer Thug); Emo Philips (Joe Earley); Jay Levy (Gandhi); Harry Kipper (Kipper Kid); Lou B. Washington (Cameraman); Vance Colvig (Bum); Nik Hagler (FCC Man); Robert K. Weiss (Bartender); Eldon G. Hallum (Spatula Husband); Sherry Engstrom (Spatula Wife); Sara Allen (Spatula Neighbor); Bob Hungerford (Sy Greenblum); John Cadenhead (Crazy Ernie); Francis M. Carlson (Blind Man); Ivan Green (Earl Ramsey); Adam Maras (Joel Miller); Travis Knight (Billy); Joseph Witt (Little Weasel); Tony Frank (Teri's Father); Billie Lee Thrash (Teri's Mother); Barry Friedman (Fletcher Cronie #1); Kevin Roden (Fletcher Cronie #2); Lisa R. Stefanic (Phyllis Weaver); Nancy Johnson (Big Edna); Debbie Mathieu (Betty); Wilma Jeanne Cummins (Little Old Lady); Cliff Stephens (Animal Deliveryman); Dr. Demento (Whipped Cream Eater); Bob Maras (Thug #3); George Fisher (Thug #4); Tony Salome (Guide #1); Joe Restivo (Guide #2); Charles Marsh (Yodeler); Belinda Bauer and Lori Wagner (Mud Wrestlers); Patrick O'Brian (Satan); Roger Callard (Conan the Librarian); Robert Frank (Timid Man); Jeff Maynard (Boy with Books); BAND: Jim West (Guitar); Steve Jay (Bass Guitar); Jon Schwartz (Drums); Kim Bullard (Keyboards).

LOS ANGELES TIMES, 7/21/89, Calendar/p. 11, Michael Wilmington

In "UHF," writer-star "Weird Al" Yankovic tries to jam dozens of movie and TV parodies into the kind of dopes-on-the-job plot that was already a self-parody in the days of the first "Police Academy." The parodies are sometimes amusing, in a talk-back-to-the-TV-screen sort of way, but the movie they're stuck in is beyond sendups.

It's another daffy, goofy, sex-crazed-guys story: "The daffy, goofy, sex-crazed guys take over a TV station." But here there isn't much sex; perhaps Yankovic's target audience is too young. These guys aren't lecherous; they're just daffy and goofy.

They race around and bang themselves on the noggin with mops and throw mustard on bikers and poodles out the window. They play with their mashed potatoes and shoot staples at each other and stick children into sandboxes full of wet oatmeal. The love interest, "Saturday Night Lives's" Victoria Jackson, might as well be in another picture. Maybve she is; halfway through this one, Yankovic breaks a date with her and she disappears until the picture's climax.

Yankovic's character, stodgily named George Newman instead of Odd Arnie or Bizarre Bob, is a congenital foul-up, constantly lost in fantasies of Spielberg movies. He takes over a failing UHF station, Channel 62, after his uncle wins it at a poker game. But in true daffy, goofy, sex-crazed guys fashion, George quickly piles up the heftiest ratings in town, despite programming shows like "Bowling for Burgers," "The Volcano Worshiper's Hour" and "Wheel of Fish," a game show whose wheel-spinner is named Vanna Whitefish.

Channel 62's superstar is the janitor, Stanley Spadowski (Michael Richards), a Jerry Lewis-style super-goon. Their nemesis is Kevin McCarthy, chewing passions to tatters as a network-affiliate czar caught in a perpetual grimace. Soon poor Stanley has been kidnaped and McCarthy is trying to foreclose the mortgage—or buy the station, or steal the deed—and a telethon is under way to raise all the money for Uncle Harvey's gambling debts.

As an actor, Yankovic alternates between screaming and staring confusedly into space. But Billy Barty, Trinidad Silva and Fran Drescher are fitfully funny. And, as Stanley, Michael Richards has one of those scarily intense mad-clown looks; he looks as if he could pick up quarters with his eyebrows.

In real life, Yankovic is a famous record parodist, sort of the Homer and Jethro of rock 'n' roll—or perhaps the Allan Sherman of MTV. (The film's director, Jay Levey, is his manager and video director.) And he has some funny ideas. The movie's highlight is a version of "The Ballad of Jed Clampett" sung to the tune of Dire Straits' "Money for Nothing." And there's a "Rambo" parody with Yankovic mowing down half the Eastern Hemisphere and the Eiffel Tower.

Yet there's something fatally wrong here. Why would someone who keeps losing himself in dream-parodies of Spielberg and Stallone movies come up with shows like "Druids on Parade" or "Name That Stain"?

The problem with "UHF" (MPAA-rated PG-13) is that everything in it is a parody. The only logic for anything that happens is that there's some new thing to make fun of—mostly inanely. It's not much of a movie. But, hey, give these daffy, goofy guys a break. Where would the film industry be without them?

NEW YORK POST, 7/21/89, p. 25, David Edelstein

As he proves in "UHF," no performer in movies has a deader deadpan than "Weird Al" Yankovic. His smooth, round face is eerily inexpressive—it's like a baby's bottom to which someone has affixed a pair of wire rims and a caterpillar. He can't even smirk wholeheartedly. Off screen, "Weird Al" might be a stitch, but as a romantic-comedy hero he's like a smudge on the lens.

Weird Al (I'm ditching the quotation marks—although I'd like to wrap them around his neck) plays George Newman, a guy with a "good imagination." After a daydream in which he's Indiana Jones dodging a boulder, fry-cook George discovers he has burned the potatoes. "Nobody here appreciates a guy with a good imagination," he laments.

No, and nobody here, either. The problem is that his good imagination teems with movies and TV shows we're sick of. (We're sick of parodies of them too—that's how old they are.) And the way Weird Al delivers the line, you don't know if he's sending up his head-in-the-clouds character or if he just can't be bothered to give a performance (or write a script).

When George's uncle wins an impoverished TV station, Channel 62, in a poker game, he gives the job of manager to his unemployed nephew. This triggers more daydreams in George, including a Weird Al music video in which boxy depictions of Beverly Hillbillies float through an abstract landscape to Dire Straits' "Money for Nothing."

It's a shame the film makers didn't ditch the story line and just serve up music-video satires and mock commercials, as in "The Groove Tube" or "Kentucky Fried Movie." But on the picture slogs, as George tries everything to pump life into the station. He hosts a local talk show. He plays a sadistic clown on a kiddie hour. (Al is big on sadism and on maltreatment of animals for laughs.)

As Channel 62's fortunes sink lower, George gets depressed, hands the mike to his retarded janitor, Stanley Spadowski (Michael Richards) and sends him out to entertain the kiddies. Surprise, twitchy Stanley's a big hit. In bars across the city people tune him in, transfixed by his stream-of-consciousness commentary. In no time Stanley drives Channel 62 to the top of the ratings, incensing the Grinchy owner (Kevin McCarthy) of top-dog Channel 8.

There are so many layers of irony here that "UHF" is hard to decipher. The station's programs are terrible, but the people go crazy for them—Channel 62 becomes a sensation. "Wheel of Fish" ("Wheel of Fortune" with fish) scores high. So do "Wonderful World of Phlegm" and "Bowling for Burgers." It's odd to see a talent like Weird Al Yankovic making sport of the public's bad taste: Why does he think he's a star?

The skits and commercials provide the movie's only life, and Al can be a heckuva parodist. But even the most uproarious bits are familiar. Weird Al sends up Sylvester Stallone (what a challenge) and has fun with a "Crazy Eddie"-style used-car salesman who threatens to club a baby seal. Emo Philips demonstrates a buzz saw and slices off his thumb, spraying George with blood. (The bit makes you appreciate Dan Aykroyd's gory hommage to Julia Child on "Saturday Night Live.")

As a writer, Yankovic has a short attention span. He doesn't know how to build a comic sequence, to top each gag—he just flings out jokes like dead fish. (This movie is the true "Wheel of Fish.") He also wastes most of his cast. "UHF" turns Victoria Jackson, who can usually be counted on to give things a lift, into a frumpy drudge. (Why couldn't she have been allowed into some of George's fantasy sequences?)

The only authentic strangeness comes from Anthony Geary as a technician called Philo; here's a deadpan that's layered, mysterious—really weird. Yankovic uses "weird" to mean "dorky creep," and that might be his problem. Weird Al just isn't weird enough.

NEWSDAY, 7/22/89, Part II/p. 17, Terry Kelleher

It's all a matter of time and money: You can pay up to seven bucks to see Weird Al Yankovic's first movie, "UHF," or you can sit home and watch an "SCTV" rerun for nothing on Nick at Nite.

The "SCTV" rerun will be better and shorter.

If you're not familiar with Yankovic's tongue-in-cheek music videos, "UHF" will show you what he can do. It will also show you what he can't do, at least not yet: write and act in a 97-minute comedy with a story line. The opening credit sequence is an "Indiana Jones" parody that includes a couple of decent sight gags. Fine, you may think. On to the next sketch.

But this is a theatrical feature, remember? It turns out we've been watching a daydream—George Newman's daydream. George Newman is a character played by Yankovic. He's a ne'er-do-well with an overactive imagination, and he can't hold a job until his uncle wins a struggling UHF television station in a poker game and puts him in charge.

OK, great. Now that the premise is established, we can get to the "SCTV"-style spoofs. And there are plenty here, many in the form of mock promos: "Conan the Librarian," "Gandhi II" (now he's a "one-man wrecking crew"), "Town Talk With George" (Yankovic's Geraldo Rivera takeoff), commercials for Spatula City and the Plots 'R Us mortuary. Some of this *is* amusing.

But if Yankovic and director/co-scenarist Jay Levey ever open a store, they ought to call it Plots Aren't Us. "UHF" keeps interrupting the fairly funny stuff to consider whether George's independent Ch. 62 will be bought up and liquidated by R.J. Fletcher (Kevin McCarthy), the ogreish owner of a network affiliate, and whether George will regain the love of his whiny girlfriend, Teri (Victoria Jackson).

McCarthy works awfully hard, to little comic effect. Jackson's responsibility is to say things like, "Oh, George, when are you going to start taking things seriously?" Outside the daydreaming, Yankovic's portrayal of George consists largely of shrugging and hair-shaking. George stages a telethon to save the station. Fletcher's minions kidnap Stanley Spadowski (Michael Richards), the moronic—make that extremely moronic—janitor who has become Ch. 62's popular kiddie-show host. It seems "UHF" will never sign off. Even the parody segments grow tiresome. After the plot is finally resolved, you'll be in no mood for a send-up of "Gone With the Wind."

Chances are you'll be gone.

Also reviewed in:
NEW YORK TIMES, 7/22/89, p. 15, Stephen Holden
VARIETY, 7/19–25/89, p. 20
WASHINGTON POST, 7/21/89, p. D7, Rita Kempley
WASHINGTON POST, 7/21/89, Weekend/p. 31, Desson Howe

UNCLE BUCK

A Universal Pictures release. *Producer:* John Hughes and Tom Jacobson. *Director:* John Hughes. *Screenplay:* John Hughes. *Director of Photography:* Ralf Bode. *Editor:* Lou Lombardo, Tony Lombardo, and Peck Prior. *Music:* Ira Newborn. *Music Editor:* Tom Kramer and Jeff Carson. *Choreographer:* Miranda Garrison. *Sound:* James Alexander. *Sound Editor:* Wylie Stateman and Tom Belford. *Production Designer:* John W. Corso. *Art Director:* Louis Mann. *Set Decorator:* Dan May. *Set Dresser:* Thomas M. Jones and Daniel B. Clancy. *Special Effects:* Jeff Jarvis. *Costumes:* Marilyn Vance-Straker. *Make-up:* Ben Nye Jr. and Jamie Weiss. *Stunt Coordinator:* James Arnett. *Running Time:* 95 minutes. *MAPP Rating:* PG.

CAST: John Candy (Uncle Buck); Jean Louisa Kelly (Tia Russell); Gaby Hoffman (Maizy Russell); Macaulay Culkin (Miles Russell); Amy Madigan (Chanice Kobolowski); Elaine Bromka (Cindy Russell); Garrett M. Brown (Bob Russell); Laurie Metcalf (Marcie Dahlgren-Frost); Jay Underwood (Bug); Brian Tarantina (Rog); Mike Starr (Pooter-the-Clown); Suzanne Shepherd (Mrs. Hogarth); Dennis Cockrum (Pal); Matt Craven (Walt Bernstein); Jerry E. Postt (Marko the Mechanic); Zak Spector (Mechanic #2); Joel Robinson (Miles' Friend #1); Colin Baumgartner (Miles' Friend #2); Eric Whiple (Miles' Friend #3); Mark Rosenthal (Party Boy #1); Doug Van Nessen (Party Boy #2); Wayne Kneeland (Party Boy #3); Gigi Casler (Party Girl in Bedroom); Gina Doctor (Party Girl #2); Rachel Thompson Perrine (Party Girl #3); Ron Payne (Maizy's Teacher); Jane Vickerilla (Teacher #1).

LOS ANGELES TIMES, 8/16/89, Calendar/p. 8, Chris Willman

In "Uncle Buck," writer-director John Hughes has devised a plot with which to fuse his two genres of choice: the clashing-family-members comedy and the tortured-teen pic.

John Candy, the titular behemoth, is the eccentric relative from blue-collar hell that no one loves (yet); When he's called in to baby-sit his stuffed-shirt brother's three progeny for a few days, the younger tykes take a back seat while Buck establishes an adversarial, then intimate, relationship with his troubled 15-year-old niece. At heart, it's really another one of Hughes' undisguised valentines to teenhood.

The overriding philosophy of most of the Hughes canon is simple: Kids are good, grown-ups aren't. But there's a little more to it than that. Corollary No. 1: Grown-ups can be good if they act like kids—hence the spontaneous charm of Uncle Buck, who feeds beer and pretzels to the family dog and who vacuums his own girth after a spirited session of raw Frosted Flakes consumption.

Corollary No. 2: Kids can be bad if they act like adults—hence the initial villainy of his niece Tia (Jean Kelly, seemingly reprising Jennifer Grey's snotty sister character in "Ferris Bueller's Day Off"), who initially attracks her keeper as an unsophisticated boob and who is trying to prove her maturity through premature sexual behavior. Uncle Buck takes up the formidable challenge of protecting her virginity, mostly through threatening her no-good boyfriend with hatchets and power drills.

Herein lies the biggest chasm between Hughes and other teen-film makers: Much as he puts impetuous adolescence on a pedestal, he tends to see sex as a threat to the young, not as a release or rite of passage. Sex is what accelerates their procession into the world of adult relationships with all the accompanying lies and rationalizations and masks. Hughes may stick Tone Loc's rap hit about engaging in the "Wild Thing" on the sound track, but he really wants his kids to just say no.

The problem with this is that we know from the outset—especially if we're familiar with Hughes' work—just how tidily all this will turn out. He can be surprisingly daring in introducing bits and pieces of tense domestic turmoil into his comedies, and this one is no exception. (Lou Lombardo, Tony Lombardo and Peck Prior did the editing, which nicely mixes tight comedic gag timing with an unusually relaxed, dramatic narrative pace.) But Hughes is usually too busy steering toward a neat, happy ending to let the intimations of nuclear family breakdowns have any real emotional sway.

Finally, "Uncle Buck" (MPAA-rated PG) has a medium-level Hughes script, only about half as good as "Planes, Trains and Automobiles," about 50 times as good as "The Great Outdoors." Before things go all awry in the final stretch, which has Buck patching things up with long-suffering gal pal Amy Madigan as well as with his family, there are some hysterical bits along the way. Not the least of these is the sight of a closed-eyed Candy scratching the family dog on the stomach and jerking his own leg in an involuntary sympathetic response, or asking his nervous sister-in-law as she leaves whether there's a plunger in the house, or 8-year-old Macaulay Culkin's deadpan Joe Friday imitation.

To get to the chuckles, most of which are well-executed, you have to wade through some of Hughes' favorite stereotypes, like the positively evil vice principal at the little girl's elementary school who calls Buck's niece "a dreamer, a silly heart." Much has been made of the autobiographical aspects of Hughes' "She's Having a Baby," but bits of this would seem even more so: Candy—who has never been more likeable—is absolutely the director's stand-in as he rails against this nasty authority figure, saying, "You so much scowl at my niece or any other kid in this school and I'll come looking for you." Like Buck's nieces and nephews, the young of America have a cinematic champion and protector.

MONTHLY FILM BULLETIN, 2/90, p. 52, Geoff Brown

In desperation, Chicago suburbanites Bob and Cindy Russell ask Bob's black sheep brother Buck to move in and take temporary charge of their three children while they make an urgent trip to Indianapolis (where Cindy's father has suffered a heart attack). Buck, a good-humoured wastrel unaccustomed to domestic life, arrives in the early hours and is soon battling with the Russells' high-tech kitchen, making the children's breakfast. The younger ones—Maizy, aged six, and Miles, eight—gradually take to Buck's unconventional ways, but fifteen-year-old Tia, who has already caused trouble with her parents, treats him with scathing contempt; he also has several run-ins with her uncouth boyfriend Bug. When Buck's long-suffering girlfriend Chanice Kobolowski phones the house, Tia spitefully tells her that Buck is busy with Marcie, their flirtatious neighbour. Arriving later to investigate, Chanice finds Marcie and the hapless Buck dancing. Buck continues to battle with the Russells' domestic appliances, and stands up vigorously to Tia's abuse. When she defiantly goes to a weekend party, Buck abandons a profitable racetrack jaunt to go in pursuit and save her virginity—only to find Bug in bed with another girl. Buck bundles Bug into the boot of his car, and once Tia is safely home gives the boy his comeuppance. By the time Bob and Cindy return from Indianapolis, Tia is contrite; Buck, in turn, looks more kindly upon the prospect of domestic bliss with the understanding Chanice.

A loud, messy, ne'er-do-well suddenly yanked from his bachelor pit to look after three young relatives in a suburbanite paradise: Uncle Buck has "sit-com pilot" written all over it. John Hughes—back once more on the Chicago beat—even separates the scenes of domestic turmoil with establishing shots of the Russell mansion, ready-made for insertion after commercial breaks (in fact, with the film having taken more than sixty million dollars at the U.S. box office, a 13-episode TV series is planned for the autumn). John Candy, of course, is adept at playing the sweetly affable oaf, whether wrestling with vacuum cleaners, drying clothes in the microwave, discovering his face has been quietly removed from his brother's wedding photos, or simply wriggling about in bed (caught in overhead shots in the manner of Robert Benchley's vintage short How to Sleep). But the film's light, amusing tone is constantly undercut by the savage nihilism of the eldest child, Tia, whose vituperations create severe problems for audience sympathy. In a film so conscious of the dual sentimental spectacle of an old rogue softened by domesticity and uptight children shedding suburban inhibitions, the miscalculation is serious and surprising. No doubt the sit-com will correct matters; it might also introduce the one recent cliché Hughes has unaccountably neglected—the adorable, burbling baby.

NEW YORK POST, 8/16/89, p. 31, David Edelstein

Posters for "Uncle Buck" show a family cowering behind a door as the fat-tornado relative (John Candy) mounts the front steps; it makes you think of those "Caddyshack"-type slob comedies about free spirits invading repressed, uptight communities.

But the ads are misleading: The film itself turns out to be distinctly minor-key, not to mention reactionary. Written and directed by John Hughes ("The Breakfast Club," "Ferris Bueller's Day Off"), it's a sober, wintry meditation about growing up and becoming a responsible person. It's an antislob-comedy slob comedy.

For one thing, Uncle Buck doesn't just show up out of the blue. He's summoned when the father of his sister-in-law Cindy (Elaine Bromka) has a heart attack and she and Buck's brother must rush to his bedside in the middle of the night, leaving their three kids behind.

This begins things on a melancholy note, and it's a troubled home anyway. Fifteen-year-old Tia (Jean Louisa Kelly) taunts her mother for moving the family to Chicago, where they have no friends. She bullies her kid brother and sister. And to prove her independence, Tia hangs out with a local sleazebag, Bug (Jay Underwood).

Who'd a' thought that messy, irresponsible, bull-in-a-china-shop Uncle Buck would save this screwed-up family? That he'd turn out to be the Superdad that Tia's never had?

The movie becomes a battle of wits between Tia and Buck, and it's serious business, loaded with sociological baggage. For Uncle Buck is a product of the counterculture. He's a ne'er-do-well. He has been seeing a woman (Amy Madigan) for eight years but has refused to marry her, calling family life old-fashioned. He wears a Russian hat, which, he loves to point out, irritates some people.

In one scene he hears a newscaster say that the communist lion has been tamed, and there's no point to the bit except to reinforce Hughes' message—Buck is all by himself. He went along with the Left because it permitted him to be self-indulgent; now, in suburbia, he understands that his stance is "a recipe for loneliness" (his girlfriend's words).

It's a neat idea to make a selfish loafer a disciplinarian and puritan by instinct. And Hughes doesn't spell out Buck's transformation—he dramatizes it cleverly.

To protect Tia's virginity, he goes after Bug with a power drill (a "Friday the 13th" image)—but hasn't he been exploiting women the same way? To protect his nephew from a clown who shows up drunk for a birthday party, he punches the bozo in the nose—but hasn't he always flouted the same family values he now seeks to defend?

These are sharp scenes. The problem is that Hughes has a TV-movie touch, with too many close-ups and too much formula plotting. He has become a lugubrious director. He tries to heave in slapstick bits for Candy, but they're laborious and alien to this material, and the pace is so glacial that "Uncle Buck" never develops any momentum.

It's a depressed piece of movie-making—grown-up in eerie ways. This Chicago could be Leningrad (it's a Leningrad of the soul), and the kids dress in black and strike alienated poses. Hughes used to identify with kids, back when anti-authoritarian movies were in vogue.

But it's a different world now—for Hughes, who's a daddy, and the nation—and he's telling the same story from the viewpoint of Ferris Bueller's principal.

Hughes hasn't totally gone over. He throws in an extraneous scene in which a female principal (with a hairy wart) tells Buck that his niece is too much of a dreamer. This allows Buck to hold forth about the importance of dreaming and irresponsibility in small children, and to make fun of the principal's wart. (It's not Hughes' classiest writing.)

He still has some comic instincts. He gets laughs by playing on Candy's cranky, demonic underbelly. And there's a scene between Buck and his sister-in-law that's a triumph of deadpan timing. Bromka, her eyes darting nervously, is curdled to her soul by the thought of big Buck and his bodily functions.

Kelly inhabits Tia completely—every time a question is addressed to her by an adult she winces as if she has been violated. And before the script stupidly trashes her, Laurie Metcalf brings a sepulchrally sexy, Bride-of-Frankenstein intensity to the ravenous divorcee across the street.

The sad thing is that the anemic, sentimental "Uncle Buck" is a personal film for Hughes—he's working from his own experience and he's really trying to express something. If he'd just fight the urge to employ thudding, slob-comedy formulas, he might find a form that suits what he has to say. He might even create one from scratch.

NEWSDAY, 8/16/89, Part II/p. 3, Mike McGrady

Whenever a career starts to lose a little zip, the first instinct is to return to a past triumph and repeat it. Repetition is the sincerest form of greed. Not only does this explain the proliferation of sequels this past summer, it also may explain why comedian John Candy and director-writer John Hughes decided to make "Uncle Buck."

Not that "Uncle Buck" is a sequel. No, this story of a lovable reprobate overseeing his brother's three children for a week is more a return trip. The basic situation ("I don't want him here," snaps his churlish suburban sister-in-law. "He doesn't have kids, he isn't married, he doesn't even work...Can you see him in this house?") enables both Hughes and Candy to attempt to re-create some of their greatest movie moments.

John Hughes' Hollywood career was firmly launched (this was well before he reinvented teenagers) with his script for "Mr. Mom," the story of an executive forced to stay home with the youngsters while his wife returned to the work force. Now Hughes returns to a similar situation, once again giving us the terrifying vision of a man in a home alone with kids—right down to, and including, major difficulties with the washing machine and love-starved neighbors.

Candy's biggest film triumph was his hilarious portrait of the unsavory, womanizing, con man brother in "Splash." Here Candy is again a confirmed bachelor who gambles, drinks, strings along his fiancee (Amy Madigan) and avoids regular employment.

With both their careers slowing down (simultaneously, in fact, with "The Great Outdoors"), they have now sought to return to the scene of their prime. Since both men so clearly know the territory, why doesn't the film generate more in the way of laughter? Partly because the construction seems so mechanical, so sitcomish, with events defining character instead of the other way around.

While Hughes has often been guilty of overreaching for a laugh, here he does so constantly. Far too often, the humor is of the rubber-crutch genre. Just as Hughes goes too far, Candy's characterization never goes far enough. We're constantly told what a reprobate Uncle Buck is, but we never see him as that. We're told he fixes horse races—but he doesn't take his three charges anywhere near a horse or a track. We're told he's a boozer and an idler, but all we see is a mountainous man who is nine-tenths heart, a sentimental slob who runs a great birthday party and takes the kids bowling and dries their laundry in the oven.

Once we begin to accept Uncle Buck's innate goodness, Hughes' script crosses us up by giving the character a sadistic streak that is both misplaced and unfunny. How could a decent sort like Candy, for example, spend long painful moments poking fun at an unfortunate growth on the assistant principal's face?

Moreover, when a young man expresses an interest in his teenage niece, he threatens both the young man's life and masculinity, terrorizing him with a hatchet and an oversized battery-powered drill before overpowering him, locking him in the trunk of his car and kidnapping him.

Needless to say, here the teenaged girl (Jean Louisa Kelly) comes to appreciate Uncle Buck's tireless efforts to protect her chastity. And through those efforts, Uncle Buck learns a bit about the essential emptiness of his ordinary life. If the ending seems to work out entirely too smoothly, rest assured it's the only thing in the movie that does.

NEWSWEEK, 9/4/89, p. 68, David Ansen

There are only two kinds of moviemaker John Hughes loves: kids and overgrown kids. Buck Russell (John Candy) is a shining example of the latter, a sweet sleazeball slob who's spent the greater part of his life playing hooky from grown-up commitments. Suddenly this big blue-collar ne'er-do-well is pressed into emergency baby-sitting duties. While his Yuppie brother and sister-in-law tend to a sick relative, Uncle Buck is summoned to the suburbs to oversee his bratty teenage niece Tia (Jean Louisa Kelly) and little Maizy and Miles (Gaby Hoffman and Macaulay Culkin). Though it's a given that the hapless Buck emerges a nurturing hero, Candy triumphs over the predictability of the plot with his finest screen performance to date. Under Hughes's sympathetic eye, this often misued comic actor finally gets to show his unique colors. Hughes's amiable, deeply conservative film (the idea of teen sex sends him into a tizzy) manages to be consistently funny without resorting to silly slapstick. It sags only in the home stretch when Hughes feels compelled to pour on the "heart".

VILLAGE VOICE, 8/22/89, p. 86, Amy Taubin

Like *Rude Awakening* (and almost every movie I've seen recently from *Batman* to *sex, lies, and videotape*), *Uncle Buck* is about some guy with hangups so huge that he can't help wearing them on his sleeve (this is supposed to endear him to the audience), who nonetheless believes he is uniquely qualified to save (i.e., impose his will on and be worshipped and adored by) everyone else in the movie. And what do you know? It all resolves in his favor—his delusions of grandeur are accepted as The Word, and he gets to indulge his particular configuration of narcissism forever. In *Uncle Buck*, John Hughes's latest stab at maturity, John Candy, in the title role, is a substitute parent who finds his purpose in life by keeping his 15-year-old niece from losing her virginity. This seemingly healthy family entertainment has a very scuzzy and barely hidden subtext.

When Mom and Dad are called away on an emergency, loaf-around Uncle Buck is drafted into taking care of their three kids. Initially leery of this lumbering two-going-on-40-year-old with his reasonable managerial voice, the younger kids are soon won over by stacks of snow-shovel-sized pancakes. But 15-year-old Tia (Jean Kelly) is repelled by Buck's backfiring, gas-belching wreck of a car, his day-at-the-track attire, and his big cigar. While this may be a bit snobbish of her, I think she's right to resist her uncle's obsessive attempts to control her private life. A staggering number of scenes in *Uncle Buck* involve Candy, looking like something out of *Driller Killer*, sneaking up on Tia and her boyfriend and threatening said boyfriend's manhood with various toolbox items. Insofar as this corresponds to a wish-fulfillment fantasy held by most fathers of teenage women, it's quite funny. The problem is that, aside from a few reaction shots of Tia pouting, glaring, and finally hurling herself into Buck's arms with a tearful "You were right," we never see her point of view. But then her function is to be a convert, not a person.

Candy has his droll moments. Hughes is pretty slick at stretching a few sitcom routines into something that passes for a feature. *Uncle Buck* is made to order for folks who believe it's both correct and easy to impose chastity on kids, and who get their rocks off by doing it. But if you're looking for family entertainment, stick to *Parenthood*, a film with admirable respect for all kinds of differences—excepting, of course, the desire not to procreate. But that's another story.

Also reviewed in:
NEW YORK TIMES, 8/16/89, p. C13, Vincent Canby
VARIETY, 8/16-22/89, p. 20
WASHINGTON POST, 8/16/89, p. D1, Rita Kempley

UNREMARKABLE LIFE, AN

An SVS Films and Continental Films Group release. *Executive Producer:* Navin Desai, Gay Mayer, and Watson Warriner. *Producer:* Amin Q. Chaudhri. *Director:* Amin Q. Chaudhri. *Screenplay:* Marcia Dinneen. *Director of Photography:* Alan Hall. *Editor:* Sandi Gerling. *Music:* Avery Sharpe. *Production Designer:* Norman B. Dodge Jr. *Costumes:* Carol Helen Beule. *Running Time:* 92 minutes. *MPAA Rating:* PG.

CAST: Patricia Neal (Frances McEllany); Shelley Winters (Evelyn); Mako (Max Chin).

LOS ANGELES TIMES, 10/27/89, Calendar/p. 10, Michael Wilmington

"An Unremarkable Life" gives us three remarkable actors—Patricia Neal, Shelley Winters and Mako—in a laudable but far-too-frail effort to revive the once-flourishing tradition of the small-town psychological family drama.

This film—about two sisters knotted together in the emotionally airless cul de sac of their family home—suggests Tennessee Wiliams, William Inge or, even more, their innumerable imitators. And like those '50s and '60s copycats, writer Marcia Dinneen and director-producer Amin Q. Chaudhri ("Tiger Warsaw") move the Freudian lyricism and family trauma of their models toward something coyer, more manageable.

It's a little chamber drama about repression. The lighting is flutey-soft. The house is a tunnel of brown corridors and oppressively neat upholstery. Within it, longtime spinster Frances McEllany (Neal) lives with her widowed sister Evelyn (Winters). Frances, whose lover died in World War II, is still a romantic, and, when she is wooed by the delightfully flirty Max Chin (Mako), a local garage worker interned during the war, her face beams with reawakened charm. Evelyn, on the other hand, hated her marriage, welcomes her imprisonment and wants to make sure Frances won't get away either—tying her down in an endless cycle of family dinners, TV shows and weekend movies. When Max cruises in, she treats him as a cross between a slob fortune hunter and a potential Fu Manchu.

This is the kind of weepy, kvetching bully role Winters loves to play, and she catches the character's racism and psychological terrorism. Then, masterfully, she turns us around in the last scene: makes us feel the woman's vulnerability and fear.

The excellent Neal is almost as good as Frances, though—heavy with long-suffering smiles—it becomes the more conventional of the two roles. And Mako could hardy be better as Max Chin. He gives the character dignity and a risque impishness, suggesting the layers of a wounded but resilient man who's made many compromises to survive and can calibrate the exact moments when lines must be drawn. These three actors supply most of "Life's" intelligence and quality. Yet, in watching them, you often feel the film makers should have gone with less obvious casting and had Winters and Neal switch parts. Going against type, Winters might have gotten something more pathetic and surprising; Neal might have been scarier and more tragic.

Chaudhri is perhaps too discreet, too respectful. This thin, unexceptional, obvious material needs more juice, more dramatic and visual resonance. There's even something awry about the time frame. In the opening scene, Evelyn is leading Frances in the Charleston—though both sisters were probably born about the time people were actually dancing it.

Perhaps Dinneen is simply remembering her '50s models—when sisters this age actually would have been recalling the Charleston. There's an occupational hazard of the Inge-Williams tradition that these film makers fall into: Just as their antagonists get self-righteous about sexual proprieties, they get self-righteous about sexual liberation.

That's what happens here; there's something almost callously happy about the resolution. The title of "An Unremarkable Life" (MPAA rated PG, despite sexual badinage) suggests that we're going to see the kind of luminous everyday parable that the late Italian scenarist Cesare Zavattini ("Umberto D") wrote so wonderfully. Instead, we get a mostly unremarkable pastiche—in which three fine actors manage, occasionally, to shine.

NEW YORK POST, 10/12/89, p. 34, Jami Bernard

Just as househunters conduct a title search to see if there is a previous claim on the property, movie makers should run prospective titles past critics to see what sort of jokes they'll be in for should the movie bomb. Alas, the makers of "An Unremarkable Life" failed to do this, so they're stuck with the sad truth: "An Unremarkable Life" is an unremarkable movie.

Not that it doesn't try for more. But not every story about small people manages to reflect the grander scheme of things. If you succeed, you get "Winesburg, Ohio." If you don't, you get "An Unremarkable Life."

Anyway, if you want to see a slow-moving story about two aging, interdependent sisters who must come to terms with their past life, future death and whether to sell the house, you can rent "The Whales of August." (Or even, by a stretch, "Whatever Happened to Baby Jane.")

In "Unremarkable," Shelley Winters in the Bette Davis role does an excellent job as the intractable sister, embittered by years of family obligations and now fearful of losing the comfortably dull routine she has established with her milder sister as they knit their days away together in the grand old house of their dead father.

Patricia Neal has the Lillian Gish role—the kinder, gentler sister, the one who is *not* a racist pig about the white neighbors' adopted Korean child, the one who at one time was (however bizarrely) a WWII fighter pilot but whose wings were clipped by the demands of her dying father. She now spends her time making preserves and doing those other colorful things that maiden old ladies supposedly do.

Well, you can imagine what they're saying over at the Bingo game when Neal's character begins keeping company with an Asian garage mechanic (Mako). Winters, tight-lipped and reproachful, sits in the dark waiting for sis like some jilted lover.

It's the kind of film a certain generation might like, because, Lord knows, there aren't many romances catering to the elderly. On the other hand, nothing happens—nothing that would give the movie a dramatic backbone, at any rate. None of the actors seem very comfortable with each other; attempts at a spirit of fun backfire most awkwardly, and the relationships simply don't ring true.

The screenplay makes the fatal mistake of assuming that banal language can somehow imbue characters with a certain universality.

Shelley Winters, playing a thoroughly dislikable character with peevish relish, is the high note.

NEWSDAY, 10/12/89, Part II/p. 5, Mike McGrady

After a screening of "An Unremarkable Life," as the crowd was dispersing into the night, I eavesdropped on one woman speaking to another: "You know, Miriam, it's a shame they don't have double features any more." While that overheard remark may seem a bit on the cryptic side, it's an accurate capsule review of the film.

What she meant was this: "An Unremarkable Life," starring old pros Patricia Neal and Shelley Winters, would have, at one time, made a nice windup to a twin bill, particularly if it were counterbalanced by, oh, a frothy musical or perhaps a sophisticated comedy. It's the kind of heavy, old-fashioned domestic drama that is infinitely more palatable when buttressed by a more lively movie and perhaps some free dinnerware.

Otherwise, this is a slightly solemn story—also, a solemnly slight story—of two elderly sisters sharing an old Victorian home in New England. They pass their days gardening, arguing, baking cookies, bickering, arranging flowers, complaining, watching television and, in general, getting on each other nerves.

When the never-married sister Frances (Patricia Neal) begins going out with a Chinese-American suitor, Max Chin (Mako), sister Evelyn (Shelley Winters) goes bonkers and attempts, with some success, to sabotage her sister's romance. Evelyn's anxiety finds its expression in the kind of bigotry ("I will not become the servant to some Chinese playboy!") that proves discouraging to both her sister and her sister's suitor. In fact, Evelyn's rampant insecurity almost ends her sister's first real romance, but love—even this kind of mild, late-blooming love—conquers all.

While Neal shows a great deal of spunky charm as the self described "old-maid school teacher," her affair proceeds in the most plodding fashion. Although she succeeds in making the mundane seem moderately interesting, the film never goes much beyond that.

The script by Marcia Dinneen, specializes in the obvious and the banal; the direction by Amin Q. Chaudri is consistently less than sprightly. As the various domestic problems are presented and worked out, it's all about as exciting as the late-night cookies and milk that one sister leaves for the other. "An Unremarkable Life," then, is a thoroughly unremarkable film, a plodding script only partially redeemed by the quality of the performances. It's definitely a "B" picture in a world that sadly, no longer has the double features that made "B" pictures watchable.

Also reviewed in:
NEW YORK TIMES, 10/12/89, p. C16, Janet Maslin
VARIETY, 9/6–12/89, p. 24
WASHINGTON POST, 11/14/89, p. C9, Rita Kempley

USED INNOCENCE

A First Run Features release. *Director:* James Benning: *Screenplay:* James Benning. *Director of Photography:* James Benning. *Running time:* 95 minutes. *MPAA Rating:* Not Rated.

NEW YORK POST, 2/22/89, p. 27, Jami Bernard

In the future, perhaps there will be no judges and juries, just committed filmmakers who will train their cameras on trumped-up murder cases and make mincemeat of them.

With the recent success and persuasiveness of "The Thin Blue Line," "A Cry in the Dark" and "The Accused," the skids are greased for James Benning's documentary "Used Innocence."

Benning takes on the case of Lawrencia Bembenek, a freshfaced ex-cop from Milwaukee who is serving a life sentence for the murder of her husband's ex-wife. All signs, and I mean *all* signs, point to Bembenek's innocence.

The filmmaker became interested in the case after spotting Bembenek's photo in a newspaper. Of course, developing a film around an attractive photo can be as shaky as convicting someone on purely circumstantial evidence, but at least from Benning's hormones arose an artistic labor of love that has a solid story of injustice at its heart, while from the trial came an indictment of a young woman whose main crime may have been to dress too well at her trial.

Bembenek's story is one that cries out for TV and movie rights. There were no eyewitnesses, no convincing motive, only a smattering of incorrect police procedures and a courtful of prosecution witnesses who admitted holding personal grudges against the defendant, or being otherwise in cahoots with possible suspects. Even Bembenek's detective husband, as likely a suspect as you'd find, was allowed to help conduct the investigation.

Enter James Benning, one of several avenging angels who have become besotted with Bembenek's blond loveliness in the course of trying to save her. Benning was not the first to see potential in the woman's story: it has had coverage in Cosmopolitan and People magazines. Along the way, Benning fell in love with his subject, and therefore his movie takes on a distinctly personal tone.

"I make films that are not very accessible," warns Benning in the first of a long correspondence. And he's right. This film doesn't twist and turn with the "Rashomon"-like narrative of "The Thin Blue Line." Instead, excerpts from the letters that went into and out of the Taycheedah Correctional Institution give "Used Innocence" its moorings. "I feel like someone has read my diary," writes Bembenek after reading a draft of the film script.

In these exchanges, all read aloud on the film's soundtrack, he tells her about his long-time lover moving out and how depressed he is; she tells him to buck up and how nice he looked during their last prison visit. Meanwhile, the screen shows only shifting clouds in the sky.

There is another long stretch in which all you see is the view from a car as it travels (and travels, and travels) all the way to the front gate of Taycheedah. Courtroom interviews are punctuated with frequent blackouts, as if the camera is blinking in astonishment at what it is recording. Visually, "Used Innocence" is a little hard on the eyes. (And if you want to read the poem that scrolls up the screen, don't sit in the last row.)

The film is exhaustive on the cause's loopholes. Hey, guys, we believe you! But ultimately, "Used Innocence" is more about James Benning and his growing attraction for his subject. That's too bad, because Benning's love life is pretty banal stuff compared to the sexy Bembenek case.

Maybe someday someone will do a documentary about something truly puzzling—like the maddening psychology of juries like the one that sent Laurie Bembenek to prison for someone else's sins.

VILLAGE VOICE, 2/28/89, p. 53, J. Hoberman

James Benning seems to have taken to heart the Adorno dictum that "every work of art is an uncommitted crime." Over the past half dozen years, Benning's interest has shifted from the self-conscious aestheticizing of the midwestern landscape to minimalist accounts of Wisconsin's most notorious would-be, mass, and/or convicted murderers: Arthur Bremer, Ed Gein, and now Lawrencia Bembenek, the subject of Used Innocence (currently at Film Forum 1).

Bembenek, a 30-year-old former Milwaukee police officer and ex-Playboy Bunny, is currently serving a life sentence; she was convicted in 1982 of murdering the ex-wife of her dashing new husband, police detective Elfred Schultz. The trial had widespread tabloid appeal—not only for Bembenek's youth and looks or for the callousness of the murder (Mrs. Schultz was executed in her bed)—but because various irregularities, including the active role Detective Schultz played in the investigation (which failed to unearth anything more than circumstantial evidence), suggest the possibility of a frame-up, or worse.

Benning's response to this apparent miscarriage of justice is perversely personal. Basically, Used Innocence documents his involvement with Bembenek. It's structured by their exchange of letters (which each reads on the soundtrack, hers underscored by a backbeat of muffled clanging, distant TV noises). Five minutes into the movie, it's clear that Benning is cultivating a crush, but, for the most part, he keeps his fantasies in check (dramatizing only the start of a strip search and a brief bit of lovemaking). Benning entertains his pen-pal with the details of his 1986 Whitney retrospective—then his girlfriend leaves him, and suddenly he's crying on Bembenek's shoulder, tacitly encouraging his Rapunzel to let down her hair. (As the movie makes apparent, Laurie gets letters from all sorts of weird dudes. Benning is just the only one offering to put her poems in a movie.)

Given their mutual (and pioneering) taste for Americanarama, it's scarcely surprising that Benning's trial film would have more than a bit in common with Errol Morris's The Thin Blue Line—the presentation of evidence as icons or props, the contemplation of enigmatic newspaper portraits and guilty landscapes, the use of actual voices in new contexts. Benning's dramatic reconstructions are more elaborate than Morris's, but his narrative sense is far sketchier. Where The Thin Blue Line was passionate and driving, Used Evidence appears self-conscious and arbitrary; although Benning goes for pathos rather than irony, his meandering presentation seems unlikely to secure his subject a new trial. (Unlike Morris, Benning is unable to offer an alternative scenario. The movie is virtually over before he gets around to mentioning the doings of detective Schultz.)

Actually, Benning's problem is less *The Thin Blue Line* than the real thing. As Morris and Schroeter and CBS realize, a sensational murder trial is the highest form of theater—the most refined mode of fiction-making. (America wouldn't be America without at least one dynamite court opera in session—a healthy chunk of the national debt must be run up providing ourselves with these spectacular shows.) Trials get people arguing and speculating, but *Used Innocence* won't. It's flat and affectless—the quintessential moment has Benning's camera peering out at the iron skies and chilly streets of suburban Wisconsin, shards of testimony resounding in his brain. Typically, this sequence ends at the prison gate.

For all its emotional tangles, *Used Innocence* is depressed—using a lengthy, single shot of a woman stenciling signs in an institutional workshop to suggest the tedium of prison life. We're each in our own prisons is Benning's banal conclusion. In the end, it makes you wonder more about his motives than Bembenek's. Literal-minded as this film is, the central question is never resolved: Who has used (or abused) whose innocence?

Also reviewed in:
NEW YORK TIMES, 2/24/89, p. C21, Janet Maslin
VARIETY, 3/22/89, p. 24

VALENTINO RETURNS

A Skouras Pictures, Inc. and Vidmark, Inc. release of an Owl Productions film. *Producer:* Peter Hoffman and David Wisnievitz. *Director:* Peter Hoffman. *Screenplay (based on his short story "Christ Has Returned to Earth and Preaches Here Nightly"):* Leonard Gardner. *Director of Photography:* Jerzy Zielinski. *Editor:* Denine Rowan. *Choreographer:* Nancy Memory. *Sound:* Lee Strosnider. *Sound Editor:* Ira Spiegel and Jeffrey Stern. *Art Director:* Woody Romine. *Set Decorator:* Kerry Longacre. *Set Dresser:* Nancy Booth. *Costumes:* Toni Spadafora. *Make-up:* Athena Demetrios. *Stunt Coordinator:* Bobby Sargent. *Running Time:* 90 minutes. *MPAA Rating:* R.

CAST: Barry Tubb (Wayne Gibbs); Frederic Forrest (Sonny Gibbs); Veronica Cartwright (Pat Gibbs); Jenny Wright (Sylvia Fuller); Macon McCalman (Leroy Fuller); Kit McDonough (Ruth Fuller); Seth Isler (Harry Ames); David Packer (Count Messner); Michael Spencer (Joe Pucci); Leonard Gardner (Lyle); Cheryl Anderson (Sharon); Jenny Gago (Teresa); Jerry Hardin (Rev. Horner); Miguel Ferrer (The Biker); Jeffrey Josephson (Balls O'Fire); Susan Falcon (Hooker); William Frankfather (Cadillac Salesman); Shirley Thomas (Cindy); John Cruz (Rainbow Club Bartender); Colleen Gillespie (Rose Room Woman); Eleanor Pledger (Rose Room Woman); Walter Richards (Virgil); Steven Wolfe (Piano Player); Yaqui Lopez (Alavaro); Roger Ice (Foreman); John Powell (Rick Kroll); Cecil Rich (Red); Julie Berriault (Verna); Hank Pericle (Hank); Frank Kanig (Beer Vendor); Devino Inocian and Ernie Valentine (Boxers); Erin Harris (Colleen); Kelli Noteman (Jackie); Ken Tompson (Auctioneer); Michael Careveo (Black Mamba Passenger); James Pack (Jailer); John Wolczynski (Booking Officer); Joan Teter (Policeman); Peter Bradley (Disc Jockey).

LOS ANGELES TIMES, 7/21/89, Calendar/p. 12, Michael Wilmington

Leonard Gardner, who helped adapt one of his own short stories into the new movie "Valentino Returns," is a writer with real presence. You can sense his point of view behind every line he writes, whether it's about about the washed-up, journeymen boxers in "Fat City," which John Huston and he made into a minor film classic in 1972, or the small-town Central California people he and director Peter Hoffman portray here.

Like "Fat City," "Valentino Returns" is about the absurdity and nightmarish underside of part of the American Dream. It's about losers who try to dream themselves into winners, big-mouths and battered women and small-town lives wasting away in the smoke and honky-tonk braggadocio of the local barrooms. But where "Fat City" came close to a tragedy of the commonplace, this movie is a teenage sex comedy, another '50s nostalgia picture. Don't let that put you off. It's slow getting started and it has flaws, but it's better-remembered and funnier than many of its competitors.

The central character, Wayne Gibbs, is played with winningly bemused understatement by ex-rodeo rider and "Lonesome Dove" co-star Barry Tubbs. He's a farm worker who has just bought a pink Cadillac that he's christened Valentino Returns, in which he intends to cruise to sex and glory. Complicating matters are his parents, an incorrigible would-be ladies' man (Frederic Forrest) and his incurably fed-up wife (Veronica Cartwright), and Wayne's pathologically unreliable buddy, Harry (Seth Isler), who claims to have an assortment of randy divorcées and hot-to-trot Swedish models on call, all or most of whom prove to be fictitious.

This familiar material becomes funny because it's such a clear-eyed look at the dreams most other teen-sex movies try to indulge. The two men closest to Wayne, his dad and Harry, cling to their fantasies with terrifying intensity, even in the face of injury or chaos. Wayne is more distanced, an observer; he sees the things others miss. There is one local girl to whom he's attracted, a fetchingly reckless blonde named Sylvia (Jenny Wright). Unfortunately, she proves to be a fireball guarded by a dragon: the town slut and daughter of a religious fanatic.

That's one of the cleverest insights of "Valentino Returns" into small-town American life: the crazy dialectic between puritanism and lechery, family and irresponsibility, home and the city's beckoning, sex-soaked nights. The key scene is a local tent-revival—the sign outside says "Christ has returned to Earth and preaches here nightly"—where Wayne and Harry run into Sylvia and her parents, and where a typically ecstatic, brow-beating sermon in interrupted by a smirking biker (Miguel Ferrer). It's typical '50s symbolism from the decade where movie biker-delinquents like Brando and James Dean became twisted Christ figures in pop mythology. But it's also a joke about the aspirations of the two pink-Cadillac cruisers, who worship the night and easy sex as fervently as their neighbors seek a savior who will banish guilt and sin.

Though the picture's control seems to improve as it goes on, first-time director Hoffman shows very little visual style. There's barely a memorable image anywhere, except perhaps the final going-down-the-road shot. But Hoffman is good with the actors. He fills the sound track with prime late-'50s rock 'n' roll, and he and his cast catch some of the restless ambience that the music fed. Tubbs, Wright, Forrest, Cartwright, Isler and many of the minor characters, including Gardner himself as Forrest's sneaky-eyed pal Lyle, have fine moments.

In some ways, Gardner is a poet of the casualties of the American Dream. But he's a poet who can smile. "Valentino Returns" (MPAA rated R for sex and language) is about people who are headed toward the smoky, beer-soaked cul-de-sacs of a "Fat City" but haven't quite reached them yet, or who have a chance—a faint chance—of breaking out. At its best, it has the giddy jocularity of a good laugh at things too deep-down rooted to cry about, too catastrophic to even try to fix.

NEW YORK POST, 7/21/89, p. 28, Jami Bernard

Fortunately, "Valentino Returns" grows on you, or you'd be plumb out of gas on a lonely stretch of highway between "American Graffiti" and all the movies in which shiny new cars take a lickin'.

The title takes its name from the flamingo-pink Cadillac that young Wayne Gibbs is paying off bit by bit with the proceeds of his tractor job in a small California town in 1958. During the course of the movie, Wayne rides about town, scoping out the babe situation with a buddy who insists he knows a Swedish divorcée who is a model and loves sex.

The search for the elusive Inga takes the guys to a biker bar, a tent prayer meeting (the movie is based on a short story called "Christ Has Returned to Earth and Preaches Here Nightly"), a barn dance (with real chicks), and some other bizarrely scenic pitstops.

Wayne ultimately settles on the ripe, sluttish daughter of a Bible-thumping egg farmer. Sylvia (Jenny Wright) is a bit on the confused side, but at least she's willing.

Despite the car and the buddies and the '50s sound track and the desperate search for horny divorcees, this is not of the teen comedy genre. It is actually a benignly satirical slice of life, thanks largely to the presence of Wayne's ultra-dysfunctional family. Dad (Frederic Forrest) is a charming cad who even gets away with a hobby of being a truly awful lounge singer. Mom (Veronica Cartwright, who was Beaver Cleaver's girl friend once upon a time) finally ditches him, leaving a note for Wayne: "Why don't you get some Chinese food for dinner. I left your father. Love, Mom."

Folks worry about "going loony" against a backdrop of dull-as-dishwater '50s small-town life.

Barry Tubb, a former champion bull-rider, made his Broadway debut in "Sweet Sue," memorable mostly for baring his butt prominently and unabashedly during the performance (he played an artist's model). He must have made a good impression on the "Valentino" film makers because he has a considerable bare-bottomed fight scene which doesn't look like it was too comfortable to film. A handsome fella, Tubb spends most of the movie looking strangely perplexed.

Wright, as the fundamentalist's sexy daughter, should not be having dates at that time of night—and certainly not in the back seat of a pink Caddy.

It may not seem like much at first, but by the time dad is giving Wayne fatherly advice on how to lie your way out of any situation, it's clear that the movie is engaging in spite of itself.

NEWSDAY, 7/21/89, Part III/p. 3, Terry Kelleher

"I'd have to be a fool to believe that story," an angry parent tells his alibiing child near the end of "Valentino Returns." Then he chooses to accept, if not believe.

This is a movie filled with fools, and you find yourself liking them for their foolishness. There's nothing new or startling here, just entertainment that sort of sneaks up and tickles you.

The time is the late '50s, the place California's San Joaquin Valley. Young Wayne Gibbs (Barry Tubb) strolls into the Cadillac showroom and slips behind the wheel of a pink, tail-finned beauty. Ah, this is the luxury vehicle that will take him to L.A., Vegas, sex, excitement — *something*. Wayne's buddy Harry (Seth Isler) seems to know numerous "divorcées" just waiting for a couple of gawky teenage studs. All Wayne has to provide is the transportation.

Closer to home, there's sexual opportunity in the person of Sylvia Fuller (Jenny Wright), the egg farmer's rather notorious daughter. Forbidden to date by her fundamentalist parents, Sylvia has a reputation for late-night rendezvous by the roadside. The trouble is, her nocturnal schedule can be embarrassingly crowded.

While he's busy coming of age, Wayne also must keep tabs on his father, whose name indicates his maturity level. Sonny Gibbs (Frederic Forrest) is first seen singing, and swaying, in a saloon: *Maybe I'm right and maybe I'm wrong/Maybe I'm weak and maybe I'm strong/Nevertheless I'm in love with you.* His crooning is pretty bad, but his fellow patrons like what they hear. Sonny seems to have that effect on people.

He's wrong and weak—no maybes about it—and his wife would have to be a fool to believe his excuses. Fed up with the boozing and philandering, Pat Gibbs (Veronica Cartwright) vows to quit Sonny for good. She moves out, but his importunity erodes her resolve. How can a woman resist a man who begs his way back into her bed, then asks for peanut butter and crackers as soon as his passion is spent?

"He has such a way about him you just have to fall for him," she explains. Well, she sees it even if we don't, and maybe she's entitled to her bit of foolishness.

To our eyes, Sonny is one part charmer, one part child and one part bum. Forrest keeps these elements in exactly the proper balance. Cartwright is consistently sympathetic, whether Pat is heeding her head or her heart. The treatment of the adults is primarily what gives "Valentino Returns" its measure of distinction, but Tubb successfully conveys Wayne's restlessness and naivete, while Wright's Sylvia manages to be ingenuous even when she's lying her pretty head off.

In his directing debut, Peter Hoffman brings a little extra sensibility to the teens-cars-nostalgia formula. Leonard Gardner, seen in two scenes as the Gibbses' card-playing friend, did a commendable job of adapting his short story for the screen. Too bad he couldn't have kept the original, unwieldy title: "Christ Has Returned to Earth and Preaches Here Nightly." (After all, would Wayne really name his new car after a silent-film star?)

Just for a hoot, Wayne and Harry stop off at a tent meeting, where the revivalist (Jerry Hardin) promises a guest appearance by Jesus Himself. The Lord misses His cue; a sardonic biker (Miguel Ferrer) barges in instead. However, Sylvia claims a sighting of the Savior later on. It's an unlikely story, but serviceable under the circumstances. What a fool believes is his or her own business.

VILLAGE VOICE, 7/25/89, p. 71, Julie Phillips

What we need to know first is, Has the pink Cadillac been used up yet as a symbol of hot times? After Elvis and Aretha and Bruce and Bernadette have had their joyrides, is there any air left in the whitewalls, any gas in the tank of the automotive love machine?

Well, maybe. In *Valentino Returns*, the eponymous Cadillac (Why Valentino? No one ever explains) is purchased on credit, in the summer of '58, by a tractor jockey named Wayne (Barry Tubb, a former junior world champion bull-rider and a mighty cute bit of hayseed beefcake), who cruises this emblem of his manhood (but an ambivalent manhood—come on, it's *pink*) through the little flat farm towns of central California. It's *American Graffiti*, only more so, and more hick: The '50s tunes are twangin' on the radio (and ringin' the cash registers for the soundtrack album), the boys are hangin' out at the stable when they're not out looking for girls, the girls are in the henhouse when they're not at the revival meetin', and when they're together, well, they're makin' love in the backseat of that fine automobile.

By day, Wayne and his best buddy Harry (Seth Isler) clean out stalls and dream of lustful divorcées. ("*This* is what she wants," Harry announces, gesturing with a pitchfork, or does he mean what he's pitching?) But the '50s are turning out not to be the time of straightforward boy-and-girlness that everyone used to say they were. Wayne's own mother (Veronica Cartwright) wants a divorce. (Her note reads, "Why don't you get some Chinese food? I've left your father. Love, Mom.") Dad (Frederic Forrest) comes home late and plays around, but the thought of Mom leaving is breaking his puny heart. Sylvia, Wayne's trampy true love (Jenny Wright), is a ball o' fire, but she lives in fear of her fundamentalist egg farmer parents and her daddy's leather belt.

Valentino is a small, uneven film, but there's something likable about it. A trip to Stockton in search of a model named Inge passes through a tent meeting, a biker bar, the town jail, the swimming hole, and possibly the only naked fight scene in celluloid history. The road to manhood winds up in family reconciliation. The pink Cadillac, beaten in its only race, breaks down. Love conquers all. Great performances from Forrest, Cartwright (she used to play the Beaver's girlfriend), and Warner help make this fluff warm and more or less convincing. And *Valentino Returns* puts its own small patch of Bondo on the body of Pink Cadillac legend.

Also reviewed in:
NEW YORK TIMES, 7/21/89, p. C9, Caryn James
VARIETY, 5/31–6/7/89, p. 35

VALMONT

An Orion Pictures release of a Claude Berri/Renn Productions (Paris)/Timothy Burrill Productions Ltd. (London) coproduction. *Producer:* Paul Rassam and Michael Hausman. *Director:* Milos Forman. *Screenplay:* Jean-Claude Carrière. *Freely adapted from "Les Liaisons Dangereuses" by:* Choderlos de Laclos. *Director of Photography:* Miroslav Ondricek. *Editor:* Alan Heim and Nena Danevic. *Music:* Christopher Palmer. *Music Editor:* John Strauss. *Choreographer:* Ann Jacoby. *Sound:* Chris Newman. *Sound Editor:* Maurice Schell. *Production Designer:* Pierre Guffroy. *Art Director:* Albert Rajau, Loula Morin, and Martina Skala. *Set Dresser:* Jacques-Albert Leguilion and Claude Suné. *Special Effects:* Garth Inns and Michel Norman. *Costumes:* Theodor Pistek. *Make-up:* Paul LeBlanc. *Running Time:* 134 minutes. *MPAA Rating:* R.

CAST: Colin Firth (Valmont); Annette Bening (Merteuil); Meg Tilly (Tourvel); Fairuza Balk (Cécile); Sian Phillips (Madame de Volanges); Jeffrey Jones (Gercourt); Henry Thomas (Danceny); Fabia Drake (Madame de Rosemonde); T.P. McKenna (Baron); Isla Blair (Baroness); Ian McNeice (Azolan); Aleta Mitchell (Victoire); Ronald Lacey (José); Vincent Schiavelli (Jean); Sandrine Dumas (Martine); Sebastien Floche (Priest); Antony Carrick (President de Tourvel); Murray Gronwall (Flea Market Salesman); Alain Frérot, Daniel Laloux, and Christian Bouillette (Thugs); John Arnold and Niels Travernier (Knights of the Maltese Order); Yvette Petit (Mother Superior); Richard De Burnchurch (Volanges' Major-domo); José Licenziato (Blind Guitar Player); Ivan Palec (Servant).

FILMS IN REVIEW, 1–2/90, p. 47, Edmond Grant

Jean-Luc Godard once proposed an interesting experiment. It would be fascinating, he suggested, to have a number of different filmmakers attempt to adapt the same story in order to view how the results varied, and how different directors shaped the material. Of course, no one took old Jean too seriously, but over the years film fans have had the opportunity to see how different filmmakers have interpreted the same plotline; most of these examples, however, were far apart in time or culturally separated (like the recent slew of American remakes of French farces). Now, within a period of one year, two vastly different adaptations of Choderlos de Laclos' classic *Les Liaisons Dangereuses* have appeared. The first, *Dangerous Liaisons* was a faithful rendition of the Christopher Hampton's theatrical version on the novel directed by

Stephen Frears; the second is a sumptuous rendering with a screenplay "freely adapted" from the novel by Buñuel collaborator Jean-Claude Carrière and direction by Milos Forman.

The two films are different in approach, but both basically stick to the outline of Laclos' novel. We see how the rogue ladies' man Valmont (in Forman's version, Colin Firth) and his female counterpart, the Marquise de Merteuil (Annette Bening), scheme to control the lives of those who surround them. Feeling betrayed as a result of her lover's imminent marriage to innocent young Cécile de Volanges, Merteuil asks Valmont to despoil the girl before she takes her marital vows. The girl, meanwhile, is enamored of her coy young musical instructor (Henry Thomas) and Valmont has plans of his own to win the affection of the demure Madame de Tourvel (Meg Tilly) and thereby win a wager with Merteuil, who says that the woman is unconquerable.

The basic plotline may be the same, but Carrière and Forman's interpretation does more to develop and broaden the scope of the material than did the film of Hampton's play. For one thing, the outlook is brighter. Where *Dangerous Liaisons* relied on witty banter to underscore the ridiculousness of some of the romantic situations, *Valmont* lets the humor rise to the surface in several wonderfully orchestrated comic sequences, such as the bold rendezvous that Merteuil schedules for the young lovers, and the masterfully played scene where Valmont confronts Merteuil bathing herself, clad only in a wet dressing gown, and demands payment on their wager. And while Frears' film emphasized the sadly tragic nature of the two leading characters, *Valmont* underscores the playfulness of their actions and takes great care to explore the spaces which they inhabit. The richness of detail that marked Forman's style in *Ragtime* and *Amadeus* returns here, as eye-catching landscapes and the requisite stately mansions alternate with colorfully decorated recreations of French street life in the 1750's. Forman goes to great lengths to let the atmosphere help carry the narrative along, such as in the scene where de Tourvel shops at a teeming market for Valmont's breakfast—the scene is almost superfluous to the storyline, but it seems to reinforce our sense of the common environment that surrounds the insular noblemen and women the story is concerned with. This exactly counters Frears' approach, which was to show the insularity of the characters' existences by having them placed only in rarified, aristocratic settings.

The somewhat irreverent attitude Forman and Carrière manifest toward their source material, first evidenced in the screen credit which reads, "freely adapted from. . .", provides the film with its greatest virtue, that of humanity. So often the film versions of classic literary works strive for such a great degree of fidelity to their source that all the life and vitality of the original work are obscured (a sin committed all too often by the "prestige" adaptations produced by the BBC). Not so with *Valmont*, which spends time leisurely developing the duplicitous interrelationships that exist between the characters. Forman and Carrière have left time for splendid bits of business, like the scene in which Valmont dances in turn with all the women who occupy his attention, working his way around gradually to his intended conquest, Madame de Tourvel.

The most significant sign of the "human touch" that Forman and Carrière have put on Laclos' original is the bristing sensuality exhibited by the characters, be it of the budding kind (Cécile), fully developed (Merteuil), or in repose (Madame de Tourvel). And though Forman takes care to invest the entire film with sensuality, he never overplays his hand. The aforementioned bathtub sequence, where Bening never actually does doff her clothing, but instead retains her soaking wet dressing gown as she climbs into bed and callously offers herself to Valmont to pay off their wager, and the moment when Valmont strokes the bared thigh of Cécile as he is dictating a letter for her—both these instances are cleverly not explicit in their erotic appeal, adding untold dimensions to the seductive games being instigated by the two "puppet masters" (Valmont and Merteuil) who rule the other characters' love lives. The fact that all these characters are of a young age (none of the four principals being over thirty, a stark contrast to Frears' version) enhances the tragic quality of their actions, underscoring the fact that very little save a broken heart, or a pathetic ending like Valmont's, can result.

Forman once again demonstrates his uncanny knack for casting (who had ever heard of F. Murray Abraham before *Amadeus*?) by choosing a sublime assortment of non-name, but still familiar, assortment of actors. Colin Firth is not overly dynamic as Valmont, but he does have the good looks and charisma needed for the role. Meg Tilly admirably fleshes out the character of Madame de Tourvel, who (as proved before in Frears' version) has little more to do than appear dewy-eyed and resist Valmont's enticements, until the final surrender to carnality. Fifteen-year-old Fairuza Balk is a fine Cécile, her coy teenage mannerisms making Valmont's seduction all the more decadent. The film's big surprise, however, is Annette Bening who looks very much like the young Diana Rigg and who miraculously incarnates Merteuil as the completely unrepentant seductrice, yet still leaves enough room in her characterization for the sad and lonely side of the character which was somewhat overemphasized in Frears' film. Bening's Merteuil is a more than equal opponent for Valmont, carefully relenting from a scheme only as it goes helplessly out of bounds, while keeping an eye out for the next opportune opening.

In the final analysis, *Valmont* proves the more exhilarating of the two contemporary adaptations of Laclos' classic. With its wealth of detail, the shimmering visual beauty of cinematographer Miroslav Ondricek's images and its fine-tuned combination of humor and eroticism, it stands as an adaptation that both does justice to its source *and* makes a few choice revisions.

LOS ANGELES TIMES, 11/17/89, Calendar/p. 1, Sheila Benson

With "Valmont" Milos Forman takes us back between the sheets of Choderlos de Laclos' great 18th-Century novel "Les Liaisons Dangereuses," back to all those seducers-with-abandon, and for a few lulling scenes he seems to be on to something.

In keeping with the period, he's dropped the age of his sexual combatants, the Marquise de Merteuil and the Vicomte de Valmont. They're now in their 20s, and their erotic machinations seem more like the careless intrigues of youth instead of the poisonous, knowing maneuvers of maturity. If it takes the "dangerous" out of the equation—and it does, oh, how it does—the reward is Annette Bening's dazzling Marquise, red-haired and purring-voiced. To have a Marquise with buoyancy and humor, whose sweet concern *might* even be sincere, is a startling idea; you can see how easily her fellow aristocrats might be taken in by this warm, beautiful young widow. In Stephen Frears' version last year, "Dangerous Liaisons," the wonder was that anyone would believe the Merteuil of Glenn Close for a second; her layers of deceit were so elaborate and so transparent.

"Valmont" *is* gorgeous, and for a while you can coast on its costumes and production details. The novel's period has been moved back 50 years, turning things into a Watteau dream. But seductive as his surfaces are, Forman's tack doesn't hold for long. His changes have muted a great tale of betrayal by intelligence and he has blunted the malign inevitability of Laclos' story.

By changing the fate of key characters, the innocent 15-year old Cécile (Fairuza Balk) and the deeply pious Madame de Tourvel (Meg Tilly), Forman and screenwriter Jean-Claude Carrière may have thought they were underlining the hypocrisy of the day. Instead, their conclusions are arch and obvious, like the wink from the elderly aunt at the film's end.

The story unfolds roughly as before: The action is set in motion by the imminent marriage of convent-educated Cécile to Gercourt, the ongoing lover of the widowed Merteuil. To get even with Gercourt (Jeffrey Jones), Merteuil schemes to have his 15-year-old's virginity taken by her confidant and equal libertine, Valmont (Colin Firth).

Valmont is bored with the assignment of seducing a child who would "probably flop on her back out of simple curiosity." Only when it becomes a bet between the two equals in deviousness does he agree to take it on. If he wins, he may claim Merteuil (although not for the first time) as payment; if he loses, he is to shut himself in a monastery and repent his sins.

Visiting the estate of his elderly aunt Madame de Rosemonde (Fabia Drake), Valmont unexpectedly finds a quarry of his own, the unshakeably faithful Tourvel, whose older husband, a judge, is away on business. This should be the story's tragic liaison, with shattering consequences; to have its effect trivialized is perhaps "Valmont's" worst sin. (Its R rating is for its ongoing seductions, sometimes accompanied by selective nudity.)

Losing the great saga of Tourvel, we spend the first third of the film on Cécile and her entanglements. And since she goes on to one of the film's newly minted social triumphs, Cécile becomes little more than a John Hughes heroine in period clothes who learns that sex is fun and you don't have to tell all. Pfui.

From the first, Forman moves to emphasize details, perhaps afraid we'd miss them. His adolescents—Balk, who *is* 15, and Henry Thomas as her well-born harp teacher, the young Chevalier Danceny—frisk about, skittering on the parquet floors. ("Return to Oz's" Dorothy and E.T.'s little pal, Elliot, as our young lovers? It's enough to make even baby boomers feel ancient.)

Danceny can't pick up two things without dropping one of them, generally his harp. It's the same "endearing" klutziness Forman used in "Amadeus" and it's even less effective here. A chevalier of that day may have been young; he was also worldly, sophisticated and cultivated, which Forman won't let Thomas play. (He can be believably steely, however.)

If we have a warm-blooded, believable Merteuil, casting Jeffrey Jones as her lover Gercourt is another mistake. Better to let Gercourt live in our imagination. Jones may be part of Forman's stock company, after his dim Emperor Josef II in "Amadeus," but why use his patented smugness here? Even taking into account Gercourt's closeness to the King, to have Merteuil involved with this popinjay makes her seem not calculating but masochistic.

Colin Firth's Valmont is pleasant, a dreadful thing to say about one of literature's most magnetic seducers. Meg Tilly's translucence is more than wasted here; for the first time, it is tiresome. It is lovely to see Sian Phillips as Cécile's rightly alarmed mother, and Fabia Drake's grand, worldly Madame de Rosemonde, forever being awakened to discover that her card-playing companions have tip-toed away, is the film's bright-eyed Dormouse.

But to consider "Valmont" in the light of Baudelaire's words on "Les Liaisons Dangereuses"—"This book, if it burns, must burn like ice"—is to see just how far down this ice has been watered.

NEW YORK, 11/20/89, p. 122, David Denby

Taken by itself, *Valmont* might have seemed a beautifully shot but rather amorphous costume extravaganza. But it can't be taken by itself, for it is yet another version of Choderlos de Laclos's brilliant novel, *Les Liaisons Dangereuses*, which was made into the superb *Dangerous Liaisons* only a year ago. That film was directed by Stephen Frears and written by Christopher Hampton. A fancy gloss on Frears's film, this one was directed by Milos Forman and written by Jean-Claude Carrière, and it's slower, more lavish, more explicit, without the first movie's thrusting adventurousness and intellectual excitement—less fun, all in all.

Valmont lacks both impudence and formal beauty. Carrière's dialogue is mostly too ordinary for prerevolutionary French aristocrats, and when it's not ordinary, it's arch. As for Forman, larking in the eighteenth century again (last time in *Amadeus*), he works up endless amounts of exuberant, powdered-wig period detail (some of it actually relevant) but works with a deficient sense of character. The two cynical aristocrats, the Marquise de Merteuil (Annette Bening) and Valmont (Colin Firth), play with the romantic affections of a young girl, Cécile (Fairuza Balk), who says that she is fifteen but looks about thirteen. Balk has a button nose, a puffy upper lip, and some baby fat. Even allowing for different sexual standards 200 years ago, there's no way any man not a pedophile could want to sleep with her, so one feels queasy when Firth goes to work on her soft little thighs.

The theater actress Annette Bening, a young, beautiful, very American-looking Merteuil, has a slow, purring style of insincerity—smiling reassurance, secret loathing—but she paces everything at the same languorous tempo, and after a while she loses our interest. Firth has a fine voice, and in conventional terms he's a more handsome Valmont than last year's John Malkovich. But Malkovich's pleasure in his own outrageous inventions carried the audience along, whereas Firth's Valmont is just a generous and high-spirited young man betrayed by Merteuil and abandoned by the others. The story now is about a youthful rake brought low—a victim.

Meg Tilly as the virtuous Madame de Tourvel is lovely—soft-voiced, diaphanous, but with a strong will. Carrière has dropped her religious scruples, however, and since her husband isn't around, we don't know what she's risking when she commits adultery with Valmont. Carrière has explained that Laclos was hampered by contemporary censorship, and that's why the wicked characters in the book are punished. But the end Carrière provides is cynical and incoherent, with no moral significance whatsoever. *Valmont* is pretty, but almost completely trivial.

NEW YORK POST, 11/17/89, p. 29, David Edelstein

Because "Valmont" is "freely adapted" from the Choderlos de Laclos novel "Les Liaisons Dangereuses," there are sure to be mean-spirited comparisons between it and last year's "Dangerous Liaisons." Too bad, because "Valmont" has much on its own to recommend it. Nice costumes, for example, and a leading lady with cute buns.

Some aspects of the plot make more sense, and the sexual chemistry between the villains far exceeds the rather icky rapport of Glenn Close and John Malkovich. It's a roomy tale de Laclos tells, and in a world where stories get repeated ad nauseam ("loser goes for it and wins," "sociopath slices up college girls"), there's space for as many "Liaisons" as the studios want to make. More, gentlemen, more!

Of course, one misses the attack of Stephen Frears' version—the thrill that accompanied its breathlessly discreet transactions, as lovers plotted their rendezvous with the steely detachment of generals. De Laclos wrote a devastating indictment of hedonism, of the impulse to separate pleasure and emotion, and the novel and the Frears/Christopher Hampton film were tragedies not of specific individuals but of a whole way of life.

Where director Milos Forman ("Amadeus"), and writer Jean-Claude Carrière excel is in popularizing the same material—so that any boob can get it—and in creating a kind of effortless lushness that pops eyes and wins awards. Until its muddled finale, "Valmont" is a sumptuous and entertaining soap opera, a $40 million "Days of Our Lives."

Its central character, the Marquise de Merteuil, is played by Annette Bening, a lovely actress with auburn hair and porcelain skin. Her Merteuil is a more plausible seductress than Close's, and she's deliciously phony—all sparkling eyes and sugar-plum-fairy smiles.

Shrewdly, Forman and Carrière dramatize the insult that sets the plot in motion—Merteuil's abandonment by her rich lover, Gercourt (Jeffrey Jones), for a 15-year-old virgin, Cécile (Fairuza Balk, who looks as if she just got out of kindergarten).

Thus, seeing the child deflowered before her wedding night is of burning importance to Merteuil. And Forman complicates matters by suggesting that the older woman may truly believe she's doing the younger a favor—educating her in the nasty ways of the world. Is Cécile strengthened or weakened by the changes she undergoes? The answer is teasingly ambiguous.

Bening is a clever actress, although her range seems narrow here—she's closer to the parade of high-cheekboned Barbie dolls who populate the soaps than Forman may have intended. Still, it's nice that she and Valmont are attracted to each other and that the audience wants them to get it on—particularly when he confronts her soaking imperiously in her bath.

As the aristocrat Valmont, Colin Firth cuts a splendid figure, offset by a cleft chin and soft, indistinct features. He seems less satanic than mischievous—not a master strategist but a young, rich wastrel who gets his kicks from sleeping with as many women as possible.

Because he has so little stature, his fall isn't of much consequence. In the novel, we're burned by that final irony: that a hedonist has been destroyed by a burst of ordinary feeling, much as the Martians in "War of the Worlds" are felled by a mere germ.

Things are, in general, pretty murky in this wind-up. The pious widow (Meg Tilly) whom Valmont seduces on a bet with Merteuil behaves oddly, and the climatic mess reveals the characters to be a bunch of spoiled, callow fools. That is clearly intentional, but the cynical jolt that sends us home is no substitute for de Laclos' decisive moral judgments. (And they are moral, not moralistic, judgments.)

At least the picture's pretty. In fact, it's hard not to gasp at the milky radiance of Miroslav Ondricek's cinematography and the silkiness of Theodor Pistek's costumes. Unlike "Amadeus," the feel of "Valmont" is airy and inviting: even when Forman heaps on the spectacle, he moves things trippingly.

As the good Catholic object of Valmont's attentions, Tilly has no wiles—as a character or an actress. She's just there, a lump. But Sian Phillips is surprisingly sympathetic as Cécile's overbearing mother, and Henry Thomas (of "E.T.") is a charmingly serious young suitor. Balk is charming, too, her baby-fat turning Valmont into the Jerry Lee Lewis of his day.

NEWSDAY, 11/17/89, Part III/p. 5, Mike McGrady

How can this be? How can two film versions of the same story—both lavishly produced, both expertly directed—be released in the space of a single year? Milos Forman, director of the 1989 version of "Les Liaisons Dangereuses"—his new title is "Valmont"—sees it this way: "That the movie industry is ready to simultaneously invest millions of dollars into two adaptations of the same subject seems healthy to me. It is a sympathetic madness."

Neither Forman nor Stephen Frears (he directed the all-too-recent "Dangerous Liaisons") is a creative slouch, and one could reasonably expect their approaches to the same material to differ. Indeed, their interpretations are wildly different, as are their styles, their characters and even their basic story structures.

With "Valmont" only the outline remains to remind us of the original Choderlos de Laclos novel that was both the scandal and the rage of France in 1782. Despite other alterations, it is still a saga of amorous skulduggery, the tale of two profligates who set off a round of intrigues that involve and threaten such innocents as a 15-year-old girl fresh from the convent, a hitherto virtuous wife and a young music instructor.

Since the film of last December was such a solid success, there seems no way to examine

"Valmont" without making comparisons. The main comparison: The Frears work was solemn, elegant, true to its source; "Valmont" is lighter in tone, ironic, more human.

If the Forman film holds any advantage at all over "Dangerous Liaisons," it may rest in the fact that it does *not* star John Malkovich as the womanizing Valmont, an act of casting that seemed as perverse as the character himself. The physically unprepossessing Malkovich turned Valmont into a mannered whiner and when he robbed the 15-year-old Cecile of her virginity, he relied on deceit, threat and brute force. British stage star Colin Firth, on the other hand, draws on an abundance of physical magnetism, wit and a boyish enthusiasm for his own womanizing; when he seduces the same Cecile, it becomes a high-spirited romp, another evening's entertainment for a romantic adept.

It is possible, however, that director Forman carries innocence too far. While Glenn Close, as the original Marquise de Merteuil, offered many layers of evil, the extravagantly bedimpled Annette Bening seems too nice, too untouched for the mammoth destructions she effects.

Not only has Forman opted for less well known actors, he has chosen a different mood. The original film was all brocaded costumes, powdered wigs and marble-walled chateaus. "Valmont" broadens horizons, bringing us into a bawdy tavern and a marketplace teeming with lowlife, lingering in a voluptuous bedchamber where a blind violinist serves up background music during milady's amorous conquests.

Forman's alterations to the original story—he comes perilously close to providing a happy ending—are sure to offend classicists. Not easily tolerated by others will be his diminishment of language. Both the original novel and last year's movie (based on the hit stage play) were formal, witty and elegant. Gone are the flowery phrases and the verbal gymnastics, gone in a conscious decision to make the people and the situation more real, more current.

While each film can be enjoyed for quite different reasons, I must cast my vote for last year's "Dangerous Liaisons" over this year's "Valmont." In so doing, I realize I'm lamenting the new film's absence of malice and acknowledging the solid entertainment value that pure evil is able to add to sexual intrigue.

NEWSWEEK, 11/20/89, p. 79, Jack Kroll

As Cicero said (or was it Sid Caesar?): *"Quis foul up magnum opus, sibi foul up."* Or: "If you screw up a masterpiece, the masterpiece will screw you up." That's what's happened with *Valmont*, which director Milos Forman ("Amadeus") and screenwriter Jean-Claude Carrière have "freely adapted" from the great 18th-century novel by Choderlos de Laclos, "Les Liaisons Dangereuses." Their handiwork is a fiasco—and a dull, draggy 2-hour-and-14-minute fiasco to boot. There was nothing dull about Christopher Hampton's stage version or Stephen Frears's 1988 movie with Glenn Close and John Malkovich. If Forman didn't want to repeat these works, he had two choices: drop the project or come up with a different, inspired angle. His version is different, all right; it's like a botched piece of plastic surgery that turns a vital human face into a blank mask of seams and tucks.

Instead of the diamond-hard, icily burning precision of Laclos, "Valmont" is flabby and tepid. The Vicomte de Valmont (Colin Firth) and the Marquise de Merteuil (Annette Bening) are no longer nihilistic seducers and destroyers of innocence but self-centered 18th-century jet-setters. With Madame de Tourvel (Meg Tilly) deprived of her profound piety, Valmont's seduction of her loses its apocalyptic evil and becomes just another romp under the duvet. The teenage Cécile (Fairuza Balk) becomes an earlier Gigi who learns that sex is fun from Valmont and gets to marry a rich suitor instead of being shunted off to a nunnery. It's as if Ophelia had gotten to marry some smorgasbord tycoon.

These changes are awful not because they're changes but because they lack the relentless logic, power and significance of the original. The satanic shenanigans of Valmont and Merteuil no longer reflect the dynamics of a corrupt society but have become nearly pointless. And to reduce this work to pointlessness is unforgivable. Especially when the film has no partially redeeming virtues of wit, irony or (despite lavish costumes and settings) true elegance. In this farrago it's hard to judge the actors: Bening's beauty and style float in a void, Firth seems callow and dumb. In this disastrous attempt at renovation Forman has kept the liaisons but not the danger.

TIME, 11/20/89, p. 92, Richard Schickel

Call it by its rightful name, *Les Liaisons Dangereuses.* Call it *Dangerous Liaisons.* Call it, if you must, *Valmont*. But in any case it looks as if we can now call it a day for stage and movie adaptations of Pierre-Ambroise-François Choderlos de Laclos's intricate, instructive novel of sexual gamesmanship among the 18th century French aristocracy. For Milos Forman and Jean-Claude Carrière, while fidding with the plot of this deliciously nasty tale, have studiously embalmed its spirit. *Valmont* arrives stiffened by the elegant, inert formalism of Forman's direction, and chilled by Carrière's all too sober respect for his source and by their mutual determination to apply modern psychological understanding to the behavior of the principal figures.

The script is almost clinically clear about why the Marquise de Merteuil (Annette Bening) and the Vicomte de Valmont (Colin Firth) embark on a campaign to debauch a 15-year-old virgin, Cécile de Volanges (Fairuza Balk). The older woman is gripped by temporary insanity because she loves the man who intends to marry the adolescent. The vicomte too has his excuses. He is possessed by a passionate nature, the ill effects of which, it is implied, are also temporary. Give the kid some time, and he will probably turn out to be an admirable citizen. Indeed, his second amorous campaign—to bed a virtuous young wife, Madame de Tourvel (Meg Tilly)—is not presented as idle and amoral womanizing but as proof of his capacity for authentic emotion. Too bad he has what we now are fond of calling "an intimacy problem," and, as a result, this affair and ultimately his life come to a bad and premature end.

How could anyone think it helpful to impose upon the behavior of a long-lost era and a vanished social class the wisdom of modern Pop psychology? It prevents the actors from tearing into their roles with the black comic gusto that Glenn Close and John Malkovich brought to their feverish performances in *Dangerous Liaisons* last year. But besides spoiling the fun, this approach blurs the work's value as a cautionary tale, capable of reminding us that motiveless malignity is a potent force in every age and one that not even Freud—let alone humanistically inclined moviemakers—can explain away.

VILLAGE VOICE, 11/21/89, p. 92, Georgia Brown

What I remember about Roger Vadim's *Les Liaisons dangereuses* is Choderlos de Laclos's shocking story and Jeanne Moreau's bruised face. I wasn't the only one seduced back in the early '60s. But that was in another country; we had been sequestered in the convent of America, producing a ripe social context. Innocence was credible then.

In last Christmas's zippy *Dangerous Liaisons*, Stephen Frears and Christopher Hampton decided to forget innocence and play evil for camp—a tactic that worked about as well as it could. When the jaded ones crashed, there was a satisfying thump. And a thump-thump-thump of the hidden romantic heart. *Liaisons*'s shocks and excitements, it's probably safe to say, were ephemeral, and the only thing lingering in aftertaste is John Malkovich's sneer. Despite the raves, I doubt anyone was seduced.

Now, trailing by a year, comes *Valmont*, Milos Forman's drawn-out collaboration with distinguished screenwriter Jean-Claude Carrière. It looks as if they want to bring back innocence. A generous, ambitious impulse.

If Frears's casting was perverse in one direction—actors teetering on the verge of self-parody—Forman's seems perverse for being so tame and pale. As archseducer Valmont, Colin Firth (a British actor suitably anemic in the creepy *Apartment Zero*) barely touches the screen. Annette Bening's homecoming queen of a Marquise de Merteuil has even less weight. Pretty in a brittle, all-American sorority girl way, Bening (whose only previous film credit is *The Great Outdoors* with John Candy and Dan Aykroyd) emits a tinkly cackle to punctuate her evildoing.

Meg (*Agnes of God*) Tilly, as the virtuous, stammering Mme. de Tourvel, at first looks so bland and sounds so dully sweet, it's hard to fathom Valmont's obsession. We watch the courtship bud while he is out punting and tries to entice her aboard his boat. When she refuses, he flops into the lake and has a water tantrum. (Forman's idea—remember Tom Hulce's Wolfie Mozart in *Amadeus*—is that childlike letting-go is not only charming but indicates genius.) With vulnerable Valmont patently in love from the beginning, Merteuil is left carrying the ball for evil and cool calculation. The deadly duo shows little rapport.

Fifteen-year-old Cécile de Volanges is shifted from the periphery to the center. She's the virgin whom Merteuil orders Valmont to seduce before the girl's arranged marriage to Merteuil's priggish lover (Jeffrey Jones). As Cécile, Fairuza Balk (born in California, not Saudi Arabia) is a plump, presexual, bug-eyed puppy dog. She clatters down marble staircases, stumbles and bumbles, and all but licks faces. (Forman's wonderful Czech comedies were populated by such mutts and mongrels. I notice in production materials that he once wrote a screenplay called *The Puppies*.)

The wholesome Cécile, fresh from the convent, is a remnant of real life, a clover in a terrarium of Venus's-flytraps. As representative of innocence, though, she's not very magnetic; it's difficult to get interested in the child's destiny. The same applies to her earnest harp teacher, Chevalier Danceny, played by *E.T.*'s Henry ("He came to *me!*") Thomas. Forman may intend a compassionate, less pompous *Liaisons*, but if so, he's got to supply more than a cast of vaguely amusing caricatures.

The test of a true *Liaisons* has to be a thrilling or devastating denouement, with desire, need, and weakness having their revenge on coldness and cynicism. But Valmont has been more or less human and sincere all along. And Merteuil in this version never really breaks. (I guess this is meant to be her tragedy.) Though there're some electric moments between Valmont and Mme. de Tourvel, the movie's final movement is lax and has a murky point of view.

The whole impression of deliberate stylelessness in *Valmont* never clarifies. Carrière's dialogue and Miroslav Ondricek's cinematography are incredibly plain. If Frears went mad with close-ups, Ondricek puts figures in a boring, washed-out middle distance. Sets—including the ostentatious love nest with dirty murals—are cluttered and monotonous. There isn't a line lively enough to quote. Obviously, this is intentional. I think that the Czech and Frenchman find our impoverished vocabulary sexy.

Also reviewed in:

NATION, 12/11/89, p. 727, Stuart Klawans
NEW REPUBLIC, 12/11/89, p. 24, Stanley Kauffmann
NEW YORK TIMES, 11/17/89, p. C20, Janet Maslin
NEW YORKER, 11/27/89, p. 105, Pauline Kael
VARIETY, 11/15/89, p. 20

VAMPIRE'S KISS

A Hemdale Film Corporation release. *Producer:* Barbara Zitwer and Barry Shills. *Director:* Robert Bierman. *Screenplay:* Joseph Minion. *Director of Photography:* Stefan Czapsky. *Editor:* Angus Newton. *Music:* Colin Towns. *Sound:* Rolf Pardula. *Sound Editor:* Robert Gavin. *Production Designer:* Christopher Nowak. *Art Director:* Ruth Ammon. *Set Decorator:* Jackie Jacobson. *Set Dresser:* Mark Hoxsie. *Costumes:* Irene Albright. *Make-up:* Hollywood DiRusso. *Special Make-up Effects:* Ed French. *Stunt Coordinator:* Peter Hock. *Running time:* 105 minutes. *MPAA Rating:* R.

CAST: Nicolas Cage (Peter Loew); Maria Conchita Alonso (Alva Restrepo); Jennifer Beals (Rachel); Elizabeth Ashley (Dr. Glazer); Kasi Lemmons (Jackie); Bob Lujan (Emilio); Jessica Lundy (Sharon); John Walker (Donald); Boris Leskin (Fantasy Cabbie); Michael Knowles (Andrew); John Michael Higgins (Ed); Jodie Markell (Joke Girl); Marc Coppola (Joke Guy); David Pierce (Theatre Guy); Amy Stiller (Theater Girl); Helen Lloyd Breed (Secretary in Ladies Room); Sol Echeverria (Alva's Mother); Jill Gatsby (Victim Girl); Rex Robbins (Sidney Langdon); Robert Dorfman (Editor #3); William DeAcutis (Editor #2); David Holbrook (Editor #1); Yanni Sfinnias (Cursing Cabbie); Rogerio Iriandade (Dr. Glazer's Lover); Robyn Kroll (Friday Secretary); Jacques Sandlescu (Ukrainian); Jorgen Schiott (Coffin Bystander); Christopher Sluka (Hanger Out); Stephen Chen (Fang Vendor); Jennifer Butt (Marriage Girl #2); Jennifer Spinner (Marriage Girl #1); Paul Sansone (Waiter); Cheryl Henry (Judy); Herschel Rosen (Man in Diner); Phil Ballou (Black Crooner); David McCarthy (Koch Bystander); Reggie Rock Bythewood (Church Bystander); Mark Oates (Apache Dancer); John Epperson (Apache Dancer); Jerry Rector (Larry); Pamela Dean Kenny (Bad Girl); Jonathan Gold (Boy).

LOS ANGELES TIMES, 6/2/89, Calendar/p. 4, Kevin Thomas

"Vampire's Kiss" is the kind of film that would self-destruct with a single false move. But in bringing Joseph Minion's mine-strewn script to the screen, British director Robert Bierman, in this theatrical feature debut, and his protean star Nicolas Cage never falter.

The result is a sleek, outrageous dark comedy that's all the funnier for constantly teetering on the brink of sheer tastelessness and silliness.

Cage is the Manhattan yuppie at his most obnoxious, a hotshot literary agent who browbeats his secretary (Maria Conchita Alonso), demanding that she concentrate on the pointless but herculean task of locating a 10-year-old missing contract. At the same time this jerk is so perplexed as to why his relationships with women are so shallow that he regularly sees a psychiatrist (cool, *soignée* Elizabeth Ashley), but he's a lousy, uncooperative patient. He's ripe for—and richly deserving of—falling victim to a sexy vampire (Jennifer Beals, perfectly cast).

As in his screenplay for Martin Scorcese's "After Hours," Minion has spun a contemporary morality play enclosed in humor and in which, in this instance, vampirism becomes a nifty metaphor for the rapaciousness of modern society. Thankfully, Bierman and Minion don't spell it out this baldly; indeed, "Vampire's Kiss" can be taken simply as a lively, imaginative fantasy.

From his first moment on the screen—it was in "Rumble Fish," in which he was gang leader Matt Dillon's treacherous lieutenant—Nicolas Cage has been full of capitvating surprises. Never before has so much been demanded of him. He must seem at once hatefully obnoxious yet pathetic in his progressive deterioration. Above all, he must *always* seem funny. Were he not, the film would be just too repellently venomous to contemplate.

But Cage carries everything with a manic intensity that plays with throwaway ease but must have required the utmost energy and concentration—not to mention spontaneity.

Alonso has a no less tricky assignment, as this most expressive of actresses succeeds in finding the humor in the mortification of the secretary. That this woman is a Latina who dares not quit her job makes it all the riskier to make her the object of such continual abuse. That the film makers get away with it is actually liberating; shrewdly, they've realized that if they proceeded timidly it would not have worked any more than soft-pedaling Cage's callous treatment of a beautiful young black woman (well-played by Kasi Lemmons) would have worked.

"Vampire's Kiss" (rated R for language, some sex) is not putting the bite on these women but on Cage's agent, whose absurd power-tripping nastiness characterizes so much of everyday life in the big city.

NEW YORK, 6/19/89, p. 68, David Debby

How would a debonair young New York literary agent behave if he thought he had been bitten by a beautiful vampire and was condemned to turn into a vampire himself? The agent (Nicolas Cage) would become more demanding, more hysterical, more manipulative and self-justifying. He would, in short, become the ultimate New Yorker.

Vampire's Kiss sets its familiar story in a realistic context: The young agent, Peter Loew, works in a high-powered office and spends his nights prowling the discos and bars, looking for love. He's a bundle of nerves, and when he can't find happiness, he complains to his shrink (Elizabeth Ashley). On the town one night, he picks up a disco doll (Jennifer Beals), and after she bites his neck in the throes of passion, he becomes convinced that she's a ghoul who has truned him into her unwilling slave. The way screenwriter Joseph Minion (*After Hours*) and young British director Robert Bierman have developed the story, it's left ambiguous whether Peter has really been vampirized or is imagining the whole thing. The *Post*'s David Edelstein, who saw the movie in an earlier version, claims that the emotional roots of Peter's dilemma were a lot clearer before the studio, Hemdale, began recutting the movie. But I found that the confusion on this point didn't destroy my great pleasure in *Vampire's Kiss*.

Whether taken as a straight horror film or as a psychological nightmare with erotic overtones, *Vampire's Kiss* mixes fable and satire in startling, and satisfying, ways. Once Peter Loew has been bitten, his new ravenousness is just an extension of his normally hyper New York life. The movie works out the familiar Nosferatu legend realistically, and the more horrifying and tragic Peter's situation, the wilder and funnier the working out becomes. In the end, Peter is reduced to walking around SoHo distraught, blood on his jaws from the previous night's search, and the passersby shrug him off as a slovenly nut case—just another New York biter. The always-thirsty Peter is every bit as suited to New York as the eccentrics in the remake of *Invasion of the Body Snatchers*, trying to hold on to their individuality, were suited to San Francisco.

Cage, with his light, hoarse voice and whipped-dog eyes, has been almost too strange for some of the ordinary-man heroes he has played (he nearly wrecked *Peggy Sue Got Married*). But as an urban swinger convinced that he requires, very late at night, a neck to bite, he's inspired. Cage doesn't spoof the vampire story the way George Hamilton did in the genial *Love at First Bite*. He makes Peter Loew an intelligent and humane man deeply horrified by what's happening to him. Yet Peter can't stop himself, and after a while, trying to provoke his secretary into murdering him, he doesn't want to stop himself. He becomes both crazy and self-hating, his situation a mix of the repulsive and the ludicrous. Here he is, the smartest young executive in New York (and Peter may be based on a well-known agent of rapacious habits), carrying plump pigeons home under his Italian suits.

Cage is still very young, only 24 when he shot the movie, and he goes all the way with his ideas; he's an actor without restraint or ballast. He gives the agent, who has long, slicked-down hair, a fey, mid-Atlantic New York-publishing accent, and the accent made me recall some of Cage's earlier performances that were verbally unsteady (physically, he's always been amazing). But the accent takes hold; Peter uses the feyness as a come-on

After Peter has been bitten, he begins goading his chaste, dutiful, and God-fearing Hispanic secretary (Maria Conchita Alonso) into working harder and harder at a ridiculous task. The goading has a demonic drive to it, and Cage, fresh in every scene, reaches outré height. Sometimes he just pitches his laugh a little too high or makes bug eyes. But he also does wild parodies of business-executive peremptoriness, punctuating his outbursts of bullying irony by thrusting out his arms or jumping on a desk. The other people in the office find him peculiar but not enough to require help—the executive could be on cocaine or just rabid in standard New York style. Director Robert Bierman and composer Colin Towns support Cage with an atmosphere of pervasive Manhattan anxiety.

Cage realizes the broadest license, but his sense of Peter as a suffering man keeps the flights from spinning out of orbit. His work is like a fantasia, a set of free musical variations, and it's painful and funny at the same time. Indeed, the whole movie stays on the high wire, never falling into low farce or ordinary screeching horror. Perhaps it's the combined tension and ambiguity, in place of the usual simplicities, that has accounted for so many of the stupidly uncomprehending reviews. Despite its problems, *Vampire's Kiss* is one of the few accomplished and original American movies released this year.

NEW YORK POST, 6/2/89, p. 23, David Edelstein

Pretentious singers bill themselves as "song stylists"; the actor Nicolas Cage, who plays a yuppie editor conviced he's a bloodsucker in the eccentric psychodrama "Vampire's Kiss," must think of himself as a "role stylist."

Cages performing has a demented, hyperbolic integrity, he lets the madness of his parts infuse him and carry him off into gaga-land. He wants to fill every moment until it bursts, and he turns his characters' tantrums into jazzy, swelling riffs.

In the process, he leaves reality in the dust, and that may turn off viewers raised on a diet of cool American realism. More dangerously, Cage doesn't take pains to make contact with an audience, so in a film as difficult or fragmented as "Vampire's Kiss" he runs the risk of acting in a vacuum.

The movie is off-putting—it's hard to get on its or Cage's wave length. Written by Joseph Minion ("After Hours"), it's another downward spiral into madness, althought this time it isn't the world that goes mad but Peter Loew (Cage), a man who can't find a way to relate to women.

Bitten in bed by a gorgeous vampire (Jennifer Beals) who may or may not be imaginary, Loew feels himself becoming a bloodsucker. By day he terrorizes a hapless secretary (Maria Conchita Alonso) in his office, bullying her obsessively over a misplaced contract; by night he haunts the streets and nightclubs, thinking of—and stalking—women.

Fascination with vampirism is clearly this lunatic's way of coping with his isolation, much as it is in George Romero's disturbing "Martin." ("Vampire's Kiss" is like a cross between "Martin" and "Bright Lights, Big City.") Hurting and subduing someone is the only means he has of making contact—the only road out of the hell of his solipsism.

The film could be a response to the new cliché, "Women—you can't live with 'em, you can't kill 'em." What you can do is ingest them, Loew concludes—drink their blood.

When I first saw "Vampire's Kiss" at an early screening (about nine months ago), the cause of Loew's craziness was torturously clear. Seeing it again recently, after it had been trimmed by its studio, Hemdale, I was horrified. Many scenes have been snipped short, and gone are most of Loew's sessions with his psychiatrist (Elizabeth Ashley).

The result is that much of the action is inexplicable. Since the audience doesn't, early on, understand what's bugging Loew, it can't get a handle on his transformation—on his rejection of a friendly, attentive lover (nicely played by Kasi Lemmons), his trashing of his apartment, his sadistic treatment of the secretary.

And people might not realize how deeply Cage connects with Loew (or "Loo," as he pronounces it), how stupendous a performance this truly is.

He's an unnerving sight. Cage's face is waxen and his eyes seem turned around, facing in. His ears stick out like a rodent's; when stalking his prey, slightly hunch-backed, he conjures up the rat-headed Max Schreck in the silent classic "Nosferatu."

But Cage also has the daring, bug-eyed grandeur of John Barrymore in "Dr. Jekyll and Mr. Hyde" and the slapstick bravura of Jerry Lewis in "The Nutty Professor." Somehow, and this is Cage's genius, the outrageous mannerisms and the inner life of his character mesh.

In the throes of his final fantasy, when Loew meets the girl of his dreams (witty Jessica Lundy) in his shrink's office, Cage is wrenching, suffused with happiness and self-possession, delivered at last.

The director, Robert Bierman, leaps back and forth from Loew's sleek, commanding fantasy self to the bloodied, whacked-out Loew on the street—talking to the air, woozily immersed in his daydream. Only then do we fully comprehend the allure of Loew's private world.

"Vampire's Kiss," in its final cut, doesn't work, but the movie is still like nothing you've ever seen. Bierman and photographer Stefan Czapsky do miraculous things with the New York skyline, framing pieces of buildings so that they look in the setting sun like battlements of a Transylvanian castle. And Colin Towns' music is sublime, a blood wedding of Gershwin and Hammer horror.

NEWSDAY, 6/2/89, Part III/p. 3, Lynn Darling

"Vampire's Kiss" begins with a nice irony: A cold-blooded sexual predator gets his comeuppance when he becomes enslaved by a beautiful, voracious ghoul in a black garter belt. From the beginning, the vampire legend has depended on its subversive sexual content; the best movies made from the myth have exploited its underlying erotic message to great effect, often in ways that mirror the prevailing mores: By the time Frank Langella played Dracula in the late '70s, the worldly decadent Count who preyed upon the virginal Lucy in Bram Stoker's Victorian novel had become her sexual liberator.

This time around, the victim is a super-yuppie literary agent whose callous self-regard incorporates a wide streak of sadism. Peter Loew (Nicolas Cage) spends his nights trolling the bars for beautiful women. To his shrink (Elizabeth Ashley), he bemoans his inability to feel anything but a fleeting passion for the women he brings home for the night. In his office, Loew spends most of his time berating a hapless secretary (Maria Conchita Alonso) who has been unable to locate a long-missing literary contract.

Loew's life begin to fall apart when he picks up Rachel (Jennifer Beals), an attractive young woman whose sexual tastes include a particularly draining sort of love bite. Soon Loew is convinced that Rachel is a vampire, and that he himself is well on his way toward becoming one.

Director Robert Bierman loads up his feature-film debut with scenes that emphasize the sexual jungle in which Loew operates—there are the trendy bars where the hunter and the hunted find one another, and even a couple of Apache dancers performing their dance of sexual conquest and violence on the street. But before long "Vampire's Kiss" drops any pretensions toward the meditation on sexual warfare it seemingly sets out to be. Instead, the movie concentrates on becoming a campy compilation of histrionics and ludicrous plotting.

Loew goes about the business of becoming a vampire with an earnest if not entirely successful dedication. He buys a cheap set of plastic vampire fangs and starts practicing his bloodletting on unsuspecting pigeons. He upends his couch and turns it into a makeshift coffin. Eventually he starts searching for victims in the crowded reaches of a Downtown discotheque, where, naturally, his wild eyes, fangs and distraught expression rate barely a backward glance.

Any claims to ambiguity, mystery, drama or suspense this movie might have made are convincingly blown out of the water by Cage's amazing bizarre performance. His eyes bugged out, his shoulders hunched, his arms launched in a continual series of spasmodic gestures, Cage makes Bela Lugosi's Dracula look like Cary Grant. Halfway through the movie, it is impossible to believe that Cage could take his performance any farther over the top; there's a certain weird fascination in watching him contradict that assumption. By comparison, Alonso's performance as the innocent secretary terrorized by Loew's increasingly mad behavior is nicely restrained, while Beals seems barely to flicker on the screen.

VILLAGE VOICE, 6/13/89, p. 68, Stuart Klawans

Having sent Griffin Dunne on a nightmare journey through Soho in *After Hours*, screenwriter Joseph Minion now sets a still more fiendish trial for the white, moneyed American male. Here is the movie that asks the question: Is there any difference between a vampire and a sexually aroused yuppie?

Peter Loew (Nicolas Cage) speaks with an affected mid-Atlantic accent, thinks of women as toys, and abuses his secretary. For this, he receives the curse of the Undead. One night, while cruising the bars, he makes the mistake of chatting up Rachel (Jennifer Beals), who turns out to have excellent taste in lingerie and a mean pair of incisors. Peter struggles; then he begins to gasp, "Yes, yes." He's discovered her at last—the woman he'll still want to see in the morning. There is, unfortunately, this little problem with the sunlight.

Nevertheless, for the first time in his life, Peter makes a commitment to a person, or whatever. Though shocked at her identity, he tries to please Rachel. If that means aspiring to Undeadness for himself, then at least he has the comfort of living in Manhattan, where you can run down the street screaming, "I'm a vampire!" and nobody will even look at you.

On one level, then, *Vampire's Kiss* is about the degradtion men will suffer for a sufficiently sexy woman. On another, it is about the infantilism that lurks behind romantic love and corporate swinishness alike. To Rachel, Peter is a hopelessly servile admirer; to his secretary Alva (Maria Conchita Alonso), he is the Boss From Hell. What links his two personas is a brattish self-satisfaction that merely becomes more pronounced during Peter's metamorphosis. Trying to become Nosferatu, he turns instead into just another obnoxious ex-preppie, wearing dark glasses and thinking he's cool.

Cage brings to the role the dumbfounded stare he used to such advantage in *Raising Arizona*, plus a heretofore unseen talent for middle-class sleaze. By far the creepiest moments of *Vampire's Kiss* are the scenes in which he browbeats Alonso; among the funniest, in a film full of delirious humor, is the scene in which he treats his psychiatrist (Elizabeth Ashley) to a sputtering, arm-waving tantrum all because she's suggested a paper in his office might have been misfiled.

When *After Hours* came out, it was natural to ask how much of the film's nasty, nervous energy came from Minion and how much from Martin Scorsese. Now we know. Robert Bierman, directing his first theatrical feature in *Vampire's Kiss*, acquits himself well, particularly when he has the wisdom to let events develop in long takes. Even so, his technique is unobtrusive enough to let you see Minion's stamp. He has proposed, in the most unsettling terms, that when some men go looking for true love, all hell's to pay. Pretty funny; pretty gruesome.

Also reviewed in:
NEW YORK TIMES, 6/2/89, p. C11, Caryn James
NEW YORKER, 6/12/89, p. 105, Pauline Kael
VARIETY, 9/21/88, p. 31
WASHINGTON POST, 6/2/89, P. D7, Hal Hinson

VERY MORAL NIGHT, A

A Hungarofilm release of a Dialog Filmstudio production. *Director:* Karoly Makk. *Screenplay (Hungarian with English subtitles):* Istvan Orkeny and Peter Bacso. *Based on the short story "The House with the Red Light" by:* Sandor Hunyady. *Director of Photography:* Janos Toth. *Editor:* Gyorgy Sivo. *Sound:* Janos Reti. *Art Director:* Tamas P. Balassa. *Set Decorator:* Tamas Vayer. *Costumes:* Emoke Czengey. *Running time:* 99 minutes. *MPAA Rating:* Not Rated.

CAST: Margit Makay (Mother); Iren Psota ("Momma"); Carla Romanelli (Bella); Gyorgyi Tarjan (Darinka); Gyorgy Cserhalmi (Kelepey).

MONTHLY FILM BULLETIN, 5/85, p. 151, Simon Ubsdell

A small town in Hungary, early this century. The girls of the local brothel return in the early evening from a visit to the theatre. Chatting excitedly and thanking "Momma", the madam, for their outing, they prepare for the coming night's work. Among the regular clients is Kelepey, a young student, known affectionately to the girls as "Doctor", who lives on a small allowance from his elderly widowed mother. He is a particular favourite with Darinka, who persuades him to stay the night when a violent storm breaks out. The following day, Momma suggests that he take up permanent residence in the house in preference to his more expensive lodgings. As a tenant, Kelepey becomes more than ever the focus of the girls' attentions, especially Darinka's.

But the idyll is interrupted one day when Kelepey's mother decides to pay him a surprise visit. Not finding her son at home, she innocently assumes the brothel to be a boarding-house, and Momma hastily orders the girls to help her sustain the illusion. The uneasy calm is shattered later that evening when the highly strung Bella tries to commit suicide, horrified at the prospect of becoming old and wrinkled like Mrs. Kelepey (though after the doctor has left, it is Mrs. Kelepey who comforts her). The bordello's clients have meanwhile begun to arrive, but the doors remain shut. Kelepey is nowhere to be found, but his mother is determined not to leave without seeing him. Two of the girls comb the town and eventually discover him at an inn watching a game of cards. He is rushed back to the bordello, but the card players decide to follow him and burst in demanding attention. Kelepey manages to extricate his mother and take her to the station without arousing her suspicions further, while Momma and the girls resume their work.

A Very Moral Night is a curious piece of work on several counts: an unexpected and disappointing exception to the courageous commitment to contemporary social and political issues of Károly Makk's more recent *Love, Behind the Brick Wall* and *Another Way*; and an oddly slight treatment of an intrinsically vigorous if undemanding theme. It has not simply retreated to the politically safe years of the early twentieth century, but regressed to the padded security of a sanitised brothel peopled with the golden-hearted whores and mild-mannered debauchees of comfortable stereotype. The essence of the Sándor Hunyady story is the stuff of low farce—ribald misunderstandings, bawdy *double entendres*, outrageous reversals. And yet Makk appears to have studiedly muted the comic potentialities of his material and aimed instead at a film of gentle pathos and faded lyriciam—an irrelevant if attractive piece of escapism.

His bright-eyed courtesans radiate an almost pubertal innocence more appropriate to a finishing school for girls, fluttering admiringly round the Miss Jean Brodie figure of "Momma", the proper procuress (she even takes her charges on improving excursions to the theatre). Darinka, climbing into bed with Kelepey, coyly insists on their both wearing nightshirts, and they duly pass a night of immaculate chastity. The transformation of the bordello into an innocent boarding-house is itself accomplished with disconcerting ease—the debauchery of the brothel is made to seem as much of an insubstantial pageant as the charade of social propriety which the girls stage with such ready fluency.

As ever, Makk shows a cunning deftness in his observation of human frailties, and an unmistakeable humanity, most strikingly evident in the magically economical performance of Margit Makay as the innocent but worldly wise Mrs. Kelepey. And there is a characteristic subtlety to the visualisation, with outstanding cinematography by János Tóth, the camera prowling voyeuristically, restlessly, through the claustrophobic darkness of the interior, peeping through parted curtains and half-opened doors, watching the wicks of oil lamps flaring and subsiding with the fitful progress of the night's business. But the prying camera has objectionable implications: the subjective technique invites us to indict the director himself as the sheepish peeping Tom. The film bears the unfortunate taint of a rather effete prurience, and its premise of a benign and enlightened matriarchy flourishing within the walls of an innocent bordello is far too coy to convince.

NEW STATESMAN, 4/12/85, p. 28, John Coleman

Compared with the magnificent *Love* (1970) and his more recent *Another Way* (1982), which was widely reckoned for its bravery in exploring a lesbian affair between an intransigent young journalist and her married colleague, the Hungarian director Karoly Makk's *A Very Moral Night* is a slight and safe entertainment for all that its setting is a brothel. Like many of his colleagues, Makk has often warily shifted the subject-matter of his films back in time: *Love* took place in the Budapest of 1953, *Another Way* was located in 1958. The "new" movie, made in 1977, is ravishingly period, small-town and—to judge from the high-buttoned clothes—early this century. Kelepey, respectfully called "Doctor" by the brothel's inmates, actually an indigent and dissolute student living off money despatched by his village mama, has a charm not too readily apparent to the spectator but swampingly sufficient for one of the whores, delicious Darinka, to write a "Dear Istvan" letter to her fiancé and for the madam herself to offer him board and lodging.

Elegantly mounted and shot, with the bordello an enticing affair of shuttered rooms opening on a courtyard and staffed by a picturesque hunchback piano-player and beautiful golden-hearted whores, the piece is a nostalgically upholstered anecdote (it originated in a short story) given its twist by the unexpected arrival of Kelepley's elderly, innocent but country-wise widowed mother (Margit Makay). During a hectic day and night the pretence is maintained that the brothel's a sedate boarding-house, local dignitaries hastily button lips and flies, to be introduced to unsuspecting Mrs Kelepey; the old woman at last departs, but not before dispensing folk comfort to a suicidal tart. Makk conducts the fairly roseate revels with panache, exploiting their pleasant possibility for innuendo ("When is bedtime?" asks Mrs K.), giving us a cut-throat card-game at a neighbouring tavern as bonus.

NEW YORK POST, 3/17/89, p. 26, Jami Bernard

"A Very Moral Night" starts out with a very immoral night, where the staff of a turn-of-the-century Hungarian brothel, clad in lace and silks and less, play hostess to the usual clientele. Breaking glass, slapped rumps, games of "horsey" fill out the evening, business as usual. At the end of the night, hostesses and patrons alike are sprawled, exhausted, in all states of undress and intoxication.

But when the staid and simple mother of the brothel's most favored permanent resident, a handsome young art student, comes to town, the girls have to play a role more outrageous than anything their clients have asked them to do—pretend they are members of an above-board boarding house, so that mom will not cut off sonny's funds.

This sets the stage for a rollicking, not quite-bawdy comedy by Karoly Makk, lushly photographed so that the screen looks as velvet as the tapestries.

Most of the fun resides in the Madam's attempts to rein in her flock as the nighttime guests begin pummeling at the door and as one of the prostitutes, afraid of growing old, attempts suicide.

Meanwhile, the innocent mother tries to make sense of this household full of very fancy linen, beautiful unmarried girls, strange comings and goings and more.

"Moral Night" is truly luscious-looking. When the movie opens, the whole house has been treated by Madam to a night at the theater; they look like any group of giggling schoolgirls dressed in their finest. Then they march upstairs to change, and as the theater clothes come off, they langorously smooth their stockings up their thighs (or "thigs," as the occasionally inept subtitles tell us), trail their fingers in lavender-scented washbasins, pin flowers in their hair, examine their own undulating bodies, and emerge fully prepared for anyone from the tentative virginal boy to the foot fetishist.

If their view of men is somewhat dim because of their line of work—one viciously kicks a john's hat off her bed after their session—they are all united by an adoring puppy-love for the student, "Doc" Kelepey. Even the Madam is taken with his charms, and he soon wheedles room and board from her for less than he has been paying at another place.

Doc's arrival on the scene energizes the ladies during the day as they cannot be energized at night. They feed him, cater to him, steal into his room to watch him sleep. They all go goofy and girlish over him. One even breaks off her engagement to a lame shoemaker back home because she so enjoys rowing on the river with Doc.

And that is why, when Doc's diminutive, inquisitive mother appears, they all pull together to try to persuade her that Doc is leading a blameless life, although certainly appearances (and manners) are against them.

There are some hilarious, understated moments as the girls make gaffes and as the countrywise mother tries to counsel the would-be suicide. Those scenes, plus an interesting take on sexuality, make "A Very Moral Night" a visual treat.

Also reviewed in:
NEW YORK TIMES, 3/17/89, p. C18, Richard Bernstein
VARIETY, 5/10/78, p. 26

VIRGIN MACHINE

A First Run Features release of a Hyena Film production. *Director:* Monika Treut. *Screenplay (German with English subtitles):* Monika Treut. *Editor:* Renate Merck. *Music:* Mona Mur, Laibach, Blazing Redheads, and Pearl Harbour. *Sound:* Alf Olbrisch. *Running time:* 85 minutes. *MPAA Rating:* Not Rated.

CAST: Ina Blum (Dorothee Müller); Marcelo Uriona (Bruno, Dorothee's Brother); Gad Klein (Heinz); Peter

Kern (Hormone Specialist); Dominique Gaspar (Dominique); Susie "Sexpert" Bright (Susie Sexpert); Shelly Mars (Ramona/Male Impersonator); Hans-Christoph Blumenberg (Man on the Phone); Carla Wood-Saivre (Woman in Hotel Room); Fakir Musafar (Man in Hotel Room); Marvin Moss (Gallery Owner); Rosanne Johnson (Waitress); Nan Kinney (Woman at Door); Steve Mobia (Taxi Driver); Fanny Fatal (Stripper); Flora Gaspar (Woman in the Kitchen); Pearl Harbour (Visitor); Mona Mur (Singer in the Bar).

LOS ANGELES TIMES, 6/2/89, Calendar/p. 4, Kevin Thomas

Don't look for fair play for men in Monika Treut's "Virgin Machine"—but then you shouldn't take this lesbian comedy from West Germany too seriously in the first place. It has its funny moments, but it also meanders.

Lovely, dark-eyed Ina Blum stars as Dorothee Müller, a young Hamburg would-be journalist who decides to research the true nature of romantic love with an amusingly Teutonic zeal. Not getting anywhere, she takes off for San Francisco, ostensibly in search of her long-absent mother, but instead she discovers her own true nature in the more uninhibited portion of the city's lesbian communtiy. No wonder she responds to these down-to-earth, free-spirited women: back home she's been having a half-hearted affair with a portly, middle-aged man and a more passionate one with her gay half-brother.

"Virgin Machine" is fairly slack and at times downright self-consciously amateurish; consequently, most welcome are the crisp presence of Susie Sexpert, who has a terrific—and hilarious—spiel on sex toys and on the joys of female strip shows for women only, and Shelly Mars, an outrageous male impersonator with whom Dorothee falls precipitously in love.

Why a woman as attractive as Dorothee should have submitted to either the boyfriend or her epicene half-brother is never clear; it would seem that, like her heroine, Treut herself succumbed to San Francisco's open ways. Somehow lesbian/feminist Treut's concern with arguing the virtues of lesbian love over heterosexual love got lost in transit. In any event, "Virgin Machine" (Times rated Mature for adult situations, some sex and nudity) ends up a good-natured, liberated sexual romp, and in this it surely succeeds.

NEW YORK POST, 2/10/89, p. 21, Jami Bernard

Dorothee is a gonzo journalist hot on the trail of one of those trendy magazine-type stories about the meaning of love. Specifically, romantic love, the kind Dorothee hopes to come to terms with by researching it.

She's not getting any answers, at least not in her native West Germany, where she's bored to tears by her fat, nose-picking ex-lover Heinz (a thankless role played by a real-life film critic), and excited by her half-brother. A hormone specialist she interviews speaks longingly of chemicals and the womb. She watches pairs of lovers with detached bafflement.

Dorothee takes off for San Francisco to continue her research and track down her mother, who fades quickly and mercifully from the script. I don't know what magazine employs this Dorothee—maybe the one from "Crocodile Dundee" that sent Linda Kozlowski to Australia to do a feature on an alligator wrestler—but there among the strip joints and the lesbian community, the journalist discovers a new kind of love.

Not romantic, necessarily, but liberating.

This is "Virgin Machine," an episodic back-&-white film from director Monika Treut, who has previously made films called "Bondage" and "Seduction: The Cruel Woman."

Treut manages a grittily picaresque tale as Dorothee gradually learns about alternative forms of sex by spying on her sado-masochistic neighbors, hanging out at a strip palace on Ladies Only night, and listening to a torch singer.

She learns the intricacles of sexual implements from "Susie Sexpert," a bespectacled traveling saleslady with a briefcase full of paraphernalia. This movie has an abundance of film critics; Sexpert plies that trade for Penthouse Forum. Maybe old film critics don't die, they just get parts in art films.

At last, Dorothee falls for male impersonator Ramona, played by performance artist Shelly Mars. The most memorable scene in the film is Mars' unflinching rendition of a man in full sexual throttle, using only a shaken bottle of warm beer to illustrate her point. Her facial expressions run the gamut from leering lust to hang-dog shame; it's a marvelous, shocking little scene that makes some of the other scenes look a little drab and puritanical by comparison.

Dorothee is played by Ina Blum, who has appeared in two Rosa von Praunheim films. Wearing a lopsided dark cap of Louise Brooks hair, Blum gradually loses the morose introspection that plagues her in the first part of the film. Once she lands in the Tenderloin, she's like a wide-eyed tourist.

Although her affair with Ramona seems to liberate her from her obsession with romantic love—and maybe from her magazine deadline as well, since she never picks up a pen—the sex scene is pretty tame compared with Mars' no-holds-barred performance. The film is uneven, and possibly more interesting in theory than in the theater.

NEWSDAY, 2/10/89, Part III/p. 3, Lynn Darling

Monika Treut has no icons—in "Virgin Machine," one woman's odyssey through her own illusions, she manages to skewer every cherished hetero- and homosexual notion about the power and the exalted status of love. There's a robust sense of humor to this movie, one that helps it over its sometimes roughshod approach to plot and transition.

"Virgin Machine" follows the adventures of Dorothee Muller (Ina Blum), an ingenuous young journalist conducting an investigation into the nature of romantic love. Muller's interest in the subject is more than academic. She's bored by the jealous attentions of her ex-lover, a doughy magazine editor, and she's a tad ambivalent about her affair with her half-brother Bruno.

Muller consults everyone from a hormone expert to the chimps in the zoo in her efforts to understand the origins of love, but it's not until she arrives in America that her research really begins to pay off. Before long, she's immersed in the more freewheeling circles of San Francisco's lesbian community, where she is initiated into the nature of her own heart.

Along the way, Muller is educated into the function and variety of sex toys by a streetside proselytizer (Susie [Sexpert] Bright), taken on a rollercoaster tour of pragmatic passion by a gorgeous male impersonator (Shellery Mars), and introduced to the other side of the footlights in a strip show performed for an appreciative all-female audience. Bit by bit, Muller's belief in the all-encompassing nature of romantic love is systematically shredded, even as her capacity for hope remains undiminished.

Treut doesn't come to a lot of meaningful conclusions through all of this, though she does give an exuberant sendoff to the idea that lesbian love is by its very nature superior to the snares and delusions inherent in any of the other varieties. But the movie's wry, ready-for-anything tone is intriguing even when Muller's adventures don't prove to be all that revelatory.

Filmed in grainy black and white and a whir of slightly manic camera angles, "Virgin Machine" comes up with an offbeat portrait of an America that looks particularly wacky and enticing after the claustrophobic, static Germany Treut presents. The spirit of the film resonates particularly through the presence of Ina Blum, whose wide-eyed adventurer is a beguiling combination of '20s vamp and '80s liberated woman.

VILLAGE VOICE, 2/14/89, p. 64, Amy Taubin

The showstopper in Monika Treut's *Virgin Machine* is Shelly Mars, a San Francisco male impersonator and stripper whose act climaxes when she sticks a well-shaken beer bottle in her boxer shorts and lets it spew. Mars's performing persona suggests an after-hours Lily Tomlin, or Patti Smith in her Keith Richard phase. But where Smith's primary means of expression—her voice—was buoyed up by a few obsessively repeated macho gestures, Mars is a mime who tells all through precise and subtle body language, tippy-toeing between irony and lewdness in a moustache, fedora, and nattily tailored suit.

Mars is one of three guides whom Dorothee (Ina Blum), the desultory heroine of *Virgin Machine*, encounters when she leaves Germany for the Oz of San Francisco in search of her long-lost mother and the meaning of love. ("I was dreaming of romantic love, that sickness my mother also had.") Dorothee, a sometime journalist, surrounds herself with chinoiserie and goes to interviews decked out in off-the-shoulder beaded thrift store numbers and Louise Brooks blackened eyelids and helmeted hair. Bicycling the Hamburg streets past grimy lowering brick buildings, she makes mental notes for a book on love, in the hope that the research will cure her of the malady. Indeed, Dorothee's life is one long *liebestod*. Relentlessly pursued by her rotund ex-boyfriend ("It didn't work with Heinz. Is that why he got so fat?"), who jealously searches her bed for other men's pubic hair, she spends her nights in a deserted bar sighing after the chanteuse (Mona Mur) or fooling around with her brother Bruno (Marcelo Fabian Uriona), singing ditties about incest ("The one that Pa did it with has done herself in"). Bruno's suggestion—that Mom would love to see her daughter—has an immediate plotploy effect. Within seconds, Dorothee is knocking on the door of a clapboard SRO, only to discover that the object of her quest ("Oh, yeah, that old German woman") has moved, leaving no forwarding address.

Dorothee takes up residence in the Tenderloin, where she watches a lot of television, peeps in on the bizarre sex rituals of her neighbors, and does some more traditional sightseeing. She meets Susie Sexpert (Susie Bright), the barker for an all-girl strip show and designer of custom-made dildoes, and Dominique (Dominique Gaspar), another displaced Gerrman whose boss, a bearded gallery owner, characterizes himself as the "king of porn." A galumphing, forthright charmer given to button-down shirts and ties, Dominique lives with her sister and her one true love—a scrappy tomcat she has rescued from the garbage. Dominique advises Dorothee to give up on romance and stick to having fun, a tactic belied by her own interest in "cupping," a blood cleansing procedure practiced by a Chinatown doc that leaves her with silver dollar-sized welts all over her body. One night, Dorothee goes to Dominique's for dinner (the entertainment—an improvised conga line—is the film's understated high point), and later, everyone goes to a "women only" club filled with butch/fem couples, many in s&m drag. There, Dorothee becomes infatuated with the debonair Mars. It's inevitable.

Treut, who also wrote the script, is an agile, intelligent director who moves easily between feverish fantasy and grubby reality. She relishes both the phrase that ironically undercuts an image (or vice versa), and the juxtaposition of incompatible points of view. In all of this, she is abetted by Elfi Mikesch's lush and evocative black-and-white cinematography.

Virgin Machine makes the most of its girls-just-want-to-have-fun moments, but backs away from its initial testing of deeper waters. Just as Dorothee abandons the search for her mother at the first obstacle, Treut gives up on her serious investigation of romance and sexuality. When Dorothee surfaces like a dazzled tourist on the wilder shores of San Francisco's lesbian community, Treut seems to be just along for the ride, having lost her critical consciousness mid-Atlantic. But please, someone, bring out the soundtrack (music by Blazing Redheads, Pearl Harbor, Laibach, and Mona Mur).

Also reviewed in:
NEW YORK TIMES, 2/10/89, p. C15, Caryn James
VARIETY, 3/1–7/89, p. 18

VOICES FROM THE ATTIC

A Jane Balfour presentation of a Siren Pictures production. *Producer:* Debbie Goodstein. *Director:* Debbie Goodstein. *Screenplay:* Debbie Goodstein and Jim Butler. *Director of Photography:* Oren Rudavsky. *Editor:* Toby Shimin. *Music:* Ken Mazur and Russ Landau. *Sound:* David Leitner. *Running Time:* 60 minutes. *MPAA Rating:* Not Rated.

NEW YORK POST, 5/12/89, p. 29, Jami Bernard

Young film maker Debbie Goodstein traveled back to the small town in Poland where her mother and 15 other relatives were sheltered in a cramped farmhouse attic for two years during World War II. They could not make noise or stand up; there were no toilets; in the winter it snowed on them and in the summer it sweltered. All but two survived.

Goodstein made this emotional pilgrimage to the attic of her mother's youth and her own subconscious along with her Aunt Sally (her mother backed out at the last minute; the trip would be too painful) and five cousins. The result is "Voices From the Attic," an intensely personal and moving documentary that seeks to understand some harsh truths and expiate long-hidden fears.

"My mother would never talk about this experience, but I knew it must have shaped her life, and I felt it shaping mine," narrates Goodstein as the brave little band sets out on its journey. "I was haunted by stories I never heard."

It turns out she and her cousins all have a fear of small, cramped places, including subways; the movie is as much about the osmosis of a parent's personal history into the subconscious of a child as about anti-Semitism and those Polish peasants who selflessly and not-so-selflessly protected Jews from the Nazis.

Sally Frishberg—or Aunt Sally—is a fearless raconteur. "It's a terribly painful subject," she says. Nevertheless, she holds kin and camera spellbound with unembroidered stories of life in that attic, and is filmed as she goes up to Mrs. Grocholski, the aging peasant woman whose attic it was, and hugs her for the first time since the war. (The woman is both touched and wounded; "You never wrote!" she complains.)

The film does not gloss over the fact that this very woman had to be bought off with everything Aunt Sally's family owned in the world before allowing them in her attic; neither does it hide the real tears that come into the woman's aged eyes when she is introduced to the offspring of the people she and her husband spared.

At least one mystery is solved by the trip—Goodstein finds out what happened to her mother's baby sister, the relative whose fate has never been discussed. The truth is a real heartbreaker, and it is the one time Aunt Sally breaks down and cries.

Anti-Semitism didn't die after the war; just as Goodstein has inherited the defiance and fear of her own parents, so have the children of the Polish village claimed their own inheritance. The visiting film crew is greeted by a "Heil, Hitler" from a boy on a bicycle and a painted swastika on the door of the old family farmhouse. If the visit to Poland is not as ultimately cathartic as maybe Goodstein had hoped, at least it sheds light on the dark corners of the attics that many inhabit all their lives.

If you have the least bit of sensitivity, you'll need a Kleenex while watching "Voices From the Attic." If your life, or those of your family, were in any way touched by the Holocaust, you'll need a whole box.

NEWSDAY, 5/12/89, Part III/p. 5, Lynn Darling

"Voices from the Attic" has a powerful story to tell: In 1942, 16 members of one Jewish family in Poland bribed a peasant family to hide them in the small attic of their farmhouse for what they thought would be a couple of weeks. They hid there for two years. Eventually, after the war, they immigrated to the United States, where they assimilated smoothly, it seemed, into the country's postwar prosperity.

But the scars cut deep, not only among the survivors, but among their children. "I was haunted by stories I had never heard," director Debbie Goodstein, a daughter of one of the survivors, says in the voice-over narration to her first film. She and her siblings and cousins inherited the trauma of their parents' ordeal: They dreamt of concentration camps, became frightened in small enclosed places, found themselves on the lookout for quick exits.

To try to make sense of the memories and fragments of experience that had helped to define her life, Goodstein traveled with five cousins and an aunt, one of the women who had survived the attic, back to the family's hometown in Poland. "Voices From the Attic" is the story of the fears Goodstein hoped to confront and the catharsis she hoped to find in the journey back.

The centerpiece of Goodstein's film is her Aunt Sally Frishberg, who was 9 years old when she went to the attic to live. A blunt, formidable woman who has learned well the harsh lessons that history has taught her, Frishberg leads the little group back into her own nightmares, ready with admirable fearlessness to confront the past.

With Frishberg leading the way, telling stories, recognizing landmarks, interviewing creased, ruddyfaced peasant women, the cousins try to give shape and gravity to the fears that have informed their lives. They walk along country roads that have probably changed little since the war; their American clothes and cameras and bags contrast tellingly with the images Frishberg conjures of their mothers and fathers walking these same roads in fear, all their worldly possessions in hand.

Goodstein is no sentimentalist: Young boys on bicycles shout "Heil Hitler" at the group as they leave one house, and word of their mission begins to circulate. Perhaps, she says, they have inherited hatred the way she and her family inherited fear.

It's too bad there aren't more such insights. This is a slight film, in part because much of what we learn about Goodstein's family and their experiences we learn second-hand, through her narration: Other than Aunt Sally, the members of her family appear only fleetingly in the film, and we get little sense of who they are, what their lives and values are like, how they perceive the collective experience that has shaped their lives. We never get to know the family well enough to understand what they take back from the long-abandoned shelter when finally they see it for themselves. The attic remains a dark and troubling symbol that never quite surrenders its secrets.

VILLAGE VOICE, 5/23/89, p. 70, Manohla Dargis

Unlike Anne Frank, Sally Frishberg survived. When she was only eight years old, she and 14 of her relatives hid from the Nazis in an open-slatted farmhouse attic measuring 10 by 15 feet, with a four-and-a-half-foot ceiling. Originally they were meant to be secreted for only a few days or, at most, a couple of weeks. They lived there—only an hour away from Auschwitz—in almost total silence for two years.

Voices From the Attic is a record of a journey back to Poland, the attic, and history, guided by Sally and filmed by her niece, Debbie Goodstein. As Sally and her children return to the village of Urzejowice, she recalls how her grandfather, who refused to believe that good Christians could be barbarians, was the only Jew in the entire village to show up for "transfer," and how the family hid for months in hollowed-out haystacks before finding—for a heavy bribe—a peasant family to take them in.

Occasionally, the visit feels almost like a group-therapy field trip. (The bouncy music of the Penguin Café Orchestra used for the score doesn't help.) These are people strenuously trying to "manage" their emotions, even as they meet with swastikas and peasants maddeningly indifferent to history—one woman, a former neighbor, tells Sally in a compensatory mode, "You suffered a lot, but now you are doing well for yourself."

At the very end of *Voices*, Goodstein explains that she wants to pass on the history of the attic to her own kids, in order to spare them the pain she and other children of Holocaust survivors experience. Early in the film her own mother says bluntly that she doesn't have to return to Poland to understand what happened, and the director's sister angrily agrees. Clearly all her life Debbie Goodstein has lived with silenced voices, yet despite the moving reminiscences of her aunt and uncles, the one important voice missing from the film, finally, is her own.

Also reviewed in:
NEW YORK TIMES, 5/12/89, p. C10, Caryn James
VARIETY, 3/15–21/89, p. 18

VOICES OF SARAFINA!

A New Yorker Films release of a Lincoln Center/Noble Enterprises production. *Executive Producer:* Gregory Mosher and Bernard Gersten. *Producer:* Bernard Gersten and Nigel Noble. *Director:* Nigel Noble. *Screenplay:* Nigel Noble. *Director of Photography:* John Hazard. *Editor:* Joan Morris. *Music:* Hugh Masekela and Mbongeni Ngema. *Running Time:* 85 minutes. *MPAA Rating:* Not Rated.

WITH: The cast of the Broadway show *Sarafina* and Miriam Makeba.

CHRISTIAN SCIENCE MONITOR, 2/28/89, p. 11, David Sterritt

One service that movies can perform quite efficiently is to bring other forms of art and entertainment closer to us. Although the Broadway theater is in one small corner of New York City, through film a Broadway show can travel anywhere. That's especially handy when the show traveled a long way to get to Broadway in the first place—like "Sarafina!," which came to the United States from South Africa.

"Voices of Sarafina!" isn't a movie version of that show, however. Rather, it's a close-up look at the people and ideas that went into it—and a revealing glimpse of South African culture from an unusual perspective.

The live show "Sarafina!" had its origins in a politically stirring event of 1976, when 15,000 schoolchildren demonstrated in Soweto, South Africa, against a new and aggressive move by the South African government: the declaration of Afrikaans as the country's official language.

Eleven years later, a number of socially alert high school students banded together at the Market Theatre in Johannesburg to create a music-theater event that would dramatize the '76 uprising. About a year and a half ago, New York's enterprising Lincoln Center produced an American edition of the show featuring a troupe of young South African performers. It earned a Tony Award nomination and is still running on Broadway.

The movie "Voices of Sarafina!" includes moments from the show, as well as vivid glances at life in poverty-ridden South African townships. More prominently, it features interviews with members of the play's cast—who go beyond their songs and dialogues to give us firsthand impressions of existence under apartheid.

Their political views are the focal point of the movie, but there's also a hearty dose of personal drama. And there's an even heartier dose of music—including *mbaqanga*, described as "the music of liberation" by the film's distributors—that captures the heartbeat of South African life.

The musical aspect of the film reaches its climax near the end, when Miriam Makeba joins the ensemble, singing and speaking of her own feelings about her country and its racial turmoil.

Watching this part of the movie, I was reminded of an earlier film about South Africa called "Come Back Africa," a brilliant portrait of life under apartheid made several years ago by Lionel Rogosin, and featuring Ms. Makeba at her most eloquent.

"Voices of Sarafina!" was directed by Nigel Noble, a New York-based documentary specialist who has won both Emmy and Academy Awards, and who obviously cares deeply about South Africa, its problems, and its future. His film isn't a brilliant work of cinema, but it has a strong emotional charge that grows from its subject and its talented cast.

The makers of "Voices of Sarafina!," including Lincoln Center-affiliated producer Bernard Gersten, expect the movie to have its broadest exposure in a shortened television version, but it's being released first by New Yorker Films as a regular theatrical picture.

It's well worth a visit for those who want to broaden their own exposure to South African history, politics, and art.

LOS ANGELES TIMES, 2/22/89, Calendar/p. 1, Sheila Benson

"Sarafina!" the stage musical dramatizing the student uprising in Soweto in 1976 performed by a troupe of young black South African schoolchildren, has not yet come to Los Angeles.

It's been busy being a hit in Manhattan since 1987. But you can get a taste of its crackling energy and the heroic commitment of its cast in "Voices of Sarafina!" a touching backstage and onstage documentary by Nigel Noble, illustrating the thoughts and experiences of these formidable young performers.

Mbongeni Ngema, their patriarchal author-director, dead serious in his black leather cap and jacket, tells one group that he expects his next words to live with them forever: On their first time away from their homeland, they must see themselves as ambassadors of black South Africa. To the free world, they must interpret life as they have known it in the townships and in schools patrolled by armed soldiers. "If you say you don't know anything, what sort of ambassadors are you?" he asks.

The 28 singers and dancers, molded into a performing family by Ngema, are phenomenal ambassadors. Strong, beautiful, sweet, smart, talented teen-agers, they grew up in the townships, mostly around Durban. As they speak of their lives at home, the contrast between their age, their extraordinary sweetness and their experience—humiliation on a daily basis, the killings of friends their own age—is almost overwhelming.

Just as you notice how potent their smiles are, one girl, probably no more than 15, explains that those smiles are part of their armor. When they are detained or beaten by South African police, their smiles come back no matter the provocation. "The black laugh," she calls it.

Wearing their stage unifrom—black derby, black sweater, starched white shirt and tie—they sing in the beautiful harmonies recognizeable from the songs of Ladysmith Black Mambazo, an infectious and haunting music known as Mbaganga, the music of liberation. ("Sarafina's!" songs are the work of Hugh Masekela and Ngema.)

Photographing a staged work that has been consciously exaggerated so that the action and the accents can be read "by the old lady in the back row on Broadway" poses a few hazards which film maker Noble hasn't solved. On stage, a couple of the performers—the schoolteacher and the boy playing Hector Peterson, the first youth shot to death at Soweto—seem grotesquely theatrical, so over-mugged that you cringe. (Then hate yourself for cringing.)

If there had been a way to take these 2,000-watt performances down just a little when they were filmed, they would have had an even greater impact. That's especially true after we've met Pat Mlaba, the quiet, intensely thoughtful actor who plays Peterson, and can contrast the power he carries in a quiet interview with the deliberate overkill he's been directed to deliver onstage.

A small portion of the crisply photographed film was shot in South Africa; there's another contrast to these scenes. As the young cast speaks movingly of their dreams, one talks about the fields and the mountains of his homeland. The shots are of the sun-baked, tin-shacked dusty township villages, as little children amuse themselves kicking a stone along the path. "I dream only of freedom," one girl says gravely, "God and our ancestors will help us."

If the film has a climax, it's the surprise visit in the green room of Miriam Makeba, in the 27th year of her exile. Apparently, none of the cast had ever seen her or even dreamed of the possibility. The presence of "Mama Zanzee," this wellspring of inspiration; *her* enormous pride in these kids who by now are weeping openly; and their spontaneous singing of "Nkosi Sikeleli Afrika" with Makeba make a scene of absolutely wracking emotion.

If the news from Johannesburg in the last week has been shocking and dispiriting and a jolt of inspiration is needed, you could find no purer, stronger source than these extraordinary, shiningly committed young people. When Makeba says, "We are a proud people, a struggling people, and we *will* win our independence," you need only look at the calm, resolute faces of this cast to know the certainty of that promise.

NEW YORK POST, 2/3/89, p. 21, David Edelstein

On stage, the musical "Sarafina!" suggests a seance on a playground. Young black South Africans bound out to enact, in song and dance, the events leading up to the 1976 massacre of students at Soweto. In the tradition of African street theater, their line readings are exaggerated and gestures extravagant; they seem less like individuals than vessels for the agony and terror of thousands of their countrymen, living and dead.

The documentary "Voices of Sarafina!" deepens this stage picture, filling in those radiant faces and conveying—in interviews—the sadness and disorientation of a childhood under apartheid, in which the young are raised to speak Afrikaans and live, in effect, as slaves.

Coincidentally, the movie does a stupendous job of capturing the magic of the theatrical event. Noble, who has many years of experience shooting concerts and stage productions, can get inisde "Sarafina!" without forsaking its sheer, overflowing theatricality. We're alternately immersed and then distanced, and the brilliant editing (by Joan Morris) corresponds not literally to the rhythms of the music ("Mbaqanga," the music of liberation) but to its emotional rhythms, its heartbeat.

Gradually, we are introduced to the performers off stage, as they describe their rehearsal process and then try to suggest —in tortured, tentative English—the firmness of their political consciousness and fragility of their emotions. They seem hesitant, battered, victims of—among other things—an education continually punctuated with gunfire and threats of imprisonment.

One young man describes, haltingly, how a woman friend was shot down beside him while fleeing the police. The damage is spiritual as well as physical. "Ever since I was born I was spoiled," he says. He cannot look at a white man without seeing an enemy, someone who despises him for reasons beyond his control. Hatred is bred into the black South African.

These are wrenching interviews, but "Voices of Sarafina!" doesn't have the tension or sense of discovery of a great documentary. What's there has been planted, and fine-tuned with an eye for Spreading the News. Coproduced by Lincoln Center (which also produced the work on stage), the movie feels more like an artful, impassioned commercial for the musical and the anti-apartheid movement as a whole. There are times you might wish that Noble had probed a little deeper.

The film, for example, doesn't touch on the sadder, less inspiring aspects of "Sarafina!"— among them an allegation that the writer/director, Mbongeni Ngema, had struck a female cast member during rehearsals. (Spokesmen for Ngema admitted that the incident had taken place, but explained it by citing "cultural differences.")

The emotional climax of "Voices of Sarafina!" is generated by another voice—exiled South African activist and singer Miriam Makeba, who tells the cast after a performance that she will die happy knowing that they are continuing what she helped to begin, "spreading the message through your music and your lovely voices...that we are a proud people and that we are a struggling people and that we will win our independence and we'll be free." Then, suddenly, she launches into an old African song called "Mama," embracing the young performers with her music as they weep.

It is an overwhelming scene. The only thing that detracts from its power is the knowledge that the cast was set up: They weren't told they were going to meet "Mama Zenze" (Mother Africa), but the movie cameras and reporters were stationed backstage, waiting to catch their spontaneous reactions. Exploitation—however noble the motives and soaring the results—cuts both ways.

NEWSDAY, 2/3/89. Part III/p. 3, Lynn Darling

They smile a lot, the young men and women who make up the cast of "Sarafina!" the musical about the 1976 Soweto uprising. And it's not long into Nigel Noble's stirring documentary, "Voices of Sarafina!" before they explain why. "Even if you cry, it doesn't help, so the better thing is to smile, no matter how hard it is," one of them says. And again, "We laugh even if someone is dead."

Back home in South Africa, they have friends and parents and brothers who have been detained and beaten. They have seen the routine of their classrooms overwhelmed by the rumble of tanks and the report of gunfire. Teenagers most of them, they have lived their lives in a state of war; among them, as they say in the movie, are 15-year-olds with the experience of 30-year-olds. They talk about their anger and their pain with luminous tolerance, given the painful simplicity of their goals: "How can I make people understand me and not hate me?" asks one young man.

"The liberation of South Africa really is in the hands of the children," says Mbongeni Ngema, the director and guiding spirit of "Sarafina!" "They're in the forefront of the struggle."

The young men and women who make up the cast of "Sarafina!" were recruited by Ngema who molded them into something of a family as well as a working unit before he brought them to the United States. The process of grooming them and preparing them continues: Never forget, Ngema tells them, that you are the ambassadors for black South Africa. The camera watches as the cast members ask questions about "what we can talk about, and what we can't talk about" in talking about South Africa; it observes them as Ngema teaches them how to project themselves so that no nuance of their message is lost even on "those old ladies on Broadway."

If anything is lost here, however, it is a sense of what these kids are like on a more personal basis. Apart from the recent allegations that Ngema has physically disciplined cast members in rehearsal, it's clear from the movie that he runs a very tight ship—the movie makes you curious to know what their relationship is to this man who brought them out of South Africa and into this extraordinary experience. The movie raises questions as well about their reaction to New York, and the violence and the volatility that affects the lives of many of the people here: They are living, after all, in a city whose children also hear gunfire just outside the classroom from time to time.

Still "Voices of Sarafina!" is an uplifting tribute to the resilience and the passion of youth, and a jolting reminder of the brutality that it must sometimes survive. Offstage interviews and scenes from the musical complement each other in building and sustaining a vibrant mood reinforced by the irresistible music. By the time the young cast members meet the exiled Miriam Makeba for the first time and raise their voices in song, it's difficult to find a dry eye either on or off the screen.

VILLAGE VOICE, 2/7/89. P. 57, Katherine Dieckmann

Though it won't dent Broadway grosses, *Voices of Sarafina!*, a documentary on the successful musical about black schoolchildren's involvement in the '76 Soweto uprising, is far more effective than the real McCoy. *Sarafina!*, a jubilant and occasionally somber look at resistance and pride, is obviously far more deserving of theatergoers' dollars than *Cats* or *Starlight Express*. But writer/director Mbongeni Ngema did too good a job when he instructed his cast to project to "those old ladies on Broadway," as he calls his theater audience in *Voices*: The children's overemphatic delivery and discomforting eagerness to please smothered heartfelt response to this well-intentioned piece.

Ngema could easily be accused of spoon-feeding a dose of guilt assuagement to biddies in furs (as well as other things, but more on that later). *Sarafina!* plays almost too perfectly on the Great White Way—though it debuted at Lincoln Center, where friends assure me that the close, pitlike space of the Mitzi E. Newhouse Theatre created an immediacy and urgency sorely lacking from the Cort Theatre's distanced balcony.

Voices of Sarafina! reaches far deeper into the emotion of the situation, or situations. Neatly excerpting the musical for non-New Yorkers who might never get to see it, the film does the show one better by personalizing the cast. *Voices* brings their faces close to us, turning a nonthreatening "celebration" with a dash of sobering drama into a direct testimonial to pain and survival. These children are entertaining in a country whose corporations have buoyed the very regime that has squashed them. While director Nigel Noble never foregrounds these connections—he could have cut the mood-setting South African footage and zeroed in on thornier issues, like what the performers make of the visible poverty and racism in New York—the paradox of the play and its performers is still apparent enough.

Equally evident is the barn-size ego of Ngema, himself a South African exile who seems to have adapted smoothly to his new land, and who rules his brood with a becalmed intensity. In a *Voice* article published last June, Erika Munk reported on charges brought against Ngema for allegedly beating female members of his cast. The situation was largely whisked away by Ngema supporters, who claimed his detractors didn't comprehend the "cultural differences" at hand (e.g., unchecked patriarchal power-tripping). From the interplay between the director and his performers, that disciplinary zeal isn't too hard to imagine. Wide-eyed, nodding children listen with rapt attention as Ngema preaches. A typical imperative: "This is the embassy, and you are the ambassadors." And I am the President/Big Daddy?

Part of the point of *Voices* is that education at home has failed South African children—it's hard to study with gunfire outside and soldiers bursting into the classroom, giving new meaning to "detention." But it's not at all clear that Ngema is a suitable teacher substitute.

Far more effective instruction comes from the young people themselves. In quiet, lilting voices and faltering English, they tell of the atrocities they've seen and how they maintain perspective. "Even if you cry," says one young man, "it doesn't help. . . . We laugh even if someone's dead." Another claims he's "spoiled"; it takes a minute to register that he doesn't mean he's *pampered*, but is saying instead that he'll never be able to look at a white without being convinced that that person hates him.

Voices of Sarafina! reaches its stirring climax with a surprise meeting between the cast and Miriam Makeba, the South African singer forced into exile who has attained Mandela-like mythic status back home. She arrives unannounced after a performance and tells the startled assemblage, in a voice heavy with sadness, how proud she is of them. Then she begins to sing a beautiful freedom song, which is broken by the sound of the children sobbing. Makeba gathers several to her and continues singing. The scene is extraordinarily powerful. Finally, it is Mama Africa, not Papa Ngema, who reminds us of the grief and optimism *Sarafina!* is meant to express.

Also reviewed in :
NATION, 2/6/89. p. 174, Stuart Klawans
NEW YORK TIMES, 2/3/89. p. C14, Janet Maslin
VARIETY, 9/28/88, p. 30
WASHINGTON POST, 4/19/89. p. D1, Hal Hinson

VOYAGE TO CYTHERA

A Centre du Cinema Grec release. *Director:* Theo Angelopoulos. *Screenplay (Greek with English subtitles):* Theo Angelopoulos, Th. Vaitinos, and T. Guerra. *Director of Photography:* Giorgios Arvanitis. *Editor:* Giorgios Triantafyllou. *Music:* Helen Karaindrou. *Production Designer:* Mikes Karapiperis. *Costumes:* Giorgios Ziakas. *Running Time:* 149 minutes. *MPAA Rating:* Not Rated.

CAST: Manos Katrakis (Spyros); Mary Chronopoulou (Voula); Dionyssis Papayannopoulos (Antonis); Dora Volanaki (Spyros's Wife); Giorgios Nezos (Panayotis); Athinodoros (Police Captain); Michalis Yannatos (Harbor Master); Akis Kareglis (Spyros); Vassilis Tsaglos (Longshoremen Union Leader); Julio Brogi (Alexandros); Despina Geroulanou (Alexandros' Wife).

NEW YORK POST, 3/31/89. p. 29, Jami Bernard

Dad is home, but never had there been a more dour homecoming. The old man (that's how he's referred to in the credits, too) is back in Greece after years and years in Russian exile. The family gathers around excitedly. "You must have many stories about Russia," they prod him. He thinks. He considers. The family waits. "It snows a lot in the winter," he mumbles finally and walks out of the room.

Okay, dad's going to be difficult to manage, and so is this movie. Right away, the old man manages to alienate his wife and exasperate his kids, especially his son, Antonis, a playwright who's been searching for his father in one way or another all his life.

"Voyage to Cythera" is a beautifully photographed, painstaking production by Greek director Theo Angelopoulos, but you'd better come to it equipped with patience, and maybe caffeine.

Never have people moved so slowly, spoken so deliberately (and sporadically), trodden so heavily as they do here. This "Voyage" seems endless.

The old man, bearded, sunken-faced, plods along carrying a satchel and a violin case as his family scampers after him uncertainly. Dad certainly has turned into something of a puzzle. Back in his old village, he remembers how to communicate with his aged friends via bird-call whistles, the Greek equivalent of the Swiss yodel or the Indian semaphore code. But when he refuses to sell his share of the mountainside to real estate developers, his former buddies cut bait: they stand outside his window yelling death threats. Anyway, the old man is not sure if he wants to stay or go. Russia, after all these years, holds a few delights for him that his long-abandoned wife isn't too thrilled about.

But can he go back to Russia? For such a quiet guy, dad is no slouch at turning people against him. Before long, Greece wants him out, but the Russians won't take him back because now he's babbling on about rotten apples, a variation on a remembered village rhyme.

Though all eyes are turned to the old man to see how he will react and what he will do next, the story is essentially told through the eyes of the grown son, a man with marital problems of his own (he's having an affair with the lead in his new play, an affair that literally spills over into the aisles). The son is haunted by the memory of his long-errant father; there is a poignantly funny scene in which dozens of wizened old men try out for a bit part in Antonis's new play by saying the words that dad will later utter, "It's me."

Just when you think the movie might be winding up, there's another hour's worth of shunting the old guy around; he's an utterly displaced person, and no one knows what to do with him. Director Angelopoulos imbues each scene with the solemnity of a funeral procession. And he has a trick of (slowly) pulling the camera back until a scene is bracketed like a haunted postcard. Visually, the movie is extraordinary. Two scenes, the sad ending shot, and the old man and his wife standing in front of their village home looking fragile, are truly heart-tugging.

The old man looks utterly ancient; perhaps he was younger when they began making this film. Certainly your own bones will be creaking by the end of it.

VILLAGE VOICE, 4/11/89, p. 64, Georgia Brown

The Odysseus story repeats with many configurations, many historical ironies, with the same country that spews out exiles harboring others. Sometimes there are actual homecomings. A master filmmaker, Theo Angelopoulos—whose films win prizes in all parts of the world yet rarely are seen in this blighted cultural garden—has made an extraordinary film about the return to Greece of a father and husband who has spent 32 years exiled in Russia. (Homer's Odysseus was absent a mere 19.) *Voyage to Cythera*, released in 1984, appears to have been on its own minijourney to our shores. How long will it take for Angelopoulos's more recent *Landscape in the Mist* to make it here?

Voyage to Cythera (taking its title from the Baudelaire poem, in which sighting the fabled isle of Aphrodite's cult shows the poet a deadly image of himself) recounts the father's return as if from the point of view of his son Telemachus—and as if Telemachus were a filmmaker, as well as a middle-aged man with a son of his own. Spyros (Manos Katrakis) is an old communist who fled to Russia after the Greek civil war because he was under a death sentence at home. Two of his three children, Alexandros (Julio Brogi) and Voula (Mary Chronopoulou); his faithful wife, Katerina (Dora Volanaki); and an old comrade, Antonis, suffer the old man's disruptive homecoming.

A brief sequence at the film's beginning shows Alexandros's young son Spyros enacting in miniature a "crime" that mimics his namesake's. The boy steals up behind a soldier, swats the stick from his hand, and takes off. With the soldier in pursuit, the boy tries a few doors (presumably neighbors'), but they're locked, and he ends up crouching behind a low gate, his head down as if praying. "This is for you...," he murmurs, reciting some names—which I take as Angelopoulos's personal dedication to political martyrs.

In the film's next phase, Alexandros wakes, dreamily drinks his coffee, and goes to an Athens film studio. In one room a large group of old men are gathered in a semicircle. One by one, the men approach a table where casting directors are seated and recite in turn the phrase, "It's me." (As each delivers the words with his own voice and emphasis, the impression grows that all individuals have these words stored, ready to say when his or her time comes.) The distracted Alexandros (who seems to dwell elsewhere) watches this procession, then wanders to another room, where a woman with whom he has been having an affair rehearses a script—words that turn up again later, as his sister's.

The line between this fictional film and *Voyage*'s narrative is left undrawn; the elision takes place so invisibly, seamlessly, that the effect is much more subtle and mysterious than an ordinary distancing. An old man selling lavender in a café is spotted by Alexandros (who focuses for the first time outside his reverie) and turns up moments later as the returning father. It is as if Angelopolous were describing a process of interior filmmaking in which casting, scripting, and images themselves have antecedents to be uncovered, remembered, rather than invented. In a stunning scene at the port, Alexandros and his sister wait for their father's boat, until, spied at a distance, the old man declares (echoes), "It's me." Enactment is reenactment; what happens, has happened.

At a family reunion in Athens, Spyros revisits his Penelope. Afraid, he is unable to recall the color of her eyes. Just as food is being served, he walks out; furious, Katerina locks herself in the kitchen. Alexandros, like a camera eye, follows his father silently to a hotel. The following day, the family drive to the mountains where their former home is. Spyros announces himself with bird calls ("the old outlaw code," interprets Katerina) that are answered by Antonis, the one comrade remaining in the village. Later. Antonis confesses that he has always coveted Katerina.

But the tale's traitorous "suitors" are actually the mass of villagers, arriving like a ragtag army to sell off their land to developers of a winter resort. "They'd sell the sky if they could," says Antonis. When Spyros refuses to sell with the rest, they threaten him for ruining their deal. His daughter is on their side: "Your generation—you took to the hills, fought, and then disappeared." She claims to be bitter for her mother's sake ("I never saw her laugh"). "One victim in this family is enough," she says, unaware that she is one victim.

At night, in a darkened room, as Spyros describes his time in exile—a passage of years until "one day a woman cooks you a meal and sews on a button...I've got three children over there"—the camera pans slowly to Katerina in the darkness on the far side of the room, and it's clear that *Voyage* is a love story. "What's she like, the other one?" Katerina asks. (The unseen presence of an alternate, inverted universe—another wife, a buried life "in another country"—is at the heart of Angelopoulos's aesthetic and his epistemology.)

This may not be a country for old men, but the young in one another's arms are more profoundly lost than their elders. Alexandros couples with his actress in the aisle of an empty theater, and Voula lets herself be screwed propped against a wall by a horny sailor. Believing in nothing, I turn to my body to feel alive, she explains to her brother, who as usual is the passive (unheroic) observer. In contrast, there is the fate of the old people in an achingly beautiful, classically formal scene.

Angelopoulos's stately, fluid direction, with his signature sequence shots, maintains a clear moral bias, rejecting cheap close-ups or prettified locations. A bare, blue tree in a winter landscape has a celestial or lunar aura, linking the film's voyage, as its very first shots do, to cosmic travel. Cythera, Venus, is also a star.

Also reviewed in:
NEW YORK TIMES, 3/31/89, p. C17, Richard Bernstein
VARIETY, 5/16/84, p. 133

WAR OF THE ROSES, THE

A Twentieth Century Fox release of a Gracie Films production. *Executive Producer:* Polly Platt and Doug Claybourne. *Producer:* James L. Brooks and Arnon Milchan. *Director:* Danny DeVito. *Screenplay:* Michael Leeson. *Based upon the novel by:* Warren Adler. *Director of Photography:* Stephen H. Burum. *Editor:* Lynzee Klingman. *Music:* David Newman. *Music Editor:* Tom Villano and Segue Music. *Sound:* Jeff Wexler and (music) Tim Boyle. *Sound Editor:* Leslie Shatz. *Production Designer:* Ida Random. *Art Director:* Mark Mansbridge. *Set Designer:* Stan Tropp, Mark Fabus, and Perry Gray. *Set Decorator:* Anne McCulley. *Special Effects:* John Frazier. *Costumes:* Gloria Gresham. *Make-up:* Stephen Abrums. *Stunt Coordinator:* Mike Runyard. *Running time:* 116 minutes. *MPAA Rating:* R.

CAST: Michael Douglas (Oliver Rose); Kathleen Turner (Barbara Rose); Danny DeVito (Gavin D' Amato); Marianne Sägebrecht (Susan); Sean Astin (Josh at 17); Heather Fairfield (Carolyn at 17); G.D. Spradlin (Harry Thurmont); Peter Donat (Larrabee); Dan Castellaneta (Man in Chair); Gloria Cromwell (Mrs. Marshall); Harlan Arnold (Mr. Dell); Mary Fogarty (Mrs. Dell); Rika Hofmann (Elke); Patricia Allison (Maureen); Peter Brocco (Elderly Mourner); Philip Perlman (Bidder at Auction); Susan Isaacs (Auctioneer's Assistant): Trenton Teigen (Josh at 10); Bethany McKinney (Carolyn at 10); Shirley Mitchell (Mrs. Dewitt); Ellen Crawford (Nurse #1); Michael Adler (Dr. Hillerman); Lisa Howard (Nurse #2); Jeff Thomas (Orderly); Jacqueline Cassell (Gavin's Secretary); Vickilyn Reynolds (Nancy/Oliver's Secretary); Eunice Suarez (Latin Woman); Julia Elliott (Latin Assistant); Tony Crane (Teenage Boy); Ryan and Shaun Wickers (Josh at 3); Catherine and Mary Donohue (Carolyn at 3); Sue Palka (Anchorwoman); Morris Jones (Anchorman); Popeye (Bennie); Tyler (Kitty Kitty); Roy Brocksmith (Mr. Fisk); Peter Hansen (Mr. Marshall); Robert Harper (Heath); Prince Hughes (Bleeding Man); Danitra Vance (Manicurist Trainee); David Wohl (Dr. Gordon).

FILMS IN REVIEW, 3/90, p. 168, Edmond Grant

The War Of The Roses is an insidious comedy that starts out playing by the rules, and gradually develops into the darkest view of American marital life ever produced by a major studio. And, not surprisingly, the nastier it gets, the funnier it gets.

Michael Douglas and Kathleen Turner play the Roses, a happy upwardly mobile couple who go through a fairy tale existence for a while. This blissful period, which extends for the film's first half, is given a menacing undertone by director/co-star Danny DeVito, via a number of strikingly intricate and often grotesque camera angles swiped from the Hitchcock canon (DeVito also paid tribute to Hitch in his first theatrical feature, *Throw Mama From The Train*). In short order, we see how the two meet, make idyllic love for a while, get married, and raise two happy, if rotund, children. All this is recounted to us by DeVito, who plays Douglas' friend and personal lawyer, telling the Roses' tale of woe to a prospective divorce client. Through the early years of marriage, Oliver (Douglas) is clearly the villain of the piece, becoming so intent on furthering his legal career that he withholds his love from Barbara (Turner). But soon the tables are turned, and Barbara turns cold, deciding that she wants a divorce on the day that her husband is rushed to an emergency ward, the presumed victim of a heart attack. From their respective cold states, the couple turn immature, as the divorce is agree to, but neither party will surrender the house that both feel they worked so hard to beautify. As the tug of war escalates, the two turn downright mean, provoking each other with a variety of outrages, until their "war" turns dangerous as Oliver barricades them both inside the house in question, instigating a kind of double edged *Shining* act, in which both husband and wife insanely stalk their stubborn ex-lovemate.

By extending the pre-"war" section of the film, one is better able to see why the couple feel they have just cause to be righteous, even to the point of childishness; also, DeVito is better able to slowly prepare the viewer for hilariously barbaric acts that are to come. The only trouble being, that the film doesn't really generate any real laughs until the two parties irrevocably split and start feuding over the house. Once the discord begins in earnest, the film picks up its pace and truly enters original territory becoming the kind of savagely dark depiction of suburbia that John Avildsen's *Neighbors* tried for and achieved only in its earlier sequences.

As the film transforms itself into a comic horror film, its true potential comes to the surface and the two leads gleefully throw themselves into their work. True, Douglas and Turner have worked together twice before, on a pair of derring-do adventure comedies (*Romancing The Stone* and *Jewel Of The Nile*), but here the two develop an almost devilish chemistry that permeates sexiness even when their characters are as imaginatively evil as they can be. Turner exudes her familiar sensuality in lethal doses, giving her character the sometime air of a dominatrix as she repeatedly physically trounces Douglas, while she retains the cold, determined air of a suburban matron (although she's at her sexiest while conducting the "war" in casual attire). Douglas does much to dignify Oliver, who emerges as somewhat of a pathetic figure as the film rolls on. Always willing to conclude the hostilities if only his ex will admit she still really loves him, he is a tragically misguided fellow, whom Douglas renders as all too human, and insanely vengeful at an adolescent level. DeVito lends nice support as Douglas' buddy, but smartly reduces his character to two running jokes (he has a big libido and is a chainsmoker) and leaves the spotlight on Turner and Douglas.

As a director, DeVito exhibits a visual style that is highly sophisticated, but also somewhat distracting. His carefully worked out composition of a good number of images cleverly echoes the work done by Hitchcock and other thriller directors, but it also unfortunately belabors some of the plotline's finer points. It is only when the truly malicious action starts that the exaggerated visuals seem entirely appropriate; earlier on, they simply seem to be drawing out the preliminaries.

Though heavy handed and somewhat slowly paced for nearly half its running time, the film does become wonderfully original when it starts to function on a subversive level. Black comedy is a rarely practiced art these days, so once it becomes apparent that the Roses are eagerly concocting ways to actually *kill* each other, it's obvious that we are being treated to a different sort of vision than those that are churned out by Spielberg's sugar coated stable of directors. It's odd to call a film that thrives on spite and vengeance refreshing, but *War Of The Roses* is exactly that. Its humor may be blunt and its message utterly ambiguous, but it qualifies as unique in this era of vehicle pictures and comedies that feature furry animals and cute toddlers.

LOS ANGELES TIMES, 12/8/89, Calendar/p. 1, Sheila Benson

If the American marriage is frail and on life support systems, then "The War of the Roses" is the sneak attack that pulls all the plugs. Pay no attention to its frenzied trailer, which makes it look like an interpersonal destruction derby. In the hands of director Danny DeVito and writer Michael Leeson, "The War of the Roses" *is* biting and vicious, a styptic pencil on the battered face of "civilized divorce." It's also thoughtful, laceratingly funny and bravely true to its own black-and-blue comic vision.

How could the marriage of Oliver and Barbara Rose go wrong? Upward bound from his first casebooks at Harvard Law School, Oliver (Michael Douglas) and outstanding college gymnast Barbara (Kathleen Turner) meet on Nantucket in a bidding war over a bit of 16th-Century Chinese ivory.

Quickly in lust, they progress to marriage, the perfect junior partnership, the perfect set of children—one boy, one girl—the perfect old Washington house, even the perfect burgeoning career for Barbara when the children are older. Then, the perfect pfffft.

The blindsided Oliver doesn't have a clue why, which is exactly the point. Although Douglas' performance has been calibrated to give some idea of Oliver's charm, particularly with his success-dressed peers, you *could* call Oliver an insensitive, workaholic, self-centered, couthless lox.

With the boss over for dinner, Oliver prods Barbara into telling a family anecdote, then cuts in to tell it faster and funnier himself. He belittles her first business steps, using her contract papers to squash a fly. Then after 18 years he wonders how Barbara, having been given *everything*, including a live-in housekeeper (the marvelous Marianne Sägebrecht, fine but underused), could possibly want anything more from life.

When it turns out that what Barbara wants is out, and waiving alimony or a share of his business, asks only for their house—which she has turned into a showplace—the lines are drawn. He would rather die than let her have it. She feels exactly the same. Then DeVito, in an evil turn as Oliver's friend and divorce lawyer, discovers a little-used statute that allows the husband to continue to reside in a contested house. Now let the mayhem begin.

Begin it does, escalating into tactics Medea might have admired—and may even have used. This is not comedy in the Ealing Studios tradition; it's comedy in the tradition of the Three Stooges armed with tire irons. It may fright the genteel, but it won't surprise anyone who saw DeVito's "Throw Momma From the Train." Because Adler's novel is better basic stuff "War" is far funnier verbally, but it's something more than punishing comedy. It's tragi-comic Cliff Notes on the death of marriage and the emptiness of perfection among the have-it-alls, and it can scare you silly.

The beauty of Leeson's script, from Warren Adler's same-named novel, is that it builds slowly to Barbara's breaking point, allowing us to wince along with her at Oliver's patronizing act. The tenacity of DeVito's direction, steady as a thumb pressing on a bruise, keeps the tone brutally consistent. If he had backed away or softened at any point, including our last sight of the Roses, the picture would have gone gurgling down the drain. Amazingly, for a film of the kinder, gentler era, DeVito (and the film's producers) stand firm.

No one will ever call DeVito a discreet director—not with his low-angle shots suggesting a weasel's-eye view of life, or his shot of Nantucket through the V of Barbara's legs as she shows-off with a headstand for Oliver's benefit. Yet DeVito also manages to suggest layers to both the potentially unlovable Roses, not only to Oliver but to Barbara as well.

Turner's Barbara may be sexually triumphant, but she is socially unsure and after all these years with Oliver, her self-esteem has vanished. She is a woman who may not have been born to money, but who has learned fast and has poured years of studying and collecting into decorating her house until it could pass any Georgetown dowager's inspection. No wonder when Barbara's finished "doing" every room, there's nothing left to hold her interest. (This house, the work of production designer Ida Random, art director Mark Mansbridge and set decorator Anne McCulley, is dead-on. It conjures up museum-perfect but sterile perfection; the essence of the slick mag drop-dead environment.)

It takes a certain nerve to serve up "The War of the Roses" (rated R for pungent language and sexual warfare) now. But if you're tired of cloying Christmas eggnog, "War" is Christmas spirits of ammonia. It'll pick you right up, leaving no nasty hangover and only a faint brackish taste in your mouth.

MONTHLY FILM BULLETIN, 3/90, p. 81, Anne Billson

Divorce lawyer Gavin D'Amato describes to a prospective client the case which ended his thirteen years of abstinence from cigarettes...Oliver Rose, a promising law student, meets Barbara, a trainee gymnast, at a Nantucket auction when they both bid for the same carved figurine. They go to bed, and subsequently get married and have two children. It seems like the perfect marriage, especially when Barbara finds the perfect house to go with it. While Oliver works hard to become senior partner at his law firm, Barbara pours all her energies into home-making and, afterwards, in starting up a catering business. But she is showing signs of dissatisfaction, and Oliver is shattered when he is rushed to hospital (with what turns out to be a hernia) and she confesses the prospect of his death had made her feel happy. Barbara files for divorce and waives her right to alimony in return for the house. But Oliver is furious when she uses as leverage the note he had written while believing himself on the verge of death ("All I am and all I have I owe to you") and, using an arcane precedent dug up by his lawyer (D'Amato), insists on moving back into their home, which they divide into territories. The relationship gets even uglier; Oliver accidentally kills Barbara's cat, and she locks him in the sauna. He saws the heels off her shoes and, in desperation, she attempts to seduce D'Amato. When Oliver disrupts an important dinner party she is holding for business clients, she destroys his beloved Morgan and feeds him pâté made from his dog. Oliver seals the two of them in the house by blocking up the doors and windows. After a number of increasingly violent encounters, they both end up trapped on the chandelier which, thanks to an earlier unrealised scheme of Barbara's, gradually pulls free of its moorings. It plummets, and they both fall to their deaths.

Whereas Danny DeVito's directorial début, *Throw Momma from the Train*, was marred by a typically Hollywood streak of sogginess (happy endings all round, and Momma dying from natural causes), one can have no such complaint about his follow-up, *The War of the Roses*. The presence of the director and his two co-stars suggests a spin-off of *Romancing the Stone*, but instead results in what is probably the bleakest portrait of a marriage since the heyday of Ingmar Bergman. Some of the exchanges, especially in the earlier part of the film, ring particularly true to life: Oliver impatiently interrupting his wife's anecdote at a dinner party, for example, or her flinching at his affected laughter.

Flying in the face of the current trend for "feelgood" endings, the film sticks to its guns to the last, when the mortally wounded Oliver attempts to hold hands with his similarly injured wife—and she brushes him away; which is enough to make the ending of *Duel in the Sun* seem positively upbeat. The presentation is stylised; DeVito delights in setting his leading players off against each other by visual means as well as verbal—camera angles and tricks of proportion which make one loom larger than the other, for instance. The violence is largely of the *Tom and Jerry* bounce-back variety (the couple look in remarkably good shape for people who have been hurled on to a hard floor from a great height), but otherwise only two concessions appear to have been made to popular sentiment.

One is the framing device by which D'Amato is seen to be telling the story; at the end he sends his prospective client packing with the unlawyerly advice that married couples should stick together through thick and thin—which gives the audience a chance to decide whether to view the entire saga as a tale which has either been inflated in the telling or made up from scratch. The other concession is a brief insert of Oliver's dog to indicate that it hasn't been made into pâté after all (even though Oliver *thinks* it has): a regrettable failure of nerve, and rather unfair to the cat which has already been sacrificed to the wheels of Oliver's Morgan. On the minus side as well is Marianne Sägebrecht's housekeeper, a character so redundant that one can only assume that DeVito took advantage of the actress' presence in the vicinity when filming began.

The film fairly summarises one of the shortcomings of modern marriage: all-consuming aspiration towards a dream of achievement (nice income, nice house, nice children) coupled with flagrant neglect of the spiritual side of things and an obsession with petty point-scoring. Though it's being presented as a black comedy, it isn't particularly funny, and one might also carp that Oliver and Barbara are such unlikeable characters that one cares little about their descent, locked in mutual antagonism, into self-destruction, though it might well be the aforementioned spiritual lack which makes them seem so brittle and unpleasant in the first place. Whatever, it confirms DeVito as one of the few mainstream film-makers who are willing (and powerful enough) to take risks.

NEW STATESMAN & SOCIETY, 3/16/90, p. 42, Suzanne Moore

At least some of the baser emotions are allowed to emerge in Danny DeVito's *The War of the Roses*. [The reference is to *The Fabulous Baker Boys*; see Moore's review of that film.] DeVito, better known as an actor, showed considerable flair for directing black comedy in *Throw Momma from the Train* and here he brings together his old pals Michael Douglas and Kathleen Turner in a film which looks at that increasingly popular activity, divorce.

They star as Oliver and Barbara Rose, a couple who on the surface of it have everything: success, kids and a beautiful home. But after 17 years of wedded bliss, Barbara realises what she hasn't got—an identity beyond being Oliver's wife. She asks for a divorce and Oliver is stunned, though the tell-tale signs have been there for a while.

Oliver cannot understand why she wants to end the marriage after all he has given her. But she cannot put a name to the problem ("I can't give you specifics"). All she wants is the house, which is the one thing Oliver won't concede, so full-scale war breaks out between them. The house and its contents symbolise their different investments. Oliver believes that it should be his, as he has paid for everything in it. Barbara believes it should be hers because she has chosen and maintained all their precious possessions. Their home is the fruit of her invisible labour and she won't part with it.

The result is a domestic horror film which echoes many of the 1940s "battle of the sexes" films. Only instead of poisonous repartee, the Roses actually slug it out physically with both partners going to extraordinary lengths to make each other leave. They kill each other's pets, he pisses on her gourmet food, she drives over his car.

This is domestic violence of a highly unusual kind, because Barbara with her background as a gymnast is more than able to meet every physical challenge. However nasty things get, this is still comedy and not real life, so he doesn't beat the shit out of her and instead admires the lengths to which she will go to destroy him. The laughs are always double-edged, deriving from a fantasy of equality (she is as strong as he is), and a sense of unease that she might not be.

Yet the most striking aspect of this modern morality tale is the house itself. It starts off as a perfect expression of a coveted lifestyle and ends up literally as a prison—the Roses have barricaded themselves in. It metamorphoses during the course of the movie from a light and spacious dream home to a strangely threatening and unfamiliar place full of dark nooks and crannies.

Turner once more proves her abilities as a comic actress, but we rarely get more than a glimpse of what has driven her character this far. Like the work she has put into the house, the source of her anger remains hidden. The film never allows her to reply to the question that DeVito, the cynical narrator of the film, says that men ask all women eventually: "What the hell is wrong with you?" But then rhetorical questions are always the most difficult to answer.

NEW YORK, 1/8/90, p. 59, David Denby

If nothing else, Danny DeVito's Punch-and-Judy hit, *The War of the Roses*, establishes that DeVito is not an impostor in the director's chair. In the early sections of the movie, as Oliver Rose (Michael Douglas) and Barbara Rose (Kathleen Turner) meet, fall in love, and get married, DeVito displays a talent for adroit camera placement, pacing, and emphasis—voilà! A director! The scenes that follow of the Roses' falling out of love—especially a nerve-racking corporate dinner party where unforgivable slights are committed—turn out to be well written, nicely acted, and psychologically convincing. A "perfect" marriage begins to come unglued under the pressure of money and success.

And there's more: DeVito gets a fully rounded performance out of Michael Douglas, whose

Oliver, a successful lawyer, is not a monster but merely an opportunist and game player who unconsciously patronizes his wife. Douglas has a talent for moral ambiguity, for bringing out the sleazy impulses in essentially decent men. The puffiness in his face can look rotten. Kathleen Turner is given an unaccountable trait—an explosive skill at gymnastics that allows her literally to jump away from troubles. Leaping or standing, Turner is fine; it's not her fault that Michael Leeson's screenplay betrays her. When she withdraws from her husband, she withdraws all the way: She won't cut him any slack, even when he's trying to make amends and get the marriage back on track. She won't even give him a straight answer. So the beautiful early balance of the movie, in which two people, perfectly in love, fall into dissatisfactions and recriminations, gets thrown out of whack—the woman goes cold and discovers a talent for bizarre and nasty tricks that comes out of nowhere.

When the Roses start playing mean—and then grisly—games with each other and the marital enmity turns into a cackling horror story, we lose interest. When people say (as many have) that *The War of the Roses* goes "too far," what they mean, I think, is that the movie abruptly changes style from realistic comedy to gothic sadism. When DeVito gets into kitty-mashing and peenie-biting, no one who's not certifiable will continue to identify with the characters. It's as if DeVito couldn't suppress himself, and a malignant little boy, hiding inside a responsible adult, has suddenly burst forth. No doubt he thinks we're all exactly like the Roses—destructive rotters under the well-mannered skin. But that is his problem.

NEW YORK POST, 12/8/89. p. 33, David Edelstein

I can't help it, I get a chill when I see the words, "A Danny DeVito Film." They appear on silk here, elegantly, but the silk turns out to be a handkerchief into which DeVito promptly blows his nose. I can almost hear him cackle, "This'll kill 'em." For a reportedly nice man, he has a lot of aggression.

"War of the Roses" is DeVito's whopper, his epic black comedy, his war movie—literally. It is loud and showy and one-note, but the actor/director has, at the very least, the courage of his convictions. The story of a bitter divorce that turns into a full-scale battle over a house ends in carnage and catastrophe. No one discovers the true meaning of Christmas.

Small wonder. Michael Douglas plays Oliver Rose, a smug, ambitious lawyer who in Nantucket meets Barbara (Kathleen Turner), the bimbo of his dreams. He trains the former gymnast to be a proper hostess; she finds and decorates (with his money) a great house; and the storybook marriage stretches prosperously into middle age.

Except Oliver is a shallow jerk who barely pays attention to Barbara, and she is a shallow jerk who wants to make something of herself now that the kids are gone. Really, they deserve each other, these gorgeous and uninteresting people.

But when he thinks he's having a heart attack, she realizes that his death would be the best thing that could happen to her, and when he recovers from what turns out to be a hiatal hernia, she sues him for divorce.

This is the start of a horror movie, and it's shown very much from the man's point-of-view: Suddenly, brrrr, the little wife goes cold on him, wants to strip him of his possessions and his manhood. (I thought of Strindberg's "The Father.")

What ensues is tit for tat and then tit for rat-tat-tat. She smashes his favorite porcelain dogs, he saws the heels off her shoe collection; he urinates in a fish dish in front of food critics and VIPs; she squashes his expensive English sports car. Favorite pets bite the dust (a Christmas motif this year). The couple takes to slugging it out, Oliver pleading for a reconciliation, Barbara begging to be left alone.

It's sophomoric and in bad taste, but I guess I'm a sophomore at heart, since I had a pretty good time hooting at how far DeVito runs with his single joke. It's not without resonance: In Hollywood, where executives make lots of money and marry beautiful women whom they keep at home, divorces are often quite bitter, and "War of the Roses" takes the idea all the way to the inner circle of hell.

Unfortunately, neither of these people has much stature or interior life, and DeVito wouldn't know how to capture it if they did. His camera is often on the floor looking up, and he goes in for splashy, hotdog effects, like the plate Turner flings at Douglas' head that seems to have its own camera.

As a director, DeVito is always on. Nothing is casually observed in his universe; you feel him always beside you, nudging you hard in the ribs. Incessant prankishness in a director can be even more wearying than humorlessness; I wanted to take away his camera and give him some crayons.

As Oliver, Douglas is cartoonishly likable—not bad but somehow generic, secondhand. Turner has energy and poise, but why can't we penetrate her mask? She's either scattered and solipsistic or ruthlessly focused. What's in-between feels unconvincing.

It's no surprise that DeVito didn't work harder to get performances from Douglas and Turner. Underneath it all, "War of the Roses" is his posion-pen letter to tall, thin, beautiful WASPs who summer on Nantucket and live in well-ordered houses. He's saying there's something warped. There's no love, only self-love. They don't scream like Italians or Jews, but the upshot is scarier when it boils over.

Maybe that's why the final joke feels so ugly and why DeVito casts himself as Oliver's lawyer, a normal, happy guy who treats his wife with loving kindness. He'd have you believe that this is good, nasty fun, but there's something weirder and more obsessive about "War of the Roses"— something DeVito never openly acknowledges. It's pay back time.

NEWSDAY, 12/8/89, Part III/p. 3, Terry Kelleher

As the opening credits run, the camera closely inspects the contours of something soft, white and inviting. A bedsheet, that's it.

But then we see "Directed by Danny DeVito," and all that whiteness turns out to be a handerchief held by DeVito, who promptly blows his nose into it.

The meaning should be plain: In "The War of the Roses," the name of the game is "gotcha." Play at your own risk.

Adapted by Michael Leeson from Warren Adler's novel, this is the story of Oliver and Barbara Rose, a husband and wife who make war, not love. When predivorce negotiations hit a wall of mutual intransigence, lawyer Oliver (Michael Douglas) and caterer Barbara (Kathleen Turner) use their exquisitely furnished home for a battleground. The conflict escalates from merely verbal hostilities to trash-and-burn destruction. No holds, including the painful leg scissors, are barred. Noncombatants, including the family cat and dog, had better take cover. To the victor goes the property, and the satisfaction of rubbing the former beloved's nose in the dirt.

We're talking about more than the usual slapstick violence here. Not only do figurines fly and cars crash, but people actually get hurt. Since "The War of the Roses" comes billed as a black comedy (just check the newspaper ad, in which Turner and Douglas exchange looks that could kill), the appropriate response would seem to be uneasy laughter. But with DeVito at the controls, we can never be too sure where this movie's headed. And the element of uncertainty is pleasing, in a perverse sort of way.

Just when you think sanity, even affection, might be creeping back into the Roses' lives, DeVito gives you the business. Rushed to the hospital and believing himself to be in the throes of a heart attack, Oliver scrawls a farewell note to Barbara that speaks of love eternal in the face of death. The crisis passes, leaving the Roses in accord on only one point: His penmanship is lousy.

Sometimes the movie fakes you the other way. Oliver and Barbara are screaming at each other; he challenges her to smash his face. Boom—she obliges. Later, Oliver invites his angry son (Sean Astin) to take a swing at him. You wait for the boom. Instead, the scene ends with the sort of hug that solves problems on sitcoms. A sentimental lapse by DeVito? More likely what's known in football as a misdirection play.

Turner and Douglas make the Roses seem really, truly, madly in hate with each other. The trouble is, they're never convincingly in love. We're shown their initial meeting, which certainly establishes the physical attraction, but the first scene from their marriage announces unequivocally that the vicious cycle of inattention (his) and frustration (hers) is well under way. "I'm more than happy—I'm married!" Oliver cries, and DeVito does everything but add the subtitle "Famous Last Words."

Admirers of DeVito's comic energy will be pleased to see the director in the role of Gavin D'Amato, a colleague in Oliver's firm who handles his divorce. However, even those who are crazy about DeVito may find D'Amato too much in evidence. The flashback structure, which has Gavin telling the cautionary tale of Oliver and Rose to a client contemplating divorce, is a major reason the movie feels overlong at two hours. And a different director might have realized that Barbara's attempted seduction of Gavin belongs on the cutting-room floor.

NEWSWEEK, 12/11/89, p. 88, David Ansen

It's been many a moon since Hollywood has produced a comedy as black as *The War of the*

Roses. And though *She-Devil* isn't in the same venomous league, it springs from a similar black lagoon of bile. Is this just coincidence, or is black comedy about to make a comeback? The feel-good Reagan years weren't conducive to a jaundiced point of view: black comedy had its heyday under the dark apocalyptic skies of the '60s, when all sacred cows were led directly to the slaughterhouse. There was no room for a "Dr. Strangelove" in the new morning declared by our national cheerleader. Instead we got Bill Murray, Eddie Murphy, "Police Academy" and the harmless high concept of "Twins."

Neither "The War of the Roses," a comedy of escalating marital warfare, nor "She-Devil," a spurned wife's revenge fantasy, harks back to the '60s satirical mode. These are about domestic, sexual demons. They go back to the romantic-comedy formulas of the '30s and '40s and attempt to twist them into grotesque new shapes. Director Danny DeVito's movie, starring Michael Douglas and Kathleen Turner, does it with brutally startling élan. Susan Seidelman's movie, with Meryl Streep and Roseanne Barr, tries to put a pastel wash over its black logic, and ends up a blur.

Adapted by Michael Leeson from Warren Adler's novel, "The War of the Roses" is a worst-case cautionary fable about divorce, a kind of slapstick "Who's Afraid of Virginia Woolf?" Oliver and Barbara rose (Douglas and Turner) have all the appurtenances of a perfect marriage. They fell in love on Nantucket when he was a brilliant Harvard law student and she was a star collegiate gymnast. They married, had two kids and, as Oliver rose to make junior partner, moved into a beautiful suburban home which Barbara has furnished with only the most exquisite antiques and objets d'art. Thinking, in his workaholic myopia, that their lives are picture perfect, Oliver is stunned one night when Barbara announces she wants a divorce. He demands to know why. "Because when I watch you eat...I just want to smash your face in,"she says, shortly before slugging him.

The real nastiness begins when Barbara announces that in lieu of alimony she wants the house and all its contents. Suddenly these sane, successful paragons of the upper middle class are fighting over property, and no holds are barred. She locks him in the sauna, he saws off the heels of her shoes. And that's just for starters. Before this battle royal reaches its hair-raising conclusion, every pretense of civility lies in ruins, along with the house.

This is funny, you ask? Indeed it is, though the laughter mixes with gasps. Certainly not everyone is going to cotton to a comedy this down and dirty. But there's no denying that Danny DeVito ("Throw Momma From the Train") is emerging as a director with a distinctive dark comic style. "The War of the Roses" unfolds in flashback, as a tall tale told by Oliver's divorce lawyer (played by DeVito) and DeVito's bold, simplified images and surprising camera angles give the story the patina of a fairy tale, albeit a nightmarish one in which no one lives happily ever after.

Douglas and Turner and DeVito worked together twice before, but never so well. This may be the most finely detailed performance Douglas has given: with delicious comic shading he shows you both Oliver's charm and his wimpishness, his mania and his confusion, and when he slurps his food you understand just why she wants to slug him. Turner, with her breathless vocal ticks and unlocatable accent, is a strangely unsettling actress: she's both a powerful and unstable presence, and in some roles you just can't get beyond her mannerisms. Here the ambiguity works to her advantage, suggesting all the inchoate rage sloshing around Barbara's restless soul. She's a formidable foe. And DeVito, with his bulldog tenacity, makes the perfect master of nasty ceremonies. "The War of the Roses" is a brave comedy to unleash on the holiday season: lovable it's not. But it snarls in your memory long after it's over.

There is one good reason, and only one, to see "She-Devil": Meryl Streep. Though she's emphasized her serious side in movies, she's an amazingly inventive comedienne, and when she's on screen as romance novelist Mary Fisher, the rich and hilariously phony "total woman" coquette, you watch her every shrug and false smile with glee. Mary is the villainess of "She Devil": she's stolen the accountant husband (Ed Begley Jr.) of Ruth (Roseanne Barr), and Ruth is going to make her pay. A spectacularly unattractive housewife with a huge mole above her lip, Ruth deliberately turns herself into the she-devil of the title and systematically sets out to destroy the lives of her wandering husband and the woman who whisked him away to her pink palace. Though they borrow many of the events of Fay Weldon's savage post-feminist novel "The Life and Loves of a She-Devil," screenwriters Barry Strugatz and Mark R. Burns take the teeth out of Weldon's fable and utterly fail to get inside their avenging angel protagonist. Barr doesn't help: though she makes a funny first impression, her flat-footed acting can most charitably be described as amateurish. Director Seidelman thrashes about in search of a tone: there's no weight to her images; the plot twists seem arbitrary and contrived. By the end you've lost interest in Ruth's revenge and can't wait until Streep gets back on screen. Watching her prod her face into new shapes in the mirror, contemplating a face-lift, you momentarily forget you're watching a mediocre movie and marvel at real comic witchcraft.

TIME, 12/11/89, p. 93, Richard Schickel

Everything had come up roses for the Roses. Oliver (Michael Douglas) has made partner at his influential law firm. Barbara (Kathleen Turner) has converted her catering service from busywork to flourishing business. The kids are trouble free and accepted by all the right schools. The last expensive antique has been placed in the last empty space in their exquisitely restored house. In other words, disaster now looms.

For the habit of discontent has been the engine driving their lives. And the only thing left to be discontented about is contentedness. Suddenly Barbara can't stand the way Oliver chews his food. Or his insistence on correcting the details when she tries to tell dinner-party stories. When he suffers what at first looks like a heart attack—it turns out to be a hiatal hernia—she cannot quite make it to the emergency room to fake anxiety and sympathy. That night, she proposes separation.

So far, so realistic. One imagines them heading for the sort of civilized divorce settlement that people with a fair amount of community property to protect generally work out. No such luck for the Roses. All kinds of good luck for moviegoers willing to follow director Danny DeVito and screenwriter Michael Leeson down an increasingly dark and comedically dangerous path. The problem is their house, symbol of everything they have struggled to achieve. Barbara is willing to forgo alimony if she can keep it. Oliver is ready to pay her almost anything if he can have it. His lawyer (nicely played by DeVito) discovers an obscure statute under which they can divorce yet continue to live under the roof on which they have lavished their truest love.

This is a terrible idea, an invitation to declare a war of attrition. It opens at a level just beyond practical joking: he saws the heel off every shoe in her closet; she totals his collection of Staffordshire. Soon enough, fires are started. And not long thereafter, the situation turns life threatening, first to household pets caught in the cross fire, then to the combatants.

What is wonderful about the film is that the filmmakers are no more willing to compromise their black comic vision of marriage than the Roses are willing to compromise their differences. Both ends are pursued to a conclusion that is bitter, surprising and utterly logical. But it is the style with which this wild farce is developed that sustains our horrified interest and keeps us laughing as the darkness gathers around Barbara and Oliver.

DeVito's transformation of a sun-splashed showplace into a haunted house is admirable, and so is his pacing. Turner is, needless to say, beautiful when she's angry—sinuous, calculating, purring before she pounces. Douglas makes something equally good of the self-righteousness and self-pity with which some males exercise territorial imperatives. And both contrive to suggest that their warfare is a kind of perverse courtship, a form of preening designed to achieve a surrender that goes far beyond the sexual. You can take or leave the implication that all marriages (and all divorces) may have that as their ultimate goal. But it would be wrong to ignore a film that blends incautious comedy and cautionary morality so expertly.

VILLAGE VOICE, 12/19/89, p. 102, Amy Taubin

Take away the framing story and *The War of the Roses* could have been the first Christmas movie that allows lonely singles who slink into multiplexes on December 25 to leave feeling smug as bugs in an Aubusson carpet. I'm sure there must be an Aubusson tucked away in the Roses' suburban palace because, really, there's everything else.

Barbara (Kathleen Turner) and Oliver (Michael Douglas)—she's a steely-thighed ex-gymnast and he has a scholarship to Harvard Law—meet at an auction, fall into bed, and discover that she's multi-orgasmic. Cut to five years later: They have two kids and a set of Baccarat, and he's about to become a partner. He's also begun to exhibit the kind of successful male superciliousness that makes her want to punch him in the teeth.

Instead, she finds a potentially perfect house and spends the next 18 years of her life and his salary cramming it with enough stuff to fill a half-dozen issues of *HG*. But even the most successful sublimations must come to an end. The kids are grown; the rooms are overflowing. She sets up a catering business and demands a divorce.

He: Is there another guy? She: No. He: A woman? She: You'd like that, wouldn't you?

Oliver (he's the same kind of passive/aggressive prick that Douglas played in *Fatal Attraction*) can't believe that Barbara doesn't love him anymore, let alone that she's demanding the house as a settlement. They dig their heels into separate bedrooms and have at each other. In the ensuing meleé a lot of china is splintered, a few rooms go up in flames, Oliver accidentally runs over Barbara's cat, and she grinds up his dog and serves it to him as pâté.

Or maybe not, because *The War of the Roses*—"a Danny DeVito film"—wants to have its dog and eat it too. What could have been a subversively antimarriage, even profeminist, black comedy about a woman who'd rather die than accommodate a man she's sick of is totally undercut by an epilogue that features DeVito as a lawyer calling the shots. After a climax that makes the end of *Duel in the Sun* look like a tea party, director DeVito cuts to lawyer DeVito advising his male client to go home and patch it up with his wife. Did he forget the point of the previous two hours—that when a woman says no, she means it?

While Douglas is suitably smarmy, Turner's saber-toothed, plush-voiced delivery runs the show. DeVito's vision, however, is strictly boilerplate polished with spit.

Also reviewed in:
NATION, 1/1/90, p. 31, Stuart Klawans
NEW YORK TIMES, 12/8/89, p. C16, Janet Maslin
VARIETY, 12/6/89, p. 32
WASHINGTON POST, 12/8/89, p. C1, Rita Kempley
WASHINGTON POST, 12/8/89, Weekend/p. 65, Desson Howe

WAR PARTY

A Hemdale Film release. *Executive Producer:* Chris Chesser and Franc Roddam. *Producer:* John Daly and Derek Gibson. *Director:* Franc Roddam. *Screenplay:* Spencer Eastman. *Director of Photography:* Brian Tufano. *Editor:* Sean Barton. *Music:* Chaz Jankel. *Sound:* Ed White. *Sound Editor:* Martin Evans. *Production Designer:* Michael Bingham. *Art Director:* Don Maskovich. *Set Designer:* Jeff Ozimek. *Set Decorator:* Tom Talbert and Julia Laughlin. *Set Dresser:* Clive A. Bowerman and William Martin. *Special Effects:* Richard O. Helmer. *Costumes:* Kathryn Morrison. *Make-up:* Matthew Mungle. *Indian Make-up:* Barbara Gilham Aubert and Alva Bird Rattler Parsons. *Stunt Coordinator:* Bud Davis. *Running time:* 96 minutes. *MPAA Rating:* R.

CAST: Billy Wirth (Sonny Crowkiller); Kevin Dillon (Skitty Harris); Tim Sampson (Warren Cutfoot); Jimmie Ray Weeks (Jay Stivic); Kevin Major Howard (Calvin Morrisey); Jerry Hardin (The Sheriff); Tantoo Cardinal (Sonny's Mother); Bill McKinney (the Mayor); Guy Boyd (Major—National Guard); R.D.Call (Posse Member No.1); William Frankfather (The Governor); M. Emmet Walsh (Colin Ditweiller); Dennis Banks (Benn Crowkiller and Dead Crow Chief); Saginaw Grant (Freddie Man Wolf); Rodney Grant (The Crow); Perry Lilley Sr. (Bubba Mad Bear); Peggy Lipton (TV Correspondent); Scott Burkholder (Lieutenant—National Guard); Matthew E. Montoya (Louis Manshadow); Jackie Old Coyote (Crystal Spooner); Dianne Debassige (Dolly Two Owls); Micole Mercurio (Jay's Wife); Billy Streater (Deputy No. 1); Wayne Waterman (George Duckworth); Cameron Thor (Lindquist); Chris Ufland (Ronnie Stivic); Monty Bass (Dennis); Richard Whitman (Harold); Jackie Parsons (B.I.A. Official); David Hart (Rookie Cop); Michael Malone (Cavalry Lieutenant); Mitch Marcus (Cavalry Major); Richard Mataisz Sr. (Bar Owner); Lon Peterson (Paramedic); Caskey Swaim (Vigilante No. 1); Dennis Rucker (Vigilante No. 2); Willy Ketchum (Vigilante No. 3); Tom Mollgard (Hotel Clerk); David Mayers (Tuxedo Salesman); Scotty Augare (Posse Member No. 2); Rusty Hendrickson (Posse Member No. 3); Tom Walter (Posse Member No. 4); Craig Hoskings (Cessna Pilot); Bud Davis (Cessna Passenger); Arthur Rooney (Deputy No. 2); Julie Rappold (Jay's Wife); Erin O'Brien (Calvin's Wife); Clyde R. Steyee (Realtor); Molly Kicking Woman (Old Indian Lady); George A. Hall III (Indian Policeman).

LOS ANGELES TIMES, 9/29/89, Calendar/p. 10, Chris Willman

The time-honored game of cowboys 'n' Indians is revived with self-consciously tragic results in "War Party," which, for all its appealing players, tense action and intriguing plot devices, is *not* the feel-good hit of the fall.

The setup is unique but strangely familiar: In modern-day Wyoming, a small band of youthful Blackfeet is being methodically hunted down in the wilderness for an ill-perceived crime against white men. Those lawmen brave or silly enough to come after them meet extremely violent resistance.

The dilemma facing the befuddled Indian heroes toward the morally ambiguous climax is whether to surrender or to fight to the finish, either way perpetuating centuries of historically gory injustice.

Yes, this is just what it sounds like: "First Blood" meets "Do the Right Thing."

The Sly-versus-Spike clash of sensibilities is an irresistibly bizarre one, but both those predecessors had queasy resolutions that were felt by many viewers to be troublesome. And terrific as much of the buildup in "War Party" is, you just know there's no conceivable way the film makers will have come up with a climax worthy of its crescendo. And you're right.

For its first half or so, though, "War Party" shapes up to be one of the shrewdest, uncanniest, nerviest action pictures of the year.

Director Franc Roddam has worked with small youth ensembles before ("Quadrophenia," "Lords of Discipline"), and there is telling detail in the way he and writer Spencer Eastman show an Indian community through the eyes of its youth, who sense that their parents have sold their souls to blend in with the white municipality but aren't quite aware just how much heritage has been shed.

These kids aren't particularly bright, or brave; like their soon-to-be-mortal-enemy Anglo counterparts in the town, they like to drink and smoke dope and indulge in casual foreplay on horseback.

A prologue portraying the systematic slaughter of an Indian tribe 100 years earlier segues into the arrival of long-haired lead player Sonny Crowkiller (Billy Wirth) in a pickup truck, listening to a rock tape that any young white stoner might have on—a quintessential '70s party anthem with Free's Paul Rodgers singing "Baby, it's all right now...we're so happy together!"

The irony in that nice touch is subtle but clear, and it's established early on that, for all the surface assimilation, there's trouble brewing between the two races that will explode in violence.

The occasion comes when a 100-year-old battle between Indians and settlers is re-enacted to lure tourists during a centennial celebration. (The ease with which the Blackfeet agree to re-create a battle in which their forefathers were wiped out is implausible, but no matter.)

One malcontent drunk decides to shoot-'em-up for real, and before anyone can figure out what happened, violence is begetting violence and history is skipping on its groove, as Wirth and Kevin Dillon and two other Indian males retreat on horseback to the woods, planeloads and truckloads of vigilante locals close behind.

The cross-cutting between hunters and prey is initially nervewracking, then drags. The appearance late in the game of a bounty hunter played by M. Emmet Walsh—a character actor who has saved many a movie—promises a pick-me-up, but he actually slows this one down, since his character has so little to do with the plot.

Offering even less of an assist is an alcoholic medicine man who plays much the same Greek-Chorus function as the town drunk in Spike Lee's movie, only far less successfully. And in this case, the final act of doing the right thing seems far more senseless than anything Lee could have concocted on a mindbendingly hot day.

Roddam and Eastman deserve credit for having the courage of their convictions in not trying to paste a sunny resolution onto their bleak (and justifiably R-rated) story. But while their "War" goes out with a literal bang, it wraps up with a symbolic whimper, one that finally seems to exploit a situation begging to be treated without warwhooping cliches or fatalism.

It's their "Party," and they'll cry if they want to; real-life Indians may be excused for failing to RSVP.

NEW YORK POST, 9/29/89, p. 24, Jami Bernard

American Indians have not gotten a very good deal from Hollywood (or from any other institution, for that matter), so it must be a victory for them to have a film in which they are the good guys, they get to play themselves and they get to right old wrongs in a cathartic replay of a historic defeat.

But "War Party" gives the American Indian a Pyrrhic victory, because it is not a very good movie, and because it reduces Indians to yet another kind of stereotype, the kind gays have been subjected to in "sensitive" films about them. Let's put it this way—movie Indians, like movie gays, do not get the girl. Metaphorically speaking, of course.

But they do get to die noble deaths, something "War Party" seems to think is an intrinsic Indian goal. (How about a noble life, instead? Or an ignoble but long life?)

When a modern-day Montana town puts on a full-costumed re-enactment of an old battle for the sake of tourist dollars, long-dormant blood feuds surface and the mock battle turns into a real one. Once the blood starts flowing, the townspeople lose their cool and embark on scalping parties that call to mind any number of redneck soirees in which the call to arms is "Yee-hah!"

Instead of being a tribute to the Indian, "War Party" uses the devastated culture as a springboard for a traditional cowboy-and-Indian chase extravaganza, with plenty of sadistic blood-lettings and shots of horses thundering over the plains.

Citing the ancient Indian battle cry, "You mess with my brothers, you mess with me"—well, they don't say "mess" in this movie, but then, neither did their ancestors—pals Billy Wirth and Kevin Dillon vow either to make a last stand or head to Canada, depending on what the old medicine man advises them.

(Kevin Dillon makes a rather Irish-looking Indian, but it's not as much an intrusion as you'd think.)

The teens, clad in traditional regalia with such modern touches as Walkmen and Twinkies, vaguely remember the teachings of the ancients, like telling time from the position of the sun, but mostly they make heap big mistakes as they go along. The movie, not knowing where to take itself after at least an hour of tiresome chase, borrows a page from "Butch Cassidy and the Sundance Kid," which only makes you feel worse about the senseless slaughter of old and the senseless movies of today.

NEWSDAY, 9/29/89, Part III/p. 3, Aileen Jacobson

"War Party" starts out like a parody of old-time westerns: The camera tracks a white feather floating down the river toward a dead Indian chief in elaborate headdress, then follows a soldier who walks past mounds of slaughtered Indians to take the chief's tomahawk to his major. A photograph is taken and the flash scares off some horses. We see the horses till they stop to graze.

But hold it. Cut to modern times: As we watch the horses graze, along comes a pickup truck, driven by a young man with long hair who's listening to loud rock music.

It's an arty way to start a movie that's full of good intentions and solemn moral tone, but slips into old movie cliches and a kind of Rambo-on-the-prairies mentality.

"War Party" is supposed to be about the way Native Americans are treated today. A century after the massacre depicted in the first scene, the Blackfeet Indians who still live near the Montana site are persuaded to stage a re-enactment to draw tourist dollars. The local white people are to play the calvary.

It all goes terribly awry when one of the white men loads his gun with real bullets to settle a score with one of the Indians. Another young Indian kills the white man and flees with a group of his friends, to be pursued by the unfailingly devious, callous and bigoted white folks of the town.

The Blackfeet, on the other hand, are unfailingly honest, brave and innocent. They also get killed in greater numbers than the whites.

Although some Native American actors are used, this is a movie made by white men, which may help to account for its distant feel. In fact, its director, Franc Roddam, is British, and in a lunatic bit of casting, one of the major Indian roles is played by pale-faced Kevin Dillon (Matt's younger brother, best known for his work in "Platoon").

The press notes for the film say Dillon's character, Skitty Harris, is 3/8 Indian and 5/8 Irish, but fractions are never mentioned in the film. Instead, Skitty is as totally committed to Indian ways as any of his friends, and you just wonder why at least one of them hasn't noticed his upturned nose or fluffy hair and asked him why he isn't on the other side.

He seems to have been thrown in as a way to attract a mainstream teenage audience. Indeed, the small group of Indian fugitives, who pledge to stand by each other till the end, often are treated in Spencer Eastman's simplistic screenplay as little more than misunderstood, alienated youth of any ethnic background. They joke about juvenile things, set up secret meetings with their girlfriends and wonder if they're famous. They play out some movie-inspired version of what it means to be brave. If it weren't for all the gore, the film could have been titled "Teen Party."

There's not much room for anyone to display acting skill, but Billy Worth has a strong screen presence as Sonny, leader of the Indian youth, and Tim Sampson is convincing as one of the comrades. Indian activist Dennis Banks, as Sonny's father and an Indian leader, is most charismatic of all, always dignified and gentle. Peggy Lipton (The Mod Squad") is good in a small role as an enterprising TV reporter—and the only white who even flinches at any of the atrocities committed on the Indians.

The film treats the idea of Indian-as-victim, white-man-as-aggressor as a new revelation, but that message is now the established one. It doesn't have to be hammered in. And it doesn't need, as part of the final apocalyptic scene, a medicine man who calls forth real lightning with his incantations. That, again, borders on parody.

VILLAGE VOICE, 10/10/89, p. 85, J. Hoberman

While Matt Dillon gives a career performance in *Drugstore Cowboy* [see Hoberman's review], younger brother Kevin maintains the family tradition of self-conscious posing—appearing, with no particular distinction, as a brash young Native American in Franc Roddam's *War Party*. A year on the shelf has not improved this botched contempo western, which immediately establishes its premise by segueing from a late 19th century Indian defeat to a sorry-looking Blackfeet reservation in present-day Montana.

The atmosphere is already heavy with free-floating hostility. Local leaders, it seems, are planning to convert the 100th anniversary of the Battle of Milk River into a gala tourist attraction, restaging the massacre with a cast of local whites and Indians. Inevitably, a disgruntled white uses the pageant as a means for settling some old scores. The battle turns real with the native aristo Sonny (Billy Wirth), his excitable sidekick (Dillon), and several other young Blackfeet forced to head for the hills, a white lynching party on their tail. "Goddam, what a mess," one law officer mournfully observes in the centennial's disastrous aftermath—and that goes double for the film.

Although a few of Roddam's early scenes have a zesty tumult reminiscent of the clash between the Mods and Rockers in the once-promising director's 1979 *Quadrophenia*, he basically lays on the ketchup to lubricate the scenario's creaky contrivances, and pumps up already clunky characterizations with Rambotic derring-do. (After bare-chested Sonny brings down a small airplane with a well-placed arrow, *War Party* begins to seem an inferior version of *First Blood*.)

There's no question where *War Party*'s sympathies lie, but, for all its aggressive liberalism and abundance of Native American extras, the movie lacks texture and nuance; it's far inferior to the splendidly eccentric *Powwow Highway*, which Warners fumbled so resoundingly earlier this year. Incidentally, connoisseurs of lost causes who attend *War Party* may note that one of the Blackfeet braves wears a Mets cap and wonder why.

Also reviewed in:
NEW YORK TIMES, 9/29/89, p. C7, Stephen Holden
VARIETY, 9/28/88, p. 17
WASHINGTON POST, 12/4/89, p. B7, Hal Hinson

WEAPONS OF THE SPIRIT

A First Run Features release of a Friends of Le Chambon production. *Producer:* Pierre Sauvage. *Director:* Pierre Sauvage. *Screenplay (English and French with English subtitles):* Pierre Sauvage. *Director of Photography:* Yves Dahan. *Editor:* Matthew Harrison. *Music:* Antonio Vivaldi, Maurice Ravel, Django Reinhardt, Ephemere Collective, and Giora Feidman. *Sound:* Patrick Baroz. *Running Time:* 90 minutes. *MPAA Rating:* Not Rated.

CAST: Joseph Atlas, Georgette Barraud, Roger Darcissac, Charles Gibert, Henri Heritier, Emma Heritier, Hilde Hillebrand, Jean Hillebrand, Lesley Maber, The Rev. Edouard Theis, and Magda Trocmé.

LOS ANGELES TIMES, 10/4/89, Calendar/p. 11, Michael Wilmington

In films today, the weapons of death and destruction are often before us. The weapons of the spirit—quieter instruments of mercy, reverence, compassion—we see much more rarely. Yet, these are what Pierre Sauvage celebrates in his inspiring documentary "Weapons of the Spirit," a chronicle of the French mountain village of Le Chambon and its extraordinary mass effort during the Nazi occupation.

Sauvage's story, told with a restraint that may make you weep, is one antidote to the blackness permeating such Holocaust documentaries as "The Sorrow and the Pity" and "Shoah." Against these now familiar portraits of widespread cowardice or complicity, Sauvage poses the ennobling example of the Chamboniers, who saved his life, the lives of his parents and of 5,000 other Jewish refugees, at least one for every inhabitant of the village.

What Le Chambon did is remarkable in itself. For the entire war, they refused to collaborate with the Nazis or their puppets, becoming, along with other mountain villages, a safe harbor for refugees. Simple mountain people, deeply Christian, many descended from France's persecuted Huguenot minority, they continuously risked death or prison to rescue people they barely knew. They shared their meager food, helped supply phony papers (forged locally and secreted in local beehives), welcomed the children into their schools and openly defied the Gestapo.

It was the pacifist pastor André Trocmé, who later died in a concentration camp, who led Le Chambon's quiet revolt and who coined the phrase of the movie's title, telling his parishioners, as France collapsed: "The responsibility of Christians is to resist the violence that will be brought to bear on their consciences ... through the weapons of the spirit." Trocmé's flock never forgot this admonition. Not one Jewish refugee was betrayed there to the Gestapo, not by Trocmé's Protestants, not by the town's Catholic minority, not by the Vichy representative, not even by the wounded German soldiers billeted at a local hotel—who probably knew, or suspected, everything. This was, for Sauvage, a vast "conspiracy of goodness" in which the unshakable faith of Le Chambon's shepherd gradually infiltrated everyone else as well.

Sauvage, a beneficiary of that goodness (another was Albert Camus, who wrote "The Plague" at a nearby farm) has obviously made this film as a partial recompense. Shot in a calm, unsentimental, elegiac style, it suggests the work of a director he admired as a critic, John Ford, in its celebration of the community, its revelation of the nobility of the commonplace, its idealism and even its sad irony: the way Le Chambon was later somewhat forgotten, even by those it saved.

Yet "Weapons of the Spirit" (Times-rated—Family) is one document—Philip Hallie's book on Le Chambon, "Lest Innocent Blood be Shed," is another—which ensures the town's remembrance: and that of these fine, brave, truly admirable people, who, though they would disclaim the role, are part of our universal conscience. Watching their extraordinary faces, we may come to realize, that, if we were all more like them, there would be no Holocausts.

NEW YORK, 9/18/89, p. 71, David Denby

One of the corrupting side effects of a catastrophe like the Holocaust is that it accustoms us so thoroughly to the prevalence of evil that we may have some difficulty in accepting the possibility of goodness. Thus the chances of creditable behavior in a future crisis are undermined. In recent years, the network of viciousness that made the Holocaust possible has been thoroughly investigated. By contrast, the occasional episodes of resistance to the Final Solution remain something of a mystery—a challenge, too, since the very existence of such episodes, however marginal or exceptional, calls into question the acquiescence in evil that so many defined as necessity.

The town of Le Chambon-sur-Lignon, in south-central France, sheltered as many as 5,000 Jews during World War II; since no other town in Vichy France practiced virtue on a comparable scale, the history of Le Chambon is as much an accusation as a stirring instance of moral courage. Why this town? The American documentary filmmaker Pierre Sauvage, who was born in Le Chambon (his Jewish parents had sought refuge there), devotes himself to this puzzle in his incisive and finally very moving *Weapons of the Spirit*. Le Chambon, it turns out, was populated largely by descendants of Huguenots, France's Protestants; the town's memory of being a persecuted minority in Catholic France was part of its communal identity. Defiance and tolerance were the poles of its moral compass: Before the war, the town had taken in refugees of the Spanish Civil War and other outcasts. And once Le Chambon acted on behalf of the Jews, its behavior created momentum—what Sauvage calls "a conspiracy of goodness." The local Vichy prefect almost certainly protected the town; the *Wehrmacht* commandant in charge of troops convalescing in Le Chambon appears to have looked the other way.

But beyond the historical and circumstantial explanations, there is a core of decency in the Chambonnais that is hard to account for. When interviewed by Sauvage, the elderly survivors of the Vichy period respond with remarkable simplicity. Their kindness appears to be instinctive, their piety a generous form of Christian witness. The Jews, they say, may not have believed in the Gospels, but they were "people of God"—the ancestors, the characters of the Old Testament. They are a modest group of heroes, these peasants and storekeepers, but there's pride in their simple assertion of right and also a somber mystique of courage, nurtured in silence and opposition through generations. Some people, they remind us, do the right thing because it's the only thing they *can* do.

NEW YORK POST, 9/1/89, p. 27, David Edelstein

In a country all too willing to turn over its Jews to Nazi occupiers, the villagers of Le Chambon-sur-Lignon in the south of France did something extraordinary: From 1940 to 1944 they gave shelter—at enormous risk—to 5,000 Jewish refugees. Miraculously, Le Chambon was never raided, although there is reason to believe officials of the puppet Vichy government and even some Nazis knew of the deception.

What happened? In the words of Pierre Sauvage, the director of "Weapons of the Spirit," there was a "conspiracy of goodness." And what Sauvage has captured, in this simple and overwhelming documentary, are the modest roots of that conspiracy. A Jew who was born in Le Chambon in the final days of the war, Sauvage has made a testament not to Judaism but to the noblest strain of Christianity.

He begins with a small, unsensational moment—a pair of Le Chambon inhabitants, Henri and Emma Heritier, who stand in front of the aged stone townhouses and shrug off the question of motive. "It was nothing" they say when asked why they did it, or, "It was just the right thing to do." As Sauvage's camera rests on them, they seem modest, diffident, remarkably uncomplicated.

You watch "Weapons of the Spirit" thinking that evil isn't really so banal (as Hannah Arendt suggested): Perhaps what it represents is human nature thrown into confusion by fear. After all, it's the rest of France that's still traumatized by World War II—by how easy, for many, collaboration came.

Le Chambon is largely composed of Huguenots—Protestants who for centuries were persecuted for their faith. As a result of that oppression, the film suggests, they developed a strong sense of right and wrong and a tradition of good works.

During the occupation, the village was led by a pastor named André Trocmé, a pacifist who opposed armed conflict with the Third Reich and, when the war was lost and a "dishonorable armistice" signed, prevailed on Le Chambon to fight quietly against the Nazi rule. The film makes plain that Trocmé (now dead) was the guiding force in this "conspiracy of goodness"—the extraordinary individual. But only in a place like Le Chambon could Trocmé's words generate prompt, unquestioning action.

It's important to understand that what happened was not a spontaneous act of heroism but the continuation of a belief—a belief that, as the Bible states, the hungry must be fed and the innocent protected. As Sauvage explores these ideas he creates a sort of anti-"Shoah" in which compassion, not hatred, lurks behind the words of ordinary Christians.

Even the Christian fundamentalists—known elsewhere for antipathy toward Judaism—took part. "Even though they didn't respect the Gospel, for us they were people of God," says one fundamentalist. "The neighbor to love as yourself is down the street."

The secret was to spell nothing out—there was a wordless communication among the villagers and their guests, many of whom moved about openly.

There's a gleeful comic tone as one farmer relays the story of how he hid false papers and passports in empty beehives, confident that Germans wouldn't stick their hands in. When the Vichy police arrived one day with empty buses to carry off Jews, Trocmé refused to turn over their names: "It's not the role of the shepherd to denounce his flock," he said. The policemen, according to a witness, were relieved that they didn't have to carry out their barbarous orders.

"Weapons of the Spirit" is rich in such stories of benign neglect or incompetence. Among them is the tale of a policeman installed in Le Chambon by the Vichy government. Officially, the young man made stern noises about Jews, but he also mingled with the townspeople and never turned in a soul. In one of the war's awful ironies, he was ultimately gunned down by resistance fighters.

Wisely, Sauvage leaves until last a visit with the family that sheltered his own parents. As he looks at pictures of himself as a baby, the movie comes full circle, back to the man whose obsession with his roots gave birth to this inspiring film.

The only aspect Sauvage leaves unexplored is the mind set of the Jews who left Le Chambon after the war and never came back, preferring to forget those years. There's no indication in the film that Sauvage's own parents didn't tell him about their ordeal until late in their lives—or that he didn't even know he was a Jew until age 18. But it's better this way. That's another, more personal story.

Ironically, Israel's most rabid, neo-conservative defenders in this country will probably balk at championing "Weapons of the Spirit." For the villagers of Le Chambon represent (in addition to Christianity) the soul of liberal activism: In this country, their descendants are the men and women who run the Sanctuary movement, which gives shelter to thousands of victims of Central American oppression. Their deeds and other good works are the true continuation of the miraculous conspiracy of goodness at Le Chambon-sur-Lignon.

NEWSDAY, 9/1/89, Part III/p. 3, Terry Kelleher

Christianity hasn't been tried and found wanting, G.K. Chesterton said early in this century. It has been found difficult and left untried.

The small French village of Le Chambon-sur-Lignon tried Christianity when it was most difficult—during the Nazi occupation of the 1940s. The inhabitants sheltered 5,000 hunted Jews—as many refugees as there were natives.

But to hear the Chambonnais tell it, the whole thing was no big deal.

"It happened so naturally—we can't understand the fuss," one elderly villager tells film maker Pierre Sauvage in "Weapons of the Spirit." "I helped simply because they needed to be helped."

Sauvage has reason to be grateful for the Chambonnais' unassuming good works. His Jewish parents fled Paris in 1943 and found their way to Le Chambon. The next year he was born in a hospital near the village. His family emigrated to New York in 1948, and not until he was 18 did Sauvage learn the circumstances of his birth.

Moved by the birth of his own son, Sauvage began the long process of making "Weapons of the Spirit" in 1980, when he was a staff producer at public television station KCET in Los Angeles. The documentary serves as Sauvage's personal "Roots" story, as well as a valuable study of courage and charity in the midst of cravenness and perfidy. The simple decency that shines through in interviews with the Chambonnais seems even more inspiring when seen against newsreel footage of Marshall Petain receiving the cheers of the collaborationist crowd.

How was it that the people of Le Chambon stood up for humanity while so many of their countrymen hastened to cooperate in Hitler's "final solution"? How did they come to be uncontaminated by what Sauvage calls "the virulent tradition of anti-Semitism that infests the very soul of Christianity"?

For one thing, they were descendants of the Huguenots, French Protestants subjected to severe persecution in the 18th Century. They knew what it meant of suffer for being different. For another, a number were fundamentalists who felt a special kinship with the Jewss through their reverence for the Old Testament.

The best explanation, however, is the most elementary: They practiced what they preached. Perhaps the most powerful moment in "Weapons of the Spirit" comes when Edouard Theis, the community's assistant pastor during the war, recites the Golden Rule—not as a shibboleth, but as an urgent injunction. as Jesus said, he that has ears, let him hear.

Theis and Pastor André Trocmé formed a stubborn "minority of two" in those days. First, as pacifists, they opposed taking arms against the German invaders. Then, as moralists, they opposed collaborating with them. Their brand of Christianity was gloriously difficult, but it only sounded impossible.

Though eminently worthwhile, "Weapons of the Spirit" lacks one cinematic ingredient: dramatic tension. The humility and matter-of-fact righteousness of the Chambonnais are commendable, but inevitably a bit monotonous. The element of conflict is introduced only when Sauvage interviews a former minister of the Vichy government, whose rationalizations would be pathetic if they weren't so appalling.

Whatever is absent from this film, you probably won't miss it. Like the people it quietly celebrates, "Weapons of the Spirit" has no need to improve on the truth.

NEWSWEEK, 9/18/89, p. 81, David Ansen

While the French Vichy government was eagerly collaborating with the Nazis—deporting, 80,000 Jews to the death camps and confirming one's blackest view of human nature—in the poor farming village of Le Chambon-sur-Lignon an altogether different response to the evils of the Holocaust occurred. There, during the war, some 5,000 Jews were saved by the inhabitants of a town that itself numbered only 5,000. How, asks filmmaker Pierre Sauvage in his moving and provocative documentary *Weapons of the Spirit,* did this "conspiracy of goodness" happen? What made Le Chambon—a town where not a single act of betrayal occurred—resist the virus that had contaminated most of Europe?

Sauvage's film is both an enquiry into the nature of goodness and a personal odyssey. The filmmaker, a Jew, was born in Le Chambon in 1944, and he returned there to interview the men and women to whom he, and so many others, owe their lives. Questioning these devout people—most of them descendants of Huguenots—about their heroic deeds, he is repeatedly faced with a similar response: "We can't understand the fuss." We helped because they needed to be helped." There is no false modesty in this. The people of Le Chambon found goodness natural, logical. What else could they do? These Protestant peasants believed that their deeds must match the words of the Old Testament. And as descendants of a greatly persecuted sect, the filmmaker suggests, their own history of oppression made them innately sympathetic to the plight of the Jews.

Though the movie makes the point that the community's effort was more a spontaneous response than an organized mission, there is no doubt that spiritual leadership was provided by pastor André Trocmé, a pacifist who, on the day after France surrendered to Germany, exhorted his flock to resist the Nazis with "the weapons of the spirit." The contagiousness of goodness even seemed to spread, curiously, to the Vichy officials and German soldiers in Chambon, who strangely failed to report what was occurring there.

There are mysteries here, which Sauvage in 90 minutes cannot fully explore. But what an extraordinary story he has revealed, one that is both enormously uplifting and, because it is so anomalous, terribly sad. In making a hopeful film about the Holocaust, Sauvage reminds us of the vast majority who lifted not a finger.

VILLAGE VOICE, 9/5/89, p. 80, Renee Tajima

The Holocaust generally conveys the sense of a grand, sweeping canvas, in the breadth of Hitler's terror machine and in the sheer mass of Jewish suffering. And so the period has inspired epic films such as *Shoah* and *Hotel Terminus.* From its title, *Weapons of the Spirit* might seem to share that lofty vision. Instead, it is a movie about simple, earthy heroes, people who seem to have been forgotten even by those they helped.

Filmmaker Pierre Sauvage returns to the place of his birth, Le Chambon-sur-Lignon, a remote French farming village known only for its intrepid winters and the 100-year period called "the Desert," when devout Huguenots were persecuted by the kings of France for their Protestant beliefs. A century later, their descendants crossed history again as 5000 Protestants provided shelter for 5000 Jewish refugees, like a blessed oasis in the middle of the Vichy-occupied country. Declares one tiny Chambonnaise woman, "It happened so naturally, we can't understand the fuss."

Despite their own poverty, the Chambonnais took in entire families as well as lone children in a quiet, unorganized network that Sauvage refers to as "a conspiracy of goodness." All this happened under the watchful eyes of France's occupiers. Nazi soldiers convalesced in a hotel right across from French resistance headquarters. Vichy police, who helped send 80,000 French Jews to the death camps, always returned from Le Chambon empty-handed. Even they, Sauvage suggests, seem to have been smitten by the beneficence of the place.

It is an astonishing story, but Sauvage's account is laid out in a conventional documentary style, à la Bill Moyers. As on-air commentator, Sauvage arrives on a train steaming toward the mountains, and through the rest of the film balances personal investment with journalistic remove. The result is a curious loss of passion. Here is a child of the Holocaust, born in hiding, who was not even told he was Jewish until the age of 18. That something ticks beneath the surface is apparent in the way Sauvage spits out the narration, especially in his descriptions of the Nazis. But the film's public television approach—interviews with two dozen-plus witnesses, preceded by the mandatory historical sequence, are illustrated by archival photos (my favorite is a portrait of a local pig named Adolf)—mutes its emotional power. *Weapons of the Spirit* is a comprehensive collective history, but it leaves one with a thirst for more personal depth.

The best films on the period have allowed us to get deep inside the moral life of an individual—

portraying the Holocaust and resistance to it as a human act, not historical aberration. What were those conflicts for the Chambonnais? The Heritiers, a peasant couple that took care of the Sauvage family, also hid false papers used by fugitive Jews who were transported to Switzerland on the underground railroad. Why, Sauvage asks, take the risk of sheltering and protecting the Jews? I don't know,'' shrugs Mrs. Heritier. "We were used to it.'' These types of answers, prevalent throughout the film, are modest and endearing, but never satisfying.

Also reviewed in:
NEW YORK TIMES 9/1/89, p. C6, Caryn James
VARIETY, 4/8/87, p. 22
WASHINGTON POST, 1/19/90, p. B1, Hal Hinson

WEEKEND AT BERNIE'S

A Twentieth Century For release of a Gladden Entertainment film. *Executive Producer:* Robert Klane and Malcolm R. Harding. *Producer:* Victor Drai. *Director:* Ted Kotcheff. *Screenplay:* Robert Klane. *Director of Photography:* François Protat. *Editor:* Joan E. Chapman. *Music:* Andy Summers. *Music Editor:* Robert Randles. *Sound:* Walter S. Hoylman. *Sound Editor:* Alan Splet. *Production Designer:* Peter Jamison. *Art Director:* Michael Novotny. *Set Designer:* Keith Burns and Dawn Serody. *Set Decorator:* Jerie Kelter. *Special Effects:* Phil Cory and Joe Digaetano. *Costumes:* Richard "Dick" Butz. *Make-up:* Barbara Palmer. *Stunt Coordinator:* Conrad Palmisano. *Running time:* 101 minutes. *MPAA Rating:* PG-13.

CAST: Andrew McCarthy (Larry Wilson); Jonathan Silverman (Richard Parker); Catherine Mary Stewart (Gwen Saunders); Terry Kiser (Bernie Lomax); Don Calfa (Paulie); Catherine Parks (Tina); Eloise Broady (Tawny); Gregory Salata (Marty); Louis Giambalvo (Vito); Ted Kotcheff (Jack Parker); Margaret Hall (Secretary); Timothy Perez (Mugger); Mark Smaltz (Security Officer); Anthony Mannino (Superintendent); Polly Segal (Woman in Elevator); Bob Horen (Maitre d'); Bruce Barbour (Beach Bum); Jason Woliner (Bratty Kid); Dan Cox (Handsome Guy); Steve Howard (Plastic Surgeon); Lorri Lindberg (Authoress); Jack Hallett (Tennis Pro); John Bennes (Harvey); Augustine Berlings (Larry's Pick-Up); Mert Hatfield (Cop); Jack Canon (Murray Rose); Nello Tare (Party Man); Joyce Bowden (Fashion Designer); Stefanos Miltsakakis (Body Builder); Dan Preston (Exercise Trainer); Jean Liles (Girl On Dock); Lisa Sherrill Gannon (Beach Girl #1); Rachel Lewis (Beach Girl #2); Dan Wargo (Party Guest); Patricia Roseman (Female Model); David Arey (Male Model); Ronald Ross (Man at Table); George Cheung (Gardner); Lou Criscuolo (First Islander); Edwin Little Dean (Water Taxi Driver); Stephen Fischer (Man on Elevator); Cindy Foster Jones (Girl at Ambulance); Richard W. Boucher (Handsome Man #2); Leslie Sternchak (Girl at Party); Tina Diane King (Girl at Party #2); Michelle Vincent (Girl on Boat).

LOS ANGELES TIMES, 7/5/89. Calendar/p. 4, Kevin Thomas

"Weekend at Bernie's'' is a one-joke comedy as fragile as a soap bubble. It never self-destructs, but because it threatens to at every turn, it unleashes so many laughs it could just end up a summer sleeper. Writer Robert Klane, who has "Where's Momma?'' among his credits, has taken an amusing premise, and director Ted Kotcheff and his young stars Andrew McCarthy and Jonathan Silverman run with it.

McCarthy's laid-back Larry and Parker's uptight Richard are decidedly junior executives at a Manhattan insurance company. So zealous is Richard that even on the hottest Saturday of the year he is reading computer printouts, when he discovers that $2 million has been paid out to a man already dead. Wow! He and Larry believe that this bit of information is sure to make their careers.

Sure enough, the top guy Bernie Lomex (Terry Kiser), slick woman-chaser and coke-sniffer, is impressed with the detective work—enough to invite the guys out for Labor Day weekend at his place in the Hamptons. It never occurs to them that maybe Richard wasn't supposed to have been such a zealous investigator. But it's Bernie who promptly winds up a corpse.

Klane ingeniously comes up with all sorts of happenings to keep Larry and Richard from contacting the police, and they soon have good reason to believe that it's imperative that everyone believe Bernie is still alive. (It's not all that hard, for apparently Bernie's pals are used to seeing him zonked out.)

No, "Weekend at Bernie's isn't the sly, darkly humorous "wandering corpse'' picture that Hitchcock's "The Trouble With Harry'' is. It can't in fact be accused of possessing so much as a shred of subtlety, but as a broad farce it's not only cleverly sustained but frequently hilarious. What's more, a weekend among the rich, the jaded and the corrupt is just the right cup of tea for an acid social satirist such as Kotcheff (who casts himself in an amusing cameo as Richard's father).

Silverman, who starred in the film of "Brighton Beach Memoirs," and McCarthy are deft and likable, but they're upstaged by Kiser. The Broadway and TV veteran may be funny as a decadent crook, but he is outright hilarious as the corpse who just never seems to stay put. Little more than seeming understandably perplexed by the frantic Richard's behavior is required of Catherine Mary Stewart, but she has a warm and lovely presence. Don Calfa and Catherine Parks get fresh laughs from those familiar gangster types, the heartless hit man and the sexpot mistress.

Production designer Peter Jamison's setting adds much to the humor, especially Bernie's high-tech beach house, big enough for a small air terminal, luxe enough for Gordon Gekko. (More detailed is Richard's parents' perfect *echt*-'50s "apartment.) As a light summer refreshment "Weekend at Bernie's" (rated an appropriate PG-13) hits the spot.

MONTHLY FILM BULLETIN, 3/90, p. 83, Kim Newman

Working overtime at weekends, Larry Wilson and Richard Parker, young employees of an insurance company, discover a two-million-dollar fraud. When they report it to their boss, Bernie Lomax, the high-living executive congratulates them by asking them out to his Long Island beach house for a celebratory weekend. Bernie, who is himself guilty of the fraud, requests that his Mafia boss associate arrange the murders of Larry and Richard. The boss, whose girlfriend is sleeping with Bernie, decrees that Larry should live but that Bernie must die. The nervous Richard asks office beauty Gwen out for a date, but it ends in disaster when he fails to pass off his father, with whom he lives, as his butler. Larry and Richard arrive at Bernie's house just after Paulie, a Mafia hit man, has murdered him. Larry, who still wants a fun weekend, convinces Richard to pretend Bernie is still alive, and when a floating party settles in Bernie's house none of the guests notice he's dead. The reluctant Richard goes along with the deception because it gives him another chance with Gwen, who lives nearby. Learning from a carelessly recorded phone call that Bernie wanted them dead, Larry and Richard further manipulate the corpse to make it seem as if Bernie is alive, which prompts Paulie to make another attempt on his life. Gwen and Richard are reconciled and, along with Larry, are pursued by an enraged Paulie, who thinks they have witnessed his final attempt at killing Bernie. Paulie is arrested, and Bernie's corpse is put aboard an ambulance. However, the gurney bed rolls off and the body ends up on the beach with Larry, Richard and Gwen.

It takes this farce nearly half its running time to set up its central premise, that the two faceless young leads, for a succession of increasingly ridiculous reasons, must try to pass off their deceased and grey-faced boss as a live swinger. Certainly coming a long way after Hitchcock's deft handling of a similar situation in *The Trouble with Harry*, *Weekend at Bernie's* opts for all the cheap humour it can wring from the concept, with Harry's mistress noisily making out with him without noticing his condition, Larry and Richard making him seem alive by tying his shoelaces to theirs and walking him around, or by having the body "ski" behind a speeding boat, with all the vacuous residents of Long Island blithely waving and chatting at the corpse. Although Terry Kiser deserves points for suffering through the corpse role much as Bruce Dern did in *The Wild Angels*, the rest of the cast mug energetically as if trying to upstage the dead character and fail entirely to create a basis for anything approaching humour. Though Ted Kotcheff and Robert Klane have at least one decent comedy apiece to their credit (*Fun with Dick and Jane, Where's Poppa?*), the central idea here is clumsily worked out, compounded by the charmlessness of the leads and the ugliness of the whole production.

NEW YORK POST, 7/5/89, p. 23, Jami Bernard

Larry and Richard have worked very hard to wangle a weekend's invitation at their boss's summer beach house, but when they arrive they find their boss has been murdered. What a drag! But why let that ruin their weekend?

This is the wacky premise of "Weekend at Bernie's." If only it had the subversive daring of the first half of "Heathers," it could have secured its place in the pantheon of black comedies. Still, despite a sophomoric teen-movie start, "Bernie" gains momentum and eventually provides a sustained level of hilarity revolving around the care and handling of Bernie's corpse.

Andrew McCarthy and Jonathan Silverman play Larry and Richard, two yuppies-in-training who discover a $2 million shortfall in the books of the insurance agency they work for. Their plan is to point out the error in order to ingratiate themselves with their boss, Bernie Lomax (Terry Kiser), so they can get a raise and rent a summer share instead of spending their weekends at gooey Tar Beach.

At this stage, the movie's aspirations look depressingly similar to those of Larry and Richard—a punch-drunk beach party with plenty of jiggle. Fortunately, Bernie is bumped off pretty early. It was he who stole the $2 million, and his plan to bring Larry and Richard out to the house to be murdered backfires when his mobster partners kill him instead for getting sloppy.

Our boys find Bernie propped up at his desk, dead as a party without a keg. "What kind of host invites you for a weekend and dies on you?" demand the boys irritably. Despite Richard's initial reservations, Larry's plan holds away; they decide to go ahead and have their fun, and report the dead body once the wild weekend is over.

It turns out Bernie was quite a party animal, so the throngs of revelers who flood his house don't seem to realize there's anything amiss. One running gag involves a neighbor who mistakes Bernie's indifference for a negotiating ploy on a car deal.

The boys move Bernie's body every now and then to make it look good, while they pursue their main objective—meeting babes. Richard has his eye on a woman from the office (Catherine Mary Stewart) on whom he's long had a crush, and Larry has his eye on anything that moves.

The real humor, though, rests on the stiff shoulders of the stiff. Terry Kiser is the funniest dead body in recent memory, as bland and implacable as a sack of potatoes when he's propped, improbably, on the couch wearing sunglasses; as loose-limbed and weak-kneed as a newborn foal when he is moved about and made to wave at passers-by. Whether lounging in a deck chair, having flies swatted off his face or going for an unplanned bit of body-surfing behind a rogue speedboat, Bernie—a dazed look of bemusement on his face—continues to be the toast of the Hamptons even after he's gone to that great sand dune in the sky.

In fact, Bernie's crowning achievement is when his mistress arrives unexpectedly, locks herself in the bedroom with him and emerges a while later with no complaints. "The guy gets laid more dead than I do alive," complains Larry.

In a series of witty sight gags, Bernie's body keeps washing up into the frame at odd moments, borne on the surf or being unearthed from a child's overzealous sand-castle play. He constantly needs vacuuming, grooming, propping and his facial expressions become more bizarrely determined as rigor mortis sets in.

Although the boys gradually become convinced that they are still targets of murder, there is nothing the slightest bit sinister about "Weekend at Bernie's." In fact, there is no edge at all. It is very difficult for the live ones, Andrew McCarthy and Jonathan Silverman, to make much of their bland-as-pap supporting roles. Most of their function is to push and pull the body around and make sarcastic asides—which are not all that sarcastic, considering they come from the pen of Robert Klane who wrote "Where's Poppa?"

As directed by Ted Kotcheff ("North Dallas Forty"), some of the slapstick scenes are right on the mark; others fall flat. The dead body is the liveliest thing on screen—luckily, in this case, that's as it should be.

NEWSDAY, 7/5/89, Part II/p. 5, Terry Kelleher

You could call "Weekend at Bernie's" a stiff. You could say it's D.O.A.

But hey, some perfectly normal people have fun with corpses.

Larry and Richard (Andrew McCarthy and Jonathan Silverman) are junior employees at a New York insurance company who discover evidence of internal fraud and report it to their sleazy boss, Bernie (Terry Kiser). He invites them to party, party, party at his beach house in the Hamptons, ostensibly as a reward for their diligence. Actually, it's Bernie who's looting the corporation, and he's planning to have Larry and Richard silenced by a Mafia hit man (Don Calfa). What Bernie doesn't know is that the hit man has higher orders to ice *him*. Larry and Richard arrive to find their host has been executed by lethal injection.

Acting out of panic and natural stupidity, Larry and Richard prop up the corpse and make believe Bernie is alive. When a "floating party" descends on the place, the summer revelers figure good ol' Bernie's simply drunk or stoned as usual.

"Doesn't anyone realize he's dead?" Richard asks Larry, as if director Ted Kotcheff hadn't already pounded the point into the sand.

All right, you say, maybe the rest of the movie gets better. But there is no rest of the movie. Larry and Richard just continue to play "Let's Pretend Bernie's Breathing," while Richard ineptly romances Gwen (Catherine Mary Stewart), a pretty intern from the office who apparently can't resist a compulsive liar. On their first date, Richard tells Gwen his parents are dead, even though they're alive. Later, he tells her Bernie is alive, even though he's dead. When Richard finally admits Bernie is dead, Gwen is understandably convinced he's alive.

If the idea of "Weekend at Bernie's" appeals to you, you'll howl when Larry and Richard pull Bernie in a little red wagon and his head bounces down the boardwalk. You'll guffaw when Larry and Richard take Bernie on a wild ride in a speedboat and wind up dragging the body in their wake. (a sure sign hilarity is in store: Richard asks Larry if he's "ever driven a boat before.")

If, on the other hand, you expect a movie to do more than milk a single crude gag, you'll wish Bernie were alive so you could kill him with your bare hands.

In the acting department, Silverman mostly aims for controlled hysteria in the Alan Arkin style. McCarthy, ordinarily the sensitive young man, seems to have been cast by mistake as a lazy lout in loud shirt and purple sneakers. Coastal North Carolina does an adequate impersonation of Long Island's East End. Oh, and Kiser makes a remarkably expressive corpse.

Fortunately for Larry and Richard, Bernie doesn't give off an unpleasant odor as the weekend wears on, which is more than can be said for Robert Klane's script. Kotcheff is capable of making good movies ("The Apprenticeship of Duddy Kravitz," "North Dallas Forty"), but with "Weekend at Bernie's" following hard on the heels of "Winter People," his name could get to be synonymous with "stiff."

VILLAGE VOICE, 7/18/89, p. 73, Julie Phillips

As movies about New York go, *Weekend at Bernie's* is one of the dumbest and tiredest of the whole huge genre. A white-boy's-eye view of summer in the city, it's the story of Larry (Andrew McCarthy) and Rich (*Brighton Beach Memoirs*'s Jonathan Silverman), a would-be East Coast Bill and Ted whining the same old New York whine: Their apartments are too small, they work too hard, they can't get girls, and they can't get out of town for the weekend.

Bernie's begins as a routine caper comedy: Our two potato-faced spastics uncover and report fraud at their company, fraud perpetrated—unbeknownst to them—by their boss, Bernie (Terry Kiser), one of the standard gang of stupid and hapless bad guys. They are invited to Bernie's beach house in the Hamptons for the weekend, with a view to their permanent disposal. On arrival, the boys find Bernie dead and his house overrun by scantily clad women. They decide not to call the cops.

Evolving through a mercifully short beach-party larval stage, *Bernie's* appears in its final form as an extended dead people joke. Bernie is washed away by the tide, recovered, used as a puppet, re-murdered twice; none of the locals ever quite catches on that Bernie is more than "just a little wasted." After enough gross dead body jokes, you begin to laugh in spite of yourself. The biggest audience response came when the boys reanchored Bernie's toupee with a staple gun.

The most pathetic aspect of this surfer movie manqué is the shoddiness of these skinny white boys' idea of a good time. The waters of the North Atlantic are gray and poisonous-looking, and the beach house is atrociously ugly, a bourgeois pleasure shack with a wet bar and a modular sofa. Bernie's party guests are all agents, large-breasted women, or aging queens; this is supposed to be funny. (As a buddy movie, *Bernie's* balances unusually large doses of both homoeroticism and homophobia.) And the object of Rich's affections (Catherine Mary Stewart) is the kind of waitress-faced, empty-headed woman that gives me chills. I know it's a tough life in the big city, but even New Yorkers should be able to come up with a better paradise than this.

Director Ted Kotcheff (*North Dallas Forty, First Blood, Winter People*) makes a cameo appearance in his underwear as Rich's pot-bellied, hairy, disgusting father. It's a revealing moment. One suspects that *Weekend at Bernie's* might not have been such an awful movie if the people who made it had had a sense of shame.

Also reviewed in:

NEW REPUBLIC, 7/31/89, p. 25, Stanley Kauffmann
NEW YORK TIMES, 7/5/89, p. C17, Stephen Holden
VARIETY, 6/28–7/4/89, p. 16
WASHINGTON POST, 7/6/89, p. D11, Hal Hinson
WASHINGTON POST, 7/7/89, Weekend/ p. 35, Joe Brown

WELCOME HOME

A Columbia Pictures release. *Executive Producer:* Don Carmody. *Producer:* Martin Ransohoff. *Director:* Franklin J. Schaffner. *Screenplay:* Maggie Kleinman. *Director of Photography:* Fred J. Koenekamp. *Editor:* Robert E. Swink. *Music:* Henry Mancini. *Music Editor:* Stephan A. Hope. *Sound:* Peter Shewchuk. *Sound Editor:* Wayne Griffin and Jane Tattersall. *Production Designer:* Dan Yarhi. *Art Director:* Dennis Davenport. *Set Decorator:* Rose Marie McSherry. *Set Dresser:* Bill Woods. *Special Effects:* Neil Trifunovich. *Costumes:* Wendy Partridge. *Make-up:* Katherine Southern. *Running time:* 96 minutes. *MPAA Rating:* R.

CAST: Kris Kristofferson (Jake); JoBeth Williams (Sarah); Sam Waterston (Woody); Brian Keith (Harry); Thomas Wilson Brown (Tyler); Trey Wilson (Colonel Barnes); J.J. (Dwayne); Ken Pogue (Senator Camden); Kieu Chinh (Leang); Matthew Beckett (Kim); Jessica Ramien (Siv); Larry Reynolds (Dr. Quayle); Nancy Beatty (Woman); Drew Comin (Little Boy); Gene Clark (Coach Wallace); Jason St. Amour (Johnson); Victor Ertmanis (Willy); Bryan Leadbeater (Drill Sergeant):

LOS ANGELES TIMES, 9/29/89, Calendar/p.4, Michael Wilmington

Something sad and fine seems to be echoing around inside the Vietnam family drama "Welcome Home." There's a compassion and sensibility splitting through the banalities of its story and dialogue, like pure tones in a dull and featureless darkness.

The last film of the late director Franklin Schaffner, it's a thinly written variation on the "Enoch Arden" theme: What would happen if a pilot, shot down over Cambodia and missing for 17 years, returned to confront his wife and her new husband? In the movie, Kris Kristofferson's Jake Robbins—a small-town football hero—is now, unsettlingly, home: an embarrassment for the service, and also for his wife (JoBeth Williams) and son (Thomas Wilson Brown), who prefer to remember him as a dead hero, enshrined on the Vietnam War Memorial.

The writer, Maggie Kleinman, fastens on her gimmick as if it were provocative and new, instead of a Victorian plot device ancient when D.W. Griffith first filmed "Arden" back in 1908. And because she's so reverent with her characters, they remain abstractions: the good but unheroic soldier; the good father (Brian Keith); the good but troubled, sensual wife; the good but threatened husband (Sam Waterston); the resentful and sharp-tongued but basically good son; the good and compassionate senator (Ken Pogue) and even—in a flood of fine fellowship—the tyrannical, deceitful, but basically good-hearted colonel (Trey Wilson) who runs the cover-up on Jake's identity.

Goodness pours from the script like cream from a country pitcher. It slops over all the inconsistencies and hoary plot devices, suffocating the life out of these people before they speak. Without this lubrication, we might wonder about Jake's patron, Sen. Camden, who seems to work without aides or a schedule, flies worldwide on a moment's notice, and decides to help Jake after they meet on a jogging track.

Kristofferson gamely plays Jake as passive. He escapes Cambodia without volition, borne to the Thailand border, unconscious, on the litter, reticent and apologetic about everything. This is a promising beginning for an offbeat character—as disaffected and wounded as the voyeur James Spader plays in the intellectual cult hit "sex, lies and videotape." But Kleinman probably doesn't see Jake in those terms. Instead, he's a victim: a poor guy, trapped in an awful war, who needs a fairy godfather of a senator to bail him out.

The script doesn't really have dramatic confrontations. It has therapeutic tableaux, where the characters make crucial life decisions and reach out for what they most need—frequently a hug. But something about it is moving, anyway.

Schaffner was dying of cancer while he directed "Welcome Home" and, in a way, you can feel him working his way toward the kind of subject he used to do best: before his Oscar for "Patton," before his submergence into big-budget liberal epics in the '70s and before his disastrous run of '80s movies—"Sphinx," "Yes, Giorgio" and "Lionheart"—that were near-parodies of his former excellence.

Here, we almost see again the Schaffner of the '50s and '60s. If the words aren't there, if the characters are too obvious, there's still a kind of relief. We can feel his simple pleasure at the chance to frame a father and son against a slowly flowing lake, or to suggest the unease of a man who will never again feel at home in his old hometown.

In parts of the film—the Kristofferson-Keith scenes, especially—there's quality that suggests the mute but sorrowful resignation the Japanese call *mono ne aware*, the guiding mood of the

Buddhist film maker Yasujiro Ozu. Mostly it's sub-surface, a matter of rhythm and image. And it can't transform "Welcome Home" (MPAA-rated R for sex and language) or save it from the script's small talk and creaky twists. But it's nice to sense that feeling, to see, at the end, even a failed attempt at the idealist themes and human stories with which Schaffner and his generation were most truly at home.

MONTHLY FILM BULLETIN, 3/90, p. 83, John Pym

Lieutenant Jake Robbins, shot down over Vietnam in 1970, turns up after 17 years in a Thai refugee camp. Separated from his Cambodian wife Leang and their two children, Kim and Siv, Jake is shipped back to Everett Air Force hospital, New York. He tracks his father Harry, now a widower, to a lakeside retreat in Vermont. Hoping simply to catch a glimpse of his son Tyler, Jake is spotted by the boy's mother, his first wife Sarah, who after Jake was reported killed in action married Woody, the owner of a lumber mill. Colonel Barnes, Jake's hospital interrogator, reports the death of Leang. One rainy day, Sarah's confusion drives her back into Jake's arms. Tyler, meanwhile, who secretly spotted Jake and his mother at their first meeting, grows sullenly uncommunicative. Sarah eventually comes clean with Woody: Jake calls at their house to confront his son. Tyler cannot accept Jake, whom he has pigeonholed as a revered memory. Jake departs, leaving unfinished business with both Sarah and Tyler. Under pressure from Senator Camden, Colonel Barnes, who up to now has behaved as though it would have been more convenient had Jake not turned up alive, gracefully surrenders the papers allowing Jake to retrieve his children from Thailand. Woody prevails on Tyler to make up with Jake. Beside the lake, under Harry's gaze, Tyler meets Kim and Siv and embraces his father.

Franklin J. Schaffner's last film begins unpromisingly in the Cambodian jungle with Leang mopping her husband's fevered brow; and it ends with the equally unpersuasive camp reunion of Jake and his two small children. In between, however, and despite its undisguised attempt to square up to a big pumped-up issue, *Welcome Home* is a well-acted and more than merely serviceable addition to the MIA Vietnam cycle. Schaffner, who after the Second World War cut his teeth in the film business as an assistant director on the *March of Time* newsreel series, has a very clear idea of how to pitch intense, if hackneyed emotional moments: the first meeting of a widower, killing time beside a lake, and the son he thought dead; the final confrontation between a teenager, who has recently been to Washington to take a rubbing from the Vietnam memorial, and the real father whom he would prefer remained dead so that his relationship with his stepfather—his *real* real father—would not be jeopardised.

The film avoids pyrotechnics in favour of a taking modesty. One could imagine the late Robert Aldrich, for example, approaching the matter-of-fact interrogation scenes in the hospital as Schaffner does: they are unreal and functional, but at the same time have a curious, old-fashioned, watchable authority—but an authority, it should be said, which evaporates the moment one stops to think about it. What does register, however, and sticks is the authority of the acting: the script plods (Sarah, for instance, comes to Jake with wet hair and a clinging shirt), but the players throughout, if never quite transcending the material, lend it moments of genuine feeling. For all the Vietnam movies which have pillaged 60s rock music, few have come up with a scene so plainly unaffected as the one here in which, to the sound of Elton John and Bernie Taupin's "Your Song", Sarah goes through the effects of another lifetime while her new husband stands outside in the shadows of the porch. All in all, not a dishonourable exit.

NEW YORK, 10/16/89, p. 75, David Denby

Franklin J. Schaffner's *Welcome Home* takes place *way* after war—seventeen years after Vietnam, when a downed American flier (Kris Kristofferson), long assumed dead, returns home and confronts his wife, who has since remarried. There's a place for this sort of earnest family stuff, in which one character after another has to "work out" his feelings about a totally contrived situation, and it's called television. No, it's called afternoon-TV soap opera. And the actors don't help. Kristofferson, retiring into the craggy monument of his face, gives a rigid performance. He acts like Abraham Lincoln's death mask.

NEW YORK POST, 9/29/89, p. 21, Jami Bernard

JoBeth Williams looks like she's seen a ghost. In fact, she has. The husband she has thought dead for the past 17 years, since he was gunned down over Cambodia, has just pulled up in a white

Porsche, and when he takes off those dark shades and reveals those ultra-blue peepers, it is unmistakably...Kris Kristofferson! Back from the dead!

"Welcome Home," evidently aspiring to be a cross between "Coming Home" and "thirtysomething," has more in common with one of those Shakespearean comedies in which mistaken identities and crossed wires compound and confound the love lives of a set of people who live in isolation from any sense of community or history. This makes it difficult to feel deeply for the problems of Air Force Lt. Jake Robbins (Kristofferson), who resurfaces years after the war with a Cambodian wife and two children in tow, and for the American wife he left behind, Sarah (Williams), who has since remarried and is raising Jake's long-lost son in middle-class serenity.

Lives and alliances are disrupted when Jake shows up. Jake's loner dad (Brian Keith) adjusts pretty quickly, but not so Sarah, who is still carrying a torch, or her new husband (Sam Waterston), a construction foreman who quickly feels the roof caving in on his comfortable life, or the confused teen-age son (Thomas Wilson Brown) who thinks mom is having an affair with the stranger in the white Porsche. (Which, in fact, she is—but Jake is more like family, no?)

Although the drama raises some of the concerns of many of the post-Vietnam movies— displacement, survivors' guilt, etc.—Jake's bizarre situation and its pat resolution have little to do with the war. Ultimately, the entire movie would have lost nothing by skipping the war angle altogether. As it is really a film about relationships and making moral choices, it could have concentrated instead on a man at war with himself, a man whose blissfully bigamous state begins to dissolve under self-scrutiny.

My being alive is not exactly cause for celebration around here," remarks Jake in the kind of wry, self-deprecating humor he develops as he finds that his presence is not only cause for alarm back home, but also the subject of top-security concerns at the Pentagon.

Theme music provided by Willie Nelson has lyrics like, "War is hell, buddy, welcome home." What is really hell for Jake is *coming* home, where ostensibly he will have to confront just who he is and just why he spent all those years in the Cambodian equivalent of middle-class comfort. ("Life couldn't have been more swell if we were sitting in f---in' Syracuse," he tells his dad, although just how swell is Syracuse?)

Sam Waterston, relegated to a hapless bit part, looks more like William Schallert every day. Williams wins the Mary Steenburgen award for warmth and caring. Kristofferson looks haggard and confused.

This is the last film, and unfortunately not the best, for director Franklin J. Schaffner ("Patton," "Planet of the Apes"), who died this summer and to whom the movie is dedicated.

NEWSDAY, 9/29/89, Part III/p. 3, Terry Kelleher

"Rambo" and "Missing in Action" used the MIA question as an excuse for mindless action. Now "Welcome Home" uses it as a pretext for endless talk. But not the diplomatic kind. The soap-opera kind.

Air Force Lt. Jake Robbins (Kris Kristofferson) was shot down over Cambodia in 1970, shortly after marrying his high school sweetheart, Sarah (JoBeth Williams). Four years later, he slipped away from his Khmer Rouge captors and took a Cambodian wife, with whom he had two children. In 1987, as the movie opens, Jake is desperately in need of medical attention, and his Cambodian family carries him on a stretcher to Thailand, where the group is forcibly separated. The woman and kids are thrown into a refugee camp; Jake is shipped Stateside.

"No bands, no parades" for this returning vet, as Willie Nelson sings in the title song. The military prefers to ignore evidence that missing American servicemen are alive in Southeast Asia. A cold-eyed colonel (the late Trey Wilson) gives Jake a "new ID," a bagful of cash and an empty promise to locate his Cambodian loved ones. In return Jake must keep quiet.

Jake later learns an elaborate coverup has been going on. Does he jet to the jungle on a Ramboesque rescue mission? No. Like a responsible citizen, he informs a U.S. senator (Ken Pogue) and the two of them confront the colonel. Do they blow the lid off this conspiracy of silence, demand a full accounting of our MIAs?

No again, because debuting screenwriter Maggie Kleinman is far more interested in personal matters. Jake finds out Sarah has a new husband, kindly Woody (Sam Waterston). He also discovers brooding Tyler (Thomas Wilson Brown), the 17-year-old son he never knew he had. Thanks to a phony plot complication—Tyler spots Sarah hugging Jake and thinks his mom's having an illicit affair—the lad gets to brood quite a lot.

Jake feels guilty for disrupting Sarah's life and being insufficiently heroic back in Cambodia. But Jake's father (Brian Keith), also kindly, feels guilty, too. "Don't think you've got a corner on the guilt market," he says. It's a bull market, that's for sure.

Meanwhile, Sarah's still attracted to Jake, and poor Woody is confused. "I wish I knew how to deal with this," he tells his wife. "How do you deal with something like this?" Yet he's not too confused to give the teenager an anti-brooding lecture. "You're going to have to deal with this, Tyler," Woody says.

Jake is actually the least verbal of the bunch. When something upsetting comes up, he tends to go for a walk. This is a fortunate trait, given Kristofferson's way with the dialogue.

"Welcome Home" was the last film for director Franklin Schaffner, who died this summer at 69 after an often distinguished career highlighted by "Patton." Schaffner got his start with live dramas in the "golden age" of television. Too bad he had to go out with something more like "As the World Turns."

VILLAGE VOICE, 10/10/89, p. 96, Manohla Dargis

Gaunt, grizzled, and sunburned, *Welcome Home*'s Kris Kristofferson actually looks like somone who's been lost in the jungle for 17 years. Shot down over Cambodia during the Vietnam War, Jake Robbins (Kristofferson) was imprisoned by the Khmer Rouge, but, after four years, managed to escape into the mountains, where he remained in hiding for 13 years. Meanwhile, back in the States, Jake was classified MIA, and his family buried a box of misidentified charred bones.

Years later, separated from his Cambodian family at a relocation camp, Jake is spirited back to the States, where the military brass is eager to keep him under wraps. (Despite some mumbled allusion to defense intelligence and cover-ups, *Welcome Home*, unlike director Franklin J. Schaffner's *Patton*, remains carefully apolitical; ultimately, the military gets off the hook.) Jake, desperate to be reunited with his Cambodian wife and children, makes a deal to keep quiet about his internment if the government will bring them to the States. He also decides to drop in on his past. As he drives his white Porsche up to his parents' spick-and-span white clapboard house, it's clear Jake is home.

At first, his mask registers as culture shock, but soon it becomes apparent that Kristofferson's emotional palette is capable of registering only the blank and the weary blank. In her thankless role as Jake's first wife, Sarah, JoBeth Williams gives a familiar turn as a sexy mom whose eyes are forever bloodshot from all her brave tears. Sam Waterston is Woody (an inside joke on his frequent stints in Allen's movies?), Sarah's second husband. He's an Alan Alda-oid replicant whose job is to mutter platitudes about family, strength, and love to his stepson, Tyler (Thomas Wilson Brown), an insufferable teenager more enamored with the Vietnam memorial than with the father who's returned.

It's easy enough to guess what will happen to all these people who manage their emotions like so much folded laundry. With such a formula, it doesn't take much imagination to figure out that Jake's Cambodian wife, Leang (Kieu Chinh), has no place in this landscape: He can only be sexual with one woman, and she's the one who matches the color of his car.

Also reviewed in:
NEW YORK TIMES, 9/29/89, p. C4, Janet Maslin
VARIETY, 5/24–30/89, p. 32
WASHINGTON POST, 9/30/89, p. C8, Rita Kempley

WE'RE NO ANGELS

A Paramount Pictures release. *Executive Producer:* Robert De Niro. *Producer:* Art Linson. *Director:* Neil Jordan. *Screenplay:* David Mamet. *Director of Photography:* Philippe Rousselot. *Editor:* Mick Audsley and Joke Van Wuk. *Music:* George Fenton. *Music Editor:* Michael Connell. *Sound:* Larry Sutton and (music) Keith Grant. *Sound Editor:* Kant Pan. *Production Designer:* Wolf Kroeger. *Art Director:* Richard Harrison. *Set Decorator:* Jim Erickson. *Special Effects:* William H. Orr. *Costumes:* Theoni V. Aldredge. *Make-up:* Ilona Herman. *Stunt Coordinator:* Vic Armstrong, Mickey Gilbert, and John Scott. *Running time:* 95 minutes. *MPAA Rating:* PG-13.

CAST: Robert De Niro (Ned); Sean Penn (Jim); Demi Moore (Molly); Hoyt Axton (Father Levesque); Bruno Kirby (Deputy); Ray McAnally (Warden); James Russo (Bobby); Wallace Shawn (Translator); John C. Reilly (Young Monk); Jay Brazeau (Sheriff); Ken Buhay (Bishop Nogulich); Elizabeth Lawrence (Mrs. Blair); Bill Murdoch (Deputy); Jessica Jickels (Rosie); Frank C. Turner (Shopkeeper); Matthew Walker (Blacksmith); Sheelah Megill (Townswoman); Sean Hoy (Workman); Lloyd Berry, David McLeod, and Richard Newman (Passersby); Frank Totino and Karen Austin (Bystanders); Antony Holland (Doctor); Sylvain Demers (Canadian Priest); Cory Dagg (Border Guard); Garwin Sanford (Prison Priest); Rick Poltaruk (Fat Monk).

FILMS IN REVIEW, 4/90, p. 233, C.M. Fiorillo

A comedy of mistaken identities, We're No Angels teams up Robert De Niro and Sean Penn—with genuinely funny results. The script, written by David Mamet, deals with the interpretive nature of miracles and has little in common with the 1955 film of the same name.

After a forced prison escape at the hands of a psychotic killer, Ned (De Niro) and Jim (Penn) seek refuge in a nearby border town where they are mistaken (!) for priests. Their attempts at crossing over into Canada—and freedom—are continuously thwarted. The duo become guests at the local monastery, impersonating the visiting holy men everyone thinks them to be.

There are some wickedly funny scenes as Ned and Jim try to pass themselves off as priests.

De Niro and Penn are devilishly charming in their first outing together. De Niro displays an endearing comic persona; Penn is refreshingly funny. An outstanding supporting cast includes Demi Moore, Bruno Kirby, John Reilly, James Russo and the late Ray McAnally. Thanks to Mamet's fine screenplay, the lead characters, as well as the minor players, are given depth and a sense of purpose. Mamet's words, as usual, are brilliant.

We're No Angels, directed by Neil Jordan (Mona Lisa), was shot in Canada. Each building of the set, designed by Wolf Kroeger (Casualties Of War), was constructed from scratch. The fictional town of Brandon echoes the poverty of the 30s. Philippe Rousselot (The Bear) is director of photography, the score is by George Fenton (Cry Freedom).

LOS ANGELES TIMES, 12/15/89. Calendar/p. 12, Michael Wilmington

In "We're No Angels," Robert De Niro and Sean Penn are cast as dim-bulb characters, reminiscent of the low-lifes in "Stranger Than Paradise," or even of the Dead End Kids. As these slow-witted, would-be streetwise goofballs try to navigate their way through the movie, their faces screw up into bizarre contortions or dissolve in empty panic.

De Niro and Penn have played dumb before. De Niro had his punchy moments in "Raging Bull" and Penn became famous doing the drug-addled surfer Spicoli in "Fast Times at Ridgemont High." But here, they're dumb on a fuller level: two guys who don't have a clue and keep miraculously faking their way along anyway.

Their arias of idiocy waiver all the way between shameless overacting and inspired foolery. But director Neil Jordan and writer David Mamet's tale of escaped convicts disguised as priests in a 1930s era Northeast border town has its charms. It's comedy about dumb luck, fortuitous grace, about two sinners redeemed by absurd awe-inspiring flukes. And, though it's a flawed work that never jells, a comedy that exposes its serious side too readily, it keeps getting eerie little grace notes.

Mamet obviously wants to suggest a kinship between the escaped cons, De Niro's Ned and Penn's Jim, and the monks who take them in. Emotionally, they're all alienated from the outside world. The cons' edginess can also be read as piety, and their jailhouse demeanor—watchful, sneaky-sly—as gravity. So there's a symbiosis. Ned and Jim grow into their roles, do good despite themselves. They're like the whiskey priest in Graham Greene's "The Power and the Glory." The cloth takes them over.

The movie is set during the Depression and the town, created from scratch by production designer Wolf Kroeger, is a dingy, muddy, wind-swept frontier city that recalls the locale of Robert Altman's "McCabe and Mrs. Miller." In this impoverished setting, even the opulent church has a leaky roof. That's why their "miraculous" Madonna seems to be crying. And, against this desperation, both the wild license of the escaped killer, Bobby (James Russo)—who can sneak a gun into an execution—and the mad despotism of the warden (the late Ray McAnally) show the frontier spirit at its scariest extreme.

Ned and Jim are innocents trapped between maniacs. They're caught between an "evil" and a "good," equally deranged and dangerous, and their only hope is to con their way across the bridge and border in the annual pilgrimage. When, like buddy-buddy Alices in a cold

Wonderland, they find an epigram on hospitality from the Bible, in the middle of wintry desolation, it's like the precursor in a fairy-tale, or parable.

"We're No Angels" is full of interesting things. It's a more intelligent, daring, textured work than many recent big studio movies. But it's a disappointment, because of the superb talent involved, not just De Niro and Penn, but cinematographer Philippe Rousselot, Mamet and Jordan. The film is less funny than it should be, less hypnotic. It never really establishes an imaginative equilibrium, and some of the performances are pitched in too broad a key.

Jordan, whose films are often brilliant on both cinematic and literary levels, fell badly with farce his last time out—the ruinously edited "High Spirits"—and his temperament may be a little too intense for this material. An Irishman, from a Catholic country, he obviously responds to the impudence of the convict-priests notion and, as "Company of Wolves" and "High Spirits" both show, he has always liked fairy tale forms. But he may be making a mistake in trying to impose his view—special, fervid, highly poetic—in even slightly formula American movies.

In a way, his sensibility never quite connects with Mamet's. Like the whimsical Bill Forsyth and the moralistic John Sayles in "Breaking In," they may even work against each other. Mamet's austerity, the almost emotionless performances he coaxes from his actors as a director, suggest a different key than the feverish, volcanic intensity Jordan likes to get. Jordan's characters sweat and batter at their bars, cry against their fate, while Mamet specializes in dry maneuvers and measured cynicism. He's more fascinated with the game, Jordan with the torment of the players.

In the friendly acting contest between De Niro and Penn, Penn makes some canny scores. De Niro takes the gruff, embittered, knit-eyebrows stance he used for his bounty hunter in "Midnight Run" and takes it further. He digs himself in, plants his face like a clenched fist, and works up four or five comic glowers and variations on wary, disguised hostility. He also has a hilarious confession scene with Bruno Kirby as a sexcrazed deputy.

But Penn's dazed Jim is a real surprise, particularly after his virulent machismo turn in "Casualties of War." Despite his rebellious, taciturn image, Penn plays him incongruously sweet. Jim's spiritual metamorphosis is a joke, but it's a tender joke infused with some awe and grace. "We're No Angels" (MPAA rated R for sex, violence, language and nudity) proves that a great ensemble is no guarantee of a great movie—but it also proves that the misses of the brilliant can still give you something extraordinary.

MONTHLY FILM BULLETIN, 6/90, p. 178, Pam Cook

1935. A state penitentiary near the Canadian border. Small-time crooks Ned and Jim are forced by psychotic killer Bobby, about to be executed, to take part in a break-out, during which Bobby, shoots two guards. Ned and Jim make their way to a town near the river which marks the border, only to find the bridge guarded by police. Taking refuge in a shop, they are mistaken for priests from the local monastery housing the famous Weeping Virgin, and take advantage of this to try to cross the bridge again. However, they are waylaid by Father Levesque, head of the monastery, who takes them for visiting scholarly priests Fathers Brown and Reilly. At the monastery, the pair don priests' raiment and endeavour to act the part, with apparent success. Jim starts to enjoy the priest's life, but Ned is anxious to escape. Ned inadvertently hears the adulterous confession of a local cop, and reluctantly accompanies him to his mistress Molly's house, where she gives them short shrift, declaring that she sleeps with men for money to support her deaf and dumb daughter Rosie, and denouncing religion as mumbo jumbo. Ned and Jim try once more to cross the bridge as priests, but are forestalled by the arrival of the brutal prison warden, who orders a house-to-house search. Taking refuge again in the monastery, Ned and Jim decide to join the procession to celebrate the Feast of our Lady of Sorrows, which crosses the bridge into Canada. However, they need an afflicted person to accompany them, and when Ned asks Molly if they can take Rosie, she demands money. They hear gunshots, and the warden claims to have captured an escaped convict. This turns out to be Bobby, who demands to see Ned in jail, where he threatens to turn in Ned and Jim for shooting the guards if they don't help him. As Jim delivers a poignant speech about the need for faith to a rapt audience assembled for the procession, Ned smuggles Bobby out of jail and hides him under the Weeping Virgin's skirts. Molly, moved by Jim's words, allows Ned to take Rosie after all, and the procession moves off. Halfway across the bridge, the police discover Bobby's escape and give chase, whereupon the convict emerges and takes Rosie hostage. In the ensuing fracas, the shrine is destroyed and the Virgin and Rosie fall into the river. Ned jumps in and saves Rosie, who is miraculously able to speak. Ned and Jim are now heroes and set off across the bridge to freedom. Ned is pursued by Molly, who declares that she is considering taking holy orders; Jim decides to return to the monastery, while Ned, Molly and Rosie cross the bridge to Canada.

We're No Angels, written by David Mamet and starring real-life buddies Robert De Niro and Sean Penn, should have been an auspicious U.S. début for Neil Jordan. Loosely based on the successful 1955 production directed by Michael Curtiz, with Humphrey Bogart, Aldo Ray and Peter Ustinov as the murderers on the run who intervene to improve the fortunes of a beleaguered family of shopkeepers, Mamet's script cynically and untidily disposes of the third member of the criminal trio until he is required for the finale, to allow the Penn/De Niro duo to dominate centre stage. Equally unconvincingly, it transposes the comedy-of-mistaken-identity narrative into a 1930s Depression-stricken religious community apparently too universally foolish to distinguish between hard-bitten convicts and gentlemen of the cloth, however flimsy the masquerade. The result is more a catalogue than a comedy of errors.

Mamet, not surprisingly, seems to have been drawn to the farcical elements of the story (the 1955 film was based on the Albert Husson play *La Cuisine des anges*), and does his best with the sequence of accidents which frustrates the attempts of crooks Ned and Jim to escape their monastery hideout and cross into Canada. However, farce relies on carefully structured and precisely timed coincidences, giving rise to frantic toing and froing in confined spaces, for which the theatre's proscenium arch provides the perfect frame. Hollywood cinema's way of telling stories by establishing ''real'' space through reverse angle shots and moving camera does not easily lend itself to the formal and intellectual pleasures of theatrical farce, and has to be ''theatricalised'' itself to work (as in *House of Games*). The Jordan of *The Company of Wolves* might have been expected to rise to this challenge; instead, he seems preoccupied with the mechanics of shooting crowd scenes and the inevitable spectacular set-piece, in which De Niro saves a child from the torrential river waters with the help of a plaster Virgin. Farce gives way to slapstick, making the religious parody, which also depends on playing the accidental against the miraculous, appear clumsy to the point of bad taste.

Indeed, the film's attitude towards religion is more than a little confused. On the one hand, like cinema, it depends on illusion and tricks to capture naive hearts and minds; on the other, the innocence required to sustain faith is blessed. The first, predictably, is encapsulated in the duplicitous figure of the Weeping Virgin, whose tears spring from a hole in the church roof where the rain leaks in, and whose skirts conceal a psychopathic killer during the climactic religious procession, but who provides the helping hand that enables Ned to save Rosie from drowning. The second resides in the young convict Jim, who finds his faith during his enforced confinement in the monastery, and finally decides, in a strangely ambiguous ending, to abandon his mentor Ned and return to the young monk who has befriended him. The cynical die-hard Ned also discovers the good within himself, protecting Molly's mute daughter Rosie in much the same way as he looks after the less-than-bright Jim. Sentimentality prevails over satire, and wit is sacrificed to a crude lampoon of an all-too-easy target.

As if to compensate for the overall formlessness, De Niro and Penn deliver mannered performances overburdened with references to cinema's mad and madcap heroes, from the Three Stooges and James Cagney to John Goodman and William Forsythe in *Raising Arizona*. De Niro looks particularly ill-at-ease, resorting to violent grimace which seem to indicate that he received minimal direction (also implied by his credit as executive producer). Penn, belying his role as the novice of the acting partnership, acquits himself better, and is reasonably convincing as his dim-witted, slack-jawed companion. Sadly, the late Ray McAnally as the insanely brutal prison warden is required to give a histrionic display which is clearly too much for him, and which adds a distressing undertone to the proceedings. Amid all the manic mugging, Demi Moore's strong and sympathetic playing of the straight-talking Molly, and Hoyt Axton's subtly urbane Father Levesque, come as a relief. Otherwise, *We're No Angels* goes down as a great opportunity squandered.

NEW STATESMAN & SOCIETY, 6/8/90, p. 44, Suzanne Moore

Contrary to popular belief, size is important. Nowhere is this more true than in the movies. The Irish director Neil Jordan has certainly fallen for the idea that bigger is better, moving up the scale in order to make big Hollywood films with big budgets and even bigger stars.

Of all the directors this might happen to, novelist turned film-maker Jordan is the most unlikely. His best films remain his 1982 debut *Angel* and *Mona Lisa*: small, personal but powerful movies.

His last film, *High Spirits*, was destroyed by post-production editing which turned what should have been inspired whimsy into little more than a series of elaborate set pieces. Jordan, however, has not been deterred. His latest effort not only stars Robert De Niro and Sean Penn but also involved constructing a small town. Written by David Mamet, seemingly on an off day, *We're No Angels* came as a package with De Niro as executive producer. It is set in 1935, with De Niro and Penn playing two loveable rogues in the living hell of a state penitentiary. Escaping almost by accident, they go on the run, trying frantically to make it over the border to Canada. Arriving at a small border town, they are mistaken for priests. That's basically it; the one joke of the movie is that the two convicts haven't got the slightest idea how to behave as holy men.

Jordan has talked of his fondness for genre bending, but *We're No Angels* most closely resembles the early comedies of silent film. De Niro and Penn are on overdrive as Laurel and Hardy, grimacing madly, looking *stoopid* at every available opportunity. In fact the film "loosely based on some of the ideas" of the 1955 movie of the same name, has an old-fashioned feel about it. That's not old-fashioned as in quaint but old-fashioned as in completely out of touch. Neither fanatical period reconstruction nor impressive sets can recreate the kind of innocence that such a story requires. Even Mamet's usual sharpness is blunted by the performances. And De Niro, so wonderfully unfunny in *The King of Comedy*, thinks he is in a pantomine rather than a film. As for Jordan, after another impersonal enterprise let us hope he realises that size isn't everything after all.

NEW YORK POST, 12/15/89, p. 41, Jami Bernard

Two escaped cons pose rather precariously as clergymen in a sleepy northern border town, 1935, in "We're No Angels," a low-key comedy filmed against the large-scale backdrop of a British Columbia winter.

Robert De Niro and Sean Penn have such an easy camaraderie and matching Brooklyn-wiseguy accents that as Ned and Jim they practically look like brothers; they pose as fathers, two priests who conveniently were lost in a snowstorm en route to the New England town where they were expected. This town's *raison d'etre* is its controversial weeping virgin shrine, which gives the local merchants a brisk business in religious trinkets.

Disguised in their priestly garb, and mumbling a lunatic collection of half-remembered, Biblical-sounding phrases in their gangster cadences, Ned and Jim hope to escape to Canada during the annual holy procession that takes the weeping virgin through customs for a day of miracle-working.

Complicating their stab at anonymity is the fact that the priests they are impersonating are authors of a famous book on the meaning of the shrine, and so the local clergy—particularly an eager young monk (John C. Reilly), and Father Levesque (Hoyt Axton)—keep entreating them for clarifications and spiritual guidance. Several times, the more inarticulate Jim (Penn) must perform impromptu blessings. In true "Being There" style, his simple words ("It's all in ya head") seem to take on larger meaning.

Meanwhile, Ned has spied a comely unwed mother undressing through her window, and is smitten. Demi Moore plays Molly, and one benefit (I suppose) of being married to Bruce Willis is that she has a mouth on her that can fillet a frozen fish. Molly's barrage of Brooklynese is for a good cause—she is determined to care for her moppet of a daughter, who is deaf. Thus far, Molly's pleas to the weeping virgin have fallen on deaf ears.

The motto of the town is a quote from the Bible: "Do not neglect to show hospitality to strangers, for thereby some have entertained angels unawares."

During the course of the movie, the two cons ostensibly perform some good works, but the men are less angels than losers. They broke jail by mistake when they found themselves in the way of another con's rush to freedom (James Russo), and the ways in which Jim inspires the young monk and Ned helps Molly's daughter are similarly haphazard. The title is right, they're no angels.

But they're not bad, either. Penn plays the sweeter of the two, a tongue-tied innocent, which is a joke on one of his earlier roles in "Bad Boys."

Some of De Niro's scenes similarly call to mind "The Mission" and "True Confessions." Now, however, he's following weeping virgins down waterfalls and hacking off leg irons in the confessional.

The humor is mild and often labored, with Penn and De Niro spending huge amounts of time searching for the right words. But De Niro's sarcastic delivery relieves the fidgeting. And then there's Wallace Shawn, who can make even a minor role as a translator hilarious, considering that half of his lines are unintelligible. The reliable Bruno Kirby plays a conscious-stricken deputy.

The production is coldly beautiful, with cinematographer Philippe Rousselot's shots of glacial countryside giving the movie a gravity and epic grandeur you wouldn't expect in a comedy. It was directed by Neil Jordan ("Mona Lisa") and written by David Mamet, loosely inspired by the '55 Humphrey Bogart prison-break comedy of the same name.

While not side-splitting, the movie is pleasurable. As Penn advises the faithful throngs, "You wanna believe in sumptin', then that's not so bad."

NEWSDAY, 12/15/89, Part III/p. 3, Mike McGrady

Ah Christmas,—traditionally, 'tis the season for Hollywood to come up with warm-hearted priests, miracle cures, maybe even a few statues weeping real tears. In the good old days, a season couldn't pass by without a "Going My Way" or "The Song of Bernadette." In fact, for a while there were so many miracle movies—remember "The Miracle of the Bells" and "The Miracle of Our Lady of Fatima"?—that film critic James Agee finally interceded: "I hereby declare myself the founding father of the Society for the Prevention of Cruelty to God."

Well, I believe the society would heartily endorse this year's miracle movie, a larky little number titled "We're No Angels," starring Robert De Niro and Sean Penn as escaped convicts who don priestly vestments to outwit the bloodhounds and posses baying for their blood.

In fact, it seems to me the only factor working against "We're No Angels" is human expectation. When you put together a cast headed by Robert De Niro and Sean Penn; then you add a top director, Neil Jordan (all but canonized for "Mona Lisa"), and you throw in a script by David Mamet, who wrote "The Untouchables" and House of Games"—when you have a package this grand, one's expectations may get a bit out of hand.

Perhaps we would do a service by first explaining what "We're No Angels" is not. It is *not* a great dramatic tour de force. It is *not* a laff-riot that will have you howling with laughter. What it is, mostly, is cute—a cute comedy with some wonderful little performances and, for those of you into seasonal observances, even a modest miracle or two.

The humor of "We're No Angels" springs from the various ludicrous positions two escaped convicts find themselves in when they try to escape by concealing their leg irons under priests cassocks.

The joke is sharpened by the fact that they are not your run-of-the-jail cons; they are stumblebums, real dese-and dose guys barely capable of carrying on civil discourse. And sharpened still further by the fact that our two cons are not passing as just any priests; they are passing as two prominent theologians, leading Catholic intellectuals visiting a small New England town to participate in the annual pageant in honor of the shrine known as "the weeping madonna." And sharpened yet again when De Niro can't resist making a play for the local bimbo (Demi Moore) who, as luck would have it, has a deaf-mute child desperately in need of a miracle cure.

Tough-guy Penn is...well...lovable, and De Niro's considerable talents, as he demonstrated in "Midnight Express," translate into comedy as readily as into drama. One of the film's high spots comes when De Niro is forced to hear a deputy sheriff's confession. Another arrives when Penn is asked to deliver the main sermon. There's a truly lovely performance by John C. Reilly as a young monk and solid support from Moore, Hoyt Axton and Wallace Shawn.

The film's slightness, I suspect, is linked to its jerry-built nature. Real-life pals De Niro and Penn, eager to appear together in a movie, let producer Art Linson know and he came up with the notion of portraying convicts on the run. David Mamet wrote a script to order and director Jordan was summoned to try his first American movie. While this may not be a system destined for greatness, it can produce an enjoyable entertainment.

NEWSWEEK, 12/25/89, p. 74, David Ansen

We're No Angels has to be the most overqualified comedy of the year. Loosely based on a tepid 1955 Humphrey Bogart comedy and set in 1935 in a wintry town near the Canadian border, it's about two bumbling escaped cons who don monks' robes and hide out in a monastery. Robert De Niro and Sean Penn play the dumb, likable louts. The distinguished David Mamet wrote the adaptation. The gifted Neil Jordan ("Mona Lisa") directed. The cinematographer, Philippe Rousselot, and the production designer, Wolf Kroeger, are among the best in the business. Needless to say, the film is extremely stylish—shot in a dark, gritty, monochromatic palette appropriate to "Mrs. Soffel" or "McCabe and Mrs. Miller." Unfortunately, it's a style utterly at odds with Mamet's foursquare, old-fashioned situational comedy: it kills the joke. Though Penn and a heavily mugging De Niro earn their share of chuckles, you leave this comedy scratching your head at the nutty incongruity of the endeavor. What were these talented people thinking?

VILLAGE VOICE, 12/26/89, p. 102, Georgia Brown

The combination of director Neil Jordan *(The Company of Wolves, High Spirits)*, writer David Mamet, and stars Robert De Niro and Sean Penn sounded promising. The result, *We're No Angels* ("not a remake of the 1955 film of the same name"), turns out to be distinguished mainly by Philippe Rousselot's superb cinematography.

When a bracingly mean convict (James Russo) breaks out of a U.S. penitentiary near Canada, two smallfry, Jim and Ned (Penn and De Niro), are swept along with him. In a border town, waiting for their chance to cross the bridge into freedom, the two former cellmates hide out with a local Catholic order that worships a statue of the Weeping Virgin (the roof leaks over her head). Most of the film's comedy centers on the improbability of mistaking these numbskulls for erudite members of the priesthood—such as the pedant played by Wallace Shawn.

Penn's "Father Brown" is a dim-witted innocent with a budding interest in matters like damnation and salvation. He often waves his hand like a child. De Niro plays the more earthbound "Father Reilly" by screwing up his face and bobbing as if he's doing an "Oriental gentleman." Demi Moore is Molly, a no-nonsense townsperson who turns tricks and takes in laundry to support her deaf-mute daughter. This is one of the flimsiest of the season's offerings.

Also reviewed in:
NATION, 1/1/90, p. 31, Stuart Klawans
NEW YORK TIMES, 12/15/89, p. C20, Vincent Canby
VARIETY, 12/13/89, p. 5
WASHINGTON POST, 12/15/89, p. D7, Hal Hinson

WHEN HARRY MET SALLY . . .

A Columbia Pictures release of a Castle Rock Entertainment/Nelson Entertainment film. *Producer:* Rob Reiner and Andrew Scheinman. *Director:* Rob Reiner. *Screenplay:* Nora Ephron. *Director of Photography:* Barry Sonnenfeld. *Editor:* Robert Leighton. *Music:* Marc Shaiman. *Sound:* Robert Eber and (music) John Richards. *Sound Editor:* Charles L. Campbell and Louis L. Edemann. *Production Designer:* Jane Musky. *Art Director:* Harold Thrasher. *Set Decorator:* George R. Nelson and Sabrina Wright-Basile. *Costumes:* Gloria Gresham. *Make-up:* Stephen Abrums, Joseph A. Campayno, Ken Chase, and Peter Montagna. *Running time:* 95 minutes. *MPAA Rating:* R.

CAST: Billy Crystal (Harry Burns); Meg Ryan (Sally Albright); Carrie Fisher (Marie); Bruno Kirby (Jess); Steven Ford (Joe); Lisa Jane Persky (Alice); Michelle Nicastro (Amanda); Gretchen Palmer (Stewardess); Robert Alan Beuth (Man on Aisle); David Burdick (9 year old Boy); Joe Viviani (Judge); Harley Kozak (Helen); Joseph Hunt (Waiter at Wedding); Kevin Rooney (Ira); Franc Luz (Julian); Tracy Reiner (Emily); Kyle Heffner (Gary); Kimberley Lamarque (Waitress); Stacey Katzin (Hostess); Estelle Reiner (Older Woman Customer); John Arceri (Christmas Tree Salesman); Peter Day (Joke Teller at Wedding).

CHRISTIAN SCIENCE MONITOR, 8/2/89, p. 11, David Sterritt

Rob Reiner is a talented director, and a funny one. His parody of rock'n'roll movies, "This Is Spinal Tap," was hilarious, and "The Princess Bride" had some wonderful moments.

I've been hoping he would tell a story that's little more substantial, though, and now I have my wish. "When Harry Met Sally..." does more than poke fun at other movies and styles, as those earlier pictures did. It pokes fun at modern American life and the kind of people you meet there—like Harry and Sally, who are as recognizable (if you're familiar with the yuppie scene) as they are amusing.

As you can guess from the title, Harry and Sally meet—it's what Hollywood calls a "cute meet"—at the beginning of the film. But don't expect romantic sparks to start flying. They're college students who need to get from the Midwest to New York, and they save money by driving there together—arguing all the way, about everything from sex to the meaning of life. Then they say goodbye, with no regrets on either side, and don't meet again for several years. This is partly because of Harry's theory that men and women can never be ordinary friends, just lovers or nothing at all.

A few chance encounters later, Harry and Sally finally do get friendly, and the story takes new emotional turns. I won't give them away because they're sometimes unexpected, and also because these changes of feeling are all the surprises Mr. Reiner has to offer in his engaging but limited movie.

This doesn't mean "When Harry Met Sally..." is as forgettable as some of the season's other films. It has its pleasures, including likable performances and (if you care to overlook some four-letter language) snappy dialogue.

It also spices its story by including staged interviews with older and wiser people who comment on the action as it unfolds—in scenes that recall movies as different as "Reds" and Chantal Akerman's new "Histoires d'Amerique," and will remind any comedy fan of Woody Allen's early "Take the Money and Run."

Reiner borrows a lot of his style from Mr. Allen, including a sunny view of New York City and a bouncy jazz-and-pop score. What he forgot to ask Woody for, regrettably, is the keen understanding of middle-class folkways that the best Allen comedies have.

Reiner is good at observing human nature, and so is Nora Ephron, who wrote the screenplay. But they don't have much to *say* about the behavior and attitudes they reproduce so carefully in their movie. If you're looking for psychological depths or insights, you'd better look somewhere else.

In the cast, Billy Crystal gives his best performance yet as Harry, and Meg Ryan is crisp and energetic in the other title role. Carrie Fisher is also a pleasure as Sally's best friend; she's at the heart of every scene she's in, without ever straining to be sexy or clever. When they're on the screen, "When Harry Met Sally..." is often fun to watch. But I'd like it more if it allowed us to understand its likable yuppies better—by exploring them instead of just putting them through their frequently predictable paces.

The movie is rated R, reflecting some vulgar words and sex-related humor.

FILMS IN REVIEW, 10/89, p. 484, Michael Buckley

This is the year's best Woody Allen film made by somebody else.

Rob Reiner directed and Nora Ephron wrote a modern battle of the sexes that spans a dozen years in the relationship of Harry (Billy Crystal) and Sally (Meg Ryan), who try to determine if they can remain friends without sex entering into it.

The movie should establish both Crystal and Ryan; he's fine in the would-be Allen role and she's wonderful as the Diane Keaton character. Bruno Kirby and Carrie Fisher nicely handle the best friends' parts.

Mainly shot in New York (or Allen's Alley), there are several crisp lines and funny situations. Despite all the Woody touches—down to a near-climactic run through the streets, a la *Manhattan*—the picture succeeds on its own.

Meg Ryan's delicatessen scene, wherein she proves to Crystal that any woman can be a good actress, is the film's funniest; however, the best line is delivered by an older female patron at the deli. Who was that lady? Estelle Reiner, the director's mother. That was a nice thing to do. Allen would have used Mae Questel.

LOS ANGELES TIMES, 7/14/89, Calendar/p. 1, Sheila Benson

Bless Harry and Sally's hearts. Over the course of their 11 years under our bemused scrutiny, they actually *talk* to each other, in splendid, risible exchanges that fly by with the speed and delicacy of a great badminton game. Bless too, director Rob Reiner and credited screenwriter Nora Ephron for ladling out the pleasure with so generous and tender a hand. It makes "When Harry Met Sally..." the summer's uncorseted, unqualified delight.

While ostensibly sorting out the question of whether men and women can be friends, before or after sex raises its lovely head, "Harry/Sally" is actually casting a hopeful and persuasive eye on romance today, on marriage even. The film's progression, with pit stops every four or five years, is separated by mock-documentary interviews as long-married couples cheerfully describe their fateful first meetings. Affection, as well as a simmering wit, is definitely in the air.

If that doesn't sound quite like the Ephron of old (certainly not the Ephron of "Heartburn," which had an undertaste so nasty you could be puckered for a month afterward), it's possibly because Reiner and Billy Crystal, longtime collaborators, reportedly added a good deal themselves during the film making. Wherever it came from, the results are charming.

No one will miss the fact that this Manhattan-based talkfest, with Gershwin on the sound track and upscale, self-scrutinizing New Yorkers on the menu, has a distinct Woody Allen flavor. Agreed. However, "Harry/Sally" has an irresistible, creakling rhythm that is Reiner's own. And is it necessarily *bad* if a film shares Allen's territory and even some of his attitudes? Sheesh!

Sally (Meg Ryan) picks up Harry (Crystal) as the two make their way in her car from the University of Chicago campus to New York. It's 1977. She's just graduated; he's just finished law school. New York, watch out.

Harry is also glued, lip, hip and anklebone, to Sally's friend Amanda in the deathless melodrama of a farewell kiss. Then—bickering all the way—Harry and Sally begin what is to be a fateful ride-sharing. Amanda, watch out.

What follows are a series of dispatches from the singles skirmishing front, upscale-New York style. They cover marriage (she's keeping her name) and divorce; living together and breaking up; affairs with married men and that full-blown horror, post-divorce dating. Rounding out the cast are Sally's best friend Marie (Carrie Fisher, possessor of one of the most deft and deadly deadpans anywhere) and Harry's buddy Jess (Bruno Kirby, perfect foil for both Harry and Marie).

As they skitter hesitantly around and then away from their fate, Ryan and Crystal's work has a delicate comic buoyancy, amazing grace in action. Crystal seems to have the edge at the opening: He may be abrasive and self-absorbed but he has the movie's funniest raunchy lines and a scorching delivery that seems to set the movie's pace. He's like a scrappy shortstop you can't take your eyes off. What becomes touching is to find that under the mouth and the razzle-dazzle there's a sweetheart, cover it though he might.

Ryan, on the other hand, grows on us from a slower start. As we meet her, 21 years old, with her exquisitely snippy nose permanently raised, she's preternaturally sure of her likes and dislikes. Easy to be put off by so much certainty—although how can you resist a girl who knows *she* wouldn't want to spend the rest of her life in Casablanca, married to a guy who runs a bar. (She maintains that Ingrid Bergman wouldn't either. "Women are very practical, which is why she gets on that plane at the end." Ah, youth.)

Fortunately, as Sally's experience grows, she blossoms and so does her faintly fey sense of humor, resulting in the movie's funniest moment, that about-to-be-infamous faked-orgasm-in-a-deli sequence. (The line that tops it—the movie's and maybe the year's best—delivered by director Reiner's mother, Estelle, was reportedly Crystal's contribution. And, frankly, none of this seems enough to give this film its R rating, when the bloody carnage of the newest Bond film walks off with a PG-13.)

Part of our fun comes from watching Harry and Sally mellow from college graduates, smug in their assurance that they know everything, to thirty-some-ers, appalled at the loneliness of the world out there, wanting to draw their wagons together in the dark and not exactly sure how to.

The other perverse giggle comes from the movie's mirror of the trends and fashions during the decade-and-a-bit it covers. It may come with a shudder of recognition. Sneer all you will at Harry's aggressively wide sideburns or Sally's 1977 flip, but keep the family album closed when you do.

There is something that remains a little superficial to "Harry and Sally." Although Harry may brood about his dark side, there are no shadowing strokes (as there were in Reiner's "Stand by Me") that might etch Harry or Sally or their milieu a little deeper. It may be a touch that people miss, or they may be grateful for the pace and the execution of the smart melee brightening the screen, the visual equivalent of Harry Connick Jr.'s Gershwin piano arrangements threaded throughout the movie.

In this perilous Summer of the Sequel, it seems churlish to want more than wit and sophistication on a bedrock of tenderness.

MONTHLY FILM BULLETIN, 12/89, p. 377, Pam Cook

1977. When they both graduate from the University of Chicago, Sally Albright gives Harry

Burns a lift to New York. Harry's pessimism is anathema to Sally; they argue constantly, parting on bad terms after Harry makes a clumsy pass, claiming that men and women can never be friends. Five years later, they meet again at the airport where Sally, now a journalist, is saying goodbye to her boyfriend Joe. Harry and Sally are on the same flight, and the old antagonism returns. Harry announces he is about to marry Helen. He invites Sally to dinner, but she declines. Five years later, Sally and Joe have broken up, while Helen wants a divorce. After Harry meets Sally in a bookshop, they go for coffee and discuss their relationships. A platonic friendship develops, and they both date other people, with more or less disastrous results. But on New Year's Eve, while dancing together, they are mutually attracted. Disturbed, they each introduce the other to their best friends, Marie and Jess, hoping that they will hit it off. However, it is Marie and Jess who hit it off. Four months later, while shopping for Marie and Jess' wedding present, Harry and Sally meet Helen and her new lover, Ira. Harry is depressed, and fights with Sally, accusing her of never getting upset about anything. Some time later, Harry gets a phone call from a distraught Sally, who has discovered that Joe is getting married. He goes to her apartment to comfort her and ends up staying the night. Upset when Harry tries to pretend the incident never happened, Sally confronts him at Jess and Marie's wedding reception. When he telephones her to apologise, she refuses to return his calls. On New Year's Eve, Sally goes to a party with Marie and Jess, while Harry wanders the streets alone and depressed. As Sally is about to leave, Harry turns up. He declares his love, and they kiss.

The recent Hollywood revival of romantic and screwball comedies with their will-they/won't-they deferral of consummation narratives smacks of contemporary sexual angst. *When Harry Met Sally*...consciously takes its cue from the couple-in-crisis comedies of an earlier period of sexual upheaval, in the split-screen telephone conversations recalling *Pillow Talk*, for instance, and in its playing off the hero's cynical world view against the heroine's almost hysterical positive attitude to everything. This playful nostalgia is certainly part of the film's appeal, although *When Harry Met Sally*...is more 80s than 60s: a certain melancholy overshadows both its humour and its romanticism.

Harry's lugubrious reflections on the disastrous outcome of human intercourse, and his insistence that men and women cannot have sex and be friends, jostle with documentary-style tableaux in which aged couples testify to the enduring power of love. These scenes punctuate Harry and Sally's intermittent encounters, which are often brief and transitory, taking place on journeys or in autumn and winter settings. Their edgy, awkward interactions, splendidly played by Meg Ryan and Billy Crystal, are always out of sync with the "normal" activities enjoyed by other couples, on New Year's Eve, for example, or at friends' dinner parties. The film harks back to classic Hollywood movies to demonstrate that the age of the romantic couple is over: the ending of *Casablanca* is a constant bone of contention between Harry and Sally, she claiming that Ingrid Bergman made the right choice, he insisting that it proves the impossibility of love between men and women surviving; and their painfully funny off-key rendition of "Surrey with the Fringe on Top" from *Oklahoma*!, while shopping for friends' wedding presents, precedes the devastating moment when Harry meets his ex-wife and her lover.

There is also a poignantly contemporary hue to the film's treatment of sex and sexual relationships. When Harry and Sally finally go to bed with one another, the moral issue is not one of sexual transgression but of how to behave now they have broken the codes of their friendship. Harry's characteristic reaction, based on cowardice, is to run away and pretend nothing has happened. Indeed, it is mostly Harry's behaviour which has to change before their relationship can progress, and it is this "lesson" that finally makes the film as much a comedy *for* the Personal Growth generation as one at its expense (compared, say, to *After Hours*). Rob Reiner directs in an intimate TV style, and with evident sympathy for both main characters (the script is partly based on his own experiences). Nora Ephron's acerbic touch is evident in a few well-aimed jibes: the couple's eventual reconciliation, in which his declaration "I love you" is returned by "I hate you" from her, goes against the grain of the happy ending, while Meg Ryan pulls off a *tour de force* in the sequence in which Sally demonstrates for Harry in a crowded restaurant what a fake orgasm sounds like. Why fake orgasms should even exist is the awkward question lurking beneath this film's light-hearted veneer.

NEW YORK, 7/24/89, p. 50, David Denby

When Harry Met Sally...may have a title that is impossible to remember (*you* try it), but it's a pretty good movie nevertheless, a bold and generally successful attempt by director Rob Reiner and writer Nora Ephron to muscle in on Woody Allen territory. Set mostly in New York among chitchatty media types, this romantic comedy poses the question "Can a man and a woman really be friends?" The answer, not a simple one, is a set of variations on companionship and love, accompanied by Louis Armstrong singing jazz, and—as a sort of bonus attraction—a series of recitations by happily married elderly couples sitting side by side on a Victorian love seat.

The couples—a sprightly bunch—are there for commentary and relief. Some of them have been married for life, others met late, but either way, as we listen to them nattering on, correcting and reinforcing one another, we get an oddly contradictory impression—that what brings people together is arbitrary and fortuitous yet at the same time entirely inevitable. These couples are truly mated; their speech patterns interlock like the floral pattern on the wallpaper behind them.

The rest of the movie illustrates the densely tangled paths a man and a woman must walk before joining hands. When Harry first meets Sally—on an overnight drive from the University of Chicago to New York in the seventies—they detest each other. Sally (Meg Ryan) is very young, very tight, extremely fussy, and rather pleased with herself; Harry (Billy Crystal) is smart and funny, but he's the kind of know-it-all who claims to understand women better than they understand themselves. He patronizes Sally, she bristles at him, and they part. In the next decade, they run into each other in New York now and then. She has become a journalist, a political consultant, and after more taunting and hissing they finally become friends. It is one of those relationships built on dissatisfaction. Sally loses a man and suffers from the feeling that she's unlovable. Harry has no trouble attracting women, but he runs through them quickly.

Through all their meetings, the same argument rattles on and on. A man and a woman, Harry says, can't truly become friends, because sex always comes into a relationship somehow, and sex changes everything; Sally disagrees. The friendship that these two have partly disproves what he's saying, but what Ephron is getting at, I think, is that Harry uses this doctrine to rationalize his failure with women. What men like him really mean is that once they've slept with a woman, they don't want to be friends with her anymore. Harry, who puts women down, learns that he has to become a woman's friend before he can become a decent lover or husband. His learning this opens the way to a berth on the love seat.

It's the most sociable of movies, with arguments aired and confidences spilled all over Manhattan. No one is caught working—it's a movie devoted to personality. Much of the writing is bright, and the direction flows easily, but the friendship of Harry and Sally, depending as it does on the American convention of mutual kvetching—you scratch my hurt and I'll scratch yours— can be a little wearisome. In one way, Harry is right: In dramatic terms, friendship is impossible, because it needs a sexual interest to keep *us* interested. In the most memorable scene, Sally demonstrates to Harry—in a deli, with amazed onlookers enjoying the show—exactly how a woman fakes an orgasm. Meg Ryan is a fine comedienne, and she gives the strenuous yet uncertain Sally an adorable smile of happiness when Sally thinks that a man really loves her. Billy Crystal is very fast, much faster than Ryan is—they don't quite go together, and that's part of the irritation of watching them parry and quip; their rhythms don't mesh. But it's good to see and hear Crystal even if, in this movie exclusively devoted to Relationships, he must constantly put brakes on his own runaway talent.

When Harry and Sally do finally go to bed, after years of talking and holding hands, they both feel strange—shocked and dismayed. This is the kind of truth about relationships that hasn't shown up in movies before. If Woody Allen is death-obsessed, thrilled by a morbid philosophy, Nora Ephron and Rob Reiner are fascinated by manners. Allen wants spiritual deliverance or at least illumination, and they want taste, style, a certain grace in behavior. Ephron sets up a protocol of romance and marriage; her comic specialty is blunt ex cathedra pronouncements, principled enunciation of eccentric social rules, large and small, and she enforces her ideas with a flicker of contempt. In this society, someone with a strong idea of how people should behave is a rarity, but, like all rule makers, Ephron arouses a spirit of revolt. *When Harry Met Sally...* is often deft, but by the end of the movie one wants to turn all its confident propositions about love and friendship upside down.

NEW YORK POST, 7/12/89. p. 23, Jami Bernard

If romance isn't as, well *romantic* as it used to be, at least we can laugh about it. "When Harry Met Sally..." is a comedy of relationships (and therefore, one might argue, a comedy of errors) that sends up every aspect of today's dating game so affectionately and hilariously you forget it's been done a zillion times. Though it chronicles a rocky road, it is made for and by people who haven't given up on love.

With their simple names, Harry and Sally are the Everyman and Everywoman of urban sigle life. Harry Burns (a cheerfully deadpan Billy Crystal) is the kind of guy who can't handle more than 30 seconds of post-coital cuddling, but who is so good in bed he can make a woman meow, so he says. One of his pet theories is that men and women cannot withstand the temptations of a platonic friendship.

His theory is tested when, straight out of college, Harry meets Sally on a ride-share to New York. Sally Albright (the precocious Meg Ryan) is meticulous, humorless, smugly confident, the kind of control freak who orders sauces, gravies and dressings "on the side."

Harry and Sally bump into each other every few years (we know Sally has loosened up when she gets a flippy new hairdo), but it is a long time before they even agree to have dinner—and then only after their relationships have failed. In no mood for new love, they're even wary of friendship.

But this is a movie that sets out to prove that, like a weed, love can get a toehold anywhere, given half a chance.

Director Rob Reiner, who was divorced when he made this movie and who met his future wife on the set, has real compassion for human foibles. His movies ("'Stand by Me," "The Princess Bride," "This Is Spinal Tap") revel in group dynamics; the heart and humor in them come from the characters and how they accommodate one another.

Nora Ephron, also a veteran of divorce (see or read *Heartburn*), wrote the screenplay. Together Reiner and Ephron move Harry and Sally like playing pieces through a cinematic boardgame where everything that could happen to two single people happens: dating, breaking up, running into the ex, being depressed, being set up by well-meaning friends. The players move on not with a roll of the dice but with a punchline.

The funniest scene is one in which the heretofore prissy Sally demonstrates—in the middle of a crowded deli—that women can fake orgasm so well that even (or particularly) a self-professed stud like Harry can't tell the difference. After her convincing display, an elderly woman at a nearby table (played by Reiner's mother) tells a waiter, I'll have what *she's* having."

The movie is interspersed with documentary-like "interviews" with elderly couples who recount how they met. These sly vignettes reveal the patterns and rules by which each couple abides. Harry and Sally's story is evidently just such an anecdote in the making.

But despite the title—with its leading ellipsis and timeless sound—this movie is unabashedly a product of its time, a definitive progress report on late-'80s love. Sally's evolution is marked by subtle and not-so-subtle nods to Goldie Hawn, Diane Keaton and Holly Hunter, themselves symbols of different eras of womanhood. In this conservative age, marriage is still a single woman's best friend, an end unto itself.

When "Harry Met Sally..." is a compendium of single-gal shorthand: Sally reads "Smart Women, Foolish Choices"; Sally goes to the salad bar (see "Crossing Delancey" for the salad bar as icon of female isolation, or maybe it's because the sneeze-guard is so photogenic); Sally's best friend keeps names of available men in a Rolodex.

Carrie Fisher and Bruno Kirby make a marvelous supporting pair as Sally and Harry's respective best friends. Fisher, a talented comic actress who always seems to be piddling away her time ("Loverboy"), plays a sucker for married men. Easygoing and uncomplicated, Kirby seems a bit blue collar to be a writer for New York magazine, but he's perfect as the disappointed and disappointing blind date for Sally. He proves that merely being available and drawing oxygen does not make one person right for another.

Reiner gives Crystal and Ryan enough leeway to find their characters themselves. Ryan goes full-throttle in two scenes—the orgasm in the deli and a wonderfully funny crying jag when she finds that her ex has married someone who was "supposed to be the transitional person, not the one." Previously, Ryan has been used as incredibly cute window dressing ("Innerspace"); this movie ought to put her in the running for better things.

Crystal adds something to his dry delivery that saves Harry from being a mere cad—watch his priceless look of claustrophobic terror after finally bedding his platonic buddy.

Ultimately, "When Harry Met Sally..." is great fun at everyone's expense, a charming, hilarious love story that will make all those bad dates you ever had seem palatable, at least for the two hours you spend in the theater.

NEWSDAY, 7/12/89, Part II/p. 3, Mike McGrady

What a relief! On the heels of the Caped Crusader and the adventurous archeologist, after a summer of ghostbusters and Star Trekkers—at long last, a non-sequel, a summertime movie purely for adults. "When Harry Met Sally...", the story of a friendship that ripens into love, vibrates with truth and humor, managing to be both emotionally involving and a four-star howler.

When Harry (Billy Crystal) first meets Sally (Meg Ryan) they are kids sharing a ride from the University of Chicago to New York. Love is no threat and, according to Harry, even friendship is an out-and-out impossibility: "Men and women can't be friends because the sex part always gets in the way."

Harry is the kind of pessimist who reads the last page of a novel first; should he die in mid-read, he'll at least know how the story came out. Sally is a play-it-safer who thinks Ingrid Bergman did the right thing in "Casablanca" by flying off with Paul Henreid and leaving Humphrey Bogart behind: "I don't want to spend the rest of my life in Casablanca married to some guy who owns a bar."

Time passes and every five years or so, a slowly maturing Harry and Sally bump into each other again. Eventually, Sally decides she would really prefer Bogart. And about that time, Harry, desperately needing a friend, tries to retract his early dictum on friendship between the sexes: "What's the statute of limitations on apologies?"

Dumped by his wife and lonely, Harry finds himself watching Spanish-language telecasts of "Leave It to Beaver" at dawn. Sally lunches with women who carry Rolodexes filled with the names of available males. "When Harry Met Sally..." is an undisguised celebration of such old-fashioned concepts as love, commitment and marriage. However, the argument is couched in such witty and with-it terms that nothing about it seems old-fashioned. Nora Ephron, writer of "Silkwood" and "Heartburn," knows these people and their common plight. There is enormous humor here, but it is never at the expense of her people; it is humor filled with empathy.

While the four central performances are first-rate (Carrie Fisher and Bruno Kirby portray Harry's and Sally's altar-bound friends), there is one that must be singled out. Ryan's talent, glimpsed in "Innerspace" and "Promised Land," here explodes in a wide-ranging role that would offer a test to any actress.

She is also directly responsible for the funniest moment I can recall in several years of steady movie-going. Harry has been brgging about his success as a love-maker; Sally wonders whether some of his romantic partners might be faking it; he assures her that he knows a fake when he hears it; she then proceeds to demonstrate a highly realistic fake orgasm—this, during supper in a crowded restaurant.

The Manhattan backdrop goes well with two dozen classic love songs like "It Had to Be You," "Our Love Is Here to Stay" and "Where or When." The film itself accomplishes precisely what the music does; it beautifully blends sentiment and sophistication. While it may bring Woody Allen's work to mind, director Rob Reiner gives "When Harry Met Sally..." its own comic life, its own solid identity.

And as Harry and Sally move closer and closer together, tears of laughter give way to a somewhat gentler mist. Because, at its heart, the film is serious, every bit as serious as Sally finally contemplating marriage: "When you realize you want to spend the rest of your life with someone, you want the rest of your life to begin as soon as possible."

NEWSWEEK, 7/17/89, p. 52, David Ansen

In the New York romantic comedy *When Harry Met Sally...* director Rob Reiner and writer Nora Ephron are wrestling with an old but pertinent question: does sex make it impossible for men and women to be true friends? They chronicle this dilemma through the 11-year relationship of Harry Burns (Billy Crystal) and Sally Albright (Meg Ryan), who meet at college in 1977, go off to pursue their own lives and reconnect 10 years later. The sharptongued, pessimist Harry—the kind of guy who reads the last page of a book first—is devastated by the breakup of his marriage; compulsive, lively Sally has just been dumped by her steady guy. These two self-conscious Yuppies are both looking for romance but they refuse to consider each other as plausible partners. Becoming bosom buddies, they delicately dance around the sexual attraction that draws them to each other but which they fear would destroy their cozy Platonic camaraderie.

"When Harry Met Sally..." can be explosively funny, as in the soon-to-be-famous scene when

Sally noisily fakes an orgasm in the middle of a crowded deli, but it is stalking subtler game. Like the neurotic urban romances of Woody Allen and James Brooks, it jests in earnest. Yet for all its wit and knowing details, the movie is strangely unsatisfying. At the crucial moment, when sex finally makes its troublesome entrance—and Harry reacts with a pathological panic that's hard to swallow—the movie becomes more schematic than real. Instead of showing us the really interesting stuff—how Harry and Sally adjust their friendship to romance—it settles for romantic-comedy convention: a sudden oh-what-a-fool-I've-been change of heart.

Part of the problem is in the casting of Crystal. Not surprisingly he handles the comedy superbly, but he's too cool and self-protective an actor to work as a romantic leading man; we want to see the inner life that hides behind the shtik. Ryan gets stronger as her character grows. She strains in the 1977 scenes and sometimes oversells her cuteness, but she blossoms into a comedienne of dazzling charm. Carrie Fisher and Bruno Kirby are delightful as Sally and Harry's confidants; even more beguiling are the series of pseudodocmentary "interviews" with old married couples celebrating connubial longevity that punctuate the drama. A movie of wonderful parts, it doesn't quite add up. In a season of rough-and-tumble entertainments, Reiner's movie is a breath of half-fresh air.

TIME, 7/31/89, p. 65, Richard Corliss

Talk is the sex of the '80s. In a time when you can hardly initiate a handshake without a note from your doctor, conversation is not just a white-collar mating dance; it is the most intimate form of safe sex. Over the telephone or a restaurant table, a man and a woman expose their emotions, exchange seminal fears and desires, make each other laugh and sob—all without touching any organ but the heart. Talk is the consummation devoutly to be wished; no wonder they call it intercourse. It is confession without penance, therapy on the cheap. It is also, in the right mouths, the last civilized popular art.

Wit, conflict, a little sex. Good stuff for a movie? Good enough for a pair of terrific movies: *When Harry Met Sally . . .*, written by Nora Ephron and directed by Rob Reiner; and *sex, lies, and videotape*, written and directed by Steven Soderbergh. Their characters are quick and engaging; they could be the *thirtysomething* folks on a good day, in a gilded mirror. As Ephron says, "People who live in cities aren't in car chases. We don't get shot at. What we mainly do is talk on the phone and have dinner." Her film and *sex, lies* serve up the urban scene at its most urbane. Clean taxis and great apartments appear in a trice, and no one's upscale job deprives him of quality time for soul scratching. But in both films the surface prettiness is just a device; it clears the cityscape of its daily detritus to focus on what matters: love. sex and friendship.

When Ephron met Reiner to discuss a script, she recalls, the director said, "I want to do a movie about two people who become friends and are really happy they become friends because they realize that if they had had sex it would have ruined everything. And they have sex and it ruins everything." Start with randy Harry (Billy Crystal) and precise Sally (Meg Ryan) in the Manhattan of your dreams, at the beginning of a beautiful friendship. But are they aware that falling in like can be as dangerous as falling in love? Reiner, who based the film partly on his life after being divorced from actress Penny Marshall, thinks he knows: "People say, *'Vive la différence,'* but it's more like a cruel joke created by God. Men and women desperately want to be with each other, but at the same time they can't stand each other and don't understand each other."

So Harry and Sally go to movies together, confide romantic traumas, even try double-dating with their respective best friends (funny Bruno Kirby and Carrie Fisher)—all the while fending off the inevitable erotic attraction. When they do surrender sexually, it is just what Harry feared. "The 'during' part was good," he admits. But postcoitally, while she glows, he glowers. He realizes that as friends they had been making love, with words and caring. Going to bed with Sally was just having sex. And now, like any guy who got what he came for, he wants out.

Like Harry and Sally, the movie is hardworking, spot on; it winepresses its conversation into epigrams. No surprise here. Reiner found wayward comedy in such genres as the rock documentary (*This Is Spinal Tap*) and the historical romance (*The Princess Bride*). Crystal, the improv master who is Reiner's closest friend—We finish each other's sentences," Crystal says, "and he finishes my lunch"—meets the challenge of making a compulsive Lothario not just likable but impishly seductive. And Ephron, a helpful Heloise of emotional heartburn, perks the script with clever answers to modern problems. How long should a man hold a woman after making love to her? "Somewhere between 30 seconds and all night." What doubt nags at any woman who lets Mr. Right get away? "You'll have to spend the rest of your life knowing that someone else is married to your husband." What is the guilty secret of married life? "No sex."

No sex? No problem. In *sex, lies, and videotape,* Soderbergh suggests that abstinence makes the heart grow fonder. Ann (Andie MacDowell) is a Baton Rouge, La., housewife too decorous to go mad. Things with her lawyer husband John (Peter Gallagher) are fine, she tells her therapist, "except I'm havin' this feeling that I don't want him to touch me." They haven't had sex for a while. At least Ann hasn't; John is pursuing an affair with her lubricious sister Cynthia (Laura San Giacomo). Curiosity is about the only thing that can be aroused in gentle Ann, and when John's chum Graham (James Spader) visits, she and he swap secrets. Hers: "I think that sex is overrated." His: "I'm impotent." They could be a couple for the '90s: the first postsexual lovers.

To describe the plot—in which we learn that Graham can reach sexual climax only while watching videotapes he has made of women's carnal confessions—is to make *sex, lies* sound like a smirking stag reel. But this is not an "adult film" in the X-rated sense; it is an adult film, "patient and subtle," in its creator's apt words. It is about men who use women by watching them, and women tired of being the object of satyric attention. What amazes is that at just 26 Soderbergh displays the three qualities associated with mature filmmakers: a unique authorial voice, a spooky camera assurance, and the easy control of ensemble acting (Andie MacDowell, start polishing your acceptance speech). Soderbergh delivers so much and promises even more.

The director of both pictures know the risk these days in mining the movie tradition of sophisticated comedy-drama that stretches from *Midnight* to *Manhattan* and *Broadcast News.* Before *sex, lies* earned raves at the U.S. Film Festival in Park City, Utah, and then won the top prize at Cannes, Soderbergh was apprehensive. "I thought the film would seem too European for an American audience," he says, "and too dialogue heavy to translate in Europe. I figured ten people would go see it four times, and that would be that." Reiner, a man Ephron describes as being "very fond of his depressions," dared to commit some small optimism on his happy set. As Meg Ryan recalls, "Rob said, "Wouldn't it be amazing to have this kind of experience, make a great movie, and have people come to see it?' "

Now people have the chance to see two comedies that waft like zephyrs through a movie summer humid with macho derring-do. In their world, romance is bruised but blooming; and the characters are so fully drawn that the moviegoer can become possessive of them, even judgmental, as he would with a friend. Would Sally have faked a fortissimo orgasm in a crowded restaurant? Would footloose Graham come back to Baton Rouge to find a love he lost nine years before? Of course they are not real people, and the difference is crucial in this talk-as-sex era. Real people talk back, act up, walk out. So let's leave the trend where it belongs: onscreen, in the season's smartest, funniest real-love films.

VILLAGE VOICE, 7/18/89, p. 68, Georgia Brown

As someone who tries not to read reviews before seeing the movie, I tend to forget that people regularly do. (Let me just say that I wasn't born a film reviewer, and I would rather not die one.) But I will try to be protective of real surprises. I was careful, for example, not to give away that Sheldon's mother turns into a moon over Manhattan in *New York Stories*—though then I saw reviews with the feat spelled out, on the grounds, I suppose, that it wasn't an ending.

When Harry Met Sally..., Rob Reiner's New York story, cheerfully gives away the whole plot in its title. Harry (Billy Crystal) meets Sally (Meg Ryan) and meets her and meets her. And then they talk about how they met. They first meet at the University of Chicago while Harry is kissing Sally's friend Amanda. This becomes a recurring image in the movie: one or the other watching a couple kiss. A minor theme is couple envy—as distinguished from sexual jealousy.

As new acquaintances, Harry and Sally drive from Chicago to New York arguing all the way. Sally, who plans to be a journalist, wears the uniform of the early '60s (Bermudas, oxford button-down shirt, shetland cardigan), although I think this is supposed to be the mid-'70s; she's straight, nasal midwestern, and a control freak. (Listen to her order a chef's salad with a string of stipulations.) Crystal's cynical deadpan Harry challenges her with the aggressiveness of a born and bred (Jewish?) New Yorker, and has fun putting her on the spot with his bluntness. He informs her that she's obviously never had great sex and that he finds her attractive. When she's offended at his coming on to her ("I'm Amanda's friend!"), he says men and women can't just be friends since sex always gets in the way.

By the time Sally drops Harry under the arch at Washington Square, the two have had it with each other, and on the soundtrack Louis Armstrong and Ella Fitzgerald are fussing," Let's Call the Whole Thing Off." *When Harry Met Sally*...(a title to throw off the rhythm of any sentence) uses song lyrics to comment directly on weather, season, and characters' moods: "Autumn in New York," "Winter Wonderland," "Isn't It Romantic," etc. (Many of these classics are performed tastefully by Harry Connick Jr.)

Years pass. Harry grows a beard; after a time, he shaves it. Sally's hairstyle loosens up, and she too develops into a cynical New Yorker. Apparently she has become a journalist, although work in this movie has been relegated to "another sphere." This is about leisure—after hours, weekends, and the pursuit of the elusive exclusive relationship. Occasionally Harry and Sally run into each other here and there—at the airport, where she's kissing her live-in boyfriend (Gerald Ford's son Steven), and at Shakespeare & Co. at the Seaport, where he's browsing in Personal Growth and she's leafing through *Smart Women/Foolish Choices*.

While recuperating from breakups and in the course of consoling each other, they finally do become friends, but not lovers. Ambivalently they watch as their respective best friends—Marie (Carrie Fisher), formerly a maker of foolish chhoices, and Jess (Bruno Kirby)—proceed to get together. Harry has amended his previous rule to read: Men and women can be friends if they're both involved with other people—which, in a sense, these two still are. Besides, Harry's and Sally's personalities clash; she continues to think of him as "the Angel of Death," and he refers to her as "Miss Hospital Corners."

Although *WHMS*...will be immediately recognizable as directly out of Woody Allen—there's New York in June and Gershwin tunes, and even black-and-white titles—Allen's comedies aren't this spic and span. Diane Keaton's WASP flake and Allen's Jewish intellectual nudge—who also have best friends and split-screen round-robin conversations—have more interesting topics of conversation. And they're funnier. *WHMS*...makes Allen's comedies look as hard to imitate as Allen's serious dramas make Bergman look. This genial romantic comedy—far from Reiner's very clever 1984 *This Is Spinal Tap*—finally seems closer to Alan Alda than to Woody.

The voice one hears more distinctly than Reiner's, or Crystal's (who's surprisingly convincing as a romantic lead), is screenwriter Nora Ephron's. *WHMS*...works by reprises, choral refrains—which is how her novel *Hearthburn* and her journalistic pieces move. Characters are defined by tics, often to do with eating. Harry chews noisily and has an unappealing way with grape seeds. Sally orders pie à la mode like this: Warm it with ice cream, ice cream if there's strawberry, whipped cream only if with real cream. I'm probably getting it wrong, and so will the waitress. A woman making such intricate demands thrives on disappointment. But finally, Sally's compulsiveness ordering meals or mailing letters (one by one, checking inside the slot each time) doesn't come to more than a bit or a shtick. These aren't really indications of personality or destiny.

Like writers of the Ann Beattie school, Ephron is a user of brand names and how-we-live-now details. Harry doesn't indulge in Mallomars or Sally nibble peanut M & M's because those companies paid for the advertising (oh, they may have anyway), but because these are the junk foods corresponding to the characters. Where identity is tied up in consumer choices, fiction may be followed as a lifestyle manual—*Heartburn* actually included recipes. Ephron's not a depressive, though, like most of the minimalists—or she's not an overt one, anyway. Perhaps the form she's intuitively inherited from her Hollywood-Broadway writer parents just happens to end on the upbeat.

Too much about *WHMS*...is derivative—and, more fatal, suffers in comparison to its sources. A documentary refrain punctuating the film—out of *Reds*, or Allen again—is lame. Old couples, reminiscing about their own first meetings, tell banal stories and their identities blur. *Casablanca*, of all movies, actually becomes a reference point in Harry and Sally's relationship. (Certain details seem seriously dated.) Woody Allen has taken a lot of flak for his romantic New York, but nothing in Allen looks as saccharine as these seasons and these locations. Reiner sentences his characters to breathe inside cliché: the Central Park Boathouse, a Sharper Image outlet, the Temple of Dendur, a Giants game where the primary colors in the stands look as if each extra were individually dressed and placed. (The batting cage is a nice touch.) There must be more even to yuppies than this.

When Sally buys a Christmas tree and struggles to carry it off into the snow, she stumbles and bumbles around too much. It's not Ryan's fault; cuteness is being asked of her because Sally hasn't much outside her quirks to define her. Crystal seems cast to provide an edge, but his tartness loses bite early on. As Harry grows more mellow and passive, he's less able to hold his own in the movie—much less in a relationship. Minimalist characters, Harry and Sally resemble figurines in a climate-controlled atrium—the kind of wonderland you shake and snow flies.

About the ending I will say only this: It is a serious mistake to show Crystal doing something beginning with R (a three-letter word ending in N) that at least two other short New York actors (W.A. and D.H.) have done enough of already.

Also reviewed in:
NEW REPUBLIC, 8/21/89, p. 26, Stanley Kauffmann
NEW YORK TIMES, 7/12/89, p. C15, Caryn James
VARIETY, 7/12–16/89, p. 24

WHEN THE WHALES CAME

A Twentieth Century Fox release of a Golden Swan production in association with Central Independent Television. *Executive Producer:* Geoffrey Wansell. *Producer:* Simon Channing-Williams. *Director:* Clive Rees. *Screenplay (based on his novel "Why the Whales Came"):* Michael Morpurgo. *Director of Photography:* Robert Paynter. *Editor:* Andrew Boulton. *Music:* Christopher Gunning. *Sound:* Peter Glossop. *Sound Editor:* John Foster. *Production Designer:* Bruce Grimes. *Art Director:* Colin Grimes. *Special Effects:* Peter Hutchinson. *Costumes:* Lindy Hemming. *Make-up:* Norma Webb and Heather Jones. *Running time:* 100 minutes. *MPAA Rating:* PG.

CAST: Irene Wilson (Molly Woodcock); Fergus Rees (The Birdman as a Boy); Paul Scofield (The Birdman); Helen Pearce (Gracie Jenkins); Max Rennie (Daniel Pender); Frederick Warder (1st Fisherman); Nicholas Jones (Vicar); Kerra Spowart (Margaret Pender); Barbara Ewing (Mary Pender); John Hallam (Treve Pender); Keith Low (2nd Fisherman); David Suchet (Will); Barbara Jefford (Auntie Mildred); Dexter Fletcher (Big Tim); Blue Philpott (Albert Pender); David Threlfall (Jack Jenkins); Helen Mirren (Clemmie Jenkins); Penny Rogers (Maisie); Derek Pearce (Fiddle Player); Susan Curnow (1st Fisherwoman); James Stedeford, Paul Thomas, and David Sherris (Big Tim's Gang); Jeremy Kemp (Mr. Wellbeloved); Joanna Bartholomew (Miss Tregarthen); Stephen Dan (Watchboy); David Quilter (Mr. Bullhead).

LOS ANGELES TIMES, 10/20/89, Calendar/p. 10, Kevin Thomas

"When the Whales Came" takes us to Britain's idyllic Isles of Scilly, where life seems unchanged through the centuries. The year, however, is 1914, and not even the beautiful island of Bryher remains untouched by the advent of the Great War. It is a time when parents start wondering, apparently for the first time, whether there really is a future for their children in a locale so remote from the modern world.

For writer Michael Morpurgo, who adapted his story "Why the Whales Came" for the screen, this time and place were nevertheless ideal for a consideration of the importance of living in harmony with nature. One of citizens of Bryher is a man (Paul Scofield) who has lived there for 60 years, having come there as a child. He believes that nature took its revenge upon the citizens of his native island of Samson, rendering it uninhabitable, after they preyed upon a school of whales that ran aground there.

Morpurgo and director Clive Rees have created a veritable paradise with their setting of splendid natural beauty and their hearty, healthy and loving people. Their point is that the people of Bryher need to become more aware of the good fortune they've seemingly always enjoyed and to respect their environment. The movie is not nearly as obvious as this sounds, and it is through two adorable children (Max Rennie, Helen Pearce) befriending the hermetic Scofield that it puts its message across.

"When the Whales Came" (rated PG, though G would seem more appropriate) is such a lovely picture, glorious-looking and fitted out with an appropriately stirring score, that one is almost afraid to give it that seemingly kiss-of-death designation, the ideal family film.

In that light, it is good to point out that no less than Helen Mirren plays Pearce's resilient mother and that this film marks one of the rare screen appearances of Scofield, one of Britain's most distinguished actors and an Oscar winner for his portrayal of Sir Thomas More in "A Man for All Seasons." It is left to him to give the film's climactic speech, and he is wonderfully persuasive. The man he plays may be reclusive, but there's nothing of the stereotypical Old Codger in his performance of a man with strong mystical beliefs.

MONTHLY FILM BULLETIN, 10/89, p. 312, Sylvia Paskin

1844: A terrible calamity has befallen the island of Samson in the Scilly Isles: a young boy and his mother are the last to give up the struggle and leave. 1914: On the neighbouring island of Bryher, ten-year-old Daniel and his friend Gracie, eight, play on the beach but are afraid of encountering the mysterious old Birdman, who is said to be mad. One day, however, they find a toy boat they have lost mysteriously returned to them, and on another occasion a beautiful carved bird, which Gracie takes to hide in the cottage where she lives with her father Jack and mother Clemmie. After a storm, they visit the Birdman's cottage, and are surprised by him there; he is stone deaf but they manage to tell him that war has broken out, and he tells them that the islanders should gather the valuable timber which the storm has washed up. This they do before the customs men come for it; the carved bird is discovered and Gracie tells her parents it was made by Daniel. Jack leaves for the war, and the Birdman begins leaving food secretly for Clemmie. The children, who have been warned by the Birdman not to set foot on Samson, are forced to land there one day when they are trapped by the tide while out fishing. They find its long-abandoned cottages and wells that have run dry. Back on Bryher, there is news of Jack's death, and Daniel's baby brother falls ill. Tim, Daniel's elder brother, inspired by the patriotic speeches of the schoolmaster, Mr. Wellbeloved, is plotting with his friends to burn down the Birdman's cottage, believing him to be a spy. Daniel overhears the plot, but before he can warn the Birdman is locked in a shed by his father for a misdemeanour. He and Gracie later find the Birdman looking at a huge stranded narwhale on the beach. He recalls the events of seventy years ago when a shoal of the whales came to Samson and were killed by the islanders. A shipwreck and other disasters followed, and the island became uninhabitable; he and his mother were the last to leave. Tim and his cronies set the Birdman's cottage alight, and when the islanders hear of the imminent appearance of the whales, they come to kill them. The Birdman and the children succeed in dissuading them, however, and fires are lit through the night to turn the whales back. The Birdman disappears; the curse is lifted and the wells on Samson run with water again. The baby recovers and Jack returns as the bells on Bryher ring in celebration.

Michael Morpurgo's children's novel, published in 1985 as *Why the Whales Came*, was inspired by a true story associated with the Scilly Island of Samson during the Napoleonic Wars. Nineteen men and boys from the island lost their lives in the wreck of a French barque which they had captured; the island never recovered from the disaster and by 1855 was uninhabited. This, presumably, is what attracted backing for the film from Sir James Goldsmith's new production company, Golden Swan, which was set up specifically to make movies from "real stories", although the film's *raison d'être*, of course, is the contemporary concern with Green issues (again notwithstanding meticulous research into and recreation of the costumes, dialect, and farming and fishing methods of the early twentieth century). Its tone is gently moralising, but for a film which carries so many positive messages it is marked by a commendable restraint, particularly with regard to the excellent performances of Helen Mirren as the resourceful Clemmie and Paul Scofield as the Birdman.

Sentimentality is offset by the presence of several less likeable characters, such as the nationalistic schoolmaster and Daniel's rough-tongued father Treve. The "aloneness" of the Birdman, who has the traditional prophetic wisdom of the shunned outsider, is paralleled by Daniel's own. Bullied by his father and neglected by his mother, he also suffers as a dreamer. But through the example of the Birdman he learns a new awareness and resilience which means, in the true spirit of children's adventure stories, that he and Gracie become the heroes of the hour and help to expiate the curse of the past. Only the second feature of commercials director Clive Rees (the first being the barely seen, buried-alive drama, *The Blockhouse*), *When the Whales Came* has a lyrical simplicity embodying a fable of sin and redemption, as well as a timely reminder of what is now at stake.

NEW YORK POST, 10/20/89, p. 30, Jami Bernard

Whales, as ponderous and rubbery as they appear, seem to find a soft spot in human hearts these days. "When the Whales Came" is a sweet, lovely, and ecologically correct fable about an island's curse and about how saving the whales somehow plays a part in lifting it.

Adapted from his novel "Why the Whales Came" by Michael Morpurgo, "Whales" is beautifully and reverently brought to the screen by director Clive Rees and an excellent cast, including Helen Mirren, and the estimable Paul Scofield as The Bridman, a sort of Boo Radley of the English Isle of Bryher.

Also, two fine young child actors, Max Rennie, who shows a lot of depth, and the angel-faced Helen Pearce (who had never acted before but just happened to be around the set when they were in pre-production), are solemn and moving as the two kids through whose eyes the gently-paced story unfolds.

On the small, windswept isle of Bryher, at the start of World War I, a tiny community goes about its meager existence as it has done for 70 years, ever since the entire population of nearby Samson Island relocated to Bryher because of a mysterious curse. There is hope for the future in the form of a new baby in their midst, but there is also the steady hardship of living off the occasional gift from the sea, like a shipwrecked boat's timber or a trap full of lobster.

The only ones having any fun, in fact, are two of the island's few children. Daniel and Gracie, who are still young enough to enjoy the simple pleasures of what is after all beach-front living. They gradually befriend the much-feared Birdman, an old recluse who takes mysterious trips in his rowboat during the island's frequent storms and who leaves the kids presents of whittled birds.

The tusked whales, or narwhals, don't come into the picture until late in the film, but even though they are played by some very realistic special-effects creations, their plight and the way in which the islanders elect to deal with it makes for one of those three-hanky endings, even if the warmest feelings you've had for fish are when they're filleted on a platter.

Most of the movie establishes the kind of life the islanders lead, which is explanation enough for what it must mean to them when something unexpected washes ashore.

The film makers take advantage of the full slate of weather provided by their location setting. The sky is by turns resort-island-blue, cold heather gray, and darkly menacing. The rocky shoreline and creaking rowboats too provide a chilly sense of isolation.

Mirren is as changeable as the weather, playing Gracie's mother with depth and sensitivity. Scofield is mesmerizing as the deaf old man who is so touched by the presence of children in his life again.

"Whales" is a sentimental movie, against which grasping '80s comedies like "The Secret of My Success" seem even sicker. Go see it and have a few sniffles.

NEWSDAY, 10/20/89, Part III/p. 5, Janice Berman

There's a certain kind of beauty in film making that comes around only rarely. It arises from the perfect combination of the innocence of childhood and the equal, primitive vulnerability of nature.

We last saw this kind of thing in Francis Ford coppola's "The Black Stallion." And only when we see "When the Whales Came," directed by Clive Rees and filmed by Robert Paynter, do we realize how much it has been missed.

"When the Whales Came," however, is a fable of an entirely different order. Filmed on lovely, desolate Bryher, one of the Isles of Scilly off the southwest coast of England, the film tells us quietly that we need to take care of nature so that nature, in turn, will protect us.

Two children, Daniel (Max Rennie) and Gracie (Helen Pearce), befriend The Birdman, as Paul Scofield's character is known, and he becomes the conscience of the piece. He is a gentle, elderly recluse who left the neighboring island of Samson as a small boy. The residents killed the narwhals—whales with long horns, like unicorns—that arrived on its shores; a curse descended on the island. And now, 70 years later—it's 1914—the Birdman has a chance to prevent the same thing from happening on Bryher.

But that moment is a long time in coming; this is not a movie that's in a rush. We have the luxury of oceans of time to delight in the play of light on the sea, time to find out about the lives of the devout, but not perfect, people who live there.

There are fine actors with terrific-looking faces in "When the Whales Came," and some of them, including the delightful little girl, Helen Pearce, are present-day residents of Bryher.

We watch them mending their nets; we see Gracie in an open boat, fishing with her father (David Threlfall) and singing a song of the sea. We take note of the love her mother (Helen Mirren) and father have for each other and for her, and we feel intensely the dark shadow the Great War casts upon this sun-dappled island.

And then there's the charm of the growing friendship between the children and the reclusive old man. A deaf woodcarver, he leaves gifts for Gracie and Daniel with messages spelled out in shells on the sand. Daniel leaves him a wooden boat. He leaves Daniel a carving knife. "Try a puffin," he suggests in shells, puffins being one of the glories the Scilly Islands.

Equally fine and enviable is the uncomplicated, unquestioning friendship of Gracie and Daniel. His father beats him too much. There's a parallel authoritarian figure in the children's off-island teacher, Mr. Wellbeloved (Jeremy Kemp); he, however, tempers his bullying with love.

So even before the whales come, and even before Daniel and Gracie help the Birdman, we've a picture of a complete community, filled with strong and self-confident figures who aren't always right.

Making the residents of Bryher aware of the difference between working with nature and usurping it will be no easy task. But when we look into the face of Scofield's Birdman, as filled with shadow and light as the island whose fate he's defending, we're filled with hope.

Also reviewed in;
NEW YORK TIMES, 10/20/89, p. C18, Janet Maslin
VARIETY, 9/6–12/89, p. 22
WASHINGTON POST, 10/20/89, p. B7, Hal Hinson

WHOOPING COUGH

A Cinephile release of a Hunnia Studio/Mafilm production. *Executive Producer:* Andras Elek. *Director:* Peter Gardos. *Screenplay (Hungarian with English subtitles):* Andras Osvat and Peter Gardos. *Director of Photography:* Tibor Mathe. *Editor:* Maria Rigo. *Music:* Janos Novak. *Sound:* Janos Reti and Istvan Sipos. *Production Designer:* Jozef Romvari. *Costumes:* Agnes Gyarmathy. *Running time:* 95 minutes. *MPAA Rating:* Not Rated.

CAST: Marcell Toth (Tomi); Eszter Karasz (Annamari); Dezso Garas (Father); Judit Hernadi (Mother); Mari Torocsik (Grandmother); Anna Feher (The Maid); Károly Eperjes (Akos).

VILLAGE VOICE, 3/21/89, p. 64, Katherine Dieckmann

This comedy-drama by Péter Gárdos is making a belated appearance in New York two years after playing the Chicago Film Festival. Set during the '56 upheaval in Hungary and seen through a young boy's eyes, it functions as a kind of prequel to Péter Gothar's *Time Stands Still*—same manual typewriter credits, coming-of-age episodes, and gliding shots down schoolhouse corridors, but lighter on that telltale sfumato. There are also shades of the kooky familial antics in Emir Kusterica's *When Father Was Away on Business*. Gárdos skillfully balances scenes of hermetic home life with evidence of outer violence, and Mari Töröcsik's chain-smoking, tough-talking grandmother is a killer combination of tenderness and spite. *Whooping Cough* feels familiar, but in this case, that's a welcome sensations.

Also reviewed in:
NEW YORK TIMES, 3/21/89, p. C20, Vincent Canby
VARIETY, 3/11/87, p. 122

WHO'S HARRY CRUMB?

A Tri-Star Pictures Release. *Executive Producer:* John Candy. *Producer:* Arnon Milchan. *Director:* Paul Flaherty. *Screenplay:* Robert Conte and Peter Martin Wortmann. *Director of Photography:* Stephen M. Katz. *Editor:* Danford B. Greene. *Music:* Michel Colombier. *Music Editor:* Ellen Segal. *Sound:* Rick Patton and (music) Frank Wolf. *Sound Editor:* Samuel C. Crutcher and Norval Crutcher. *Production Designer.* Trevor Williams. *Art Director:* Stephen Geaghan. *Set Decorator:* Elizabeth Wilcox. *Set Dresser:* Gordon Brunner,

Douglas Robert Carnegie, and Peter Mills. *Special Effects:* Gene Grigg. *Costumes:* Jerry R. Allen. *Make-up:* Jan Newman. *Make-up Prosthetics:* Steve LaPorte. *Stunt Coordinator:* Bill Ferguson. *Running time:* 87 minutes. *MPAA Rating:* PG-13.

CAST: John Candy (Harry Crumb); Jeffrey Jones (Eliot Draisen); Annie Potts (Helen Downing); Tim Thomerson (Vince Barnes); Barry Corbin (P.J. Downing); Shawnee Smith (Nikki Downing); Valri Bromfield (Detective Casey); Doug Steckler (Dwayne); Renee Coleman (Jennifer Downing); Wesley Mann (Tim); Tamsin Kelsey (Marie); Joe Flaherty (Doorman); Fiona Roeske (Crumb Receptionist); Lori O'Byrne (Karen); Michele Goodger (Mrs. MacIntyre); Beverley Elliott (Joanne); P.Lynn Johnson (Kelly); Peter Yunker (Jeffrey Brandt); Brenda Crichlow (Suki's Salon Receptionist); Garwin Sanford (Dennis Kimball); Tony Dakota (Freddy); Rob Morton (Airport Cop); Marcel Maillard (Chauffeur); Leslie Ewen (Airport X-Ray Guard); Manny Perry (Cop in Car); Gaye Heatherington (Lover); Patrick McKenna (TV Man); Daliah Bache (TV Woman); Eve Smith (Elderly Woman); Tino Insana (Smokey); Frank T. Hernandez and Fran Casado (Salesmen); Cyndi Lee Rice (Stewardess); Lyle Alzado (Man in Apartment); Deanna Oliver (Woman in Apartment); Ira Miller (Accountant); Stephen Young (Interior Decorator).

LOS ANGELES TIMES, 2/3/89, Calendar/p. 10, Kevin Thomas

"Who's Harry Crumb?"—he's John Candy as the klutziest detective since Peter Sellers' Inspector Clouseau. In this pleasantly silly private-eye spoof, Crumb is a grand poseur, shamelessly self-important, slow on the uptake yet good of heart and not the complete fool he so often seems.

He's in constant battle with objects inanimate and otherwise. Doors swing back to smack him in the nose, paper shredders make quick work of his ties, and supposedly stationary exercise bikes have a way of running out of control when he places his considerable bulk upon them. Seeing himself as a master of disguise, he dares to don jockey silks. Don't ask how he manages to end up on top of a ceiling fan. In short, imagine Oliver Hardy playing Philip Marlowe.

You can be sure that a 90 million-year-old fossilized pterodactyl egg is in grave danger in his presence. The egg is the special treasure of the smarmy head of Crumb & Crumb (Jeffrey Jones), who has his own reasons for summoning Harry, feckless grandson of the detective agency's founder, to Los Angeles to help out in a kidnaping case in which a beautiful heiress (Renee Coleman) is being held for a $10-million ransom.

Writers Robert Conte and Peter Martin Wortmann have come up with a gallery of deliciously skewered private-eye stereotypes. There's the heiress' enigmatic father (Barry Corbin); her outrageously sluttish and greedy stepmother (Annie Potts, a sexy comic delight); Potts' rugged but thick-headed tennis-pro lover (Tim Thomerson); the laziest, most insolent butler you ever saw (Wesley Mann), and Crumb's special nemesis, a super uptight cop (Valri Bromfield).

Most important is the kidnaped woman's teen-age sister Nikki (Shawnee Smith, a real winner), who teams up with Crumb and in doing so emerges from the shadow of her adored glamorous sibling. The film's free-wheeling nonsense is nicely anchored in the mutually sustaining friendship that develops between Crumb and Nikki. Director Paul Flaherty brings to the film consistent good judgment and deftness.

When so much that passes for comedy these days is the humor of unrelieved crassness and elaborate mayhem—costing fortunes in special effects and involving legions of stunt people—it's easy to oversell a light and modest laugh-out-loud entertainment like "Who's Harry Crumb?"(rated PG-13 for mild raunchiness). Still, you're left glad that Candy, a sweet-natured clown who never loses his innate dignity, bows off leaving open the clear possibility of further adventures for Harry Crumb.

MONTHLY FILM BULLETIN, 7/89, p. 219, Geoff Brown

Harry Crumb, fat-headed grandson of the founder of a prestigious detective agency, is summoned from the Mid-West to the Los Angeles head office to work on the kidnapping of multi-millionaire P.J. Downing's daughter Jennifer. Crumb believes his hour has finally come, but the agency boss Eliot Draisen has assigned him to the case only to cover his own tracks. For Draisen arranged the kidnapping himself, and plans to use the ransom money as bait to capture Helen, Downing's young nymphomaniac wife. Helen, however, only has eyes for Vince Barnes, a country club Romeo; together they plan to take possession of Downing's fortune by arranging his accidental death. A ransom note for ten million dollars arrives at the Downing mansion, where Crumb prowls around to little effect, though he finds a useful ally in Jennifer's younger sister Nikki. Crumb lives dangerously: he falls through the skylight spying on Helen at the Yacht Club, tumbles down an air conditioning vent while observing Vince's apartment, and skirts death driving Downing's car after Vince has tampered with the brakes. The cumulative evidence points to Helen and Vince; Crumb, disguised as a jockey, tries to nail them at the racetrack rendezvous arranged for the ransom exchange. But Draisen takes charge of the money and drives to the airport, where Vince, in close pursuit, snatches his suitcase and trusses him up in a storage cupboard. Crumb and Nikki apprehend Vince just before his plane takes off for Buenos Aires; then Draisen, discovered in the cupboard, confesses the kidnapping to the amazed Crumb. With the case triumphantly solved, Crumb is made president of the firm.

A typical gag sequence in *Who's Harry Crumb?* finds John Candy peering through binoculars from the Yacht Club roof at the prime suspects in his kidnapping case. He slides down, crashes through a skylight, and lands on a revolving ceiling fan in the restaurant below. Many spins later, Candy lurches through the chairs and tables, grasping diners' heads for support and snaring a loose toupée. He then totters outside and belly-flops with an enormous splash into the waiting water. Not since Frank Tashlin's heyday has a Hollywood comedy been so designed to look like a cartoon. Elsewhere, director Paul Flaherty (a past associate of Candy's on the Canadian spoof comedy series *Second City TV*) treats his balloon-like hero as an animated blob, bouncing undented from innumerable physical adventures with ventilator shafts, scaffolding, runaway cars, exercise bikes and paper shredders—every prop in the gagman's armoury.

Aside from its strength as a live-action cartoon, *Who's Harry Crumb?* cannot boast many claims to originality. As with Leslie Nielsen's character in *The Naked Gun*, Harry Crumb is a prime example of the Comic Hero as Impervious Idiot, bumbling through a deadpan genre parody; one gag brings a specific echo of Nielsen's *contretemps* with Ricardo Montalban's fishtank. In his penchant for outrageous disguises, Crumb is also kid brother to *Fletch* (though minus Chevy Chase's slick patter): along the way, Candy gets kitted out as a Hungarian hairdresser with shaved head and turquoise suit, a turbaned Indian (with regrettable accent), an outsized jockey, and a reborn Mae West in flaming pink. Unlike *Fletch*, or indeed *Fletch Lives*, the motivating plot contains little mystery to tantalise audiences: an early scene clearly establishes Draisen, the agency boss, as the kidnapper. The wholesale reliance on burlesque foolery and cartoon antics is also monotonous at times, but Candy's benign clowning and straight-faced treatment of the silliest lines reap modest rewards.

NEW YORK POST, 2/4/89, p. 21, David Edelstein

"Who's Harry Crumb?" is the story of a guy who puts on silly disguises and tries to sneak into places where he's not wanted. Personally, I find this an extremely fertile subject for comedy, but the movie treats its audience like cretins who need to be nudged in the ribs when it's time for them to laugh. Even the 12-year-olds in back of me were insulted.

The picture begins with a beautiful young woman (Renee Coleman) taking off her clothes and getting chloroformed in the middle of a mud massage. It's a promising start. She's an heiress, it turns out, and the apple of her daddy's eye. But to solve the kidnapping, the head of the detective agency, Draisen (Jeffrey Jones), calls in Harry Crumb (John Candy), who has been exiled for incompetence to the firm's Tulsa branch.

Why summon a nincompoop? Because Draisen himself is the kidnapper, and is confident that the clumsy, pretentious fool won't get anywhere near the truth. But we know better, don't we?

Red hair brushed back in a mini-pompadour, head waggling with know-it-all assurance, Candy's Harry has a tendency to fall off buildings, get blown out of air shafts and make pronouncements of staggering idiocy. He's so dumb he thinks an enlarged photo of a woman's head and shoulders is a photo of a giant woman. He's so dumb he thinks the ransom notes—composed of individual letters from magazine headlines—are the work of one eccentric typewriter. ("Find that crazy typewriter and you've found your kidnapper.")

That's actually not a bad line, but even the picture's good jokes have a way of reverberating in the theater's tomb-like silence. "Who's Harry Crumb?" borrows its tone from the "Pink Panther" films, but it's closer to a "Pink Elephant" movie, and I'm not just talking about Candy's girth. The slapstick is so lumbering that you have time to look at your watch in mid-gag. A universe in which everything goes disastrously wrong is, finally, as boring as one in which everything goes right.

The picture groans with broad, stereotypical characters, among them the heiress' greedy-nympho stepmother (Annie Potts) and her thick-witted tennis-pro lover (Tim Thomerson). The actors are bearable, however, and Shawnee Smith—as the plainer, neglected daughter who tags along after Crumb—has an appealingly down-to-earth delivery. But other performers are degraded, especially Valri Bromfield as a policewoman—her aura of competence guarantees she'll be referred to as "butch."

Director Paul Flaherty worked with Candy as a writer for Second City TV (his brother Joe has a cameo in "Who's Harry Crumb?"), and you'd think he'd have more taste, that he wouldn't settle for a script in which the only targets were stupidity and clumsiness. SCTV, after all, was the most exhilarating hallucination of TV ever to appear on TV, and while it made wicked fun of both American and Canadian culture, it had a healthy respect for its own viewers.

What's saddest about "Who's Harry Crumb?" is how comfortable Candy seems condescending to his audience. (He's also the executive producer, so he presumably had more than a little creative control.) With the exception of "Splash," his work since SCTV has consisted of slob comedies like "Armed and Dangerous," "Summer Rental" and "The Great Outdoors."

Writing creative obituaries for the gifted performers of SCTV is not my idea of a good time, but that's the American cinema for you—a place where comic artists lose touch with the source of their greatness. Four years ago, I'd have laughed if someone told me a John Candy film would be something to dread. Today I've stopped laughing.

NEWSDAY, 2/3/89, Part III/p. 5, Mike McGrady

For weeks now the ads have been asking, "Who's Harry Crumb?" Even as the question is asked, it is answered because each ad carries the familiar, friendly, well-meaning, earnestly lovable features of the larger-than-life John Candy. Since we know *who* Harry Crumb is, we must now address a slightly more complicated question: *What* is Harry Crumb?

Well, for starters, Harry Crumb, a bumbling private eye, is distantly related to the old (circa 1975 to 1983) Canadian television series that first brought Candy to our attention. That was, of course, "SCTV," an imaginative and offbeat cult favorite that could go from excruciatingly funny to simply excruciating in a matter of seconds. Director Paul Flaherty (his only other film was "18 Again") is another "SCTV"veteran as is his brother, comic Joe Flaherty, who also appears in this film.

As long as we've started with lineage, we must observe that Harry Crumb is also a blood relative of Inspector Clouseau of "Pink Panther" fame. That same smug self-satisfaction, that same blind sincerity, that same well-meaning ignorance, that same tendency to trip and destroy everything within eyesight.

And that same aptitude for detection. Consider Crumb's analysis of a ransom note, one of those ransom notes constructed from letters that have been snipped from headlines and magazine covers and pasted on a page. The intrepid Crumb studies the note, ponders deeply, gives the waiting police officials his considered opinion.

"You find that crazy typewriter," he finally announces, "and you'll find your kidnapper."

What is "Harry Crumb"? It is...silly, unrelievedly silly. Perhaps the approach to humor can best be described as haphazard. No potentially comic notion, no matter how childish or asinine, is ignored.

So it is that the desk in Harry Crumb's detective office features a small decorative orange tree. When a client visits, oranges start falling from the tree, first singly, then in multiples. Thereafter, throughout the movie, one must keep a wary eye out for falling oranges. Yes, definitely a haphazard approach to humor.

"Harry Crumb" can also be, at odd moments, hilarious. I do mean odd moments. The funniest scenes in the film involve brief walk-ons by a young unknown, Wesley Mann, portraying a lazy butler with sleep-filled eyes and surly disposition.

"I suppose this'd be a good time for coffee," his employer suggests.

"Oh, great,"he groans, "now I suppose *everyone'll* want some."

Maybe you had to be there. Whenever things slow down, which does happen, Candy appears in yet another outlandish disguise. The final disguise, the most outlandish and funniest, calls for man-mountain Candy to disguise himself as a jockey and mingle with all those other little fellows at a race track while purebreds roll their eyes in terror.

The story itself is little more than a string supporting some highly elaborate sight gags. Some of these uncaptioned cartoons—especially one that has Candy riding a speeding ceiling fan—will be remembered long after the rest of the movie is forgotten sometime early next week.

VILLAGE VOICE, 2/14/89, p. 70, Bruce Handy

Who's Harry Crumb? is another comedy, almost as awful, almost as sloppy, and it squanders far more talent—at least in front of the camera (which I suppose makes it the more offensive movie). [The reference is to *Her Alibi*.] It's a *Pink Panther*-esque knockoff—a *"Pink Panther* substance," to borrow the terminology of corporate fake-cheese makers—and John Candy plays the bumbling, destructive detective, hauling his girth around from telegraphed gag to telegraphed gag. (This is the kind of movie where nearly every scene is built around a prominently placed breakaway prop.) The teeth-gnashing boss honors have been done by Jeffrey Jones, the improbably long-nosed actor who turns up in everything (he was the principal in *Ferris Bueller's Day Off*, the intruding house buyer in *Beetlejuice*); unfortunately, the talented Jones has turned up in this very same role too many times before—he's getting tired, and tiresome. On the other hand, Annie Potts, as a gold-digging wife, manages to put an interesting bitter spin on even her most achingly unsubtle lines. (And the actress has a lot to be bitter about here.) Paul Flaherty (*18 Again!*) directed, indifferently, and the *Harry Crumb* production notes say that he used to work with Candy on *SCTV*—which is a very sad note to end on. If Candy, who executive-produced *Harry Crumb*, doesn't watch it, he's going to be remembered as a bad film comedian (*Summer Rental* and *Armed and Dangerous* come to mind) rather than as a great TV one. Wearing out his welcome, he'll become the Gene Wilder of his generation—that is, if fellow Canadian Dan Aykroyd hasn't already copped the honors.

Also reviewed in:
NEW YORK TIMES, 2/3/89, p. C14, Janet Maslin
VARIETY, 2/8–14/89, p. 20
WASHINGTON POST, 2/4/89, p. G6, Richard Harrington

WINTER PEOPLE

A Columbia Pictures release of a Nelson Entertainment production. *Producer:* Robert H. Solo. *Director:* Ted Kotcheff. *Screenplay:* Carol Sobieski. *Based on the novel by:* John Ehle. *Director of Photography:* François Protat. *Editor:* Thom Noble. *Music:* John Scott. *Music Editor:* Steve Livingston and Ken Johnson. *Sound:* Robert Gravenor and (music) Leslie Shatz. *Sound Editor:* Alan Splet. *Production Designer:* Ron Foreman. *Art Director:* Charles Butcher. *Set Decorator:* Leslie Morales. *Set Dresser:* Randall R. Milazzo, Richard Dearborn, and Denise Dugally. *Special Effects:* John Stirber. *Costumes:* Ruth Morley. *Make-up:* Richard Arrington. *Stunt Coordinator:* Eddy Donno. *Running time:* 110 minutes. *MPAA Rating:* PG-13.

CAST: Kurt Russell (Wayland Jackson); Kelly McGillis (Collie Wright); Lloyd Bridges (William Wright); Mitchell Ryan (Drury Campbell); Amelia Burnette (Paula Jackson); Eileen Ryan (Annie Wright); Lanny Flaherty (Gudger Wright); Don Michael Paul (Young Wright); David Dwyer (Milton Wright); Jeffrey Meek (Cole Campbell); Bill Gribble (Skeet Campbell); Wallace Merck (Harmon Campbell); Walker Averitt (Margaret Campbell); Dashiell Coleman (Jonathan Wright); Barbara Freeman (Mavis McGregor); Gary Bullock (Mr. McGregor); Ivan Green (Mr. Crawford); Lucile Dew McIntyre (Mrs. Crawford); Judy Simpson Cook (Gudger's Wife); James Eric (Bartering Man); Rebecca Koon (Bartering Woman); Dick Parkinson (Campbell Man #1); Stacy Moore (Campbell Man #2).

LOS ANGELES TIMES, 4/13/89, Calendar/p. 1, Sheila Benson

"Winter People," which opens the AFI/Fest tonight and plays in selected theaters beginning Friday, has so many arresting characters and facets that when it begins to go completely haywire it's like watching someone you've become rather fond of come unglued.

Carol Sobieski's screenplay, adapted from the carefully wrought novel of North Carolina regional novelist John Ehle, sets a father and young daughter from more citified Pennsylvania down in the middle of an isolated Smoky Mountains community, mid-Depression time. Wayland Jackson (Kurt Russell) is a decent, gentle, humorous man with patience enough to make clocks, which happens to be his trade. Recently widowed and only now coming out of it, he is the devoted father to a ferocious, outspoken 10-year-old daughter, Paula (splendid newcomer Amelia Burnette).

When their car gets stuck in a country stream, father and daughter stumble down through misty woods onto a remote mountain compound belonging to Collie Wright (Kelly McGillis) a notably suspicious woman, and her beautiful, 6-month-old son, Jonathan.

Collie, it seems, is a pridefully unmarried mother, although she has kept the father's identity secret. (It doesn't take vast detective work to ferret out the man however; if you remember the Hatfields and the McCoys or Romeo and Juliet you might have a clue.)

Having this baby has alienated Collie from her mother, but not her patriarchal father (Lloyd Bridges) or her three brothers: the weak, guilt-ridden storekeeper Gudger (Lanny Flaherty), stocky blacksmith Milton (David Dwyer), or Young (Don Michael Paul), obviously the youngest, a handsome, traveling, all-purpose hell-raiser.

Almost instantly, Jackson and Paula are taken up by the lonely Collie, although the specter of the baby's father, who may return at any moment, hangs over their growing involvement. Jackson, whom Collie quarters in an outbuilding, is introduced to this close-knit mountain community and even persuades the Wright clan to back the building of an enormous clock tower in the center of town.

Sobieski's dialogue is respectful of Ehle's beautifully written North Carolina talk, expanding it at times inventively. But, excepting nicely played scenes between Jackson, Collie and Paula, the tone that director Ted Kotcheff has set begins to seems ludicrous.

Don Michael Paul has been encouraged to play the lusty Young like every amateur auditioning for the role of the Rainmaker in a bus-and-truck touring company. The baby's father looks and acts like a slathering, backwoods Rasputin. It makes it impossible to imagine Collie with him more than once, and theirs was supposed to be a love affair that went on for more than two years. The suspicion rises that this off-beat property may be condemned.

It's a feeling that gets stronger with our first introduction to the Campbell clan, rivals to the Wrights and headed by elder Drury Campbell (Mitchell Ryan). They're first seen robbing and vandalizing the Jackson's stranded car like a pack of howling, bearded degenerates. Granted that these hunters and trappers are nearly barbaric in the novel; they still cannot be played like the North Carolina branch of Faulkner's vicious, inbred Snopes family, or the film and its relationships are in deep trouble.

Ehle has written with the utmost precision, neatly delineating country people and their beautiful, oppressive surroundings with loving attention. It's important that the Campbell and Wright patriarchs be imposing, nuanced figures. Kotcheff slurps effects onto his canvas with strokes broad enough to cover a barn.

And what, in heaven's name, attracted Kurt Russell to a role where he could be upstaged by a 10-year-old, by an imitation Rainmaker or by a raving backwoods madman?)

The melodrama does plays itself out with an uncommon number of unexpected twists. However, Collie's extraordinary decision near the close of the story snaps what credulity we may still be hanging onto. It's an essentially literary device that may hold up better on a page than on a screen. Or better on any page than on *this* screen.

Collie's action is like an inversion of the famous Faulkner story in "Knight's Gambit," which became the poignant film "Tomorrow" and may—still—contain one of Robert Duvall's greatest performances. It centers around a lovingly raised child taken over by a brutish, vicious family. Because of the way the Campbells have been drawn here, Collie's act, difficult enough to understand under any circumstances, becomes absolutely unthinkable.

Finally, in a last indignity, the film makers graft a sunshine-through-the-tears ending onto Ehle's stoic, entirely fitting conclusion, a horse-trading session between the patriarchs which conveys continuity, birthright and dynasty. (Writer Sobieski cannot be entirely removed from responsibility here, since she was also the supervising producer, under the principal producer, Robert Solo.)

"The Winter People" (rated PG-13 for some of its brutality and rough language) is nevertheless a handsomely realized production. Its production designer Ron Foreman has made details like Gudger's store realistic but never quaint; the work of cinematographer François Protat ("The Hitchhiker," "Joshua Then and Now") is exquisite and subdued without calling attention to itself, as is the succinct work of editor Thom Noble.

And given the improbable demands of her part, McGillis makes a heroic Collie, although the notion of her wild unbridled passion for the baby's ruttish father seems to fall a little short of, say, Cathy's for Heathcliff. For my money, the movie's most intriguing performance is by the young, matter-of-fact Amelia Burnette who, in the freezing cold, manages lines like "I can't move my fingers" without a hint of whining. Atta girl.

MONTHLY FILM BULLETIN, 2/90, P. 53, Geoff Brown

The 1930s, during a harsh winter. After his wife's death, clockmaker Wayland Johnson sets out to make a new home with his young daughter Paula. When their car breaks down in the South Appalachian mountains, Wayland walks to a log cabin for shelter; there he finds Collie Wright, a fiercely independent unmarried mother, whose family play a prominent part in the life of their valley community. The Wrights' sworn enemies are the Campbells, hunters and trappers who live in the hills. Depite herself, Collie falls for the gentle Wayland. To rid himself of his "outsider" status, he joins in the community annual bear hunt, proving his courage by killing a charging bear. Through Collie's urging, her father William offers Wayland the job of making a clock for the town's steeple. With Wayland finally accepted by the community, Cole Campbell—youngest and wildest of the Campbell clan, and the secret father of Collie's baby Jonathan—bursts back into Collie's life, seeking to continue their former passionate affair. During a vicious fight with Wayland and Collie's brothers, he is drowned in the river; the Campbells demand an eye for an eye. Collie visits Drury Campbell, the family's patriarch, admitting her affair with Cole and offering full custody of Jonathan in return for peace. She returns in a daze, alone, and takes to her bed. Months pass. Wayland ventures to ask the Campbells if Jonathan could visit at Easter, when he is due to marry Collie; Drury Campbell refuses, and sends him off with gunfire. But on Collie and Wayland's wedding day, Drury rides into town; his heart melted, he gives Jonathan back.

"There really is no other movie like this," Ted Kotcheff declares in the film's production notes. Viewers of *The Trail of the Lonesome Pine, Tol'able David* and other backwoods romances of the 1920s may well disagree; though *Winter People* certainly has little competition among contemporary fare. Kotcheff and his team struggle to resurrect their genre, staging the confrontations between the brutal, hairy Campbells, the snarling Wrights, and the fierce North Carolina winter landscapes with wildly overdramatic compositions, lighting and music. But there is far more energy here than sense, or sensibility: the material remains a corpse dug up for no good reason. Among the luckless cast, Lloyd Bridges is on vigorous form, puffing away at the pipe of wisdom as the Wright patriarch, but Kelly McGillis cannot prevent Collie, the embattled unmarried mother, from becoming a hollow stereotype. Kurt Russell is left with the wimp's part: a gentle clock-tinkering townie in the gun-toting backwoods, muttering from time to time about his childhood "back home in Norway". Even he appears signally unconvinced.

NEW YORK POST, 4/14/89, p. 37, David Edelstein

"Winter People" casts Kurt Russell as a bookish, gentle 1920s widower who fashions wondrous clocks out of wood and metal. Quite a stroke of casting. Did Don Johnson turn the filmmakers down? Was Bruce Willis unavailable?

They did snare Kelly McGillis for the role of an ornery Southern hillbilly with an illegitimate son. ("Ah wuz cry-zee" is how she accounts for her youthful indiscretion.) Casting this outrageous couldn't have been a mere fluke; the movie might have been dreamed up by drag queens over bowls of hashish.

Painfully earnest and often howlingly funny, "Winter People" sets Wayland Jackson (Russell) and his daughter Paula (Amelia Burnette), down in backwoods North Carolina, where their jalopy stalls in a creek.

In a nearby house lives Collie Wright (McGillis) and her baby boy. Although she's hostile at first to their plea for shelter from the cold, Collie's heart is finally moved by the little girl's pig (that is not a misprint), and she agrees to let the trio (father, daughter, pig) bunk down in her shack.

With his books and civilized ways and his dream of building a clock tower on the church, Wayland doesn't exactly fit snugly into the community. But he ingratiates himself with Collie's father (Lloyd Bridges, wagging his head sagely, as if contemplating a run for the presidency), and he proves his manhood in a bear hunt by leaping on the back of a grizzly. (He also proves some other things.)

All would go swimmingly were it not for the baby's dad, Cole Campbell (Jeffrey Meek), a member of the barbarous, hirsute Campbell clan across the river and one jealous sumbitch.

Cole doesn't have Russell's Alan Alda-ish ways with the ladies. For instance, his idea of chivalry is grabbing the hair on the back of Collie's neck and mashing her mouth against his. With his long hair and tongue-wagging insolence, Meek acts less hillbilly than heavy metal.

No wonder Collie falls hard for sweet Wayland, even if the romance stirs things up. But that's not unusual—heavy and glum as she looks, she's a slave to those womanly emotions. As her brother Gudger (Lanny Flaherty) puts it, "Yer always gettin' into trouble, always gettin' others into trouble, always ploughin' yer own furrow." You said a mouthful there, Gudger.

"Winter People" is one of those turkeys that puts a critic in Texas Chainsaw Massacre mode, so before this bloodbath goes much further I ought to say that it isn't an evil sort of movie. It's less manipulative than many big-studio pictures, and it regards violence not as a turn-on but as horrifying and unnecessary. Just when you're set for a climatic massacre of the bad guys (as in "Straw Dogs") the movie substitutes...friendship. Brotherhood. Patty-cake.

Which will probably leave audiences hissing. Such are the perils of bravely abandoning a formula.

"Winter People" isn't really meant as an action film. Written by Carol Sobieski, it's a woman's picture about paying the price for feminine passion, and it builds to an act of self-sacrifice that's genuinely wrenching.

Alas, the movie was directed by a man (Ted Kotcheff) whose greatest successes have been macho flicks like "First Blood." Whatever gold there is in Sobieski's script (not much), Kotcheff's not the guy to mine it. He and photographer François Protat give the woods and streams an icy, wide-screen grandeur, but for all the depth and verisimilitude they might as well have cast Santa and his elves.

McGillis has clearly taken some acting classes since she rattled her way through "The Accused." I know because she's doing exercises from Stanislavski 101 on screen.

She sculpts the air. She employs Sense Memory. When she is called on by Cole's father (Mitchell Ryan) to prove carnal knowledge of his son by naming the locations of his moles ("On his...right hip...On the inside of his...thigh") the audience watches entranced. There hasn't been acting this hypnotically terrible since the glory days of "Dark Shadows."

McGillis had a lightness and wit back in "Reuben, Reuben" and "Witness," but if she doesn't watch herself, she's going to bounce Karen Black from every drag-queen repertoire in the country.

NEWSDAY, 4/14/89, Part III/p. 5, Mike McGrady

The central figure in "Winter People" is Wayland Jackson (Kurt Russell), a likable, mildmannered clockmaker who finds himself stranded in the middle of hillbilly country where many unpleasant things happen to him in not-rapid-enough succession.

For example: Wayland's truck stalls in the middle of an icy stream where it is looted and destroyed by the Campbell clan, as clear a collection of genetic misfits as ever graced the large screen; when they apply a bullwhip to the woman (Kelly McGillis) kind enough to give him shelter, Wayland stands by helplessly.

Wayland next engages an enraged bear in hand-to-hand combat, followed by brutal fistfights with hillbillies from both clans. Then he is beaten bloody by a young giant who has amorous designs on McGillis and who also shotguns the clockmaker's most elaborate clock. Finally, after ducking bullets and risking freezing during a fight in an icy river, Wayland is asked to leave the territory. He says, "It's been the best part of my life so far to be here."

His tough little daughter (Amelia Burnette) is not so easily impressed, and I can only second her sentiments when she points out, "We should have gone to Philadelphia, Papa."

"Winter People," a somber, well-intentioned, stupid melodrama, invites—no, first invites, then demands—laughter in all the wrong places. As a rule, critics are loathe to reveal their sentiments in advance of their reviews, and the theaterful of reviewers and journalists restrained themselves as long as humanly possible. But by the end of this film—about the time a mother was sacrificing her baby in exchange for peace between the clans—merriment was universal and giggles were giving way to guffaws.

No need to pinpoint one specific failing—in this case there's enough blame to go around. The Carol Sobieski script, based on a John Ehle novel and directed with undue reverence by Ted Kotcheff, has all the delicacy of vintage "Snuffy Smith"comic strips. While I can't help liking Kurt Russell and Kelly McGillis, their recent performances are placing an undue strain on my affection. But this is one of those movies where everything, up to and including John Scott's background music, is abysmal.

Let me qualify that. I kind of, sort of, almost liked Amelia Burnette as Wayland's little girl. At least I fully subscribed to her sentiments about hill country. On the whole, *I'd* rather be in Philadelphia, too.

VILLAGE VOICE, 4/25/89, p. 68, Amy Taubin

It was well past the halfway point at the preview of *Winter People* when the first titters broke. Once they started, there was no containing them. We were laughing not only at the absurdity of the film but at having sat in dutiful silence for, oh, so very long. I passed most of that time trying to imagine why anyone had invested money and energy in the kind of regional period melodrama that earns fledgling playwrights their first rejections. About the only thing I could come up with was that someone reasoned (in not atypical Hollywood fashion) that Kelly McGillis, having appeared in a successful movie where she played an Amish woman (*Witness*), could be inched over a few states into the Ozarks, and lightning would strike twice. McGillis, who plays the mother of an illegitimate child, fathered by the bear-hunting—and very hirsute—son of her father's mortal enemy, is rescued from her loneliness by a sensitive clockmaker (Kurt Russell) who, being Norwegian, is accustomed to swimming in cold water and therefore able to defeat the hairy hulk when they finally fight it out on the ice floes—but you don't want to hear any of this. McGillis really locks her jaw on the part, which bodes ill for her career. She plays most of it for pioneer-woman-style self-reliance, but when her ex comes around, she gets this look on her face like my favorite female cat did when the male who knocked her up came too close—defiance nipped in the bud by plain old physical fear. Not uninteresting, though not worth the agony of the other 115 minutes.

Also reviewed in:
NEW YORK TIMES, 4/14/89, p. C12, Caryn James
VARIETY, 4/12–18/89, p. 7
WASHINGTON POST, 4/14/89, p. C1, Hal Hinson

WIRED

A Taurus Entertainment release. *Producer:* Edward S. Feldman and Charles R. Meeker. *Director:* Larry Peerce. *Screenplay:* Earl Mac Rauch. *Based on the book "Wired: The Short Life and Fast Times of John Belushi" by:* Bob Woodward. *Director of Photography:* Tony Imi. *Editor:* Eric Sears. *Music:* Basil Poledouris. *Music Editor:* Christopher Kennedy. *Choreographer:* Joanne DeVito. *Sound:* Robert Wald and (music) Tim Boyle. *Sound Editor:* Cecelia Hall. *Production Designer:* Brian Eatwell. *Art Director:* Richard F. Mays. *Set Designer:* Sally Thornton. *Set Decorator:* Susan Emshwiller. *Costumes:* Chari Feldman. *Make-up:* Robin Beauchesne. *Running time:* 108 minutes. *MPAA Rating:* R.

CAST: Michael Chiklis (John Belushi); Ray Sharkey (Angel Velasquez); J.T. Walsh (Bob Woodward); Patti D'Arbanville (Cathy Smith); Lucinda Jenney (Judy Belushi); Alex Rocco (Arnie Fromson); Gary Groomes (Dan Aykroyd); Jere Burns (Lou); Clyde Kusatsu (Coroner); Tom Bower and Earl Billings (Detectives); Dakin Matthews ("Washington Post" Editor); J.C. Quinn (Comedy Coach); Steve Vinovich (Studio Executive); Matthew Faison (Doctor Robbins); Jon Snyder (Film Director); Finis Henderson III (Morgue Attendant); Amy Michelson (Photographer); Blake Clard (Jenkins); Scott Plank (Herb Axelson); Brooke McCarter (Punk Rocker); Paul Ben-Victor (Perino); Richard Feldman (Studio Page); Ned Bellamy (Forrest); John Apicella (Loading Supervisor); Joe Urla (Stage Manager); Diane Behrens (Typist); Roger Rook (Coroner's Assistant); Ron Perkins (Record Producer); Drew Pillsbury (Morgue Nurse); Charles Holman (SNL Cast Member); Nancy DeCarl (Hotel Manager); Keith Joe Dick (Man in Club); Pete Willcox (Elvis Impersonator); A.C. Meadows (Colonel Impersonator): Billy Preston (Himself); Neil Portnow (Band Leader, "King Bee"); Michael Ruff, Cliff Hugo, David Williams, Bruce Wallenstein, Marc Caz Macino, Ralph Humphrey, Jimmy Haslip, Buzzy Feiten, Richard Elliott, Keith Joe Dick and Allan Thomas (Blues Brothers and SNL Bands).

CHRISTIAN SCIENCE MONITOR, 8/29/89, p. 10, David Sterritt

John Belushi was a new kind of comedian, with a style so powerful that it took over and transformed every entertainment he decided to honor with his bearlike presence.

His brand of wild, look-Ma-no-brains humor became nationally famous on "Saturday Night Live," ushering in a kind of irreverent farce hitherto unknown on television.

Since movies represent the highest rung of show-biz success, everyone knew he'd tackle Hollywood sooner or later, and when he did—in "Animal House," another boffo exercise in excess—the results reflected *his* personality more than that of National Lampoon magazine, which presented the film, or that of John Landis, who directed it. He was a slob, and he loved being a slob, and his audience loved him for it. His stardom was assured.

All might have gone brilliantly for Mr. Belushi if his on-screen personality had been just an act cooked up by a mature and self-aware performer. Sadly, his private life was mired in the same kind of freeform outrageousness that marked his public persona, and his career was ended by a drug overdose.

His completed TV shows and movies (from "Animal House" and "Blues Brothers" to "Continental Divide" and "Old Boyfriends") still have plenty of admirers. But in today's drug-aware climate, Belushi tends to be remembered with very mixed feelings. Which is a problem for any biographer who wants to chronicle his life and times in a way that will have Belushi-style entertainment value.

How do you make a movie about a man whose idea of fun made him rich and famous for a few years, but eventually landed him in the morgue? "Wired," the new bio-pic directed by Larry Peerce, uses two maneuvers in facing this challenge: It loads the action with Belushi's own kind of pitchblack humor, and it makes his death not the sad finale but the running theme of the entire story. In a move that Belushi would surely have approved, Mr. Peerce and screenwriter Earl MacRauch make his corpse (animatedly played by Michael Chiklis) the hero of their tale, revisiting the people and places of his life in a last attempt to understand what happened to him. This has an odd effect—reminding us constantly of Belushi's unfortunate fate, yet approaching it from a bizarre angle that makes the whole situation seem farcical.

This strategy is apparently an attempt at pleasing every possible moviegoer. The reasoning seems to be that Belushi detractors will applaud the constant (and cautionary) emphasis on his death, while his admirers will wallow in the zany energy with which it's splashed across the screen.

The picture certainly succeeds at reproducing Belushi's manic energy and wired-up sensibility. But it fails to give any meaningful insights into a couple of issues that must be dealt with if his biography is to have any enduring value: How did the qualities of energy and nonconformism come to be so overdeveloped in his personality, and why didn't he learn to modify them as he grew and presumably matured?

Answers to those questions might have turned "Wired" into a probing and even valuable film. As it stands, it's a shallow and often boorish entertainment that trades more in voyeurism than understanding.

Peerce keeps the action of "Wired" moving with surprising vigor, considering that much of his past work (from "One Potato, Two Potato" to "The Other Side of the Mountain") has been in the soap-opera genre.

The generally able cast includes J. T. Walsh and Patti D'Arbanville as well as Ray Sharkey, who's memorable as an angelic taxi driver. Toni Imi photographed the film, which is based on a best-seller by one-time Watergate reporter Bob Woodward, and Basil Poledouris composed the score.

"Wired" is rated R for various reasons, including raunchy language.

LOS ANGELES TIMES, 8/25/89, Calendar/p. 1, Michael Wilmington

You can't know. You don't know what it's like to be me.

—John Belushi

Does anyone know? Any time? In "Wired," a movie based, very roughly, on Bob Woodward's book on the meteoric career and drug-overdose death of John Belushi, the film makers try for a multileveled hipster exposé: a whacked-out docudrama, "Citizen Kane" squeezed through "Saturday Night Live" and basted with National Lampoon blood and bile.

Unlike Woodward, who projected little or zero simpatico for his subject, scenarist Earl Mac Rauch and director Larry Peerce are obviously trying to make the kind of movie Belushi himself might have had fun doing. They want to pump it full of his trademarks: the kamikaze humor, calculated outrage, show-biz in-jokes and explosive honesty. But it's too weird a task, too black a show. When they try to jam in sentiment and uplift, "Wired" starts overloading, blowing its circuits.

Like "Saturday Night Live," the movie jokes about death, kids or impersonates the famous, zips back and forth from sketch to sketch, throws in a rock act, winks and leers and then tries to slug us with a little heart. It begins with rapid, sock-in-the-eye juxtapositions: Belushi (Michael Chiklis) in his hated bee outfit, an off-screen conversation on casting him in "Wired" ("No man, he's dead!"), and then Belushi mysteriously revived and sweating from the morgue. Outside, he hails Ray Sharkey as Angel Velasquez, a Puerto Rican cabbie and fellow overdose victim: a cross between a junkie philosopher and Clarence the Guardian Angel in "It's a Wonderful Life."

It's Angel's job, apparently, to show the increasingly freaked-out John where he went wrong. He spins his rider quickly though TV success; the chaotic, highstakes atmosphere of his movies; his home life with wife Judy (Lucinda Jenney, a fine job) and his on-the-road antics with best buddy and comic partner Dan Aykroyd (Gary Groomes, another fine job).

This grisly cab ride is also interspersed with the dour investigations of the movie's Bob Woodward (J.T. Walsh), a just-the-facts-ma'am journalist put on the case by Judy to uncover the whole truth. Woodward, Angel and Belushi, in his morgue robe, all zip in and out of the same reality planes—occasionally, some of them hail the others on the street—and the movie skitters restlessly through scenes re-created from Woodward's book as well as imaginary "Saturday Night Live" routines and grotesque fantasies, erupting like paranoid flip-outs through the joked-up docudrama.

It's a last-gasp, punch-you-in-the-ribs, anything-for-a-laugh-or-sob movie—and it tries to punch things up to the same quasi-cocaine energy level that characterized a lot of '70s show-biz and movie humor. But there's a difference. In the crack-ravaged, freebase-plagued '80s, this tune hits sourer notes—though the movie's oddball edge, slopped up with soap-opera twinges, plays less like a cautionary drug tale than a punked-out Remembrance of Flings Past.

Now the movie's Belushi, instead of slamming fate's door with a coke-and-heroin speedball administered by scruffy death angel Cathy Smith (a scarily low-key performance by Patti D'Arbanville), seems doomed far earlier. The movie has a schizoid, lurching drive. It's about death's wild ride—playing out your string, dancing over the edge—and also about sweet vulnerable, lovable John, wasted by his appetites.

Chiklis, the 25-year-old unknown who plays Belushi, captures this duality very well. He gives an intensely empathetic performance—awash in sweat, rage and desperation—that subtly suggests the real Belushi and elevates him to myth. Chiklis doesn't have Belushi's waggling eyebrows, but he gets the mix of *machismo* and delicacy. His skin looks transparent, bruisable: the skin of a corpse, an addict, a victim.

Chiklis also gets Belushi's maniacal spontaneity. Playing against Sharkey's stylized Angel—a cold-eyed, wised-up spritzer who turns all his y's defiantly into j's ("So what jou want?")—he has the look of a man lowered over the flames. Playing against Groomes' warm, sloppy-grinning Aykroyd, he has a tender camaraderie. (This is the relationship that should have been caught in the actual Belushi-and-Aykroyd movies.) In the book, Belushi was trapped in the terse, white sidewalks of Woodward's prose, the police-blotter flatness and austerity. Here Rauch and Peerce let him answer Woodward's "You did it to yourself, John." The dying face blazes out, with a cop-hater's contempt. Even his sweat drops seem accusatory.

Reading Woodward's book, you might have expected the movie to be a "Lost Weekend" on uppers. But Rauch, who also co-wrote "New York, New York" and "Buckaroo Banzai," tries to take it further with this intricate, double-chase structure: Woodward and Belushi careening toward each other over the messy terrain of his life. He gets points for audacity and director Larry Peerce some for emotion. But the movie keeps pulling up short.

The names are changed: John Landis turns into an anonymous manic beanpole of a director; Belushi manager Bernie Brillstein and assistant Joel Briskin are renamed. And Belushi's super-agent, Michael Ovitz, disappears completely, like God, somewhere above the unseen skyline.

There may be a tendency to reject "Wired" on the simplest grounds. (That isn't John! That isn't Danny!) But the crippling flaw in the film lies in its mix of surface daring and inner funk. Inside, it keeps flinching. What the film never suggests—what Woodward barely suggests either—is that two addictions may have been involved in Belushi's destruction: one to cocaine; one, by others, to deals.

Belushi, like many media rebels, began as an outlaw and ended as a commodity—a tormented commodity. That's part of the story "Wired" (MPAA-rated R for drug use, sex and language) misses: the addictions of commerce. Shouldn't the deal always be secondary to the work, the image to the man, the business to the audience, the per diem to *carpe diem*? You would think John Belushi, who worshiped the instant, would never have gotten trapped in the concrete of his own image. You would think the movie of his life would never get shot up with tricks and evasion. And you would think a great clown would never let a deal or a ruined deal—or a high—seal him off forever from the people who wanted to laugh with him. But...*nooooooooooooo.*

MONTHLY FILM BULLETIN, 10/89, 312, Geoff Brown

March 5, 1982. The body of comedian John Belushi is discovered in a Los Angeles hotel and taken to the mortuary. Hearing the news, Bob Woodward, of *The Washington Post*, contemplates writing a series of articles about the wayward performer. Back in the morgue, an astonished Belushi wakes up on the slab and lurches into his after-life, fleeing to a cab driven by his guardian angel Velasquez, who escorts him on a whirlwind tour of his past. At his Greenwich Village apartment, Belushi's dependence on drugs puts a strain on his relationship with his wife Judy; at the NBC television studios, Belushi and his close friend Dan Aykroyd join the cast of *Saturday Night Live*, developing characters like the Blues Brothers. With the co-operation of Judy Belushi, Woodward embarks on a fullscale biography. He reads transcripts of police interviews with Cathy Smith, the drug pusher who visited Belushi hours before he died; he interviews Arnie Fromson, Belushi's manager who realised drugs were the only way to ensure Belushi stayed alert for an engagement. The dead Belushi and Velasquez continue their odyssey. In Chicago, in 1972, he performs his famous samurai sketch; arriving in Hollywood, he makes a huge impression in *National Lampoon's Animal House*. Aware of his reckless behaviour, Belushi makes a pact with Aykroyd: if one of them dies young, there should be no tears. In his final months, Belushi becomes increasingly difficult to control. He hides away at the Hotel Château Marmont, well supplied with drugs and alcohol, endeavouring to finish a script. Cathy Smith supplies him with heroin and leaves; then Bob Woodward materialises, coolly observing the final hours of a self-destructive genius.

Any Hollywood fears that *Wired* would follow Bob Woodward and document the community's widespread drug use have proved completely unfounded. Though their film version regurgitates stray incidents and lines of recalled dialogue, Larry Peerce and writer Earl Mac Rauch go out of their way to avoid direct resemblance to Woodward's book. There is also little resemblance to any other Hollywood bio-pic. Where else in film history does the biographical target regain life on the mortuary slab, to be driven through his career highlights—half bemused, half appalled—by an equally dead Puerto Rican taxi driver? Where else does the subject's posthumous biographer become part of the drama, stalking through scenes, icy and unsympathetic, goading the victim even on his deathbed? "Why the needles?" Woodward asks insistently. "I can't breathe; breathe for me, Woodward", Belushi says, fading fast.

In real life, Woodward's method of resuscitating Belushi was by meticulously charting his life's downward spiral through extensive interviews, plus the minutiae of diaries, credit card receipts and such. Peerce and Mac Rauch, however, reduce Woodward's catalogue to a fantasy comic-strip jumble, with only a token bearing on documented events. The bustling film and TV communities that nurtured Belushi's virtues and vices have shrunk to a few names and shadows. In this version, Dan Aykroyd appears as Belushi's more-or-less straight sidekick, trying to keep his buddy clean, sane and sober; personal manager Bernie Brillstein has become "Arnie Fromson"; while John Landis is depicted as a nameless film director with a beard. Even Belushi's routines emerge garbled: one *Saturday Night Live* recreation pointlessly conflates the Conehead sketches (in which Belushi never appeared) with his celebrated Nixon-Kissinger routine.

Amid all this whirling fuzziness, newcomer Michael Chiklis makes a creditable stab at conveying Belushi's passion and childlike naivety; he also provides a workable visual facsimile. Yet in neither the shards of Belushi's routines nor the script's own attempts at grotesque black farce is Chiklis/Belushi actually *funny*. Without that saving grace, Belushi easily seems—in the words of the Los Angeles cop interviewed by Woodward—"Just another fat junkie who went belly-up". According to the filmmakers, they aimed at bringing warmth and a celebratory note to Woodward's book, while providing—of course—"a very strong antidrug statement". But how do you inject warmth if the humour falls flat? How can you be fiercely anti-drugs when Belushi's abuse is shrouded in shadow and fantasy? By the time *Wired* completed its lengthy journey through lawyers' offices, two directors (Robert Markowitz was first slated, in 1984), and the scriptwriter's eccentric brain, any point to the exercise was well and truly lost.

NEW STATESMAN & SOCIETY, 10/13/89, p. 45, Suzanne Moore

Nothing in the world makes me feel more like taking drugs than the combined spectacle of Lady Diana and Nancy Reagan telling me to "just say no". I accept that this unhealthy attitude may indicate some severe personality disorder and, believe me, I've tried to get over it. This week, for instance, I went to yet another anti-drug movie in the hope that somehow I would see the light. Instead I saw *Wired,* the film based on the life (and death) of American comedian, John Belushi.

Belushi, star of *Saturday Night Live, Animal House* and *The Blues Brothers,* died in 1982 from a drug overdose. A mixture of cocaine and heroin known as a speedball finally did him in. His death—neither the first nor last in Hollywood—seemed to reverberate around the community. Even Belushi, famed for his excesses, had finally proved to be mortal. And worse, he died doing what so many of them enjoyed doing.

It's an unlikely story for Bob Woodward, the journalist who broke the Watergate scandal and author of *All the Presidents Men,* to pursue. But the result of relentless investigation produced not just a series of articles but a book—*Wired: the short life and times of John Belushi.* The book—scrupulously researched, every source authenticated, every chance conversation documented—is a major indictment of the "Hollywood system".

Belushi may have been responsible for his own death but it certainly would not have been possible without the lavish care and attention of a cast of Hollywood hangers-on. These varied from the pathetic Cathy Smith, the woman who supplied drugs to many of the inner circle (and who fixed Belushi his final high) to the big names such as Robert De Niro, Hugh Hefner and Chevy Chase.

Because so many people were implicated in Woodward's book, *Wired,* the film has taken years to get off the ground. Legal action and threatened libel suits have meant that, though now completed, the film is completely devoid of what made the book worth reading: there are no intimate tales of Hollywood Babylon here. Instead we get a clumsily banal portrait of a minor talent bent on self-destruction. Anything that might be worth saying about drugs/addiction/the star system/fame/the tacit agreement between producers, managers and agents that keeps people like Belushi well supplied with drugs, cannot be said.

Belushi himself is presented as comic genius. Certainly he was emblematic for a generation of Americans who considered themselves "alternative". The height of his fame was in the late seventies as *Saturday Night Live* peaked and he made *Animal House.* It's difficult now to understand the significance of *Saturday Night Live* but, in the context of American TV, it continually pushed the boundaries of what was considered acceptable. Its knowing, in-joke humour made constant references to drug use which thrilled its young audience. You had to be stoned to laugh at most of the jokes. Veering between political satire and infantile humour it may now seem unwatchable and unfunny but it was unlike anything else on TV and made stars of Belushi, Chevy Chase and Dan Aykroyd.

Wired makes the awful mistake of trying to duplicate the "classic" sketches which made Belushi such a cult. Despite Michael Chiklis's careful impersonation, they just look embarrassing. The biggest laugh to be had in the film is from the dubious comparison of Belushi to the brilliant Lenny Bruce. Apart from their drug habits they couldn't be further apart. Belushi's appeal lay in his physicality, almost Neanderthal at times, his ability to appeal to the lowest common denominator. Playing the slobbish Bluto in *Animal House,* he takes the logic of consumption to the extreme—eating, drinking, farting and belching excessively.

Belushi lived up to image. A friend remarked, "he wants to grab the world and snort it." Cocaine seemed the ideal drug and it was in plentiful supply. Cocaine didn't fuck you up—quite the opposite. It made you work better, feel clear-headed and clever. Just what a comic under pressure needed to get the edge, the sharpness necessary for a great performance. Drugs, Belushi maintained, helped him to stay alert to the comic possibilities of every situation. It's a pity then, that, often by the time he got on stage, he could barely stand.

As the film shows through two very awkward scenes using flashbacks, Belushi soon deteriorated into a selfish junkie. The fact that he was famous didn't make this process any more interesting. The fact that he was always given enough cash to buy drugs by producers, concerned that without them he might have fucked up a recording deal, is glossed over.

Belushi's story is of a pre-clean and sober Hollywood. Today everyone is now busy polishing their own detox stories—Carrie Fisher, who features prominently in the book, is having her tale of drug abuse turned into a movie titled *Postcards from the Edge*. Not a day goes by without some star confessing an addiction of one sort or another. Belushi once said that shooting up was "like kissing God". But who needs God when you can be born again at the Betty Ford clinic? The most unfortunate part of this spiritual conversion is that you have to spend the rest of your life mouthing anti-drug slogans which are about as helpful as they are inane.

Mind you, some of them seemed just as stupid before they gave up the chemicals. Robert De Niro, apparently so steeped in The Method, thought it was a good idea to use real heroin when Belushi was shooting a drug-taking scene so that the emotions expressed would be truthful. It's just as well the script didn't require a road accident. *Wired* doesn't go into such details though it remains voyeuristically fascinated with the paraphernalia of drug abuse. The camera is as fixated on the needle and spoon as any addict and, as usual, heroin is treated with a special awe.

It's almost as if you can take cocaine through your nostrils until your brain is falling out but look at smack and you die instantly. The media seem to need the bogeyman of drugs at a time when the old enemies like "reds under the beds" are fading away. Drug dealers represent the ultimate evil that figure in every major contemporary thriller. As Schwarzenegger and James Bond fight the international drug trade, so will George Bush who, like his predecessor, knows that life always imitates art. Drug dealing may be one of the most enterprising and efficient forms of capitalism, creating insatiable demands and wrecking lives, but it is not the root of *all* evil.

The "war against drugs" cannot be won by simplistic moralising. Legalisation is now being mooted in the most unlikely places (Judge Pickles has even cottoned on) as it is realised that current policies don't have a hope of succeeding. People working day to day with drug users are now discussing drug addiction in new ways. Rather than the usual "addiction as disease" syndrome, they are talking about patterns of drug use with many people spending a few years taking drugs and then coming off them by their mid-thirties as their lifestlye changes.

Hollywood, like most governments, would still prefer to deal with the drug problem with repressive methods. This repression leads to hysteria: it leads to bad movies like *Wired* and bad moves like the recent raid on Broadwater Farm. No one is arguing that drugs are a "good thing" but when "just saying no" clearly doesn't work, perhaps we should have the courage to "just say yes".

NEW YORK POST, 8/25/89, p. 21, David Edelstein

The remarkable thing about all the recent films purporting to document the drug culture of the '70s and early '80s is that watching them, you'd have no idea why anyone ever did drugs. With all the nosebleeds and coughing fits and swollen veins, it looks so relentlessly painful...

Doubtless this pleases the media's moral watchdogs (some of whom howl in these pages), but the approach can't illuminate the causes of addiction, which in this society run deeper than mere hedonism. Drugs can kill you, but they also fill a void and offer a (false) sense of potency; before enslaving, they liberate. The best anti-drug movie will be the one that begins by making the case *for* drugs.

It will not be "Wired," the John Belushi story based on Bob Woodward's 1984 chronicle. This film is just awful; my jaw dropped so far I thought I'd need surgery to reconnect it. The hipper it tries to be, the more pathetically unhip it seems—its like those inept, church-produced playlets you see on Sundays at 7 a.m. (usually after partying all Saturday night).

The movie opens with Belushi (Michael Chiklis) lying dead in L.A.'s Chateau Marmont. After he's lugged to the morgue in a body bag, an attendant leaves a piece of food on top of him; suddenly, the corpse grabs the snack and stuffs it into its mouth. (The audience watched this in dead silence.)

Belushi awakes in horror, scampers naked around the morgue, then emerges into the night in a hastily fashioned toga, eager to return to his life. He hails a cab and is pleased when the Puerto Rican driver (Ray Sharkey) recognizes him; "I know joo," says Sharkey. "I seen you in a movie. You played a coke addict, but you died in the end."

This puzzles Belushi, who never played an addict. Then he finds the doors are locked. "My friends call me Angel," says the cabbie, by way of explanation.

Somehow "Wired" tops this hilarious overture—it turns into a long harangue against Belushi's ghost for his selfish ways and bad habits. In the end, the movie says, he wasn't so special; he was "just another fat junkie who went belly up." Penetrating stuff.

The film makes no connections between Belushi's art—which was dependent on excess and danger—and the way he lived. It pretends to, of course, cross-cutting from his ghost to his life to his performances on "Saturday Night Live" to a poker-faced Bob Woodward (J.T. Walsh) retracing his steps.

Because of all this leaping around, there are no sustained sequences. Director Larry Peerce and writer Earl Mac Rauch can stay in the shallows while making believe their work is avant-garde; they're trying to pass off their weaknesses as a bold artistic choice. They toss in gonzo gags, like the one in which the dead Belushi looks up at his Japanese coroner and sees first a samurai, then a Benihana chef. But then old Angel returns, and it's back to Sunday school.

Belushi brought the threat of explosion with him when he acted. He was the wild card that "Saturday Night Live"—which traded on its liveness—needed, and the show's creators exploited it even as they worried about his health and sanity.

He threw himself totally into his comedy, often frightening you with the risks he took. Yet what was funny was not his ferocity but a certain daintiness that accompanied it; he endeared himself with quick flashes of a tender, poetic soul.

Chiklis looks soft at the start—this isn't a guy who (like Belushi) could have been an all-conference middle linebacker. He gets Belushi's mannerisms (especially in the musical numbers) but not the danger that went with them; he's fundamentally sweet.

Yet he's a personable performer and (amazingly, considering his lines) he creates a convincing human being. Toward the end, as the bloated, flaming-eyed Belushi snorts lines in the Chateau Marmont, he's even a ringer for the star, and the scenes acquire a "You Are There" eeriness.

Bewilderingly, though, we spend as much time with Woodward as we do with Belushi. The real Woodward is known to be chummy and obsequious, but this guy is a cipher, ashen and blobby in his gray suit. Discussing the story with Judy Belushi (Lucinda Jenney), he tells her he needs access to "the paper trail of John Belushi's life." (Sounds sexy, eh?)

Throughout, the film makers attempt to turn Woodward into a titan of Belushi's calibre—they even have the ghost of Belushi exclaiming that he'll go down in history now that Bob Woodward is writing a book about him.

The mistake, of course, was using the book as the basis for anything. It's an easy read, but thematically "Wired" has no organization—it stays far outside its subject, as if Woodward disapproved of his subject so much that he couldn't begin to empathize (a biographer's greatest challenge).

There are moments when the movie makers get at something deeper. In a wonderful scene, a Chicago comedy coach (J.C. Quinn) roars at the young Belushi that stand-up comedy is pure aggression—it's letting the demons loose. ("Make 'em hemorrhage!" he screams.)

The coach is right, and this aesthetic fueled the greatest comic of the last quarter-century—Richard Pryor, who also burned himself out. (The complicated question is whether Pryor would have been as brilliant without this attitude—and the drugs that went with it.)

"Wired" is even more laughable than Pryor's misbegotten "Jo Jo Dancer." In the last half-hour Woodward and Belushi converge—a mighty meeting. Woodward paces around the Chateau Marmont bungalow and watches Cathy Smith (Patti D'Arbanville) inject Belushi, who turns to the camera and says: "How 'bout you, Woody? You wanna hit?" He didn't, but I was ready for one.

The movie scores points off Hollywood for hypocrisy. It shows how drugs were built into Belushi's contracts and lingers on (otherwise pointless) scenes in which Judy tells Woodward she wants people to see her husband as he was and agent Bernie Brillstein (here "Arnie Fromson") encourages Woodward to make his projected article a book. They later attacked that book. And "Wired" nearly didn't get made, allegedly because of a campaign by superagent Mike Ovitz.

The efforts to suppress "Wired" make it all the more clear how short the film falls. This could have been a knockout portrait of the perils of modern celebrity—an eye-opener. But the culture will have to be a lot more grown up about drugs if that movie is ever to be made.

NEWSDAY, 8/25/89, Part III/p. 5, Mike McGrady

"Wired," a portrait of the late comic John Belushi as an unfunny, piggish, loud-mouthed cokehead, once again brings to mind Mark Antony's funeral oration for the fallen Caesar: "The evil that men do lives after them. The good is oft interred with their bones."

Anyone unfamiliar with Belushi's comic genius will watch this stupid little film and wonder why on earth anyone would care about this belching, beer-guzzling, coke-snorting, egomaniacal creep. The movie offers no reason to quarrel with a hard-bitten cop who sums up Belushi's life and death this way: "He's just another fat junkie who went belly-up."

It couldn't have been easy, making an entire film centered on one of the most creative comics in recent history without a single giggle, without so much as a smile. Oh, the on-screen audiences seem to be enjoying the Belushi-imitator's performance; his every gesture results in convulsions of hilarity and frenzies of applause. Only the audience in the movie theater will sit stony-faced, wondering how it missed the joke.

Not only is "Wired" unfunny, there are absolutely no insights into the comic's death, or answers to the why of his death by overdose at age 33. As if aware of this key failing, the moviemakers have an actor (J.T. Walsh) portraying reporter Bob Woodward, who warns Belushi's widow not to expect too much: "We'll find out something. But maybe we won't. You have to be prepared for that."

Among the strange choices made by the moviemakers is to have Woodward, who wrote the book the movie is based on, wandering through Belushi's life, at times even exchanging conversation with the late comic. Another strange choice is to bring Belushi back to life, assign him a Puerto Rican angel and have him witness such events as his own autopsy. Describing the moviemakers—Larry Peerce directed and Earl Mac Rauch wrote the script—can be left to Antony's unimprovable funeral oration: "O judgment! Thou art fled to brutish beasts and men have lost their reason."

Let me see, are there any unanswered questions? Some will doubtless be curious about whether unknown actor Michael Chiklis can maintain a Belushi imitation for the length of a feature film. No, not for an instant. Copying a few mannerisms is hardly enough; he doesn't capture an ounce of Belushi's humanity, not a flicker of his creativity.

Will *anyone* be happy with this ill-advised flick? The only people I can imagine are film critics assigned to prepare annual worst-10 lists. Only nine more to go.

NEWSWEEK, 9/4/89, p. 68, David Ansen

You've proably heard by now of all the heavy Hollywood artillery aimed at keeping Bob Woodward's John Belushi biography from reaching the screen. Well, the Friends of Belushi needn't have worried: this tedious, unenlightening tale of showbiz excess self-destructs faster than its famous hero. Screenwriter Earl Mac Rauch obviously wanted to invoke some of the anarchic Belushi spirit by using such gonzo devices as a guardian angel (Ray Sharkey, with a Hispanic accent) who takes Belushi's ghost on a tour of his misspent life. The effect is more embarrassing than outrageous. Switching to a "Citizen Kane" tactic, the movie also doggedly trails the glum Woodward (J.T. Walsh) as he tries to get to the source of Belushi's demons. His earth-shattering conclusion: there's no mystery here, he did it to himself. Dramatically, "Wired" has nowhere to go, and director Larry Peerce treads murky water for two hours, serving up mirthless copies of old "Saturday Night Live" skits, meaningless glimpses of Belushi's private life and enough drug-induced night sweats for a "Just Say No" campaign. Michael Chiklis works hard—oh so hard—to bring the comic back to life; it's not his fault that "Wired" plays as flat as a smashed Conehead. No mystery here either: the movie OD's on banality.

TIME, 8/28/89, p. 64, Richard Corliss

Well, they sure could have called it *Weird*. After all, the main characters in this bonkers biopic are two people John Belushi never met during his brief, explosive life: Bob Woodward, the actor's biographer, and John Belushi dead. You have to cherish the daredevil idiocy of a movie whose climax is a parody of Woodward's legendary deathbed chat with CIA director William Casey. The journalist visits the hotel room where Belushi took his fatal overdose and hallucinates an interview with the dying star. "Breathe for me, Woodward!" the samurai comic cries. And it's hard to hate a docudrama in which Cathy Smith, Belushi's last drug source, materializes in the straight-arrow reporter's fantasy and asks, "How 'bout you, Woody? You want a hit?"

If Woodward does want a hit, he is unlikely to get one from this turkey, overstuffed as it is with mad ambitions and bad karma. *Wired* wants to turn the story of the *Saturday Night Live* comedian and gonzo movie star into a cautionary fable about celebrity in the fast lane—and never mind that some powerful people in the movie business were not eager to see the picture made or released. Reprising Belushi's career without being able to use clips or skits from his most famous work should be challenge enough. But nooo! *Wired* insists on merging the complex flash back devices of two favorite old movies. So on one swerving narrative track, Woodward (J.T. Walsh), like the reporter in *Citizen Kane,* gets dirty dish from the star's friends. On the other, an angel of death (Ray Sharkey), a hipster version of the guardian angel in *It's a Wonderful Life,* escorts the dead Belushi (Michael Chiklis) to the scenes of his ebullient crimes.

Woodward's best seller, though it traced Belushi's last days with a doggedness that would have done the Evangelists proud, was a turgid read that had little feeling for its subject and found no broad meaning in it. At least adapter Earl Mac. Rauch (*The Adventures of Buckaroo Banzai*) knows that the only way to pin Belushi and Hollywood is to wax satiric and surrealistic. When the dead Belushi prowls his old haunts in a morgue sheet that looks like a toga out of the *Animal House* closet, the film almost has style to match its guts. So does Chiklis' boldly percussive performance. But *Wired*'s take on Belushi is so lame and gross that it validates the verdict of a cop in the movie: "He's just another fat junkie who went belly-up."

Was he? Not exactly, though the distinction eludes *Wired.* Professionally, Belushi was a gifted TV sketch artist who found the wide-screen format confining. Personally, he was a middle-class white kid with an anarchic urge to play the cool black jazzman—so he partied and bullied and ODed just like his heroes. Early death was only the last piece of the legend this blues brother created for himself. In the film's one good laugh, a physician elicits Belushi's pharmaceutical history and then asks, deadpan, "Next of kin?" Belushi was delivered to his humongous family of fans, who mourned a talent that went up in free-basing flames. But where do you send a killer-B movie like *Wired*, with many enemies and no mourners?

VILLAGE VOICE, 8/29/89, p. 63, Georgia Brown

It's interesting to contemplate a time when doing cocaine becomes unfashionable, nay, even stigmatized, on the grounds that the drug has decimated whole cultures and environments—certain Latin American countries, for example, and New York City. The impulse to save (e.g., seals, elephants, Alaskan waterways) might be extended to the average citizen of Colombia or Crown Heights. (I may have missed something, but I didn't notice that the recent benefit at BAM linked Amazon rain forest devastation to coca growing.) So far, individual demand and consumption are conveniently disassociated from the ethics and tactics of suppliers.

This got off my chest, I turn to *Wired*—a curious representation of the short unhappy life of John Belushi, talented comic, who overdosed at 33 in an era before the one fantasized above. The movie looks as if it's been sabotaged, not by Michael Ovitz and CAA, or by Belushi's friends, or even by a major drug cartel, but by interests closer to the conception phase. Cautionary stories are unlikely to make good movies, but you'd be hard-pressed to find a script as excruciatingly lame as this one, directed by Larry Peerce. Earl Mac Rauch is credited as screenwriter, but the co-writer of Scorsese's *New York, New York* and writer of *The Adventures of Buckaroo Banzai* probably can't be solely responsible for all the clinkers that will have audiences wincing, groaning, and guffawing. One of *Wired*'s (unintentionally) funny lines comes when a disembodied voice whispers to the pudgy, somnambulistic reporter Bob Woodward (J.T. Walsh, who's a far cry from Robert Redford), "It's not an article, it's book!" It's not a movie, I would say, it's a dog.

For sheer clumsiness the film faithfully matches its source, Woodward's solemn, fatuous book. Many of the movie's dopiest lines are transposed indirectly (usually with a context change) from *Wired* the bestseller. Someone who writes as badly as Woodward shouldn't use a fictionalizing method—setting scences and simulating conversations based on interviews with one party. (You may recall Nixon and Kissinger on bended knee.)

Wired the movie attempts a further foray into style, inventing a meta- or subfiction with Woodward the investigative reporter as a character floating through the plot. By the last scenes the reporter achieves an intimacy with his subject that accounts for characters addressing him directly, out of the reconstructed past. "How 'bout you, Woody? You want a hit?" teases Cathy Smith (Patti D'Arbanville), about to administer Belushi's (Michael Chiklis) fatal dose.

Not content with just one fancy narrative tack, the filmmakers supply an alternate (intentionally) comic one: Belushi wakes up in the morgue, and after wolfing down a sandwich left on his stomach by an attendant, races outside in his sheet to hail a taxi. The cab turns out to be driven by his guardian angel—Puerto Rican for no other reason than to pun on his name, Angel Velasquez. (Ray Sharkey's impersonation is guaranteed to make Spanish-speakers cringe.) Angel conducts his reluctant fare (shades of Bill Murray in *Scrooged*) on a trip through his brief adult life, and tries to convince John that he's no longer among the living. "We dead, brother. We both dead." Why this task should be so difficult, like many things in the movie, is inexplicable.

These two incompatible plots—featuring the reporter and the angel—intertwine arbitrarily until colliding embarrassingly on Belushi's deathbed. "Breathe for me, Woodward!" begs Belushi, having finally accepted that he's dying. It's here at last that Woodward gets to pose directly the overwhelming question. A contradiction, you see, has baffled the reporter since Judy Belushi (Lucinda Jenney) initially asked him to solve the riddle of her husband's death. And so he asks, "If you hated needles, how come you were using them?" John, Judy told him, was *afraid* of needles.

No doubt *Wired*'s filmmakers, setting out, had precedents in mind—movies from *The Jolson Story* to *The Rose*. But hiring actors to impersonate Belushi and Dan Aykroyd (Gary Groomes) doing their *Saturday Night Live* routines—or variations on these—was almost bound to look foolish and redundant when one can turn on cable and watch repeats. The imitations aren't so bad, they're just gratuitous.

Why did Woodward take on Belushi's biography in the first place? Other than the coincidence, mentioned occasionally, that they are from the same hometown, Wheaton, Illinois? An obvious reason (outside of money) is that he intended to create a reporter's portrait of a certain stratum of the drug culture. Woodward's bent clearly is not psychoanalytic (Belushi's childhood rates maybe three paragraphs out of some 500 pages), and he has no ability to bring people to life; the only value his account has is as an oddly written journalistic record of a social world in which drugs play a major part. In this one aspect, the book—impressing by sheer volume—is frightening. The movie—aspiring to cuteness and entertainment—doesn't begin to get this down.

Also reviewed in:
NEW YORK TIMES, 8/25/89, p. C14, Vincent Canby
VARIETY, 8/9–15/89, p. 20
WASHINGTON POST, 8/25/89, p. D1, Rita Kempley
WASHINGTON POST, 8/25/89, Weekend/p. 33, Desson Howe

WIZARD, THE

A Universal Pictures release of a Finnegan-Pinchuk Company production. *Executive Producer:* Lindsley Parsons Jr. *Producer:* David Chisholm and Ken Topolsky. *Director:* Todd Holland. *Screenplay:* David Chisholm. *Director of Photography:* Robert Yeoman. *Editor:* Tom Finan. *Music:* J. Peter Robinson. *Music Editor:* Michael Dittrick. *Sound:* Morteza Rezvani. *Sound Editor:* J. Paul Huntsman. *Production Designer:* Michael Mayer. *Art Director:* Rob Sissman. *Set Designer:* Bobby Strohmeyer. *Set Decorator:* Claire J. Bowin. *Set Dresser:* Quinn Monahan. *Special Effects:* Eddie Surkin. *Costumes:* Scilla Andreen-Hernandez. *Make-up:* Lynne Eagan. *Stunt Coordinator:* James Halty. *Running time:* 97 minutes. *MPAA Rating:* PG.

CAST: Luke Edwards (Jimmy); Vincent Leahr (Tate); Wendy Phillips (Christine); Dea McAllister (Counselor); Sam McMurray (Bateman); Beau Bridges (Sam); Fred Savage (Corey); Christian Slater (Nick); Will Seltzer (Putnam); Roy Conrad (Bus Clerk); Jenny Lewis (Haley); Roderick Dexter (Trucker #1); Ray Bickel (Trucker #2); Chuck Skinner (Grease Monkey); W.K. Cowan (Salesman #1); William C. Thompson (Salesman #2); Sonny Dukes (Biker); T. Dan Hopkins (Old Navajo); Jason Oliver (Tough Teen #1); Rowdy Metzger (Tough Teen #2); Preston Scott Lee (Tough Teen #3); Beth Grant (Diner Manager); Gregor Hesse (Younger Boy); Jackey Vinson (Lucas); Tom Kerley (Pinball Teen); Frank McRae (Spanky); Gene Skillen (Stickman); Blair Anthony (Hotel Security); Thomas Stanczyk (Rick the Video Counselor); Jacqueline Lear (Bubblegum Girl); Valana C. Hatter (Diner Waitress); Roderick Dexter (Wrecking Yard Man); Terri Lynn Neish (Poolside Waitress); Lee Arenberg (Armageddon Registrar); Steven Grives (Armageddon Announcer); Marisa Desimone (Mora Grissom); Zed James Frizzelle (Lucas' Buddy); Jim Pirri (Studio Tour Guide); David D'Ovidio (Armageddon Official).

LOS ANGELES TIMES, 12/15/89, Calendar/p. 18, Michael Wilmington

Video games, and the kids obsessed with them, are the main subjects of "The Wizard." But is it inevitable that the movie itself become a video game, with the movie-makers ramming us through the story, trying to jam down all our buttons?

"Rain Man" may be one of the models for "The Wizard," but the treatment is closer to "Pac-man." The characters don't really interact. They keep moving forward, gobbling up the plot as they go. By the time they've moved from the Nevada deserts to the gaudy glamour centers of Los Angeles, for a championship called Video Armageddon, the story has been chewed to pieces.

"The Wizard" is bright, fast and energetic, but there's not much real life to it. It's another movie that's disappeared into its own marketing hook: Three kids on the road, living and loving, racing toward personal redemption and video ascension.

In the movie, brothers Corey (Fred Savage) and Jimmy (Luke Edwards) flee from their desert homes to save the socially-alienated Jimmy from an institution. Though they're brothers, they live apart: Corey with his rowdy blue-collar dad Sam (Beau Bridges) and brother Nick (Christian Slater); Jimmy his with his prim mother (Wendy Phillips) and prickly stepfather (Sam McMurray) in an uptight yuppie environment that's driving him buggy.

Soon, there's a set of criss-crossing, cross-class pursuits. Dad and brother are after them in a pickup truck; Mom and Step-dad have hired a Blue Meanie of a Bounty Hunter (Will Seltzer), who practically cackles with villainy, while engaging in a set of Laurel-and-Hardy car-destruction duels with Sam and Nick.

Improbably, the kids run into their main game competitor at a truckstop: video genius Lucas (Jackey Vinson), with his power glove and "spaghetti western" intro. Filling out the road team—playing Dorothy Lamour to their Bob and Bing—is the feisty Haley (Jenny Lewis), whose kissing lesson for the swaggering Corey provides one of the film's few highlights.

Producer-writer David Chisholm knows all the road movie archetypes. Rock music pumps up the backgrounds, the children are rescued by truckers and bikers. But perhaps he knows them too well. "The Wizard" not only recalls the basic situation of "Rain Man." It also recalls "Midnight Run," "Twins" "Things Change," "Hollywood or Bust"—all those other "on the road" movies where a glib smoothie (like Savage) and an awkward or shy natural genius (Edwards) flee through the desert, pursued by authority figures or crooks and heading toward gambling cities and jackpots.

There's not a speck of originality or a squib of spontaneity in this kiddie-kiddie "buddy-buddy" movie. Director Todd Holland, making his feature debut, is a recent UCLA Film School graduate; Chisholm is active on TV. They both show a certain superficial verve, but the script is too frail for a movie, too dense for a video game. And most of the actors are too good for this picture.

At the end, "The Wizard" (MPAA rated PG) virtually becomes a trailer-advertisement for Universal Studios—with everybody racing wildly though the studio's amusement park trying to find Video Armageddon. There may be some symbolic significance in that, but it's probably not wise to dwell on it.

NEW YORK POST, 12/15/89, p. 43, Jami Bernard

It looks like one, walks like one, and quacks like one, but "The Wizard" is neither a duck nor a movie, technically speaking. It is a commercial for the Universal Studios tour and for the latest Nintendo video game, and the pitchmen just happen to be actors, including Beau Bridges, Christian Slater and Fred Savage.

In fact, if you show up at theaters early enough, you'll get a free Nintendo magazine, which looks, walks and quacks like a magazine, but is just another advertisement for Nintendo products. If you feel strongly that moviegoers should not have to pay to see ads, then you'll want to skip this one.

Buried inside this big fat commercial is a sentimental, pleasantly mediocre story about a broken family that comes to terms with each other when one of the sons, a charismatic adolescent (Savage), runs off with his newly institutionalized half-brother, a solemn, troubled child (Luke Edwards).

Soon the rest of the family is in earnest pursuit, including the divorced father (Bridges), the uncaring new stepfather (Sam McMurray), the alienated teen son (Slater), the hapless mother (Wendy Phillips), plus a ruthless finder of lost children (Will Seltzer).

The troubled one, Jimmy, turns out to be a wizard, the kind of idiot savant the Who anointed with their song "Pinball Wizard." But this isn't the '60s, so Jimmy is a whiz instead at video games, specifically Nintendo ones.

With his gift and his brother's finagling, plus his brother's new friend, a feisty girl they've come across in their travels (Jenny Lewis), they scam up enough money to make their way to the national video championships in California.

Yes, it's a "Rain Man" for the kiddie set. Perhaps there was no time to develop a unique story-line, what with all those video games blinking and buzzing in the filmmakers' heads.

The movie is a virtual catalog of Nintendo products; the climax pits the fragile Jimmy against the reigning champ in a bloodless bout of Super Mario Brothers, the latest version.

If you think there are a lot of buttons to push on a video game, that's nothing compared to the buttons they push in "The Wizard." The kids' isolation and need for creative expression are carefully designed to manipulate the targeted audience into buying what the movie is selling: Nintendo games to soothe every ill.

And just in time for Christmas, fancy that!

NEWSDAY, 12/15/89, Part III/p. 3, Terry Kelleher

The key line comes early in "The Wizard," when Corey (Fred Savage) marvels at an accomplishment by Jimmy (Luke Edwards), his little half-brother:

"You got fifty thousand on Double Dragon?!"

If you're the type who thinks the Super Mario Brothers are related to the governor of New York, you're in trouble from here on. But if Nintendo is your idea of Nirvana, and even a super-dumb plot couldn't possibly spoil your enjoyment of any movie with a video-game angle, "The Wizard" should be enough to lure you out of the arcade and into the neighboring multiplex.

Quick, the tangled background: Sam (Beau Bridges) and Christine (Wendy Phillips) are ex-spouses. Sam lives with Corey and Nick (Christian Slater), his sons by the woman he was married to before Christine. Christine, now wed to a jerk (Sam McMurray), has custody of Jimmy.

Jimmy seems to know only the word "California," frequently runs away from home and compulsively builds pyramids a la Richard Dreyfuss in "Close Encounters of the Third Kind." Says the jerk: "We're thinking about putting him in an institution...a home."

When Corey gets wind of this plan, he's understandably upset. "They're talking about putting him in...a home," he says to his father.

Corey slips out of the house, hides in a Hostess Cake truck (nice commercial for Hostess) and rides to "the home," out of which he snatches Jimmy. Naturally, they head for California, hooking up with a girl wanderer named Haley (Jenny Lewis).

Haley, too, is wowed by Jimmy's video-game prowess. "Think they'd put him in a home after he won...*this?*" she asks Corey, dramatically producing the brochure for a $50,000 video-game tournament to be held soon in Los Angeles.

En route to L.A., the kids raise funds through video-game hustling. Sam and Nick are in hot pursuit. So is Putnam (Will Seltzer), a mercenary runaway-hunter hired by the jerk. For fun, Sam repeatedly smashes his pickup into Putnam's car. Meanwhile, Sam becomes addicted to Teenage Mutant Ninja Turtles. It's a swell way to pass the time when he and Nick aren't busy bonding.

Back to the kids, who are busy sharing secrets. Turns out Jimmy was traumatized by the drowning death of his twin sister, and now carries her effects everywhere in his lunch box. And Haley's mother has a destructive gambling habit. She should try a more benign addiction, like video games.

After a three-day training stop in Reno and extensive telephonic briefings from the Nintendo Game-Playing Department (nice commercial for Nintendo), Jimmy and his handlers are ready for "Video Armageddon," held at Universal City Studios (nice commercial for Universal, makers of "The Wizard" and other fine films). The tournament features a screaming, chanting crowd and a screaming, near-satanic emcee. The outcome, long delayed, is predictable.

This is the first starring movie role for Savage, who demonstrates his appeal weekly on TV's "The Wonder Years," an infinitely more intelligent vehicle. He and Lewis are engaging together, but David Chisholm's script provides Savage with too little to do gives the audience plenty of chance to stare at fuzzy video screens and try to follow the figures that flit across them. Sorry, no joystick at your seat.

VILLAGE VOICE, 12/26/89, p. 114, Stuart Klawans

For all its deadliness, though, *Family Business* can at least claim to be a movie. [See Klawans' review.] *The Wizard* is an advertisement.

Imagine the Las Vegas section of *Rain Man*, with video games instead of black-jack and a Dumbo-eared nine-year-old substituting for Dustin Hoffman. The main purpose of telling us this kid's story, so far as I can tell, is to announce the arrival of Nintendo's new game, "Super Mario Bros. 3." But, even in an era of diminished expectations, this doesn't seem quite sufficient for a picture; so the filmmakers have also thrown in a pitch for the Universal Studios tour. That's *The Wizard*.

And yet no description of the product, however exhaustive, could be complete without mentioning the presence of Fred Savage, who has achieved fame on television as the more normal-looking of the kids on *The Wonder Years*. He's used here for his credibility with the eight-to-12 set, more or less like Michael J. Fox selling Diet Pepsi. He also helps put across the filmmakers' attitudes about sexual and racial roles, which are somewhere to the right of what you'd find in your average Shirley Temple vehicle.

Also reviewed in:
NEW YORK TIMES, 12/15/89, p. C30, Janet Maslin
VARIETY, 12/20/89, p. 23
WASHINGTON POST, 12/15/89, p. D7, Rita Kempley

WONDERLAND

A Vestron Pictures release of a Granada Film in association with Ideal Communications Films and Television. *Producer:* Steve Morrison. *Director:* Philip Saville. *Screenplay:* Frank Clarke. *Director of Photography:* Dick Pope. *Editor:* Richard Bedford. *Music:* Hans Zimmer. *Music Editor:* Geoff Hogg. *Sound:* Tony Jackson. *Sound Editor:* Anthony Sloman. *Production Designer:* David Brockhurst. *Art Director:* Diana Johnstone. *Set Dresser:* Aly Burge. *Special Effects:* Diane Pfister. *Costumes:* Jane Brown. *Make-up:* Sula Loizou. *Stunt Coordinator:* Peter Diamond. *Running time:* 103 minutes. *MPAA Rating:* R.

CAST: Emile Charles (Eddie); Tony Forsyth (Michael); Robert Stephens (Vincent); Clare Higgins (Eve); Bruce Payne (Echo); Robbie Coltrane (Annabelle); Carsten Norgaard (Dolphin Man); Kim Christie (Jean); Louis Embrick (Billy); Joseph Carrington (Ray); Julie Graham (Hazel); Paula Ann Bland (Beverley); Niven Boyd (Dave); Clare Parker (Young Jean); Caroline Milmoe (Lillie); Forbes Collins ("John Schlesinger"); Malcolm Frederick (Truck Driver); Albie Woodington (PC—Brighton); Jame McMartin (PC—Fruit Machine); Paul Netterfield (DJ—Fruit Machine); Jason Cunliffe (1st Lad—Fruit Machine); Mark Birch (2nd Lad—Fruit Machine); Anton Brookes (Thug); Mandy Walsh (Fat Woman at Party); David Bauckham (Security Man); Liz Stooke (TV Reporter).

LOS ANGELES TIMES, 7/21/89, Calendar/p. 12, Chris Willman

Life is fraught with peril for the two 16-year-old English heroes of "Wonderland," and not just because they're the only witnesses to a grisly murder at a gay disco. They themselves are homosexual, which leaves them prey to cruel peers, macho fathers and aging seducers, not to mention, of course, that machete-wielding, mascara-wearing homicidal hit man who's trying to track them down.

Director Philip Saville's slickly made film is part social drama, part suspense thriller, part Silly Putty. Inasmuch as it attempts to be a thriller trailing teens on the run from a mad killer, "Wonderland" is not all that far removed from the old kid-witness-in-peril theme of "The Window" or "Cloak and Dagger," updated to include menacing drag queens as well as musunderstanding parents and law figures. But it strives for a more resonant fate for its outcast protagonists.

Young, innocent, persecuted and gay, these two kids are so hemmed in by society and circumstance that they sort of remind you, in a symbolic sort of way, of course, of... caged dolphins.

Dolphins? Say what? Everyone's favorite New Age sea mammals as emblems of wounded gay pride? Indeed, this is the movie's pivotal and unwieldy symbolic connection, and where the script by Frank Clarke ("Letter to Brezhnev") finally turns unforgivably loopy. The purpose of these porpoises—part of the show at a Marineland-like seaside emporium called Wonderland—is to represent the limited recourses of our heroes. The script reminds us of this by having one of the young protagonists keep talking to the brainy fish, saying things like "I'm like you, you know—trapped."

Yes, we know, and for a while, we care, thanks to some fine acting and intriguing setups. As Eddie, the more naive and effeminately mannered of the two leads, Emile Charles manages to essay a genuine innocent set adrift; his fascination with the campier side of show biz and gay culture seems born out of delight, not decadence. The more street-wise of the pair is Tony Forsyth, equally effective as Michael, a blustery but golden-hearted tough who will sleep with whomever he has to to survive.

Their temporary savior is Robert Stephens, playing an aging opera star whose fondness for young men brings him to take the boys in at his beachside residence; his transition from good guy to victimizer to victim is quite touching. Not so sympathetic is his sort-of paramour, Clare Higgins, nearly as nasty a seductress here as in the "Hellraiser" pictures.

If only we had just these characters to contend with—but the splish-splash of plot elements gets more turbulent. There's that icy blond killer out there, sharpening his blades as he goes, moving in a preternatural slow motion that is the sole province of filmic maniacs and that would get him a loitering citation in real life. And there are the dolphins. And then the killer meets up with the dolphins, and we're off into lulu land, never to return.

Not until the jaw-dropping ending is it possible to suspect just how profoundly ludicrous the otherwise promising "Wonderland" (MPAA-rated R) is going to turn out. It wouldn't be giving too much away to reveal that one of the heroes leaves his mortally wounded pal bleeding alone, at length, in order to participate in a dolphin liberation—which may please the most extreme of animal-rights activists, but which leaves the rest of the audience wondering what happened to the old ideal of fetching paramedics for one's buddy.

"Save the humans!" could be our rallying cry; better yet, rescue reason.

MONTHLY FILM BULLETIN, 11/88, p. 330, Anne Billson

Berated by his father for his camp behaviour and liking for opera and old movies, seventeen-year-old Eddie runs away from his Liverpool home and joins his friend Michael, a street-wise hustler who is also on the run. The boys spend an evening at a night-club, where Michael wins a disco dance competition. Later, both boys witness the murder of Annabelle, the club's transvestite host, by Echo, a killer hired by local gangsters. They manage to escape, although Eddie is fascinated by Echo, who resembles the green-eyed stranger who appears in his recurring dreams about dolphins. The boys take refuge in a hotel where Vincent, an opera singer, is giving a recital. While Eddie enthuses to Vincent about his singing, Michael steals money from the guests' coats. His is caught redhanded by Eve, Vincent's business manager, who agrees not to turn him over to the authorities in exchange for sexual favours for both her and Vincent. The boys are accordingly taken to Brighton, where the singer is contracted to make some cassette-tape commercials. Unaware of the sordid nature of the deal his friend has made, Eddie wanders into the dolphinarium and is horrified to find a dolphin called Sooty being forced to perform degrading tricks. He leaves in disgust and is befriended by Jean, an animal rights activist who is planning to kidnap the dolphin and set it free. Michael attempts to blackmail Vincent. Echo, meanwhile, has followed the boys to Brighton, and beats Vincent up. Upset because he believes Michael guilty of the assault, Eddie breaks into the dolphinarium and swims in the pool with Sooty. He is attacked and stabbed by Echo, but Michael and Sooty combine forces to drown the killer. With Jean's help, Michael hijacks the truck in which Sooty has been placed by his owners and drives it into the sea. Sooty saves his liberator from drowning, and Michael returns to comfort Eddie as he dies.

As seems to be the case with virtually every low-budget British film these days, *The Fruit Machine* suffers from a fatal lack of genre constraint and narrative discipline. Frank Clarke's ideas shoot off in all directions—so much so that the audience is left dangling on a variety of different threads, wondering which one they should be following. The film starts out as domestic sit-com, with Eddie's mother recalling her moment of near-glory when auditioning for a role in *Saturday Night and Sunday Morning* (the memory is garbled: she thinks the director was John Schlesinger, whereas, as her husband points out, "It was directed by a woman—Karel Reisz), then veers off into a gangland thriller, a male buddy movie, a socio-realist commentary on modern sexual mores, and an animal-rightist wish-fulfilment fantasy.

Clarke has stated that he hopes *The Fruit Machine* "does for gay people what *Letter to Brezhnev* did for the Russians". The group that comes out on top here, however, is undoubtedly the cetaceans. Sooty and his pals are accorded an inordinate amount of sentimental screen time in which they are presented both as a symbol of the mysterious male fantasy figure (Sooty transforms periodically into a naked man, most notably during an idyllic skinny-dipping sequence) and as a thuddingly obvious metaphor for Eddie's social predicament ("I'm like you, you see—

trapped"). Despite Clarke's best effort, his homosexual characters come across as every bit as stereotyped as those in films less sympathetic to his cause. Eddie is the senstivie artistic type, sexually innocent but hopelessly obsessed by the mysterious macho man of his dreams. Michael is the Mr. Sloane-ish rent-boy, Vincent the homosexual artist past his physical prime, and Annabelle the burly building-site worker who moonlights in a frock.

Vincent and Eve, introduced as if they were going to be pivotal characters, are discarded as soon as they have transported the boys to the promised land of Brighton. Michael, whose petty thievery and sexual opportunism do not mark him out as a particularly endearing young hero, is largely overshadowed by Eddie, whose fey brand of romanticism eventually seems not so much innocent as simple-minded. The story suggests that creatures as sensitive as he cannot survive in the modern world, as though romanticism and realism were always mutually exclusive. The audience's identification with and affection for these characters is repeatedly over-estimated, with farcical results. In the final death scene, Michael cradles his stricken chum in his arms and (instead of summoning the medical attention so obviously required) croons "Running Wild" from *Some Like It Hot* as Eddie gives up the ghost.

NEW YORK POST, 4/28/89, p. 31, Jami Bernard

Free a dolphin, save a soul. "Wonderland," about two gay teens in Liverpool who run away, have adventures, cross wits with a maniac ninja killer and commune with mammals, draws a murky connection between homosexuality and the fish-bowl life of trained dolphins. It's a weird, uncertain movie, socially and ecologically "correct" but pretty hard to fathom.

Eddie (Emile Charles) and Michael (Tony Forsyth) are platonic pals who want to escape their respective gay bashing environments. Eddie is the sensitive one, a handsome, naive 16-year-old whose white mother watches romances on TV while eating bonbons and having a good cry, and whose black father is irritated by Eddie's "unmanly" grace and theatrical flair. Michael is the more pragmatic of the two, a hustler pent up in a home for juvenile delinquents.

Off they run for parts unknown, starting with a neon-drenched theme nightclub called The Fruit Machine where the two boys make the transvestite scene and then witness the murder of their cross-dressed hostess (a decidedly un-fey Robbie Coltrane in gingham). The contract killer, a blond ninja swordsman, has the cool, chiseled looks and glowing cat's-eyes of a guy who could have gotten into The Fruit Machine without paying the cover charge.

He spots the lads and, to prove that he is going to find them and tear them to pieces, he pulls one eye down by the lower lid. Where I grew up that was street slang for "sike," or "rank out," meaning "you're a sucker." Here it means "I'm gonna git you, sucka."

The boys are scared, and fall in with an old closet-queen opera singer on his way to Brighton. There Michael services his host and his host's conniving female agent (separate sessions), while Eddie wanders off blissfully to watch the dolphins at a nearby marine show called Wonderland.

Not only does Eddie identify with Flipper ("It's not a fish—it's a creature!" he keeps insisting), but he also has a dream-lover (who looks suspiciously like the maniac killer had he chosen a more pleasant profession) who shows up for some nude aquatics with Eddie and company. You, me, the dolphins—it's heaven on earth! Almost as good as singing Eddie's favorite Marilyn Monroe tune: "*Running wild, lost control...feeling gay, restless too.*"

The swirling underwater scenes are pleasingly, languidly shot, the camera gliding in and out and upside down like another dolphin. The scenes with the two lads have a similar in-synch feeling that makes their friendship a durable enough premise for a movie, and Emile Charles as Eddie is especially ingratiating.

On the other hand, the dolphin metaphor is baffling, the movie's ending unconvincing and lazily melodramatic. ("*Swim! Swim for your life!*") Director Philip Saville, a former actor who directed the excellent BBC version of "The Life and Loves of a She-Devil," does not seem to know whether his fish are swimming upstream, down or into a net. Without the slasher angle, "Wonderland" has the same comically gritty ambiance of "Letter to Brezhnev," also written by screenwriter Frank Clarke. But enter the ninja, and exit the fun and the fish (OK, the *creature*). "Wonderland" needed just a little more time on the drawing board, or the spawning ground.

NEWSDAY, 4/28/89, Part III/p. 5, Lynn Darling

Eddie (Emile Charles) and Michael (Tony Forsyth) are 16-year-old misfits, unable to find a place among the orderly categories in which the world in Liverpool would like to fit them.

Eddie is a dreamy, sensitive product of a querulous, racially mixed marriage; his mother lives in a fantasy world of regret and maudlin self-pity over her long-lost youth and beauty, while his father can only express his concern for his son through his harsh attempts to make a man of him.

Michael is tougher, more acquainted with the brutality of the world—he's run away from the detention center in which his stepmother has confined him—and knows how to scrape along on the furtive desires of older men.

They are already outsiders, trying to make the best of a bad bargain, armed only with their friendship and a hopefulness that has survived all the blows the world has dealt them. That isn't enough, of course, but it's all they've got. At times grittily realistic, at times extravagantly lyric, "Wonderland" isn't an easy movie to like.

Overly symbolic and often incredible in its plotline, the movie manages to stumble as often as it flies. But "Wonderland" is always intriguing, brooding on its themes of alienation, sexual dispossession and despair with compelling passion and intensity. The movie forces you to accept it on its own terms, warts, wildness and all.

The two friends talk their way into a gay nightclub, where at the end of a long night they are inadvertent witnesses to a brutal murder. Pursued by the assassin (Bruce Payne) they make their way to Brighton, befriended by a predatory, aging opera star (Robert Stephens) and his equally licentious business manager (Clare Higgins). There, at the tacky, little aquatic park Wonderland, Eddie pursues a sense of kinship and connection with the performing bottle-nosed dolphins.

"Wonderland" isn't a movie that leaves much to subtlety. Eddie's identification with the trapped, abused dolphins, also living in a world foreign to their nature, is made glaringly obvious. But the movie also takes some wonderful chances, reveling in a sensual fantasy that reaches its culmination when Eddie dives into the dolphins' pool to swim naked with them.

Other gambles work less well. The blond, sinister assassin (with identity problems of his own) is not only particularly inept in his attempt to kill a couple of frightened teenagers, but becomes thoroughly ridiculous in a scene in which he flourishes his knife in rhythmic, ritual movement while clothed in nothing but a pair of diaphanous black pajamas.

Still, "Wonderland" stays afloat, despite the clunkers in plot and script, thanks to the grit and innocence of its two co-stars, and to the consistently fine look of the film, which alternates between a soft, fleshly moodiness and an atmosphere of ominous mystery.

VILLAGE VOICE, 5/2/89, p. 80, Elliott Stein

Wonderland's credits seemed promising. This first film produced by English Granada TV specifically for theatrical release was written by Fred Clarke (*Letter to Brezhnev*) and directed by Philip Saville, who helmed the remarkable TV miniseries *The Life and Loves of a She-Devil*. They've created a schizoid tale, an ecological gay adventure-thriller involving two insouciant adolescent best buddies from Liverpool who run off together, wind up in Brighton, and soon find themselves in the direst of straits. Though most of the characters are stereotyped, the Liverpudlian sections are fast-paced and entertaining. But the script goes totally bonkers during the later sequences, leading to a bathetic climax featuring the most ludicrous death scene within memory. If the movie's heart's in the right place, its head is more than a wee bit muddled.

The chums are Eddie (Emile Charles), a naive, shy, and idealistic kid whose brutal father bashes him to "straighten him out"; and Michael (Tony Forsyth), a brash, streetwise hustler. One night, though underage, they charm their way into a lively nightclub called the Fruit Machine (the original British release title), where Michael strips down to his well-filled boxers and wins a dance contest, and they witness the machete murder of the club's drag-queen mother hen. With the homophobic psycho in hot pursuit, the boys flee to the seaside as part of the entourage of a lubricious, over-the-hill operatic tenor.

The film manages to turn into a sort of campy *Turtle Diary* when Eddie—who has been haunted by a hunky fantasy Dolphin Man creature who appears to him in dreams and lavatory visions— attempts to free the dolphins in a Marineland-type show and return them to the sea. The animals' captivity is apparently intended as a metaphor for the oppression of homosexuals. Ouch! Although Charles and Forsyth are extremely engaging, and the intense nonsexual bonding of the two little scudders is well-observed and often moving, *Wonderland*, if rarely boring, is an unruly mess.

Also reviewed in:
NEW YORK TIMES, 4/28/89, p. C10, Vincent Canby
VARIETY, 6/1/88, p. 12
WASHINGTON POST, 6/3/89, p. C13, Hal Hinson

WORTH WINNING

A Twentieth Century Fox release of an A & M Films production. *Executive Producer:* Tom Joyner. *Producer:* Gil Friesen and Dale Pollock. *Director:* Will Mackenzie. *Screenplay:* Josann McGibbon and Sara Parriott. *Based on the movel by:* Dan Lewandowski. *Director of Photography:* Adam Greenberg. *Editor:* Sidney Wolinsky. *Music:* Patrick Williams. *Music Editor:* Sally Boldt. *Sound:* Dave McMillan and (music) Humberto Gatica. *Sound Editor:* Bob Newlan. *Production Designer:* Lilly Kilvert. *Art Director:* Jon Hutman. *Set Designer:* David Klassen. *Set Decorator:* Linda Spheeris. *Special Effects:* King Hernandez. *Costumes:* Robert Blackman. *Make-up:* Lona Jeffers and Fred Blau. *Stunt Coordinator:* Norman Howell and Doug Coleman. *Running time:* 95 minutes. *MPAA Rating:* PG-13.

CAST: Mark Harmon (Taylor Worth); Madeleine Stowe (Veronica Briskow); Lesley Ann Warren (Eleanor Larimore); Maria Holvöe (Erin Cooper); Mark Blum (Ned Braudy); Andrea Martin (Claire Braudy); Tony Longo (Terry Childs); Alan Blumenfeld (Howard Lattimore); Devin Ratray (Howard Lattimore Jr.); David Brenner (Celebrity Auctioneer); Jon Korkes (Sam); Brad Hall (Eric); Shannon Lawrence (Chloe Braudy); Todd Cameron Brown (Owen Braudy); Russ Bolinger (Gus); Joan Severance (Lizbette); Emily Kuroda (Cory Chu); Karen Newman (Amy); John Walcutt (Chip); Rick Hurst (Big Bouncin' Bob); Meg Wyllie (Granny); Arthur Malet (Ticket Taker); John Carter (Mr. Cooper); Nancy Glass (Channel 8 Newscaster); Thomas Bellin (Minister); Catherine M. Cummings (Box Office Woman); Phillip Simon (Maitre d'); Micah Rowe (Bryan); Andrew McCullough (Stage Manager); Robert Mayon (Sportscaster); Marcy Shelton (Track Cashier); Cari Lightfoot (Ticket Seller); Gerald J. Wilson (Video Tech).

LOS ANGELES TIMES, 10/27/89, Calendar/p. 8, Kevin Thomas

What makes "Worth Winning" so depressing is that so much effort and talent has been expended on such a bad idea. It's hard to imagine how the film makers thought they could make palatable, let alone amusing, the spectacle of a seasoned playboy accepting a bet that he can get three women to accept his proposal of marriage within three months.

This cruel notion would work in a dark Buñuelian satire—a sort of "Indiscreet Charm of the Bourgeoisie"—but "Worth Winning" means to be a sleek send-'em-home-happy romantic comedy, even though it is the stuff of "Dangerous Liaisons."

You can understand why Philadelphia psychiatrist Ned Braudy (Mark Blum) proposes the bet to his pal Taylor Worth (Mark Harmon), a handsome TV weatherman and local celebrity. Although not fully admitting it, Ned is jealous of the happy-go-lucky Taylor's endless string of casual conquests and decides that his friend needs to experience some emotional pain. (Ned really is the physician in need of healing himself.) Taylor is actually dubious about the plan, recognizing its potential for hurt, if not to himself, then to the women Ned has selected for him to conquer. Taylor, however, succumbs to male vanity and to the possibility of winning a genuine Picasso, which Ned has put up as the prize. (Never mind that the painting is an heirloom belonging to Ned's wife.)

As directed by TV veteran Will Mackenzie (in his feature debut), "Worth Winning" proceeds with clockwork precision. Taylor turns on the charm to a Philadelphia Eagles receptionist (beautiful and talented newcomer Maria Holvöe), to a rich, sex-starved matron (Lesley Ann Warren) and to a sharp-tongued but vulnerable concert pianist (Madeleine Stowe).

No question about it, Harmon and his three leading ladies are terrific. In adapting Dan Lewandowski's novel, writers Josann McGibbon and Sara Parriott have made sure that none of the women are defenseless airheads but bright, attractive women with plenty of humor and resourcefulness. Each is worth Taylor's efforts, and Harmon has the easy style and confidence to be a thoroughly convincing seducer.

But "Worth Winning" doesn't acknowledge that it's really saying that it's OK for rich, famous and sexy men to get away with just about anything with women with no more than a slap on the wrist. Filmed entirely in settings of luxury and privilege, including exteriors in Philadelphia's handsome, restored Society Hill district, "Worth Winning" (rated a decidedly lenient PG-13) tells us more about contemporary values than it may have intended; when all is said and done, it endorses rather than criticizes the male attitudes and behavior it depicts.

NEW YORK POST, 10/27/89, p. 25, Jami Bernard

People Magazine once voted Mark Harmon the sexiest man on earth. Frankly, I can't see why. Didn't this guy once play serial killer Ted Bundy? What's worse, in "Worth Winning"—which is not much worth seeing—he plays one of those woman-hating lotharios whose relationships last two months before he goes out for a fresh kill. With his snide asides to the camera a la "Ferris Bueller," Harmon's character is not easy to like.

And in this movie, Harmon is completely charmless as he takes up his buddies on a sick bet to get three beautiful women to agree to marry him within three months. The proposal and acceptance has to be videotaped as proof. If he wins, he gets his friend's Picasso. If he loses, he loses his fishing cottage.

In any case, when the bet is over, he gets to walk away from three trusting women, one of whom will have already chosen the color of her bridesmaids' dresses. What a side-splitter.

The friends believe that he'll lose the bet, that someone "will give him the gift of heartache," and that it is only then that the confirmed bachelor will settle down. It's a malicious, misogynist comedy.

Some of which might have been forgiven if it weren't so boring. The laughs are few and the characters without much individual appeal. Harmon plays Taylor Worth, a local TV weatherman who is such a dunce on the air it's incredible these women would fall for him. Lesley Ann Warren is a libidinous married woman. Maria Holvöe is a naive, gorgeous mascot for a football team. And Madeleine Stowe is the brainy, sexy concert pianist for whom Taylor eventually falls when he discovers that playing "Olympic mice" in bed with her can be fun.

The first sign of trouble is the opening credits, where Harmon is superimposed against a cloud-filled blue sky as small squares bearing portions of women float by, subject to his approval. If he dislikes a leg or breast or thigh floating by, he zaps them with a TV remote control device, until he has created the perfect woman, who of course is just an assemblage of the appropriate legs, breasts, thighs, etc.

Even though he ostensibly learns that a real woman is more than the sum of her parts, the one he falls for just happens to be insanely accomplished, beautiful, smart, secure, fun and smart-mouthed. Taylor, the newly perfect man, is duplicitous, insensitive, sexually unfaithful, prone to smoking huge cigars (always a problem sign), and so territorial he won't allow his girlfriend to move his bed up against the window.

The wife of Taylor's best friend (Mark Blum), luscious Joan Severance has a walk-on as a jilted girlfriend, one of the many who can't get enough punishment from Taylor, and David Brenner appears mysteriously at the end as himself and has one funny line.

It is amazing to learn that the script for this lame diatribe against women was written by two of that gender. Perhaps they consoled themselves that the brief revenge scenes near the end redeem the preceding, or perhaps their script started out more tongue in cheek than what appears on the screen. In any case, Hollywood must be a place where you can easily sell your own kind down the river.

NEWSDAY, 10/27/89, Part III/p. 5, Janice Berman

Mark Harmon, who vanished from "St. Elsewhere" as a rake plowed under by heterosexual AIDS, hasn't learned his lesson at all. This time, as weatherman Taylor Worth in "Worth Winning," he's sleeping with two women. How Philly's most eligible bachelor has managed to keep his pants zipped in the presence of No. 3 is sort of fudged over, but any lech who sees this unfunny comedy is likely to feel that two out of three ain't bad.

There are three women because Taylor's best buddy, a shrink named Ned Braudy (Mark Blum), bets him he can't get all three women (whom he has selected from among the assortment of ample curves and flowing manes that populate this flick) to accept a marriage proposal. Let us pause here to note that Dr. Ned has bet his wife's (Andrea Martin, whose talent is wasted) Picasso.

And the fun begins, as Taylor drives his yupped-out BMW convertible from one assignation to another, wooing and winning, lying and laying. Busy, busy, busy.

Harmon seems untaxed and uninspired by his role. The movie is filled with casual asides from Taylor to the audience. But from watching "Burns and Allen," I knew George Burns, and Mark Harmon is no George Burns.

And this is no madcap comedy, no "Philadelphia Story," aborted wedding notwithstanding, no "When Harry Met Sally...," restaurant confessions—um, notwithstanding.

The tip-off to "Worth Winning" is the title sequence, when women are electronically cut into segments and their body parts shuffled around. This is at least initially Taylor's notion of women; they're interchangeable in all aspects.

He does, however, end up being more involved with one of his quarry than he had anticipated. The woman he likes is the only one who thinks and acts like a normal human being, even though when she has him to a dinner party, she's wearing a dress that's ridiculously revealing.

OK, forget the dress. Forget that almost every woman in the movie is wearing clothes that are too tight, or that every time this lamebrained weatherman goes on the air, women flock around him.

If we forget all that, maybe we could say that there has been some symbolic gesture toward (aargh) commitment.

But balance that against those enormous cigars the guys smoke at their poker game, and it's easy to tell which symbol has the upper hand.

Also reviewed in:
NEW YORK TIMES, 10/27/89, p. C8, Janet Maslin
VARIETY, 11/1/89, p. 34
WASHINGTON POST, 10/28/89, p. C9. Hal Hinson

YAABA

A New Yorker Films release of an Arcadia Films (Paris)/Les Films de L'Avenir (Ouagadougou)/Thelma Film AG (Zurich) production. *Producer:* Freddy Denaes, Pierre-Alain Meier, and Idrissa Ouedraogo. *Director:* Idrissa Ouedraogo. *Screenplay (Mooré with English Subtitles):* Idrissa Ouedraogo. *Director of Photography:* Matthias Kälin. *Editor:* Loredana Cristelli. *Music:* Francis Bebey. *Sound:* Jean-Paul Mugel. *Running time:* 90 minutes. *MPAA Rating:* Not Rated.

CAST: Fatimata Sanga (Yaaba); Noufou Ouedraogo (Bila); Roukietou Barry (Nopoko); Adama Ouedraogo (Kougri); Amadé Toure (Tibo); Sibidou Ouedraogo (Poko); Adama Sidibe (Razougou); Rasmané Ouedraogo (Noaga).

CHRISTIAN SCIENCE MONITOR, 10/24/89, p. 11, David Sterritt

When people around the world talk about movies, Hollywood is the first place they usually think of. And one of the last might be Africa, since developing countries there produce fewer films than nations on some other continents.

Yet films are produced in African countries, and some of them reach out to moviegoers in far distant lands. Senegalese director Ousmano Sembene has made several internationally successful films, and his latest, "Camp de Thiaroye," has appeared in various festivals recently, even though it's not one of his best efforts. Other filmmakers from Africa who have drawn widespread attention include Souleymane Cisse of Mali, who made "Brightness"; Ngangura Mweze of Zaire, who codirected "La Vie est belle"; and Désiré Ecaré of the Ivory Coast, who made "Faces of Women." There's even a film festival every other year in Burkina Faso (which used to be known as Upper Volta).

Once in a while—not nearly often enough—an African picture gets commercially distributed in the United States, attracting the notice of popular audiences as well as internationally-minded critics. That's happening this season with a movie from Burkina Faso, written and directed by a talented filmmaker named Idrissa Ouedraogo. It's called "Yaaba," and it's now playing commercially in the US after a successful showing at the New York Film Festival. It also won the international critics prize at this year's Cannes film festival, and has become a hit in Paris, where it's been playing in six different theaters.

In the language of Burkina Faso, known as Mooré, "yaaba" means grandmother, and one of the main characters is an old woman who's been given that nickname. But she's not an ordinary old woman. The people in her village have decided she's a witch who brings them bad luck, and she's been forced to live in exile on the fringe of the community.

Children sometimes see more clearly than their parents, though, and a little boy and girl make friends with the outcast. They're the ones who call her Yaaba, and they pay visits to her in secret. The plot reaches a turning point when these children get into a fight with some rough kids, and one of Yaaba's friends is badly injured. Yaaba helps save her, and the child's mother finally sees the truth about the old woman, leading to a bittersweet ending.

"Yaaba" doesn't have much talk in it, partly because Burkina Faso has many different dialects from village to village. Since the filmmaker wanted his movie to be widely understandable, he made it as visual as possible, relying more on images than words. This is helpful to audiences who don't speak Mooré, and it's also cinematically refreshing, at a time when many conventional films rely all too much on people chattering to one another instead of giving us creative and expressive imagery.

Also welcome is the warm humanity of the picture. In the past, African films have often emphasized political messages as a way of asserting independence and reacting against the colonialism that has plagued Africa. By contrast, "Yaaba" is a shining example of the new wave in African cinema, which doesn't want to be just African but worldwide in its appeal. It isn't a fancy or melodramatic film, and it moves rather slowly, especially if you compare it with hyperactive Hollywood pictures. But it glows with gentleness and charm, and it offers solid proof that moviemaking is alive and well on the African continent.

LOS ANGELES TIMES, 5/25/90, Calendar/p. 8, Sheila Benson

A young boy and girl run across the vast, rosy-brick colored landscape at the opening of "Yaaba;" we see them in the same shot at the close. All that will have taken place in between is a world of understanding.

"Yaaba's" power sneaks up on you. At first it seems as spare as the airy African Savannah where it unfolds. It's only with a little distance from its muted beauty that the plan of the film becomes clear.

Writer-director Idrissa Ouedraogo won the International Critics' Prize at Cannes last year for this tender film, his second feature, which he set in a village in Burkina Faso near the one in which he was born. (Before 1984, Burkina Faso had been the French colony of Upper Volta.) Not a fable, a myth or a fairy tale, "Yaaba" concerns the human comedy, told in terms of the greatest elegance and simplicity.

Plot is not what drives the film. Like a warm-country "McCabe and Mrs. Miller," most of this is life overheard, caught a little on the bias. This remote African town might be a rural French village or a Spanish one—with its town drunk, its village beauty, its handsome widower, its parents, both stubborn and sensible and its old, old woman thought to be a witch.

She is the proud, outcast Sana (Fatimata Sanga), her gray hair cropped close to her skull, her rare smile an utter surprise. The film's two main children, 12-year-old motherless Bila (Noufou Ouedraogo) and budding beauty Nopoko (Roukietou Barry), his cousin and closest friend, meet her on a forbidden visit to the cemetery as they pay their respects to Bila's mother's grave. In this setting and later, the children discover that this "witch" is a humorous, neat old party, innocent of everything of which she's been accused.

Bila in particular takes to her. He brings her the present of a filched rooster and as they share its stringy roasted bones he calls her Yaaba, grandmother. It coaxes forth that smile: "That's the first time someone has called me grandmother," she says, "and it makes me very happy."

The rest of his village is in no hurry to change their opinion that she is a witch and the source of their ills, particularly Nopoko's short-tempered father. It will become a life-and-death matter when one of the children becomes seriously ill and no one will accept Yaaba's advice about a cure. But director Ouedraogo is in no hurry to trot out a pat solution; he is having too good a time creating fine, quiet, wryly knowledgeable portraits from around the village.

The town drunk turns out to be also the wisest man in the place. His beautiful wife, probably wooed by his wits originally, is now repulsed by his drinking, while the impotence it brings on makes her prey to the local con artist. The town scold is also the mother of the three most impossible children in the place, while its most severe father is married to the most thoughtful—and effective—wife. And all of them are observed by the village voyeur, whose worldly "Ah! that's life!" punctuates every spied lovemaking or adultery. His tolerance for human frailties, however, doesn't slow him down one split-second from broadcasting the news everywhere.

This is the sort of rich mix of foibles that delighted Jean Renoir and seems to fairly energize Ouedraogo, whose work with this cast of non-professionals—many of whom are from his family—is flawless. Equally moving and lyrical is the lighting camerawork of Matthias Kälin and the delicately haunting music of Francis Bebey.

"Yaaba" (Times-rated: Family) closes elegiacally. In the film's cemetery scene, director Ouedraogo noted the broken cooking pots of the dead, placed simply on top of their rounded grave sites. There is the sense at the end of his film of another cracked and empty vessel, its usefulness on this Earth over, its contents passed on to a younger soul and an infinite feeling of universality and closure.

MONTHLY FILM BULLETIN, 1/90, p. 25, James Leahy

Two young cousins, Bila and Nopoko, are in the village cemetery pouring a libation for Nopoko's dead mother, watched by Sana, an elderly woman reputed to be a witch. Back in the village a food store is on fire, and Sana is blamed, particularly by the woman Pegda. Only Noaga, the village drunk, speaks in defence of the old woman. Bila, too, tries to defend Sana to his father, Kougri. As a result, he is forbidden to visit the cemetery. A fight breaks out when Bila protects Sana against stones thrown by Pegda's three children. Tibo, Nopoko's father, breaks it up, but is accused by Pegda of helping to attack her children. That night Koudi tries to arouse her husband Noaga to make love and when it fails, goes to meet her clandestine lover, Razougou. Bila steals a chicken to give to Sana, who is moved when he calls her "Yaaba" (Grandmother). Nopoko sneaks on Bila to his father, who punishes him, but his mother Poko supports him. Nopoko comes to Bila's aid when they are ambushed by Pegda's children, and is cut on the wrist by a knife. As a punishment, Pegda's husband throws her and her children out. Nopoko is taken ill with tetanus, and an expensive healer who comes to the village claims that a witch has stolen her soul. Only Bila and Noaga are not taken in. The villagers march on Yaaba's hut demanding Nopoko's soul back and, finding it empty, burn it. Bila promises to build her a new home. They set off to see Taryam, the great herbalist, but Kougri spots them and makes Bila come back. When Yaaba arrives, Taryam collects herbs for a potion. When they deliver it, however, only Noaga recognises Taryam, and Kougri charges Yaaba with having created work for her friend. Poko sends Bila to retrieve the medicine from the healer, and secretly they does Nopoko until she is well again. While the villagers celebrate Nopoko's father Tibo's wedding, Koudi slips away to join Razougou. The village's elderly "Peeping Tom" denounces the lovers and Razougou is chased off, but Koudi, unashamed, publicly tells her husband what she thinks of him. The next morning, Poko gives Bila food for Yaaba, but she has died in the night. Noaga helps Bila and Nopoko to bury her and explains how the death of her parents left her isolated from the rest of the village. Bila knew this already, and Nopoko is angry that he did not tell her. He apologises, giving her a bracelet that was a gift from Yaaba.

Yaaba has been described by one observer as a film calculated to please the European audience and by another as clearly influenced by *Pather Panchali*, the film that brought Bengali-language cinema international acclaim. Certainly any film which is centred on the playfully competitive friendship of two such compelling children as Bila and particularly Nopoko runs the risk of being dismissed as an appeal to the sentimentality of the metropolitan audience. However, it would be a mistake to ignore the way in which the narrative is firmly rooted in the problems and social organisation of African village life, producing particular resonances for Africans. For example, Sana's isolation derives from the fact that she has been an orphan since infancy, without kin to connect her to society, or descendents who would care for her and call her "Yaaba".

Similarly, as cousins, Bila and Nopoko would be expected to marry. Thus Nopoko's coyness about revealing her nakedness when the two children bathe at the waterhole has a specific meaning, while Bila's offer of Nopoko to Pegda's eldest son as a bride is a way of teasing his future wife. Bila himself, who stands for clear-sightedness cutting through pretence and hypocrisy, offers a hopeful model for the next generation. It is important that he is able to act effectively and, in alliance with his mother Poko, who also believes in the need for change, save Nopoko's life. Even more important is the fact that such insight involves a return to traditional wisdom and practices. Through the character of Taryam, Idrissa Ouedraogo suggests that traditional healing is based on knowledge which is in danger of being lost, partly due to charlatans who play on time-honoured superstitions for their own profit.

Bila's intelligence allows him to separate what is sustaining in tradition from what is destructive in custom. Moreover, his judgments are based in a developing and maturing human tolerance. When he and Yaaba spot the illicit lovers Koudi and Razougou, he says what Koudi is doing is wrong. Yaaba responds that she may have her reasons. After Yaaba's death, Bila uses the same words to defend Koudi against Nopoko's condemnation of her behaviour, showing that he has learnt and profited from his relationship with the old woman he tried to integrate into his unyielding community.

NEW STATESMAN & SOCIETY, 2/2/90, p. 44, Suzanne Moore

Is it really fair to compare a film made in one of the poorest countries in the world with a $37 million production by one of Hollywood's flashiest directors? No of course not. But *Yaaba*, made in Burkina Faso, a country with no film-making infrastructure will have to compete with Ridley Scott's *Black Rain*. [See Moore's review of *Black Rain*.] Such is the democracy of the marketplace.

In fact this week's releases seem deliberately chosen to highlight the inequities of "the system". First we have the big boys. Brain de Palma's *Casualties of War* is another hugely expensive guilt-tripping Vietnam movie. Then there is Scott's *Black Rain* set in Japan, *Yaaba* from Africa and *Piravi* from Kerala in India. *Yaaba* and *Piravi* will, no doubt, be lumped together as "Third Cinema" though actually Kerala has a thriving film culture unlike Burkina Faso.

Yaaba, directed by Idrissa Ouedraogo, with its clear images, its wide open spaces and faith in storytelling is a million miles away from the cluttered frames of Hollywood. *Yaaba* means grandmother and the plot concerns the relationship between an old woman and a young boy. But underneath the deceptive simplicity of the film we see a complex portrait of village existence. Though these people have nothing—no electricity, few possesions—Ouedraogo never simplifies their emotional life.

One wonders what Ridley Scott would have done in the brilliant light of this red desert landscape. Could he bear one frame of a film not to be stuffed with *things* and reflections of things? How could he even contemplate a movie without smokey light filtering though grey-blue venetian blinds? For Ridley is a former ad man, the designer director par excellence. This obsession with surface has produced some of the best and most influential movies of the last ten years. Both *Blade Runner* and *Alien* looked fantastic and had the added extra of exciting plots. *Black Rain* simply looks fantastic.

It is set largely is Osaka, which will no doubt interest those who are in the business of constructing the cyberpunk canon. *Blade Runner*'s vision of a future American city was swarming with Asiatic influence and Chiba City, one of the locations of William Gibson's seminal novel *Neuromancer*, was also in Osaka. Yet Scott's explanation for choosing Osaka over Tokyo is based on practicalities—it was an easier place to film in. Here, in this empire of neon signs, the previous influences of his films can be foregrounded and you can't help feeling that, like so many of us, he is far happier dealing with Japan as *the future* rather than dealing with it in the present.

The plot itself is as old as they come. Two New York cops witness a murder and are assigned to take the killer back to the Japanese police in Osaka. It's another cop-out-of-water scenario with the culture clash played for all its worth. Michael Douglas plays the hard cop Nick, an unlikeable macho bore who watches his partner, the soft cop, get disembowelled by a gang of Japanese maniacs on motorbikes. They are all members of the Yakusa, "the Jap mob" which is crudely portrayed here as a more exotic version of the Mafia. After the death of his buddy, Nick reluctantly teams up with his Japanese counterpart, the cautious and honest Masahiro and ends up teaching him a thing or two about American philosophy summed up here as "sometimes you have to go for it".

As dubious and racist as this film is, full of lines like "Isn't there a nip in this building who speaks fucking English?" (which hasn't stopped it being acclaimed in Japan itself), it is undeniably first-class entertainment. It is slick, loud and full of thoroughly enjoyable, mindless violence. Every frame is crammed with surface and superficial detail, steam and light. Every puddle is spotlit, every pair of sunglasses dazzling.

Yet underneath all these shining surfaces there is an emptiness that is not just the emptiness of a formula plot but a sense of foreboding. America doesn't know how to deal with Japan. It cannot accept that it is no longer itself the centre of the world. And it cannot begin to accept that it has been beaten at its own game, rather than by some commie plot. Japan has made capitalism *work*.

The central relationship of *Black Rain*, between Nick and Masahiro, is a crumbling assertion of American superiority. Nick cannot come to terms with the Japanese code—the stereotype of membership of a group being more important than individual desires. Nick sees Japan as a mere imitator, a country full of repression and with no originality. There is nothing more alien to the American ethos than the idea of a voluntary rather than an enforced collectivity. Nick's is the desperate voice of rugged individualism, a man who refuses "to play by the rules". Japan is full of rules that are incomprehensible to him. And then we have the Yakusa who are actually fighting over counterfeit money. It is almost an admission that Japan cannot only produce goods more efficently than the west, but that it can now make its own dollars. America is redundant which is why this movie makes such a conspicuous and botched effort to turn us back to the American way.

Outside the fiction of the film, Japan is actually buying into the fiction-making machine of Hollywood. Sony has recently taken over some of the major studios. As the sun rises in the east, the American debt crisis grows. The only female character in the film, naturally enough a glamourous American bargirl on the make, describes her relationship with the country as a love-hate one.

But *Black Rain* is full of very little love for Japan. It is fear that drives it, and the Japanese themselves are portrayed as the ultimate *Aliens*. Instead the film mouths its t-shirt slogan, "Sometimes you have to go for it", as jingoistic compensation for what even the American government is having to come to terms with: that sometimes it's too late. Someone else has already gone for it and is winning.

NEW YORK POST, 10/6/89, p. 28, David Edelstein

They call her a witch, the crone who lives on the outskirts of the desert village; they say she's the cause of their various misfortunes. Here, on a remote savanna in Africa's Burkina Faso, this outcast (Fatimata Sanga) lives quietly, drifting across the brown, arid landscape like a ghost—so wizened and sticklike that she might indeed be a phantom.

She isn't, however. When the children of the village throw rocks at her, she does not cry, but bleeds.

One little boy, Bila (Noufou Ouedraogo), doesn't take part in the ridicule; he knows in his heart she is innocent of witchcraft. Although forbidden to see her, Bila steals away and brings her food. He calls her "Yaaba," which means "grandmother."

"Yaaba," which won the International Critics Prize at the 1989 Cannes Film Festival, is a Swiss-French-Burkina Faso co-production, written and directed by 35-year-old African Idrissa Ouedraogo.

In a culture known for its moralism and superstition, the Paris-educated Ouedraogo has made a liberal, enlightened tear-jerker about respect for someone who's different. It's no coincidence that at the New York Film Festival, where "Yaaba" premiered, it was shown the day after D.W. Griffith's "Intolerance."

As drama, "Yaaba" isn't exciting. Tidy and predictable, it's the sort of movie critics dub "a rare fable" because it's so elementary on the level of storytelling.

We know that Yaaba's "magic" will be vindicated, that the charlatan who suggests that the villagers burn down her hut will get his comeuppance. We can predict that, at one point, Yaaba will display not only great wisdom but the sort of progressive tolerance that others have denied her. We can guess the three-handkerchief ending.

Yet the movie's images transcend its conventional plotting. Chief among those is Sanga herself. Her head is shaved, and she is bare-chested—her breasts now long, tubular flaps of skin. Yaaba cuts a lean, stark figure on the gray-blue horizon—she seems the very embodiment of loneliness.

As Bila, Noufou Ouedraogo is lithe and waggish; he moves beautifully and delivers his lines with what seems (the movie is in Moore, so it's hard to say for sure) a trace of mockery. He loves Yaaba, but he's also a bit embarrassed about that love, so he teases her and plays with her—he goes against the picture's sentimental grain.

The other acting is variable, and there's a faint whiff of Afro-European gentility (generally absent in this extraordinary New York Film Festival year). But disliking "Yaaba" would be like spitting on your grandmother or clubbing a baby seal. There's just no call for that kind of behavior.

NEWSDAY, 10/6/89, Part III/p. 5, Mike McGrady

Film festivals can be broadening. You not only see films from Earth's farthest corners, you simultaneously see a picture of how other people live. Films being shown at the New York Film Festival, for example, include one from France ("Monsieur Hire") [see McGrady's review] and another from Burkina Faso ("Yaaba").

And where, you might well ask, is Burkina Faso? First clue, it used to be known as Upper Volta. No help? OK, the easiest way to find Burkina Faso is to head for the Ivory Coast and hang a left.

Perhaps it will come as no surprise to hear that "Yaaba" is the first film ever to make the trip all the way from Burkina Faso (or Upper Volta, for that matter) to the New York Film Festival. It also traveled to Cannes, where earlier this year it walked off with the International Critics' Prize.

Writer-director Idrissa Ouedraogo, shooting in 35mm for the first time, does not use professional actors in his film, possibly because Burkina Faso has no professional actors listed among its nearly 7 million residents. The two young leads happen to be his wife's cousins and the other actors include friends and neighbors. Ouedraogo does not use a script when making a movie because his performers don't understand the concept of a script, and it is much easier, to use the vernacular of our own culture, to wing it.

"Yaaba,"which opens a commercial run today at the Lincoln Art, is the story of two young cousins, a boy and a girl, who befriend an aged outcast, a pariah who lives alone. Although the villagers have rejected the old woman, the youngsters become her protectors. When the girl comes down with tetanus, the old woman brings a healer able to cure her with what is apparently a magic potion.

The film is as simple and basic as the family legend it's based on, and much of its value comes from what it tells us about a different part of the world. What do we learn about Burkina Faso? Well, we can see that it's a tropical savanna, a desert-like plain marked by clumps of vegetation. The conditions for life are, well primitive—the little girls play jacks with pebbles and volunteer firemen combat house fires by carrying clay basins of water to the inferno.

We learn further that in Burkina Faso not all blind beggars are blind, not all new brides are faithful and not all husbands are sober. One more conclusion: The people of Burkina Faso enjoy movies that are slow-moving, primitive, simple and even a bit simplistic.

SIGHT & SOUND, Spring 1990, p. 133, Jill Forbes

It might seem remarkable for Burkina Faso, one of the poorest countries in Africa, to have a film industry, and yet five Burkinabe films were shown at the recent Pan African film festival. And it is not in any way to detract from Idrissa Ouedraogo's *Yaaba* to suggest that it has partly attracted international attention on this score. The other source of *Yaaba*'s appeal, however, is its capacity to evoke universal truths by recounting simple events and so to transcend the confines of village, state or even continent.

The "Yaaba" or grandmother of the title is honorary—"No one has ever called me that before," she says to young Bila who gives her this affectionate nickname. They are not related. Indeed, Yaaba is a village outcast, a wizened, sun-dried old woman who keeps her distance from the cluster of mud huts that form Bila's village and who is widely believed to be a witch of some kind. Ignoring their families' injunctions to stay clear, Bila and his cousin Nopoko strike up a friendship with the old lady which is based on the special empathy that often arises between the very old and the very young. This friendship stands them in good stead when, after a fight with some other children, Nopoko is stabbed with a rusty knife and contracts tetanus. Through Bila's intercession, Yaaba is finally allowed, after other remedies have failed, to introduce her friend the healer to the village and Nopoko is cured.

Of course, part of the fear she inspires is fear of her knowledge, which derives both from her age and her habitation. Hovering just outside the village that excludes her, she is well placed to see the comings and goings others do not see. In particular, the fact that Kougri has become exasperated with her alcoholic husband and has finally succumbed to the advances of Razougou. Everyone knows she owed her husband loyalty, but "we should not judge her," says Yaaba, "she has her reasons." In this way, the old woman becomes an other worldly presence, a serene contrast to the domestic interactions in the village which, though they are observed with considerable affection and humour, are essentially trivial: the women usually retire in mock offence to their huts until they get their own way.

Much of the village business in fact concerns matters of life and death, the arranging of marriages, a wedding party, the fear that Nopoko may die, yet all these things are made relative by Yaaba's distant and somehow timeless overview. The film is structured in such a way as to suggest the cycle of life, death and renewal. It opens and closes with the identical shot of children running away from the camera across the dusty landscape, a shot which at the beginning of the film is followed, and at the end is preceded, by an episode where they tend a grave. The fact that at the end of the film the grave is Yaaba's points not to the end of the life-cycle so much as the end of the narrative, the implication being that there is a resemblance between film-maker and Yaaba that is based on distance or wisdom or both.

This, in turn, introduces another aspect of *Yaaba* which is both worrying and appealing. Ouedraogo's slightly distanced and affectionate view of his compatriots may be explained by the fact that he is already in his mid-thirties (not a beginner, therefore) but, more important, by the long training that took him first to Kiev and later to the IDHEC film school in Paris. Like many other African film-makers—Ousmane Sembène springs to mind—he has benefited from the cultural aid with which France has bolstered her post-imperialist presence in Africa. Furthermore, Ouedraogo was not merely trained in France, but he also raised the money for this film from European, and especially Swiss, sources, something for which he has been strongly criticised by other African film-makers. This has simultaneously ensured adequate distribution for *Yaaba* and allowed it production values acceptable to European cinema and television.

But it has also made the film strangely anachronistic. Watching *Yaaba* is like opening one of Jean de Brunhoff's stories of Babar the Elephant and seeing the colonial experience schematised, sanitised and narrated with affectionate comedy for the amusement of European children. There, as it were, are all the trappings we expect: the oasis, the river to bathe in, the circular houses built from mud, the costumes, the dances, the old lady who is both faith healer and guru. It is the studied innocence, above all, which is part of the charm of both this film and of Babar, lifting them both literally outside time.

There is something both very accomplished and very odd about a capacity to look at one's own country so dispassionately and to adopt the style and manners of an outsider. The literary genre was popular in the eighteenth century and *Yaaba* is a not too distant descendant of it, hence the classicism of its narrative. However, in this case the relationship between looker and looked-at is not neutral, for in order to portray his people thus Ouedraogo has had to adopt the coloniser's point of view.

Are we therefore to assimilate the film-maker and the wise old woman, as the film implies, making the observer's point of view one of knowledge to which the youngsters aspire? Conversely, do we consider that the African film-maker has a particularly contradictory role to play in attempting to valorise the simple and the universal by means of the most sophisticated of tools? Looked at in this way *Yaaba* becomes an even more fascinating film, both a moving and accomplished narrative of life in a poor African village and a poignant image of modernisation.

VILLAGE VOICE, 10/10/89, p. 90, Georgia Brown

Manhood is a rocky road in Idrissa Ouedraogo's *Yaaba*. Or rather a dry and dusty one. The parched savannah of Burkina Faso (until 1984 called Upper Volta) is the setting for this spare coming-of-age tale, which opens and closes on a lyrical image of a boy chasing a girl across the desert. Women seem to be in possession of deeper secrets than men. Men improvise and play catch-up.

To catch the girl Nopoko, Bila shrewdly takes up with a bald crone who wears only a long skirt and glides around the brush outside his village. Significantly, Nopoko first uses the old woman to find Bila in a hide-and-seek game, and Bila appropriates her, calls her *Yaaba* (grandmother), as if he intuits her special powers. The villagers call her a witch, but she turns out simply to have uncommon sense. Bila watches the village men have trouble keeping women and probably realizes that he can use more help than they can offer.

Ouedraogo, who trained at IDHEC in Paris, films with nonprofessional actors—both 12-year-old bright-eyes are his wife's cousins—and in the Mooré dialect of his native village. He points out that Burkina Faso has over 40 dialects, and "if you want your films to be understood, they must be very expressive and visual. No dialogue, no commentary, just mise-en-scène." Language in *Yaaba* functions musically, complementing the lively score. Repeating the addressed person's name at the beginning of sentences seems to be the custom, but it also keeps up a kind of rhythmic punctuation. In *Yaaba*, Ouedraogo stays with simple, elemental materials, composing out of daily life and textures, such as sand, clay, and skin, the wrinkled and the unwrinkled.

Also reviewed in:
NEW REPUBLIC, 11/13/89, p. 23, Stanley Kauffmann
NEW YORK TIMES, 10/4/89, p. C18, Janet Maslin
VARIETY, 5/17–23/89, p. 39
WASHINGTON POST, 1/26/90, p. B7, Hal Hinson

YOUNG EINSTEIN

A Warner Bros. release of a Serious Productions film. *Executive Producer:* Graham Burke and Ray Beattie. *Producer:* Yahoo Serious, Warwick Ross, and David Roach. *Director:* Yahoo Serious. *Screenplay:* Yahoo Serious and David Roach. *Director of Photography:* Jeff Darling. *Editor:* Yahoo Serious. *Music:* William Motzig, Martin Armiger, and Tommy Tycho. *Music Editor:* David Roach. *Sound:* Geoff Grist, Max Hensser, Paul Brincat, and (music) Robin Gray, Mike Stavrou, and Nick Launay. *Sound Editor:* Annie Breslin and Ashley Grenville. *Art Director:* Steve Marr, Laurie Faen, Colin Gibson, and Ron Highfield. *Special Effects:* Patrick Fitzgerald, Steve Courtley, Laurie Faen, and Pauline Grebert. *Costumes:* Susan Bowden. *Make-up:* Sherry Hubbard, Robin Pickering, Angela Conti, and Wendy Sainsbury. *Stunt Coordinator:* Yahoo Serious. *Running time:* 90 minutes. *MPAA Rating:* PG.

Cast: Yahoo Serious (Albert Einstein); Odile Le Clezio (Marie Curie); John Howard (Preston Preston); Peewee Wilson (Mr. Einstein); Su Cruickshank (Mrs. Einstein); Lulu Pinkus (The Blonde); Kaarin Fairfax (Brunette); Michael Lake (Manager); Jonathan Coleman (Wolfgang Bavarian); Johnny McCall (Rudy Bavarian); Michael Blaxland (Desk Clerk); Ray Fogo (Bright Clerk); Terry Pead and Alice Pead (Inventor Couple); Frank McDonald (Nihilist); Tony Harvey (Bursar); Tim Elliot (Lecturer); Ray Winslade (Droving Student); Ian "Danno" Rogerson (Randy Student); Wendy De Waal (Prudish Student); P.J. Voeten (Chinese Student); Warren Coleman (Lunatic Professor); Glenn Butcher (Ernest Rutherford); Steve Abbott (Brian Asprin); Russell Cheek (Nurse); Warwick Irwin (Gate Guard); Keith Heygate (Scientists's Guard); Roger Ward (Cat Pie Cook); Michael Matou and Ted Reid (Asylum Guards); Martin Raphael (Crazed Lunatic); Max Meldrum (Mr. Curie); Rose Jackson (Mrs. Curie); Basil Clarke (Charles Darwin); Adam Bowen (Marconi); Esben Strom (Wilbur Wright); Tim McKew (Sigmund Freud); Phillipa Baker (Freud's Mother); Geoff Aldridge and Hugh Wayland (Lumière Brothers); Ian James Tait (Thomas Edison); Aku Kadogo (African Lady); Margot Ross (Emotional Mother); Madeleine Ross (Baby Scientist); Nick Conroy (Clark Gable); Michael Shirley (Admiral Shackleton); Ollie Hall and Christian Manon (Darwin's Bodyguards); John Even Hughes (Drunk); Johnny McCall (Tasmanian Devil); Megan Shapcott, Inge Burke, and Georgie Parker (Country Girl Fans); David Ngoom (Aboriginal Dancer); Wick Wilson (News Cameraman); David Roach and Colin Gibson (Country Yokels).

FILMS IN REVIEW, 12/89, p. 621, Janet Halverson

A film clip used in the TV Commercial portrays young Albert as a hayseed Harpo lookalike sitting in a tin washtub on his front porch. His knees poke out and he grimaces with concentration as he fiddles on his viola. He stops to remove some dishes from their communal bath as his parents (Su Cruickshank, Peewee Wilson) look on benignly. The porch overlooks the verdant, dramatically steep hills of Tasmania, where they are apple growers. A viola string snaps and Albert considers it.

This imagery didn't move masses of moviegoers into U.S. theaters. It seemed to borrow from its betters: Harpo, L'il Abner, Amadeus at his most tiresome; fission hairdos right out of William Blake. Why was this dud a superhit Down Under?

Yahoo Serious, writer, actor (young Albert), director and producer, tells an unorthodox version of Einstein's early life. In 1905 the wild-haired office clerk challenges common sense with his Theory of Relativity. He has left home to go to Sydney to patent $E = mc^2$, which came to him while devising a way to force bubbles into his father's home-brewed beer. In 1906 he transforms his viola into the first electric guitar and invents rock 'n' roll music.

On his way to Sydney, an epic journey which reveals the variety and beauty of the Australian landscape, Albert falls for brilliant, beautiful, plucky Marie Curie (Odile Le Clezio), a young French (!) scientist, who returns his love. (She's nothing like the young Pole Greer Garson beatified years ago, though just as smart and good. On the same train ride Albert meets archvillain Preston Preston (John Howard), who runs the patent office in Sydney, and who will scheme to steal Albert's Theory.

After consignment to an insane asylum, which keeps all the bright and original thinkers out of trouble, Albert escapes in time to get to Paris to save an international convention of scientists from perishing at the detonation of the first atomic bomb. (Preston has accidentally created it in an attempt to build a beer-brewing device from plans he stole from Albert.)

Young Einstein has a broad and hyperactive cartoonlike quality. It is populated by endearing furry and feathered and scaly creatures with whom Albert relates amiably. And there are wonderful human characters, lots of adventure, colorful Edwardian sets and costumes and some food for thought about the meaning of it all. Possibly there is one kitchen sink too many, though not the one stacked ozone-layer high with applecore-laden plates.

A kindly, lively, funny picture, *Young Einstein* deserved a better chance.

LOS ANGELES TIMES, 8/4/89, Calendar/p. 13, Chris Willman

This summer, moviegoers get to choose between two explanations of the origin of rock 'n' roll. In "Great Balls of Fire," Jerry Lee Lewis peers into the black heart of the night and finds sin, sex rhythm and boogie-woogie. Then there's the revisionist view of "Young Einstein," in which rock springs forth full blown as the instant result of a white man's scientific formula.

To a generation of kids who've grown up on research-driven radio hits and formulaic music videos, it's understandable that the latter genesis will probably seem like the true one.

"Young Einstein" comes to America as the last stop on a world-domination whistle-stop tour, having already proven a surprise smash hit in most of the Earth's cinematic territories—especially its country of origin, Australia, where it broke all box-office records. And, frankly, its unrepentant goofiness may make you a little afraid for—or of—these countries.

Can anyone who worried about the mental health of France after that whole Jerry Lewis medal business fail to be deeply alarmed over the popular deification of director/writer/star Yahoo Serious in the lands Down Under?

The Lewis connection is a real one, thanks to Serious' characterization of his title genius as a bumbler who falls out of windows while putting on his pants. (His grown-up sexlessness may also remind you of Pee-wee Herman.) The legend of Albert Einstein's feeble school record and apparent absent-mindedness are no doubt what inspired Serious to conceive an entire movie in which the budding scientist stumbles into brilliant discoveries by happenstance and accident. Young Al is so naive he doesn't know his cheap hotel is actually a brothel. He can't conceive that his atom-splitting inventions might ever be used for evil purposes. Oh yes, he also invents surfing *and* rock, which, for this picture's target audience, are far more significant achievements than any old theory of relativity.

For any number of reasons, "Young Einstein" just may be the best movie of the summer for the young'uns. Neither Grail water nor battery acid causes anyone's face to melt and, moreover, it has a genuine sweetness rarely found even in pre-teen-oriented pix.

It could serve as a sort of healing salve for outcast kids with its lesson that even if your hair is unkempt, you can't keep a job, you're bumbling, gangly and shy and everyone laughs at your ideas, you may still turn out to be the greatest mind of your generation and drive the girls wild to boot. There are less healthy morals for kids in this year's PG collection, to be sure.

Adults may have more of a problem, not so much for the ludicrous bending of history as much as the unerring silliness of so many time-worn gags. In Serious' scenario, Einstein's theories eventually land him in a lunatic asylum, where his girlfriend, Marie Curie (Odile Le Clezio), comes to visit him dressed as a man. When they kiss, in the oldest drag gag known to man or "Yentl," the fellow inmates look on in homophobic horror. And the dialogue never gets much beyond the level of: "Science, eh? I'm keenly interested." "Pleased to meet you, Keenly!"

Serious fares far better as a first-time director who knows better than to place too much time or weight on any one gag. "Einstein" has a handsome period look, even when director of photography Jeff Darling is shooting the musical montages that periodically break up the action. The pop-song choices include savvy picks from the catalogs of such fine Aussie outfits as the Models, the Lime Spider, Big Pig and Paul Kelly, and one of the picture's loopiest, best moments has Serious spontaneously breaking into dance alongside a troop of Hare Krishnas to the tune of the Saints' sprightly "The Music Goes Round My Head."

If Serious only used rock as incongruous source music instead of a subject, he wouldn't get into so much trouble. It may not be too grouchy to complain that movies like this and "Back to the Future" steer close to racism when they lightheartedly try to steal the origins of rock away from the ethnic forces that shaped it. (Serious does include a shot of a bushman playing a pipe while he sings the line about "my man a-wailin' sax" in the climactic version of Chuck Berry's "Rock 'n' Roll Music," which, if meant as his nod to black culture, is a pretty insensitive one.)

However, it's just about impossible to dislike a movie in which examples of the hero's pacifism include his risking his life to save kitties from being baked to death inside a pie. And even through his abundance of bad jokes, Serious manages to rack up more good will than bad, as a deadpan comic actor whose voice seems to be evolving into puberty with each line reading. Perhaps it's wrong to expect more out of what is essentially a children's film; the title is, after all, "Young Einstein," not "Thirtysomething Einstein." Still, grown-ups may wish the level of sophistication here were more Monty Python and less Monkees, more *yahoo* and less *yikes*.

MONTHLY FILM BULLETIN, 10/89, p. 313, Kim Newman

Tasmania, 1905. Albert Einstein, the eccentric offspring of an apple farmer, is asked by his father to come up with a way of putting bubbles in beer. Formulating a theory of relativity and splitting a beer atom, he produces a great explosion and, as a side effect, succeeds in putting a head on the local flat brew. He departs for Sydney to patent his formula, and along the way meets Marie Curie, a Nobel prize-winning physicist, and Preston Preston, a slimy scientific entrepreneur. In Sydney, Einstein moves into a hotel on Lonely Street and is snubbed by the patents office, which Preston runs. Meanwhile, Preston takes his formula to a firm of Bavarian beer brewers and puts it into action. Einstein and Marie fall in love, and she gets him a position in the patents office from which Preston fires him. Einstein passes the time by inventing the surfboard and the electric guitar, and Preston arranges for him to be incarcerated in an insane asylum. Preston builds a gigantic atomic beer barrel which Marie tells him is dangerous. When Einstein refuses to do anything to prevent this, Marie leaves for Europe, accusing him of being a man of thought not action. Einstein escapes from the asylum and travels to Paris, where Preston is unveiling his barrel to Charles Darwin at the 1906 Science Academy Awards. Picking up Marie along the way, Einstein arrives just as the barrel is going critical and threatening to explode. He plugs in his electric guitar and defuses the energy in the barrel by playing rock 'n' roll music. Later, Einstein and Marie return in triumph to Tasmania.

After *Crocodile Dundee*, *Young Einstein* has proved domestically to be the most successful Australian comedy of all time. If Paul Hogan's brain child became an international success thanks to some discreet pruning and a studied air of affable blandness, it is hard to imagine Yahoo Serious' spikier, sillier, more enervating project repeating the trick. Serious' Einstein is a frizzy-haired, knock-kneed loon in shorts who divides his time between physics theorems and rock 'n' roll, all the while strenuously trying to win over an audience with his winsome whining. It is obvious that Serious aspires to be a comic creation like Paul Reubens' Pee-wee Herman, and to that extent surrounds himself with trusty sidekicks like his stout-hearted parents, the denizens of Lonely Street and various distinguished scientists (Edison, Marconi, Rutherford, the Wright Brothers, etc.) in the asylum and at the Science Academy Awards, not to mention paraphernalia like his makeshift electric guitar, the ever-present apples, a surfboard hewn from a log, a pocket-filling compass, a cockatoo and a scrap of paper with the Theory of Relativity scrawled on it. The film, however, misfires on every cod-scientific cylinder, emerging as something akin to the mod Victorian farragoes of the late 60s (*The Best House in London*, *The Assassination Bureau*) in its mix of sloppy farce, period name-dropping (Darwin comes accompanied by a beagle, and the awards ceremony is being filmed by two stereotypical Frenchmen, the Lumière brothers) and eyeball-rolling obviousness. Amid the mess, one or two jokes—the preparation of a kitten pie in the asylum, a cameo appearance by a Warner Bros.-style Tasmanian Devil—work, but most of the gags fall flat. When Einstein announces that he intends to turn his formulae over to the governments of the world and Marie protests that they might use them to create atomic weapons, the hero ingenuously grins and says, "If you can't trust the governments of the world, then who can you trust?" This doggy, rather smug benevolence runs throughout *Young Einstein* which, for all its studied and very tiresome whackiness, is completely without sex, violence or drug abuse. The result is a film which manages to be innocuous and appalling at the same time.

NEW YORK POST, 8/4/89, P. 23, Jami Bernard

Picture Albert Einstein as a young man, socially awkward, famous hair askew but not yet gray, using—what was it, 10 percent of his brain?—to discover the Theory of Relativity and other scientific truths on a lark. That is the promising premise of "Young Einstein," a juvenile comedy that uses just 10 percent of its potential.

In this movie's scheme of fractured history, young Albert is a Tasmanian apple farmer's son whose first discovery of note is how to put bubbles in brew by splitting the beer atom. He goes on to surf his way to the wave-particle theory of light, and electrifies his viola to stun the outback with a new type of music he dubs "roll 'n' rock."

When some kill-joy complains that Einstein's famous equation (which everyone pronounces as "em") is "an affront to common sense," the inventor is nonplused. "That's relativity!" he shrugs cheerfully.

As portrayed by the physically agile Australian comic actor Yahoo Serious—he adopted the dopey name and evidently thinks of it as a goof on society, but there's something obnoxious about it, like the kid who wants too much to be noticed—Albert is a gangly magnet for pratfalls and misunderstandings, his fair standing on end like one of those science projects for static electricity, his clothes baggy and clownish in a way that really gets preschoolers going.

The movie has been a sensation in its native Australia, but despite America's hunger for shrimp-on-the-barbie films for Down Under, this one fails to translate. Serious has an underlying earnestness that shows he is serious about comedy, but hard work does not necessarily yield belly laughs. When Einstein splits the beer atom, the outhouse cum laboratory goes kaboom, and Albert appears in smoking black-face with his first frothy brew—that's the kind of physical humor that swings the boy genius from one misadventure to the next.

"I'm keenly interested," says a lunatic asylum inmate, one of the few people to respond to Einstein's theories. "Pleased to meet you, Keenly," says Serious in the kind of dull joke that may have once upon a time touched off his own name-change.

A would-be auteur, Serious wrote, directed, produced, starred and did many of his own stunts, Buster Keaton-style. But the wild-eyed actor is an acquired taste, much like the first bubbly beer must have been. Serious acts largely with his hair, bobbing it about his thin, earnest face, making this Albert Einstein an idiot savant who stumbles upon Big Truths while munching apples, happily ignorant of the world around him.

The quixotic, peripatetic plot pits the conventional (bad guy steals formula to start his own brewery) against the unconventional (Einstein has a romantic meeting of the minds with Marie Curie). Like "Insignificance," where Marilyn Monroe trades ideas with Einstein for an afternoon, "Young Einstein" creates such what-if situations as a Paris science expo that gathers all the great minds of the turn of the century in one room. Once there, they don't exchange ideas after all; even "Bill & Ted's Excellent Adventure" attempted to show some interaction among its historical figures.

Serious plays fast and loose with history—crediting Einstein with one of Newton's theories, for instance (if high school science serves me correctly)—which frees him up for lunacy. Unfortunately, it is not an inspired lunacy. The stunts, like falling backward out a window, are done in a workmanlike but not terribly hilarious way.

Many of the sight gags have been seen before—knitting a woolen sweater right off a sheep's back, crashing through a roof into a newly risen cake, etc. With no less than Einstein as an inspiration for a movie, surely the result should be a little more imaginative? The only laugh I recall is when the French Nobel laureate leaves behind only a croissant by which to be remembered. (Marie Curie, played by Odile Le Clezio, is Nobel-caliber window dressing, exclaiming *"C'est incroyable"* at everything.)

The last thing the film does is prove the Big Bang theory—which is that most movies don't feel they're on solid footing unless they wrap up with a big-bang finish. Even with its cerebral subject, "Young Einstein" is not a comedy of ideas, but of pratfalls.

NEWSDAY, 8/4/89, part III/p. 3, Mike McGrady

In its native Australia, "Young Einstein" opened to a bigger box office than "Raiders of the Lost Ark" or "Rambo." It drew longer lines than "Ghostbusters" or "Star Wars." It is, at this writing, the fourth-largest Down Under movie hit of all time. Although this is a phenomenon that surpasses all human understanding, this much can be said with some certainty: Those hordes of ticket buyers were not there out of any great love of history.

Writer-director-producer-star Yahoo Serious (not his original name) plays a young Albert Einstein (not his original life) who is here seen as a boy on the island of Tasmania. Young Einstein has what would seem to be a gift for science, and simple everyday occurrences are apt to trigger this kind of idle musing: "For every action there is an opposite and equal reaction."

Young Einstein's dad, an apple grower, does not particularly understand his wild-haired son's gift for invention or, for that matter, much about the world of science.

"So, see, Dad," Albert says, "I want to be a physicist."

"What do they grow?" the father asks with charming rural innocence.

The father's idea of a worthwhile invention would be something to add bubbles to the flat beers of that era. In trying to please his father, Al comes up with the formula: "$E = mc^2$" And what is that? "The formula for splitting beer atoms."

There is enough such silliness to qualify "Young Einstein" as a Pee-wee Herman movie without

Pee-wee Herman, which is not altogether a bad idea. It also includes a romance with a sexy young Marie Curie (Odile Le Clezio). While strolling with her beside the Australian seashore, young Albert has another of his insights. "If only time could stand still," he murmurs romantically. Then: "That's it! The theory of relativity!"

"Did you just think of that?" she asks, in naked admiration.

"Yes."

The greatest discoveries of this century come to Albert in the most modest of circumstances. In dashing off a letter home, he's apt to add this kind of postscript: "P.S. I think I've just discovered the key to the universe."

Whether one is responsive to this kind of humor or not depends on many diverse factors— factors such as one's education, background, intellect, cultural attainment, level of inebriation and so forth. At one point in the film—Sigmund Freud's strict mother slaps down her son's hand with a stern, "Don't pick your nose!"—I laughed. That was the only time. But then I don't laugh much at Pee-wee Herman movies either.

In truth, the historical inaccuracies didn't bother me all that much. With just one exception. If Yahoo Serious decides to credit Einstein with inventing the electric guitar, that's OK with me. I can even accept the thought of him whittling a log down into the world's first surfboard. Only at one point does Serious overstep all bounds of propriety—that's when he credits Einstein with inventing a new form of music. The great scientist deeply regretted his role in the development of the A-bomb; how on earth might he feel about inventing rock and roll as well?

VILLAGE VOICE, 8/15/89, P. 69, J. Hoberman

Humor being relative, each culture has its own unexportable film comics. Germans worship Otto Waalkes, Japanese swear by the eternal Tora-san, Brits used to revel in the dread "Carry On" ensemble, Italians—and *Cahiers du Cinéma*—are knocked out by Nanni Moretti. (Our current example is Ernest, or maybe Chevy Chase.) The Australians, as you're doubtless aware, are wild for Yahoo Serious—a knock-kneed, wide-eyed, open-mouthed dude with a coiffure like a sunburst and an utter willingness to prance about on camera, thrashing along with some recycled Chuck Berry, or just snapping his suspenders on the beat. The joke is that, in *Young Einstein* at least, this latest superhero from the land of Mad Max, Paul Cox, and Crocodile Dundee, is supposed to be a titan of intellect.

According to *Variety, Young Einstein*—which Serious cowrote, directed, and starred in (introducing himself, bowl on head, in the process of creating his electroshock hairdo) is the fourth largest grossing movie in Australian history, right behind *Crocs I* and *II*, and *E.T.*, and Serious is something of a culture hero (an Australian *Time* cover boy, an Australian *60 Minutes* autointerview). Five years in the making, *Young Einstein* was originally completed in mid-1986 and consequently received four nominations for the Australian Film Awards (screenplay, music, sound, and cinematography). Afterwards, a decision was made to reedit and reshoot the film (supplying a more upbeat ending, natch), Warner Bros. coming on the scene as international distributor.

Who will ever forget the moment in *Close Encounters* when an awestruck scientist reverently theorizes that Albert Einstein was "one of them" (i.e., came from outer space)? Still, the joke that an innocent rube from the isle of Tasmania (a primordial landscape that may be something like Australia's Australia) is the world's greatest genius (and $E = mc^2$ a formula for putting bubbles in beer) will only carry Yahoo Serious so far. *Young Einstein* is mainly a mixture of wacky stunts and corny sight gags (in order to learn physics, Young Einstein catapults himself into the stratosphere). But just as the 18th century Jewish sage known as the Gaon of Vilna supposedly came up with calculus while sitting on the crapper, the Tasmanian genius invents rock'n'roll in his spare time. Unable to patent his brewing technique or theory of relativity, he moves into a hotel on Lonely Street and, idly watching some kiddies play hopscotch, is inspired to lay down a few chords on his electrified viola. While he's at it, he carves the first surfboard too, hoping to impress his girlfriend Marie Curie.

A semi-pert Diane to Young Einstein's beanpole Woody, Mme. Curie (Odile Le Clezio) shows great underwear and a boundless appreciation for our hero. *Young Einstein* turns unexpectedly sweet when the pair start waxing enthusiastic about black holes and subatomic particles. (Their conversation suggests the dialogue in Roberto Rossellini's austere, deadpan biopics of Socrates or

Blaise Pascal.) For the most part, however, *Young Einstein*'s nonslapstick wit is strictly sub-*Rocky and Bullwinkle*: Low as most of the humor is, you need a modicum of quiz show background to appreciate Marconi's dialect broadcast of the 1906 Science Academy Awards at which Charles Darwin arrives with the Beagle in tow (arf!).

The fact is, Yahoo does take himself seriously. "I embraced that Marcel Duchamp-Andy Warhol ethic [sic] that art is what one decides it shall be," he told *The New York Times* of his early art school career. Then inspiration struck: "Here's this wonderful collusion of painting, music, literature, acting, theater and photography in this really young art form called movies." (It's sure not as young as it used be but, hey, maybe that's just me.) As innocent in his way as his trailblazing alter-ego, Serious recalled being "surprised to discover that film was in fact a language."

You may be nearly as surprised to discover that *Young Einstein* has a political agenda. Not only is Yahoo's outfit a late '60s mishmash—with a garish cacaphony of paisleys, checks and stripes amplifying his frizzed-out electric 'fro—so is his thinking. After the film's villainous bureaucrat Preston Preston (John Howard) has Young E committed to a mental hospital, the inmates inform him that his formula is actually a blueprint for universal destruction. At the screening I attended, judiciously padded by the film's publicist with at least a dozen high school kids, this information provoked yawns, while Yahoo's ostentatious squelch, "If you can't trust the governments of the world, who can you trust?" fell flat on the floor and lay there accusingly for the rest of the flick.

Serious fun to be sure. *Young Einstein* is even well shot—too much so for my taste. (Given its dopey, knockabout humor, this movie really should be shoddier.) The look is as anonymous as its protagonist's is individualized. The fact is, a predilection for the funky chicken aside, Serious has no stylistic tics. His greatest quirk is a fondness for light classic music, scoring a scene of his mother knitting a sheep to something like Grieg's "Peer Gynt" suite. Little bugs and creatures are ubiquitous here; every other scene has an animal tethered to it—a kangaroo grazing on campus, an apple orchard invaded by a Tasmanian Devil.

It's impossible to dismiss a movie in which some clown defuses an atomic bomb while doing Chuck Berry splits in Tasmanian lederhosen. Still, you only have to compare the vaudeville in *Young Einstein* to that of the Quad's current midnight offering, *Tales of the Gimli Hospital*, to see the difference between Yahoo's would-be wack-o-rama and a genuinely eccentric film sensibility.

Also reviewed in:
NEW YORK TIMES, 8/4/89, p. C13, Caryn James
VARIETY, 10/12/88, p. 18
WASHINGTON POST, 8/4/89, p. B1, Rita Kempley

ZOU ZOU

A Kino International release. *Executive Producer:* Arys Nissotti. *Director:* Marc Allégret. *Screenplay (French with English subtitles):* Pepito Abatino. *Adaptation:* Carlo Rim. *Director of Photography:* Michel Kelber, Louis Née, Boris Kaufman, and Jacques Mercanton. *Music:* Vincent Scotto, Georges Van Parys, and Al Romanis. *Sound:* Antoine Archimbeaud. *Set Designer:* Lazare Meerson. *Running time:* 92 minutes. *MPAA Rating:* Not Rated.

CAST: Josephine Baker (Zou Zou); Jean Gabin (Jean); Yvette Lebon (Claire): Pierre Larquey (Old Mélé); Illa Meery (Miss Barbara, the Leading Lady): Teddy Michaud (Julot); Madeleine Guitty and Marcel Vallée (M. Trompe); Andree Wendler and Serge Grave (Baby Jean).

NEW YORK POST, 2/10/89, p. 19, Jerry Tallmer

Oh my, for a little girl from the slums of St. Louis, she sure had the world by the tail. By 1927, shaking her bananas in the Folies Bergère, walking her leopard on a leash down the Champs Elysées, she had received 40,000 love letters, 2,000 of them proposing marriage.

Her name was Josephine Baker. America never quite dug her—not to the extent that Paris did, and Europe.

When she was 60 or thereabouts, I saw her singing, dancing, wisecracking, preening herself, on a Broadway stage. "I suppose you want to know where we came from," she told her audience as she patted her tummy, her flanks, her etc. "We came from Christian Dior of Paris, of course." "Astonishing," I wrote, "Astonishing isn't in it."

For those who were perhaps not yet born for that even, or who missed the 1987 Arts & Entertainment documentary, here is a second chance. For two weeks starting today, Film Forum 2 on Watts Street is offering a double-bill of Josephine Baker in two of her best movies, "Zou Zou" (1934) and "Princess Tam Tam" (1935), in new 35-mm prints newly subtitled.

The 7:10 p.m. screening of "Princess Tam Tam" will be introduced by Jean-Claude Baker, proprietor of Chez Josephine, a restaurant on 43nd Street's Theater Row named for his mother's nightclub on the Rue Pigalle. Jean-Claude is No. 4 of her 11 adopted children from eight different national backgrounds.

Both these films are semi-autobiographical.

In "Zou Zou," directed by Marc. Allégret (the year after he'd directed Raimu & Co. in Pagnol's "Fanny"), a 28-year-old Josephine Baker plays a poor laundress who carries the torch for her half-brother, played by the great Jean Gabin. She works her way up in music halls and becomes the toast of Paris.

Much like Josephine herself, who had mugged her way into prominence in the chorus of Noble Sissle's "Shuffle Along" while still in her teens. And who, according to Film Forum programmer Bruce Goldstein, had a half-brother in real life she was crazy about.

"Princess Tam Tam," directed by Edmond Greville, opens with a novelist played by Albert Prejean having a fight with his wife. "We'll go to Africa," he says. The picture cuts to Tunisia, and there's Josephine, barefoot, a peasant, stealing something. The novelist takes her back to Paris, makes her a lady—the Pygmalion story—which, again, for that little girl from the slums of St. Louis, wasn't too far off the mark.

But to sketch the foregoing is to omit everything that counts, *i.e.*, Josephine herself. Listen to Donald Bogle in his "Brown Sugar" (Harmony Books), a look back at America's black female superstars:

"Baker—with her daring (she was going topless long before it was fashionable), her imagination, her outlandish costumes, her gorgeous chocolate shoulders—was a one-woman extravaganza, the most shameless assertive form of self-pride any audience, black or white, had ever seen.

"Throughout the Twenties she toured the great European capitals—Berlin, Budapest, Amsterdam, London, Madrid—and epitomized the new freedom and festivity with a hint of decadence always just beneath the surface. And before anyone knew it, she had taken America's flapper spirit to new heights and in an unexpected direction."

Film Forum's Goldstein: "In an era when most black women in films were doing maids and mammies, these pictures were vehicles, designed for "La Bakairr." Her name comes on before the title of the movie, and you get goose pimples. It's like Clark Gable in "Gone With the Wind." The occasion for this run is Black History Month, but I didn't need that. I would have done it any month.

NEWSDAY, 2/10/89, Part III/p. 5, Bruce Eder

[*Zou Zou* was reviewed jointly with *Princess Tam Tam;* see Eder's review of that film.]

VILLAGE VOICE, 2/14/89, p. 64, Amy Taubin

[*Zou Zou* was reviewed jointly with *Princess Tam Tam*; see Taubin's review of that film.]

Also reviewed in:
NEW YORK TIMES, 2/10/89, p. C13, Vincent Canby

ADDENDUM

The following reviews arrived too late to be included in previous issues of FILM REVIEW ANNUAL. The issues of FILM REVIEW ANNUAL in which the credits and film reviews appear are given in parenthesis after the name of the film.

ALIENS *(Film Review Annual, 1987)*

JUMP CUT, No. 35, 4/90, p. 85, Christine Anne Holmlund

[*Aliens* was reviewed jointly with *Down and Out in Beverly Hills;* see Holmlund's review in this Addendum.]

BLACK RAIN (JAPAN) *(Film Review Annual, 1990)*

NEW STATESMAN & SOCIETY, 7/6/90, p. 36, Suzanne Moore

Shohei Imamura's film Black Rain may share a name with Ridley Scott's racist thriller but it couldn't be more different. The black rain of the title refers to the deadly radioactive substance that fell from the clouds following the bombing of Hiroshima. While Scott uses this to superficially explain anti-American feeling among the Japanese, by the end of the film you realise that it's actually a device to sanction aggressive anti-Japanese feeling. Imamura's film, on the other hand, simply charts the after-effects of the bomb.

Shot in timeless black and white, the film focuses on Yasuko and her family, who are caught up in those terrible events of August 1945. She and her aunt and uncle survive, though she is caught in the black rain. They trudge through what was once Hiroshima, surrounded by the dying—their skin hanging off them like tattered clothes.

Next time we see Yasuko it is five years later and she has reached marrying age. Yet one potential groom after another drops her as soon as they find out she was in Hiroshima. She has become an untouchable. Even the medical certificate that her uncle obtains for her means nothing.

Imamura is at his best in dealing with the total powerlessness and incomprehension of this "community bound by the bomb". Even as the tumours start to appear the local people believe that fresh carp blood will keep them healthy. But as the film moves slowly and inevitably to its terrible conclusion, the stoicism of Yasuko and her family starts to become wearing.

There is no anger in this film, only a kind of martyrdom. The women are particularly long-suffering, though Imamura is known for his attempts to break down the stereotyped portrayal of Japanese women.

Everything is coated in a dull humanism which becomes numbing. Though *Black Rain* reminds us of just how wrong the bombing of Hiroshima was—and who now thinks otherwise?—it ignores the specifics of the situation. As awful as it was, this wasn't an event that happened outside of history but from its very centre. Japan was at war; the imperialist rampages visited on China and Korea are nowhere mentioned here. For many of its victims the bomb indeed did come out of the blue. But surely if we are to prevent such an atrocity occurring again we have to understand how it happened. Moral condemnation alone is about as effective as the rickety umbrellas that the peasants used to shield themselves from the fall-out.

CANDY MOUNTAIN *(Film Review Annual, 1989)*

MONTHLY FILM BULLETIN, 1/90, p. 10, Tom Milne

Julius, a musician more ambitious than talented, sees a chance of boosting his dream of launching his own group when he overhears rock star Keith Burns and his business associates talking about Elmore Silk, a fabled guitar-maker who dropped out and disappeared, and whose guitars (if he has continued working) would be priceless. Never having heard of Elmore but assuring Keith that he's an old friend, Julius negotiates a $2,000 advance, with another thousand to come if he finds Elmore. Ditched by his long-suffering girlfriend Darlene, who drives off in "his" car (which she paid for), Julius hitches a ride from a van driver (who sticks him for $50) to the home of Elmore's brother Al. A wealthy, world-weary musician, Al treats him to a night of drunken harangues before pointing him in the direction of Elmore's daughter Alice. Driving a T-Bird sold to him by Al for $1,000 as part of the deal, Julius finds Alice living near Niagara Falls in a trailer park with her quarrelsome husband Henry, an out-of-work, wheelchair-bound musician, and their unhappy daughter. In return for Elmore's address, Julius is forced to swap the T-Bird for an old VW van, which breaks down as he heads into Canada. On payment of $175, a garage man trades him an ancient Chevy, which he runs into a parked boat somewhere in the Canadian wilds. Claiming that he was trespassing, Archie (the local JP) and his son Huey (the constable) jail him under the impression that he is a bounty hunter. Finally allowed to proceed, minus Chevy and $100 (all he claims to have left), Julius hitches a ride to the address given by Alice, to find a lonely Frenchwoman, Cornelia, looking after her dying mother. The ever-restless Elmore, she explains moved on after living with her for a while. Inviting Julius to share her bed that night, Cornelia secures him a lift the next day in a school bus going to the small seaboard town where Elmore may still be. At the address, Julius finds a room full of new guitars, and eventually meets Elmore, who—juggling two women and evidently about to move on—merely smiles as Julius explains his quest. Unaware that Elmore has made a deal with the Japanese—in return for a substantial monthly payment for life, he has contracted to supply twelve guitars, destroy the rest, and make no more—Julius watches in bafflement as Elmore consigns his priceless guitars to the bonfire. Gloomily, Julius sets off to hitchhike home.

"Life ain't no candy mountain", says the kindly van driver who offers Candide/Julius his first lift down the road, a cracker-barrel sage who demonstrates the truth of his own dictum that you have to take the rough with the smooth by suddenly demanding a $50 reward for his act of charity. This, in other words, is another trip down the well-worn road-movie trail where disillusionment for dreams and aspirations lies in wait just over the rainbow.

Though handled throughout with the off-beat, eccentric eye one associates with both Robert Frank and Rudy Wurlitzer (we first meet Julius trying to reclaim his guitar from a uniformed security cop, who comes on like a ferocious mugger in defending his borrowed treasure at gunpoint), it looks as though *Candy Mountain* is going to settle for the usual cautionary tale about fame, fortune and the bleak vistas of the world of pop. Julius' first two encounters, with Elmore Silk's brother and son-in-law, musicians both, are certainly pointed enough: one a star left high and dry on a pinnacle of achievement (a wonderfully acerbic portrait of aimless disenchantment from Tom Waits), rattling around like a wayward pinball in the luxurious wastes of his home, trying to sidetrack his boredom with drink and golf on the lawn; the other a loser, his wheelchair equally haphazardly driven by raging resentments at the riches which are giving his trailer-park junkyard the go-by.

Crucial to Julius' odyssey, however, is his laconically inconsequential encounter, on a lonely, snowy road somewhere across the Canadian border, with a very old man, out for a constitutional and glad of a lift for the rest of his short way home. His tranquil presence and patriarchal mien, complete to the white fringe whiskers of Victorian days, might suggest a symbol of stability, of roots sent down deep and firm into the earth over which Julius is drifting. The patriarchal aspect is rather knocked on the head when Julius makes conversation by asking if he has any children. "Nope", the old man grins, "Not as yet..." Instead, oddly, he sets one dreaming of the world of Herman Melville, and one would scarcely be surprised to hear him say, "Call me Ishmael", or launch into one of Father Mapple's sermons.

Irrelevant to the action, over in a minute or two, this sequence nevertheless adds a dimension to the film: not precisely a sense of the past, but a shift away from the present into a kind of timelessness of *other* values. And look back from it, one begins to see in a different light some, at least, of the rip-offs to which Julius has been subjected. The garage man who settles for $175 when Julius (lying) pleads that the asking price of $200 is all the money he has, is probably moved by a spirit of generosity; so too, perhaps—who knows?—is Al Silk in capriciously selling him a car surely worth more than the $1,000 he asks for out of the $2,000 Julius confesses to having. From this point on, Julius' journey becomes part *éducation sentimentale*, part involuntary intrusion into the secret places of other people's lives, and part mystical experience whose mystique he never quite fathoms. At the end, standing on the bleak, windswept cliffs overlooking the Atlantic, watching in mingled exhilaration and dispossession as Elmore burns his guitars, Julius is a sadder man, perhaps even a wiser one, but still a wanderer in the dark.

What he fails to read, as he doggedly follows in Elmore's footsteps, are the signs (often embedded in the songs on the soundtrack) pointing to the trail of bitterness and betrayal Elmore left in passing. Once more caught up with, once more preparing to move on, Elmore is assumed by the Japanese businesswoman (not to mention Julius himself) to have accepted her lifetime security deal so that he can "be a free man on the open road". Ever the anti-romantic, Elmore is quick to set the record straight: "I say freedom don't have much to do with the road, one way or the other". He is in fact more accurately defined by the song associated with him: "The devil jumped a hawk and made him too nervous to fly/All that hawk could do was lay down and cry". Contrariwise, Elmore listens, with wistful envy, as the ebullient Rita MacNeil sings in a local club: "You will meet the hands that give, the ones that take/Everybody needs a place to keep them warm, to keep them safe".

Elmore, in other words, is a hawk jumped by the devil of success, henceforward assailed by demands (from commercial interests, from people who love him) which he is unwilling, or possibly constitutionally unable, to respond to. Akin in a sense to Graham Greene's burnt-out case (the contract by which he escapes, skyrocketing the value of his guitars by guaranteeing their rarity, is tantamount to a certification of his own death), he can only keep on running. With Julius acting as his own Homer, committing a series of messages for Elmore to a pocket tape-recorder and interweaving them with flights of fancy about his own heroic expectations, his odyssey is a delight in several ways: the marvellous string of performances achieved through unorthodox casting that slyly incorporates a whole slew of musicians; the brilliance with which Frank and Wurlitzer ring the visual and verbal changes on the encounters—inconsequential, enigmatic, emotionally charged or simply bizarre—littering Julius' path; and, not least, the complexity with which the music is interwoven from background to foreground and back again until it becomes a protagonist in its own right. *Candy Mountain* may perhaps be summed up (in Robert Frank's words) as the story of a young man who "realises he will have to make his own way through life". But its parts are always much more than this sum.

CITY OF SADNESS, A *(Film Review Annual, 1990)*

MONTHLY FILM BULLETIN, 6/90, p. 152, Tony Rayns

On August 15, 1945, Japan's fifty-one-year colonial rule in Taiwan ends and the island reverts to China's sovereignty. The Lin family, headed by elderly widower Lin Ah-Lu, is one of countless many forced by the change in government to reorder its affairs. In Keelung, Lin and his eldest son Wen-Heung (both prominent in local gangster circles) refurbish their Japanese-style night-club and reopen it as the "Little Shanghai". Lin's second son is missing (presumed dead) on forced service with the Japanese army's medical corps in the Philippines, and his third son Wen-Leung returns home from working as a translator for the Japanese in Shanghai with a nervous breakdown and is confined to hospital. Lin's youngest son, Wen-Ching, deaf and mute since a childhood accident, runs a small photo-studio in Kimguichui, in the mountains above Keelung. Through his teacher friend Wu Hinoe, Wen-Ching meets a group of intellectuals—Messrs. He, Xie, Lin and Wu—who gather in his home to discuss politics; he also befriends Hinoe's sister Hinomi when she takes a nursing job in the Kimguichui Miners' Hospital. Hinomi bids a sad farewell to her Japanese friend Shizuko, one of the last to be repatriated to Japan. Seemingly recovered from his mental problems, Wen-Leung joins Ah Ga (one of Wen-Heung's gangster associates) in a meeting with black-marketeers from Shanghai, who propose that he use his family's trading connections to smuggle contraband goods to the Mainland. Despite the unsolved murder of "Red Monkey", another of Ah Ga's gangster friends, Wen-Leung decides to go behind his elder brother's back and makes a private deal with the Shanghainese. When Wen-Heung finds out, he overcomes his rage and diplomatically consults other local gang bosses to calm the situation. But when Wen-Leung is arrested as a suspected wartime collaborator, Wen-Heung is forced to turn to the Mainlanders for help in getting him released. Wen-Leung eventually returns home a broken man, his mind in ruins. On February 28, 1947, Wen-Ching accompanies Hinoe on a trip to Taipei, where they are caught up in the rioting that follows an army massacre of unarmed demonstrators calling for Taiwanese independence. Hinoe is injured in the fracas; he takes Hinomi back to their parents' home for safety, and then disappears into the mountains to join a group of guerrillas fighting the Kuomintang (KMT) government. Martial law is declared and many (including, briefly, Wen-Ching) are arrested. Some months later, Wen-Ching secretly visits Hinoe's encampment and finds him married and determined to continue the fight against oppressive and autocratic government. Hinoe urges Wen-Ching to marry Hinomi. Anxiety and paranoia hang heavy over the community in Keelung. Ah Ga picks a fight with Mainland gangster Kim Tsua; the incident escalates, and both Wen-Heung and Ah Ga are killed in knife fights. Soon after Wen-Heung's funeral, Wen-Ching marries Hinomi; in the spring of 1949, they have a baby. Wen-Ching still works as a photographer, giving money to and passing messages for the resistance. One day word comes that the guerrilla encampment has been raided by the army; Hinoe is dead. As winter approaches, Hinomi writes to Wen-Heung's daughter Ah Shueh that Wen-Ching has been arrested again; she can get no word of his fate. In Keelung, the Little Shanghai has few customers and the only men left in the household are the senile Lin Ah-Lu and the insane Wen-Leung. In December 1949, the Mainland falls to the Communists and Chiang Kai-Shek's KMT government retreats to Taiwan. Taipei is proclaimed the "temporary" capital of the Republic of China.

Despite winning the Golden Lion at last year's Venice Film Festival, *A City of Sadness* has not had an easy passage into Western distribution: most critics and audiences apparently find it too dauntingly long and complex for comfort. In Taiwan, by contrast, the film's unprecedented candour in facing up to a shameful and previously taboo period in the island's history earned it an astonishing box-office success, no doubt boosted by attacks in the conservative press. The British distributor has prefaced the film with a long roller title that aims to clarify the historical background and introduce the main characters, but it's clear that the film can never have the same meaning and impact abroad that is has at home. Foreign appreciation of Hou's vision is bound to be keyed to its aesthetic qualities rather than its social and political acumen.

A City of Sadness is a demanding film for any audience, not least because it pushes Hou Xiaoxian's long take/fixed angle aesthetic further than his earlier films, but its governing precepts are anything but obscure. It defines its central thrust through metaphors of light and darkness. It opens on a note of cautious optimism, with the (off-screen) birth of a child who is named Kang-Ming ("Light"), and closes on a note of weary resignation, with an image of the deserted Little Shanghai night-club lit by a flickering lightbulb that is obviously about to give out. The opening, in particular, indicates the way that Hou will use his simple, visual metaphors to merge domestic incident with national event. The birth is heard from the darkened adjoining room where the anxious father Wen-Heung paces to and fro under a single, inadequate light; but the sounds of parturition have to compete on the sound-track with the radio relay of Emperor Hirohito's speech announcing the Japanese surrender and his own abdication from divine status. The same palpable sense of gloom and confusion hangs over the closing image, which emphasises the fundamental tawdriness of the night-club (from the moment the last pane of cheap, coloured glass was puttied into place, it was never more than a provincial fantasy of metropolitan glitz). The image's sense of impending extinction also picks up the forlorn mood of the preceding sequence, in which dinner is silently served to the geriatric patriarch and his only surviving son. Captions are superimposed over these opening and closing sequence, bracketing the film's time span and pointing up August 1945 and December 1949 as two "new beginnings" in Taiwan's history; the final shots make it unnecessary for the second caption to mention that martial-law repression lasted until three years ago.

The film, then, amounts to Hou's attempt to account for the forty years under martial law. Based on extensive first-hand research, it uncovers a repressed history and recreates the social and political chaos of the late 1940s in order to ask implicit questions about how, why and where Taiwan went wrong. It doesn't entirely avoid portentousness as it works through this project—the Sakamotoesque score, for instance, sometimes shouts when it should whisper—but the film certainly never lapses into the kind of ponderous didacticism that characterises, say, Angelopoulous' equivalent forays into the darker corners of Greek history.

The strength of Hou's aesthetic is that it allows him to keep a certain distance from his plot and characters. As usual, he focuses on domestic situations and views his characters with evident warmth and sympathy, but the built-in distance prevents him from becoming enbroiled in the small melodramas of everyday life and at the same time helps to direct attention towards the larger constructions that can be inferred from everything that is shown and heard. "Distance" here means not only Hou's well known predilection for medium and long shots, the great majority of them taken from a fixed angle, but also a pattern of ellipses that is new in his cinema. Throughout the film, Hou cuts away from action at a moment when its emotional tension is still unresolved, leaving plot threads dangling but using carried-over sound to maintain the emotional continuity. This strategy seems inherently risky, and there are moments when Hou's grip on his narrative falters; but an occasional fudging of plot points is a small price to pay for the overall success in keeping both the wood and the trees in focus. (It's worth noting in passing that Hou was no doubt emboldened to make his experiments with sound by having continuous synch-sound recording at his disposal for the first time.)

Allegory plays no part in the film's design, but it's clear that the central characters—particularly the four sons of the Lin family, one of whom never appears—do represent diverse aspects of the Taiwanese predicament in the late 1940s, or perhaps diverse responses to events in which they can never be more than pawns. Wen-Heung, the eldest, has emerged from the years of Japanese occupation with a keen sense of his personal and professional role in life. He speaks Japanese, wears Japanese working-class clothes and used to run a Japanese-style night-club, but thinks of himself as a native Taiwanese-Chinese, working within a gangster's clearly defined code of honour. He is outraged by the ruthless and unprincipled behaviour of the Mainlanders he has to deal with, and is ultimately driven close to despair by his inability to hold his extended family together (that is, his inability to fulfil the burden of his family role as eldest son). His death at the hands of a Mainland thug is thus synonymous with the eclipse of the social values he stood for, a process that was of course exacerbated when Taipei became the KMT's seat of government in 1949.

At the opposite pole, the youngest son Wen-Ching has withdrawn from family life, partly because the childhood accident that left him deaf and mute has cut him off from conventional communication, but also because his "delicate" temperament (as a small boy, he used to delight in copying the gestures of the heroines in local operas) never meshed with his father and elder brother's robust masculinity. Pursuing typically intellectual interests, he has no reason to think of his own identity as a Taiwanese in political terms until his "literary" friends draw him into the struggle for Taiwanese independence. His disappearance into a KMT prison, almost certainly to face execution, hints at the enormity of the reign of terror that heralded Chiang Kai-Shek's arrival in Taiwan.

In these terms, the unseen second son and the third son Wen-Leung stand for the millions of Taiwanese men who were dragged into the Pacific War by the Japanese. The second son, the first in the family to receive higher education, was a doctor pressed into field service with the Japanese army; his widow keeps his hospital clinic spotless for his wished-for return, as if the skills he attained cannot be cancelled out. Wen-Leung, on the other hand, *willingly* served the Japanese in Shanghai; he evidently took after his eldest brother's criminal proclivities, but lacked Wen-Heung's strength of character. Why was he a collaborator? The film sidesteps the question, presumably in the interests of making him all the more representative of the countless Taiwanese who simply went with the flow, lacking any real sense of their political position during the war. No character in the film is in full control of his or her own destiny, but none is as weak-willed and helpless as Wen-Leung.

It is easy enough to extrapolate these character sketches from the film, but Hou admits no scene that merely establishes character. People are often mentioned before they appear, but they are invariably already caught up in events by the time they enter the film's action. Relationships, familial and otherwise, are never explained but required to emerge naturally from the stream of events and conversations. In short, Hou's method is to construct a panorama of characters and incidents in which no one has privileged status. The avoidance of conventioned scene-setting and character-sketching is another facet of the refusal to get bogged down in domestic drama; like the visual compositions and the narrative ellipses, it helps the film to find the generalities beyond the specifics.

Hou would not have been able to get away with such oblique strategies if *A City of Sadness* lacked a solid, underlying structure. The concept that underpins the entire film is itself rather daring: Hou proposes a secret kinship between the gangster underworld and the political underground, as if to suggest that secrecy and subterfuge are endemic parts of Taiwanese identity. Wen-Heung's gangster milieu is drawn as lovingly as anything in the films of Jean-Pierre Melville, and the workings of the traditional gangster code are seen as a viable form of social organisation.

Equally, the free-thinking dissidents who cluster around Wen-Ching are seen as quintessential modern Chinese intellectuals: drinking, exchanging polemics, singing nostalgic songs and, when driven to it, taking up arms in the best traditions of the May Fourth Movement. (It is hardly accidental that these characters are played by people like H.T. Jan, the film's executive producer, Wu Nianzhen, the scriptwriter, and Zhang Dachun, Taiwan's best young novelist; nor is it an accident that Wu Nianzhen gives himself all the ripest anti-KMT lines, and has enormous fun delivering them.) In both cases, Mainland China is the origin of the trouble that will reduce them to chaos. The gangster underworld is decimated by Wen-Leung's misbegotten alliance with unscrupulous thugs from Shanghai. And the political underground is shattered by Mainland troops in the wake of the notorious February 28 Incident, when unarmed demonstrators were massacred in Taipei while calling for Taiwanese independence.

In some ways, *A City of Sadness* builds directly on the foundations of Hou's earlier films. It develops their perception of a society in which the men act while the women have no choice but to stand aside and watch; like *Daughter of the Nile*, it uses the device of a voice-over (here, excerpts from Hinomi's diaries) from the point of view of a powerless, marginalised woman. It extends Hou's fascination with neo-primitive film form by using Wen-Ching's handicaps as an excuse to recreate silent-movie narrative, complete with extensive inter-titles, to render the notes he writes and receives in his "conversations" with Hinomi. Even the gangster/intellectual dichotomy could be related to films like *The Boys from Fengkuei* and *The Time to Live and the Time to Die*, where characters face the choice between knife fights and books.

In other ways, though, the film marks another considerable step forward in Hou's career. To analyse the ways that it works, as above, is to risk undervaluing its textural richness (each image is painstakingly detailed), its emotional complexity (Chen Song-yong and Tony Leung head a phalanx of indelible performances), and its admirable refusal to descend to easy judgments. Taiwan suddenly finds itself enjoying the freedoms that China equally suddenly finds itself denied, and Hou has risen to the occasion by making the only Chinese film of 1989 that extends the parameters of the "New Chinese Cinema". Its balance between the personal and the political is spectacular and exemplary, as if a brilliant miniaturist had miraculously filled a huge canvas.

Also reviewed in:
NEW REPUBLIC, 6/11/90, p. 26, Stanley Kauffmann

CLEAN AND SOBER *(Film Review Annual, 1989)*

MONTHLY FILM BULLETIN, 6/90, p. 161, Tim Pulleine

Daryl Poynter is a Philadelphia real-estate salesman who has become addicted to cocaine as well as alcohol, and has "borrowed" $92,000 of his employers' money to play the stock exchange in hopes of alleviating his debts. But the investments do not pay off and half the money is lost. Daryl's situation worsens when the woman with whom he has spent the night suffers a heart attack from cocaine use; police are called and she is taken to hospital. Daryl attempts to fly to Canada, but finds his credit card is not in good standing. Hearing a radio commercial for Causeway House, a drug rehabilitation centre, he enrols as a temporary means of vanishing. His counsellor, Craig, detects the insincerity of his motives and subsequently expels him from the programme. But after Daryl fails in attempts either to obtain more cocaine or to raise any funds (trying to persuade his mother to remortgage his parents' home), he regains admittance to the centre; there a colleague, Martin, brings news that the girlfriend's overdose has proved fatal. Daryl becomes more responsive to fellow inmates, among them his teenage room-mate Donald, and Charlie, a working-class woman employed at a steel plant who lives with the incipiently violent Lenny. Daryl is released into the care of an ex-addict "sponsor", Richard Dirks, who advocates his sorting out the issue of the missing money with his boss, Kramer. When he eventually does, Kramer tells him that though he will not be prosecuted if he makes restitution, there is no chance of his regaining his job. Meanwhile, Daryl has visited Charlie at home, where he is dismayed to find Lenny still using drugs. Daryl and Charlie become friends and then lovers, but Daryl's attempt to persuade her to leave Lenny and live with him provokes a row. She leaves, but subsequently decides to drive back to his apartment; as she sniffs cocaine at the wheel, she is involved in a collision and killed. Richard tells the grieving Daryl that blaming himself is only a form of evasion. Later, at an "addicts anonymous" meeting, Daryl gives a public accounting for his actions and is awarded a pin for remaining "clean and sober" for thirty days.

Clean and Sober contains various elements of a social-problem melodrama, examining drug dependency in the milieu not of some "exotic" sub-culture but of workaday office and factory life in Philadelphia. But these co-exist with, and are mainly subordinated to, a study in psychological dynamics of the sort represented by, say, the earlier films of Bob Rafelson. (The device of opening the film with an enigmatic direct-to-camera monologue by M. Emmet Walsh, which is only later identified as a "confession" to an AA meeting, strikes at the outset an odd reminder of *The King of Marvin Gardens.*) The third factor in the equation of *Clean and Sober*, however, is the casting of Michael Keaton, with its calculated contradiction of his association (the film was, of course, made before *Batman*) with eccentrically humorous roles. Not the least arresting aspect of the film, in fact, is how closely the scenario risks resemblance to the kind of "wise guy" black comedy in which its star might have been expected to be found. These go beyond incidental bits of business ("Drink up", says Daryl as he hands over a urine sample) to scenes like that in which he tries to persuade his parents to give up the roof over their heads on his behalf.

Hovering intimations of comedy, though, are constantly denied, and the darker texture correspondingly emphasised, by tone and context. This becomes grimly evident in the very first scene in which Daryl appears, as he starts to make "comically" exaggerated sexual advances to his bedmate, only to discover that she is a virtual corpse. Though a first directorial venture, *Clean and Sober* yokes its assorted components into a convincing whole through a confidently wrought style—sustained use of close-ups, exclusion of establishing shots, emphatic editing, restricted colour palette, and compression of focal depth. If these traits suit the 30s-style determinism and self-help doctrine of the film's sociology, they also serve, perhaps more importantly, to enhance a sense of sustained subjectivity. And for all the careful ordinariness of the surroundings, the performances transcend naturalism, in the floridly elaborated "character" drawing of Walsh and Morgan Freeman as well as in the Method-ish intensity of Keaton (the theatricality inherent in the overall effect is wittily acknowledged in the closing sequence, when Daryl's confessional address is punctuated by shots of the "audience" applauding).

The figure so far not mentioned is Charlie, who only enters the action about halfway through but is subsequently crucial to its working out. In fact, the film accommodates what amounts to a two-part structure. Boldly challenging schematism head-on, the drama is constructed so that it is when Daryl is at the lowest ebb of his decline (when he learns of his girlfriend's death from drugs) that he is able to look outside himself and perceive Charlie's vulnerability. To an extent, the latter half adheres to the not unfamiliar pattern of a protagonist who regenerates himself by assuming responsibility for a fellow unfortunate, and one who in this case proves to have found greater difficulty than himself in kicking the habit. But the relationship between Daryl and Charlie retains an abrasive individuality, the class divide between them pointed up by some jaggedly written dialogue.

Further, the arbitrariness of Charlie's death contradicts any ready-made resolution, even as it subliminally reinforces (the shot of Charlie sniffing cocaine just before the accident rhymes with the earlier one of Daryl drinking vodka at the wheel of his car before entering the clinic) a sense of predetermination. And in turn, the theme of moral self-reliance is ironically complicated via Richard's subsequent accusation that Daryl is avoiding facing up to his very *lack* of culpability. This scene, bridging the car crash and the coda of Daryl's "thirty day" speech, serves to emphasise the precariousness of the ending. The ambiguity, along with the film's prevailing circularity, is reasserted in the closing image of car headlights being turned on outside the meeting hall. The photographic effect is of candles being lighted in the darkness, yet at the same time we recall the very first words spoken in the film, when Richard describe to the AA his memories of standing on a street corner, peering into the lights of oncoming cars as he feverishly awaited the arrival of his drug connection.

CREATOR (*Film Review Annual, 1986*)

MONTHLY FILM BULLETIN, 7/90, p. 193, Tom Milne

Harry Wolper, a brilliant, eccentric research biologist at the University Medical Center, despises convention, paperwork and the academic mind. In pursuit of a private project to reproduce his beloved wife Lucy from cells preserved since she died ten years ago, he misappropriates an expensive piece of equipment ordered by his arch-enemy, Dr. Sid Kuhlenbeck; and as an assistant he hijacks Boris Lafkin, a promising student earmarked by Sid for his own department (the main inducement being Harry's artful claim to know the girl, a complete stranger, who vanished after Boris trailed her to the lab, certain that he had at last found his dream girl). Bemused when Harry explains the crazy project he is to work on, Boris is moved by the love that inspired it; ignoring Sid's warning that the association may jeopardise his academic future, he pledge himself to Harry's cause; and is rewarded when Harry contrives to come up with the name of his dream girl, Barbara Spencer. While Boris and Barbara discover that the attraction is mutual, Harry meets Meli, an unhappy girl ditched by her lover, and is able to reassure her that she is not pregnant. The grateful Meli, promptly falling in love with Harry, agrees to provide him with the female eggs he needs to regrow Lucy from her cells. Meanwhile, snooping around the lab in hopes of discrediting Harry, Sid finds evidence of the misappropriated equipment and has it disconnected. The Lucy project is set back to square one; Harry is to be put out to grass at Northfield, a research facility for superannuated faculty members which has no finance available for research; Boris decides to try to salvage his own career; and Meli leaves, discouraged by Harry's undiminished determination to resurrect Lucy. Suddenly Barbara falls ill and goes into a coma; when tests reveal that nothing can be done, her parents agree with Sid that her life support system should be turned off. But refusing to accept the verdict, backed up by Harry, Boris stays with Barbara, pleading until at last she miraculously opens her eyes. Moved, Harry consigns Lucy's remaining cells to the ocean and declares his love for Meli. When Harry moves to Northfield, everyone else goes along—even the disgruntled Sid—since the funding committee has decided that the finance goes where Harry goes.

Jeremy Leven's adaptation of his own novel starts with several strikes against it, not least its habit of indulging in dialogue requiring delivery with a flourish of capital letters. "You know what our problem is around here?" Harry demands rhetorically, "Too many Machines. We're missing the Big Picture". The message, of course, concerns caring, that ubiquitous curse of Hollywood sentimentality in the 80s. This is heralded by a scene in which, with stuffy Sid arguing that the hospital is meant for humans, Harry busily and humanely gets on with the business of operating on a pet chimp brought in by its distressed owner. And it is finally rammed home, with an inordinate weight of special pleading, in the climactic sequence where a young man's devotion rescues his beloved from the jaws of death.

Such medical reprieves from deep coma are of course not unknown to medical history; what is objectionable here, quite apart from the milking of emotion and the scoring of cheap satirical points, is the inappropriateness. In a wacky context where the mad professor is trying to regrow his wife from seed like a pot plant, and his assistant is woken every morning by a home-made robot spouting homilies about Mozart's achievements at his age and reminders to resume his quest "for the Ultimate Female", the debate with grief-stricken parents about turning off their daughter's life support seems like an unwarranted intrusion of reality.

Surprisingly, *Creator* nevertheless emerges as more likeable than not, thanks to performances of delightful fantasy from all four leads (even if Peter O'Toole, here playing God's *alter ego*, as usual seems rather too brimful of self-satisfaction). If the film is ultimately pointless (or worse), at least Ivan Passer's handling of the romantic complications—Vincent Spano and Virginia Madsen frustrated by uncertainty as to how to proceed in dishonouring the platonic pact made when she became homeless and he offered to share his flat; Mariel Hemingway and O'Toole sundered by her perception of herself as a nymphomaniac, he of himself as monogamously bonded to a memory—offers a pleasing reminder of the more complex ramifications of the triangle relationship in *Cutter's Way*.

CRIMES AND MISDEMEANORS (*Film Review Annual, 1990*)

SIGHT & SOUND, Summer 1990, p. 207, Richard Combs

The Woody Allen *oeuvre* as a whole—developing, at its steady film-a-year pace, into the most fascinating in American cinema—is divided into three parts. There are those films in which Allen himself features, such a compulsive source of self-denigrating one-liners that the films easily disappear into one-joke black holes like *Zelig*. Then there are those films in which he doesn't appear, where the worries about the meaninglessness of existence, the terrors of non-existence, are dispersed among an all-star art-house cast, who make high drama out of these previously comic phobias. And finally there are those works, initially *Hannah and Her Sisters* and now *Crimes and Misdemeanors*, which contain both a film with and one without Woody Allen.

The relationship between the two is bound to be uneasy—Woody in his part of the film trying to wisecrack himself and his anxieties off the screen, while in the other he creates an unembarrassed theatrical space for his characters' *Weltschmerz*. In the one, afraid of being thought self-important, he is always trying to puncture pretension; in the other, afraid of not being thought serious, he is always trying to locate *the* fears of modern consciousness. *Crimes and Misdemeanors* is clearly raising the stakes over *Hannah* in this respect. Where the latter worried about love and commitment, the puzzling vagaries of the human heart, *Crimes* goes for life and death, a man's relationship to his God. Where *Hannah* nodded to Chekhov, *Crimes* takes its title from Dostoevsky, the loss of "punishment" being both the self-denigrating joke this time around (in a modern, relativistic world it's always possible to plea-bargain for a lesser offence, a misdemeanour) and the heart of the moral matter.

The protagonist of this side of the film is Dr Judah Rosenthal (Martin Landau), respected ophthalmologist, upstanding citizen, loving family man and cultured individual, who is driven to instigate a murder. By a series of steps he daren't think about while he is taking them, he agrees that his mistress of two years (Anjelica Huston), who is now refusing to accept a tucked-away non-existence, can only be dealt with via a final solution. Judah has a convenient black-sheep brother who so deals with her, but he also has a religious Jewish upbringing whose precepts about absolute justice and an all-seeing God increasingly haunt him. His shock is to discover, not only that a lightning bolt fails to strike him, but he doesn't even feel bad forever. That the most awful things can be done and lived with.

On the other side is Clifford Stern (Allen), an aspiring film-maker whose honourable mention at the Cincinnati Documentary Film Festival, and his earnest commitment to Real Values, cut little ice with his wife or his TV producer brother-in-law Lester (Alan Alda). The latter is the primary representative of the world of false values, a fount of pseudo-profound formulas ("Comedy is tragedy—plus time"), non-stop ideas for new series (which he dictates into a pocket recorder), and so impervious to Clifford's scorn that he even offers him the job of directing a TV feature about himself ("a creative mind at work"). This at least introduces Clifford to soul mate Halley Reed (Mia Farrow), associate producer of the show, who tells him that the creative mind she really wanted to document was Gabriel Garcia Marquez. In return, Clifford shows her his uncompleted film about an unregarded sage for our time, Louis Levy (Martin Bergmann), who has genuinely profound things to say about the human condition.

To the extent that Judah and Clifford's stories work as separate, self-contained essays on the theme of moral choices and consequences, both remain naggingly unsatisfying. In the first case, this has to do with Allen's weakness as a straight dramatist, and in the second with his self-indulgence as a comic. Judah's scenes with his mistress, their wrangling in the present with occasional flashbacks to happier days, outline the dilemma without giving it much substance, even being (despite a generally fine performance by Landau) off-key in the higher dramatic reaches. Similarly, all the play on eyes—God's, Judah's, even those of another brother-in-law of Clifford's, Ben (Sam Waterston), who is going blind but has the firmest moral convictions of anyone in the film—seems like the kind of pseudo-profound motif one might find in one of Lester's shows. The snugness of Judah's plight becomes a smugness in the case of Clifford, as he and Halley engage in self-congratulatory banter about Garcia Marquez or Professor Levy, or discover that they share that other enthusiasm of the "authentic" soul, a love of old movies.

When these two stories cross each other, however, something else comes into play. Although Judah and Clifford don't meet until the film's final scene (the wedding of Ben's daughter), Allen uses clips from the movies Clifford watches to cut occasionally between them. The clips might be rather obvious jokes about Judah's problems, either marital (*Mr and Mrs Smith*) or murderous (*Happy Go Lucky*), except that Clifford's comment at one point, "This sort of thing only happens in the movies", works as a more complex irony, an acknowledgment even of his intellectual smugness.

The perfection he finds in cinema, the satisfaction of art, makes him not merely a sympathetic nebisch, too sensitive ever to succeed, but an escapist—like the heroine of *The Purple Rose of*

Cairo, or like Judah himself, who admits he was living in a dream world until he stumbled into his current mess. The "doubling" of Judah and Clifford's stories gives the film a different theme—incompleteness is all, the incompleteness of moral systems, of art, even of one's sense of personal guilt. *Crimes and Misdemeanors* itself becomes incomplete—self-contradictory, ramshackle, often strangely adrift. But through it Allen finds a way forward from such "perfectly" achieved, self-cancelling conceits as *Zelig*.

DEAD HEAT (*Film Review Annual, 1989*)

MONTHLY FILM BULLETIN, 1/90, p. 11, Kim Newman

Los Angeles. Detectives Roger Mortis and Doug Bigelow are investigating a series of robberies committed by apparently invulnerable thieves. Rebecca Smythers, Mortis' Coroner girlfriend, claims the jewel raiders are reanimated corpses, but Dr. McNab, her boss, ridicules the idea. A trace element on the bodies of twice-dead heist men leads the detectives to Dante Pharmaceuticals, where they are shown around by PR woman Randi James. Investigating on his own, Bigelow tangles with a reanimated monster and, during a violent shoot-out, Mortis is shoved into a killing chamber and suffocated. Using a machine in the Dante plant, Rebecca brings Mortis back to life, but she diagnoses a progressive decay which will kill him again within twelve hours. Mortis and Bigelow track down Randi, who is trying to escape, and survive a shoot-out with a couple of zombies. Randi leads them to Thule, a Chinese restaurateur, who tries to kill them by unleashing a roomful of reanimated meat. Following up a clue found at the Dante plant, the detectives deduce that the firm, a private think tank run by the supposedly deceased Arthur P. Loudermilk, has been using the promise of the resurrection machine to cheat ageing millionaires of their fortunes. Bigelow is murdered, and Randi, who confesses that she is herself a zombie, rots before Mortis' eyes. Mortis deduces that McNab is part of the conspiracy, and confronts him. McNab, who has just killed Rebecca, locks Mortis in an ambulance to perish, but the detective manages to escape. He shoots his way into the reanimation chamber, where Loudermilk and McNab are giving a sales pitch, and McNab tries to turn Bigelow's newly raised corpse against his friend. Bigelow remembers who Mortis is, and the zombie cops kill McNab and, despite the pleas and offers of Loudermilk, destroy the machine. Knowing they will soon decay, they walk into the night...

The problem of the lazy comic approach that has blighted the late 80s horror film is more than amply demonstrated by *Dead Heat*, which combines the current craze for bizarre cop team-ups with the *Re-Animator/Return of the Living Dead* brand of slapstick zombie gore. A TV clip, plus the character name Bigelow, signals the plot's essential derivation from *DOA*, but while the idea of a briefly reanimated corpse spending his last twelve hours before he decays trying to track down his killer is promising, the film keeps interrupting the race-against-time to set up another major special-effects sequence or to crack jokes which interrupt the suspenseful tone. The most elaborately bizarre scene has Keye Luke reviving a roomful of meat, which leads to such disturbing images as a butchered cow carcass stumping after a victim and Treat Williams wrestling with a reanimated liver. However, this FX bonanza has been dropped into the film even though it violates the script's logic by suggesting that each scrap of a reanimated corpse can stay alive when the initial shoot-out has proved that the zombies *can* be killed, and contradicts the supposedly definitive finale by showing that the reanimation machine at the Dante plant isn't the only one in the city.

As the elitist brains behind the scheme, whose philosophy is "God didn't mean for rich people to die, and if He did, we can buy Him off", Vincent Price doesn't make much of his one big scene, and Darren McGavin's toupeed coroner doesn't really fill in for him on the villainy front. Treat Williams and Joe Piscopo banter endlessly, taking only a few scenes to lament the misery of their situations ("I can't live my entire life in six hours"), exchanging wisecracks about holding death-day parties and contradicting the police academy ruling that "a dead cop can't be a good cop", before wandering off to decompose together with "this could be the end of a beautiful friendship". But the overwhelmingly light tone sits ill with a storyline that involves the casual death of every sympathetic character—Rebecca is especially ill-used as a throwaway, unreanimated corpse, while Randi's spectacular putrefaction is a triumph of special effects rendered meaningless by uncommitted acting.

DISTANT VOICES, STILL LIVES (*Film Review Annual, 1989*)

CINEASTE, Vol. XVII, No. 3, 1990, p. 42, Leonard Quart

Distant Voices, Still Lives is a remarkable autobiographical film, every frame and feeling of which is built on the most primal, painful, and personal of memories. It is a low budget work (produced by The British Film Institute for about a million pounds), unmediated by genre conventions, star turns, or special effects.

Directed and written by Terence Davies, the film deals with the life of his working class family in Liverpool during the Forties and Fifties. The memories he resurrects are unsentimental and chilling—a claustrophobic, sometimes brutalizing world, with little chance for escape. There are moments of real pleasure—both private and communal—but they never quite compensate for the generally oppressive and grim lives the family and their friends lead.

The film is divided into two sections shot two years apart. The anguished first half, *Distant Voices*, centers around the authoritarian, raging father (Pete Postlethwaite), his death and funeral, and the marriage of his sharp-tongued, angry daughter Eileen (Angela Walsh). The second, which is more melancholy than harrowing in tone, focuses on pub songfests and the marriage of the quieter, more inward son Tony (Deal Williams). Even in the second half, however, the traumatic memory of the father survives, moving Tony to break down into tears right after his wedding.

Distant Voices, Still Lives is not a conventional social realist film detailing through a traditional narrative the social texture and behavior of a working class world. Davies does recreate the physical surfaces of his past—the worn, gray row houses, the brightly-lit local pub, and the dark brown interior of the movie palace. The film purposely bleaches out primary colors and shoots within a brown tonal range so the past is not prettified or romanticized.

Davies eschews a linear narrative for elliptically cutting back and forth in time, and many of his shots are carefully constructed and highly stylized, almost turning scenes into still photos and static tableaus. The film includes lengthy, recurring shots of the house's front door, windows, and inside staircase, with voices heard off-screen—Davies conjuring up a past from which he may want to remember only fragments—rather than fully developed sequences. It's as if the essence of the past can be distilled in the image of a front door covered with a Christmas wreath, or a slow, evocative pan across row houses on Christmas Eve; there seems to be no need or desire on Davies's part for more detailed exposition. There are also striking images of the entire screen filled with umbrellas bobbing in the rain—a homage to Hitchcock's *Foreign Correspondent*—an overhead shot of Tony and his brother-in-law seemingly free-falling through a glass roof which shatters like a block of ice, and a final haunting image of his mother, one of his sisters and her husband, receding into the darkness of the past.

The film is permeated with music which acts as a counterpoint to the narrative. In Davies's words, the music becomes "on occasions the narrative itself." The family and their friends sing a great deal both in the pub and at various family celebrations. The songs include "Barney Google," "Buttons and Bows," "Up a Lazy River," and "My Yiddisher Momma"—mostly Forties' and Fifties' popular American music. They sing for a variety of reasons: to forget and escape their constricted lives; as a substitute for the direct communication of feeling (they are never truly articulate or at ease with spoken language); and for the pure joy and warmth of communal singing.

Besides singing, the family has other popular culture diversions and manufactured dreams which provide comfort, make their lives a bit more bearable, and help create a shared culture. There is radio on Sunday afternoons—the second section of the film opens with a montage of various family members raptly listening in their homes to typical sports, comedy, and music programming. And there are the movies—Davies remembers his sisters going regularly to the local movie palace, and crying copious tears at the romantic bathos of *Love is a Many Splendored Thing*.

Davies recalls that long-gone, traditional working class culture with great affection. Despite his homage to both that cohesive culture and to the emotional strength of his mother and sisters, the past remains basically an agonizing one. His father may have moments of tranquility—singing "When Irish Eyes are Smiling" while calmly grooming his horse—and he's even capable of tenderness—blessing his sleeping children on Christmas Eve—but from the latter scene the film makes an abrupt cut to his violently knocking all the dishes off the table. The most memorable images of the father show him bullying and bellowing, locking his young son out of the house one night, and beating his wife senseless. His behavior seems unmotivated and arbitrary. He has no capacity for introspection, and the film offers no social or psychological explanations for his actions.

The victimized mother (Freda Dowie) is often depressed—constantly frightened that something will set the father off shouting and swinging his fists. When asked by one of her daughters why she married their father, however, she can only simply and poignantly reply: "He was a good dancer." While the scene develops, we can hear on the soundtrack the voice of Ella Fitzgerald singing "Taking a Chance on Love." The irony inherent in juxtaposing a song about happy endings with this hateful marriage may be too obvious, but in Davies's film it seamlessly intensifies the feeling of heartbreaking desolation which pervades the film's first section.

In "Still Lives," marital life is less brutal and ominous, but still alienating. One sister, Maisie (Lorraine Ashbourne), marries a decent, sympathetic man, but the marriages of Eileen and her friends are essentially unhappy ones. Eileen marries a porcine-looking man, for whom she ultimately has contempt. They live in her grandmother's house with her father's crazy brother—a life that finally extinguishes any sense of personal possibility which might have survived her father's tirades and tyranny. Her once spirited, lively friends are no better off—married to men who either intimidate and control them, or who devote most of their passion to football, the horses, and drinking with 'the boys' at the pub.

The worlds of working class Liverpool men and women are separate ones. Their marriages bitterly repeat many of the patterns of the previous generation. While one of Eileen's friends, Jingles (Marie Jelliman), suffers silently, Eileen, though just as entrapped in her marriage, changes the pattern a bit by constantly carping at and putting down her husband.

Distant Voices, Still Lives resonates most powerfully on an emotional and visceral level. It's a film of images and voices, not ideas or words. Davies resurrects his memories without really providing cultural or psychological interpretations for the way his family lived. That world is a given, the experience speaking solely in its own terms and no other.

What Davies has achieved is an unsparing and lyrical recreation of both the rich texture of working class culture, and a family life filled with ineluctable sorrow. Davies's clear-eyed recollections don't attempt to soften the ache and anguish of the past. Through the filter of memory, however, he has composed a series of luminous visual and aural images which transforms that misery into an immutable experience.

Also reviewed in:
NEW REPUBLIC, 8/28/89, p. 27, Stanley Kauffmann
NEW YORK TIMES, 8/13/89, p. 57, Vincent Canby
NEW YORKER, 9/4/89, p. 88, Terrence Rafferty
WASHINGTON POST, 9/1/89, p. B1, Hal Hinson
WASHINGTON POST, 9/1/89, Weekend/p. 31, Desson Howe

DOWN AND OUT IN BEVERLY HILLS (*Film Review Annual, 1987*)

JUMP CUT, No. 35, 4/90, p. 85, Christine Anne Holmlund

A New Cold War rages on movie screens across the United States. Scores of recent Hollywood films, most of them genre films, pit the United States against Russia or against Russian satellites. The films also marshall U.S. and Allied support behind U.S. foreign and domestic policy. *Top Gun* (Scott: 1986), *Heartbreak Ridge* (Eastwood: 1986), *White Nights* (Hackford: 1985), *The Highlander* (Mulcahy: 1986). *Red Dawn* (Milius: 1984) and the three Rambo films (*First Blood* Kotcheff: 1982), *Rambo: First Blood, Part II* (Cosmatos: 1986) and *Rambo III* (Stallone: 1988) represent a few, obvious examples of this widespread and diverse phenomenon. Other, less overtly xenophobic and chauvinistic films also inscribe and articulate New Cold War concerns.

Despite much talk about New Cold War films as a current Hollywood trend, few critics understand the scope and functioning of New Cold War ideology in movies. All too often, both the popular press and more academically oriented film critics dismiss these films as manipulative and "bad," overlooking the films' value as entertainment. Such critics emphasize ideological containment and ignore the possibility of counter-hegemonic readings. Even Andrew Britton's perceptive "Reaganite Entertainment" occasionally succumbs to these tendencies. Britton focuses on films made in the late 70s and 80s, and he interprets them in light of what he calls Reaganite ideology. He does acknowledge that "the films' negation or recuperation of history has the effect of a potential weakness as well as a strength." Yet he concludes that in these films Reaganite ideology emerges victorious, if empty. His analysis glosses over contradictions within the film texts, and it ignores the divergent reactions found among individual audience members and among audience subgroups defined by race, sex, class, sexuality and subculture.[1]

The films' success does not simply result from their enthusiastically presenting a New Cold War. Their strongest appeal often comes from the way they revert to earlier U.S. value systems, or from how they include value systems implicitly or overtly opposed to New Cold War tenets. In other words, these films contain something for everyone. Ideology becomes embedded in and interwoven with entertainment. Cultural diversity and division are not just ignored, they are integrated into the film fictions. As a resut, these movies are not simply expressions of New Cold War ideology, they also *constitute* it and *undercut* it in the process of incorporating a variety of personal and social anxieties and desires into a representational mode.

I examine here three recent Hollywood films to explore this process. I have chosen to analyze *Down and Out in Beverly Hills* (Mazursky: 1985), *Rocky IV* (Stallone: 1985) and *Aliens* (Cameron: 1986) for two reasons. First, they are either sequels or remakes. While we could dismiss them as purely formulaic, we can use the fact that they are sequels and remakes to grasp the historical dimensions of how Hollywood cinema has inscribed New Cold War ideology. How films incorporate new cultural, historical and ideological material becomes more than usually obvious when we compare sequels and remakes to each other and to the original films.

Second, each film represents different genre mixes—one is satire and farce; another, sports and adventure; and the third, horror and science fiction. In spite of such genre variety, all three films rely on a New Cold War's premise and promise for their plots, characters, and/or settings. The genre range demonstrates the phenomenon's pervasiveness at the same time that it helps us identify the elements which constitute this ideology.

To analyze these films, I will concentrate on how roles within the family, relations of race and class, and relations between the dominant culture and yuppie and punk subcultures serve as nodal points for cinema to elaborate current ideological concerns. In New Cold War films like these, I will argue, economic fears become rewritten as sexual dilemmas, and white subcultures and racial minorities become subsumed within or behind the white middle class family. Yet the presence of strong female, non-white and/or counter-cultural characters does indicate that social change has occurred and is occurring. Like a thread that runs throughout their fictions, all three films depict a resurgent United States' posture of strength, yet the films also refer constantly to fear of weakness. Memories about both Vietnam and social protest coexist and collide as cinematic fictions use the past and future to shore up, disguise or replace the present.

For us as activists and critics, these films provide an opportunity to raise crucial political, theoretical questions. Why are these films so successful at the box office? Why do women as well as men, blacks as well as whites relish Rambo, Rocky and Ripley? Do such films merely inscribe the ideology of a dominant, right-wing, New Cold War—or Reaganite ideology, as Britton suggests—or is their message broader and more contradictory? How, where, and why might audience reactions differ? These questions and their answers would not just indicate relations among author, text, and reader but also a possibility of and necessity for social and political resistance and change.

TROUBLE IN PARADISE:
DOWN AND OUT IN BEVERLY HILLS

At first sight Paul Mazursky's comedy, *Down and Out in Beverly Hills*, does not seem to have anything to do with the New Cold War. A remake over fifty years later of Jean Renoir's pre-

Popular Front film, *Boudu Sauve des Eaux* (Boudu Saved From Drowning, 1932), Mazursky's film gently satirizes the guilty complacence of Beverly Hills nouveaux riches and North American consumer culture in general without overtly addressing questions of foreign or domestic policy or, as Renoir's film does, without hinting at possibilities for class solidarity and structural change. Instead, *Down and Out* uses the family to act out and cover up New Cold War desires and anxieties. In *Down and Out in Beverly Hills*, the Whiteman family acts both progressively and traditionally, capable under strong paternal leadership of absorbing any and all subcultures, from punks to gays to blacks to Mexicans and a host of others. In much the same way, the political rhetoric of the Carter and Reagan administrations appealed nostalgically to the security the nuclear family supposedly offered. In this way the government deflected attention from the economic and political gains achieved by the women's, black and gay movements of the 1960s and 70s and weakened the appeal of counter-cultural movements like the hippies and the punks. Within the political framework of the late 70s to late 80s, governmental allusions to both domestic prosperity and Soviet threat sidestepped the economic and political challenges posed by First World countries or power blocs (Japan, OPEC, Europe, etc.). It also inhibited understanding the indigenous threats to U.S. dominance in Latin America, Africa and Asia.

The politics of *Down and Out* are more liberal or at least more contradictory. The film both acknowledges and subsumes sexual, racial, class and national difference. Yet in the broader context of New Cold War rhetoric, fluctuations like these commonly occur because liberals and conservatives do not stand necessarily opposed. On the contrary, as sociologist Alan Wolfe convincingly argues, the myth of a New Cold War has its political origins in the semi-conscious alliance between liberals and the radical right which has dominated U.S. politics since World War II.[2]

Down and Out in Beverly Hills takes as its subject, homelessness, a favorite theme of the mid 1980s. Dave Whiteman (Richard Dreyfuss) and his family adopt a street person, Jerry Baskin (Nick Nolte) when Jerry tries to drown himself in their swimming pool. Although Dave tries to convince Jerry to go straight and get a job, Jerry refuses, preferring to lounge around the house, drink lo-cal sodas, play the piano, and screw Dave's neurotic wife (Bette Midler), his Mexican maid (Elizabeth Peña) and his anorexic daughter (Tracy Nelson). Despite the comic mishaps Jerry provokes, at the end of the film the Whiteman family welcomes him as one of its members, but not having him marry into it.

Ostensibly class difference lies at the heart of *Down and Out*'s humor. Yet like so many Hollywood films, this film finally remains indifferent to class. unlike the tramp in *Boudu*, Mazursky's bum does not function so disruptively within the family. Just the fact that the director chose the family swimming pool rather than the Pacific ocean for Jerry's suicide attempt indicates how Mazursky domesticated and privatized the politics of the original *Boudu*. There M. Lestingois (Charles Granval) rescues Boudu (Michel Simon) in a public setting. Renoir structured his film around class difference in 1930s France. As Christopher Faulkner puts it, in *Boudu*, "the whole point...is to preserve the sense of the incompatibility of two social classes and the irrevocable barriers between them."[3]

Similarly, Jerry and Boudu have opposed characterizations. As befits the first R-rated film from the Disney studios, Jerry seems amazingly well-bred, capable of reciting Shakespeare and playing Debussy. As a result, several critics have remarked that Jerry functions more like an innocent apolitical left-over hippie than a social pariah or anarchist (Corliss; O'Brien, Ap. 11, 1986). In contrast, Boudu not only has no cultural savoir faire, as Michel Simon portrays the character, he even has difficulty walking a straight line. The two films also have radically different endings. *Down and Out*'s narrative, in contrast to *Boudu*'s, does not need to marry Jerry off to the maid, and thus has no need to confront a threat of "miscegenation," a spectre which vies with homosexuality for the title "all-time worst nightmare" in the squeaky clean universe of Disney thought. Jerry's extraordinary sexual appeal, virility and promiscuity might exclude him from Disneyland, but in the context of a Disney film for adults, they guarantee heterosexuality—on which the Disney empire rests.[4] By ending with Jerry's return to the family, *Down and Out* rejects *Boudu*'s most utopian and anarchic moment. At the end of the original film, Boudu literally jumps ship to return to the river and a bum's happy life. The final shots even suggest a kind of carefree lumpen solidarity—a line of bums file past Notre Dame Cathedral singing Boudu's theme song, "Sur les bords de la Seine."[5]

Like *Bob and Carol and Ted and Alice*, Mazursky's first film (1969), *Down and Out in Beverly Hills* deals far more with middle class sexual dilemmas than with conspicuous consumption or class relations. Because *Down and out* defines all problems in sexual, not economic terms, class never really presents a problem. Dressed in an expensive lounging outfit and surrounded by objets d'art, Barb Whiteman explains to Jerry: "I used to go shopping for gratification. But that's like sex without a climax, you know." For Barb, sex, not money, remains the real issue. Jerry the bum has the answer to her needs: he knows the rules better than anyone. A 1980s Lady Chatterley's lover, he gives Barb the climax she's been craving, and he solves all the other family members' problems as well. He brings the gay punk son, Max (Evan Richards), out of the closet, persuades the anorexic daughter to eat, turns the Mexican maid on to Che and Mao, befriends the dog, and eases Dave's guilt at being so rich, all without ever getting at the economic and/or social roots of their or his problems.

Of course *Boudu*, like *Down and Out*, worries about a decline in masculinity, virility and/or sexuality in the middle classes. M. Lestingois and Dave Whiteman are both wimps. However, the images in *Down and Out* insist on the fact, constantly contrasting Richard Dreyfuss' skinny little body with Nick Nolte's hulking frame in medium two shots. In *Boudu*, as Janet Walker and Luli McCarroll argue, the middle classes repress sexuality; in *Down and Out*, the middle class extends the range of "tolerable" sexuality. Indeed, because *Down and Out* translates all social ills as sexual problems, the film becomes a kind of Freudian "talking cure" for 1980s America. Going the New Cold War patriarchal family one better, the ending offers us two dads for the price of one: Jerry joins Dave Whiteman as head of the family. Trapped in the narrow hallways of the Lestingois house, Boudu remains a destructive child; in the wide open spaces of the Whiteman mansion, Jerry stays on there as an understanding, tolerant, contented, virile father who knows best.

Down and Out is so preoccupied with creating one big happy family that it ends up promoting the wealth it sets out to mock.[6] As in countless other Hollywood films, economic anxiety becomes contained and displaced by an insistence that money isn't everything and that the poor often live happier than the rich.[7] When Jerry takes Dave to the beach to meet his friends and sing folk songs, they seem more like Boy Scouts on an overnight or hippies at a hootenanny than impoverished street people. And in this film about poverty and homelessness, only the rich daughter feels hunger. In the present context of world economics, this is absurd. It is funny only to those who do not face need. As one critic writes about Dave Whiteman's boast, "I ate garbage last night, Barb, and I loved it!": "The movie had better find its audience in this country, because no one else in the world would possibly understand it." (Denby, Feb. 3, 1986)

The mystification of poverty which pervades *Down and Out in Beverly Hills* functions today to justify right wing domestic policies fueled by the myth of the New Cold War, specifically abolishing welfare programs and instituting a regressive income tax. At the same time, however, it suggests U.S. nostalgia for the economic security of the 60s and 70s. The decision to portray Jerry Baskin as a cultured hippie rather than as a bona fide street person stands as a case in point. Hippies could afford to turn on, tune in and drop out. As the sons and daughters of the middle classes, they posed no real threat to society. "[*Down and Out*] isn't about the U.S. middle class reaching out to understand something ugly and terrifying, but reaching out to one of its own," comments Tom O'Brien (Ap. 11, 1986). Like many 60s hippies, Jerry returns to his middle class roots, becomes a yuppie, serves as a consultant and, after a feeble attempt at emancipation, returns at the end of the film to drink a cup of Cappucino with the Whiteman family. Gone is Renoir's fondness for "le gros rouge" (cheap red wine), that mark of proletarian culture and male bonding.

The need for consensus at home thus stands as a major message in *Down and Out in Beverly Hills*, and one which marks it as a New Cold War film. Like Jerry the hippie, gay and punk subcultures and a variety of racial subgroups become integrated into the Whiteman family. The working class origins and anti-bourgeois stance of the punks, provocatively analyzed by Dick Hebdige in *Subculture*, become mere fashion statements in *Down and Out in Beverly Hills*. Jerry reassures Max about his choice of lipstick: "You can go with more orange, definitely more orange." At the end of the film, Max gets welcomed back into the family fold. His homosexuality seems just a problem of communication, not a real problem, and his punk identity remains coded in consumer terms rather than as social criticism.

Similarly, the film both emphasizes and negates the reality of racial discrimination. It shows racial minorities visible everywhere, and everyone—Blacks, Chicanos, Iranians, Japanese, Chinese—seems happy, healthy and wealthy. The Mexican maid and the Japanese gardener have status as part of the family and enjoy financial success to boot. The maid has her own credit card while the gardener owns a condo in Hawaii. No question of deportation here: these are *our* aliens. Servants, business associates, workers or friends—everyone loves the Whitemans.

However, the sheer repetition of this cheery message reveals the anxiety which underlies New Cold War rhetoric. The threat posed to U.S. economic dominance by other countries, more overtly acknowledged in a film like *Gung Ho* (Howard: 1986), becomes contained in *Down and Out* by trotting out earlier myths of racial and cultural assimilation, success and love. The narrative structure depends on Thanksgiving and Christmas, holidays symbolic of U.S. benevolence. A madcap chase scene during the Whiteman's Christmas party even unites everyone—the family, their Black and Iranian neighbors, Japanese friends, a delegation of Chinese industrialists and a Mexican mariachi band—in the swimming pool from which Dave rescued Jerry at the beginning of the film.

The racism which lurks beneath much of *Down and Out*'s humor does surface abruptly, if briefly, when Dave and Jerry visit Dave's hanger factory in Tiajuana. The sequence begins as a tribute to the wonders of technology: we see machines in close-up magically pump out hangers. Dave explains to Jerry that low cost (i.e. little human labor) means high profits. He boasts that his workers stay happy because he provides such a good health care package, then calls a Mexican worker over and orders him to show his teeth and smile. The image vividly recalls slave markets.

The film depicts bourgeois fears of the working class and lumpen proletariat most obviously, and less mixed up with liberal messages of equality, when the narrative approaches questions of sexuality, health and class. "He might have herpes!" Barb shrills when Dave gives Jerry mouth to mouth resuscitation. Only when Jerry is "made over" does he really exude fitness, and only then can he heal others. The 1980s fear of sexually transmitted diseases did not concern the characters in Renoir's film.

Down and Out, like *Soul Man* (Miner: 1986) and other recent comedies, skillfully combines the 70s message that it is OK to "do your own thing" with a more conservative 80s message that anything goes as long as white male access to social power structures remains guaranteed. By foregrounding sexuality and acknowledging if backpedalling race, class and subculture, *Down and Out* speaks to the New Cold War being fought on the U.S. domestic front and with U.S. allies, at the same time that it points to the continuing influence of 60s and 70s countercultures and political movements. Though the film has no allusions to a Soviet threat and virtually no allusions to the seditious seductiveness of Marxist philosophy (aside from the shots of the voluptuous Mexican maid reading Mao), other fears and fantasies of today's resurgent U.S. do occur, among them the challenges of foreign economic competition, the need to stay physically and psychologically in shape, and the continuing dream of the United States as a melting pot where everyone comes out white, male and middle class.

Nonetheless, through its tolerance of deviant subcultures *Down and Out* goes far beyond what the right-wing proponents of a New Cold War ideology would ever accept. By diluting the purity of the New Cold War myth, *Down and Out in Beverly Hills* broadens its appeal at the same time that it guts the politics of the counter-cultural and/or subcultural ideologies on which it also draws. In this film, opportunities for audience identification with and distance from both the narrative and the images are multiple and complex. With such a mixed bag of tricks, small wonder the *Down and Out* has enjoyed such box office success, while *Boudu* provoked a riot at its premiere and closed after only three days (Sensonske, Martin).

PATRIARCHS MEET PUNKS;
ROCKY IV AND FOREIGN WAR

Unlike *Down and Out in Beverly Hills*, *Rocky IV* is instantly identifiable as a New Cold War film. The plot blatantly pits Us against Them, the U.S. against the U.S.S.R.. It incarnates in the bulky shapes of Rocky Balboa (Sylvester Stallone) and Ivan Drago (Dolph Lundgren) the New Cold War tenet that an increasingly ominous Soviet presence threatens U.S. economic and political interests. Like *Down and Out*, *Rocky IV* weaves domestic issues relating to the family, gender roles, race and subcultures in with an obvious obsession with foreign policy. More than *Down and Out*, though, the film tries, in Andrew Britton's terms, to "mandate. . .choral support" from the audience, to unite a wide variety of subgroups in support of its basically ultra-right wing message.

Yet because the film tackles so much within the simplistic framework of the highly formulaic Rocky series, contradictions occasionally emerge to fissure its conservative message. Tania

Modleski has claimed that open-endedness and an absence of plot and character development in recent formula and genre films inhibit audience identification and jeopardize the construction of the bourgeois ego. Such a claim may or may not hold true for the diverse audiences of the Rocky films; clearly, *Rocky IV* flouts audience expectations as much as it fulfills them. Audiences think they know what they will get from a film labelled *Rocky IV*, both because it is a sequel and because it so obviously fits into the action-adventure genre. Viewers pay for a story and pictures which will once again demonstrate Rocky's macho prowess.[8] But *Rocky IV* deviates in certain key ways from the rest of the series. Unlike in the other films, narrative tension here centers on Rocky's fear of weakness and aging. The plot is more overtly political, with the training and fight sequences set in Russia. And Rocky's opponent is white, not black. Although *Rocky III* also asks whether Rocky still "has the eye of the tiger," the question there is phrased in personal, not national or international terms. In *Rocky IV*, in contrast, conservative phobias vie with conservative fantasies for screen time.

In *Rocky IV*, Rocky Balboa, archetypal explorer, retraces his steps, going from the New World to the Old. He returns to the ring in Russia on Christmas day to avenge the death of his best friend, Apollo Creed (Carl Weathers) at the hands of Soviet superhero Ivan Drago. As in *Down and Out* but far more paradoxically so, the film once again invokes the myth of Christmas as the holiday of peace and harmony, now to disguise U.S. aggression. Throughout the film, the cultural and political differences between the U.S. and the U.S.S.R. are emphasized and exaggerated. As in all the Rocky films, *Rocky IV* begins with a fight sequence, but here it looks stylized and abstract, a series of extreme close-ups of a red, white and blue boxing glove pounding into and then in slow motion pulverizing a red glove decorated with a yellow hammer and sickle. Later lengthy parallel-editing sequences show Rocky training in Siberian ice and snow, running up mountains, chopping wood and lifting his friends on his back while Drago receives steroid injections and works out in a Moscow gym equipped with the latest body-building machines. Newspaper and magazine headlines, TV news commentaries, and real-life sports commentators like Warner Wolf are interwoven in the film narrative to document the authenticity of the final fictional battle. In this way the narrative simultaneously acknowledges, frames and subsumes history and reality.[9]

The outcome of the final battle never remains in doubt. While Rocky and Apollo fought to a draw in *Rocky*, the first film in the series (Avildsen: 1976), Rocky has won every fight since: first against Apollo in *Rocky II* (Stallone: 1979), then against Clubber Lang (Mr. T) in *Rocky III* (Stallone: 1982). Both audiences and critics recognize Rocky's mythic qualities. He represents the U.S. dream that, with hard work, courage and faith, a working class ethnic man can make good, especially in the realms of sports or entertainment.

But *Rocky IV* represents a significant departure from the rest of the series' emphasis on class, race and upward mobility. The original film is typical of an early 70s variant of success-myth films in which, as Chuck Kleinhans puts it, "the working-class origins [of the heroes] are central to the narrative." *Rocky IV* combines Rocky's traditionally-based persona with that of the New Cold War hero, Rambo. Gone are the long shots of the first film which anchor Rocky in the space and time of mid 70s Philadelphia working class neighborhoods. Gone too, the comparatively rich dialogue and the portrayal of Rocky and his pals as losers. Like the characters protrayed by Clint Eastwood, Arnold Schwarzenegger/and Chuck Norris, Stallone's fourth Rocky and his Rambo represent tough, invincible warriors, always ready to fight the good fight though they have almost nothing to say about it. Apollo's almost monosyllabic eloquence before his exhibition bout with Drago sums up the film's message. As the sound track from Rocky blares in the background, Apollo tells Rocky,

> You can't change what you really are. We have to be right in the middle of the action 'cuz we the warriors. And without some damn war to fight....

Spectacle is more important than speech in the action-adventure genre as a whole, it is true. But in in referring to this film even more than to the other *Rocky* films, critics overwhelmingly labeled *Rocky* a cartoon or comic strip character, so devoid do his actions seem of psychological motivation (Goldman; Kroll; Denby, Dec. 12, 86; Schickel, Dec. 9, 1986). Rather than articulate New Cold War concerns, Rocky embodies them. "I just gotta do what I gotta do," he tells Adrian.

Worries about the shape and status of the male body replace class, sex and even romance as major narrative concerns. In *Rocky IV*, Rocky's body and the body politic become presented as identical, while Rocky's more important fight is internal, not external. In true 80s right-wing fashion, discipline and freedom are presented as two sides of the same coin, with individualism (good) pitted against self-indulgence (bad). (Wolfe) The real narrtive crisis thus occurs towards the middle of the film not during the final fight scene, as Rocky wonders whether he should or could fight again.

A montage of clips from the earlier films, slow-motion shots of the Drago/Apollo fight, and close-ups of Rocky in his car are coupled with pounding rock lyrics. The images clearly label his earlier victories as past, while the words of the song stress his present dilemma:

> There's no easy way out.
> There's no short cut home.
> There's no easy way out.
> Giving in can be wrong.

The sounds of rock'n roll and the rhythmic editing of music videos replace the religious iconography of the earlier films, and offer hope of Rocky's rejuvenation if not resurrection.

Pre-fight Soviet rhetoric plays on U.S. fears of inadequacy. "The defeat of this little champ [Rocky] will be a perfect example of how pathetically weak your society has become," says the chief Soviet trainer at a press conference. In response, the training sequences repetitively display Stallone's muscular body as tauter and leaner than ever before while the narrative describes Rocky's regimen as a return to nature and pioneer values. The film uses conventional, ideologically coded and ideologically loaded rites of purification which the warrior hero must undergo. In this way, New Cold War rhetoric becomes fused with macho anxieties and earlier U.S. myths.

Like *Down and Out, Rocky IV* seemingly associates weakness with capitalist accumulation. The film contains this weakness by proposing yuppies as a kind of effete, emasculated, pseudo-class, unworthy of organized opposition. Ultimately both films condone and promote materialism. "This house, the cars and all the stuff we've got, that ain't everything," Rocky explains to Adrian, echoing her admonitions to him in *Rocky III*. To prove his sincerity, he temporarily and rhetorically gives up all his wealth and thereby proves he is worthy of it. Fond of dichotomy, like all action/adventure films, *Rocky IV* posits a world where punks square off against yuppies. Like many other recent genre movies—*Highlander* (Mulcahy: 1986), *The Terminator* (Cameron: 1984) and *Bladerunner* (Scott: 1982) to name just three—*Rocky IV* employs the punk subculture's insistence on visual style for its own narrative and spectacular ends. The bad guys, Drago and his Russian wife, Ludmilla (Brigitte Nielsen), are costumed as punks. They have short, spikey hair cuts, they wear fashionably chic punk clothes with padded shoulders, and Ludmilla wears two earrings on one ear. Extreme low angle close-ups position Drago as a monster, while medium shots and long shots stress his enormous size and suggest he is part man, part machine.

The negative characteristics of late capitalism in the United States simply become displaced on to a visibly different, threatening Other.[10] The film's paranoid insistence on dichotomy denies the complexity and fragmentation of social life in advanced capitalist countries. Instead the oppositions between yuppies and punks become, to quote Fredric Jameson, "a privileged representational shorthand for grasping a network of power and control too difficult for our minds and imaginations to grasp...." The casting of tall, blond Scandinavians—ideal Aryan übermenschen—as Russians collapses history still further. In *Rocky IV*'s visual logic, Reds equal Nazis.

So much does the film rely on dualism that it has room for only one enemy. All subgroups and subcultures except punks rally to Rocky's side. As in *Down and Out in Beverly Hills*, not only women and children but even blacks become part of the big happy U.S. family which Rocky heads, though here domestic affairs play second fiddle to foreign policy.

Nowhere does this become more apparent than in the film's portrayal of blacks. Unlike all the other *Rocky* films and even more than in *Down and Out in Beverly Hills*, race does not pose a problem in *Rocky IV*. Apollo eagerly enlists in the New Cold War, responding to Drago's challenge when Rocky turns it down. Apollo's Las Vegas exhibition bout with Drago is a masterpiece of spectacle, shot in reds, whites and blues and replete with dancing girls, fireworks and rock music. Mr. Soul himself, James Brown, belts out "Livin' in America" as Apollo prances out, dressed in his Uncle Sam costume from *Rocky II*. The more blatant racism of the earlier films surfaces only in Apollo's cocky lack of preparation and prefight macho posturing. Because in this film Apollo acts both foolishly and bravely, blacks and whites in the audience can mourn his death with Rocky and vow a common vengeance. At the same time the story line absolves whites and

Rocky of guilt since the underlying message remains: Apollo deserved to die because he was unprepared and weak.

As for women, all the *Rocky* films assign them roles only within in the context of the family—as wives, sisters and mothers. *Rocky IV* adds to traditional family values an ideological agenda. The family becomes just another sports arena for broadcasting New Cold War messages, and politics replace relationships and romance. "I fight so you don't have to fight," Rocky tells his son. The interactions between Rocky and Adrian, a prime focus of the first film and still important in the second and third, here recede into the background. While Adrian initially shows great concern for Rocky's welfare, ultimately she realizes her country's honor is at stake and joins her husband as he trains in Russia.

Reaction shots of Adrian, Ludmilla and Apollo's wife pepper the fight sequences. The way Ludmilla is filmed adds a layer of ambiguity to the film's clear-cut ideological message. The film shows her far more often in close-up and extreme close-up than Adrian; she looks far more glamorous and exotic; and she has the larger speaking role. Indeed, she speaks for her man, who thereby loses a degree of male power. For women in the audience, the conflict between spectacle and narrative—the one favoring the villainness, the other the heroine—offers a choice of female characters with whom to identify, at the partial expense of ideological unity.

Thanks to the multiple ideological concerns *Rocky IV* contains within its formulaic narrative, Rocky's final victory pleases everyone. Small wonder that almost half the audience for *Rocky IV* is over 25 and almost half is female (Goldman). Part of the film's charm derives from its predictability.[11] By round fifteen, blacks and whites, young and old, women and men, yuppies and punks in the movie theater all chant "Rocky! Rocky! Rocky! Rocky!" along with the Russians in the film. The decibel level of their enthusiasm exceeds that of all the earlier films. Even Drago finally adopts U.S. values and asserts himself as an anti-authoritarian, individualist punk. "I fight to win—for me!" he bellows at the KGB agent who has been berating him, then throws the agent bodily out of the ring.

Constantly shifting camera set-ups, reaction shots, camera angles and pans draw everyone into the action. Rocky's final victory speech has a brilliant incoherence, managing to appeal to pacifists and Cold War advocates alike. His words reflect the average U.S. citizen's mistrust of government bureaucracy and fear of nuclear war. At the same time, the images offer us the satisfaction of knowing that David can beat Goliath. With elaborate and inarticulate pauses, panting all the while, Rocky says:

> Thank you. I came here tonight and I didn't know what to expect. I seen a lot of people hatin' me and I didn't know what to feel about that so I guess I didn't like you much none either. During this fight I seen a lot of changin'. The way u'se felt about me and the way I felt about you. In here there were two guys killin' each other, but I guess that's better than 20 million. What I'm tryin' to say is, that if I can change and you can change, everybody can change!

Even the Politburo must stand and cheer. The United States is not only resurgent, it is victorious. Humanism and aggression stand side by side in this closing sequence, just as they do in the rhetoric of the New Cold War. History becomes collapsed. *Rocky* replaces the casualty figures of nuclear annihilation with the 20 million dead of the Second World War. The film delivers its good-will Christmas message of hope on U.S. terms, but it masks those terms by ending as it began, with the nuclear family. In this way, Rocky's last words and the film's images echo those of *Rocky II*. But now Rocky's message of love goes out to his son, not to Adrian, as the boy sits at home in front of the TV: "I just want to say one thing to my kid who should be home sleepin'. Merry Christmas, kid! I love you!"

As in *Down and Out in Beverly Hills*, the final emphasis shifts from the specific problems of New Cold War U.S.A. to enduring patriarchal power. But new subcultures and subgroups have been integrated into the family, distorting and reinforcing the New Cold War ideology predicated on those values. Personal history replaces international history, and the way is paved for sequels to come.

FEMINISM MEETS IMPERIALISM:
ALIENS AND NEW COLD WAR IN SPACE

Aliens similarly embeds its references to current foreign policy concerns within the nuclear family. But here, unlike *Rocky IV, Down and Out in Beverly Hills* and most other New Cold War films, the hero is a woman, albeit one with an androgynous name: Ripley (Sigourney Weaver). In the context of an action-adventure *cum* science fiction *cum* horror film like *Aliens*, the presence of a central female character who emerges successful had strong is exceptional. The switch from male to female hero indicates the extent to which feminism has infiltrated film and changed daily life.

At the same time, Ripley remains a token. Her status as hero focuses attention on sex roles at the expense of international—in this case, intergalactic—politics. Indeed, the film's strategy could be defined as a perverse reversal of the early 1970s feminist maxim, "the personal is political." In *Aliens*, even more than in *Down and Out* and *Rocky IV*, the political becomes rewritten as and restricted to the personal. With the exception of the sound track, every aspect of the film, from the mise-en-scene to the plot to the characters, remains tied to female sexuality, which in turn becomes defined via motherhood.

In actuality *Aliens'* storyline rests on the premise of a foreign threat to U.S. imperialist economic interests far more openly than *Down and Out* does and far more ominously than *Rocky IV*. It also critiques, as the original *Alien* (Scott: 1979) also does, these interests' callous inhumanity. In *Alien*, however, this inhumanity grounds the entire film. Big business (the Company) and technology (the ship's computer and the robot/scientist) seem allied as much if not more against the crew members themselves, who are slated to die, as against the aliens, who will merely be captured and brought back to the United States. Thus, while female sexuality remains a major concern in *Alien*, the film deals with other issues.[12] In *Aliens*, in contrast, the overt political overtone of the film's beginning recede into the background and become subplots as soon as Ripley and the Marines leave the earth. Big business less obviously represents the bad guy because audience antipathy stays focused on a single individual, Carter Burke (Paul Reiser), the yuppie company representative.[13] The sequel vindicates technology. The robot, Bishop, (Lance Henriksen) initially an object of fear, becomes a hero, more "human" than the space ships and the advanced weapons systems but just as synonymous with progress."

Aliens begins where *Alien* left off, with Ripley and her cat deep in hypersleep somewhere in outer space. On her return to earth 57 years later, Ripley confronts the same profit-hungry corporation which in the first film engineered the destruction of her ship and crew. Despite her protests, a new generation of corporate executives perfunctorily terminates the investigation of the earlier disaster. But when an entire colony of U.S. settlers on a remote planet is mysteriously wiped out, the company turns to Ripley for help. After much debate, Burke persuades her to accompany him and a Marine rescue force as an advisor.

When Ripley, Burke and the Marines arrive at the colony, they discover a waif-like little girl nicknamed Newt (Carrie Henn). She alone has evaded the aliens by hiding in the air and heating ducts of the settlers' bioworld. Ripley feels a kinship with Newt, the only other person to have experienced and survived an alien attack. Their relationship quickly deepens. In shot/reverse shots, close-ups and medium two-shots, the film chronicles an awakening mother/daughter bond between the two. As the aliens come ever closer, Ripley repeatedly risks her own life to save Newt. The most dramatic example of motherly self-sacrifice occurs near the end of the film. Even though the planet is about to explode, Ripley returns, alone but armed with every weapon in the Marine arsenal, to rescue Newt from the clutches of the giant serpent-like mother alien. She sets the alien's eggs on fire and wisks Newt back to the space ship/womb just in time.

In *Alien* Ripley's maternal qualities are suggested only by her love for her cat, Jonesy. In *Aliens*, in contrast, Ripley incarnates heroism and motherhood for both ultra-conservatives and feminists. Her devotion to her child has clear appeal to right-wing proponents of traditional sexual politics at the same time as her independence, autonomy and androgyny fly in the face of conservative ideas of what a woman is and should be. Feminists, on the other hand, champion Ripley because she stands on her own two feet, yet does not hesitate to care. Also, she successfully combines blue-collar and managerial skills (she works as a loader before becoming a military advisor). By going it alone, against gender stereotypes and all odds, Ripley proves single mothers can be successful parents.

This brings a welcome change from the nurturing male single parent movies of the late 70s and early 80s like *Kramer vs. Kramer* (Benton: 1979), *Mr. Mom* (Dragoti: 1983) and even *Beyond the Thunderdome* (Miller: 1985). Like Mad Max, Ripley is not just a single parent, she is also a child finder—a quintessentially 1980s concern. She seems more adept than either Kramer, Mr. Mom or Mad Max at juggling the dual pressures of work and family which confront and tantalize the majority of women, not just feminists, in the 1980s. Anxious to improve their economic status while often still wanting traditional female roles as mothers and/or wives, women today must more than ever negotiate and resolve societal contradictions within their personal live. They often have educational preparation and high expectations, but affirmative action has failed them, social services have been gutted, and pay inequities continue unabated. By identifying with Ripley, women find not only hope for success, but also, consciously or unconciously, the satisfaction of vengeance.

As a character Ripley is assigned phallic attributes at the same time as she is clearly marked as heterosexual. The narrative hints at a romance between her and Hicks, the nicest male Marine (Michael Biehn).[14] In *Aliens* as in Alien, she periodically functions as a reassuring female fetish object. In her underwear, as Barbara Creed notes, her "body is pleasurable and reassuring to look at. She signifies the 'acceptable' form and shape of woman." Most of the time, however, Ripley wears baggy clothing and moves assertively. When she climbs into her loader machine to fight the mother alien, all her femininity disappears: she becomes a man. One of *Aliens'* mixed messages is thus very similar to the messages of *Down and Out in Beverly Hills* and *Rocky IV*. To act, one must have muscles and one must, if not be a man, at least masquerade as a man. In fact, several critics have referred to Ripley as "Rambolina" (Kopkind, Korpivaara, Crouchet, Small, Kael). On some level, all three films encapsulate what women and men of the 1980s know: society still defines success in male terms.

The film similarly incorporates ambiguous portrayals of the secondary female characters. The depiction of Vasquez (Jenette Goldstein), a career soldier who out-machos everyone, offers the clearest example of the film's play with sexual politics. "Hey, Vasquez, have you ever been mistaken for a man?" a male Marine asks as she effortlessly executes a series of overhand chin-ups. "No, have you?" she replies. Throughout the film she not only defies sex roles, she also challenges the definition of female sexuality as heterosexuality. With her muscles, her red bandana and her aggressive stance, Goldstein plays the character as dyke, Latin American revolutionary, and U.S. career soldier rolled into one. The narrative insists on Vasquez' heroism. Like Apollo in *Rocky IV*, she volunteers for the toughest assignments, and at the end she resolutely sacrifices herself for her comrades and her country. Nowhere does *Aliens* mention the possibility of a direct bonding between women other than that between mother and daughter. What "bonding" exists between Ripley and Vasquez is mediated through nationality. They are on the same side in an imperialist war, not sisters or lovers. Because the film hints that Vasquez is gay but emphasizes her courage, the character appeals to a wide spectrum of audience members, from radical lesbians to arch conservatives.

On the whole *Aliens* is more concerned with the traditional female body than with androgynous or masculine female bodies. Women are linked with reproduction, sexuality and carnality throughout the film. These associations become most obvious when projected onto the aliens or transposed to the background sets. In *Alien* the enemy "mother" is the ship's computer, not a female creature. There the mise-en-scene betrays the film's preoccupation with the riddle of femininity more than the design of the monsters does. They look like sexless blobs. In the attack on the near-naked Ripley at the end of the movie, they become male rapists. In *Aliens*, in contrast, the monsters are insects, ruled over by a queen. As Penelope Tarratt notes in Monsters from the Id," science fiction films often couple insect fear with a dread of the phallic mother as they reenact repressed sexual desires.

Ripley wreaks vengeance against a creature distinctly coded in terms of male-defined femininity. The alien mother's snarling mouth represents a veritable *vagina dentata*. Feminists may interpret this bad mother in terms of right-wing women who live to breed and to attack others who do not share their reproductive agenda.[15] Such an interpretation is possible given the film's feminist leanings. However, the overriding effect of the alien queen's portrayal as a "single mother" is to displace and subsume women's rebellion against patriarchal power structures and men onto an archetypal myth of Woman, and to direct women viewers' anger against other women. Seen in this light, Ripley's killing of the alien queen appeals to men as much if not more than it appeals to women, for by it Ripley protects men from their dread of women.[16]

In the final analysis, *Aliens'* ideological slipperiness stems less from its blend of misogyny and feminism than from its combining these traits with militarism and imperialism. The film hides international politics behind personal and family politics more skillfully than either *Down and Out* or *Rocky IV* do. Not surprisingly, critics ignore *Aliens'* militaristic and imperialist premises while discussing or at least mentioning such premises in reviews of other science fiction and adventure films, whether *Rocky IV, Raiders of the Lost Ark* (Spielberg: 1981) or *Star Wars* (Lucas: 1977).

Critics may debate *Aliens'* attitudes towards women and Woman, but the right of Ripley, the U.S. Marines and the "terraformers" to occupy and colonize another world goes largely unquestioned (Kopkind; Creed; Ansen; O'Toole; Schickel, July 28, 1986).

In many ways *Aliens* has a far more bellicose narrative than either *Down and Out in Beverly Hills* or *Rocky IV*. Sexuality, war and colonization constantly overlap, especially in the substrata of the film. The sets (the space ships and the artificially constructed, self-contained world of the colonists) resemble wombs, as they did in *Alien* (Creed, 1986). More overtly than in *Alien*, they also evoke colonialism and the jungles of Vietnam. The artificial bio-world of the settlers is dark, shot in blues and greys, claustrophic, full of tunnels and pipes, hot and often steamy. With their guns pointing out in front of them, the Marines seem like penises impregnating the colony, sperm searching for alien eggs, and warriors seeking to protect imperialist interests by destroying the enemy. The portrayal of the aliens also links sexuality and war. Their unexpected and violent emergence from their victims' stomachs suggests a combined fantasy of how babies are born, invasion and occupation all at once. The incredibly rapid growth of these "babies," their tails and the sticky white secretions they leave behind suggest erections, penises and ejaculation while also inscribing right wing fears of widespread and uncontrollable popular uprisings.

As in *Down and Out* and *Rocky IV*, domestic and foreign policy issues become tightly entwined. Once again, a Hollywood film mobilizes women, blacks, Latinos, proletarians and punks in support of colonialism and imperialism. The multi-racial mix of the Marines recalls the extended family in *Down and Out* and the united front of blacks and whites in *Rocky IV*. Everyone functions in peak physical shape, with the exception of Burke, who looks flat-chested and thin. But as with *Rocky IV*'s emphasis on training and fitness, *Aliens'* insistence on bodybuilding betrays the United States' anxiety that, as in Beirut and Vietnam, it will once again be caught off guard or found unprepared. Fear of contagion by AIDS-like diseases replaces fear of aging or weakness, perhaps because *Aliens* deals with colonialism (Kopkind).[17] As Edward Saïd notes, the association of the colonial other with disease, insanity and sexuality typifies colonial discourse.

As in other New Cold War films, the film invokes the iconography of yuppie and punk subcultures to create a world of clear-cut binary oppositions. But while in *Rocky IV* "yuppie" signified weakness to overcome, here it signifies cowardice and treachery to wipe out. Burke, the yuppie, becomes the depository of the negative characteristics of U.S. imperialism, much as Drago and Ludmilla, the punks, do in *Rocky IV*. In *Aliens* the underlying binary structures simply become reversed. The film valorizes punks; here, the Marines, not the Russians, sport spike haircuts, chains and black fingerless gloves.

Lighting, camera angle and movement, editing, music and ambient sound all encourage and reinforce jingoist audience identification with Ripley and the Marines as good Americans. Flares and napalm blasts provide bursts of white, while reds and blues flood the screen during moments of crisis. Low angle shots, a constantly moving camera and rapid editing leave little time for thought. As in *The Terminator*, Cameron's first film, another ominous surprise awaits just around the corner. Drums, gunfire, explosions, screams and yells echo, conveying a sense of urgency and danger.

Allusions to other war films and references to U.S. military involvement in Vietnam and Cambodia, absent from *Alien*, permeate *Aliens*. A scene reminiscent of *The Deer Hunter* (Cimino: 1978) evokes the U.S. soldiers' boredom and jaded search for thrills in Vietnam. For example, as lunchtime entertainment, the robot "Bishop" stabs a knife between the outstretched fingers of a Marine's hand. *Aliens'* characterization of the Marines as insubordinate, combat-wise troops led by an incompetent lieutenant replays a cliché found in Vietnam war films from *Apocalypse Now* (Coppola: 1979) to *Full Metal Jacket* (Kubrick: 1987) and *Platoon* (Stone: 1987). Here the lieutenant's refusal to let the Marines stalking the aliens fire because they are under a nuclear reactor recalls not only the field experiences of Marines in Vietnam but also the helplessness of the Marines in Beirut. And the hurried departure of Ripley, Newt, Hicks and Bishop in the space shuttle calls to mind the last minute airlifts from both Saigon and Phnom Penh.

Aliens goes far beyond other, more realist, war films. Because it blends science fiction, action-adventure and horror genres, fantasies replace facts and outweigh fears. The film tells us that not only can the United States win imperialist wars but even survive nuclear ones. In this film, conventional weapons prove insufficient, as in Vietnam, but in space nuclear weapons presumably can function safely and successfully. The film conveys none of the terror of nuclear annihilation which permeated science fiction movies of the 1950s. When only Burke's voice urges restraint, to nuke or not to nuke never even becomes a question.

Aliens' conclusion, like that of countless other New Cold War films, evades facing societal and political problems by apparently returning to traditional values. "I like to think the real message [of *Aliens*] is love," Sigourney Weaver has said (Schickel, July 28, 1986). The film's final sequence recalls those of *Down and Out in Beverly Hills* and *Rocky IV*. Ripley tucks Newt into her sleeping pod, and assures the girl that at last it's, "safe to dream." Their mother/daughter relationship ensures imperialism's continuation, just as the father/son relationship does in *Rockey IV*. To depict Ripley as nurturer justifies and masks the film's violence and promotes a New Cold War characterization of U.S. foreign policy as defensive, not aggressive.

Contradictions inevitably remain. In many ways they become heightened because, unlike *Rocky IV* or *Down and Out in Beverly Hills, Aliens* takes the economic and political gains of an *oppositional* movement—the women's movement—as its raison d'etre. The portrayal of Ripley and Vasquez as strong, independent, likeable women warriors threatens the patriarchal values on which New Cold War ideology relies even as the film collapses feminism into imperialism. *Aliens* does use many stereotypical images of women as mothers, daughters, bitches and bull dykes. But for all its fondness for convention, it acknowledges that motherhood *has* changed, and that women's identities and roles *have* multiplied. In this film as in society, victory in Vietnam is patently a fiction; single, working women are demonstrably a fact. The dread and the desires attaching to women and to war operate here on different registers. *Aliens'* mass appeal—and its subversive potential—lie in the gaps and bridges it creates and negotiates between the two levels.

CONCLUSION

Because they belong to different genres, *Down and Out in Beverly Hills, Rocky IV* and *Aliens* seem to address different questions and to work in different ways. Closer examination reveals the films have much in common. All three employ, promote, dilute and dissolve a New Cold War ideology specific to the United States of the late 70s and 80s, an ideology absent from the original film or the preceding films in the series. All three replace the political with the personal, rewrite economic concerns as sexual problems, and end by returning to tradition. Drawing on earlier romance and success myths, all three films disguise military aggression as nurturance and love, even as they dramatize the need for domestic unity in the face of external threat.

But the fact that these films promote nationalism, patriarchy and imperialism ultimately means less than their obsessive organization of current fears and fantasies surrounding sexual, racial, subcultural and class difference. Contradictions constantly emerge which point up ambivalences in New Cold War ideology itself, perched precariously as it is between conservativism and liberalism, the old and the new. Because the films attempt not only to address but also to entertain a variety of subgroups and subcultures in their intended audience, they undercut and extend right-wing ideology. In particular, the films incorporate references to oppositional movements of the 1960s, 70s and 80s and construct alternative points of identification. When *Down and Out in Beverly Hills, Rocky IV, Aliens* and films like them include blacks, gays lesbians, punks, Mexicans, Japanese, and other subgroups within the traditional nuclear family, when they promote working mothers as single heads of household, and acknowledge or even excuse male insecurities, they dilute and occasionally undermine the purity of New Cold War rhetoric.

The very effort these films make to transcribe and channel current social contexts so as to ensure a unified audience response betrays the existence of multiple audience responses, and hints at the continuing appeal of progressive political movements. In the final analysis, the mixed ideological messages and confused styles of address characteristic of *Down and Out in Beverly Hills, Rocky IV* and *Aliens* demonstrate that subgroups and subcultures have become more, not less important in today's film audiences and in society as a whole. There are several "correct" responses to these films, and these responses are anticipated by the film text and in excesses that point beyond the text.

These films do not merely bracket reality by solipsistically referring to themselves and other media products, as Andrew Britton argues. they do not merely construct entertainment as separate from and in opposition to life. Britton's concentration on the film texts he analyzes works against his exploring how audiences use these texts, and his methodology blinds him to the contradictions contained within the films. Looked at from the point of view of the audience, the very category "entertainment" proves more complicated than critics usually acknowledge. Since individual audience members have different relations to labor, gender, sexuality, race and subcultures, viewers also have different relations to, expectations of, and uses for entertainment.[18] As Gina Marchetti argues with reference to the functioning of class and ideology in *The A-Team*, popular films like these address, subsume and reconcile audience differences in order to make money, yet the contradictions they raise cannot be completely contained. Rather than emphasize, as Britton does, the monolithic pervasiveness of "Reaganite" or New Cold War ideology in today's film texts, we should, to quote James Collins,

> take into account the centring power of individual discourses, [and] the power of individuals to make choices regarding those discourses. While a unitary culture may have disappeared, unitary discourses constructing very specific subjects have only intensified.

Marxist and feminist mass media critics face a difficult task.How do we map the intersections, overlays and divergences among mass culture, dominant ideologies, representation and history, while neither denying nor oversimplifying the category of the subject? I would maintain it is too soon to characterize and categorize the relations between today's popular films and society as fixed, or to view a priori any form of popular culture as "bad" and manipulative. To do so means ignoring points of opposition and vulnerability which inevitably exist within, and despite, dominant discourses. Instead, as Dana Polan suggests, we should engage in an ongoing analysis which studies individual texts within their larger intertextuality, and within the overall operations of capitalism today. In this spirit I have analyzed New Cold War ideology in *Down and Out in Beverly Hills*, *Rocky IV* and *Aliens*. I secretly hope, of course, that in sequels and remakes to come, aliens will populate Beverly Hills and cheer as Ripley razes Rocky.
while neither denying nor oversimplifying the category of the subject? I would maintain it is too

NOTES

[1] Britton's pessimistic view of contemporary popular films is typical of much Marxist postmodernist criticism where the high modernist novel or the classic Hollywood film are taken as models and norms. See, for example, Jameson.

Recently, of course, critics of postmodern mass media have begun to recognize that individual audience members and subgroups within film audiences can and do resist dominant ideological messages, even while consuming and/or enjoying them. See, for example, Collins and essays in Modleski, ed..

[2] Noam Chomsky gives a more detailed description of the New Cold War's many manifestations and consequences today.

[3] Faulkner perceptively argues, however, that while Boudu is a film about class difference, it is not a film about class conflict. He categorizes the film's humor as, in Roland Barthes' terms, "inoculative" rather than subversive, maintaining that Renoir never identifies or accuses the economic structures on which bourgeois cultural hegemony rest.

[4] For an analysis of sexuality, class and feminism in an earlier Disney film, see my article on *The North Avenue Irregulars* (dir. Bilson, 1979).

[5] In ending with the tramp's successful conversion to a bourgeois, Mazursky's film is far more faithful to the original play by Rene Fauchois than Renoir's *Boudu*. See Sesonske, Faulkner for discussions of the shifts between Renoir's film and Fauchois' play.

[6] The banality and gentility of Mazursky's critique of the dominant organization of gender, sexuality and class become obvious when compared with John Water's acerbic send up of Baltimore's lower middle classes in *Polyester* (1979).

[7] See Robin Woods' article, "Ideology, Genre, Auteur," for a list of values and assumptions of U.S. capitalist ideology which pervade classic Hollywood film. More specifically, *Down and Out in Beverly Hills* participates in what Chuck Kleinhans calls "the sophisticated or ironic success myth in which the price of material success is shown to be spiritual and social emptiness. We could call this the bourgeois failure myth, or the sour-grapes version of the naive success myth."

[8] Stallone's reliance on New Cold War ideology is especially blatant in *Rambo III*. Set in Soviet-occupied Afghanistan, *Rambo III* bombed at the box office, in good part because it was released shortly after the Soviets announced they were withdrawing troops and ultimately pulling out of the country.

[9] In contrast, few audience members of *Down and Out* realize it is based on an earlier French

film. Jameson stated (1984) that remakes as *re*makes provide us with a kind of "pseudo-historical depth" as "the history of aesthetic styles displaces real history," This needs nuancing in the case of *Down and Out*. Any connotation of pastness" predicated on intertextuality is on the whole lost on the viewing public because the original is an older, *foreign*, film.

[10] Indeed, in a *People* magazine interview (Jerome), Stallone speaks of Drago in the way that Europeans, Third World peoples and even many U.S. citizens would speak of the United States: "Drago represents technology, big business, machines, and international politics."

[11] Britton maintains that predictability is the main source of pleasure in 80s films. While this may be true of the *Rocky* films and other blatantly New Cold War films, he fails to account for the widespread distribution and popular success of films which are considerably more ideologically volatile, like Susan Seidelman's *Desperately Seeking Susan* (1984).

[12] Barbara Creed's article, "Horror and the Monstrous Feminine," (1986) is typical of the tendency in feminist criticism to focus on gender and sexuality at the expense of race and imperialism. Creed reads *Alien* against Kristeva's theories of abjection. She argues that *Alien* in particular and horror films in general inscribe both an archaic mother (here: the womb/the black hole) and a phallic mother (here: the aliens). Her analysis is fruitful but limited to analyzing "a complex representation of the monstrous-feminine in terms of the maternal figure as perceived within a patriarchal ideology."

[13] As Jim Naureckas notes in this review of the film, the reference to Carter is significant: "[Burke's] unusual first name may be taken as a swipe at detente—he wants to profit from the Aliens, not destroy them." See also Ernest Larsen in a similar discussion of the corporation's control over the first *Alien* spaceship crew.

[14] Hicks is in fact the only man to survive, albeit thanks to Ripley and blinded in one eye (castrated).

[15] An example is Margaret Atwood's depiction of ruling class women in the feminist dystopia, *The Handmaid's Tale*.

[16] Few reviewers except Naureckas acknowledge *Aliens'* appeals to a male fear of women, preferring to concentrate on Ripley's feminism. For the original psychoanalytic analysis, see Karen Horney.

[17] The same fear of sexually transmitted diseases appears in *Witches of Eastwick* (Miller: 1987) where for the first time a heroine suffers from herpes.

[18] Kleinhans concludes "Working Class Heroes" with a similar observation: "When we talk about film audience we always mean an aggregate of various audiences, which can be described by distinguishing their nationality, language, sex, class, race, religion, age, occupation or political views. In other words, there is never a homogeneous audience for a Hollywood film." John Fiske argues that audience identification with elements of popular TV shows occurs not between the individual viewer and one or more of the characters, but at the level of the discursive structures of the TV text. Such an understanding of identification "recognizes that [the] play of similarity and difference along the axes of nation, race, class, gender, power, work, etc. [in the text] fits with the discursive structure of the reading subject."

REFERENCES

Ansen, David, "Terminating the Aliens," *Newsweek* 108.3 (July 21, 1986)

Atwood, Margaret, *The Handmaid's Tale* (Boston: Houghton Mifflin, 1986)

Britton, Andrew, "Blissing Out: The Politics of Reagantite Entertainment," *Movie* 31-32 (Winter 1986)

Chomsky, Noam, *Towards a New Cold War: Essays on the Current Crisis and How We Got There* (New York: Pantheon, 1982)

Collins, James, "Postmodernism and Cultural Practice: Redefining the Parameters," *Screen* 28.2 (Spring 1987)

Corliss, Rich, "Sugary Satire," *Time* 27.4 (January 27, 1986)

Creed, Barbara, "From Here to Modernity: Feminism and Postmodernism," *Screen* 28.2 (Spring 1987)

Creed, Barbara, "Horror and the Monstrous-Feminine: An Imaginary Abjection," *Screen* 27.1 (January-February 1986)

Crouchet, Bruce, "Aliens," *Cinefantastique* 16.3 (July 1986)

Denby, David, "Angst at the Top," *New York* 19.5 (February 3, 1986)

Denby, David, "Cartoon God, Fallen Idol," *New York* 18.48 (December 9, 1985)

Faulkner, Christopher, *The Social Cinema of Jean Renoir* (Princeton: Princeton University Press, 1986)

Fiske, John, *Television Culture* (London: Methuen, 1987)

Goldman, Peter, "Rocky and Rambo," *Newsweek* 106.26 (December 23, 1985)

Grant, Barry, ed. *Flim Genre Reader* (Austin: Univ. of TX, 1986)

Hebdige, Dick, *Subculture: The Meaning of Style* (London: Methuen, 1979)

Holmlund, Christine, "Tots to Tanks: Walt Disney Presents Feminism for the Family," *Social Text* 1.2 (Summer 1979)

Horney, Karen, The Dread of Woman," *Feminine Psychology* (New York: W.W. Norton & Co., 1967)

Jameson, Frederic, "Postmodernism and Consumer Society," *The Anti-Aesthetic*, ed. Hal Foster (Port Townsend, WA: Bay Press, 1983)

Jameson, Fredric, "Postmodernism or the Cultural Logic of Late Capitalism," *New Left Review* 146 (July-August 1984)

Jerome, Jim, "Screen," *People Weekly* 24.24 (December 9, 1985)

Kael, Pauline, "The Current Cinema," New Yorker 62 (August 11, 1986)

Kleinhans, Chuck, "Working-Class Film Heroes: Junior Johnson, Evel Knievel and the Film Audience," JUMP CUT 2 (1974), reprinted in *JUMP CUT: Hollywood, Politics and Counter Cinema*, ed. Peter Steven (Praegar: New York, 1985)

Kopkind, Andrew, "The Fly, Aliens," *The Nation* (september 20, 1986)

Korpivaara, Ari, "Roll Over Rambo," *Ms.* 15.3 (September 1986)

Kroll, Jack, "Socking It to the Russians," *Newsweek* 106.24 (December 9, 1985)

Larsen, Earnest, "Alien and Dawn of the Dead: High-Tech Horror," JUMP CUT 21 (November 1979)

Marchetti, Gina, "Class, Ideology and Commercial Television: An Analysis of The A-Team," *Journal of Film and Video* 39 (Spring 1987)

Martin, John W, *The Golden Age of French Cinema* (Boston: Twayne, 1983)

Modleski, Tania, "The Terror of Pleasure: The Contemporary Horror Film and Postmodern Theory," Modleski, Tania, ed., *Studies in Entertainment* (Bloomington: Indiana University Press, 1986)

Naureckas Jim, "*Aliens:* Mother and the Teeming Hordes," JUMP CUT 32 (April 1986)

O'Brien, John, "Tomfoolery 10, Satire 0," *National Review* 38.5 (March 28, 1986)

O'Brien, Tom, "Comedy High and Low," *Commonweal* 113.7 (April 11, 1986)

O'Brien, Tom, Review of *Rocky IV, Commonweal* 113.1 (January 17, 1986)

O'Toole, Lawrence, "*Aliens,*" *Maclean's* 99.30 (July 28, 1986)

Polan, Dana, "Brief Encounters: Mass Culture and The Evacuation of Sense" in Modleski, ed.

Saïd, Edward, *Orientalism* (New York: Vintage, 1979)

Schickel, Richard, "Help! They're Back!," *Time* 128.4 (July 28, 1986)

Schickel, Richard, "Win the Battle, Lose the War," *Time* 126.23 (December 9, 1985)

Sesonske, Alexandre, *Jean Renoir* (Cambridge: Harvard University Press, 1980)

Small, Michael, "Sigourney Weaver Leads an *Alien* Box Office Invasion," *People Weekly* 26.10 (September 8, 1986)

Tarratt, Penelope, "Monsters from the Id," in Grant, ed.

Walker, Janet and McCarroll, Luli, "Renoir on the Bridge: A Reading of *Boudu Saved From Drowning*," *Wide Angle* 4.4 (1981)

Wolfe, Alan, "Society, Liberalism and the Radical Right," *New Left Review* 128 (July-August 1981)

Woods, Robin, "Ideology, Genre, Auteur," in Grant, ed.

ERNEST SAVES CHRISTMAS (*Film Review Annual, 1989*)

MONTHLY FILM BULLETIN, 12/89, p. 365, Richard Combs

December 23. Santa Claus arrives in Orlando, Florida, having decided that his advanced years and failing memory (he has had the job of bringing joy to the world's children since 1889) necessitate his passing on his mantle and toy sack to someone else. He has chosen Joe Carruthers, whose television programme for children has recently been cancelled. From the airport, Santa is taken on a hair-raising ride to the Orlando Children's Museum by the manically good-natured Ernest P. Worrell, who also finds himself taking charge of a runaway teenage girl calling herself Harmony. Santa's efforts to approach Carruthers are frustrated by the latter's smooth-talking agent Marty, who wants to launch him on a movie career with a part in a current production, *Christmas Slay*. Santa is eventually jailed as a vagrant and nuisance, and has to be sprung by Ernest and Harmony posing as a pair of governmental snoopers into the prison system. Ernest smuggles Santa into the film studio to see Carruthers by posing as a snake-farm wrangler, but Carruthers is already being groomed for his film role. He has second thoughts when he realises it is to be a monster/slasher movie, but time is running out on Santa's Christmas Eve deadline. Ernest rushes back to the airport to collect Santa's reindeer, which have now begun climbing the ceiling to the consternation of two baggage handlers. Two of Santa's helper elves also arrive, and they and Ernest board the sleigh to rendezvous with Santa at the children's museum. Seeing them flash through the sky, Carruthers finally backs out of the movie deal, and Harmony, who has meanwhile taken off with Santa's sack of goodies, also has second thoughts and returns to the museum. After a wild ride, Ernest turns up with the sleigh and the terrified elves, and Carruthers is officially invested as the future Santa.

Ernest Saves Christmas is the latest dismal episode in the takeover by the product-placement movie of American films for children. Individual merchandise may be less conspicuous here than in *Mac and Me*, perhaps, though the opening images of Santa Claus come courtesy of Coca-Cola, and the cab driven with bruising abandon by the central character of course sports its own advertising hoarding. But *Ernest* is the feature-length extension of the commercials created by the Nashville agency of Garden & Cherry around the meddling, muddling character of Ernest P. Worrell, and in the movie's gallumphing style, senior executive and now director John Cherry never lets one forget it. (Knowledge of the commercials is, as it were, inscribed in the movie, particularly with a scene in which a subjective camera stands in for Ernest's unseen friend Vernon, baffling to the uninitiated.) Jim Varney's relentless grimacing and all-over-the-place slapstick looks like a desperate attempt to fill out a ninety-minute "spot", and it's hard to tell whether the random skits that punctuate his performance (some Pee-Wee Herman mincing, a Paul Hogan-ish snake farmer) are intended as spoofs of or demented commercials for the originals.

EVERYBODY'S ALL-AMERICAN (*Film Review Annual, 1989*)

MONTHLY FILM BULLETIN, 3/90, p. 84, John Pym

1957: Gavin Grey, a star Louisiana college football player, joins the hard world of the

Washington Redskins. He refuses sponsorship from car-dealer Bolling Kiely and invests in the Grey Ghost Inn managed by college teammate Edward Lawrence. Years pass and marriage to Babs Rogers, a former Magnolia Queen, turns decidedly flat. Meanwhile, Donnie McCaslin, the nephew to whom Gavin has often entrusted the neglected Babs, makes his way up the academic ladder; and Narvel Blue, a poor but determined kitchen-hand, rejects a career in pro-football and joins the Civil Rights movement. Lawrence is murdered and thrown through a window, a sign, Narvel informs Gavin, of the mob settling a bad debt. Kiely becomes the controlling partner in the inn. On his retirement from the Redskins, Gavin celebrates with the team and Donnie and Babs at last make love. Gavin joins a synthetic turf company: his job being to regale clients with his feats as the legendary "Grey Ghost". Having quarrelled with Kiely for neglecting the inn, Gavin attempts a comeback with the Denver Broncos: he is, however, a scarred has-been. Narvel, now a businessman and coming politician, employs the grateful Babs as his personal assistant. At a 1981 college reunion, Gavin guesses at Babs' infidelity; at a commemorative diner, however, he acknowledges the importance of their love.

Jessica Lange, Dennis Quaid and Timothy Hutton—all awkwardly aging down—play out a slow-footed romantic Southern saga. Babs discovers the pleasure of work and responsibility; Gavin the emptiness of fame; Donnie (saddled with the nickname "Cake") the prospective pleasure of an East Coast marriage. The setting is principally the Louisiana of supermarket fiction and the secondary characters, signposts along the long route of the plot, are devoid of individuality: the hero-worshipping car-dealer; the inadequate saloon-keeper; the patient black man waiting for his day. Although apparently taking the story at least half seriously, director Taylor Hackford offers a few light moments: the Magnolia Queen's wedding night being the most enjoyable, followed as it is by an obvious cut to the unseemly ruck of a pro-football game. Hemlines, hairdos and dance fads mark the passing years, along with some dog-eared snippets of actuality footage: a corsage from the attic.

FAR NORTH (*Film Review Annual, 1989*)

MONTHLY FILM BULLETIN, 3/90, p. 69, Richard Combs

When her father Bertrum is thrown from a buggy being pulled wildly by their old farm horse Mel, Kate returns to Minnesota to visit him in hospital. She fears this may be her last chance to reach some understanding with the intractable old man, but he is still scathing about the life she is trying to make for herself in the "big city", suspects that, though unattached, she is pregnant (his other daughter Rita, also unmarried, has remained on the family farm with her teenage daughter Jilly), and insists that she must shoot Mel. Kate sees this as the latest of the tests that he has always set her (to make her a surrogate son), but returning to the farm tentatively tries out the rifle, to Rita's disgust (she is determined to save Mel). While resentment and jealousy simmers between the sisters, Jilly's nighttime escapades add to the family tensions. Kate and Rita's mother Amy has grown fey and distracted, displaced by the collapse of the traditionally male-centred farm life that has made Bertrum so embittered, leaving a female clannishness about to be reasserted in an upcoming one-hundredth birthday party for Gramma. In hospital, Bertrum vents his anger at all the disappointments of his life on placid Uncle Dane (an alcoholic, in hospital for drying out), while Rita and Kate clash again over the latter's attempt to carry out her father's instructions, and Mel escapes into the woods. Rita sends Jilly to look for him, but when Kate finds him on the road after returning from a visit to her father, the sisters take the horse out to find Jilly. Realising that he will have to shoot Mel himself, Bertrum discharges himself from hospital and starts to walk back to the farm, trailed by Uncle Dane. In the woods, at night, where Kate and Rita have found Jilly necking with a boy, and settled their own differences after nearly coming to blows, Bertrum sees the women on horseback as a ghostly visitation, and rushes off in terror. He collapses, trying to make a last stand against the life which he feels has turned on him, and is carried back to the farm on Mel. While Gramma's birthday party takes place as a virtually all-female affair, Bertrum leads Mel out to the fields with his rifle.

Far North, Sam Shepard's début as director of his own original screenplay, has those clean but pushy dramatic lines, the visual straightforwardness and determination to say it all (or nearly all) through the actors that one expects when playwrights turn film-makers. The straightforwardness is not the same as the visual economy, the compression, one would expect from an experienced film director, but the particular spareness of Shepard's own theme and aesthetic, all those etiolated spaces where love or some similarly mysterious conjunction took place eons ago, has obligingly taken the imprint of some experienced film-makers in the past. One wonders if the clean contours of *Far North* will inevitably house ghosts, if Shepard's Shepard will resemble Wenders' or Robert Altman's.

As it happens, the ghosts come from much further afield than that, a wild and woolly bunch, with Shepard's theatrical figures, even at their most familiar—another demonstration that the family that squabbles together, stays together—destabilised by the raw Minnesota landscapes, tottering about the frozen edge of Lake Superior. The film insists on the locked-in wintry cussedness of its landscapes, their barbaric mysteriousness, to such an extent that they end up making the drama strange, or feeding strange bits of cinema into the theatre. This could be Arthur Miller with forests courtesy of Tarkovsky, or William Inge mingled with tipsy parts of David Lynch. The latter's timber country is more north-west, but it inspires a similar edge of the wilderness/edge of consciousness feeling, which seems to have left the inhabitants rather hypnotised. And what could be more Lynchian than Shepard's grandmother, or great-grandmother, who in one feverish montage leads this distaff family in a reversion to their hitherto unguessed Finnish roots, incanting over a railway timetable as she worries about who will make it to her hundredth birthday party?

If these wilder moments bespeak the true Shepard, or the True North, there's a dismaying amount of conventional engineering in the plot to produce them. The four-way family conflicts work like separate playlets—separated first of all by the credit-sequence accident that puts Charles Durning's patriarch Bertrum in hospital—which remain too over-driven and under-powered to keep the film going at more than a sluggish pace. Daughter Kate (Jessica Lange) returns from the perhaps not-too-successful life she has made for herself in the city, to find her father testing her as of yore (he wants her to shoot the horse, an old farm favourite, that put him in hospital); Kate is immediately at loggerheads with the sister, Rita (Tess Harper), who has stayed on the farm, over the issue of the horse and unresolved items of sibling rivalry; mother (Ann Wedgeworth) meanwhile wanders round vacantly, preparig huge breakfasts for the long-gone table of menfolk, and back on the ward, Bertrum vents the backed-up spleen of a lifetime on the only other extant male member of the family, docile, alcoholic Uncle Dane (Donald Moffat). Inevitably, Bertrum will discharge himself and stump off back to the farm, a Falstaff-sized ghost in his hospital gown, heading for a ghostly confrontation in the woods with his two daughters, who have been chasing the errant horse and reach a reconciliation of sorts riding him home (three a-horse, with Rita's equally errant adolescent daughter).

At which point, the playlets coalesce into something madder, something that conjures the cussedness of the landscape, the life it sucks away and the stubborn forms it gives back. Conjures, that is, in Bertrum's mind when, "haunted" by the sight of the three women on horseback, and now pursued by a finally exasperated Uncle Dane (from his wife's side of the family), he slips into his own incantation of the roots of these woes, the feral lineaments of life in the far north: "That's where they got it—the tribes...the Mongols...barbarian women". The film responds with a montage of this dementia—wild staring eyes, savages on horses—leading to its final celebratory scene, grandma's birthday party, several generations of placid matriarchy, while Bertrum leads the horse off into the snow to do the man's job he had tried to confer on his daughter. If the result is an inevitably unstable mix of generational conflict, via hallucination *and* the well-made play, it's fascinating for the rhymes, projections and displacements it contains. Altman's Shepard is here, or Altman's pre-Shepard in *3 Women* (where a purely female life force is putting out strange roots in the desert). And through this affinity one might see Shepard displacing himself in *Far North*, the self who featured in pieces in *Motel Chronicles*, confronting, like Kate, an intractable father (with accompanying photographs, in which Shepard Snr. Looks a little like the old Western actor Arthur Hunnicutt), and a stubborn masculine hold on the far South. "My dad lives alone on the desert. He says he doesn't fit with people".

NEW STATESMAN & SOCIETY, 2/9/90, p. 44, Suzanne Moore

Sam Shepard is the thinking women's Sylvester Stallone. He's rough and tough but cool enough to appear on the front of Italian *Vogue*. What's more, old "cowboy mouth" writes plays that maul every myth of American culture. He writes about being drunk and howling at the moon, about loving your country and hating your family and about the bare essentials of life—horses and guns. *Far North* is the first movie that he has directed—a peculiar mishmash of sentiment and stereotype that feels far too stagey ever to work properly. It's almost a parody of a Sam Shepard play. There is the proud and beautiful daughter who goes home to the woods of Minnesota because her father has had an accident. The old man wants her to "shoot his hoss". Her Mama is strictly doolally (lace collars and far away looks). Her teenage niece is a would-be nympho.

The motif, if there is one, seems to be the recurring question: "Where have all the men gone?" Which may possibly say something about the breakdown of American culture. Or maybe it's a quasi-feminist statement, because judging from this lot, wherever they have gone the women are better off without them.

FRESH HORSES (*Film Review Annual, 1989*)

MONTHLY FILM BULLETIN, 7/90, p. 197, John Pym

Matt Larkin, a well-to-do engineering student at the University of Cincinnati, is introduced by his friend Tipton to an older woman, Jean McBaine, who presides over a ramshackle bohemian household across the Kentucky border. Matt, who works part-time as a bingo-caller, is infatuated by the mysterious Jewel, an abused waif apparently sheltering under Jean's wing, and after searching his heart breaks his engagement to surgeon's daughter Alice Price. Matt courts Jewel warily. One evening, while Jewel is in Lexington, allegedly visiting her mother, Tipton tells Matt that his twenty-year-old girlfriend is in fact sixteen and has a husband in the Navy. Recriminations ensue, with Matt visiting Tipton's cousin Gary, a lawyer, to discuss the cost of a divorce, Jewel finding a picture of Alice in Matt's bedroom, and Matt's unsuspecting father coming upon his son and the angry Jewel. Matt and Jewel consummate their affair in a disused railroad shack. Learning from his friend Sproles that Jewel's husband, Green, is suspected of murder, Matt gives Jewel money to pay for a divorce. Their affair cools, however, and hits bottom one night when Jewel discovers the disconsolate Matt and a party of girls, including the importunate Ellen, roasting marshmallows in the shack. Later, it is reported that Jewel has been "raped" by Green and his father. An edgy confrontation between Matt and Green ends with Jewel's declaration that she wants rid of them both. Sometime later, at a Cincinnati Winterfest, Jewel introduces the resigned but still love-struck Matt to her new boyfriend.

This soulful, overladen love story, doomed from reel one, reunites the young stars of *Pretty in Pink*, Molly Ringwald and Andrew McCarthy. Derived from his off-Broadway, one-set play, Larry Ketron's script retains some now redundant theatrical devices, notably the messengers Tipton and Sproles entering with off-screen bad news. The atmosphere of the deserted funfair through which the lovers at one point maunder (echoing Matt's state of mind and, perhaps, the destiny of his inventive engineering ambitions), the vacancy of rural Kentucky and the gleam of rainswept Cincinnati, where money appears to buy a particularly arid sort of pleasure, are arrestingly conveyed. The trouble, though, is an awful lot of heart-searching on Matt's part and an awful lot of bygone agony and injustice on Jewel's, which, despite the patently sincere performances, simply fail to persuade.

GRAND HIGHWAY, THE (*Film Review Annual, 1989*)

MONTHLY FILM BULLETIN, 2/89, p. 49, Tom Milne

Claire, a Parisienne approaching the term of her pregnancy while her husband is working as a waiter in Nice for the season, arranges to park her nine-year-old son Louis with her old friend Marcelle in Brittany. Unaware that the somewhat uncouth man who offers to help with their luggage on the walk from the station is Marcelle's husband Pelo, Claire primly ignores him; and that night the tearfully abandoned Louis, whose bedroom looks out on the cemetery, is terrified when Pelo, returning from a drunken spree, playfully pretends to be a ghost. Marcelle, however, proves kinder than she seemed, and Louis soon finds a friend and mentor in the slightly older Martine, a neighbour's child. Admiring a carved wooden wagon which Martine warns him to leave alone since Pelo made it and won't let anyone touch it, Louis is thrilled when Pelo gives it to him as a toy; and with Pelo apologising for the ghost incident, their relationship progresses by leaps and bounds. Louis nevertheless remains baffled—even after Martine imparts what she knows of the facts of life—by the violent scenes at night when Pelo returns drunk and batters vainly on Marcelle's door. The marital rift in fact dates from the death in childbirth of their son—who would have been the same age as Louis—and now provokes competition for Louis' love. Not really understanding when Pelo explains, Louis is more preoccupied by worries as to why his mother hasn't come to collect him and whether he will ever see his father again. In despair when the cynical Martine explains about adultery and divorce, Louis climbs to the church roof (where he had once reluctantly followed Martine on a dare), crying his hatred of them all when the frightened Pelo tries to talk him down. Seeing a car and thinking his mother has arrived, Louis slips, but is saved from falling by Pelo. Soon after learning that he now has a baby brother, Louis is happily reunited with his mother; and saying goodbye to the disconsolate Martine, he departs for Paris, leaving Pelo and Marcelle reconciled but again bereft of a child.

Travelling well-worn paths that lead back to *Jeux Interdits* and beyond, this is the standard tale of childish sensibilities in premature conflict with the harsh realities of life, signposted none too subtly by the glimpse of a rabbit being bled through the eye and flayed that greets the arrival of a somewhat tiresomely snivelling Louis in the Breton village. This moment of rustic truth proves, however, to be merely a convenient peg on which to hang a strand of Disneyish sentimentality about furry things, with the boy fearfully hovering over a pet rabbit in its hutch, anxiously insisting that he prefers fish to meat, and finally taking the rabbit up to the church roof to share in his desperate protest against an uncaring world. Bawdily and healthily cynical, his chum Martine provides some welcome distraction, notably when she introduces the terrified Louis to the joys of viewing the world from the rooftops, her requirement that he complete the rite by peeing through a gargoyle's mouth crowned by unexpected benediction when his offering rains upon a nun passing beneath.

The locations also lend the film an undeniable charm, most potent in scenes where nothing of any dramatic moment is going on: the curé shambling ponderously down the main street, soutane unbuttoned in the summer sun, nose in breviary yet still alert for childish misdemeanour; the encounter with the bizarre old frog lady on her way back from a trip to the ponds; the family seeing the doctor's car go by, followed as if on cue—"If the curé passes I'll be making a coffin tomorrow", Pelo had remarked—by the priest on his bike, then the gravedigger with his tools, heralding the demise (of an old lady) no one has mentioned but the entire community has clearly been expecting. It is when the plot intrudes its clumsy contrivances that the film loses its grip. Worst of these is the laborious presentation of the fraught relationship between Marcelle and Pelo as a "mystery", eventually resolved (though with more explanations to come) by the discovery of a nursery kept locked as a shrine. One might almost be watching some half-hearted Gothic romance, although the film is desperately serious in its melodramatics.

HARLEM NIGHTS (*Film Review Annual, 1990*)

MONTHLY FILM BULLETIN, 7/90, p. 199, Verina Glaessner

Harlem, 1918. A young boy delivers some cigarettes to Sugar Ray, who runs a sleazy back-room craps dive. When one of the players objects to the boy's presence, and threatens him and Sugar Ray with a knife, he is shot dead by the boy. Twenty years later, Ray is the owner of the glitzy Club Sugar Ray, which the boy, now known as Quick, helps him to run. Ray is under pressure to close down by Bugsy Calhoune, a mobster who runs a number of rival establishments, and by Sergeant Cantone, a cop on Calhoune's payroll. Ray is in favour of pulling out but Quick would rather fight, and when he receives a letter from Dominique, the mistress of Calhoune's henchman Tony Smalls, suggesting a meeting, Quick (who has already been attracted to Dominique) accepts. Ray rejects an offer from Cantone to split the profits of the club three ways between themselves and Calhoune, and at the meeting with Dominique, Quick turns down a similar offer from the mobsters to work for them. But when Tony Smalls is killed for having double-crossed Calhoune, Quick is suspected of the deed by Smalls' brother Tommy. A chase ensues and Quick kills Tommy and his two henchmen. Ray then puts into action a plan to rob Calhoune of his gambling take, and tricks the gangster into betting on the wrong boxer in the World Title fight by leading him to believe he has fixed the contest. Calhoune has meanwhile ordered Dominique to kill Quick, but after they have made love at Calhoune's mansion, Quick shoots her. One of Ray's prostitutes,

Sunshine, lures Calhoune's pick-up man Richie to a meeting, where they are apprehended by Ray and Quick, disguised as policemen, on the pretext that they are taking Sunshine in on heroin charges. When two genuine policemen turn up, the pair are forced to let Richie go; but in the confusion, the police unknowingly make off with the bag containing Calhoune's money, while Richie delivers a bag containing not heroin but sugar to his boss. Ray and Quick lure Cantone into a derelict bank building and lock him in the safe. Seeking revenge, Calhoune makes for Ray's home, realising too late that he has been set up. The house explodes. Ray, Quick and the rest of the Club Sugar Ray are safely on the other side of the river, having made enough money on the fight to relocate.

Harlem Nights, roughly moving in on *Cotton Club* territory, is a sad film, afflicted with an inarticulateness every bit as crippling as that which afflicts the punch-drunk World Title holder Jack Jenkins. Where there should be sure-fire, "street-cred" repartee, there are only half-a-dozen very familiar slang interjections. Where there should be some kind of over-arching moral sense of "*les mains sales*", there is only an ineffectual attempt to draw a line between big-time operators and club-owners like Richard Pryor's put-upon Sugar Ray. But in a film where squeezing a trigger is as routine as squeezing a toothpaste tube, we remain to be convinced. It is sad to see actress Della Reese (as Ray's resident madam, Vera) so misused, and Pryor himself reduced to what looks like catatonia.

HIGH SPIRITS (*Film Review Annual, 1989*)

FILMS IN REVIEW, 2/89, p. 106, Nathaniel Bird

The latest of the simple minded assembly line comedies is *High Spirits*, by writer/director Neil Jordan (*Mona Lisa*), from whom one might have expected better things. But one can just picture the glee of the studio executives: Remember how well they did with a guy falling in love with Daryl Hannah as a mermaid? Well, how about a guy falling for Daryl Hannah as a ghost?

This formulaic, narrow mindedly high concept movie has Steve Guttenberg unhappily married to Patty D'Arbanville, vacationing in Peter O'Toole's ancestral Irish castle, now a decaying hotel, where O'Toole is trying ineptly to bolster profits by faking a haunted atmosphere to entice American tourists. Predictably, a few authentic spirits unexpectedly appear, notably a ghostly 18th Century Irish lass (Hannah), who is cursed to continuously re-enact her wedding night tragedy when she was murdered by her suspicious bride-groom (Liam Neeson, who is becoming the ubiquitous cinema Irishman). And when Guttenberg accidentally interrupts the nightly murder routine—the inevitable happens.

The comic supernatural/fantasy film does have respectable and engaging antecedents, dating all the way back to Georges Melies at the turn of the century, but this is a pallid, limp step child. The movie plods on unimaginatively, with no attempt to use the meeting of two eras as a source of humor, as Guttenberg evinces no interest in either the past or the hereafter, and Hannah slips right into a miniskirt with no hint of culture shock. Unlike the defter *Splash*, where the filmmaker could elicit laughs just from the heroine's gazing bewilderedly at a maniacal stereo equipment commercial, *High Spirits* instead throws in special effects, loud music and shrieking, one dimensional characters to create the illusion of comic excitement, disguising the absence of audience laughter.

The one touch of elegance is provided by O'Toole, who, especially when first seen repeating a string of vulgar epithets, makes one yearn for the more intelligent comedies of years past.

HOME AND THE WORLD, THE (*Film Review Annual, 1986*)

FILM QUARTERLY, Winter 1989-90, p. 40, Darius Cooper

In India, a woman's identity never belongs to her. It is wholly defined by her relationship to others. The patriarchal Indian tradition always forces her to play what it deems the appropriate role of the daughter/sister/wife/mistress/daughter within the narrow confines of the Indian family structure. The role of "wife" is a particularly constricting one, and Satyajit Ray in his latest film *The Home and the World* sets out to explore how Bimala, his heroine, struggles to redefine herself as "wife" and "mistress" in a determined effort to free herself from the traditional definitions of these two roles as imposed and insisted upon by her husband Nikhil and her lover Sandip.

Ray's film, to a large extent, is a faithful adaptation of Rabindranath Tagore's novel of the same name which was published in 1919. The film very sensitively portrays a wife's confused passion, a husband's misguided nobility, and a lover's shrewd exploitation of these qualities to suit his own selfish and Machiavellian ends. Both husband and wife suffer, but since the lover conveniently exits, and the husband pays the price by getting killed, it is the wife who ultimately gets victimized by the powerful, Hindu forces of the period's male hegemony.

In Tagore's novel, there were three distinct points of view—Bimala's, Nikhil's, and Sandip's. In the film, however, it is Bimala who significantly becomes the focus of Satyajit Ray's gaze. We see her seduced by two different worlds, in which her liberation is promised but never delivered. Each world, and the culture it personifies, becomes in the film a strategic *mirror*, in which both men try to impose their own version of the Hindu woman they want Bimala to become. Their ownership of Bimala is determined by the measure of success that each achieves. The mirroring device becomes the film's central motif, and Ray uses it masterfully to chronicle the painful odyssey of a woman whose image is never fated to be her own.

The first mirror in the film, in which Bimala is made to function, is the Anglophile world of the English governess, Miss Gilby. Nikhil hires her to teach his wife the English language, Highland songs, piano playing, and the attainment of proper British etiquette as observed in social rituals, like the correct pouring of tea for invited guests. Miss Gilby teaches Bimala a particular English song that becomes, in the film, a very important leitmotif of this Doll's House universe:

Tell me the tales that to me were so dear
Long long ago, long long ago.
Sing me the songs that I wanted to hear
Long long ago, long ago.

When Ray frames only Miss Gilby singing this song, it evokes, very poignantly, this Englishwoman's own, isolated condition, expressing her longing for the green shores of England. Then when Ray cuts to Bimala singing this song alone in the frame, it designates Bimala's forced emancipation from her Indian moorings, and enunciates her educative progress in obtaining some kind of mastery over another culture's language and customs. But when Ray focuses in the next shot on both women singing this song in unison within the same frame, we see the divided selves of each, confronting one another. Although they belong to separate cultures, the women share a common identity since both are controlled by Nikhil. One is playing the role of "teacher" and the other is playing the role of "student" for this zamindar. Later, after Bimala has been smitten by her first glimpse of Sandip and is preparing herself in her bedroom to invite him for tea the next day, we see her singing the same song she has been taught. As she sings it, she picks up Sandip's portrait from the mantlepiece, and directly addresses it with a very suggestive verse from the song we have not hear before:

Now that you're come
All my grief is removed.
Let me forget that
So long you have wooed.

Ray very shrewdly alerts us to the new direction that Bimala's eros is going to take. Nikhil is present in the room and watching her; and through this song, Bimala is already indicating to him that she is unwilling to be the recipient of his suffocating kind of love, and that she would like to be wooed by another man. Ray strengthens this resolve through carefully planted Hindu signifiers. When Nikhil, irritated by this English song, asks Bimala to sing a Bengali song, Bimala switches to a Mira bhajan (devotional song), in which that famous married Rajput princess openly confesses her love for Krishna and asks this love god to come quickly and consummate her passion. By fusing the Sandip/Krishna icons, Bimala's yearning to explore eros with another man is established. Earlier on, Bimala had introduced this idea very daringly to Nikhil (and us) by declaring that she "envied Draupadi with her five husbands," (Draupadi was the joint wife of the five Pandava brothers in the Indian epic, *The Mahabharata*, and she was loved and was enjoyed by each without conflicts or jealousy.)

Bimala's unique position in Ray's text lies in her honesty in recording, like a Bengali Lady Genji, the intimate details of the psychological struggle between her eroding loyalty towards her husband and her increasing fascination with his best friend. This is conveyed through her frequent voice-overs. Both Nikhil and Sandip are viewed through her sensitive consciousness. From Bimala's point of view, Nikhil is presented as an Apollonian figure who is noble but in many ways unapproachable, whereas Sandip emerges as the Dionysian force who, in spite of being potentially threatening, satisfies a lot of her repressed and unspoken desires. Ray positions Bimala in the same way as Tennyson had placed Guinevere in *Idylls of the King*. Nikhil is the Arthur figure, the noble zamindar who, in his lofty ideals, sets up difficult standards of morality in devotion, behavior, and motivations. Sandip is the Lancelot figure bringing temptation, heat, and color into Bimala's life, making her illicit eros glitter in the dark.

Nikhil creates a tiny Camelot for Bimala and himself. Initially attracted and comforted by this safe site, Bimala soon tires of it. Like Arthur, Nikhil displays a lot of unstained virtues. He does not drink or womanize. He brings Miss Gilby to educate and introduce Bimala to the modern age where the English language with its manners and customs reigns. He adorns Bimala with the colored garments of modern fashion. Whatever she asks for, he gives. He remains consecrated for her, at all times, like a prince, so full of perfection and personification of the thoroughly good man that he loses his mystery and the challenge of personality that sustain and nurture a marriage. The excitement of manliness, which is absent from this Camelot, is provided by Sandip when he comes to Bimala's neighborhood with his followers to preach the doctrine of Swadeshi. Ray positions Bimala, with the other women, sitting behind a screen to hear what Sandip has to say. Into this *mise-en-scène* Sandip makes a grand entry, seated in a big chair, which is hoisted on the shoulders of ten or twelve youths. When he begins to speak, Ray shows Bimala impatiently pushing away the screen from before her face. From this moment Sandip becomes the consuming object of her gaze. What is courageous on Bimala's part is her utter willingness to be swept away in a Laurentian roar of fire, passion, and flood. She understands the nature of this current on which she is so precariously balanced, and she boldly advances and retreats on it "open eyed." She comes to acknowledge it openly in the true spirit of that other spiritual sister of hers—Charulata.

As the typical nineteenth-century, aristocratic, Bengali housewife, in Ray's 1964 film, Charu was forced to function within the traditional boundaries that her position as a Hindu wife in the patriarchal joint-family structure allowed. She was expected to stitch (which we saw her doing in the film's credit sequence, embroidering a "B" on her husband's handkerchief); supervise all domestic chores; serve meals to her husband; and cultivate her idle moments in the practice of gently feminine pastimes like playing cards, embroidery, reading, playing the piano, and decorating herself for her spouse. Writing, of course, was a male prerogative, and both Amal, her lover and Bhupati, her husband, felt very threatened when Charu's writing got published for the first time in an important Bengali literary journal. It was very daring then, on Charu's part to signal her emancipation from such a routine by boldly expressing her attraction towards her husband's younger cousin, Amal. And this was made explicit to us by Ray in the "garden," overflowing with the writing and recitation of poetry, bright sunshine, and deep lurking passions.

In that scene, Amal is on the ground, writing and reading; and Charu is seated on a swing, observing him. This sunlit garden becomes a very important strategic spot in the film, where we see Charu's conscious definition of her hidden desires, not only presented to us, but also to herself. Ray, however, has implied the ultimate direction of this gaze all along: the embroidered exercise-book that she had stitched for Amal, and on which he is now writing his poems solely for her; the brand-new slippers she has hidden in her cupboard, and which she hopes to surprise him with; her insistence that Amal eat only the betel-leaf, which she prepares; her mending of all his torn clothes. All these small events occur so innocuously in the film that Amal, the spectator, and even Charu, seem to miss the real intent till this consistent gaze of Charu's fuses them together.

By shooting the entire scene from Charu's vantage point on the swing, Ray conveys very accurately and subtly the changes of desire occurring wihtin her at this crucial moment. We only see what Charu's gaze selects for herself and us. The exuberance of the editing, every time Charu's feet hit the ground while she is on the swing, literally and psychologically elevates her desires to ascending levels of bliss. The dizzying see-saw reflects the blur of her own passions, precariously at tilt, here, in the newly found outdoor sanctum. After she stops swinging, a cool and collected Charu now trains her lorgnette brazenly on Amal. As his magnified face appears in close-up prominently before her, we realize that Charu has confronted herself openly and freely with her forbidden desires.

Following Charu's example, Bimala's eros enables her to make an important distinction between the "emancipation" that Nikhil offers her and the "infatuation" which Sandip overpowers her with. She opts for the latter since she finds her presence more authenticated by it. As an emancipated wife, she felt decorated and constantly surveyed by Nikhil, especially in all the ways she was constantly asked to manifest her presence to him. As an infatuated woman, however, the surveyor in herself is given free reign to express how *she* would like to appear to the lover which her eros has chosen. Then when her presence is newly appreciated, Bimala can transform herself into an active and attractive object of vision, instead of appearing as a passive, decorative object.

Although Nikhil wants to free Bimala in the style of the "great women [as he tells his widowed sister-in-law] who were never in purdah," he adds, in a patriarchal manner, that "man must have his fancies too." Ray establishes his patriarchal intent when he shows Nikhil watching the spectacle of Bimala preparing herself for him before her bedroom mirror. He has forced a narcissism on her, and we see Bimala constantly making and unmaking herself as the sexual object for her lord and master. When Sandip meets Bimala for the first time at tea the next day, he imposes another kind of narcissism on her by granting her the twin titles of "Mother Goddess" and "Queen Bee." Her "feminine intuition," which Nikhil regularly teases her about, is quick to acknowledge Sandip's dual personification of her femininity: as the powerful "mother," who can preserve and nurture, *and* as the sexual "queen," who can attract and entice. In the emancipatory mirror, offered by Nikhil, we are made to witness a woman who is reduced to a decorative object. When we see Sandip granting Bimala the privilege of infatuation, we see how Bimala is provided with an opportunity to express herself for the first time as an attractive object for a man whom *her* eros has chosen. But even in Sandip's emancipatory mirror, she is reduced to functioning as a sexual prisoner. He woos her endlessly with his public oratory of the Swadeshi cause, only because he wants her to sexually surrender herself to him. Ray positions his heroine tragically, thus, between the mirrors of one man's ineffectual enlightenment, and another's sybaritic, sexual politics.

The *mise-en-scène* during the tea sequence establishes Bimala's growing attraction towards Sandip. He is gradually shown as becoming the consuming object of her gaze. And Ray registers this evocatively by a careful arrangement of tracking shots and slow zooms that first draw Bimala's eros to the surface, and then target it on the man as a sexual object. Ray places Nikhil and Bimala on the sofa together. Sandip sits opposite them on a chair. Abruptly, we see Sandip getting up to sing a stirring patriotic song. This song is aimed directly at Bimala. As he sings, the camera is focused directly on Sandip from behind Nikhil's head. It slowly tracks, till it comes to rest behind Bimala's head. Then, from her perspective, Ray slowly and very unobtrusively zooms in on Sandip's passionate, singing face. A reverse zoom follows, this time from Sandip to Bimala's face, completely enthralled by his song. As the zooms accelerate, they are intercut with medium shots of all three of them, in which Nikhil is often seen removing his glasses and wiping them. Such an action brilliantly registers the gradual loss of the wife from the husband's gaze. The repeated zooms, on the other hand, seem to bring Bimala and Sandip closer together in an implied space from which Nikhil has been evicted.

In another scene between Sandip and Bimala, Ray registers their growing awareness of each other through the important signifier of a particular brand of British cigarette that Sandip is shown smoking. For all his *swadeshi* politics (in which the banning of all English goods was the most distinctive principle), Sandip cannot bear to smoke an Indian brand. He smokes a popular British brand in which a "Pompadour" logo on the cigarette packet is represented by a flirtatious lady in a large, flouncing dress. Although Bimala has been told by Nikhil that "our Sandip has had many affairs of the heart with women, not all of them *swadeshi*," she coquettishly picks up the "Pompadour" packet, stares at the lady on it, and then, in a sly whisper, murmurs half to herself and half to Sandip; "I know you won the hearts of many..." leaving the sentence deliberately unfinished. With this wonderfully staged moment, Ray displays Bimala wanting to prove to Sandip that *swadeshi* women, like herself, can be as attractive and as seductive as that British lady with the flouncing dress on the cigarette packet. And the fact that she is dressed in this scene in a very bold red saree, only for his benefit, emphasizes this sexual claim, for a red saree is exactly what a traditional Bengali woman wears on the day of her marriage. She is actually hinting to Sandip that she is preparing herself for her seduction. So the next time when they meet, Sandip confirms this expectation by telling Bimala that the thrill of politics is far inferior to the thrill a man like him feels when faced with the challenge of "winning the heart of a woman" like her.

Another revealing scene between the two enables Ray to express the confusion and arrest that assail both partners temporarily before they can make their actual plunge into illicit passion. The moment occurs when Bimala says that she is prepared to offer Sandip any amount of money for the *swadeshi* cause, should he need it. Although the offer is genuine, there is a deeper implication. The gender roles of a normally active Sandip and a quietly passive Bimala are suddenly reversed in this scene. It is Bimala who is now constantly shown circling the stationary Sandip. She seems to be completely absorbed by his presence. We can sense her desire to elicit from him a response to her offer, in which politics and desire are powerfully comingled. The normally ebullient Sandip is shown in a completely stunned posture as Bimala continues to literally make circles round him. When he fails to respond to this new version of Bimala, she resignedly moves to go, thereby prompting him to finally act in the way she has wanted him to all along. He runs and blocks her exit and grasps her hands. She does not resist because she wants him to control this relationship from now on. She has literally put herself into his strong arms. The dominant positions in Sandip's patriarchal mirror have changed; Ray allows his heroine a brief victory before the storm breaks, and Bimala is confronted by Sandip's true designs.

When Bimala goes to present the gold sovereigns (which she has stolen from her husband's treasury) to Sandip, Ray shows him unable to restrain himself. Fascinated by the gold, we see him spring forward as if to embrace Bimala. Repulsed by his avariciousness, Bimala pushes him away. This is the crucial moment in the film when Bimala sees Sandip in his true colors and realizes that all his rhetoric and vows of love have been mere bluster. She thinks she is liberated from his "snaky coils" and is saved but this proves to be merely an illusion. Having triumphed over her lover (she pushes him so violently that he staggers backwards, hitting his head on the edge of a marble table before dropping to the floor half-dazed) Bimala feels uncertain in the re-establishing of connubial ties with her husband Nikhil. Under the harsh censure of the Hindu tradition on one hand, and the "noble generosity" with which she thinks Nikhil accepts her back, Bimala finds her femininity crushed and confused by guilt, which now forces her to constantly re-evaluate her position as a woman in the resumed role of the fallen wife. She longs to revert to her Camelot state again, but it is too late.

In her essay, "When the Woman Looks," Linda Williams points out that the most instructive moment in narrative cinema occurs

> when the "good girl" heroines are granted the power of the look.... [As Mary Ann Doane suggests,] "the woman's exercise of an active investigating gaze can only be simultaneous with her own victimization." The woman's gaze is punished, in other words, by narrative processes that transform curiosity and desire into masochistic fantasy.*

When a repentant Bimala weeps uncontrollably before her bedroom mirror, Nikhil takes her into his arms but refuses to block her tear-stained image, reflected in the mirror. He wants that image to portray to Bimala her fall from grace, not only in his eyes, but in her own eyes too. It is only then that he can offer her the patriarchal privilege of his forgiveness. Ray endorses this privileged male position, most remarkably, in the film's final scene when he reduces Bimala to the position of widow through three apocalyptic dissolves. Ray's presentation very powerfully inscribes how Hinduism finally fixes Bimala and strips her of her femininity and womanhood. From the rich wife of a zamindar with luxurious hair, expensive clothes, and bedecked jewelery, the Hindu forces of her age's history reduce her, in these three cruel dissolves, to a weeping widow with shaven hair, a plain saree, and an unadorned self. This ending is more shattering than Tagore's. In the novel, Nikhil's funeral pyre had very significantly provided Bimala with a cathartic purification in her state of widowhood. Through this purification Tagore had redeemed Bimala, whose eros had plunged her into the forbidden fires of desire for another man, and had finally made her attain a defiant, stoical stance where she feared neither herself nor anybody else. Ray's final image of Bimala is just the opposite. Ray ends his film with Bimala completely emptied of her essential, female self before the all-pervasive and judgmental forces of Hinduism. Ray makes Bimala the inevitable victim of her period's history which finally forces her to occupy a position which is neither at home nor in the world of her time.

NOTE

* Linda Williams, "When the Woman Looks" in Re-Vision: *Essays in Feminist Film Criticism*, ed. by Mary Anne Doane, Patricia Mellencamp, Linda Williams. (Los Angeles: American Film Institute, 1984), p. 85.

HOTEL TERMINUS (*Film Review Annual, 1989*)

FILMS IN REVIEW, 1/89, p. 42, Kevin Lewis

Marcel Ophuls' latest exploration of the Nazi mind could be taken as a companion piece to his *The Sorrow And The Pity*, but it is a more complex and ambitious undertaking than the earlier masterwork. Whereas *Sorrow* was comfortably set in an historical time frame—the occupation of France during World War II—and concerned the question of French collaboration, *Hotel Terminus* is more universal and far reaching in its inquiry into ethics and expediency. The film is four-and-a-half hours long, but it is never boring. It is a vast mosaic of humanity, complete with selective memory and twisted motivations.

Klaus Barbie was a Nazi war criminal convicted of committing actrocities in Lyons, France. Nevertheless, the American Counter Intelligence Corps (C.I.C.) felt he could be useful and claimed ignorance of his crimes. When the French condemned him *in absentia*, he was allowed to disappear to Bolivia in 1951 until his extradition by the French in 1983.

Barbie isn't interviewed on camera, nor is his testimony heard during his 1987 trial. Instead, Ophuls superbly creates a documentary done in the style of *Citizen Kane*, relating his narrative through the words of Barbie's victims, business associates, his left wing lawyer, his Nazi colleagues, and his American employers. These interviews are horrifying and sleazy because they are the personal, intimate observations of ordinary people. Ophuls has stated that he doesn't believe in the "banality of evil" approach of Hannah Arendt. but it is shocking to see the shallowness of emotions expressed, the self-absorption shown, and the threadbare rationalizations offered by the participants. Ophuls in concerned with the lack of true morality—one sees how evil flourished because of the indifference or blindness of others. Many of the "man in the street" interviews dwell on the fact that forty years have gone by and this appears to be ancient history to most of them. The most telling interview in the film is with Johannes Schneider-Merck, the Peruvian importer-exporter, whom Barbie cheated on a business deal. Merck thought he was a friend of Barbie's, and, judging from his interview, he suspected that Barbie (who called himself Klaus Altmann) was a hunted war criminal. He only betrayed Barbie to Simon Wiesenthal when he felt he'd been swindled.

The overriding question in the film is: Why did America shield Barbie? Though Ophuls doesn't challenge the now retired American intelligence officers on camera, the impression is left that they secretly admired Barbie. Eugene Kolb, Barbie's former superior, is glib about Barbie's faults. Attorney Allan Ryan. Jr., of the U.S. Department of Justice, wrote what is referred to as the Ryan Report on the case, and is rough on the C.I.C.'s rationale. He recommended that the U.S. apologize to France.

In a deeply disturbing sense, the message of the film is that business is business and morals are morals, and never the twain shall meet. Klaus Barbie, who ironically almost entered the priesthood, was the ultimate organization man, and for that reason he was usually respected by the people he dealt with. In France, Barbie's business was death and the elimination of the Resistance. Wtih the Americans, it was information. In Bolivia, it was the masterminding of spy networks for Hugo Banzer Suarez, the dictator. Marcel Ophuls, with this film, shows us that, alas, Barbie did not operate alone.

HOUSE OF BERNARDA ALBA, THE (*Film Review Annual, 1989*)

MONTHLY FILM BULLETIN, 3/90, p. 63, Tom Milne

Having buried her husband, Bernarda Alba, a figure of wealth and consequence in the village, returns to the house where her senile mother is kept confined largely to the attic. Ignoring the warnings of her trusty servant Poncia, Bernarda announces an eight-year period of strict mourning during which her five unmarried daughters—Angustias, Martirio, Magdalena, Adela and Amelia—will not be permitted to leave the house. Frustration flares into resentment when the sisters learn that Angustias, the eldest at thirty-nine, is to be allowed to entertain a suitor for her hand. Martirio, particularly embittered because Bernarda has swiftly terminated her own 'unsuitable' romance with a farmer's son, consoles herself with the knowledge that the spinsterish Angustias—only child of Bernarda's first husband, and commanding a much larger dowry than her sisters—is being wooed by handsome, twenty-five-year-old Pepe El Romano only because of her money. But it is the secretive Adela, already enamoured of Pepe, who takes action, despite a cautionary scene witnessed by the household: an unmarried girl who allegedly killed her baby is pursued and lynched by villagers in the street outside. Undeterred, Adela starts waylaying Pepe after his authorised evening visits to Angustias, eventually making love with him in the stables. Spying on the lovers, unable to contain her jealousy, Martirio summons her mother. Adela is defiant; Pepe bolts in the confusion; and Bernarda, firing two wild shots after him as he flees, announces that he is dead. Defying her mother, the repentant Martirio insists that Pepe got away. Locking herself in her room, Adela nevertheless hangs herself. Bernarda orders that the body be cut down and dressed as a virgin, so that no rumours of shame will be voiced.

Lorca's last play, completed a couple of months before his death in the early days of the Spanish Civil War, obviously had powerful relevance to a society caught between the oppressively tradition-bound régime of the past and the Fascist dictatorship of the future. Now that this immediate context has receded, what we are left with is more in the nature of a family drama: powerful and even chilling, but interesting less for its major theme of the destructiveness of tyranny than for certain side issues. The housekeeper Poncia, for example, looms initially as a monument of peasant common sense, with her earthy attitude to sex and marriage healthily counteracting Bernarda's fanatical puritanism. Then in a startling reversal during the street lynching scene, hers is the voice calling loudest for the sinner to be hounded to death; it's as potent an illustration as any of the way in which ignorance and superstition turn essentially worthy souls into puppets of dictatorship.

That the play still works as magnificently as it does on stage is due to the brilliant severity of Lorca's conception: a stark clash of black on white in which the mourning women, trapped within four walls, are inexorably squeezed of their last drop of life. Mario Camus, doing commendably little opening out (an introductory view of the village, the funeral service in church, glimpses of the lynching), remains faithful to Lorca's text throughout, directs with taste and discretion, and coaxes creditable performances from the entire cast. The play nevertheless *does* open out, inexorably and almost inadvertently, destroying Lorca's single-minded intensity along with the dark poetry of despair it breeds.

Contributing to the sense of flabbiness are a number of symbolic asides (a bird languishing in a cage; three of the girls staring at a rutting stallion); several unnecessary reminders that men are excluded from this microcosm (male mourners served drinks outside the house while the camera stays with the women paying their respects inside; a shadowy glimpse or two of Pepe flitting by in the night); some very obvious day-for-night shooting (particularly disruptive in the context of stark contrasts); and above all, a plethora of shots in which the various girls moon disconsolately in different rooms, and which do more to dissipate tension than to raise the temperature of frustration and despair. What ultimately emerges is a perilously straight-faced cousin to those eccentrically Gothic tales of hot-house sex so beloved of writers chronicling America's Deep South. As such, it has its moments; as Lorca, it rates only Beta double minus.

HUNGARIAN FAIRY TALE, A (*Film Review Annual, 1989*)

LOS ANGELES TIMES, 6/7/89, Calendar/p. 4, Kevin Thomas

Gyula Gazdag's "A Hungarian Fairy Tale" is one of those magical films in which events are totally unexpected, yet responses to them seem exactly right.

In this dark political satire and fable of the absurd that questions the nature of identity, everybody is confronted with increasingly perplexing and surreal circumstances. Gazdag's grasp of human nature is as impressive as his style, and his imagination is nothing short of dazzling. "A Hungarian Fairy Tale" will surely rank among the year's best films.

One of the most critical and talented of the younger generation of Hungarian film makers, Gazdag begins with a droll tone designed to throw us off balance (where we remain for the rest of the film). Carried away by a production of Mozart's "The Magic Flute," a lovely young woman with a Mona Lisa smile (Mária Varga) embarks upon a night of love with a stranger that results in her giving birth to a baby boy whom she calls Andris. The entire film turns upon a curious quirk in Hungarian law that requires that every child must have a father listed on his birth certificate. If the father is unknown, then his identity must be invented.

Suddenly, the now-adolescent Andris (Dávid Vermes) must seek out this non-existent father and is plunged into adventure. At the same time, the clerk (Frantisek Husák), who helped Andris' mother come up with a name, occupation and address for the boy's father, snaps and starts destroying piles upon piles of records, which propels him into his own odyssey.

On one level Gazdag, who wrote his film with Miklós Györffy, takes a bemused look at the workings of fate; on another, he skewers bureaucratic society in which the individual has no existence apart from his papers and official records. Watching this film at first stirs up all those paranoid fears one has of losing one's wallet, but Gazdag takes us much father: In a spirit of anarchy, he argues that our only real hope is somehow to escape from society entirely. "A Hungarian Fairy Tale' depicts the warmest of impulses at constant odds with the coldest of rules and regulations.

Shot in glorious black-and-white and accompanied throughout by themes from "The Magic Flute," "A Hungarian Fairy Tale' moves swiftly from one keenly perceptive and dryly witty vignette to the next, which serves to anchor Gazdag's flights of fancy in everyday reality. Vermes, who has the look of a 12-year-old Brando, sustains the film with his heart-wrenching portrayal of the bewildered yet increasingly resilient Andris. The gaunt Husák is engaging as the similarly single-minded clerk, and late in the film Eszter Csákányi adds her strong maternal presence as a woman determined to help Andris even if he does point a rifle at her. The concentration of these actors and others is unflagging, and the world of the ironically titled "A Hungarian Fairy Tale' (Times-rated Mature for complex, intense themes) into which they and Gazdag take us is too familiar for confort.

MONTHLY FILM BULLETIN, 8/89, p. 239, Philip Strick

After a performance of The Magic Flute, a young Hungarian woman, Maria, meets a handsome stranger. The result of their brief encounter is a boy, Andris, whom Maria raises alone. One day she is summoned to the child custody department fo the local council where a sympathetic clerk, Antal Orbán, explains to her that the law requires a father's name to be entered on the boy's birth certificate. Together they invent a parent, calling him Orbán as a convenient surname. Some years later, while Andris is at school, Maria is accidentally killed in the street; told that as an orphan he will have to go into a children's home, the boy decides he can avoid this by finding his father. He send a telegram to the name and address given on the birth certificate and goes into hiding to await his parent's arrival. Coincidentally, the "real" Orbán has at last given up his job in disgust; he devotes himself to removing from various archives the birth documents he has had to compile over the years and destroying them. In the course of his travels he is arrested and sent briefly to an asylum but contrives to be released and continues his mission. Meanwhile Andris, with no word from his father, travels to the town of Ujhely to find him. Unsuccessful and despairing, he is befriended by the mother and stepfather of a small girl, Tünde; they trace an address for him, a small isolated cottage, but nobody is at home so they offer him a bed for the night. Afraid that his hosts might hand him over to the authorities, the boy slips away and mingles with other schoolchildren next day during an outdoor weaponry class. He steals a rifle, returns to the cottage, and waits for its owner to appear; this turns out to be a youg woman who, unintimidated by the gun, offers to help Andris in his quest. After some adventures involving a routine security check, which an old lady helps them avoid, they find themselves on a train where Orbán is furtively destroying his latest batch of recovered documents. Andris shoots a sinister character in one of the carriages, the train comes to a halt, and with Orbán and the young woman he makes his escape across country amid fusillades from their pursuers. Under the supervision of the three handmaidens from The Magic Flute, they reach a giant statue of an eagle, which flies off with them aboard.

Every Hungarian child, whether born in or out of wedlock, is required by law to have two named parents. Any name will do, so long as the record supports the popular and well-substantiated belief that it takes two to procreate. This tactful ordinance, designed to ensure that no child need feel disadvantaged (while preserving at the same time Hungary's reputation, should anyone ask, as a bastion of legitimacy), is cited by Gyula Gazdag as the inspiration for his film: "It's a white lie with an unassailable humanistic motive, and also an absurdity which illustrates a special Hungarian way of thinking". An easy target to hit, one would imagine, and for the first third of his film Gazdag aligns his sights for a decisive broadside: the father of a newborn child is unknown, a weary clerk puts his own name on the birth certificate, and all is well until, abruptly motherless, the boy needs desperately to contact his fictitious parent. The situation must actually have occurred on more than one occasion, and a neo-realist documentary style suggests itself as the simplest way of allowing the inevitable consequences of bureaucratic doublethink to emerge.

Gazdag has indeed opted for neo-realist monochrome, but nothing else about his oddly-designated "fairy tale" is at all predictable. No sooner is the boy launched on his search than the film interrupts itself with a parallel pilgrimage in which the registry clerk walks out of his job and indulges in self-inflicted penance by tracking down and destroying all the documents he faked on the government's behalf over the years. In that he has in a sense adopted a paternalistic role, we can expect him to cross the boy's path eventually, but by the time they meet there has been such a confusion of other encounters that the purpose of their partnership has become totally opaque. The boy acquires a rifle, a limitless supply of ammunition, and a mother-substitute, and the adventure turns into an inexplicable scramble of deaths and chases culminating in the poorly processed take-off of a rusting statue of an eagle (glimpsed in the background in various earlier scenes), the three of them cheerily on its back. This may have something to do with a special Hungarian way of thinking (the eagle is mythologically connected to the appearance of the first Hungarian kings and arrival in the promised land), but its relevance is well disguised; it is certainly absurd.

Compounding the fantasy, Gazdag weaves in an assortment of references to *The Magic Flute*, presumably as an inducement to plumb some hidden depths. Dealing as it does with misguided parents and baffling legal restrictions, the opera might offer helpful points of connection; but with ruthless misapplication Gazdag severs them all. The opening romance, in tune with Mozart, is suitably thwarted, but then the links fall aparts: the lovers disappear form the text (although the "Pamina" figure, the boy's mother, is in due course seen in limbo in his pleasantly macabre dream), and the birds of Papageno take over as, in a cruel joke, pigeons dislodge a fatal brick, and wings come to the rescue at the end. The escaping trio celebrate their departure to the accompaniment of the Queen of the Night's three handmaidens, but the silliness of this final apparition is beyond redemption. As with the example of the butterfly brooch, which comes and goes in the action without resolving itself as a meaningful symbol, we must conclude that Gazdag, whatever his protestations, has merely constructed an elaborately trivial comedy with no ulterior purpose.

Also reviewed in:
NATION, 2/6/89. p. 175, Stuart Klawans
WASHINGTON POST, 5/19/89, p. D7, Hal Hinson
WASHINGTON POST, 5/19/89, Weekend/p. 41, Desson Howe

HYPOTHESIS OF A STOLEN PAINTING (*Film Review Annual, 1988*)

LOS ANGELES TIMES, 11/13/89, Calendar/p. 3, Kevin Thomas

Chilean emigré experimental film maker Raul Ruiz's 70-minute "Hypothesis of a Stolen Painting" (1978) is at once a dryly amusing mystery and a sly parody on tedious, officious art history documentaries and on the whole notion that art can be explained."

An elderly, garrulous art collector (Jean Rougeul) shows us his collection of seven paintings of the (fictitious) 19th-Century artist Frederic Tonnere that caused a great scandal when they were exhibited a century ago. Seemingly unconnected, they look to be the very kind of academic art that the Impressionists were sweeping away. In any event, the collector says he has imagined a missing eighth painting that explains how all the paintings are connected to reveal what caused the scandal. We discover that the grand salon where he displays his Tonneres is part of an immense old Paris mansion in which *tableaux vivants* bring the paintings alive. "What fascinated me the most," Ruiz has said, "is this chasm between the ideas that you have of things and the things that you see."

IMAGINE: JOHN LENNON (*Film Review Annual, 1989*)

FILMS IN REVIEW, 2/89, p. 103, C.M. Fiorillo

John Lennon was 40 years old when he was assassinated. Of those 40 years, 100 minutes of film culled from 200 hours of footage have been consolidated to define his life. It was a daunting task. The result is *Imagine: John Lennon*, produced by David L. Wolper and directed by Andrew Solt. Their documentary, for the most part narrated by Lennon himself, takes a restrained look at the career and personal life of one of the musical geniuses of our time. It concluded with his murder: John Lennon was shot to death outside his New York City apartment on December 8, 1980.

The hours of videotape filmed at Tittenhurst Park Estate in Ascot, England, in 1971 during the recording sessions for the "Imagine" album are the heart of Wolper's documentary. From there, the film moves forward and back, retracing the life of John Lennon. It is a brilliant ensemble of black and white and color video clips taken from (sometimes fuzzy) newsreels and theatrical films. Wolper also splices in scenes from Lennon's home movies, sometimes professionally shot, other times of remarkably poor quality and rendered all the more poignant. In some instances the filmmakers have devised video montages from black and white and color photographs to make a striking moving image.

The audio portion on *Imagine: John Lennon* include radio and television interviews given by Lennon as well as talking head interviews and voice-overs from those closest to the singer, namely, his family: wife Yoko, ex-wife Cynthia, sons Julian and Sean, and Aunt Mimi. (Voices notably absent: George, Ringo, and Paul.)

Then, of course, there's the music, Nearly three dozen songs interlace the film, from early Beatles classics such as "Love Me Do" to later gems such as "Revolution," "Don't Let Me Down," and Across The Universe," from solo Lennon efforts during the Plastic Ono Band days such as "How Do You Sleep?" to rock 'n' roll oldies such as "Stand By Me;" from comeback charmers such as "(Just Like) Starting Over" to the brilliant "Imagine." If not for the film itself, the documentary should be "watched" in order to hear so many terrific Beatles and Lennon tunes in one sitting.

Although Lennon made beautiful music, he was not a saint. And Wolper doesn't entirely gloss over the man's life. He dutifully presents the vibrant, cynical wit as well as the angry outbursts in the recording studio. There is on display, however, more of the caring, loving John, the John who offers food to a drifter who sleeps in his garden, the John who preaches love and peace, than the John who lashed out at not-so-nice interviewers and estranged ex-partner Paul McCartney, and the John who created havoc and headlines in Los Angeles during his 14-month "lost weekend" separation from Yoko.

The result of the work of Wolper and Solt, as well as co-writer/producer Sam Egan and film editor Bert Lovitt, is an entertaining, if not enlightening, production. *Imagine: John Lennon* offers little new information on the singer for his ardent admirers. It is, rather, a loving tribute to a man who gave so much of himself and his life to the world, only to have everything selfishly snatched away by a deranged "fan."

IRON EAGLE II (*Film Review Annual, 1989*)

MONTHLY FILM BULLETIN, 4/89, p. 114, Kim Newman

A Middle Eastern country with a dangerously unstable régime is on the point of bringing on-line a nuclear missile base which is viewed as a threat by both the Pentagon and the Kremlin. General Stillmore, who is personally opposed to Soviet-American military co-operation, orders Brigadier General Charles "Chappy" Sinclair to liaise in Israel with his Russian counterpart Vladimir Vardovsky. A hand-picked team of American and Russian pilots and ground support has been assembled to train under Sinclair and Vardovsky for a "surgical" mission to destroy the nuclear base. Captain Matt Cooper, whose best friend was recently shot down over Alaskan Soviet air space, is especially prejudiced against the Soviets, but finds himself attracted to a Russian pilot, Valeri Zuyeniko. Major Bush suffers from claustrophobia and is killed when he flies into a box canyon similar to one the mission will have to fly through. Suspicious because records of Bush's handicap have been removed from his file, Chappy confronts Stillmore, who admits that his Russian counterpart and he have specifically assembled a team of unreliables who will be unable to co-operate. Stillmore's plan is to drop an atom bomb on the missile base, killing thousands of innocent people in the vicinity. Chappy assembles the team, who have been grounded following Bush's death and several brawls, and they all volunteer to disobey orders and and go through with the mission. Chappy and Vardovsky lead the ground assault team who destroy the missile base's ground-to-air defences, whereupon Cooper, Valeri and the other pilots destroy the base from the air. The nuclear strike is called off and Chappy and Cooper volunteer to go to Moscow as part of an exchange programme.

Following *Red Heat* in its use of resurgent détente as a background for simple shoot-'em-up action, *Iron Eagle II* is a mix of the absurdly tactful—the villains of the piece are never specifically identified as Iranians, although since the maps shown locate their missile base to the East of the Persian Gulf there can be little doubt of their identity—and the simply absurd. The ploy whereby Stillmore and a Russian general co-operate on a nuclear bombing mission because they hate the very idea of Soviet-American military co-operation is typical of the script's general ludicrousness. In the air, it's all a matter of having Clay Lacy, aerial photographer of *Top Gun*, recreate the finale of *Star Wars*, which was itself derivative of aviation movies. And on the ground, the training of the international misfits is a low-key reworking of the *Dirty Dozen* formula, with a wise-cracking capitalist pilot trying to sell blankets to the Russian soldiers, an assortment of broad caricatures squabbling but then deciding they love each other after all, and Sharon H. Brandon proving even less convincing as a Soviet air ace than Janet Leigh in *Jet Pilot*.

JUDGMENT IN BERLIN (*Film Review Annual, 1989*)

MONTHLY FILM BULLETIN, 4/90, p. 109, Farrah Anwar

East Berlin, 1978. Hans Schuster, a West Berlin engineer, is arranging the escape to the West of his lover Sigrid Radke, her young daughter Marina, and her friend Helmut Thiele (whose own wife and children are already in West Berlin). They plan to travel by ship from Gdansk to Hamburg, but Schuster is arrested at the German/Polish border with their false papers and passports. With the help of a toy gun, Helmut and Sigrid then hijack a Polish plane and force it to land in West Berlin. Eight of their fellow passengers seek immediate asylum, but Helmut, Sigrid and Marina are arrested. The East German government insists that they be either extradited or prosecuted, and the the U.S. is asked by the West German government to oversee the trial. Judge Herbert J. Stern is flown in to preside over the courthouse (which although situated in Germany will function as an American court of law), and he insists that the accused be tried before a jury, as guaranteed by the American Constitution, despite efforts by the U.S. government to have the case treated as a political rather than judicial matter. Meanwhile, in East Berlin, Schuster is told by a Russian officer, Uri Andreyev, that he cannot be tried until the hijacking case is resolved. The case against Sigrid is dropped when her counsel, Bernard Hellring, proves that she was coerced into giving a confession to U.S. official Heller. Thiele's trial begins unpromisingly when the Polish air crew testify that he used excessive threats and violence to persuade them to land in West Germany. But it transpires that they have been instructed as to what evidence to give by the Polish prosecutor general, and a fellow passenger, Guenther X, eventually testifies on Thiele's behalf that the crew knew the gun was a toy and deflected the flight voluntarily. Thiele is found not guilty on all charges except that of "taking an unlawful hostage"; despite a request by the U.S. government that he be handed over for at least four years, Stern sentences him to time already served and thus frees him immediately. Sigrid and Hans Schuster remain separated by the Berlin Wall.

"Remember they're not bad guys, just people doing their duty", opines Judge Hubert J. Stern (whose real-life account of this trial formed the basis of *Judgment in Berlin*), about the American prosecutors facing him in a German court. (It's a sentiment which echoes, in a different courtroom context, the ingenuousness of the child narrator in *To Kill a Mockingbird*, when she apologises for not feeling any animosity towards the lawyer opposing her father: "I'm sorry that I can't provide any drama in this respect; if I did it would not be true".) Unfortunately, the makers of *Judgment* have ignored the point and gone for more traditionally full-blooded courtroom melodrama, with heroes and villains rather than the guilty and innocent. This is a pity because the film does begin with a convincing sense of the desperation that obviously marks the lives of the refugees, and its factual basis is rife with ironies and political duplicities which should have been to its advantage. But all subtleties are cast aside with the entrance of the judge (Martin Sheen, with heart visibly palpitating on his sleeve) and his good wife (the film is punctuated with the couple in various states of undress and duress as Stern explains the major plot developments to her). With Sheen and Sam Wanamaker (as Sigrid's counsel) chewing up the scenery, it soon becomes clear that just as Sigrid and Helmut became pawns in the super-power tussle, their screen counterparts will remain in the wings of these star turns. With the arrival of the sneeringly two-dimensional state prosecutors, all the courtroom clichés fall neatly into place and the eventual verdict and sentencing are never in doubt (though the film attempts to drum up some tension by keeping Mrs. Stern in the dark on the eve of the judgment). Indeed, so loaded are the dice against the U.S. Justice Department, that one can't help but feel a twinge of sympathy for them as they struggle in vain to do evil against the invincibly liberal Judge Stern.

LADY IN WHITE *(Film Review Annual, 1989)*

LOS ANGELES TIMES, 4/22/88, Calendar/p. 8, Sheila Benson

For all its supernatural vein, "Lady in White" has an engaging, Hardy Boys feeling about it and, in Lukas Haas, probably the screen's most irresistible performer this side of Kermit the Frog. And every ounce of Master Haas' adorability will be put to the test, because "Lady in White" is also a virtual junkyard of mismatched ideas and elements, thrown up on the screen in a friendly, haphazard fashion.

There is What Lukas Saw in the Cloakroom (a mysterious, transparent little girl), What Happened to Lukas in the Cloakroom (near-death by unseen hands), and What Lukas Found in the Cloakroom (that would be telling). And that's only the warm-up.

This is played against genuinely warm scenes of Italian family comedy, probably coming straight from the boyhood memories of Frank LaLoggia, the film's writer, director, co-producer, composer and arranger. There are also genuinely appalling camera flourishes and directorial touches, like the handling of the grade-school teacher or Haas' two chums, and some pretty amazing scripting, like that point-blank assassination or the mind-boggling identity of the multiple murderer, let alone his motives. Those too, come from LaLoggia, who obviously went to a lot of movies when he was growing up and forgot all the right ones.

"Lady in White" also has swooping supernatural visitations, mostly from a mother and child spirit aching to be reunited. Since these goings-on take place in a town roughly the size of Santa Monica, it's hard to know how they've been missing each other all these eons.

There are other excellent actors in this impenetrable thicket. Alex Rocco as Haas' father, Len Cariou as the family's lifelong friend, Katherine Helmond as a sort of vanilla float, Jason Presson as Haas' affectionate older brother and Henry Harris as the school janitor. Somehow you suspect that all of them had a lot more fun making this PG-13-rated picture than we have sitting through it.

MONTHLY FILM BULLETIN, 6/89, p. 183, Anne Billson

On a visit to his home town of Willowpoint Falls, Frankie Scarlatti remembers an incident in his childhood which inspired him to become a writer of ghost stories...

Halloween, 1962: At the end of the school day, Frankie is locked in the cloakroom by his classmates Donald and Louie. After dreaming about his dead mother's funeral, he wakes to see a ghostly re-enactment of the murder of a little girl, Melissa Ann Montgomery. Shortly afterwards, an attempt is made on Frankie's life, and Harold Williams, the school's back janitor, is arrested for the murders of Melissa (in 1951) and ten other children (in the intervening years). While recovering from his ordeal, Frankie again sees Melissa's ghost, which appears to be searching for its mother. Realising that the murderer dropped incriminating evidence down a drain in the cloakroom, Frankie collects all the items he finds there. Later, he accompanies Donald and Louie on a trip to Widow's Peak, a clifftop which is reputed to be haunted by a lady in white. The boys venture into a seemingly uninhabited cottage but are frightened away by a mysterious woman in white. Frankie confides in his elder brother Gino (who also sees Melissa's ghost) and, after another re-enactment of the murder, follows the ghostly trail to Widow's Peak, where he sees Melissa being thrown off the cliff, and the spirit of a grief-stricken Mrs. Montgomery emerging from the cottage and throwing herself after her daughter's corpse. Williams is freed due to lack of evidence, but is shot dead by the mother of one of the murdered children. Gino does some investigating of his own, and finds that the object which the murderer dropped was a class ring belonging to Phil, a close friend of Mr. Scarlatti's. Frankie, meanwhile, is practising his archery with Phil and, hearing him whistle Melissa's favourite tune, realises that he is the murderer. Pursued by Phil, he flees to the cottage, where Phil is attacked by the woman in white, who turns out to be Amanda Harper, Melissa's aunt. As the cottage goes up in flames, Phil strangles Amanda and is about to throw Frankie from Widow's Peak when he is startled by the ghost of Melissa's mother, whom Frankie watches being finally, and happily, reunited with her dead daughter. Phil refuses Mr. Scarlatti's offer of help and falls to his death from the cliff.

Like *Stand by Me*, *Lady in White* concerns a writer's recollections of a crucial point in his life, mixing nostalgia for an idyllic childhood with his gradual realisation that the world is a darker place than it had first appeared. Willowpoint Falls is initially presented as an idealised small town, part-Capra and part-Spielberg, where the inhabitants make up one big happy family, with the Scarlattis, eccentric grandparents and all, as the happiest family of all—and, as in the typical Spielbergian setting, the young protagonist is missing (in both senses of the word) one of his parents. It is only later that the charming facade cracks to show hints of the corruption beneath: Phil, the friendly substitute uncle who has been accepted into the bosom of the family, is revealed as a child molester and murderer, while the unfortunate Harold Williams becomes a victim to the incipient racism which is occasionally glimpsed, in its fully fledged form, on televisions news bulletins from the Deep South. Fear of the unknown, and of the supernatural in particular, is thus replaced by more concrete terrors: the threat which comes from within, from the family itself and from the eruption of prejudice and destruction into everyday life.

Melissa's first ghostly appearance, as she trustingly follows the invisible murderer into the cloakroom and sings her favourite song for him before being strangled, is genuinely chilling. Frankie, who has already been introduced as a sensitive child with an active imagination (in class, he reads out the monster story he has written), is able to accept this manifestation unconditionally, and we see it through his eyes. In the later stages, an over-complicated plot perhaps produces one mysterious figure in white too many flitting around on Widow's Peak, while due to an all-round lack of suspects, the murderer's identity becomes fairly obvious early on. The scene in which Melissa and her mother are reunited also wallows in twinkling stardust and syrupy music, though it does suggest that Frankie, by engineering the reunion, has in some way come to terms with the loss of his own mother and the idea of mortality. On the whole, this is a satisfyingly spooky tale which works on a variety of levels: as a ghost story, a murder mystery, a family drama and a portrayal of childish innocence pricked by the first glimmerings of maturity.

LAIR OF THE WHITE WORM, THE (*Film Review Annual, 1989*)

FILMS IN REVIEW, 2/89, p. 102, William K. Everson

Bram Stoker's last novel was a difficult one to read. (So was his *Dracula* for that matter, but the effort paid off). Ken Russell has been fairly faithful to the *spirit* of that novel however, and has been *relatively* restrained in curbing his own tendencies to bravura shock sequences. (They're there, in some startling montage sequences, but in content, length and frequency of appearance they're far more disciplined than in the usual Russell film). True, the plot offers more blood, nudity and devil worship detail than would ever have been countenanced in the classic horror films of the early '30s, but this film does in some way resemble them in its essential simplicity, in its fairly clear cut characters, and in its willingness to let the story develop in its own time and fashion. There is no excess of incident or action, and the climatic set piece, while very satisfactory, is not overdone in terms of special effects. (Most contemporary horror films would have considered it "not enough," and added a second climax). There's a nice sense of casual black humor running through it all, the extensive English rural location work adds a kind of chilling realism, and Stoker's stock Van Helsing character is pleasingly reincarnated in modern terms. The worm/snake motif that runs throughout is also made kin to vampiric mythology, allowing the *very* classy villainess (Amanda Donohoe) to be menacing, sensuous *and* funny. There's also an excellent performance from a (to me) newcomer named Hugh Grant, who has the wit to play his role along Dennis Price lines without once camping it up. If only there was a market for serious new actors in the Colman/Price/Herbert Marshall tradition, his career would be made.

The only disappointment: after a thoroughly satisfying excursion into (relatively) dignified horror, the film adds the now seemingly inevitable post-climax epilogue, indicating that evil *will* triumph and that everything is about to be recycled. After a story that we've been persuaded to take comparatively seriously, and characters that we've learned to like and who have triumphed in time honored tradition, it's a pointless wrap up and the film would be much better off without it.

MONTHLY FILM BULLETIN, 4/89, p. 115, Kim Newman

The Peak District. Scots archaeologist Angus Flint unearths a mysterious reptile skull on a Roman site at Mercy Farm, a property run by Eve and Mary Trent, two young girls orphaned by their parents' recent unexplained disappearance. Angus suspects that the skull is connected to the legend of the D'Ampton Worm a monstrous dragon reputed to have been killed by Sir John D'Ampton. Erny, the local policeman, investigates reports of a prowler near Temple House and is bitten by a snake. He is saved by Lady Sylvia Marsh, who has returned unexpectedly, and who sucks out the poison. Lady Sylvia, an immortal snake-vampire, steals the skull from Mercy Farm while Angus and Mary are joining a search for the missing Trents, which has been restarted since the discovery of Mr. Trent's watch in Stone Rigg cavern. Sylvia, who needs to make a virgin sacrifice to the snake god Dionyn, lures Kevin, a boy scout, back to her estate, but has to drown him suddenly when she is visited by Lord James D'Ampton, the descendant of Sir John. James, Angus and the Trent girls suspect that the dragon—Dionyn—still lives, and that Sylvia is its high priestess. Using snake charmer's music, they lure Sylvia out of her house, so Angus and Mary can investigate. However, the vampire they find is actually Mrs. Trent, whom James has to cut in two. Sylvia kidnaps Eve, intending her to be the sacrifice, and in a battle with Erny, who has become Sylvia's acolyte, Angus kills the constable. While James supervises the pumping of poison gas into Stone Rigg cavern, Mary and Angus try to rescue Eve. Mary is tied up and Angus bitten by Sylvia. But Angus has had an antidote to the venom prepared and manages to push Sylvia into the jaws of Dionyn, rescue Eve and blow up the monster. The laboratory, however, has given Angus the wrong serum, and he finds himself falling prey to the vampire urge...

Ken Russell has always been drawn to the horror genre in a half-ashamed sort of way: Wagner sprouts fangs in his *Lisztomania*, the spectres of Dr. Jekyll and Mr. Hyde and of *The Outer Limits* haunt *Altered States*, *The Devils* is the direct descendant of *Witchfinder General*, *Crimes of Passion* feels a lot like *Belle de Jour* meets *Psycho*, and *Gothic*, although well in line with his series of biographies of erratic geniuses, comes on rather like a remake without music of *The Rocky Horror Picture Show*. *The Lair of the White Worm* dispenses with the tatters of literary or cultural respectabilty that adorn these film and goes literally for the throat, not only by adapting Bram Stoker's last, worst and strangest novel, but also by adopting many of Hammer Films' strategies in their various assaults on English Gothic sensibilities. Russell has approached *Lair* as the work of "someone who has a good idea in his head but didn't have the capacity to put it properly on paper." Unfortunately, he has disdained to elaborate in any interesting way on the material—for instance, by drawing on the tactics of H.P. Lovecraft in some of his works which share the same themes—and simply mounts the whole thing as a charade with video-worthy dollops of nudity and gore to leaven the laughs.

The film opens with the distinctive titling favoured by Hammer: coloured Gothic lettering against a green and pleasant background. And the playing of Peter Capaldi, Hugh Grant, Catherine Oxenberg (whose Northern accent is audibly dubbed) and Sammi Davis is precisely as makeshift and insipid as that of the juveniles of *Dracula Has Risen from the Grave* or *Lust for a Vampire,* while the yokels in the background are as willing as any mittel European villagers to go on a monster hunt at a word from the lord of the manor. For some reason, although computers are glimpsed in the background and we are led to believe that the setting is the late 1980s, the dialogue is littered with 60s slang—characters have "bad trips", are "freaked out", think perversions are "kinky", and lament that they should "get their act together"—and many of the background details ring as laughably false as the mod haircuts on the Victorian in *Taste the Blood of Dracula* or the variety of British regional accents found in Transylvanian peasants in *Frankenstein Created Woman.*

If the intention was to make a deliberately and comically terrible film, it's a shame that Russell saw fit to let only one of his cast—he admirable Amanda Donohoe—in on the joke, and that the standard comic relief of Stratford Johns' grumbling butler is so thuddingly unfunny. Ms. Donohoe, however, is a worthy vampire lady, and whenever Sylvia is on screen, showing off her incredibly bizarre and snake-like wardrobe, the film comes to life. Her drowning of the boy scout in the sunken bath by prodding his venom-paralysed body under the soapy water with the toe of her black, thigh-length fetish boot is one of the few genuinely creepy-funny-sexy notes sounded in what is generally a pedestrian, smirking movie. Russell leaves his signature on the trippy dream sequences, which involve naked and painted girls or nuns being raped by Roman soldiers while a huge snake strangles Jesus on the cross, or Sylvia and Eve as cat-fighting stewardesses showing their suspenders to James in a private jet. But he proves incapable of handling straight suspense, horror or supernatural sequences.

NEW STATESMAN & SOCIETY, 3/17/89, P. 42, Suzanne Moore

If, in the alphabet of cinema, A is for Art film, B is for the equally important B-movie. And Ken Russell, uncomfortably pretentious in the first category, is undoubtedly a master of the second. For what he makes are not B-movies made strange by hindsight, full of the joys of wooden acting, repressed sexuality and daft dialogue, but contemporary films that hover between the tastelessly bad and the cultishly good.

In this respect, his latest effort *Lair of the White Worm* is a winner, Based (very loosely) on a Bram Stoker novel, the film draws upon olde English legends about giant worms, snakes and serpents that terrorised the land before the coming of Christianity. The "worm" turns up again in modern England when a young archaeologist, Angus, discovers a peculiar skull in the garden of two orphaned sisters, Mary and Eve. Strange goings-on in the locality lead Angus, the girls and the local aristo, Lord James D' Ampton, to the mysterious Lady Sylvia Marsh. For not only does Lady Sylvia have a penchant for outfits that would make a drag queen blush, she is, on the side, a part-time reptile.

Amanda Donohoe has great fun vamping around in negligés and thigh-length boots, sinking her fangs into innocent boy scouts. The rest of the cast look as though they've already been half paralysed as they monotonously explain the plot to one another.

The whole thing is a marvellous excuse for the usual Ken Russell trademarks—nuns, suspenders, a spot of pagan ritual and, of course, the dildoes—but none of it really matters as the film is so patently silly. The director himself claims that it's his intention "to keep an audience guessing as to whether I'm being serious or not."

Lair of the White Worm, like Russell's other recent films, is, above all, a very English movie; its humour is part of the camp tradition that runs through both the Carry On films and Hammer Horror. And Russell, a man for whom a symbol is clearly something with which to make as loud a noise as possible, proves once again that he is spiritually closer to Benny Hill than Fellini.

Enough has already been said about his use of women, which actually strikes me as no worse and, at times, more sophisticated than in most contemporary horror movies. And the moment when Lady Sylvia, weird contact lenses in place and fangs out, straps on a hugely ornate dildoe with which to deflower the appallingly virginal Catherine Oxenberg (yes! it's Alexis's daughter from *Dynasty*), lifts this movie out of the realms of the ridiculous into the sublime.

LANDLORD BLUES *(Film Review Annual, 1989)*

VILLAGE VOICE, 6/6/89, p. 65, Manohla Dargis

Neighborhood's a lot better, huh?"
"It was always okay."

Cheap rent, and the desire for it, are atavisms. Holding on to a decent lease in Super Luxury Condo Land can be a feat of romantic heroism, or desperation. The bittersweet adventure of tenant life on the Lower East Side is chronicled in Jacob Burckhardt's modest, offbeat comedy, *Landlord Blues*. Rough around the edges, the shoestring production re-creates the area as a Naked City freak house: Colombian mobster, hitmen for hire, malevolent landlords.

George (Mark Boone Jr.) lives in the back of his bicycle shop. (The store's interior is modeled on the real George's bike shop on East 12th.) He's being squeezed by his landlord, Streck (played with sleazy aplomb by Richard Litt), to make way for tonier occupants, maybe a gallery (already an anachronism since by now many art spaces have either folded or relocated). Streck, a Michael Milken in vitro, is a second-generation, small-time entrepreneur who supplements his 'burb lifestyle with a coke-peddling sideline. He's your Landlord From Hell, evicting old ladies and screwing junkie tenants when they can't make the rent, prowling the East Village in a white Lincoln Town Car fueled by greedy ambition. ("In five years the neighborhood will be bigger than Madison Avenue.")

Landlord Blues is peppered with bad jokes (the Polish safecracker who ties up the safe and blows the guard), idiosyncratic verité touches, familiar streets and characters. Like cowriter William Gordy, Burckhardt is a local, and the film is filled with downtown faces. There's Carmelita Tropicana in an offscreen cameo, incidental music by members of the Lounge Lizards, and a guest appearance by the filmmaker's father, avant-gardist Rudy Burckhardt, as a grizzled native (identified in the credits as Kokoschka's nephew).

There's no sentimentalizing the good fight. George's tougher-than-leather lawyer (Nona Hendryx, who sings the film's anthem) is no match for Streck's arsonist, played with laid-back cool by area artist George Schneeman. (He also wrote the original story upon which the screenplay is based.) Our hero and his cronies—including a boozing cabbie played by painter Bill Rice, the Chill Wills of Lower East Side cheapies—are forced to push the battle to extremes. Salvation may come through the squats, though that route is uncertain. In fiction, the menace comes from Streck and his brethren, who are waiting for abandoned buildings to be renovated before reappropriating them. In fact, as the recent Avenue B fiasco proved, the true threat is from realty's handmaiden, the city itself.

Also reviewed in:
NATION, 6/19/89, p. 862, Stuart Klawans

LAST EMPEROR, THE (*Film Review Annual, 1988*)

FILM QUARTERLY, Winter 1988–89, p. 47, Fatimah Tobing Rony

There seem to be two responses to Bernardo Bertolucci's *The Last Emperor*. One is typified by a remark I overheard as I left the theater: "I loved it! And I learned so much about history too." The other is characterized by a *New York Times* article which, in its obsession with verisimilitude, set out to prove the historical *in*accuracy of the film.[1] Perhaps these concerns with the film's true-to-lifeness should not be surprising. With its extravagantly ornamental sets and multicolored costumed "cast of thousands," *The Last Emperor* harkens back to Hollywood epics à la Cecil B. De Mille. Unlike De Mille, however, Bertolucci has openly rejected the ideal of historical accuracy. As Bertolucci remarked concerning the film's pre-production research: "We had to know the entire truth before we could *choose* to be unfaithful to it."[2]

To focus only on *The Last Emperor's* verisimilitude is therefore misguided at best: a more interesting approach to the historical film is to examine its faculty of engaging the viewer in a game of *belief and disbelief*. As Jean-Louis Comolli has written, the historical film is a *game*, one which stretches the audience's belief in cinema's fictional apparatus to its utmost. Comolli writes, "The simulacrum does not fool a 'passive' spectator (there are no 'passive spectators'): The spectator has to participate in his own fooling; the simulacrum is the *means* whereby he is helped to fool himself."[3] It is the foregrounding of this game of belief and disbelief within *The Last Emperor* which I would like to explore in this review—a game which, no matter how self-reflexive, ultimately does not liberate the viewer from the "shackles" of spectatorship nor move the film beyond the confines of a certain dangerous tradition of film history and orientalist historiography.

Past films by Bertolucci have shown an awareness of ideology as not only a set of political beliefs imposed from above, but as a way in which one experiences the world and perceives reality. *The Conformist* (1970) and *The Spider's Stratagem* (1970) implicitly critique the "naturalness" of film, showing it to be a cultural apparatus which constructs individuals as ideological subjects, fabricating a reality that appears unified and ahistorical.[4] Like the protagonists Marcello Clerici (Jean-Louis Trintignant) in *The Conformist* and Athos Magnani (Giulio Brogi) in *The Spider's Stratagem* who are entrapped in the ideological screens of fascist history, the emperor Pu Yi is both subject of and subject to history. Although the narrative of Pu Yi's life is presented in a coherent, chronological form—beginning with his arrest in 1950, and then proceeding through flashbacks through his entire life—Pu Yi (John Lone) is also presented as an allegorical figure for the ideal film spectator, produced as a subject-effect, seduced by the fetishism of film.

Like another story about an emperor, Hans Christian Andersen's "The Emperor's New Clothes,"[5] *The Last Emperor* is a story about surface and the act of looking. In Andersen's fairy tale, the magical cloth does not exist. Instead the weaving is the *story* that the two swindlers tell the emperor, a story which becomes a veil: the emperor and his subjects see that they do not see but are afraid to admit their own "stupidity" or "incompetence." Believing in the clothes covers the fear shared by both the emperor and his subjects of being caught "naked," the fear that they cannot trust their own eyes. Like the film viewer who fetishizes the cinematic apparatus, the emperor and his subjects fetishize the "magical" cloth. The new clothes are both a sign of fullness and coherence, and a lie hiding a fear of inadequacy or nakedness.

Bertolucci's *The Last Emperor* is also a weaving, a story which embroiders upon theories of film spectatorship and fetishism. As a fabric, it too consists of a telling. Bertolucci's film *exposes* the fetishism of ideology and film spectatorship, constructed as the film is out of screens superimposed on screens, veils covering veils in rich brocaded clothes. The veils or screens exist not only in the court of the Forbidden City, but also later in the screens of ideology of Manchukuo, and of the Maoist re-education camp; they also parallel the screen onto which a film is projected. Like the ideal film spectator who both sees the fabricated nature of cinema and yet denies it at the same time in order to enjoy watching the film, Pu Yi deludes himself into thinking that he is master of his own domain, when in fact he is merely a symbol and puppet manipulated for the benefit on various political regimes.

The visual style and narrative of the film is composed of screens of ideologies, mirroring the way in which the relations of subjectivity, lack, and spectatorship are conceptualized by Bertolucci. The first screen is the billowing yellow canopy that fascinates the three-year-old Pu Yi, who runs out of the Hall of Supreme Harmony into the bright sunlight on the first day of his reign, and is suddenly greeted by thousands of kowtowing courtiers. A second screen is the long white sheet that prevents the eunuchs from touching the adolescent Pu Yi as they play together. These playmates appear only as shadows from the point of view of Pu Yi; the white sheet brings to mind both the movie screen and the wall in Plato's cave. A third screen is part of yet another game: Pu Yi and his two wives play hide and seek under a silk sheet—as we viewers only see their shapes while simultaneously an unseen fire, like the fire in Plato's cave, blazes in the Forbidden City's storerooms, set by the eunuchs who are afraid that Pu Yi will discover their thefts. The final screen is the crisp, red flag of Mao's Red Guard, waved by the zealous marching youth of the Cultural Revolution.

Pu Yi's imprisonment is a necessary component of his desire, since only *within* the prison can he be emperor. Like the fetishism of the ideal film spectator described by Metz, his desire is sustained by a game in which he oscillates between belief (Yes, I am emperor) and disbelief (No, I am not emperor). The psychoanalytic underpinnings of his desire are revealed in his fixation on returning to the mother and his search for origins, a return perhaps to the Imaginary: Pu Yi is seen repeatedly running after a fleeing mother figure, first his wet nurse, then upon his mother's death, and finally when his wife is forced to an asylum. Always held back by lackeys, his return to the mother is never successful, as indeed it cannot be: his overriding desire is to remain emperor.

Pu Yi's desire to be emperor, even a puppet emperor, is molded by the needs of the particular regime in power. Because Pu Yi is an emperor, he must abide by certain rules, akin to those of the model film viewer. His is a royal body that Pu Yi himself learns to objectify: he is rigid and impassive; he never uses the pronoun "I," referring to himself in the third person or as the royal "we"; and as emperor he is supposed to see all, but no one may look at him. Like the film viewer who, identifying with the camera, comes to believe that s/he is in the position of the "transcendental eye," Pu Yi thinks he is all-perceiving when in fact he is only allowed to see what his captors want him to see. Since no one may look at him, since no one else may wear the royal yellow, and since no other men are allowed to live in the palace of the Forbidden City, Pu Yi cannot see any representation of himself. He never sees himself in the clothes of another, or in the gaze of another, flattened as a representation within that gaze, just as the film viewer does not find his or her body reflected in the mirror that is the movie screen.

As the Lord Chamberlain tells the tutor Mr. Johnston (Peter O'Toole), Pu Yi is a symbol of great importance. As symbol, therefore, he not only figures for the textually produced viewer, but for the object of spectatorship itself. In every regime, Pu Yi is under a surveillance by a power that monitors and contains him. His first overseer is of course the Lord Chamberlain, with the eunuchs. The architecture of the Forbidden City moreover is conducive to voyeurism: doorways are framed by doorways, rooms lie within rooms, and the palace is its own *mise-en-abyme*.

Pu Yi's next important overseer is Johnston. He is also a voyeur: it is Johnston who watches Pu Yi play the screen game with the eunuchs and Johnston who photographs him before he leaves the Forbidden City, a neat trope for his particular objectification of the emperor. Johnston introduced Pu Yi to western education and western ideas of reform, and yet he keeps Pu Yi ignorant of the political realities of revolution. Instead Johnston encourages his passion for superficial reform like western fads, clothes, tennis, etc.

After his years of tutoring under Johnston, Pu Yi is forced to leave the Forbidden City by Jiang Jie-Shi's (Chiang Kai-Shek's) troops, but his blindness to the imperatives of political reform and to the fact that his monarchy is indeed obsolete is symbolized by his wearing of dark glasses, and his stumbling walk as he goes outside the palace gate for the first time. He thus leaves the first prison only to enter another one. The Japanese become Pu Yi's third overseers by convincing him that they will help him become emperor again. The sequences with the Japanese, reminiscent of the *mise-en-scène* of The Conformist, are replete with the signifiers of "fascinating fascism," to use Susan Sontag's term, from the grey and black interior architecture of his new palace, combining sterile modernity and kitsch, to the playboy Pu Yi's smooth rendition of "Am I Blue?", like a crooner in an Italian white-telephone film.

The new palace is another theater of shadows, a fascist prison for the deluded Pu Yi who refuses to perceive the imperialist motives of his puppet masters. The coronation ball is a dramatic metaphor for this new prison/cave: we see Amikasu (Ryuichi Sakamoto) directing cameramen as the harsh lighting used for filming creates a chiaroscuro world where the dancers cast large shadows. Only Pu Yi's wife, Wan Jung (Joan Chen) protests their imprisonment. Her self-destructive resistance is characterized by the sequence in which she eats lotus blossoms petal by petal as her husband greets the Japanese dignitaries, thereby calling attention to her and Pu Yi's role in Manchukuo as mere "lotus eaters."

Just as Pu Yi came to know that he was not really Emperor of China in the Forbidden City, he becomes increasingly aware of his manipulation by the Japanese, but in both cases he is immobilized by his own desire to be emperor. Although the monochromatic khaki world of the Fushun prison, a re-education camp for Mao's new order, is a starkly different environment, it does parallel his earlier prisons. Once again we have a place of surveillance, this time tied to our own viewing of the film. Our voyeurism is pointed out by our identification with the point-of-view peephole shot of the governor watching Pu Yi having his shoes tied by his former valet. Like the governor, we too desire to learn the truth about Pu Yi.

In many ways, the governor seems to be the best of Pu Yi's overseers. As the governor tells the prisoners in his orientation speech: "We believe that men are good. We believe that the only way to change is to stare at the truth." Yet Bertolucci subverts any idealist notions that man has the ability to see the truth. In one crucial scene Pu Yi made explicitly into a cinematic spectator, viewing a film composed of newsreel footage of Japanese atrocities in China and Manchukuo. But it is only when Pu Yi sees an image of *himself* that he stands, entranced, staring straight at his own mass-produced portrait. This "moment of truth" is immediately undermined, since the next shot is of the hailing hands of a rally, as if to highlight the notion that ideology hails the subject, fabricates a unified reality, reminding one of Louis Althusser's statement: "All ideology hails or interpellates concrete individuals as concrete subjects."[6] There is no child to cry out that the emperor hasn't got anything on, because ultimately there is no royal body, no referent of truth but only clothes, its signs.[7]

The final screen is that of China during the Cultural Revolution. Instead of the chanting golden-robed monks of the Forbidden City, there are Mao Zedong's marching, bullying children. The aging Pu Yi protests to these children that the governor "is a teacher, a good teacher," only to be ignored. The red flag waves, symbol of another blinding ideology; a group of uniformed girls in red arm bands march in a circle, to the accompaniment of accordionists lined up under a mural depicting the beaming face of Chairman Mao in the sun. In Plato's allegory the sun represented the light of truth, the Good; here the sun is just another propagandistic symbol of power. The movement of the girls in a circle with the red-flag-waving youth in the middle repeats the circular chase of the young Pu Yi and his brother Pu Chieh, and this choreographed use of screens is important because it represents the ultimate inescapability of ideology. Just as Marcello was caught in a swirling circle of dancers in *The Conformist*, Pu Yi never comes to any ultimate truth, but is always trapped within a circle.

So far in this review, I too may appear to be seduced by the visual splendor and conceptual sophistication of Bertolucci's latest work. I would like to argue now that although Bertolucci has created a film that exposes the woven screens of shadows and nesting boxes which constitutes both history and film spectatorship, at the center of the film is also a *lack*, an emptiness of a particular ideological nature.

To begin, the last screen of ideology which I discussed, that of the cruelty and theater of Maoist China, seems a little too transparent to me. What it reveals is another screen of ideology: that of the current Chinese government's support of the film through its granting of unprecedented permission for on-site shooting. The governor of the prison is even played by the actor and director Ying Ruocheng, Deputy Minister of Culture. A critical perspective on the Cultural Revolution is welcome to the present government with its program of economic reforms, and it is only because of these reforms that a western film-maker like Bertolucci would be allowed to film in China at all. This unfavorable representation of Maoist China also reveals a shift in Bertolucci's stance as an Italian Marxist intellectual who at one point was sympathetic to Mao but seems now to have shifted allegiances.[8]

Secondly, *The Last Emperor*, which after all is a work financed by Western capital, must be posited within a tradition of Hollywood realism and the epic film, especially in the ways it reflects orientalist historiography. At the film's conclusion, the horde of western tourists who invade the Hall of Supreme Harmony reminds us that we too have been tourists in Pu Yi's life. The seamlessness of the film is ruptured here, and we are abruptly brought back to our own time. Yet for all its implied critique of the filmic apparatus, Bertolucci's film, as a narratival, chronological story of the life of one man, still constructs a classical subject-effect through the strategies of mainstream realist Hollywood cinema—witness the many marks of "authenticity," whether it be the inserted titles of place and date, or the logic of the continuity editing. The self-reflexive foregrounding of the apparatus of film does not challenge the essential game of belief and disbelief: Bertolucci allows us to disbelieve, as if winking at us—yes, it is only a game—in order that we may believe just a little bit longer. *The Last Emperor* is an airtight box that only contains boxes within boxes (Pu Yi's life, after all, spans the history of cinema), and I find the ending to be an excuse for what is basically still a realist film.

Moreover, *The Last Emperor* simulates the Hollywood epic films—it is a simulation of a simulation—through its self-reflexive style of realism. The difference between Cecil B. De Mille and Bertolucci is that at some level De Mille invoked the rubric of historical accuracy as a marketing strategy for his films. But despite De Mille's efforts, the Hollywood looks and accents of his actors, of course, always gave the film away. Bertolucci, on the other hand, is aware of the impossibility of historical authenticity, and thus he highlights the surface of history. The problem is that in creating another film about surface spectacle and Orientalism, Bertolucci feeds into some dangerous myths about China. Perhaps the epic, the spectacular Hollywood historical film, may be characterized as a representation of a power struggle, usually an essentialist Manichean struggle for some kind of empire, some kind of hegemony—a battle of ideologies. In lavish Hollywood spectacles like those of De Mille, there are usually implicit or explicit struggles between East and West, the barbaric versus the civilized, with the civilized always winning at the end. Although *The Last Emperor* tries to subvert the De Mille style of representing history by containing within the film a self-reflexive critique of film, it does not escape from one major problem: colonialist attitudes. *The Last Emperor's* opium-dream-like oneiricism, although self-conscious, descends into old stereotypes about China and Orientalism: that is, Oriental cruelty, sensuality, and lack of rationality. The West has traditionally thought of itself as the site of substance and the Orient as one of *surface*; the fetishism of the film for dazzling silks, brocades, and embroidery still promotes an attitude that after all underneath the Orient's silky sleeves there is nothing there.

While Pu Yi was in his box of shadows, tremendous changes transformed China from the Middle Kingdom into the People's Republic of China. As the production history of *The Last Emperor* shows, moreover, the transformation continues, this time with the bourgeoisification of China. John Powers relates an interesting anecdote: in between takes of one scene, Chinese soldiers, hired as extras for the scene involving rebelling students, listened to disco and took pictures of themselves with cameras hidden underneath their costumes.[9] May we then think of Bertolucci himself as a last emperor? The irony of the title *The Last Emperor* is that in trying to get away from looking for the referent, for truth, for the causes of effects—this is a film about the *last* emperor, the title has nothing to do with originals—this film which tries to subvert the ideological apparatus of film ends up hiding behind an old ideological screen, and a pernicious one at that. If Pu Yi is a model for the ideal film spectator, we do not become the last emperors, aware of our production as subject-effects. Instead, the old empire continues, albeit under a new surface.

NOTES

[1] Richard Bernstein, "Is 'The Last Emperor' Truth or Propaganda?'', *New York Times* (May 8, 1988), Cl, 33.

[2] John Powers, "Last Tango in Beijing," *America Film*, November 1987, Vol. XIII, No. 2, 40.

[3] Jean-Louis Comolli, "Historical Fiction: A Body Too Much, " *Screen* 19, no. 2 (Summer 1978), 46.

[4] Jodi Hauptmann has written an unpublished paper that explores the relation of the story of Plato's cave to *The Conformist*, entitled "Slaves to Shadows: The Allegory of Plato's Cave in *The Conformist*."

[5] Hans Christian Andersen, *Eighty Fairy Tales*, trans. R. P. Keigwin (New York: Pantheon, 1982), 64–68. For my interpretation of "The Emperor's New Clothes" I am indebted in part to Shoshana Felman's class lectures on the same fairy tale.

[6] Louis Althusser, "Ideology and Ideological State Apparatuses (Notes Towards an Investigation," trans. Ben Brewster, *Lenin and Philosophy and Other Essays* (New York and London: Monthly Review Press, 1971), 173.

[7] Ettore Scola's *La Nuit de Varennes* (1982) is arguably more successful in foregrounding the game of the historical film because of its playfulness. Scola does not show the body of the king at all, but shows us only the king's red inauguration coat, dwelling instead on the *discourse* centered around the king, the conversations held within the coach.

[8] See Robert Philip Koller's chapter on Godard, and Bertolucci's early politics in his chapter, "Versus Godard,' "*Bernardo Bertolucci* (London: British Film Institute, 1985), 11–35.

[9] Powers, 40.

LAST TEMPTATION OF CHRIST, THE (*Film Review Annual, 1989*)

JUMP CUT, No. 35, 4/90, p. 108, Lisa DiCaprio

Despite its religious detractors, *The Last Temptation* celebrates Christ's life. It affirms his teachings and sacrifice. In rather traditional terms, director Martin Scorsese depicts Christ's departure from basic tenets of Old Testament Judaism: Jesus' transformation of the angry and even wrathful God of the Israelites into a compassionate and merciful one embracing the entire human race, his condemnation of animal sacrifice and the money changers in the temple, and his opposition to open revolt as the only solution to the Roman domination of Israel. Instead, Jesus argues with Judas (Harvey Keitel) that love must replace hatred: "The circle of sin must be broken or else it will only be repeated." The soul, argues Jesus, is the foundation of the body—not the reverse, as Judas maintains.

For Scorsese, a Catholic, this film derives from his preoccupation with exploring the issues of sin and redemption in modern life, first exemplified in *Mean Street*. So why all the furor? *The Last Temptation* has received official condemnation from the Catholic Church, full-page ads in the *New York Times* by fundamentalist groups detailing "blasphemous" scenes in the film, and widespread protests, some aimed at stopping its production by Universal Pictures. In many ways, this protest replays (in a magnified way) the reaction which met the Greek publication of the Kazantzakis novel on which the screenplay is based. At that time, the Greek Orthodox Church attempted to excommunicate Kazantzakis, and in April of 1954, the Pope placed *The Last Temptation* on the Index of censored works.

What is new in *The Last Temptation* cinematic version of the Christ story—and that which fundamentalists find most objectionable—is the process by which Christ finally accepts his role as redeemer of the human race. At the film's outset, we see a passage from the Prologue to the novel in which Kazantzakis states that all his life Christ has been consumed by the "incessant, merciless battle between the spirit and the flesh." This battle is at the center of *The Last Temptation* and it is portrayed in fully human terms, including a dream sequence in which Christ (about to die on the cross) imagines himself being as the husband of Mary Magdalene (Barbara Hershey) and the father of several children, rather than being crucified on the cross.

This probing into Christ's personal life has received special attack. A protest leaflet handed out in front of New York's Ziegfeld Theater condemns the film as an "indecent, audacious, insolent, arrogant and improper inquiry into the private, sacred life of Jesus." The private life of Jesus, however, is precisely what *The Last Temptation* aims to explore, rather than repeat the sanitized version of Christ presented in such Biblical epics as last year's television special, *Jesus of Nazareth*.

In his introduction to one of Kazantzakis' earlier works, *The Saviors of God* (1927), Kimon Friar writes that Kazantzakis "had brooded long on the ultimate spiritual significance and martyrdom of Christ stripped of dogmatic and ceremonious ritual. . . ." It is just such a Christ which we encounter in *The Last Temptation*—one who is indecisive, fearful of dying, followed by shadows, and without a clear understanding of the mission assigned to him by God. "I am a liar, I am a hypocrite. I am afraid of everything. Lucifer is inside of men," states Jesus at a particularly anguished moment. He is even shown experiencing sexual fantasies about Mary Magdalene—considered a sin in the eyes of the Catholic Church.

By contrast, the film depicts Judas as sure of himself—a Zealot who criticizes Christ for making the crosses on which the Romans will crucify Jews accused of sedition. And Christ regards Judas as the strongest of all his disciples the one on whom Christ must rely to betray him: "We're bringing God and man together. Without that there will be no redemption. You have to kill me."

Despite its reversing the traditional relationship between Christ and Judas, the film does not portray Christ simply as a weakling. Instead, Willem Dafoe (much acclaimed for his Christ-like performance as Sargeant—in *Platoon*) brings to Scorsese's Christ just the proper combination of divine inspiration and human weakness which the film demands. However, the portrayal of such weakness strikes at the very heart of the most enduring resolution of the paradox of Christ as both human and divine: the Augustinian view that Christ represented humanity in its perfected, rather than actual form.

Did Christ suffer as man or as God? Did he have "two-natures" or one? How was the union of man and God in Christ to be interpreted? These questions the Church confronted in the first few centuries of tis existence, as it consolidated itself ideologically and organizationally. In his recent study, *Jesus Through the Centuries*, historian and theologian Jaroslav Pelikan shows how the solution offered by St. Augustine was an idealization of Christ as man. Grappling with issues related to the fall of humanity, St. Augustine not only came up with the doctrine of original sin, but he also determined that "Jesus was, then, not only the image of divinity, but the image of humanity as it had originally been intended to be and as through him it could now become; he was in this sense the 'ideal man.' " Christ, according to Augustine, was human insofar as he was the Word made flesh, but his humanity reflected the future perfection of "man." In *The Last Temptation*, the tables are turned on this concept of Christ one traditionally associated with Christianity. Instead, the film portrays Christ in two dimensions: as humanity is in its "fallen condition'' and as humans can become through their belief in God. And the struggle between the spirit and the flesh—otherwise reserved for mere mortals—thereby become transferred to the figure of Christ himself.

Myths, as Joseph Campbell emphasized, need constant updating or they can lose their meaning. As the film shows, this mythologizing began with the apostles, themselves. In the film, for example, Paul confronts a living Christ who has renounced his mission, that Christ calls Paul's description of his crucifixion a lie: "I live like a man now. For the first time I enjoy it." Paul replies that the only hope for Christ's believers lies in the resurrected Jesus: "You started all this. Now you can't stop it. You don't know how much people need God. My Jesus is much more important and powerful than you."

In *The Last Temptation*, the myth of Christ takes on a new and contemporary shapes. The film depicts Christ almost as an anti-hero, whose final sacrifice is all the more meaningful because it comes as the product of intense personal struggle. As Christ finally acknowledges that the "guardian angel" who promised him life was really Satan in disguise, Christ asks for and receives a second chance. "It is accomplished," are Christ's final words when that moment arrives. Despite all previous vacillation, he dies as Christos Rex—Christ triumphant. In that moment, the narrative conclusion depends on a decidedly Christian ideal of sacrifice and spiritual transcendence which Scorsese's right-wing critics are unable (or unwilling) to appreciate.

Unfortunately, however, some of the film's power is diminished by its technical and conceptual weaknesses. At times the dialogue seems stilted and even undermines its own seriousness by playing on historical hindsight, as when the other apostles refer to Peter as "solid as a rock." On a visual level, the film degenerates into Hollywood extravaganza as it aims to capture certain Biblical highlights. Dafoe's distinctly Aryan features also detract from the film's faithfulness to time and place, although in this instance Scorsese is only following a long-standing artistic precedent of representing Christ through the blinders of Western white culture.

Overall, however, *The Last Temptation* may very well represent the crowning of Scorsese's carer. The film for the most part succeeds in challenging certain tenets of Christianity in order to capture what Scorsese considers to be Christianity's essence. Even non-believer and/or those raised outside of the Christian tradition stand to gain much from viewing the film. Although we may not share Kazantzakis' particular obsession with the mind/body split, we can all appreciate the desire to transform our ordinary existence—with all its material requirements—into something more meaningful than its own maintenance or reproduction. This, then, may be the real (Catholic as Universal) lesson of Christ's Passion which *The Last Temptation* aims to convey: the desire and ability of each of us (as mortals) to transform that which decays and dies into something permanent, the mundane into the spiritual—the ordinary into the extraordinary.[1]

NOTES

[1] Coincidentally with the release of *The Last Temptation*, new historical evidence indicates that Kazantzakis' rendition of a Christ who maintains an ascetic existence in order to fulfill his Christian mission (rather than out of any view that sexuality is sinful) may very well be close to historical reality. In *Adam, Eve, and the Serpent*, Elaine Pagels concludes that the concept of original sin (and all that it entails) overturned views held by early Christians on the relationship between sexuality and moral freedom. Pagels contends that prior to Augustine, "Christians regarded *freedom* as the primary message of *Genesis 1-3* [the story of Adam and Eve]—freedom in its many forms, including free will, freedom from demonic powers, freedom from social and sexual obligations, freedom from tyrannical government and from fate; and self-mastery as the source of such freedom." Later, with Augustine, self-mastery as a basis for moral freedom was destroyed as "Adam's sin. . .corrupted our experience of sexuality (which Augustine tended to identify with original sin), and made us incapable of genuine political freedom." If Pagels is correct, *The Last Temptation* may represent a rather brilliant example of art imitating life.

LE JUPON ROUGE (*Film Review Annual, 1989*)

VILLAGE VOICE, 6/13/89, p. 63, C. Carr

Geneviève Lefebvre's *Le Jupon Rouge* is a complicated story about the fragility of both life and relationships. In the opening sequence, Manuela (Marie-Christine Barrault) leaves her boyfriend at the airport, and it soon becomes clear that she has always put romance second to political work. She assists an older woman named Bacha (Alida Valli), a Holocaust survivor who's become an internationally renowned activist. "Survivors' lives are ruined," announces Bacha, who seems to be at peace only when addressing the cruelest issues—the "disappeared," apartheid, torture. When Manuela begins a love affair with another woman, Bacha finds a cruelty in her own nature that she had probably never confronted before. "You with that girl brings out the worst in me," she finally admits to Manuela.

All of the characters remain sympathetic and multidimensional, largely because the acting is good. And their situation is beyond the easy remedies of political correctness. The script makes Manuela a bit too enigmatic, however. We never understand her history with Bacha, or what motivates her political commitments, or why she chooses to be secretive with her lover. However, I prefer mystery to pat answers. And the characters in *Le Jupon Rouge* seem to be looking for answers that could take a lifetime to unravel: Did I deserve to survive? Do I deserve to love?

MONKEY SHINES (*Film Review Annual, 1989*)

MONTHLY FILM BULLETIN, 2/90, p. 45, Kim Newman

Pittsburgh. Allan Mann, a law student and college athlete, is struck by a truck while training. Dr. Wiseman, a specialist, tells him that his spinal cord is shattered, and that he is unable to help him. Now a quadriplegic, Allan suffers a series of emotional shocks, as his girlfriend Linda leaves him for his doctor, and his smothering mother Dorothy moves in to run his life, bringing with her Maryanne, an unsympathetic nurse. Geoffrey Fisher, a researcher in craniology, introduces Allan to Melanie Parker, an animal trainer who specialises in tutoring capuchin monkeys as household help for the disabled. Melanie gives Allan a monkey called Ella, whom Geoffrey has unethically injected with a serum made from human cranial fluid in an attempt to make her smarter, and she soon replaces Maryanne as the invalid's nurse, driving her rival from the house by killing Maryanne's pet bird. However, Allan and Ella develop a psychic link, and Ella picks up on Allan's latent hostilities, leaving the house one night to cause a fire in which Dr. Wiseman and Linda are killed. Geoffrey has an inkling of what's going on, and pushes himself harder—keeping himself going with drugs—to research the problem. Meanwhile, Allan and Melanie become romantically involved, and Ella is made jealous. She causes Dorothy's death and, feeling rejected by Allan, goes wild, disabling Geoffrey when he tries to intervene, and trying to stab Melanie with a hypodermic syringe. Allan tries to protect the unconscious Melanie and himself with only his mouth and, in defeating Ella, manages to move his hand, indicating that he could recover. But his bad dreams about the monkey continue...

Like David Cronenberg and Larry Cohen, George Romero has fiercely cherished his independence from Hollywood, always working on his home turf and from original screenplays, putting up with the occasional box-office disappointment to pursue his own vision untrammelled by the conventional studio wisdom as to what a horror movie ought to be. This, financed by Orion but shot in Pittsburgh with Romero's usual collaborators, is at once his first major-studio project and his first literary adaptation (*Creepshow* was mainly based on *unpublished* Stephen King stories). Adapted from British writer Michael Stewart's scientific thriller—the original has an Oxford setting—*Monkey Shines* has suffered from a little tampering (after previews, a regulation last-minute gratuitous shock was added to the otherwise subtly effective ending), but for the most part his style transfers seamlessly to the mainstream.

Significantly, he has subsequently announced that he intends to leave the thankless task of remaking his seminal *Night of the Living Dead* to his master make-up protégé Tom Savini, while he tackles another underrated, understated British suspense shocker, Bernard Taylor's *Mummy's Boys*.

There are echoes in the basic premise—mixing monkeys with cranial fluid—of such mad-science chestnuts as *The Monster and the Girl* or *The Strange Case of Dr. Rx* and the various versions of *Donovan's Brain*, while the terror-by-simian angle was recently explored, far less successfully, in the killer-chimp picture *Link* (1986). But the high-tech approach to an outmoded horror theme signals a more serious attempt to deal with the frontiers of science. While this has a tighter storyline than most of Romero's scattershot horrors, restricted to its major setting by the lead character's quadriplegia, the director-writer's personality shows through in the gradual build-up of unbearable tension and the profane, pithy dialogue. A good fifteen to twenty minutes longer that the average horror film, it dares to begin slowly, concentrating on the characterisations. The treatment of disability is especially sensitive, particularly in the tactfully filmed sex scene between the crippled Allan and the able-bodied Melanie, and the essential situation, without too much in the way of actual horror (the murders are very ambiguously presented), carefully set up.

However, after it has worked up a head of narrative steam, the film pulls a marvellously sustained finale as Ella fumbles with hypodermic needles near the heroine's eyes, the drug-addled scientist is torn between saving his friend and his reputation, and the paralysed hero has to find convincing ways of defending himself with only his head. John Pankow's Geoffrey cleverly straddles the fence, being at once a traditional mad movie boffin and a credible modern scientist in the fast-talking vein of William Hurt in *Altered States*, using drugs to keep awake as he toils in a spotless laboratory among shrieking monkeys and struggling with his credibly mixed motives. The finale avoids the distastefulness of most disabled-in-distress movies by taking the time to establish a characterisation for the hero that doesn't depend on his quadriplegia. Audrey Hepburn's 'super blind lady' in *Wait Until Dark* was that and nothing more, while Allan is a crankier, wittier hero, railing against his restrictions but believably overcoming them in the end. Jason Beghe is marvellous in an obviously restricted role, signalling this mindlink with the jungle creature by talking and spitting like Marlon Brando, while Ella the monkey (albeit once or twice replaced by a puppet) outdoes her rival in *Link* in displaying an astonishing variety of responses and turning into a credibly malicious character.

PEDDLER, THE *(Film Review Annual, 1990)*

FILM QUARTERLY, Spring 1990, p. 38, William Johnson

Few Westerners going to see a recent Iranian film produced by the Organization for the Propagation of Islamic Thought would expect to find technical sophistication, a script inspired in part by a European story, and a vision of post-revolutionary Tehran so bleak that none of the characters, including the faithful at a mosque, commands affection or respect. I have no idea what *The Peddler* means to its maker or to its Iranian viewers—the questionnaire I sent in care of the Tehran Film Office went unanswered—but over here its grim brilliance confronts the image of Iran as a totalitarian theocracy. The news release issued by the Film Society of Lincoln Center had it right: *The Peddler* was the revelation of the 1989 New Directors/New Films festival. It was in some ways the most surprising film of the year.

The film consists of three tenuously connected episodes. The first, "The Happy Child," is based on a story by Alberto Moravia. A poor married couple who are cousins live in an abandoned bus with their four children, all of whom have some physical handicap. The wife is about to give birth again, and the husband believes the baby will be physically sound if brought up in better circumstances. The parents try unsuccessfully to have the baby boy kept at the hospital. They then leave him in a basket in front of a mosque, hoping for a well-to-do foster parent, but a beggar woman takes him as a prop to enhance her appeal. The parents retrieve the baby and place the basket inside the mosque near two prosperous-looking men, who merely peek in it and then continue discussing business. Finally the father leaves the baby at the estate of a wealthy man he once worked for, and the couple go home contented. But the baby is not accepted: the episode ends with him back in the hospital—in a ward for retarded children.

The second episode, "The Birth of an Old Woman," focuses on a man who lives with his mother, a woman so ancient and decrepit that she can neither move nor speak. As the son prepares meals, cleans the apartment and trundles his mother about in her wheelchair, he delivers a continuous litany of wishes and complaints, saying among other things that he could find a good job and get married if she were dead. They live solely on her pension, which he leaves the apartment once a month to collect. This time, returning home with food and her drugs, he is knocked unconscious by a car. Passers-by—including the couple from Episode 1—pretend to help but steal his purchases. Two men in a van—who will reappear in Episode 3—say they will take him to a hospital but instead drive out of the city, rob him, and dump him on the road. Meanwhile the mother sits in her wheelchair on the balcony, where the son had left her. At midnight she fades away, to reappear as a little girl in a passing carriage. Eventually the son returns home and resumes his chores and monologue as if the mother were still alive.

In Episode 3, "The Peddler," a young man is selling stolen shirts for a criminal gang when he is hustled away by two other gang members—the men who robbed the son in Episode 2. A brief flashback reveals that the peddler saw the two execute another member, and he is afraid that he too is about to be silenced. At one point he jumps out of the van, starts to run and is shot down—but this turns out to be the first of several scenes, all ending with the peddler's death, that appear real but represent his terrified imagination. He is taken to a cafe where the gang boss talks with him for a while before leading him down to the basement. The boss shows other stolen goods that the gang is now expanding into, and then says that the peddler is not reliable. The two strongarm men reappear. The peddler dodges them, fights back, and bursts through a wall to the street. But this escape is only imagined: he enters a hearse with no driver, passes the carriage with the little girl/mother from Episode 2, and sees the executed man apparently alive. The peddler collapses and is back in the basement, dead.

By itself, the overlapping of characters between episodes is superficial, but there are other, more significant linkes. Episode 2 begins with a small crowd pursuing an old man and jeering, "He's crazy!" This pursuit leads to the sidewalk below the son's and mother's apartment, where the son harangues them, plays a trumpet and drum and engages them in a brief water fight. Following upon the scene of the retarded children that closes Episode 1, these incidents suggest what the "happy child" may eventually become—a "crazy" man or an obsessive eccentric. Midway through Episode 2, Makhmalbaf inserts a scene in which a car cuts across a busy street and the driver is dragged out by an angry crowd, and this apparent digression may foreshadow the peddler's fear when driven off in Episode 3.

There are at least two general progressions throughout the film. Virtually all of Episode 1 is realistic, with no unusual camera setups or lighting effects and with fairly sparse dialogue against a background of natural sounds. Only at the end is there an expressionistic flourish as the camera dollies back from the baby in its hospital crib to reveal the retarded children all around, while disembodied laughter echoes on the sound track. Most of Episode 2 is realistic, too, but involves more dramatic contrasts: crowds and busy streets with their confusion of sounds, the enclosed apartment with the son's monologue and the mother's silence. Toward the end the episode dips into fantasy, beginning as the uncanny silence of the mother on the balcony is broken by the midnight chimes of the clock, which (in another touch of expressionism) shift into slow motion. After the mother's transformation into the young girl in the carriage, the arrival of the son returns the film to apparent realism: but now he is living a fantasy in which his mother is still alive. This foreshadows the strategy of Episode 3, which quickly compromises its apparent realism by revealing parts of it as imagined. The contrasts here are even stronger than in Episode 2: the static crowd in the market; the speedy van ride, accompanied by heavy incidental music; the soft, sinister speech of the crime boss amid the echoing chatter of the cafe. Eventually, with its Bergmanesque death sequence, the episode travels further into fantasy than Episode 2; and even when it returns to realism with the peddler's dead body there is an accompaniment of suspenseful music that modulates without a break into an ethereal chorale. This introduces an odd coda in which the camera circles around what appears to be a fetus in a jar. Recalling as it does the Star Child at the end of *2001*, the coda points to the birth of a new life beyond the reality that the central characters have all found too painful to confront.

The progression from realism to fantasy is reflected in the film's lighting and sound levels. Episode 1 begins in the extensive waste lot where the married cousins live: it is daytime and the sun is shining in a broad expanse of blue sky. The whole of the episode takes place in the daytime, but it ends indoors, in the ward for retarded children. Except for the disembodied laughter at the end, the sounds are casual and unemphatic. Episode 2 begins outdoors, also in the daytime, and includes a lengthy exterior sequence in which the son collects the check and is robbed. Much of the action, however, takes place in the dark-walled apartment where mother and son live, and the episode ends at night. The sounds are generally louder (crowds, street traffic, trumpet and drum) or more insistent (the son's monologue) than anything in Episode 1. Episode 3 begins in gray exteriors, proceeds into a dimly lit cafe and descends to an even more dimly lit basement; the peddler's final fantasy, in which he breaks out into the world of the dead, takes place on nighttime street. Meanwhile, in several key scenes, incidental music adds its weight to the emphatic natural sounds and dialogue. Thus the three episodes form an overlapping progression from light to dark in the image, from light to heavy in the sound.

I am in no position to relate *The Peddler* to Iranian film making in general, since I have seen only one other film made in Iran—Sohrab Shahid Saless's prerevolutionary *A Simple Event* (1973)—and two postrevolutionary films made in US by exiles—Parviz Sayyad's *The Mission* (1983) and Ghasem Ebrahimian's *The Suitor* (1988). The partly annotated list of films in Bahman Maghsoudlou's *Iranian Cinema* (New York, 1987) suggests that most prerevolutionary commercial production was heavily influenced by Hollywood, since it featured many remakes of American films (including such unlikely inspiration as *Cape Fear and Cat Ballou*). *A Simple Event*, however, focused like *The Peddler* on the bleak underside of life: its central character, the only son of poor parents, is caught between the demands of school work and the work he has to do for his family; almost incidentally, his mother dies. Although Saless's style suggests neorealism rather than Makhmalbaf's sophisticated eclecticism, he gives his film a powerful formal shape by having his young protagonist move everywhere at a trot—as if the pressure of poverty and labor is hurrying him visibly from childhood to premature old age.

One of the exiles' films, *The Suitors*, throws into relief the problem of appreciating a film made in a different culture. The narrative of *The Suitors* stems directly from the slaughtering of a sheep in the bathroom of a New York City apartment shared by a group of Iranians. The killing is shown obliquely, so that quite possibly it did not take place in reality. In *The Peddler*, by contrast, Episode 3 opens with a frontal view of the cutting of a sheep's throat on a balcony; the dripping of blood onto the courtyard below leads the camera down to the peddler. While the makers of *The Suitors* may have taken American sensibilities into account, no such issue existed for Makhmalbaf. Other parts of the film may seem callous toward humans: in Episode 1, actually deformed children play the cousins' offspring and actually retarded childred appear in the hospital sequences. Yet beyond such prickly details, the film shows a continual sympathy for marginal members of society—the poor and the ignorant, the eccentric and the unfortunate, the old and the intimidated.

Certainly *The Peddler* carries no overtones of the fanaticism that Khomeini's Iran displayed to the outside world—its transcendental rage not only against the Great Satan but also against its secular neighbor Iraq, its universal contract on Salman Rushdie, etc. The one incident that suggests xenophobia (of a kind that could happen almost anywhere) shows the police singling out Afghans for suspicion of the first killing in Episode 3, when a flashback has already made it clear that they are innocent. Similarly, the film offers no approval of the Muslim fundamentalism that strains this non-believer's tolerance. Although the few women who appear are subordinate, as in Iranian reality, Makhmalbaf presents this with a touch of irony: the husband in Episode 1 petulantly blames his wife for the failure of the mosque attempt that had been his idea. The mother in Episode 2, mute and paralyzed, may even be taken as the *reductio ad absurdum* of Khomeini's ideal woman; and Makhmalbaf in a sense liberates her at the end by showing the healthy young girl she once had been.

All of these cultural and social issues raise a critical questions: Is *The Peddler* of interest only because it offer a glimpse into a country that has made itself forbiddingly enigmatic? Certainly that glimpse adds to its interest; certainly, too, the film's eclectic style and dark vision would seem less striking if it came from a Western country. But it is meaningless to separate these apparent incidentals from the film's "essence." In retrospect, after the first surprise has passed, *The Peddler* remains a powerful memory. As hard as it may be to like, this is an easy film to admire.

ROCKY IV *(Film Review Annual, 1986)*

JUMP CUT, No. 35, 4/90, p. 85, Christine Anne Holmlund

[*Rocky IV* was reviewed jointly with *Down and Out in Beverly Hills;* see Holmlund's review in this addendum.]

SCANDAL (*Film Review Annual, 1990*)

FILM QUARTERLY, Summer 1990, p. 17, Paul Thomas

Whether or not most films can be said to be orchestrated around the "male gaze," Michael Caton-Jones's elegant film *Scandal* is orchestrated around nothing else. It may be one of the most voyeuristic films yet made. It falls short as an exposé either of the Profumo affair in general or of the framing and suicide of its real victim, Stephen Ward, in particular. But the film is very much an exposé all the same, an exposé of seeing and being seen.

The key moment in *Scandal* comes as Ward (John Hurt) is being interrogated, not very gently, bu the police. By this stage he knew he was the man who knew too much and that, as a result, he was "for the drop." For him, the Profumo affair had not ended with the resignation of John Profumo from Harold Macmillan's Conservative government. Ward had already started to spill the beans about the affair's "security aspect" and had to be stopped. Criminal proceedings and, if possible, conviction, could discredit his word in advance. The police, acting on instructions, were on the lookout for as many offenses as possible with which Ward could be charged. The more mud thrown, the more chance that some of it would stick. On being told in the course of his interrogation of the number of people the police claimed were ready to testify against him (147: Christine Keeler alone was to be interviewed 24 times) and of the "filth" they had succeeded in raking up at the same time ("real pox-ridden harlots" and all) Ward, on edge, snaps off the side of the eyeglasses he is nervously toying with. "Oh dear, look at that," says his interrogator, neatly specifying what Ward will no longer be able to do very easily. (We later see Ward in his kitchen, fastening together his glasses with scotch tape, which he throws across the room in frustration; he is to wear the taped-together glasses at his trial.) Ward, if he was guilty of anything at all, was guilty of observation. Looking, or (if you will) leering and ogling are not normally considered indictable offenses in British courts of law, but they do shade over into voyeurism, as Ward seems to have been well aware. The master-stroke of *Scandal* is that Michael Caton-Jones makes sure that, watching it, we as spectators become aware of our own voyeurism too.

Ward like looking at women, particularly women who liked being looked at. He had, in the words of the "Indian doctor" *Scandal* leaves unnamed (though his identify has long been known), "the most highly trained eye in London" for doing so. Ward's evident pleasure in looking at women, which up till this point in the film had been our pleasure too, is now snapped, broken, and is not to be regained. Ward's sense of sight, and through it ours as spectators, had been privileged in the earlier part of *Scandal*. But from this point onwards nothing Ward sees through his broken glasses is going to bring him any pleasure, least of all seeing Christine Keeler (Joanne Whalley-Kilmer) from the dock when he is on trial. *Scandal* untowardly romanticizes Ward's relationship with Keeler throughout, to the point of having her change the color of her hair (shades of *Vertigo*) in his bathroom. In the film, they exchange warm glances when Keeler is on the witness-stand; in reality, Keeler too "shopped" (i.e., betrayed) Ward, perjured herself in court, and went to jail.

The pivotal scene where Ward nervously breaks his glasses is prefigured aptly enough by two parallel sequences seen from his point of view. These stand out visually and stylistically from the rest of *Scandal* by being shot in natural sunlight on the streets of London near where Ward lived. The first is at the beginning of the film, after the titles. We see Stephen Ward not just happy to be alive but glowing, beaming with happiness. (Anyone who thinks ecstasy a hard emotion for John Hurt to convey will have his or her preconceptions shattered right away.) Ward's eye is caught by an attractive young woman riding a bicycle. His gaze follows her around a corner. The camera pans slowly to the right. The young woman is showing some leg. We know what Ward is thinking. We are thinking it ourselves.

This sequence is reprised later in the film. By this stage, Profumo has resigned in disgrace from his position as War Minister in the cabinet, having admitted lying in a personal statement to that *sanctum sanctorum*, the House of Commons, about the "propriety" of his past relationship with Christine Keeler; and Eugene Ivanov, the Russian naval attaché who had also had a liaison with Keeler at Ward's (and, it was later to transpire, MI5's) instigation, had been recalled to the Soviet Union. Once again Ward, whose friends are now being encouraged by the police to desert him in droves, is out on the street, scanning the "talent," seeking solace in what he sees. Once again, we see from his point of view a young woman on a bicycle, and once again the camera pans to the right, following her round the corner. Only this time Ward's pleasure (and ours) is abruptly blocked. The camera comes to rest on the figure of the plainclothes police officer we've already seen picking off Ward's friends one by one. "Hello, Stephen," he says, as though he already knew him; his unappealing features fill the screen and obstruct Ward's view—then, and thereafter: for the remainder of the film, and for the rest of Ward's life.

Scandal's artful figuration of the visual or specular is carefully judged, and helps hold the film together. It begins but does not end with Ward, who was an artist (he drew pictures at the Adolph Eichmann trial in Tel Aviv for the *Daily Telegraph* and is shown in *Scandal* sketching portraits at his own at the Old Bailey) as well as an osteopath with friends in high places. Both Christine Keeler and Mandy Rice-Davies (Bridget Fonda) also evidently relished the sexuality of looking, being looked at and seeing themselves in photographs. (The ostensible ambition of these would-be *demi-mondaines* was to become "models.") This is pointed up nicely by another sequence that stands out visually from the rest of the film, where Christine and Mandy get tarted up for a night on the town, at the Twenty-One Club, identified by Mandy as a "knocking shop." For a few glorious moments the screen is alive with garter-belts, thighs, breasts, and lipstick applied in extreme close-up. This would be a soft-porn interlude and nothing more but for the highly ad-agency nature of the photography and the fact that Christine and Mandy are not undressing but dressing—dressing up with a vengeance, literally girding their loins for the battle of the sexes. This, to pile delight on delight, turns out to involve a hilarious threesome with "Douglas Fairfax Junior" (sic) during which Mandy and Christine can't stop giggling at their own attempts to simulate moans of pleasure of the required kind. The music on the sound track as they dress up is the Shadows' "Apache," a tune whose Red-Indians-and-warpaint motif recalls the "Running Bear" dancing-girl sequence we've already seen the two women help perform at Murray's Club.

Scandal is more generally an orgy not of sex—what we see is pretty tame by present-day standards—but of the specular. Its characters see and define themselves in the gaze of others. They see themselves and portray themselves as they would like others to see them—Profumo in this mental hall of mirrors as the blameless statesman with "an army to run," Lord Astor as the victim of circumstances, Christine and Mandy as girls out for a good time, Ivanov as the impartial judge of British capitalist decadence. Only the notoriously indiscreet Ward has nothing to hide, at least as this film portrays him; it is others who want him silenced, others for whom Ward's eventual suicide was to prove mightily convenient. Profumo may have been the war hero turned War Minister, but it was Ward who died that others might live.

Scandal penetrates all these various delusions and hypocrisies by using the apparently "realistic" device of the still-camera-within-the-frame. It does so, up to a point, to good effect. For the daytime swimming-pool sequence at Cliveden we see the action (including Profumo's planting an incriminating kiss on Keeler's thigh as she is riding on his shoulders, noticed by his wife) through the viewfinder of an ordinary pocket camera. But more usually it is press cameras that punctuate the action, and freeze it into monochrome stills. The stills then become a kind of record or reportage, and the film by extension a kind of semi-documentary report, as though the camera (unlike virtually every character in the film) does not and could not lie. The trouble is, however, that these monochrome freeze-frames also in effect try to pin down and locate the Profumo affair, distancing it from us as though it all took place in a bygone era when "procurement" (one of the charges levelled against Stephen Ward) had nothing to do with Pentagon weapons contracts and everything to do with vice and prostitution. It is in its attempts at distancing that *Scandal* is at its least convincing. Its own drawbacks, and for that matter its own history, reveal just how long-lasting and lingering, and not at all how remote and short-lived, the Profumo affair has been, from its own day down to our own.

In that perspective, *Scandal* is a cautious and carefully judged film—perhaps *too* much so. Unlike its characters, it resists easy temptations. The Profumo affair may have been a spectacle of sorts, a *grand guignol* as well as a masquerade, but *Scandal* goes to great lengths to avoid the spectacular. Even Ward's trial, *the* trial of the sixties in Britain, is dramatically muted (except when Mandy Rice-Davies is in the witness-box, stealing the show). We have no Mervyn Griffith-Jones describing Ward as "this filthy fellow," no Justice Marshall mistaking Mandy Rice-Davies for Marilyn Monroe—or observing, quite rightly, that Ward had been "abandoned in his extremity," no least by the pusillanimous Lord Astor, who is as conspicuous in his absence from the film version as he was from the real one. *Scandal* deliberately and consistently plays down and de-melodramatizes the political scandal that is its subject. The Profumo affair was, after all, a sensational mélange of politics, sex, vice, espionage, hypocrisy in high and low places, and betrayal. It had, on top of these, sub-plots involving national security, race, class, money, sleaze, disinformation and cover-up (do these sound familiar?).

Of all these, it is betrayal that comes through most consistently, though (it could be argued) not forcefully enough. The style of the film is not forceful at all, but low-key and lackluster; even the early night-club sequences at Murray's are sleazy rather than garish, gaudy but deadpan. Interiors throughout the film, and there are plenty of these, are generally lit in pink or blue (blue being the color of the Conservative party, and pink that of Mandy Rice-Davies's get-up at Ward's trial) and are meticulously reconstructed. Real locations—Wimpole Mews (where Stephen Ward lived), Cliveden (Lord Astor's country seat), the *cottage orné* which Ward rented from Astor—appear to have been used wherever possible. Others—Christine Keeler's mother's home (a converted railway carriage in Wraysbury), the interior of Ward's flat, Murray's Club—are painstakingly reconstructed in a beautiful job (Simon Holland's) of set design.

But, in the end, verisimilitude is one thing, veracity another, as the Profumo affair in its way indicated, and as *Scandal*, perhaps despite itself, shows all over again. By perpetuating half-truths the film is rather eerily in keeping with its subject-matter; a few caveats are in order to set the record straighter, if not straight. Ward at first publicly, on TV, backed up Profumo's mendacious denial of any "impropriety" with Keeler, only to backtrack subsequently, though one would guess neither this, nor the fact that the peppy Many Rice-Davies attempted suicide, from seeing *Scandal*. There again, it is interesting to speculate why the film never goes for the jugular of the Establishment. It could in principle have done so without making of Ward a gentle and blameless tragic hero. Would it not have been quite enough to have portrayed Ward as what he was, someone who was hounded to death, someone thrown to the wolves, someone ritually sacrificed in one of the most disgraceful travesties of British justice the other side of Ulster, someone who killed himself in transparent conviction of his own innocence and of the guilt of others?

Nor is this the only place where *Scandal* backs off where it could have hit home. Profumo's lying statement before the Commons is rendered accurately (though his wife's presence in the Visitor's Gallery is not hinted at), but here again it's a case of the truth but not the whole truth. The film glosses over the fact that Profumo had been dragged out of bed the night before the big day by four of his cabinet colleagues and his lawyer in order to draw up his "personal" statement, which was in reality a collective product. *Scandal's* version of the speech as delivered in the Commons interestingly enough omits the final paragraph. ("I shall not hesitate to issue writs for libel and slander if scandalous allegations are repeated outside the House.") The reaseon for this omission is not simply that *Scandal* is concerned to portray Profumo as hapless, weak, and confused (Ian McKellan looks uncomfortable in the role, in a very well-acted film), while his words smack of a "manly" bravado—let my skulking detractors come out from behind the skirts of parliamentary privilege, and I'll see they get what's coming to them. (Profumo subsequently sued both *Paris-Match* and *Tempo Illustrado*, accepting £50 from the latter in an out-of-court settlement.)

It's hard not to conclude that the real reason for *Scandal's* reluctance to approach the subject of libel is the same kowtowing to absurdly restrictive press and libel laws that stymied and prevented reporting of the Profumo affair in the first place. It is after all a matter of record that one recent book on the Profumo/Ward scandal, one that can freely be read anywhere else in the world, was recalled from libraries and bookshops in the UK and actually pulped (shades of *Spycatcher*), simply because one of the police officers who had interrogated Ward, and who was believed dead, turned up alive and kicking in Australia. He promptly and successfully sued the authors and publisher for defamation. The success of this figure, who actually features in *Scandal*, helps explain why the Profumo affair defies any attempt at historical distancing, or pinning down. It casts a long shadow. *Scandal* started life as a projected TV mini-series from which British TV backed down and pulled out when it was already in production. We can only speculate why, but I have my suspicions, which are helped along by the eponymous "Indian doctor" and "Douglas Fairfax, Junior." As it stands, the film, sad to say, frequently betrays its fragmented, episodic origins: chronology and narrative are often muddy, and characters drop in and out unexplained, like uninvited guests. (That Peter Rachman, Mandy Rice-Davies's loathesome slum-lord lover, was dead by the time of Ward's trial is never mentioned.) A TV mini-series might have set these lapses to rights, but this we shall never know; "Masterpiece Theatre," I'm afraid, is going to have to make do with something else, something more "British." (How about yet another re-run of "Yes, Minister"? It might just fit the bill.)

At the end of *Scandal* a couple of messages, each of them a half-truth, roll onto the screen. Taken together, they suggest not just how murky the Profumo affair still remains, but also that it's not yet even over. We are told first that in November 1964 Macmillan's government fell, "exhausted by the scandal." True enough, although nothing we have seen in *Scandal*, which ends with Ward's suicide in July 1963, has any immediate bearing on the end of this particular, unsavory era. Most of the events portrayed in the film took place in 1961, but became public knowledge only after Ward's death. What came in between July 1963 and November 1964 was not just a bloodied Macmillan's desperate attempts to sit on the Philby scandal, where real, heavy-duty espionage was involved, but also the Denning Report of September 1963. This piece of whitewash had its terms of reference restricted to the (unknowable) "security aspects" of the Profumo affair, which were held in all seriousness to exclude Ward (even though we now know that Ward had helped the MI5 set up what was supposed to be a "honey trap" for Ivanov, whose name had been forwarded by the Russian defector Oleg Penkovsky, with Keller). The Denning Report succeeded in prolonging the Profumo affair it was supposed to have put to rest, and became part of the scandal it was supposed to have explained away.

The second half-truth that rolls up on the screen before the credits take us out and away tells us of the date of Stephen Ward's funeral and adds that "nobody came." True enough; but a wreath was sent by (among others) Kenneth Tynan, John Osborne, Arnold Wesker, Joe Orton, and Penelope Gilliat, who signed a card "to Stephen Ward, victim of hypocrisy." It does not diminish Ward, but it does diminish this film, to point out that we are not yet done with this self-same hypocrisy.

TORCH SONG TRILOGY *(Film Review Annual, 1989)*

CINEASTE, Vol. XVII, No. 3, 1990, p. 47, Jude Schwendenwien

The movie version of Harvey Fierstein's award-winning play, *Torch Song Trilogy*, can easily claim a place as a landmark film in gay cinema. Fierstein, with the help of director Paul Bogart, has convincingly demonstrated that a film dealing with the issue of homosexuality can be accessible to a general audience without sacrificing honest content. While the specter of AIDS has cast a negative pall on prior homosexual-oriented films like *An Early Frost* and *Parting Glances*, and films like *Maurice* and *Prick Up Your Ears* stress unhappiness and unfulfillment surrounding gay relationships, *Torch Song Trilogy* strikes a proper balance and a sense of universality.

In press releases, the plot is described as follows: "*Torch Song Trilogy* is the funny and poignant story of a gay New Yorker's search for love and respect in a heterosexual world." There are some inaccuracies to that description. Fierstein's character, Arnold Beckoff, does not hold a typical job in a straight-oriented environment. Instead, he performs in cabarets as the feisty, gravel-voiced drag diva Virginia Hamm. Politically, Beckoff is not an assimilationist—a gay individual who assumes the codes and mannerisms of straight behavior to gain acceptance in mainstream society. Fierstein could have explored the tension felt by a character deliberately going against the grain of heterosexual society. What Fierstein and Beckoff do allow is the entrance of straight elements into this homosexual content (i.e., his mother, his former bisexual lover Ed who cannot come out of the closet). Beckoff earns a good living as a drag queen performer, even more money than his father (much to the father's annoyance). On this level, we never really see Beckoff gain acceptance as a homosexual because we don't see a complete picture of resistance.

For this reason, *Torch Song Trilogy* lacks a certain edge that could have made it a potent statement on homosexual life since the Stonewall riots. Yet somehow the movie works. If Fierstein achieves anything, he successfully proves a salient point about humanity—that difference is actually the norm if people would just pay attention. Beckoff is a man who can be completely forthright with his emotions. Fierstein is a more theatrical than cinematic performer—he tends to overdo every emotional high and low, embellishing his speeches with little facial tics and broad mannerisms. Nevertheless, the Fierstein charisma is affecting and memorable, constituting the true heart of the film. Above all, Arnold Beckoff is a survivor. Fierstein proves that an individual is strong when he or she listens to an inner directive and accepts one's true identity. While Beckoff at times comes across as vulnerable and fragile, he still demonstrates the strength to give his obtrusive mother (played at fever pitch by Ann Bancroft) and ultimatum to accept him as he is or leave his life forever.

Fierstein and Bogart strive for a clarity and fluidity that make the film immensely watchable and enjoyable. Fierstein can deal with the disaffected nature of casual gay encounters—at one point he states that he has slept with hundreds of men and not one has ever said (believably), "Arnold, I love you"—yet his basic need for love and affection is a human trait understood by straights and gays alike. Likewise, the film never attempts to gloss over the more graphic aspects of gay promiscuity—for example, Arnold enters the back room of a Seventies gay bar for an anonymous sexual encounter. Fierstein and Bogart simply treat this incident as an aspect of human behavior unknown to many people. In light of the present AIDS crisis, such a representation of rampant promiscuity might seem irresponsible, but Fierstein views *Torch Song Trilogy* as an honest document of the times as he saw them.

As entertainment goes, *Torch Song Trilogy* is well-done, maybe even too much so. Paul Bogart, a veteran of sitcom television, directs with a perky, clean style. Histrionics and melodrama frequently take over, but at all times Fierstein's scintillating wit shines through. Of course, Fierstein is quite a romantic. Is the idyllic union between Arnold and Alan (a young model played by Matthew Broderick) too cozy to believe? Yes, it seems so, until we see Alan's propensity for infidelity with Arnold's married ex-lover Ed (played by the wholesome-looking Brian Kerwin). Yet Fierstein is also a realist, showing us the devastating effects of homophobia in the fatal beating of Alan by streetpunks.

Torch Song Trilogy never portrays homosexuals as stereotypes or parodies. Fierstein does not write from a ghettoized point of view, so Bogart's sensibility fits well with this open-minded perspective. We can all, gay or straight, sympathize with Beckoff's search for love and respect in the world. As such, *Torch Song Trilogy* is a gay man's story that hits home with all people.

YEELEN (*Film Review Annual, 1988*)

VILLAGE VOICE, 4/18/89, p. 71, Elliott Stein

The stereotyped image of African cinema is one of films about poverty—a bit boring, but sincere—whose technical clumsiness should be overlooked in deference to the nobility of their sentiments. The clichés don't apply to *Brightness (Yeelen)*, an astonishing work of great virtuosity, arguably the most beautiful African film ever made. Its director, Souleymane Cissé, born 1940 in Mali's capital, Bamako, spent five years at film school in Moscow, where he studied with Eisenstein's ex-pupil, Mark Donskoi. *Brightness* is his fourth feature. (Cissé's *Baara* [April 19] and *The Wind* [April 26] are being screened at the Collective.)

The film is set in a remote era, among the Bambara, before the coming of Europeans to Africa. It follows the trajectory of a long initiation rite: Nianankoro, the young hero, must learn the science of the gods, knowledge that will help him make his way in the world. Soma, his father, does not want to be supplanted and refuses to pass along his knowledge—he's preparing to immolate an albino human and a dog in order to destroy Nianankoro. "My son, your father is a terror," the youth's mother warns. He flees his father's wrath and goes on a journey to meet his uncle, acquiring a wife and fathering a son of his own along the way. The uncle presents him with a magical wooden "wing" so that he can do battle with Soma's mystical pestle. At their final encounter, both son and father are destroyed by the "brightness" generated by their magic machines. When the light dies down, Nianankoro's naked child unearths two giant eggs in the sand—sharing of knowledge and the regeneration of the world will proceed from them.

A plot summary can do little justice to the sumptuousness of this enchanting and fluently directed road movie, which is full of broad, sweeping landscapes of swamp and plain. Jean-Noël Ferragut's breathtaking cinematography bathes the film in an uncanny soft golden light. Cissé's uncluttered directorial style is a model of visual shorthand—in brief shots, objects somehow seem to evoke states of grace. Since there are no stage companies in Mali, Cissé simply found his performers by wandering through towns and villages. Most of the actors are nonprofessionals who cannot read; all are remarkable. The young hero is played by Issiaka Kane, bright of eye and long of limb, discovered by the director at a Bamako neighborhood dance contest. His graceful force impresses during physical and verbal duels, when the curtly percussive Bambaran language rings out as the characters "sing like the divine hyenas."

There are moments in *Brightness* that suggest the Oedipus story, the son-father struggles of Cronus and Zeus, and, closer to home, *2001* and *Star Wars*. These are first thoughts, a tentative gloss on an extraordinary closed world that seems to embody universal passions and myths of creation.

AWARDS

ACADEMY OF MOTION PICTURE ARTS AND SCIENCES
62nd Annual Academy Awards—March 26, 1990

BEST PICTURE—*Driving Miss Daisy*
Other Nominees: *Born on the Fourth of July; Dead Poets Society; Field of Dreams; My Left Foot*

BEST ACTOR—Daniel Day-Lewis in *My Left Foot*
Other Nominees: Kenneth Branagh in *Henry V;* Tom Cruise in *Born on the Fourth of July;* Morgan Freeman in *Driving Miss Daisy;* Robin Williams in *Dead Poets Society*

BEST ACTRESS — Jessica Tandy in *Driving Miss Daisy*
Other Nominees: Isabelle Adjani in *Camille Claudel;* Pauline Collins in *Shirley Valentine;* Jessica Lange in *Music Box;* Michelle Pfeiffer in *The Fabulous Baker Boys*

BEST SUPPORTING ACTOR—Denzel Washington in *Glory*
Other Nominees: Danny Aiello in *Do the Right Thing;* Dan Aykroyd in *Driving Miss Daisy; Marlon Brando* in *A Dry White Season;* Martin Landau in *Crimes and Misdemeanors*

BEST SUPPORTING ACTRESS—Brenda Fricker in *My Left Foot*
Other Nominees: Anjelica Huston in *Enemies, A Love Story;* Lena Olin in *Enemies, A Love Story;* Julia Roberts in *Steel Magnolias;* Dianne Wiest in *Parenthood*

BEST DIRECTOR—Olivers Stone for *Born on the Fourth of July*
Other Nominess: Woody Allen for *Crimes and Misdemeanors;* Peter Weir for *Dead Poets Society;* Kenneth Branagh for *Henry V;* Jim Sheridan for *My Left Foot*

BEST FOREIGN-LANGUAGE FILM—*Cinema Paradiso* (Italy)
Other Nominees: *Camille Claudel* (France); *Jesus of Montreal* (Canada); *Santiago, the Story of His New Life* (Puerto Rico); *Waltzing Regitze* (Denmark)

BEST ORIGINAL SCREENPLAY—Tom Schulman for *Dead Poets Society*

Other Nominees: Woody Allen for *Crimes and Misdemeanors;* Spike Lee for *Do the Right Thing;* Steven Soderbergh for *sex, lies, and videotape;* Nora Ephron for *When Harry Met Sally. . .*

BEST ADAPTED SCREENPLAY—Alfred Uhry for *Driving Miss Daisy*
Other Nominees: Oliver Stone and Ron Kovic for *Born on the Fourth of July;* Roger L. Simon and Paul Mazursky for *Enemies, A Love Story;* Phil Alden for *Field of Dreams;* Jim Sheridan and Shane Connaughton for *My Left Foot*

BEST CINEMATOGRAPHY—Freddie Francis for *Glory*
Other Nominees: Mikael Salomon for *The Abyss;* Haskell Wexler for *Blaze;* Robert Richardson for *Born on the Fourth of July;* Michael Ballhaus for *The Fabulous Baker Boys*

BEST FILM EDITING—David Brenner and Joe Hutshing for *Born on the Fourth of July*
Other Nominees: Noëlle Boisson for *The Bear;* Mark Warner for *Driving Miss Daisy;* William Steinkamp for *The Fabulous Baker Boys;* Steven Rosenblum for *Glory*

BEST ART DIRECTION—Anton Furst with set decoration by Peter Young for *Batman*
Other Nominees: Leslie Dilley with set decoration by Anne Kuljian for *The Abyss;* Dante Ferretti with set decoration by Francesca Lo Schiavo for *The Adventures of Baron Munchausen;* Bruno Rubeo with set decoration by Crispian Sallis for *Driving Miss Daisy;* Norman Garwood with set decoration by Garrett Lewis for *Glory*

BEST COSTUME DESIGN—Phyllis Dalton for *Henry V*
Other Nominees: Gabriella Pescucci for *The Adventures of Baron Munchausen;* Elizabeth McBride for *Driving Miss Daisy;* Joe I. Tompkins for *Harlem Nights;* Theodor Pistek for *Valmont*

BEST MAKE-UP—Manlio Rocchetti for *Driving Miss Daisy*
Other Nominees: Maggie Weston and Fabrizio Sforza for *The Adventures of Baron Munchausen;* Dick Smith, Ken Diaz, and Greg Nelson for *Dad*

BEST ORIGINAL SCORE—Alan Menken for *The Little Mermaid*
Other Nominees: John Williams for *Born on the Fourth of July;* David Grusin for *The Fabulous Baker Boys;* James Horner for *Field of Dreams;* John Williams for *Indiana Jones and the Last Crusade*

BEST ORIGINAL SONG—"Under the Sea" from *The Little Mermaid*, music by Alan Menken and lyrics by Howard Ashman
Other Nominees: "After All" from *Chances Are*, music by Tom Snow and lyrics by Dean Pitchford; "The Girl Who Used to Be Me" from *Shirley*

Valentine, music by Marvin Hamlisch and lyrics by Alan and Marilyn Bergman; "I Love to See You Smile" from *Parenthood*, music and lyrics by Randy Newman; "Kiss the Girl" from *The Little Mermaid*, music by Alan Menken and lyrics by Howard Ashman

BEST SOUND—Donald O. Mitchell, Gregg C. Rudloff, Elliot Tyson, and Russell Williams 2d for *Glory*
Other Nominees: Don Bassman, Kevin F. Cleary, Richard Overton, and Lee Orloff for *The Abyss;* Donald O. Mitchell, Kevin O'Connell, Greg Russell, and Keith A. Wester for *Black Rain;* Michael Minkler, Gregory H. Watkins, Wylie Stateman, and Tod O. Maitland for *Born on the Fourth of July;* Ben Burtt, Gary Summers, Shawn Murphy, and Tony Dawe for *Indiana Jones and the Last Crusade*

BEST SOUND EDITING—Ben Burtt and Richard Hymns for *Indiana Jones and the Last Crusade*
Other Nominees: Milton C. Burrow and William L. Manger for *Black Rain;* Robert Henderson and Alan Robert Murray for *Lethal Weapon 2*

BEST VISUAL EFFECTS—John Bruno, Dennis Muren, Hoyt Yeatmen, and Dennis Skotak for *The Abyss*
Other Nominees: Richard Conway and Kent Houston for *The Adventures of Baron Munchausen;* Ken Ralston, Michael Lantieri, John Bell, and Steve Gawley for *Back to the Future, Part II*

BEST DOCUMENTARY FEATURE—*Common Threads: Stories From the Quilt*
Other Nominees: *Adam Clayton Powell; Crack USA: Country Under Siege; For All Mankind; Super Chief: The Life and Legacy of Earl Warren*

BEST DOCUMENTARY SHORT—*The Johnstown Flood*
Other Nominees: *Fine Food, Fine Pastries, Open 6 to 9; Yad Vashem: Preserving the Past to Ensure the Future*

BEST ANIMATED SHORT—*Balance*
Other Nominees: *Cow; The Hill Farm*

BEST LIVE-ACTION SHORT—*Work Experience*
Other Nomineess: *Amazon Diary; The Childeater*

HONORARY AND SPECIAL AWARDS
Honorary Award to Akira Kurosawa for lifetime achievement.
Jean Hersholt Humanitarian Award to Howard W. Koch, producer and director.
Gordon E. Sawyer Award to Pierre Angenieux for "invention of the zoom lens."

NATIONAL SOCIETY OF FILM CRITICS
January 7, 1990

BEST PICTURE—*Drugstore Cowboy*

BEST ACTOR—Daniel Day-Lewis in *My Left Foot*

BEST ACTRESS—Michelle Pfeiffer in *The Fabulous Baker Boys*

BEST SUPPORTING ACTOR—Beau Bridges in *The Fabulous Baker Boys*

BEST SUPPORTING ACTRESS—Anjelica Huston in *Enemies, A Love Story*

BEST DIRECTOR—Gus Van Sant Jr. for *Drugstore Cowboy*

BEST SCREENPLAY—Gus Van Sant Jr. and Daniel Yost for *Drugstore Cowboy*

BEST CINEMATOGRAPHY—Michael Ballhaus for *The Fabulous Baker Boys*

BEST DOCUMENTARY FILM—Michael Moore for *Roger & Me*

NEW YORK FILM CRITICS CIRCLE
January 14, 1990

BEST PICTURE—*My Left Foot*

BEST ACTOR—Daniel Day-Lewis in *My Left Foot*

BEST ACTRESS—Michelle Pfeiffer in *The Fabulous Baker Boys*

BEST SUPPORTING ACTOR—Alan Alda in *Crimes and Misdemeanors*

BEST SUPPORTING ACTRESS—Lena Olin in *Enemies, A Love Story*

BEST DIRECTOR—Paul Mazursky for *Enemies, A Love Story*

BEST SCREENPLAY—Gus Van Sant Jr. and Daniel Yost for *Drugstore Cowboy*

BEST CINEMATOGRAPHY—Ernest Dickerson for *Do the Right Thing*

BEST FOREIGN-LANGUAGE FILM— *Story of Women* (France)

BEST DOCUMENTARY—*Roger & Me*

BEST FIRST-TIME DIRECTOR—Kenneth Branagh for *Henry V*

GOLDEN GLOBE
47th Annual Awards—January 20, 1990

BEST PICTURE (drama)—*Born on the Fourth of July*

BEST PICTURE (comedy or musical)—*Driving Miss Daisy*

BEST ACTOR (drama)—Tom Cruise in *Born on the Fourth of July*

BEST ACTOR (comedy or musical)—Morgan Freeman in *Driving Miss Daisy*

BEST ACTRESS (drama)—Michelle Pfeiffer in *The Fabulous Baker Boys*

BEST ACTRESS (comedy or musical)—Jessica Tandy in *Driving Miss Daisy*

BEST SUPPORTING ACTOR—Denzel Washington in *Glory*

BEST SUPPORTING ACTRESS—Julia Roberts in *Steel Magnolias*

BEST DIRECTOR—Oliver Stone for *Born on the Fourth of July*

BEST SCREENPLAY—Oliver Stone and Ron Kovic for *Born on the Fourth of July*

BEST ORIGINAL SCORE—Alan Menken for *The Little Mermaid*

BEST ORIGINAL SONG—"Under the Sea" from *The Little Mermaid*, music by Alan Menken and lyrics by Howard Ashman

BEST FOREIGN-LANGUAGE FILM—*Cinema Paradiso* (Italy)

LOS ANGELES FILM CRITICS ASSOCIATION
December 16, 1989

BEST PICTURE—*Do the Right Thing*

BEST ACTOR—Daniel Day-Lewis in *My Left Foot*

BEST ACTRESS—(tie) Andie MacDowell in *sex, lies, and videotape* and Michelle Pfeiffer in *The Fabulous Baker Boys*

BEST SUPPORTING ACTOR—Danny Aiello in *Do the Right Thing*

BEST SUPPORTING ACTRESS—Brenda Fricker in *My Left Foot*

BEST DIRECTOR—Spike Lee for *Do the Right Thing*

BEST SCREENPLAY—Gus Van Sant Jr. and Daniel Yost for *Drugstore Cowboy*

BEST CINEMATOGRAPHY—Michael Ballhaus for *The Fabulous Baker Boys*

BEST SCORE—Bill Lee and contributing artists for *Do the Right Thing*

BEST FOREIGN FILM—(tie) *Story of Women* (France) and *Distant Voices, Still Lives* (Great Britain)

BEST DOCUMENTARY FILM—*Roger & Me*

INDEPENDENT/EXPERIMENTAL AWARD—Gregg Araki for *The Long Weekend O'Despair*

CAREER ACHIEVEMENT AWARD—Stanley Donen

NEW GENERATION AWARD—Laura San Giacomo

SPECIAL ANIMATION AWARD—John Musker and Ron Clements for *The Little Mermaid*

SPECIAL AWARD—The Margaret Herrick Library of the Academy of Motion Picture Arts and Sciences, "whose holdings and special collections have significantly contributed to the advancement of film scholarship."

NATIONAL BOARD OF REVIEW
David Wark Griffith Award—December 13, 1989

BEST PICTURE—*Driving Miss Daisy*
Other Selections: *Henry V; sex, lies, and videotape; The Fabulous Baker Boys; My Left Foot; Dead Poets Society; Crimes and Misdemeanors; Born on the Fourth of July; Glory; Field of Dreams*

BEST ACTOR—Morgan Freeman in *Driving Miss Daisy*

BEST ACTRESS—Michelle Pfeiffer in *The Fabulous Baker Boys*

BEST SUPPORTING ACTOR—Alan Alda in *Crimes and Misdemeanors*

BEST SUPPORTING ACTRESS—Mary Stuart Masterson in *Immediate Family*

BEST DIRECTOR—Kenneth Branagh for *Henry V*

BEST FOREIGN FILM—*Story of Women*
Other Selections: *Camille Claudel; La Lectrice; Chocolat; Little Thief*

SPECIAL AWARDS
Robert A. Harris for the restoration of *Lawrence of Arabia.*
Molly Haskell and Andrew Sarris for film criticism.
Robert Giroux for "six decades of distinguished efforts on behalf of film.

CANNES FILM FESTIVAL
42nd Annual Awards—May 23, 1989

BEST PICTURE (Golden Palm Award)—*sex, lies, and videotape*

BEST DIRECTOR—Emir Kusturica for *Time of the Gypsies*

BEST ACTOR—James Spader in *sex, lies, and videotape*

BEST ACTRESS—Meryl Streep in *A Cry in the Dark*

SPECIAL GRAND JURY PRIZE—(tie) *Too Beautiful for You* and *Cinema Paradiso*

JURY PRIZE—*Jesus of Montreal*

CAMERA D'OR—*My 20th Century*

BEST SHORT SUBJECT—*50 Years*

TECHNICAL ACHIEVEMENT—Shohei Imamura for *Black Rain* (Japan)

BEST ARTISTIC CONTRIBUTION—*Mystery Train*

INDEX

CAST

McKinnon, Ray, 339
McKone, Vivienne, 606
MacLachlan, Andrew, 10, 407
McLain, Antoinette, 548
MacLaine, Shirley, 1252
McLaughlin, Sheila, 1140
McLaughlin-Gray, Jack, 825
McLean, Andrew, 1248
MacLean, Dwayne, 328
McLean, Hilda, 961
McLeod, David, 1430
McLeod, Duncan, 104
MacLeod, Margaret-Anne, 1291
MacLeod, Murray, 93
McLiam, Eanna, 883
McManus, Michael, 1225
McMartin, James, 1468
MacMillan, Andrew, 911
McMillan, Kenneth, 1318
MacMilliam, Ashlee, 622
McMullen, Cliff, 182
McMullen, Sam, 1046
McMurray, Sam, 1465
McNab, Angie, 1006
McNally, Terrence E., 369
McNamara, Dermot A., 428
McNamara, J. Patrick, 104, 533
McNamara, Pat, 723
McNamara, Peter, 476
McNamara, William, 326, 326
McNeice, Ian, 1381
MacNeill, Peter, 1006, 1059
McNicol, Peter, 500
McNinch, Thelma, 1245
McQueen, Armelia, 945
McRae, Frank, 436, 751, 1465
McTavish, Graham, 407, 477
McTeer, Janet, 551
McTighe, Michael, 134
MacVittie, Bruce, 134, 669
McWilliams, David, 219
McWilliams, Robin, 1196
Madden, Sharon, 1362
Maddox, James, 413
Madigan, Amy, 454, 1370
Madonna, 130
Madorsky, Bryan, 981
Madrid, Robert, 1056
Madsen, Jarry, 1143
Madsen, Virginia, 555
Maeda, Gin, 1333
Magaloni, Honorato, 751
Magarian, Andrew, 216
Maghsoudlou, Bahman, 1276
Magnuson, Ann, 185, 573
Magoondi, Yahoots, 1318
Magrath, Gavin, 51
Maguelon, Pierre, 773
Maguire, Brian, 617
Maguire, Ellen, 328
Maguire, Leonard, 357
Mahler, Bruce, 1024
Mahmud-Bey, Shiek, 1143
Mahoney, John, 1103
Maidment, Steve, 240
Maier, Tom, 99
Maillard, Huguette, 1261
Maillard, Marcel, 1449
Maines, Eleanor, 797

Mainprize, James, 669, 844
Maistre, François, 1261
Majewicz, Steven, 1209
Makay, Margit, 1392
Makeba, Miriam, 1399
Mako, 1374
Makoni, Tinashe, 357
Malden, Jennifer Scott, 1108
Maldonado, Usimon, 692
Male, Jayne, 332
Malet, Arthur, 1472
Malikyan, Kervork, 640
Malina, Judith, 398, 573
Malinowski, Chester, 240
Mallard, Gladys, 1252
Malmuth, Bruce, 723
Malone, Michael, 1414
Maloney, Michael, 1225
Maloney, Peter, 806
Malpas, George, 93, 640
Maltseva, Marina, 410
Mamayeva, N., 410
Mamberti, Sergio, 1083
Manahan, Anna, 22
Mancini, Dennis, 182
Mandylor, Costas, 1341
Mangikian, Rev. Yegishe, 697
Manierka, Peter, 1206
Manimanzi, Anna, 357
Mankuma, Blu, 622, 797
Mann, Andrea, 233, 472, 622, 797
Mann, Traci, 1340
Mann, Wesley, 56, 1449
Manni, Vic, 1056
Manning,Ruth, 185
Mannino, Anthony, 1422
Mannino, Janet, 557
Manoff, Dinah, 130, 1245
Manolikakis, Andreas, 615
Manon, Christian, 1481
Mañon, Juan Karlos, 954
Manos, George, 240
Mantello, Joe, 225
Manzoni, Anthony, 1036
Mapother, William R., 134
Maranzana, Mario, 704
Maras, Adam, 1367
Maras, Bob, 1367
Maras, Slavica, 1248
Marbury, Magda Szekely, 871
Marcel, Kelly, 524
Marcelic, Eugen, 1248
Marciano, David, 543, 731
Marcinek, Douglas, 871
Marcus, Mitch, 1414
Mardirosian, Tom, 911
Mardis, Bobby, 617
Marengo, Mario, 1206
Marenkov, V., 410
Margolin, Janet, 500
Margulies, David, 500
Marie, Camille, 956
Marie, Louisa, 971
Marie, Madeleine, 157, 1261
Marin, Cheech, 501, 1095, 1349
Marin, Jason, 768
Mario, Annie, 1268
Marioni, Ray, 1036
Mark, Dana, 971
Markell, Jodie, 891, 1388

Markkula, Jorma, 44
Markle, Paul, 384
Markley, Walter, 961
Marko, Monica, 234
Marley, Cedella, 836
Marley, Rita, 836
Marlowe, Curtiss, 565
Maroff, Bob, 653
Marot, Irene, 288, 496
Marques, Juana, 1326
Marquez, Roberto Martin, 810
Marrocco, Gino, 1206
Mars, Kenneth, 768, 1024
Mars, Shelly, 1395
Marsh, Charles, 1367
Marsh, Mae, 657
Marsh, Walter, 622
Marshall, Clare, 1036
Marshall, David, Anthony, 790
Marshall, E.G., 901
Marshall, Larry, 1173
Marshall, Rick, 1245
Marshall, William, Jay, 225
Martana, Bob, 225, 449
Martin, Andrea, 1095, 1472
Martin, Dan, 166
Martin, Deborah, 1349
Martin, George, 277
Martin, Jo, 476, 407
Martin, Kellie, 1349
Martin, Marji, 1191
Martin, Nan, 38
Martin, Richard, 1326
Martin, Rosemary, 332, 357
Martin, Sharlene, 490
Martin, Steve, 971
Martin, Vincent, 1267
Martin, W.T., 595
Martinez, A, 1173, 1027
Martinez, Evangelina Sosa, 947
Martinez, Jerry, 1295
Martinez, Roberto Sosa, 947
Martini, Ettore, 10
Martot, Pierre, 1261
Martusz, Jean-Michel, 1268
Mash, Jurgen, 1261
Ma Shao-chun, 1095
Mask, Ace, 1062
Masnata, Laura, 1324
Mason, Madison, 442
Massari, Léa, 868
Massey, Daniel, 1108
Massey, Jamila, 524
Massey, Marisol, 1138
Massey, Walter, 663
Masters, Rick, 134
Masterson, Mary Stuart, 182
Masterson, Rod, 124
Mastrantonio, Mary Elizabeth, 1, 669
Mastroianni, Armand, 1056
Masuoka, Toru, 1300
Mataisz, Richard Sr., 1414
Matanky, Gary, 653
Matheson, Chris, 104
Matheson, David, 384
Matheson, Tim, 1231
Mathews, Jon, 38
Mathews, Tony, 1108
Mathias, Anna, 1024
Mathieu, Debbie, 1367

Mathios, Steve, 277
Matou, Michael, 1481
Matsuda, Yusaku, 113
Mattera, Phil, 384
Matthews, Dakin, 419, 1456
Matthews, Hilary, 971
Matthews, Jon, 565, 565
Matthews, Michael, 1191
Maude-Roxby, Roddy, 606
Maur-Thorp, Sarah, 386
Mauri, Paco, 1083
Max, 1173, 729
Maxwell, Don, 937, 1209
Maxwell, Paul, 640
May, Walker, 1252
Mayers, David, 1414
Maynard, Jeff, 1367
Mayo-Chandler, Karen, 956
Mayon, Robert, 1472
Mayron, Gale, 134, 134, 557
Mayron, Melanie, 185
Mays, Joanna, 606
Mazursky, Paul, 398, 1120
Mazzola, Anthony, 93
Mbandu, Kongo, 189
Means, Mike, 1027
Mears, Michael, 1036
Medeiros, Glenn, 686
Medlock, Ken, 680
Meek, Barbara, 1138
Meek, Jeffrey, 679, 1452
Meery, Illa, 1486
Megill, Sheelah, 1430
Mehler, Edward, 605
Meier, Barry, 844
Meillon, John, 413
Mein, Simon, 277
Meisner, Gunter, 628
Meldrum, Max, 1481
Meldrum, Wendel, 694
Mele, Nick, 937
Melford, Jill, 386
Melhuse, Peder, 1024
Meligan, David, 653
Mellor, Christie, 565
Melto, Morgan Biscomb, 930
Melvazzi, Gino, 606
Melville, Pauline, 606
Melvin, Murray, 219
Mendelson, Aaron, 565
Mendoza, Jaclyn, 1003
Menken, Robin, 1120
Mercado, Jose, 847
Merchant, Ann, 1282
Merck, Wallace, 1452
Mercurio, Micole, 513, 604, 1414
Merlin, Yvette, 880
Merovitz, Shirley, 398
Mesa, Elio, 295
Mesman, Bill, 124
Messinger, M., 364
Metas, Christopher, 941
Metcalf, Laurie, 1370
Metonidze, Veroniko, 46
Metzger, Rowdy, 1465
Metzler, Jim, 941, 947
Meyer, Emmy, 1338
Meyers, Adrian, 67
Meyers, Bruce, 822
Mezzogiorno, Vittorio, 822
Mgcina, Sophie, 357
Miao, Cora, 375
Michael, 38, 67

Michaels, Gordon, 806
Michaels, Julie, 1066
Michaels, Marie, 1359
Michaud, Teddy, 1486
Michell, Calvin, 836
Michelson, Amy, 1456
Middleton, Barbara, 1282
Midkiff, Dale, 997
Miki, Norihei, 107
Mikuni, Rentaro, 1308
Milano, Alyssa, 1231
Milaris, Julia, 825
Milazzo, Joe, 994
Miles, Ben, 496
Miles, Marc, 1027
Miles, Sylvia, 1173
Miles, Will, 640
Milford, Penelope, 565
Milhaud, Sylvie, 1335
Milhoan, Michael, 454
Military, Frank, 267
Miller, Betty, 595
Miller, Dennis, 413
Miller, Dick, 152, 435
Miller, Ira, 1449
Miller, Joel, 663
Miller, John, 993
Miller, Joshua, 1313
Miller, Katherine E., 669
Miller, Larry, 1318
Miller, Linda Eve, 1362
Miller, Marilou, 810
Miller, Matt, 1338, 1340
Miller, Maxine, 328
Miller, Penelope Ann, 267
Miller, R.J., 216
Miller, Stephen E., 233, 267, 622
Miller, Vera, 398
Millinar, Rod, 272
Mills, Christopher W., 134
Mills, Keith R., 467
Mills, Richard, 841
Mills-Cockell, Juno, 981
Milmoe, Caroline, 818, 1468
Miltsakakis, Stefanos, 257, 1422
Min Luong, 513
Minces, Luis, 1324
Mindja, Essindi, 190
Minns, Bryon, 134
Minor, Bob, 516
Minor, Willie, 134
Minsker, Andy, 738
Minter, Kelly, 847, 937
Minyon, Michelle, 825
Miou-Miou, 708
Miquel, Joëlle, 483
Mironocv, Alexander, 779
Mirren, Helen, 1445
Mitchell, Aleta, 1381
Mitchell, Billy J., 640
Mitchell, Heather, 413
Mitchell, Mitch, 676
Mitchell, Shirley, 1406
Mitchell-Smith, Ilan, 197
Mitrovic, Drago, 1248
Mixon, Alan, 586
Miyagima, Eri, 1279
Miyamoto, Nobuko, 1308
Miyori, Kim, 99, 810
Mizuhara, Rie, 1279
Mlynarczyk, Wikor, 1341
Mobia, Steve, 1395

PRODUCERS

DIRECTORS

SCREENWRITERS

CINEMATOGRAPHERS

EDITORS

MUSIC

PRODUCTION CREW

Oliart, Veronica, 701
Oliney, Alan, 543, 617
Oliosi, Jose, 831
Onodera, Osamu, 1308
Oppewall, Jeannine, 38, 871, 1089
Orbom, Eric, 1024
O'Reilly, Valli, 185, 1231
Orlikoff, Lee, 56
Orloff, Lee, 1, 813
Orr, Bill, 797
Orr, William H., 233, 1429
Orsatti, Ernie, 692
Orsatti, Frank, 790
Ortega, Kenny, 1167
Ortiz, Hiram, 557
Osmo, Ben, 272
Ottarr, Geir, 489
Overton, Al, 1251
Owen, Chris, 163
Ozimek, Jeff, 1414

Pacelli, Joseph G., 56
Padilla, Daniel, 701
Pain, Keith, 516
Paley, Alan, 606
Palk, Anthony, 267
Palmer, Barbara, 844, 1422
Palmisano, Conrad, 1143, 1348, 1362, 1422
Pan, Kant, 1429
Paolo, Lyn, 390
Papa, Tony, 659
Papalia, Gregory, 500
Paprocka, Izabela, 1341
Pardula, Rolf, 1388
Parker, Art, 267
Parker, Gale, 533
Parker, Gary, 328
Parker, Ralph, 797
Parks, Stan, 113, 182
Parra, Antonio, 11
Parrondo, Gil, 436
Parrott, Hayward, 844
Parsons, Alva Bird Rattler, 1414
Partridge, Lily, 1016
Partridge, Wendy, 1426
Pasternak, Vladimir, 779
Pasztor, Beatrix Aruna, 130, 348
Patch, Karen, 99
Patchett, Byron, 211
Paterson, Candy, 1186
Paterson, Vincent, 836
Patton, Rick, 1448
Paul, Victor, 93, 434
Paull, Lawrence G., 543
Payne, James W., 586
Pearl, Linda, 216, 954
Peckham, Linda, 1279
Pedemonte, Theresa, 103
Pennell, Peter, 11, 1036
Pepiot, Ken, 152
Peraza, Michael A. Jr., 768
Perez, Jose, 436
Perovic, Nada, 253
Perry, Clive, 1291
Pescucci, Gabriella, 11, 548
Peters, Randy, 454
Peters-Hollingsworth, Kathryn, 617
Pethig, Hazel, 496
Petrovic, Nemanja, 253

Pfister, Diane, 1468
Phillipe et Gaston, 1034
Phillips, Bill, 357
Phillips, Bob, 1191
Phillips, Erica Edell, 824, 1352
Picerni, Charles, 731, 1066
Pickering, Robin, 1481
Pickrell, Gregory, 765
Pickwoad, Michael, 219, 606
Pilcher, Jim, 1313
Piller, Tony, 56
Pinezich, Lyn, 1196
Pirmez, Emily, 831
Pischiutta, Adriano, 11
Pisoni, Edward, 663, 1252
Pistek, Theodor, 1381
Pittman, Craig H., 134
Pizzini, Denise, 597
Plain, Andrew, 413
Plaxton, James, 536
Pochron, Jon, 419
Point, Florentino, 701
Poladian, Michael, 697
Polar Bear, 1167
Polizzi, Lauren, 523, 533
Poll, Lee, 1252
Pollack, Bernie, 790, 1295
Polyakh, Natalya, 779
Pomeroy, John, 22
Pomeroy-Cook, Lorna, 22
Port, Nina, 130
Porter, Bobby, 622, 1032
Portnow, Neil, 1456
Post, John, 941, 956, 1056
Powell, Anthony, 640
Powell, Sandy, 476
Poyner, John, 575
Precht, Andrew, 1
Preston, Billy, 1456
Preston, Ward, 1367
Price, Mathew, 1359
Pritchett, John, 38, 836, 1305
Proix, Franck, 190
Provost, Larry, 935
Pugatch, Yuri, 409
Purcell, Graham, 413
Purcell, William, Oliver, 134

Quaglio, Laurent, 82

Rae, Ted, 937
Raineri, Anna Rita, 1313
Rajau, Albert, 1381
Rajk, Laszlo, 481
Ralston, Ken, 56
Ramsey, Carol, 1214
Ramsey, Nina, 911, 971
Randall, William J., 442
Randolph, Virginia, 731
Random, Ida, 604, 1405
Rangel, Germinal, 357
Rankin, John, 56
Rapisarda, Bruno, 1093
Ratliff, E. Scott, 555
Ray, Brenda, 211
Razatos, Spiro, 1056
Razzi, Massimo, 11
Rea, Bill, 824
Read, Brian, 836
Reade, Dick, 903
Rebman, Cindy, 694

Redbourn, Michael, 847, 1191
Rees, Kim, 97
Reeves, Brian, 467
Reidy, Michael, 997
Reiner, Susan, 941
Reinhart, John, 292, 824
Rejas, Miguel, 1335
Reti, Janos, 1392, 1448
Reusch, Christa, 1245
Reynolds, Carleton E., 277
Reynolds, Richard, 604
Rezvani, Morteza, 847, 1465
Ribeiro de Abreu, Renaldo, 1267
Ribier, Pascal, 483
Ricard, Dominic, 384
Rice, Stephen, 1313
Richard, Michael, 981
Richards, Ethel Robins, 810
Richards, John, 768, 1127, 1251, 1435
Richardson, Edward, 123
Richardson, John, 751
Richardson, Kimberley, 622
Richwood, Frank, 653
Rifkin, Jay, 113, 339
Ringwood, Bob, 67
Ritenour, Scott, 947
Riva, J. Michael, 731, 1295
Rizzo, Gary H., 1348
Robb-King, Peter, 640
Roberts, Grant, 689
Robertson, Stuart, 911
Robinson, Jane, 1108
Rocchetti, Manlio, 148, 339, 548
Rochester, Art, 1103
Rodgers, Mic, 731
Rodis-Jamero, Nilo, 1237
Rogalla, Erica, 871
Roland, Hans, 292, 603
Roman, Voytek, 1248
Romanac, Nick, 813
Romine, Woody, 1378
Romvari, Jozef, 537, 1448
Rondell, Ron, 586
Ronne, David, 1237
Rose, Penny, 1270
Rosenberg, Philip, 428, 669
Rosenfeld, Hilary, 1341
Rosenstock, Scott, 993
Rosone, Jean, 1362
Ross, Jerry, 679, 810
Ross, Morga, 476
Rosse, Steve, 301
Roth, Ann, 428, 586, 669
Roth, Dena, 216
Roth, Sonja, 1299
Rousseau, Patrick, 663
Rowe, David, 436
Rowsell, Arthur, 981
Roysden, Thomas L., 259
Rubeo, Bruno, 134, 339, 947
Rubino, Beth, 1200
Rubino, Carmine, 659
Rudolf, Gene, 557, 679, 844
Ruff, Michael, 1456
Ruhm, Jane, 1103
Runyan, Mike, 1405
Rupp, Jacob, 622
Ruskin, Judy, 134

Russel-Van Lierop, Toy, 722, 1143
Rutledge, Robert R., 1295
Ryack, Rita, 653, 993
Ryan, Christopher, 472
Ryba, Tom, 961
Ryder, James, 1153
Ryder, Winston, 715, 806
Rylander, Eric, 390
Ryrie, Elizabeth, 189

Sabat, James, 113, 240, 911
Sabbatini, Enrico, 947
Sable, Dan, 653, 911, 1214
Sabo, Michael, 449
Sacco, Roseanna, 708
Sadoff, Marty, 847
Sage, Jefferson, 130
Sainsbury, Wendy, 1481
Sakaguchi, Takeharu, 20
Saklad, Steve, 947
Salazar, Rita, 871
Saldanhà, Jorge, 831
Sallid, Otis, 1206
Sallis, Crispian, 339
Samson, Kim, 765
Sandberg, Eric H., 1362
Sanders, Suzanne Parker, 1191
Sandin, Judi, 1032
Sands, Dennis S., 1, 56, 93, 99, 1348
Santandrea-Cull, Theresa, 1225
Sapunova, A., 745
Sargent, Bobby, 1378
Savelyev, V., 745
Scaife, Hugh, 166
Schaper, Bob, 1103
Scharinger, Gerlinde, 211
Schedler, Al, 797
Schell, Maurice, 166, 225, 738, 1245, 1381
Schiefelbein, John, 413
Schierholz, Peg, 947
Schilling, Rob, 510
Schirmer, William H., 653
Schiro, Art, 689
Schmelzle, Hans-Jurgen, 82
Schmidt, Joanne, 1153
Schmidt, Rick, 867
Schmidt-Feng, Morgan, 867
Schneider, Phillip, 1359
Schnell, Curtis, 250
Schoneberg, Andy, 954
Schoppe, James L., 1138
Schulenberg, Robert, 956
Schultz, Karen, 1214
Schulze, Lisa, 956
Schutt, Debra, 851
Schwob, Oliver, 697
Scott, Elisabeth, 956
Scott, Elliot, 640
Scott, Jeanette, 1200
Scott, John, 1429
Scott, Walter, 56, 930
Seguin, François, 841
Selk, Alan J., 257, 557
Selmer, Anne, 436
Sen, Jupiter, 219
Serious, Yahoo, 1481
Serody, Dawn, 257, 1422

Seymour, Sharon, 555
Shabtay, Michal, 388
Shaff, Amy, 728
Shanahan, James, 944
Shapkaits, E., 745
Sharkey, Paul, 386
Sharpe, Don, 67, 663
Shatz, Leslie, 1405, 1452
Shavers, Edward, 467
Shaw, Lindy, 1046
Sheldon, Greg, 1095
Shell, Maurice, 428
Shelley, Bob, 339
Shepard, Sekou, 1338, 1340
Shewchuk, Peter, 1426
Shircore, Jenny, 406, 966
Shohan, Naomi, 1191
Shorkey, Kathy, 1167
Shorr, Richard, 1191
Shostrom, Mark, 292
Silverman, Adam, 824
Sim, Gordon, 1127
Simmons, Brian, 551
Simon, Mark, 987
Simoni, Dario, 715
Simpson, Danielle, 216
Simpson, George, 152
Singelis, James T., 1143
Sinivia, Adriano, 704
Sipos, Istvan, 1448
Sissman, Rob, 1465
Skala, Martina, 1381
Skinner, William Ladd, 747, 790
Slodki, Naomi, 1032
Sloman, Anthony, 1468
Smart, Tony, 11
Smith, Christina, 113, 123, 1252
Smith, Dick, 259
Smith, Eddie, 301
Smith, Gord, 881, 134
Smith, J. Grey, 134
Smith, Jane, 956
Smith, Peter Lansdown, 442
Smith, Roy Forge, 103
Smith, Scott, 944, 961
Smolek, Jeff, 152, 987
Snyder, David L., 1183
Snyder, Dawn, 454
Soderbergh, Steven, 1153
Soletti, Frank, 1140
Solylo, Jeff, 1291
Sonski, Paul, 56
Soraci, Jesse, 189
Sosalla, David, 597
Soupios, Meredith, 891
Southern, Katherine, 1006, 1426
Sowder, Cynthia, 1027
Spadafora, Toni, 1378
Spader, Victoria, 185, 1153
Specter, Ronnie, 419
Spencer, James, 152
Spencer, Noriko, 413
Spencer, Norris, 113
Spheeris, Linda, 1472
Spiegel, Ira, 1378
Spier, Carol, 1058, 1206
Spirson, Jon, 523
Spisak, Neil, 669, 933
Splet, Alan, 277, 1422, 1452
Spriggs, Austen, 883, 883

CUMULATIVE TITLE INDEX
1981-1990

Big Trouble	116	(87)
Big Trouble	1693	(89)
Big Trouble in Little China	119	(87)
Bigfoot and the Hendersons (see Harry and the Hendersons)		(88)
Bigger Splash, A	148	(85)
Biggles	189	(89)
Bill And Ted's Excellent Adventure	103	(90)
Bill Cosby—"Himself"	102	(84)
Billy Galvin	146	(88)
Biloxi Blues	191	(89)
Biquefarre	150	(85)
Bird	198	(89)
Birdy	152	(85)
Birgitt Haas Must Be Killed	86	(83)
Bizet's Carmen	161	(85)
Black Cauldron, The	96	(86)
Black Goddess	76	(81)
Black Joy	124	(87)
Black Marble, The	76	(81)
Black Moon Rising	126	(87)
Black Rain (Japan)	107	(90)
Black Rain (Japan)	1488	(90)
Black Rain (United States)	113	(90)
Black Shack Alley (see Sugar Cane Alley)		(85)
Black Stallion Returns, The	103	(84)
Black Sun 731	122	(90)
Black Widow	149	(88)
Black and White	148	(88)
Black and White Like Day and Night	95	(82)
Blade Runner	91	(83)
Blaise Pascal	81	(81)
Blame It on Rio	170	(85)
Blaze	123	(90)
Bleak Moments	82	(81)
Bless Their Little Hearts	176	(85)
Blind	163	(88)
Blind Alley (see Perfect Strangers)		(87)
Blind Date	164	(88)
Blind Trust	171	(88)
Bliss	129	(87)
Blob, The	210	(89)
Blood Beach	98	(82)
Blood Diner	174	(88)
Blood Feud	82	(81)
Blood Simple	104	(86)
Blood Wedding	101	(82)
Bloodhounds of Broadway	130	(90)
Bloodsport	213	(89)
Bloody Kids	85	(81)
Blow Out	106	(82)
Blow Out	1420	(83)
Blue City	134	(87)
Blue Iguana, The	215	(89)
Blue Lagoon, The	86	(81)

Metropolis	880	(85)
Metropolitan Avenue	805	(87)
Michael Kohlhaas	621	(81)
Micki & Maude	887	(85)
Middle Age Crazy	623	(81)
Middleman, The	622	(81)
Midnight Crossing	941	(89)
Midnight Run	943	(89)
Midsummer Night's Sex Comedy, A	737	(83)
Mighty Quinn, The	836	(90)
Mike's Murder	894	(85)
Mikey and Nicky	809	(86)
Milagro Beanfield War, The	950	(89)
Miles From Home	959	(89)
Milk and Honey	841	(90)
Millennium	844	(90)
Million Dollar Mystery	979	(88)
Miracle Mile	847	(90)
Mirror, The	740	(84)
Mirror Crack'd, The	626	(81)
Mischief	812	(86)
Mishima: A Life in Four Chapters	814	(86)
Miss Firecracker	851	(90)
Miss Mary	808	(87)
Miss...or Myth?	982	(88)
Missing	750	(83)
Missing in Action	898	(85)
Missing in Action 2: The Beginning	828	(86)
Mission, The	742	(84)
Mission, The	900	(85)
Mission, The	814	(87)
Mission, The	1716	(88)
Missionary, The	765	(83)
Mississippi Blues	830	(86)
Mississippi Burning	964	(89)
Mr. Love	826	(87)
Mr. Mom	744	(84)
Mr. North	977	(89)
Mr. Universe	858	(90)
Misunderstood	904	(85)
Mix-Up	828	(87)
Mixed Blood	832	(86)
Modern Girls	831	(87)
Modern Problems	715	(82)
Modern Romance	717	(82)
Moderns, The	983	(89)
Mommie Dearest	721	(82)
Mon Oncle d'Amerique	629	(81)
Mona Lisa	834	(87)
Mondo New York	990	(89)
Money Juggler, The	861	(90)
Money Pit, The	845	(87)
Monkey Grip	747	(84)
Monkey Shines: An Experiment in Fear	993	(89)